MAP PAGES

DEN FINLAND

ESTONIA

LATVIA

UNGARY MOLDOVA

UKRAINE

ATIA ROMANIA

SERBIA

BULG

LBANIA GEORGIA

GREECE TURKEY ARM. AZER. TURKMENISTAN UZBEKISTAN

KAZAKHSTAN

KYRGYZSTAN

TAJIK.

RUSSIA

MONGOLIA

NORTH KOREA

SOUTH KOREA

JAPAN

SYRIA

IRAQ

JORDAN

IRAN

AFGHAN.

CHINA

BYA EGYPT

KUWAIT

SAUDI ARABIA

QATAR

U.A.E.

OMAN

PAKISTAN

NEPAL

BANGLA-DESH

BURMA

LAOS

TAIWAN

Tropic of Cancer

PACIFIC OCEAN

HAD SUDAN

YEMEN

ERITREA

DJIBOUTI

INDIA

THAILAND

CAMB.

VIETNAM

PHILIPPINES

CENTRAL AFRICAN REP

SOUTH SUDAN

ETHIOPIA

SOMALIA

SRI LANKA

UGANDA KENYA

CONGO (DEM. REP OF THE)

RWANDA

BURUNDI

TANZANIA

INDIAN OCEAN

MALAYSIA

INDONESIA

PAPUA NEW GUINEA

Equator

OLA

ZAMBIA MALAWI

MOZAMBIQUE

MADAGASCAR

E. TIMOR

BIA

ZIMBABWE

BOTSWANA

SWAZILAND

SOUTH AFRICA

LESOTHO

AUSTRALIA

Tropic of Capricorn

NEW ZEALAND

SYMBOLS

ADMINISTRATION			PHYSICAL FEATURES		
International boundaries	Internal boundaries	**PERU** Country names	Perennial streams	Intermittent lakes	▲ 8848 Elevations in metres
International boundaries (undefined or disputed)	National parks	KENT Administrative area names	Intermittent streams	Swamps and marshes	▼ 8500 Sea depths in metres
International boundaries show the *de facto* situation where there are rival claims to territory			Sand deserts	Permanent ice and glaciers	*1134* Height of lake surface above sea level in metres

The Royal Geographical Society

ESSENTIAL WORLD ATLAS

PHILIP'S

PHILIP'S would like to thank **Richard Chiles** and the staff at
NPA Satellite Mapping, Edenbridge, Kent, UK (www.npa.cgg.com)
for sourcing and processing the satellite imagery that appears in the atlas.

Published in Great Britain in 2013 by Philip's,
a division of Octopus Publishing Group Limited
(www.octopusbooks.co.uk)
Endeavour House, 189 Shaftesbury Avenue, London WC2H 8JY
An Hachette UK Company (www.hachette.co.uk)

Copyright © 2013 Philip's
Reprinted 2014

Cartography by Philip's

ISBN 978–1–84907–293–9

A CIP catalogue record for this book is available from the British Library.

Printed in Hong Kong

Details of other Philip's titles and services can be found on our website at:
www.philips-maps.co.uk

Front cover image: Anton Balazh / Shutterstock

USER GUIDE

The reference maps which form the main body of this atlas have been prepared in accordance with the highest standards of international cartography to provide an accurate and detailed representation of the Earth. The scales and projections used have been carefully chosen to give balanced coverage of the world, while emphasizing the most densely populated and economically significant regions. A hallmark of Philip's mapping is the use of hill shading and relief colouring to create a graphic impression of landforms: this makes the maps exceptionally easy to read. However, knowledge of the key features employed in the construction and presentation of the maps will enable the reader to derive the fullest benefit from the atlas.

MAP SEQUENCE

The atlas covers the Earth continent by continent: first Europe; then its land neighbour Asia (mapped north before south, in a clockwise sequence), then Africa, Australia and Oceania, North America and South America. This is the classic arrangement adopted by most cartographers since the 16th century. For each continent, there are maps at a variety of scales. First, physical relief

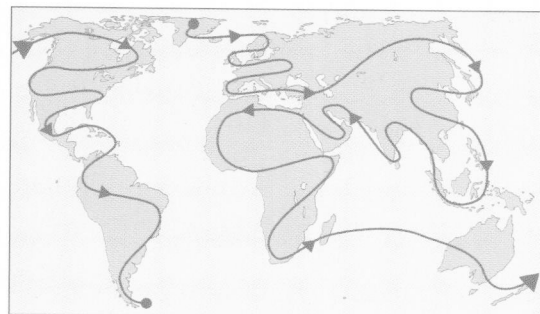

and political maps of the whole continent; then a series of larger-scale maps of the regions within the continent, each followed, where required, by still larger-scale maps of the most important or densely populated areas. The governing principle is that by turning the pages of the atlas, the reader moves steadily from north to south through each continent, with each map overlapping its neighbours.

MAP PRESENTATION

With very few exceptions (for example, for the Arctic and Antarctica), the maps are drawn with north at the top, regardless of whether they are presented upright or sideways on the page. In the borders will be found the map title; a locator diagram showing the area covered; continuation arrows showing the page numbers for maps of adjacent areas; the scale; the projection used; the degrees of latitude and longitude; and the letters and figures used in the index for locating place names and geographical features. Physical relief maps also have a height reference panel identifying the colours used for each layer of contouring.

MAP SYMBOLS

Each map contains a vast amount of detail which can only be conveyed clearly and accurately by the use of symbols. Points and circles of varying sizes locate and identify the relative importance of towns and cities; different styles of type are employed for administrative, geographical and regional place names to aid identification. A variety of pictorial symbols denote landforms such as glaciers, marshes and coral reefs, and man-made structures including roads, railways, airports and canals. International borders are shown by red lines. Where neighbouring countries are in dispute, for example in parts of the Middle East, the maps show the *de facto* boundary between nations, regardless of the legal or historical situation. The symbols are explained on the front endpaper of the atlas.

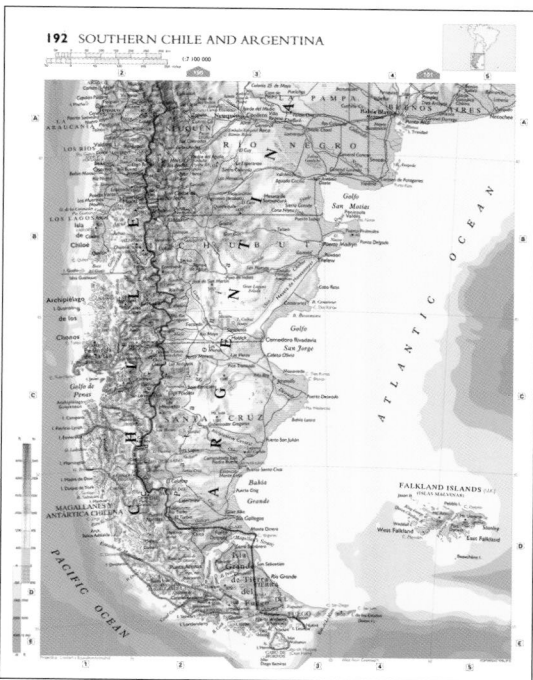

MAP SCALES

1:16 000 000
1 inch = 252 statute miles

The scale of each map is given in the numerical form known as the 'representative fraction'. The first figure is always one, signifying one unit of distance on the map; the second figure, usually in millions, is the number by which the map unit must be multiplied to give the equivalent distance on the Earth's surface. Calculations can easily be made in centimetres and kilometres, by dividing the Earth units figure by 100 000 (i.e. deleting the last five 0s). Thus 1:1 000 000 means 1 cm = 10 km. The calculation for inches and miles is more laborious, but 1 000 000 divided by 63 360 (the number of inches in a mile) shows that 1:1 000 000 means approximately 1 inch = 16 miles. The table below provides distance equivalents for scales down to 1:50 000 000.

LARGE SCALE		
1:1 000 000	1 cm = 10 km	1 inch = 16 miles
1:2 500 000	1 cm = 25 km	1 inch = 39.5 miles
1:5 000 000	1 cm = 50 km	1 inch = 79 miles
1:6 000 000	1 cm = 60 km	1 inch = 95 miles
1:8 000 000	1 cm = 80 km	1 inch = 126 miles
1:10 000 000	1 cm = 100 km	1 inch = 158 miles
1:15 000 000	1 cm = 150 km	1 inch = 237 miles
1:20 000 000	1 cm = 200 km	1 inch = 316 miles
1:50 000 000	1 cm = 500 km	1 inch = 790 miles
SMALL SCALE		

MEASURING DISTANCES

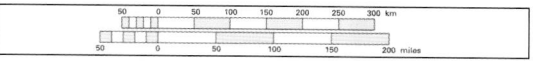

Although each map is accompanied by a scale bar, distances cannot always be measured with confidence because of the distortions involved in portraying the curved surface of the Earth on a flat page. As a general rule, the larger the map scale (that is, the lower the number of Earth units in the representative fraction), the more accurate and reliable will be the distance measured. On small-scale maps such as those of the world and of entire continents, measurement may only be accurate

along the 'standard parallels', or central axes, and should not be attempted without considering the map projection.

MAP PROJECTIONS

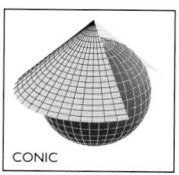  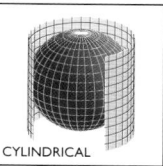

Unlike a globe, no flat map can give a true scale representation of the world in terms of area, shape and position of every region. Each of the numerous systems that have been devised for projecting the curved surface of the Earth on to a flat page involves the sacrifice of accuracy in one or more of these elements. The variations in shape and position of landmasses such as Alaska, Greenland and Australia, for example, can be quite dramatic when different projections are compared. For this atlas, the guiding principle has been to select projections that involve the least distortion of size and distance. The projection used for each map is noted in the border. Most fall into one of three categories – conic, azimuthal or cylindrical – whose basic concepts are shown above. Each involves plotting the forms of the Earth's surface on a grid of latitude and longitude lines, which may be shown as parallels, curves or radiating spokes.

LATITUDE AND LONGITUDE

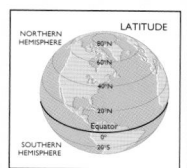 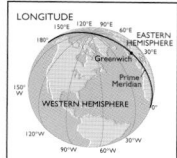 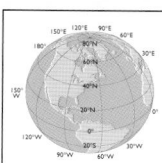

Accurate positioning of individual points on the Earth's surface is made possible by reference to the geometrical system of latitude and longitude. Latitude *parallels* are drawn west–east around the Earth and numbered by degrees north and south of the equator, which is designated 0° of latitude. Longitude *meridians* are drawn north–south and numbered by degrees east and west of the *prime meridian*, 0° of longitude, which passes through Greenwich in England. By referring to these co-ordinates and their subdivisions of minutes (1/60th of a degree) and seconds (1/60th of a minute), any place on Earth can be located to within a few hundred metres. Latitude and longitude are indicated by blue lines on the maps; they are straight or curved according to the projection employed. Reference to these lines is the easiest way of determining the relative positions of places on different maps, and for plotting compass directions.

NAME FORMS

For ease of reference, both English and local name forms appear in the atlas. Oceans, seas and countries are shown in English throughout the atlas; country names may be abbreviated to their commonly accepted form (for example, Germany, not The Federal Republic of Germany). Conventional English forms are also used for place names on the smaller-scale maps of the continents. However, local name forms are used on all large-scale and regional maps, with the English form given in brackets only for important cities – the large-scale map of Russia and Northern Asia thus shows Moskva (Moscow). For countries which do not use a Roman script, place names have been transcribed according to the systems adopted by the British and US Geographic Names Authorities. For China, the Pin Yin system has been used, with some more widely known forms appearing in brackets, as with Beijing (Peking). Both English and local names appear in the index, the English form being cross-referenced to the local form.

CONTENTS

WORLD STATISTICS

COUNTRIES 8

CITIES 9

CLIMATE 10–11

PHYSICAL DIMENSIONS 12–13

IMAGES OF EARTH

LONDON, UNITED KINGDOM 16

AMSTERDAM, NETHERLANDS 17

ROME, ITALY 18

ISTANBUL, TURKEY 19

MUMBAI, INDIA 20

SINGAPORE CITY, SINGAPORE 21

BEIJING, CHINA 22

TOKYO, JAPAN 23

NOUAKCHOTT, MAURITANIA 24

CAIRO, EGYPT 25

JUBA, SOUTH SUDAN 26

CAPE TOWN, SOUTH AFRICA 27

SYDNEY, AUSTRALIA 28

CHRISTCHURCH, NEW ZEALAND 29

VANCOUVER, CANADA 30

QUÉBEC, CANADA 31

NEW YORK CITY, USA 32

CHICAGO, USA 33

SAN FRANCISCO, USA 34

LAS VEGAS, USA 35

MEXICO CITY, MEXICO 36

PANAMA CANAL, PANAMA 37

SANTIAGO, CHILE 38

RIO DE JANEIRO, BRAZIL 39

OCEAN SEAFLOORS

ARCTIC OCEAN SEAFLOOR 41

ATLANTIC OCEAN SEAFLOOR 42–43

PACIFIC OCEAN SEAFLOOR 44–45

INDIAN OCEAN SEAFLOOR 46

SOUTHERN OCEAN SEAFLOOR 47

WORLD MAPS

THE WORLD: PHYSICAL 50–51
1:84 000 000

THE WORLD: POLITICAL 52–53
1:84 000 000

ARCTIC OCEAN 54
1:31 100 000

ANTARCTICA 55
1:31 100 000

ATLANTIC OCEAN 56
1:45 000 000

GREENLAND 57
1:11 100 000

EUROPE

EUROPE: PHYSICAL 58
1:17 800 000

EUROPE: POLITICAL 59
1:17 800 000

SCANDINAVIA 60–61
1:5 300 000
Iceland 1:5 300 000
Færoe Islands 1:5 300 000

DENMARK AND SOUTHERN SWEDEN 62–63
1:2 200 000

IRELAND 64
1:1 800 000

SCOTLAND 65
1:1 800 000
Orkney Islands 1:1 800 000
Shetland Islands 1:1 800 000

ENGLAND AND WALES 66–67
1:1 800 000
Isles of Scilly 1:1 800 000

BRITISH ISLES 68
1:4 400 000

NETHERLANDS, BELGIUM
AND LUXEMBOURG 69
1:2 200 000

NORTHERN FRANCE 70–71
1:2 200 000

SOUTHERN FRANCE 72–73
1:2 200 000

CENTRAL EUROPE 74–75
1:4 400 000

GERMANY AND SWITZERLAND 76–77
1:2 200 000

AUSTRIA, CZECH REPUBLIC
AND SLOVAK REPUBLIC 78–79
1:2 200 000

HUNGARY, ROMANIA AND
THE LOWER DANUBE 80–81
1:2 200 000

POLAND AND THE SOUTHERN BALTIC 82–83
1:2 200 000

BALTIC STATES, BELARUS
AND UKRAINE 84–85
1:4 400 000

THE VOLGA BASIN AND
THE CAUCASUS 86–87
1:4 400 000

WESTERN SPAIN AND PORTUGAL 88–89
1:2 200 000

EASTERN SPAIN 90–91
1:2 200 000
Menorca 1:2 200 000

NORTHERN ITALY, SLOVENIA
AND CROATIA 92–93
1:2 200 000

SOUTHERN ITALY 94–95
1:2 200 000

THE BALKANS 96–97
1:2 200 000

SOUTHERN GREECE AND
WESTERN TURKEY 98–99
1:2 200 000

THE BALEARICS, THE CANARIES
AND MADEIRA 100
1:900 000 / 1:1 800 000

MALTA, CRETE, CORFU, RHODES
AND CYPRUS 101
1:900 000 / 1:1 200 000

ASIA

ASIA: PHYSICAL 102
1:44 400 000

ASIA: POLITICAL 103
1:44 400 000

TURKEY AND TRANSCAUCASIA 104–105
1:4 400 000

RUSSIA AND NORTHERN ASIA 106–107
1:17 800 000

KAZAKHSTAN AND CENTRAL ASIA 108–109
1:8 900 000

CHINA AND THE FAR EAST 110–111
1:13 300 000
Hong Kong, Macau and Shenzhen 1:890 000

JAPAN **112–113**
1:4 400 000
Ryukyu Islands 1:4 400 000

NORTHERN CHINA AND KOREA **114–115**
1:5 300 000

SOUTHERN CHINA AND TAIWAN **116–117**
1:5 300 000
Hainan 1:5 300 000

INDONESIA AND THE PHILIPPINES **118–119**
1:11 100 000
Java and Madura 1:6 700 000
Bali 1:1 800 000

MAINLAND SOUTH-EAST ASIA **120–121**
1:5 300 000
Ko Phuket 1:900 000
Ko Samui 1:900 000
Pinang 1:900 000
Singapore 1:900 000

SOUTH ASIA **122–123**
1:8 900 000

NORTHERN INDIA, PAKISTAN
AND NEPAL **124–125**
1:5 300 000
Jammu and Kashmir 1:5 300 000

SOUTHERN INDIA AND SRI LANKA **126–127**
1:5 300 000
Lakshadweep Islands 1:5 300 000
Andaman and Nicobar Islands 1:5 300 000

THE MIDDLE EAST **128–129**
1:6 200 000

THE NEAR EAST **130**
1:2 200 000

ARABIA AND THE HORN OF AFRICA **131**
1:13 300 000

AFRICA

AFRICA: PHYSICAL **132**
1:37 300 000

AFRICA: POLITICAL **133**
1:37 300 000

NORTHERN AFRICA **134–135**
1:13 300 000
Azores 1:13 300 000
Cape Verde Islands 1:8 900 000

MOROCCO, ALGERIA AND TUNISIA **136**
1:7 100 000

EGYPT **137**
1:7 100 000

WEST AFRICA **138–139**
1:7 100 000

CENTRAL AND SOUTHERN AFRICA **140–141**
1:13 300 000
Seychelles 1:2 200 000
Réunion 1:2 200 000
Mauritius 1:2 200 000
Comoros 1:7 100 000
Madagascar 1:13 300 000

EAST AFRICA **142–143**
1:7 100 000

SOUTHERN AFRICA **144–145**
1:7 100 000

INDIAN OCEAN **146**
1:45 000 000

AUSTRALIA AND OCEANIA

AUSTRALIA AND OCEANIA:
PHYSICAL AND POLITICAL **147**
1:44 400 000

WESTERN AUSTRALIA **148–149**
1:7 100 000

EASTERN AUSTRALIA **150–151**
1:7 100 000
Whitsunday Islands 1:2 200 000
Tasmania 1:7 100 000
Torres Strait 1:7 100 000

SOUTH-EASTERN AUSTRALIA **152–153**
1:3 500 000

NEW ZEALAND – NORTH ISLAND **154**
1:3 100 000
Fiji 1:5 300 000

NEW ZEALAND – SOUTH ISLAND **155**
1:3 100 000
Tahiti and Moorea 1:900 000
Chatham Islands 1:3 100 000

PACIFIC OCEAN **156–157**
1:48 000 000

NORTH AMERICA

NORTH AMERICA: PHYSICAL **158**
1:31 100 000

NORTH AMERICA: POLITICAL **159**
1:31 100 000

CANADA **160–161**
1:13 300 000
Northern Canada 1:13 300 000

WESTERN CANADA **162–163**
1:6 200 000

EASTERN CANADA **164–165**
1:6 200 000

UNITED STATES **166–167**
1:13 300 000
Hawai'i 1:13 300 000
Alaska 1:13 300 000

UNITED STATES – WEST **168–169**
1:6 250 000

CENTRAL AND SOUTHERN
CALIFORNIA AND
WESTERN WASHINGTON **170–171**
1:2 200 000

UNITED STATES – MIDWEST
AND NORTH-EAST **172–173**
1:6 250 000

NORTH-EASTERN UNITED STATES **174–175**
1:2 200 000

UNITED STATES – SOUTH **176–177**
1:6 250 000

SOUTH-EASTERN UNITED STATES **178–179**
1:2 200 000

MEXICO **180–181**
1:7 100 000

CENTRAL AMERICA AND
THE WEST INDIES **182–183**
1:7 100 000
Jamaica 1:2 700 000
Guadeloupe 1:1 800 000
Martinique 1:1 800 000
Puerto Rico 1:2 700 000
Virgin Islands 1:1 800 000
St Lucia 1:890 000
Barbados 1:890 000

SOUTH AMERICA

SOUTH AMERICA: PHYSICAL **184**
1:31 100 000

SOUTH AMERICA: POLITICAL **185**
1:31 100 000

SOUTH AMERICA – NORTH **186–187**
1:14 200 000
Trinidad and Tobago 1:2 200 000

PERU AND THE CENTRAL ANDES **188**
1:7 100 000

NORTH-EASTERN BRAZIL **189**
1:7 100 000

CENTRAL SOUTH AMERICA **190–191**
1:7 100 000

SOUTHERN CHILE AND ARGENTINA **192**
1:7 100 000

INDEX TO WORLD
MAPS **193–288**

WORLD STATISTICS: COUNTRIES

This alphabetical list includes the principal countries and territories of the world. If a territory is not completely independent, the country it is associated with is named. The area figures give the total area of land, inland water and ice. The population figures are 2012 estimates where available. The annual income is the Gross Domestic Product per capita in US dollars. The figures are the latest available, usually 2012 estimates.

Country/Territory	Area km² Thousands	Area miles² Thousands	Population Thousands	Capital	Annual Income US $
Afghanistan	652	252	30,420	Kabul	1,000
Albania	28.7	11.1	3,003	Tirana	8,000
Algeria	2,382	920	37,367	Algiers	7,500
American Samoa (US)	0.20	0.08	55	Pago Pago	8,000
Andorra	0.47	0.18	85	Andorra La Vella	37,200
Angola	1,247	481	18,056	Luanda	6,200
Anguilla (UK)	0.10	0.04	15	The Valley	12,200
Antigua & Barbuda	0.44	0.17	89	St John's	17,500
Argentina	2,780	1,074	42,192	Buenos Aires	18,200
Armenia	29.8	11.5	2,970	Yerevan	5,600
Aruba (Netherlands)	0.19	0.07	108	Oranjestad	21,800
Australia	7,741	2,989	22,016	Canberra	42,400
Austria	83.9	32.4	8,220	Vienna	42,500
Azerbaijan	86.6	33.4	9,494	Baku	10,700
Azores (Portugal)	2.2	0.86	236	Ponta Delgada	15,000
Bahamas	13.9	5.4	316	Nassau	31,300
Bahrain	0.69	0.27	1,248	Manama	28,200
Bangladesh	144	55.6	161,084	Dhaka	2,000
Barbados	0.43	0.17	288	Bridgetown	25,500
Belarus	208	80.2	9,644	Minsk	16,000
Belgium	30.5	11.8	10,438	Brussels	38,100
Belize	23.0	8.9	328	Belmopan	8,400
Benin	113	43.5	9,599	Porto-Novo	1,700
Bermuda (UK)	0.05	0.02	69	Hamilton	69,900
Bhutan	47.0	18.1	717	Thimphu	6,500
Bolivia	1,099	424	10,290	La Paz/Sucre	5,000
Bosnia-Herzegovina	51.2	19.8	3,879	Sarajevo	8,300
Botswana	582	225	2,098	Gaborone	16,800
Brazil	8,514	3,287	199,321	Brasília	12,000
Brunei	5.8	2.2	409	Bandar Seri Begawan	50,500
Bulgaria	111	42.8	7,038	Sofia	14,200
Burkina Faso	274	106	17,275	Ouagadougou	1,400
Burma (Myanmar)	677	261	54,585	Rangoon/Naypyidaw	1,400
Burundi	27.8	10.7	10,557	Bujumbura	600
Cambodia	181	69.9	14,953	Phnom Penh	2,400
Cameroon	475	184	20,130	Yaoundé	2,300
Canada	9,971	3,850	34,300	Ottawa	41,500
Canary Is. (Spain)	7.2	2.8	1,682	Las Palmas/Santa Cruz	19,900
Cape Verde Is.	4.0	1.6	524	Praia	4,100
Cayman Is. (UK)	0.26	0.10	53	George Town	43,800
Central African Republic	623	241	5,057	Bangui	800
Chad	1,284	496	10,976	Ndjaména	2,000
Chile	757	292	17,067	Santiago	18,400
China	9,597	3,705	1,343,240	Beijing	9,100
Colombia	1,139	440	45,239	Bogotá	10,700
Comoros	2.2	0.86	737	Moroni	1,300
Congo	342	132	4,366	Brazzaville	4,700
Congo (Dem. Rep. of the)	2,345	905	73,599	Kinshasa	400
Cook Is. (NZ)	0.24	0.09	11	Avarua	9,100
Costa Rica	51.1	19.7	4,636	San José	12,600
Croatia	56.5	21.8	4,480	Zagreb	18,100
Cuba	111	42.8	11,075	Havana	9,900
Curaçao (Netherlands)	0.44	0.17	146	Willemstad	15,000
Cyprus	9.3	3.6	1,138	Nicosia	26,900
Czech Republic	78.9	30.5	10,177	Prague	27,200
Denmark	43.1	16.6	5,543	Copenhagen	37,700
Djibouti	23.2	9.0	774	Djibouti	2,700
Dominica	0.75	0.29	73	Roseau	14,600
Dominican Republic	48.5	18.7	10,089	Santo Domingo	9,600
East Timor	14.9	5.7	1,144	Dili	9,500
Ecuador	284	109	15,224	Quito	8,800
Egypt	1,001	387	83,688	Cairo	6,600
El Salvador	21.0	8.1	6,091	San Salvador	7,700
Equatorial Guinea	28.1	10.8	685	Malabo	20,200
Eritrea	118	45.4	6,086	Asmara	800
Estonia	45.1	17.4	1,275	Tallinn	21,200
Ethiopia	1,104	426	91,196	Addis Ababa	1,200
Falkland Is. (UK)	12.2	4.7	3	Stanley	55,400
Faroe Is. (Denmark)	1.4	0.54	49	Tórshavn	30,500
Fiji	18.3	7.1	890	Suva	4,800
Finland	338	131	5,263	Helsinki	36,500
France	552	213	65,631	Paris	35,500
French Guiana (France)	90.0	34.7	203	Cayenne	8,300
French Polynesia (France)	4.0	1.5	275	Papeete	18,000
Gabon	268	103	1,608	Libreville	17,300
Gambia, The	11.3	4.4	1,840	Banjul	1,900
Georgia	69.7	26.9	4,571	Tbilisi	5,900
Germany	357	138	81,306	Berlin	39,100
Ghana	239	92.1	24,652	Accra	3,300
Gibraltar (UK)	0.006	0.002	29	Gibraltar Town	43,000
Greece	132	50.9	10,768	Athens	25,100
Greenland (Denmark)	2,176	840	58	Nuuk	38,400
Grenada	0.34	0.13	109	St George's	14,100
Guadeloupe (France)	1.7	0.66	453	Basse-Terre	7,900
Guam (US)	0.55	0.21	160	Agana	15,000
Guatemala	109	42.0	14,099	Guatemala City	5,200
Guinea	246	94.9	10,885	Conakry	1,100
Guinea-Bissau	36.1	13.9	1,629	Bissau	1,100
Guyana	215	83.0	742	Georgetown	8,000
Haiti	27.8	10.7	9,802	Port-au-Prince	1,300
Honduras	112	43.3	8,297	Tegucigalpa	4,600
Hungary	93.0	35.9	9,958	Budapest	19,800
Iceland	103	39.8	313	Reykjavik	39,400
India	3,287	1,269	1,205,074	New Delhi	3,900
Indonesia	1,905	735	248,645	Jakarta	5,000
Iran	1,648	636	78,869	Tehran	13,100
Iraq	438	169	31,129	Baghdad	4,600
Ireland	70.3	27.1	4,722	Dublin	41,700
Israel	20.6	8.0	7,591	Jerusalem	32,200
Italy	301	116	61,261	Rome	30,100
Ivory Coast (Côte d'Ivoire)	322	125	21,952	Yamoussoukro	1,700
Jamaica	11.0	4.2	2,889	Kingston	9,100
Japan	378	146	127,368	Tokyo	36,200
Jordan	89.3	34.5	6,509	Amman	6,000
Kazakhstan	2,725	1,052	17,522	Astana	13,900
Kenya	580	224	43,013	Nairobi	1,800
Kiribati	0.73	0.28	102	Tarawa	5,900
Korea, North	121	46.5	24,589	Pyŏngyang	1,800
Korea, South	99.3	38.3	48,861	Seoul	32,400
Kosovo	10.9	4.2	1,837	Pristina	7,400
Kuwait	17.8	6.9	2,646	Kuwait City	43,800
Kyrgyzstan	200	77.2	5,497	Bishkek	2,400

Country/Territory	Area km² Thousands	Area miles² Thousands	Population Thousands	Capital	Annual Income US $
Laos	237	91.4	6,586	Vientiane	3,000
Latvia	64.6	24.9	2,192	Riga	18,100
Lebanon	10.4	4.0	4,140	Beirut	15,900
Lesotho	30.4	11.7	1,930	Maseru	2,000
Liberia	111	43.0	3,888	Monrovia	700
Libya	1,760	679	5,613	Tripoli	13,300
Liechtenstein	0.16	0.06	37	Vaduz	89,400
Lithuania	65.2	25.2	3,526	Vilnius	20,100
Luxembourg	2.6	1.0	509	Luxembourg	80,700
Macedonia (FYROM)	25.7	9.9	2,082	Skopje	10,900
Madagascar	587	227	22,005	Antananarivo	1,000
Madeira (Portugal)	0.78	0.30	241	Funchal	25,800
Malawi	118	45.7	16,323	Lilongwe	900
Malaysia	330	127	29,180	Kuala Lumpur/Putrajaya	16,900
Maldives	0.30	0.12	394	Malé	8,700
Mali	1,240	479	15,494	Bamako	1,100
Malta	0.32	0.12	410	Valletta	26,100
Marshall Is.	0.18	0.07	68	Majuro	2,500
Martinique (France)	1.1	0.43	436	Fort-de-France	14,400
Mauritania	1,026	396	3,359	Nouakchott	2,100
Mauritius	2.0	0.79	1,313	Port Louis	15,600
Mayotte (France)	0.37	0.14	231	Mamoudzou	4,900
Mexico	1,958	756	114,975	Mexico City	15,300
Micronesia, Fed. States of	0.70	0.27	106	Palikir	2,200
Moldova	33.9	13.1	3,657	Kishinev	3,500
Monaco	0.001	0.0004	31	Monaco	63,400
Mongolia	1,567	605	3,180	Ulan Bator	5,400
Montenegro	14.0	5.4	657	Podgorica	11,700
Montserrat (UK)	0.10	0.39	5	Brades	8,500
Morocco	447	172	32,309	Rabat	5,300
Mozambique	802	309	23,516	Maputo	1,200
Namibia	824	318	2,166	Windhoek	7,800
Nauru	0.02	0.008	9	Yaren	5,000
Nepal	147	56.8	29,891	Katmandu	1,300
Netherlands	41.5	16.0	16,731	Amsterdam/The Hague	42,300
New Caledonia (France)	18.6	7.2	260	Nouméa	15,000
New Zealand	271	104	4,328	Wellington	28,800
Nicaragua	130	50.2	5,728	Managua	3,300
Niger	1,267	489	16,345	Niamey	900
Nigeria	924	357	170,124	Abuja	2,700
Northern Mariana Is. (US)	0.46	0.18	51	Saipan	12,500
Norway	324	125	4,707	Oslo	55,300
Oman	310	119	3,090	Muscat	28,500
Pakistan	796	307	190,291	Islamabad	2,900
Palau	0.46	0.18	21	Melekeok	8,100
Panama	75.5	29.2	3,510	Panamá	15,300
Papua New Guinea	463	179	6,310	Port Moresby	2,700
Paraguay	407	157	6,542	Asunción	6,100
Peru	1,285	496	29,550	Lima	10,700
Philippines	300	116	103,775	Manila	4,300
Poland	323	125	38,415	Warsaw	21,000
Portugal	88.8	34.3	10,781	Lisbon	23,000
Puerto Rico (US)	8.9	3.4	3,691	San Juan	16,300
Qatar	11.0	4.2	1,952	Doha	102,800
Réunion (France)	2.5	0.97	788	St-Denis	6,200
Romania	238	92.0	21,849	Bucharest	12,800
Russia	17,075	6,593	142,518	Moscow	17,700
Rwanda	26.3	10.2	11,690	Kigali	1,400
St Kitts & Nevis	0.26	0.10	51	Basseterre	15,500
St Lucia	0.54	0.21	162	Castries	13,300
St Vincent & Grenadines	0.39	0.15	104	Kingstown	11,900
Samoa	2.8	1.1	194	Apia	6,200
San Marino	0.06	0.02	32	San Marino	36,200
São Tomé & Príncipe	0.96	0.37	183	São Tomé	2,300
Saudi Arabia	2,150	830	26,535	Riyadh	25,700
Senegal	197	76.0	12,970	Dakar	1,900
Serbia	77.5	29.9	7,277	Belgrade	10,500
Seychelles	0.46	0.18	90	Victoria	26,200
Sierra Leone	71.7	27.7	5,486	Freetown	1,400
Singapore	0.68	0.26	5,353	Singapore City	60,900
Slovak Republic	49.0	18.9	5,483	Bratislava	24,300
Slovenia	20.3	7.8	1,997	Ljubljana	28,600
Solomon Is.	28.9	11.2	585	Honiara	3,400
Somalia	638	246	10,086	Mogadishu	600
South Africa	1,221	471	48,810	Cape Town/Pretoria	11,300
Spain	498	192	47,043	Madrid	30,400
Sri Lanka	65.6	25.3	21,481	Colombo	6,100
Sudan	1,886	728	34,207	Khartoum	2,400
Sudan, South	620	239	10,625	Juba	900
Suriname	163	63.0	560	Paramaribo	12,300
Swaziland	17.4	6.7	1,387	Mbabane	5,300
Sweden	450	174	9,104	Stockholm	41,700
Switzerland	41.3	15.9	7,926	Berne	45,300
Syria	185	71.5	22,531	Damascus	5,100
Taiwan	36.0	13.9	23,235	Taipei	38,500
Tajikistan	143	55.3	7,768	Dushanbe	2,200
Tanzania	945	365	46,913	Dodoma	1,700
Thailand	513	198	67,091	Bangkok	10,000
Togo	56.8	21.9	6,961	Lomé	1,100
Tonga	0.65	0.25	106	Nuku'alofa	7,500
Trinidad & Tobago	5.1	2.0	1,226	Port of Spain	20,400
Tunisia	164	63.2	10,733	Tunis	9,700
Turkey	775	299	79,749	Ankara	15,000
Turkmenistan	488	188	5,055	Ashkhabad	8,500
Turks & Caicos Is. (UK)	0.43	0.17	46	Cockburn Town	11,500
Tuvalu	0.03	0.01	11	Fongafale	3,300
Uganda	241	93.1	33,641	Kampala	1,400
Ukraine	604	233	44,854	Kiev	7,600
United Arab Emirates	83.6	32.3	5,314	Abu Dhabi	49,000
United Kingdom	242	93.4	63,047	London	36,700
United States of America	9,629	3,718	313,847	Washington, DC	49,800
Uruguay	175	67.6	3,316	Montevideo	15,800
Uzbekistan	447	173	28,394	Tashkent	3,500
Vanuatu	12.2	4.7	256	Port-Vila	4,900
Venezuela	912	352	28,048	Caracas	13,200
Vietnam	332	128	91,519	Hanoi	3,500
Virgin Is. (UK)	0.15	0.06	31	Road Town	38,500
Virgin Is. (US)	0.35	0.13	105	Charlotte Amalie	14,500
Wallis & Futuna Is. (France)	0.20	0.08	15	Mata-Utu	3,800
Yemen	528	204	24,772	Sana'	2,200
Zambia	753	291	13,817	Lusaka	1,700
Zimbabwe	391	151	12,620	Harare	500

WORLD STATISTICS: CITIES

This list shows the principal cities with more than 850,000 inhabitants. The figures are taken from the most recent census or estimate available, usually 2012, and as far as possible are the population of the metropolitan area or urban agglomeration. The list includes Metropolitan Statistical Areas from the United States 2010 Census. All the figures are in thousands. Local name forms have been used for the smaller cities (for example, Thessaloniki).

AFGHANISTAN
Kabul 3,097

ALGERIA
Algiers 2,916

ANGOLA
Luanda 5,068
Huambo 1,098

ARGENTINA
Buenos Aires 13,528
Córdoba 1,556
Rosario 1,283
Mendoza 1,072
San Miguel de Tucumán 868

ARMENIA
Yerevan 1,116

AUSTRALIA
Sydney 4,543
Melbourne 3,961
Brisbane 2,039
Perth 1,649
Adelaide 1,198

AUSTRIA
Vienna 1,720

AZERBAIJAN
Baku 2,123

BANGLADESH
Dhaka 15,391
Chittagong 5,239
Khulna 1,781
Rajshahi 932

BELARUS
Minsk 1,861

BELGIUM
Brussels 1,949
Antwerpen 959

BENIN
Cotonou 924

BOLIVIA
Santa Cruz 1,719
La Paz 1,715

BRAZIL
São Paulo 20,395
Rio de Janeiro 11,990
Belo Horizonte 5,910
Pôrto Alegre 4,115
Salvador 3,940
Recife 3,890
Fortaleza 3,740
Curitiba 3,490
Campinas 2,835
Brasília 2,330
Belém 2,205
Goiânia 2,155
Vitória 1,825
Santos 1,820
Manaus 1,802
Natal 1,315
São Luís 1,275
Guarulhos 1,222
Maceió 1,190
Joinville 1,065
Florianópolis 1,040
João Pessoa 1,010
Teresina 911
Duque de Caxias 855

BULGARIA
Sofia 1,174

BURKINA FASO
Ouagadougou 2,053

BURMA (MYANMAR)
Rangoon 4,457
Mandalay 1,063
Naypyidaw 1,060

CAMBODIA
Phnom Penh 1,550

CAMEROON
Douala 2,449
Yaoundé 2,432

CANADA
Toronto 5,573
Montréal 3,856
Vancouver 2,267
Calgary 1,216
Ottawa 1,208
Edmonton 1,142

CHAD
Ndjamena 1,079

CHILE
Santiago 6,355
Valparaiso 931

CHINA
Shanghai 20,208
Beijing 15,594
Guangzhou, Guangdong 10,849
Shenzhen 10,630
Chongqing 9,977
Wuhan 9,158
Tianjin 8,744
Dongguan, Guangdong 7,280
Hong Kong 7,122
Chengdu 6,670
Foshan 6,486
Nanjing, Jiangsu 5,866
Harbin 5,687
Shenyang 5,568
Hangzhou 5,448
Xi'an, Shaanxi 4,975
Shantou 4,175
Zhengzhou 3,964
Qingdao 3,797
Jinan, Shandong 3,697
Changchun 3,694
Taiyuan, Shanxi 3,495
Kunming 3,472
Suzhou, Jiangsu 3,463
Wuxi, Jiangsu 3,366
Dalian 3,335
Changsha 3,335
Ürümqi 3,123
Hefei 3,012
Fuzhou, Fujian 2,897
Xiamen 2,880
Zhongshan 2,862
Shijiazhuang 2,841
Zibo 2,797
Ningbo 2,755
Wenzhou 2,733
Lanzhou 2,555
Guiyang 2,525
Nanchang 2,411
Changzhou, Jiangsu 2,405
Jinxi 2,268
Xuzhou 2,242
Nanning 2,136
Nanchong 2,046
Wanxian 1,963
Baotou 1,953
Jilin 1,942
Tangshan 1,927
Huzhou 1,856
Weifang 1,752
Anshan 1,694
Tianmen 1,676
Shangqiu 1,650
Lu'an 1,647
Haikou 1,624
Qiqihar 1,616
Daqing 1,603
Yangzhou 1,603
Xinghua 1,587
Luoyang 1,575
Pingxiang 1,562
Yantai 1,557
Xiantao 1,528
Hohhot 1,499
Linyi 1,454
Xianyang 1,450
Luzhou 1,447
Neijiang 1,441
Huainan 1,436
Changde 1,429
Suining, Sichuan 1,401
Datong 1,390
Liuzhou 1,390
Fushun 1,379
Xintai 1,334
Yancheng 1,330
Heze 1,318
Yiyang 1,318
Huai'an 1,316
Handan 1,306
Tai'an 1,276
Suqian 1,258
Jining, Shandong 1,246
Chifeng 1,238
Jingmen 1,228
Nanyang 1,227
Yuzhou 1,226
Xining 1,225
Zaozhuang 1,211
Zaoyang 1,210
Tianshui 1,199
Yueyang 1,184
Yongzhou 1,182
Baoding 1,177
Mudanjiang 1,171
Liupanshui 1,149
Anyang 1,144
Leshan 1,143
Hengyang 1,135
Jiangmen 1,130
Xiaoshan 1,130
Yixing 1,129
Yinchuan 1,119
Quanzhou 1,097
Zigong 1,087
Putian 1,084
Zhangjiakou 1,072
Jinzhou 1,070
Fuyu 1,068
Jixi 1,067
Yulin 1,060
Mianyang 1,052
Zhuzhou 1,047
Xinyang 1,045
Pingdingshan 1,041
Zhanjiang 1,041
Xinyi, Jiangsu 1,022
Lianyungang 1,017
Linqing 1,009
Jiamusi 1,006
Xiangfan 1,006
Huaibei 1,005
Guilin 992
Dongying 989
Benxi 980
Xiangtan 979
Puning 945
Xiangxiang 936
Zhangjiagang 936
Baoji 933
Xinyu 932
Yichun, Heilongjiang 916
Qinhuangdao 913
Yichun, Jiangxi 890
Zhaotong 879
Yuyao 876
Jinzhou 865
Anshun 864
Shaoguan 856
Xuanzhou 851

COLOMBIA
Bogotá 8,743
Medellín 3,694
Cali 2,453
Barranquilla 1,900
Bucaramanga 1,120
Cartagena 988

CONGO
Brazzaville 1,611

CONGO (DEM. REP. OF THE)
Kinshasa 8,798
Lubumbashi 1,556
Mbuji-Mayi 1,504
Kananga 888

COSTA RICA
San José 1,511

CROATIA
Zagreb 1,067

CUBA
Havana 2,116

CZECH REPUBLIC
Prague 1,276

DENMARK
Copenhagen 1,206

DOMINICAN REPUBLIC
Santo Domingo 2,191
Santiago de los Caballeros 804

ECUADOR
Guayaquil 2,287
Quito 1,622

EGYPT
Cairo 11,169
Alexandria 4,494
Shubrâ el Kheima 937

EL SALVADOR
San Salvador 1,605

ETHIOPIA
Addis Ababa 2,979

FINLAND
Helsinki 1,134

FRANCE
Paris 10,620
Marseilles 1,489
Lyons 1,488
Lille 1,042
Nice 991
Toulouse 933
Bordeaux 852

GEORGIA
Tbilisi 1,121

GERMANY
Berlin 3,462
Hamburg 1,796
Munich 1,364
Cologne 1,006

GHANA
Accra 2,573
Kumasi 2,019

GREECE
Athens 3,414
Thessaloniki 883

GUATEMALA
Guatemala City 1,168

GUINEA
Conakry 1,786

HAITI
Port-au-Prince 2,207

HONDURAS
Tegucigalpa 1,088

HUNGARY
Budapest 1,737

INDIA
Delhi 22,654
Mumbai 19,744
Kolkata 14,402
Chennai 8,784
Bangalore 8,614
Hyderabad 7,837
Ahmedabad 6,425
Pune 5,100
Surat 4,661
Jaipur 3,102
Kanpur 2,928
Lucknow 2,926
Nagpur 2,511
Indore 2,188
Coimbatore 2,180
Patna 2,059
Bhopal 1,900
Vadodara 1,829
Agra 1,763
Vishakhapatnam 1,746
Ludhiana 1,622
Kochi 1,620
Nashik 1,579
Vijayawada 1,511
Madurai 1,472
Varanasi 1,443
Meerut 1,434
Rajkot 1,406
Jamshedpur 1,346
Faridabad 1,330
Srinagar 1,285
Ghaziabad 1,277
Jabalpur 1,273
Asansol 1,248
Allahabad 1,223
Aurangabad 1,201
Dhanbad 1,200
Amritsar 1,190
Solapur 1,155
Jodhpur 1,149
Raipur 1,140
Ranchi 1,137
Gwalior 1,111
Guwahati 1,075
Bhilainagar-Durg 1,069
Chandigarh 1,034
Thiruvananthapuram 1,030
Tiruchirapalli 1,028
Kota 1,013
Trivandrum 1,010
Calicut 1,007
Mysore 991
Bareilly 990
Tiruppur 982
Hubli-Dharwad 950
Salem 925
Aligarh 919
Moradabad 900
Bhubaneswar 891
Jalandhar 880
Bhiwandi 859
Jammu 857

INDONESIA
Jakarta 9,769
Surabaya 2,787
Bandung 2,429
Medan 2,118
Semarang 1,573
Palembang 1,455
Makassar 1,387
Batam 1,034
Bogor 978
Pekanbaru 955
Bandar Lampung 900
Denpasar 850

IRAN
Tehran 7,304
Mashhad 2,713
Karaj 1,635
Esfahan 1,781
Tabriz 1,509
Shiraz 1,321
Ahvaz 1,082
Qom 1,065
Kermanshah 851

IRAQ
Baghdad 6,036
Mosul 1,494
Irbil 1,039
Basra 942
As Sulaymaniyah 867

IRELAND
Dublin 1,121

ISRAEL
Tel Aviv-Yafo 3,381
Haifa 1,054

ITALY
Rome 3,298
Milan 2,909
Naples 2,373
Turin 1,613
Palermo 915

IVORY COAST (CÔTE D'IVOIRE)
Abidjan 4,288
Yamoussoukro 966

JAMAICA
Kingston 875

JAPAN
Tokyo 13,159
Yokohama 3,689
Osaka 2,665
Nagoya 2,264
Sapporo 1,916
Kobe 1,544
Kyoto 1,474
Fukuoka 1,463
Kawasaki 1,426
Saitama 1,222
Hiroshima 1,174
Kitakyushu 1,011
Sendai 1,008
Hamamatsu 1,000
Naha 970
Chiba 961

JORDAN
Amman 1,179

KAZAKHSTAN
Almaty 1,426

KENYA
Nairobi 3,363
Mombasa 1,040

KOREA, NORTH
Pyŏngyang 2,843

KOREA, SOUTH
Seoul 9,888
Busan 3,372
Incheon 2,884
Daegu 2,447
Daejeon 1,538
Gwangju 1,503
Seongnam 1,353
Suwon 1,159
Ulsan 1,100
Goyang 988
Bucheon 932

KUWAIT
Kuwait City 2,406

LEBANON
Beirut 2,022

LIBYA
Tripoli 1,127
Benghazi 1,114

MADAGASCAR
Antananarivo 1,987

MALAWI
Lilongwe 870
Blantyre 860

MALAYSIA
Kuala Lumpur 1,556
Klang 1,190
Johore Bharu 1,045

MALI
Bamako 2,037

MEXICO
Mexico City 20,446
Guadalajara 4,525
Monterrey 4,213
Puebla 2,335
Tijuana 1,820
Toluca 1,748
León 1,653
Ciudad Juárez 1,338
Torreón 1,242
Querétaro 1,143
San Luis Potosí 1,061
Mérida 1,040
Aguascalientes 957
Mexicali 957
Acapulco 883
Chihuahua 874

MONGOLIA
Ulan Bator 1,184

MOROCCO
Casablanca 3,046
Rabat 1,843
Fès 1,088
Marrakesh 939

MOZAMBIQUE
Maputo 1,150

NEPAL
Katmandu 1,015

NETHERLANDS
Amsterdam 1,056
Rotterdam 1,014

NEW ZEALAND
Auckland 1,452

NICARAGUA
Managua 1,165

NIGER
Niamey 1,297

NIGERIA
Lagos 11,223
Kano 3,375
Ibadan 2,949
Abuja 2,153
Port Harcourt 1,894
Kaduna 1,524
Benin City 1,359
Ogbomosho 1,075
Aba 866
Maiduguri 851

NORWAY
Oslo 915

PAKISTAN
Karachi 13,876
Lahore 7,566
Faisalabad 3,038
Rawalpindi 2,026
Multan 1,775
Gujranwala 1,767
Hyderabad 1,701
Peshawar 1,523
Quetta 903
Islamabad 856

PANAMA
Panamá 1,426

PARAGUAY
Asunción 2,139

PERU
Lima 9,130

PHILIPPINES
Manila 11,862
Davao 1,565
Zamboanga 884
Cebu 855

POLAND
Warsaw 1,723
Lódz 910

PORTUGAL
Lisbon 2,843
Porto 1,367

PUERTO RICO
San Juan 2,475

ROMANIA
Bucharest 1,937

RUSSIA
Moscow 11,621
St Petersburg 4,866
Novosibirsk 1,478
Yekaterinburg 1,355
Nizhniy Novgorod 1,245
Samara 1,166
Omsk 1,156
Kazan 1,147
Chelyabinsk 1,135
Rostov 1,092
Ufa 1,064
Volgograd 1,022
Perm 991
Krasnoyarsk 980
Voronezh 894

RWANDA
Kigali 1,004

SAUDI ARABIA
Riyadh 5,451
Jedda 3,578
Mecca 1,591
Medina 1,142
Dammam 941

SENEGAL
Dakar 3,035

SERBIA
Belgrade 1,135

SIERRA LEONE
Freetown 1,007

SINGAPORE
Singapore City 5,188

SOMALIA
Mogadishu 1,554

SOUTH AFRICA
Johannesburg 3,844
Cape Town 3,562
Durban 3,012
Pretoria 1,501
Vereeniging 1,200
Port Elizabeth 1,119

SPAIN
Madrid 6,574
Barcelona 5,570

SRI LANKA
Colombo 2,115

SUDAN
Khartoum 4,632

SWEDEN
Stockholm 1,385

SWITZERLAND
Zürich 1,194

SYRIA
Aleppo 3,164
Damascus 2,650
Homs 1,369
Hamah 933

TAIWAN
Taipei 2,730
Kaohsiung 1,560
T'aichung 1,244
Tainan 1,205

TANZANIA
Dar es Salaam 3,588

THAILAND
Bangkok 8,426
Samut Prakan 1,212

TOGO
Lomé 1,524

TUNISIA
Tunis 2,385

TURKEY
Istanbul 11,253
Ankara 4,194
Izmir 2,927
Bursa 1,713
Adana 1,468
Gaziantep 1,198
Konya 1,057
Antalya 907

UGANDA
Kampala 1,659

UKRAINE
Kiev 2,829
Kharkov 1,451
Dnepropetrovsk 1,100
Odessa 1,010
Donetsk 959

UNITED ARAB EMIRATES
Dubai 1,978
Abu Dhabi 942
Sharjah 983

UNITED KINGDOM
London 9,005
Birmingham 2,272
Manchester 2,213
Liverpool 1,519
Glasgow 1,137
Newcastle-upon-Tyne 874

UNITED STATES OF AMERICA
New York 19,016
Los Angeles 12,945
Chicago 9,505
Dallas–Fort Worth 6,527
Houston 6,087
Philadelphia 5,992
Washington, DC 5,704
Miami 5,670
Atlanta 5,359
Boston 4,591
San Francisco 4,391
San Bernadino 4,305
Detroit 4,286
Phoenix–Mesa 4,263
Seattle 3,500
Minneapolis–St Paul 3,318
San Diego 3,140
Tampa–St Petersburg 2,825
St Louis 2,817
Baltimore 2,729
Denver 2,600
Pittsburgh 2,360
Portland 2,263
San Antonio 2,195
Sacramento 2,176
Orlando 2,171
Cincinnati 2,138
Cleveland 2,068
Kansas City 2,053
Las Vegas 1,970
San Jose 1,865
Columbus 1,858
Charlotte 1,795
Austin 1,784
Indianapolis 1,779
Norfolk–Virginia Beach 1,680
Nashville 1,617
Providence 1,600
Milwaukee 1,562
Jacksonville 1,360
Memphis 1,326
Louisville 1,295
Oklahoma 1,278
Richmond 1,269
Hartford 1,213
New Orleans 1,191
Raleigh 1,163
Salt Lake City 1,145
Buffalo 1,134
Birmingham 1,132
Rochester 1,055
Tucson 989
Honolulu 964
Tulsa 947
Fresno 943
Stamford 926
Albuquerque 899
Omaha 877
Albany 871
New Haven 861

URUGUAY
Montevideo 1,672

UZBEKISTAN
Tashkent 2,227

VENEZUELA
Caracas 3,242
Maracaibo 2,310
Valencia 1,866
Barquisimeto 1,245
Maracay 1,115

VIETNAM
Ho Chi Minh City 6,405
Hanoi 2,955
Can Tho 1,004
Haiphong 925

YEMEN
Sana' 2,419

ZAMBIA
Lusaka 1,802

ZIMBABWE
Harare 1,542

WORLD STATISTICS: CLIMATE

Rainfall and temperature figures are provided for more than 70 cities around the world. As climate is affected by altitude, the height of each city is shown in metres beneath its name. For each location, the top row of figures shows the total rainfall or snow in millimetres, and the bottom row the average temperature in degrees Celsius; the total annual rainfall and average annual temperature are at the end of the rows. The map opposite shows the city locations.

CITY	JAN.	FEB.	MAR.	APR.	MAY	JUNE	JULY	AUG.	SEPT.	OCT.	NOV.	DEC.	YEAR
EUROPE													
Athens, Greece	62	37	37	23	23	14	6	7	15	51	56	71	402
107 m	10	10	12	16	20	25	28	28	24	20	15	11	18
Berlin, Germany	42	33	41	37	54	69	56	58	45	37	44	55	571
55 m	-1	0	4	9	14	17	19	18	15	9	5	1	9
Istanbul, Turkey	87	71	63	43	33	25	24	24	44	71	85	107	655
14 m	5	6	7	11	16	20	23	23	20	16	12	8	14
Lisbon, Portugal	111	110	69	54	44	16	3	4	33	62	93	103	702
77 m	11	12	14	16	17	20	22	23	21	18	14	12	17
London, UK	54	40	37	37	46	45	57	59	49	57	64	48	593
5 m	4	5	7	9	12	16	18	17	15	11	8	5	11
Málaga, Spain	61	51	62	46	26	5	1	3	29	64	64	62	474
33 m	12	13	16	17	19	29	25	26	23	20	16	13	18
Moscow, Russia	39	38	36	37	53	58	88	71	58	45	47	54	624
156 m	-13	-10	-4	6	13	16	18	17	12	6	-1	-7	4
Odessa, Ukraine	57	62	30	21	34	34	42	37	37	13	35	71	473
64 m	-3	-1	2	9	15	20	22	22	18	12	9	1	10
Paris, France	56	46	35	42	57	54	59	64	55	50	51	50	619
75 m	3	4	8	11	15	18	20	19	17	12	7	4	12
Rome, Italy	71	62	57	51	46	37	15	21	63	99	129	93	744
17 m	8	9	11	14	18	22	25	25	22	17	13	10	16
Shannon, Ireland	94	67	56	53	61	57	77	79	86	86	96	117	929
2 m	5	5	7	9	12	14	16	16	14	11	8	6	10
Stockholm, Sweden	43	30	25	31	34	45	61	76	60	48	53	48	554
44 m	-3	-3	-1	5	10	15	18	17	12	7	3	0	7
ASIA													
Bangkok, Thailand	8	20	36	58	198	160	160	175	305	206	66	5	1,397
2 m	26	28	29	30	29	29	28	28	28	28	26	25	28
Beirut, Lebanon	191	158	94	53	18	3	3	3	5	51	132	185	892
34 m	14	14	16	18	22	24	27	28	26	24	19	16	21
Colombo, Sri Lanka	89	69	147	231	371	224	135	109	160	348	315	147	2,365
7 m	26	26	27	28	28	27	27	27	27	27	26	26	27
Harbin, China	6	5	10	23	43	94	112	104	46	33	8	5	488
160 m	-18	-15	-5	6	13	19	22	21	14	4	-6	-16	3
Ho Chi Minh, Vietnam	15	3	13	43	221	330	315	269	335	269	114	56	1,984
9 m	26	27	29	30	29	28	28	28	27	27	27	26	28
Hong Kong, China	33	46	74	137	292	394	381	361	257	114	43	31	2,162
33 m	16	15	18	22	26	28	28	28	27	25	21	18	23
Jakarta, Indonesia	300	300	211	147	114	97	64	43	66	112	142	203	1,798
8 m	26	26	27	27	27	27	27	27	27	27	27	26	27

CITY	JAN.	FEB.	MAR.	APR.	MAY	JUNE	JULY	AUG.	SEPT.	OCT.	NOV.	DEC.	YEAR
ASIA (continued)													
Kabul, Afghanistan	34	60	68	72	23	1	6	2	2	4	19	22	313
1,815 m	-3	-1	6	13	18	22	25	24	20	14	7	3	12
Karachi, Pakistan	13	10	8	3	3	18	81	41	13	<3	3	5	196
4 m	19	20	24	28	30	31	30	29	28	28	24	20	26
Kolkata, India	10	31	36	43	140	297	325	328	252	114	20	5	1,600
6 m	20	22	27	30	30	30	29	29	29	28	23	19	26
Manama, Bahrain	8	18	13	8	3	0	0	0	0	0	18	18	81
5 m	17	18	21	25	29	32	33	34	31	28	24	19	26
Mumbai, India	3	3	3	3	18	485	617	340	264	64	13	3	1,809
11 m	24	24	26	28	30	29	27	27	27	28	27	26	27
New Delhi, India	23	18	13	8	13	74	180	172	117	10	3	10	640
218 m	14	17	23	28	33	34	31	30	29	26	20	15	25
Omsk, Russia	15	8	8	13	31	51	51	51	28	25	18	20	318
85 m	-22	-19	-12	-1	10	16	18	16	10	1	-11	-18	-1
Qazaly, Kazakhstan	10	10	13	13	15	5	5	8	8	10	13	15	125
63 m	-12	-11	-3	6	18	23	25	23	16	8	-1	-7	7
Shanghai, China	48	58	84	94	94	180	147	142	130	71	51	36	1,135
7 m	4	5	9	14	20	24	28	28	23	19	12	7	16
Singapore	252	173	193	188	173	173	170	196	178	208	254	257	2,413
10 m	26	27	28	28	28	28	28	27	27	27	27	27	27
Tehran, Iran	46	38	46	36	13	3	3	3	3	8	20	31	246
1,220 m	2	5	9	16	21	26	30	29	25	18	12	6	17
Tokyo, Japan	48	74	107	135	147	165	142	152	234	208	97	56	1,565
6 m	3	4	7	13	17	21	25	26	23	17	11	6	14
Ulan Bator, Mongolia	3	3	3	5	10	28	76	51	23	5	5	3	208
1,325 m	-26	-21	-13	-1	6	14	16	14	8	-1	-13	-22	-3
Verkhoyansk, Russia	5	5	3	5	8	23	28	25	13	8	8	5	134
100 m	-50	-45	-32	-15	0	12	14	9	2	-15	-38	-48	-17
AFRICA													
Addis Ababa, Ethiopia	3	3	25	135	213	201	206	239	102	28	3	0	1,151
2,450 m	19	20	20	20	19	18	18	19	21	22	21	20	20
Antananarivo, Madag.	300	279	178	53	18	8	8	10	18	61	135	287	1,356
1,372 m	21	21	21	19	18	15	14	15	17	19	21	21	19
Cairo, Egypt	5	4	4	1	1	0	0	0	0	1	4	6	26
116 m	13	15	18	21	25	28	28	28	26	24	20	15	22
Cape Town, S. Africa	15	8	18	48	79	84	89	66	43	31	18	10	508
17 m	21	21	20	17	14	13	12	13	14	16	18	19	17
Jo'burg, S. Africa	114	109	89	38	25	8	8	8	23	56	107	125	709
1,665 m	20	20	18	16	13	10	11	13	16	18	19	20	16

CITY	JAN.	FEB.	MAR.	APR.	MAY	JUNE	JULY	AUG.	SEPT.	OCT.	NOV.	DEC.	YEAR

AFRICA (continued)

CITY	JAN.	FEB.	MAR.	APR.	MAY	JUNE	JULY	AUG.	SEPT.	OCT.	NOV.	DEC.	YEAR
Khartoum, Sudan	3	3	3	3	3	8	53	71	18	5	3	0	158
390 m	24	25	28	31	33	34	32	31	32	32	28	25	29
Kinshasa, Congo (D.R.)	135	145	196	196	158	8	3	3	31	119	221	142	1,354
325 m	26	26	27	27	26	24	23	24	25	26	26	26	25
Lagos, Nigeria	28	46	102	150	269	460	279	64	140	206	69	25	1,836
3 m	27	28	29	28	28	26	26	25	26	26	28	28	27
Lusaka, Zambia	231	191	142	18	3	3	3	0	3	10	91	150	836
1,277 m	21	22	21	21	19	16	16	18	22	24	23	22	21
Monrovia, Liberia	31	56	97	216	516	973	996	373	744	772	236	130	5,138
23 m	26	26	27	27	26	25	24	25	25	25	26	26	26
Nairobi, Kenya	38	64	125	211	158	46	15	23	31	53	109	86	958
820 m	19	19	19	19	18	16	16	16	18	19	18	18	18
Timbuktu, Mali	1	0	0	1	4	16	54	74	29	4	0	0	183
301 m	22	24	28	32	34	35	32	30	32	31	28	23	29
Tunis, Tunisia	64	51	41	36	18	8	3	8	33	51	48	61	419
66 m	10	11	13	16	19	23	26	27	25	20	16	11	18
Walvis Bay, Namibia	3	5	8	3	3	3	3	3	3	3	3	3	23
7 m	19	19	19	18	17	16	15	14	14	15	17	18	18

AUSTRALIA, NEW ZEALAND AND ANTARCTICA

CITY	JAN.	FEB.	MAR.	APR.	MAY	JUNE	JULY	AUG.	SEPT.	OCT.	NOV.	DEC.	YEAR
Alice Springs, Aust.	43	33	28	10	15	13	8	8	8	18	31	38	252
579 m	29	28	25	20	15	12	12	14	18	23	26	28	21
Christchurch, NZ	56	43	48	48	66	66	69	48	46	43	48	56	638
10 m	16	16	14	12	9	6	6	7	9	12	14	16	11
Darwin, Australia	386	312	254	97	15	3	3	3	13	51	119	239	1,491
30 m	29	29	29	29	28	26	25	26	28	29	30	29	28
Mawson, Antarctica	11	30	20	10	44	180	4	40	3	20	0	0	362
14 m	0	−5	−10	−14	−15	−16	−18	−18	−19	−13	−5	−1	−11
Perth, Australia	8	10	20	43	130	180	170	149	86	56	20	13	881
60 m	23	23	22	19	16	14	13	13	15	16	19	22	18
Sydney, Australia	89	102	127	135	127	117	117	76	73	71	73	73	1,181
42 m	22	22	21	18	15	13	12	13	15	18	19	21	17

NORTH AMERICA

CITY	JAN.	FEB.	MAR.	APR.	MAY	JUNE	JULY	AUG.	SEPT.	OCT.	NOV.	DEC.	YEAR
Anchorage, USA	20	18	15	10	13	18	41	66	66	56	25	23	371
40 m	−11	−8	−5	2	7	12	14	13	9	2	−5	−11	2
Chicago, USA	51	51	66	71	86	89	84	81	79	66	61	51	836
251 m	−4	−3	2	9	14	20	23	22	19	12	5	−1	10
Churchill, Canada	15	13	18	23	32	44	46	58	51	43	39	21	402
13 m	−28	−26	−20	−10	−2	6	12	11	5	−2	−12	−22	−7
Edmonton, Canada	25	19	19	22	43	77	89	78	39	17	16	25	466
676 m	−15	−10	−5	4	11	15	17	16	11	6	−4	−10	3
Honolulu, USA	104	66	79	48	25	18	23	28	36	48	64	104	643
12 m	23	18	19	20	22	24	25	26	26	24	22	19	22
Houston, USA	89	76	84	91	119	117	99	99	104	94	89	109	1,171
12 m	12	13	17	21	24	27	28	29	26	22	16	12	21

NORTH AMERICA (continued)

CITY	JAN.	FEB.	MAR.	APR.	MAY	JUNE	JULY	AUG.	SEPT.	OCT.	NOV.	DEC.	YEAR
Kingston, Jamaica	23	15	23	31	102	89	38	91	99	180	74	36	800
34 m	25	25	25	26	26	28	28	28	27	27	26	26	26
Los Angeles, USA	79	76	71	25	10	3	3	3	5	15	31	66	381
95 m	13	14	14	16	17	19	21	22	21	18	16	14	17
Mexico City, Mexico	13	5	10	20	53	119	170	152	130	51	18	8	747
2,309 m	12	13	16	18	19	19	17	18	18	16	14	13	16
Miami, USA	71	53	64	81	173	178	155	160	203	234	71	51	1,516
8 m	20	20	22	23	25	27	28	28	27	25	22	21	24
Montréal, Canada	72	65	74	74	66	82	90	92	88	76	81	87	946
57 m	−10	−9	−3	−6	13	18	21	20	15	9	2	−7	6
New York City, USA	94	97	91	81	81	84	107	109	86	89	76	91	1,092
96 m	−1	−1	3	10	16	20	23	23	21	15	7	1	11
St Louis, USA	58	64	89	97	114	114	89	86	81	74	71	64	1,001
173 m	0	1	7	13	19	24	26	26	22	15	8	2	14
San José, Costa Rica	15	5	20	46	229	241	211	241	305	300	145	41	1,798
1,146 m	19	19	21	21	22	21	21	21	21	20	20	19	20
Vancouver, Canada	154	115	101	60	52	45	32	41	67	114	150	182	1,113
14 m	3	5	6	9	12	15	17	17	14	10	6	4	10
Washington, DC, USA	86	76	91	84	94	99	112	109	94	74	66	79	1,064
22 m	1	2	7	12	18	23	25	24	20	14	8	3	13

SOUTH AMERICA

CITY	JAN.	FEB.	MAR.	APR.	MAY	JUNE	JULY	AUG.	SEPT.	OCT.	NOV.	DEC.	YEAR
Antofagasta, Chile	0	0	0	3	3	3	5	3	3	3	3	0	13
94 m	21	21	20	18	16	15	14	14	15	16	18	19	17
Buenos Aires, Arg.	122	123	154	107	92	50	53	63	78	139	131	103	1,215
27 m	23	23	21	17	13	9	10	11	13	15	19	22	16
Lima, Peru	3	3	3	3	5	5	8	8	8	3	3	3	41
120 m	23	24	24	22	19	17	17	16	17	18	19	21	20
Manaus, Brazil	249	231	262	221	170	84	58	38	46	107	142	203	1,811
44 m	28	28	28	27	28	28	28	28	29	29	29	28	28
Paraná, Brazil	287	236	239	102	13	3	3	5	28	127	231	310	1,582
260 m	23	23	23	23	23	21	21	22	24	24	24	23	23
Rio de Janeiro, Brazil	125	122	130	107	79	53	41	43	66	79	104	137	1,082
61 m	26	26	25	24	22	21	21	21	21	22	23	25	23

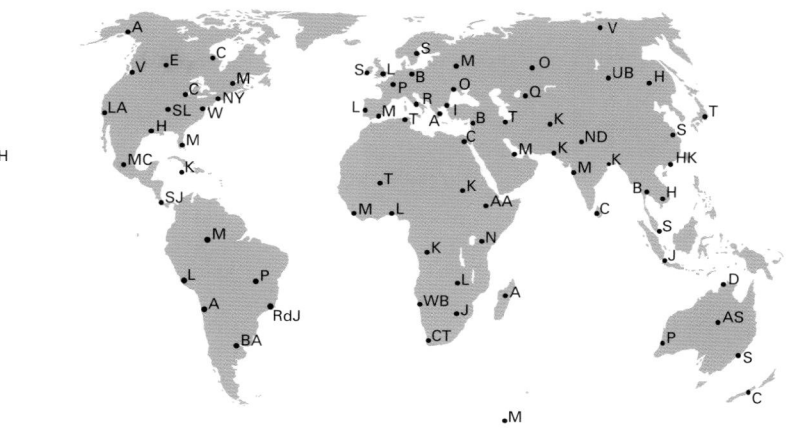

WORLD STATISTICS: PHYSICAL DIMENSIONS

Each topic list is divided into continents and within a continent the items are listed in order of size. The bottom part of many of the lists is selective in order to give examples from as many different countries as possible. The order of the continents is as in the atlas, Europe through to South America. The world top ten are shown in square brackets; in the case of mountains this has not been done because the world top 30 are all in Asia. The figures are rounded as appropriate.

WORLD, CONTINENTS, OCEANS

THE WORLD

	km²	miles²	%
The World	509,450,000	196,672,000	–
Land	149,450,000	57,688,000	29.3
Water	360,000,000	138,984,000	70.7
Asia	44,500,000	17,177,000	29.8
Africa	30,302,000	11,697,000	20.3
North America	24,241,000	9,357,000	16.2
South America	17,793,000	6,868,000	11.9
Antarctica	14,100,000	5,443,000	9.4
Europe	9,957,000	3,843,000	6.7
Australia and Oceania	8,557,000	3,303,000	5.7
Pacific Ocean	155,557,000	60,061,000	46.4
Atlantic Ocean	76,762,000	29,638,000	22.9
Indian Ocean	68,556,000	26,470,000	20.4
Southern Ocean	20,327,000	7,848,000	6.1
Arctic Ocean	14,056,000	5,427,000	4.2

SEAS

PACIFIC

	km²	miles²
South China Sea	2,974,600	1,148,500
Bering Sea	2,268,000	875,000
Sea of Okhotsk	1,528,000	590,000
East China and Yellow Sea	1,249,000	482,000
Sea of Japan	1,008,000	389,000
Gulf of California	162,000	62,500
Bass Strait	75,000	29,000

ATLANTIC

	km²	miles²
Caribbean Sea	2,766,000	1,068,000
Mediterranean Sea	2,516,000	971,000
Gulf of Mexico	1,543,000	596,000
Hudson Bay	1,232,000	476,000
North Sea	575,000	223,000
Black Sea	462,000	178,000
Baltic Sea	422,170	163,000
Gulf of St Lawrence	238,000	92,000

INDIAN

	km²	miles²
Red Sea	438,000	169,000
Persian Gulf	239,000	92,000

MOUNTAINS

EUROPE

		m	ft
Elbrus	Russia	5,642	18,510
Dykh Tau	Russia	5,203	17,070
Shkhara	Russia/Georgia	5,201	17,064
Koshtan Tau	Russia	5,152	16,903
Kazbek	Russia/Georgia	5,047	16,558
Pushkin	Russia/Georgia	5,033	16,512
Katyn Tau	Russia/Georgia	4,979	16,335
Shota Rustaveli	Russia/Georgia	4,860	15,945
Mont Blanc	France/Italy	4,808	15,774
Monte Rosa	Italy/Switzerland	4,634	15,203
Dom	Switzerland	4,545	14,911
Liskamm	Switzerland	4,527	14,852
Weisshorn	Switzerland	4,505	14,780
Tebulos	Russia/Georgia	4,492	14,737
Taschorn	Switzerland	4,490	14,730
Matterhorn/Cervino	Italy/Switzerland	4,478	14,691
Mont Maudit	France/Italy	4,465	14,649
Bazar Dyuzi	Russia/Azerbaijan	4,462	14,639
Grandes Jorasses	France/Italy	4,208	13,806
Jungfrau	Switzerland	4,158	13,642
Barre des Ecrins	France	4,102	13,458
Gran Paradiso	Italy	4,061	13,323
Piz Bernina	Italy/Switzerland	4,049	13,284
Eiger	Switzerland	3,970	13,025
Grossglockner	Austria	3,797	12,457
Mulhacén	Spain	3,478	11,411
Etna	Italy	3,323	10,902
Zugspitze	Germany	2,962	9,718
Olympus	Greece	2,917	9,570
Galdhøpiggen	Norway	2,469	8,100
Ben Nevis	UK	1,344	4,408

ASIA

		m	ft
Everest	China/Nepal	8,850	29,035
K2 (Godwin Austen)	China/Kashmir	8,611	28,251
Kanchenjunga	India/Nepal	8,598	28,208
Lhotse	China/Nepal	8,516	27,939
Makalu	China/Nepal	8,481	27,824
Cho Oyu	China/Nepal	8,201	26,906
Dhaulagiri	Nepal	8,167	26,795
Manaslu	Nepal	8,156	26,758
Nanga Parbat	Kashmir	8,126	26,660
Annapurna	Nepal	8,078	26,502
Gasherbrum	China/Kashmir	8,068	26,469
Broad Peak	China/Kashmir	8,051	26,414
Xixabangma Feng	China	8,012	26,286
Gayachung Kang	Nepal	7,897	25,909
Himalchuli	Nepal	7,893	25,896
Disteghil Sar	Kashmir	7,885	25,869
Nuptse	Nepal	7,879	25,849
Kangbachen	Nepal	7,858	25,781
Khunyang Chhish	Kashmir	7,852	25,761
Masherbrum	Kashmir	7,821	25,659
Nanda Devi	India	7,817	25,646
Rakaposhi	Kashmir	7,788	25,551
Batura	Kashmir	7,785	25,541
Namche Barwa	China	7,782	25,531
Kamet	India	7,756	25,447
Soltoro Kangri	Pakistan	7,742	25,400
Gurla Mandhata	China	7,728	25,354
Trivor	Pakistan	7,720	25,328
Kongur Shan	China	7,719	25,324
Jannu	Nepal	7,710	25,295
Tirich Mir	Pakistan	7,690	25,229
K'ula Shan	Bhutan/China	7,543	24,747
Pik Imeni Ismail Samani	Tajikistan	7,495	24,590
Demavend	Iran	5,604	18,386
Ararat	Turkey	5,165	16,945
Gunong Kinabalu	Malaysia (Borneo)	4,101	13,455
Yu Shan	Taiwan	3,952	12,966
Fuji-San	Japan	3,776	12,388

AFRICA

		m	ft
Kilimanjaro	Tanzania	5,895	19,340
Mt Kenya	Kenya	5,199	17,057
Ruwenzori (Margherita)	Uganda/Congo (D.R.)	5,109	16,762
Meru	Tanzania	4,565	14,977
Ras Dashen	Ethiopia	4,533	14,872
Karisimbi	Rwanda/Congo (D.R.)	4,507	14,787
Mt Elgon	Kenya/Uganda	4,321	14,176
Batu	Ethiopia	4,307	14,130
Guna	Ethiopia	4,231	13,882
Toubkal	Morocco	4,165	13,665
Irhil Mgoun	Morocco	4,071	13,356
Mt Cameroun	Cameroon	4,070	13,353
Amba Ferit	Ethiopia	3,875	13,042
Pico del Teide	Spain (Tenerife)	3,718	12,198
Thabana Ntlenyana	Lesotho	3,482	11,424
Emi Koussi	Chad	3,415	11,204
Mt aux Sources	Lesotho/South Africa	3,282	10,768
Piton des Neiges	Réunion	3,069	10,069

OCEANIA

		m	ft
Puncak Jaya	Indonesia	4,884	16,024
Puncak Trikora	Indonesia	4,730	15,518
Puncak Mandala	Indonesia	4,702	15,427
Mt Wilhelm	Papua New Guinea	4,508	14,790
Mauna Kea	USA (Hawai'i)	4,205	13,796
Mauna Loa	USA (Hawai'i)	4,169	13,678
Aoraki Mt Cook	New Zealand	3,753	12,313
Mt Popomanaseu	Solomon Islands	2,439	8,002
Mt Orohena	French Polynesia (Tahiti)	2,241	7,352
Mt Kosciuszko	Australia	2,228	7,310

NORTH AMERICA

		m	ft
Mt McKinley (Denali)	USA (Alaska)	6,194	20,321
Mt Logan	Canada	5,959	19,551
Pico de Orizaba	Mexico	5,610	18,405
Mt St Elias	USA/Canada	5,489	18,008
Popocatépetl	Mexico	5,452	17,887

NORTH AMERICA (continued)

		m	ft
Mt Foraker	USA (Alaska)	5,304	17,401
Iztaccihuatl	Mexico	5,230	17,159
Mt Lucania	Canada	5,226	17,146
Mt Steele	Canada	5,073	16,644
Mt Bona	USA (Alaska)	5,005	16,420
Mt Blackburn	USA (Alaska)	4,996	16,391
Mt Sanford	USA (Alaska)	4,949	16,237
Mt Wood	Canada	4,840	15,880
Nevado de Toluca	Mexico	4,690	15,387
Mt Fairweather	USA (Alaska)	4,663	15,298
Mt Hunter	USA (Alaska)	4,442	14,573
Mt Whitney	USA	4,418	14,495
Mt Elbert	USA	4,399	14,432
Mt Harvard	USA	4,395	14,419
Mt Rainier	USA	4,392	14,409
Blanca Peak	USA	4,372	14,344
Longs Peak	USA	4,345	14,255
Tajumulco	Guatemala	4,220	13,845
Grand Teton	USA	4,197	13,770
Mt Waddington	Canada	4,019	13,186
Mt Robson	Canada	3,954	12,972
Chirripó Grande	Costa Rica	3,819	12,529
Pico Duarte	Dominican Rep.	3,175	10,417

SOUTH AMERICA

		m	ft
Aconcagua	Argentina	6,962	22,841
Ojos del Salado	Argentina/Chile	6,863	22,615
Monte Pissis	Argentina	6,793	22,287
Nevado Huascarán	Peru	6,768	22,205
Cerro Bonete	Argentina	6,759	22,175
Cerro Llullaillaco	Argentina/Chile	6,739	22,110
Cerro Mercedario	Argentina/Chile	6,720	22,047
Yerupaja	Peru	6,632	21,758
Nevado de Tres Cruces	Argentina/Chile	6,620	21,719
Tupungato	Argentina/Chile	6,570	21,555
Sajama	Bolivia	6,520	21,391
Coropuna	Peru	6,425	21,079
Illimani	Bolivia	6,402	21,004
Ausangate	Peru	6,384	20,945
Nevado de Cachi	Argentina	6,380	20,932
Cerro del Toro	Argentina	6,380	20,932
Siula Grande	Peru	6,356	20,853
Chimborazo	Ecuador	6,310	20,702
Incahuasi	Argentina/Chile	6,218	20,400
Alpamayo	Peru	5,947	19,511
Cerro Galan	Argentina	5,912	19,396
Cotapaxi	Ecuador	5,896	19,344
Pico Cristóbal Colón	Colombia	5,775	18,947
Pico Bolivar	Venezuela	4,981	16,342

ANTARCTICA

		m	ft
Vinson Massif		4,897	16,066
Mt Kirkpatrick		4,528	14,855
Mt Markham		4,349	14,268

OCEAN DEPTHS

ATLANTIC OCEAN

	m	ft	
Puerto Rico (Milwaukee) Deep	8,604	28,232	[7]
Cayman Trench	7,680	25,197	[10]
Gulf of Mexico	5,203	17,070	
Mediterranean Sea	5,121	16,801	
Black Sea	2,211	7,254	
North Sea	660	2,165	
Baltic Sea	463	1,519	
Hudson Bay	258	846	

INDIAN OCEAN

	m	ft
Java Trench	7,450	24,442
Red Sea	2,635	8,454
Persian Gulf	73	239

PACIFIC OCEAN

	m	ft	
Mariana Trench	11,022	36,161	[1]
Tonga Trench	10,882	35,702	[2]
Japan Trench	10,554	34,626	[3]
Kuril Trench	10,542	34,587	[4]
Mindanao Trench	10,497	34,439	[5]
Kermadec Trench	10,047	32,962	[6]

PACIFIC OCEAN (continued)

	m	ft	
Peru–Chile Trench	8,050	26,410	[8]
Aleutian Trench	7,822	25,662	[9]

ARCTIC OCEAN

	m	ft
Molloy Deep	5,608	18,399

SOUTHERN OCEAN

	m	ft
South Sandwich Trench	7,235	23,737

LAND LOWS

		m	ft
Caspian Sea	Europe	−28	−92
Dead Sea	Asia	−422	−1,384
Lake Assal	Africa	−156	−512
Lake Eyre North	Oceania	−16	−52
Death Valley	North America	−86	−282
Laguna del Carbón	South America	−105	−344

RIVERS

EUROPE

		km	miles
Volga	Caspian Sea	3,700	2,300
Danube	Black Sea	2,850	1,770
Ural	Caspian Sea	2,535	1,575
Dnieper	Black Sea	2,285	1,420
Kama	Volga	2,030	1,260
Don	Black Sea	1,990	1,240
Pechora	Arctic Ocean	1,790	1,110
Oka	Volga	1,480	920
Belaya	Kama	1,420	880
Dniester	Black Sea	1,400	870
Vyatka	Kama	1,370	850
Rhine	North Sea	1,320	820
Northern Dvina	Arctic Ocean	1,290	800
Desna	Dnieper	1,190	740
Elbe	North Sea	1,145	710
Vistula	Baltic Sea	1,090	675
Loire	Atlantic Ocean	1,020	635

ASIA

		km	miles	
Yangtse	Pacific Ocean	6,380	3,960	[3]
Yenisey–Angara	Arctic Ocean	5,550	3,445	[5]
Huang Ho	Pacific Ocean	5,464	3,395	[6]
Ob–Irtysh	Arctic Ocean	5,410	3,360	[7]
Mekong	Pacific Ocean	4,500	2,800	[9]
Amur	Pacific Ocean	4,442	2,760	
Lena	Arctic Ocean	4,402	2,735	
Irtysh	Ob	4,250	2,640	
Yenisey	Arctic Ocean	4,090	2,540	
Ob	Arctic Ocean	3,680	2,285	
Indus	Indian Ocean	3,100	1,925	
Brahmaputra	Indian Ocean	2,900	1,800	
Syrdarya	Aral Sea	2,860	1,775	
Salween	Indian Ocean	2,800	1,740	
Euphrates	Indian Ocean	2,700	1,675	
Vilyuy	Lena	2,650	1,645	
Kolyma	Arctic Ocean	2,600	1,615	
Amudarya	Aral Sea	2,540	1,578	
Ural	Caspian Sea	2,535	1,575	
Ganges	Indian Ocean	2,510	1,560	
Si Kiang	Pacific Ocean	2,100	1,305	
Irrawaddy	Indian Ocean	2,010	1,250	
Tarim–Yarkand	Lop Nur	2,000	1,240	
Tigris	Indian Ocean	1,900	1,180	

AFRICA

		km	miles	
Nile	Mediterranean	6,695	4,160	[1]
Congo	Atlantic Ocean	4,670	2,900	[8]
Niger	Atlantic Ocean	4,180	2,595	
Zambezi	Indian Ocean	3,540	2,200	
Oubangi/Uele	Congo (D.R.)	2,250	1,400	
Kasai	Congo (D.R.)	1,950	1,210	
Shaballe	Indian Ocean	1,930	1,200	
Orange	Atlantic Ocean	1,860	1,155	
Cubango	Okavango Delta	1,800	1,120	
Limpopo	Indian Ocean	1,770	1,100	
Senegal	Atlantic Ocean	1,640	1,020	
Volta	Atlantic Ocean	1,500	930	

AUSTRALIA

		km	miles
Murray–Darling	Southern Ocean	3,750	2,330
Darling	Murray	3,070	1,905
Murray	Southern Ocean	2,575	1,600
Murrumbidgee	Murray	1,690	1,050

NORTH AMERICA

		km	miles	
Mississippi–Missouri	Gulf of Mexico	5,971	3,710	[4]
Mackenzie	Arctic Ocean	4,240	2,630	
Missouri	Mississippi	4,088	2,540	

NORTH AMERICA (continued)

		km	miles
Mississippi	Gulf of Mexico	3,782	2,350
Yukon	Pacific Ocean	3,185	1,980
Rio Grande	Gulf of Mexico	3,030	1,880
Arkansas	Mississippi	2,340	1,450
Colorado	Pacific Ocean	2,330	1,445
Red	Mississippi	2,040	1,270
Columbia	Pacific Ocean	1,950	1,210
Saskatchewan	Lake Winnipeg	1,940	1,205
Snake	Columbia	1,670	1,040
Churchill	Hudson Bay	1,600	990
Ohio	Mississippi	1,580	980
Brazos	Gulf of Mexico	1,400	870
St Lawrence	Atlantic Ocean	1,170	730

SOUTH AMERICA

		km	miles	
Amazon	Atlantic Ocean	6,450	4,010	[2]
Paraná–Plate	Atlantic Ocean	4,500	2,800	[10]
Purus	Amazon	3,350	2,080	
Madeira	Amazon	3,200	1,990	
São Francisco	Atlantic Ocean	2,900	1,800	
Paraná	Plate	2,800	1,740	
Tocantins	Atlantic Ocean	2,750	1,710	
Orinoco	Atlantic Ocean	2,740	1,700	
Paraguay	Paraná	2,550	1,580	
Pilcomayo	Paraná	2,500	1,550	
Araguaia	Tocantins	2,250	1,400	
Juruá	Amazon	2,000	1,240	
Xingu	Amazon	1,980	1,230	
Ucayali	Amazon	1,900	1,180	
Uruguay	Plate	1,610	1,000	

LAKES

EUROPE

		km²	miles²
Lake Ladoga	Russia	17,700	6,800
Lake Onega	Russia	9,700	3,700
Saimaa system	Finland	8,000	3,100
Vänern	Sweden	5,500	2,100

ASIA

		km²	miles²	
Caspian Sea	Asia	371,000	143,000	[1]
Lake Baikal	Russia	30,500	11,780	[8]
Tonlé Sap	Cambodia	20,000	7,700	
Lake Balkhash	Kazakhstan	18,500	7,100	
Dongting Hu	China	12,000	4,600	
Aral Sea	Kazakhstan/Uzbekistan	6,800	2,620	
Issyk Kul	Kyrgyzstan	6,200	2,400	
Lake Urmia	Iran	5,900	2,300	
Koko Nur	China	5,700	2,200	
Poyang Hu	China	5,000	1,900	
Lake Khanka	China/Russia	4,400	1,700	
Lake Van	Turkey	3,500	1,400	

AFRICA

		km²	miles²	
Lake Victoria	East Africa	68,000	26,300	[3]
Lake Tanganyika	Central Africa	33,000	13,000	[6]
Lake Malawi/Nyasa	East Africa	29,600	11,430	[9]
Lake Chad	Central Africa	25,000	9,700	
Lake Bangweulu	Zambia	9,840	3,800	
Lake Turkana	Ethiopia/Kenya	8,500	3,290	
Lake Volta	Ghana	8,480	3,270	
Lake Kariba	Zambia/Zimbabwe	5,380	2,150	
Lake Albert	Uganda/Congo (D.R.)	5,300	2,050	
Lake Nasser	Egypt/Sudan	5,250	2,030	
Lake Mweru	Zambia/Congo (D.R.)	4,920	1,900	
Lake Kyoga	Uganda	4,430	1,710	
Lake Tana	Ethiopia	3,620	1,400	
Lake Cabora Bassa	Mozambique	2,750	1,070	
Lake Rukwa	Tanzania	2,600	1,000	
Lake Mai-Ndombe	Congo (D.R.)	2,300	890	

AUSTRALIA

		km²	miles²
Lake Eyre	Australia	8,900	3,400
Lake Torrens	Australia	5,800	2,200
Lake Gairdner	Australia	4,800	1,900

NORTH AMERICA

		km²	miles²	
Lake Superior	Canada/USA	82,350	31,800	[2]
Lake Huron	Canada/USA	59,600	23,010	[4]
Lake Michigan	USA	58,000	22,400	[5]
Great Bear Lake	Canada	31,800	12,280	[7]
Great Slave Lake	Canada	28,500	11,000	[10]
Lake Erie	Canada/USA	25,700	9,900	
Lake Winnipeg	Canada	24,400	9,400	
Lake Ontario	Canada/USA	19,500	7,500	
Lake Nicaragua	Nicaragua	8,200	3,200	
Lake Athabasca	Canada	8,100	3,100	
Smallwood Reservoir	Canada	6,530	2,520	
Reindeer Lake	Canada	6,400	2,500	
Nettilling Lake	Canada	5,500	2,100	

SOUTH AMERICA

		km²	miles²
Lake Titicaca	Bolivia/Peru	8,300	3,200
Lake Poopo	Bolivia	2,800	1,100

ISLANDS

EUROPE

		km²	miles²	
Great Britain	UK	229,880	88,700	[8]
Iceland	Atlantic Ocean	103,000	39,800	
Ireland	Ireland/UK	84,400	32,600	
Novaya Zemlya (N.)	Russia	48,200	18,600	
Spitsbergen	Norway	39,000	15,100	
Novaya Zemlya (S.)	Russia	33,200	12,800	
Sicily	Italy	25,500	9,800	
Sardinia	Italy	24,000	9,300	
Nordaustlandet	Norway	15,000	5,600	
Corsica	France	8,700	3,400	
Crete	Greece	8,350	3,200	
Sjælland	Denmark	6,850	2,600	

ASIA

		km²	miles²	
Borneo	South-east Asia	744,360	287,400	[3]
Sumatra	Indonesia	473,600	182,860	[6]
Honshu	Japan	230,500	88,980	[7]
Sulawesi (Celebes)	Indonesia	189,000	73,000	
Java	Indonesia	126,700	48,900	
Luzon	Philippines	104,700	40,400	
Mindanao	Philippines	101,500	39,200	
Hokkaido	Japan	78,400	30,300	
Sakhalin	Russia	74,060	28,600	
Sri Lanka	Indian Ocean	65,600	25,300	
Taiwan	Pacific Ocean	36,000	13,900	
Kyushu	Japan	35,700	13,800	
Hainan	China	34,000	13,100	
Timor	South-east Asia	33,600	13,000	
Shikoku	Japan	18,800	7,300	
Halmahera	Indonesia	18,000	6,900	
Ceram	Indonesia	17,150	6,600	
Sumbawa	Indonesia	15,450	6,000	
Flores	Indonesia	15,200	5,900	
Samar	Philippines	13,100	5,100	
Negros	Philippines	12,700	4,900	
Bangka	Indonesia	12,000	4,600	
Palawan	Philippines	12,000	4,600	
Panay	Philippines	11,500	4,400	
Sumba	Indonesia	11,100	4,300	
Mindoro	Philippines	9,750	3,800	

AFRICA

		km²	miles²	
Madagascar	Indian Ocean	587,040	226,660	[4]
Socotra	Indian Ocean	3,600	1,400	
Réunion	Indian Ocean	2,500	965	
Tenerife	Atlantic Ocean	2,350	900	
Mauritius	Indian Ocean	1,865	720	

OCEANIA

		km²	miles²	
New Guinea	Indonesia/Papua NG	821,030	317,000	[2]
New Zealand (S.)	Pacific Ocean	150,500	58,100	
New Zealand (N.)	Pacific Ocean	114,700	44,300	
Tasmania	Australia	67,800	26,200	
New Britain	Papua New Guinea	37,800	14,600	
New Caledonia	Pacific Ocean	19,100	7,400	
Viti Levu	Fiji	10,500	4,100	
Hawai'i	Pacific Ocean	10,450	4,000	
Bougainville	Papua New Guinea	9,600	3,700	
Guadalcanal	Solomon Islands	6,500	2,500	
Vanua Levu	Fiji	5,550	2,100	
New Ireland	Papua New Guinea	3,200	1,200	

NORTH AMERICA

		km²	miles²	
Greenland	Atlantic Ocean	2,175,600	839,800	[1]
Baffin Island	Canada	508,000	196,100	[5]
Victoria Island	Canada	212,200	81,900	[9]
Ellesmere Island	Canada	212,000	81,800	[10]
Cuba	Caribbean Sea	110,860	42,800	
Newfoundland	Canada	110,680	42,700	
Hispaniola	Dominican Rep./Haiti	76,200	29,400	
Banks Island	Canada	67,000	25,900	
Devon Island	Canada	54,500	21,000	
Melville Island	Canada	42,400	16,400	
Vancouver Island	Canada	32,150	12,400	
Somerset Island	Canada	24,300	9,400	
Jamaica	Caribbean Sea	11,400	4,400	
Puerto Rico	Atlantic Ocean	8,900	3,400	
Cape Breton Island	Canada	4,000	1,500	

SOUTH AMERICA

		km²	miles²
Tierra del Fuego	Argentina/Chile	47,000	18,100
Falkland Islands (East)	Atlantic Ocean	6,800	2,600
South Georgia	Atlantic Ocean	4,200	1,600
Galapagos (Isabela)	Pacific Ocean	2,250	870

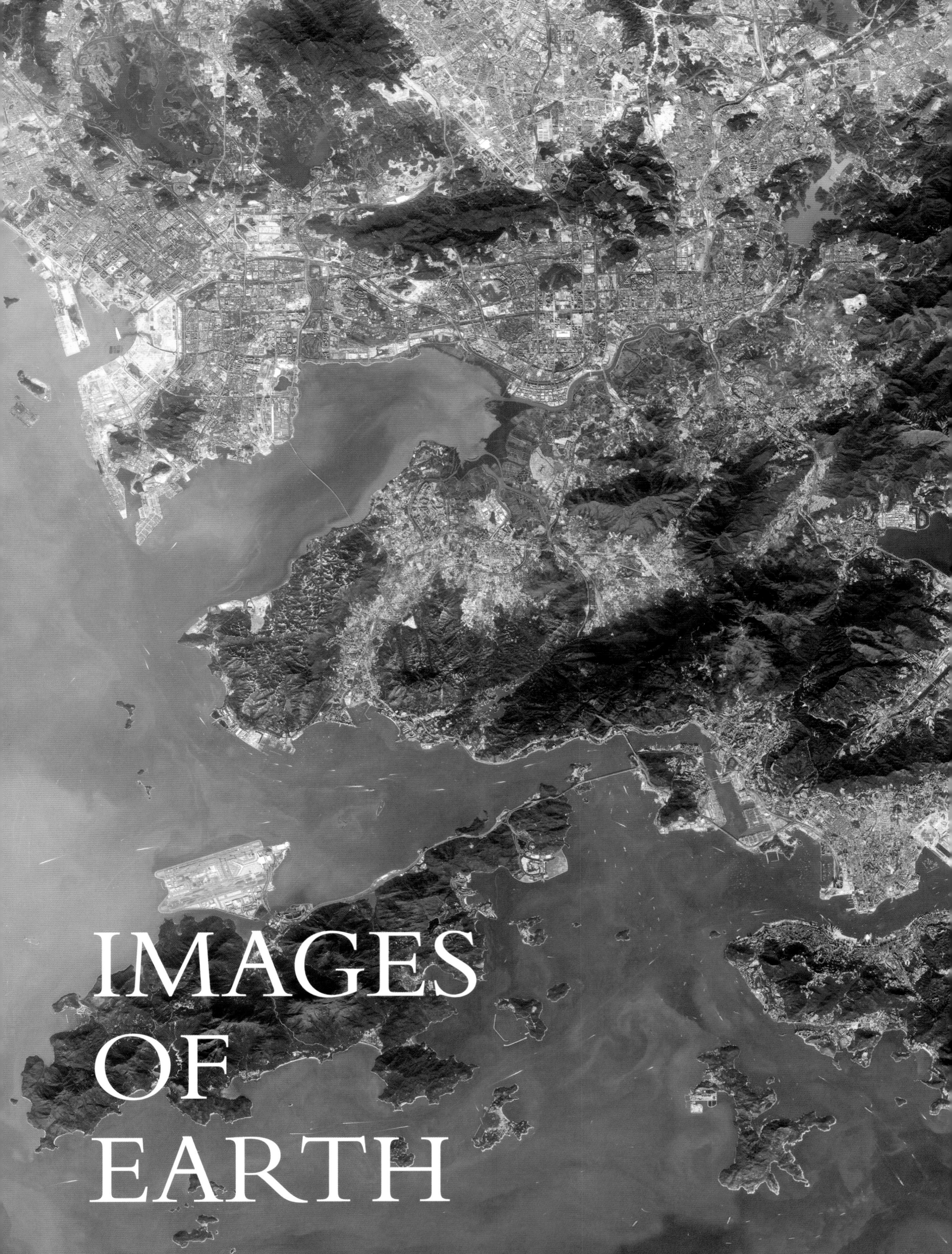

IMAGES
OF
EARTH

This image covers one of the most dynamic areas in the world, Hong Kong, with Shenzhen to its north. Hong Kong became a major port and international financial centre during the period of British rule and retains a special status as a Special Administrative Region (SAR) with a high degree of economic autonomy, including the retention of the Hong Kong dollar. To its north Shenzhen was established by China as a Special Economic Zone (SEZ) in 1979, to attract foreign industry and investment. This has proved very successful and communications between the two have also improved, as can be seen by the sinuous Shenzhen Bay Bridge in the middle of the left-hand page. [Map page 117]
Source: RapidEye/NPA Satellite Mapping

The River Thames snakes from Chelsea Bridge in the west to Tower Bridge in the east in this image covering both the West End and the City of London. Despite having a population in excess of 8 million people, there are still many parks and open spaces around the city centre. St James's Park and Green Park, together with Buckingham Palace and its gardens, can be seen at centre left of the image, and, on the western edge, parts of Hyde Park and Regent's Park can also be seen. Just below the page title, at top centre, the newly developing area around Kings Cross and St Pancras railway stations can be seen. In addition, the low sun shows clearly the shadows of The Shard and the chimney of Tate Modern as well as the many high-rise buildings in the City. [Map page 67]
Source: GeoEye/NPA Satellite Mapping

As both the capital and the largest city in the Netherlands, with over 1 million inhabitants, Amsterdam is a major commercial and cultural centre. Its name is derived from its position at the mouth of the River Amstel, flowing in from the south. The urban area is split by the Nordzeekanaal, which connects the Ijsselmeer to the North Sea. There is also the important Rijnkanaal, which links it with the major inland waterways of Europe via the River Rhine. The ancient core of the settlement is to the south, where the concentric rings of the famous canal system can be seen. This network is evidence of city planning to accommodate and service a fast-rising population in the 17th century. [Map page 69]
Source: RapidEye/NPA Satellite Mapping

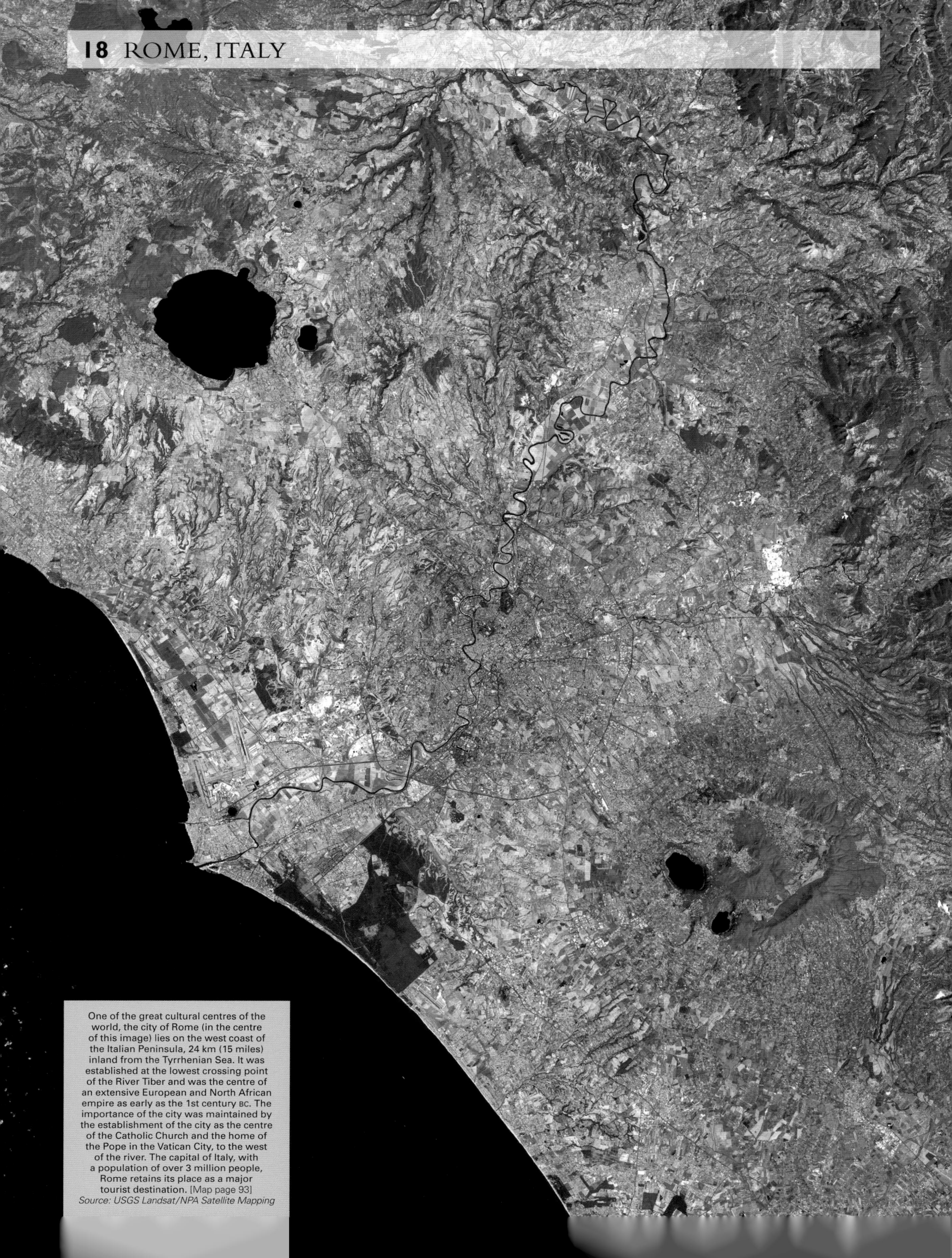

One of the great cultural centres of the world, the city of Rome (in the centre of this image) lies on the west coast of the Italian Peninsula, 24 km (15 miles) inland from the Tyrrhenian Sea. It was established at the lowest crossing point of the River Tiber and was the centre of an extensive European and North African empire as early as the 1st century BC. The importance of the city was maintained by the establishment of the city as the centre of the Catholic Church and the home of the Pope in the Vatican City, to the west of the river. The capital of Italy, with a population of over 3 million people, Rome retains its place as a major tourist destination. [Map page 93]
Source: USGS Landsat/NPA Satellite Mapping

The city of Istanbul was formerly known as Constantinople and, before that, as Byzantium. It is split by the narrow stretch of water running from north to south called the Bosporus. This forms the continental boundary between Europe and Asia, connecting the Black Sea, to the north, to the Sea of Marmara, thence to the Mediterranean. It is because of this strategic position between the east–west (land) and north–south (sea) trade routes that the city has been important for such a long time. Under the Ottoman Empire it was the capital city of Turkey, but in 1923 this was moved to Ankara. Currently, over 11 million people live in Istanbul, the largest city in Turkey. [Map page 104]
Source: USGS Landsat/NPA Satellite Mapping

Also known as Bombay, Mumbai is the largest and most important commercial city in India, with a population of 20 million people. Its harbour is the best in the country, and the new port, built in 1989 and called Nhava Sheva (on the right-hand side of the image), handles 65% of the country's total container traffic. The growth of cotton weaving, and the opening of the Suez Canal in 1869, cemented its position as India's most important trading port. Diversifying into areas such as engineering and information technology, the city is also the centre of the highly successful Hindi movie industry, or 'Bollywood', which exports its products around the world. [Map page 126]
Source: RapidEye/NPA Satellite Mapping

Three countries can be seen in this image. At the top, partially covered by cloud, is the southern end of Malaysia; the large island just below is the independent city state of Singapore; and the islands at the bottom of the image are part of Indonesia. Singapore has developed a fast-growing economy based on being the focus of south-east Asian shipping routes and on the trans-shipment of goods between the Far East and the West. As a result, it is one of the world's major ports and much new development, by reclaiming land from the sea, can be seen in the south. The city state is one of the world's wealthiest countries, with a population of over 5 million people. [Map page 121]
Source: RapidEye/NPA Satellite Mapping

Beijing, also known as Peking, is the capital and cultural centre of China, with a population of over 15 million people. It is situated at the northern end of the North China Plain and has a hot, dry climate. Water supply is an ongoing problem for such a large city, as too are air pollution and dust storms. At the centre of the built-up area in this image can be seen the small rectangle of the Forbidden City, the palace compound built from the 14th century onwards. The city is the terminus of several new high-speed railway lines, and Beijing Capital International Airport, clearly visible in this image to the north-east of the city, is now the second busiest airport in the world. [Map page 114]
Source: USGS Landsat/NPA Satellite Mapping

At the head of Tokyo Bay, the capital city forms the centre of one of the world's most densely populated areas. With its satellites of Kawasaki and Yokohama, the population of over 34 million people makes this metropolitan area the world's largest 'megacity'. Owing to the shortage of space for expansion, much development takes place on areas reclaimed from the sea, such as Haneda International Airport, visible at the mouth of the Tama River, towards the south-west of the image. The area is prone to earthquakes, and in 1923 the Great Kanto Earthquake devastated the city, killing 143,000 people. Consequently, modern buildings are reinforced to withstand seismic activity. [Map page 113]
Source: RapidEye/NPA Satellite Mapping

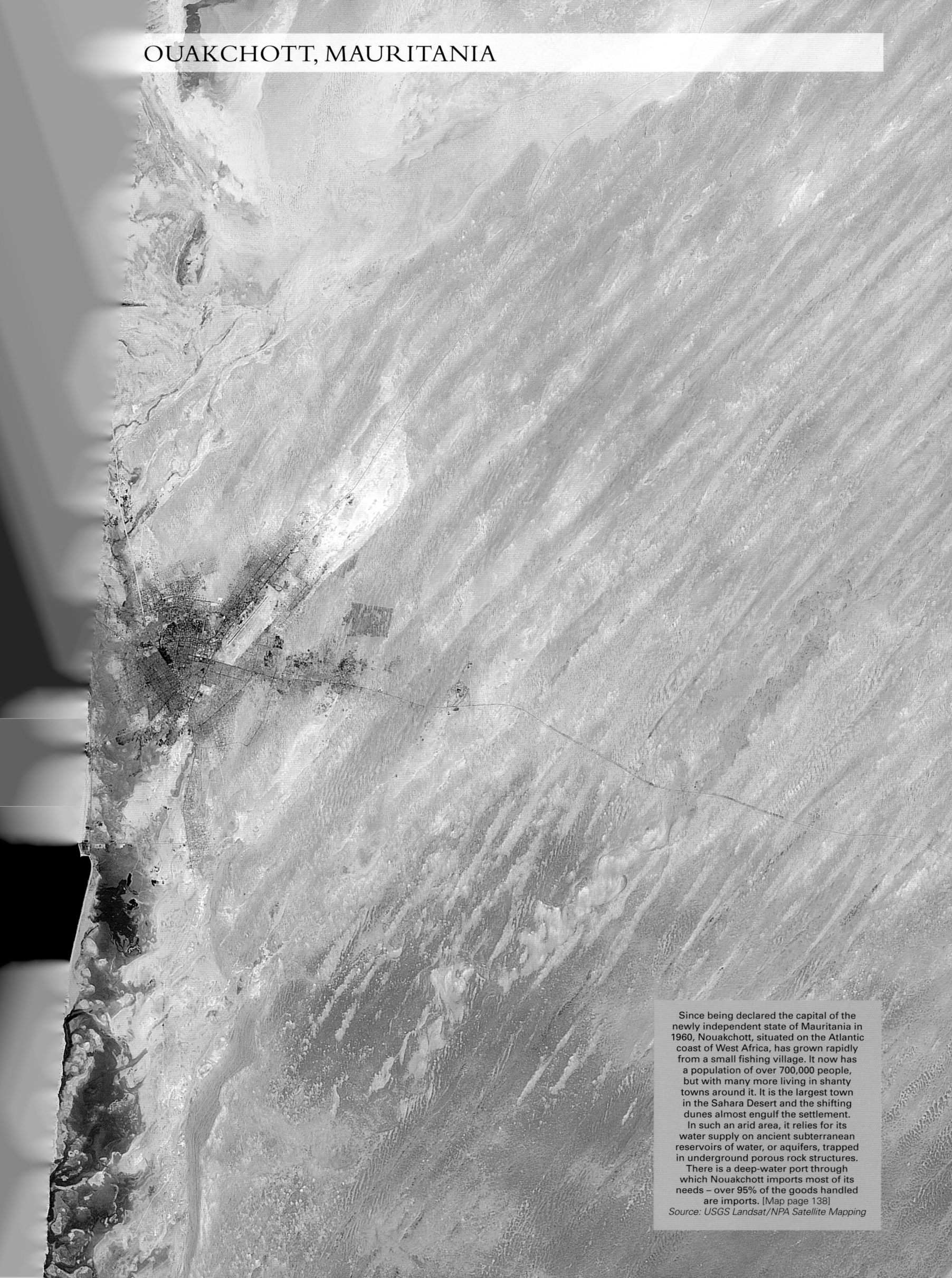

OUAKCHOTT, MAURITANIA

Since being declared the capital of the newly independent state of Mauritania in 1960, Nouakchott, situated on the Atlantic coast of West Africa, has grown rapidly from a small fishing village. It now has a population of over 700,000 people, but with many more living in shanty towns around it. It is the largest town in the Sahara Desert and the shifting dunes almost engulf the settlement.
In such an arid area, it relies for its water supply on ancient subterranean reservoirs of water, or aquifers, trapped in underground porous rock structures.
There is a deep-water port through which Nouakchott imports most of its needs – over 95% of the goods handled are imports. [Map page 138]
Source: USGS Landsat/NPA Satellite Mapping

The largest city in Africa, with over 11 million inhabitants, Cairo evolved in a strategic location on the eastern bank of the River Nile just below its delta, 165 km (100 miles) from the Mediterranean Sea. This image clearly shows the differences between the arid desert areas to the south-east and south-west, the fertile lands of the Nile flood plain, and the urban area itself. Air pollution from vehicle emissions and industry is a major concern in this rapidly expanding metropolitan area. To ease congestion, three metro lines have been built. The shadows of the Pyramids on the Giza Plateau can be seen at the bottom left of the image, showing the modern city's links with Ancient Egypt. [Map page 137]
Source: RapidEye/NPA Satellite Mapping

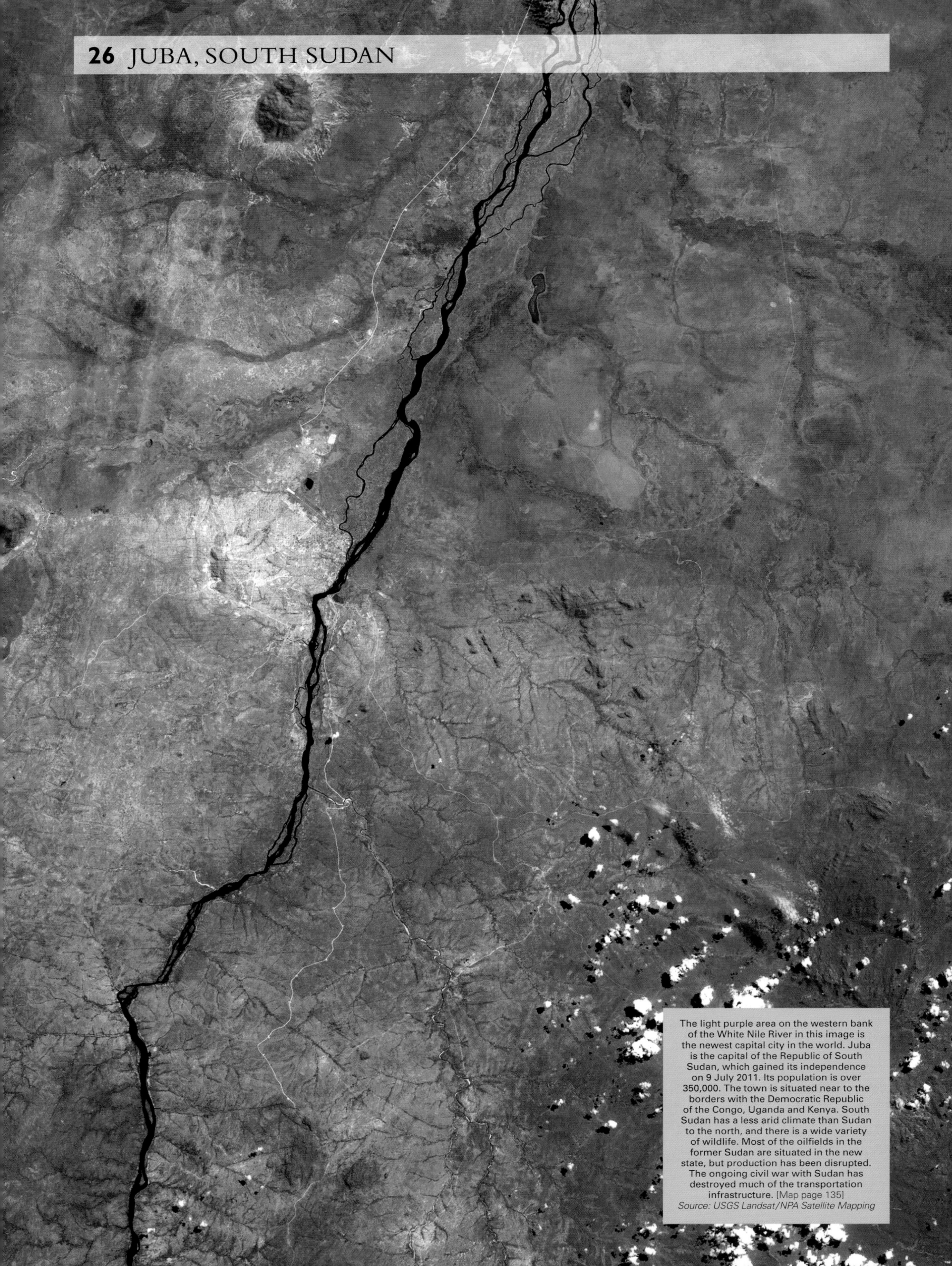

The light purple area on the western bank of the White Nile River in this image is the newest capital city in the world. Juba is the capital of the Republic of South Sudan, which gained its independence on 9 July 2011. Its population is over 350,000. The town is situated near to the borders with the Democratic Republic of the Congo, Uganda and Kenya. South Sudan has a less arid climate than Sudan to the north, and there is a wide variety of wildlife. Most of the oilfields in the former Sudan are situated in the new state, but production has been disrupted. The ongoing civil war with Sudan has destroyed much of the transportation infrastructure. [Map page 135]
Source: USGS Landsat/NPA Satellite Mapping

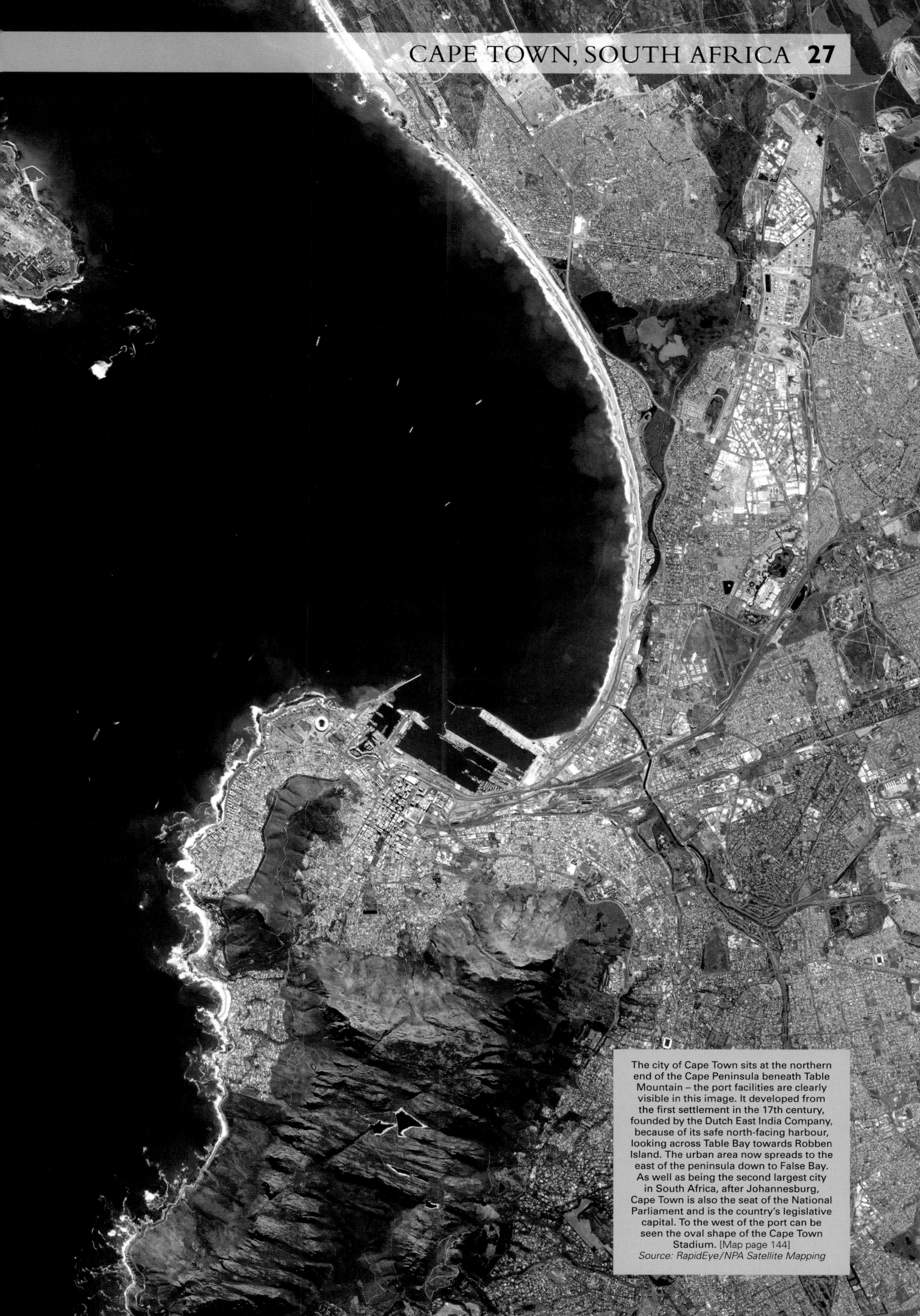

The city of Cape Town sits at the northern end of the Cape Peninsula beneath Table Mountain – the port facilities are clearly visible in this image. It developed from the first settlement in the 17th century, founded by the Dutch East India Company, because of its safe north-facing harbour, looking across Table Bay towards Robben Island. The urban area now spreads to the east of the peninsula down to False Bay. As well as being the second largest city in South Africa, after Johannesburg, Cape Town is also the seat of the National Parliament and is the country's legislative capital. To the west of the port can be seen the oval shape of the Cape Town Stadium. [Map page 144]
Source: RapidEye/NPA Satellite Mapping

Sydney is the largest city in Australia, with a population of over 4.5 million inhabitants. It was founded at the end of the 18th century at Sydney Cove on the south shore of Port Jackson, the northern of the two enclosed bays seen here. It has since spread inland along the valley of the Parramatta River and to the south, to Botany Bay. The image covers the main central business district from the Sydney Harbour Bridge down to the runways of Australia's busiest airport, Sydney Kingsford Smith. On the Pacific coast, at the southern end of the pointed peninsula, the white sands and sheltered bay of Bondi Beach can be seen. As the financial and commercial centre for the whole country, the city has a vibrant cultural life. [Map page 153]
Source: RapidEye/NPA Satellite Mapping

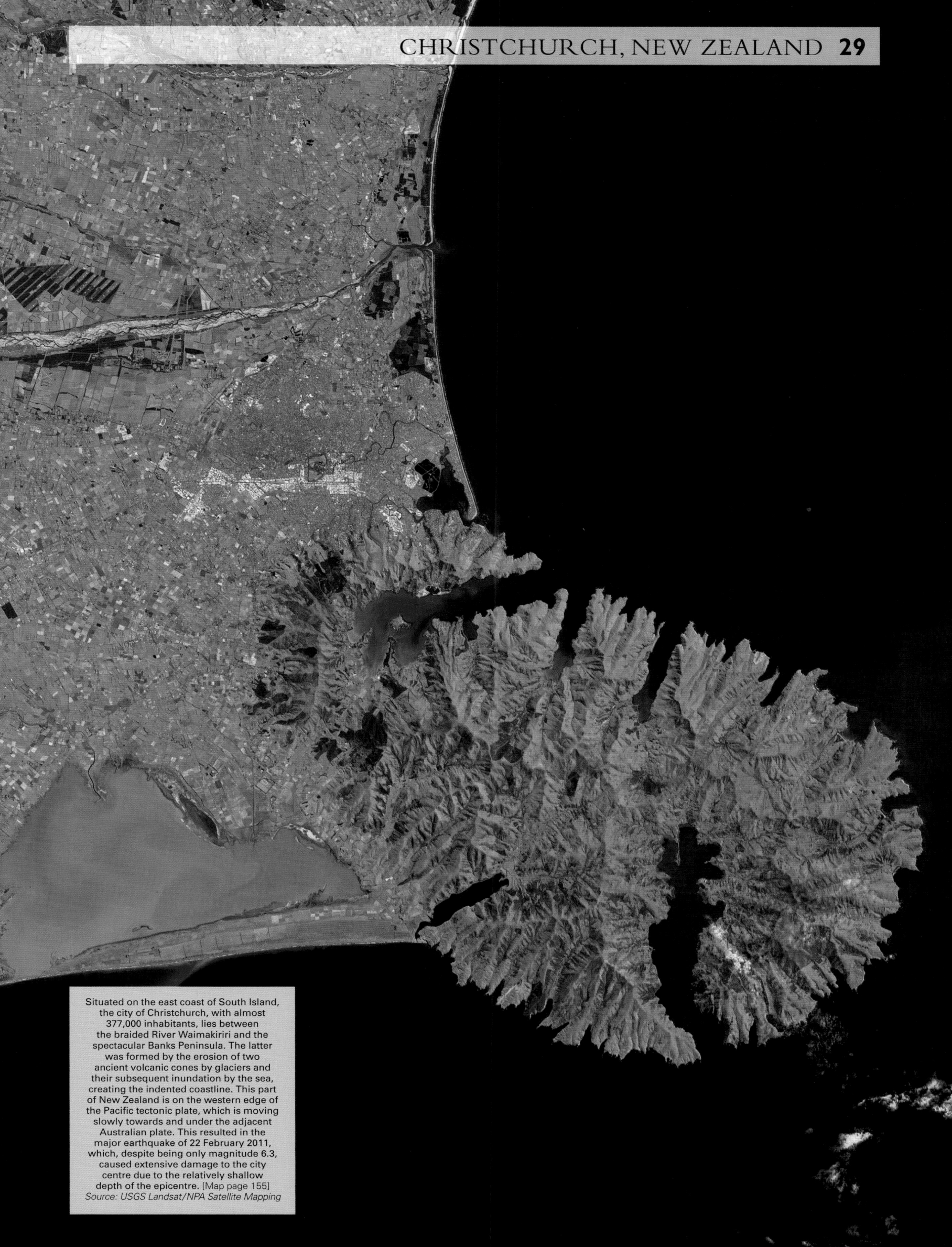

Situated on the east coast of South Island, the city of Christchurch, with almost 377,000 inhabitants, lies between the braided River Waimakiriri and the spectacular Banks Peninsula. The latter was formed by the erosion of two ancient volcanic cones by glaciers and their subsequent inundation by the sea, creating the indented coastline. This part of New Zealand is on the western edge of the Pacific tectonic plate, which is moving slowly towards and under the adjacent Australian plate. This resulted in the major earthquake of 22 February 2011, which, despite being only magnitude 6.3, caused extensive damage to the city centre due to the relatively shallow depth of the epicentre. [Map page 155]
Source: USGS Landsat/NPA Satellite Mapping

On the north side of the Fraser River delta, the settlement grew up in the second half of the 19th century around its fine, natural harbour. It developed as the western railhead of the Canadian Pacific Railroad and is now the terminus of the Trans-Canada Highway, which crosses on the easternmost of the two road bridges visible here to the north. Vancouver is the largest cargo port in Canada. The larger metropolitan area of the city is home to over 2.25 million people. Downtown Vancouver is at the southern end of the peninsula which projects northwards and separates Vancouver Harbour from Burrard Inlet. The wooded area at the northern end is Stanley Park, which is connected to West and North Vancouver via the Lions Gate Bridge. [Map page 162]
Source: RapidEye/NPA Satellite Mapping

Québec was founded as a trading post in 1608, at the narrowest point of the St Lawrence River, just to the south-west of the Île d'Orléans, and is one of the oldest cities in North America. Strategically, the city controlled the movement of shipping between the Atlantic Ocean and the Great Lakes, and consequently developed fortifications on the cliffs of Cape Diamond, 97 m (320 ft) above the river. The port is 1,370 km (850 miles) from the Atlantic, 2,404 km (1,495 miles) from Duluth, and 2,252 km (1,400 miles) from Chicago. It has a population of over 500,000 people and is the capital city of the French-speaking province of the same name. [Map page 165]
Source: RapidEye/NPA Satellite Mapping

This image covers parts of New York City (to the east) and Jersey City (to the west). Flowing from the north, the Hudson River divides them, and the elongated island of Manhattan with Central Park at its heart is clearly visible. It is the centre of the most densely populated metropolitan area in the United States, with a population in excess of 19 million people. To the south-east is the end of Long Island, on which the suburbs of Brooklyn and Queens are situated. South-west of Manhattan are two small islands: the first is Ellis Island, where the early immigrants first disembarked, and beyond that is Liberty Island, where the famous Statue of Liberty is located. [Map page 175]
Source: RapidEye/NPA Satellite Mapping

Situated on the south-western shore of Lake Michigan, Chicago is the centre of the third largest metropolitan area in the United States, with a population of over 9.5 million people. The central area of the agglomeration, known by some as 'Chicagoland', can be seen on the lake shore. It developed as a major transport focus for the Midwest, with complex road and rail networks radiating out to its rich agricultural hinterland. It also developed as a large port, trading these commodities on a global scale. Chicago boasts the fifth busiest airport in the world, O'Hare International, which handles over 66.6 million passengers a year and which can be seen towards the north-west of the city. [Map page 172]
Source: USGS Landsat/NPA Satellite Mapping

The northern end of the 'Bay Area' is shown: hilly San Francisco is at the top end of the southern peninsula, with the Golden Gate Bridge connecting it to Sausalito to the north. Alcatraz Island, former home of the infamous prison, can be seen as a small island to the east of the bridge. On the opposite shore, connected by the double-decker Bay Bridge, are Oakland and Berkeley. Founded by the Spanish at the end of the 18th century, the town expanded rapidly with the Californian Gold Rush in the mid-19th century. Sitting close by the San Andreas Fault, the city was destroyed by an earthquake and subsequent fire in 1906, and there was further major earthquake damage in 1989. [Map page 170]
Source: RapidEye/NPA Satellite Mapping

The city is situated in a basin within the Mojave Desert in Nevada. Known worldwide for its night life and gambling, Las Vegas has also become a popular destination for retired people and families. The population of the metropolitan area is now almost 2 million people. To the east of the grid-pattern layout of the town lies the Hoover Dam, formerly known as Boulder Dam, which was built across the Colorado River in 1935. The lake behind the dam is known as Lake Mead, the largest man-made reservoir in the United States. It is used for flood control, irrigation, and hydroelectric-power generation in the region, but recent dry years have resulted in reduced water levels. [Map page 171]
Source: USGS Landsat/NPA Satellite Mapping

With a population of over 23 million people for the continuous metropolitan area visible here, Mexico City is one of North America's most important commercial centres. It was originally founded by the Aztecs in 1325, on an island in Lake Texcoco, which has dried up over time. The city sits in a valley some 2,240 m (7,350 ft) above sea level. The relentless growth of the urban area has resulted in both air pollution and water-supply problems. To the south-east of the city can be seen three towering snow-covered volcanic peaks. The southernmost of these is Popocatépetl, an active volcano 5,452 m (17,887 ft) high, which has two glaciers near its summit. [Map page 181]
Source: USGS Landsat/NPA Satellite Mapping

The Panama Canal, originally dug between 1904–14, crosses between the Caribbean Sea, to the north of the image, and the Pacific Ocean in the south. Paradoxically, therefore, the Pacific entrance is to the east of the Caribbean entrance. Panama City, the capital of Panama, is at the Pacific end of the canal. The canal has until recently been able to handle the world's largest cargo vessels, carrying up to 5,000 containers, thus cutting the ocean passage time between Asia and the eastern USA. It is now being upgraded so that by the end of 2015 it will be able to handle the latest vessels – these can carry a maximum load of 12,000 containers. [Map page 182]
Source: USGS Landsat/NPA Satellite Mapping

Santiago, the capital city of Chile, lies at the foot of the Andes in the country's fertile central valley at an altitude of 520 m (1,706 ft), some 60 km (37 miles) south-east of the main port of Valparaíso. To the east the mountains rise to over 6,000 m (20,000 ft). The boundary with Argentina runs north–south along the watershed some 75 km (46 miles) to the east. The city, which was founded as early as 1541, expanded rapidly to its current population of over 6 million inhabitants. This has resulted in some air pollution and smog problems, particularly during the winter months. The Mapocho River divides the city, flowing from the Andes to the Pacific Ocean. [Map page 190]
Source: USGS Landsat/NPA Satellite Mapping

Situated on the west side of the mouth of the Guanabara Bay, Rio de Janeiro is the most visited city in the southern hemisphere. It is famous for its beaches (Copacabana and Ipanema, both at the western entrance to the bay), its carnivals, the Sugar Loaf Mountain, and the famous Cristo Redentor (Christ the Redeemer) statue. It has a hot, humid climate with a mean daily temperature of 24°C (75°F), and was the capital city of Brazil until 1960, when the newly built capital Brasília superseded it. It is the second largest manufacturing centre in Brazil, after São Paulo, and a major port. The metropolitan area has a population of almost 11 million people. [Map page 191]
Source: USGS Landsat/NPA Satellite Mapping

OCEAN SEAFLOORS

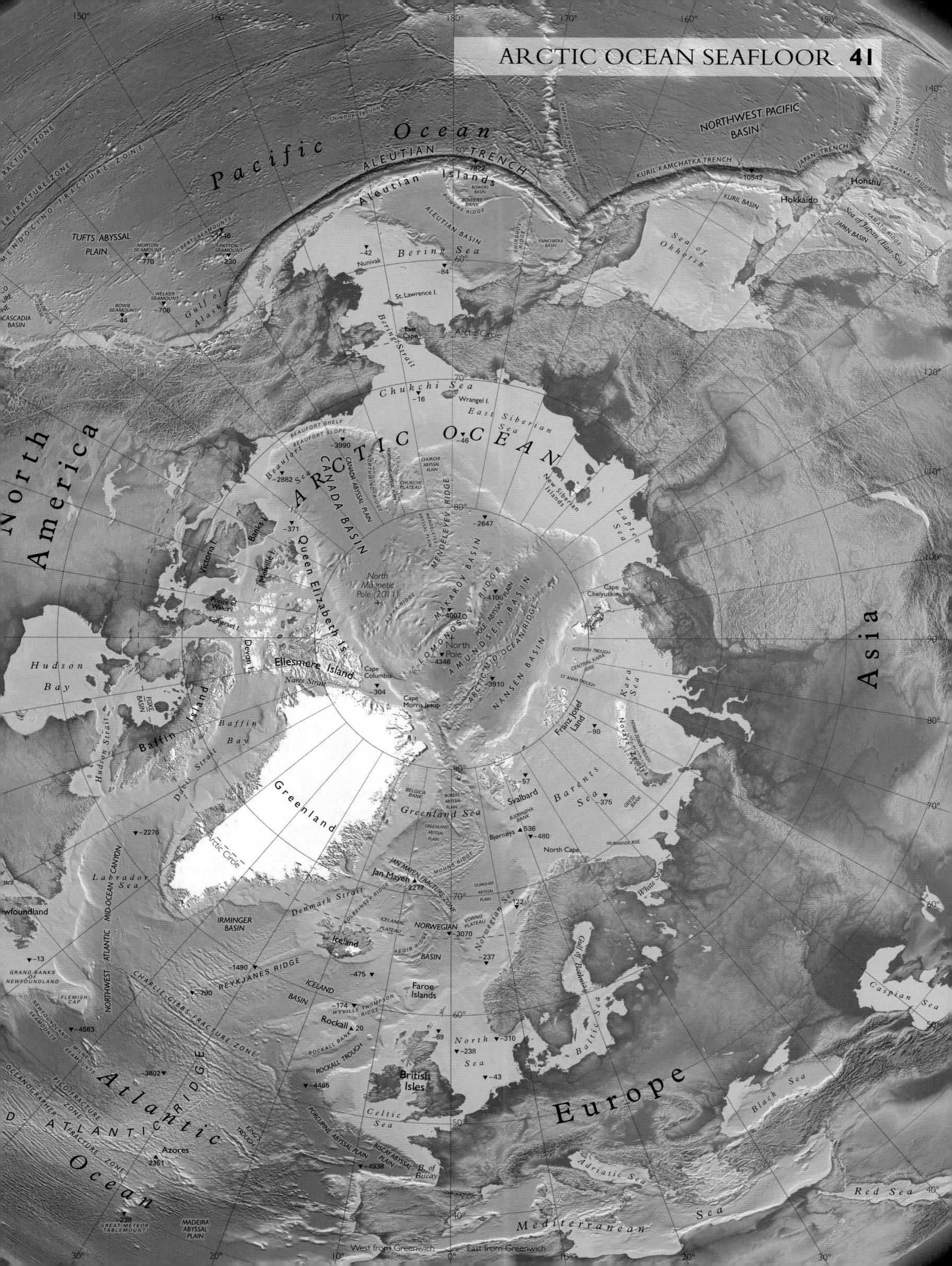

Pacific Ocean

NORTHWEST PACIFIC BASIN

ALEUTIAN TRENCH

Aleutian Islands

BOWERS RIDGE
BOWERS BANK
BOWERS BASIN

KURIL-KAMCHATKA TRENCH

−10542

JAPAN TRENCH

Honshu

NANKAI TROUGH

Hokkaido

KURIL BASIN

−7822

SHIRSHOV RIDGE

KAMCHATKA BASIN

Sea of Okhotsk

Sea of Japan (East Sea)

JAPAN BASIN

CHINOOK TROUGH

MENDOCINO FRACTURE ZONE

FRACTURE ZONE

TUFTS ABYSSAL PLAIN

MORTON SEAMOUNT −770

−648

GILBERT SEAMOUNTS

PATTON SEAMOUNT 230

ALEUTIAN BASIN

Bering Sea

−42 Nunivak

−84

St. Lawrence I.

Bering Strait

East Cape

Arctic Circle

WELKER SEAMOUNT −708

BOWIE SEAMOUNT −44

Gulf of Alaska

CASCADIA BASIN

Chukchi Sea −16

Wrangel I.

East Siberian Sea

−46

New Siberian Islands

Laptev Sea

North America

BEAUFORT SHELF
BEAUFORT SLOPE

−3990

Beaufort Sea

−2882

CANADA BASIN

NORTHWIND RIDGE
NORTHWIND ESCARPMENT

CHUKCHI ABYSSAL PLAIN

CHUKCHI PLATEAU

MENDELEEV RIDGE

MENDELEEV ABYSSAL PLAIN

−2647

Cape Chelyuskin

ARCTIC OCEAN

−371

Banks I.

Victoria I.

Melville I.

Queen Elizabeth Is.

ALPHA RIDGE

North Magnetic Pole (2011) +

MAKAROV BASIN

−4007

−4100

LOMONOSOV RIDGE

POLE ABYSSAL PLAIN

AMUNDSEN BASIN

NANSEN BASIN

−3910

VOZONIN TROUGH

CENTRAL KARA RISE

ST. ANNA TROUGH

Kara Sea

Asia

Prince of Wales I.

Somerset I.

Devon I.

Ellesmere Island

Cape Columbia −304

Nares Strait

North Pole −4346

+

ARCTIC MID-OCEAN RIDGE

Franz Josef Land −90

Novaya Zemlya

Hudson Bay

FOXE BASIN

Baffin Island

Devon Strait

Baffin Bay

Cape Morris Jesup

Cape

80°

−57

Svalbard

Barents Sea −375

GEESE BANK

Hudson Strait

−2276

Greenland

Arctic Circle

BELGICA BANK

BOREAS ABYSSAL PLAIN

GREENLAND ABYSSAL PLAIN

Greenland Sea

BJØRNØYA BANK

Bjørnøya 536

−480

North Cape

MURMANSK RISE

White Sea

Gulf of Bothnia

Labrador Sea

NORTHWEST ATLANTIC MID-OCEAN CANYON

IRMINGER BASIN

Denmark Strait

JAN MAYEN FRACTURE ZONE

Jan Mayen 277

MOHNS RIDGE

DUMSHAF ABYSSAL PLAIN

Norwegian Sea −122

Newfoundland

−13

GRAND BANKS OF NEWFOUNDLAND

KOLBEINSEY RIDGE

ICELANDIC PLATEAU

NORWEGIAN

VORING PLATEAU

−3070

Iceland

−1490

REYKJANES RIDGE

ICELAND BASIN

−475

BASIN

−237

Baltic Sea

FLEMISH CAP

CHARLIE GIBBS FRACTURE ZONE

−790

AEGIR RIDGE

−174

WYVILLE THOMPSON RIDGE

Faroe Islands

NEWFOUNDLAND SEAMOUNTS

MINES SEAMOUNTS

−4563

Rockall 20

ROCKALL BANK

−69

−310

North

−238

Sea

Black Sea

OCEANOGRAPHER FRACTURE ZONE

−3802

PICO FRACTURE ZONE

MID-ATLANTIC RIDGE

ROCKALL TROUGH

−4465

British Isles

−43

Caspian Sea

Azores 2361

KING'S TROUGH

PORCUPINE ABYSSAL PLAIN

BISCAY ABYSSAL PLAIN

−4938

Celtic Sea

B. of Biscay

Europe

Adriatic Sea

Red Sea

MADEIRA ABYSSAL PLAIN

GREAT METEOR TABLEMOUNT 238

Mediterranean Sea

West from Greenwich

East from Greenwich

Atlantic Ocean

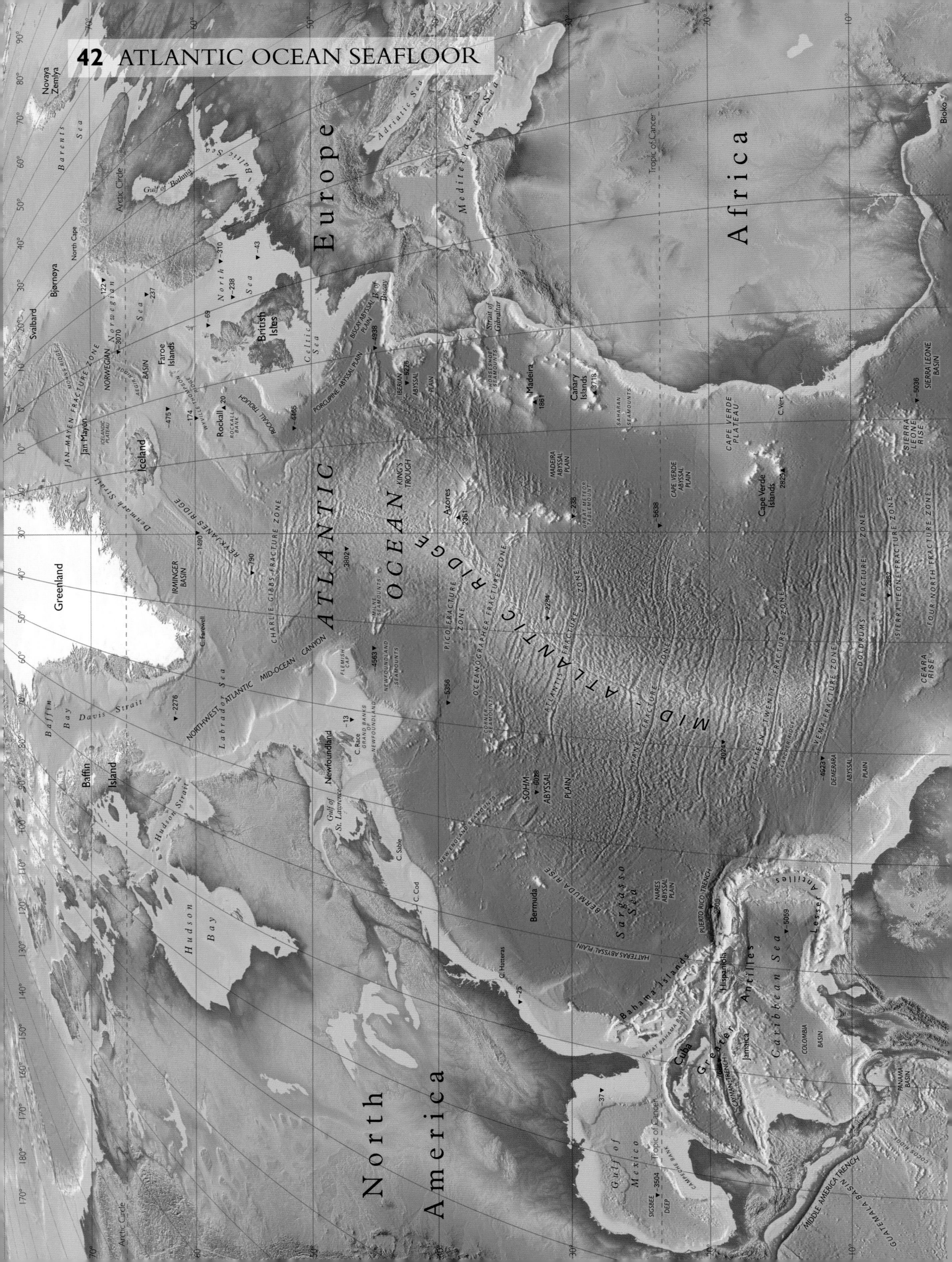

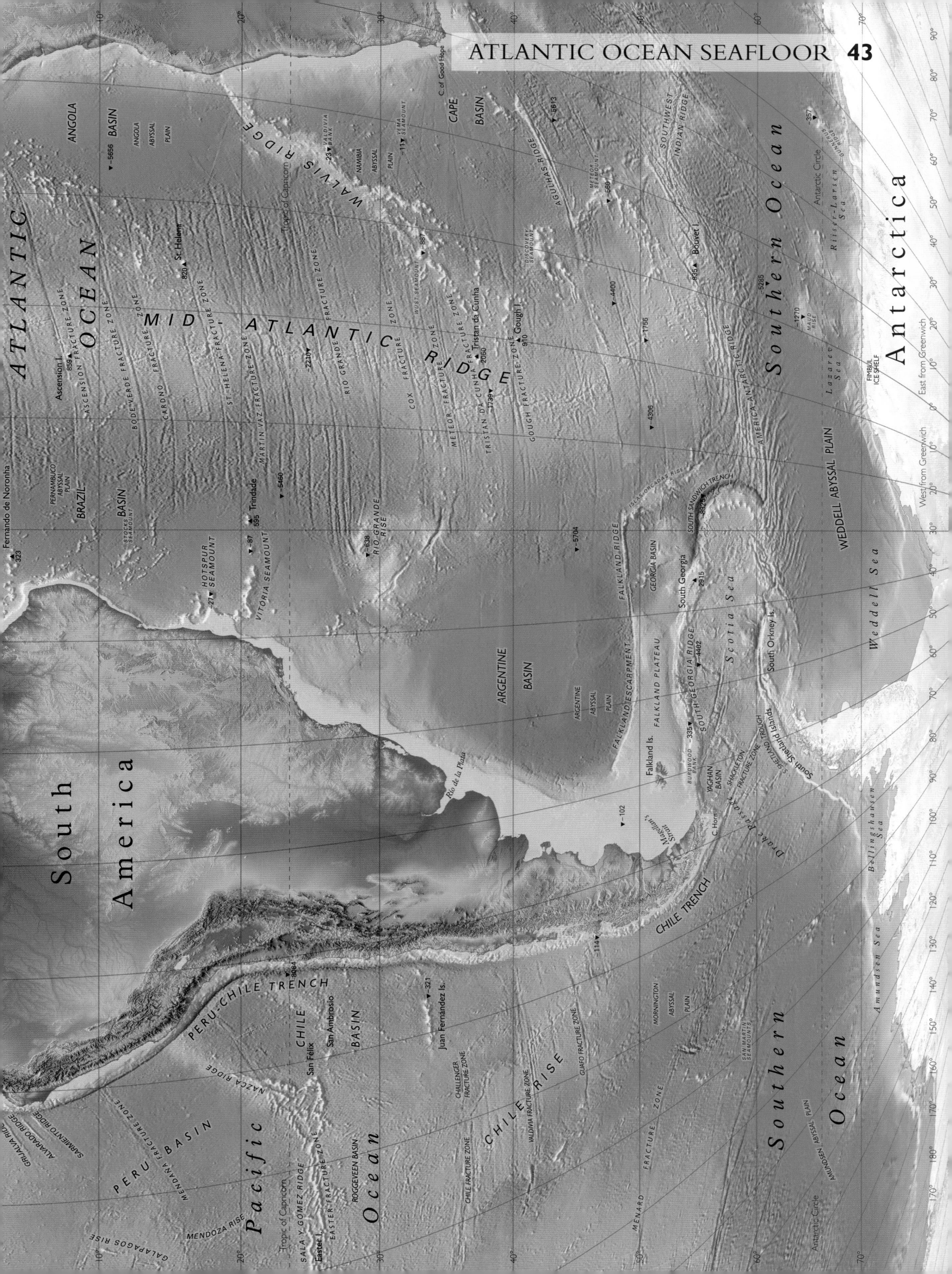

ATLANTIC

ANGOLA

ANGOLA BASIN

▼-5656

ANGOLA ABYSSAL PLAIN

NAMIBIA ABYSSAL PLAIN

VALDIVIA BANK

-23▼

-2210▼

St. Helena

820▲

Ascension I. 859▲

Fernando de Noronha

PERNAMBUCO ABYSSAL PLAIN

BRAZIL

▲-323

BRAZIL BASIN

STOCKS SEAMOUNT

HOTSPUR SEAMOUNT

-27▼

VITORIA SEAMOUNT

Trindade 595▲

-5460▼

-87▼

-638▼

RIO GRANDE RISE

-5704▼

O C E A N

M I D - A T L A N T I C

WALVIS RIDGE

ASCENSION FRACTURE ZONE

BODE VERDE FRACTURE ZONE

CARDNO FRACTURE ZONE

ST. HELENA FRACTURE ZONE

MARTIN VAZ FRACTURE ZONE

VALDIVIA FRACTURE ZONE

RIO GRANDE FRACTURE ZONE

COX FRACTURE ZONE

METEOR FRACTURE ZONE

GOUGH FRACTURE ZONE

VEMA SEAMOUNT

-11▼

WÜST SEAMOUNT

TRISTAN DA CUNHA FRACTURE ZONE

Tristan da Cunha 2060▲

-1799▼

Gough I. 910▲

C. of Good Hope

CAPE BASIN

AGUILHAS RIDGE

-5613▼

DISCOVERY SEAMOUNT

METEOR SEAMOUNT

-660▼

-4400▼

R I D G E

-887▼

-1766▼

-4306▼

SOUTHWEST INDIAN RIDGE

Bouvet I. 935▲

-5285▼

-1270▼

MAUD RISE

-357▲

Antarctic Circle

RIISER-LARSEN ICE SHELF

Riiser-Larsen Sea

FIMBUL ICE SHELF

East from Greenwich

Lazaret Sea

Southern Ocean

Antarctica

ISLAS ORCADAS RISE

SOUTH SANDWICH TRENCH

-8325▼

South Georgia

2915▲

-335▼

GEORGIA BASIN

South Orkney Is.

SCOTIA SEA

SOUTH GEORGIA RIDGE

-4402▼

South Shetland Islands

AMERICA-ANTARCTIC RIDGE

WEDDELL ABYSSAL PLAIN

Weddell Sea

FALKLAND RIDGE

FALKLAND ESCARPMENT

FALKLAND PLATEAU

Falkland Is.

ARGENTINE BASIN

ARGENTINE ABYSSAL PLAIN

Río de la Plata

-102▼

BURDWOOD BANK

YAGHAN BASIN

SHACKLETON FRACTURE ZONE

SHETLAND TROUGH

C. Horn

Magellan Strait

Drake Passage

Bellingshausen Sea

Amundsen Sea

Southern

South

America

CHILE

San Felix

San Ambrosio

Juan Fernández Is.

-321▼

Tropic of Capricorn

Easter I.

PERU-CHILE TRENCH

-3064▲

PERU BASIN

ROGGEVEEN BASIN

MENDOZA RISE

GALAPAGOS RISE

GRIJALVA RISE

ALVARADO RIDGE

SARMIENTO RIDGE

SALA Y GOMEZ RIDGE

NAZCA RIDGE

EASTER FRACTURE ZONE

MENDAÑA FRACTURE ZONE

CHILE RIDGE

CHILE FRACTURE ZONE

CHALLENGER FRACTURE ZONE

VALDIVIA FRACTURE ZONE

GUAFO FRACTURE ZONE

CHILE RISE

MORNINGTON ABYSSAL PLAIN

MENARD FRACTURE ZONE

VALDIVIA FRACTURE ZONE

SAN MARTIN SEAMOUNTS

CHILE TRENCH

-114▼

Pacific Ocean

Ocean

AMUNDSEN ABYSSAL PLAIN

Antarctic Circle

West from Greenwich

Arctic Circle

Asia

Bering Sea

St. Lawrence I.

ALEUTIAN BASIN

Sea of Okhotsk
~1000

Kamchatka

BOWERS RIDGE
BOWERS BANK
BOWERS BASIN

ALEUTIAN ISLANDS

ALEUTIAN TRENCH

CHIROCK TROUGH

KURIL BASIN

KURIL KAMCHATKA TRENCH

KAMCHATKA

EMPEROR SEAMOUNT CHAIN

HESS RISE

EMPEROR TROUGH

Hokkaido
~10542

NORTHWEST PACIFIC BASIN

SHATSKY RISE
~2450

Sea of Japan (East Sea)

YAMATO RIDGE
JAPAN BASIN

Honshu
~841

JAPAN TRENCH

Midway Is. ~13

HAWAII

Yellow Sea

East China Sea

NANKAI TROUGH

IZU OGASAWARA TRENCH

BONIN TRENCH

PALAU KYUSHU RIDGE

MARIANA RIDGE

MARIANA TROUGH

MARIANA TRENCH

MID-PACIFIC SEAMOUNTS

MAPMAKERS SEAMOUNTS

MAGELLAN SEAMOUNTS

Tropic of Cancer

Taiwan

OKINAWA SHOTO TRENCH
NANSEI SHOTO RIDGE
NANSEI SHOTO TRENCH

PHILIPPINE

Hainan

Gulf of Tonkin

South China Sea

Luzon

SOUTH CHINA BASIN

Bay of Bengal

Maudin Sun

Andaman Is. 732

ANDAMAN SEA
ANDAMAN BASIN
~4267

Nicobar Is. ▲642

Ceylon

Dondra Head

Gulf of Thailand

PALAWAN TROUGH

Philippine Islands
~10057

Mindanao

PHILIPPINE TRENCH

PHILIPPINE BASIN

WEST MARIANA BASIN

CHALLENGER DEEP ~11022

EAST MARIANA BASIN

Palau Is.

PALAU TRENCH
AP TRENCH

CAROLINE SEAMOUNTS

Marshall Is.

MARSHALL SEAMOUNTS

CENTRAL PACIFIC BASIN

Micronesia

PACIFIC

Sulu Sea
SULU BASIN

~22

SUNDA SHELF

Celebes Sea
CELEBES BASIN

EAURIPIK RISE

Pohnpei 791

WEST CAROLINE BASIN

EAST CAROLINE BASIN

MELANESIAN BASIN

Phoenix Is.

NINETYEAST RIDGE

COCOS BASIN

MENTAWAI BASIN

Sumatra

MAKASSAR STRAIT
SOUTH MAKASSAR BASIN

Celebes

Borneo

SERAM SEA

NORTH BANDA BASIN

BANDA SEA

New Guinea

Bismarck Sea
New Britain

ONTONG JAVA PLATEAU

SOLOMON RISE

Melanesia

CEYLON PLAIN
~1550

AFANASY NIKITIN SEAMOUNT

MID-INDIAN OCEAN BASIN

Java Sea

Sunda Str.

Java

FLORES SEA

SOUTH BANDA BASIN

Timor

Arafura Sea

ARAFURA SHELF

Torres Str.

PAPUA PLATEAU

NEW BRITAIN TRENCH ~8940

Solomon Sea

SOUTH SOLOMON TRENCH

~8322
~9165

Samoa I.

Indian Ocean

Cocos Is.

OSBORN PLATEAU

INVESTIGATOR RIDGE

SUNDA TRENCH (JAVA TRENCH)
SUNDA TROUGH ~7125

Christmas I. ▲61

ROO RISE

~6204

Timor Sea

ARAFURA SHELF

SAHUL SHELF

Gulf of Carpentaria

Great Barrier Reef

CORAL SEA BASIN

QUEENSLAND PLATEAU

Coral Sea

POCKLINGTON TROUGH

Espiritu Santo

New Caledonia

WEST FIJI BASIN

Fiji Is.

~570

NORTH AUSTRALIAN BASIN

GASCOGNE PLAIN

EXMOUTH PLATEAU

North West C.
CUVIER BASIN

WALLABY PLATEAU

CUVIER PLATEAU

C. Inscription

Australia

NEW HEBRIDES TRENCH

LORD HOWE SEAMOUNT CHAIN

NORFOLK RIDGE

NEW CALEDONIA RISE

Norfolk I. ▲319

SOUTH FIJI BASIN

~10822

Tropic of Capricorn

WHARTON BASIN

EAST INDIAMAN RIDGE

BATAVIA KNOLL

GULDEN DRAAK KNOLL

PERTH BASIN

NATURALISTE FRACTURE ZONE

BROUWER SEAMOUNT ~5745

NATURALISTE PLATEAU
C. Leeuwin

DIAMANTINA FRACTURE ZONE ~6602

LORD HOWE RISE

HAWKE TROUGH

COLVILLE RIDGE

TONGA TRENCH

KERMADEC TRENCH

~10047

SOUTH FIJI BASIN

BROKEN RIDGE

Amsterdam I. ▲881

St. Paul Is. ▲284

SOUTH AUSTRALIAN BASIN

Bass Str.

Tasman Sea

Tasmania

TASMAN ABYSSAL PLAIN

EAST TASMAN PLATEAU

CHALLENGER PLATEAU

TASMAN BASIN

North I.

New Zealand

CHATHAM RISE

Chatham

DEL CAÑO RISE

Crozet Is. ▲1090
~4590

SOUTHEAST INDIAN RIDGE

Kerguelen Is. ▲1850

274

Heard I. ▲2745

KERGUELEN PLATEAU

South I.

BOUNTY TROUGH

Bounty Is. ~60
BOUNTY PLATEAU

Antipodes I.

Auckland Is.

CAMPBELL PLATEAU

Campbell I. ▲272

BOLLONS SEAMOUNT

SNARES SEAMOUNT

Macquarie I.

AUSTRALIAN-ANTARCTIC DISCORDANCE

AUSTRALIAN-ANTARCTIC BASIN

SOUTH INDIAN ABYSSAL PLAIN ~4650

Dumont d'Urville Sea

~6240

MACQUARIE RIDGE

~6800

CONRAD RISE

LENA SEAMOUNT

ELAN BANK

~6739

ENDERBY ABYSSAL PLAIN

VALDIVIA ABYSSAL PLAIN

AMERY BASIN

C. Borley

5325

PRINCESS ELIZABETH TROUGH

Davis Sea

Vincennes Bay

Paulding Bay

Porpoise Bay

Prydz Bay

Balleny Is.

Scott I. ~50

Southern Ocean

Antarctic Circle

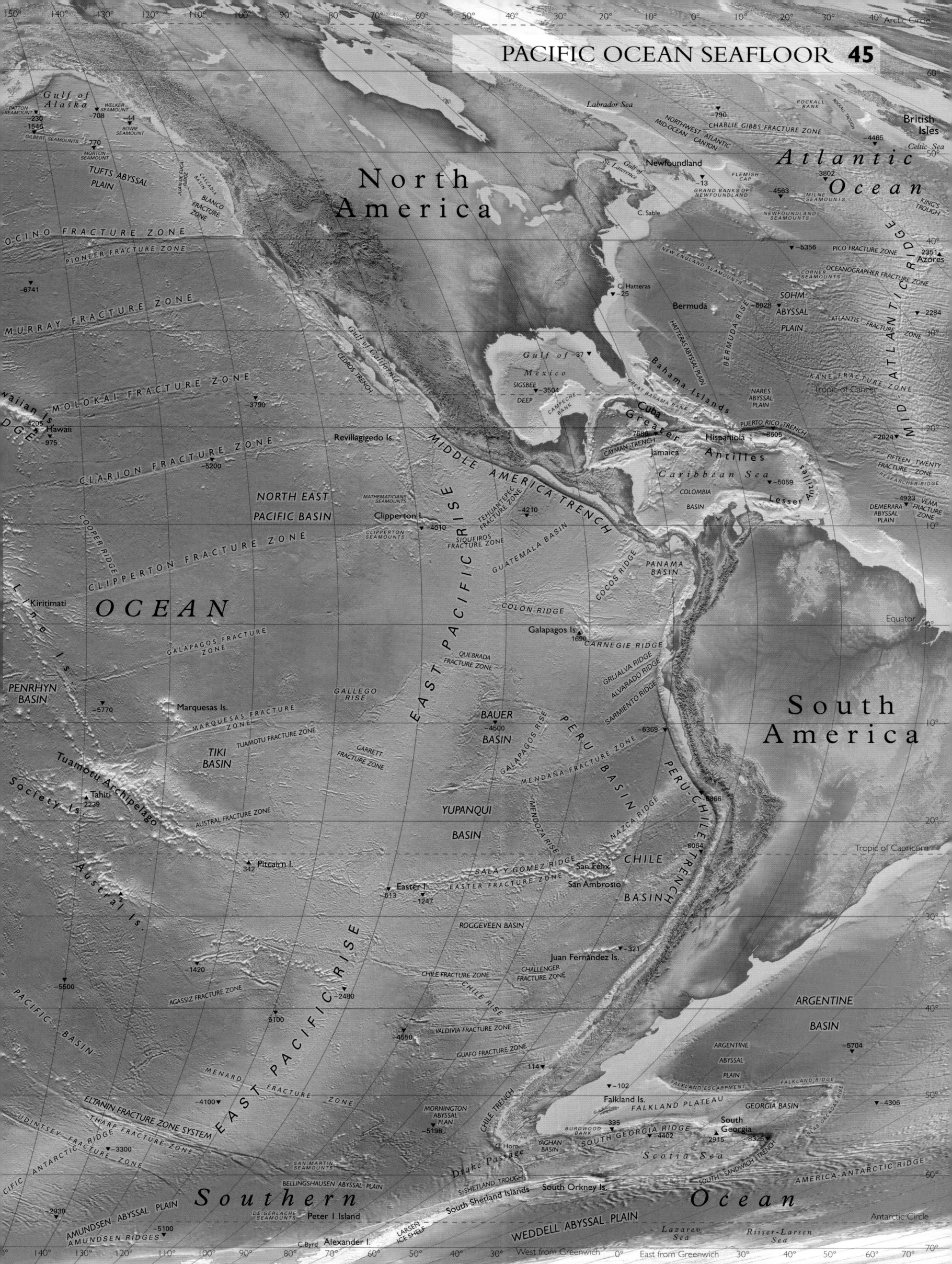

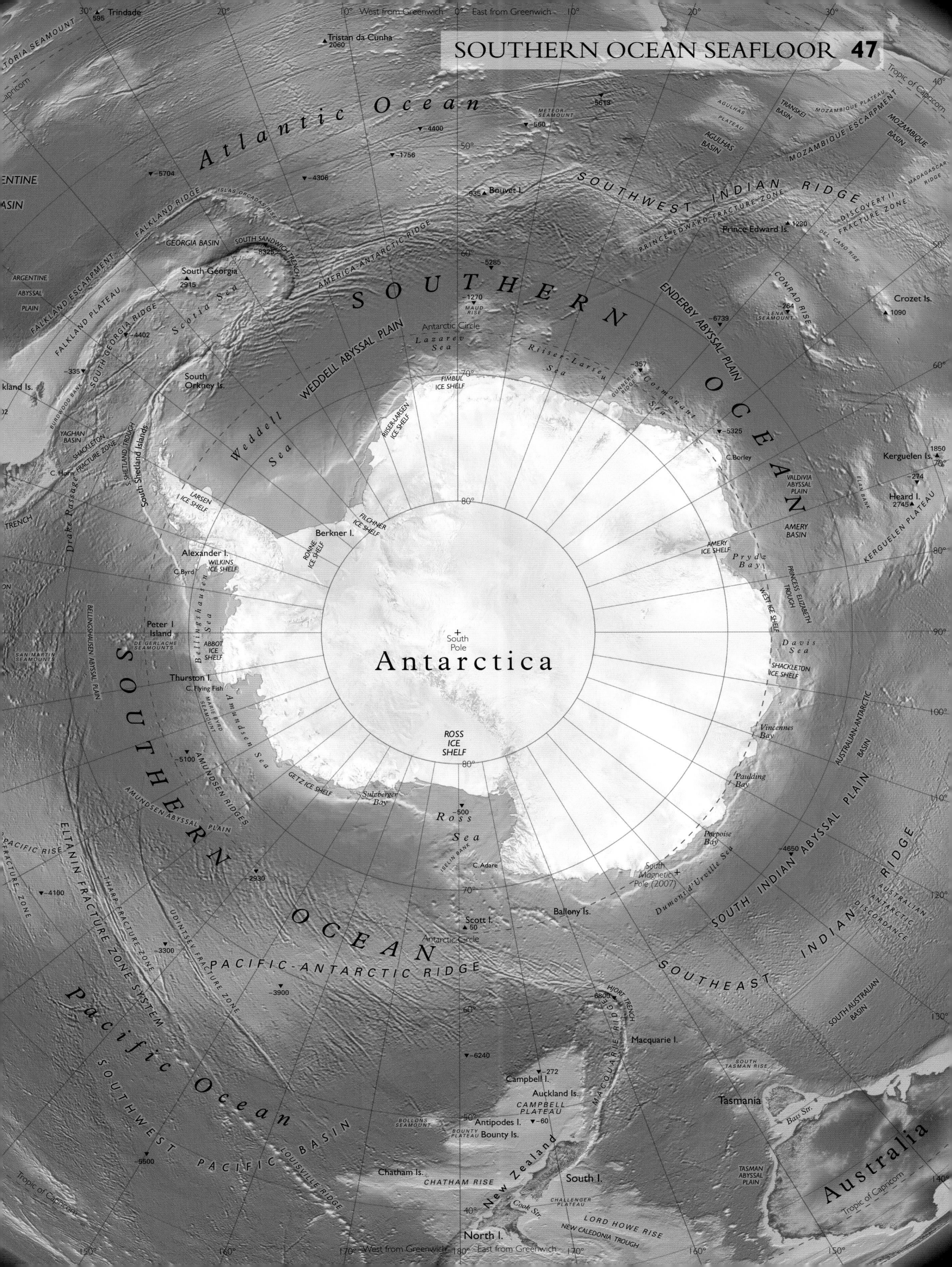

30° Trinidade
595
20°
10° West from Greenwich
0° East from Greenwich
10°
20°
30°
40° Tropic of Capricorn

Tristan da Cunha
2060

▼ -5613

Atlantic Ocean

-5704 ▼
▼ -4400
MADAGASCAR RIDGE

ORIA SEAMOUNT
-4306 ▼
50°
-560 ▼
METEOR SEAMOUNT
-935 ▲ Bouvet I.
AGULHAS PLATEAU
TRANSKEI BASIN
MOZAMBIQUE PLATEAU
MOZAMBIQUE ESCARPMENT
MOZAMBIQUE BASIN

Capricorn
-1756 ▼
SOUTHWEST INDIAN RIDGE
AGULHAS BASIN

ENTINE
FALKLAND RIDGE
ISLAS ORCADAS RISE
SOUTH SANDWICH TRENCH
-8326
AMERICA-ANTARCTIC RIDGE
PRINCE EDWARD FRACTURE ZONE
DISCOVERY II FRACTURE ZONE
DEL CANO RISE

GEORGIA BASIN
▼ -5285
Prince Edward Is. ▲ 1230

ARGENTINE ABYSSAL PLAIN
South Georgia
2915 ▲
Scotia Sea
S O U T H E R N
ENDERBY ABYSSAL PLAIN
CONRAD RISE
2264 ▲
LENA SEAMOUNT
Crozet Is.

FALKLAND ESCARPMENT
SOUTH GEORGIA RIDGE
-4402 ▼
-1270 MAUD RISE
Antarctic Circle
▼ -6739
▲ 1090

kland Is.
-335 ▼
BURDWOOD BANK
South Orkney Is.
Lazarev Sea
Riiser-Larsen Sea
▼ -357
GUNNERUS RIDGE
COSMONAUT SEA
Kerguelen Is. 1850

02
YAGHAN BASIN
SHACKLETON FRACTURE ZONE
FIMBUL ICE SHELF
O C E A N
C. Borley
▼ -5325
-214 ▼

C. Horn
S. SHETLAND ISLANDS
Drake Passage Fracture Zone
Weddell Sea
WEDDELL ABYSSAL PLAIN
RIISER-LARSEN ICE SHELF
70°
VALDIVIA ABYSSAL PLAIN
ELAN BANK
Heard I.
2745 ▲

TRENCH
LARSEN ICE SHELF
80°
FILCHNER ICE SHELF
Berkner I.
AMERY ICE SHELF
Prydz Bay
AMERY BASIN
KERGUELEN PLATEAU

Alexander I.
WILKINS ICE SHELF
C. Byrd
RONNE ICE SHELF
South Pole
Antarctica
WEST ICE SHELF
PRINCESS ELIZABETH TROUGH
90°

Bellingshausen Sea
Peter I Island
DE GERLACHE SEAMOUNTS
ABBOT ICE SHELF
Davis Sea
SHACKLETON ICE SHELF

SAN MARTIN SEAMOUNTS
BELLINGSHAUSEN ABYSSAL PLAIN
Thurston I.
C. Flying Fish
ROSS ICE SHELF
Vincennes Bay
100°
AUSTRALIAN-ANTARCTIC BASIN

ON
MARIE BYRD SEAMOUNT
Amundsen Sea
Paulding Bay

S O U T H E R N
▼ -5100
AMUNDSEN RIDGES
80°
110°

EAST PACIFIC RISE
ELTANIN FRACTURE ZONE SYSTEM
AMUNDSEN ABYSSAL PLAIN
GETZ ICE SHELF
Sulzberger Bay
Ross Sea
▼ -500
Porpoise Bay

FRACTURE ZONE
THARP FRACTURE ZONE
-2930 ▼
ISELIN BANK
South Magnetic Pole (2007) +
Dumont d'Urville Sea
-4650 ▼
SOUTH INDIAN ABYSSAL PLAIN
120°

-4100 ▼
UDINTSEV FRACTURE ZONE
70°
C. Adare
AUSTRALIAN-ANTARCTIC DISCORDANCE
RIDGE

Pacific Ocean
-3300 ▼
O C E A N
Ballen Is.
Scott I.
50 ▲
Antarctic Circle
SOUTHEAST
SOUTH AUSTRALIAN BASIN
130°

PACIFIC-ANTARCTIC RIDGE
-3900 ▼
HJORT TRENCH
6800
MACQUARIE RIDGE
INDIAN

SOUTHWEST PACIFIC BASIN
LOUISVILLE RIDGE
-6240 ▼
Macquarie I.
SOUTH TASMAN RISE

-5500 ▼
BOLLONS SEAMOUNT
Campbell I.
-272 ▲
Auckland Is.
CAMPBELL PLATEAU
Tasmania
BASS STR.
TASMAN ABYSSAL PLAIN

Tropic of Capricorn
Chatham Is.
BOUNTY PLATEAU
Antipodes I.
-60 ▼
Bounty Is.
New Zealand
South I.
LORD HOWE RISE
Australia

CHATHAM RISE
COOK STR.
CHALLENGER PLATEAU
NEW CALEDONIA TROUGH

North I.
170° West from Greenwich
180° East from Greenwich
170°
160°
150°

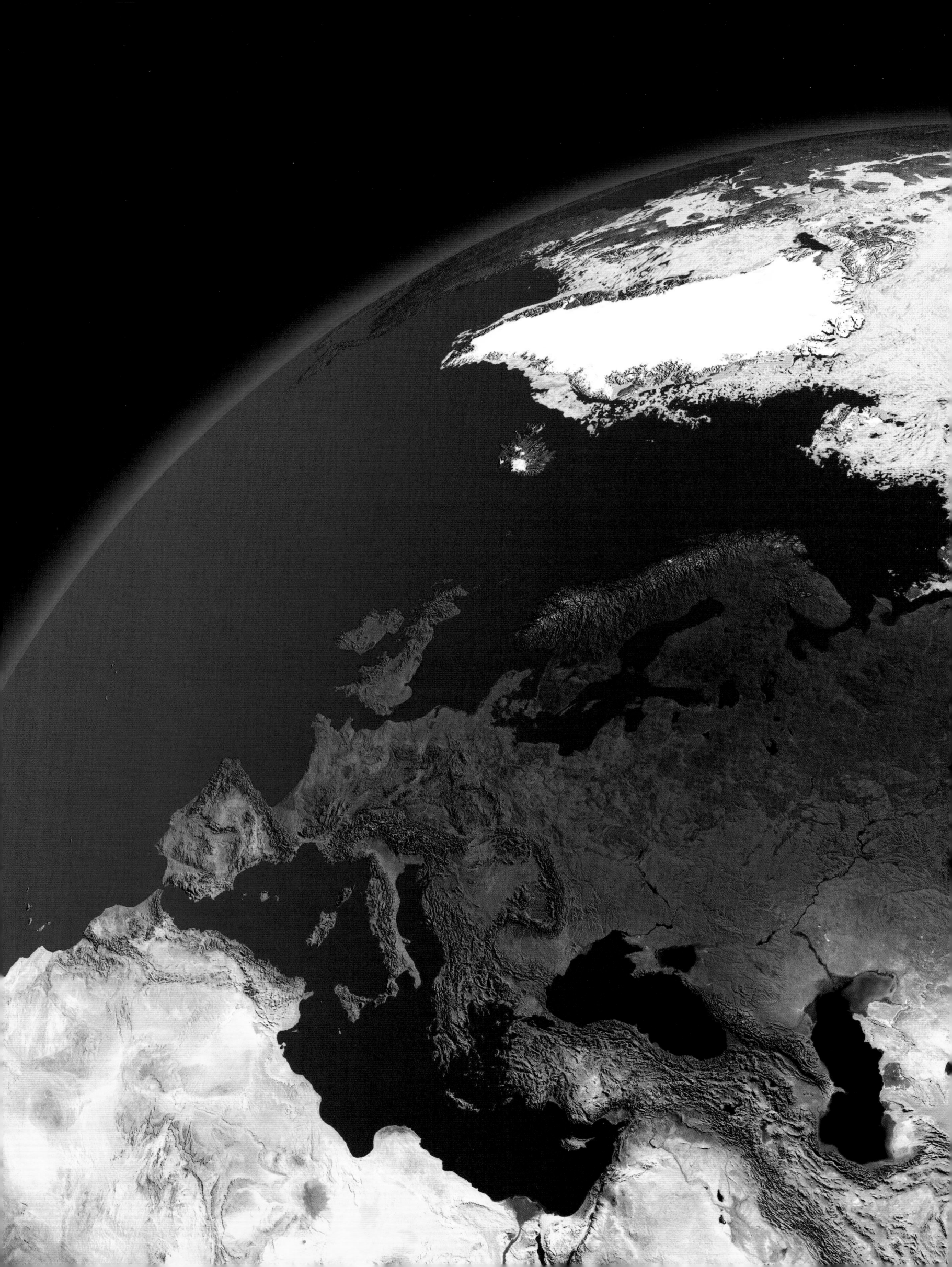

WORLD
MAPS

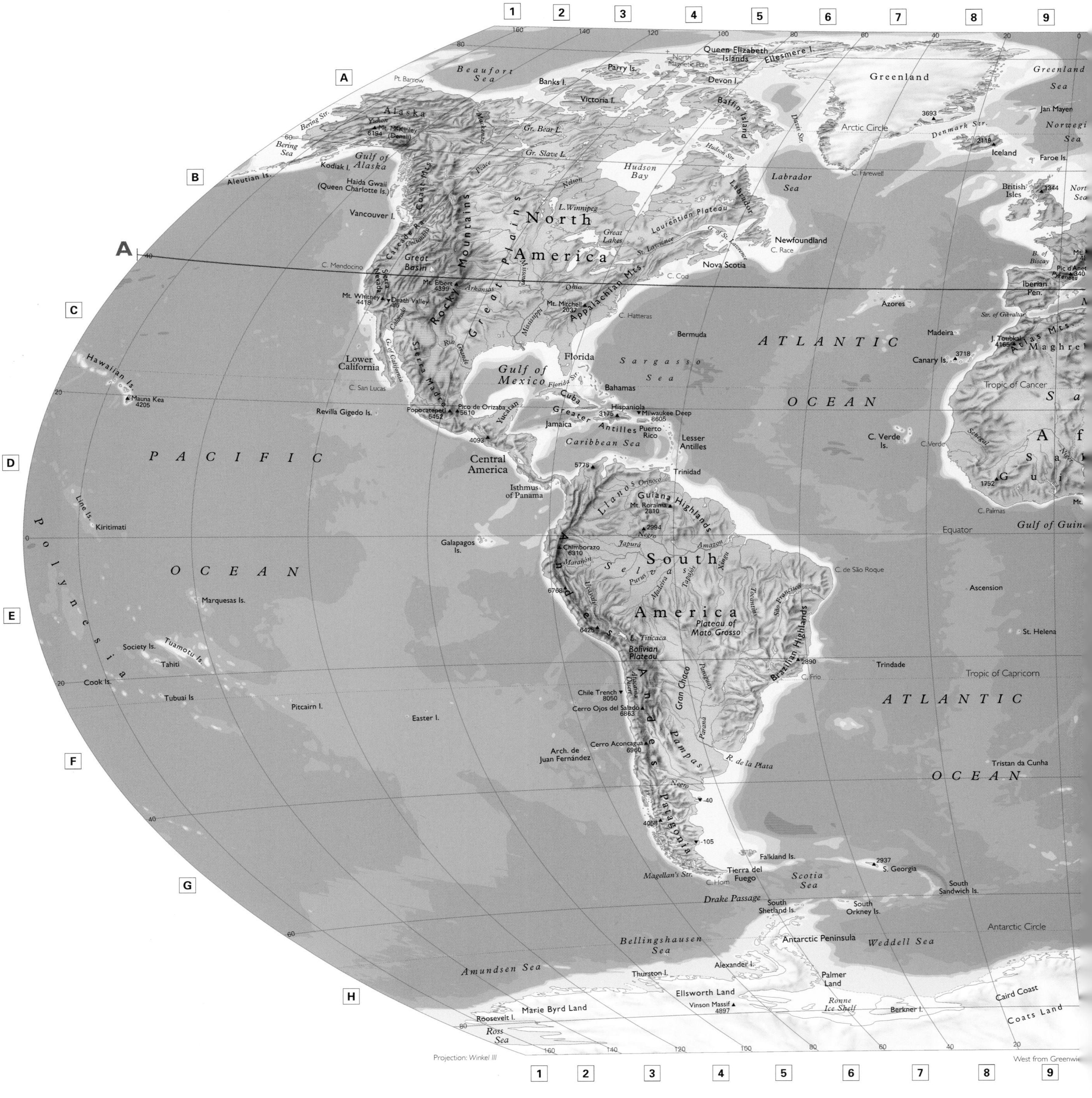

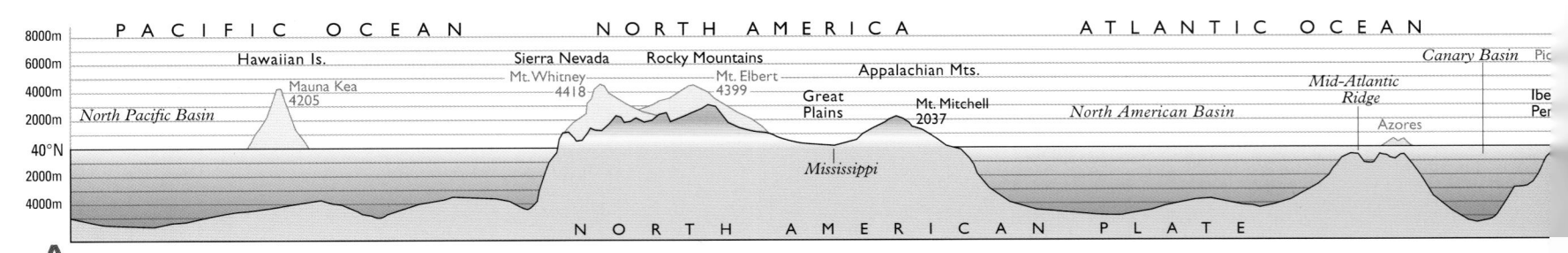

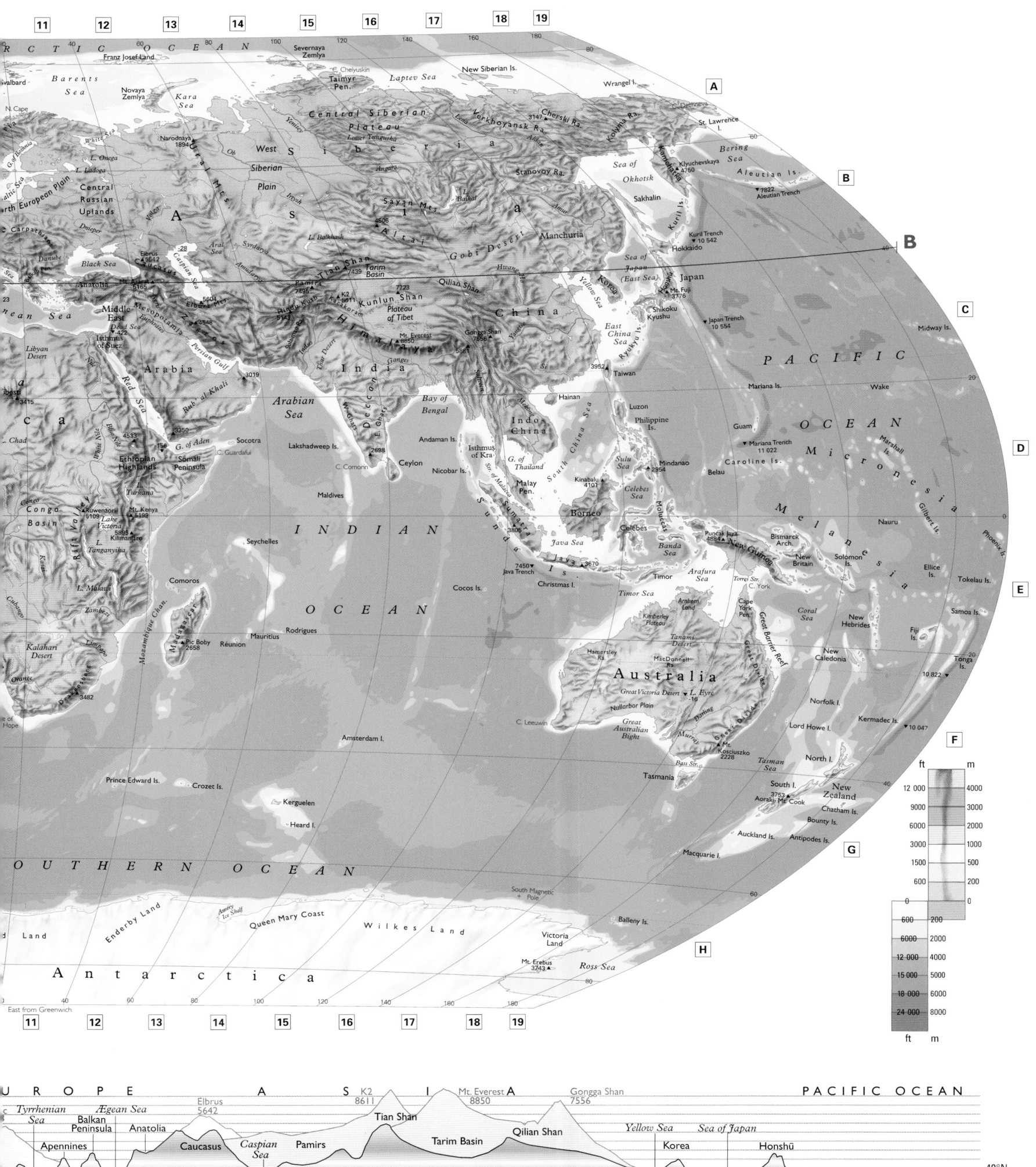

Equatorial Scale 1:84 000 000

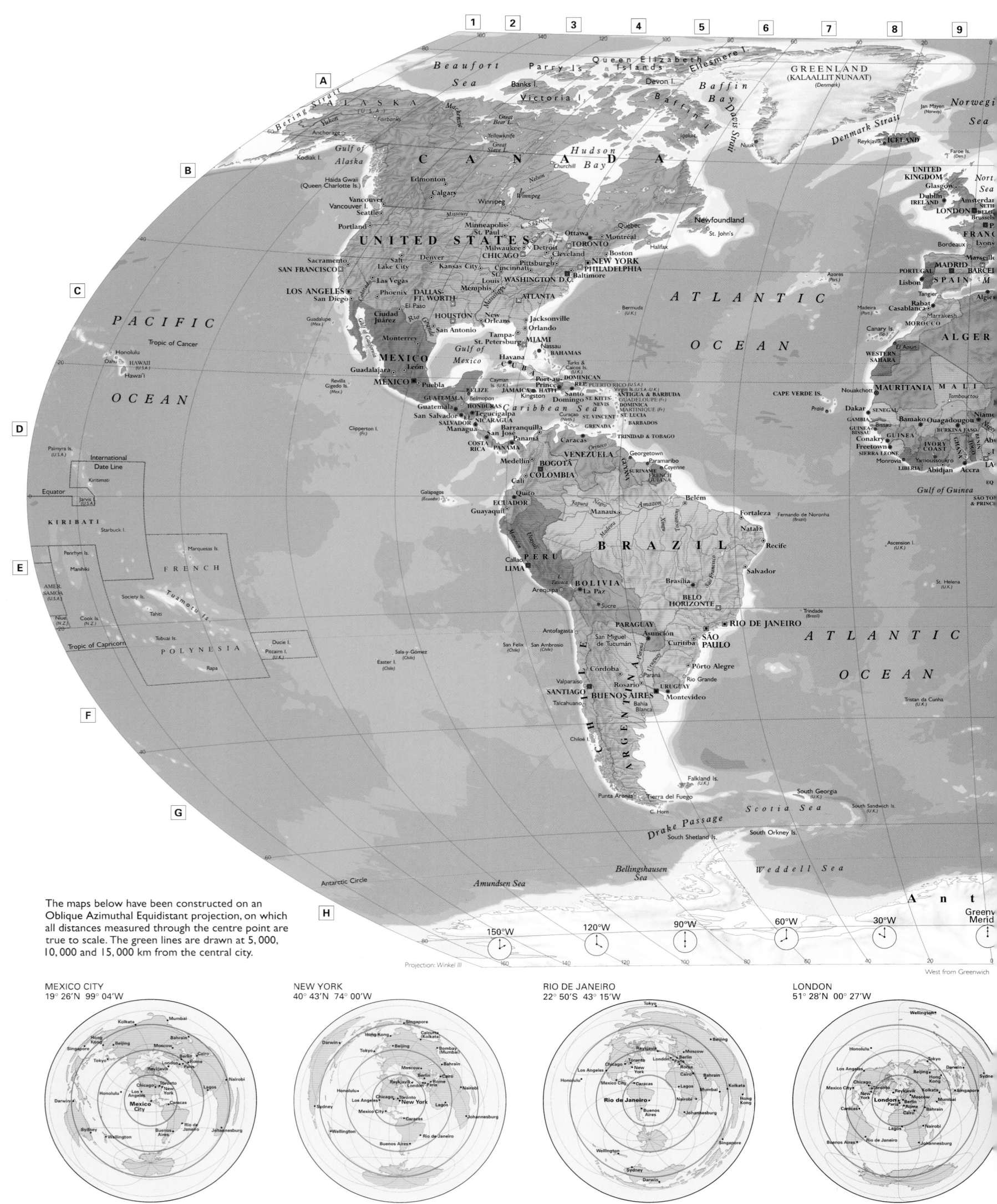

1 **2** **3** **4** **5** **6** **7** **8** **9**

Beaufort Sea
Parry Is.
Queen Elizabeth Islands
Ellesmere I.
GREENLAND
(KALAALLIT NUNAAT)
(Denmark)
Jan Mayen (Norway)
Norwegian Sea

Banks I.
Devon I.
Baffin Bay
Bering Strait
Yukon
ALASKA (U.S.A.)
Anchorage
Fairbanks
Victoria I.
Mackenzie
Great Bear L.
Yellowknife
Great Slave L.
Baffin I.
Davis Strait
Iqaluit
Nuuk
Denmark Strait
Reykjavik ICELAND
Faroe Is. (Den.)

Kodiak I.
Gulf of Alaska
Haida Gwaii (Queen Charlotte Is.)
C A N A D A
Hudson Bay
Churchill
Newfoundland
St. John's

UNITED KINGDOM
Glasgow
North Sea
Dublin
IRELAND
LONDON
Amsterdam NETH.
Brussels BELG.

Vancouver I.
Vancouver
Seattle
Portland
Edmonton
Calgary
Winnipeg
L. Winnipeg
Nelson
Ottawa
Montréal
TORONTO
Québec
Halifax

UNITED STATES
Minneapolis-St. Paul
Milwaukee
CHICAGO
Detroit
Cleveland
Boston
NEW YORK
PHILADELPHIA
Baltimore
WASHINGTON D.C.

FRANCE
Bordeaux
Lyons
Marseille

Sacramento
SAN FRANCISCO
Salt Lake City
Denver
Kansas City
St. Louis
Cincinnati
Pittsburgh

ATLANTIC OCEAN

PORTUGAL
Lisbon
MADRID
SPAIN
BARCE

LOS ANGELES
San Diego
Las Vegas
Phoenix
DALLAS-FT. WORTH
Memphis
ATLANTA

Bermuda (U.K.)
Azores (Port.)

Tangiers
Rabat
Casablanca
MOROCCO
ALGER

PACIFIC OCEAN

Tropic of Cancer

El Paso
Ciudad Juárez
Rio Grande
HOUSTON
New Orleans
Jacksonville
Orlando
MIAMI
Tampa-St. Petersburg
Nassau
BAHAMAS

Madeira (Port.)
Canary Is. (Sp.)
El Aaiún
WESTERN SAHARA

Honolulu
Oahu HAWAII (U.S.A.)
Hawai'i

Guadalupe (Mex.)
Gulf of Mexico
Havana
CUBA
Turks & Caicos Is. (U.K.)

Nouakchott
MAURITANIA
MALI

Revilla Gigedo Is. (Mex.)

Guadalajara
León
MEXICO
Puebla
MÉXICO
CAPE VERDE IS.
Praia
Dakar
SENEGAL

BELIZE
Belmopan
Cayman Is.
JAMAICA
Kingston
Port-au-Prince
HAITI
DOMINICAN REP.
PUERTO RICO (U.S.A.)
Santo Domingo
Virgin Is. (U.S.A.-U.K.)
ANTIGUA & BARBUDA
ST. KITTS & NEVIS
GUADELOUPE (Fr.)
DOMINICA
MARTINIQUE (Fr.)
ST. LUCIA

GAMBIA
GUINEA-BISSAU
Conakry
GUINEA
Freetown
SIERRA LEONE
Monrovia
LIBERIA
IVORY COAST
Bamako
Ouagadougou
BURKINA FASO
Niam
GHANA
Yamoussoukro
Abidjan
Accra

Clipperton I. (Fr.)

GUATEMALA
Guatemala
San Salvador
SALVADOR
HONDURAS
Tegucigalpa
NICARAGUA
Managua
San José
COSTA RICA
PANAMA
Panama
Caribbean Sea
Curaçao (Neth.)
ST. VINCENT
GRENADA
BARBADOS
TRINIDAD & TOBAGO

EQ

Palmyra Is. (U.S.A.)

International Date Line
Kiritimati

Barranquilla
Medellín
Cali
BOGOTÁ
COLOMBIA
Caracas
VENEZUELA
Georgetown
Paramaribo
SURINAME
Cayenne
FRENCH GUIANA
GUYANA
Orinoco

Gulf of Guinea
SÃO TOMÉ & PRÍNCIPE

Equator
Jarvis I. (U.S.A.)

KIRIBATI
Starbuck I.

Galápagos (Ecuador)
Quito
ECUADOR
Guayaquil
Japurá
Negro
Manaus
Amazon
Belém
Fortaleza
Fernando de Noronha (Brazil)
Natal

Ascension I. (U.K.)

Penrhyn Is.
Manihiki

FRENCH

Marquesas Is.

PERU
Callao
LIMA
Juruá
Purus
B R A Z I L
Madeira
Tapajós
Xingu
Tocantins
São Francisco
Recife
Salvador

St. Helena (U.K.)

AMER. SAMOA (U.S.A.)
Niue (N.Z.)
Cook Is. (N.Z.)

Society Is.
Tahiti
Tuamotu Is.
POLYNESIA

BOLIVIA
La Paz
Sucre
Arequipa
Brasília
BELO HORIZONTE

Tropic of Capricorn

Tubuai Is.
Rapa
Ducie I. (U.K.)
Pitcairn I. (U.K.)

Easter I. (Chile)
Sala-y-Gómez (Chile)

San Félix (Chile)
San Ambrosio (Chile)
Antofagasta

PARAGUAY
Asunción
San Miguel de Tucumán
Curitiba
SÃO PAULO
RIO DE JANEIRO
Pôrto Alegre
Rio Grande

Trindade (Brazil)

ATLANTIC OCEAN

Córdoba
Rosario
Paraná
Paraguay
Uruguay
URUGUAY
C H I L E
A R G E N T I N A
Valparaíso
SANTIAGO
BUENOS AIRES
Montevideo
Bahía Blanca
Talcahuano

Tristan da Cunha (U.K.)

Chiloé I.

Falkland Is. (U.K.)
South Georgia (U.K.)

Punta Arenas
Tierra del Fuego
C. Horn
Drake Passage
Scotia Sea
South Shetland Is.
South Orkney Is.
South Sandwich Is. (U.K.)

Antarctic Circle
Amundsen Sea
Bellingshausen Sea
Weddell Sea

A n t

The maps below have been constructed on an Oblique Azimuthal Equidistant projection, on which all distances measured through the centre point are true to scale. The green lines are drawn at 5,000, 10,000 and 15,000 km from the central city.

H

150°W   120°W   90°W   60°W   30°W   Greenwich Meridian

Projection: Winkel III

West from Greenwich

MEXICO CITY
19° 26'N 99° 04'W

NEW YORK
40° 43'N 74° 00'W

RIO DE JANEIRO
22° 50'S 43° 15'W

LONDON
51° 28'N 00° 27'W

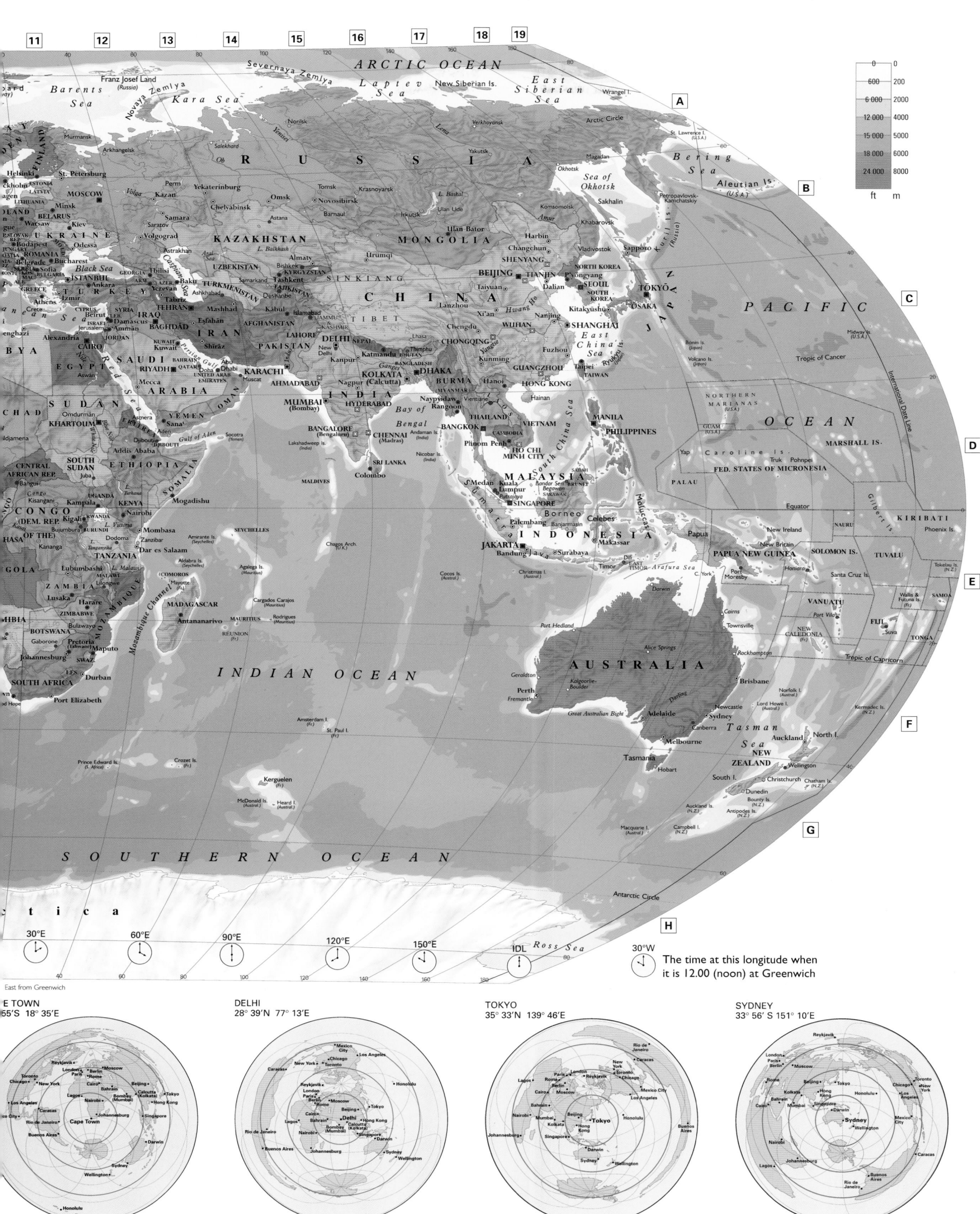

11   12   13   14   15   16   17   18   19

ARCTIC OCEAN

Franz Josef Land
(Russia)

Barents
Sea

Novaya
Zemlya

Severnaya Zemlya

Kara Sea

Laptev
Sea

New Siberian Is.

East
Siberian
Sea

Wrangel I.

Arctic Circle

Murmansk

Arkhangelsk

Norilsk

Verkhoyansk

St. Lawrence I.
(U.S.A.)

FINLAND

Helsinki

St. Petersburg

Perm

Yekaterinburg

Ob

Salekhard

Yakutsk

Magadan

Sea of
Okhotsk

Bering
Sea

ESTONIA

LATVIA

MOSCOW

Kazan

R U S S I A

Tomsk

Krasnoyarsk

Petropavlovsk-
Kamchatsky

Aleutian Is.
(U.S.A.)

Minsk

Volga

Yenisey

Irkutsk

Okhotsk

Khabarovsk

Amur

Warsaw

BELARUS

Samara

Omsk

Novosibirsk

L. Baikal

Ulan Ude

Komsomolsk

UKRAINE

Kiev

Odessa

Saratov

KAZAKHSTAN

Barnaul

MONGOLIA

Ulan Bator

Sakhalin

Vladivostok

Sapporo

ROMANIA

Bucharest

Volgograd

Astrakhan

Aral
Sea

L. Balkhash

Almaty

Harbin

Changchun

SHENYANG

NORTH KOREA

Pyongyang

Kuril Is.
(Russia)

BULGARIA

Black Sea

GEORGIA

Tbilisi

Baku

Bishkek

Urumqi

BEIJING

TIANJIN

Dalian

SEOUL

SOUTH
KOREA

TOKYO

OSAKA

ISTANBUL

Ankara

ARM.
AZER.

UZBEKISTAN

Tashkent

Samarkand

KYRGYZSTAN

S I N K I A N G

Taiyuan

Hwang Ho

Kitakyushu

PACIFIC

TURKEY

Izmir

Athens

GREECE

CYPRUS

SYRIA

Beirut

LEB.
Damascus

Tabriz

TURKMENISTAN

Ashkhabad

TAJIKISTAN

Dushanbe

C H I N A

Lanzhou

Xi'an

Nanjing

WUHAN

SHANGHAI

East
China
Sea

Bonin Is.
(Japan)

Midway Is.
(U.S.A.)

Mediterranean Sea

Jerusalem

ISRAEL

Amman

JORDAN

Baghdad

TEHRAN

Esfahan

Kabul

Islamabad

AFGHANISTAN

JAMMU &
KASHMIR

TIBET

Lhasa

Chengdu

Chongqing

Fuzhou

Taipei

TAIWAN

Volcano Is.
(Japan)

Tropic of Cancer

LIBYA

Alexandria

CAIRO

Shiraz

Persian Gulf

Kuwait

KUWAIT

BAHRAIN

QATAR

Doha

Abu Dhabi

UNITED ARAB
EMIRATES

Muscat

IRAN

IRAQ

LAHORE

PAKISTAN

DELHI

New
Delhi

Kanpur

NEPAL

Katmandu

BHUTAN

Thimphu

BANGLADESH

DHAKA

Kunming

GUANGZHOU

HONG KONG

Hainan

International Date Line

EGYPT

SAUDI
ARABIA

RIYADH

KARACHI

AHMADABAD

Nagpur

Ganges

KOLKATA
(Calcutta)

BURMA
(MYANMAR)

Naypyidaw

Hanoi

NORTHERN
MARIANAS
(U.S.A.)

Aswan

Mecca

Red Sea

MUMBAI
(Bombay)

I N D I A

HYDERABAD

Bay of
Bengal

Rangoon

Vientiane

THAILAND

BANGKOK

VIETNAM

MANILA

GUAM
(U.S.A.)

MARSHALL IS.

CHAD

SUDAN

Omdurman

KHARTOUM

YEMEN

Sana'a

Aden

Gulf of Aden

Socotra
(Yemen)

BANGALORE
(Bengaluru)

Lakshadweep
(India)

CHENNAI
(Madras)

Andaman Is.
(India)

CAMBODIA

Pinom Penh

HO CHI
MINH CITY

Nicobar Is.
(India)

OCEAN

Yap

Caroline Is.

Truk
(F.S.M.)

Pohnpei

FED. STATES OF MICRONESIA

DJIBOUTI

Djibouti

Addis Ababa

SOUTH
SUDAN

Juba

ETHIOPIA

SOMALIA

SRI LANKA

Colombo

MALDIVES

MALAYSIA

Kuala
Lumpur

Putrajaya

SINGAPORE

Medan

SABAH

Bandar Seri
Begawan

BRUNEI

SARAWAK

PALAU

Equator

NAURU

Gilbert Is.

KIRIBATI

Phoenix Is.

CENTRAL
AFRICAN REP.

Bangui

UGANDA

Kampala

KENYA

Nairobi

Mogadishu

Seychelles

Amirante Is.
(Seychelles)

Chagos Arch.
(U.K.)

Palembang

Banjarmasin

Borneo

Celebes

Moluccas

I N D O N E S I A

Papua

New Ireland

New Britain

SOLOMON IS.

TUVALU

CONGO
(DEM. REP.
OF THE)

Kisangani

RWANDA

Kigali

BURUNDI

Bujumbura

L. Victoria

Dodoma

Zanzibar

TANZANIA

Mombasa

Dar es Salaam

Aldabra Is.
(Seychelles)

Agalega Is.
(Mauritius)

JAKARTA

Bandung

Java

Surabaya

Dili

EAST
TIMOR

Timor

Arafura Sea

C. York

Makassar

PAPUA NEW GUINEA

Port
Moresby

Honiara

Santa Cruz Is.

Tokelau
(N.Z.)

ANGOLA

ZAMBIA

Lubumbashi

Kananga

MALAWI

Lilongwe

COMOROS

Mayotte
(Fr.)

Cargados Carajos
(Mauritius)

Christmas I.
(Austral.)

Cocos Is.
(Austral.)

Darwin

Cairns

Townsville

NEW
CALEDONIA
(Fr.)

VANUATU

Port Vila

Wallis &
Futuna (Fr.)

SAMOA

Lusaka

Harare

ZIMBABWE

MADAGASCAR

Antananarivo

MAURITIUS

Rodrigues
(Mauritius)

Port Hedland

Rockhampton

FIJI

Suva

TONGA

ZAMBIA

BOTSWANA

Bulawayo

Pretoria

Gaborone

MOZAMBIQUE

Mozambique Channel

Maputo

SWAZ.

RÉUNION
(Fr.)

Amsterdam I.
(Fr.)

St. Paul I.
(Fr.)

Alice Springs

AUSTRALIA

Brisbane

Newcastle

Sydney

Norfolk I.
(Austral.)

Lord Howe I.
(Austral.)

Tropic of Capricorn

SOUTH AFRICA

Johannesburg

Pretoria

LES.

Durban

Port Elizabeth

C. of Good Hope

Prince Edward Is.
(S. Africa)

Crozet Is.
(Fr.)

INDIAN OCEAN

Geraldton

Perth

Fremantle

Kalgoorlie-
Boulder

Great Australian Bight

Adelaide

Canberra

Melbourne

Darling

Tasman
Sea

Auckland

North I.

Kermadec Is.
(N.Z.)

Kerguelen
(Fr.)

McDonald Is.
(Austral.)

Heard I.
(Austral.)

Tasmania

Hobart

South I.

NEW
ZEALAND

Wellington

Christchurch

Chatham Is.
(N.Z.)

SOUTHERN   OCEAN

Dunedin

Bounty Is.
(N.Z.)

Auckland Is.
(N.Z.)

Antipodes Is.
(N.Z.)

Macquarie I.
(Austral.)

Campbell I.
(N.Z.)

A n t a r c t i c a

Antarctic Circle

Ross Sea

A

B

C

D

E

F

G

H

0   0
600   200
6 000 2000
12 000 4000
15 000 5000
18 000 6000
24 000 8000
ft   m

30°E   60°E   90°E   120°E   150°E   IDL

East from Greenwich

30°W

The time at this longitude when
it is 12.00 (noon) at Greenwich

CAPE TOWN
33° 55'S 18° 35'E

DELHI
28° 39'N 77° 13'E

TOKYO
35° 33'N 139° 46'E

SYDNEY
33° 56' S 151° 10'E

54 ARCTIC OCEAN

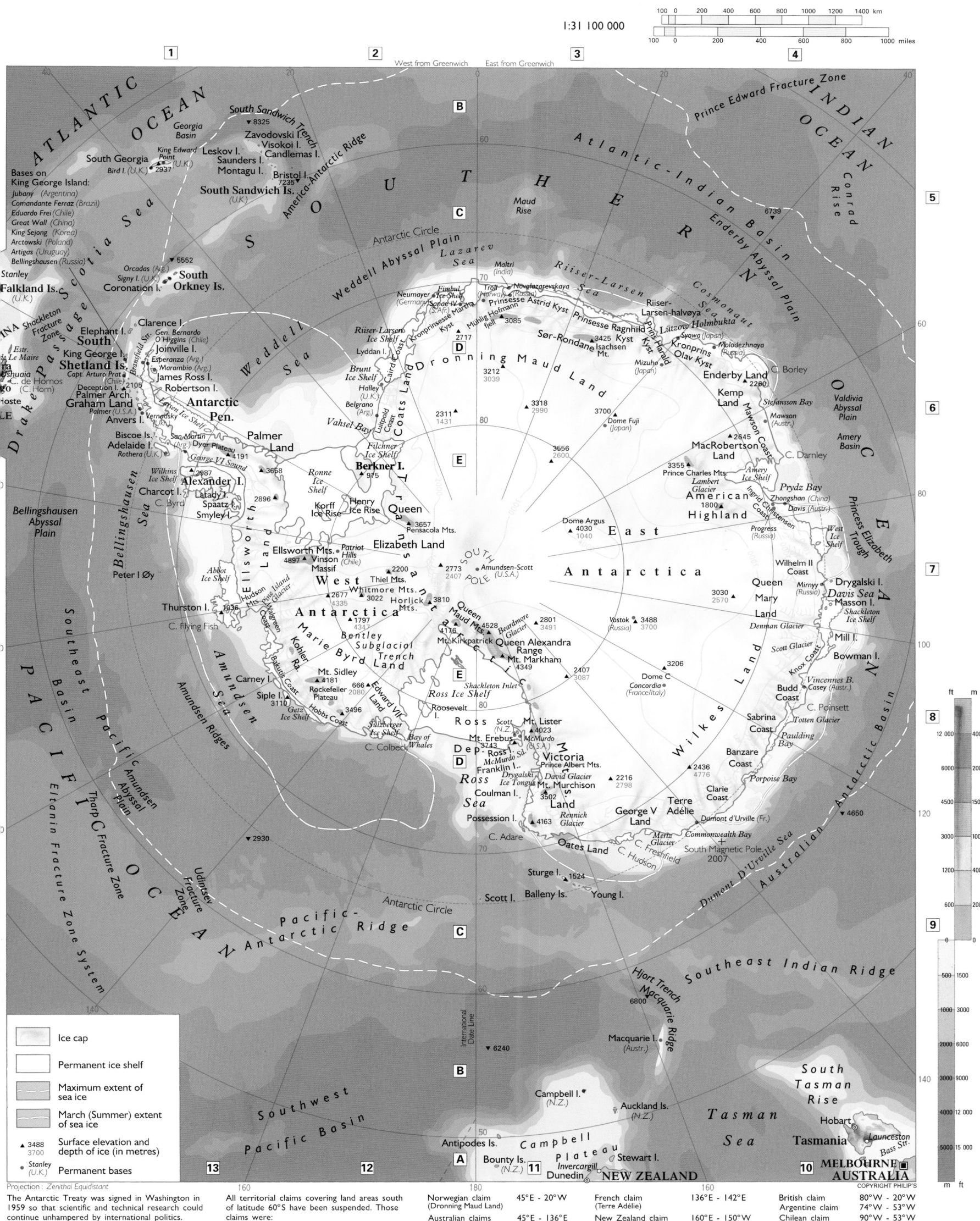

1:31 100 000

The Antarctic Treaty was signed in Washington in 1959 so that scientific and technical research could continue unhampered by international politics.

All territorial claims covering land areas south of latitude 60°S have been suspended. Those claims were:

Norwegian claim (Dronning Maud Land)	45°E – 20°W	French claim (Terre Adélie)	136°E – 142°E
Australian claims	45°E – 136°E 142°E – 160°E	New Zealand claim (Ross Dependency)	160°E – 150°W
		British claim	80°W – 20°W
		Argentine claim	74°W – 53°W
		Chilean claim	90°W – 53°W

Projection: Zenithal Equidistant

Equatorial Scale 1:45 000 000

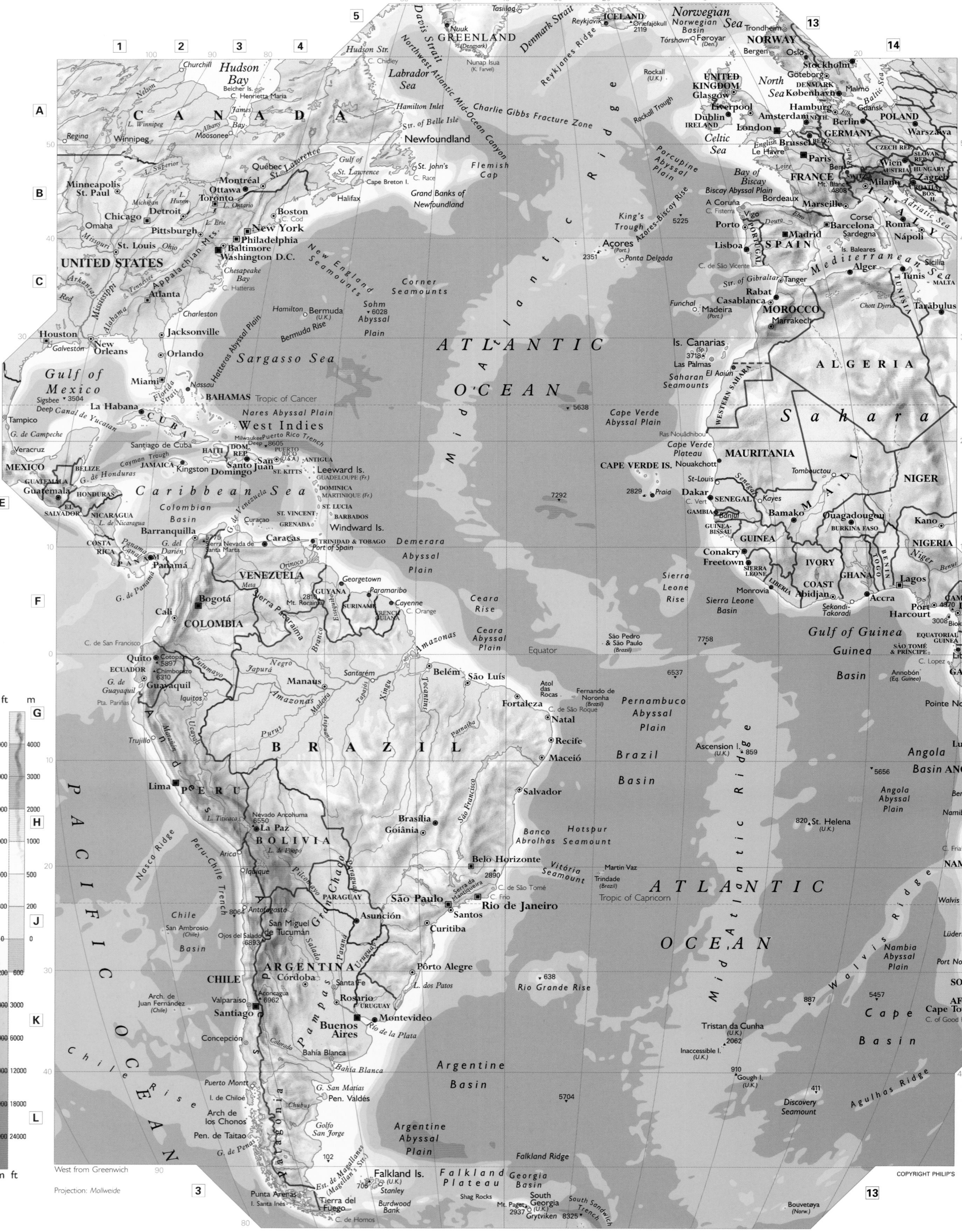

GREENLAND (Denmark)

Davis Strait
Nuuk
Tasiilaq
Hudson Str.
C. Chidley
Nunap Isua (K. Farvel)
Denmark Strait
Reykjavík
ICELAND
Öræfajökull 2119
Norwegian Basin
Norwegian Sea
Tórshavn
Føroyar (Den.)
Trondheim
NORWAY
Bergen
Oslo
Stockholm
Göteborg
Malmö
DENMARK
København

Churchill
Hudson Bay
Belcher Is.
C. Henrietta Maria
James Bay
L. Winnipeg
C A N A D A
Regina
Winnipeg
Moosonee
Hamilton Inlet
Labrador Sea
Northwest Atlantic Mid-Ocean Canyon
Rockall (U.K.)
Rockall Trough
UNITED KINGDOM
Glasgow
Liverpool
Dublin
IRELAND
North Sea
DENMARK
Hamburg
Gdańsk
Berlin
POLAND
Warszawa
GERMANY

St. of Belle Isle
Newfoundland
Charlie Gibbs Fracture Zone
Porcupine Abyssal Plain
Celtic Sea
Amsterdam
NETH.
London
Brussel
BELG.
Le Havre
Paris
FRANCE
CZECH REP.
SLOVAK REP.
AUSTRIA HUNGARY

L. Superior
Minneapolis
St. Paul
L. Michigan
L. Huron
L. Ontario
L. Erie
Détroit
Toronto
Ottawa
Montréal
Québec
St-Laurent
Gulf of St. Lawrence
Cape Breton I.
C. Race
St. John's
Flemish Cap
Grand Banks of Newfoundland
King's Trough
Azores-Biscay Rise
5225
Bay of Biscay
Biscay Abyssal Plain
Mt. Blanc 4808
Milano
ITALY
Zagreb
CROATIA
BOS.

Chicago
Omaha
Pittsburgh
St. Louis
Ohio
Missouri
UNITED STATES
New York
Philadelphia
Baltimore
Washington D.C.
Boston
C. Cod
Halifax
New England Seamounts
Corner Seamounts
A Coruña
C. Fisterra
Bordeaux
Marseille
Barcelona
Sardegna
Corse
Roma
Nápoli

Appalachian Mts.
Arkansas
Red
Atlanta
Alabama
Charleston
Jacksonville
C. Hatteras
Chesapeake Bay
Hamilton
Bermuda (U.K.)
Sohm 6028 Abyssal Plain
Bermuda Rise
Açores (Port.)
2351
Ponta Delgada
Porto
Vigo
Douro
PORTUGAL
SPAIN
Lisboa
Madrid
Mediterranean Sea
Alger
Tunis
Sicilia
MALTA
TUNISIA

Houston
Galveston
New Orleans
Orlando
Miami
Sargasso Sea
Hatteras Abyssal Plain
A T L A N T I C
O C E A N
Is. Canarias (Sp.)
3718
Las Palmas
Saharan Seamounts
Funchal
Madeira (Port.)
C. de São Vicente
Str. of Gibraltar
Tanger
Rabat
Casablanca
MOROCCO
Marrakech
Chott Djerid
Tarābulus
ALGERIA

Gulf of Mexico
Sigsbee 3504
Deep
Canal de Yucatan
La Habana
CUBA
Tampico
G. de Campeche
Veracruz
BAHAMAS
Nassau
Tropic of Cancer
Nares Abyssal Plain
West Indies
5638
Cape Verde Abyssal Plain
Ras Nouâdhibou
S a h a r a

MEXICO
GUATEMALA
BELIZE
G. de Honduras
Cayman Trough
Santiago de Cuba
JAMAICA
Kingston
HAITI
DOM. REP.
Santo Domingo
San Juan
PUERTO RICO (U.S.A.)
Milwaukee Deep 8605
Puerto Rico Trench
ANTIGUA
ST. KITTS
GUADELOUPE (Fr.)
DOMINICA
MARTINIQUE (Fr.)
Cape Verde Plateau
MAURITANIA
Tombouctou
NIGER

Guatemala
HONDURAS
EL SALVADOR
NICARAGUA
L. de Nicaragua
COSTA RICA
Panamá Canal
Panamá
PANAMA
Barranquilla
Caribbean Sea
Colombian Basin
G. de Venezuela
Curaçao
ST. VINCENT
GRENADA
BARBADOS
ST. LUCIA
Windward Is.
Leeward Is.
TRINIDAD & TOBAGO
Port of Spain
Demerara Abyssal Plain
2829 Praia
7292
CAPE VERDE IS.
St-Louis
Dakar
C. Vert
SENEGAL
GAMBIA
Banjul
GUINEA-BISSAU
Bamako
Kayes
M A L I
Ouagadougou
BURKINA FASO
Kano
NIGERIA

Cali
Bogotá
COLOMBIA
Sierra Nevada de Santa Marta
G. del Darién
575
Caracas
VENEZUELA
Georgetown
GUYANA
Mt. Roraima 2810
Paramaribo
SURINAME
Cayenne
FRENCH GUIANA
C. Orange
Ceara Rise
Sierra Leone Rise
Conakry
Freetown
GUINEA
SIERRA LEONE
LIBERIA
IVORY COAST
Monrovia
Sierra Leone Basin
Abidjan
GHANA
Accra
TOGO
BENIN
Lagos
Sekondi-Takoradi
Port Harcourt
3008
Bioko
4070
GULF of GUINEA
EQUATORIAL GUINEA
SÃO TOMÉ & PRÍNCIPE

C. de San Francisco
Quito
ECUADOR
Cotopaxi 5897
Chimborazo 6310
G. de Guayaquil
Guayaquil
Pta. Pariñas
Iquitos
Negro
Japurá
Putumayo
Manaus
B R A Z I L
Santarém
Amazonas
Belém
São Luís
Ceara Abyssal Plain
Equator
São Pedro & São Paulo (Brazil)
7758
6537
Fernando de Noronha (Brazil)
Atol das Rocas
C. de São Roque
Fortaleza
Natal
Guinea Basin
Annobón (Eq. Guinea)
Pointe Noire
GABON
Libr.

Trujillo
Lima
PERU
Amazonas
Ucayali
Madeira
Purus
Juruá
Madre
Xingu
Tapajós
Tocantins
Pernambuco Abyssal Plain
Recife
Maceió
Brazil Basin
Ascension I. (U.K.) 859
Angola Basin
Lua
ANG.
5656

La Paz
Nevado Ancohuma 6550
L. Titicaca
BOLIVIA
Arica
São Francisco
Brasília
Goiânia
Salvador
Banco Abrolhos
Hotspur Seamount
820 St. Helena (U.K.)
Angola Abyssal Plain
Namibe
Beng.

Iquique
Antofagasta 8064
San Ambrosio (Chile)
Ojos del Salado 6893
Nazca Ridge
Peru-Chile Trench
Belo Horizonte
2890
Vitória Seamount
Martin Vaz
Trindade (Brazil)
2890
C. de São Tomé
Tropic of Capricorn
A T L A N T I C
O C E A N
NAM.

Arch. de Juan Fernández (Chile)
Valparaíso
Santiago
CHILE
Aconcagua 6962
Córdoba
San Miguel de Tucumán
ARGENTINA
Pilcomayo
PARAGUAY
Asunción
Gran Chaco
Paraná
Salado
Uruguai
São Paulo
Santos
Curitiba
Pôrto Alegre
C. Frio
Rio de Janeiro
638
Rio Grande Rise
5704
Lüderitz
Port Noll
Nambia Abyssal Plain
Walvis Ridge
Walvis Ridge

Concepción
Rosario
Santa Fe
URUGUAY
Montevideo
Buenos Aires
Río de la Plata
Pampas
Colorado
Bahía Blanca
L. dos Patos
887
5457
Tristan da Cunha (U.K.) 2062
Inaccessible I. (U.K.)
910
Gough I. (U.K.)
411
Discovery Seamount
Cape Basin
Cape Town
AFR.
C. of Good H.
SOU.

Puerto Montt
Arch de los Chonos
Pen. de Taitao
P A C I F I C
O C E A N
Chile Rise
Est. de Magallanes (Magellan Str.)
Punta Arenas
I. Santa Inés
Tierra del Fuego
C. de Hornos
G. San Matías
Pen. Valdés
Chubut
Golfo San Jorge
G. de Penas
102
Argentine Basin
Argentine Abyssal Plain
Falkland Is. (U.K.)
706
Stanley
Falkland Plateau
Burdwood Bank
Georgia Basin
Shag Rocks
South Georgia (U.K.)
Mt. Paget 2937
Grytviken
8325
South Sandwich Trench
Bouvetøya (Nor.)
Agulhas Ridge

ft m
12000 4000
9000 3000
6000 2000
3000 1000
1500 500
600 200
0 0
200 600
1000 3000
2000 6000
4000 12000
6000 18000
8000 24000
m ft

West from Greenwich
Projection: Mollweide

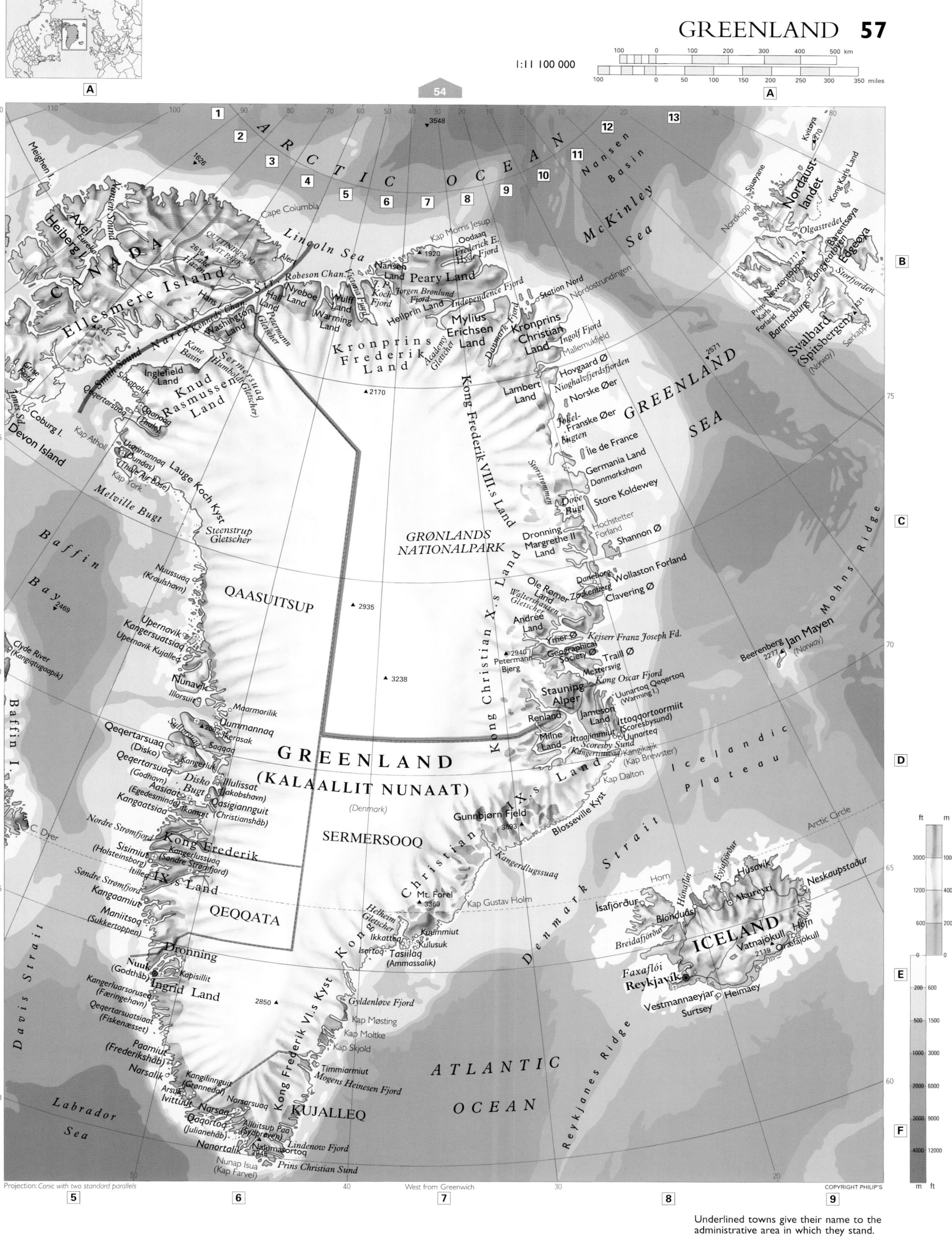

1:11 100 000

Projection: Conic with two standard parallels

COPYRIGHT PHILIP'S

Underlined towns give their name to the administrative area in which they stand.

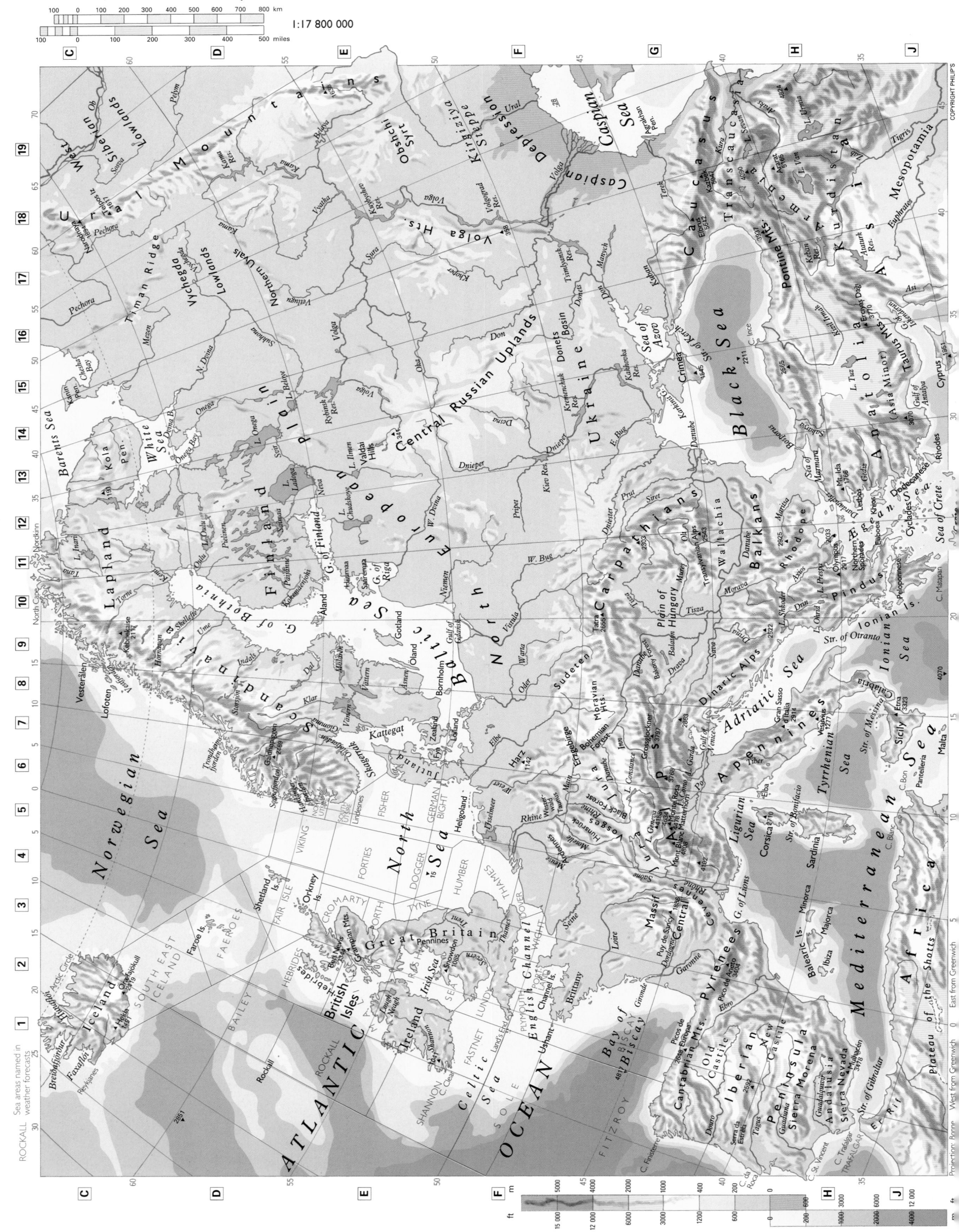

1:17 800 000

COPYRIGHT PHILIPS

Projection: Bonne

1:17 800 000

100 0 100 200 300 400 500 600 700 800 km

100 0 100 200 300 400 500 miles

■ LONDON Capital Cities

COPYRIGHT PHILIP'S

Projection: Bonne

West from Greenwich   East from Greenwich

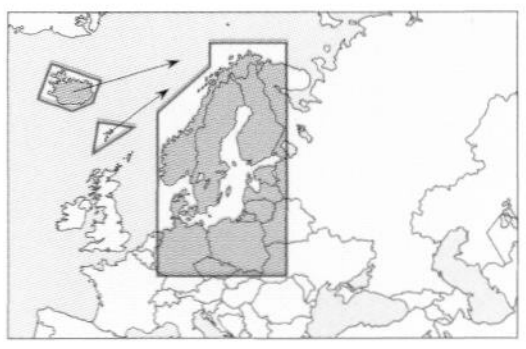

1:5 300 000

50 0 25 50 75 100 125 150 175 km

50 0 25 50 75 100 125 miles

106

| | A | | B | | C | | D | | E | | F |

BARENTS SEA

R U S S I A

KARELIA

F I N L A N D

L a p p l a n d

L A P L A N D

N O R W A Y

S W E D E N

Arctic Circle

Murmansk · Kola · Severomorsk · Polyarnyy

Vardø · Vadsø · Varangerhalvøya · Tanafjorden

Nordkapp · Magerøya · Hammerfest · Nordkinnhalvøya

Tromsø · Narvik · Vesterålen · Lofoten

Kiruna · Gällivare · Luleå · Boden · Piteå · Skellefteå · Umeå

Oulu · Kokkola · Vaasa (Vasa) · Pori · Rauma

Rovaniemi · Kemi · Tornio · Haparanda

Östersund · Sundsvall · Trondheim · Steinkjer · Namsos

Gulf of Bothnia

ATLANTIC OCEAN

ICELAND on same scale

Reykjavík · Keflavík · Akureyri · Vatnajökull · Hekla · Faxaflói · Breiðafjörður

---

FÆROE ISLANDS on same scale

Tórshavn · Streymoy · Eysturoy · Suðuroy · Vágar · Sandoy

Føroyar (Faeroe Is.) (Den.)

Projection: Conical with two standard parallels

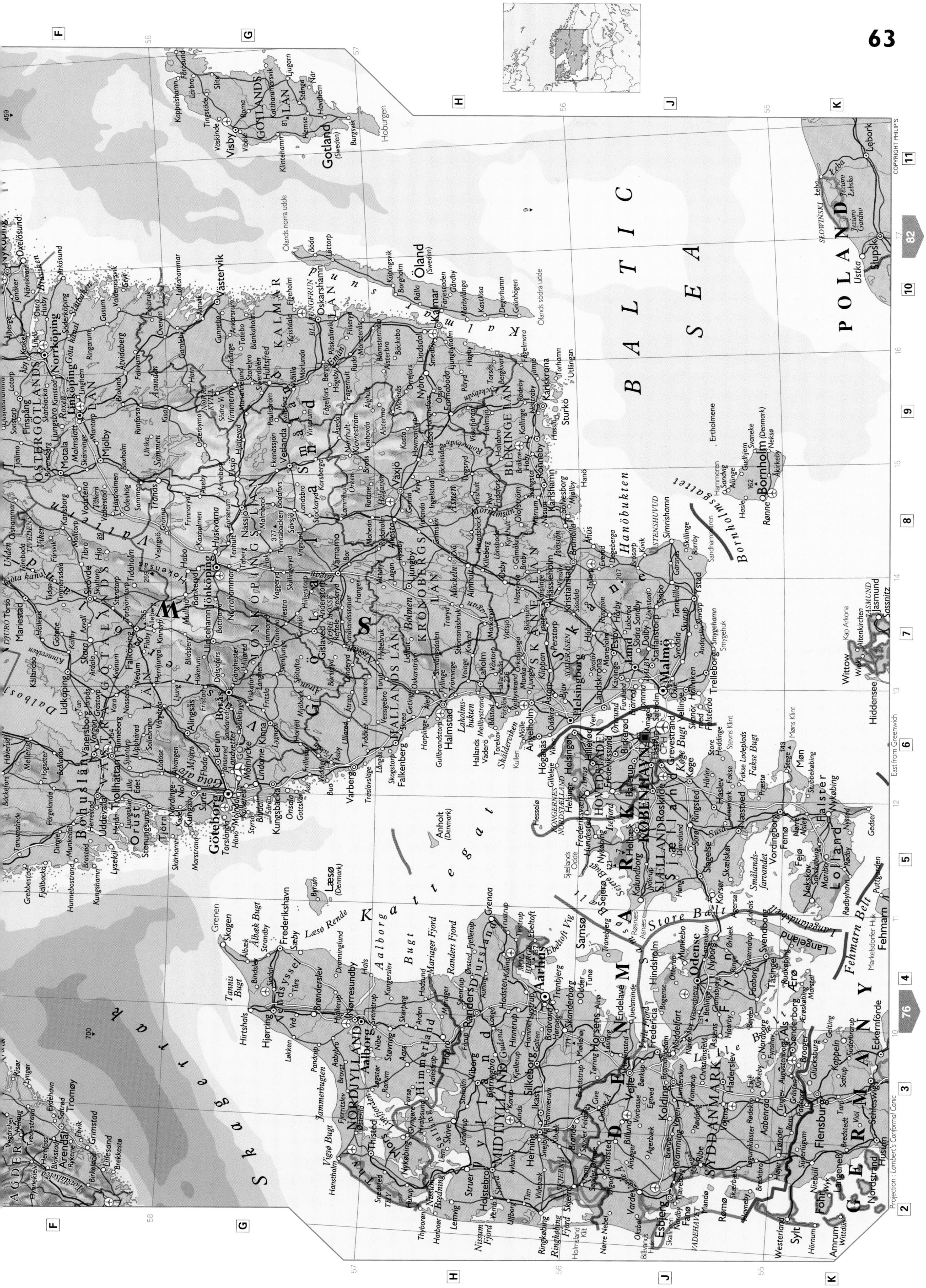

BALTIC SEA

POLAND

GERMANY

DENMARK

Gotland (Sweden)

GOTLANDS LÄN

Öland (Sweden)

KALMAR LÄN

BLEKINGE LÄN

KRONOBERGS LÄN

SKÅNE LÄN

HALLANDS LÄN

JÖNKÖPINGS LÄN

ÖSTERGÖTLANDS LÄN

VÄSTRA GÖTALANDS LÄN

Småland

Bornholm (Denmark)

Bornholmsgattet

Hanöbukten

Kattegat

Skagerrak

Aalborg Bugt

Læsø Rende

NORDJYLLAND

MIDTJYLLAND

SYDDANMARK

SJÆLLAND

København

Göteborg

Malmö

Aarhus

Odense

Norrköping

Linköping

Kalmar

Växjö

Karlskrona

Helsingborg

Lund

Roskilde

Store Bælt

Fehmarn Belt

Lolland

Falster

Møn

Fyn

Ærø

Projection: Lambert's Conformal Conic

East from Greenwich

1:1 800 000

10 0 10 20 30 40 50 60 70 80 km
10 0 10 20 30 40 50 miles

Key to Scottish unitary authorities on map

1 CITY OF ABERDEEN
2 DUNDEE CITY
3 WEST DUNBARTONSHIRE
4 EAST DUNBARTONSHIRE
5 CITY OF GLASGOW
6 INVERCLYDE
7 RENFREWSHIRE
8 EAST RENFREWSHIRE
9 NORTH LANARKSHIRE
10 FALKIRK
11 CLACKMANNANSHIRE
12 WEST LOTHIAN
13 CITY OF EDINBURGH
14 MIDLOTHIAN

ORKNEY IS. on same scale

ORKNEY
North Ronaldsay
Papa Westray
Westray
Rousay
Eday
Sanday
Stronsay
Brough Hd.
Mainland
Stromness
Kirkwall
Shapinsay
Hoy
Scapa Flow
St. Mary's
Burray
South Ronaldsay
Burwick
Dunnet Hd.
Stroma
Pentland Firth
Duncansby Head
John o' Groats
Thurso
Sinclair's Bay

SHETLAND IS. on same scale

Muckle Flugga
Unst
Haroldswick
Yell Sound
Esha Ness
Yell
Fetlar
Sullom Voe
Ulsta
Out Skerries
Voe
Whalsay
St. Magnus Bay
Papa Stour
Walls
Scalloway
Lerwick
Bressay
Foula
West Burra
Boddam
Sumburgh Hd.

Main map

Pentland Firth
Scapa Flow
Hoy
Burwick
C. Wrath
Dunnet Hd.
Stroma
John o' Groats
Durness
L. Eriboll
Strathy Pt.
Dounreay
Thurso
Halkirk
Caithness
Tongue
Ben Hope 927
Reay Forest
Eddrachillis B.
Handa
Sutherland
Highlands
Naver
Wick
Lybster
Sinclair's Bay
Noss Hd.
Ord of Caithness
Helmsdale
Pt. of Stoer
Enard B.
Rubha Coigeach
L. Assynt
Lochinver
Ben More Assynt 998
961
705
Brora
Loch Shin
Lairg
Oykel
Bonar Bridge
Golspie
L. Laxford
115
Butt of Lewis
Flannan Is.
Gallan Hd.
Stornoway
Broad Bay
Eye Peninsula
Lewis
Scarp
Taransay
799
Clisham
Tarbert
Harris
Toe Hd.
Pabbay
Berneray
(WESTERN ISLES)
EILEAN SIAR
North Uist
Lochmaddy
Grimsay
Benbecula
Ardivachar Pt.
Baleshare
South Uist
Ben Mhor 620
Wiay
Lochboisdale
Eriskay
Castlebay
Barra
Vatersay
Sandray
Barra Hd. 268
the Hebrides
North Minch
Little Minch
L. Seaforth
Sound of Harris
Rubha Hunish
Uig
Dunvegan
L. Snizort
Skye
Portree
Raasay
Rona
L. Bracadale
Cuillin Hills 992
Scalpay
Cuillin Sound
L. Gairloch
Gairloch
L. Ewe
L. Maree 1053
Greenstone Pt.
Gruinard B.
L. Broom
Ullapool
L. Fannich
Ben Wyvis 1045
Garron
Strathpeffer
Dingwall
Muir of Ord
Beauly
Cromarty
Dornoch Firth
Tarbat Ness
Tain
Invergordon
Alness
Moray Firth
Lossiemouth
Portknockie
Portsoy
Rosehearty
Kinnairds Hd.
Fraserburgh
Burghead
Elgin
Buckie
Cullen
Banff
Macduff
Aberchirder
Turriff
Rattray Hd.
Peterhead
Nairn
Forres
MORAY
Rothes
Fochabers
Keith
Huntly
Deveron
Buchan
Oldmeldrum
Ellon
Cruden Bay
Buchan Ness
Inverness
Drumnadrochit
Loch Ness
Charlestown of Aberlour
Dufftown
Grantown-on-Spey
Inverurie
Kintore
Westhill
Dyce
Aberdeen
Girdle Ness
ABERDEENSHIRE
Strath Spey
Aviemore
Cairn Gorm 1245
CAIRNGORMS
Ben Macdhui 1309
Alford
Aboyne
Banchory
Peterculter
Stonehaven
L. Shiel
Kyle of Lochalsh
Dornie
Stromeferry
Carn Eige 1182
Glen Affric
1068
Glen Moriston
Fort Augustus
Monadhliath Mts.
Kingussie
Newtonmore
Carn Ban 941
1121
Lochnagar 1154
Ballater
Braemar
Forest of Atholl
N. Esk
Inverbervie
Laurencekirk
Brechin
Mallaig
Arisaig
L. Morar
Glen Garry
L. Arkaig
1128
Glen Spean
Spean Bridge
Fort William
Ben Nevis 1344
Kinlochleven
Glen Coe
Ballachulish
Rannoch Moor
1148
L. Rannoch
Blair Atholl
Pitlochry
Kirriemuir
Forfar
Montrose
Arbroath
Carnoustie
Monifieth
Firth of Tay
ANGUS
S. Esk
Garry
PERTH AND KINROSS
Aberfeldy
Ben Lawers 1214
Dunkeld
Blairgowrie
Alyth
455
Coupar Angus
Scone
Perth
Dundee
Tayport
Leuchars
St. Andrews
Fife Ness
NORTH SEA
Rùm (Rhum)
Eigg
Muck
Pt. of Ardnamurchan
Morvern
Sound of Mull
Tobermory
Coll
Tiree
Passage of Tiree
Staffa
Ulva
Mull
Ben More 966
Iona
Kerrera
Oban
Lismore
L. Linnhe
L. Etive
Ben Cruachan 1126
Loch Awe
Crianlarich
Ben More 1174
Killin
Crieff
Auchterarder
Comrie
983
Ben Vorlich
Callander
Auchtermuchty
Cupar
FIFE
Falkland
Glenrothes
Leven
Buckhaven
Anstruther
Colonsay
Oronsay
Scarba
Luing
Loch Lomond
LOCH LOMOND AND THE TROSSACHS
Ben Lomond 973
Aberfoyle
Ochil Hills
Kinross
Dunfermline
Dollar
Alloa
Clackmannan
Kirkcaldy
North Berwick
Dunbar
Firth of Forth
ARGYLL AND BUTE
Inveraray
Lochgilphead
Loch Fyne
Rubh' a' Mhail
Ardnave Pt.
Islay
Bowmore
Port Ellen
Rhinns Pt.
Mull of Oa
720
Tarbert
Gigha
Kintyre
Helensburgh
Dumbarton
Alexandria
Clydebank
Greenock
Gourock
Port Glasgow
Rothesay
Bute
Dunoon
GLASGOW
Paisley
Stirling
Bannockburn
Denny
Grangemouth
Bo'ness
Falkirk
Cumbernauld
Kirkintilloch
Airdrie
Coatbridge
Motherwell
Hamilton
East Kilbride
Wishaw
Carluke
Lanark
Strathaven
Biggar
Livingston
EDINBURGH
Musselburgh
Haddington
EAST LOTHIAN
St. Abb's Head
Eyemouth
Dalkeith
Bonnyrigg
Penicuik
651
Moorfoot Hills
Peebles
Pentland Hills
Lammermuir Hills
535
Duns
Coldstream
Tweed
Berwick-upon-Tweed
Campbeltown
Mull of Kintyre
Firth of Clyde
Goat Fell 874
Brodick
Arran
Kilbrannan Sd.
NORTH AYRSHIRE
Ardrossan
Saltcoats
Kilwinning
Irvine
Troon
Prestwick
Ayr
Kilmarnock
EAST AYRSHIRE
Cumnock
Maybole
Girvan
Ailsa Craig
Dalmellington
SOUTH AYRSHIRE
733
Sanquhar
SOUTH LANARKSHIRE
Broad Law 840
Galashiels
Melrose
Selkirk
Jedburgh
SCOTTISH BORDERS
Hawick
Eildon Hills
Kelso
The Cheviot 816
Cheviot Hills
Wooler
Alnwick
Almouth
Amble
Morpeth
NORTHUMBERLAND
Merrick
New Galloway
Dumfries & Galloway
Lochmaben
Lockerbie
Moffat
Langholm
Gretna
ENGLAND
Newcastle-upon-Tyne
Gateshead
Blaydon
Stanley
Consett
Durham
Crook
Bishop Auckland
Hexham
Haltwhistle
Carlisle
CUMBRIA
Kielder Water
BORDER
North Tyne
931
Cross Fell 893
Alston
Penrith
Appleby-in-Westmorland
Barnard Castle
Brough
Stranraer
Portpatrick
Newton Stewart
Gatehouse of Fleet
Castle Douglas
Dalbeattie
Kirkcudbright
Wigtown
Whithorn
Burrow Hd.
Mull of Galloway
Luce Bay
L. Ryan
Cairnryan
Wigtown B.
Dumfries
Annan
Solway Firth
Silloth
Aspatria
Maryport
Workington
Cockermouth
Keswick
Derwent Water
Skiddaw 931
Ullswater
Helvellyn 950
Whitehaven
St. Bees Hd.
Stromness
NORTHERN IRELAND
Larne
Carrickfergus
Bangor
Donaghadee
Newtownards
Holywood
Belfast
Belfast L.
Cushendall
Garron Pt.
269
North Channel
Galloway

ATLANTIC OCEAN

Sea of the Hebrides

Inner Hebrides

Outer Hebrides

Jura
Sd. of Jura
Colonsay

HIGHLAND

Grampian Mountains

Strathmore

Sidlaw Hills

Southern Uplands

ft m
3000 1000
1500 500
600 200
300 100
0 0
50 150
100 300
200 600
500 1500
1000 3000
m ft

Projection: Lambert's Conformal Conic
West from Greenwich
COPYRIGHT PHILIP'S

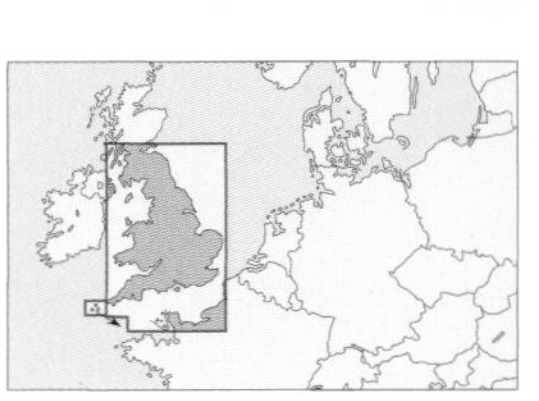

10 0 10 20 30 40 50 60 70 80 km
10   20   30   40   50 miles

1:1 800 000

Key to English unitary authorities on map

25 HARTLEPOOL
26 DARLINGTON
27 STOCKTON-ON-TEES
28 MIDDLESBROUGH
29 REDCAR AND CLEVELAND
30 BLACKPOOL
31 BLACKBURN WITH DARWEN
32 HALTON
33 WARRINGTON
34 KINGSTON UPON HULL
35 NORTH EAST LINCOLNSHIRE
36 STOKE-ON-TRENT
37 TELFORD AND WREKIN
38 DERBY CITY
39 CITY OF NOTTINGHAM
40 LEICESTER CITY
41 RUTLAND
42 PETERBOROUGH
43 MILTON KEYNES
44 LUTON
45 NORTH SOMERSET
46 CITY OF BRISTOL
47 BATH AND NORTH EAST SOMERSET
48 SWINDON
49 READING
50 WOKINGHAM
51 WINDSOR AND MAIDENHEAD
52 SLOUGH
53 BRACKNELL FOREST
54 THURROCK
55 SOUTHEND-ON-SEA
56 MEDWAY
57 PLYMOUTH
58 TORBAY
59 POOLE
60 BOURNEMOUTH
61 SOUTHAMPTON
62 PORTSMOUTH
63 BRIGHTON AND HOVE
64 BEDFORD
65 CENTRAL BEDFORDSHIRE
66 CHESHIRE WEST AND CHESTER
67 CHESHIRE EAST

Key to Welsh unitary authorities on map

15 SWANSEA
16 NEATH PORT TALBOT
17 BRIDGEND
18 RHONDDA CYNON TAFF
19 MERTHYR TYDFIL
20 CAERPHILLY
21 BLAENAU GWENT
22 TORFAEN
23 CARDIFF
24 NEWPORT

NORTH SEA

IRISH SEA

North Channel

NORTHERN IRELAND

SCOTLAND

ENGLAND

WALES

ISLE OF MAN

The Wash

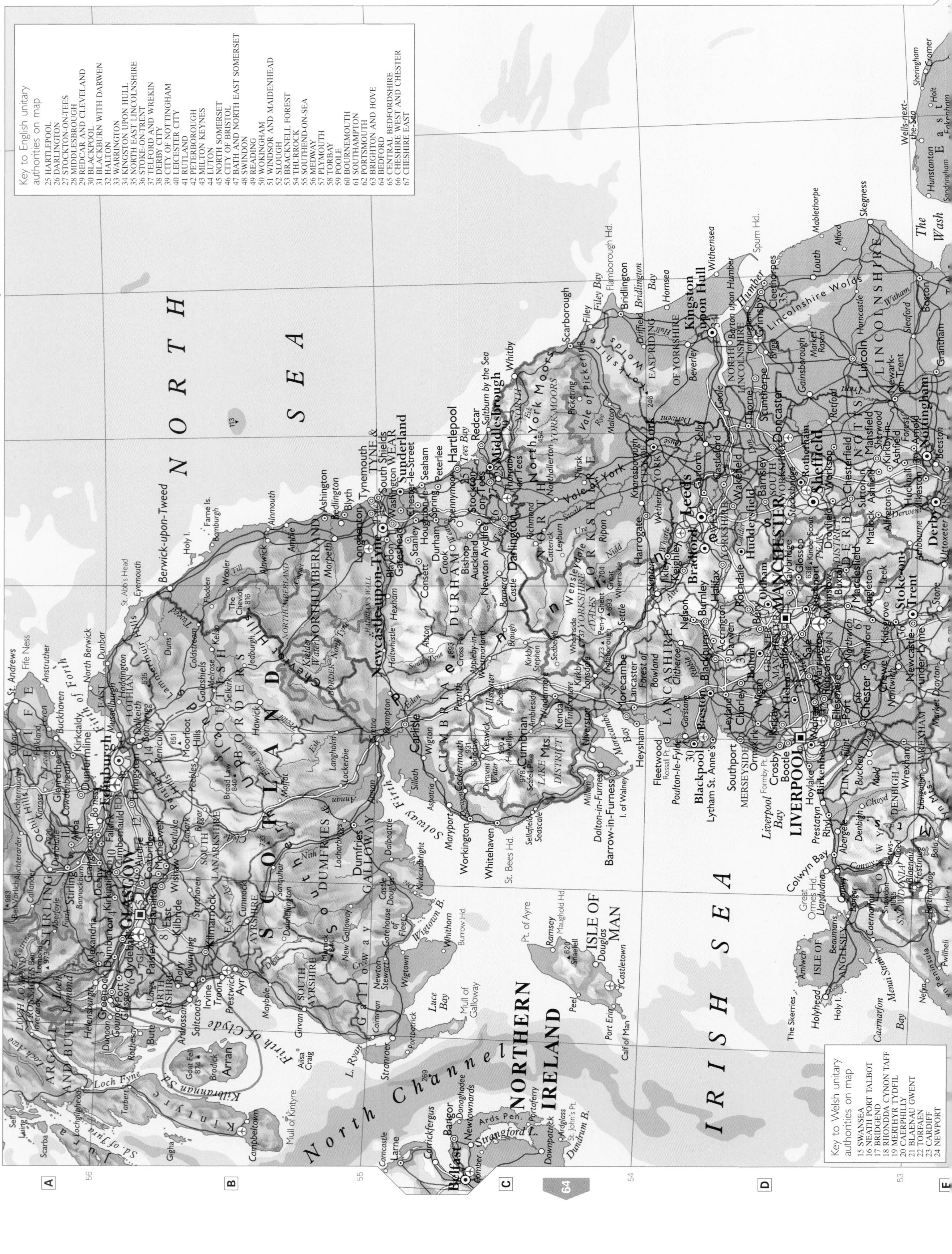

Projection : Lambert's Conformal Conic

ISLES OF SCILLY
on same scale

ISLES OF SCILLY

1:4 400 000

ATLANTIC OCEAN

Shetland Is.
(U.K.)
Yell
Unst
Fetlar
458
Foula
Mainland
Lerwick
Fair Isle

Orkney Is.
Westray
Sanday
Stronsay
Mainland
Kirkwall
Hoy
South
Ronaldsay

C. Wrath
Pentland Firth
Thurso
Wick
Helmsdale

Lewis
Stornoway
North Minch
Harris
St. Kilda
(U.K.)
North
Uist
Benbecula
South Uist
Barra
Skye
992
Outer Hebrides
Sea of the Hebrides
Inner Hebrides
1182
North West Highlands
Golspie
Lairg
Tain
Invergordon
Dingwall
Inverness
Nairn
Elgin
Buckie
Banff
Fraserburgh
Peterhead
Huntly
L. Ness
Glen Mor
Aviemore
CAIRNGORMS
Don
Inverurie
Aberdeen

1081
Fort William
Ben Nevis
1344
Dee
1311
Ballater
Stonehaven
SCOTLAND
Grampian Mts.
Montrose
Forfar
Arbroath
Dundee
St. Andrews

Rum
Eigg
Coll
Tobermory
966
Mull
Iona
Tiree
Colonsay
Oban
L. Awe
L. Fyne
L. LOMOND & TROSSACHS
1214
L. Lomond
973
Stirling
Glenrothes
Perth
Kirkcaldy
Dunfermline
Dunbar

Jura
Islay
Dumbarton
Greenock
Paisley
GLASGOW
Motherwell
East Kilbride
Hamilton
EDINBURGH
Berwick-upon-Tweed

Arran
Campbeltown
Irvine
Kilmarnock
Ayr
Southern Uplands
840
Galashiels
Jedburgh
816
Cheviot Hills
Alnwick

N O R T H   S E A

238

NORTHUMBERLAND
Newcastle-upon-Tyne
South Shields
Sunderland
Gateshead
Hexham
Durham
Hartlepool
Redcar
Middlesbrough
Stockton-on-Tees
Darlington
N. YORK MOORS
Scarborough

Malin Hd.
North Channel
Buncrana
Letterkenny
Coleraine
Derry/Londonderry
Ballymena
Larne
GLENVEAGH
Lifford
Antrim
Bangor
Donegal
Omagh
Lough
Neagh
Lisburn
BELFAST
Portadown
Lurgan
NORTHERN IRELAND
Ulster
Lower L.
Erne
Enniskillen
Armagh
Newry
Mull of
Galloway
Clones
852
Kirkcudbright
Dumfries
Annan
Carlisle

Firth of Clyde

Stranraer
Workington
Whitehaven
Cumbrian Mts.
893
978
LAKE DISTRICT
Pennines

Achill I.
Ballina
Castlebar
L. Conn
Sligo
Leitrim
Cavan
Castleblaney
Dundalk
Drogheda
820
Douglas
I. of Man
Barrow-in-Furness
Lancaster
YORKSHIRE DALES
Bridlington

Westport
L. Mask
Connemara
Lough
Corrib
Roscommon
Longford
Athlone
Lough
Ree
Mullingar
Kells
Boyne
Blackpool
Preston
Burnley
Keighley
Harrogate
York
Beverley
Kingston upon Hull

Galway B.
Aran Is.
GALWAY
Ballinasloe
Birr
DUBLIN
Dun Laoghaire
Holyhead
Anglesey
Southport
Bolton
Bradford
Leeds
Halifax
Huddersfield
Barnsley
Doncaster
Rotherham
Grimsby
Scunthorpe
Humber

Ennis
BURREN
Lough
Derg
Tullamore
Portlaoise
Athy
Carlow
Bray
Colwyn Bay
1085
Snowdon
Wrexham
Chester
Crewe
PEAK
DISTRICT
Stockport
Chesterfield
Sheffield
Nottingham
Lincoln
Skegness
Boston
THE WASH

Kilrush
Shannon
Limerick
Nenagh
Thurles
Kilkenny
Pwllheli
SNOWDONIA
Shrewsbury
Telford
Stafford
Derby
Stoke-on-Trent
Grantham
Trent
King's Lynn
THE BROADS
Cromer
Great Yarmouth

953
Dingle
Tralee
920
Clonmel
Carrick-on-Suir
Wexford
Rosslare
Cardigan
Bay
Aberystwyth
Cambrian Mts.
Welshpool
Wolverhampton
BIRMINGHAM
886
Coventry
Rugby
Nuneaton
Leicester
Corby
Peterborough
Ely
Thetford
Bury St. Edmunds
Lowestoft

1041
Carrantuohill
Macgillycuddy's Reeks
Killarney
Mallow
Blackwater
Waterford
Dungarvan
WALES
Redditch
Worcester
Hereford
Royal
Leamington Spa
Northampton
Bedford
Milton Keynes
Cambridge
Ipswich
Felixstowe
Colchester

Valencia
Bandon
Cork
Cobh
Kinsale
Youghal
Carmarthen
BRECON
BEACONS
Merthyr Tydfil
Neath
Cwmbran
Gloucester
Cheltenham
COTSWOLD HILLS
Oxford
Hemel
Hempstead
High Wycombe
Luton
Harlow
Stevenage
Watford
Chelmsford
Basildon
Southend-on-Sea

C. Clear
99
PEMBROKESHIRE
COAST
Haverfordwest
Milford Haven
Pembroke
Fishguard
Llanelli
Swansea
Port Talbot
Rhondda
Cardiff
Newport
Bristol
Bath
Swindon
Newbury
Reading
LONDON
Slough
Chatham
Margate
Canterbury
Maidstone
Dover

St. George's Channel
Bristol Channel
Barry
Weston-super-Mare
Basingstoke
Guildford
Reigate
Crawley
Ashford
Folkestone
Str. of Dover
Gris
Nez

CELTIC
SEA
618
DARTMOOR
EXMOOR
Barnstaple
Bude
Taunton
Yeovil
Salisbury
NEW
FOREST
Southampton
Winchester
SOUTH
DOWNS
Fareham
Havant
Worthing
Brighton
Eastbourne
Hastings

Newquay
Truro
St. Austell
Exmouth
Torbay
Bournemouth
Poole
Weymouth
Newport
Isle of
Wight
Portsmouth
C.
Gris
Nez

Land's End
Penzance
Falmouth
Isles of Scilly
Plymouth

E n g l i s h   C h a n n e l

I R I S H   S E A

UNITED
KINGDOM

ENGLAND

L i v e r p o o l
Warrington
Oldham
MANCHESTER
LIVERPOOL
Blackburn
Bolton

Projection: Conical with two standard parallels
West from Greenwich
East from Greenwich
COPYRIGHT PHILIP'S

N O R W
Bergen
Askøyna
Stord
Bømlo
Haugesund
Kopervik
Åkrahamn
Stavan

NETHERLAND
's-Gravenhage
(Den Haag)
Hoek van Holland
ROTTERD
Haa

BELGIU
BRUSS
(Bruxe)
LILLE
Gent
Antwe
Brugge
Oostende
Zeebrugge
Vlissingen

FRANCE
Alderney
C. de la
Hague
Pte. de
Barfleur
Cherbourg-
Octeville
Volognes
Guernsey
St. Peter
Port
Sark
St. Helier
Jersey
Channel Is.
(U.K.)
Cotentin
Caen
Bayeux
Lisieux
Elbeuf
Seine
Rouen
Le Havre
Bolbec
Trouville-sur-Mer
Fécamp
Dieppe
Le Tréport
33
Abbeville
Amiens
Picardie
Pays de
Caux
Boulogne-
sur-Mer
Le Touquet-
Paris-Plage
St-Omer
Béthune
Bruay-la-
Buissière
Lens
St. Quentin
Laon
Cambrai
Valenciennes
Tournai

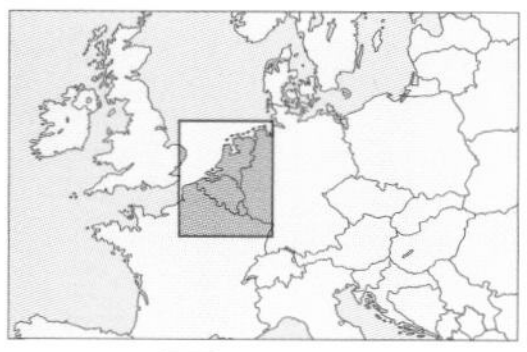

1:2 200 000

10 0 10 20 30 40 50 60 70 80 90 km
10 0 10 20 30 40 50 60 miles

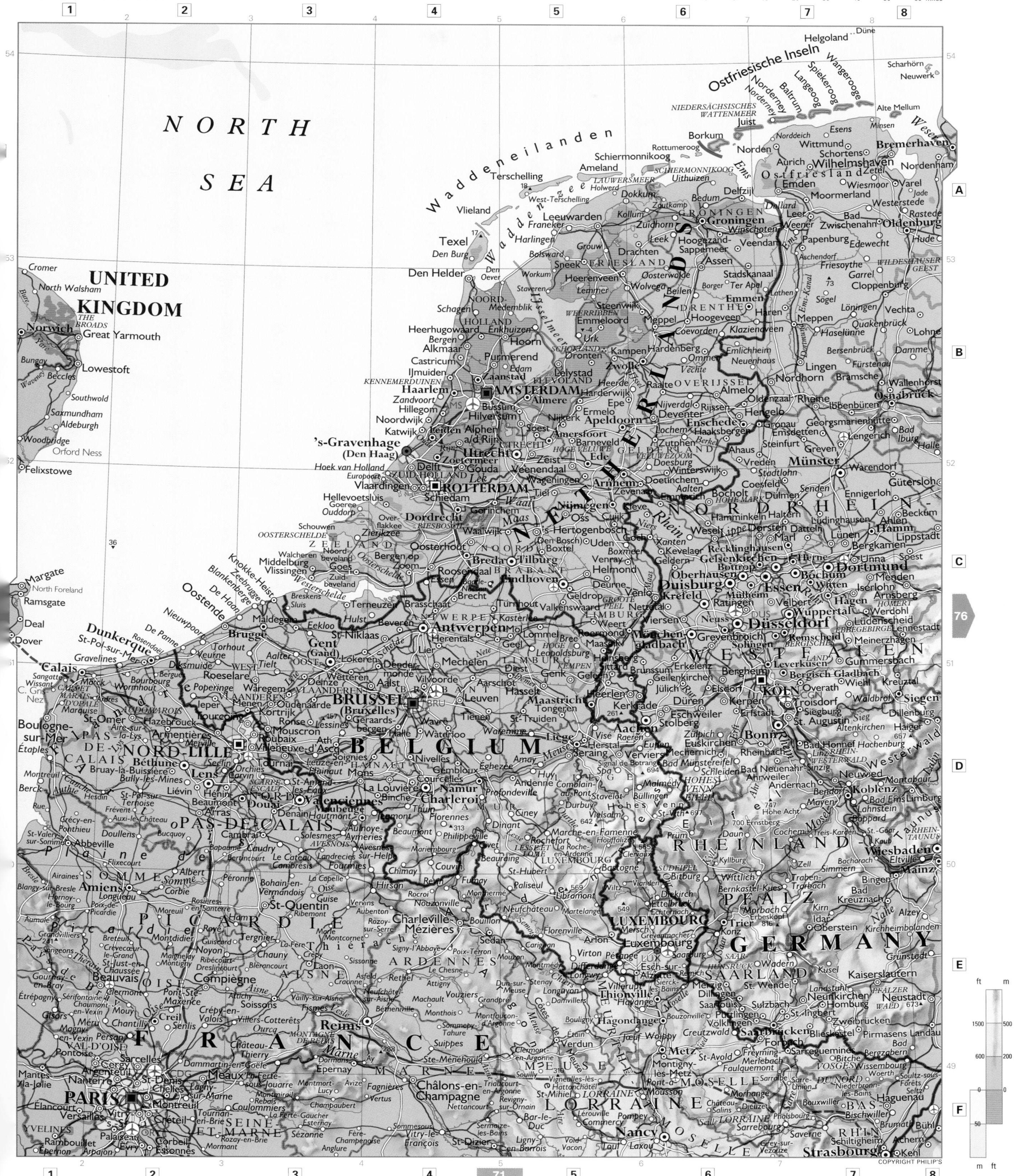

NORTH SEA

UNITED KINGDOM

NETHERLANDS

BELGIUM

GERMANY

FRANCE

LUXEMBOURG

High-speed rail routes

Underlined towns give their name to the administrative area in which they stand.

COPYRIGHT PHILIP'S

1:2 200 000

10 0 10 20 30 40 50 60 70 80 90 km
10 0 10 20 30 40 50 60 miles

UNITED KINGDOM

English Channel

ATLANTIC

OCEAN

Projection : Lambert's Conformal Conic

West from Greenwich

DÉPARTEMENTS IN THE PARIS AREA
1 Ville de Paris   3 Val-de-Marne
2 Seine-St-Denis   4 Hauts-de-Seine

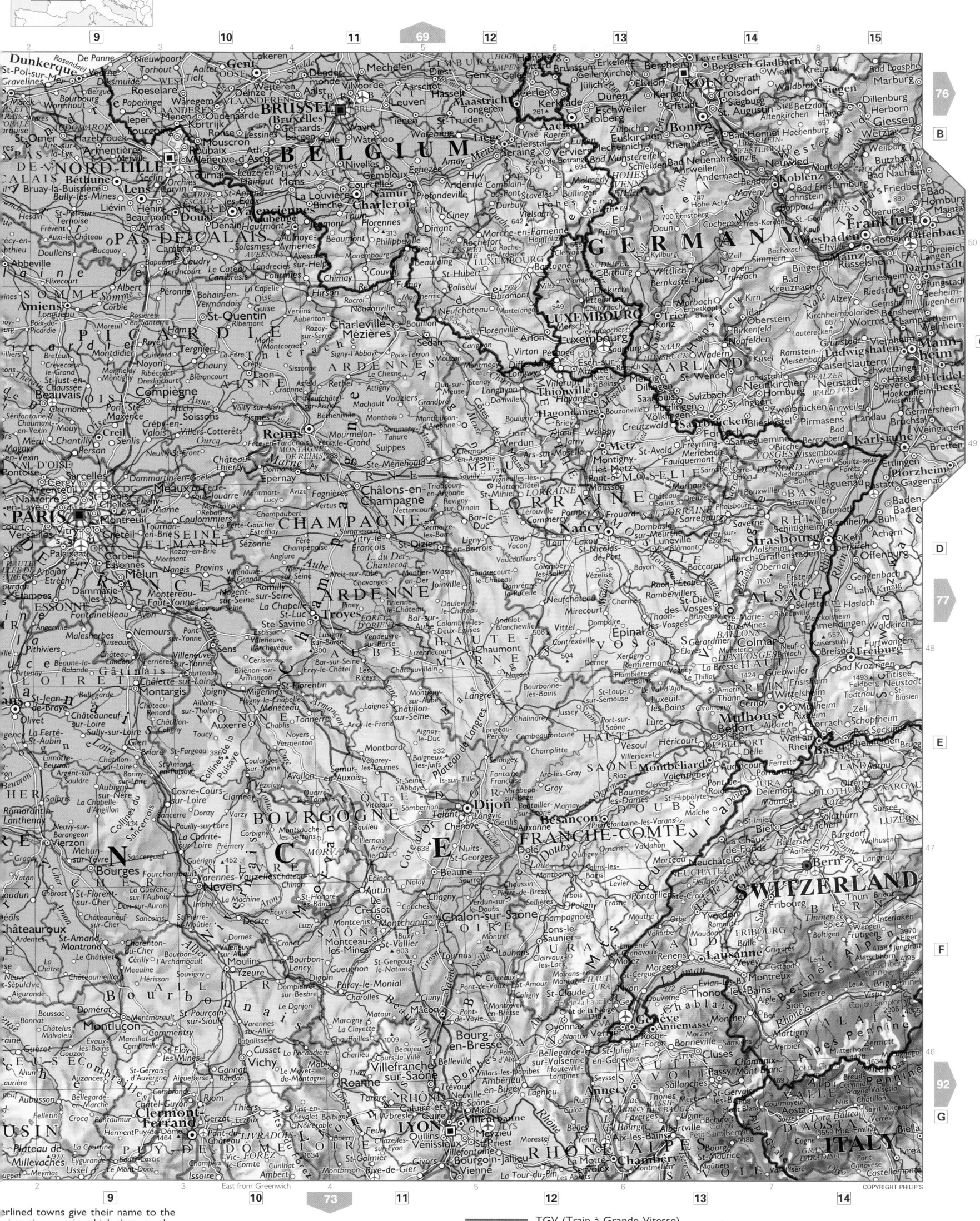

Underlined towns give their name to the
administrative area in which they stand.

—— TGV (Train à Grande Vitesse)

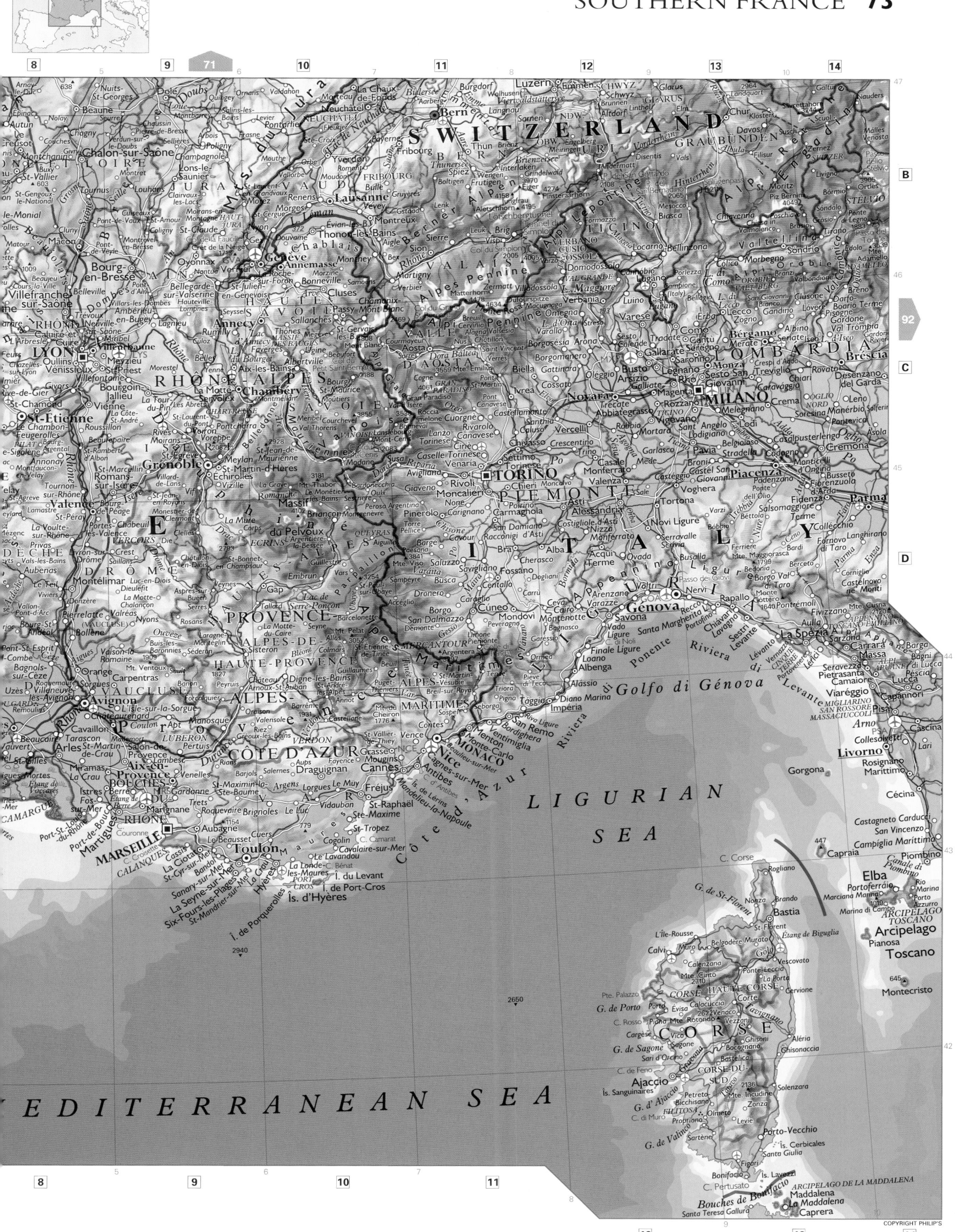

1:4 400 000

Projection: Conical with two standard parallels

NORTH SEA

BALTIC SEA

ADRIATIC SEA

UNITED KINGDOM

NETHERLANDS

BELGIUM

LUXEMBOURG

FRANCE

GERMANY

DENMARK

SWITZERLAND

AUSTRIA

ITALY

SLOVENIA

CZECH

Major cities and places (selection):

Norwich, Cromer, Great Yarmouth, Lowestoft, Ipswich, Felixstowe, Harwich, Margate, Dover, Calais, Dunkerque, Boulogne-sur-Mer, Zeebrugge, Oostende, Den Helder, Alkmaar, Hoorn, Haarlem, **AMSTERDAM**, Leiden, 's-Gravenhage (Den Haag), **ROTTERDAM**, Dordrecht, Breda, Tilburg, Eindhoven, Groningen, Leeuwarden, Assen, Emmen, Zwolle, Deventer, Apeldoorn, Arnhem, Utrecht, Almere, Gouda, Hoek van Holland, Vlissingen, Gent, Brugge, Antwerpen, **BRUSSELS (Bruxelles)**, Mechelen, Leuven, Namur, Charleroi, Liège, Verviers, Mons, Tournai, **LILLE**, Maastricht, Aachen, **KÖLN (Cologne)**, **Bonn**, Düren, Koblenz, Düsseldorf, Solingen, Wuppertal, Essen, Bochum, **Dortmund**, Gelsenkirchen, Oberhausen, Duisburg, Krefeld, Mönchengladbach, Münster, Osnabrück, Bielefeld, Herford, Hamm, Paderborn, Kassel, Göttingen

HAMBURG, Bremen, Bremerhaven, Cuxhaven, Wilhelmshaven, Emden, Oldenburg, Delmenhorst, Lübeck, Kiel, Flensburg, Schleswig, Neumünster, Rostock, Stralsund, Greifswald, Schwerin, Lüneburg, Hannover, Wolfsburg, Braunschweig, Hildesheim, Salzgitter, Magdeburg, **BERLIN**, Potsdam, Brandenburg, Oranienburg, Frankfurt, Cottbus, Dessau, Halle, Leipzig, Dresden, Chemnitz, Gera, Jena, Erfurt, Weimar, Eisenach, Gotha, Zwickau, Plauen, Hof, Bautzen, Görlitz

Szczecin, Świnoujście, Kołobrzeg, Koszalin, Stargard, Gorzów Wielkopolski, **PRAHA (Prague)**, Plzeň, České Budějovice, Liberec, Ústí nad Labem, Karlovy Vary, Kladno, Cheb, Domažlice

Reims, Paris, Créteil, Épernay, Châlons-en-Champagne, Troyes, Sens, Auxerre, Dijon, Besançon, Belfort, Mulhouse, Colmar, Strasbourg, Haguenau, Saverne, Nancy, Metz, Thionville, Verdun, Sedan, Charleville-Mézières, Saarbrücken, Karlsruhe, Mannheim, Heidelberg, Ludwigshafen, Mainz, Wiesbaden, Frankfurt, Darmstadt, Worms, Speyer, Kaiserslautern, Trier, Würzburg, Nürnberg, Fürth, Erlangen, Regensburg, Ingolstadt, Augsburg, **MÜNCHEN (Munich)**, Ulm, Stuttgart, Reutlingen, Tübingen, Pforzheim, Heilbronn, Aalen, Rosenheim, Kempten, Kaufbeuren, Passau, Landshut

Bern, Basel, Zürich, Winterthur, Sankt Gallen, Luzern, Genève, Lausanne, Montreux, Sion, Chur, Davos, Sankt Moritz, Bellinzona, Locarno, Lugano, Vaduz

Innsbruck, Salzburg, Linz, Wels, Steyr, Graz, Klagenfurt, Villach, Lienz, Kufstein, Bregenz

Lyon, Saint-Étienne, Grenoble, Chambéry, Annecy, Valence, Montélimar, Avignon, Nîmes, Arles, Aix-en-Provence, **MARSEILLE**, Toulon, Hyères, Cannes, Antibes, **NICE**, **MONACO**, Monte-Carlo, Menton, San Remo, Imperia, Savona, **Génova**, La Spezia, Carrara, Massa, Viareggio, **Pisa**, **Firenze (Florence)**, **SAN MARINO**, Rimini, Forlì, Cesena, Ravenna, **Bologna**, Modena, Reggio nell'Emilia, Parma, Piacenza, Cremona, Mantova, **MILANO (Turin)**, **TORINO (Turin)**, Novara, Vercelli, Alessandria, Asti, Cuneo, Savona, Genova, Como, Lecco, Bergamo, Brescia, Verona, Vicenza, Padova, **Venezia (Venice)**, Treviso, Trento, Bolzano, Merano, Udine, Gorizia, Trieste, **LJUBLJANA**, Kranj, Celje, Rijeka, Pula, Zadar

Golfo di Génova, Golfo di Venézia

Deutsche Bucht, Kieler Bucht, Mecklenburger Bucht, Stettiner Haff, Rügen, Usedom, Wolin, Fehmarn, Sylt, Föhr, Nordfriesische Inseln, Ostfriesische Inseln, Helgoland, Terschelling, Texel, Ameland

Mont Blanc, Matterhorn, Jungfrau, Gran Paradiso, Monte Rosa, Großglockner, Zugspitze, Brenner P., Mte. Cimone, Mt. Ventoux, Mt. Mézenc

Rivers: Elbe, Weser, Ems, Rhein, Ruhr, Lippe, Mosel, Main, Neckar, Donau, Isar, Inn, Lech, Saar, Seine, Marne, Aisne, Oise, Rhône, Saône, Doubs, Po, Adige, Oder, Havel, Spree, Mulde, Saale

MASSIF CENTRAL

ALPES

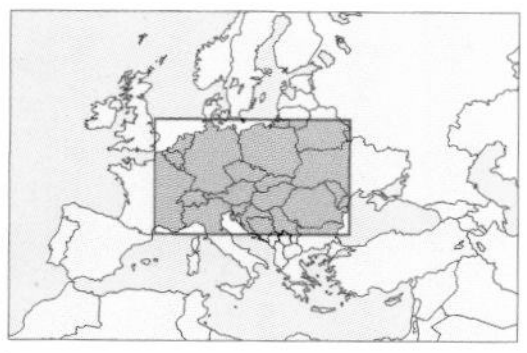

10 11 12 **61** 13 14 15 **84** 16

Zatoka *Gdańska* Kaliningrad (Russia) Vilnius LITHUANIA MAHILYOW BELARUS

Gdynia Gdańsk Elbląg MINSK

LITHUANIA
BELARUS
HRODNA
MINSK
HOMYEL
Homyel

Białystok

BREST
Brest
Pripet Marsh
PRYPYATSKY

WARSZAWA (Warsaw)

P O L A N D

Łódź

Lublin

VOLYN RIVNE

KYYIV (Kiev)

ZHYTOMYR

Kraków

Lviv (Lvov) U K R A I N E

LVIV
Ternopil TERNOPIL
KHMELNYTSKYY
Khmelnytskyy VINNYTSYA
Vinnytsya

SLOVAK REP.
Bratislava

Košice ZAKARPATTYA

Chernivtsi CHERNIVTSI M O L D O V A

Chișinău (Kishinev)
Tiraspol

H U N G A R Y

BUDAPEST

Debrecen

Satu Mare
Baia Mare

Oradea

Cluj-Napoca

R O M A N I A

Târgu Mureș

Iași

Bacău

Timișoara

Arad

Sibiu Brașov

Galați

Brăila

BELGRAD (Belgrade)

SERBIA

Craiova

BUCUREȘTI (Bucharest)

Constanța

BOSNIA-HERZEGOVINA

Sarajevo

BULGARIA

9 10 11 12 13 14 15

East from Greenwich COPYRIGHT PHILIP'S

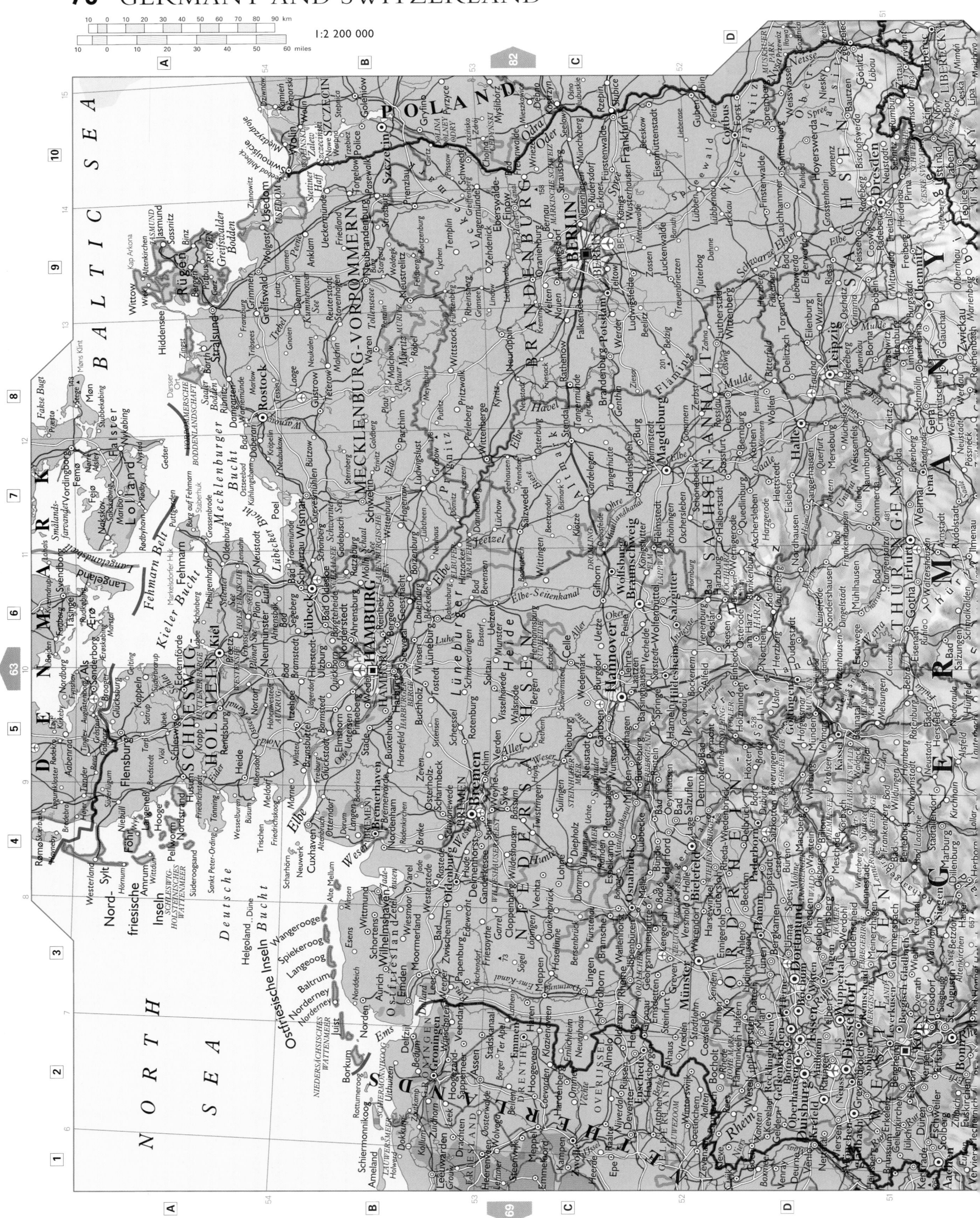

1:2 200 000

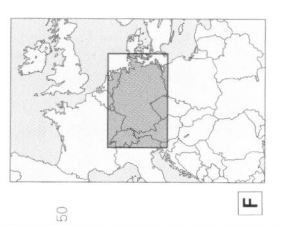

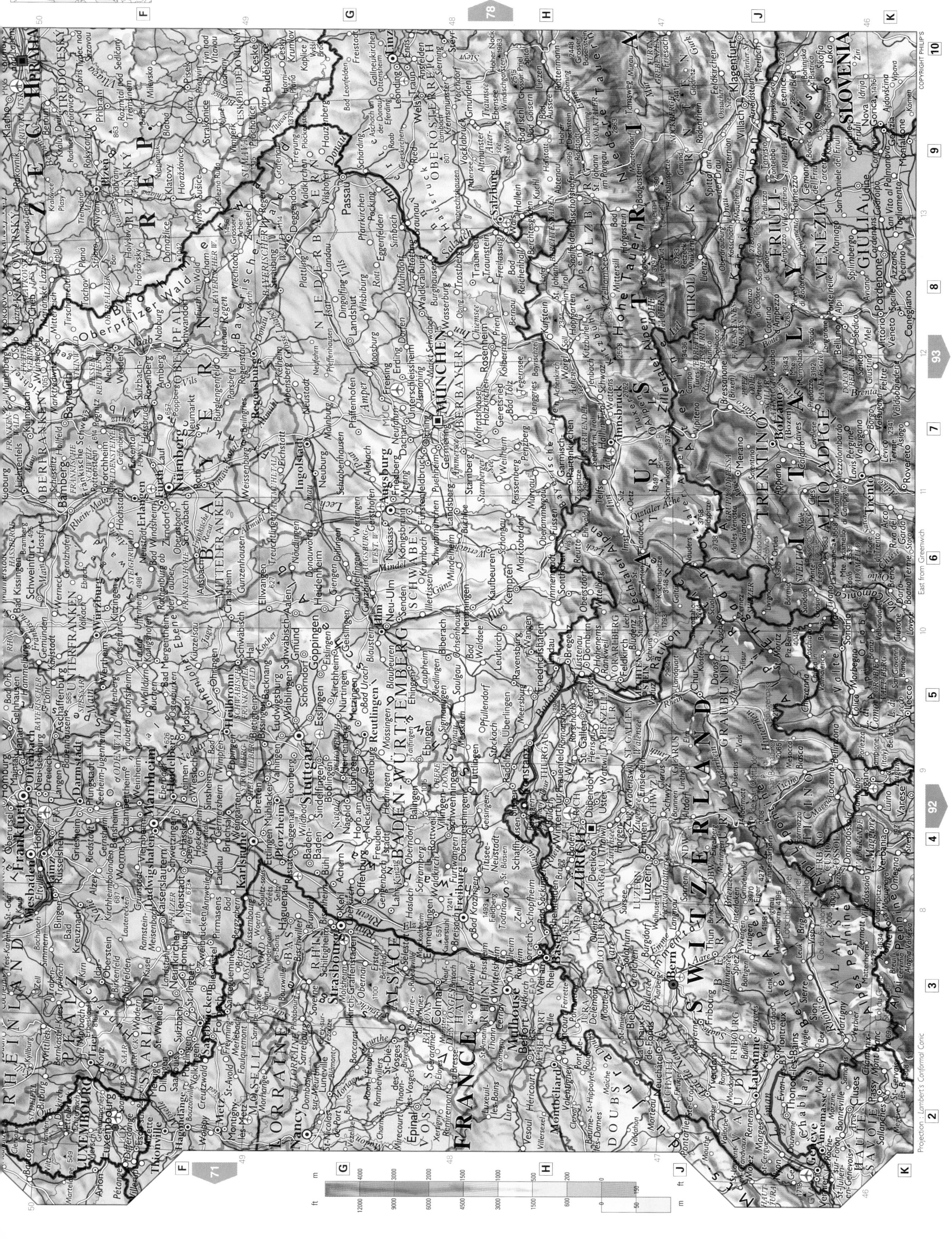

Underlined towns give their name to the administrative area in which they stand.
High-speed rail routes
Projection: Lambert's Conformal Conic
COPYRIGHT PHILIP'S
East from Greenwich
SWITZERLAND
FRANCE
LUXEMBOURG
SLOVENIA
BADEN-WÜRTTEMBERG
BAYERN
TIROL
ALSACE
LORRAINE
GRAUBÜNDEN
TRENTINO-ALTO ADIGE
FRIULI-VENEZIA GIULIA
SAARLAND
MÜNCHEN
ZÜRICH
BERN
STRASBOURG
Stuttgart
Innsbruck
Salzburg
Nürnberg
Frankfurt
Luxembourg
Genève
Lausanne
Mulhouse
Bolzano
Trento
Augsburg
Ulm
Karlsruhe
Mannheim
Regensburg
Passau
Linz
Plzeň
Ingolstadt

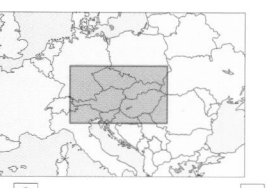

Underlined towns give their name to the administrative area in which they stand.

1:2 200 000

Administrative divisions in Croatia:
1 Brodsko-Posavska   5 Osječko-Baranjska   9 Vukovarsko-Srijemska
2 Koprivničko-Križevačka   6 Požeško-Slavonska
4 Međimurska   8 Virovitičko-Podravska

Underlined towns give their name to the administrative area in which they stand.

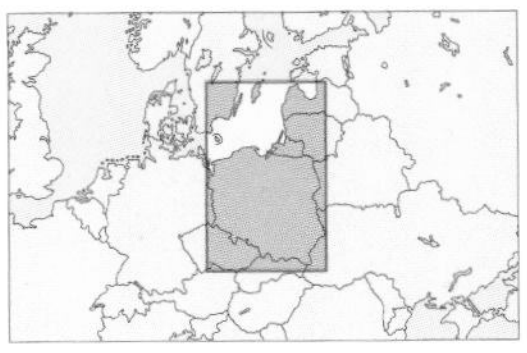

1:2 200 000

10 0 10 20 30 40 50 60 70 80 90 km

10 0 10 20 30 40 50 60 miles

Gulf of Riga

LATVIA

LITHUANIA

SWEDEN

BALTIC SEA

POLAND

KALININGRAD (Russia)

Riga
Jūrmala
Jelgava
Šiauliai
Telšiai
Plungė
Tauragė
Klaipėda
Palanga
Neringa
Curonian Spit
Kaunas
Marijampolė
Kaliningrad
Elbląg
Malbork
Gdynia
Sopot
Gdańsk
Zatoka Gdańska
Hel
Władysławowo
Puck
Wejherowo
Lębork
Kartuzy
Kościerzyna
Tczew
Starogard
Słupsk
Ustka
Koszalin
Darłowo
Kołobrzeg
Białogard

Gotland (Sweden)
Visby
Öland (Sweden)
Kalmar
Karlskrona
Bornholm (Denmark)
Rønne

Ventspils
Liepāja

POMORSKIE
WARMIŃSKO-MAZURSKIE
ZACHODNIO-POMORSKIE

Neman
Nemunas
Wisła

Underlined towns give their name to the administrative area in which they stand.

COPYRIGHT PHILIP'S

Projection: Lambert's Conformal Conic

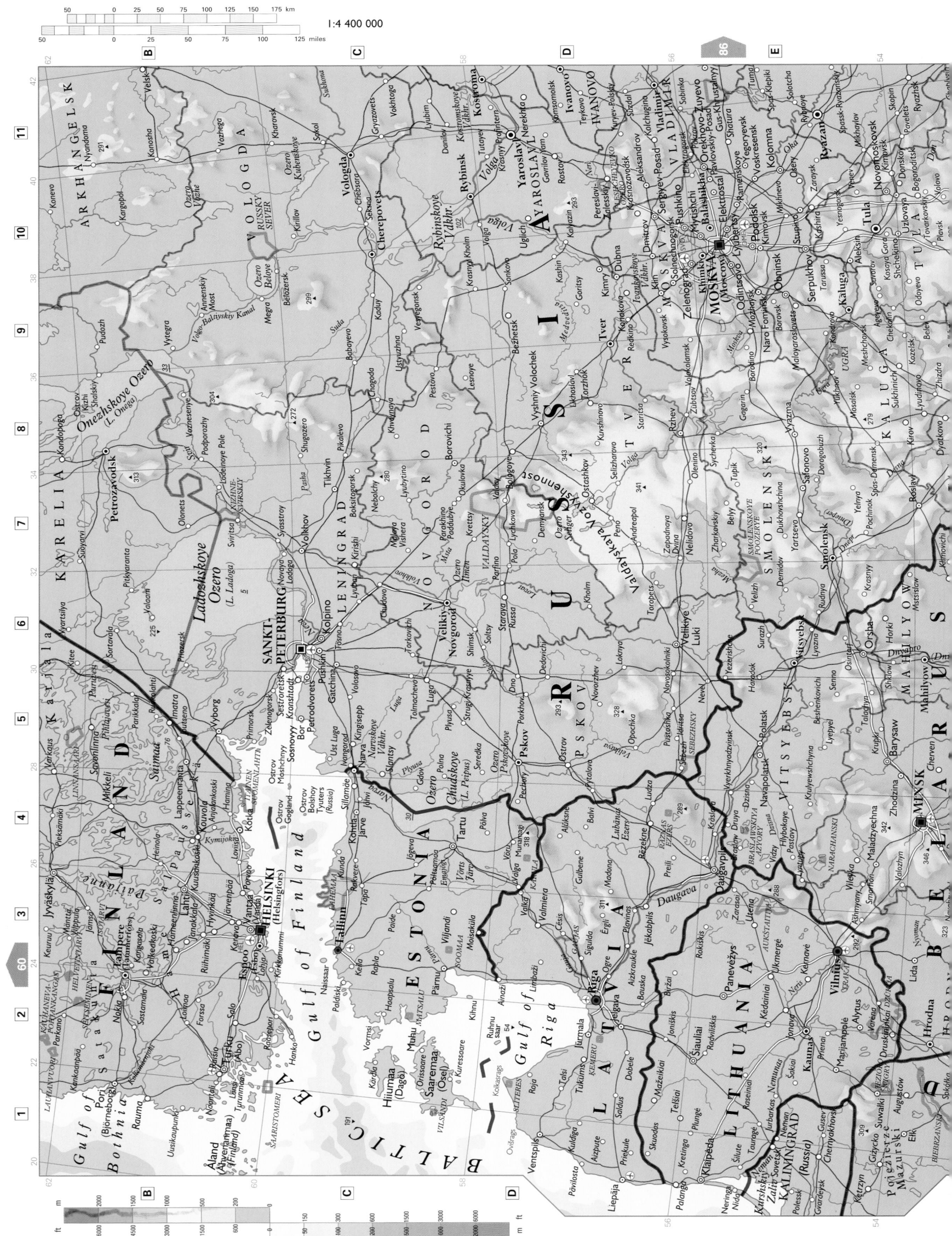

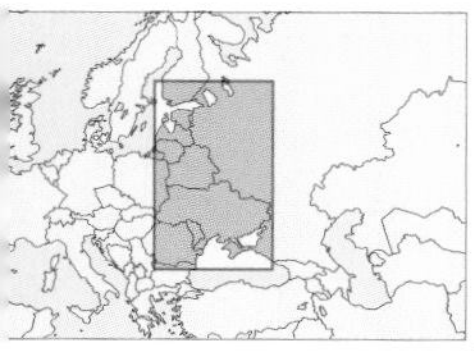

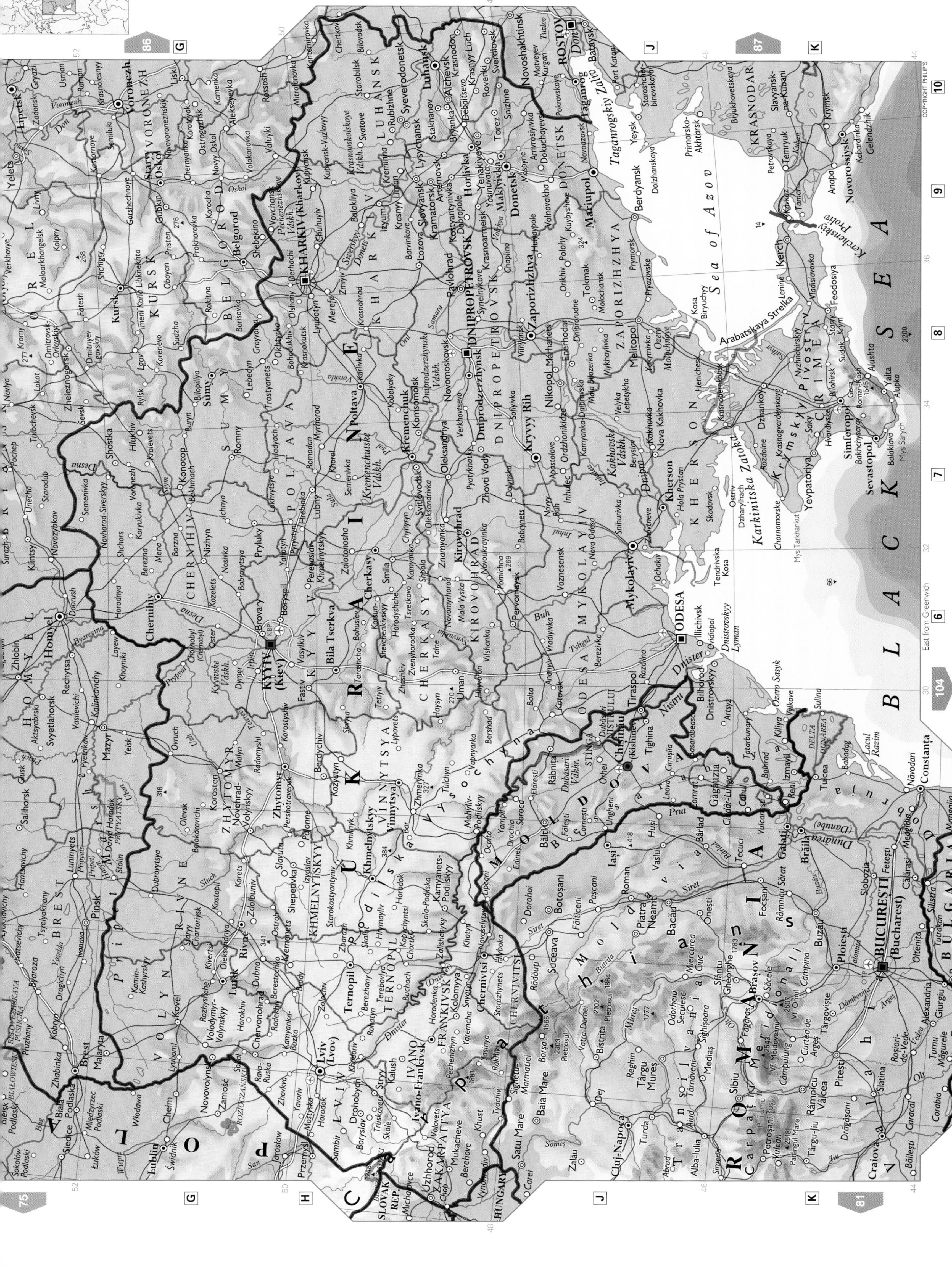

U K R A I N E

B L A C K   S E A

Sea of Azov

BULGARIA

ROMANIA

MOLDOVA

SLOVAK REP.

HUNGARY

KRASNODAR

O R E L

KURSK

BELGOROD

SUMY

VORONEZH

POLTAVA

KHARKIV

LUHANSK

DONETSK

ZAPORIZHZHYA

DNIPROPETROVSK

KIROVOHRAD

CHERKASY

KYYIV

CHERNIHIV

ZHYTOMYR

VINNYTSYA

KHMELNYTSKYY

TERNOPIL

LVIV

IVANO-FRANKIVSK

ZAKARPATTYA

CHERNIVTSI

ODESA

MYKOLAYIV

KHERSON

CRIMEA

VOLYN

RIVNE

BREST

HOMYEL

Taganrogskiy Zaliv

Kerchenskiy Proliv

Karkinitska Zatoka

ROSTOV

Voronezh

Kursk

Belgorod

Sumy

Poltava

KHARKIV (Kharkov)

Luhansk

Donetsk

Mariupol

Zaporizhzhya

DNIPROPETROVSK

Kryvyy Rih

Kherson

Mykolayiv

ODESA

Kirovohrad

Cherkasy

Bila Tserkva

KYYIV (Kiev)

Chernihiv

Homyel

Mazyr

Zhytomyr

Vinnytsya

Khmelnytskyy

Ternopil

Rivne

Lutsk

Lviv (Lvov)

Ivano-Frankivsk

Chernivtsi

Simferopol

Sevastopol

Yalta

Feodosiya

Kerch

Novorossiysk

Krasnodar

BUCUREŞTI (Bucharest)

Constanţa

Dnister

Dnipro

Desna

Prut

Danube

Projection: Conical with two standard parallels

East from Greenwich

COPYRIGHT PHILIP'S

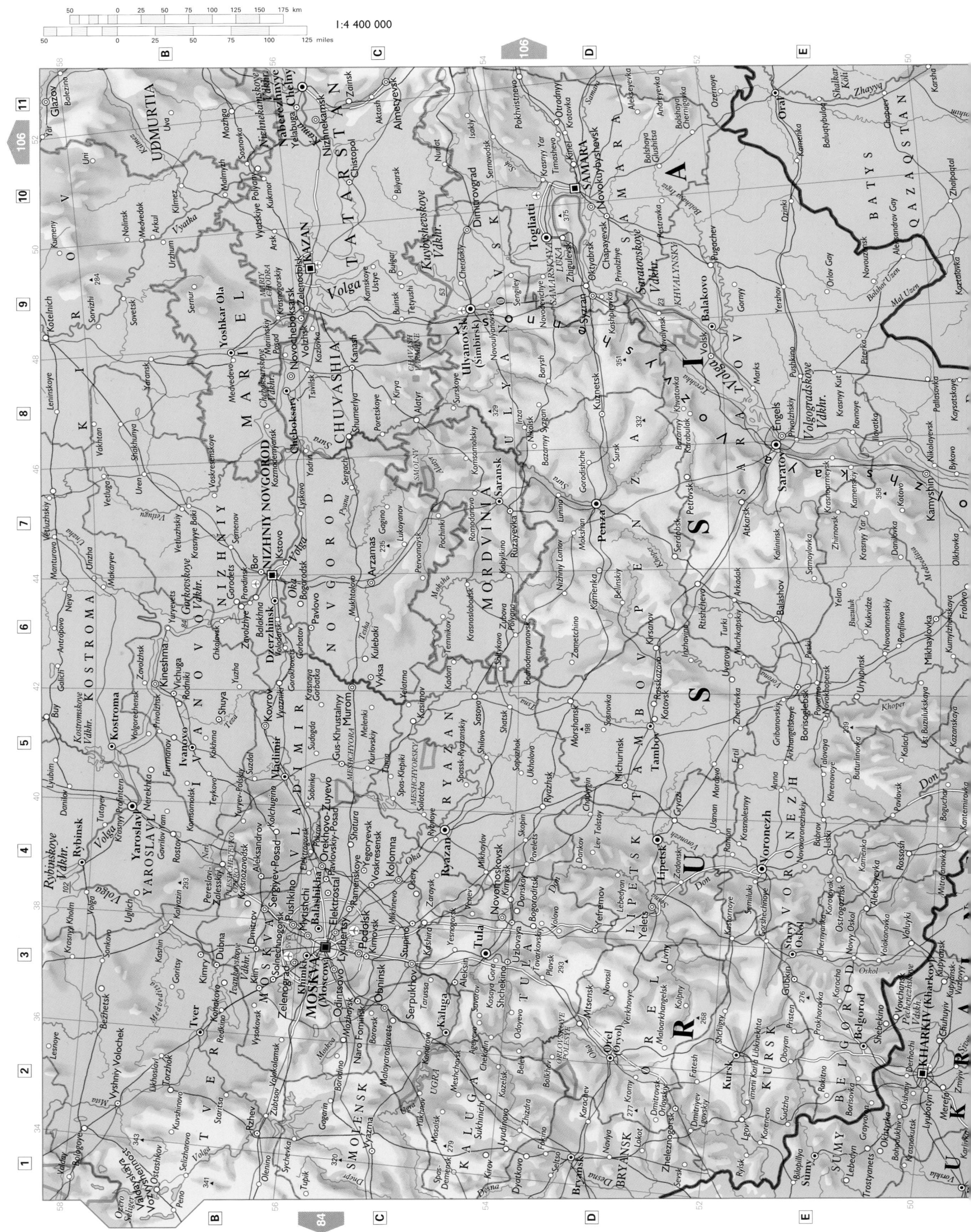

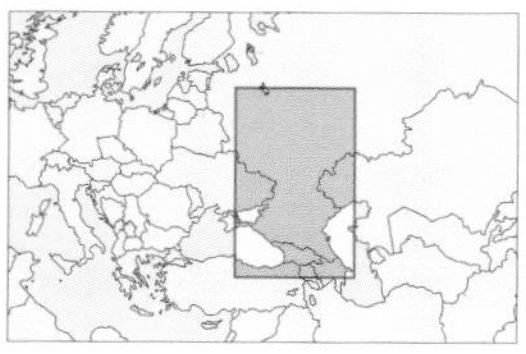

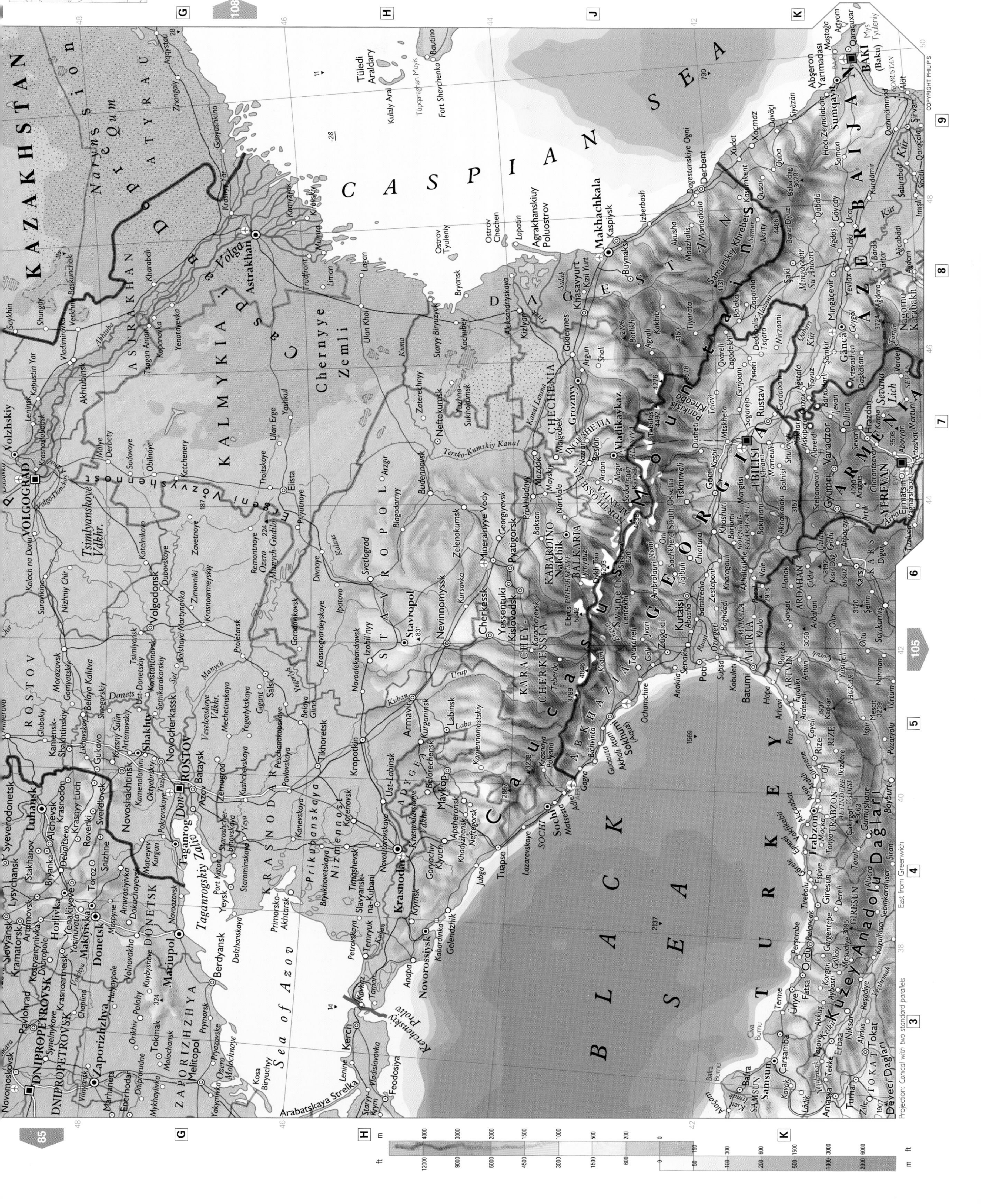

CASPIAN SEA

BLACK SEA

Sea of Azov

KAZAKHSTAN

AZERBAIJAN

ARMENIA

GEORGIA

TURKEY

KALMYKIA

ASTRAKHAN

CHERNYYE ZEMLI

STAVROPOL

KRASNODAR

ROSTOV

DONETSK

ZAPORIZHZHYA

DNIPROPETROVSK

CHECHENIA

INGUSHETIA

DAGESTAN

NORTH OSSETIA

KABARDINO-BALKARIA

KARACHEY-CHERKESSIA

ADYGEA

ABKHAZIA

SOUTH OSSETIA

AJARIA

Caucasus

Greater Caucasus

Prikaspiyskaya Nizmennost

Kuzey Anadolu Dağları

Naryn Qum

Baskunchak

Tsimlyanskoye Vdkhr.

Volga-Don

Volga

Don

Major towns (selected):

VOLGOGRAD, Astrakhan, ROSTOV, Novocherkassk, Shakhty, Taganrog, Krasnodar, Stavropol, Nevinnomyssk, Armavir, Maykop, SOCHI, Tuapse, Novorossiysk, Anapa, Kerch, Feodosiya, Mariupol, Berdyansk, Melitopol, Tokmak, ZAPORIZHZHYA, DNIPROPETROVSK, DONETSK, Makiyivka, Horlivka, Luhansk, Syeverodonetsk, Kramatorsk, Slovyansk, Volzhskiy, Volgodonsk, Elista, Cherkessk, Mineralnyye Vody, Pyatigorsk, Kislovodsk, Yessentuki, Prokhladnyy, Nalchik, Mozdok, Vladikavkaz, Nazran, Grozny, Argun, Gudermes, Khasavyurt, Buynaksk, Makhachkala, Kaspiysk, Izberbash, Derbent, BAKI (Baku), Sumqayit, Gäncä, Mingäçevir, TBILISI, Rustavi, Kutaisi, Batumi, Poti, YEREVAN, Gyumri, Vanadzor, TRABZON, SAMSUN, Ordu, Giresun, Rize

Caucasus Mts.

Elbrus 5642

Dykh Tau

Kazbek 5047

El'brus

Araks

Kür

Kura

Kuban

Terek

Sulak

Samur

Terek-Kumskiy Kanal

Volga-Don

East from Greenwich

Projection: Conical with two standard parallels

Grid references: G H J K / 3 4 5 6 7 8 9

10 0 10 20 30 40 50 60 70 80 90 km

1:2 200 000

10 0 10 20 30 40 50 60 miles

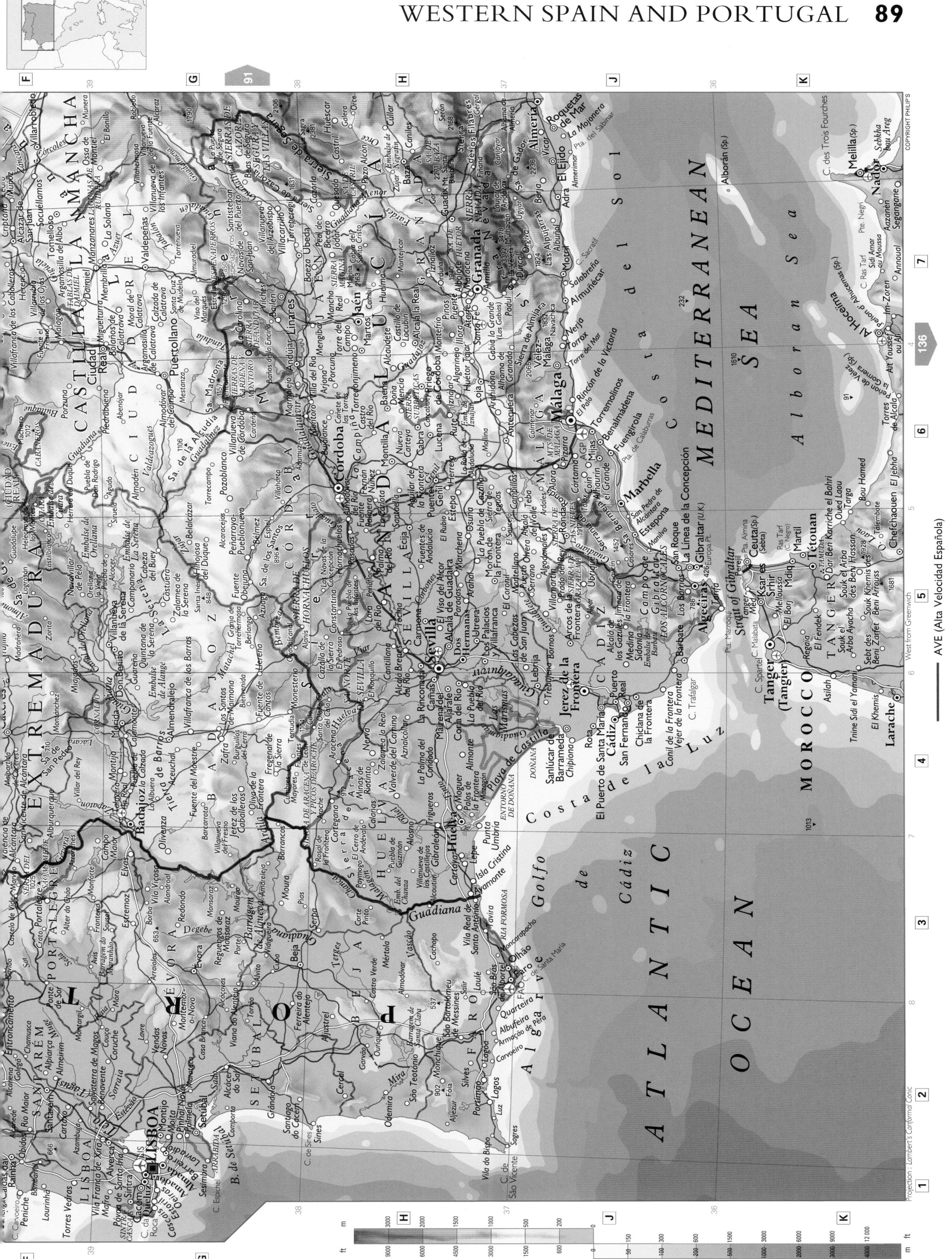

1:2 200 000

1:2 200 000

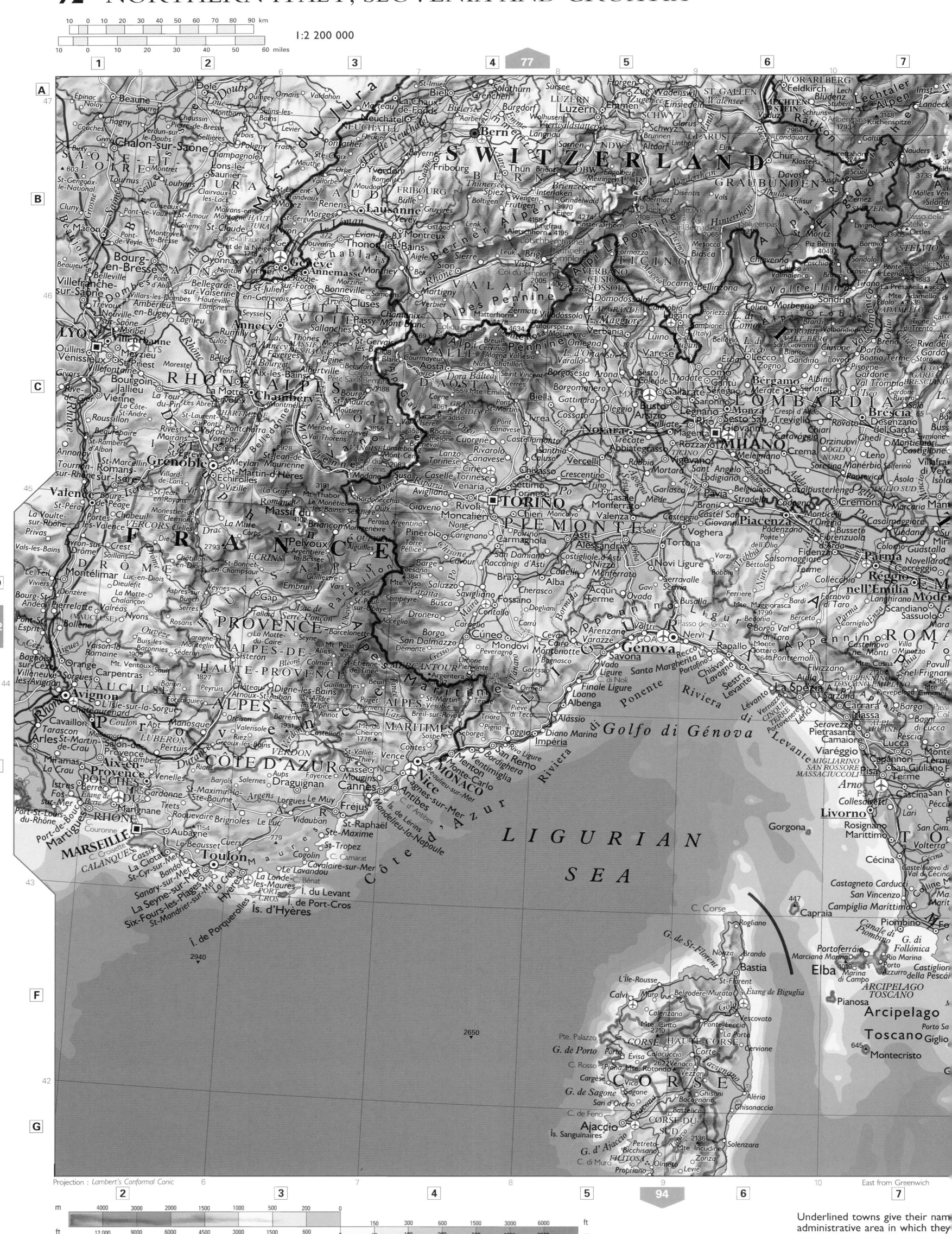

Projection : Lambert's Conformal Conic

East from Greenwich

Underlined towns give their nam
administrative area in which they

Administrative divisions in Croatia:
- ...sko-Posavska
- 4 Medimurska
- 8 Viroviticko-Podravska
- ...vnicko-Krizevacka
- 6 Pozesko-Slavonska
- 10 Zagrebacka
- ...nsko-Zagorska
- 7 Varazdinska

—————— TAV (Treno Alta Velocità)

COPYRIGHT PHILIP'S

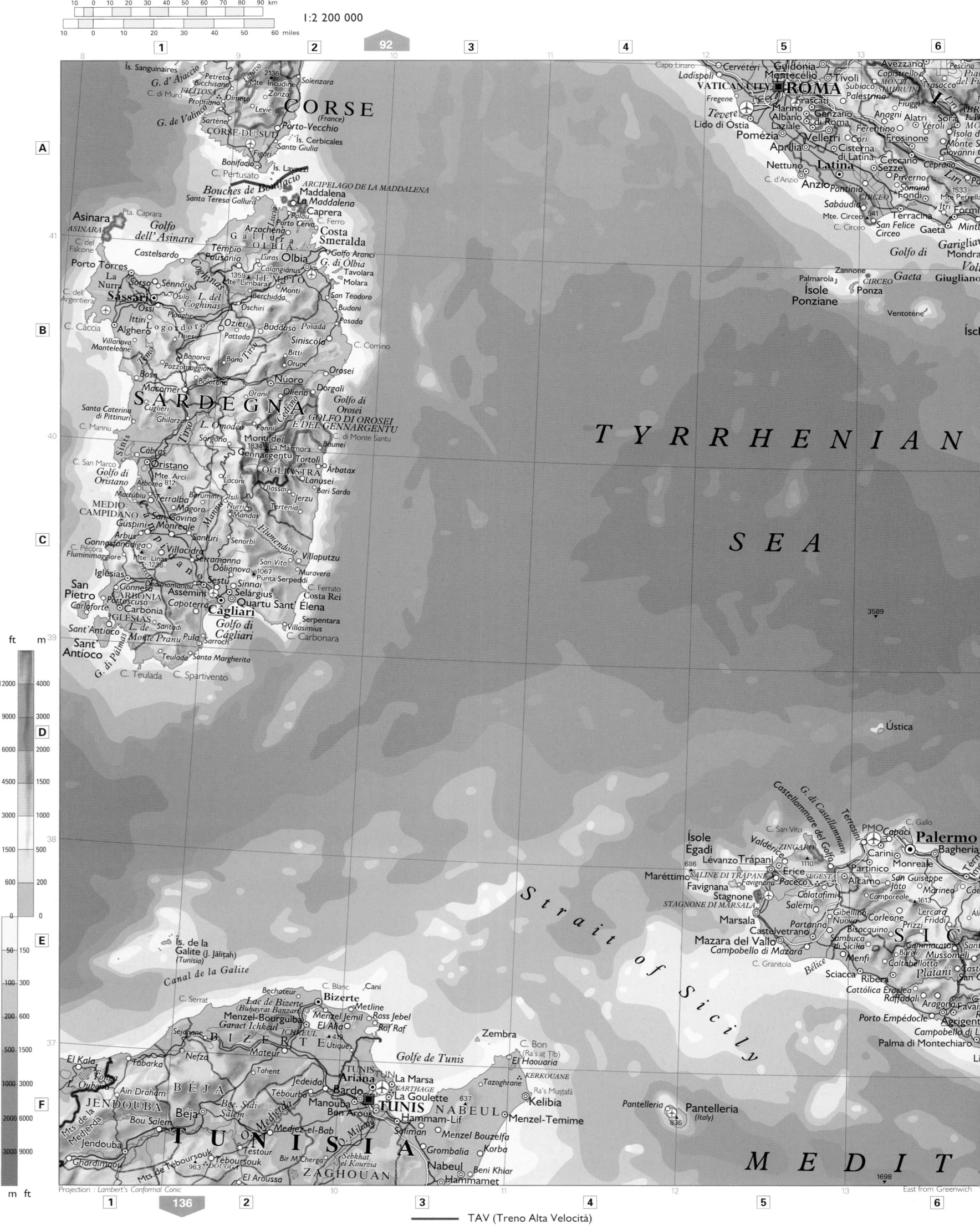

1:2 200 000

TAV (Treno Alta Velocità)

Projection : Lambert's Conformal Conic

East from Greenwich

TYRRHENIAN

SEA

Strait of Sicily

CORSE
(France)

CORSE-DU-SUD

SARDEGNA

TUNISIA

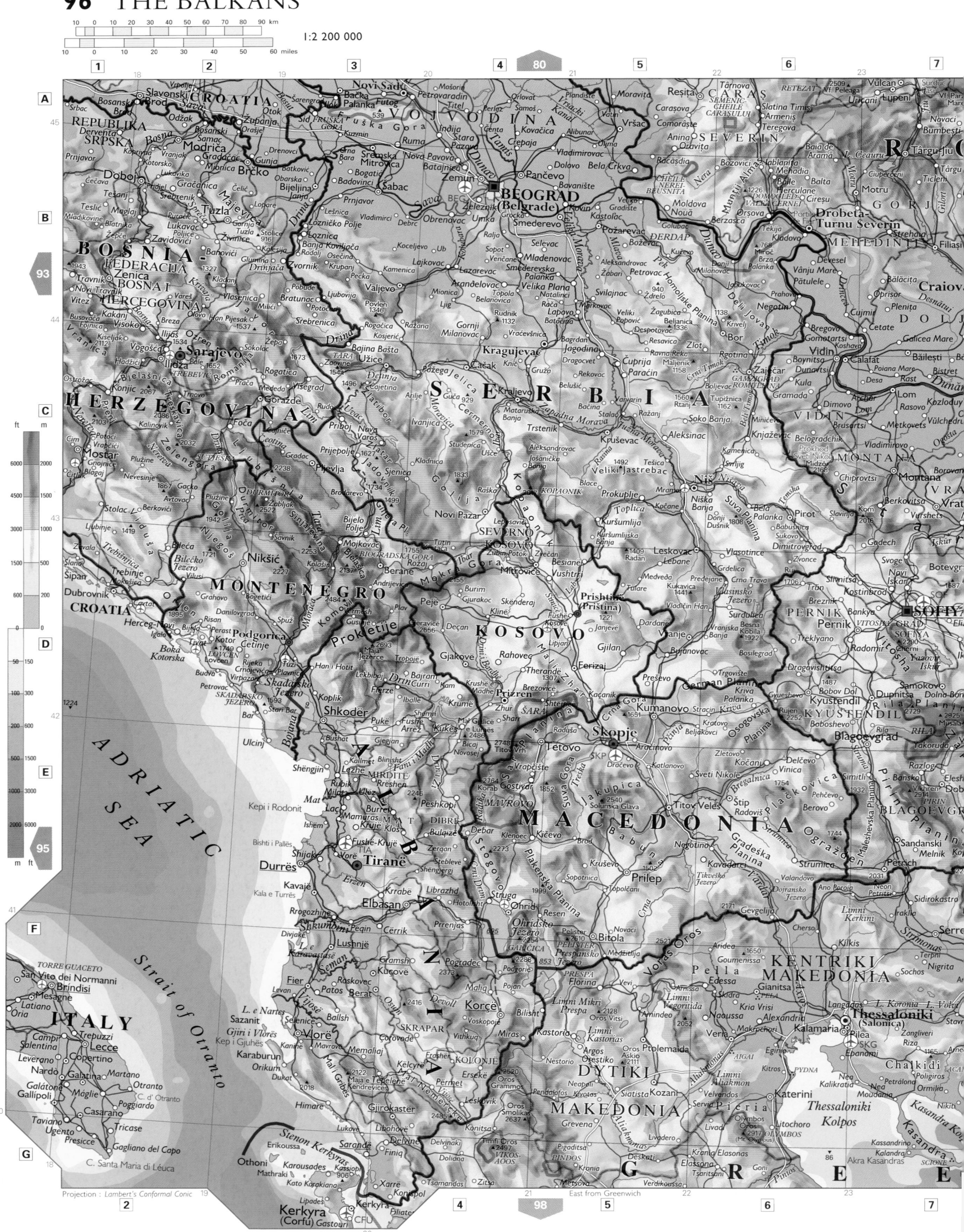

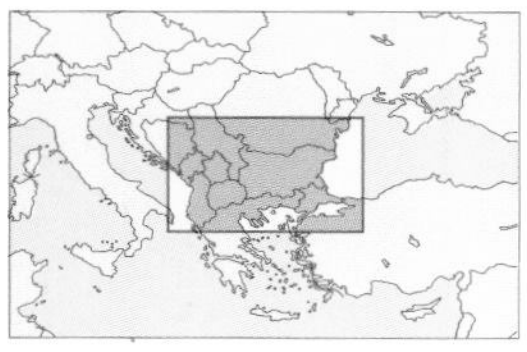

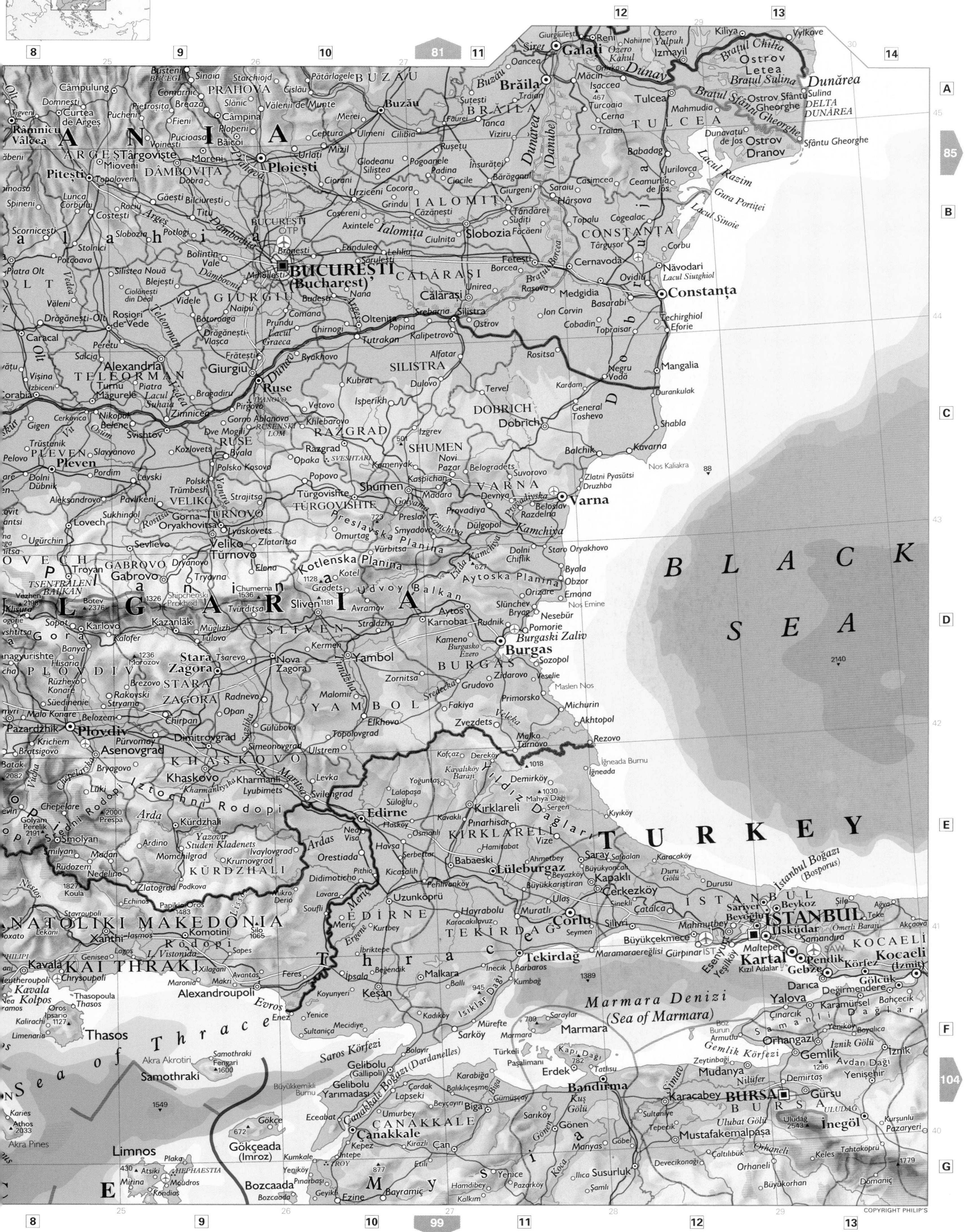

BLACK SEA

TURKEY

BULGARIA

Marmara Denizi (Sea of Marmara)

Sea of Thrace

DELTA DUNĂREA

ROMANIA

Major places: Bucureşti (Bucharest), Ploieşti, Buzău, Brăila, Galaţi, Constanţa, Mangalia, Ruse, Giurgiu, Pleven, Veliko Tŭrnovo, Gabrovo, Shumen, Varna, Burgas, Sliven, Stara Zagora, Yambol, Plovdiv, Pazardzhik, Asenovgrad, Khaskovo, Kŭrdzhali, Edirne, Kırklareli, Lüleburgaz, Çorlu, Tekirdağ, İstanbul, Üsküdar, Kartal, Gebze, Kocaeli (İzmit), Gölcük, Yalova, Bursa, İnegöl, Bandırma, Gemlik, Mudanya, Çanakkale, Gelibolu (Gallipoli), Alexandroupoli, Komotini, Xanthi, Kavala, Samothraki, Thasos, Limnos

Underlined towns give their name to the administrative area in which they stand.

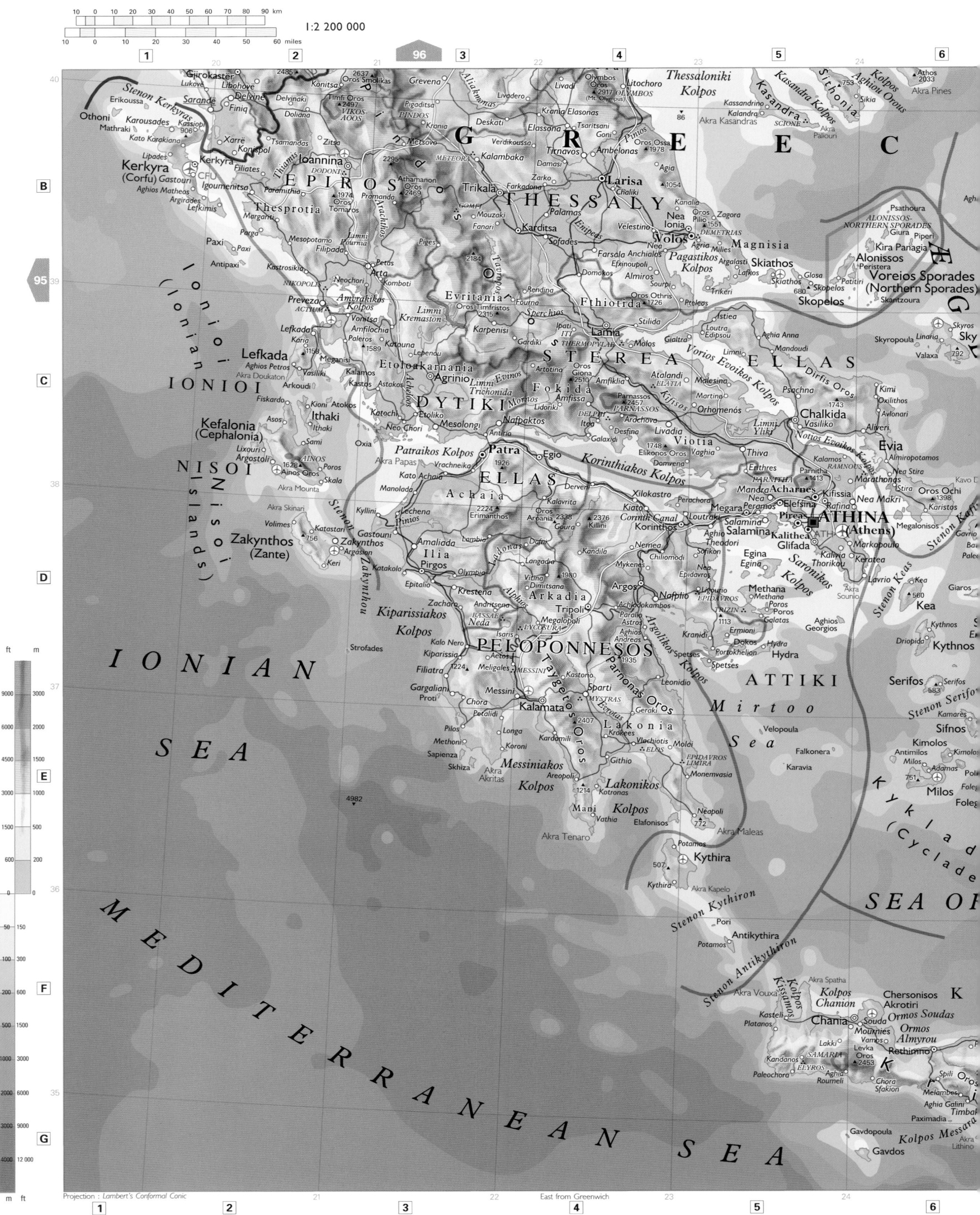

1:2 200 000

Projection : Lambert's Conformal Conic

East from Greenwich

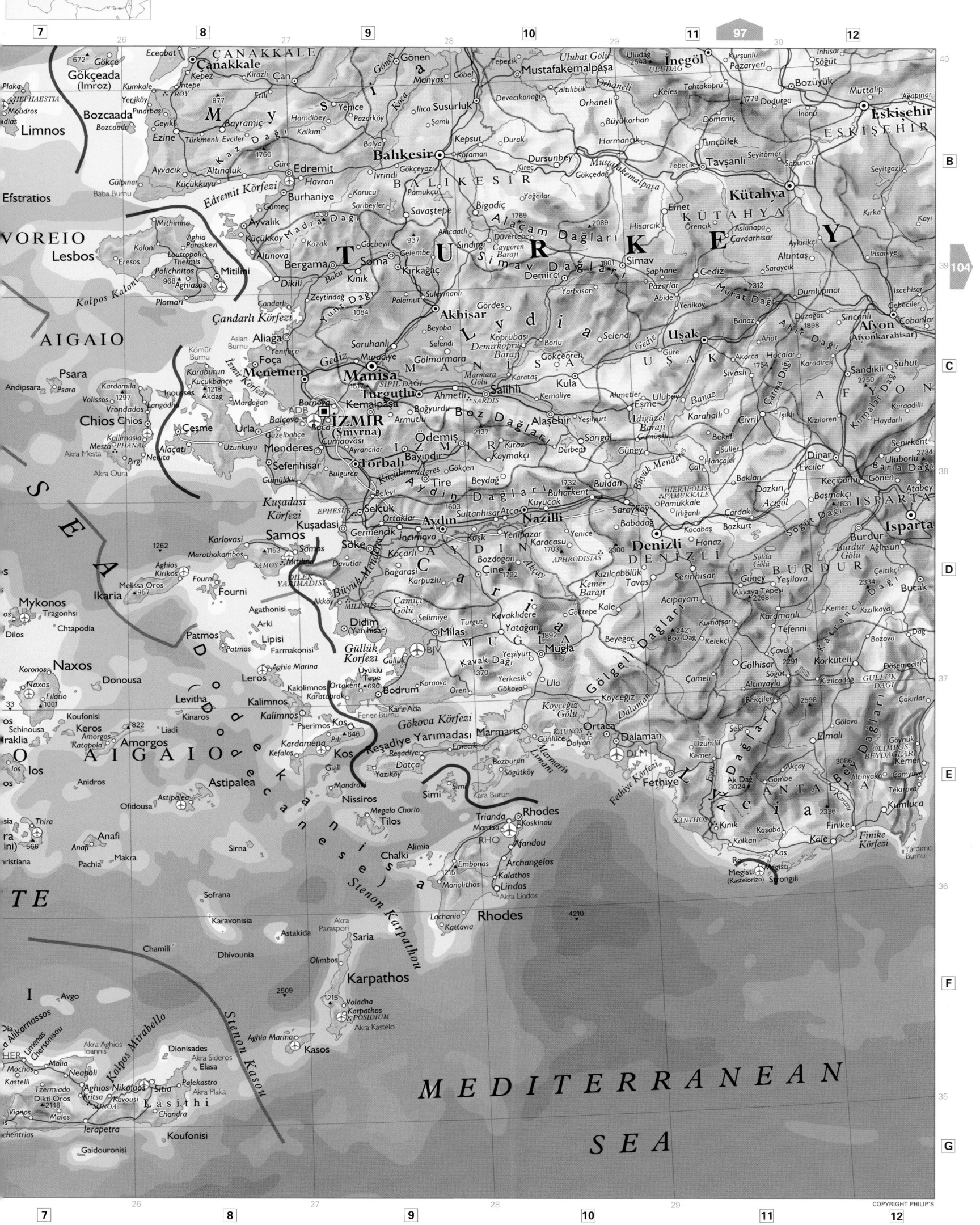

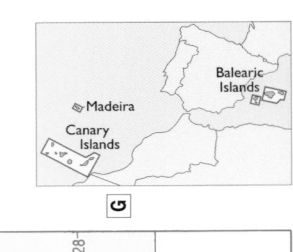

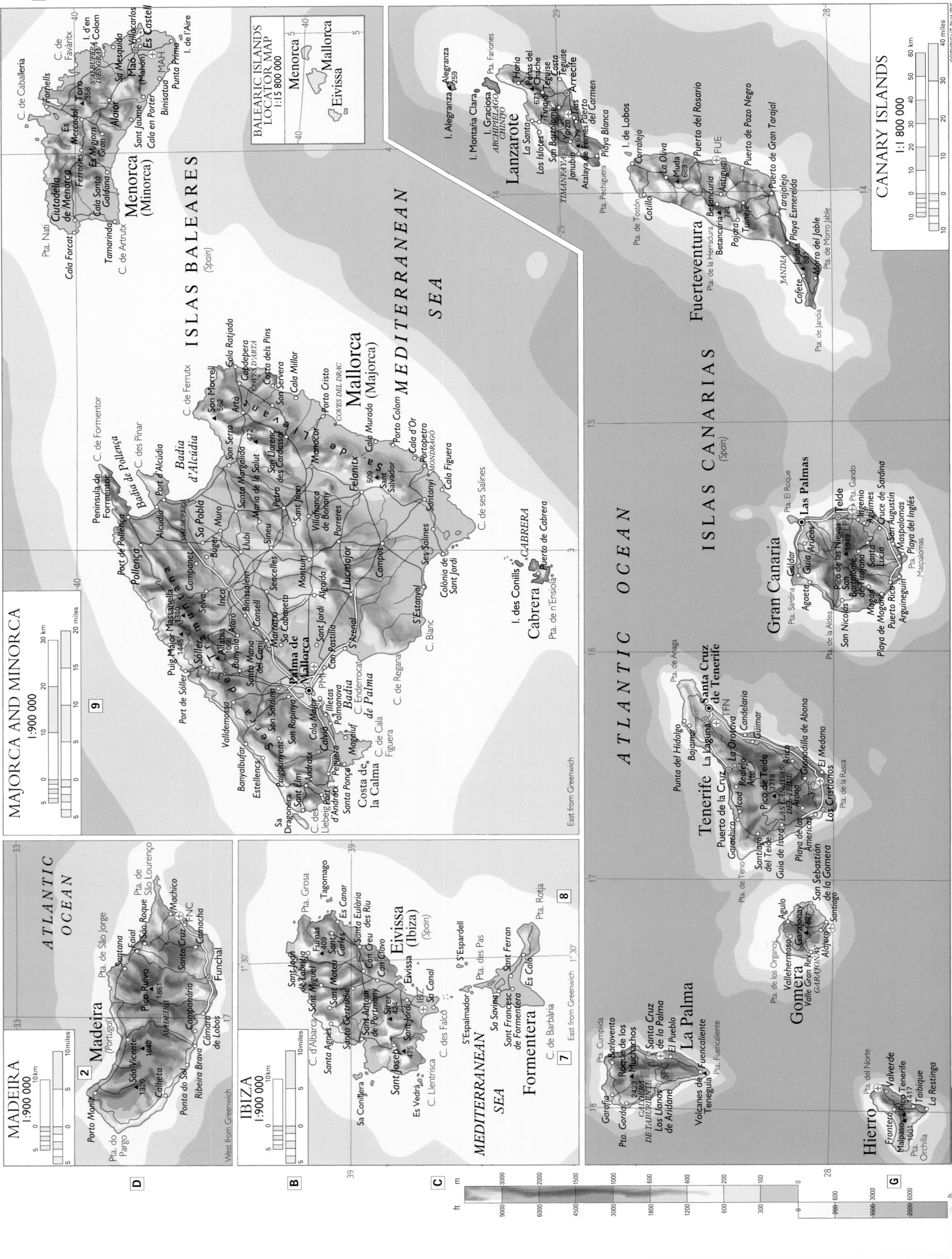

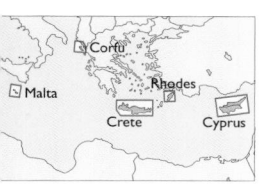

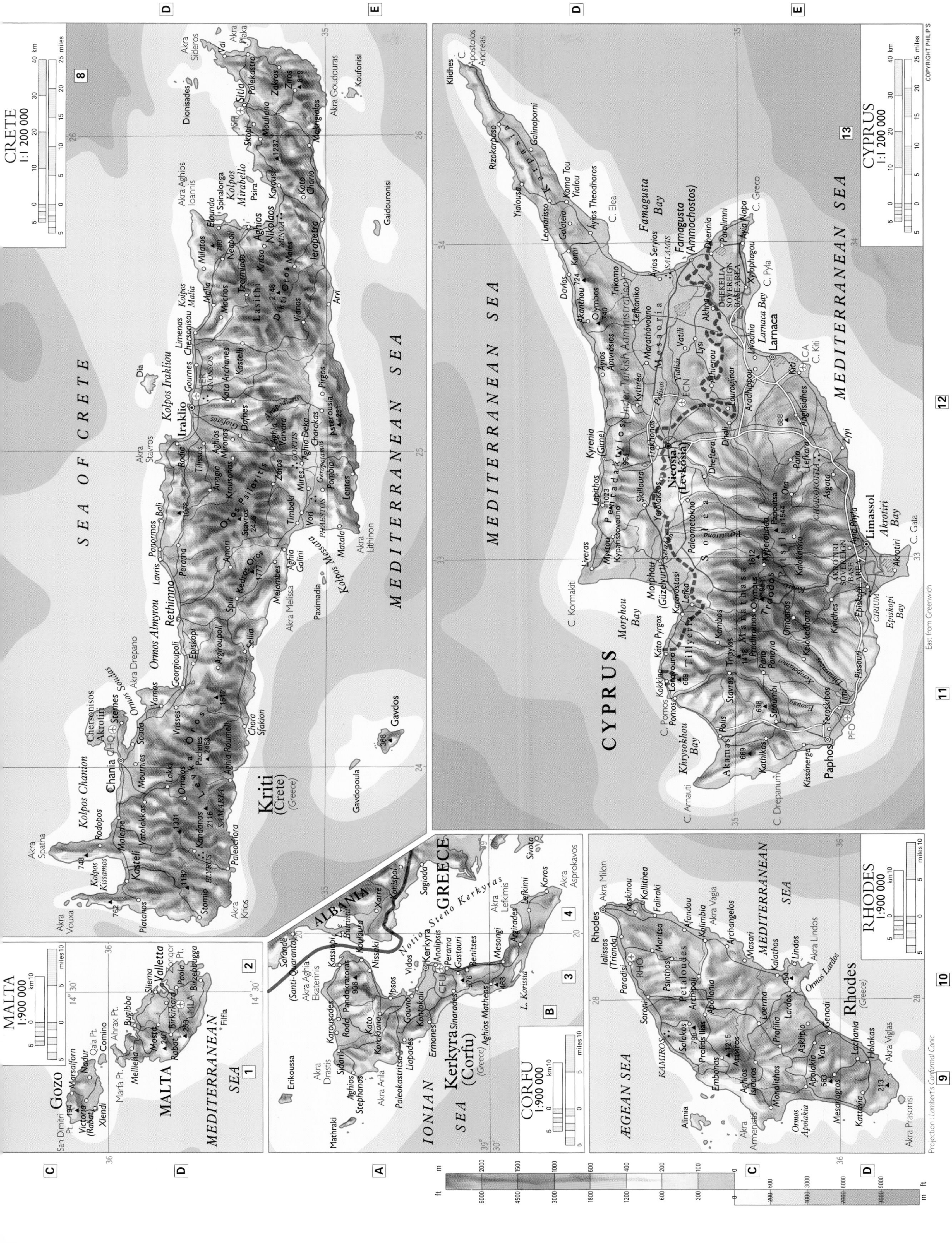

1:44 400 000

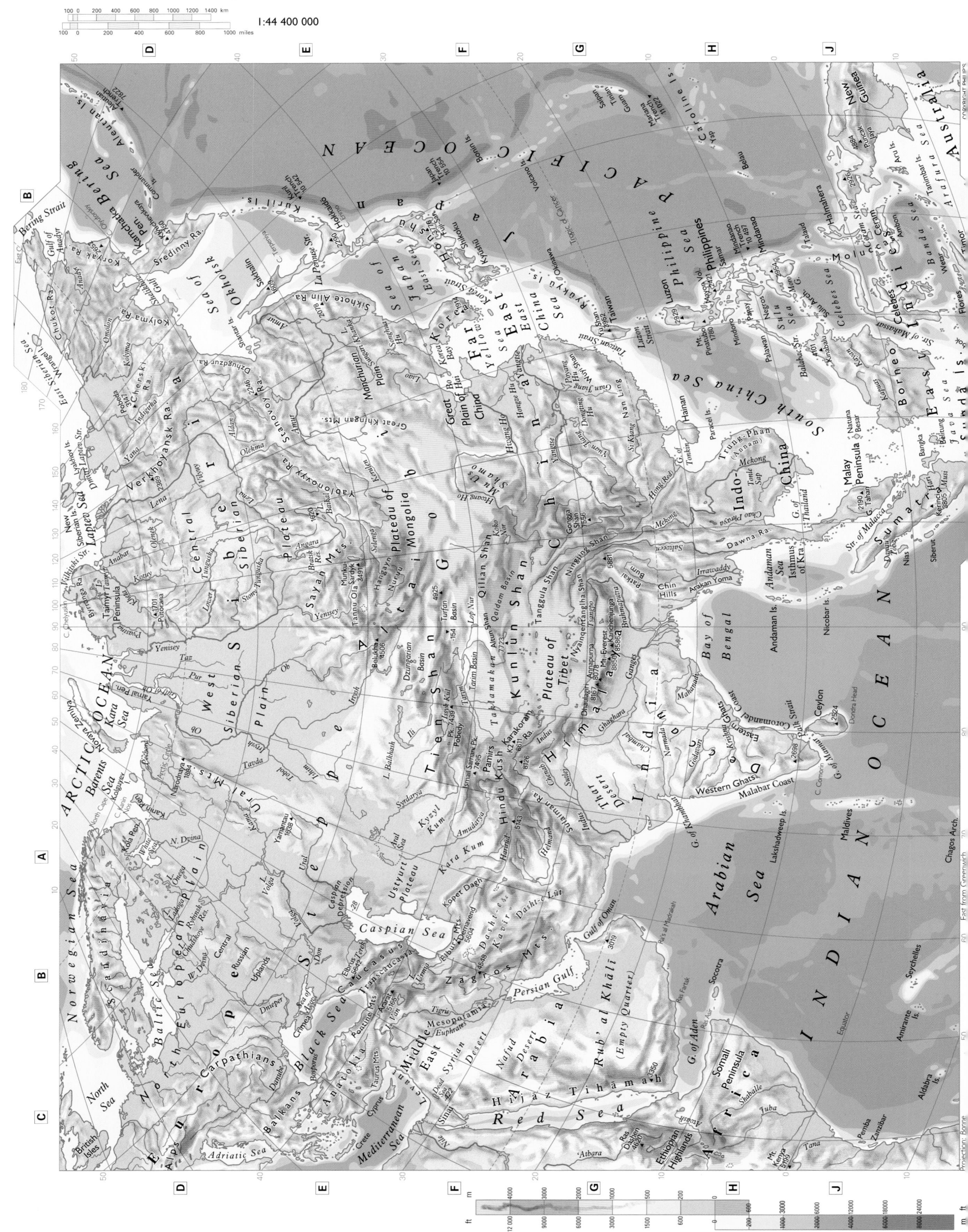

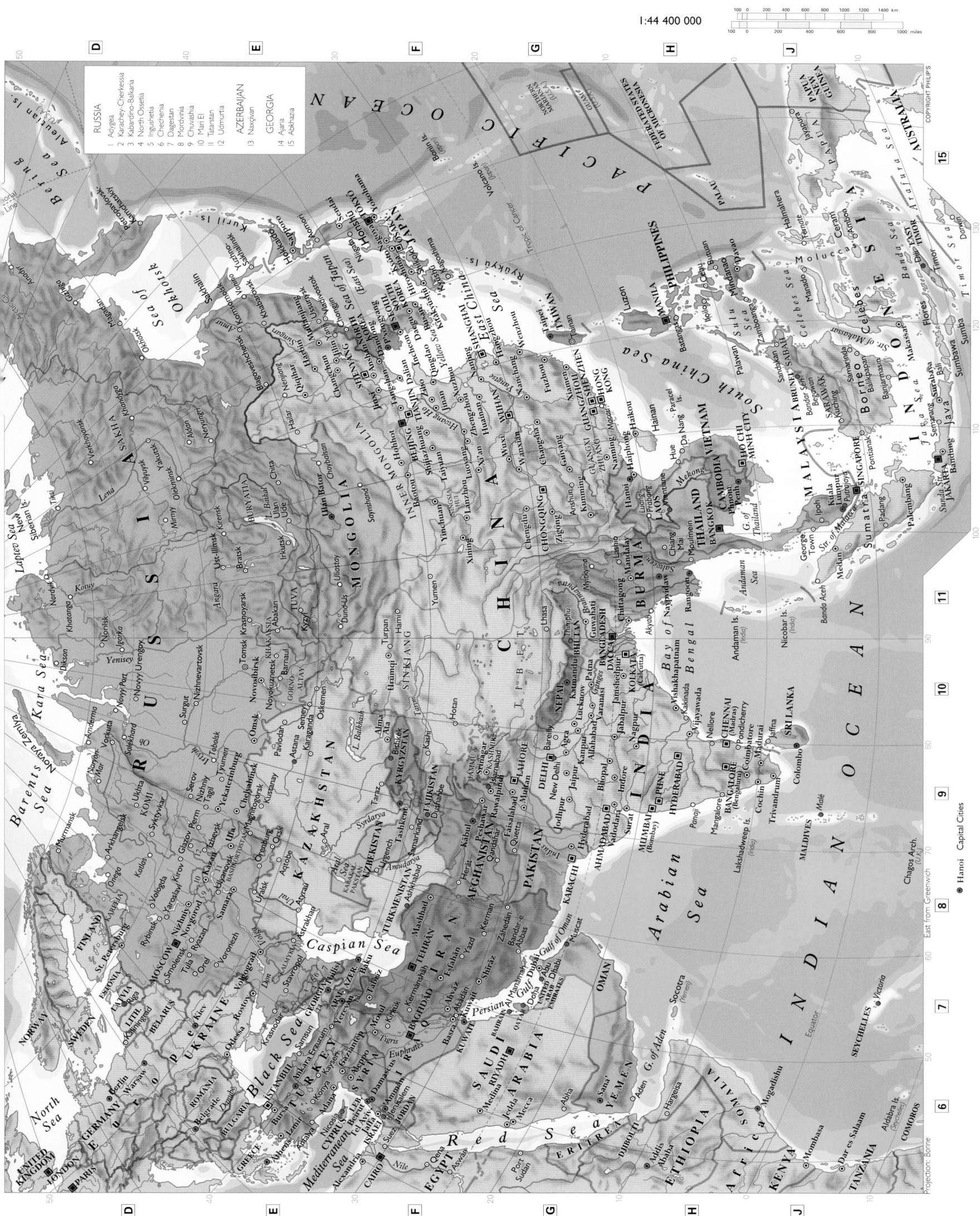

1:44 400 000

100 0 200 400 600 800 1000 1200 1400 km
100 0   200   400   600   800   1000 miles

RUSSIA
1 Adygea
2 Karachey-Cherkessia
3 Kabardino-Balkaria
4 North Ossetia
5 Ingushetia
6 Chechenia
7 Dagestan
8 Mordvinia
9 Chuvashia
10 Mari El
11 Tatarstan
12 Udmurtia
AZERBAIJAN
13 Naxçivan
GEORGIA
14 Ajaria
15 Abkhazia

● Hanoi   Capital Cities

COPYRIGHT PHILIP'S

Projection: Bonne

East from Greenwich

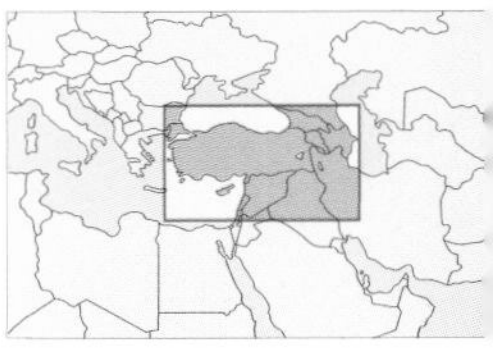

1 : 4 400 000

50   0   25   50   75   100   125   150   175 km
50   0   25   50   75   100   125 miles

BULGARIA

B L A C K   S E A

Stara Zagora
Yambol
Burgas
Aytos
Nos Emine
Elkhovo
Michurin
Kırklareli
Edirne
Igneada
Igneada Burnu
Demirköy
Kilimli
Zonguldak
Ereğli
Karabük
Bartın
Amasra
Cide
Kurucaşile
Çatalzeytin
İnebolu
Abana
Ayancık
Erfelek
Sinop
Gerze
İnce Burun
Bafra Burnu
SAMSUN
Samsun
Terme
Ünye
Fatsa

İSTANBUL
Kartal
Kocaeli (İzmit)
Sakarya (Adapazarı)
Sea of Marmara
Marmara Denizi
BURSA
Bursa
ESKİŞEHİR
Eskişehir
Kütahya
KÜTAHYA
ANKARA
Kırıkkale
ÇANKIRI
ÇORUM
Çorum
TOKAT
Tokat
SİVAS
Sivas

İZMİR (Smyrna)
Manisa
MANİSA
AYDIN
DENİZLİ
Denizli
MUĞLA
ISPARTA
Isparta
BURDUR
Burdur
KONYA
Konya
KARAMAN
Karaman (Laranda)
NİĞDE
Niğde
KAYSERİ
Kayseri
NEVŞEHİR
Nevşehir
AKSARAY
Aksaray
ADANA
Adana
İÇEL
İçel (Mersin)
Tarsus
GAZİANTEP
Gaziantep (Antep)
KAHRAMANMARAŞ
Kahramanmaraş
HATAY
İskenderun
Antalya
Antalya Körfezi

GREECE
Rhodes
Lindos
Karpathos
Kasos

CYPRUS
Nicosia
Kyrenia
Famagusta
Larnaca
Limassol
Morphou
Paphos
Troodos
Akrotiri
Episkopi
(Under Turkish Administration)
Rizokarpaso
Apostolos Andreas

M E D I T E R R A N E A N   S E A

LEBANON
Tarābulus (Tripoli)
BAYRŪT (Beirut)
Saydā
Şūr
DIMASHQ (Damascus)
HIMŞ (Homs)
HAMĀH
Al Lādhiqīyah (Latakia)

ISRAEL
HEFA (Haifa)
TEL AVIV-YAFO
Netanya
Hadera
Nābulus
WEST BANK
Jerusalem
Ashdod
Ashqelon
AMMAN
JORDAN

Projection: Conical with two standard parallels

97
99
130

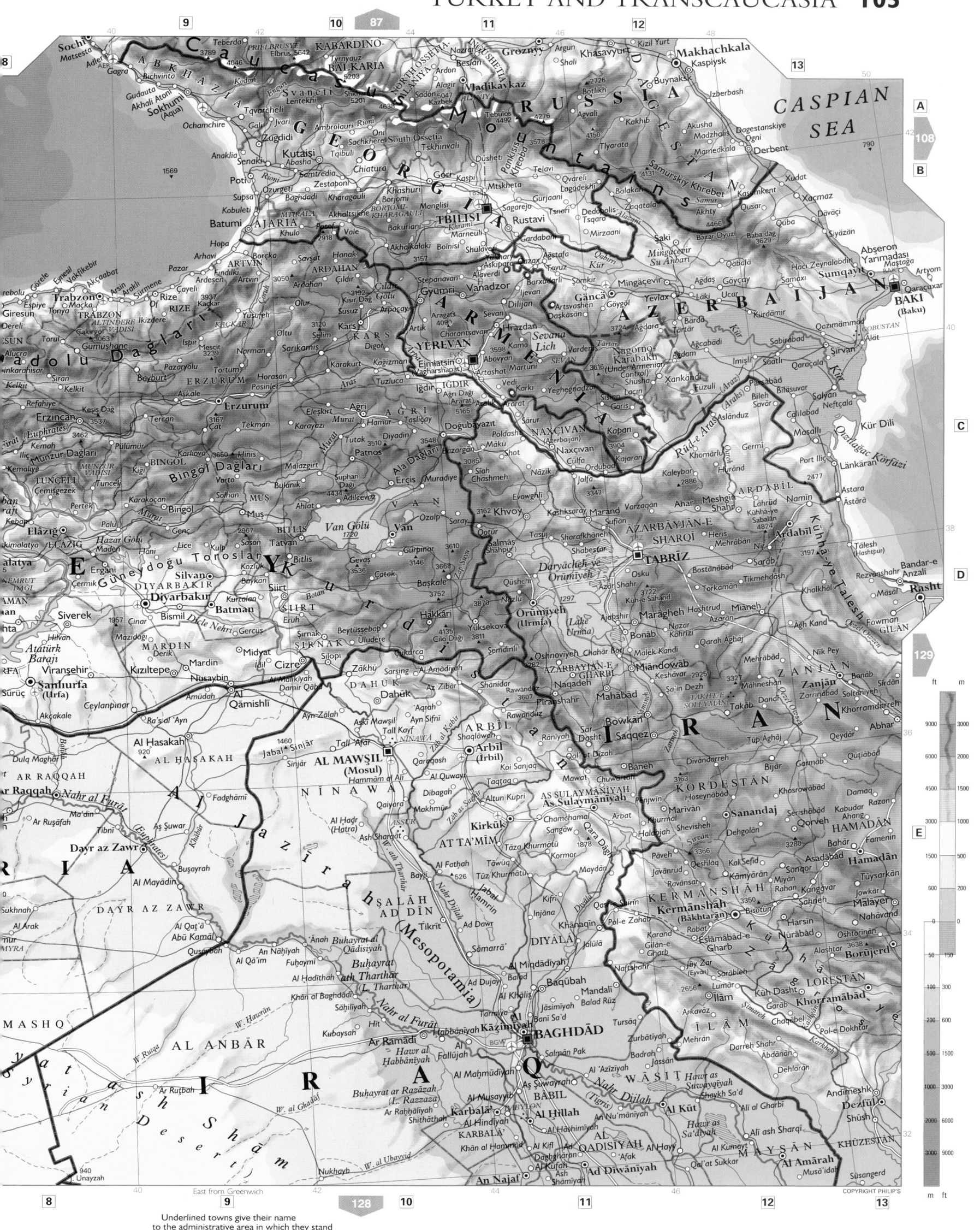

Underlined towns give their name
to the administrative area in which they stand

East from Greenwich

COPYRIGHT PHILIP'S

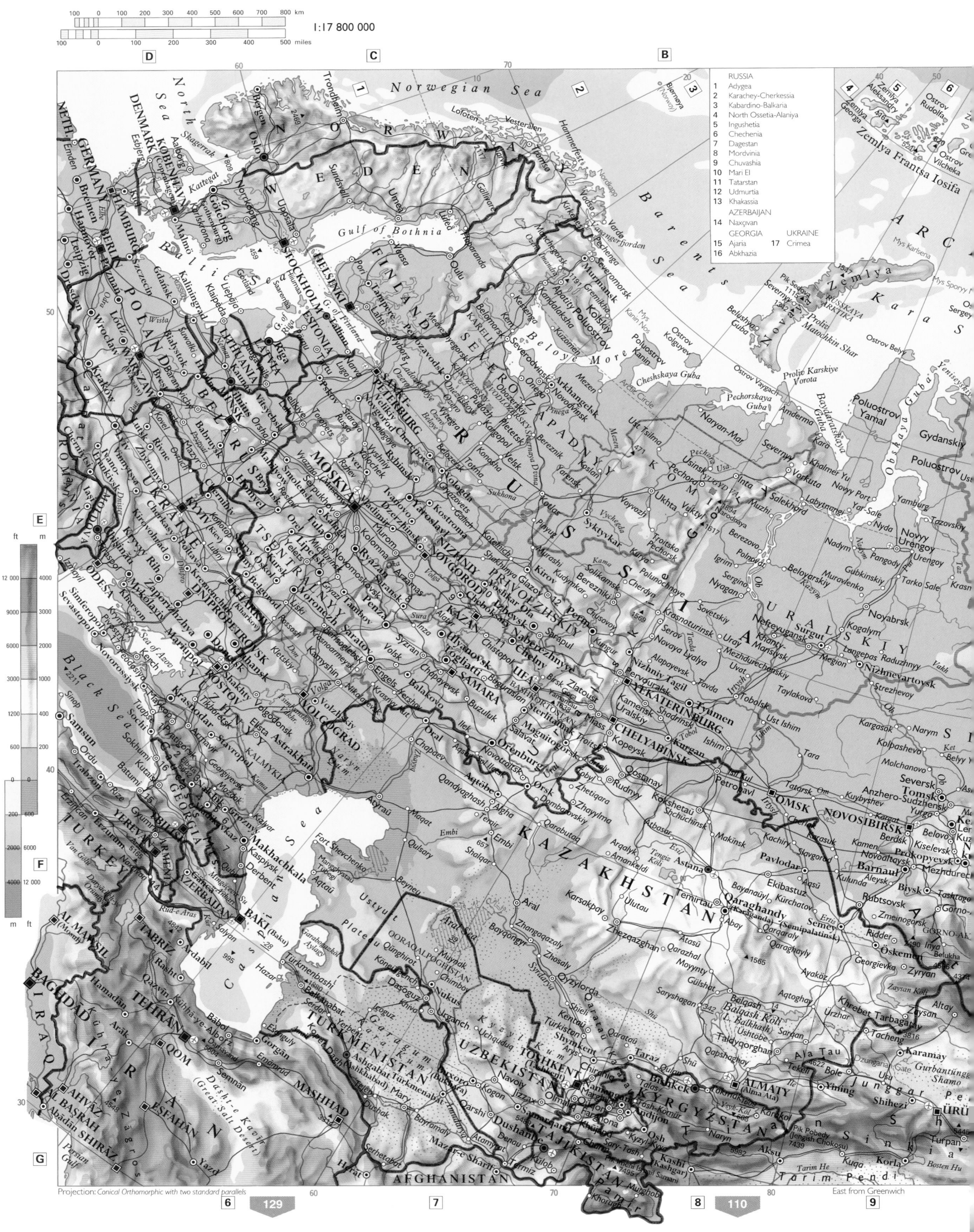

1:17 800 000

	RUSSIA
1	Adygea
2	Karachey-Cherkessia
3	Kabardino-Balkaria
4	North Ossetia-Alaniya
5	Ingushetia
6	Chechenia
7	Dagestan
8	Mordvinia
9	Chuvashia
10	Mari El
11	Tatarstan
12	Udmurtia
13	Khakassia
	AZERBAIJAN
14	Naxçivan
	GEORGIA	UKRAINE
15	Ajaria	17 Crimea
16	Abkhazia

Projection: Conical Orthomorphic with two standard parallels

East from Greenwich

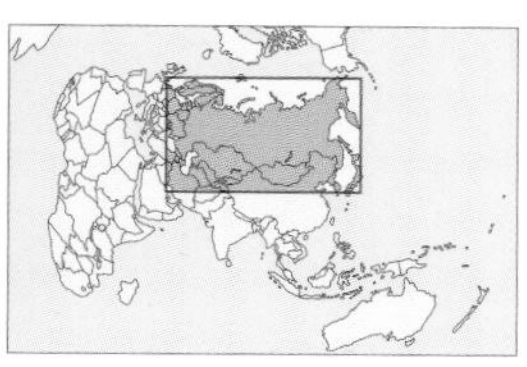

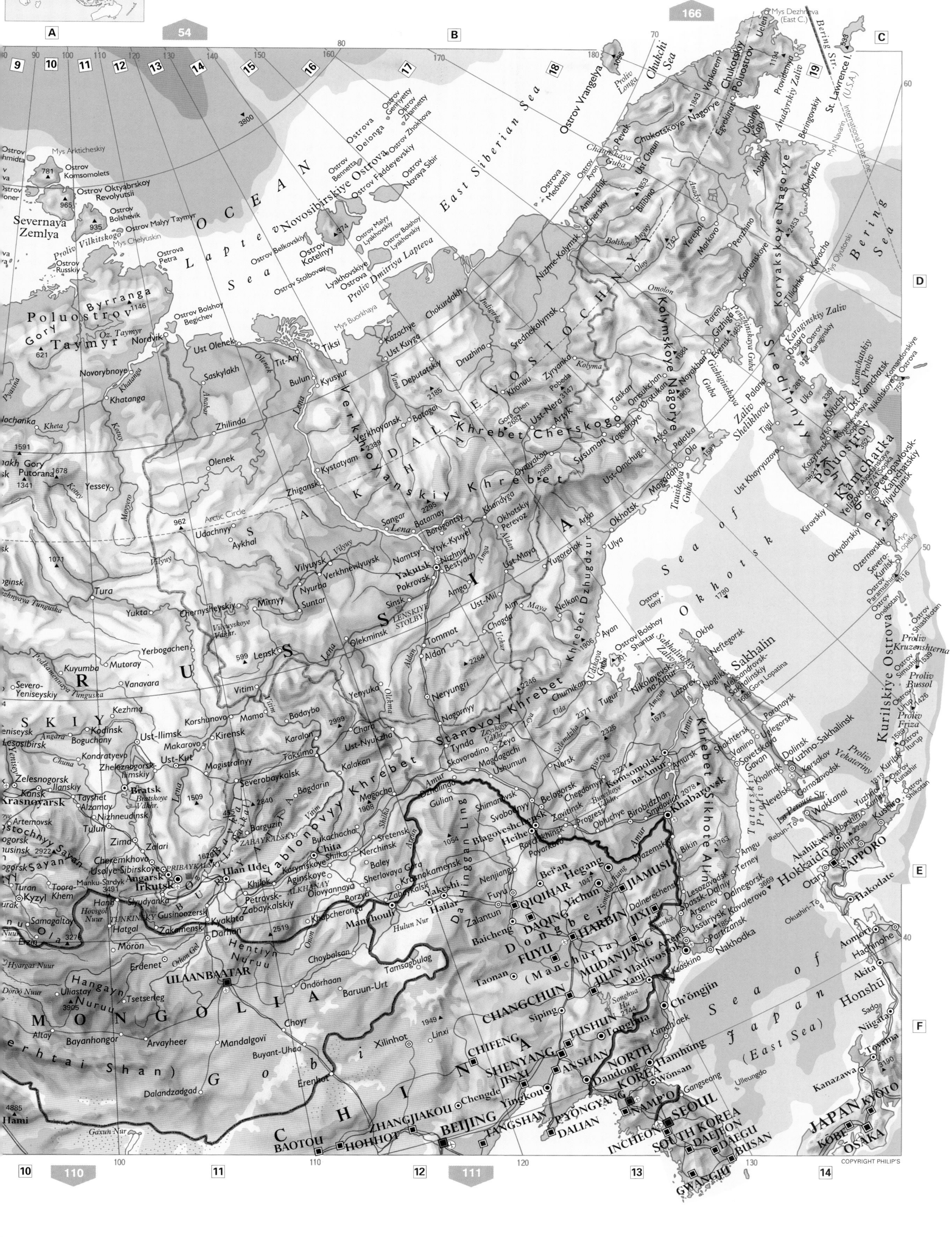

ARCTIC OCEAN

Laptev Sea

East Siberian Sea

Chukchi Sea

Bering Sea

Sea of Okhotsk

Sea of Japan (East Sea)

Severnaya Zemlya

Novosibirskiye Ostrova

Poluostrov Taymyr

Gory Byrranga

Ostrov Vrangelya

Poluostrov Kamchatka

Kurilskiye Ostrova

Sakhalin

Hokkaidō

Honshū

R U S S I A

MONGOLIA

CHINA

NORTH KOREA

SOUTH KOREA

JAPAN

ULAANBAATAR

BEIJING

SEOUL

PYONGYANG

HARBIN

SHENYANG

CHANGCHUN

Vladivostok

Khabarovsk

Komsomolsk-na-Amur

Yakutsk

Irkutsk

Bratsk

Krasnoyarsk

Gobi

Manchuria

COPYRIGHT PHILIP'S

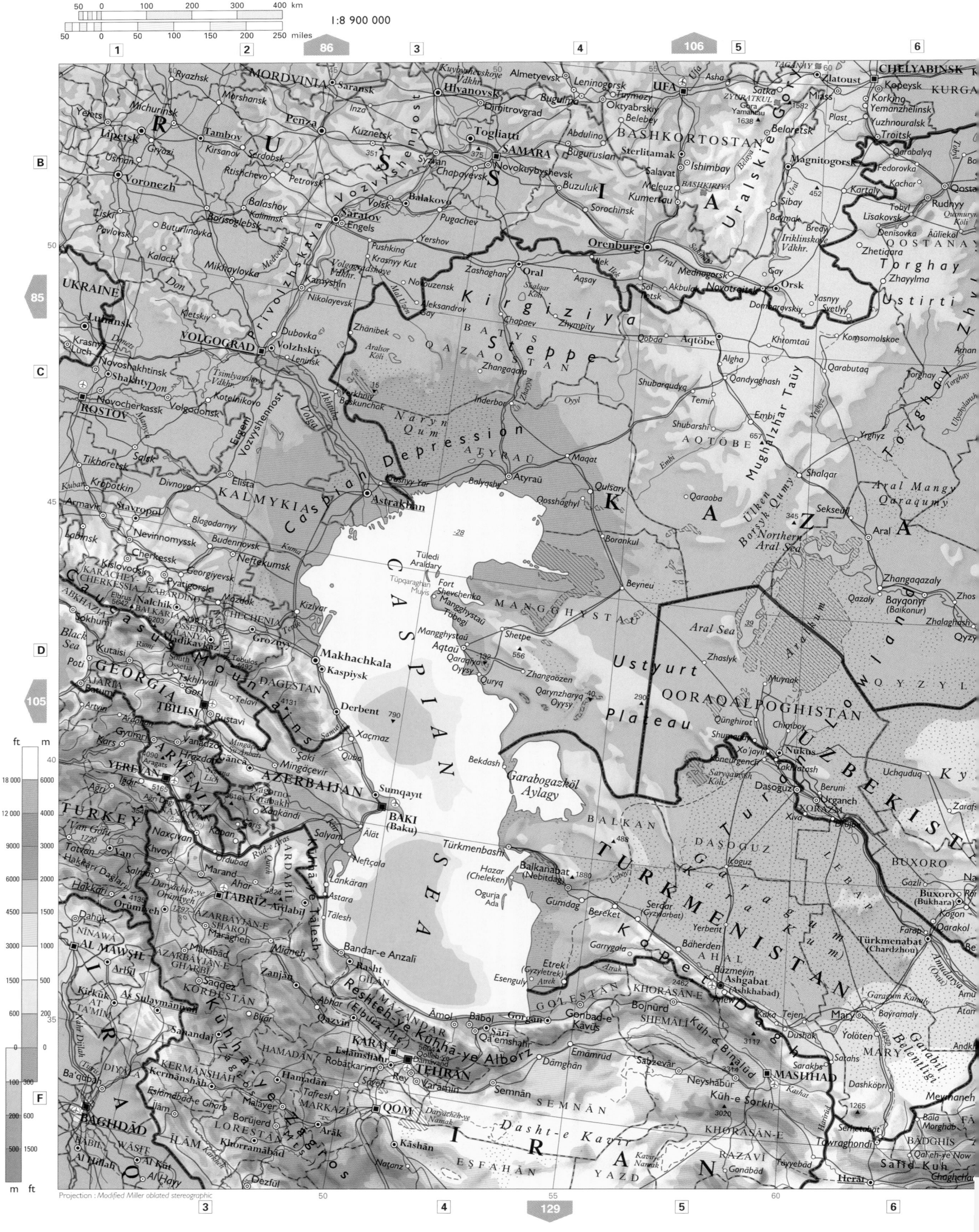

1:8 900 000

Projection : Modified Miller oblated stereographic

Underlined towns give their name to the
administrative area in which they stand.

1:13 300 000

Projection: Bonne

East from Greenwich

RUSSIA

Sakhalin

Khabarovsk

Khrebet Sikhote Alin

HOKKAIDO
SAPPORO

QIQIHAR

HARBIN

JIAMUSI

JILIN
MUDANJIANG

CHANGCHUN

Vladivostok

SEA OF
JAPAN
(EAST SEA)

HONSHU

SENDAI

NORTH
KOREA

P'YONGYANG

TŌKYŌ
KAWASAKI
YOKOHAMA

NAGOYA

BEIJING
(Peking)

TANGSHAN

TIANJIN SHI
TIANJIN

SEOUL
SOUTH
KOREA

INCHEON

KYOTO
ŌSAKA
HAMAMATSU

TAIYUAN

SHIJIAZHUANG

DAEJEON

DAEGU
ULSAN

KŌBE
Sakai

YELLOW

SEA

BUSAN

HIROSHIMA

SHIKOKU

QINGDAO

GWANGJU

KITAKYUSHU

FUKUOKA

KYŪSHŪ

JAPAN

NANJING

SHANGHAI SHI

SHANGHAI

HANGZHOU

NINGBO

EAST CHINA

SEA

PACIFIC

OCEAN

WUHAN

CHANGSHA

TAIZHOU

WENZHOU

Tropic of Cancer

FUZHOU

T'AIPEI
T'AICHUNG

GUANGZHOU
(Canton)

XIAMEN

TAIWAN

KAOHSIUNG

FOSHAN

SHANTOU

SHENZHEN
HONG KONG
(Xianggang)

Macau

SOUTH CHINA

SEA

HAIKOU

HAINAN

PHILIPPINES

HONG KONG, MACAU AND SHENZHEN
1:890 000

GUANGDONG

SHENZHEN

ZHONGSHAN

ZHUHAI

Macau
(Aomen)

Pearl
River
Bridge

Zhujiang Kou
(Mouth of the Pearl)

HONG KONG
(Xianggang)
Hong Kong
Island

Kowloon
(Jiulong)

Victoria

Lantau Island
(Tai Yue Shan)

COPYRIGHT PHILIP'S

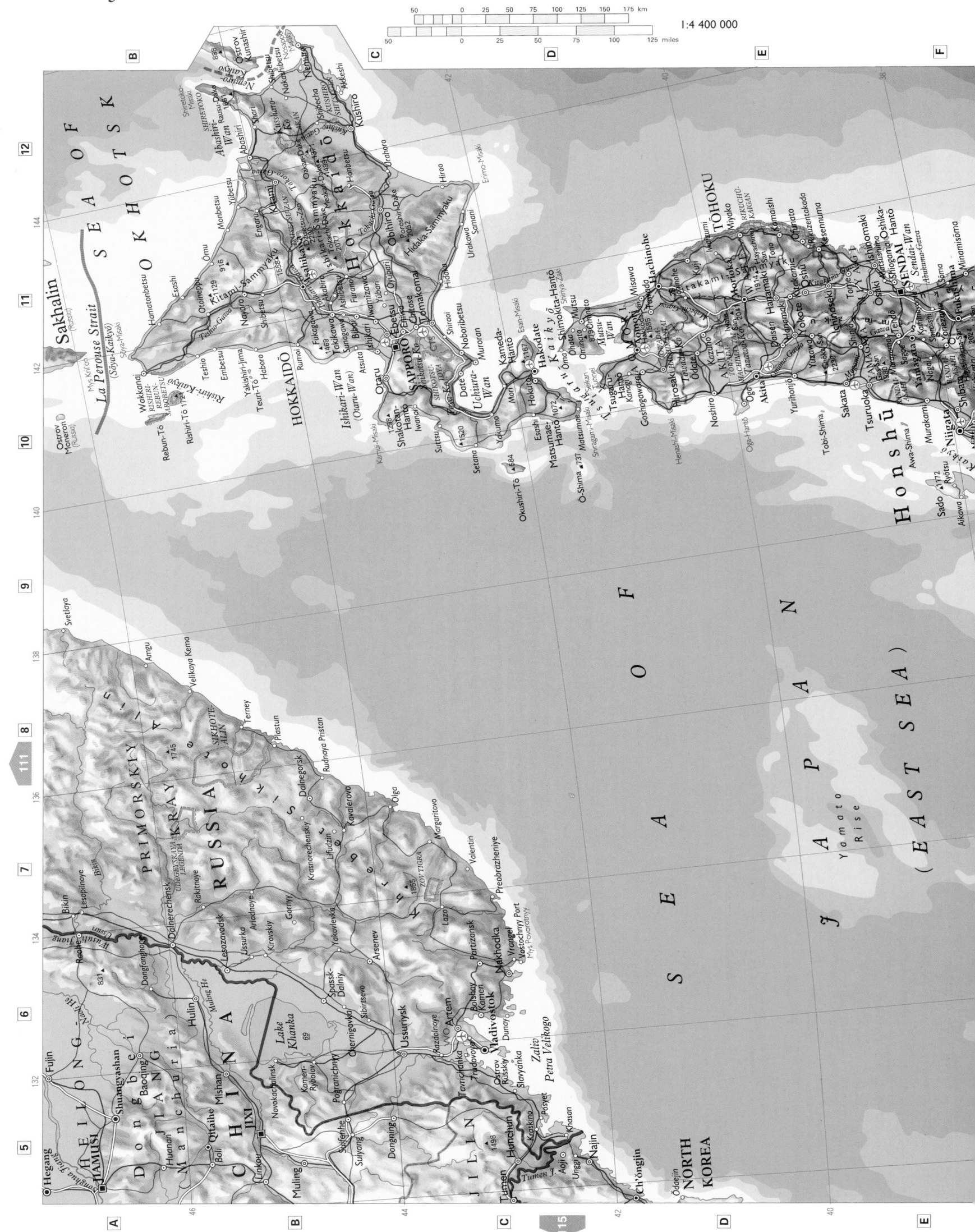

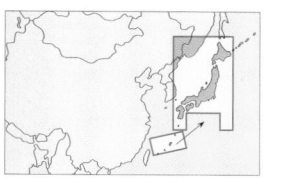

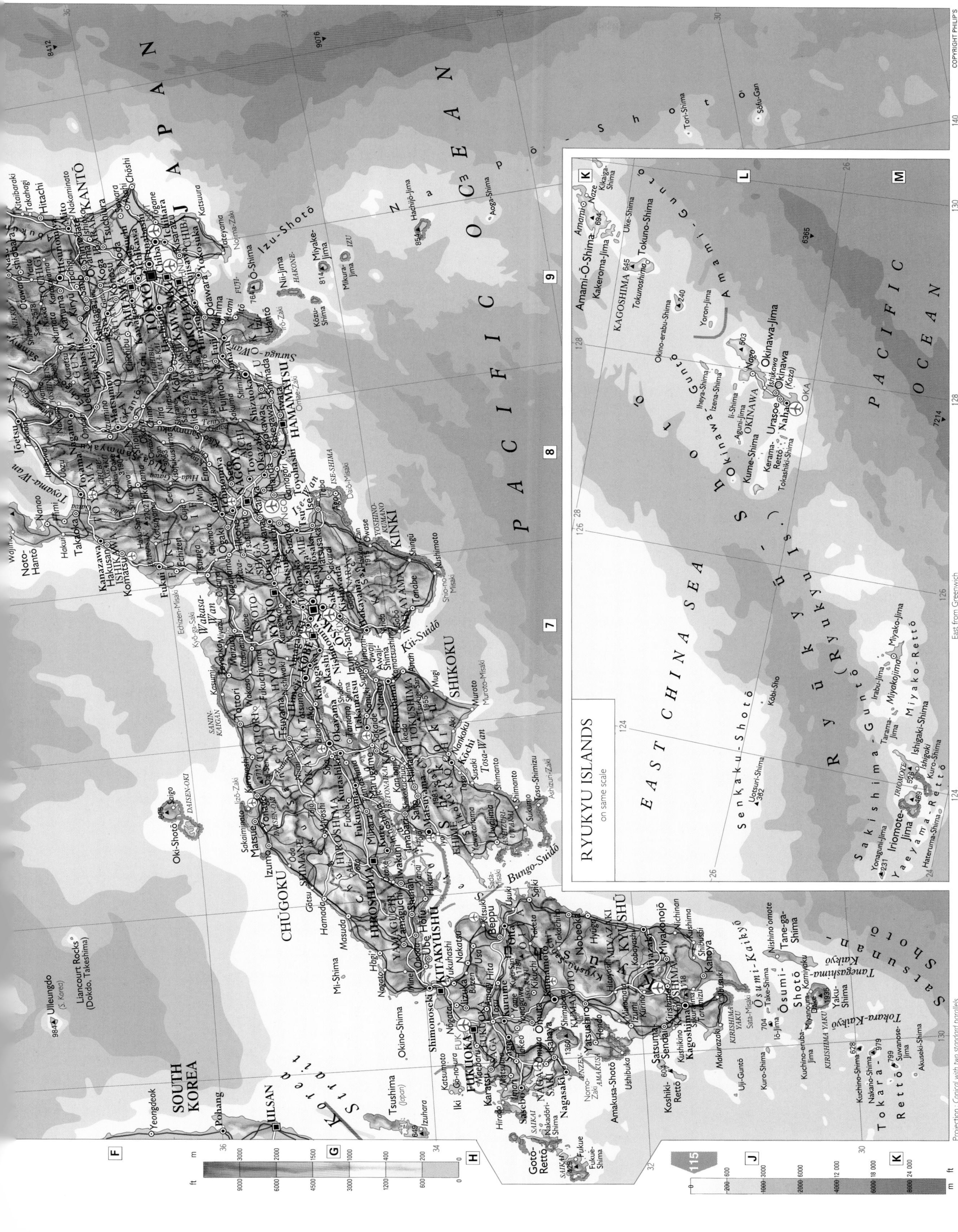

JAPAN

PACIFIC OCEAN

SOUTH KOREA

EAST CHINA SEA

RYUKYU ISLANDS
on same scale

Ryūkyū (Ryukyu)

Amami-Guntō

Okinawa-Guntō

Sakishima-Guntō

Yaeyama-Rettō

Miyako-Rettō

Senkaku-Shotō

PACIFIC OCEAN

KANTŌ

TOKYO

KINKI

CHŪGOKU

SHIKOKU

KYUSHU

East from Greenwich

COPYRIGHT PHILIP'S

Projection: Conical with two standard parallels

ft	m
9000	3000
6000	2000
4500	1500
3000	1000
1200	400
600	200
0	0

m	ft
200–600	
2000	6000
4000	12 000
6000	18 000
8000	24 000

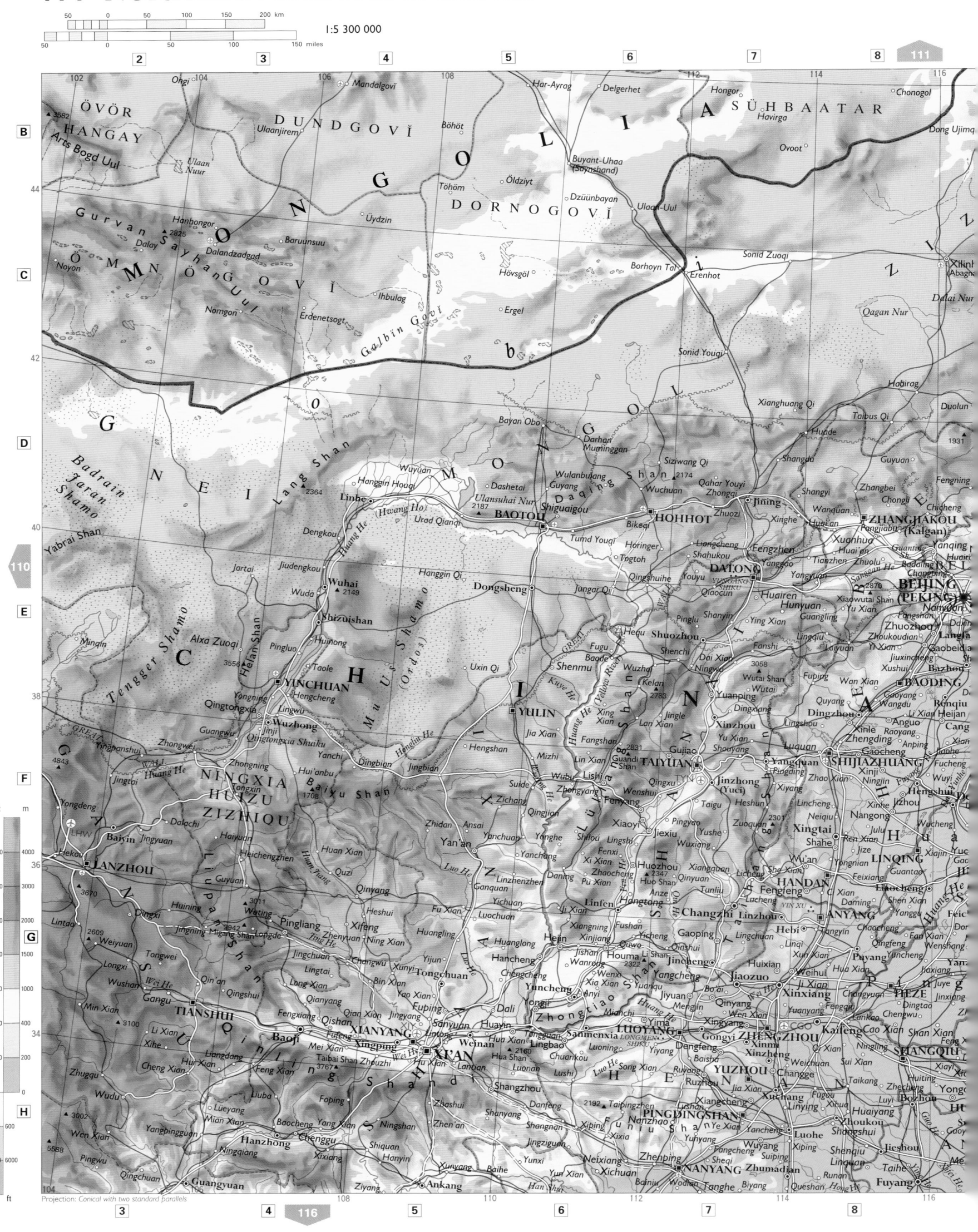

1:5 300 000

Projection: Conical with two standard parallels

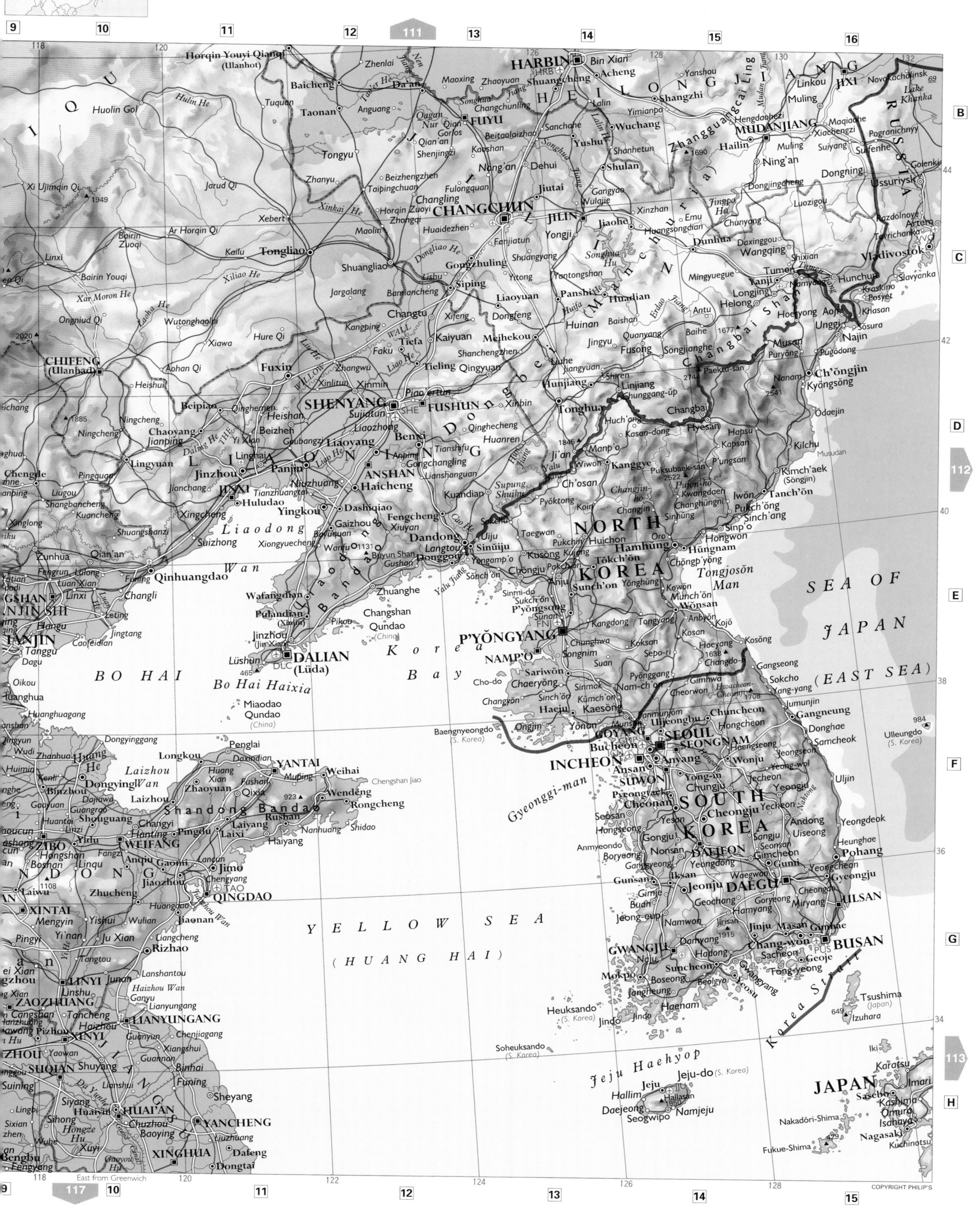

118
B

Horqin Youyi Qianqi
(Ulanhot)
Baicheng
Zhenlai
Maoxing
Zhaoyuan
Da'an
HARBIN
Bin Xian
Yanshou
Linkou
HXI
Novokachalinsk
69
Lake
Khanka

Huolin Gol
Tuquan
Qagan Nur Qian Qi
Songhua
Changchunling
Shuangcheng
Acheng
Shangzhi
Yimianpo
Hengdaohezi
MUDANJIANG
Xiaochengzi
Maqiaohe
Pogranichnyy
RUSSIA
44

Xi Ujimqin Qi
1949
Jarud Qi
Tongyu
Beitaoloizhai
FUYU
Sanchahe
Yushu
Shanhetun
Wuchang
Hailin
Muling
Suiyang
Sufenhe
Golenki
Ussuriysk

Bairin Zuoqi
Zhanyu
Beizhengzhen
Fulongquan
Nong'an
Dehui
1690
Ning'an
Dongjingcheng
Luozigou
Razdolnoye

Ar Horqin Qi
Kailu
Taipingchuan
Horqin Zuoyi
Zhongqi
Changling
CHANGCHUN
Jiutai
JILIN
Jiaohe
Huangsongdian
Emu
Jingpo Ha
Chunyang
Dongning
VLADIVOSTOK
Arte'm

Linxi
Xar Moron He
Liaoha He
Shuangliao
Jargalang
Bamiancheng
Gongzhuling
Yitong
Shuangyang
Panshi
Huadian
Mingyuegue
Antu
Helong
Longjing
Yanji
Tumen
Hunchun
Kraskino
Posyet
Slavyanka

2020
Ongniud Qi
Wutonghaolu
Siping
Liaoyuan
Xifeng
Dongfeng
Huinan
Baishan
Quanyang
Baihe
1677
Musan
Puryong
Pugodong
Najin

CHIFENG
(Ulanhad)
Aohan Qi
Changtu
Kangping
Meihekou
Shanchengzhen
Jingyu
Fusong
Songjianghe
Changbai
2541
Najin

Ningcheng
1885
Heishui
Fuxin
Zhangwu
Faku
Tiefa
Kaiyuan
Qingyuan
Tieling
Hunjiang
Linjiang
Huch'ang
Paektu-san
2744
Hyesan
Kimch'aek

Chengde
1108
Pingquan
Jianping
Chaoyang
Jinxi
SHENYANG
Sujiatun
FUSHUN
Qinghecheng
Huanren
1846
Ji'an
Manp'o
Kasan-dong
Kapsan
P'ungsan
Odaejin

Lingyuan
Jianchang
Lingyuan
Liugou
Beipiao
Qinghemen
Heishan
Beizhen
Liaoyang
Anping
Gongchangling
Tianshifu
Kuandian
Ch'osan
Wiwon
Kwangdaeng
Changjin-ho
Pujon-ho
Sinhung
Musudan

Xinglong
Shangbancheng
Kuancheng
Xingcheng
HXI
Tianzhuangtai
ANSHAN
Haicheng
Niuzhuang
Benxi
Changlangtze
Lianshanguan
Kuandian
Pyoktong
Koin
Changjin
Changhungni
Iwon
Tanch'on
Pukch'ong
Sinch'ang

Zunhua
Qian'an
Huludao
Jinzhou
Panjin
Dashiqiao
Yingkou
Fengcheng
Xiuyan
Cao He
Supung Shuiku
Pukchin
Huichon
Oro
Hamhung
Hongwon
Chongp'yong
40

Fengrun
Fining
Qinhuangdao
Suizhong
Gaizhou
Boyang
1131
Xiongyuecheng
Dandong
Uiju
Sinuiju
Songamp'o
Kusong
Kujang
Tokch'on
Sinp'o
Hamhung

Changli
Wafangdian
Gushan
Buryu Shan
Donggou
Taegwan
Anju
Sunch'on
Yonghung
Wonsan
SEA OF JAPAN

TIANJIN
Leting
Pulandian
(Xinjin)
Changshan
Zhuanghe
Yalu Jiang
Sinmi-do
Sukch'on
P'yongsong
Kangdong
Tongyang
Anbyon
Kojo
E

Tanggu
Dagu
Jinzhou
(Jin Xian)
Pikou
Qundao
(China)
Sunan
Chunghwa
Koksan
Sepo-ri
Changdo-g
Hoeyang
Kosong
Gangseong

Caofeidian
LUshun
DALIAN
(Luda)
465
DLC
Cho-do
P'YONGYANG
NAMP'O
Sariwon
Chaeryong
Pyonggang
Hwachean-
Cheorwon
1708
Sokcho
Yang-yang
38

Miaodao Qundao
(China)
Korea
Bay
Sinch'on
Kumch'on
Nam-ch'on
Gimhwa
Ulleungdo
(S. Korea)
984

BO HAI
Bo Hai Haixia
Changyon
Haeju
Kaesong
Panmunjom
Uijeongbu
Chuncheon
Hongcheon
Jumunjin
Gangneung
F

Huanghua
Dongyinggang
Longkou
Penglai
Baengnyeongdo
(S. Korea)
Ongjin
Yonan
Munsan
GOYANG
SEOUL
SEONGNAM
Hoengseong
Donghae
Samcheok

Huang He
Laizhou
Wan
Daxindian
YANTAI
Weihai
Chengshan Jiao
Gyeonggi-man
INCHEON
Bucheon
Anyang
Wonju
Yeong-wol
Uljin

DongyingWan
Zhaoyuan
Muping
Ansan
SUWON
Yong-in
Yecheon

Binzhou
Dajuang
Huang
Xian
Fushan
Qixia
923
Wendeng
Pyongtaek
Cheonan
Chungju
Yeongju
Yeongdeok
36

ZIBO
Changyi
Hanting
Pingdu
Laiyang
Rushan
Rongcheng
Seosan
Cheongju
Yecheon
SOUTH
KOREA
Heunghae
Pohang

WEIFANG
Gaomi
Jimo
Laixi
Shidao
Hongseong
Gongju
DAEJEON
Sangju
Seonsan
Uiseong
Andong

Linqu
Anqiu
Jiaozhou
Chengyang
TAO
QINGDAO
Haiyang
Nanhuang
Anmyeondo
Boryeong
Nonsan
Yeongdong
Gimcheon
Gumi
Yeongcheon
Gyeongju

XINTAI
Mengyin
Yishui
Wulian
Jiaonan Wan
Boryeong
Gangyeong
Iksan
Jeonju
Waegwan
DAEGU
Miryang
ULSAN
G

Pingyi
Yi'nan
Ju Xian
Huangdao
Gunsan
Gimje
Geochang
Goryeong
Gyeongsan
Changnyeong

ZAOZHUANG
Cangshan
Tancheng
Rizhao
Tongtou
YELLOW SEA
(HUANG HAI)
Jeong-eup
Namwon
Hamyang
Jinju
Masan
Gimhae
BUSAN
Chang-won
PUS

LINYI
Junan
Lanshantou
Haizhou Wan
Gwangju
Naju
Hadong
Sacheon
Tong-yeong
Geoje
Korea Strait

XINYI
Guanyun
Chenjiagang
LIANYUNGANG
Haizhou
Pizhou
Xiangshui
Heuksando
(S. Korea)
Jindo
Mokpo
Suncheon
Boseong
Beolgyo
Gwangyang
Yeosu
649
Tsushima
(Japan)
Izuhara
34

SUQIAN
Shuyang
Binhai
Guannan
Soheuksando
(S. Korea)
113

Siyang
Lianshui
Funing
Sheyang
Jeju Haehyop
JAPAN
Iki
Karatsu
Imari

Huai'an
HUAI'AN
Chuzhou
Baoying
Jiuzhuang
YANCHENG
Baoying
Hallim
Jeju
Jeju-do
(S. Korea)
Hallasan
Namjeju
Daejeong
Seogwipo
Nakadori-Shima
Omuro
Isahaya
Sasebo
Kashima
NAGASAKI
Kuchinotsu

XINGHUA
Hongze Hu
Dafeng
Dongtai
Fukue-Shima
429
Fengyang

East from Greenwich

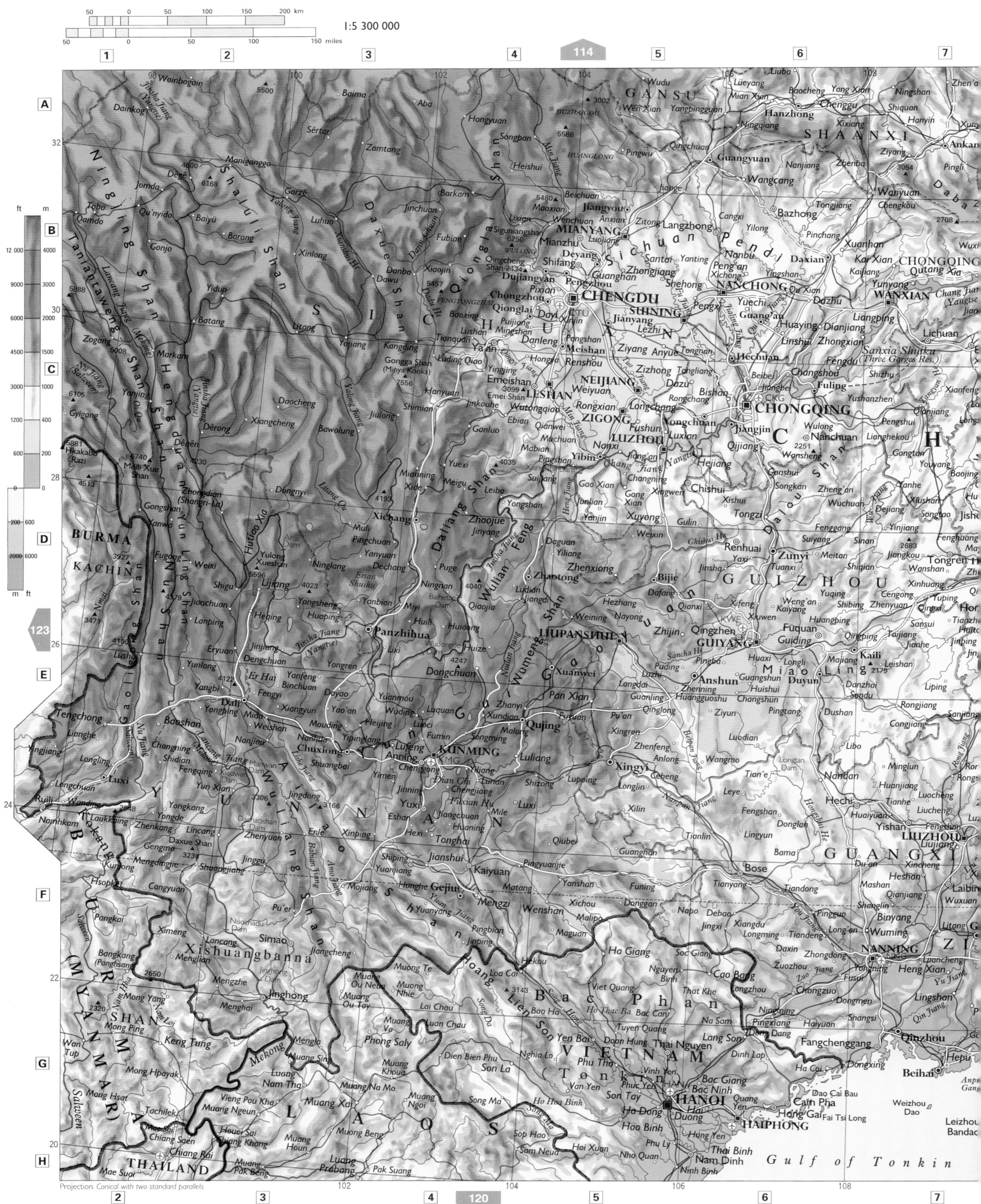

1:5 300 000

Projection: Conical with two standard parallels

1:11 100 000

Projection: Mercator

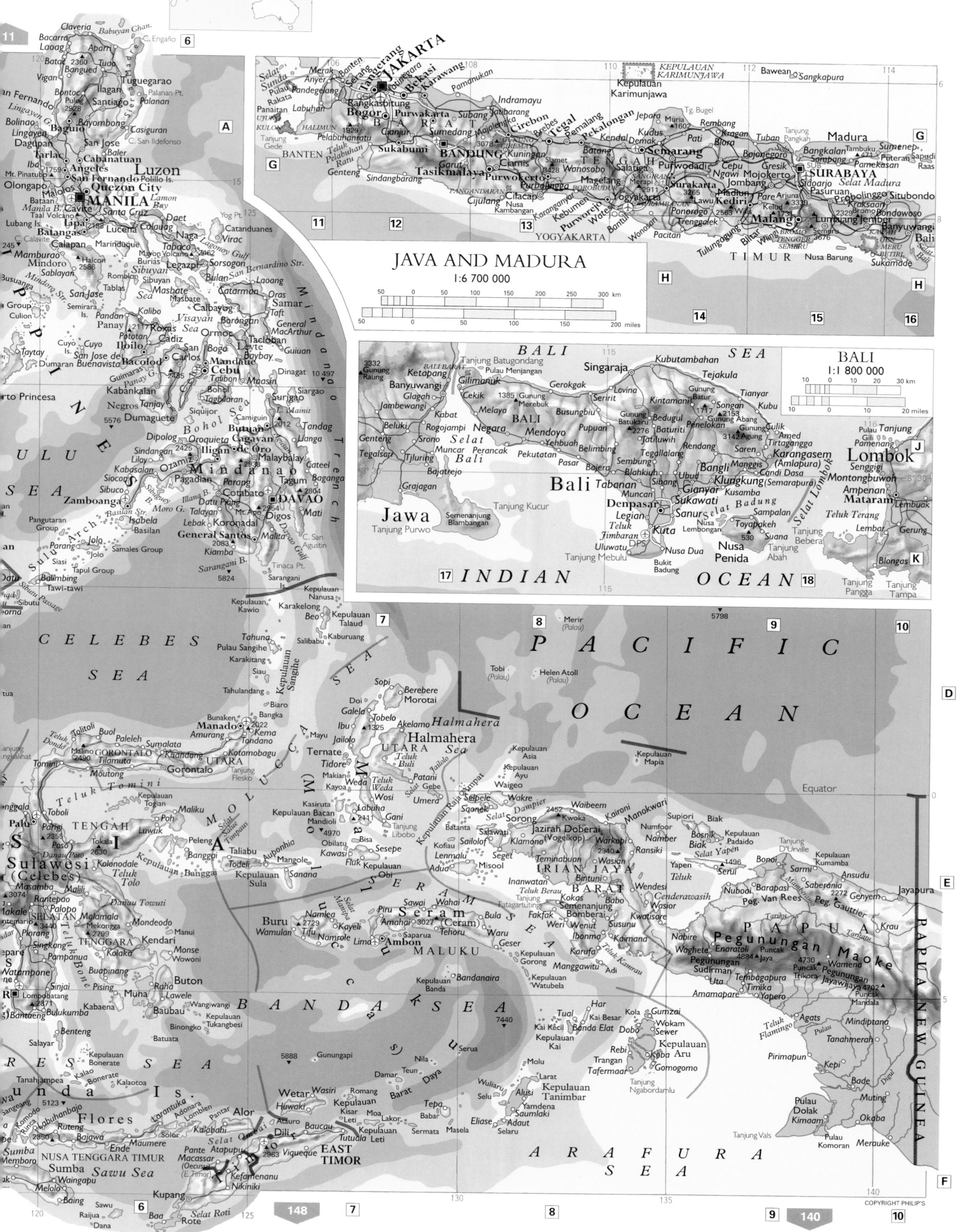

JAVA AND MADURA
1:6 700 000

BALI
1:1 800 000

1:5 300 000

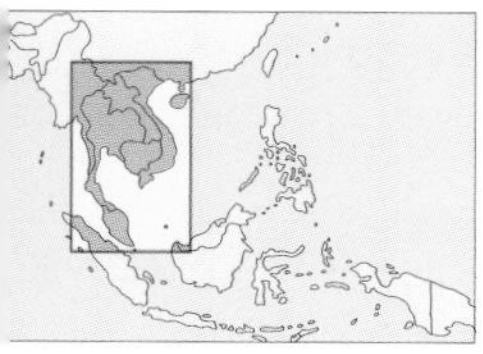

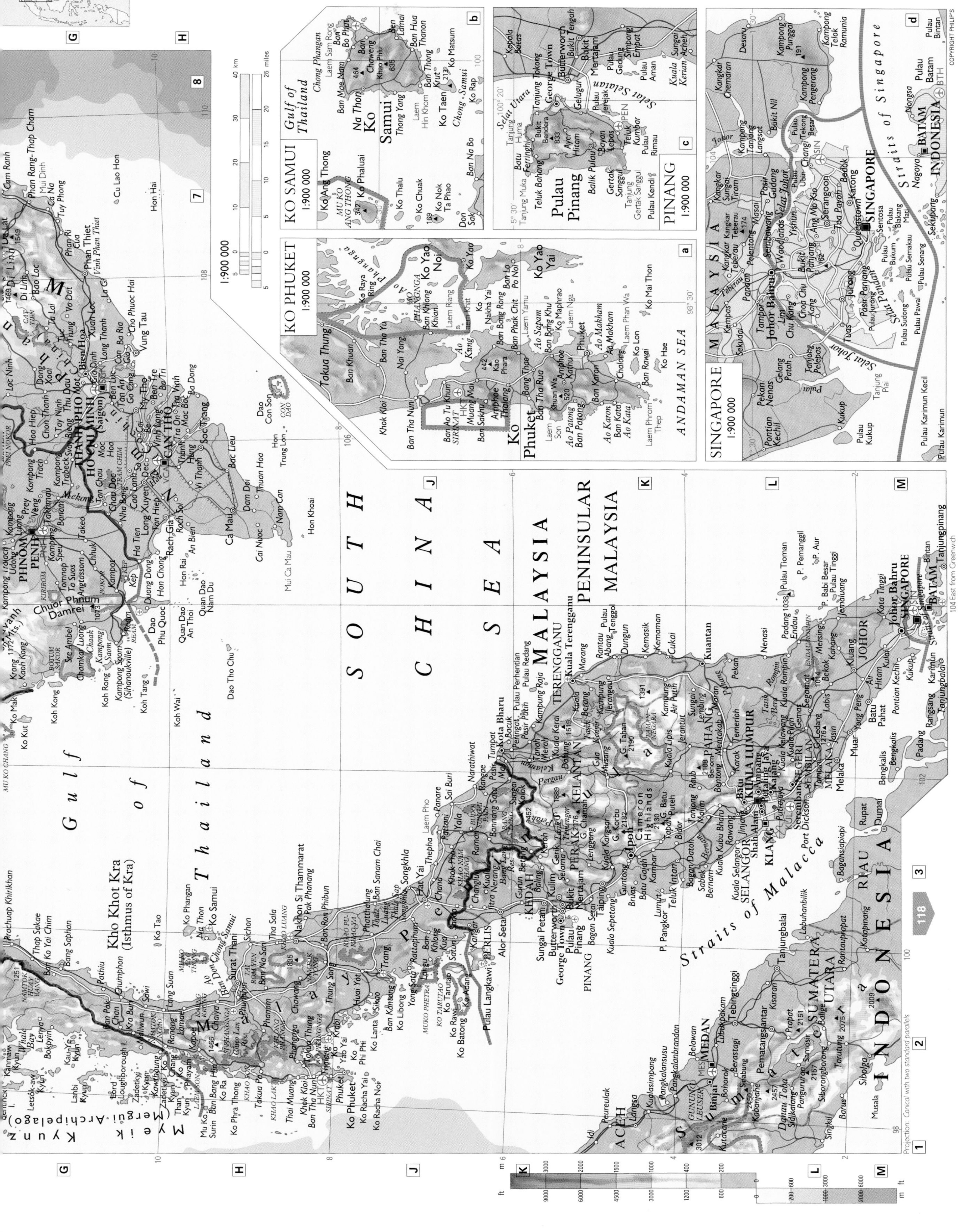

Inset Maps

KO SAMUI 1:900 000

PINANG (Pulau Pinang) 1:900 000

KO PHUKET 1:900 000

SINGAPORE 1:900 000

Major Labels

Gulf of Thailand

SOUTH CHINA SEA

ANDAMAN SEA

Gulf of Thailand

PENINSULAR MALAYSIA

MALAYSIA

Straits of Malacca

Straits of Singapore

Kho Khot Kra (Isthmus of Kra)

Myeik Archipelago (Mergui Archipelago)

Ko Samui

Pulau Pinang

Ko Phuket

SINGAPORE

INDONESIA

SUMATERA UTARA

ACEH

RIAU

BATAM

KUALA LUMPUR

JOHOR

Johor Bahru

George Town

Butterworth

HO CHI MINH (Saigon)

PHNOM PENH

Mekong

Projection: Conical with two standard parallels

104 East from Greenwich

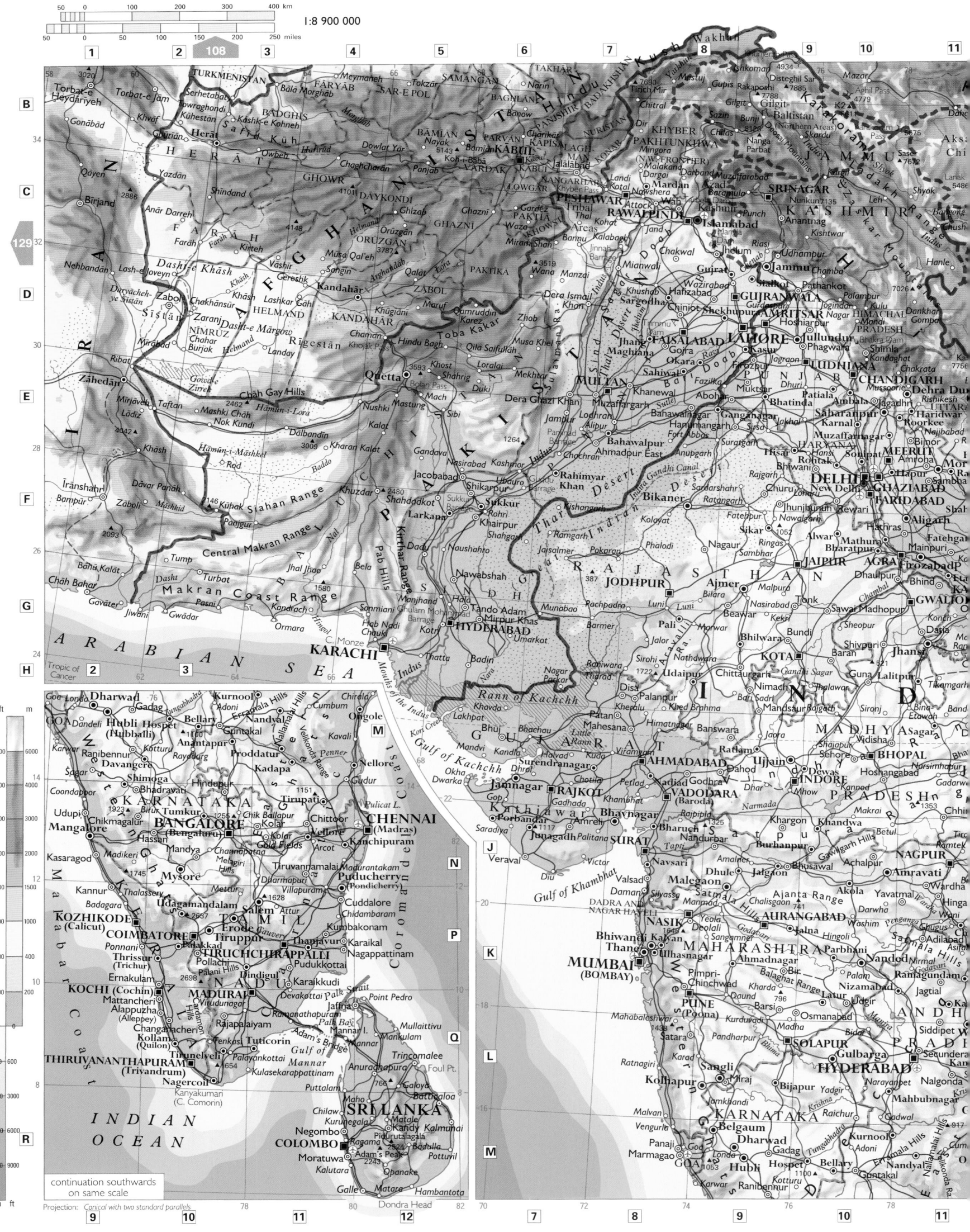

1:8 900 000

50 0 100 200 300 400 km

50 0 50 100 150 200 250 miles

continuation southwards on same scale

Projection: *Conical with two standard parallels*

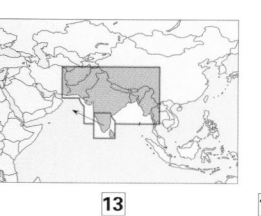

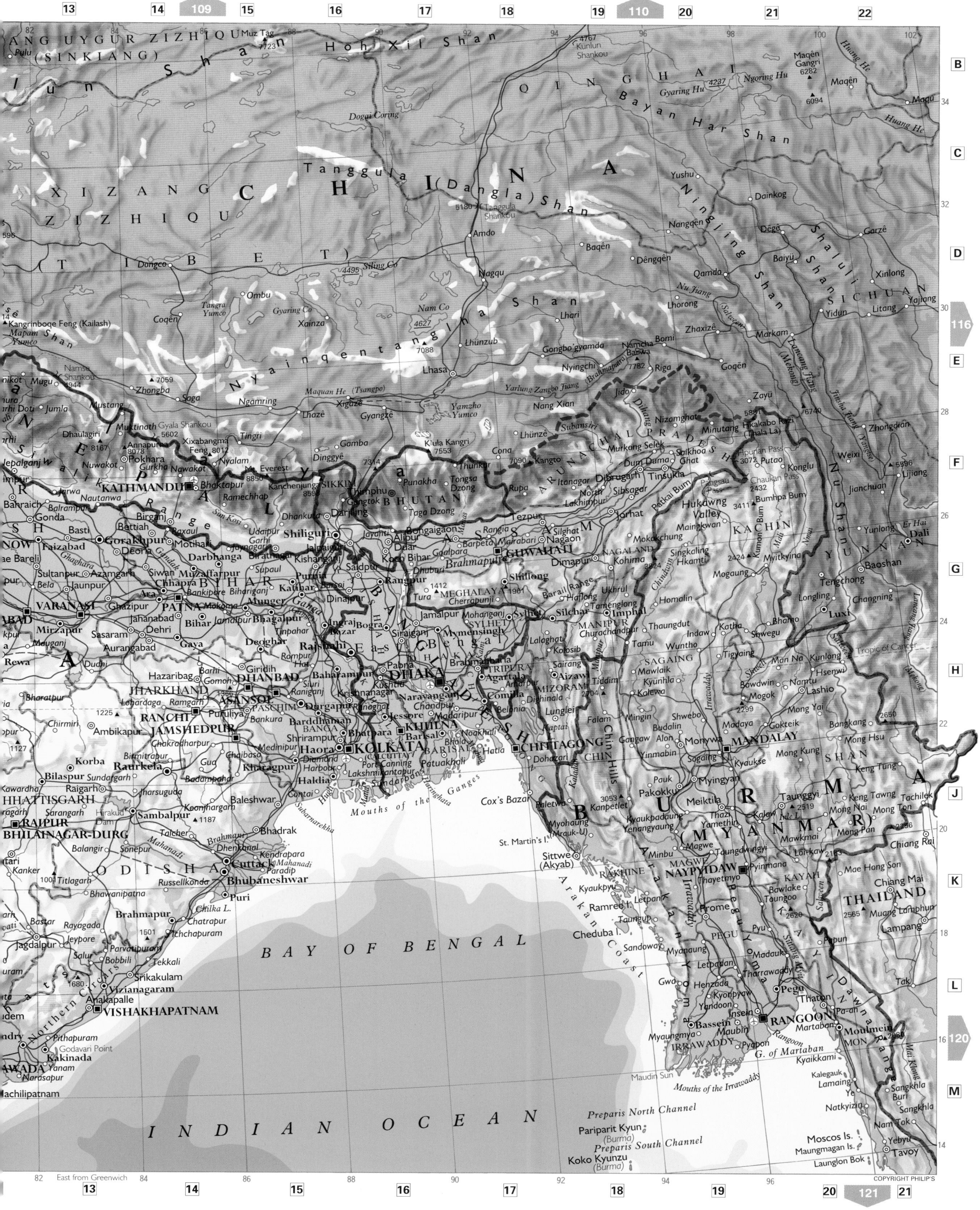

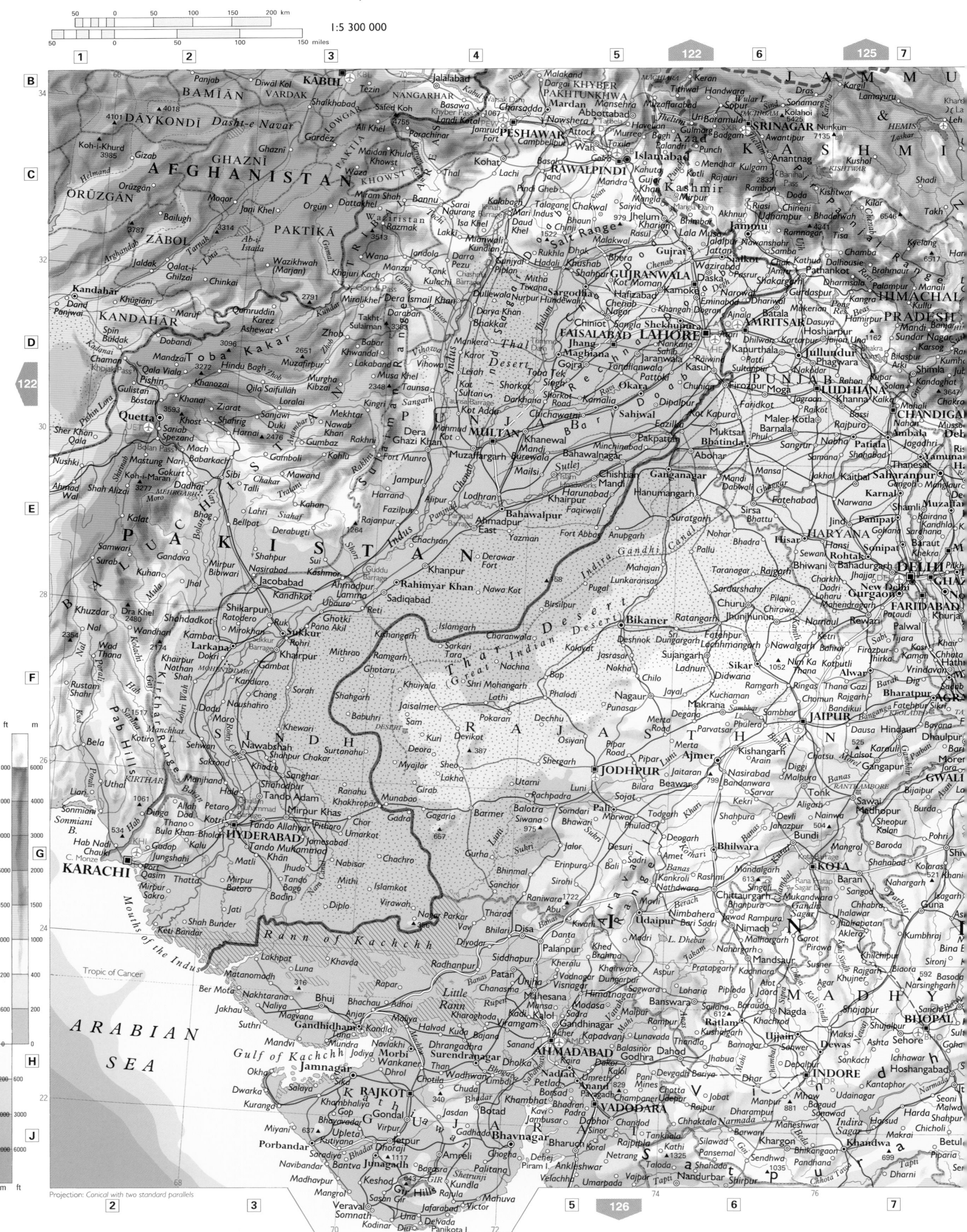

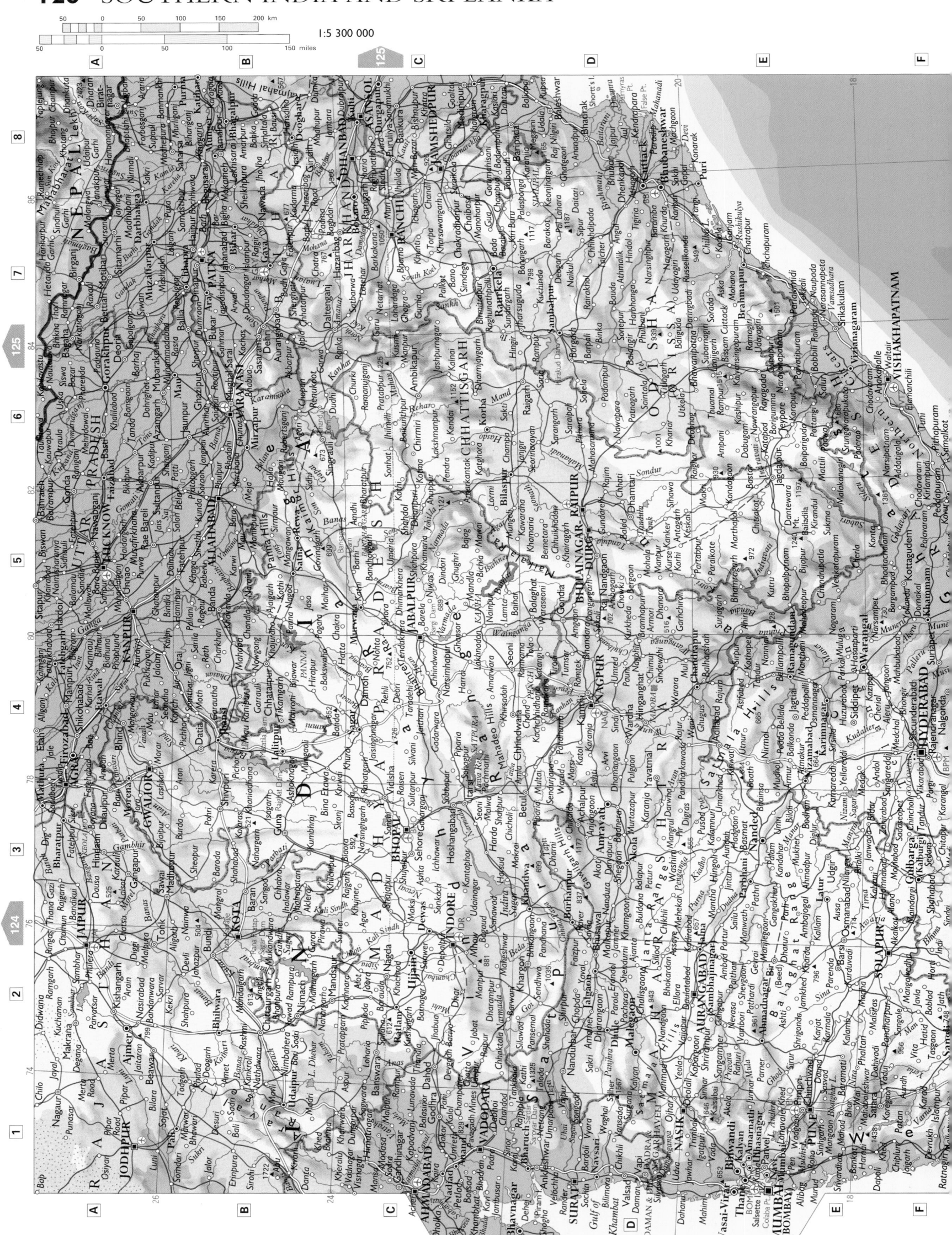

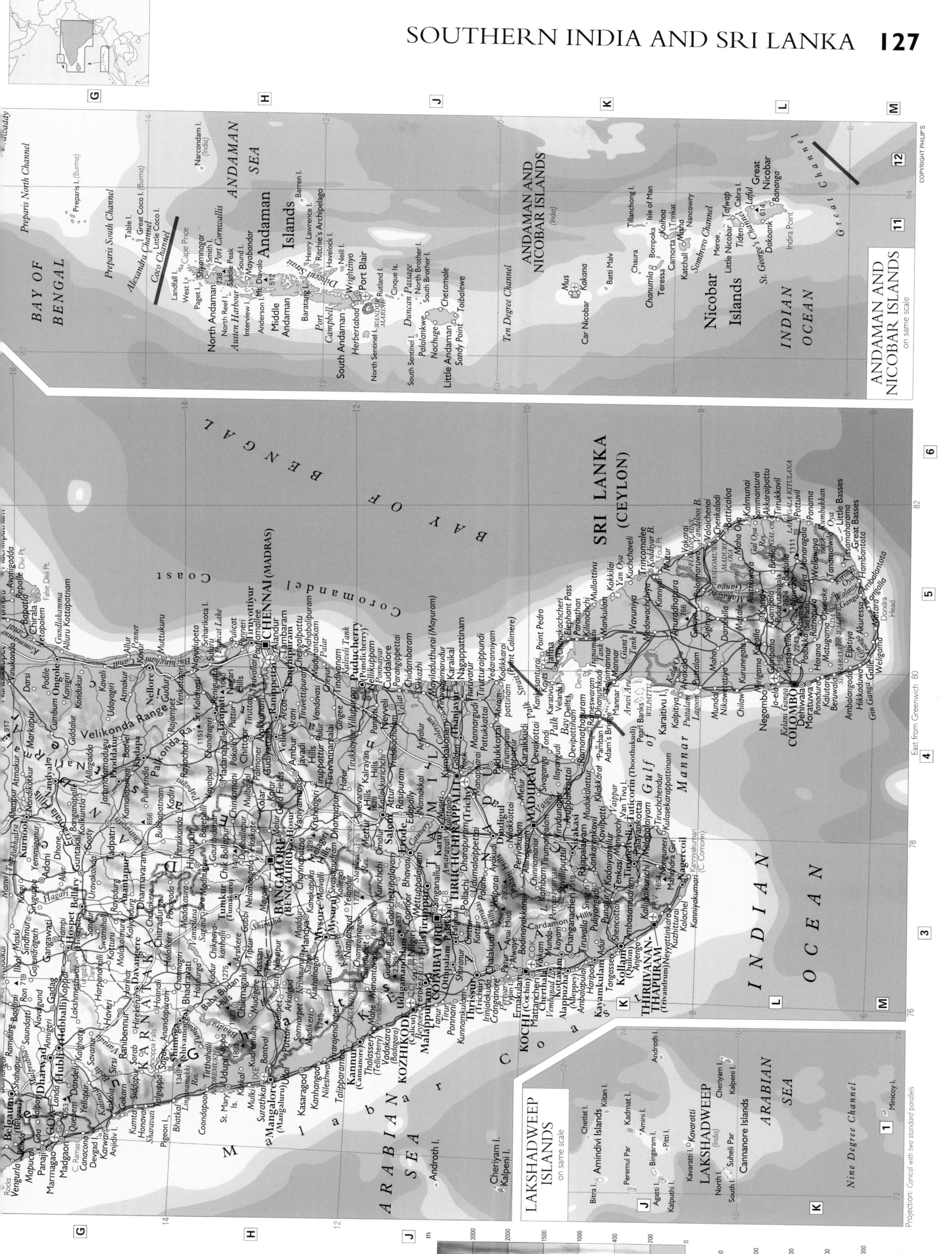

ANDAMAN AND NICOBAR ISLANDS
(India)

ANDAMAN AND
NICOBAR ISLANDS
on same scale

LAKSHADWEEP
ISLANDS
on same scale

LAKSHADWEEP
(India)

Projection: Conical with two standard parallels

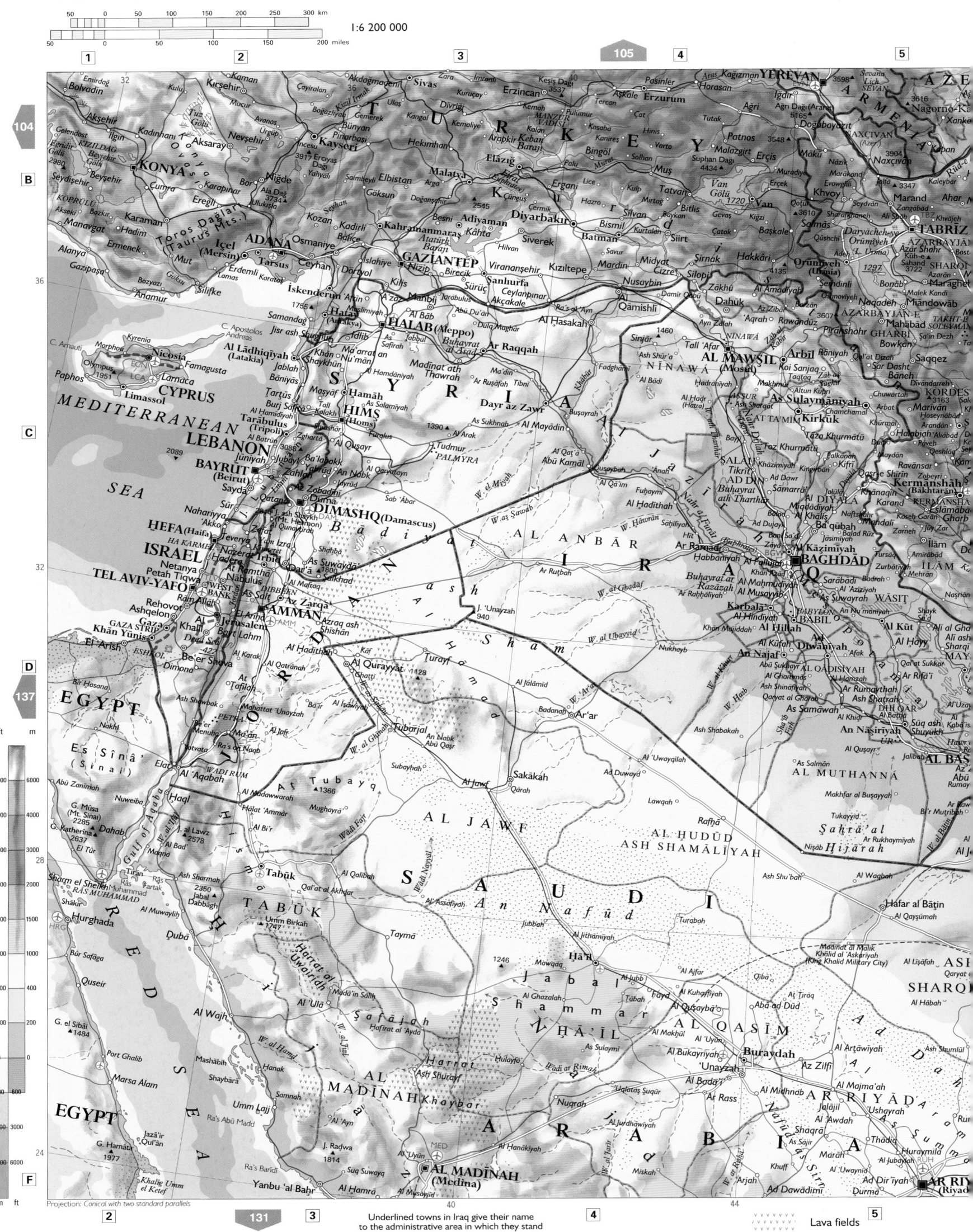

1:6 200 000

Underlined towns in Iraq give their name
to the administrative area in which they stand

Lava fields

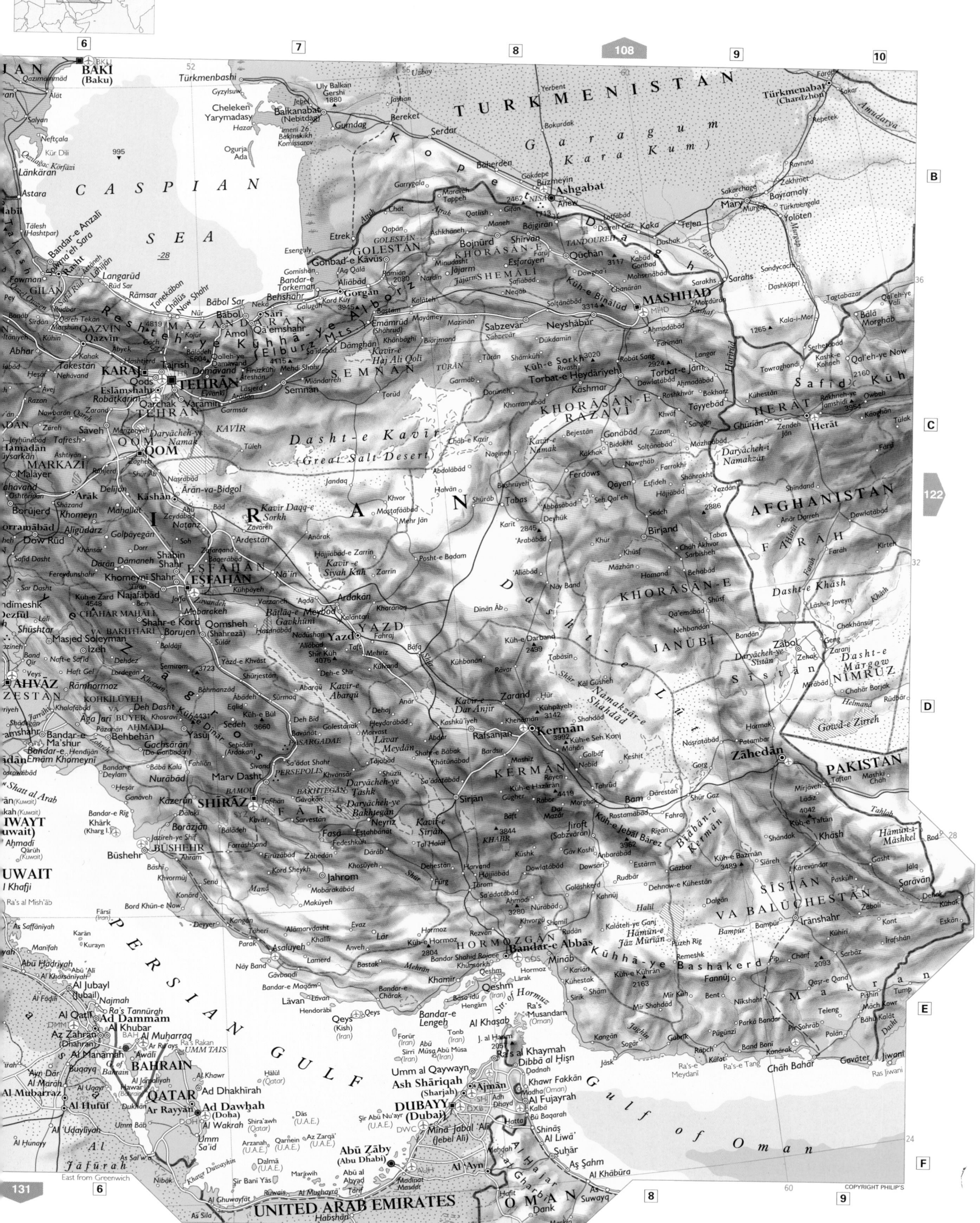

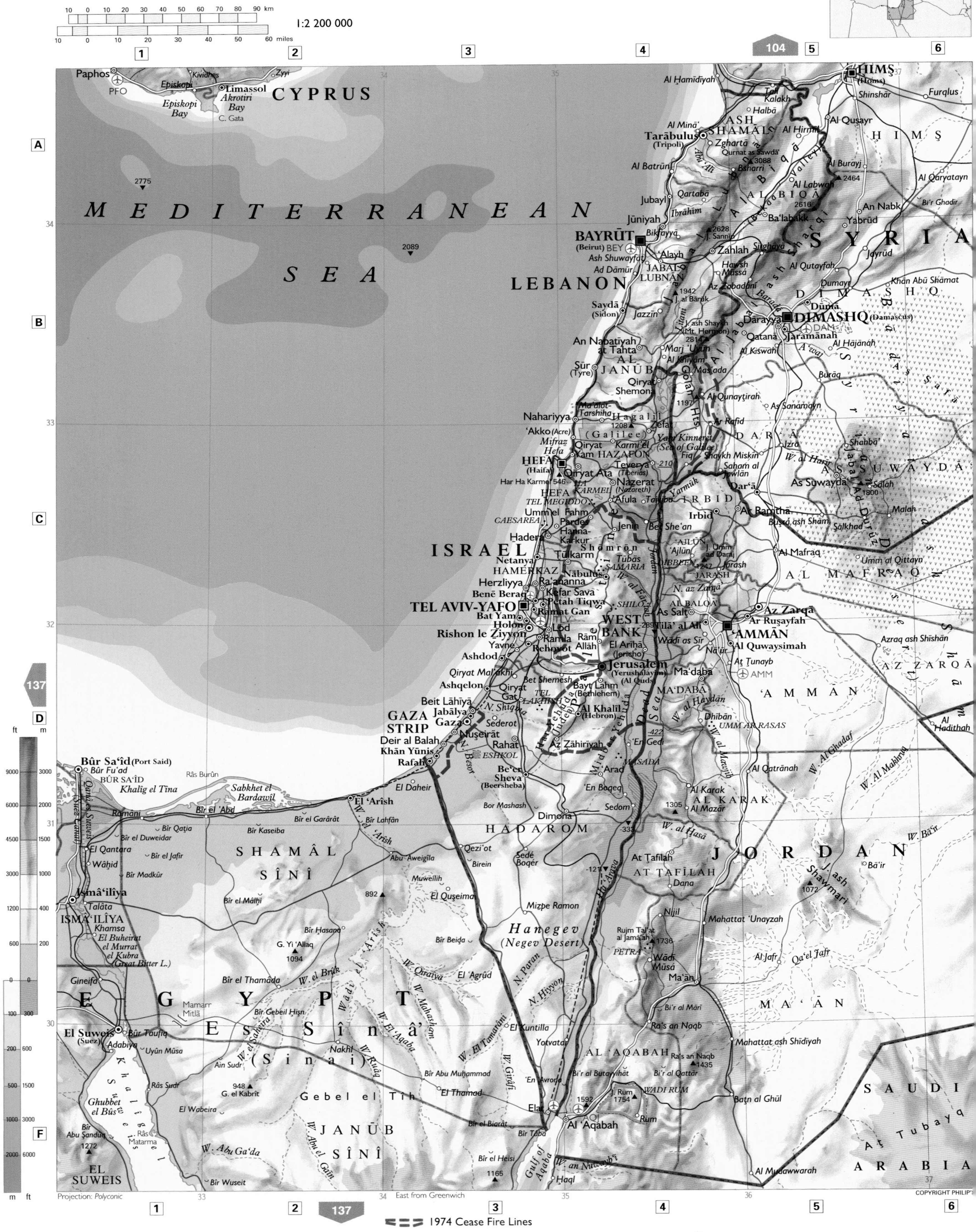

1:2 200 000

10 0 10 20 30 40 50 60 70 80 90 km
10 0 10 20 30 40 50 60 miles

MEDITERRANEAN SEA

CYPRUS
Paphos • PFO • Episkopi • Kividhes • Zyyi
Limassol • Akrotiri Bay • Episkopi Bay • C. Gata

2775 ▽
2089 ▽

LEBANON
Al Ḥamīdīyah • Al Mīnā • Ṭarābulus (Tripoli) • Al Baṭrūn • Jubayl • Ibrāhīm • Jūniyah
BAYRŪT (Beirut) BEY • Ash Shuwayfāt • Ad Dāmūr • Saydā (Sidon) • Jazzīn
An Nabaṭīyah at Taḥta • Ṣūr (Tyre) • Qiryat Shemona

SYRIA
Al Hirmil • Zgharta • Qurnat as Sawdā 3088 • Bsharri • Al Labwah • Al Qusayr
2616 • Baʿlabakk • Yabrūd • An Nabk • Bir Ghadir • Al Qaryatayn • 2464 • Al Burayj
2628 • Sannīn • Biktayyā • ʿAlayh • Zahlah • Silghāyā • Dumayr • Khān Abū Shāmat
DIMASHQ (Damascus) • Darayyā • Qatana • Jaramānah • Al Ḥājānah • Al Kiswah
Marj ʿUyūn • Az Zabadānī • Al Qutayfah • **DIMASHQ**
Burāq • As Sanamayn • 1197 • Al Qunayṭirah • Izraʿ • Ar Rafid • Shaykh Miskīn
Darʿā • As Suwaydā • Shahbā • 1800 • Malaḥ • Buṣrā ash Shām • Ṣalkhad

ISRAEL
Nahariyya • Maʿalot-Tarshiha • 1208 • Hagalil (Galilee) • ʿAkko (Acre) • Mifraz Hefa
Qiryat Yam • Karmiʾel • HAZAFON • Yam Kinneret (Sea of Galilee) • Tevorya (Tiberias) • Fiq
HEFA (Haifa) • Qiryat Ata • Har Ha Karmel 546 • Nazerat (Nazoreth) • HA KARMEL
HEFA • TEL MEGIDDO • Afula • Taiyba • Nazerat
Umm el Fahm • CAESAREA • Hanna-Karkur • Pardes • Jenin • Bet Sheʾan
Hadera • Shomrôn • Ṭūbās • SAMARIA • ʿAjlūn • Umm ad Daraj • Jarash
Netanya • Ṭūlkarm • Nabulus • IBBĪN • JARASH
HAMERKAZ • Raʾanana • Kefar Sava • N. az Zurqā • Al Balqāʾ
Herzliyya • Benē Beraq • Petah Tiqwa • SHILON • As Salṭ • Wādi as Sīr
TEL AVIV-YAFO • Ramat Gan • 2814 • ʿIlāʾ ʿAlī
Bat Yam • Holon • Lod • Rām Allāh • El Arīḥā (Jericho) • Naʿūr
Rishon le Ziyyon • Ramla • **WEST BANK** • Maʿdaba
Yavne • Rehovot • Bet Shemesh • **Jerusalem** (Yerushalayim) (Al Quds)
Ashdod • Qiryat Malakhi • Bayt Laḥm (Bethlehem) • MAʿDABA • Dhiban
Qiryat Gat • TEL LAKHISH • Al Khalīl (Hebron) • UMM AR RASAS
Ashqelon • Beit Lāhiyā • Jabālya • N. Shiqa • ʿEn Gedi • Dhiban
GAZA STRIP • Gaza • Sederot • Az Zāhirīyah • 422 • Dead Sea
Nuṣeirāt • Rahat • ESHKOL • Arad • MASADA
Deir al Balah • Khān Yūnis • Beʾer Sheva (Beersheba) • Sedom
Rafah • Be'er Sheva • Dimona • HADAROM • En Boqeq

EGYPT
Bûr Saʿîd (Port Said) • Bûr Fuʾad • BÛR SAʿÎD • Râs Burûn • Sabkhet el Bardawîl
El ʿArîsh • Ed Daheir • El Daheir • W. el ʿArîsh
Români • Bîr el ʿAbd • Bîr el Garârât • Bîr Lahfân • Abu Aweigila • Qezîʿot • Birein
El Qantara • Bîr Qaṭia • Bîr el Duweidar • Bîr el Jafir • El Quseima • Sedé Boqér
Ismâʿilîya • Wâḥid • Bîr Madkûr • 892 • Muweilih • Mizpe Ramon
ISMÂʿILÎYA • Ṭalâta • Khamsa • Bîr Hasana • 121
El Buheirat el Murrat el Kubra (Great Bitter L.) • Bîr Beiḍa • Hanegev (Negev Desert)
Gineifa • G. Yi ʿAllaq 1094 • Bîr el Thamâda • W. el Brûk • El ʿAgrûd • N. Paran
SHAMÂL SÎNÎ

El Suweis (Suez) • Bûr Taufiq • Adabiya • Uyûn Mûsa • Ain Sudr • Nakhl
ES SÎNÂʾ (Sinai) • 948 G. el Kabrît • El Thamad • W. el Aqaba
Mamarr Miṭla • El Thamâd • Yotvata • AL AQABAH
Râs Sudr • Ghubbet el Bûs • Ras Matarma • W. Abu Muhammad • Bîr al Butayliḥat
1272 • **JANÛB SÎNÎ** • W. Abu Gaʿda • W. Abuʾl Gûn • Bîr el Heisi • 1165

EL SUWEIS • Bîr Abu Sandûq • Bîr Wuseit • Al Muḍawwarah

JORDAN
Al Mafraq • AL MAFRAQ • Umm al Qittayn • Umm ar Ruṣayfah
AMMAN • Az Zarqā • Ar Ruṣayfah • Azraq ash Shīshān
Al Quwaysimah • AMM • ʿAMMAN • AZ ZARQĀ
At Tunayb • Maʿdaba • W. al Ḥaydān • Al Hadithah
MAʿDĀB • 1305 • Al Qaṭrānah • Al Qaṭrānah
Al Karak • ALKARAK • Al Mazār • W. Al Mūjib
At Ṭafīlah • Dana • AT TAFĪLAH • W. al Ḥasā • W. Baʿir • Bâʿir
JORDAN • Njil • Mahaṭṭat ʿUnayzah • MAʿĀN
Rujm Talʿat al Jamāʿīn 1738 • PETRA • Wādi Mūsa • Al Jafr • Qaʿel Jafr
1072 J. ash Shawmari • Maʿân • Baṭn al Ghûl • Mahaṭṭat ash Shīdiyah
Raʾs an Naqb • 1435 • Raʾs an Naqb • Elat • 1592 • 1754 Rum • WADI RUM • Rum
Al ʿAqabah • Al Aqaba • At Ṭubayq

SAUDI ARABIA
Ḥaql • At Ṭubayq

HIMS
ḤIMṢ (Homs) • Al Hamīdīyah • Tall • Kalakh • Shinshār • Furqlus • HIMṢ • Bir Ghadir

IRBID
Irbid • Ar Ramtha • Ajlūn • Jarash

COPYRIGHT PHILIP'S

Projection: Polyconic

East from Greenwich

◄═══ 1974 Cease Fire Lines

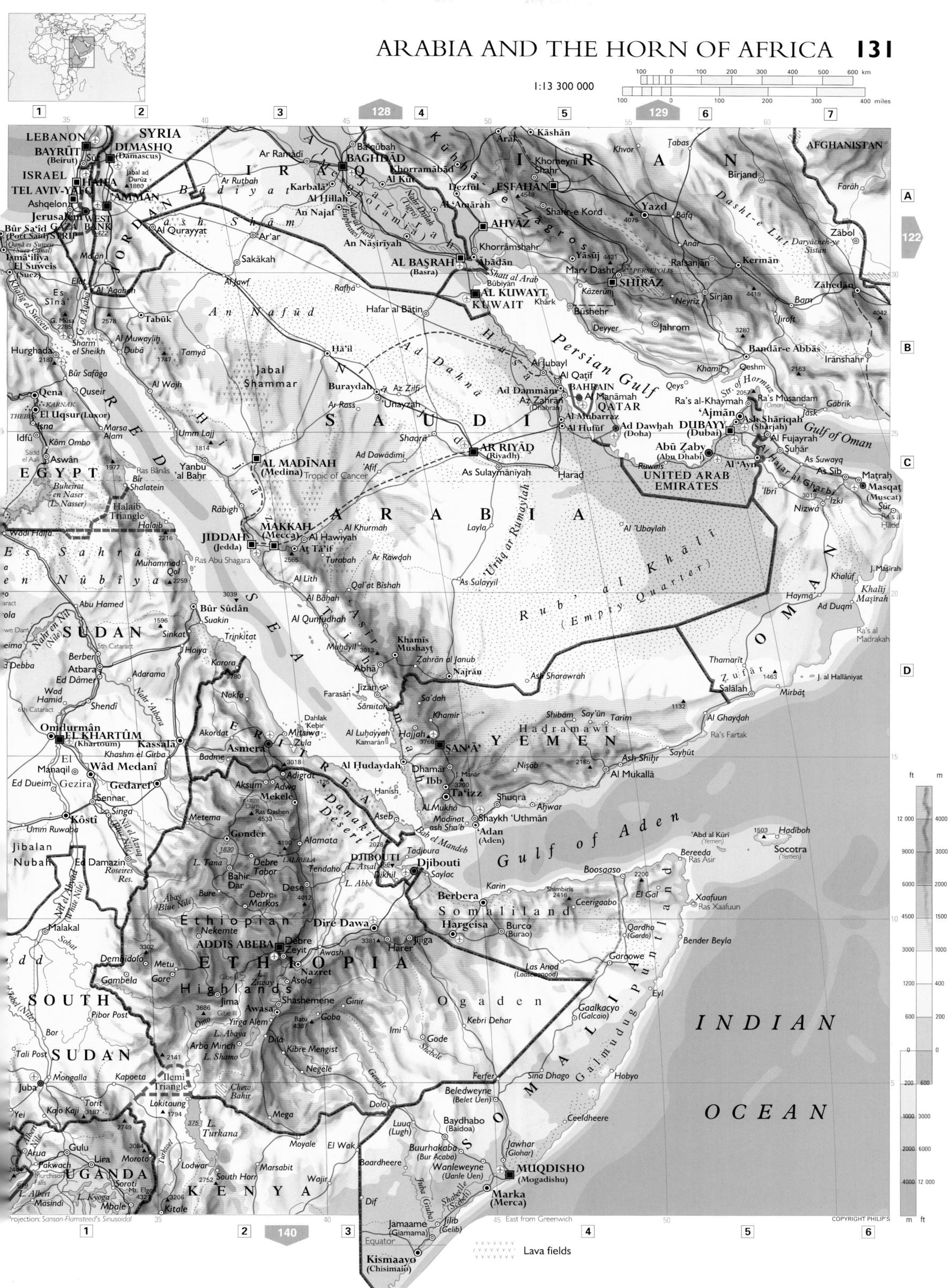

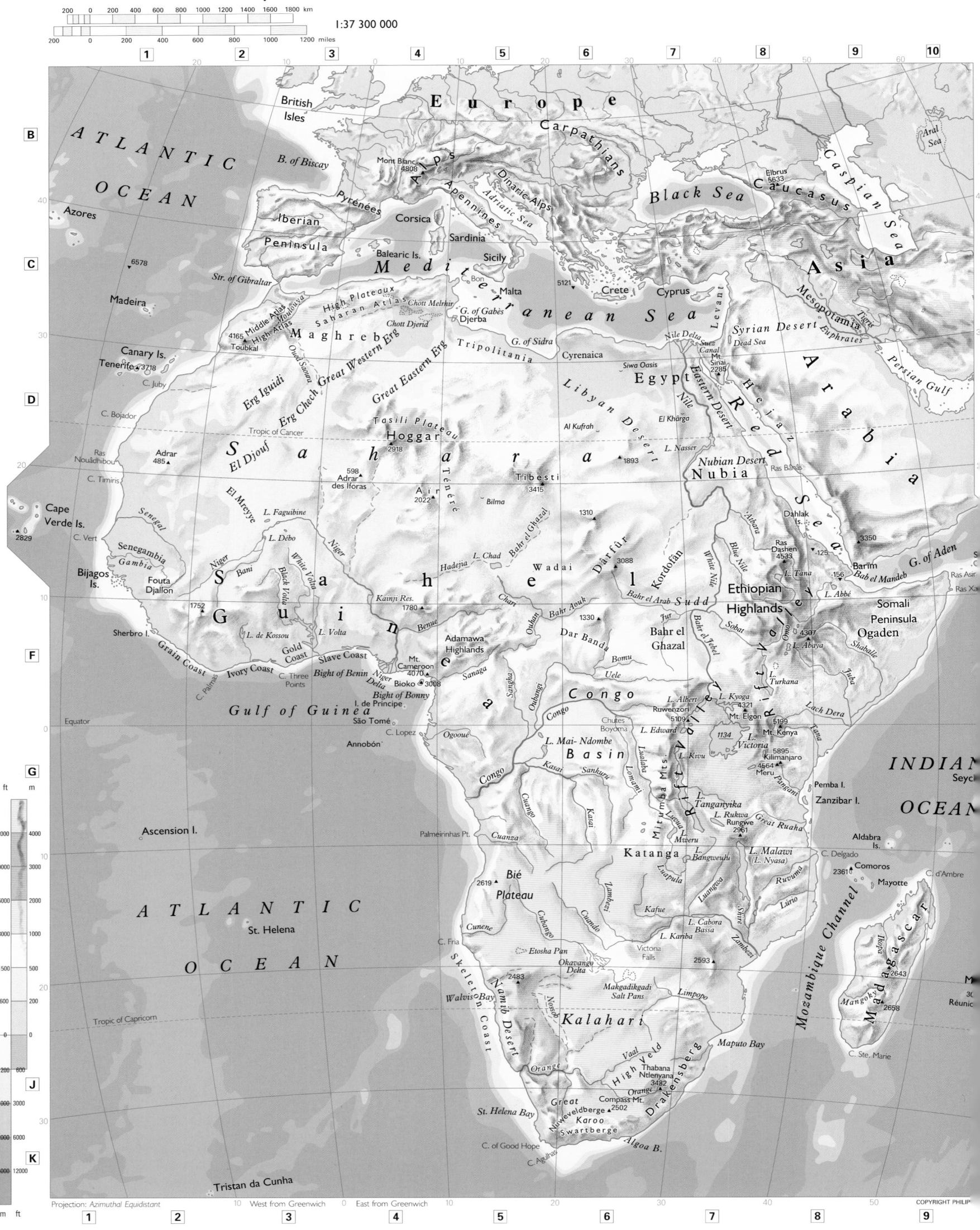

1:37 300 000

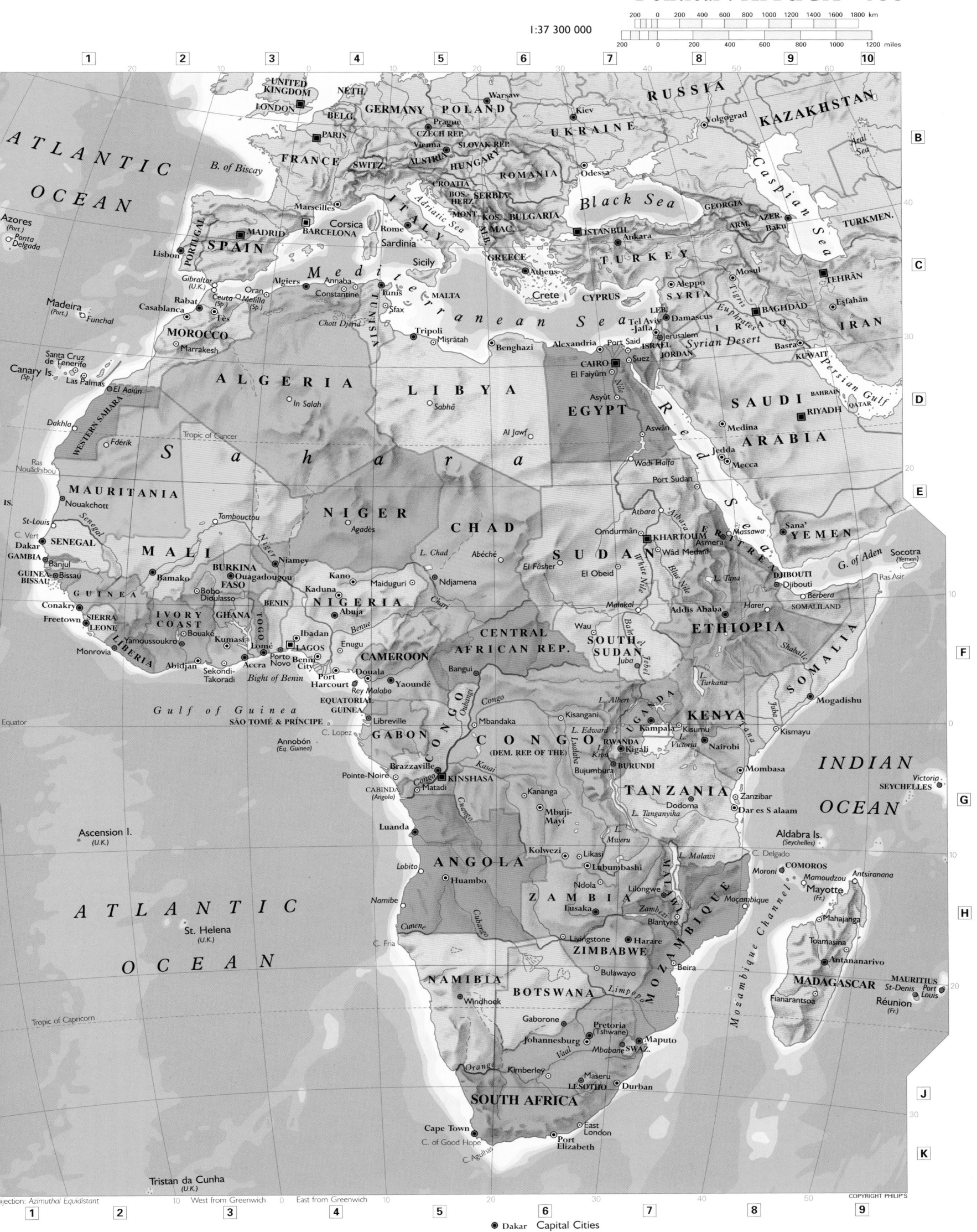

1:37 300 000

● Dakar Capital Cities

Projection: Azimuthal Equidistant

COPYRIGHT PHILIP'S

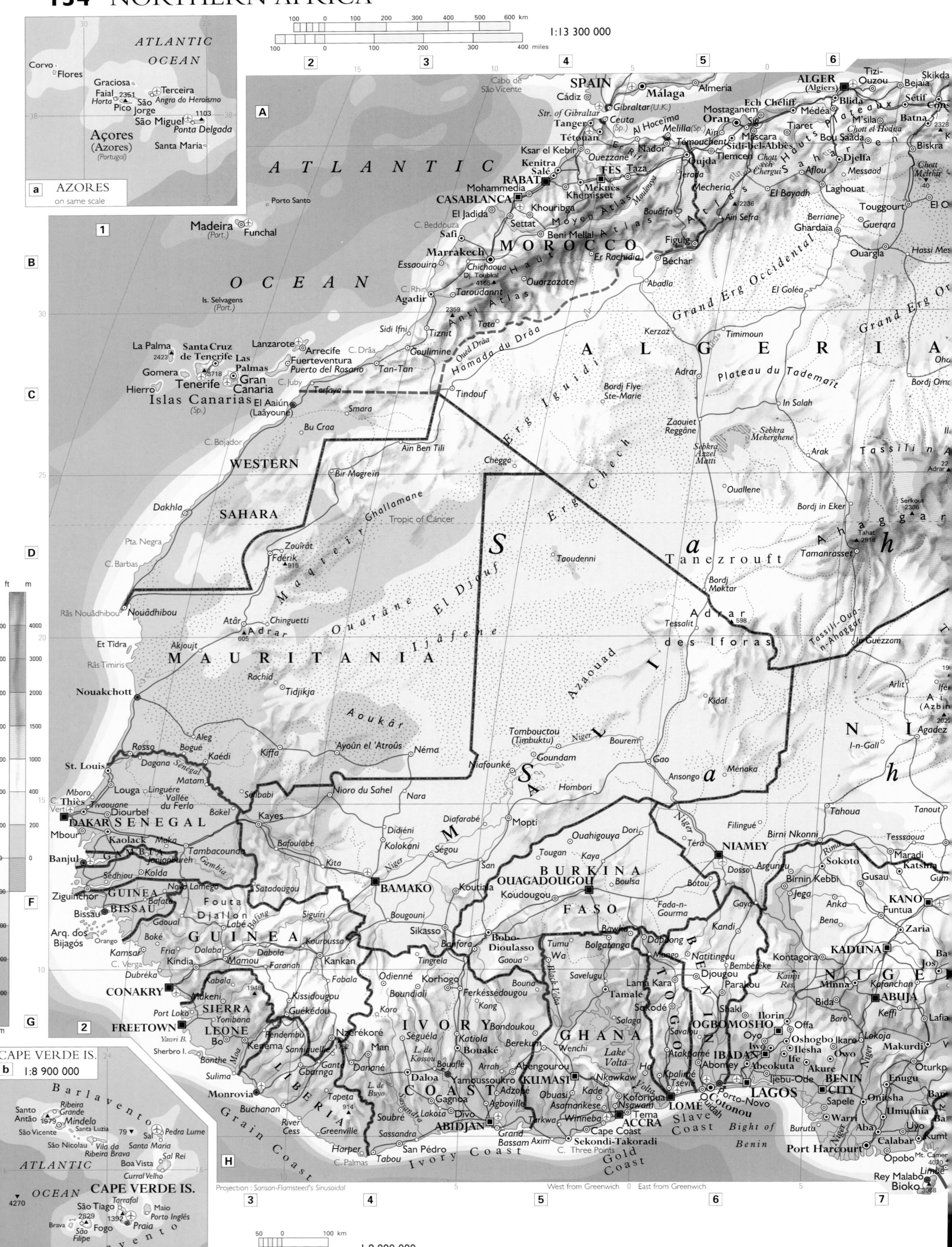

1:13 300 000

100   0   100   200   300   400   500   600 km

100   0   100   200   300   400 miles

Projection : Sanson-Flamsteed's Sinusoidal

b CAPE VERDE IS.
1:8 900 000

CAPE VERDE IS.

1:8 900 000

50   0   100 km

50   0   50 miles

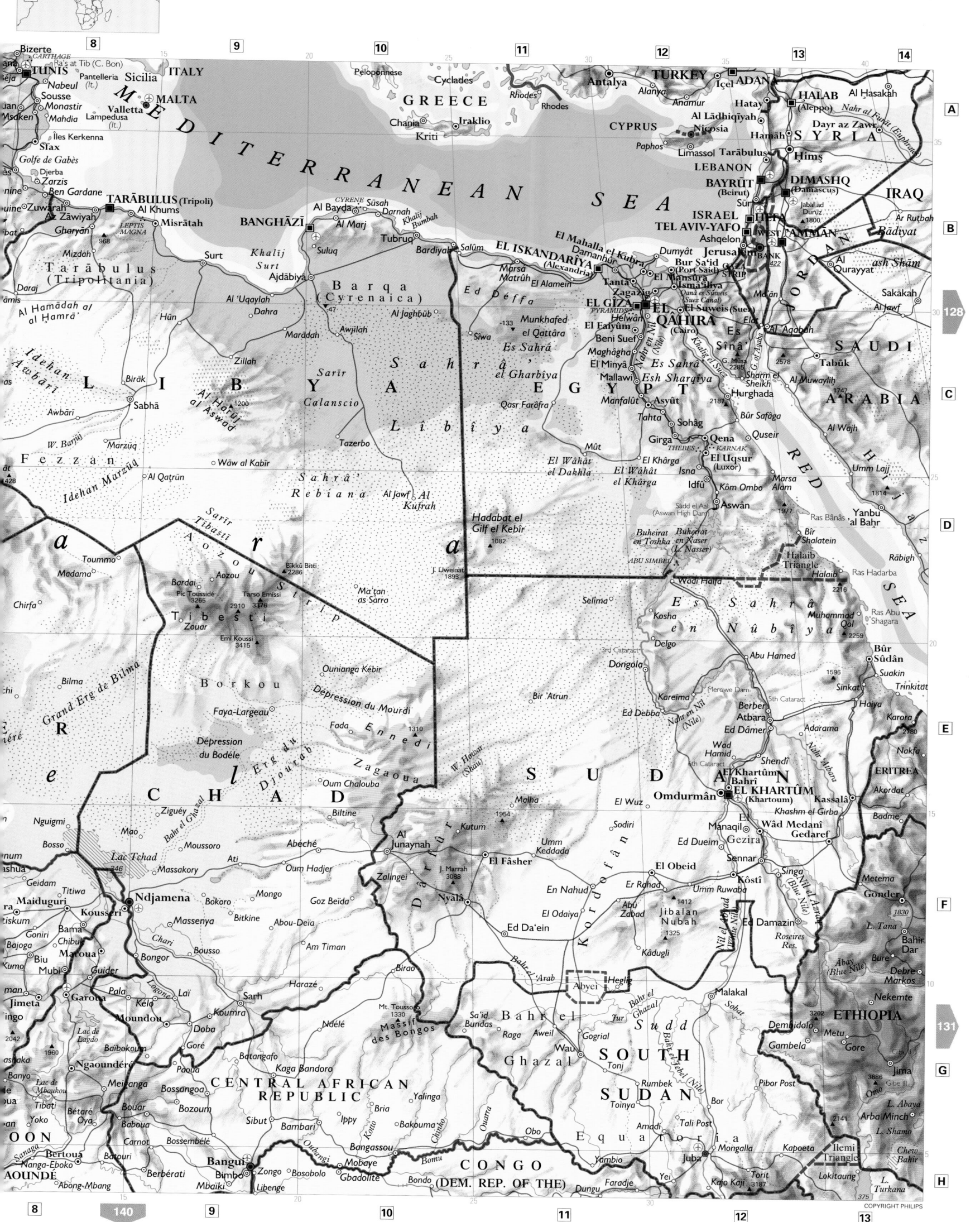

Lava fields

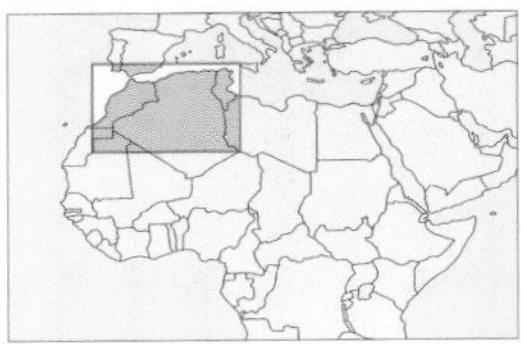

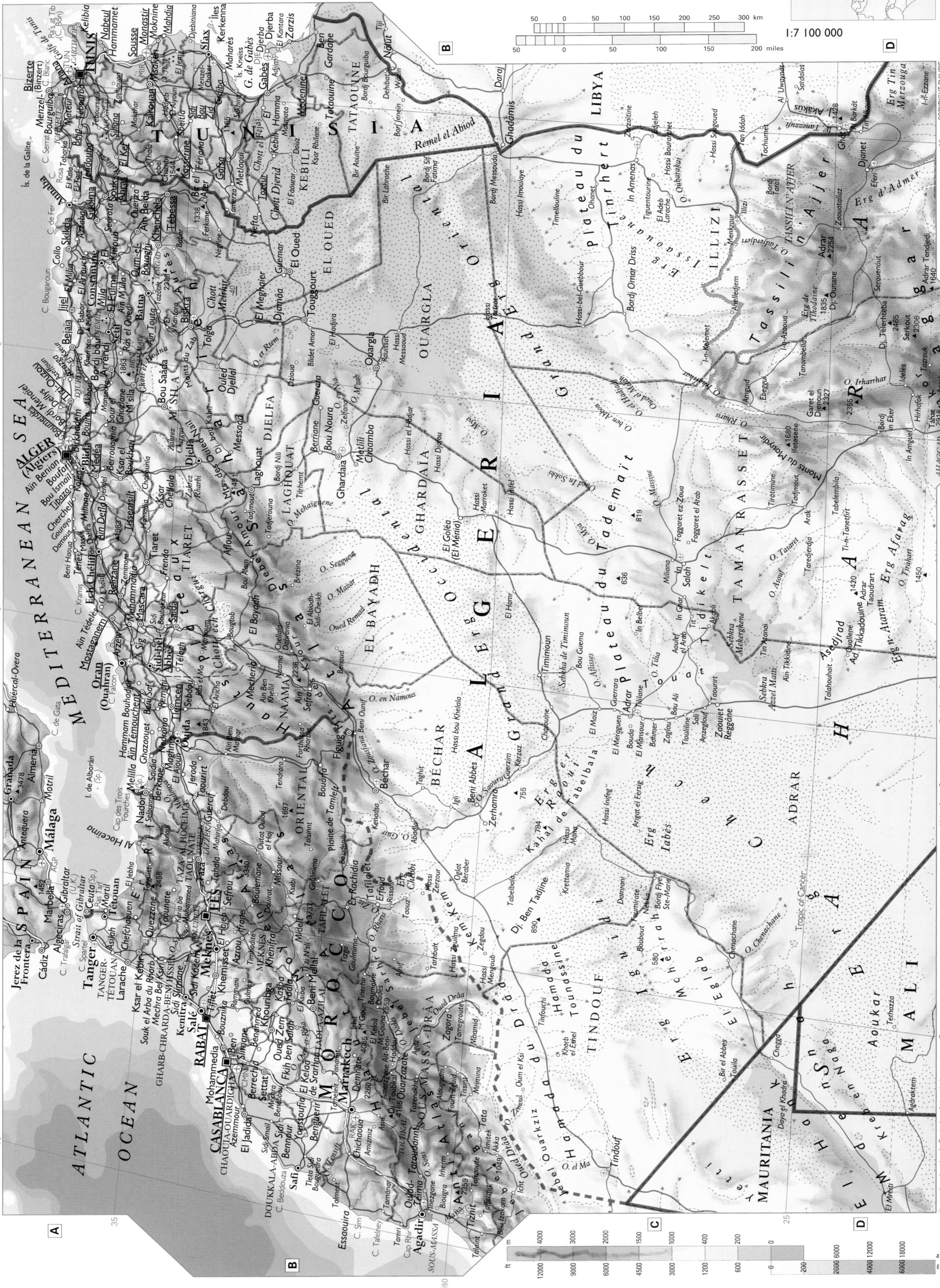

1:7 100 000

MEDITERRANEAN SEA

ATLANTIC OCEAN

TUNISIA

ALGERIA

MOROCCO

LIBYA

MALI

MAURITANIA

SPAIN

Tunis
Bizerte (Binzert)
Nabeul
Sousse
Sfax
Gabès
Kairouan
Tébessa
Constantine
ALGER (Algiers)
Oran (Ouahran)
Béchar
Ouargla
El Oued
Touggourt
Ghardaïa
Laghouat
Tiaret
Tlemcen
Oujda
Fès
Meknès
RABAT
Casablanca
Marrakech
Agadir
Tindouf
Reggane
Adrar
In Salah
Tamanrasset
Djanet
Ghadamis
Ghat

Málaga
Granada
Almería
Gibraltar
Tanger
Tétouan
Ceuta
Melilla

Tropic of Cancer

Plateau du Tinrhert
Tassili n'Ajjer
Erg Chech
Grand Erg Oriental
Grand Erg Occidental
Plateau du Tademaït
Hamada du Draa
Sahara

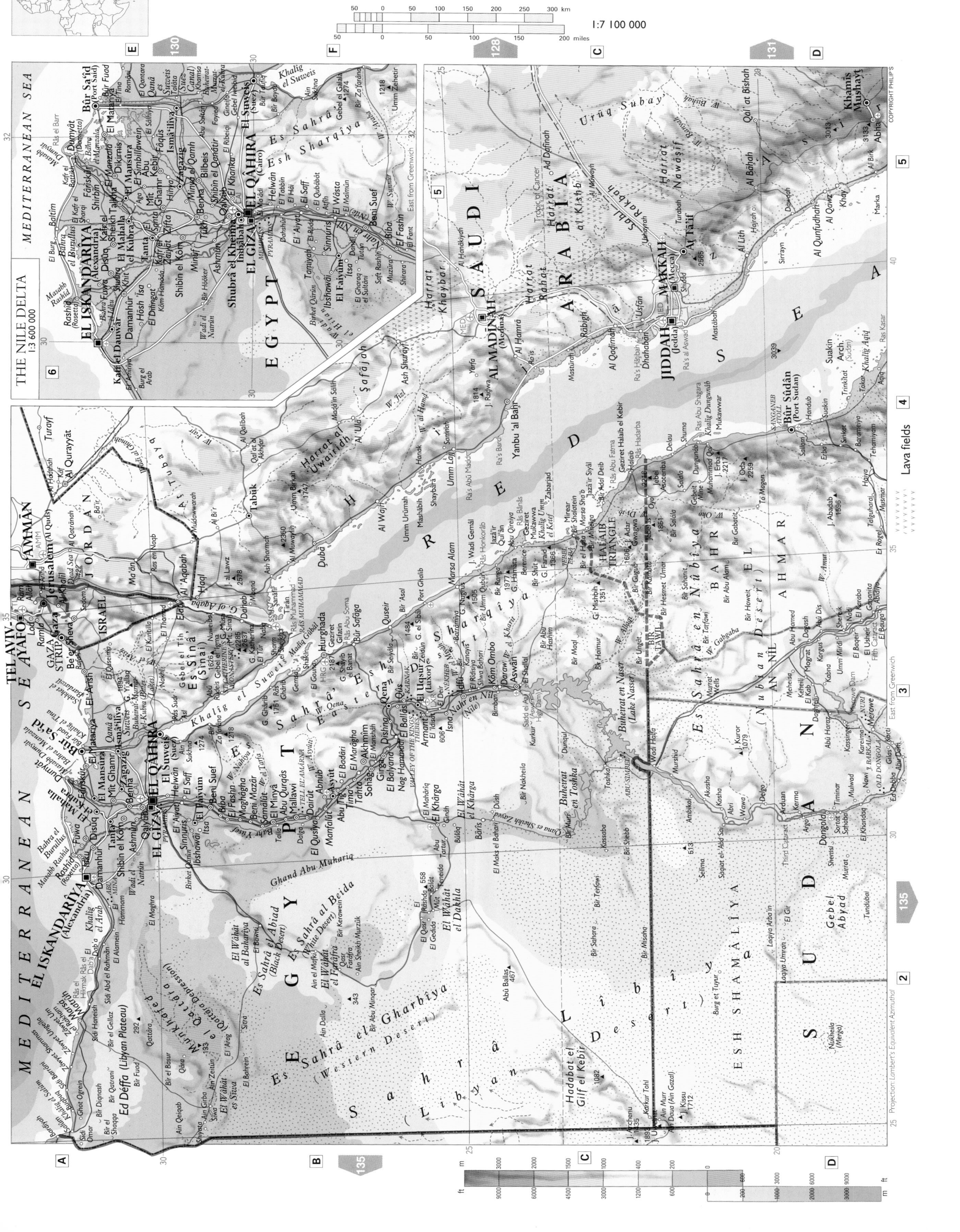

50 0 50 100 150 200 250 300 km

1:7 100 000

50 0 50 100 150 200 miles

THE NILE DELTA
1:3 600 000

MEDITERRANEAN SEA

MEDITERRANEAN SEA

EGYPT

SAUDI ARABIA

JORDAN

ISRAEL

SUDAN

RED SEA

Es Sahrâ esh Sharqîya (Eastern Desert)

Es Sahrâ el Gharbîya (Western Desert)

Sahrâ' Lîbîya (Libyan Desert)

Es Sahrâ en Nûbîya (Nubian Desert)

EL QÂHIRA (Cairo)

EL ISKANDARÎYA (Alexandria)

EL GÎZA

AL MADÎNAH (Medina)

MAKKAH (Mecca)

JIDDAH (Jedda)

Bûr Sûdân (Port Sudan)

AMMAN

TEL AVIV–YÂFO

Jerusalem (Al Quds)

Khamîs Mushayt

BIR TAWIL

HALA'IB TRIANGLE

Lava fields

Tropic of Cancer

East from Greenwich

COPYRIGHT PHILIP'S

Projection: Lambert's Equivalent Azimuthal

1:7 100 000

50 0 50 100 150 200 250 300 km
50 0 50 100 150 200 miles

134

Projection : Lambert's Equivalent Azimuthal

Underlined towns give their name to the
administrative area in which they stand.

Administrative divisions in Ivory Coast:
1 Dix-Huit Montagnes   4 Lagunes   7 Moyen-Comoé
2 Fromager   5 Marahoué   8 Sud-Bandama
3 Haut-Sassandra   6 Moyen-Cavally   9 Sud-Comoé

West from

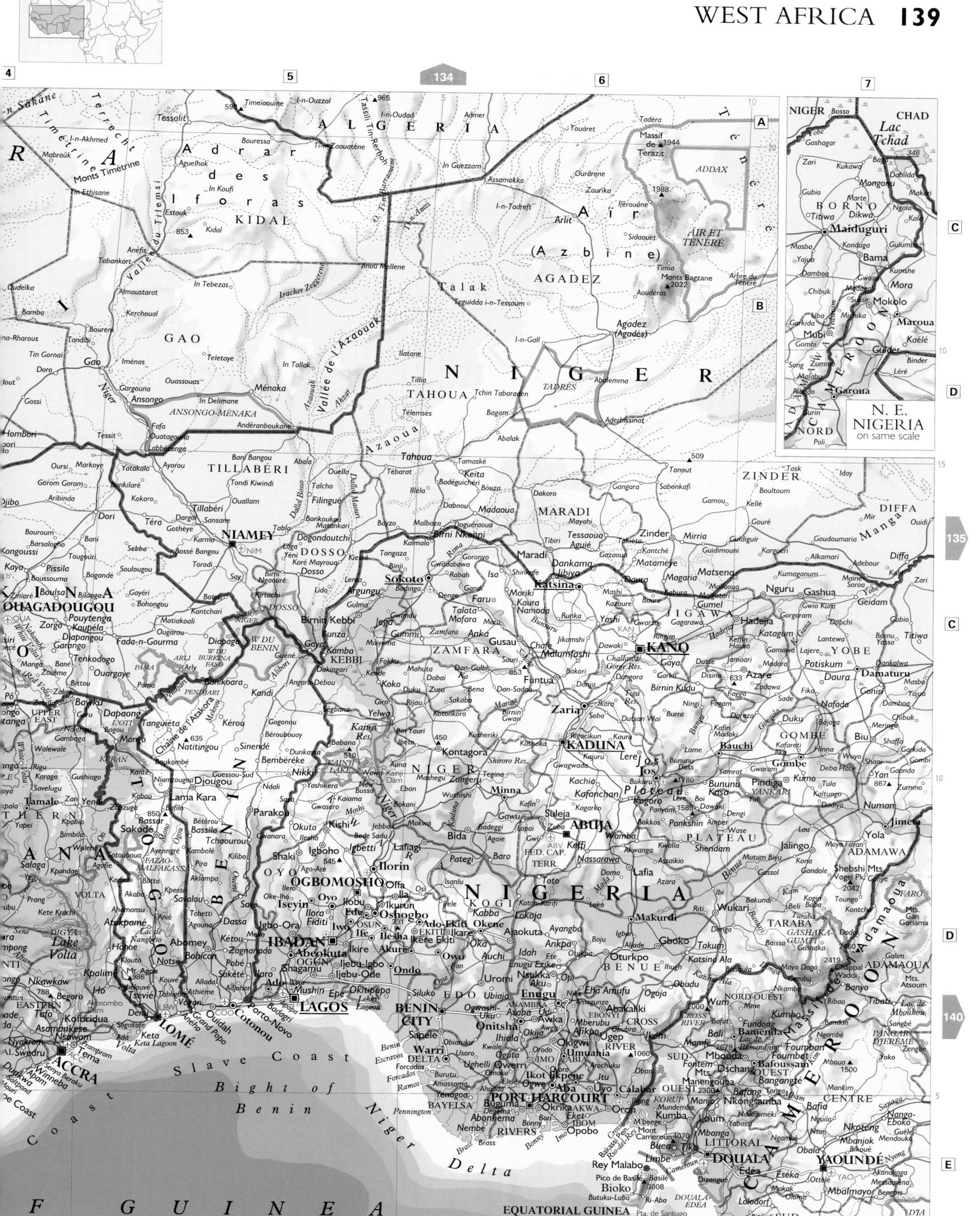

N. E.
NIGERIA
on same scale

East from Greenwich

COPYRIGHT PHILIP'S

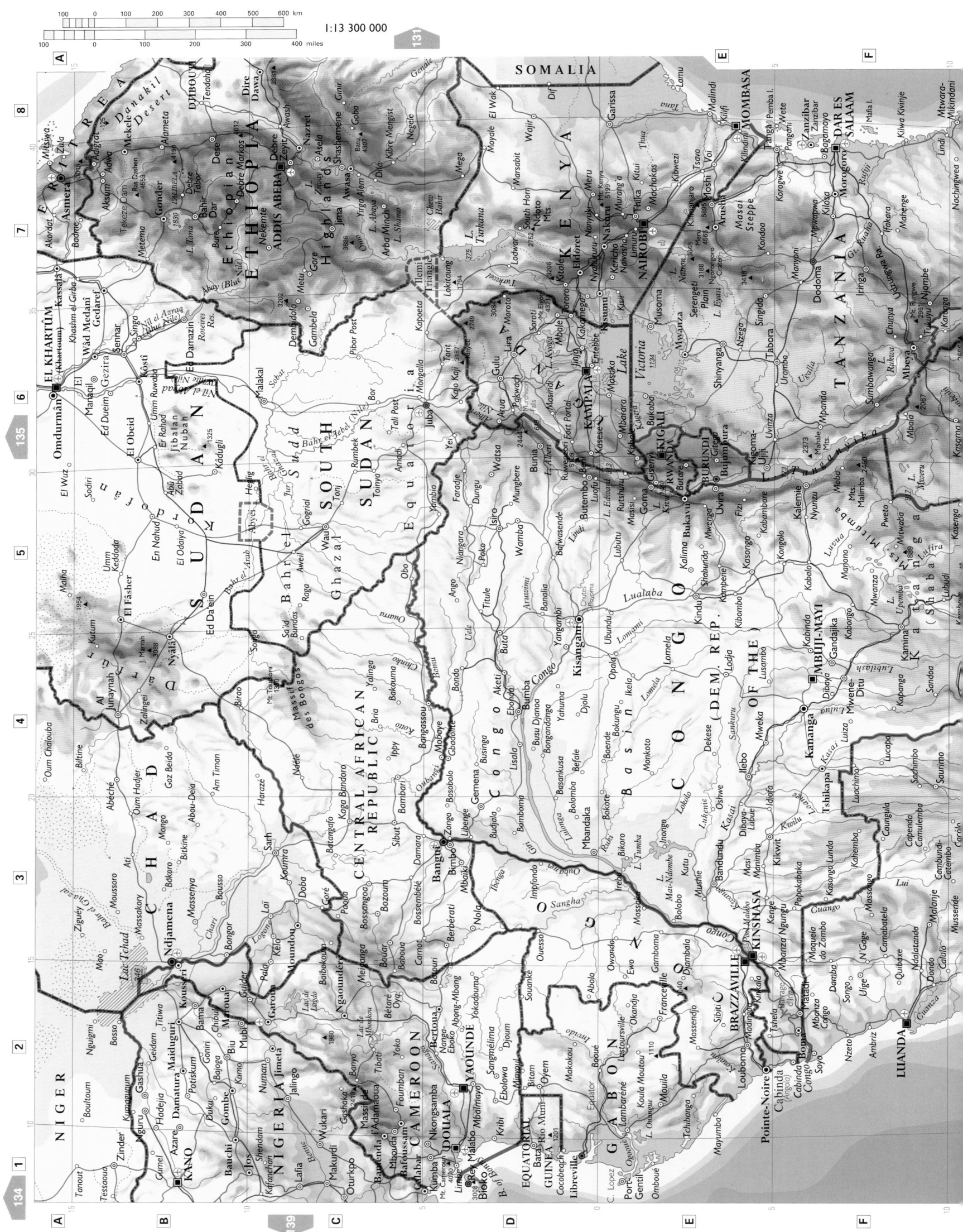

1:13 300 000

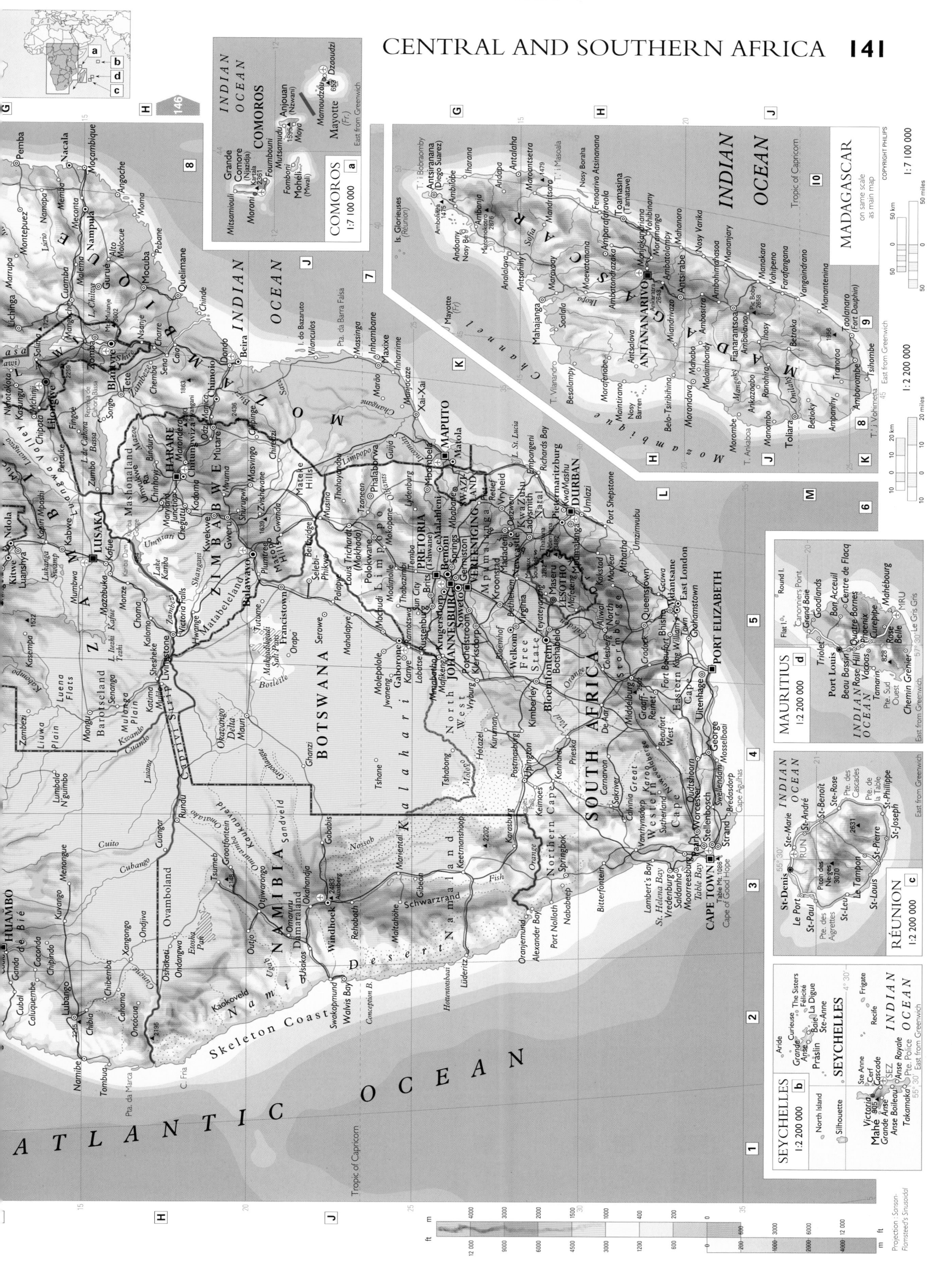

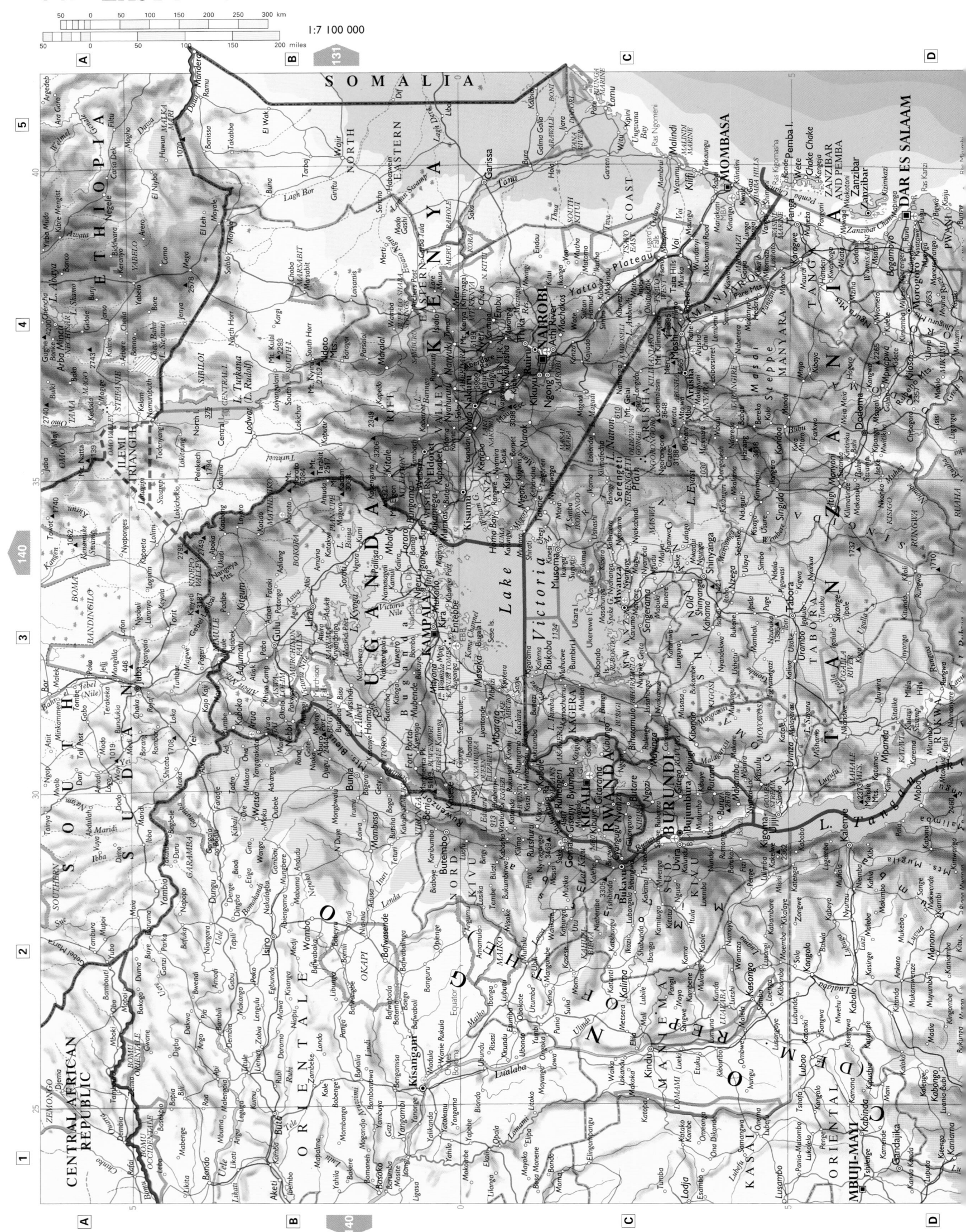

1:7 100 000

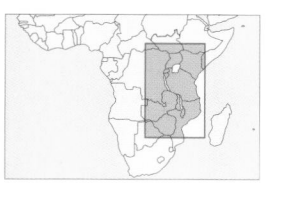

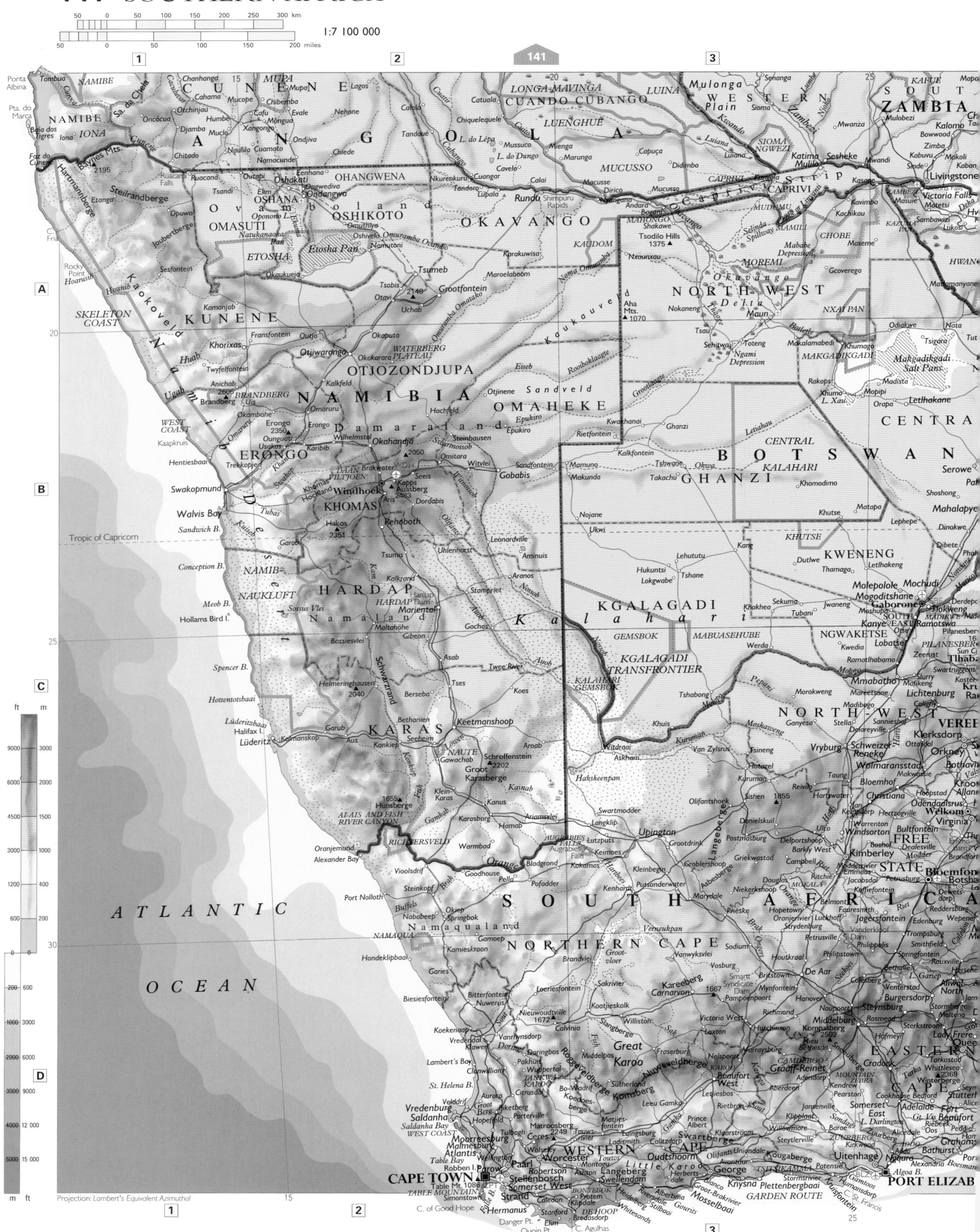

1:7 100 000

Projection: Lambert's Equivalent Azimuthal

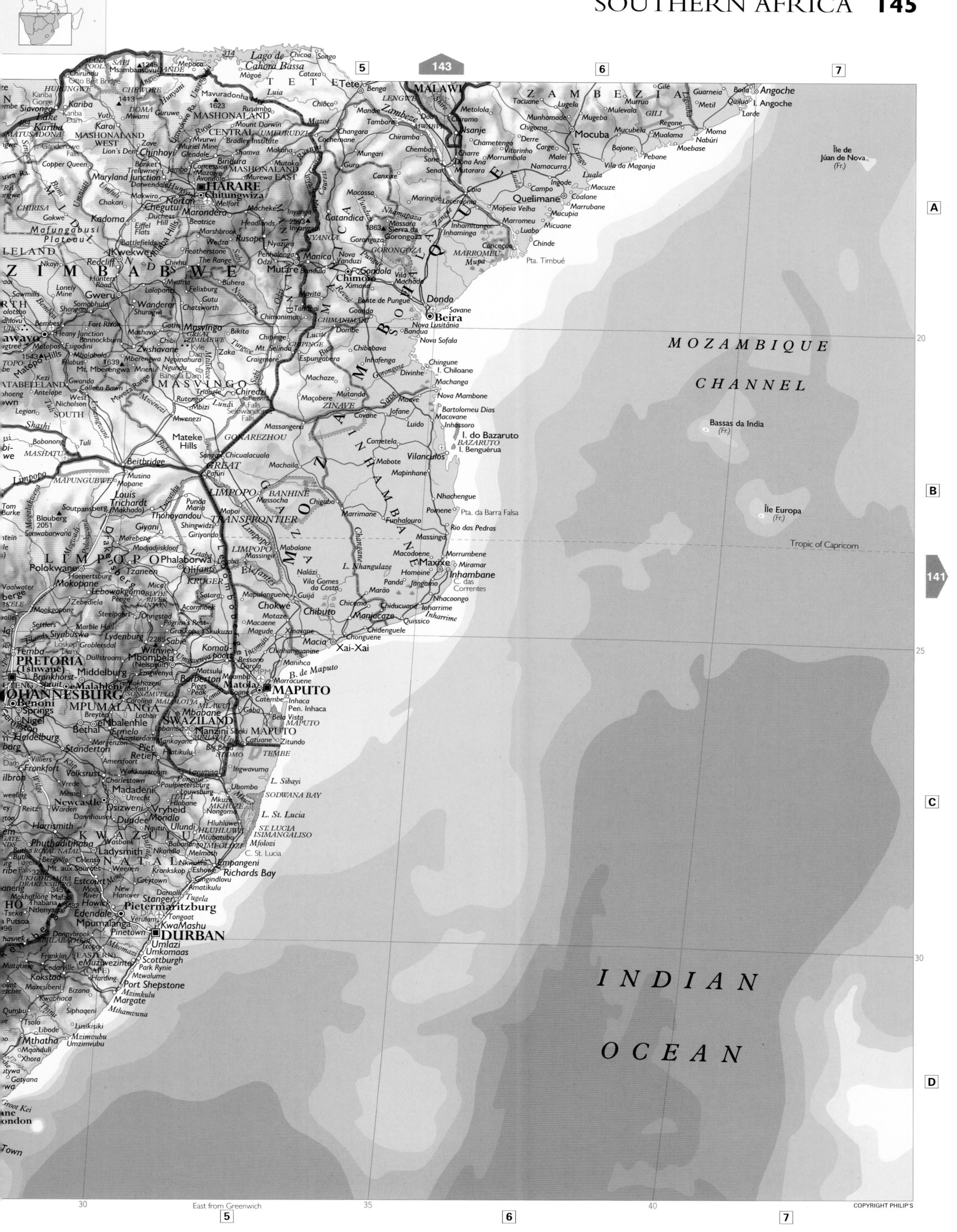

ZAMBEZIA

Lago de Chicoa Songo
Cahora Bassa Môgöe
314
SAFI
POOLS
Mepoca
1245
Chirundu
Otto Beit Bridge
ANDE
Mavuradonha Ra.
Luia
Chióco
TETE Tete Benga
Zambeze Qoo MWABU
Metolola Tacuane Gilé Angoche
MALAWI Nsanje Chiromo Munhamade Lugela Regone I. Angoche
HUNGWE Kariba Kariba Yuti Guruwe Mount Darwin Rusambo Mandie Chigoma Mocuba Mulevala GILI Metil Moma
Siavonga Gorge Dam DOMA Ra. Mazoe Changara Tambara Chiramba Chemba Cargo Derre Pebane Nabúri
Lake 1413 Karoi 1623 MASHONALAND Bradley Chicoane Senat Dona Ana Morrumbala Namacurra Vila de Maganja Moebase
Kariba MASHONALAND CENTRAL UMFURUDZI Institute Cochemane Mutarara Ingode Luala
WEST Chinhoyi Muriel Mine Shamva Makaha Guro Canxixe Maringue Locorôngia Coia Mopeia Velha Coalane
Copper Queen Lion's Den Glendale Concession Mazoe Macossa Quelimane
Maryland Junction Banket Trelawney Bindura MASHONALAND Catandica Nhamapasa Inhaminga Marromeu Mucupia
Norton Avondale EAST Mutoko Murewa GORONGOZA Marrubane Micuane
HARARE Chitungwiza 1863 Gorongoza Cançeção Chinde
Chegutu Marondera Headlands Inyanga Nova Sierra da MARROMEU Chinde
Kadoma Cheshire Beatrice Marshbrook Nyanga Vanduzi Gorongoza Mupa Pta. Timbué
Featherstone Wedza 2593 Gondola Vila
Rusape NYANGA Manica Machado
Kwekwe Redcliff Eiffel Flats The Range Chivhu Odzi Chimoio Dondo
ZIMBABWE Gweru Somabhula Lalapansi Myarra Felixburg Gutu Buhera Mavita Ximana Pante de Pungue Savane
Shangani Shurugwi Chatsworth Chimanimani Beira
Wanderer Mbizo Nova Lusitânia
Hunters Lonely CHIPINGE Dombe Nova Sofala
Road Mine Fort Rixon Mashava GREAT Bikita Chipinge Mt. Selinda Bandua
Esigodini ZIMBABWE Chibi Chimanimani Chibabava
Matopos 1543 Dan Mberengwa Ngomahura Zaka Turgwe Espungabera Chingune I. Chiloane
Mbalabala 1639 Mt. Mberengwa Ngundu Machaze Machanga MOZAMBIQUE
Kezi Mneni Craignear Nova Mambone
MASVINGO Rutenga Lundi Mapoge ZINAVE Moove Bartolomeu Dias CHANNEL
Gwanda Colleen Bawn Chiredzi Zaka Macoyne
Antelope Triangle Selowandoma Covane Divinhe Inhassoro
SOUTH Nicholson Mwenezi Falls Massangena Jofane Machanga
Shashi Mateke Mwenezi Cometela Luido I. do Bazaruto
Bobonong Hills GONAREZHOU Nhachengue Vilanculos BAZARUTO
Songa Chicualacuala Machaila I. Benguérua
Beitbridge GREAT Mabote Mapinhane
Musina Pafuri Mahenye
Mopane LIMPOPO Massocha Marrime Pomene
Louis Punda BANHINE Chigubo Funhalouro Pta. da Barra Falsa
Trichardt Maria TRANSFRONTIER Massinga Rio das Pedras
Blouberg (Makhado) Giyani KRUGER Nalázi Macovane Inhambane
2051 Thohoyandou Shingwidzi Homoíne Miramar
Soutpansberg Giriyondo Macoodene Morrumbene C. das Correntes
LIMPOPO Phalaborwa Letaba Olifants L. Nhangueze Maxixe Nhacoongo
Polokwane Olifants Massingir Vila Gomes Pandá Jangamo
Haenertsburg Mica Elefantes da Costa Marão
Mokopane Tzaneen Penge Chokwe Guijá Chicamo Chiducuane Inharrime
Lebowakgomo Setara Mazambene Quissico
Marble Hall Gravelotte Acornhoek Macaene Xinavane Magude Chidenguele
Zebediela Ohrigstad Pilgrim's Rest Skukuza Manjacaze
Steelpoort Graskop Chibuto Chonguene
Siyabuswa Sabie Chibuto
Lydenburg Witrivier Komati Macia Xai-Xai
Loskop 2285 poort Incomati Chihanguanine
Groblersdal Mbombela Nsikazi Ressano Nhanica
Dullstroom (Nelspruit) Barberton Garcia
Middelburg Machadodorp Matsulu Marracuene
PRETORIA Bronkhorst Piggs Peak MPM
(Tshwane) spruit Malalane Peak B. de Maputo Catembe
Kempton (Belfast) SWAZILAND Barberton Matola MAPUTO Pen. Inhaca
JOHANNESBURG Caroline Lothair MLAWULA Mbabane Sheki Pen. Inhaca
Benoni Springs Ermelo Manzini MAPUTO Bela Vista
Nigel Mbalenhle Retief Piet Namaacha Catuane Zitundo
Heidelburg Bethal Mkhazeni Hlatikulu NDUMO TEMBE Big Bend
Standerton Amersfoort Lavumisa Ingwavuma
Villiers Wakkerstroom Pongola Ubombo L. Sibayi
Frankfort Volksrust Paulpietersburg Louwsburg Mbazwana SODWANA BAY
Vrede Memel Charlestown Vryheid KwaMbonambi
Reitz Warden Newcastle Utrecht Mondlo IMPALA MKHUZE L. St. Lucia
Dannhauser Hlobane Ngotshe Mtubatuba ST. LUCIA
Harrismith Madadeni Nqutu Ulundi Hluhluwe ISIMANGALISO
Dundee HLUHLUWE C. St. Lucia
Phuthaditjhaba Osizweni Babanango Nkwalini Nongoma Mfolozi
KWAZULU Vryheid Melmoth Empangeni
Bergville Ladysmith Ntambanana Eshowe Gingindlovu Richards Bay
Butha ROYAL NATAL NATAL Kranskop Amatikulu
Mt. aux Escourt Weenen Nkandla Stanger
Sources Colenso Greytown Darnall
Mokhotlong UKHAHLAMBA Mooi Tugela
Thabana DRAKENSBERG New Hanover Howick Tongaat
3482 Moor River Pietermaritzburg Verulam
Ntsikeni Edendale KwaMashu
Mpumalanga Pinetown DURBAN
Donnybrook Umlazi
Franklin Umkomaas
Cedarville eMuzizweni Scottburgh
Kokstad Harding Park Rynie
Maxesibeni Bizana Mtwalume
Qumbu Kwabhaca Port Shepstone
Libode Siphageni Margate
Mthatha Lusikisiki Mzimkulu Mamvuna
Mqanduli Mzimvubu
Xhora Tsolo

MOZAMBIQUE CHANNEL

Île de Júan de Nova (Fr.)

Bassas da India (Fr.)

Île Europa (Fr.)

Tropic of Capricorn

INDIAN OCEAN

20

25

30

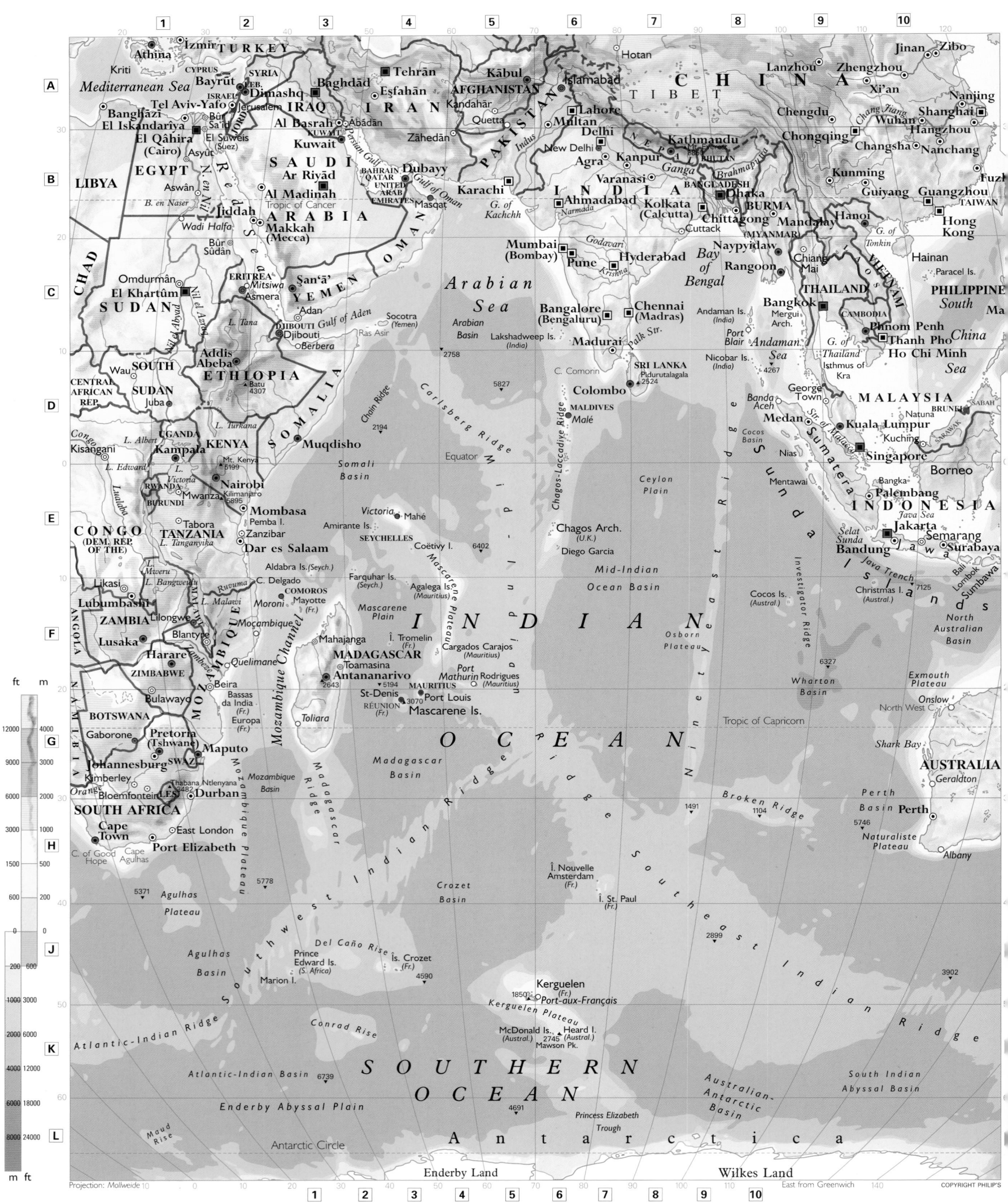

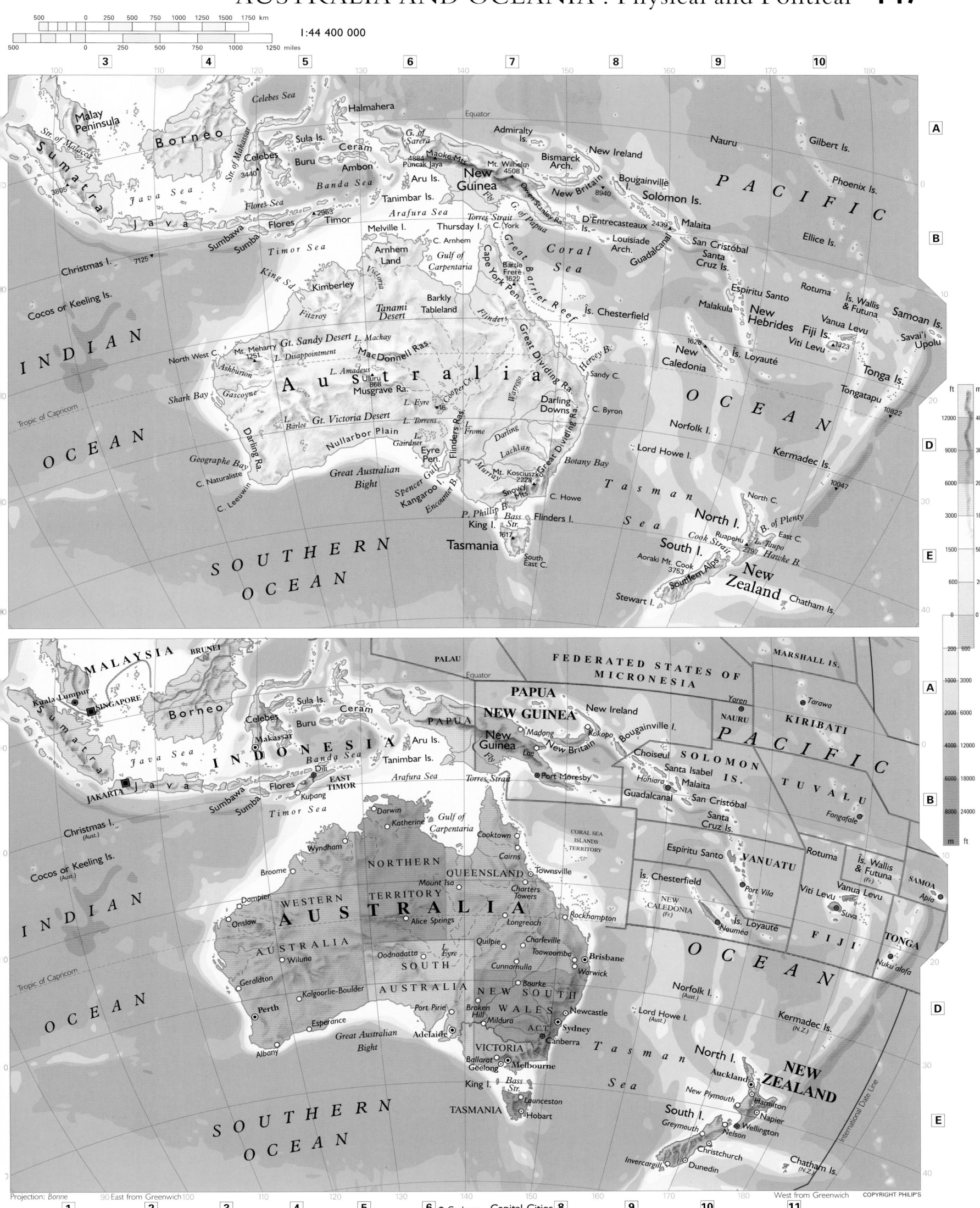

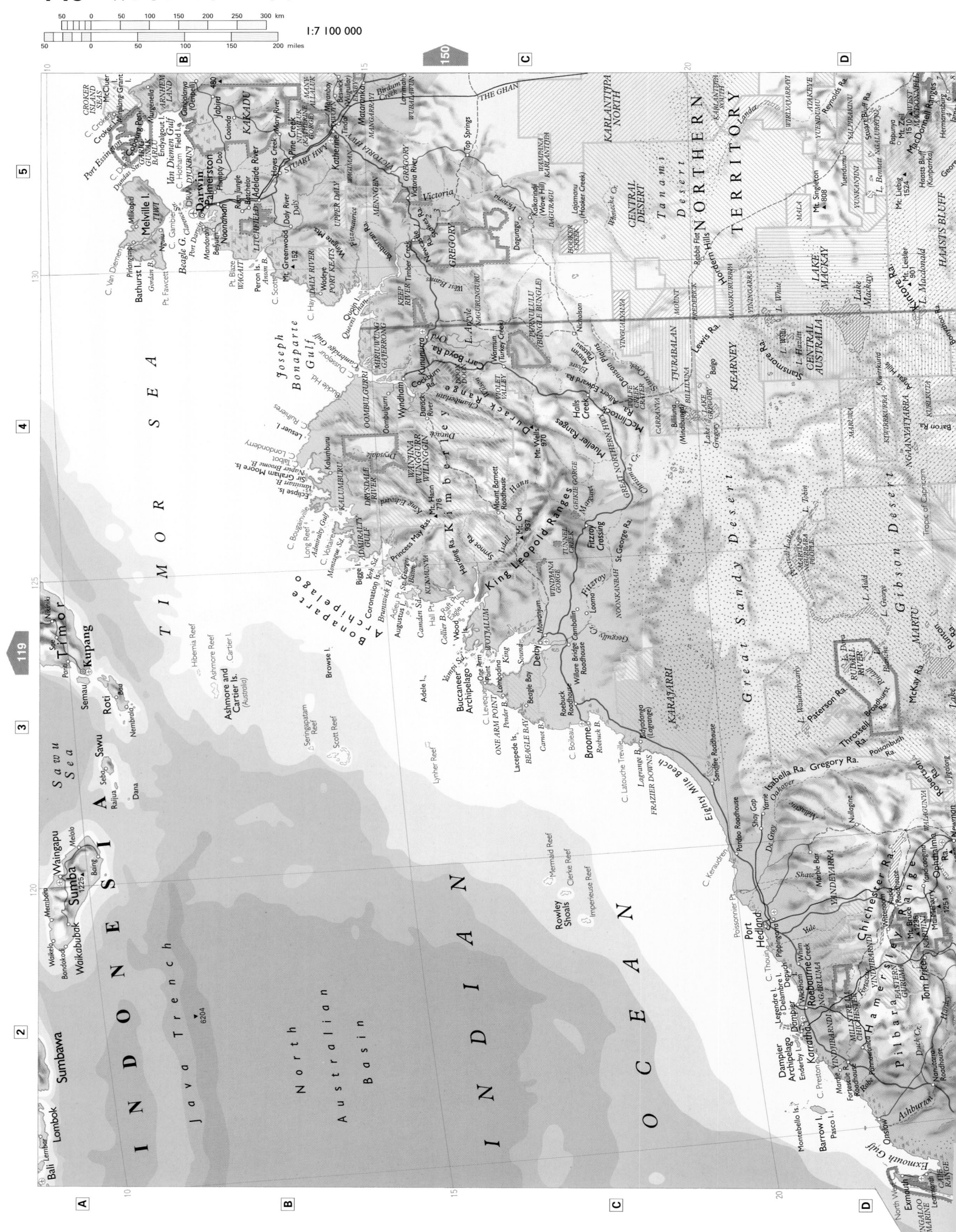

1:7 100 000

150

119

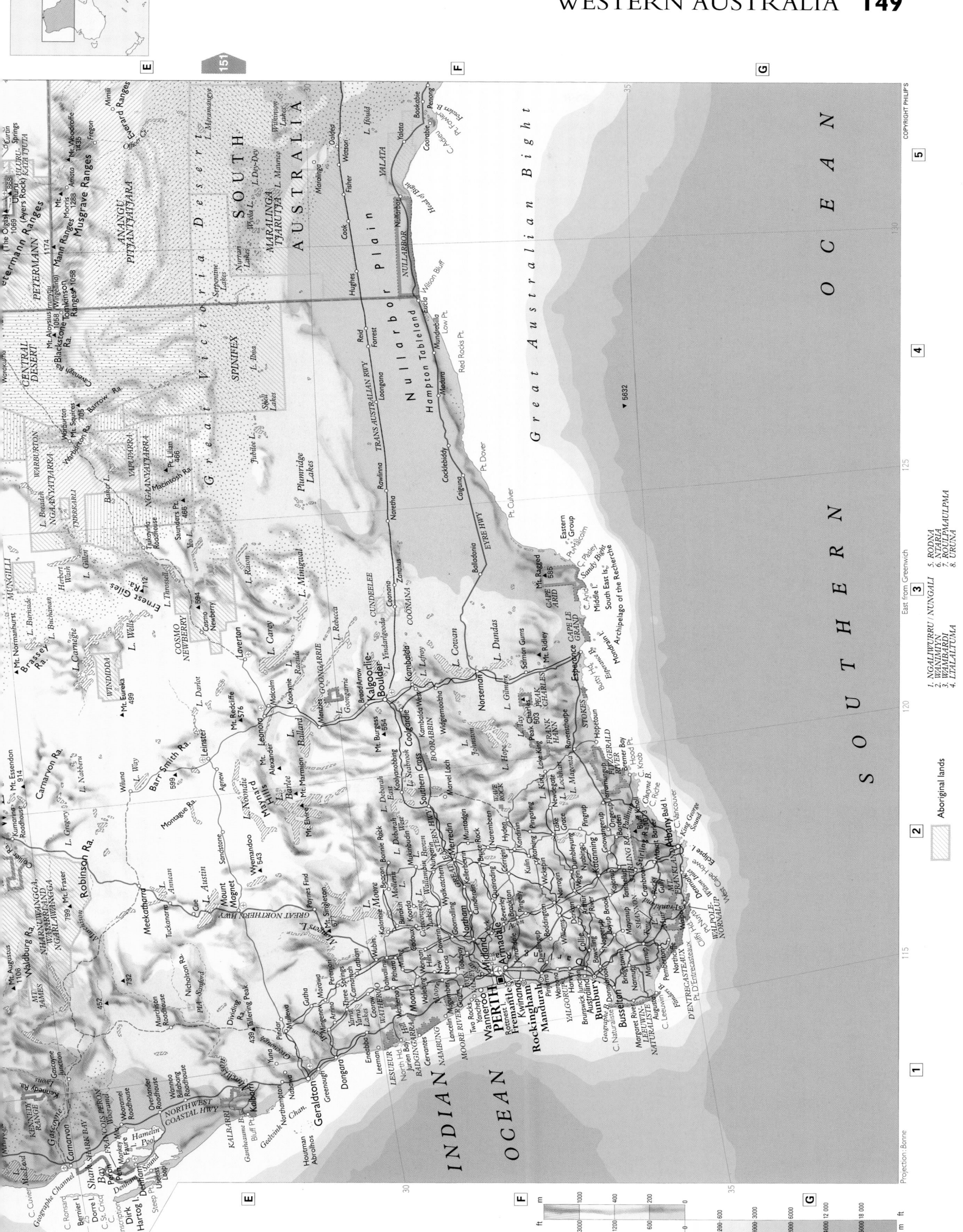

Projection: Bonne

East from Greenwich

Aboriginal lands

1. NGALIWURRU / NUNGALI
2. WANIMYN
3. WAMBARDI
4. LYALALITUMA
5. RODNA
6. NTARIA
7. ROULPMAULPMA
8. URUNA

INDIAN OCEAN

SOUTHERN OCEAN

Great Australian Bight

SOUTH AUSTRALIA

m
ft
1000 — 3000
400 — 1200
200 — 600
0 — 0
0 — 0
200 — 600
2000 — 6000
4000 — 12 000
6000 — 18 000

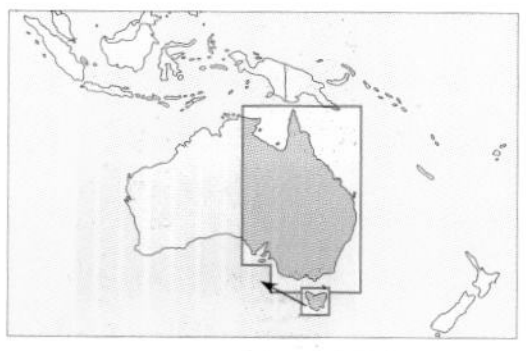

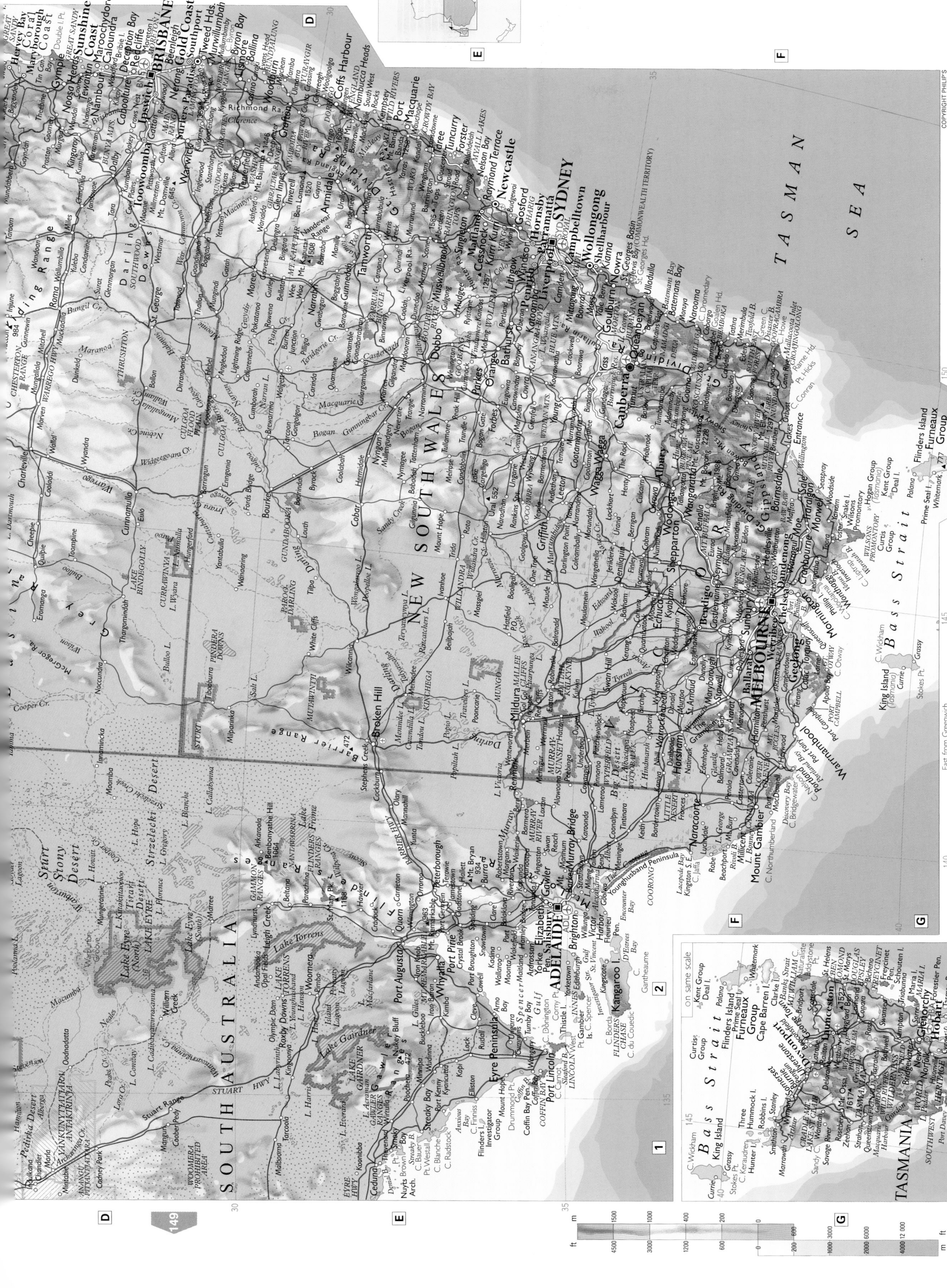

COPYRIGHT PHILIP'S

Projection: Borne

Aboriginal lands

on same scale

TASMAN SEA

NEW SOUTH WALES

SOUTH AUSTRALIA

VICTORIA

TASMANIA

BRISBANE

SYDNEY

Canberra

MELBOURNE

ADELAIDE

Hobart

Bass Strait

1:3 500 000

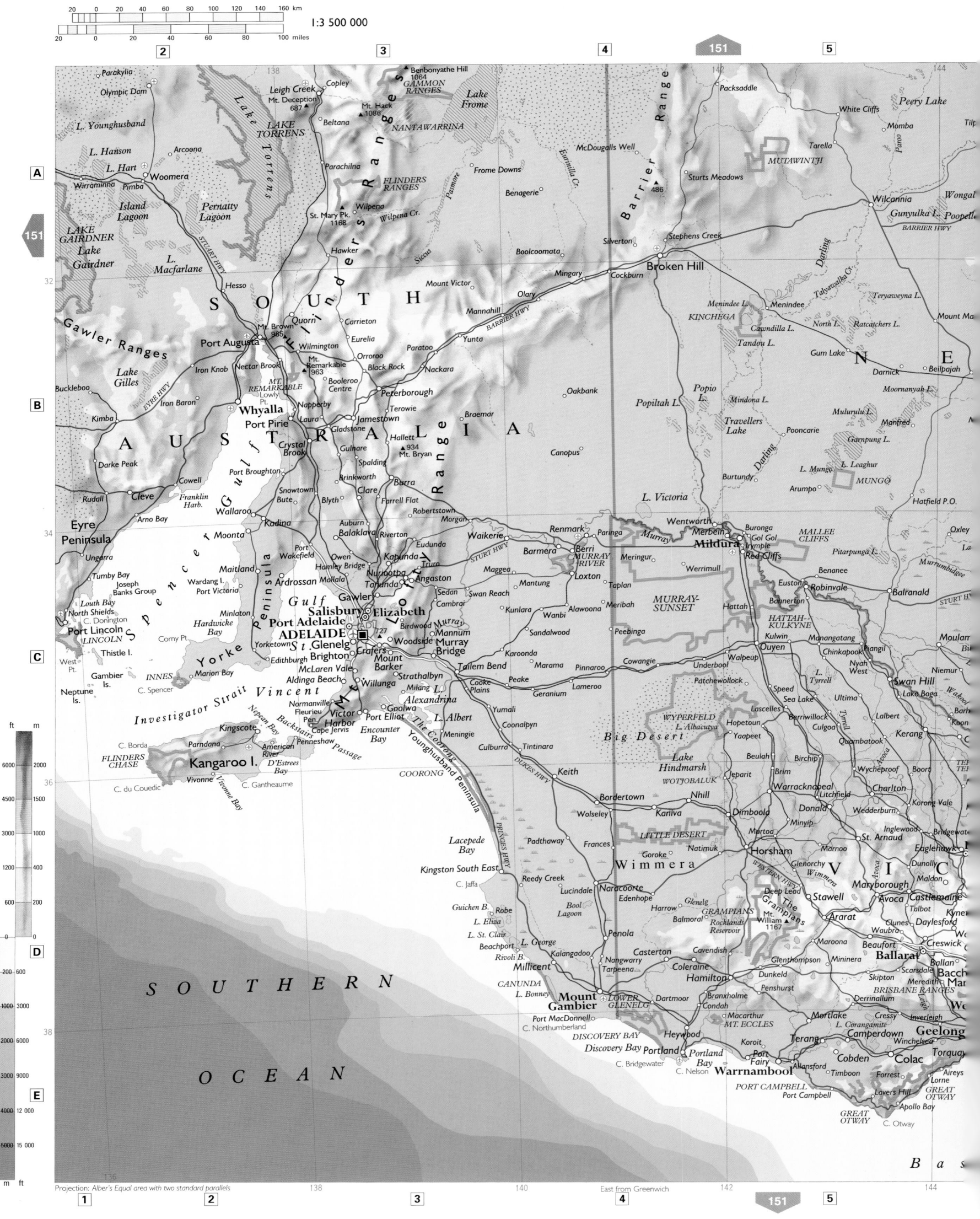

Aboriginal lands

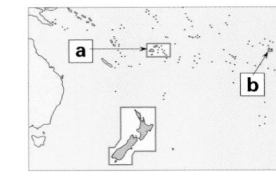

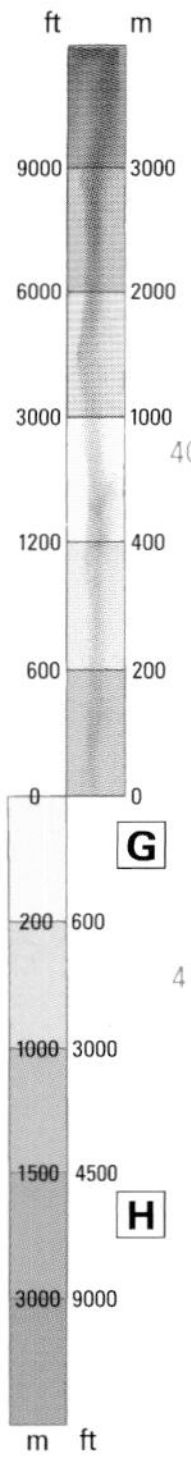

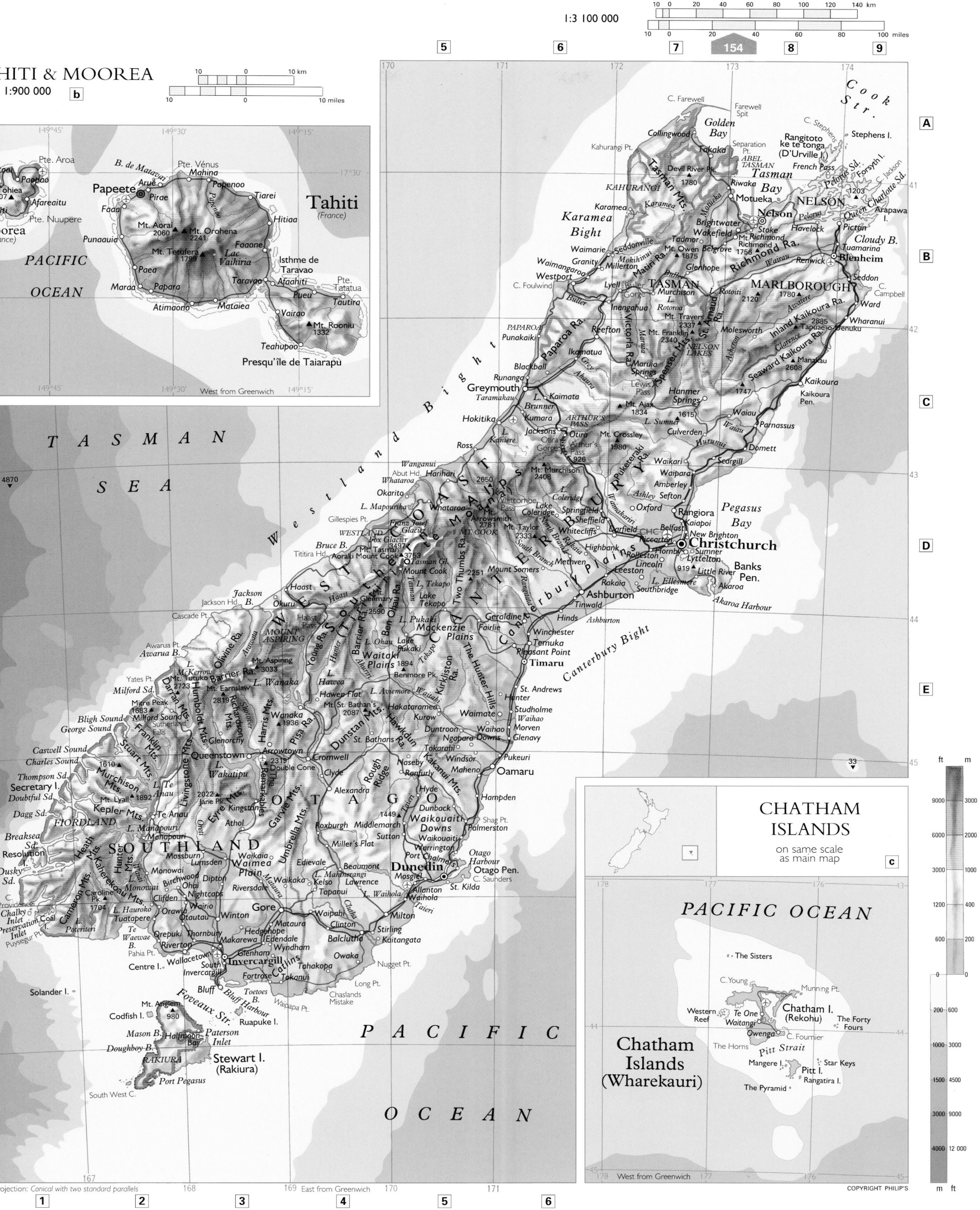

R U S S I A

Moskva
Volga
Yekaterinburg
Tomsk
Novosibirsk
Astana (Aqmola)
Semey
Irkutsk
Oz. Baykal
Chita
Lena
Ob'
Blagoveshchensk
Amur
Khabarovsk
Okhotsk
Sea of Okhotsk
Poluostrov Kamchatka
Shirshov Ridge
Komandorskiye Ostrova (Russia)
Near Is. (U.S.A.)
Petropavlovsk-Kamchatskiy
Aleutian Basin
Aleut...
7822
Aleutian Trench

KAZAKHSTAN
Aral Sea
Balqash Köl
Almaty
Toshkent
KYRGYZSTAN
TAJIKISTAN
Altai
MONGOLIA
Ulaanbaatar
Ürümqi
Changchun
Harbin
Shenyang
NORTH KOREA
Sapporo
Hakodate
La Perouse Str.
Kurilskiye Ostrova
Kuril'skiye Ostrova
Kuril-Kamchatka Trench
10,542
Emperor Seamount Chain
Northwest

AFGHANISTAN
Kabul
Srinagar
PAKISTAN
Lahore
Delhi
Kanpur
Indus
Himalaya
Kunlun Shan
XIZANG
Lhasa
8850 Mt. Everest
NEPAL
Brahmaputra
Ganga
C H I N A
Beijing
Tianjin
Taiyuan
Lanzhou
Xi'an
Dalian
Qingdao
Seoul
SOUTH KOREA
Nagoya
Kyoto
Osaka
Kitakyushū
Kyūshū
Shikoku
Sendai
Tōkyō
Yokohama
JAPAN
Fiji-San 3776
Sea of Japan
10,554
Japan Trench
Shatsky Rise
Pacific
Basin
Midway (U.S.A.)

INDIA
Hyderabad
Chennai (Madras)
Kolkata (Calcutta)
Dhaka
BANGLADESH
BURMA
Mandalay
Irrawaddy
Salween
Kunming
Chongqing
Wuhan
Hangzhou
Changsha
Fuzhou
Guangzhou
Hong Kong
Macau
Nanjing
Shanghai
East China Sea
Yellow Sea
Huang He
Chang J.
Taipei
TAIWAN
Ryūkyū-retto (Japan)
Okinawa
Lisianski (U.S.A.)
Minami-Tori-Shima (Japan)
Kazan-Rettō (Japan)
Iwo-Jima (Japan)
Ogasawara Gunto (Japan)
Kyushu-Palau Ridge
Shichito-Ozima-Ridge
Mid-Pacific Mou...
Wake I. (U.S.A.)
P

SRI LANKA
Colombo
Bay of Bengal
Rangoon
Bangkok
THAILAND
G. of Thailand
Phnom Penh
CAMBODIA
VIETNAM
Thanh Pho Ho Chi Minh
Andaman Is. (India)
Nicobar Is. (India)
LAOS
Hanoi
Hainan
Luzon
Manila
Mindoro
Samar 10,497
Paracel Is.
C. Engano
Philippine Sea
PHILIPPINES
Palawan
Mekong
South China Sea
West Mariana Basin
Philippine Basin
NORTHERN MARIANAS (U.S.A.)
Tinian
Saipan
East Mariana Basin
GUAM (U.S.A.)
Challenger 11,022 Deep
Mariana Trench
Micronesia
MARSHALL IS.
Bikini Atoll
Enewetak Atoll
Ralik Chain
Ratak Chain
Kwajalein
Majuro
Jaluit I.
Ce
International Date Line

MALAYSIA
PEN. MALAYSIA
Kuala Lumpur
Singapore
Sumatera
Palembang
Jakarta
Surabaya
Java Sea
Jawa
Borneo
SARAWAK
BRUNEI
SABAH
Celebes Sea
Sulu Sea
Mindanao
Davao
4101
Sulawesi
Makassar
Halmahera
Seram
Buru
Maluku
Banda Sea
Flores Sea
Flores
Sumbawa
Sumba
Bali
Selat Sunda
Sunda Islands
I N D O N E S I A
Mindanao Trench
Yap
Caroline Is.
Melekeok
PALAU
West Caroline Basin
Eauripik Rise
FED. STATES OF MICRONESIA
East Caroline Basin
Chuuk
Pohnpei
Palikir
Micronesia
Melanesian Basin
Solomon Rise
Tarawa
Butaritari
Yaren
NAURU
Banaba
Gilbert Is.
Howland Bake...
Phoenix Is.
Abar...
Ende...
O
Pa...
K

INDIAN OCEAN
Cocos Is. (Austral.)
Christmas I. (Austral.)
Ninety East Ridge
Wharton Basin
North Australian Basin
Broken Ridge
Exmouth Plateau
North West C.
Broome
Darwin
C. Arnhem
Gulf of Carpentaria
Cairns
Townsville
Mount Isa
Alice Springs
L. Eyre
Geraldton
Perth Basin
Perth
Naturaliste Plateau
Albany
Great Australian Bight
Adelaide
Canberra
Sydney
Murray
Darling
Mt. Kosciuszko 2228
AUSTRALIA
Torres Strait
C. York
Port Moresby
Lae
New Guinea
PAPUA
Puncak Jaya 4884
PAPUA NEW GUINEA
Admiralty Is.
New Ireland
Bismarck Arch.
New Britain
Kokopo
Bougainville
8940
SOLOMON IS.
Honiara
Guadalcanal
Louisiade Arch.
Santa Cruz Is. 9165
Coral Sea Basin
Coral Sea
Great Barrier Reef
Great Dividing Ra.
Rockhampton
Brisbane
Middleton Reef
Lord Howe I. (Austral.)
Norfolk I. (Austral.)
Melanesia
VANUATU
Espíritu Santo
Port Vila
Île Chesterfield
7570
NEW CALEDONIA (Fr.)
Nouméa
Îs. Loyauté
New Caledonia Ridge
Norfolk Ridge
Lord Howe Rise
West Fiji Basin
Vanua Levu
Viti Levu
Suva
FIJI
Fongafale
TUVALU
Rotuma
Îs. Wallis & Futuna (Fr.)
Nuku'alofa
South Fiji Basin
Kermadec Is. (N.Z.)
Kerma... Trench 10,047
East Tasman Plateau
Tasman Sea
Tasman Basin
South Tasman Rise
Bass Str.
Tasmania
Hobart
Melbourne
Middleton
10,822
To...
Tr...
South Fiji Basin

NEW ZEALAND
Auckland
Wellington
Cook Strait
Christchurch
Ch...
Bounty Trough
Aoraki Mt. Cook 3753
Dunedin
Invercargill
Bounty I. (N.Z.)
Antipodes Is. (N.Z.)
Campbell Rise
Auckland Is. (N.Z.)
Campbell I. (N.Z.)
Macquarie I. (Austral.)

Île St. Paul (Fr.)
Nouvelle Amsterdam (Fr.)
Mid-Indian Ridge
Mid-Indian Ridge
SOUTHERN OCEAN
Île Crozet (Fr.)
Kerguelen (Fr.)
Heard I. (Austral.)

ft | m
12 000 | 4000
9000 | 3000
6000 | 2000
3000 | 1000
1500 | 500
600 | 200
0 | 0
600 | 200
3000 | 1000
6000 | 2000
12 000 | 4000
18 000 | 6000
24 000 | 8000
m | ft

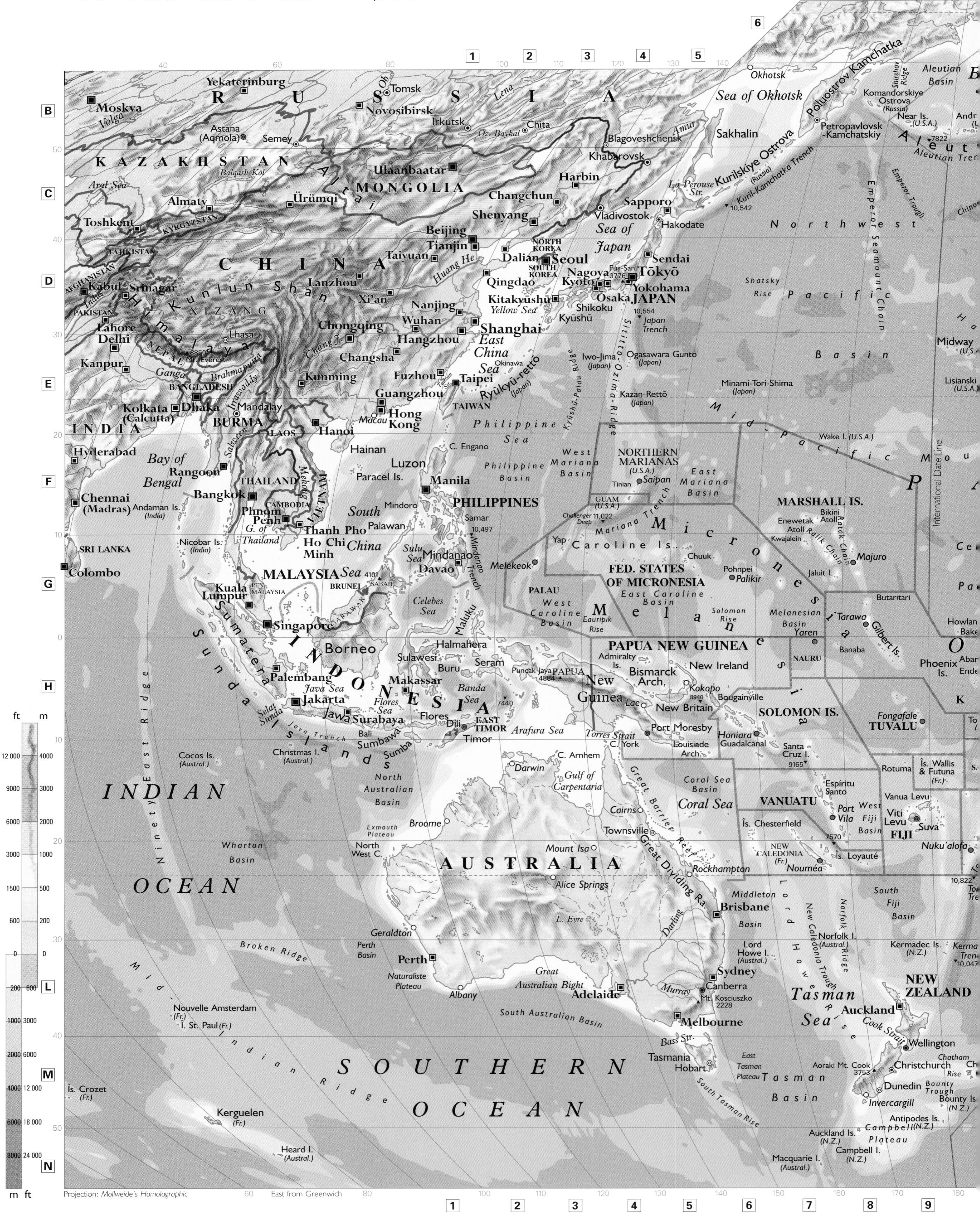

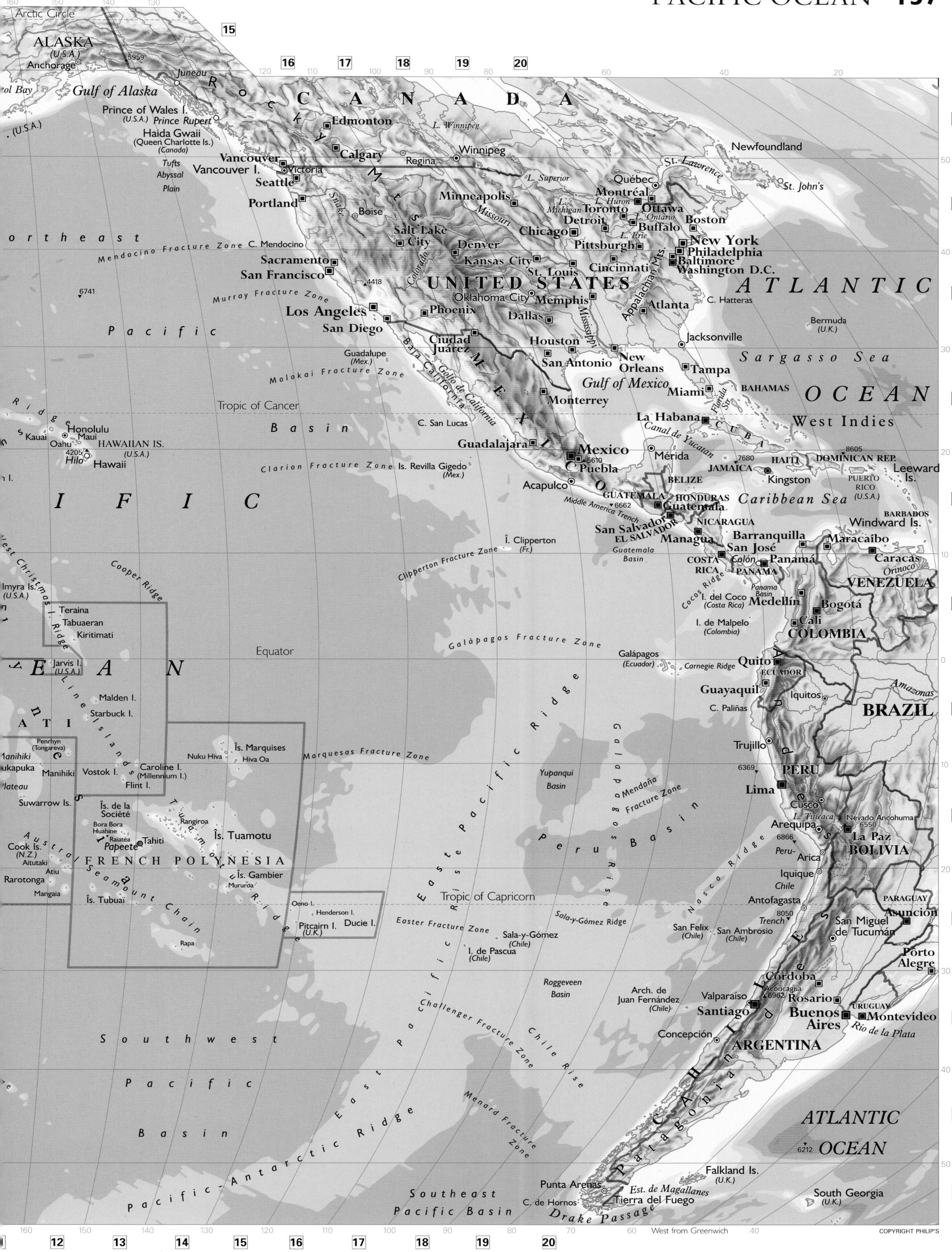

ALASKA
(U.S.A.)
Anchorage

Arctic Circle

Gulf of Alaska

Prince of Wales I.
(U.S.A.) Prince Rupert
Haida Gwaii
(Queen Charlotte Is.)
(Canada)

CANADA

Edmonton

Calgary

L. Winnipeg

Winnipeg

Regina

Newfoundland

St. Lawrence

Québec

St. John's

Tufts
Abyssal
Plain

Vancouver
Vancouver I.
Victoria
Seattle

Portland

Boise

Snake

L. Superior

Montréal

Ottawa

Boston

L. Huron
L. Michigan

Toronto
Detroit

Minneapolis

Missouri

Chicago

Pittsburgh

Buffalo
L. Erie
L. Ontario

New York

Philadelphia
Baltimore
Washington D.C.

ATLANTIC

ortheast

Mendocino Fracture Zone C. Mendocino

Sacramento
San Francisco

4418

UNITED STATES

Denver
Kansas City

St. Louis

Oklahoma City Memphis

Cincinnati

Appalachian Mts.

Atlanta

C. Hatteras

6741

Pacific

Murray Fracture Zone

Los Angeles
San Diego

Phoenix

Dallas

Houston

Bermuda
(U.K.)

Guadalupe
(Mex.)

Ciudad
Juárez

San Antonio

New
Orleans

Jacksonville

Tampa

Sargasso Sea

OCEAN

Molokai Fracture Zone

Baja California

Gulf of Mexico

Miami

BAHAMAS

West Indies

Tropic of Cancer

Basin

C. San Lucas

Gulf of California

Monterrey

La Habana

CUBA

E

Ridge

Honolulu
Oahu Maui
Kauai HAWAIIAN IS.
4205 (U.S.A.)
Hilo Hawaii

Guadalajara

Mexico
5610
Puebla

Mérida

Canal de Yucatán

7680

HAITI

8605

DOMINICAN REP.

Leeward
Is.

Clarion Fracture Zone

Is. Revilla Gigedo
(Mex.)

Acapulco

O

GUATEMALA

JAMAICA

Kingston

PUERTO
RICO
(U.S.A.)

IFIC

Î. Clipperton
(Fr.)

Middle America Trench

HONDURAS

Guatemala

Caribbean Sea

BARBADOS

Windward Is.

Clipperton Fracture Zone

6662

San Salvador
EL SALVADOR

NICARAGUA
Managua

Barranquilla

San José

Maracaibo

Caracas

Imyra Is.
(U.S.A.)

Cooper Ridge

Guatemala
Basin

COSTA
RICA

Colón
PANAMA

Panamá

I. del Coco
(Costa Rica)

Panama
Basin

Medellín

VENEZUELA

EAN

Teraina
Tabuaeran
Kiritimati

I. de Malpelo
(Colombia)

Cali
COLOMBIA

G

Equator

Galápagos Fracture Zone

Galápagos
(Ecuador)

Carnegie Ridge

Quito
ECUADOR

Bogotá

Jarvis I.
(U.S.A.)

Malden I.

Guayaquil

Iquitos

Amazonas

ATI

Starbuck I.

C. Paliñas

BRAZIL

H

Manihiki
ukapuka

Penrhyn
(Tongareva)
Manihiki

Vostok I.

Caroline I.
(Millennium I.)
Flint I.

Nuku Hiva

Îs. Marquises
Hiva Oa

Marquesas Fracture Zone

Trujillo

Plateau

Suwarrow Is.

PERU

6369

Suwarrow Is.

Yupanqui
Basin

Mendaña
Fracture Zone

Lima

Cusco
L. Titicaca

Îs. de la
Société
Bora Bora
Huahine
Raiatéa Tahiti
Papeete

Rangiroa

Îs. Tuamotu

Peru Basin

Arequipa

Nevado Ancohuma
6550

J

Cook Is.
(N.Z.)
Aitutaki
Rarotonga
Atiu
Mangaia

Austral

FRENCH POLYNESIA

Seamount Chain

Îs. Gambier
Mururoa

6866

Peru-
Arica

Nazca Ridge

La Paz
BOLIVIA

Îs. Tubuai

Tropic of Capricorn

Iquique
Chile

Oeno I.

Henderson I.
Ducie I.

Antofagasta

PARAGUAY

K

Rapa

Pitcairn I.
(U.K.)

Easter Fracture Zone

Sala-y-Gómez
(Chile)

Sala-y-Gómez Ridge

San Felix
(Chile)

San Ambrosio
(Chile)

8050
Trench

Asunción

San Miguel
de Tucumán

I. de Pascua
(Chile)

Córdoba

Aconcagua
6962

Porto
Alegre

Roggeveen
Basin

Arch. de
Juan Fernández
(Chile)

Valparaíso
Santiago

Rosario

Buenos
Aires

URUGUAY
Montevideo
Río de la Plata

L

Southwest

Pacific

Pacific-Antarctic Ridge

East Pacific Ridge

Challenger Fracture Zone

Concepción

Chile Rise

Menard Fracture Zone

ARGENTINA

Patagonian

Cordillera

ATLANTIC

M

Basin

Southeast
Pacific Basin

Punta Arenas
C. de Hornos

Est. de Magallanes
Tierra del Fuego

Drake Passage

Falkland Is.
(U.K.)

6212

South Georgia
(U.K.)

OCEAN

N

100 0 200 400 600 800 1000 1200 1400 km

1:31 100 000

100 0 200 400 600 800 1000 miles

ft m

9000 3000

6000 2000

3000 1000

1500 500

600 200

0 0

-200 600

1000 3000

2000 6000

4000 12000

6000 18000

8000 24000

m ft

Projection: Bonne

West from Greenwich

COPYRIGHT PHILIP'S

1:31 100 000

100 0   200   400   600   800   1000 1200 1400 km

100 0   200   400   600   800   1000 miles

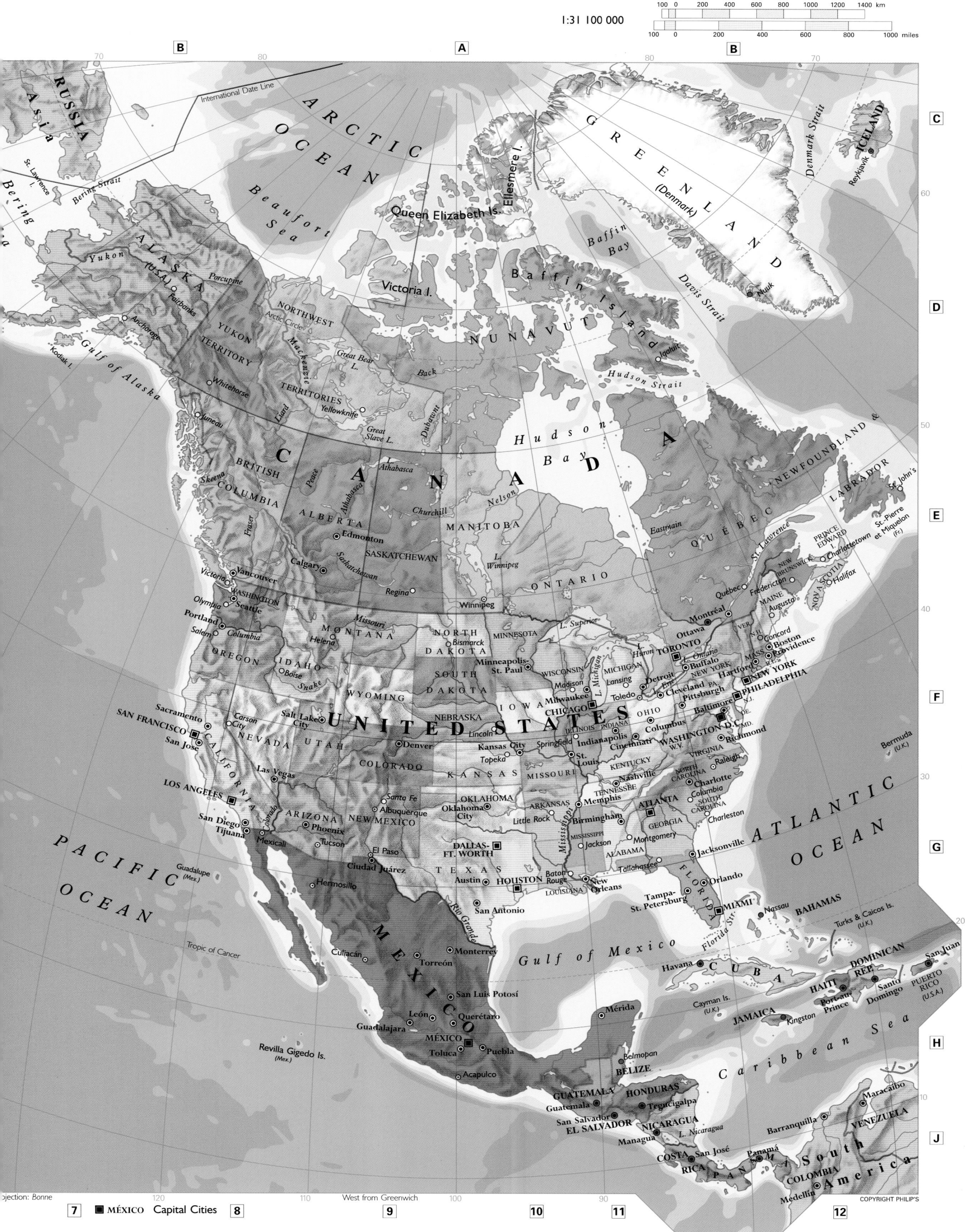

B   A   B   C

RUSSIA

Asia

Bering

St. Lawrence I.

Bering Strait

ARCTIC   OCEAN

International Date Line

Beaufort

Sea

Queen Elizabeth Is.

Ellesmere I.

GREENLAND

(Denmark)

Denmark Strait

ICELAND

Reykjavik

60

ALASKA

(USA)

Yukon

Fairbanks

Porcupine

Anchorage

Kodiak I.

Gulf of Alaska

Juneau

Whitehorse

YUKON

TERRITORY

Arctic Circle

NORTHWEST

Mackenzie

Great Bear L.

Victoria I.

Baffin Island

Baffin
Bay

Davis Strait

Nuuk

D

Liard

TERRITORIES

Yellowknife

Great Slave L.

NUNAVUT

Back

Dubawnt

Iqaluit

Hudson Strait

50

BRITISH

COLUMBIA

Skeena

Fraser

Peace

CANADA

Athabasca

ALBERTA

Edmonton

Athabasca

Saskatchewan

Nelson

Churchill

MANITOBA

Hudson

Bay

QUÉBEC

Eastmain

St. Lawrence

NEWFOUNDLAND &

LABRADOR

St. John's

St-Pierre
et Miquelon
(Fr.)

E

Victoria

Vancouver

Calgary

SASKATCHEWAN

Regina

L.
Winnipeg

Winnipeg

ONTARIO

PRINCE
EDWARD
I.

Charlottetown

NEW
BRUNSWICK

NOVA
SCOTIA

Halifax

Québec

Fredericton

40

WASHINGTON

Olympia

Seattle

Portland

Salem

Columbia

OREGON

Helena

MONTANA

Missouri

IDAHO

Boise

Snake

WYOMING

NORTH
DAKOTA

Bismarck

SOUTH
DAKOTA

MINNESOTA

Minneapolis-
St. Paul

WISCONSIN

Madison

Milwaukee

L. Superior

L.
Huron

L. Michigan

MICHIGAN

Lansing

Detroit

Ottawa

TORONTO

L.
Ontario

Buffalo

NEW
YORK

Montréal

VER.

MAINE

Augusta

N.H. Concord

Boston

MASS.

Providence

Hartford

NEW YORK

F

Sacramento

SAN FRANCISCO

San Jose

Carson
City

NEVADA

Salt Lake
City

UTAH

Denver

COLORADO

NEBRASKA

Lincoln

IOWA

Kansas City

Topeka

St.
Louis

ILLINOIS

CHICAGO

INDIANA

Indianapolis

Springfield

OHIO

Columbus

Cincinnati

Cleveland

Pittsburgh

PA.

Erie

Baltimore

WASHINGTON D.C.

MD.

Richmond

DE.

N.J.

PHILADELPHIA

Bermuda
(U.K.)

30

LOS ANGELES

San Diego

CALIFORNIA

Las Vegas

Santa Fe

ARIZONA

Phoenix

Tucson

NEW
MEXICO

Albuquerque

El Paso

OKLAHOMA

Oklahoma
City

KANSAS

MISSOURI

Little Rock

ARKANSAS

Memphis

TENNESSEE

Nashville

KENTUCKY

VIRGINIA

W.V.

Raleigh

NORTH
CAROLINA

Charlotte

Columbia

SOUTH
CAROLINA

Charleston

ATLANTIC

OCEAN

G

PACIFIC

OCEAN

Tijuana

Mexicali

Guadalupe
(Mex.)

Ciudad Juárez

Hermosillo

Rio Grande

Monterrey

TEXAS

DALLAS-
FT. WORTH

Austin

San Antonio

HOUSTON

LOUISIANA

Baton
Rouge

New
Orleans

MISSISSIPPI

Jackson

ALABAMA

Montgomery

Birmingham

GEORGIA

ATLANTA

Tallahassee

Jacksonville

FLORIDA

Orlando

Tampa-
St. Petersburg

MIAMI

Florida Str.

BAHAMAS

Nassau

Turks & Caicos Is.
(U.K.)

20

Tropic of Cancer

Culiacán

Torreón

MÉXICO

San Luis Potosí

León

Querétaro

Guadalajara

MÉXICO

Toluca

Puebla

Acapulco

Gulf of Mexico

Havana

CUBA

Cayman Is.
(U.K.)

JAMAICA

Kingston

HAITI

Port-au-
Prince

DOMINICAN
REP.

Santo
Domingo

PUERTO
RICO
(U.S.A.)

San Juan

Caribbean

Sea

Mérida

H

Revilla Gigedo Is.
(Mex.)

BELIZE

Belmopan

GUATEMALA

Guatemala

San Salvador

EL SALVADOR

HONDURAS

Tegucigalpa

NICARAGUA

Managua

L. Nicaragua

COSTA
RICA

San José

PANAMA

Barranquilla

Maracaibo

VENEZUELA

COLOMBIA

Medellín

South

America

10

J

Projection: Bonne

West from Greenwich

COPYRIGHT PHILIP'S

7   ■ MÉXICO Capital Cities   8   9   10   11   12

120   110   100   90   80

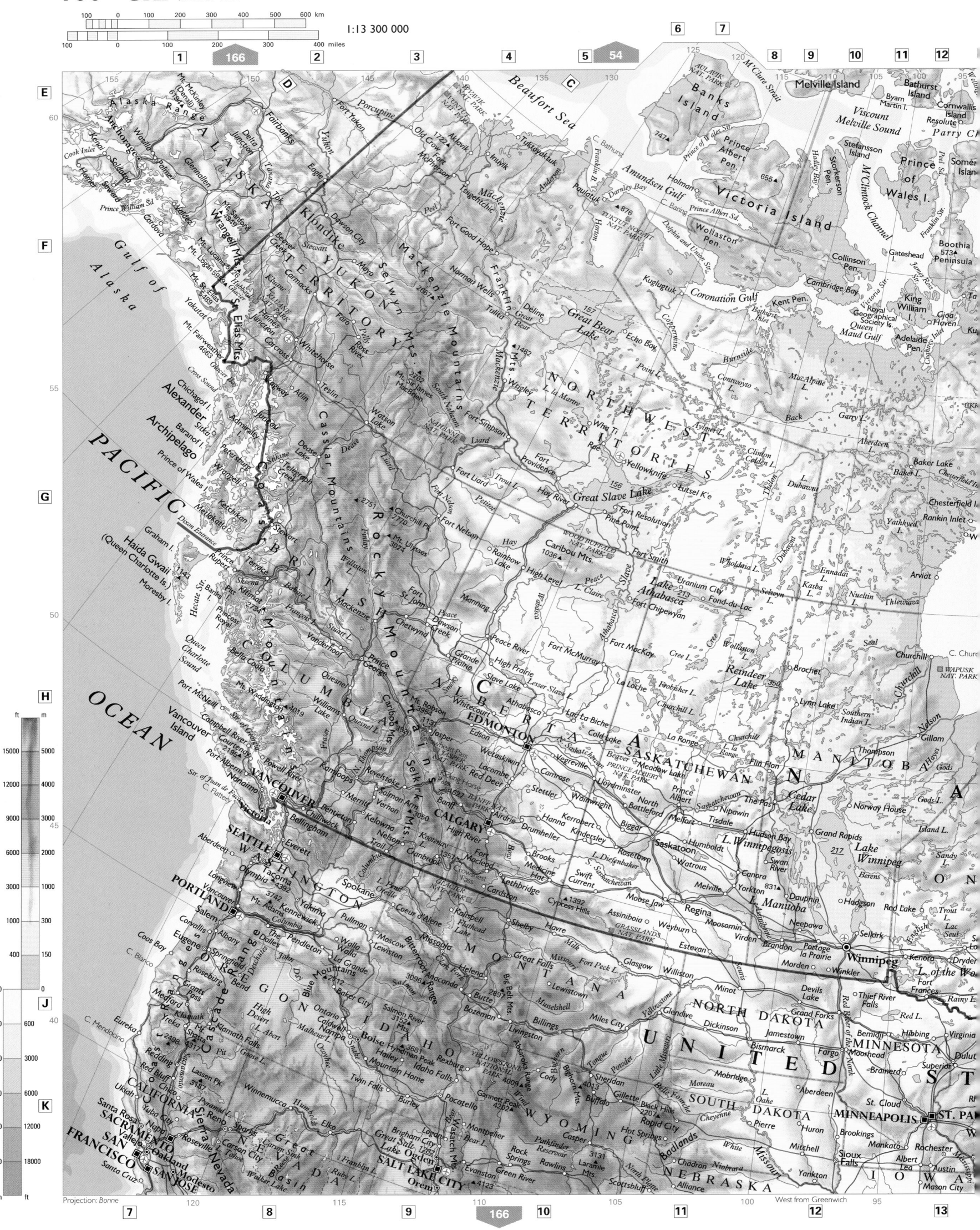

15 16 17 18 19 20 21

NORTHERN CANADA
continuation northwards on same
scale as main map

54
57

120 115 110 105 100 95 90 85 80 75 70 65 60 55 50 45 40

8 9 10 11 12 13 14 15 16 17 18 19

A
B
C
D
E
F
G
H
J

North Magnetic Pole
+ 2011
1626

ARCTIC OCEAN

C. Columbia
Lincoln Sea
Kronprins Frederik Land
2170

GREENLAND (KALAALLIT NUNAAT)
(Denmark)

QUTTINIRPAAQ NAT. PARK
2616
Barbeau Pk.
Alert
Nyeboe Land
Sermersuaq
(Humboldt Gletscher)

C. Thomas Hubbard
Meighen I.
Lake Hazen
Petermann Gletscher

Peary Channel
C. Isachsen
Greely Fjord
Eureka
Knud Rasmussen Land

Borden Island
Sverdrup Islands
Axel Heiberg Island
2210
Kane Basin
Qegertarsuaq (Thule)

Brock I.
Mackenzie King I.
Ellef Ringnes Island
Amund Ringnes
Norwegian Bay
Cornwall
Graham
Prince of Wales Icefield
Qaanaaq (Thule)
Ujummannaq (Dundas)
Kap York

Prince Patrick Island
N.W.T.
King Christian I.
Lougheed I.
Emerald I.

Queen Elizabeth Islands
NUNAVUT
Grinnell Pen.
Grise Fiord
Coburg I.
Lauge Koch Kyst

Eglinton I.
776
Parry Islands
Melville Island
Bathurst Island
Byam Martin I.
Cornwallis Island
Resolute
Lowther
Jones Sound
Devon Island
1951

Melville Bugt
2469

Viscount Melville Sound
Parry Channel
Lancaster Sound

Stefansson Island
Prince of Wales I.
Somerset Island
Peel Sd.
Prince Regent Inlet
Brodeur Pen.
Arctic Bay
Nanisivik
SIRMILIK NAT. PARK
1951
Bylot I.
Pond Inlet
Baffin Bay

Main map:

Lancaster Sound
GREENLAND (Denmark)
Baffin Bay
2469
Nunavik

Bylot I.
Eclipse Sd.
Pond Inlet
C. Adair
Clyde River
Davis Strait

SIRMILIK NAT. PARK
1951
Nanisivik
Borden Pen.

Baffin Island
C. Raper
Home B.

Igloolik
Rowley I.
Hall Beach
Prince Charles I.
Air Force I.
AUYUITTUQ NAT. PARK
2147
Cumberland Peninsula
Qikiqtarjuaq
C. Dyer

Foxe Basin
Spicer Is.
Koukdjuak
Nettilling L.
Pangnirtung
Cumberland Sd.
Hoare B.
C. Mercy

Melville Peninsula
Taverner Bay
Amadjuak L.

NUNAVUT
Repulse Bay
Vansittart I.
C. Dorchester
Foxe Pen.
Hall Peninsula
Meta Incognita Peninsula
Frobisher Bay

Southampton I.
Coral Harbour
Bell Pen.
Mill I.
Salisbury
Kinngait
Iqaluit
Kimmirut
Resolution I.

Coats I.
Nottingham I.
Charles I.
Salluit
Hudson Strait
C. Chidley
Killiniq
TORNGAT MTS. NAT. PARK

Mansel I.
Digges Is.
Ivujivik
642
Quaqtaq
Akpatok I.
1652
Mt. Caubvick

Kangiqsujuaq
Cratère du Nouveau-Québec 657
Kangirsuk
Ungava Bay
Torngat Mts.
Hebron
Smith I.
Péninsule d'Ungava
Arnaud
Kangiqsualujjuaq
Nain
Labrador

Puvirnituq
L. Payne
Feuilles
Kuujjuaq
George
Hopedale
Labrador Sea
3809

Ottawa Is.
257
Inukjuak
Baleine
C. Harrison

Mélèzes
Rigolet
Cartwright
Port Hope Simpson
NEWFOUNDLAND & LABRADOR

Sleeper Is.
King George Is.
L. Minto
L. à l'Eau Claire
Smallwood Res.
North West River
Happy Valley-Goose Bay
128
Belle Isle
St. Anthony

Sanikiluaq
Bakers Dozen Is.
Grande Baleine
L. Bienville
Schefferville
Kawawachikamach
Churchill
Churchill Falls
Str. of Belle Isle
Baie Verte
Grey Is.

Belcher Is.
C. Henrietta Maria
Kanaaupscow
Petitsikapau L.
Esker
Ashuanipi
Deer Lake
Long Range Mts.
Notre Dame B.
Lewisporte
Bonavista

James Bay
Pte. Louis XIV
Chisasibi
La Grande
Labrador City
Fermont
Natashquan
Corner Brook
835
Grand Falls-Windsor
Gander
Trinity B.
Carbonear

Twin Is.
Akimiski I.
Wemindji
Eastmain
Eastman
Rupert
L. Mistassini
Gagnon
Mts. Otish
1135
Groulx
1104 Mts.
Moisie
Havre-St-Pierre
Î. d'Anticosti
Stephenville
Newfoundland
St. John's
Placentia
Avalon Pen.
C. Race

Attawapiskat
Charlton I.
Waskaganish
L. Albanel
Romaine
St-Augustin
Dét. de Jacques-Cartier
Placentia B.
Marystown

Fort Albany
Nottaway
Rés. Gouin
Sept-Îles
320
Port-Cartier
Dét. d'Honguedo
Gaspé
Gulf of St. Lawrence
Cabot Strait
Channel-Port-aux-Basques
C. Ray

Moosonee
Harricana
Bell
Chibougamau
Dolbeau-Mistassini
Alma
Baie-Comeau
1268
Pén. de la Gaspésie
Matane
Îs. de la Madeleine

Nakina
Kenogami
Cochrane
Amos
L. Matagami
Matagami
Chicoutimi
Rimouski
Campbellton
Bathurst
PRINCE EDWARD
Cape Breton I.
Sydney
Glace Bay

Geraldton
Hearst
Kapuskasing
Rés. Cabonga
Roberval
Jonquière
1172
Rivière-du-Loup
Grand Falls
Miramichi
Summerside
Charlottetown
Port Hawkesbury
New Antigonish

Marathon
Oba
Kirkland Lake
Val-d'Or
La Tuque
St-Jean
Edmundston
NEW BRUNSWICK
Moncton
Amherst
Truro
Glasgow

Bay
Wawa
Timmins
Chapleau
New Liskeard
Rouyn-Noranda
Shawinigan
Trois-Rivières
Thetford Mines
St-Georges
Woodstock
Fredericton
NOVA SCOTIA
New Glasgow
Dartmouth
Halifax

Sault Ste. Marie
Elliot Lake
Sudbury
North Bay
Mont-Laurier
Joliette
St-Hyacinthe
Sherbrooke
MAINE
Saint John
Bay of Fundy
Kentville
Bridgewater

Manistique
Georgian Bay
Parry Sound
Pembroke
MONTRÉAL
Granby
Champlain
Bangor
Digby
Liverpool

L. Superior
183
Sault Ste. Marie
Manitoulin
Huntsville
OTTAWA
Hull
Outaouais
Augusta
Yarmouth
C. Sable

Petoskey
Lake Huron
Owen Sound
Orillia
Peterborough
Kingston
Brockville
VERMONT
Montpelier
Portland
NEW HAMPSHIRE
Concord
Manchester

Traverse City
Georgian Bay
Barrie
Belleville
1629
Adirondack Mts.
Burlington
Lewiston
Lowell

Cadillac
Green Bay
Owen Sound
Oshawa
L. Ontario
ROCHESTER
Syracuse
Albany
MASS.
BOSTON
C. Cod

Sheboygan
L. Michigan
TORONTO
Kitchener
Hamilton
Niagara Falls
BUFFALO
NEW YORK
Springfield
R.I.
PROVIDENCE
CONN.
HARTFORD

MILWAUKEE
Grand Rapids
Flint
Sarnia
London
Erie
PENNSYLVANIA
Elmira
Binghamton
New Haven

Lansing
DETROIT
Windsor
L. Erie
CLEVELAND
Toledo

14 16 17 18 19 20

COPYRIGHT PHILIP'S

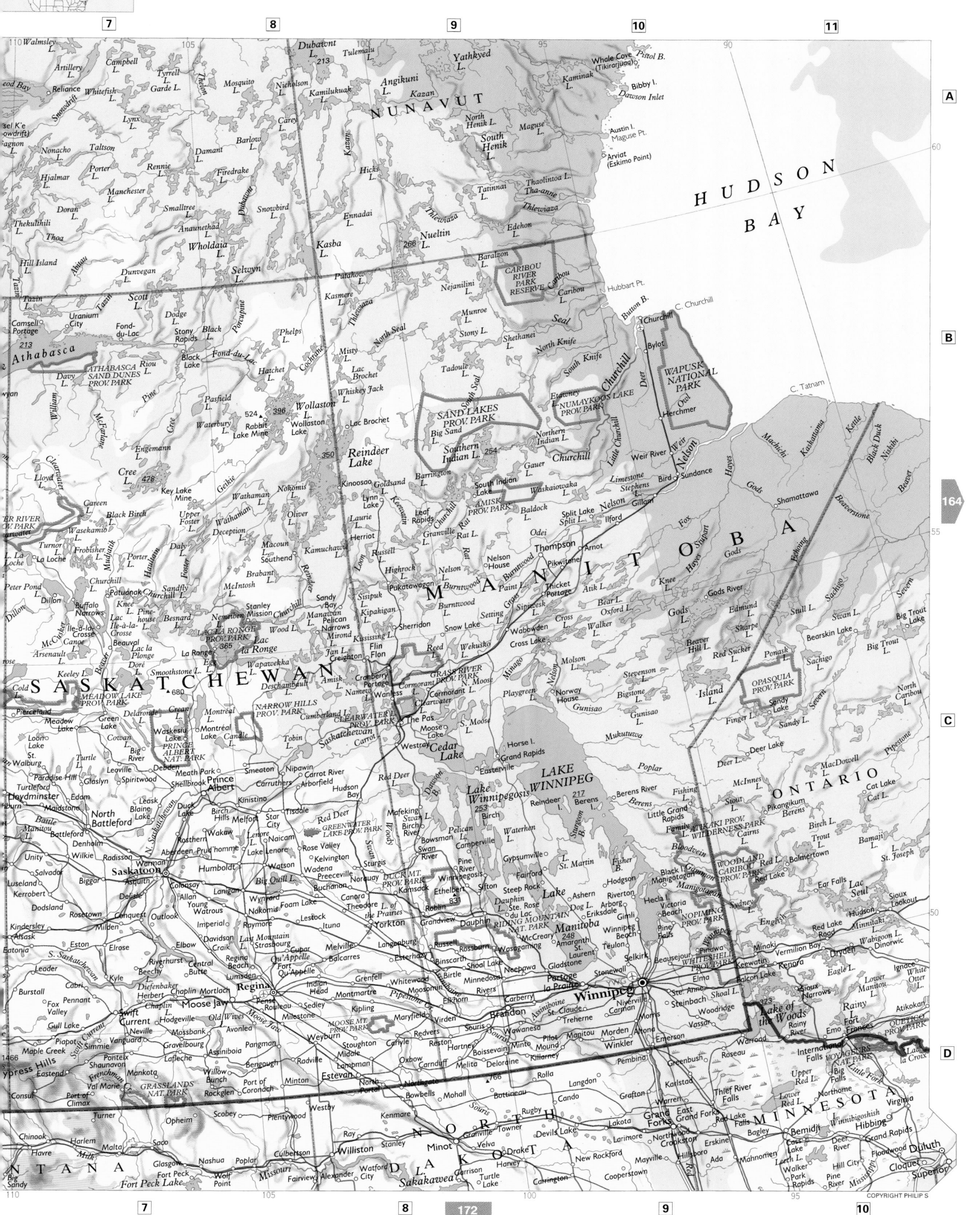

HUDSON BAY

NUNAVUT

SASKATCHEWAN

MANITOBA

ONTARIO

MINNESOTA

NORTH DAKOTA

MONTANA

LAKE WINNIPEG

Lake Winnipegosis

Cedar Lake

Reindeer Lake

Lake Athabasca

WAPUSK NATIONAL PARK

CARIBOU RIVER PARK RESERVE

SAND LAKES PROV. PARK

NUMAYKOOS LAKE PROV. PARK

GRASS RIVER PROV. PARK

OPASQUIA PROV. PARK

WOODLAND CARIBOU PROV. PARK

NOPIMING PROV. PARK

WHITESHELL PROV. PARK

PRINCE ALBERT NAT. PARK

MEADOW LAKE PROV. PARK

GRASSLANDS NAT. PARK

DUCK MT. PROV. PARK

RIDING MOUNTAIN NAT. PARK

Winnipeg

Regina

Saskatoon

Prince Albert

Brandon

Churchill

Moose Jaw

Thompson

Flin Flon

The Pas

Dauphin

Yorkton

Selkirk

Lake of the Woods

1:13 300 000

100 0 100 200 300 400 500 600 km
100 0 100 200 300 400 miles

| 11 | 12 | 13 | 14 | 16 | 160 | 17 |

G

40

H

J

35

K

PACIFIC OCEAN

Inset map

Anchorage → Washington D.C. 3363 miles 5412 km
Anchorage → San Francisco 2010 miles 3234 km
Anchorage → Honolulu 2785 miles 4482 km
San Francisco → Washington D.C. 2438 miles 3923 km
Honolulu → San Francisco 2395 miles 3854 km

Tropic of Cancer

West from Greenwich

Alaska map

ALASKA
on same scale

107

RUSSIA

Koryakskoye Nagorye

BERING SEA

Aleutian Islands

Near Islands
Rat Islands
Andreanof Islands
Fox Islands

CHUKCHI SEA

ARCTIC OCEAN

Bering Strait

International Date Line

St. Lawrence I. (U.S.A.)

St. Matthew I.

Nunivak I.

Pribilof Is.

St. Paul I.
St. George I.

Yukon Delta

Kuskokwim Mountains

Bristol Bay

Alaska Peninsula

Kodiak I.

Gulf of Alaska

North Slope

Brooks Range

A L A S K A (U.S.A.)

Yukon Flats

Alaska Range

Mt. McKinley (Denali) 6194

Chugach Mts.

Anchorage

Fairbanks

Projection: Albers' Equal Area with two standard parallels

West from Greenwich

| 4 | 5 | 6 | 7 | 8 | 9 | 10 | 11 | 12 |

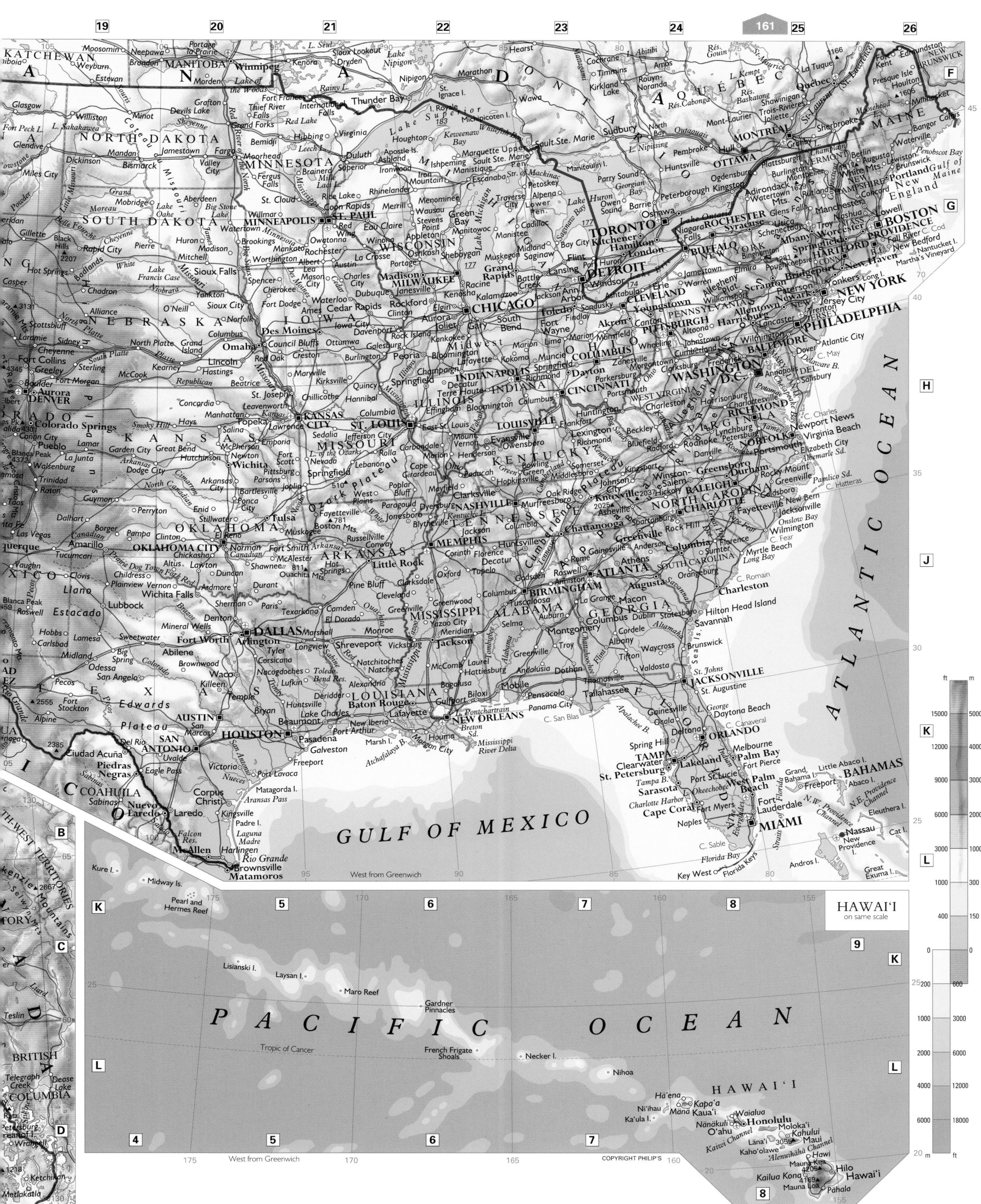

KATCHEWAN
MANITOBA
Winnipeg
Lake of the Woods
CANADA
QUÉBEC
NEW BRUNSWICK

NORTH DAKOTA
MINNESOTA
ONTARIO
MAINE

SOUTH DAKOTA
MINNEAPOLIS
ST. PAUL
WISCONSIN
Lake Superior
Lake Michigan
Lake Huron
TORONTO
OTTAWA
MONTRÉAL

NEBRASKA
IOWA
MILWAUKEE
CHICAGO
DETROIT
Lake Erie
CLEVELAND
BUFFALO
ROCHESTER
NEW YORK
BOSTON
PROVIDENCE
HARTFORD

DENVER
Colorado Springs
KANSAS
KANSAS CITY
ST. LOUIS
INDIANAPOLIS
OHIO
COLUMBUS
PITTSBURGH
PHILADELPHIA
BALTIMORE
WASHINGTON D.C.

Pueblo
OKLAHOMA
OKLAHOMA CITY
Tulsa
MISSOURI
LOUISVILLE
CINCINNATI
KENTUCKY
WEST VIRGINIA
VIRGINIA
RICHMOND
NORFOLK

Amarillo
ARKANSAS
Little Rock
MEMPHIS
NASHVILLE
TENNESSEE
NORTH CAROLINA
RALEIGH
CHARLOTTE

Lubbock
DALLAS
Fort Worth
Arlington
BIRMINGHAM
ATLANTA
SOUTH CAROLINA
Charleston

TEXAS
AUSTIN
SAN ANTONIO
HOUSTON
LOUISIANA
Baton Rouge
MISSISSIPPI
ALABAMA
GEORGIA
Savannah
JACKSONVILLE

COAHUILA
Nuevo Laredo
Laredo
Brownsville
Matamoros
NEW ORLEANS
GULF OF MEXICO
ORLANDO
TAMPA
St. Petersburg
FLORIDA
MIAMI
BAHAMAS

ATLANTIC OCEAN

HAWAI'I
on same scale

5 **6** **7** **8** **9**

Pearl and Hermes Reef
Lisianski I.
Laysan I.
Maro Reef
Gardner Pinnacles

P A C I F I C   O C E A N

Tropic of Cancer
French Frigate Shoals
Necker I.
Nihoa
HAWAI'I
Honolulu
O'ahu
Maui
Hawai'i
Hilo

4 **5** **6** **7** **8**

West from Greenwich

COPYRIGHT PHILIP'S

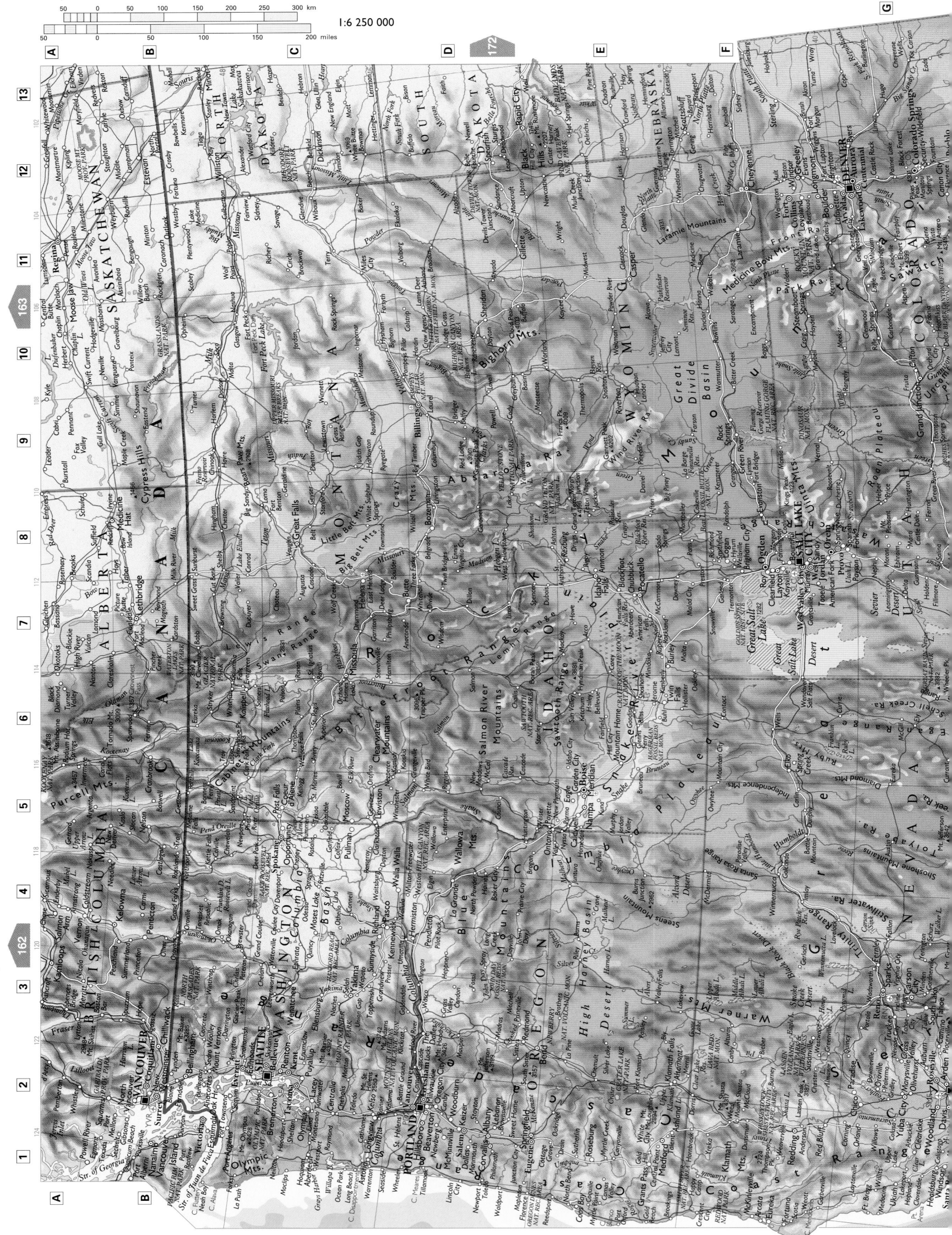

1:6 250 000

Lava fields

Projection: Albers' Equal Area with two standard parallels

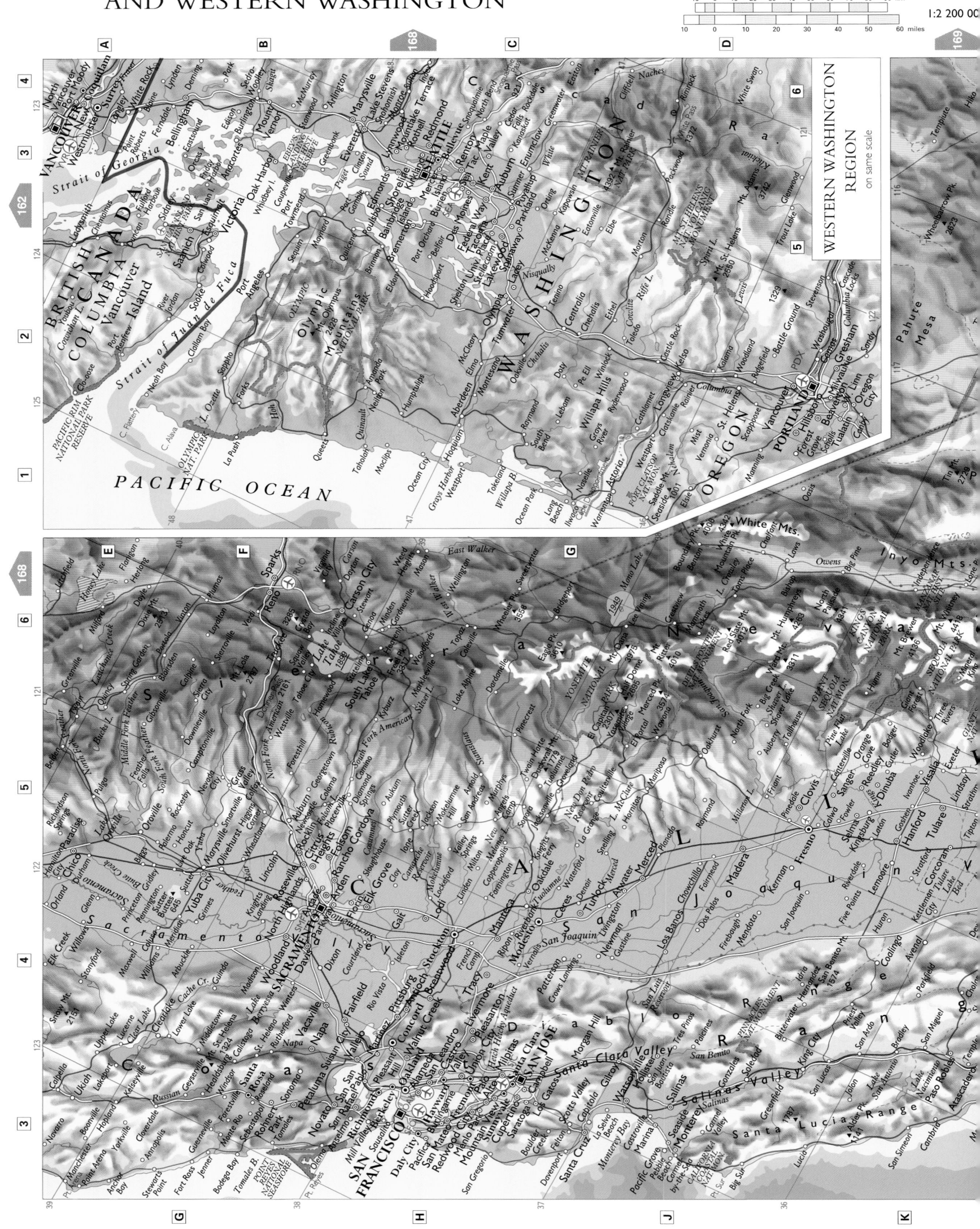

1:2 200 000

WESTERN WASHINGTON REGION
on same scale

Lava fields

West from Greenwich

Projection: Bonne

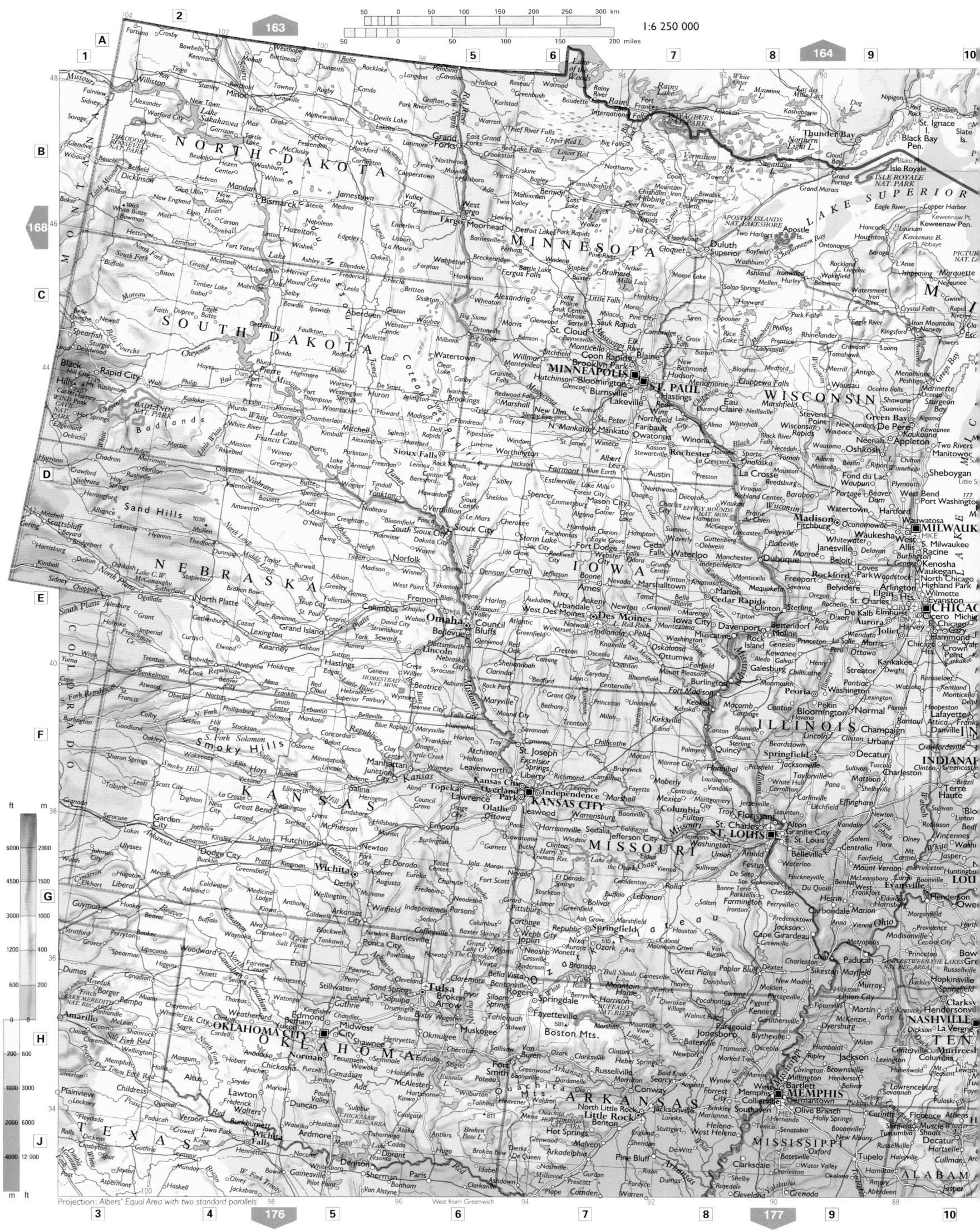

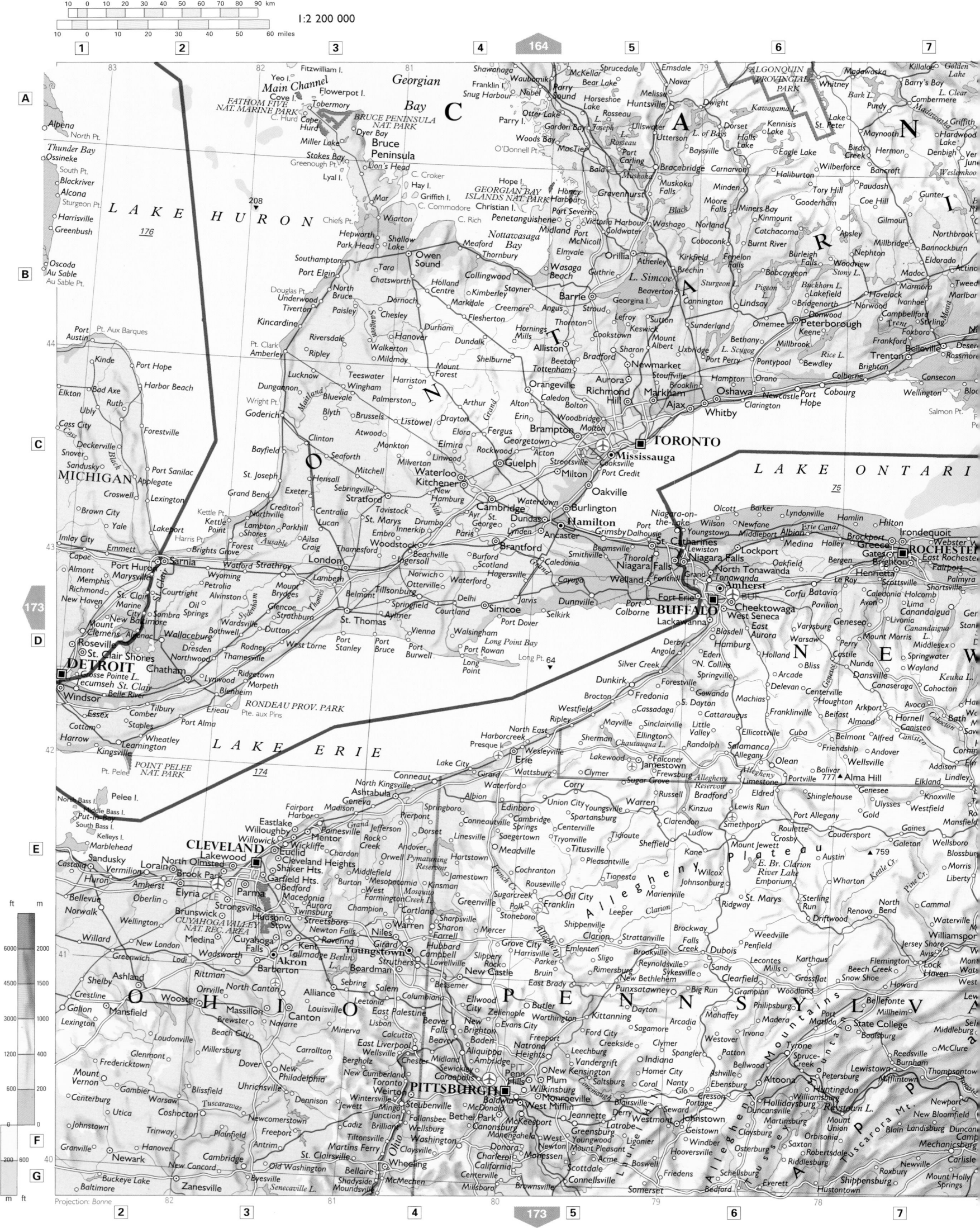

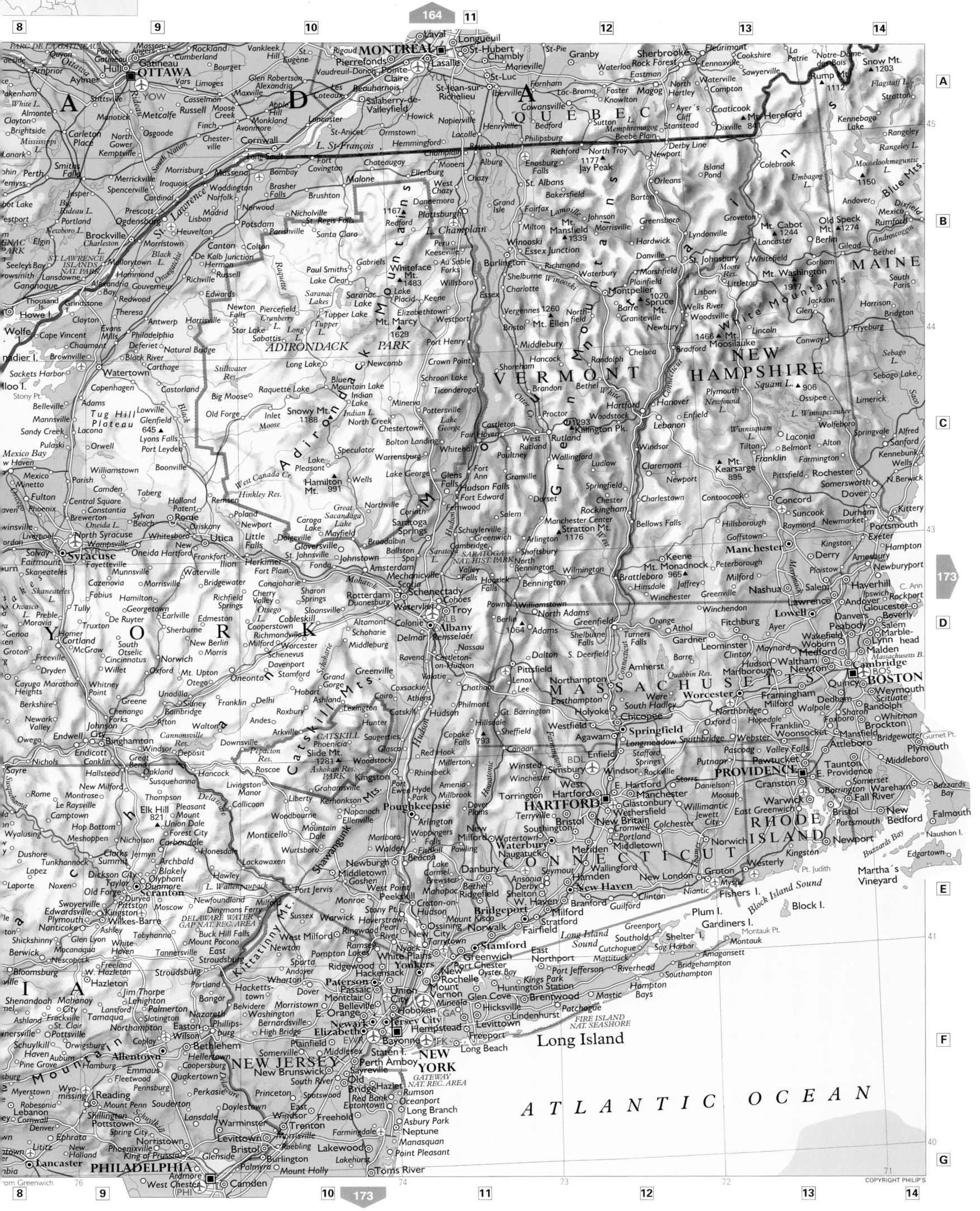

50   0   50   100   150   200   250   300 km

1:6 250 000

50   0   50   100   150   200 miles

1:2 200 000

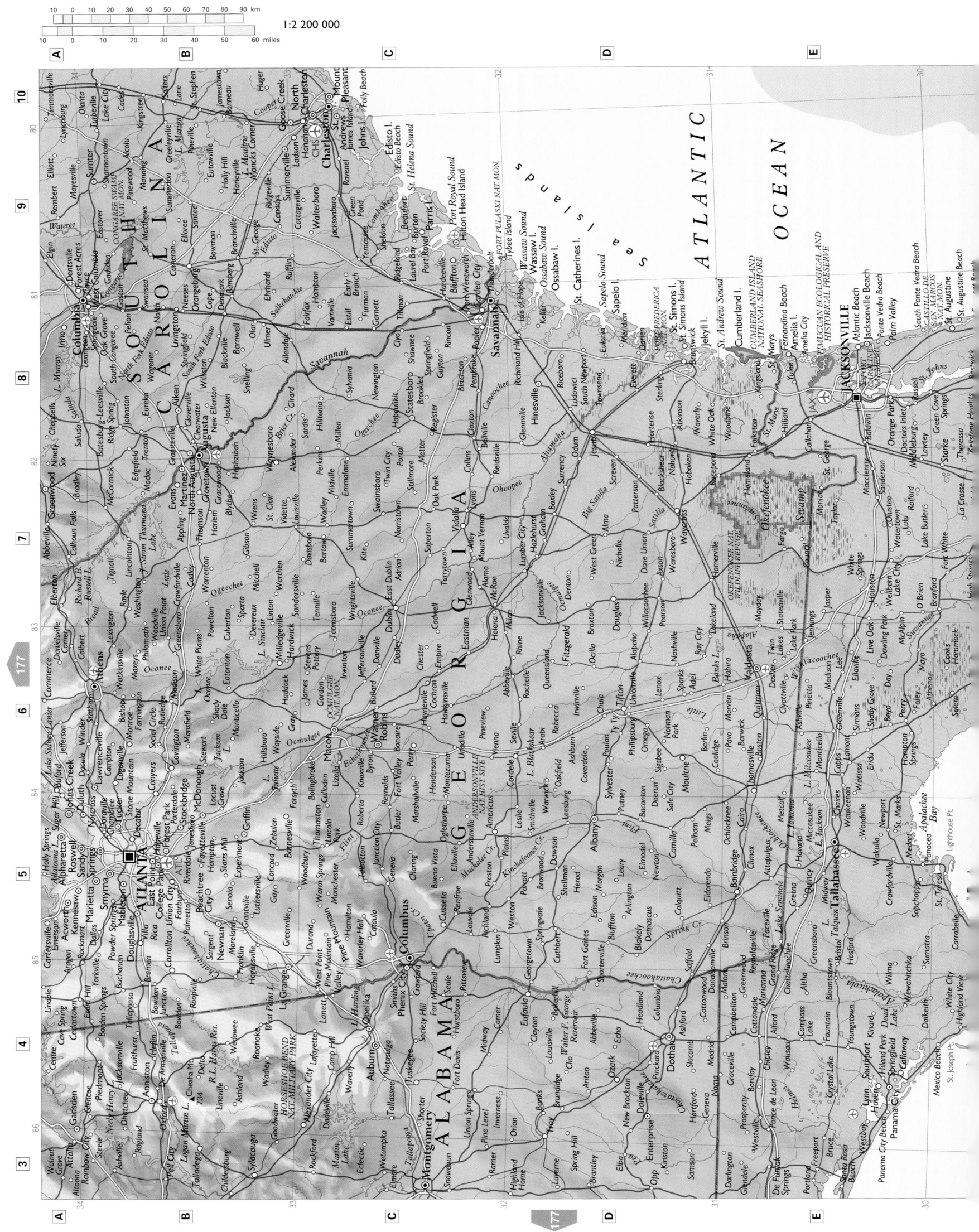

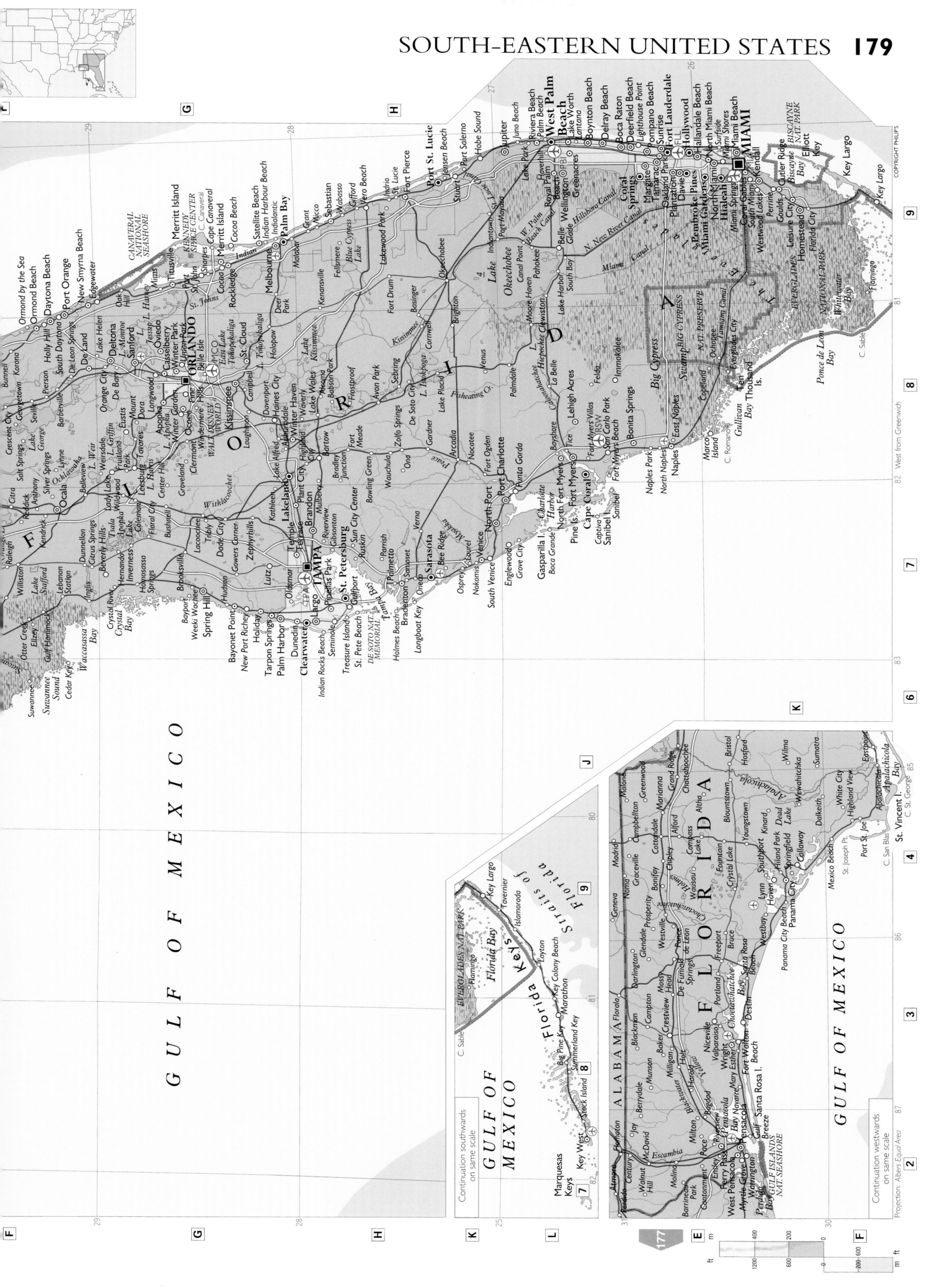

GULF OF MEXICO

FLORIDA

Continuation southwards
on same scale

Continuation westwards
on same scale

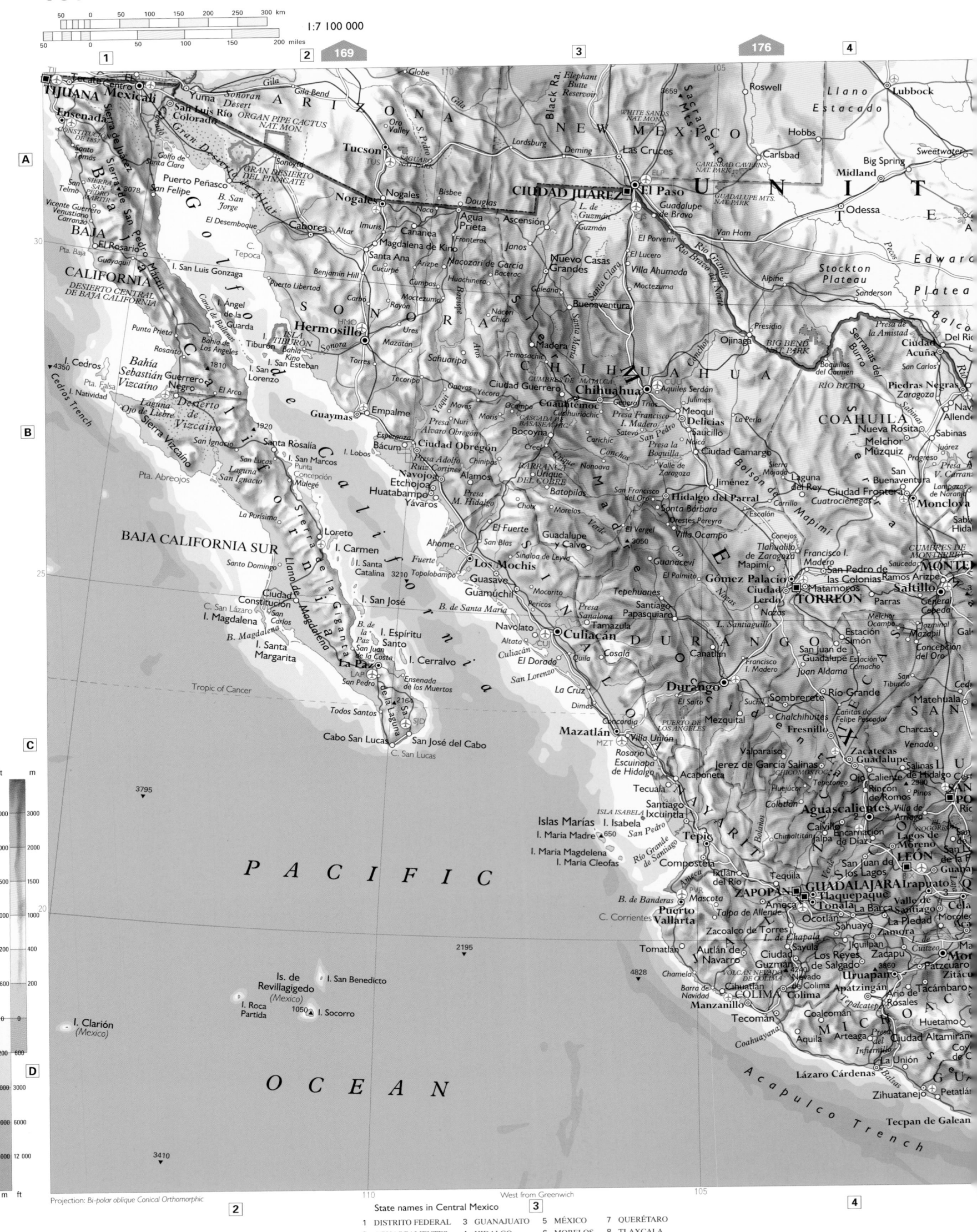

1:7 100 000

50 0 50 100 150 200 250 300 km
50 0 50 100 150 200 miles

Projection: Bi-polar oblique Conical Orthomorphic

ft m
9000 3000
6000 2000
4500 1500
3000 1000
1200 400
600 200
0 0
200 600
1000 3000
2000 6000
4000 12 000
m ft

West from Greenwich

State names in Central Mexico

| 1 DISTRITO FEDERAL | 3 GUANAJUATO | 5 MÉXICO | 7 QUERÉTARO |
| 2 AGUASCALIENTES | 4 HIDALGO | 6 MORELOS | 8 TLAXCALA |

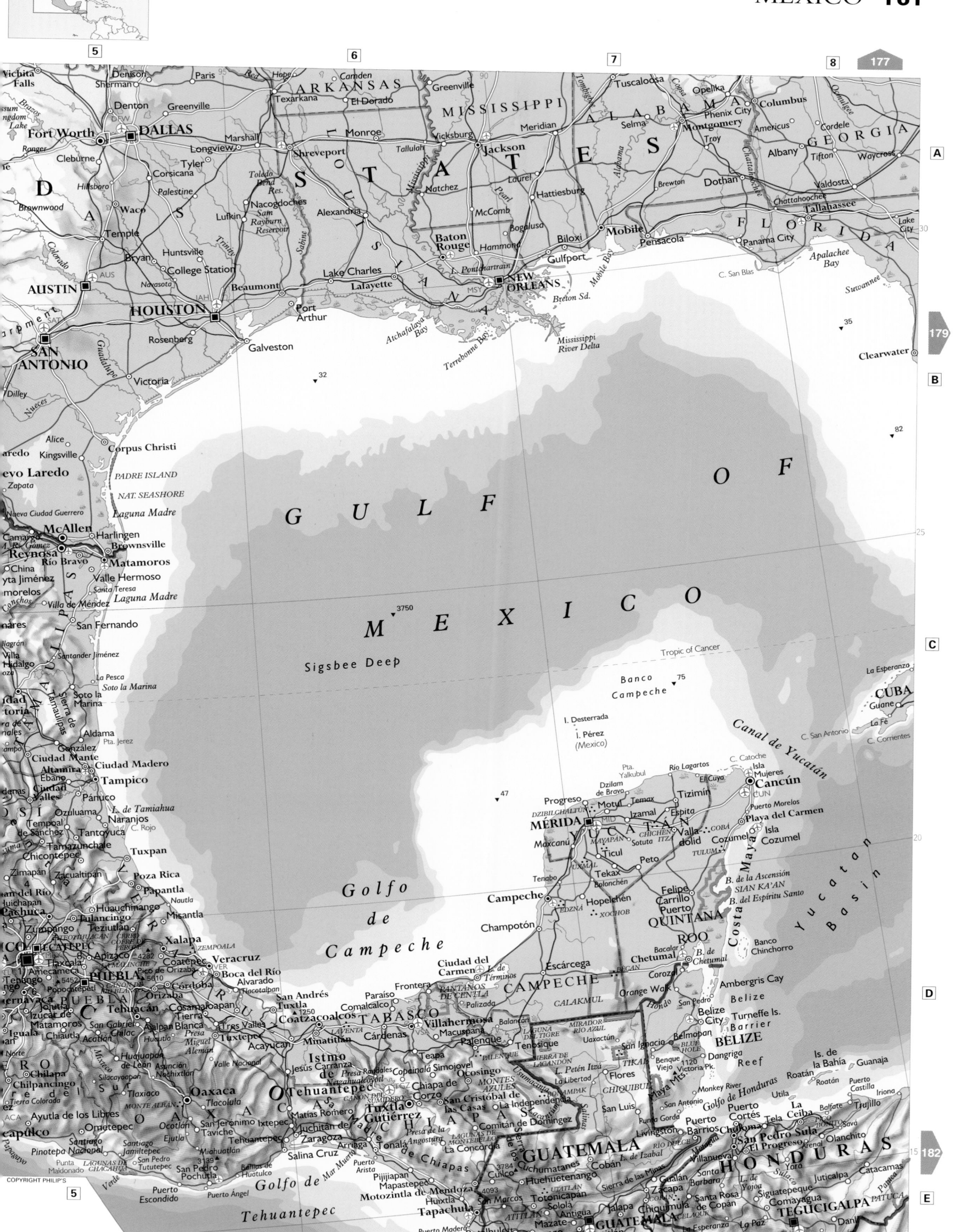

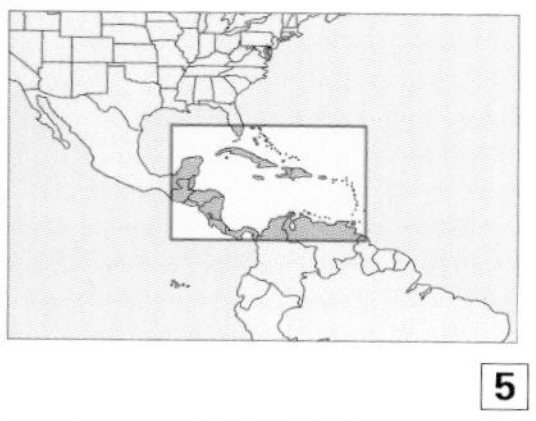

Inset maps

PUERTO RICO (d) 1:2 700 000
10 0 10 20 30 40 50 km
10 0 10 20 30 miles

ATLANTIC OCEAN
PUERTO RICO (U.S.A.)
Pta. Aguijereada · Isabela · Barceloneta · Arecibo · Manatí · Vega · Baja · Río Grande
Aguadilla · San Sebastián · Utuado · Bayamón · SAN JUAN · Carolina · Fajardo · Dewey
Mayagüez · Adjuntas · Cordillera Central · Caguas · Humacao · Naguabo · Culebra · Vieques
San Germán · Cerro de Punta 1338 · Mts. de Uroyan · Yauco · Cayey · Coamo · Yabucoa · Esperanza
Pta. Aguila · Guánica · Ponce · Guayama · I. Caja de Muertos

VIRGIN ISLANDS (e) 1:1 800 000
10 0 10 20 30 km
10 0 10 20 miles
Rufling Pt. · The Settlement · Anegada · East Pt.
Virgin Islands (U.K.)
Jost Van Dyke I. · Great Camanoe · Virgin Gorda · Spanish Town
Virgin Is. (U.S.A.) · Hans Lollik I. · Guana I. · 521 · Road Town · Tortola
Charlotte Amalie · Cruz Bay · St. John I. · Peter I.
St. Thomas I. · VIRGIN IS.

ST. LUCIA (f) 1:890 000
5 0 10 km
5 0 5 10 miles
Cap Point · Pte. Hardy
Gros Islet · Esperance Bay
Castries · Marquis
Girard
Anse la Raye · Canaries · Millet · Dennery
Soufrière · Mt. Gimie 950
Soufrière Bay · 750 Petit Piton · Micoud · Trou Gras Pt.
Gros Piton Pt. · 796 Gros Piton · Vierge Pt.
Choiseul · UVF · ST. LUCIA
Laborie · Vieux Fort · C. Moule à Chique

BARBADOS (g) 1:890 000
5 0 10 km
5 0 10 miles
ATLANTIC OCEAN
Crab Hill · North Point · Spring Hall
Fustic · Portland · Boscobelle
Speightstown · Belleplaine · 245
Westmoreland · Bathsheba · 340 · BARBADOS
Alleynes Bay · Mt. Hillaby · Hillcrest
Holetown · Martin's Bay
Jackson · Bridgefield · Massiah Street
Black Rock · Ellerton · Edey · Ragged Pt.
Bridgetown · Ivy · Oistins · Six Cross Roads
Carlisle Bay · BGI · The Crane
Worthing · Oistins Bay · St. Martins
South Point · Chancery Lane

Main map

ATLANTIC OCEAN

Town · Bight · Cat I. · Salvador I. · Conception I. · Rum Cay · Long I.
Clarence Town · Samana Cay
Tropic of Cancer
Crooked I. · Plana Cays · Mayaguana I.
Albert Town · Snug Corner · Acklins I.
Mira por vos Cay
Hogsty Reef · Little Inagua I.
Lake Rose · Great Inagua I.
Matthew Town · INAGUA
Moa · ALEJANDRO DE HUMBOLDT · Baracoa
Tanamo · Maisi · Pta. de Maisi · Paso de los Vientos (Windward Passage)
Î. de la Tortue
Cap-Haïtien · Monte Cristi · LA ISABELA · Santiago de los Caballeros · San Francisco de Macorís
Puerto Rico Trench · Milwaukee Deep 8605
Jean Rabel · Port-de-Paix · Puerto Plata · La Vega · Nagua · Samaná
Fort Liberté · Navidad Bank
Fort · Gonaïves · Central · Pico Duarte 3175 · Sánchez · Sabana de la Mar
Foux · G. de la Gonâve · Hinche · Hato Mayor · C. Engaño
Jérémie · Î. de la Gonâve · HAITI · San Juan · San Pedro de Macorís · Highey
Dame · St-Marc · PORT-AU-PRINCE · DOMINICAN REP. · La Romana
Massif de la Hotte · Petit Goave · Jacmel · 2680 · L. Enriquillo · SANTO DOMINGO · Isla Saona
Les Cayes · Aquin · SIERRA DE BAHORUCO · Barahona · San Cristóbal · B. de Yuma · I. Mona (U.S.A.)
Pointe-à-Gravois · Î. à Vache · Pedernales
Hispaniola · PUERTO RICO (U.S.A.)

Bayamón · SAN JUAN · Carolina · Virgin Gorda · Anegada · Virgin Is. (U.K.) · Sombrero (U.K.)
Aguadilla · Arecibo · 1338 · Fajardo · St. Thomas · Road Town · Tortola · Anguilla (U.K.)
Mayagüez · Ponce · Caguas · Culebra · Charlotte Amalie · Virgin Is. (U.S.A.) · St.-Martin (Fr.)
Guayama · Vieques · Christiansted · St. Maarten (Neth.) · St.-Barthélemy (Fr.)
Frederiksted · St. Croix (U.S.A.) · St. Eustatius (Neth.) · Barbuda
Basseterre · St. Liamuiga 1156 · ANTIGUA & BARBUDA
Nevis · ST. KITTS & NEVIS · St. John's · Antigua
Redonda · Soufrière · Montserrat · Hills · Ste-Rose · Le Moule · La Désirade
(U.K.) · 914 · GUADELOUPE (Fr.) · Pointe-à-Pitre
Portsmouth · 1447 · Basse-Terre · Marie-Galante (Fr.) · Grand-Bourg
Morne Diablotin · DOMINICA · I. des Saintes (Fr.) · Dominica Passage
Roseau · MORNE TROIS PITONS · DOM · Martinique Passage
Mt. Pelée 1397 · Ste-Marie
Fort-de-France · Le Robert · Rivière-Pilote · MARTINIQUE (Fr.)
FDF · St. Lucia Channel
Castries · ST. LUCIA
Soufrière · UVF · St. Vincent Passage
Soufrière 1234 · St. Vincent
SVD · Kingstown · ST. VINCENT & THE GRENADINES
Bequia · The Grenadines
Canouan · Tobago · BARBADOS
Bridgetown · BGI · Speightstown · 340
Carriacou · St. George's · GRENADA · GND · 840

CARIBBEAN SEA
Antilles · Muertas Trough 5500
Beata Ridge · 4530
Venezuelan Basin · 5420
Colombian Basin
I. de Aves (Venezuela)
Aves Ridge
Leeward Islands · Lesser Antilles · Windward Islands · Grenada Basin
ABC Islands · Lesser Antilles
Aruba (Neth.) · Oranjestad · AUA · Curaçao · Willemstad · CUR · Bonaire
I. Las Aves (Ven.) · I. Orchila (Ven.) · I. Blanquilla (Ven.) · Is. Los Hermanos (Ven.)
Pta. Gallinas · Is. Los Roques (Ven.) · Is. Los Testigos (Ven.)
I. La Tortuga (Ven.) · I. de Margarita · NUEVA ESPARTA · La Asunción · Porlamar · Tobago
COLOMBIA · GUAJIRA · MACUIRA · Pta. Espada · Pen. de Paraguaná · Puerto Cumarebo · Cerro El Copey 920 · Scarborough
Santa Marta · Ríohacha · Uribia · Maicao · Punto Fijo · MÉDANOS DE CORO · Cariaco · Carúpano · Güiria · Galera Point
TAYRONA · SA. NEVADA DE SANTA MARTA · Pen. de la Guajira · Punta Cardón · La Vela · I. La Tortuga · La Blanquilla · Arima · Trinidad
SOLEDAD · Ciénaga · San Rafael · FALCÓN · Mene de Mauroa · Tucacas · HENRI PITTIER · Maiquetía · Cumaná · SUCRE · Pozo Claro · Río Claro · TRINIDAD & TOBAGO
Santa Rita · La Concepción · LARA · San Felipe · Puerto Cabello · CARACAS · Carúpano · Cariaco · POS · Port of Spain · 940
MARACAIBO · MAR · Cabimas · Ciudad Ojeda · CARABOBO · MARACAY · Los Teques · MIRANDA · Río Chico · La Cruz · Barcelona · Caripito · Serpent's Mouth
VALLEDUPAR · Villa del Rosario · Machiques · Lago de Maracaibo · BARQUISIMETO · VALENCIA · Villa de Cura · San Juan de los Morros · El Sombrero · 2640 · Caicara · Maturín · MARIUSA DELTA
MAGDALENA · Plato · CÉSAR · ZULIA · Mene Grande · YARACUY · ARAURE · GUARICO · Valle de la Pascua · ANZOÁTEGUI · Santa María de Ipire · Anaco · Cantaura · El Tigre · MONAGAS · Tucupita · AMACURO
Calamar · El Banco · MÉRIDA · SA. NEVADA · Barinas · PORTUGUESA · Guanare · Calabozo · Soledad · Ciudad Guayana
Mompós · Magangué · NORTE DE SANTANDER · 4981 · Pico Bolívar · Libertad · BARINAS · San Fernando de Apure · Sierra Imataca · El Pao
Ayapel · Ocaña · Cúcuta · TÁCHIRA · Santa Bárbara · San Carlos · VENEZUELA · Achaguas · Orinoco · Ciudad Bolívar · Upata · El Callao
Caucasia · Simití · Bruzual · Apure · Caicara · Mapire · Embalse de Guri · Guasipati · Tumeremo

COPYRIGHT PHILIP'S

(elevation scale in feet and metres)
ft: 600 6000 12 000 18 000 24 000
m: 200 2000 4000 6000 8000

Projection: Lambert's Azimuthal Equal Area

COPYRIGHT PHILIP'S

1:31 100 000

Projection: Lambert's Azimuthal Equal Area

COPYRIGHT PHILIP'S

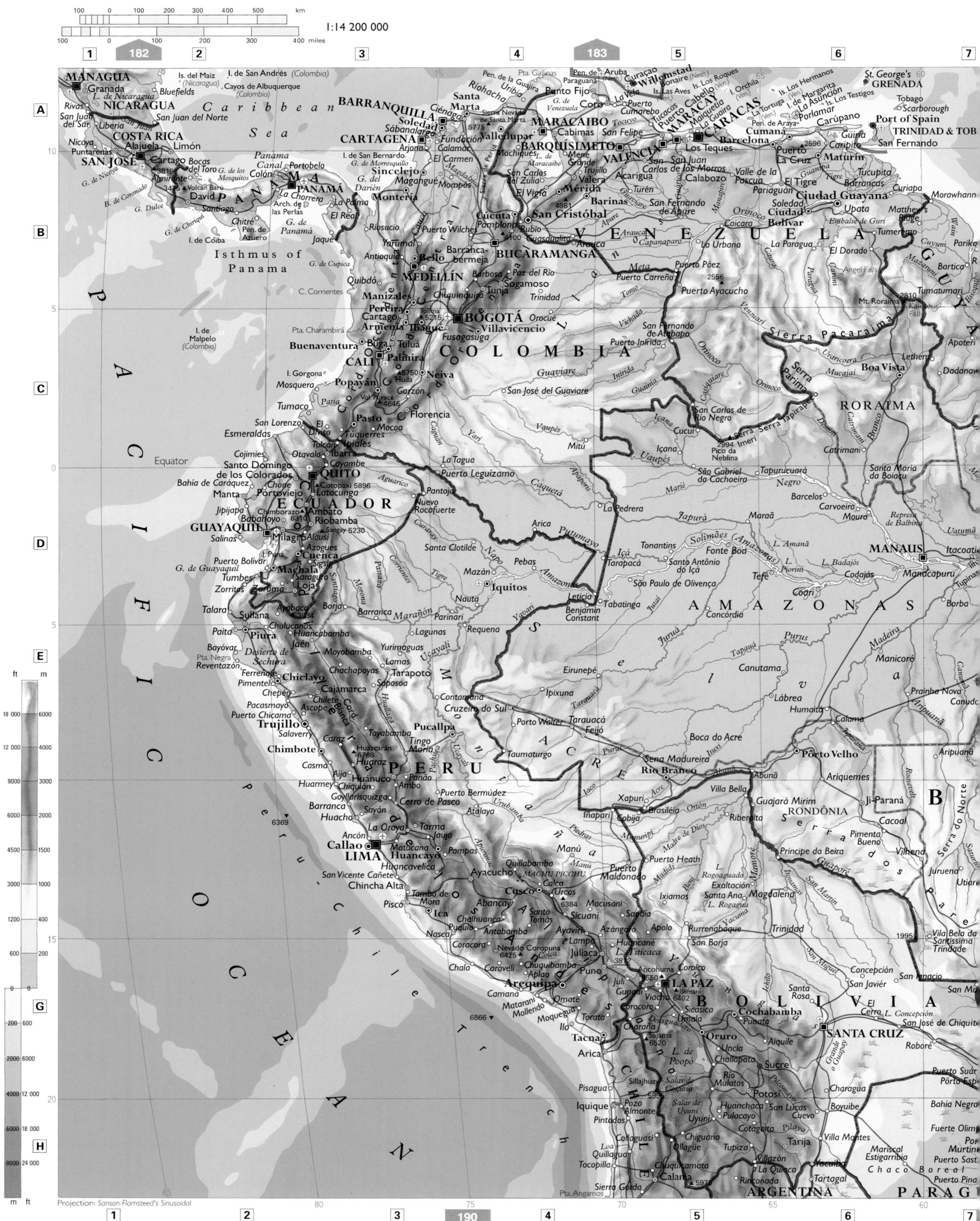

1:14 200 000

Projection: Sanson-Flamsteed's Sinusoidal

TRINIDAD AND TOBAGO
1:2 200 000

10 0 10 20 30 40 50 km
10 0 10 20 30 miles

J

Tobago
North Pt.
Charlotteville
Castara 585 Little
Plymouth Main Ridge Tobago
Buccoo Reef Roxborough
Crown Pt. Scarborough
Rockly Bay

11

ATLANTIC

OCEAN

K

VENEZUELA
Pen. de
Paria
Macuro Maraval
Corozal
Pt.
Monos I.
La Vache Pt.
Chupara Pt.
Blanchisseuse
Maracas Bay
Matelot
Sans Souci
Northern Range
936 940 Mt. Aripo
Toco
Galera Pt.
Redhead
Salybia
Güiria
Port
of
Spain
San
Juan
Tunapuna
Arima
Valencia
Matura
Bay
Chaguanas
Caroni
Talparo
Sangre Grande
Upper Manzanilla
Nariva
Swamp
Cocos
Bay

Golfo de Paria
Couva
Point Lisas
Otaheite Bay
San Fernando
Brighton
Guapo Bay
La Brea
Point Fortin
Cedros Bay
Bonasse
Icacos Pt.
Erin Pt.
Palo Seco
Rio Claro
Guataro Pt.
Gasparillo
Princes Town
Penal
Pitch
Lake
Siparia
Basse Terre
Moruga
La Lune
304 Trinity
Hills
Mayaro
Mayaro Bay
Guayaguayare
Galeota Pt.

Trinidad

ATLANTIC
OCEAN

Serpent's Mouth
VENEZUELA Pta. Bombedor

West from Greenwich

L

ATLANTIC

OCEAN

Paramaribo
Nieuw Amsterdam
Moengo St-Laurent du Maroni
Albina Iracoubo
Sinnamary
Kourou
Cayenne
W. J. Van
Blommestein
Meer
Kaw
C. Orange
SURINAME FRENCH
GUIANA St-Georges
Oiapoque
Camopi

Equator

São Pedro &
São Paulo
(Braz.)

0

Serra
Tumucumaque
AMAPÁ
Meriumã
Macapá
Mazagão
Afuá Chaves
I. Caviana
I. Mexiana
C. Maguarinho
Curuçá Salinópolis
Soure
I. de Maracá
Araguari
Amapá

D

Óbidos
Monte
Alegre Prainha
Alenquer
Santarém Belterra
Brasília Legal
Altamira
Aveiro
I. Grande
de Gurupá
Almeirim
Porto de Moz
Gurupá Breves
Cametá Baião
I. de
Marajó
Vigia Bragança
Castanhal Turiaçu
Abaetetuba
BELÉM
Curralinho
Viseu
Cururupu
Pinheiro
Alcântara
São Luís
Barreirinhas
Rosário
Itapecuru-
Mirim
Parnaíba
Tutóia
Luís Correia
Camocim
PARÁ
Tucuruí
Brejo
Viana
Santa Inês
Bacabal
Pedreiras
Codó
Caxias
Coroatá
Piripiri
Granja Itapipoca
Sobral
Maranguape
Cascavel
Acaraú
Caucaia
FORTALEZA
Baturité
Russas
Aracati
Areia Branca
Macau
Ceará-Mirim
Atol
das Rocas
(Braz.)
Fernando de Noronha
(Braz.)

5

Marabá
Maranhão
Imperatriz
Barra
do Corda
Colinas
Teresina
Campo
Maior
Oiticica
Quixadá
Ipu
Crateús
Senador Pompeu
Caraúbas
Mossoró
RIO GRANDE
DO NORTE
NATAL
Canguaretama

E

Conceição do
Araguaia
Araguaína
Carolina
Estreito
Porto Franco
Tocantinópolis
Loreto
Floriano
Nova Iorque
Uruçuí
Picos
Oeiras
Amarante
Valença
do Piauí
São João
do Piauí
PIAUÍ
Chapada do Araripe
Crato
Juazeiro
do Norte
Cajazeiras
Iguatu
Cedro
Sousa
Patos
Currais
Novos
Alagoa
Grande
Mamanguape
Cabedelo
JOÃO PESSOA
Campina
Grande
Caruaru
Olinda
RECIFE
Jaboatão

10

Araguacema
Pedro Afonso
Santa
Filomena
PARAÍBA
Salgueiro
Petrolina
Paulistana
Remanso
Casa Nova
Juazeiro
PERNAMBUCO
Garanhuns
Pesqueira
Palmares
Rio Largo
MACEIÓ
Arapiraca
Penedo

6059

Palmas
Porto Nacional
Miracema
do Tocantins
Represa de
Sobradinho
São
Francisco
Senhor-do-
Bonfim
Jacobina
Mundo
Novo
Propriá
SERGIPE
ALAGOAS
Aracaju
São Cristóvão
Estância

F

BRAZIL
TOCANTINS
Santa Isabel
do Morro
Gurupi
Peixe
Paranã
Taguatinga
Campos Belos
São
Domingos
Barreiras
Ibotirama
Xique-Xique
Barra
Santa Maria
da Vitória
Bom Jesus
da Lapa
BAHÍA
Itaberaba
Feira de
Santana
Serra
do Sincorá
Valença
Nazaré
Cachoeira
Castro
Alves
Santo Amaro
SALVADOR
Alagoinhas
Queimadas
Seminha
B. de Todos os Santos

15

GROSSO
Cuiabá
Santo Antonio
Rondonópolis
Planalto do
Mato Grosso
Niquelândia
1678
Aruanã
Uruaçu
Posse
Carinhanha
Januária
Monte Azul
Condeúba
Brumado
Vitória da
Conquista
Jequié
Ubaitaba
Ilhéus
Canavieiras
Belmonte
Porto Seguro

G

GOIÁS
Cuiabá
Barra do Garças
Coxim
GROSSO
DO SUL
Jataí
Rio Verde
Itumbiara
Quirinópolis
Goiás
Anápolis
GOIÂNIA
Alto Araguaia
Morrinhos
Catalão
DIST.
FED.
BRASÍLIA
Formosa
Luziânia
São Francisco
Paracatu
Pirapora
João Pinheiro
Patos de
Minas
Montes
Claros
Salinas
Araçuaí
Diamantina
Teófilo Otoni
Nanuque
Pedra Azul
Jequitinhonha
Itamaraju
Prado
Caravelas
Conceição da Barra
Banco dos
Abrolhos

27

20

Campo
Grande
Santa Fé de Sul
Água Clara
Três Lagoas
Panorama
Presidente Epitácio
Andradina
Araçatuba
Birigüi
Penápolis
Ituiutaba
Uberlândia
Araguari
Uberaba
Frutal
Prata
Araxá
Ibiá
Curvelo
Paracatu
Sête Lagoas
MINAS GERAIS
BELO HORIZONTE
Sabará
Ouro
Pico da
Bandeira
2890
Colatina
Ipatinga
Itabira
Cataguazes
Governador
Valadares
Nova
Venécia
Linhares
São
Mateus
VITÓRIA
Vila Velha
Cachoeiro de Itapemirim
Trindade
(Braz.)
Martin Vaz
(Braz.)

H

Presidente
Prudente
Marília
Assis
Bauru
Jaú
Piracicaba
Limeira
Botucatu
CAMPINAS
Araraquara
São Carlos
Catanduva
Rio Preto
São José do
Barretos
Ribeirão Preto
Franca
Guaxupé
Caldas
Passos
Divinópolis
Lima
Conselheiro
Lafaiete
Ponte
Nova
Ouro
Prêto
Barbacena
São João
del Rei
Juiz de Fora
Três Rios
Volta
Redonda
Petrópolis
Nova Friburgo
Campos
Cabo Frio
Niterói
RIO DE JANEIRO

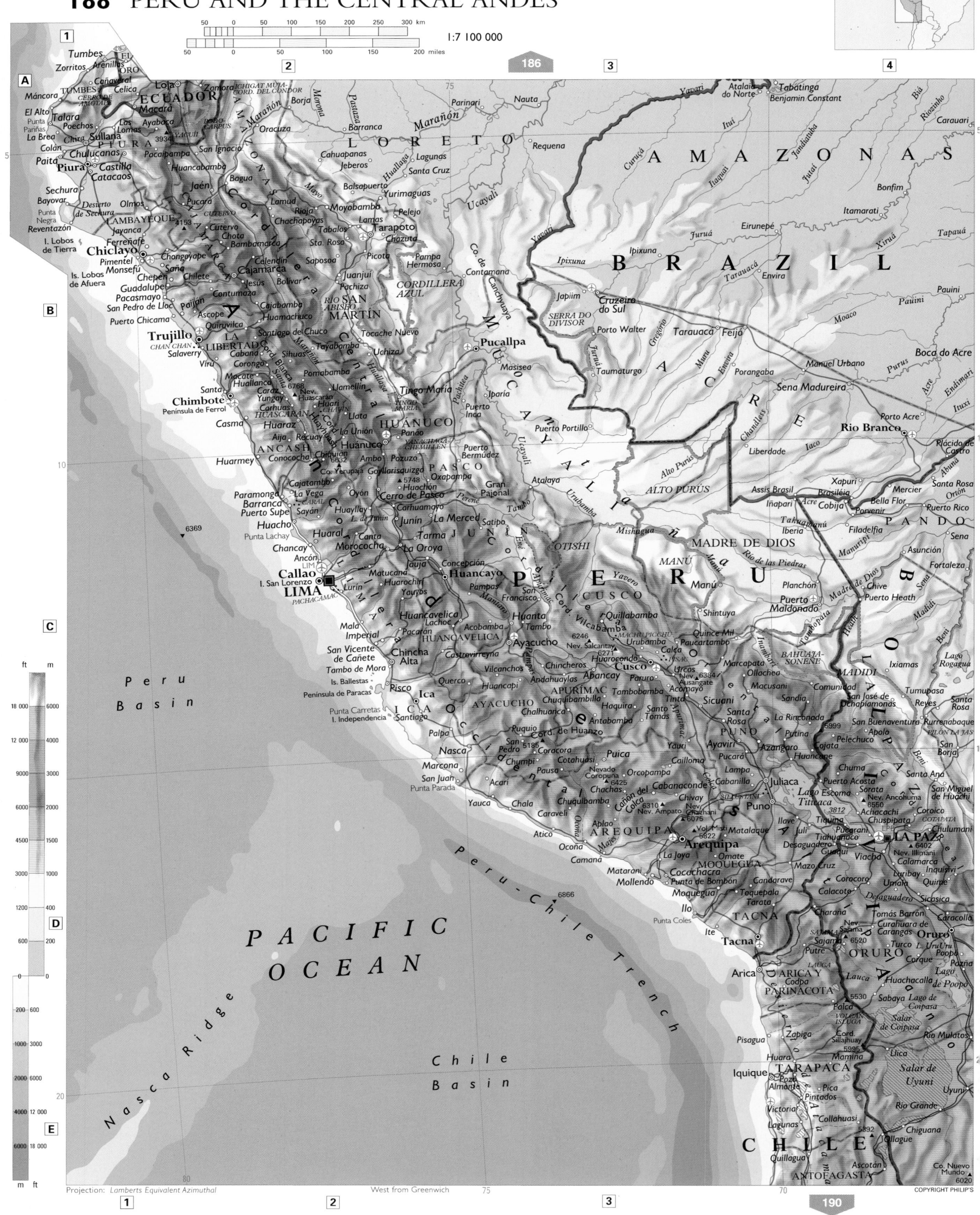

50 0 50 100 150 200 250 300 km

1:7 100 000

50 0 50 100 150 200 miles

186

PACIFIC
OCEAN

Peru
Basin

Chile
Basin

Peru-Chile Trench

Nasca Ridge

A M A Z O N A S

B R A Z I L

A C R E

B O L I V I A

P E R U

PANDO

MADRE DE DIOS

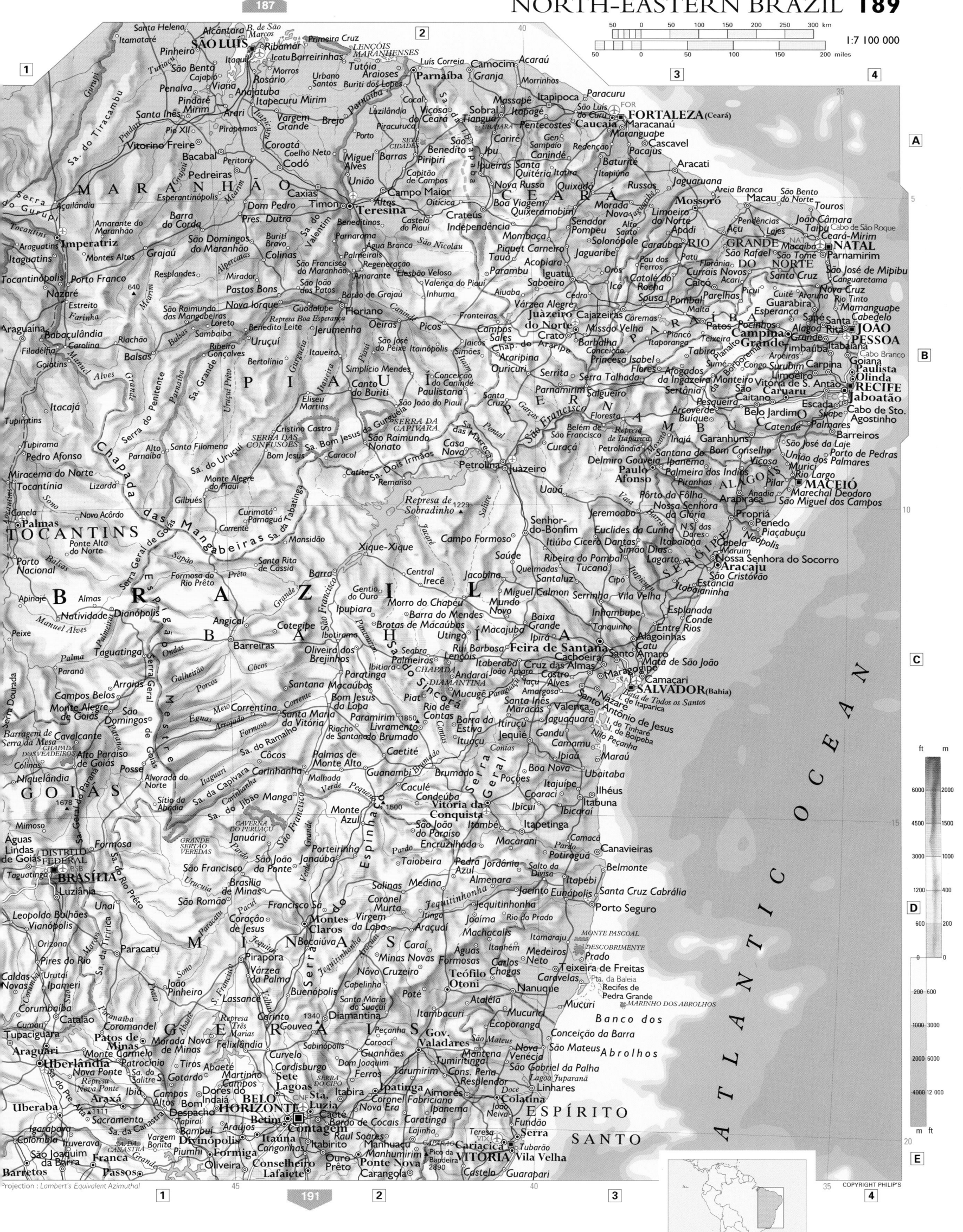

50 0 50 100 150 200 250 300 km
1:7 100 000
50 0 50 100 150
200 miles

1

2

3

4

A

B

C

D

E

B. de São Marcos
Santa Helena
Itamataré
Alcântara
Primeira Cruz
SÃO LUÍS
Pinheiro
Ribamar
Icatu
Barreirinhas
LENÇÓIS
MARANHENSES
Tutóia
Luís Correia
Camocim
Acaraú
Itaqui
São Bento
Araioses
Morros
Urbano
Santos
Buriti dos Lopes
Parnaíba
Granja
Morrinhos
Itapipoca
Paracuru
Cajapió
Penalva
Viana
Anajatuba
Itapecuru Mirim
Rosário
Araioses
Cocal
Luzilândia
Viçosa
do Ceará
Sobral
Itapagé
Massapê
Caucaia
FORTALEZA (Ceará)
Pindaré
Mirim
Piracuruca
Tianguá
Pentecostes
São Luís
do Curu
Maracanaú
Maranguape
Santa Inês
Vitorino Freire
Bacabal
Peritoró
Codó
Brejo
Porto
Piripiri
Cariré
Jpu
Sampaio
Redenção
Canindé
Pacajus
Cascavel
Pindaré
Coroatá
Coelho Neto
Miguel
Alves
Barras
Benedito
de Campos
Ibiapina
Santa
Quitéria
Itatira
Baturité
Itapiúna
Aracati

MARANHÃO
Pedreiras
União
Campo Maior
Nova Russa
Quixadá
Russas
Jaguaruana
Açailândia
Esperantinópolis
Dom Pedro
Pres. Dutra
Timon
Teresina
Altos
Castelo
do Piauí
Boa Viagem
Oiticica
Morada
Nova
CEARÁ
Areia Branca
Macau
São Bento
do Norte
Touros
Amarante
do Maranhão
Grajaú
Caxias
Benedítinos
Crateús
Quixeramobim
Senador
Pompeu
Solonópole
Caraúbas
Pau dos
Ferros
Apodi
Limoeiro
do Norte
Açu
Pendências
São Tomé
Cabo de São Roque
Imperatriz
Montes Altos
São Domingos
do Maranhão
Buriti
Bravo
Agua Branca
Parnarama
Independência
Mombaça
Piquet Carneiro
Tauá
Acopiara
Iguatu
Orós
Icó
Jaguaribe
Catolé do
Rocha
Sousa
Patu
Florânia
São Rafael
Currais Novos
Santa Cruz
Lajes
João Câmara
Taipu
Ceará-Mirim
NATAL
Tocantinópolis
Porto Franco
Colinas
São Francisco
do Maranhão
Elesbão Veloso
Valença do Piauí
Inhuma
Saboeiro
Aiuaba
Várzea Alegre
Cedro
Fronteiras
Campos
Sales
RIO
GRANDE
DO
NORTE
Acari
Caicó
Parelhas
Picuí
Cuité
Parnamirim
Nazaré
Araguaína
Farinha
Estreito
Nova Iorque
Guadalupe
Floriano
Picos
**Juazeiro
do Norte**
Crato
Jaicós
Chap. do
Araripe
Missão Velha
Barbalha
Araripina
Ouricuri
Cajazeiras
Côremas
Piancó
Pombal
Malta
Patos
Pocinhos
Esperança
Araruna
Mamanguape
Rio Tinto
Guarabira
Tocantínia
Miracema do Norte
Babaculândia
Carolina
Filadélfia
Goiatins
Balsas
Loreto
Benedito Leite
Uruçuí
Ribeiro Gonçalves
Bertolínia
Simplício Mendes
Conceição do Canindé
Paulistana
Serra
Cruz
Serrita
Parnamirim
Salgueiro
Sertânia
Flores
Afogados
da Ingazeira
Teixeira
Princesa Isabel
Itaporanga
Planalto
Tabira
Sumé
Monteiro
Congo
Vitória de S. Antão
Caruaru
Surubim
Carpina
Goiana
Paulista
**JOÃO
PESSOA**
Cabo Branco
RECIFE
Olinda
Jaboatão
Araguaína
Tupiratins
Tupirama
Pedro Afonso
Palmas
Represa de
Sobradinho
Remanso
Casa
Nova
Petrolina
Juazeiro
Uauá
Belém de
São Francisco
Floresta
Delmiro Gouveia
Paulo
Afonso
Piranhas
Arcoverde
Buíque
Belo Jardim
Pesqueira
Caitano
Garanhuns
Bom Conselho
São José da Laje
Murici
Rio Largo
MACEIÓ
Marechal Deodoro
São Miguel dos Campos
Porto de Pedras
União dos Palmares
Palmeira dos Índios
Ipanema
Santana do
Ipanema
Piaçabuçu
Penedo
Pilar
Anadia
Arapiraca
Propriá
Neópolis

PIAUÍ
TOCANTINS
GOIÁS
BRASÍLIA
DISTRITO
FEDERAL
MINAS GERAIS
BAHIA
PERNAMBUCO
ALAGOAS
SERGIPE
ARACAJU
São Cristóvão
Estância
Itabaianinha
Tobias Barreto
Lagarto
Simão Dias
Itabaiana
N.S. das
Dores
Capela
Maruim
Nossa Senhora do Socorro
Cícero Dantas
Ribeira do Pombal
Tucano
Cipó
Jeremoabo
Euclides da Cunha
Monte Santo
Senhor-
do-Bonfim
Campo Formoso
Jaguarari
Juazeiro
Sento Sé
Xique-Xique
Barra
Santa Rita
de Cássia
Formosa do
Rio Prêto
Corrente
Mansidão
Gilbués
Curimatá
Parnaguá
Alvorada do
Norte
Posse
Niquelândia
Colinas
Barragem de
Serra da Mesa
Cavalcante
Alto Paraíso
de Goiás
Minaçu
Dianópolis
Almas
Natividade
Peixe
Arraias
Taguatinga
Campos Belos
Monte Alegre
de Goiás
São
Domingos
Paranã
Palma
Manuel Alves
Novo Acôrdo
Lizarda
Monte Alegre
do Piauí
Corrente
São Raimundo
Nonato
Serra da
Capivara
Bom Jesus
da Lapa
Malhada
Carinhanha
Manga
Januária
São Francisco
Porteirinha
Taiobeiras
Salinas
Medina
Rio Pardo
de Minas
Encruzilhada
Macarani
Canavieiras
Belmonte
Santa Cruz
Cabrália
Porto Seguro
Eunápolis
Itabela
Itamaraju
Prado
Teixeira de Freitas
Caravelas
Nanuque
Mucuri
Montanha
Ecoporanga
Conceição da Barra
São Mateus
Nova Venécia
Linhares
ESPÍRITO
SANTO
VITÓRIA
Vila Velha
Guarapari
Cariacica
Serra
Fundão
Colatina
Aimorés
Gov. Valadares
Resplendor
Mantena
Teófilo
Otoni
Itambacuri
Carlos Chagas
Malacacheta
Águas
Formosas
Araçuaí
Minas Novas
Diamantina
Capelinha
Jequitinhonha
Almenara
Jordânia
Itaobim
Pedra
Azul
Salto da
Divisa
Jacinto

ATLANTIC OCEAN

ft   m
6000 2000
4500 1500
3000 1000
1200 400
600   200
0   0
200   600
1000 3000
2000 6000
4000 12000
m   ft

Projection: Lambert's Equivalent Azimuthal

COPYRIGHT PHILIP'S

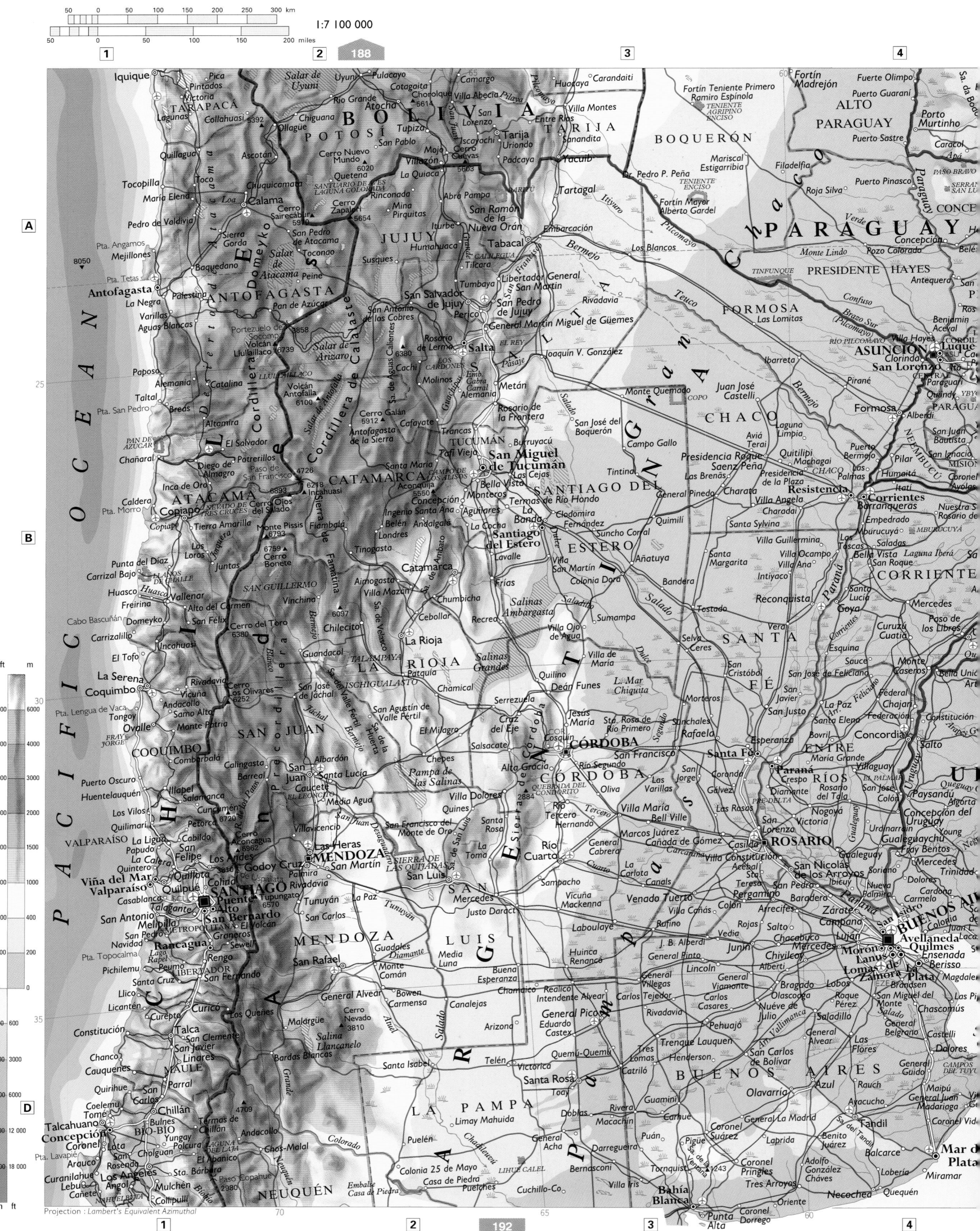

ATLANTIC

OCEAN

50   0   50   100 150 200 250 300 km

1:7 100 000

50   0   50   100   150
200 miles

FALKLAND ISLANDS (U.K.)
(ISLAS MALVINAS)

ATLANTIC OCEAN

PACIFIC OCEAN

ft   m

9000   3000

6000   2000

4500   1500

3000   1000

1200   400

600   200

0   0

200   600

1000   3000

2000   6000

4000   12 000

m   ft

Projection : Lambert's Equivalent Azimuthal

COPYRIGHT PHILIP

West from Greenwich

INDEX TO WORLD MAPS

HOW TO USE THE INDEX

e index contains the names of all the principal places and features shown on the World Maps. ch name is followed by an additional entry in italics giving the country or region within which it ocated. The alphabetical order of names composed of two or more words is governed primarily the first word, then by the second, and then by the country or region name that follows. This is example of the rule:

Mir *Niger*		14°5N 11°59E	**139** C7
Mīr Kūh *Iran*		26°22N 58°55E	**129** E8
Mīr Shahdād *Iran*		26°15N 58°29E	**129** E8
Mira *Italy*		45°26N 12°8E	**93** C9

ysical features composed of a proper name (Erie) and a description (Lake) are positioned habetically by the proper name. The description is positioned after the proper name and is ally abbreviated:

Erie, L. *N. Amer.*	42°15N 81°0W	**174** D4

ere a description forms part of a settlement or administrative name, however, it is always tten in full and put in its true alphabetical position:

Mount Isa *Australia*	20°42S 139°26E	**150** C2

mes beginning with M' and Mc are indexed as if they were spelled Mac. Names beginning are alphabetized under Saint, but Sankt, Sint, Sant', Santa and San are all spelt in full and are habetized accordingly. If the same place name occurs two or more times in the index and all are in same country, each is followed by the name of the administrative subdivision in which it is located.

e geographical co-ordinates which follow each name in the index give the latitude and longitude of h place. The first co-ordinate indicates latitude – the distance north or south of the Equator. The ond co-ordinate indicates longitude – the distance east or west of the Greenwich Meridian. Both tude and longitude are measured in degrees and minutes (there are 60 minutes in a degree).

e latitude is followed by N(orth) or S(outh) and the longitude by E(ast) or W(est).

e number in bold type which follows the geographical co-ordinates refers to the number of the p page where that feature or place will be found. This is usually the largest scale at which the ce or feature appears.

e letter and figure that are immediately after the page number give the grid square on the p page, within which the feature is situated. The letter represents the latitude and the figure longitude. A lower-case letter immediately after the page number refers to an inset map on t page.

some cases the feature itself may fall within the specified square, while the name is outside. is is usually the case only with features that are larger than a grid square.

ers are indexed to their mouths or confluences, and carry the symbol ➝ after their names. e following symbols are also used in the index: ■ country, ☑ overseas territory or dependency, irst-order administrative area, △ national park, ⌂ other park (provincial park, nature erve or game reserve), ☼ Australian Aborginal land, ✕ (LHR) principal airport (and location ntifier).

HOW TO PRONOUNCE PLACE NAMES

English-speaking people usually have no difficulty in reading and pronouncing correctly English place names. However, foreign place name pronunciations may present many problems. Such problems can be minimized by following some simple rules. However, these rules cannot be applied to all situations, and there will be many exceptions.

1. In general, stress each syllable equally, unless your experience suggests otherwise.
2. Pronounce the letter 'a' as a broad 'a' as in 'arm'.
3. Pronounce the letter 'e' as a short 'e' as in 'elm'.
4. Pronounce the letter 'i' as a cross between a short 'i' and long 'e', as the two 'i's in 'California'.
5. Pronounce the letter 'o' as an intermediate 'o' as in 'soft'.
6. Pronounce the letter 'u' as an intermediate 'u' as in 'sure'.
7. Pronounce consonants hard, except in the Romance-language areas where 'g's are likely to be pronounced softly like 'j' in 'jam'; 'j' itself may be pronounced as 'y'; and 'x's may be pronounced as 'h'.
8. For names in mainland China, pronounce 'q' like the 'ch' in 'chin', 'x' like the 'sh' in 'she', 'zh' like the 'j' in 'jam', and 'z' as if it were spelled 'dz'. In general, pronounce 'a' as in 'father', 'e' as in 'but', 'i' as in 'keep', 'o' as in 'or', and 'u' as in 'rule'.

Moreover, English has no diacritical marks (accent and pronunciation signs), although some languages do. The following is a brief and general guide to the pronunciation of those most frequently used in the principal Western European languages.

		Pronunciation as in
French	é	day and shows that the 'e' is to be pronounced; e.g. Orléans.
	è	mare
	î	used over any vowel and does not affect pronunciation; shows contraction of the name, usually omission of 's' following a vowel.
	ç	's' before 'a', 'o' and 'u'.
	ë, ï, ü	over 'e', 'i' and 'u' when they are used with another vowel and shows that each is to be pronounced.
German	ä	fate
	ö	fur
	ü	no English equivalent; like French 'tu'.
Italian	à, é	over vowels and indicates stress.
Portuguese	ã, õ	vowels pronounced nasally.
	ç	boss
	á	shows stress.
	ô	shows that a vowel has an 'i' or 'u' sound combined with it.
Spanish	ñ	canyon
	ü	pronounced as 'w' and separately from adjoining vowels.
	á	usually indicates that this is a stressed vowel.

ABBREVIATIONS

C.T. – Australian Capital Territory	El Salv. – El Salvador	Man. – Manitoba	Okla. – Oklahoma	Sask. – Saskatchewan
R. – Autonomous Region	Eq. Guin. – Equatorial Guinea	Mass. – Massachusetts	Ont. – Ontario	Scot. – Scotland
ghan. – Afghanistan	Est. – Estrecho	Md. – Maryland	Or. – Orientale	Sd. – Sound
. – Africa	Falk. Is. – Falkland Is.	Me. – Maine	Oreg. – Oregon	Sev. – Severnaya
. – Alabama	Fd. – Fjord	Medit. S. – Mediterranean Sea	Os. – Ostrov	Sib. – Siberia
a. – Alberta	Fla. – Florida	Mich. – Michigan	Oz. – Ozero	Sprs. – Springs
er. – America(n)	Fr. – French	Minn. – Minnesota	P. – Pass, Passo, Pasul, Pulau	St. – Saint
. – Antilles	G. – Golfe, Golfo, Gulf, Guba,	Miss. – Mississippi	P.E.I. – Prince Edward Island	Sta. – Santa
h. – Archipelago	Gebel	Mo. – Missouri	Pa. – Pennsylvania	Ste. – Sainte
z. – Arizona	Ga. – Georgia	Mont. – Montana	Pac. Oc. – Pacific Ocean	Sto. – Santo
k. – Arkansas	Gt. – Great, Greater	Mozam. – Mozambique	Papua N.G. – Papua New Guinea	Str. – Strait, Stretto
Oc. – Atlantic Ocean	Guinea-Biss. – Guinea-Bissau	Mt.(s) – Mont, Montaña, Mountain	Pass. – Passage	Switz. – Switzerland
– Baie, Bahía, Bay, Bucht, Bugt	H.K. – Hong Kong	Mte. – Monte	Peg. – Pegunungan	Tas. – Tasmania
. – British Columbia	H.P. – Himachal Pradesh	Mti. – Monti	Pen. – Peninsula, Péninsule	Tenn. – Tennessee
ngla. – Bangladesh	Hants. – Hampshire	N. – Nord, Norte, North, Northern,	Phil. – Philippines	Terr. – Territory, Territoire
r. – Barrage	Harb. – Harbor, Harbour	Nouveau, Nahal, Nahr	Pk. – Peak	Tex. – Texas
.-H. – Bosnia-Herzegovina	Hd. – Head	N.B. – New Brunswick	Plat. – Plateau	Tg. – Tanjung
– Cabo, Cap, Cape, Coast	Hts. – Heights	N.C. – North Carolina	Prov. – Province, Provincial	Trin. & Tob. – Trinidad & Tobago
.R. – Central African Republic	I.(s). – Île, Ilha, Insel, Isla, Island,	N. Cal. – New Caledonia	Pt. – Point	U.A.E. – United Arab Emirates
Prov. – Cape Province	Isle	N. Dak. – North Dakota	Pta. – Ponta, Punta	U.K. – United Kingdom
lif. – California	Ill. – Illinois	N.H. – New Hampshire	Pte. – Pointe	U.S.A. – United States of America
. – Catarata	Ind. – Indiana	N.I. – North Island	Qué. – Québec	Univ. – University, Université,
at. – Central	Ind. Oc. – Indian Ocean	N.J. – New Jersey	Queens. – Queensland	Universidad
an. – Channel	Ivory C. – Ivory Coast	N. Mex. – New Mexico	R. – Rio, River	Ut. P. – Uttar Pradesh
lo. – Colorado	J. – Jabal, Jebel	N.S. – Nova Scotia	R.I. – Rhode Island	Va. – Virginia
nn. – Connecticut	Jaz. – Jazīrah	N.S.W. – New South Wales	Ra. – Range	Vdkhr. – Vodokhranilishche
rd. – Cordillera	Junc. – Junction	N.W.T. – North West Territory	Raj. – Rajasthan	Vdskh. – Vodoskhovyshche
– Creek	K. – Kap, Kapp	N.Y. – New York	Recr. – Recreational, Récréatif	Vf. – Vírful
ech. – Czech Republic	Kans. – Kansas	N.Z. – New Zealand	Reg. – Region	Vic. – Victoria
. – District of Columbia	Kep. – Kepulauan	Nac. – Nacional	Rep. – Republic	Vol. – Volcano
. – Delaware	Ky. – Kentucky	Nat. – National	Res. – Reserve, Reservoir	Vt. – Vermont
n. – Democratic	L. – Lac, Lacul, Lago, Lagoa, Lake,	Nebr. – Nebraska	Rhld-Pfz. – Rheinland-Pfalz	W. – Wadi, West
p. – Dependency	Limni, Loch, Lough	Neths. – Netherlands	S. – South, Southern, Sur	W. Va. – West Virginia
s. – Desert	La. – Louisiana	Nev. – Nevada	Si. Arabia – Saudi Arabia	Wall. & F. Is. – Wallis and Futuna Is.
t. – Détroit	Ld. – Land	Nfld & L.. – Newfoundland and	S.C. – South Carolina	Wash. – Washington
t. – District	Liech. – Liechtenstein	Labrador	S. Dak. – South Dakota	Wis. – Wisconsin
– Djebel	Lux. – Luxembourg	Nic. – Nicaragua	S.I. – South Island	Wlkp. – Wielkopolski
m. Rep. – Dominican Republic	Mad. P. – Madhya Pradesh	O. – Oued, Ouadi	S. Leone – Sierra Leone	Wyo. – Wyoming
– East	Madag. – Madagascar	Occ. – Occidentale	Sa. – Serra, Sierra	Yorks. – Yorkshire

A

A Baiuca *Spain* 43°19N 8°29W **88** B2
A Baña = San Vicenzo *Spain* 42°58N 8°46W **88** C2
A Cañiza *Spain* 42°13N 8°16W **88** C2
A Carballa *Spain* 43°13N 8°54W **88** B2
A Carreira *Spain* 43°21N 8°12W **88** B2
A Coruña *Spain* 43°20N 8°25W **88** B2
A Coruña □ *Spain* 43°10N 8°30W **88** B2
A Cruz do Incio *Spain* 42°39N 7°21W **88** C3
A Estrada *Spain* 42°43N 8°27W **88** C2
A Feira do Monte *Spain* 43°12N 7°34W **88** B3
A Fonsagrada *Spain* 43°8N 7°4W **88** B3
A Guarda *Spain* 41°56N 8°52W **88** D2
A Gudiña *Spain* 42°4N 7°8W **88** C3
A Pobre *Spain* 42°58N 7°3W **88** C3
A Ramallosa *Spain* 42°45N 8°30W **88** C2
A Rúa *Spain* 42°24N 7°6W **88** C3
A Serra de Outes *Spain* 42°52N 8°55W **88** C2
A Shau *Vietnam* 16°6N 107°22E **120** D6
Aabenraa *Denmark* 55°3N 9°25E **63** J3
Aabybro *Denmark* 57°10N 9°44E **63** G3
Aachen *Germany* 50°45N 6°6E **76** E2
Aalborg *Denmark* 57°2N 9°54E **63** G3
Aalborg Bugt *Denmark* 56°50N 10°35E **63** H4
Aalen *Germany* 48°51N 10°6E **77** G6
Aalestrup *Denmark* 56°42N 9°29E **63** H3
Aalst *Belgium* 50°56N 4°2E **69** D4
Aalten *Neths.* 51°56N 6°35E **69** C6
Aalter *Belgium* 51°5N 3°28E **69** C3
Äänekoski *Finland* 62°36N 25°44E **60** E21
Aarau *Switz.* 47°23N 8°4E **77** H4
Aarberg *Switz.* 47°2N 7°16E **77** H3
Aare → *Switz.* 47°33N 8°14E **77** H4
Aargau □ *Switz.* 47°26N 8°10E **77** H4
Aarhus *Denmark* 56°8N 10°11E **63** H4
Aars *Denmark* 56°48N 9°30E **63** H3
Aarschot *Belgium* 50°59N 4°49E **69** D4
Aasiaat *Greenland* 68°43N 52°56W **57** D5
Aba *China* 32°59N 101°42E **116** A3
Aba *Dem. Rep. of the Congo* 3°58N 30°17E **142** B3
Aba *Nigeria* 5°10N 7°19E **139** D6
Abaco I. *Bahamas* 26°25N 77°10W **182** A4
Abadab, J. *Sudan* 18°54N 35°56E **137** D4
Ābādān *Iran* 30°22N 48°20E **129** D6
Ābādeh *Iran* 31°8N 52°40E **129** D7
Abadín *Spain* 43°21N 7°29W **88** B3
Abadla *Algeria* 31°2N 2°45W **136** B3
Abaeté *Brazil* 19°9S 45°27W **189** D1
Abaeté → *Brazil* 18°2S 45°12W **189** D1
Abaetetuba *Brazil* 1°40S 48°50W **187** D9
Abagnar Qi = Xilinhot *China* 43°52N 116°2E **114** C9
Abah, Tanjung *Indonesia* 8°46S 115°38E **119** K18
Abai *Paraguay* 25°58S 55°54W **191** B4
Abakaliki *Nigeria* 6°22N 8°2E **139** D6
Abakan *Russia* 53°40N 91°10E **109** B12
Abala *Niger* 14°56N 3°22E **139** C5
Abalak *Niger* 15°22N 6°21E **139** B6
Abalemma *Niger* 16°12N 7°50E **139** B6
Abana *Turkey* 41°59N 34°1E **104** B6
Abancay *Peru* 13°35S 72°55W **188** C3
Abang, Gunung *Indonesia* 8°16S 115°25E **119** J18
Abano Terme *Italy* 45°22N 11°46E **93** C8
Abarán *Spain* 38°12N 1°23W **91** G3
Abariringa *Kiribati* 2°50S 171°40W **156** H10
Abarqū *Iran* 31°10N 53°20E **129** D7
Abasha *Georgia* 42°11N 42°13E **87** J6
Abashiri *Japan* 44°0N 144°15E **112** B12
Abashiri-Wan *Japan* 44°0N 144°30E **112** C12
Abaújszántó *Hungary* 48°16N 21°12E **80** B6
Abava → *Latvia* 57°6N 21°54E **82** A8
Ābay = Nîl el Azraq → *Sudan* 15°38N 32°31E **135** E12
Abay *Kazakhstan* 49°38N 72°53E **109** C8
Abaya, L. *Ethiopia* 6°30N 37°50E **131** F2
Abaza *Russia* 52°39N 90°6E **109** B12
Abbadia di Fiastra ⌓ *Italy* 43°12N 13°24E **93** E10
Abbadia San Salvatore *Italy* 42°53N 11°41E **93** F8
'Abbāsābād *Iran* 33°34N 58°23E **129** C8
Abbay = Nîl el Azraq → *Sudan* 15°38N 32°31E **135** E12
Abbaye, Pt. *U.S.A.* 46°58N 88°8W **172** B9
Abbé, L. *Ethiopia* 11°8N 41°47E **131** E3
Abbeville *France* 50°6N 1°49E **71** B8
Abbeville *Ala., U.S.A.* 31°34N 85°15W **178** D4
Abbeville *Ga., U.S.A.* 31°59N 83°18W **178** D6
Abbeville *La., U.S.A.* 29°58N 92°8W **176** G8
Abbeville *S.C., U.S.A.* 34°11N 82°23W **178** A7
Abbeyfeale *Ireland* 52°23N 9°18W **64** D2
Abbeyleix *Ireland* 52°54N 7°22W **64** D4
Abbiategrasso *Italy* 45°24N 8°54E **92** C5
Abbot Ice Shelf *Antarctica* 73°0S 92°0W **55** D16
Abbotsford *Canada* 49°5N 122°20W **162** D4
Abbottabad *Pakistan* 34°10N 73°15E **124** B5
Abbou, O. ben → *Algeria* 28°32N 5°14E **136** C5
ABC Islands *W. Indies* 12°15N 69°0W **183** D6
Abd al Kūrī *Yemen* 12°5N 52°20E **131** E5
Ābdānān *Iran* 32°56N 47°28E **105** F12
Ābdar *Iran* 30°16N 55°19E **129** D7
'Abdolābād *Iran* 34°12N 56°30E **129** C8
Abdulino *Russia* 53°42N 53°40E **108** B4
Abdulpur *Bangla.* 24°15N 88°59E **125** G13
Abéché *Chad* 13°50N 20°35E **135** F10
Abejar *Spain* 41°48N 2°47W **90** D2
Abel Tasman △ *N.Z.* 40°59S 173°3E **155** A8
Abengourou *Ivory C.* 6°42N 3°27W **138** D4
Abenójar *Spain* 38°53N 4°21W **89** G6
Åbenrå = Aabenraa *Denmark* 55°3N 9°25E **63** J3
Abensberg *Germany* 48°48N 11°51E **77** G7
Abeokuta *Nigeria* 7°3N 3°19E **139** D5
Aberaeron *U.K.* 52°15N 4°15W **67** E3
Aberayron = Aberaeron *U.K.* 52°15N 4°15W **67** E3
Aberchirder *U.K.* 57°34N 2°37W **65** D6
Abercorn *Australia* 25°12S 151°5E **151** D5
Abercrombie River △ *Australia* 34°5S 149°40E **153** C8
Aberdare *U.K.* 51°43N 3°27W **67** F4
Aberdare △ *Kenya* 0°22S 36°44E **142** C4
Aberdare Ra. *Kenya* 0°15S 36°50E **142** C4
Aberdaugleddau = Milford Haven *U.K.* 51°42N 5°7W **67** F2
Aberdeen *Australia* 32°9S 150°56E **153** B9
Aberdeen *Canada* 52°20N 106°8W **163** C7
Aberdeen *China* 22°14N 114°8E **111** a
Aberdeen *S. Africa* 32°28S 24°2E **144** D3
Aberdeen *U.K.* 57°9N 2°5W **65** D6
Aberdeen *Idaho, U.S.A.* 42°57N 112°50W **168** E7
Aberdeen *Md., U.S.A.* 39°31N 76°10W **173** F15
Aberdeen *Miss., U.S.A.* 33°49N 88°33W **177** E10
Aberdeen *S. Dak., U.S.A.* 45°28N 98°29W **172** C4
Aberdeen *Wash., U.S.A.* 46°59N 123°50W **170** D3
Aberdeen, City of □ *U.K.* 57°10N 2°10W **65** D6
Aberdeen L. *Canada* 64°30N 99°0W **160** E12
Aberdeenshire □ *U.K.* 57°17N 2°36W **65** D6
Aberdovey = Aberdyfi *U.K.* 52°33N 4°3W **67** E3
Aberdyfi *U.K.* 52°33N 4°3W **67** E3
Aberfeldy *U.K.* 56°37N 3°51W **65** E5
Aberfoyle *U.K.* 56°11N 4°23W **65** E4
Abergavenny *U.K.* 51°49N 3°1W **67** F4
Abergele *U.K.* 53°17N 3°35W **66** D4
Abergwaun = Fishguard *U.K.* 52°0N 4°58W **67** E3
Aberhonddu = Brecon *U.K.* 51°57N 3°23W **67** F4
Abermaw = Barmouth *U.K.* 52°44N 4°4W **66** E3
Abernathy *U.S.A.* 33°50N 101°51W **176** E4
Aberpennar = Mountain Ash *U.K.* 51°40N 3°23W **67** F4
Abert, L. *U.S.A.* 42°38N 120°14W **168** E3
Abertawe = Swansea *U.K.* 51°37N 3°57W **67** F4
Aberteifi = Cardigan *U.K.* 52°5N 4°40W **67** E3
Aberystwyth *U.K.* 52°25N 4°5W **67** E3
Abhā *Si. Arabia* 18°0N 42°34E **137** D5
Abhar *Iran* 36°9N 49°13E **105** D13
Abhayapuri *India* 26°24N 90°38E **125** F14
Abia □ *Nigeria* 5°30N 7°35E **139** D6
Abide *Turkey* 38°55N 29°20E **99** C11
Abidiya *Sudan* 18°18N 34°3E **137** D3
Abidjan *Ivory C.* 5°26N 3°58W **138** D4
Abilene *Kans., U.S.A.* 38°55N 97°13W **172** F5
Abilene *Tex., U.S.A.* 32°28N 99°43W **176** E5
Abingdon *U.K.* 51°40N 1°17W **67** F6
Abingdon *U.S.A.* 36°43N 81°59W **173** G13
Abington Reef *Australia* 18°0S 149°35E **150** B4
Abiod, Remel el *Tunisia* 31°45N 9°35E **136** B5
Abisko △ *Sweden* 68°18N 18°44E **60** B18
Abitau → *Canada* 59°53N 109°3W **163** B7
Abitibi → *Canada* 51°3N 80°55W **164** B3
Abitibi, L. *Canada* 48°40N 79°40W **164** C4
Abkhaz Republic = Abkhazia □ *Georgia* 43°12N 41°5E **87** J5
Abkhazia □ *Georgia* 43°12N 41°5E **87** J5
Abminga *Australia* 26°8S 134°51E **151** D1
Abnûb *Egypt* 27°18N 31°4E **137** B3
Åbo = Turku *Finland* 60°30N 22°19E **84** B2
Abohar *India* 30°10N 74°10E **124** D6
Aboisso *Ivory C.* 5°30N 3°5W **138** D4
Abomey *Benin* 7°10N 2°5E **139** D5
Abong-Mbang *Cameroon* 4°0N 13°8E **140** D2
Abonnema *Nigeria* 4°41N 6°49E **139** E6
Abony *Hungary* 47°12N 20°3E **80** C5
Aboso *Ghana* 5°23N 1°57W **138** D4
Abou-Deïa *Chad* 11°20N 19°20E **135** F9
Abovyan *Armenia* 40°16N 44°37E **87** K7
Aboyne *U.K.* 57°4N 2°47W **65** D6
Abra Pampa *Argentina* 22°43S 65°42W **190** A2
Abraham L. *Canada* 52°15N 116°35W **162** C5
Abrantes *Portugal* 39°24N 8°7W **89** F2
Abreojos, Pta. *Mexico* 26°50N 113°40W **180** B2
Abri *Sudan* 20°50N 30°27E **137** C3
Abrolhos, Banco dos *Brazil* 18°0S 38°0W **189** D3
Abrud *Romania* 46°19N 23°5E **80** D8
Abruzzo □ *Italy* 42°15N 14°0E **93** F10
Absaroka Range *U.S.A.* 44°45N 109°50W **168** D9
Abşeron Yarımadası *Azerbaijan* 40°28N 49°57E **87** K9
Abtenau *Austria* 47°33N 13°21E **78** D6
Abu *India* 24°41N 72°50E **124** G5
Abū al Abyad *U.A.E.* 24°11N 53°50E **129** E7
Abū al Khaşīb *Iraq* 30°25N 48°0E **128** D5
Abū 'Alī *Si. Arabia* 27°20N 49°27E **129** E6
Abū 'Alī → *Lebanon* 34°25N 35°50E **130** A4
Abû Ballas *Egypt* 24°26N 27°36E **137** C2
Abu Dhabi = Abū Ẓāby *U.A.E.* 24°28N 54°22E **129** E7
Abû Dis *Sudan* 19°12N 33°38E **137** D3
Abū Du'ān *Syria* 36°25N 38°15E **105** D8
Abu el Gaīn, W. → *Egypt* 29°35N 33°30E **130** F2
Abu Fatma, Ras *Sudan* 22°25N 36°25E **137** C4
Abu Ga'da, W. → *Egypt* 29°15N 32°53E **130** F1
Abū Ḩadrīyah *Si. Arabia* 27°20N 48°58E **129** E6
Abu Hamed *Sudan* 19°32N 33°13E **137** D3
Abû Haraz *Sudan* 19°8N 32°18E **137** D3
Abū Kamāl *Syria* 34°30N 41°0E **105** E9
Abu Kebîr *Egypt* 30°43N 31°40E **137** E7
Abū Madd, Ra's *Si. Arabia* 24°50N 37°7E **128** E3
Abu Mena = Abu Mina *Egypt* 30°51N 29°40E **137** E6
Abu Mina *Egypt* 30°51N 29°40E **137** E6
Abū Mūsā *U.A.E.* 25°52N 55°3E **129** E7
Abū Qaşr *Si. Arabia* 30°21N 38°34E **128** D3
Abu Qireiya *Egypt* 24°5N 35°28E **137** C4
Abu Qurqâs *Egypt* 28°1N 30°44E **137** F7
Abu Shagara, Ras *Sudan* 21°4N 37°19E **137** C4
Abu Simbel *Egypt* 22°18N 31°40E **137** C3
Abu Soma, Râs *Egypt* 26°51N 33°58E **137** B3
Abū Şukhayr *Iraq* 31°54N 44°30E **105** G11
Abu Sultân *Egypt* 30°24N 32°21E **137** E8
Abu Tig *Egypt* 27°4N 31°15E **137** B3
Abû Zabad *Sudan* 12°25N 29°10E **135** F11
Abū Ẓāby *U.A.E.* 24°28N 54°22E **129** E7
Abū Zeydābād *Iran* 33°54N 51°45E **129** C6
Abuja *Nigeria* 9°5N 7°32E **139** D6
Abukuma-Gawa → *Japan* 38°6N 140°52E **112** E10
Abukuma-Sammyaku *Japan* 37°30N 140°45E **112** F10
Abunã *Brazil* 9°40S 65°20W **186** E5
Abunã → *Brazil* 9°41S 65°20W **186** E5
Aburo *Dem. Rep. of the Congo* 2°4N 30°53E **142** B3
Abut Hd. *N.Z.* 43°7S 170°15E **155** D5
Åby *Sweden* 58°40N 16°10E **63** F10
Aby, Lagune *Ivory C.* 5°15N 3°14W **138** D4
Abyei ⧄ *Sudan* 9°30N 28°30E **135** G11
Ābyek *Iran* 36°4N 50°33E **129** B6
Academy Gletscher *Greenland* 82°2N 34°0W **57** A7
Acadia △ *U.S.A.* 44°20N 68°13W **173** C19
Açailândia *Brazil* 4°57S 47°30W **189** A1
Acajutla *El Salv.* 13°36N 89°50W **182** D2
Acámbaro *Mexico* 20°2N 100°44W **180** D4
Acanthus *Greece* 40°27N 23°47E **96** F7
Acaponeta *Mexico* 22°30N 105°22W **180** C3
Acapulco *Mexico* 16°51N 99°55W **181** D5
Acaraí, Serra *Brazil* 1°50N 57°50W **186** C7
Acaraú *Brazil* 2°53S 40°7W **189** A2
Acari *Brazil* 6°31S 36°38W **189** B3
Acarí *Peru* 15°25S 74°36W **188** D3
Acarigua *Venezuela* 9°33N 69°12W **186** B5
Acatlán *Mexico* 18°12N 98°3W **181** D5
Acayucán *Mexico* 17°57N 94°55W **181** D6
Accéglio *Italy* 44°28N 7°0E **92** D4
Accomac *U.S.A.* 37°43N 75°40W **173** G16
Accous *France* 43°0N 0°36W **72** E3
Accra *Ghana* 5°35N 0°6W **139** D4
Accrington *U.K.* 53°45N 2°22W **66** D5
Acebal *Argentina* 33°20S 60°50W **190** C3
Aceh □ *Indonesia* 4°15N 97°30E **118** D1
Acerra *Italy* 40°57N 14°22E **95** B7
Aceuchal *Spain* 38°39N 6°30W **89** G4
Achacachi *Bolivia* 16°3S 68°43W **188** D4
Achaia *Greece* 38°5N 21°45E **98** C3
Achalpur *India* 21°22N 77°32E **126** D3
Achao *Chile* 42°28S 73°30W **192** B2
Acharnes *Greece* 38°5N 23°44E **98** C5
Acheloos → *Greece* 38°19N 21°7E **98** C3
Acheng *China* 45°30N 126°58E **115** B14
Achenkirch *Austria* 47°32N 11°45E **78** D4
Achensee *Austria* 47°26N 11°45E **78** D4
Achentrias *Greece* 34°59N 25°13E **99** G7
Acher *India* 23°10N 72°32E **124** H5
Achern *Germany* 48°37N 8°4E **77** G4
Acheron → *N.Z.* 42°16S 173°4E **155** C8
Achill Hd. *Ireland* 53°58N 10°15W **64** C1
Achill I. *Ireland* 53°58N 10°1W **64** C1
Achim *Germany* 53°1N 9°3E **76** B5
Achinsk *Russia* 56°20N 90°20E **107** D10
Achladokambos *Greece* 37°31N 22°35E **98** D4
Acıgöl *Turkey* 37°50N 29°50E **99** D11
Acıpayam *Turkey* 37°26N 29°22E **99** D11
Acireale *Italy* 37°37N 15°10E **95** E8
Ackerman *U.S.A.* 33°19N 89°11W **177** E10
Acklins I. *Bahamas* 22°30N 74°0W **183** B5
Acme *Canada* 51°33N 113°30W **162** C6
Acme *U.S.A.* 40°8N 79°26W **174** F5
Acobamba *Peru* 12°52S 74°35W **188** C3
Acomayo *Peru* 13°55S 71°38W **188** C3
Aconcagua, Cerro *Argentina* 32°39S 70°0W **190** C2
Aconquija, Mt. *Argentina* 27°0S 66°0W **190** B2
Acopiara *Brazil* 6°6S 39°27W **189** B3
Açores, Is. dos *Atl. Oc.* 38°0N 27°0W **134** a
Acornhoek *S. Africa* 24°37S 31°2E **145** B5
Acquapendente *Italy* 42°44N 11°52E **93** F8
Acquasanta Terme *Italy* 42°46N 13°24E **93** F10
Acquasparta *Italy* 42°41N 12°33E **93** F9
Acquaviva delle Fonti *Italy* 40°54N 16°50E **95** B9
Ácqui Terme *Italy* 44°41N 8°28E **92** D5
Acraman, L. *Australia* 32°2S 135°23E **151** E2
Acre = 'Akko *Israel* 32°55N 35°4E **130** C4
Acre □ *Brazil* 9°1S 71°0W **188** B3
Acre → *Brazil* 8°45S 67°22W **188** B4
Acri *Italy* 39°29N 16°23E **95** C9
Acs *Hungary* 47°42N 18°2E **80** C3
Actinolite *Canada* 44°32N 77°19W **174** B7
Actium *Greece* 38°57N 20°45E **98** C2
Acton *Canada* 43°38N 80°3W **174** C4
Açu *Brazil* 5°34S 36°54W **189** B3
Acworth *U.S.A.* 34°4N 84°41W **178** A5
Ad Dafinah *Si. Arabia* 23°18N 41°58E **137** C5
Ad Daghghāran *Iraq* 32°8N 44°55E **105** G11
Ad Dahnā *Si. Arabia* 24°30N 48°10E **131** C4
Ad Dammām *Si. Arabia* 26°20N 50°5E **129** E6
Ad Dāmūr *Lebanon* 33°43N 35°27E **130** B4
Ad Dawādimī *Si. Arabia* 24°35N 44°15E **128** E5
Ad Dawḩah *Qatar* 25°15N 51°35E **129** E6
Ad Dawr *Iraq* 34°27N 43°47E **105** E10
Ad Dhakhīrah *Qatar* 25°44N 51°33E **129** E6
Ad Dir'īyah *Si. Arabia* 24°44N 46°35E **128** E5
Ad Dīwānīyah *Iraq* 32°0N 45°0E **105** F11
Ad Dujayl *Iraq* 33°51N 44°14E **105** F11
Ad Duwayd *Si. Arabia* 30°15N 42°17E **128** D4
Ada *Ghana* 5°44N 0°40E **139** D5
Ada *Serbia* 45°49N 20°9E **80** E5
Ada *Minn., U.S.A.* 47°18N 96°31W **172** B5
Ada *Okla., U.S.A.* 34°46N 96°41W **176** D6
Adabiya *Egypt* 29°53N 32°28E **130** F1
Adair, C. *Canada* 71°30N 71°34W **161** C17
Adaja → *Spain* 41°32N 4°52W **88** D6
Adak *U.S.A.* 51°45N 176°45W **166** E4
Adak I. *U.S.A.* 51°45N 176°45W **166** E4
Adam, Mt. *Falk. Is.* 51°34S 60°4W **192** D4
Adamaoua □ *Cameroon* 6°30N 13°30E **139** D7
Adamaoua, Massif de l' *Cameroon* 7°20N 12°20E **139** D7
Adamawa □ *Nigeria* 9°20N 12°30E **139** D7
Adamawa Highlands = Adamaoua, Massif de l' *Cameroon* 7°20N 12°20E **139** D7
Adamello, Mte. *Italy* 46°9N 10°30E **92** B7
Adamello ⌓ *Italy* 46°4N 10°28E **92** B7
Adaminaby *Australia* 36°0S 148°45E **153** D8
Adams *Mass., U.S.A.* 42°38N 73°7W **175** D11
Adams *N.Y., U.S.A.* 43°49N 76°1W **175** C8
Adams *Wis., U.S.A.* 43°57N 89°49W **172** D9
Adams, Mt. *U.S.A.* 46°12N 121°30W **170** D5
Adam's Bridge *Sri Lanka* 9°15N 79°40E **127** K4
Adams L. *Canada* 51°10N 119°40W **162** C5
Adam's Peak *Sri Lanka* 6°48N 80°30E **127** L5
Adamuz *Spain* 38°2N 4°32W **89** G6
'Adan *Yemen* 12°45N 45°0E **131** E4
Adana *Turkey* 37°0N 35°16E **104** D6
Adana □ *Turkey* 37°0N 35°30E **104** D6
Adanero *Spain* 40°56N 4°36W **88** E6
Adang, Ko *Thailand* 6°33N 99°18E **121** J2
Adapazarı = Sakarya *Turkey* 40°48N 30°25E **104** B4
Adar Gwagwa, J. *Sudan* 22°15N 35°20E **137** C4
Adarama *Sudan* 17°10N 34°52E **135** E12
Adare *Ireland* 52°34N 8°47W **64** D3
Adare, C. *Antarctica* 71°0S 171°0E **55** D11
Adaut *Indonesia* 8°8S 131°7E **119** F8
Adavale *Australia* 25°52S 144°32E **151** D3
Adda → *Italy* 45°8N 9°53E **92** C6
Addatigala *India* 17°31N 82°3E **126** F6
Addis Ababa = Addis Abeba *Ethiopia* 9°2N 38°42E **131** F2
Addis Abeba *Ethiopia* 9°2N 38°42E **131** F2
Addison *U.S.A.* 42°1N 77°14W **174** D7
Addo *S. Africa* 33°32S 25°45E **144** D4
Addo △ *S. Africa* 33°30S 25°50E **144** D4
Adebour *Niger* 13°17N 11°50E **139** C7
Ādeh *Iran* 37°42N 45°11E **128** B5
Adel *U.S.A.* 31°8N 83°25W **178** D6
Adel Bagrou *Mauritania* 15°29N 6°57W **138** B3
Adelaide *Australia* 34°52S 138°30E **152** C3
Adelaide *S. Africa* 32°42S 26°20E **144** D4
Adelaide I. *Antarctica* 67°15S 68°30W **55** C17
Adelaide Pen. *Canada* 68°15N 97°30W **160** D12
Adelaide River *Australia* 13°15S 131°7E **148** B5
Adelaide Village *Bahamas* 25°0N 77°31W **182** A4
Adelanto *U.S.A.* 34°35N 117°22W **171** L9
Adele I. *Australia* 15°32S 123°9E **148** C3
Adélie, Terre *Antarctica* 68°0S 140°0E **55** C10
Adelie Land = Adélie, Terre *Antarctica* 68°0S 140°0E **55** C10
Adelong *Australia* 35°16S 148°4E **153** C8
Adelsk *Belarus* 53°24N 23°47E **82** E10
Ademuz *Spain* 40°5N 1°13W **90** E3
Aden = 'Adan *Yemen* 12°45N 45°0E **131** E4
Aden, G. of *Ind. Oc.* 12°30N 47°30E **131** E4
Adendorp *S. Africa* 32°15S 24°30E **144** D3
Aderbissinat *Niger* 15°34N 7°54E **139** B6
Adh Dhayd *U.A.E.* 25°17N 55°53E **129** E7
Adhoi *India* 23°26N 70°32E **124** H4
Adi *Indonesia* 4°15S 133°30E **119** E8
Adieu, C. *Australia* 32°0S 132°10E **149** F5
Adieu Pt. *Australia* 15°14S 124°35E **148** C3
Adige → *Italy* 45°9N 12°20E **93** C9
Adigrat *Ethiopia* 14°20N 39°26E **131** E2
Adıgüzel Barajı *Turkey* 38°13N 29°14E **99** C11
Adilabad *India* 19°33N 78°20E **126** E4
Adilcevaz *Turkey* 38°47N 42°43E **105** C10
Adirondack ⌓ *U.S.A.* 44°0N 74°20W **175** C10
Adirondack Mts. *U.S.A.* 44°0N 74°0W **175** C10
Adis Abeba = Addis Abeba *Ethiopia* 9°2N 38°42E **131** F2
Adıyaman *Turkey* 37°45N 38°16E **105** D8
Adıyaman □ *Turkey* 37°30N 38°10E **105** D8
Adjim *Tunisia* 33°47N 10°50E **136** B6
Adjohon *Benin* 6°41N 2°32E **139** D5
Adjud *Romania* 46°7N 27°10E **81** D12
Adjumani *Uganda* 3°20N 31°50E **142** B3
Adjuntas *Puerto Rico* 18°10N 66°43W **183** d
Adlavik Is. *Canada* 55°0N 58°40W **165** B8
Adler *Russia* 43°28N 39°52E **87** J4
Admer *Algeria* 20°21N 5°27E **139** A6
Admer, Erg d' *Algeria* 24°0N 9°5E **136** D5
Admiralty G. *Australia* 14°20S 125°55E **148** B4
Admiralty Gulf ☼ *Australia* 14°16S 125°52E **148** B4
Admiralty I. *U.S.A.* 57°30N 134°30W **162** B2
Admiralty Inlet *Canada* 72°30N 86°0W **161** C14
Admiralty Is. *Papua N. G.* 2°0S 147°0E **147** B7
Adnan Menderes, İzmir ✈ (ADB) *Turkey* 38°23N 27°6E **99** C9
Ado *Nigeria* 6°36N 2°56E **139** D5
Ado-Ekiti *Nigeria* 7°38N 5°12E **139** D6
Adolfo González Chaves *Argentina* 38°2S 60°5W **190** D3
Adolfo Ruiz Cortines, Presa *Mexico* 27°15N 109°6W **180** B3
Adonara *Indonesia* 8°15S 123°5E **119** F6
Adoni *India* 15°33N 77°18E **127** G3
Adony *Hungary* 47°6N 18°52E **80** C3
Adour → *France* 43°32N 1°32W **72** E2
Adra *India* 23°30N 86°42E **125** H12
Adra *Spain* 36°43N 3°3W **89** J7
Adrano *Italy* 37°40N 14°50E **95** E7
Adrar *Algeria* 27°51N 0°19W **136** C3
Adrar *Mauritania* 20°30N 7°30W **134** D3
Adrar □ *Algeria* 25°45N 1°0E **136** C4
Adrar □ *Mauritania* 21°0N 10°0W **138** A3
Adrar des Iforas *Africa* 19°40N 1°40E **139** B5
Ádria *Italy* 45°3N 12°3E **93** C9
Adrian *Ga., U.S.A.* 32°33N 82°35W **178** C7
Adrian *Mich., U.S.A.* 41°54N 84°2W **173** E11
Adrian *Tex., U.S.A.* 35°16N 102°40W **176** D3
Adriatic Sea *Medit. S.* 43°0N 16°0E **58** G9
Adua *Indonesia* 1°45S 129°50E **119** E7
Adur *India* 9°8N 76°40E **127** K3
Adwa *Ethiopia* 14°15N 38°52E **131** E2
Adygea □ *Russia* 45°0N 40°0E **87** H5
Adzhar Republic = Ajaria □ *Georgia* 41°30N 42°0E **87** K6
Adzopé *Ivory C.* 6°7N 3°49W **138** D4
Aegae = Aigai *Greece* 40°28N 22°19E **96** F6
Ægean Sea *Medit. S.* 38°30N 25°0E **99** C7
Aerhtai Shan *Mongolia* 46°40N 92°45E **109** C12
Ærø *Denmark* 54°52N 10°25E **63** K4
Ærøskøbing *Denmark* 54°53N 10°24E **63** K4
Aetdia-Akarnania = Etoloakarnania *Greece* 38°45N 21°18E **98** C3
Aetos *Greece* 37°15N 21°50E **98** D3
Afaahiti *Tahiti* 17°45S 149°17W **155** b
'Afak *Iraq* 32°4N 45°15E **105** F11
Afandou *Greece* 36°18N 28°12E **101** C10
Afarag, Erg *Algeria* 23°50N 2°47E **136** D4
Afghanistan ■ *Asia* 33°0N 65°0E **122** C4
Afikpo *Nigeria* 5°53N 7°54E **139** D6
Aflisses, O. → *Algeria* 28°40N 0°50E **136** C4
Aflou *Algeria* 34°7N 2°3E **136** B4
Afogados da Ingàzeira *Brazil* 7°45S 37°39W **189** B3
Afognak I. *U.S.A.* 58°15N 152°30W **166** D9
Afragóla *Italy* 40°55N 14°18E **95** B7
Afram → *Ghana* 7°0N 0°52W **139** D4
Africa 10°0N 20°0E **132** E6
'Afrīn *Syria* 36°32N 36°50E **104** D7
Afşin *Turkey* 38°14N 36°55E **104** C7
Afton *N.Y., U.S.A.* 42°14N 75°32W **175** D9
Afton *Wyo., U.S.A.* 42°44N 110°56W **168** E8
Afuá *Brazil* 0°15S 50°20W **187** D8
'Afula *Israel* 32°37N 35°17E **130** C4
Afyon *Turkey* 38°45N 30°33E **99** C12
Afyon □ *Turkey* 38°25N 30°30E **99** C12
Afyonkarahisar = Afyon *Turkey* 38°45N 30°33E **99** C12
Aga *Egypt* 30°55N 31°10E **137** E7
Āgā Jarī *Iran* 30°42N 49°50E **129** D6
Agadés = Agadez *Niger* 16°58N 7°59E **139** B6
Agadez *Niger* 16°58N 7°59E **139** B6
Agadir *Morocco* 30°28N 9°55W **136** B2
Agaete *Canary Is.* 28°6N 15°43W **100** F4
Agaie *Nigeria* 9°1N 6°18E **139** D6
Agalega Is. *Mauritius* 11°0S 57°0E **146** F4
Ağapınar *Turkey* 39°48N 30°47E **99** B12
Agar *India* 23°40N 76°2E **124** H7
Agar → *India* 21°0N 82°57E **126** D6
Agartala *India* 23°50N 91°23E **123** H17
Agăş *Romania* 46°28N 26°15E **81** D11
Agassiz *Canada* 49°14N 121°46W **162** D4
Agassiz Icecap *Canada* 80°15N 76°0W **161** A16
Agats *Indonesia* 5°33S 138°0E **119** F9
Agatti I. *India* 10°50N 72°12E **127** J1
Agattu I. *U.S.A.* 52°25N 173°35E **166** E2
Agawam *U.S.A.* 42°5N 72°37W **175** D12
Agbélouvé *Togo* 6°35N 1°14E **139** D5
Agboville *Ivory C.* 5°55N 4°15W **138** D4
Ağcabädi *Azerbaijan* 40°5N 47°27E **87** K8
Ağdam *Azerbaijan* 40°0N 46°58E **87** K8
Ağdara *Azerbaijan* 40°13N 46°49E **87** K8
Ağdaş *Azerbaijan* 40°44N 47°22E **87** K8
Agde *France* 43°19N 3°28E **72** E7
Agde, C. d' *France* 43°16N 3°28E **72** E7
Agdz *Morocco* 30°47N 6°30W **136** B2
Agdzhabedi = Ağcabädi *Azerbaijan* 40°5N 47°27E **87** K8
Agen *France* 44°12N 0°38E **72** D4
Agerbæk *Denmark* 55°36N 8°48E **63** J2
Agersø *Denmark* 55°13N 11°12E **63** J5
Ageyevo *Russia* 54°10N 36°27E **84** E9
Aggteleki △ *Hungary* 48°27N 20°36E **80** B5
Āgh Kand *Iran* 37°15N 48°4E **105** D13
Aghathonisi *Greece* 37°28N 27°0E **99** D8
Aghia Anna *Greece* 38°52N 23°24E **98** C5
Aghia Deka *Greece* 35°3N 24°58E **101** D6
Aghia Ekaterinis, Akra *Greece* 39°50N 19°50E **101** A3
Aghia Galini *Greece* 35°6N 24°41E **101** D6
Aghia Marina *Kasos, Greece* 35°27N 26°53E **99** F8
Aghia Marina *Leros, Greece* 37°11N 26°48E **99** D8
Aghia Paraskevi *Greece* 39°14N 26°21E **99** B8
Aghia Roumeli *Greece* 35°14N 23°58E **98** F5
Aghia Varvara *Greece* 35°8N 25°1E **101** D7
Aghiasos *Greece* 39°5N 26°23E **99** B8
Aghio Theodori *Greece* 37°55N 23°9E **98** D5
Aghion Oros □ *Greece* 40°25N 24°6E **97** F8
Aghios Andreas *Greece* 37°21N 22°45E **98** D4
Aghios Efstratios *Greece* 39°34N 24°58E **98** B6
Aghios Georgios *Greece* 37°28N 23°57E **98** D5
Aghios Ioannis, Akra *Greece* 35°20N 25°40E **101** D7
Aghios Isidoros *Greece* 36°9N 27°51E **101** C9
Aghios Kirikos *Greece* 37°34N 26°17E **99** D8
Aghios Matheos *Greece* 39°30N 19°47E **101** B3
Aghios Mironas *Greece* 35°15N 25°1E **99** F7
Aghios Nikolaos *Greece* 35°11N 25°41E **101** D7
Aghios Petros *Greece* 38°40N 20°36E **98** C2
Aghios Stephanos *Greece* 39°46N 19°39E **101** A3
Aghiou Orous, Kolpos *Greece* 40°6N 24°0E **96** F7
Aghireşu *Romania* 46°53N 23°15E **81** D8
Agia *Greece* 39°43N 22°45E **98** B4
Aginskoye *Russia* 51°6N 114°32E **107** D12
Agjert *Mauritania* 16°23N 9°17W **138** B3
Ağlasun *Turkey* 37°39N 30°31E **99** D12
Agly → *France* 42°46N 3°3E **72** F7
Agnéby □ *Ivory C.* 6°0N 4°15W **138** D4
Agnew *Australia* 28°1S 120°31E **149** E3
Agnibilékrou *Ivory C.* 7°10N 3°11W **138** D4
Agnita *Romania* 45°59N 24°40E **81** E9
Agnone *Italy* 41°48N 14°22E **93** G11
Ago-Are *Nigeria* 8°30N 3°25E **139** D5
Agofie *Ghana* 8°27N 0°15E **139** D5
Agogna → *Italy* 45°4N 8°54E **92** C5
Agoitz = Aoiz *Spain* 42°46N 1°22W **90** C3
Agön *Sweden* 61°34N 17°23E **62** C11
Agon-Coutainville *France* 49°2N 1°34W **70** C5
Ágordo *Italy* 46°18N 12°2E **93** B9
Agori *India* 24°33N 82°57E **125** G10
Agouna *Benin* 7°39N 1°47E **139** D5
Agout → *France* 43°47N 1°41E **72** E5
Agra *India* 27°17N 77°58E **124** F7
Agrakhanskiuy Poluostrov *Russia* 43°42N 47°36E **87** J8
Agramunt *Spain* 41°48N 1°6E **90** D6
Ágreda *Spain* 41°51N 1°55W **90** D3
Ağri *Turkey* 39°44N 43°3E **105** C10
Ağri □ *Turkey* 39°45N 43°5E **105** C10
Agri → *Italy* 40°13N 16°44E **95** B9
Ağrı Dağı *Turkey* 39°50N 44°15E **105** C11
Ağri Karakose = Ağri *Turkey* 39°44N 43°3E **105** C10
Agria *Greece* 39°20N 23°1E **98** B5
Agrigento *Italy* 37°19N 13°34E **94** E6
Agrinio *Greece* 38°37N 21°27E **98** C3
Agrópoli *Italy* 40°21N 14°59E **95** B7
Ağstafa *Azerbaijan* 41°7N 45°27E **87** K7
Água Branca *Brazil* 5°50S 42°40W **189** B2
Agua Caliente *Mexico* 32°29N 116°59W **171** N10
Agua Caliente Springs *U.S.A.* 32°56N 116°19W **171** N10
Água Clara *Brazil* 20°25S 52°45W **187** H8
Agua Fria ⌓ *U.S.A.* 34°14N 112°0W **169** J8
Agua Hechicera *Mexico* 32°28N 116°15W **171** N10
Agua Prieta *Mexico* 31°18N 109°34W **180** A3
Aguada Cecilio *Argentina* 40°51S 65°51W **192** B3
Aguadilla *Puerto Rico* 18°26N 67°10W **183** d
Aguadulce *Panama* 8°15N 80°32W **182** E3
Aguanga *U.S.A.* 33°27N 116°51W **171** M10
Aguanish *Canada* 50°14N 62°2W **165** B7
Aguanish → *Canada* 50°13N 62°5W **165** B7
Aguapey → *Argentina* 29°7S 56°36W **190** B4
Aguaray Guazú → *Paraguay* 24°47S 57°19W
Aguarico → *Ecuador* 0°59S 75°11W
Aguaro-Guariquito △ *Venezuela* 8°20N 66°35W
Aguas → *Spain* 41°20N 0°30W
Aguas Blancas *Chile* 24°15S 69°55W
Aguas Calientes, Sierra de *Argentina* 25°26S 66°40W
Águas Formosas *Brazil* 17°5S 40°57W
Águas Lindas de Goiás *Brazil* 15°46S 48°15W
Aguascalientes *Mexico* 21°53N 102°18W
Aguascalientes □ *Mexico* 22°0N 102°20W
Agudo *Spain* 38°59N 4°52W
Águeda *Portugal* 40°34N 8°27W
Agueda → *Spain* 41°2N 6°56W
Aguelhok *Mali* 19°29N 0°52E
Aguié *Niger* 13°31N 7°46E
Aguila, Punta *Puerto Rico* 17°57N 67°13W
Aguilafuente *Spain* 41°13N 4°7W
Aguilar de Campóo *Spain* 42°47N 4°15W
Aguilar de la Frontera *Spain* 37°31N 4°40W
Aguilares *Argentina* 27°26S 65°35W
Águilas *Spain* 37°23N 1°35W
Agüimes *Canary Is.* 27°58N 15°27W
Aguja, C. de la *Colombia* 11°18N 74°12W
Agujereada, Pta. *Puerto Rico* 18°30N 67°8W
Agulhas, C. *S. Africa* 34°52S 20°0E
Agulhas Ridge *Atl. Oc.* 42°0S 15°0E
Agulo *Canary Is.* 28°11N 17°12W
Agung, Gunung *Indonesia* 8°20S 115°28E
Aguni-Jima *Japan* 26°30N 127°10E
Agur *Uganda* 2°28N 32°55E
Agusan → *Phil.* 9°0N 125°30E
Ağva *Turkey* 41°8N 29°51E
Agvali *Russia* 42°36N 46°8E
Aha Mts. *Botswana* 19°45S 21°0E
Ahaggar *Algeria* 23°0N 6°30E
Ahaggar △ *Algeria* 23°0N 4°50E
Ahai Dam *China* 27°21N 100°30E
Ahal □ *Turkmenistan* 37°0N 57°0E
Ahamansu *Ghana* 7°38N 0°35E
Ahar *Iran* 38°35N 47°0E
Ahat *Turkey* 38°39N 29°47E
Ahaura → *N.Z.* 42°21S 171°34E
Ahaus *Germany* 52°4N 7°0E
Ahelledjem *Algeria* 26°37N 6°58E
Ahimanawa Ra. *N.Z.* 39°3S 176°30E
Ahipara B. *N.Z.* 35°5S 173°5E
Ahir Dağı *Turkey* 38°45N 30°10E
Ahiri *India* 19°30N 80°0E
Ahlat *Turkey* 38°45N 42°29E
Ahlen *Germany* 51°45N 7°53E
Ahmad Wal *Pakistan* 29°18N 65°58E
Ahmadabad *India* 23°0N 72°40E
Aḩmadābād *Khorāsān, Iran* 35°3N 60°50E
Aḩmadābād *Khorāsān, Iran* 35°49N 59°42E
Aḩmadī *Iran* 27°56N 56°42E
Ahmadnagar *India* 19°7N 74°46E
Ahmadpur *India* 18°40N 76°57E
Ahmadpur East *Pakistan* 29°12N 71°10E
Ahmadpur Lamma *Pakistan* 28°19N 70°3E
Ahmedabad = Ahmadabad *India* 23°0N 72°40E
Ahmednagar = Ahmadnagar *India* 19°7N 74°46E
Ahmetbey *Turkey* 41°26N 27°34E
Ahmetler *Turkey* 38°28N 29°5E
Ahmetli *Turkey* 38°32N 27°57E
Ahoada *Nigeria* 5°8N 6°36E
Ahome *Mexico* 25°55N 109°11W
Ahoskie *U.S.A.* 36°17N 76°59W
Ahr → *Germany* 50°32N 7°16E
Ahram *Iran* 28°52N 51°16E
Ahrax Pt. *Malta* 36°0N 14°22E
Ahrensbök *Germany* 54°2N 10°35E
Ahrensburg *Germany* 53°40N 10°13E
Ahuachapán *El Salv.* 13°54N 89°52W
Ahun *France* 46°4N 2°5E
Ahuriri → *N.Z.* 44°31S 170°12E
Åhus *Sweden* 55°56N 14°18E
Ahvāz *Iran* 31°20N 48°40E
Ahvenanmaa = Åland *Finland* 60°15N 20°0E
Aḩwar *Yemen* 13°30N 46°40E
Ahzar → *Mali* 15°30N 3°20E
Ai → *India* 26°26N 90°44E
Ai-Ais *Namibia* 27°54S 17°59E
Ai-Ais and Fish River Canyon △ *Namibia* 24°45S 17°15E
Aichach *Germany* 48°27N 11°8E
Aichi □ *Japan* 35°0N 137°15E
Aigai *Greece* 40°28N 22°19E
Aigle *Switz.* 46°18N 6°58E
Aignay-le-Duc *France* 47°40N 4°43E
Aigoual, Mt. *France* 44°8N 3°35E
Aigre *France* 45°54N 0°1E
Aigrettes, Pte. des *Réunion* 21°3S 55°13E
Aiguá *Uruguay* 34°13S 54°46W
Aigueperse *France* 46°3N 3°13E
Aigues → *France* 44°7N 4°43E
Aigues-Mortes *France* 43°35N 4°12E
Aigues-Mortes, G. d' *France* 43°31N 4°3E
Aigües-Tortes i Estany de St. Maurici △ *Spain* 42°38N 0°31E
Aiguilles *France* 44°47N 6°51E
Aiguillon *France* 44°18N 0°21E
Aigurande *France* 46°27N 1°49E
Aihui = Heihe *China* 50°10N 127°30E
Aija *Peru* 9°50S 77°45W
Aikawa *Japan* 38°2N 138°15E
Aiken *U.S.A.* 33°34N 81°43W
Ailao Shan *China* 24°0N 101°20E
Aileron *Australia* 22°39S 133°20E
Ailey *U.S.A.* 32°11N 82°34W

nt-sur-Tholon
ance 47°52N 3°20E 71 E10
k Canada 55°11N 59°18W 165 A8
Craig Canada 43°8N 81°33W 174 C3
Craig U.K. 55°15N 5°6W 65 F3
Russia 59°0N 133°55E 107 D14
ogasta Argentina 28°33S 66°50W 190 B2
orés Brazil 19°30S 41°4W 189 D2
☐ France 46°5N 5°20E 71 F12
→ France 45°45N 5°11E 73 C9
Beïda Algeria 35°50N 7°29E 136 A5
Ben Khellil Algeria 33°15N 0°49W 136 B3
Ben Tili Mauritania 25°59N 9°27W 134 C4
Beni Mathar Morocco 34°1N 2°0W 136 B3
Benian Algeria 36°48N 2°55E 136 A4
Dalla Egypt 27°20N 27°23E 137 B2
Defla Algeria 36°16N 1°58E 136 A4
Defla ☐ Algeria 36°10N 2°10E 136 A4
l Mafki Egypt 27°30N 28°15E 137 B2
Birba Egypt 29°20N 25°14E 137 B2
'Ilia Algeria 36°2N 6°35E 136 A5
Murr Sudan 21°50N 25°9E 137 C2
Deiqab Egypt 29°42N 24°55E 137 B1
efra Algeria 32°47N 0°37W 136 B3
Sheikh Murzûk
gypt 26°47N 27°45E 137 B2
Sudr Egypt 29°50N 33°6E 130 F2
Sukhna Egypt 29°32N 32°20E 137 F8
Tédelès Algeria 36°0N 0°21E 136 A4
Témouchent Algeria 35°16N 1°8W 136 A3
Témouchent ☐
eria 35°20N 1°5W 136 A3
Tikkidine Algeria 25°33N 1°24E 136 C4
Touta Algeria 35°26N 5°54E 136 A5
eitûn Egypt 29°10N 25°48E 137 B2
orah Morocco 34°37N 3°32W 136 B3
ni Latvia 57°50N 24°24E 84 D3
s Oros Greece 38°9N 20°40E 98 C2
worth U.S.A. 42°33N 99°52W 172 D4
le Bolivia 18°10S 65°10W 186 G5
iger 18°30N 8°0E 139 B6
Ténéré ⌂ Niger 18°12N 9°56E 139 B6
orce I. Canada 67°58N 74°5W 161 D17
itam Malaysia 1°55N 103°11E 121 M4
nes France 49°58N 1°55E 71 C8
ie Canada 51°18N 114°2W 162 C6
ie U.K. 55°52N 3°57W 65 F5
→ France 49°18N 4°49E 71 C11
→ U.K. 53°43N 0°55W 66 D7
I. de l' Spain 39°48N 4°16E 100 B11
sur-la-Lys France 50°37N 2°22E 71 B9
sur-l'Adour France 43°42N 0°15W 72 E3
s Inlet Australia 38°29S 144°5E 152 E6
Beach Australia 20°16S 148°43E 150 b
ult France 46°50N 0°8W 70 F6
→ Germany 49°49N 10°58E 77 F6
☐ Chile 46°30S 73°0W 192 C2
☐ France 49°42N 3°40E 71 C10
→ France 49°26N 2°50E 71 C9
dia 25°54N 79°14E 125 G8
en Haddou Morocco 31°3N 7°7W 136 B2
a, Sierra de Spain 38°35N 0°24W 91 G4
n U.S.A. 46°32N 93°42W 172 B7
aki Cook Is. 18°52S 159°45W 157 J12
oa Brazil 6°38S 40°7W 189 B2
Romania 46°19N 23°44E 81 D8
n-Provence France 43°32N 5°27E 73 E9
n-Chapelle = Aachen
many 50°45N 6°6E 76 E2
es-Bains France 45°41N 5°53E 73 C9
sur-Vienne France 45°47N 1°9E 72 C5
a = Egina Greece 37°45N 23°26E 98 D5
wl India 23°40N 92°44E 123 H18
say France 46°44N 1°38W 70 F5
aukle Latvia 56°36N 25°11E 84 D3
te Latvia 56°43N 21°40E 82 B8
vakamatsu Japan 37°30N 139°56E 112 F9
hir Iran 37°28N 45°54E 105 D11
io France 41°55N 8°40E 73 G12
io, G. d' France 41°52N 8°40E 73 G12
→ Uganda 2°52N 31°16E 142 B3
arh India 24°52N 80°16E 125 G9
an Mexico 18°22N 97°15W 181 D5
a India 20°30N 75°48E 126 D2
a Ra. India 20°28N 75°50E 126 D2
cuta Nigeria 7°28N 6°42E 139 D6
Rep. = Ajaria ☐
rgia 41°30N 42°0E 87 K6
a ☐ Georgia 41°30N 42°0E 87 K6
Canada 43°50N 79°1W 174 C5
Mt. N.Z. 42°35S 172°5E 155 C7
iyâ Libya 30°54N 20°4E 135 B10
ščina Slovenia 45°54N 13°54E 93 C10
Hungary 47°4N 17°31E 80 C2
n Jordan 32°18N 35°47E 130 C4
n ☐ Jordan 32°18N 35°47E 130 C4
n U.A.E. 25°25N 55°30E 129 E7
r India 26°28N 74°37E 124 F6
a India 31°50N 74°48E 124 D6
.S.A. 32°22N 112°52W 169 K7
. de Spain 43°31N 3°35W 88 B7
ağ Turkey 36°30N 29°32E 99 E11
ağlar Turkey 39°32N 36°12E 104 C7
ağları Turkey 36°30N 29°30E 99 E11
ovurak Russia 51°11N 90°36E 109 B12
a Togo 8°10N 1°2E 139 D5
ira Japan 43°33N 142°5E 112 C11
li Algeria 26°49N 1°31E 136 C4
emika Obrucheva, Khrebet
sia 51°50N 96°0E 109 B13
era △ Rwanda 1°31S 30°33E 142 C3
kot India 17°32N 76°13E 126 F3
nas Cyprus 35°3N 32°18E 101 D11
△ Japan 43°20N 144°20E 112 C12
thou Cyprus 35°22N 33°45E 101 D12
ca Turkey 38°35N 29°35E 99 C11
oa N.Z. 43°49S 172°55E 155 D7
oa Harbour N.Z. 43°50S 172°55E 155 D7
ha Sudan 21°10N 30°32E 137 C3
hi Japan 34°45N 134°58E 113 G7
rpur Bihar, India 24°39N 83°58E 125 G10
rpur Ut. P., India 26°25N 82°32E 125 F10
u Algeria 36°31N 4°31E 136 A4
lak Russia 51°11N 55°37E 108 B5
abat Turkey 41°1N 39°34E 105 B8
dağ Turkey 38°27N 37°43E 104 C7
kale Turkey 36°41N 38°56E 105 D8
koca Turkey 41°5N 31°8E 104 B4
ova Turkey 41°31N 29°57E 97 E13
y Turkey 36°36N 29°45E 99 E11
y → Turkey 37°50N 28°15E 99 D10
Akdağ Turkey 38°33N 26°30E 99 C8
Akdağmadeni Turkey 39°39N 35°53E 104 C6
Akdoğan = Lysi Cyprus 35°6N 33°41E 101 D12
Akelamo Indonesia 1°35N 129°40E 119 D7
Åkers styckebruk
Sweden 59°15N 17°5E 62 E11
Åkersberga Sweden 59°29N 18°18E 62 E12
Akeru → India 17°25N 80°5E 126 F5
Aketi
Dem. Rep. of the Congo 2°38N 23°47E 140 D4
Akhali Atoni Georgia 43°7N 40°50E 87 J5
Akhalkalaki Georgia 41°27N 43°25E 87 K6
Akhaltsikhe Georgia 41°40N 43°0E 87 K6
Akhisar Turkey 38°56N 27°48E 99 C9
Akhmîm Egypt 26°31N 31°47E 137 B3
Akhna Cyprus 35°3N 33°47E 101 D12
Akhnur India 32°52N 74°45E 125 C6
Akhtopol Bulgaria 42°6N 27°56E 97 D11
Akhtuba → Russia 47°41N 46°55E 87 G8
Akhtubinsk Russia 48°13N 46°7E 87 F8
Akhty Russia 41°30N 47°45E 87 K8
Akhtyrka = Okhtyrka
Ukraine 50°25N 35°0E 85 G8
Aki Japan 33°30N 133°54E 113 H6
Akimiski I. Canada 52°50N 81°30W 164 B3
Akıncı Burnu Turkey 36°19N 35°46E 104 D6
Akıncılar = Louroujina
Cyprus 35°0N 33°28E 101 E12
Akiōta Japan 34°36N 132°19E 113 G6
Åkirkeby Denmark 55°4N 14°55E 63 J8
Akita Japan 39°45N 140°7E 112 E10
Akita ☐ Japan 39°40N 140°30E 112 E10
Akjoujt Mauritania 19°45N 14°15W 138 B2
Akka Mali 15°24N 4°11W 138 B4
Akka Morocco 29°22N 8°9W 136 C2
Akkaraipattu Sri Lanka 7°13N 81°51E 127 L5
Akkaya Tepesi Turkey 37°25N 29°38E 99 D11
Akkeshi Japan 43°2N 144°51E 112 C12
'Akko Israel 32°55N 35°4E 130 C4
Akköy Turkey 37°29N 27°15E 99 D9
Akkuş Turkey 40°47N 37°0E 104 B7
Aklampa Benin 8°15N 2°10E 139 D5
Aklavik Canada 68°12N 135°0W 160 D4
Aklera India 24°26N 76°32E 124 G7
Akmenė Lithuania 56°15N 22°45E 82 B9
Akmenrags Latvia 56°50N 21°4E 82 B8
Akmonte = Almonte
Spain 37°13N 6°38W 89 H4
Aknoul Morocco 34°40N 3°55W 136 B3
Akō Japan 34°45N 134°24E 113 G7
Ako Nigeria 10°19N 10°48E 139 C7
Akola Maharashtra, India 20°42N 77°2E 126 D3
Akola Maharashtra, India 19°32N 74°3E 126 E2
Akonolinga Cameroon 3°50N 12°18E 139 E7
Akor Mali 14°59N 6°58W 138 C3
Akordat Eritrea 15°30N 37°40E 131 D2
Akosombo Dam Ghana 6°20N 0°5E 139 D5
Akot India 21°10N 77°10E 126 D3
Akoupé Ivory C. 6°23N 3°54W 138 D4
Akpatok I. Canada 60°25N 68°8W 161 E18
Åkrahamn Norway 59°15N 5°10E 61 G11
Akranes Iceland 64°19N 22°5W 60 D2
Akreïjit Mauritania 18°19N 9°11W 138 B3
Akritas, Akra Greece 36°43N 21°54E 98 E3
Akron Colo., U.S.A. 40°10N 103°13W 168 F12
Akron Ohio, U.S.A. 41°5N 81°31W 174 E3
Akrotiri Cyprus 34°36N 32°57E 101 E11
Akrotiri, Akra Greece 40°26N 25°27E 97 F9
Akrotiri Bay Cyprus 34°35N 33°10E 101 E12
Aksai Chin China 35°15N 79°55E 125 B8
Aksaray Turkey 38°25N 34°2E 104 C6
Aksaray ☐ Turkey 38°20N 33°45E 104 C5
Aksay = Aqsay
Kazakhstan 51°11N 53°0E 108 B4
Akşehir Turkey 38°18N 31°30E 104 C4
Akşehir Gölü Turkey 38°30N 31°25E 104 C4
Akstafa = Ağstafa
Azerbaijan 41°7N 45°27E 87 K7
Aksu China 41°5N 80°10E 109 D10
Aksu → Turkey 36°52N 30°57E 104 D4
Aksu He → China 40°26N 80°59E 109 D10
Aksum Ethiopia 14°5N 38°40E 131 E2
Aktash Russia 55°2N 52°0E 86 C11
Akto China 39°5N 75°59E 109 E9
Aktsyabrski Belarus 52°38N 28°53E 75 B15
Aktyubinsk = Aqtöbe
Kazakhstan 50°17N 57°10E 108 B5
Aku Nigeria 6°40N 7°18E 139 D6
Akure Nigeria 7°15N 5°5E 139 D6
Akuressa Sri Lanka 6°5N 80°29E 127 L5
Akureyri Iceland 65°40N 18°6W 60 D4
Akuseki-Shima Japan 29°27N 129°37E 113 K4
Akusha Russia 42°18N 47°30E 87 J8
Akwa-Ibom ☐ Nigeria 4°30N 7°30E 139 E6
Akwanga Nigeria 8°55N 8°23E 139 D6
Akyab = Sittwe
Burma 20°18N 92°45E 123 J18
Akyazı Turkey 40°40N 30°38E 104 B4
Al 'Adan = 'Adan
Yemen 12°45N 45°0E 131 E4
Al Aḩsā = Hasa
Si. Arabia 25°50N 49°0E 129 E6
Al Ajfar Si. Arabia 27°26N 43°0E 128 E4
Al Amādīyah Iraq 37°5N 43°30E 105 D10
Al 'Amārah Iraq 31°55N 47°15E 105 G12
Al Anbār ☐ Iraq 33°25N 42°0E 128 C4
Al 'Aqabah Jordan 29°31N 35°0E 130 F4
Al 'Aqabah ☐ Jordan 29°30N 35°0E 130 F4
Al Arak Syria 34°38N 38°35E 105 E8
Al 'Aramah Si. Arabia 25°30N 46°0E 128 E5
Al 'Artāwīyah
Si. Arabia 26°31N 45°20E 128 E5
Al 'Āşimah = 'Ammān ☐
Jordan 31°40N 36°30E 130 D5
Al 'Assāfīyah Si. Arabia 28°17N 38°59E 128 D3
Al 'Awdah Si. Arabia 25°32N 45°41E 128 E5
Al 'Ayn Si. Arabia 25°4N 38°6E 128 E3
Al 'Ayn U.A.E. 24°15N 55°45E 129 E7
Al 'Azīzīyah Iraq 32°54N 45°4E 105 F11
Al Bāb Syria 36°23N 37°29E 104 D7
Al Bad' Si. Arabia 28°28N 35°1E 128 D2
Al Bada'i' Si. Arabia 26°2N 43°33E 128 E4
Al Bādī Iraq 35°56N 41°32E 128 C4
Al Bāḩah Si. Arabia 20°1N 41°28E 137 C5
Al Baḩrah Kuwait 29°40N 47°52E 128 D5
Al Baḩral Mayyit = Dead Sea
Asia 31°30N 35°30E 130 D4
Al Balqā' ☐ Jordan 32°5N 35°45E 130 C4
Al Bārūk, J. Lebanon 33°39N 35°40E 130 B4
Al Başrah Iraq 30°30N 47°50E 128 D5
Al Baţḩā Iraq 31°6N 45°53E 128 D5
Al Batrūn Lebanon 34°15N 35°40E 130 A4
Al Bayḑā Libya 32°50N 21°44E 135 B10
Al Biqā Lebanon 34°10N 36°10E 130 A5
Al Bi'r Si. Arabia 28°51N 36°16E 128 D3
Al Bukayrīyah Si. Arabia 26°9N 43°40E 128 E4
Al Burayj Syria 34°15N 36°46E 130 A5
Al Faḑilī Si. Arabia 26°58N 49°10E 129 E6
Al Fallūjah Iraq 33°20N 43°55E 105 F10
Al Fatḩah Iraq 35°3N 43°33E 105 E10
Al Fāw Iraq 30°0N 48°30E 129 D6
Al Fujayrah U.A.E. 25°7N 56°18E 129 E8
Al Ghadaf, W. →
Jordan 31°26N 36°43E 130 D5
Al Ghammās Iraq 31°45N 44°37E 128 D5
Al Ghazālah Si. Arabia 26°48N 41°19E 128 E4
Al Ghuwayfāt U.A.E. 24°10N 51°38E 129 E6
Al Ḩadīthah Iraq 34°0N 41°13E 105 E10
Al Ḩadīthah Si. Arabia 31°28N 37°8E 130 D6
Al Ḩaḑr Iraq 35°35N 42°44E 105 E10
Al Ḩājānah Syria 33°20N 36°33E 130 B5
Al Ḩajar al Gharbī
Oman 24°10N 56°15E 129 E8
Al Ḩāmad Si. Arabia 31°30N 39°30E 128 D3
Al Ḩamdānīyah Syria 35°25N 36°50E 128 C3
Al Ḩamīdīyah Syria 34°42N 35°57E 130 A4
Al Ḩammār Iraq 30°57N 46°51E 128 D5
Al Ḩamrā' Si. Arabia 24°2N 38°55E 128 E3
Al Ḩamzah Iraq 31°43N 44°58E 128 D5
Al Ḩanākīyah
Si. Arabia 24°51N 40°31E 128 E4
Al Harūj al Aswad Libya 27°0N 17°10E 135 C9
Al Ḩasakah Syria 36°35N 40°45E 105 D9
Al Ḩasakah ☐ Syria 36°40N 40°50E 105 D9
Al Hāshimīyah Iraq 32°22N 44°39E 105 G11
Al Ḩayy Iraq 32°5N 46°5E 105 F12
Al Ḩijarah Asia 30°0N 44°0E 128 D4
Al Ḩillah Iraq 32°30N 44°25E 105 F11
Al Hindīyah Iraq 32°30N 44°10E 105 F11
Al Hirmil Lebanon 34°26N 36°24E 130 A5
Al Hoceïma Morocco 35°8N 3°58W 136 A3
Al Ḩudaydah Yemen 14°50N 43°0E 131 E3
Al Ḩudūd ash Shamālīyah ☐
Si. Arabia 29°10N 42°30E 128 D4
Al Hufūf Si. Arabia 25°25N 49°45E 129 E6
Al Ḩumayḑah
Si. Arabia 29°14N 34°56E 128 D2
Al Ḩunayy Si. Arabia 25°58N 48°45E 129 E6
Al Īsāwīyah Si. Arabia 30°43N 37°59E 128 D3
Al Jafr Jordan 30°18N 36°14E 130 E5
Al Jāfūrah Si. Arabia 25°0N 50°15E 129 E7
Al Jaghbūb Libya 29°42N 24°38E 135 C10
Al Jahrah Kuwait 29°25N 47°40E 128 D5
Al Jalāmīd Si. Arabia 31°20N 40°6E 128 D3
Al Jamalīyah Qatar 25°37N 51°5E 129 E6
Al Janūb ☐ Lebanon 33°20N 35°20E 130 B4
Al Jawf Libya 24°10N 23°24E 135 D10
Al Jawf Si. Arabia 29°55N 39°40E 128 D3
Al Jawf ☐ Si. Arabia 29°30N 39°30E 128 D3
Al Jazair = Algeria ■
Africa 28°30N 2°0E 136 C4
Al Jazirah Iraq 33°30N 44°0E 105 E10
Al Jithāmīyah Si. Arabia 27°41N 41°43E 128 E4
Al Jubayl Si. Arabia 27°0N 49°50E 129 E6
Al Jubaylah Si. Arabia 24°55N 46°25E 128 E5
Al Jubb Si. Arabia 27°11N 42°17E 128 E4
Al Junaynah Sudan 13°27N 22°45E 135 F10
Al Kabā'ish Iraq 30°58N 47°0E 128 D5
Al Karak Jordan 31°11N 35°42E 130 D4
Al Karak ☐ Jordan 31°0N 36°0E 130 E5
Al Kāẓimīyah Iraq 33°22N 44°18E 105 F11
Al Khābūrah Oman 23°57N 57°5E 129 F8
Al Khafji Si. Arabia 28°24N 48°29E 129 E6
Al Khalīl West Bank 31°32N 35°6E 130 D4
Al Khāliş Iraq 33°49N 44°32E 105 F11
Al Kharsānīyah
Si. Arabia 27°13N 49°18E 129 E6
Al Khaşab Oman 26°14N 56°15E 129 E8
Al Khawr Qatar 25°41N 51°30E 129 E6
Al Khiḑr Iraq 31°12N 45°33E 128 D5
Al Khiyām Lebanon 33°20N 35°36E 130 B4
Al Khubar Si. Arabia 26°17N 50°12E 129 E6
Al Khums Libya 32°40N 14°17E 135 B8
Al Khurmah Si. Arabia 21°54N 42°3E 131 C3
Al Kifl Iraq 32°13N 44°22E 105 G11
Al Kiswah Syria 33°23N 36°14E 130 B5
Al Kūfah Iraq 32°2N 44°24E 105 F11
Al Kufrah Libya 24°17N 23°15E 135 D10
Al Kuhayfīyah Si. Arabia 27°12N 43°3E 128 E4
Al Kumayt Iraq 32°2N 46°52E 105 G12
Al Kūt Iraq 32°30N 46°0E 105 F11
Al Kuwayt Kuwait 29°30N 48°0E 128 D5
Al Labwah Lebanon 34°11N 36°20E 130 A5
Al Lādhiqīyah Syria 35°30N 35°45E 104 E6
Al Lādhiqīyah ☐ Syria 35°45N 36°0E 104 E6
Al Līth Si. Arabia 20°9N 40°15E 137 C5
Al Liwā' Oman 24°31N 56°36E 129 E8
Al Luḩayyah Yemen 15°45N 42°40E 131 D3
Al Madīnah Iraq 30°57N 47°16E 128 D5
Al Madīnah Si. Arabia 24°35N 39°52E 128 E3
Al Mafraq Jordan 32°17N 36°14E 130 C5
Al Mafraq ☐ Jordan 32°17N 36°15E 130 C5
Al Maghreb = Morocco ■
N. Afr. 32°0N 5°50W 134 B4
Al Maḩmūdīyah Iraq 33°3N 44°21E 105 F11
Al Majma'ah Si. Arabia 25°57N 45°22E 128 E5
Al Makhruq, W. →
Jordan 31°28N 37°0E 130 D6
Al Makḩūl Si. Arabia 26°37N 42°39E 128 E4
Al Mālikīyah Syria 37°10N 42°8E 105 D10
Al Manāmah Bahrain 26°10N 50°30E 129 E6
Al Maqwa' Kuwait 29°10N 47°59E 128 D5
Al Maraḩ Si. Arabia 25°35N 49°35E 129 E6
Al Marj Libya 32°25N 20°30E 135 B10
Al Maţlā Kuwait 29°24N 47°40E 128 D5
Al Mawşil Iraq 36°15N 43°5E 105 D10
Al Mayādin Syria 35°1N 40°27E 105 E9
Al Mazār Jordan 31°4N 35°41E 130 D4
Al Midhnab Si. Arabia 25°50N 44°18E 128 E5
Al Minā' Lebanon 34°24N 35°49E 130 A4
Al Miqdādīyah Iraq 34°0N 45°0E 105 E11
Al Mubarraz Si. Arabia 25°30N 49°40E 129 E6
Al Mudawwarah Jordan 29°19N 36°0E 130 F5
Al Mughayrā' U.A.E. 24°5N 53°32E 129 E7
Al Muḩarraq Bahrain 26°15N 50°40E 129 E6
Al Mukallā Yemen 14°33N 49°2E 131 E4
Al Mukhā Yemen 13°18N 43°15E 131 E3
Al Musayjīd Si. Arabia 24°5N 39°5E 128 E3
Al Musayyib Iraq 32°49N 44°20E 105 F11
Al Muthanná ☐ Iraq 30°30N 45°15E 128 D5
Al Muwayh Si. Arabia 22°41N 41°37E 137 C5
Al Muwaylih Si. Arabia 27°40N 35°30E 128 E2
Al Owuho = Otukpa
Nigeria 7°9N 7°41E 139 D6
Al Qādisīyah ☐ Iraq 32°0N 45°0E 128 D5
Al Qā'im Iraq 34°21N 41°7E 105 E9
Al Qalībah Si. Arabia 28°24N 37°42E 128 D3
Al Qāmishlī Syria 37°2N 41°14E 105 D9
Al Qaryatayn Syria 34°12N 37°13E 130 A6
Al Qaşīm ☐ Si. Arabia 26°0N 43°0E 128 E4
Al Qaţ'ā Syria 34°40N 40°48E 105 E9
Al Qaţīf Si. Arabia 26°35N 50°0E 129 E6
Al Qatrānah Jordan 31°12N 36°6E 130 D5
Al Qaţrūn Libya 24°56N 15°3E 135 D9
Al Qawz Si. Arabia 18°58N 41°26E 137 D5
Al Qayşūmah Si. Arabia 28°20N 46°7E 128 D5
Al Quds = Jerusalem
Israel/West Bank 31°47N 35°10E 130 D4
Al Qunayţirah Syria 33°5N 35°45E 130 B4
Al Qunfudhah Si. Arabia 19°3N 41°4E 137 D5
Al Qurayyāt Si. Arabia 31°20N 37°20E 128 D3
Al Qurnah Iraq 31°1N 47°25E 128 D5
Al Quşayr Iraq 30°39N 45°50E 128 D5
Al Quşayr Syria 34°31N 36°34E 130 A5
Al Qutayfah Syria 33°44N 36°36E 130 B5
Al Quwayr Iraq 36°2N 43°29E 105 D10
Al Quwaysimah Jordan 31°55N 35°57E 130 D4
Al 'Ubaylah Si. Arabia 21°59N 50°57E 131 C5
Al 'Uḑaylīyah Si. Arabia 25°8N 49°18E 129 E6
Al 'Ulā Si. Arabia 26°35N 38°0E 128 E3
Al 'Uqayr Si. Arabia 25°40N 50°15E 129 E6
Al 'Uwaynid Si. Arabia 24°50N 46°0E 128 E5
Al 'Uwayqīlah
Si. Arabia 30°30N 42°10E 128 D4
Al 'Uyūn Ḩijāz,
Si. Arabia 24°33N 39°35E 128 E3
Al 'Uyūn Najd,
Si. Arabia 26°30N 43°50E 128 E4
Al 'Uzayr Iraq 31°19N 47°25E 128 D5
Al Wajh Si. Arabia 26°10N 36°30E 128 E3
Al Wakrah Qatar 25°10N 51°40E 129 E6
Al Waqbah Si. Arabia 28°48N 45°33E 128 D5
Al Wari'āh Si. Arabia 27°51N 47°25E 128 E5
Al Yaman = Yemen ■
Asia 15°0N 44°0E 131 E3
Ala Italy 45°45N 11°0E 92 C8
Ala Archa △
Kyrgyzstan 42°32N 74°28E 109 D8
Ala Dağ Turkey 37°44N 35°9E 128 B2
Ala Dağları Turkey 39°15N 43°33E 105 C10
Ala Tau Asia 45°30N 80°40E 109 C10
Ala Tau Shankou = Dzungarian
Gate Asia 45°10N 82°0E 109 C10
Alabama ☐ U.S.A. 33°0N 87°0W 177 E11
Alabama → U.S.A. 31°8N 87°57W 177 F11
Alabaster U.S.A. 33°15N 86°49W 177 E11
Alaca Turkey 40°10N 34°51E 104 B6
Alacaatlı Turkey 39°15N 28°3E 99 B10
Alaçam Turkey 41°36N 35°36E 104 B6
Alaçam Dağları Turkey 39°18N 28°49E 99 B10
Alacant = Alicante
Spain 38°23N 0°30W 91 G4
Alaçatı Turkey 38°15N 26°22E 99 C8
Alachua U.S.A. 29°47N 82°30W 178 F7
Alaejos Spain 41°18N 5°13W 88 D5
Alagir Russia 43°3N 44°14E 87 J7
Alagna Valsésia Italy 45°51N 7°56E 92 C4
Alagoa Grande Brazil 7°3S 35°35W 189 B3
Alagoas ☐ Brazil 9°0S 36°0W 189 B3
Alagoinhas Brazil 12°7S 38°20W 189 C3
Alagón Spain 41°46N 1°12W 90 D3
Alagón → Spain 39°44N 6°53W 88 F4
Alaheaieatnu = Altaelva →
Norway 69°54N 23°17E 60 B20
Alai Range Asia 39°45N 72°0E 109 E8
Alaior Spain 39°57N 4°8E 100 B11
Alajero Canary Is. 28°3N 17°13W 100 F2
Alajuela Costa Rica 10°2N 84°8W 182 D3
Alaknanda → India 30°8N 78°36E 125 D8
Alakol Kazakhstan 46°0N 81°5E 109 C10
Alakurtti Russia 66°58N 30°25E 60 C24
Alamarvdasht Iran 27°37N 52°59E 129 E7
Alameda Calif., U.S.A. 37°46N 122°15W 170 H4
Alameda N. Mex.,
U.S.A. 35°11N 106°37W 169 J10
Alamo Ga., U.S.A. 32°9N 82°47W 178 C7
Alamo Nev., U.S.A. 37°22N 115°10W 171 H11
Alamogordo U.S.A. 32°54N 105°57W 169 K11
Alamos Mexico 27°1N 108°56W 180 B3
Alamosa U.S.A. 37°28N 105°52W 169 H11
Alampur India 15°55N 78°6E 127 G4
Åland Finland 60°15N 20°0E 61 F19
Aland India 17°36N 76°35E 126 F3
Alandroal Portugal 38°41N 7°24W 89 G3
Ålands hav Europe 60°0N 19°30E 61 G18
Alandsbro Sweden 62°40N 17°51E 62 B11
Alandur India 13°0N 80°15E 127 H5
Alange, Embalse d' Spain 38°45N 6°18W 89 G4
Alanis Spain 38°3N 5°43W 89 G5
Alaniya = North Ossetia-
Alaniya ☐ Russia 43°30N 44°30E 87 J7
Alaniya △ Russia 42°55N 44°30E 87 J7
Alanya Turkey 36°38N 32°0E 104 D5
Alapaha U.S.A. 31°23N 83°13W 178 D6
Alapayevsk Russia 57°52N 61°42E 106 D7
Alappuzha India 9°30N 76°28E 127 K3
Alar del Rey Spain 42°38N 4°20W 88 C6
Alaraz Spain 40°45N 5°17W 88 E5
Alarcón, Embalse de
Spain 39°36N 2°10W 90 F2
Alaró Spain 39°42N 2°47E 100 B9
Alaşehir Turkey 38°23N 28°30E 99 C10
Alashtar Iran 33°51N 48°15E 105 F13
Alaska ☐ U.S.A. 64°0N 154°0W 166 C9
Alaska, G. of Pac. Oc. 58°0N 145°0W 160 F3
Alaska Peninsula
U.S.A. 56°0N 159°0W 166 D8
Alaska Range U.S.A. 62°50N 151°0W 160 E1
Alássio Italy 44°0N 8°10E 92 E5
Ālāt Azerbaijan 39°58N 49°25E 87 L9
Alatau Shan = Ala Tau
Asia 45°30N 80°40E 109 C10
Alatri Italy 41°43N 13°21E 93 G10
Alatyr Russia 54°55N 46°35E 86 C8
Alatyr → Russia 54°52N 46°36E 86 C8
Alausí Ecuador 2°0S 78°50W 186 D3
Álava ☐ Spain 42°48N 2°28W 90 C2
Alava, C. U.S.A. 48°10N 124°44W 170 B2
Alaverdi Armenia 41°15N 44°37E 87 K7
Alavo = Alavus Finland 62°35N 23°36E 60 E20
Alavus Finland 62°35N 23°36E 60 E20
Alawa ✪ Australia 15°42S 134°39E 150 B1
Alawoona Australia 34°45S 140°30E 152 C4
Alayawarra ✪
Australia 22°0S 134°30E 150 C1
'Alayh Lebanon 33°46N 35°33E 130 B4
Alayköy = Yerolakkos
Cyprus 35°11N 33°15E 101 D12
Alazani → Azerbaijan 41°5N 46°40E 87 K8
Alba Italy 44°42N 8°2E 92 D5
Alba ☐ Romania 46°10N 23°30E 81 D8
Alba Adriática Italy 42°50N 13°56E 93 F10
Alba de Tormes Spain 40°50N 5°30W 88 E5
Alba-Iulia Romania 46°8N 23°39E 81 D8
Albac Romania 46°28N 22°58E 80 D7
Albacete Spain 39°0N 1°50W 91 F3
Albacete ☐ Spain 38°50N 2°0W 91 G3
Albacutya, L. Australia 35°45S 141°58E 152 C4
Ålbæk Denmark 57°36N 10°25E 63 G4
Ålbæk Bugt Denmark 57°35N 10°40E 63 G4
Albaida Spain 38°51N 0°31W 91 G4
Albalate de las Nogueras
Spain 40°22N 2°18W 90 E2
Albalate del Arzobispo
Spain 41°6N 0°31W 90 D4
Alban France 43°53N 2°28E 72 E6
Albanel, L. Canada 50°55N 73°12W 164 B5
Albania ■ Europe 41°0N 20°0E 96 E4
Albano Laziale Italy 41°44N 12°39E 93 G9
Albany Australia 35°1S 117°58E 149 G2
Albany Ga., U.S.A. 31°35N 84°10W 178 D5
Albany N.Y., U.S.A. 42°39N 73°45W 175 D11
Albany Oreg., U.S.A. 44°38N 123°6W 168 D2
Albany Tex., U.S.A. 32°44N 99°18W 176 E5
Albany → Canada 52°17N 81°31W 164 B3
Albarca, C. d' Spain 39°4N 1°22E 100 B7
Albardón Argentina 31°20S 68°30W 190 C2
Albarracín Spain 40°25N 1°26W 90 E3
Albarracín, Sierra de
Spain 40°30N 1°30W 90 E3
Albatera Spain 38°11N 0°52W 91 G4
Albâtre, Côte d' France 49°55N 0°50E 70 C7
Albatross B. Australia 12°45S 141°30E 150 A3
Albatross Pt. N.Z. 38°7S 174°44E 154 E3
Albegna → Italy 42°30N 11°11E 93 F8
Albemarle U.S.A. 35°21N 80°12W 177 D14
Albemarle Sd. U.S.A. 36°5N 76°0W 177 C16
Albenga Italy 44°3N 8°13E 92 D5
Alberche → Spain 39°58N 4°46W 88 F6
Alberdi Paraguay 26°14S 58°20W 190 B4
Albères, Mts. France 42°28N 2°56E 72 F6
Ålberga Sweden 58°44N 16°35E 63 F10
Alberga → Australia 27°6S 135°33E 151 D2
Albersdorf Germany 54°8N 9°17E 76 A5
Albert France 50°0N 2°38E 71 C9
Albert, L. Africa 1°30N 31°0E 142 B3
Albert, L. Australia 35°30S 139°10E 152 C3
Albert Edward Ra.
Australia 18°17S 127°57E 148 C4
Albert Lea U.S.A. 43°39N 93°22W 172 D7
Albert Nile → Uganda 3°36N 32°2E 142 B3
Albert Town Bahamas 22°37N 74°33W 183 B5
Alberta ☐ Canada 54°40N 115°0W 162 C6
Alberti Argentina 35°1S 60°16W 190 D3
Albertinia S. Africa 34°11S 21°34E 144 D3
Albertirsa Hungary 47°14N 19°37E 80 C4
Alberto de Agostini △
Chile 54°38S 71°37W 192 D2
Alberton Canada 46°50N 64°0W 165 C7
Albertville France 45°40N 6°22E 73 C10
Albertville U.S.A. 34°16N 86°13W 177 D11
Albi France 43°56N 2°9E 72 E6
Albia U.S.A. 41°2N 92°48W 172 E7
Albina Suriname 5°37N 54°15W 187 B8
Albina, Ponta Angola 15°52S 11°44E 144 A1
Albino Italy 45°46N 9°47E 92 C6
Albion Mich., U.S.A. 42°15N 84°45W 173 D11
Albion Nebr., U.S.A. 41°42N 98°0W 172 E4
Albion Pa., U.S.A. 41°53N 80°22W 174 E4
Albocásser Spain 40°21N 0°1E 90 E5
Albolote Spain 37°14N 3°39W 89 H7
Alborán Medit. S. 35°57N 3°0W 89 K7
Alboran Sea Medit. S. 36°0N 3°30W 89 K7
Alborea Spain 39°17N 1°24W 91 F3
Ålborg = Aalborg Denmark 57°2N 9°54E 63 G3
Ålborg Bugt = Aalborg Bugt
Denmark 56°50N 10°35E 63 H4
Alborz, Reshteh-ye Kūhhā-ye
Iran 36°0N 52°0E 129 C7
Albox Spain 37°23N 2°8W 91 H2
Albufeira Portugal 37°5N 8°15W 89 H2
Albula → Switz. 46°38N 9°28E 77 J5
Albuñol Spain 36°48N 3°11W 89 J7
Albuquerque U.S.A. 35°5N 106°39W 169 J10
Albuquerque, Cayos de
Caribbean 12°10N 81°50W 182 D3
Alburg U.S.A. 44°59N 73°18W 175 B11
Alburno, Mte. Italy 40°33N 15°17E 95 B8
Alburquerque Spain 39°15N 6°59W 89 F4
Albury Australia 36°3S 146°56E 153 D7
Alby Sweden 62°30N 15°28E 62 B9
Alcácer do Sal Portugal 38°22N 8°33W 89 G2
Alcáçovas Portugal 38°23N 8°9W 89 G2
Alcalá de Guadaira
Spain 37°20N 5°50W 89 H5
Alcalá de Henares Spain 40°28N 3°22W 88 E7
Alcalá de los Gazules
Spain 36°29N 5°43W 89 J5
Alcalá de Xivert Spain 40°19N 0°13E 90 E5
Alcalá del Júcar Spain 39°12N 1°26W 91 F3
Alcalá del Río Spain 37°31N 5°59W 89 H5
Alcalá del Valle Spain 36°54N 5°10W 89 J5
Alcalá la Real Spain 37°27N 3°57W 89 H7
Álcamo Italy 37°59N 12°55E 94 E5
Alcanadre Spain 42°24N 2°7W 90 C2
Alcanadre → Spain 41°43N 0°12W 90 D4
Alcanar Spain 40°33N 0°28E 90 E5
Alcanede Portugal 39°25N 8°49W 89 F2
Alcanena Portugal 39°27N 8°40W 89 F2
Alcañices Spain 41°41N 6°21W 88 D4
Alcañiz Spain 41°2N 0°8W 90 D4
Alcântara Brazil 2°20S 44°30W 189 A2
Alcántara Spain 39°41N 6°57W 88 F4
Alcántara, Embalse de
Spain 39°44N 6°50W 88 F4
Alcantarilla Spain 37°59N 1°12W 91 H3
Alcaracejos Spain 38°24N 4°58W 89 G6
Alcaraz Spain 38°40N 2°29W 91 G2
Alcaraz, Sierra de Spain 38°40N 2°20W 91 G2
Alcaudete Spain 37°35N 4°5W 89 H6
Alcázar de San Juan
Spain 39°24N 3°12W 89 F7
Alchevsk Ukraine 48°30N 38°45E 85 H10
Alcira = Alzira Spain 39°9N 0°30W 91 F4
Alcobaça Portugal 39°32N 8°58W 89 F2
Alcobendas Spain 40°32N 3°38W 88 E7
Alcolea del Pinar Spain 41°2N 2°28W 90 D2
Alcoma U.S.A. 27°54N 81°29W 179 H8
Alcorcón Spain 40°20N 3°48W 88 E7
Alcoutim Portugal 37°25N 7°28W 89 H3
Alcova U.S.A. 42°34N 106°43W 168 E10
Alcoy Spain 38°43N 0°30W 91 G4
Alcubierre, Sierra de
Spain 41°45N 0°22W 90 D4
Alcublas Spain 39°48N 0°43W 90 F4
Alcúdia Spain 39°51N 3°7E 100 B10
Alcúdia, B. d' Spain 39°47N 3°15E 100 B10
Alcúdia, Sierra de la
Spain 38°34N 4°30W 89 G6
Aldabra Is. Seychelles 9°22S 46°28E 133 G8
Aldama Mexico 22°55N 98°4W 181 C5
Aldan Russia 58°40N 125°30E 107 D13
Aldan → Russia 63°28N 129°35E 107 C13
Aldea, Pta. de la
Canary Is. 28°0N 15°50W 100 G4
Aldeburgh U.K. 52°10N 1°37E 67 E9
Alder Pk. U.S.A. 35°53N 121°22W 170 K5
Alderney U.K. 49°42N 2°11W 67 H5
Aldershot U.K. 51°15N 0°44W 67 F7
Aldinga Beach
Australia 35°17S 138°27E 152 C3
Åled Sweden 56°44N 12°57E 63 H6
Aledo U.S.A. 41°12N 90°45W 172 E8
Aleg Mauritania 17°3N 13°55W 138 B2
Alegranza Canary Is. 29°23N 13°32W 100 E6
Alegranza, I. Canary Is. 29°23N 13°32W 100 E6
Alegre Brazil 20°50S 41°30W 191 A7
Alegrete Brazil 29°40S 56°0W 191 B4
Aleksandriya = Oleksandriya
Kirovohrad, Ukraine 48°42N 33°3E 85 H7
Aleksandriya = Oleksandriya
Rivne, Ukraine 50°37N 26°19E 75 C14
Aleksandriyskaya
Russia 43°58N 47°14E 87 J8
Aleksandrov Russia 56°23N 38°44E 84 D10
Aleksandrov Gay Russia 50°9N 48°34E 86 E9
Aleksandrovac Serbia 43°28N 21°3E 96 C5
Aleksandrovac Serbia 44°28N 21°13E 96 B5
Aleksandrovka = Oleksandrivka
Ukraine 48°55N 32°20E 85 H7
Aleksandrovo Bulgaria 43°14N 24°51E 97 C8
Aleksandrovsk-Sakhalinskiy
Russia 50°50N 142°20E 111 A17
Aleksandrów Kujawski
Poland 52°53N 18°43E 83 F5
Aleksandrów Łódźki
Poland 51°49N 19°17E 83 G6
Aleksandry, Zemlya
Russia 80°25N 48°0E 106 A5
Alekseyevka Samara,
Russia 52°35N 51°17E 86 D10
Alekseyevka Voronezh,
Russia 50°43N 38°40E 85 G10
Aleksin Russia 54°31N 37°9E 84 E9
Aleksinac Serbia 43°31N 21°42E 96 C5
Além Paraíba Brazil 21°52S 42°41W 191 A7
Alemania Argentina 25°40S 65°30W 190 B2
Alemania Chile 25°10S 69°55W 190 B2
Alençon France 48°27N 0°4E 70 D7
Alenquer Brazil 1°56S 54°46W 187 D8
'Alenuihähä Channel
U.S.A. 20°30N 156°0W 167 L8
Alépé Ivory C. 5°29N 3°40W 138 D4
Aleppo = Ḩalab Syria 36°10N 37°15E 104 D7
Alerce Andino △ Chile 41°33S 72°29W 192 B2
Alerce Costero △ Chile 40°10S 73°30W 192 B2
Aléria France 42°5N 9°26E 73 F13
Alert Canada 83°2N 60°0W 161 A20
Aleru India 17°39N 79°3E 126 F4
Alès France 44°9N 4°5E 73 D8
Aleşd Romania 47°3N 22°22E 80 C7
Alessándria Italy 44°54N 8°37E 92 D5
Ålesund Norway 62°28N 6°12E 60 E12
Alet-les-Bains France 42°59N 2°14E 72 F6
Aletschhorn Switz. 46°28N 8°0E 77 J4
Aleutian Basin Pac. Oc. 57°0N 177°0E 156 B9
Aleutian Is. Pac. Oc. 52°0N 175°0W 156 B10
Aleutian Range U.S.A. 60°0N 154°0W 166 D9
Aleutian Trench
Pac. Oc. 48°0N 180°0E 54 D17
Alexander Ga., U.S.A. 33°1N 81°53W 178 B8
Alexander N. Dak.,
U.S.A. 47°51N 103°39W 172 B2
Alexander, Mt.
Australia 28°58S 120°16E 149 E3
Alexander Arch. U.S.A. 56°0N 136°0W 160 F4
Alexander Bay S. Africa 28°40S 16°30E 144 C2
Alexander City U.S.A. 32°56N 85°58W 178 C4
Alexander I. Antarctica 69°0S 70°0W 55 C17
Alexandra Australia 37°8S 145°40E 153 D6
Alexandra N.Z. 45°14S 169°25E 155 F4
Alexandra Channel
Burma 14°7N 93°13E 127 G11
Alexandra Falls
Canada 60°29N 116°18W 162 A5
Alexandria = El Iskandarîya
Egypt 31°13N 29°58E 137 H6
Alexandria B.C.,
Canada 52°35N 122°27W 162 C4
Alexandria Ont.,
Canada 45°19N 74°38W 175 A10
Alexandria Romania 43°57N 25°24E 81 G10
Alexandria S. Africa 33°38S 26°28E 144 D4
Alexandria U.K. 55°59N 4°35W 65 F4
Alexandria La., U.S.A. 31°18N 92°27W 176 F8
Alexandria Minn.,
U.S.A. 45°53N 95°22W 172 C6
Alexandria S. Dak.,
U.S.A. 43°39N 97°47W 172 D5
Alexandria Va., U.S.A. 38°49N 77°5W 173 F15
Alexandria Bay U.S.A. 44°20N 75°55W 175 B9
Alexandrina, L.
Australia 35°25S 139°10E 152 C3
Alexandroupoli Greece 40°50N 25°54E 97 F9
Alexis → Canada 52°33N 56°8W 165 B8
Alexis Creek Canada 52°10N 123°20W 162 C4
Aley → Russia 52°51N 83°6E 109 B10
Aleysk Russia 52°40N 83°0E 109 B10
Alfabia Spain 39°44N 2°44E 100 B9
Alfambra Spain 40°33N 1°5W 90 E3
Alfândega da Fé Portugal 41°20N 6°59W 88 D4
Alfaro Spain 42°10N 1°50W 90 C3
Alfatar Bulgaria 43°59N 27°13E 97 C11
Alfeld Germany 51°59N 9°50E 76 D5
Alfenas Brazil 21°20S 46°10W 191 A6

Alföld Hungary 46°30N 20°0E 80 D5
Alfonsine Italy 44°30N 12°3E 93 D9
Alford Aberds., U.K. 57°14N 2°41W 65 D6
Alford Lincs., U.K. 53°15N 0°10E 66 D8
Alford U.S.A. 30°42N 85°24W 178 E4
Alfred Maine, U.S.A. 43°29N 70°43W 175 C14
Alfred N.Y., U.S.A. 42°16N 77°48W 174 D7
Alfredton N.Z. 40°41S 175°54E 154 G4
Alfreton U.K. 53°6N 1°24W 66 D6
Alfta Sweden 61°21N 16°4E 62 C10
Algaida Spain 39°33N 2°53E 100 B9
Algar Spain 36°40N 5°39W 89 J5
Ålgård Norway 58°46N 5°53E 61 G11
Algarinejo Spain 37°19N 4°9W 89 H6
Algarve Portugal 36°58N 8°20W 89 J2
Algeciras Spain 36°9N 5°28W 89 J5
Algemesí Spain 39°11N 0°27W 91 F4
Alger Algeria 36°42N 3°8E 136 A4
Alger □ Algeria 36°45N 3°10E 91 a8
Alger ✈ (ALG) Algeria 36°39N 3°13E 91 a8
Algeria ■ Africa 28°30N 2°0E 136 C4
Algha Kazakhstan 49°53N 57°20E 108 C5
Ålghult Sweden 57°0N 15°35E 63 G9
Algiers = Alger Algeria 36°42N 3°8E 136 A4
Algoa B. S. Africa 33°50S 25°45E 144 D4
Algodonales Spain 36°54N 5°24W 89 J5
Algodor → Spain 39°55N 3°53W 88 F7
Algoma U.S.A. 44°36N 87°26W 172 C10
Algona U.S.A. 43°4N 94°14W 172 D6
Algonac U.S.A. 42°37N 82°32W 174 D2
Algonquin △ Canada 45°50N 78°30W 164 C4
Algorta Spain 43°21N 2°59W 90 B2
Algorta Uruguay 32°25S 57°24W 190 C4
Alhama de Almería
  Spain 36°57N 2°34W 89 J8
Alhama de Aragón
  Spain 41°18N 1°54W 90 D3
Alhama de Granada
  Spain 37°0N 3°59W 89 H7
Alhama de Murcia Spain 37°51N 1°25W 91 H3
Alhambra U.S.A. 34°5N 118°7W 171 L8
Alhaurín el Grande
  Spain 36°39N 4°41W 89 J6
Alhucemas = Al Hoceïma
  Morocco 35°8N 3°58W 136 A3
'Alī al Gharbī Iraq 32°30N 46°45E 105 F12
'Alī ash Sharqī Iraq 32°7N 46°44E 105 F12
'Alī Bayramlı = Şirvan
  Azerbaijan 39°59N 48°52E 87 L3
'Alī Khēl Afghan. 33°57N 69°43E 124 C3
'Alī Shāh Iran 38°9N 45°50E 128 B5
Ália Italy 37°47N 13°43E 94 E6
'Alīābād Golestān, Iran 36°40N 54°33E 129 B7
'Alīābād Khorāsān, Iran 32°30N 57°30E 129 C8
'Alīābād Kordestān, Iran 35°4N 46°58E 128 C5
'Alīābād Yazd, Iran 31°41N 53°49E 129 D7
Aliade Nigeria 7°18N 8°29E 139 D6
Aliaga Spain 40°40N 0°42W 90 E4
Aliağa Turkey 38°47N 26°59E 99 C8
Aliakmonas → Greece 40°30N 22°36E 96 F6
Alibag India 18°38N 72°56E 126 E1
Alibori → Benin 11°56N 3°17E 139 C5
Alibunar Serbia 45°5N 20°57E 80 E5
Alicante Spain 38°23N 0°30W 91 G4
Alicante □ Spain 38°30N 0°37W 91 G4
Alicante ✈ (ALC) Spain 38°17N 0°33W 91 G4
Alice S. Africa 32°48S 26°55E 144 D4
Alice U.S.A. 27°45N 98°5W 176 H5
Alice → Queens.,
  Australia 24°2S 144°50E 150 C3
Alice → Queens.,
  Australia 15°35S 142°20E 150 B3
Alice, Punta Italy 39°24N 17°9E 95 C10
Alice Arm Canada 55°29N 129°31W 162 B3
Alice Springs Australia 23°40S 133°50E 150 C1
Alicedale S. Africa 33°15S 26°4E 144 D4
Aliceville U.S.A. 33°8N 88°9W 177 E10
Alicudi Italy 38°33N 14°20E 95 D7
Aliganj India 27°30N 79°10E 125 F8
Aligarh Raj., India 25°55N 76°15E 124 G6
Aligarh Ut. P., India 27°55N 78°10E 124 F8
Alīgūdarz Iran 33°25N 49°45E 129 C6
Alijó Portugal 41°16N 7°27W 88 D3
Alimia Greece 36°16N 27°43E 101 C9
Alingsås Sweden 57°56N 12°31E 63 G6
Alipur Pakistan 29°25N 70°55E 124 E4
Alipur Duar India 26°30N 89°35E 123 F16
Aliquippa U.S.A. 40°37N 80°15W 174 E4
Alishan Taiwan 23°31N 120°48E 117 F13
Aliste → Spain 41°34N 5°58W 88 D5
Alitus = Alytus Lithuania 54°24N 24°3E 84 E3
Aliveri Greece 38°24N 24°2E 98 C5
Aliwal North S. Africa 30°45S 26°45E 144 D4
Alix Canada 52°24N 113°11W 162 C6
Aljezur Portugal 37°18N 8°49W 89 H2
Aljustrel Portugal 37°55N 8°10W 89 H2
Alkamari Niger 13°27N 11°10E 139 C7
Alkhanay → Russia 51°0N 113°30E 107 D12
Alkmaar Neths. 52°37N 4°45E 69 B4
All American Canal
  U.S.A. 32°45N 115°15W 171 N11
Allada Benin 6°41N 2°9E 139 D5
Allagadda India 15°8N 78°30E 127 G4
Allagash → U.S.A. 47°5N 69°3W 173 B19
Allah Dad Pakistan 25°38N 67°34E 124 G2
Allahabad India 25°25N 81°58E 125 G9
Allan Canada 51°53N 106°4W 163 C7
Allanche France 45°14N 2°57E 72 C6
Allanridge S. Africa 27°45S 26°40E 144 C4
Allansford Australia 38°26S 142°39E 152 E5
Allanton U.K. 55°53N 5°7W 155 E3
Allaqi, Wadi → Egypt 23°7N 32°47E 137 C3
Allariz Spain 42°11N 7°50W 88 C3
Allassac France 45°15N 1°29E 72 C5
Allatoona L. U.S.A. 34°10N 84°44W 178 A5
Ålleberg Sweden 58°8N 13°36E 63 F7
Allegany U.S.A. 42°6N 78°30W 174 D6
Allegheny → U.S.A. 40°27N 80°1W 174 F5
Allegheny Mts.
  U.S.A. 38°15N 80°10W 173 F13
Allegheny Plateau
  U.S.A. 41°30N 78°0W 173 E14
Allegheny Res. U.S.A. 41°50N 79°0W 174 E6
Allègre France 45°12N 3°41E 72 C7
Allègre, Pte. Guadeloupe 16°22N 61°46W 182 b
Allen Argentina 38°35S 67°50W 192 A3
Allen, Bog of Ireland 53°15N 7°0W 64 C5
Allen, L. Ireland 54°8N 8°4W 64 B3
Allendale U.S.A. 33°1N 81°18W 178 B8
Allende Mexico 28°20N 100°51W 180 B4

Allentown U.S.A. 40°37N 75°29W 175 F9
Allentsteig Austria 48°41N 15°20E 78 C8
Alleppey = Alappuzha
  India 9°30N 76°28E 127 K3
Allepuz Spain 40°29N 0°44W 90 E4
Aller → Germany 52°56N 9°12E 76 C5
Alleynes B. Barbados 13°13N 59°39W 183 g
Alliance Nebr., U.S.A. 42°6N 102°52W 172 D2
Alliance Ohio, U.S.A. 40°55N 81°6W 174 F3
Allier □ France 46°25N 2°40E 71 F9
Allier → France 46°57N 3°4E 71 F10
Alliford Bay Canada 53°12N 131°58W 162 C2
Alligator Pond Jamaica 17°52N 77°34W 182 a
Allinagaram India 10°2N 77°30E 127 J3
Allinge Denmark 55°17N 14°50E 63 J8
Alliston Canada 44°9N 79°52W 174 B5
Alloa U.K. 56°7N 3°47W 65 E5
Allones France 48°20N 1°40E 70 D8
Allora Australia 28°2S 152°0E 151 D5
Allos France 44°15N 6°38E 73 D10
Alluitsup Paa Greenland 60°30N 45°35W 57 E6
Allur India 14°40N 80°4E 127 G5
Alluru Kottapatnam
  India 15°24N 80°7E 127 G5
Alma Canada 48°35N 71°40W 165 C5
Alma Ga., U.S.A. 31°33N 82°28W 178 D7
Alma Kans., U.S.A. 39°1N 96°17W 172 F5
Alma Mich., U.S.A. 43°23N 84°39W 173 D11
Alma Nebr., U.S.A. 40°6N 99°22W 172 E4
Alma Wis., U.S.A. 44°20N 91°55W 172 C8
Alma Ata = Almaty
  Kazakhstan 43°15N 76°57E 109 D9
Alma Hill U.S.A. 42°2N 78°0W 174 D7
Almacelles Spain 41°43N 0°27E 90 D5
Almada Portugal 38°41N 9°8W 89 G1
Almadén Australia 17°22S 144°40E 150 B3
Almadén Spain 38°49N 4°52W 89 G6
Almalyk = Olmaliq
  Uzbekistan 40°50N 69°35E 109 D7
Almanor, L. U.S.A. 40°14N 121°9W 168 F3
Almansa Spain 38°51N 1°5W 91 G3
Almanza Spain 42°39N 5°3W 88 C5
Almanzor, Pico Spain 40°15N 5°18W 88 E5
Almanzora → Spain 37°14N 1°50W 91 H3
Almas Brazil 11°33S 47°9W 189 C11
Almaş, Munţii Romania 44°49N 22°12E 80 F7
Almaty Kazakhstan 43°15N 76°57E 109 D9
Almaty □ Kazakhstan 44°30N 78°0E 109 D9
Almazán Spain 41°30N 2°30W 90 D2
Almazora Spain 39°57N 0°3W 90 F4
Almeirim Brazil 1°30S 52°34W 187 D8
Almeirim Portugal 39°12N 8°37W 89 F2
Almelo Neths. 52°22N 6°42E 69 B6
Almenar de Soria Spain 41°43N 2°12W 90 D2
Almenara Brazil 16°11S 40°42W 189 D2
Almenara Spain 39°46N 0°14W 90 F4
Almenara, Sierra de
  Spain 37°34N 1°32W 91 H3
Almendra, Embalse de
  Spain 41°10N 6°5W 88 D4
Almendralejo Spain 38°41N 6°26W 89 G4
Almere Neths. 52°20N 5°15E 69 B5
Almería Spain 36°52N 2°27W 91 H2
Almería □ Spain 37°20N 2°20W 91 H2
Almería, G. de Spain 36°41N 2°28W 91 J2
Älmhult Sweden 56°33N 14°8E 63 H8
Almirante Panama 9°10N 82°30W 182 E3
Almirante Montt, G.
  Chile 51°52S 72°50W 192 D2
Almiropotamos Greece 38°16N 24°11E 98 C6
Almiros Greece 39°11N 22°45E 98 B4
Almodóvar Portugal 37°31N 8°2W 89 H2
Almodóvar del Campo
  Spain 38°43N 4°10W 89 G6
Almodóvar del Río Spain 37°48N 5°1W 89 H5
Almond → U.S.A. 42°19N 77°44W 174 D7
Almont U.S.A. 42°55N 83°3W 174 D1
Almonte Canada 45°14N 76°12W 175 A8
Almonte Spain 37°13N 6°38W 89 H4
Almora India 29°38N 79°40E 125 E8
Almoradí Spain 38°7N 0°46W 91 G4
Almorox Spain 40°14N 4°24W 88 E6
Almoustarat Mali 17°35N 0°8E 139 B5
Älmsta Sweden 59°58N 18°50E 62 E12
Almudévar Spain 42°3N 0°35W 90 C4
Almuñécar Spain 36°43N 3°41W 89 J7
Almunge Sweden 59°53N 18°3E 62 E12
Almuradiel Spain 38°32N 3°28W 89 G7
Almus Turkey 40°22N 36°54E 104 B7
Almvik Sweden 57°49N 16°30E 63 G10
Almyrou, Ormos
  Greece 35°23N 24°20E 101 D6
Alness U.K. 57°41N 4°16W 65 D4
Alnif Morocco 31°10N 5°8W 136 B2
Alnmouth U.K. 55°24N 1°37W 66 B6
Alnwick U.K. 55°24N 1°42W 66 B6
Aloi Uganda 2°16N 33°10E 142 B3
Alon Burma 22°12N 95°5E 123 H19
Alonissos Greece 39°12N 23°50E 98 B5
Alonnisos-Northern Sporades △
  Greece 39°15N 24°5E 98 B6
Alor Indonesia 8°15S 124°30E 119 F6
Alor Setar Malaysia 6°7N 100°22E 121 J3
Álora Spain 36°49N 4°46W 89 J6
Alosno Spain 37°33N 7°7W 89 H3
Alot India 23°56N 75°40E 124 H6
Alougoum Morocco 30°17N 6°56W 136 B2
Aloysius, Mt. Australia 26°0S 128°38E 149 E4
Alpaugh U.S.A. 35°53N 119°29W 170 K7
Alpedrinha Portugal 40°6N 7°27W 88 E3
Alpena U.S.A. 45°4N 83°27W 174 A1
Alpercatas → Brazil 6°2S 44°19W 189 B2
Alpes-de-Haute-Provence □
  France 44°8N 6°10E 73 D10
Alpes-Maritimes □
  France 43°55N 7°10E 73 E11
Alpha Australia 23°39S 146°37E 150 C4
Alpha Ridge Arctic 84°0N 118°0W 54 A2
Alpharetta U.S.A. 34°5N 84°18W 178 A5
Alphen aan den Rijn
  Neths. 52°7N 4°40E 69 B4
Alphios → Greece 37°15N 21°30E 98 D3
Alpiarça Portugal 39°15N 8°35W 89 F2
Alpine Ariz., U.S.A. 33°51N 109°9W 169 K9
Alpine Calif., U.S.A. 32°50N 116°46W 171 N10
Alpine Tex., U.S.A. 30°22N 103°40W 176 G3
Alpine → Australia 36°56S 148°10E 153 D7
Alps Europe 46°30N 9°30E 74 C5
Alpu Turkey 39°46N 30°58E 104 C4

Alpurrurulam
  Australia 20°59S 137°50E 150 C2
Alqueta, Barragem do
  Portugal 38°20N 7°25W 89 G3
Alrø Denmark 55°52N 10°5E 63 J4
Als Denmark 54°59N 9°55E 63 K3
Alsace □ France 48°15N 7°25E 71 D14
Alsask Canada 51°21N 109°59W 163 C7
Alsek → U.S.A. 59°10N 138°12W 162 B1
Alsfeld Germany 50°44N 9°16E 76 E5
Alsta Norway 65°58N 12°40E 60 D15
Alsterbro Sweden 56°57N 15°55E 63 H9
Alstermo Sweden 56°58N 15°38E 63 H9
Alston U.K. 54°49N 2°25W 66 C5
Alta Norway 69°57N 23°10E 60 B20
Alta, Sierra Spain 40°31N 1°30W 90 E3
Alta Gracia Argentina 31°40S 64°30W 190 C3
Alta Murgia △ Italy 40°55N 16°30E 95 B9
Alta Sierra U.S.A. 35°42N 118°33W 171 K8
Altaelva → Norway 69°54N 23°17E 60 B20
Altafjorden Norway 70°5N 23°5E 60 A20
Altai = Aerhtai Shan
  Mongolia 46°40N 92°45E 109 C12
Altai = Gorno-Altay □
  Russia 51°0N 86°0E 109 B11
Altai → Russia 50°30N 85°30E 109 B11
Altamaha → U.S.A. 31°20N 81°20W 178 E8
Altamira Brazil 3°12S 52°10W 187 D8
Altamira Chile 25°47S 69°51W 190 B2
Altamira Mexico 22°24N 97°55W 181 C5
Altamira, Cuevas de
  Spain 43°20N 4°5W 88 B6
Altamont U.S.A. 42°42N 74°2W 175 D10
Altamura Indonesia 3°20S 128°55E 119 E7
Altanbulag Mongolia 50°16N 106°30E 110 A10
Altar Mexico 30°43N 111°44W 180 A2
Altar, Gran Desierto de
  Mexico 31°50N 114°10W 180 B2
Altata Mexico 24°40N 107°55W 180 C3
Altavista U.S.A. 37°6N 79°17W 173 G14
Altay China 47°48N 88°10E 109 C11
Altay Mongolia 46°22N 96°15E 110 B8
Altdorf Switz. 46°52N 8°36E 77 J4
Alte Mellum Germany 53°43N 8°10E 76 B4
Altea Spain 38°38N 0°2W 91 G4
Altenberg Germany 50°45N 13°45E 76 E9
Altenbruch Germany 53°49N 8°46E 76 B4
Altenkirchen
  Mecklenburg-Vorpommern,
  Germany 54°38N 13°22E 76 A9
Altenkirchen Rhld-Pfz.,
  Germany 50°41N 7°39E 76 E3
Altenmarkt Austria 47°43N 14°39E 78 D7
Alter do Chão Portugal 39°12N 7°40W 89 F3
Altha U.S.A. 30°34N 85°8W 178 E4
Altınkaya Barajı
  Turkey 41°18N 35°30E 104 B6
Altınoluk Turkey 39°34N 26°45E 99 B8
Altınova Turkey 39°12N 26°47E 99 B8
Altıntaş Turkey 39°4N 30°7E 99 B12
Altınyaka Turkey 36°33N 30°20E 99 E12
Altınyayla Turkey 37°0N 29°33E 99 D11
Altiplano Bolivia 17°0S 68°0W 188 D4
Altkirch France 47°37N 7°15E 71 E14
Altmühl → Germany 48°54N 11°52E 77 G7
Altmühltal △ Germany 48°54N 11°28E 77 G7
Altmunster Austria 47°54N 13°45E 78 D6
Alto Adige = Trentino-Alto
  Adige □ Italy 46°30N 11°0E 93 B8
Alto Araguaia Brazil 17°15S 53°20W 187 G8
Alto Cuchumatanes =
  Cuchumatanes, Sierra de los
  Guatemala 15°35N 91°25W 182 C1
Alto del Carmen Chile 28°46S 70°30W 190 B1
Alto Douro Portugal 41°6N 7°47W 88 D3
Alto Garça Bresciano □
  Italy 45°42N 10°38E 92 C7
Alto Ligonha Mozam. 15°30S 38°11E 143 F4
Alto Molocue Mozam. 15°50S 37°35E 143 F4
Alto Paraguay □
  Paraguay 21°0S 58°30W 190 A4
Alto Paraíso de Goiás
  Brazil 14°7S 47°31W 189 C1
Alto Paraná □
  Paraguay 25°30S 54°50W 191 B5
Alto Parnaíba Brazil 9°6S 45°57W 189 B1
Alto Purús → Peru 10°55S 70°28W 188 B3
Alto Río Senguerr
  Argentina 45°2S 70°50W 192 C2
Alto Santo Brazil 5°31S 38°15W 189 B3
Alto Tajo □ Spain 40°44N 2°30W 90 E2
Alton Canada 43°54N 80°5W 174 C4
Alton U.K. 51°9N 0°59W 67 F7
Alton Ill., U.S.A. 38°53N 90°11W 172 F8
Alton N.H., U.S.A. 43°27N 71°13W 175 C13
Altoona Ala., U.S.A. 34°2N 86°20W 178 A4
Altoona Pa., U.S.A. 40°31N 78°24W 174 F6
Altos Brazil 5°3S 42°28W 189 B2
Altötting Germany 48°12N 12°39E 77 G8
Altsasu = Alsasua Spain 42°54N 2°10W 90 C2
Altstätten Switz. 47°22N 9°33E 77 H5
Altun Kupri Iraq 35°45N 44°9E 105 E11
Altun Shan China 38°30N 88°0E 109 E11
Alturas U.S.A. 41°29N 120°32W 168 F3
Altus U.S.A. 34°38N 99°20W 176 D5
Altyn-Emel △
  Kazakhstan 44°40N 78°26E 109 D9
Alūksne Latvia 57°24N 27°3E 84 D4
Alunda Sweden 60°4N 18°5E 62 D12
Alupka Ukraine 44°23N 34°2E 85 K8
Alur India 15°24N 77°15E 127 K4
Alushta Ukraine 44°40N 34°25E 85 K8
Alusi Indonesia 7°35S 131°40E 119 F8
Alustante Spain 40°36N 1°40W 90 E3
Alutgama Sri Lanka 6°26N 79°59E 127 L4
Alutnwara Sri Lanka 7°29N 80°55E 127 L5
Aluva = Alwaye India 10°8N 76°24E 127 J3
Alva U.S.A. 36°48N 98°40W 176 C5
Alvängen Sweden 57°58N 12°8E 63 G6
Alvão □ Portugal 41°22N 7°48W 88 D3
Alvarado Mexico 18°46N 95°46W 181 D5
Alvarado U.S.A. 32°24N 97°13W 176 E6
Alvaro Obregón, Presa
  Mexico 27°52N 109°52W 180 B3

Älvdalen Sweden 61°13N 14°4E 62 C8
Alvear Argentina 29°5S 56°30W 190 B4
Alverca Portugal 38°56N 9°1W 89 G1
Alvesta Sweden 56°54N 14°35E 63 H8
Älvkarleby Sweden 60°34N 17°26E 62 D11
Alvord Desert U.S.A. 42°30N 118°25W 168 E4
Älvros Sweden 62°3N 14°38E 62 B8
Älvsbyn Sweden 65°40N 21°0E 60 D19
Alwar India 27°38N 76°34E 124 F7
Alwaye India 10°8N 76°24E 127 J3
Alxa Zuoqi China 38°50N 105°40E 114 E3
Alyangula Australia 13°55S 136°30E 150 A2
Alyata = Ālät Azerbaijan 39°58N 49°25E 87 L9
Alyth U.K. 56°38N 3°13W 65 E5
Alytus Lithuania 54°24N 24°3E 84 E3
Alzada U.S.A. 45°2N 104°25W 168 D11
Alzamay Russia 55°33N 98°39E 107 D10
Alzey Germany 49°45N 8°7E 77 F4
Alzira Spain 39°9N 0°30W 91 F4
Am Timan Chad 11°0N 20°10E 135 F10
Amādalen Sweden 61°20N 14°42E 62 C8
Amadeus, L. Australia 24°54S 131°0E 149 D5
Amadi
  Dem. Rep. of the Congo 3°40N 26°40E 142 B2
Amadi South Sudan 5°29N 30°25E 135 G12
Amadjuak L. Canada 65°0N 71°8W 161 C17
Amadora Portugal 38°45N 9°13W 89 G1
Amagansett U.S.A. 40°59N 72°9W 175 F12
Amagasaki Japan 34°42N 135°23E 113 G7
Amager Denmark 55°36N 12°35E 63 J6
Amagi Japan 33°25N 130°39E 113 H5
Amagunze Nigeria 6°20N 7°40E 139 D6
Amahai Indonesia 3°20S 128°55E 119 E7
Amaiun-Maia Spain 43°12N 1°29W 90 B3
Amakusa = Hondo
  Japan 32°27N 130°12E 113 H5
Amakusa-Shotō Japan 32°15N 130°10E 113 H5
Åmål Sweden 59°3N 12°42E 62 E6
Amalfi Italy 40°38N 14°36E 95 B7
Amaliada Greece 37°47N 21°22E 98 D3
Amalner India 21°5N 75°5E 126 D2
Amamapare Indonesia 4°53S 136°38E 119 E9
Amambaí Brazil 23°5S 55°13W 191 A4
Amambaí → Brazil 23°22S 53°56W 191 A5
Amambay □ Paraguay 23°0S 56°0W 191 A4
Amambay, Cordillera de
  S. Amer. 23°0S 55°45W 191 A4
Amami Japan 28°22N 129°27E 113 K4
Amami-Guntō Japan 27°16N 129°21E 113 L4
Amami-Ō-Shima
  Japan 28°16N 129°21E 113 K4
Aman, Pulau Malaysia 5°16N 100°24E 121 c
Amaná, L. Brazil 2°35S 64°40W 186 D6
Amanat → India 24°7N 84°4E 125 G11
Amanda Park U.S.A. 47°28N 123°55W 170 C3
Amankeldi Kazakhstan 50°10N 65°10E 108 D7
Amantea Italy 39°8N 16°4E 95 C9
Amapá Brazil 2°5N 50°50W 187 C8
Amapá □ Brazil 1°40N 52°0W 187 C8
Amarante Brazil 6°14S 42°50W 189 B2
Amarante Portugal 41°16N 8°5W 88 D2
Amarante do Maranhão
  Brazil 5°36S 46°45W 189 B1
Amaranth Canada 50°36N 98°43W 163 C9
Amaravati → India 11°0N 78°15E 127 J4
Amareleja Portugal 38°12N 7°13W 89 G3
Amargosa Brazil 13°2S 39°36W 189 C3
Amargosa → U.S.A. 36°14N 116°51W 171 J10
Amargosa Desert
  U.S.A. 36°40N 116°30W 171 J10
Amargosa Range
  U.S.A. 36°20N 116°45W 171 J10
Amari Greece 35°13N 24°40E 101 D6
Amarillo U.S.A. 35°13N 101°50W 176 D4
Amarkantak India 22°40N 81°45E 125 H9
'Amārna, Tell el Egypt 27°38N 30°52E 137 B3
Amarnath India 19°12N 73°22E 126 E1
Amaro, Mte. Italy 42°5N 14°5E 93 F11
Amarpur India 25°5N 87°0E 125 G12
Amarwara India 22°18N 79°10E 124 H8
Amasra Turkey 41°45N 32°23E 104 B5
Amassama Nigeria 5°1N 6°2E 139 D6
Amasya Turkey 40°40N 35°50E 104 B6
Amasya □ Turkey 40°40N 35°50E 104 B6
Amata Australia 26°9S 131°9E 149 E5
Amatikulu S. Africa 29°3S 31°33E 145 D5
Amatitlán Guatemala 14°29N 90°38W 182 D1
Amatrice Italy 42°38N 13°17E 93 F10
Amay Belgium 50°33N 5°19E 69 D5
Amazon = Amazonas →
  S. Amer. 0°5S 50°0W 187 D8
Amazonas □ Brazil 5°0S 65°0W 186 D6
Amazonas □ Peru 5°0S 78°0W 188 E3
Amazonas → S. Amer. 0°5S 50°0W 187 D8
Ambad India 19°38N 75°50E 126 E2
Ambah India 26°43N 78°13E 124 F8
Ambahijollo India 20°40N 80°43E 126 D5
Ambahta India 29°53N 77°9E 124 E7
Ambajogai India 18°44N 76°23E 126 E3
Ambala India 30°23N 76°56E 124 D7
Ambalangoda Sri Lanka 6°15N 80°5E 127 L5
Ambalapulai India 9°25N 76°25E 127 K3
Ambalavao Madag. 21°50S 46°56E 141 J9
Ambanja Madag. 13°40S 48°27E 141 G9
Ambarchik Russia 69°40N 162°20E 107 C17
Ambato Ecuador 1°5S 78°42W 186 D3
Ambato, Sierra de
  Argentina 28°25S 66°10W 190 B3
Ambato Boeny Madag. 16°28S 46°43E 141 H8
Ambatofinandrahana
  Madag. 20°33S 46°48E 141 J9
Ambatolampy Madag. 19°20S 47°35E 141 H9
Ambatondrazaka
  Madag. 17°55S 48°28E 141 H9
Ambelonas Greece 39°45N 22°22E 98 B4
Amberg Germany 49°26N 11°52E 77 F7
Ambergris Cay Belize 18°0N 87°55W 181 D7
Ambérieu-en-Bugey
  France 45°57N 5°20E 73 C9
Amberley Canada 44°2N 81°42W 174 B3
Amberley N.Z. 43°9S 172°44E 155 D7
Ambert France 45°33N 3°44E 72 C7
Ambidédi Mali 14°35N 11°47W 138 C2
Ambikapur India 23°15N 83°15E 125 H10
Ambikol Sudan 21°20N 30°50E 137 D3
Ambilobé Madag. 13°10S 49°3E 141 G9
Amble U.K. 55°20N 1°36W 66 B6
Ambleside U.K. 54°26N 2°58W 66 C5

Ambohitra Madag. 12°30S 49°10E 141 G9
Amboise France 47°24N 1°2E 70 E8
Ambon Indonesia 3°43S 128°12E 119 E7
Amboseli, L. Kenya 2°40S 37°10E 142 C4
Amboseli △ Kenya 2°37S 37°13E 142 C4
Ambositra Madag. 20°31S 47°25E 141 J9
Ambovombe Madag. 25°11S 46°5E 141 K9
Amboy U.S.A. 34°33N 115°45W 171 L11
Amboyna Cay
  S. China Sea 7°50N 112°50E 118 C4
Ambridge U.S.A. 40°36N 80°14W 174 F4
Ambriz Angola 7°48S 13°8E 140 F2
Ambrolauri Georgia 42°31N 43°9E 105 A10
Ambur India 12°48N 78°43E 127 H4
Amchitka I. U.S.A. 51°32N 179°0E 166 E3
Amderma Russia 69°45N 61°30E 108 A10
Amdhi India 23°51N 81°27E 125 H9
Amdo China 32°20N 91°40E 110 E7
Ameca Mexico 20°33N 104°2W 180 C4
Ameca → Mexico 20°41N 105°18W 180 C3
Amecameca de Juárez
  Mexico 19°8N 98°46W 181 D5
Amed Indonesia 8°19S 115°39E 119 J18
Ameland Neths. 53°27N 5°45E 69 A5
Amélia Italy 42°33N 12°25E 93 F9
Amelia City U.S.A. 30°35N 81°28W 178 E8
Amelia I. U.S.A. 30°40N 81°25W 178 E8
Amendolara Italy 39°57N 16°35E 95 C9
Amenia U.S.A. 41°51N 73°33W 175 E11
America-Antarctica Ridge
  S. Ocean 59°0S 16°0W 55 B2
American Falls U.S.A. 42°47N 112°51W 168 E7
American Falls Res.
  U.S.A. 42°47N 112°52W 168 E7
American Fork
  U.S.A. 40°23N 111°48W 168 F8
American Highland
  Antarctica 73°0S 75°0E 55 D6
American River
  Australia 35°47S 137°46E 152 C2
American Samoa ☑
  Pac. Oc. 14°20S 170°0W 157 J11
Americana Brazil 22°45S 47°20W 191 A6
Americus U.S.A. 32°4N 84°14W 178 D3
Amersfoort Neths. 52°9N 5°23E 69 B5
Amersfoort S. Africa 26°59S 29°53E 145 C4
Amery Basin S. Ocean 68°15S 74°30E 55 C6
Amery Ice Shelf
  Antarctica 69°30S 72°0E 55 C6
Amerzgane Morocco 31°4N 7°14W 136 B2
Ames U.S.A. 42°2N 93°37W 172 D7
Amesbury U.S.A. 42°51N 70°56W 175 D14
Amet India 25°18N 73°56E 124 G5
Amfiklia Greece 38°38N 22°35E 98 C4
Amfilochia Greece 38°52N 21°9E 98 C3
Amfipoli Greece 40°48N 23°52E 96 F7
Amfissa Greece 38°32N 22°22E 98 C4
Amga Russia 60°50N 132°0E 107 C14
Amga → Russia 62°38N 134°32E 107 C14
Amgaon India 21°22N 80°22E 125 J6
Amguid Algeria 26°26N 5°22E 136 C6
Amgun → Russia 52°56N 139°38E 107 D14
Amherst Canada 45°48N 64°8W 165 C7
Amherst Mass.,
  U.S.A. 42°23N 72°31W 175 D12
Amherst N.Y., U.S.A. 42°59N 78°48W 174 D6
Amherst Ohio, U.S.A. 41°24N 82°14W 174 E2
Amherst I. Canada 44°8N 76°43W 175 B8
Amherstburg Canada 42°6N 83°6W 164 D3
Amiata, Mte. Italy 42°53N 11°37E 93 F8
Amidon U.S.A. 46°29N 103°19W 172 B2
Amiens France 49°54N 2°16E 71 C9
Amindeo Greece 40°42N 21°42E 96 F5
Amindivi Is. India 11°23N 72°23E 127 J1
Amini I. India 11°6N 72°45E 127 J1
Aminuis Namibia 23°43S 19°21E 144 B2
Amīrābād Iran 33°20N 46°16E 128 C5
Amirante Is. Seychelles 6°0S 53°0E 102 J7
Amisk L. Canada 54°35N 102°15W 163 C8
Amistad, Presa de la
  Mexico 29°26N 101°3W 180 B4
Amistad △ U.S.A. 29°32N 101°12W 176 G4
Amite U.S.A. 30°44N 90°30W 177 F9
Amizmiz Morocco 31°12N 8°15W 136 B2
Amla India 21°56N 78°7E 124 J8
Amlapura Indonesia 8°27S 115°37E 119 J18
Amli I. U.S.A. 52°4N 173°30W 166 E5
Amlwch U.K. 53°24N 4°20W 66 D3
'Ammān Jordan 31°57N 35°52E 130 D4
'Ammān □ Jordan 31°40N 36°30E 130 D5
'Ammān ✈ (AMM)
  Jordan 31°50N 36°0E 130 D5
Ammanford U.K. 51°48N 3°59W 67 F4
Ammassalik = Tasiilaq
  Greenland 65°40N 37°20W 57 D7
Ammerån → Sweden 63°9N 16°13E 62 A10
Ammersee Germany 48°0N 11°7E 77 G7
Ammochostos = Famagusta
  Cyprus 35°8N 33°55E 101 D12
Ammon U.S.A. 43°28N 111°58W 168 E8
Amnat Charoen
  Thailand 15°51N 104°38E 120 E5
Amnura Bangla. 24°37N 88°25E 125 G13
Amo Jiang → China 23°30N 100°45E 122 F3
Åmol Iran 36°23N 52°20E 129 B7
Amorgos Greece 36°50N 25°57E 98 D7
Amory U.S.A. 33°59N 88°29W 177 E10
Amos Canada 48°35N 78°5W 164 C4
Åmot Norway 59°57N 9°54E 61 G13
Åmot Sweden 60°58N 16°27E 62 D10
Amotsdal Norway 59°37N 8°26E 61 G13
Amoy = Xiamen
  China 24°25N 118°4E 117 F12
Ampang Malaysia 3°8N 101°45E 121 L3
Ampani India 19°38N 82°48E 127 E5
Ampanihy Madag. 24°40S 44°45E 141 J8
Ampato, Nevado Peru 15°0S 71°50W 188 D3
Ampenan Indonesia 8°35S 116°13E 119 K19
Amper → Germany 48°29N 11°55E 77 G7
Amphitrite Group
  S. China Sea 16°50N 112°20E 118 A4
Amphoe Kathu Thailand 7°55N 98°21E 121 a

Amphoe Thalang Thailand 8°1N 98°20E 121 a
Amposta Spain 40°43N 0°34E 90 E6
Amqui Canada 48°28N 67°27W 165 C6
Amrabad India 16°23N 78°50E 126 F4
Amravati India 20°55N 77°45E 126 D4
Amreli India 21°35N 71°17E 126 J7
Amritsar India 31°35N 74°57E 124 D6
Amroha India 28°53N 78°30E 124 E8
Amrum Germany 54°38N 8°21E 76 A4
Amsterdam Neths. 52°23N 4°54E 69 B4
Amsterdam U.S.A. 42°56N 74°11W 175 D10
Amsterdam ✈ (AMS)
  Neths. 52°18N 4°45E 69 B4
Amsterdam, Î. = Nouvelle
  Amsterdam, Î.
  Ind. Oc. 38°30S 77°30E 14 J9
Amstetten Austria 48°7N 14°51E 78 C7
'Amūdah Syria 37°6N 40°55E 128 A4
Amudarya →
  Turkmenistan 37°53N 65°15E 109 E6
Amukta Pass U.S.A. 52°0N 171°0W 166 E5
Amund Ringnes I.
  Canada 78°20N 96°25W 161 B9
Amundsen Abyssal Plain
  S. Ocean 65°0S 125°0W 55 C13
Amundsen Basin Arctic 87°30N 80°0E 54 A8
Amundsen Gulf Canada 71°0N 124°0W 160 B7
Amundsen Ridges
  S. Ocean 69°15S 123°0W 55 C14
Amundsen-Scott
  Antarctica 90°0S 166°0E 55 E
Amundsen Sea
  Antarctica 72°0S 115°0W 55 D15
Amungen Sweden 61°10N 15°40E 62 C9
Amuntai Indonesia 2°28S 115°25E 118 E5
Amur → Russia 52°56N 141°10E 107 D15
Amur, W. → Sudan 18°56N 33°34E 137 D3
Amurang Indonesia 1°5N 124°40E 119 D6
Amurrio Spain 43°3N 3°0W 90 B2
Amursk Russia 50°14N 136°54E 107 D14
Amusco Spain 42°10N 4°28W 88 C6
Amvrakikos Kolpos
  Greece 39°0N 20°55E 98 C2
Amvrosiyivka Ukraine 47°43N 38°30E 85 C8
Amyderya = Amudarya →
  Uzbekistan 37°53N 65°15E 109 E6
An Bang, Dao = Amboyna Cay
  S. China Sea 7°50N 112°50E 118 C4
An Bien Vietnam 9°45N 105°0E 121 H5
An Hoa Vietnam 15°40N 108°5E 120 E7
An Khe Vietnam 13°57N 108°51E 120 E7
An Nabatīyah at Tahta
  Lebanon 33°23N 35°27E 130 B4
An Nabk Syria 34°2N 36°44E 130 B5
An Nafūd Si. Arabia 28°15N 41°0E 106 E4
An Nāşirīyah Iraq 34°26N 41°33E 128 C4
An Najaf Iraq 32°3N 44°15E 106 F6
An Nāşirīyah Iraq 31°0N 46°15E 106 F6
An Nhon = Binh Dinh
  Vietnam 13°55N 109°7E 120 E7
An Nīl □ Sudan 19°30N 33°0E 137 E3
An Nu'ayrīyah
  Si. Arabia 27°30N 48°30E 106 E6
An Nu'mānīyah Iraq 32°32N 45°25E 106 F6
An Ros = Rush Ireland 53°31N 6°6W 64 C5
An Thoi, Quan Dao
  Vietnam 9°58N 104°0E 121 H4
Anabar → Russia 73°8N 113°36E 107 B12
Anaconda U.S.A. 46°8N 112°57W 168 C7
Anacortes U.S.A. 48°30N 122°37W 170 B4
Anadarko U.S.A. 35°4N 98°15W 176 D5
Anadia Brazil 9°42S 36°18W 189 C4
Anadia Portugal 40°26N 8°27W 88 E2
Anadolu Turkey 39°0N 30°0E 99 C5
Anadyr Russia 64°35N 177°20E 107 C18
Anadyr → Russia 64°55N 176°5E 107 C18
Anadyrskiy Zaliv
  Russia 64°0N 180°0E 107 C19
Anafi Greece 36°22N 25°48E 98 E7
Anaga, Pta. de
  Canary Is. 28°34N 16°9W 52 F3
Anagni Italy 41°44N 13°9E 94 A5
'Ānah Iraq 34°25N 42°0E 106 E4
Anaheim U.S.A. 33°50N 117°55W 171 M9
Anahim Lake Canada 52°28N 125°18W 162 C3
Anai Mudi India 10°12N 77°4E 127 J3
Anaimalai Hills India 10°20N 76°40E 127 J3
Anajatuba Brazil 3°16S 44°37W 189 B2
Anakapalle India 17°42N 83°6E 127 F6
Anakie Australia 23°32S 147°45E 150 C4
Anaklia Georgia 42°22N 41°35E 105 A7
Analalava Madag. 14°35S 48°0E 141 G9
Analipsis Greece 39°36N 19°55E 101 B3
Anambar → Pakistan 30°15N 68°50E 124 D3
Anambas, Kepulauan
  Indonesia 3°20N 106°30E 118 D3
Anambas Is. = Anambas,
  Kepulauan Indonesia 3°20N 106°30E 118 D3
Anamosa U.S.A. 42°7N 91°17W 172 D8
Anamur Turkey 36°8N 32°58E 104 D5
Anan Japan 33°54N 134°40E 113 H7
Anand India 22°32N 72°59E 126 D1
Anandapuram India 14°5N 73°30E 127 H2
Anandpur India 21°16N 86°13E 125 J12
Ananes Greece 36°33N 24°9E 98 E6
Anangu Pitjantjatjara ♢
  Australia 27°0S 132°0E 149 E5
Anantapur India 14°39N 77°42E 127 H3
Anantnag India 33°45N 75°10E 124 B6
Anapa Russia 44°55N 37°25E 85 D8
Anápolis Brazil 16°15S 48°50W 187 G9
Anapu → Brazil 1°53S 50°53W 187 D8
Anār Iran 30°55N 55°13E 129 D7
Anārak Iran 33°25N 53°40E 129 C7
Anas → India 23°26N 74°0E 124 H5
Anatolia = Anadolu
  Turkey 39°0N 30°0E 99 C5
Anatoliki Makedonia kai
  Thraki □ Greece 41°10N 24°50E 96 F7
Añatuya Argentina 28°20S 62°50W 190 B3
Anatye ♢ Australia 22°30S 135°30E 150 C2
Anaunethad L.
  Canada 60°55N 104°25W 163 A8
Anbyon N. Korea 39°1N 127°35E 114 E14

ares, Sierra dos
  ain   42°51N 6°52W **88** C4
ares △ Spain   42°50N 6°40W **88** C4
ash □ Peru   9°30S 77°45W **188** B2
aster Canada   43°13N 79°59W **174** C5
enis France   47°21N 1°10W **70** E5
ho, Canal Chile   50°0S 74°20W **192** B2
hor Bay U.S.A.   38°48N 123°34W **170** G4
horage U.S.A.   61°13N 149°54W **166** D2
huras Spain   39°29N 4°50W **89** F6
huthengu India   8°40N 76°46E **127** K3
i China   39°20N 116°40E **114** D4
ohuma, Nevado
  olivia   16°0S 68°50W **188** D4
ón Peru   11°50S 77°10W **188** C2
ona Italy   43°38N 13°30E **93** E10
ud Chile   42°0S 73°50W **192** B2
y-le-Franc France   47°46N 4°10E **71** E11
a China   46°24N 125°19E **111** B14
acollo Argentina   37°10S 70°42W **190** D1
acollo Chile   30°14S 71°46W **190** C1
ahuaylas Peru   13°40S 73°25W **188** C3
algalá Argentina   27°40S 66°30W **190** B2
alsnes Norway   62°35N 7°43E **60** E12
alucía □ Spain   37°35N 5°0W **89** H6
ain   37°35N 5°0W **89** H6
alusia U.S.A.   31°18N 86°29W **177** F11
aman Is. Ind. Oc.   10°0N 93°0E **127** K11
aman & Nicobar Is. □
  dia   10°0N 93°0E **127** K11
aman Sea Ind. Oc.   13°0N 96°0E **118** B1
apa Madag.   14°39S 49°39E **141** G9
ara Namibia   18°2S 21°9E **144** A3
araí Brazil   12°48S 41°20W **189** C2
elot-Blancheville
  ance   48°15N 5°18E **71** D12
enes Norway   69°19N 16°18E **60** B17
enne Belgium   50°28N 5°5E **69** D5
éranboukane Mali   15°26N 3°12E **139** B5
ermatt Switz.   46°38N 8°35E **77** J4
ernach Germany   50°26N 7°26E **76** F3
ernos-les-Bains
  ance   44°44N 1°6W **72** D2
erslöv Sweden   55°26N 13°19E **63** E3
erson Australia   38°31S 145°26E **153** E6
erson Alaska,
  .S.A.   64°25N 149°15W **166** C10
erson Calif.,
  S.A.   40°27N 122°18W **168** F2
erson Ind., U.S.A.   40°10N 85°41W **173** E11
erson Mo., U.S.A.   36°39N 94°27W **172** G6
erson S.C., U.S.A.   34°31N 82°39W **177** D13
erson → Canada   69°42N 129°0W **160** D6
erson I. India   12°46N 92°43E **127** H11
ersonville □ U.S.A. 32°12N 84°9W **178** D5
erstorp Sweden   57°19N 13°39E **63** G7
es U.S.A.   42°12N 74°47W **175** D10
es, Cord. de los
  Amer.   20°0S 68°0W **188** E4
fjorden Norway   69°10N 16°20E **60** B17
hra, L. India   18°54N 73°32E **126** E1
hra Pradesh □ India 18°0N 79°0E **126** F4
jon Uzbekistan   41°10N 72°15E **109** D8
jon □ Uzbekistan   40°45N 72°20E **109** D8
kithira = Antikythira
  eece   35°52N 23°15E **98** F5
meshk Iran   32°27N 48°21E **105** F13
milos = Antimilos
  eece   36°47N 24°12E **98** E6
paros = Antiparos
  eece   37°0N 25°3E **99** D7
paxoi = Antipaxi
  eece   39°9N 20°13E **98** B2
zhan = Andijon
  bekistan   41°10N 72°15E **109** D8
 khvoy Afghan.   36°52N 65°8E **109** C7
n Spain   43°13N 2°1W **90** B2
oany Madag.   13°25S 48°16E **141** G9
ola India   17°51N 78°4E **126** F4
ola India   16°57N 76°50E **126** F3
ong S. Korea   36°40N 128°43E **115** F15
orra N. Korea   40°59N 0°28W **90** E4
orra ■ Europe   42°30N 1°30E **72** F5
orra La Vella Andorra 42°31N 1°32E **72** E5
over U.K.   51°12N 1°29W **67** F6
over Maine,
  .S.A.   44°38N 70°45W **175** B14
over Mass., U.S.A.   42°40N 71°8W **175** D13
over N.J., U.S.A.   40°59N 74°45W **175** F10
over Ohio, U.S.A.   41°36N 80°34W **174** E4
over Russia   69°10N 15°50E **60** B16
radina Brazil   20°54S 51°23W **187** H8
ratx Spain   39°39N 2°25E **100** B9
eaof Reel S.A.   51°30N 176°0W **166** E4
eapol Russia   56°40N 32°17E **84** D7
ée Land Greenland   78°0N 20°0W **57** C8
ews S.C., U.S.A.   33°27N 79°34W **177** C15
ews Tex., U.S.A.   32°19N 102°33W **176** E3
eyevka Russia   52°19N 51°55E **86** D10
zo Italy   41°13N 16°17E **95** A9
rijevica Montenegro 42°45N 19°48E **96** C4
ritsena Greece   37°29N 21°52E **98** D3
os Greece   37°29N 21°52E **98** D3
os I. Bahamas   24°30N 78°0W **182** B4
os Town Bahamas   24°43N 77°47W **182** B4
oscoggin →
  .S.A.   44°6N 69°54W **175** C14
roth I. India   10°50N 73°41E **127** J1
rychów Poland   49°51N 19°18E **83** J6
selv Norway   69°4N 18°34E **60** B18
ijar Spain   38°30N 6°52W **89** G6
alo Angola   11°25S 16°45E **144** G3
y Sweden   57°48N 14°49E **63** G8
s Mali   18°2S 0°36E **139** B5
gada Br. Virgin Is. 18°45N 64°20W **183** e
gada, B. Argentina   40°20S 62°20W **192** B4
Indies   18°15N 63°45W **183** C7
gada Passage
  Indies   18°15N 63°45W **183** C7
o Togo   6°12N 1°34W **139** D5
o Argentina   38°0S 68°45W **192** A3
ni-Noi Moldova   46°52N 29°15E **81** D14
o, Pico de Spain   42°37N 0°40E **90** C5
o Turkmenistan   37°52N 58°31E **108** E5
  China   27°21N 114°40E **117** D10

Ang Mo Kio Singapore 1°23N 103°50E **121** d
Ang Thong Thailand   14°35N 100°31E **120** E3
Ang Thong, Ko Thailand 9°37N 99°41E **121** b
Ang Thong, Mu Ko △
  Thailand   9°40N 99°43E **121** b
Angamos, Punta Chile 23°1S 70°32W **190** A1
Angara → Russia   58°5N 94°20E **107** D10
Angara-Débou Benin   11°19N 3°3E **139** C5
Angarsk Russia   52°30N 104°0E **110** A9
Angas Hills Australia 23°0S 127°50E **148** D4
Angaston Australia   34°30S 139°8E **152** C3
Ånge Sweden   62°31N 15°35E **62** B9
Ángel, Salto = Angel Falls
  Venezuela   5°57N 62°30W **186** B6
Ángel de la Guarda, I.
  Mexico   29°20N 113°25W **180** B2
Angel Falls Venezuela 5°57N 62°30W **186** B6
Angeles Phil.   15°9N 120°33E **119** A6
Ängelholm Sweden   56°15N 12°50E **63** H6
Angellala Creek →
  Australia   26°25S 146°14E **153** A4
Angels Camp U.S.A.   38°4N 120°32W **170** G6
Ängelsberg Sweden   59°58N 16°0E **62** E10
Ångermanälven →
  Sweden   63°0N 17°20E **62** A11
Ångermanland Sweden 63°36N 17°45E **60** E17
Angermünde Germany   53°0N 14°0E **76** B9
Angers Canada   50°13N 75°29W **175** A9
Angers France   47°30N 0°35W **70** E6
Angerville France   48°19N 2°0E **71** D9
Ångesån → Sweden   66°16N 22°47E **60** C20
Angical Brazil   12°0S 44°42W **189** C2
Angikuni L. Canada   62°12N 99°59W **163** A9
Angkor Cambodia   13°22N 103°50E **120** F4
Angledool Australia 29°5S 147°55E **151** D4
Anglem, Mt. N.Z.   46°45S 167°53E **155** G2
Anglés France   41°57N 2°38E **90** D7
Anglesey U.K.   53°17N 4°20W **66** D3
Anglesey, Isle of □ U.K. 53°16N 4°18W **66** D3
Anglet France   43°29N 1°31W **72** E2
Angleton U.S.A.   29°10N 95°26W **176** G7
Anglin → France   46°42N 0°52E **72** B4
Anglisidhes Cyprus   34°51N 33°27E **101** E12
Angmagssalik = Tasiilaq
  Greenland   65°40N 37°20W **57** D7
Ango
  Dem. Rep. of the Congo 4°10N 26°5E **142** B2
Angoche Mozam.   16°8S 39°55E **143** F4
Angoche, I. Mozam.   16°20S 39°50E **143** F4
Angol Chile   37°56S 72°45W **190** D1
Angola Ind., U.S.A. 41°38N 85°0W **173** E11
Angola N.Y., U.S.A. 42°38N 79°2W **174** D5
Angola ■ Africa   12°0S 18°0E **141** G3
Angola Abyssal Plain
  Atl. Oc.   15°0S 2°0E **56** H12
Angola Basin Atl. Oc. 15°0S 3°0E **56** H12
Angoulême France   45°39N 0°10E **72** C4
Angoumois France   45°50N 0°25E **72** C4
Angra do Heroísmo
  Azores   38°39N 27°13W **134** a
Angra dos Reis Brazil 23°0S 44°10W **191** A7
Angrapa → Russia   54°37N 21°54E **82** D8
Angren Uzbekistan   41°1N 70°12E **109** D8
Angtassom Cambodia   11°1N 104°41E **121** G5
Angu
  Dem. Rep. of the Congo 3°23N 24°30E **142** B1
Anguang China   45°15N 123°45E **115** B12
Anguilla □ W. Indies 18°14N 63°5W **183** C7
Angul India   20°51N 85°6E **126** D7
Anguo China   38°28N 115°15E **114** C8
Angurugu Australia   14°0S 136°25E **150** A2
Angus Canada   44°19N 79°53W **174** B5
Angus □ U.K.   56°46N 2°56E **65** E6
Angwa → Zimbabwe   16°0S 30°23E **145** A5
Anhandui → Brazil   21°46S 52°9W **191** A5
Anhanguera Brazil   18°27S 48°12W **191** A6
Anholt Denmark   56°42N 11°33E **63** H5
Anhua China   28°23N 111°12E **117** C8
Anhui □ China   32°0N 117°0E **117** B11
Anhwei = Anhui □
  China   32°0N 117°0E **117** B11
Anichab Namibia   21°0S 14°46E **144** B1
Anidros Greece   36°38N 25°43E **99** F7
Anié Togo   7°42N 1°8E **139** D5
Animas U.S.A.   36°43N 108°13W **169** H9
Anin Burma   15°36N 97°50E **120** E1
Anina Romania   45°6N 21°51E **80** E6
Aninoasa Romania   44°47N 24°10E **81** F9
Anjalankoski Finland 60°45N 26°51E **64** B4
Anjangaon India   21°10N 77°20E **126** D3
Anjar = Anchuthengu
  India   8°40N 76°46E **127** K3
Anji China   30°46N 119°40E **117** B12
Anjidiv I. India   14°40N 74°10E **127** G2
Anjou France   47°20N 0°15W **70** E6
Anjouan Comoros Is. 12°15S 44°20E **141** a
Anju N. Korea   39°36N 125°40E **115** E13
Anka Nigeria   12°13N 5°58E **139** C6
Ankaboa, Tanjona
  Madag.   21°58S 43°20E **141** J8
Ankang China   32°40N 109°1E **116** A5
Ankara Turkey   39°57N 32°54E **104** C5
Ankara □ Turkey   39°55N 32°50E **104** C5
Ankaratra Madag.   19°25S 47°12E **141** H9
Ankarsrum Sweden   57°41N 16°20E **63** G10
Ankazoabo Madag.   22°18S 44°31E **141** J8
Ankeny U.S.A.   41°44N 93°36W **172** E7
Anklam Germany   53°51N 13°41E **76** B9
Ankleshwar India   21°38N 73°3E **126** D1
Ankola India   14°40N 74°18E **127** G2
Ankoro
  Dem. Rep. of the Congo 6°45S 26°55E **142** D2
Ankpa Nigeria   7°22N 7°38E **139** D6
Anlong China   25°2N 105°27E **116** E5
Anlong Veng Cambodia 14°14N 104°5E **120** E5
Anlu China   31°15N 113°45E **117** B9
Anmyeondo S. Korea   36°25N 126°25E **115** F14
Ann Sweden   63°19N 12°33E **62** A6
Ann, C. U.S.A.   42°38N 70°35W **175** D14
Ann Arbor U.S.A.   42°17N 83°45W **173** D12
Anna Russia   51°28N 40°23E **86** D6
Anna U.S.A.   37°28N 89°15W **172** G9
Annaba Algeria   36°50N 7°46E **136** A5
Annaba □ Algeria   36°50N 7°46E **136** A5
Annaberg-Buchholz
  Germany   50°34N 13°0E **76** E9
Annalee → Ireland   54°2N 7°24W **64** B4
Annam = Trung-Phan
  Vietnam   17°0N 109°0E **120** D6

Annamitique, Chaîne
  Asia   17°0N 106°0E **120** D6
Annan U.K.   54°59N 3°16W **65** G5
Annan → U.K.   54°58N 3°16W **65** G5
Annapolis U.S.A.   38°59N 76°30W **173** F15
Annapolis Royal
  Canada   44°44N 65°32W **165** D6
Annapurna Nepal   28°34N 83°50E **125** E10
Annean, L. Australia 26°54S 118°14E **149** E2
Anneberg Sweden   57°29N 12°4E **63** E7
Annecy France   45°55N 6°8E **73** C10
Annecy, Lac d' France 45°52N 6°10E **73** C10
Annemasse France   46°12N 6°16E **71** F13
Annenskiy Most Russia 60°45N 37°10E **84** B9
Anning China   24°55N 102°26E **116** E4
Anniger India   15°26N 75°26E **127** G2
Anning China   24°55N 102°26E **116** E4
Anniston U.S.A.   33°39N 85°50W **178** B4
Annobón Atl. Oc.   1°25S 5°36E **133** G4
Annonay France   45°15N 4°40E **73** C8
Annot France   43°58N 6°38E **73** E10
Annotto B. Jamaica   18°17N 76°45W **182** a
Ånnsjön Sweden   63°19N 12°34E **62** A6
Annville U.S.A.   40°20N 76°31W **175** F8
Ano Poroia Greece   41°17N 23°2E **96** E7
Ano Siros Greece   37°29N 24°56E **98** D6
Anogia Greece   35°16N 24°52E **101** D6
Anou Mellene Mali   17°19N 0°33E **139** B5
Anoumaba Ivory C.   6°23N 4°38W **138** D4
Anping Hebei, China 38°15N 115°30E **114** E8
Anping Liaoning, China 41°5N 123°30E **115** C12
Anpu Gang China   21°25N 109°50E **116** G7
Anqing China   30°30N 117°3E **117** B11
Anqiu China   36°25N 119°10E **115** F10
Anren China   26°43N 113°18E **117** D9
Ansager Denmark   55°43N 8°45E **63** J2
Ansai China   36°50N 109°20E **114** F5
Ansan S. Korea   37°21N 126°52E **115** F14
Ansbach Germany   49°28N 10°34E **77** F6
Anse Boileau Seychelles 4°43S 55°29E **141** b
Anse la Raye St. Lucia 13°55N 61°3W **183** f
Anse Royale Seychelles 4°44S 55°31E **141** b
Ansfelden Austria   48°12N 14°17E **78** C7
Anshan China   41°5N 122°58E **115** D12
Anshun China   26°18N 105°57E **116** D5
Ansião Portugal   39°56N 8°27W **88** F2
Ansley U.S.A.   41°18N 99°23W **172** E4
Ansó Spain   42°51N 0°48W **90** C4
Ansoáin Spain   42°50N 1°38W **90** C3
Anson B. Australia   13°20S 130°6E **148** B5
Ansongo Mali   15°25N 0°35E **139** B5
Ansongo-Ménaka △
  Mali   15°3N 1°37E **139** B5
Ansonia U.S.A.   41°21N 73°5W **175** E11
Anstruther U.K.   56°14N 2°41W **65** E6
Ansudu Indonesia   2°11S 139°22E **119** E9
Antabamba Peru   14°40S 73°0W **188** C3
Antagarh India   20°6N 81°9E **126** D5
Antakya = Hatay
  Turkey   36°14N 36°10E **104** D7
Antalaha Madag.   14°57S 50°20E **141** G10
Antalya Turkey   36°52N 30°45E **104** D4
Antalya □ Turkey   36°50N 30°45E **104** D4
Antalya Körfezi Turkey 36°15N 31°30E **104** D4
Antananarivo Madag. 18°55S 47°31E **141** H9
Antarctic Pen. Antarctica 67°0S 60°0W **55** C18
Antarctica   90°0S 0°0S **55** E3
Antelope Zimbabwe   21°2S 28°31E **143** G2
Antep = Gaziantep
  Turkey   37°6N 37°23E **104** D7
Antequera Paraguay   24°8S 57°7W **190** A4
Antequera Spain   37°5N 4°33W **89** H6
Antero, Mt. U.S.A.   38°41N 106°15W **168** G10
Anthony Fla., U.S.A. 29°18N 82°7W **177** F10
Anthony Kans., U.S.A. 37°9N 98°2W **172** G4
Anthony N. Mex.,
  U.S.A.   32°0N 106°36W **169** K10
Anti Atlas Morocco   30°0N 8°30W **136** C2
Anti-Lebanon = Sharqi, Al Jabal
  ash Lebanon   33°40N 36°10E **130** B5
Antibes France   43°34N 7°6E **73** E11
Antibes, C. d' France 43°31N 7°7E **73** E11
Anticosti, Î. d' Canada 49°30N 63°0W **165** C7
Antifer, C. d' France 49°41N 0°10E **70** C7
Antigo U.S.A.   45°9N 89°9W **172** C9
Antignonish Canada   45°38N 61°58W **165** D7
Antigua Canary Is.   28°24N 14°1W **100** F5
Antigua Guatemala   14°34N 90°41W **182** D1
Antigua W. Indies   17°0N 61°50W **183** C7
Antigua & Barbuda ■
  W. Indies   17°20N 61°48W **183** C7
Antigua Colombia   6°40N 75°55W **186** B3
Antiparos Greece   37°0N 25°3E **99** D7
Antipaxi Greece   39°9N 20°13E **98** B2
Antipodes Is. Pac. Oc. 49°45S 178°40E **156** M9
Antlers U.S.A.   34°14N 95°37W **176** D7
Antofagasta Chile   23°50S 70°30W **190** A1
Antofagasta □ Chile 24°0S 69°0W **190** A2
Antofagasta de la Sierra
  Argentina   26°5S 67°20W **190** B2
Antofalla Argentina 25°30S 68°5W **190** B2
Antofalla, Salar de
  Argentina   25°40S 67°45W **190** B2
Anton U.S.A.   33°49N 102°10W **176** E3
Antonina Brazil   25°26S 48°42W **191** B6
Antrain France   48°28N 1°30W **70** D5
Antrim U.K.   54°43N 6°14W **64** B5
Antrim □ U.K.   40°7N 81°21W **174** F3
Antrim U.S.A.   55°3N 6°14W **64** A5
Antrim, Mts. of U.K. 55°3N 6°14W **64** A5
Antrim Plateau
  Australia   18°8S 128°20E **148** C4
Antrodoco Italy   42°25N 13°5E **93** F10
Antropovo Russia   58°25N 43°6E **86** A6
Antsalova Madag.   18°40S 44°37E **141** H8
Antsiranana Madag.   12°25S 49°20E **141** G9
Antsohihy Madag.   14°50S 47°59E **141** G9
Antu China   42°30N 128°20E **115** C15

Antwerp = Antwerpen
  Belgium   51°13N 4°25E **69** C4
Antwerp U.S.A.   44°12N 75°37W **175** B9
Antwerpen Belgium   51°13N 4°25E **69** C4
Antwerpen □ Belgium 51°15N 4°40E **69** C4
Anupgarh India   29°10N 73°10E **124** E5
Anuppur India   23°8N 81°41E **125** H9
Anuradhapura Sri Lanka 8°22N 80°28E **127** K5
Anurrete ◌ Australia 20°50S 135°38E **150** C2
Anveh Iran   27°23N 54°11E **129** E7
Anvers = Antwerpen
  Belgium   51°13N 4°25E **69** C4
Anvers I. Antarctica 64°30S 63°40W **55** C17
Anwen China   29°4N 120°26E **117** C13
Anxi Fujian, China   25°2N 118°12E **117** E12
Anxi Gansu, China   40°30N 95°43E **110** C8
Anxian China   31°40N 104°25E **116** B5
Anxious B. Australia 33°24S 134°45E **151** E1
Anyama Ivory C.   5°30N 4°3W **138** D4
Anyang China   36°5N 114°21E **114** F8
Anyang S. Korea   37°23N 126°55E **115** F14
Anyer Indonesia   6°4S 105°53E **119** G11
Anyi Jiangxi, China 28°49N 115°25E **117** C10
Anyi Shanxi, China   35°2N 111°2E **114** G6
Anyuan China   25°9N 115°21E **117** E10
Anyue China   30°9N 105°50E **116** B5
Anza U.S.A.   33°35N 116°39W **171** M10
Anze China   36°10N 112°12E **114** F7
Anzegloul Algeria   26°50N 0°1E **136** C4
Anzhero-Sudzhensk
  Russia   56°10N 86°0E **106** D9
Ánzio Italy   41°27N 12°37E **94** A5
Ao Makham Thailand   7°50N 98°24E **121** a
Ao Phangnga △ Thailand 8°10N 98°32E **121** a
Aoga-Shima Japan   32°28N 139°46E **113** H9
Aohan Qi China   43°18N 119°43E **115** C10
Aoiz Spain   42°46N 1°22W **90** C3
Aoji N. Korea   42°31N 130°23E **115** C16
Aomen = Macau
  China   22°12N 113°33E **117** F9
Aomori Japan   40°45N 140°45E **112** D10
Aomori □ Japan   40°45N 140°40E **112** D10
Aonla India   28°16N 79°11E **125** E8
Aoraki Mount Cook
  N.Z.   43°36S 170°9E **155** D5
Aorai, Mt. Tahiti   17°34S 149°30W **155** b
Aorangi Ra. N.Z.   41°28S 175°22E **154** H4
Aosta Italy   45°45N 7°20E **92** C4
Aotea Harbour N.Z.   38°0S 174°50E **154** E3
Aotearoa = New Zealand
  Oceania   40°0S 176°0E **154** G5
Aoudéras Niger   17°45N 8°20E **139** B6
Aoukâr Mauritania   17°40N 10°0W **138** B3
Aoulef el Arab Algeria 26°55N 1°2E **136** C4
Aozou, Couloir d' Chad 22°0N 19°0E **135** D9
Apá → S. Amer.   22°6S 58°2W **190** A4
Apache U.S.A.   34°54N 98°22W **176** D5
Apache Junction
  U.S.A.   33°25N 111°33W **169** K8
Apalachee B. U.S.A. 30°0N 84°0W **178** F5
Apalachicola U.S.A. 29°43N 84°59W **178** F5
Apalachicola →
  U.S.A.   29°43N 84°58W **178** F5
Apalachicola B. U.S.A. 29°40N 85°0W **178** F3
Apam Ghana   5°19N 0°42W **139** D4
Apapa Nigeria   6°26N 3°21E **139** D5
Apaporis → Colombia 1°23S 69°25W **186** D5
Aparados da Serra △
  Brazil   29°10S 50°8W **191** B5
Aparri Phil.   18°22N 121°38E **119** A6
Apateu Romania   46°36N 21°47E **80** D6
Apatin Serbia   45°40N 18°59E **80** E4
Apatity Russia   67°34S 33°22E **60** C25
Apatula = Finke
  Australia   25°34S 134°35E **150** D1
Apatzingán Mexico   19°5N 102°21W **180** D4
Apeldoorn Neths.   52°13N 5°57E **69** B5
Apen Germany   53°13N 7°48E **76** B3
Apennines = Appennini
  Italy   44°30N 10°0E **92** D7
Aphrodisias Turkey   37°42N 28°46E **99** D10
Api Nepal   30°0N 80°57E **110** F5
Apia Samoa   13°50S 171°50W **147** C11
Apiacás, Serra dos Brazil 9°50S 57°0W **186** E7
Apiaí Brazil   11°31S 48°18W **189** C1
Apinajé Brazil   11°31S 48°18W **189** C1
Apiti N.Z.   39°58S 175°54E **154** F4
Apizaco Mexico   19°25N 98°8W **181** D5
Aplao Peru   16°0S 72°40W **188** D3
Apo, Mt. Phil.   6°53N 125°14E **119** C7
Apodi Brazil   5°39S 37°48W **189** C4
Apolakia Greece   36°5N 27°48E **101** D9
Apolakia, Ormos Greece 36°5N 27°45E **101** D9
Apolda Germany   51°2N 11°32E **76** D7
Apollo Bay Australia 38°45S 143°40E **152** E5
Apollonia = Susah
  Libya   32°52N 21°59E **135** B10
Apollonia Greece   36°35N 27°58E **101** C9
Apolo Bolivia   14°30S 68°30W **188** C4
Apopa El Salv.   13°48N 89°10W **182** D2
Apopka U.S.A.   28°40N 81°31W **179** G8
Apopka, L. U.S.A.   28°38N 81°37W **179** G8
Aporé → Brazil   19°27S 50°57W **187** G8
Apostle Is. U.S.A.   47°0N 90°40W **172** B8
Apostle Islands △
  U.S.A.   46°55N 91°0W **172** B8
Apóstoles Argentina 28°0S 56°0W **191** B4
Apostolos Andreas, C.
  Cyprus   35°42N 34°35E **101** D13
Apostolovo Ukraine   47°39N 33°39E **85** J7
Apoteri Guyana   4°2N 58°32W **186** C7
Appalachian Mts.
  U.S.A.   38°0N 80°0W **173** G14
Appelbo Sweden   60°29N 14°1E **62** D8
Appennini Italy   44°30N 10°0E **92** D7
Appennino Lucano-Val d'Agri-
  Lagonegrese △ Italy 40°15N 16°10E **95** B8
Appennino Ligure Italy 44°30N 9°0E **92** D6
Appennino Tosco-Emiliano △
  Italy   44°30N 10°0E **92** D7
Appenzell-Ausser Rhoden □
  Switz.   47°23N 9°23E **77** H5
Appenzell-Inner Rhoden □
  Switz.   47°20N 9°25E **77** H5
Appiano Italy   46°28N 11°15E **93** B8

Apple Hill Canada   45°13N 74°46W **175** A10
Apple Valley U.S.A. 34°32N 117°14W **171** L9
Appleby-in-Westmorland
  U.K.   54°35N 2°29W **66** C5
Appledore U.S.A.   51°3N 4°13W **67** F3
Appleton U.S.A.   44°16N 88°25W **172** C9
Appling U.S.A.   33°33N 82°19W **178** B7
Approuague →
  Fr. Guiana   4°30N 51°57W **187** C8
Apricena Italy   41°47N 15°27E **93** G12
Aprília Italy   41°36N 12°39E **94** A5
Apsheronsk Russia   44°28N 39°42E **85** H5
Apsley Canada   44°45N 78°6W **174** B6
Apt France   43°53N 5°24E **73** E9
Apuane, Alpi Italy   44°7N 10°14E **92** D7
Apucarana Brazil   23°55S 51°33W **191** A5
Apulia = Púglia □ Italy 41°15N 16°30E **95** B9
Apure → Venezuela   7°37N 66°25W **186** B5
Apurímac □ Peru   14°30S 73°0W **188** C3
Apurímac → Peru   12°17S 73°56W **188** C3
Apuseni, Munții
  Romania   46°30N 22°45E **80** D7
Āq Qālā Iran   37°10N 54°30E **129** B7
Aqaba = Al 'Aqabah
  Jordan   29°31N 35°0E **130** F4
Aqaba, G. of Red Sea 29°0N 34°40E **128** D2
'Aqabah, Khalīj al = Aqaba, G. of
  Red Sea   29°0N 34°40E **128** D2
Aqadyr Kazakhstan   48°17N 74°16E **108** C8
Āqchah Afghan.   36°56N 66°11E **128** E7
'Aqdā Iran   32°26N 53°37E **129** C7
Aqīg Sudan   18°14N 38°12E **137** D4
Aqiq, Khalīg Sudan   18°20N 38°10E **137** D4
Ao Makham Thailand   7°50N 98°24E **121** a
Aqköl Kazakhstan   51°59N 70°56E **108** B8
Aqmola = Astana
  Kazakhstan   51°10N 71°30E **108** B8
Aqrah Iraq   36°46N 43°45E **105** C10
Aqsay Kazakhstan   51°11N 53°0E **108** B6
Aqshatau Kazakhstan 47°59N 74°3E **108** C8
Aqsū Ongtüstik Qazaqstan,
  Kazakhstan   42°25N 69°50E **108** D7
Aqsū Pavlodar,
  Kazakhstan   52°2N 76°55E **108** B9
Aqsüek Kazakhstan   44°37N 74°30E **108** C8
Aqtaū Mangghystaū,
  Kazakhstan   43°39N 51°12E **108** D4
Aqtaū Qaraghandy,
  Kazakhstan   50°14N 73°3E **108** B8
Aqtöbe Kazakhstan   50°17N 57°10E **108** B5
Aqtoghay Kazakhstan 46°57N 79°40E **108** C9
Aqua = Sokhumi Georgia 43°0N 41°0E **87** J5
Aquidauana Brazil   20°30S 55°50W **187** H7
Aquila Mexico   18°36N 103°30W **180** D4
Aquileia Italy   45°46N 13°22E **93** C10
Aquiles Serdán
  Mexico   28°36N 105°53W **180** B3
Aquin Haiti   18°16N 73°24W **183** C5
Aquitaine □ France   44°25N 0°30W **72** D3
Ar Horqin Qi China   43°45N 120°0E **115** C11
Ar Rafid Syria   32°57N 35°52E **130** C4
Ar Rabbāḥ Syria   34°50N 36°0E **130** C4
Ar Ramādī Iraq   33°25N 43°20E **105** F10
Ar Ramthā Jordan   32°34N 36°0E **130** C5
Ar Raqqah Syria   35°59N 39°8E **105** E8
Ar Raqqah □ Syria   35°30N 39°10E **105** D8
Ar Rashidiya = Er Rachidia
  Morocco   31°58N 4°20W **136** B3
Ar Rass Si. Arabia   25°50N 43°40E **128** E4
Ar Rawdah Si. Arabia 25°0N 43°40E **128** E4
Ar Rayyan Qatar   25°17N 51°25E **129** E6
Ar Rifā'i Iraq   31°50N 46°10E **128** D5
Ar Riyāḍ Si. Arabia 24°41N 46°42E **128** E5
Ar Ru'ays Qatar   26°8N 51°12E **129** E6
Ar Rukhaymīyah Iraq 29°22N 45°38E **128** D5
Ar Rumaythah Iraq   31°31N 45°12E **128** D5
Ar Ruṣāfah Syria   35°45N 38°49E **105** E8
Ar Ruṭbah Iraq   33°0N 40°15E **128** C4
Ara India   25°35N 84°32E **125** G11
Ara Arc → Australia 24°19N 86°30W **177** D11
'Arab, Bahr el →
  South Sudan   9°0N 29°30E **135** G11
Arab, Khalīg el Egypt 30°55N 29°0E **137** B8
Arab, Shatt al → Asia 29°57N 48°34E **128** D6
'Araba, W. → Egypt   30°0N 33°2E **137** B8
'Arabābād Iran   33°2N 57°41E **129** C8
Araban Turkey   37°28N 37°44E **104** D7
Arabatskaya Strelka
  Ukraine   45°40N 35°0E **85** K8
Arabba Italy   46°30N 11°52E **93** B8
Arabi Si. Arabia   31°50N 83°44W **178** D6
Arabia Asia   25°0N 45°0E **102** F6
Arabian Basin Ind. Oc. 11°30N 65°0E **146** C5
Arabian Desert = Es Sahrâ' Esh
  Sharqīya Egypt   27°30N 32°30E **137** C3
Arabian Gulf = Persian Gulf
  Asia   27°0N 50°0E **129** E6
Arabian Sea Ind. Oc. 16°0N 65°0E **102** G8
Araç Turkey   41°15N 33°21E **104** B5
Aracaju Brazil   10°55S 37°4W **189** D4
Aracati Brazil   4°30S 37°44W **189** C4
Araçatuba Brazil   21°10S 50°30W **191** A5
Aracena Spain   37°53N 6°38W **89** H4
Aracena, Sierra de Spain 37°50N 6°50W **89** H4
Arachova Greece   38°28N 22°35E **98** C4
Aračinovo Macedonia 42°1N 21°34E **96** D5
Araçuaí Brazil   16°52S 42°4W **189** E3
Araçuaí → Brazil   16°46S 42°2W **189** E3
'Arad Israel   31°15N 35°12E **130** D4
Arad Romania   46°10N 21°20E **80** D6
Arad □ Romania   46°20N 21°30E **80** D6
Arādān Iran   35°21N 52°30E **129** C7
Aradhippou Cyprus   34°57N 33°36E **101** E12
Arafura Sea E. Indies 9°0S 135°0E **147** B6
Aragats Armenia   40°30N 44°15E **87** K7
Aragón □ Spain   41°25N 0°40W **90** D4
Aragón → Spain   42°13N 1°44W **90** C3
Aragona Italy   37°24N 13°27E **94** G6
Araguacema Brazil   8°50S 49°20W **187** E9
Araguaia → Brazil   5°21S 48°41W **187** E9
Araguaína Brazil   7°12S 48°12W **187** E9
Araguari Brazil   18°38S 48°11W **189** E1
Araguari → Brazil   1°15N 49°55W **187** C9
Araguatins Brazil   5°38S 48°7W **189** C1
Arahal Spain   37°15N 5°33W **89** H5
Arain India   26°27N 75°2E **124** F6
Araioses Brazil   2°53S 41°55W **189** C3
Arak Algeria   25°20N 3°45E **136** C4
Arāk Iran   34°0N 49°40E **128** C5
Arakan = Rakhine □
  Burma   19°0N 94°15E **123** K18

Arakan Coast Burma   19°0N 94°0E **123** K19
Arakan Yoma Burma   20°0N 94°40E **123** K19
Arakkonam India   13°7N 79°43E **126** G4
Araklı Turkey   41°6N 40°2E **105** B9
Araks = Aras, Rūd-e →
  Asia   40°5N 48°29E **105** B13
Araks → Asia   39°10N 47°10E **108** A5
Aral Kazakhstan   46°41N 61°45E **108** C6
Aral Mangy Qaraqumy
  Kazakhstan   46°50N 63°10E **108** C6
Aral Sea Asia   45°0N 58°20E **108** C5
Aral Tengizi = Aral Sea
  Asia   45°0N 58°20E **108** C5
Aralık Turkey   39°52N 44°31E **105** C11
Aralkum = Aral
  Kazakhstan   44°30N 60°0E **108** C6
Aralsk = Aral
  Kazakhstan   46°41N 61°45E **108** C6
Aralskoye More = Aral Sea
  Asia   45°0N 58°20E **108** C5
Aralsor, Ozero = Aralsor Köli
  Kazakhstan   49°5N 48°12E **87** F9
Aralsor Köli Kazakhstan 49°5N 48°12E **87** F9
Aramac Australia   22°58S 145°14E **150** C4
Aran → India   19°55N 78°12E **126** E4
Aran, Val de Spain   42°50N 0°55E **90** C5
Aran I. = Arranmore
  Ireland   55°0N 8°30W **64** A3
Aran Is. Ireland   53°6N 9°38W **64** C2
Aranda de Duero Spain 41°39N 3°42W **88** D7
Arandán Iran   35°23N 46°55E **128** C5
Aranga N.Z.   35°44S 173°40E **154** B4
Arani India   12°43N 79°19E **127** H4
Aranjuez Spain   40°1N 3°40W **88** E7
Aranos Namibia   24°9S 19°7E **144** B2
Aransas Pass U.S.A. 27°55N 97°9W **176** H6
Aranyaprathet
  Thailand   13°41N 102°30E **120** F4
Araouane Mali   18°55N 3°30W **138** B4
Arapahoe U.S.A.   40°18N 99°54W **172** E4
Arapawa I. N.Z.   41°11S 174°17E **155** F5
Arapey Grande →
  Uruguay   30°55S 57°49W **190** C4
Arapgir Turkey   39°5N 38°30E **105** C8
Arapiraca Brazil   9°45S 36°39W **189** D3
Arapis, Akra Greece 40°27N 24°0E **97** F8
Arapongas Brazil   23°29S 51°28W **191** A5
Arapuni N.Z.   38°4S 175°39E **154** E4
Ar'ar Si. Arabia   30°59N 41°2E **128** D4
Araranguá Brazil   29°0S 49°30W **191** B6
Araraquara Brazil   21°50S 48°0W **187** H9
Araras, Serra das Brazil 25°0S 53°10W **191** B5
Ararat Armenia   39°48N 44°50E **116** C5
Ararat Australia   37°16S 142°58E **152** C3
Ararat, Mt. = Ağrı Dağı
  Turkey   39°50N 44°15E **105** C11
Arari Brazil   3°28S 44°47W **189** A2
Araria India   26°9N 87°33E **125** F12
Araripe, Chapada do
  Brazil   7°20S 40°0W **189** D3
Araripina Brazil   7°33S 40°34W **189** D3
Araruama, L. de Brazil 22°53S 42°12W **191** A7
Araruna Brazil   6°52S 35°44W **189** D4
Aras, Rūd-e → Asia   40°5N 48°29E **105** B13
Aratāne Mauritania   18°24N 8°32W **138** B3
Arauca Colombia   7°0N 70°40W **186** B4
Arauca → Venezuela   7°24N 66°35W **186** B5
Arauco Chile   37°16S 73°25W **190** D1
Araújos Brazil   19°56S 45°14W **189** C1
Aravalli Range India 25°0N 73°30E **124** G5
Arawa → Kenya   1°24S 40°9E **142** C5
Arawata → N.Z.   44°0S 168°40E **155** E2
Araxá Brazil   19°35S 46°55W **189** E2
Araya, Pen. de
  Venezuela   10°40N 64°0W **186** A6
Arba Minch Ethiopia 6°0N 37°30E **137** F2
Arbat Iraq   35°25N 45°35E **105** C11
Árbatax Italy   39°56N 9°42E **94** C2
Arbil Iraq   36°15N 44°5E **105** D11
Arbil □ Iraq   36°20N 44°0E **105** D11
Arboga Sweden   59°24N 15°52E **62** E9
Arbois France   46°55N 5°46E **71** F12
Arboréa Italy   39°46N 8°35E **94** C1
Arborfield Canada   53°6N 103°39W **163** C8
Arborg Canada   50°54N 97°13W **163** C9
Arbre du Ténéré Niger 17°50N 10°0E **139** B7
Arbroath U.K.   56°34N 2°35W **65** E6
Arbuckle U.S.A.   39°1N 122°3W **170** F4
Arbus Italy   39°30N 8°33E **94** C1
Arc → France   45°34N 6°12E **73** C10
Arc-lès-Gray France 47°28N 5°34E **71** E12
Arcachon France   44°40N 1°10W **72** D2
Arcachon, Bassin d'
  France   44°42N 1°10W **72** D2
Arcade U.S.A.   42°32N 78°25W **174** D6
Arcadia = Arkadia
  Greece   37°30N 22°0E **98** D4
Arcadia Fla., U.S.A. 27°13N 81°52W **179** H8
Arcadia La., U.S.A. 32°33N 92°55W **176** E8
Arcadia Pa., U.S.A. 40°47N 78°51W **174** F6
Arcanum U.S.A.   40°52N 124°5W **168** F1
Arcévia Italy   43°30N 12°56E **93** E9
Archanes Greece   35°16N 25°11E **101** D7
Archangel = Arkhangelsk
  Russia   64°38N 40°36E **106** C5
Archangelos Greece   36°13N 28°7E **101** C10
Archar Bulgaria   43°50N 22°54E **96** C6
Archbold U.S.A.   41°30N 75°32W **175** F8
Archena Spain   38°9N 1°16W **91** G3
Archer → Australia   13°28S 141°41E **150** A3
Archer B. Australia 13°20S 141°30E **150** A3
Archer Bend = Mungkan
  Kandju △ Australia 13°35S 142°52E **150** A3
Archers Post Kenya   0°35N 37°35E **142** B4
Arches △ U.S.A.   38°45N 109°25W **168** G9
Archipel-de-Mingan △
  Canada   50°13N 63°10W **165** B7
Archipiélago Chinijo △
  Canary Is.   29°20N 13°30W **100** E6
Archipiélago Los Roques △
  Venezuela   11°50N 66°44W **183** D6
Arci, Mte. Italy   39°47N 8°44E **94** C1
Arcidosso Italy   42°52N 11°33E **93** F8
Arcila = Asilah Morocco 35°29N 6°0W **136** A2
Arcipelago de la Maddalena △
  Italy   41°14N 9°24E **94** A2
Arcipelago Toscano △
  Italy   42°45N 10°15E **92** F7
Arcis-sur-Aube France 48°32N 4°10E **71** D11

Arckaringa Cr. → *Australia* 28°10S 135°22E **151** D2
Arco *Italy* 45°55N 10°53E **92** C7
Arco *U.S.A.* 43°38N 113°18W **168** E7
Arcoona *Australia* 31°2S 137°1E **152** A2
Arcos de Jalón *Spain* 41°12N 2°16W **90** D2
Arcos de la Frontera *Spain* 36°45N 5°49W **89** J5
Arcos de Valdevez *Portugal* 41°55N 8°22W **88** D2
Arcot *India* 12°53N 79°20E **127** H4
Arcoverde *Brazil* 8°25S 37°4W **189** B3
Arcozelo *Portugal* 40°32N 7°47W **88** E3
Arctic Bay *Canada* 73°1N 85°7W **161** C14
Arctic Mid-Ocean Ridge *Arctic* 87°0N 90°0E **54** A
Arctic Ocean *Arctic* 78°0N 160°0W **54** B18
Arctic Red River = Tsiigehtchic *Canada* 67°15N 134°0W **160** D5
Arctowski *Antarctica* 62°30S 58°0W **55** C18
Arda → *Bulgaria* 41°40N 26°30E **97** E10
Arda → *Italy* 45°2N 10°2E **92** C7
Ardabīl *Iran* 38°15N 48°18E **105** C13
Ardabīl □ *Iran* 38°15N 48°20E **129** B6
Ardahan *Turkey* 41°7N 42°41E **105** B10
Ardahan □ *Turkey* 41°10N 42°50E **105** B10
Ardakān = Sepīdān *Iran* 30°20N 52°5E **129** D7
Ardakān *Iran* 32°19N 53°59E **129** C7
Ardala *Sweden* 58°22N 13°19E **63** F7
Ardales *Spain* 36°53N 4°51W **89** J6
Ardara *Ireland* 54°46N 8°25W **64** B3
Ardas → *Greece* 41°40N 26°30E **97** E10
Ardèche □ *France* 44°42N 4°16E **73** D8
Ardèche → *France* 44°16N 4°39E **73** D8
Ardee *Ireland* 53°52N 6°33W **64** C5
Arden *Canada* 44°43N 76°56W **174** B8
Arden *Denmark* 56°46N 9°52E **63** H3
Arden *Calif., U.S.A.* 38°36N 121°33W **170** G5
Arden *Nev., U.S.A.* 36°1N 115°14W **171** J11
Ardenne *Belgium* 49°50N 5°5E **69** E5
Ardennes = Ardenne *Belgium* 49°50N 5°5E **69** E5
Ardennes □ *France* 49°35N 4°40E **71** C11
Ardentes *France* 46°45N 1°50E **71** F8
Arderin *Ireland* 53°2N 7°39W **64** C4
Ardeşen *Turkey* 41°12N 41°2E **105** B9
Ardestān *Iran* 33°20N 52°25E **129** C7
Ardfert *Ireland* 52°20N 9°47W **64** D2
Ardglass *U.K.* 54°16N 5°36W **64** B6
Ardhéa = Aridea *Greece* 40°58N 22°3E **96** F6
Ardila → *Portugal* 38°12N 7°28W **89** G3
Ardino *Bulgaria* 41°34N 25°9E **97** E9
Ardivachar Pt. *U.K.* 57°23N 7°26W **65** D1
Ardlethan *Australia* 34°22S 146°53E **153** C7
Ardmore *Okla., U.S.A.* 34°10N 97°8W **176** D6
Ardmore *Pa., U.S.A.* 40°2N 75°17W **175** F9
Ardnamurchan, Pt. of *U.K.* 56°43N 6°14W **65** E2
Ardnave Pt. *U.K.* 55°53N 6°20W **65** F2
Ardon *Russia* 43°10N 44°18E **87** J7
Ardore *Italy* 38°11N 16°10E **95** D9
Ardres *France* 50°50N 1°59E **71** B8
Ardrossan *Australia* 34°26S 137°53E **152** C2
Ardrossan *U.K.* 55°39N 4°49W **65** F4
Ards Pen. *U.K.* 54°33N 5°34W **64** B6
Arduan *Sudan* 19°54N 30°20E **137** D3
Ardud *Romania* 47°37N 22°52E **80** C7
Åre *Sweden* 63°22N 13°15E **62** A7
Arecibo *Puerto Rico* 18°29N 66°43W **183** d
Areia Branca *Brazil* 5°0S 37°0W **189** A3
Arena, Pt. *U.S.A.* 38°57N 123°44W **170** G3
Arenal *Honduras* 15°21N 86°50W **182** C2
Arenales, Cerro *Chile* 47°5S 73°40W **192** C2
Arenas = Las Arenas *Spain* 43°17N 4°50W **88** B6
Arenas de San Pedro *Spain* 40°12N 5°5W **88** E5
Arendal *Norway* 58°28N 8°46E **61** G13
Arendsee *Germany* 52°52N 11°27E **76** C7
Arenys de Mar *Spain* 41°35N 2°33E **90** D7
Arenzano *Italy* 44°24N 8°41E **92** D5
Areopoli *Greece* 36°40N 22°22E **98** E4
Arequipa *Peru* 16°20S 71°30W **188** D3
Arequipa □ *Peru* 16°0S 72°50W **188** D3
Arès *France* 44°47N 1°8W **72** D2
Arévalo *Spain* 41°3N 4°43W **88** D6
Arezzo *Italy* 43°25N 11°53E **93** E8
Arga *Turkey* 38°21N 37°59E **128** B3
Arga → *Spain* 42°18N 1°47W **90** C3
Argalasti *Greece* 39°13N 23°13E **98** B5
Argamasilla de Alba *Spain* 39°8N 3°5W **89** F7
Argamasilla de Calatrava *Spain* 38°44N 4°4W **89** G6
Arganda del Rey *Spain* 40°19N 3°26W **88** E7
Arganil *Portugal* 40°13N 8°3W **88** E2
Argarapa ✪ *Australia* 22°20S 134°58E **150** C1
Argelès-Gazost *France* 43°0N 0°6W **72** E3
Argelès-sur-Mer *France* 42°34N 3°1E **72** F7
Argens → *France* 43°24N 6°44E **73** E10
Argent, Côte d' *France* 44°15N 1°30W **72** D2
Argent-sur-Sauldre *France* 47°33N 2°25E **71** E9
Argenta *Canada* 50°11N 116°56W **162** C5
Argenta *Italy* 44°37N 11°50E **93** D8
Argentan *France* 48°45N 0°1W **70** D6
Argentário, Mte. *Italy* 42°24N 11°9E **93** F8
Argentat *France* 45°6N 1°56E **72** C5
Argentera *Italy* 44°12N 7°5E **92** D4
Argenteuil *France* 48°56N 2°15E **71** D9
Argentia *Canada* 47°18N 53°58W **165** C9
Argentiera, C. dell' *Italy* 40°44N 8°8E **94** B1
Argentina ■ *S. Amer.* 35°0S 66°0W **185** G4
Argentine Abyssal Plain *Atl. Oc.* 46°0S 52°0W **56** L6
Argentine Basin *Atl. Oc.* 45°0S 45°0W **56** L7
Argentino, L. *Argentina* 50°10S 73°0W **192** D2
Argenton-les-Vallées *France* 46°59N 0°27W **70** F6
Argenton-sur-Creuse *France* 46°36N 1°30E **71** F8
Argeş □ *Romania* 45°0N 24°45E **81** F9
Argeş → *Romania* 44°5N 26°38E **81** F11
Arghandab → *Afghan.* 31°30N 64°15E **124** D1
Argirades *Greece* 39°27N 19°58E **101** B3
Argiroupoli *Greece* 35°17N 24°20E **101** D6
Argo *Sudan* 19°28N 30°30E **137** D3
Argolikos Kolpos *Greece* 37°20N 22°52E **98** D4
Argonne *France* 49°10N 5°0E **71** C12
Argos *Greece* 37°40N 22°43E **98** D4
Argos Orestiko *Greece* 40°27N 21°18E **96** F5
Argostoli *Greece* 38°11N 20°29E **98** C2
Arguedas *Spain* 42°11N 1°36W **90** C3
Arguello, Pt. *U.S.A.* 34°35N 120°39W **171** L6
Arguineguín *Canary Is.* 27°46N 15°41W **100** G4
Argun *Russia* 43°18N 45°52E **87** J7
Argun → *Russia* 53°20N 121°28E **111** A13
Argungu *Nigeria* 12°40N 4°31E **139** C5
Argus Pk. *U.S.A.* 35°52N 117°26W **171** K9
Argyle, L. *Australia* 16°20S 128°40E **148** C4
Argyll & Bute □ *U.K.* 56°13N 5°28W **65** E3
Arhavi *Turkey* 41°21N 41°18E **105** B9
Århus = Aarhus *Denmark* 56°8N 10°11E **63** H4
Aria *N.Z.* 38°33S 175°0E **154** E4
Ariadnoye *Russia* 45°8N 134°25E **112** B7
Ariamsvlei *Namibia* 28°9S 19°51E **144** C2
Ariana *Tunisia* 36°52N 10°12E **136** A6
Ariana □ *Tunisia* 36°50N 9°52E **136** A5
Ariano Irpino *Italy* 41°9N 15°5E **95** A8
Aribinda *Burkina Faso* 14°17N 0°52W **139** C4
Arica *Chile* 18°32S 70°20W **188** D3
Arica *Colombia* 2°0S 71°50W **186** D4
Arica y Parinacota □ *Chile* 17°40S 69°50W **188** D4
Arico *Canary Is.* 28°9N 16°29W **100** F3
Arid, C. *Australia* 34°1S 123°10E **149** F3
Arida *Japan* 34°5N 135°8E **113** G7
Aride *Seychelles* 4°13S 55°40E **141** b
Aridea *Greece* 40°58N 22°3E **96** F6
Ariège □ *France* 42°56N 1°30E **72** F5
Ariège → *France* 43°30N 1°25E **72** E5
Arieş → *Romania* 46°24N 23°20E **81** D8
Arigat el Fersig *Algeria* 27°35N 2°7W **136** C3
Arīḩā *Israel* 31°51N 35°27E **137** A4
Arila, Akra *Greece* 39°43N 19°39E **101** A3
Arilje *Serbia* 43°44N 20°7E **96** C4
Arima *Trin. & Tob.* 10°38N 61°17W **183** D7
Arinos → *Brazil* 10°25S 58°20W **186** F7
Ario de Rosales *Mexico* 19°12N 101°43W **180** D4
Ariogala *Lithuania* 55°16N 23°28E **82** C10
Aripo, Mt. *Trin. & Tob.* 10°45N 61°15W **187** K15
Aripuanã *Brazil* 9°25S 60°30W **186** E6
Aripuanã → *Brazil* 5°7S 60°25W **186** E6
Ariquemes *Brazil* 9°55S 63°6W **186** E6
Arisaig *U.K.* 56°55N 5°51W **65** E3
Arish, W. el → *Egypt* 31°9N 33°49E **137** E8
Aristazabal I. *Canada* 52°40N 129°10W **162** C3
Ariton *U.S.A.* 31°36N 85°43W **178** D4
Ariyalur *India* 11°8N 79°8E **127** J4
Ariza *Spain* 41°19N 2°3W **90** D2
Arizaro, Salar de *Argentina* 24°40S 67°50W **190** A2
Arizona *Argentina* 35°45S 65°25W **190** D2
Arizona □ *U.S.A.* 34°0N 112°0W **169** J8
Arizpe *Mexico* 30°20N 110°10W **180** A2
'Arjah *Si. Arabia* 24°43N 44°17E **128** E5
Arjäng *Sweden* 59°24N 12°8E **62** E6
Arjeplog *Sweden* 66°3N 17°54E **60** C17
Arjepluovve = Arjeplog *Sweden* 66°3N 17°54E **60** C17
Arjona *Colombia* 10°14N 75°22W **186** A3
Arjona *Spain* 37°56N 4°4W **89** H6
Arjuna *Indonesia* 7°49S 112°34E **119** G15
Arka *Russia* 60°15N 142°0E **107** C15
Arkadak *Russia* 51°58N 43°30E **86** E6
Arkadelphia *U.S.A.* 34°7N 93°4W **176** D8
Arkadia *Greece* 37°30N 22°20E **98** D4
Arkaig, L. *U.K.* 56°59N 5°10W **65** E3
Arkalgud *India* 12°46N 76°3E **127** H3
Arkalyk = Arqalyk *Kazakhstan* 50°13N 66°50E **109** B7
Arkansas □ *U.S.A.* 35°0N 92°30W **176** D8
Arkansas → *U.S.A.* 33°47N 91°4W **176** E9
Arkansas City *U.S.A.* 37°4N 97°2W **172** G5
Arkaroola *Australia* 30°20S 139°22E **151** E2
Arkavāz *Iran* 33°22N 46°35E **105** F12
Arkhangelsk *Russia* 64°38N 40°36E **106** C5
Arkhangelskoye *Russia* 51°32N 40°58E **86** E5
Arki *Greece* 37°24N 26°44E **99** D8
Arki *India* 31°9N 76°58E **124** D7
Arklow *Ireland* 52°48N 6°10W **64** D5
Arkona, Kap *Germany* 54°42N 13°26E **76** A9
Arkösund *Sweden* 58°29N 16°56E **63** F10
Arkoudi *Greece* 38°33N 20°43E **98** C2
Arkport *U.S.A.* 42°24N 77°42W **174** D7
Arkticheskiy, Mys *Russia* 81°10N 95°0E **107** A10
Arkul *Russia* 57°17N 50°3E **86** B10
Arkville *U.S.A.* 42°9N 74°37W **175** D10
Ärla *Sweden* 59°17N 16°40E **62** E10
Arlanda, Stockholm ✈ (ARN) *Sweden* 59°41N 17°56E **62** E11
Arlanza → *Spain* 42°6N 4°9W **88** C6
Arlanzón → *Spain* 42°3N 4°17W **88** C6
Arlbergpass *Austria* 47°9N 10°12E **78** D3
Arlbergtunnel *Austria* 47°9N 10°12E **78** D3
Arles *France* 43°41N 4°40E **73** E8
Arli *Burkina Faso* 11°35N 1°28E **139** C5
Arli △ *Burkina Faso* 11°35N 1°28E **139** C5
Arlington *S. Africa* 28°1S 27°53E **145** C4
Arlington *Ga., U.S.A.* 31°26N 84°44W **178** D5
Arlington *N.Y., U.S.A.* 41°42N 73°54W **175** E11
Arlington *Oreg., U.S.A.* 45°43N 120°12W **168** D3
Arlington *S. Dak., U.S.A.* 44°22N 97°8W **172** C5
Arlington *Tex., U.S.A.* 32°44N 97°6W **176** E6
Arlington *Va., U.S.A.* 38°53N 77°7W **173** F15
Arlington *Vt., U.S.A.* 43°5N 73°9W **175** C11
Arlington *Wash., U.S.A.* 48°12N 122°8W **170** B4
Arlington Heights *U.S.A.* 42°5N 87°59W **172** D10
Arlit *Niger* 19°0N 7°38E **134** E7
Arlon *Belgium* 49°42N 5°49E **69** E5
Arlparra *Australia* 22°11S 134°30E **150** C1
Arltunga *Australia* 23°26S 134°41E **150** C1
Armação de Pêra *Portugal* 37°6N 8°22W **89** H2
Armadale *Australia* 32°9S 116°0E **149** F2
Armagh *U.K.* 54°21N 6°39W **64** B5
Armagh □ *U.K.* 54°18N 6°37W **64** B5
Armagnac *France* 43°50N 0°10E **72** E4
Armançon → *France* 47°59N 3°30E **71** E10
Armando Bermudez △ *Dom. Rep.* 19°3N 71°0W **183** C5
Armant *Egypt* 25°37N 32°32E **137** B3
Armatree *Australia* 31°26S 148°28E **153** A8
Armavir *Russia* 45°2N 41°7E **87** H5
Armenia *Colombia* 4°35N 75°45W **186** C3
Armenia ■ *Asia* 40°20N 45°0E **87** K7
Armeniş *Romania* 45°13N 22°17E **80** E7
Armenistis, Akra *Greece* 36°8N 27°42E **101** C9
Armentières *France* 50°40N 2°50E **71** B9
Armidale *Australia* 30°30S 151°40E **153** A9
Armilla *Spain* 37°9N 3°37W **89** H7
Armori *India* 20°28N 79°59E **126** D4
Armorique ⌂ *France* 48°22N 3°50W **70** D3
Armour *U.S.A.* 43°19N 98°21W **172** D4
Armstrong *B.C., Canada* 50°25N 119°10W **162** C5
Armstrong *Ont., Canada* 50°18N 89°4W **164** B2
Armur *India* 18°48N 78°16E **126** E4
Armutlu *Bursa, Turkey* 40°31N 28°50E **97** F12
Armutlu *İzmir, Turkey* 38°24N 27°34E **99** C9
Arnarfjörður *Iceland* 65°48N 23°40W **60** D2
Arnaud → *Canada* 59°59N 69°46W **161** F18
Arnauti, C. *Cyprus* 35°6N 32°17E **101** D11
Arnay-le-Duc *France* 47°10N 4°27E **71** E11
Arnea *Greece* 40°30N 23°38E **96** F7
Arnedillo *Spain* 42°13N 2°14W **90** C2
Arnedo *Spain* 42°12N 2°5W **90** C2
Arnett *U.S.A.* 36°8N 99°46W **176** C5
Arnhem *Neths.* 51°58N 5°55E **69** C5
Arnhem, C. *Australia* 12°20S 137°30E **150** A2
Arnhem B. *Australia* 12°20S 136°10E **150** A2
Arnhem Land *Australia* 13°10S 134°30E **150** A1
Arnhem Land ✪ *Australia* 12°50S 134°50E **150** A1
Arnissa *Greece* 40°47N 21°49E **96** F5
Arno → *Italy* 43°41N 10°17E **92** E7
Arno Bay *Australia* 33°54S 136°34E **152** B2
Arnold *U.K.* 53°1N 1°7W **66** D6
Arnold *Calif., U.S.A.* 38°15N 120°21W **170** G6
Arnold *Mo., U.S.A.* 38°26N 90°23W **172** F8
Arnoldstein *Austria* 46°33N 13°43E **78** E6
Arnon → *France* 47°13N 2°1E **71** E9
Arnot *Canada* 55°56N 96°41W **163** B9
Arnøya *Norway* 70°9N 20°40E **60** A19
Arnprior *Canada* 45°26N 76°21W **175** A8
Arnsberg *Germany* 51°24N 8°5E **76** D4
Arnsberger Wald ⌂ *Germany* 51°25N 8°20E **76** D4
Arnstadt *Germany* 50°50N 10°56E **76** E6
Aroab *Namibia* 26°41S 19°39E **144** C2
Aroania Oros *Greece* 37°56N 22°12E **98** D4
Aroche *Spain* 37°56N 6°57W **89** H4
Arochuku *Nigeria* 5°21N 7°54E **139** D6
Aroeiras *Brazil* 7°31S 35°41W **189** B3
Arolsen *Germany* 51°23N 9°2E **76** D5
Aron *India* 25°57N 77°56E **124** G6
Aron → *France* 46°50N 3°28E **71** F10
Arona *Canary Is.* 28°6N 16°40W **100** F3
Arona *Italy* 45°46N 8°34E **92** C5
Aros → *Mexico* 29°9N 107°57W **180** B3
Arousa, Ría de → *Spain* 42°28N 8°57W **88** C2
Arpa → *Asia* 39°28N 44°56E **105** C11
Arpaçay *Turkey* 40°50N 43°19E **105** B10
Arpajon *France* 48°36N 2°15E **71** D9
Arpajon-sur-Cère *France* 44°53N 2°28E **72** D6
Arpaşu de Jos *Romania* 45°47N 24°37E **81** E9
Arqalyk *Kazakhstan* 50°13N 66°50E **109** B7
Arrah = Ara *India* 25°35N 84°32E **125** G11
Arrah *Ivory C.* 6°40N 3°58W **138** D4
Arraias *Brazil* 12°56S 46°57W **189** C1
Arraiolos *Portugal* 38°44N 7°59W **89** G3
Arran *U.K.* 55°34N 5°12W **65** F3
Arranmore *Ireland* 55°0N 8°30W **64** A3
Arras *France* 50°17N 2°46E **71** B9
Arrasate *Spain* 43°4N 2°30W **90** B2
Arrats → *France* 44°6N 0°52E **72** D4
Arreau *France* 42°54N 0°22E **72** F4
Arrecife *Canary Is.* 28°57N 13°37W **100** F6
Arrecifes *Argentina* 34°6S 60°9W **190** C3
Arrée, Mts. d' *France* 48°26N 3°55W **70** D3
Arresø *Denmark* 55°58N 12°6E **63** J6
Arriaga *Mexico* 16°14N 93°54W **181** D6
Arribes del Duero ⌂ *Spain* 41°11N 6°39W **88** D4
Arrilalah *Australia* 23°43S 143°54E **150** C3
Arrino *Australia* 29°30S 115°40E **149** E2
Arriondas *Spain* 43°23N 5°11W **88** B5
Arrojado → *Brazil* 13°24S 44°20W **189** C2
Arromanches-les-Bains *France* 49°20N 0°38W **70** C6
Arronches *Portugal* 39°8N 7°16W **89** F3
Arros → *France* 43°40N 0°2W **72** E3
Arrow, L. *Ireland* 54°3N 8°19W **64** B3
Arrowsmith, Mt. *N.Z.* 43°20S 170°55E **155** D5
Arrowtown *N.Z.* 44°57S 168°50E **155** E3
Arroyo de la Luz *Spain* 39°30N 6°38W **89** F4
Arroyo Grande *U.S.A.* 35°7N 120°35W **171** K6
Ars *Iran* 37°9N 47°46E **128** B5
Ars-sur-Moselle *France* 49°5N 6°4E **71** C13
Arsenault L. *Canada* 55°6N 108°32W **163** B7
Arsenev *Russia* 44°10N 133°15E **112** B6
Arsiero *Italy* 45°48N 11°21E **93** C8
Arsikere *India* 13°15N 76°15E **127** H3
Arsin *Turkey* 41°8N 39°55E **105** B8
Arsk *Russia* 56°10N 49°50E **86** B9
Årsunda *Sweden* 60°31N 16°45E **62** D10
Arta *Greece* 39°8N 21°2E **98** B3
Artà *Spain* 39°41N 3°21E **100** B10
Artà, Coves d' *Spain* 39°40N 3°24E **100** B10
Artashat *Armenia* 40°0N 44°35E **105** B11
Arteaga *Mexico* 18°28N 102°25W **180** D4
Arteixo = A Baiuca *Spain* 43°19N 8°29W **88** B2
Artem = Artyom *Azerbaijan* 40°28N 50°20E **87** K10
Artem *Russia* 43°22N 132°13E **112** C6
Artemovsk *Russia* 54°45N 93°35E **107** D10
Artemovsk *Ukraine* 48°35N 38°0E **85** H9
Artemovskiy *Russia* 47°45N 40°16E **87** G5
Artenay *France* 48°5N 1°50E **71** D8
Artern *Germany* 51°22N 11°18E **76** D7
Artesa de Segre *Spain* 41°54N 1°3E **90** D6
Artesia = Mosomane *Botswana* 24°2S 26°19E **144** B4
Artesia *U.S.A.* 32°51N 104°24W **169** K11
Arthington *Liberia* 6°35N 10°45W **138** D2
Arthur *Canada* 43°50N 80°32W **174** C4
Arthur → *Australia* 41°2S 144°40E **151** G3
Arthur Cr. → *Australia* 22°30S 136°25E **150** C2
Arthur Pt. *Australia* 22°7S 150°3E **150** C5
Arthur River *Australia* 33°20S 117°2E **149** F2
Arthur's Pass *N.Z.* 42°54S 171°35E **155** C6
Arthur's Pass △ *N.Z.* 42°53S 171°42E **155** C6
Arthur's Town *Bahamas* 24°38N 75°42W **183** B4
Artigas *Antarctica* 62°30S 58°0W **55** C18
Artigas *Uruguay* 30°20S 56°30W **190** C4
Artik *Armenia* 40°38N 43°58E **87** K6
Artillery L. *Canada* 63°9N 107°52W **163** A7
Artois *France* 50°20N 2°30E **71** B9
Artotina *Greece* 38°42N 22°2E **98** C4
Artova *Turkey* 40°5N 36°28E **104** B7
Artrutx, C. de *Spain* 39°55N 3°49E **100** B10
Arts Bogd Uul *Mongolia* 44°40N 102°20E **114** B2
Artsvashen *Armenia* 40°38N 45°30E **105** B11
Artsyz *Ukraine* 46°4N 29°26E **81** D14
Artux *China* 39°40N 76°10E **109** E9
Artvin *Turkey* 41°14N 41°44E **105** B9
Artvin □ *Turkey* 41°10N 41°50E **105** B9
Artyk *Russia* 64°12N 145°6E **107** C15
Artyom *Azerbaijan* 40°28N 50°20E **87** K10
Aru, Kepulauan *Indonesia* 6°0S 134°30E **119** F8
Aru Is. = Aru, Kepulauan *Indonesia* 6°0S 134°30E **119** F8
Arua *Uganda* 3°1N 30°58E **142** B3
Aruanã *Brazil* 14°54S 51°10W **187** F8
Aruba ☒ *W. Indies* 12°30N 70°0W **183** D6
Arucas *Canary Is.* 28°7N 15°32W **100** F4
Arudy *France* 43°7N 0°28W **72** E3
Arué *Tahiti* 17°31S 149°30W **155** b
Arumpo *Australia* 33°48S 142°55E **152** B5
Arun → *Nepal* 26°55N 87°10E **125** F12
Arun → *U.K.* 50°49N 0°33W **67** G7
Arunachal Pradesh □ *India* 28°0N 95°0E **123** F19
Aruppukkottai *India* 9°31N 78°8E **127** K4
Arusha *Tanzania* 3°20S 36°40E **142** C4
Arusha □ *Tanzania* 3°20S 36°30E **142** C4
Arusha △ *Tanzania* 3°16S 36°47E **142** C4
Arusha Chini *Tanzania* 3°32S 37°20E **142** C4
Aruvi → *Sri Lanka* 8°48N 79°53E **127** K4
Aruwimi → *Dem. Rep. of the Congo* 1°13N 23°36E **142** B1
Arvada *Colo., U.S.A.* 39°48N 105°5W **168** G11
Arvada *Wyo., U.S.A.* 44°39N 106°8W **168** D10
Arvakalu *Sri Lanka* 8°20N 79°58E **127** K4
Arvayheer *Mongolia* 46°15N 102°48E **110** B9
Arve → *France* 46°11N 6°8E **71** F13
Arvi *Greece* 34°59N 25°28E **101** E7
Arvi *India* 20°59N 78°16E **126** D4
Arviat *Canada* 61°6N 93°59W **163** A10
Arvidsjaur *Sweden* 65°35N 19°10E **60** D18
Arvika *Sweden* 59°40N 12°36E **62** E6
Arvin *U.S.A.* 35°12N 118°50W **171** K8
Arwal *India* 25°15N 84°41E **125** G11
Arxan *China* 47°11N 119°57E **111** B12
Åryd *Sweden* 56°49N 14°59E **63** H8
Arys *Kazakhstan* 42°26N 68°48E **109** D7
Arzachena *Italy* 41°5N 9°23E **94** A2
Arzamas *Russia* 55°27N 43°55E **86** C6
Arzanah *U.A.E.* 24°47N 52°34E **129** E7
Arzew *Algeria* 35°50N 0°23W **136** A3
Arzgir *Russia* 45°18N 44°23E **87** H7
Arzignano *Italy* 45°31N 11°20E **93** C8
Arzúa *Spain* 42°56N 8°9W **88** C2
Aš *Czech Rep.* 50°13N 12°12E **78** A5
Ås *Sweden* 63°15N 14°34E **62** A8
As Pontes de García Rodríguez *Spain* 43°27N 7°50W **88** B3
Aş Şafā *Syria* 33°10N 37°0E **130** B6
As Saffānīyah *Si. Arabia* 27°55N 48°50E **129** E6
As Safīrah *Syria* 36°5N 37°21E **104** D7
Aş Şahm *Oman* 24°10N 56°53E **129** E8
As Sājir *Si. Arabia* 25°11N 44°36E **128** E5
As Salamīyah *Syria* 35°1N 37°2E **104** E7
As Salmān *Iraq* 30°30N 44°32E **128** D5
As Salt *Jordan* 32°2N 35°43E **130** C4
As Sal'w'a *Qatar* 24°23N 50°50E **129** E6
As Samāwah *Iraq* 31°15N 45°15E **128** D5
As Sanamayn *Syria* 33°3N 36°10E **130** B5
As Sila' *U.A.E.* 24°4N 51°45E **129** E6
As Sukhnah *Syria* 34°52N 38°52E **105** E8
As Sulaymānīyah *Iraq* 35°35N 45°29E **105** E11
As Sulaymānīyah □ *Iraq* 35°50N 45°30E **105** E11
As Sulaymī *Si. Arabia* 26°17N 41°21E **128** E4
As Sulayyil *Si. Arabia* 20°27N 45°34E **131** C4
As Summān *Si. Arabia* 25°0N 47°0E **128** E5
Aş Şuwar *Syria* 35°30N 40°38E **105** E9
As Suwaydā' *Syria* 32°40N 36°30E **130** C5
As Suwaydā' □ *Syria* 32°45N 36°45E **130** C5
As Suwayq *Oman* 23°51N 57°26E **129** F8
Aş Şuwayrah *Iraq* 32°55N 45°0E **105** F11
Åsa *Sweden* 57°21N 12°8E **63** G6
Asab *Namibia* 25°30S 18°0E **144** C2
Asaba *Nigeria* 6°12N 6°38E **139** D6
Asad, Buḩayrat al *Syria* 36°0N 38°15E **105** D8
Asadābād *Iran* 34°47N 48°7E **105** E13
Asafo *Ghana* 6°20N 2°40W **138** D4
Asahi *Japan* 35°43N 140°39E **113** E10
Asahi-Gawa → *Japan* 34°36N 133°58E **113** G6
Asahigawa = Asahikawa *Japan* 43°46N 142°22E **112** C11
Asahikawa *Japan* 43°46N 142°22E **112** C11
Asaluyeh *Iran* 27°29N 52°37E **129** E7
Asamankese *Ghana* 5°50N 0°40W **139** D4
Asan → *India* 26°37N 78°24E **125** F8
Asansol *India* 23°40N 87°1E **125** H12
Åsarna *Sweden* 62°39N 14°22E **62** B8
Asbesberge *S. Africa* 29°0S 23°0E **144** C3
Asbestos *Canada* 45°47N 71°58W **165** C5
Asbury Park *U.S.A.* 40°13N 74°1W **175** F10
Åsby *Sweden* 57°14N 12°18E **63** G6
Ascea *Italy* 40°8N 15°11E **95** B8
Ascensión *Mexico* 31°6N 107°59W **180** A3
Ascensión, B. de la *Mexico* 19°40N 87°30W **181** D7
Ascension I. *Atl. Oc.* 7°57S 14°23W **133** G2
Aschach an der Donau *Austria* 48°22N 14°2E **78** C7
Aschaffenburg *Germany* 49°58N 9°6E **77** F5
Aschendorf *Germany* 53°3N 7°19E **76** B3
Aschersleben *Germany* 51°45N 11°29E **76** D7
Asciano *Italy* 43°14N 11°33E **93** E8
Áscoli Piceno *Italy* 42°51N 13°34E **93** F10
Áscoli Satriano *Italy* 41°11N 15°32E **95** A8
Ascope *Peru* 7°46S 79°8W **188** B2
Ascotán *Chile* 21°45S 68°17W **190** A2
Aseb *Eritrea* 13°0N 42°40E **131** E3
Åseda *Sweden* 57°10N 15°20E **63** G9
Asedjrad *Algeria* 24°51N 1°29E **136** D4
Asela *Ethiopia* 8°0N 39°0E **131** F2
Åsen *Sweden* 61°17N 13°50E **62** C7
Asenovgrad *Bulgaria* 42°1N 24°51E **97** D8
Asfeld *France* 49°27N 4°5E **71** C11
Asfûn el Matâ'na *Egypt* 25°26N 32°30E **137** B3
Aşgabat = Ashgabat *Turkmenistan* 37°58N 58°24E **129** B8
Asgata *Cyprus* 34°46N 33°15E **101** E12
Ash Fork *U.S.A.* 35°13N 112°29W **169** J7
Ash Grove *U.S.A.* 37°19N 93°35W **172** G7
Ash Shabakah *Iraq* 30°49N 43°39E **128** D4
Ash Shamāl □ *Lebanon* 34°25N 36°0E **130** A5
Ash Shāmīyah *Iraq* 31°55N 44°35E **105** G11
Ash Shāriqah *U.A.E.* 25°23N 55°26E **129** E7
Ash Sharmah *Si. Arabia* 28°1N 35°16E **128** D2
Ash Sharqāt *Iraq* 35°27N 43°16E **105** E10
Ash Shaţrah *Iraq* 31°30N 46°10E **128** D5
Ash Shawbak *Jordan* 30°32N 35°34E **128** D2
Ash Shiḩr *Yemen* 14°45N 49°36E **131** E4
Ash Shināfīyah *Iraq* 31°35N 44°39E **128** D5
Ash Shu'bah *Si. Arabia* 28°54N 44°44E **128** D5
Ash Shumlūl *Si. Arabia* 26°31N 47°20E **128** E5
Ash Shūr'a *Iraq* 35°58N 43°13E **128** C4
Ash Shurayf *Si. Arabia* 25°43N 39°14E **128** E3
Ash Shuwayfāt *Lebanon* 33°45N 35°30E **130** B4
Asha *Russia* 55°0N 57°16E **108** B5
Ashanti □ *Ghana* 7°30N 1°30W **139** D4
Ashbourne *U.K.* 53°2N 1°43W **66** D6
Ashburn *U.S.A.* 31°43N 83°39W **178** D6
Ashburton *N.Z.* 43°53S 171°48E **155** D6
Ashburton → *Australia* 21°40S 114°56E **148** D1
Ashburton, North Branch → *N.Z.* 43°54S 171°44E **155** D6
Ashburton, South Branch → *N.Z.* 43°54S 171°44E **155** D6
Ashcroft *Canada* 50°40N 121°20W **162** C4
Ashdod *Israel* 31°49N 34°35E **130** D3
Ashdown *U.S.A.* 33°40N 94°8W **176** E7
Asheboro *U.S.A.* 35°43N 79°49W **177** D15
Ashern *Canada* 51°11N 98°21W **163** C9
Asherton *U.S.A.* 28°27N 99°46W **176** G5
Asheville *U.S.A.* 35°36N 82°33W **177** D13
Ashewat *Pakistan* 31°22N 68°32E **124** D3
Asheweig → *Canada* 54°17N 87°12W **164** B2
Ashford *Australia* 29°15S 151°3E **151** D5
Ashford *U.K.* 51°8N 0°53E **67** F8
Ashford *U.S.A.* 31°11N 85°14W **178** D4
Ashgabat *Turkmenistan* 37°58N 58°24E **129** B8
Ashhurst *N.Z.* 40°16S 175°45E **154** G4
Ashibetsu *Japan* 43°31N 142°11E **112** C11
Ashikaga *Japan* 36°28N 139°29E **113** F9
Ashington *U.K.* 55°11N 1°33W **66** B6
Ashizuri-Uwakai △ *Japan* 32°56N 132°32E **113** H6
Ashizuri-Zaki *Japan* 32°44N 133°0E **113** H6
Ashkarkot *Afghan.* 33°3N 67°58E **124** C2
Ashkhabad = Ashgabat *Turkmenistan* 37°58N 58°24E **129** B8
Āshkhāneh *Iran* 37°26N 56°55E **129** B8
Ashland *Ala., U.S.A.* 33°16N 85°50W **178** B4
Ashland *Kans., U.S.A.* 37°11N 99°46W **172** G4
Ashland *Ky., U.S.A.* 38°28N 82°38W **173** F12
Ashland *Maine, U.S.A.* 46°38N 68°24W **173** B19
Ashland *Mont., U.S.A.* 45°36N 106°16W **168** D10
Ashland *Ohio, U.S.A.* 40°52N 82°19W **174** F2
Ashland *Oreg., U.S.A.* 42°12N 122°43W **168** E2
Ashland *Pa., U.S.A.* 40°45N 76°22W **175** F8
Ashland *Va., U.S.A.* 37°46N 77°29W **173** G15
Ashland *Wis., U.S.A.* 46°35N 90°53W **172** B8
Ashley *N. Dak., U.S.A.* 46°2N 99°22W **172** B4
Ashley *Pa., U.S.A.* 41°12N 75°55W **175** E9
Ashley → *N.Z.* 43°17S 172°44E **155** D7
Ashmore and Cartier Is. *Ind. Oc.* 12°15S 123°0E **148** B3
Ashmore Reef *Australia* 12°14S 123°5E **148** B3
Ashmûn *Egypt* 30°18N 30°58E **137** E7
Ashmyany *Belarus* 54°26N 25°52E **75** A13
Ashokan Res. *U.S.A.* 41°56N 74°13W **175** E10
Ashoknagar *India* 24°34N 77°43E **126** B3
Ashqelon *Israel* 31°42N 34°35E **130** D3
Ashta *India* 23°1N 76°43E **124** H7
Ashtabula *U.S.A.* 41°52N 80°47W **174** E4
Ashti *Maharashtra, India* 21°12N 78°11E **126** D4
Ashti *Maharashtra, India* 18°50N 75°15E **126** E2
Āshtiyān *Iran* 34°31N 50°0E **129** C6
Ashton *S. Africa* 33°50S 20°5E **144** D3
Ashton *U.S.A.* 44°4N 111°27W **168** D8
Ashuanipi, L. *Canada* 52°45N 66°15W **165** B6
Ashuapmushuan → *Canada* 48°37N 72°20W **164** C5
Ashur = Assur *Iraq* 35°27N 43°15E **105** E10
Ashville *Ala., U.S.A.* 33°50N 86°15W **178** B4
Ashville *Fla., U.S.A.* 30°37N 83°39W **178** E6
Ashville *Pa., U.S.A.* 40°34N 78°33W **174** F6
'Āṣī → *Asia* 36°1N 35°59E **104** D6
Asia 45°0N 75°0E **102** E9
Asia, Kepulauan *Indonesia* 1°0N 131°13E **119** D8
Asiago *Italy* 45°52N 11°30E **93** C8
Asifabad *India* 19°20N 79°24E **126** E4
Asilah *Morocco* 35°29N 6°0W **136** A2
Asinara *Italy* 41°4N 8°16E **94** A1
Asinara, G. dell' *Italy* 41°0N 8°30E **94** A1
Asino *Russia* 57°0N 86°0E **106** D9
Asipovichy *Belarus* 53°19N 28°33E **75** B15
'Asīr *Si. Arabia* 18°40N 42°30E **137** D5
Asir, Ras *Somalia* 11°55N 51°10E **131** E5
Aska *India* 19°2N 84°42E **126** E7
Aşkale *Turkey* 39°55N 40°41E **105** C9
Askersund *Sweden* 58°53N 14°55E **63** F8
Askham *S. Africa* 26°59S 20°47E **144** C3
Askī Mawşil *Iraq* 36°30N 42°45E **105** D10
Askim *Norway* 59°35N 11°10E **61** G14
Askio, Oros *Greece* 40°25N 21°35E **96** F5
Askja *Iceland* 65°3N 16°48W **60** D5
Asklipio *Greece* 36°4N 27°56E **101** C9
Askøyna *Norway* 60°29N 5°10E **60** F11
Asl *Egypt* 29°33N 32°44E **137** F8
Aslan Burnu *Turkey* 38°44N 26°45E **99** C8
Aslanapa *Turkey* 39°13N 29°52E **99** B11
Asländuz *Iran* 39°26N 47°24E **105** C12
Asmara = Asmera *Eritrea* 15°19N 38°55E **131** D2
Asmera *Eritrea* 15°19N 38°55E **131** D2
Asnæs *Denmark* 55°40N 11°0E **63** J4
Åsnen *Sweden* 56°37N 14°45E **63** H8
Asni *Morocco* 31°17N 7°58W **136** B2
Aso Kujū △ *Japan* 32°53N 131°6E **113** H5
Åsola *Italy* 45°13N 10°24E **92** C7
Asos *Greece* 38°22N 20°33E **98** C2
Asoteriba, Jebel *Sudan* 21°51N 36°30E **137** C4
Asouf, O. → *Algeria* 25°40N 2°8E **136** C4
Aspatria *U.K.* 54°47N 3°19W **66** C4
Aspe *Spain* 38°20N 0°40W 9
Aspen *U.S.A.* 39°11N 106°49W 168
Aspendos *Turkey* 36°54N 31°7E 10
Aspermont *U.S.A.* 33°8N 100°14W 17
Aspet *France* 43°1N 0°48E 7
Aspiring, Mt. *N.Z.* 44°23S 168°46E 15
Aspres-sur-Buëch *France* 44°32N 5°44E 7
Asprokavos, Akra *Greece* 39°21N 20°6E 10
Aspromonte △ *Italy* 38°9N 15°58E 9
Aspur *India* 23°58N 74°7E 12
Asquith *Canada* 52°8N 107°13W 16
Assab = Aseb *Eritrea* 13°0N 42°40E 13
Assâba □ *Mauritania* 16°40N 11°40W 13
Assâba, Massif de l' *Mauritania* 16°10N 11°45W 13
Assagny △ *Ivory C.* 5°10N 4°48W 13
Assaikio *Nigeria* 8°34N 8°55E 13
Assal, L. *Djibouti* 11°40N 42°26E 13
Assam □ *India* 26°0N 93°0E 12
Assamakka *Niger* 19°21N 5°38E 13
Assateague Island ⌂ *U.S.A.* 38°15N 75°10W 17
Assaye *India* 20°15N 75°53E 12
Asse *Belgium* 50°24N 4°10E 6
Assekrem *Algeria* 23°16N 5°49E 13
Assémini *Italy* 39°17N 9°0E 9
Assen *Neths.* 53°0N 6°35E 6
Assens *Denmark* 55°16N 9°55E 6
Assini *Ivory C.* 5°9N 3°17W 13
Assiniboia *Canada* 49°40N 105°59W 16
Assiniboine → *Canada* 49°53N 97°8W 16
Assiniboine, Mt. *Canada* 50°52N 115°39W 16
Assis *Brazil* 22°40S 50°20W 19
Assis Brasil *Brazil* 10°55S 69°32W 18
Assisi *Italy* 43°4N 12°37E 9
Assur *Iraq* 35°27N 43°15E 10
Assynt, L. *U.K.* 58°10N 5°3W 6
Astaffort *France* 44°4N 0°40E 7
Astakida *Greece* 35°53N 26°50E 9
Astakos *Greece* 38°32N 21°5E 9
Astana *Kazakhstan* 51°10N 71°30E 10
Āstāneh *Iran* 37°17N 49°59E 12
Astara *Azerbaijan* 38°30N 48°50E 10
Āstārā *Iran* 38°20N 48°52E 10
Astarabad = Gorgān *Iran* 36°55N 54°30E 12
Asterousia *Greece* 34°59N 25°3E 10
Asti *Italy* 44°54N 8°12E 9
Astipalea *Greece* 36°32N 26°22E 9
Astorga *Spain* 42°29N 6°8W 8
Astoria *U.S.A.* 46°11N 123°50W 17
Åstorp *Sweden* 56°6N 12°55E 6
Astrakhan *Russia* 46°25N 48°5E 8
Astrakhan □ *Russia* 47°45N 46°20E 8
Astrebla Downs *Australia* 24°12S 140°34E 15
Astudillo *Spain* 42°12N 4°22W 8
Asturias □ *Spain* 43°15N 6°0W 8
Asturias ✈ (OVD) *Spain* 43°33N 6°3W 8
Asunción *Bolivia* 11°46S 67°50W 18
Asunción *Paraguay* 25°10S 57°30W 19
Asunción Nochixtlán *Mexico* 17°28N 97°14W 18
Åsunden *Sweden* 58°0N 15°51E 6
Aswa → *Uganda* 3°43N 31°55E 14
Aswa-Lolim ⌂ *Uganda* 2°43N 31°35E 14
Aswad, Ra's al *Si. Arabia* 21°20N 39°0E 13
Aswân *Egypt* 24°4N 32°57E 13
Aswan High Dam = Sadd el Aali *Egypt* 23°54N 32°54E 13
Asyût *Egypt* 27°11N 31°4E 13
Asyûti, Wadi → *Egypt* 27°11N 31°16E 13
Aszód *Hungary* 47°39N 19°28E 8
At-Bashy *Kyrgyzstan* 41°10N 75°48E 1
At Ţafilah *Jordan* 30°45N 35°30E 13
At Ţafilah □ *Jordan* 30°45N 35°30E 13
At Tā'if *Si. Arabia* 21°5N 40°27E 13
At Ta'mīm □ *Iraq* 35°30N 44°20E 12
At Ţirāq *Si. Arabia* 27°19N 44°33E 12
Aţ Ţubayq *Si. Arabia* 29°30N 37°0E 12
Aţ Ţunayb *Jordan* 31°48N 35°57E 13
Atabey *Turkey* 37°57N 30°39E 9
Atacama □ *Chile* 27°30S 70°0W 19
Atacama, Desierto de *Chile* 24°0S 69°20W 19
Atacama, Salar de *Chile* 23°30S 68°20W 19
Atakeye ✪ *Australia* 22°30S 133°45E 14
Atakor *Algeria* 23°27N 5°31E 13
Atakpamé *Togo* 7°31N 1°13E 13
Atalandi *Greece* 38°39N 22°58E 9
Atalaya *Peru* 10°45S 73°50W 18
Atalaya de Femes *Canary Is.* 28°56N 13°47W 1
Ataléia *Brazil* 18°3S 41°6W 18
Atami *Japan* 35°5N 139°4E 11
Atamyrat *Turkmenistan* 37°50N 65°12E 1
Atapuerca, Cueva de *Spain* 42°22N 3°32W 8
Atapupu *Indonesia* 9°0S 124°51E 1
Atâr *Mauritania* 20°30N 13°5W 13
Ataram, Erg n- *Algeria* 23°57N 2°0E 13
Atarfe *Spain* 37°13N 3°40W 8
Atari *Pakistan* 30°56N 74°2E 12
Atascadero *U.S.A.* 35°29N 120°40W 17
Atasū *Kazakhstan* 48°30N 71°0E 10
Atatürk, İstanbul ✈ (IST) *Turkey* 40°59N 28°49E 9
Atatürk Barajı *Turkey* 37°28N 38°30E 10
Atauro *E. Timor* 8°10S 125°30E 1
Ataviros *Greece* 36°12N 27°50E 10
Atbara *Sudan* 17°42N 33°59E 13
'Atbara, Nahr → *Sudan* 17°40N 33°56E 1
Atbasar *Kazakhstan* 51°48N 68°20E 1
Atbashi = At-Bashy *Kyrgyzstan* 41°10N 75°48E 1
Atça *Turkey* 37°53N 28°13E 9
Atchafalaya B. *U.S.A.* 29°25N 91°25W 1
Atchison *U.S.A.* 39°34N 95°7W 1
Atebubu *Ghana* 7°47N 1°0W 1
Ateca *Spain* 41°20N 1°49W 9
Aterno → *Italy* 42°11N 13°51E 9
Āteshān *Iran* 35°35N 52°37E 1
Atesine, Alpi *Italy* 46°55N 11°30E 1
Atessa *Italy* 42°4N 14°27E 1
Atfih *Egypt* 29°25N 31°15E 1
Ath *Belgium* 50°38N 3°47E 1
Athabasca *Canada* 54°45N 113°20W 1

abasca → Canada 58°40N 110°50W 163 B6
abasca, L. Canada 59°15N 109°15W 163 B7
abasca Sand Dunes ⌂
nada 59°4N 108°43W 163 B7
garh India 20°32N 85°37E 126 D7
amanon Oros Greece 39°30N 21°26E 98 B3
boy Ireland 53°36N 6°56W 64 C5
na U.S.A. 29°59N 83°30W 178 F6
enry Ireland 53°18N 8°44W 64 C3
ens = Athina Greece 37°58N 23°43E 98 D5
ens Ala., U.S.A. 34°48N 86°58W 177 D11
ens Ga., U.S.A. 33°57N 83°23W 178 B6
ens N.Y., U.S.A. 42°16N 73°49W 175 D11
ens Ohio, U.S.A. 39°20N 82°6W 173 F12
ens Pa., U.S.A. 41°57N 76°31W 175 E8
ens Tenn., U.S.A. 35°27N 84°36W 177 D12
ens Tex., U.S.A. 32°12N 95°51W 176 E7
erley Canada 44°37N 79°20W 174 B5
erton Australia 17°17S 145°30E 150 B4
River Kenya 1°28S 36°58E 142 C4
éme Benin 6°37N 1°40E 139 D5
enou Cyprus 35°3N 33°32E 101 D12
na Greece 37°58N 23°43E 98 D5
na ✕ (ATH) Greece 37°56N 23°56E 98 D5
nai = Athina Greece 37°58N 23°43E 98 D5
one Ireland 53°25N 7°56W 64 C4
malik India 20°43N 84°32E 126 D7
i India 16°44N 75°6E 126 F2
i N.Z. 45°30S 168°35E 155 F3
l U.S.A. 42°36N 72°14W 175 D12
ll, Forest of U.K. 56°51N 3°50W 65 E5
ll, Kap Greenland 76°25N 69°30W 57 B4
lville Canada 47°59N 66°43W 165 C6
s Greece 40°9N 24°22E 97 F8
Ireland 53°0N 7°0W 64 C5
had 13°13N 18°20E 135 F9
k Uganda 3°12N 32°2E 142 B3
muri N.Z. 38°24S 176°5E 154 E5
Peru 16°14S 73°40W 188 D3
nza Spain 41°12N 2°52W 90 D2
L. Canada 55°15N 96°0W 163 B9
aki ⌂ Canada 51°30N 95°31W 163 C9
ameg → Canada 52°30N 82°46W 164 B3
okan Canada 48°45N 91°37W 164 C1
onak L. Canada 52°40N 64°32W 165 B7
aono Tahiti 17°46S 149°28W 155 b
ampattinam India 10°28N 79°20E 127 J4
Cook Is. 20°0S 158°10W 157 J12
Russia 60°50N 151°48E 107 C16
I. U.S.A. 52°7N 174°30W 166 E5
ırsk Russia 51°55N 45°2E 86 E7
nson Ga., U.S.A. 31°13N 81°47W 178 D8
nson Nebr., U.S.A. 42°32N 98°59W 172 D4
nta Ga., U.S.A. 33°45N 84°23W 178 B5
nta Tex., U.S.A. 33°7N 94°10W 176 E7
nta Hartsfield-Jackson Int. ✕
TL) U.S.A. 33°38N 84°26W 178 B5
ntic U.S.A. 41°24N 95°1W 172 E6
ntic Beach U.S.A. 30°20N 81°24W 178 E8
ntic City U.S.A. 39°21N 74°27W 173 F16
ntic-Indian Basin
tarctica 60°0S 30°0E 55 B4
ntic Ocean 0°0 20°0W 56 F8
ntis S. Africa 33°34S 18°29E 144 D2
s Mts. = Haut Atlas
orocco 32°30N 5°0W 136 B3
Canada 59°31N 133°41W 162 B2
, L. Canada 59°26N 133°45W 162 B2
⌂ Canada 59°10N 134°30W 162 B2
akur Andhra Pradesh,
dia 18°45N 78°39E 126 E4
akur Andhra Pradesh,
dia 14°37N 79°40E 127 G4
akur Andhra Pradesh,
dia 15°53N 78°35E 127 G4
ore U.S.A. 31°2N 87°29W 179 D2
a U.S.A. 34°23N 96°8W 176 D6
os Greece 38°28N 20°49E 98 C2
a U.S.A. 35°19N 117°37W 171 K9
asuk U.S.A. 70°28N 157°24W 166 A8
→ Bangla. 24°7N 89°22E 125 G13
k = Atrek →
rkmenistan 37°35N 53°58E 129 B8
n Sweden 57°7N 12°57E 63 G6
n → Sweden 56°53N 12°30E 63 H6
uli India 28°2N 78°20E 124 E8
k → Turkmenistan 37°35N 53°58E 129 B8
Italy 42°35N 13°58E 93 F10
ki Greece 39°56N 25°13E 99 B7
um, Mts. Cameroon 6°41N 12°57E 139 D7
ta Japan 43°24N 141°26E 112 C10
lla U.S.A. 34°1N 86°6W 178 A3
peu Laos 14°48N 106°50E 120 E6
pulgus U.S.A. 30°45N 84°29W 178 E5
wapiskat Canada 52°56N 82°24W 164 B3
wapiskat →
nada 52°57N 82°18W 164 B3
wapiskat L.
nada 52°18N 87°54W 164 B2
rsee Austria 47°55N 13°32E 78 D6
ca = Attiki □ Greece 37°10N 23°40E 98 D5
ca Ind., U.S.A. 40°18N 87°15W 172 E10
ca Ohio, U.S.A. 41°4N 82°53W 174 E2
chy France 49°25N 3°3E 71 C10
gny France 49°28N 4°35E 71 C11
kamagen L. Canada 55°0N 66°30W 165 B6
ki □ Greece 37°10N 23°40E 98 D5
eboro U.S.A. 41°57N 71°17W 175 E13
ck Pakistan 33°52N 72°20E 124 C5
pu = Attapeu
os 14°48N 106°50E 120 E6
I. U.S.A. 52°55N 172°55E 166 E2
nga Australia 30°55S 150°50E 153 A9
r India 11°35N 78°30E 127 J4
el → Argentina 36°17S 66°50W 190 D2
a Uganda 2°7N 32°20E 142 B3
dabreg Sweden 58°12N 16°0E 63 F10
ater U.S.A. 37°21N 120°37W 170 H6
ood Canada 43°40N 81°1W 174 C3
ood U.S.A. 39°48N 101°3W 172 F3
rau Kazakhstan 47°5N 52°0E 108 C4
Sable U.S.A. 44°25N 83°20W 174 B1
Sable → U.S.A. 44°25N 83°20W 173 C12
Sable Forks
S.A. 44°27N 73°41W 175 B11
Sable Pt. U.S.A. 44°20N 83°20W 174 B1
s Honduras 15°29N 84°20W 182 C3
sberg Namibia 22°37S 17°13E 144 B2
agne France 43°17N 5°37E 73 E9
e □ France 48°15N 4°10E 71 D11
e → France 48°34N 3°43E 71 D10
Aubenas France 44°37N 4°24E 73 D8
Aubenton France 49°50N 4°12E 71 C11
Auberry U.S.A. 37°7N 119°29W 170 H7
Aubigny-sur-Nère France 47°30N 2°24E 71 E9
Aubin France 44°33N 2°15E 72 D6
Aubrac, Mts. d' France 44°40N 3°2E 72 D7
Auburn Australia 34°1S 138°42E 152 C3
Auburn Ala., U.S.A. 32°36N 85°29W 178 C4
Auburn Calif., U.S.A. 38°54N 121°4W 170 G5
Auburn Ind., U.S.A. 41°22N 85°4W 173 E11
Auburn Maine, U.S.A. 44°6N 70°14W 173 C18
Auburn N.Y., U.S.A. 42°56N 76°34W 175 D8
Auburn Nebr., U.S.A. 40°23N 95°51W 172 E6
Auburn Pa., U.S.A. 40°36N 76°6W 175 F8
Auburn Wash., U.S.A. 47°18N 122°14W 170 C4
Auburn Ra. Australia 25°15S 150°30E 151 D5
Auburndale U.S.A. 28°4N 81°48W 179 G8
Aubusson France 45°57N 2°11E 72 C6
Auce Latvia 56°28N 22°53E 82 B9
Auch France 43°39N 0°36E 72 E4
Auchi Nigeria 7°6N 6°13E 139 D6
Auchterarder U.K. 56°18N 3°41W 65 E5
Auchtermuchty U.K. 56°18N 3°13W 65 E5
Auckland N.Z. 36°52S 174°46E 154 C3
Auckland □ N.Z. 36°50S 175°0E 154 C3
Auckland Is. Pac. Oc. 50°40S 166°5E 156 N8
Aude □ France 43°8N 2°28E 72 E6
Aude → France 43°13N 3°14E 72 E7
Auden Canada 50°14N 87°53W 164 B2
Auderville France 49°43N 1°57W 70 C5
Audierne France 48°1N 4°34W 70 D2
Audincourt France 47°30N 6°50E 71 E13
Audomarois ⌂ France 50°50N 2°30E 71 B9
Audubon U.S.A. 41°43N 94°56W 172 E6
Aue Germany 50°35N 12°41E 76 E8
Auerbach Germany 50°30N 12°24E 76 E8
Augathella Australia 25°48S 146°35E 151 D4
Aughnacloy U.K. 54°25N 6°59W 64 B5
Aughrim Ireland 53°18N 8°19W 64 C3
Augrabies Falls
S. Africa 28°35S 20°20E 144 C3
Augrabies Falls △
S. Africa 28°40S 20°22E 144 C3
Augsburg Germany 48°25N 10°52E 77 G6
Augsburg-Westliche Wälder ⌂
Germany 48°22N 10°40E 77 G6
Augusta Australia 34°19S 115°9E 149 F2
Augusta Italy 37°13N 15°13E 95 E8
Augusta Ark., U.S.A. 35°17N 91°22W 176 D9
Augusta Ga., U.S.A. 33°28N 81°58W 178 B8
Augusta Kans., U.S.A. 37°41N 96°59W 172 G5
Augusta Maine,
U.S.A. 44°19N 69°47W 173 C19
Augusta Mont., U.S.A. 47°30N 112°24W 168 C7
Augustenborg Denmark 54°57N 9°53E 63 K3
Augustów Poland 53°51N 23°0E 82 E9
Augustus, Mt.
Australia 24°20S 116°50E 149 D2
Augustus I. Australia 15°20S 124°30E 148 C3
Aujuittuq = Grise Fiord
Canada 76°25N 82°57W 161 B15
Aukrug ⌂ Germany 54°5N 9°45E 76 A5
Aukštaitija △ Lithuania 55°15N 26°0E 61 J22
Aukum U.S.A. 38°34N 120°43W 170 G6
Aul India 20°41N 86°39E 126 D8
Aulavik △ Canada 73°42N 119°55W 160 C8
Auld, L. Australia 22°25S 123°50E 148 D3
Äülïeköl Kazakhstan 52°32N 62°45E 108 B6
Aulifeltet Norway 60°30N 11°21E 62 D5
Aulla Italy 44°12N 9°58E 92 D6
Aulnay France 46°2N 0°22W 72 B3
Aulne → France 48°17N 4°16W 70 D2
Aulnoye-Aymeries
France 50°12N 3°50E 71 B10
Ault France 50°8N 1°26E 70 B8
Ault U.S.A. 40°35N 104°44W 168 F11
Aulus-les-Bains France 42°49N 1°19E 72 F5
Aumale France 49°46N 1°46E 71 C8
Aumont-Aubrac France 44°43N 3°17E 72 D7
Auna Nigeria 10°9N 4°42E 139 C5
Aundah India 19°32N 77°3E 126 E3
Aundh India 17°33N 74°23E 126 F2
Aunging Denmark 56°26N 10°22E 63 H4
Aunis France 46°5N 0°50W 72 B3
Auponhia Indonesia 1°58S 125°27E 119 E7
Aups France 43°37N 6°15E 73 E10
Aur, Pulau Malaysia 2°35N 104°10E 121 L5
Auraiya India 26°28N 79°33E 125 F8
Aurangabad Bihar,
India 24°45N 84°18E 125 G11
Aurangabad Maharashtra,
India 19°50N 75°23E 126 E2
Auray France 47°40N 2°59W 70 E4
Aurès Algeria 35°8N 6°30E 136 A5
Aurich Germany 53°28N 7°28E 76 B3
Aurillac France 44°55N 2°26E 72 D6
Auronzo di Cadore Italy 46°33N 12°26E 93 B9
Aurora Canada 44°0N 79°28W 174 C5
Aurora S. Africa 32°40S 18°29E 144 D2
Aurora Colo., U.S.A. 39°43N 104°49W 168 G11
Aurora Ill., U.S.A. 41°45N 88°19W 172 E9
Aurora Mo., U.S.A. 36°58N 93°43W 172 G7
Aurora N.Y., U.S.A. 42°45N 76°42W 175 D8
Aurora Nebr., U.S.A. 40°52N 98°0W 172 E5
Aurora Ohio, U.S.A. 41°21N 81°20W 174 E3
Aurukun Australia 13°20S 141°45E 150 A3
Aurukun ⊙ Australia 13°36S 141°48E 150 A3
Aus Namibia 26°35S 16°12E 144 C2
Ausa India 18°15N 76°30E 126 E3
Ausable → Canada 43°19N 81°46W 174 C3
Auschwitz = Oświęcim
Poland 50°2N 19°11E 83 H6
Auski Roadhouse
Australia 22°22S 118°41E 148 D2
Austen Harbour India 12°55N 92°45E 127 H11
Austerlitz = Slavkov u Brna
Czech Rep. 49°10N 16°52E 79 B9
Austin Minn., U.S.A. 43°40N 92°58W 172 D7
Austin Nev., U.S.A. 39°30N 117°4W 168 G5
Austin Pa., U.S.A. 41°38N 78°6W 174 E6
Austin Tex., U.S.A. 30°17N 97°45W 176 F6
Austin, L. Australia 27°40S 118°0E 149 E2
Austin I. Canada 61°10N 94°0W 163 A10
Austra Norway 65°8N 11°55E 60 D14
Austral Is. = Tubuaï, Îs.
French Polynesia 25°0S 150°0W 157 K13
Austral Seamount Chain
Pac. Oc. 24°0S 150°0W 157 K13
Australia ■ Oceania 23°0S 135°0E 147 D6
Australian-Antarctic Basin
S. Ocean 60°0S 120°0E 55 C9
Australian Capital Territory □
Australia 35°30S 149°0E 153 C8
Australind Australia 33°17S 115°42E 149 F2
Austria ■ Europe 47°0N 14°0E 78 E7
Austvågøya Norway 68°20N 14°40E 60 B16
Auterive France 43°21N 1°29E 72 E5
Authie → France 50°22N 1°38E 71 B8
Authon-du-Perche
France 48°12N 0°54E 70 D7
Autlán de Navarro
Mexico 19°46N 104°22W 180 D4
Autun France 46°58N 4°17E 71 F11
Auvergne □ France 45°20N 3°15E 72 C7
Auvergne, Mts. d' France 45°20N 2°55E 72 C6
Auvézère → France 45°12N 0°50E 72 C4
Auxerre France 47°48N 3°32E 71 E10
Auxi-le-Château France 50°15N 2°8E 71 B9
Auxonne France 47°10N 5°20E 71 E12
Auyuittuq △ Canada 67°30N 66°0W 161 D18
Auzances France 46°2N 2°30E 71 F9
Auzangate, Nevado
Peru 13°47S 71°13W 188 C3
Av-Dovurak Russia 51°17N 91°35E 107 D10
Ava U.S.A. 36°57N 92°40W 172 G7
Avachinskaya Sopka
Russia 53°15N 158°50E 107 D16
Avallon France 47°30N 3°53E 71 E10
Avalon U.S.A. 33°21N 118°20W 171 M8
Avalon Pen. Canada 47°30N 53°20W 165 C9
Avanigadda India 16°0N 80°56E 127 G5
Avanos Turkey 38°43N 34°51E 104 C6
Avantas Greece 40°57N 25°56E 97 F9
Avaré Brazil 23°4S 48°58W 191 A6
Avawatz Mts. U.S.A. 35°40N 116°30W 171 K10
Avdan Dağı Turkey 40°23N 29°46E 97 F13
Aveiro Brazil 3°10S 55°5W 187 D7
Aveiro Portugal 40°37N 8°38W 88 E2
Aveiro □ Portugal 40°40N 8°35W 88 E2
Āvej Iran 35°40N 49°15E 129 C6
Avellaneda Argentina 34°40S 58°22W 190 C4
Avellino Italy 40°54N 14°47E 95 B7
Avenal U.S.A. 36°0N 120°8W 170 K6
Aversa Italy 40°58N 14°12E 95 B7
Avery U.S.A. 47°15N 115°49W 168 C6
Aves, I. de W. Indies 15°45N 63°55W 183 C7
Aves, Is. las Venezuela 12°0N 67°30W 183 D6
Avesnes-sur-Helpe
France 50°8N 3°55E 71 B10
Avesnois ⌂ France 50°10N 3°45E 71 B10
Avesta Sweden 60°9N 16°10E 62 D10
Aveyron □ France 44°22N 2°45E 72 D6
Aveyron → France 44°5N 1°16E 72 D5
Avezzano Italy 42°2N 13°25E 93 F10
Avgo Greece 35°33N 25°37E 99 F7
Aviá Terai Argentina 26°45S 60°50W 190 B3
Aviano Italy 46°4N 12°36E 93 B9
Aviemore U.K. 57°12N 3°50W 65 D5
Aviemore, L. N.Z. 44°37S 170°18E 155 E5
Avigliana Italy 45°5N 7°23E 92 C4
Avigliano Italy 40°44N 15°43E 95 B8
Avignon France 43°57N 4°50E 73 E8
Ávila Spain 40°39N 4°43W 88 E6
Ávila □ Spain 40°30N 5°0W 88 E6
Ávila, Sierra de Spain 40°40N 5°15W 88 E5
Avila Beach U.S.A. 35°11N 120°44W 171 K6
Avilés Spain 43°35N 5°57W 88 B5
Aviño Spain 43°36N 8°8W 88 B2
Avintes Portugal 41°7N 8°33W 88 D2
Avis Portugal 39°4N 7°53W 89 F3
Avis U.S.A. 41°11N 77°19W 174 E7
Avísio → Italy 46°7N 11°5E 92 B8
Avissawella Sri Lanka 6°56N 80°11E 127 L5
Aviz = Avis Portugal 39°4N 7°53W 89 F3
Avize France 48°59N 4°1E 71 D11
Avlonari Greece 38°31N 24°8E 98 C6
Avlum Denmark 56°16N 8°47E 63 H2
Avoca Australia 37°5S 143°26E 152 D5
Avoca U.S.A. 42°25N 77°25W 174 D7
Avoca → Australia 35°40S 143°43E 152 C5
Avoca → Ireland 52°48N 6°10W 64 D5
Avola Canada 51°45N 119°19W 162 C5
Avola Italy 36°56N 15°7E 95 F8
Avon U.S.A. 42°55N 77°45W 174 D7
Avon → Australia 31°40S 116°7E 149 F2
Avon → Bristol, U.K. 51°29N 2°41W 67 F5
Avon → Dorset, U.K. 50°44N 1°46W 67 G6
Avon → Warks., U.K. 52°0N 2°8W 67 E5
Avon Park U.S.A. 27°36N 81°31W 179 H8
Avondale Zimbabwe 17°43S 30°58E 143 F3
Avonlea Canada 50°0N 105°0W 163 D8
Avonmore Canada 45°10N 74°58W 175 A10
Avonmouth U.K. 51°30N 2°42W 67 F5
Avramov Bulgaria 42°45N 26°38E 97 D10
Avranches France 48°40N 1°20W 70 D5
Avre → France 48°47N 1°22E 70 D8
Avrig Romania 45°43N 24°21E 81 E9
Avrillé France 47°30N 0°35W 70 E6
Avtovac Bos.-H. 43°9N 18°35E 96 C2
Awa-Shima Japan 38°27N 139°14E 112 E9
A'waj → Syria 33°23N 36°20E 130 B5
Awaji-Shima Japan 34°30N 134°50E 113 G7
'Awālī Bahrain 26°0N 50°30E 129 E6
Awantipur India 33°55N 75°3E 125 C6
Awanui N.Z. 35°4S 173°17E 154 B2
Awarja → India 17°5N 76°15E 126 F3
Awarua B. N.Z. 44°28S 168°4E 155 E3
Awarua Pt. N.Z. 44°15S 168°5E 155 E3
Awasa Ethiopia 7°2N 38°28E 131 F2
Awash Ethiopia 9°1N 40°10E 131 F3
Awaso Ghana 6°15N 2°22W 138 D4
Awat China 40°35N 80°24E 109 D10
Awatere → N.Z. 41°37S 174°10E 155 B9
Awbārī Libya 26°46N 12°57E 135 C8
Awbārī, Idehan Libya 27°10N 11°30E 135 C8
Awe, L. U.K. 56°17N 5°16W 65 E3
Awgu Nigeria 6°4N 7°24E 139 D6
Awjilah Libya 29°8N 21°7E 135 C10
Awka Nigeria 6°12N 7°5E 139 D6
Ax-les-Thermes France 42°44N 1°50E 72 F5
Axat France 42°48N 2°13E 72 F6
Axe → U.K. 50°42N 3°4W 67 F5
Axel Heiberg I. Canada 80°0N 90°0W 161 B14
Axim Ghana 4°51N 2°15W 138 E4
Axintele Romania 44°37N 26°47E 81 F11
Axios → Greece 40°57N 22°35E 96 F6
Axminster U.K. 50°46N 3°0W 67 G4
Axson U.S.A. 31°17N 82°44W 178 D7
Axvall Sweden 58°23N 13°34E 63 F7
Ay France 49°3N 4°1E 71 C11
Ayabaca Peru 4°40S 79°53W 188 A2
Ayabe Japan 35°20N 135°20E 113 G7
Ayacucho Argentina 37°5S 58°20W 190 D4
Ayacucho Peru 13°0S 74°0W 188 C3
Ayacucho □ Peru 14°0S 74°0W 188 C3
Ayaguz = Ayaköz
Kazakhstan 48°10N 80°10E 109 C10
Ayakkum Hu China 37°30N 89°20E 109 E11
Ayaköz Kazakhstan 48°10N 80°10E 109 C10
Ayaköz → Kazakhstan 46°40N 79°14E 109 C9
Ayakudi India 10°28N 77°56E 127 J3
Ayamé Ivory C. 5°35N 3°9W 138 D4
Ayamonte Spain 37°12N 7°24W 89 H3
Ayan Russia 56°30N 138°16E 107 D14
Ayancık Turkey 41°57N 34°35E 104 B6
Ayangba Nigeria 7°31N 7°8E 139 D6
Ayas Turkey 40°2N 32°21E 104 B5
Ayaviri Peru 14°50S 70°35W 188 C3
Āybak Afghan. 36°15N 68°5E 109 E7
Aybastı Turkey 40°41N 37°23E 104 B7
Aydarköl Uzbekistan 40°50N 67°10E 109 D7
Aydın Turkey 37°51N 27°51E 104 D2
Aydın □ Turkey 37°50N 28°0E 99 D9
Aydın Dağları Turkey 38°0N 28°0E 99 D10
Aydingkol Hu China 42°40N 89°15E 109 D11
Ayenngré Togo 8°40N 1°1E 139 D5
Ayer U.S.A. 42°34N 71°35W 175 D13
Ayer Hitam Malaysia 5°24N 100°16E 121 c
Ayerbe Spain 42°17N 0°41W 90 C4
Ayer's Cliff Canada 45°10N 72°3W 175 A12
Ayers Rock = Uluru
Australia 25°23S 131°5E 149 E5
Ayeyarwady = Irrawaddy →
Burma 15°50N 95°6E 123 M19
Áyia Napa Cyprus 34°59N 34°0E 101 E13
Áyia Phyla Cyprus 34°43N 33°1E 101 E12
Áyios Amvrósios
Cyprus 35°20N 33°35E 101 D12
Áyios Seryios Cyprus 35°12N 33°53E 101 D12
Áyios Theodhoros
Cyprus 35°22N 34°1E 101 D13
Áyios Yeóryios = Aghios Georgios
Greece 37°28N 23°57E 98 D5
Aykhal Russia 66°0N 111°30E 107 C12
Aykirikçi Turkey 39°8N 30°9E 99 B12
Aylesbury U.K. 51°49N 0°49W 67 F7
Aylmer Canada 42°46N 80°59W 174 D4
Aylmer, L. Canada 64°5N 108°30W 160 E10
'Ayn, Wādī al Oman 22°15N 55°28E 129 F7
Ayn Dār Si. Arabia 25°55N 49°10E 129 E7
Ayn Sifnī Iraq 36°41N 43°20E 105 D10
Ayn Zālah Iraq 36°45N 42°35E 105 D10
Ayna Spain 38°34N 2°3W 91 G2
Ayolas Paraguay 27°10S 56°59W 190 B4
Ayon, Ostrov Russia 69°50N 169°0E 107 C17
Ayora Spain 39°3N 1°3W 91 F3
Ayorou Niger 14°53N 1°0E 139 C5
'Ayoûn el 'Atroûs
Mauritania 16°38N 9°37W 138 B3
Ayr Australia 19°35S 147°25E 150 B4
Ayr Canada 43°17N 80°27W 174 C4
Ayr U.K. 55°28N 4°38W 65 F4
Ayr → U.K. 55°28N 4°38W 65 F4
Ayrancı Turkey 37°21N 33°41E 104 D5
Ayrancılar Turkey 38°15N 27°18E 99 C9
Ayre, Pt. of I. of Man 54°25N 4°21W 66 C3
Ayribaba Turkmenistan 37°50N 66°34E 109 E7
Ayton Australia 15°56S 145°22E 150 B4
Aytos Bulgaria 42°42N 27°16E 97 D11
Aytoska Planina
Bulgaria 42°45N 27°30E 97 D11
Ayu, Kepulauan
Indonesia 0°35N 131°5E 119 D8
Ayutla Guatemala 14°40N 92°10W 182 D1
Ayutla de los Libres
Mexico 16°54N 99°13W 181 D5
Ayutthaya = Phra Nakhon Si
Ayutthaya Thailand 14°25N 100°30E 120 E3
Ayvacık Turkey 39°36N 26°24E 104 C2
Ayvalık Turkey 39°20N 26°46E 99 B8
Az Zabadānī Syria 33°43N 36°5E 130 B5
Az Zāhirīyah
West Bank 31°25N 34°58E 130 D3
Az Zahrān Si. Arabia 26°10N 50°7E 129 E6
Az Zarqā Jordan 32°5N 36°4E 130 C5
Az Zarqā' U.A.E. 24°53N 53°4E 129 E7
Az Zarqā □ Jordan 32°5N 36°4E 130 C5
Az Zāwiyah Libya 32°52N 12°56E 135 B8
Az Zibār Iraq 36°52N 44°4E 105 D11
Az Zilfī Si. Arabia 26°12N 44°52E 128 E5
Az Zubayr Iraq 30°26N 47°40E 128 D5
Azad Kashmir □
Pakistan 33°50N 73°50E 125 C5
Azahar, Costa del Spain 40°0N 0°5E 90 F5
Azambuja Portugal 39°4N 8°51W 89 F2
Azamgarh India 26°5N 83°13E 125 F10
Azangaro Peru 14°55S 70°13W 188 C3
Azaoua Niger 15°50N 4°0E 139 B5
Azaouad Mali 19°0N 3°0W 138 B4
Azaouak → Mali 15°30N 3°18E 139 B5
Azaouak, Vallée de l'
Mali 15°50N 3°20E 139 B5
Āzār Shahr Iran 37°45N 45°59E 105 D11
Azara Nigeria 8°22N 9°12E 139 D6
Azarān Iran 37°25N 47°16E 105 D12
Azärbayjan = Azerbaijan ■
Asia 40°20N 48°0E 87 K9
Āzarbāyjān-e Gharbī □
Iran 37°0N 44°30E 128 B5
Āzarbāyjān-e Sharqī □
Iran 37°20N 47°0E 128 B5
Azare Nigeria 11°55N 10°10E 139 C7
Azay-le-Rideau France 47°16N 0°30E 70 E7
A'zāz Syria 36°36N 37°4E 104 D7
Azazga Algeria 36°48N 4°22E 136 A4
Azbine = Aïr Niger 18°30N 8°0E 139 B6
Azeffoun Algeria 36°51N 4°26E 136 A4
Azemmour Morocco 33°20N 9°20W 136 B2
Azerbaijan ■ Asia 40°20N 48°0E 87 K9
Azkoien = Peralta Spain 42°20N 1°48W 90 C3
Aznalcóllar Spain 37°32N 6°17W 89 H4
Azogues Ecuador 2°35S 78°0W 186 D3
Azores = Açores, Is. dos
Atl. Oc. 38°0N 27°0W 134 a
Azores-Biscay Rise
Atl. Oc. 42°0N 20°0W 56 B9
Azov Russia 47°3N 39°25E 87 G4
Azov, Sea of Europe 46°0N 36°30E 85 J9
Azovskoye More = Azov, Sea of
Europe 46°0N 36°30E 85 J9
Azpeitia Spain 43°12N 2°19W 90 B2
Azraq ash Shīshān
Jordan 31°50N 36°49E 130 D5
Azrou Morocco 33°28N 5°19W 136 B2
Aztec U.S.A. 36°49N 107°59W 169 H10
Azua de Compostela
Dom. Rep. 18°25N 70°44W 183 C5
Azuaga Spain 38°16N 5°39W 89 G5
Azuara Spain 41°15N 0°53W 90 D4
Azuer → Spain 39°8N 3°36W 89 F7
Azuero, Pen. de Panama 7°30N 80°30W 182 E3
Azuga Romania 45°27N 25°33E 81 E10
Azul Argentina 36°42S 59°43W 190 D4
Azumino Japan 36°20N 137°50E 113 F8
Azur, Côte d' France 43°25N 7°10E 73 E11
Azusa U.S.A. 34°8N 117°52W 171 L9
Azzaba Algeria 36°48N 7°6E 136 A5
Azzano Décimo Italy 45°52N 12°56E 93 C9
Azzel Matti, Sebkra
Algeria 26°10N 0°43E 136 C4

B

Ba Be △ Vietnam 22°25N 105°37E 120 A5
Ba Don Vietnam 17°45N 106°26E 120 D6
Ba Dong Vietnam 9°40N 106°33E 121 H6
Ba Ngoi Vietnam 11°54N 109°10E 121 G7
Ba Ria Vietnam 10°30N 107°10E 121 G6
Ba Tri Vietnam 10°2N 106°36E 121 G6
Ba Vi △ Vietnam 21°1N 105°22E 120 B5
Ba Xian = Bazhou
China 39°8N 116°22E 114 E9
Baa Indonesia 10°50S 123°0E 148 B3
Baalbek = Ba'labakk
Lebanon 34°0N 36°10E 130 B5
Baamonde Spain 43°7N 7°44W 88 B3
Baardheere Somalia 2°20N 42°27E 131 G3
Baarle-Nassau Belgium 51°27N 4°56E 69 C4
Bab el Mandeb Red Sea 12°35N 43°25E 131 E3
Baba Bulgaria 42°44N 23°59E 96 D7
Bābā, Koh-i- Afghan. 34°30N 67°0E 109 F7
Baba Budan Hills India 13°30N 75°44E 127 H2
Baba Burnu Turkey 39°29N 26°2E 99 B8
Baba dag Azerbaijan 41°0N 48°19E 87 K9
Bābā Kalū Iran 30°7N 50°49E 129 D6
Babaçulândia Brazil 7°13S 47°46W 189 B1
Babadag Romania 44°53N 28°44E 81 F13
Babadağ Turkey 37°49N 28°52E 99 D10
Babaeski Turkey 41°26N 27°6E 97 E11
Babahoyo Ecuador 1°40S 79°30W 186 D3
Babai = Sarju → India 27°21N 81°23E 125 F9
Babai → Nepal 28°10N 82°21E 125 E10
Babana Nigeria 10°31N 3°46E 139 C5
Babar Algeria 35°10N 7°6E 136 A5
Babar Indonesia 8°0S 129°30E 119 F7
Babar Pakistan 31°7N 69°32E 124 D3
Babarkach Pakistan 29°45N 68°0E 124 E3
Babayevo Russia 59°24N 35°55E 84 C8
Babb U.S.A. 48°51N 113°27W 168 B7
Babenhausen Germany 49°57N 8°57E 77 F4
Băbeni Romania 44°59N 24°11E 81 F9
Baberu India 25°33N 80°43E 125 G9
Babi Besar, Pulau
Malaysia 2°25N 103°59E 121 L4
Babia Gora Europe 49°38N 19°38E 83 J6
Babian Jiang → China 22°55N 101°47E 116 F3
Bābil □ Iraq 32°30N 44°30E 128 C5
Babimost Poland 52°10N 15°49E 83 F2
Babinda Australia 17°20S 145°56E 150 B4
Babine Canada 55°22N 126°37W 162 B3
Babine → Canada 55°45N 127°44W 162 B3
Babine L. Canada 54°48N 126°0W 162 C3
Babiogórski △ Poland 49°38N 19°39E 83 J6
Babo Indonesia 2°30S 133°30E 119 E8
Babócsa Hungary 46°2N 17°21E 80 D2
Bābol Iran 36°40N 52°50E 129 B7
Bābol Sar Iran 36°45N 52°45E 129 B7
Babor, Dj. Algeria 36°31N 5°25E 136 A5
Baborów Poland 50°7N 18°1E 83 H5
Baboua C.A.R. 5°49N 14°58E 140 C2
Babruysk Belarus 53°10N 29°15E 75 B15
Babson Park U.S.A. 27°49N 81°32W 179 H8
Babuhri India 26°49N 69°43E 124 F3
Babuna Macedonia 41°30N 21°40E 96 E5
Babura Nigeria 12°51N 8°59E 139 C6
Babusar Pass Pakistan 35°12N 73°59E 125 B5
Babušnica Serbia 43°7N 22°27E 96 C6
Babuyan Chan. Phil. 18°40N 121°30E 119 A6
Babylon Iraq 32°34N 44°22E 105 F11
Bač Serbia 45°29N 19°17E 80 E4
Bâc → Moldova 46°55N 29°26E 81 D14
Bac Can Vietnam 22°8N 105°49E 116 F5
Bac Giang Vietnam 21°16N 106°11E 116 G6
Bac Lieu Vietnam 9°17N 105°43E 121 H5
Bac Ninh Vietnam 21°13N 106°4E 116 G6
Bac Phan Vietnam 22°0N 105°0E 116 G5
Bacabal Brazil 4°15S 44°45W 189 A2
Bacalar Mexico 18°43N 88°27W 181 D7
Bacan, Kepulauan
Indonesia 0°35S 127°30E 119 E7
Bacarra Phil. 18°15N 120°37E 119 A6
Bacău Romania 46°35N 26°55E 81 D11
Bacău □ Romania 46°30N 26°45E 81 D11
Baccarat France 48°28N 6°42E 71 D13
Bacchus Marsh
Australia 37°43S 144°27E 152 D6
Bacerac Mexico 30°18N 108°50W 180 A3
Băceşti Romania 46°50N 27°11E 81 D12
Bach Long Vi, Dao
Vietnam 20°10N 107°40E 120 B6
Bach Ma △ Vietnam 16°11N 107°49E 120 D6
Bacharach Germany 50°3N 7°44E 77 E3
Bachhwara India 25°35N 85°54E 125 G11
Bachu China 39°46N 78°34E 109 E9
Bačina Serbia 43°42N 21°23E 96 C5
Back → Canada 65°10N 104°0W 160 D11
Bačka Palanka Serbia 45°17N 19°27E 80 E4
Bačka Topola Serbia 45°49N 19°39E 80 E4
Bäckebo Sweden 56°53N 16°4E 63 H10
Bäckefors Sweden 58°48N 12°9E 63 F6
Bäckhammar Sweden 59°10N 14°11E 62 E8
Bački Petrovac Serbia 45°29N 19°32E 80 E4
Backnang Germany 48°56N 9°26E 77 G5
Backstairs Passage
Australia 35°40S 138°5E 152 C3
Bacolod Phil. 10°40N 122°57E 119 B6
Baconton U.S.A. 31°23N 84°10W 178 D5
Bacqueville-en-Caux
France 49°47N 1°0E 70 C8
Bács-Kiskun □ Hungary 46°43N 19°30E 80 D4
Bácsalmás Hungary 46°8N 19°17E 80 D4
Bacuk Malaysia 6°4N 102°25E 121 J4
Bácum Mexico 27°33N 110°5W 180 B2
Bād Iran 33°41N 52°1E 129 C7
Bad → U.S.A. 44°21N 100°22W 172 C3
Bad Aussee Austria 47°43N 13°45E 78 D6
Bad Axe U.S.A. 43°48N 83°0W 174 C2
Bad Bergzabern Germany 49°6N 7°59E 77 F3
Bad Berleburg Germany 51°2N 8°26E 76 D4
Bad Bevensen Germany 53°5N 10°35E 76 B6
Bad Bramstedt Germany 53°55N 9°53E 76 B5
Bad Brückenau Germany 50°18N 9°47E 77 E5
Bad Doberan Germany 54°6N 11°53E 76 A7
Bad Driburg Germany 51°43N 9°1E 76 D5
Bad Ems Germany 50°20N 7°43E 77 E3
Bad Frankenhausen
Germany 51°21N 11°5E 76 D7
Bad Freienwalde
Germany 52°46N 14°1E 76 C10
Bad Goisern Austria 47°38N 13°38E 78 D6
Bad Harzburg Germany 51°52N 10°34E 76 D6
Bad Hersfeld Germany 50°52N 9°42E 76 E5
Bad Hofgastein Austria 47°17N 13°6E 78 D6
Bad Homburg Germany 50°13N 8°38E 77 E4
Bad Honnef Germany 50°38N 7°13E 76 E3
Bad Iburg Germany 52°10N 8°3E 76 C4
Bad Ischl Austria 47°44N 13°38E 78 D6
Bad Kissingen Germany 50°11N 10°4E 77 E6
Bad Königshofen
Germany 50°17N 10°28E 77 E6
Bad Kreuznach Germany 49°50N 7°51E 77 F3
Bad Krozingen Germany 47°54N 7°42E 77 H3
Bad Laasphe Germany 50°56N 8°25E 76 E4
Bad Langensalza
Germany 51°5N 10°38E 76 D6
Bad Lauterberg Germany 51°38N 10°28E 76 D6
Bad Leonfelden Austria 48°31N 14°18E 78 C7
Bad Liebenwerda
Germany 51°31N 13°24E 76 D9
Bad Mergentheim
Germany 49°28N 9°42E 77 F5
Bad Münstereifel
Germany 50°33N 6°46E 76 E2
Bad Nauheim Germany 50°21N 8°43E 77 E4
Bad Neuenahr-Ahrweiler
Germany 50°32N 7°5E 76 E3
Bad Neustadt Germany 50°18N 10°13E 77 E6
Bad Oeynhausen
Germany 52°12N 8°46E 76 C4
Bad Oldesloe Germany 53°48N 10°22E 76 B6
Bad Orb Germany 50°12N 9°22E 77 E5
Bad Pyrmont Germany 51°59N 9°16E 76 D5
Bad Reichenhall
Germany 47°43N 12°54E 77 H8
Bad Säckingen Germany 47°33N 7°56E 77 H3
Bad Salzuflen Germany 52°5N 8°45E 76 C4
Bad Salzungen Germany 50°48N 10°14E 76 E6
Bad Sankt Leonhard
Austria 46°58N 14°47E 78 E7
Bad Schwartau Germany 53°55N 10°41E 76 B6
Bad Segeberg Germany 53°56N 10°17E 76 B6
Bad Tölz Germany 47°45N 11°34E 77 H7
Bad Urach Germany 48°29N 9°23E 77 G5
Bad Vöslau Austria 47°58N 16°12E 79 D9
Bad Waldsee Germany 47°55N 9°45E 77 H5
Bad Wildungen Germany 51°6N 9°7E 76 D5
Bad Wimpfen Germany 49°13N 9°11E 77 F5
Bad Windsheim
Germany 49°36N 10°25E 77 F6
Bad Zwischenahn
Germany 53°12N 8°1E 76 B4
Bada Barabil India 22°7N 85°24E 125 H11
Badagara = Vadakara
India 11°35N 75°40E 127 J2
Badagri Nigeria 6°25N 2°55E 139 D5
Badain Jaran Shamo
China 40°23N 102°0E 110 C9
Badajós, L. Brazil 3°15S 62°50W 186 D6
Badajoz Spain 38°50N 6°59W 89 G4
Badajoz □ Spain 38°40N 6°30W 89 G4
Badakhshān □ Afghan. 36°30N 71°0E 109 E8
Badaling China 40°20N 116°0E 114 D9
Badalona Spain 41°26N 2°15E 90 D7
Badalzai Afghan. 29°50N 65°35E 124 E1
Badami India 15°55N 75°41E 127 G2
Badampahar India 22°10N 86°10E 126 C8
Badanah Si. Arabia 30°58N 41°30E 128 D4
Badarinath India 30°45N 79°30E 125 D8
Badas, Kepulauan
Indonesia 0°45N 107°5E 118 D3
Baddo → Pakistan 28°0N 64°20E 122 F4
Bade Indonesia 7°10S 139°35E 119 F9
Badeggi Nigeria 9°1N 6°8E 139 D6
Badéguichéri Niger 14°30N 5°22E 139 C6
Baden Austria 48°1N 16°13E 79 C9
Baden Switz. 47°28N 8°18E 77 H4
Baden U.S.A. 40°38N 80°14W 174 F4
Baden-Baden Germany 48°44N 8°13E 77 G4
Baden-Württemberg □
Germany 48°20N 8°40E 77 G4
Badgam India 34°1N 74°45E 125 B6
Badgastein Austria 47°7N 13°9E 78 D6
Badger Canada 49°0N 56°4W 165 C8
Badger U.S.A. 36°38N 119°1W 170 J7
Bādghīs □ Afghan. 35°0N 63°0E 108 F6
Badgingarra △
Australia 30°23S 115°22E 149 F2
Badia Polésine Italy 45°5N 11°29E 93 C8
Badiar △ Guinea 13°37N 13°11W 138 C2
Badin Pakistan 24°38N 68°54E 124 G3
Badinka ⌂ Mali 13°31N 9°29W 138 C3
Badlands U.S.A. 43°55N 102°30W 172 D2
Badlands △ U.S.A. 43°38N 102°56W 172 D2
Badme N. Afr. 14°43N 37°48E 131 E2
Badnera India 20°48N 77°44E 126 D3
Badogo Mali 11°2N 8°13W 138 C3
Badoumbé Mali 13°42N 10°15W 138 C2
Badrah Iraq 33°6N 45°58E 105 F11
Badrain Jaran Shamo
China 40°40N 103°20E 114 D2
Badrinath India 30°44N 79°29E 125 D8
Badu Australia 10°7S 142°11E 150 a
Badulla Sri Lanka 7°1N 81°7E 127 L5
Badung, Bukit
Indonesia 8°49S 115°10E 119 K18
Badung, Selat
Indonesia 8°40S 115°22E 119 K18
Badvel India 14°45N 79°3E 127 G4
Baena Spain 37°37N 4°20W 89 H6
Baengnyeongdo
S. Korea 37°57N 124°40E 115 F13
Baerami Australia 32°27S 150°27E 153 B9
Baetov Kyrgyzstan 41°13N 74°54E 109 D8
Baeza Spain 37°57N 3°25W 89 H7

Bafang Cameroon 5°9N 10°11E 139 D7
Bafatá Guinea-Biss. 12°8N 14°40W 138 C2
Baffin B. N. Amer. 72°0N 64°0W 158 B13
Baffin I. Canada 68°0N 75°0W 161 D17
Bafia Cameroon 4°40N 11°10E 139 E7
Bafilo Togo 9°22N 1°22E 139 D5
Bafing □ Ivory C. 8°20N 7°40W 138 D3
Bafing → Mali 13°49N 10°50W 138 C2
Bafing △ Mali 12°38N 10°28W 138 C2
Bafliyūn Syria 36°37N 36°59E 128 B3
Bafoulabé Mali 13°50N 10°55W 138 C2
Bafoussam Cameroon 5°28N 10°25E 139 D7
Bāfq Iran 31°40N 55°25E 129 D7
Bafra Turkey 41°34N 35°54E 104 B6
Bafra Burnu Turkey 41°45N 36°2E 104 B7
Bāft Iran 29°15N 56°38E 129 D8
Bafut Cameroon 6°6N 10°2E 139 D7
Bafwasende Dem. Rep. of the Congo 1°3N 27°5E 142 B2
Bagaha India 27°6N 84°5E 126 A7
Bagalkot India 16°10N 75°40E 127 F2
Bagam Niger 15°43N 6°35E 139 B6
Bagamoyo Tanzania 6°28S 38°55E 142 D4
Bagan Datoh Malaysia 3°59N 100°47E 121 L3
Bagan Serai Malaysia 5°1N 100°32E 121 K3
Baganga Phil. 7°34N 126°33E 119 C7
Bagani Namibia 18°7S 21°41E 144 A3
Bagansiapiapi Indonesia 2°12N 100°50E 118 D2
Bagasra India 21°30N 71°0E 124 J4
Bagaud India 21°30N 75°53E 124 H6
Bagdad Calif., U.S.A. 34°35N 115°53W 171 L11
Bagdad Fla., U.S.A. 30°36N 87°2W 179 E2
Bagdarin Russia 54°26N 113°36E 107 D12
Bagé Brazil 31°20S 54°15W 191 C5
Bagenalstown Ireland 52°42N 6°58W 64 D5
Bagepalli India 13°47N 77°47E 127 H3
Bageshwar India 29°51N 79°46E 125 E8
Bagevadi India 16°35N 75°58E 126 F2
Baggs U.S.A. 41°2N 107°39W 168 F10
Bagh Pakistan 33°59N 73°45E 125 G9
Baghain → India 25°32N 81°1E 125 G9
Baghdād Iraq 33°20N 44°23E 105 F11
Baghdadi Georgia 42°4N 42°49E 105 A10
Bagheria Italy 38°5N 13°30E 94 D6
Baghlān Afghan. 32°12N 68°46E 109 F7
Baghlān □ Afghan. 36°0N 68°30E 109 E7
Bagley U.S.A. 47°32N 95°24W 172 B6
Baglung Nepal 28°16N 83°36E 125 E10
Bagnara Cálabra Italy 38°17N 15°48E 95 D8
Bagnasco Italy 44°18N 8°2E 92 D5
Bagnères-de-Bigorre France 43°5N 0°9E 72 E4
Bagnères-de-Luchon France 42°47N 0°38E 72 F4
Bagni di Lucca Italy 44°1N 10°35E 92 D7
Bagno di Romagna Italy 43°50N 11°57E 93 E8
Bagnoles-de-l'Orne France 48°32N 0°25W 70 D6
Bagnols-sur-Cèze France 44°10N 4°36E 73 D8
Bagnorégio Italy 42°37N 12°6E 93 F9
Bago = Pegu Burma 17°20N 96°29E 123 L20
Bagodar India 24°5N 85°52E 125 G11
Bagrationovsk Russia 54°23N 20°39E 82 D7
Bagrdan Serbia 44°5N 21°11E 96 B5
Bagua Peru 5°35S 78°22W 186 E2
Baguio Phil. 16°26N 120°34E 119 A6
Bagyurdu Turkey 38°25N 27°41E 99 C9
Bagzane, Monts Niger 17°43N 8°45E 139 B6
Bahabón de Esguerva Spain 41°52N 3°43W 88 D7
Bahadurganj India 26°16N 87°49E 125 F12
Bahadurgarh India 28°40N 76°57E 124 E7
Bahama, Canal Viejo de W. Indies 22°10N 77°30W 182 B4
Bahamas ■ N. Amer. 24°0N 75°0W 183 B5
Bahār Iran 34°54N 48°26E 105 E13
Baharampur India 24°2N 88°27E 125 G13
Baharu Pandan = Pandan Malaysia 1°32N 103°46E 121 d
Bahawalnagar Pakistan 30°0N 73°15E 124 E5
Bahawalpur Pakistan 29°24N 71°40E 124 E4
Bahçe Turkey 37°13N 36°34E 104 D7
Bahçecik Turkey 40°41N 29°44E 97 F13
Bäherden Turkmenistan 38°25N 57°26E 129 B8
Baheri India 28°45N 79°34E 125 E8
Bahgul → India 27°45N 79°36E 125 F8
Bahi Tanzania 5°58S 35°21E 142 D4
Bahi Swamp Tanzania 6°10S 35°0E 142 D4
Bahía = Salvador Brazil 13°0S 38°30W 189 C3
Bahía □ Brazil 12°0S 42°0W 189 C2
Bahía, Is. de la Honduras 16°45N 86°15W 182 C2
Bahía Blanca Argentina 38°35S 62°13W 190 D3
Bahía de Caráquez Ecuador 0°40S 80°27W 186 D2
Bahía de Los Angeles Mexico 28°56N 113°34W 180 B2
Bahía Honda Cuba 22°54N 83°10W 182 B3
Bahía Kino Mexico 28°47N 111°58W 180 B2
Bahía Laura Argentina 48°10S 66°30W 192 C3
Bahía Mansa Chile 40°33S 73°46W 192 D2
Bahía Negra Paraguay 20°5S 58°5W 186 H7
Bahir Dar Ethiopia 11°37N 37°10E 131 E2
Bahmanzād Iran 31°15N 51°47E 129 D6
Bahmer Algeria 27°32N 0°10W 136 C3
Bahraich India 27°38N 81°37E 125 F9
Bahrain ■ Asia 26°0N 50°35E 129 E6
Bahror India 27°51N 76°20E 124 F7
Bāhū Kalāt Iran 25°43N 61°25E 129 E9
Bai Mali 13°35N 3°28W 138 C4
Bai Bung, Mui = Ca Mau, Mui Vietnam 8°38N 104°44E 121 H5
Bai Thuong Vietnam 19°54N 105°23E 120 C5
Baia de Aramă Romania 45°0N 22°50E 80 E7
Baia Mare Romania 47°40N 23°35E 81 C8
Baia-Sprie Romania 47°41N 23°43E 81 C8
Baião Brazil 2°40S 49°40W 187 D9
Baïbokoum Chad 7°46N 15°43E 135 G9
Baicheng Jilin, China 45°38N 122°42E 115 B12
Baicheng Xinjiang Uygur, China 41°46N 81°52E 109 D10
Băicoi Romania 45°3N 25°52E 81 E10
Baidoa = Baydhabo Somalia 3°8N 43°30E 131 G3
Baie-Comeau Canada 49°12N 68°10W 165 C6
Baie-St-Paul Canada 47°28N 70°32W 165 C5
Baie Ste-Anne Seychelles 4°18S 55°45E 141 b
Baie-Trinité Canada 49°25N 67°20W 165 C6
Baie Verte Canada 49°55N 56°12W 165 C8

Baignes-Ste-Radegonde France 45°23N 0°25W 72 C3
Baigneux-les-Juifs France 47°31N 4°39E 71 E11
Baihar India 22°6N 80°33E 125 H9
Baihe Hubei, China 32°50N 110°5E 117 A8
Baihe Jilin, China 42°27N 128°9E 115 C15
Baihetan Dam China 27°11N 102°54E 116 D4
Ba'ijī Iraq 35°0N 43°30E 105 E10
Baijnath India 25°55N 79°37E 125 E8
Baikal, L. = Baykal, Oz. Russia 53°0N 108°0E 107 D11
Baikonur = Bayqonyr Kazakhstan 45°40N 63°20E 108 C6
Baikunthpur India 23°15N 82°33E 125 H10
Bailadila, Mt. India 18°43N 81°15E 126 E5
Baile Átha Cliath = Dublin Ireland 53°21N 6°15W 64 C5
Baile Átha Fhirdhia = Ardee Ireland 53°52N 6°33W 64 C5
Baile Átha Í = Athy Ireland 53°0N 7°0W 64 C5
Baile Átha Luain = Athlone Ireland 53°25N 7°56W 64 C4
Baile Átha Troim = Trim Ireland 53°33N 6°48W 64 C5
Baile Brígín = Balbriggan Ireland 53°37N 6°11W 64 C5
Băile Govora Romania 45°3N 24°11E 81 E9
Băile Herculane Romania 44°53N 22°26E 80 F7
Băile Olănești Romania 45°12N 24°14E 81 E9
Baile Sear = Baleshare U.K. 57°31N 7°22W 65 D1
Băile Tușnad Romania 46°9N 25°51E 81 D10
Bailén Spain 38°8N 3°48W 89 G7
Băilești Romania 44°1N 23°20E 81 F8
Bailhongal India 15°55N 74°53E 127 G2
Bailieborough Ireland 53°56N 6°59W 64 C5
Baima China 33°0N 100°26E 116 A3
Bain-de-Bretagne France 47°50N 1°40W 70 E5
Bainbridge Ga., U.S.A. 30°55N 84°35W 178 E5
Bainbridge N.Y., U.S.A. 42°18N 75°29W 175 D9
Bainbridge Island U.S.A. 47°38N 122°32W 170 C4
Baine China 42°0N 128°0E 111 C14
Baing Indonesia 10°14S 120°34E 119 F6
Bainiu China 32°50N 112°15E 117 A9
Baiona Spain 42°6N 8°52W 88 C2
Bā'ir Jordan 30°45N 36°55E 130 E5
Bairiki = Tarawa Kiribati 1°30N 173°0E 156 G9
Bairin Youqi China 43°30N 118°35E 115 C10
Bairin Zuoqi China 43°58N 119°15E 115 C10
Bairnsdale Australia 37°48S 147°36E 153 F7
Baisha China 34°20N 112°32E 114 G7
Baisha Li China 19°12N 109°20E 117 a
Baishan = Hunjiang China 41°54N 126°26E 115 D14
Baishan China 42°43N 127°14E 115 C14
Baissa Nigeria 7°14N 10°38E 139 D7
Baitadi Nepal 29°35N 80°25E 125 E9
Baitarani → India 20°45N 86°48E 126 D8
Baixa Grande Brazil 11°57S 40°11W 189 C2
Baixa Limia-Sierra do Xurés Spain 41°59N 8°2W 88 D2
Baiyin China 36°45N 104°14E 114 F3
Baiyü China 31°16N 98°50E 116 B2
Baiyu Shan China 37°15N 107°30E 114 F4
Baj Baj India 22°30N 88°5E 125 H13
Baja Hungary 46°12N 18°59E 80 D3
Baja, Pta. Mexico 29°58N 115°49W 180 B1
Baja California Mexico 31°10N 115°12W 180 A1
Baja California □ Mexico 30°0N 115°0W 180 B2
Baja California Sur □ Mexico 25°50N 111°50W 180 B2
Bajag India 22°40N 81°21E 125 H9
Bajamar Canary Is. 28°33N 16°20W 100 F3
Bajana India 23°7N 71°49E 124 H4
Bajatrejo Indonesia 8°29S 114°19E 119 J17
Bajawa Indonesia 8°47S 120°59E 119 F6
Bajera Indonesia 8°31S 115°2E 119 J18
Bäjgīrān Iran 37°36N 58°24E 129 B8
Bajimba, Mt. Australia 29°17S 152°6E 151 D5
Bajina Bašta Serbia 43°58N 19°35E 96 C3
Bajmok Serbia 45°57N 19°24E 80 E4
Bajo Boquete Panama 8°46N 82°27W 182 E3
Bajo Caracoles Argentina 47°27S 70°56W 192 C2
Bajo Nuevo Caribbean 15°40N 78°50W 182 C4
Bajoga Nigeria 10°57N 11°20E 139 C7
Bajool Australia 23°40S 150°35E 150 C5
Bak Hungary 46°43N 16°51E 80 D1
Bakar Croatia 45°18N 14°32E 93 C11
Bakasi Pen. Cameroon 4°42N 8°20E 139 D6
Bakel Senegal 14°56N 12°20W 138 C2
Baker Calif., U.S.A. 35°16N 116°4W 171 K10
Baker Fla., U.S.A. 30°48N 86°41W 179 E3
Baker Mont., U.S.A. 46°22N 104°17W 168 C2
Baker, Canal Chile 47°45S 74°4W 192 C1
Baker, L. Canada 64°0N 96°0W 160 D12
Baker, Mt. U.S.A. 48°50N 121°49W 168 B3
Baker City U.S.A. 44°47N 117°50W 168 D5
Baker I. Pac. Oc. 0°10N 176°35W 156 G10
Baker I. U.S.A. 55°20N 133°40W 162 B2
Baker L. Canada 26°54S 126°5E 149 E4
Baker Lake Canada 64°20N 96°3W 160 D12
Bakerhill U.S.A. 31°47N 85°18W 178 D4
Bakers Creek Australia 21°13S 149°7E 150 C4
Bakers Dozen Is. Canada 56°45N 78°45W 164 A4
Bakersfield Calif., U.S.A. 35°23N 119°1W 171 K8
Bakersfield Vt., U.S.A. 44°45N 72°48W 175 B12
Bakharden = Bäherden Turkmenistan 38°25N 57°26E 129 B8
Bakhchysaray Ukraine 44°40N 33°45E 85 K7
Bakhmach Ukraine 51°10N 32°45E 85 G7
Bākhtarān = Kermānshāh Iran 34°23N 47°0E 105 E12
Bākhtarān □ = Kermānshāh □ Iran 34°0N 46°30E 105 E12
Bakhtegān, Daryācheh-ye Iran 29°40N 53°50E 129 D7
Bakhtegān △ Iran 29°51N 53°44E 129 D7
Bakı Azerbaijan 40°29N 49°56E 87 K9
Bakırdaği Turkey 38°55N 35°27E 104 D6
Bakkafjörður Iceland 66°2N 14°48W 60 C6

Bakkagerði Iceland 65°31N 13°49W 60 D7
Baklan Turkey 38°0N 29°36E 99 C11
Bako Ivory C. 9°8N 7°40W 138 D3
Bakony Hungary 47°10N 17°30E 80 C2
Bakony Forest = Bakony Hungary 47°10N 17°30E 80 C2
Bakori Nigeria 11°34N 7°25E 139 C6
Bakouma C.A.R. 5°40N 22°56E 140 C4
Baksan Russia 43°42N 43°32E 87 J6
Bakswaho India 24°15N 79°18E 125 G8
Baku = Bakı Azerbaijan 40°29N 49°56E 87 K9
Bakundi Nigeria 8°2N 10°9E 139 D7
Bakuriani Georgia 41°44N 43°31E 105 B10
Bakutis Coast Antarctica 74°0S 120°0W 55 D15
Baky = Bakı Azerbaijan 40°29N 49°56E 87 K9
Bala Canada 45°1N 79°37W 174 A5
Bala Senegal 14°1N 13°8W 138 C2
Balâ Turkey 39°32N 33°6E 104 C5
Bala U.K. 52°54N 3°36W 66 E4
Bālā Morghāb Afghan. 35°35N 63°20E 108 E6
Balabac I. Phil. 8°0N 117°0E 118 C5
Balabac Str. E. Indies 7°53N 117°5E 118 C5
Balabagh Afghan. 34°25N 70°12E 124 B4
Ba'labakk Lebanon 34°0N 36°10E 130 B5
Balabalangan, Kepulauan Indonesia 2°20S 117°30E 118 E5
Bălăcița Romania 44°23N 23°8E 81 F8
Balad Iraq 34°0N 44°9E 105 F11
Balad Rūz Iraq 33°42N 45°5E 105 F11
Bālādeh Fārs, Iran 29°17N 51°56E 129 D6
Bālādeh Māzandaran, Iran 36°12N 51°48E 129 B6
Balaghat India 21°49N 80°12E 126 D5
Balaghat Ra. India 18°50N 76°30E 126 E3
Balaguer Spain 41°50N 0°50E 90 D5
Balakän Azerbaijan 41°43N 46°24E 87 K8
Balakhna Russia 56°25N 43°32E 86 B6
Balaklava Australia 34°7S 138°22E 152 C3
Balaklava Ukraine 44°30N 33°30E 85 K7
Balakliya Ukraine 49°28N 36°55E 85 H9
Balakovo Russia 52°4N 47°55E 86 D8
Balamau India 27°10N 80°21E 125 F9
Balan Romania 46°39N 25°49E 81 D10
Balancán Mexico 17°48N 91°32W 181 D6
Balashikha Russia 55°48N 37°58E 84 E9
Balashov Russia 51°30N 43°10E 86 E6
Balasinor India 22°57N 73°23E 124 H5
Balasore = Baleshwar India 21°35N 87°3E 126 D8
Balassagyarmat Hungary 48°4N 19°15E 80 B4
Balât Egypt 25°36N 29°19E 137 B2
Balaton Hungary 46°50N 17°40E 80 D2
Balaton-Felvidéki △ Hungary 46°52N 17°30E 80 C2
Balatonboglár Hungary 46°46N 17°40E 80 D2
Balatonfüred Hungary 46°58N 17°54E 80 D2
Balatonszentgyörgy Hungary 46°41N 17°19E 80 D2
Balazote Spain 38°54N 2°9W 91 G2
Balbina, Represa de Brazil 2°0S 59°30W 186 D7
Balboa Panama 8°57N 79°34W 182 E4
Balbriggan Ireland 53°37N 6°11W 64 C5
Balcarce Argentina 38°0S 58°10W 190 D4
Balcarres Canada 50°50N 103°35W 163 C8
Bălcești Romania 44°37N 23°57E 81 F8
Balchik Bulgaria 43°28N 28°11E 97 C12
Balclutha N.Z. 46°15S 169°45E 155 G4
Balcones Escarpment U.S.A. 29°30N 99°15W 176 G5
Balçova Turkey 38°22N 27°4E 99 C9
Bald I. Australia 34°57S 118°27E 149 F2
Bald Knob U.S.A. 35°19N 91°34W 176 D9
Baldock L. Canada 56°33N 97°57W 163 B9
Baldwin Fla., U.S.A. 30°18N 81°59W 178 E4
Baldwin Mich., U.S.A. 43°54N 85°51W 173 D11
Baldwin Pa., U.S.A. 40°21N 79°58W 174 F5
Baldwinsville U.S.A. 43°10N 76°20W 175 C8
Baldy Peak U.S.A. 33°54N 109°34W 169 K9
Bale Croatia 45°4N 13°46E 93 C10
Baleares, Is. Spain 39°30N 3°0E 90 B10
Balearic Is. = Baleares, Is. Spain 39°30N 3°0E 90 B10
Baleia, Pta. da Brazil 17°40S 39°7W 189 D3
Baleine → Canada 58°15N 67°40W 165 A6
Baleine, Petite R. de la → Canada 56°0N 76°45W 164 A4
Băleni Romania 45°48N 27°51E 81 E12
Baler Phil. 15°46N 121°34E 119 A6
Baleshare U.K. 57°31N 7°22W 65 D1
Baleshwar India 21°35N 87°3E 126 D8
Baley Russia 51°36N 116°37E 107 D12
Balezino Russia 58°2N 53°6E 86 B11
Balfate Honduras 15°48N 86°25W 182 C2
Balgo Australia 20°9S 127°58E 148 D4
Balharshah India 19°50N 79°23E 126 E4
Bali Cameroon 5°54N 10°0E 139 D7
Bali Greece 35°25N 24°47E 101 D6
Bali India 25°11N 73°17E 124 G5
Bali Indonesia 8°20S 115°0E 119 J18
Bali □ Indonesia 8°20S 115°0E 119 J18
Bali, Selat Indonesia 8°18S 114°25E 119 J17
Balí, Selat △ Indonesia 8°12S 114°15E 119 J17
Bali Sea Indonesia 8°0S 115°0E 119 J17
Balia S. Leone 7°48N 11°1W 138 D2
Baliapal India 21°40N 87°17E 125 J12
Baligród Poland 49°20N 22°17E 83 J9
Balik Pulau Malaysia 5°21N 100°14E 121 c
Balıkeşir Turkey 39°39N 27°53E 99 B9
Balıkeşir □ Turkey 39°45N 28°0E 99 B9
Balıklıçeşme Turkey 40°31N 27°2E 99 F11
Balıkpapan Indonesia 1°10S 116°55E 118 E5
Baling Malaysia 5°41N 100°55E 121 K3
Balinge Sweden 60°6N 17°57E 77 G4
Balingen Germany 48°16N 8°51E 74 G4
Balingian Romania 46°41N 21°54E 80 D6
Balintang Channel Phil. 19°50N 121°46E 119 A6
Balipara India 26°50N 92°45E 125 F18
Baliza Brazil 16°0S 52°20W 187 G8
Balkan □ Turkmenistan 40°0N 54°30E 108 E5
Balkan Mts. = Stara Planina Bulgaria 43°15N 23°0E 96 C7
Balkanabat Turkmenistan 39°30N 54°22E 129 B7
Balkh Afghan. 36°44N 66°47E 109 E7
Balkh □ Afghan. 36°30N 67°0E 109 E7

Balkhash = Balqash Kazakhstan 46°50N 74°50E 106 E8
Balkhash, Ozero = Balqash Köli Kazakhstan 46°0N 74°50E 109 C8
Balkonda India 18°52N 78°21E 126 E4
Balladonia Australia 32°27S 123°51E 149 F3
Balladonia Ireland 53°55N 8°34W 64 C3
Ballan Australia 37°33S 144°13E 152 D6
Ballarat Australia 37°33S 143°50E 152 D6
Ballard, L. Australia 29°20S 120°40E 149 E3
Ballater U.K. 57°3N 3°3W 65 D5
Ballé Mali 15°18N 8°33W 138 B2
Ballena, Canal de Mexico 29°10N 113°29W 180 B2
Balleny Is. Antarctica 66°30S 163°0E 55 C11
Balleroy France 49°11N 0°50W 70 C6
Ballerup Denmark 55°43N 12°21E 63 J6
Ballestas, Is. Peru 13°44S 76°25W 188 C2
Ballia India 25°46N 84°12E 125 G11
Ballina Australia 28°50S 153°31E 151 D5
Ballina Ireland 54°7N 9°9W 64 B2
Ballinasloe Ireland 53°20N 8°13W 64 C3
Ballincollig Ireland 51°53N 8°33W 64 E3
Ballinger U.S.A. 31°45N 99°57W 176 F5
Ballinrobe Ireland 53°38N 9°13W 64 C2
Ballinskelligs B. Ireland 51°48N 10°13W 64 E1
Ballon France 48°10N 0°14E 70 D7
Ballons des Vosges △ France 48°0N 7°0E 71 E14
Ballsh Albania 40°36N 19°44E 96 F3
Ballston Spa U.S.A. 43°0N 73°51W 175 D11
Ballyboghil Ireland 53°32N 6°16W 64 C5
Ballybunion Ireland 52°31N 9°40W 64 D2
Ballycanew Ireland 52°37N 6°19W 64 D5
Ballycastle U.K. 55°12N 6°15W 64 A5
Ballyclare U.K. 54°46N 6°0W 64 B5
Ballycroy △ Ireland 54°5N 9°50W 64 B2
Ballydehob Ireland 51°34N 9°28W 64 E2
Ballygawley U.K. 54°27N 7°2W 64 B4
Ballyhaunis Ireland 53°46N 8°46W 64 C3
Ballyheige Ireland 52°23N 9°49W 64 D2
Ballymena U.K. 54°52N 6°17W 64 B5
Ballymoney U.K. 55°5N 6°31W 64 A5
Ballymote Ireland 54°5N 8°31W 64 B3
Ballynahinch U.K. 54°24N 5°54W 64 B6
Ballyporeen Ireland 52°16N 8°6W 64 D3
Ballyquintin Pt. U.K. 54°20N 5°30W 64 B6
Ballyshannon Ireland 54°30N 8°11W 64 B3
Balmaceda Chile 46°0S 71°50W 192 C2
Balmaseda Spain 43°11N 3°12W 90 B1
Balmazújváros Hungary 47°37N 21°21E 80 C6
Balmertown Canada 51°4N 93°41W 163 C10
Balmoral Australia 37°15S 141°48E 152 D4
Balmorhea U.S.A. 30°59N 103°45W 176 F3
Balneário Camboriú Brazil 26°59S 48°38W 191 B6
Balochistan = Baluchistan □ Pakistan 27°30N 65°0E 122 F4
Balod India 20°44N 81°13E 126 D5
Balonne → Australia 28°47S 147°56E 151 D4
Balotra India 25°50N 72°14E 124 G5
Balpyq Bī Kazakhstan 44°52N 78°12E 109 D9
Balqash Kazakhstan 46°50N 74°50E 106 E8
Balqash Köli Kazakhstan 46°0N 74°50E 109 C8
Balrampur India 27°30N 82°20E 125 F10
Balranald Australia 34°38S 143°33E 152 C5
Bals Romania 44°22N 24°5E 81 F9
Balsapuerto Peru 5°48S 76°33W 188 E2
Balsas Maranhão, Brazil 7°15S 44°35W 189 B2
Balsas → Mexico 17°55N 102°10W 180 D4
Balsas del Norte Mexico 18°0N 99°46W 181 D5
Bålsta Sweden 59°35N 17°30E 62 E11
Balta Ukraine 47°54N 29°45E 81 C14
Baltaköl Kazakhstan 43°7N 67°46E 109 D7
Baltanás Spain 41°56N 4°15W 88 D6
Bălți Moldova 47°48N 27°58E 81 C12
Baltic Sea Europe 57°0N 19°0E 63 H8
Baltīm Egypt 31°35N 31°10E 137 E7
Baltimore Ireland 51°29N 9°22W 64 F2
Baltimore Md., U.S.A. 39°17N 76°36W 173 F15
Baltimore Ohio, U.S.A. 39°51N 82°36W 174 G2
Baltinglass Ireland 52°56N 6°43W 64 D5
Baltit Pakistan 36°15N 74°40E 125 A6
Baltiysk Russia 54°41N 19°58E 82 D6
Baltrum Germany 53°43N 7°24E 76 B3
Baluchistan □ Pakistan 27°30N 65°0E 122 F4
Baluqtybulaq Kazakhstan 50°51N 51°9E 86 E10
Balurghat India 25°15N 88°44E 125 G13
Balvi Latvia 57°8N 27°15E 84 D4
Balya Turkey 39°44N 27°35E 99 B9
Balykchy Kyrgyzstan 42°26N 76°12E 109 D9
Balyqshy Kazakhstan 47°4N 51°52E 108 C4
Bam Iran 29°7N 58°14E 129 D8
Bama China 24°8N 107°12E 116 E6
Bama Nigeria 11°33N 13°41E 139 C7
Bamaga Australia 10°50S 142°25E 150 A3
Bamaji L. Canada 51°9N 91°25W 164 B1
Bamako Mali 12°34N 7°55W 138 C3
Bamba Mali 17°5N 1°24W 139 B4
Bambamarca Peru 6°45S 78°45W 188 E2
Bambara Maoundé Mali 13°26N 4°3W 138 B4
Bambari C.A.R. 5°40N 20°35E 140 C4
Bambaroo Australia 18°50S 146°10E 150 B4
Bamberg Germany 49°54N 10°54E 74 F6
Bamberg U.S.A. 33°18N 81°2W 178 D6
Bambesi Ethiopia 9°45N 34°40E 139 ...
Bambey Senegal 14°42N 16°28W 138 C1
Bambili Dem. Rep. of the Congo 3°40N 26°0E 142 B5
Bamboi Ghana 8°13N 2°1W 138 D4
Bambuí Brazil 20°1S 45°58W 191 A6
Bamburgh U.K. 55°37N 1°43W 66 B6
Bamenda Cameroon 5°57N 10°11E 139 D7
Bamfield Canada 48°45N 125°10W 162 D3
Bāmiān Afghan. 34°49N 67°49E 109 E7
Bāmiān □ Afghan. 35°0N 67°0E 109 E7
Bamiancheng China 43°15N 124°2E 115 C13
Bamkin Cameroon 6°3N 11°27E 139 D7
Bamou C.A.R. 3°29N 26°0E 142 B5
Bampūr Iran 27°15N 60°21E 129 E9
Bampūr → Iran 27°24N 59°30E 129 E9
Ban Burkina Faso 14°5N 2°27W 138 C4
Ban Ao Tu Khun Thailand 8°9N 98°20E 121 a

Ban Ban Laos 19°31N 103°30E 120 C4
Ban Bang Hin Thailand 9°32N 98°35E 121 H2
Ban Bang Khu Thailand 7°57N 98°23E 121 a
Ban Bang Rong Thailand 8°3N 98°25E 121 a
Ban Bo Phut Thailand 9°33N 100°2E 121 b
Ban Chaweng Thailand 9°32N 100°3E 121 b
Ban Chiang Thailand 17°30N 103°10E 120 D4
Ban Chiang Klang Thailand 19°25N 100°55E 120 C3
Ban Choho Thailand 15°2N 102°9E 120 E4
Ban Dan Lan Hoi Thailand 17°0N 99°35E 120 D2
Ban Don = Surat Thani Thailand 9°6N 99°20E 121 H2
Ban Don Vietnam 12°53N 107°48E 120 F6
Ban Don, Ao → Thailand 9°20N 99°25E 121 H2
Ban Dong Thailand 19°30N 100°59E 120 C3
Ban Hong Thailand 18°18N 98°50E 120 C2
Ban Hua Thanon Thailand 9°26N 100°1E 121 b
Ban Kantang Thailand 7°25N 99°31E 121 J2
Ban Karon Thailand 7°51N 98°18E 121 a
Ban Kata Thailand 7°50N 98°18E 121 a
Ban Keun Laos 18°22N 102°35E 120 C4
Ban Khai Thailand 12°46N 101°18E 120 F3
Ban Kheun Laos 20°13N 101°7E 120 B3
Ban Khlong Khian Thailand 8°10N 98°26E 121 a
Ban Khlong Kua Thailand 6°57N 100°8E 121 J3
Ban Khuan Thailand 8°20N 98°25E 121 a
Ban Ko Yai Chim Thailand 11°17N 99°26E 121 G2
Ban Laem Thailand 13°13N 99°59E 120 F2
Ban Lamai Thailand 9°28N 100°3E 121 b
Ban Lao Ngam Laos 15°28N 106°10E 120 E6
Ban Le Kathe Thailand 15°49N 98°53E 120 E2
Ban Lo Po Noi Thailand 8°1N 98°34E 121 a
Ban Mae Chedi Thailand 19°11N 99°31E 120 C2
Ban Mae Nam Thailand 9°34N 99°59E 121 b
Ban Mae Sariang Thailand 18°10N 97°56E 120 C1
Ban Mê Thuôt = Buon Ma Thuot Vietnam 12°40N 108°3E 120 F7
Ban Mi Thailand 15°3N 100°32E 120 E3
Ban Na Bo Thailand 9°19N 99°41E 121 b
Ban Na San Thailand 8°53N 99°52E 121 H2
Ban Na Tong Laos 20°56N 101°47E 120 B3
Ban Nam Bac Laos 20°38N 102°20E 120 B4
Ban Nammi Laos 17°7N 104°48E 120 D5
Ban Nong Bok Laos 17°5N 104°48E 120 D5
Ban Nong Pling Thailand 15°40N 100°10E 120 E3
Ban Pak Chan Thailand 10°32N 98°51E 121 G2
Ban Patong Thailand 7°54N 98°18E 121 a
Ban Phai Thailand 16°4N 102°44E 120 D4
Ban Phak Chit Thailand 8°9N 98°24E 121 a
Ban Pong Thailand 13°50N 99°55E 120 F2
Ban Rawai Thailand 7°47N 98°20E 121 a
Ban Ron Phibun Thailand 8°9N 99°51E 121 H2
Ban Sakhu Thailand 8°4N 98°18E 121 a
Ban Sanam Chai Thailand 7°33N 100°25E 121 J3
Ban Tak Thailand 17°2N 99°4E 120 D2
Ban Tako Thailand 14°5N 102°40E 120 E4
Ban Tha Nun Thailand 8°12N 98°18E 121 a
Ban Tha Rua Thailand 8°0N 98°22E 121 a
Ban Tha Yu Thailand 8°17N 98°22E 121 a
Ban Thong Krut Thailand 9°25N 99°57E 121 b
Ban Xien Kok Laos 20°54N 100°39E 120 B3
Ban Yen Nhan Vietnam 20°57N 106°2E 120 B6
Banaba Kiribati 0°45S 169°50E 156 H8
Banagher Ireland 53°11N 7°59W 64 C3
Banalia Dem. Rep. of the Congo 1°32N 25°5E 142 B5
Banam Cambodia 11°20N 105°17E 121 G5
Banamba Mali 13°29N 7°22W 138 C3
Banana Australia 24°28S 150°8E 150 C5
Bananal, I. do Brazil 11°30S 50°30W 187 F8
Banaras = Varanasi India 25°22N 83°0E 125 G10
Banas → Gujarat, India 23°45N 71°25E 124 H4
Banas → Mad. P., India 24°15N 81°30E 125 G9
Bânâs, Ras Egypt 23°57N 35°59E 137 D4
Banaz Turkey 38°44N 29°46E 99 C11
Banaz → Turkey 38°46N 29°4E 99 C11
Banbridge U.K. 54°22N 6°16W 64 B5
Banbury U.K. 52°4N 1°20W 67 E6
Banchory U.K. 57°3N 2°29W 65 D6
Bancroft Canada 45°3N 77°51W 174 A7
Band Romania 46°30N 24°25E 81 D9
Band Boni Iran 25°30N 59°33E 129 E8
Band Qīr Iran 31°39N 48°53E 129 D6
Banda Mad. P., India 24°3N 78°57E 125 G8
Banda Maharashtra, India 15°49N 73°53E 127 G1
Banda Ut. P., India 25°30N 80°26E 125 G9
Banda, Kepulauan Indonesia 4°37S 129°50E 119 E7
Banda Aceh Indonesia 5°35N 95°20E 118 C1
Banda Banda, Mt. Australia 31°10S 152°28E 153 A10
Banda Elat Indonesia 5°40S 133°5E 119 F8
Banda Is. = Banda, Kepulauan Indonesia 4°37S 129°50E 119 E7
Banda Sea Indonesia 6°0S 130°0E 119 F7
Bandai-Asahi △ Japan 37°38N 140°4E 112 F10
Bandai-San Japan 37°36N 140°4E 112 F10
Bandama → Ivory C. 6°32N 5°30W 138 D3
Bandama Blanc → Ivory C. 6°55N 5°9W 138 D3
Bandama Rouge → Ivory C. 6°55N 5°9W 138 D3
Bandān Iran 31°23N 60°44E 129 D9
Bandanaira Indonesia 4°32S 129°54E 119 E7
Bandanwara India 26°9N 74°38E 124 F6
Bandar = Machilipatnam India 16°12N 81°8E 127 F5
Bandar-e Abbās Iran 27°15N 56°15E 129 E8
Bandar-e Anzalī Iran 37°30N 49°30E 105 D13
Bandar-e Bushehr = Büshehr Iran 28°55N 50°55E 129 D6
Bandar-e Chārak Iran 26°45N 54°20E 129 E7
Bandar-e Deylam Iran 30°5N 50°10E 129 D6
Bandar-e Emām Khomeynī Iran 30°30N 49°5E 129 D6
Bandar-e Lengeh Iran 26°35N 54°58E 129 E7

Bandar-e Maqām Iran 26°56N 53°29E 129 E7
Bandar-e Ma'shur Iran 30°35N 49°10E 129 D6
Bandar-e Rīg Iran 29°29N 50°38E 129 D6
Bandar-e Torkeman Iran 37°0N 54°10E 129 B7
Bandar Labuan Malaysia 5°20N 115°14E 118 C5
Bandar Lampung Indonesia 5°20S 105°10E 118 F3
Bandar Maharani = Muar Malaysia 2°3N 102°34E 121 L4
Bandar Penggaram = Batu Pahat Malaysia 1°50N 102°56E 121 L4
Bandar Seri Begawan Brunei 4°52N 115°0E 118 C5
Bandar Shahid Rajaee Iran 27°7N 56°4E 129 E8
Bandar Sri Aman Malaysia 1°15N 111°32E 118 D4
Bandawe Malawi 11°58S 34°5E 143 G6
Bande Spain 42°3N 7°58W 88 C3
Bandeira, Pico da Brazil 20°26S 41°47W 191 A7
Bandera Argentina 28°55S 62°20W 190 B3
Banderas, B. de Mexico 20°40N 105°25W 180 C3
Bandhavgarh India 23°40N 81°2E 125 H9
Bandhavgarh △ India 23°45N 81°10E 125 H9
Bandi → India 26°12N 75°47E 124 F6
Bandia → India 19°2N 80°28E 126 E5
Bandiagara Mali 14°12N 3°29W 138 C4
Bandikui India 27°3N 76°34E 124 F7
Bandipur △ India 11°45N 76°30E 127 J3
Bandırma Turkey 40°20N 28°0E 99 B10
Bandjarmasin = Banjarmasin Indonesia 3°20S 114°35E 118 E4
Bandol France 43°8N 5°46E 73 E12
Bandon Ireland 51°44N 8°44W 64 E3
Bandon → Ireland 51°43N 8°37W 64 E3
Bandula Mozam. 19°0S 33°7E 143 H6
Bandundu Dem. Rep. of the Congo 3°15S 17°22E 140 E3
Bandung Indonesia 6°54S 107°36E 118 F3
Bané Burkina Faso 11°42N 0°15W 138 C4
Băneasa Romania 45°56N 27°55E 81 E12
Bāneh Iran 35°59N 45°53E 105 D12
Banes Cuba 21°0N 75°42W 183 B4
Banff Canada 51°10N 115°34W 162 C5
Banff U.K. 57°40N 2°33W 65 D6
Banff △ Canada 51°30N 116°15W 162 C5
Banfora Burkina Faso 10°40N 4°40W 138 C4
Bang Fai → Laos 16°57N 104°45E 120 D5
Bang Hieng → Laos 16°10N 105°10E 120 D5
Bang Krathum Thailand 16°34N 100°18E 120 D3
Bang Lamung Thailand 13°3N 100°56E 120 F3
Bang Lang △ Thailand 5°58N 101°19E 121 d
Bang Lang Res. Thailand 6°6N 101°17E 121 d
Bang Mun Nak Thailand 16°2N 100°23E 120 D3
Bang Pa In Thailand 14°14N 100°35E 120 E3
Bang Rakam Thailand 16°45N 100°7E 120 D3
Bang Saphan Thailand 11°14N 99°28E 121 G2
Bang Thao Thailand 7°59N 98°18E 121 a
Bangaduni I. India 21°34N 88°52E 125 J13
Bangala Dam Zimbabwe 21°7S 31°25E 143 J6
Bangalore India 12°59N 77°40E 127 H3
Banganapalle India 15°19N 78°14E 127 G3
Banganga → India 27°6N 77°25E 124 F7
Bangangté Cameroon 5°8N 10°32E 139 D7
Bangaon India 23°0N 88°47E 125 H13
Bangassou C.A.R. 4°55N 23°7E 140 D4
Banggai Indonesia 1°34S 123°30E 119 E6
Banggai, Kepulauan Indonesia 1°40S 123°30E 119 E6
Banggai Arch. = Banggai, Kepulauan Indonesia 1°40S 123°30E 119 E6
Banggi, Pulau Malaysia 7°17N 117°12E 118 C5
Banghāzī Libya 32°11N 20°3E 135 B10
Bangka Sulawesi, Indonesia 1°50N 125°5E 119 D7
Bangka Sumatera, Indonesia 2°0S 105°50E 118 E3
Bangka, Selat Indonesia 2°30S 105°30E 118 E3
Bangka-Belitung □ Indonesia 2°30S 107°0E 118 E3
Bangkalan Indonesia 7°2S 112°46E 118 F4
Bangkinang Indonesia 0°18N 101°5E 118 D2
Bangko Indonesia 2°5S 102°9E 118 E2
Bangkok Thailand 13°45N 100°35E 120 F3
Bangkok, Bight of Thailand 12°55N 100°30E 120 F3
Bangla = Paschimbanga □ India 23°0N 88°0E 125 H13
Bangladesh ■ Asia 24°0N 90°0E 125 G17
Bangli Indonesia 8°27S 115°21E 119 J18
Bangong Co India 33°45N 78°43E 125 B8
Bangor Down, U.K. 54°40N 5°40W 64 B6
Bangor Gwynedd, U.K. 53°14N 4°8W 66 D3
Bangor Maine, U.S.A. 44°48N 68°46W 173 C19
Bangor Pa., U.S.A. 40°52N 75°13W 175 E9
Bangued Phil. 17°40N 120°37E 119 A6
Bangui C.A.R. 4°23N 18°35E 140 D3
Banguru Dem. Rep. of the Congo 0°30N 27°10E 142 B5
Bangweulu, L. Zambia 11°0S 30°0E 142 G6
Bangweulu Swamp Zambia 11°20S 30°15E 142 G6
Banhine △ Mozam. 22°49S 32°55E 143 J6
Bani Burkina Faso 13°43N 0°10W 138 C4
Bani Dom. Rep. 18°16N 70°22W 183 C5
Bani → Mali 14°30N 4°12W 138 C4
Bani, Djebel Morocco 29°16N 8°0W 132 C4
Bani Bangou Niger 15°3N 2°25E 138 B5
Banī Sa'd Iraq 33°34N 44°32E 105 F11
Banihal Pass India 33°30N 75°12E 125 C6
Banikoara Benin 11°18N 2°25E 139 C5
Banissa Kenya 3°55N 40°19E 145 A5
Bāniyās Syria 35°10N 36°0E 130 A4
Banja Luka Bos.-H. 44°49N 17°11E 96 B2
Banjar India 31°38N 77°21E 124 D7
Banjar → India 22°36N 80°22E 125 H8
Banjarmasin Indonesia 3°20S 114°35E 118 E4
Banjul The Gambia 13°28N 16°40W 138 C1
Banka India 24°53N 86°55E 125 G12
Bankas Mali 14°4N 3°31W 138 C4
Bankeryd Sweden 57°53N 14°6E 63 H6
Banket Zimbabwe 17°27S 30°19E 143 H6

ankilaré Niger 14°35N 0°44E 139 C5
ankipore India 25°35N 85°10E 123 G14
ankot India 17°58N 73°2E 126 F1
anks U.S.A. 31°49N 85°51W 178 D4
anks I. = Moa Australia 10°11S 142°16E 150 a
anks I. B.C., Canada 53°20N 130°0W 162 C3
anks I. N.W.T., Canada 73°15N 121°30W 160 C7
anks L. U.S.A. 31°2N 83°6W 178 D6
anks Pen. N.Z. 43°45S 173°15E 155 D8
anks Str. Australia 40°40S 148°10E 151 G4
ankura India 23°11N 87°18E 125 H12
ankya Bulgaria 42°43N 23°8E 96 D7
anmankhi India 25°53N 87°11E 125 G12
ann ➝ Armagh, U.K. 54°30N 6°31W 64 B5
ann ➝ L'derry., U.K. 55°8N 6°41W 64 A5
annalec France 47°57N 3°42W 70 E3
annang Sata Thailand 6°16N 101°16E 121 J3
annerton Australia 34°42S 142°47E 152 C5
anning U.S.A. 33°56N 116°53W 171 M10
annockburn Canada 44°39N 77°33W 174 B7
annockburn U.K. 56°5N 3°55W 65 E5
annockburn Zimbabwe 20°17S 29°48E 143 G2
annu Pakistan 33°0N 70°18E 122 C7
ano India 22°40N 84°55E 125 H11
añolas = Banyoles Spain 42°16N 2°44E 90 C7
anon France 44°2N 5°38E 73 D9
años de la Encina Spain 38°10N 3°46W 89 G7
años de Molgas Spain 42°15N 7°40W 88 C3
anovce nad Bebravou Slovak Rep. 48°44N 18°16E 79 C11
anovići Bos.-H. 44°25N 18°32E 80 F3
ansagar Dam India 24°11N 81°17E 126 B5
ansgaon India 26°33N 83°21E 125 F10
anská Bystrica Slovak Rep. 48°46N 19°14E 79 C12
anská Štiavnica Slovak Rep. 48°25N 18°55E 79 C11
ansko Bulgaria 41°52N 23°28E 96 E7
anskobystrický ☐ Slovak Rep. 48°20N 19°0E 79 C12
answara India 23°32N 74°24E 124 H6
antaeng Indonesia 5°32S 119°56E 119 F5
antaji ➝ Nigeria 8°6N 10°5E 139 D7
anteay Prei Nokor Cambodia 11°56N 105°40E 121 G5
anten ☐ Indonesia 6°30S 106°0E 119 G11
antry Ireland 51°41N 9°27W 64 E2
antry B. Ireland 51°37N 9°44W 64 E2
antva India 21°29N 70°12E 124 J4
antval India 12°55N 75°0E 127 H2
anya Bulgaria 42°33N 24°50E 97 D8
anya, Pta. de la Spain 40°33N 0°36E 90 E5
anyak, Kepulauan Indonesia 2°10N 97°10E 118 D1
anyalbufar Spain 39°42N 2°31E 100 B9
anyeres de Mariola Spain 38°44N 0°38W 91 G4
anyo Cameroon 6°52N 11°45E 139 D7
anyoles Spain 42°16N 2°44E 90 C7
anyuls-sur-Mer France 42°28N 3°8E 72 F7
anyuwangi Indonesia 8°13S 114°21E 119 J17
anzare Coast Antarctica 68°0S 125°0E 55 C9
Ha Vietnam 22°11N 104°21E 116 F5
Lac Vietnam 22°57N 105°40E 120 A5
Loc Vietnam 11°32N 107°48E 121 G6
'an China 22°34N 113°52E 111 a
cheng China 33°12N 106°56E 116 A6
de China 39°1N 111°5E 114 E6
di China 39°38N 117°20E 115 E9
ding China 38°50N 115°28E 114 E8
ji China 34°20N 107°5E 114 G4
jing China 28°45N 109°41E 116 C7
kang China 31°54N 111°12E 117 B8
shan Shanghai, China 31°24N 121°28E 117 B13
shan Yunnan, China 25°10N 99°5E 116 E2
tou China 40°32N 110°2E 114 D6
ulé ➝ Mali 12°36N 9°45W 138 C3
xing China 30°24N 102°50E 116 B4
ying China 33°17N 119°20E 115 H10
you = Ledong China 18°41N 109°5E 117 a
India 27°23N 72°18E 124 F5
atla India 15°55N 80°30E 127 G5
aume France 50°7N 2°50E 71 B9
erābād Iran 33°2N 51°58E 129 C6
qūbah Iraq 33°45N 44°50E 105 F11
uedano Chile 23°20S 69°52W 190 A2
Montenegro 42°8N 19°6E 96 D3
Ukraine 49°4N 27°40E 75 D14
Bigha India 25°21N 85°47E 125 G11
Harbor U.S.A. 44°23N 68°13W 173 C19
le-Duc France 48°47N 5°10E 71 D12
sur-Aube France 48°14N 4°40E 71 D11
sur-Seine France 48°7N 4°20E 71 D11
India 25°16N 81°43E 125 G9
Romania 47°2N 27°3E 81 C12
Banki India 26°55N 81°12E 125 F9
abai Indonesia 2°32S 115°34E 118 E5
aboo U.S.A. 43°28N 89°45W 172 D9
acoa Cuba 20°20N 74°30W 183 B5
adā ➝ Syria 33°33N 36°34E 130 B5
adero Argentina 33°52S 59°29W 190 C4
adine Australia 30°56S 149°4E 153 A8
aga U.S.A. 46°47N 88°30W 172 B9
aganul Romania 44°49N 27°31E 81 F12
agoi Kenya 1°47N 36°47E 142 B4
ah ➝ India 27°42N 77°5E 124 F6
ahona Dom. Rep. 18°13N 71°7W 183 C5
ail Range India 25°15N 93°20E 123 G18
ajas, Madrid ✈ (MAD) Spain 40°26N 3°34W 88 E7
akaldo Spain 43°18N 2°59W 90 B2
akar ➝ India 24°7N 86°14E 125 G12
akee △ Australia 31°37S 151°53E 153 A9
akot India 21°33N 84°59E 125 J11
akpur India 22°47N 88°21E 125 H13
alaba Australia 24°13S 149°50E 150 C4
alla Spain 42°53N 7°15W 88 C3
alzon L. Canada 60°0N 98°3W 163 B9
amati India 18°11N 74°33E 126 E2
amba India 20°25N 85°23E 126 D7
ameiya Sudan 18°32N 36°38E 137 D4
amula India 34°15N 74°20E 125 B6
an India 25°9N 76°40E 124 G7
an ➝ Pakistan 25°13N 68°17E 124 G3
añain Spain 42°48N 1°40W 90 C3
anavichy Belarus 53°10N 26°0E 75 B14
ani Burkina Faso 13°9N 3°51W 138 C4
Baranof U.S.A. 57°5N 134°50W 162 B2
Baranof I. U.S.A. 57°0N 135°0W 160 F4
Baranów Sandomierski Poland 50°29N 21°30E 83 H8
Baranya ☐ Hungary 46°0N 18°15E 80 E3
Barão de Cocais Brazil 19°56S 43°28W 189 D2
Barão de Grajaú Brazil 6°45S 43°1W 189 B2
Baraolt Romania 46°5N 25°34E 81 D10
Baraona Spain 41°17N 2°39W 90 D2
Barapasi Indonesia 2°15S 137°5E 119 E9
Barasat India 22°46N 88°31E 125 H13
Barat Daya, Kepulauan Indonesia 7°30S 128°0E 119 F7
Baratang I. India 12°13N 92°45E 127 H11
Barataria B. U.S.A. 29°20N 89°55W 177 G10
Barauda India 23°33N 75°15E 124 H6
Baraut India 29°13N 77°7E 124 E7
Barbacena Brazil 21°15S 43°56W 191 A7
Barbados ■ W. Indies 13°10N 59°30W 183 g
Barbalha Brazil 7°19S 39°17W 189 B3
Barban Croatia 45°5N 14°2E 93 C11
Barbària, C. de Spain 38°39N 1°24E 100 C7
Barbaros Turkey 40°54N 27°27E 97 F11
Barbas, C. W. Sahara 22°20N 16°42W 134 D2
Barbastro Spain 42°2N 0°5E 90 C5
Barbate Spain 36°13N 5°56W 89 J5
Barbeau Pk. Canada 81°54N 75°1W 161 A16
Barberino di Mugello Italy 44°0N 11°15E 93 E8
Barberton S. Africa 25°42S 31°2E 145 C5
Barberton U.S.A. 41°1N 81°39W 174 E3
Barberville U.S.A. 29°11N 81°26W 179 F8
Barbezieux-St-Hilaire France 45°28N 0°9W 72 C3
Barbosa Colombia 5°57N 73°37W 186 B4
Barbourville U.S.A. 36°52N 83°53W 173 G12
Barbuda W. Indies 17°30N 61°40W 183 C7
Bârca Romania 43°59N 23°36E 81 G8
Barcaldine Australia 23°43S 145°6E 150 C4
Barcarrota Spain 38°31N 6°51W 89 G4
Barcellona Pozzo di Gotto Italy 38°9N 15°13E 95 D8
Barcelona Spain 41°22N 2°10E 90 D7
Barcelona Venezuela 10°10N 64°40W 186 A6
Barcelona ☐ Spain 41°30N 2°0E 90 D7
Barcelona ✈ (BCN) Spain 41°18N 2°5E 90 D7
Barceloneta Puerto Rico 18°27N 66°32W 183 d
Barcelonette France 44°23N 6°40E 73 D10
Barcelos Brazil 1°0S 63°0W 186 D6
Barcin Poland 52°52N 17°55E 83 F4
Barclayville Liberia 4°48N 8°10W 138 E3
Barcoo ➝ Australia 25°30S 142°50E 150 D3
Barcs Hungary 45°58N 17°28E 80 E2
Barczewo Poland 53°50N 20°42E 82 E7
Bärdä Azerbaijan 40°25N 47°10E 87 K8
Barda del Medio Argentina 38°45S 68°11W 192 A3
Bardaï Chad 21°25N 17°0E 135 D9
Bardas Blancas Argentina 35°49S 69°45W 190 D2
Bardawîl, Sabkhet el Egypt 31°10N 33°15E 130 D2
Barddhaman India 23°14N 87°39E 125 H12
Bardejov Slovak Rep. 49°18N 21°15E 79 B14
Bardera = Baardheere Somalia 2°20N 42°27E 131 G3
Bardi Italy 44°38N 9°44E 92 D6
Bardīyah Libya 31°45N 25°5E 135 B10
Bardoli India 21°12N 73°5E 126 D1
Bardolino Italy 45°33N 10°43E 92 C7
Bardonécchia Italy 45°5N 6°42E 92 C3
Bardsey I. U.K. 52°45N 4°47W 66 E3
Bardstown U.S.A. 37°49N 85°28W 173 G11
Bareilly India 28°22N 79°27E 125 E8
Barela India 23°6N 80°3E 125 H9
Barellan Australia 34°16S 146°24E 153 C7
Barentin France 49°33N 0°58E 70 C7
Barenton France 48°38N 0°50W 70 D6
Barents Sea Arctic 73°0N 39°0E 54 B9
Barentsøya Svalbard 78°25N 21°20E 57 B13
Barfleur France 49°40N 1°17W 70 C5
Barfleur, Pte. de France 49°42N 1°16W 70 C5
Barga Italy 44°4N 10°29E 92 D7
Bargara Australia 24°50S 152°25E 150 C5
Bargarh India 21°20N 83°37E 126 D6
Bargas Spain 39°56N 4°3W 88 F6
Barge Italy 44°43N 7°20E 92 D4
Bargi Dam India 22°59N 80°0E 126 C5
Bargo Australia 34°18S 150°35E 153 C9
Bargteheide Germany 53°44N 10°14E 76 B6
Barguzin Russia 53°37N 109°37E 107 D11
Barh India 25°29N 85°46E 125 G11
Barhaj India 26°18N 83°44E 125 F10
Barham Australia 35°36S 144°8E 152 C6
Barharwa India 24°52N 87°47E 125 G12
Barhi India 24°15N 85°25E 125 G11
Bari India 26°39N 77°39E 124 F7
Bari Italy 41°8N 16°51E 95 A9
Bari Doab Pakistan 30°20N 73°0E 124 D5
Bari Sadri India 24°28N 74°30E 124 G6
Bari Sardo Italy 39°50N 9°38E 94 C2
Barīdī, Ra's Si. Arabia 24°17N 37°31E 128 E3
Barīm Yemen 12°39N 43°25E 132 E8
Barinas Venezuela 8°36N 70°15W 186 B4
Baring, C. Canada 70°0N 117°30W 160 D8
Baringo, L. Kenya 0°47N 36°16E 142 B4
Baripada India 21°57N 86°45E 126 D8
Bârîs Egypt 24°42N 30°31E 137 C3
Barisal Bangla. 22°45N 90°20E 123 H17
Barisal ☐ Bangla. 22°45N 90°20E 123 H17
Barisan, Pegunungan Indonesia 3°30S 102°15E 118 E2
Barito ➝ Indonesia 4°0S 114°50E 118 E4
Baritú △ Argentina 23°43S 64°40W 190 A3
Barjac France 44°20N 4°22E 73 D8
Barjols France 43°34N 6°2E 73 E10
Barjūj, Wadi ➝ Libya 25°26N 12°12E 135 C8
Bark L. Canada 45°27N 77°51W 174 A7
Barkakana India 23°37N 85°29E 125 H11
Barkal, J. Sudan 18°32N 31°50E 137 D3
Barkam China 31°51N 102°28E 116 B4
Barker U.S.A. 43°20N 78°33W 174 C6
Barkley, L. U.S.A. 37°1N 88°14W 177 C10
Barkley Sound Canada 48°50N 125°10W 162 D3
Barkly East S. Africa 30°58S 27°33E 144 D4
Barkly Homestead Australia 19°52S 135°50E 150 B2
Barkly Tableland Australia 17°50S 136°40E 150 B2
Barkly West S. Africa 28°5S 24°31E 144 C3
Barkol Kazak Zizhixian China 43°37N 93°2E 110 C7
Barla Dağı Turkey 38°5N 30°40E 99 C12
Bârlad Romania 46°15N 27°38E 81 D12
Bârlad ➝ Romania 45°38N 27°32E 81 E12
Barlee, L. Australia 29°15S 119°30E 149 E2
Barlee, Mt. Australia 24°38S 128°13E 149 D4
Barletta Italy 41°19N 16°17E 95 A9
Barlinek Poland 53°0N 15°15E 83 F2
Barlovento Canary Is. 28°48N 17°48W 100 F2
Barlovento C. Verde Is. 17°0N 25°0W 134 b
Barlow L. Canada 62°0N 103°0W 163 A8
Barmedman Australia 34°9S 147°21E 153 C7
Barmer India 25°45N 71°20E 124 G4
Barmera Australia 34°15S 140°28E 152 C4
Barmouth U.K. 52°44N 4°4W 66 E3
Barmstedt Germany 53°47N 9°46E 76 B5
Barna ➝ India 25°21N 83°3E 125 G10
Barnagar India 23°7N 75°19E 124 H6
Barnala India 30°23N 75°33E 124 D6
Barnard ➝ Australia 31°34S 151°25E 153 A9
Barnard Castle U.K. 54°33N 1°55W 66 C6
Barnato Australia 31°38S 145°0E 153 A6
Barnaul Russia 53°20N 83°40E 109 B10
Barnes Australia 36°2S 144°49E 152 D6
Barnesville Ga., U.S.A. 33°3N 84°9W 178 B5
Barnesville Minn., U.S.A. 46°43N 96°28W 172 B5
Barnet ☐ U.K. 51°38N 0°9W 67 F7
Barneveld Neths. 52°7N 5°36E 69 B5
Barneville-Cartevert France 49°23N 1°46W 70 C5
Barnhart U.S.A. 31°8N 101°10W 176 F4
Barnsley U.K. 53°34N 1°27W 66 D6
Barnstable U.S.A. 41°42N 70°18W 173 E18
Barnstaple U.K. 51°5N 4°4W 67 F3
Barnstaple Bay = Bideford Bay U.K. 51°5N 4°20W 67 F3
Barnwell U.S.A. 33°15N 81°23W 178 B8
Baro Nigeria 8°35N 6°18E 139 D6
Baroda = Vadodara India 22°20N 73°10E 124 H5
Baroda India 25°29N 76°35E 124 G7
Baroe S. Africa 33°13S 24°33E 144 D3
Baron Ra. Australia 23°30S 127°45E 148 D4
Barong China 31°3N 99°20E 116 B2
Barotseland Zambia 15°0S 24°0E 141 H4
Barouéli Mali 13°4N 6°50W 138 C3
Barpali India 21°11N 83°35E 126 D6
Barpeta India 26°20N 91°10E 123 F17
Barqa Libya 27°0N 23°0E 135 C10
Barques, Pt. Aux U.S.A. 44°4N 82°58W 174 B2
Barquísimeto Venezuela 10°4N 69°19W 186 A5
Barr, Ras el Egypt 31°32N 31°50E 137 E7
Barr Smith Range Australia 27°4S 120°20E 149 E3
Barra Brazil 11°5S 43°10W 189 C2
Barra Gambia 13°28N 16°32W 138 C1
Barra U.K. 57°0N 7°29W 65 E1
Barra, Sd. of U.K. 57°4N 7°25W 65 D1
Barra da Estiva Brazil 13°38S 41°19W 189 C2
Barra de Navidad Mexico 19°12N 104°41W 180 D4
Barra do Corda Brazil 5°30S 45°10W 189 B1
Barra do Garças Brazil 15°54S 52°16W 187 G8
Barra do Mendes Brazil 11°43S 42°4W 189 C2
Barra do Piraí Brazil 22°30S 43°50W 191 A7
Barra Falsa, Pta. da Mozam. 22°58S 35°37E 145 B6
Barra Hd. U.K. 56°47N 7°40W 65 E1
Barra Mansa Brazil 22°35S 44°12W 191 A7
Barraba Australia 30°21S 150°35E 153 A9
Barrackpur = Barakpur India 22°47N 88°21E 125 H13
Barrafranca Italy 37°22N 14°12E 95 E7
Barrāmīya Egypt 25°4N 33°47E 137 B3
Barranca Lima, Peru 10°45S 77°50W 188 C2
Barranca Loreto, Peru 4°50S 76°50W 186 D3
Barranca del Cobre ⌓ Mexico 27°18N 107°40W 180 B3
Barrancabermeja Colombia 7°0N 73°50W 186 B4
Barrancas Venezuela 8°55N 62°5W 186 B6
Barrancos Portugal 38°10N 6°58W 89 G4
Barranqueras Argentina 27°30S 59°0W 190 B4
Barranquilla Colombia 11°0N 74°50W 186 A4
Barras Brazil 4°15S 42°18W 189 A2
Barraute Canada 48°26N 77°38W 164 C4
Barre Mass., U.S.A. 42°25N 72°6W 175 D12
Barre Vt., U.S.A. 44°12N 72°30W 175 B12
Barreal Argentina 31°33S 69°28W 190 C2
Barreiras Brazil 12°8S 45°0W 189 C2
Barreirinhas Brazil 2°30S 42°50W 189 A2
Barreiro Portugal 38°39N 9°5W 89 G1
Barreiros Brazil 8°49S 35°12W 189 B3
Barrême France 43°57N 6°23E 73 E10
Barren, Nosy Madag. 18°25S 43°40E 141 H8
Barren I. India 12°16N 93°51E 127 H11
Barretos Brazil 20°30S 48°35W 189 E1
Barrhead Canada 54°10N 114°24W 162 C6
Barrie Canada 44°24N 79°40W 174 B5
Barrier, C. N.Z. 36°25S 175°32E 154 C4
Barrier Ra. Australia 31°0S 141°30E 152 A4
Barrier Ra. Otago, N.Z. 44°15S 169°32E 155 E4
Barrier Ra. W. Coast, N.Z. 44°30S 168°30E 155 E3
Barrière Canada 51°12N 120°7W 162 C4
Barrineau Park U.S.A. 30°42N 87°26W 179 E2
Barrington U.S.A. 41°44N 71°18W 175 E13
Barrington L. Canada 56°55N 100°15W 163 B8
Barrington Tops Australia 32°6S 151°28E 153 B9
Barrington Tops △ Australia 32°4S 151°25E 153 B9
Barringun Australia 29°1S 145°41E 151 D4
Barron U.S.A. 45°24N 91°51W 172 C8
Barrow U.S.A. 71°18N 156°47W 166 A8
Barrow ➝ Ireland 52°25N 6°58W 64 D5
Barrow, Pt. U.S.A. 71°23N 156°29W 166 A8
Barrow Creek Australia 21°30S 133°55E 150 C1
Barrow I. Australia 20°45S 115°20E 148 D2
Barrow-in-Furness U.K. 54°7N 3°14W 66 C4
Barrow Pt. Australia 14°20S 144°40E 150 A3
Barrow Ra. Australia 26°0S 127°40E 149 E4
Barrow Str. Canada 74°20N 95°0W 161 C13
Barruecopardo Spain 41°4N 6°40W 88 D4
Barruelo de Santullán Spain 42°54N 4°17W 88 C6
Barry U.K. 51°24N 3°16W 67 F4
Barry's Bay Canada 45°29N 77°41W 174 A7
Barsalogho Burkina Faso 13°25N 1°3W 139 C4
Barsat Pakistan 36°10N 72°45E 125 A5
Barsham Syria 35°21N 40°33E 105 E9
Barshatas Kazakhstan 48°10N 78°39E 109 C9
Barsi India 18°10N 75°50E 126 E2
Barsinghausen Germany 52°18N 9°28E 76 C5
Barsoi India 25°48N 87°57E 123 G15
Barstow U.S.A. 34°54N 117°1W 171 L9
Barth Germany 54°22N 12°42E 76 A8
Bartica Guyana 6°25N 58°40W 186 B7
Bartin Turkey 41°38N 32°21E 104 B5
Bartle Frere Australia 17°27S 145°50E 150 B4
Bartlesville U.S.A. 36°45N 95°59W 176 C7
Bartlett Calif., U.S.A. 36°29N 118°2W 170 J8
Bartlett Tenn., U.S.A. 35°12N 89°52W 177 D10
Bartlett, L. Canada 63°5N 118°20W 162 A5
Bartolomeu Dias Mozam. 21°10S 35°8E 143 G4
Barton U.S.A. 44°45N 72°11W 175 B12
Barton upon Humber U.K. 53°41N 0°25W 66 D7
Bartoszyce Poland 54°15N 20°55E 82 D7
Bartow Fla., U.S.A. 27°54N 81°50W 179 H8
Bartow Ga., U.S.A. 32°53N 82°29W 178 C7
Barú, Volcan Panama 8°55N 82°35W 182 E3
Barumba Dem. Rep. of the Congo 1°3N 23°37E 142 B1
Barúmini Italy 39°42N 8°59E 94 C1
Barung, Nusa Indonesia 8°30S 113°30E 119 H15
Baruth Germany 52°4N 13°30E 76 C9
Baruun Urt Mongolia 46°46N 113°15E 111 B11
Baruunsuu Mongolia 43°43N 105°35E 114 C3
Barvinkove Ukraine 48°57N 37°0E 85 H9
Barwani India 22°2N 74°57E 124 H6
Barwice Poland 53°44N 16°21E 82 E3
Barwick U.S.A. 30°54N 83°44W 178 E6
Barxudarlı Azerbaijan 41°0N 45°14E 105 B11
Barycz ➝ Poland 51°42N 16°15E 83 G3
Barysaw Belarus 54°17N 28°28E 75 A15
Barysh Russia 53°39N 47°8E 86 D8
Barzān Iraq 36°55N 44°3E 128 B5
Bârzava Romania 46°7N 21°59E 80 D6
Bas-Rhin ☐ France 48°40N 7°30E 71 D14
Bas-Sassandra ☐ Ivory C. 5°30N 7°0W 138 D3
Bašaid Serbia 45°38N 20°25E 80 E5
Bāsa'idū Iran 26°35N 55°20E 129 E7
Basal Pakistan 33°33N 72°13E 124 C5
Basankusa Dem. Rep. of the Congo 1°5N 19°50E 140 D3
Basarabeasca Moldova 46°21N 28°58E 81 D13
Basarabi Romania 44°10N 28°26E 81 F13
Basarabia = Bessarabiya Moldova 47°0N 28°10E 75 E15
Basauri Spain 43°13N 2°53W 90 B2
Basawa Afghan. 34°15N 70°50E 124 B4
Bascuñán, C. Chile 28°52S 71°35W 190 B1
Basel Switz. 47°35N 7°35E 77 H3
Basel Euroairport ✈ (EAP) France 47°36N 7°33E 71 E14
Basel-Landschaft ☐ Switz. 47°26N 7°45E 77 H3
Basento ➝ Italy 40°20N 16°49E 95 B9
Bashākerd, Kūhhā-ye Iran 26°42N 58°35E 129 E8
Bashaw Canada 52°35N 112°58W 162 C6
Bāshī Iran 28°41N 51°4E 129 D6
Bashkand = Artsvashen Armenia 40°38N 45°30E 105 B11
Bashkir Republic = Bashkortostan ☐ Russia 54°0N 57°0E 108 B5
Bashkiriya △ Russia 52°58N 56°30E 108 B5
Bashkortostan ☐ Russia 54°0N 57°0E 108 B5
Bashtanivka Ukraine 45°46N 29°29E 81 E14
Basilan I. Phil. 6°35N 122°0E 119 C6
Basilan Str. Phil. 6°50N 122°0E 119 C6
Basildon U.K. 51°34N 0°28E 67 F8
Basilé Eq. Guin. 3°42N 8°48E 139 E6
Basilé, Pico de Eq. Guin. 3°36N 8°49E 139 E6
Basilicata ☐ Italy 40°30N 16°30E 95 B9
Basim = Washim India 20°3N 77°0E 126 D3
Basin U.S.A. 44°23N 108°2W 168 D9
Basinger U.S.A. 27°23N 81°2W 179 H8
Basingstoke U.K. 51°15N 1°5W 67 F6
Baška Croatia 44°58N 14°45E 93 D11
Başkale Turkey 38°2N 43°59E 105 C10
Baskatong, Rés. Canada 46°46N 75°50W 164 C4
Basle = Basel Switz. 47°35N 7°35E 77 H3
Başmakçı Turkey 37°54N 30°1E 99 D12
Basmat India 19°15N 77°12E 126 E3
Basoda India 23°52N 77°54E 124 H7
Basoko Dem. Rep. of the Congo 1°16N 23°40E 142 B1
Basque, Côte France 43°50N 2°0W 72 E2
Basque, Pays France 43°15N 1°20W 72 E2
Basque Provinces = País Vasco ☐ Spain 42°50N 2°45W 90 C2
Basra = Al Başrah Iraq 30°30N 47°50E 128 D5
Bass Str. Australia 39°15S 146°30E 151 F4
Bassae Greece 37°26N 21°53E 98 D3
Bassano Canada 50°48N 112°20W 162 C6
Bassano del Grappa Italy 45°46N 11°44E 93 C8
Bassar Togo 9°19N 0°57E 139 D5
Bassas da India Ind. Oc. 22°0S 39°0E 143 G4
Basse-Normandie ☐ France 48°45N 0°30W 70 D6
Basse-Pointe Martinique 14°52N 61°8W 182 c
Basse Santa-Su Gambia 13°13N 14°15W 138 C2
Basse-Terre Guadeloupe 16°0N 61°44W 182 b
Basse Terre Trin. & Tob. 10°7N 61°19W 187 K15
Bassein Burma 16°45N 94°30E 123 L19
Basses, Pte. des Guadeloupe 15°52N 61°17W 182 b
Basseterre St. Kitts & Nevis 17°17N 62°43W 183 C7
Bassett U.S.A. 42°35N 99°32W 172 D4
Bassi India 30°44N 76°21E 124 D7
Bassigny France 48°0N 5°30E 71 E12
Bassikounou Mauritania 15°55N 6°1W 138 B3
Bassila Benin 9°1N 1°46E 139 D5
Bassum Germany 52°50N 8°40E 76 C4
Båstad Sweden 56°25N 12°51E 63 H6
Bastak Iran 27°15N 54°25E 129 E7
Baştām Iran 36°29N 55°4E 129 B7
Bastar India 19°15N 81°40E 126 E5
Bastelica France 42°1N 9°3E 73 F13
Basti India 26°52N 82°55E 125 F10
Bastia France 42°40N 9°30E 73 F13
Bastogne Belgium 50°1N 5°43E 69 D5
Bastrop La., U.S.A. 32°47N 91°55W 176 E9
Bastrop Tex., U.S.A. 30°7N 97°19W 176 F6
Basuo = Dongfang China 18°50N 108°33E 117 a
Bat Yam Israel 32°2N 34°44E 130 C3
Bata Eq. Guin. 1°57N 9°50E 140 D1
Bata Romania 46°1N 22°4E 80 D7
Bataan ☐ Phil. 14°40N 120°25E 119 B6
Batabanó Cuba 22°41N 82°18W 182 B3
Batabanó, G. de Cuba 22°30N 82°30W 182 B3
Batac Phil. 18°3N 120°34E 119 A6
Batagai Russia 67°38N 134°38E 107 C14
Batajnica Serbia 44°54N 20°17E 96 B4
Batak Bulgaria 41°57N 24°12E 97 E8
Batala India 31°48N 75°12E 124 D6
Batalha Portugal 39°40N 8°50W 88 F2
Batam Indonesia 1°10N 104°2E 121 d
Batama Dem. Rep. of the Congo 0°58N 26°33E 142 B2
Batamay Russia 63°30N 129°15E 107 C13
Batang China 30°1N 99°0E 116 B2
Batang Indonesia 6°55S 109°45E 119 G13
Batangafo C.A.R. 7°25N 18°20E 140 C3
Batangas Phil. 13°35N 121°10E 119 B6
Batanta Indonesia 0°55S 130°40E 119 E8
Batatais Brazil 20°54S 47°37W 191 A6
Batavia U.S.A. 43°0N 78°11W 174 D6
Bataysk Russia 47°3N 39°45E 85 J10
Batchelor Australia 13°4S 131°1E 148 B5
Batdambang Cambodia 13°7N 103°12E 120 F4
Batemans B. Australia 35°40S 150°12E 153 C9
Batemans Bay Australia 35°44S 150°11E 153 C9
Batesburg-Leesville U.S.A. 33°54N 81°33W 178 B8
Batesville Ark., U.S.A. 35°46N 91°39W 176 D9
Batesville Miss., U.S.A. 34°19N 89°57W 177 D10
Batesville Tex., U.S.A. 28°58N 99°37W 176 G5
Bath Canada 44°11N 76°47W 175 B8
Bath U.K. 51°23N 2°22W 67 F5
Bath Maine, U.S.A. 43°55N 69°49W 173 D19
Bath N.Y., U.S.A. 42°20N 77°19W 174 D7
Bath & North East Somerset ☐ U.K. 51°21N 2°27W 67 F5
Batheay Cambodia 11°59N 104°57E 121 G5
Bathsheba Barbados 13°13N 59°32W 183 g
Bathurst Australia 33°25S 149°31E 153 B8
Bathurst Canada 47°37N 65°43W 165 C6
Bathurst S. Africa 33°30S 26°50E 144 D4
Bathurst, C. Canada 70°34N 128°0W 160 C6
Bathurst B. Australia 14°16S 144°25E 150 A3
Bathurst Harb. Australia 43°15S 146°10E 151 G4
Bathurst I. Australia 11°30S 130°10E 148 B5
Bathurst I. Canada 76°0N 100°30W 161 B11
Bathurst Inlet Canada 66°50N 108°1W 160 D10
Batie Burkina Faso 9°53N 2°53W 138 D4
Batiki Fiji 17°48S 179°10E 154 a
Batken Kyrgyzstan 40°3N 70°50E 109 D8
Batken ☐ Kyrgyzstan 39°50N 71°0E 109 E8
Batlow Australia 35°31S 148°9E 153 C8
Batman Turkey 37°55N 41°5E 105 D9
Baţn al Ghūl Jordan 29°36N 35°56E 130 F4
Batna Algeria 35°34N 6°15E 136 A5
Batna ☐ Algeria 35°30N 5°55E 136 A5
Batočina Serbia 44°7N 21°5E 96 B5
Batoka Zambia 16°45S 27°15E 143 F2
Baton Rouge U.S.A. 30°27N 91°11W 176 F9
Batong, Ko Thailand 6°32N 99°12E 121 J2
Bátonyterenye Hungary 47°59N 19°50E 80 C4
Batopilas Mexico 27°1N 107°44W 180 B3
Batouri Cameroon 4°30N 14°25E 140 D2
Båtsfjord Norway 70°38N 29°39E 60 A23
Batsi Greece 37°52N 24°47E 98 D6
Battambang = Batdambang Cambodia 13°7N 103°12E 120 F4
Batti Malv India 8°50N 92°51E 127 K11
Batticaloa Sri Lanka 7°43N 81°45E 127 L5
Battipáglia Italy 40°37N 14°58E 95 B7
Battle U.K. 50°55N 0°30E 67 G8
Battle ➝ Canada 52°43N 108°15W 163 C7
Battle Creek U.S.A. 42°19N 85°11W 173 D11
Battle Ground U.S.A. 45°47N 122°32W 170 E4
Battle Harbour Canada 52°16N 55°35W 165 B8
Battle Lake U.S.A. 46°17N 95°43W 172 B6
Battle Mountain U.S.A. 40°38N 116°56W 168 F5
Battlefields Zimbabwe 18°37S 29°47E 143 F2
Battleford Canada 52°45N 108°15W 163 C7
Battonya Hungary 46°16N 21°3E 80 D6
Batu Ethiopia 6°55N 39°45E 131 F2
Batu Malaysia 3°15N 101°40E 121 L3
Batu, Kepulauan Indonesia 0°30S 98°25E 118 E1
Batu Ferringhi Malaysia 5°28N 100°15E 121 c
Batu Gajah Malaysia 4°28N 101°3E 121 K3
Batu Is. = Batu, Kepulauan Indonesia 0°30S 98°25E 118 E1
Batu Pahat Malaysia 1°50N 102°56E 121 M4
Batu Puteh, Gunung Malaysia 4°15N 101°31E 121 K3
Batuata Indonesia 6°12S 122°42E 119 F6
Batugondang, Tanjung Indonesia 8°6S 114°29E 119 J17
Batukaru, Gunung Indonesia 8°20S 115°5E 119 J18
Batumi Georgia 41°39N 41°44E 87 K5
Batur, Gunung Indonesia 8°14S 115°23E 119 J18
Batura Sar Pakistan 36°30N 74°31E 125 A6
Baturaja Indonesia 4°11S 104°15E 118 E2
Baturité Brazil 4°28S 38°45W 189 A3
Baturiti Indonesia 8°19S 115°11E 119 J18
Batys Qazaqstan ☐ Kazakhstan 50°0N 50°0E 108 C3
Bau Malaysia 1°25N 110°9E 118 D4
Baubau Indonesia 5°25S 122°38E 119 F6
Baucau E. Timor 8°27S 126°27E 119 F7
Bauchi Nigeria 10°22N 9°48E 139 C6
Bauchi ☐ Nigeria 10°30N 10°0E 139 C7
Baud France 47°52N 3°1W 70 E3
Bauda India 20°50N 84°25E 126 D7
Baudette U.S.A. 48°43N 94°36W 172 A6
Bauer, C. Australia 32°44S 134°4E 151 E1
Bauhinia Australia 24°35S 149°18E 150 C4
Baukau = Baucau E. Timor 8°27S 126°27E 119 F7
Bauld, C. Canada 51°38N 55°26W 161 G20
Baume-les-Dames France 47°22N 6°22E 71 E13
Baunatal Germany 51°14N 9°24E 76 D5
Baunei Italy 40°2N 9°40E 94 B2
Baure Nigeria 12°52N 8°50E 139 C6
Bauru Brazil 22°10S 49°0W 191 A6
Bausi India 24°48N 87°1E 125 G12
Bauska Latvia 56°24N 24°15E 82 B11
Bautino Kazakhstan 44°35N 50°14E 87 H10
Bautzen Germany 51°10N 14°26E 76 D10
Bauya S. Leone 8°12N 12°38W 138 D2
Bavānāt Iran 30°28N 53°27E 129 D7
Bavanište Serbia 44°49N 20°55E 80 F5
Bavaria = Bayern ☐ Germany 48°50N 12°0E 77 G7
Båven Sweden 59°0N 16°56E 62 E10
Bavispe ➝ Mexico 29°15N 109°11W 180 B3
Baw Baw △ Australia 37°50S 146°17E 153 D7
Bawdwin Burma 23°5N 97°20E 123 H20
Bawean Indonesia 5°46S 112°35E 118 F4
Bawku Ghana 11°3N 0°19W 139 C4
Bawlakhe Burma 19°11N 97°21E 123 K20
Bawolung China 28°50N 101°16E 116 C3
Baxley U.S.A. 31°47N 82°21W 178 D7
Baxter U.S.A. 46°21N 94°17W 172 B6
Baxter Springs U.S.A. 37°2N 94°44W 172 G6
Baxter State ⌓ U.S.A. 46°5N 68°57W 173 B19
Bay City Mich., U.S.A. 43°36N 83°54W 173 D12
Bay City Tex., U.S.A. 28°59N 95°58W 176 G7
Bay Minette U.S.A. 30°53N 87°46W 177 F11
Bay of Plenty ☐ N.Z. 38°0S 177°0E 154 D5
Bay Roberts Canada 47°36N 53°16W 165 C9
Bay St. Louis U.S.A. 30°19N 89°20W 177 F10
Bay Springs U.S.A. 31°59N 89°17W 177 F10
Bay View N.Z. 39°25S 176°50E 154 F5
Baya Dem. Rep. of the Congo 11°53S 27°25E 143 E2
Bayamo Cuba 20°20N 76°40W 182 B4
Bayamón Puerto Rico 18°24N 66°9W 183 d
Bayan Har Shan China 34°0N 98°0E 110 E8
Bayan Hot = Alxa Zuoqi China 38°50N 105°40E 114 E3
Bayan Lepas Malaysia 5°17N 100°16E 121 c
Bayan Obo China 41°52N 109°59E 114 D5
Bayan-Ovoo = Erdenetsogt Mongolia 42°55N 106°5E 114 C4
Bayana India 26°55N 77°18E 124 F7
Bayanaūyl Kazakhstan 50°45N 75°45E 109 B9
Bayanhongor Mongolia 46°8N 102°43E 110 B9
Bayard N. Mex., U.S.A. 32°46N 108°8W 169 K9
Bayard Nebr., U.S.A. 41°45N 103°20W 172 E2
Baybay Phil. 10°40N 124°55E 119 B6
Bayburt Turkey 40°15N 40°20E 105 B9
Bayburt ☐ Turkey 40°35N 39°25E 105 B8
Baydaratskaya Guba Russia 69°0N 67°30E 106 C7
Baydhabo Somalia 3°8N 43°30E 131 G3
Bayelsa ☐ Nigeria 4°30N 6°0E 139 E6
Bayerische Alpen Germany 47°35N 11°30E 77 H7
Bayerische Rhön ⌓ Germany 50°15N 10°5E 77 E6
Bayerischer Spessart ⌓ Germany 49°58N 10°15E 77 F6
Bayerischer Wald Germany 48°56N 12°50E 77 G8
Bayern ☐ Germany 48°50N 12°0E 77 G7
Bayeux France 49°17N 0°42W 70 C6
Bayfield Canada 43°34N 81°42W 174 C3
Bayfield U.S.A. 46°49N 90°49W 172 B8
Bayındır Turkey 38°13N 27°39E 99 C9
Baykal, Oz. Russia 53°0N 108°0E 107 D11
Baykan Turkey 38°7N 41°44E 105 C9
Baymak Russia 52°36N 58°19E 108 B5
Baynes Mts. Namibia 17°15S 13°0E 144 A1
Bayombong Phil. 16°30N 121°10E 119 A6
Bayon France 48°30N 6°20E 71 D13
Bayona = Baiona Spain 42°6N 8°52W 88 C2
Bayonet Point U.S.A. 28°20N 82°41W 179 G7
Bayonne France 43°30N 1°28W 72 E2
Bayonne U.S.A. 40°40N 74°6W 175 F10
Bayovar Peru 5°50S 81°0W 188 B1
Bayport U.S.A. 28°32N 82°39W 179 G7
Bayqonyr Kazakhstan 45°40N 63°20E 108 C6
Bayram-Ali = Baýramaly Turkmenistan 37°37N 62°10E 129 B9
Baýramaly Turkmenistan 37°37N 62°10E 129 B9
Bayramiç Turkey 39°48N 26°36E 99 B8
Bayreuth Germany 49°56N 11°35E 77 F7
Bayrischzell Germany 47°41N 12°0E 77 H8
Bayrūt Lebanon 33°53N 35°31E 130 B4
Bays, L. of Canada 45°15N 79°4W 174 A5
Bayshore U.S.A. 26°43N 81°50W 179 J8
Baysville Canada 45°9N 79°7W 174 A5
Bayt Lahm West Bank 31°43N 35°12E 130 D4
Baytik Shan China 45°15N 90°50E 109 C12
Baytown U.S.A. 29°43N 94°59W 176 G7
Bayuquan China 40°16N 122°8E 115 D12
Bayzo Niger 13°52N 4°35E 139 C5
Baza Spain 37°30N 2°47W 89 H8
Bazar Dyuzi Russia 41°12N 47°50E 87 K8
Bazardüzü = Bazar Dyuzi Russia 41°12N 47°50E 87 K8
Bāzargān Iran 39°22N 44°26E 105 C11
Bazarny Karabulak Russia 52°20N 46°29E 86 D8
Bazarnyy Syzgan Russia 53°45N 46°40E 86 D8
Bazaruto, I. do Mozam. 21°40S 35°28E 145 B6
Bazaruto △ Mozam. 21°42S 35°26E 145 B6
Bazas France 44°27N 0°13W 72 D3
Bazhong China 31°52N 106°46E 116 B6
Bazhou China 39°8N 116°22E 114 E9
Bazmān, Kūh-e Iran 28°4N 60°1E 129 D9
Baztan = Elizondo Spain 43°12N 1°30W 90 B3
Bé, Nosy Madag. 13°25S 48°15E 141 G9
Beach U.S.A. 46°58N 104°0W 172 B2
Beach City U.S.A. 40°39N 81°35W 174 F3
Beachport Australia 37°29S 140°0E 152 D4
Beachville Canada 43°5N 80°49W 174 C4
Beachy Hd. U.K. 50°44N 0°15E 67 G8
Beacon Australia 30°26S 117°52E 149 F2
Beacon U.S.A. 41°30N 73°58W 175 E11
Beaconsfield Australia 41°11S 146°48E 151 G4
Beagle, Canal S. Amer. 55°0S 68°30W 192 E3
Beagle Bay Australia 16°58S 122°40E 148 C3
Beagle Bay ☼ Australia 16°53S 122°40E 148 C3
Beagle G. Australia 12°15S 130°25E 148 B5
Béal an Átha = Ballina Ireland 54°7N 9°9W 64 B2

Béal Átha na Sluaighe =
  Ballinasloe Ireland   53°20N 8°13W 64 C3
Beals Cr. → U.S.A.   53°20N 100°51W 176 C4
Beamsville Canada   43°12N 79°28W 174 C5
Bear → Calif., U.S.A.   38°56N 121°36W 170 G5
Bear → Utah, U.S.A.   41°30N 112°8W 166 G17
Béar, C. France   42°31N 3°8E 72 E7
Bear I. Ireland   51°38N 9°50W 64 E2
Bear L. Canada   55°8N 96°0W 163 B9
Bear L. U.S.A.   41°59N 111°21W 168 F8
Bear Lake Canada   45°27N 79°35W 174 A5
Beardmore Canada   49°36N 87°57W 164 C2
Beardmore Glacier
  Antarctica   84°30S 170°0E 55 E11
Beardstown U.S.A.   40°1N 90°26W 172 E8
Bearma → India   24°20N 79°51E 125 G8
Béarn France   43°20N 0°30W 72 E3
Bearpaw Mts. U.S.A.   48°12N 109°30W 168 B9
Bearskin Lake Canada   53°58N 91°2W 164 B1
Beas → India   31°10N 74°59E 124 D6
Beas de Segura Spain   38°15N 2°53W 89 G8
Beasain Spain   43°3N 2°11W 90 B2
Beata, C. Dom. Rep.   17°40N 71°30W 183 D5
Beata, I. Dom. Rep.   17°34N 71°31W 183 C5
Beatrice U.S.A.   40°16N 96°45W 172 E5
Beatrice Zimbabwe   18°15S 30°55E 143 F3
Beatrice, C. Australia   14°20S 136°55E 150 A2
Beatton → Canada   56°15N 120°45W 162 B4
Beatton River Canada   57°26N 121°20W 162 B4
Beatty U.S.A.   36°54N 116°46W 170 J10
Beau Bassin Mauritius   20°13S 57°27E 141 d
Beaucaire France   43°48N 4°39E 73 E8
Beauce, Plaine de la
  France   48°10N 1°45E 71 D8
Beauceville Canada   46°13N 70°46W 165 C5
Beauchêne, I. Falk. Is.   52°55S 59°15W 192 D5
Beaudesert Australia   27°59S 153°0E 151 D5
Beaufort Australia   37°25S 143°25E 152 D5
Beaufort Malaysia   5°30N 115°40E 118 C5
Beaufort N.C., U.S.A.   34°43N 76°40W 177 D16
Beaufort S.C., U.S.A.   32°26N 80°40W 178 C9
Beaufort Sea Arctic   72°0N 140°0W 158 B5
Beaufort West S. Africa   32°18S 22°36E 144 D3
Beaugency France   47°47N 1°38E 71 E8
Beauharnois Canada   45°20N 73°52W 175 A11
Beaujeu France   46°10N 4°35E 71 F11
Beaujolais France   46°0N 4°22E 71 F11
Beaulieu → Canada   62°3N 113°11W 162 A6
Beaulieu-sur-Dordogne
  France   44°58N 1°50E 72 D5
Beaulieu-sur-Mer
  France   43°42N 7°20E 73 E11
Beauly U.K.   57°30N 4°28W 65 D4
Beauly → U.K.   57°29N 4°27W 65 D4
Beaumaris U.K.   53°16N 4°6W 66 D3
Beaumont Belgium   50°15N 4°14E 69 D4
Beaumont N.Z.   45°50N 169°33E 155 F4
Beaumont Calif.,
  U.S.A.   33°57N 116°59W 171 M9
Beaumont Tex., U.S.A.   30°5N 94°6W 176 F7
Beaumont-de-Lomagne
  France   43°53N 1°0E 72 E5
Beaumont-du-Périgord
  France   44°45N 0°46E 72 D4
Beaumont-le-Roger
  France   49°4N 0°47E 70 C7
Beaumont-sur-Sarthe
  France   48°13N 0°8E 70 D7
Beaune France   47°2N 4°50E 71 E11
Beaune-la-Rolande France   48°4N 2°25E 71 D9
Beaupré Canada   47°3N 70°54W 165 C5
Beaupréau France   47°12N 1°0W 70 E6
Beauraing Belgium   50°7N 4°57E 69 D4
Beaurepaire France   45°22N 5°1E 73 C9
Beausejour Canada   50°5N 96°35W 163 C9
Beauvais France   49°25N 2°8E 71 C9
Beauval Canada   55°9N 107°37W 163 B7
Beauvoir-sur-Mer France   46°55N 2°2W 70 F4
Beauvoir-sur-Niort
  France   46°12N 0°30W 72 B3
Beaver Okla., U.S.A.   36°49N 100°31W 176 C4
Beaver Pa., U.S.A.   40°42N 80°19W 174 F4
Beaver Utah, U.S.A.   38°17N 112°38W 168 G7
Beaver → B.C.,
  Canada   59°52N 124°20W 162 B4
Beaver → Ont., Canada   55°55N 87°48W 164 A2
Beaver → Sask.,
  Canada   55°26N 107°45W 163 B7
Beaver → U.S.A.   36°35N 99°30W 176 C5
Beaver City U.S.A.   40°8N 99°50W 172 E4
Beaver Creek Canada   63°0N 141°0W 160 B3
Beaver Dam U.S.A.   43°28N 88°50W 172 D9
Beaver Falls U.S.A.   40°46N 80°20W 174 F4
Beaver Hill L. Canada   54°5N 94°50W 163 C10
Beaver I. U.S.A.   45°40N 85°33W 173 C11
Beavercreek U.S.A.   39°43N 84°11W 173 F11
Beaverhill L. Canada   53°27N 112°32W 162 C6
Beaverlodge Canada   55°11N 119°29W 162 B5
Beaverton →
  Canada   54°59N 89°25W 164 B2
Beaverton Canada   44°26N 79°9W 174 B5
Beaverton U.S.A.   45°29N 122°48W 170 E4
Beawar India   26°3N 74°18E 124 F6
Bebedouro Brazil   21°0S 48°25W 191 A6
Bebera, Tanjung
  Indonesia   8°4S 115°51E 119 K18
Bebra Germany   50°59N 9°48E 78 E5
Becán Mexico   18°34N 89°31W 181 D7
Bécancour Canada   46°20N 72°26W 173 B17
Beccles U.K.   52°27N 1°35E 67 E9
Bečej Serbia   45°36N 20°3E 88 B5
Beceni Romania   45°23N 26°48E 81 E11
Becerreá Spain   42°51N 7°10W 88 C3
Béchar Algeria   31°38N 2°18W 136 B3
Béchar □ Algeria   30°15N 3°5E 136 B4
Becharof L. U.S.A.   57°56N 156°23W 166 D8
Becharre = Bsharri
  Lebanon   34°15N 36°0E 130 A5
Bechyně Czech Rep.   49°17N 14°29E 78 B7
Beckley U.S.A.   37°47N 81°11W 173 G13
Beckum Germany   51°45N 8°2E 78 D4
Beclean Romania   47°11N 24°11E 81 C9
Bečov nad Teplou
  Czech Rep.   50°5N 12°49E 78 A5
Bečva → Czech Rep.   49°31N 17°20E 79 B10
Bédar Spain   37°11N 1°59W 91 H3
Bédarieux France   43°37N 3°10E 72 E7
Beddouza, C. Morocco   32°33N 9°8E 76 B4
Bederkesa Germany   53°37N 8°50E 78 B4
Bedford Canada   45°7N 72°59W 175 A12

Bedford S. Africa   32°40S 26°10E 144 D4
Bedford U.K.   52°8N 0°28W 67 E7
Bedford Ind., U.S.A.   38°52N 86°29W 172 F10
Bedford Iowa, U.S.A.   40°40N 94°44W 172 E6
Bedford Ohio, U.S.A.   41°23N 81°32W 174 E3
Bedford Pa., U.S.A.   40°1N 78°30W 174 F6
Bedford Va., U.S.A.   37°20N 79°31W 173 G14
Bedford □ U.K.   52°4N 0°28W 67 E7
Bedford, C. Australia   15°14S 145°21E 150 A4
Bedków Poland   51°36N 19°44E 83 G6
Bednja → Croatia   46°20N 16°52E 93 B13
Bednodemyanovsk
  Russia   53°55N 43°15E 86 D6
Bedok Singapore   1°19N 103°56E 121 d
Bedónia Italy   44°30N 9°38E 92 D6
Bedourie Australia   24°30S 139°30E 150 C2
Bedti → India   14°50N 74°44E 127 G2
Bedum Neths.   53°18N 6°36E 69 A6
Bedzin Poland   50°19N 19°7E 83 H6
Bee Ridge U.S.A.   27°17N 82°29W 179 H7
Beebe Plain Canada   45°1N 72°9W 175 A12
Beech Creek U.S.A.   41°5N 77°36W 174 E7
Beechworth Australia   36°22S 146°43E 153 D7
Beechy Canada   50°53N 107°24W 163 C7
Beed = Bir India   19°4N 75°46E 126 E2
Beef I. Br. Virgin Is.   18°26N 64°30W 183 e
Beelitz Germany   52°14N 12°58E 78 C8
Beenleigh Australia   27°43S 153°10E 151 D5
Be'er Menuha Israel   30°19N 35°8E 128 D3
Be'er Sheva Israel   31°15N 34°48E 130 D3
Beersheba = Be'er Sheva
  Israel   31°15N 34°48E 130 D3
Beeskow Germany   52°10N 14°15E 78 C10
Beestekraal S. Africa   25°23S 27°38E 145 C4
Beeston U.K.   52°56N 1°14W 66 E6
Beeton Canada   44°5N 79°47W 174 B5
Beetzendorf Germany   52°42N 11°6E 78 C7
Beeville U.S.A.   28°24N 97°45W 176 G6
Befale
  Dem. Rep. of the Congo   0°25N 20°45E 140 D4
Bega Australia   36°41S 149°51E 153 D8
Bega, Canalul Romania   45°37N 20°46E 80 E5
Bégard France   48°38N 3°18W 70 D3
Beğendik Turkey   40°55N 26°34E 97 F10
Begoro Ghana   6°23N 0°23E 139 D4
Begusarai India   25°24N 86°9E 125 G12
Behābād Iran   32°24N 59°47E 129 C8
Behala India   22°30N 88°18E 125 H13
Behbehān Iran   30°30N 50°15E 129 D6
Behm Canal U.S.A.   55°10N 131°0W 162 B2
Behshahr Iran   36°45N 53°35E 129 B7
Bei Jiang → China   23°2N 112°58E 117 F9
Bei Shan China   41°30N 96°0E 110 C8
Bei'an China   48°10N 126°20E 111 B14
Beibei China   29°47N 106°22E 116 C6
Beichuan China   31°55N 104°39E 116 B5
Beihai China   21°28N 109°6E 116 G7
Beijing China   39°53N 116°21E 114 C9
Beijing □ China   39°55N 116°20E 114 C9
Beilen Neths.   52°52N 6°27E 69 B6
Beiliu China   22°41N 110°21E 117 F8
Beilngries Germany   49°2N 11°28E 77 F7
Beilpajah Australia   32°54S 143°52E 152 B5
Beinn na Faoghla = Benbecula
  U.K.   57°26N 7°21W 65 D1
Beipan Jiang → China   24°55N 106°5E 116 E6
Beipiao China   41°52N 120°32E 115 D11
Beira Mozam.   19°50S 34°52E 143 F3
Beirut = Bayrūt
  Lebanon   33°53N 35°31E 130 B4
Beiseker Canada   51°23N 113°32W 162 C6
Beit Lekhem = Bayt Lahm
  West Bank   31°43N 35°12E 130 D4
Beitaolaizhao China   44°58N 125°58E 115 B13
Beitbridge Zimbabwe   22°12S 30°0E 143 G3
Beiuș Romania   46°40N 22°21E 80 D7
Beizhen = Binzhou
  China   37°20N 118°2E 115 F10
Beizhen China   41°38N 121°54E 115 D11
Beizhengzhen China   44°31N 123°30E 115 B12
Beja Portugal   38°2N 7°53W 89 G3
Béja Tunisia   36°43N 9°12E 136 A5
Beja □ Portugal   37°55N 7°55W 89 H3
Béja □ Tunisia   36°40N 9°29E 136 A5
Bejaïa Algeria   36°42N 5°2E 136 A5
Bejaïa □ Algeria   36°40N 4°55E 136 A4
Béjar Spain   40°23N 5°46W 88 B5
Bejestān Iran   34°30N 58°5E 129 C8
Bekaa Valley = Al Biqā
  Lebanon   34°10N 36°10E 130 A5
Bekasi Indonesia   6°14S 106°59E 119 G12
Bekçiler Turkey   36°56N 29°44E 99 E11
Bekdash Turkmenistan   41°34N 52°32E 108 D4
Békés Hungary   46°47N 21°9E 80 D6
Békés □ Hungary   46°45N 21°0E 80 D6
Békéscsaba Hungary   46°40N 21°5E 80 D6
Bekili Turkey   38°17N 29°27E 99 C11
Bekok Malaysia   2°20N 103°7E 121 L4
Bekwai Ghana   6°30N 1°34W 139 D4
Bela India   25°50N 82°0E 125 G10
Bela Pakistan   26°12N 66°20E 124 F2
Bela Bela S. Africa   24°51S 28°19E 145 B4
Bela Crkva Serbia   44°55N 21°27E 80 F6
Bela Palanka Serbia   43°13N 22°17E 96 C6
Bela Vista Brazil   22°12S 56°20W 190 A4
Bela Vista Mozam.   26°10S 32°44E 145 C5
Bélábre France   46°34N 1°8E 72 B5
Belalcázar Spain   38°35N 5°10W 89 G5
Belan → India   24°2N 81°45E 125 G9
Belanovica Serbia   44°15N 20°33E 80 E5
Belarus ■ Europe   53°30N 27°0E 75 D14
Belau = Palau ■ Palau   7°30N 134°30E 156 G5
Belawan Indonesia   3°33N 98°32E 118 D1
Belaya → Russia   54°40N 56°0E 108 B5
Belaya Glina Russia   46°5N 40°48E 87 G5
Belaya Kalitva Russia   48°13N 40°50E 87 F5
Belaya Tserkov = Bila Tserkva
  Ukraine   49°45N 30°10E 75 D16
Belaya Zemlya, Ostrova
  Russia   81°36N 62°18E 106 A7
Belcești Romania   47°19N 27°7E 81 C12
Belchatów Poland   51°21N 19°22E 83 H6
Belcher Is. Canada   56°15N 78°45W 164 A3
Belchite Spain   41°18N 0°43W 90 B6
Belden U.S.A.   40°2N 121°17W 170 E5
Belebey Russia   54°7N 54°7E 86 D9
Beledweyne Somalia   4°30N 45°5E 131 G4
Belém Brazil   1°20S 48°30W 187 D9

Belém de São Francisco
  Brazil   8°46S 38°58W 189 D3
Belén Argentina   27°40S 67°5W 190 B2
Belén Paraguay   23°30S 57°6W 190 A4
Belen Turkey   36°31N 36°10E 130 C4
Belen U.S.A.   34°40N 106°46W 169 J10
Belene Bulgaria   43°39N 25°10E 97 C11
Bélesta France   42°55N 1°56E 72 F5
Belet Uen = Beledweyne
  Somalia   4°30N 45°5E 131 G4
Belev Russia   53°50N 36°5E 84 F9
Belevi Turkey   38°0N 27°28E 99 C9
Belfair U.S.A.   47°27N 122°50W 170 C4
Belfast = eMakhazeni
  S. Africa   25°42S 30°2E 145 C5
Belfast N.Z.   43°27S 172°39E 155 D7
Belfast U.K.   54°37N 5°56W 64 B6
Belfast Maine, U.S.A.   44°26N 69°1W 173 C19
Belfast N.Y., U.S.A.   42°21N 78°7W 174 D6
Belfast L. U.K.   54°40N 5°50W 64 B6
Belfield U.S.A.   46°53N 103°12W 172 B2
Belford France   47°38N 6°50E 71 E13
Belfort, Territoire de □
  France   47°40N 6°55E 71 E13
Belfry U.S.A.   45°9N 109°1W 168 D9
Belgaum India   15°55N 74°35E 127 G2
Belgavi = Belgaum
  India   15°55N 74°35E 127 G2
Belgioioso Italy   45°10N 9°19E 92 C6
Belgium ■ Europe   50°30N 5°0E 69 D4
Belgodère France   42°35N 9°1E 73 F13
Belgorod Russia   50°35N 36°35E 85 G9
Belgorod □ Russia   50°45N 36°45E 85 G9
Belgorod-Dnestrovskiy =
  Bilhorod-Dnistrovskyy
  Ukraine   46°11N 30°23E 85 J6
Belgrade = Beograd
  Serbia   44°50N 20°37E 96 B4
Belgrade U.S.A.   45°47N 111°11W 168 D8
Belgrano Antarctica   77°52S 34°37W 55 D1
Belhaven U.S.A.   35°33N 76°37W 177 D16
Béli Guinea-Biss.   11°51N 13°55W 138 C2
Beli Nigeria   7°52N 10°55E 139 D7
Beli Manastir Croatia   45°45N 18°36E 80 E3
Beli Timok → Serbia   43°53N 22°14E 96 C6
Bélice → Italy   37°35N 12°55E 94 E5
Belimbing Indonesia   8°24S 115°2E 119 J18
Belinskiy Russia   53°0N 43°25E 86 D6
Belinyu Indonesia   1°35S 105°50E 118 E3
Beliton Is. = Belitung
  Indonesia   3°10S 107°50E 118 E3
Belitung Indonesia   3°10S 107°50E 118 E3
Beliu Romania   46°30N 22°0E 80 D6
Belize ■ Cent. Amer.   17°0N 88°30W 181 D7
Belize Barrier Reef Belize   17°9N 88°3W 181 D7
Belize City Belize   17°25N 88°10W 181 D7
Beljakovci Macedonia   42°6N 21°59E 96 D5
Beljanica Serbia   44°8N 21°43E 96 B5
Belkovskiy, Ostrov
  Russia   75°32N 135°44E 107 B14
Bell → Canada   49°48N 77°38W 164 C4
Bell L. Canada   50°46N 55°35W 165 B8
Bell-Irving → Canada   56°12N 129°5W 162 B3
Bell Peninsula Canada   63°50N 82°0W 161 E15
Bell Ville Argentina   32°40S 62°40W 190 C3
Bella Italy   40°45N 15°32E 95 B8
Bella Bella Canada   52°10N 128°10W 162 C3
Bella Coola Canada   52°25N 126°40W 162 C3
Bella Flor Bolivia   11°9S 67°49W 188 C4
Bella Unión Uruguay   30°15S 57°40W 190 C4
Bella Vista Corrientes,
  Argentina   28°33S 59°0W 190 B4
Bella Vista Tucuman,
  Argentina   27°10S 65°25W 190 B2
Bellac France   46°7N 1°3E 72 B5
Bellágio Italy   45°59N 9°15E 92 C6
Bellaire U.S.A.   40°1N 80°45W 174 F4
Bellária Italy   44°9N 12°28E 93 D9
Bellary India   15°10N 76°56E 127 G3
Bellata Australia   29°53S 149°46E 151 D4
Belle Fourche →
  U.S.A.   44°26N 102°18W 172 C2
Belle Glade U.S.A.   26°41N 80°40W 179 J9
Belle-Île France   47°20N 3°10W 70 E3
Belle Isle Canada   51°57N 55°25W 165 B8
Belle Isle, Str. of
  Canada   51°30N 56°30W 165 B8
Belle Plaine U.S.A.   41°54N 92°17W 172 E7
Belle River Canada   42°18N 82°43W 174 D2
Belle Yella Liberia   7°24N 10°0W 138 D3
Belledonne France   45°20N 6°10E 73 C10
Bellefontaine U.S.A.   40°22N 83°46W 173 E12
Bellefonte U.S.A.   40°55N 77°47W 174 F7
Bellegarde France   46°7N 4°45E 71 F11
Bellegarde-en-Marche
  France   45°59N 2°18E 72 C6
Bellegarde-sur-Valserine
  France   46°4N 5°50E 71 F12
Bellême France   48°22N 0°34E 70 D7
Belleoram Canada   47°31N 55°25W 165 C8
Belleplaine Barbados   13°15N 59°34W 183 g
Belleview U.S.A.   29°4N 82°3W 179 F7
Belleville Canada   44°10N 77°23W 174 B7
Belleville France   46°7N 4°45E 71 F11
Belleville Ill., U.S.A.   38°31N 89°59W 172 F9
Belleville Kans., U.S.A.   39°50N 97°38W 172 F5
Belleville N.Y., U.S.A.   43°46N 76°10W 175 C9
Belleville-sur-Vie France   46°51N 1°26W 70 F4
Bellevue Canada   49°35N 114°22W 162 D6
Bellevue Idaho, U.S.A.   43°28N 114°16W 168 E6
Bellevue Nebr., U.S.A.   41°9N 95°54W 172 E6
Bellevue Ohio, U.S.A.   41°17N 82°51W 174 E2
Bellevue Wash.   47°37N 122°12W 170 C4
Belley France   45°46N 5°41E 73 C9
Bellin = Kangirsuk
  Canada   60°0N 70°0W 161 F18
Bellinge Denmark   55°16N 10°20E 63 J4
Bellingen Australia   30°25S 152°50E 153 A10
Bellingham U.S.A.   48°46N 122°29W 170 B4
Bellingshausen Abyssal Plain
  S. Ocean   65°0S 90°0W 55 C16
Bellingshausen Sea
  Antarctica   66°0S 80°0W 55 C17

Bello Colombia   6°20N 75°33W 186 B3
Bellows Falls U.S.A.   43°8N 72°27W 175 C12
Bellpat Pakistan   29°0N 68°5E 124 E3
Bellpuig Spain   41°37N 1°1E 90 D6
Belluno Italy   46°9N 12°13E 93 B9
Bellville U.S.A.   32°9N 81°59W 178 C8
Bellwood U.S.A.   40°36N 78°20W 174 F6
Bélmez Spain   38°17N 5°17W 89 G5
Belmont Australia   33°4S 151°42E 153 B9
Belmont Canada   42°53N 81°5W 174 D3
Belmont S. Africa   29°28S 24°22E 144 C3
Belmont U.S.A.   42°14N 78°2W 174 D6
Belmonte Brazil   16°0S 39°0W 189 D3
Belmonte Portugal   40°21N 7°20W 88 B3
Belmopan Belize   17°18N 88°30W 181 D7
Belmullet Ireland   54°14N 9°58W 64 B2
Belo Horizonte Brazil   19°55S 43°56W 189 D2
Belo Jardim Brazil   8°20S 36°26W 189 D3
Belo-Tsiribihina Madag.   19°40S 44°30E 141 H8
Belogorsk = Bilohirsk
  Ukraine   45°3N 34°35E 85 K8
Belogorsk Russia   51°0N 128°20E 107 D13
Belogradchik Bulgaria   43°53N 22°42E 96 C6
Belogradets Bulgaria   43°22N 27°18E 97 C11
Beloit Kans., U.S.A.   39°28N 98°6W 172 F4
Beloit Wis., U.S.A.   42°31N 89°2W 172 D9
Belokorovichi Ukraine   51°7N 28°2E 75 C15
Belomorsk Russia   64°35N 34°54E 106 C4
Belonia India   23°15N 91°30E 123 H17
Belopolye = Bilopillya
  Ukraine   51°14N 34°20E 85 G8
Belorechensk Russia   44°46N 39°52E 87 H4
Beloretsk Russia   53°58N 58°24E 108 B5
Belorussia = Belarus ■
  Europe   53°30N 27°0E 75 B14
Beloslav Bulgaria   43°11N 27°42E 97 C11
Belousovka Kazakhstan   50°8N 82°31E 109 B10
Belovezhskaya Pushcha =
  Białowieski □ Poland   52°43N 23°50E 83 F10
Belovo Bulgaria   42°13N 24°1E 97 D8
Belovo Russia   54°30N 86°0E 109 B11
Beloyarskiy Russia   63°42N 66°40E 106 C7
Beloye, Ozero Russia   60°10N 37°35E 84 B9
Beloye More Russia   66°30N 38°0E 58 B13
Belozem Bulgaria   42°12N 25°2E 97 D9
Belozersk Russia   60°1N 37°45E 84 B9
Belpasso Italy   37°35N 14°58E 95 E7
Belpre U.S.A.   39°17N 81°34W 173 F13
Belrain India   28°23N 80°55E 125 E9
Belt U.S.A.   47°23N 110°55W 168 C8
Beltana Australia   30°48S 138°25E 152 A3
Belterra Brazil   2°45S 55°0W 187 D8
Beltinci Slovenia   46°37N 16°20E 93 B13
Belton U.S.A.   31°3N 97°28W 176 F6
Belton L. U.S.A.   31°6N 97°28W 176 F6
Beltsy = Bălți Moldova   47°48N 27°58E 81 C12
Belturbet Ireland   54°6N 7°26W 64 B4
Belukha Russia   49°50N 86°50E 109 C11
Beluran Malaysia   5°48N 117°35E 118 C5
Beluša Slovak Rep.   49°5N 18°17E 79 B11
Belušić Serbia   43°50N 21°10E 96 C5
Belvedere Maríttimo
  Italy   39°37N 15°52E 95 C8
Belvedere France   44°46N 1°0E 72 D5
Belvidere N.J., U.S.A.   40°50N 75°5W 175 F9
Belvís de la Jara Spain   39°45N 4°57W 88 F6
Belyando → Australia   21°38S 146°50E 150 C4
Belyando Crossing
  Australia   21°32S 146°51E 150 C4
Belyuen Australia   12°34S 130°42E 148 B5
Belyy Russia   55°49N 33°3E 84 C7
Belyy, Ostrov Russia   73°30N 71°0E 106 B8
Belyy Yar Russia   58°26N 84°39E 106 D9
Belyye Vody = Aqsū
  Kazakhstan   42°25N 69°50E 109 D7
Belz Ukraine   50°23N 23°26E 83 H11
Belz Poland   50°23N 23°26E 83 H11
Belżyce Poland   51°11N 22°17E 83 G9
Belzoni U.S.A.   33°11N 90°29W 177 E9
Bemaraha △ Madag.   18°40S 44°45E 141 H8
Bembéréke Benin   10°11N 2°43E 139 C6
Bembesi Zimbabwe   20°0S 28°58E 143 G2
Bembesi → Zimbabwe   18°57S 27°47E 143 F2
Bembézar → Spain   37°45N 5°13W 89 H5
Bembibre Spain   42°37N 6°25W 88 C4
Bemboka △ Australia   36°35S 149°41E 153 D8
Bemetara India   21°42N 81°32E 125 J9
Bemidji U.S.A.   47°28N 94°53W 172 B6
Ben Iran   32°32N 50°45E 129 C6
Ben Boyd △ Australia   37°0S 149°55E 153 D8
Ben Cruachan U.K.   56°26N 5°8W 65 E3
Ben Dearg U.K.   57°47N 4°56W 65 D4
Ben En △ Vietnam   19°37N 105°30E 120 C5
Ben Gardane Tunisia   33°11N 11°11E 136 B6
Ben Halls Gap △
  Australia   31°37S 151°1E 153 A9
Ben Hope U.K.   58°25N 4°36W 65 C4
Ben Lawers U.K.   56°32N 4°14W 65 E4
Ben Lomond N.S.W.,
  Australia   30°1S 151°43E 151 E5
Ben Lomond Tas.,
  Australia   41°38S 147°42E 151 G4
Ben Lomond U.K.   56°11N 4°38W 65 E4
Ben Lomond △
  Australia   41°33S 147°42E 151 G4
Ben Luc Vietnam   10°39N 106°29E 121 G6
Ben Macdhui U.K.   57°4N 3°40W 65 D5
Ben Mhor U.K.   57°15N 7°18W 65 D1
Ben More Argyll & Bute,
  U.K.   56°26N 6°1W 65 E2
Ben More Stirling, U.K.   56°23N 4°32W 65 E4
Ben More Assynt U.K.   58°8N 4°52W 65 C4
Ben Nevis U.K.   56°48N 5°1W 65 E3
Ben Ohau Ra. N.Z.   44°1S 170°4E 155 D5
Ben Quang Vietnam   17°3N 106°55E 120 D6
Ben Slimane Morocco   33°38N 7°7W 136 B3
Ben Tadjine, Djebel
  Algeria   29°0N 3°30W 136 C3
Ben Tre Vietnam   10°14N 106°23E 121 G6
Ben Vorlich U.K.   56°21N 4°14W 65 E4
Ben Wyvis U.K.   57°40N 4°35W 65 D4
Bena Nigeria   11°20N 5°50E 139 C6
Benaco, L. di = Garda, L. di
  Italy   45°40N 10°41E 92 C7
Benagerie Australia   31°25S 140°22E 152 A4
Benahmed Morocco   33°4N 7°9W 136 B3
Benalla Australia   36°30S 146°0E 153 D7
Benalmádena Spain   36°36N 4°34W 89 J6

Benambra, Mt.
  Australia   36°31S 147°34E 153 D7
Benanee Australia   34°31S 142°52E 152 C5
Benares = Varanasi
  India   25°22N 83°0E 125 G10
Bénat, C. France   43°5N 6°22E 73 E10
Benavente Portugal   38°59N 8°49W 89 G2
Benavente Spain   42°2N 5°43W 88 C5
Benavides de Órbigo
  Spain   42°30N 5°54W 88 C5
Benavides U.S.A.   27°36N 98°25W 176 H5
Benbecula U.K.   57°26N 7°21W 65 D1
Benbonyathe Hill
  Australia   30°25S 139°11E 152 A3
Bend U.S.A.   44°4N 121°19W 168 D3
Bendemeer Australia   30°53S 151°8E 153 A9
Bender Beyla Somalia   9°30N 50°48E 131 F5
Bendery = Tighina
  Moldova   46°50N 29°30E 81 E16
Bendigo Australia   36°40S 144°15E 152 D6
Bendorf Germany   50°25N 7°35E 76 E3
Benē Beraq Israel   32°6N 34°51E 130 C3
Benedito Leite Brazil   7°13S 44°34W 189 D2
Bénéna Mali   13°9N 4°17W 138 C4
Benešov Czech Rep.   49°46N 14°41E 78 B7
Benevento Italy   41°8N 14°45E 95 A7
Benfeld France   48°22N 7°34E 71 D14
Beng Mealea
  Cambodia   13°28N 104°14E 120 F5
Benga Mozam.   16°11S 33°40E 143 F3
Bengal, Bay of Ind. Oc.   15°0N 90°0E 123 M17
Bengaluru = Bangalore
  India   12°59N 77°40E 127 H3
Bengbis Cameroon   3°27N 12°36E 139 E7
Bengbu China   32°58N 117°20E 117 A11
Benghazi = Banghāzī
  Libya   32°11N 20°3E 135 B10
Bengkalis Indonesia   1°30N 102°10E 121 M4
Bengkulu Indonesia   3°50S 102°12E 118 E2
Bengkulu □ Indonesia   3°48S 102°16E 118 E2
Bengough Canada   49°25N 105°10W 163 D7
Bengtsfors Sweden   59°2N 12°14E 62 E6
Benguela Angola   12°37S 13°25E 141 G2
Benguerir Morocco   32°16N 7°56W 136 B3
Benguérua, I. Mozam.   21°58S 35°28E 145 B6
Benha Egypt   30°26N 31°8E 137 E7
Beni
  Dem. Rep. of the Congo   0°30N 29°27E 142 B2
Beni → Bolivia   10°23S 65°24W 186 F5
Beni Abbès Algeria   30°5N 2°5W 136 B3
Beni Hammad Algeria   35°49N 4°47E 136 A4
Beni Haoua Algeria   36°30N 1°30E 136 A4
Beni Mazâr Egypt   28°32N 30°44E 137 C7
Beni Mellal Morocco   32°21N 6°21W 136 B3
Beni Ounif Algeria   32°0N 1°10W 136 B3
Beni Saf Algeria   35°17N 1°15W 136 A3
Beni Suef Egypt   29°5N 31°6E 137 C7
Beniah L. Canada   63°23N 112°17W 162 A6
Benicarló Spain   40°23N 0°23E 90 E5
Benicássim Spain   40°3N 0°9E 90 E5
Benidorm Spain   38°33N 0°9W 91 G4
Benin ■ Africa   10°0N 2°0E 139 C5
Benin → Nigeria   5°55N 5°4E 139 D6
Benin, Bight of W. Afr.   5°0N 3°0E 139 E5
Benin City Nigeria   6°20N 5°31E 139 D6
Benito Juárez Argentina   37°40S 59°43W 190 D4
Benjamin Aceval
  Paraguay   24°58S 57°34W 190 A4
Benjamin Constant
  Brazil   4°40S 70°15W 186 D4
Benjamin Hill Mexico   30°9N 111°7W 180 A2
Benkelman U.S.A.   40°3N 101°32W 172 E3
Benkovac Croatia   44°2N 15°37E 93 D12
Benmore Pk. N.Z.   44°25S 170°8E 155 E5
Bennett Canada   59°51N 135°0W 162 B2
Bennett, L. Australia   22°50S 131°2E 148 D5
Bennetta, Ostrov
  Russia   76°21N 148°56E 107 B15
Bennettsville U.S.A.   34°37N 79°41W 177 D15
Bennichâb
  Mauritania   19°32N 15°12W 138 B1
Bennington N.H.,
  U.S.A.   43°0N 71°55W 175 C11
Bennington Vt.,
  U.S.A.   42°53N 73°12W 175 D11
Bénodet France   47°53N 4°7W 70 E2
Benom Malaysia   3°50N 102°6E 121 L4
Benoni S. Africa   26°11S 28°18E 145 C4
Benoud Algeria   32°20N 0°16E 136 B4
Benque Viejo del Carmen
  Belize   17°5N 89°8W 181 D7
Bensheim Germany   49°40N 8°38E 77 F4
Benson Ariz., U.S.A.   31°58N 110°18W 169 L8
Benson Minn., U.S.A.   45°19N 95°36W 172 C6
Bent Iran   26°20N 59°31E 129 E8
Benteng Indonesia   6°10S 120°30E 119 F6
Bentinck I. Australia   17°3S 139°35E 150 B2
Bentinck I. Burma   11°45N 98°3E 121 G2
Bentley Subglacial Trench
  Antarctica   80°0S 115°0W 55 E15
Bento Gonçalves Brazil   29°10S 51°31W 191 B5
Benton Ark., U.S.A.   34°34N 92°35W 176 D8
Benton Calif., U.S.A.   37°48N 118°32W 170 H8
Benton Ill., U.S.A.   38°0N 88°55W 172 F9
Benton La., U.S.A.   32°42N 93°44W 176 E7
Benton Harbor U.S.A.   42°6N 86°27W 172 D10
Bentong Malaysia   3°31N 101°55E 121 L3
Bentonville U.S.A.   36°22N 94°13W 176 C7
Benue □ Nigeria   7°20N 8°45E 139 D6
Benue → Nigeria   7°48N 6°46E 139 D6
Benxi China   41°20N 123°48E 115 D12
Beo Indonesia   4°25N 126°50E 119 D7
Beograd Serbia   44°50N 20°37E 96 B4
Beograd ✈ (BEG) Serbia   44°50N 20°17E 96 B4
Beoumi Ivory C.   7°45N 5°23W 138 D3
Beppu Japan   33°15N 131°30E 113 H5
Beqa Fiji   18°23S 178°8E 154 a
Beqaa Valley = Al Biqā
  Lebanon   34°10N 36°10E 130 A5
Ber Mota India   23°27N 68°34E 124 H3
Berach → India   25°15N 75°2E 124 G6
Berane Montenegro   42°51N 19°52E 96 D3
Berat Albania   40°43N 19°59E 96 E2
Berau → Tanjungredeb
  Indonesia   2°9N 117°29E 118 C5

Berau, Teluk Indonesia   2°30S 132°30E 1
Berber Sudan   18°0N 34°0E 1
Berbera Somalia   10°30N 45°2E 1
Berbérati C.A.R.   4°15N 15°40E 1
Berbice → Guyana   6°20N 57°32W 1
Berceto Italy   44°31N 9°51E
Berchida Italy   40°47N 9°10E
Berchtesgaden Germany   47°38N 13°0E
Berchtesgaden △
  Germany   47°34N 12°55E
Berck France   50°25N 1°36E
Berdichev = Berdychiv
  Ukraine   49°57N 28°30E 1
Berdsk Russia   54°47N 83°2E 10
Berdyansk Ukraine   46°45N 36°50E 8
Berdychiv Ukraine   49°57N 28°30E 8
Berea U.S.A.   37°34N 84°17W 17
Berebere Somalia   2°25N 128°45E 1
Bereeda Somalia   11°45N 51°0E 1
Berehomet Ukraine   48°10N 25°19E 8
Berehove Ukraine   48°15N 22°35E 8
Bereket Turkmenistan   39°16N 55°32E 1
Berekum Ghana   7°29N 2°34W 1
Berenice Egypt   24°2N 35°25E 1
Berens → Canada   52°25N 97°2W 1
Berens I. Canada   52°18N 97°18W 1
Berens River Canada   52°25N 97°0W 1
Beresford Australia   32°50S 151°40E 1
Beresford U.S.A.   43°5N 96°47W 1
Berestechko Ukraine   50°22N 25°5E 8
Berești Romania   46°6N 27°50E 8
Beretău → Romania   47°10N 21°50E 8
Berettyó → Hungary   46°59N 21°7E
Berettyóújfalu Hungary   47°13N 21°33E
Bereza = Byaroza
  Belarus   52°31N 24°51E 8
Berezhany Ukraine   49°26N 24°58E 8
Berezina = Byarezina →
  Belarus   52°33N 30°14E 7
Berezivka Ukraine   47°14N 30°55E 8
Berezna Ukraine   51°35N 31°46E
Bereznik Russia   62°51N 42°40E 1
Berezniki Russia   59°24N 56°46E 1
Berezovka Russia   64°0N 65°0E 1
Berezyne Ukraine   46°14N 29°12E 8
Berga Spain   42°6N 1°48E
Berga Sweden   57°14N 16°3E
Bergama Turkey   39°8N 27°11E
Bérgamo Italy   45°41N 9°43E
Bergaon India   20°41N 80°27E 1
Bergara Spain   43°6N 2°24W
Bergby Sweden   60°57N 17°2E
Berge Norway   59°34N 8°10E
Bergedorf Germany   53°28N 10°6E
Bergeforsen Sweden   62°32N 17°23E
Bergen Mecklenburg-Vorpommern,
  Germany   54°25N 13°25E
Bergen Niedersachsen,
  Germany   52°49N 9°57E
Bergen Neths.   52°40N 4°43E
Bergen Norway   60°20N 5°20E
Bergen op Zoom Neths.   51°28N 4°18E
Bergerac France   44°51N 0°30E
Bergheim Germany   50°57N 6°38E
Bergholz U.S.A.   40°31N 80°53W 1
Bergisch Gladbach
  Germany   50°59N 7°8E
Bergisches Land ○
  Germany   51°0N 7°30E
Bergkamen Germany   51°37N 7°38E
Bergkvara Sweden   56°23N 16°5E
Bergshamra Sweden   59°38N 18°37E
Bergsjö Sweden   61°59N 17°3E
Bergstrasse-Odenwald ○
  Germany   49°45N 5°55E
Bergues France   50°58N 2°24E
Bergviken Sweden   61°15N 16°40E
Bergville S. Africa   28°52S 29°18E 1
Berhala, Selat Indonesia   1°0S 104°15E 1
Berhampore = Baharampur
  India   24°2N 88°27E 1
Berhampur = Brahmapur
  India   19°15N 84°54E 1
Berheci → Romania   45°58N 27°28E 8
Bering Glacier
  U.S.A.   60°20N 143°30W 1
Bering Sea Pac. Oc.   58°0N 171°0W 1
Bering Strait Pac. Oc.   65°30N 169°0W 1
Beringovskiy Russia   63°3N 179°19E 10
Berisso Argentina   34°56S 57°50W 1
Berja Spain   36°50N 2°56W
Berkane Morocco   34°52N 2°20W
Berkeley U.S.A.   37°51N 122°16W 1
Berkner I. Antarctica   79°30S 50°0W 5
Berkovitsa Bulgaria   43°16N 23°8E
Berkshire U.S.A.   42°19N 76°11W 1
Berkshire Downs U.K.   51°33N 1°29W
Berlanga Spain   38°17N 5°50W
Berlanga, I. Portugal   39°25N 9°30W
Berlanga de Duero Spain   41°28N 2°50W
Berlin Germany   52°31N 13°23E 7
Berlin Ga., U.S.A.   31°4N 83°37W 1
Berlin Md., U.S.A.   38°20N 75°13W 1
Berlin N.H., U.S.A.   44°28N 71°11W 1
Berlin N.Y., U.S.A.   42°42N 73°23W 1
Berlin Wis., U.S.A.   43°58N 88°57W 1
Berlin □ Germany   52°31N 13°23E 7
Berlin, L. U.S.A.   41°3N 81°0W 1
Bermagui Australia   36°25S 150°4E 1
Bermejo → Formosa,
  Argentina   26°51S 58°23W 1
Bermejo → San Juan,
  Argentina   32°30S 67°30W 1
Bermejo, Paso = Uspallata, P. de
  Argentina   32°37S 69°22W 1
Bermeo, L. Canada   53°35N 68°55W 1
Bermeo Spain   43°25N 2°47W
Bermillo de Sayago Spain   41°22N 6°8W
Bermuda ☑ Atl. Oc.   32°18N 64°45W 1
Bermuda Rise Atl. Oc.   32°30N 65°0W
Bern Switz.   46°57N 7°28E 7
Bern □ Switz.   46°45N 7°40E
Bernalda Italy   40°24N 16°44E
Bernalillo U.S.A.   35°18N 106°33W 1
Bernardo de Irigoyen
  Argentina   26°15S 53°40W 1
Bernardo O'Higgins △
  Chile   48°50S 75°36W 1
Bernardsville U.S.A.   40°43N 74°34W 1
Bernasconi Argentina   37°55S 63°44W 1

au Bayern, Germany 47°47N 12°22E 77 H8
au Brandenburg,
rmany 52°40N 13°35E 76 C9
ay France 49°5N 0°35E 70 C7
burg Germany 51°47N 11°44E 76 D7
dorf Austria 47°59N 16°1E 78 D9
e = Bern Switz. 46°57N 7°28E 77 J3
e = Bern □ Switz. 46°45N 7°40E 77 J3
er Alpen Switz. 46°27N 7°35E 77 J3
eray U.K. 57°43N 7°11W 65 D1
ier I. Australia 24°50S 113°12E 149 D1
ina, Piz Switz. 46°20N 9°54E 77 J5
kastel-Kues Germany 49°55N 7°3E 77 F3
ubouay Benin 10°34N 2°46E 139 C5
un Czech Rep. 49°57N 14°5E 78 B7
unka → Czech Rep. 50°0N 14°22E 78 B7
vo Macedonia 41°38N 22°51E 96 E6
, Étang de France 43°27N 5°5E 73 E9
-l'Étang France 43°27N 5°10E 73 E9
chid Morocco 33°18N 7°36W 136 B2
Australia 34°14S 140°35E 152 C4
ane Algeria 32°50N 3°46E 136 B4
dale Australia 36°22S 148°48E 153 D8
gan Australia 35°38S 145°49E 153 C6
willock Australia 35°36S 142°59E 152 C5
uaghia Algeria 36°10N 2°53E 136 A4
Australia 34°46S 150°43E 153 C9
France 46°50N 2°0E 71 F8
Is. Bahamas 25°40N 77°50W 182 A4
dale U.S.A. 30°53N 87°3W 179 E2
essa, L. U.S.A. 38°31N 122°6W 170 G4
ville U.S.A. 36°22N 93°34W 176 C8
ba Namibia 26°0S 17°46E 144 C2
nbrück Germany 52°34N 7°56E 76 C3
nad Ukraine 48°22N 29°31E 81 B14
mirans Spain 42°54N 8°38W 88 C2
hold U.S.A. 48°19N 101°44W 172 A3
oud U.S.A. 40°19N 105°5W 168 F11
ncourt France 50°5N 2°58E 71 B9
linia Brazil 7°38S 43°57W 189 B2
ua Cameroon 4°30N 13°45E 140 D2
aghboy B. Ireland 53°22N 9°54W 64 C2
i Uzbekistan 41°41N 60°45E 108 D6
i Sri Lanka 6°30N 80°0E 127 L4
ick U.S.A. 41°3N 76°14W 175 E8
ick-upon-Tweed
. 55°46N 2°0W 66 B6
yn Mts. U.K. 52°54N 3°26W 66 E4
slav Ukraine 46°50N 33°30E 85 J7
sa Romania 44°39N 21°58E 80 F6
ence Hungary 46°12N 17°11E 80 D2
Pakistan 35°4N 73°56E 125 B5
ampy Madag. 16°43S 44°29E 141 H8
nçon France 47°15N 6°2E 71 E13
Indonesia 2°40S 116°0E 118 E5
enkovichi Belarus 55°2N 29°29E 84 E5
në Kosovo 42°54N 21°10E 96 D5
a Serbia 45°8N 20°6E 80 E5
n Russia 43°15N 44°28E 87 J7
a Kobila Serbia 42°31N 22°10E 96 D6
ard L. Canada 55°25N 106°0W 163 B7
Turkey 37°41N 37°52E 104 D7
r, N. → Egypt 31°28N 34°22E 130 D3
rabiya Moldova 47°0N 28°10E 75 E15
rabka = Basarabeasca
oldova 46°21N 28°58E 81 D13
ges France 44°18N 4°8E 73 D8
mer Ala., U.S.A. 33°24N 86°58W 177 E11
mer Mich., U.S.A. 46°29N 90°3W 172 B8
mer Pa., U.S.A. 40°59N 80°30W 174 F4
n France 49°18N 1°0W 70 C6
nes-sur-Gartempe
ance 46°6N 1°22E 72 B5
ick Australia 14°34S 132°53E 148 B5
ick ✪ Australia 14°31S 132°51E 148 B5
he'an Israel 32°30N 35°30E 130 C4
hemesh Israel 31°44N 35°0E 130 D4
ncuria Canary Is. 28°25N 14°3W 100 F5
nzos Spain 43°15N 8°12W 88 B2
é Oya Cameroon 5°40N 14°5E 140 C2
a Spain 39°35N 0°28W 91 F4
ou Benin 9°12N 2°16E 139 D5
l S. Africa 26°27S 29°28E 145 C4
anien Namibia 26°31S 17°8E 144 C2
any Canada 44°11N 78°34W 174 B6
any Mo., U.S.A. 40°16N 94°2W 172 E6
any Okla., U.S.A. 35°31N 97°38W 176 D6
el Alaska, U.S.A. 60°48N 161°45W 166 C7
el Conn., U.S.A. 41°22N 73°25W 175 E11
el Maine, U.S.A. 44°25N 70°47W 175 B14
el Vt., U.S.A. 43°50N 72°38W 175 C12
el Park U.S.A. 40°19N 80°2W 174 F4
enville France 49°18N 4°23E 71 C11
er = Bayt Lahm
st Bank 31°43N 35°12E 130 D4
ehem S. Africa 28°14S 28°18E 145 C4
ehem U.S.A. 40°37N 75°23W 175 F9
ulie S. Africa 30°30S 25°59E 144 D4
une France 50°30N 2°38E 71 B9
une → France 49°53N 1°9E 70 C8
ngra Australia 34°45S 147°51E 153 C7
Brazil 19°58S 44°13W 189 D2
ky Madag. 23°48S 44°20E 141 J8
ng Malaysia 1°24N 111°31E 118 D4
ng Thailand 5°45N 101°5E 121 K3
ota Australia 25°45S 140°42E 150 D3
aqdala Kazakhstan 45°45N 70°30E 109 C8
ka Madag. 23°16S 46°0E 141 J9
amites Canada 48°56N 68°40W 165 C6
amites → Canada 48°56N 68°38W 165 C6
ndorf U.S.A. 41°32N 90°30W 172 E8
ah India 26°48N 84°33E 125 F11
a Sweden 58°55N 16°38E 63 F10
la Italy 44°47N 9°36E 92 D6
India 21°58N 77°59E 126 D3
s-y-Coed U.K. 53°5N 3°48W 66 D4
Spain 39°56N 0°12W 90 F4
lorf Germany 50°46N 7°52E 76 E3
France 44°6N 6°59E 73 D10
ah Australia 35°58S 142°29E 152 C5
ah Mich., U.S.A. 44°38N 86°6W 172 C10
ah N. Dak., U.S.A. 47°16N 101°47W 172 B3
ron → France 47°29N 1°15E 70 E8
ren Belgium 51°12N 4°16E 69 C4
rley Australia 32°9S 116°56E 149 F2
rley U.K. 53°51N 0°26W 66 D7
rly U.S.A. 42°33N 70°53W 175 D14
rly Hills Calif.,
S.A. 34°5N 118°24W 171 L8
rly Hills Fla.,
S.A. 28°55N 82°28W 179 G7

Beverungen Germany 51°39N 9°22E 76 D5
Bewas → India 23°59N 79°21E 125 H8
Bewdley Canada 44°5N 78°19W 174 B6
Bex Switz. 46°15N 7°1E 77 J3
Bexhill U.K. 50°51N 0°29E 67 G8
Bey Dağları Turkey 36°38N 30°29E 99 E12
Beyānlū Iran 36°0N 47°51E 128 C5
Beyazköy Turkey 41°21N 27°42E 97 E11
Beyçayırı Turkey 40°15N 26°35E 97 F10
Beydağ Turkey 38°5N 28°13E 99 C10
Beyeğaç Turkey 37°14N 28°53E 99 D10
Beyin Ghana 5°1N 2°41W 138 D4
Beykoz Turkey 41°7N 29°7E 97 E13
Beyla Guinea 8°30N 8°38W 138 D3
Beynat France 45°8N 1°44E 72 C5
Beyneu Kazakhstan 45°18N 55°9E 108 C5
Beyoba Turkey 38°48N 27°47E 99 C9
Beyoğlu Turkey 41°1N 28°58E 97 E12
Beypazarı Turkey 40°10N 31°56E 104 B4
Beypore → India 11°10N 75°47E 127 J2
Beyşehir Turkey 37°41N 31°43E 104 D4
Beyşehir Gölü Turkey 37°41N 31°33E 104 D4
Beytüşşebap Turkey 37°35N 43°10E 105 D10
Bezdan Serbia 45°50N 18°57E 80 E3
Bezhetsk Russia 57°47N 36°39E 84 D9
Béziers France 43°20N 3°12E 72 E7
Bezwada = Vijayawada
India 16°31N 80°39E 126 F5
Bhabua India 25°3N 83°37E 125 G10
Bhachau India 23°20N 70°16E 124 H4
Bhadar → Gujarat,
India 22°17N 72°20E 124 H5
Bhadar → Gujarat,
India 21°27N 69°47E 124 J3
Bhadarwah India 32°58N 75°46E 125 C6
Bhadgaon = Bhaktapur
Nepal 27°38N 85°24E 125 F11
Bhadohi India 25°25N 82°34E 125 G10
Bhadra India 29°8N 75°14E 124 E6
Bhadra → India 14°0N 75°20E 127 H2
Bhadrachalam India 17°40N 80°53E 126 F5
Bhadrak India 21°10N 86°30E 126 D8
Bhadran India 22°19N 72°6E 124 H5
Bhadravati India 13°49N 75°40E 127 H2
Bhag Pakistan 29°2N 67°49E 124 E2
Bhagalpur India 25°10N 87°0E 125 G12
Bhagirathi → Paschimbanga,
India 23°25N 88°23E 125 H13
Bhagirathi → Uttarakhand,
India 30°8N 78°35E 125 D8
Bhainsa India 19°10N 77°58E 126 E3
Bhakkar Pakistan 31°40N 71°5E 124 D4
Bhakra Dam India 31°30N 76°45E 124 D7
Bhaktapur Nepal 27°38N 85°24E 125 F11
Bhalki India 18°2N 77°13E 126 E3
Bhamo Burma 24°15N 97°15E 123 G20
Bhamragarh India 19°30N 80°40E 126 E5
Bhandara India 21°5N 79°42E 126 D4
Bhanpura India 24°31N 75°44E 124 G6
Bhanrer Ra. India 23°40N 79°45E 125 H8
Bhaptiahi India 26°19N 86°44E 125 F12
Bharat = India ■ Asia 20°0N 78°0E 122 K11
Bharatpur Chhattisgarh,
India 23°44N 81°46E 125 H9
Bharatpur Raj., India 27°15N 77°30E 124 F7
Bharatpur Nepal 27°34N 84°10E 125 F11
Bharno India 23°14N 84°53E 125 H11
Bharraig = Barra U.K. 57°0N 7°29W 65 E1
Bharraig, Caolas = Barra, Sd. of
U.K. 57°4N 7°25W 65 D1
Bharuch India 21°47N 73°0E 126 D1
Bhatarsaigh = Vatersay
U.K. 56°55N 7°32W 65 E1
Bhatghar L. India 18°10N 73°48E 126 E1
Bhatinda India 30°15N 74°57E 124 D6
Bhatkal India 13°58N 74°35E 127 H2
Bhatpara India 22°50N 88°25E 125 H13
Bhattu India 29°36N 75°19E 124 E6
Bhaun Pakistan 32°55N 72°40E 124 C5
Bhaunagar = Bhavnagar
India 21°45N 72°10E 126 D1
Bhavani India 11°27N 77°43E 127 J3
Bhavnagar India 21°45N 72°10E 126 D1
Bhawanipatna India 19°55N 83°10E 126 E6
Bhawari India 25°42N 73°4E 124 G5
Bhayavadar India 21°51N 70°15E 124 J4
Bhearnaraigh = Berneray
U.K. 57°43N 7°11W 65 D1
Bhera Pakistan 32°29N 72°57E 124 C5
Bheri → Nepal 28°47N 81°18E 125 E9
Bhikangaon India 21°52N 75°57E 124 J6
Bhilai = Bhilainagar-Durg
India 21°13N 81°26E 126 D5
Bhilainagar-Durg India 21°13N 81°26E 126 D5
Bhilsa = Vidisha India 23°28N 77°53E 124 H7
Bhilwara India 25°25N 74°38E 124 G6
Bhima → India 16°25N 77°17E 126 F3
Bhimavaram India 16°30N 81°30E 127 F5
Bhimbar Pakistan 32°59N 74°3E 125 C6
Bhind India 26°30N 78°46E 125 F8
Bhinga India 27°43N 81°56E 125 F9
Bhinmal India 25°0N 72°15E 124 G5
Bhisho S. Africa 32°50S 27°23E 144 D4
Bhiwandi India 19°20N 73°0E 126 E1
Bhiwani India 28°50N 76°9E 124 E7
Bhogava → India 22°26N 72°20E 124 H5
Bhojpur Nepal 27°10N 87°3E 125 F12
Bhokardan India 20°16N 75°46E 126 D2
Bhola Bangla. 22°45N 90°35E 123 H17
Bholari Pakistan 25°19N 68°13E 124 G3
Bhongir India 17°30N 78°56E 126 F4
Bhopal India 23°20N 77°30E 124 H7
Bhopalpatnam India 18°52N 80°23E 126 E5
Bhor India 18°12N 73°53E 126 E1
Bhuban India 20°53N 85°50E 126 D7
Bhubaneshwar India 20°15N 85°50E 126 D7
Bhuj India 23°15N 69°49E 124 H3
Bhumiphol Res.
Thailand 17°20N 98°40E 120 D2
Bhusawal India 21°3N 75°46E 126 D2
Bhutan ■ Asia 27°25N 90°30E 123 F17
Biafra, B. of = Bonny, Bight of
Africa 3°30N 9°20E 139 E6
Biak Indonesia 1°10S 136°6E 119 E9
Biała Poland 50°24N 17°40E 83 H4
Biała → Poland 50°3N 20°55E 83 H7
Biała Piska Poland 53°37N 22°5E 82 E9
Biała Podlaska Poland 52°4N 23°6E 83 F10
Biała Rawska Poland 51°48N 20°29E 83 G7
Białobrzegi Poland 51°39N 20°57E 83 G7
Białogard Poland 54°2N 15°58E 82 D2

Białowieski △ Poland 52°43N 23°50E 83 F10
Białowieża Poland 52°41N 23°49E 83 F10
Biały Bór Poland 53°53N 16°51E 82 E3
Białystok Poland 53°10N 23°10E 83 E10
Biancavilla Italy 37°38N 14°52E 95 E7
Bianco Italy 38°5N 16°9E 95 D9
Biankouma Ivory C. 7°50N 7°40W 138 D3
Biaora India 23°56N 76°56E 124 H7
Bīārjmand Iran 36°6N 55°53E 129 B7
Biaro Indonesia 2°5N 125°26E 119 D7
Biarritz France 43°29N 1°33W 72 E2
Biasca Switz. 46°22N 8°58E 77 J4
Biba Egypt 28°55N 31°0E 137 F7
Bibai Japan 43°19N 141°52E 112 C10
Bibbiena Italy 43°42N 11°49E 93 E8
Bibby I. Canada 61°55N 93°0W 163 A10
Bibei → Spain 42°24N 7°13W 88 C3
Biberach Germany 48°5N 9°47E 77 G5
Bibiani Ghana 6°30N 2°8W 138 D4
Bibile Sri Lanka 7°10N 81°25E 127 L5
Bibungwa
Dem. Rep. of the Congo 2°40S 28°15E 142 C2
Bicaj Albania 41°58N 20°25E 96 E4
Bicaz Romania 46°53N 26°5E 81 D11
Bicazu Ardelean
Romania 46°51N 25°56E 81 D10
Biccari Italy 41°23N 15°12E 95 A8
Bicester U.K. 51°54N 1°9W 67 F6
Bicheno Australia 41°52S 148°18E 151 G4
Bichia India 22°27N 80°42E 125 H9
Bichvinta Georgia 43°9N 40°21E 87 J5
Bickerton I. Australia 13°45S 136°10E 150 A2
Bicske Hungary 47°29N 18°38E 80 C3
Bid = Bir India 19°4N 75°46E 126 E2
Bida Nigeria 9°3N 5°58E 139 D6
Bidar India 17°55N 77°35E 126 F3
Biddeford U.S.A. 43°30N 70°28W 173 D18
Bideford U.K. 51°1N 4°13W 67 F3
Bideford Bay U.K. 51°5N 4°20W 67 F3
Bidhuna India 26°49N 79°31E 125 F8
Bīdokht Iran 34°20N 58°46E 129 C8
Bidor Malaysia 4°6N 101°15E 121 K3
Bidyadanga Australia 18°45S 121°43E 148 C3
Bie Sweden 59°5N 16°12E 62 E10
Bié, Planalto de Angola 12°0S 16°0E 141 G3
Bieber U.S.A. 41°7N 121°8W 168 F3
Biebrza → Poland 53°13N 22°25E 83 E9
Biebrzański △ Poland 53°36N 22°45E 82 E9
Biecz Poland 49°44N 21°15E 83 J8
Biel Switz. 47°8N 7°14E 77 H3
Bielawa Poland 50°43N 16°37E 83 H3
Bielefeld Germany 52°1N 8°33E 76 C4
Bielersee Switz. 47°6N 7°5E 77 H3
Biella Italy 45°34N 8°3E 92 C5
Bielsk Podlaski Poland 52°47N 23°12E 83 F10
Bielsko-Biała Poland 49°50N 19°2E 83 J6
Bien Hoa Vietnam 10°57N 106°49E 121 G6
Bienne = Biel Switz. 47°8N 7°14E 77 H3
Bienvenida Spain 38°18N 6°12W 89 G4
Bienville, L. Canada 55°5N 72°40W 164 A5
Bierné France 47°48N 0°33W 70 E6
Bierun Poland 50°6N 19°6E 83 H6
Bierutów Poland 51°7N 17°32E 83 G4
Biesbosch △ Neths. 51°45N 4°48E 69 C4
Biescas Spain 42°37N 0°20W 90 C4
Biese → Germany 52°53N 11°46E 76 C7
Biesiesfontein S. Africa 30°57S 17°58E 144 D2
Bieszczadzki △ Poland 49°5N 22°43E 83 J9
Bietigheim-Bissingen
Germany 48°58N 9°8E 77 G5
Bieżuń Poland 52°58N 19°55E 83 F6
Biferno → Italy 41°59N 15°2E 93 G12
Big → Canada 54°50N 58°55W 165 B8
Big B. = Awarua B.
N.Z. 44°28S 168°4E 155 E3
Big B. Canada 55°43N 60°35W 165 A7
Big Bear City U.S.A. 34°16N 116°51W 171 L10
Big Bear Lake U.S.A. 34°15N 116°56W 171 L10
Big Belt Mts. U.S.A. 46°30N 111°25W 168 C8
Big Bend Swaziland 26°50S 31°58E 145 C5
Big Bend △ U.S.A. 29°20N 103°5W 176 G3
Big Black → U.S.A. 32°3N 91°4W 177 E9
Big Blue → U.S.A. 39°35N 96°34W 172 F5
Big Buddha
Hong Kong, China 22°15N 113°54E 111 a
Big Creek U.S.A. 37°11N 119°14W 170 H7
Big Cypress ⌂ U.S.A. 26°0N 81°10W 179 J8
Big Cypress Swamp
U.S.A. 26°15N 81°30W 179 J8
Big Desert Australia 35°45S 141°10E 151 F3
Big Falls U.S.A. 48°12N 93°48W 172 A7
Big Fork → U.S.A. 48°31N 93°43W 172 A7
Big Horn Mts. = Bighorn Mts.
U.S.A. 44°25N 107°0W 168 D10
Big I. Canada 61°7N 116°45W 162 A5
Big Lake U.S.A. 31°12N 101°28W 176 F4
Big Moose U.S.A. 43°49N 74°58W 175 C10
Big Muddy Cr. →
U.S.A. 48°8N 104°36W 168 B11
Big Pine U.S.A. 37°10N 118°17W 170 H8
Big Pine Key U.S.A. 24°40N 81°21W 179 L8
Big Piney U.S.A. 42°32N 110°7W 168 E8
Big Quill L. Canada 51°55N 104°30W 163 C8
Big Rapids U.S.A. 43°42N 85°29W 173 D11
Big Rideau L. Canada 44°40N 76°15W 175 B8
Big River Canada 53°50N 107°0W 163 C7
Big Run U.S.A. 40°57N 78°55W 174 F6
Big Sable Pt. U.S.A. 44°3N 86°1W 172 C10
Big Salmon →
Canada 61°52N 134°55W 162 A2
Big Sand L. Canada 57°45N 99°45W 163 B9
Big Sandy U.S.A. 48°11N 110°7W 168 B8
Big Sandy → U.S.A. 38°25N 82°36W 173 F12
Big Sandy Cr. = Sandy Cr. →
U.S.A. 41°51N 109°47W 168 F9
Big Sandy Cr. →
U.S.A. 38°7N 102°29W 168 G12
Big Satilla Cr. → U.S.A. 31°27N 82°3W 178 D7
Big Sioux → U.S.A. 42°29N 96°27W 172 D5
Big South Fork ⌂
U.S.A. 36°27N 84°47W 177 C12
Big Spring U.S.A. 32°15N 101°28W 176 E4
Big Stone City U.S.A. 45°18N 96°28W 172 C5
Big Stone Gap U.S.A. 36°52N 82°47W 173 G12
Big Stone L. U.S.A. 45°18N 96°27W 172 C5
Big Sur U.S.A. 36°15N 121°48W 170 J5
Big Timber U.S.A. 45°50N 109°57W 168 D9
Big Trout L. Canada 53°40N 90°0W 164 B2
Big Trout Lake Canada 53°45N 90°0W 164 B2
Biğa Turkey 40°13N 27°14E 97 F11
Biga → Turkey 40°20N 27°14E 97 F11

Bigadiç Turkey 39°22N 28°7E 99 B10
Biganos France 44°39N 0°59W 72 D3
Biggar Canada 52°4N 108°0W 163 C7
Biggar U.K. 55°38N 3°32W 65 F5
Bigge I. Australia 14°35S 125°10E 148 B4
Biggenden Australia 25°31S 152°4E 151 D5
Biggleswade U.K. 52°5N 0°14W 67 E7
Biggs U.S.A. 39°25N 121°43W 170 F5
Bighorn U.S.A. 46°10N 107°27W 168 C10
Bighorn → U.S.A. 46°10N 107°28W 168 C10
Bighorn Canyon ⌂
U.S.A. 45°10N 108°0W 168 D10
Bighorn L. U.S.A. 44°55N 108°15W 168 D9
Bighorn Mts. U.S.A. 44°25N 107°0W 168 D10
Bignona Senegal 12°52N 16°14W 138 C1
Bigorre France 43°10N 0°5E 72 E4
Bigstone L. Canada 53°42N 95°44W 163 C9
Biguglia, Étang de
France 42°36N 9°29E 73 F13
Bigwa Tanzania 7°10S 39°10E 142 D4
Bihać Bos.-H. 44°49N 15°57E 93 D12
Bihar India 25°5N 85°40E 125 G11
Bihar □ India 25°0N 86°0E 125 G12
Biharamulo Tanzania 2°25S 31°25E 142 C3
Biharamulo ⌂ Tanzania 2°24S 31°26E 142 C3
Bihariganj India 25°44N 86°59E 125 G12
Biharkeresztes Hungary 47°8N 21°44E 80 C6
Bihor □ Romania 47°0N 22°10E 80 D7
Bihor, Munţii Romania 46°29N 22°47E 80 D7
Bijagós, Arquipélago dos
Guinea-Biss. 11°15N 16°10W 138 C1
Bijaipur India 26°2N 77°20E 124 F7
Bijapur Chhattisgarh,
India 18°50N 80°50E 126 E5
Bijapur Karnataka, India 16°50N 75°55E 126 F2
Bījār Iran 35°52N 47°35E 105 E12
Bijauri Nepal 28°6N 82°20E 125 E10
Bijawar India 24°38N 79°30E 125 G8
Bijela Montenegro 42°28N 18°39E 96 D2
Bijeljina Bos.-H. 44°46N 19°14E 80 F4
Bijelo Polje Montenegro 43°1N 19°45E 96 C3
Bijie China 27°20N 105°16E 116 D5
Bijnor India 29°27N 78°11E 124 E8
Bikaner India 28°2N 73°18E 124 E5
Bikapur India 26°30N 82°7E 125 F10
Bikeqi China 40°43N 111°20E 114 D6
Bikfayyā Lebanon 33°55N 35°41E 130 B4
Bikin Russia 46°50N 134°20E 112 A7
Bikin → Russia 46°51N 134°2E 112 A7
Bikini Atoll Marshall Is. 12°0N 167°30E 156 F8
Bikita Zimbabwe 20°6S 31°41E 145 B5
Bīkkū Bīttī Libya 22°0N 19°12E 135 D9
Bikoué Cameroon 3°55N 11°50E 139 E7
Bila Tserkva Ukraine 49°45N 30°10E 75 D16
Bilanga Burkina Faso 12°40N 0°1W 139 C4
Bilara India 26°14N 73°53E 124 F5
Bilaspur Chhattisgarh,
India 22°2N 82°15E 125 H10
Bilaspur Punjab, India 31°19N 76°50E 124 D7
Biläsuvar Azerbaijan 39°27N 48°32E 105 C13
Bilauk Taungdan
Thailand 13°0N 99°0E 120 F2
Bilauri Nepal 28°41N 80°21E 125 E9
Bilbao Spain 43°16N 2°56W 90 B2
Bilbao ✕ (BIO) Spain 43°18N 2°57W 90 B2
Bilbeis Egypt 30°25N 31°34E 137 E7
Bilbo = Bilbao Spain 43°16N 2°56W 90 B2
Bilbor Romania 47°6N 25°30E 81 C10
Bilche-Zolote Ukraine 48°47N 25°53E 81 B10
Bilciureşti Romania 44°44N 25°48E 81 F10
Bíldudalur Iceland 65°41N 23°36W 60 D2
Bílé Karpaty Europe 49°5N 18°0E 79 B11
Bileća Bos.-H. 42°53N 18°27E 96 D2
Bilecik Turkey 40°5N 30°5E 104 B4
Bilecik □ Turkey 40°0N 30°0E 104 B3
Bilećko Jezero Bos.-H. 42°54N 18°28E 96 D2
Bileh Savār Iran 39°21N 48°21E 105 C13
Biłgoraj Poland 50°33N 22°42E 83 H9
Bilgram India 27°11N 80°2E 125 F9
Bilhaur India 26°51N 80°5E 125 F9
Bilhorod-Dnistrovskyy
Ukraine 46°11N 30°23E 85 J6
Bilibino Russia 68°3N 166°20E 107 C17
Bilibiza Mozam. 12°30S 40°20E 143 E5
Bilimora India 20°45N 72°57E 126 D1
Bilisht Albania 40°37N 21°2E 96 F5
Billabong Cr. →
Australia 35°5S 144°2E 152 C6
Billdal Sweden 57°35N 11°57E 63 G5
Billiluna Australia 19°37S 127°41E 148 C4
Billings U.S.A. 45°47N 108°30W 168 D9
Billiton Is. = Belitung
Indonesia 3°10S 107°50E 118 E3
Billsta Sweden 63°20N 18°28E 62 A12
Billund Denmark 55°44N 9°6E 63 J3
Bilma Niger 18°50N 13°30E 135 E8
Bilma, Grand Erg de
Niger 18°30N 14°0E 135 E8
Bilo Gora Croatia 45°53N 17°15E 80 E2
Biloela Australia 24°24S 150°31E 150 C5
Bilohirsk Ukraine 45°3N 34°35E 85 K8
Biloli India 18°46N 77°44E 126 E3
Bilopillya Ukraine 51°14N 34°20E 85 G8
Bilovodsk Ukraine 49°13N 39°36E 85 H10
Biloxi U.S.A. 30°24N 88°53W 177 F10
Bilpa Morea Claypan
Australia 25°0S 140°0E 150 D3
Biltine Chad 14°40N 20°50E 135 F10
Bilyarsk Russia 54°58N 50°22E 86 C10
Bim Son Vietnam 20°4N 105°51E 120 B5
Bima Indonesia 8°22S 118°49E 119 F5
Bimban Egypt 24°24N 32°54E 137 C3
Bimberi Pk. Australia 35°44S 148°51E 153 C8
Bimbila Ghana 8°54N 0°5E 139 D5
Bimbo C.A.R. 4°15N 18°33E 140 D3
Bimini Is. Bahamas 25°42N 79°25W 182 A4
Bin Xian Heilongjiang,
China 45°42N 127°32E 115 B14
Bin Xian Shaanxi, China 35°2N 108°4E 114 G5
Bin Yauri Nigeria 10°46N 4°45E 139 C5
Bina-Etawah India 24°13N 78°14E 124 G8
Binalong Australia 34°40S 148°39E 153 C8
Bīnālūd, Kūh-e Iran 36°30N 58°30E 129 B8
Binatang = Bintangau
Malaysia 2°10N 111°40E 118 D4
Binche Belgium 50°26N 4°10E 69 D4
Binchuan China 25°42N 100°38E 116 E3
Binder Chad 9°56N 14°27E 139 D7
Bindki India 26°2N 80°36E 125 F9
Bindslev Denmark 57°33N 10°11E 63 G4
Bindura Zimbabwe 17°18S 31°18E 143 F3

Binéfar Spain 41°51N 0°18E 90 D5
Bingara Australia 29°52S 150°36E 151 D5
Bingaram I. India 10°56N 72°17E 127 J1
Bingen Germany 49°57N 7°55E 77 F3
Bingerville Ivory C. 5°18N 3°49W 138 D4
Bingham U.S.A. 45°3N 69°53W 173 C19
Binghamton U.S.A. 42°6N 75°55W 175 D9
Bingöl Turkey 38°53N 40°29E 105 C9
Bingöl □ Turkey 38°55N 40°30E 105 C9
Bingöl Dağları Turkey 39°16N 41°9E 105 C9
Bingsjö Sweden 61°1N 15°39E 62 C9
Binh Dinh Vietnam 13°55N 109°7E 120 F7
Binh Son Vietnam 15°20N 108°40E 120 E7
Binhai China 34°2N 119°49E 115 G10
Binic France 48°46N 2°50W 70 D4
Binisatua Spain 39°50N 4°11E 100 B11
Binissalem Spain 39°41N 2°50E 100 B9
Binjai Indonesia 3°20N 98°30E 118 D3
Binji Nigeria 13°10N 4°55E 139 C5
Binka India 21°2N 83°48E 126 D6
Binnaway Australia 31°28S 149°24E 153 A8
Binongko Indonesia 5°57S 124°2E 119 F6
Binscarth Canada 50°37N 101°17W 163 C8
Bintan Indonesia 1°0N 104°0E 118 D2
Bintangau Malaysia 2°10N 111°40E 118 D4
Bintulu Malaysia 3°10N 113°0E 118 D4
Bintuni Indonesia 2°7S 133°32E 119 E8
Binyang China 23°12N 108°47E 116 F7
Binz Germany 54°24N 13°35E 76 A9
Binzert = Bizerte Tunisia 37°15N 9°50E 136 A5
Binzhou China 37°20N 118°2E 115 F10
Bio Bío □ Chile 37°35S 72°0W 190 D1
Biobío → Chile 36°49S 73°10W 190 D1
Biograd na Moru
Croatia 43°56N 15°29E 93 E12
Biogradska Gora △
Montenegro 42°55N 19°40E 96 D3
Bioko Eq. Guin. 3°30N 8°40E 139 E6
Biokovo Croatia 43°23N 17°0E 93 E14
Biougra Morocco 30°15N 9°14W 136 B2
Bipindi Cameroon 3°6N 10°30E 139 E7
Bir India 19°4N 75°46E 126 E2
Bir Abu Hashim Egypt 23°42N 34°6E 137 C3
Bir Abu Minqar Egypt 26°33N 27°33E 137 B2
Bir Abu Muḥammad
Egypt 29°44N 34°14E 130 F3
Bîr Adal Deib Sudan 22°35N 36°10E 137 C4
Bi'r al Butayyihāt
Jordan 29°47N 35°20E 130 F4
Bi'r al Mārī Jordan 30°4N 35°33E 130 E4
Bi'r al Qattār Jordan 29°47N 35°32E 130 F4
Bir Aouine Tunisia 32°25N 9°18E 136 B5
Bîr 'Asal Egypt 25°55N 34°20E 137 B3
Bir Atrun Sudan 18°15N 26°40E 137 D2
Bîr Beiḍa Egypt 30°25N 34°29E 130 E3
Bîr Diqnash Egypt 31°3N 25°23E 137 A2
Bir el Abbes Algeria 26°7N 6°9W 136 C2
Bîr el 'Abd Egypt 31°2N 33°0E 130 D2
Bir el Ater Algeria 34°46N 8°3E 136 B5
Bîr el Basur Egypt 29°51N 25°49E 137 B2
Bîr el Biarât Egypt 29°30N 34°43E 130 F3
Bîr el Duweidar Egypt 30°56N 32°32E 130 E1
Bîr el Garârât Egypt 31°3N 33°34E 130 D2
Bîr el Gellaz Egypt 30°50N 26°40E 137 A2
Bîr el Heisi Egypt 29°22N 34°36E 130 F3
Bîr el Jafir Egypt 30°50N 32°41E 130 E1
Bîr el Mâlḥi Egypt 30°38N 33°19E 130 E2
Bîr el Shaqqa Egypt 30°54N 25°1E 137 A2
Bîr el Thamâda Egypt 30°12N 33°27E 130 E2
Bîr Fuad Egypt 30°35N 26°28E 137 A2
Bîr Gebeil Ḥiṣn Egypt 30°2N 33°18E 130 E2
Bi'r Ghadīr Syria 34°6N 37°3E 130 A6
Bîr Haimur Egypt 22°45N 33°40E 137 C3
Bîr Ḥasana Egypt 30°29N 33°46E 130 E2
Bîr Hôôker Egypt 30°22N 30°21E 137 E7
Bîr Kanayis Egypt 24°59N 33°15E 137 C3
Bîr Kaseiba Egypt 31°0N 33°17E 130 E2
Bîr Kerawein Egypt 27°10N 28°25E 137 B2
Bîr Lahfân Egypt 31°0N 33°51E 130 E2
Bir Lahrache Algeria 32°1N 8°12E 136 B5
Bîr Madkûr Egypt 30°44N 32°33E 130 E1
Bîr Maql Egypt 23°7N 33°40E 137 C3
Bîr Mîneiga Sudan 22°47N 35°12E 137 C4
Bîr Misaha Egypt 22°13N 27°59E 137 C2
Bir Mogreïn Mauritania 25°10N 11°25W 134 C3
Bîr Murr Egypt 23°28N 30°10E 137 C3
Bi'r Muṭribah Kuwait 29°54N 47°17E 128 D5
Bîr Nakheila Egypt 24°1N 30°50E 137 C3
Bîr Qaṭia Egypt 30°58N 32°45E 130 E1
Bîr Qatrani Egypt 30°55N 26°10E 137 A2
Bîr Ranga Egypt 24°25N 35°15E 137 C4
Bîr Sahara Egypt 22°54N 28°40E 137 C2
Bîr Seiyâla Egypt 26°10N 33°50E 137 B3
Bir Shalatein Egypt 23°5N 35°25E 137 C4
Bîr Shebb Egypt 22°25N 29°40E 137 C2
Bîr Shût Egypt 23°50N 35°15E 137 C4
Bîr Terfawi Egypt 22°57N 28°55E 137 C2
Bîr Umm Qubûr Egypt 24°35N 34°2E 137 C3
Bîr Ungât Egypt 22°8N 33°48E 137 C3
Bîr Za'farâna Egypt 29°10N 32°40E 137 F8
Bîr Zeidûn Egypt 25°45N 33°40E 137 B3
Birāk Libya 27°31N 14°20E 135 C8
Biramfêro Guinea 11°40N 9°10W 138 C3
Biratnagar Nepal 26°27N 87°17E 125 F12
Birawa
Dem. Rep. of the Congo 2°20S 28°48E 142 C2
Birch → Canada 58°28N 112°17W 162 B6
Birch Hills Canada 52°59N 105°25W 163 C7
Birch I. Canada 52°26N 99°54W 163 C9
Birch L. N.W.T., Canada 62°4N 116°33W 162 A5
Birch L. Ont., Canada 51°23N 92°18W 164 B1
Birch Mts. Canada 57°30N 113°10W 162 B6
Birch River Canada 52°24N 101°6W 163 C8
Birchip Australia 35°56S 142°55E 152 C5
Birchiş Romania 45°58N 22°9E 80 E7
Birchwood N.Z. 45°55S 167°53E 155 F2
Bird Canada 56°30N 94°13W 163 B10
Bird I. = Aves, I. de
W. Indies 15°45N 63°55W 183 C7
Bird I. S. Georgia 54°0S 38°3W 55 B1
Birds Creek Canada 45°6N 77°52W 174 A7
Birdsville Australia 25°51S 139°20E 150 D2
Birdum Cr. → Australia 15°14S 133°0E 148 C5
Birdwood Australia 34°51S 138°58E 152 C3
Birecik Turkey 37°2N 38°0E 105 D8
Birein Israel 30°50N 34°28E 130 E3
Bireuen Indonesia 5°14N 96°39E 118 C1
Birganj Nepal 27°1N 84°52E 125 F11
Birifo Gambia 13°30N 14°0W 138 C2
Birigüi Brazil 21°18S 50°16W 191 A5
Bīrjand Iran 32°53N 59°13E 129 C8

Birka Sweden 59°20N 17°32E 62 E11
Birkenfeld Germany 49°38N 7°9E 77 F3
Birkenhead U.K. 53°23N 3°2W 66 D4
Birkerød Denmark 55°50N 12°25E 63 J6
Birket Qârûn Egypt 29°30N 30°40E 137 F7
Birkfeld Austria 47°21N 15°45E 78 D8
Birkhadem Algeria 36°43N 3°3E 136 A4
Bîrlad = Bârlad
Romania 46°15N 27°38E 81 D12
Birmingham U.K. 52°29N 1°52W 67 E6
Birmingham U.S.A. 33°31N 86°48W 177 E11
Birmingham Int. ✕ (BHX)
U.K. 52°26N 1°45W 67 E6
Birmitrapur India 22°24N 84°46E 126 C7
Birni Ngaouré Niger 13°5N 2°51E 139 C5
Birni Nkonni Niger 13°55N 5°15E 139 C6
Birnin Gwari Nigeria 11°0N 6°45E 139 C6
Birnin Kebbi Nigeria 12°32N 4°12E 139 C5
Birnin Kudu Nigeria 11°30N 9°29E 139 C6
Birobidzhan Russia 48°50N 132°50E 111 B15
Birr Ireland 53°6N 7°54W 64 C4
Birrie → Australia 29°43S 146°37E 151 D4
Birsilpur India 28°11N 72°15E 124 E5
Birsk Russia 55°25N 55°30E 106 D6
Birtle Canada 50°30N 101°5W 163 C8
Birur India 13°30N 75°55E 122 N9
Biryuchiy Ukraine 46°10N 35°0E 85 J8
Biržai Lithuania 56°11N 24°45E 84 D3
Birżebbugga Malta 35°50N 14°32E 101 D2
Bisa Indonesia 1°15S 127°28E 119 E7
Bisáccia Italy 41°1N 15°22E 95 A8
Bisacquino Italy 37°42N 13°15E 94 E6
Bisalpur India 28°14N 79°48E 125 E8
Bisbee U.S.A. 31°27N 109°55W 169 L9
Biscarrosse France 44°22N 1°20W 72 D2
Biscarrosse et de Parentis, Étang
de France 44°21N 1°10W 72 D2
Biscay, B. of Atl. Oc. 45°0N 2°0W 58 F5
Biscay Abyssal Plain
Atl. Oc. 45°0N 8°0W 56 B11
Biscayne ⌂ U.S.A. 25°25N 80°12W 179 K9
Biscayne B. U.S.A. 25°40N 80°12W 179 K9
Biscéglie Italy 41°14N 16°30E 95 A9
Bischheim France 48°37N 7°46E 71 D14
Bischofshofen Austria 47°26N 13°14E 78 D6
Bischofswerda Germany 51°7N 14°10E 76 D10
Bischwiller France 48°46N 7°50E 71 D14
Biscoe Is. Antarctica 66°0S 67°0W 55 C17
Biscotasing Canada 47°18N 82°9W 164 C3
Biševo Croatia 42°57N 16°3E 93 F13
Bishah, W. →
Si. Arabia 21°24N 43°26E 137 C5
Bishan China 29°33N 106°12E 116 C6
Bishkek Kyrgyzstan 42°54N 74°46E 109 D8
Bishnupur India 23°8N 87°20E 125 H12
Bisho = Bhisho S. Africa 32°50S 27°23E 144 D4
Bishop Calif., U.S.A. 37°22N 118°24W 170 H8
Bishop Ga., U.S.A. 33°49N 83°26W 178 B6
Bishop Tex., U.S.A. 27°35N 97°48W 176 H6
Bishop Auckland U.K. 54°39N 1°40W 66 C6
Bishop's Falls Canada 49°2N 55°30W 165 C8
Bishop's Stortford U.K. 51°52N 0°10E 67 F8
Bisignano Italy 39°31N 16°17E 95 C9
Bisina, L. Uganda 1°38N 33°56E 142 B3
Biskra Algeria 34°50N 5°44E 136 B5
Biskra □ Algeria 34°40N 5°25E 136 B5
Biskupiec Poland 53°53N 20°58E 82 E7
Bismarck U.S.A. 46°48N 100°47W 172 B3
Bismarck Arch.
Papua N. G. 2°30S 150°0E 147 B7
Bismark Germany 52°40N 11°33E 76 C7
Bismil Turkey 37°51N 40°40E 105 D9
Biso Uganda 1°44N 31°26E 142 B3
Bison U.S.A. 45°31N 102°28W 172 C2
Bīsotūn Iran 34°23N 47°26E 105 E12
Bispgården Sweden 63°2N 16°40E 62 A10
Bissagos = Bijagós, Arquipélago
dos Guinea-Biss. 11°15N 16°10W 138 C1
Bissam Cuttack India 19°31N 83°31E 126 E6
Bissau Guinea-Biss. 11°45N 15°45W 138 C1
Bissaula Nigeria 7°0N 10°27E 139 D7
Bissikrima Guinea 10°50N 10°58W 138 C2
Bissorã Guinea-Biss. 12°16N 15°35W 138 C1
Bistcho L. Canada 59°45N 118°50W 162 B5
Bistreţ Romania 43°54N 23°23E 81 G8
Bistrica = Ilirska-Bistrica
Slovenia 45°34N 14°14E 93 C11
Bistriţa Romania 47°9N 24°35E 81 C9
Bistriţa → Romania 46°30N 26°57E 81 D11
Bistriţa Năsăud □
Romania 47°15N 24°30E 81 C9
Bistriţei, Munţii
Romania 47°15N 25°40E 81 C10
Biswan India 27°29N 81°2E 125 F9
Bisztynek Poland 54°8N 20°53E 82 D7
Bitam Gabon 2°5N 11°25E 140 D2
Bitburg Germany 49°58N 6°31E 77 F2
Bitche France 49°2N 7°25E 71 C14
Bithynia Turkey 40°40N 31°0E 104 B4
Bitkine Chad 11°59N 18°13E 135 F9
Bitlis Turkey 38°20N 42°3E 105 C10
Bitlis □ Turkey 38°20N 42°5E 105 C10
Bitola Macedonia 41°1N 21°20E 96 E5
Bitolj = Bitola Macedonia 41°1N 21°20E 96 E5
Bitonto Italy 41°6N 16°41E 95 A9
Bitra I. India 11°33N 72°9E 127 J1
Bitter Creek U.S.A. 41°33N 108°33W 168 F9
Bitter L. = Buheirat-Murrat-el-
Kubra Egypt 30°18N 32°26E 137 E8
Bitterfeld Germany 51°37N 12°20E 76 D8
Bitterfontein S. Africa 31°1S 18°32E 144 D2
Bitterroot → U.S.A. 46°52N 114°7W 168 C6
Bitterroot Range
U.S.A. 46°0N 114°20W 168 D6
Bitterwater U.S.A. 36°23N 121°0W 170 J6
Bitti Italy 40°29N 9°23E 94 B2
Bittou Burkina Faso 11°17N 0°18W 139 C4
Biu Nigeria 10°40N 12°3E 139 C7
Bivolari Romania 47°31N 27°27E 81 C12
Bivolu, Vf. Romania 47°16N 25°58E 81 C10
Biwa-Ko Japan 35°15N 136°10E 113 G8
Biwabik U.S.A. 47°32N 92°21W 172 B7
Bixad Romania 47°56N 23°28E 81 C8
Bixby U.S.A. 35°57N 95°53W 176 D7
Biya → Russia 52°25N 85°0E 109 B11
Biyang China 32°38N 113°21E 114 H7
Biysk Russia 52°40N 85°0E 109 B11
Bizana S. Africa 30°50S 29°52E 145 D4
Bizen Japan 34°43N 134°8E 113 G7
Bizerte Tunisia 37°15N 9°50E 136 A5
Bizerte □ Tunisia 37°5N 9°35E 136 A5

204 Bjargtangar
INDEX TO WORLD MA

Bjargtangar Iceland 65°30N 24°30W 60 D1
Bjärnum Sweden 56°17N 13°43E 63 H7
Bjästa Sweden 63°12N 18°29E 62 A12
Bjelasica Montenegro 42°50N 19°40E 96 D3
Bjelašnica Bos.-H. 43°43N 18°9E 80 G3
Bjelovar Croatia 45°56N 16°49E 93 C13
Bjerringbro Denmark 56°23N 9°39E 63 H3
Björbo Sweden 60°27N 14°44E 62 D8
Björklinge Sweden 60°2N 17°33E 62 D11
Björkö Sweden 59°52N 19°2E 62 E13
Björneborg = Pori Finland 61°29N 21°48E 84 B1
Björneborg Sweden 59°14N 14°16E 62 E8
Bjørnevatn Norway 69°40N 30°0E 60 B24
Bjørnøya Arctic 74°30N 19°0E 54 B8
Bjursås Sweden 60°44N 15°25E 62 D9
Bjuv Sweden 56°5N 12°55E 63 H6
Bla Mali 12°56N 5°47W 138 C3
Blå Jungfrun △ Sweden 57°16N 16°47E 63 G10
Blace Serbia 43°18N 21°17E 96 C5
Blachownia Poland 50°49N 18°56E 83 H5
Black = Da → Vietnam 21°15N 105°20E 116 G5
Black → Canada 44°42N 79°19W 174 B5
Black → Ariz., U.S.A. 33°44N 110°13W 169 K8
Black → Ark., U.S.A. 35°38N 91°20W 176 D9
Black → La., U.S.A. 31°16N 91°50W 176 F9
Black → Mich., U.S.A. 42°59N 82°27W 174 D2
Black → N.Y., U.S.A. 43°59N 76°4W 175 C8
Black → Wis., U.S.A. 43°57N 91°22W 172 D8
Black Bay Pen. Canada 48°38N 88°21W 164 C2
Black Birch L. Canada 56°53N 107°45W 163 B7
Black Canyon of the Gunnison ⌂ U.S.A. 38°40N 107°35W 168 G10
Black Diamond Canada 50°45N 114°14W 162 C6
Black Duck → Canada 56°51N 89°2W 164 A2
Black Forest = Schwarzwald Germany 48°30N 8°20E 77 G4
Black Forest U.S.A. 39°0N 104°43W 168 G11
Black Hd. Ireland 53°9N 9°16W 64 C2
Black Hills U.S.A. 44°0N 103°45W 172 D2
Black I. Canada 51°12N 96°30W 163 C9
Black L. Canada 59°12N 105°15W 163 B7
Black L. Mich., U.S.A. 45°28N 84°16W 173 C11
Black L. N.Y., U.S.A. 44°31N 75°36W 175 B9
Black Lake Canada 59°11N 105°20W 163 B7
Black Mesa U.S.A. 36°58N 102°58W 176 C3
Black Mountain Australia 30°18S 151°39E 153 A9
Black Mt. = Mynydd Du U.K. 51°52N 3°50W 67 F4
Black Mts. U.K. 51°55N 3°7W 67 F4
Black Range U.S.A. 33°15N 107°50W 169 K10
Black River Jamaica 18°0N 77°50W 182 a
Black River U.S.A. 44°0N 75°47W 175 C9
Black River Falls U.S.A. 44°18N 90°51W 172 C8
Black Rock Australia 32°50S 138°44E 152 B3
Black Rock Barbados 13°7N 59°37W 183 g
Black Rock Desert U.S.A. 41°10N 118°50W 168 F4
Black Sea Eurasia 43°30N 35°0E 58 G12
Black Tickle Canada 53°28N 55°45W 165 B8
Black Volta → Africa 8°41N 1°33W 138 D4
Black Warrior → U.S.A. 32°32N 87°51W 177 E11
Blackall Australia 24°25S 145°45E 150 C4
Blackball N.Z. 42°22S 171°26E 155 C6
Blackbraes △ Australia 19°10S 144°10E 150 B3
Blackbull Australia 17°55S 141°45E 150 B3
Blackburn U.K. 53°45N 2°29W 66 D5
Blackburn, Mt. U.S.A. 61°44N 143°26W 166 C11
Blackburn with Darwen □ U.K. 53°45N 2°29W 66 D5
Blackdown Tableland △ Australia 23°52S 149°8E 150 C4
Blackfoot U.S.A. 43°11N 112°21W 168 E7
Blackfoot → U.S.A. 46°52N 113°53W 168 C7
Blackfoot Res. U.S.A. 42°55N 111°39W 168 E8
Blackman U.S.A. 30°56N 86°38W 179 E3
Blackpool U.K. 53°49N 3°3W 66 D4
Blackpool □ U.K. 53°49N 3°3W 66 D4
Blackriver U.S.A. 44°46N 83°17W 174 B1
Blacks Harbour Canada 45°3N 66°49W 165 C6
Blacksburg U.S.A. 37°14N 80°25W 173 G13
Blacksheat U.S.A. 31°18N 82°14W 178 D7
Blackshear, L. U.S.A. 31°51N 83°56W 178 D6
Blacksod B. Ireland 54°6N 10°0W 64 B1
Blackstairs Mt. Ireland 52°33N 6°48W 64 D5
Blackstone U.S.A. 37°5N 78°0W 173 G14
Blackstone Ra. Australia 26°0S 128°30E 149 E4
Blackville U.S.A. 33°22N 81°16W 178 B8
Blackwater = West Road → Canada 53°18N 122°53W 162 C4
Blackwater Australia 23°35S 148°53E 150 C4
Blackwater → Meath, Ireland 53°39N 6°41W 64 C4
Blackwater → Waterford, Ireland 52°4N 7°52W 64 D4
Blackwater → U.K. 54°31N 6°35W 64 B5
Blackwater → U.S.A. 30°36N 87°2W 179 E2
Blackwell U.S.A. 36°48N 97°17W 176 C6
Blackwells Corner U.S.A. 35°37N 119°47W 171 K7
Bladensburg △ Australia 22°30S 142°59E 150 C3
Blaenau Ffestiniog U.K. 53°0N 3°56W 66 E4
Blaenau Gwent □ U.K. 51°48N 3°12W 67 F4
Blåfjella-Skjækerfjella △ Norway 64°15N 13°8E 60 D15
Blagaj Bos.-H. 43°16N 17°55E 96 C1
Blagnac France 43°37N 1°23E 72 E5
Blagnac, Toulouse ✈ (TLS) France 43°37N 1°22E 72 E5
Blagodarnyy Russia 45°7N 43°37E 87 H6
Blagoevgrad Bulgaria 42°2N 23°5E 96 D7
Blagoevgrad □ Bulgaria 42°2N 23°5E 96 D7
Blagoveshchensk Russia 50°20N 127°30E 111 A14
Blahkiuh Indonesia 8°31S 115°12E 119 J18
Blain France 47°29N 1°45W 70 E5
Blain U.S.A. 40°20N 77°31W 174 F7
Blaine Minn., U.S.A. 45°10N 93°13W 172 C7
Blaine Wash., U.S.A. 48°59N 122°45W 170 B4
Blaine Lake Canada 52°51N 106°52W 163 C7
Blair U.S.A. 41°33N 96°8W 172 E5
Blair Athol Australia 22°42S 147°31E 150 C4
Blair Atholl U.K. 56°46N 3°50W 65 E5
Blairgowrie U.K. 56°35N 3°21W 65 E5
Blairsden U.S.A. 39°47N 120°37W 170 F6
Blairsville U.S.A. 40°26N 79°16W 174 F5
Blaj Romania 46°10N 23°57E 81 D8
Blakang Mati, Pulau Singapore 1°15N 103°50E 121 d
Blake Pt. U.S.A. 48°11N 88°25W 172 A9
Blakely Ga., U.S.A. 31°23N 84°56W 178 D5
Blakely Pa., U.S.A. 41°28N 75°37W 175 E9
Blambangan, Semenanjung Indonesia 8°42S 114°29E 119 K17
Blâmont France 48°35N 6°50E 71 D13
Blanc, C. Spain 39°21N 2°51E 100 B9
Blanc, C. Tunisia 37°15N 9°56E 136 A5
Blanc, Mont Europe 45°48N 6°50E 73 C10
Blanca, B. Argentina 39°10S 61°30W 192 A4
Blanca, Cord. Peru 9°10S 77°35W 186 E3
Blanca, Costa Spain 38°25N 0°10W 91 G4
Blanca Peak U.S.A. 37°35N 105°29W 169 H11
Blanche, C. Australia 33°1S 134°9E 151 E1
Blanche, L. S. Austral., Australia 29°15S 139°40E 151 D2
Blanche, L. W. Austral., Australia 22°25S 123°17E 148 D3
Blanchisseuse Trin. & Tob. 10°48N 61°18W 187 K15
Blanco S. Africa 33°55S 22°23E 144 D3
Blanco U.S.A. 30°6N 98°25W 176 F5
Blanco → Argentina 30°20S 68°42W 190 C2
Blanco, C. Costa Rica 9°34N 85°8W 182 E2
Blanco, C. U.S.A. 42°51N 124°34W 168 E1
Blanda → Iceland 65°37N 20°9W 60 D3
Blandford Forum U.K. 50°51N 2°9W 67 G5
Blanding U.S.A. 37°37N 109°29W 169 H9
Blanes Spain 41°40N 2°48E 90 D7
Blangy-sur-Bresle France 49°55N 1°37E 71 C8
Blanice → Czech Rep. 49°10N 14°5E 78 B7
Blankaholm Sweden 57°36N 16°31E 63 G10
Blankenberge Belgium 51°20N 3°9E 69 C3
Blankenburg Germany 51°47N 10°57E 76 D6
Blanquefort France 44°55N 0°38W 72 D3
Blanquilla, I. Venezuela 11°51N 64°37W 183 D7
Blanquillo Uruguay 32°53S 55°37W 191 C4
Blansko Czech Rep. 49°22N 16°40E 79 B9
Blantyre Malawi 15°45S 35°0E 143 F4
Blarney Ireland 51°56N 8°33W 64 E3
Blasdell U.S.A. 42°48N 78°50W 174 D6
Błaszki Poland 51°38N 18°30E 83 G5
Blatná Czech Rep. 49°25N 13°52E 78 B6
Blato Croatia 42°56N 16°48E 93 F13
Blaubeuren Germany 48°24N 9°46E 77 G5
Blaustein Germany 48°25N 9°53E 77 G5
Blåvands Huk Denmark 55°33N 8°4E 63 J2
Blaydon U.K. 54°58N 1°42W 66 C6
Blaye France 45°8N 0°40W 72 C3
Blaye-les-Mines France 44°1N 2°8E 72 D6
Blayney Australia 33°32S 149°14E 153 B8
Blaze, Pt. Australia 12°56S 130°11E 148 B5
Błażowa Poland 49°53N 22°7E 83 J9
Bleckede Germany 53°17N 10°43E 76 B6
Bled Slovenia 46°27N 14°7E 93 B11
Bleiburg Austria 46°35N 14°49E 78 E7
Blejeşti Romania 44°19N 25°27E 81 F10
Blekinge Sweden 56°25N 15°20E 61 H16
Blekinge län □ Sweden 56°20N 15°20E 63 H9
Blenheim Canada 42°20N 82°0W 174 D3
Blenheim N.Z. 41°38S 173°57E 155 B8
Bléone → France 44°5N 6°0E 73 D10
Blérancourt France 49°31N 3°9E 71 C10
Bletchley U.K. 51°59N 0°44W 67 F7
Bleus, Monts Dem. Rep. of the Congo 1°30N 30°30E 142 B3
Blida Algeria 36°30N 2°49E 136 A4
Blida □ Algeria 36°35N 3°0E 136 A4
Blidet Amor Algeria 32°59N 5°58E 136 B5
Blidö Sweden 59°37N 18°53E 62 E12
Blidsberg Sweden 57°56N 13°30E 63 G7
Blieskastel Germany 49°14N 7°12E 77 F3
Bligh Sound N.Z. 44°47S 167°32E 155 E2
Bligh Water Fiji 17°0S 178°0E 154 a
Blind River Canada 46°10N 82°58W 164 C3
Blinisht Albania 41°52N 19°59E 96 E3
Bliss Idaho, U.S.A. 42°56N 114°57W 168 E6
Bliss N.Y., U.S.A. 42°34N 78°15W 174 D6
Blissfield U.S.A. 40°24N 81°58W 174 F3
Blitar Indonesia 8°5S 112°11E 119 H15
Blitchton U.S.A. 32°12N 81°26W 178 C8
Blitta Togo 8°23N 1°6E 139 D5
Block I. U.S.A. 41°11N 71°35W 175 E13
Block Island Sd. U.S.A. 41°15N 71°40W 175 E13
Bloemfontein S. Africa 29°6S 26°7E 144 C4
Bloemhof S. Africa 27°38S 25°32E 144 C4
Blois France 47°35N 1°20E 70 E8
Blomskog Sweden 59°16N 12°2E 62 E6
Blomstermåla Sweden 56°59N 16°21E 63 H10
Blönduós Iceland 65°40N 20°12W 60 D3
Blongas Indonesia 8°53S 116°2E 119 K19
Blonie Poland 52°12N 20°37E 83 F7
Bloodvein → Canada 51°47N 96°43W 163 C9
Bloody Foreland Ireland 55°10N 8°17W 64 A3
Bloomer U.S.A. 45°6N 91°29W 172 C8
Bloomfield Canada 43°59N 77°14W 174 C7
Bloomfield Iowa, U.S.A. 40°45N 92°25W 172 E7
Bloomfield N. Mex., U.S.A. 36°43N 107°59W 169 H10
Bloomfield Nebr., U.S.A. 42°36N 97°39W 172 D5
Bloomington Ill., U.S.A. 40°28N 89°0W 172 E9
Bloomington Ind., U.S.A. 39°10N 86°32W 172 F10
Bloomington Minn., U.S.A. 44°50N 93°17W 172 C7
Bloomsburg U.S.A. 41°0N 76°27W 175 F8
Bloomsbury Australia 20°48S 148°38E 150 b
Blora Indonesia 6°57S 111°25E 119 G14
Blossburg U.S.A. 41°41N 77°4W 174 E7
Blosseville Kyst Greenland 68°50N 26°30W 57 D8
Blouberg S. Africa 23°8S 28°59E 145 B4
Blountstown U.S.A. 30°27N 85°3W 178 E4
Bludenz Austria 47°10N 9°50E 78 D2
Blue Cypress L. U.S.A. 27°44N 80°45W 179 H9
Blue Earth U.S.A. 43°38N 94°6W 172 D6
Blue Hole △ Belize 17°24N 87°30W 182 C2
Blue Lagoon △ Zambia 15°28S 27°26E 143 F2
Blue Mesa Res. U.S.A. 38°28N 107°20W 168 G10
Blue Mountain Lake U.S.A. 43°51N 74°27W 175 C10
Blue Mountain Pk. Jamaica 18°3N 76°36W 182 a
Blue Mt. U.S.A. 40°30N 76°30W 175 F8
Blue Mts. Australia 33°40S 150°15E 153 B9
Blue Mts. Jamaica 18°3N 76°36W 182 a
Blue Mts. Maine, U.S.A. 44°50N 70°35W 175 B14
Blue Mts. Oreg., U.S.A. 45°0N 118°20W 168 D4
Blue Mts. △ Australia 34°2S 150°15E 153 C9
Blue Mud B. Australia 13°30S 136°0E 150 A2
Blue Mud Bay ☼ Australia 13°25S 136°2E 150 A2
Blue Nile = Nîl el Azraq → Sudan 15°38N 32°31E 135 E12
Blue Rapids U.S.A. 39°41N 96°39W 172 F5
Blue Ridge U.S.A. 36°40N 80°50W 173 G13
Blue River Canada 52°6N 119°18W 162 C5
Bluefield U.S.A. 37°15N 81°17W 173 G13
Bluefields Nic. 12°20N 83°50W 182 D3
Bluevale Canada 43°51N 81°15W 174 C3
Bluff Australia 23°35S 149°4E 150 C4
Bluff N.Z. 46°37S 168°20E 155 G3
Bluff U.S.A. 37°17N 109°33W 169 H9
Bluff Harbour N.Z. 46°36S 168°21E 155 G3
Bluff Knoll Australia 34°24S 118°15E 149 F2
Bluff Pt. Australia 27°50S 114°5E 149 E1
Bluffton Ga., U.S.A. 31°31N 84°52W 178 D5
Bluffton Ind., U.S.A. 40°44N 85°11W 173 E11
Bluffton S.C., U.S.A. 32°14N 80°52W 178 C9
Blumenau Brazil 27°0S 49°0W 191 B6
Blunt U.S.A. 44°31N 99°59W 172 C4
Bly U.S.A. 42°24N 121°3W 168 E3
Blyde River Canyon ⌂ S. Africa 24°37S 31°2E 145 B5
Blyth Australia 33°49S 138°28E 152 B3
Blyth Canada 43°44N 81°26W 174 C3
Blyth U.K. 55°8N 1°31W 66 B6
Blythe Calif., U.S.A. 33°37N 114°36W 171 M12
Blythe Ga., U.S.A. 33°17N 82°12W 178 B7
Blytheville U.S.A. 35°56N 89°55W 177 D10
Bo S. Leone 7°55N 11°50W 138 D2
Bo Duc Vietnam 11°58N 106°50E 121 G6
Bo Hai China 39°0N 119°0E 115 E10
Bo Hai Haixia Asia 38°25N 121°10E 115 E11
Bo Xian = Bozhou China 33°55N 115°41E 114 H8
Boa Esperança, Represa Brazil 6°50S 43°50W 189 B2
Boa Nova Brazil 14°22S 40°10W 189 C2
Boa Viagem Brazil 5°7S 39°44W 189 B3
Boa Vista Brazil 2°48N 60°30W 186 C6
Boa Vista C. Verde Is. 16°0N 22°49W 134 b
Boaco Nic. 12°29N 85°35W 182 D2
Bo'ai China 35°10N 113°3E 114 G7
Boal Spain 43°25N 6°49W 88 B4
Boalsburg U.S.A. 40°47N 77°49W 174 F7
Boane Mozam. 26°6S 32°19E 145 C5
Boao China 19°8N 110°34E 117 a
Boardman U.S.A. 41°2N 80°40W 174 E4
Boath India 19°20N 78°20E 126 E4
Bobadah Australia 32°19S 146°41E 153 B7
Bobai China 22°17N 109°59E 116 F7
Bobbili India 18°35N 83°30E 126 E6
Bóbbio Italy 44°46N 9°23E 92 D6
Bobcaygeon Canada 44°33N 78°33W 174 B6
Boblad India 17°13N 75°26E 126 F2
Böblingen Germany 48°40N 9°1E 77 G5
Bobo-Dioulasso Burkina Faso 11°8N 4°13W 138 C4
Bobolice Poland 53°58N 16°37E 82 E3
Boboņong Botswana 21°58S 28°20E 145 B4
Boboshevo Bulgaria 42°9N 23°0E 96 D7
Bobov Dol Bulgaria 42°20N 23°0E 96 D6
Bóbr → Poland 52°4N 15°4E 83 F2
Bobraomby, Tanjon' i Madag. 12°40S 49°10E 141 G9
Bobrov Russia 51°5N 40°2E 86 E5
Bobrovytsya Ukraine 50°45N 31°23E 85 G6
Bobruysk = Babruysk Belarus 53°10N 29°15E 75 B15
Bobrynets Ukraine 48°4N 32°5E 85 H7
Boby, Pic Madag. 22°12S 46°55E 141 J9
Boca del Rio Mexico 19°5N 96°4W 181 D5
Boca do Acre Brazil 8°50S 67°27W 188 B4
Boca Grande U.S.A. 26°45N 82°16W 179 J7
Boca Raton U.S.A. 26°21N 80°5W 179 J9
Bocaiúva Brazil 17°7S 43°49W 189 D2
Bocanda Ivory C. 7°5N 4°31W 138 D4
Bocas del Dragón = Dragon's Mouths Trin. & Tob. 11°0N 61°50W 187 K15
Bocas del Toro Panama 9°15N 82°20W 182 E3
Boceguillas Spain 41°20N 3°39W 88 D7
Bochmanivka Ukraine 47°40N 29°34E 81 C14
Bochnia Poland 49°58N 20°27E 83 J7
Bocholt Germany 51°50N 6°36E 76 D2
Bochum = Senwabarana S. Africa 23°17S 29°7E 145 B4
Bochum Germany 51°28N 7°13E 76 D3
Bockenem Germany 52°1N 10°8E 76 C6
Bočki Poland 52°39N 23°3E 83 F10
Bocognano France 42°5N 9°4E 73 F13
Bocoyna Mexico 27°52N 107°35W 180 B3
Bocşa Romania 45°21N 21°47E 80 E6
Boda Dalarna, Sweden 61°1N 15°13E 62 C9
Böda Kalmar, Sweden 57°15N 17°3E 63 G11
Boda Västernorrland, Sweden 62°52N 16°39E 62 B10
Bodafors Sweden 57°48N 14°23E 63 G8
Bodaybo Russia 57°50N 114°0E 107 D12
Boddam U.K. 59°56N 1°17W 65 B7
Boddington Australia 32°50S 116°30E 149 F2
Bode Sadu Nigeria 9°0N 4°47E 139 D5
Bodega Bay U.S.A. 38°20N 123°3W 170 G3
Boden Sweden 65°50N 21°42E 60 D19
Bodensee Europe 47°35N 9°25E 77 H5
Bodenteich Germany 52°50N 10°42E 76 C6
Bodh Gaya India 24°41N 84°59E 125 G11
Bodhan India 18°40N 77°44E 126 E3
Bodinayakkanur India 10°2N 77°10E 127 J3
Bodinga Nigeria 12°58N 5°10E 139 C6
Bodmin U.K. 50°28N 4°43W 67 G3
Bodmin Moor U.K. 50°33N 4°36W 67 G3
Bodø Norway 67°17N 14°24E 60 C16
Bodrog → Hungary 48°11N 21°22E 80 B6
Bodrum Turkey 37°3N 27°30E 99 D9
Bódva → Hungary 48°19N 20°45E 80 B5
Boën France 45°44N 4°1E 73 C8
Boende Dem. Rep. of the Congo 0°24S 21°12E 140 E4
Boeotia = Viotia Greece 38°20N 23°0E 98 C5
Boerne U.S.A. 29°47N 98°44W 176 G5
Boesmans → S. Africa 33°42S 26°39E 144 D4
Boffa Guinea 10°16N 14°3W 138 C2
Bogalusa U.S.A. 30°47N 89°52W 177 F10
Bogan → Australia 30°20S 146°55E 153 A7
Bogan Gate Australia 33°7S 147°49E 153 B7
Bogandé Burkina Faso 13°2N 0°8W 139 C4
Bogantungan Australia 23°41S 147°17E 150 C4
Bogata U.S.A. 33°28N 95°13W 176 E7
Bogatić Serbia 44°51N 19°30E 96 B3
Boğazkale Turkey 40°2N 34°37E 104 B6
Boğazlıyan Turkey 39°11N 35°14E 104 C6
Bogda Shan China 43°35N 89°40E 109 D11
Bogen Sweden 60°4N 12°33E 62 D6
Bogense Denmark 55°34N 10°5E 63 J4
Bogetići Montenegro 42°41N 18°58E 96 D2
Boggabilla Australia 28°36S 150°24E 151 D5
Boggabri Australia 30°45S 150°5E 153 A9
Boggeragh Mts. Ireland 52°2N 8°55W 64 D3
Boglan = Solhan Turkey 38°57N 41°3E 105 C9
Bognor Regis U.K. 50°47N 0°40W 67 G7
Bogo Phil. 11°3N 124°0E 119 B6
Bogodukhov = Bohodukhiv Ukraine 50°9N 35°33E 85 G8
Bogong, Mt. Australia 36°47S 147°17E 153 D7
Bogor Indonesia 6°36S 106°48E 118 F3
Bogoroditsk Russia 53°47N 38°8E 84 F10
Bogorodsk Russia 56°4N 43°30E 86 B6
Bogoso Ghana 5°38N 2°3W 138 D4
Bogotá Colombia 4°34N 74°0W 186 C4
Bogotol Russia 56°15N 89°50E 106 D9
Bogou Togo 10°40N 0°12E 139 C5
Bogra Bangla. 24°51N 89°22E 123 G16
Boguchany Russia 58°40N 97°30E 107 D10
Boguchar Russia 49°55N 40°32E 86 F5
Bogué Mauritania 16°45N 14°10W 138 B2
Boguszów-Gorce Poland 50°45N 16°12E 83 H3
Bohain-en-Vermandois France 49°59N 3°28E 71 C10
Bohdan Ukraine 48°2N 24°22E 81 B9
Bohemian Forest = Böhmerwald Germany 49°8N 13°14E 77 F9
Bohena Cr. → Australia 30°17S 149°42E 153 A8
Bohinjska Bistrica Slovenia 46°17N 14°1E 93 B11
Böhmerwald Germany 49°8N 13°14E 77 F9
Bohmte Germany 52°22N 8°19E 76 C4
Bohodukhiv Ukraine 50°9N 35°33E 85 G8
Bohol □ Phil. 9°50N 124°10E 119 C6
Bohol Sea Phil. 9°0N 124°0E 119 C6
Bohongou Burkina Faso 12°30N 0°40E 139 C5
Bőhönye Hungary 46°25N 17°28E 80 D2
Bohorodchany Ukraine 48°48N 24°32E 81 B9
Bohorok Indonesia 3°30N 98°12E 121 L2
Böhöt Mongolia 45°13N 108°16E 114 B5
Bohu China 41°58N 86°37E 109 D11
Bohuslän Sweden 58°25N 12°0E 63 F5
Bohuslav Ukraine 49°33N 30°56E 85 H6
Boi Nigeria 9°35N 9°27E 139 D6
Boi, Pta. do Brazil 23°55S 45°15W 191 A6
Boiaçu Brazil 0°27S 61°46W 186 D6
Boigu Australia 9°16S 142°13E 150 a
Boileau, C. Australia 17°40S 122°7E 148 C3
Boipariguda India 18°46N 82°26E 126 E6
Boipeba, I. de Brazil 13°39S 38°55W 189 C3
Boiro Spain 42°39N 8°54W 88 C2
Boise U.S.A. 43°37N 116°13W 168 E5
Boise City U.S.A. 36°44N 102°31W 176 C3
Boissevain Canada 49°15N 100°5W 163 D8
Böite → Italy 46°5N 12°5E 93 B9
Boitzenburg Germany 53°16N 13°35E 76 B9
Boizenburg Germany 53°23N 10°43E 76 B6
Bojador, C. W. Sahara 26°0N 14°30W 134 C3
Bojana → Albania 41°52N 19°22E 96 E3
Bojano Italy 41°29N 14°29E 95 A7
Bojanowo Poland 51°43N 16°42E 83 G3
Bøjden Denmark 55°6N 10°7E 63 J4
Bojnūrd Iran 37°30N 57°20E 129 B8
Bojonegoro Indonesia 7°11S 111°54E 119 G14
Boju Nigeria 7°22N 7°55E 139 D6
Boka Serbia 45°22N 20°52E 80 E5
Boka Kotorska Montenegro 42°23N 18°32E 96 D2
Bokala Ivory C. 8°31N 4°33W 138 D4
Bokani Nigeria 9°28N 5°10E 139 D6
Bokaro India 23°46N 85°55E 125 H11
Boké Guinea 10°56N 14°17W 138 C2
Bokhara → Australia 29°55S 146°42E 151 D4
Bokkos Nigeria 9°17N 9°1E 139 D6
Boknafjorden Norway 59°14N 5°40E 61 G11
Bokor △ Cambodia 10°50N 104°1E 121 G5
Bokora △ Uganda 2°12N 31°32E 142 B3
Bokoro Chad 12°25N 17°14E 135 F9
Bokpyin Burma 11°18N 98°42E 121 G2
Boksitogorsk Russia 59°22N 33°50E 84 C7
Bokungu Dem. Rep. of the Congo 0°35S 22°50E 140 E4
Bol Croatia 43°18N 16°38E 93 E13
Bolama Guinea-Biss. 11°30N 15°30W 138 C1
Bolan → Pakistan 28°38N 67°42E 124 E2
Bolan Pass Pakistan 29°50N 67°20E 122 E5
Bolaños → Mexico 21°12N 104°5W 180 C4
Bolaños de Calatrava Spain 38°54N 3°40W 89 G7
Bolayır Turkey 40°31N 26°45E 97 F10
Bolbec France 49°30N 0°30E 70 C7
Boldājī Iran 31°56N 51°3E 129 D6
Boldeşti-Scăeni Romania 45°3N 26°2E 81 E11
Bole China 44°55N 81°37E 109 C10
Bole Ghana 9°3N 2°23W 138 D4
Bolekhiv Ukraine 49°0N 23°57E 75 D12
Bolesławiec Poland 51°17N 15°37E 83 G2
Bolgatanga Ghana 10°44N 0°53W 139 C4
Bolgrad = Bolhrad Ukraine 45°40N 28°32E 81 E13
Bolhrad Ukraine 45°40N 28°32E 81 E13
Bolinao Phil. 16°23N 119°54E 119 A5
Bolingbroke U.S.A. 32°57N 83°48W 178 C6
Bolintin-Vale Romania 44°27N 25°46E 81 F10
Bolivar Peru 7°18S 77°48W 188 B2
Bolivar Mo., U.S.A. 37°37N 93°25W 172 G7
Bolivar N.Y., U.S.A. 42°4N 78°10W 174 D6
Bolivar Tenn., U.S.A. 35°12N 89°0W 177 D10
Bolívar, Pico Venezuela 8°32N 71°2W 183 E5
Bolivia ■ S. Amer. 17°6S 64°0W 186 G6
Bolivian Plateau = Altiplano Bolivia 17°0S 68°0W 188 D4
Boljevac Serbia 43°51N 21°58E 96 C5
Bolkhov Russia 53°25N 36°0E 84 F9
Bolków Poland 50°55N 16°6E 83 H3
Bollebygd Sweden 57°40N 12°35E 63 G6
Bollène France 44°18N 4°45E 73 D8
Bollnäs Sweden 61°21N 16°24E 62 C10
Bollon Australia 28°2S 147°29E 151 D4
Bollstabruk Sweden 62°59N 17°40E 62 B11
Bolmen Sweden 56°55N 13°40E 63 H7
Bolnisi Georgia 41°26N 44°32E 87 K7
Bolobo Dem. Rep. of the Congo 2°6S 16°20E 140 E3
Bologna Italy 44°29N 11°20E 93 D8
Bologna ✈ (BLQ) Italy 44°32N 11°16E 93 D8
Bologoye Russia 57°55N 34°5E 84 D8
Bolomba Dem. Rep. of the Congo 0°35N 19°0E 140 D3
Bolonchén Mexico 20°1N 89°45W 181 D7
Bolótana Italy 40°20N 8°52E 94 B1
Boloven, Cao Nguyen Laos 15°10N 106°30E 120 E6
Bolpur India 23°40N 87°45E 125 H12
Bolsena Italy 42°39N 11°59E 93 F8
Bolsena, L. di Italy 42°36N 11°56E 93 F8
Bolshakovo Russia 54°53N 21°40E 82 D8
Bolshaya Chernigovka Russia 52°6N 50°52E 86 D10
Bolshaya Glushitsa Russia 52°28N 50°30E 86 D10
Bolshaya Martynovka Russia 47°19N 41°37E 87 G5
Bolshaya Vradiyevka Ukraine 47°50N 30°40E 85 J6
Bolshevik, Ostrov Russia 78°30N 102°0E 107 B11
Bolshoy Anyuy → Russia 68°30N 160°49E 107 C17
Bolshoy Begichev, Ostrov Russia 74°20N 112°30E 107 B12
Bolshoy Kamen Russia 43°7N 132°19E 112 C6
Bolshoy Kavkas = Caucasus Mountains Eurasia 42°50N 44°0E 87 J7
Bolshoy Lyakhovskiy, Ostrov Russia 73°35N 142°0E 107 B15
Bolshoy Tyuters, Ostrov Russia 59°51N 27°13E 84 C4
Bolsward Neths. 53°3N 5°32E 69 A5
Bolt Head U.K. 50°12N 3°48W 67 G4
Boltaña Spain 42°28N 0°4E 90 C5
Boltigen Switz. 46°38N 7°24E 77 J3
Bolton Canada 43°54N 79°45W 174 C5
Bolton U.K. 53°35N 2°26W 66 D5
Bolton Landing U.S.A. 43°32N 73°35W 175 C11
Bolu Turkey 40°45N 31°35E 104 B4
Bolu □ Turkey 40°40N 31°30E 104 B4
Bolungavík Iceland 66°9N 23°15W 60 C2
Boluo China 23°3N 114°21E 117 F10
Bolvadin Turkey 38°45N 31°4E 104 C4
Bolzano Italy 46°31N 11°22E 93 B8
Bom Conselho Brazil 9°10S 36°41W 189 B3
Bom Despacho Brazil 19°43S 45°15W 189 D1
Bom Jesus Brazil 9°4S 44°22W 189 B2
Bom Jesus da Gurguéia, Serra Brazil 9°0S 43°0W 189 B2
Bom Jesus da Lapa Brazil 13°15S 43°25W 189 C2
Boma Dem. Rep. of the Congo 5°50S 13°4E 140 F2
Bomaderry Australia 34°52S 150°37E 153 C9
Bombala Australia 36°56S 149°15E 153 D8
Bombarral Portugal 39°15N 9°9W 89 F1
Bombay = Mumbai India 18°56N 72°50E 126 E1
Bombay U.S.A. 44°56N 74°34W 175 B10
Bombedor, Pta. Venezuela 9°53N 61°37W 187 L15
Bomberai, Semenanjung Indonesia 3°0S 133°0E 119 E8
Bomboma Dem. Rep. of the Congo 2°25N 18°55E 140 D3
Bombombwa Dem. Rep. of the Congo 1°40N 25°40E 142 B2
Bomi China 29°50N 95°45E 110 F8
Bomi Hills Liberia 7°1N 10°38W 138 D2
Bomili Dem. Rep. of the Congo 1°45N 27°5E 142 B2
Bømlo Norway 59°37N 5°13E 61 G11
Bomokandi → Dem. Rep. of the Congo 3°39N 26°8E 142 B2
Bompoka India 8°15N 93°13E 127 K11
Bomu → C.A.R. 4°40N 22°30E 140 D4
Bon, C. = Ra's aţ Tib Tunisia 37°1N 11°2E 136 A6
Bon Acceuil Mauritius 20°10S 57°39E 141 d
Bon Echo ⌂ Canada 44°55N 77°16W 174 B7
Bon Sar Pa Vietnam 12°24N 107°35E 120 F6
Bonāb Āżarbājān-e Sharqī, Iran 37°20N 46°4E 105 D12
Bonāb Zanjān, Iran 36°35N 48°41E 105 D13
Bonaigarh India 21°50N 84°57E 125 J11
Bonaire U.S.A. 32°33N 83°36W 178 C6
Bonaire W. Indies 12°10N 68°15W 183 D6
Bonampak Mexico 16°44N 91°5W 181 D6
Bonang Australia 37°11S 148°41E 153 D8
Bonanza Nic. 13°54N 84°35W 182 D3
Bonaparte Arch. Australia 14°0S 124°30E 148 B3
Boñar Spain 42°52N 5°19W 88 C5
Bonar Bridge U.K. 57°54N 4°20W 65 D4
Bonasse Trin. & Tob. 10°5N 61°54W 187 K15
Bonaventure Canada 48°5N 65°32W 165 C6
Bonavista Canada 48°40N 53°5W 165 C9
Bonavista, C. Canada 48°42N 53°5W 165 C9
Bonavista B. Canada 48°45N 53°25W 165 C9
Bondeno Italy 44°53N 11°25E 93 D8
Bondo Dem. Rep. of the Congo 3°55N 23°53E 142 B1
Bondokodi Indonesia 9°33S 119°0E 148 A2
Bondoukou Ivory C. 8°2N 2°47W 138 D4
Bondowoso Indonesia 7°55S 113°49E 119 G15
Bone, Teluk Indonesia 4°10S 120°50E 119 E6
Bonerate Indonesia 7°25S 121°5E 119 F6
Bonerate, Kepulauan Indonesia 6°30S 121°10E 119 F6
Bo'ness U.K. 56°1N 3°37W 65 E5
Bonete, Cerro Argentina 27°55S 68°40W 190 B2
Bong Son = Hoai Nhon Vietnam 14°28N 109°1E 120 E7
Bongaigaon India 26°28N 90°34E 110 F7
Bongandanga Dem. Rep. of the Congo 1°24N 21°3E 140 D4
Bongor Chad 10°35N 15°20E 135 F9
Bongos, Massif des C.A.R. 8°40N 22°25E
Bongouanou Ivory C. 6°42N 4°15W
Bonham U.S.A. 33°35N 96°11W
Boni Mali 15°3N 2°10W
Boni ⌂ Kenya 1°35S 41°18E
Boni Italia France 41°24N 9°10E
Bonifacio, Bouches de Medit. S. 41°12N 9°15E
Bonifay U.S.A. 30°47N 85°41W
Bonin Is. = Ogasawara Gunto Pac. Oc. 27°0N 142°0E
Bonita Springs U.S.A. 26°21N 81°47W
Bonkoukou Niger 14°0N 3°15E
Bonn Germany 50°46N 7°6E
Bonnat France 46°20N 1°54E
Bonne Terre U.S.A. 37°55N 90°33W
Bonneau U.S.A. 33°16N 79°58W
Bonners Ferry U.S.A. 48°42N 116°19W
Bonnétable France 48°11N 0°25E
Bonneval France 45°22N 7°3E
Bonneval-sur-Arc France 48°11N 1°24E
Bonneville France 46°4N 6°24E
Bonney, L. Australia 37°50S 140°20E
Bonnie Doon Australia 37°2S 145°53E
Bonnie Rock Australia 30°29S 118°22E
Bonny Nigeria 4°25N 7°13E
Bonny → Nigeria 4°20N 7°10E
Bonny, Bight of Africa 3°30N 9°20E
Bonny Hills Australia 31°36S 152°51E
Bonny-sur-Loire France 47°33N 2°50E
Bonnyrigg U.K. 55°53N 3°6W
Bonnyville Canada 54°20N 110°45W
Bonoi Italy 40°25N 9°2E
Bonoi Indonesia 1°45S 137°41E
Bonorva Italy 40°25N 8°46E
Bonsall U.S.A. 33°16N 117°14W
Bontang Indonesia 0°10N 117°30E
Bontebok △ S. Africa 34°5S 20°28E
Bonthe S. Leone 7°30N 12°33W
Bontoc Phil. 17°7N 120°58E
Bonyeri Ghana 5°1N 2°46W
Bonyhád Hungary 46°18N 18°32E
Bonython Ra. Australia 23°40S 128°45E
Booderee △ Australia 35°12S 150°42E
Boodjamulla △ Australia 18°15S 138°6E
Bookabie Australia 31°50S 132°41E
Booker U.S.A. 36°27N 100°32W
Bool Lagoon Australia 37°7S 140°40E
Boola Guinea 8°22N 8°41W
Booleroo Centre Australia 32°53S 138°21E
Booligal Australia 33°58S 144°53E
Böön Tsagaan Nuur Mongolia 45°35N 99°9E
Boonah Australia 27°58S 152°41E
Boone Iowa, U.S.A. 42°4N 93°53W
Boone N.C., U.S.A. 36°13N 81°41W
Booneville Ark., U.S.A. 35°8N 93°55W
Booneville Miss., U.S.A. 34°39N 88°34W
Boonville Calif., U.S.A. 39°1N 123°22W
Boonville Ind., U.S.A. 38°3N 87°16W
Boonville Mo., U.S.A. 38°58N 92°44W
Boonville N.Y., U.S.A. 43°29N 75°20W
Boorabbin △ Australia 31°30S 120°10E
Boorindal Australia 30°22S 146°11E
Boorowa Australia 34°28S 148°44E
Boort Australia 36°7S 143°46E
Boosaaso Somalia 11°12N 49°18E
Boothia, Gulf of Canada 71°0N 90°0W
Boothia Pen. Canada 71°0N 94°0W
Bootle U.K. 53°28N 3°1W
Booué Gabon 0°5S 11°55E
Boppard Germany 50°13N 7°35E
Boquilla, Presa de la Mexico 27°31N 105°30W
Boquillas del Carmen Mexico 29°11N 102°58W
Bor Czech Rep. 49°41N 12°45E
Bor Russia 56°28N 43°59E
Bor Serbia 44°5N 22°7E
Bor South Sudan 6°10N 31°40E
Bor Sweden 57°9N 14°10E
Bor Turkey 37°54N 34°32E
Bor Mashash Israel 31°7N 34°50E
Bora Bora French Polynesia 16°30S 151°45W
Borah Peak U.S.A. 44°8N 113°47W
Boraha, Nosy Madag. 16°50S 49°55E
Borankul Kazakhstan 46°11N 54°25E
Borås Sweden 57°43N 12°56E
Borāzjān Iran 29°22N 51°10E
Borba Brazil 4°12S 59°34W
Borba Portugal 38°50N 7°26W
Borborema, Planalto da Brazil 7°0S 37°0W
Borcea Romania 44°20N 27°45E
Borçka Turkey 41°25N 41°41E
Bord Khūn-e Now Iran 28°3N 51°28E
Borda, C. Australia 35°45S 136°34E
Bordeaux France 44°50N 0°36W
Bordeaux ✈ (BOD) France 44°50N 0°35W
Borden Australia 34°3S 118°12E
Borden-Carleton Canada 46°18N 63°47W
Borden I. Canada 78°30N 111°30W
Borden Pen. Canada 73°0N 83°0W
Borden Springs U.S.A. 33°56N 85°28W
Border Ranges △ Australia 28°24S 152°56E
Borders = Scottish Borders □ U.K. 55°35N 2°50W
Bordertown Australia 36°19S 140°45E
Borðeyri Iceland 65°12N 21°6W
Bordighera Italy 43°46N 7°39E
Bordj bou Arreridj Algeria 36°4N 4°45E
Bordj Bourguiba Tunisia 32°12N 10°2E
Bordj Flye Ste-Marie Algeria 27°19N 2°32W
Bordj in Eker Algeria 24°9N 5°3E
Bordj Menaïel Algeria 36°46N 3°43E
Bordj Messouda Algeria 30°12N 9°25E
Bordj Mokhtar Algeria 21°20N 0°56E
Bordj Nili Algeria 33°28N 3°2E
Bordj Omar Driss Algeria 28°10N 6°40E

Sif Fatima Algeria 31°6N 8°41E 136 B5
Tarat Algeria 25°55N 9°3E 136 C4
amwood U.K. 51°40N 0°15W 67 F7
Wielkopolski
nd 51°54N 17°11E 83 G4
sberg Sweden 58°34N 15°17E 63 F9
= Porvoo Finland 60°24N 25°40E 84 B3
mpad India 19°37N 80°52E 126 F5
rnes Iceland 64°32N 21°55W 60 D3
fjellet Norway 65°20N 13°45E 60 D15
r Neths. 52°54N 6°44E 69 B6
r U.S.A. 35°39N 101°24W 176 D4
olm Sweden 56°52N 16°39E 63 H10
a Italy 38°49N 16°30E 95 D9
San Dalmazzo
44°20N 7°30E 92 D4
San Lorenzo Italy 43°57N 11°23E 93 E8
Val di Taro Italy 44°29N 9°46E 92 D6
Valsugana Italy 46°3N 11°27E 93 B8
manero Italy 45°42N 8°28E 92 C5
rose Italy 42°11N 13°13E 93 F10
sésia Italy 45°43N 8°16E 92 C5
yn Tal Mongolia 43°50N 111°58E 114 C6
igeria 4°42N 7°21E 139 E6
amma India 19°33N 82°33E 126 E6
nane Laos 18°33N 103°43E 120 C4
glebsk Russia 51°27N 42°5E 86 E6
v = Barysaw
rus 54°17N 28°28E 75 A15
vka Russia 50°36N 36°1E 85 G9
neïn Tunisia 31°45N 10°9E 136 B6
Peru 4°20S 77°40W 186 D3
Spain 41°48N 1°34W 90 D3
Blancas = Les Borges
nques Spain 41°31N 0°52E 90 D5
ni Georgia 41°48N 43°28E 87 K6
p Denmark 55°39N 9°39E 63 J3
u Chad 18°15N 18°50E 135 E9
m Germany 53°34N 6°40E 76 B2
nge Sweden 60°29N 15°26E 62 D9
, C. Antarctica 66°15S 52°30E 55 C5
Turkey 38°44N 28°27E 99 C10
da → Italy 44°23N 8°13E 92 D5
o Italy 46°28N 10°22E 92 B7
Germany 51°7N 12°29E 76 D8
Sulinowo Poland 53°32N 16°36E 82 E3
o E. Indies 1°0N 115°0E 118 D5
olm Denmark 55°10N 15°0E 63 J8
olmsgattet Europe 55°15N 14°20E 63 J8
□ Nigeria 11°30N 10°30E 139 C7
s Spain 36°48N 5°42W 89 J5
va Turkey 38°27N 27°14E 99 C9
Yassa Nigeria 12°14N 12°25E 139 C7
udur △
nesia 7°36S 110°12E 119 G14
ino Russia 55°31N 35°40E 84 E8
ino Ukraine 46°18N 29°15E 81 D14
ontsy Russia 62°42N 131°8E 107 C14
oro Shan China 44°6N 83°10E 109 D10
no Burkina Faso 11°45N 2°58W 138 C4
U.S.A. 35°0N 117°39W 171 L9
gan Phil. 11°37N 125°26E 119 B7
u Ivory C. 8°46N 7°30W 138 D3
an Bulgaria 43°27N 23°45E 96 C7
ichi Russia 58°25N 33°55E 84 C7
sk Russia 55°12N 36°24E 84 E9
skoy Kazakhstan 53°48N 64°9E 108 B6
y Sweden 55°27N 14°10E 63 J8
go Springs
A. 33°15N 116°23W 171 M10
l Spain 40°4N 0°4W 90 E4
okane Ireland 53°0N 8°7W 64 D3
loola Australia 16°4S 136°17E 150 B2
Cluj, Romania 46°56N 23°40E 81 D8
Maramureș,
nania 47°41N 24°50E 81 C9
d India 22°25N 72°54E 124 H5
Romania 46°57N 25°34E 81 D10
chiv Ukraine 48°48N 23°25E 81 B11
d-Abaúj-Zemplén □
ngary 48°20N 21°0E 80 B6
es-Orgues France 45°24N 2°29E 72 C6
a = Bole China 44°55N 81°37E 109 C10
U.K. 52°29N 4°2W 67 E3
an Sweden 62°45N 13°50E 62 B7
erd Iran 33°55N 48°50E 105 F13
ong S. Korea 36°21N 126°36E 115 F14
ya Ukraine 49°4N 23°0E 83 J10
lav Ukraine 49°18N 23°28E 83 J10
pil Ukraine 50°21N 30°59E 85 G6
omi = Borjomi
rgia 41°48N 43°28E 87 K6
a Ukraine 51°18N 32°26E 85 G7
a Russia 50°24N 116°31E 111 A12
Italy 40°18N 8°30E 94 B1
ska Dubica
.-H. 45°10N 16°50E 93 C13
ska Gradiška
.-H. 45°10N 17°15E 80 E2
ska Kostajnica
.-H. 45°11N 16°33E 93 C13
ska Krupa
.-H. 44°53N 16°10E 93 D13
nski Brod Bos.-H. 45°10N 18°0E 80 E2
nski Novi Bos.-H. 45°2N 16°22E 93 C13
nski Petrovac
.-H. 44°35N 16°21E 93 D13
nski Šamac Bos.-H. 45°3N 18°29E 80 E3
nsko Grahovo
.-H. 44°12N 16°26E 93 D13
stle U.K. 50°41N 4°42W 67 G3
bbelle Barbados 13°17N 59°35W 183 g
hina 23°53N 106°35E 116 F6
ang S. Korea 34°46N 127°5E 115 G14
an China 36°28N 117°49E 115 F9
of S. Africa 28°31S 25°13E 144 C4
rūyeh Iran 33°50N 57°30E 129 C8
egrad Serbia 42°30N 22°27E 96 D6
ovice Czech Rep. 49°29N 16°40E 79 B9
a → Bos.-H. 45°4N 18°29E 80 E3
a i Hercegovina = Bosnia-
rzegovina ■ Europe 44°0N 18°0E 80 G2
a-Herzegovina ■
rope 44°0N 18°0E 80 G2
k Indonesia 1°5S 136°10E 119 E9
olo
n. Rep. of the Congo 4°15N 19°50E 140 D3
orus = İstanbul Boğazı
key 41°5N 29°3E 97 E13
ue Farms U.S.A. 35°51N 106°42W 169 J10
Bosra = Buşra ash Shām
Syria 32°30N 36°25E 130 C5
Bossangoa C.A.R. 6°35N 17°30E 140 C3
Bossé Bangou Niger 13°20N 1°18E 139 C5
Bossier City U.S.A. 32°31N 93°44W 176 E8
Bossiesvlei Namibia 25°1S 16°44E 144 C2
Bosso Niger 13°43N 13°19E 139 C7
Bosso, Dallol → Niger 12°25N 2°50E 139 C5
Bossol, Proliv Russia 46°30N 151°0E 107 E16
Bostan Pakistan 30°26N 67°2E 124 D2
Bostānābād Iran 37°50N 46°50E 105 D12
Bosten Hu China 41°55N 87°40E 109 D11
Boston U.K. 52°59N 0°2W 66 E7
Boston Ga., U.S.A. 30°47N 83°47W 178 E6
Boston Mass., U.S.A. 42°22N 71°3W 175 D13
Boston Bar Canada 49°52N 121°30W 162 D4
Boston Mts. U.S.A. 35°42N 93°15W 176 D8
Bostwick U.S.A. 29°46N 81°38W 178 F8
Bosumtwi, L. Ghana 6°30N 1°25W 139 D4
Bosut → Croatia 45°20N 18°45E 80 E3
Boswell Canada 49°28N 116°45W 162 D5
Boswell U.S.A. 40°10N 79°2W 174 F5
Botad India 22°15N 71°40E 124 H4
Botan → Turkey 37°57N 42°2E 105 D10
Botany B. Australia 33°58S 151°11E 147 E8
Botene Laos 17°35N 101°12E 120 D3
Botev Bulgaria 42°44N 24°52E 97 D8
Botevgrad Bulgaria 42°55N 23°47E 96 D7
Bothaville S. Africa 27°23S 26°34E 144 C4
Bothnia, G. of Europe 62°0N 20°0E 60 F19
Bothwell Australia 42°20S 147°1E 151 G4
Bothwell Canada 42°38N 81°52W 174 D3
Boticas Portugal 41°41N 7°40W 88 D3
Botletle → Botswana 20°10S 23°15E 144 B3
Botlikh Russia 42°39N 46°11E 87 J8
Botna → Moldova 46°45N 29°34E 81 D14
Botoroaga Romania 44°8N 25°32E 81 F10
Botoșani Romania 47°42N 26°41E 81 C11
Botoșani □ Romania 47°50N 26°50E 81 C11
Botou Burkina Faso 12°42N 1°59E 139 C5
Botou China 38°4N 116°34E 114 E9
Botricello Italy 38°56N 16°51E 95 D9
Botro Ivory C. 7°51N 5°19W 138 D3
Botshabelo S. Africa 29°14S 26°44E 144 C4
Botswana ■ Africa 22°0S 24°0E 144 B3
Bottineau U.S.A. 48°50N 100°27W 172 A3
Bottnaryd Sweden 57°47N 13°50E 63 G7
Bottrop Germany 51°31N 6°58E 76 D2
Botucatu Brazil 22°55S 48°30W 191 A6
Botum Sakor △
Cambodia 11°5N 103°15E 121 G4
Botwood Canada 49°6N 55°23W 165 C8
Bou Alam Algeria 33°50N 1°26E 136 B4
Bou Ali Algeria 27°11N 0°4W 136 C3
Bou Djébéha Mali 18°25N 2°45W 138 B4
Bou Guema Algeria 28°49N 0°19E 136 C4
Bou Ismaïl Algeria 36°38N 2°42E 136 A4
Bou Izakarn Morocco 29°12N 9°46W 136 C2
Boû Naga Mauritania 18°49N 13°20W 138 B2
Bou Noura Algeria 32°29N 3°43E 136 B4
Boû Rjeïmât Mauritania 19°4N 15°3W 138 B1
Bou Saâda Algeria 35°11N 4°9E 136 A4
Bou Salem Tunisia 36°45N 9°2E 136 A5
Bouaflé Ivory C. 7°1N 5°47W 138 D3
Bouaké Ivory C. 7°40N 5°2W 138 D3
Bouar C.A.R. 6°0N 15°40E 140 C3
Bouârfa Morocco 32°32N 1°58W 136 B3
Boubout Algeria 27°26N 4°30W 136 C3
Boucaut B. Australia 12°0S 134°25E 150 A1
Bouches-du-Rhône □
France 43°37N 5°2E 73 E9
Boucle de Baoulé △ Mali 13°53N 9°0W 138 C3
Boucles de la Seine Normande ⌂
France 49°32N 0°35E 70 C7
Bouctouche Canada 46°30N 64°45W 165 C7
Bouda Algeria 27°50N 0°27W 136 C3
Boudenib Morocco 31°59N 3°31W 136 B3
Boufarik Algeria 36°34N 2°58E 136 A4
Bougainville, C.
Australia 13°57S 126°4E 148 B4
Bougainville I.
Papua N. G. 6°0S 155°0E 147 B8
Bougainville Reef
Australia 15°30S 147°5E 150 B4
Bougaroun, C. Algeria 37°6N 6°30E 136 A5
Bougie = Bejaïa Algeria 36°42N 5°2E 136 A5
Bougouni Mali 11°30N 7°20W 138 C3
Bougtob Algeria 34°2N 0°5E 136 B4
Bouillon Belgium 49°44N 5°3E 69 E5
Bouïra Algeria 36°20N 3°59E 136 A4
Bouïra □ Algeria 36°15N 3°55E 136 A4
Boukombé Benin 10°13N 1°9E 139 C5
Boulal Mali 15°8N 8°21W 138 B3
Boulazac France 45°10N 0°47E 72 C4
Boulder Colo., U.S.A. 40°1N 105°17W 168 F11
Boulder Mont., U.S.A. 46°14N 112°7W 168 C7
Boulder City U.S.A. 35°58N 114°49W 171 K12
Boulder Creek U.S.A. 37°7N 122°7W 170 H4
Boulder Dam = Hoover Dam
U.S.A. 36°1N 114°44W 171 K12
Bouli Mauritania 15°17N 12°18W 138 B2
Boulia Australia 22°52S 139°51E 150 C2
Bouligny France 49°17N 5°45E 71 C12
Boulogne → France 47°12N 1°47W 70 E5
Boulogne-sur-Gesse
France 43°18N 0°38E 72 E4
Boulogne-sur-Mer France 50°42N 1°36E 71 B8
Bouloire France 47°59N 0°45E 70 E7
Boulouli Mali 15°30N 9°25W 138 B3
Boulsa Burkina Faso 12°39N 0°34W 139 C4
Boultoum Niger 14°45N 10°25E 139 C7
Bouma △ Fiji 16°50S 179°52W 154 a
Boumalne Dadès
Morocco 31°25N 6°0W 136 B2
Boûmdeïd Mauritania 17°25N 11°50W 138 B2
Boumerdès Algeria 36°46N 3°28E 136 A4
Boumerdès □ Algeria 36°45N 3°40E 136 A4
Boun Neua Laos 21°38N 101°54E 120 B3
Boun Tai Laos 21°23N 101°58E 120 B3
Bouna Ivory C. 9°10N 3°0W 138 D4
Boundary Peak
U.S.A. 37°51N 118°21W 170 H8
Boundiali Ivory C. 9°30N 6°20W 138 D3
Bountiful U.S.A. 40°53N 111°52W 168 F8
Bounty Is. Pac. Oc. 48°0S 178°30E 156 M9
Bounty Trough Pac. Oc. 46°0S 178°0E 156 M9
Boura Mali 12°25N 4°33W 138 C4
Bourbon-Lancy France 46°37N 3°45E 71 F10
Bourbon-l'Archambault
France 46°36N 3°4E 71 F10
Bourbonnais France 46°28N 3°0E 71 F10
Bourbonne-les-Bains
France 47°54N 5°45E 71 E12
Bourbourg France 50°56N 2°12E 71 B9
Bourdel L. Canada 56°43N 74°10W 164 A5
Bourem Mali 17°0N 0°24W 139 B4
Bourg France 45°3N 0°34W 72 C3
Bourg-Argental France 45°18N 4°32E 73 C8
Bourg-de-Péage France 45°2N 5°3E 73 C9
Bourg-en-Bresse France 46°13N 5°12E 71 F12
Bourg-Lastic France 45°39N 2°35E 72 C6
Bourg-Madame France 42°26N 1°55E 72 F5
Bourg-St-Andéol France 44°23N 4°39E 73 D8
Bourg-St-Maurice
France 45°35N 6°46E 73 C10
Bourganeuf France 45°57N 1°45E 72 C5
Bourgas = Burgas
Bulgaria 42°33N 27°29E 97 D11
Bourges France 47°9N 2°25E 71 E9
Bourget Canada 45°26N 75°9W 175 A9
Bourget, Lac du France 45°44N 5°52E 73 C9
Bourgneuf, B. de France 47°3N 2°10W 70 E4
Bourgneuf-en-Retz France 47°2N 1°58W 70 E5
Bourgogne □ France 47°0N 4°50E 71 F11
Bourgoin-Jallieu France 45°36N 5°17E 73 C9
Bourgueil France 47°17N 0°10E 70 E7
Bourke Australia 30°8S 145°55E 151 E4
Bourne U.K. 52°47N 0°22W 66 E7
Bournemouth U.K. 50°43N 1°52W 67 G6
Bournemouth □ U.K. 50°43N 1°52W 67 G6
Bouroum Burkina Faso 13°37N 0°39W 139 C4
Bouse U.S.A. 33°56N 114°0W 171 M13
Boussac France 46°22N 2°13E 71 F9
Boussé Burkina Faso 12°39N 1°53W 139 C4
Bousso Chad 10°34N 16°52E 135 F9
Boussouma
Burkina Faso 12°52N 1°13W 139 C4
Boutilimit Mauritania 17°45N 14°40W 138 B2
Boutonne → France 45°54N 0°50W 72 C3
Bouvet I. = Bouvetøya
Antarctica 54°26S 3°24E 56 M12
Bouvetøya Antarctica 54°26S 3°24E 56 M12
Bouxwiller France 48°49N 7°27E 71 D14
Bouza Niger 14°29N 6°2E 139 C6
Bouznika Morocco 33°46N 7°6W 136 B2
Bouzonville France 49°17N 6°32E 71 C13
Bova Marina Italy 37°56N 15°55E 95 E8
Bovalino Italy 38°10N 16°10E 95 D9
Bovec Slovenia 46°20N 13°33E 93 B10
Bovill U.S.A. 46°51N 116°24W 168 C5
Bovino Italy 41°15N 15°20E 95 A8
Bovril Argentina 31°21S 59°26W 190 C4
Bow → Canada 49°57N 111°41W 162 C6
Bow Island Canada 49°50N 111°23W 168 B8
Bowbells U.S.A. 48°48N 102°15W 172 A2
Bowdle U.S.A. 45°27N 99°39W 172 C4
Bowdon U.S.A. 33°32N 85°15W 178 B4
Bowdon Junction
U.S.A. 33°40N 85°9W 178 B4
Bowelling Australia 33°25S 116°30E 149 F2
Bowen Argentina 35°0S 67°31W 190 D2
Bowen Australia 20°0S 148°16E 150 J6
Bowen Mts. Australia 37°0S 147°50E 153 D7
Bowers Basin Pac. Oc. 53°45N 176°0E 54 D16
Bowers Ridge Pac. Oc. 54°0N 180°0E 54 D17
Bowie Ariz., U.S.A. 32°19N 109°29W 169 K9
Bowie Tex., U.S.A. 33°34N 97°51W 176 E6
Bowkān Iran 36°31N 46°12E 105 D12
Bowland, Forest of U.K. 54°0N 2°30W 66 D5
Bowling Green Fla.,
U.S.A. 27°38N 81°50W 179 H8
Bowling Green Ky.,
U.S.A. 36°59N 86°27W 172 G10
Bowling Green Ohio,
U.S.A. 41°23N 83°39W 173 E12
Bowling Green, C.
Australia 19°19S 147°25E 150 B4
Bowling Green Bay △
Australia 19°26S 146°57E 150 B4
Bowman N. Dak.,
U.S.A. 46°11N 103°24W 172 B2
Bowman S.C., U.S.A. 33°21N 80°41W 178 B9
Bowman I. Antarctica 65°0S 104°0E 55 C8
Bowmanville = Clarington
Canada 43°55N 78°41W 174 C6
Bowmore U.K. 55°45N 6°17W 65 F2
Bowral Australia 34°26S 150°27E 153 C9
Bowraville Australia 30°37S 152°52E 151 E5
Bowron → Canada 54°3N 121°50W 162 C4
Bowron Lake ⌂
Canada 53°10N 121°5W 162 C4
Bowser L. Canada 56°30N 129°30W 162 B3
Bowsman Canada 52°14N 101°12W 163 C8
Bowwood Zambia 17°5S 26°20E 143 F2
Box Cr. → Australia 34°10S 143°50E 151 E3
Boxholm Sweden 58°12N 15°3E 63 F9
Boxmeer Neths. 51°38N 5°56E 69 C5
Boxtel Neths. 51°36N 5°20E 69 C5
Boyabat Turkey 41°28N 34°47E 104 B6
Boyalıca Turkey 40°29N 29°33E 97 F13
Boyang China 29°0N 116°38E 117 C11
Boyany Ukraine 48°17N 26°8E 81 B11
Boyce U.S.A. 31°23N 92°40W 176 F8
Boyd U.S.A. 30°11N 83°37W 178 E6
Boyd L. Canada 52°46N 76°42W 164 B4
Boyle Canada 54°35N 112°49W 162 C6
Boyle Ireland 53°59N 8°18W 64 C3
Boyne → Ireland 53°43N 6°15W 64 C5
Boyne, Bend of the
Ireland 53°41N 6°27W 64 C5
Boyne City U.S.A. 45°13N 85°1W 173 C11
Boynitsa Bulgaria 43°58N 22°32E 96 C6
Boynton Beach U.S.A. 26°32N 80°4W 179 J9
Boyoma, Chutes
Dem. Rep. of the Congo 0°35N 25°23E 142 B2
Boysen Res. U.S.A. 43°25N 108°11W 168 E9
Boyuibe Bolivia 20°25S 63°17W 186 G6
Boyup Brook Australia 33°50S 116°23E 149 F2
Boz Burun Turkey 40°32N 28°46E 97 F12
Boz Dağ Turkey 37°18N 29°11E 99 D11
Boz Dağları Turkey 38°20N 28°0E 99 C10
Bozburun Turkey 36°43N 28°4E 99 E10
Bozcaada Turkey 39°49N 26°3E 104 C2
Bozdoğan Turkey 37°40N 28°17E 99 D10
Bozeman U.S.A. 45°41N 111°2W 168 D8
Bozen = Bolzano Italy 46°31N 11°22E 93 B8
Boževac Serbia 44°32N 21°24E 96 B5
Bozhou China 33°55N 115°41E 114 H8
Bozkır Turkey 37°11N 32°14E 104 D5
Bozkurt Turkey 37°50N 29°37E 99 D11
Bozouls France 44°28N 2°43E 72 D6
Bozoum C.A.R. 6°25N 16°35E 140 C3
Bozova Antalya, Turkey 37°13N 30°18E 99 D12
Bozova Sanliurfa, Turkey 37°21N 38°32E 105 D8
Bozovici Romania 44°56N 22°1E 80 F7
Bozüyük Turkey 39°54N 30°3E 99 B12
Bozyazı Turkey 36°6N 33°0E 128 B2
Bra Italy 44°42N 7°51E 92 D4
Braås Sweden 57°4N 15°3E 63 G9
Brabant □ Belgium 50°46N 4°30E 69 D4
Brabant L. Canada 55°58N 103°43W 163 B8
Brabrand Denmark 56°9N 10°7E 63 H4
Brač Croatia 43°20N 16°40E 93 E13
Bracadale, L. U.K. 57°20N 6°30W 65 D2
Bracciano Italy 42°6N 12°10E 93 F9
Bracciano, L. di Italy 42°7N 12°14E 93 F9
Bracebridge Canada 45°2N 79°19W 174 A5
Bracieux France 47°30N 1°30E 70 E8
Bräcke Sweden 62°45N 15°26E 62 B9
Brackettville U.S.A. 29°19N 100°25W 176 G4
Bracki Kanal Croatia 43°24N 16°40E 93 E13
Bracknell U.K. 51°25N 0°43W 67 F7
Bracknell Forest □ U.K. 51°25N 0°44W 67 F7
Brad Romania 46°10N 22°50E 80 D7
Brádano → Italy 40°23N 16°51E 95 B9
Bradenton U.S.A. 27°30N 82°34W 179 H7
Bradford Canada 44°7N 79°34W 174 B5
Bradford U.K. 53°47N 1°45W 66 D6
Bradford Pa., U.S.A. 41°58N 78°38W 174 E6
Bradford Vt., U.S.A. 43°59N 72°9W 175 C12
Bradley Ark., U.S.A. 33°6N 93°39W 176 E8
Bradley Calif., U.S.A. 35°52N 120°48W 170 K6
Bradley Institute
Zimbabwe 17°7S 31°25E 143 F3
Bradley Junction
U.S.A. 27°48N 81°59W 179 H8
Brady U.S.A. 31°9N 99°20W 176 F5
Brædstrup Denmark 55°58N 9°37E 63 J3
Braemar Australia 33°12S 139°35E 152 B3
Braeside Canada 45°28N 76°24W 175 A8
Braga Portugal 41°35N 8°25W 88 D2
Braga □ Portugal 41°30N 8°30W 88 D2
Bragadiru Romania 43°46N 25°31E 81 G10
Bragado Argentina 35°2S 60°27W 190 D3
Bragança Brazil 1°0S 47°2W 187 D9
Bragança Portugal 41°48N 6°50W 88 D4
Bragança □ Portugal 41°30N 6°45W 88 D4
Bragança Paulista
Brazil 22°55S 46°32W 191 A6
Brahestad = Raahe
Finland 64°40N 24°28E 60 D21
Brahmanbaria Bangla. 23°58N 91°15E 123 H17
Brahmani → India 20°39N 86°46E 126 D8
Brahmapur India 19°15N 84°54E 126 E7
Brahmaputra → Asia 23°40N 90°35E 125 H13
Braich-y-pwll U.K. 52°47N 4°46W 66 E3
Braidwood Australia 35°27S 149°49E 153 C8
Brăila Romania 45°19N 27°59E 81 E12
Brăila □ Romania 45°5N 27°30E 81 E12
Brainerd U.S.A. 46°22N 94°12W 172 B6
Braintree U.K. 51°53N 0°34E 67 F8
Braintree U.S.A. 42°13N 71°0W 175 D14
Brak → S. Africa 29°35S 22°55E 144 C3
Brake Germany 53°20N 8°28E 76 B4
Brakel Germany 51°42N 9°11E 76 D5
Brakna □ Mauritania 17°0N 13°20W 138 B2
Bräkne-Hoby Sweden 56°14N 15°6E 63 H9
Brakwater Namibia 22°28S 17°3E 144 B2
Brålanda Sweden 58°34N 12°21E 63 F6
Bramberg Germany 50°6N 10°40E 77 E6
Bramdrupdam Denmark 55°31N 9°28E 63 J3
Bramhapuri India 20°36N 79°52E 126 D4
Bramming Denmark 55°28N 8°42E 63 J2
Brämön Sweden 62°14N 17°40E 62 B11
Brampton Canada 43°45N 79°45W 174 C5
Brampton U.K. 54°57N 2°44W 66 C5
Brampton I. Australia 20°49S 149°16E 150 b
Bramsche Germany 52°24N 7°59E 76 C3
Branchville U.S.A. 33°15N 80°49W 178 B9
Branco → Brazil 1°20S 61°50W 186 D6
Branco, C. Brazil 7°9S 34°47W 189 B4
Brandberg Namibia 21°10S 14°33E 144 B1
Brandberg ⌂ Namibia 21°10S 14°30E 144 B1
Brande Denmark 55°57N 9°8E 63 J3
Brandenburg = Neubrandenburg
Germany 53°33N 13°15E 76 B9
Brandenburg Germany 52°25N 12°33E 76 C8
Brandenburg □ Germany 52°50N 13°0E 76 C9
Brandfort S. Africa 28°40S 26°30E 144 C4
Brando France 42°47N 9°27E 73 F13
Brandon Canada 49°50N 99°57W 163 D9
Brandon Fla., U.S.A. 27°56N 82°17W 179 H7
Brandon Vt., U.S.A. 43°48N 73°6W 175 C11
Brandon B. Ireland 52°17N 10°8W 64 D1
Brandon Mt. Ireland 52°15N 10°15W 64 D1
Brandsen Argentina 35°10S 58°15W 190 D4
Brandvlei S. Africa 30°25S 20°30E 144 D3
Brandýs nad Labem
Czech Rep. 50°10N 14°40E 78 A7
Brănești Romania 44°27N 26°20E 81 F11
Branford Conn., U.S.A. 41°17N 72°49W 175 E12
Branford Fla., U.S.A. 29°58N 82°56W 178 F7
Braniewo Poland 54°25N 19°50E 82 D6
Bransfield Str. Antarctica 63°0S 59°0W 55 C18
Brańsk Poland 52°45N 22°50E 83 F9
Branson U.S.A. 36°39N 93°13W 172 G7
Brantford Canada 43°10N 80°15W 174 C4
Brantley U.S.A. 31°35N 86°16W 178 D3
Brantôme France 45°22N 0°39E 72 C4
Branxholme Australia 37°52S 141°49E 152 D4
Branxton Australia 32°38S 151°21E 153 B9
Branzi Italy 46°1N 9°46E 92 B6
Bras d'Or L. Canada 45°50N 60°50W 165 C7
Brasher Falls U.S.A. 44°49N 74°47W 175 B10
Brasil = Brazil ■ S. Amer. 12°0S 50°0W 187 F9
Brasil, Planalto Brazil 18°0S 46°30W 184 E6
Brasiléia Brazil 11°0S 68°45W 188 C4
Brasília Distrito Federal,
Brazil 15°47S 47°55W 189 D1
Brasília Minas Gerais,
Brazil 16°12S 44°26W 189 D2
Brasília Legal Brazil 3°49S 55°36W 187 D7
Braslaw Belarus 55°38N 27°0E 84 E4
Braslawskiya Azyory △
Belarus 55°36N 27°3E 84 E4
Braslovče Slovenia 46°21N 15°3E 93 B12
Brașov Romania 45°38N 25°35E 81 E10
Brașov □ Romania 45°45N 25°15E 81 E10
Brass Nigeria 4°35N 6°14E 139 E6
Brass → Nigeria 4°15N 6°13E 139 E6
Brassac-les-Mines France 45°24N 3°20E 72 C7
Brasschaat Belgium 51°19N 4°27E 69 C4
Brassey, Banjaran
Malaysia 5°0N 117°15E 118 D5
Brassey Ra. Australia 25°8S 122°15E 149 E3
Brasstown Bald
U.S.A. 34°53N 83°49W 177 D13
Brastad Sweden 58°23N 11°30E 63 F5
Brastavățu Romania 43°55N 24°24E 81 G9
Bratan = Morozov
Bulgaria 42°30N 25°10E 97 D9
Brateș Romania 45°50N 26°4E 81 E11
Bratislava Slovak Rep. 48°10N 17°7E 79 C10
Bratislava M.R. Štefánik ✕ (BTS)
Slovak Rep. 48°11N 17°9E 79 C10
Bratislavský □
Slovak Rep. 48°15N 17°20E 79 C10
Bratsigovo Bulgaria 42°1N 24°22E 97 D8
Bratsk Russia 56°10N 101°30E 107 D11
Bratskoye Vdkhr.
Russia 56°0N 101°40E 107 D11
Brattleboro U.S.A. 42°51N 72°34W 175 D12
Bratunac Bos.-H. 44°13N 19°21E 80 F4
Braunau Austria 48°15N 13°3E 78 C6
Braunschweig Germany 52°15N 10°31E 76 C6
Braunton U.K. 51°7N 4°10W 67 F3
Brava C. Verde Is. 15°0N 24°40W 134 b
Brava, Costa Spain 41°30N 3°0E 90 D8
Bravicea Moldova 47°22N 28°27E 81 C13
Bråviken Sweden 58°38N 16°32E 63 F10
Bravo del Norte, Rio = Grande,
Rio → N. Amer. 25°58N 97°9W 176 J6
Brawley U.S.A. 32°59N 115°31W 171 N11
Bray Ireland 53°13N 6°7W 64 C5
Bray, Mt. Australia 14°0S 134°30E 150 A1
Bray-sur-Seine France 48°25N 3°14E 71 D10
Brazeau → Canada 52°55N 115°14W 162 C5
Brazil U.S.A. 39°32N 87°8W 172 F10
Brazil ■ S. Amer. 12°0S 50°0W 187 F9
Brazil Basin Atl. Oc. 15°0S 25°0W 56 H9
Brazilian Highlands = Brasil,
Planalto Brazil 18°0S 46°30W 184 E6
Brazo Sur → S. Amer. 25°21S 57°42W 190 B4
Brazos → U.S.A. 28°53N 95°23W 176 G7
Brazzaville Congo 4°9S 15°12E 140 E3
Brčko Bos.-H. 44°54N 18°46E 80 F3
Brda → Poland 53°8N 18°8E 83 E5
Brdy Czech Rep. 49°43N 13°55E 78 B6
Bré = Bray Ireland 53°13N 6°7W 64 C5
Breaden, L. Australia 25°51S 125°28E 149 E4
Breaksea Sd. N.Z. 45°35S 166°35E 155 F1
Bream B. N.Z. 35°56S 174°28E 154 B3
Bream Hd. N.Z. 35°51S 174°36E 154 B3
Bream Tail N.Z. 36°3S 174°36E 154 C3
Breas Chile 25°29S 70°24W 190 B1
Breaza Romania 45°11N 25°40E 81 E10
Brebes Indonesia 6°52S 109°3E 119 G13
Brechin Canada 44°32N 79°10W 174 B5
Brechin U.K. 56°44N 2°39W 65 E6
Brecht Belgium 51°21N 4°38E 69 C4
Breckenridge Colo.,
U.S.A. 39°29N 106°3W 168 G10
Breckenridge Minn.,
U.S.A. 46°16N 96°35W 172 B5
Breckenridge Tex.,
U.S.A. 32°45N 98°54W 176 E5
Breckland U.K. 52°30N 0°40E 67 E8
Brecknock, Pen. Chile 54°35S 71°30W 192 D2
Břeclav Czech Rep. 48°46N 16°53E 79 C9
Brecon U.K. 51°57N 3°23W 67 F4
Brecon Beacons U.K. 51°53N 3°26W 67 F4
Brecon Beacons △ U.K. 51°50N 3°30W 67 F4
Breda Neths. 51°35N 4°45E 69 C4
Bredaryd Sweden 57°10N 13°45E 63 G7
Bredasdorp S. Africa 34°33S 20°2E 144 D3
Bredbo Australia 35°58S 149°10E 153 C8
Bredebro Denmark 55°4N 8°50E 63 J2
Bredstedt Germany 54°37N 8°55E 76 A4
Bredy Russia 52°26N 60°21E 108 B6
Bree Belgium 51°8N 5°35E 69 C5
Bregalnica → Macedonia 41°43N 22°9E 96 E6
Bregenz Austria 47°30N 9°45E 78 D2
Bregovo Bulgaria 44°9N 22°39E 96 B6
Bréhal France 48°53N 1°30W 70 D5
Bréhat, Î. de France 48°51N 3°0W 70 D4
Breiðafjörður Iceland 65°15N 23°15W 60 D2
Breil-sur-Roya France 43°56N 7°31E 73 E11
Breisach Germany 48°1N 7°36E 77 G3
Brejo Brazil 3°41S 42°47W 189 A2
Bremen Germany 53°4N 8°47E 76 B4
Bremen U.S.A. 33°43N 85°9W 178 B4
Bremen □ Germany 53°4N 8°50E 76 B4
Bremer Bay Australia 34°21S 119°20E 149 F2
Bremer I. Australia 12°5S 136°45E 150 A2
Bremerhaven Germany 53°33N 8°36E 76 B4
Bremerton U.S.A. 47°34N 122°37W 170 C4
Bremervörde Germany 53°29N 9°8E 76 B5
Brenes Spain 37°32N 5°54W 89 H5
Brenham U.S.A. 30°10N 96°24W 176 F6
Brenne France 46°44N 1°14E 72 B5
Brenne ⌂ France 46°40N 1°15E 72 B5
Brennerpass Austria 47°2N 11°30E 78 D4
Breno Italy 45°57N 10°18E 92 C7
Brent U.S.A. 32°56N 87°10W 177 E11
Brenta → Italy 45°11N 12°18E 93 C9
Brentwood U.K. 51°37N 0°19E 67 F8
Brentwood Calif.,
U.S.A. 37°56N 121°42W 170 H5
Brentwood N.Y.,
U.S.A. 40°47N 73°15W 175 F11
Bréscia Italy 45°33N 10°15E 92 C7
Breskens Neths. 51°23N 3°33E 69 C3
Breslau = Wrocław Poland 51°5N 17°5E 83 G4
Bresle → France 50°4N 1°22E 70 B8
Bressanone Italy 46°43N 11°39E 93 B8
Bressay U.K. 60°9N 1°6W 65 A7
Bresse France 46°50N 5°10E 71 F12
Bressuire France 46°51N 0°30W 70 F6
Brest Belarus 52°10N 23°40E 75 B12
Brest France 48°24N 4°31W 70 D2
Brest □ Belarus 52°30N 26°10E 75 B13
Brest-Litovsk = Brest
Belarus 52°10N 23°40E 75 B12
Bretagne □ France 48°10N 3°0W 70 D3
Bretçu Romania 46°7N 26°18E 81 D11
Bretenoux France 44°54N 1°51E 72 D5
Breteuil Eure, France 48°50N 0°57E 70 D7
Breteuil Oise, France 49°38N 2°18E 71 C9
Breton Canada 53°7N 114°28W 162 C6
Breton, Pertuis France 46°17N 1°25W 72 B2
Breton Sd. U.S.A. 29°35N 89°15W 177 G10
Brett, C. N.Z. 35°10S 174°20E 154 B3
Bretten Germany 49°2N 8°42E 77 F4
Breuil-Cervinia Italy 45°56N 7°38E 92 C4
Brevard U.S.A. 35°14N 82°44W 177 D13
Breves Brazil 1°40S 50°29W 187 D8
Brewarrina Australia 30°0S 146°51E 151 E4
Brewer U.S.A. 44°48N 68°46W 173 C19
Brewer, Mt. U.S.A. 36°44N 118°28W 170 J8
Brewerville Liberia 6°26N 10°47W 138 D2
Brewster N.Y., U.S.A. 41°24N 73°36W 175 E11
Brewster Ohio, U.S.A. 40°43N 81°36W 174 F3
Brewster Wash., U.S.A. 48°6N 119°47W 168 B4
Brewster, Kap = Kangikajik
Greenland 70°7N 22°0W 57 C8
Brewton U.S.A. 31°7N 87°4W 177 F11
Breyten S. Africa 26°16S 30°0E 145 C5
Breza Bos.-H. 44°2N 18°16E 80 F3
Brežice Slovenia 45°54N 15°35E 93 C12
Brézina Algeria 33°4N 1°14E 136 B4
Březnice Czech Rep. 49°32N 13°57E 78 B6
Breznik Bulgaria 42°44N 22°55E 96 D6
Brezno Slovak Rep. 48°50N 19°40E 79 C12
Brezoi Romania 45°21N 24°15E 81 E9
Brezovicë Kosovo 42°15N 21°3E 96 D5
Brezovo Bulgaria 42°21N 25°5E 97 D9
Bria C.A.R. 6°30N 21°58E 140 C4
Briançon France 44°54N 6°39E 73 D10
Briare France 47°38N 2°45E 71 E9
Briático Italy 38°43N 16°2E 95 D9
Bribie I. Australia 27°0S 153°10E 151 D5
Bribri Costa Rica 9°38N 82°50W 182 E3
Briceni Moldova 48°22N 27°6E 81 B12
Bricquebec France 49°28N 1°38W 70 C5
Bridgefield Barbados 13°9N 59°36W 183 g
Bridgehampton
U.S.A. 40°56N 72°19W 175 F12
Bridgend U.K. 51°30N 3°34W 67 F4
Bridgend □ U.K. 51°36N 3°36W 67 F4
Bridgenorth Canada 44°23N 78°23W 174 B6
Bridgeport Calif.,
U.S.A. 38°15N 119°14W 170 G7
Bridgeport Conn.,
U.S.A. 41°11N 73°12W 175 E11
Bridgeport N.Y., U.S.A. 43°9N 75°58W 175 C9
Bridgeport Nebr.,
U.S.A. 41°40N 103°6W 172 E2
Bridgeport Tex., U.S.A. 33°13N 97°45W 176 E6
Bridger U.S.A. 45°18N 108°55W 168 D9
Bridgeton U.S.A. 39°26N 75°14W 173 F16
Bridgetown Australia 33°58S 116°7E 149 F2
Bridgetown Barbados 13°6N 59°37W 183 g
Bridgetown Canada 44°55N 65°18W 165 D6
Bridgewater Tas.,
Australia 42°44S 147°14E 151 G4
Bridgewater Vic.,
Australia 36°36S 143°59E 152 D5
Bridgewater Canada 44°25N 64°31W 165 D7
Bridgewater Mass.,
U.S.A. 41°59N 70°58W 175 E14
Bridgewater N.Y.,
U.S.A. 42°53N 75°15W 175 D9
Bridgewater, C.
Australia 38°23S 141°23E 152 E4
Bridgnorth U.K. 52°32N 2°25W 67 E5
Bridgton U.S.A. 44°3N 70°42W 175 B14
Bridgwater U.K. 51°8N 2°59W 67 F5
Bridgwater B. U.K. 51°15N 3°15W 67 F4
Bridlington U.K. 54°5N 0°12W 66 C7
Bridlington B. U.K. 54°4N 0°10W 66 C7
Bridport Australia 40°59S 147°23E 151 G4
Bridport U.K. 50°44N 2°45W 67 G5
Briec France 48°6N 4°0W 70 D2
Brienne-le-Château
France 48°24N 4°30E 71 D11
Brienon-sur-Armançon
France 47°59N 3°38E 71 E10
Brienz Switz. 46°46N 8°2E 77 J4
Brienzersee Switz. 46°44N 7°53E 77 J3
Brier Cr. → U.S.A. 32°44N 81°26W 178 C8
Brière ⌂ France 47°22N 2°13W 70 E4
Brig Switz. 46°18N 7°59E 77 J3
Brigg U.K. 53°34N 0°28W 66 D7
Brigham City U.S.A. 41°31N 112°1W 168 F7
Bright Australia 36°42S 146°56E 153 D7
Brighton Australia 35°5S 138°30E 152 C3
Brighton Canada 44°2N 77°44W 174 B7
Brighton Trin. & Tob. 10°15N 61°39W 187 K15
Brighton U.K. 50°49N 0°7W 67 G7
Brighton Fla., U.S.A. 27°14N 81°6W 179 H8
Brighton N.Y., U.S.A. 43°8N 77°34W 174 C7
Brightside Canada 45°7N 76°29W 175 A8
Brightwater N.Z. 41°22S 173°9E 155 B8
Brignogan-Plage France 48°40N 4°20W 70 D2
Brignoles France 43°25N 6°5E 73 E10
Brihuega Spain 40°45N 2°52W 90 E2
Brikama Gambia 13°15N 16°45W 138 C1
Brilliant U.S.A. 40°15N 80°39W 174 F4
Brilon Germany 51°23N 8°35E 76 D4
Brim Australia 36°3S 142°27E 152 D5
Brindabella △ Australia 35°14S 148°55E 153 C8
Bríndisi Italy 40°39N 17°55E 95 B10
Brinje Croatia 44°59N 15°9E 93 D12
Brinkley U.S.A. 34°53N 91°12W 176 D9
Brinkworth Australia 33°42S 138°26E 152 B3
Brinnon U.S.A. 47°41N 122°54W 170 C4
Brinson U.S.A. 30°59N 84°44W 178 E5
Brion, Î. Canada 47°46N 61°26W 165 C7
Brionne France 49°11N 0°43E 70 C7
Brionski Croatia 44°55N 13°45E 93 D10
Brioude France 45°18N 3°24E 72 C7
Briouze France 48°42N 0°23W 70 D6
Brisay Canada 54°26N 70°31W 165 B5
Brisbane Australia 27°25S 153°2E 151 D5
Brisbane → Australia 27°24S 153°9E 151 D5
Brisbane Ranges △
Australia 37°47S 144°16E 152 D6
Brisbane Water △
Australia 33°26S 151°23E 153 B9
Brisighella Italy 44°13N 11°46E 93 D8
Bristol U.K. 51°26N 2°35W 67 F5
Bristol Conn., U.S.A. 41°40N 72°57W 175 E12
Bristol Fla., U.S.A. 30°26N 84°59W 178 E5
Bristol Pa., U.S.A. 40°6N 74°51W 175 F10
Bristol R.I., U.S.A. 41°40N 71°16W 175 E13
Bristol Tenn., U.S.A. 36°36N 82°11W 177 C13
Bristol Vt., U.S.A. 44°8N 73°4W 175 B11
Bristol, City of □ U.K. 51°27N 2°36W 67 F5
Bristol B. U.S.A. 58°0N 160°0W 166 D8
Bristol Channel U.K. 51°18N 4°30W 67 F3
Bristol I. Antarctica 58°45S 28°0W 55 B1
Bristol L. U.S.A. 34°28N 115°41W 171 L11
Bristow U.S.A. 35°50N 96°23W 176 D6

Britain = Great Britain Europe 54°0N 2°15W 58 E5
British Columbia □ Canada 55°0N 125°15W 162 C3
British Indian Ocean Terr. = Chagos Arch. ☒ Ind. Oc. 6°0S 72°0E 146 E6
British Isles Europe 54°0N 4°0W 68 D5
British Mts. N. Amer. 68°50N 140°0W 166 B12
British Virgin Is. ☒ W. Indies 18°30N 64°30W 183 e
Brits S. Africa 25°37S 27°48E 145 C4
Britstown S. Africa 30°37S 23°30E 144 D3
Britt Canada 45°46N 80°34W 164 C3
Brittany = Bretagne □ France 48°10N 3°0W 70 D3
Britton U.S.A. 45°48N 97°45W 172 C5
Brive-la-Gaillarde France 45°10N 1°32E 72 C5
Briviesca Spain 42°32N 3°19W 88 C7
Brixen = Bressanone Italy 46°43N 11°39E 93 B8
Brixham U.K. 50°23N 3°31W 67 G4
Brnaze Croatia 43°41N 16°40E 93 E13
Brnenský □ Czech Rep. 49°10N 16°40E 79 B9
Brno Czech Rep. 49°10N 16°35E 79 B9
Broach = Bharuch India 21°47N 73°0E 126 D1
Broad → Ga., U.S.A. 33°59N 82°39W 178 B7
Broad → S.C., U.S.A. 34°1N 81°4W 177 D14
Broad Arrow Australia 30°23S 121°15E 149 F3
Broad B. U.K. 58°14N 6°18W 65 C2
Broad Haven Ireland 54°20N 9°55W 64 B2
Broad Law U.K. 55°30N 3°21W 65 F5
Broad Pk. = Faichan Kangri India 35°48N 76°34E 125 B7
Broad Sd. Australia 22°0S 149°45E 150 C4
Broadalbin U.S.A. 43°4N 74°12W 175 C10
Broadback → Canada 51°21N 78°52W 164 B4
Broadford Australia 37°14S 145°4E 153 D6
Broadhurst Ra. Australia 22°30S 122°30E 148 D3
Broads, The U.K. 52°45N 1°30E 66 E9
Broadus U.S.A. 45°27N 105°25W 168 D11
Brøager Denmark 54°53N 9°40E 63 K3
Broby Sweden 56°15N 14°4E 63 H8
Brocēni Latvia 56°42N 22°32E 82 B9
Brochet Canada 57°53N 101°40W 163 B8
Brochet, L. Canada 58°36N 101°35W 163 B8
Brock I. Canada 77°52N 114°19W 161 B9
Brocken Germany 51°47N 10°37E 76 D6
Brockelhurst Australia 32°9S 148°38E 153 B8
Brocklesby Australia 35°48S 146°40E 153 C7
Brockport U.S.A. 43°13N 77°56W 174 C7
Brockton U.S.A. 42°5N 71°1W 175 D13
Brockville Canada 44°35N 75°41W 175 B9
Brockway Mont., U.S.A. 47°18N 105°45W 168 C11
Brockway Pa., U.S.A. 41°15N 78°47W 174 E6
Brocton U.S.A. 42°23N 79°26W 174 D5
Brod Macedonia 41°32N 21°17E 96 E5
Brodarevo Serbia 43°14N 19°44E 96 C3
Brodeur Pen. Canada 72°30N 88°10W 161 C14
Brodick U.K. 55°35N 5°9W 65 F3
Brodnica Poland 53°15N 19°25E 83 E6
Brody Ukraine 50°5N 25°10E 75 C13
Brogan U.S.A. 44°15N 117°31W 168 D5
Broglie France 49°2N 0°30E 70 C7
Brok Poland 52°43N 21°52E 83 F8
Broken Arrow U.S.A. 36°3N 95°48W 176 C7
Broken Bow Nebr., U.S.A. 41°24N 99°38W 172 E4
Broken Bow Okla., U.S.A. 34°2N 94°44W 176 D7
Broken Bow Lake U.S.A. 34°9N 94°40W 176 D7
Broken Hill Australia 31°58S 141°29E 152 A4
Broken Ridge Ind. Oc. 30°0S 94°0E 156 L1
Broken River Ra. Australia 21°0S 148°22E 150 b
Brokind Sweden 58°13N 15°42E 63 F9
Bromley □ U.K. 51°24N 0°2E 67 F8
Bromo, Gunung Indonesia 7°56N 112°57E 119 H15
Bromo Tengger Semeru △ Indonesia 7°56S 112°57E 119 H15
Bromölla Sweden 56°5N 14°28E 63 H8
Bromsgrove U.K. 52°21N 2°2W 67 E5
Brønderslev Denmark 57°16N 9°57E 63 G3
Brong-Ahafo □ Ghana 7°50N 2°0W 138 D4
Broni Italy 45°4N 9°16E 92 C6
Bronkhorstspruit S. Africa 25°46S 28°45E 145 C4
Brønnøysund Norway 65°28N 12°14E 60 D15
Bronson U.S.A. 29°27N 82°39W 179 F7
Bronte Italy 37°47N 14°50E 95 E7
Bronwood U.S.A. 31°50N 84°22W 178 D5
Brook Park U.S.A. 41°23N 81°48W 174 E4
Brookhaven U.S.A. 31°35N 90°26W 177 F9
Brookings Oreg., U.S.A. 42°3N 124°17W 168 E1
Brookings S. Dak., U.S.A. 44°19N 96°48W 172 C5
Brooklet U.S.A. 32°23N 81°40W 178 C8
Brooklin Canada 43°55N 78°55W 174 C6
Brooklyn Park U.S.A. 45°6N 93°23W 172 C7
Brooks Canada 50°35N 111°55W 162 C6
Brooks Range U.S.A. 68°0N 152°0W 166 B9
Brooksville U.S.A. 28°33N 82°23W 179 G7
Brookton Australia 32°22S 117°0E 149 F2
Brookville U.S.A. 41°10N 79°5W 174 E5
Broom, L. U.K. 57°55N 5°15W 65 D3
Broome Australia 18°0S 122°15E 148 C3
Broons France 48°20N 2°16W 70 D4
Brora U.K. 58°0N 3°52W 65 C5
Brora → U.K. 58°0N 3°51W 65 C5
Brørup Denmark 55°29N 9°1E 63 J2
Brösarp Sweden 55°43N 14°6E 63 J8
Brosna → Ireland 53°14N 7°58W 64 C4
Broşteni Mehedinţi, Romania 44°45N 22°59E 80 F7
Broşteni Suceava, Romania 47°14N 25°43E 81 C10
Brotas de Macaúbas Brazil 12°0S 42°38W 189 C2
Brothers U.S.A. 43°49N 120°36W 168 E3
Brou France 48°13N 1°11E 70 D8
Brouage France 45°52N 1°4W 72 C2
Brough U.K. 54°32N 2°18W 66 C5
Brough Hd. U.K. 59°8N 3°20W 65 B5
Broughton Island = Qikiqtarjuaq Canada 67°33N 63°0W 161 D19
Broumov Czech Rep. 50°35N 16°20E 79 A9
Brovary Ukraine 50°34N 30°48E 85 G6
Brovst Denmark 57°6N 9°31E 63 G3
Brown, L. Australia 31°5S 118°15E 149 F2
Brown, Mt. Australia 32°30S 138°0E 152 B3
Brown, Pt. Australia 32°32S 133°50E 151 E1
Brown City U.S.A. 43°13N 82°59W 174 C2
Brown Willy U.K. 50°35N 4°37W 67 G3
Brownfield U.S.A. 33°11N 102°17W 176 E3
Browning U.S.A. 48°34N 113°1W 168 B7
Brownsville Oreg., U.S.A. 44°24N 122°59W 168 D2
Brownsville Pa., U.S.A. 40°1N 79°53W 174 F5
Brownsville Tenn., U.S.A. 35°36N 89°16W 177 D10
Brownsville Tex., U.S.A. 25°54N 97°30W 176 J6
Brownville U.S.A. 44°0N 75°59W 175 C9
Brownwood U.S.A. 31°43N 98°59W 176 F5
Browse I. Australia 14°7S 123°33E 148 B3
Broxton U.S.A. 31°38N 82°53W 178 D7
Bruas Malaysia 4°30N 100°47E 121 K3
Bruay-la-Buissière France 50°29N 2°33E 71 B9
Bruce, Mt. Australia 22°37S 118°8E 148 D2
Bruce B. N.Z. 43°35S 169°42E 155 D4
Bruce Pen. Canada 45°0N 81°30W 174 B3
Bruce Peninsula △ Canada 45°14N 81°36W 174 A3
Bruce Rock Australia 31°52S 118°8E 149 F2
Bruche → France 48°34N 7°43E 71 D14
Bruchsal Germany 49°7N 8°35E 77 F4
Bruck an der Leitha Austria 48°1N 16°47E 79 C9
Bruck an der Mur Austria 47°24N 15°16E 78 D8
Brue → U.K. 51°13N 2°59W 67 F5
Bruges = Brugge Belgium 51°13N 3°13E 69 C3
Brugg Switz. 47°29N 8°11E 77 H4
Brugge Belgium 51°13N 3°13E 69 C3
Bruin U.S.A. 41°3N 79°43W 174 E5
Brûk, W. el → Egypt 30°15N 33°50E 130 E2
Bruksvallarna Sweden 62°38N 12°27E 62 B6
Brûlé Canada 53°15N 117°58W 162 C5
Brûlé, L. Canada 53°35N 64°4W 165 B7
Brûlon France 47°58N 0°15W 70 E6
Brumado Brazil 14°14S 41°40W 189 C2
Brumado → Brazil 14°13S 41°40W 189 C2
Brumath France 48°43N 7°40E 71 D14
Brumunddal Norway 60°53N 10°56E 60 F14
Brundidge U.S.A. 31°43N 85°49W 178 D4
Bruneau U.S.A. 42°53N 115°48W 168 E6
Bruneau → U.S.A. 42°56N 115°57W 168 E6
Bruneck = Brunico Italy 46°48N 11°56E 93 B8
Brunei = Bandar Seri Begawan Brunei 4°52N 115°0E 118 D5
Brunei ■ Asia 4°50N 115°0E 118 D5
Brunflo Sweden 63°5N 14°50E 62 A8
Brunico Italy 46°48N 11°56E 93 B8
Brunnen Switz. 46°59N 8°37E 77 J4
Brunner, L. N.Z. 42°37S 171°27E 155 C6
Brunnsberg Sweden 61°17N 13°56E 62 C8
Brunsbüttel Germany 53°53N 9°6E 76 B5
Brunssum Neths. 50°57N 5°59E 69 D5
Brunswick = Braunschweig Germany 52°15N 10°31E 76 C6
Brunswick Ga., U.S.A. 31°10N 81°30W 178 D8
Brunswick Maine, U.S.A. 43°55N 69°58W 173 D19
Brunswick Md., U.S.A. 39°19N 77°38W 173 F15
Brunswick Mo., U.S.A. 39°26N 93°8W 172 F7
Brunswick Ohio, U.S.A. 41°14N 81°51W 174 E3
Brunswick, Pen. de Chile 53°30S 71°30W 192 D2
Brunswick B. Australia 15°15S 124°50E 148 C3
Brunswick Junction Australia 33°15S 115°50E 149 F2
Brunt Ice Shelf Antarctica 75°30S 25°0W 55 D2
Bruntál Czech Rep. 49°59N 17°27E 79 B10
Brus Laguna Honduras 15°47N 84°35W 182 C3
Brusartsi Bulgaria 43°40N 23°5E 96 C7
Brush U.S.A. 40°15N 103°37W 168 F12
Brushton U.S.A. 44°50N 74°31W 175 B10
Brusio Switz. 46°14N 10°8E 77 J6
Brusque Brazil 27°5S 49°0W 191 B6
Brussel Belgium 50°51N 4°21E 69 D4
Brussel ✕ (BRU) Belgium 50°54N 4°29E 69 D5
Brussels = Brussel Belgium 50°51N 4°21E 69 D4
Brussels Canada 43°44N 81°15W 174 C3
Brusy Poland 53°53N 17°43E 82 E4
Bruthen Australia 37°42S 147°50E 153 D7
Bruxelles = Brussel Belgium 50°51N 4°21E 69 D4
Bruyères France 48°10N 6°40E 71 D13
Bruz France 48°1N 1°46W 70 D5
Brwinów Poland 52°9N 20°40E 83 F7
Bryagovo Bulgaria 41°58N 25°8E 97 E9
Bryan Ohio, U.S.A. 41°28N 84°33W 173 E11
Bryan Tex., U.S.A. 30°40N 96°22W 176 F6
Bryan, Mt. Australia 33°30S 139°5E 152 B3
Bryanka Ukraine 48°32N 38°45E 85 H10
Bryansk Bryansk, Russia 53°13N 34°25E 85 F8
Bryansk Dagestan, Russia 44°20N 47°10E 87 H8
Bryansk □ Russia 53°10N 33°10E 85 F7
Bryce Canyon △ U.S.A. 37°30N 112°10W 169 H7
Bryne Norway 58°44N 5°38E 61 G11
Bryson City U.S.A. 35°26N 83°27W 177 D13
Bryukhovetskaya Russia 45°48N 39°0E 85 K10
Brza Palanka Serbia 44°28N 22°27E 96 B6
Brzeg Poland 50°52N 17°30E 83 H4
Brzeg Dolny Poland 51°16N 16°41E 83 G3
Brześć Kujawski Poland 52°36N 18°55E 83 F5
Brzesko Poland 49°59N 20°34E 83 J7
Brzeziny Poland 51°49N 19°42E 83 G6
Brzozów Poland 49°41N 22°3E 83 J9
Bsharri Lebanon 34°15N 36°0E 130 A5
Bū Baqarah U.A.E. 25°35N 56°25E 129 E8
Bu Craa W. Sahara 26°45N 12°50W 134 C3
Bū Ḩasā U.A.E. 23°30N 53°20E 129 F7
Bua Fiji 16°48S 178°37E 154 a
Bua Sweden 57°14N 12°7E 63 G6
Bua → Malaysia 12°45S 34°16E 143 E3
Bua Yai Thailand 15°33N 102°26E 120 E4
Buan S. Korea 35°44N 126°44E 115 G14
Buapinang Indonesia 4°40S 121°30E 119 E6
Buba Guinea-Biss. 11°40N 14°59W 138 C2
Bubanza Burundi 3°6S 29°23E 142 C2
Bubaque Guinea-Biss. 11°16N 15°51W 138 C1
Bubi → Zimbabwe 22°20S 31°7E 145 B5
Būbiyān Kuwait 29°45N 48°15E 129 D6
Buca Fiji 16°38S 179°52E 154 a
Buca Turkey 38°22N 27°11E 99 C9
Bucak Turkey 37°28N 30°36E 99 D12
Bucaramanga Colombia 7°0N 73°0W 186 B4
Bucasia Australia 21°2S 149°10E 150 b
Buccaneer Arch. Australia 16°7S 123°20E 148 C3
Buccino Italy 40°38N 15°22E 95 B8
Buccoo Reef Trin. & Tob. 11°10N 60°51W 187 J16
Bucecea Romania 47°47N 26°28E 81 C11
Bucegi △ Romania 45°25N 25°25E 81 E10
Buchach Ukraine 49°5N 25°25E 75 D13
Buchan Australia 37°30S 148°12E 153 D8
Buchan U.K. 57°32N 2°21W 65 D6
Buchan Ness U.K. 57°29N 1°46W 65 D7
Buchanan Canada 51°40N 102°45W 163 C8
Buchanan Liberia 5°57N 10°2W 138 D2
Buchanan U.S.A. 33°48N 85°11W 178 B4
Buchanan, L. Queens., Australia 21°35S 145°52E 150 C4
Buchanan, L. W. Austral., Australia 25°33S 123°2E 149 E3
Buchanan, L. U.S.A. 30°45N 98°25W 176 F5
Buchanan Cr. → Australia 19°13S 136°33E 150 B2
Buchans Canada 48°50N 56°52W 165 C8
Bucharest = Bucureşti Romania 44°27N 26°10E 81 F11
Buchen Germany 49°32N 9°20E 77 F5
Bucheon S. Korea 37°28N 126°45E 115 F14
Buchholz Germany 53°19N 9°52E 76 B5
Buchloe Germany 48°1N 10°44E 77 G6
Buchon, Pt. U.S.A. 35°15N 120°54W 170 K6
Buciumi Romania 47°3N 23°1E 80 C8
Buck Hill Falls U.S.A. 41°11N 75°16W 175 E9
Bückeburg Germany 52°16N 9°2E 76 C5
Buckeye Lake U.S.A. 39°55N 82°29W 174 G2
Buckhannon U.S.A. 39°0N 80°8W 173 F13
Buckhaven U.K. 56°11N 3°3W 65 E5
Buckhorn L. Canada 44°29N 78°23W 174 B6
Buckie U.K. 57°41N 2°58W 65 D6
Buckingham Canada 45°37N 75°24W 164 C4
Buckingham U.K. 51°59N 0°57W 67 F7
Buckingham B. Australia 12°10S 135°40E 150 A2
Buckingham Canal India 14°0N 80°5E 127 H5
Buckinghamshire □ U.K. 51°53N 0°55W 67 F7
Buckle Hd. Australia 14°26S 127°52E 148 B4
Buckleboo Australia 32°54S 136°12E 152 B2
Buckley U.K. 53°10N 3°5W 66 D4
Buckley → Australia 20°10S 138°49E 150 C2
Bucklin U.S.A. 37°33N 99°38W 172 G4
Bucks L. U.S.A. 39°54N 121°12W 170 F5
Bucquoy France 50°9N 2°43E 71 B9
Bucureşti Romania 44°27N 26°10E 81 F11
Bucureşti Otopeni ✕ (OTP) Romania 44°30N 26°11E 81 F11
Bucyrus U.S.A. 40°48N 82°59W 173 E12
Budacu, Vf. Romania 47°7N 25°41E 81 C10
Budalin Burma 22°20N 95°10E 123 H19
Budaörs Hungary 47°27N 18°57E 80 C3
Budapest Hungary 47°29N 19°3E 80 C4
Budapest □ Hungary 47°29N 19°5E 80 C4
Budapest ✕ (BUD) Hungary 47°26N 19°14E 80 C4
Budaun India 28°5N 79°10E 125 E8
Budawang △ Australia 35°10S 150°12E 153 C9
Budd Coast Antarctica 68°0S 112°0E 55 C8
Budderoo △ Australia 35°40S 150°41E 153 C9
Budduso Italy 40°35N 9°15E 94 B2
Bude U.K. 50°49N 4°34W 67 G3
Budennovsk Russia 44°50N 44°10E 87 H7
Budeşti Romania 44°13N 26°30E 81 F11
Budeyi Ukraine 48°3N 29°16E 81 B14
Budge Budge = Baj Baj India 22°30N 88°5E 125 H13
Budgewoi Australia 33°13S 151°34E 153 B9
Budia Spain 40°38N 2°46W 90 E2
Büdingen Germany 50°16N 9°7E 77 E5
Budjala Dem. Rep. of the Congo 2°50N 19°40E 140 D3
Budo-Sungai Padi △ Thailand 6°19N 101°42E 121 J3
Budoni Italy 40°40N 9°45E 94 B2
Búdrio Italy 44°32N 11°32E 93 D8
Budva Montenegro 42°17N 18°50E 96 D2
Budzyń Poland 52°54N 16°59E 83 F3
Bue Cameroon 4°10N 9°9E 139 E6
Buellton U.S.A. 34°37N 120°12W 171 L6
Buena Esperanza Argentina 34°45S 65°15W 190 C2
Buena Park U.S.A. 33°52N 117°59W 171 M9
Buena Vista Colo., U.S.A. 38°51N 106°8W 168 G10
Buena Vista Ga., U.S.A. 32°19N 84°31W 178 C5
Buena Vista Va., U.S.A. 37°44N 79°21W 173 G14
Buena Vista Lake Bed U.S.A. 35°12N 119°18W 171 K7
Buenaventura Colombia 3°53N 77°4W 186 C3
Buenaventura Mexico 29°51N 107°29W 180 B3
Buendia, Embalse de Spain 40°25N 2°43W 90 E2
Buenópolis Brazil 17°54S 44°11W 189 D2
Buenos Aires Argentina 34°36S 58°22W 190 C4
Buenos Aires Costa Rica 9°10N 83°20W 182 E3
Buenos Aires □ Argentina 36°30S 60°0W 190 D4
Buenos Aires, L. = General Carrera, L. S. Amer. 46°35S 72°0W 192 C2
Buffalo Mo., U.S.A. 37°39N 93°6W 172 G7
Buffalo N.Y., U.S.A. 42°53N 78°53W 174 D6
Buffalo Okla., U.S.A. 36°50N 99°38W 176 C5
Buffalo S. Dak., U.S.A. 45°35N 103°33W 172 C2
Buffalo Wyo., U.S.A. 44°21N 106°42W 168 D10
Buffalo → Canada 60°5N 115°5W 162 A5
Buffalo → S. Africa 28°43S 30°37E 145 C5
Buffalo ⌂ U.S.A. 36°14N 92°36W 176 C8
Buffalo Head Hills Canada 57°25N 115°55W 162 B5
Buffalo L. Alta., Canada 52°27N 112°54W 162 C6
Buffalo L. N.W.T., Canada 60°12N 115°25W 162 A5
Buffalo Narrows Canada 55°51N 108°29W 163 B7
Buffalo Springs ⌂ Kenya 0°32N 37°35E 142 B4
Buffels → S. Africa 29°36S 17°3E 144 C2
Buford U.S.A. 34°7N 83°59W 178 A6
Bug = Buh → Ukraine 46°59N 31°58E 85 J6
Bug → Poland 52°31N 21°5E 83 F8
Buga Colombia 4°0N 76°15W 186 C3
Bugala I. Uganda 0°40S 32°20E 142 C3
Buganda Uganda 0°0 31°30E 142 C3
Buganga Uganda 0°3S 32°0E 142 C3
Bugeat France 45°36N 1°55E 72 C5
Bugel, Tanjung Indonesia 6°26S 111°3E 119 G14
Búger Spain 39°45N 2°59E 100 B9
Bugibba Malta 35°57N 14°25E 101 D1
Bugojno Bos.-H. 44°2N 17°25E 80 F2
Bugsuk I. Phil. 8°12N 117°18E 118 C5
Bugulma Russia 54°33N 52°48E 108 B4
Buguma Nigeria 4°42N 6°55E 139 E6
Bugungu ⌂ Uganda 2°17N 31°50E 142 B3
Buguruslan Russia 53°39N 52°26E 108 B4
Buh → Ukraine 46°59N 31°58E 85 J6
Buharkent Turkey 37°58N 28°44E 99 D10
Buheirat-Murrat-el-Kubra Egypt 30°18N 32°26E 137 E8
Buhera Zimbabwe 19°18S 31°29E 145 A5
Bühl Germany 48°40N 8°8E 77 G4
Buhl U.S.A. 42°36N 114°46W 168 E6
Buhuşi Romania 46°41N 26°45E 81 D11
Bui △ Ghana 8°21N 2°21W 138 D4
Buila-Vanturariţa △ Romania 45°15N 24°0E 81 E8
Builth Wells U.K. 52°9N 3°25W 67 E4
Buinsk Russia 55°0N 48°18E 86 C9
Buique Brazil 8°37S 37°9W 189 B3
Buir Nur Mongolia 47°50N 117°42E 111 B12
Buis-les-Baronnies France 44°17N 5°16E 73 D9
Buitrago del Lozoya Spain 40°58N 3°38W 88 E7
Bujalance Spain 37°54N 4°23W 89 H6
Bujanovac Serbia 42°28N 21°44E 96 D5
Bujaraloz Spain 41°29N 0°10W 90 D4
Buje Croatia 45°24N 13°39E 93 C10
Buji China 22°37N 114°5E 111 a
Bujumbura Burundi 3°16S 29°18E 142 C2
Bük Hungary 47°22N 16°45E 80 C1
Buk Poland 52°21N 16°30E 83 F3
Bukachacha Russia 52°55N 116°50E 107 D12
Bukama Dem. Rep. of the Congo 9°10S 25°50E 143 D2
Bukavu Dem. Rep. of the Congo 2°20S 28°52E 142 C2
Bukene Tanzania 4°15S 32°48E 142 C3
Bukhara = Buxoro Uzbekistan 39°48N 64°25E 108 E6
Bukhoro = Buxoro Uzbekistan 39°48N 64°25E 108 E6
Bukhtarma Res. = Zaysan Kŏli Kazakhstan 48°0N 83°0E 109 C10
Bukima Tanzania 1°50S 33°25E 142 C3
Bukit Bendera Malaysia 5°25N 100°15E 121 c
Bukit Mertajam Malaysia 5°22N 100°28E 121 c
Bukit Nil Malaysia 1°22N 104°12E 121 d
Bukit Tengah Malaysia 5°22N 100°25E 121 c
Bukittinggi Indonesia 0°20S 100°20E 118 E2
Bükk Hungary 48°0N 20°30E 80 B5
Bukkapatnam India 14°14N 77°46E 127 G3
Bükki △ Hungary 48°3N 20°30E 80 B5
Bukoba Tanzania 1°20S 31°49E 142 C3
Bukum, Pulau Singapore 1°14N 103°46E 121 d
Bukuru Nigeria 9°42N 8°48E 139 D6
Bukuya Uganda 0°40N 31°52E 142 B3
Būl, Kuh-e Iran 30°48N 52°45E 129 D7
Bula Guinea-Biss. 12°7N 15°43W 138 C1
Bula Indonesia 3°6S 130°30E 119 E8
Bülach Switz. 47°31N 8°32E 77 H4
Bŭlaevo Kazakhstan 54°54N 70°26E 109 B8
Bulahdelah Australia 32°23S 152°13E 153 B10
Bulan Phil. 12°40N 123°52E 119 B6
Bulancak Turkey 40°56N 38°14E 105 B8
Bulanık Turkey 39°4N 42°14E 105 C10
Bûlâq Egypt 25°10N 30°38E 137 B3
Bulawayo Zimbabwe 20°7S 28°32E 143 G2
Buldan Turkey 38°2N 28°50E 99 C10
Buldana India 20°30N 76°18E 126 D3
Buldir I. U.S.A. 52°21N 175°56E 166 E3
Bulenga Ghana 9°56N 2°12W 138 D4
Bulgan Mongolia 48°45N 103°34E 110 B9
Bulgar Russia 54°57N 49°4E 86 C9
Bulgaria ■ Europe 42°35N 25°30E 97 D9
Bulgheria, Monte Italy 40°4N 15°26E 95 B8
Bulgurca Turkey 38°9N 27°9E 99 C9
Buli, Teluk Indonesia 0°48N 128°25E 119 D7
Buliluyan, C. Phil. 8°20N 117°15E 118 C5
Bulkley → Canada 55°15N 127°40W 162 B3
Bull Shoals L. U.S.A. 36°22N 92°35W 176 C8
Bullaque → Spain 38°59N 4°17W 89 G6
Bullard U.S.A. 32°38N 83°30W 178 C6
Bullas Spain 38°2N 1°40W 91 G3
Bulle Switz. 46°37N 7°3E 77 J3
Buller → N.Z. 41°44S 171°36E 155 B6
Buller, Mt. Australia 37°10S 146°28E 153 D7
Buller Gorge N.Z. 41°40S 172°10E 155 B7
Bulleringa △ Australia 17°39S 143°56E 150 B3
Bullhead City U.S.A. 35°8N 114°32W 171 K12
Bulli Australia 34°15S 150°57E 153 C9
Büllingen Belgium 50°25N 6°16E 69 D6
Bullock Creek Australia 17°43S 144°31E 150 B3
Bulloo → Australia 28°43S 142°30E 151 D3
Bulloo L. Australia 28°43S 142°25E 151 D3
Bulls N.Z. 40°10S 175°24E 154 G4
Bully-les-Mines France 50°27N 2°44E 71 B9
Bulman Australia 13°39S 134°20E 150 A1
Bulnes Chile 36°42S 72°19W 190 D1
Bulqizë Albania 41°30N 20°21E 96 E4
Bulsar = Valsad India 20°40N 72°58E 126 D1
Bultfontein S. Africa 28°18S 26°10E 144 C4
Bulukumba Indonesia 5°33S 120°11E 119 F6
Bulun Russia 70°37N 127°30E 107 B13
Bulungkol China 38°36N 74°58E 109 E8
Bumba Dem. Rep. of the Congo 2°13N 22°30E 140 D4
Bumbah, Khalīj Libya 32°20N 23°15E 135 B10
Bumbeşti-Jiu Romania 45°10N 23°24E 81 E8
Bumbiri I. Tanzania 1°40S 31°55E 142 C3
Bumbuna S. Leone 9°2N 11°49W 138 D2
Bumhpa Bum Burma 26°51N 97°14E 123 F20
Bumi → Zimbabwe 17°0S 28°20E 143 F2
Buna Kenya 2°58N 39°30E 142 B4
Bunaken Indonesia 1°37N 124°46E 119 D6
Bunazi Tanzania 1°3S 31°23E 142 C3
Bunbury Australia 33°20S 115°35E 149 F2
Bunclody Ireland 52°39N 6°40W 64 D5
Buncrana Ireland 55°8N 7°27W 64 A4
Bundaberg Australia 24°54S 152°22E 151 C5
Bundanoon Australia 34°40S 150°16E 153 C9
Bünde Germany 52°11N 8°35E 76 C4
Bundey → Australia 21°46S 135°37E 150 C2
Bundi India 25°30N 75°35E 124 G6
Bundjalung △ Australia 29°16S 153°21E 151 D5
Bundoran Ireland 54°28N 8°18W 64 B3
Bundure Australia 35°10S 146°1E 153 C7
Bung Kan Thailand 18°23N 103°37E 120 C4
Bunga → Nigeria 11°23N 9°56E 139 C6
Bungay U.K. 52°27N 1°28E 67 E9
Bungendore Australia 35°14S 149°30E 153 C8
Bungil Cr. → Australia 27°5S 149°5E 151 D4
Bungle Bungle = Purnululu △ Australia 17°20S 128°20E 148 C4
Bungo-Suidō Japan 33°0N 132°15E 113 H6
Bungoma Kenya 0°34N 34°34E 142 B3
Bungotakada Japan 33°35N 131°25E 113 H5
Bungu Tanzania 7°35S 39°0E 142 D4
Bunia Dem. Rep. of the Congo 1°35N 30°20E 142 B3
Bunji Pakistan 35°45N 74°40E 125 B6
Bunkie U.S.A. 30°57N 92°11W 176 F8
Bunnell U.S.A. 29°28N 81°16W 179 F8
Bunnythorpe N.Z. 40°16S 175°39E 154 G4
Buñol Spain 39°25N 0°47W 91 F4
Bunsuru → Nigeria 13°21N 6°23E 139 C5
Buntok Indonesia 1°40S 114°58E 118 E4
Bununu Dass Nigeria 10°5N 9°31E 139 C6
Bununu Kasa Nigeria 9°51N 9°32E 139 D6
Bunya Mts. △ Australia 26°51S 151°34E 151 D5
Bünyan Turkey 38°51N 35°51E 104 C6
Bunyola Spain 39°41N 2°42E 100 B9
Bunyu Indonesia 3°35N 117°50E 118 D5
Bunza Nigeria 12°8N 4°0E 139 C5
Buol Indonesia 1°15N 121°32E 119 D6
Buon Brieng Vietnam 13°9N 108°12E 120 F7
Buon Ho Vietnam 12°57N 108°18E 120 F7
Buon Ma Thuot Vietnam 12°40N 108°3E 120 F7
Buong Long Cambodia 13°44N 106°59E 120 F6
Buorkhaya, Mys Russia 71°50N 132°40E 107 B14
Buqayq Si. Arabia 26°0N 49°45E 129 E6
Buqbuq Egypt 31°29N 25°29E 137 A2
Bur Acaba = Buurhakaba Somalia 3°12N 44°20E 131 G3
Bûr Fuad Egypt 31°15N 32°20E 137 E8
Bûr Safâga Egypt 26°43N 33°57E 128 E2
Bûr Sa'îd Egypt 31°16N 32°18E 137 E8
Bûr Sûdân Sudan 19°32N 37°9E 137 D4
Bûr Taufiq Egypt 29°54N 32°32E 137 F8
Bura Kenya 1°4S 39°58E 142 C4
Burakin Australia 30°31S 117°10E 149 F2
Burang China 30°15N 81°10E 110 E5
Burao = Burco Somalia 9°32N 45°32E 131 F4
Burāq Syria 33°11N 36°29E 130 B5
Burathum Nepal 28°4N 84°50E 125 E11
Buraydah Si. Arabia 26°20N 43°59E 128 E4
Burbank U.S.A. 34°12N 118°18W 171 L8
Burcher Australia 33°30S 147°16E 153 B7
Burco Somalia 9°32N 45°32E 131 F4
Burda India 25°50N 77°35E 124 G7
Burdekin → Australia 19°38S 147°25E 150 B4
Burdur Turkey 37°45N 30°17E 99 D12
Burdur □ Turkey 37°45N 30°0E 99 D12
Burdur Gölü Turkey 37°44N 30°10E 99 D12
Burdwan = Barddhaman India 23°14N 87°39E 125 H12
Burdwood Bank Atl. Oc. 54°0S 59°0W 56 M6
Bure Ethiopia 10°40N 37°4E 131 E2
Bure → U.K. 52°38N 1°43E 66 E9
Burela Spain 43°39N 7°24W 88 B3
Büren Germany 51°33N 8°35E 76 D4
Bureskoye Vdkhr. Russia 50°16N 130°20E 107 D14
Bureya → Russia 49°27N 129°30E 107 E13
Burford Canada 43°7N 80°27W 174 C4
Burg Germany 52°16N 11°51E 76 C7
Burg auf Fehmarn Germany 54°28N 11°9E 76 A7
Burg el Arab Egypt 30°54N 29°32E 137 E6
Burg et Tuyur Sudan 20°55N 27°56E 137 C2
Burg Stargard Germany 53°29N 13°18E 76 B9
Burgas Bulgaria 42°33N 27°29E 97 D11
Burgas □ Bulgaria 42°30N 27°20E 97 D11
Burgaski Zaliv Bulgaria 42°30N 27°39E 97 D11
Burgdorf Germany 52°27N 10°1E 76 C6
Burgdorf Switz. 47°3N 7°37E 77 H3
Burgenland □ Austria 47°20N 16°20E 79 D9
Burgeo Canada 47°37N 57°38W 165 C8
Burgersdorp S. Africa 31°0S 26°20E 144 D4
Burgess, Mt. Australia 30°50S 121°5E 149 F3
Burghausen Germany 48°9N 12°49E 77 G8
Burghead U.K. 57°43N 3°30W 65 D5
Búrgio Italy 37°36N 13°17E 94 E6
Burglengenfeld Germany 49°12N 12°2E 77 F8
Burgohondo Spain 40°26N 4°47W 88 E6
Burgos Spain 42°21N 3°41W 88 C7
Burgos □ Spain 42°21N 3°42W 88 C7
Burgstädt Germany 50°54N 12°49E 76 E8
Burgsvik Sweden 57°3N 18°19E 63 G12
Burguillos del Cerro Spain 38°23N 6°35W 89 G4
Burgundy = Bourgogne □ France 47°0N 4°50E 71 F11
Burhaniye Turkey 39°30N 26°58E 99 B8
Burhanpur India 21°18N 76°14E 126 D3
Burhi Gandak → India 25°20N 86°37E 125 G12
Burhner → India 22°43N 80°31E 125 H9
Burias I. Phil. 12°55N 123°5E 119 B6
Burica, Pta. Costa Rica 8°3N 82°51W 182 E3
Burien U.S.A. 47°28N 122°20W 170 C4
Burigi, L. Tanzania 2°2S 31°22E 142 C3
Burigi ⌂ Tanzania 2°20S 31°6E 142 C3
Burim Kosovo 42°45N 20°24E 96 D4
Burin Canada 47°1N 55°14W 165 C8
Buriram Thailand 15°0N 103°0E 120 E4
Buriti Bravo Brazil 5°50S 43°50W 189 B2
Buriti dos Lopes Brazil 3°10S 41°52W 189 A2
Burkburnett U.S.A. 34°6N 98°34W 176 D5
Burke → Australia 23°12S 139°33E 150 C2
Burke Chan. Canada 52°10N 127°30W 162 C3
Burketown Australia 17°45S 139°33E 150 B2
Burkina Faso ■ Africa 12°0N 1°0W 138 C4
Burk's Falls Canada 45°37N 79°24W
Burlada Spain 42°49N 1°36W
Burleigh Falls Canada 44°33N 78°12W
Burley U.S.A. 42°32N 113°48W
Burlingame U.S.A. 37°35N 122°21W
Burlington Canada 43°18N 79°45W
Burlington Colo., U.S.A. 39°18N 102°16W
Burlington Iowa, U.S.A. 40°49N 91°14W
Burlington Kans., U.S.A. 38°12N 95°45W
Burlington N.C., U.S.A. 36°7N 79°26W
Burlington N.J., U.S.A. 40°4N 74°51W
Burlington Vt., U.S.A. 44°29N 73°12W
Burlington Wash., U.S.A. 48°28N 122°20W
Burlington Wis., U.S.A. 42°41N 88°17W
Burma ■ Asia 21°0N 96°30E
Burnaby I. Canada 52°25N 131°19W
Burnet U.S.A. 30°45N 98°14W
Burney U.S.A. 40°53N 121°40W
Burnham U.S.A. 40°38N 77°34W
Burnham-on-Sea U.K. 51°14N 3°0W
Burnie Australia 41°4S 145°56E
Burnley U.K. 53°47N 2°14W
Burns U.S.A. 43°35N 119°3W
Burns Junction U.S.A. 42°47N 117°51W
Burns Lake Canada 54°14N 125°45W
Burnside → Canada 66°51N 108°4W
Burnside, L. Australia 25°22S 123°0E
Burnsville U.S.A. 44°47N 93°17W
Burnt River Canada 44°41N 78°42W
Burntwood → Canada 56°8N 96°34W
Burntwood L. Canada 55°22N 100°26W
Buronga Australia 34°18S 142°20E
Burqān Kuwait 29°0N 47°57E
Burqin China 47°43N 87°0E
Burra Australia 33°40S 138°55E
Burra Nigeria 11°0N 8°56E
Burragorang, L. Australia 33°52S 150°37E
Burray U.K. 58°51N 2°54W
Burrel Albania 41°36N 20°1E
Burren △ Ireland 53°9N 9°5W
Burren Junction Australia 30°7S 148°58E
Burrendong, L. Australia 32°45S 149°10E
Burriana Spain 39°50N 0°4W
Burrinjuck, L. Australia 35°0S 148°36E
Burro, Serranías del Mexico 28°56N 102°5W
Burrow Hd. U.K. 54°41N 4°24W
Burrowa-Pine Mountain △ Australia 36°6S 147°45E
Burrum Coast △ Australia 25°13S 152°36E
Burruyacú Argentina 26°30S 64°40W
Burry Port U.K. 51°41N 4°15W
Bursa Turkey 40°15N 29°5E
Bursa □ Turkey 40°10N 29°5E
Burseryd Sweden 57°12N 13°17E
Burstall Canada 50°39N 109°54W
Burton Ohio, U.S.A. 41°28N 81°8W
Burton S.C., U.S.A. 32°26N 80°43W
Burton, L. Canada 54°45N 78°20W
Burton upon Trent U.K. 52°48N 1°38W
Burtundy Australia 33°45S 142°15E
Buru Indonesia 3°30S 126°30E
Burullus, Bahra el Egypt 31°25N 31°0E
Burûn, Râs Egypt 31°14N 33°7E
Burundi ■ Africa 3°15S 30°0E
Bururi Burundi 3°57S 29°37E
Burutu Nigeria 5°20N 5°29E
Burwell U.S.A. 41°47N 99°8W
Burwick U.K. 58°45N 2°58W
Bury U.K. 53°35N 2°17W
Bury St. Edmunds U.K. 52°15N 0°43E
Buryatia □ Russia 53°0N 110°0E
Bürylbaytal Kazakhstan 44°56N 74°0E
Buryn Ukraine 51°13N 33°50E
Burzenin Poland 51°28N 18°47E
Busalla Italy 44°34N 8°57E
Busan S. Korea 35°5N 129°0E
Busango Swamp Zambia 14°15S 25°45E
Busaso = Boosaaso Somalia 11°12N 49°18E
Buşayrah Syria 35°9N 40°26E
Busca Italy 44°31N 7°29E
Bushat Albania 41°58N 19°34E
Būshehr Iran 28°55N 50°55E
Būshehr □ Iran 28°20N 51°45E
Bushenyi Uganda 0°35S 30°10E
Bushire = Būshehr Iran 28°55N 50°55E
Bushnell U.S.A. 28°40N 82°7W
Bushtyna Ukraine 48°3N 23°28E
Busie Ghana 10°29N 2°22W
Businga Dem. Rep. of the Congo 3°16N 20°59E
Büsingen Germany 47°42N 8°41E
Busko-Zdrój Poland 50°28N 20°42E
Busovača Bos.-H. 44°6N 17°53E
Buşra ash Shām Syria 32°30N 36°25E
Busselton Australia 33°42S 115°15E
Busseto Italy 44°59N 10°2E
Bussière-Badil France 45°39N 0°36E
Bussolengo Italy 45°28N 10°51E
Bussum Neths. 52°16N 5°10E
Bustamante, B. Argentina 45°5S 66°18W
Buşteni Romania 45°24N 25°32E
Busto, C. Spain 43°34N 6°28W
Busto Arsízio Italy 45°37N 8°51E
Busu Djanoa Dem. Rep. of the Congo 1°43N 21°23E
Busuanga I. Phil. 12°10N 120°0E
Büsum Germany 54°7N 8°51E
Busungbiu Indonesia 8°16S 114°58E
Buta Dem. Rep. of the Congo 2°50N 24°53E
Butare Rwanda 2°31S 29°52E
Butaritari Kiribati 3°30N 174°0E
Bute Australia 33°51S 138°0E
Bute U.K. 55°48N 5°2W
Bute Inlet Canada 50°40N 124°53W
Butemba Uganda 1°9N 31°37E

ıbo
ı. Rep. of the Congo 0°9N 29°18E 142 B2
ıi Romania 46°19N 22°7E 80 D7
ıa Italy 37°11N 14°11E 95 E7
ı Kenya 0°13N 34°30E 142 B3
ı-Buthe Lesotho 28°47S 28°14E 145 C4
ıa Uganda 1°50N 31°20E 142 B3
· Ga., U.S.A. 32°33N 84°14W 178 C5
· Mo., U.S.A. 38°16N 94°20W 172 F6
· Pa., U.S.A. 40°52N 79°54W 174 F5
ı Indonesia 5°0S 122°45E 119 E6
Mont., U.S.A. 46°0N 112°32W 168 C7
Nebr., U.S.A. 42°58N 98°51W 172 D4
Creek → U.S.A. 39°12N 121°56W 170 F5
·worth = Gcuwa
rica 32°20S 28°11E 145 D4
·worth Malaysia 5°24N 100°23E 121 c
vant Ireland 52°14N 8°40W 64 D3
eld, Mt. Australia 24°45S 128°9E 149 D4
n B. Canada 58°45N 94°23W 163 B10
nwillow U.S.A. 35°24N 119°28W 171 K7
Hd. Australia 33°54S 121°9E 149 F3
n Phil. 8°57N 125°33E 119 C7
u-Luba Eq. Guin. 3°29N 8°33E 139 E6
g = Buton
nesia 5°0S 122°45E 119 E6
inovka Russia 50°50N 40°35E 86 E5
al Nepal 27°33N 83°31E 125 F10
ach Germany 50°25N 8°40E 77 E4
w Germany 53°50N 11°58E 76 B7
akaba Somalia 3°12N 44°20E 131 G3
Duar India 27°45N 89°35E 125 F13
· India 25°34N 83°58E 125 G10
o Uzbekistan 39°48N 64°25E 108 E6
hude Germany 53°28N 9°39E 76 B5
n U.K. 53°16N 1°54W 66 D6
France 46°44N 4°40E 71 F11
ussia 58°28N 41°28E 86 A5
t-Uhaa
ıgolia 44°55N 110°11E 114 B6
aksk Russia 42°48N 47°7E 87 J8
Ivory C. 6°21N 7°5W 138 D3
L. de Ivory C. 6°16N 7°10W 138 D3
Menderes →
ey 37°28N 27°11E 99 D9
çekmece Turkey 41°2N 28°35E 97 E12
kariştiran
ey 41°18N 27°33E 97 E11
kemikli Burnu
ey 40°18N 26°14E 97 F10
kkonuk = Komi
rus 35°24N 34°0E 101 D13
korhan Turkey 39°46N 28°56E 99 B10
kyoncalı Turkey 41°20N 27°55E 97 E11
n Shan China 40°4N 122°43E 115 D12
çais France 46°54N 1°25E 70 F8
Romania 45°10N 26°50E 81 E11
□ Romania 45°20N 26°30E 81 E11
→ Romania 45°26N 27°44E 81 E12
, Pasul Romania 45°35N 26°12E 81 E11
Japan 33°35N 131°5E 113 H5
Croatia 45°24N 13°58E 93 C10
→ Mozam. 19°50S 34°43E 143 F3
ı Romania 45°38N 21°36E 80 E6
eýin Turkmenistan 38°33N 58°12E 129 B8
uk Russia 52°48N 52°12E 108 B4
uk → Russia 50°15N 42°7E 86 E6
rds Bay U.S.A. 41°45N 70°37W 175 E14
Mkubwa Zambia 13°8S 28°38E 143 E2
Δ Uganda 1°2S 29°42E 142 C2
Ruse, Bulgaria 43°28N 25°44E 97 C9
Varna, Bulgaria 42°53N 27°55E 97 D11
Slatina Bulgaria 43°26N 23°58E 96 C7
Martin I.
ıda 75°15N 104°15W 161 B11
zina → Belarus 52°33N 30°14E 75 B16
za Belarus 52°31N 24°51E 75 B13
s = Jubayl Lebanon 34°5N 35°39E 130 A4
wa Poland 51°1N 22°36E 83 G9
na Poland 51°7N 18°12E 83 G5
szcz Poland 53°10N 18°0E 83 E5
ussia = Belarus ■
pe 53°30N 27°0E 75 B14
U.S.A. 39°43N 104°14W 168 G11
ille U.S.A. 39°58N 81°32W 174 G3
l Δ Australia 22°52S 150°45E 150 C5
na Belarus 53°31N 30°14E 75 B16
v = Bykhaw
rus 53°31N 30°14E 75 B16
vo Russia 49°50N 45°25E 86 F7
U.S.A. 33°8N 110°7W 169 K8
Canada 58°25N 94°8W 163 B10
I. Canada 73°13N 78°34W 161 C16
n U.S.A. 32°11N 90°15W 177 E9
C. Antarctica 69°38S 76°7W 55 C17
k Australia 30°40S 146°27E 153 A7
U.S.A. 32°39N 83°46W 178 C6
, C. Australia 28°43S 153°38E 151 D5
Bay Australia 28°43S 153°37E 151 D5
nga, Gory Russia 75°0N 100°0E 107 B11
nga Mts. = Byrranga, Gory
sia 75°0N 100°0E 107 B11
Denmark 57°16N 11°0E 63 G5
Sweden 64°57N 21°11E 60 D19
älven → Sweden 64°57N 21°13E 60 D19
rtsya Ukraine 48°27N 24°14E 81 B9
yca → Dolnośląskie,
nd 51°12N 16°55E 83 G3
yca → Lubelskie,
nd 51°21N 22°46E 83 G9
yca Kłodzka
nd 50°19N 16°39E 83 H3
Slovak Rep. 49°13N 18°34E 79 B11
Ukraine 48°38N 24°28E 81 B9
n Poland 50°25N 18°54E 83 H5
n Odrzański Poland 51°44N 15°48E 83 G2
Poland 54°10N 17°30E 82 D4
ba Rwanda 1°35S 30°4E 142 C3
Czech Rep. 48°58N 17°18E 79 C10
→ Poland 52°25N 20°15E 83 E7
McConaughy, L.
A. 41°14N 101°40W 172 E3
Vietnam 18°45N 105°45E 120 C5
ı Vietnam 9°7N 105°8E 121 H5
au, Mui Vietnam 8°38N 104°44E 121 H5
Vietnam 11°20N 108°54E 121 G7
apé Paraguay 25°23S 57°5W 190 B4
Caaguazú Δ Paraguay 26°5S 55°31W 191 B4
Caála Angola 12°46S 15°30E 141 G3
Caamaño Sd. Canada 52°55N 129°25W 162 C3
Caazapá Paraguay 26°8S 56°19W 190 B4
Caazapá □ Paraguay 26°10S 56°0W 191 B4
Cabana Peru 8°25S 78°5W 188 B2
Cabana de Bergantiños = A
Carballa Spain 43°13N 8°54W 88 B2
Cabanaconde Peru 15°38S 71°58W 188 D3
Cabañaquinta Spain 43°10N 5°38W 88 B5
Cabanatuan Phil. 15°30N 120°58E 119 A6
Cabañeros ⌂ Spain 39°18N 4°35W 89 F6
Cabanes Spain 40°9N 0°2E 90 E5
Cabanilla Peru 15°36S 70°28W 188 D3
Cabano Canada 47°40N 68°56W 165 C6
Čabar Croatia 45°36N 14°39E 93 C11
Cabazon U.S.A. 33°55N 116°47W 171 M10
Cabedelo Brazil 7°0S 34°50W 189 B4
Cabeza del Buey Spain 38°44N 5°13W 89 G5
Cabezón de la Sal Spain 43°18N 4°14W 88 B6
Cabhán, An = Cavan
Ireland 54°0N 7°22W 64 B4
Cabildo Chile 32°30S 71°5W 190 C1
Cabimas Venezuela 10°23N 71°25W 186 A4
Cabinda Angola 5°33S 12°11E 140 F2
Cabinda □ Angola 5°0S 12°30E 140 F2
Cabinet Mts. U.S.A. 48°10N 115°50W 168 B6
Cabo Blanco Argentina 47°15S 65°47W 192 C3
Cabo de Gata-Níjar ⌂
Spain 36°51N 2°6W 91 J2
Cabo de Hornos Δ
Chile 55°42S 67°20W 192 E3
Cabo de Santo Agostinho
Brazil 8°20S 34°55W 189 B4
Cabo Frio Brazil 22°51S 42°3W 191 A7
Cabo Pantoja Peru 1°0S 75°10W 186 D3
Cabo Raso Argentina 44°20S 65°15W 192 B3
Cabo San Lucas
Mexico 22°53N 109°54W 180 C3
Cabo Verde = Cape Verde Is. ■
Atl. Oc. 16°0N 24°0W 134 b
Cabonga, Réservoir
Canada 47°20N 76°40W 164 C4
Cabool U.S.A. 37°7N 92°6W 172 G7
Caboolture Australia 27°5S 152°58E 151 D5
Cabora Bassa Dam = Cahora
Bassa, Lago de
Mozam. 15°20S 32°50E 143 F3
Caborca Mexico 30°37N 112°6W 180 A2
Cabot, Mt. U.S.A. 44°30N 71°25W 175 B13
Cabot Hd. Canada 45°14N 81°17W 174 A3
Cabot Str. Canada 47°15N 59°40W 165 C8
Cabourg France 49°17N 0°7W 70 C6
Cabra Spain 37°30N 4°28W 89 H6
Cabra del Santo Cristo
Spain 37°42N 3°16W 89 H7
Cabra I. India 7°18N 93°50E 127 L11
Cábras Italy 39°56N 8°32E 94 C1
Cabrera Spain 39°8N 2°57E 100 B9
Cabrera, Sierra de la
Spain 42°12N 6°40W 88 C4
Cabrera Δ Spain 39°13N 2°53E 91 F7
Cabri Canada 50°35N 108°25W 163 C7
Cabriel → Spain 39°14N 1°3W 91 F3
Cacabelos Spain 42°36N 6°44W 88 C4
Caçador Brazil 26°47S 51°0W 191 B5
Čačak Serbia 43°54N 20°20E 96 C4
Caçapava do Sul Brazil 30°30S 53°30W 191 C5
Càccamo Italy 37°56N 13°40E 94 E6
Cacém Portugal 38°46N 9°18W 89 G1
Cáceres Brazil 16°5S 57°40W 186 G7
Cáceres Spain 39°26N 6°23W 89 F4
Cáceres □ Spain 39°45N 6°0W 88 F5
Cache Bay Canada 46°22N 80°0W 164 C4
Cache Cr. → U.S.A. 38°42N 121°42W 170 G5
Cache Creek Canada 50°48N 121°19W 162 C4
Cacheu Guinea-Biss. 12°14N 16°8W 138 C1
Cachi Argentina 25°5S 66°10W 190 B2
Cachimbo, Serra do
Brazil 9°30S 55°30W 187 E7
Cachinal de la Sierra
Chile 24°58S 69°32W 190 A2
Cachoeira Brazil 12°30S 39°0W 189 C3
Cachoeira do Sul Brazil 30°3S 52°53W 191 C5
Cachoeiro de Itapemirim
Brazil 20°51S 41°7W 191 A7
Cachopo Portugal 37°20N 7°49W 89 H3
Cacine Guinea-Biss. 11°8N 14°57W 138 C1
Cacoal Brazil 11°32S 61°18W 186 F6
Cacólo Angola 10°9S 19°21E 140 G3
Caconda Angola 13°48S 15°8E 141 G3
Caculé Brazil 14°30S 42°13W 189 C2
Cadaqués Spain 42°17N 3°17E 90 C8
Čadca Slovak Rep. 49°26N 18°45E 79 B11
Caddo U.S.A. 34°7N 96°16W 176 D6
Cader Idris U.K. 52°42N 3°53W 67 E4
Cadereyta de Jiménez
Mexico 25°36N 100°0W 180 B5
Cades U.S.A. 33°47N 79°47W 178 B10
Cadí, Serra del Spain 42°17N 1°42E 90 C6
Cadí-Moixeró ⌂ Spain 42°17N 1°44E 90 C3
Cadibarrawirracanna, L.
Australia 28°52S 135°27E 151 D2
Cadillac France 44°38N 0°20W 72 D3
Cadillac U.S.A. 44°15N 85°24W 173 C11
Cadiz Phil. 10°57N 123°15E 119 B6
Cádiz Spain 36°30N 6°20W 89 J4
Cadiz Calif., U.S.A. 34°30N 115°28W 171 L11
Cadiz Ohio, U.S.A. 40°22N 81°0W 174 F4
Cádiz □ Spain 36°36N 5°45W 89 J5
Cádiz, G. de Spain 36°40N 7°0W 89 J3
Cadiz L. U.S.A. 34°18N 115°24W 171 L11
Cadley U.S.A. 33°32N 82°40W 178 B7
Cadney Park Australia 27°55S 134°3E 151 D1
Cadomin Canada 53°2N 117°20W 162 C5
Cadotte Lake Canada 56°26N 116°23W 162 B5
Cadours France 43°44N 1°2E 72 E5
Cadoux Australia 30°46S 117°7E 149 F2
Cadwell U.S.A. 32°20N 83°3W 178 C6
Caen France 49°10N 0°22W 70 C6
Caerdydd = Cardiff U.K. 51°29N 3°10W 67 F4
Caerfyrddin = Carmarthen
U.K. 51°52N 4°19W 67 F3
Caergybi = Holyhead
U.K. 53°18N 4°38W 66 D3
Caernarfon U.K. 53°8N 4°16W 66 D3
Caernarfon B. U.K. 53°4N 4°40W 66 D3
Caernarvon = Caernarfon
U.K. 53°8N 4°16W 66 D3
Caerphilly U.K. 51°35N 3°13W 67 F4
Caerphilly □ U.K. 51°37N 3°12W 67 F4
Caesarea Israel 32°30N 34°53E 130 C3
Caeté Brazil 19°55S 43°40W 189 D2
Caetité Brazil 13°50S 42°32W 189 C2
Cafayate Argentina 26°2S 66°0W 190 B2
Cafu Angola 16°30S 15°8E 144 A2
Cagayan de Oro Phil. 8°30N 124°40E 119 C6
Cagli Italy 43°33N 12°39E 93 E9
Cágliari Italy 39°13N 9°7E 94 C2
Cágliari, G. di Italy 39°8N 9°11E 94 C2
Cagnano Varano Italy 41°49N 15°47E 93 G12
Cagnes-sur-Mer France 43°40N 7°9E 73 E11
Caguán → Colombia 0°8S 74°18W 186 D4
Caguas Puerto Rico 18°14N 66°2W 183 d
Caha Mts. Ireland 51°45N 9°40W 64 E2
Cahama Angola 16°17S 14°19E 144 A1
Cahir Ireland 52°22N 7°56W 64 D4
Cahirciveen Ireland 51°56N 10°14W 64 E1
Cahora Bassa, Lago de
Mozam. 15°20S 32°50E 143 F3
Cahore Pt. Ireland 52°33N 6°12W 64 D5
Cahors France 44°27N 1°27E 72 D5
Cahuapanas Peru 5°15S 77°0W 188 B2
Cahul Moldova 45°50N 28°15E 81 E13
Cai Bau, Dao Vietnam 21°10N 107°27E 116 G6
Cai Be Vietnam 10°20N 106°2E 121 G6
Cai Nuoc Vietnam 8°56N 105°1E 121 H5
Caia Mozam. 17°51S 35°24E 143 F4
Caianda Angola 11°2S 23°31E 143 E1
Caibarién Cuba 22°30N 79°30W 182 B4
Caicara Venezuela 7°38N 66°10W 186 B5
Caicó Brazil 6°20S 37°0W 189 B3
Caicos Is.
Turks & Caicos 21°40N 71°40W 183 B5
Caicos Passage
W. Indies 22°45N 72°45W 183 B5
Caidian China 30°35N 114°2E 117 B10
Caiguna Australia 32°16S 125°29E 149 F4
Cailloma Peru 15°9S 71°45W 188 D3
Căinari Moldova 46°41N 29°3E 81 D14
Caird Coast Antarctica 75°0S 25°0W 55 D1
Cairn Gorm U.K. 57°7N 3°39W 65 D5
Cairngorm Mts. U.K. 57°6N 3°42W 65 D5
Cairngorms Δ U.K. 57°10N 3°50W 65 D5
Cairnryan U.K. 54°59N 5°1W 65 G3
Cairns Australia 16°57S 145°45E 150 B4
Cairns L. Canada 51°42N 94°30W 163 C10
Cairo = El Qâhira Egypt 30°2N 31°13E 137 E7
Cairo Ga., U.S.A. 30°52N 84°13W 178 E5
Cairo Ill., U.S.A. 37°0N 89°11W 172 G9
Cairo N.Y., U.S.A. 42°18N 74°0W 175 D10
Cairo Montenotte Italy 44°23N 8°16E 92 D5
Caiseal = Cashel Ireland 52°30N 7°53W 64 D4
Caisleán an Bharraigh = Castlebar
Ireland 53°52N 9°18W 64 C2
Caithness U.K. 58°25N 3°35W 65 C5
Caithness, Ord of U.K. 58°8N 3°36W 65 C5
Caja de Muertos, I.
Puerto Rico 17°54N 66°32W 183 d
Cajabamba Peru 7°38S 78°4W 188 B2
Cajamarca Peru 7°5S 78°28W 188 B2
Cajamarca □ Peru 6°15S 78°50W 188 B2
Cajapió Brazil 2°58S 44°48W 189 A2
Cajarc France 44°29N 1°50E 72 D5
Cajatambo Peru 10°30S 77°2W 188 C2
Cajazeiras Brazil 6°52S 38°30W 189 B3
Čajetina Serbia 43°47N 19°42E 96 C3
Çakirgol Turkey 40°33N 39°40E 105 B8
Çakırlar Turkey 36°52N 30°33E 99 E12
Čakovec Croatia 46°23N 16°26E 93 B13
Çal Turkey 38°4N 29°23E 99 C11
Cala Spain 37°59N 6°21W 89 H4
Cala → Spain 37°38N 6°5W 89 H4
Cala Cadolar, Punta de = Rotja,
Pta. Spain 38°38N 1°35E 91 G6
Cala d'Or Spain 39°23N 3°14E 100 B10
Cala en Porter Spain 39°52N 4°8E 100 B11
Cala Figuera Spain 39°20N 3°10E 100 B10
Cala Figuera, C. de Spain 39°27N 2°31E 100 B9
Cala Forcat Spain 40°0N 3°47E 100 B10
Cala Major Spain 39°33N 2°37E 100 B9
Cala Mezquida = Sa Mesquida
Spain 39°55N 4°16E 100 B11
Cala Millor Spain 39°35N 3°22E 100 B10
Cala Murada Spain 39°27N 3°17E 100 B10
Cala Ratjada Spain 39°43N 3°27E 100 B10
Cala Santa Galdana
Spain 39°56N 3°58E 100 B10
Calabar Nigeria 4°57N 8°20E 139 E6
Calabogie Canada 45°18N 76°43W 175 A8
Calabozo Venezuela 9°0N 67°28W 186 B5
Calábria □ Italy 39°0N 16°30E 95 C9
Calábria Δ Italy 39°6N 16°35E 95 C9
Calaburras, Pta. de Spain 36°30N 4°38W 89 J6
Calaceite Spain 41°1N 0°11E 90 D5
Calacoto Bolivia 17°16S 68°38W 188 D4
Calacuccia France 42°21N 9°1E 73 F13
Calafat Romania 43°58N 22°59E 80 G7
Calafell Spain 41°11N 1°34E 90 D6
Calahorra Spain 42°18N 1°59W 90 C3
Calais France 50°57N 1°56E 71 B8
Calais U.S.A. 45°11N 67°17W 173 C20
Calakmul ⌂ Mexico 18°14N 89°48W 181 D7
Calalaste, Cord. de
Argentina 25°0S 67°0W 190 B2
Calama Brazil 8°0S 62°50W 186 E6
Calama Chile 22°30S 68°55W 190 A2
Calamar Colombia 10°15N 74°55W 186 A4
Calamarca Bolivia 16°55S 68°9W 188 D4
Calamian Group Phil. 11°50N 119°55E 119 B5
Calamocha Spain 40°50N 1°17W 90 E3
Calamonte Spain 38°53N 6°23W 89 G4
Călan Romania 45°44N 22°59E 80 E7
Calañas Spain 37°40N 6°53W 89 H4
Calanda Spain 40°56N 0°15W 90 E4
Calang Indonesia 4°37N 95°37E 118 D1
Calangiánus Italy 40°56N 9°11E 94 B2
Calanques Δ France 43°14N 5°30E 73 E9
Calanscio, Sarīr Libya 27°30N 22°30E 135 C10
Calapan Phil. 13°25N 121°7E 119 B6
Călăraşi Moldova 47°16N 28°19E 81 C13
Călăraşi Romania 44°12N 27°20E 81 F12
Călăraşi □ Romania 44°10N 27°0E 81 F12
Calasparra Spain 38°14N 1°41W 91 G3
Calatafimi Italy 37°55N 12°52E 94 E5
Calatayud Spain 41°20N 1°40W 90 D3
Călăţele Romania 46°46N 23°1E 80 D8
Calato = Kalathos Greece 36°9N 28°8E 99 E10
Calauag Phil. 13°55N 122°15E 119 B6
Calavà, C. Italy 38°11N 14°55E 95 D7
Calavite, C. Phil. 13°26N 120°20E 119 B6
Calbayog Phil. 12°4N 124°38E 119 B6
Calca Peru 13°22S 72°0W 188 C3
Calcasieu L. U.S.A. 29°55N 93°18W 176 G8
Calcium U.S.A. 44°1N 75°50W 175 B9
Calcutta = Kolkata
India 22°34N 88°21E 125 H13
Calcutta U.S.A. 40°40N 80°34W 174 F4
Caldaro Italy 46°25N 11°14E 93 B8
Caldas da Rainha Portugal 39°24N 9°8W 89 F1
Caldas de Reis Spain 42°36N 8°39W 88 C2
Caldas Novas Brazil 17°45S 48°38W 189 D1
Calder → U.K. 53°44N 1°22W 66 D6
Caldera Chile 27°5S 70°55W 190 B1
Caldera de Taburiente Δ
Canary Is. 28°43N 17°52W 100 F2
Caldwell Idaho, U.S.A. 43°40N 116°41W 168 E5
Caldwell Kans., U.S.A. 37°2N 97°37W 172 G5
Caldwell Tex., U.S.A. 30°32N 96°42W 176 F6
Caledon Canada 43°51N 79°51W 174 C5
Caledon S. Africa 34°14S 19°26E 144 D2
Caledon → S. Africa 30°31S 26°5E 144 D4
Caledon B. Australia 12°45S 137°0E 150 A2
Caledonia Canada 43°7N 79°58W 174 C5
Caledonia U.S.A. 42°58N 77°51W 174 D7
Calella Spain 41°37N 2°40E 90 D7
Calemba Angola 16°0S 15°44E 144 A2
Calen Australia 20°56S 148°48E 150 b
Calenzana France 42°31N 8°51E 73 F12
Caleta Olivia Argentina 46°25S 67°25W 192 C3
Caletones Chile 34°6S 70°27W 190 C1
Calexico U.S.A. 32°40N 115°30W 171 N11
Calf of Man I. of Man 54°3N 4°48W 66 C3
Calgary Canada 51°0N 114°10W 162 C6
Calheta Madeira 32°44N 17°11W 100 D2
Calhoun U.S.A. 34°30N 84°57W 177 D12
Calhoun Falls U.S.A. 34°6N 82°36W 178 A7
Cali Colombia 3°25N 76°35W 186 C3
Calicut = Kozhikode
India 11°15N 75°43E 127 J2
Cálida, Costa Spain 37°30N 1°30W 91 H3
Caliente U.S.A. 37°37N 114°31W 169 H6
California Mo., U.S.A. 38°38N 92°34W 172 F7
California Pa., U.S.A. 40°4N 79°54W 174 F5
California □ U.S.A. 37°30N 119°30W 170 H7
California, Baja, T.N. = Baja
California □ Mexico 30°0N 115°0W 180 B2
California, Baja, T.S. = Baja
California Sur □
Mexico 25°50N 111°50W 180 B2
California, G. de Mexico 27°0N 111°0W 180 B2
California City U.S.A. 35°10N 117°55W 171 K9
California Hot Springs
U.S.A. 35°51N 118°41W 171 K8
Cälilabad Azerbaijan 39°12N 48°29E 105 C13
Calilegua Δ Argentina 25°36S 64°50W 190 B3
Călimăneşti Romania 45°14N 24°20E 81 E9
Călimani, Munţii
Romania 47°12N 25°0E 81 C10
Călimani Δ Romania 47°7N 25°10E 81 C10
Calingasta Argentina 31°15S 69°30W 190 C2
Calipatria U.S.A. 33°8N 115°31W 171 M11
Calistoga U.S.A. 38°35N 122°35W 170 G4
Calitri Italy 40°54N 15°26E 95 B8
Calitzdorp S. Africa 33°33S 21°42E 144 D3
Callabonna, L.
Australia 29°40S 140°5E 151 D3
Callac France 48°25N 3°27W 70 D3
Callahan U.S.A. 30°34N 81°50W 178 E8
Callan Ireland 52°32N 7°24W 64 D4
Callander U.K. 56°15N 4°13W 65 E4
Callao Peru 12°3S 77°8W 188 C2
Callaway U.S.A. 30°8N 85°36W 178 E4
Callicoon U.S.A. 41°46N 75°3W 175 E9
Calling Lake Canada 55°15N 113°12W 162 B6
Calliope Australia 24°0S 151°16E 150 C5
Callosa de Segura Spain 38°7N 0°53W 91 G4
Callosa d'En Sarrià Spain 38°40N 0°8W 91 G4
Calma, Costa de la Spain 39°28N 2°26E 100 B9
Calne U.K. 51°26N 2°0W 67 F6
Calola Angola 16°25S 17°48E 144 A2
Calonge Spain 41°52N 3°5E 90 D8
Caloosahatchee →
U.S.A. 26°31N 82°1W 179 J7
Calore → Italy 41°11N 14°28E 95 A7
Caloundra Australia 26°45S 153°10E 151 D5
Calpe Spain 38°39N 0°3E 91 G5
Calpella U.S.A. 39°14N 123°12W 170 F3
Calpine U.S.A. 39°40N 120°27W 170 F6
Calstock Canada 49°47N 84°9W 164 C3
Caltabellotta Italy 37°34N 13°13E 94 E6
Caltagirone Italy 37°14N 14°31E 95 E7
Caltanissetta Italy 37°29N 14°4E 95 E7
Çaltılıbük Turkey 39°57N 28°36E 97 G12
Caluire-et-Cuire France 45°48N 4°52E 71 G11
Calulo Angola 10°1S 14°56E 140 G2
Caluso Italy 45°18N 7°53E 92 C4
Calvados □ France 49°5N 0°15W 70 C6
Calvert → Australia 16°17S 137°44E 150 B2
Calvert I. Canada 51°30N 128°0W 162 C3
Calvert Ra. Australia 24°0S 122°30E 148 D3
Calvi France 42°34N 8°45E 73 F12
Calvià Spain 39°34N 2°31E 100 B9
Calvillo Mexico 21°51N 102°43W 180 C4
Calvinia S. Africa 31°28S 19°45E 144 D2
Calvo, Mte. Italy 41°44N 15°46E 93 G12
Calwa U.S.A. 36°42N 119°46W 170 J7
Calzada Almuradiel = Almuradiel
Spain 38°32N 3°28W 89 G7
Calzada de Calatrava
Spain 38°42N 3°46W 89 G7
Cam → U.K. 52°21N 0°16E 67 E8
Cam Lam = Ba Ngoi
Vietnam 11°54N 109°10E 121 G7
Cam Pha Vietnam 21°7N 107°18E 116 G6
Cam Ranh Vietnam 11°54N 109°12E 121 G7
Cam Xuyen Vietnam 18°15N 106°0E 120 C6
Camabatela Angola 8°20S 15°26E 140 F3
Camaçã Brazil 15°24S 39°30W 189 D3
Camaçari Brazil 12°41S 38°18W 189 C3
Camacha Madeira 32°41N 16°49W 100 D3
Camacupa Angola 11°58S 17°22E 141 G3
Camagüey Cuba 21°20N 77°55W 182 B4
Camaiore Italy 43°56N 10°18E 92 E7
Camamu Brazil 13°57S 39°7W 189 C3
Camaná Peru 16°30S 72°50W 188 D3
Camanche Res. U.S.A. 38°14N 121°1W 170 G6
Camaquã Brazil 30°51S 51°49W 191 C5
Camaquã → Brazil 31°17S 51°47W 191 C5
Câmara de Lobos
Madeira 32°39N 16°59W 100 D3
Camarat, C. France 43°12N 6°41E 73 E10
Çamardı Turkey 37°49N 34°58E 104 D6
Camarès France 43°49N 2°53E 72 E6
Camaret-sur-Mer France 48°16N 4°37W 70 D2
Camargo Mexico 26°19N 98°50W 181 B5
Camargue France 43°34N 4°34E 73 E8
Camargue ⌂ France 43°30N 4°30E 73 E8
Camarillo U.S.A. 34°13N 119°2W 171 L7
Camariñas Spain 43°8N 9°12W 88 B1
Camarón, C. Honduras 16°0N 85°5W 182 C2
Camarones Argentina 44°50S 65°40W 192 B3
Camarones, B.
Argentina 44°45S 65°35W 192 B3
Camas Spain 37°24N 6°2W 89 H4
Camas U.S.A. 45°35N 122°24W 170 E4
Camas Valley U.S.A. 43°2N 123°40W 168 E2
Camballin Australia 17°59S 124°12E 148 C3
Cambará Brazil 23°2S 50°5W 191 A5
Cambay = Khambhat
India 22°23N 72°33E 124 H5
Cambay, G. of = Khambhat, G. of
India 20°45N 72°30E 122 J8
Cambil Spain 37°40N 3°33W 89 H7
Cambo-les-Bains France 43°22N 1°23W 72 E2
Cambodia ■ Asia 12°15N 105°0E 120 F5
Camborne U.K. 50°12N 5°19W 67 G2
Cambrai Australia 34°40S 139°16E 152 C3
Cambrai France 50°11N 3°14E 71 B10
Cambre Spain 43°17N 8°20W 88 B2
Cambria U.S.A. 35°34N 121°5W 170 K5
Cambrian Mts. U.K. 52°3N 3°57W 67 E4
Cambridge Canada 43°23N 80°15W 174 C4
Cambridge Jamaica 18°18N 77°54W 182 a
Cambridge N.Z. 37°54S 175°29E 154 D4
Cambridge U.K. 52°12N 0°8E 67 E8
Cambridge Mass.,
U.S.A. 42°23N 71°7W 175 D13
Cambridge Minn.,
U.S.A. 45°34N 93°13W 172 C7
Cambridge N.Y., U.S.A. 43°2N 73°22W 175 C11
Cambridge Nebr.,
U.S.A. 40°17N 100°10W 172 E3
Cambridge Ohio, U.S.A. 40°2N 81°35W 174 F3
Cambridge Bay
Canada 69°10N 105°0W 160 D11
Cambridge G.
Australia 14°55S 128°15E 148 B4
Cambridge Springs
U.S.A. 41°48N 80°4W 174 E4
Cambridgeshire □ U.K. 52°25N 0°7W 67 E7
Cambrils Spain 41°8N 1°3E 90 D6
Cambuci Brazil 21°35S 41°55W 191 A7
Cambundi-Catembo
Angola 10°10S 17°35E 140 G3
Camdeboo Δ S. Africa 32°28S 24°25E 144 D3
Camden Australia 34°1S 150°43E 153 C9
Camden Ala., U.S.A. 31°59N 87°17W 177 F11
Camden Ark., U.S.A. 33°35N 92°50W 176 E8
Camden Maine, U.S.A. 44°13N 69°4W 173 C19
Camden N.J., U.S.A. 39°55N 75°7W 175 G9
Camden N.Y., U.S.A. 43°20N 75°45W 175 C9
Camden S.C., U.S.A. 34°16N 80°36W 177 D14
Camden Sd. Australia 15°27S 124°25E 148 C3
Camdenton U.S.A. 38°1N 92°45W 172 F7
Camelford U.K. 50°37N 4°42W 67 G3
Çameli Turkey 37°5N 29°24E 99 D11
Camenca Moldova 48°3N 28°42E 81 B13
Camerino Italy 43°8N 13°4E 93 E10
Camerón Chile 53°38S 69°39W 192 D3
Cameron Ariz., U.S.A. 35°53N 111°25W 169 J8
Cameron La., U.S.A. 29°48N 93°20W 176 G8
Cameron Mo., U.S.A. 39°44N 94°14W 172 F6
Cameron S.C., U.S.A. 33°34N 80°43W 178 B9
Cameron Tex., U.S.A. 30°51N 96°59W 176 F6
Cameron Highlands
Malaysia 4°27N 101°22E 121 K3
Cameron Hills Canada 59°48N 118°0W 162 B5
Cameron Mts. N.Z. 46°1S 167°0E 155 G2
Cameroon ■ Africa 6°0N 12°30E 135 G7
Camerota Italy 40°2N 15°22E 95 B8
Cameroun → Cameroon 4°0N 9°35E 139 E6
Cameroun, Mt. Cameroon 4°13N 9°10E 139 E6
Cametá Brazil 2°12S 49°30W 187 D9
Çamiçi Gölü Turkey 37°29N 27°28E 99 D9
Camilla U.S.A. 31°14N 84°12W 178 D5
Caminha Portugal 41°50N 8°50W 88 D2
Camino U.S.A. 38°44N 120°41W 170 G6
Camlıbel = Myrtou
Cyprus 35°18N 33°4E 101 D12
Cammal U.S.A. 41°24N 77°28W 174 E7
Cammarata Italy 37°38N 13°38E 94 E6
Camocim Brazil 2°55S 40°50W 189 A2
Camonica, Val Italy 46°0N 10°20E 92 B7
Camooweal Australia 19°56S 138°7E 150 B2
Camooweal Caves Δ
Australia 20°1S 138°11E 150 C2
Camopi Fr. Guiana 3°12N 52°17W 187 C8
Camorta India 8°8N 93°30E 127 K11
Camp Hill Ala., U.S.A. 32°48N 85°39W 178 C4
Camp Hill Pa., U.S.A. 40°14N 76°55W 174 F8
Camp Nelson U.S.A. 36°8N 118°39W 171 J8
Camp Pendleton
U.S.A. 33°13N 117°24W 171 M9
Camp Verde U.S.A. 34°34N 111°51W 169 J8
Camp Wood U.S.A. 29°40N 100°1W 176 G4
Campagna Italy 40°40N 15°6E 95 B8
Campana Argentina 34°10S 58°55W 190 C4
Campana, I. Chile 48°20S 75°20W 192 C1
Campanário Madeira 32°39N 17°2W 100 D2
Campanario Spain 38°52N 5°36W 89 G5
Campanet Spain 39°46N 2°58E 100 B9
Campània □ Italy 41°0N 14°30E 95 B7
Campas del Tuyú Δ
Argentina 36°17S 56°50W 190 D4
Campbell S. Africa 28°48S 23°44E 144 C3
Campbell Calif., U.S.A. 37°17N 121°57W 170 H5
Campbell Fla., U.S.A. 28°16N 81°27W 179 G8
Campbell Ohio, U.S.A. 41°5N 80°37W 174 E4
Campbell, C. N.Z. 41°47S 174°18E 155 B9
Campbell I. Pac. Oc. 52°30S 169°0E 156 N8
Campbell L. Canada 63°14N 106°55W 163 A7
Campbell Plateau
S. Ocean 50°0S 170°0E 55 A11
Campbell River Canada 50°5N 125°20W 162 C3
Campbellford Canada 44°18N 77°48W 174 B7
Campbellpur Pakistan 33°46N 72°26E 124 C5
Campbellsville U.S.A. 37°21N 85°20W 173 G11
Campbellton Canada 47°57N 66°43W 165 C6
Campbellton U.S.A. 30°57N 85°24W 178 E4
Campbelltown
Australia 34°4S 150°49E 153 C9
Campbeltown U.K. 55°26N 5°36W 65 F3
Campeche Mexico 19°51N 90°32W 181 D6
Campeche □ Mexico 19°0N 90°30W 181 D6
Campeche, Golfo de
Mexico 19°30N 93°0W 181 D6
Câmpeni Romania 46°22N 23°3E 80 D8
Camperdown Australia 38°14S 143°9E 152 E5
Camperville Canada 51°59N 100°9W 163 C8
Campi Salentina Italy 40°24N 18°1E 95 B11
Câmpia Turzii Romania 46°34N 23°53E 81 D8
Campidano Italy 39°30N 8°47E 94 C1
Campíglia Marittima
Italy 43°4N 10°37E 92 E7
Campillo de Altobuey
Spain 39°36N 1°49W 91 F3
Campillos Spain 37°4N 4°51W 89 H6
Câmpina Romania 45°10N 25°45E 81 E10
Campina Grande Brazil 7°20S 35°47W 189 B3
Campinas Brazil 22°50S 47°0W 191 A6
Campione Italy 45°58N 8°58E 73 C12
Campli Italy 42°43N 13°41E 93 F10
Campo Spain 42°25N 0°24E 90 C5
Campo de Criptana Spain 39°24N 3°7W 89 F7
Campo de Gibraltar
Spain 36°15N 5°25W 89 J5
Campo de los Alisos Δ
Argentina 27°15S 66°0W 190 B2
Campo Formoso Brazil 10°30S 40°20W 189 C2
Campo Grande Brazil 20°25S 54°40W 187 H8
Campo Maior Brazil 4°50S 42°12W 189 A2
Campo Maior Portugal 39°2N 7°7W 89 F3
Campo Mourão Brazil 24°3S 52°22W 191 A5
Campo Túres Italy 46°53N 11°55E 93 B8
Campobasso Italy 41°34N 14°39E 95 A7
Campobello di Licata
Italy 37°15N 13°55E 94 E6
Campobello di Mazara
Italy 37°38N 12°45E 94 E5
Campofelice di Roccella
Italy 37°59N 13°53E 94 E6
Campomarino Italy 41°57N 15°2E 93 G12
Camporeale Italy 37°54N 13°6E 94 E6
Camporrobles Spain 39°39N 1°24W 90 F3
Campos Brazil 21°50S 41°20W 191 A7
Campos Spain 39°26N 3°1E 100 B10
Campos Altos Brazil 19°47S 46°10W 189 D1
Campos Belos Brazil 13°10S 47°3W 189 C1
Campos del Paraiso = Carrascosa
del Campo Spain 40°2N 2°45W 90 E2
Campos Novos Brazil 27°21S 51°50W 191 B5
Campos Sales Brazil 7°4S 40°23W 189 B2
Camprodon Spain 42°19N 2°23E 90 C7
Campton Fla., U.S.A. 30°53N 86°31W 179 E3
Campton Ga., U.S.A. 33°52N 83°43W 178 B6
Camptonville U.S.A. 39°27N 121°3W 170 F5
Camptown U.S.A. 41°44N 76°14W 175 E8
Câmpulung Argeş,
Romania 45°17N 25°3E 81 E10
Câmpulung Suceava,
Romania 47°32N 25°30E 81 C10
Câmpuri Romania 46°0N 26°50E 81 D11
Campville U.S.A. 29°40N 82°7W 178 F7
Camrose Canada 53°0N 112°50W 162 C6
Camsell Portage
Canada 59°37N 109°15W 163 B7
Çamyuva Turkey 36°30N 30°30E 99 E12
Çan Turkey 40°2N 27°3E 97 F11
Can Clavo Spain 38°57N 1°27E 100 C7
Can Creu Spain 38°58N 1°28E 100 C7
Can Gio Vietnam 10°25N 106°58E 121 G6
Can Pastilla Spain 39°32N 2°42E 100 B9
Can Tho Vietnam 10°2N 105°46E 121 G5
Canaan U.S.A. 42°2N 73°20W 175 D11
Canacona India 15°1N 74°4E 127 G2
Canada ■ N. Amer. 60°0N 100°0W 160 G11
Canada Abyssal Plain
Arctic 80°0N 140°0W 54 B18
Canada Basin Arctic 75°0N 145°0W 54 B18
Cañada de Gómez
Argentina 32°40S 61°30W 190 C3
Canadian U.S.A. 35°55N 100°23W 176 D4
Canadian → U.S.A. 35°28N 95°3W 176 D7
Canadian Shield Canada 53°0N 75°0W 158 D12
Canadys U.S.A. 33°3N 80°37W 178 B9
Canajoharie U.S.A. 42°54N 74°35W 175 D10
Çanakkale Turkey 40°8N 26°24E 97 F10
Çanakkale □ Turkey 40°10N 26°25E 97 F10
Çanakkale Boğazı
Turkey 40°17N 26°32E 97 F10
Canal Flats Canada 50°10N 115°48W 162 C5
Canal Point U.S.A. 26°52N 80°38W 179 J9
Canalejas Argentina 35°15S 66°34W 190 D2
Canals Argentina 33°35S 62°53W 190 C3
Canals Spain 38°58N 0°35W 91 G4
Canandaigua U.S.A. 42°54N 77°17W 174 D7
Canandaigua L. U.S.A. 42°47N 77°19W 174 D7
Cananea Mexico 31°0N 110°18W 180 A2
Canarias, Is. Atl. Oc. 28°30N 16°0W 100 F4
Canaries St. Lucia 13°55N 61°4W 183 f
Canarreos, Arch. de los
Cuba 21°35N 81°40W 182 B3
Canary Is. = Canarias, Is.
Atl. Oc. 28°30N 16°0W 100 F4
Canaseraga U.S.A. 42°27N 77°45W 174 D7
Canastra, Serra da
Brazil 20°0S 46°20W 189 E1
Canatlán Mexico 24°31N 104°47W 180 C4
Canaveral, C. U.S.A. 28°27N 80°32W 179 G9
Canaveral ⌂ U.S.A. 28°28N 80°34W 179 G9
Cañaveruelas Spain 40°24N 2°38W 90 E2
Canavieiras Brazil 15°39S 39°0W 189 D3
Canbelego Australia 31°32S 146°18E 153 A7
Canberra Australia 35°15S 149°8E 153 C8
Canby Calif., U.S.A. 41°27N 120°52W 168 F3
Canby Minn., U.S.A. 44°43N 96°16W 172 C5
Canby Oreg., U.S.A. 45°16N 122°42W 170 E4
Cancale France 48°40N 1°50W 70 D5
Canche → France 50°31N 1°39E 71 B8
Canchyuaya, Cordillera de
Peru 7°30S 74°0W 188 B3
Cancún Mexico 21°8N 86°44W 181 C7
Candanchú Spain 42°47N 0°32W 90 C4
Candarave Peru 17°15S 70°13W 188 D3
Çandarlı Turkey 38°56N 26°56E 99 C8
Çandarlı Körfezi Turkey 38°52N 26°55E 99 C8
Candás Spain 43°35N 5°45W 88 B5
Candé France 47°34N 1°2W 70 E5
Candela Italy 41°8N 15°31E 95 A8
Candelaria Argentina 27°29S 55°44W 191 B4
Candelaria Canary Is. 28°22N 16°22W 100 F3
Candelario ⌂ Spain 40°20N 5°46W 88 E5
Candeleda Spain 40°10N 5°14W 88 E5

Candelo *Australia* 36°47S 149°43E 153 D8
Candi Dasa *Indonesia* 8°30S 115°34E 119 J18
Candia = Iraklio *Greece* 35°20N 25°12E 101 D7
Candia, Sea of = Crete, Sea of
  Greece 36°0N 25°0E 99 E7
Candle L. *Canada* 53°50S 105°18W 163 C17
Candlemas I. *Antarctica* 57°3S 26°40W 55 B1
Cando *U.S.A.* 48°32N 99°12W 172 A4
Canela *Brazil* 10°15S 48°25W 189 C1
Canelli *Italy* 44°43N 8°17E 92 D5
Canelones *Uruguay* 34°32S 56°17W 191 C4
Canet de Mar *Spain* 41°35N 2°35E 90 D7
Canet-Plage *France* 42°41N 3°2E 72 F7
Cañete *Chile* 37°50S 73°30W 190 D1
Cañete *Spain* 40°3N 1°54W 90 E3
Cañete de las Torres
  Spain 37°53N 4°19W 89 H6
Cangas *Spain* 42°16N 8°47W 88 C2
Cangas de Onís *Spain* 43°21N 5°8W 88 B5
Cangas del Narcea *Spain* 43°10N 6°32W 88 B4
Cangnan *China* 27°30N 120°23E 117 D13
Cangshan *China* 34°50N 118°2E 115 G10
Canguaretama *Brazil* 6°20S 35°5W 189 B3
Canguçu *Brazil* 31°22S 52°43W 191 C5
Canguçu, Serra do
  Brazil 31°20S 52°40W 191 C5
Cangxi *China* 31°47N 105°59E 116 B5
Cangyuan *China* 23°12N 99°14E 116 F2
Cangzhou *China* 38°19N 116°52E 114 E9
Caniapiscau →
  Canada 56°40N 69°30W 165 A6
Caniapiscau, L. *Canada* 54°10N 69°55W 165 B6
Canicattì *Italy* 37°21N 13°51E 94 E6
Canicattini Bagni *Italy* 37°3N 15°4E 95 E8
Canigou *France* 42°31N 2°27E 72 F6
Caniles *Spain* 37°26N 2°43W 89 H8
Canim Lake *Canada* 51°47N 120°54W 162 C4
Canindé *Brazil* 4°22S 39°19W 189 A3
Canindé → *Brazil* 6°15S 42°52W 189 B2
Canindeyu □ *Paraguay* 24°10S 55°0W 191 A5
Canino *Italy* 42°28N 11°45E 93 F8
Canisteo *U.S.A.* 42°16N 77°36W 174 D7
Canisteo → *U.S.A.* 42°7N 77°8W 174 D7
Cañitas de Felipe Pescador
  Mexico 23°36N 102°43W 180 C4
Cañizal *Spain* 41°12N 5°22W 88 D5
Canjáyar *Spain* 37°1N 2°44W 89 H8
Çankırı *Turkey* 40°40N 33°37E 104 B5
Çankırı □ *Turkey* 40°40N 33°30E 104 B5
Cankuzo *Burundi* 3°10S 30°31E 142 C3
Canmore *Canada* 51°7N 115°18W 162 C5
Cann River *Australia* 37°35S 149°7E 153 D8
Canna *U.K.* 57°3N 6°33W 65 D2
Cannanore = Kannur
  India 11°53N 75°27E 127 J2
Cannanore Is. *India* 10°30N 72°30E 127 J1
Cannes *France* 43°32N 7°1E 73 E11
Canning Town = Port Canning
  India 22°23N 88°40E 125 H13
Cannington *Canada* 44°20N 79°2W 174 B5
Cannòbio *Italy* 46°4N 8°42E 92 B5
Cannock *U.K.* 52°41N 2°1W 67 E5
Cannonball →
  U.S.A. 46°26N 100°35W 172 B3
Cannondale Mt.
  Australia 25°13S 148°57E 150 D4
Cannonsville Res.
  U.S.A. 42°4N 75°22W 175 D9
Cannonvale *Australia* 20°17S 148°43E 150 b
Canoas *Brazil* 29°56S 51°11W 191 B5
Canoe L. *Canada* 55°10N 108°15W 163 B7
Cañon City *U.S.A.* 38°27N 105°14W 168 G11
Cañón de Río Blanco △
  Mexico 18°43N 97°15W 181 D5
Cañón del Río Lobos △
  Spain 41°46N 3°28W 88 D7
Canonniers Pt. *Mauritius* 20°2S 57°32E 141 d
Canoochee → *U.S.A.* 31°59N 81°19W 178 D8
Canopus *Australia* 33°29S 140°42E 152 B4
Canora *Canada* 51°40N 102°30W 163 C8
Canosa di Púglia *Italy* 41°13N 16°4E 95 A9
Canowindra *Australia* 33°35S 148°38E 153 B8
Canso *Canada* 45°20N 61°0W 165 C7
Canso, Str. of *Canada* 45°20N 61°0W 165 C7
Canta *Peru* 11°29S 76°37W 188 C2
Cantabria □ *Spain* 43°10N 4°0W 88 B7
Cantabria, Sierra de
  Spain 42°40N 2°30W 90 C2
Cantabrian Mts. = Cantábrica,
  Cordillera *Spain* 43°0N 5°10W 88 C5
Cantábrica, Cordillera
  Spain 43°0N 5°10W 88 C5
Cantal □ *France* 45°5N 2°45E 72 C6
Cantal, Plomb du *France* 45°3N 2°45E 72 C6
Cantanhede *Portugal* 40°20N 8°36E 88 E2
Cantavieja *Spain* 40°31N 0°25W 90 E4
Čantavir *Serbia* 45°55N 19°46E 80 E4
Cantemir *Moldova* 46°17N 28°14E 81 D13
Canterbury *Australia* 25°23S 141°53E 150 D3
Canterbury *U.K.* 51°16N 1°6E 67 F9
Canterbury □ *N.Z.* 43°45S 171°19E 155 E4
Canterbury Bight *N.Z.* 44°16S 171°55E 155 E6
Canterbury Plains
  N.Z. 43°55S 171°22E 155 D6
Cantil *U.S.A.* 35°18N 117°58W 171 K9
Cantillana *Spain* 37°36N 5°50W 89 H5
Canto do Buriti *Brazil* 8°7S 42°58W 189 B2
Canton = Guangzhou
  China 23°6N 113°13E 117 F9
Canton Ga., *U.S.A.* 34°14N 84°29W 177 D12
Canton Ill., *U.S.A.* 40°33N 90°2W 172 E8
Canton Miss., *U.S.A.* 32°37N 90°2W 177 E9
Canton Mo., *U.S.A.* 40°8N 91°32W 172 E8
Canton N.Y., *U.S.A.* 44°36N 75°10W 175 B9
Canton Ohio, *U.S.A.* 40°48N 81°23W 174 F3
Canton S. Dak., *U.S.A.* 43°18N 96°35W 172 D5
Canton L. *U.S.A.* 36°6N 98°35W 176 C5
Cantonment *U.S.A.* 30°37N 87°20W 179 E2
Cantù *Italy* 45°44N 9°8E 92 C6
Canudos *Brazil* 7°13S 58°5W 186 E7
Canumã → *Brazil* 3°55S 59°10W 186 D7
Canunda △ *Australia* 37°42S 140°16E 152 B4
Canutama *Brazil* 6°30S 64°20W 186 E6
Canutillo *U.S.A.* 31°55N 106°36W 176 F1
Canvey *U.K.* 51°31N 0°37E 67 F8
Canyon *U.S.A.* 34°59N 101°55W 176 D4
Canyon De Chelly △
  U.S.A. 36°10N 109°20W 169 H9
Canyonlands △ *U.S.A.* 38°15N 110°0W 169 G9

Canyons of the Ancients △
  U.S.A. 37°30N 108°55W 169 H9
Canyonville *U.S.A.* 42°56N 123°17W 168 E2
Cao Bang *Vietnam* 22°40N 106°15E 116 F6
Cao He → *China* 40°10N 124°32E 115 D13
Cao Lanh *Vietnam* 10°27N 105°38E 121 G5
Cao Xian *China* 34°50N 115°35E 114 G8
Caofeidian *China* 38°56N 118°32E 115 E10
Cáorle *Italy* 45°36N 12°53E 93 C9
Cap-aux-Meules
  Canada 47°23N 61°52W 165 C7
Cap-Chat *Canada* 49°6N 66°40W 165 C6
Cap-de-la-Madeleine
  Canada 46°22N 72°31W 164 C5
Cap-Haïtien *Haiti* 19°40N 72°20W 183 C5
Cap Pt. *St. Lucia* 14°7N 60°57W 183 f
Capac *U.S.A.* 43°1N 82°56W 174 D2
Capáccio *Italy* 40°25N 15°5E 95 B8
Capaci *Italy* 38°10N 13°14E 94 D6
Capanaparo → *Venezuela* 7°1N 67°7W 186 B5
Capánnori *Italy* 43°50N 10°34E 92 E7
Caparaó △ *Brazil* 20°25S 41°46W 189 E2
Capbreton *France* 43°39N 1°26W 72 E2
Capdenac *France* 44°34N 2°5E 72 D6
Capdepera *Spain* 39°42N 3°26E 90 F8
Cape → *Australia* 20°59S 146°51E 150 C4
Cape Arid △ *Australia* 33°58S 123°13E 149 F3
Cape Barren I.
  Australia 40°25S 148°15E 151 G4
Cape Basin *Atl. Oc.* 34°0S 7°0W 56 K12
Cape Breton Highlands △
  Canada 46°50N 60°40W 165 C7
Cape Breton I. *Canada* 46°0N 60°30W 165 C7
Cape Canaveral *U.S.A.* 28°24N 80°36W 179 G9
Cape Charles *U.S.A.* 37°16N 76°1W 174 G8
Cape Coast *Ghana* 5°5N 1°15W 139 D4
Cape Cod △ *U.S.A.* 41°56N 70°6W 173 E18
Cape Coral *U.S.A.* 26°33N 81°57W 179 J8
Cape Crawford
  Australia 16°41S 135°43E 150 B2
Cape Dorset = Kinngait
  Canada 64°14N 76°32W 161 E16
Cape Fear → *U.S.A.* 33°53N 78°1W 177 E15
Cape Girardeau *U.S.A.* 37°19N 89°32W 172 G9
Cape Hatteras △
  U.S.A. 35°30N 75°28W 177 D17
Cape Hillsborough △
  Australia 20°54S 149°2E 150 b
Cape Jervis *Australia* 35°40S 138°5E 152 C3
Cape Le Grand △
  Australia 33°54S 122°26E 149 F3
Cape Lookout △
  U.S.A. 34°35N 76°25W 177 D16
Cape May *U.S.A.* 38°56N 74°56W 173 F16
Cape May Point
  U.S.A. 38°56N 74°58W 173 F16
Cape Melville △
  Australia 14°26S 144°28E 150 A3
Cape Mount △ *Liberia* 6°44N 11°24W 138 D2
Cape Range △ *Australia* 22°3S 114°0E 148 D1
Cape St. George
  Canada 48°28N 59°14W 165 C8
Cape Tormentine
  Canada 46°8N 63°47W 165 C7
Cape Town *S. Africa* 33°55S 18°22E 144 D2
Cape Upstart △
  Australia 19°45S 147°48E 150 B4
Cape Verde Abyssal Plain
  Atl. Oc. 23°0N 26°0W 56 D9
Cape Verde Is. ■ *Atl. Oc.* 16°0N 24°0W 134 b
Cape Verde Plateau
  Atl. Oc. 18°0N 20°0W 56 E10
Cape Vincent *U.S.A.* 44°8N 76°20W 175 B8
Cape York Peninsula
  Australia 12°0S 142°30E 150 A3
Capela *Brazil* 10°30S 37°0W 189 C3
Capelinha *Brazil* 17°42S 42°31W 189 E2
Capella *Australia* 23°2S 148°1E 150 C4
Capendu *France* 43°11N 2°31E 72 E6
Capertree *Australia* 33°6S 149°58E 153 C8
Capestang *France* 43°20N 3°2E 72 E7
Capesterre-Belle-Eau
  Guadeloupe 16°4N 61°36W 182 b
Capesterre-de-Marie-Galante
  Guadeloupe 15°53N 61°14W 182 b
Capim → *Brazil* 1°40S 47°47W 189 D2
Capistrello *Italy* 41°57N 13°23E 93 G10
Capitan *U.S.A.* 33°35N 105°35W 169 K11
Capitán Aracena, I.
  Chile 54°0S 71°20W 192 D2
Capitán Arturo Prat
  Antarctica 63°0S 61°0W 55 C17
Capitán Pastene *Chile* 38°13S 73°1W 192 A2
Capitão de Campos
  Brazil 4°26S 41°33W 189 B2
Capitol Reef △ *U.S.A.* 38°15N 111°10W 169 G8
Capítola *U.S.A.* 36°59N 121°57W 170 J5
Capivara, Serra da
  Brazil 14°35S 45°0W 189 C2
Capizzi *Italy* 37°51N 14°29E 95 E7
Capoche → *Mozam.* 15°35S 33°0E 143 F3
Capodichino, Nápoli ✈ (NAP)
  Italy 40°51N 14°16E 95 B7
Capodistria = Koper
  Slovenia 45°31N 13°44E 93 C10
Caporetto = Kobarid
  Slovenia 46°15N 13°30E 93 B10
Capoterra *Italy* 39°11N 8°58E 94 C1
Cappadocia *Turkey* 39°0N 35°0E 104 C6
Capps *U.S.A.* 30°24N 83°54W 178 E6
Capraia *Italy* 43°2N 9°50E 92 E6
Caprara, Pta. *Italy* 41°7N 8°19E 94 A1
Caprarola *Italy* 42°19N 12°14E 93 F9
Caprera *Italy* 41°12N 9°28E 94 A2
Capri *Italy* 40°33N 14°14E 95 B7
Capricorn Coast
  Australia 23°16S 150°49E 150 C5
Capricorn Group
  Australia 23°30S 151°55E 150 C5
Capricorn Ra.
  Australia 23°20S 116°50E 148 D2
Caprino Veronese *Italy* 45°36N 10°47E 92 C7
Caprivi □ *Namibia* 18°0S 23°0E 144 A3
Caprivi Strip *Namibia* 18°0S 23°0E 144 A3
Caps et Marais d'Opale □
  France 50°40N 2°0E 71 B9
Captains Flat *Australia* 35°35S 149°27E 153 C8
Captieux *France* 44°18N 0°16W 72 D3
Captiva *U.S.A.* 26°31N 82°11W 179 J7

Capulin Volcano △
  U.S.A. 36°47N 103°58W 176 C3
Caquetá → *Colombia* 1°15S 69°15W 186 D5
Car Nicobar *India* 9°10N 92°47E 127 K11
Caracal *Romania* 44°8N 24°22E 81 F9
Caracas *Venezuela* 10°30N 66°55W 186 A5
Caracol *Belize* 16°45N 89°6W 182 C2
Caracol *Mato Grosso do Sul,*
  Brazil 22°18S 57°1W 190 A4
Caracol *Piauí, Brazil* 9°15S 43°22W 189 B2
Caracollo *Bolivia* 17°39S 67°10W 188 G5
Caragabal *Australia* 33°49S 147°45E 153 B8
Carágüli *Italy* 44°25N 7°26E 92 D4
Carahue *Chile* 38°43S 73°12W 192 A2
Caraí *Brazil* 17°12S 41°42W 189 D2
Carajás *Brazil* 6°5S 50°23W 187 E8
Carajás, Serra dos *Brazil* 6°0S 51°30W 187 E8
Caral *Peru* 10°53S 77°31W 188 C2
Carangola *Brazil* 20°44S 42°5W 189 E2
Caransebeş *Romania* 45°28N 22°18E 80 E7
Carantec *France* 48°40N 3°55W 70 D3
Caraquet *Canada* 47°48N 64°57W 165 C6
Caraş Severin □
  Romania 45°10N 22°10E 80 E7
Caraşova *Romania* 45°11N 21°51E 80 E6
Caratasca, L. de
  Honduras 15°20N 83°40W 182 C3
Caratinga *Brazil* 19°50S 42°10W 189 E2
Caraúbas *Brazil* 5°43S 37°33W 189 B3
Caravaca de la Cruz *Spain* 38°8N 1°52W 91 G3
Caravággio *Italy* 45°30N 9°38E 92 C6
Caravela *Guinea-Biss.* 11°30N 16°30W 138 C1
Caravelas *Brazil* 17°45S 39°15W 189 D3
Caraveli *Peru* 15°45S 73°25W 188 C3
Caravelle, Presqu'île de la
  Martinique 14°46N 60°48W 182 c
Caraz *Peru* 9°3S 77°47W 188 B2
Carazinho *Brazil* 28°16S 52°46W 191 B5
Carballino = O Carballiño
  Spain 42°26N 8°5W 88 C2
Carballo *Spain* 43°13N 8°41W 88 B2
Carberry *Canada* 49°50N 99°25W 163 D9
Carbó *Mexico* 29°42N 110°58W 180 B2
Carbón, L. del
  Argentina 49°35S 68°21W 192 C3
Carbonara, C. *Italy* 39°6N 9°31E 94 C2
Carbondale *Colo.,*
  U.S.A. 39°24N 107°13W 168 G10
Carbondale *Ill., U.S.A.* 37°44N 89°13W 172 G9
Carbondale *Pa., U.S.A.* 41°35N 75°30W 175 D9
Carbonear *Canada* 47°42N 53°13W 165 C9
Carboneras *Spain* 36°59N 1°53W 91 J3
Carboneras de Guadazón
  Spain 39°54N 1°50W 90 F3
Carbónia *Italy* 39°10N 8°30E 94 C1
Carbonne *France* 43°18N 1°11E 72 E5
Carcabuey *Spain* 37°27N 4°17W 89 H6
Carcagente = Carcaixent
  Spain 39°8N 0°28W 91 F4
Carcaixent *Spain* 39°8N 0°28W 91 F4
Carcajou *Canada* 57°47N 117°6W 162 B5
Carcarana →
  Argentina 32°27S 60°48W 190 C3
Carcasse, C. *Haiti* 18°30N 74°28W 183 C5
Carcassonne *France* 43°13N 2°20E 72 E6
Carcoar *Australia* 33°36S 149°8E 153 B8
Carcross *Canada* 60°13N 134°45W 162 A2
Çardak *Çanakkale,*
  Turkey 40°26N 26°43E 97 F10
Çardak *Denizli, Turkey* 37°49N 29°39E 99 D11
Cardamom Hills *India* 9°30N 77°15E 127 K3
Cardamon Mts. = Kravanh,
  Chuor Phnum
  Cambodia 12°0N 103°32E 121 G4
Cardeña *Spain* 38°16N 4°20W 89 G6
Cárdenas *Cuba* 23°0N 81°30W 182 B3
Cárdenas *San Luis Potosí,*
  Mexico 22°0N 99°38W 181 C5
Cárdenas *Tabasco,*
  Mexico 17°59N 93°22W 181 D6
Cardener → *Spain* 41°41N 1°51E 90 D6
Cardenete *Spain* 39°46N 1°41W 90 F3
Cardiel, L. *Argentina* 48°55S 71°10W 192 C2
Cardiff *U.K.* 51°29N 3°10W 67 F4
Cardiff *U.K.* 51°31N 3°12W 67 F4
Cardiff-by-the-Sea
  U.S.A. 33°1N 117°17W 171 M9
Cardigan *U.K.* 52°5N 4°40W 67 E3
Cardigan B. *U.K.* 52°30N 4°30W 67 E3
Cardinal *Canada* 44°47N 75°23W 175 B9
Cardona *Spain* 41°56N 1°40E 90 D6
Cardona *Uruguay* 33°53S 57°18W 190 C4
Cardoso, Ilha do *Brazil* 25°8S 47°58W 191 A6
Cardston *Canada* 49°15N 113°20W 162 D6
Cardwell *Australia* 18°14S 146°2E 150 B4
Careen L. *Canada* 57°0N 108°11W 163 B7
Carei *Romania* 47°40N 22°29E 80 C7
Careiro *Brazil* 3°19N 1°15W 70 C5
Carey, L. *Australia* 29°0S 122°15E 149 E3
Carey, L. *Canada* 62°12N 102°55W 163 A8
Careysburg *Liberia* 6°34N 10°30W 138 D2
Cargados Carajos *Ind. Oc.* 17°0S 59°0E 146 F4
Cargèse *France* 42°7N 8°35E 73 F12
Carhaix-Plouguer
  France 48°18N 3°36W 70 D3
Carhuamayo *Peru* 10°51S 76°4W 188 C2
Carhuas *Peru* 9°15S 77°39W 188 B2
Carhué *Argentina* 37°10S 62°50W 190 D3
Caria *Turkey* 37°20N 28°10E 99 D10
Cariacica *Brazil* 20°16S 40°25W 189 E2
Cariati *Italy* 39°30N 16°57E 95 C9
Caribbean Sea *W. Indies* 15°0N 75°0W 183 D5
Cariboo Mts. *Canada* 53°0N 121°0W 162 C4
Caribou → *Man.,*
  Canada 59°20N 94°44W 163 B10
Caribou → *N.W.T.,*
  Canada 61°27N 125°45W 162 A3
Caribou I. *Canada* 47°22N 85°49W 164 C2
Caribou Is. *Canada* 61°55N 113°15W 162 A6
Caribou L. *Man.,*
  Canada 59°21N 96°10W 163 B9
Caribou L. *Ont., Canada* 50°25N 89°5W 164 B2
Caribou Mts. *Canada* 59°12N 115°40W 162 B5
Caribou River △
  Canada 59°35N 95°50W 163 B9
Caríbou = Dimitrovgrad
  Serbia 43°22N 22°48E 96 C6
Carichíc *Mexico* 27°56N 107°3W 180 B3
Carignan *France* 49°38N 5°10E 71 C12

Carignano *Italy* 44°55N 7°40E 92 D4
Carinda *Australia* 30°28S 147°41E 153 A7
Cariñena *Spain* 41°20N 1°13W 90 D3
Carinhanha *Brazil* 14°15S 44°46W 189 C2
Carinhanha → *Brazil* 14°20S 43°47W 189 C2
Carini *Italy* 38°8N 13°11E 94 D6
Cariño *Spain* 43°45N 7°52W 88 B3
Carínola *Italy* 41°11N 13°58E 94 A6
Carinthia = Kärnten □
  Austria 46°52N 13°30E 78 E6
Caripito *Venezuela* 10°8N 63°6W 186 A6
Cariré *Brazil* 3°57S 40°27W 189 A2
Carlet *Spain* 39°14N 0°31W 91 F4
Carleton, Mt. *Canada* 47°23N 66°53W 165 C6
Carleton Place *Canada* 45°8N 76°9W 175 A8
Carletonville *S. Africa* 26°23S 27°22E 144 D4
Carlin *U.S.A.* 40°43N 116°7W 168 F5
Carlingford L. *U.K.* 54°3N 6°9W 64 B5
Carlinville *U.S.A.* 39°17N 89°53W 172 F9
Carlisle *U.K.* 54°54N 2°56W 66 C5
Carlisle *U.S.A.* 40°12N 77°12W 174 F7
Carlisle B. *Barbados* 13°5N 59°37W 183 g
Carlisle I. *Australia* 20°49S 149°18E 150 b
Carlit, Pic *France* 42°35N 1°55E 72 F5
Carloforte *Italy* 39°8N 8°18E 94 C1
Carlos Casares
  Argentina 35°32S 61°20W 190 D3
Carlos Chagas *Brazil* 17°43S 40°45W 189 D2
Carlos Tejedor
  Argentina 35°25S 62°25W 190 D3
Carlow *Ireland* 52°50N 6°56W 65 D5
Carlow □ *Ireland* 52°43N 6°50W 65 D5
Carlsbad *Calif., U.S.A.* 33°10N 117°21W 171 M9
Carlsbad *N. Mex.,*
  U.S.A. 32°25N 104°14W 169 K11
Carlsbad Caverns △
  U.S.A. 32°10N 104°35W 169 K11
Carlsberg Ridge *Ind. Oc.* 10°N 66°0E 146 D5
Carluke *U.K.* 55°45N 3°50W 65 F5
Carlyle *Canada* 49°40N 102°20W 163 D8
Carmacks *Canada* 62°5N 136°16W 160 E4
Carmagnola *Italy* 44°51N 7°43E 92 D4
Carman *Canada* 49°30N 98°0W 163 D9
Carmarthen *U.K.* 51°52N 4°19W 67 F3
Carmarthen B. *U.K.* 51°40N 4°30W 67 F3
Carmarthenshire □ *U.K.* 51°55N 4°13W 67 F3
Carmaux *France* 44°3N 2°10E 72 D6
Carmel *U.S.A.* 41°26N 73°41W 175 E11
Carmel, Mt. = Ha Karmel, Har
  Israel 32°46N 35°3E 130 C4
Carmel-by-the-Sea
  U.S.A. 36°33N 121°55W 170 J5
Carmel Valley *U.S.A.* 36°29N 121°43W 170 J5
Carmelo *Uruguay* 34°0S 58°20W 190 C4
Carmen *Bolivia* 11°40S 67°51W 188 C4
Carmen *Paraguay* 27°13S 56°12W 191 B4
Carmen, I. *Mexico* 25°57N 111°12W 180 B2
Carmen de Patagones
  Argentina 40°50S 63°0W 192 B4
Cármenes *Spain* 42°58N 5°34W 88 C5
Carmensa *Argentina* 35°15S 67°40W 190 D2
Carmi *Australia* 21°55S 149°24E 150 C4
Carmi *U.S.A.* 38°5N 88°10W 172 F9
Carmila *Australia* 21°55S 149°24E 150 C4
Carmona *Costa Rica* 10°0N 85°15W 182 E2
Carmona *Spain* 37°28N 5°42W 89 H5
Carn Ban *U.K.* 57°7N 4°15W 65 D4
Carn Eige *U.K.* 57°17N 5°8W 65 D3
Carnac *France* 47°35N 3°6W 70 E3
Carnamah *Australia* 29°41S 115°53E 149 E2
Carnarvon *Australia* 24°51S 113°42E 149 D1
Carnarvon *Canada* 45°3N 78°41W 174 A6
Carnarvon *S. Africa* 30°56S 22°8E 144 D3
Carnarvon △ *Australia* 24°54S 148°2E 150 D4
Carnarvon Ra. *Queens.,*
  Australia 25°15S 148°30E 150 D4
Carnarvon Ra. *W. Austral.,*
  Australia 25°20S 120°45E 149 E3
Carnatic *India* 9°40N 77°50E 127 K3
Carndonagh *Ireland* 55°16N 7°15W 64 A4
Carnduff *Canada* 49°10N 101°50W 163 D8
Carnegie *U.S.A.* 40°24N 80°5W 174 F4
Carnegie, L. *Australia* 26°5S 122°30E 149 E3
Carnegie Ridge *Pac. Oc.* 1°0S 85°0W 157 H19
Carney I. *Antarctica* 73°57S 121°0W 55 D14
Carnic Alps = Karnische Alpen
  Europe 46°36N 13°0E 78 E6
Carniche Alpi = Karnische Alpen
  Europe 46°36N 13°0E 78 E6
Carnot *C.A.R.* 4°59N 15°56E 140 D3
Carnot, C. *Australia* 34°57S 135°38E 151 E2
Carnot B. *Australia* 17°20S 121°30E 148 C3
Carnoustie *U.K.* 56°30N 2°42W 65 E6
Carnsore Pt. *Ireland* 52°10N 6°22W 65 D5
Caro *U.S.A.* 43°29N 83°24W 173 D12
Caroga Lake *U.S.A.* 43°8N 74°28W 175 C10
Carol City *U.S.A.* 25°56N 80°14W 177 J14
Carolina *Brazil* 7°10S 47°30W 189 B2
Carolina *Puerto Rico* 18°23N 65°58W 183 d
Carolina *S. Africa* 26°5S 30°6E 145 D5
Caroline I. *Kiribati* 9°58S 150°13W 157 H12
Caroline Is. *Micronesia* 8°0N 150°0E 156 G6
Caroline Pk. *N.Z.* 45°57S 167°15E 155 E1
Carolina, Pte. des
  Réunion 21°9S 55°51E 141 c
Caroni *Trin. & Tob.* 10°34N 61°23W 187 K15
Caroni → *Venezuela* 8°21N 62°43W 186 B6
Caronie = Nébrodi, Monti
  Italy 37°54N 14°35E 95 E7
Caroona *Australia* 31°24S 150°26E 153 A9
Carpathians *Europe* 49°30N 21°0E 75 D11
Carpaţii Meridionali
  Romania 45°30N 25°0E 81 E9
Carpentaria, G. of
  Australia 14°0S 139°0E 150 A2
Carpentras *France* 44°3N 5°2E 73 D9
Carpi *Italy* 44°47N 10°53E 92 D7
Carpina *Brazil* 7°51S 35°15W 189 B3
Cărpineni *Moldova* 46°46N 28°22E 81 D13
Carpinteria *U.S.A.* 34°24N 119°31W 171 L7
Carpio *Spain* 41°13N 5°7W 88 D5
Carr Boyd Ra.
  Australia 16°15S 128°35E 148 C4
Carra, L. *Ireland* 53°41N 9°14W 64 C1
Carrabelle *U.S.A.* 29°51N 84°40W 178 F5
Carraig Mhachaire Rois =
  Carrickmacross
  Ireland 53°59N 6°43W 64 C5
Carraig na Siúire = Carrick-on-
  Suir *Ireland* 52°21N 7°24W 64 D4

Carral *Spain* 43°14N 8°21W 88 B2
Carranya ◇ *Australia* 19°13S 127°46E 148 C4
Carrara *Italy* 44°5N 10°6E 92 D7
Carrascosa del Campo
  Spain 40°2N 2°45W 90 E2
Carrauntoohill *Ireland* 52°0N 9°45W 64 D2
Carretas, Punta *Peru* 14°12S 76°17W 188 C2
Carriacou *St. Barbados* 12°30N 61°30W 183 k
Carrick-on-Shannon
  Ireland 53°57N 8°7W 64 C3
Carrick-on-Suir *Ireland* 52°21N 7°24W 64 D4
Carrickfergus *U.K.* 54°43N 5°49W 64 B6
Carrickmacross *Ireland* 53°59N 6°43W 64 C5
Carrieton *Australia* 32°25S 138°31E 152 B3
Carrigaline *Ireland* 51°48N 8°23W 64 E3
Carrillo *Mexico* 26°54N 103°55W 180 B4
Carrington *U.S.A.* 47°27N 99°8W 172 B4
Carrión → *Spain* 41°53N 4°32W 88 D6
Carrión de los Condes
  Spain 42°20N 4°37W 88 C6
Carrizal Bajo *Chile* 28°5S 71°20W 190 B1
Carrizalillo *Chile* 29°5S 71°30W 190 B1
Carrizo Cr. →
  U.S.A. 36°55N 103°55W 169 H12
Carrizo Plain △
  U.S.A. 35°11N 119°47W 170 K7
Carrizo Springs *U.S.A.* 28°31N 99°52W 176 G5
Carrizozo *U.S.A.* 33°38N 105°53W 169 K11
Carroll *U.S.A.* 42°4N 94°52W 172 D7
Carrollton *Ga., U.S.A.* 33°35N 85°5W 178 D4
Carrollton *Ill., U.S.A.* 39°18N 90°24W 172 F8
Carrollton *Ky., U.S.A.* 38°41N 85°11W 173 F11
Carrollton *Mo., U.S.A.* 39°22N 93°30W 172 F7
Carrollton *Ohio, U.S.A.* 40°34N 81°5W 174 F3
Carron → *U.K.* 57°53N 4°22W 65 D4
Carron, L. *U.K.* 57°22N 5°35W 65 D3
Carrot → *Canada* 53°50N 101°17W 163 C8
Carrot River *Canada* 53°17N 103°35W 163 C8
Carrouges *France* 48°34N 0°10W 70 D6
Carrù *Italy* 44°29N 7°52E 92 D4
Carruthers *Canada* 52°52N 109°16W 163 C7
Çarşamba *Turkey* 41°11N 36°44E 104 B7
Çarşöli *Italy* 42°6N 13°5E 93 F10
Carson *Calif., U.S.A.* 33°49N 118°16W 171 M8
Carson *N. Dak., U.S.A.* 46°25N 101°34W 172 B3
Carson → *U.S.A.* 39°45N 118°40W 170 F8
Carson City *U.S.A.* 39°10N 119°46W 170 F7
Carson Sink *U.S.A.* 39°50N 118°25W 168 G4
Cartagena *Colombia* 10°25N 75°33W 186 A3
Cartagena *Spain* 37°38N 0°59W 91 H4
Cartago *Colombia* 4°45N 75°55W 186 C3
Cartago *Costa Rica* 9°50N 83°55W 182 E3
Cártama *Spain* 36°43N 4°39W 89 J6
Cartaxo *Portugal* 39°10N 8°47W 89 F2
Cartaya *Spain* 37°16N 7°9W 89 H3
Cartersville *U.S.A.* 34°10N 84°48W 178 C3
Carterton *N.Z.* 41°2S 175°31E 154 F4
Carthage *Tunisia* 36°52N 10°20E 94 F3
Carthage *Ill., U.S.A.* 40°25N 91°8W 172 E8
Carthage *Mo., U.S.A.* 37°11N 94°19W 172 G6
Carthage *N.Y., U.S.A.* 43°59N 75°37W 175 C9
Carthage *Tex., U.S.A.* 32°9N 94°20W 176 E7
Cartier I. *Australia* 12°31S 123°29E 148 B3
Cartwright *Canada* 53°41N 56°58W 165 B8
Caruaru *Brazil* 8°15S 35°55W 189 B3
Carúpano *Venezuela* 10°39N 63°15W 186 A6
Caruthersville *U.S.A.* 36°11N 89°39W 172 G9
Carvin *France* 50°30N 2°57E 71 B9
Carvoeiro *Brazil* 1°30S 61°59W 186 D6
Carvoeiro, C. *Portugal* 39°21N 9°24W 89 F1
Cary *U.S.A.* 35°47N 78°46W 177 D15
Cas-gwent = Chepstow
  U.K. 51°38N 2°41W 67 F5
Casa, Pas de la = Envalira, Port d'
  Europe 42°32N 1°40E 90 C6
Casa Branca *Portugal* 38°29N 8°12W 89 G2
Casa de Piedra
  Argentina 38°5S 67°28W 190 D2
Casa de Piedra, Embalse
  Argentina 38°5S 67°32W 190 D2
Casa Grande *U.S.A.* 32°53N 111°45W 169 K8
Casa Nova *Brazil* 9°25S 41°5W 189 B2
Casablanca *Chile* 33°20S 71°25W 190 C1
Casablanca *Morocco* 33°36N 7°36W 136 B4
Casablanca □ *Morocco* 33°38N 7°30W 136 B4
Casacalenda *Italy* 41°44N 14°51E 93 G11
Casale Monferrato *Italy* 45°8N 8°27E 92 C5
Casalmaggiore *Italy* 44°59N 10°26E 92 D7
Casalpusterlengo *Italy* 45°11N 9°39E 92 C6
Casamance → *Senegal* 12°33N 16°46W 138 C1
Casarano *Italy* 40°0N 18°10E 95 B11
Casares *Spain* 36°27N 5°16W 89 J5
Casas Ibáñez *Spain* 39°17N 1°30W 91 F3
Casasimanro *Spain* 39°22N 2°3W 91 F2
Casatejada *Spain* 39°54N 5°40W 88 F5
Casaviejo *Spain* 40°17N 4°46W 88 E6
Cascada de Basaseachic △
  Mexico 28°9N 108°15W 180 B3
Cascade *Seychelles* 4°39S 55°29E 141 b
Cascade *Idaho, U.S.A.* 44°31N 116°2W 168 D5
Cascade *Mont., U.S.A.* 47°16N 111°42W 168 C8
Cascade Locks *U.S.A.* 45°40N 121°54W 170 E5
Cascade Pt. *N.Z.* 44°1S 168°20E 155 E2
Cascade Ra. *U.S.A.* 47°0N 121°30W 170 D5
Cascade Res. *U.S.A.* 44°32N 116°3W 168 D5
Cascades, Pte. des
  Réunion 21°9S 55°51E 141 c
Cascais *Portugal* 38°41N 9°25W 89 G1
Cascavel *Ceará, Brazil* 4°7S 38°14W 189 A3
Cascavel *Paraná, Brazil* 24°57S 53°28W 191 A5
Cáscina *Italy* 43°41N 10°33E 92 E7
Casco B. *U.S.A.* 43°45N 70°0W 173 D18
Caselle Torinese *Italy* 45°10N 7°39E 92 C4
Caserta *Italy* 41°4N 14°20E 95 A7
Casey *Antarctica* 66°0S 76°0E 55 C8
Caseyr, Raas = Asir, Ras
  Somalia 11°55N 51°10E 131 E5
Cashel *Ireland* 52°30N 7°53W 64 D4
Casiguran *Phil.* 16°22N 122°7E 119 A6
Casilda *Argentina* 33°10S 61°10W 190 C3
Casimcea *Romania* 44°45N 28°23E 81 F13
Casino *Australia* 28°52S 153°3E 153 A9
Casiquiare → *Venezuela* 2°1N 67°7W 186 C5
Casitas *Brazil* 10°5S 80°39W 188 A1
Čáslav *Czech Rep.* 49°54N 15°22E 78 D8
Casma *Peru* 9°30S 78°20W 188 B2
Casmalia *U.S.A.* 34°50N 120°32W 171 L6
Casola Valsénio *Italy* 44°12N 11°40E 93 D8
Cásoli *Italy* 42°7N 14°18E 93 F11

Caspe *Spain* 41°14N 0°1W
Caspe *Spain* 42°51N 106°19W 1
Caspian Depression
  Eurasia 47°0N 48°0E
Caspian Sea *Eurasia* 43°0N 50°0E
Cass City *U.S.A.* 43°36N 83°10W
Cass Lake *U.S.A.* 47°23N 94°3
Cassà de la Selva *Spain* 41°53N 2°52E
Cassadaga *U.S.A.* 42°20N 79°19W
Cassano allo Iónio *Italy* 39°47N 16°20E
Casselberry *U.S.A.* 28°41N 81°20W
Casselman *Canada* 45°19N 75°5W
Casselton *U.S.A.* 46°54N 97°13W
Cassiar Mts. *Canada* 59°30N 130°30W
Cassino *Italy* 41°30N 13°49E
Cassis *France* 43°14N 5°32E
Cassville *U.S.A.* 36°41N 93°52W
Castagneto Carducci
  Italy 43°9N 10°36E
Castaic *U.S.A.* 34°30N 118°38W
Castalia *U.S.A.* 41°24N 82°49W
Castanhal *Brazil* 1°18S 47°55W
Castara *Trin. & Tob.* 11°17N 60°42W 1
Castéggio *Italy* 45°0N 9°7E
Castejón de Monegros
  Spain 41°37N 0°15W
Castèl del Monte *Italy* 41°5N 16°16E
Castèl San Giovanni *Italy* 41°47N 14°6E
Castèl San Giovanni *Italy* 45°4N 9°26E
Castèl San Pietro Terme
  Italy 44°24N 11°35E
Castelbuono *Italy* 37°56N 14°5E
Castelfidardo *Italy* 43°28N 13°33E
Castelfiorentino *Italy* 43°36N 10°58E
Castelfranco Véneto
  Italy 45°40N 11°55E
Casteljaloux *France* 44°19N 0°6E
Castell-Nedd = Neath
  U.K. 51°39N 3°48W
Castellabate *Italy* 40°17N 14°57E
Castellammare, G. di
  Italy 38°8N 12°54E
Castellammare del Golfo
  Italy 38°1N 12°53E
Castellammare di Stábia
  Italy 40°42N 14°29E
Castellamonte *Italy* 45°23N 7°42E
Castellane *France* 43°50N 6°31E
Castellana *Italy* 40°53N 17°10E
Castelli *Argentina* 36°7S 57°47W
Castellón de la Plana □
  Spain 39°58N 0°3W
Castellote *Spain* 40°48N 0°15W
Castellóuro *Italy* 41°50N 14°43E
Castelnau-de-Médoc
  France 45°2N 0°48W
Castelnau-Magnoac
  France 43°17N 0°31E
Castelnaudary *France* 43°20N 1°58E
Castelnovo ne' Monti
  Italy 44°26N 10°24E
Castelnuovo di Val di Cécina
  Italy 43°12N 10°59E
Castelo *Brazil* 20°33S 41°14W
Castelo Branco *Portugal* 39°50N 7°31W
Castelo Branco □
  Portugal 39°52N 7°45W
Castelo de Paiva *Portugal* 41°2N 8°16W
Castelo de Vide *Portugal* 39°25N 7°27W
Castelo do Piauí *Brazil* 5°20S 41°33W
Castelsardo *Italy* 40°55N 8°43E
Castelsarrasin *France* 44°2N 1°7E
Casteltérmini *Italy* 37°32N 13°39E
Castelvetrano *Italy* 37°41N 12°47E
Casterton *Australia* 37°30S 141°30E
Castets *France* 43°52N 1°9W
Castiglion Fiorentino
  Italy 43°20N 11°55E
Castiglione del Lago *Italy* 43°7N 12°3E
Castiglione della Pescáia
  Italy 42°46N 10°53E
Castiglione delle Stiviere
  Italy 45°23N 10°29E
Castilblanco *Spain* 39°17N 5°5W
Castile *U.S.A.* 42°38N 78°3W 1
Castilla *Peru* 5°12S 80°38W 1
Castilla, Playa de *Spain* 37°0N 6°33W
Castilla-La Mancha □
  Spain 39°30N 3°30W
Castilla y Leon □ *Spain* 42°0N 5°0W
Castillo de Locubín *Spain* 37°32N 3°56W
Castillo de San Marcos □
  U.S.A. 29°54N 81°19W
Castillon-en-Couserans
  France 42°56N 1°1E
Castillonès *France* 44°39N 0°37E
Castillos *Uruguay* 34°12S 53°52W 1
Castle Dale *U.S.A.* 39°13N 111°1W
Castle Douglas *U.K.* 54°56N 3°56W
Castle Rock *Colo.,*
  U.S.A. 39°22N 104°51W 1
Castle Rock *Wash.,*
  U.S.A. 46°17N 122°54W
Castlebar *Ireland* 53°52N 9°18W
Castlebay *U.K.* 56°57N 7°31W
Castleblayney *Ireland* 54°7N 6°44W
Castlecliff *N.Z.* 39°57S 175°5E
Castlecomer *Ireland* 52°48N 7°14W
Castlederg *U.K.* 54°43N 7°35W
Castleford *U.K.* 53°43N 1°21W
Castlegar *Canada* 49°20N 117°40W
Castlemaine *Australia* 37°2S 144°12E
Castlemaine *Ireland* 52°10N 9°42W
Castlepoint *N.Z.* 40°54S 176°15E
Castlepollard *Ireland* 53°41N 7°19W
Castlerea *Ireland* 53°46N 8°29W
Castlereagh →
  Australia 30°12S 147°32E
Castlereagh B.
  Australia 12°10S 135°10E
Castleton *U.S.A.* 43°37N 73°11W 1
Castleton-on-Hudson
  U.S.A. 42°31N 73°45W 1
Castletown I. of Man *U.K.* 54°5N 4°38W
Castletown Bearhaven
  Ireland 51°39N 9°55W
Castor *Canada* 52°15N 111°50W

r → Canada 53°24N 78°58W 164 B4
rland U.S.A. 43°53N 75°31W 175 C9
es France 43°37N 2°13E 72 E6
cum Neths. 52°33N 4°40E 69 B4
es St. Lucia 14°2N 60°58W 183 f
il Spain 37°48N 2°46W 89 H8
o Brazil 24°45S 50°0W 191 A6
o Chile 42°30S 73°50W 192 B2
o Alves Brazil 12°46S 39°33W 189 C3
o del Río Spain 37°41N 4°29W 89 H6
o-Urdiales Spain 43°23N 3°11W 88 B7
o Valley U.S.A. 37°41N 122°5W 170 H4
o Verde Portugal 37°1N 8°4W 89 H2
ojeriz Spain 42°17N 4°9W 88 C6
opol Spain 43°32N 7°0W 88 B4
oreale Italy 38°6N 15°12E 95 D8
ovillari Italy 39°49N 16°12E 95 C9
oville U.S.A. 36°46N 121°45W 170 J5
ovirreyna Peru 13°20S 75°18W 188 C2
era Spain 38°43N 5°37W 89 G5
ell Sound N.Z. 44°59S 167°8E 155 E2
urkey 39°40N 41°3E 105 C9
a, Dao Vietnam 20°50N 107°0E 120 B6
a △ Vietnam 20°47N 107°3E 120 B6
Bahamas 24°30N 75°30W 183 B4
, Canada 51°40N 91°50W 164 B1
ake Canada 51°40N 91°50W 164 B1
ien △ Vietnam 11°25N 107°17E 121 G6
Slovak Rep. 47°58N 18°38E 79 D11
amas Honduras 14°54N 85°56W 182 D2
aos Peru 5°20S 80°45W 188 B1
guases Brazil 21°23S 42°39W 191 A7
Turkey 38°1N 43°8E 105 C10
ağzı Turkey 41°30N 31°59E 104 B4
ão Brazil 18°10S 47°57W 189 D1
ca Turkey 41°8N 28°27E 97 E12
na Canada 48°31N 53°4W 165 C9
na Chile 25°13S 69°43W 190 B2
na U.S.A. 32°30N 110°50W 169 K8
onia = Cataluña □
41°40N 1°15E 90 D6
uña □ Spain 41°40N 1°15E 90 D6
zeytin Turkey 41°57N 34°12E 104 B6
marca Argentina 28°30S 65°50W 190 B2
marca □ Argentina 27°0S 65°50W 190 B2
nduanes □ Phil. 13°50N 124°20E 119 B6
nduva Brazil 21°5S 48°58W 191 A6
nia Italy 37°30N 15°6E 95 E8
nia, G. di Italy 37°24N 15°9E 95 E8
nzaro Italy 38°54N 16°35E 95 D9
rman Phil. 12°28N 124°35E 119 B6
umbo-Bari △
ombia 9°3N 73°12W 183 E5
ula U.S.A. 32°39N 84°52W 178 C5
acoma Canada 44°44N 78°19W 174 B6
Phil. 7°47N 126°24E 119 C7
nbe Mozam. 26°0S 32°33E 145 C5
ade Brazil 8°40S 35°43W 189 B3
ham U.K. 51°15N 0°4W 67 F7
ir na Mart = Westport
and 53°48N 9°31W 64 C2
cart Australia 36°52S 149°24E 153 D8
cart S. Africa 32°18S 27°10E 144 D4
edral City
A. 33°47N 116°28W 171 M10
edral Rock △
stralia 30°24S 152°15E 153 A10
amet U.S.A. 46°12N 123°23W 170 D3
Guinea-Biss. 11°17N 15°15W 138 C1
Brazil 9°31S 43°1W 189 B2
ttsburg U.S.A. 38°25N 82°36W 173 F12
s N.Z. 46°22S 169°17E 155 G4
ı Dağı Turkey 38°25N 29°50E 99 C11
che, C. Mexico 21°35N 87°5W 181 C7
é do Rocha Brazil 6°21S 37°45W 189 B3
, Mte. Italy 43°28N 12°42E 93 E9
ó Argentina 36°26S 63°24W 190 D3
mani Brazil 0°27N 61°41W 186 C6
mani → Brazil 0°28N 61°44W 186 C6
ill U.S.A. 42°14N 73°52W 175 D11
ill ⌂ U.S.A. 42°8N 74°39W 175 D10
ill Mts. U.S.A. 42°10N 74°25W 175 D10
Mt. Australia 13°49S 134°23E 150 A1
ngus U.S.A. 42°20N 78°52W 174 D6
rick U.K. 54°23N 1°37W 66 C6
lica Italy 43°58N 12°44E 92 E9
lica Eraclea Italy 37°26N 13°24E 94 E6
Brazil 12°21S 38°23W 189 C3
ala Angola 16°25S 19°2E 144 A2
ane Mozam. 26°48S 32°18E 145 C5
Mozam. 13°45S 35°30E 143 E4
vick, Mt. = Iberville, Mt. d'
ada 58°50N 63°50W 161 F19
a → Colombia 8°54N 74°28W 186 B4
aia Brazil 3°40S 38°35W 189 A3
asus Mountains
asia 42°50N 44°0E 87 J7
ete Argentina 31°38S 68°20W 190 C2
ete Spain 38°42N 1°2W 91 G3
ry France 50°7N 3°22E 71 B10
se Mts. Mozam. 15°14S 30°33E 143 F3
es France 48°18N 2°10W 70 D4
ònia Italy 38°23N 16°24E 95 D9
gula Angola 8°26S 18°38E 140 F3
uenes Chile 36°0S 72°22W 190 D1
a → Venezuela 7°38N 64°53W 186 B6
esi → Mozam. 17°8S 33°0E 143 F3
ani Moldova 46°38N 29°25E 81 D14
apscal Canada 48°19N 67°12W 165 C6
sade France 44°10N 1°33E 72 D5
se-Méjean France 44°18N 3°42E 72 D7
ses du Quercy ⌂
ance 44°35N 1°35E 72 D5
erets France 42°52N 0°8W 72 F3
ery → India 11°9N 78°52E 127 J4
, Pays de France 49°38N 0°35E 70 C7
de' Tirreni Italy 40°42N 14°42E 95 B7
do → Portugal 41°32N 8°48W 88 D2
grande del Cassibile ⌂
y 36°58N 15°6E 95 F8
illon France 43°50N 5°2E 73 E9
laire-sur-Mer
ance 43°10N 6°33E 73 E10
lcante Brazil 13°48S 47°30W 189 C1
lese Italy 46°17N 11°27E 93 B8
lier U.S.A. 48°48N 97°37W 172 A5
lla = Cavally →
ica 4°22N 7°32W 138 E3
lla △ Liberia 5°8N 7°20W 138 D3
lli Is. N.Z. 35°0S 173°58E 154 B2
lly → Africa 4°22N 7°32W 138 E3
Cavan Ireland 54°0N 7°22W 64 B4
Cavan □ Ireland 54°1N 7°16W 64 C4
Cavárzere Italy 45°8N 12°5E 93 C9
Çavdarhisar Turkey 39°12N 29°37E 99 B11
Çavdır Turkey 37°10N 29°42E 99 D11
Cave Creek U.S.A. 33°50N 111°57W 169 K8
Cave Spring U.S.A. 34°6N 85°20W 178 A4
Cavelleria, C. de Spain 40°5N 4°5E 100 A11
Cavenagh Ra.
Australia 26°12S 127°55E 149 E4
Cavendish Australia 37°31S 142°2E 152 D5
Caverna do Peruaçu △
Brazil 15°0S 44°35W 189 D2
Caviana, I. Brazil 0°10N 50°10W 187 C8
Cavite Phil. 14°29N 120°54E 119 B6
Cavnic Romania 47°40N 23°52E 81 C8
Cavour Italy 44°47N 7°22E 92 D4
Cavtat Croatia 42°35N 18°13E 96 D2
Cawndilla L. Australia 32°30S 142°15E 152 B5
Cawnpore = Kanpur
India 26°28N 80°20E 125 F9
Caxias Brazil 4°55S 43°20W 189 A2
Caxias do Sul Brazil 29°10S 51°10W 191 B5
Çay Turkey 38°35N 31°1E 104 C4
Cay Sal Bank Bahamas 23°45N 80°0W 182 B4
Cayambe Ecuador 0°3N 78°8W 186 C3
Cayce U.S.A. 33°58N 81°4W 178 B8
Çaycuma Turkey 41°25N 32°4E 104 B5
Çayeli Turkey 41°5N 40°45E 105 B9
Cayenne Fr. Guiana 5°5N 52°18W 187 B8
Cayey Puerto Rico 18°7N 66°10W 183 d
Caygören Barajı Turkey 39°15N 28°12E 99 B10
Cayiralan Turkey 39°17N 35°38E 104 C6
Cayirova = Áyios Theodhoros
Cyprus 35°22N 34°1E 101 D13
Caylus France 44°15N 1°47E 72 D5
Cayman Brac
Cayman Is. 19°43N 79°49W 182 C4
Cayman Is. ☒
W. Indies 19°40N 80°30W 182 C3
Cayman Trench
Caribbean 17°0N 83°0W 158 H11
Cayres France 44°55N 3°48E 72 D7
Cayuga Canada 42°59N 79°50W 174 D5
Cayuga U.S.A. 42°54N 76°44W 175 D8
Cayuga Heights U.S.A. 42°27N 76°29W 175 D8
Cayuga L. U.S.A. 42°41N 76°41W 175 D8
Cazalla de la Sierra Spain 37°56N 5°45W 89 H5
Căzănești Romania 44°36N 27°3E 81 F12
Cazaubon France 43°56N 0°3W 72 E3
Cazaux et de Sanguinet, Étang de
France 44°29N 1°10W 72 D2
Cazenovia U.S.A. 42°56N 75°51W 175 D9
Cazères France 43°13N 1°5E 72 E5
Cazin Bos.-H. 44°57N 15°57E 93 D12
Čazma Croatia 45°45N 16°39E 93 C13
Cazombo Angola 11°54S 22°56E 141 G4
Cazorla Spain 37°55N 3°2W 89 H7
Cazorla, Sierra de Spain 38°5N 2°55W 89 G8
Cea → Spain 42°0N 5°36W 88 C5
Ceahlău △ Romania 46°58N 25°55E 81 D10
Ceamurlia de Jos
Romania 44°43N 28°47E 81 F13
Ceanannus Mor = Kells
Ireland 53°44N 6°53W 64 C5
Ceará = Fortaleza Brazil 3°45S 38°35W 189 A3
Ceará □ Brazil 5°0S 40°0W 189 B3
Ceara Abyssal Plain
Atl. Oc. 0°0 36°30W 56 F7
Ceará-Mirim Brazil 5°38S 35°25W 189 B3
Ceara Rise Atl. Oc. 4°30N 43°30W 56 F7
Ceatharlach = Carlow
Ireland 52°50N 6°56W 64 D5
Ceauru, L. Romania 44°58N 23°11E 81 F8
Cébaco, I. de Panama 7°33N 81°9W 182 E3
Cebollar Argentina 29°10S 66°35W 190 B2
Cebollera, Sierra Spain 42°0N 2°30W 90 D2
Cebreros Spain 40°27N 4°28W 88 E6
Cebu Phil. 10°18N 123°54E 119 B6
Čečava Bos.-H. 44°42N 17°44E 80 F2
Ceccano Italy 41°34N 13°20E 94 A6
Cece Hungary 46°46N 18°39E 80 D3
Cechi Ivory C. 6°15N 4°25W 138 D4
Cecil Plains Australia 27°30S 151°11E 151 D5
Cécina Italy 43°19N 10°31E 92 E7
Cécina → Italy 43°18N 10°29E 92 E7
Ceclavín Spain 39°50N 6°45W 88 F4
Cedar → U.S.A. 41°17N 91°21W 172 E8
Cedar City U.S.A. 37°41N 113°4W 169 H7
Cedar Creek Res. U.S.A. 32°11N 96°4W 176 E6
Cedar Falls Iowa,
U.S.A. 42°32N 92°27W 172 D7
Cedar Falls Wash.,
U.S.A. 47°25N 121°45W 170 C5
Cedar Key U.S.A. 29°8N 83°2W 179 F6
Cedar L. Canada 53°10N 100°0W 163 C9
Cedar Park U.S.A. 30°30N 97°49W 176 F6
Cedar Rapids U.S.A. 41°59N 91°40W 172 E8
Cedartown U.S.A. 34°1N 85°15W 178 A4
Cedarvale Canada 55°1N 128°22W 162 B3
Cedarville S. Africa 30°23S 29°3E 145 D4
Cedeira Spain 43°39N 8°2W 88 B2
Cedral Mexico 23°50N 100°45W 180 C4
Cedrino → Italy 40°11N 9°24E 94 B2
Cedro Brazil 6°34S 39°3W 189 B3
Cedros, I. Mexico 28°12N 115°15W 180 B1
Cedros B. Trin. & Tob. 10°16N 61°54W 187 K15
Ceduna Australia 32°7S 133°46E 151 E1
Cedynia Poland 52°53N 14°12E 83 F1
Cée Spain 42°57N 9°10W 88 C1
Ceel Gaal Somalia 10°58N 50°20E 131 E5
Ceel Waaq Kenya 2°49N 40°56E 140 D8
Ceeldheere Somalia 3°50N 47°8E 131 G4
Ceerigaabo Somalia 10°35N 47°20E 131 E4
Cefalù Italy 38°2N 14°1E 95 D7
Cega → Spain 41°33N 4°46W 88 D6
Cegléd Hungary 47°11N 19°47E 80 C4
Céglie Messápica Italy 40°39N 17°31E 95 B10
Cehegín Spain 38°6N 1°48W 91 G3
Ceheng China 24°58N 105°48E 116 E5
Cehu-Silvaniei Romania 47°24N 23°9E 81 C8
Ceica Romania 46°53N 22°10E 80 D7
Ceira → Portugal 40°13N 8°16W 88 E2
Çekerek Turkey 40°4N 35°29E 104 B6
Cekik Indonesia 8°12S 114°27E 119 J17
Čelákovice Czech Rep. 50°10N 14°46E 78 A7
Celano Italy 42°5N 13°33E 93 F10
Celanova Spain 42°9N 7°58W 88 C3
Celaque △ Honduras 14°30N 88°43W 182 D2
Celaya Mexico 20°31N 100°37W 180 C4
Celbridge Ireland 53°20N 6°32W 64 C5
Celebes = Sulawesi
Indonesia 2°0S 120°0E 119 E6
Celebes Sea Indonesia 3°0N 123°0E 119 D6
Celendín Peru 6°52S 78°10W 188 B2
Čelić Bos.-H. 44°43N 18°49E 80 F3
Celina U.S.A. 40°33N 84°35W 173 E11
Celinac Bos.-H. 44°44N 17°22E 80 F2
Celje Slovenia 46°16N 15°18E 93 B12
Celldömölk Hungary 47°16N 17°10E 80 C2
Celle Germany 52°37N 10°4E 76 C6
Celorico da Beira
Portugal 40°38N 7°24W 88 E3
Celtic Sea Atl. Oc. 50°9N 9°34W 68 F2
Çeltikçi Turkey 37°32N 30°29E 99 D12
Çemişgezek Turkey 39°3N 38°56E 105 C8
Cenderawasih, Teluk
Indonesia 3°0S 135°20E 119 E9
Cengong China 27°13N 108°44E 116 D7
Ceno → Italy 44°43N 10°5E 92 D7
Centallo Italy 44°30N 7°35E 92 D4
Centelles Spain 41°50N 2°14E 90 D7
Centennial U.S.A. 39°34N 104°52W 168 G11
Center N. Dak., U.S.A. 47°7N 101°18W 172 B3
Center Tex., U.S.A. 31°48N 94°11W 176 F7
Center Hill U.S.A. 28°38N 82°3W 179 G7
Centerburg U.S.A. 40°18N 82°42W 174 F2
Centerville Calif.,
U.S.A. 36°44N 119°30W 170 J7
Centerville Iowa, U.S.A. 40°44N 92°52W 172 E7
Centerville Pa., U.S.A. 40°3N 79°59W 174 F5
Centerville Tenn.,
U.S.A. 35°47N 87°28W 177 D11
Centerville Tex., U.S.A. 31°16N 95°59W 176 F7
Cento Italy 44°43N 11°17E 93 D8
Central = Tsentralnyy □
Russia 52°0N 40°0E 106 D4
Central Brazil 11°8S 42°8W 189 C2
Central □ Botswana 22°0S 26°30E 144 B4
Central □ Ghana 5°30N 1°0W 139 D4
Central □ Kenya 0°30S 37°30E 142 C4
Central □ Malawi 13°30S 33°30E 143 E3
Central □ Zambia 14°25S 28°50E 143 E2
Central, Cordillera
Colombia 5°0N 75°0W 186 C4
Central, Cordillera
Costa Rica 10°10N 84°5W 182 D3
Central, Cordillera
Dom. Rep. 19°15N 71°0W 183 C5
Central, Cordillera Peru 7°0S 77°30W 188 B2
Central, Cordillera
Puerto Rico 18°8N 66°35W 183 d
Central African Rep. ■
Africa 7°0N 20°0E 135 G9
Central America
America 12°0N 85°0W 158 H11
Central Australia ◎
Australia 22°30S 128°30E 148 D4
Central Bedfordshire □
U.K. 52°5N 0°20W 67 E7
Central Butte Canada 50°48N 106°31W 163 C7
Central City Colo.,
U.S.A. 39°48N 105°31W 168 G11
Central City Ky.,
U.S.A. 37°18N 87°7W 172 G10
Central City Nebr., U.S.A. 41°7N 98°0W 172 E4
Central Desert ◎
Australia 19°56S 130°46E 148 C5
Central I. Kenya 3°30N 36°0E 142 B4
Central Island △ Kenya 2°33N 36°1E 142 B4
Central Japan Int. ✕ (NGO)
Japan 34°53N 136°45E 113 G8
Central Kalahari ⌂
Botswana 22°36S 23°58E 144 B3
Central Makran Range
Pakistan 26°30N 64°15E 122 F4
Central Pacific Basin
Pac. Oc. 8°0N 175°0W 156 G10
Central Patricia Canada 51°30N 90°9W 164 B1
Central Point U.S.A. 42°23N 122°55W 168 E2
Central Russian Uplands
Europe 54°0N 36°0E 58 E13
Central Siberian Plateau
Russia 65°0N 105°0E 102 B12
Central Square U.S.A. 43°17N 76°9W 175 C8
Centralia Canada 43°17N 81°28W 174 C3
Centralia Ill., U.S.A. 38°32N 89°8W 172 F9
Centralia Mo., U.S.A. 39°13N 92°8W 172 F7
Centralia Wash.,
U.S.A. 46°43N 122°58W 170 D4
Centre U.S.A. 34°9N 85°41W 178 A4
Centre □ Cameroon 4°35N 12°0E 139 E7
Centre de Flacq
Mauritius 20°12S 57°43E 141 d
Centreville N.Y., U.S.A. 42°28N 78°14W 174 D6
Centreville Pa., U.S.A. 41°44N 79°45W 174 E5
Century U.S.A. 30°58N 87°16W 179 E2
Cenxi China 22°57N 110°57E 117 F8
Čeotina → Bos.-H. 43°36N 18°50E 96 C2
Cephalonia = Kefalonia
Greece 38°15N 20°30E 98 C2
Čepin Croatia 45°32N 18°34E 80 E3
Ceprano Italy 41°33N 13°31E 94 A6
Ceptura Romania 45°1N 26°21E 81 E11
Cepu Indonesia 7°9S 111°35E 119 G14
Ceram = Seram
Indonesia 3°10S 129°0E 119 E7
Ceram Sea = Seram Sea
Indonesia 2°30S 128°30E 119 E7
Cerbère France 42°26N 3°10E 72 F7
Cerbicales, Îs. France 41°33N 9°22E 73 G13
Cercal Portugal 37°48N 8°40W 89 H2
Cerdanya Spain 42°22N 1°35E 90 C6
Cère → France 44°55N 1°49E 72 D5
Cerea Italy 45°12N 11°13E 93 C8
Ceredigion □ U.K. 52°16N 4°15W 67 E3
Ceres Argentina 29°55S 61°55W 190 B3
Ceres S. Africa 33°21S 19°18E 144 D2
Ceres U.S.A. 37°35N 120°57W 170 H6
Ceresio, L. di = Lugano, L. di
Switz. 46°0N 9°0E 92 C6
Céret France 42°30N 2°42E 72 F6
Cerf Seychelles 4°38S 55°40E 141 b
Cergy France 49°2N 2°4E 71 C9
Cerignola Italy 41°17N 15°53E 95 A8
Cerigo = Kythira Greece 36°8N 23°0E 98 E5
Cérilly France 46°37N 2°50E 71 F9
Cerisiers France 48°8N 3°30E 71 D10
Cerizay France 46°50N 0°40W 70 F6
Çerkeş Turkey 40°49N 32°52E 104 B5
Çerkezköy Turkey 41°17N 28°0E 97 E12
Cerknica Slovenia 45°48N 14°21E 93 C11
Cerkovica Bulgaria 43°41N 24°50E 97 C8
Cermerno Serbia 43°35N 20°25E 96 C4
Çermik Turkey 38°8N 39°26E 105 C8
Cerna Romania 45°4N 28°17E 81 E13
Cerna → Romania 44°38N 23°58E 81 F8
Cernavodă Romania 44°22N 28°3E 81 F13
Cernay France 47°44N 7°10E 71 E14
Cernik Croatia 45°17N 17°22E 80 E2
Cërrik Albania 41°2N 19°58E 96 E3
Cerralvo, I. Mexico 24°15N 109°55W 180 C3
Cerritos Mexico 22°25N 100°16W 180 C4
Cerro Chato Uruguay 33°6S 55°8W 191 C4
Cerro Cofre de Perote △
Mexico 19°29N 97°8W 181 D5
Cerro Corá △ Paraguay 22°35S 56°2W 191 A4
Cerro de Pasco Peru 10°45S 76°10W 188 C2
Cerro el Copey △
Venezuela 10°59N 63°53W 183 D7
Cerro Hoya △ Panama 7°17N 80°45W 182 E3
Cerro Saroche △
Venezuela 10°8N 69°38W 183 D6
Cerro Sombrero Chile 52°45S 69°15W 192 D3
Cerros Colorados, Embalse
Argentina 38°30S 68°50W 192 A3
Certaldo Italy 43°33N 11°2E 92 E8
Cervaro → Italy 41°30N 15°52E 95 A8
Cervati, Monte Italy 40°17N 15°29E 95 B8
Cerventes Australia 30°31S 115°3E 149 F2
Cervera Spain 41°40N 1°16E 90 D6
Cervera de Pisuerga
Spain 42°51N 4°30W 88 C6
Cervera del Río Alhama
Spain 42°2N 1°58W 90 C3
Cervéteri Italy 42°0N 12°6E 93 F9
Cérvia Italy 44°15N 12°22E 93 D9
Cervignano del Friuli
Italy 45°49N 13°20E 93 C10
Cervinara Italy 41°1N 14°37E 95 A7
Cervione France 42°20N 9°29E 73 F13
Cervo Spain 43°40N 7°24W 88 B3
Cesarò Italy 37°50N 14°38E 95 E7
Cesena Italy 44°8N 12°15E 93 D9
Cesenático Italy 44°12N 12°24E 93 D9
Cēsis Latvia 57°18N 25°15E 84 D3
Česká Lípa Czech Rep. 50°45N 14°30E 78 A7
Česká Rep. = Czech Rep. ■
Europe 50°0N 15°0E 78 B8
Česká Třebová
Czech Rep. 49°54N 16°27E 79 B9
České Budějovice
Czech Rep. 48°55N 14°25E 78 C7
České Švýcarsko △
Czech Rep. 50°50N 14°15E 78 A7
České Velenice
Czech Rep. 48°45N 14°57E 78 C7
Českobudějovický □
Czech Rep. 49°10N 14°30E 78 B7
Českomoravská Vrchovina
Czech Rep. 49°30N 15°40E 78 B8
Český Brod Czech Rep. 50°4N 14°52E 78 A7
Český Krumlov
Czech Rep. 48°43N 14°21E 78 C7
Český Těšín Czech Rep. 49°45N 18°39E 79 B11
Česma → Croatia 45°35N 16°29E 93 C13
Çeşme Turkey 38°20N 26°23E 99 C8
Cessnock Australia 32°50S 151°21E 153 B9
Cesson-Sévigné France 48°7N 1°36W 70 D5
Cestas France 44°44N 0°41W 72 D3
Cestos → Liberia 5°40N 9°10W 138 D3
Cestos Sehnkwehn △
Liberia 5°40N 9°10W 138 D3
Cetate Romania 44°7N 23°2E 80 F8
Cetin Grad Croatia 45°9N 15°45E 93 C12
Cetina → Croatia 43°26N 16°42E 93 E13
Cetinje Montenegro 42°23N 18°59E 96 D2
Cetraro Italy 39°31N 15°55E 95 C8
Ceuta N. Afr. 35°52N 5°18W 134 A4
Ceva Italy 44°23N 8°2E 92 D5
Cévennes France 44°10N 3°50E 72 D7
Cévennes △ France 44°15N 3°45E 72 D7
Ceyhan Turkey 37°4N 35°47E 104 D6
Ceyhan → Turkey 36°38N 35°40E 104 D6
Ceylanpınar Turkey 36°50N 40°2E 105 D9
Ceylon = Sri Lanka ■
Asia 7°30N 80°50E 127 L5
Ceylon Plain Ind. Oc. 4°0S 82°0E 146 E7
Cèze → France 44°6N 4°43E 73 D8
Cha-am Thailand 12°48N 99°58E 120 F2
Chabanais France 45°52N 0°48E 72 C4
Chabeuil France 44°54N 5°3E 73 D9
Chablais France 46°20N 6°36E 71 F13
Chablis France 47°47N 3°48E 71 E10
Chabounia Algeria 35°30N 2°38E 136 A4
Chacabuco Argentina 34°40S 60°27W 190 C3
Chacao, Canal Chile 41°47S 73°42W 192 B2
Chachani, Nevado
Peru 16°11S 71°31W 188 D3
Chachapoyas Peru 6°15S 77°50W 188 B2
Chachasp Peru 15°30S 72°15W 188 D3
Chachoengsao Thailand 13°42N 101°5E 120 F3
Chachran Pakistan 28°55N 70°30E 124 E4
Chachro Pakistan 25°5N 70°15E 124 G4
Chaco □ Argentina 26°30S 61°0W 190 B3
Chaco □ Paraguay 26°0S 60°0W 190 B4
Chaco → U.S.A. 36°46N 108°39W 169 H9
Chaco △ Argentina 27°0S 59°30W 190 B4
Chaco Boreal S. Amer. 22°0S 60°0W 186 H6
Chaco Culture ⌂
U.S.A. 36°3N 107°58W 169 H10
Chacon, C. U.S.A. 54°42N 132°0W 162 C2
Chad ■ Africa 15°0N 17°15E 135 F8
Chad, L. = Tchad, L.
Chad 13°30N 14°30E 135 F8
Chadileuvú →
Argentina 37°46S 66°0W 190 D2
Chadiza Zambia 14°45S 32°27E 143 E3
Chadron U.S.A. 42°50N 103°0W 172 D2
Chadyr-Lunga = Ciadâr-Lunga
Moldova 46°3N 28°51E 81 D13
Chae Hom Thailand 18°43N 99°35E 120 C2
Chae Son △ Thailand 18°42N 99°20E 120 C2
Chaem → Thailand 18°11N 98°38E 120 C2
Chaeryŏng N. Korea 38°24N 125°36E 115 E13
Chafe Nigeria 11°59N 6°50E 139 C6
Chagai Hills = Chāh Gay Hills
Afghan. 29°30N 64°0E 122 E3
Chagda Russia 58°45N 130°38E 107 D14
Chagdo Kangri China 34°15N 84°10E 109 F10
Chaghcharān Afghan. 34°31N 65°15E 109 F7
Chagny France 46°57N 4°45E 71 F11
Chagoda Russia 59°10N 35°15E 84 C8
Chagos Arch. ☒ Ind. Oc. 6°0S 72°0E 146 E6
Chagos-Laccadive Ridge
Ind. Oc. 3°0N 73°0E 146 D6
Chagres △ Panama 9°33N 79°37W 182 E4
Chaguanas
Trin. & Tob. 10°30N 61°26W 187 K15
Chāh Ākhvor Iran 32°41N 59°40E 129 C8
Chāh Bahar Iran 25°20N 60°40E 129 E9
Chāh-e Kavīr Iran 34°29N 56°52E 129 C8
Chāh Gay Hills Afghan. 29°30N 64°0E 122 E3
Chahār Borj Iran 37°6N 45°59E 105 D11
Chahār Borjak Afghan. 30°17N 62°3E 122 D3
Chahār Mahāll va Bakhtīarī □
Iran 32°0N 49°0E 129 C6
Chai Badan Thailand 15°12N 101°8E 120 E3
Chaibasa India 22°42N 85°49E 125 H11
Chaillé-les-Marais France 46°25N 1°2W 72 B2
Chain Ridge Ind. Oc. 6°0N 54°0E 146 D4
Chainat Thailand 15°11N 100°8E 120 E3
Chainpur Nepal 27°17N 87°19E 125 F12
Chaires U.S.A. 30°26N 84°7W 178 E5
Chaitén Chile 42°55S 72°43W 192 B2
Chaiya Thailand 9°23N 99°14E 121 H2
Chaiyaphum Thailand 15°48N 102°2E 120 E4
Chaj Doab Pakistan 32°15N 73°0E 124 C5
Chajari Argentina 30°42S 58°0W 190 C4
Chak Amru Pakistan 32°22N 75°11E 124 C6
Chakar → Pakistan 29°29N 68°2E 124 E3
Chakari Zimbabwe 18°5S 29°51E 145 A4
Chake Chake Tanzania 5°15S 39°45E 142 D4
Chakhānsūr Afghan. 31°10N 62°0E 122 D3
Chakonipau, L. Canada 56°18N 68°30W 165 A6
Chakradharpur India 22°45N 85°40E 125 H11
Chakrata India 30°42N 77°51E 124 D7
Chakwal Pakistan 32°56N 72°53E 124 C5
Chala Peru 15°48S 74°20W 188 D3
Chalais France 45°16N 0°3E 72 C4
Chalakudi India 10°18N 76°20E 127 J3
Chalchihuites Mexico 23°29N 103°53W 180 C4
Chalcis = Chalkida
Greece 38°27N 23°42E 98 C5
Châlette-sur-Loing France 48°1N 2°44E 71 D9
Chaleur B. Canada 47°55N 65°30W 165 C6
Chalfant U.S.A. 37°32N 118°21W 170 H8
Chalhuanca Peru 14°15S 73°15W 188 C3
Chaliki Greece 39°36N 22°30E 98 B4
Chalindrey France 47°43N 5°26E 71 E12
Chaling China 26°58N 113°30E 117 D9
Chalisgaon India 20°30N 75°10E 126 D2
Chalk River Canada 46°1N 77°27W 164 C4
Chalkar, Ozero = Shalkar Köli
Kazakhstan 50°35N 51°47E 86 E10
Chalki Greece 36°17N 27°35E 99 E9
Chalkida Greece 38°27N 23°42E 98 C5
Chalkidiki Greece 40°25N 23°20E 96 F7
Chalky Inlet N.Z. 46°3S 166°31E 155 G1
Challakere India 14°19N 76°39E 127 G3
Challans France 46°50N 1°52W 70 F5
Challapata Bolivia 18°53S 66°50W 186 G5
Challawa Gorge Res.
Nigeria 11°54N 8°25E 139 C6
Challenger Deep
Pac. Oc. 11°30N 142°0E 156 F6
Challenger Fracture Zone
Pac. Oc. 35°0S 105°0W 157 L17
Challis U.S.A. 44°30N 114°14W 168 D6
Chalmette U.S.A. 29°56N 89°57W 177 G10
Chaloem Rattanakosin △
Thailand 14°40N 99°17E 120 E2
Chalon-sur-Saône
France 46°48N 4°50E 71 F11
Chalong Thailand 7°50N 98°22E 121 a
Chalonnes-sur-Loire
France 47°20N 0°45W 70 E6
Châlons-en-Champagne
France 48°58N 4°20E 71 D11
Chálten, Cerro = Fitz Roy, Cerro
Argentina 49°17S 73°5W 192 C2
Châlus France 45°39N 0°58E 72 C4
Chālūs Iran 36°38N 51°26E 129 B6
Cham Germany 49°13N 12°39E 77 F8
Cham, Cu Lao Vietnam 15°57N 108°30E 120 E7
Chama U.S.A. 36°54N 106°35W 169 H10
Chamaicó Argentina 35°3S 64°58W 190 D3
Chaman Pakistan 30°58N 66°25E 122 D5
Chamba India 32°35N 76°10E 124 C7
Chamba Tanzania 11°37S 37°0E 143 E4
Chambal → India 26°29N 79°15E 125 F8
Chamberlain U.S.A. 43°49N 99°20W 172 D4
Chamberlain →
Australia 15°30S 127°54E 148 C4
Chamberlain L.
U.S.A. 46°14N 69°19W 173 B19
Chambers U.S.A. 35°11N 109°26W 169 J9
Chambersburg U.S.A. 39°56N 77°40W 173 F15
Chambéry France 45°34N 5°55E 73 C9
Chambeshi → Zambia 11°53S 29°48E 140 G6
Chambi, Jebel Tunisia 35°11N 8°39E 136 A5
Chamblee U.S.A. 33°53N 84°18W 178 B5
Chambly Canada 45°27N 73°17W 175 A11
Chambord Canada 48°25N 72°6W 165 C5
Chamboulive France 45°26N 1°42E 72 C5
Chamchamal Iraq 35°32N 44°50E 105 E11
Chamela Mexico 19°32N 105°5W 180 D3
Chamical Argentina 30°22S 66°27W 190 C2
Chamili Greece 35°50N 26°15E 99 F8
Chamkar Luong
Cambodia 11°0N 103°45E 121 G4
Chamoli India 30°24N 79°21E 125 D8
Chamonix-Mont Blanc
France 45°55N 6°51E 73 C10
Chamouchuane =
Ashuapmushuan →
Canada 48°37N 72°20W 164 C5
Champa India 22°2N 82°43E 125 H10
Champagne Canada 60°49N 136°30W 162 A1
Champagne France 48°40N 4°20E 71 D11
Champagnole France 46°45N 5°55E 71 F12
Champaign U.S.A. 40°7N 88°15W 172 E9
Champaner India 22°29N 73°32E 124 H5
Champassak Laos 14°53N 105°52E 120 E5
Champaubert France 48°50N 3°45E 71 D10
Champawat India 29°20N 80°6E 125 E9
Champdeniers-St-Denis
France 46°29N 0°25W 72 B3
Champdoré, L. Canada 55°55N 65°49W 165 A6
Champeix France 45°37N 3°8E 72 C7
Champion U.S.A. 41°19N 80°51W 174 E4
Champlain U.S.A. 44°59N 73°27W 175 B11
Champlain, L. U.S.A. 44°40N 73°20W 175 B11
Champlitte France 47°32N 5°31E 71 E12
Champotón Mexico 19°21N 90°43W 181 D6
Champua India 22°5N 85°40E 125 H11
Chamrajnagar India 11°52N 76°52E 127 J3
Chamusca Portugal 39°21N 8°29W 89 F2
Chan Chan Peru 8°7S 79°0W 188 B2
Chana Thailand 6°55N 100°44E 121 J3
Chañaral Chile 26°23S 70°40W 190 B1
Chanārān Iran 36°39N 59°6E 129 B8
Chanasma India 23°44N 72°5E 124 H5
Chancay Peru 11°32S 77°25W 188 C2
Chancery Lane Barbados 13°3N 59°30W 183 g
Chanco Chile 35°44S 72°32W 190 D1
Chand India 21°57N 79°7E 125 J8
Chandan Chauki India 28°33N 80°47E 125 E9
Chandannagar India 22°52N 88°24E 125 H13
Chandausi India 28°27N 78°49E 125 E8
Chandeleur Is. U.S.A. 29°55N 88°57W 177 G10
Chandeleur Sd. U.S.A. 29°55N 89°0W 177 G10
Chandigarh India 30°43N 76°47E 124 D7
Chandil India 22°58N 86°3E 125 H12
Chandler Australia 27°0S 133°19E 151 D1
Chandler Canada 48°18N 64°46W 165 C7
Chandler Ariz., U.S.A. 33°18N 111°50W 169 K8
Chandler Okla., U.S.A. 35°42N 96°53W 176 D6
Chandless → Brazil 9°8S 69°51W 188 B4
Chandod India 21°59N 73°28E 124 J5
Chandpur Bangla. 23°8N 90°45E 123 H17
Chandra Greece 35°3N 26°8E 99 F8
Chandragiri India 13°35N 79°19E 127 H4
Chandrapur India 19°57N 79°25E 126 E4
Chandrupatla India 18°33N 80°24E 126 E5
Chānf Iran 26°38N 60°29E 129 E9
Chang Pakistan 26°59N 68°30E 124 F3
Chang, Ko Thailand 12°0N 102°23E 121 G4
Chang, Ko Thailand 9°50N 98°27E 121 H2
Ch'ang Chiang = Chang Jiang →
China 31°48N 121°10E 117 B13
Chang Jiang →
China 31°48N 121°10E 117 B13
Chang-won S. Korea 35°16N 128°37E 115 G15
Changan China 22°48N 113°48E 111 a
Changanacheri India 9°25N 76°31E 127 K3
Changanassery = Changanacheri
India 9°25N 76°31E 127 K3
Changane → Mozam. 24°30S 33°30E 145 B5
Changbai China 41°25N 128°5E 115 D15
Changbai Shan China 42°20N 129°0E 115 C15
Changchiak'ou = Zhangjiakou
China 40°48N 114°55E 114 D8
Ch'angchou = Changzhou
China 31°47N 119°58E 117 B12
Changchun China 43°57N 125°17E 115 C13
Changchunling
China 45°18N 125°27E 115 B13
Changde China 29°4N 111°35E 117 C8
Changdo-ri N. Korea 38°30N 127°40E 115 E14
Changfeng China 32°28N 117°10E 117 A11
Changge China 34°13N 113°46E 114 G7
Changhai = Shanghai
China 31°15N 121°26E 117 B13
Changhua China 30°12N 119°12E 117 B12
Changhua Taiwan 24°2N 120°30E 117 E13
Changhŭngni
N. Korea 40°24N 128°19E 115 D15
Changi Singapore 1°23N 103°59E 121 d
Changi, Singapore ✕ (SIN)
Singapore 1°23N 103°59E 121 M4
Changji China 44°1N 87°19E 109 D11
Changjiang China 19°20N 108°55E 117 a
Changjiang Shuiku
China 22°29N 113°27E 111 a
Changjin N. Korea 40°23N 127°15E 115 D14
Changjin-ho N. Korea 40°30N 127°15E 115 D14
Changle China 25°59N 119°27E 117 E12
Changli China 39°40N 119°13E 115 E10
Changling China 44°20N 123°58E 115 B12
Changlun Malaysia 6°25N 100°26E 121 J3
Changning Hunan,
China 26°28N 112°22E 117 D9
Changning Sichuan,
China 28°40N 104°56E 116 C5
Changning Yunnan,
China 24°45N 99°30E 116 E2
Changping China 40°14N 116°12E 114 D9
Changsha China 28°12N 113°0E 117 C9
Changshan China 28°55N 118°27E 117 C12
Changshan Qundao
China 39°11N 122°32E 115 E12
Changshou China 29°50N 107°4E 116 C6
Changshu China 31°38N 120°43E 117 B13
Changshun China 26°3N 106°25E 116 D6
Changtai China 24°35N 117°42E 117 E11
Changting China 25°50N 116°22E 117 E11
Changtu China 42°46N 124°6E 115 C13
Changuinola Panama 9°26N 82°31W 182 E3
Changwu Guangxi Zhuangzu,
China 23°25N 111°17E 117 F8
Changwu Shaanxi,
China 35°10N 107°45E 114 G4
Changxing China 31°0N 119°55E 117 B12
Changyang China 30°30N 111°10E 117 B8
Changyi China 36°40N 119°30E 115 F10
Changyŏn N. Korea 38°15N 125°6E 115 E13
Changyuan China 35°15N 114°42E 114 G8
Changzhi China 36°10N 113°6E 114 F7
Changzhou China 31°47N 119°58E 117 B12
Chanhanga Angola 16°0S 14°8E 144 A1
Chania Greece 35°30N 24°4E 101 D6
Chanion, Kolpos Greece 35°33N 23°55E 101 D5
Chanlar = Goygöl
Azerbaijan 40°37N 46°12E 87 K8
Channagiri India 14°2N 75°56E 127 G2
Channapatna India 12°40N 77°15E 127 H3
Channel Is. U.K. 49°19N 2°24W 67 H5
Channel Is. U.S.A. 33°40N 119°15W 171 M7
Channel Islands △
U.S.A. 34°0N 119°24W 171 L7
Channel-Port aux Basques
Canada 47°30N 59°9W 165 C8
Channel Tunnel Europe 51°0N 1°30E 67 F9
Channing U.S.A. 35°41N 102°20W 176 D3
Chantada Spain 42°36N 7°46W 88 C3
Chanthaburi Thailand 12°38N 102°12E 120 F4
Chantilly France 49°12N 2°29E 71 C9
Chantonnay France 46°40N 1°3W 70 F5
Chantrey Inlet
Canada 67°48N 96°20W 160 D12
Chanumla India 8°19N 93°5E 127 K11
Chanute U.S.A. 37°41N 95°27W 172 G6
Chany, Ozero Russia 54°49N 77°29E 106 D8
Chanza → Spain 37°32N 7°30W 89 H3

Chao Hu China 31°30N 117°30E **117 B11**
Chao Phraya →
  Thailand 13°40N 100°31E **120 F3**
Chao Phraya Lowlands
  Thailand 15°30N 100°0E **120 E3**
Chaocheng China 36°4N 115°37E **114 F8**
Chaohu China 31°38N 117°50E **117 B11**
Chaouia-Ouardigha □
  Morocco 33°0N 7°30W **136 B2**
Chaoyang Guangdong,
  China 23°17N 116°30E **117 F11**
Chaoyang Liaoning,
  China 41°35N 120°22E **115 D11**
Chaozhou China 23°42N 116°32E **117 F11**
Chapada Diamantina △
  Brazil 12°52S 41°30W **189 C2**
Chapada dos Veadeiros △
  Brazil 14°0S 47°30W **189 C1**
Chapaev Kazakhstan 50°25N 51°10E **86 E10**
Chapais Canada 49°47N 74°51W **164 C5**
Chapala Mozam. 15°50S 37°35E **143 F4**
Chapala, L. de Mexico 20°15N 103°0W **180 C4**
Chapayevsk Russia 53°0N 49°40E **86 D9**
Chapecó Brazil 27°14S 52°41W **191 B5**
Chapel Hill U.S.A. 35°55N 79°4W **177 D15**
Chapleau Canada 47°50N 83°24W **164 C3**
Chaplin Canada 50°28N 106°40W **163 C7**
Chaplin L. Canada 50°22N 106°36W **163 C7**
Chaplino Ukraine 48°8N 36°15E **85 H9**
Chaplygin Russia 53°15N 40°0E **84 F11**
Chappell U.S.A. 41°6N 102°28W **172 E2**
Chappells U.S.A. 34°11N 81°52W **178 A8**
Chapra = Chhapra
  India 25°48N 84°44E **125 G11**
Chaqābel Iran 33°16N 47°30E **105 F12**
Chara Russia 56°54N 118°20E **107 D12**
Charadai Argentina 27°35S 59°55W **190 B4**
Charagua Bolivia 19°45S 63°10W **186 G6**
Charakas Greece 35°1N 25°7E **101 D7**
Charambirá, Punta
  Colombia 4°16N 77°32W **186 C3**
Charaña Bolivia 17°30S 69°25W **188 D4**
Charantsavan Armenia 40°35N 44°41E **87 K7**
Charanwala India 27°51N 72°10E **124 F5**
Charata Argentina 27°13S 61°14W **190 B3**
Charcas Mexico 23°8N 101°7W **180 C4**
Charcot I. Antarctica 70°0S 70°0W **55 C17**
Chard U.K. 50°52N 2°58W **67 G5**
Chardon U.S.A. 41°35N 81°12W **174 E3**
Chardzhou = Türkmenabat
  Turkmenistan 39°6N 63°34E **129 B9**
Charente □ France 45°50N 0°16E **72 C4**
Charente → France 45°57N 1°5W **72 C2**
Charente-Maritime □
  France 45°45N 0°45W **72 C3**
Charenton-du-Cher
  France 46°44N 2°39E **71 F9**
Chari → Chad 12°58N 14°31E **135 F8**
Chārīkār Afghan. 35°0N 69°10E **109 E7**
Charing U.S.A. 32°28N 84°22W **178 C5**
Chariton U.S.A. 41°1N 93°19W **172 E7**
Chariton → U.S.A. 39°19N 92°58W **172 F7**
Chärjew = Türkmenabat
  Turkmenistan 39°6N 63°34E **129 B9**
Charkhari India 25°24N 79°45E **125 G8**
Charkhi Dadri India 28°37N 76°17E **124 E7**
Charleroi Belgium 50°24N 4°27E **69 D4**
Charleroi U.S.A. 40°9N 79°57W **174 F5**
Charles, C. U.S.A. 37°7N 75°58W **173 G16**
Charles, Peak
  Australia 32°52S 121°11E **149 F3**
Charles City U.S.A. 43°4N 92°41W **172 D7**
Charles de Gaulle, Paris ✈ (CDG)
  France 49°0N 2°32E **71 D9**
Charles I. Canada 62°39N 74°15W **161 E17**
Charles L. Canada 59°50N 110°33W **163 B6**
Charles Sound N.Z. 45°2S 167°4E **155 F2**
Charles Town U.S.A. 39°17N 77°52W **173 F15**
Charlesbourg Canada 46°51N 71°16W **173 B18**
Charleston Ill., U.S.A. 39°30N 88°10W **172 F9**
Charleston Miss., U.S.A. 34°1N 90°4W **177 D9**
Charleston Mo., U.S.A. 36°55N 89°21W **172 G9**
Charleston S.C.,
  U.S.A. 32°46N 79°56W **178 C10**
Charleston W. Va.,
  U.S.A. 38°21N 81°38W **173 F13**
Charleston L. Canada 44°32N 76°0W **175 B9**
Charleston Peak
  U.S.A. 36°16N 115°42W **171 J11**
Charlestown Ireland 53°58N 8°48W **64 C3**
Charlestown S. Africa 27°26S 29°53E **145 C4**
Charlestown Ind.,
  U.S.A. 38°27N 85°40W **173 F11**
Charlestown N.H.,
  U.S.A. 43°14N 72°25W **175 C12**
Charlestown of Aberlour
  U.K. 57°28N 3°14W **65 D5**
Charleville Australia 26°24S 146°15E **151 D4**
Charleville Ireland 52°21N 8°40W **64 D3**
Charleville-Mézières
  France 49°44N 4°40E **71 C11**
Charlevoix U.S.A. 45°19N 85°16W **173 C11**
Charlie Gibbs Fracture Zone
  Atl. Oc. 52°45N 35°30W **56 A8**
Charlieu France 46°10N 4°10E **71 F11**
Charlotte Mich.,
  U.S.A. 42°34N 84°50W **173 D11**
Charlotte N.C., U.S.A. 35°13N 80°50W **177 D14**
Charlotte Vt., U.S.A. 44°19N 73°16W **175 B11**
Charlotte Amalie
  U.S. Virgin Is. 18°21N 64°56W **183 e**
Charlotte Harbor U.S.A. 26°57N 82°4W **179 J7**
Charlotte L. Canada 52°12N 125°19W **162 C3**
Charlottenberg Sweden 59°54N 12°17E **63 E14**
Charlottesville U.S.A. 38°2N 78°30W **173 F14**
Charlottetown Nfld. & L.,
  Canada 52°46N 56°7W **165 B8**
Charlottetown P.E.I.,
  Canada 46°14N 63°8W **165 C7**
Charlotteville
  Trin. & Tob. 11°20N 60°33W **187 J16**
Charlton Australia 36°16S 143°24E **152 D5**
Charlton I. Canada 52°0N 79°20W **164 B4**
Charmes France 48°22N 6°17E **71 D13**
Charny Canada 46°43N 71°15W **165 C5**
Charolles France 46°27N 4°16E **71 F11**
Chârost France 47°1N 2°7E **71 F9**
Charouine Algeria 29°0N 0°15W **136 C5**
Charre Mozam. 17°13S 35°10E **143 F4**
Charroux France 46°9N 0°25E **72 B4**

Charsadda Pakistan 34°7N 71°45E **124 B4**
Charters Towers
  Australia 20°5S 146°13E **150 C4**
Chartres France 48°29N 1°30E **70 D8**
Chartreuse ⌀ France 45°22N 5°42E **73 C9**
Charysh → Russia 52°22N 83°45E **109 D10**
Chascomús Argentina 35°30S 58°0W **190 D4**
Chase Canada 50°50N 119°41W **162 C5**
Chasefu Zambia 11°55S 33°8E **143 E3**
Chashma Barrage
  Pakistan 32°27N 71°20E **124 C4**
Chaslands Mistake
  N.Z. 46°38S 169°22E **155 G4**
Chasseneuil-sur-Bonnieure
  France 45°52N 0°29E **72 C4**
Chât Iran 37°59N 55°16E **129 B7**
Chatal Balkan = Udvoy Balkan
  Bulgaria 42°50N 26°50E **97 D10**
Château-Arnoux-St-Auban
  France 44°6N 6°0E **73 D10**
Château-Chinon France 47°4N 3°56E **71 E10**
Château-d'Olonne
  France 46°30N 1°44W **72 B2**
Château-du-Loir France 47°40N 0°25E **70 E7**
Château-Gontier France 47°50N 0°48W **70 E6**
Château-la-Vallière
  France 47°30N 0°20E **70 E7**
Château-Landon France 48°8N 2°40E **71 D9**
Château-Renard France 47°56N 2°55E **71 E9**
Château-Renault France 47°36N 0°56E **70 E7**
Château-Salins France 48°50N 6°30E **71 D13**
Château-Thierry France 49°3N 3°20E **71 C10**
Châteaubourg France 48°7N 1°25W **70 D5**
Châteaubriant France 47°43N 1°23W **70 E5**
Châteaudun France 48°3N 1°20E **70 D8**
Chateaugay U.S.A. 44°56N 74°5W **175 B10**
Châteaugiron France 48°3N 1°30W **70 D5**
Châteauguay, L. Canada 56°26N 70°3W **165 A5**
Châteaulin France 48°11N 4°8W **70 D2**
Châteaumeillant France 46°35N 2°12E **71 F9**
Châteauneuf-du-Faou
  France 48°11N 3°50W **70 D3**
Châteauneuf-sur-Charente
  France 45°36N 0°3W **72 C3**
Châteauneuf-sur-Cher
  France 46°52N 2°18E **71 F9**
Châteauneuf-sur-Loire
  France 47°52N 2°13E **71 E9**
Châteaurenard France 43°53N 4°51E **73 E8**
Châteauroux France 46°50N 1°40E **71 F8**
Châteauvillain France 48°2N 4°55E **71 D11**
Châteaux, Pte. des
  Guadeloupe 16°15N 61°10W **182 b**
Châtel-Guyon France 45°55N 3°4E **72 C7**
Châtelaillon-Plage France 46°5N 1°5W **72 B2**
Châtellerault France 46°50N 0°30E **70 F7**
Châtelus-Malvaleix France 46°18N 2°1E **71 F9**
Chatham = Miramichi
  Canada 47°2N 65°28W **165 C6**
Chatham Canada 42°24N 82°11W **174 D2**
Chatham U.K. 51°22N 0°32E **67 F8**
Chatham U.S.A. 42°21N 73°36W **175 D11**
Chatham, I. Chile 50°40S 74°25W **192 D2**
Chatham Is. Pac. Oc. 44°0S 176°40W **155 c**
Chatham Rise Pac. Oc. 43°30S 180°0E **156 M10**
Châtillon Italy 45°45N 7°37E **92 C4**
Châtillon-Coligny France 47°50N 2°51E **71 E9**
Châtillon-en-Diois France 44°41N 5°29E **73 D9**
Châtillon-sur-Indre
  France 46°59N 1°10E **70 F8**
Châtillon-sur-Loire
  France 47°35N 2°44E **71 E9**
Châtillon-sur-Seine
  France 47°50N 4°33E **71 E11**
Chatmohar Bangla. 24°15N 89°15E **125 G13**
Chatra India 24°12N 84°56E **125 G11**
Chatrapur India 19°22N 85°2E **126 E7**
Chats, L. des Canada 45°30N 76°20W **175 A8**
Chatsu India 26°36N 75°57E **124 F6**
Chatsworth Canada 44°27N 80°54W **174 B4**
Chatsworth Zimbabwe 19°38S 31°13E **143 F3**
Châttagâm = Chittagong
  Bangla. 22°19N 91°48E **123 H17**
Chattahoochee U.S.A. 30°42N 84°51W **178 E5**
Chattahoochee →
  U.S.A. 30°54N 84°57W **178 E5**
Chattanooga U.S.A. 35°3N 85°19W **177 D12**
Chatteris U.K. 52°28N 0°2E **67 E8**
Chatturat Thailand 15°40N 101°51E **120 E3**
Chau Doc Vietnam 10°42N 105°7E **121 G5**
Chaudes-Aigues France 44°51N 3°1E **72 D7**
Chauffailles France 46°13N 4°20E **71 F11**
Chaukan Pass Burma 27°8N 97°10E **123 F20**
Chaumont France 48°7N 5°8E **71 D12**
Chaumont U.S.A. 44°4N 76°8W **175 B8**
Chaumont-en-Vexin
  France 49°16N 1°53E **71 C8**
Chaumont-sur-Loire
  France 47°29N 1°11E **70 E8**
Chaunay France 46°13N 0°9E **72 B4**
Chaunskaya G. Russia 69°0N 169°0E **107 C17**
Chauny France 49°37N 3°12E **71 C10**
Chaura India 8°27N 93°2E **127 K11**
Chausey, Îs. France 48°52N 1°49W **70 D5**
Chaussin France 46°59N 5°22E **71 F12**
Chautara Nepal 27°46N 85°42E **125 F11**
Chautauqua L. U.S.A. 42°10N 79°24W **174 D5**
Chauvigny France 46°34N 0°39E **70 F7**
Chauvin Canada 52°45N 110°10W **163 C6**
Chavakachcheri
  Sri Lanka 9°30N 80°9E **127 K5**
Chavanges France 48°30N 4°34E **71 D11**
Chavash Varmane △
  Russia 54°50N 47°10E **86 C8**
Chaves Brazil 0°15S 49°55W **187 D9**
Chaves Portugal 41°45N 7°32W **88 D3**
Chavin Peru 9°35S 77°10W **188 B2**
Chawang Thailand 8°25N 99°30E **121 H2**
Chazelles-sur-Lyon
  France 45°39N 4°22E **73 C8**
Chazuta Peru 6°30S 76°0W **188 B2**
Chazy U.S.A. 44°53N 73°26W **175 B11**
Cheaha Mt. U.S.A. 33°29N 85°49W **178 B4**
Cheb Czech Rep. 50°9N 12°28E **78 A5**
Chebbi, Erg Africa 31°12N 3°58W **136 B3**
Cheboksarskoye Vdkhr.
  Russia 56°13N 46°58E **86 B8**
Cheboksary Russia 56°8N 47°12E **86 B8**
Cheboygan U.S.A. 45°39N 84°29W **173 C11**
Chebsara Russia 59°10N 38°59E **84 C10**
Chech, Erg Africa 25°0N 2°15W **136 D5**

Chechelnyk Ukraine 48°13N 29°22E **81 B14**
Chechen, Ostrov Russia 43°59N 47°40E **87 H8**
Chechenia □ Russia 43°30N 45°29E **87 J7**
Checheno-Ingush Republic =
  Chechenia □ Russia 43°30N 45°29E **87 J7**
Chechnya = Chechenia □
  Russia 43°30N 45°29E **87 J7**
Chęciny Poland 50°46N 20°28E **83 H7**
Checotah U.S.A. 35°28N 95°31W **176 D7**
Chedabucto B. Canada 45°25N 61°8W **165 C7**
Cheduba I. Burma 18°45N 93°40E **123 K18**
Cheektowaga U.S.A. 42°54N 78°45W **174 D6**
Cheepie Australia 26°33S 145°0E **151 D4**
Chef-Boutonne France 46°7N 0°4W **72 B3**
Chefchaouen Morocco 35°9N 5°15W **136 A2**
Chegdomyn Russia 51°7N 133°1E **107 D14**
Chegga Mauritania 25°27N 5°40W **134 C4**
Chegutu Zimbabwe 18°10S 30°14E **143 F3**
Chehalis U.S.A. 46°40N 122°58W **170 D4**
Chehalis → U.S.A. 46°57N 123°50W **170 D3**
Cheile Bicazului-Hăşmaş △
  Romania 46°55N 25°50E **83 D10**
Cheile Nerei-Beusniţa △
  Romania 44°56N 21°52E **80 F6**
Cheiron, Mt. du France 43°49N 6°58E **73 E10**
Cheju = Jeju S. Korea 33°31N 126°32E **115 H14**
Cheju-do = Jeju-do
  S. Korea 33°29N 126°34E **115 H14**
Cheju Str. = Jeju Haehyop
  S. Korea 33°53N 126°30E **115 H14**
Chek Lap Kok China 22°18N 113°56E **111 a**
Chek Lap Kok ✈ (HKG)
  China 22°19N 113°57E **111 a**
Chekalin Russia 54°10N 36°10E **84 E9**
Chekhovo Russia 54°33N 20°43E **82 D7**
Chekiang = Zhejiang □
  China 29°0N 120°0E **117 C13**
Chela, Sa. da Angola 16°20S 13°20E **144 A1**
Chelan U.S.A. 47°51N 120°1W **168 C3**
Chelan, L. U.S.A. 48°11N 120°30W **168 B3**
Cheleken = Hazar
  Turkmenistan 39°34N 53°16E **108 E4**
Cheleken Yarymadasy
  Turkmenistan 39°30N 53°15E **129 B7**
Chelforó Argentina 39°0S 66°33W **192 A3**
Chéliff, O. → Algeria 36°0N 0°8E **136 A4**
Chelkar = Shalqar
  Kazakhstan 47°48N 59°39E **108 C5**
Chellala Dahrania Algeria 33°2N 0°1E **136 B4**
Chelles France 48°53N 2°35E **71 D9**
Chelm Poland 51°8N 23°30E **83 G10**
Chełmno Poland 53°20N 18°30E **83 E5**
Chelmsford U.K. 51°44N 0°29E **67 F8**
Chełmża Poland 53°10N 18°39E **83 E5**
Chelsea Australia 38°5S 145°8E **153 E6**
Chelsea U.S.A. 43°59N 72°27W **175 C12**
Cheltenham U.K. 51°54N 2°4W **67 F5**
Chelva Spain 39°45N 1°0W **90 F4**
Chelyabinsk Russia 55°10N 61°24E **108 A6**
Chelyuskin, C. = Chelyuskin, Mys
  Russia 77°30N 103°0E **107 B11**
Chelyuskin, Mys
  Russia 77°30N 103°0E **107 B11**
Chemainus Canada 48°55N 123°42W **170 B3**
Chemba Mozam. 17°9S 34°53E **141 H6**
Chembar = Belinskiy
  Russia 53°0N 43°25E **86 D6**
Chemillé France 47°14N 0°45W **70 E6**
Chemin Grenier
  Mauritius 20°29S 57°28E **141 d**
Chemnitz Germany 50°51N 12°54E **78 E8**
Chemult U.S.A. 43°14N 121°47W **168 E3**
Chen, Gora Russia 65°16N 141°50E **107 C15**
Chenab → Pakistan 30°23N 71°2E **124 D4**
Chenab Nagar Pakistan 31°45N 72°55E **124 D5**
Chenachane Algeria 26°0N 4°15W **136 C3**
Chenachane, O. →
  Algeria 25°20N 3°20W **136 C3**
Chenango Forks
  U.S.A. 42°15N 75°51W **175 D9**
Chenchiang = Zhenjiang
  China 32°11N 119°26E **117 A12**
Cheney U.S.A. 47°30N 117°35W **168 C5**
Cheng Xian China 33°43N 105°42E **114 H3**
Chengalpattu India 12°42N 79°58E **127 H4**
Chengbu China 26°18N 110°16E **117 D8**
Chengcheng China 35°8N 109°56E **114 G5**
Chenghai China 23°30N 116°42E **117 F11**
Chengjiang China 24°39N 103°0E **116 E4**
Chengkou China 31°54N 108°31E **116 B7**
Chengmai China 19°50N 109°58E **117 a**
Chengshan Jiao
  China 37°25N 122°44E **115 F12**
Ch'engtu = Chengdu
  China 30°38N 104°2E **116 B5**
Chengwu China 34°58N 115°50E **114 G8**
Chengyang China 36°18N 120°21E **115 F11**
Chenjiagang China 34°23N 119°47E **115 G10**
Chenkaladi Sri Lanka 7°47N 81°35E **127 L5**
Chennai India 13°8N 80°19E **127 H5**
Chenôve France 47°16N 5°1E **71 E12**
Chenxi China 28°2N 110°12E **117 C8**
Chenzhou China 25°47N 113°1E **117 E9**

Cheraw U.S.A. 34°42N 79°53W **177 D15**
Cherbourg-Octeville
  France 49°39N 1°40W **70 C5**
Cherchell Algeria 36°35N 2°12E **136 A4**
Cherdakly Russia 54°25N 48°50E **86 C9**
Cherdyn Russia 60°24N 56°29E **106 C6**
Cheremkhovo Russia 53°8N 103°1E **110 A9**
Cheremushki Russia 54°35N 58°0W **190 D4**
Cherepanovo Russia 54°15N 83°30E **109 B10**
Cherepovets Russia 59°5N 37°55E **84 C9**
Chergui, Chott ech
  Algeria 34°21N 0°25E **136 B4**
Chergui, Zahrez Algeria 35°11N 3°31E **136 A4**
Cherial India 17°55N 78°59E **126 F4**
Cheriyam I. India 10°9N 73°40E **127 J1**
Cherikov = Cherykaw
  Belarus 53°32N 31°20E **75 B16**
Cherkasy Ukraine 49°27N 32°4E **85 H7**
Cherkasy □ Ukraine 48°55N 30°50E **85 H5**
Cherkessk Russia 44°15N 42°5E **87 H6**
Cherla India 18°5N 80°49E **126 E5**
Cherlak Russia 54°15N 74°55E **109 B8**
Chernaya Russia 70°30N 89°10E **107 B9**
Chernelytsya Ukraine 48°49N 25°26E **81 B10**
Cherni Bulgaria 42°35N 23°18E **96 D7**
Chernigov = Chernihiv
  Ukraine 51°28N 31°20E **85 G6**
Chernihiv Ukraine 51°28N 31°20E **85 G6**
Chernihiv □ Ukraine 51°10N 32°5E **85 G7**
Chernivtsi Chernivtsi,
  Ukraine 48°15N 25°52E **81 B10**
Chernivtsi Vinnyts'ka,
  Ukraine 48°32N 28°9E **81 B13**
Chernivtsi □ Ukraine 48°25N 25°30E **81 B10**
Chernobyl = Chornobyl
  Ukraine 51°20N 30°15E **75 C16**
Chernogorsk Russia 53°49N 91°18E **109 B12**
Chernomorskoye =
  Chornomorske
  Ukraine 45°31N 32°40E **85 K7**
Chernovtsy = Chernivtsi
  Ukraine 48°15N 25°52E **81 B10**
Chernyakhovsk Russia 54°36N 21°48E **82 D8**
Chernyanka Russia 50°56N 37°49E **85 G9**
Chernysheyskiy
  Russia 63°0N 112°30E **107 C12**
Chernyye Zemli Russia 46°10N 46°0E **87 H8**
Cherokee Iowa, U.S.A. 42°45N 95°33W **172 D6**
Cherokee Okla., U.S.A. 36°45N 98°21W **176 C5**
Cherokee Village
  U.S.A. 36°18N 91°31W **176 C9**
Cherokees, Grand Lake O' The
  U.S.A. 36°28N 95°0W **176 C7**
Cherquenco Chile 38°35S 72°0W **192 A2**
Cherrapunji India 25°17N 91°47E **125 G17**
Cherry Valley U.S.A. 42°48N 74°45W **175 D10**
Cherskiy Russia 68°45N 161°18E **107 C17**
Cherskogo Khrebet
  Russia 65°0N 143°0E **107 C15**
Cherso Greece 41°5N 22°47E **96 D6**
Chersonisos Greece 35°18N 25°22E **101 D7**
Chersonisos Akrotiri
  Greece 35°30N 24°10E **101 D6**
Chertkovo Russia 49°25N 40°19E **85 H11**
Cherven Belarus 53°45N 28°28E **75 B15**
Cherven-Bryag Bulgaria 43°17N 24°7E **97 C8**
Chervonoarmiyske
  Ukraine 45°47N 28°44E **81 E13**
Chervonohrad Ukraine 50°25N 24°10E **75 C13**
Cherwell → U.K. 51°44N 1°14W **67 F6**
Cherykaw Belarus 53°32N 31°20E **75 B16**
Chesapeake U.S.A. 36°49N 76°16W **173 G15**
Chesapeake B. U.S.A. 38°0N 76°10W **173 F14**
Cheshire East □ U.K. 53°15N 2°15W **66 D5**
Cheshire West and Chester □
  U.K. 53°15N 2°40W **66 D5**
Cheshskaya Guba
  Russia 67°20N 47°0E **106 C5**
Cheshunt U.K. 51°43N 0°1W **67 F7**
Chesil Beach U.K. 50°37N 2°33W **67 G5**
Chesley Canada 44°17N 81°5W **174 B3**
Cheste Spain 39°30N 0°41W **91 F4**
Chester U.K. 53°12N 2°53W **66 D5**
Chester Calif., U.S.A. 40°19N 121°14W **168 F3**
Chester Ga., U.S.A. 32°24N 83°9W **178 D6**
Chester Ill., U.S.A. 37°55N 89°49W **172 G9**
Chester Mont., U.S.A. 48°31N 110°58W **168 B8**
Chester Pa., U.S.A. 39°51N 75°22W **173 F16**
Chester S.C., U.S.A. 34°43N 81°12W **177 D14**
Chester Vt., U.S.A. 43°16N 72°36W **175 C12**
Chester W. Va., U.S.A. 40°37N 80°34W **174 F4**
Chester-le-Street U.K. 54°51N 1°34W **66 C6**
Chesterfield U.K. 53°15N 1°25W **66 D6**
Chesterfield, Îs. N. Cal. 19°52S 158°15E **147 C8**
Chesterfield Inlet
  Canada 63°30N 90°45W **160 E13**
Chesterton Ra.
  Australia 25°30S 147°27E **151 D4**
Chesterton Range △
  Australia 26°16S 147°22E **151 D4**
Chestertown U.S.A. 39°13N 76°4W **173 F14**
Chesterville Canada 45°6N 75°14W **175 A9**
Chesuncook L. U.S.A. 46°0N 69°21W **173 C19**
Chéticamp Canada 46°37N 60°59W **165 C7**
Chetlat I. India 11°42N 72°42E **127 J1**
Chetrosu Moldova 48°5N 27°54E **81 B12**
Chetumal Mexico 18°30N 88°20W **181 D7**
Chetumal, B. de
  Cent. Amer. 18°40N 88°10W **181 D7**
Chetwynd Canada 55°45N 121°36W **162 B4**
Cheung Chau China 22°13N 114°1E **111 a**
Chevanceaux France 45°18N 0°14W **72 C3**
Cheviot, The U.K. 55°29N 2°9W **66 B5**
Cheviot Hills U.K. 55°20N 2°30W **66 B5**
Cheviot Ra. Australia 25°20S 143°45E **150 D3**
Chew Bahir Ethiopia 4°40N 36°50E **135 G12**
Chewelah U.S.A. 48°17N 117°43W **168 B5**
Chewore △ Zimbabwe 16°0S 29°52E **143 F2**
Cheyenne Okla., U.S.A. 35°37N 99°40W **176 D5**
Cheyenne Wyo.,
  U.S.A. 41°8N 104°49W **168 F11**
Cheyenne → U.S.A. 44°41N 101°18W **172 C3**
Cheyenne Wells
  U.S.A. 38°49N 102°21W **168 G12**
Cheyne B. Australia 34°35S 118°50E **149 F2**
Cheyur India 12°21N 80°0E **127 H5**
Chhabra India 24°40N 76°54E **124 G7**
Chhaktala India 22°6N 74°11E **124 H6**
Chhapra India 25°48N 84°44E **125 G11**

Chhata India 27°42N 77°30E **124 F7**
Chhatarpur Jharkhand,
  India 24°23N 84°11E **125 G11**
Chhatarpur Mad. P.,
  India 24°55N 79°35E **125 G8**
Chhati Mozam. 20°47N 81°40E **126 D5**
Chhattisgarh □ India 22°0N 82°0E **125 J10**
Chhep Cambodia 13°45N 105°24E **120 F5**
Chhindwara Mad. P.,
  India 23°3N 79°29E **125 H8**
Chhindwara Mad. P.,
  India 22°2N 78°59E **125 H7**
Chhlong Cambodia 12°15N 105°58E **120 F5**
Chhota Tawa → India 22°14N 76°36E **124 H7**
Chhoti Kali Sindh →
  India 24°2N 75°31E **124 G6**
Chhuikhadan India 21°32N 81°22E **125 J9**
Chhuk Cambodia 10°46N 104°28E **121 G5**
Chi → Thailand 15°11N 104°43E **120 E5**
Chi Thanh Vietnam 13°45N 109°16E **120 F7**
Chiai Taiwan 23°29N 120°25E **117 F13**
Chiali Taiwan 23°9N 120°10E **117 F13**
Chianciano Terme Italy 43°2N 11°49E **93 E8**
Chiang Dao, Doi
  Thailand 19°23N 98°54E **120 C2**
Chiang Kham
  Thailand 19°32N 100°18E **120 C3**
Chiang Khan Thailand 17°52N 101°36E **120 D3**
Chiang Khong
  Thailand 20°17N 100°24E **116 G3**
Chiang Mai Thailand 18°47N 98°59E **120 C2**
Chiang Rai Thailand 19°52N 99°50E **116 G3**
Chiang Saen Thailand 20°16N 100°5E **116 G3**
Chianti Italy 43°32N 11°25E **93 E8**
Chiapa de Corzo Mexico 16°42N 93°0W **181 D6**
Chiapas □ Mexico 16°30N 92°30W **181 D6**
Chiapas, Sa. Madre de
  Mexico 15°40N 93°0W **181 D6**
Chiaramonte Gulfi Italy 37°2N 14°42E **95 E7**
Chiaravalle Italy 43°36N 13°19E **93 E10**
Chiaravalle Centrale
  Italy 38°41N 16°25E **95 D9**
Chiari Italy 45°32N 9°56E **92 C6**
Chiatura Georgia 42°15N 43°17E **87 A6**
Chiautla de Tapia
  Mexico 18°18N 98°36W **181 D5**
Chiávari Italy 44°19N 9°19E **92 D6**
Chiavenna Italy 46°19N 9°24E **92 B6**
Chiba Japan 35°30N 140°7E **113 G10**
Chiba □ Japan 35°30N 140°20E **113 G10**
Chibabava Mozam. 20°17S 33°35E **145 B5**
Chibemba Cunene, Angola 15°48S 14°8E **141 H2**
Chibemba Huila, Angola 16°20S 15°20E **144 A2**
Chibi Zimbabwe 20°18S 30°25E **145 B5**
Chibia Angola 15°10S 13°42E **141 H2**
Chibougamau Canada 49°56N 74°24W **164 C5**
Chibougamau, L.
  Canada 49°50N 74°20W **164 C5**
Chibuk Nigeria 10°52N 12°50E **139 C7**
Chibuto Mozam. 24°40S 33°33E **145 B5**
Chic-Chocs, Mts.
  Canada 48°55N 66°0W **165 C6**
Chicacole = Srikakulam
  India 18°14N 83°58E **126 E6**
Chicago U.S.A. 41°52N 87°38W **172 E10**
Chicago Heights
  U.S.A. 41°30N 87°38W **172 E10**
Chichagof I. U.S.A. 57°30N 135°30W **160 F4**
Chichaoua Morocco 31°32N 8°44W **136 B3**
Chichawatni Pakistan 30°32N 72°42E **124 D5**
Chichén-Itzá Mexico 20°40N 88°35W **181 C7**
Chicheng China 40°55N 115°55E **114 D8**
Chichester U.K. 50°50N 0°47W **67 G7**
Chichester Ra.
  Australia 22°12S 119°15E **148 D2**
Chichibu Japan 35°59N 139°10E **113 F9**
Chichibu-Tama-Kai △
  Japan 35°52N 138°42E **113 G9**
Ch'ich'ihaerh = Qiqihar
  China 47°26N 124°0E **111 B13**
Chicholi India 22°1N 77°40E **124 H8**
Chickasaw △ U.S.A. 34°26N 97°0W **176 D6**
Chickasha U.S.A. 35°3N 97°58W **176 D6**
Chiclana de la Frontera
  Spain 36°26N 6°9W **89 J4**
Chiclayo Peru 6°42S 79°50W **188 B2**
Chico U.S.A. 39°44N 121°50W **170 F5**
Chico → Chubut,
  Argentina 44°0S 67°0W **192 B3**
Chico → Santa Cruz,
  Argentina 50°0S 68°30W **192 D3**
Chicoa Mozam. 15°36S 32°20E **143 F3**
Chicomo Mozam. 24°31S 34°6E **145 B5**
Chicomostoc Mexico 22°28N 102°46W **180 C4**
Chicontepec Mexico 20°58N 98°10W **181 C5**
Chicopee U.S.A. 42°9N 72°37W **175 D12**
Chicoutimi Canada 48°28N 71°5W **165 C5**
Chicualacuala Mozam. 22°6S 31°42E **145 B5**
Chidambaram India 11°20N 79°45E **127 J4**
Chidenguele Mozam. 24°55S 34°11E **145 B5**
Chidley, C. Canada 60°23N 64°26W **161 E19**
Chiducuane Mozam. 24°35S 34°25E **145 B5**
Chiede Angola 17°15S 16°22E **144 A2**
Chiefland U.S.A. 29°29N 82°52W **179 F7**
Chiefs Pt. Canada 44°41N 81°18W **174 B3**
Chiem Hoa Vietnam 22°12N 105°17E **120 A5**
Chiemsee Germany 47°53N 12°28E **78 H8**
Chiengi Zambia 8°45S 29°10E **143 D2**
Chiengmai = Chiang Mai
  Thailand 18°47N 98°59E **120 C2**
Chienti → Italy 43°18N 13°45E **93 E10**
Chieri Italy 45°1N 7°49E **92 C4**
Chiers → France 49°39N 4°59E **71 C11**
Chiesa in Valmalenco
  Italy 46°16N 9°51E **92 B6**
Chiese → Italy 45°8N 10°25E **92 C7**
Chieti Italy 42°21N 14°10E **93 F11**
Chièvres Belgium 50°35N 3°48E **69 D3**
Chifeng China 42°18N 118°58E **115 C10**
Chigirin Ukraine 49°4N 32°38E **85 H7**
Chignecto B. Canada 45°30N 64°40W **165 C7**
Chiguana Bolivia 21°0S 67°58W **190 A2**
Chigwell U.K. 51°37N 0°6E **67 F8**
Chihli, G. of = Bo Hai
  China 39°0N 119°0E **115 E10**
Chihuahua Mexico 28°38N 106°5W **180 B3**
Chihuahua □ Mexico 28°30N 106°0W **180 B3**
Chiili = Shieli
  Kazakhstan 44°20N 66°15E **108 C7**
Chik Bollapur India 13°25N 77°45E **127 H3**

Chikalda India 21°24N 77°19E **12...**
Chikhli Ahmadabad, India 20°45N 73°4E **12...**
Chikhli Maharashtra,
  India 20°20N 76°18E **12...**
Chikmagalur India 13°15N 75°45E **12...**
Chiknayakanhalli
  India 13°26N 76°37E **12...**
Chikodi India 16°26N 74°38E **12...**
Chilanga Malawi 16°2S 34°50E **14...**
Chilanga Zambia 15°33S 28°16E **14...**
Chilapa Mexico 17°36N 99°10W **18...**
Chilas Pakistan 35°25N 74°5E **12...**
Chilaw Sri Lanka 7°30N 79°50E **12...**
Chilcotin → Canada 51°44N 122°23E **16...**
Childers Australia 25°15S 152°17E **15...**
Childersburg U.S.A. 33°16N 86°21W **17...**
Childress U.S.A. 34°25N 100°13W **17...**
Chile ■ S. Amer. 35°0S 72°0W **19...**
Chile Chico Chile 46°33S 71°44W **19...**
Chile Rise Pac. Oc. 38°0S 92°0W **15...**
Chilecito Argentina 29°10S 67°30W **19...**
Chilete Peru 7°10S 78°50W **18...**
Chilia, Braţul →
  Romania 45°14N 29°42E **8...**
Chilik → Kazakhstan 43°33N 78°17E **1...**
Chililabombwe Zambia 12°18S 27°43E **1...**
Chilim Pakistan 35°5N 75°5E **1...**
Chilin = Jilin China 43°44N 126°30E **1...**
Chiliomodi Greece 37°48N 22°51E **9...**
Chilka L. India 19°40N 85°25E **1...**
Chilko → Canada 52°0N 123°40W **1...**
Chilko L. Canada 51°20N 124°10W **1...**
Chillagoe Australia 17°7S 144°33E **1...**
Chillán Chile 36°40S 72°10W **1...**
Chillicothe Ill., U.S.A. 40°55N 89°29W **1...**
Chillicothe Mo., U.S.A. 39°48N 93°33W **1...**
Chillicothe Ohio,
  U.S.A. 39°20N 82°59W **1...**
Chilliwack Canada 49°10N 121°54W **1...**
Chilo India 27°25N 73°32E **1...**
Chiloane, I. Mozam. 20°40S 34°55E **1...**
Chiloé, I. de Chile 42°30S 73°50W **1...**
Chiloé △ Chile 42°11S 73°59N **1...**
Chilpancingo Mexico 17°33N 99°30W **1...**
Chiltern Australia 36°10S 146°36E **1...**
Chiltern Hills U.K. 51°40N 0°53W **6...**
Chilton U.S.A. 44°2N 88°10W **1...**
Chilubi Zambia 11°5S 29°58E **1...**
Chilubula Zambia 10°14S 30°51E **1...**
Chilumba Malawi 10°28S 34°12E **1...**
Chilung Taiwan 25°3N 121°45E **1...**
Chilwa, L. Malawi 15°15S 35°40E **1...**
Chimaltitán Mexico 21°35N 103°50W **1...**
Chimán Panama 8°45N 78°40W **1...**
Chimanimani Zimbabwe 19°48S 32°52E **1...**
Chimanimani △
  Zimbabwe 19°48S 33°0E **1...**
Chimay Belgium 50°3N 4°20E **6...**
Chimayo U.S.A. 36°0N 105°56W **1...**
Chimba Zambia 9°54S 31°28E **1...**
Chimborazo Ecuador 1°29S 78°55W **1...**
Chimbote Peru 9°0S 78°35W **1...**
Chimboy Uzbekistan 42°57N 59°47E **1...**
Chimkent = Shymkent
  Kazakhstan 42°18N 69°36E **1...**
Chimoio Mozam. 19°4S 33°30E **1...**
Chimpembe Zambia 9°31S 29°33E **1...**
Chimur India 20°30N 79°23E **1...**
Chin □ Burma 22°0N 93°0E **1...**
Chin Hills Burma 22°30N 93°30E **1...**
Chin Ling Shan = Qinling Shandi
  China 33°50N 108°10E **1...**
China Mexico 25°42N 99°14W **1...**
China ■ Asia 30°0N 110°0E **1...**
China, Great Plain of
  Asia 35°0N 115°0E **1...**
China Lake U.S.A. 35°44N 117°37W **1...**
Chinan = Jinan China 36°38N 117°1E **1...**
Chinandega Nic. 12°35N 87°12W **1...**
Chinati Peak U.S.A. 29°57N 104°29W **1...**
Chincha Alta Peru 13°25S 76°7W **1...**
Chinchaga → Canada 58°53N 118°20W **1...**
Chincheros Peru 13°30S 73°44W **1...**
Chinchilla Australia 26°45S 150°38E **1...**
Chinchilla de Monte Aragón
  Spain 38°53N 1°40W **9...**
Chincholi India 17°28N 77°26E **1...**
Chinchorro, Banco
  Mexico 18°35N 87°22W **1...**
Chinchou = Jinzhou
  China 41°5N 121°3E **1...**
Chincoteague U.S.A. 37°56N 75°23W **1...**
Chinde Mozam. 18°35S 36°30E **1...**
Chindwin → Burma 21°26N 95°15E **1...**
Chineni India 33°2N 75°15E **1...**
Chinga Mozam. 15°13S 38°35E **1...**
Chingola Zambia 12°31S 27°53E **1...**
Chingole Malawi 13°4S 34°17E **1...**
Ch'ingtao = Qingdao
  China 36°5N 120°20E **1...**
Chinguetti Mauritania 20°25N 12°24W **1...**
Chingune Mozam. 20°33S 34°58E **1...**
Chinhanguanine
  Mozam. 25°21S 32°30E **1...**
Chinhoyi Zimbabwe 17°20S 30°8E **1...**
Chiniot Pakistan 31°45N 73°0E **1...**
Chinipas Mexico 27°23N 108°32W **1...**
Chinji Pakistan 32°42N 72°22E **1...**
Chinju = Jinju
  S. Korea 35°12N 128°2E **1...**
Chinkapook Australia 35°11S 142°57E **1...**
Chinko → C.A.R. 4°50N 23°53E **1...**
Chinle U.S.A. 36°9N 109°33W **1...**
Chinmen Taiwan 24°26N 118°19E **1...**
Chinmen Tao Taiwan 24°26N 118°12E **1...**
Chinnampo = Namp'o
  N. Korea 38°52N 125°10E **1...**
Chino Japan 35°59N 138°9E **1...**
Chino U.S.A. 33°59N 117°41W **1...**
Chino Valley U.S.A. 34°45N 112°27W **1...**
Chinook U.S.A. 48°35N 109°14W **1...**
Chinook Trough
  Pac. Oc. 44°0N 175°0W **15...**
Chinsali Zambia 10°30S 32°2E **1...**
Chinsura = Chunchura
  India 22°53N 88°27E **12...**
Chintalapudi India 17°4N 80°59E **12...**
Chintamani India 13°26N 78°3E **12...**

ióggia Italy 45°13N 12°17E 93 C9
ios Greece 38°27N 26°9E 99 C8
ipata Zambia 13°38S 32°28E 143 E3
ipercaeni Moldova 47°31N 28°50E 81 C13
ipindo Angola 13°49S 15°48E 141 G3
ipinge Zimbabwe 20°13S 32°28E 143 G3
ipinge ⌖ Zimbabwe 20°14S 33°0E 143 G3
ipiona Spain 36°44N 6°26W 89 J4
ipley U.S.A. 30°47N 85°32W 178 E4
iplun India 17°31N 73°34E 126 F1
ipman Canada 46°6N 65°53W 165 C6
ipoka Malawi 13°57S 34°28E 143 E3
ippenham U.K. 51°27N 2°6W 67 F5
ippewa → U.S.A. 44°25N 92°5W 172 C7
ippewa Falls U.S.A. 44°56N 91°24W 172 C8
ipping Norton U.K. 51°56N 1°32W 67 F6
iprovtsi Bulgaria 43°24N 22°52E 96 C6
iputneticook Lakes
N. Amer. 45°35N 67°35W 173 C20
iquián Peru 10°10S 77°0W 188 C2
iquibul ⌖ Belize 16°49N 88°52W 182 C2
iquimula Guatemala 14°51N 89°37W 182 D2
iquinquira Colombia 5°37N 73°50W 186 B4
ir → Russia 48°30N 43°0E 87 F6
irala India 15°50N 80°26E 127 G5
iramba Mozam. 16°55S 34°39E 143 F3
irawa India 28°14N 75°42E 124 E6
rchiq Uzbekistan 41°29N 69°35E 109 D7
redzi Zimbabwe 21°0S 31°38E 143 H5
iricahua ⌂ U.S.A. 32°0N 109°20W 169 K9
iricahua Peak
U.S.A. 31°51N 109°18W 169 L9
irikof I. U.S.A. 55°50N 155°40W 166 D8
riquí, G. de Panama 8°0N 82°10W 182 E3
riquí, L. de Panama 9°10N 82°0W 182 E3
irisa ⌖ Japan 17°53S 28°15E 143 F2
imbabwe 21°10S 32°12E 143 G3
rmri India 23°15N 82°20E 125 H10
rnogi Romania 44°7N 26°32E 81 F11
rpan Bulgaria 42°10N 25°19E 97 D9
rripó Grande, Cerro
Costa Rica 9°29N 83°29W 182 E3
rundu Zimbabwe 16°3S 28°50E 145 A4
isamba Zambia 14°55S 28°20E 143 E2
sapani Nepal 28°37N 81°16E 125 E9
sasibi Canada 53°50N 79°0W 164 B4
ishan Taiwan 22°44N 120°31E 117 F13
isholm Canada 54°55N 114°10W 162 C6
isholm U.S.A. 47°29N 92°53W 172 B7
ishtian Mandi
akistan 29°50N 72°55E 124 E5
shui China 28°30N 105°42E 116 C5
shui He → China 28°49N 105°50E 116 C5
simaio = Kismaayo
omalia 0°22S 42°32E 131 H3
simba Falls Zambia 10°12S 30°56E 143 E3
şinău Moldova 47°2N 28°50E 81 C13
şinău ✈ (KIV)
Moldova 47°3N 28°46E 81 C13
sineu Criş Romania 46°32N 22°27E 80 D6
sone → Italy 44°49N 7°25E 92 D4
sos Mts. U.S.A. 29°5N 103°15W 176 G3
stopol Russia 55°25N 50°38E 86 C10
a Russia 52°0N 113°35E 111 A11
apur India 17°10N 77°5E 126 C3
ipa Malawi 9°41S 33°19E 143 D3
oso Japan 42°49N 141°39E 112 C10
radurga India 14°14N 76°24E 127 E3
rakot India 19°10N 81°40E 126 E5
ral Pakistan 35°50N 71°56E 122 B7
ravati → India 14°45N 78°15E 127 G4
rata Pakistan 7°59N 80°27W 182 E3
tagong Bangla. 22°19N 91°48E 123 H17
tagong □ Bangla. 24°5N 91°0E 123 G17
taurgarh India 20°44N 74°38E 124 G6
toor India 13°15N 79°5E 127 H4
tur India 10°40N 76°45E 127 J3
ungwiza Zimbabwe 18°0S 31°6E 143 F3
asi Italy 43°1N 11°57E 93 E8
a Spain 39°27N 0°41W 91 F4
asso Italy 45°11N 7°53E 92 C4
ay Peru 15°40S 71°30W 188 D3
e Bolivia 12°23S 68°35W 188 C4
hu Zimbabwe 19°2S 30°52E 143 F3
ilcoy Argentina 34°55S 60°0W 190 C4
vanda Tanzania 11°23S 34°55E 143 E3
i China 22°0N 112°58E 117 G9
arira Zimbabwe 17°36S 27°45E 143 F2
arira ⌖ Zimbabwe 17°44S 27°12E 143 F2
ela Zambia 13°8S 25°0E 143 E2
lov = Orenburg
ssia 51°45N 55°6E 108 B5
lovsk Russia 56°50N 43°10E 86 B6
mec nad Cidlinou
ch Rep. 50°9N 15°29E 78 A4
ielnik Poland 52°20N 20°43E 83 E9
lo N. Korea 38°30N 124°40E 115 E13
Phuoc Hai
tnam 10°26N 107°18E 121 G6
Chu Kang
gapore 1°22N 103°41E 121 d
e △ Botswana 18°37S 24°23E 144 A4
iánow Poland 51°27N 15°55E 82 E2
iwel Poland 53°29N 15°21E 82 E2
olate Mts.
S.A. 33°15N 115°15W 171 M11
awhatchee →
.A. 30°25N 86°8W 178 E3
awhatchee B.
.A. 30°20N 86°20W 179 E3
varam Andhra Pradesh,
va 16°2N 80°42E 127 F5
varam Andhra Pradesh,
va 17°27N 81°46E 126 F5
ecz Poland 52°24N 19°2E 83 F6
w Czech Rep. 50°15N 12°48E 78 A5
ziez Poland 52°58N 16°58E 83 F3
e Choel Argentina 39°11S 65°40W 192 A3
hã Zandi Iran 31°21N 48°32E 129 C6
eul St. Lucia 13°47N 61°3W 183 f
eul Solomon Is. 7°0S 156°40E 147 B8
: Mexico 26°43N 108°17W 180 B3
ice Poland 52°58N 14°25E 82 F1
ow Poland 53°42N 17°32E 82 E4
Chai Thailand 14°44N 102°10E 120 E4
Canyon Res.
.A. 28°30N 98°20W 176 G5

Chokurdakh Russia 70°38N 147°55E 107 B15
Chokwé Mozam. 24°32S 32°59E 145 C5
Cholame U.S.A. 35°44N 120°18W 170 K6
Cholet France 47°4N 0°52W 70 E6
Cholguan Chile 37°10S 72°3W 190 D1
Choma Zambia 16°48S 26°59E 143 F2
Chomun India 27°15N 75°40E 124 F6
Chomutov Czech Rep. 50°28N 13°23E 78 A6
Chon Buri Thailand 13°21N 101°1E 120 F3
Chon Thanh Vietnam 11°24N 106°36E 121 G6
Chone Ecuador 0°40S 80°0W 186 D3
Chong Kai Cambodia 13°57N 103°35E 120 F4
Chong Mek Thailand 15°10N 105°27E 120 E5
Chong Phangan Thailand 9°39N 100°0E 121 b
Chong Samui Thailand 9°21N 99°50E 121 b
Chongde China 30°32N 120°26E 117 B13
Ch'ŏngjin N. Korea 41°47N 129°50E 115 D15
Chŏngju N. Korea 39°40N 125°5E 115 E13
Chongli China 40°58N 115°15E 114 D8
Chongming China 31°38N 121°23E 117 B13
Chongming Dao
China 31°40N 121°30E 117 B13
Chongori Rock Art
Malawi 14°17S 34°16E 143 E3
Chongoyape Peru 6°35S 79°25W 188 B2
Chŏngp'yŏng
N. Korea 39°47N 127°23E 115 E14
Chongqing Chongqing,
China 29°35N 106°25E 116 C6
Chongqing Sichuan,
China 30°38N 103°40E 116 B4
Chongren China 27°46N 116°3E 117 D11
Chongwe Mozam. 25°3S 33°49E 145 C5
Chongyang Zambia 15°4S 28°42E 143 F2
Chongyi China 25°45N 114°29E 117 E10
Chongzuo China 22°23N 107°20E 116 C6
Chonogol Mongolia 45°54N 115°22E 114 B8
Chonos, Arch. de los
Chile 45°0S 75°0W 192 C2
Chop Ukraine 48°26N 22°12E 80 B7
Chopda India 21°20N 75°15E 126 D2
Chopim → Brazil 25°35S 53°5W 191 B5
Chor Pakistan 25°31N 69°46E 124 G3
Chora Greece 37°3N 21°42E 98 D3
Chora Sfakion Greece 35°15N 24°9E 101 D6
Chorbat La India 34°42N 76°37E 125 B7
Chorley U.K. 53°39N 2°38W 66 D5
Chorna Ukraine 47°36N 29°20E 81 C14
Chornobyl Ukraine 51°20N 30°15E 75 C16
Chornomorske Ukraine 45°31N 32°40E 85 K7
Chorolque, Cerro
Bolivia 20°59S 66°5W 190 A2
Choroszcz Poland 53°10N 22°59E 83 E9
Chorregon Australia 22°40S 143°32E 150 C3
Chorro el Indio ⌂
Venezuela 7°43N 72°9W 183 E5
Chortkiv Ukraine 49°2N 25°46E 75 D13
Chorzele Poland 53°15N 20°55E 83 E7
Chorzów Poland 50°18N 18°57E 83 H5
Chos-Malal Argentina 37°20S 70°15W 190 D1
Ch'osan N. Korea 40°50N 125°47E 115 D13
Choszczno Poland 53°7N 15°25E 82 E2
Chota Peru 6°33S 78°39W 188 B2
Choteau U.S.A. 47°49N 112°11W 168 C7
Chotěboř Czech Rep. 49°43N 15°40E 78 B8
Chotila India 22°23N 71°15E 124 H4
Chotta Udepur India 22°19N 74°1E 124 H6
Chowchilla U.S.A. 37°7N 120°16W 170 H6
Choybalsan Mongolia 48°4N 114°30E 111 B11
Choyr Mongolia 46°24N 108°30E 111 B10
Chrisoupoli Greece 40°59N 24°42E 97 F8
Christchurch N.Z. 43°33S 172°47E 155 D7
Christchurch U.K. 50°44N 1°47W 67 G6
Christian I. Canada 44°50N 80°12W 174 B4
Christian Sd. U.S.A. 55°56N 134°40W 167 D13
Christiana Greece 36°14N 25°13E 99 E7
Christiana S. Africa 27°52S 25°8E 144 C4
Christiansfeld Denmark 55°21N 9°29E 63 F3
Christianshåb = Qasigiannguit
Greenland 68°50N 51°18W 57 D5
Christiansted
U.S. Virgin Is. 17°45N 64°42W 183 C7
Christie B. Canada 62°32N 111°10W 163 A6
Christina → Canada 56°40N 111°3W 163 B6
Christmas Cr. →
Australia 18°29S 125°23E 148 C4
Christmas I. = Kiritimati
Kiribati 1°58N 157°27W 157 G12
Christmas I. Ind. Oc. 10°30S 105°40E 146 F9
Christopher, L.
Australia 24°49S 127°42E 149 D4
Chrudim Czech Rep. 49°58N 15°43E 78 B8
Chrzanów Poland 50°10N 19°21E 83 H6
Chtapodia Greece 37°24N 25°54E 99 D7
Chtimba Malawi 10°35S 34°13E 143 E3
Chū = Shū →
Kazakhstan 45°0N 67°44E 109 D7
Chū = Shū →
Kazakhstan 45°0N 67°44E 109 D7
Chu → Vietnam 19°53N 105°45E 120 C5
Chu Lai Vietnam 15°28N 108°45E 120 E7
Chu Mom Ray △
Vietnam 14°29N 107°38E 120 E6
Chu Se Vietnam 13°40N 108°8E 120 E7
Chuadanga Bangla. 23°38N 88°51E 125 H13
Chuak, Ko Thailand 9°49N 99°41E 121 b
Ch'uanchou = Quanzhou
China 24°55N 118°34E 117 E12
Chuankou China 34°20N 110°59E 116 G6
Chubbuck U.S.A. 42°55N 112°28W 168 E7
Chūbu □ Japan 36°45N 137°30E 113 F8
Chūbu-Sangaku △
Japan 36°30N 137°40E 113 F8
Chubut □ Argentina 43°30S 69°0W 192 B3
Chubut → Argentina 43°20S 65°5W 192 B3
Chuchi L. Canada 55°12N 124°30W 162 B4
Chuda India 22°29N 71°41E 124 H4
Chudovo Russia 59°10N 31°41E 84 C6
Chudskoye, Ozero
Russia 58°13N 27°30E 84 C4
Chugach Mts. U.S.A. 60°45N 147°0W 166 C10
Chūgoku □ Japan 35°0N 133°0E 113 G6
Chūgoku-Sanchi Japan 35°0N 133°0E 113 G6

Chuguyev = Chuhuyiv
Ukraine 49°55N 36°45E 85 H9
Chugwater U.S.A. 41°46N 104°50W 168 F11
Chuhuyiv Ukraine 49°55N 36°45E 85 H9
Chuka Kenya 0°20S 37°39E 142 C4
Chukchi Plateau Arctic 78°0N 165°0W 54 B17
Chukchi Sea Russia 68°0N 175°0W 107 C19
Chukotskiy Mys
Russia 64°14N 173°9W 166 C5
Chukotskiy Poluostrov
Russia 66°0N 174°0W 166 B5
Chukotskoye Nagorye
Russia 68°0N 175°0E 107 C18
Chula U.S.A. 31°33N 83°32W 178 D6
Chula Vista U.S.A. 32°38N 117°5W 171 N9
Chulband → India 20°40N 79°54E 126 D4
Chulucanas Peru 5°8S 80°10W 188 B1
Chulumani Bolivia 16°24S 67°31W 188 D4
Chulym → Russia 57°43N 83°51E 106 D9
Chum Phae Thailand 16°40N 102°6E 120 D4
Chum Saeng Thailand 15°55N 100°15E 120 E3
Chuma Bolivia 15°24S 68°56W 188 D4
Chumar India 32°40N 78°35E 125 C8
Chumbicha Argentina 29°0S 66°10W 190 B2
Chumerna Bulgaria 42°45N 25°55E 97 D9
Chumikan Russia 54°40N 135°10E 107 D14
Chumphon Thailand 10°35N 99°14E 121 G2
Chumpi Peru 15°4S 73°46W 188 D3
Chumuare Mozam. 14°31S 31°50E 143 E3
Chuna → Russia 57°47N 94°37E 107 D10
Chun'an China 29°35N 119°3E 117 C12
Chuncheon S. Korea 37°58N 127°44E 115 F14
Chunchura India 22°53N 88°27E 125 H13
Chunga Zambia 15°0S 26°2E 143 F2
Chunggang-ŭp
N. Korea 41°48N 126°48E 115 D14
Chunghwa N. Korea 38°52N 125°47E 115 E13
Chungju S. Korea 36°58N 127°58E 115 F14
Chungking = Chongqing
China 29°35N 106°25E 116 C6
Chungli Taiwan 24°57N 121°13E 117 E13
Chungt'iaoshan = Zhongtiao
Shan China 35°0N 111°10E 114 G6
Chungyang Shanmo
Taiwan 23°10N 121°0E 117 F13
Chunian Pakistan 30°57N 74°0E 124 D6
Chunya Tanzania 8°30S 33°27E 143 D3
Chunyang China 43°38N 129°23E 115 C15
Chupara Pt.
Trin. & Tob. 10°49N 61°22W 187 K15
Chuquibamba Peru 15°47S 72°44W 188 D3
Chuquibambilla Peru 14°7S 72°41W 188 C3
Chuquicamata Chile 22°15S 69°0W 190 A2
Chur Switz. 46°52N 9°32E 77 J5
Churachandpur India 24°20N 93°40E 123 G18
Church Stretton U.K. 52°32N 2°48W 67 E5
Churchill Australia 38°19S 146°25E 153 E7
Churchill Canada 58°47N 94°11W 163 B10
Churchill → Man.,
Canada 58°47N 94°12W 163 B10
Churchill → Nfld. & L.,
Canada 53°19N 60°10W 165 B7
Churchill, C. Canada 58°46N 93°12W 163 B10
Churchill Falls Canada 53°36N 64°19W 165 B7
Churchill L. Canada 55°55N 108°20W 163 B7
Churchill Pk. Canada 58°10N 125°10W 162 B3
Churki India 23°50N 83°12E 125 H10
Churu India 28°20N 74°50E 124 E6
Churún Merú = Angel Falls
Venezuela 5°57N 62°30W 186 B6
Chushal India 33°40N 78°40E 125 C8
Chuska Mts. U.S.A. 36°15N 108°50W 169 H9
Chusovoy Russia 58°22N 57°50E 106 D6
Chuspipata Bolivia 16°18S 67°48W 188 D4
Chust Uzbekistan 41°0N 71°13E 109 D8
Chute-aux-Outardes
Canada 49°7N 68°24W 165 C6
Chuuk = Truk
Micronesia 7°25N 151°46E 156 G7
Chuvash Republic = Chuvashia □
Russia 55°30N 47°0E 86 C8
Chuvashia □ Russia 55°30N 47°0E 86 C8
Chuwārtah Iraq 35°43N 45°34E 105 E11
Chuxiong China 25°2N 101°28E 116 E3
Chüy □ Kyrgyzstan 42°55N 75°15E 109 D9
Chüy Uruguay 33°41S 53°27W 191 C5
Chüy □ Kyrgyzstan 42°25N 75°16E 109 D9
Chuzhou China 32°29N 118°42E 117 A12
Chynadiyeve Ukraine 48°29N 22°50E 80 B7
Ci Xian China 36°20N 114°25E 114 F8
Ciacova Romania 45°35N 21°10E 80 E6
Ciadâr-Lunga Moldova 46°3N 28°51E 81 D13
Ciamis Indonesia 7°20S 108°21E 119 G13
Cianjur Indonesia 6°49S 107°8E 119 G12
Cianorte Brazil 23°37S 52°37W 191 A5
Cibola U.S.A. 33°17N 114°42W 171 M12
Çiçekdağı Turkey 39°36N 34°24E 104 C6
Cicero U.S.A. 41°51N 87°44W 172 E10
Cicero Dantas Brazil 10°36S 38°23W 189 C3
Cicia Fiji 17°45S 179°18W 154 a
Cidacos → Spain 42°21N 1°38W 90 C3
Cide Turkey 41°53N 33°1E 104 B5
Ciéagas del Catatumbo △
Venezuela 9°25N 71°54W 183 E5
Ciechanów Poland 52°52N 20°38E 83 F7
Ciechanowiec Poland 52°40N 22°31E 83 F9
Ciechocinek Poland 52°53N 18°45E 83 F5
Ciego de Ávila Cuba 21°50N 78°50W 182 B4
Ciénaga Colombia 11°1N 74°15W 186 A4
Cienfuegos Cuba 22°10N 80°30W 182 B3
Cierp-Gaud France 42°55N 0°40E 72 F4
Cies, Is. Spain 42°12N 8°55W 88 C2
Cieszanów Poland 50°14N 23°8E 83 H10
Cieszyn Poland 49°45N 18°35E 83 J5
Cieza Spain 38°17N 1°23W 91 G3
Çifteler Turkey 39°22N 31°2E 104 C4
Cifuentes Spain 40°47N 2°37W 90 E2
Cihanbeyli Turkey 38°40N 32°55E 104 C5
Cihuatlán Mexico 19°14N 104°35W 180 D4
Cijara, Embalse de Spain 39°18N 4°52W 89 C5
Cijara → Spain 39°18N 4°35W 89 F6
Cijulang Indonesia 7°42S 108°27E 119 G13
Cilacap Indonesia 7°43S 109°0E 119 G13
Çıldır Turkey 41°7N 43°8E 105 B10
Çıldır Gölü Turkey 41°15N 43°15E 105 B10
Cili China 29°30N 111°8E 117 C8
Cilibia Romania 45°4N 27°4E 81 E12
Cilicia Turkey 36°30N 35°0E 104 D5

Cill Airne = Killarney
Ireland 52°4N 9°30W 64 D2
Cill Chainnigh = Kilkenny
Ireland 52°39N 7°15W 64 D4
Cill Dara = Kildare Ireland 53°9N 6°55W 64 C5
Cill Droichid = Celbridge
Ireland 53°20N 6°32W 64 C5
Cill Mhantáin = Wicklow
Ireland 52°59N 6°3W 64 D5
Çilo Dağı Turkey 37°28N 43°55E 105 D10
Cima U.S.A. 35°14N 115°30W 171 K11
Cimarron Kans.,
U.S.A. 37°48N 100°21W 172 G3
Cimarron N. Mex.,
U.S.A. 36°31N 104°55W 169 H11
Cimarron → U.S.A. 36°10N 96°17W 172 G6
Cimişlia Moldova 46°34N 28°44E 81 D13
Cimone, Mte. Italy 44°12N 10°42E 92 D7
Çınar Turkey 37°46N 40°19E 105 D9
Cinca → Spain 41°26N 0°21E 90 D5
Cincar Bos.-H. 43°55N 17°5E 80 G2
Cincinnati U.S.A. 39°9N 84°27W 173 F11
Cincinnatus U.S.A. 42°33N 75°54W 175 D9
Çine Turkey 37°37N 28°2E 99 D10
Ciney Belgium 50°18N 5°5E 68 D5
Cíngoli Italy 43°23N 13°10E 93 E10
Cinigiano Italy 42°53N 11°24E 93 F8
Cinque I. India 11°16N 92°42E 127 J11
Cinque Terre ✠ Italy 44°8N 9°54E 73 F12
Cinto, Mte. France 42°24N 8°54E 73 F12
Cintruénigo Spain 42°5N 1°49W 90 C3
Ciocile Romania 44°49N 27°14E 81 F12
Ciolăneşti din Deal
Romania 44°19N 25°5E 81 F10
Ciorani Romania 44°45N 26°25E 81 F11
Ciovo Croatia 43°30N 16°17E 93 E13
Cipó Brazil 11°6S 38°31W 189 C3
Cipolletti Argentina 38°56S 67°59W 192 A3
Circeo, Mte. Italy 41°14N 13°3E 94 A6
Çırçır Turkey 40°3N 36°47E 104 C7
Circle Alaska, U.S.A. 65°50N 144°4W 166 B11
Circle Mont., U.S.A. 47°25N 105°35W 168 C11
Circleville U.S.A. 39°36N 82°57W 173 F12
Cirebon Indonesia 6°45S 108°32E 118 F3
Cirencester U.K. 51°43N 1°57W 67 F6
Cireşu Romania 44°47N 22°31E 80 F7
Cirey-sur-Vezouze
France 48°35N 6°57E 71 D13
Ciríe Italy 45°14N 7°36E 92 C4
Círium Cyprus 34°40N 32°53E 101 E11
Ciró Italy 39°23N 17°3E 95 C10
Ciró Marina Italy 39°22N 17°8E 95 C10
Ciron → France 44°36N 0°18W 72 D3
Cirebon = Cireşu 32°23N 98°59W 176 E5
Ciscoa U.S.A. 47°10N 105°35W 168 C11
Cislău Romania 45°14N 26°20E 81 E11
Cisna Poland 49°12N 22°20E 83 J9
Cisnădie Romania 45°42N 24°9E 81 E9
Cisterna di Latina Italy 41°35N 12°49E 94 A5
Cisternino Italy 40°44N 17°26E 95 B10
Cistierna Spain 42°48N 5°7W 88 C5
Citeli-Ckaro = Dedoplis Tsqaro
Georgia 41°33N 46°0E 87 K8
Citlaltépetl = Orizaba, Pico de
Mexico 18°58N 97°15W 181 D5
Citra U.S.A. 29°25N 82°7W 179 F7
Citrus Heights U.S.A. 38°42N 121°17W 170 G5
Citrus Springs U.S.A. 29°2N 82°27W 179 F7
Città del Vaticano = Vatican
City ■ Europe 41°54N 12°27E 93 G9
Città della Pieve Italy 42°57N 12°1E 93 F9
Città di Castello Italy 43°27N 12°14E 93 E9
Città Sant' Angelo Italy 42°32N 14°5E 93 F11
Cittadella Italy 45°39N 11°47E 93 C8
Cittaducale Italy 42°23N 12°57E 93 F9
Cittanova Italy 38°21N 16°5E 95 D9
Ciuc, Munţii Romania 46°35N 26°5E 81 D11
Ciucaş, Vf. Romania 45°31N 25°56E 81 E11
Ciucea Romania 46°57N 22°49E 80 D7
Ciuciulea Moldova 47°40N 27°29E 81 C12
Ciuciuleni Moldova 47°2N 28°25E 81 C13
Ciudad Acuña Mexico 29°18N 100°55W 180 B4
Ciudad Altamirano
Mexico 18°20N 100°40W 180 D4
Ciudad Anáhuac
Mexico 27°14N 100°7W 180 B4
Ciudad Bolívar Venezuela 8°5N 63°36W 186 B6
Ciudad Camargo
Mexico 27°40N 105°10W 180 B3
Ciudad Cortés Costa Rica 8°55N 84°0W 182 E3
Ciudad de México
Mexico 19°24N 99°9W 181 D5
Ciudad del Carmen
Mexico 18°38N 91°50W 181 D6
Ciudad del Este
Paraguay 25°30S 54°50W 191 B5
Ciudad Delicias = Delicias
Mexico 28°13N 105°28W 180 B3
Ciudad Frontera
Mexico 26°56N 101°27W 180 B4
Ciudad Guayana
Venezuela 8°0N 62°30W 186 B6
Ciudad Guerrero
Mexico 28°33N 107°30W 180 B3
Ciudad Guzmán
Mexico 19°41N 103°29W 180 D4
Ciudad Juárez Mexico 31°44N 106°29W 180 A3
Ciudad Lerdo Mexico 25°32N 103°32W 180 B4
Ciudad Madero Mexico 22°19N 97°50W 181 C5
Ciudad Mante Mexico 22°44N 98°59W 181 C5
Ciudad Obregón
Mexico 27°29N 109°56W 180 B3
Ciudad Real Spain 38°59N 3°55W 89 G7
Ciudad Real □ Spain 38°59N 3°55W 89 G7
Ciudad Rodrigo Spain 40°35N 6°32W 88 E4
Ciudad Valles Mexico 21°59N 99°1W 181 C5
Ciudad Victoria Mexico 23°44N 99°8W 181 C5
Ciulniţa Romania 44°26N 27°22E 81 F12
Ciumeghiu Romania 46°44N 21°35E 80 D6
Ciuperceni Romania 44°54N 23°48E 80 F8
Civa Burnu Turkey 41°21N 36°38E 104 B7
Cividale del Friuli Italy 46°6N 13°25E 93 C10
Civita Castellana Italy 42°17N 12°24E 93 F9
Civitanova Marche
Italy 43°18N 13°44E 93 E10
Civitavécchia Italy 42°6N 11°48E 93 F8
Civray France 46°10N 0°17E 72 B4
Çivril Turkey 38°20N 29°43E 99 C11
Cixerri → Italy 39°17N 8°59E 94 C1

Cixi China 30°17N 121°9E 117 B13
Cizre Turkey 37°19N 42°10E 105 D10
Clackmannanshire □
U.K. 56°10N 3°43W 65 E5
Clacton-on-Sea U.K. 51°47N 1°11E 67 F9
Claire → France 46°47N 0°33E 70 F7
Claire, L. Canada 58°35N 112°5W 162 B6
Clairton U.S.A. 40°18N 79°53W 174 F5
Clairvaux-les-Lacs
France 46°35N 5°45E 71 F12
Claise → France 46°56N 0°42E 72 B5
Clallam Bay U.S.A. 48°15N 124°16W 170 B2
Clamecy France 47°28N 3°30E 71 E10
Clanton U.S.A. 32°51N 86°38W 178 E2
Clanwilliam S. Africa 32°11S 18°52E 144 C2
Clara → France 53°21N 7°37W 64 C4
Clare Australia 33°50S 138°37E 152 B3
Clare U.S.A. 43°49N 84°46W 173 D11
Clare □ Ireland 52°45N 9°0W 64 D3
Clare → Ireland 53°20N 9°2W 64 C2
Clare I. Ireland 53°47N 10°0W 64 C1
Claremont Calif., U.S.A. 34°6N 117°43W 171 L9
Claremont N.H.,
U.S.A. 43°23N 72°20W 175 C12
Claremont Pt. Australia 14°1S 143°41E 150 A3
Claremore U.S.A. 36°19N 95°36W 176 C7
Claremorris Ireland 53°45N 9°0W 64 C3
Clarence → Australia 29°25S 153°22E 151 D5
Clarence → N.Z. 42°10S 173°56E 155 D5
Clarence, I. Chile 54°0S 72°0W 192 D2
Clarence I. Antarctica 61°10S 54°0W 55 C18
Clarence Str. Australia 12°0S 131°0E 148 B5
Clarence Town
Bahamas 23°6N 74°59W 183 B5
Clarendon Pa., U.S.A. 41°47N 79°6W 174 E5
Clarendon Tex.,
U.S.A. 34°56N 100°53W 176 D4
Clarenville Canada 48°10N 54°1W 165 C9
Claresholm Canada 50°2N 113°33W 162 D6
Clarie Coast Antarctica 68°0S 135°0E 55 C9
Clarinda U.S.A. 40°44N 95°2W 172 E6
Clarington Canada 43°55N 78°41W 174 C6
Clarion Iowa, U.S.A. 42°44N 93°44W 172 D7
Clarion Pa., U.S.A. 41°13N 79°23W 174 E5
Clarion → U.S.A. 41°7N 79°41W 174 E5
Clarion Fracture Zone
Pac. Oc. 20°0N 120°0W 158 H7
Clarion Fracture Zone
Pac. Oc. 19°0N 120°0W 157 G16
Clark, Pt. Canada 44°4N 81°45W 174 B3
Clark Fork U.S.A. 48°9N 116°11W 168 B5
Clark Fork → U.S.A. 48°9N 116°15W 168 B5
Clarkdale U.S.A. 34°46N 112°3W 169 J7
Clark City Canada 50°12N 66°38W 165 B6
Clarke I. Australia 40°32S 148°10E 151 G4
Clarke Ra. Australia 20°40S 148°30E 150 b
Clarks Fork Yellowstone →
U.S.A. 45°32N 108°50W 168 D9
Clark's Harbour
Canada 43°25N 65°38W 165 D6
Clarks Hill L. = J. Strom
Thurmond L. U.S.A. 33°40N 82°12W 178 B7
Clarks Summit U.S.A. 41°30N 75°42W 175 E9
Clarksburg U.S.A. 39°17N 80°30W 173 F13
Clarksdale U.S.A. 34°12N 90°35W 179 D9
Clarkston U.S.A. 46°25N 117°3W 168 C5
Clarksville Ark., U.S.A. 35°28N 93°28W 176 D8
Clarksville Tenn.,
U.S.A. 36°32N 87°21W 177 C11
Clarksville Tex., U.S.A. 33°37N 95°3W 176 E7
Clatskanie U.S.A. 46°6N 123°12W 170 D3
Claude U.S.A. 35°7N 101°22W 176 D4
Clavering Ø Greenland 74°15N 21°0W 57 C8
Claxton U.S.A. 32°10N 81°55W 179 D8
Clay U.S.A. 38°17N 121°10W 170 G5
Clay Center U.S.A. 39°23N 97°8W 172 F5
Claypool U.S.A. 33°25N 110°51W 169 K8
Claysburg U.S.A. 40°17N 78°27W 174 F6
Claysville U.S.A. 40°7N 80°25W 174 F4
Clayton Canada 45°11N 76°19W 175 A8
Clayton Ala., U.S.A. 31°53N 85°27W 178 F3
Clayton N. Mex.,
U.S.A. 36°27N 103°11W 169 H12
Clayton N.Y., U.S.A. 44°14N 76°5W 175 B8
Clear, C. Ireland 51°25N 9°32W 64 E2
Clear Hills Canada 56°40N 119°30W 162 B5
Clear L. U.S.A. 41°56N 122°6W 168 F2
Clear L. Ireland 51°26N 9°30W 64 E2
Clear Lake Iowa, U.S.A. 43°8N 93°23W 172 D7
Clear Lake S. Dak.,
U.S.A. 44°45N 96°41W 172 C5
Clear Lake Res. U.S.A. 41°56N 121°5W 168 F3
Clearfield Pa., U.S.A. 41°2N 78°27W 174 E6
Clearfield Utah, U.S.A. 41°7N 112°2W 168 F7
Clearlake U.S.A. 38°57N 122°38W 170 G4
Clearwater Canada 51°38N 120°2W 162 C4
Clearwater U.S.A. 27°59N 82°48W 179 H7
Clearwater → Alta.,
Canada 52°22N 114°57W 162 C6
Clearwater → Alta.,
Canada 56°44N 111°23W 163 B6
Clearwater L. Canada 53°34N 99°49W 163 C9
Clearwater Lake ⌂
Canada 54°0N 101°0W 163 C8
Clearwater Mts. U.S.A. 46°5N 115°20W 168 C6
Clearwater River ⌂
Canada 56°55N 109°10W 163 B7
Cleburne U.S.A. 32°21N 97°23W 176 E6
Clee Hills U.K. 52°26N 2°35W 67 E5
Cleethorpes U.K. 53°33N 0°3W 66 D7
Cleeve Cloud U.K. 51°56N 2°0W 67 F6
Clelles France 44°50N 5°38E 73 D9
Clemson U.S.A. 34°41N 82°50W 177 D13
Clerke Reef Australia 17°22S 119°20E 148 C2
Clermont Australia 22°49S 147°39E 150 C4
Clermont France 49°23N 2°24E 71 C9
Clermont-en-Argonne
France 49°5N 5°4E 71 C12
Clermont-Ferrand France 45°46N 3°4E 72 C7
Clermont-l'Hérault
France 43°38N 3°26E 72 E7
Clervaux Lux. 50°4N 6°2E 68 D6
Cles Italy 46°22N 11°2E 92 B8
Cleve Australia 33°43S 136°30E 152 B2
Clevedon U.K. 51°26N 2°52W 67 F5
Cleveland Miss., U.S.A. 33°45N 90°43W 179 D9
Cleveland Ohio, U.S.A. 41°29N 81°41W 174 E3

Cleveland Okla., U.S.A. 36°19N 96°28W 176 C6
Cleveland Tenn.,
U.S.A. 35°10N 84°53W 177 D12
Cleveland Tex., U.S.A. 30°21N 95°5W 176 F7
Cleveland, C. Australia 19°11S 147°1E 150 B4
Cleveland, Mt. U.S.A. 48°56N 113°51W 168 B7
Cleveland Heights
U.S.A. 41°31N 81°33W 174 E3
Clevelândia Brazil 26°24S 52°23W 191 B5
Clew B. Ireland 53°50N 9°49W 64 C2
Clewiston U.S.A. 26°45N 80°56W 179 H7
Clifden Ireland 53°29N 10°1W 64 C1
Clifden N.Z. 46°1S 167°42E 155 G2
Cliffy Hd. Australia 35°1S 116°29E 149 G2
Cliftin Australia 27°59S 151°53E 151 D5
Clifton Ariz., U.S.A. 33°3N 109°18W 169 K9
Clifton Colo., U.S.A. 39°7N 108°25W 168 G9
Clifton Tex., U.S.A. 31°47N 97°35W 176 F6
Clifton Beach Australia 16°46S 145°39E 150 B4
Climax U.S.A. 30°53N 84°26W 178 F5
Clinch → U.S.A. 35°53N 84°29W 177 D12
Clingmans Dome
U.S.A. 35°34N 83°30W 177 D13
Clint U.S.A. 31°35N 106°14W 176 F1
Clinton B.C., Canada 51°6N 121°35W 162 C4
Clinton Ont., Canada 43°37N 81°32W 174 C3
Clinton N.Z. 46°12S 169°23E 155 G4
Clinton Ark., U.S.A. 35°36N 92°28W 176 D8
Clinton Conn., U.S.A. 41°17N 72°32W 175 E12
Clinton Ill., U.S.A. 40°9N 88°57W 172 E9
Clinton Ind., U.S.A. 39°40N 87°24W 172 F10
Clinton Iowa, U.S.A. 41°51N 90°12W 172 E8
Clinton Mass., U.S.A. 42°25N 71°41W 175 D13
Clinton Miss., U.S.A. 32°20N 90°20W 179 E9
Clinton Mo., U.S.A. 38°22N 93°46W 172 F7
Clinton N.C., U.S.A. 35°0N 78°22W 177 D15
Clinton Okla., U.S.A. 35°31N 98°58W 176 D5
Clinton S.C., U.S.A. 34°29N 81°53W 177 D14
Clinton Tenn., U.S.A. 36°6N 84°8W 177 C12
Clinton Wash., U.S.A. 47°59N 122°21W 170 C4
Clinton, C. Australia 22°30S 150°45E 150 C5
Clinton Colden L.
Canada 63°58N 107°27W 160 C10
Clio U.S.A. 31°43N 85°37W 178 D4
Clipperton, Î.
Pac. Oc. 10°18N 109°13W 157 F17
Clipperton Fracture Zone
Pac. Oc. 19°0N 122°0W 157 G16
Clisham U.K. 57°58N 6°49W 65 D2
Clisson France 47°5N 1°16W 70 E5
Clitheroe U.K. 53°53N 2°22W 66 D5
Clive N.Z. 39°36S 176°58E 154 F5
Clo-oose Canada 48°39N 124°49W 170 B2
Cloates, Pt. Australia 22°43S 113°40E 148 D1
Clocolan S. Africa 28°55S 27°34E 145 C4
Clodomira Argentina 27°35S 64°14W 190 B3
Clogheen Ireland 52°17N 7°56W 64 D4
Clogher Hd. Ireland 53°48N 6°14W 64 C5
Clonakilty Ireland 51°37N 8°53W 64 E3
Clonakilty B. Ireland 51°35N 8°51W 64 E3
Cloncurry Australia 20°40S 140°28E 150 C3
Cloncurry Ireland 53°25N 6°48W 64 C5
Cloncurry →
Australia 18°37S 140°40E 150 B3
Clondalkin Ireland 53°19N 6°25W 64 C5
Clones Ireland 54°11N 7°15W 64 B4
Clonmel Ireland 52°21N 7°42W 64 D4
Cloppenburg Germany 52°51N 8°1E 76 C4
Cloquet U.S.A. 46°43N 92°28W 172 B7
Clorinda Argentina 25°16S 57°45W 190 B4
Cloud Peak U.S.A. 44°23N 107°11W 168 D10
Cloudcroft U.S.A. 32°58N 105°45W 169 K11
Cloudy B. N.Z. 41°25S 174°10E 155 B9
Cloverdale U.S.A. 38°48N 123°1W 170 G4
Clovis Calif., U.S.A. 36°49N 119°42W 170 J7
Clovis N. Mex., U.S.A. 34°24N 103°12W 169 J12
Cloyes-sur-le-Loir France 48°0N 1°14E 70 E8
Cloyne Ireland 51°51N 8°13W 64 E3
Cluain Meala = Clonmel
Ireland 52°21N 7°42W 64 D4
Club Terrace Australia 37°35S 148°58E 153 D8
Cluj □ Romania 46°45N 23°30E 81 D8
Cluj-Napoca Romania 46°47N 23°38E 81 D8
Clunes Australia 37°20S 143°45E 152 D5
Cluny France 46°26N 4°38E 71 F11
Cluses France 46°5N 6°35E 71 F13
Clusone Italy 45°53N 9°57E 92 C6
Clutha → N.Z. 46°20S 169°49E 155 G2
Clwyd → U.K. 53°19N 3°31W 66 D4
Clyde N.Z. 45°12S 169°20E 155 F4
Clyde → U.K. 55°55N 4°30W 65 F4
Clyde River Canada 70°30N 68°30W 161 C18
Clydebank U.K. 55°54N 4°23W 65 F4
Clymer N.Y., U.S.A. 42°1N 79°37W 174 D5
Clymer Pa., U.S.A. 40°40N 79°1W 174 D5
Cneo U.S.A. 32°29N 81°16W 178 C8
Côa → Portugal 41°5N 7°6W 88 D2
Coachella U.S.A. 33°41N 116°10W 171 M10
Coachella Canal
U.S.A. 32°43N 114°57W 171 N12
Coahoma U.S.A. 32°18N 101°18W 176 E4
Coahuayana →
Mexico 18°41N 103°45W 180 D4
Coahuila □ Mexico 27°0N 102°0W 180 B4
Coal → Canada 59°39N 126°57W 162 B3
Coal I. N.Z. 46°8S 166°40E 155 G1
Coalane Mozam. 17°48S 37°2E 143 F4
Coalcomán Mexico 18°47N 103°9W 180 D4
Coaldale Canada 49°45N 112°35W 162 D6
Coalgate U.S.A. 34°32N 96°13W 176 D6
Coalinga U.S.A. 36°9N 120°21W 170 J6
Coalisland U.K. 54°33N 6°42W 64 B5
Coalville U.S.A. 52°44N 1°23W 66 E6
Coalville U.S.A. 40°55N 111°24W 168 F8
Coamo Puerto Rico 18°5N 66°22W 183 d
Coaraci Brazil 14°39S 39°33W 189 C3
Coari Brazil 4°8S 63°7W 186 D6
Coast □ Kenya 3°20S 39°45E 142 C4
Coast Mts. Canada 55°0N 129°20W 162 C3
Coast Ranges U.S.A. 39°0N 123°0W 170 G4
Coatbridge U.K. 55°52N 4°6W 65 F4
Coatepec Mexico 19°27N 96°58W 181 D5
Coatepeque Guatemala 14°46N 91°55W 182 D1
Coatesville U.S.A. 39°59N 75°50W 173 F16
Coaticook Canada 45°10N 71°46W 175 A13

Coats I. *Canada* 62°30N 83°0W 161 E15
Coats Land *Antarctica* 77°0S 25°0W 55 D1
Coatzacoalcos *Mexico* 18°7N 94°25W 181 D6
Cobá *Mexico* 20°31N 87°45W 181 C7
Cobadin *Romania* 44°5N 28°13E 81 F13
Cobalt *Canada* 47°25N 79°42W 164 C4
Cobán *Guatemala* 15°30N 90°21W 182 C1
Çobanlar *Turkey* 38°41N 30°47E 99 C12
Cobar *Australia* 31°27S 145°48E 153 A4
Cobargo *Australia* 36°20S 149°55E 153 D8
Cobbannah *Australia* 37°37S 147°13E 153 D7
Cobberas, Mt.
  Australia 36°53S 148°12E 153 D8
Cobden *Australia* 38°20S 143°3E 152 E5
Cobh *Ireland* 51°51N 8°17W 64 E3
Cóbh, An = Cobh *Ireland* 51°51N 8°17W 64 E3
Cobija *Bolivia* 11°0S 68°50W 188 C4
Cobleskill *U.S.A.* 42°41N 74°29W 175 D10
Coboconk *Canada* 44°39N 78°48W 174 B6
Cobourg *Canada* 43°58N 78°10W 174 C6
Cobourg Pen.
  Australia 11°20S 132°15E 148 B5
Cobram *Australia* 35°54S 145°40E 153 C6
Cóbué *Mozam.* 12°0S 34°58E 143 E3
Coburg *Germany* 50°15N 10°58E 77 E6
Coburg I. *Canada* 75°57N 79°26W 161 B16
Coca *Spain* 41°13N 4°32W 88 D6
Cocachacra *Peru* 17°5S 71°45W 188 D3
Cocal *Brazil* 3°28S 41°34W 189 A2
Cocanada = Kakinada
  India 16°57N 82°11E 126 F6
Cocentaina *Spain* 38°45N 0°27W 91 G4
Cochabamba *Bolivia* 17°26S 66°10W 186 G5
Cochem *Germany* 50°9N 7°9E 77 E3
Cochemane *Mozam.* 17°0S 32°54E 143 F3
Cochin = Kochi *India* 9°58N 76°20E 127 K3
Cochin China = Nam-Phan
  Vietnam 10°30N 106°0E 121 G6
Cochran *U.S.A.* 32°23N 83°21W 178 C6
Cochrane *Alta.,*
  Canada 51°11N 114°30W 162 C6
Cochrane *Ont., Canada* 49°0N 81°0W 164 C3
Cochrane *Chile* 47°15S 72°33W 192 C2
Cochrane → *Canada* 59°0N 103°40W 163 B8
Cochrane, L. *Chile* 47°10S 72°0W 192 C2
Cochranton *U.S.A.* 41°31N 80°3W 174 E4
Cockburn *Australia* 32°5S 141°0E 152 B4
Cockburn, Canal *Chile* 54°30S 72°0W 192 D2
Cockburn I. *Canada* 45°55N 83°22W 164 C3
Cockburn Ra. *Australia* 15°46S 128°0E 148 C4
Cockermouth *U.K.* 54°40N 3°22W 66 C4
Cocklebiddy *Australia* 32°0S 126°3E 149 F4
Cockpit Country, The
  Jamaica 18°15N 77°45W 182 a
Coco → *Cent. Amer.* 15°0N 83°8W 182 D3
Coco, I. del *Pac. Oc.* 5°25N 87°55W 157 G19
Coco Channel *Asia* 13°45N 93°10E 127 H11
Cocoa *U.S.A.* 28°21N 80°44W 179 G9
Cocoa Beach *U.S.A.* 28°19N 80°37W 179 G9
Cocobeach *Gabon* 0°59N 9°34E 140 D1
Cocoparra △ *Australia* 34°10S 146°12E 153 C7
Cocora *Romania* 44°45N 27°3E 81 F12
Côcos *Brazil* 14°10S 44°33W 189 C2
Côcos → *Brazil* 12°44S 44°48W 189 C2
Cocos B. *Trin. & Tob.* 10°24N 61°2W 187 K15
Cocos Basin *Ind. Oc.* 1°0N 94°0E 146 D8
Cocos = Coco, I. del
  Pac. Oc. 5°25N 87°55W 157 G19
Cocos Is. *Ind. Oc.* 12°10S 96°55E 146 F8
Cocos Ridge *Pac. Oc.* 2°0N 89°0W 157 G19
Cod, C. *U.S.A.* 42°5N 70°10W 173 D18
Codajás *Brazil* 3°55S 62°0W 186 D6
Codfish I. *N.Z.* 46°47S 167°38E 155 G2
Codigoro *Italy* 44°49N 12°8E 93 D9
Codlea *Romania* 45°42N 25°27E 81 E10
Codó *Brazil* 4°30S 43°55W 189 A2
Codogno *Italy* 45°9N 9°42E 92 C6
Codróipo *Italy* 45°58N 12°59E 93 C10
Codru, Munţii *Romania* 46°30N 22°15E 80 D7
Cody *U.S.A.* 44°32N 109°3W 168 D9
Coe Hill *Canada* 44°52N 77°50W 174 B7
Coelemu *Chile* 36°30S 72°48W 190 D1
Coelho Neto *Brazil* 4°15S 43°0W 189 A2
Coen *Australia* 13°52S 143°12E 150 A3
Coesfeld *Germany* 51°56N 7°10E 76 D3
Coetivy I. *Seychelles* 7°8S 56°16E 146 E4
Coeur d'Alene *U.S.A.* 47°41N 116°46W 168 C5
Coeur d'Alene L.
  U.S.A. 47°32N 116°49W 168 C5
Coevorden *Neths.* 52°40N 6°44E 69 B6
Cofete *Canary Is.* 28°6N 14°23W 100 F5
Coffeyville *U.S.A.* 37°2N 95°37W 172 G6
Coffin B. *Australia* 34°38S 135°28E 151 E2
Coffin Bay *Australia* 34°37S 135°29E 151 E2
Coffin Bay △ *Australia* 34°34S 135°19E 151 E2
Coffin Bay Peninsula
  Australia 34°32S 135°15E 151 E2
Coffs Harbour
  Australia 30°16S 153°5E 153 A10
Cofrentes *Spain* 39°13N 1°5W 91 F3
Cogalnic = Kohylnyk →
  Ukraine 45°49N 29°40E 81 E14
Cogealac *Romania* 44°36N 28°36E 81 F13
Coghinas → *Italy* 40°55N 8°48E 94 B1
Coghinas, L. del *Italy* 40°46N 9°3E 94 B2
Cognac *France* 45°41N 0°20W 72 C3
Cogne *Italy* 45°37N 7°21E 92 C4
Cogolin *France* 43°15N 6°29E 73 E10
Cogolludo *Spain* 40°59N 3°10W 90 E1
Cohocton *U.S.A.* 42°30N 77°30W 174 D7
Cohocton → *U.S.A.* 42°9N 77°6W 174 D7
Cohoes *U.S.A.* 42°46N 73°42W 175 D11
Cohuna *Australia* 35°45S 144°15E 152 C6
Coiba, I. de *Panama* 7°30N 81°40W 182 E3
Coig → *Argentina* 51°0S 69°10W 192 D3
Coigeach, Rubha *U.K.* 58°6N 5°26W 65 D7
Coihaique *Chile* 45°30S 71°45W 192 C2
Coimbatore *India* 11°2N 76°59E 127 J3
Coimbra *Brazil* 19°55S 57°48W 186 G6
Coimbra *Portugal* 40°15N 8°27W 88 E2
Coimbra □ *Portugal* 40°12N 8°25E 88 E2
Coin *Spain* 36°40N 4°48W 89 J6
Coipasa, L. de *Bolivia* 19°12S 68°7W 188 D4
Coipasa, Salar de
  Bolivia 19°26S 68°9W 188 D4
Cojata *Peru* 15°2S 69°22S 188 D4
Cojimies *Ecuador* 0°20N 80°0W 186 C2
Cojocna *Romania* 46°45N 23°50E 81 D8
Cojutepequé *El Salv.* 13°41N 88°54W 182 D2
Čoka *Serbia* 45°57N 20°12E 80 E5

Cokeville *U.S.A.* 42°5N 110°57W 168 E8
Colaba Pt. *India* 18°53N 72°48E 126 E1
Colac *Australia* 38°21S 143°35E 152 E5
Colachel = Kolachel
  India 8°10N 77°15E 127 K3
Colán *Peru* 5°0S 81°0W 188 B1
Colatina *Brazil* 19°32S 40°37W 189 D2
Colbert *U.S.A.* 34°2N 83°13W 178 A6
Colborne *Canada* 44°0N 77°53W 174 C7
Colby *U.S.A.* 39°24N 101°3W 172 F3
Colca → *Peru* 15°55S 72°30W 186 G4
Colca, Cañón del *Peru* 15°50S 72°20W 188 D3
Colchester *U.K.* 51°54N 0°55E 67 F8
Colchester *U.S.A.* 41°35N 72°20W 175 E12
Cold L. *Canada* 54°33N 110°5W 163 C7
Cold Lake *Canada* 54°27N 110°10W 163 C7
Coldstream *Canada* 50°13N 119°11W 162 C5
Coldstream *U.K.* 55°39N 2°15W 65 F6
Coldwater *Canada* 44°42N 79°40W 174 B5
Coldwater *Kans.,*
  U.S.A. 37°16N 99°20W 172 G4
Coldwater *Mich.,*
  U.S.A. 41°57N 85°0W 173 E11
Coleambally *Australia* 34°49S 145°52E 153 C6
Colebrook *U.S.A.* 44°54N 71°30W 175 B13
Coleman *Canada* 49°40N 114°30W 162 D6
Coleman *Fla., U.S.A.* 28°48N 82°4W 179 G7
Coleman *Tex., U.S.A.* 31°50N 99°26W 176 F5
Coleman → *Australia* 15°6S 141°38E 150 B3
Colenso *S. Africa* 28°44S 29°50E 145 C4
Coleraine *Australia* 37°36S 141°40E 152 D4
Coleraine *U.K.* 55°8N 6°41W 64 A5
Coleridge, L. *N.Z.* 43°17S 171°30E 155 D6
Colesberg *S. Africa* 30°45S 25°5E 144 D4
Coleville *U.S.A.* 38°34N 119°30W 170 G7
Colfax *Calif., U.S.A.* 39°6N 120°57W 170 F6
Colfax *La., U.S.A.* 31°31N 92°42W 176 F8
Colfax *Wash., U.S.A.* 46°53N 117°22W 168 C5
Colhué Huapi, L.
  Argentina 45°30S 69°0W 192 C3
Colibaşi = Mioveni
  Romania 44°56N 24°54E 81 F9
Colibaşi *Moldova* 45°43N 28°11E 81 E13
Cólico *Italy* 46°8N 9°22E 92 B6
Coligny *France* 46°23N 5°21E 71 F12
Coligny *S. Africa* 26°17S 26°15E 145 C4
Colima *Mexico* 19°14N 103°43W 180 D4
Colima □ *Mexico* 19°10N 104°0W 180 D4
Colima, Nevado de
  Mexico 19°33N 103°38W 180 D4
Colina *Chile* 33°13S 70°45W 190 C1
Colina do Norte
  Guinea-Biss. 12°28N 15°0W 138 C2
Colinas *Goiás, Brazil* 14°0S 48°2W 189 C1
Colinas *Maranhão, Brazil* 6°0S 44°10W 189 B2
Colindres *Spain* 43°24N 3°27W 88 B7
Coll *U.K.* 56°39N 6°34W 65 E2
Collaguasi *Chile* 21°5S 68°45W 190 A2
Collarada, Peña di *Spain* 42°43N 0°29W 90 C4
Collarenebri *Australia* 29°33S 148°34E 151 D4
Colle di Val d'Elsa *Italy* 43°25N 11°6E 92 C8
Colléchio *Italy* 44°35N 10°13E 92 D7
Colleen Bawn *Zimbabwe* 21°0S 29°12E 143 G2
College *U.S.A.* 64°52N 147°49W 166 C10
College Park *U.S.A.* 33°39N 84°27W 178 B5
College Station *U.S.A.* 30°37N 96°21W 176 F6
Collesalvetti *Italy* 43°34N 10°27E 92 C7
Colli Euganei △ *Italy* 45°18N 11°43E 93 C8
Collie *N.S.W., Australia* 31°41S 148°18E 153 A8
Collie *W. Austral.,*
  Australia 33°22S 116°8E 149 F2
Collier B. *Australia* 16°10S 124°15E 148 C3
Collier Ra. *Australia* 24°45S 119°10E 149 D2
Collier Range △
  Australia 24°39S 119°7E 149 D2
Collierville *U.S.A.* 35°3N 89°40W 177 D10
Collina, Passo di *Italy* 44°2N 10°56E 92 D7
Collingwood *Canada* 44°29N 80°13W 174 B4
Collingwood *N.Z.* 40°41S 172°40E 155 A7
Collins *Canada* 50°17N 89°27W 164 B2
Collins *U.S.A.* 32°11N 82°7W 178 C7
Collins Bay *Canada* 44°14N 76°36W 175 B8
Collinson Pen.
  Canada 69°58N 101°24W 160 D11
Collinsville *Australia* 20°30S 147°56E 150 C4
Collipulli *Chile* 37°55S 72°30W 190 D1
Collo *Algeria* 36°58N 6°37E 136 A5
Collooney *Ireland* 54°11N 8°29W 64 B3
Colmar *France* 48°5N 7°20E 71 D14
Colmars *France* 44°11N 6°39E 73 D10
Colmenar *Spain* 36°54N 4°20W 89 J6
Colmenar de Oreja *Spain* 40°6N 3°25W 88 E7
Colmenar Viejo *Spain* 40°39N 3°47W 88 E7
Colo → *Australia* 33°25S 150°52E 153 B9
Cologne = Köln *Germany* 50°56N 6°57E 76 E2
Colom, I. d'en *Spain* 39°58N 4°16E 100 B11
Colóm *Mexico* 18°34N 120°53W 170 G6
Colomb-Béchar = Béchar
  Algeria 31°38N 2°18W 136 B3
Colombey-les-Belles
  France 48°32N 5°54E 71 D12
Colombey-les-Deux-Églises
  France 48°13N 4°50E 71 D11
Colômbia *Brazil* 20°10S 48°40W 189 E1
Colombia ■ *S. Amer.* 3°45N 73°0W 186 C4
Colombian Basin
  Caribbean 14°0N 76°0W 182 D4
Colombo *Sri Lanka* 6°56N 79°58E 127 L4
Colomiers *France* 43°36N 1°21E 72 E5
Colón *B. Aires, Argentina* 33°53S 61°7W 190 C3
Colón *Entre Rios,*
  Argentina 32°12S 58°10W 190 C4
Colón *Cuba* 22°42N 80°54W 182 B3
Colón *Panama* 9°20N 79°54W 182 E4
Colón, Arch. de *Ecuador* 0°0 91°0W 184 D1
Colonia 25 de Mayo
  Argentina 37°48S 67°41W 192 A3
Colònia de Sant Jordi
  Spain 39°19N 2°59E 100 B9
Colonia del Sacramento
  Uruguay 34°25S 57°50W 190 C4
Colonia Dora *Argentina* 28°34S 62°59W 190 B3
Colonial Beach *U.S.A.* 38°15N 76°58W 173 F15
Colonie *U.S.A.* 42°43N 73°50W 175 D11
Colonna, C. *Italy* 39°2N 17°12E 95 C10
Colonsay *Canada* 51°59N 105°52W 163 C7
Colonsay *U.K.* 56°5N 6°12W 65 E2
Colorado □ *U.S.A.* 39°30N 105°30W 168 G11
Colorado → *Argentina* 39°50S 62°8W 192 A4

Colorado → *N. Amer.* 31°45N 114°40W 169 L6
Colorado → *U.S.A.* 28°36N 95°59W 176 G7
Colorado City *U.S.A.* 32°24N 100°52W 176 E4
Colorado Plateau
  U.S.A. 37°0N 111°0W 169 H8
Colorado River Aqueduct
  U.S.A. 33°50N 117°23W 171 L12
Colorado Springs
  U.S.A. 38°50N 104°49W 168 G11
Colorno *Italy* 44°56N 10°23E 92 D7
Colotlán *Mexico* 22°6N 103°16W 180 C4
Colquitt *U.S.A.* 31°10N 84°44W 178 D5
Colstrip *U.S.A.* 45°53N 106°38W 168 D10
Colton *U.S.A.* 44°33N 74°56W 175 B10
Columbia *Ala., U.S.A.* 31°18N 85°7W 178 D4
Columbia *Ky., U.S.A.* 37°6N 85°18W 173 G11
Columbia *Miss.,*
  U.S.A. 31°15N 89°50W 177 F10
Columbia *Mo., U.S.A.* 38°57N 92°20W 172 F7
Columbia *Pa., U.S.A.* 40°2N 76°30W 175 F8
Columbia *S.C., U.S.A.* 34°0N 81°2W 178 A8
Columbia *Tenn., U.S.A.* 35°37N 87°2W 177 D8
Columbia → *N. Amer.* 46°15N 124°5W 170 D2
Columbia, C. *Canada* 83°6N 69°57W 161 A18
Columbia, District of □
  U.S.A. 38°55N 77°0W 173 F15
Columbia, Mt. *Canada* 52°8N 117°20W 162 C5
Columbia Basin *U.S.A.* 46°45N 119°5W 168 C4
Columbia Falls *U.S.A.* 48°23N 114°11W 168 B6
Columbia Mts. *Canada* 52°0N 119°0W 162 C5
Columbia Plateau
  U.S.A. 44°0N 117°30W 168 E5
Columbiana *U.S.A.* 40°53N 80°42W 174 F4
Columbretes, Is. *Spain* 39°50N 0°50E 90 F5
Columbus *Ga., U.S.A.* 32°28N 84°59W 178 C5
Columbus *Ind., U.S.A.* 39°13N 85°55W 173 F11
Columbus *Kans.,*
  U.S.A. 37°10N 94°50W 172 G6
Columbus *Miss.,*
  U.S.A. 33°30N 88°25W 177 E10
Columbus *Mont.,*
  U.S.A. 45°38N 109°15W 168 D9
Columbus *N. Mex.,*
  U.S.A. 31°50N 107°38W 169 L10
Columbus *Nebr., U.S.A.* 41°26N 97°22W 172 E6
Columbus *Ohio, U.S.A.* 39°58N 83°0W 173 F12
Columbus *Tex., U.S.A.* 29°42N 96°33W 176 G6
Colunga *Spain* 43°29N 5°16W 88 B5
Colusa *U.S.A.* 39°13N 122°1W 170 F4
Colville *U.S.A.* 48°33N 117°54W 168 B5
Colville → *U.S.A.* 70°25N 150°30W 166 A9
Colville, C. *N.Z.* 36°29S 175°21E 154 C4
Colville Channel *N.Z.* 36°25S 175°27E 154 C4
Colwood *Canada* 48°26N 123°29W 170 B3
Colwyn Bay *U.K.* 53°18N 3°44W 66 D4
Comácchio *Italy* 44°42N 12°11E 93 D9
Comalcalco *Mexico* 18°16N 93°13W 181 D6
Comallo *Argentina* 41°0S 70°5W 192 B2
Comana *Romania* 44°10N 26°10E 81 F11
Comanche *U.S.A.* 31°54N 98°36W 176 F5
Comandante Ferraz
  Antarctica 62°30S 58°0W 55 C18
Comandante Luis Piedrabuena
  Argentina 49°59S 68°54W 192 C3
Comăneşti *Romania* 46°25N 26°26E 81 D11
Comarnic *Romania* 45°15N 25°38E 81 E10
Comayagua *Honduras* 14°25N 87°37W 182 D2
Combahee → *U.S.A.* 32°31N 80°31W 178 C9
Combara *Australia* 31°10S 148°22E 153 A8
Combarbalá *Chile* 31°11S 71°2W 190 C1
Combe Martin *U.K.* 51°12N 4°3W 67 F3
Combeaufontaine
  France 47°38N 5°54E 71 E12
Comber *Canada* 42°14N 82°33W 174 D2
Comber *U.K.* 54°33N 5°45W 64 B6
Combermere *Canada* 45°22N 77°37W 174 A7
Comblain-au-Pont
  Belgium 50°29N 5°35E 69 D5
Combourg *France* 48°25N 1°46W 70 D5
Comboyne *Australia* 31°34S 152°27E 153 A10
Combrailles *France* 46°8N 2°8E 71 F9
Combronde *France* 45°58N 3°5E 72 C7
Comer *Ala., U.S.A.* 32°2N 85°23W 178 C4
Comer *Ga., U.S.A.* 34°4N 83°8W 178 A6
Comeragh Mts. *Ireland* 52°18N 7°34W 64 D4
Comet *Australia* 23°36S 148°38E 150 C4
Comilla *Bangla.* 23°28N 91°10E 123 H17
Comino *Malta* 36°1N 14°20E 101 C1
Comino, C. *Italy* 40°32N 9°49E 94 B2
Cómiso *Italy* 36°56N 14°36E 95 F7
Comitán de Domínguez
  Mexico 16°15N 92°8W 181 D6
Commentry *France* 46°20N 2°46E 71 F9
Commerce *Ga., U.S.A.* 34°12N 83°28W 178 A6
Commerce *Tex., U.S.A.* 33°15N 95°54W 176 E7
Commercy *France* 48°43N 5°34E 71 D12
Committee B. *Canada* 68°30N 86°30W 161 D14
Commodore, C. *Canada* 44°47N 80°54W 174 B4
Commonwealth B.
  Antarctica 67°0S 144°0E 55 C10
Commoron Cr. →
  Australia 28°22S 150°8E 151 D5
Communism Pk. = imeni Ismail
  Samani, Pik *Tajikistan* 39°0N 72°2E 109 E8
Como *Italy* 45°47N 9°5E 92 C6
Como, L. di *Italy* 46°0N 9°11E 92 B6
Comodoro Rivadavia
  Argentina 45°50S 67°40W 192 C3
Comoé → *Ivory C.* 5°12N 3°44W 138 D4
Comoé △ *Ivory C.* 9°23N 4°10W 138 D4
Comorâşte *Romania* 45°10N 21°35E 80 E6
Comorin, C. = Kannyakumari
  India 8°4N 77°40E 127 K3
Comoros ■ *Ind. Oc.* 12°10S 44°15E 141 a
Comox *Canada* 49°42N 124°55W 162 D4
Compass Lake *U.S.A.* 30°36N 85°24W 178 F4
Compiègne *France* 49°24N 2°50E 71 C9
Comporta *Portugal* 38°22N 8°46W 89 G2
Compostela *Brazil* 20°10S 48°40W 189 E1
Comprida, I. *Brazil* 24°50S 47°42W 191 A6
Compton *Canada* 45°14N 71°49W 175 B13
Compton *U.S.A.* 33°53N 118°13W 171 M8
Comrat *Moldova* 46°18N 28°40E 81 E13
Comrie *U.K.* 56°22N 3°58W 65 E5
Comstock *U.S.A.* 29°41N 101°10W 176 G4
Con Cuong *Vietnam* 19°2N 104°54E 120 C5
Con Dao △ *Vietnam* 8°42N 106°35E 121 H6
Con Son, Dao *Vietnam* 8°41N 106°37E 121 H6
Cona Niyeu *Argentina* 41°58S 67°0W 192 B3
Conakry *Guinea* 9°29N 13°49W 138 D2
Conara *Australia* 41°50S 147°26E 151 E4

Conargo *Australia* 35°16S 145°10E 153 C6
Concarneau *France* 47°52N 3°56W 70 E3
Conceição *Brazil* 7°33S 38°31W 189 B3
Conceição *Mozam.* 18°47S 36°7E 143 F4
Conceição da Barra
  Brazil 18°35S 39°45W 189 D3
Conceição do Araguaia
  Brazil 8°0S 49°2W 187 E9
Conceição do Canindé
  Brazil 7°54S 41°34W 189 B2
Concepción *Argentina* 27°20S 65°35W 190 B2
Concepción *Bolivia* 16°15S 62°8W 186 G6
Concepción *Chile* 36°50S 73°0W 190 D1
Concepción *Paraguay* 23°22S 57°26W 190 A4
Concepción *Peru* 11°54S 75°19W 188 C2
Concepción □ *Chile* 37°0S 72°30W 190 D1
Concepción, Est. de
  Chile 50°30S 74°55W 192 D2
Concepción, L. *Bolivia* 17°20S 61°20W 186 G6
Concepción, Pta.
  Mexico 26°53N 111°50W 180 B2
Concepción del Oro
  Mexico 24°38N 101°25W 180 C4
Concepción del Uruguay
  Argentina 32°35S 58°20W 190 C4
Conception, Pt.
  U.S.A. 34°27N 120°28W 171 L6
Conception B. *Canada* 47°45N 53°0W 165 C9
Conception B. *Namibia* 23°55S 14°22E 144 B1
Conception I. *Bahamas* 23°52S 75°9W 183 B4
Concession *Zimbabwe* 17°27S 30°56E 143 F3
Conchas Dam *U.S.A.* 35°22N 104°11W 169 J11
Conches-en-Ouche
  France 48°58N 0°56E 70 D7
Concho *U.S.A.* 34°28N 109°36W 169 J9
Concho → *U.S.A.* 31°34N 99°43W 176 F5
Conchos → *Chihuahua,*
  Mexico 29°35N 104°25W 180 B4
Conchos → *Tamaulipas,*
  Mexico 24°55N 97°38W 181 B5
Concord *Calif., U.S.A.* 37°59N 122°2W 170 H4
Concord *Ga., U.S.A.* 33°5N 84°26W 178 C5
Concord *N.C., U.S.A.* 35°25N 80°35W 177 D14
Concord *N.H., U.S.A.* 43°12N 71°32W 175 C13
Concordia *Antarctica* 75°6S 123°23E 55 D9
Concordia *Argentina* 31°20S 58°2W 190 C4
Concórdia *Amazonas,*
  Brazil 4°36S 66°36W 186 D5
Concórdia *Sta. Catarina,*
  Brazil 27°14S 52°1W 191 B5
Concordia *Mexico* 23°17N 106°4W 180 C3
Concordia *U.S.A.* 39°34N 97°40W 172 F5
Concrete *U.S.A.* 48°32N 121°45W 168 B3
Condah *Australia* 37°57S 141°44E 152 D4
Condamine *Australia* 26°56S 150°9E 151 D5
Condat *France* 45°21N 2°46E 72 C6
Conde *Brazil* 11°49S 37°37W 189 C3
Condé-sur-Noireau
  France 48°51N 0°33W 70 D6
Condeúba *Brazil* 14°52S 42°0W 189 D2
Condobolin *Australia* 33°4S 147°6E 153 B7
Condom *France* 43°57N 0°22E 72 E4
Condon *U.S.A.* 45°14N 120°11W 168 D3
Conegliano *Italy* 45°53N 12°18E 93 C9
Conejera, I. = Conills, I. des
  Spain 39°11N 2°58E 100 B9
Conejos *Mexico* 26°14N 103°53W 180 B4
Conemaugh → *U.S.A.* 40°28N 79°19W 174 F5
Conero △ *Italy* 43°32N 13°35E 93 C10
Confolens *France* 46°2N 0°40E 72 B4
Confuso → *Paraguay* 25°9S 57°34W 190 B4
Congaree △ *U.S.A.* 33°44N 80°38W 178 B9
Congaree → *U.S.A.* 33°47N 80°47W 178 B9
Congaz *Moldova* 46°7N 28°36E 81 D13
Congdon *Australia* 16°10S 124°18E 148 C3
Conghua *China* 23°36N 113°31E 117 F9
Congjiang *China* 25°43N 108°52E 118 E7
Congleton *U.K.* 53°10N 2°13W 66 D5
Congo → *Brazil* 7°48S 36°40W 189 B3
Congo (Brazzaville) = Congo ■
  Africa 1°0S 16°0E 140 E3
Congo (Kinshasa) = Congo, Dem.
  Rep. of the ■ *Africa* 3°0S 23°0E 140 E4
Congo ■ *Africa* 1°0S 16°0E 140 E3
Congo → *Africa* 6°4S 12°24E 140 F2
Congo, Dem. Rep. of the ■
  Africa 3°0S 23°0E 140 E4
Congo Basin *Africa* 0°10S 24°30E 140 E4
Congonhas *Brazil* 20°30S 43°52W 189 E2
Congress *U.S.A.* 34°9N 112°51W 169 J7
Conguillío △ *Chile* 38°40S 71°42W 192 A2
Conil de la Frontera
  Spain 36°17N 6°10W 89 J4
Conills, I. des *Spain* 39°11N 2°58E 100 B9
Conimbla △ *Australia* 33°45S 148°28E 153 B8
Coniston *Canada* 46°29N 80°51W 164 C3
Conjeeveram = Kanchipuram
  India 12°52N 79°45E 127 H4
Conklin *Canada* 55°38N 111°5W 163 B6
Conklin → *U.S.A.* 42°2N 75°49W 175 D9
Conn, L. *Ireland* 54°3N 9°15W 64 B2
Connacht □ *Ireland* 53°43N 9°12W 64 C2
Conneaut *U.S.A.* 41°57N 80°34W 174 E4
Conneautville *U.S.A.* 41°45N 80°22W 174 E4
Connecticut □ *U.S.A.* 41°30N 72°45W 175 E12
Connecticut →
  U.S.A. 41°16N 72°20W 175 E12
Connell *U.S.A.* 46°40N 118°52W 168 C4
Connellsville *U.S.A.* 40°1N 79°35W 174 F5
Connemara *Ireland* 53°29N 9°45W 64 C2
Connemara △ *Ireland* 53°32N 9°52W 64 C2
Connerré *France* 48°3N 0°30E 70 D7
Connors Ra. *Australia* 21°40S 149°10E 150 C4
Conococha *Peru* 10°7S 77°18W 188 B2
Conques *France* 44°36N 2°23E 72 D6
Conquest *Canada* 51°32N 107°14W 163 C7
Conrad *U.S.A.* 48°10N 111°57W 168 B8
Conran, C. *Australia* 37°49S 148°44E 153 D8
Conroe *U.S.A.* 30°19N 95°27W 176 F7
Consecon *Canada* 44°0N 77°31W 174 C7
Conselheiro Lafaiete
  Brazil 20°40S 43°48W 189 E2
Conselheiro Pena
  Brazil 19°10S 41°30W 189 D2
Consell *Spain* 39°40N 2°49E 100 B9
Conselve *Italy* 45°14N 11°49E 93 C8
Consett *U.K.* 54°51N 1°50W 66 C6
Consort *Canada* 52°1N 110°46W 163 C6

Constance = Konstanz
  Germany 47°40N 9°10E 77 H5
Constance, L. = Bodensee
  Europe 47°35N 9°25E 77 H5
Constanţa *Romania* 44°14N 28°38E 81 F13
Constanţa □ *Romania* 44°15N 28°15E 81 F13
Constantina *Spain* 37°51N 5°40W 89 H5
Constantine *Algeria* 36°25N 6°42E 136 A5
Constantine □ *Algeria* 36°30N 6°40E 136 A5
Constitución *Chile* 35°20S 72°30W 190 D1
Constitución *Uruguay* 31°0S 57°50W 190 C4
Constitución de 1857 △
  Mexico 32°4N 115°55W 180 A1
Consuegra *Spain* 39°28N 3°36W 89 F7
Consul *Canada* 49°20N 109°30W 163 D7
Contact *U.S.A.* 41°46N 114°45W 168 F6
Contagem *Brazil* 19°55S 44°6W 189 D2
Contai *India* 21°54N 87°46E 125 J12
Contamana *Peru* 7°19S 74°55W 188 B3
Contas → *Brazil* 14°17S 39°1W 189 C3
Contes *France* 43°49N 7°19E 73 E11
Contocook *U.S.A.* 43°13N 71°45W 175 C13
Contra Costa *Mozam.* 25°9S 33°30E 145 C5
Contres *France* 47°24N 1°26E 70 E8
Contrexéville *France* 48°10N 5°53E 71 D12
Contumaza *Peru* 7°23S 78°57W 188 B2
Contwoyto L. *Canada* 65°42N 110°50W 160 D9
Conversano *Italy* 40°58N 17°7E 95 B10
Conway = Conwy *U.K.* 53°17N 3°50W 66 D4
Conway = Conwy →
  U.K. 53°17N 3°50W 66 D4
Conway *Australia* 20°24S 148°41E 150 b
Conway *Canada* 44°6N 76°54W 174 B8
Conway *Ark., U.S.A.* 35°5N 92°26W 176 D8
Conway *N.H., U.S.A.* 43°59N 71°7W 175 C13
Conway *S.C., U.S.A.* 33°51N 79°3W 177 E15
Conway, C. *Australia* 20°34S 148°46E 150 b
Conway, L. *Australia* 28°17S 135°35E 151 D2
Conwy □ *U.K.* 53°17N 3°50W 66 D4
Conwy *U.K.* 53°17N 3°50W 66 D4
Conwy □ *U.K.* 53°10N 3°44W 66 D4
Conwy → *U.K.* 53°17N 3°50W 66 D4
Conyers *U.S.A.* 33°40N 84°1W 178 B5
Cooch Behar = Koch Bihar
  India 26°22N 89°29E 123 F16
Cooinda *Australia* 13°15S 130°5E 148 B5
Cook *Australia* 30°37S 130°25E 149 F5
Cook *U.S.A.* 47°51N 92°41W 172 B7
Cook, B. *Chile* 55°10S 70°0W 192 E3
Cook, C. *Canada* 50°8N 127°55W 162 C3
Cook, Mt. = Aoraki Mount Cook
  N.Z. 43°36S 170°9E 155 D5
Cook Inlet *U.S.A.* 60°0N 152°0W 166 D9
Cook Is. ■ *Pac. Oc.* 17°0S 160°0W 157 J12
Cook Strait *N.Z.* 41°15S 174°29E 154 B3
Cooke Plains *Australia* 35°23S 139°34E 152 C3
Cookeville *U.S.A.* 36°10N 85°30W 177 C12
Cookhouse *S. Africa* 32°44S 25°47E 144 D4
Cooks Hammock *U.S.A.* 29°56N 83°17W 178 F6
Cooks Harbour *Canada* 51°36N 55°52W 165 B8
Cookshire *Canada* 45°25N 71°38W 175 A13
Cookstown *Canada* 44°11N 79°42W 174 B5
Cookstown *U.K.* 54°38N 6°45W 64 B5
Cooksville *Canada* 43°35N 79°39W 174 C5
Cooktown *Australia* 15°30S 145°16E 150 B4
Coolabah *Australia* 31°1S 146°43E 153 A7
Cooladdi *Australia* 26°37S 145°23E 153 A4
Coolah *Australia* 31°48S 149°41E 153 A8
Coolah Tops △
  Australia 31°52S 150°0E 153 A9
Coolamon *Australia* 34°46S 147°8E 153 C7
Coolaney *Ireland* 54°9N 8°36W 64 B3
Coolgardie *Australia* 30°55S 121°8E 149 F3
Coolidge *Ariz., U.S.A.* 32°59N 111°31W 169 K8
Coolidge *Ga., U.S.A.* 31°1N 83°52W 178 D6
Coolidge Dam *U.S.A.* 33°10N 110°32W 169 K8
Cooma *Australia* 36°12S 149°8E 153 D8
Coon Rapids *U.S.A.* 45°9N 93°19W 172 C7
Coonabarabran
  Australia 31°14S 149°18E 153 A8
Coonalpyn *Australia* 35°43S 139°52E 152 C3
Coonamble *Australia* 30°56S 148°27E 153 A8
Coonana *Australia* 31°0S 123°0E 149 F3
Coonana ✪ *Australia* 30°51S 122°53E 149 F3
Coonarr *Australia* 13°42N 74°40E 127 H2
Coondapoor *India* 13°42N 74°40E 127 H2
Cooninie, L. *Australia* 26°4S 139°59E 151 D2
Cooper *U.S.A.* 33°23N 95°42W 176 E7
Cooper → *U.S.A.* 32°50N 79°56W 178 C9
Cooper Cr. →
  Australia 28°29S 137°46E 151 D2
Cooper Ridge *Pac. Oc.* 10°0N 150°30W 157 G12
Cooperstown *N. Dak.,*
  U.S.A. 47°27N 98°8W 172 B4
Cooperstown *N.Y.,*
  U.S.A. 42°42N 74°56W 175 D10
Coopracambra △
  Australia 37°20S 149°20E 153 D8
Coorabie *Australia* 31°54S 132°18E 149 F5
Coorong, The
  Australia 35°50S 139°20E 152 C3
Coorow *Australia* 29°53S 116°2E 149 E2
Cooroy *Australia* 26°22S 152°54E 151 D5
Coos Bay *U.S.A.* 43°22N 124°13W 168 E1
Coosa → *U.S.A.* 32°30N 86°16W 177 E11
Cootamundra *Australia* 34°36S 148°1E 153 C8
Cootehill *Ireland* 54°4N 7°5W 64 B4
Copahue Paso *Argentina* 37°49S 71°8W 190 D1
Copainalá *Mexico* 17°4N 93°18W 181 D6
Copake *U.S.A.* 42°7N 73°31W 175 D11
Copán *Honduras* 14°50N 89°9W 182 D2
Cope *U.S.A.* 39°40N 102°51W 168 G12
Cope, Colo., U.S.A. 39°40N 102°51W 168 G12
Cope, C. *Spain* 37°26N 1°28W 91 H3
Copeland *U.S.A.* 25°57N 81°22W 179 H8
Copenhagen = København
  Denmark 55°40N 12°26E 63 J6
Copertino *Italy* 40°16N 18°3E 95 B11
Copiapó *Chile* 27°30S 70°20W 190 B1
Copiapó → *Chile* 27°19S 70°56W 190 B1
Coplay *U.S.A.* 40°44N 75°29W 175 F9
Copley *Australia* 30°36S 138°26E 151 E2
Copo △ *Argentina* 25°53S 61°41W 190 B3
Copp L. *Canada* 60°14N 114°40W 162 A6
Copparo *Italy* 44°54N 11°49E 93 D8
Coppename → *Suriname* 5°48N 55°55W 187 B7

Copper Canyon = Barranca del
  Cobre △ *Mexico* 27°18N 107°40W 171
Copper Center
  U.S.A. 61°58N 145°18W 166 D11
Copper Harbor *U.S.A.* 47°28N 87°53W 172
Copper Queen
  Zimbabwe 17°29S 29°18E 143
Copperas Cove *U.S.A.* 31°8N 97°54W 176
Copperbelt □ *Zambia* 13°15S 27°30E 143
Coppermine = Kugluktuk
  Canada 67°50N 115°5W 160
Coppermine →
  Canada 67°49N 116°4W 160
Copperopolis *U.S.A.* 37°58N 120°38W 170
Copşa Mică *Romania* 46°7N 24°15E 81
Coquet → *U.K.* 55°20N 1°32W 66 B6
Coquille *U.S.A.* 43°11N 124°11W 168
Coquimbo *Chile* 30°0S 71°20W 190
Coquimbo □ *Chile* 31°0S 71°0W 190
Coquitlam *Canada* 49°17N 122°45W 170
Corabia *Romania* 43°48N 24°30E 81
Coração de Jesus
  Brazil 16°43S 44°22W 189
Coracora *Peru* 15°5S 73°45W 188
Coraki *Australia* 28°59S 153°17E 153
Coral *U.S.A.* 40°29N 79°10W 174
Coral Bay *Australia* 23°8S 113°46E 149
Coral Gables *U.S.A.* 25°43N 80°16W 179
Coral Harbour *Canada* 64°8N 83°10W 161
Coral Sea *Pac. Oc.* 15°0S 150°0E 150
Coral Sea Basin *Pac. Oc.* 14°0S 152°0E 150
Coral Sea Islands Terr. □
  Australia 20°0S 155°0E 150
Coral Springs *U.S.A.* 26°16N 80°16W 179
Corangamite, L.
  Australia 38°0S 143°30E 152
Coraopolis *U.S.A.* 40°31N 80°10W 174
Corato *Italy* 41°9N 16°25E 95
Corbeil-Essonnes *France* 48°36N 2°26E 70
Corbett △ *India* 29°30N 79°0E 124
Corbie *France* 49°54N 2°30E 70
Corbières *France* 42°55N 2°35E 72
Corbigny *France* 47°16N 3°40E 70
Corbin *U.S.A.* 36°57N 84°6W 173
Corbones → *Spain* 37°36N 5°39W 89
Corbu *Romania* 44°25N 28°39E 81
Corby *U.K.* 52°30N 0°41W 67
Corcaigh = Cork *Ireland* 51°54N 8°29W 64
Corcoran *U.S.A.* 36°6N 119°33W 170
Corcovado △ *Chile* 43°25S 72°45W 192
Corcovado △ *Costa Rica* 8°33N 83°35W 182
Cordele *U.S.A.* 31°58N 83°47W 178
Cordell *U.S.A.* 35°17N 98°59W 176
Cordenòns *Italy* 45°59N 12°42E 93
Cordes-sur-Ciel *France* 44°4N 1°57E 72
Cordillera Azul △ *Peru* 7°30S 76°30W 188
Cordisburgo *Brazil* 19°7S 44°21W 189
Córdoba *Argentina* 31°20S 64°10W 190
Córdoba *Mexico* 18°53N 96°56W 181
Córdoba *Spain* 37°50N 4°50W 89
Córdoba □ *Argentina* 31°22S 64°15W 190
Córdoba □ *Spain* 38°5N 5°0W 89
Córdoba, Sierra de
  Argentina 31°10S 64°25W 190
Cordova *U.S.A.* 60°33N 145°45W 166
Corella *Spain* 42°7N 1°48W 90
Corella → *Australia* 19°34S 140°47E 150
Coremas *Brazil* 7°1S 37°58W 189
Corentyne → *S. Amer.* 5°55S 57°20W 187
Corfield *Australia* 21°40S 143°21E 150
Corfu = Kerkyra *Greece* 39°38N 19°50E 97
Corfu *U.S.A.* 42°57N 78°24W 174
Corfu ✈ (CFU) *Greece* 39°35N 19°54E 97
Corfu, Str. of = Kerkyras, Notio
  Steno *Greece* 39°34N 20°0E 97
Corgo = O Corgo *Spain* 42°56N 7°25W 88
Cori *Italy* 41°39N 12°55E 94
Coria *Spain* 39°58N 6°33W 88
Coria del Río *Spain* 37°16N 6°3W 89
Coricudgy *Australia* 32°51S 150°24E 153
Coriglíano Cálabro *Italy* 39°36N 16°31E 95
Coringa Is. *Australia* 16°58S 149°58E 150
Corinth = Korinthos
  Greece 37°56N 22°55E 97
Corinth *Miss., U.S.A.* 34°56N 88°31W 177
Corinth *N.Y., U.S.A.* 43°15N 73°49W 175
Corinth, G. of = Korinthiakos
  Kolpos *Greece* 38°16N 22°30E 97
Corinth Canal *Greece* 37°58N 23°0E 97
Corinto *Brazil* 18°20S 44°30W 189
Corinto *Nic.* 12°30N 87°10W 182
Cork *Ireland* 51°54N 8°29W 64
Cork □ *Ireland* 51°57N 8°40W 64
Cork Harbour *Ireland* 51°47N 8°16W 64
Corlay *France* 48°20N 3°5W 70
Corleone *Italy* 37°49N 13°18E 94
Corleto Perticara *Italy* 40°24N 16°2E 95
Çorlu *Turkey* 41°11N 27°49E 97
Cormack L. *Canada* 60°56N 121°37W 162
Cormòns *Italy* 45°58N 13°28E 93
Cormorant *Canada* 54°14N 100°35W 163
Cormorant L. *Canada* 54°15N 100°50W 163
Corn Is. = Maíz, Is. del
  Nic. 12°15N 83°4W 182
Cornalvo △ *Spain* 39°1N 6°13W 89
Corner Brook *Canada* 48°57N 57°58W 165
Corner Inlet *Australia* 38°45S 146°20E 153
Corner Seamounts
  Atl. Oc. 35°0N 52°0W 10
Corneşti *Moldova* 47°21N 28°1E 81
Corníglio *Italy* 44°29N 10°5E 92
Corning *Ark., U.S.A.* 36°25N 90°35W 176
Corning *Calif., U.S.A.* 39°56N 122°11W 170
Corning *Iowa, U.S.A.* 40°59N 94°44W 172
Corning *N.Y., U.S.A.* 42°9N 77°3W 174
Corno Grande *Italy* 42°28N 13°34E 94
Cornwall *Canada* 45°2N 74°44W 175
Cornwall *U.S.A.* 40°17N 76°25W 175
Cornwall □ *U.K.* 50°26N 4°40W 67
Cornwall I. *Canada* 77°37N 94°38W 161
Cornwallis I. *Canada* 75°8N 95°0W 161
Cornwell □ *U.S.A.* 50°0 52°0W 10
Corny Pt. *Australia* 34°55S 137°0E 152
Coro *Venezuela* 11°25N 69°41W 186
Coroaci *Brazil* 18°35S 42°17W 189
Coroatá *Brazil* 4°8S 44°0W 189
Corocoro *Bolivia* 17°15S 68°28W 188
Coroico *Bolivia* 16°0S 67°50W 188
Coromandel *Brazil* 18°28S 47°13W 189

mandel *N.Z.* 36°45S 175°31E **154** C4
mandel Coast *India* 12°30N 81°0E **127** H5
mandel Pen. *N.Z.* 37°0S 175°45E **154** C4
mandel Ra. *N.Z.* 37°0S 175°40E **154** C4
na *Calif., U.S.A.* 33°53N 117°34W **171** M9
na *N. Mex.,* 34°15N 105°36W **169** J11
nado *U.S.A.* 32°41N 117°10W **171** N9
sta Rica 9°0N 83°40W **182** E3
nados, B. de 41°40S 74°0W **192** B2
nados, G. de los
ile
exico 32°26N 117°19W **171** N9
nation *Canada* 52°5N 111°27W **162** C6
nation Gulf
nada 68°25N 110°0W **160** D10
nation I. *Antarctica* 60°45S 46°0W **55** C18
stralia 14°57S 124°55E **148** B3
nda *Argentina* 31°58S 60°56W **190** C3
nel *Chile* 35°0S 73°10W **190** D1
nel Bogado
raguay 27°11S 56°18W **190** B4
nel Dorrego 38°40S 61°10W **190** D3
nel Fabriciano
azil 19°31S 42°38W **189** D2
nel Murta *Brazil* 16°37S 42°11W **189** D2
nel Oviedo
raguay 25°24S 56°30W **190** B4
nel Pringles 38°0S 61°30W **190** D3
nel Suárez 37°30S 61°52W **190** D3
nel Vidal 37°28S 57°45W **190** D4
ngo *Peru* 8°30S 77°53W **188** B2
puna, Nevado 15°30S 72°41W **188** D3
vodë *Albania* 40°31N 20°14E **96** F4
awa *Australia* 35°58S 146°21E **153** C7
zal □ *Belize* 18°23N 88°22W **181** D7
zal Pt.
n. & Tob. 10°45N 61°37W **187** K15
s *France* 44°50N 5°56E **73** D9
us *Argentina* 27°10S 55°30W **191** B4
us Christi *U.S.A.* 27°47N 97°24W **176** M6
S.A.
a *Bolivia* 18°20S 67°41W **188** D4
al *Chile* 39°52S 73°26W **192** A2
al de Almaguer
in 39°45N 3°10W **88** F7
alejo *Canary Is.* 28°43N 13°53W **100** F6
aun Pen. *Ireland* 53°54N 9°54W **64** C2
ggio *Italy* 44°46N 10°47E **92** D7
inte *Brazil* 10°27S 45°10W **189** C1
ente → *Brazil* 13°8S 43°28W **189** C2
ntes, C. das
nzam. 24°6S 35°34E **145** B6
eze □ *France* 13°20S 44°39W **189** C2
eze → *France* 45°20N 1°45E **72** C5
ente → *Brazil* 45°10N 1°28E **72** C5
ds, L. *Ireland* 53°27N 9°16W **64** C2
dônia *Italy* 43°15N 13°30E **93** E10
entes *Argentina* 27°30S 58°45W **190** B4
entes □ *Argentina* 28°0S 57°0W **190** B4
entes → *Peru* 3°43S 74°35W **188** B3
entes, C. *Colombia* 12°28N …
entes, C. *Cuba* 21°43N 84°30W **182** B3
entes, C. *Mexico* 20°25N 105°42W **180** C3
gan *U.S.A.* 31°0N 94°52W **176** F7
verton *Guyana* 5°55N 57°20W **186** B7
gong *Australia* 36°12S 147°53E **153** D7
yong *Australia* 36°12S 147°53E **153** D7
e □ *France* 43°1N 9°0E **73** G13
e, C. *France* 43°1N 9°0E **73** G13
e → *France* 42°14N 9°10E **73** G13
e-du-Sud □ *France* 41°45N 9°0E **73** G13
ca = Corse □ *France* 42°0N 9°0E **73** G13
cana *U.S.A.* 32°6N 96°28W **176** E6
France 42°19N 9°11E **73** G13
a Pinto *Portugal* 37°42N 7°29W **89** H3
egana *Spain* 37°52S 6°49W **89** H4
s, Mar de = California, G. de
exico 27°0N 111°0W **180** B2
ez *U.S.A.* 37°21N 108°35W **169** H9
naidh, Inis = Enniscorthy
land 52°30N 6°34W **64** C5
na d'Ampezzo *Italy* 46°32N 12°8E **93** B7
and *N.Y., U.S.A.* 42°36N 76°11W **175** D8
and *Ohio, U.S.A.* 41°20N 80°44W **174** E4
na *Italy* 43°16N 11°59E **93** E8
bal → *Guinea-Biss.* 11°57N 15°5W **138** C2
he *Portugal* 38°57N 8°30W **89** G2
h → *Turkey* 41°38N 41°38E **87** K5
m *Turkey* 40°30N 34°57E **104** B6
m □ *Turkey* 40°40N 35°0E **104** B6
mbá *Brazil* 19°0S 57°30W **186** G7
mbá → *Brazil* 18°19S 48°55W **189** D1
mba *Brazil* 18°9S 48°43W **189** D1
nd *Romania* 46°30N 25°13E **81** D10
nna = A Coruña
llis *U.S.A.* 44°34N 123°16W **168** D2
nada 25°30N 74°3W **164** B5
Azores 39°43N 31°8W **134** a
don *U.S.A.* 40°46N 93°19W **172** E7
la *Mexico* 23°20N 106°41W **180** C3
maloapan de Carpio
exico 18°22N 95°48W **181** D5
nza *U.S.A.* 39°18N 16°15E **95** D9
reni *Romania* 44°38N 26°35E **81** F11
octon *U.S.A.* 40°16N 81°51W **174** F3
o Newberry
stralia 27°30S 122°54E **149** E3
o Newberry □
stralia 27°30S 122°53E **149** E3
onaut Sea *S. Ocean* 66°30S 40°0E **55** C5
e-Cours-sur-Loire
Junction *U.S.A.* 36°3N 117°57W **171** J9
S.A. 33°53N 117°44W **171** J9
Pk., *U.S.A.* 36°19N 116°50W **171** J10
Argentina 31°5S 64°30W **190** C3

Cossato *Italy* 45°34N 8°10E **92** C5
Cossé-le-Vivien *France* 47°57N 0°54W **70** E6
Cosson → *France* 47°30N 1°15E **70** E8
Costa dels Pins *Spain* 39°38N 3°26E **100** B10
Costa Mesa *U.S.A.* 33°38N 117°55W **171** N9
Costa Rica ■ *Cent. Amer.* 10°0N 84°0W **182** E3
Costa Teguise *Canary Is.* 29°0N 13°10W **100** F6
Costesti *Romania* 44°40N 24°53E **81** F9
Costigliole d'Asti *Italy* 44°48N 8°11E **92** D5
Cosumnes → *U.S.A.* 38°16N 121°26W **170** G5
Coswig *Sachsen, Germany* 51°7N 13°34E **76** D9
Coswig *Sachsen-Anhalt,*
  Germany 51°53N 12°27E **76** D8
Cotabato *Phil.* 7°14N 124°15E **119** C6
Cotacajes → *Bolivia* 16°0S 67°1W **188** D4
Cotagaita *Bolivia* 20°45S 65°40W **190** A2
Cotahuasi *Peru* 15°12S 72°50W **188** D3
Côte-d'Ivoire = Ivory Coast ■
  Africa 7°30N 5°0W **138** D4
Côte-d'Or □ *France* 47°30N 4°50E **71** E11
Coteau des Prairies
  U.S.A. 45°20N 97°50W **172** C5
Coteau du Missouri
  U.S.A. 47°0N 100°0W **172** B4
Cotegipe *Brazil* 12°2S 44°15W **189** C2
Cotentin *France* 49°15N 1°30W **70** C5
Côtes de Meuse *France* 48°25N 2°40W **70** D4
Côtes-d'Armor □ *France* 48°25N 2°40W **70** D4
Côtes-du-Nord = Côtes-
  d'Armor □ *France* 48°25N 2°40W **70** D4
Cotiella *Spain* 42°31N 0°19E **90** C5
Cotillo *Canary Is.* 28°41N 14°1W **100** F5
Cotiujeni *Moldova* 47°51N 28°33E **81** C13
Cotonou *Benin* 6°20N 2°25E **139** D5
Cotopaxi *Ecuador* 0°40S 78°30W **186** D4
Cotronei *Italy* 39°9N 16°47E **95** C9
Cotswold Hills *U.K.* 51°42N 2°10W **67** F5
Cottage Grove *U.S.A.* 43°48N 123°3W **168** E2
Cottageville *U.S.A.* 32°56N 80°29W **178** C9
Cottam *Canada* 42°8N 82°45W **174** D2
Cottbus *Germany* 51°45N 14°20E **76** D10
Cottondale *U.S.A.* 30°48N 85°23W **178** E4
Cottonwood *Ala., U.S.A.* 31°3N 85°18W **178** D4
Cottonwood *Ariz.,*
  U.S.A. 34°45N 112°1W **169** J7
Cotulla *U.S.A.* 28°26N 99°14W **176** G5
Coubre, Pte. de la *France* 45°42N 1°15W **72** C2
Couches *France* 46°53N 4°30E **71** F11
Couço *Portugal* 38°58N 8°17W **89** G2
Coudersport *U.S.A.* 41°46N 78°1W **174** E6
Couedic, C. du *Australia* 36°5S 136°40E **152** D2
Couëron *France* 47°13N 1°44W **70** E5
Couesnon → *France* 48°38N 1°32W **70** C5
Couhé *France* 46°17N 0°11E **72** B4
Coulanges-sur-Yonne
  France 47°31N 3°33E **71** E10
Coulee City *U.S.A.* 47°37N 119°17W **168** C4
Coulee Dam Nat. Recr. Area =
  Lake Roosevelt →
  U.S.A. 48°5N 118°14W **168** B4
Coulman I. *Antarctica* 73°35S 170°0E **55** D11
Coulommiers *France* 48°50N 3°3E **71** D10
Coulon → *France* 43°51N 5°6E **73** E9
Coulonge → *Canada* 45°52N 76°46W **164** C4
Coulonges-sur-l'Autize
  France 46°29N 0°36W **72** B3
Coulounieix-Chamiers
  France 45°11N 0°42E **72** C4
Coulterville *U.S.A.* 37°43N 120°12W **170** H6
Council *Alaska, U.S.A.* 64°53N 163°41W **166** C7
Council *Idaho, U.S.A.* 44°44N 116°26W **168** D5
Council Bluffs *U.S.A.* 41°16N 95°52W **172** E6
Council Grove *U.S.A.* 38°40N 96°29W **172** F5
Coupeville *U.S.A.* 48°13N 122°41W **170** B4
Courantyne = Corentyne →
  S. Amer. 5°50N 57°8W **186** B7
Courcelles *Belgium* 50°28N 4°22E **69** D4
Courchevel *France* 45°25N 6°36E **73** C10
Courçon *France* 46°15N 0°50W **72** B3
Courmayeur *Italy* 45°47N 6°58E **92** C2
Couronne, C. *France* 43°19N 5°3E **73** E9
Cours-la-Ville *France* 46°7N 4°19E **71** F11
Coursan *France* 43°14N 3°4E **72** E7
Courseulles-sur-Mer
  France 49°20N 0°29W **70** C6
Courtenay *Canada* 49°45N 125°0W **162** D4
Courtenay *France* 48°2N 3°3E **71** D10
Courtland *Canada* 42°51N 80°38W **174** D4
Courtland *U.S.A.* 38°20N 121°34W **170** G5
Courtrai = Kortrijk
  Belgium 50°50N 3°17E **69** D3
Courtright *Canada* 42°49N 82°28W **174** D2
Coushatta *U.S.A.* 32°1N 93°21W **176** F8
Coutances *France* 49°3N 1°28W **70** C5
Coutras *France* 45°3N 0°8W **72** C3
Coutts Crossing
  Australia 29°49S 152°55E **151** D5
Couva *Trin. & Tob.* 10°25N 61°27W **187** K15
Couvin *Belgium* 50°3N 4°29E **69** D4
Covarrubias *Spain* 42°4N 3°31W **88** C7
Covasna *Romania* 45°50N 26°10E **81** E11
Covasna □ *Romania* 45°50N 26°0E **81** E10
Cove I. *Canada* 45°17N 81°44W **174** A3
Coventry *U.K.* 52°25N 1°28W **67** E6
Coverdale *Portugal* 31°38N 83°58W **178** D6
Covilhã *Portugal* 40°17N 7°31W **88** E3
Covington *Ga., U.S.A.* 33°36N 83°51W **178** C6
Covington *Ky., U.S.A.* 39°5N 84°30W **173** F11
Covington *Tenn.,*
  U.S.A. 35°34N 89°39W **177** D10
Covington *Va., U.S.A.* 37°47N 79°59W **173** G14
Cowal, L. *Australia* 33°40S 147°25E **153** B7
Cowan, L. *Australia* 31°45S 121°45E **149** F3
Cowan L. *Canada* 54°0N 107°15W **167** C7
Cowangie *Australia* 35°12S 141°26E **152** C4
Cowansville *Canada* 45°14N 72°46W **175** A12
Coward Springs
  Australia 29°24S 136°49E **151** D2
Cowcowing Lakes
  Australia 30°55S 117°20E **149** F2
Cowdenbeath *U.K.* 56°7N 3°21W **65** E5
Cowell *Australia* 33°39S 136°56E **152** B2
Cowes *Australia* 38°28S 145°14E **153** C6
Cowes *U.K.* 50°45N 1°18W **67** G6
Cowichan L. *Canada* 48°53N 124°17W **170** B2
Cowlitz → *U.S.A.* 46°6N 122°55W **170** D4
Cowra *Australia* 33°49S 148°42E **153** B8
Cox *Spain* 38°8N 0°53W **91** G4
Coxilha Grande *Brazil* 28°18S 51°30W **191** B5
Coxim *Brazil* 18°30S 54°55W **187** G8

Cox's Bazar *Bangla.* 21°26N 91°59E **123** J17
Coyah *Guinea* 9°42N 13°22W **138** D2
Coyote Wells *U.S.A.* 32°44N 115°58W **171** N11
Coyuca de Benitez
  Mexico 17°2N 100°4W **181** D4
Coyuca de Catalán
  Mexico 18°20N 100°39W **180** D4
Cozad *U.S.A.* 40°52N 99°59W **172** E4
Cozes *France* 45°34N 0°49W **72** C3
Cozia □ *Romania* 45°25N 24°16E **81** E9
Cozumel *Mexico* 20°31N 86°55W **181** C7
Cozumel, Isla *Mexico* 20°30N 86°40W **181** C7
Crab Hill *Barbados* 13°19N 59°38W **183** g
Cracow = Kraków
  Poland 50°4N 19°57E **83** H6
Cracow *Australia* 25°17S 150°17E **151** D5
Craddock Channel
  N.Z. 36°10S 175°13E **154** C4
Cradle Mt.-Lake St. Clair △
  Australia 41°49S 147°56E **151** G4
Cradock *Australia* 32°6S 138°31E **152** B2
Cradock *S. Africa* 32°8S 25°36E **144** D4
Crafers *Australia* 35°0S 138°42E **152** C3
Craig *U.S.A.* 40°31N 107°33W **168** F10
Craigavon *U.K.* 54°27N 6°23W **64** B5
Craigieburn *Australia* 37°38S 144°56E **153** D6
Craigmore *Zimbabwe* 20°28S 32°50E **143** G3
Craik *Canada* 51°3N 105°49W **167** C7
Crailsheim *Germany* 49°8N 10°5E **77** F6
Craiova *Romania* 44°21N 23°48E **81** F8
Cramsie *Australia* 23°20S 144°15E **150** C3
Cranberry L. *U.S.A.* 44°11N 74°50W **175** B10
Cranberry Portage
  Canada 54°35N 101°23W **163** C8
Cranbrook *Australia* 34°18S 117°33E **149** F2
Cranbrook *Canada* 49°30N 115°46W **162** D5
Crandon *U.S.A.* 45°34N 88°54W **172** C9
Crane *Oreg., U.S.A.* 43°25N 118°35W **168** E4
Crane *Tex., U.S.A.* 31°24N 102°21W **176** F3
Crane, The *Barbados* 13°6N 59°27W **183** g
Cranganore *India* 10°13N 76°13E **127** J3
Cranston *U.S.A.* 41°47N 71°26W **175** E13
Craon *France* 47°50N 0°58W **70** E6
Craonne *France* 49°27N 3°46E **71** C10
Craponne-sur-Arzon
  France 45°19N 3°51E **72** C7
Crasna *Romania* 46°32N 27°51E **81** D12
Crasna → *Romania* 47°44N 22°35E **80** C7
Crasnei, Munţii *Romania* 47°0N 23°20E **81** C8
Crater L. *U.S.A.* 42°56N 122°6W **168** E2
Crater Lake △ *U.S.A.* 42°55N 122°10W **168** E2
Craters of the Moon △
  U.S.A. 43°25N 113°30W **168** E7
Crateús *Brazil* 5°10S 40°39W **189** B2
Crati → *Italy* 39°43N 16°31E **95** C9
Crato *Brazil* 7°10S 39°25W **189** B3
Crato *Portugal* 39°16N 7°39W **89** F3
Craven, L. *Canada* 54°20N 76°56W **164** B4
Crawford *Ala., U.S.A.* 32°27N 85°11W **178** C4
Crawford *Nebr.,*
  U.S.A. 42°41N 103°25W **172** D2
Crawfordsville *U.S.A.* 40°2N 86°54W **172** E10
Crawfordville *Fla.,*
  U.S.A. 30°11N 84°23W **178** E5
Crawfordville *Ga.,*
  U.S.A. 33°33N 82°54W **178** B7
Crawley *U.K.* 51°7N 0°11W **67** F7
Crazy Mts. *U.S.A.* 46°12N 110°20W **168** C8
Crean L. *Canada* 54°5N 106°9W **163** C7
Crécy-en-Ponthieu
  France 50°15N 1°53E **71** B8
Crediton *Canada* 43°17N 81°33W **174** C3
Crediton *U.K.* 50°47N 3°40W **67** G4
Cree → *Canada* 58°57N 105°47W **163** B7
Cree → *U.K.* 54°55N 4°25W **65** G4
Cree L. *Canada* 57°30N 106°30W **163** B7
Creede *U.S.A.* 37°51N 106°56W **169** H10
Creekside *U.S.A.* 40°40N 79°11W **174** F5
Creel *Mexico* 27°45N 107°38W **180** B3
Creemore *Canada* 44°19N 80°6W **174** B4
Creighton *Canada* 54°45N 101°54W **163** C8
Creighton *U.S.A.* 42°28N 97°54W **172** D5
Creil *France* 49°15N 2°29E **71** C9
Crema *Italy* 45°22N 9°41E **92** C6
Cremona *Italy* 45°7N 10°2E **92** C7
Crepaja *Serbia* 45°1N 20°38E **80** E5
Crépy *France* 49°37N 3°32E **71** C10
Crépy-en-Valois *France* 49°14N 2°54E **71** C9
Cres *Croatia* 44°58N 14°25E **93** D11
Crescent Beach *U.S.A.* 29°46N 81°15W **178** F8
Crescent City *Calif.,*
  U.S.A. 41°45N 124°12W **168** F1
Crescent City *Fla.,*
  U.S.A. 29°26N 81°31W **178** F8
Crescent Group
  S. China Sea 16°30N 111°40E **118** A4
Crescent Hd.
  Australia 31°11S 152°59E **153** A10
Crescent L. *U.S.A.* 29°28N 81°30W **178** F8
Crescentino *Italy* 45°11N 8°6E **92** C5
Crespi d'Adda *Italy* 45°35N 9°32E **92** C6
Crespo *Argentina* 32°2S 60°19W **190** C3
Cresson *U.S.A.* 40°28N 78°36W **174** F6
Cressy *Australia* 38°2S 143°40E **152** C5
Crest *France* 44°44N 5°2E **73** D9
Crestline *Calif., U.S.A.* 34°14N 117°18W **171** L9
Crestline *Ohio, U.S.A.* 40°47N 82°44W **174** F2
Creston *Canada* 49°10N 116°31W **162** D5
Creston *Calif., U.S.A.* 35°32N 120°33W **170** K6
Creston *Iowa, U.S.A.* 41°4N 94°22W **172** E7
Crestview *Calif.,*
  U.S.A. 37°46N 118°58W **170** H8
Crestview *Fla., U.S.A.* 30°46N 86°34W **178** F3
Creswick *Australia* 37°25S 143°58E **152** D5
Crêt de la Neige *France* 46°16N 5°58E **71** F12
Crete = Kríti *Greece* 35°15N 25°0E **101** D7
Crete *U.S.A.* 40°38N 96°58W **172** E5
Crete, Sea of *Greece* 36°0N 25°0E **99** F7
Créteil *France* 48°47N 2°27E **71** D9
Creus, C. de *Spain* 42°20N 3°19E **90** C8
Creuse □ *France* 46°0N 2°0E **72** B5
Creuse → *France* 47°0N 0°34E **72** B4
Creutzwald *France* 49°12N 6°42E **71** C13
Creuzburg *Germany* 51°3N 10°14E **76** D6
Crèvecœur-le-Grand
  France 49°37N 2°5E **71** C9
Crevillent *Spain* 38°12N 0°48W **91** G4
Crewe *U.K.* 53°6N 2°26W **66** D5
Crewkerne *U.K.* 50°53N 2°48W **67** G5
Crianlarich *U.K.* 56°24N 4°37W **65** E4
Criciúma *Brazil* 28°40S 49°23W **191** B6

Cricova *Moldova* 47°8N 28°52E **81** C13
Crieff *U.K.* 56°22N 3°50W **65** E5
Crikvenica *Croatia* 45°11N 14°40E **93** C11
Crimea □ *Ukraine* 45°30N 33°10E **85** K8
Crimean Pen. = Krymskyy
  Pivostriv *Ukraine* 45°0N 34°0E **85** K8
Crimmitschau *Germany* 50°48N 12°24E **76** E8
Cristino Castro *Brazil* 8°49S 44°13W **189** B2
Cristuru Secuiesc
  Romania 46°17N 25°2E **81** D10
Crişul Alb → *Romania* 46°42N 21°17E **80** D6
Crişul Negru →
  Romania 46°42N 21°16E **80** D6
Crişul Repede →
  Romania 46°55N 20°59E **80** D5
Criuleni *Moldova* 47°13N 29°10E **81** C14
Crivitz *Germany* 53°34N 11°39E **76** B7
Crna → *Macedonia* 41°33N 21°59E **96** E5
Crna Gora = Montenegro ■
  Europe 42°40N 19°20E **96** C3
Crna Gora *Macedonia* 42°10N 21°30E **96** D5
Crna Reka = Crna →
  Macedonia 41°33N 21°59E **96** E5
Crni Drim → *Macedonia* 41°17N 20°40E **96** E4
Crni Timok → *Serbia* 43°53N 22°15E **96** C6
Crnojleva Planina = Zhar, Mali
  Kosovo 42°20N 21°0E **96** D5
Črnomelj *Slovenia* 45°33N 15°10E **93** C12
Croagh Patrick *Ireland* 53°46N 9°40W **64** C2
Croajingolong △
  Australia 37°45S 149°26E **153** D8
Croatia ■ *Europe* 45°20N 16°0E **93** C13
Crocker, Banjaran
  Malaysia 5°40N 116°30E **118** C5
Crockett *U.S.A.* 31°19N 95°27W **176** F7
Crocodile = Umgwenya →
  Mozam. 25°14S 32°18E **145** C5
Crocodile → *S. Africa* 24°12S 26°53E **144** B4
Crocodile Is. *Australia* 12°3S 134°58E **150** A1
Crocq *France* 45°52N 2°21E **72** C6
Crohy Hd. *Ireland* 54°55N 8°26W **64** B3
Croisette, C. *France* 43°14N 5°22E **73** E9
Croisic, Pte. du *France* 47°19N 2°31W **70** E4
Croix, L. la *Canada* 48°20N 92°15W **164** C1
Croker, C. *Australia* 10°58S 132°35E **148** B5
Croker, C. *Canada* 44°58N 80°59W **174** B4
Croker I. *Australia* 11°12S 132°32E **148** B5
Croker Islands Seas ♦
  Australia 11°20S 132°30E **148** B5
Cromarty *U.K.* 57°40N 4°2W **65** D4
Cromer *U.K.* 52°56N 1°17E **66** E9
Cromwell *N.Z.* 45°3S 169°14E **155** F4
Cromwell *U.S.A.* 41°36N 72°39W **175** E12
Cronat *France* 46°43N 3°40E **71** F10
Cronulla *Australia* 34°3S 151°8E **153** B9
Crook *U.K.* 54°43N 1°45W **66** C6
Crooked → *Canada* 54°50N 122°54W **162** C4
Crooked → *U.S.A.* 44°32N 121°16W **168** D3
Crooked I. *Bahamas* 22°50N 74°10W **183** B5
Crooked Island Passage
  Bahamas 22°55N 74°35W **183** B5
Crookston *Minn.,*
  U.S.A. 47°47N 96°37W **172** B5
Crookston *Nebr.,*
  U.S.A. 42°56N 100°45W **172** D3
Crookwell *Australia* 34°28S 149°24E **153** C8
Cropane-Micone △ *Italy* 38°31N 16°18E **95** D9
Crosby *U.K.* 53°30N 3°3W **66** D4
Crosby *N. Dak., U.S.A.* 48°55N 103°18W **172** A2
Crosbyton *U.S.A.* 33°40N 101°14W **176** E4
Crosia *Italy* 39°35N 16°45E **95** C9
Cross → *Nigeria* 4°42N 8°21E **139** E6
Cross City *U.S.A.* 29°38N 83°7W **179** F6
Cross Fell *U.K.* 54°43N 2°28W **66** C5
Cross L. *Canada* 54°45N 97°30W **163** C9
Cross Lake *Canada* 54°37N 97°47W **163** C9
Cross River □ *Nigeria* 6°0N 8°0E **139** D6
Cross Sound *U.S.A.* 58°0N 135°0W **160** F4
Crossett *U.S.A.* 33°8N 91°58W **176** F9
Crosshaven *Ireland* 51°47N 8°17W **64** E3
Crossley, Mt. *N.Z.* 42°50S 172°5E **155** C7
Crossmaglen *Ireland* 54°5N 6°36W **64** B5
Crossmolina *Ireland* 54°6N 9°20W **64** B2
Crossville *U.S.A.* 35°57N 85°2W **177** D12
Croswell *U.S.A.* 43°16N 82°37W **174** C2
Croton-on-Hudson
  U.S.A. 41°12N 73°55W **175** E11
Crotone *Italy* 39°5N 17°8E **95** C10
Crow → *Canada* 59°41N 124°20W **162** B4
Crow Agency *U.S.A.* 45°36N 107°28W **168** D10
Crow Hd. *Ireland* 51°35N 10°9W **64** E1
Crowdy Bay △
  Australia 31°45S 152°45E **153** A10
Crowell *U.S.A.* 33°59N 99°43W **176** E5
Crowl Cr. → *Australia* 32°0S 145°30E **153** B6
Crowley *U.S.A.* 30°13N 92°22W **176** F8
Crowley, L. *U.S.A.* 37°35N 118°42W **170** H8
Crown Point *Ind.* 41°25N 87°22W **172** E10
Crown Point *N.Y.* 43°57N 73°26W **175** C11
Crownpoint *U.S.A.* 35°41N 108°9W **169** J9
Crows Landing *U.S.A.* 37°23N 121°6W **170** H5
Crows Nest *Australia* 27°16S 152°4E **151** D5
Crowsnest Pass
  Canada 49°40N 114°40W **162** D6
Croydon *Australia* 18°13S 142°14E **150** B3
Croydon □ *U.K.* 51°22N 0°5W **67** F7
Crozet, Îs. *Ind. Oc.* 46°27S 52°0E **146** J4
Crozet Basin *Ind. Oc.* 39°0S 60°0E **146** K5
Crozon *France* 48°15N 4°30W **70** D2
Cruce de Sardina
  Canary Is. 27°52N 15°22W **100** G4
Crushen *Ireland* 52°57N 8°53W **64** D3
Cruz, C. *Cuba* 19°50N 77°50W **182** C4
Cruz Alta *Brazil* 28°40S 53°40W **191** B5
Cruz Bay *U.S. Virgin Is.* 18°20N 64°48W **183** e
Cruz das Almas *Brazil* 12°0S 39°6W **189** D3
Cruz del Eje *Argentina* 30°45S 64°50W **190** C3
Cruzeiro *Brazil* 18°45S 44°11W **189** D2
Cruzeiro do Oeste *Brazil* 23°46S 53°4W **191** A5
Cruzeiro do Sul *Brazil* 7°35S 72°35W **188** B3
Cry L. *Canada* 58°45N 129°0W **162** B3
Crystal Bay *U.S.A.* 39°15N 120°0W **170** F7
Crystal Brook
  Australia 33°21S 138°12E **152** B3
Crystal City *U.S.A.* 28°41N 99°50W **176** G5

Crystal Falls *U.S.A.* 46°5N 88°20W **172** B9
Crystal Lake *U.S.A.* 30°26N 85°42W **178** E4
Crystal River *U.S.A.* 28°54N 82°35W **179** G7
Crystal Springs *U.S.A.* 31°59N 90°21W **177** F9
Csenger *Hungary* 47°50N 22°41E **80** C7
Csongrád *Hungary* 46°43N 20°12E **80** D5
Csongrád □ *Hungary* 46°32N 20°15E **80** D5
Csorna *Hungary* 47°38N 17°18E **80** D2
Csurgo *Hungary* 46°16N 17°9E **80** D2
Cu Lao Hon *Vietnam* 10°54N 108°18E **121** G7
Cua Rao *Vietnam* 19°16N 104°27E **120** C5
Cuácua → *Mozam.* 17°54S 37°0E **143** F4
Cuamato *Angola* 17°2S 15°7E **144** A2
Cuamba *Mozam.* 14°45S 36°22E **143** F4
Cuando → *Angola* 17°30S 23°15E **141** H4
Cuando Cubango □
  Angola 16°25S 20°0E **144** A3
Cuangar *Angola* 17°36S 18°39E **144** A2
Cuango = Kwango →
  Dem. Rep. of the Congo 3°14S 17°22E **140** E3
Cuanza → *Angola* 9°21S 13°9E **140** F2
Cuarto → *Argentina* 33°25S 63°2W **190** C3
Cuatrociénegas *Mexico* 26°59N 102°5W **180** B4
Cuauhtémoc *Mexico* 28°25N 106°52W **180** B3
Cuba *Portugal* 38°10N 7°54W **89** G3
Cuba *N. Mex., U.S.A.* 36°1N 107°4W **169** H10
Cuba *N.Y., U.S.A.* 42°13N 78°17W **174** D6
Cuba ■ *W. Indies* 22°0N 79°0W **182** B4
Cubango → *Africa* 18°50S 22°25E **144** A3
Çubuk *Turkey* 40°14N 33°3E **104** B5
Cuc Phuong △
  Vietnam 20°17N 105°38E **120** B5
Cuchillo-Co *Argentina* 38°26S 64°40W **190** D2
Cuchumatanes, Sierra de los
  Guatemala 15°35N 91°25W **182** C1
Cuckfield *U.K.* 51°1N 0°8W **67** F7
Cucuí *Brazil* 1°12N 66°50W **186** C5
Cucurpé *Mexico* 30°20N 110°43W **180** A2
Cúcuta *Colombia* 7°54N 72°31W **186** B4
Cudalbi *Romania* 45°46N 27°41E **81** E12
Cuddalore *India* 11°46N 79°45E **127** J4
Cuddapah = Kadapa
  India 14°30N 78°47E **127** G4
Cuddapan, L. *Australia* 25°45S 141°26E **150** D3
Cudgewa *Australia* 36°10S 147°42E **153** D7
Cudillero *Spain* 43°33N 6°9W **88** B4
Cue *Australia* 27°25S 117°54E **149** E2
Cuéllar *Spain* 41°23N 4°21W **88** D6
Cuenca *Ecuador* 2°50S 79°9W **186** D3
Cuenca *Spain* 40°5N 2°10W **90** E2
Cuenca, Serranía de
  Spain 39°55N 1°50W **90** E3
Cuenca Alta del Manzanares △
  Spain 40°50N 3°55W **88** E7
Cuerda del Pozo, Embalse de la
  Spain 41°51N 2°44W **90** D2
Cuernavaca *Mexico* 18°55N 99°15W **181** D5
Cuero *U.S.A.* 29°6N 97°17W **176** G6
Cuers *France* 43°14N 6°5E **73** E10
Cueva de la Quebrada del Toro △
  Venezuela 10°46N 69°3W **183** D6
Cuevas del Almanzora
  Spain 37°18N 1°58W **91** H3
Cuevo *Bolivia* 20°15S 63°30W **186** H6
Cugir *Romania* 45°48N 23°25E **81** E8
Cuglieri *Italy* 40°11N 8°34E **94** B1
Cugnaux *France* 43°32N 1°20E **72** E5
Cuiabá *Brazil* 15°30S 56°0W **187** G7
Cuiabá → *Brazil* 17°5S 56°36W **187** G7
Cuihangcun *China* 22°27N 113°32E **111** a
Cuijk *Neths.* 51°44N 5°50E **69** C5
Cuilapa *Guatemala* 14°16N 90°18W **182** D1
Cuillin Hills *U.K.* 57°13N 6°15W **65** D2
Cuillin Sd. *U.K.* 57°4N 6°20W **65** D2
Cuilo = Kwilu →
  Dem. Rep. of the Congo 3°22S 17°22E **140** E3
Cuiseaux *France* 46°30N 5°22E **71** F12
Cuité *Brazil* 6°29S 36°9W **189** B3
Cuito → *Angola* 18°1S 20°48E **144** A3
Cuitzeo, L. de *Mexico* 19°55N 101°5W **180** D4
Cujmir *Romania* 44°13N 22°57E **80** F7
Cukai *Malaysia* 4°13N 103°25E **121** K4
Çukurca *Turkey* 37°14N 43°36E **105** D10
Culbertson *U.S.A.* 48°9N 104°31W **168** B11
Culburra *N.S.W.,*
  Australia 34°56S 150°46E **153** C9
Culburra *S. Austral.,*
  Australia 35°50S 139°58E **152** C3
Culcairn *Australia* 35°41S 147°3E **153** C7
Culebra *Puerto Rico* 18°19N 65°18W **183** d
Culebra, Sierra de la
  Spain 41°55N 6°20W **88** D4
Culfa *Azerbaijan* 38°57N 45°38E **105** C11
Culgoa → *Australia* 29°56S 146°20E **151** D4
Culgoa Flood Plain △
  Australia 28°58S 147°5E **151** D4
Culiacán *Mexico* 24°48N 107°24W **180** C3
Culiacán → *Mexico* 24°30N 107°42W **180** C3
Culik *Indonesia* 8°21S 115°37E **119** J18
Culion *Phil.* 11°54N 119°58E **119** B6
Cúllar *Spain* 37°35N 2°34W **89** H8
Cullarin Ra. *Australia* 34°30S 149°30E **153** C8
Cullen *U.K.* 57°42N 2°49W **65** D6
Cullen Bullen *Australia* 33°18S 150°2E **153** B9
Cullen Pt. *Australia* 11°57S 141°54E **150** A3
Cullera *Spain* 39°9N 0°17W **91** F4
Cullman *U.S.A.* 34°11N 86°51W **177** D11
Cullompton *U.K.* 50°51N 3°24W **67** G4
Culoz *France* 45°47N 5°46E **73** C9
Culpeper *U.S.A.* 38°30N 78°0W **173** F14
Culuene → *Brazil* 12°56S 52°51W **187** F8
Culver, Pt. *Australia* 32°54S 124°43E **149** F3
Culverden *N.Z.* 42°47S 172°49E **155** C7
Culverton *U.S.A.* 33°4N 82°47W **178** C7
Cumaná *Venezuela* 10°30N 64°5W **186** A6
Cumaovasi *Turkey* 38°4N 27°6E **99** D9
Cumari *Brazil* 18°16S 48°11W **189** D1
Cumberland *B.C.,*
  Canada 49°40N 125°0W **162** D4
Cumberland *Ont.,*
  Canada 45°29N 75°24W **175** A9
Cumberland → *U.S.A.* 36°15N 87°0W **177** C11
Cumberland L., *U.S.A.* 36°52N 85°9W **173** G11
Cumberland Gap △
  U.S.A. 36°36N 83°40W **173** G12

Cumberland I. *U.S.A.* 30°50N 81°25W **178** E8
Cumberland Is.
  Australia 20°35S 149°10E **150** b
Cumberland Island △
  U.S.A. 30°51N 81°24W **178** E8
Cumberland L. *Canada* 54°3N 102°18W **163** C8
Cumberland Pen.
  Canada 67°0N 64°0W **161** D19
Cumberland Plateau
  U.S.A. 36°0N 85°0W **177** D12
Cumberland Sd.
  Canada 65°30N 66°0W **161** D18
Cumbernauld *U.K.* 55°57N 3°58W **65** F5
Cumborah *Australia* 29°40S 147°45E **151** D4
Cumbres de Majalca △
  Mexico 28°48N 106°30W **180** B3
Cumbres de Monterrey △
  Mexico 25°26N 100°25W **180** B4
Cumbres Mayores *Spain* 38°4N 6°39W **89** G4
Cumbria □ *U.K.* 54°42N 2°52W **66** C5
Cumbrian Mts. *U.K.* 54°30N 3°0W **66** C5
Cumbum *India* 15°40N 79°10E **127** G4
Cuminá → *Brazil* 1°30S 56°0W **187** D7
Cummings Mt. *U.S.A.* 35°2N 118°34W **171** K8
Cummins *Australia* 34°16S 135°43E **151** E2
Cumnock *Australia* 32°59S 148°46E **153** B8
Cumnock *U.K.* 55°28N 4°17W **65** F4
Cumpas *Mexico* 30°2N 109°48W **180** B3
Cumplida, Pta.
  Canary Is. 28°50N 17°48W **100** F2
Çumra *Turkey* 37°34N 32°45E **104** D5
Cuncumén *Chile* 31°53S 70°38W **190** C1
Cundeelee ♦ *Australia* 30°43S 123°25E **149** F3
Cunderdin *Australia* 31°37S 117°12E **149** F2
Cunene → *Angola* 17°20S 11°50E **144** A1
Cúneo *Italy* 44°23N 7°32E **92** D4
Cung Son *Vietnam* 13°2N 108°58E **120** F7
Çüngüş *Turkey* 38°13N 39°17E **128** B3
Cunillera, I. = Sa Conillera
  Spain 38°59N 1°13E **100** C7
Cunlhat *France* 45°38N 3°32E **72** C7
Cunnamulla *Australia* 28°2S 145°38E **151** D4
Cuorgnè *Italy* 45°23N 7°39E **92** C4
Cupar *Canada* 50°57N 104°10W **163** C8
Cupar *U.K.* 56°19N 3°1W **65** E5
Cupcini *Moldova* 48°6N 27°23E **81** B12
Cupertino *U.S.A.* 37°19N 122°2W **170** H4
Cupica, G. de *Colombia* 6°25N 77°30W **186** B3
Čuprija *Serbia* 43°57N 21°26E **96** C5
Curaçá *Brazil* 8°59S 39°54W **189** B3
Curaçao *W. Indies* 12°10N 69°0W **183** D6
Curacautín *Chile* 38°26S 71°53W **192** A2
Curahuara de Carangas
  Bolivia 17°52S 68°26W **188** D3
Curanilahue *Chile* 37°29S 73°28W **190** D1
Curaray → *Peru* 2°20S 74°5W **186** D4
Cure → *France* 47°40N 3°41E **71** E10
Curepipe *Mauritius* 20°19S 57°31E **141** d
Curepto *Chile* 35°8S 72°1W **190** D1
Curia *Portugal* 40°22N 8°22E **88** E2
Curiapo *Venezuela* 8°33N 61°5W **186** B6
Curicó *Chile* 34°55S 71°20W **190** C1
Curieuse *Seychelles* 4°15S 55°44E **141** b
Curimatá *Brazil* 10°25S 44°17W **189** C2
Curinga *Italy* 38°49N 16°19E **95** D9
Curitiba *Brazil* 25°20S 49°10W **191** B6
Curitibanos *Brazil* 27°18S 50°36W **191** B5
Curlewis *Australia* 31°7S 150°16E **153** A9
Curonian Lagoon = Kurshskiy
  Zaliv *Russia* 55°9N 21°6E **82** C8
Curonian Spit *Europe* 55°20N 20°55E **82** C7
Currabubula *Australia* 31°16S 150°44E **153** A9
Currais Novos *Brazil* 6°13S 36°30W **189** B3
Curral Velho *C. Verde Is.* 16°8N 22°48W **134** b
Curralinho *Brazil* 1°45S 49°46W **187** D9
Currane, L. *Ireland* 51°50N 10°4W **64** E1
Currant *U.S.A.* 38°44N 115°28W **168** G6
Curraweena *Australia* 30°47S 145°54E **153** A6
Currawinya △
  Australia 28°55S 144°27E **151** D3
Current → *U.S.A.* 36°15N 90°55W **177** D9
Currie *Australia* 39°56S 143°53E **151** F3
Currie *U.S.A.* 40°16N 114°45W **168** F6
Curtea de Argeş
  Romania 45°12N 24°42E **81** E9
Curtici *Romania* 46°21N 21°18E **80** D6
Curtin Springs
  Australia 25°20S 131°45E **149** E5
Curtis *U.S.A.* 40°38N 100°31W **172** E3
Curtis Group *Australia* 39°30S 146°37E **151** F4
Curtis I. *Australia* 23°35S 151°10E **150** C5
Curuápanema → *Brazil* 2°25S 55°2W **187** D7
Curuçá *Brazil* 0°43S 47°50W **187** D9
Curuçá → *Brazil* 4°27S 71°23W **188** A3
Curuguaty *Paraguay* 24°31S 55°42W **191** A4
Çürüksu Çayi = Büyük
  Menderes → *Turkey* 37°28N 27°11E **99** D9
Curup *Indonesia* 3°26S 102°13E **118** E2
Cururupu *Brazil* 1°50S 44°50W **187** D10
Curuzú Cuatiá
  Argentina 29°50S 58°5W **190** B4
Curvelo *Brazil* 18°45S 44°27W **189** D2
Cusco □ *Peru* 13°32S 72°0W **188** D3
Cusco □ *Peru* 13°31S 71°59W **188** D3
Cushendall *U.K.* 55°5N 6°4W **64** A5
Cushing *U.S.A.* 35°59N 96°46W **176** D6
Cushing, Mt. *Canada* 57°35N 126°57W **162** B3
Cusihuiríáchic
  Mexico 28°14N 106°50W **180** B3
Cusna, Mte. *Italy* 44°17N 10°23E **92** D7
Cusset *France* 46°8N 3°28E **71** F10
Cusseta *U.S.A.* 32°18N 84°46W **178** C5
Custer *U.S.A.* 43°46N 103°36W **172** D2
Cut Bank *U.S.A.* 48°38N 112°20W **168** B7
Cutchogue *U.S.A.* 41°1N 72°30W **175** E12
Cuthbert *U.S.A.* 31°46N 84°48W **178** D5
Cutler *U.S.A.* 36°31N 119°17W **170** J7
Cutler Ridge *U.S.A.* 25°35N 80°20W **179** K9
Cutro *Italy* 39°2N 16°59E **95** C9
Cuttaburra →
  Australia 29°43S 144°22E **151** D3
Cuttack *India* 20°25N 85°57E **126** D7
Cuvier, C. *Australia* 23°14S 113°22E **149** D1
Cuvier I. *N.Z.* 36°27S 175°50E **154** C4
Cuxhaven *Germany* 53°51N 8°41E **76** B4
Cuyahoga Falls *U.S.A.* 41°8N 81°29W **174** E3
Cuyahoga Valley △
  U.S.A. 41°24N 81°33W **174** E3
Cuyo *Phil.* 10°51N 121°2E **119** B6

Cuyuni → *Guyana* 6°23N 58°41W **186** B7
Cuzco = Cusco *Peru* 13°32S 72°0W **188** C3
Čvrsnica *Bos.-H.* 43°36N 17°35E **80** G2
Cwmbran *U.K.* 51°39N 3°2W **67** F4
Cyangugu *Rwanda* 2°29S 28°54E **142** C2
Cybinka *Poland* 52°12N 14°46E **83** F1
Cyclades = Kyklades
Greece 37°0N 24°30E **98** E6
Cygnet *Australia* 43°8S 147°1E **151** G4
Cynthiana *U.S.A.* 38°23N 84°18W **173** F11
Cypress Hills *Canada* 49°40N 109°30W **163** D7
Cypress Hills ○
Canada 49°40N 109°30W **163** D7
Cyprus ■ *Asia* 35°0N 33°0E **101** E12
Cyrenaica = Barqa
Libya 27°0N 23°0E **135** C10
Cyrene *Libya* 32°53N 21°52E **135** B10
Czaplinek *Poland* 53°34N 16°14E **82** E3
Czar *Canada* 52°27N 110°50W **163** C6
Czarna → *Łódzkie,*
Poland 51°18N 19°55E **83** G6
Czarna → *Świętokrzyskie,*
Poland 50°28N 21°21E **83** H8
Czarna Białostocka
Poland 53°18N 23°17E **83** E10
Czarna Woda *Poland* 53°51N 18°6E **82** E5
Czarne *Poland* 53°42N 16°58E **82** E3
Czarnków *Poland* 52°55N 16°38E **83** F3
Czech Rep. ■ *Europe* 50°0N 15°0E **78** B8
Czechowice-Dziedzice
Poland 49°54N 18°59E **83** J5
Czempiń *Poland* 52°9N 16°43E **83** F3
Czeremcha *Poland* 52°31N 23°21E **83** F10
Czersk *Poland* 53°46N 17°58E **82** E4
Czerwieńsk *Poland* 52°1N 15°23E **83** F2
Czerwionka-Leszczyny
Poland 50°7N 18°37E **83** H5
Częstochowa *Poland* 50°49N 19°7E **83** H6
Człopa *Poland* 53°6N 16°6E **83** E3
Człuchów *Poland* 53°41N 17°22E **82** E4
Czyżew-Osada *Poland* 52°48N 22°19E **83** F9

D

Da → *Vietnam* 21°15N 105°20E **116** G5
Da Hinggan Ling *China* 48°0N 121°0E **111** B13
Da Lat *Vietnam* 11°56N 108°25E **121** G7
Da Nang *Vietnam* 16°4N 108°13E **120** D7
Da Qaidam *China* 37°50N 95°15E **110** D8
Da Yunhe → *Hopei,*
China 39°10N 117°10E **115** E9
Da Yunhe → *Jiangsu,*
China 34°25N 120°5E **117** A12
Da'an *China* 45°30N 124°7E **115** B13
Daan Viljoen △ *Namibia* 22°2S 16°45E **144** B2
Dab'a, Ras el *Egypt* 31°3N 28°31E **137** E6
Daba Shan *China* 32°0N 109°0E **116** B7
Dabai *Nigeria* 11°25N 5°15E **139** C6
Dabakala *Ivory C.* 8°15N 4°20W **138** D4
Dabas *Hungary* 47°11N 19°19E **80** C4
Dabbagh, Jabal
Si. Arabia 27°52N 35°45E **128** E2
Dabhoi *India* 22°10N 73°20E **124** H5
Dąbie *Poland* 52°5N 18°50E **83** F5
Dabie Shan *China* 31°20N 115°20E **117** B10
Dabilda *Cameroon* 12°45N 14°35E **139** C7
Dabnou *Niger* 14°10N 5°22E **139** C6
Dabola *Guinea* 10°50N 11°5W **138** C2
Dabou *Ivory C.* 5°20N 4°23W **138** D4
Daboya *Ghana* 9°30N 1°20W **138** D4
Dabravolya *Belarus* 52°55N 23°59E **83** F10
Dąbrowa Białostocka
Poland 53°40N 23°21E **82** E10
Dąbrowa Górnicza
Poland 50°15N 19°10E **83** H6
Dąbrowa Tarnowska
Poland 50°10N 20°59E **83** H7
Dabu *China* 24°22N 116°41E **117** E11
Dabugam *India* 19°27N 82°26E **126** E6
Dabung *Malaysia* 5°23N 102°1E **121** K4
Dacca = Dhaka
Bangla. 23°43N 90°26E **125** H14
Dachang *China* 32°13N 118°45E **117** A12
Dachaoshan Dam
China 24°1N 100°22E **116** E3
Dachau *Germany* 48°15N 11°26E **77** G7
Dachigam △ *India* 34°10N 75°0E **124** B6
Dachstein, Hoher
Austria 47°28N 13°35E **78** D6
Dačice *Czech Rep.* 49°5N 15°26E **78** B8
Dacre *Canada* 45°22N 76°57W **174** A8
Dacula *U.S.A.* 33°59N 83°54W **178** B6
Dadanawa *Guyana* 2°50N 59°30W **186** C7
Daday *Turkey* 41°28N 33°27E **104** B5
Dade City *U.S.A.* 28°22N 82°11W **179** E7
Dadès, Oued →
Morocco 30°58N 6°44W **136** B2
Dadeville *U.S.A.* 32°50N 85°46W **178** C4
Dadhar *Pakistan* 29°28N 67°39E **124** E2
Dadiya *Nigeria* 9°35N 11°24E **139** D7
Dadnah *U.A.E.* 25°32N 56°22E **129** E8
Dadra & Nagar Haveli □
India 20°5N 73°0E **126** D1
Dadri = Charkhi Dadri
India 28°37N 76°17E **124** E7
Dadu *Pakistan* 26°45N 67°45E **124** F2
Dadu He → *China* 29°31N 103°46E **116** C4
Daegu *S. Korea* 35°50N 128°37E **115** G15
Daejeon *S. Korea* 36°20N 127°28E **115** F14
Daejeong *S. Korea* 33°8N 126°17E **115** H14
Daet *Phil.* 14°2N 122°55E **119** B6
Dafang *China* 27°9N 105°39E **116** D5
Dafeng *China* 33°12N 120°45E **117** A13
Dafnes *Greece* 35°13N 25°3E **101** D7
Dafni *Greece* 37°48N 22°1E **98** D4
Dağ *Turkey* 37°12N 30°31E **99** D12
Dagana *Senegal* 16°30N 15°35W **138** B1
Dagash *Sudan* 19°19N 33°25E **137** D3
Dagestan □ *Russia* 42°30N 47°0E **87** J8
Dagestanskiye Ogni
Russia 42°6N 48°12E **87** J9
Dagg Sd. *N.Z.* 45°23S 166°45E **155** F1
Daggett *U.S.A.* 34°52N 116°52W **171** L10
Daghestan Republic =
Dagestan □ *Russia* 42°30N 47°0E **87** J8
Daghfeli *Sudan* 19°18N 32°40E **137** D3
Dağlıq Qarabağ =
Nagorno-Karabakh □
Azerbaijan 39°55N 46°45E **105** C12

Dagö = Hiiumaa *Estonia* 58°50N 22°45E **88** C2
Dagu *China* 38°59N 117°40E **115** E9
Daguan *China* 27°43N 103°56E **116** D4
Dagupan *Phil.* 16°3N 120°20E **119** A6
Daguragu *Australia* 17°33S 130°30E **148** C5
Daguragu ○ *Australia* 17°24S 130°48E **148** C5
Dahab *Egypt* 28°31N 34°31E **128** D2
Dahanu *India* 19°58N 72°44E **126** E1
Dahivadi *India* 17°43N 74°33E **126** F2
Dahlak Kebir *Eritrea* 15°50N 40°10E **131** D3
Dahlenburg *Germany* 53°11N 10°44E **76** B6
Dahlonega *U.S.A.* 34°32N 83°59W **177** D13
Dahme *Germany* 51°52N 13°25E **76** D9
Dahod *India* 22°50N 74°15E **124** H6
Dahong Shan *China* 31°25N 113°0E **117** B9
Dahongliutan *China* 35°45N 79°20E **125** B8
Dahra *Libya* 29°30N 17°50E **135** C9
Dahra *Senegal* 15°22N 15°30W **138** B1
Dahra, Massif de *Algeria* 36°7N 1°21E **136** A4
Dahshūr *Egypt* 29°45N 31°14E **137** F7
Dahūk *Iraq* 36°50N 43°1E **105** D10
Dahūk □ *Iraq* 36°50N 42°50E **105** D10
Dai Hao *Vietnam* 18°1N 106°25E **120** C6
Dai-Sen *Japan* 35°22N 133°32E **113** G6
Dai Shan *China* 30°25N 122°10E **117** B14
Dai Xian *China* 39°4N 112°58E **114** E7
Daicheng *China* 38°42N 116°38E **114** E9
Daikondi = Dāykondī □
Afghan. 34°0N 66°0E **122** C5
Dailekh *Nepal* 28°50N 81°44E **125** E9
Daimiel *Spain* 39°5N 3°35W **89** F7
Daingean *Ireland* 53°18N 7°17W **64** C4
Daingean, An = Dingle
Ireland 52°9N 10°17W **64** D1
Dainkog *China* 32°30N 97°58E **116** A1
Daintree *Australia* 16°20S 145°20E **150** B4
Daintree ○ *Australia* 16°8S 145°2E **150** B4
Daiō-Misaki *Japan* 34°15N 136°45E **113** G8
Dairût *Egypt* 27°34N 30°43E **137** B3
Daisen *Japan* 39°27N 140°29E **112** E10
Daisen-Oki △ *Japan* 35°23N 133°34E **113** G6
Daisetsu-Zan *Japan* 43°30N 142°57E **112** C11
Daisetsu-Zan △
Japan 43°30N 142°55E **112** C11
Daitari *India* 21°10N 85°46E **126** D7
Daiyun Shan *China* 25°50N 118°15E **117** E12
Dajarra *Australia* 21°42S 139°30E **150** C2
Dajiawa *China* 37°9N 119°0E **115** F10
Dajin Chuan → *China* 31°16N 101°59E **116** B4
Dak Dam *Cambodia* 12°20N 107°21E **120** F6
Dak Nhe *Vietnam* 15°28N 107°48E **120** E6
Dak Pek *Vietnam* 15°4N 107°44E **120** E6
Dak Song *Vietnam* 12°19N 107°35E **121** F6
Dak Sui *Vietnam* 14°55N 107°43E **120** E6
Dakar *Senegal* 14°34N 17°29W **138** C1
Dakar □ *Senegal* 14°45N 17°20W **138** C1
Dakhla *W. Sahara* 23°50N 15°53W **134** D2
Dakhla, El Wâhât el
Egypt 25°30N 28°50E **137** B2
Dakingari *Nigeria* 11°37N 4°1E **139** C5
Dakoank *India* 7°2N 93°43E **127** L11
Dakor *India* 22°45N 73°11E **124** H5
Dakoro *Niger* 14°31N 6°46E **139** C6
Dakota City *U.S.A.* 42°25N 96°25W **172** D5
Đakovica = Gjakovë
Kosovo 42°22N 20°26E **96** D4
Đakovo *Croatia* 45°19N 18°24E **80** E3
Dala-Järna *Sweden* 60°33N 14°26E **62** D8
Dalaba *Guinea* 10°47N 12°12W **138** C2
Dalachi *China* 36°48N 105°0E **114** F3
Dalai Nur *China* 43°20N 116°45E **114** C9
Dālakī *Iran* 29°26N 51°17E **129** D6
Dalälven → *Sweden* 60°12N 16°43E **62** D10
Dalaman *Turkey* 36°41N 28°43E **99** E10
Dalaman → *Turkey* 36°41N 28°43E **99** E10
Dalandzadgad
Mongolia 43°27N 104°30E **114** C3
Dalap-Uliga-Darrit = Majuro
Marshall Is. 7°9N 171°12E **156** G9
Dalarna *Sweden* 61°0N 14°0E **62** D8
Dalarnas län □ *Sweden* 61°0N 14°15E **62** D8
Dalay *Mongolia* 43°28N 103°30E **114** C2
Dālbandīn *Pakistan* 29°0N 64°23E **124** E4
Dalbeattie *U.K.* 54°56N 3°50W **65** G5
Dalbeg *Australia* 20°16S 147°18E **150** C4
Dalbosjön *Sweden* 58°40N 12°45E **63** F6
Dalby *Australia* 27°10S 151°17E **151** D5
Dalby *Sweden* 55°40N 13°22E **63** J7
Dalby Söderskog △
Sweden 55°41N 13°21E **63** J7
Dale City *U.S.A.* 38°38N 77°19W **173** F15
Dale Hollow L. *U.S.A.* 36°32N 85°27W **177** C12
Daleville *U.S.A.* 31°19N 85°43W **178** D4
Dalga *Egypt* 27°39N 30°41E **137** B3
Dalgán *Iran* 27°31N 59°19E **129** E8
Dalhart *U.S.A.* 36°4N 102°31W **176** C3
Dalhousie *Canada* 48°5N 66°26W **165** C6
Dalhousie *India* 32°38N 75°58E **124** C6
Dali *Shaanxi, China* 34°48N 109°58E **114** G5
Dali *Yunnan, China* 25°40N 100°10E **116** E3
Dalian *China* 38°50N 121°40E **115** E11
Daliang Shan *China* 28°0N 102°45E **116** D4
Daling He → *China* 40°55N 121°40E **115** D11
Dâliyat el Karmel *Israel* 32°43N 35°2E **130** C4
Dalj *Croatia* 45°29N 18°59E **80** E3
Dalkeith *U.K.* 55°54N 3°4W **65** F5
Dalkeith *U.K.* 30°0N 85°9W **178** E4
Dalkey *Ireland* 53°16N 6°6W **64** C5
Dallas *Ga., U.S.A.* 33°55N 84°51W **178** B5
Dallas *Oreg., U.S.A.* 44°55N 123°19W **168** D2
Dallas *Tex., U.S.A.* 32°47N 96°48W **176** E6
Dalles, The *U.S.A.* 45°36N 121°10W **168** D3
Dalmā *U.A.E.* 24°30N 52°20E **129** E7
Dalmacija *Croatia* 43°20N 17°0E **93** E13
Dalmas, L. *Canada* 53°30N 71°50W **165** B5
Dalmatia = Dalmacija
Croatia 43°20N 17°0E **93** E13
Dalmau *India* 26°4N 81°2E **125** F9
Dalmellington *U.K.* 55°19N 4°23W **65** F4
Dalmeny *Australia* 36°5S 150°8E **153** D9
Dalnegorsk *Russia* 44°32N 135°33E **112** B7
Dalnerechensk *Russia* 45°50N 133°40E **112** B6
Dalny = Dalian
China 38°50N 121°40E **115** E11
Daloa *Ivory C.* 7°0N 6°30W **138** D3
Dalou Shan *China* 28°0N 106°30E **116** D5
Dalry *U.K.* 55°42N 4°43W **65** F4
Dalrymple, L. *Australia* 20°40S 147°0E **150** C4
Dalrymple, Mt. *Australia* 21°1S 148°39E **150** C4
Dals Långed *Sweden* 58°56N 12°18E **63** F6
Dalsjöfors *Sweden* 57°46N 13°5E **63** G7

Dalsland *Sweden* 58°50N 12°15E **63** F6
Dalton *Ga., U.S.A.* 34°46N 84°58W **177** D12
Dalton *Mass., U.S.A.* 42°28N 73°11W **175** D11
Dalton *Nebr., U.S.A.* 41°25N 102°58W **172** E2
Dalton, Kap *Greenland* 69°25N 24°3W **57** D8
Dalton-in-Furness *U.K.* 54°10N 3°11W **66** C4
Dalvík *Iceland* 65°58N 18°32W **60** D4
Dālvadis = Jokkmokk
Sweden 66°35N 19°50E **60** C18
Dalwallinu *Australia* 30°17S 116°40E **149** F2
Daly → *Australia* 13°35S 130°19E **148** B5
Daly City *U.S.A.* 37°42N 122°27W **170** H4
Daly L. *Canada* 56°32N 105°39W **163** B7
Daly River *Australia* 13°46S 130°42E **148** B5
Daly River-Port Keats ○
Australia 14°13S 129°36E **148** B4
Daly Waters *Australia* 16°15S 133°24E **150** B1
Dam Doi *Vietnam* 8°50N 105°12E **121** H5
Dam Ha *Vietnam* 21°21N 107°36E **120** B6
Damachova *Belarus* 51°45N 23°36E **83** G10
Daman *India* 20°25N 72°57E **126** D1
Daman & Diu □ *India* 20°25N 72°58E **126** D1
Dāmaneh *Iran* 33°1N 50°29E **129** C6
Damanhûr *Egypt* 31°0N 30°30E **137** E7
Damant L. *Canada* 61°45N 105°5W **163** A7
Damaq *Iran* 35°25N 48°49E **105** E13
Damar *Indonesia* 7°7S 128°40E **119** F7
Damara *C.A.R.* 4°58N 18°42E **140** D3
Damaraland *Namibia* 20°0S 15°0E **144** B2
Damascus = Dimashq
Syria 33°30N 36°18E **130** B5
Damascus *U.S.A.* 31°18N 84°43W **178** D5
Damasi *Greece* 39°43N 22°11E **98** B4
Damaturu *Nigeria* 11°45N 11°55E **139** C7
Damāvand *Iran* 35°47N 52°0E **129** C7
Damāvand, Qolleh-ye
Iran 35°56N 52°10E **129** C7
Damba *Angola* 6°44S 15°20E **140** F3
Dâmbovița □ *Romania* 45°0N 25°30E **81** F10
Dâmbovița → *Romania* 44°12N 26°26E **81** F11
Dâmbovnic →
Romania 44°28N 25°18E **81** F10
Dambulla *Sri Lanka* 7°51N 80°39E **127** L5
Dame Marie *Haiti* 18°34N 74°26W **183** C5
Dāmghān *Iran* 36°10N 54°17E **129** B7
Dāmienești *Romania* 46°44N 26°59E **81** D11
Damietta = Dumyât
Egypt 31°24N 31°48E **137** E7
Damin *China* 36°15N 115°6E **114** F8
Dāmir Qābū *Syria* 36°58N 41°51E **128** B4
Dammam = Ad Dammām
Si. Arabia 26°20N 50°5E **129** E6
Dammarie-les-Lys *France* 48°31N 2°39E **71** D9
Dammartin-en-Goële
France 49°3N 2°41E **71** C9
Damme *Germany* 52°32N 8°11E **76** C4
Damodar → *India* 23°17N 87°35E **125** H12
Damoh *India* 23°50N 79°28E **125** H8
Damous *Algeria* 36°31N 1°42E **136** A4
Dampier *Australia* 20°41S 116°42E **148** D2
Dampier, Selat *Indonesia* 0°40S 131°0E **119** E8
Dampier Arch.
Australia 20°38S 116°32E **148** D2
Damrani *Algeria* 27°45N 2°56W **136** C3
Damrei, Chuor Phnum
Cambodia 11°30N 103°0E **121** G4
Damvillers *France* 49°20N 5°21E **71** C12
Damyang *S. Korea* 35°19N 126°59E **115** G14
Dan-Gulbi *Nigeria* 11°40N 6°15E **139** C6
Dan-Sadau *Nigeria* 11°17N 6°29E **139** C6
Dana *Indonesia* 11°0S 121°15E **119** F6
Dana *Jordan* 30°41N 35°37E **130** E4
Dana *Nepal* 28°32N 83°37E **125** E10
Dana, L. *Canada* 50°53N 77°20W **164** B4
Dana, Mt. *U.S.A.* 37°54N 119°12W **170** H7
Danakil Desert *Ethiopia* 12°45N 41°0E **131** E3
Danané *Ivory C.* 7°16N 8°9W **138** D3
Danba *China* 30°54N 101°48E **116** B3
Danbury *U.S.A.* 41°24N 73°28W **175** E11
Danby L. *U.S.A.* 34°13N 115°5W **171** L11
Dand *Afghan.* 31°28N 65°32E **124** D1
Dande → *Zimbabwe* 15°56S 30°16E **143** F3
Dandeldhura *Nepal* 29°20N 80°35E **125** E9
Dandeli *India* 15°5N 74°30E **127** G2
Dandenong *Australia* 38°0S 145°15E **153** E6
Dandi *Iran* 36°32N 47°57E **105** D12
Dandong *China* 40°10N 124°20E **115** D13
Daneborg *Greenland* 74°18N 20°14W **57** C8
Danfeng *China* 33°45N 110°25E **114** H6
Dang → *Chad* 9°10N 15°18E **139** D9
Dangan Liedao *China* 22°2N 114°8E **117** F10
Dangé-St-Romain *France* 46°56N 0°36E **72** B4
Dangé-ni *Ethiopia* 11°18N 36°56E **131** E4
Danger Is. = Pukapuka
Cook Is. 10°53S 165°49W **157** J11
Danger Pt. *S. Africa* 34°40S 19°17E **144** E2
Dangla Shan = Tanggula Shan
China 32°40N 92°10E **110** E7
Dangrek, Mts. = Dangrek,
Phnom *Thailand* 14°...N 104°0E **120** E5
Dangrek, Phnom
Thailand 14°20N 104°0E **120** E5
Dangriga *Belize* 17°0N 88°13W **181** D7
Dangshan *China* 34°27N 116°22E **114** G9
Dangtu *China* 31°32N 118°25E **117** B12
Dangyang *China* 30°52N 111°44E **117** B8
Daniel *U.S.A.* 42°52N 110°4W **168** E8
Daniel's Harbour
Canada 50°13N 57°35W **165** B8
Danielskuil *S. Africa* 28°11S 23°33E **144** D3
Danielson *U.S.A.* 41°48N 71°53W **175** E13
Danielsville *U.S.A.* 34°8N 83°13W **178** B6
Danilov *Russia* 58°16N 40°13E **84** C11
Danilovgrad *Montenegro* 42°38N 19°9E **96** C3
Danilovka *Russia* 50°25N 44°12E **86** E7
Daning *China* 36°28N 110°45E **114** F6
Danja *Nigeria* 11°21N 7°31W **139** C6
Danjiangkou *China* 32°31N 111°30E **114** H6
Danjiangkou Shuiku
China 32°37N 111°30E **117** A8
Dank *Oman* 23°33N 56°16E **129** F8
Dankalwa *Nigeria* 11°52N 12°12E **139** C7
Dankama *Nigeria* 13°20N 7°44E **139** C6
Dankhar Gompa *India* 32°10N 78°10E **124** C8

Dankov *Russia* 53°20N 39°5E **84** F10
Danleng *China* 30°1N 103°31E **116** B4
Danlí *Honduras* 14°4N 86°35W **182** D2
Danmark = Denmark ■
Europe 55°45N 10°0E **63** J3
Danmark Fjord
Greenland 81°30N 22°0W **57** A8
Danmarkshavn
Greenland 76°45N 18°50W **57** B9
Dannemora *U.S.A.* 44°43N 73°44W **175** B11
Dannenberg *Germany* 53°6N 11°5E **76** B7
Dannevirke *N.Z.* 40°12S 176°8E **154** G5
Dannhauser *S. Africa* 28°0S 30°3E **145** C5
Danshui *U.S.A.* 42°34N 77°42W **174** D7
Danta *India* 24°11N 72°46E **124** G5
Dantan *India* 21°57N 87°20E **125** J12
Dante = Xaafuun
Somalia 10°25N 51°16E **131** E5
Dantewara *India* 18°54N 81°21E **126** E5
Danube = Dunărea →
Europe 45°20N 29°40E **81** E14
Danvers *U.S.A.* 42°34N 70°56W **175** D14
Danville *Ga., U.S.A.* 32°37N 83°15W **178** C6
Danville *Ill., U.S.A.* 40°8N 87°37W **172** E2
Danville *Ky., U.S.A.* 37°39N 84°46W **173** G11
Danville *Pa., U.S.A.* 40°58N 76°37W **175** E8
Danville *Va., U.S.A.* 36°36N 79°23W **173** G14
Danville *Vt., U.S.A.* 44°25N 72°9W **175** B12
Danyang *China* 32°0N 119°31E **117** B12
Danzhai *China* 26°11N 107°48E **116** D5
Danzhou *China* 19°31N 109°33E **117** a
Danzig = Gdańsk *Poland* 54°22N 18°40E **82** D5
Dão → *Portugal* 40°20N 8°11W **88** E2
Dao Xian *China* 25°36N 111°31E **117** E8
Daocheng *China* 29°0N 100°10E **116** C3
Daoud = Aïn Beïda
Algeria 35°50N 7°29E **136** A5
Daoukro *Ivory C.* 7°10N 3°58W **138** D4
Dapaong *Togo* 10°55N 0°16E **139** C5
Dapchi *Nigeria* 12°32N 11°31E **139** C7
Dapoli *India* 17°46N 73°11E **126** F1
Daqing *China* 46°35N 125°0E **111** B13
Daqing Shan *China* 40°40N 111°0E **114** D6
Daqq-e Sorkh, Kavīr
Iran 33°45N 52°50E **129** C7
Daqu Shan *China* 30°25N 122°20E **117** B14
Dar Banda *Africa* 8°0N 23°0E **132** F6
Dar el Beida = Casablanca
Morocco 33°36N 7°36W **136** B2
Dar es Salaam *Tanzania* 6°50S 39°12E **142** D4
Dar Mazār *Iran* 29°14N 57°20E **129** D8
Dar'ā *Syria* 32°36N 36°7E **130** C5
Dar'ā □ *Syria* 32°55N 36°10E **130** C5
Dārāb *Iran* 28°50N 54°30E **129** D7
Daraban *Pakistan* 31°44N 70°20E **124** D4
Darabani *Romania* 48°10N 26°39E **81** B11
Daraj *Libya* 30°10N 10°28E **135** B8
Dārān *Iran* 32°59N 50°24E **129** C6
Daravica = Gjeravicë
Kosovo 42°32N 20°8E **96** D4
Daraw *Egypt* 24°22N 32°51E **137** C3
Dārayyā *Syria* 33°28N 36°15E **130** B5
Darazo *Nigeria* 11°1N 10°24E **139** C7
Darband *Pakistan* 34°20N 72°50E **124** B5
Darband, Kūh-e *Iran* 31°34N 57°8E **129** D8
Darbhanga *India* 26°15N 85°55E **125** F11
D'Arcy *Canada* 50°33N 122°29W **162** C4
Darda *Croatia* 45°40N 18°41E **80** E3
Dardanel *Kosovo* 42°35N 21°35E **96** D5
Dardanelle *Ark., U.S.A.* 35°13N 93°9W **176** D8
Dardanelle *Calif.,
U.S.A.* 38°20N 119°50W **170** G7
Dardanelles = Çanakkale Boğazı
Turkey 40°17N 26°32E **97** F10
Darende *Turkey* 38°35N 37°30E **104** C7
Dārestān *Iran* 29°9N 58°42E **129** D8
Darfield *N.Z.* 43°29S 172°7E **155** D7
Darfo-Boario Terme
Italy 45°53N 10°11E **92** C7
Dârfûr *Sudan* 13°40N 24°0E **135** F10
Dargai *Pakistan* 34°25N 71°55E **124** B4
Dargaville *N.Z.* 35°57S 173°52E **154** B4
Dargol *Niger* 13°54N 1°22E **139** C5
Darhan *Mongolia* 49°37N 106°21E **110** B10
Darhan Muminggan
China 41°40N 110°28E **114** D6
Darica *Turkey* 40°45N 29°23E **104** B3
Darién □ *Panama* 7°36N 77°57W **182** E4
Darién, G. del *Colombia* 9°0N 77°0W **186** B3
Darién □ *Panama* 7°36N 77°57W **182** E4
Dariganga = Ovoot
Mongolia 45°21N 113°45E **114** B7
Daringbadi *India* 19°54N 84°8E **126** E7
Darjeeling = Darjiling
India 27°3N 88°18E **125** F13
Darjiling *India* 27°3N 88°18E **125** F13
Darkan *Australia* 33°20S 116°43E **149** F2
Darke Peak *Australia* 33°27S 136°12E **152** B2
Darkhana *Pakistan* 30°39N 72°11E **124** D5
Darkot Pass *Pakistan* 36°45N 73°26E **124** A5
Darling → *Australia* 34°4S 141°54E **152** C4
Darling Downs
Australia 27°30S 150°30E **151** D5
Darling Ra. *Australia* 32°30S 116°20E **149** F2
Darlington *U.K.* 54°32N 1°33W **66** C6
Darlington *Fla., U.S.A.* 30°57N 86°3W **178** D3
Darlington *S.C.,
U.S.A.* 34°18N 79°52W **177** D15
Darlington, L. *S. Africa* 33°10S 25°9E **144** E4
Darlington Point
Australia 34°37S 146°1E **153** C7
Darlot, L. *Australia* 27°48S 121°35E **149** E3
Darłowo *Poland* 54°25N 16°25E **82** D3
Dârmănești *Bacău,
Romania* 46°21N 26°33E **81** D11

Dârmănești *Suceava,
Romania* 47°44N 26°9E **81** C11
Darnah *Libya* 32°40N 22°35E **135** B10
Darnall *S. Africa* 29°23S 31°18E **145** D5
Darney *France* 48°5N 6°2E **71** D13
Darnick *Australia* 32°48S 143°38E **153** B5
Darnley, C. *Antarctica* 68°0S 69°0E **55** C6
Darnley B. *Canada* 69°30S 123°30W **160** D7
Daroca *Spain* 41°9N 1°25W **90** D3
Darou-Mousti *Senegal* 15°3N 16°3W **138** B1
Darr → *Australia* 23°39S 143°50E **150** C3
Darra Pezu *Pakistan* 32°19N 70°44E **124** C4

Darran Mts. *N.Z.* 44°37S 167°59E **155** E2
Darreh Shahr *Iran* 33°7N 47°22E **105** F12
Darrequeira *Argentina* 37°42S 63°10W **190** D3
Darrington *U.S.A.* 48°15N 121°36W **168** B3
Darsi *India* 15°46N 79°44E **127** G4
Darsser Ort *Germany* 54°28N 12°32E **76** A8
Dart → *U.K.* 50°24N 3°39W **67** G4
Dartford *U.K.* 51°26N 0°13E **67** F8
Dartmoor *Australia* 37°56S 141°19E **152** D4
Dartmoor *U.K.* 50°38N 3°57W **67** G4
Dartmoor △ *U.K.* 50°37N 3°59W **67** G4
Dartmouth *Canada* 44°40N 63°30W **165** D7
Dartmouth *U.K.* 50°21N 3°36W **67** G4
Dartmouth, L. *Queens.,
Australia* 26°4S 145°18E **151** D4
Dartmouth, L. *Vic.,
Australia* 36°34S 147°32E **153** D7
Dartuch, C. = Artrutx, C. de
Spain 39°55N 3°49E **100** B10
Daruvar *Croatia* 45°35N 17°14E **80** E2
Darvaza *Turkmenistan* 40°11N 58°24E **87** K9
Darvel, Teluk = Lahad Datu,
Telok *Malaysia* 4°50N 118°20E **119** D5
Darvi *Mongolia* 46°27N 94°7E **110** C12
Darwen *U.K.* 53°42N 2°29W **66** D5
Darwendale *Zimbabwe* 17°41S 30°33E **145** A5
Darwha *India* 20°15N 77°45E **126** D3
Darwin *Australia* 12°25S 130°51E **148** B5
Darwin *U.S.A.* 36°15N 117°35W **171** J9
Darwin, Mt. *Chile* 54°47S 69°55W **192** D3
Darya Khan *Pakistan* 31°48N 71°6E **124** D4
Daryapur *India* 20°55N 77°20E **126** D3
Daryoi Amu = Amudarya →
Uzbekistan 43°58N 59°34E **108** D5
Dās *U.A.E.* 25°20N 53°30E **129** E7
Dashen, Ras *Ethiopia* 13°8N 38°26E **131** E4
Dasher *U.S.A.* 30°45N 83°13W **178** E6
Dashetai *China* 41°0N 109°5E **114** D5
Dashiqiao *China* 40°38N 122°30E **115** D12
Dashkānu = Daşkäsän
Azerbaijan 40°25N 46°0E **87** K7
Dashköpri *Turkmenistan* 36°16N 62°8E **129** B9
Dasht → *Pakistan* 25°10N 61°40E **122** G2
Daska *Pakistan* 32°20N 74°20E **124** C6
Daşkäsän *Azerbaijan* 40°25N 46°0E **87** K7
Daşoguz *Turkmenistan* 41°49N 59°58E **108** D5
Dassa *Benin* 7°46N 2°14E **139** D5
Dasuya *India* 31°49N 75°38E **124** C6
Datça *Turkey* 36°46N 27°40E **99** E9
Date *Japan* 42°28N 140°52E **112** C10
Datia *India* 25°39N 78°27E **125** G8
Datian *China* 25°40N 117°50E **117** E11
Datong *Anhui, China* 30°48N 117°44E **117** B11
Datong *Qinghai, China* 36°20N 102°50E **110** D9
Datong *Shanxi, China* 40°6N 113°18E **114** D7
Dattakhel *Pakistan* 32°54N 69°46E **124** C3
Dattapur = Dhamangaon
India 20°48N 78°9E **126** D4
Datteln *Germany* 51°39N 7°21E **76** D3
Datu, Tanjung *Indonesia* 2°5N 109°39E **118** D3
Datu Piang *Phil.* 7°2N 124°30E **119** C6
Datuk, Tanjong = Datu, Tanjung
Indonesia 2°5N 109°39E **118** D3
Daud Khel *Pakistan* 32°53N 71°34E **124** C4
Daudnagar *India* 25°2N 84°24E **125** G11
Daugava → *Latvia* 57°4N 24°3E **88** B4
Daugavpils *Latvia* 55°53N 26°32E **84** E4
Daulatabad *India* 19°57N 75°15E **126** E2
Daulpur *India* 26°45N 77°59E **124** F7
Daun *Germany* 50°11N 6°49E **77** E2
Daund *India* 18°26N 74°40E **126** E2
Daung Kyun *Burma* 12°13N 98°4E **121** F1
Dauphin *Canada* 51°9N 100°5W **163** C8
Dauphin, L. *Canada* 40°22N 76°56W **174** F8
Dauphin, L. *Canada* 51°20N 99°45W **163** C8
Dauphiné *France* 45°15N 5°25E **73** C9
Daura *Borno, Nigeria* 11°31N 11°24E **139** C7
Daura *Katsina, Nigeria* 13°2N 8°21E **139** C6
Dausa *India* 26°52N 76°20E **124** F7
Dāvaçi *Azerbaijan* 41°15N 48°57E **87** K9
Davangere *India* 14°25N 75°55E **127** G2
Davao *Phil.* 7°0N 125°40E **119** C7
Davao G. *Phil.* 6°30N 125°48E **119** C7
Dāvar Panāh = Sarāvān
Iran 27°25N 62°15E **129** E9
Davenport *Calif.,
U.S.A.* 37°1N 122°12W **170** H4
Davenport *Fla., U.S.A.* 28°10N 81°36W **179** E8
Davenport *Iowa, U.S.A.* 41°32N 90°35W **172** E8
Davenport *Wash.,
U.S.A.* 47°39N 118°9W **168** C4
Davenport Ra.
Australia 20°28S 134°0E **150** C1
Davenport Range △
Australia 20°36S 134°22E **150** C1
Daventry *U.K.* 52°16N 1°10W **67** E6
David *Panama* 8°30N 82°30W **182** E3
David City *U.S.A.* 41°15N 97°8W **172** E5
David Glacier
Antarctica 75°20S 162°0E **55** D11
David Gorodok = Davyd Haradok
Belarus 52°4N 27°8E **75** B14
Davidson *Canada* 51°16N 105°59W **163** C7
Davidson Mts.
U.S.A. 68°40N 142°22W **166** B11
Davis *Antarctica* 68°34S 77°55E **55** C6
Davis *U.S.A.* 38°33N 121°44W **170** G5
Davis Dam *U.S.A.* 35°12N 114°34W **171** K12
Davis Inlet *Canada* 55°50N 60°59W **165** A7
Davis Mts. *U.S.A.* 30°50N 103°55W **176** E3
Davis Sea *Antarctica* 66°0S 92°0E **55** C7
Davis Str. *N. Amer.* 65°0N 58°0W **161** D19
Davison *U.S.A.* 43°2N 83°31W **173** D12
Davlos *Cyprus* 35°25N 33°54E **101** D12
Davos *Switz.* 46°48N 9°49E **75** C5
Davy L. *Canada* 58°53N 108°18W **163** B7
Davyd Haradok *Belarus* 52°4N 27°8E **75** B14
Davutlar *Turkey* 37°43N 27°17E **99** D9
Davy L. *Canada* 58°53N 108°18W **163** B7
Dawaki *Bauchi, Nigeria* 10°3N 9°28E **139** D7
Dawaki *Kano, Nigeria* 11°37N 8°1E **139** C6
Dawei = Tavoy *Burma* 14°2N 98°12E **120** E1
Dawes Ra. *Australia* 24°40S 150°40E **150** C5
Dawlish *U.K.* 50°35N 3°28W **67** G4
Dawna Ra. *Burma* 16°30N 98°30E **120** D2
Dawros Hd. *Ireland* 54°50N 8°33W **64** B3
Dawson *Canada* 64°10N 139°30W **160** E6
Dawson, I. *Chile* 53°50S 70°50W **192** D2
Dawson B. *Canada* 52°53N 100°49W **163** C8
Dawson City *Canada* 64°10N 139°30W **160** E6

Dawson Creek
Canada 55°45N 120°15W [cut]
Dawson Inlet *Canada* 61°50N 93°25W [cut]
Dawson Ra. *Australia* 24°30S 149°48E [cut]
Dawu *Hubei, China* 31°34N 114°7E [cut]
Dawu *Sichuan, China* 30°55N 101°10E [cut]
Dax *France* 43°44N 1°3W [cut]
Daxian *China* 31°15N 107°23E [cut]
Daxin *China* 22°50N 107°11E [cut]
Daxindian *China* 37°30N 120°50E [cut]
Daxing *China* 39°47N 116°24E [cut]
Daxinggou *China* 43°25N 129°40E [cut]
Daxue Shan *Sichuan,
China* 30°30N 101°30E [cut]
Daxue Shan *Yunnan,
China* 23°42N 99°48E [cut]
Day *U.S.A.* 30°12N 83°17W [cut]
Dayao *China* 25°43N 101°20E [cut]
Dayet en Naharat *Mali* 17°39N 3°10W [cut]
Dayia *China* 30°41N 103°29E [cut]
Dāykondī □ *Afghan.* 34°0N 66°0E [cut]
Daylesford *Australia* 37°21S 144°9E [cut]
Dayong *China* 29°11N 110°30E [cut]
Dayr az Zawr *Syria* 35°20N 40°5E [cut]
Dayr az Zawr □ *Syria* 34°50N 40°10E [cut]
Daysland *Canada* 52°50N 112°20W [cut]
Dayton *Nev., U.S.A.* 39°14N 119°36W [cut]
Dayton *Ohio, U.S.A.* 39°45N 84°12W [cut]
Dayton *Pa., U.S.A.* 40°53N 79°15W [cut]
Dayton *Tenn., U.S.A.* 35°30N 85°1W [cut]
Dayton *Wash., U.S.A.* 46°19N 117°59W [cut]
Dayton *Wyo., U.S.A.* 44°53N 107°16W [cut]
Daytona Beach *U.S.A.* 29°13N 81°1W [cut]
Dayu *China* 25°24N 114°22E [cut]
Dayville *U.S.A.* 44°28N 119°32W [cut]
Dazhu *China* 30°41N 107°15E [cut]
Dazkırı *Turkey* 37°57N 29°52E [cut]
Dazu *China* 29°40N 105°42E [cut]
De Aar *S. Africa* 30°39S 24°0E [cut]
De Armanville *U.S.A.* 33°38N 85°45W [cut]
De Bary *U.S.A.* 28°54N 81°18W [cut]
De Funiak Springs
U.S.A. 30°43N 86°7W [cut]
De Grey → *Australia* 20°12S 119°13E [cut]
De Haan *Belgium* 51°16N 3°2E [cut]
De Hoop △ *S. Africa* 34°30S 20°28E [cut]
De Kalb Junction
U.S.A. 44°30N 75°16W [cut]
De Land *U.S.A.* 29°2N 81°18W [cut]
De Leon *U.S.A.* 32°7N 98°32W [cut]
De Leon Springs *U.S.A.* 29°7N 81°21W [cut]
De Long Mts. *U.S.A.* 68°10N 163°30W [cut]
De Panne *Belgium* 51°6N 2°34E [cut]
De Pere *U.S.A.* 44°27N 88°4W [cut]
De Queen *U.S.A.* 34°2N 94°21W [cut]
De Quincy *U.S.A.* 30°27N 93°26W [cut]
De Ruyters *U.S.A.* 42°45N 75°53W [cut]
De Smet *U.S.A.* 44°23N 97°33W [cut]
De Soto *U.S.A.* 38°8N 90°34W [cut]
De Soto City *U.S.A.* 27°27N 81°24W [cut]
De Tour Village *U.S.A.* 46°0N 83°56W [cut]
De Witt *U.S.A.* 34°18N 91°20W [cut]
Dead L. *U.S.A.* 30°10N 85°10W [cut]
Dead Sea *Asia* 31°30N 35°30E [cut]
Deadman B. *U.S.A.* 29°30N 83°30W [cut]
Deadwood *U.S.A.* 44°23N 103°44W [cut]
Deadwood L. *Canada* 59°10N 128°30W [cut]
Deal *U.K.* 51°13N 1°25E [cut]
Deal I. *Australia* 39°30S 147°20E [cut]
Dealesville *S. Africa* 28°41S 25°44E [cut]
De'an *China* 29°21N 115°46E [cut]
Dean → *Canada* 52°49N 126°58W [cut]
Dean, Forest of *U.K.* 51°45N 2°33W [cut]
Dean Chan. *Canada* 52°30N 127°15W [cut]
Deán Funes *Argentina* 30°20S 64°20W [cut]
Dease → *Canada* 59°56N 128°32W [cut]
Dease L. *Canada* 58°40N 130°5W [cut]
Dease Lake *Canada* 58°25N 130°6W [cut]
Death Valley *U.S.A.* 36°15N 116°50W [cut]
Death Valley △ *U.S.A.* 36°29N 117°6W [cut]
Death Valley Junction
U.S.A. 36°20N 116°25W [cut]
Deatnu = Tana →
Norway 70°30N 28°14E [cut]
Deauville *France* 49°23N 0°2E [cut]
Deba *Spain* 43°18N 2°21W [cut]
Deba Habe *Nigeria* 10°14N 11°20E [cut]
Debagram *India* 23°41N 88°18E [cut]
Debaltsevo *Ukraine* 48°22N 38°26E [cut]
Debao *China* 23°21N 106°46E [cut]
Debar *Macedonia* 41°31N 20°30E [cut]
Debden *Canada* 53°30N 106°50W [cut]
Debdou *Morocco* 33°59N 3°0W [cut]
Debica *Poland* 50°2N 21°25E [cut]
Deblin *Poland* 51°34N 21°50E [cut]
Deblo *Poland* 52°44N 14°41E [cut]
Débo, L. *Mali* 15°14N 4°15W [cut]
DeBolt *Canada* 55°12N 118°1W [cut]
Deborah East, L.
Australia 30°45S 119°30E [cut]
Deborah West, L.
Australia 30°45S 119°5E [cut]
Debre Serbia* 44°38N 19°53E [cut]
Debre Markos *Ethiopia* 10°20N 37°40E [cut]
Debre Tabor *Ethiopia* 11°50N 38°26E [cut]
Debre Zeyit *Ethiopia* 8°50N 39°0E [cut]
Debrecen *Hungary* 47°33N 21°42E [cut]
Debrzno *Poland* 53°31N 17°14E [cut]
Deçan *Kosovo* 42°32N 20°17E [cut]
Decatur *Ala., U.S.A.* 34°36N 86°59W [cut]
Decatur *Ga., U.S.A.* 33°46N 84°17W [cut]
Decatur *Ill., U.S.A.* 39°51N 88°57W [cut]
Decatur *Ind., U.S.A.* 40°50N 84°56W [cut]
Decazeville *France* 44°34N 2°15E [cut]
Deccan *India* 18°0N 79°0E [cut]
Deception, Mt.
Australia 30°42S 138°16E [cut]
Deception Bay
Australia 27°10S 153°5E [cut]
Deception I. *Antarctica* 63°0S 60°15W [cut]
Deception L. *Canada* 56°33N 104°13W [cut]
Dechang *China* 27°25N 102°10E [cut]
Dechhu *India* 26°46N 72°20E [cut]
Děčín *Czech Rep.* 50°47N 14°12E [cut]
Deckerville *U.S.A.* 43°32N 82°44W [cut]
Decollatura *Italy* 39°3N 16°21E [cut]
Decorah *U.S.A.* 43°18N 91°48W [cut]

Romania 46°56N 24°50E **81** D9
eece = Alexandroupoli
agach = Alexandroupoli
Greece 35°25N 25°54E **97** F9
nam U.S.A. 42°15N 71°10W **175** D13
polis Tsqaro Georgia 41°33N 46°0E **87** K8
ougou Burkina Faso 3°30N 3°25W **138** C4
ovichi Russia 57°32N 29°56E **84** D5
a Malawi 14°20S 34°42E **143** E3
▸ Aberds., U.K. 57°9N 2°5W **65** D6
▸ Dumf. & Gall., U.K. 54°51N 4°3W **65** G4
▸ Wales, U.K. 53°22N 3°17W **66** D4
B. Canada 61°15N 116°35W **162** A5
ina 22°27N 113°55E **111** a
Lead Australia 37°0S 142°43E **152** D5
owater Australia 29°25S 151°51E **151** D5
▸ Canada 58°23N 94°13W **163** B10
L. Canada 52°40N 94°20W **163** C10
nada 49°11N 57°27W **165** C8
Lake Nfld. & L.,
nada 52°36N 94°20W **163** C10
Lodge U.S.A. 46°24N 112°44W **168** C7
Park Fla., U.S.A. 28°6N 80°54W **179** D9
Park Wash.,
S.A. 47°57N 117°28W **168** C5
River U.S.A. 47°20N 93°48W **172** B7
agun Australia 19°16S 146°33E **150** B4
field Beach U.S.A. 26°19N 80°6W **179** D9
ance U.S.A. 41°17N 84°22W **173** E11
ana India 26°50N 74°20E **124** F6
China 31°44N 98°39E **116** D2
ebe ▸ Portugal 38°13N 7°29W **89** G3
berga Sweden 55°51N 14°5E **63** J8
elas Canada 47°30N 68°35W **165** C6
ma Nigeria 4°50N 6°48E **139** E6
erfors Sweden 59°15N 14°27E **62** E8
erhamn Sweden 56°20N 16°24E **63** H10
gendorf Germany 48°50N 12°57E **77** G8
▸ Pakistan 31°3N 73°21E **124** D5
rmenlik = Kythréa
yprus 35°15N 33°29E **101** D12
Bid Iran 30°39N 53°11E **129** D7
Dasht Iran 30°47N 50°33E **129** D6
e Shīr Iran 31°29N 53°45E **129** D7
aj Iran 30°42N 54°53E **129** D7
ak Iran 27°11N 62°37E **129** E9
dez Iran 31°43N 50°17E **129** D6
ej India 21°44N 72°40E **124** J5
golān Iran 28°30N 55°35E **129** D7
wala Sri Lanka 6°50N 79°51E **127** L4
orān Iran 32°41N 47°16E **105** F12
now-e Kūhestān
Iran 27°58N 58°32E **129** E8
a Dun India 30°20N 78°4E **124** D8
i India 24°50N 84°15E **125** G11
a China 25°26N 118°14E **117** F12
ai China 44°30N 125°45E **115** B13
ze Belgium 50°59N 3°22E **70** C3
al Balah Gaza Strip 31°25N 34°21E **130** D3
Romania 47°10N 23°52E **81** C8
Sweden 59°35N 13°29E **62** E7
ang China 28°18N 108°7E **116** C7
u ▸ Zimbabwe 18°4S 26°42E **144** A4
alb U.S.A. 41°56N 88°46W **172** E9

m. Rep. of the Congo 3°24S 21°24E **140** E4
caño Rise Ind. Oc. 45°15S 44°15E **146** J3
Mar U.S.A. 32°58N 117°16W **171** N9
Norte U.S.A. 37°41N 106°21W **169** H10
mbre I. Australia 20°26S 117°5E **148** D2
Rio U.S.A. 29°22N 100°54W **176** G4
no Peak U.S.A. 35°46N 119°15W **171** K7
no U.S.A. 35°12N 112°22W **168** G7
reyville S. Africa 26°41S 25°26E **144** D4
ronde L. Canada 54°3N 107°3W **163** C7
van U.S.A. 42°38N 88°39W **172** D9
ware U.S.A. 40°18N 83°4W **173** E12
ware □ U.S.A. 39°0N 75°20W **173** F8
ware ▸ U.S.A. 39°15N 75°20W **175** G9
ware B. U.S.A. 39°0N 75°10W **173** F8
ware Water Gap △
S.A. 41°0N 74°55W **175** E10
a Canada 56°56N 71°28W **165** B5
rück Germany 51°46N 8°34E **76** D4
evo Macedonia 41°58N 22°46E **96** E6
gate Australia 37°45 148°56E **153** D8
mont Switz. 47°22N 7°20E **77** H3
Neths. 52°1N 4°22E **69** B4
I. Sri Lanka 9°30N 79°40E **127** K4
ijl Neths. 53°20N 6°55E **69** A6
ada, Punta Chile 52°28S 69°32W **192** D3
ado, C. Mozam. 10°45S 40°40E **143** E5
erhet Mongolia 45°50N 110°30E **114** B6
o Sudan 22°0N 80°30E **137** C3
i Canada 42°51N 80°30W **174** D4
i India 28°39N 77°13E **124** E7
i La., U.S.A. 32°28N 91°30W **176** E9
i N.Y., U.S.A. 42°17N 74°55W **175** D10
jovan Serbia 44°13N 22°9E **96** B6
e Canada 51°38N 112°23W **162** C6
ce Turkey 40°45N 34°15E **104** C6
as Mexico 28°13N 105°28W **180** B3
ān Iran 33°59N 50°40E **129** C6
e Canada 65°11N 123°25W **160** D7
ngha China 29°34S 27°34E **140** D8
zsch Germany 51°31N 12°0E **76** D8
erance I. N.G. 9°31S 141°34E **150** a
City U.S.A. 31°56N 105°12W **169** K11
Rapids U.S.A. 43°50N 96°43W **172** D6
rance 47°30N 7°2E **71** C7
ys Algeria 36°57N 3°57E **136** A4
rance 42°37N 73°47W **175** C11
nenhorst Germany 53°39N 8°37E **76** B4
niro Gouveia Brazil 9°24S 38°6W **189** B3
ce Croatia 45°53N 14°50E **93** C11
ga, Ostrava
raine 76°40N 149°20E **107** B15
raine Australia 41°30S 146°40E **151** G4
raine = Dilos Greece 37°23N 25°15E **98** D7
hi Greece 40°36N 86°41W **172** E10
hos U.S.A. 40°51N 84°21W **173** E11
ortshoop S. Africa 28°22S 24°20E **144** D3

Delray Beach U.S.A. 26°28N 80°4W **179** J9
Delsbo Sweden 61°48N 16°32E **62** C10
Delta Ala., U.S.A. 33°26N 85°42W **178** B4
Delta Colo., U.S.A. 38°44N 108°4W **168** G9
Delta Utah, U.S.A. 39°21N 112°35W **168** G7
Delta □ Nigeria 5°30N 6°0E **139** D6
Delta del Ebre ▸ Spain 40°43N 0°43E **90** C6
Delta del Po ▸ Italy 44°50N 12°15E **93** D9
Delta du Saloum △
Senegal 13°42N 16°43W **138** C1
Delta Dunărea ◠
Romania 45°15N 29°25E **81** E14
Delta Junction U.S.A. 64°2N 145°44W **160** E2
Deltebre Spain 40°43N 0°43E **90** C5
Deltona U.S.A. 28°54N 81°16W **179** G8
Delungra Australia 29°39S 150°51E **151** D5
Delvada India 20°46N 71°2E **124** J4
Delvinaki Greece 39°57N 20°32E **98** B2
Delvinë Albania 39°59N 20°6E **96** G4
Demak Indonesia 6°53S 110°38E **119** G14
Demanda, Sierra de la
Spain 42°15N 3°0W **90** C2
Demavend = Damāvand,
Qolleh-ye Iran 35°56N 52°10E **129** C7
Dembia C.A.R. 4°56N 23°53E **142** B1
Dembia
Dem. Rep. of the Congo 3°33N 25°48E **142** B2
Dembidolo Ethiopia 8°34N 34°50E **131** F1
Demchok India 32°42N 79°29E **125** C8
Demer ▸ Belgium 50°57N 4°42E **69** D4
Demerara Abyssal Plain
Atl. Oc. 10°0N 48°0W **56** F7
Demetrias Greece 39°22N 23°1E **98** B5
Demidov Russia 55°16N 31°30E **84** E6
Deming N. Mex.,
U.S.A. 32°16N 107°46W **169** K10
Deming Wash., U.S.A. 48°50N 122°13W **170** B4
Demini ▸ Brazil 0°46S 62°56W **186** D6
Demirci Turkey 39°2N 28°38E **99** B10
Demirköprü Barajı
Turkey 38°42N 28°25E **99** C10
Demirköy Turkey 41°49N 27°45E **97** E11
Demmin Germany 53°54N 13°2E **76** B9
Demnate Morocco 31°44N 6°59W **136** B2
Demonte Italy 44°19N 7°17E **92** D4
Demopolis U.S.A. 32°31N 87°50W **177** E11
Dempo Indonesia 4°2S 103°15E **118** E2
Demyansk Russia 57°40N 32°27E **84** D7
Den Bosch = 's-Hertogenbosch
Neths. 51°42N 5°17E **69** C5
Den Burg Neths. 53°3N 4°47E **69** A4
Den Chai Thailand 17°59N 100°4E **120** D3
Den Haag = 's-Gravenhage
Neths. 52°7N 4°17E **69** B4
Den Helder Neths. 52°57N 4°45E **69** B4
Den Oever Neths. 52°56N 5°2E **69** B5
Denain France 50°20N 3°22E **71** B10
Denair U.S.A. 37°32N 120°48W **170** H6
Denali = McKinley, Mt.
U.S.A. 63°4N 151°0W **160** E1
Denau = Denov
Uzbekistan 38°16N 67°54E **109** E7
Denbigh Canada 45°8N 77°15W **174** A7
Denbigh U.K. 53°12N 3°25W **66** D4
Denbighshire □ U.K. 53°8N 3°22W **66** D4
Dendang Indonesia 3°7S 107°56E **118** E3
Dendermonde Belgium 51°2N 4°5E **69** C4
Dengchuan China 25°59N 100°3E **116** E3
Denge Nigeria 12°52N 5°21E **139** C6
Dengfeng China 34°25N 113°2E **114** G7
Dengi Nigeria 9°25N 9°55E **139** D6
Dengkou China 40°18N 106°55E **114** D4
Denguélé □ Ivory C. 9°45N 7°30W **138** D3
Dengzhou China 32°34N 112°4E **117** A9
Denham Australia 25°56S 113°31E **149** E1
Denham, Mt. Jamaica 18°13N 77°32W **182** a
Denham Ra. Australia 21°55S 147°46E **150** C4
Denham Sd. Australia 25°45S 113°15E **149** E1
Denholm Canada 52°39N 108°1W **163** C7
Denia Spain 38°49N 0°8E **91** G5
Denial B. Australia 32°14S 133°32E **151** E1
Deniliquin Australia 35°30S 144°58E **153** C6
Denimoo = Fort Resolution
Canada 61°10N 113°40W **162** A6
Denison Iowa, U.S.A. 42°1N 95°21W **172** D6
Denison Tex., U.S.A. 33°45N 96°33W **176** E6
Denison Plains
Australia 18°35S 128°0E **148** C4
Deniskova Kazakhstan 52°27N 61°39E **108** D6
Deniyaya Sri Lanka 6°21N 80°33E **127** L5
Denizli Turkey 37°42N 29°2E **99** D11
Denizli □ Turkey 37°45N 29°5E **99** D11
Denman Glacier
Antarctica 66°45S 99°25E **5** C7
Denmark Australia 34°59S 117°25E **149** F2
Denmark U.S.A. 33°19N 81°9W **178** B8
Denmark ■ Europe 55°45N 10°0E **63** J3
Denmark Str. Atl. Oc. 66°0N 30°0W **57** D8
Dennery St. Lucia 13°55N 60°54W **183** f
Dennison U.S.A. 40°24N 81°19W **174** F3
Denny U.K. 56°1N 3°55W **65** E5
Denov Uzbekistan 38°16N 67°54E **109** E7
Denpasar ✈ (DPS)
Indonesia 8°44S 115°10E **119** K18
Denton Ga., U.S.A. 31°44N 82°42W **178** D7
Denton Mont., U.S.A. 47°19N 109°57W **168** C8
Denton Tex., U.S.A. 33°13N 97°8W **176** E6
D'Entrecasteaux, Pt.
Australia 34°50S 115°57E **149** F2
D'Entrecasteaux △
Australia 34°20S 115°33E **149** F2
D'Entrecasteaux Is.
Papua N. G. 9°0S 151°0E **147** B8
Dentsville U.S.A. 34°4N 80°58W **178** B8
Denu Ghana 6°4N 1°8E **139** D5
Denver Colo., U.S.A. 39°42N 104°59W **168** G11
Denver Pa., U.S.A. 40°14N 76°8W **175** F8
Deoband India 19°53N 82°44E **126** D6
Deobhog India 19°53N 82°44E **126** D6
Deodrug India 16°26N 76°52E **127** L3
Deogarh Odisha, India 21°32N 84°45E **126** D7
Deogarh Raj., India 25°32N 73°54E **124** G5
Deoghar India 24°30N 86°42E **125** G12
Deolali India 19°58N 73°50E **124** K4
Deoli = Devli India 25°50N 75°20E **124** G6
Deora India 26°22N 70°55E **124** F4

Deori India 23°24N 79°1E **125** H8
Deoria India 26°31N 83°48E **125** F10
Deosai Mts. Pakistan 35°40N 75°0E **125** B6
Depalpur India 22°51N 75°33E **124** H6
Deposit U.S.A. 42°4N 75°25W **175** D9
Depuch I. Australia 20°37S 117°44E **148** D2
Deputatskiy Russia 69°18N 139°54E **107** C14
Dêqên China 28°34N 98°51E **116** C2
Deqing China 23°8N 111°42E **117** F8
Der-Chantecoq, L. du
France 48°35N 4°40E **71** D11
Dera Ghazi Khan
Pakistan 30°5N 70°43E **124** D4
Dera Ismail Khan
Pakistan 31°50N 70°50E **124** D4
Derabugti Pakistan 29°2N 69°9E **124** E3
Derawar Fort Pakistan 28°46N 71°20E **124** E4
Derbent Russia 42°5N 48°15E **87** F8
Derbent Turkey 38°11N 28°33E **99** C10
Derby U.K. 52°56N 1°28W **66** E6
Derby Conn., U.S.A. 41°19N 73°5W **175** E11
Derby Kans., U.S.A. 37°33N 97°16W **172** G5
Derby N.Y., U.S.A. 42°41N 78°58W **174** D6
Derby City □ U.K. 52°56N 1°28W **66** E6
Derby Line U.S.A. 45°0N 72°6W **175** B12
Derbyshire □ U.K. 53°11N 1°38W **66** D6
Derdap △ Serbia 44°40N 22°23E **96** B6
Derdepoort S. Africa 24°38S 26°24E **144** B4
Derecske Hungary 47°20N 21°33E **80** C6
Dereham U.K. 52°41N 0°57E **67** E8
Dereköy Turkey 41°55N 27°21E **97** E11
Dereli Turkey 40°44N 38°26E **105** B8
Derg ▸ U.K. 54°44N 7°26W **64** B6
Derg, L. Ireland 53°0N 8°20W **64** D3
Dergachi = Derhachi
Ukraine 50°9N 36°11E **85** G9
Derhachi Ukraine 50°9N 36°11E **85** G9
Deridder U.S.A. 30°51N 93°17W **176** F8
Derik Turkey 37°21N 40°18E **105** D9
Derinkuyu Turkey 38°22N 34°45E **104** C6
Dermantsi Bulgaria 43°8N 24°17E **97** C8
Dermott U.S.A. 33°32N 91°26W **176** E9
Dêrong China 28°44N 99°9E **116** C2
Derrinallum Australia 37°57S 143°15E **152** D5
Derry = Londonderry
U.K. 55°0N 7°20W **64** B4
Derry = Londonderry □
U.K. 55°0N 7°20W **64** B4
Derry N.H., U.S.A. 42°53N 71°19W **175** D13
Derry Pa., U.S.A. 40°20N 79°18W **174** F5
Derryveagh Mts. Ireland 54°56N 8°11W **64** B3
Derval France 47°40N 1°41W **70** E5
Derveni Greece 38°8N 22°25E **98** C4
Derventa Bos.-H. 44°59N 17°55E **80** F2
Derwent ▸ Cumb., U.K. 54°39N 3°33W **66** C4
Derwent ▸ Derby, U.K. 52°57N 1°28W **66** E6
Derwent ▸ N. Yorks.,
U.K. 53°45N 0°58W **66** D7
Derwent Water U.K. 54°35N 3°9W **66** C4
Derzhavīnsk Kazakhstan 51°6N 66°19E **109** B7
Derzhavīnsk, Mys
Russia 66°5N 169°40W **107** C19
Dezhou China 37°26N 116°18E **114** F9
Des Moines Iowa,
U.S.A. 41°35N 93°37W **172** E7
Des Moines N. Mex.,
U.S.A. 36°46N 103°50W **169** H12
Des Moines Wash.,
U.S.A. 47°24N 122°19W **170** C4
Des Moines ▸ U.S.A. 40°23N 91°25W **172** E8
Desa Ethiopia 13°15N 38°8E **131** E2
Desaguadero ▸
Argentina 34°30S 66°46W **190** C2
Desaguadero ▸ Bolivia 16°35S 69°5W **188** G4
Desantne Ukraine 45°34N 29°32E **81** E14
Desaru Malaysia 1°31N 104°17E **121** d2
Descanso, Pta. Mexico 32°21N 117°3W **171** N9
Descartes France 46°59N 0°42E **72** B4
Deschaillons-sur-St-Laurent
Canada 46°32N 72°7W **165** C5
Deschambault L.
Canada 54°50N 103°30W **163** C8
Deschutes ▸ U.S.A. 45°38N 120°55W **168** D3
Dese Ethiopia 11°5N 39°40E **131** E2
Deseado, C. Chile 52°45S 74°42W **192** D2
Desenzano del Garda
Italy 45°28N 10°32E **92** C7
Deseronto Canada 44°12N 77°3W **174** B7
Desert Center U.S.A. 33°43N 115°24W **171** M11
Desert Hot Springs
U.S.A. 33°58N 116°30W **171** M10
Desfina Greece 38°25N 22°31E **98** C4
Deshnok India 27°48N 73°21E **124** F5
Desierto Central de Baja
California □
Mexico 29°40N 114°50W **180** B2
Deskati Greece 39°55N 21°49E **96** G5
Desna ▸ Ukraine 50°33N 30°32E **75** C16
Desnăţui ▸ Romania 43°53N 23°35E **81** F8
Desolación, I. Chile 53°0S 74°0W **192** D2
Despeñaperros, Paso
Spain 38°24N 3°30W **89** D4
Despeñaperros ◠ Spain 38°23N 3°32W **89** D4
Despotiko Greece 36°57N 24°58E **98** E6
Despotovac Serbia 44°6N 21°30E **96** B5
Dessau Germany 51°51N 12°14E **76** D8
Dessye = Dese Ethiopia 11°5N 39°40E **131** E2
D'Estrees B. Australia 35°55S 137°45E **152** C2
Desuri India 25°18N 73°35E **124** G5
Desvres France 50°40N 1°48E **71** B8
Det Udom Thailand 14°54N 105°5E **120** E5
Deta Romania 45°24N 21°13E **80** B6
Detinja ▸ Serbia 43°51N 20°5E **96** C4
Detmold Germany 51°56N 8°52E **76** D4
Detour, Pt. U.S.A. 45°40N 86°40W **172** C10
Detroit U.S.A. 42°19N 83°12W **174** D1
Detroit Lakes U.S.A. 46°49N 95°51W **172** B6
Detva Slovak Rep. 48°33N 19°25E **79** C12
Deua △ Australia 35°32S 149°46E **153** C4
Deurne Neths. 51°27N 5°49E **69** C5
Deutsch-Luxemburgischer ◠
Germany 49°58N 6°12E **77** F7
Deutsche Bucht Germany 54°15N 8°0E **76** A4
Deutschland = Germany ■
Europe 51°0N 10°0E **76** D6

Deutschlandsberg
Austria 46°49N 15°14E **78** E8
Deux-Sèvres □ France 46°35N 0°20W **70** F6
Deva Romania 45°53N 22°55E **80** E7
Devakottai India 9°55N 78°45E **127** K4
Devaprayag India 30°13N 78°35E **125** D8
Devarkonda India 16°42N 78°56E **126** F4
Dévaványa Hungary 47°2N 20°59E **80** C5
Deveci Dağları Turkey 40°6N 36°15E **104** B7
Devecikonağı Turkey 39°55N 28°34E **99** C12
Devecser Hungary 47°6N 17°26E **80** C2
Develi Turkey 38°23N 35°29E **104** C6
Devereux U.S.A. 33°13N 83°5W **178** B6
Deveron ▸ U.K. 57°41N 2°32W **65** D6
Devesel Romania 44°28N 22°41E **80** F7
Devgad I. India 14°48N 74°5E **127** G2
Devgarh India 16°23N 73°23E **127** F1
Devgadh Bariya India 22°40N 73°55E **124** H5
Devi ▸ India 11°59N 86°24E **126** E8
Devikot India 26°42N 71°12E **124** F4
Devil River Pk. N.Z. 40°56S 172°37E **155** A7
Devils Den U.S.A. 35°46N 119°58W **170** K7
Devils Hole = Death Valley △
U.S.A. 36°29N 117°6W **171** J9
Devils Lake U.S.A. 48°7N 98°52W **172** A4
Devils Paw Canada 58°47N 134°0W **162** B2
Devils Postpile △
U.S.A. 37°37N 119°5W **170** H7
Devil's Pt. Sri Lanka 9°26N 80°6E **127** K5
Devils Tower U.S.A. 44°35N 104°42W **168** D11
Devils Tower △
U.S.A. 44°48N 104°55W **168** D11
Devin Bulgaria 41°44N 24°24E **97** E8
Devine U.S.A. 29°8N 98°54W **176** G5
Devizes U.K. 51°22N 1°58W **67** F6
Devli India 25°50N 75°20E **124** G6
Devnya Bulgaria 43°13N 27°33E **97** C11
Devoll ▸ Albania 40°57N 20°15E **96** F4
Devon Canada 53°24N 113°44W **162** C6
Devon □ U.K. 50°50N 3°40W **67** G4
Devon I. Canada 75°10N 85°0W **161** B15
Devonport Australia 41°10S 146°22E **151** G4
Devonport N.Z. 36°49S 174°49E **155** B5
Devrek Turkey 41°13N 31°57E **104** B4
Devrekâni Turkey 41°36N 33°50E **104** B5
Devrez ▸ Turkey 41°6N 34°25E **104** B6
Devrukh India 17°3N 73°37E **126** F1
Dewas India 22°59N 76°3E **124** H7
Dewetsdorp S. Africa 29°33S 26°39E **144** C4
Dewey Puerto Rico 18°18N 65°18W **183** d
Dexing China 28°46N 117°30E **117** C11
Dexter Maine, U.S.A. 45°1N 69°18W **173** C19
Dexter Mo., U.S.A. 36°48N 89°57W **172** G9
Dexter N. Mex.,
U.S.A. 33°12N 104°22W **169** K11
Dey-Dey, L. Australia 29°12S 131°4E **149** E5
Deyang China 31°3N 104°27E **116** B5
Deyhūk Iran 33°15N 57°30E **129** C8
Deyyer Iran 27°55N 51°55E **129** E6
Dez ▸ Iran 31°39N 48°52E **105** F13
Dezadeash L. Canada 60°28N 136°58W **162** A1
Dezfūl Iran 32°20N 48°30E **105** F13
Dezhneva, Mys
Russia 66°5N 169°40W **107** C19
Dezhou China 37°26N 116°18E **114** F9
Dhadhar ▸ India 24°56N 85°24E **125** G11
Dhahaban Si. Arabia 21°58N 39°3E **137** C4
Dhahiriya = Az Zāhirīyah
West Bank 31°25N 34°58E **130** D3
Dhahran = Az Zahrān
Si. Arabia 26°10N 50°7E **129** E6
Dhak Pakistan 32°25N 72°33E **124** C5
Dhaka Bangla. 23°43N 90°26E **125** H14
Dhaka □ Bangla. 24°25N 90°25E **125** G14
Dhali Cyprus 35°1N 33°25E **101** D12
Dhamangaon India 20°48N 78°9E **126** J10
Dhamār Yemen 14°30N 44°20E **131** E3
Dhampur India 29°19N 78°33E **125** E8
Dhamra ▸ India 20°47N 86°58E **126** B8
Dhamtari India 20°42N 81°35E **126** D5
Dhanbad India 23°50N 86°30E **125** H12
Dhangarhi Nepal 28°55N 80°40E **125** E9
Dhankuta Nepal 26°55N 87°40E **125** F12
Dhanora India 20°20N 80°22E **126** B5
Dhanpuri India 23°13N 81°30E **125** H9
Dhanushkodi India 9°11N 79°24E **127** K4
Dhar India 22°35N 75°26E **124** H6
Dharampur India 20°32N 73°17E **124** H6
Dharamsala = Dharmsala
India 32°16N 76°23E **124** C7
Dharan Nepal 26°49N 87°17E **125** F12
Dharangaon India 21°1N 75°16E **126** D2
Dharapuram India 10°45N 77°34E **127** J3
Dhariwal India 31°57N 75°19E **124** D6
Dharla ▸ Bangla. 25°46N 89°42E **125** G13
Dharmapuri India 12°10N 78°10E **127** H4
Dharmavaram India 14°29N 77°44E **127** G3
Dharmjaygarh India 22°28N 83°13E **125** H10
Dharmsala India 32°16N 76°23E **124** C7
Dharni India 21°33N 76°53E **124** J7
Dharug △ Australia 33°20S 151°2E **153** B9
Dharur India 18°3N 76°8E **126** E3
Dharwad India 15°30N 75°4E **127** G2
Dhasan ▸ India 25°48N 79°24E **124** G8
Dhaulagiri Nepal 28°39N 83°28E **125** E10
Dhebar, L. India 24°10N 74°0E **124** G6
Dheftera Cyprus 35°5N 33°16E **101** D12
Dhenkanal India 20°45N 85°35E **126** B7
Dherinia Cyprus 35°3N 33°57E **101** D12
Dheskáti = Deskati
Greece 39°55N 21°49E **96** G5
Dhī Qār □ Iraq 31°0N 46°15E **105** F12
Dhiarrizos ▸ Cyprus 34°41N 32°34E **101** E11
Dhībān Jordan 31°30N 35°46E **130** D4
Dhilwan India 31°31N 75°21E **124** D6
Dhimarkhera India 23°28N 80°22E **125** H9
Dholka India 22°44N 72°29E **124** H5
Dhomokós =Domokos
Greece 39°10N 22°18E **98** B4
Dhond = Daund India 18°26N 74°40E **126** E2
Dhone India 15°25N 77°53E **127** G3
Dhoraji India 21°45N 70°37E **124** J4
Dhorpatan Nepal 28°29N 83°4E **125** E10
Dhragonisi = Tragonhsi
Greece 37°7N 25°29E **98** D7
Dhrangadhra India 22°59N 71°31E **124** H4
Dhrol India 22°33N 70°25E **124** H4
Dhubab Yemen 12°57N 43°34E **131** F3
Dhuburi India 26°2N 89°59E **125** F13
Dhule India 20°58N 74°50E **124** J6
Di-ib, W. ▸ Sudan 22°38N 36°6E **137** C4

Di Linh Vietnam 11°35N 108°4E **121** G7
Di Linh, Cao Nguyen
Vietnam 11°30N 108°0E **121** G7
Dia Greece 35°28N 25°14E **101** D7
Diabakania Guinea 10°38N 10°58E **138** C3
Diablo Range U.S.A. 37°20N 121°25W **170** J5
Diafarabé Mali 14°9N 4°57W **138** C4
Diala Mali 14°10N 9°58W **138** C3
Dialakoro Mali 12°18N 7°54W **138** C3
Dialakoto Senegal 13°21N 13°19W **138** C2
Diallassagou Mali 13°47N 3°41W **138** C4
Diamante Argentina 32°5S 60°40W **190** C3
Diamante Italy 39°41N 15°49E **95** C8
Diamante ▸ Argentina 34°30S 66°46W **190** C2
Diamantina Brazil 18°17S 43°40W **189** D2
Diamantina ▸
Australia 26°45S 139°10E **151** D2
Diamantina △
Australia 23°33S 141°23E **150** C3
Diamantino Brazil 14°30S 56°30W **187** D7
Diamond Bar U.S.A. 34°1N 117°48W **171** L9
Diamond Harbour
India 22°11N 88°14E **125** H13
Diamond Is. Australia 17°25S 151°5E **150** B5
Diamond Mts. U.S.A. 39°40N 115°50W **168** G6
Diamond Springs
U.S.A. 38°42N 120°49W **170** G6
Diamou Mali 14°5N 11°16W **138** C2
Dian Chi China 24°50N 102°42E **116** E4
Dianalund Denmark 55°32N 11°30E **63** J5
Dianbai China 21°30N 111°0E **117** G8
Diancheng China 21°30N 111°4E **117** G8
Dianjiang China 30°24N 107°20E **116** B6
Diano Marina Italy 43°54N 8°5E **92** E5
Dianópolis Brazil 11°38S 46°50W **187** F9
Dianra Ivory C. 8°45N 6°14W **138** D3
Diaoyu Dao = Senkaku-Shotō
E. China Sea 25°45N 123°30E **113** M1
Diaoyu Tai = Senkaku-Shotō
E. China Sea 25°45N 123°30E **113** M1
Diapaga Burkina Faso 12°5N 1°46E **139** C5
Diapangou Burkina Faso 12°5N 0°10W **138** C5
Diariguila Guinea 10°35N 10°2W **138** C2
Diavolo, Mt. India 12°40N 92°56E **127** H11
Diba = Dibbā al Ḩiṣn
U.A.E. 25°45N 56°16E **129** E8
Dibagah Iraq 35°52N 43°48E **105** C10
Dibai India 28°13N 78°15E **124** E8
Dibaya
Dem. Rep. of the Congo 6°30S 22°57E **140** F4
Dibaya-Lubue
Dem. Rep. of the Congo 4°12S 19°54E **140** E3
Dibbā al Ḩiṣn U.A.E. 25°45N 56°16E **129** E8
Dibbeen △ Jordan 32°20N 35°45E **130** C4
D'Iberville, Lac Canada 55°55N 73°15W **164** A5
Dibete Botswana 23°45S 26°32E **144** B4
Dibrugarh India 27°29N 94°55E **123** F19
Dickens U.S.A. 33°37N 100°50W **176** E4
Dickinson U.S.A. 46°53N 102°47W **172** B2
Dickson U.S.A. 36°5N 87°23W **177** C11
Dickson City U.S.A. 41°28N 75°36W **175** E9
Dicle Baraji Turkey 38°20N 40°11E **105** C9
Dicle Nehri ▸ Turkey 37°44N 41°10E **105** D9
Dicomano Italy 43°53N 11°31E **93** E8
Didiéni Mali 13°53N 8°6W **138** C3
Didim Turkey 37°22N 27°16E **99** D9
Didimotiko Turkey 41°22N 26°29E **97** F10
Didsbury Canada 51°35N 114°10W **162** C6
Didwana India 27°23N 74°36E **124** F6
Die France 44°47N 5°22E **73** D9
Diébougou Burkina Faso 11°0N 3°15W **138** C4
Diecke Guinea 7°27N 8°54W **138** D3
Diefenbaker, L. Canada 51°0N 106°55W **163** C7
Diego de Almagro Chile 26°22S 70°3W **190** B1
Diego Garcia Ind. Oc. 7°50S 72°50E **146** E6
Diego Ramírez, Islas
Chile 56°30S 68°44W **192** E3
Diego Suarez = Antsiranana
Madag. 12°25S 49°20E **141** G9
Diekirch Lux. 49°52N 6°10E **69** E6
Diéma Mali 14°32N 9°12W **138** C3
Diembéring Senegal 12°29N 16°47W **138** C1
Diemelsee ◠ Germany 51°20N 8°46E **76** D4
Dien Ban Vietnam 15°53N 108°16E **120** E7
Dien Bien Phu Vietnam 21°20N 103°0E **116** D4
Dien Chau, Vinh
Vietnam 19°0N 105°55E **120** C5
Dien Khanh Vietnam 12°15N 109°6E **121** F7
Diepholz Germany 52°37N 8°22E **76** B4
Dieppe France 49°54N 1°4E **70** C8
Dierks U.S.A. 34°7N 94°1W **176** D7
Diest Belgium 50°58N 5°4E **69** D5
Dietikon Switz. 47°24N 8°24E **77** H4
Dieulefit France 44°33N 5°4E **73** D9
Dieuze France 48°49N 6°43E **71** D13
Dif Somalia 0°59N 40°58E **131** G3
Diffa Niger 13°18N 12°36E **139** C7
Diffa □ Niger 14°0N 12°30E **139** C7
Differdange Lux. 49°31N 5°54E **69** F5
Dig India 27°28N 77°20E **124** F7
Digba
Dem. Rep. of the Congo 4°25N 25°48E **142** B2
Digby Canada 44°38N 65°50W **165** D6
Digges Is. Canada 62°40N 77°50W **161** E16
Diggi India 26°22N 75°26E **124** F6
Dighinala Bangla. 23°15N 92°5E **125** H18
Dighton U.S.A. 38°29N 100°28W **172** F3
Diglur India 18°34N 77°33E **126** E3
Digna Mali 14°48N 8°10W **138** C3
Digne-les-Bains France 44°5N 6°12E **73** D10
Digoin France 46°29N 4°1E **72** F7
Digor Turkey 40°22N 43°25E **105** B10
Digos Phil. 6°45N 125°20E **119** C7
Digranes Iceland 66°4N 14°44W **60** C6
Digras India 20°7N 77°42E **126** J10
Digul ▸ Indonesia 7°7S 138°42E **149** B10
Digya ◠ Ghana 7°15N 0°0W **139** D5
Dihang = Brahmaputra ▸
Asia 23°40N 90°35E **125** H13
Dijlah, Nahr ▸ Asia 31°0N 47°25E **128** D5
Dijon France 47°20N 5°3E **71** E12
Dikhil Djibouti 11°8N 42°20E **131** E3
Dikili Turkey 39°4N 26°53E **99** C8
Dikirnis Egypt 31°9N 31°35E **130** H7
Dikkil = Dikhil Djibouti 11°8N 42°20E **131** E3
Dikodougou Ivory C. 9°4N 5°45W **138** D3
Diksmuide Belgium 51°2N 2°52E **69** C2
Dikson Russia 73°40N 80°5E **106** B9
Dikti Oros Greece 35°8N 25°22E **101** D7
Dikwa Nigeria 12°4N 13°30E **139** C7
Dila Ethiopia 6°21N 38°22E **131** F2

Dilek Yarimadisi △
Turkey 37°40N 27°10E **99** D9
Dili E. Timor 8°39S 125°34E **119** F7
Diligent Strait India 12°11N 92°57E **127** H11
Dilijan Armenia 40°46N 44°57E **87** K7
Dilinata Greece 38°13N 20°31E **98** C2
Dilj Croatia 45°29N 18°1E **80** E3
Dillenburg Germany 50°43N 8°17E **76** E4
Dilley U.S.A. 28°40N 99°10W **176** G5
Dilli = India 28°39N 77°13E **124** E7
Dilli Mali 15°1N 7°40W **138** C3
Dillingen Bayern,
Germany 48°36N 10°30E **77** G6
Dillingen Saarland,
Germany 49°22N 6°43E **77** F2
Dillingham U.S.A. 59°3N 158°28W **166** D8
Dillon Canada 55°56N 108°35W **163** B7
Dillon Mont., U.S.A. 45°13N 112°38W **168** D7
Dillon S.C., U.S.A. 34°25N 79°22W **177** D15
Dillon ▸ Canada 55°56N 108°56W **163** B7
Dillsburg U.S.A. 40°7N 77°2W **174** F7
Dilolo
Dem. Rep. of the Congo 10°28S 22°18E **140** G4
Dilos Greece 37°23N 25°15E **98** D7
Dilove Ukraine 47°56N 24°11E **81** C9
Dimapur India 25°54N 93°45E **116** F4
Dimas Mexico 23°43N 106°47W **180** C3
Dimashq Syria 33°30N 36°18E **130** B5
Dimashq □ Syria 33°30N 36°30E **130** B5
Dimbaza S. Africa 32°50S 27°14E **145** D4
Dimbokro Ivory C. 6°45N 4°46W **138** D4
Dimboola Australia 36°28S 142°7E **152** D5
Dîmbovița = Dâmbovița ▸
Romania 44°12N 26°26E **81** F11
Dimbulah Australia 17°8S 145°4E **150** B4
Dimitrovgrad Bulgaria 42°5N 25°35E **97** D9
Dimitrovgrad Russia 54°14N 49°39E **86** C9
Dimitrovgrad Serbia 43°2N 22°48E **96** C6
Dimitrovo = Pernik
Bulgaria 42°35N 23°2E **96** C7
Dimitsana Greece 37°36N 22°3E **98** D4
Dimmitt U.S.A. 34°33N 102°19W **176** D3
Dimona Israel 31°2N 35°1E **130** D4
Dinagat I. Phil. 10°10N 125°40E **119** F7
Dinajpur Bangla. 25°33N 88°43E **123** G16
Dinan France 48°28N 2°2W **70** D4
Dīnān Āb Iran 32°4N 56°49E **129** C8
Dinant Belgium 50°16N 4°55E **69** D4
Dinapur India 25°38N 85°5E **125** G11
Dinar Turkey 38°5N 30°10E **99** C12
Dīnār, Kūh-e Iran 30°42N 51°46E **129** D6
Dinara Planina Croatia 44°0N 16°30E **93** C13
Dinard France 48°38N 2°6W **70** D4
Dinaric Alps = Dinara Planina
Croatia 44°0N 16°30E **93** C13
Dinbych = Denbigh U.K. 53°12N 3°25W **66** D4
Dinbych-y-Pysgod = Tenby
U.K. 51°40N 4°42W **67** F3
Dindanko Mali 14°8N 9°30W **138** C3
Dindi ▸ India 16°24N 78°15E **127** F4
Dindigul India 10°25N 78°0E **127** J4
Dindori India 22°57N 81°5E **125** H9
Ding Xian = Dingzhou
China 38°30N 114°59E **114** E8
Dinga Pakistan 25°26N 67°10E **124** G2
Ding'an China 19°42N 110°19E **117** a
Dingbian China 37°35N 107°32E **114** F4
Dingelstädt Germany 51°18N 10°19E **76** D6
Dingle Sweden 58°32N 11°35E **63** F5
Dingle B. Ireland 52°9N 10°17W **64** D1
Dingle Pen. Ireland 52°12N 10°5W **64** D1
Dingmans Ferry
U.S.A. 41°13N 74°55W **175** E10
Dingnan China 24°45N 115°0E **117** E10
Dingo Australia 23°38S 149°19E **150** C4
Dingolfing Germany 48°37N 12°30E **77** G8
Dingtao China 35°5N 115°35E **114** G8
Dinguiraye Guinea 11°18N 10°49W **138** C2
Dingwall U.K. 57°36N 4°26W **65** D4
Dingxi China 35°30N 104°33E **114** G3
Dingxiang China 38°30N 112°58E **114** E7
Dingyuan China 32°32N 117°41E **117** A11
Dingzhou China 38°30N 114°59E **114** E8
Dinh, Mui Vietnam 11°22N 109°1E **121** G7
Dinh Lap Vietnam 21°33N 107°6E **116** G6
Dinin ▸ Ireland 52°43N 7°19W **64** D4
Dinira △ Venezuela 9°57N 70°6W **183** E5
Dinokwe Botswana 23°29S 26°37E **144** B4
Dinorwic Canada 49°41N 92°30W **163** D10
Dinosaur △ Canada 50°47N 111°30W **162** C6
Dinosaur △ U.S.A. 40°30N 108°45W **168** F9
Dinuba U.S.A. 36°32N 119°23W **170** J7
Diö Sweden 56°37N 14°15E **63** H8
Diodar India 12°23N 6°50E **138** G3
Dioka Mali 14°57N 10°4W **138** C2
Diongoï Mali 14°38N 8°34W **138** C3
Dionisiades Greece 35°20N 26°10E **101** D8
Diósgyör Hungary 48°7N 20°43E **80** C5
Diosig Romania 47°18N 22°2E **80** C7
Diougani Mali 14°9N 2°44W **138** C4
Diouloulou Senegal 13°5N 16°38W **138** C1
Dioura Mali 14°9N 5°12W **138** C3
Diourbel Senegal 14°39N 16°12W **138** C1
Diourbel □ Senegal 14°45N 16°15W **138** C1
Dipalpur Pakistan 30°40N 73°39E **124** D5
Dipkarpaz = Rizokarpaso
Cyprus 35°36N 34°23E **101** D13
Diplo Pakistan 24°35N 69°35E **124** G3
Dipolog Phil. 8°36N 123°20E **119** C6
Dipperu △ Australia 21°56S 148°42E **150** C4
Dipton N.Z. 45°54S 168°22E **155** F2
Dir Pakistan 35°8N 71°59E **123** B13
Diré Mali 16°20N 3°25W **138** B4
Dire Dawa Ethiopia 9°35N 41°45E **131** F3
Dirfis Oros Greece 38°40N 23°54E **98** C5
Diriamba Nic. 11°51N 86°19W **182** E2
Dirk Hartog I. Australia 25°50S 113°5E **149** E1
Dirranbandi Australia 28°33S 148°17E **151** D4
Disa India 24°18N 72°10E **124** G4
Disappointment, C.
U.S.A. 46°18N 124°5W **170** D2
Disappointment, L.
Australia 23°20S 122°40E **148** D3
Disaster B. Australia 37°15S 149°58E **153** D8
Discovery B. China 22°18N 114°1E **111** a
Discovery Bay △
Australia 38°9S 141°16E **152** D4
Discovery Seamount
Atl. Oc. 42°0S 0°10E **56** L12

216 Disentis Muster

INDEX TO WORLD MA

Disentis Muster *Switz.* 46°42N 8°50E **77** J4
Dishna *Egypt* 26°9N 32°32E **137** B3
Disina *Nigeria* 11°35N 9°50E **139** C6
Disko = Qeqertarsuaq *Greenland* 69°45N 53°30W **57** D5
Disko Bugt *Greenland* 69°10N 52°0W **57** D5
Disna = Dzisna → *Belarus* 55°34N 28°12E **84** E5
Disneyland Hong Kong *China* 22°18N 114°2E **111** a
Diss *U.K.* 52°23N 1°7E **67** E9
Disteghil Sar *Pakistan* 36°20N 75°12E **125** A6
District of Columbia □ *U.S.A.* 38°55N 77°0W **173** F15
Distrito Federal □ *Brazil* 15°45S 47°45W **189** D1
Distrito Federal □ *Mexico* 19°15N 99°10W **181** D5
Disûq *Egypt* 31°8N 30°35E **137** E7
Diu *India* 20°45N 70°58E **124** J4
Dīvāndarreh *Iran* 35°55N 47°2E **105** E12
Dives → *France* 49°18N 0°7W **70** C6
Dives-sur-Mer *France* 49°18N 0°8W **70** C6
Divi Pt. *India* 15°59N 81°9E **127** G5
Divichi = Däväçi *Azerbaijan* 41°15N 48°57E **87** K9
Divide *U.S.A.* 45°45N 112°45W **168** D7
Dividing Ra. *Australia* 27°45S 116°0E **149** E2
Divinópolis *Brazil* 20°10S 44°54W **189** E2
Divjake *Albania* 41°0N 19°32E **96** F3
Divnoye *Russia* 45°55N 43°21E **87** H6
Divo *Ivory C.* 5°48N 5°15W **138** D3
Divriği *Turkey* 39°22N 38°7E **105** C8
Dīwāl Kol *Afghan.* 34°23N 67°52E **124** B2
Dix-Huit Montagnes □ *Ivory C.* 7°30N 7°40W **138** D3
Dixie Mt. *U.S.A.* 39°55N 120°16W **170** F6
Dixie Union *U.S.A.* 31°20N 82°28W **178** D7
Dixon *Calif., U.S.A.* 38°27N 121°49W **170** G5
Dixon *Ill., U.S.A.* 41°50N 89°29W **172** E9
Dixon Entrance *U.S.A.* 54°30N 132°0W **160** G5
Dixville *Canada* 45°4N 71°46W **175** A13
Diyadin *Turkey* 39°33N 43°40E **105** C10
Diyālá □ *Iraq* 33°45N 44°50E **128** C5
Diyālá → *Iraq* 33°13N 44°30E **105** F11
Diyarbakır *Turkey* 37°55N 40°18E **105** D9
Diyarbakır □ *Turkey* 38°0N 40°10E **105** D9
Diyodar *India* 24°8N 71°50E **124** G4
Dizangué *Cameroon* 3°46N 9°59E **139** E6
Djakarta = Jakarta *Indonesia* 6°9S 106°52E **118** F3
Djamâa *Algeria* 33°32N 5°59E **136** B5
Djamba *Angola* 16°45S 13°58E **144** A1
Djambala *Congo* 2°32S 14°30E **140** E2
Djanet *Algeria* 24°35N 9°32E **136** D5
Djawa = Jawa *Indonesia* 7°0S 110°0E **118** F3
Djebel Tazzeka △ *Morocco* 34°6N 4°11W **136** B3
Djebiniana *Tunisia* 35°1N 11°0E **136** A6
Djelfa *Algeria* 34°40N 3°15E **136** B4
Djelfa □ *Algeria* 34°20N 3°40E **136** B4
Djema *C.A.R.* 6°3N 25°15E **142** A2
Djémila *Algeria* 36°19N 5°44E **136** A5
Djendel *Algeria* 36°15N 2°25E **136** A4
Djenné *Mali* 14°0N 4°30W **138** C4
Djenoun, Garet el *Algeria* 25°4N 5°31E **136** C5
Djerba *Tunisia* 33°48N 10°54E **136** B6
Djerba, Î. de *Tunisia* 33°50N 10°48E **135** B8
Djerid, Chott *Tunisia* 33°42N 8°30E **136** B5
Djibo *Burkina Faso* 14°9N 1°35W **139** C4
Djibouti *Djibouti* 11°30N 43°5E **131** E3
Djibouti ■ *Africa* 12°0N 43°0E **131** E3
Djolu *Dem. Rep. of the Congo* 0°35N 22°5E **140** D4
Djoudj △ *Senegal* 16°24N 16°14W **138** B1
Djougou *Benin* 9°40N 1°45E **139** D5
Djoum *Cameroon* 2°41N 12°35E **140** D2
Djourab, Erg du *Chad* 16°40N 18°50E **135** E9
Djugu *Dem. Rep. of the Congo* 1°55N 30°35E **142** B3
Djukbinj △ *Australia* 12°11S 131°2E **148** B5
Djúpivogur *Iceland* 64°39N 14°17W **60** D6
Djurås *Sweden* 60°34N 15°8E **62** D9
Djurdjura △ *Algeria* 36°20N 4°15E **136** A4
Djurö △ *Sweden* 58°52N 13°28E **63** F7
Djursland *Denmark* 56°27N 10°45E **63** H4
Dmitriya Lapteva, Proliv *Russia* 73°0N 140°0E **107** B15
Dmitriyev Lgovskiy *Russia* 52°10N 35°0E **85** F8
Dmitrov *Russia* 56°25N 37°32E **84** D9
Dmitrovsk-Orlovskiy *Russia* 52°29N 35°10E **85** F8
Dnepr = Dnipro → *Ukraine* 46°30N 32°18E **85** J7
Dneprodzerzhinsk = Dniprodzerzhynsk *Ukraine* 48°32N 34°37E **85** H8
Dneprodzerzhinskoye Vdkhr. = Dniprodzerzhynske Vdskh. *Ukraine* 48°49N 34°8E **85** H8
Dnepropetrovsk = Dnipropetrovsk *Ukraine* 48°30N 35°0E **85** H8
Dneprorudnoye = Dniprorudne *Ukraine* 47°21N 34°58E **85** J8
Dnestr = Dnister → *Europe* 46°18N 30°17E **75** E16
Dnieper = Dnipro → *Ukraine* 46°30N 32°18E **85** J7
Dniester = Dnister → *Europe* 46°18N 30°17E **75** E16
Dnipro → *Ukraine* 46°30N 32°18E **85** J7
Dniprodzerzhynsk *Ukraine* 48°32N 34°37E **85** H8
Dniprodzerzhynske Vdskh. *Ukraine* 48°49N 34°8E **85** H8
Dnipropetrovsk *Ukraine* 48°30N 35°0E **85** H8
Dnipropetrovsk □ *Ukraine* 48°15N 34°50E **85** H8
Dniprorudne *Ukraine* 47°21N 34°58E **85** J8
Dnister → *Europe* 46°18N 30°17E **75** E16
Dnistrovskyy Lyman *Ukraine* 46°15N 30°17E **85** J6
Dno *Russia* 57°50N 29°58E **84** D5
Dnyapro = Dnipro → *Ukraine* 46°30N 32°18E **85** J7
Do Gonbadān = Gachsārān *Iran* 30°15N 50°45E **129** D6
Doaktown *Canada* 46°33N 66°8W **165** C6
Doan Hung *Vietnam* 21°30N 105°10E **116** G5
Doba *Chad* 8°40N 16°50E **135** G9
Dobandi *Pakistan* 31°13N 66°50E **124** D2
Dobbiaco *Italy* 46°44N 12°14E **93** B9
Dobbyn *Australia* 19°44S 140°2E **150** B3
Dobczyce *Poland* 49°52N 20°25E **83** J7
Dobele *Latvia* 56°37N 23°16E **82** B10
Dobele □ *Latvia* 56°35N 23°5E **82** B10
Döbeln *Germany* 51°6N 13°7E **76** D9
Doberai, Jazirah *Indonesia* 1°25S 133°0E **119** E8
Dobiegniew *Poland* 52°59N 15°45E **83** F2
Doblas *Argentina* 37°5S 64°0W **190** D3
Dobo *Indonesia* 5°45S 134°15E **119** F8
Doboj *Bos.-H.* 44°46N 18°4E **80** F3
Dobra *Wielkopolskie, Poland* 51°55N 18°37E **83** G5
Dobra *Zachodnio-Pomorskie, Poland* 53°34N 15°20E **82** E2
Dobra *Dâmbovita, Romania* 44°52N 25°40E **81** F10
Dobra *Hunedoara, Romania* 45°54N 22°36E **80** E7
Dobre Miasto *Poland* 53°58N 20°26E **82** E7
Dobreşti *Romania* 46°51N 22°18E **80** D7
Dobrich *Bulgaria* 43°37N 27°49E **97** C11
Dobrich □ *Bulgaria* 43°37N 27°49E **97** C11
Dobrinishta *Bulgaria* 41°49N 23°34E **96** E7
Dobřiš *Czech Rep.* 49°46N 14°10E **78** B7
Dobrodzień *Poland* 50°45N 18°25E **83** H5
Dobromyl *Ukraine* 49°34N 22°46E **83** J9
Dobron *Ukraine* 48°25N 22°23E **80** B7
Dobropole *Ukraine* 48°25N 37°2E **85** H9
Dobrovolsk *Russia* 54°46N 22°31E **82** D9
Dobruja *Europe* 44°30N 28°15E **81** F13
Dobrush *Belarus* 52°25N 31°22E **75** B16
Dobrzany *Poland* 53°22N 15°25E **82** E2
Dobrzyń nad Wisłą *Poland* 52°39N 19°22E **83** F6
Doc, Mui *Vietnam* 17°58N 106°30E **120** D6
Doce → *Brazil* 19°37S 39°49W **189** D3
Docker River = Kaltukatjara *Australia* 24°52S 129°5E **149** D4
Docksta *Sweden* 63°3N 18°18E **62** A12
Doctor Arroyo *Mexico* 23°40N 100°11W **180** C4
Doctor Pedro P. Peña *Paraguay* 22°27S 62°21W **190** A3
Doctors Inlet *U.S.A.* 30°6N 81°47W **178** E8
Doda *India* 33°10N 75°34E **125** C6
Doda, L. *Canada* 49°25N 75°13W **164** C4
Doda Betta *India* 11°24N 76°44E **127** J3
Dodballapur *India* 13°18N 77°32E **127** H3
Dodecanese = Dodekanisa *Greece* 36°35N 27°0E **99** E8
Dodekanisa *Greece* 36°35N 27°0E **99** E8
Dodge City *U.S.A.* 37°45N 100°1W **172** G3
Dodge L. *Canada* 59°50N 105°36W **163** B7
Dodgeville *U.S.A.* 42°58N 90°8W **172** D8
Dodo *Cameroon* 7°30N 12°3E **139** D7
Dodoma *Tanzania* 6°8S 35°45E **142** D4
Dodoma □ *Tanzania* 6°0S 36°0E **142** D4
Dodoni *Greece* 39°40N 20°46E **98** B2
Dodori ⌂ *Kenya* 1°55S 41°7E **142** C5
Dodsland *Canada* 51°50N 108°45W **163** C7
Dodson *U.S.A.* 48°24N 108°15W **168** B9
Dodurga *Turkey* 39°49N 29°57E **99** B11
Doerun *U.S.A.* 31°19N 83°55W **178** D6
Doesburg *Neths.* 52°1N 6°9E **69** B6
Doetinchem *Neths.* 51°59N 6°18E **69** C6
Dog Creek *Canada* 51°35N 122°14W **162** C4
Dog I. *U.S.A.* 29°48N 84°36W **178** F5
Dog L. *Man., Canada* 51°2N 98°31W **163** C9
Dog L. *Ont., Canada* 48°48N 89°30W **164** C2
Doğanşehir *Turkey* 38°5N 37°53E **104** C7
Dogliani *Italy* 44°32N 7°56E **92** D4
Dogondoutchi *Niger* 13°38N 4°2E **139** C5
Dogran *Pakistan* 31°48N 73°35E **124** D5
Doğubayazıt *Turkey* 39°31N 44°5E **105** C11
Doguéraoua *Niger* 14°0N 5°31E **139** C6
Doha = Ad Dawḩah *Qatar* 25°15N 51°35E **129** E6
Dohazari *Bangla.* 22°10N 92°5E **123** H18
Dohrighat *India* 26°16N 83°31E **125** F10
Doi *Indonesia* 2°14N 127°49E **119** D7
Doi Inthanon *Thailand* 18°35N 98°29E **120** C2
Doi Inthanon △ *Thailand* 18°33N 98°34E **120** C2
Doi Khuntan △ *Thailand* 18°33N 99°14E **120** C2
Doi Luang *Thailand* 18°30N 101°0E **120** C3
Doi Luang △ *Thailand* 19°22N 99°35E **120** C2
Doi Phukha △ *Thailand* 19°8N 101°9E **120** C3
Doi Saket *Thailand* 18°52N 99°9E **120** C2
Doi Suthep Pui △ *Thailand* 18°49N 98°53E **120** C2
Doi Toa *Thailand* 17°55N 98°30E **120** D2
Dois Irmãos, Sa. *Brazil* 9°0S 42°30W **189** B2
Dojransko Jezero *Macedonia* 41°13N 22°44E **96** E6
Dokdo = Liancourt Rocks *Asia* 37°15N 131°52E **113** F5
Dokkum *Neths.* 53°20N 5°59E **69** A5
Dokos *Greece* 37°20N 23°20E **98** D5
Dokri *Pakistan* 27°25N 68°7E **124** F3
Dokuchayevsk *Ukraine* 47°44N 37°40E **85** J9
Dol-de-Bretagne *France* 48°34N 1°47W **70** D5
Dolak, Pulau *Indonesia* 8°0S 138°30E **119** F9
Dolbeau-Mistassini *Canada* 48°53N 72°14W **165** C5
Dole *France* 47°7N 5°31E **71** E12
Dolenji Logatec = Logatec *Slovenia* 45°56N 14°15E **93** C11
Dolgellau *U.K.* 52°45N 3°53W **66** E4
Dolgelley = Dolgellau *U.K.* 52°45N 3°53W **66** E4
Dolhasca *Romania* 47°26N 26°36E **81** C11
Doliana *Greece* 39°54N 20°32E **98** B2
Dolianova *Italy* 39°22N 9°10E **94** C2
Dolinsk *Russia* 47°21N 142°48E **107** E15
Dolinskaya = Dolynska *Ukraine* 48°6N 32°46E **85** H7
Dolj □ *Romania* 44°10N 23°30E **81** F8
Dollard *Neths.* 53°20N 7°10E **69** A7
Dolna Banya *Bulgaria* 42°18N 23°44E **96** D7
Dolni Chiflik *Bulgaria* 42°59N 27°43E **97** D11
Dolni Dŭbnik *Bulgaria* 43°24N 24°26E **97** C8
Dolnośląskie □ *Poland* 51°10N 16°30E **83** G3
Dolný Kubín *Slovak Rep.* 49°12N 19°18E **79** B12
Dolo *Ethiopia* 4°11N 42°3E **131** G3
Dolo *Italy* 45°25N 12°5E **93** C9
Dolomites = Dolomiti *Italy* 46°23N 11°51E **93** B8
Dolomiti *Italy* 46°23N 11°51E **93** B8
Dolomiti Bellunesi △ *Italy* 46°10N 12°5E **93** B9
Dolores *Argentina* 36°20S 57°40W **190** D4
Dolores *Uruguay* 33°34S 58°15W **190** C4
Dolores *U.S.A.* 37°28N 108°30W **169** H9
Dolores → *U.S.A.* 38°49N 109°17W **168** G9
Dolovo *Serbia* 44°55N 20°52E **80** F5
Dolphin, C. *Falk. Is.* 51°10S 59°0W **192** D5
Dolphin and Union Str. *Canada* 69°5N 114°45W **160** D9
Dolsk *Poland* 51°59N 17°3E **83** G4
Dolyna *Ukraine* 48°58N 24°1E **81** B9
Dolynska *Ukraine* 48°6N 32°46E **85** H7
Dolynske *Ukraine* 47°32N 29°55E **81** C14
Dolzhanskaya *Russia* 46°37N 37°48E **85** J9
Dom Joaquim *Brazil* 18°57S 43°16W **189** D2
Dom Pedrito *Brazil* 31°0S 54°40W **191** C5
Dom Pedro *Brazil* 4°59S 44°27W **189** A2
Doma *Nigeria* 8°25N 8°18E **139** D6
Doma ⌂ *Zimbabwe* 16°28S 30°12E **143** F3
Domaniç *Turkey* 39°48N 29°36E **99** B11
Domariaganj → *India* 26°17N 83°44E **125** F10
Domasi *Malawi* 15°15S 35°22E **143** F4
Domažlice *Czech Rep.* 49°28N 12°58E **78** B5
Dombarovskiy *Russia* 50°46N 59°32E **106** D6
Dombås *Norway* 62°4N 9°8E **60** E13
Dombasle-sur-Meurthe *France* 48°38N 6°21E **71** D13
Dombes *France* 45°58N 5°0E **73** C9
Dombóvár *Hungary* 46°21N 18°9E **80** D3
Dombrád *Hungary* 48°13N 21°54E **80** B6
Dome Argus *Antarctica* 80°50S 76°30E **55** E6
Dome C. *Antarctica* 75°12S 123°37E **55** D9
Dome Fuji *Antarctica* 77°20S 39°45E **55** D5
Domel I. = Letsôk-aw Kyun *Burma* 11°30N 98°25E **121** G2
Domérat *France* 46°21N 2°32E **71** F9
Domett *N.Z.* 42°53S 173°12E **155** C8
Domeyko *Chile* 29°0S 71°0W **190** B1
Domeyko, Cordillera *Chile* 24°30S 69°0W **190** A2
Domfront *France* 48°37N 0°40W **70** D6
Dominador *Chile* 24°21S 69°20W **190** A2
Dominica ■ *W. Indies* 15°20N 61°20W **183** C7
Dominica Passage *W. Indies* 15°10N 61°20W **183** C7
Dominican Rep. ■ *W. Indies* 19°0N 70°30W **183** C5
Dömitz *Germany* 53°8N 11°15E **76** B7
Domme *France* 44°48N 1°12E **72** D5
Domneşti *Romania* 45°12N 24°50E **81** E9
Domodóssola *Italy* 46°7N 8°17E **92** B5
Domogled-Valea Cernei △ *Romania* 44°52N 22°27E **80** F7
Domokos *Greece* 39°10N 22°18E **98** B4
Dompaire *France* 48°14N 6°14E **71** D13
Dompierre-sur-Besbre *France* 46°31N 3°41E **71** F10
Dompim *Ghana* 5°10N 2°5W **138** D4
Domrémy-la-Pucelle *France* 48°26N 5°40E **71** D12
Domvena *Greece* 38°15N 22°59E **98** C4
Domville, Mt. *Australia* 28°1S 151°15E **151** D5
Domžale *Slovenia* 46°9N 14°35E **93** B11
Don → *India* 16°20N 76°15E **127** F3
Don → *Russia* 47°4N 39°18E **85** J10
Don → *Aberds., U.K.* 57°11N 2°5W **65** D6
Don → *S. Yorks., U.K.* 53°41N 0°52W **66** D7
Don, C. *Australia* 11°18S 131°46E **148** B5
Don Benito *Spain* 38°53N 5°51W **89** G5
Don Figuereroa Mts. *Jamaica* 18°5N 77°36W **182** a
Don Sak *Thailand* 9°18N 99°41E **121** b
Dona Ana = Nhamaabué *Mozam.* 17°25S 35°5E **143** F4
Doña Mencía *Spain* 37°33N 4°21W **89** H6
Donaghadee *U.K.* 54°39N 5°33W **64** B6
Donaghmore *Ireland* 52°52N 7°36W **64** D4
Donald *Australia* 36°23S 143°0E **152** D5
Donaldsonville *U.S.A.* 30°6N 90°59W **176** F9
Donalsonville *U.S.A.* 31°3N 84°53W **178** D5
Doñana △ *Spain* 36°59N 6°23W **89** J4
Donau = Dunărea → *Europe* 45°20N 29°40E **81** E14
Donau → *Austria* 48°10N 17°0E **79** C10
Donau Auen △ *Austria* 48°8N 16°44E **79** C9
Donaueschingen *Germany* 47°56N 8°29E **77** H4
Donauwörth *Germany* 48°43N 10°47E **77** G6
Doncaster *U.K.* 53°32N 1°6W **66** D6
Dondo *Angola* 9°45S 14°25E **140** F2
Dondo *Mozam.* 19°33S 34°46E **143** F3
Dondo, Teluk *Indonesia* 0°50N 120°30E **119** D6
Dondra Head *Sri Lanka* 5°55N 80°40E **127** M5
Donduşeni *Moldova* 48°14N 27°36E **81** B12
Donegal *Ireland* 54°39N 8°5W **64** B3
Donegal □ *Ireland* 54°53N 8°0W **64** B4
Donegal B. *Ireland* 54°31N 8°49W **64** B3
Donets → *Russia* 47°33N 40°55E **87** G5
Donets Basin *Ukraine* 49°0N 38°0E **58** F13
Donetsk *Ukraine* 48°0N 37°45E **85** J9
Donetsk □ *Ukraine* 48°0N 37°30E **85** H9
Dong Ba Thin *Vietnam* 12°8N 109°13E **121** F7
Dong Dang *Vietnam* 21°54N 106°42E **116** G6
Dong Giam *Vietnam* 19°25N 105°31E **120** C5
Dong Ha *Vietnam* 16°55N 107°8E **120** D6
Dong Hene *Laos* 16°40N 105°18E **120** D5
Dong Hoi *Vietnam* 17°29N 106°36E **120** D6
Dong Jiang → *China* 23°6N 114°0E **117** F10
Dong Khe *Vietnam* 22°26N 106°27E **120** A6
Dong Phayayen *Thailand* 14°20N 101°22E **120** E3
Dong Ujimqin Qi *China* 45°32N 116°55E **114** B9
Dong Van *Vietnam* 23°16N 105°22E **120** A5
Dong Xoai *Vietnam* 11°32N 106°55E **121** G6
Donga *Nigeria* 7°45N 10°2E **139** D7
Donga → *Nigeria* 8°20N 9°58E **139** D7
Dong'an *China* 26°23N 111°12E **117** D8
Dongara *Australia* 29°14S 114°57E **149** E1
Dongargarh *India* 21°10N 80°40E **126** D5
Dongbei *China* 45°0N 125°0E **115** D13
Dongchuan *China* 26°8N 103°1E **116** D4
Donges *France* 47°18N 2°4W **70** E4
Dongfang *China* 18°50N 108°33E **117** a
Dongfeng *China* 42°40N 125°34E **115** C13
Donggala *Indonesia* 0°30S 119°40E **119** E5
Donggan *China* 23°22N 105°9E **116** F5
Donggang *China* 39°52N 124°10E **115** E13
Dongguan *China* 22°58N 113°44E **117** F9
Dongguang *China* 37°50N 116°30E **114** F9
Donghae *S. Korea* 37°29N 129°7E **115** F15
Donghai Dao *China* 21°0N 110°15E **117** G8
Dongjingcheng *China* 44°5N 129°10E **115** B15
Dongkou *China* 27°6N 110°35E **117** D8
Donglan *China* 24°30N 107°21E **116** E6
Dongliao He → *China* 42°58N 123°32E **115** C12
Dongliu *China* 30°13N 116°55E **117** B11
Dongmen *China* 22°20N 107°48E **116** F6
Dongning *China* 44°2N 131°5E **115** B16
Dongnyi *China* 28°3N 100°15E **116** C3
Dongola *Sudan* 19°9N 30°22E **137** D3
Dongping *China* 35°55N 116°20E **114** G9
Dongsha Dao *S. China Sea* 20°45N 116°43E **111** G12
Dongshan *China* 23°43N 117°30E **117** F11
Dongsheng *China* 39°50N 110°0E **114** E6
Dongtai *China* 32°51N 120°21E **117** A13
Dongting Hu *China* 29°18N 112°45E **117** C9
Dongtou *China* 27°51N 121°10E **117** D13
Dongxiang *China* 28°11N 116°34E **117** C11
Dongxing *China* 21°34N 108°0E **116** G7
Dongyang *China* 29°13N 120°15E **117** C13
Dongying *China* 37°37N 118°37E **115** F10
Dongyinggang *China* 37°55N 118°58E **115** F10
Dongzhi *China* 30°9N 117°0E **117** B11
Donington, C. *Australia* 34°45S 136°0E **152** C2
Doniphan *U.S.A.* 36°37N 90°50W **172** G8
Donja Stubica *Croatia* 45°59N 15°59E **93** C12
Donji Dušnik *Serbia* 43°12N 22°5E **96** C6
Donji Miholjac *Croatia* 45°45N 18°10E **80** E3
Donji Milanovac *Serbia* 44°28N 22°6E **96** B6
Donji Vakuf *Bos.-H.* 44°8N 17°24E **80** F2
Dønna *Norway* 66°6N 12°30E **60** C15
Donna *U.S.A.* 26°9N 98°4W **176** H5
Donnacona *Canada* 46°41N 71°41W **165** C5
Donnelly's Crossing *N.Z.* 35°42S 173°38E **154** B2
Donner Pass *U.S.A.* 39°19N 120°20W **170** F6
Donnybrook *Australia* 33°34S 115°48E **149** F2
Donnybrook *S. Africa* 29°59S 29°48E **145** C4
Donora *U.S.A.* 40°11N 79°52W **174** F5
Donostia = Donostia-San Sebastián *Spain* 43°17N 1°58W **90** B3
Donostia-San Sebastián *Spain* 43°17N 1°58W **90** B3
Donousa *Greece* 37°8N 25°48E **99** D7
Donskoy *Russia* 53°55N 38°15E **84** F10
Donwood *Canada* 44°19N 78°16W **174** B6
Donzère *France* 44°28N 4°43E **73** D8
Donzy *France* 47°20N 3°6E **71** E10
Dookie *Australia* 36°20S 145°41E **153** D6
Doomadgee *Australia* 17°56S 138°49E **150** B2
Doomadgee ✪ *Australia* 17°56S 138°49E **150** B2
Doon → *U.K.* 55°27N 4°39W **65** F4
Doon Doon ✪ *Australia* 16°18S 128°14E **148** C4
Dora, L. *Australia* 22°0S 123°0E **148** D3
Dora Báltea → *Italy* 45°11N 8°3E **92** C5
Dora Ripária → *Italy* 45°5N 7°44E **92** C4
Doran L. *Canada* 61°13N 108°6W **163** A7
Doraville *U.S.A.* 33°54N 84°17W **178** B5
Dorchester *U.K.* 50°42N 2°27W **67** G5
Dorchester, C. *Canada* 65°27N 77°27W **161** D16
Dordabis *Namibia* 22°52S 17°38E **144** B2
Dordogne □ *France* 45°5N 0°40E **72** C4
Dordogne → *France* 45°2N 0°36W **72** C3
Dordrecht *Neths.* 51°48N 4°39E **69** C4
Dordrecht *S. Africa* 31°20S 27°3E **144** D4
Dore → *France* 45°50N 3°35E **72** C7
Dore, Mts. *France* 45°32N 2°50E **72** C6
Doré L. *Canada* 54°46N 107°17W **163** C7
Dores do Indaiá *Brazil* 19°27S 45°36W **189** D1
Dorfen *Germany* 48°15N 12°8E **77** G8
Dorgali *Italy* 40°17N 9°35E **94** B2
Dori *Burkina Faso* 14°3N 0°2W **139** C4
Doring → *S. Africa* 31°54S 18°39E **144** D2
Doringbos *S. Africa* 31°59S 19°16E **144** D2
Dorking *U.K.* 51°14N 0°19W **67** F7
Dormaa-Ahenkro *Ghana* 7°15N 2°52W **138** D4
Dormans *France* 49°4N 3°38E **71** C10
Dornakal *India* 17°27N 80°10E **126** F5
Dornbirn *Austria* 47°25N 9°45E **78** D2
Dornes *France* 46°48N 3°18E **71** F10
Dorneşti *Romania* 47°52N 26°1E **81** C11
Dornie *U.K.* 57°17N 5°31W **65** D3
Dornoch *Canada* 44°18N 80°51W **174** B4
Dornoch *U.K.* 57°53N 4°2W **65** D4
Dornoch Firth *U.K.* 57°51N 4°4W **65** D4
Dornogovĭ □ *Mongolia* 44°0N 110°0E **114** C6
Doro *Mali* 16°9N 0°51W **139** B4
Doro, Kavo *Greece* 38°9N 24°38E **98** C6
Dorog *Hungary* 47°42N 18°45E **80** C3
Dorogobuzh *Russia* 54°50N 33°18E **84** E7
Dorohoi *Romania* 47°56N 26°23E **81** C11
Döröö Nuur *Mongolia* 48°0N 93°0E **109** C12
Dorr *Iran* 33°17N 50°38E **129** C6
Dorre I. *Australia* 25°13S 113°12E **149** E1
Dorrigo *Australia* 30°20S 152°44E **153** A10
Dorrigo △ *Australia* 30°22S 152°47E **153** A10
Dorris *U.S.A.* 41°58N 121°55W **168** F3
Dorset *Canada* 45°14N 78°54W **174** A6
Dorset *Ohio, U.S.A.* 41°40N 80°40W **174** E4
Dorset *Vt., U.S.A.* 43°15N 73°5W **175** C11
Dorset □ *U.K.* 50°45N 2°26W **67** G5
Dorsten *Germany* 51°40N 6°58E **76** D2
Dortmund *Germany* 51°30N 7°28E **76** D3
Dortmund-Ems-Kanal → *Germany* 51°50N 7°26E **76** D3
Dörtyol *Turkey* 36°50N 36°13E **104** D7
Dorum *Germany* 53°41N 8°34E **76** B4
Doruma *Dem. Rep. of the Congo* 4°42N 27°33E **142** B2
Dorūneh *Iran* 35°10N 57°18E **129** C8
Dos Bahías, C. *Argentina* 44°58S 65°32W **192** B3
Dos Hermanas *Spain* 37°16N 5°55W **89** H5
Dos Palos *U.S.A.* 36°59N 120°37W **170** J6
Döşemealtı *Turkey* 37°4N 30°36E **99** D12
Dosso *Niger* 13°0N 3°13E **139** C5
Dosso □ *Niger* 13°30N 3°30E **139** C5
Dosso ⌂ *Niger* 12°36N 2°36E **139** C5
Dostyq *Kazakhstan* 45°15N 82°29E **109** C10
Dothan *U.S.A.* 31°13N 85°24W **178** D4
Doty *U.S.A.* 46°38N 123°17W **170** D3
Douai *France* 50°21N 3°4E **71** B10
Douako *Guinea* 9°45N 10°8W **138** D2
Douala *Cameroon* 4°0N 9°45E **139** E6
Douarnenez *France* 48°6N 4°21W **70** D2
Doubabougou *Mali* 14°13N 7°59W **138** C3
Double Cone *N.Z.* 45°4S 168°49E **155** F3
Double Island Pt. *Australia* 25°56S 153°11E **151** D5
Double Mountain Fork → *U.S.A.* 33°16N 100°0W **176** E4
Doubrava → *Czech Rep.* 50°2N 15°20E **78** A8
Doubs □ *France* 47°10N 6°20E **71** E13
Doubs → *France* 46°53N 5°1E **71** F12
Doubtful Sd. *N.Z.* 45°20S 166°49E **155** F1
Doubtless B. *N.Z.* 34°55S 173°26E **154** A2
Doudeville *France* 49°43N 0°47E **70** C7
Doué-la-Fontaine *France* 47°11N 0°16W **70** E6
Douentza *Mali* 14°58N 2°48W **138** C4
Douentza ⌂ *Mali* 15°40N 2°25W **138** B4
Dougga *Tunisia* 36°25N 9°13E **136** A5
Doughboy B. *N.Z.* 47°2S 167°40E **155** H2
Douglas *Canada* 45°31N 76°56W **174** A8
Douglas *I. of Man* 54°10N 4°28W **66** C3
Douglas *S. Africa* 29°4S 23°46E **144** C3
Douglas *Ariz., U.S.A.* 31°21N 109°33W **169** L9
Douglas *Ga., U.S.A.* 31°31N 82°51W **178** D7
Douglas *Wyo., U.S.A.* 42°45N 105°24W **168** E11
Douglas Apsley △ *Australia* 41°45S 148°11E **151** G4
Douglas Chan. *Canada* 53°40N 129°20W **162** C3
Douglas Pt. *Canada* 44°19N 81°37W **174** B3
Douglasville *U.S.A.* 33°45N 84°45W **178** B5
Douirat *Morocco* 33°2N 4°11W **136** B3
Doukaton, Akra *Greece* 38°34N 20°33E **98** C2
Doukkala-Abda □ *Morocco* 32°10N 8°50W **136** B2
Doulevant-le-Château *France* 48°23N 4°55E **71** D11
Doullens *France* 50°10N 2°20E **71** B9
Doumen *China* 22°10N 113°18E **117** F9
Douna *Mali* 13°13N 6°0W **138** C3
Dounreay *U.K.* 58°35N 3°44W **65** C5
Dourada, Serra *Brazil* 13°10S 48°45W **189** C1
Dourados *Brazil* 22°9S 54°50W **191** A5
Dourados → *Brazil* 21°58S 54°18W **191** A5
Dourados, Serra dos *Brazil* 23°30S 53°30W **191** A5
Dourdan *France* 48°30N 2°1E **71** D9
Douro → *Europe* 41°8N 8°40W **88** D2
Douvaine *France* 46°19N 6°16E **71** F13
Douz *Tunisia* 33°25N 9°0E **136** B5
Douze → *France* 43°54N 0°30W **72** E3
Dove → *U.K.* 52°51N 1°36W **66** E6
Dove Creek *U.S.A.* 37°46N 108°54W **169** H9
Dover *Australia* 43°18S 147°2E **151** G4
Dover *U.K.* 51°7N 1°19E **67** F9
Dover *Del., U.S.A.* 39°10N 75°32W **173** F16
Dover *N.H., U.S.A.* 43°12N 70°56W **175** C14
Dover *N.J., U.S.A.* 40°53N 74°34W **175** F10
Dover *Ohio, U.S.A.* 40°32N 81°29W **174** F3
Dover, Pt. *Australia* 32°32S 125°32E **149** F4
Dover, Str. of *Europe* 51°0N 1°30E **67** G9
Dover-Foxcroft *U.S.A.* 45°11N 69°13W **173** C19
Dover Plains *U.S.A.* 41°43N 73°35W **175** E11
Dovey = Dyfi → *U.K.* 52°32N 4°3W **67** E3
Dovhe *Ukraine* 48°22N 23°17E **81** B8
Dovrefjell *Norway* 62°15N 9°33E **60** E13
Dovrefjell-Sunndalsfjella △ *Norway* 62°23N 9°11E **60** E13
Dow Rūd *Iran* 33°28N 49°4E **129** C6
Dowa *Malawi* 13°38S 33°58E **143** E3
Dowagiac *U.S.A.* 41°59N 86°6W **172** E10
Dowerin *Australia* 31°12S 117°2E **149** F2
Dowgha'i *Iran* 36°54N 58°32E **129** B8
Dowlatābād *Kermān, Iran* 28°20N 56°40E **129** D8
Dowlatābād *Khorāsān, Iran* 35°16N 59°29E **129** C8
Dowling Park *U.S.A.* 30°15N 83°15W **178** E6
Down □ *U.K.* 54°23N 6°2W **64** B5
Downey *Calif., U.S.A.* 33°56N 118°9W **171** M8
Downey *Idaho, U.S.A.* 42°26N 112°7W **168** E7
Downham Market *U.K.* 52°37N 0°23E **67** E8
Downieville *U.S.A.* 39°34N 120°50W **170** F6
Downpatrick *U.K.* 54°20N 5°43W **64** B6
Downpatrick Hd. *Ireland* 54°20N 9°21W **64** B2
Downsville *U.S.A.* 42°5N 75°0W **175** D10
Downton, Mt. *Canada* 52°42N 124°52W **162** C4
Dowsārī *Iran* 28°25N 57°59E **129** D8
Doxato *Greece* 41°9N 24°16E **97** E8
Doyle *U.S.A.* 40°2N 120°6W **170** E6
Doylestown *U.S.A.* 40°21N 75°10W **175** F9
Dozois, Rés. *Canada* 47°30N 77°5W **164** C4
Dra Khel *Pakistan* 27°58N 66°45E **124** F2
Drâa, C. *Morocco* 28°47N 11°0W **134** C3
Drâa, Hamada du *Algeria* 28°0N 7°0W **136** C2
Drâa, Oued → *Morocco* 28°40N 11°10W **136** C1
Drac → *France* 45°12N 5°42E **73** C9
Drac, Coves del *Spain* 39°31N 3°19E **100** B10
Dračevo *Macedonia* 41°56N 21°31E **96** E5
Drachten *Neths.* 53°7N 6°5E **69** A6
Drăgănești *Moldova* 47°43N 28°15E **81** C13
Drăgănești-Olt *Romania* 44°9N 24°32E **81** F9
Drăgănești-Vlașca *Romania* 44°5N 25°33E **81** F10
Dragaš = Sharr *Kosovo* 42°5N 20°41E **96** D4
Drăgășani *Romania* 44°39N 24°17E **81** F9
Dragichyn *Belarus* 52°15N 25°8E **75** B13
Dragocvet *Serbia* 43°58N 21°15E **96** C5
Dragon's Mouths *Trin. & Tob.* 11°0N 61°50W **187** K15
Dragovishtitsa *Bulgaria* 42°22N 22°39E **96** D6
Draguignan *France* 43°32N 6°27E **73** E10
Drahove *Ukraine* 48°14N 23°33E **81** B8
Drain *U.S.A.* 43°40N 123°19W **168** E2
Drake *U.S.A.* 47°55N 100°23W **172** B3
Drake Passage *S. Ocean* 58°0S 68°0W **55** B17
Drakensberg *S. Africa* 31°0S 28°0E **145** D4
Drama *Greece* 41°9N 24°10E **97** E8
Drammen *Norway* 59°42N 10°12E **61** G14
Drangajökull *Iceland* 66°9N 22°15W **60** C2
Dranov, Ostrov *Romania* 44°55N 29°30E **81** F14
Dras *India* 34°25N 75°48E **125** B6
Drastis, Akra *Greece* 39°48N 19°40E **101** A3
Drau = Drava → *Croatia* 45°33N 18°55E **80** E3
Drava → *Croatia* 45°33N 18°55E **80** E3
Dravograd *Slovenia* 46°36N 15°5E **93** B12
Drawa → *Poland* 52°52N 15°59E
Drawieński △ *Poland* 53°6N 15°58E
Drawno *Poland* 53°13N 15°46E
Drawsko Pomorskie *Poland* 53°35N 15°50E
Drayton *Canada* 43°46N 80°40W
Drayton Valley *Canada* 53°12N 114°58W
Dreieich *Germany* 50°1N 8°41E
Drenthe □ *Neths.* 52°52N 6°40E
Drepano, Akra *Greece* 35°28N 24°14E
Drepanum, C. *Cyprus* 34°54N 32°19E
Dresden *Canada* 42°35N 82°11W
Dresden *Germany* 51°3N 13°44E
Dresden *U.S.A.* 42°41N 76°57W
Dreux *France* 48°44N 1°23E
Drezdenko *Poland* 52°50N 15°49E
Driffield *U.K.* 54°0N 0°26W
Driftwood *U.S.A.* 41°20N 78°8W
Driggs *U.S.A.* 43°44N 111°6W
Drin → *Albania* 42°1N 19°38E
Drin i Zi → *Albania* 41°37N 20°28E
Drina → *Bos.-H.* 44°53N 19°21E
Drincea → *Romania* 44°20N 22°55E
Drinjača → *Bos.-H.* 44°15N 19°8E
Driopida *Greece* 37°25N 24°26E
Drissa = Vyerkhnyadzvinsk *Belarus* 55°45N 27°58E
Drniš *Croatia* 43°51N 16°10E
Drøbak *Norway* 59°39N 10°39E
Drobeta-Turnu Severin *Romania* 44°39N 22°41E
Drobin *Poland* 52°42N 19°58E
Drochia *Moldova* 48°2N 27°48E
Drogheda *Ireland* 53°43N 6°22W
Drogichin = Dragichyn *Belarus* 52°15N 25°8E
Drogobych = Drohobych *Ukraine* 49°20N 23°30E
Drohiczyn *Poland* 52°24N 22°39E
Drohobych *Ukraine* 49°20N 23°30E
Droichead Átha = Drogheda *Ireland* 53°43N 6°22W
Droichead na Bandan = Bandon *Ireland* 51°44N 8°44W
Droichead Nua = Newbridge *Ireland* 53°11N 6°48W
Droitwich *U.K.* 52°16N 2°8W
Drôme □ *France* 44°38N 5°15E
Drôme → *France* 44°46N 4°46E
Dromedary, C. *Australia* 36°17S 150°10E
Drómling ⌂ *Germany* 52°29N 11°5E
Dromore *Down, U.K.* 54°25N 6°9W
Dromore *Tyrone, U.K.* 54°31N 7°28W
Dromore West *Ireland* 54°15N 8°52W
Dronero *Italy* 44°28N 7°22E
Dronfield *U.K.* 53°19N 1°27W
Dronne → *France* 45°2N 0°9W
Dronning Ingrid Land *Greenland* 64°25N 52°5W
Dronning Maud Land *Antarctica* 72°30S 12°0E
Dronninglund *Denmark* 57°10N 10°19E
Dronten *Neths.* 52°32N 5°43E
Dropt → *France* 44°35N 0°6W
Drosendorf *Austria* 48°52N 15°37E
Droué *France* 48°3N 1°6E
Drouin *Australia* 38°10S 145°53E
Drujba *Uzbekistan* 41°13N 61°18E
Druk Yul = Bhutan ■ *Asia* 27°25N 90°30E
Drumbo *Canada* 43°16N 80°35W
Drumcliff *Ireland* 54°20N 8°29W
Drumheller *Canada* 51°25N 112°40W
Drummond *U.S.A.* 46°40N 113°9W
Drummond I. *U.S.A.* 46°1N 83°39W
Drummond Pt. *Australia* 34°9S 135°16E
Drummond Ra. *Australia* 23°45S 147°10E
Drummondville *Canada* 45°55N 72°25W
Drumright *U.S.A.* 35°59N 96°36W
Druskininkai *Lithuania* 54°3N 23°58E
Drut → *Belarus* 53°8N 30°5E
Druya *Belarus* 55°45N 27°28E
Druzhba *Bulgaria* 43°15N 28°1E
Druzhina *Russia* 68°14N 145°18E
Drvar *Bos.-H.* 44°21N 16°23E
Drvenik *Croatia* 43°27N 16°3E
Drwęca → *Poland* 53°0N 18°42E
Dry Harbour Mts. *Jamaica* 18°19N 77°24W
Dry Tortugas *U.S.A.* 24°38N 82°55W
Dryander △ *Australia* 20°13S 148°34E
Dryanovo *Bulgaria* 42°59N 25°28E
Dryden *Canada* 49°47N 92°50W
Dryden *U.S.A.* 42°30N 76°18W
Drygalski I. *Antarctica* 66°0S 92°0E
Drygalski Ice Tongue *Antarctica* 75°24S 163°30E
Drysdale → *Australia* 13°59S 126°51E
Drysdale I. *Australia* 11°41S 136°0E
Drysdale River △ *Australia* 14°56S 127°2E
Drzewica *Poland* 51°27N 20°29E
Drzewiczka → *Poland* 51°36N 20°36E
Dschang *Cameroon* 5°32N 10°3E
Du Gué → *Canada* 57°21N 70°45W
Du He → *China* 32°48N 110°40E
Du Quoin *U.S.A.* 38°1N 89°14W
Du'an *China* 23°59N 108°3E
Duanesburg *U.S.A.* 42°45N 74°11W
Duaringa *Australia* 23°42S 149°42E
Duarte, Pico *Dom. Rep.* 19°2N 70°59W
Dubai = Dubayy *U.A.E.* 25°18N 55°20E
Dubăsari *Moldova* 47°15N 29°10E
Dubăsari Vdkhr. *Moldova* 47°30N 29°0E
Dubawnt → *Canada* 64°33N 100°6W
Dubawnt L. *Canada* 63°8N 101°28W
Dubayy *U.A.E.* 25°18N 55°20E
Dubbo *Australia* 32°11S 148°35E
Dube → *Liberia* 5°16N 7°29W
Dubele *Dem. Rep. of the Congo* 2°56N 29°35E
Dübendorf *Switz.* 47°24N 8°37E
Dubica *Croatia* 45°11N 16°48E
Dublin *Ireland* 53°21N 6°15W

ublin *Ga., U.S.A.* 32°32N 82°54W **178** C2
ublin *Tex., U.S.A.* 32°5N 98°21W **176** E5
ublin □ *Ireland* 53°24N 6°20W **64** C5
ublin ✈ (DUB) *Ireland* 53°26N 6°15W **64** C5
ubna *Russia* 56°44N 37°10E **84** D9
ubnica nad Váhom
  Slovak Rep. 48°58N 18°11E **79** C11
ubno *Ukraine* 50°25N 25°45E **75** C13
ubois *Idaho, U.S.A.* 44°10N 112°14W **168** D7
uBois *Pa., U.S.A.* 41°7N 78°46W **174** E6
ubossary = Dubăsari
  Moldova 47°15N 29°10E **81** C14
ubove *Ukraine* 48°10N 23°53E **81** B8
ubovka *Russia* 49°5N 44°50E **87** F7
ubovskoye *Russia* 47°28N 42°46E **87** G6
ubrajpur *India* 23°48N 87°25E **125** H12
ubréka *Guinea* 9°46N 13°31W **138** D2
ubrovitsa = Dubrovytsya
  Ukraine 51°31N 26°35E **75** C14
ubrovnik *Croatia* 42°39N 18°6E **96** D2
ubrovytsya *Ukraine* 51°31N 26°35E **75** C14
ubuque *U.S.A.* 42°30N 90°41W **172** D8
ubysa → *Lithuania* 55°5N 23°26E **82** C10
uc Tho *Vietnam* 18°32N 105°35E **120** C5
uchang *China* 29°18N 116°12E **117** C11
uchesne *U.S.A.* 40°10N 110°24W **168** F8
uchess *Australia* 21°20S 139°50E **150** C2
ucie I. *Pac. Oc.* 24°40S 124°48W **157** K15
uck → *U.S.A.* 36°2N 87°52W **174** G4
uck Cr. → *Australia* 22°37S 116°53E **148** D2
uck Lake *Canada* 52°50N 106°16W **163** C7
uck Mountain △
  Canada 51°45N 101°0W **163** C8
uckwall, Mt. *U.S.A.* 37°58N 120°7W **170** H6
uderstadt *Germany* 51°31N 10°15E **76** D6
udhi *India* 24°15N 83°10E **125** G10
udinka *Russia* 69°30N 86°13E **107** C9
udley *U.K.* 52°31N 2°5W **67** E5
udley *U.S.A.* 32°32N 83°5W **178** C6
udna → *India* 19°17N 76°54E **126** E3
udwa *India* 28°30N 80°41E **125** E9
udwa △ *India* 28°30N 80°40E **125** E9
uékoué *Ivory C.* 6°40N 7°15W **138** D3
ueñas *Spain* 41°52N 4°33W **88** D6
uero = Douro → *Europe* 41°8N 8°40W **88** D2
uffown *Switz.* 45°56N 7°52E **77** K3
ufourspitz *Switz.* 45°56N 7°52E **77** K3
ugi Otok *Croatia* 44°0N 15°3E **93** C13
ugo Selo *Croatia* 45°51N 16°18E **93** C13
uisburg *Germany* 51°26N 6°45E **76** D4
uiwelskloof = Modjadjiskloof
  S. Africa 23°42S 30°10E **145** B5
uiyangyan *China* 31°2N 103°38E **116** B4
ukat *Albania* 40°16N 19°32E **96** F3
ukdamïn *Iran* 35°59N 57°43E **129** C8
ukelský Průsmyk
  Slovak Rep. 49°25N 21°42E **79** B14
ukhän *Qatar* 25°25N 50°50E **129** E6
ukhovshchina *Russia* 55°15N 32°27E **84** C7
uki *Pakistan* 30°14N 68°25E **122** D6
ukla *Poland* 49°30N 21°35E **83** J8
uku *Bauchi, Nigeria* 10°43N 10°43E **139** C7
uku *Sokoto, Nigeria* 11°11N 4°55E **139** C5
ulan *China* 36°0N 97°11E **110** D8
ulce *U.S.A.* 36°56N 107°0W **169** H10
ulce → *Argentina* 30°32S 62°33W **190** C3
ulce, G. *Costa Rica* 8°40N 83°20W **182** E3
ulf *Iraq* 35°7N 45°51E **128** C5
ulgopol *Bulgaria* 43°3N 27°22E **97** C11
ulia *China* 39°2N 116°55E **114** E9
ulgopol *Bulgaria* 43°3N 27°22E **97** C11
ullewa *Pakistan* 31°50N 71°25E **124** D4
ulstroom *S. Africa* 25°27S 30°7E **145** C5
ulmen *Germany* 51°49N 7°17E **76** D3
ulovo *Bulgaria* 43°48N 27°9E **97** C11
ul Maghär *Syria* 36°22N 38°39E **105** D8
uluth *Ga., U.S.A.* 34°0N 84°9W **178** A5
uluth *Minn., U.S.A.* 46°47N 92°6W **172** B7
um Dum *India* 22°39N 88°26E **125** H13
uma *Duma India* 27°40N 95°40E **123** F19
umä *Syria* 33°34N 36°24E **130** B5
umaguete *Phil.* 9°17N 123°15E **119** C6
umai *Indonesia* 1°35N 101°28E **118** D2
umaran *Phil.* 10°33N 119°50E **119** B5
umas *Ark., U.S.A.* 33°53N 91°29W **179** H9
umas *Tex., U.S.A.* 35°52N 101°58W **176** D4
umayr *Syria* 33°39N 36°42E **130** B5
umbarton *U.K.* 55°57N 4°33W **65** F4
umbier *Slovak Rep.* 48°56N 19°38E **79** C12
umbleyung *Australia* 33°17S 117°42E **149** F2
umbrăveni *Romania* 46°14N 24°34E **81** D9
umfries *U.K.* 55°4N 3°37W **65** F5
umfries & Galloway □
  U.K. 55°9N 3°58W **65** F5
uniręşti *Romania* 45°33N 26°35E **81** E11
unka *India* 24°12N 87°15E **125** G12
ulupinar *Turkey* 38°45N 30°0E **99** E5
unmer *Germany* 52°31N 8°20E **76** C4
ümmer → *Germany* 52°31N 8°21E **76** C4
unoine → *Canada* 46°13N 77°51W **164** C4
unoine, L. *Canada* 46°55N 77°55W **164** C4
unont d'Urville
  Antarctica 66°40S 140°0E **55** C10
unont d'Urville Sea
  Ocean 63°30S 138°0E **55** C9
unyât *Egypt* 31°24N 31°48E **137** E7
unyât, Masabb *Egypt* 31°28N 31°51E **137** E7
u Dealgan = Dundalk
  Ireland 54°1N 6°24W **64** B5
u Garbhán = Dungarvan
  Ireland 52°5N 7°37W **64** D4
u Laoghaire *Ireland* 53°17N 6°8W **64** C5
u-le-Palestel *France* 46°18N 1°39E **72** B4
u-sur-Auron *France* 46°53N 2°33E **71** F9
u-sur-Meuse *France* 49°23N 5°11E **71** C12
a = Dunărea →
  Europe 45°20N 29°40E **81** E14
a-Drava △ *Hungary* 46°15N 18°50E **80** D3
-völgyi-főcsatorna
  Hungary 46°40N 19°14E **80** D4
aföldvár *Hungary* 46°50N 18°57E **80** D3
agiri *U.S.A.* 30°31N 79°52E **125** D8
aj = Dunărea →
  Europe 45°20N 29°40E **81** E14
ajec → *Poland* 50°15N 20°44E **83** H7
ajská Streda
  Slovak Rep. 48°0N 17°37E **79** D10
akeszi *Hungary* 47°37N 19°8E **80** C4
apataj *Hungary* 46°39N 19°4E **80** D4
área → *Europe* 45°20N 29°40E **81** E14
újváros *Hungary* 46°58N 18°57E **80** D3

Dunav = Dunărea →
  Europe 45°20N 29°40E **81** E14
Dunavaţu de Jos
  Romania 44°59N 29°13E **81** F14
Dunavtsi *Bulgaria* 43°57N 22°53E **96** C6
Dunay *Russia* 42°52N 132°22E **112** C6
Dunayivtsi *Ukraine* 48°54N 26°50E **81** B11
Dunback *N.Z.* 45°23S 170°36E **155** F5
Dunbar *U.K.* 56°0N 2°31W **65** E6
Dunbar, L. *U.S.A.* 32°43N 109°46W **169** K9
Duncan *Canada* 48°45N 123°40W **170** B3
Duncan *Ariz., U.S.A.* 32°43N 109°6W **169** K9
Duncan *Okla., U.S.A.* 34°30N 97°57W **176** D6
Duncan, L. *Canada* 62°51N 113°58W **162** A6
Duncan Passage *India* 11°0N 92°0E **127** J11
Duncan Town
  Bahamas 22°15N 75°45W **182** B4
Duncannon *U.S.A.* 40°23N 77°2W **174** F7
Duncansby Head *U.K.* 58°38N 3°1W **65** C5
Duncansville *U.S.A.* 40°25N 78°26W **174** F6
Dund-Us *Mongolia* 48°1N 91°38E **109** C12
Dundaga *Latvia* 57°31N 22°21E **82** A9
Dundalk *Canada* 44°10N 80°24W **174** B4
Dundalk *Ireland* 54°1N 6°24W **64** B5
Dundalk *U.S.A.* 39°15N 76°31W **173** F15
Dundalk Bay *Ireland* 53°55N 6°15W **64** C5
Dundas = Uummannaq
  Greenland 77°33N 68°52W **57** B4
Dundas *Canada* 43°17N 79°59W **174** C5
Dundas, L. *Australia* 32°35S 121°50E **149** F3
Dundas I. *Canada* 54°30N 130°50W **162** C2
Dundas Str. *Australia* 11°15S 131°35E **148** B5
Dundee *S. Africa* 28°11S 30°15E **145** C5
Dundee *U.K.* 56°28N 2°59W **65** E6
Dundee *U.S.A.* 42°32N 76°59W **174** D8
Dundee City □ *U.K.* 56°30N 2°58W **65** E6
Dundgovĭ □ *Mongolia* 45°10N 106°0E **114** B4
Dundrum *U.K.* 54°16N 5°52W **64** B6
Dundrum B. *U.K.* 54°13N 5°47W **64** B6
Dunedin *N.Z.* 45°50S 170°33E **155** F5
Dunedin *U.S.A.* 28°1N 82°46W **179** G7
Dunedoo *Australia* 32°0S 149°25E **153** A8
Dunfanaghy *Ireland* 55°11N 7°58W **64** A4
Dunfermline *U.K.* 56°5N 3°27W **65** E5
Dungannon *Canada* 43°51N 81°36W **174** C3
Dungannon *U.K.* 54°31N 6°46W **64** B5
Dungarpur *India* 23°52N 73°45E **124** H5
Dungarvan *Ireland* 52°5N 7°37W **64** D4
Dungarvan Harbour
  Ireland 52°4N 7°35W **64** D4
Dungeness *U.K.* 50°54N 0°59E **67** G8
Dunginen *U.K.* 54°56N 6°56W **64** B5
Dunglow *Ireland* 54°57N 8°21W **64** B3
Dungog *Australia* 32°22S 151°46E **153** B9
Dungu
  Dem. Rep. of the Congo 3°40N 28°32E **142** B2
Dungun *Malaysia* 4°45N 103°25E **121** K4
Dungunâb *Sudan* 21°10N 37°9E **137** C4
Dungunâb, Khalîg
  Sudan 21°5N 37°12E **137** C4
Dunhua *China* 43°20N 128°14E **115** C15
Dunhuang *China* 40°8N 94°36E **110** C7
Dunk I. *Australia* 17°59S 146°29E **150** B4
Dunkassa *Benin* 10°21N 3°10E **139** C5
Dunkeld *Queens.,*
  Australia 33°25S 149°29E **155** L4
Dunkeld *Vic., Australia* 37°40S 142°22E **152** D5
Dunkeld *U.K.* 56°34N 3°35W **65** E5
Dunkerque *France* 51°2N 2°20E **71** A9
Dunkery Beacon *U.K.* 51°9N 3°36W **67** F4
Dunkirk = Dunkerque
  France 51°2N 2°20E **71** A9
Dunkirk *U.S.A.* 42°29N 79°20W **174** D5
Dunkwa *Central, Ghana* 6°0N 1°47W **138** D4
Dunkwa *Central, Ghana* 5°30N 1°0W **139** D4
Dunleary = Dún Laoghaire
  Ireland 53°17N 6°8W **64** C5
Dunleer *Ireland* 53°50N 6°24W **64** C5
Dunmanus B. *Ireland* 51°31N 9°50W **64** E2
Dunmanway *Ireland* 51°43N 9°6W **64** E2
Dunmarra *Australia* 16°42S 133°25E **150** B1
Dunmore *U.S.A.* 41°25N 75°38W **175** E9
Dunmore East *Ireland* 52°9N 7°0W **64** D5
Dunmore Town
  Bahamas 25°30N 76°39W **182** A4
Dunn *U.S.A.* 35°19N 78°37W **177** D15
Dunnellon *U.S.A.* 29°3N 82°28W **179** F7
Dunnet Hd. *U.K.* 58°40N 3°21W **65** C5
Dunning *U.S.A.* 41°50N 100°6W **172** E3
Dunnville *Canada* 42°54N 79°36W **174** D5
Dunolly *Australia* 36°51S 143°44E **152** D5
Dunoon *U.K.* 55°57N 4°56W **65** F4
Dunqul *Egypt* 23°26N 31°37E **137** C3
Duns *U.K.* 55°47N 2°20W **65** F6
Dunseith *U.S.A.* 48°50N 100°3W **172** A3
Dunshaughlin *Ireland* 53°31N 6°33W **64** C5
Dunsmuir *U.S.A.* 41°13N 122°16W **168** F2
Dunstable *U.K.* 51°53N 0°32W **67** F7
Dunstan Mts. *N.Z.* 44°53S 169°35E **155** E4
Dunster *Canada* 53°8N 119°50W **162** C5
Duntroon *N.Z.* 44°51S 170°40E **155** F5
Dunvegan *U.K.* 57°27N 6°35W **65** D2
Dunvegan L. *Canada* 60°8N 107°10W **163** A7
Duolun *China* 42°12N 116°28E **114** C9
Duomula *China* 34°8N 82°29E **109** F10
Duong Dong *Vietnam* 10°13N 103°58E **121** G4
Dupree *U.S.A.* 45°4N 101°35W **172** C3
Dupuyer *U.S.A.* 48°13N 112°30W **168** B7
Duque de Caxias *Brazil* 22°46S 43°18W **191** A7
Duque de York, I.
  Chile 50°37S 75°25W **192** D1
Durack → *Australia* 15°33S 127°52E **148** C4
Durack Ra. *Australia* 16°50S 127°40E **148** C4
Durack River
  Australia 15°32S 127°39E **148** C4
Durağan *Turkey* 41°25N 35°3E **104** B6
Durak *Turkey* 39°42N 28°17E **99** E3
Durakovac = Gjurakoc
  Kosovo 42°43N 20°21E **96** C2
Durance → *France* 43°55N 4°45E **73** E8
Durand *Ga., U.S.A.* 32°55N 84°46W **178** C5
Durand *Wis., U.S.A.* 44°38N 91°58W **172** C8
Durango *Mexico* 24°3N 104°39W **180** C4
Durango *U.S.A.* 37°16N 107°53W **169** H10
Durango □ *Mexico* 24°50N 105°20W **180** C4
Durankulak *Bulgaria* 43°41N 28°32E **97** C12
Durant *Miss., U.S.A.* 33°4N 89°51W **179** J10
Durant *Okla., U.S.A.* 33°59N 96°25W **176** E6
Duratón → *Spain* 41°37N 4°7W **88** D6

Durazno *Uruguay* 33°25S 56°31W **190** C4
Durazzo = Durrës
  Albania 41°19N 19°28E **96** E3
Durban *France* 42°59N 2°49E **72** F6
Durban *S. Africa* 29°49S 31°1E **145** C5
Durban ✈ (DIA)
  S. Africa 29°37S 31°7E **145** C5
Durbuy *Belgium* 50°21N 5°28E **69** D5
Dúrcal *Spain* 36°59N 3°34W **89** E7
Đurđevac *Croatia* 46°2N 17°3E **80** D2
Düren *Germany* 50°48N 6°29E **76** E2
Durg = Bhilainagar-Durg
  India 21°13N 81°26E **126** D5
Durgapur *India* 23°30N 87°20E **125** H12
Durham *Canada* 44°10N 80°49W **174** B4
Durham *U.K.* 54°47N 1°34W **66** C6
Durham *Calif., U.S.A.* 39°39N 121°48W **170** F5
Durham *N.C., U.S.A.* 35°59N 78°54W **177** D15
Durham *N.H., U.S.A.* 43°8N 70°56W **175** C14
Durham □ *U.K.* 54°42N 1°45W **66** C6
Durlas = Thurles *Ireland* 52°41N 7°49W **64** D4
Durleşti *Moldova* 47°1N 28°46E **81** C13
Durmä *Si. Arabia* 24°37N 46°8E **128** E5
Durmitor *Montenegro* 43°10N 19°0E **96** C2
Durmitor △ *Montenegro* 43°10N 19°0E **96** C2
Durness *U.K.* 58°34N 4°45W **65** C4
Durrës *Albania* 41°19N 19°28E **96** E3
Durrow *Ireland* 52°51N 7°24W **64** D4
Dursey I. *Ireland* 51°36N 10°12W **64** E1
Dursley *U.K.* 51°40N 2°21W **67** F5
Dursunbey *Turkey* 39°35N 28°37E **99** B10
Durtal *France* 47°40N 0°18W **70** E6
Duru
  Dem. Rep. of the Congo 4°14N 28°50E **142** B2
Duru Gölü *Turkey* 41°20N 28°35E **97** E12
Durusu *Turkey* 41°18N 28°41E **97** E12
Durûz, Jabal ad *Jordan* 32°35N 36°40E **130** C5
D'Urville, Tanjung
  Indonesia 1°28S 137°54E **119** E9
D'Urville I. *N.Z.* 40°50S 173°55E **155** A8
Duryea *U.S.A.* 41°20N 75°45W **175** E9
Dũsh *Egypt* 24°35N 30°41E **137** C3
Dushak *Turkmenistan* 37°13N 60°1E **129** B9
Dushan *China* 25°48N 107°30E **116** E6
Dushanbe *Tajikistan* 38°33N 68°48E **109** F7
Dusheti *Georgia* 42°10N 44°42E **87** J7
Dusky Sd. *N.Z.* 45°47S 166°30E **155** F1
Dussejour, C. *Australia* 14°45S 128°13E **148** B4
Düsseldorf *Germany* 51°14N 6°47E **76** D2
Düsseldorf Rhein-Ruhr ✈ (DUS)
  Germany 51°17N 6°46E **76** D2
Dusti *Tajikistan* 37°20N 68°40E **109** E7
Dusznik-Zdrój *Poland* 50°24N 16°24E **83** H3
Dutch Harbor *U.S.A.* 53°53N 166°32E **166** E6
Dutlwe *Botswana* 23°58S 23°46E **144** A3
Dutsan Wai *Nigeria* 10°50N 8°10E **139** C6
Dutse *Nigeria* 11°46N 9°20E **139** C6
Dutton *Canada* 42°39N 81°30W **174** D3
Dutton → *Australia* 20°44S 143°10E **150** C3
Dutywa *S. Africa* 32°8S 28°18E **145** D4
Duved *Sweden* 63°23N 12°55E **62** A6
Düvertepe *Turkey* 39°14N 28°27E **99** B10
Duwayhin, Khawr
  U.A.E. 24°20N 51°25E **129** E6
Duyfken Pt. *Australia* 12°33S 141°38E **150** A3
Duyun *China* 26°18N 107°29E **116** D6
Düzağaç *Turkey* 38°48N 30°10E **99** C12
Duzce = Akhna *Cyprus* 35°3N 33°47E **101** D12
Düzce *Turkey* 40°50N 31°10E **104** B4
Düzce □ *Turkey* 40°50N 31°10E **104** B4
Düziçi *Turkey* 37°15N 36°28E **104** D7
Dve Mogili *Bulgaria* 43°35N 25°55E **97** C9
Dvina, Severnaya →
  Russia 64°32N 40°30E **58** C14
Dvinsk = Daugavpils
  Latvia 55°53N 26°32E **84** E4
Dvor *Croatia* 45°4N 16°22E **93** C13
Dvůr Králové nad Labem
  Czech Rep. 50°27N 15°50E **78** A8
Dwarka *India* 22°18N 69°8E **124** H3
Dwellingup *Australia* 32°43S 116°4E **149** F2
Dwight *Canada* 45°20N 79°1W **174** A5
Dwight *U.S.A.* 41°5N 88°26W **172** E9
Dyakove *Ukraine* 48°1N 23°0E **80** B7
Dyatkovo *Russia* 53°40N 34°27E **84** F8
Dyatlovo = Dzyatlava
  Belarus 53°28N 25°28E **75** B13
Dyce *U.K.* 57°13N 2°12W **65** D6
Dyer, C. *Canada* 66°37N 61°16W **161** D19
Dyer Bay *Canada* 45°10N 81°20W **174** A3
Dyer Plateau
  Antarctica 70°45S 65°30W **55** D17
Dyersburg *U.S.A.* 36°3N 89°23W **177** C10
Dyfi → *U.K.* 52°32N 4°3W **67** E3
Dyje → *Czech Rep.* 48°37N 16°56E **79** C9
Dykh Tau *Russia* 43°3N 43°8E **87** J6
Dymer *Ukraine* 50°47N 30°18E **75** C16
Dynów *Poland* 49°50N 22°11E **83** J9
Dysart *Australia* 22°32S 148°23E **150** C4
Dytiki Ellas □ *Greece* 38°30N 21°45E **97** E9
Dyviziya *Ukraine* 45°55N 29°59E **81** E14
Dzaoudzi *Mayotte* 12°47S 45°16E **141** a
Dzavhan → *Mongolia* 48°0N 96°0E **109** C13
Dzavhan Gol →
  Mongolia 48°54N 93°23E **110** B7
Dzerzhinsk *Russia* 56°14N 43°30E **86** B6
Dzhalal-Abad = Jalal-Abad
  Kyrgyzstan 40°56N 73°0E **109** D8
Dzhalinda *Russia* 53°26N 124°0E **107** D13
Dzhizak = Jizzax
  Uzbekistan 40°6N 67°50E **109** D7
Dzhugdzur, Khrebet
  Russia 57°30N 138°0E **107** D14
Dzhulynk *Ukraine* 48°26N 29°45E **81** B14
Dzhvari = Jvari *Georgia* 42°42N 42°4E **87** J6
Dzhankoy *Ukraine* 45°40N 34°20E **85** K8
Dzhankoy *Kazakhstan* 49°25N 46°50E **86** F8
Dzharylhach, Ostriv
  Ukraine 46°2N 32°55E **85** J7
Dzhetygara = Zhitiqara
  Kazakhstan 52°11N 61°12E **108** C6
Dzhezkazgan = Zhezqazghan
  Kazakhstan 47°44N 67°40E **109** D7
Dzhizak = Jizzax
  Uzbekistan 40°6N 67°50E **109** D7
Dzhugdzur, Khrebet
  Russia 57°30N 138°0E **107** D14
Dzhvari = Jvari *Georgia* 42°42N 42°4E **87** J6
Dzhyr Mongolia 45°35N 95°23E **110** B7
Dzhankoy *Ukraine* 45°40N 34°20E **85** K8
Dziadowa Kłoda *Poland* 51°16N 17°42E **81** A11
Dzialdowo *Poland* 53°15N 20°15E **83** E7
Dzialoszyce *Poland* 50°22N 20°20E **83** H7
Dzialoszyn *Poland* 51°6N 18°50E **83** G5
Dzibilchaltún *Mexico* 21°10N 89°35W **181** C7
Dzierzgoń *Poland* 53°58N 19°20E **82** E6
Dzierżoniów *Poland* 50°45N 16°39E **83** H3
Dzilam de Bravo
  Mexico 21°24N 88°53W **181** C7
Dzioua *Algeria* 33°14N 5°14E **136** B5
Dzisna *Belarus* 55°34N 28°12E **84** E5
Dzisna → *Belarus* 55°34N 28°12E **84** E5
Dziwnów *Poland* 54°2N 14°45E **82** B1
Dzūkija □ *Lithuania* 54°10N 24°30E **61** J21
Dzungarian Basin = Junggar
  Pendi *China* 44°30N 86°0E **109** D11
Dzungarian Gate *Asia* 45°10N 82°0E **109** D10
Dzur *Mongolia* 49°39N 95°46E **109** C13
Dzüünbayan *Mongolia* 44°29N 110°2E **114** B6
Dzüünharaa
  Mongolia 48°52N 106°28E **110** B10
Dzüünmod *Mongolia* 47°45N 106°58E **110** B10
Dzyarzhynsk *Belarus* 53°40N 27°1E **75** B14
Dzyatlava *Belarus* 53°28N 25°28E **75** B13

E

E.C. Manning △
  Canada 49°5N 120°45W **162** D4
Eabamet L. *Canada* 51°30N 87°46W **164** B2
Eabametoong *Canada* 51°30N 88°0W **164** B2
Éadan Doire = Edenderry
  Ireland 53°21N 7°4W **64** C4
Eads *U.S.A.* 38°29N 102°47W **168** G12
Eagar *U.S.A.* 34°6N 109°17W **169** J9
Eagle *Alaska, U.S.A.* 64°47N 141°12W **166** C3
Eagle *Colo., U.S.A.* 39°39N 106°50W **168** G10
Eagle → *Canada* 53°36N 57°26W **165** B8
Eagle Butte *U.S.A.* 45°0N 101°10W **172** C3
Eagle Grove *U.S.A.* 42°40N 93°54W **172** D7
Eagle L. *Canada* 49°42N 93°13W **163** D10
Eagle L. *Calif., U.S.A.* 40°39N 120°45W **168** F3
Eagle L. *Maine, U.S.A.* 46°20N 69°22W **173** B19
Eagle Lake *Canada* 45°8N 78°29W **174** A6
Eagle Lake *Maine,*
  U.S.A. 47°3N 68°36W **173** B19
Eagle Lake *Tex., U.S.A.* 29°35N 96°20W **176** G6
Eagle Mountain
  U.S.A. 33°49N 115°27W **171** M11
Eagle Nest *U.S.A.* 36°33N 105°16W **169** H11
Eagle Pass *U.S.A.* 28°43N 100°30W **176** G4
Eagle Pk. *U.S.A.* 38°10N 119°25W **170** G7
Eagle Pt. *Australia* 16°11S 124°23E **148** C3
Eagle River *Mich.,*
  U.S.A. 47°25N 88°18W **172** B9
Eagle River *Wis.,*
  U.S.A. 45°55N 89°15W **172** C9
Eaglehawk *Australia* 36°44S 144°15E **152** D6
Eagles Mere *U.S.A.* 41°25N 76°33W **175** E8
Ealing □ *U.K.* 51°31N 0°20W **67** F7
Ear Falls *Canada* 50°38N 93°13W **163** C10
Earlimart *U.S.A.* 35°53N 119°16W **171** K7
Earlville *U.S.A.* 42°44N 75°32W **175** D9
Early Branch *U.S.A.* 32°45N 80°55W **178** C9
Earn → *U.K.* 56°21N 3°18W **65** E5
Earn, L. *U.K.* 56°23N 4°13W **65** E4
Earnslaw, Mt. *N.Z.* 44°32S 168°27E **155** E2
Earth *U.S.A.* 34°14N 102°24W **176** D3
Easley *U.S.A.* 34°50N 82°36W **177** D13
East → *U.S.A.* 40°42N 73°58W **175** F11
East Angus *Canada* 45°30N 71°40W **165** C5
East Antarctica *Antarctica* 80°0S 90°0E **55** D7
East Aurora *U.S.A.* 42°46N 78°37W **174** D6
East Ayrshire □ *U.K.* 55°26N 4°11W **65** F4
East Bengal *Bangla.* 24°0N 90°0E **123** G17
East Beskids = Vychodné Beskydy
  Europe 49°20N 22°0E **79** B15
East Brady *U.S.A.* 40°59N 79°37W **174** F5
East Branch Clarion River L.
  U.S.A. 41°35N 78°35W **174** E6
East C. = Dezhneva, Mys
  Russia 66°5N 169°40W **107** C19
East C. *N.Z.* 37°42S 178°35E **154** B7
East Caroline Basin
  Pac. Oc. 4°0N 146°45E **156** G6
East Chicago *U.S.A.* 41°38N 87°27W **172** E10
East China Sea *Asia* 30°0N 126°0E **111** F14
East Coulee *Canada* 51°23N 112°27W **162** C6
East Dereham = Dereham
  U.K. 52°41N 0°57E **67** E8
East Dublin *U.S.A.* 32°32N 82°52W **178** C7
East Dunbartonshire □
  U.K. 55°57N 4°13W **65** F4
East Falkland *Falk. Is.* 51°30S 58°30W **192** D5
East Grand Forks
  U.S.A. 47°56N 97°1W **172** B5
East Greenwich
  U.S.A. 41°40N 71°27W **175** E13
East Grinstead *U.K.* 51°7N 0°0 **67** F8
East Hartford *U.S.A.* 41°46N 72°39W **175** E12
East Haydon *Australia* 18°0S 141°30E **150** B3
East Helena *U.S.A.* 46°35N 111°56W **168** C8
East Indies *Asia* 0°0 102°0E **102** J14
East Kilbride *U.K.* 55°47N 4°11W **65** F4
East Lamma Channel
  China 22°14N 114°9E **111** a
East Lansing *U.S.A.* 42°44N 84°29W **173** D11
East Liverpool *U.S.A.* 40°37N 80°35W **174** F4
East London *S. Africa* 33°0S 27°55E **145** D4
East Lothian □ *U.K.* 55°58N 2°44W **65** F6
East Main = Eastmain
  Canada 52°10N 78°30W **164** B4
East Mariana Basin
  Pac. Oc. 12°0N 153°0E **156** F7
East Naples *U.S.A.* 26°8N 81°46W **179** H8
East Northport *U.S.A.* 40°53N 73°20W **175** F11
East Orange *U.S.A.* 40°46N 74°12W **175** F10
East Pacific Rise
  Pac. Oc. 15°0S 110°0W **157** J17
East Palatka *U.S.A.* 29°39N 81°36W **179** F7
East Palestine *U.S.A.* 40°50N 80°33W **174** F4
East Pine *Canada* 55°48N 120°12W **162** B4
East Point *U.S.A.* 33°41N 84°26W **178** B4
East Providence
  U.S.A. 41°49N 71°23W **175** E13
East Pt. *Br. Virgin Is.* 18°40N 64°18W **183** e
East Pt. *Canada* 46°27N 61°58W **165** C7
East Renfrewshire □
  U.K. 55°46N 4°21W **65** F4

East Retford = Retford
  U.K. 53°19N 0°56W **66** D7
East Riding of Yorkshire □
  U.K. 53°55N 0°30W **66** D7
East Rochester *U.S.A.* 43°7N 77°29W **174** C7
East St. Louis *U.S.A.* 38°37N 90°9W **172** F8
East Schelde = Oosterschelde →
  Neths. 51°33N 4°0E **69** C4
East Sea = Japan, Sea of
  Asia 40°0N 135°0E **112** E7
East Siberian Sea
  Russia 73°0N 160°0E **107** B17
East Stroudsburg *U.S.A.* 41°1N 75°11W **175** E9
East Sussex □ *U.K.* 50°56N 0°19E **67** G8
East Tasman Plateau
  Pac. Oc. 43°30S 152°0E **156** M7
East Tawas *U.S.A.* 44°17N 83°29W **173** C12
East Timor ■ *Asia* 8°50S 126°0E **119** F7
East Toorale *Australia* 30°27S 145°28E **151** E4
East Walker →
  U.S.A. 38°52N 119°10W **170** G7
East Windsor *U.S.A.* 40°17N 74°34W **175** F10
Eastbourne *N.Z.* 41°19S 174°55E **154** H3
Eastbourne *U.K.* 50°46N 0°18E **67** G8
Eastend *Canada* 49°32N 108°50W **163** D7
Easter Fracture Zone
  Pac. Oc. 25°0S 115°0W **157** K16
Easter I. = Pascua, I. de
  Chile 27°7S 109°23W **157** K17
Eastern □ *Ghana* 6°30N 0°30W **139** D4
Eastern □ *Kenya* 0°0 38°30E **142** C4
Eastern □ *S. Leone* 8°15N 11°0W **138** D2
Eastern Cape □ *S. Africa* 32°0S 26°0E **144** D4
Eastern Cr. →
  Australia 20°40S 141°35E **150** C3
Eastern Desert = Es Sahrâ' Esh
  Sharqîya *Egypt* 27°30N 32°30E **137** B3
Eastern Ghats *India* 14°0N 78°50E **127** H4
Eastern Group = Lau Group
  Fiji 17°0S 178°30W **154** a
Eastern Group
  Australia 33°30S 124°30E **149** F3
Eastern Guruma ◌
  Australia 22°0S 117°0E **148** D2
Eastern Transvaal = Mpumalanga □
  S. Africa 26°0S 30°0E **145** C5
Easterville *Canada* 53°8N 99°49W **163** C9
Easthampton *U.S.A.* 42°16N 72°40W **175** D12
Eastlake *U.S.A.* 41°40N 81°26W **174** E3
Eastleigh *U.K.* 50°58N 1°21W **67** G6
Eastmain *Canada* 52°10N 78°30W **164** B4
Eastmain → *Canada* 52°27N 78°26W **164** B4
Eastman *Canada* 45°18N 72°19W **175** A12
Eastman *U.S.A.* 32°12N 83°11W **178** C6
Easton *Md., U.S.A.* 38°47N 76°5W **173** F15
Easton *Pa., U.S.A.* 40°41N 75°13W **175** F9
Easton *Wash., U.S.A.* 47°14N 121°11W **170** C5
Eastport *U.S.A.* 44°56N 67°0W **173** C20
Eastpoint *U.S.A.* 29°44N 84°53W **178** F5
Eastport *U.S.A.* 44°56N 67°0W **173** C20
Eastsound *U.S.A.* 48°42N 122°55W **170** B4
Eaton *U.S.A.* 40°32N 104°42W **168** F11
Eatonia *Canada* 51°13N 109°25W **163** C7
Eatonton *U.S.A.* 33°20N 83°23W **178** B6
Eatontown *U.S.A.* 40°19N 74°4W **175** F10
Eatonville *U.S.A.* 46°52N 122°16W **170** D4
Eau Claire *U.S.A.* 44°49N 91°30W **172** C8
Eau Claire, L. à l'
  Canada 56°10N 74°25W **164** A5
Eauripik Rise *Pac. Oc.* 2°0N 142°0E **156** G6
Eauze *France* 43°53N 0°7E **72** E4
Eban *Nigeria* 9°40N 4°50E **139** D5
Ebano *Mexico* 22°13N 98°24W **181** C5
Ebbegebirge △ *Germany* 51°10N 7°50E **76** D3
Ebbw Vale *U.K.* 51°46N 3°12W **67** F4
Ebeltoft *Denmark* 56°12N 10°41E **63** H4
Ebeltoft Vig *Denmark* 56°10N 10°35E **63** H4
Ebensburg *U.S.A.* 40°29N 78°44W **174** F6
Ebensee *Austria* 47°48N 13°46E **78** D6
Eber Gölü *Turkey* 38°38N 31°11E **104** C4
Eberswalde-Finow
  Germany 52°50N 13°49E **76** C9
Ebetsu *Japan* 43°7N 141°34E **112** C10
Ebey's Landing △
  U.S.A. 48°12N 122°41W **170** B4
Ebian *China* 29°11N 103°13E **116** C4
Ebingen *Germany* 48°13N 9°1E **77** G5
Ebinur Hu *China* 44°55N 82°55E **109** D10
Eboli *Italy* 40°39N 15°2E **95** B8
Ebolowa *Cameroon* 2°55N 11°10E **139** E7
Ebonda
  Dem. Rep. of the Congo 2°12N 22°21E **140** D4
Ebonyi □ *Nigeria* 6°20N 8°0E **139** D6
Ebrach *Germany* 49°51N 10°29E **77** F6
Ebre = Ebro → *Spain* 40°43N 0°54E **90** B5
Ébrié, Lagune *Ivory C.* 5°12N 4°26W **138** D4
Ebro → *Spain* 40°43N 0°54E **90** B5
Ebro, Embalse del *Spain* 43°0N 3°58W **88** C7
Ebstorf *Germany* 53°2N 10°24E **76** B6
Ecatepec de Morelos
  Mexico 19°36N 99°3W **181** D5
Ecbatana = Hamadān
  Iran 34°52N 48°32E **105** E13
Eceabat *Turkey* 40°11N 26°21E **97** F10
Ech Chéliff *Algeria* 36°10N 1°20E **136** A4
Ech Chéliff □ *Algeria* 36°15N 1°30E **136** A4
Echchonnee
  U.S.A. 32°39N 83°36W **178** C6
Echigo-Sammyaku
  Japan 36°50N 139°50E **113** F9
Echinos *Greece* 41°16N 25°1E **97** D9
Échirolles *France* 45°9N 5°45E **73** D9
Echizen *Japan* 35°59N 136°10E **113** G8
Echizen-Misaki *Japan* 35°59N 135°57E **113** G7
Echmiadzin = Ejmiatsin
  Armenia 40°12N 44°19E **87** K7
Echo *Canada* 55°6N 117°55W **160** D8
Echo Bay N.W.T.,
  Canada 66°5N 117°55W **160** D8
Echo Bay *Ont., Canada* 46°29N 84°4W **164** C3
Echoing → *Canada* 55°51N 92°5W **164** B1
Echternach *Lux.* 49°49N 6°25E **69** E6
Echuca *Australia* 36°10S 144°45E **153** D6
Écija *Spain* 37°30N 5°10W **89** H5
Eckental *Germany* 49°35N 11°12E **77** F7
Eckernförde *Germany* 54°28N 9°50E **76** A5

Eclectic *U.S.A.* 32°38N 86°2W **178** C3
Eclipse I. *Australia* 35°5S 117°58E **149** G2
Eclipse Is. *Australia* 13°54S 126°19E **148** B4
Eclipse Sd. *Canada* 72°38N 79°0W **161** C16
Éccommoy *France* 47°50N 0°17E **70** E7
Ecoporanga *Brazil* 18°23S 40°50W **189** D2
Écouché *France* 48°42N 0°10W **70** D6
Écrins △ *France* 44°54N 6°18E **73** D10
Ecuador ■ *S. Amer.* 2°0S 78°0W **186** D3
Écueillé *France* 47°5N 1°21E **70** E8
Ed *Sweden* 58°55N 11°55E **63** F5
Ed Da'ein *Sudan* 11°26N 26°9E **140** A5
Ed Damazin *Sudan* 11°46N 34°21E **135** F12
Ed Dâmer *Sudan* 17°27N 34°0E **135** E12
Edam *Canada* 53°11N 108°46W **163** C7
Edam *Neths.* 52°31N 5°3E **69** B5
Edane *Sweden* 59°38N 12°49E **62** E6
Edapally *India* 11°19N 78°3E **127** J4
Eday *U.K.* 59°11N 2°47W **65** B6
Eddrachillis B. *U.K.* 58°17N 5°14W **65** C3
Eddystone *U.K.* 50°11N 4°16E **67** G3
Eddystone Pt.
  Australia 40°59S 148°20E **151** G4
Ede *Neths.* 52°4N 5°40E **69** B5
Ede *Nigeria* 7°45N 4°29E **139** D5
Édéa *Cameroon* 3°51N 10°9E **139** E7
Edebäck *Sweden* 60°25N 13°32E **62** D7
Edehon L. *Canada* 60°25N 97°15W **163** A9
Edelény *Hungary* 48°18N 20°44E **80** B5
Eden *Australia* 37°3S 149°55E **153** D8
Eden *N.C., U.S.A.* 36°29N 79°53W **177** C15
Eden *N.Y., U.S.A.* 42°39N 78°55W **174** D6
Eden *Tex., U.S.A.* 31°13N 99°51W **176** F5
Eden → *U.K.* 54°57N 3°1W **66** C4
Edenburg *S. Africa* 29°43S 25°58E **144** C4
Edendale *N.Z.* 46°19S 168°48E **155** G3
Edendale *S. Africa* 29°39S 30°18E **145** C5
Edenderry *Ireland* 53°21N 7°4W **64** C4
Edenhope *Australia* 37°4S 141°7E **152** C3
Edenton *U.S.A.* 36°4N 76°39W **177** C16
Edenville *S. Africa* 27°37S 27°34E **145** C4
Eder → *Germany* 51°12N 9°28E **76** D5
Eder-Stausee *Germany* 51°10N 8°57E **76** D4
Edessa *Greece* 40°48N 22°5E **96** F6
Edewecht *Germany* 53°8N 7°58E **76** B3
Edfu = Idfû *Egypt* 24°55N 32°49E **137** C3
Edgar *U.S.A.* 40°22N 97°58W **172** E5
Edgartown *U.S.A.* 41°23N 70°31W **175** E14
Edge Hill *U.S.A.* 52°8N 1°26W **67** E6
Edgecumbe *N.Z.* 37°59S 176°47E **154** D5
Edgefield *U.S.A.* 33°47N 81°56W **178** B8
Edgeley *U.S.A.* 46°22N 98°43W **172** B4
Edgemont *U.S.A.* 43°18N 103°50W **172** D2
Edgeøya *Svalbard* 77°45N 22°30E **54** B9
Edgewater *U.S.A.* 28°59N 80°54W **179** G9
Édhessa = Edessa *Greece* 40°48N 22°5E **96** F6
Edievale *N.Z.* 45°49S 169°22E **155** F4
Edina *Liberia* 6°0N 10°10W **138** D2
Edina *U.S.A.* 40°10N 92°11W **172** E7
Edinboro *U.S.A.* 41°52N 80°8W **174** E4
Edinburg *U.S.A.* 26°18N 98°10W **176** H5
Edinburgh *U.K.* 55°57N 3°13W **65** F5
Edinburgh ✈ (EDI) *U.K.* 55°54N 3°22W **65** F5
Edinburgh, City of □
  U.K. 55°57N 3°17W **65** F5
Edineţ *Moldova* 48°9N 27°18E **81** B12
Edirne *Turkey* 41°40N 26°34E **97** E10
Edirne □ *Turkey* 41°12N 26°30E **97** E10
Edison *Ga., U.S.A.* 31°34N 84°44W **178** D3
Edison *Wash., U.S.A.* 48°33N 122°27W **170** B4
Edisto → *U.S.A.* 32°29N 80°21W **178** C9
Edisto Beach *U.S.A.* 32°29N 80°20W **178** C9
Edisto I. *U.S.A.* 32°35N 80°20W **178** C9
Edithburgh *Australia* 35°5S 137°43E **152** C2
Edjeleh *Algeria* 28°38N 9°50E **136** C7
Edmeston *U.S.A.* 42°42N 75°15W **175** D9
Edmond *U.S.A.* 35°39N 97°29W **176** D6
Edmonds *U.S.A.* 47°48N 122°22W **170** C4
Edmonton *Australia* 17°2S 145°46E **150** B4
Edmonton *Canada* 53°30N 113°30W **162** C6
Edmund L. *Canada* 54°45N 93°17W **164** B1
Edmundston *Canada* 47°23N 68°20W **165** C6
Edna *U.S.A.* 28°59N 96°39W **176** G6
Edo □ *Nigeria* 6°30N 6°0E **139** D6
Edolo *Italy* 46°10N 10°21E **92** B7
Edremit *Turkey* 39°34N 27°0E **99** B9
Edremit Körfezi *Turkey* 39°30N 26°45E **99** B8
Edsbro *Sweden* 59°54N 18°29E **62** E12
Edsbruk *Sweden* 58°1N 16°29E **63** F10
Edsbyn *Sweden* 61°23N 15°49E **62** C9
Edson *Canada* 53°35N 116°28E **162** C5
Eduardo Castex
  Argentina 35°50S 64°18W **190** D3
Eduardo Frei *Antarctica* 62°30S 58°0W **55** C18
Edward → *Australia* 35°5S 143°30E **152** C5
Edward, L. *Africa* 0°25S 29°40E **142** C2
Edward VII Land
  Antarctica 80°0S 150°0W **55** E13
Edwards *Calif., U.S.A.* 34°50N 117°40W **171** L9
Edwards *N.Y., U.S.A.* 44°20N 75°15W **175** B9
Edwards Plateau
  U.S.A. 30°45N 101°20W **176** F4
Edwardsville *U.S.A.* 41°15N 75°56W **175** E9
Edzná *Mexico* 19°39N 90°19W **181** D6
Edzo *Canada* 62°49N 116°4W **162** A5
Eeklo *Belgium* 51°11N 3°33E **69** C3
Eenhana *Namibia* 17°30S 16°23E **144** A2
Eesti = Estonia ■ *Europe* 58°30N 25°30E **84** C3
Eferding *Austria* 48°18N 14°1E **78** D7
Effigy Mounds △ *U.S.A.* 43°5N 91°11W **172** D8
Eforie *Romania* 44°1N 28°37E **81** F13
Efxinoupoli *Greece* 39°12N 22°48E **98** B4
Ega → *Spain* 42°19N 1°55W **90** C3
Égadi, Ísole *Italy* 37°55N 12°16E **94** E5
Egan Range *U.S.A.* 39°35N 114°55W **168** G6
Eganville *Canada* 45°32N 77°5W **174** A7
Egedesminde = Aasiaat
  Greenland 68°43N 52°56W **57** D5
Eger = Cheb *Czech Rep.* 50°9N 12°28E **78** A5
Eger *Hungary* 47°53N 20°27E **80** C5
Eger → *Hungary* 47°38N 20°50E **80** C5
Egersund *Norway* 58°26N 6°1E **61** G12
Egg L. *Canada* 55°5N 105°30W **163** B7
Eggegebirge Südlicher Teutoburger Wald □
  Germany 51°40N 8°59E **76** D4

Eggenburg *Austria* 48°38N 15°50E **78 C8**
Eggenfelden *Germany* 48°23N 12°46E **77 G8**
Éghezée *Belgium* 50°35N 4°55E **69 D4**
Egilsstaðir *Iceland* 65°16N 14°25W **60 D6**
Egina *Greece* 37°45N 23°26E **98 D5**
Eginio *Greece* 40°28N 22°28E **96 F6**
Egio *Greece* 38°15N 22°5E **98 C4**
Égletons *France* 45°24N 2°3E **72 C6**
Eglinton I. *Canada* 75°48N 118°30W **161 B8**
Egmont *Canada* 49°45N 123°56W **162 D4**
Egmont, C. *N.Z.* 39°16S 173°45E **154 F2**
Egmont, Mt. = Taranaki, Mt. *N.Z.* 39°17S 174°5E **154 F3**
Egmont △ *N.Z.* 39°17S 174°4E **154 F3**
Egra *India* 21°54N 87°32E **125 J12**
Eğridir *Turkey* 37°52N 30°51E **104 D4**
Eğridir Gölü *Turkey* 37°53N 30°50E **104 D4**
Egtved *Denmark* 55°38N 9°18E **63 J3**
Éguas → *Brazil* 13°26S 44°14W **189 C2**
Éguzon-Chantôme *France* 46°27N 1°33E **71 F8**
Egvekinot *Russia* 66°19N 179°50W **107 C19**
Egyek *Hungary* 47°39N 20°52E **80 C5**
Egypt ■ *Africa* 28°0N 31°0E **137 F7**
Eha Amufu *Nigeria* 6°30N 7°46E **139 D6**
Ehime □ *Japan* 33°30N 132°40E **113 H6**
Ehingen *Germany* 48°16N 9°43E **77 G5**
Ehrenberg *U.S.A.* 33°36N 114°31W **171 M12**
Ehrhardt *U.S.A.* 33°6N 81°1W **178 D8**
Ehrwald *Austria* 47°24N 10°56E **78 D3**
Eibar *Spain* 43°11N 2°28W **90 B2**
Eichstätt *Germany* 48°54N 11°11E **77 G7**
Eider → *Germany* 54°19N 8°57E **76 A4**
Eidsvold *Australia* 25°25S 151°12E **151 D5**
Eidsvoll *Norway* 60°19N 11°14E **61 F14**
Eielson *U.S.A.* 64°40N 147°4W **166 C10**
Eifel *Germany* 50°15N 6°50E **77 E2**
Eiffel Flats *Zimbabwe* 18°20S 30°0E **143 F3**
Eiger *Switz.* 46°34N 8°1E **92 B5**
Eigg *U.K.* 56°54N 6°10W **65 E2**
Eighty Mile Beach *Australia* 19°30S 120°40E **148 C3**
Eil, L. *U.K.* 56°51N 5°16W **65 E3**
Eildon *Australia* 37°14S 145°55E **153 D6**
Eildon, L. *Australia* 37°10S 146°0E **153 D7**
Eilean Siar □ *U.K.* 57°30N 7°10W **65 D1**
Eilenburg *Germany* 51°27N 12°36E **76 D8**
Einasleigh *Australia* 18°32S 144°5E **150 B3**
Einasleigh → *Australia* 17°30S 142°17E **150 B3**
Einbeck *Germany* 51°49N 9°53E **76 D5**
Eindhoven *Neths.* 51°26N 5°28E **69 C5**
Einsiedeln *Switz.* 47°7N 8°46E **77 H4**
Eire = Ireland ■ *Europe* 53°50N 7°52W **64 C4**
Eiríksjökull *Iceland* 64°46N 20°24W **60 D3**
Eiriosgaigh = Eriskay *U.K.* 57°4N 7°18W **65 D1**
Eirunepé *Brazil* 6°35S 69°53W **188 B4**
Eiseb → *Namibia* 20°33S 20°59E **144 B2**
Eisenach *Germany* 50°58N 10°19E **76 E6**
Eisenberg *Germany* 50°58N 11°54E **76 E7**
Eisenerz *Austria* 47°32N 14°54E **78 D7**
Eisenhüttenstadt *Germany* 52°9N 14°38E **76 C10**
Eisenkappel *Austria* 46°29N 14°36E **78 E7**
Eisenstadt *Austria* 47°51N 16°31E **79 D9**
Eisfeld *Germany* 50°25N 10°54E **77 E6**
Eisleben *Germany* 51°32N 11°32E **76 D7**
Eislingen *Germany* 48°41N 9°42E **77 G5**
Eivissa *Spain* 38°54N 1°26E **100 C7**
Eixe, Serra do *Spain* 42°0N 6°54W **88 C4**
Ejea de los Caballeros *Spain* 42°7N 1°9W **90 C3**
Ejmiatsin *Armenia* 40°12N 44°19E **87 K7**
Ejura *Ghana* 7°23N 1°15W **139 D4**
Ejutla *Mexico* 16°34N 96°44W **181 D5**
Ekalaka *U.S.A.* 45°53N 104°33W **168 D11**
Ekaterinburg = Yekaterinburg *Russia* 56°50N 60°30E **106 D7**
Ekenäs = Raasepori *Finland* 60°0N 23°26E **84 B2**
Ekenässjön *Sweden* 57°28N 15°1E **63 G9**
Ekerö *Sweden* 59°16N 17°45E **62 E11**
Eket *Nigeria* 4°38N 7°56E **139 E6**
Eketahuna *N.Z.* 40°38S 175°43E **154 G4**
Ekibastuz *Kazakhstan* 51°50N 75°10E **108 D9**
Ekiti □ *Nigeria* 7°25N 5°20E **139 D6**
Ekoli *Dem. Rep. of the Congo* 0°23S 24°13E **142 C1**
Ekoln *Sweden* 59°45N 17°37E **62 E11**
Ekshärad *Sweden* 60°10N 13°30E **62 D7**
Eksjö *Sweden* 57°40N 14°58E **63 G8**
Ekuma → *Namibia* 18°40S 16°2E **144 A2**
Ekwan → *Canada* 53°12N 82°15W **164 B3**
Ekwan Pt. *Canada* 53°16N 82°7W **164 B3**
El Aaiún *W. Sahara* 27°9N 13°12W **134 C3**
El Abanico *Chile* 37°20S 71°31W **190 D1**
El Abiodh-Sidi-Cheikh *Algeria* 32°53N 0°31E **136 B4**
El Adeb Larache *Algeria* 27°22N 8°52E **136 C5**
El 'Agrûd *Egypt* 30°14N 34°24E **130 E3**
El Aioun *Morocco* 34°33N 2°30W **136 B4**
El 'Aiyat *Egypt* 29°36N 31°15E **137 F7**
El Alamein *Egypt* 30°48N 28°58E **137 C6**
El Alto *Peru* 4°15S 81°14W **188 A1**
El 'Aqaba, W. → *Egypt* 30°7N 33°54E **130 E2**
El 'Arag *Egypt* 28°40N 26°20E **137 C6**
El Aricha *Algeria* 34°13N 1°10W **136 B4**
El Arîhã *West Bank* 31°52N 35°27E **130 C4**
El 'Arîsh *Egypt* 31°8N 33°50E **130 D2**
El 'Arîsh, W. → *Egypt* 31°8N 33°47E **130 D2**
El Arrouch *Algeria* 36°37N 6°53E **136 A5**
El Asnam = Ech Chéliff *Algeria* 36°10N 1°20E **136 A4**
El Astillero *Spain* 43°24N 3°49W **88 B7**
El Badâri *Egypt* 27°4N 31°25E **137 B3**
El Bahrein *Egypt* 28°30N 26°25E **137 C3**
El Ballâs *Egypt* 26°2N 32°43E **137 B3**
El Balyana *Egypt* 26°10N 32°3E **137 B3**
El Baqeir *Sudan* 30°40N 33°40E **137 C3**
El Barco de Ávila *Spain* 40°21N 5°31W **88 E5**
El Bayadh *Algeria* 33°40N 1°1E **136 B4**
El Bayadh □ *Algeria* 33°10N 1°0E **136 B4**
El Bierzo *Spain* 42°45N 6°30W **88 C4**
El Bluff *Nic.* 11°59N 83°40W **182 D3**
El Bolsón *Argentina* 41°58S 71°30W **192 B2**
El Bonillo *Spain* 38°57N 2°35W **91 C4**
El Burgo de Osma *Spain* 41°35N 3°4W **90 D1**
El Cain *Argentina* 41°43S 68°31W **192 B3**
El Cajon *U.S.A.* 32°48N 116°58W **171 N10**
El Calafate *Argentina* 50°19S 72°15W **192 D2**
El Campello *Spain* 38°26N 0°24W **91 G4**
El Campo *U.S.A.* 29°12N 96°16W **176 G6**
El Capitan *U.S.A.* 37°44N 119°38E **170 H7**
El Carbón *Honduras* 15°25N 85°32W **182 C2**
El Carmen *Colombia* 9°43N 75°8W **186 B3**
El Centro *U.S.A.* 32°48N 115°34W **171 N11**
El Cerro *Bolivia* 17°30S 61°40W **186 D5**
El Cerro de Andévalo *Spain* 37°45N 6°57W **89 H4**
El Compadre *Mexico* 32°20N 116°14W **171 N10**
El Corcovado *Argentina* 43°25S 71°35W **192 B2**
El Coronil *Spain* 37°5N 5°38W **89 H5**
El Cuy *Argentina* 39°55S 68°25W **192 A3**
El Cuyo *Mexico* 21°31N 87°41W **181 C7**
El Dab'a *Egypt* 31°0N 28°27E **137 E7**
El Daheir *Egypt* 31°13N 34°10E **130 D3**
El Deir *Egypt* 25°25N 32°20E **137 B3**
El Descanso *Mexico* 32°12N 116°58W **171 N10**
El Desemboque *Mexico* 30°33N 113°1W **180 A2**
El Dilingat *Egypt* 30°50N 30°31E **137 E7**
El Diviso *Colombia* 1°22N 78°14W **186 C3**
El Djouf *Mauritania* 21°25N 6°40W **134 D4**
El Dorado *Mexico* 24°17N 107°21W **180 C3**
El Dorado *Ark., U.S.A.* 33°12N 92°40W **176 E8**
El Dorado *Kans., U.S.A.* 37°49N 96°52W **172 G5**
El Dorado *Venezuela* 6°55N 61°37W **186 B6**
El Dorado Springs *U.S.A.* 37°52N 94°1W **172 G6**
El Eglab *Algeria* 26°20N 4°30W **136 C3**
El Ejido *Spain* 36°47N 2°49W **89 J8**
El Escorial *Spain* 40°35N 4°7W **88 E6**
El Espinar *Spain* 41°43N 4°15W **88 D6**
El Eulma *Algeria* 36°9N 5°42E **136 A5**
El Faiyûm *Egypt* 29°19N 30°50E **137 F7**
El Faoura *Tunisia* 33°22N 8°45E **136 B1**
El Fâsher *Sudan* 13°33N 25°26E **135 F11**
El Fashn *Egypt* 28°50N 30°54E **137 F7**
El Ferrol = Ferrol *Spain* 43°29N 8°15W **88 B2**
El Fuerte *Mexico* 26°25N 108°39W **180 B3**
El Gedida *Egypt* 25°40N 28°30E **137 B2**
El Geneina = Al Junaynah *Sudan* 13°27N 22°45E **135 F10**
El Geteina □ *Sudan* 15°0N 33°0E **135 F12**
El Gir *Sudan* 19°50N 28°18E **137 D2**
El Giza *Egypt* 30°0N 31°12E **137 F7**
El Gogorrón △ *Mexico* 21°49N 100°57W **180 C4**
El Goléa *Algeria* 30°30N 2°50E **136 B4**
El Gouna *Egypt* 27°5N 33°47E **137 B3**
El Guácharo △ *Venezuela* 10°8N 63°21W **183 D7**
El Guache △ *Venezuela* 9°45N 69°30W **183 E6**
El Hadjira *Algeria* 32°36N 5°30E **136 B5**
El Hâi *Egypt* 29°39N 31°18E **137 F7**
El Hajeb *Morocco* 33°43N 5°13W **136 B2**
El Hamma *Tunisia* 33°54N 9°48E **136 B5**
El Hammam *Egypt* 30°52N 29°25E **137 E6**
El Homr *Algeria* 29°43N 1°45E **136 C4**
El 'Idisât *Egypt* 25°30N 32°35E **137 B3**
El Iskandarîya *Egypt* 31°13N 29°58E **137 H6**
El Istiwa'iya *Sudan* 5°0N 28°0E **135 G11**
El Jadida *Morocco* 33°11N 8°17W **136 B2**
El Jardal *Honduras* 14°54N 88°50W **182 D2**
El Jebha *Morocco* 35°11N 4°43W **136 A3**
El Jem *Tunisia* 35°18N 10°48E **136 B2**
El Kab *Sudan* 19°27N 32°46E **137 D3**
El Kafr el Sharqi *Egypt* 31°16N 31°10E **137 E7**
El Kala *Algeria* 36°53N 8°26E **136 A5**
El Kantara *Algeria* 35°14N 5°45E **136 A5**
El Kantara *Tunisia* 33°45N 10°58E **136 B6**
El Karaba *Sudan* 18°32N 33°41E **137 D3**
El Kef *Tunisia* 36°12N 8°47E **136 A5**
El Kef □ *Tunisia* 36°0N 9°0E **136 A5**
El Kelaâ de Srahna *Morocco* 32°4N 7°27W **136 B2**
El Kelaâ M'Gouna *Morocco* 31°14N 6°7W **136 B2**
El Khandaq *Sudan* 18°30N 30°30E **137 D3**
El Khanka *Egypt* 30°13N 31°21E **137 E7**
El Khârga *Egypt* 25°30N 30°33E **137 B3**
El Khartûm *Sudan* 15°31N 32°35E **135 E12**
El Khartûm Bahri *Sudan* 15°40N 32°31E **135 E12**
El Khroub *Algeria* 36°10N 6°55E **136 A5**
El Kseur *Algeria* 36°46N 4°49E **136 A4**
El Ksiba *Morocco* 32°45N 6°1W **136 B3**
El Kuntilla *Egypt* 30°1N 34°45E **130 E3**
El Leoncito △ *Argentina* 31°58S 69°10W **190 C2**
El Lucero *Mexico* 30°37N 106°31W **180 A3**
El Maestrazgo *Spain* 40°30N 0°25W **90 E4**
El Maghra *Egypt* 30°15N 28°55E **137 E6**
El Mahalla el Kubra *Egypt* 31°0N 31°0E **137 E7**
El Mahârîq *Egypt* 25°35N 30°35E **137 B3**
El Maïmûn *Egypt* 29°14N 31°15E **137 F7**
El Maitén *Argentina* 42°3S 71°10W **192 B2**
El Maiz *Algeria* 28°19N 0°9W **136 C3**
El Maks el Bahari *Egypt* 24°30N 30°40E **137 C3**
El Malpais △ *U.S.A.* 34°53N 108°0W **169 J10**
El Manshâh *Egypt* 26°26N 31°50E **137 B3**
El Mansour *Algeria* 27°47N 0°14W **136 C3**
El Mansûra *Egypt* 31°0N 31°19E **137 E7**
El Manzala *Egypt* 31°16N 31°56E **137 E7**
El Maragha *Egypt* 26°35N 31°10E **137 B3**
El Masnou *Spain* 41°28N 2°20E **90 D7**
El Matarîya *Egypt* 31°15N 32°0E **137 E7**
El Medano *Canary Is.* 28°3N 16°32W **100 F3**
El Meghaier *Algeria* 33°55N 5°58E **136 B5**
El Ménia = El Goléa *Algeria* 30°30N 2°50E **136 B4**
El Meragven △ *Algeria* 28°0N 0°7W **136 C3**
El Milagro *Argentina* 30°59S 65°59W **190 C3**
El Minyâ *Egypt* 28°7N 30°33E **137 F7**
El Monte *U.S.A.* 34°4N 118°1W **171 L8**
El Montseny *Spain* 41°55N 2°25E **90 D7**
El Mreyye *Mauritania* 18°0N 6°0W **138 B3**
El Obeid *Sudan* 13°8N 30°10E **135 F11**
El Odaiya *Sudan* 12°8N 28°12E **135 F11**
El Oro *Mexico* 19°50N 100°7W **181 D4**
El Oued *Algeria* 33°20N 6°58E **136 B5**
El Oued □ *Algeria* 33°10N 7°15E **136 B5**
El Palmar △ *Argentina* 31°45N 106°29W **180 F1**
El Paso *U.S.A.* 31°45N 106°29W **176 F1**
El Paso de Robles = Paso Robles *U.S.A.* 35°38N 120°41W **170 K6**
El Pedernoso *Spain* 39°29N 2°45W **91 C4**
El Pedroso *Spain* 37°51N 5°45W **89 H5**
El Pinacate y Gran Desierto de Altar = Gran Desierto del Pinacate △ *Mexico* 31°51N 113°32W **180 A2**
El Pobo de Dueñas *Spain* 40°46N 1°39W **90 E3**
El Portal *U.S.A.* 37°41N 119°47W **170 H7**
El Porvenir *Mexico* 31°15N 105°51W **180 A3**
El Prat Barcelona ✈ (BCN) *Spain* 41°18N 2°5E **90 D7**
El Prat de Llobregat *Spain* 41°19N 2°5E **90 D7**
El Progreso *Honduras* 15°26N 87°51W **182 C2**
El Pueblo *Canary Is.* 28°36N 17°47W **100 F2**
El Puente del Arzobispo *Spain* 39°48N 5°10W **88 F5**
El Puerto de Santa María *Spain* 36°36N 6°13W **89 J4**
El Qâhira *Egypt* 30°2N 31°13E **137 F7**
El Qantara *Egypt* 30°51N 32°20E **130 E1**
El Qasr *Egypt* 25°44N 28°42E **137 B2**
El Qubâbât *Egypt* 29°28N 31°16E **137 F7**
El Quseima *Egypt* 30°40N 34°15E **130 E3**
El Qusîya *Egypt* 27°29N 30°44E **137 B3**
El Râshda *Egypt* 25°36N 28°57E **137 B2**
El Real de Santa María *Panama* 8°0N 77°40W **186 B3**
El Reno *U.S.A.* 35°32N 97°57W **176 D6**
El Rey △ *Argentina* 24°40S 64°34W **190 A3**
El Ridisiya *Egypt* 24°56N 32°51E **137 C3**
El Rio *U.S.A.* 34°14N 119°10W **171 L7**
El Ronquillo *Spain* 37°44N 6°10W **89 H4**
El Roque, Pta. *Canary Is.* 28°10N 15°25W **100 F4**
El Rosario *Mexico* 30°1N 115°45W **180 A1**
El Rubio *Spain* 37°22N 5°0W **89 H5**
El Saff *Egypt* 29°34N 31°16E **137 F7**
El Salto *Mexico* 23°47N 105°22W **180 C3**
El Salvador ■ *Cent. Amer.* 13°50N 89°0W **182 D2**
El Sauce *Nic.* 13°0N 86°40W **182 D2**
El Saucejo *Spain* 37°4N 5°6W **89 H5**
El Shallal *Egypt* 24°0N 32°53E **137 C3**
El Simbillawein *Egypt* 30°48N 31°13E **137 E7**
El Suweis *Egypt* 29°58N 32°31E **137 F8**
El Tabbin *Egypt* 29°47N 31°18E **137 F7**
El Tamarâni, W. → *Egypt* 30°7N 34°43E **130 E3**
El Tarf *Algeria* 36°46N 8°19E **136 A5**
El Tarf □ *Algeria* 36°45N 8°10E **136 A5**
El Thamad *Egypt* 29°40N 34°28E **130 F3**
El Tigre *Venezuela* 8°44N 64°15W **186 B6**
El Tîh, Gebel *Egypt* 29°40N 33°50E **130 F2**
El Tîna *Egypt* 31°3N 32°22E **137 E8**
El Tofo *Chile* 29°22S 71°18W **190 B1**
El Tránsito *Chile* 28°52S 70°17W **190 B1**
El Tûr *Egypt* 28°14N 33°36E **128 D2**
El Turbio *Argentina* 51°45S 72°5W **192 D2**
El Uqsur *Egypt* 25°41N 32°38E **137 B3**
El Valle → *Spain* 37°56N 1°6W **91 H3**
El Vendrell *Spain* 41°10N 1°30E **90 D6**
El Vergel *Mexico* 26°28N 106°22W **180 B3**
El Vigía *Venezuela* 8°38N 71°39W **186 B4**
El Viso del Alcor *Spain* 37°23N 5°43W **89 H5**
El Wabeira *Egypt* 29°34N 33°6E **130 F2**
El Wuz *Sudan* 15°5N 30°7E **135 E12**
Elafonisos *Greece* 36°29N 22°56E **98 E4**
Elamanchili *India* 17°33N 82°50E **126 F6**
Élancourt *France* 48°47N 1°58E **71 D8**
Elands *Australia* 31°37S 152°20E **153 A10**
Elasa *Greece* 35°18N 26°21E **99 F8**
Elassona *Greece* 39°53N 22°12E **98 B4**
Elat *Israel* 29°30N 34°56E **130 F3**
Elatia *Greece* 38°37N 22°46E **98 C4**
Eláziğ *Turkey* 38°37N 39°14E **105 C8**
Eláziğ □ *Turkey* 38°40N 39°15E **105 C8**
Elba *Italy* 42°46N 10°17E **92 F7**
Elba *U.S.A.* 31°25N 86°4W **178 D3**
Elbasan *Albania* 41°9N 20°9E **96 E4**
Elbe *U.S.A.* 46°45N 122°10W **170 D4**
Elbe → *Europe* 53°50N 9°0E **76 B5**
Elbe-Seitenkanal *Germany* 52°45N 10°32E **76 C6**
Elbert, Mt. *U.S.A.* 39°7N 106°27W **168 G10**
Elberton *U.S.A.* 34°7N 82°52W **178 A7**
Elbeuf *France* 49°17N 1°2E **70 C8**
Elbing = Elbląg *Poland* 54°10N 19°25E **82 D6**
Elbistan *Turkey* 38°13N 37°15E **104 C7**
Elbląg *Poland* 54°10N 19°25E **82 D6**
Elbow *Canada* 51°7N 106°35W **163 C7**
Elbrus *Russia* 43°21N 42°30E **87 J6**
Elburz Mts. = Alborz, Reshteh-ye Kühhā-ye *Iran* 36°0N 52°0E **129 C7**
Elche *Spain* 38°15N 0°42W **91 G4**
Elche de la Sierra *Spain* 38°27N 2°3W **91 G2**
Elcho I. *Australia* 11°55S 135°45E **150 A2**
Elda *Spain* 38°29N 0°47W **91 G4**
Eldama Ravine *Kenya* 0°3N 35°43E **142 B4**
Elde → *Germany* 53°7N 11°15E **76 B7**
Eldon *Mo., U.S.A.* 38°21N 92°35W **172 F7**
Eldon *Wash., U.S.A.* 47°33N 123°3W **170 C3**
Eldora *U.S.A.* 42°22N 93°5E **172 D7**
Eldorado *Argentina* 26°28S 54°43W **191 B5**
Eldorado *Canada* 44°35N 77°31W **174 B7**
Eldorado *Ill., U.S.A.* 37°49N 88°26W **172 G9**
Eldorado *Tex., U.S.A.* 30°52N 100°36W **176 F4**
Eldorendo *U.S.A.* 31°3N 84°39W **178 D5**
Eldoret *Kenya* 0°30N 35°17E **142 B4**
Eldred *U.S.A.* 41°58N 78°23W **174 E6**
Elea, C. *Cyprus* 35°19N 34°4E **101 D13**
Eleanora, Pk. *Australia* 32°57S 121°9E **149 F3**
Elefantes → *Africa* 24°10S 32°40E **145 C5**
Elefantes, G. *Chile* 46°28S 73°49W **192 C2**
Elefsina *Greece* 38°4N 23°26E **98 C5**
Eleftherios Venizelos ✈ (ATH) *Greece* 37°53N 23°56E **98 D5**
Elektrogorsk *Russia* 55°56N 38°50E **84 E10**
Elektrostal *Russia* 55°41N 38°32E **84 E10**
Elele *Nigeria* 5°5N 6°50E **139 D6**
Elemi Triangle = Ilemi *Africa* 5°0N 35°20E **142 B4**
Elena *Bulgaria* 42°55N 25°53E **97 D9**
Elephant Butte Res. *U.S.A.* 33°9N 107°11W **169 K10**
Elephant I. *Antarctica* 61°0S 55°0W **55 C18**
Elephant Pass *Sri Lanka* 9°35N 80°25E **127 K5**
Elesbão Veloso *Brazil* 6°13S 42°8W **189 D5**
Eleshnitsa *Bulgaria* 41°52N 23°36E **96 E7**
Eleskirt *Turkey* 39°50N 42°5E **105 C10**
Eleuthera I. *Bahamas* 25°0N 76°20W **182 A4**
Eleutheroupoli *Greece* 40°52N 24°20E **97 F8**
Elgin *Canada* 44°36N 76°13W **175 B8**
Elgin *U.K.* 57°39N 3°19W **65 D5**
Eltham *N.Z.* 39°26S 174°19E **154 F3**
Elgin *Ill., U.S.A.* 42°2N 88°17W **172 D9**
Elgin *N. Dak., U.S.A.* 46°24N 101°51W **172 B3**
Elgin *Oreg., U.S.A.* 45°34N 117°55W **168 D5**
Elgin *S.C., U.S.A.* 34°10N 80°48W **178 A5**
Elgin *Tex., U.S.A.* 30°21N 97°22W **176 F6**
Elgoibar *Spain* 43°13N 2°24W **90 B2**
Elgon, Mt. *Africa* 1°10N 34°30E **142 B3**
Elikonos Oros *Greece* 38°18N 22°45E **98 C4**
Elim *Namibia* 17°48S 15°31E **144 A2**
Elim *S. Africa* 34°35S 19°45E **144 D2**
Elin Pelin *Bulgaria* 42°40N 23°36E **96 D7**
Elis = Ilia *Greece* 37°45N 21°35E **98 D3**
Eliseu Martins *Brazil* 8°13S 43°42W **189 D5**
Eliza, L. *Australia* 37°15S 139°50E **152 C3**
Elizabeth *Australia* 34°42S 138°41E **152 C2**
Elizabeth *U.S.A.* 40°39N 74°12W **175 F10**
Elizabeth City *U.S.A.* 36°18N 76°14W **177 C16**
Elizabethton *U.S.A.* 36°21N 82°13W **177 C13**
Elizabethtown *Ky., U.S.A.* 37°42N 85°52W **173 G11**
Elizabethtown *N.Y., U.S.A.* 44°13N 73°36W **175 B11**
Elizabethtown *Pa., U.S.A.* 40°9N 76°36W **175 F8**
Elizondo *Spain* 43°12N 1°30W **90 B3**
Elk *Poland* 53°50N 22°21E **82 E9**
Elk → *Canada* 49°11N 115°14W **162 D5**
Elk → *Poland* 53°41N 22°28E **82 E9**
Elk City *U.S.A.* 35°25N 99°25W **176 D5**
Elk Creek *U.S.A.* 39°36N 122°32W **170 F4**
Elk Grove *U.S.A.* 38°25N 121°22W **170 G5**
Elk Island △ *Canada* 53°35N 112°59W **162 C6**
Elk Lake *Canada* 47°40N 80°25W **164 C3**
Elk Point *Canada* 53°54N 110°55W **162 C6**
Elk River *Idaho, U.S.A.* 46°47N 116°11W **168 C5**
Elk River *Minn., U.S.A.* 45°18N 93°35W **172 C7**
Elkedra → *Australia* 21°8S 136°22E **150 C2**
Elkhart *Ind., U.S.A.* 41°41N 85°58W **173 E11**
Elkhart *Kans., U.S.A.* 37°0N 101°54W **172 G3**
Elkhorn *Canada* 49°59N 101°14W **163 D8**
Elkhorn → *U.S.A.* 41°8N 96°19W **172 E5**
Elkhovo *Bulgaria* 42°10N 26°35E **97 D10**
Elkin *U.S.A.* 36°15N 80°51W **177 C14**
Elkins *U.S.A.* 38°55N 79°51W **173 F14**
Elkland *U.S.A.* 41°59N 77°19W **174 E7**
Elko *Canada* 49°20N 115°10W **162 D5**
Elko *U.S.A.* 40°50N 115°46W **168 F6**
Elkton *U.S.A.* 43°49N 81°1W **174 C1**
Ellas = Greece ■ *Europe* 40°0N 23°0E **98 B3**
Ellaville *Fla., U.S.A.* 30°23N 83°10W **178 E6**
Ellaville *Ga., U.S.A.* 32°14N 84°19W **178 D5**
Ellef Ringnes I. *Canada* 78°30N 102°2W **161 B11**
Ellen, Mt. *U.S.A.* 44°9N 72°56W **175 B12**
Ellenburg *U.S.A.* 44°54N 73°48N 175 **175 B11**
Ellendale *U.S.A.* 46°0N 98°32W **172 B4**
Ellensburg *U.S.A.* 46°59N 120°34W **168 C3**
Ellenville *U.S.A.* 41°43N 74°24W **175 E10**
Ellerton *Barbados* 13°7N 59°33W **183 g**
Ellery, Mt. *Australia* 37°28S 148°47E **153 D8**
Ellesmere, L. *N.Z.* 43°47S 172°28E **155 D7**
Ellesmere I. *Canada* 79°30N 80°0W **161 B16**
Ellesmere Island = Quttinirpaaq △ *Canada* 82°13N 72°13W **161 A17**
Ellesmere Port *U.K.* 53°17N 2°54W **66 D5**
Ellice Is. = Tuvalu ■ *Pac. Oc.* 8°0S 178°0E **147 B10**
Ellicottville *U.S.A.* 42°17N 78°40W **174 D6**
Ellington *U.S.A.* 42°13N 79°6W **174 D5**
Elliot *Australia* 17°33S 133°32E **150 B1**
Elliot *S. Africa* 31°22S 27°48E **145 D4**
Elliot Lake *Canada* 46°25N 82°35W **164 C3**
Elliotdale = Xhora *S. Africa* 31°55S 28°38E **145 D4**
Elliott *Key, U.S.A.* 25°27N 80°12W **179 K9**
Ellis *U.S.A.* 38°56N 99°34W **172 F4**
Elliston *Australia* 33°39S 134°53E **151 E1**
Ellisville *U.S.A.* 31°36N 89°12W **177 F10**
Ellon *U.K.* 57°22N 2°4W **65 D6**
Ellora *India* 20°1N 75°10E **126 D2**
Ellore = Eluru *India* 16°48N 81°8E **126 F5**
Ellsworth *Kans., U.S.A.* 38°44N 98°14W **172 F4**
Ellsworth *Maine, U.S.A.* 44°33N 68°25W **173 C19**
Ellsworth Land *Antarctica* 76°0S 89°0W **55 D16**
Ellsworth Mts. *Antarctica* 78°30S 85°0W **55 D16**
Ellwangen *Germany* 48°57N 10°8E **77 G6**
Ellwood City *U.S.A.* 40°52N 80°17W **174 F4**
Ellzey *U.S.A.* 29°19N 82°49W **179 F7**
Elm *Switz.* 46°54N 9°10E **77 J5**
Elm-Lappwald △ *Germany* 52°15N 10°50E **76 C6**
Elma *U.S.A.* 47°0N 123°25W **170 D3**
Elma *Canada* 49°52N 95°55W **163 D9**
Elmadağ *Turkey* 39°55N 33°14E **104 C5**
Elmalı *Turkey* 36°44N 29°56E **99 E11**
Elmhurst *U.S.A.* 41°53N 87°56W **172 E10**
Elmina *Ghana* 5°5N 1°21W **139 D4**
Elmira *Canada* 43°36N 80°33W **174 C4**
Elmira *U.S.A.* 42°6N 76°48W **174 D8**
Elmira Heights *U.S.A.* 42°8N 76°50W **174 D8**
Elmodel *U.S.A.* 31°21N 84°29W **178 D5**
Elmore *Australia* 36°30S 144°37E **152 D6**
Elmore *U.S.A.* 32°48N 115°49W **171 N11**
Elmshorn *Germany* 53°43N 9°40E **76 B5**
Elmwood *Canada* 44°15N 81°10W **174 C4**
Elne *France* 42°36N 2°58E **72 F6**
Elora *Canada* 43°41N 80°26W **174 C4**
Elos *Greece* 36°46N 22°43E **98 E4**
Elounda *Greece* 35°16N 25°42E **101 D7**
Éloyes *France* 48°6N 6°36E **71 D13**
Elphin *Canada* 44°55N 76°37W **175 B8**
Elpitiya *Sri Lanka* 6°17N 80°10E **127 L5**
Elrose *Canada* 51°12N 108°0W **163 C7**
Elsas *Canada* 48°32N 82°55W **164 C3**
Elsdorf *Germany* 50°55N 6°34E **76 E2**
Elsie *U.S.A.* 45°52N 123°36W **170 E3**
Elsinore = Helsingør *Denmark* 56°2N 12°35E **63 H6**
Elster → *Germany* 51°25N 11°57E **76 D7**
Elsterwerda *Germany* 51°27N 13°31E **76 D9**
Eltanin Fracture Zone System *S. Ocean* 54°0S 130°0W **55 B14**
Elton *Russia* 49°5N 46°52E **87 F8**
Elton, Ozero *Russia* 49°5N 46°42E **87 F8**
Eltville *Germany* 50°2N 8°7E **77 E4**
Eluru *India* 16°48N 81°8E **126 F5**
Elvas *Portugal* 38°50N 7°10W **89 G3**
Elven *France* 47°44N 2°36W **70 E4**
Elverum *Norway* 60°53N 11°34E **60 F14**
Elvire → *Australia* 17°51S 128°11E **148 C4**
Elvire, Mt. *Australia* 29°22S 119°36E **149 E2**
Elvo → *Italy* 45°23N 8°21E **92 C5**
Elwell, L. = Tiber Res. *U.S.A.* 48°19N 111°6W **168 B8**
Elwood *Ind., U.S.A.* 40°17N 85°50W **173 E11**
Elwood *Nebr., U.S.A.* 40°36N 99°52W **172 E4**
Elx = Elche *Spain* 38°15N 0°42W **91 G4**
Ely *U.K.* 52°24N 0°16E **67 E8**
Ely *Minn., U.S.A.* 47°55N 91°51W **172 B8**
Ely *Nev., U.S.A.* 39°15N 114°54W **168 G6**
Elyria *U.S.A.* 41°22N 82°7W **174 E2**
Elyros *Greece* 35°15N 23°45E **98 F5**
Elz → *Germany* 48°18N 7°44E **77 G3**
Emajõgi → *Estonia* 58°25N 27°20E **84 C4**
eMakhazeni *S. Africa* 25°42S 30°2E **145 D5**
eMalahleni *S. Africa* 25°51S 29°14E **145 D4**
Emāmrūd *Iran* 36°30N 55°0E **129 B7**
Emån → *Sweden* 57°8N 16°30E **63 G10**
eMbalenhle *S. Africa* 26°32S 29°4E **145 D4**
Embarcación *Argentina* 23°10S 64°0W **190 A3**
Embetsu *Japan* 44°44N 141°47E **112 B10**
Embi *Kazakhstan* 48°50N 58°8E **108 C5**
Embi → *Kazakhstan* 46°55N 53°28E **108 C4**
Embonas *Greece* 36°13N 27°51E **101 C9**
Embro *Canada* 43°9N 80°54W **174 C4**
Embrun *France* 44°34N 6°30E **73 D10**
Embu *Kenya* 0°32S 37°38E **142 C4**
Emden *Germany* 53°21N 7°12E **76 B3**
Emei Shan *China* 29°32N 103°46E **116 C4**
Emeishan *China* 29°31N 103°23E **116 C4**
Emerald *Australia* 23°32S 148°10E **150 C4**
Emerald *U.S.A.* 76°48N 114°10W **161 B9**
Émeraude, Côte d' *France* 48°45N 2°40W **70 D4**
Emerson *Canada* 49°0N 97°10W **163 D9**
Emet *Turkey* 39°20N 29°15E **99 B11**
Emgwenya *S. Africa* 25°40S 30°18E **145 D5**
Emi Koussi *Chad* 19°45N 18°55E **135 E9**
Emilia-Romagna □ *Italy* 44°45N 11°0E **92 D8**
Emilius, Mte. *Italy* 45°45N 7°20E **92 C4**
Emin *China* 46°34N 83°36E **109 C10**
Eminabad *Pakistan* 32°2N 74°8E **124 C6**
Emine, Nos *Bulgaria* 42°40N 27°56E **97 D11**
Emirdağ *Turkey* 39°2N 31°8E **104 C4**
Emissi, Tarso *Chad* 21°27N 18°36E **135 D9**
Emlenton *U.S.A.* 41°11N 79°43W **174 E5**
Emlichheim *Germany* 52°37N 6°51E **76 C2**
Emmaboda *Sweden* 56°37N 15°32E **63 H9**
Emmalane *U.S.A.* 32°46N 82°0W **178 D7**
Emmastad *Neths.* 29°2S 25°15E **144 D3**
Emmaus *S. Africa* 40°32N 75°30W **175 F9**
Emme → *Switz.* 47°14N 7°32E **77 H3**
Emmeloord *Neths.* 52°44N 5°46E **69 B5**
Emmen *Neths.* 52°48N 6°57E **69 B6**
Emmen *Switz.* 47°5N 8°18E **77 H4**
Emmendingen *Germany* 48°7N 7°51E **77 G3**
Emmerich *Germany* 51°50N 6°12E **76 D2**
Emmetsburg *U.S.A.* 43°7N 94°41W **172 D6**
Emmett *Idaho, U.S.A.* 43°52N 116°30W **168 E5**
Emmett *Mich., U.S.A.* 42°59N 82°46W **174 D1**
Emmiganuru = Yemmiganur *India* 15°44N 77°29E **127 G3**
Emmonak *U.S.A.* 62°47N 164°31W **166 C7**
Emo *Canada* 48°38N 93°50W **163 D10**
Emőd *Hungary* 47°57N 20°47E **80 C5**
Emona *Bulgaria* 42°43N 27°53E **97 D11**
Empalme *Mexico* 27°58N 110°51W **180 B2**
Empangeni *S. Africa* 28°50S 31°52E **145 D5**
Empedrado *Argentina* 28°0S 58°46W **190 B4**
Emperor Seamount Chain *Pac. Oc.* 40°0N 170°0E **156 D9**
Emperor Trough *Pac. Oc.* 43°0N 175°30E **156 C9**
Empire *U.S.A.* 32°21N 83°18W **178 C6**
Empoli *Italy* 43°43N 10°57E **92 E7**
Emporia *Kans., U.S.A.* 38°25N 96°11W **172 F5**
Emporia *Va., U.S.A.* 36°42N 77°32W **173 G15**
Emporium *U.S.A.* 41°31N 78°14W **174 E6**
Empress *Canada* 50°57N 110°0W **163 C7**
Empty Quarter = Rub' al Khālī *Si. Arabia* 19°0N 48°0E **131 D4**
Ems → *Germany* 53°20N 7°12E **76 B3**
Emsdale *Canada* 45°32N 79°19W **174 A5**
Emsdetten *Germany* 52°10N 7°31E **76 C3**
Emu *China* 43°40N 128°6E **115 C15**
Emu Park *Australia* 23°13S 150°50E **150 C5**
eMuziwezinto *S. Africa* 30°15S 30°45E **145 D5**
'En 'Avrona *Israel* 29°43N 35°0E **130 F4**
'En Boqeq *Israel* 31°12N 35°21E **129 D4**
'En Gedi *Israel* 31°28N 35°23E **129 D4**
En Nahud *Sudan* 12°45N 28°25E **135 F11**
Ena *Japan* 35°25N 137°25E **113 G8**
Enånger *Sweden* 61°30N 17°9E **62 C11**
Enard B. *U.K.* 58°5N 5°20W **65 C3**
Enare träsk = Inarijärvi *Finland* 69°0N 28°0E **60 B23**
Enarotali *Indonesia* 3°55S 136°21E **119 E9**
Encampment *U.S.A.* 41°12N 106°47W **168 E10**
Encantadas, Serra *Brazil* 30°40S 53°0W **191 C5**
Encarnación *Paraguay* 27°15S 55°50W **191 B4**
Encarnación de Díaz *Mexico* 21°31N 102°14W **180 C4**
Enchi *Ghana* 5°53N 2°48W **138 D4**
Encinitas *U.S.A.* 33°3N 117°17W **171 M9**
Encino *U.S.A.* 34°39N 105°28W **169 J11**
Encounter B. *Australia* 35°45S 138°45E **152 C2**
Encruzilhada *Brazil* 15°31S 40°54W **189 D2**
Encs *Hungary* 48°20N 21°8E **80 B6**
Endako *Canada* 54°6N 125°2W **162 C3**
Endau *Kenya* 1°18S 38°31E **142 C4**
Endau Rompin △ *Malaysia* 2°27N 103°45E **121 L4**
Ende *Indonesia* 8°45S 121°40E **119 F6**
Endeavour Str. *Australia* 10°45S 142°0E **150 A3**
Endelave *Denmark* 55°46N 10°18E **63 J4**
Enderbury *Kiribati* 3°8S 171°5W **150**
Enderby *Canada* 50°35N 119°10W **162 D5**
Enderby Abyssal Plain *S. Ocean* 60°0S 40°0E **5**
Enderby I. *Australia* 20°35S 116°30E **148 D2**
Enderby Land *Antarctica* 66°0S 53°0E **5**
Enderlin *U.S.A.* 46°38N 97°36E **172 B5**
Enderrocat, C. *Spain* 39°28N 2°43E **100**
Endicott *U.S.A.* 42°6N 76°4W **175 D8**
Endicott Mts. *U.S.A.* 68°0N 152°0W **166**
Endimari → *Brazil* 8°46S 66°7W **188 B5**
Endwell *U.S.A.* 42°6N 76°2W **175 D8**
Endyalgout I. *Australia* 11°40S 132°35E **150 A1**
Ené → *Peru* 11°10S 74°18W **188**
Eneabba *Australia* 29°49S 115°16E **149 E2**
Enerhodar *Ukraine* 47°30N 34°48E **87 J8**
Enewetak Atoll *Marshall Is.* 11°30N 162°15E **158**
Enez *Turkey* 40°45N 26°5E **97 F10**
Enfer, Pte. d' *Martinique* 14°22N 60°54W **184**
Enfield *Canada* 44°56N 63°32W **109**
Enfield *Conn., U.S.A.* 41°58N 72°36W **175**
Enfield *N.C., U.S.A.* 36°11N 77°41W **177**
Enfield *N.H., U.S.A.* 43°39N 72°9W **175**
Engadin *Switz.* 46°45N 10°10E **7**
Engaño, C. *Dom. Rep.* 18°30N 68°20W **183**
Engaño, C. *Phil.* 18°35N 122°23E **119**
Engaru *Japan* 44°3N 143°31E **112 B11**
Engcobo = Ngcobo *S. Africa* 31°37S 28°0E **14**
Engelberg *Switz.* 46°48N 8°26E **77**
Engels *Russia* 51°28N 46°6E **8**
Engelsberg = Ängelsberg *Sweden* 59°58N 16°0E **62**
Engemann L. *Canada* 58°0N 106°55W **16**
Enggano *Indonesia* 5°20S 102°40E **12**
England *U.S.A.* 34°33N 91°58W **17**
England □ *U.K.* 53°0N 2°0W **6**
Englee *Canada* 50°45N 56°5W **16**
Englehart *Canada* 47°49N 79°52W **164**
Englewood *U.S.A.* 26°58N 82°21W **179**
English → *Canada* 49°12N 91°5W **163**
English Bazar = Ingraj Bazar *India* 24°58N 88°10E **125**
English Channel *Europe* 50°0N 2°0W **67**
English Company's Is., The *Australia* 11°50S 136°32E **150**
English River *Canada* 49°14N 91°0W **164**
Engures ezers *Latvia* 57°10N 23°6E **8**
Enguri → *Georgia* 42°27N 41°38E **8**
Enid *U.S.A.* 36°24N 97°53W **17**
Enipeas → *Greece* 39°22N 22°17E **9**
Eniwa *Japan* 43°0N 141°30E **112**
Enkhuizen *Neths.* 52°42N 5°17E **69**
Enköping *Sweden* 59°37N 17°4E **62**
Enle *China* 24°0N 101°9E **11**
Enna *Italy* 37°34N 14°16E **9**
Ennadai L. *Canada* 60°58N 101°20W **16**
Ennedi *Chad* 17°15N 22°0E **13**
Enngonia *Australia* 29°21S 145°50E **15**
Ennigerloh *Germany* 51°50N 8°2E **7**
Ennis *Ireland* 52°51N 8°59W **6**
Ennis *Mont., U.S.A.* 45°21N 111°44W **16**
Ennis *Tex., U.S.A.* 32°20N 96°38W **17**
Enniscorthy *Ireland* 52°30N 6°34W **6**
Enniskillen *U.K.* 54°21N 7°39W **6**
Ennistimon *Ireland* 52°57N 9°17W **6**
Enns *Austria* 48°14N 14°32E **7**
Enns → *Austria* 48°14N 14°32E **7**
Eno *Finland* 62°47N 30°10E **6**
Enosburg Falls *U.S.A.* 44°55N 72°48W **17**
Enping *China* 22°16N 112°21E **11**
Enriquillo, L. *Dom. Rep.* 18°20N 71°40W **18**
Enschede *Neths.* 52°13N 6°53E **6**
Ensenada *Argentina* 34°55S 57°55W **19**
Ensenada *Chile* 41°12S 72°33W **19**
Ensenada *Mexico* 31°52N 116°37W **18**
Ensenada de los Muertos *Mexico* 23°59N 109°51W **18**
Enshi *China* 30°18N 109°29E **11**
Ensiola, Pta. de n' *Spain* 39°7N 2°55E **10**
Ensisheim *France* 47°50N 7°20E **7**
Ensley *U.S.A.* 30°31N 87°16W **17**
Entebbe *Uganda* 0°4N 32°28E **14**
Enterprise *Canada* 60°47N 115°45W **16**
Enterprise *Ala., U.S.A.* 31°19N 85°51W **17**
Enterprise *Oreg., U.S.A.* 45°25N 117°17W **16**
Entorno de Doñana △ *Spain* 37°0N 6°26W **8**
Entrance, The *Australia* 33°21S 151°30E **15**
Entraygues-sur-Truyère *France* 44°38N 2°35E **7**
Entre Ríos *Bolivia* 21°30S 64°25W **19**
Entre Ríos □ *Argentina* 30°30S 58°30W **19**
Entrepeñas, Embalse de *Spain* 40°34N 2°42W **9**
Entroncamento *Portugal* 39°28N 8°28W **8**
Enugu *Nigeria* 6°30N 7°30E **13**
Enugu □ *Nigeria* 6°30N 7°30E **13**
Enugu Ezike *Nigeria* 7°0N 7°29E **13**
Enumclaw *U.S.A.* 47°12N 121°59W **17**
Envalira, Port d' *Europe* 42°33N 1°43E **9**
Envermeu *France* 49°53N 1°15E **7**
Enviken *Sweden* 60°49N 15°56E **6**
Envira *Brazil* 7°18S 70°15W **18**
Envira → *Brazil* 7°18S 70°13W **18**
Enying *Hungary* 46°56N 18°15E **8**
Enza → *Italy* 44°54N 10°31E **9**
Eochaill = Youghal *Ireland* 51°56N 7°52W **6**
Éólie, Ís. *Italy* 38°30N 14°57E **9**
Epanomi *Greece* 40°25N 22°59E **9**
Epe *Neths.* 52°21N 5°59E **6**
Epe *Nigeria* 6°36N 3°59E **13**
Épernay *France* 49°3N 3°56E **7**
Épernon *France* 48°35N 1°40E **7**
Ephesus *Turkey* 37°55N 27°22E **9**
Ephraim *U.S.A.* 39°22N 111°35W **16**
Ephrata *Pa., U.S.A.* 40°11N 76°11W **17**
Ephrata *Wash., U.S.A.* 47°19N 119°33W **16**
Epidaurus = Epidavros *Greece* 37°40N 23°7E **9**
Epidavros *Greece* 37°40N 23°7E **9**
Epidavros Limira *Greece* 36°46N 23°0E **9**
Épila *Spain* 41°36N 1°17W **9**
Épinac *France* 46°59N 4°31E **7**
Épinal *France* 48°10N 6°27E **7**

ros □ Greece 39°30N 20°30E 98 B2
kopi Cyprus 34°40N 32°54E 101 E11
kopi Greece 35°20N 24°20E 101 D6
kopi Bay Cyprus 34°35N 32°50E 101 E11
alio Greece 37°37N 21°30E 98 D3
alock, L. Australia 36°52S 144°34E 152 D6
an = Appiano Italy 46°28N 11°15E 93 B8
ingen Germany 49°8N 8°53E 77 F4
om U.K. 51°19N 0°16W 67 F7
kiro Namibia 21°40S 19°9E 144 B2
atoria = El Istiwa'iya
udan 5°0N 28°0E 135 G11
atorial Guinea ■ Africa 2°0N 8°0E 140 D1
ai China 25°48N 100°11E 116 E3
achidia Morocco 31°58N 4°20W 136 B3
ahad Sudan 12°45N 30°32E 135 F12
if Morocco 35°1N 4°1W 136 A3
ogel Sudan 18°10N 35°25E 137 D4
lea Italy 45°35N 12°40E 93 C9
ndol India 20°56N 75°20E 126 D2
wadi Myit = Irrawaddy →
urma 15°50N 95°6E 123 M19
wadi Myitwanya = Irrawaddy,
louths of the
urma 15°30N 95°0E 123 M19
wan △ Thailand 14°25N 98°58E 120 E2
Italy 45°48N 9°15E 92 C6
Sudan 19°5N 36°51E 137 D4
, J. Sudan 20°48N 36°47E 137 C4
a Turkey 40°42N 36°36E 104 B7
ng Shan China 42°50N 84°59E 109 D10
skopf Germany 49°44N 7°2E 77 F3
= Arbil Iraq 36°15N 44°5E 105 D11
k Turkey 38°39N 43°36E 128 B4
s Turkey 39°2N 43°21E 105 C10
yaş Dağı Turkey 38°30N 35°30E 128 B2
Hungary 47°22N 18°56E 80 C3
o Jiang → China 42°37N 128°0E 115 C14
k Turkey 40°23N 27°47E 97 F11
mli Turkey 36°36N 34°19E 104 D6
n = Ulaan-Uul
ongolia 46°4N 100°49E 114 B6
net Mongolia 49°2N 104°5E 110 B9
netsogt Mongolia 42°55N 106°5E 114 C4
ng Germany 48°18N 11°54E 77 G7
e → France 47°13N 1°32W 70 E5
us, Mt. Antarctica 77°35S 167°0E 55 D11
him Brazil 27°35S 52°15W 191 B5
li Konya, Turkey 37°31N 34°4E 104 D6
li Zonguldak, Turkey 41°15N 31°24E 104 B4
Monti Italy 37°20N 14°20E 95 E7
hot China 43°48N 112°2E 114 C7
→ Spain 41°26N 4°45W 88 D6
os Greece 39°11N 25°57E 99 B7
mentaū Kazakhstan 51°37N 73°6E 109 B8
ek Turkey 41°53N 34°55E 104 B6
nisdam S. Africa 28°30S 26°50E 144 C4
ud Morocco 31°30N 4°15W 136 B3
adt Germany 50°50N 6°50E 76 E2
→ Germany 51°11N 6°44E 76 D2
rt Germany 50°58N 11°2E 76 E7
ni Turkey 38°17N 39°49E 105 C8
Mongolia 43°8N 109°5E 114 C5
e → Turkey 41°1N 26°22E 97 E10
ni Vozvyshennost
ussia 47°0N 44°0E 87 G7
Latvia 56°54N 25°38E 84 D3
n He = Argun →
ssia 53°20N 121°28E 111 A13
n Youqi China 50°15N 120°11E 111 A13
n Taiwan 23°54N 120°22E 117 F13
→ Spain 42°3N 5°44W 88 C5
ll, L. U.K. 58°30N 4°42W 65 C4
Italy 38°2N 12°35E 94 D5
U.S.A. 30°18N 83°45W 178 E6
U.S.A. 42°8N 80°5W 174 D4
L. N. Amer. 42°15N 81°0W 174 D4
Canal U.S.A. 43°5N 78°43W 174 C7
u Canada 42°16N 81°57W 174 D3
u = Ceerigaabo
malia 10°35N 47°20E 131 E4
oussa Greece 39°53N 19°34E 101 A3
sdale Canada 50°52N 98°7W 163 C9
anthos Greece 37°57N 21°50E 98 D3
o-Misaki Japan 41°50N 143°15E 112 D11
Canada 43°35N 80°7W 174 C4
Pt. Trin. & Tob. 10°3N 61°39W 187 K15
pura India 25°9N 73°3E 124 G5
ay U.K. 57°4N 7°18W 65 D1
res Greece 38°13N 23°20E 98 C5
ea ■ Africa 14°0N 38°30E 131 D2
→ Portugal 39°40N 7°1W 88 F3
ch-Tam Pass Asia 39°46N 74°2E 109 E8
lenz Germany 51°4N 6°19E 76 D2
er Germany 52°25N 13°44E 76 C9
ngen Germany 49°36N 11°0E 77 F6
unda Australia 25°14S 133°12E 150 D1
elo Neths. 52°18N 5°35E 69 B5
elo S. Africa 26°31S 29°59E 145 C4
enek Turkey 38°36N 33°0E 104 D5
oni Greece 37°23N 23°15E 98 D5
ones Greece 39°37N 19°46E 101 A3
oupoli Greece 37°28N 24°57E 98 D6
kulam India 9°59N 76°22E 127 K3
→ Ireland 54°30N 8°16W 64 B3
, Lower L. U.K. 54°28N 7°47W 64 B4
, Upper L. U.K. 54°14N 7°32W 64 B4
France 48°18N 0°56W 70 D6
st Giles Ra.
stralia 27°0S 123°45E 149 E3
tberg Germany 50°13N 6°47E 77 E2
e India 11°24N 77°45E 127 J3
nanga Australia 26°40S 143°11E 151 D3
go Namibia 21°39S 15°58E 144 B2
go □ Namibia 22°20S 15°0E 144 B2
y France 48°38N 2°29W 70 D4
mala Hills India 15°30N 78°15E 127 G4
nteria Spain 43°19N 1°54W 90 B3
al Ireland 55°2N 8°6W 64 A3
undra △
stralia 37°20S 148°47E 153 D8
Hd. Ireland 54°17N 10°0W 64 B1
kë Albania 40°22N 20°40E 96 F4
ine U.S.A. 47°40N 96°0W 172 B6
in France 48°25N 7°38E 71 D14
China 46°30N 90°5E 109 C12
n Shuiku China 27°5N 101°52E 116 D3
olmene Denmark 55°19N 15°11E 63 J9
Russia 51°55N 40°50E 86 E5
= Irtysh → Russia 61°4N 68°52E 106 C7
Kazakhstan 53°20N 75°27E 109 B9
Ertis → Kazakhstan 47°52N 84°16E 109 C10
Eruh Turkey 37°46N 42°13E 105 D10
Ervy-le-Châtel France 48°2N 3°55E 71 D10
Erwin U.S.A. 36°9N 82°25W 177 C13
Eryuan China 26°7N 99°57E 116 D2
Erzgebirge Germany 50°27N 12°55E 76 E8
Erzin Russia 50°15N 95°10E 109 B13
Erzincan Turkey 39°46N 39°30E 105 C8
Erzincan □ Turkey 39°45N 39°30E 105 C8
Erzurum Turkey 39°57N 41°15E 105 C9
Erzurum □ Turkey 39°55N 41°15E 105 C9
Es Caló Spain 38°40N 1°30E 100 C8
Es Canar Spain 39°2N 1°36E 100 B8
Es Mercadal Spain 39°59N 4°5E 100 B11
Es Migjorn Gran Spain 39°57N 4°3E 100 B11
Es Sahrâ al Beida Egypt 27°50N 28°45E 137 B2
Es Sahrâ' Esh Sharqîya
Egypt 27°30N 32°30E 137 B3
Es Sînâ' Egypt 29°0N 34°0E 130 F2
Es Vedrà Spain 38°52N 1°12E 100 C7
Esambo
Dem. Rep. of the Congo 3°48S 23°30E 142 C1
Esan-Misaki Japan 41°40N 141°10E 112 D10
Esashi Hokkaidō, Japan 44°56N 142°35E 112 B11
Esashi Hokkaidō, Japan 41°52N 140°7E 112 D10
Esbjerg Denmark 55°29N 8°29E 63 J2
Esbo = Espoo Finland 60°12N 24°40E 84 B3
Escada Brazil 8°22S 35°8W 189 B3
Escalante U.S.A. 37°47N 111°36W 169 H8
Escalante → U.S.A. 37°24N 110°57W 169 H8
Escalón Mexico 26°45N 104°20W 180 B4
Escambia → U.S.A. 30°32N 87°11W 179 E2
Escanaba U.S.A. 45°45N 87°4W 172 C10
Escárcega Mexico 18°37N 90°43W 181 D6
Esch-sur-Alzette Lux. 49°32N 6°0E 69 E6
Eschede Germany 52°44N 10°14E 76 C6
Eschwege Germany 51°11N 10°2E 76 D6
Eschweiler Germany 50°49N 6°15E 76 E2
Esco Bolivia 15°40S 69°8W 188 D4
Escondido U.S.A. 33°7N 117°5W 171 M9
Escravos → Nigeria 5°35N 5°10E 139 D6
Escuinapa de Hidalgo
Mexico 22°50N 105°50W 180 C3
Escuintla Guatemala 14°20N 90°48W 182 D1
Eséka Cameroon 3°41N 10°44E 139 E7
Eşen → Turkey 36°27N 29°16E 99 E11
Esenguly Turkmenistan 37°37N 53°59E 108 E4
Esens Germany 53°38N 7°36E 76 B3
Esentepe = Áyios Amvrósios
Cyprus 35°20N 33°35E 101 D12
Esenyurt Turkey 41°3N 28°48E 97 E12
Esera → Spain 42°6N 0°15E 90 C5
Eşfahān Iran 32°39N 51°43E 129 C6
Eşfahān □ Iran 32°50N 51°50E 129 C6
Esfarāyen Iran 37°4N 57°30E 129 B8
Esfideh Iran 33°39N 59°46E 129 C8
Esgueva → Spain 41°40N 4°43W 88 D6
Esh Sham = Dimashq
Syria 33°30N 36°18E 130 B5
Esh Shamâlîya □ Sudan 19°0N 29°0E 137 D2
Esha Ness U.K. 60°29N 1°38W 65 A7
Eshan China 24°11N 102°24E 116 E4
Esher U.K. 51°21N 0°20W 67 F7
Eshkäshem = Ishkashim
Tajikistan 36°44N 71°37E 109 E8
Eshkol △ Israel 31°20N 34°30E 130 D3
Eshowe S. Africa 28°50S 31°30E 145 C5
Esiama Ghana 4°56N 2°25W 138 E4
Esigodini Zimbabwe 20°18S 28°56E 145 B4
Esil = Ishim → Russia 57°45N 71°10E 106 D8
Esil Kazakhstan 51°57N 66°24E 109 B7
Esino → Italy 43°39N 13°22E 93 E10
Esk → Dumf. & Gall., U.K. 54°58N 3°2W 65 G5
Esk → N. Yorks., U.K. 54°30N 0°37W 66 C7
Eskān Iran 26°48N 63°9E 129 E9
Esker Siding Canada 53°53N 66°25W 165 B6
Eskifjörður Iceland 65°3N 13°55W 60 D7
Eskilsäter Sweden 58°57N 13°10E 63 F7
Eskilstuna Sweden 59°22N 16°32E 62 E10
Eskimalatya Turkey 38°24N 38°22E 105 C8
Eskimo Point = Arviat
Canada 61°6N 93°59W 163 A10
Eskişehir Turkey 39°50N 30°30E 99 B12
Eskişehir □ Turkey 39°40N 31°0E 99 B12
Esla → Spain 41°29N 6°3W 88 D4
Eslāmābād-e Gharb
Iran 34°10N 46°30E 105 E12
Eslāmshahr Iran 35°40N 51°10E 129 C6
Eslöv Sweden 55°50N 13°20E 63 J7
Eşme Turkey 38°23N 28°58E 99 C10
Esmeralda, I. Chile 48°55S 75°25W 192 C1
Esmeraldas Ecuador 1°0N 79°40W 186 C3
Esna = Isna Egypt 25°17N 32°30E 137 B3
Esnagi L. Canada 48°36N 84°33W 164 C3
Esom Hill U.S.A. 33°57N 85°23W 178 B4
Espalion France 44°32N 2°47E 72 D6
España = Spain ■ Europe 39°0N 4°0W 59 H5
Espanola Canada 46°15N 81°46W 164 C3
Espanola U.S.A. 35°59N 106°5W 169 J10
Esparreguera Spain 41°33N 1°52E 90 D6
Esparza Costa Rica 9°59N 84°40W 182 E3
Espelkamp Germany 52°24N 8°36E 76 C4
Esperança Brazil 7°1S 35°51W 189 B3
Esperance Australia 33°45S 121°55E 149 F3
Esperance B. Australia 33°48S 121°55E 149 F3
Esperance Harbour
St. Lucia 14°4N 60°55W 183 f
Esperantinópolis Brazil 4°53S 44°53W 189 A2
Esperanza Antarctica 65°0S 55°0W 55 C18
Esperanza Santa Cruz,
Argentina 51°1S 70°49W 192 D2
Esperanza Santa Fe,
Argentina 31°29S 61°3W 190 C3
Esperanza Puerto Rico 18°6N 65°28W 183 d
Espéraza France 42°56N 2°14E 72 F6
Espichel, C. Portugal 38°22N 9°16W 89 G1
Espiel Spain 38°11N 5°1W 89 G5
Espigão, Serra do
Brazil 26°35S 50°30W 191 B5
Espinar Peru 14°51S 71°24W 188 C3
Espinazo, Sierra del = Espinhaço,
Serra do Brazil 17°30S 43°30W 189 D2
Espinhaço, Serra do
Brazil 17°30S 43°30W 189 D2
Espinho Portugal 41°1N 8°38W 88 D2
Espinilho, Serra do
Brazil 28°30S 55°0W 191 B5
Espinosa de los Monteros
Spain 43°5N 3°34W 88 B7
Espirito Santo □ Brazil 20°0S 40°45W 189 E2
Espírito Santo do Pinhal
Brazil 22°10S 46°46W 191 A6
Espíritu Santo Vanuatu 15°15S 166°50E 147 C9
Espíritu Santo, B. del
Mexico 19°20N 87°35W 181 D7
Espíritu Santo, I.
Mexico 24°30N 110°22W 180 C2
Espita Mexico 21°1N 88°19W 181 C7
Espiye Turkey 40°56N 38°43E 105 B8
Esplanada Brazil 11°47S 37°57W 189 C3
Espoo Finland 60°12N 24°40E 84 B3
Espuña, Sierra de Spain 37°51N 1°35W 91 H3
Espungabera Mozam. 20°29S 32°45E 145 B5
Esquel Argentina 42°55S 71°20W 192 B2
Esquimalt Canada 48°26N 123°25W 170 B3
Esquina Argentina 30°0S 59°30W 190 C4
Essaouira Morocco 31°32N 9°42W 136 B2
Essen Belgium 51°28N 4°28E 69 C4
Essen Germany 51°28N 7°2E 76 D3
Essendon, Mt. Australia 25°0S 120°29E 149 E3
Essequibo → Guyana 6°50N 58°30W 186 B7
Essex Canada 42°10N 82°49W 174 D2
Essex Calif., U.S.A. 34°44N 115°15W 171 L11
Essex N.Y., U.S.A. 44°19N 73°21W 175 B11
Essex □ U.K. 51°54N 0°27E 67 F8
Essex Junction U.S.A. 44°29N 73°7W 175 B11
Esslingen Germany 48°44N 9°18E 77 G5
Essonne □ France 48°30N 2°20E 71 D9
Estaca de Bares, C. de
Spain 43°46N 7°42W 88 B3
Estación Camacho
Mexico 24°25N 102°18W 180 C4
Estación Simón
Mexico 24°42N 102°35W 180 C4
Estadilla Spain 42°4N 0°16E 90 C5
Estados, I. de Los
Argentina 54°40S 64°30W 192 D4
Estagel France 42°47N 2°40E 72 F6
Eşţahbānāt Iran 29°8N 54°4E 129 D7
Estância Brazil 11°16S 37°26W 189 C3
Estancia U.S.A. 34°46N 106°4W 169 J10
Estancia Monte León
Argentina 50°14S 68°55W 192 D3
Estārm Iran 28°21N 58°21E 129 D8
Estarreja Portugal 40°45N 8°35W 88 E2
Estats, Pic d' Spain 42°40N 1°24E 90 C6
Estcourt S. Africa 29°0S 29°53E 145 C4
Este Italy 45°14N 11°39E 93 C8
Este △ Dom. Rep. 18°14N 68°42W 183 C6
Esteli Nic. 13°9N 86°22W 182 D2
Estella Spain 42°40N 2°2W 90 C2
Estellencs Spain 39°39N 2°29E 100 B9
Estena → Spain 39°23N 4°44W 89 F6
Estepa Spain 37°17N 4°52W 89 H6
Estepona Spain 36°24N 5°7W 89 J5
Esterhazy Canada 50°37N 102°5W 163 C8
Esternay France 48°44N 3°33E 71 D10
Esterri d'Aneu Spain 42°38N 1°5E 90 C6
Estevan Canada 49°10N 102°59W 163 D8
Estevan Group Canada 53°3N 129°38W 162 C3
Estherville U.S.A. 43°24N 94°50W 172 D6
Estill U.S.A. 32°45N 81°15W 178 C8
Estissac France 48°16N 3°48E 71 D10
Eston Canada 51°8N 108°40W 163 C7
Estonia ■ Europe 58°30N 25°30E 84 C3
Estoril Portugal 38°42N 9°23W 89 G1
Estouk Mali 18°14N 1°2E 139 B5
Estreito Brazil 6°32S 47°25W 187 E9
Estreito Maranhão, Brazil 6°34S 47°27W 189 B1
Estrela, Serra da Portugal 40°10N 7°45W 88 E3
Estrella Spain 38°25N 3°35W 89 G7
Estremoz Portugal 38°51N 7°39W 89 G3
Estrondo, Serra do Brazil 7°20S 48°0W 187 E9
Esztergom Hungary 47°47N 18°44E 80 C3
Et Tidra Mauritania 19°45N 16°20W 138 B1
Etah India 27°35N 78°40E 125 F8
Étain France 49°13N 5°38E 71 C12
Étampes France 48°26N 2°10E 71 D9
Etanga Namibia 17°55S 13°0E 144 A1
Étaples France 50°30N 1°39E 71 B8
Etawah India 26°48N 79°6E 125 F8
Etawney L. Canada 57°50N 96°50W 163 B9
Etchojoa Mexico 26°55N 109°38W 180 B3
Ete Nigeria 7°2N 7°28E 139 D6
eThekwini = Durban
S. Africa 29°49S 31°1E 145 C5
Ethel U.S.A. 46°32N 122°46W 170 D4
Ethelbert Canada 51°32N 100°25W 163 C8
Ethiopia ■ Africa 8°0N 40°0E 131 F3
Ethiopian Highlands
Ethiopia 10°0N 37°0E 131 F2
Etili Turkey 39°59N 26°54E 97 G10
Etive, L. U.K. 56°29N 5°10W 65 E3
Etna Italy 37°50N 14°55E 95 E7
Etoile
Dem. Rep. of the Congo 11°33S 27°30E 143 E2
Etoliko Greece 38°26N 21°21E 98 C3
Etolin Strait U.S.A. 60°20N 165°15W 166 C6
Etoloakarnania Greece 38°45N 21°18E 98 C3
Etosha △ Namibia 19°0S 16°0E 144 A2
Etosha Pan Namibia 18°40S 16°30E 144 A2
Etowah U.S.A. 35°20N 84°32W 177 D12
Étréchy France 48°30N 2°12E 71 D9
Etrek Turkmenistan 37°36N 54°46E 129 B7
Étrépagny France 49°18N 1°36E 71 C8
Étretat France 49°42N 0°12E 70 C7
Etropole Bulgaria 42°50N 24°0E 97 D8
Ettelbruck Lux. 49°51N 6°5E 69 E6
Ettlingen Germany 48°56N 8°25E 77 G4
Ettrick Water → U.K. 55°31N 2°55W 65 F6
Etuku
Dem. Rep. of the Congo 3°42S 25°45E 142 C2
Etulia Moldova 45°32N 28°27E 81 E13
Etzná-Tixmucuy = Edzná
Mexico 19°39N 90°19W 181 D6
Eu France 50°3N 1°26E 70 B8
Euboea = Evia Greece 38°30N 24°0E 98 C6
Euchareena Australia 32°57S 149°6E 153 B8
Eucla Australia 31°41S 128°52E 149 F4
Euclid U.S.A. 41°34N 81°32W 174 E3
Euclides da Cunha
Brazil 10°31S 39°1W 189 C3
Eucumbene, L.
Australia 36°2S 148°40E 153 D8
Eudora U.S.A. 33°7N 91°16W 176 E9
Eudunda Australia 34°12S 139°7E 152 C3
Eufaula Ala., U.S.A. 31°54N 85°9W 178 D4
Eufaula Okla., U.S.A. 35°17N 95°35W 176 D7
Eufaula L. U.S.A. 35°18N 95°21W 176 D7
Eugene U.S.A. 44°5N 123°4W 168 D2
Eugowra Australia 33°22S 148°24E 153 B8
Eulo Australia 28°10S 145°3E 151 D4
Eulonia U.S.A. 31°32N 81°26W 178 D8
Eumungerie Australia 31°56S 148°36E 153 A8
Eungella △ Australia 20°57S 148°40E 150 b
Eunice La., U.S.A. 30°30N 92°25W 176 F8
Eunice N. Mex.,
U.S.A. 32°26N 103°10W 169 K12
Eupen Belgium 50°37N 6°3E 69 D6
Euphrates = Furāt, Nahr al →
Asia 31°0N 47°25E 128 D5
Eure □ France 49°10N 1°0E 70 C8
Eure → France 49°18N 1°12E 70 C8
Eure-et-Loir □ France 48°22N 1°30E 70 D8
Eureka Canada 80°0N 85°56W 161 B14
Eureka Calif., U.S.A. 40°47N 124°9W 168 F1
Eureka Kans., U.S.A. 37°49N 96°17W 172 G5
Eureka Mont., U.S.A. 48°53N 115°3W 168 B6
Eureka Nev., U.S.A. 39°31N 115°58W 168 G6
Eureka S.C., U.S.A. 33°42N 81°46W 178 B8
Eureka S. Dak., U.S.A. 45°46N 99°38W 172 C4
Eureka, Mt. Australia 26°35S 121°35E 149 E3
Eureka Sd. Canada 79°0N 85°0W 161 B15
Eurelia Australia 32°33S 138°35E 152 B3
Eurinilla Cr. →
Australia 30°53S 140°11E 152 A4
Euroa Australia 36°44S 145°35E 153 D6
Euroairport ✈ (EAP)
France 47°36N 7°33E 71 E14
Europa, Île Ind. Oc. 22°20S 40°22E 145 B7
Europa, Picos de Spain 43°10N 4°49W 88 B6
Europa, Pt. Gib. 36°3N 5°21W 89 J5
Europe 50°0N 20°0E 58 E10
Europoort Neths. 51°57N 4°10E 69 C4
Euskadi = País Vasco □
Spain 42°50N 2°45W 90 C2
Euskirchen Germany 50°39N 6°48E 76 E2
Eustis U.S.A. 28°51N 81°41W 179 G8
Euston Australia 34°30S 142°46E 152 C5
Eutawville U.S.A. 33°24N 80°21W 178 B9
Eutin Germany 54°8N 10°36E 76 A6
Eutsuk L. Canada 53°20N 126°45W 162 C3
Evale Angola 16°33S 15°44E 144 A2
Evans U.S.A. 40°23N 104°41W 168 F11
Evans, L. Canada 50°50N 77°0W 164 B4
Evans City U.S.A. 40°46N 80°4W 174 F4
Evans Head Australia 29°7S 153°27E 151 D5
Evansburg Canada 53°36N 114°59W 162 C5
Evanston Ill., U.S.A. 42°3N 87°40W 172 D10
Evanston Wyo.,
U.S.A. 41°16N 110°58W 168 F8
Evansville U.S.A. 37°58N 87°35W 172 G10
Évaux-les-Bains France 46°12N 2°29E 71 F9
Evaz Iran 27°46N 53°59E 129 E7
Evciler Afyon, Turkey 38°4N 29°54E 99 C11
Evciler Çanakkale, Turkey 39°47N 26°4E 99 B8
Eveleth U.S.A. 47°28N 92°32W 172 B7
Evensk Russia 62°12N 159°30E 107 C16
Everard, L. Australia 31°30S 135°0E 151 E2
Everard Ranges
Australia 27°5S 132°28E 149 E5
Everest, Mt. Nepal 28°5N 86°58E 125 E12
Everett Ga., U.S.A. 31°24N 81°38W 178 D8
Everett Pa., U.S.A. 40°1N 78°23W 174 F6
Everett Wash., U.S.A. 47°59N 122°12W 170 C4
Everglades, The U.S.A. 25°50N 81°0W 179 K9
Everglades △ U.S.A. 25°30N 81°0W 179 K9
Everglades City U.S.A. 25°52N 81°23W 179 K8
Evergreen Ala., U.S.A. 31°26N 86°57W 177 F11
Evergreen Mont.,
U.S.A. 48°14N 114°17W 168 B6
Everöd Sweden 55°53N 14°5E 63 J8
Everson Australia 36°25S 146°33E 153 D7
Evertsberg Sweden 61°8N 13°58E 62 C7
Evesham U.K. 52°6N 1°56W 67 E6
Evia Greece 38°30N 24°0E 98 C6
Évian-les-Bains France 46°24N 6°35E 71 F13
Evinos → Greece 38°27N 21°40E 98 C3
Évisa France 42°15N 8°48E 73 F12
Evje Norway 58°36N 7°51E 61 G12
Évora Portugal 38°33N 7°57W 89 G3
Évora □ Portugal 38°33N 7°50W 89 G3
Evowghlī Iran 38°43N 45°13E 105 C11
Évreux France 49°3N 1°8E 70 C8
Evritania Greece 39°5N 21°30E 98 B3
Évron France 48°10N 0°24W 70 D6
Evros → Greece 41°40N 26°34E 97 F10
Evrotas → Greece 36°50N 22°40E 98 E4
Évry France 48°38N 2°27E 71 D9
Évvoia = Evia Greece 38°30N 24°0E 98 C6
Ewe, L. U.K. 57°49N 5°38W 65 D3
Ewing U.S.A. 42°16N 98°21W 172 D4
Ewo Congo 0°48S 14°45E 140 E2
Exaltación Bolivia 13°10S 65°20W 186 F5
Excelsior Springs
U.S.A. 39°20N 94°13W 172 F6
Excideuil France 45°20N 1°4E 72 C5
Exe → U.K. 50°41N 3°29W 67 G4
Exeter Canada 43°21N 81°29W 174 C3
Exeter U.K. 50°43N 3°31W 67 G4
Exeter Calif., U.S.A. 36°18N 119°9W 170 J7
Exeter N.H., U.S.A. 42°59N 70°57W 175 D14
Exmoor U.K. 51°12N 3°45W 67 F4
Exmoor △ U.K. 51°8N 3°42W 67 F4
Exmouth Australia 21°54S 114°10E 148 D1
Exmouth U.K. 50°37N 3°25W 67 G4
Exmouth G. Australia 22°15S 114°15E 148 D1
Exmouth Plateau
Ind. Oc. 19°0S 114°0E 156 J3
Expedition △ Australia 25°41S 149°7E 151 D4
Expedition Ra.
Australia 24°30S 149°12E 150 C4
Experiment = Highland Mills
U.S.A. 33°17N 84°17W 178 B5
Extremadura □ Spain 39°30N 6°5W 89 F4
Exuma Sound
Bahamas 24°30N 76°20W 182 B4
Eyasi, L. Tanzania 3°30S 35°0E 142 C4
Eye Pen. U.K. 58°13N 6°10W 65 C2
Eyemouth U.K. 55°52N 2°5W 65 F6
Eygues = Aigues →
France 44°7N 4°43E 73 D8
Eygurande France 45°40N 2°26E 71 G9
Eyjafjallajökull Iceland 63°38N 19°36W 60 E4
Eyjafjörður Iceland 66°15N 18°30W 60 C4
Eyl Somalia 8°0N 49°50E 131 F4
Eymet France 44°40N 0°25E 72 D4
Eymoutiers France 45°40N 1°45E 72 C5
Eynesil Turkey 41°4N 39°9E 105 B8
Eyre (North), L.
Australia 28°30S 137°20E 151 D2
Eyre (South), L.
Australia 29°18S 137°25E 151 D2
Eyre → France 44°39N 1°1W 72 D2
Eyre, L. Australia 29°30S 137°26E 147 D6
Eyre Mts. N.Z. 45°25S 168°25E 155 F3
Eyre Pen. Australia 33°30S 136°17E 152 C1
Eysturoy Færoe Is. 62°13N 6°54W 60 E9
Eyvān = Jūy Zar Iran 33°50N 46°18E 105 F12
Eyvānkī Iran 35°24N 51°56E 129 C6
Ezcaray Spain 42°19N 3°0W 90 C1
Ežerėlis Lithuania 54°53N 23°37E 82 D10
Ezhou China 30°23N 114°50E 117 B10
Ezine Turkey 39°48N 26°20E 99 B8
Ezouza → Cyprus 34°44N 32°27E 101 E11

F

F.Y.R.O.M. = Macedonia ■
Europe 41°53N 21°40E 96 E5
Faaa Tahiti 17°34S 149°35W 155 b
Faaborg Denmark 55°6N 10°15E 63 J4
Faaone Tahiti 17°40S 149°21W 155 b
Fabala Guinea 9°44N 9°5W 138 D3
Fabens U.S.A. 31°30N 106°10W 176 F1
Fabero Spain 42°46N 6°37W 88 C4
Fabius U.S.A. 42°50N 75°59W 175 D9
Fabriano Italy 43°20N 12°54E 93 E9
Făcăeni Romania 44°32N 27°53E 81 F12
Faceville U.S.A. 30°45N 84°38W 178 E5
Fachi Niger 18°6N 11°34E 135 E8
Facundo Argentina 45°18S 69°58W 192 C3
Fada Chad 17°13N 21°34E 135 E10
Fada-n-Gourma
Burkina Faso 12°10N 0°30E 139 C5
Fadd Hungary 46°28N 18°49E 80 D3
Faddeyevskiy, Ostrov
Russia 76°0N 144°0E 107 B15
Fadghāmī Syria 35°53N 40°52E 105 E9
Faenza Italy 44°17N 11°53E 93 D8
Færingehavn =
Kangerluarsoruseq
Greenland 63°45N 51°27W 57 E5
Færoe Is. = Føroyar ☒
Atl. Oc. 62°0N 7°0W 60 F9
Fafa Mali 15°22N 0°48E 139 B5
Fafe Portugal 41°27N 8°11W 88 D2
Fagam Nigeria 11°1N 10°1E 139 C7
Făgăraş Romania 45°48N 24°58E 81 E9
Făgăraş, Munţii
Romania 45°40N 24°40E 81 E9
Fågelfors Sweden 57°12N 15°51E 63 H9
Fågelmara Sweden 56°16N 15°58E 63 H9
Fagerhult Sweden 57°8N 15°40E 63 G9
Fagersta Sweden 60°1N 15°46E 62 D9
Făget Romania 45°52N 22°10E 80 E7
Făget, Munţii Romania 47°40N 23°10E 81 C8
Faggo Nigeria 11°21N 9°57E 139 C6
Fagnano, L. Argentina 54°30S 68°0W 192 D3
Fagnières France 48°58N 4°20E 71 D11
Faguibine, L. Mali 16°45N 4°0W 138 B4
Fahlīān Iran 30°11N 51°28E 129 D6
Fahraj Kermān, Iran 29°0N 59°0E 129 D8
Fahraj Yazd, Iran 31°46N 54°36E 129 D7
Fai Tsi Long Vietnam 21°0N 107°30E 116 G6
Faial Azores 38°34N 28°42W 134 a
Faial Madeira 32°47N 16°53W 100 D3
Faichan Kangri India 35°48N 76°34E 125 B7
Fair Haven N.Y.,
U.S.A. 43°18N 76°42W 175 C8
Fair Haven Vt., U.S.A. 43°36N 73°16W 175 C11
Fair Hd. U.K. 55°14N 6°9W 64 A5
Fair Isle U.K. 59°32N 1°38W 68 B6
Fair Oaks U.S.A. 38°39N 121°16W 170 G5
Fairbanks Alaska,
U.S.A. 64°51N 147°43W 160 E2
Fairbanks Fla., U.S.A. 29°44N 82°16W 178 F7
Fairburn U.S.A. 33°34N 84°35W 178 B5
Fairbury U.S.A. 40°8N 97°11W 172 E5
Fairfax S.C., U.S.A. 32°59N 81°15W 178 C8
Fairfax Vt., U.S.A. 44°40N 73°1W 175 B11
Fairfield Australia 33°53S 150°57E 153 B9
Fairfield Calif., U.S.A. 38°15N 122°3W 170 G4
Fairfield Conn., U.S.A. 41°9N 73°16W 175 E11
Fairfield Idaho, U.S.A. 43°21N 114°44W 168 E6
Fairfield Ill., U.S.A. 38°23N 88°22W 172 F9
Fairfield Iowa, U.S.A. 40°56N 91°57W 172 E8
Fairfield Tex., U.S.A. 31°44N 96°10W 176 F6
Fairford Canada 51°37N 98°38W 163 C9
Fairhope U.S.A. 30°31N 87°54W 177 F11
Fairlie N.Z. 44°5S 170°49E 155 E5
Fairmead U.S.A. 37°5N 120°10W 170 H6
Fairmont Minn., U.S.A. 43°39N 94°28W 172 D6
Fairmont W. Va.,
U.S.A. 39°29N 80°9W 173 F13
Fairmount Calif.,
U.S.A. 34°45N 118°26W 171 L8
Fairmount N.Y., U.S.A. 43°5N 76°12W 175 C8
Fairplay U.S.A. 39°15N 106°2W 168 G10
Fairport U.S.A. 43°6N 77°27W 174 C7
Fairport Harbor U.S.A. 41°45N 81°17W 174 E3
Fairview Canada 56°5N 118°25W 162 B5
Fairview Mont.,
U.S.A. 47°51N 104°3W 168 C11
Fairview Okla., U.S.A. 36°16N 98°29W 176 C5
Fairweather, Mt.
U.S.A. 58°55N 137°32W 162 B1
Faisalabad Pakistan 31°30N 73°5E 124 D5
Faith U.S.A. 45°2N 102°2W 172 C2
Faizabad India 26°45N 82°10E 125 F10
Faizpur India 21°14N 75°49E 126 D2
Fajardo Puerto Rico 18°20N 65°39W 183 d
Fajr, W. → Si. Arabia 29°10N 38°10E 128 D3
Fakenham U.K. 52°51N 0°51E 66 E8
Fåker Sweden 63°0N 14°34E 62 A8
Fakfak Indonesia 2°55S 132°18E 119 E8
Fakiya Bulgaria 42°10N 27°6E 97 D11
Fakobli Ivory C. 7°23N 7°23W 138 D3
Fakse Denmark 55°15N 12°8E 63 J6
Fakse Bugt Denmark 55°11N 12°15E 63 J6
Fakse Ladeplads Denmark 55°11N 12°9E 63 J6
Faku China 42°32N 123°21E 115 C12
Falaba S. Leone 9°54N 11°22W 138 D2
Falaise France 48°54N 0°12W 70 D6
Falakro Oros Greece 41°15N 23°58E 96 E7
Falam Burma 23°0N 93°45E 123 H18
Fălciu Romania 46°17N 28°7E 81 D13
Falcó, C. des Spain 38°50N 1°23E 100 C7
Falcon, C. Algeria 35°50N 0°50W 136 A3
Falcón, Presa Mexico 26°35N 99°10W 181 B5
Falcon Lake Canada 49°42N 95°15W 163 D9
Falcon Res. U.S.A. 26°34N 99°10W 176 H5
Falconara Marittima
Italy 43°37N 13°24E 93 E10
Falcone, C. del Italy 40°58N 8°12E 94 B1
Falconer U.S.A. 42°7N 79°12W 174 D5
Faléa Mali 12°16N 11°17W 138 C2
Falémé → Senegal 14°46N 12°14W 138 C2
Falerum Sweden 58°8N 16°13E 63 F10
Faleshty = Făleşti
Moldova 47°32N 27°44E 81 C12
Făleşti Moldova 47°32N 27°44E 81 C12
Falfurrias U.S.A. 27°14N 98°9W 176 H5
Falher Canada 55°44N 117°15W 162 B5
Faliraki Greece 36°22N 28°12E 101 C10
Falkenberg Germany 51°35N 13°14E 76 D9
Falkenberg Sweden 56°54N 12°30E 63 H6
Falkensee Germany 52°34N 13°4E 76 C9
Falkirk U.K. 56°0N 3°47W 65 F5
Falkirk □ U.K. 55°58N 3°49W 65 F5
Falkland U.K. 56°16N 3°12W 65 E5
Falkland, East, I.
Falk. Is. 51°40S 58°30W 192 D5
Falkland, West, I.
Falk. Is. 51°40S 60°0W 192 D5
Falkland Is. ☒ Atl. Oc. 51°30S 59°0W 192 D5
Falkland Plateau Atl. Oc. 51°0S 50°0W 56 M7
Falkland Ridge Atl. Oc. 49°20S 40°0W 56 L8
Falkland Sd. Falk. Is. 52°0S 60°0W 192 D5
Falkonera Greece 36°50N 23°52E 98 E5
Falköping Sweden 58°12N 13°33E 63 F7
Fall River U.S.A. 41°43N 71°10W 175 E13
Fallbrook U.S.A. 33°23N 117°15W 171 M9
Fallon U.S.A. 39°28N 118°47W 168 G4
Falls City U.S.A. 40°3N 95°36W 172 E6
Falls Creek U.S.A. 41°9N 78°48W 174 E6
Falmouth Jamaica 18°30N 77°40W 182 a
Falmouth U.K. 50°9N 5°5W 67 G2
Falmouth U.S.A. 41°33N 70°37W 175 E14
Falsa, Pta. Mexico 27°51N 115°3W 180 B1
False B. S. Africa 34°15S 18°40E 144 D2
False Divi Pt. India 15°43N 80°50E 127 G5
False Pt. India 20°18N 86°48E 126 D8
Falso, C. Honduras 15°12N 83°21W 182 C3
Falster Denmark 54°45N 11°55E 63 K5
Fălticeni Romania 47°21N 26°20E 81 C11
Falun Sweden 60°37N 15°37E 62 D9
Famagusta Cyprus 35°8N 33°55E 101 D12
Famagusta Bay Cyprus 35°15N 34°0E 101 D13
Famatina, Sierra de
Argentina 27°30S 68°0W 190 B2
Famenin Iran 35°5N 48°58E 105 E13
Family L. Canada 51°54N 95°27W 163 C9
Famoso U.S.A. 35°37N 119°12W 171 K7
Fan Xian China 35°55N 115°38E 114 G8
Fana Mali 13°0N 6°56W 138 C3
Fanad Hd. Ireland 55°17N 7°38W 64 A4
Fanari Greece 39°24N 21°47E 98 B3
Fánes-Sénnes-Braies ⌂
Italy 46°38N 12°4E 93 B9
Fang Thailand 19°55N 99°13E 120 C2
Fang Xian China 32°3N 110°40E 117 A8
Fangchang China 31°5N 118°4E 117 B12
Fangcheng China 33°18N 112°59E 114 H7
Fangchenggang China 21°42N 108°21E 116 G7
Fangliao Taiwan 22°22N 120°38E 117 F13
Fangshan Beijing, China 39°41N 116°0E 114 E9
Fangshan Shanxi, China 38°3N 111°25E 114 E6
Fangzi China 36°33N 119°10E 115 F10
Fani i Madh → Albania 41°56N 20°16E 96 E4
Fanjiatun China 43°40N 125°15E 115 C13
Fanling China 22°30N 114°8E 111 a
Fannich, L. U.K. 57°38N 4°59W 65 D4
Fannūj Iran 26°35N 59°38E 129 E8
Fanø Denmark 55°25N 8°25E 63 J2
Fano Italy 43°50N 13°1E 93 E10
Fanshi China 39°12N 113°20E 114 E7
Fao = Al Fāw Iraq 30°0N 48°30E 129 D6
Faqirwali Pakistan 29°27N 73°0E 124 E5
Fâqûs Egypt 30°44N 31°47E 137 E7
Far East = Dalnevostochnyy □
Russia 67°0N 140°0E 107 C14
Far East Asia 40°0N 130°0E 102 E14
Fara in Sabina Italy 42°12N 12°43E 93 F9
Faradje
Dem. Rep. of the Congo 3°50N 29°45E 142 B2
Farafangana Madag. 22°49S 47°50E 141 J9
Farafenni Gambia 13°34N 15°36W 138 C1
Farâfra, El Wâhât el
Egypt 27°15N 28°20E 137 B2
Farāh Afghan. 32°20N 62°7E 122 C3
Farāh □ Afghan. 32°25N 62°10E 122 C3
Faraid, Gebel Egypt 23°33N 35°19E 137 C4
Farako Ivory C. 10°45N 6°50W 138 D4
Faramana Burkina Faso 11°56N 4°45W 138 C4
Faranah Guinea 10°3N 10°45W 138 C2
Farap Turkmenistan 39°9N 63°36E 108 E6
Farasān, Jazā'ir
Si. Arabia 16°45N 41°55E 131 D3
Farasan Is. = Farasān, Jazā'ir
Si. Arabia 16°45N 41°55E 131 D3
Fardes → Spain 37°35N 3°0W 89 H7
Fareham U.K. 50°51N 1°11W 67 G6
Farewell, C. N.Z. 40°29S 172°43E 155 A7
Farewell C. = Nunap Isua
Greenland 59°48N 43°55W 57 F6
Farewell Spit N.Z. 40°35S 173°0E 155 A8
Färgelanda Sweden 58°34N 12°0E 63 F5
Farghona Uzbekistan 40°23N 71°19E 109 D8
Farghona □ Uzbekistan 40°30N 71°15E 109 D8
Farghona Vodiysi Asia 40°46N 71°30E 109 D8
Fargo Ga., U.S.A. 30°41N 82°34W 178 E7
Fargo N. Dak., U.S.A. 46°53N 96°48W 172 B5
Fār'iah, W. al →
West Bank 32°12N 35°27E 130 C4
Faribault U.S.A. 44°18N 93°16W 172 C7
Faridabad India 28°26N 77°19E 124 E6
Faridkot India 30°44N 74°45E 124 D6
Faridpur Bangla. 23°15N 89°55E 125 H13
Faridpur India 28°13N 79°33E 125 E8
Färila Sweden 61°48N 15°50E 62 C9
Farim Guinea-Biss. 12°27N 15°9W 138 C1
Farīmān Iran 35°40N 59°49E 129 C8
Farinha → Brazil 6°51S 47°30W 189 B1
Fariones, Pta.
Canary Is. 29°13N 13°28W 100 E6
Fâriskûr Egypt 31°20N 31°43E 137 E7
Färjestaden Sweden 56°39N 16°27E 63 H10
Farkadona Greece 39°36N 22°4E 98 B4
Farleigh Australia 21°4S 149°8E 150 b
Farmakonisi Greece 37°17N 27°5E 99 D9
Farmerville U.S.A. 32°47N 92°24W 176 E8

Farmingdale *U.S.A.* 40°12N 74°10W **175** F10
Farmington *Canada* 55°54N 120°30W **162** B4
Farmington *Calif.,*
U.S.A. 37°55N 120°59W **170** H6
Farmington *Ga., U.S.A.* 33°47N 83°26W **178** B6
Farmington *Maine,*
U.S.A. 44°40N 70°9W **173** C18
Farmington *Mo.,*
U.S.A. 37°47N 90°25W **172** G8
Farmington *N.H.,*
U.S.A. 43°24N 71°4W **175** C13
Farmington *N. Mex.,*
U.S.A. 36°44N 108°12W **169** H9
Farmington *Utah.*
U.S.A. 40°59N 111°53W **168** F8
Farmington →
U.S.A. 41°51N 72°38W **175** E12
Farmville *U.S.A.* 37°18N 78°24W **173** G14
Färnäs *Sweden* 61°0N 14°39E **62** D8
Farne Is. *U.K.* 55°38N 1°37W **66** B6
Färnebofjärden △
Sweden 60°10N 16°48E **62** D10
Farnham *Canada* 45°17N 72°59W **175** A12
Farnham, Mt. *Canada* 50°29N 116°30W **162** C5
Faro *Brazil* 2°10S 56°39W **187** D7
Faro *Canada* 62°11N 133°22W **160** E5
Faro *Portugal* 37°2N 7°55W **89** H3
Fårö *Sweden* 57°55N 19°5E **63** G13
Faro □ *Portugal* 37°12N 8°10W **89** H2
Faro ✈ (FAO) *Portugal* 37°2N 7°57W **89** H3
Fårösund *Sweden* 57°52N 19°2E **63** G13
Farquhar, C. *Australia* 23°50S 113°36E **149** D1
Farquhar Is. *Seychelles* 11°0S 52°0E **146** F4
Farrars Cr. →
Australia 25°35S 140°43E **150** D3
Farrāshband *Iran* 28°57N 52°5E **129** D7
Farrell *U.S.A.* 41°13N 80°30W **174** E4
Farrell Flat *Australia* 33°48S 138°48E **152** B3
Farrokhī *Iran* 33°50N 59°31E **129** C8
Farruch, C. = Ferrutx, C. de
Spain 39°47N 3°21E **100** B10
Farrukhabad *India* 27°24N 79°34E **126** A4
Färs □ *Iran* 29°30N 55°0E **129** D7
Farsala *Greece* 39°17N 22°23E **98** B4
Fārsī *Iran* 27°58N 50°11E **129** E6
Farso *Denmark* 56°46N 9°19E **63** H3
Farson *U.S.A.* 42°7N 109°26W **168** E9
Farsund *Norway* 58°5N 6°55E **61** G12
Fartak, Rās *os. Arabia* 28°5N 34°34E **128** D2
Fartak, Ra's *Yemen* 15°38N 52°15E **131** D5
Fârtăneşti *Romania* 45°49N 27°59E **81** E12
Fartura, Serra da
Brazil 26°21S 52°52W **191** B5
Faru *Nigeria* 12°48N 6°12E **139** C6
Fārūj *Iran* 37°14N 58°14E **129** B8
Fårup *Denmark* 56°33N 9°51E **63** H3
Farvel, Kap = Nunap Isua
Greenland 59°48N 43°55W **57** F6
Farwell *U.S.A.* 34°23N 103°2W **176** D3
Fāryāb □ *Afghan.* 36°0N 65°0E **109** E7
Fasā *Iran* 29°0N 53°39E **129** D7
Fasano *Italy* 40°50N 17°22E **95** B10
Fassa *Mali* 13°26N 8°15W **138** C3
Fastiv *Ukraine* 50°7N 29°57E **75** C15
Fastnet Rock *Ireland* 51°22N 9°37W **64** E2
Fastov = Fastiv *Ukraine* 50°7N 29°57E **75** C15
Fatagartuting, Tanjung
Indonesia 2°46S 131°57E **119** E8
Fatehabad *Haryana,*
India 29°31N 75°27E **124** E6
Fatehabad *Ut. P., India* 27°1N 78°19E **124** F8
Fatehgarh *India* 27°25N 79°35E **124** F8
Fatehpur *Bihar, India* 24°38N 85°14E **125** G11
Fatehpur *Raj., India* 28°0N 74°40E **124** F6
Fatehpur *Ut. P., India* 25°56N 81°13E **125** F9
Fatehpur *Ut. P., India* 27°10N 81°13E **125** F9
Fatehpur Sikri *India* 27°6N 77°40E **124** F6
Fatesh *Russia* 52°8N 35°57E **85** F8
Fathom Five △ *Canada* 45°17N 81°40W **174** A3
Fatick *Senegal* 14°19N 16°27W **138** C1
Fatick □ *Senegal* 14°15N 16°30W **138** C1
Fatima *Canada* 47°24N 61°53W **165** C7
Fátima *Portugal* 39°37N 8°39W **89** F2
Fatoya *Guinea* 11°37N 9°10W **138** C3
Fatsa *Turkey* 41°2N 37°31E **104** B7
Faucille, Col de la *France* 46°22N 6°2E **71** F13
Faulkton *U.S.A.* 45°2N 99°8W **172** C4
Faulquemont *France* 49°3N 6°36E **71** C13
Faure I. *Australia* 25°52S 113°50E **149** E1
Fǎurei *Romania* 45°6N 27°19E **81** E12
Fauresmith *S. Africa* 29°44S 25°17E **144** C4
Fauske *Norway* 67°17N 15°25E **60** C16
Favara *Italy* 37°19N 13°39E **94** E6
Favǎritx, C. de *Spain* 40°0N 4°15E **100** B11
Faverges *France* 45°45N 6°17E **73** C10
Favignana *Italy* 37°56N 12°20E **94** E5
Favignana, I. *Italy* 37°56N 12°19E **94** E5
Fawcett, Pt. *Australia* 11°46S 130°2E **148** B5
Fawn → *Canada* 55°20N 87°35W **164** A2
Fawnskin *U.S.A.* 34°16N 116°56W **171** L10
Faxaflói *Iceland* 64°29N 23°0W **60** D2
Faxälven → *Sweden* 63°13N 17°13E **62** A10
Faya-Largeau *Chad* 17°58N 19°6E **135** E9
Fayd *Si. Arabia* 27°1N 42°52E **128** E4
Fayence *France* 43°38N 6°42E **73** E10
Fayette *Ala., U.S.A.* 33°41N 87°50W **177** E11
Fayette *Mo., U.S.A.* 39°9N 92°41W **172** F7
Fayette *N.Y., U.S.A.* 42°48N 76°48W **175** D8
Fayetteville *Ark., U.S.A.* 36°4N 94°10W **176** C7
Fayetteville *Ga., U.S.A.* 33°27N 84°27W **178** B5
Fayetteville *N.C.,*
U.S.A. 35°3N 78°53W **177** D15
Fayetteville *N.Y., U.S.A.* 43°1N 76°0W **175** C9
Fayetteville *Tenn.,*
U.S.A. 35°9N 86°34W **177** D11
Fayied *Egypt* 30°18N 32°16E **137** E8
Faylakah *Kuwait* 29°27N 48°20E **129** D6
Fayón *Spain* 41°15N 0°20E **90** D5
Fazao-Malfakassa △
Togo 8°45N 0°50E **139** D5
Fazilka *India* 30°27N 74°2E **124** D6
Fazilpur *Pakistan* 29°18N 70°29E **124** E5
Fdérik *Mauritania* 22°40N 12°45W **134** D3
Feakle *Ireland* 52°56N 8°40W **64** D3
Feale → *Ireland* 52°27N 9°37W **64** D2
Fear, C. *U.S.A.* 33°50N 77°58W **177** E16
Feather → *U.S.A.* 38°47N 121°36W **170** G4
Feather Falls *U.S.A.* 39°36N 121°16W **170** F5
Featherston *N.Z.* 41°6S 175°20E **154** H4
Featherstone *Zimbabwe* 18°42S 30°55E **143** F3
Fécamp *France* 49°45N 0°22E **70** C7

Fedala = Mohammedia
Morocco 33°44N 7°21W **136** B2
Federación *Argentina* 31°0S 57°55W **190** C4
Féderal *Argentina* 30°57S 58°48W **190** C4
Federal Capital Terr. □
Nigeria 9°0N 7°10E **139** D6
Federal Way *U.S.A.* 47°18N 122°19W **170** C4
Fedeshküh *Iran* 28°49N 53°50E **129** D7
Fehérgyarmat *Hungary* 47°58N 22°30E **80** C7
Fehmarn *Germany* 54°27N 11°7E **76** A7
Fehmarn Belt *Europe* 54°35N 11°20E **63** K5
Fehmarn Belt = Fehmarn Belt
Europe 54°35N 11°20E **63** K5
Fei Xian *China* 35°18N 117°59E **115** C9
Feicheng *China* 36°14N 116°45E **114** F9
Feidong *China* 32°0N 117°35E **117** B11
Feijó *Brazil* 8°9S 70°21W **188** B3
Feilding *N.Z.* 40°13S 175°35E **154** G4
Feira de Santana
Brazil 12°15S 38°57W **189** C3
Feixi *China* 31°43N 117°59E **117** B11
Feixiang *China* 36°30N 114°45E **114** F8
Fejaj, Chott el *Tunisia* 33°52N 9°14E **136** B5
Fejér □ *Hungary* 47°9N 18°30E **80** C3
Fejo *Denmark* 54°55N 11°30E **63** K5
Feke *Turkey* 37°48N 35°56E **104** D6
Felanitx *Spain* 39°28N 3°9E **100** B10
Felda *Malaysia* 26°34N 81°28W **179** J8
Feldbach *Austria* 46°57N 15°52E **78** E8
Feldberg *Baden-W.,*
Germany 47°52N 8°0E **77** H3
Feldberg *Mecklenburg-Vorpommern,*
Germany 53°20N 13°25E **76** B9
Feldkirch *Austria* 47°15N 9°37E **78** D2
Feldkirchen *Austria* 46°44N 14°6E **78** E7
Félicité *Seychelles* 4°19S 55°52E **141** b
Felipe Carrillo Puerto
Mexico 19°38N 88°3W **181** D7
Felixburg *Zimbabwe* 19°29S 30°51E **145** A5
Felixlândia *Brazil* 18°47S 44°55W **189** D2
Felixstowe *U.K.* 51°58N 1°23E **67** F9
Felletin *France* 45°53N 2°11E **72** C6
Fellingsbro *Sweden* 59°26N 15°37E **62** E9
Fellsmere *U.S.A.* 27°46N 80°36W **179** H9
Felton *U.S.A.* 37°3N 122°4W **170** H4
Feltre *Italy* 46°1N 11°54E **93** B8
Femer Bælt = Fehmarn Bælt
Europe 54°35N 11°20E **63** K5
Femø *Denmark* 54°58N 11°33E **63** K5
Femunden *Norway* 62°10N 11°53E **60** E14
Femundsmarka △
Norway 62°18N 12°6E **60** E15
Fen He → *China* 35°36N 110°42E **114** G6
Fene *Spain* 43°27N 8°9W **88** B2
Fenelon Falls *Canada* 44°32N 78°45W **174** B6
Fener Burnu *Turkey* 36°58N 27°18E **99** E9
Feng Xian *Jiangsu,*
China 34°43N 116°35E **114** G9
Feng Xian *Shaanxi,*
China 33°54N 106°40E **114** H4
Fengari *Greece* 40°25N 25°32E **97** F9
Fengcheng *Jiangxi,*
China 28°12N 115°48E **117** C10
Fengcheng *Liaoning,*
China 40°28N 124°5E **115** D13
Fengdu *China* 29°55N 107°48E **116** C6
Fengfeng *China* 36°28N 114°8E **114** F8
Fenggang *China* 27°57N 107°47E **116** D6
Fenghua *China* 29°40N 121°25E **117** C13
Fenghuang *China* 27°57N 109°29E **116** D7
Fengjie *China* 31°3N 109°31E **116** B7
Fengkai *China* 23°24N 111°30E **117** F8
Fengkang *Taiwan* 22°12N 120°41E **117** F13
Fengle *China* 31°29N 112°29E **117** B9
Fenglin *Taiwan* 23°45N 121°26E **117** F13
Fengning *China* 41°10N 116°33E **114** D9
Fengqing *China* 24°38N 99°55E **116** E2
Fengqiu *China* 35°2N 114°25E **114** G8
Fengrun *China* 39°48N 118°8E **115** E10
Fengshan *Guangxi Zhuangzu,*
China 24°39N 109°15E **116** E7
Fengshan *Guangxi Zhuangzu,*
China 24°31N 107°3E **116** E6
Fengshan *Taiwan* 22°38N 120°21E **117** F13
Fengshun *China* 23°46N 116°10E **117** F11
Fengtai *China* 32°50N 116°40E **117** A11
Fengtongzhai △ *China* 30°32N 102°54E **116** B4
Fengxiang *China* 34°29N 107°25E **114** G4
Fengxin *China* 28°41N 115°18E **117** C10
Fengyang *China* 32°51N 117°29E **117** A11
Fengyi *China* 25°37N 100°20E **116** E3
Fengzhen *China* 40°25N 113°2E **114** D7
Feno, C. de *France* 41°58N 8°33E **73** G12
Fenoarivo Atsinanana
Madag. 17°22S 49°25E **141** H9
Fens, The *U.K.* 52°38N 0°2W **66** E7
Fensmark *Denmark* 55°17N 11°48E **63** J5
Fenton *U.S.A.* 42°48N 83°42W **173** D12
Fenxi *China* 36°40N 111°31E **114** F6
Fenyang *China* 37°18N 111°48E **114** F6
Fenyi *China* 27°45N 114°47E **117** D10
Feodosiya *Ukraine* 45°2N 35°16E **85** K8
Fer, C. de *Algeria* 37°3N 7°10E **136** A6
Ferbane *Ireland* 53°16N 7°50W **64** C4
Ferdows *Iran* 33°58N 58°2E **129** C8
Fère-Champenoise
France 48°45N 3°59E **71** D10
Fère-en-Tardenois
France 49°10N 3°30E **71** C10
Ferentino *Italy* 41°42N 13°15E **93** G10
Feres *Greece* 40°53N 26°10E **97** F10
Ferfer *Somalia* 5°4N 45°9E **131** F4
Fergana = Farghona
Uzbekistan 40°23N 71°19E **109** D8
Fergana Range *Asia* 41°0N 73°0E **109** D8
Fergus *Canada* 43°43N 80°24W **174** C4
Fergus Falls *U.S.A.* 46°17N 96°4W **172** B5
Fériana *Tunisia* 34°59N 8°33E **136** B5
Feričanci *Croatia* 45°32N 18°0E **80** E2
Ferihegy, Budapest ✈ (BUD)
Hungary 47°26N 19°14E **80** C5
Ferizaj *Kosovo* 42°23N 21°10E **96** D5
Ferkane *Algeria* 34°37N 7°26E **136** B6
Ferkéssédougou *Ivory C.* 9°35N 5°6W **138** D3
Ferlach *Austria* 46°32N 14°18E **78** E7
Ferland *Canada* 50°19N 88°27W **164** B2
Ferlo, Vallée du
Senegal 15°15N 14°14W **138** B2

Ferlo-Nord □ *Senegal* 15°43N 14°0W **138** B2
Ferlo-Sud □ *Senegal* 15°43N 14°0W **138** B2
Fermanagh □ *U.K.* 54°21N 7°40W **64** B4
Fermo *Italy* 43°9N 13°43E **93** E10
Fermont *Canada* 52°47N 67°5W **165** B6
Fermoselle *Spain* 41°19N 6°27W **88** D4
Fermoy *Ireland* 52°9N 8°16W **64** D3
Fernán Núñez *Spain* 37°40N 4°44W **89** H6
Fernández *Argentina* 27°55S 63°50W **190** B3
Fernandina Beach
U.S.A. 30°40N 81°27W **178** E8
Fernando de Noronha
Brazil 4°0S 33°10W **187** D12
Fernando Póo = Bioko
Eq. Guin. 3°30N 8°40E **139** E6
Ferndale *Canada* 44°58N 81°17W **174** B3
Ferndale *U.S.A.* 48°51N 122°36W **170** B4
Fernie *Canada* 49°30N 115°5W **162** D5
Fernlees *Australia* 23°51S 148°7E **154** C4
Fernley *U.S.A.* 39°36N 119°15W **168** G4
Fernwood *U.S.A.* 43°16N 73°38W **175** C11
Feroke *India* 11°9N 75°46E **127** J2
Ferozepore = Firozpur
India 30°55N 74°40E **124** D6
Ferrandina *Italy* 40°29N 16°27E **95** B9
Ferrara *Italy* 44°50N 11°35E **93** D8
Ferrato, C. *Italy* 39°18N 9°38E **94** C2
Ferreira do Alentejo
Portugal 38°4N 8°6W **89** G2
Ferreñafe *Peru* 6°42S 79°50W **188** B2
Ferrerías *Spain* 39°59N 4°1E **100** B11
Ferret, C. *France* 44°38N 1°15W **72** D2
Ferrette *France* 47°30N 7°20E **71** E14
Ferriday *U.S.A.* 31°38N 91°33W **176** F9
Ferrières *France* 44°40N 9°30E **92** D6
Ferro, Capo *Italy* 41°9N 9°31E **94** A2
Ferrol *Spain* 43°29N 8°15W **88** B2
Ferrol, Pen. de *Peru* 9°10S 78°35W **188** B2
Ferron *U.S.A.* 39°5N 111°8W **168** G8
Ferros *Brazil* 19°14S 43°2W **189** D2
Ferrutx, C. de *Spain* 39°47N 3°21E **100** B10
Ferry Pass *U.S.A.* 30°31N 87°13W **179** E2
Ferryland *Canada* 47°2N 52°53W **165** C9
Fertile *U.S.A.* 47°32N 96°17W **172** B5
Fertő-Hanság △
Hungary 47°25N 16°50E **80** C1
Fertőszentmiklós
Hungary 47°35N 16°53E **80** C1
Fès *Morocco* 34°0N 5°0W **136** B3
Fès □ *Morocco* 34°1N 5°0W **136** B3
Fessenden *U.S.A.* 47°39N 99°38W **172** B4
Festus *U.S.A.* 38°13N 90°24W **172** F8
Feteşti *Romania* 44°22N 27°51E **81** F12
Fethiye *Turkey* 36°36N 29°6E **99** E11
Fethiye Körfezi *Turkey* 36°40N 28°50E **99** E10
Fetlar *U.K.* 60°36N 0°52W **65** A8
Feuilles → *Canada* 58°47N 70°4W **161** F17
Feurs *France* 45°45N 4°13E **73** C8
Feyzābād *Afghan.* 37°7N 70°33E **109** E8
Fez = Fès *Morocco* 34°0N 5°0W **136** B3
Fezzan *Libya* 27°0N 13°0E **135** C8
Fiambalá *Argentina* 27°45S 67°37W **190** B2
Fianarantsoa *Madag.* 21°26S 47°5E **141** J9
Fichtelgebirge *Germany* 50°2N 11°55E **77** E7
Fichtelgebirge □ *Germany* 50°8N 12°0E **77** E8
Ficksburg *S. Africa* 28°51S 27°53E **145** C4
Fidenza *Italy* 44°52N 10°3E **92** D7
Fiditi *Nigeria* 7°45N 3°53E **139** D5
Field → *Australia* 23°48S 138°0E **150** C2
Field I. *Australia* 12°5S 132°23E **148** B5
Fieni *Romania* 45°8N 25°25E **81** E10
Fier *Albania* 40°43N 19°33E **96** F3
Fierzë *Albania* 42°15N 20°1E **96** D4
Fife □ *U.K.* 56°16N 3°1W **65** E5
Fife Ness *U.K.* 56°17N 2°35W **65** E6
Fifth Cataract *Sudan* 18°22N 33°50E **137** D3
Figari *France* 41°29N 9°7E **73** G12
Figeac *France* 44°37N 2°2E **72** D6
Figeholm *Sweden* 57°22N 16°33E **63** G10
Figline Valdarno *Italy* 43°37N 11°28E **93** E8
Figtree *Zimbabwe* 20°22S 28°20E **143** G2
Figueira Castelo Rodrigo
Portugal 40°57N 6°58W **88** E4
Figueira da Foz *Portugal* 40°7N 8°54W **88** E2
Figueiró dos Vinhos
Portugal 39°55N 8°16W **88** F2
Figueres *Spain* 42°18N 2°58E **90** C7
Figuig *Morocco* 32°5N 1°11W **136** B3
Fiji ■ *Pac. Oc.* 17°20S 179°0E **154** a
Fika *Nigeria* 11°15N 11°13E **139** C7
Filabres, Sierra de los
Spain 37°13N 2°20W **89** H8
Filabusi *Zimbabwe* 20°34S 29°20E **145** B4
Filadelfia *Bolivia* 11°20S 68°46W **188** C4
Filadélfia *Brazil* 7°21S 47°30W **189** B1
Filadelfia *Italy* 38°47N 16°17E **95** D9
Filadelfia *Paraguay* 22°21S 60°2W **190** A3
Fil'akovo *Slovak Rep.* 48°17N 19°50E **79** C12
Filchner Ice Shelf
Antarctica 79°0S 40°0W **55** D1
Filey *U.K.* 54°12N 0°18W **66** C7
Filey B. *U.K.* 54°12N 0°15W **66** C7
Filfla *Malta* 35°47N 14°24E **101** D1
Filiaşi *Romania* 44°33N 23°31E **81** F8
Filiates *Greece* 39°38N 20°16E **98** B2
Filiatra *Greece* 37°9N 21°35E **98** D3
Filicudi *Italy* 38°35N 14°33E **95** D7
Filingué *Niger* 14°21N 3°22E **139** C5
Filiouri → Lissós →
Greece 41°15N 25°40E **97** E9
Filipada *Greece* 39°12N 20°58E **98** B3
Filipstad *Sweden* 59°43N 14°9E **62** E8
Filitosa *France* 41°45N 8°52E **73** G12
Fillmore *Calif., U.S.A.* 34°24N 118°55W **171** L8
Fillmore *Utah, U.S.A.* 38°58N 112°20W **168** G7
Filotio *Greece* 37°3N 25°30E **97** D7
Filottrano *Italy* 43°26N 13°21E **93** E10
Filyos Çayı → *Turkey* 41°35N 32°10E **104** B5
Fin *Mali* 13°15N 8°46W **138** C3
Finale Emília *Italy* 44°50N 11°18E **93** D8
Finale Lígure *Italy* 44°10N 8°20E **92** D5
Finch *Canada* 45°11N 75°7W **175** A9
Finch Hatton *Australia* 20°25S 148°39E **150** C4
Findhorn → *U.K.* 57°38N 3°38W **65** D5
Fındıklı *Turkey* 41°16N 41°9E **105** B9
Findlay *U.S.A.* 41°2N 83°39W **173** E12

Fine *U.S.A.* 44°14N 75°8W **175** B9
Finger L. *Canada* 53°33N 93°30W **164** B1
Finger Lakes *U.S.A.* 42°40N 76°30W **175** D8
Fingoè *Mozam.* 15°55S 31°50E **143** F3
Finike *Turkey* 36°21N 30°10E **99** E12
Finike Körfezi *Turkey* 36°17N 30°16E **99** E12
Finiq *Albania* 39°54N 20°3E **96** G4
Finistère □ *France* 48°20N 4°0W **70** D3
Finisterre = Fisterra
Spain 42°54N 9°16W **88** C1
Finisterre, C. = Fisterra, C.
Spain 42°50N 9°19W **88** C1
Finke *Australia* 25°34S 134°35E **150** D1
Finke Gorge △
Australia 24°8S 132°49E **148** D5
Finland ■ *Europe* 63°0N 27°0E **60** E22
Finland, G. of *Europe* 60°0N 26°0E **84** C3
Finlay → *Canada* 57°0N 125°10W **162** B3
Finley *Australia* 35°38S 145°35E **153** C6
Finley *U.S.A.* 47°31N 97°50W **172** B5
Finn → *Ireland* 54°51N 7°28W **64** B4
Finnerödja *Sweden* 58°57N 14°24E **63** F8
Finnigan, Mt.
Australia 15°49S 145°17E **150** B4
Finniss, C. *Australia* 33°8S 134°51E **151** E1
Finnmark *Norway* 69°37N 23°57E **60** B20
Finnsnes *Norway* 69°14N 18°0E **60** B18
Finspäng *Sweden* 58°43N 15°47E **63** F9
Finsteraarhorn *Switz.* 46°31N 8°10E **77** J4
Finsterwalde *Germany* 51°37N 13°42E **76** D9
Fiora → *Italy* 42°20N 11°34E **93** F8
Fiordland △ *N.Z.* 45°46S 167°0E **155** F2
Fiorenzuola d'Arda *Italy* 44°56N 9°55E **92** D6
Fīq *Syria* 32°46N 35°41E **130** C4
Firat = Furāt, Nahr al →
Asia 31°0N 47°25E **128** D5
Fire Island △ *U.S.A.* 40°38N 73°8W **175** F11
Firebag → *Canada* 57°45N 111°21W **163** B6
Firebaugh *U.S.A.* 36°52N 120°27W **170** J6
Firedrake L. *Canada* 61°25N 104°30W **163** A8
Firenze *Italy* 43°46N 11°15E **93** E8
Firenze Amerigo Vespucci ✈
(FLR) *Italy* 43°49N 11°13E **93** E8
Firenze Pisa ✈ (PSA)
Italy 43°40N 10°22E **92** E7
Firenzuola *Italy* 44°7N 11°23E **93** D8
Firk, Sha'ib → *Iraq* 30°59N 44°34E **128** D5
Firmi *France* 44°33N 2°19E **72** D6
Firminy *France* 45°23N 4°18E **73** C8
Firozabad *India* 27°10N 78°25E **125** F8
Firozpur *India* 30°55N 74°40E **124** D6
Firozpur-Jhirka *India* 27°48N 76°57E **124** F7
Fīrūzābād *Iran* 28°52N 52°35E **129** D7
Fīrūzkūh *Iran* 35°50N 52°50E **129** C7
Firvale *Canada* 52°27N 126°13W **162** C3
Fish → *Namibia* 28°7S 17°10E **144** C2
Fish → *S. Africa* 31°30S 20°16E **144** D3
Fish River Canyon
Namibia 27°40S 17°35E **144** C2
Fisheating Cr. →
U.S.A. 26°57N 81°7W **179** J8
Fisher B. *Canada* 51°35N 97°13W **163** C9
Fishers I. *U.S.A.* 41°15N 72°0W **175** E13
Fishguard *U.K.* 52°0N 4°58W **67** E3
Fishing L. *Canada* 52°10N 95°24W **163** C9
Fishkill *U.S.A.* 41°32N 73°54W **175** E11
Fiskardo *Greece* 38°30N 20°37E **98** C2
Fiskenæsset = Qeqertarsuatsiaat
Greenland 63°5N 50°45W **57** E5
Fismes *France* 49°20N 3°40E **71** C10
Fisterra *Spain* 42°54N 9°16W **88** C1
Fisterra, C. *Spain* 42°50N 9°19W **88** C1
Fitchburg *Mass.,*
U.S.A. 42°35N 71°48W **175** D13
Fitchburg *Wis., U.S.A.* 42°58N 89°28W **172** D9
Fitz Roy *Argentina* 47°0S 67°0W **192** C3
Fitz Roy, Cerro
Argentina 49°17S 73°5W **192** C2
Fitzgerald *Canada* 59°51N 111°36W **162** B6
Fitzgerald *U.S.A.* 31°43N 83°15W **178** D6
Fitzgerald River △
Australia 33°53S 119°55E **149** F3
Fitzmaurice →
Australia 14°45S 130°5E **148** B5
Fitzroy → *Queens.,*
Australia 23°32S 150°52E **150** C5
Fitzroy → *W. Austral.,*
Australia 17°31S 123°35E **148** C3
Fitzroy Crossing
Australia 18°9S 125°38E **148** C4
Fitzwilliam I. *Canada* 45°30N 81°45W **174** A3
Fiume = Rijeka *Croatia* 45°20N 14°21E **93** C11
Fiumicino, Roma ✈ (FCO)
Italy 41°48N 12°15E **93** G9
Five Points *U.S.A.* 36°26N 120°6W **170** J6
Fivizzano *Italy* 44°14N 10°8E **92** D7
Fizi *Dem. Rep. of the Congo* 4°17S 28°55E **142** C2
Fjällbacka *Sweden* 58°36N 11°17E **63** F5
Fjällnäs *Sweden* 62°36N 12°11E **62** B6
Fjärdhundra *Sweden* 59°47N 16°56E **62** E10
Fjellerup *Denmark* 56°29N 10°34E **63** H4
Fjerritslev *Denmark* 57°5N 9°15E **63** G3
Fjugesta *Sweden* 59°11N 14°52E **62** E8
Fkih ben Salah *Morocco* 32°32N 6°45W **136** B2
Flagler *Canada* 51°12N 111°39W **162** C6
Flagler Beach *U.S.A.* 29°29N 81°8W **178** F7
Flagstaff *U.S.A.* 35°12N 111°39W **169** J8
Flagstaff L. *U.S.A.* 45°12N 70°18W **175** A14
Flaherty I. *Canada* 56°15N 79°15W **164** A4
Flåm *Norway* 60°50N 7°7E **60** F12
Flambeau → *U.S.A.* 45°18N 91°14W **172** C8
Flamborough Hd. *U.K.* 54°7N 0°5W **66** C7
Fláming *Germany* 52°0N 13°0E **76** C8
Flaming Gorge △
U.S.A. 41°10N 109°25W **168** F9
Flaming Gorge Res.
U.S.A. 41°10N 109°25W **168** F9
Flamingo, Teluk
Indonesia 5°30S 138°0E **119** F9
Flanders = Flandre
Europe 50°50N 2°30E **71** B9
Flandre *Europe* 50°50N 2°30E **71** B9
Flandre-Occidentale = West-
Vlaanderen □ *Belgium* 51°0N 3°0E **69** D2
Flandre-Orientale = Oost-
Vlaanderen □ *Belgium* 51°0N 3°50E **69** C3
Flandreau *U.S.A.* 44°3N 96°36W **172** C5
Flanigan *U.S.A.* 40°10N 119°53W **170** E7
Flannan Is. *U.K.* 58°9N 7°52W **65** C1
Flåsjön *Sweden* 64°5N 15°40E **60** D16

Flat → *Canada* 61°33N 125°18W **162** A3
Flat I. *Mauritius* 19°53S 57°35E **141** d
Flat I., *S. China Sea* 10°49N 115°49E **118** B5
Flat Pt. *N.Z.* 41°14S 175°57E **154** H4
Flathead L. *U.S.A.* 47°51N 114°8W **168** C6
Flattery, C. *Australia* 14°58S 145°21E **150** A4
Flattery, C. *U.S.A.* 48°23N 124°29W **170** B2
Flatwoods *U.S.A.* 38°31N 82°43W **173** F12
Fleetwood *Canada* 49°27N 75°49W **175** F9
Fleetwood *U.K.* 53°55N 3°1W **66** D4
Flekkefjord *Norway* 58°18N 6°39E **61** G12
Flemington *U.S.A.* 41°7N 77°28W **174** E7
Flemish Cap *Atl. Oc.* 47°0N 45°0W **56** B7
Flen *Sweden* 59°4N 16°35E **62** E10
Flensburg *Germany* 54°47N 9°27E **76** A5
Flers *France* 48°47N 0°33W **70** D6
Flesherton *Canada* 44°16N 80°33W **174** B4
Flesko, Tanjung
Indonesia 0°29N 124°30E **119** D6
Fleurance *France* 43°52N 0°40E **72** E4
Fleurie, Côte *France* 49°25N 0°40W **70** C6
Fleurier *Switz.* 46°54N 6°35E **77** J2
Fleurieu Pen. *Australia* 35°40S 138°5E **152** C3
Flevoland □ *Neths.* 52°30N 5°30E **69** B5
Flin Flon *Canada* 54°46N 101°53W **163** C8
Flinders → *Australia* 17°36S 140°36E **150** B3
Flinders B. *Australia* 34°19S 115°19E **149** F2
Flinders Chase △
Australia 35°50S 136°42E **152** C2
Flinders Group
Australia 14°11S 144°15E **150** A3
Flinders I. *S. Austral.,*
Australia 33°44S 134°41E **151** E1
Flinders I. *Tas., Australia* 40°0S 148°0E **151** G4
Flinders Ranges
Australia 31°30S 138°30E **152** B3
Flinders Ranges △
Australia 31°30S 138°40E **152** B3
Flinders Reefs
Australia 17°37S 148°31E **150** B4
Flint *U.K.* 53°15N 3°8W **66** D4
Flint *U.S.A.* 43°1N 83°41W **173** D12
Flint → *U.S.A.* 30°57N 84°34W **178** E5
Flint I. *Kiribati* 11°26S 151°48W **157** J12
Flintshire □ *U.K.* 53°17N 3°17W **66** D4
Fliseryd *Sweden* 57°6N 16°15E **63** G10
Flix *Spain* 41°14N 0°32E **90** D5
Flixecourt *France* 50°1N 2°5E **71** B9
Floby *Sweden* 58°8N 13°20E **63** F7
Floda *Sweden* 57°49N 12°22E **63** G6
Flodden *U.K.* 55°37N 2°8W **66** B5
Flogny-la-Chapelle
France 47°57N 3°57E **71** E10
Floodplains △ *Sri Lanka* 8°10N 81°10E **127** K5
Floodwood *U.S.A.* 46°56N 92°55W **172** B7
Flora *U.S.A.* 38°40N 88°29W **172** F9
Florac *France* 44°20N 3°37E **72** D7
Florahome *U.S.A.* 29°44N 81°54W **178** F8
Floral City *U.S.A.* 28°45N 82°17W **179** G7
Florala *U.S.A.* 31°0N 86°20W **177** F11
Florânia *Brazil* 6°8S 36°49W **189** B3
Florence = Firenze *Italy* 43°46N 11°15E **93** E8
Florence *Ala., U.S.A.* 34°48N 87°41W **177** D11
Florence *Ariz., U.S.A.* 33°2N 111°23W **169** K8
Florence *Colo., U.S.A.* 38°23N 105°8W **168** G11
Florence *Oreg., U.S.A.* 43°58N 124°7W **168** D1
Florence *S.C., U.S.A.* 34°12N 79°46W **177** D15
Florence, L. *Australia* 28°53S 138°9E **151** D2
Florencia *Colombia* 1°36N 75°36W **186** C2
Florennes *Belgium* 50°15N 4°35E **69** D4
Florensac *France* 43°23N 3°28E **72** E7
Florenville *Belgium* 49°40N 5°19E **69** E5
Flores *Azores* 39°26N 31°13W **134** a
Flores *Brazil* 7°51S 37°59W **189** B3
Flores *Guatemala* 16°59N 89°50W **182** C2
Flores *Indonesia* 8°35S 121°0E **119** F6
Flores → *U.S.A.* 29°20N 126°10W **182** C3
Flores Sea *Indonesia* 6°30S 120°0E **119** F6
Floreşti *Moldova* 47°53N 28°17E **81** C13
Floresville *U.S.A.* 29°8N 98°10W **176** G5
Floriano *Brazil* 6°50S 43°0W **189** B2
Florianópolis *Brazil* 27°30S 48°30W **191** B6
Florida *Cuba* 21°32N 78°14W **182** B4
Florida *Uruguay* 34°7S 56°10W **191** C4
Florida □ *U.S.A.* 28°0N 82°0W **178** G7
Florida, Straits of *U.S.A.* 25°0N 80°0W **182** B4
Florida B. *U.S.A.* 25°0N 80°45W **179** K9
Florida City *U.S.A.* 25°27N 80°29W **179** K9
Florida Keys *U.S.A.* 24°40N 81°0W **179** L9
Floridia *Italy* 37°5N 15°9E **95** E8
Florin *U.S.A.* 38°30N 121°24W **170** G5
Florina *Greece* 40°48N 21°26E **96** F5
Florissant *U.S.A.* 38°47N 90°19W **172** F8
Florø *Norway* 61°35N 5°1E **60** F11
Flower Station *Canada* 45°10N 76°41W **175** A8
Flowerpot I. *Canada* 45°18N 81°38W **174** A3
Floydada *U.S.A.* 33°59N 101°20W **176** E4
Fluk *Indonesia* 1°42S 127°44E **119** E7
Flúmen → *Spain* 41°43N 0°9W **90** D4
Flumendosa → *Italy* 39°26N 9°37E **94** C2
Fluminimaggiore *Italy* 39°26N 8°30E **94** C1
Flushing = Vlissingen
Neths. 51°26N 3°34E **69** C3
Fluvià → *Spain* 42°12N 3°7E **90** C8
Fly → *Papua N. G.* 8°25S 143°0E **147** B7
Flying Fish, C.
Antarctica 72°6S 102°29W **55** D15
Foam Lake *Canada* 51°40N 103°32W **163** C8
Foča *Bos.-H.* 43°31N 18°47E **96** C2
Foça *Turkey* 38°39N 26°56E **99** C8
Fochabers *U.K.* 57°37N 3°6W **65** D5
Focşani *Romania* 45°41N 27°15E **81** E12
Fodécontéa *Guinea* 10°50N 14°32W **138** C2
Fogang *China* 23°52N 113°30E **117** F9
Foggaret ez Zoua *Algeria* 27°13N 2°49E **136** C4
Fóggia *Italy* 41°27N 15°34E **95** A8
Foggo *Nigeria* 11°21N 9°57E **139** C7
Foglia → *Italy* 43°57N 12°54E **93** E9
Fogo *Canada* 49°43N 54°17W **165** C9
Fogo *C. Verde Is.* 15°0N 24°20W **134** b
Fogo I. *Canada* 49°40N 54°5W **165** C9
Föhr *Germany* 54°43N 8°30E **76** A4
Fóia *Portugal* 37°19N 8°37W **89** H2
Foix *France* 42°58N 1°38E **72** F5
Fojnica *Bos.-H.* 43°59N 17°51E **96** C2
Fokida □ *Greece* 38°30N 22°15E **98** C4
Fokino *Russia* 53°30N 34°22E **84** E5
Fokku *Nigeria* 11°36N 4°32E **139** C5

Folda *Nord-Trøndelag,*
Norway 64°32N 10°30E **6**...
Folda *Nordland, Norway* 67°38N 14°50E **6**...
Földeák *Hungary* 46°19N 20°30E ...
Folegandros *Greece* 36°40N 24°55E ...
Foley *Botswana* 21°34S 27°21E **1**...
Foley *U.S.A.* 30°24N 87°41W **1**...
Foley *Ala., U.S.A.* 30°4N 83°32W **1**...
Foleyet *Canada* 48°15N 82°25W **1**...
Folgefonna *Norway* 60°3N 6°23E **6**...
Foligno *Italy* 42°57N 12°42E ...
Folkestone *U.K.* 51°5N 1°12E ...
Folkston *U.S.A.* 30°50N 82°0W **1**...
Follansbee *U.S.A.* 40°19N 80°35W **1**...
Follónica *Italy* 42°55N 10°45E ...
Follónica, G. di *Italy* 42°54N 10°43E ...
Folsom *U.S.A.* 38°40N 121°9W **1**...
Folsom L. *U.S.A.* 38°42N 121°9W **1**...
Folteşti *Romania* 45°45N 28°3E **8**...
Fomboni *Comoros Is.* 12°18S 43°46E ...
Fond du Lac *Canada* 59°19N 107°12W **1**...
Fond du Lac *U.S.A.* 43°47N 88°27W **1**...
Fond-du-Lac →
Canada 59°17N 106°0W **1**...
Fonda *U.S.A.* 42°57N 74°22W **1**...
Fondi *Italy* 41°21N 13°25E ...
Fonfría *Spain* 41°37N 6°9W ...
Fongafale *Tuvalu* 8°31S 179°13E **1**...
Fonni *Italy* 40°7N 9°15E ...
Fonsagrada = A Fonsagrada
Spain 43°8N 7°4W ...
Font-Romeu-Odeillo-Via
France 42°31N 2°2E ...
Fontaine-Française
France 47°32N 5°21E **7**...
Fontainebleau *France* 48°24N 2°40E ...
Fontana *U.S.A.* 34°6N 117°26W **1**...
Fontana, L. *Argentina* 44°55S 71°30W **1**...
Fontas → *Canada* 58°14N 121°48W **1**...
Fonte Boa *Brazil* 2°33S 66°0W **1**...
Fontem *Cameroon* 5°32N 9°52E **1**...
Fontenay-le-Comte
France 46°28N 0°48W ...
Fontenelle Res. *U.S.A.* 42°1N 110°3W **1**...
Fontur *Iceland* 66°23N 14°32W **6**...
Fonyód *Hungary* 46°44N 17°33E ...
Foochow = Fuzhou
China 26°5N 119°16E **11**...
Foping *China* 33°41N 108°0E **1**...
Foraker, Mt. *U.S.A.* 62°58N 151°24W **1**...
Forbach *France* 49°10N 6°52E **7**...
Forbesganj *India* 26°17N 87°18E **12**...
Forbes *Australia* 33°22S 148°5E **1**...
Forcados *Nigeria* 5°26N 5°26E **1**...
Forcados → *Nigeria* 5°25N 5°19E **1**...
Forcalquier *France* 43°58N 5°47E ...
Forchheim *Germany* 49°43N 11°4E **7**...
Ford City *Calif., U.S.A.* 35°9N 119°27W **1**...
Ford City *Pa., U.S.A.* 40°46N 79°32W **1**...
Førde *Norway* 61°27N 5°53E **6**...
Fords Bridge *Australia* 29°41S 145°29E **1**...
Fordyce *U.S.A.* 33°49N 92°25W **1**...
Forécariah *Guinea* 9°28N 13°10W **1**...
Forel, Mt. *Greenland* 66°52N 36°55W **5**...
Foremost *Canada* 49°26N 111°34W **1**...
Forest *Canada* 43°6N 82°0W **1**...
Forest *U.S.A.* 32°22N 89°29W **1**...
Forest Acres *U.S.A.* 34°1N 80°58W **1**...
Forest City *Iowa, U.S.A.* 43°16N 93°39W **1**...
Forest City *N.C.,*
U.S.A. 35°20N 81°52W **1**...
Forest City *Pa., U.S.A.* 41°39N 75°28W **1**...
Forest Grove *U.S.A.* 45°31N 123°7W **1**...
Forest Park *U.S.A.* 33°37N 84°22W **1**...
Forestburg *Canada* 52°35N 112°1W **1**...
Foreste Casentinesi-Monte
Falterona-Campigna △
Italy 43°50N 11°48E ...
Foresthill *U.S.A.* 39°1N 120°49W **1**...
Forestier Pen. *Australia* 42°58N 147°52E **1**...
Forestville *Canada* 48°48N 69°2W **1**...
Forestville *Calif.,*
U.S.A. 38°28N 122°54W **1**...
Forestville *N.Y., U.S.A.* 42°28N 79°10W **1**...
Forêt d'Orient △ *France* 48°16N 4°19E **7**...
Forez, Mts. du *France* 45°40N 3°50E ...
Forfar *U.K.* 56°39N 2°53W **6**...
Forillon △ *Canada* 48°46N 64°12W **1**...
Forks *U.S.A.* 47°57N 124°23W **1**...
Forksville *U.S.A.* 41°29N 76°35W **1**...
Forlì *Italy* 44°13N 12°3E ...
Forli-Cesena □ *Italy* 44°10N 12°20E ...
Forman *U.S.A.* 46°7N 97°38W **1**...
Formazza *Italy* 46°22N 8°26E ...
Formby Pt. *U.K.* 53°33N 3°6W **6**...
Formentera *Spain* 38°43N 1°27E ...
Formentor, C. de *Spain* 39°58N 3°13E **1**...
Formentor, Pen. de
Spain 39°56N 3°11E **1**...
Former Yugoslav Republic of
Macedonia = Macedonia ■
Europe 41°53N 21°40E ...
Fórmia *Italy* 41°15N 13°37E ...
Formiche, L. *Brazil* 20°27S 45°25W **1**...
Formigine *Italy* 44°37N 10°51E ...
Formosa = Taiwan ■
Asia 23°30N 121°0E **11**...
Formosa *Argentina* 26°15S 58°10W **1**...
Formosa *Brazil* 15°32S 47°20W **1**...
Formosa □ *Argentina* 25°0S 60°0W **1**...
Formosa, Serra *Brazil* 12°0S 55°0W **1**...
Formosa B. = Ungwana B.
Kenya 2°45S 40°20E **1**...
Formosa do Rio Prêto
Brazil 11°2S 45°3W **1**...
Fornells *Spain* 40°3N 4°7E **1**...
Fornos de Algodres
Portugal 40°38N 7°32W ...
Fornovo di Taro *Italy* 44°42N 10°6E ...
Foroshogna △ *Norway* 62°39N 10°41E **6**...
Føroyar ☑ *Atl. Oc.* 62°0N 7°0W ...
Forres *U.K.* 57°37N 3°37W **6**...
Forrest *Vic., Australia* 38°33S 143°47E **1**...
Forrest *W. Austral.,*
Australia 30°51S 128°6E **1**...
Forrest, Mt. *Australia* 24°48S 127°45E **1**...
Forrest City *U.S.A.* 35°1N 90°47W **1**...
Fors *Sweden* 60°14N 16°20E **6**...
Forsayth *Australia* 18°33S 143°34E **1**...

orserum *Sweden* 57°42N 14°30E **63** G8
orshaga *Sweden* 59°33N 13°29E **62** E7
orslöv *Sweden* 56°21N 12°48E **63** H6
orsmo *Sweden* 63°16N 17°11E **62** A11
orssa *Finland* 60°49N 23°38E **84** B2
orst *Germany* 51°45N 14°37E **76** D10
orster *Australia* 32°12S 152°31E **153** B10
orsvik *Sweden* 58°35N 14°26E **63** F8
orsyth *Ga., U.S.A.* 33°2N 83°56W **178** B6
orsyth *Mont.,*
  U.S.A. 46°16N 106°41W **168** C10
orsyth I. *N.Z.* 40°58S 174°5E **155** A9
ort Abbas *Pakistan* 29°12N 72°52E **124** E5
ort Albany *Canada* 52°15N 81°35W **164** B3
ort Assiniboine
  Canada 54°20N 114°45W **162** C6
ort Augustus *U.K.* 57°9N 4°42W **65** D4
ort Beaufort *S. Africa* 32°46S 26°40E **144** D4
ort Benton *U.S.A.* 47°49N 110°40W **168** B8
ort Bragg *U.S.A.* 39°26N 123°48W **168** G2
ort Bridger *U.S.A.* 41°19N 110°23W **168** F8
ort Caroline ⌂ *U.S.A.* 30°23N 81°30W **178** E8
ort Chipewyan
  Canada 58°42N 111°8W **163** B6
ort Clatsop = Lewis and Clark △
  U.S.A. 46°8N 123°53W **170** D3
ort Collins *U.S.A.* 40°35N 105°5W **168** F11
ort-Coulonge *Canada* 45°50N 76°45W **164** C4
ort Covington
  U.S.A. 44°59N 74°29W **175** B10
ort Dauphin = Taolanaro
  Madag. 25°2S 47°0E **141** K9
ort Davis *Ala., U.S.A.* 32°15N 85°43W **178** C4
ort Davis *Tex., U.S.A.* 30°35N 103°54W **176** F3
ort-de-France
  Martinique 14°36N 61°5W **182** c
ort Defiance *U.S.A.* 35°45N 109°5W **169** J9
ort Dodge *U.S.A.* 42°30N 94°11W **172** D6
ort Drum *U.S.A.* 27°32N 80°48W **179** M5
ort Edward *U.S.A.* 43°16N 73°35W **175** C11
ort Erie *Canada* 42°54N 78°56W **174** D6
ort Fairfield *U.S.A.* 46°46N 67°50W **173** B20
ort Frances *Canada* 48°36N 93°24W **163** D10
ort Franklin = Déline
  Canada 65°11N 123°25W **160** D7
ort Frederica ⌂
  U.S.A. 31°13N 81°23W **178** D8
ort Gaines *U.S.A.* 31°36N 85°3W **178** D4
ort Garland *U.S.A.* 37°26N 105°26W **169** H11
ort George = Chisasibi
  Canada 53°50N 79°0W **164** B4
ort Good Hope
  Canada 66°14N 128°40W **160** D6
ort Hancock *U.S.A.* 31°18N 105°51W **176** F2
ort Hope = Eabametoong
  Canada 51°30N 88°0W **164** B2
ort Irwin *U.S.A.* 35°16N 116°41W **171** K10
ort Kent *U.S.A.* 47°15N 68°36W **173** B19
ort Klamath *U.S.A.* 42°42N 122°0W **168** D3
ort Laramie *U.S.A.* 42°13N 104°31W **168** E11
ort Lauderdale *U.S.A.* 26°7N 80°8W **179** J9
ort Liard *Canada* 60°14N 123°30W **162** A3
ort Liberté *Haiti* 19°42N 71°51W **183** C5
ort Lupton *U.S.A.* 40°5N 104°49W **168** F11
ort MacKay *Canada* 57°12N 111°41W **162** B6
ort Macleod *Canada* 49°45N 113°30W **162** D6
ort McMurray
  Canada 56°44N 111°7W **162** B6
ort McPherson
  Canada 67°30N 134°55W **160** D5
ort Madison *U.S.A.* 40°38N 91°27W **172** E8
ort Matanzas ⌂
  U.S.A. 29°43N 81°14W **178** F8
ort Meade *U.S.A.* 27°45N 81°48W **179** H8
ort Mitchell *U.S.A.* 32°20N 85°1W **178** C4
ort Morgan *U.S.A.* 40°15N 103°48W **168** F12
ort Myers *U.S.A.* 26°39N 81°52W **179** J8
ort Myers Beach
  U.S.A. 26°27N 81°52W **179** J8
ort Myers Villas
  U.S.A. 26°33N 81°52W **179** J8
ort Nelson *Canada* 58°50N 122°44W **162** B4
ort Nelson → *Canada* 59°32N 124°0W **162** B4
ort Norman = Tulita
  Canada 64°57N 125°30W **160** E6
ort Ogden *U.S.A.* 27°5N 81°58W **179** H8
ort Payne *U.S.A.* 34°26N 85°43W **177** D12
ort Peck *U.S.A.* 48°1N 106°27W **168** B10
ort Peck Dam *U.S.A.* 48°0N 106°26W **168** C10
ort Peck L. *U.S.A.* 48°0N 106°26W **168** C10
ort Pierce *U.S.A.* 27°27N 80°20W **179** H10
ort Pierre *U.S.A.* 44°21N 100°22W **172** C3
ort Plain *U.S.A.* 42°56N 74°37W **175** C10
ort Portal *Uganda* 0°40N 30°20E **142** B3
ort Providence
  Canada 61°3N 117°40W **162** A5
ort Pulaski ⌂ *U.S.A.* 32°2N 80°56W **178** C9
ort Qu'Appelle
  Canada 50°45N 103°50W **163** C8
ort Resolution
  Canada 61°10N 113°40W **162** A6
ort Rixon *Zimbabwe* 20°2S 29°17E **143** G2
ort Ross *U.S.A.* 38°32N 123°13W **170** G3
ort Rupert = Waskaganish
  Canada 51°30N 78°40W **164** B4
ort St. James *Canada* 54°30N 124°10W **162** C4
ort St. John *Canada* 56°15N 120°50W **162** B4
ort Saskatchewan
  Canada 53°40N 113°8W **162** C6
ort Scott *U.S.A.* 37°50N 94°42W **172** G6
ort Severn *Canada* 56°0N 87°40W **164** A2
ort Shevchenko
  Kazakhstan 44°35N 50°23E **87** H10
ort Simpson *Canada* 61°52N 121°23W **162** A4
ort Smith *Canada* 60°0N 111°51W **162** A6
ort Smith *U.S.A.* 35°23N 94°25W **177** D7
ort Stockton *U.S.A.* 30°53N 102°53W **176** F3
ort Sumner *U.S.A.* 34°28N 104°15W **169** J11
ort Thompson *U.S.A.* 44°3N 99°26W **172** C4
ort Union ⌂ *U.S.A.* 35°54N 105°1W **169** J11
ort Valley *U.S.A.* 32°33N 83°53W **178** C5
ort Vermilion *Canada* 58°24N 116°0W **162** B5
ort Walton Beach
  U.S.A. 30°25N 86°36W **179** D1
ort Ware *Canada* 57°26N 125°41W **162** B3
ort Wayne *U.S.A.* 41°4N 85°9W **173** E11
ort White *U.S.A.* 29°55N 82°43W **178** F8
ort Worth *U.S.A.* 32°43N 97°19W **176** E6
ort Yates *U.S.A.* 46°5N 100°38W **172** B3
ort Yukon *U.S.A.* 66°34N 145°16W **160** D2

Fortaleza *Bolivia* 12°6S 66°49W **188** C4
Fortaleza *Brazil* 3°45S 38°35W **189** A3
Forteau *Canada* 51°28N 56°58W **165** B8
Fortescue → *Australia* 21°0S 116°4E **148** D2
Fortescue River Roadhouse
  Australia 21°17S 116°8E **148** D2
Forth → *U.K.* 56°9N 3°50W **65** E5
Forth, Firth of *U.K.* 56°5N 2°55W **65** E6
Fortín Uno *Argentina* 38°50S 65°18W **192** A3
Fortore → *Italy* 41°55N 15°17E **93** G12
Fortrose *N.Z.* 46°38S 168°45E **155** G3
Fortrose *U.K.* 57°35N 4°9W **65** D4
Fortuna *Spain* 38°11N 1°7W **91** G3
Fortuna *Calif., U.S.A.* 40°36N 124°9W **168** F1
Fortuna *N. Dak.,*
  U.S.A. 48°55N 103°47W **172** A2
Fortune *Canada* 47°4N 55°50W **165** C8
Fortune B. *Canada* 47°30N 55°22W **165** C8
Forür *Iran* 26°17N 54°32E **129** E7
Fos-sur-Mer *France* 43°26N 4°56E **73** E8
Fosen *Norway* 63°50N 10°20E **60** E14
Foshan *China* 23°3N 113°9E **117** F9
Fosnavåg *Norway* 62°22N 5°38E **60** E11
Foso *Ghana* 5°43N 1°15W **139** D4
Fossano *Italy* 44°33N 7°43E **92** D4
Fossil *U.S.A.* 45°0N 120°9W **168** D3
Fossil Butte ⌂ *U.S.A.* 41°50N 110°27W **168** F8
Fossombrone *Italy* 43°41N 12°48E **93** E9
Foster *Australia* 38°40S 146°15E **153** F7
Foster *Canada* 45°17N 72°30W **175** A12
Foster → *Canada* 55°47N 105°49W **163** B7
Fostoria *U.S.A.* 41°10N 83°25W **173** E12
Fouesnant *France* 47°53N 4°1W **70** E2
Fougères *France* 48°21N 1°14W **70** D5
Foul Pt. *Sri Lanka* 8°35N 81°18E **127** K5
Foula *U.K.* 60°10N 2°5W **65** A6
Foulalaba *Mali* 10°40N 7°20W **138** C3
Foulness I. *U.K.* 51°36N 0°55E **67** F8
Foulwind, C. *N.Z.* 41°45S 171°28E **155** D4
Foum Zguid *Morocco* 30°2N 6°59W **136** B4
Foumban *Cameroon* 5°45N 10°50E **139** D7
Foumbot *Cameroon* 5°31N 10°28E **139** D7
Foumbouni *Comoros Is.* 11°51S 43°29E **141** a
Foumirate *Algeria* ... **136** A6
Foundiougne *Senegal* 14°5N 16°32W **138** C1
Fountain *Colo.,*
  U.S.A. 38°41N 104°42W **168** G11
Fountain *Fla., U.S.A.* 30°29N 85°25W **178** F4
Fountain Hills *U.S.A.* 33°37N 111°43W **169** K8
Fountain Springs
  U.S.A. 35°54N 118°51W **171** K8
Four Mountains, Is. of
  U.S.A. 53°0N 170°0W **166** C5
Fourchambault *France* 47°0N 3°3E **71** K10
Fouriesburg *S. Africa* 28°38S 28°14E **144** C4
Fourmies *France* 50°1N 4°2E **71** B11
Fourna *Greece* 39°3N 21°52E **98** B3
Fourni *Greece* 37°36N 26°32E **99** D8
Fours *France* 46°50N 3°42E **71** F10
Fouta Djallon *Guinea* 11°20N 12°10W **138** C2
Foux, Cap-à- *Haiti* 19°43N 73°27W **183** C5
Foveaux Str. *N.Z.* 46°42S 168°10E **155** G3
Fowey *U.K.* 50°20N 4°39W **67** G3
Fowler *Calif., U.S.A.* 36°38N 119°41W **170** J7
Fowler *Colo., U.S.A.* 38°8N 104°2W **168** G11
Fowlers B. *Australia* 31°59S 132°34E **149** F5
Fowman *Iran* 37°13N 49°19E **105** D13
Fox → *Canada* 56°3N 93°18W **163** B10
Fox Creek *Canada* 54°24N 116°48W **162** C5
Fox Is. *U.S.A.* 53°0N 168°0W **166** C6
Fox Lake *Canada* 58°28N 114°31W **162** B6
Fox Valley *Canada* 50°30N 109°25W **163** C7
Foxboro *Canada* 44°14N 77°26W **174** B7
Foxboro *U.S.A.* 42°4N 71°16W **175** D13
Foxdale *Australia* 20°22S 148°35E **150** b
Foxe Basin *Canada* 66°0N 77°0W **161** C6
Foxe Chan. *Canada* 65°0N 80°0W **161** C6
Foxe Pen. *Canada* 65°0N 76°0W **161** C6
Foxen *Sweden* 59°25N 11°55E **62** E5
Foxford *Ireland* 53°59N 9°7W **64** C2
Foxton *N.Z.* 40°29S 175°18E **154** G4
Foyle, Lough *U.K.* 55°7N 7°4W **64** A4
Foynes *Ireland* 52°37N 9°7W **64** D2
Foz *Spain* 43°33N 7°20W **88** A3
Foz do Cunene *Angola* 17°15S 11°48E **144** A1
Foz do Gregório *Brazil* 6°47S 70°44W **188** B3
Foz do Iguaçu *Brazil* 25°30S 54°30W **191** B5
Frackville *U.S.A.* 40°47N 76°14W **175** F8
Fraga *Spain* 41°32N 0°21E **90** D5
Fraile Muerto *Uruguay* 32°31S 54°32W **191** C5
Framingham *U.S.A.* 42°18N 71°24W **175** D13
Frampol *Poland* 50°41N 22°40E **83** H9
Franca *Brazil* 20°33S 47°30W **189** E1
Francavilla al Mare
  Italy 42°25N 14°17E **93** F11
Francavilla Fontana
  Italy 40°32N 17°35E **95** B10
France ■ *Europe* 47°0N 3°0E **59** F6
Frances *Australia* 36°41S 140°55E **152** D4
Frances → *Canada* 60°16N 129°10W **162** A3
Frances L. *Canada* 61°23N 129°30W **162** A3
Franceville *Gabon* 1°40S 13°32E **140** E2
Franche-Comté □
  France 46°50N 5°55E **71** F12
Francis Case, L. *U.S.A.* 43°4N 98°34W **172** D5
Francisco Beltrão *Brazil* 26°5S 53°4W **191** B5
Francisco Ignacio Madero
  Coahuila, Mexico 25°48N 103°18W **180** B4
Francisco Ignacio Madero
  Durango, Mexico 24°26N 104°18W **180** C4
Francisco Sá *Brazil* 16°28S 43°30W **189** D2
Francistown *Botswana* 21°7S 27°33W **145** C4
Francofonte *Italy* 37°14N 14°53E **95** E7
François *Canada* 47°35N 56°45W **165** C8
François L. *Canada* 54°0N 125°30W **162** C3
Francois Peron △
  Australia 25°42S 113°33E **149** E1
Francs Pk. *U.S.A.* 43°58N 109°20W **168** E9
Franeker *Neths.* 53°12N 5°33E **69** A5
Frank Hann △
  Australia 32°52S 120°19E **149** F3
Frankenberg *Germany* 51°3N 8°48E **76** D4
Frankenberg *Germany*
  51°5N 11°30E **77** E7
Frankford *Canada* 44°12N 77°36W **174** B7
Frankfort *S. Africa* 27°17S 28°30E **145** C4
Frankfort *Ind., U.S.A.* 40°17N 86°31W **172** E10
Frankfort *Kans., U.S.A.* 39°42N 96°25W **172** F5
Frankfort *Ky., U.S.A.* 38°12N 84°52W **173** F11
Frankfort *N.Y., U.S.A.* 43°2N 75°4W **175** C9
Frankfurt *Brandenburg,*
  Germany 52°20N 14°32E **76** C10
Frankfurt *Hessen, Germany* 50°7N 8°41E **77** E4
Frankfurt ✈ (FRA)
  Germany 50°1N 8°34E **77** E4
Fränkische Alb *Germany* 49°10N 11°23E **77** F7
Fränkische Rezat →
  Germany 49°11N 11°1E **77** F7
Fränkische Saale →
  Germany 50°3N 9°42E **77** E5
Fränkische Schweiz
  Germany 49°50N 11°16E **77** F7
Fränkische Schweiz-Veldensteiner
  Forst ⌂ *Germany* 49°45N 11°27E **77** F7
Frankland → *Australia* 35°0S 116°48E **149** G2
Franklin *Ga., U.S.A.* 33°17N 85°6W **178** B4
Franklin *Ky., U.S.A.* 36°43N 86°35W **172** G10
Franklin *La., U.S.A.* 29°48N 91°30W **179** G9
Franklin *Mass., U.S.A.* 42°5N 71°24W **175** D13
Franklin *N.H., U.S.A.* 43°27N 71°39W **175** C13
Franklin *N.Y., U.S.A.* 42°20N 75°9W **175** D9
Franklin *Nebr., U.S.A.* 40°6N 98°57W **172** E4
Franklin *Pa., U.S.A.* 41°24N 79°50W **174** E5
Franklin *Tenn., U.S.A.* 35°55N 86°52W **177** C11
Franklin *W. Va.,*
  U.S.A. 38°39N 79°20W **173** F14
Franklin B. *Canada* 69°45N 126°0W **160** C7
Franklin D. Roosevelt L.
  U.S.A. 48°18N 118°9W **168** B4
Franklin-Gordon Wild Rivers △
  Australia 42°19S 145°51E **151** G4
Franklin Harb.
  Australia 33°43S 136°55E **152** B2
Franklin I. *Antarctica* 76°10S 168°30E **55** D11
Franklin I. *Canada* 45°24N 80°20W **174** A4
Franklin L. *U.S.A.* 40°25N 115°22W **168** F6
Franklin Mts. *Canada* 65°0N 125°0W **160** D6
Franklin Mts. *N.Z.* 44°55S 167°45E **155** F1
Franklin Str. *Canada* 72°0N 96°0W **160** C12
Franklinton *U.S.A.* 30°51N 90°9W **177** F9
Franklinville *U.S.A.* 42°20N 78°27W **174** D6
Franklyn Mt. *N.Z.* 42°4S 172°42E **155** C7
Frankston *Australia* 38°8S 145°8E **153** E6
Fränö *Sweden* 62°55N 17°50E **62** B11
Fransfontein *Namibia* 20°12S 15°1E **144** B2
Frenchman Cr. →
  U.S.A. 40°14N 100°50W **172** E3
Fränsta *Sweden* 62°30N 16°11E **62** B10
Frantsa Iosifa, Zemlya
  Arctic 82°0N 55°0E **106** A6
Franz *Canada* 48°25N 84°30W **164** C3
Franz Josef Land = Frantsa Iosifa,
  Zemlya *Arctic* 82°0N 55°0E **106** A6
Franz Josef Strauss ✈ (MUC)
  Germany 48°21N 11°47E **77** G7
Franzburg *Germany* 54°11N 12°51E **76** A8
Frascati *Italy* 41°48N 12°41E **93** G9
Fraser *U.S.A.* 42°32N 82°57W **174** D2
Fraser → *B.C., Canada* 49°7N 123°11W **170** A3
Fraser → *Nfld. & L.,*
  Canada 56°39N 62°10W **165** A7
Fraser, Mt. *Australia* 25°35S 118°20E **149** E2
Fraser I. *Australia* 25°15S 153°10E **151** D5
Fraser Lake *Canada* 54°0N 124°50W **162** C4
Fraserburg *S. Africa* 31°55S 21°30E **144** E3
Fraserburgh *U.K.* 57°42N 2°1W **65** D6
Fraserdale *Canada* 49°55N 81°37W **164** C3
Frasertown *N.Z.* 38°58S 177°28E **154** E6
Frashër *Albania* 40°23N 20°30E **96** F4
Frasne *France* 46°50N 6°10E **71** F13
Frauenfeld *Switz.* 47°34N 8°54E **77** H4
Fray Bentos *Uruguay* 33°10S 58°15W **190** C4
Fray Jorge △ *Chile* 30°42S 71°40W **190** C1
Frazier Downs ○
  Australia 18°48S 121°42E **148** C3
Frechilla *Spain* 42°8N 4°50W **88** C6
Fredericia *Denmark* 55°34N 9°45E **63** J3
Frederick *Md., U.S.A.* 39°25N 77°25W **173** F15
Frederick *Okla., U.S.A.* 34°23N 99°1W **176** D5
Frederick *S. Dak.,*
  U.S.A. 45°50N 98°31W **172** C4
Frederick E. Hyde Fjord
  Greenland 83°25N 29°0W **57** A8
Fredericksburg *Pa.,*
  U.S.A. 40°27N 76°26W **175** F8
Fredericksburg *Tex.,*
  U.S.A. 30°16N 98°52W **176** F5
Fredericksburg *Va.,*
  U.S.A. 38°18N 77°28W **173** F15
Fredericktown *Mo.,*
  U.S.A. 37°34N 90°18W **172** G8
Fredericktown *Ohio,*
  U.S.A. 40°29N 82°33W **174** F2
Frederico Westphalen
  Brazil 27°22S 53°24W **191** B5
Fredericton *Canada* 45°57N 66°40W **165** C6
Fredericton Junction
  Canada 45°41N 66°40W **165** C6
Frederikshåb = Paamiut
  Greenland 62°0N 49°43W **57** E6
Frederikshamn = Hamina
  Finland 60°34N 27°12E **84** B4
Frederikshavn *Denmark* 57°28N 10°31E **63** G4
Frederikssund *Denmark* 55°50N 12°3E **63** J6
Frederiksted
  U.S. Virgin Is. 17°43N 64°53W **183** C7
Frederiksværk *Denmark* 55°58N 12°4E **63** J6
Fredonia *Ariz., U.S.A.* 36°57N 112°32W **169** H7
Fredonia *Kans., U.S.A.* 37°32N 95°49W **172** G6
Fredonia *N.Y., U.S.A.* 42°26N 79°20W **174** D5
Fredrikstad *Norway* 59°13N 10°57E **63** G14
Free State □ *S. Africa* 28°30S 27°0E **144** C4
Freehold *U.S.A.* 40°16N 74°17W **175** F10
Freeland *U.S.A.* 41°1N 75°54W **175** E9
Freels, C. *Nfld. & L.,*
  Canada 49°15N 53°30W **165** C9
Freels, C. *Nfld. & L.,*
  Canada 46°37N 53°32W **165** C9
Freeman *Calif., U.S.A.* 35°35N 117°53W **171** K9
Freeman *S. Dak.,*
  U.S.A. 43°21N 97°26W **172** D5
Freeport *Bahamas* 26°30N 78°47W **182** A4
Freeport *Fla., U.S.A.* 30°30N 86°8W **178** F3

Freeport *Ill., U.S.A.* 42°17N 89°36W **172** D9
Freeport *N.Y., U.S.A.* 40°39N 73°35W **175** F11
Freeport *Ohio, U.S.A.* 40°12N 81°15W **174** F3
Freeport *Tex., U.S.A.* 40°41N 79°41W **174** F5
Freeport *Tex., U.S.A.* 28°57N 95°21W **176** E7
Freetown *S. Leone* 8°30N 13°17W **138** D2
Freeville *U.S.A.* 42°30N 76°20W **175** D8
Frégate, L. de la
  Canada 53°15N 74°45W **164** B5
Fregenal de la Sierra
  Spain 38°10N 6°39W **89** G4
Fregene *Italy* 41°51N 12°12E **93** G9
Fregon *Australia* 26°45S 132°1E **149** E5
Fréhel, C. *France* 48°40N 2°20W **70** D4
Freiberg *Germany* 50°55N 13°20E **76** D8
Freibourg = Fribourg
  Switz. 46°49N 7°9E **77** J3
Freiburg *Baden-W.,*
  Germany 47°59N 7°51E **77** H3
Freiburg *Niedersachsen,*
  Germany 53°49N 9°16E **76** B5
Freilassing *Germany* 47°50N 12°58E **77** H8
Freire *Chile* 38°54S 72°38W **192** A2
Freirina *Chile* 28°30S 71°10W **190** B1
Freising *Germany* 48°24N 11°45E **77** G7
Freistadt *Austria* 48°30N 14°30E **77** G8
Freital *Germany* 51°1N 13°39E **76** D9
Fréjus *France* 43°25N 6°44E **73** E10
Fremantle *Australia* 32°7S 115°47E **149** F2
Fremont *Calif., U.S.A.* 37°32N 121°57W **170** H4
Fremont *Mich., U.S.A.* 43°28N 85°57W **172** D3
Fremont *Nebr., U.S.A.* 41°26N 96°30W **172** E5
Fremont *Ohio, U.S.A.* 41°21N 83°7W **173** E12
Fremont → *U.S.A.* 38°24N 110°42W **168** G8
French Camp *U.S.A.* 37°53N 121°16W **170** H5
French Cays = Plana Cays
  Bahamas 22°38N 73°30W **183** B5
French Creek →
  U.S.A. 41°24N 79°50W **174** E5
French Frigate Shoals
  U.S.A. 23°45N 166°10W **167** L6
French Guiana ☑
  S. Amer. 4°0N 53°0W **187** C8
French I. *Australia* 38°20S 145°22E **153** F6
French Island △
  Australia 38°20S 145°22E **153** F6
French Mts. *Canada* 72°0N 96°0W **160** C12
French Pass *N.Z.* 40°55S 173°55E **155** D5
French Polynesia ☑
  Pac. Oc. 20°0S 145°0W **157** J13
French Riviera = Azur, Côte d'
  France 43°25N 7°10E **73** E11
Frenchman Cr. →
  N. Amer. 48°31N 107°10W **168** B10
Frenchman Cr. →
  U.S.A. 40°14N 100°50W **172** E3
Frenda *Algeria* 35°2N 1°1E **136** A4
Frenštát pod Radhoštěm
  Czech Rep. 49°33N 18°13E **79** B11
Fresco *Ivory C.* 5°3N 5°31W **138** D3
Fresco → *Brazil* 7°15S 51°30W **187** E8
Freshfield, C.
  Antarctica 68°25S 151°10E **55** C10
Fresnay-sur-Sarthe *France* 48°17N 0°1E **70** D7
Fresnillo *Mexico* 23°10N 102°53W **180** C4
Fresno *U.S.A.* 36°44N 119°47W **170** J7
Fresno Alhándiga *Spain* 40°42N 5°37W **88** E5
Fresno Res. *U.S.A.* 48°36N 109°57W **168** B9
Freudenstadt *Germany* 48°27N 8°24E **77** G8
Frévent *France* 50°15N 2°17E **71** B9
Frew → *Australia* 20°0S 135°38E **150** C2
Frewsburg *U.S.A.* 42°3N 79°10W **174** D5
Freycinet △ *Australia* 42°11S 148°19E **151** G4
Freycinet Pen.
  Australia 42°0S 148°25E **151** G4
Freyming-Merlebach
  France 49°8N 6°48E **71** C13
Freyung *Germany* 48°48N 13°31E **77** G9
Fria *Guinea* 10°27N 13°38W **138** C2
Fria, C. *Namibia* 18°0S 12°0E **144** A1
Friant *U.S.A.* 36°59N 119°43W **170** J7
Fuḥaymī *Iraq* 34°12N 42°20E **105** E10
Fuhlsbüttel, Hamburg ✈ (HAM)
  Germany 53°35N 9°59E **76** B5
Fuidhaigh = Wiay *U.K.* 57°24N 7°13W **65** D1
Fuji *Japan* 35°9N 138°39E **113** G9
Fuji-Hakone-Izu △
  Japan 35°15N 138°45E **113** G9
Fuji-San *Japan* 35°22N 138°44E **113** G9
Fuji-Yoshida *Japan* 35°30N 138°46E **113** G9
Fujian □ *China* 26°0N 118°0E **117** D12
Fujin *China* 47°16N 132°1E **115** B15
Fujinomiya *Japan* 35°10N 138°40E **113** G9
Fujisawa *Japan* 35°22N 139°29E **113** G9
Fujiyama, Mt. = Fuji-San
  Japan 35°22N 138°44E **113** G9
Fukagawa *Japan* 43°43N 142°2E **112** C11
Fukien = Fujian □ *China* 26°0N 118°0E **117** D12
Fukuchiyama *Japan* 35°19N 135°9E **113** G7
Fukue *Japan* 32°41N 128°51E **113** H4
Fukue-Shima *Japan* 32°40N 128°45E **113** H4
Fukui *Japan* 36°5N 136°10E **113** F8
Fukui □ *Japan* 36°0N 136°12E **113** G8
Fukuoka *Japan* 33°39N 130°21E **113** H5
Fukuoka □ *Japan* 33°30N 131°0E **113** H5
Fukushima *Japan* 37°44N 140°28E **112** F10
Fukushima □ *Japan* 37°30N 140°15E **112** F10
Fukuyama *Japan* 34°35N 133°20E **113** G6
Fulacunda *Guinea-Biss.* 11°43S 15°3W **138** C2
Fulaga *Fiji* 19°8S 178°33W **154** a
Fulan → *Sweden* 61°18N 13°4E **62** C7
Fulda *Germany* 50°32N 9°40E **76** E5
Fulda → *Germany* 51°25N 9°39E **76** D5
Fulford Harbour
  Canada 48°47N 123°27W **170** B3
Fulleborn *Papua N. G.* ...
Fullerton *Calif.,*
  U.S.A. 33°53N 117°56W **171** M9
Fullerton *Nebr., U.S.A.* 41°22N 97°58W **172** E5
Fulton *Mo., U.S.A.* 38°52N 91°57W **172** F8
Fulton *N.Y., U.S.A.* 43°19N 76°25W **175** C8
Fulufjället *Sweden* 61°32N 12°41E **62** C6
Fumay *France* 49°58N 4°42E **71** C11
Fumel *France* 44°30N 0°58E **72** D4
Fumin *China* 25°10N 102°20E **116** E4
Frómista *Spain* 42°16N 4°25W **88** C6
Funabashi *Japan* 35°45N 140°0E **113** G10
Funafuti = Fongafale
  Tuvalu 8°31S 179°13E **147** B10

Fronteira *Portugal* 39°3N 7°39W **89** F3
Fronteiras *Brazil* 7°5S 40°37W **189** B2
Frontenac → *Canada* 44°32N 90°53W **175** B8
Frontera *Canary Is.* 27°47N 17°59W **100** G2
Frontera *Mexico* 18°32N 92°38W **181** D6
Frontignan *France* 43°27N 3°45E **72** E7
Frosinone *Italy* 41°38N 13°19E **94** A6
Frostburg *U.S.A.* 39°39N 78°56W **173** F14
Frostisen *Norway* 68°14N 17°10E **60** B17
Frostproof *U.S.A.* 27°45N 81°32W **179** H8
Frøya *Norway* 63°43N 8°40E **60** E13
Fruita *U.S.A.* 39°9N 108°44W **168** G9
Fruithurst *U.S.A.* 33°44N 85°26W **178** B4
Fruitland *U.S.A.* 38°51N 81°43W **170** B8
Frumoasa *Romania* 46°28N 25°48E **81** D10
Frunze = Bishkek
  Kyrgyzstan 42°54N 74°46E **109** D8
Frunzivka *Ukraine* 47°20N 29°45E **81** C14
Fruška Gora *Serbia* 45°7N 19°30E **80** E4
Fruška Gora △ *Serbia* 45°8N 19°40E **96** A3
Frutal *Brazil* 20°0S 49°0W **187** H9
Frutigen *Switz.* 46°35N 7°38E **77** J3
Frýdek-Místek
  Czech Rep. 49°40N 18°20E **79** B11
Frýdlant *Czech Rep.* 50°56N 15°9E **78** A8
Fryeburg *U.S.A.* 44°1N 70°59W **175** B14
Fryvaldov = Jeseník
  Czech Rep. 50°14N 17°8E **79** A10
Fthiótida *Greece* 38°50N 22°25E **98** B4
Fu Xian = Wafangdian
  China 39°38N 121°58E **115** E11
Fu Xian *China* 36°0N 109°20E **114** G5
Fu'an *China* 27°11N 119°36E **117** D12
Fubian *China* 31°17N 102°22E **116** B4
Fucécchio *Italy* 43°44N 10°48E **92** E7
Fucheng *China* 37°50N 116°10E **114** F9
Fuchou = Fuzhou
  China 26°5N 119°16E **117** D12
Fuchū *Japan* 34°34N 133°14E **113** G6
Fuchuan *China* 24°50N 111°5E **117** E8
Fuchun Jiang → *China* 30°5N 120°5E **117** B13
Fúcino, Piana del *Italy* 42°1N 13°31E **93** F10
Fuding *China* 27°20N 120°12E **117** D13
Fuencaliente *Spain* 38°25N 4°18W **89** G6
Fuencaliente, Pta.
  Canary Is. 28°27N 17°51W **100** F2
Fuengirola *Spain* 36°32N 4°41W **89** J6
Fuenlabrada *Spain* 40°17N 3°48W **88** E7
Fuensalida *Spain* 40°3N 4°12W **88** E6
Fuente-Álamo *Spain* 38°44N 1°24W **91** G3
Fuente-Álamo de Murcia
  Spain 37°42N 1°6W **91** H3
Fuente de Cantos *Spain* 38°15N 6°18W **89** G4
Fuente del Maestre *Spain* 38°31N 6°28W **89** G4
Fuente el Fresno *Spain* 39°14N 3°46W **89** F7
Fuente Obejuna *Spain* 38°15N 5°25W **89** G5
Fuente Palmera *Spain* 37°42N 5°6W **89** H5
Fuentes de Andalucía
  Spain 37°28N 5°20W **89** H5
Fuentes de Ebro *Spain* 41°31N 0°38W **90** D4
Fuentes de León *Spain* 38°5N 6°32W **89** G4
Fuentesaúco *Spain* 41°15N 5°30W **88** D5
Fuerte → *Mexico* 25°54N 109°22W **180** B3
Fuerte Olimpo *Paraguay* 21°0S 57°51W **190** A4
Fuerteventura
  Canary Is. 28°30N 14°0W **100** F6
Fuerteventura ✈ (FUE)
  Canary Is. 28°24N 13°52W **100** F6
Fufeng *China* 34°22N 108°0E **114** G5
Fugong *China* 27°5N 98°47E **116** D2
Fugou *China* 34°3N 114°25E **116** A8
Fugu *China* 39°2N 111°3E **114** E6
Fuhai *China* 47°2N 87°25E **109** C11
Funan *China* 32°39N 115°42E **117** A10
Funäsdalen *Sweden* 62°33N 12°32E **62** B6
Funchal *Madeira* 32°38N 16°54W **100** D3
Funchal ✈ (FNC)
  Madeira 32°42N 16°45W **100** D3
Fundación *Colombia* 10°31N 74°11W **186** A4
Fundão *Brazil* 19°55S 40°24W **189** D2
Fundão *Portugal* 40°8N 7°30W **88** E3
Fundong *Cameroon* 6°15N 10°16E **139** D7
Fundu Moldovei
  Romania 47°32N 25°24E **81** C10
Fundulea *Romania* 44°28N 26°31E **81** F10
Fundy, B. of *Canada* 45°0N 66°0W **165** D6
Fundy △ *Canada* 45°35N 65°10W **165** C6
Funhalouro *Mozam.* 23°3S 34°25E **145** B5
Funing *Hebei, China* 39°53N 119°12E **115** E10
Funing *Jiangsu, China* 33°45N 119°50E **115** H10
Funing *Yunnan, China* 23°35N 105°45E **116** F5
Funiu Shan *China* 33°30N 112°20E **114** H7
Funsi *Ghana* 10°21N 1°54W **138** C4
Funtua *Nigeria* 11°30N 7°18E **139** C6
Fuping *Hebei, China* 38°48N 114°12E **114** E8
Fuping *Shaanxi, China* 34°42N 109°10E **114** G5
Fuqing *China* 25°41N 119°21E **117** E12
Fuquan *China* 26°40N 107°27E **116** D6
Furano *Japan* 43°21N 142°23E **112** C11
Furāt, Nahr al → *Asia* 31°0N 47°25E **128** D5
Fürg *Iran* 28°18N 55°13E **129** D7
Furman *U.S.A.* 32°41N 81°11W **178** C8
Furmanov *Russia* 57°10N 41°6E **86** B6
Furnás *Spain* 39°3N 1°32E **100** B8
Furnas, Represa de
  Brazil 20°50S 45°30W **191** A6
Furneaux Group
  Australia 40°10S 147°50E **151** G4
Furqlus *Syria* 34°36N 37°8E **130** A6
Fürstenau *Germany* 52°31N 7°40E **76** C3
Fürstenberg *Germany* 53°10N 13°8E **76** B9
Fürstenfeld *Austria* 47°3N 16°3E **78** B9
Fürstenfeldbruck
  Germany 48°11N 11°15E **77** G7
Fürstenwalde *Germany* 52°22N 14°3E **76** C10
Fürth *Germany* 49°28N 10°59E **77** F6
Fürth im Wald *Germany* 49°18N 12°50E **77** F8
Furtwangen *Germany* 48°2N 8°12E **77** G4
Furudal *Sweden* 61°10N 15°11E **62** C9
Furukawa = Ōsaki
  Japan 38°34N 140°58E **112** E10
Furulund *Sweden* 55°46N 13°6E **63** J7
Furuvik *Sweden* 61°38N 17°20E **62** D11
Fury and Hecla Str.
  Canada 69°56N 84°0W **161** D15
Fusagasugá *Colombia* 4°21N 74°22W **186** C4
Fuscaldo *Italy* 39°25N 16°2E **95** C9
Fushan *Shandong,*
  China 37°30N 121°15E **115** F11
Fushan *Shanxi, China* 35°58N 111°51E **114** G6
Fushë Arrëz *Albania* 42°4N 20°2E **96** B4
Fushë Kosovë *Kosovo* 42°40N 21°5E **96** C5
Fushë Krujë *Albania* 41°30N 19°43E **96** E3
Fushun *Liaoning,*
  China 41°50N 123°56E **115** D12
Fushun *Sichuan, China* 29°13N 104°52E **116** C5
Fusong *China* 42°20N 127°15E **115** C14
Füssen *Germany* 47°34N 10°42E **77** H6
Fustic *Barbados* 13°16N 59°38W **183** g
Fusui *China* 22°40N 107°56E **116** F6
Futian *China* 22°32N 114°4E **111** a
Futog *Serbia* 45°15N 19°42E **80** E4
Futrono *Chile* 40°8S 72°24W **192** B2
Fuwa *Egypt* 31°33N 30°43E **137** B12
Fuxian Hu *China* 24°30N 102°53E **116** E4
Fuxin *China* 42°5N 121°48E **115** C11
Fuyang *Anhui, China* 33°0N 115°48E **117** A10
Fuyang *Zhejiang, China* 30°5N 119°57E **117** B12
Fuyang He → *China* 38°12N 117°0E **114** E9
Fuying Dao *China* 26°34N 120°9E **117** D13
Fuyong *China* 22°40N 113°49E **111** a
Fuyu *Heilongjiang,*
  China 47°49N 124°27E **111** B13
Fuyu *Jilin, China* 45°12N 124°43E **115** B13
Fuyuan *China* 48°20N 134°5E **115** B16
Fuyun *China* 47°0N 89°28E **109** C11
Füzesgyarmat *Hungary* 47°6N 21°14E **80** C6
Fuzhou = Linchuan
  China 27°57N 116°15E **117** D11
Fuzhou *China* 26°5N 119°16E **117** D12
Füzuli *Azerbaijan* 39°36N 47°8E **105** C12
Fyn *Denmark* 55°20N 10°30E **63** J4
Fyne, L. *U.K.* 55°59N 5°23W **65** F3
Fynshav *Denmark* 54°59N 9°59E **63** J3

G

Ga *Ghana* 9°47N 2°30W **138** D4
Gaalkacyo *Somalia* 6°30N 47°30E **131** F4
Gaanda *Nigeria* 10°10N 12°27E **139** C7
Gabas → *France* 43°46N 0°42W **72** E3
Gabba *Australia* 9°45S 142°38E **150** a
Gabela *Angola* 11°0S 14°24E **140** G2
Gabès *Tunisia* 33°53N 10°2E **136** B6
Gabès □ *Tunisia* 33°35N 9°30E **136** B5
Gabès, G. de *Tunisia* 34°0N 10°30E **136** B6
Gabgaba, W. → *Egypt* 22°10N 33°5E **137** C3
Gabia la Grande *Spain* 37°8N 3°40W **89** H7
Gąbin *Poland* 52°23N 19°41E **83** F6
Gabon ■ *Africa* 0°10S 10°0E **140** E2
Gaborone *Botswana* 24°45S 25°57E **144** B4
Gabriels *U.S.A.* 44°26N 74°12W **175** B10
Gābrīk *Iran* 25°44N 58°28E **129** E8
Gabrovo *Bulgaria* 42°52N 25°19E **97** D9
Gacé *France* 48°49N 0°20E **70** D7
Gāch Sār *Iran* 36°7N 51°19E **129** B6
Gachsārān *Iran* 30°15N 50°45E **129** D6
Gacko *Bos.-H.* 43°10N 18°33E **96** C7
Gad Hinglaj *India* 16°14N 74°21E **127** F2
Gadag *India* 15°30N 75°45E **127** F2
Gadap *Pakistan* 25°5N 67°28E **124** G2
Gadarwara *India* 22°50N 78°50E **125** H8
Gadebusch *Germany* 53°42N 11°7E **76** B6
Gadhada *India* 22°0N 71°35E **124** J4
Gádor, Sierra de *Spain* 36°57N 2°45W **89** H8
Gadra *Pakistan* 25°40N 70°38E **124** G4
Gadsden *Ala., U.S.A.* 34°1N 86°1W **178** B3
Gadsden *S.C., U.S.A.* 33°51N 80°46W **178** B5
Gadwal *India* 16°10N 77°50E **127** F3
Gadyach = Hadyach
  Ukraine 50°21N 34°0E **85** G10
Găești *Romania* 44°48N 25°19E **81** F10
Gaeta *Italy* 41°12N 13°35E **94** A6

Gaeta, G. di Italy 41°6N 13°30E 94 A6
Gaffney U.S.A. 35°5N 81°39W 177 D14
Gafsa Tunisia 34°24N 8°43E 136 B5
Gafsa □ Tunisia 34°30N 8°48E 136 B5
Gagarawa Nigeria 12°25N 9°32E 139 C6
Gagaria India 25°43N 70°46E 124 G4
Gagarin Russia 55°38N 35°0E 84 E8
Găgăuzia □ Moldova 46°10N 28°40E 81 D13
Gaggenau Germany 48°48N 8°18E 77 G4
Gagino Russia 55°15N 45°1E 86 C7
Gagliano del Capo Italy 39°50N 18°22E 95 C11
Gagnef Sweden 60°36N 15°5E 62 D9
Gagnoa Ivory C. 6°56N 6°16W 138 D3
Gagnon Canada 51°50N 68°5W 165 B6
Gagnon, L. Canada 62°3N 110°27W 163 A6
Gagra Georgia 43°20N 40°10E 87 J5
Gahini Rwanda 1°50S 30°30E 142 C3
Gahmar India 25°27N 83°49E 125 G10
Gai Xian = Gaizhou China 40°22N 122°20E 115 D12
Gaidouronisi Greece 34°53N 25°41E 101 F7
Gail U.S.A. 32°46N 101°27W 176 E4
Gail → Austria 46°36N 13°53E 78 E6
Gaillac France 43°54N 1°54E 72 E5
Gaillimh = Galway Ireland 53°17N 9°3W 64 C2
Gaillon France 49°10N 1°20E 70 C8
Gaimán Argentina 43°10S 65°25W 192 B3
Gaines U.S.A. 41°46N 77°35W 174 E7
Gainesville Fla., U.S.A. 29°40N 82°20W 179 F7
Gainesville Ga., U.S.A. 34°18N 83°50W 177 D13
Gainesville Mo., U.S.A. 36°36N 92°26W 172 G7
Gainesville Tex., U.S.A. 33°38N 97°8W 176 E6
Gainsborough U.K. 53°24N 0°46W 66 D7
Gairdner, L. Australia 31°30S 136°0E 152 A2
Gairloch U.K. 57°43N 5°41W 65 D3
Gairloch, L. U.K. 57°43N 5°45W 65 D3
Gaizhou China 40°22N 122°20E 115 D12
Gaj Croatia 45°28N 17°3E 80 E2
Gaj → Pakistan 26°26N 67°21E 124 F2
Gajendragarh India 15°44N 75°59E 127 G2
Gakuch Pakistan 36°7N 73°45E 125 A5
Gal Oya △ Sri Lanka 7°0N 81°20E 127 L5
Gal Oya Res. Sri Lanka 7°5N 81°30E 127 L5
Galâla, Gebel el Egypt 29°21N 32°22E 137 F8
Galán, Cerro Argentina 25°55S 66°52W 190 B2
Galana → Kenya 3°9S 40°8E 142 C5
Galanta Slovak Rep. 48°11N 17°45E 79 C10
Galapagar Spain 40°36N 3°58W 88 E7
Galápagos = Colón, Arch. de Ecuador 0°0 91°0W 184 D1
Galapagos Fracture Zone Pac. Oc. 3°0N 110°0W 157 G17
Galapagos Rise Pac. Oc. 15°0S 95°0W 157 J18
Galashiels U.K. 55°37N 2°49W 65 F6
Galatas Greece 37°30N 23°26E 98 D5
Galatea N.Z. 38°24S 176°45E 154 E5
Galateia Cyprus 35°25N 34°4E 101 D13
Galaţi Romania 45°27N 28°2E 81 E13
Galaţi □ Romania 45°45N 27°30E 81 E12
Galatia Turkey 39°30N 33°0E 104 C5
Galatina Italy 40°10N 18°10E 95 B11
Galátone Italy 40°9N 18°4E 95 B11
Galax U.S.A. 36°40N 80°56W 173 G13
Galaxidi Greece 38°22N 22°23E 98 C4
Galbīn Govĭ Mongolia 43°0N 107°0E 114 C4
Galcaio = Gaalkacyo Somalia 6°30N 47°30E 131 F4
Galdhøpiggen Norway 61°38N 8°18E 60 F13
Galeana Chihuahua, Mexico 30°7N 107°38W 180 A3
Galeana Nuevo León, Mexico 24°50N 100°4W 180 A3
Galela Indonesia 1°50N 127°49E 119 D7
Galeota Pt. Trin. & Tob. 10°8N 60°59W 187 K16
Galera Spain 37°45N 2°33W 91 H2
Galera, Pta. Chile 39°59S 73°43W 192 A2
Galera Pt. Trin. & Tob. 10°49N 60°54W 183 D7
Galesburg U.S.A. 40°57N 90°22W 172 E8
Galestan △ Iran 37°30N 56°0E 129 B8
Galeton U.S.A. 41°44N 77°39W 174 E7
Galheirão → Brazil 12°23S 45°5W 189 C1
Gali Georgia 42°37N 41°46E 87 J5
Galicea Mare Romania 44°4N 23°19E 81 F8
Galich Russia 58°22N 42°24E 86 A6
Galiche Bulgaria 43°34N 23°53E 96 C7
Galicia □ Spain 42°43N 7°45W 88 C3
Galičica △ Macedonia 41°2N 20°55E 96 E4
Galilee = Hagalil Israel 32°53N 35°18E 130 C4
Galilee, L. Australia 22°20S 145°50E 150 C4
Galilee, Sea of = Yam Kinneret Israel 32°45N 35°35E 130 C4
Galim Cameroon 7°6N 12°25E 139 D7
Galina Pt. Jamaica 18°24N 76°58W 182 a
Galinoporni Cyprus 35°31N 34°18E 101 D13
Galion U.S.A. 40°44N 82°47W 174 F2
Galite, Îs. de la Tunisia 37°30N 8°59E 136 A5
Galiuro Mts. U.S.A. 32°30N 110°20W 169 K8
Galiwinku Australia 12°2S 135°34E 150 A2
Gallan Hd. U.K. 58°15N 7°2W 65 C1
Gallarate Italy 45°40N 8°48E 92 C5
Gallatin U.S.A. 36°24N 86°27W 177 C11
Galle Sri Lanka 6°5N 80°10E 127 L5
Gállego → Spain 41°39N 0°51W 90 D4
Gallegos → Argentina 51°35S 69°0W 192 D3
Galley Hd. Ireland 51°32N 8°55W 64 E3
Galliate Italy 45°29N 8°42E 92 C5
Gallinas, Pta. Colombia 12°28N 71°40W 186 A4
Gallipoli = Gelibolu Turkey 40°28N 26°43E 97 F10
Gallipoli Italy 40°3N 17°58E 95 B10
Gallipolis U.S.A. 38°49N 82°12W 173 F12
Gällivare Sweden 67°9N 20°40E 60 C19
Gallneukirchen Austria 48°21N 14°25E 78 C7
Gällö Sweden 62°55N 15°13E 62 B9
Gallo, C. Italy 38°13N 13°19E 94 D6
Gallocanta, L. de Spain 40°58N 1°30W 90 E3
Galloo I. U.S.A. 43°55N 76°25W 175 C8
Galloway U.K. 55°1N 4°29W 65 F4
Galloway, Mull of U.K. 54°39N 4°52W 65 G4
Gallup U.S.A. 35°32N 108°45W 169 J9
Gallur Spain 41°52N 1°19W 90 D3
Gallura Italy 41°5N 9°20E 94 A2
Galmudug Somalia 6°30N 48°0E 131 F4
Galong Australia 34°37S 148°34E 153 C8
Galoya Sri Lanka 8°10N 80°55E 127 K5
Galt U.S.A. 38°15N 121°18W 170 G5
Galten Denmark 56°9N 9°54E 63 H3
Galtür Austria 46°58N 10°11E 78 E3
Galty Mts. Ireland 52°22N 8°10W 64 D3
Galtymore Ireland 52°21N 8°11W 64 D3
Galugāh Iran 36°43N 53°48E 129 B7
Galva U.S.A. 41°10N 90°3W 172 E8
Galvarino Chile 38°24S 72°47W 192 A2
Galve de Sorbe Spain 41°13N 3°10W 90 D1
Galveston U.S.A. 29°18N 94°48W 176 G7
Galveston B. U.S.A. 29°36N 94°50W 176 G7
Gálvez Argentina 32°0S 61°14W 190 C3
Galway Ireland 53°17N 9°3W 64 C2
Galway □ Ireland 53°22N 9°1W 64 C2
Galway B. Ireland 53°13N 9°10W 64 C2
Gam → Vietnam 21°55N 105°12E 120 B5
Gamagōri Japan 34°50N 137°14E 113 G8
Gamawa Nigeria 12°10N 10°31E 139 C7
Gambaga Ghana 10°30N 0°28W 139 C4
Gambat Pakistan 27°17N 68°26E 124 F3
Gambhir → India 26°58N 77°27E 124 F6
Gambia ■ W. Afr. 13°25N 16°0W 138 C1
Gambia → W. Afr. 13°28N 16°34W 138 C1
Gambier U.S.A. 40°22N 82°23W 174 F2
Gambier, C. Australia 11°56S 130°57E 148 B5
Gambier, Îs. French Polynesia 23°8S 134°58W 157 K14
Gambier Is. Australia 35°3S 136°30E 152 C2
Gambo Canada 48°47N 54°13W 165 C9
Gamboli Pakistan 29°53N 68°24E 124 E3
Gamboma Congo 1°55S 15°52E 140 E3
Gamka → S. Africa 33°18S 21°39E 144 D3
Gamkab → Namibia 28°4S 17°54E 144 C2
Gamla Uppsala Sweden 59°54N 17°40E 62 E11
Gamlakarleby = Kokkola Finland 63°50N 23°8E 60 E20
Gamleby Sweden 57°54N 16°24E 63 G10
Gammon → Canada 51°24N 95°44W 163 C9
Gammon Ranges △ Australia 30°38S 139°8E 151 E2
Gamou Niger 14°20N 9°55E 139 C6
Gampaha Sri Lanka 7°5N 79°59E 127 L4
Gampola Sri Lanka 7°10N 80°34E 127 L5
Gamtoos → S. Africa 33°58S 25°1E 144 D4
Gamzigrad-Romuliana Serbia 43°53N 22°11E 96 C6
Gan France 43°12N 0°27W 72 E3
Gan Gan Argentina 42°30S 68°10W 192 B3
Gan Goriama, Mts. Cameroon 7°44N 12°45E 139 D7
Gan Jiang → China 29°15N 116°0E 117 C11
Ganado U.S.A. 35°43N 109°33W 169 J9
Gananita Sudan 18°22N 33°50E 137 D3
Gananoque Canada 44°20N 76°10W 175 B8
Ganāveh Iran 29°35N 50°35E 129 D6
Gäncä Azerbaijan 40°45N 46°20E 87 K8
Gancheng China 18°51N 108°37E 117 a
Gand = Gent Belgium 51°2N 3°42E 69 C3
Ganda Angola 13°3S 14°35E 141 G2
Gandajika Dem. Rep. of the Congo 6°46S 23°58E 140 F4
Gandak → India 25°39N 85°13E 125 G11
Gandava Pakistan 28°32N 67°32E 124 E2
Gander Canada 48°58N 54°35W 165 C9
Gander L. Canada 48°58N 54°35W 165 C9
Ganderkesee Germany 53°2N 8°32E 76 B4
Ganderowe Falls Zimbabwe 17°20S 29°10E 143 F2
Gandesa Spain 41°3N 0°26E 90 D5
Gandhi Sagar India 24°40N 75°40E 124 G6
Gandhinagar India 23°15N 72°45E 124 H5
Gandi Nigeria 12°55N 5°49E 139 C6
Gandia Spain 38°58N 0°9W 91 G4
Gandino Italy 45°49N 9°54E 92 C6
Gando, Pta. Canary Is. 27°55N 15°22W 100 G4
Gandole Nigeria 8°28N 11°35E 139 D7
Gandu Brazil 13°45S 39°30W 189 C3
Ganêb Mauritania 18°29N 10°8W 138 B2
Ganedidalem = Gani Indonesia 0°48S 128°14E 119 E7
Ganga → India 23°20N 90°30E 125 H14
Ganga Sagar India 21°38N 88°5E 125 J13
Gangafani Mali 14°20N 2°20W 138 C4
Gangakher India 18°57N 76°45E 126 E3
Gangan → India 28°38N 78°58E 125 E8
Ganganagar India 29°56N 73°56E 124 E5
Gangapur Maharashtra, India 19°41N 75°1E 126 E2
Gangapur Raj., India 26°32N 76°49E 124 F7
Gangara Niger 14°35N 8°29E 139 C6
Gangaw Burma 22°5N 94°5E 123 H19
Gangawati India 15°30N 76°36E 127 G3
Gangdisê Shan China 31°20N 81°0E 125 D9
Ganges = Ganga → India 23°20N 90°30E 125 H14
Ganges Canada 48°51N 123°31W 162 D4
Ganges France 43°56N 3°42E 72 E7
Ganges, Mouths of the India 21°30N 90°0E 125 J14
Ganggyeong S. Korea 36°10N 127°0E 115 F14
Gänghester Sweden 57°42N 13°1E 63 G7
Gangi Italy 37°48N 14°12E 95 E7
Gângiova Romania 43°54N 23°50E 81 G8
Gangneung S. Korea 37°45N 128°54E 115 F15
Gangoh India 29°46N 77°18E 124 E7
Gangotri India 30°50N 79°10E 125 D8
Gangotri △ India 30°50N 79°10E 125 D8
Gangseong S. Korea 38°24N 128°30E 115 E15
Gangtok India 27°20N 88°37E 123 F16
Gangu China 34°40N 105°15E 114 G3
Gangyao China 44°12N 126°37E 115 B14
Gani Indonesia 0°48S 128°14E 119 E7
Ganj India 27°45N 78°57E 125 F8
Ganjam India 19°23N 85°4E 126 E7
Ganluo China 28°58N 102°59E 116 C4
Ganmain Australia 34°47S 147°1E 153 C7
Gannat France 46°7N 3°11E 71 F10
Gannett Peak U.S.A. 43°11N 109°39W 168 E9
Ganquan China 36°20N 109°20E 114 F5
Gänserdorf Austria 48°20N 16°43E 79 C9
Ganshui China 28°40N 106°40E 116 C6
Gansu □ China 36°0N 104°0E 114 G3
Ganta Liberia 7°15N 8°59W 138 D3
Gantheaume, C. Australia 36°4S 137°32E 152 D2
Gantheaume B. Australia 27°40S 114°10E 149 E1
Gantsevichi = Hantsavichy Belarus 52°49N 26°30E 75 B14
Ganye Nigeria 8°25N 12°4E 139 D7
Ganyem = Genyem Indonesia 2°46S 140°12E 119 E10
Ganyu China 34°50N 119°8E 115 G10
Ganyushkino Kazakhstan 46°35N 49°20E 87 G9
Ganzhou China 25°51N 114°56E 117 E10
Gao Mali 16°15N 0°5W 139 B4
Gao Xian China 28°21N 104°32E 116 C5
Gao'an China 28°26N 115°17E 117 C10
Gaobeidian China 39°19N 115°51E 114 E8
Gaocheng China 38°2N 114°49E 114 E8
Gaochun China 31°20N 118°49E 117 B12
Gaohebu China 30°43N 116°49E 117 B11
Gaokeng China 27°40N 113°58E 117 D9
Gaolan Dao China 21°55N 113°10E 117 G9
Gaoligong Shan China 24°45N 98°45E 116 E2
Gaomi China 36°20N 119°42E 115 F10
Gaoping China 35°45N 112°55E 114 G7
Gaotang China 36°50N 116°15E 114 F9
Gaoua Burkina Faso 10°20N 3°8W 138 C4
Gaoual Guinea 11°45N 13°25W 138 C2
Gaoxiong = Kaohsiung Taiwan 22°35N 120°16E 117 F13
Gaoyang China 38°40N 115°45E 114 E8
Gaoyao China 23°3N 112°27E 117 F9
Gaoyou China 32°47N 119°26E 117 A12
Gaoyou Hu China 32°45N 119°20E 117 A12
Gaoyuan China 37°8N 117°58E 115 F9
Gaozhou China 21°58N 110°50E 117 G8
Gap France 44°33N 6°5E 73 D10
Gapat → India 24°30N 82°28E 125 G10
Gapuwiyak Australia 12°25S 135°43E 150 A2
Gar China 32°10N 79°58E 110 E4
Gara, L. Ireland 53°57N 8°26W 64 C3
Garāb Iran 33°27N 47°16E 105 F12
Garabogazköl Aylagy Turkmenistan 41°0N 53°30E 108 D4
Garachico Canary Is. 28°22N 16°46W 100 F3
Garachiné Panama 8°0N 78°12W 182 E4
Garafia Canary Is. 28°48N 17°57W 100 F2
Garagum Turkmenistan 39°30N 60°0E 129 B8
Garah Australia 29°5S 149°38E 151 D4
Garajonay Canary Is. 28°7N 17°14W 100 F2
Garajonay △ Canary Is. 28°7N 17°14W 100 F2
Garamba △ Dem. Rep. of the Congo 4°10N 29°40E 142 B2
Garango Burkina Faso 11°48N 0°34W 139 C4
Garanhuns Brazil 8°50S 36°30W 189 B3
Garautha India 25°34N 79°18E 125 G8
Garawa ☉ Australia 16°43S 136°51E 150 B2
Garawe Liberia 4°35N 8°0W 138 E3
Garba Tula Kenya 0°30N 38°32E 142 B4
Garberville U.S.A. 40°6N 123°48W 168 F2
Garbiyang India 30°8N 80°54E 125 D9
Garbsen Germany 52°26N 9°31E 76 C5
Garças → Brazil 8°43S 39°41W 189 B3
Gard □ France 44°2N 4°10E 73 D8
Gard → France 43°51N 4°37E 73 E8
Garda, L. di Italy 45°40N 10°41E 92 C7
Gardabani Georgia 41°27N 45°5E 87 K7
Gardanne France 43°27N 5°27E 73 E9
Gårdby Sweden 56°36N 16°38E 63 H10
Garde L. Canada 62°50N 106°13W 163 A7
Gardelegen Germany 52°32N 11°24E 76 C7
Garden City Ga., U.S.A. 32°6N 81°9W 178 C8
Garden City Kans., U.S.A. 37°58N 100°53W 172 G3
Garden City Tex., U.S.A. 31°52N 101°29W 176 F4
Garden Grove U.S.A. 33°47N 117°55W 171 M9
Gardens of Stone △ Australia 33°14S 150°11E 153 B9
Gardēz Afghan. 33°37N 69°9E 124 C3
Gardiki Greece 38°50N 21°55E 98 C3
Gardiner Maine, U.S.A. 44°14N 69°47W 173 C19
Gardiner Mont., U.S.A. 45°2N 110°22W 168 D8
Gardiners I. U.S.A. 41°6N 72°6W 175 E12
Gardner Fla., U.S.A. 27°21N 81°48W 179 H8
Gardner Mass., U.S.A. 42°34N 71°59W 175 D13
Gardner Canal Canada 53°27N 128°8W 162 C3
Gardner Pinnacles U.S.A. 25°0N 167°55W 167 L6
Gardnerville U.S.A. 38°56N 119°45W 170 G7
Gardno, Jezioro Poland 54°40N 17°7E 82 D4
Gardo = Qardho Somalia 9°30N 49°6E 131 F4
Gardone Riviera Italy 45°37N 10°34E 92 C7
Gardone Val Trómpia Italy 45°41N 10°11E 92 C7
Gárdony Hungary 47°12N 18°39E 80 C3
Gares = Puente la Reina Spain 42°40N 1°49W 90 C3
Garešnica Croatia 45°36N 16°56E 93 C13
Garéssio Italy 44°12N 8°2E 92 D5
Garey U.S.A. 34°53N 120°19W 171 L6
Garfield U.S.A. 47°1N 117°9W 168 C5
Garforth U.K. 53°47N 1°24W 66 D6
Gargaliani Greece 37°4N 21°38E 98 D3
Gargan, Mt. France 45°37N 1°39E 72 C5
Gargano △ Italy 41°43N 15°52E 93 G12
Gargantua, C. Canada 47°36N 85°2W 173 B11
Gargett Australia 21°9S 148°46E 150 b
Gargouna Mali 15°56N 0°13E 139 B5
Gargždai Lithuania 55°43N 21°24E 82 C8
Garhchiroli India 20°10N 80°0E 126 D5
Garibaldi ⌂ Canada 49°50N 122°40W 162 D4
Garies S. Africa 30°32S 17°59E 144 D2
Garig Gunak Barlu △ Australia 11°26S 131°58E 148 B5
Garigliano → Italy 41°13N 13°45E 94 A6
Garissa Kenya 0°25S 39°40E 142 C4
Garkida Nigeria 10°27N 12°36E 139 C7
Garko Nigeria 11°45N 8°53E 139 C6
Garland Tex., U.S.A. 32°54N 96°38W 176 E6
Garland Utah, U.S.A. 41°45N 112°10W 168 F7
Garlasco Italy 45°12N 8°55E 92 C5
Garliava Lithuania 54°49N 23°52E 82 D10
Garlin France 43°33N 0°16W 72 E3
Garmāb Semnān, Iran 35°25N 56°45E 129 C8
Garmāb Zanjān, Iran 35°50N 48°11E 105 E13
Garmisch-Partenkirchen Germany 47°30N 11°6E 77 H7
Garmsār Iran 35°20N 52°25E 129 C7
Garner U.S.A. 43°6N 93°36W 172 D7
Garnett U.S.A. 38°17N 95°14W 172 F6
Garnpung L. Australia 33°25S 143°10E 152 B5
Garo Hills India 25°30N 90°30E 125 G14
Garoe = Garoowe Somalia 8°25N 48°33E 131 F4
Garonne → France 45°2N 0°36W 72 C3
Garonne, Canal Latéral à la France 44°15N 0°18E 72 D4
Garoowe Somalia 8°25N 48°33E 131 F4
Garot India 24°19N 75°41E 124 G6
Garou, L. Mali 16°2N 2°45W 138 B4
Garoua Cameroon 9°19N 13°21E 139 D7
Garpenberg Sweden 60°19N 16°12E 62 D10
Garphyttan Sweden 59°18N 14°56E 62 E8
Garrauli India 25°5N 79°22E 125 G8
Garrel Germany 52°57N 8°1E 76 C4
Garrison Mont., U.S.A. 46°31N 112°49W 168 C7
Garrison N. Dak., U.S.A. 47°40N 101°25W 172 B3
Garrison Res. = Sakakawea, L. U.S.A. 47°30N 101°25W 172 B3
Garron Pt. U.K. 55°3N 5°59W 64 A6
Garrovillas de Alconétar Spain 39°40N 6°33W 89 F4
Garrucha Spain 37°11N 1°49W 91 H3
Garry → U.K. 56°44N 3°47W 65 E5
Garry, L. Canada 65°58N 100°18W 160 D11
Garrygala Turkmenistan 38°31N 56°29E 129 B8
Garsen Kenya 2°20S 40°5E 142 C5
Gärsnäs Sweden 55°32N 14°10E 63 J8
Garson L. Canada 56°19N 110°2W 163 B6
Garstang U.K. 53°55N 2°46W 66 D5
Gartempe → France 46°47N 0°49E 72 B4
Gartz Germany 53°13N 14°23E 76 B10
Garu Ghana 10°55N 0°11W 139 C4
Garu India 23°40N 84°14E 125 H11
Garub Namibia 26°37S 16°0E 144 C2
Garut Indonesia 7°14S 107°53E 119 G12
Garvão Portugal 37°42N 8°21W 89 H2
Garvie Mts. N.Z. 45°30S 168°50E 155 F3
Garwa = Garoua Cameroon 9°19N 13°21E 139 D7
Garwa India 24°11N 83°47E 125 G10
Garwolin Poland 51°55N 21°38E 83 G8
Gary U.S.A. 41°36N 87°20W 172 E10
Garz Germany 54°19N 13°20E 76 A9
Garzê China 31°38N 100°1E 116 B3
Garzón Colombia 2°10N 75°40W 186 C3
Gas-San Japan 38°32N 140°1E 112 E10
Gasan Kuli = Esenguly Turkmenistan 37°37N 53°59E 108 E4
Gascogne France 43°45N 0°20E 72 E4
Gascogne, G. de Europe 44°0N 2°0W 72 E2
Gascony = Gascogne France 43°45N 0°20E 72 E4
Gascoyne → Australia 24°52S 113°37E 149 D1
Gascoyne Junction Australia 25°2S 115°17E 149 E2
Gascueña Spain 40°18N 2°31W 90 E2
Gashagar Nigeria 13°22N 12°47E 139 C7
Gashaka Nigeria 7°20N 11°29E 139 D7
Gashaka-Gumti △ Nigeria 7°23N 11°34E 139 D7
Gasherbrum Pakistan 35°40N 76°40E 125 B7
Gashua Nigeria 12°54N 11°0E 139 C7
Gaspar Str. = Gelasa, Selat Indonesia 2°50S 107°0E 118 E3
Gasparilla I. U.S.A. 26°46N 82°16W 179 J7
Gasparillo Trin. & Tob. 10°18N 61°26W 187 K15
Gaspé Canada 48°52N 64°30W 165 C7
Gaspé, C. de Canada 48°48N 64°7W 165 C7
Gaspé Pen. = Gaspésie, Pén. de la Canada 48°45N 65°40W 165 C6
Gaspésie, Pén. de la Canada 48°45N 65°40W 165 C6
Gaspésie ⌂ Canada 48°55N 66°10W 165 C6
Gassan Burkina Faso 12°49N 3°12W 138 C4
Gassol Nigeria 8°34N 10°25E 139 D7
Gasteiz = Vitoria-Gasteiz Spain 42°50N 2°41W 90 C2
Gaston U.S.A. 33°49N 81°5W 178 B8
Gastonia U.S.A. 35°16N 81°11W 177 D14
Gastouni Greece 37°51N 21°15E 98 D3
Gastouri Greece 39°34N 19°54E 98 B1
Gastre Argentina 42°20S 69°15W 192 B3
Gästrikland Sweden 60°45N 16°40E 62 D10
Gata, C. Cyprus 34°34N 33°2E 101 E12
Gata, C. de Spain 36°41N 2°13W 91 J2
Gata, Sierra de Spain 40°20N 6°45W 88 E4
Gataga → Canada 58°35N 126°59W 162 B3
Gătaia Romania 45°26N 21°30E 80 E6
Gatchina Russia 59°35N 30°9E 84 C6
Gatehouse of Fleet U.K. 54°53N 4°12W 65 G4
Gates U.S.A. 43°9N 77°42W 174 C7
Gateshead U.K. 54°57N 1°35W 66 C6
Gateshead I. Canada 70°36N 100°26W 160 C11
Gatesville U.S.A. 31°26N 97°45W 176 F6
Gateway ⌂ U.S.A. 40°38N 73°51W 175 F11
Gaths Zimbabwe 20°2S 30°32E 143 G3
Gâtinais France 48°5N 2°40E 71 D9
Gâtine, Hauteurs de France 46°35N 0°45W 72 B3
Gatineau Canada 45°29N 75°39W 175 A9
Gatineau → Canada 45°27N 75°42W 164 C4
Gatineau △ Canada 45°40N 76°0W 164 C4
Gattinara Italy 45°37N 8°22E 92 C5
Gatton Australia 27°32S 152°17E 151 D5
Gatún, L. Panama 9°7N 79°56W 182 E4
Gatwick, London ✈ (LGW) U.K. 51°10N 0°11W 67 F7
Gatyana S. Africa 32°16S 28°31E 145 D4
Gau Fiji 18°2S 179°18E 154 a
Gaucín Spain 36°31N 5°19W 89 J5
Gauer L. Canada 57°0N 97°50W 163 B9
Gauhati = Guwahati India 26°10N 91°45E 123 F17
Gauja → Latvia 57°10N 24°16E 84 D3
Gaujas △ Latvia 57°10N 24°50E 61 H21
Gaula → Norway 63°21N 10°14E 60 E14
Gaurdak = Gowurdak Turkmenistan 37°50N 66°4E 109 E7
Gauri Phanta India 28°41N 80°36E 125 E9
Gauribidanur India 13°37N 77°32E 127 H3
Gaustatoppen Norway 59°48N 8°40E 61 G13
Gauteng □ S. Africa 26°0S 28°0E 145 C4
Gāv Koshī Iran 28°38N 57°12E 129 D8
Gāvakān Iran 29°37N 53°10E 129 D7
Gavarnie France 42°44N 0°1W 72 F3
Gavāter Iran 25°10N 61°31E 129 E9
Gāvbandī Iran 27°12N 53°4E 129 E7
Gavdopoula Greece 34°56N 24°0E 101 E6
Gavdos Greece 34°50N 24°5E 101 E6
Gavi Italy 44°41N 8°49E 92 D5
Gavião Portugal 39°28N 7°56W 89 F3
Gaviota U.S.A. 34°29N 120°13W 171 L6
Gāvkhūnī, Bāţlāq-e Iran 32°6N 52°52E 129 C7
Gävle Sweden 60°40N 17°9E 62 D11
Gävleborgs län □ Sweden 61°30N 16°15E 62 C10
Gävlebukten Sweden 60°40N 17°20E 62 D11
Gavorrano Italy 42°55N 10°54E 92 F7
Gavray France 48°55N 1°20W 70 D5
Gavrilov Yam Russia 57°18N 39°49E 84 D10
Gavrio Greece 37°54N 24°44E 98 D6
Gawachab Namibia 27°4S 17°55E 144 C2
Gawilgarh Hills India 21°15N 76°45E 126 D3
Gawler Australia 34°30S 138°42E 152 C3
Gawler Ranges Australia 32°30S 135°45E 152 B2
Gawu Nigeria 9°14N 6°52E 139 D6
Gaxun Nur China 42°22N 100°30E 110 C9
Gay Russia 51°27N 58°27E 108 B5
Gay U.S.A. 33°6N 84°35W 178 B5
Gaya India 24°47N 85°4E 125 G11
Gaya Niger 11°52N 3°28E 139 C5
Gaya Nigeria 11°57N 9°0E 139 C6
Gayéri Burkina Faso 12°39N 0°29E 139 C5
Gaylord U.S.A. 45°2N 84°41W 173 C11
Gayndah Australia 25°35S 151°32E 151 D5
Gaysin = Haysyn Ukraine 48°57N 29°25E 81 B14
Gayvoron = Hayvoron Ukraine 48°22N 29°52E 81 B14
Gaza Gaza Strip 31°30N 34°28E 130 D3
Gaza □ Mozam. 23°10S 32°45E 145 B5
Gaza Strip ■ Asia 31°29N 34°25E 130 D3
Gazanjyk = Bereket Turkmenistan 39°16N 55°32E 129 B7
Gazaoua Niger 13°32N 7°55E 139 C6
Gāzbor Iran 28°5N 58°51E 129 D8
Gazi Dem. Rep. of the Congo 1°3N 24°30E 142 B1
Gaziantep Turkey 37°6N 37°23E 104 D7
Gaziantep □ Turkey 37°0N 37°0E 104 D7
Gazimağusa = Famagusta Cyprus 35°8N 33°55E 101 D12
Gazipaşa Turkey 36°16N 32°18E 104 D5
Gazli Uzbekistan 40°8N 63°27E 108 D6
Gbadolite Dem. Rep. of the Congo 4°17N 21°1E 140 D4
Gbarnga Liberia 7°19N 9°13W 138 D3
Gboko Nigeria 7°17N 9°4E 139 D6
Gcoverega Botswana 19°8S 24°18E 144 A3
Gcuwa S. Africa 32°20S 28°11E 145 D4
Gdańsk Poland 54°22N 18°40E 82 D5
Gdańsk ✈ (GDN) Poland 54°22N 18°30E 82 D5
Gdańska, Zatoka Poland 54°30N 19°20E 82 D6
Gdov Russia 58°48N 27°55E 84 C4
Gdynia Poland 54°35N 18°33E 82 D5
Geba → Guinea-Biss. 11°46N 15°36W 138 C1
Gebe Indonesia 0°5N 129°25E 119 D7
Gebeciler Turkey 38°46N 30°46E 99 C12
Gebeit Mine Sudan 21°3N 36°29E 137 C4
Gebel Abyad Sudan 19°0N 28°0E 137 D2
Gebel Iweibid Egypt 30°8N 32°13E 137 E8
Gebze Turkey 40°47N 29°25E 97 F13
Geçitkale = Lefkoniko Cyprus 35°18N 33°44E 101 D12
Gedaref Sudan 14°2N 35°28E 135 F13
Gede, Tanjung Indonesia 6°46S 105°12E 119 G11
Gediz Turkey 39°1N 29°24E 99 B11
Gediz → Turkey 38°35N 26°48E 99 C8
Gèdre France 42°47N 0°2E 72 F4
Gedser Denmark 54°35N 11°55E 63 K5
Gedung, Pulau Malaysia 5°17N 100°23E 121 c
Geegully Cr. → Australia 18°32S 123°41E 148 C3
Geel Belgium 51°10N 4°59E 69 C4
Geelong Australia 38°10S 144°22E 152 E6
Geelvink B. = Cenderawasih, Teluk Indonesia 3°0S 135°20E 119 E9
Geelvink Chan. Australia 28°30S 114°0E 149 E1
Geesthacht Germany 53°26N 10°22E 76 B6
Geidam Nigeria 12°57N 11°57E 139 C7
Geikie → Canada 57°45N 103°52W 163 B8
Geikie Gorge △ Australia 18°3S 125°41E 148 C4
Geilenkirchen Germany 50°57N 6°7E 76 E2
Geisingen Germany 47°54N 8°38E 77 H4
Geislingen Germany 48°37N 9°50E 77 G5
Geistown U.S.A. 40°18N 78°52W 174 F6
Geita Tanzania 2°48S 32°12E 142 C3
Gejiu China 23°20N 103°10E 116 F4
Gel, Meydān-e Iran 29°4N 54°50E 129 D7
Gela Italy 37°4N 14°15E 95 E7
Gela, G. di Italy 37°0N 14°20E 95 F7
Gelahun Liberia 7°55N 10°28W 138 D2
Gelang Patah Malaysia 1°27N 103°35E 121 d
Gelasa, Selat Indonesia 2°50S 107°0E 118 E3
Gelderland □ Neths. 52°5N 6°10E 69 B6
Geldern Germany 51°31N 6°20E 76 D2
Geldrop Neths. 51°25N 5°32E 69 C5
Geleen Neths. 50°57N 5°49E 69 D5
Gelehun S. Leone 8°20N 11°40W 138 D2
Gelembe Turkey 39°10N 27°50E 99 B9
Gelendost Turkey 38°7N 31°1E 104 C4
Gelendzhik Russia 44°33N 38°10E 85 K10
Gelib = Jilib Somalia 0°29N 42°46E 131 G3
Gelibolu Turkey 40°28N 26°43E 97 F10
Gelibolu Yarımadası Turkey 40°20N 26°30E 97 F10
Gelidonya Burnu Turkey 36°12N 30°24E 104 D4
Gelnhausen Germany 50°11N 9°11E 77 E5
Gelnica Slovak Rep. 48°51N 20°55E 79 C13
Gelsenkirchen Germany 51°32N 7°6E 76 D3
Gelting Germany 54°45N 9°53E 76 A5
Gelugur Malaysia 5°22N 100°18E 121 c
Gemas Malaysia 2°37N 102°36E 121 L4
Gembloux Belgium 50°34N 4°43E 69 D4
Gembu Nigeria 6°42N 11°10E 139 D7
Gemena Dem. Rep. of the Congo 3°13N 19°48E 140 D3
Gemerek Turkey 39°15N 36°10E 104 C7
Gemikonağı = Karavostasi Cyprus 35°8N 32°50E 101 D11
Gemla Sweden 56°52N 14°39E 63 H8
Gemlik Turkey 40°26N 29°9E 97 F13
Gemlik Körfezi Turkey 40°25N 28°55E 97 F12
Gemona del Friuli Italy 46°16N 13°9E 93 B10
Gemsa Egypt 27°39N 33°35E 137 B3
Gemsbok △ Botswana 25°5S 21°1E 144 C3
Gemünden Germany 50°3N 9°42E 77 E5
Genadi Greece 36°2N 27°56E 101 C9
Genale → Ethiopia 6°2N 39°1E 131 F2
Genç Turkey 38°44N 40°34E 105 C9
Gençay France 46°23N 0°23E 72 B4
General Acha Argentina 37°20S 64°38W 190 D3
General Alvear B. Aires, Argentina 36°0S 60°0W 190 D4
General Alvear Mendoza, Argentina 35°0S 67°40W 190
General Artigas Paraguay 26°52S 56°16W 190
General Belgrano Argentina 36°35S 58°47W 190
General Bernardo O'Higgins Antarctica 63°0S 58°3W 55 C
General Cabrera Argentina 32°53S 63°52W 190
General Carrera, L. S. Amer. 46°35S 72°0W 192
General Cepeda Mexico 25°21N 101°22W 180
General Conesa Argentina 40°6S 64°25W 192
General Guido Argentina 36°40S 57°50W 190
General Juan Madariaga Argentina 37°0S 57°0W 190
General La Madrid Argentina 37°17S 61°20W 190
General Lorenzo Vintter Argentina 40°45S 64°26W 192
General MacArthur Phil. 11°18N 125°28E 119
General Martin Miguel de Güemes Argentina 24°50S 65°0W 190
General Pico Argentina 35°45S 63°50W 190
General Pinedo Argentina 27°15S 61°20W 190
General Pinto Argentina 34°45S 61°50W 190
General Roca Argentina 39°2S 67°35W 192
General Sampaio Brazil 4°2S 39°29W 189
General Santos Phil. 6°5N 125°14E 119
General Toshevo Bulgaria 43°42N 28°6E 97
General Treviño Mexico 26°14N 99°29W 181
General Trías Mexico 28°21N 106°22W 180
General Viamonte Argentina 35°1S 61°3W 190
General Villegas Argentina 35°5S 63°0W 190
General Vintter, L. Argentina 43°55S 71°40W 192
Genesee Idaho, U.S.A. 46°33N 116°56W 168
Genesee Pa., U.S.A. 41°59N 77°54W 174
Genesee → U.S.A. 43°16N 77°36W 174
Geneseo Ill., U.S.A. 41°27N 90°9W 172
Geneseo N.Y., U.S.A. 42°48N 77°49W 174
Geneva = Genève Switz. 46°12N 6°9E 7
Geneva Ala., U.S.A. 31°2N 85°52W 178
Geneva Ga., U.S.A. 32°35N 84°33W 178
Geneva N.Y., U.S.A. 42°52N 76°59W 174
Geneva Nebr., U.S.A. 40°32N 97°36W 17
Geneva Ohio, U.S.A. 41°48N 80°57W 174
Geneva, L. = Léman, L. Europe 46°26N 6°30E 71
Genève Switz. 46°12N 6°9E 7
Gengenbach Germany 48°24N 8°1E 7
Gengma China 23°32N 99°20E 11
Genhe China 50°47N 121°31E 111
Genichesk = Henichesk Ukraine 46°12N 34°50E 8
Genil → Spain 37°42N 5°19W 8
Genisea Greece 41°1N 24°57E 9
Genk Belgium 50°58N 5°32E 6
Genlis France 47°11N 5°12E 71
Gennargentu, Mti. del Italy 40°1N 9°19E 9
Gennes France 47°20N 0°17W 7
Genoa = Gènova Italy 44°25N 8°57E 9
Genoa Australia 37°29S 149°35E 15
Genoa N.Y., U.S.A. 42°40N 76°32W 17
Genoa Nebr., U.S.A. 41°27N 97°44W 17
Genoa Nev., U.S.A. 39°2N 119°50W 17
Genoa → Argentina 44°55S 70°5W 19
Génova Italy 44°25N 8°57E 9
Génova ✈ (GOA) Italy 44°25N 8°56E 9
Génova, G. di Italy 44°0N 9°0E 9
Genriyetty, Ostrov Russia 77°6N 156°30E 107
Gent Belgium 51°2N 3°42E 6
Genteng Jawa Barat, Indonesia 7°22S 106°24E 119
Genteng Jawa Timur, Indonesia 8°22S 114°9E 11
Genthin Germany 52°25N 12°9E 7
Gentio do Ouro Brazil 11°25S 42°30W 18
Genyem Indonesia 2°46S 140°12E 119
Genzano di Lucánia Italy 40°51N 16°2E 9
Genzano di Roma Italy 41°42N 12°41E 9
Geoagiu Romania 45°55N 23°12E 8
Geochang S. Korea 35°41N 127°55E 115
Geographe B. Australia 33°30S 115°15E 14
Geographe Chan. Australia 24°30S 113°0E 14
Geographical Society Ø Greenland 72°57N 23°15W 5
Geokchay = Göyçay Azerbaijan 40°42N 47°43E
Georga, Zemlya Russia 80°30N 49°0E 1
George S. Africa 33°58S 22°29E 14
George → Canada 58°49N 66°10W 16
George, L. N.S.W., Australia 35°10S 149°25E 1
George, L. S. Austral., Australia 37°25S 140°0E 1
George, L. W. Austral., Australia 22°45S 123°40E 14
George, L. Uganda 0°5N 30°10E 1
George, L. Fla., U.S.A. 29°17N 81°36W 1
George, L. N.Y., U.S.A. 43°37N 73°33W 17
George Gill Ra. Australia 24°22S 131°45E 1
George Pt. Australia 20°6S 148°36E
George River = Kangiqsualujjuaq Canada 58°30N 65°59W 16
George Sound N.Z. 44°52S 167°25E 1
George Town Australia 41°6S 146°49E 1
George Town Bahamas 23°33N 75°47W 1
George Town Cayman Is. 19°20N 81°24W 1
George Town Malaysia 5°25N 100°20E
George V Land Antarctica 69°0S 148°0E 5
George VI Sound Antarctica 71°0S 68°0W 5

orge West *U.S.A.* 28°20N 98°7W **176** G5
Gambia 13°30N 14°47W **138** C2
orgetown = Janjanbureh
orgetown *Australia* 18°17S 143°33E **150** B3
Canada 43°40N 79°56W **174** C5
orgetown *Ont.,*
orgetown *P.E.I.,*
Canada 46°13N 62°24W **165** C7
orgetown *Guyana* 6°50N 58°12W **186** B7
orgetown *Calif.,*
U.S.A. 38°54N 120°50W **170** G6
orgetown *Colo.,*
U.S.A. 39°42N 105°42W **168** G11
orgetown *Fla.,*
U.S.A. 29°23N 81°38W **179** F8
orgetown *Ga., U.S.A.* 31°53N 85°6W **178** D4
orgetown *Ky.,*
U.S.A. 38°13N 84°33W **173** F11
orgetown *N.Y.,*
U.S.A. 42°46N 75°44W **175** D9
orgetown *Ohio,*
U.S.A. 38°52N 83°54W **173** F12
orgetown *S.C.,*
U.S.A. 33°23N 79°17W **177** E15
orgetown *Tex.,*
U.S.A. 30°38N 97°41W **176** F6
orgia □ *U.S.A.* 32°50N 83°15W **178** C6
orgia ■ *Asia* 42°0N 43°0E **87** J6
N. Amer. 49°25N 124°0W **170** A3
orgia Basin *S. Ocean* 50°45S 35°30W **55** B1
orgian B. *Canada* 45°15N 81°0W **174** A4
orgian Bay Islands △
Canada 44°53N 79°52W **174** B5
rgiĕvka
Kazakhstan 49°19N 84°34E **109** C10
rgina → *Australia* 23°30S 139°47E **150** C2
rgina I. *Canada* 22°24N 79°17W **174** B5
rgioupoli *Greece* 35°20N 24°15E **101** D6
rgiyevsk *Russia* 44°12N 43°28E **87** H6
rgsmarienhütte
Germany 52°13N 8°3E **76** E4
Germany 50°53N 12°4E **76** E8
aardsbergen *Belgium* 50°45N 3°53E **69** D3
aki *Greece* 37°0N 22°42E **98** D4
al, Serra *Bahia, Brazil* 11°55S 41°0W **189** C2
al, Serra *Goiás,*
Brazil 11°15S 46°30W **189** C1
al, Serra *Sta. Catarina,*
Brazil 26°25S 50°0W **191** B6
al de Goiás, Serra
Brazil 12°0S 46°0W **189** C1
al do Paraná, Serra
Brazil 15°0S 47°30W **189** D1
aldine *N.Z.* 44°5S 171°15E **155** E6
aldton *Australia* 47°36N 110°16W **168** C8
aldton *Australia* 28°48S 114°32E **149** E1
anium *Australia* 44°44N 87°1W **164** C2
anium *Australia* 35°23S 140°11E **152** C4
ardmer *France* 48°3N 6°50E **71** D13
ine, Mt. *U.S.A.* 61°35N 152°27W **166** C9
ine *Australia* 35°1N 143°52E **152** B3
de Turkey 37°44N 28°27E **99** D10
shk *Japan* 31°47N 64°35E **122** D4
tsried *Germany* 47°51N 11°28E **77** H7
al *Spain* 37°7N 2°31W **91** H2
k *Malaysia* 5°50N 101°15E **121** K3
ng *U.S.A.* 41°50N 103°40W **172** E2
ach *U.S.A.* 40°39N 119°21W **168** F4
achovský štít
Slovak Rep. 49°11N 20°7E **79** B13
nan Bight = Deutsche Bucht
Germany 54°15N 8°0E **76** A4
an Planina
Macedonia 42°20N 22°0E **96** D6
ania Land
eenland 77°5N 19°30W **57** B9
ansen Landing
nada 55°43N 124°40W **162** B4
antown *U.S.A.* 35°5N 89°49W **177** D10
any ■ *Europe* 51°0N 10°0E **76** E6
encik *Turkey* 37°52N 27°37E **99** D9
nering *Germany* 48°8N 11°22E **77** G7
ersheim *Germany* 49°45N 8°22E **77** F4
I *Iran* 39°1N 48°35E **105** C13
iston *S. Africa* 26°13S 28°10E **145** C4
ika-Lumo *Spain* 43°19N 2°40W **90** B2
sheim *Germany* 49°45N 8°30E **77** F4
Japan 35°48N 137°14E **113** G8
gery *Australia* 35°50S 147°1E **153** C7
cgak *Indonesia* 8°1S 114°27E **119** J17
zhofen *Germany* 51°38N 8°31E **76** D4
a = Girona *Spain* 41°58N 2°46E **90** D7
potamos → *Greece* 35°3N 24°50E **101** D6
ard Canada 50°30N 117°17W **162** C5
gong *Australia* 34°46S 150°47E **153** C9
→ *France* 43°35N 3°0E **72** E4
→ *France* 44°9N 0°39E **72** D4
eld *Germany* 50°27N 9°56E **76** E5
ppa Falls *India* 14°12N 74°46E **127** G2
hofen *Germany* 48°25N 10°53E **77** G6
k Sanggul
Malaysia 5°17N 100°12E **121** c
k Sanggul, Tanjung
alaysia 5°16N 100°11E **121** c
ong *Indonesia* 8°43S 116°7E **119** K19
t *France* 45°48N 3°8E **72** C7
Turkey 41°48N 35°12E **104** B6
ce *Germany* 51°38N 8°31E **76** D4
Indonesia 3°50S 130°54E **119** E8
→ *Italy* 44°24N 7°33E **92** D4
e *Spain* 40°18N 3°43E **91** C4
ge *Sweden* 56°49N 12°44E **63** H6
sburg N.Dak. *U.S.A.* 39°50N 77°14W **173** F15
ge *S. Dak.,*
A. 45°1N 99°57W **172** C4
. = Algorta *Spain* 43°21N 2°59W **90** B2
ce Shelf *Antarctica* 75°0S 130°0W **55** D14
e *Australia* 32°22S 148°50E **153** E9
Turkey 38°15N 43°6E **105** C10
adan *France* 44°40N 3°40E **72** D7
ilija *Macedonia* 41°9N 22°0E **96** D6
a → *Spain* 38°53N 6°57W **89** G4
ance 46°21N 6°3E **71** F13
ce France 39°48N 26°12E **99** B8
ville *U.S.A.* 38°42N 122°54W **170** G4
ada Dam *China* 40°20N 111°20E **117** B8

Ghadāf, W. al → *Iraq* 32°56N 43°30E **105** F10
Ghadāmis *Libya* 30°11N 9°29E **135** B8
Ghaggar → *India* 29°30N 74°53E **124** E6
Ghaghara → *India* 25°45N 84°40E **125** G11
Ghaghat → *Bangla.* 25°19N 89°38E **125** G13
Ghagra *India* 23°17N 84°33E **125** H11
Ghallamane *Mauritania* 23°15N 10°0W **134** D4
Ghana ■ *W. Afr.* 8°0N 1°0W **139** D4
Ghanpokhara *Nepal* 28°17N 84°14E **125** E11
Ghansor *India* 22°39N 80°1E **125** H9
Ghanzi *Botswana* 21°50S 21°34E **144** B3
Ghanzi □ *Botswana* 22°0S 22°30E **144** B3
Gharb-Chrarda-Beni Hssen □
Morocco 35°35N 6°0W **136** A2
Gharbîya, Es Sahrâ el
Egypt 27°40N 26°30E **137** B2
Ghardaïa *Algeria* 32°20N 3°37E **136** B4
Ghardaïa □ *Algeria* 31°5N 3°10E **136** B4
Ghârib, G. *Egypt* 28°6N 32°54E **137** F8
Gharyān *Libya* 32°10N 13°0E **135** B8
Ghāt *Libya* 24°59N 10°11E **135** D8
Ghatal *India* 22°40N 87°46E **125** H12
Ghatampur *India* 26°8N 80°13E **125** F9
Ghatgaon *India* 21°24N 85°53E **126** D7
Ghatprabha → *India* 16°15N 75°20E **127** F2
Ghats, Eastern *India* 14°0N 78°50E **127** H4
Ghats, Western *India* 14°0N 75°0E **127** H2
Ghatsila *India* 22°36N 86°29E **125** H12
Ghaţţī *Si. Arabia* 31°16N 37°31E **128** D3
Ghawdex = Gozo *Malta* 36°3N 14°15E **101** C1
Ghazal, Bahr el → *Chad* 13°0N 15°47E **135** F9
Ghazal, Bahr el →
South Sudan 9°31N 30°25E **135** G12
Ghazaouet *Algeria* 35°8N 1°50W **136** A3
Ghaziabad *India* 28°42N 77°26E **124** E7
Ghazipur *India* 25°38N 83°35E **125** G10
Ghazni *Afghan.* 33°30N 68°28E **124** C3
Ghazni □ *Afghan.* 32°10N 68°20E **122** C6
Ghedi *Italy* 45°24N 10°16E **92** C7
Ghelari *Romania* 45°38N 22°45E **80** E7
Ghent = Gent *Belgium* 51°2N 3°42E **69** C3
Gheorghe Gheorghiu-Dej = Oneşti
Romania 46°17N 26°47E **81** D11
Gheorgheni *Romania* 46°43N 25°41E **81** D10
Gherla *Romania* 47°2N 23°57E **81** C8
Ghidigeni *Romania* 46°3N 27°30E **81** D12
Ghilarza *Italy* 40°7N 8°50E **94** B1
Ghimeş-Făget *Romania* 46°35N 26°22E **81** D11
Ghînah, Wâdî al →
Si. Arabia 30°27N 38°14E **128** D3
Ghisonaccia *France* 42°1N 9°26E **73** F13
Ghisoni *France* 42°8N 9°12E **73** F13
Ghizar → *Pakistan* 36°15N 73°43E **125** A5
Ghod → *India* 18°30N 74°35E **126** E2
Ghogha *India* 21°40N 72°20E **126** J8
Ghot Ogrein *Egypt* 31°10N 25°20E **137** A2
Ghotaru *India* 27°20N 70°1E **124** F4
Ghotki *Pakistan* 28°5N 69°21E **124** E3
Ghowr □ *Afghan.* 34°0N 64°20E **122** C4
Ghughri *India* 22°39N 80°41E **125** H9
Ghugus *India* 19°58N 79°12E **126** E4
Ghulam Mohammad Barrage
Pakistan 25°30N 68°20E **124** G3
Ghūrīān *Afghan.* 34°17N 61°25E **122** C3
Gia Dinh *Vietnam* 10°49N 106°42E **121** G6
Gia Lai = Plei Ku
Vietnam 13°57N 108°0E **120** F7
Gia Nghia *Vietnam* 11°58N 107°42E **121** G6
Gia Ngoc *Vietnam* 14°50N 108°58E **120** E7
Gia Vuc *Vietnam* 14°42N 108°34E **120** E7
Giali *Greece* 36°41N 27°11E **99** E9
Gialtra *Greece* 38°51N 22°59E **98** C4
Giamama = Jamaame
Somalia 0°4N 42°44E **131** G3
Gianitsa *Greece* 40°46N 22°24E **96** F6
Giannutri *Italy* 42°15N 11°6E **92** F8
Giant Forest *U.S.A.* 36°36N 118°43W **170** J8
Giant Mts. = Krkonoše
Czech Rep. 50°50N 15°35E **78** A8
Giant Sequoia △
U.S.A. 36°10N 118°35W **170** K8
Giants Causeway *U.K.* 55°16N 6°29W **64** A5
Giant's Tank *Sri Lanka* 8°51N 80°2E **127** K5
Gianyar *Indonesia* 8°32S 115°20E **119** K18
Giarabub = Al Jaghbūb
Libya 29°42N 24°38E **135** C10
Giarre *Italy* 37°43N 15°11E **95** E8
Giaveno *Italy* 45°2N 7°21E **92** C4
Gibara *Cuba* 21°9N 76°11W **182** B4
Gibbon *U.S.A.* 40°45N 98°51W **172** E4
Gibe II *Ethiopia* 8°0N 37°0E **131** F2
Gibe III *Ethiopia* 7°0N 37°30E **131** F2
Gibellina Nuova *Italy* 37°47N 12°58E **94** E5
Gibeon *Namibia* 25°9S 17°43E **144** C2
Gibraléon *Spain* 37°23N 6°58W **89** H4
Gibraltar ☑ *Europe* 36°7N 5°22W **89** J5
Gibraltar, Str. of *Medit. S.* 35°55N 5°40W **89** K5
Gibraltar Range △
Australia 29°31S 152°19E **151** D5
Gibson *U.S.A.* 33°14N 82°36W **178** B7
Gibson Desert *Australia* 24°0S 126°0E **148** D4
Gibsons *Canada* 49°24N 123°32W **162** D4
Gibsonton *U.S.A.* 27°51N 82°23W **179** H17
Gibsonville *U.S.A.* 39°46N 120°54W **170** F6
Giddalur *India* 15°20N 78°57E **127** G4
Giddings *U.S.A.* 30°11N 96°56W **176** F6
Giebnegáisi = Kebnekaise
Sweden 67°53N 18°33E **60** C18
Gien *France* 47°40N 2°36E **71** E9
Giengen *Germany* 48°37N 10°14E **77** G6
Giessen *Germany* 50°36N 8°41E **77** F4
Gīfan *Iran* 37°54N 57°28E **129** B8
Gifatin, Geziret *Egypt* 27°10N 33°50E **137** E8
Gifford *U.S.A.* 27°40N 80°25W **179** H9
Gifhorn *Germany* 52°29N 10°32E **76** C6
Gift Lake *Canada* 55°53N 115°49W **162** B5
Gifu *Japan* 35°30N 136°45E **113** G8
Gifu □ *Japan* 35°40N 137°0E **113** G8
Gigant *Russia* 46°28N 41°20E **87** G5
Giganta, Sa. de la
Mexico 26°0N 111°39W **180** B2
Gigen *Bulgaria* 43°40N 24°28E **97** C8
Gigha *U.K.* 55°42N 5°44W **65** F3
Giglio *Italy* 42°20N 10°52E **92** F7
Gignac *France* 43°39N 3°32E **72** E7
Gigüela → *Spain* 39°8N 3°44W **89** F7
Gijón *Spain* 43°32N 5°42W **88** B5
Gikongoro *Rwanda* 2°28S 29°34E **142** C2

Gil I. *Canada* 53°12N 129°15W **162** C3
Gila → *U.S.A.* 32°43N 114°33W **169** K6
Gila Bend *U.S.A.* 32°57N 112°43W **169** K7
Gila Bend Mts. *U.S.A.* 33°10N 113°0W **169** K7
Gila Cliff Dwellings △
U.S.A. 33°12N 108°16W **169** K9
Gīlān □ *Iran* 37°0N 50°0E **129** B6
Gīlān-e Gharb *Iran* 34°8N 45°55E **105** E11
Gilău *Romania* 46°45N 23°23E **81** D8
Gilbert → *Australia* 16°35S 141°15E **150** B3
Gilbert Is. *Kiribati* 1°0N 172°0E **147** A10
Gilbert River *Australia* 18°9S 142°52E **150** B3
Gilbert Seamounts
Pac. Oc. 52°50N 150°10W **54** D18
Gilbués *Brazil* 9°50S 45°21W **189** B1
Gilead *U.S.A.* 44°24N 70°59W **175** B14
Gilf el Kebir, Hadabat el
Egypt 23°50N 25°50E **137** C2
Gilford I. *Canada* 50°40N 126°30W **162** C3
Gilgandra *Australia* 31°43S 148°39E **153** A8
Gilgil *Kenya* 0°30S 36°20E **142** C4
Gilgit *India* 35°50N 74°15E **125** B6
Gilgit → *Pakistan* 35°44N 74°37E **125** B6
Gilgit-Baltistan □
Pakistan 36°30N 73°0E **125** A5
Gilgunnia *Australia* 32°26S 146°2E **153** B7
Gili *Indonesia* 8°10S 114°26E **119** J17
Gilimanuk *Indonesia* 8°10S 114°26E **119** J17
Giljeva Planina *Europe* 43°9N 20°0E **97** C4
Gillam *Canada* 56°20N 94°40W **163** B10
Gilleleje *Denmark* 56°8N 12°19E **63** H6
Gillen, L. *Australia* 26°11S 124°38E **149** E3
Gilles, L. *Australia* 32°50S 136°45E **152** B2
Gillespies Pt. *N.Z.* 43°24S 169°49E **155** D4
Gillette *U.S.A.* 44°18N 105°30W **168** D11
Gilliat *Australia* 20°40S 141°28E **150** C3
Gillingham *U.K.* 51°23N 0°33E **67** F8
Gilmer *U.S.A.* 32°44N 94°57W **176** E7
Gilmore, L. *Australia* 32°29S 121°37E **149** F3
Gilmour *Canada* 44°48N 77°37W **174** B7
Gilort → *Romania* 44°38N 23°32E **81** E8
Gilroy *U.S.A.* 37°1N 121°34W **170** H5
Gimcheon *S. Korea* 36°11N 128°4E **115** F15
Gimhae *S. Korea* 35°14N 128°53E **115** G15
Gimhwa *S. Korea* 38°17N 127°28E **115** E14
Gimje *S. Korea* 35°48N 126°45E **115** G14
Gimli *Canada* 50°40N 97°0W **163** C9
Gimone → *France* 44°0N 1°6E **72** E5
Gimont *France* 43°38N 0°52E **72** E4
Gin → *Sri Lanka* 6°5N 80°7E **127** L5
Gin Gin *Australia* 25°0S 151°58E **151** D5
Ginâh *Egypt* 25°21N 30°30E **137** B3
Gineifa *Egypt* 30°12N 32°25E **137** E8
Gingee *India* 12°15N 79°25E **127** H4
Gingin *Australia* 31°22S 115°54E **149** F2
Gingindlovu *S. Africa* 29°2S 31°30E **145** C5
Ginir *Ethiopia* 7°6N 40°40E **131** F3
Ginosa *Italy* 40°35N 16°45E **95** B9
Ginzo de Limia = Xinzo de Limia
Spain 42°3N 7°47W **88** C3
Giofyros → *Greece* 35°20N 25°6E **101** D7
Giohar = Jawhar
Somalia 2°48N 45°30E **131** G4
Gióia, G. di *Italy* 38°30N 15°45E **95** D8
Gióia del Colle *Italy* 40°48N 16°55E **95** B9
Gióia Táuro *Italy* 38°25N 15°54E **95** D8
Gioiosa Iónica *Italy* 38°20N 16°18E **95** D9
Gioiosa Marea *Italy* 38°10N 14°54E **95** D7
Giona, Oros *Greece* 38°38N 22°14E **98** C4
Giovi, Passo dei *Italy* 44°33N 8°57E **92** D5
Giovinazzo *Italy* 41°11N 16°40E **95** A9
Gippsland *Australia* 37°52S 147°0E **153** D7
Gir → *India* 21°0N 71°0E **124** J4
Gir Hills *India* 21°0N 71°0E **124** J4
Girab *India* 26°2N 70°38E **124** F4
Girâfi, W. → *Egypt* 29°58N 34°39E **130** F3
Giraltovce *Slovak Rep.* 49°7N 21°32E **79** B14
Girard *St. Lucia* 13°59N 60°57W **183** D7
Girard *Ga., U.S.A.* 33°3N 81°43W **178** B7
Girard *Kans., U.S.A.* 37°31N 94°51W **172** G6
Girard *Ohio, U.S.A.* 41°9N 80°42W **174** E4
Girardville *U.S.A.* 40°48N 76°19W **174** E4
Girdle Ness *U.K.* 57°9N 2°3W **65** D6
Giresun *Turkey* 40°55N 38°30E **105** B8
Giresun □ *Turkey* 40°30N 38°0E **105** B8
Girga *Egypt* 26°17N 31°55E **137** D3
Giri → *India* 30°28N 77°41E **124** D7
Giridih *India* 24°10N 86°21E **125** G12
Girifalco *Italy* 38°49N 16°25E **95** D9
Giriftu *Kenya* 1°59N 39°46E **142** B4
Girilambone *Australia* 31°16S 146°57E **153** A7
Girne = Kyrenia
Cyprus 35°20N 33°20E **101** D12
Giro *Nigeria* 11°7N 4°42E **139** C5
Giromagny *France* 47°45N 6°50E **71** E13
Giron = Kiruna *Sweden* 67°52N 20°15E **60** C19
Girona *Spain* 41°58N 2°46E **90** D7
Girona □ *Spain* 42°11N 2°30E **90** D7
Gironde □ *France* 44°45N 0°30W **72** D3
Gironde → *France* 45°32N 1°7W **72** C2
Gironella *Spain* 42°2N 1°53E **90** D6
Girraween △ *Australia* 28°46S 151°54E **151** D5
Girringun △ *Australia* 18°15S 145°32E **150** B4
Giru *Australia* 19°30S 147°5E **150** B4
Girvan *U.K.* 55°14N 4°51W **65** F4
Gisborne *Australia* 37°29S 144°36E **152** D6
Gisborne *N.Z.* 38°39S 178°5E **154** E7
Gisborne □ *N.Z.* 38°30S 178°0E **154** E7
Gisenyi *Rwanda* 1°41S 29°15E **142** C2
Gislaved *Sweden* 57°19N 13°32E **63** H7
Gisors *France* 49°15N 1°47E **71** C8
Gitarama *Rwanda* 2°4S 29°47E **142** C2
Gitega *Burundi* 3°26S 29°56E **142** C2
Githio = Juba →
Somalia 1°30N 42°35E **131** G3
Giuba = Juba →
Giugliano in Campania
Italy 40°56N 14°12E **95** B7
Giulianova *Italy* 42°45N 13°57E **92** F10
Giura *Greece* 39°23N 24°10E **98** B6
Giurgeni *Romania* 44°45N 27°48E **81** F12
Giurgiu *Romania* 43°52N 25°57E **81** G10
Giurgiu □ *Romania* 44°20N 26°0E **81** F10
Giurgiuleşti *Moldova* 45°29N 28°12E **81** E13
Give *Denmark* 55°51N 9°13E **63** J3
Givet *France* 50°8N 4°49E **71** B11
Givors *France* 45°35N 4°45E **73** C8
Givry *France* 46°41N 4°46E **71** F11
Giyani *S. Africa* 23°19S 30°43E **145** B5

Giza = El Gîza *Egypt* 30°0N 31°12E **137** F7
Giza Pyramids *Egypt* 29°58N 31°9E **137** F7
Gizab *Afghan.* 33°22N 66°17E **124** C1
Gizhiga *Russia* 62°3N 160°30E **107** C17
Gizhiginskaya Guba
Russia 61°0N 158°0E **107** C16
Gizycko *Poland* 54°2N 21°48E **82** D8
Gizzeria *Italy* 38°59N 16°12E **95** D9
Gjakovë *Kosovo* 42°22N 20°26E **96** D4
Gjalicë e Lumës, Mal.
Albania 42°22N 20°26E **96** C4
Gjegjan *Albania* 41°58N 20°3E **96** E4
Gjeravicë *Kosovo* 42°32N 20°8E **96** D4
Gjilan *Kosovo* 42°27N 21°28E **96** D5
Gjirokastër *Albania* 40°7N 20°10E **96** F4
Gjoa Haven *Canada* 68°38N 95°53W **160** D12
Gjøvik *Norway* 60°47N 10°43E **60** F14
Gjuhês, Kep i *Albania* 40°28N 19°15E **96** F3
Gjurakoc *Kosovo* 42°43N 20°29E **96** D4
Glace Bay *Canada* 46°11N 59°58W **165** C8
Glacier △ *Canada* 51°15N 117°30W **162** C5
Glacier △ *U.S.A.* 48°42N 113°48W **168** B7
Glacier Bay *U.S.A.* 58°40N 136°0W **160** F4
Glacier Bay △ *U.S.A.* 58°45N 136°30W **162** B1
Glacier Peak *U.S.A.* 48°7N 121°7W **168** B3
Gladewater *U.S.A.* 32°33N 94°56W **176** E7
Gladstone *Queens.,*
Australia 23°52S 151°16E **150** C5
Gladstone *S. Austral.,*
Australia 33°15S 138°22E **152** B3
Gladstone *Canada* 50°13N 98°57W **163** C9
Gladstone *U.S.A.* 45°51N 87°1W **172** C9
Gladwin *U.S.A.* 43°59N 84°29W **173** D11
Glafsfjorden *Sweden* 59°30N 12°37E **62** E6
Glagah *Indonesia* 8°13S 114°18E **119** J17
Głagów Małopolski
Poland 50°10N 21°56E **83** H8
Glåma = Glomma →
Norway 59°12N 10°57E **61** G14
Gláma *Iceland* 65°48N 23°0W **60** D2
Glamis *U.K.* 32°55N 115°5W **171** N11
Glamoč *Bos.-H.* 44°3N 16°51E **93** D13
Glamorgan, Vale of □
U.K. 51°28N 3°25W **67** F4
Glamsbjerg *Denmark* 55°17N 10°6E **63** J4
Glarus *Switz.* 47°3N 9°4E **77** F5
Glarus □ *Switz.* 47°0N 9°5E **77** F5
Glasco *Kans., U.S.A.* 39°22N 97°50W **172** F5
Glasgow *U.K.* 55°51N 4°15W **65** F4
Glasgow *Ky., U.S.A.* 37°0N 85°55W **173** G11
Glasgow *Mont.,*
U.S.A. 48°12N 106°38W **168** B10
Glasgow, City of □ *U.K.* 55°51N 4°12W **65** F4
Glasgow Int. ✈ (GLA)
U.K. 55°51N 4°21W **65** F4
Glaslyn *Canada* 53°22N 108°21W **163** C7
Glastonbury *U.K.* 51°9N 2°43W **67** F5
Glastonbury *U.S.A.* 41°43N 72°37W **175** E12
Glauchau *Germany* 50°49N 12°31E **76** E8
Glava *Sweden* 59°33N 12°35E **62** E6
Glavice *Croatia* 43°43N 16°41E **93** E13
Glazov *Russia* 58°9N 52°40E **86** A11
Gleichen *Canada* 50°52N 113°3W **162** C6
Gleisdorf *Austria* 47°6N 15°44E **78** D8
Gleiwitz = Gliwice
Poland 50°22N 18°41E **83** H5
Glen *U.S.A.* 44°7N 71°11W **175** B13
Glen Affric *U.K.* 57°17N 5°1W **65** D3
Glen Afton *N.Z.* 37°37S 175°4E **154** D4
Glen Canyon *U.S.A.* 37°30N 110°40W **169** H8
Glen Canyon △ *U.S.A.* 37°15N 111°0W **169** H8
Glen Canyon Dam
U.S.A. 36°57N 111°29W **169** H8
Glen Coe *U.K.* 56°40N 5°0W **65** E3
Glen Cove *U.S.A.* 40°51N 73°38W **175** F11
Glen Garry *U.K.* 57°3N 5°7W **65** D3
Glen Innes *Australia* 29°44S 151°44E **151** D5
Glen Lyon *U.S.A.* 41°10N 76°5W **175** E8
Glen Massey *N.Z.* 37°38S 175°2E **154** D4
Glen Mor *U.K.* 57°9N 4°37W **65** D4
Glen Moriston *U.K.* 57°11N 4°52W **65** D4
Glen Robertson
Canada 45°22N 74°30W **175** A10
Glen Spean *U.K.* 56°53N 4°40W **65** E4
Glen Ullin *U.S.A.* 46°49N 101°50W **172** B3
Glénan, Îs. de *France* 47°42N 4°0W **70** E3
Glenavy *N.Z.* 44°54S 171°7E **155** E6
Glenbeigh *Ireland* 52°3N 9°58W **64** D2
Glenburn *Australia* 37°27S 145°26E **153** D6
Glencoe *Canada* 42°45N 81°43W **174** D3
Glencoe *S. Africa* 28°11S 30°11E **145** C5
Glencoe *Ala., U.S.A.* 33°57N 85°56W **178** B4
Glencoe *Minn., U.S.A.* 44°46N 94°9W **172** C6
Glencolumbkille *Ireland* 54°43N 8°42W **64** B3
Glendale *Ariz., U.S.A.* 33°32N 112°11W **169** K7
Glendale *Calif., U.S.A.* 34°9N 118°15W **171** L8
Glendale *Fla., U.S.A.* 30°52N 86°7W **178** E3
Glendale *Zimbabwe* 17°22S 31°5E **143** F3
Glendive *U.S.A.* 47°7N 104°43W **168** C11
Glendo *U.S.A.* 42°30N 105°2W **168** E11
Glenelg *Australia* 34°58S 138°31E **152** C3
Glenelg → *Australia* 38°4S 140°59E **152** E4
Glenfield *U.S.A.* 43°43N 75°24W **175** C9
Glengad Hd. *Ireland* 55°20N 7°10W **64** A4
Glengarriff *Ireland* 51°45N 9°34W **64** E2
Glenham *N.Z.* 46°26S 168°52E **155** G3
Glenhope *N.Z.* 41°40S 172°38E **155** D5
Glenmary, Mt. *N.Z.* 43°55S 169°55E **155** D4
Glenmorgan *Australia* 27°14S 149°42E **151** D4
Glennallen *U.S.A.* 62°7N 145°33W **160** E2
Glennamaddy *Ireland* 53°37N 8°33W **64** C3
Glenns Ferry *U.S.A.* 42°57N 115°18W **168** E6
Glennville *U.S.A.* 31°56N 81°56W **178** D8
Glenora *Canada* 58°7N 131°35W **162** B2
Glenora Canada 48°16S 147°18E **151** G4
Glenorchy *Tas.,*
Australia 42°49S 147°18E **151** G4
Glenorchy *Vic.,*
Australia 36°55S 142°41E **152** D5
Glenorchy *N.Z.* 44°51S 168°24E **155** E3
Glenore *Australia* 17°50S 141°12E **150** B3
Glenreagh *Australia* 30°2S 153°1E **151** E5
Glenrock *U.S.A.* 42°52N 105°52W **168** E11
Glenrothes *U.K.* 56°12N 3°10W **65** E5
Glens Falls *U.S.A.* 43°19N 73°39W **175** C11
Glenside *U.S.A.* 40°6N 75°9W **175** F9
Glenthompson
Australia 37°38S 142°35E **152** D5

Glenties *Ireland* 54°48N 8°17W **64** B3
Glenveagh △ *Ireland* 55°3N 8°1W **64** A3
Glenville *U.S.A.* 38°56N 80°50W **173** F13
Glenwood *Canada* 49°0N 54°58W **165** C9
Glenwood *Ark., U.S.A.* 34°20N 93°33W **176** D8
Glenwood *Iowa, U.S.A.* 41°3N 95°45W **172** E6
Glenwood *Wash.,*
U.S.A. 45°39N 95°23W **172** C6
Glenwood *Wash.,*
U.S.A. 46°1N 121°17W **170** D5
Glenwood Springs
U.S.A. 39°33N 107°19W **168** G10
Glettinganes *Iceland* 65°30N 13°37W **60** D7
Glifada *Greece* 37°52N 23°45E **98** D5
Glimåkra *Sweden* 56°19N 14°7E **63** H8
Glin *Ireland* 52°34N 9°17W **64** D2
Glina *Croatia* 45°20N 16°6E **93** C13
Glinojeck *Poland* 52°49N 20°21E **82** E7
Globe *U.S.A.* 33°24N 110°47W **169** K8
Glodeanu Siliştea
Romania 44°50N 26°48E **81** F11
Glodeni *Moldova* 47°45N 27°31E **81** C12
Glödnitz *Austria* 46°53N 14°7E **78** E7
Gloggnitz *Austria* 47°41N 15°56E **78** D8
Głogów *Poland* 51°37N 16°5E **83** G3
Głogówek *Poland* 50°21N 17°53E **83** H4
Glomma → *Norway* 59°12N 10°57E **61** G14
Glorieuses, Îs. *Ind. Oc.* 11°30S 47°20E **141** G9
Glosa *Greece* 39°10N 23°45E **98** B5
Glossop *U.K.* 53°27N 1°56W **66** D6
Gloucester *Australia* 32°0S 151°59E **153** B9
Gloucester *U.K.* 51°53N 2°15W **67** F5
Gloucester *U.S.A.* 42°37N 70°40W **175** D14
Gloucester I. *Australia* 20°0S 148°30E **150** b
Gloucester Island △
Australia 20°0S 148°30E **150** b
Gloucester Point
U.S.A. 37°15N 76°30W **173** G15
Gloucestershire □ *U.K.* 51°46N 2°15W **67** F5
Gloversville *U.S.A.* 43°3N 74°21W **175** C10
Glovertown *Canada* 48°40N 54°3W **165** C9
Gloverville = Warrenville
U.S.A. 33°33N 81°48W **178** B8
Glowno *Poland* 51°59N 19°42E **83** G6
Głubczyce *Poland* 50°13N 17°52E **83** H4
Głubokiy *Russia* 48°35N 40°25E **87** F5
Głubokoe *Kazakhstan* 50°8N 82°18E **109** B10
Glubokoye = Hlybokaye
Belarus 55°10N 27°45E **84** E4
Głuchołazy *Poland* 50°19N 17°24E **83** H4
Glücksburg *Germany* 54°50N 9°33E **76** A5
Glückstadt *Germany* 53°45N 9°25E **76** B5
Glukhov = Hlukhiv
Ukraine 51°40N 33°58E **85** G7
Glusk *Belarus* 52°53N 28°41E **75** B15
Głuszyca *Poland* 50°41N 16°23E **83** H3
Glyn Ebwy = Ebbw Vale
U.K. 51°46N 3°12W **67** F4
Glyngøre *Denmark* 56°46N 8°52E **63** H2
Gmünd *Kärnten, Austria* 46°54N 13°31E **78** E6
Gmünd *Niederösterreich,*
Austria 48°45N 15°0E **78** D8
Gmunden *Austria* 47°55N 13°48E **78** D6
Gnarp *Sweden* 62°3N 17°16E **62** B11
Gnesta *Sweden* 59°3N 17°17E **62** E11
Gniew *Poland* 53°50N 18°50E **82** E5
Gniewkowo *Poland* 52°54N 18°25E **83** E5
Gniezno *Poland* 52°30N 17°35E **83** F4
Gnjilane = Gjilane *Kosovo* 42°28N 21°29E **96** D5
Gnoien *Germany* 53°58N 12°41E **76** B8
Gnosjö *Sweden* 57°22N 13°43E **63** G7
Gnowangerup
Australia 33°58S 117°59E **149** F2
Go Cong *Vietnam* 10°22N 106°40E **121** G6
Gō-no-ura *Japan* 33°44N 129°40E **113** H4
Goa *India* 15°33N 73°59E **127** G1
Goa □ *India* 15°33N 73°59E **127** G1
Goalen Hd. *Australia* 36°33S 150°4E **153** D9
Goalpara *India* 26°10N 90°40E **125** F17
Goaltor *India* 22°43N 87°10E **125** H12
Goalundo Ghat
Bangla. 23°50N 89°47E **125** H13
Goaso *Ghana* 6°36N 2°30W **138** D4
Goat Fell *U.K.* 55°38N 5°11W **65** F3
Goba *Ethiopia* 7°1N 39°59E **131** F2
Goba *Mozam.* 26°15S 32°13E **145** D5
Gobabis *Namibia* 22°30S 19°0E **144** C2
Göbel *Turkey* 40°0N 28°9E **97** F12
Gobernador Gregores
Argentina 48°46S 70°15W **192** C2
Gobi *Asia* 44°0N 110°0E **114** C6
Gobichettipalayam
India 11°31N 77°21E **127** J3
Gobō *Japan* 33°53N 135°10E **113** H7
Gobustan *Azerbaijan* 40°7N 49°22E **105** B13
Göçbeyli *Turkey* 39°13N 27°25E **99** B9
Goch *Germany* 51°41N 6°9E **76** D2
Gochas *Namibia* 24°59S 18°55E **144** B2
Godavari → *India* 16°25N 82°18E **126** F6
Godavari Pt. *India* 17°0N 82°20E **126** F6
Godbout *Canada* 49°20N 67°38W **165** C6
Godda *India* 24°50N 87°13E **125** G12
Godech *Bulgaria* 43°1N 23°4E **96** C7
Goderich *Canada* 43°45N 81°41W **174** C3
Goderville *France* 49°38N 0°22E **70** C7
Godhavn = Qeqertarsuaq
Greenland 69°15N 53°38W **57** C5
Godhra *India* 22°49N 73°40E **124** H5
Gödöllő *Hungary* 47°38N 19°25E **80** C4
Godoy Cruz *Argentina* 32°56S 68°52W **194** C2
Gods → *Canada* 56°22N 92°51W **164** A1
Gods L. *Canada* 54°40N 94°15W **164** A1
Gods River *Canada* 54°50N 94°5W **164** A1
Godthåb = Nuuk
Greenland 64°10N 51°35W **57** C5
Goeie Hoop, Kaap die = Good
Hope, C. of *S. Africa* 34°24S 18°30E **144** C2
Goéland, L. au *Canada* 49°50N 76°48W **164** C4
Goélands, L. aux
Canada 55°27N 64°17W **165** A7
Goeree *Neths.* 51°50N 4°0E **69** C3
Goes *Neths.* 51°30N 3°55E **69** C3
Goffstown *U.S.A.* 43°1N 71°36W **175** C13
Gogama *Canada* 47°35N 81°43W **164** C3
Gogebic, L. *U.S.A.* 46°30N 89°35W **172** B9
Gogland, Os. *Russia* 60°5N 26°52E **63** E22
Gogolin *Poland* 50°30N 18°0E **83** H5
Gogonou *Benin* 10°50N 2°50E **139** C5
Gogra = Ghaghara →
India 25°45N 84°40E **125** G11
Gogrial *South Sudan* 8°30N 28°0E **135** G11
Gogui *Mali* 15°32N 9°25W **138** B3
Gohana *India* 29°8N 76°42E **124** E7
Goharganj *India* 23°1N 77°41E **124** H7
Goi → *India* 22°4N 74°46E **124** H6
Goiana *Brazil* 7°33S 34°59W **189** B4
Goiânia *Brazil* 16°43S 49°20W **187** G9
Goiás *Brazil* 15°55S 50°10W **187** G8
Goiás □ *Brazil* 12°10S 48°0W **187** F9
Goiatins *Brazil* 7°42S 47°12W **189** B1
Goio-Erê *Brazil* 24°12S 53°1W **191** A5
Góis *Portugal* 40°10N 8°6W **88** E2
Gojō *Japan* 34°21N 135°42E **113** G7
Gojra *Pakistan* 31°10N 72°40E **124** D5
Gokak *India* 16°11N 74°52E **127** F2
Gokarn *India* 14°33N 74°17E **127** G2
Gökçe *Turkey* 40°10N 25°55E **97** F9
Gökçeada *Turkey* 40°10N 25°50E **97** F9
Gökçedağ *Turkey* 39°33N 28°56E **99** B10
Gökçen *Turkey* 38°7N 27°53E **99** C9
Gökçeören *Turkey* 38°37N 28°35E **99** C10
Gökçeyazı *Turkey* 39°40N 27°44E **99** B9
Gökırmak → *Turkey* 41°25N 35°8E **104** B6
Gökova *Turkey* 38°28N 27°17E **99** D10
Gökova Körfezi *Turkey* 36°55N 27°50E **99** E9
Göksu → *Turkey* 36°19N 34°5E **104** D6
Göksun *Turkey* 38°3N 36°30E **104** C7
Gokteik *Burma* 22°26N 97°0E **123** H20
Göktepe *Turkey* 37°25N 28°34E **99** D10
Gokurt *Pakistan* 29°40N 67°26E **124** E2
Gokwe *Zimbabwe* 18°7S 28°58E **143** F2
Gol Gol *Australia* 34°12S 142°14E **152** C5
Gola *India* 28°3N 80°32E **125** E9
Golakganj *India* 26°8N 89°52E **125** F13
Golan Heights = Hagolan
Syria 33°0N 35°45E **130** C4
Golanci *Poland* 52°57N 17°18E **83** E4
Goläshkerd *Iran* 27°59N 57°16E **129** E8
Golaya Pristen = Hola Prystan
Ukraine 46°29N 32°32E **85** J7
Gölbaşı *Adıyaman,*
Turkey 37°43N 37°25E **104** D7
Gölbaşı *Ankara, Turkey* 39°47N 32°49E **104** C5
Golconda *India* 17°24N 78°23E **126** F4
Golconda *U.S.A.* 40°58N 117°30W **168** F5
Gölcük *Kocaeli, Turkey* 40°42N 29°48E **97** F13
Gölcük *Niğde, Turkey* 38°14N 34°47E **104** C6
Gold *U.S.A.* 41°52N 77°50W **174** E7
Gold Beach *U.S.A.* 42°25N 124°25W **168** E1
Gold Coast *W. Afr.* 4°0N 1°40W **139** E4
Gold Hill *U.S.A.* 42°26N 123°3W **168** E2
Gold River *Canada* 49°46N 126°3W **162** D3
Goldap *Poland* 54°19N 22°18E **82** D9
Goldberg *Germany* 53°35N 12°4E **76** B8
Golden *Canada* 51°20N 116°59W **162** C5
Golden B. *N.Z.* 40°40S 172°50E **155** D4
Golden Gate *U.S.A.* 37°48N 122°29W **169** H2
Golden Gate Highlands △
S. Africa 28°40S 28°40E **145** C4
Golden Hinde *Canada* 49°40N 125°44E **162** D3
Golden Lake *Canada* 45°34N 77°21W **174** A7
Golden Rock *India* 10°45N 78°48E **127** J4
Golden Spike △
U.S.A. 41°37N 112°33W **168** F7
Golden Vale *Ireland* 52°33N 8°17W **64** D3
Goldendale *U.S.A.* 45°49N 120°50W **168** D3
Goldfield *U.S.A.* 37°42N 117°14W **169** H5
Goldsand L. *Canada* 57°2N 101°8W **163** B8
Goldsboro *U.S.A.* 35°23N 77°59W **177** D16
Goldsmith *U.S.A.* 31°59N 102°37W **176** F3
Goldthwaite *U.S.A.* 31°27N 98°34W **176** F5
Golega *Portugal* 39°24N 8°29W **89** F2
Goleniów *Poland* 53°35N 14°50E **82** E1
Golestán □ *Iran* 37°20N 55°25E **129** B7
Golestának *Iran* 30°36N 54°14E **129** D7
Goleta *U.S.A.* 34°27N 119°50W **171** L7
Golfito *Costa Rica* 8°41N 83°5W **182** E3
Golfo Aranci *Italy* 40°59N 9°38E **94** B2
Golfo de Santa Clara
Mexico 31°42N 114°30W **180** A2
Golfo di Orosei e del
Gennargentu △ *Italy* 40°5N 9°15E **94** B2
Gölgeli Dağları *Turkey* 37°10N 28°55E **99** D10
Gölhisar *Turkey* 37°7N 29°35E **99** D11
Goliad *U.S.A.* 28°40N 97°23W **176** G6
Golija *Montenegro* 43°5N 18°45E **96** C2
Golija *Serbia* 43°22N 20°15E **96** C4
Golina *Poland* 52°15N 18°4E **83** F5
Gölköy *Turkey* 40°41N 37°37E **104** B7
Göllersdorf *Austria* 48°29N 16°7E **78** C9
Gölmarmara *Turkey* 38°42N 27°56E **99** C9
Golmud *China* 36°25N 94°53E **110** D7
Golo → *France* 42°31N 9°32E **73** F13
Golpāyegān *Iran* 33°27N 50°18E **129** C6
Golpazarı *Turkey* 40°16N 30°18E **104** B4
Golra *Pakistan* 33°37N 72°56E **124** C5
Golspie *U.K.* 57°58N 3°59W **65** D5
Golub-Dobrzyń *Poland* 53°7N 19°2E **83** E6
Golubac *Serbia* 44°38N 21°38E **96** B5
Golyam Perelik *Bulgaria* 41°36N 24°33E **97** E8
Golyama Kamchiya →
Bulgaria 43°10N 27°55E **97** C11
Goma
Dem. Rep. of the Congo 1°37S 29°10E **142** C2
Gomal Pass *Pakistan* 31°56N 69°20E **124** D3
Gomati → *India* 25°32N 83°11E **125** G10
Gombari
Dem. Rep. of the Congo 2°45N 29°3E **142** B2
Gombe *Nigeria* 10°19N 11°2E **139** C7
Gombe □ *Nigeria* 10°36N 11°8E **139** C7
Gombe *Turkey* 36°39N 29°38E **99** E11
Gombe → *Tanzania* 4°38S 31°40E **142** D3
Gombe Stream △
Tanzania 4°38S 29°37E **142** C2
Gombi *Nigeria* 10°12N 12°30E **139** C7
Gomel = Homyel
Belarus 52°28N 31°0E **75** B16
Gomera *Canary Is.* 28°7N 17°14W **100** F2
Gómez Palacio
Mexico 25°34N 103°30W **180** B4
Gomfi *Greece* 39°26N 21°36E **98** B3
Gomishān *Iran* 37°4N 54°6E **129** B7
Gommern *Germany* 52°14N 11°50E **76** C7
Gomogomo *Indonesia* 6°39S 134°43E **119** F8
Gomotartsi *Bulgaria* 44°7N 22°45E **96** B6
Gompa = Ganta *Liberia* 7°15N 8°59W **138** D3
Gonābād *Iran* 34°15N 58°45E **129** C8

Gonaïves *Haiti* 19°20N 72°42W **183** C5
Gonarezhou △
Zimbabwe 21°32S 31°55E **143** G3
Gonâve, G. de la *Haiti* 19°29N 72°42W **183** C5
Gonâve, Île de la *Haiti* 18°51N 73°3W **183** C5
Gonbad-e Kāvūs *Iran* 37°20N 55°25E **129** B7
Gönc *Hungary* 48°28N 21°14E **80** B6
Gonda *India* 27°9N 81°58E **125** F19
Gondal *India* 21°58N 70°52E **124** J4
Gonder *Ethiopia* 12°39N 37°30E **131** E2
Gondia *Mozam.* 21°23N 80°10E **126** D5
Gondola *Mozam.* 19°10S 33°37E **143** F3
Gondomar *Portugal* 41°10N 8°35W **88** D2
Gondrecourt-le-Château
France 48°31N 5°30E **71** D12
Gönen *Balıkesir, Turkey* 40°6N 27°39E **97** F11
Gönen *Isparta, Turkey* 37°57N 30°31E **99** D12
Gönen → *Turkey* 40°6N 27°39E **97** F11
Gong Xian *China* 28°23N 104°47E **116** C5
Gong'an *China* 30°7N 112°12E **117** B9
Gongbei *China* 22°12N 113°32E **111** a
Gongchangling *China* 41°7N 123°27E **115** D12
Gongcheng *China* 24°50N 110°49E **117** E8
Gongga Shan *China* 29°40N 101°55E **116** C3
Gonggar *China* 29°23N 91°7E **110** F7
Gongguan *China* 21°48N 109°36E **116** G7
Gonghe *China* 36°18N 100°32E **110** D9
Gongju *S. Korea* 36°27N 127°7E **115** F14
Gongliu *China* 43°28N 82°8E **109** D10
Gongming *China* 22°47N 113°53E **111** a
Gongola → *Nigeria* 9°30N 12°4E **139** D7
Gongolgon *Australia* 30°21S 146°54E **151** E4
Gongshan *China* 27°43N 98°29E **116** D2
Gongtan *China* 28°55N 108°20E **116** C7
Gongyi *China* 34°45N 112°58E **114** G7
Gongzhuling *China* 43°30N 124°40E **115** C13
Goni *Spain* 39°52N 22°29E **98** B4
Goniadz *Poland* 53°30N 22°44E **82** E9
Goniri *Nigeria* 11°30N 12°15E **139** C7
Gonjo *China* 30°52N 98°17E **116** B2
Gonnesa *Italy* 39°16N 8°28E **94** C1
Gonnosfanádiga *Italy* 39°29N 8°39E **94** C1
Gonzales *Calif., U.S.A.* 36°30N 121°26W **170** J5
Gonzales *Tex., U.S.A.* 29°30N 97°27W **176** G6
González *Mexico* 22°48N 98°25W **181** C5
Goobang △ *Australia* 33°0S 148°32E **153** B8
Good Hope, C. of
S. Africa 34°24S 18°30E **144** D2
Good Hope Lake
Canada 59°16N 129°18W **162** B3
Gooderham *Canada* 44°54N 78°21W **174** B6
Goodhouse *S. Africa* 28°57S 18°13E **144** C2
Gooding *U.S.A.* 42°56N 114°43W **168** E6
Goodland *U.S.A.* 39°21N 101°43W **172** F3
Goodlands *Mauritius* 20°2S 57°39E **141** d
Goodlow *Canada* 56°20N 120°8W **162** B4
Goodooga *Australia* 29°3S 147°28E **151** D4
Goodsprings *U.S.A.* 35°49N 115°27W **171** K11
Goodwater *U.S.A.* 33°4N 86°3W **178** B3
Goole *U.K.* 53°42N 0°53W **66** D7
Goolgowi *Australia* 33°58S 145°41E **153** B6
Goolwa *Australia* 35°30S 138°47E **152** C3
Goomalling *Australia* 31°15S 116°49E **149** F2
Goomeri *Australia* 26°12S 152°6E **151** D5
Goonda *Mozam.* 19°48S 33°57E **143** F3
Goondiwindi *Australia* 28°30S 150°21E **151** D5
Goongarrie, L. *Australia* 30°3S 121°9E **149** F3
Goongarrie △ *Australia* 30°7S 121°30E **149** F3
Goonyella *Australia* 21°4S 147°58E **150** C4
Goose → *Canada* 53°20N 60°35W **165** B7
Goose Creek *U.S.A.* 32°59N 80°2W **178** C9
Goose L. *U.S.A.* 41°56N 120°26W **168** F3
Gooty *India* 15°7N 77°41E **127** G3
Gop *India* 22°5N 69°50E **124** H3
Gopalganj *India* 26°28N 84°30E **125** F11
Göppingen *Germany* 48°42N 9°39E **77** G5
Gor *Spain* 37°23N 2°58W **89** H8
Góra *Dolnośląskie, Poland* 51°40N 16°31E **83** G3
Góra *Mazowieckie, Poland* 52°39N 20°6E **83** F7
Góra Kalwaria *Poland* 51°59N 21°14E **83** G8
Gorakhpur *India* 26°47N 83°23E **125** F10
Goražde *Bos.-H.* 43°38N 18°58E **80** G3
Gorbatov *Russia* 56°12N 43°2E **86** B6
Gorbea *Spain* 43°1N 2°50W **90** B2
Gorczański △ *Poland* 49°30N 20°10E **83** J7
Gorda, Pta. *Canary Is.* 28°45N 18°0W **100** F2
Gorda, Pta. *Nic.* 14°20N 83°10W **182** D3
Gordan B. *Australia* 11°35S 130°10E **148** B5
Gördes *Turkey* 38°54N 28°17E **99** C10
Gordon *Ga., U.S.A.* 32°54N 83°20W **178** C6
Gordon *Nebr., U.S.A.* 42°48N 102°12W **172** D2
Gordon → *Australia* 42°27S 145°30E **154** G4
Gordon, I. *Chile* 54°55S 69°30W **192** D3
Gordon Bay *Canada* 45°12N 79°47W **174** A5
Gordon L. *Alta.,
Canada* 56°30N 110°25W **163** B6
Gordon L. *N.W.T.,
Canada* 63°5N 113°11W **162** A6
Gordonvale *Australia* 17°5S 145°50E **150** B4
Goré *Chad* 7°59N 16°31E **135** G9
Gore *Ethiopia* 8°12N 35°32E **131** F2
Gore *N.Z.* 46°5S 168°58E **155** G3
Gore Bay *Canada* 45°57N 82°28W **164** D3
Gorée, Île de *Senegal* 14°40N 17°23W **138** C1
Görele *Turkey* 41°2N 39°0E **105** B8
Göreme *Turkey* 38°35N 34°52E **104** C6
Gorey *Ireland* 52°41N 6°18W **64** D5
Gorg *Iran* 29°29N 59°43E **129** D8
Gorgān *Iran* 36°55N 54°30E **129** B7
Gorgol □ *Mauritania* 15°45N 13°0W **138** B2
Gorgona *Italy* 43°26N 9°54E **92** E6
Gorgona, I. *Colombia* 3°0N 78°10W **186** C3
Gorgoram *Nigeria* 12°40N 10°45E **139** C7
Gorham *U.S.A.* 44°23N 71°10W **175** B13
Gori *Georgia* 42°0N 44°7E **87** J7
Goribidnur = Gauribidanur
India 13°37N 77°32E **127** H3
Goriganga → *India* 29°45N 80°23E **125** E9
Gorinchem *Neths.* 51°50N 4°59E **69** C4
Goris *Armenia* 39°31N 46°22E **105** C12
Goritsy *Russia* 57°4N 36°43E **86** B9
Gorizia *Italy* 45°56N 13°37E **93** C10
Gorj □ *Romania* 45°5N 23°25E **81** E8
Gorki = Horki *Belarus* 54°17N 30°59E **84** E6
Gorkiy = Nizhniy Novgorod
Russia 56°20N 44°0E **86** B7
Gorkovskoye Vdkhr.
Russia 57°2N 43°4E **86** B6
Gorleston *U.K.* 52°35N 1°44E **67** E9
Gorlice *Poland* 49°35N 21°11E **83** J8
Görlitz *Germany* 51°9N 14°58E **76** D10

Gorlovka = Horlivka
Ukraine 48°19N 38°5E **85** H10
Gorman *U.S.A.* 34°47N 118°51W **171** L8
Gorna Dzhumayo = Blagoevgrad
Bulgaria 42°2N 23°5E **96** D7
Gorna Oryakhovitsa
Bulgaria 43°7N 25°40E **97** C9
Gornja Radgona
Slovenia 46°40N 16°2E **93** B13
Gornja Tuzla *Bos.-H.* 44°35N 18°46E **80** F3
Gornji Grad *Slovenia* 46°20N 14°52E **93** B11
Gornji Milanovac *Serbia* 44°3N 20°29E **96** B4
Gornji Vakuf *Bos.-H.* 43°57N 17°34E **80** G2
Gorno Ablanovo
Bulgaria 43°37N 25°43E **97** C9
Gorno-Altay □ *Russia* 51°0N 86°0E **109** B11
Gorno-Altaysk *Russia* 51°50N 86°5E **109** B11
Gornyak *Russia* 50°59N 81°27E **109** B10
Gornyatskiy *Russia* 48°18N 40°56E **87** F5
Gornyy *Primorsk,
Russia* 44°57N 133°59E **112** B6
Gornyy *Saratov, Russia* 51°50N 48°30E **86** E9
Gorodenka = Horodenka
Ukraine 48°41N 25°29E **81** B10
Gorodets *Russia* 56°38N 43°28E **86** B6
Gorodishche = Horodyshche
Ukraine 49°17N 31°27E **85** H6
Gorodishche *Russia* 53°13N 45°40E **86** D7
Gorodnya = Horodnya
Ukraine 51°55N 31°33E **85** G6
Gorodok = Haradok
Belarus 55°30N 30°3E **84** E6
Gorodok = Horodok
Ukraine 49°46N 23°32E **75** D12
Gorodovikovsk *Russia* 46°8N 41°58E **87** G5
Goroke *Australia* 36°43S 141°29E **152** D4
Gorokhov = Horokhiv
Ukraine 50°30N 24°45E **75** C13
Gorokhovets *Russia* 56°13N 42°39E **86** B6
Gorom Gorom
Burkina Faso 14°26N 0°14W **139** C4
Goromonzi *Zimbabwe* 17°52S 31°22E **143** F3
Gorong, Kepulauan
Indonesia 3°59S 131°25E **119** E8
Gorongose → *Mozam.* 20°30S 34°40E **145** B5
Gorongoza *Mozam.* 18°44S 34°2E **143** F3
Gorongoza, Sa. da
Mozam. 18°27S 34°2E **143** F3
Gorongoza △ *Mozam.* 18°50S 34°29E **145** A5
Gorontalo *Indonesia* 0°35N 123°5E **119** D6
Gorontalo □ *Indonesia* 0°50N 122°20E **119** D6
Goronyo *Nigeria* 13°29N 5°39E **139** C6
Górowo Iławeckie
Poland 54°17N 20°30E **82** D7
Gorron *France* 48°25N 0°50W **70** D6
Gorshechnoye *Russia* 51°31N 38°2E **85** G10
Gort *Ireland* 53°3N 8°49W **64** C3
Gortis *Greece* 35°4N 24°58E **101** D6
Gorumahisani *India* 22°20N 86°24E **126** C8
Goryachiy Klyuch *Russia* 44°38N 39°8E **87** H4
Goryeong *S. Korea* 35°44N 128°15E **115** G15
Gorzkowice *Poland* 51°13N 19°36E **83** G6
Górzno *Poland* 53°12N 19°38E **83** E6
Gorzów Śląski *Poland* 51°3N 18°22E **83** G5
Gorzów Wielkopolski
Poland 52°43N 15°15E **83** F2
Gosford *Australia* 33°23S 151°18E **153** B9
Goshen *Calif., U.S.A.* 36°21N 119°25W **170** J7
Goshen *Ind., U.S.A.* 41°35N 85°50W **173** E11
Goshen *N.Y., U.S.A.* 41°24N 74°20W **175** E10
Goshogawara *Japan* 40°48N 140°27E **112** D10
Goslar *Germany* 51°54N 10°25E **76** D6
Gospić *Croatia* 44°35N 15°23E **93** D12
Gosport *U.K.* 50°48N 1°9W **67** G6
Gossas *Senegal* 14°28N 16°0W **138** C1
Gosse → *Australia* 19°32S 134°37E **150** B1
Gossi *Mali* 15°48N 1°20W **139** B4
Gostivar *Macedonia* 41°48N 20°57E **96** E4
Gostyń *Poland* 51°50N 17°3E **83** G4
Gostynin *Poland* 52°26N 19°29E **83** F6
Göta älv → *Sweden* 57°42N 11°54E **63** G5
Göta kanal *Sweden* 58°30N 15°58E **63** F10
Götaland *Sweden* 57°30N 14°30E **63** G8
Göteborg *Sweden* 57°43N 11°59E **63** G5
Götene *Sweden* 58°32N 13°30E **63** F7
Goteşti *Moldova* 46°9N 28°10E **81** D13
Gotha *Germany* 50°56N 10°42E **76** E6
Gothenburg = Göteborg
Sweden 57°43N 11°59E **63** G5
Gothenburg *U.S.A.* 40°56N 100°10W **172** E3
Gothèye *Niger* 13°52N 1°34E **139** C5
Gotland *Sweden* 57°30N 18°33E **63** G12
Gotlands län □ *Sweden* 57°15N 18°30E **63** G12
Gotō = Fukue *Japan* 32°41N 128°51E **113** H4
Gotō-Rettō *Japan* 32°55N 129°5E **113** H4
Gotse Delchev *Bulgaria* 41°36N 23°46E **96** E7
Gotska Sandön *Sweden* 58°24N 19°15E **63** F13
Gōtsu *Japan* 35°0N 132°14E **113** G6
Göttero, Monte *Italy* 44°22N 9°42E **92** D6
Göttingen *Germany* 51°31N 9°55E **76** D5
Gottskär *Sweden* 57°25N 12°2E **63** G6
Gottwald = Zmiyev
Ukraine 49°39N 36°27E **85** H9
Gottwaldov = Zlín
Czech Rep. 49°14N 17°40E **79** B10
Goubangzi *China* 41°20N 121°52E **115** D11
Gouda *Neths.* 52°1N 4°42E **69** B4
Goudiri *Senegal* 14°15N 12°45W **138** C2
Goudoumaria *Niger* 13°40N 11°10E **139** C7
Goudouras, Akra *Greece* 34°59N 26°6E **101** E8
Gouéké *Guinea* 8°2N 8°43W **138** D3
Gough I. *Atl. Oc.* 40°10S 9°45W **56** L11
Gouin, Rés. *Canada* 48°35N 74°40W **164** C5
Gouitafla *Ivory C.* 7°30N 5°53W **138** D3
Goulburn *Australia* 34°44S 149°44E **153** C8
Goulburn Is. *Australia* 11°40S 133°20E **150** A1
Goulburn River △
Australia 32°19S 150°10E **153** B9
Goulds *U.S.A.* 25°34N 80°23W **179** H5
Goulia *Ivory C.* 10°1N 7°11W **138** C3
Goulimine *Morocco* 28°56N 10°0W **134** C3
Goulmima *Morocco* 31°41N 4°57W **136** B3
Goumbou *Mali* 15°2N 7°25W **138** B3
Goumenissa *Greece* 40°56N 22°37E **96** D6
Goundam *Mali* 16°27N 3°40W **138** B4
Goura *Greece* 37°56N 22°20E **98** D4

Gouraya *Algeria* 36°31N 1°56E **136** A4
Gourbassi *Mali* 13°24N 11°38W **138** C2
Gourdon *France* 44°44N 1°23E **72** D5
Gouré *Niger* 14°0N 10°10E **139** C7
Gourin *France* 48°8N 3°37W **70** D3
Gourma-Rharous *Mali* 16°55N 1°50W **139** B4
Gournay-en-Bray *France* 49°29N 1°44E **71** C8
Gournes *Greece* 35°19N 25°16E **101** D7
Gourock *U.K.* 55°57N 4°49W **65** F4
Gourock Ra. *Australia* 36°0S 149°25E **153** D8
Goursi *Burkina Faso* 12°42N 2°37W **138** C4
Gouvea *Brazil* 18°27S 43°44W **189** D2
Gouverneur *U.S.A.* 44°20N 75°28W **175** B9
Gouvia *Greece* 39°39N 19°50E **101** A3
Gove Peninsula
Australia 12°17S 136°49E **150** A2
Governador Valadares
Brazil 18°15S 41°57W **189** D2
Governor's Harbour
Bahamas 25°10N 76°14W **182** A4
Goviĭaltay □ *Mongolia* 46°30N 96°0E **109** C13
Govindgarh *India* 24°23N 81°18E **125** G9
Gowan Ra. *Australia* 25°0S 145°0E **150** D4
Gowanda *U.S.A.* 42°28N 78°56W **174** D6
Gower *U.K.* 51°35N 4°10W **67** F3
Gowers Corner *U.S.A.* 28°20N 82°30W **179** G7
Gowna, L. *Ireland* 53°51N 7°34W **64** C4
Gowurdak *Turkmenistan* 37°50N 66°4E **109** E7
Goya *Argentina* 29°10S 59°10W **190** B4
Goyang *S. Korea* 37°39N 126°50E **115** F14
Goyder Lagoon
Australia 27°3S 138°58E **151** D2
Goygöl *Azerbaijan* 40°37N 46°12E **87** K8
Goyllarisquizga *Peru* 10°31S 76°24W **188** C2
Göynük *Antalya, Turkey* 36°41N 30°33E **99** E12
Göynük *Bolu, Turkey* 40°24N 30°48E **104** B4
Göz Beïda *Chad* 12°10N 21°20E **135** F10
Gozdnica *Poland* 51°28N 15°4E **83** G2
Gozo *Malta* 36°3N 14°15E **101** C1
Graaff-Reinet *S. Africa* 32°13S 24°32E **144** D3
Grabo *Ivory C.* 4°57N 7°30W **138** D3
Grabow *Germany* 53°17N 11°34E **76** B7
Grabów nad Prosną
Poland 51°31N 18°7E **83** G5
Gračac *Croatia* 44°18N 15°57E **93** D12
Gračanica *Bos.-H.* 44°43N 18°18E **80** F3
Graçay *France* 47°10N 1°50E **71** E6
Graceville *U.S.A.* 30°58N 85°31W **178** F4
Gracewood *U.S.A.* 33°22N 82°2W **178** B7
Gracias a Dios, C.
Honduras 15°0N 83°10W **182** D3
Graciosa *Azores* 39°4N 28°0W **134** a
Graciosa, I. *Canary Is.* 29°15N 13°32W **100** E6
Grad Sofiya □ *Bulgaria* 42°35N 23°20E **96** D7
Gradac *Montenegro* 42°23N 19°9E **96** C3
Gradačac *Bos.-H.* 44°52N 18°26E **80** F3
Gradeška Planina
Macedonia 41°30N 22°15E **96** E6
Gradets *Bulgaria* 42°46N 26°30E **97** D10
Gradišče *Slovenia* 46°37N 15°50E **93** B12
Grădiştea de Munte
Romania 45°37N 23°13E **81** E8
Grado *Italy* 45°40N 13°23E **93** C10
Grado *Spain* 43°23N 6°4W **88** B4
Grady *U.S.A.* 34°49N 103°19W **169** J12
Graeca, Lacul *Romania* 44°5N 26°10E **81** F11
Grafenau *Germany* 48°51N 13°22E **77** G9
Gräfenberg *Germany* 49°39N 11°15E **77** G7
Grafham Water *U.K.* 52°19N 0°18W **67** E7
Grafton *Australia* 29°38S 152°58E **151** D5
Grafton *N. Dak., U.S.A.* 48°25N 97°25W **172** A5
Grafton *W. Va., U.S.A.* 39°21N 80°2W **173** F13
Graham *Canada* 49°20N 90°30W **164** C1
Graham *Ga., U.S.A.* 31°50N 82°30W **178** D7
Graham *Tex., U.S.A.* 33°6N 98°35W **176** E5
Graham, Mt. *U.S.A.* 32°42N 109°52W **169** K9
Graham Bell, Ostrov = Greem-
Bell, Ostrov *Russia* 81°0N 62°0E **106** A7
Graham I. *B.C.,
Canada* 53°40N 132°30W **162** C2
Graham I. *Nunavut,
Canada* 77°25N 90°30W **161** B13
Graham Land *Antarctica* 65°0S 64°0W **55** C17
Grahamstown *S. Africa* 33°19S 26°31E **144** D4
Grahamsville *U.S.A.* 41°51N 74°33W **175** E10
Grahovo *Montenegro* 42°40N 18°40E **96** D2
Graïba *Tunisia* 34°30N 10°13E **136** B6
Graie, Alpi *Europe* 45°30N 7°10E **73** C11
Grain Coast *W. Afr.* 4°20N 10°0W **138** E3
Grajagan *Indonesia* 8°35S 114°13E **119** K17
Grajaú *Brazil* 5°50S 46°4W **189** B1
Grajaú → *Brazil* 3°41S 44°48W **189** A2
Grajewo *Poland* 53°39N 22°30E **82** E9
Gramada *Bulgaria* 43°49N 22°39E **96** C8
Gramat *France* 44°48N 1°43E **72** D5
Grammichele *Italy* 37°13N 14°38E **95** E7
Grámmos, Óros *Greece* 40°18N 20°47E **96** F4
Grampian □ *U.K.* 57°20N 2°55W **66** d
Grampian Highlands = Grampian
Mts. *U.K.* 56°50N 4°0W **65** E5
Grampian Mts. *U.K.* 56°50N 4°0W **65** E5
Grampians, The
Australia 37°15S 142°20E **152** D5
Grampians △
Australia 37°15S 142°28E **152** D5
Gramsh *Albania* 40°52N 20°12E **96** F4
Gran Altiplanicie Central
Argentina 49°0S 69°30W **192** F3
Gran Canaria
Canary Is. 27°55N 15°35W **100** G4
Gran Chaco *S. Amer.* 25°0S 61°0W **190** B3
Gran Desierto del Pinacate △
Mexico 31°51N 113°32W **180** A2
Gran Laguna Salada
Argentina 44°24S 67°23W **192** B3
Gran Pajonal *Peru* 10°45S 74°38E **188** C2
Gran Paradiso *Italy* 45°33N 7°17E **92** C4
Gran Sasso d'Itália
Italy 42°27N 13°42E **93** F10
Gran Sasso e Monti Della Laga △
Italy 42°32N 13°22E **93** F10
Granada *Nic.* 11°58N 86°0W **182** D2
Granada *Spain* 37°10N 3°35W **89** H7
Granada *U.S.A.* 38°4N 102°19W **168** G12
Granada □ *Spain* 37°18N 3°0W **89** H7
Granadilla de Abona
Canary Is. 28°7N 16°33W **100** F3
Granard *Ireland* 53°47N 7°30W **64** C4

Granbury *U.S.A.* 32°27N 97°47W **176** E6
Granby *Canada* 45°25N 72°45W **175** A12
Granby *U.S.A.* 40°5N 105°56W **168** F11
Grand → *Canada* 42°51N 79°34W **174** D5
Grand → *Mo., U.S.A.* 39°23N 93°7W **172** F7
Grand → *S. Dak.,
U.S.A.* 45°40N 100°45W **172** C3
Grand Bahama I.
Bahamas 26°40N 78°30W **182** A4
Grand Baie *Mauritius* 20°0S 57°35E **141** d
Grand Bank *Canada* 47°6N 55°48W **165** C8
Grand Bassam *Ivory C.* 5°10N 3°49W **138** D4
Grand Bend *Canada* 43°18N 81°45W **174** C3
Grand Béréby *Ivory C.* 4°38N 6°55W **138** E3
Grand-Bourg
Guadeloupe 15°53N 61°19W **182** b
Grand Canal = Da Yunhe →
China 39°10N 117°10E **115** E9
Grand Canyon *U.S.A.* 36°3N 112°9W **169** H7
Grand Canyon △
U.S.A. 36°15N 112°30W **169** H7
Grand Canyon-Parashant □
U.S.A. 36°30N 113°45W **169** H7
Grand Cayman
Cayman Is. 19°20N 81°20W **182** C3
Grand Cess *Liberia* 4°40N 8°12W **138** E3
Grand Coulee *U.S.A.* 47°57N 119°0W **168** C4
Grand Coulee Dam
U.S.A. 47°57N 118°59W **168** C4
Grand Falls *Canada* 47°3N 67°44W **165** C6
Grand Falls-Windsor
Canada 48°56N 55°40W **165** C8
Grand Forks *Canada* 49°0N 118°30W **162** D5
Grand Forks *U.S.A.* 47°55N 97°3W **172** B5
Grand Gorge *U.S.A.* 42°21N 74°29W **175** D10
Grand Haven *U.S.A.* 43°4N 86°13W **172** D10
Grand I. *Mich., U.S.A.* 46°31N 86°40W **172** B10
Grand I. *N.Y., U.S.A.* 43°0N 78°58W **174** D6
Grand Island *U.S.A.* 40°55N 98°21W **172** E4
Grand Isle *La., U.S.A.* 29°14N 90°0W **177** G9
Grand Isle *Vt., U.S.A.* 44°43N 73°18W **175** B11
Grand Junction *U.S.A.* 39°4N 108°33W **168** G9
Grand L. *N.B., Canada* 45°57N 66°7W **165** C6
Grand L. *Nfld. & L.,
Canada* 49°0N 57°30W **165** C8
Grand L. *Nfld. & L.,
Canada* 53°40N 60°30W **165** B7
Grand L. *U.S.A.* 29°55N 92°47W **176** G8
Grand Lahou *Ivory C.* 5°10N 5°5W **138** D3
Grand Lake *U.S.A.* 40°15N 105°49W **168** F11
Grand-Lieu, L. de *France* 47°6N 1°40W **70** E5
Grand Manan I.
Canada 44°45N 66°52W **165** D6
Grand Marais *Mich.,
U.S.A.* 46°40N 85°59W **173** B11
Grand Marais *Minn.,
U.S.A.* 47°45N 90°25W **164** C1
Grand-Mère *Canada* 46°36N 72°40W **164** C5
Grand Popo *Benin* 6°15N 1°57E **139** D5
Grand Portage *U.S.A.* 47°58N 89°41W **172** B9
Grand Prairie *U.S.A.* 32°44N 96°59W **176** E6
Grand Rapids *Canada* 53°12N 99°19W **163** C9
Grand Rapids *Mich.,
U.S.A.* 42°58N 85°40W **173** D11
Grand Rapids *Minn.,
U.S.A.* 47°14N 93°31W **172** B7
Grand Ridge *U.S.A.* 30°43N 85°1W **178** E4
Grand St-Bernard, Col du
Europe 45°50N 7°10E **73** K3
Grand Staircase-Escalante □
U.S.A. 37°25N 111°33W **169** H8
Grand Teton *U.S.A.* 43°54N 110°50W **168** E8
Grand Teton △
U.S.A. 43°50N 110°50W **168** E8
Grand Union Canal *U.K.* 52°7N 0°53W **67** E7
Grandas *Spain* 43°13N 6°53W **88** B4
Grande → *Jujuy,
Argentina* 24°20S 65°2W **190** A2
Grande → *Mendoza,
Argentina* 36°52S 69°45W **190** D2
Grande → *Bolivia* 15°51S 64°39W **186** G6
Grande → *Bahia,
Brazil* 11°30S 44°30W **189** C2
Grande → *Minas Gerais,
Brazil* 20°6S 51°4W **191** H8
Grande, B. *Argentina* 50°30S 68°20W **192** D3
Grande, Rio →
N. Amer. 25°58N 97°9W **176** J6
Grande, Serra *Piauí,
Brazil* 8°0S 45°10W **189** B1
Grande, Serra *Tocantins,
Brazil* 11°15S 46°30W **189** C1
Grande Anse *Seychelles* 4°18S 55°45E **141** b
Grande Baleine →
Canada 55°16N 77°47W **164** A4
Grande Cache *Canada* 53°53N 119°8W **162** C5
Grande Casse, Pte. de la
France 45°24N 6°49E **73** C10
Grande Comore
Comoros Is. 11°35S 43°20E **141** a
Grande-Entrée *Canada* 47°30N 61°40W **165** C7
Grande Prairie
Canada 55°10N 118°50W **162** B5
Grande-Rivière *Canada* 48°26N 64°30W **165** C7
Grande Sertão Veredas △
Brazil 15°10S 45°40W **189** D1
Grande-Terre
Guadeloupe 16°20N 61°25W **182** b
Grande-Vallée *Canada* 49°14N 65°8W **165** C6
Grande Vigie, Pte. de la
Guadeloupe 16°32N 61°27W **182** b
Grandfalls *U.S.A.* 31°20N 102°51W **176** F3
Grândola *Portugal* 38°12N 8°35W **89** G2
Grandpré *France* 49°20N 4°50E **71** C11
Grands Causses △ *France* 44°5N 2°58E **72** D6
Grands-Jardins
Canada 47°41N 70°51W **165** C5
Grandview *Canada* 51°10N 100°42W **163** C8
Grandview *U.S.A.* 46°15N 119°54W **168** C4
Grandvilliers *France* 49°40N 1°57E **71** C8
Graneros *Chile* 34°5S 70°45W **190** C1
Grangemouth *U.K.* 56°1N 3°42W **65** E5
Granger *U.S.A.* 41°35N 109°58W **168** F9
Grängesberg *Sweden* 60°6N 15°1E **63** F9
Grangeville *U.S.A.* 45°56N 116°7W **168** D5
Granisle *Canada* 54°53N 126°13W **162** C3
Granit Rose, Côte *France* 48°50N 4°10W **70** D2
Granite City *U.S.A.* 38°42N 90°8W **172** F8

Granite Falls *U.S.A.* 44°49N 95°33W **172** C6
Granite L. *Canada* 48°8N 57°5W **165** C8
Granite Mt. *U.S.A.* 33°5N 116°28W **171** M10
Granite Pk. *U.S.A.* 45°10N 109°48W **168** D9
Graniteville S.C.,
U.S.A. 33°34N 81°49W **178** B8
Graniteville *Vt., U.S.A.* 44°8N 72°29W **175** B12
Granitola, C. *Italy* 37°33N 12°39E **94** E5
Granity *N.Z.* 41°39S 171°51E **155** B6
Granja *Brazil* 3°7S 40°50W **189** A2
Granja de Moreruela
Spain 41°48N 5°44W **88** D5
Granja de Torrehermosa
Spain 38°19N 5°35W **89** G5
Gränna *Sweden* 58°1N 14°28E **63** F8
Granollers *Spain* 41°39N 2°18E **90** D7
Gransee *Germany* 53°1N 13°8E **76** B9
Grant *Fla., U.S.A.* 27°56N 80°32W **179** G7
Grant *Nebr., U.S.A.* 40°50N 101°43W **172** E3
Grant, Mt. *U.S.A.* 38°34N 118°48W **168** G4
Grant City *U.S.A.* 40°29N 94°25W **172** E6
Grant I. *Australia* 11°10S 132°52E **148** B5
Grant Range *U.S.A.* 38°30N 115°25W **168** G6
Grantham *U.K.* 52°55N 0°38W **66** E7
Grantown-on-Spey *U.K.* 57°20N 3°36W **65** D5
Grants *U.S.A.* 35°9N 107°52W **169** J10
Grants Pass *U.S.A.* 42°26N 123°19W **168** E2
Grantsville *U.S.A.* 40°36N 112°28W **168** F7
Grantville *U.S.A.* 33°14N 84°50W **178** B5
Granville *France* 48°50N 1°35W **70** D5
Granville *N. Dak.,
U.S.A.* 48°16N 100°47W **172** A3
Granville *N.Y., U.S.A.* 43°24N 73°16W **175** C11
Granville *Ohio, U.S.A.* 40°4N 82°31W **174** F2
Granville L. *Canada* 56°18N 100°30W **163** B8
Graskop *S. Africa* 24°56S 30°49E **145** B5
Gräsö *Sweden* 60°28N 18°35E **62** D12
Grass → *Canada* 56°3N 96°33W **163** B9
Grass Range *U.S.A.* 47°2N 108°48W **168** C9
Grass River △ *Canada* 54°40N 100°50W **163** C8
Grass Valley *Calif.,
U.S.A.* 39°13N 121°4W **170** F4
Grass Valley *Oreg.,
U.S.A.* 45°22N 120°47W **168** D3
Grassano *Italy* 40°38N 16°17E **95** B9
Grasse *France* 43°38N 6°56E **73** E10
Grassflat *U.S.A.* 41°0N 78°6W **174** E6
Grasslands △ *Canada* 49°11N 107°38W **163** D7
Grassy *Australia* 40°3S 144°5E **151** G3
Gråsten *Denmark* 54°55N 9°35E **63** K3
Grästorp *Sweden* 58°20N 12°40E **63** F7
Gratkorn *Austria* 47°8N 15°21E **78** D8
Graubünden □ *Switz.* 46°45N 9°30E **77** J5
Graulhet *France* 43°45N 1°59E **72** E5
Graus *Spain* 42°11N 0°20E **90** C5
Grave, Pte. de *France* 45°34N 1°4W **72** C2
Gravelbourg *Canada* 49°50N 106°35W **163** D7
Gravelines *France* 51°1N 2°10E **71** A9
's-Gravenhage *Neths.* 52°7N 4°17E **69** B4
Gravenhurst *Canada* 44°52N 79°20W **174** B5
Gravesend *Australia* 29°35S 150°20E **151** D5
Gravesend *U.K.* 51°26N 0°22E **67** F8
Gravina in Púglia *Italy* 40°49N 16°25E **95** B9
Gravois, Pointe-à- *Haiti* 16°15N 73°56W **183** C5
Gravona → *France* 41°58N 8°45E **73** G12
Gray *France* 47°27N 5°35E **71** E12
Gray *U.S.A.* 33°1N 83°32W **178** B6
Grayling *U.S.A.* 44°40N 84°43W **173** C11
Grays *U.K.* 51°28N 0°21E **67** F8
Grays Harbor *U.S.A.* 46°59N 124°1W **170** D2
Grays L. *U.S.A.* 43°4N 111°26W **168** E8
Grays River *U.S.A.* 46°21N 123°37W **170** D3
Grayvoron *Russia* 50°29N 35°41E **85** G8
Graz *Austria* 47°4N 15°27E **78** D8
Grdelica *Serbia* 42°55N 22°3E **96** D6
Greasy L. *Canada* 62°55N 122°12W **162** A4
Great Abaco I. = Abaco I.
Bahamas 26°25N 77°10W **182** A4
Great Artesian Basin
Australia 23°0S 144°0E **150** C3
Great Australian Bight
Australia 33°30S 130°0E **149** F5
Great Bahama Bank
Bahamas 23°15N 78°0W **182** B4
Great Barrier I. *N.Z.* 36°11S 175°25E **154** C4
Great Barrier Reef
Australia 18°0S 146°50E **150** B4
Great Barrier Reef ○
Australia 20°0S 150°0E **150** B4
Great Barrington
U.S.A. 42°12N 73°22W **175** D11
Great Basalt Wall △
Australia 19°52S 145°43E **150** B4
Great Basin *U.S.A.* 40°0N 117°0W **168** G5
Great Basin △ *U.S.A.* 38°56N 114°15W **168** G6
Great Bear → *Canada* 65°0N 126°0W **160** B7
Great Bear L. *Canada* 65°30N 120°0W **160** B7
Great Belt = Store Bælt
Denmark 55°20N 11°0E **63** J4
Great Bend *Kans.,
U.S.A.* 38°22N 98°46W **172** F4
Great Bend *Pa., U.S.A.* 41°58N 75°45W **175** E9
Great Blasket I. *Ireland* 52°6N 10°32W **64** D1
Great Britain *Europe* 54°0N 2°15W **58** E5
Great Camanoe
Br. Virgin Is. 18°30N 64°35W **183** e
Great Channel *Asia* 6°0N 94°0E **127** L11
Great Coco I. = Koko Kyunzu
Burma 14°7N 93°22E **127** G11
Great Codroy *Canada* 47°51N 59°16W **165** C8
Great Divide, The = Great
Dividing Ra. *Australia* 23°0S 146°0E **150** C4
Great Divide Basin
U.S.A. 42°0N 108°0W **168** E9
Great Dividing Ra.
Australia 23°0S 146°0E **150** C4
Great Driffield = Driffield
U.K. 54°0N 0°26W **66** C7
Great Exuma I.
Bahamas 23°30N 75°50W **182** B4
Great Falls *U.S.A.* 47°30N 111°17W **168** C8
Great Fish = Groot-Vis →
S. Africa 33°28S 27°5E **144** D4
Great Guana Cay
Bahamas 24°0N 76°20W **182** B4
Great Himalayan △
India 31°30N 77°30E **124** D7
Great Inagua I.
Bahamas 21°0N 73°20W **183** B5

Great Indian Desert = Thar Desert
India 28°0N 72°0E **1**
Great Karoo *S. Africa* 31°55S 21°0E **1**
Great Khingan Mts. = Da
Hinggan Ling *China* 48°0N 121°0E **11**
Great Lake *Australia* 41°50S 146°40E **1**
Great Lakes *N. Amer.* 46°0N 84°0W **18**
Great Limpopo Transfrontier △
Africa 23°0S 31°45E **1**
Great Malvern *U.K.* 52°7N 2°18W
Great Miami → *U.S.A.* 39°7N 84°49W **1**
Great Nicobar *India* 7°0N 93°50E **1**
Great Ormes Head *U.K.* 53°20N 3°52W
Great Otway △
Australia 38°50S 143°50E **1**
Great Ouse → *U.K.* 52°48N 0°21E
Great Palm I. *Australia* 18°45S 146°40E **1**
Great Pedro Bluff
Jamaica 17°51N 77°44W
Great Pee Dee →
U.S.A. 33°21N 79°10W **1**
Great Plains *N. Amer.* 47°0N 105°0W
Great Ruaha →
Tanzania 7°56S 37°52E **1**
Great Sacandaga L.
U.S.A. 43°6N 74°16W **1**
Great Saint Bernard Pass = Grand
St-Bernard, Col du
Europe 45°50N 7°10E **7**
Great Salt Desert = Kavīr, Dasht-e
Iran 34°30N 55°0E **1**
Great Salt L. *U.S.A.* 41°15N 112°40W **1**
Great Salt Lake Desert
U.S.A. 40°50N 113°30W **1**
Great Salt Plains L.
U.S.A. 36°45N 98°8W **1**
Great Sand Dunes △
U.S.A. 37°48N 105°45W **1**
Great Sandy △
Australia 26°13S 153°2E **1**
Great Sandy Desert
Australia 21°0S 124°0E **1**
Great Sangi = Sangihe, Pulau
Indonesia 3°35N 125°30E **1**
Great Scarcies → *S. Leone* 9°0N 13°0W **1**
Great Sea Reef *Fiji* 16°15S 179°0E **1**
Great Sitkin I. *U.S.A.* 52°3N 176°6W **1**
Great Skellig *Ireland* 51°47N 10°33W **1**
Great Slave L. *Canada* 61°23N 115°38W **1**
Great Smoky Mts. △
U.S.A. 35°40N 83°40W **1**
Great Stour = Stour →
U.K. 51°18N 1°22E **1**
Great Victoria Desert
Australia 29°30S 126°30E **1**
Great Wall *Antarctica* 62°30S 58°0W **1**
Great Wall *China* 38°30N 109°30E **1**
Great Whernside *U.K.* 54°10N 1°58W
Great Yarmouth *U.K.* 52°37N 1°44E
Great Zab = Zāb al Kabīr →
Iraq 36°1N 43°24E **1**
Great Zimbabwe
Zimbabwe 20°16S 30°54E **1**
Greater Antilles
W. Indies 17°40N 74°0W
Greater London □ *U.K.* 51°31N 0°6W
Greater Manchester □
U.K. 53°30N 2°15W
Greater Sunda Is.
Indonesia 7°0S 112°0E
Grebbestad *Sweden* 58°42N 11°15E **1**
Grebenka = Hrebinka
Ukraine 50°9N 32°22E **1**
Greco, C. *Cyprus* 34°57N 34°5E **1**
Greco, Mte. *Italy* 41°48N 13°58E **1**
Gredos, Sierra de *Spain* 40°20N 5°0W **1**
Greece □ *Europe* 40°0N 23°0E **1**
Greeley *Colo., U.S.A.* 40°25N 104°42W **1**
Greeley *Nebr., U.S.A.* 41°33N 98°32W **1**
Greeleyville *U.S.A.* 33°40N 79°59W **1**
Greely Fd. *Canada* 80°30N 85°0W **1**
Greem-Bell, Ostrov
Russia 81°0N 62°0E **1**
Green → *Ky., U.S.A.* 37°54N 87°30W **1**
Green → *Utah, U.S.A.* 38°11N 109°53W **1**
Green B. *U.S.A.* 45°0N 87°30W **1**
Green Bay *U.S.A.* 44°31N 88°0W **1**
Green C. *Australia* 37°13S 150°1E **1**
Green Cove Springs
U.S.A. 29°59N 81°42W **1**
Green I. = Lütao
Taiwan 22°40N 121°30E **1**
Green Lake *Canada* 54°17N 107°47W **1**
Green Mts. *U.S.A.* 43°45N 72°45W **1**
Green Pond *U.S.A.* 32°44N 80°37W **1**
Green River *Utah,
U.S.A.* 38°59N 110°10W **1**
Green River *Wyo.,
U.S.A.* 41°32N 109°28W **1**
Green Valley *U.S.A.* 31°52N 110°56W **1**
Greenacres *U.S.A.* 26°38N 80°7W **1**
Greenbank *U.S.A.* 48°6N 122°34W **1**
Greenbush *Mich.,
U.S.A.* 44°35N 83°19W **1**
Greenbush *Minn.,
U.S.A.* 48°42N 96°11W **1**
Greencastle *U.S.A.* 39°38N 86°52W **1**
Greene *U.S.A.* 42°20N 75°46W **1**
Greeneville *U.S.A.* 36°10N 82°50W **1**
Greenfield *Calif.,
U.S.A.* 36°19N 121°15W **1**
Greenfield *Calif., U.S.A.* 35°15N 119°0W **1**
Greenfield *Ind., U.S.A.* 39°47N 85°46W **1**
Greenfield *Iowa, U.S.A.* 41°18N 94°28W **1**
Greenfield *Mass.,
U.S.A.* 42°35N 72°36W **1**
Greenfield *Mo., U.S.A.* 37°25N 93°51W **1**
Greenfield Park
Canada 45°29N 73°28W **1**
Greenland ☒ *N. Amer.* 66°0N 45°0W **1**
Greenland Sea *Arctic* 73°0N 10°0W **1**
Greenock *U.K.* 55°57N 4°46W **1**
Greenore *Ireland* 54°1N 6°9W **1**
Greenore Pt. *Ireland* 52°14N 6°19W **1**
Greenough *Australia* 28°58S 114°43E **1**
Greenough →
Australia 28°51S 114°38E **1**
Greenough Pt. *Canada* 44°58N 81°26W **1**
Greenport *U.S.A.* 41°6N 72°22W **1**
Greensboro *Fla., U.S.A.* 30°34N 84°45W **1**

nsboro Ga., U.S.A. 33°35N 83°11W 178 B6
nsboro N.C.,
.A. 36°4N 79°48W 177 C15
nsburg Vt.,
.A. 44°36N 72°18W 175 B12
nsburg Ind.,
.A. 39°20N 85°29W 173 F11
nstone = Geraldton
ada 49°44N 87°10W 164 C2
nstone Pt. U.K. 57°55N 5°37W 65 D3
nvale Australia 18°59S 145°7E 150 B4
nville Liberia 5°1N 9°6W 138 D3
nville Ala., U.S.A. 31°50N 86°38W 177 F11
nville Calif., U.S.A. 40°8N 120°57W 170 E6
nville Fla., U.S.A. 30°28N 83°38W 178 E6
nville Ga., U.S.A. 33°2N 84°43W 178 B5
nville Maine,
.A. 45°28N 69°35W 173 C19
nville Mich.,
.A. 43°11N 85°15W 173 D11
nville Miss., U.S.A. 33°24N 91°4W 177 E9
nville Mo., U.S.A. 37°8N 90°27W 172 G8
nville N.C.,
.A. 35°37N 77°23W 177 D16
nville N.H.,
.A. 42°46N 71°49W 175 D13
nville N.Y., U.S.A. 42°25N 74°1W 175 D10
nville Ohio, U.S.A. 40°6N 84°38W 173 E11
nville Pa., U.S.A. 41°24N 80°23W 174 E4
nville S.C., U.S.A. 34°51N 82°24W 177 D13
nville Tex., U.S.A. 33°8N 96°7W 176 E6
nwater Lake ○
ada 52°32N 103°30W 163 C8
nwich Conn.,
.A. 41°2N 73°38W 175 E11
nwich N.Y.,
.A. 43°5N 73°30W 175 C11
nwich Ohio, U.S.A. 41°2N 82°31W 174 E2
nwich □ U.K. 51°29N 0°1E 67 F8
nwood Canada 49°10N 118°40W 162 D5
nwood Ark.,
.A. 35°13N 94°16W 176 D7
nwood Fla., U.S.A. 30°52N 85°10W 178 E4
nwood Ind., U.S.A. 39°37N 86°7W 172 F10
nwood Miss.,
.A. 33°31N 90°11W 177 E9
nwood S.C.,
.A. 34°12N 82°10W 178 A7
nwood, Mt.
ralia 13°48S 130°4E 148 B5
ie Ivory C. 6°48N 6°43W 138 D3
ério ➤ Brazil 6°50S 70°46W 188 B3
ory U.S.A. 43°14N 99°26W 172 D4
ory ➤ Australia 17°53S 139°17E 150 B2
ory, L. S. Austral.,
ralia 28°55S 139°0E 151 D2
ory, L. W. Austral.,
ralia 20°0S 127°40E 148 D4
ory, L. W. Austral.,
ralia 25°38S 119°58E 149 E2
ory △ Australia 15°38S 131°15E 148 C5
ory Downs
ralia 18°35S 138°45E 150 B2
ory Ra. Queens.,
ralia 19°30S 143°40E 150 B3
ory Ra. W. Austral.,
ralia 21°20S 121°12E 148 D3
enberg Germany 53°6N 13°57E 76 B9
swald Germany 54°5N 13°23E 76 A9
swalder Bodden
many 54°12N 13°35E 76 A9
Austria 48°14N 14°51E 78 C7
Germany 50°39N 12°10E 76 E8
ikha Russia 67°59N 39°47E 106 C4
ada Denmark 56°25N 10°53E 63 H4
ada U.S.A. 33°47N 89°49W 177 E10
ade ■ W. Indies 12°10N 61°40W 183 D7
ade France 43°47N 1°17E 72 E5
adines, The
Vincent 12°40N 61°20W 183 D7
chen Switz. 47°12N 7°24E 77 H3
en Denmark 57°44N 10°40E 63 G4
ell Australia 33°52S 148°8E 153 B8
ell Canada 50°30N 102°56W 163 C8
ville, C. Australia 12°0S 143°13E 150 A3
Chan.
ada 53°40N 129°46W 162 C3
-les-Bains France 43°45N 5°52E 73 E9
am U.S.A. 36°30N 122°25W 170 E4
k Indonesia 7°13S 112°38E 119 G15
a U.K. 55°0N 3°3W 65 F5
a Fla., U.S.A. 30°37N 84°40W 178 E5
a La., U.S.A. 29°54N 90°3W 179 H9
Strand Denmark 55°34N 12°18E 63 J6
ena Argentina 52°6N 7°37E 76 C3
ena Greece 40°4N 21°25E 96 F5
enbroich Germany 51°5N 6°35E 76 D2
enmacher Lux. 49°41N 6°26E 69 E6
esmühlen Germany 53°52N 11°12E 76 B7
➤ Canada 47°24N 57°6W 165 C8
➤ N.Z. 42°27S 171°12E 155 C6
C. Australia 13°0S 136°35E 150 A2
Is. Canada 50°50N 55°35W 161 G20
Ra. Australia 27°0S 143°30E 151 D3
ull U.S.A. 44°30N 108°3W 168 D9
nouth N.Z. 42°29S 171°13E 155 C6
stones Ireland 53°9N 6°5W 64 C5
own U.S.A. 41°45S 175°29E 154 H4
novskiy Russia 51°28N 41°50E 86 E5
s, Mal i Albania 40°17N 19°45E 96 F3
ey U.S.A. 39°22N 121°42W 170 F5
wastad S. Africa 28°49S 23°15E 144 D3
heim Germany 49°51N 8°33E 77 F4
kirchen Austria 48°16N 13°48E 78 D6
U.S.A. 33°15N 84°16W 178 B5
n, L. U.S.A. 28°52N 81°51W 179 G8
th Australia 34°18S 146°2E 153 C17
th Canada 45°50N 77°10W 174 A7
ull U.S.A. 44°30N 108°55W 178 B4
ols France 44°23N 0°2W 72 D3
aylov = Hrymayliv
aine 49°20N 26°5E 75 D14
eripol Moldova 47°9N 29°18E 81 C14

Grimma Germany 51°14N 12°43E 76 D8
Grimmen Germany 54°7N 13°3E 76 A9
Grimsay U.K. 57°29N 7°14W 65 D1
Grimsby Canada 43°12N 79°34W 174 C5
Grimsby U.K. 53°34N 0°5W 66 D7
Grímsey Iceland 66°33N 17°58W 60 C5
Grimshaw Canada 56°10N 117°40W 162 B5
Grímsstaðir Norway 58°20N 8°35E 61 G13
Grindelwald Switz. 46°38N 8°2E 77 J4
Grindsted Denmark 55°46N 8°55E 63 J2
Grindstone I. U.S.A. 44°17N 76°27W 175 B8
Grindu Romania 44°44N 26°50E 81 F11
Grinnell U.S.A. 41°45N 92°43W 172 E7
Grinnell Pen. Canada 76°40N 95°0W 161 B13
Grintavec Slovenia 46°22N 14°32E 93 B11
Griomasaigh = Grimsay
U.K. 57°29N 7°14W 65 D1
Gris-Nez, C. France 50°52N 1°35E 71 B8
Grise Fiord Canada 76°25N 82°57W 161 B15
Grisolles France 43°49N 1°19E 72 E5
Grisons = Graubünden □
Switz. 46°45N 9°30E 77 J5
Grisslehamn Sweden 60°5N 18°49E 62 D12
Grmeč Planina Bos.-H. 44°43N 16°16E 93 D13
Groais I. Canada 50°55N 55°35W 165 B8
Grobiņa Latvia 56°33N 21°10E 82 B8
Groblersdal S. Africa 25°15S 29°25E 145 C4
Grobming Austria 47°27N 13°54E 78 D6
Grocka Serbia 44°40N 20°42E 96 B4
Gródek Poland 53°6N 23°40E 83 E10
Grodków Poland 50°43N 17°21E 83 H4
Grodno = Hrodna
Belarus 53°42N 23°52E 82 E10
Grodzisk Mazowiecki
Poland 52°7N 20°37E 83 F7
Grodzisk Wielkopolski
Poland 52°15N 16°22E 83 F3
Grodzyanka = Hrodzyanka
Belarus 53°31N 28°42E 75 B15
Groesbeck U.S.A. 31°31N 96°32W 176 F6
Groix France 47°38N 3°29W 70 E3
Groix, Î. de France 47°38N 3°28W 70 E3
Grójec Poland 51°50N 20°58E 83 G7
Gronau Niedersachsen,
Germany 52°5N 9°47E 76 C5
Gronau Nordrhein-Westfalen,
Germany 52°12N 7°2E 76 C3
Grong Norway 64°25N 12°8E 60 D15
Grönhögen Sweden 56°16N 16°24E 63 H10
Groningen Neths. 53°15N 6°35E 69 A6
Groningen □ Neths. 53°16N 6°40E 69 A6
Grønlands △ Greenland 75°0N 35°0W 57 C7
Grønnedal = Kangilinnguit
Greenland 61°20N 47°57W 57 E6
Groom U.S.A. 35°12N 101°6W 176 D4
Groot ➤ S. Africa 33°45S 24°36E 144 E3
Groot-Berg ➤ S. Africa 32°47S 18°8E 144 D2
Groot-Brakrivier
S. Africa 34°2S 22°18E 144 E3
Groot Karasberge
Namibia 27°20S 18°40E 144 C2
Groot-Kei ➤ S. Africa 32°41S 28°22E 145 D4
Groot-Vis ➤ S. Africa 33°28S 27°5E 144 E4
Grootdrink S. Africa 28°33S 21°42E 144 C3
Groote Eylandt
Australia 14°0S 136°40E 150 A2
Groote Peel ○ Neths. 51°22N 5°49E 69 C5
Grootfontein Namibia 19°31S 18°6E 144 A2
Grootlaagte ➤ Africa 20°55S 21°27E 144 A3
Grootvloer ➤ S. Africa 30°0S 20°40E 144 B3
Gros C. Canada 61°59N 113°32W 162 A6
Gros Islet St. Lucia 14°5N 60°58W 183 f
Gros Morne △ Canada 49°40N 57°50W 165 C8
Gros Piton St. Lucia 13°49N 61°5W 183 f
Gros Piton Pt. St. Lucia 13°49N 61°5W 183 f
Grósio Italy 46°18N 10°4E 92 B7
Grosne ➤ France 46°42N 4°56E 71 F11
Grossa, Pta. Spain 39°6N 1°36E 100 B8
Grosse Point U.S.A. 42°23N 82°54W 173 D12
Grossenbrode Germany 54°21N 11°4E 76 A7
Grossenhain Germany 51°17N 13°32E 76 D9
Grosser Arber Germany 49°6N 13°8E 77 F9
Grosser Plöner See
Germany 54°10N 10°22E 76 A6
Grosseto Italy 42°46N 11°8E 93 F8
Grossgerungs Austria 48°34N 14°57E 78 C7
Grossglockner Austria 47°5N 12°40E 78 D5
Groswater B. Canada 54°20N 57°40W 165 B8
Groton Conn., U.S.A. 41°21N 72°5W 175 E12
Groton N.Y., U.S.A. 42°36N 76°22W 175 D8
Groton S. Dak., U.S.A. 45°27N 98°6W 172 C4
Grottáglie Italy 40°32N 17°26E 95 B10
Grottaminarda Italy 41°4N 15°2E 95 A8
Grottammare Italy 42°59N 13°52E 93 F10
Grouard Mission
Canada 55°33N 116°9W 162 B5
Grouin, Pte. du France 48°43N 1°51W 70 D5
Groundhog ➤ Canada 48°45N 82°58W 164 C3
Grouw Neths. 53°5N 5°51E 69 A5
Grove City Fla., U.S.A. 26°56N 82°19W 179 J7
Grove City Pa., U.S.A. 41°10N 80°5W 174 E4
Grove Hill U.S.A. 31°42N 87°47W 177 F11
Groveland Calif.,
U.S.A. 37°50N 120°14W 170 H6
Groveland Fla., U.S.A. 28°34N 81°51W 179 G8
Grover Beach U.S.A. 35°7N 120°37W 171 K6
Groves U.S.A. 29°57N 93°54W 176 G7
Groveton U.S.A. 44°36N 71°31W 175 B13
Grovetown U.S.A. 33°33N 82°12W 178 B7
Grožnjan Croatia 45°22N 13°43E 93 C10
Groznyy Russia 43°20N 45°45E 87 J7
Grubišno Polje Croatia 45°44N 17°12E 80 B2
Grudovo Bulgaria 42°21N 27°10E 97 C12
Grudusk Poland 53°30N 20°38E 83 E7
Grudziądz Poland 53°30N 18°47E 83 E5
Gruinard B. U.K. 57°56N 5°35W 65 D3
Gruissan France 43°8N 3°7E 72 E7
Grumo Áppula Italy 41°1N 16°43E 95 A9
Grums Sweden 59°22N 13°5E 62 E7
Grünberg Germany 50°36N 8°58E 76 E4
Gründau Germany 50°10N 9°9E 77 E5
Grundy Center U.S.A. 42°22N 92°47W 172 D7
Grünstadt Germany 49°34N 8°9E 77 F4
Gruppo di Tessa ○ Italy 46°47N 11°0E 92 B8
Gruvberget Sweden 61°6N 16°11E 62 C10
Gruver U.S.A. 36°16N 101°24W 176 C4
Gruyères Switz. 46°35N 7°4E 77 J3
Gruža Serbia 43°54N 20°46E 96 C4
Gryazi Russia 52°30N 39°58E 85 F10
Gryazovets Russia 58°50N 40°10E 84 C11

Grybów Poland 49°36N 20°55E 83 J7
Grycksbo Sweden 60°40N 15°29E 62 D9
Gryfice Poland 53°55N 15°13E 82 E2
Gryfino Poland 53°16N 14°29E 83 E1
Gryfów Śląski Poland 51°2N 15°24E 83 G2
Gryt Sweden 58°12N 16°48E 63 F10
Grythyttan Sweden 59°41N 14°32E 62 E8
Grytviken S. Georgia 54°19S 36°33W 56 M8
Gua India 22°18N 85°20E 125 H11
Gua Musang Malaysia 4°53N 101°58E 121 K3
Guabún, Pta. Chile 41°48S 74°2W 192 B2
Guacanayabo, G. de
Cuba 20°40N 77°20W 182 B4
Guachípas ➤
Argentina 25°40S 65°30W 190 B2
Guadajoz ➤ Spain 37°50N 4°51W 89 H6
Guadalajara Mexico 20°40N 103°20W 180 C4
Guadalajara Spain 40°37N 3°12W 90 E1
Guadalajara □ Spain 40°47N 2°30W 90 E2
Guadalaviar = Turia ➤
Spain 39°27N 0°19W 91 F4
Guadalcanal
Solomon Is. 9°32S 160°12E 147 B9
Guadalcanal Spain 38°5N 5°52W 89 G5
Guadalén ➤ Spain 38°5N 3°32W 89 G7
Guadales Argentina 34°30S 67°55W 190 C2
Guadalimar ➤ Spain 36°35N 6°13W 89 J4
Guadalmena ➤ Spain 38°5N 3°28W 89 G7
Guadalmez ➤ Spain 38°46N 5°4W 89 G5
Guadalquivir ➤ Spain 36°47N 6°22W 89 J4
Guadalupe = Guadeloupe ☑
W. Indies 16°15N 61°40W 182 b
Guadalupe Brazil 6°44S 43°47W 189 B2
Guadalupe Mexico 22°45N 102°31W 180 C4
Guadalupe Spain 39°27N 5°17W 89 F5
Guadalupe U.S.A. 34°58N 120°34W 171 L6
Guadalupe ➤ U.S.A. 28°27N 96°47W 176 G6
Guadalupe, Sierra de
Spain 39°28N 5°30W 89 F5
Guadalupe de Bravo
Mexico 31°23N 106°7W 180 A3
Guadalupe I. Pac. Oc. 29°0N 118°50W 158 G8
Guadalupe Mts. △
U.S.A. 31°40N 104°30W 176 F2
Guadalupe Peak
U.S.A. 31°50N 104°52W 176 F2
Guadalupe y Calvo
Mexico 26°6N 106°58W 180 B3
Guadarrama, Sierra de
Spain 41°0N 4°0W 88 E7
Guadeloupe ☑ W. Indies 16°50N 62°15W 182 b
Guadeloupe △
Guadeloupe 16°10N 61°40W 182 b
Guadeloupe Passage
W. Indies 16°50N 62°15W 183 C7
Guadiamar ➤ Spain 36°55N 6°24W 89 J4
Guadiana ➤ Portugal 37°14N 7°22W 89 H3
Guadiana Menor ➤
Spain 37°56N 3°15W 89 H7
Guadiaro ➤ Spain 36°17N 5°17W 89 J5
Guadiato ➤ Spain 37°48N 5°5W 89 H5
Guadiela ➤ Spain 40°22N 2°49W 90 E2
Guadix Spain 37°18N 3°11W 89 H7
Guafo, Boca del Chile 43°35S 74°0W 192 B2
Guafo, I. Chile 43°35S 74°50W 192 B2
Guaico Trin. & Tob. 10°35N 61°9W 187 K15
Guainía □ Colombia 2°1N 67°7W 186 C5
Guaíra Brazil 24°5S 54°10W 191 A5
Guaíra ➤ Paraguay 25°45S 56°30W 190 B4
Guaire = Gorey Ireland 52°41N 6°18W 64 D5
Guaitecas, Is. Chile 44°0S 74°30W 192 B2
Guajará-Mirim Brazil 10°50S 65°20W 186 F5
Guajira, Pen. de la
Colombia 12°0N 72°0W 186 A4
Gualán Guatemala 15°8N 89°22W 182 C2
Gualdo Tadino Italy 43°14N 12°47E 93 E9
Gualeguay Argentina 33°10S 59°14W 190 C4
Gualeguaychú
Argentina 33°3S 59°31W 190 C4
Gualequay ➤
Argentina 33°19S 59°39W 190 C4
Gualicho, Salina
Argentina 40°25S 65°20W 192 B3
Guam ☑ Pac. Oc. 13°27N 144°45E 156 F6
Guamblin, I. Chile 44°50S 75°0W 192 B2
Guaminí Argentina 37°1S 62°28W 190 D3
Guamúchil Mexico 25°28N 108°6W 180 B3
Guana I. Br. Virgin Is. 18°30N 64°30W 183 e
Guanabacoa Cuba 23°8N 82°18W 182 B3
Guanacaste, Cordillera de
Costa Rica 10°40N 85°4W 182 D2
Guanacaste △
Costa Rica 10°51N 85°30W 182 D2
Guanaceví Mexico 25°56N 105°57W 180 B3
Guanahani = San Salvador I.
Bahamas 24°0N 74°30W 183 B5
Guanaja Honduras 16°30N 85°55W 182 C2
Guanajay Cuba 22°56N 82°42W 182 B3
Guanajuato Mexico 21°1N 101°15W 180 C4
Guanajuato □ Mexico 21°0N 101°0W 180 C4
Guanambi Brazil 14°13S 42°47W 189 C2
Guandacol Argentina 29°30S 68°40W 190 B2
Guandi Shan China 37°53N 111°29E 114 F6
Guane Cuba 22°10N 84°7W 182 B3
Guang'an China 30°28N 106°35E 116 B6
Guangchang China 26°50N 116°21E 117 D11
Guangde China 30°54N 119°25E 117 B12
Guangdong □ China 23°0N 113°0E 117 F9
Guangfeng China 28°24N 118°21E 117 C12
Guanghua = Laohekou
China 32°22N 111°38E 116 A7
Guangling China 39°47N 114°17E 116 E8
Guangmao Shan China 24°5N 98°17E 116 E2
Guangnan China 24°17N 105°0E 116 E5
Guangning China 23°40N 112°22E 117 F9
Guangrao China 37°5N 118°25E 115 F10
Guangshui China 31°37N 114°0E 117 B10
Guangshun China 26°8N 106°21E 116 D6
Guangwu China 37°48N 105°57E 114 F3
Guangxi Zhuangzu Zizhiqu □
China 24°0N 109°0E 116 F7
Guangyuan China 32°26N 105°51E 114 H3
Guangze China 27°30N 117°12E 117 D11
Guangzhou China 23°6N 113°13E 117 F9
Guanhães Brazil 18°45S 42°57W 189 D2
Guánica Puerto Rico 17°58N 66°55W 183 d
Guanipa ➤ Venezuela 9°56N 62°26W 186 B6
Guanling China 25°56N 105°35E 116 E5

Guannan China 34°8N 119°21E 115 G10
Guantánamo Cuba 20°10N 75°14W 183 B4
Guantánamo B. Cuba 19°59N 75°10W 183 C4
Guanting Shuiku
China 40°14N 115°35E 114 D8
Guanyang China 25°30N 111°8E 117 E8
Guanyun China 34°20N 119°18E 115 G10
Guapay = Grande ➤
Bolivia 15°51S 64°39W 186 G6
Guápiles Costa Rica 10°10N 83°46W 182 D3
Guapo B. Trin. & Tob. 10°12N 61°41W 187 K15
Guaporé Brazil 28°51S 51°54W 191 B5
Guaporé ➤ Brazil 11°55S 65°4W 186 F5
Guaqui Bolivia 16°41S 68°54W 186 G5
Guara, Sierra de Spain 42°19N 0°15W 90 C4
Guarabira Brazil 6°51S 35°29W 189 B3
Guaramacal △
Venezuela 9°13N 70°12W 183 E5
Guarapari Brazil 20°40S 40°30W 189 D3
Guarapuava Brazil 25°20S 51°30W 191 B5
Guaratinguetá Brazil 22°49S 45°9W 191 A6
Guaratuba Brazil 25°53S 48°38W 191 B6
Guarda Portugal 40°32N 7°20W 88 E3
Guarda □ Portugal 40°40N 7°20W 88 E3
Guardafui, C. = Asir, Ras
Somalia 11°55N 51°10E 131 E5
Guardamar del Segura
Spain 38°5N 0°39W 91 G4
Guardavalle Italy 38°31N 16°30E 95 C9
Guárdia Sanframondi
Italy 41°15N 14°36E 95 A7
Guardiagrele Italy 42°11N 14°13E 93 F11
Guardo Spain 42°47N 4°50W 88 C6
Guareña Spain 38°51N 6°6W 89 G4
Guareña ➤ Spain 41°29N 5°23W 88 D5
Guárico □ Venezuela 8°40N 66°35W 186 B5
Guarujá Brazil 24°2S 46°25W 191 A6
Guarulhos Brazil 23°29S 46°33W 191 A6
Guasave Mexico 25°34N 108°27W 180 B3
Guasdualito Venezuela 7°15N 70°44W 186 B4
Guastalla Italy 44°55N 10°39E 92 D7
Guatemala Guatemala 14°40N 90°22W 182 D1
Guatemala ■
Cent. Amer. 15°40N 90°30W 182 C1
Guatemala Basin
Pac. Oc. 11°0N 95°0W 157 F18
Guatemala Trench
Pac. Oc. 14°0N 95°0W 158 H10
Guatopo △ Venezuela 10°5N 66°30W 183 D6
Guatuaro Pt.
Trin. & Tob. 10°19N 60°59W 187 K16
Guaviare □ Colombia 4°3N 67°44W 186 C5
Guaxupé Brazil 21°10S 47°5W 191 A6
Guayaguayare
Trin. & Tob. 10°8N 61°2W 187 K15
Guayama Puerto Rico 17°59N 66°7W 183 d
Guayaneco, Arch.
Chile 47°45S 75°10W 192 C1
Guayaquil Ecuador 2°15S 79°52W 186 D3
Guayaquil Mexico 29°59N 115°4W 180 B1
Guayaquil, G. de Ecuador 3°10S 81°0W 186 D2
Guaymas Mexico 27°56N 110°54W 180 B2
Guba
Dem. Rep. of the Congo 10°38S 26°27E 143 E2
Gûbâl, Madîq Egypt 34°0N 34°0E 137 B3
Gubbi India 13°19N 76°56E 127 H3
Gúbbio Italy 43°21N 12°35E 93 E9
Guben Germany 51°57N 14°42E 76 D10
Gubin Poland 51°57N 14°43E 83 G1
Gubio Nigeria 12°30N 12°42E 139 C7
Gubkin Russia 51°17N 37°32E 85 G9
Gubkinskiy Russia 64°27N 76°36E 106 C8
Gucheng China 32°20N 111°30E 117 A8
Gudalur India 11°30N 76°29E 127 J3
Gudata Georgia 43°7N 40°32E 87 J5
Gudbrandsdalen
Norway 61°33N 10°10E 60 F14
Guddu Barrage
Pakistan 28°30N 69°50E 124 E3
Gudená ➤ Denmark 56°29N 10°13E 63 H4
Gudermes Russia 43°24N 46°5E 87 J8
Gudhjem Denmark 55°12N 14°58E 63 J8
Gudivada India 16°30N 81°3E 127 F5
Gudiyattam India 12°57N 78°55E 127 H4
Gudur India 14°12N 79°55E 127 G4
Guebwiller France 47°55N 7°12E 71 E14
Guecho = Algorta Spain 43°21N 2°59W 90 B2
Guékédou Guinea 8°40N 10°5W 138 D2
Guélengdeng Chad 10°34N 15°22E 139 B8
Guelma Algeria 36°25N 7°29E 136 A5
Guelma □ Algeria 36°25N 7°25E 136 A5
Guelmine = Goulimine
Morocco 28°56N 10°0W 134 C3
Guelph Canada 43°35N 80°20W 174 C4
Guemar Algeria 33°30N 6°49E 136 B5
Guéméné-Penfao France 47°38N 1°50W 70 E5
Guéméné-sur-Scorff
France 48°4N 3°13W 70 D3
Guéné Benin 11°44N 3°16E 139 C5
Guer France 47°54N 2°8W 70 E4
Güer Aike Argentina 51°39S 69°35W 192 D3
Guérande France 47°20N 2°26W 70 E4
Guerara Algeria 32°51N 4°22E 136 B4
Guercif Morocco 34°14N 3°21W 136 B4
Guéret France 46°11N 1°51E 71 F8
Guérigny France 47°6N 3°10E 71 E10
Guernica = Gernika-Lumo
Spain 43°19N 2°40W 90 B2
Guernsey U.S.A. 42°16N 104°45W 168 E11
Guernsey ☑ U.K. 49°26N 2°35W 67 H5
Guerrara Algeria 28°5N 0°8E 136 C5
Guerrero □ Mexico 17°30N 100°0W 181 D5
Guerzim Algeria 29°39N 1°40W 136 C4
Guessou-Sud Benin 10°3N 2°38E 139 C5
Gueugnon France 46°36N 4°4E 71 F11
Guéyo Ivory C. 5°5N 6°5W 138 D3
Gúghər Iran 29°28N 56°27E 129 D8
Guglionesi Italy 41°55N 14°55E 93 G11
Gui Jiang ➤ China 23°30N 111°15E 117 F8
Guia Canary Is. 28°8N 15°38E 100 F4
Guia de Isora
Canary Is. 28°12N 16°46W 100 F3
Guia Lopes da Laguna
Brazil 21°26S 56°7W 191 A4
Guiana Highlands
S. Amer. 5°10N 60°40W 184 C4
Güney Burdur, Turkey 37°39N 29°42E 99 D11
Güney Denizli, Turkey 38°9N 29°4E 99 C10

Güneydoğu Toroslar
Turkey 38°20N 40°30E 105 C9
Gungal Australia 32°17S 150°32E 153 B9
Gunisao ➤ Canada 53°56N 97°53W 163 C9
Gunisao L. Canada 53°33N 96°15W 163 C9
Gunjur Gambia 13°12N 16°44W 138 C1
Gunjyal Pakistan 32°20N 71°55E 124 C4
Günlüce Turkey 36°50N 28°20E 99 E10
Gunma □ Japan 36°30N 138°20E 113 F9
Gunnarskog Sweden 59°49N 12°34E 62 E6
Gunnbjørn Fjeld
Greenland 68°55N 29°47W 57 D8
Gunnebo Sweden 57°44N 16°32E 63 G10
Gunnedah Australia 30°59S 150°15E 153 B9
Gunnewin Australia 25°59S 148°33E 151 D4
Gunningbar Cr. ➤
Australia 31°14S 147°6E 153 A7
Gunnison Colo.,
U.S.A. 38°33N 106°56W 168 G10
Gunnison Utah, U.S.A. 39°9N 111°49W 168 G8
Gunnison ➤ U.S.A. 39°4N 108°35W 168 G9
Gunsan S. Korea 35°59N 126°45E 115 G14
Guntakal India 15°11N 77°27E 127 G3
Gunter Canada 44°52N 77°32W 174 B7
Guntersville U.S.A. 34°21N 86°18W 177 D11
Guntong Malaysia 4°36N 101°3E 121 K3
Guntur India 16°23N 80°30E 127 F5
Gunung Ciremay △
Indonesia 6°53S 108°24E 119 G13
Gunungapi Indonesia 6°45S 126°30E 119 F7
Gunungsitoli Indonesia 1°15N 97°30E 118 D1
Gunupur India 19°5N 83°50E 126 E6
Günz ➤ Germany 48°27N 10°16E 77 G6
Gunza Angola 10°50S 13°50E 140 G2
Günzburg Germany 48°26N 10°17E 77 G6
Gunzenhausen Germany 49°7N 10°44E 77 F6
Guo He ➤ China 32°59N 117°10E 117 A11
Guoyang China 33°32N 116°12E 114 H9
Gupis Pakistan 36°15N 73°20E 125 A5
Gura Humorului
Romania 47°35N 25°53E 81 C10
Gura-Teghii Romania 45°30N 26°25E 81 E11
Gurahonţ Romania 46°16N 22°21E 80 D7
Gurbantünggüt Shamo
China 45°8N 87°20E 109 C11
Gurdaspur India 32°5N 75°31E 124 C6
Gurdon U.S.A. 33°55N 93°9W 176 E8
Güre Balıkesir, Turkey 39°36N 26°54E 99 B8
Güre Uşak, Turkey 38°39N 29°10E 99 C11
Gurgaon India 28°27N 77°1E 124 E7
Gürgentepe Turkey 40°51N 37°50E 104 D6
Gurghiu, Munţii
Romania 46°41N 25°15E 81 D10
Gurgueia ➤ Brazil 6°50S 43°24W 189 B2
Gurha India 25°12N 71°39E 124 G4
Guri, Embalse de
Venezuela 7°50N 62°52W 186 B6
Gurin Nigeria 9°5N 12°54E 139 D7
Gurjaani Georgia 41°43N 45°52E 87 K7
Gurk ➤ Austria 46°35N 14°31E 78 E7
Gurkha Nepal 28°5N 84°40E 125 E11
Gurla Mandhata = Naimona'nyi
Feng China 30°26N 81°18E 125 D9
Gurley Australia 29°45S 149°48E 151 D4
Gurnet Point U.S.A. 42°1N 70°34W 175 D14
Guro Mozam. 17°26S 32°38E 143 F3
Gürpınar İstanbul,
Turkey 40°59N 28°37E 97 F12
Gürpınar Van, Turkey 38°18N 43°25E 105 C10
Gürsu Turkey 40°13N 29°11E 97 F13
Gurué Mozam. 15°25S 36°58E 143 F4
Gurun Malaysia 5°49N 100°27E 121 K3
Gürün Turkey 38°43N 37°15E 104 C7
Gurupá Brazil 1°25S 51°35W 187 D8
Gurupá, I. Grande de
Brazil 1°25S 51°45W 187 D8
Gurupi Brazil 11°43S 49°4W 187 F9
Gurupi ➤ Brazil 1°13S 46°6W 187 D9
Gurupi, Serra do Brazil 5°0S 47°50W 189 B1
Guruwe Zimbabwe 16°40S 30°42E 145 A5
Gurvan Sayhan Uul
Mongolia 43°50N 104°0E 114 C9
Guryev = Atyraū
Kazakhstan 47°5N 52°0E 108 C4
Guryevsk Russia 47°20N 38°8E 87 J10
Gus-Khrustalnyy Russia 55°42N 40°44E 86 C5
Gusau Nigeria 12°12N 6°40E 139 C6
Gusev Russia 54°35N 22°10E 82 D9
Gushan China 39°50N 123°35E 115 E12
Gushgy = Serhetabat
Turkmenistan 35°20N 62°18E 129 C9
Gushi China 32°11N 115°41E 117 A10
Gushiago Ghana 9°55N 0°15W 139 D4
Gusinje Montenegro 42°35N 19°50E 96 D3
Gusinoozersk Russia 51°16N 106°27E 107 D11
Güspini Italy 39°32N 8°37E 94 C1
Güssing Austria 47°3N 16°20E 78 D9
Gustav Holm, Kap
Greenland 66°36N 34°15W 57 D7
Gustavus U.S.A. 58°25N 135°44W 162 B1
Gustine U.S.A. 37°16N 121°0W 170 H6
Güstrow Germany 53°47N 12°10E 76 B8
Gusum Sweden 58°16N 16°30E 63 F10
Guta = Kolárovo
Slovak Rep. 47°54N 18°0E 79 D10
Gütersloh Germany 51°54N 8°24E 76 D4
Guthalungra Australia 19°52S 147°50E 150 B4
Guthrie Canada 44°28N 79°32W 174 B5
Guthrie Okla., U.S.A. 35°53N 97°25W 176 D6
Guthrie Tex., U.S.A. 33°37N 100°19W 176 E4
Gutian China 26°28N 118°43E 117 D12
Guttenberg U.S.A. 42°47N 91°6W 172 D8
Gutu Zimbabwe 19°41S 31°9E 145 A5
Guwahati India 26°10N 91°45E 123 F17
Guy Fawkes River △
Australia 30°0S 152°20E 151 E5
Guyana ■ S. Amer. 5°0N 59°0W 186 C7
Guyane française = French
Guiana ☑ S. Amer. 4°0N 53°0W 187 C8
Guyang China 41°0N 110°5E 114 D6
Guyenne France 44°30N 0°40E 72 D4
Guymon U.S.A. 36°41N 101°29W 176 C4
Guyra Australia 30°15S 151°40E 151 E5
Guyton U.S.A. 32°20N 81°24W 178 C8
Guyuan Hebei, China 41°37N 115°40E 114 D8
Guyuan Ningxia Huizu,
China 36°0N 106°20E 114 F4
Guzar Uzbekistan 38°36N 66°15E 109 E7
Güzelbahçe Turkey 38°21N 26°54E 99 C8

Güzelyurt = Morphou
  Cyprus 35°12N 32°59E 101 D11
Guzhang *China* 28°42N 109°58E 116 C7
Guzhen *China* 33°22N 117°18E 115 H9
Guzmán, L. de *Mexico* 31°20N 107°30W 180 A3
Gvardeysk *Russia* 54°39N 21°5E 82 D8
Gvardeyskoye *Ukraine* 45°7N 34°1E 85 K8
Gwa *Burma* 17°36N 94°34E 123 L19
Gwaai *Zimbabwe* 19°15S 27°45E 143 F2
Gwaai → *Zimbabwe* 18°5S 26°52E 143 F2
Gwabegar *Australia* 30°37S 148°59E 153 A8
Gwadabawa *Nigeria* 13°28N 5°15E 139 C6
Gwädar *Pakistan* 25°10N 62°18E 122 G3
Gwagwada *Nigeria* 10°15N 7°15E 139 C6
Gwai Haanas △
  Canada 52°21N 131°26W 162 C2
Gwalior *India* 26°12N 78°10E 124 F8
Gwanara *Nigeria* 8°55N 3°9E 139 D5
Gwanda *Zimbabwe* 20°55S 29°0E 143 G2
Gwandu *Nigeria* 12°30N 4°41E 139 C5
Gwane
  Dem. Rep. of the Congo 4°45N 25°48E 142 B2
Gwangju *S. Korea* 35°9N 126°54E 115 G14
Gwangyang *S. Korea* 34°56N 127°41E 115 G14
Gwanju = Gwangju
  S. Korea 35°9N 126°54E 115 G14
Gwaram *Nigeria* 10°15N 10°25E 139 C7
Gwarzo *Nigeria* 12°20N 8°55E 139 C6
Gwasero *Nigeria* 9°29N 3°30E 139 D5
Gwda → *Poland* 53°3N 16°44E 83 E3
Gweebarra B. *Ireland* 54°51N 8°23W 64 B3
Gweedore *Ireland* 55°3N 8°14W 64 A3
Gweru *Zimbabwe* 19°28S 29°45E 143 F2
Gwi *Nigeria* 9°0N 7°10E 139 D6
Gwinn *U.S.A.* 46°19N 87°27W 172 B10
Gwio Kura *Nigeria* 12°40N 11°2E 139 C7
Gwoza *Nigeria* 11°5N 13°40E 139 C7
Gwydir → *Australia* 29°27S 149°48E 151 D4
Gwynedd □ *U.K.* 52°52N 4°10W 66 E3
Gyandzha = Gäncä
  Azerbaijan 40°45N 46°20E 87 K8
Gyangzê *China* 29°5N 89°47E 110 F6
Gyaring Hu *China* 34°50N 97°40E 110 E8
Gydanskiy Poluostrov
  Russia 70°0N 78°0E 106 C8
Gyeonggi-man
  S. Korea 37°0N 125°30E 115 F13
Gyeongju *S. Korea* 35°51N 129°14E 115 G15
Gyldenløve Fjord
  Greenland 64°15N 40°30W 57 E6
Gympie *Australia* 26°11S 152°38E 151 C5
Gyomaendröd *Hungary* 46°56N 20°50E 80 D5
Gyöngyös *Hungary* 47°48N 19°56E 80 C4
Györ *Hungary* 47°41N 17°40E 80 C2
Györ-Moson-Sopron □
  Hungary 47°40N 17°20E 80 C2
Gypsum Pt. *Canada* 61°53N 114°35W 162 A6
Gypsumville *Canada* 51°45N 98°40W 163 C9
Gyueshevo *Bulgaria* 42°14N 22°28E 96 D6
Gyula *Hungary* 46°38N 21°17E 80 D6
Gyumri *Armenia* 40°47N 43°50E 87 K6
Gyzylarbat = Serdar
  Turkmenistan 39°4N 56°23E 129 B8
Gyzyletrek = Etrek
  Turkmenistan 37°36N 54°46E 129 B7
Gzhatsk = Gagarin
  Russia 55°38N 35°0E 84 E8

H

H. Neely Henry L.
  U.S.A. 33°55N 86°2W 178 B3
Ha 'Arava → *Israel* 30°50N 35°20E 130 E4
Ha Coi *Vietnam* 21°26N 107°46E 116 G6
Ha Dong *Vietnam* 20°58N 105°46E 116 G5
Ha Giang *Vietnam* 22°50N 104°59E 116 F5
Ha Karmel, Har *Israel* 32°44N 35°3E 130 C4
Ha Karmel △ *Israel* 32°45N 35°5E 130 C4
Ha Long = Hong Gai
  Vietnam 20°57N 107°5E 116 G6
Ha Long, Vinh *Vietnam* 20°56N 107°3E 120 B6
Ha Tien *Vietnam* 10°23N 104°29E 121 G5
Ha Tinh *Vietnam* 18°20N 105°54E 120 C5
Ha Trung *Vietnam* 19°58N 105°50E 120 C5
Haakon VII Topp = Beerenberg
  Norway 71°0N 8°20W 57 C10
Haaksbergen *Neths.* 52°9N 6°45E 69 B6
Haapsalu *Estonia* 58°56N 23°30E 64 C2
Haarby *Denmark* 55°13N 10°7E 63 J4
Haarlem *Neths.* 52°23N 4°39E 69 B4
Haast *N.Z.* 43°51S 169°1E 155 C4
Haast → *N.Z.* 43°50S 169°2E 155 C4
Haast Pass *N.Z.* 44°6S 169°21E 155 C4
Haasts Bluff *Australia* 23°22S 132°0E 148 D5
Haasts Bluff ◌
  Australia 23°39S 130°43E 148 D5
Hab → *Pakistan* 24°53N 66°41E 124 G3
Hab Nadi Chauki
  Pakistan 25°0N 66°50E 124 G2
Habahe *China* 48°3N 86°23E 109 C11
Habaswein *Kenya* 1°2N 39°30E 142 B4
Habay *Canada* 58°50N 118°44W 162 B5
Ḥabbānīyah *Iraq* 33°17N 43°29E 105 F10
Ḥabbānīyah, Hawr al
  Iraq 33°17N 43°29E 105 F10
Habibas, Îles *Algeria* 35°44N 1°8W 91 A3
Habichtswald ◌ *Germany* 51°18N 9°15E 76 D5
Habirag *China* 42°17N 115°42E 114 C8
Habo *Sweden* 57°55N 14°6E 63 G8
Haboro *Japan* 44°22N 141°42E 112 B10
Ḥabshān *U.A.E.* 23°50N 53°37E 129 F7
Hachenburg *Germany* 50°40N 7°49E 76 E3
Hachijō-Jima *Japan* 33°5N 139°45E 113 H9
Hachiman = Gujō
  Japan 35°45N 136°57E 113 G8
Hachinohe *Japan* 40°30N 141°29E 112 D10
Hachiōji *Japan* 35°40N 139°20E 113 G9
Hacı Zeynalabdin
  Azerbaijan 40°37N 49°33E 87 K9
Hacıbektaş *Turkey* 38°56N 34°33E 104 C6
Hacılar *Turkey* 38°38N 35°26E 104 C6
Hack, Mt. *Australia* 30°45S 138°50E 152 B2
Hackås *Sweden* 62°55N 14°30E 62 B8
Hackensack *U.S.A.* 40°52N 74°4W 175 F10
Hackettstown *U.S.A.* 40°51N 74°50W 175 F10
Håckrenmagasinet
  Sweden 63°15N 13°20E 62 C7
Hadali *Pakistan* 32°16N 72°11E 124 C5
Hadarba, Ras *Sudan* 22°4N 36°51E 137 D4
Hadarom □ *Israel* 31°0N 35°0E 130 E4

Ḥadd, Ra's al *Oman* 22°35N 59°50E 131 C6
Haddington *U.K.* 55°57N 2°47W 65 F6
Haddock *U.S.A.* 33°2N 83°26W 177 D7
Hadejia *Nigeria* 12°30N 10°5E 139 C7
Hadejia → *Nigeria* 12°50N 10°51E 139 C7
Hadera *Israel* 32°27N 34°55E 130 C3
Hadera, N. → *Israel* 32°28N 34°52E 130 C3
Haderslev *Denmark* 55°15N 9°30E 63 J3
Hadgaon *India* 19°30N 77°40E 126 E3
Hadhramaut = Ḥaḍramawt □
  Yemen 15°30N 49°30E 131 D4
Ḥaḍībū *Yemen* 12°39N 54°2E 131 E5
Hadilik *China* 37°56N 86°6E 109 E11
Hadım *Turkey* 36°58N 32°26E 104 D5
Hadjadj, O. el → *Algeria* 28°18N 5°20E 136 C5
Hadjeb el Aïoun *Tunisia* 35°21N 9°32E 136 A5
Hadley B. *Canada* 72°31N 108°12W 160 C10
Hadong *S. Korea* 35°5N 127°44E 115 G14
Ḥaḍramawt □ *Yemen* 15°30N 49°30E 131 D4
Hadrian's Wall *U.K.* 55°0N 2°30W 66 B5
Hadsten *Denmark* 56°19N 10°3E 63 H4
Hadsund *Denmark* 56°44N 10°8E 63 H4
Hadyach *Ukraine* 50°21N 34°0E 85 G8
Hae, Ko *Thailand* 7°44N 98°22E 121 a
Haeju *N. Korea* 38°3N 125°45E 115 E13
Hā'ena *U.S.A.* 22°14N 159°34W 167 L8
Haenam *S. Korea* 34°34N 126°35E 115 G14
Haenertsburg *S. Africa* 24°0S 29°50E 145 B4
Haerhpin = Harbin
  China 45°48N 126°40E 115 B14
Hafar al Bāṭin
  Si. Arabia 28°32N 45°52E 128 D5
Hafik *Turkey* 39°51N 37°23E 104 C7
Ḥafirat al 'Aydā
  Si. Arabia 26°26N 39°12E 128 E3
Ḥafit *Oman* 23°59N 55°49E 129 F7
Hafizabad *Pakistan* 32°5N 73°40E 124 C5
Haflong *India* 25°10N 93°5E 125 G18
Haft Gel *Iran* 31°30N 49°32E 129 D6
Hagalil *Israel* 32°53N 35°18E 130 C4
Hagari → *India* 15°40N 77°0E 127 G3
Hagby *Sweden* 56°34N 16°11E 63 H10
Hagemeister I. *U.S.A.* 58°39N 160°54W 166 D7
Hagen *Germany* 51°21N 7°27E 76 D3
Hagenow *Germany* 53°26N 11°12E 76 B7
Hagerman *U.S.A.* 33°7N 104°20W 169 K11
Hagerman Fossil Beds ◌
  U.S.A. 42°48N 114°57W 168 E6
Hagerstown *U.S.A.* 39°39N 77°43W 173 F15
Hagersville *Canada* 42°58N 80°3W 174 D4
Hagetmau *France* 43°39N 0°37W 72 E3
Hagfors *Sweden* 60°3N 13°45E 62 D7
Hagi *Japan* 34°30N 131°22E 113 G5
Hagolan *Syria* 33°0N 35°45E 130 C4
Hagondange *France* 49°16N 6°11E 71 C13
Hags Hd. *Ireland* 52°57N 9°28W 64 D2
Hague, C. de la *France* 49°44N 1°56W 70 C5
Hague, The = 's-Gravenhage
  Neths. 52°7N 4°17E 69 B4
Haguenau *France* 48°49N 7°47E 71 D14
Hahira *U.S.A.* 30°59N 83°22W 178 E6
Hai Duong *Vietnam* 20°56N 106°19E 116 G6
Hai'an *Guangdong, China* 20°18N 110°11E 117 a
Hai'an *Jiangsu, China* 32°37N 120°27E 117 A13
Haicheng *China* 40°50N 122°45E 115 D12
Haida Gwaii *Canada* 53°20N 132°10W 162 C2
Haidar Khel *Afghan.* 33°58N 68°38E 124 C3
Haidarâbâd = Hyderabad
  India 17°22N 78°29E 126 F4
Haidargarh *India* 26°37N 81°22E 125 F9
Haifa = Ḥefa *Israel* 32°46N 35°0E 130 C4
Haifeng *China* 22°58N 115°10E 117 F10
Haiger *Germany* 50°43N 8°12E 76 E4
Haikou *China* 20°1N 110°16E 117 a
Ḥā'il *Si. Arabia* 27°28N 41°45E 128 E4
Ḥā'il □ *Si. Arabia* 26°40N 41°40E 128 E4
Hailar *China* 49°10N 119°38E 111 B12
Hailey *U.S.A.* 43°31N 114°19W 168 E6
Haileybury *Canada* 47°30N 79°38W 164 C4
Hailin *China* 44°37N 129°30E 115 B15
Hailing Dao *China* 21°35N 111°47E 117 G8
Hailun *China* 47°28N 126°50E 111 B14
Hailuoto *Finland* 65°3N 24°45E 60 D21
Haimen *Guangdong, China* 23°15N 116°38E 117 F11
Haimen *Jiangsu, China* 31°52N 121°10E 117 B13
Hainan □ *China* 19°0N 109°30E 117 a
Hainan Dao *China* 19°0N 109°30E 117 a
Hainan Str. = Qiongzhou Haixia
  China 20°10N 110°15E 117 a
Hainaut □ *Belgium* 50°30N 4°0E 69 D4
Hainburg *Austria* 48°9N 16°56E 79 C9
Haines *Alaska, U.S.A.* 59°14N 135°26W 162 B1
Haines *Oreg., U.S.A.* 44°55N 117°56W 168 D5
Haines City *U.S.A.* 28°7N 81°38W 179 G8
Haines Junction
  Canada 60°45N 137°30W 162 A1
Hainfeld *Austria* 48°3N 15°48E 78 C8
Haining *China* 30°28N 120°40E 117 B13
Haiphong *Vietnam* 20°47N 106°41E 116 G6
Haitan Dao *China* 25°30N 119°45E 117 E12
Haiti ■ *W. Indies* 19°0N 72°30W 183 C5
Haiya *Sudan* 18°20N 36°21E 137 G4
Haiyan *Qinghai, China* 36°53N 100°59E 110 D9
Haiyan *Zhejiang,
  China* 30°28N 120°58E 117 B13
Haiyang *China* 36°47N 121°9E 115 F11
Haiyuan *Guangxi Zhuangzu,
  China* 22°46N 107°35E 116 F6
Haiyuan *Ningxia Huizu,
  China* 36°35N 105°52E 114 F3
Haizhou Wan *China* 34°50N 119°20E 115 G10
Haj Ali Qoli, Kavīr *Iran* 34°56N 55°15E 129 C8
Hajdú-Bihar □ *Hungary* 47°30N 21°30E 80 C6
Hajdúböszörmény
  Hungary 47°40N 21°30E 80 C6
Hajdúdorog *Hungary* 47°48N 21°30E 80 C6
Hajdúháza *Hungary* 47°30N 21°42E 80 C6
Hajdúnánás *Hungary* 47°50N 21°26E 80 C6
Hajdúsámson *Hungary* 47°37N 21°45E 80 C6
Hajdúszoboszló *Hungary* 47°27N 21°22E 80 C6
Haji Ibrahim *Iraq* 36°40N 44°30E 105 D11
Hajipur *India* 25°45N 85°13E 125 G11
Ḥajjah *Yemen* 15°42N 43°36E 131 D4
Ḥajjiābād *Iran* 28°19N 55°55E 129 D7
Ḥajjiābād-e Zarrīn *Iran* 33°9N 54°51E 129 C7
Hajnówka *Poland* 52°47N 23°35E 83 F10

Hakansson, Mts.
  Dem. Rep. of the Congo 8°40S 25°45E 143 D2
Hakataramea *N.Z.* 44°43S 170°30E 155 E5
Hakkâri *Turkey* 37°34N 43°44E 105 G11
Hakkâri □ *Turkey* 37°30N 44°0E 105 D10
Hakkâri Dağları
  Turkey 38°2N 42°58E 105 C10
Hakken-Zan *Japan* 34°10N 135°54E 113 G7
Hakkōda San *Japan* 40°40N 140°50E 112 D10
Hakodate *Japan* 41°45N 140°44E 112 D10
Hakos *Namibia* 23°13S 16°21E 144 B2
Haksberg *Sweden* 60°1N 15°12E 62 D9
Hakskeenpan *S. Africa* 26°48S 20°13E 144 C3
Haku-San *Japan* 36°9N 136°46E 113 F8
Haku-San △ *Japan* 36°15N 136°45E 113 F8
Hakui *Japan* 36°53N 136°47E 113 F8
Hakusan *Japan* 36°31N 136°34E 113 F8
Hala *Pakistan* 25°43N 68°20E 122 G6
Ḥalab *Syria* 36°10N 37°15E 104 D7
Ḥalab □ *Syria* 36°10N 37°10E 104 D7
Ḥalabjah *Iraq* 35°10N 45°58E 105 E11
Halaib *Sudan* 22°12N 36°30E 137 C4
Halaib Triangle *Africa* 22°30N 35°20E 137 C4
Ḥalat 'Ammār *Si. Arabia* 29°10N 36°4E 128 D3
Halbā *Lebanon* 34°34N 36°6E 130 A5
Halberstadt *Germany* 51°54N 11°3E 76 D7
Halcombe *N.Z.* 40°8S 175°30E 154 D4
Halcon, Mt. *Phil.* 13°16N 121°0E 119 B6
Halde Fjäll = Haltiatunturi
  Finland 69°17N 21°18E 60 B19
Halden *Norway* 59°9N 11°23E 61 G14
Haldensleben *Germany* 52°17N 11°24E 76 C7
Haldia *Bangla.* 22°1N 88°3E 125 H13
Haldwani *India* 29°31N 79°30E 125 E8
Hale → *Australia* 24°56S 135°53E 150 C2
Halesowen *U.K.* 52°27N 2°3W 67 E5
Halesworth *U.K.* 52°20N 1°31E 67 E9
Haleyville *U.S.A.* 34°14N 87°37W 177 D11
Half Assini *Ghana* 5°1N 2°50W 138 D4
Half Dome *U.S.A.* 37°44N 119°32E 170 H7
Halfeti *Turkey* 37°15N 37°52E 104 D7
Halfmoon Bay *N.Z.* 46°50S 168°5E 155 G2
Halfway → *Canada* 56°12N 121°32W 162 B4
Halia *India* 24°50N 82°19E 125 G10
Haliak → *India* 24°50N 82°19E 125 G10
Haliki = Chalki *Greece* 36°17N 27°35E 99 E9
Halikida = Chalkida
  Greece 38°27N 23°42E 98 C5
Halkidiki = Chalkidiki
  Greece 40°25N 23°20E 96 F7
Halkirk *U.K.* 58°30N 3°29W 65 C5
Hall Beach *Canada* 68°46N 81°12W 161 D15
Hall in Tirol *Austria* 47°17N 11°30E 78 D4
Hall Pen. *Canada* 63°30N 66°0W 161 E18
Hall Pt. *Australia* 15°40S 124°23E 148 C3
Hallabro *Sweden* 56°22N 15°5E 63 H9
Halland □ *Sweden* 57°8N 12°47E 61 H15
Hallandale Beach
  U.S.A. 25°58N 80°8W 179 K9
Hallands län □ *Sweden* 57°0N 12°40E 63 H6
Hallands Väderö *Sweden* 56°27N 12°34E 63 H6
Hallandsås *Sweden* 56°22N 13°0E 63 H7
Ḥallāniyat, Jazā'ir al
  Oman 17°30N 55°58E 131 D6
Hallasan *S. Korea* 33°22N 126°32E 115 H14
Hällbybrunn *Sweden* 59°24N 16°25E 62 E10
Halle *Belgium* 50°44N 4°13E 69 D4
Halle *Nordrhein-Westfalen,
  Germany* 52°3N 8°22E 76 C4
Halle *Sachsen-Anhalt,
  Germany* 51°30N 11°56E 76 D7
Hällefors *Sweden* 59°47N 14°31E 62 E8
Hälleforsnäs *Sweden* 59°10N 16°30E 62 E10
Hallein *Austria* 47°40N 13°5E 78 D6
Hällekis *Sweden* 58°38N 13°27E 63 F7
Hallen *Sweden* 63°11N 14°4E 62 A8
Hallett *Australia* 33°25S 138°55E 152 B3
Hallettsville *U.S.A.* 29°27N 96°57W 176 G6
Halley *Antarctica* 75°35S 26°39W 55 D1
Hallia → *India* 16°55N 79°20E 126 F4
Hallim *S. Korea* 33°24N 126°15E 115 H14
Hallingdalselva →
  Norway 60°23N 9°35E 60 F13
Hallingskarvet △
  Norway 60°37N 7°45E 60 F12
Hallock *U.S.A.* 48°47N 96°57W 172 A5
Halls Creek *Australia* 18°16S 127°38E 148 C4
Halls Gap *Australia* 37°8S 142°34E 151 F3
Halls Lake *Canada* 45°7N 78°45W 174 A6
Hallsberg *Sweden* 59°5N 15°7E 62 E9
Hallstahammar *Sweden* 59°38N 16°15E 62 E10
Hallstatt *Austria* 47°33N 13°38E 78 D6
Hallstavik *Sweden* 60°5N 18°37E 62 D12
Hallstead *U.S.A.* 41°58N 75°45W 175 E9
Halmahera *Indonesia* 0°40N 128°0E 119 D7
Halmahera Sea *Indonesia* 0°20N 130°0E 119 D7
Halmeu *Romania* 47°57N 23°2E 80 C8
Halmstad *Sweden* 56°41N 12°52E 63 H6
Halong Bay = Ha Long, Vinh
  Vietnam 20°56N 107°3E 120 B6
Halq el Oued = La Goulette
  Tunisia 36°50N 10°18E 94 F3
Hals *Denmark* 57°0N 10°18E 63 H4
Hälsingborg = Helsingborg
  Sweden 56°3N 12°42E 63 H6
Hälsingland *Sweden* 61°40N 16°5E 62 C10
Halstad *U.S.A.* 47°21N 96°50W 172 B5
Halstead *U.K.* 51°57N 0°40E 67 F8
Haltern *Germany* 51°44N 7°11E 76 D3
Haltiatunturi *Finland* 69°17N 21°18E 60 B19
Halton □ *U.K.* 53°22N 2°45W 66 D5
Haltwhistle *U.K.* 54°58N 2°26W 66 C5
Ḥalūl *Qatar* 25°40N 52°40E 129 E7
Halvad *India* 23°1N 71°11E 124 H7
Halvān *Iran* 33°57N 56°15E 129 C8
Ham *France* 49°45N 3°4E 71 C10
Hamab *Namibia* 28°7S 19°16E 144 D2
Hamada *Japan* 34°56N 132°4E 113 G6
Hamadān *Iran* 34°52N 48°32E 105 E13
Hamadān □ *Iran* 35°0N 49°0E 105 F13
Hamadia *Algeria* 35°28N 1°57E 136 A4
Ḥamāh *Syria* 35°5N 36°40E 104 D7
Ḥamāh □ *Syria* 35°10N 37°0E 104 D7

Hamamatsu *Japan* 34°45N 137°45E 113 G8
Hamar *Norway* 60°48N 11°7E 60 F14
Hamâta, Gebel *Egypt* 24°17N 35°0E 128 E2
Hamatonbetsu *Japan* 45°10N 142°20E 112 B11
Hambantota *Sri Lanka* 6°10N 81°10E 127 L5
Hamber ◌ *Canada* 52°20N 118°0W 162 C5
Hamburg *Germany* 53°33N 9°59E 76 B5
Hamburg *Ark., U.S.A.* 33°14N 91°48W 176 E9
Hamburg *N.Y., U.S.A.* 42°43N 78°50W 174 D6
Hamburg *Pa., U.S.A.* 40°33N 75°59W 175 F9
Hamburg □ *Germany* 53°30N 10°0E 76 B5
Hamburg Fuhlsbüttel ✈ (HAM)
  Germany 53°39N 9°59E 76 B5
Ḥamd, W. al →
  Si. Arabia 24°55N 36°20E 128 E3
Hamden *U.S.A.* 41°23N 72°54W 175 E12
Hamdibey *Turkey* 39°50N 27°15E 99 B9
Häme *Finland* 61°38N 25°10E 60 F21
Hämeenlinna *Finland* 61°0N 24°28E 84 B3
Hamélé *Ghana* 10°56N 2°45W 138 C4
Hamelin Pool *Australia* 26°22S 114°20E 149 E1
Hameln *Germany* 52°6N 9°21E 76 C5
Hamerkaz □ *Israel* 32°15N 34°55E 130 C3
Hamersley Ra.
  Australia 22°0S 117°45E 148 D2
Hamhŭng *N. Korea* 39°54N 127°30E 115 E14
Hami *China* 42°55N 93°25E 110 C7
Hamilton *Australia* 37°45S 142°2E 151 F3
Hamilton *Bermuda* 32°17N 64°47W 56 C5
Hamilton *Canada* 43°15N 79°50W 174 D5
Hamilton *N.Z.* 37°47S 175°19E 154 D4
Hamilton *U.K.* 55°46N 4°2W 65 F4
Hamilton *Ala., U.S.A.* 34°9N 87°59W 177 D11
Hamilton *Ga., U.S.A.* 32°45N 84°53W 178 C5
Hamilton *Mont.,
  U.S.A.* 46°15N 114°10W 168 C6
Hamilton *N.Y., U.S.A.* 42°50N 75°33W 175 D9
Hamilton *Ohio, U.S.A.* 39°24N 84°34W 173 F11
Hamilton *Tex., U.S.A.* 31°42N 98°7W 176 F5
Hamilton →
  *Queens.,
  Australia* 23°30S 139°47E 150 C2
Hamilton → *S. Austral.,
  Australia* 26°40S 135°19E 151 D2
Hamilton City *U.S.A.* 39°45N 122°1W 170 F4
Hamilton I. *Australia* 20°21S 148°56E 150 b
Hamilton Inlet *Canada* 54°0N 57°30W 165 B8
Hamilton Mt. *U.S.A.* 43°25N 74°22W 175 C10
Hamina *Finland* 60°34N 27°12E 84 B4
Hamirpur *H.P., India* 31°41N 76°31E 124 D7
Hamirpur *Ut. P., India* 25°57N 80°9E 125 G9
Hamitabat *Turkey* 41°30N 27°17E 97 E11
Hamlet *U.S.A.* 34°53N 79°42W 177 D15
Hamley Bridge
  Australia 34°17S 138°35E 152 C3
Hamlin = Hameln
  Germany 52°6N 9°21E 76 C5
Hamlin *N.Y., U.S.A.* 43°17N 77°55W 174 C7
Hamlin *Tex., U.S.A.* 32°53N 100°8W 176 E4
Hamm *Germany* 51°40N 7°50E 76 D3
Hammām al Alīl *Iraq* 36°9N 43°15E 105 D10
Hammam Bouhadjar
  Algeria 35°23N 0°58W 136 A3
Hammamet *Tunisia* 36°24N 10°38E 136 A6
Hammâm, Hawr al *Iraq* 30°47N 46°35E 128 D5
Hammarstrand *Sweden* 63°7N 16°20E 62 A10
Hammelburg *Germany* 50°6N 9°53E 77 E5
Hammenen *Denmark* 56°8N 9°53E 63 H3
Hammerfest *Norway* 70°39N 23°41E 60 A20
Hamminkeln *Germany* 51°43N 6°35E 76 D2
Hammond *Ind.,
  U.S.A.* 41°38N 87°30W 172 E10
Hammond *La., U.S.A.* 30°30N 90°28W 177 F9
Hammond *N.Y., U.S.A.* 44°27N 75°42W 175 B9
Hammondsport *U.S.A.* 42°25N 77°13W 174 D7
Hammonton *U.S.A.* 39°39N 74°48W 173 F16
Hampden *N.Z.* 45°18S 170°50E 155 F5
Hampi *India* 15°18N 76°28E 127 G3
Hampshire □ *U.K.* 51°7N 1°23W 67 F6
Hampshire Downs *U.K.* 51°15N 1°10W 67 F6
Hampton *N.B., Canada* 45°32N 65°51W 165 D6
Hampton *Ont., Canada* 43°58N 78°45W 174 C6
Hampton *Ark., U.S.A.* 33°32N 92°28W 176 E8
Hampton *Iowa, U.S.A.* 42°45N 93°13W 172 D7
Hampton *N.H., U.S.A.* 42°57N 70°50W 175 D14
Hampton *S.C., U.S.A.* 32°52N 81°7W 178 C8
Hampton *Va., U.S.A.* 37°2N 76°21W 173 G15
Hampton Bays *U.S.A.* 40°53N 72°30W 175 F12
Hampton Springs
  U.S.A. 30°5N 83°40W 178 E6
Hampton Tableland
  Australia 32°0S 127°0E 149 F4
Hamra *Sweden* 61°39N 14°59E 62 C8
Ḥamrin, Jabal *Iraq* 34°30N 44°30E 105 E11
Hamur *Turkey* 39°37N 43°3E 105 C10
Hamyang *S. Korea* 35°30N 127°42E 115 G14
Han i Hotit *Albania* 42°19N 19°27E 96 D3
Han Jiang → *China* 23°25N 116°40E 117 F11
Han Shui → *China* 30°34N 114°17E 117 B10
Hanahan *U.S.A.* 32°55N 80°0W 178 C10
Hanak *Si. Arabia* 25°32N 37°0E 128 E3
Hanak *Turkey* 41°14N 42°50E 105 B10
Hanamaki *Japan* 39°23N 141°7E 112 E10
Hanang *Tanzania* 4°30S 35°25E 142 C4
Hanau *Germany* 50°7N 8°56E 77 E4
Hanbogd = Ihbulag
  Mongolia 43°11N 107°10E 114 C4
Hançalar *Turkey* 38°8N 29°24E 99 C11
Hâncești *Moldova* 46°50N 28°36E 81 D13
Hancheng *China* 35°31N 110°25E 114 G6
Hanchuan *China* 30°40N 113°50E 117 B9
Hancock *Mich., U.S.A.* 47°8N 88°35W 172 B9
Hancock *N.Y., U.S.A.* 41°57N 75°17W 175 E9
Hancock *Vt., U.S.A.* 43°55N 72°50W 175 B13
Handa *Japan* 34°53N 136°55E 113 G8
Handan *China* 36°35N 114°28E 114 F8
Handeni *Tanzania* 5°25S 38°2E 142 D4
Handlová *Slovak Rep.* 48°45N 18°35E 83 C10
Handub *Sudan* 19°15N 37°16E 137 D4
Handwara *India* 34°21N 74°20E 124 B9
Hanegev *Israel* 30°50N 35°0E 130 E4
Hanford *U.S.A.* 36°20N 119°39E 170 J7
Hanford Reach ◌
  U.S.A. 46°40N 119°30W 168 C4
Hang Chat *Thailand* 18°20N 99°21E 120 C2
Hangang → *S. Korea* 37°50N 126°30E 115 F14
Hangayn Nuruu
  Mongolia 47°30N 99°0E 110 B8

Hangchou = Hangzhou
  China 30°18N 120°11E 117 B13
Hanger *Sweden* 57°6N 13°58E 63 G7
Hangnga Somalia* 9°30N 44°2E
Hanggin Houqi *China* 40°58N 107°4E 114 D4
Hanggin Qi *China* 39°52N 108°50E 114 E5
Hangu *China* 39°18N 117°53E 115 E9
Hangzhou *China* 30°18N 120°11E 117 B13
Hangzhou Wan
  China 30°15N 120°45E 117 B13
Hanh *Mongolia* 51°32N 100°35E 110 A9
Hanhöhiy Uul
  Mongolia 49°30N 94°30E 109 C12
Hanhongor *Mongolia* 43°55N 104°28E 114 C3
Hania = Chania *Greece* 35°30N 24°4E 101 D6
Ḥanīdh *Si. Arabia* 24°55N 36°20E 128 E3
Ḥaniš *Yemen* 13°45N 42°46E 131 E3
Haniska *Slovak Rep.* 48°37N 21°15E 79 C14
Hanjiang *China* 25°26N 119°6E 117 E12
Hankinson *U.S.A.* 46°4N 96°54W 172 B5
Hankö *Finland* 59°50N 22°57E 84 C2
Hankou *China* 30°35N 114°30E 117 B10
Hanksville *U.S.A.* 38°22N 110°43W 168 G8
Hanle *India* 32°42N 79°4E 125 C8
Hanmer Springs *N.Z.* 42°32S 172°50E 155 C7
Hann → *Australia* 17°26S 126°17E 148 C4
Hann, Mt. *Australia* 15°45S 126°0E 148 C4
Hanna *U.S.A.* 51°40N 111°54W 162 C6
Hanna *U.S.A.* 41°52N 106°34W 168 F10
Hannah B. *Canada* 51°40N 80°0W 164 B4
Hannibal *Mo., U.S.A.* 39°42N 91°22W 172 F8
Hannibal *N.Y., U.S.A.* 43°19N 76°35W 175 C8
Hannik *Sudan* 18°12N 32°20E 137 D3
Hannover *Germany* 52°22N 9°46E 76 C5
Hanö *Sweden* 56°1N 14°50E 63 H8
Hanöbukten *Sweden* 55°35N 14°30E 63 H8
Hanoi *Vietnam* 21°5N 105°55E 116 G5
Hanover = Hannover
  Germany 52°22N 9°46E 76 C5
Hanover *Canada* 44°9N 81°2W 174 B3
Hanover *S. Africa* 31°4S 24°29E 144 D3
Hanover *N.H., U.S.A.* 43°42N 72°17W 175 C12
Hanover *Ohio, U.S.A.* 40°4N 82°16W 174 F2
Hanover *Pa., U.S.A.* 39°48N 76°59W 173 F15
Hanover, I. *Chile* 51°0S 74°50W 192 G2
Hans Lollik I.
  U.S. Virgin Is. 18°24N 64°53W 183 e
Hansdiha *India* 24°36N 87°5E 125 G12
Hanshou *China* 28°56N 111°50E 117 C8
Hansi *H.P., India* 32°27N 77°50E 124 C7
Hansi *Haryana, India* 29°10N 75°57E 124 E6
Hanson, L. *Australia* 31°0S 136°15E 152 B2
Hansweert *Neths.* 51°26N 3°54E 69 D3
Hanson I. *U.S.A.* 29°30N 81°16W 175 B11
Hanting *China* 36°46N 119°12E 115 F10
Hantsavichy *Belarus* 52°49N 26°30E 75 B14
Hanumangarh *India* 29°35N 74°19E 124 E6
Hanyin *China* 32°54N 108°28E 114 H5
Hanyuan *China* 29°21N 102°40E 116 C4
Hanzhong *China* 33°10N 107°1E 116 A6
Hanzhuang *China* 34°33N 117°23E 115 G9
Haora *India* 22°34N 88°18E 125 H13
Haoxue *China* 30°3N 112°24E 117 B9
Haparanda *Sweden* 65°52N 24°8E 60 D21
Haparanda Skärgård ◌
  Sweden 65°35N 23°44E 60 D20
Hapeville *U.S.A.* 33°39N 84°24W 178 B5
Happy *U.S.A.* 34°45N 101°52W 176 D4
Happy Camp *U.S.A.* 41°48N 123°23W 168 F2
Happy Valley-Goose Bay
  Canada 53°15N 60°20W 165 B7
Hapsu *N. Korea* 41°13N 128°51E 115 D15
Hapur *India* 28°45N 77°45E 124 E7
Haql *Si. Arabia* 29°10N 34°58E 130 F3
Haquira *Peru* 14°14S 72°12W 188 C3
Har *Indonesia* 5°16S 133°14E 119 F8
Har Hu *China* 38°20N 97°38E 110 D8
Har Us Nuur *Mongolia* 48°0N 92°0E 109 C12
Har Yehuda *Israel* 31°35N 34°57E 130 D3
Harad *Si. Arabia* 24°22N 49°0E 128 E5
Haradok *Belarus* 55°30N 30°3E 84 E6
Häradsbäck *Sweden* 56°38N 14°47E 63 H8
Haramosh *Pakistan* 35°50N 74°54E 125 B6
Haranomachi = Minamisōma
  Japan 37°38M 140°58E 112 F10
Harar = Harer *Ethiopia* 9°20N 42°8E 133 G3
Harare *Zimbabwe* 17°43S 31°2E 143 F3
Harazé *Chad* 9°57N 20°48E 135 G10
Harbel *Liberia* 6°16N 10°20W 138 D2
Harbhanga *India* 20°38N 84°36E 126 D7
Harbin *China* 45°48N 126°40E 115 B14
Harbiye *Turkey* 36°10N 36°8E 104 D7
Harbo *Sweden* 60°7N 17°12E 62 D11
Harboøre *Denmark* 56°38N 8°10E 63 H2
Harbor Beach *U.S.A.* 43°51N 82°39W 174 C2
Harborcreek *U.S.A.* 42°9N 79°57W 174 D5
Harbour Breton
  Canada 47°29N 55°50W 165 C8
Harbour Deep *Canada* 50°25N 56°32W 165 B8
Harburg *Germany* 53°27N 9°58E 76 B5
Harburger Berge ◌
  Germany 53°26N 9°51E 76 B5
Harda *India* 22°27N 77°5E 124 H7
Hardangerfjorden *Norway* 60°5N 6°0E 61 F12
Hardangervidda *Norway* 60°7N 7°20E 60 F12
Hardap □ *Namibia* 24°0S 17°0E 144 B2
Hardap Dam *Namibia* 24°32S 17°50E 144 B2
Hardeeville *U.S.A.* 32°17N 81°5W 178 C8
Hardenberg *Neths.* 52°34N 6°37E 69 B6
Harderwijk *Neths.* 52°21N 5°38E 69 B5
Hardey → *Australia* 22°45S 116°8E 148 D2
Hardin *U.S.A.* 45°44N 107°37W 168 D10
Harding *S. Africa* 30°35S 29°55E 145 E4
Harding Ra. *Australia* 16°17S 124°55E 148 C3
Hardisty *Canada* 52°40N 111°18W 162 C6
Hardoi *India* 27°26N 80°6E 125 F9
Hardwar = Haridwar
  India 29°58N 78°9E 124 E8
Hardwick *Ga., U.S.A.* 33°4N 83°14W 178 C6
Hardwick *Vt., U.S.A.* 44°30N 72°22W 175 B12
Hardwick B.
  Australia 34°55S 137°0E 152 C2
Hardwood Lake
  Canada 45°12N 77°26W 174 A7
Hardy, Pen. *Chile* 55°30S 68°20W 192 H3
Hardy, Pte. *St. Lucia* 14°6N 60°56W 183 f
Hare B. *Canada* 51°15N 55°45W 165 B8

Haren *Germany* 52°47N 7°13E 76 C3
Harer *Ethiopia* 9°20N 42°8E 133 G3
Harfleur *France* 49°30N 0°10E 70 B7
Hargeisa *Somalia* 9°30N 44°2E 132 F3
Harghita □ *Romania* 46°30N 25°30E 81 C7
Harghita, Munții
  Romania 46°25N 25°35E 81 C7
Hargshamn *Sweden* 60°12N 18°30E 62 D12
Hari → *Indonesia* 1°16S 104°5E 118 E2
Haria *Canary Is.* 29°8N 13°32W 48 F6
Haridwar *India* 29°58N 78°9E 124 E8
Harihari *N.Z.* 43°9S 170°33E 155 D3
Hariharpur Garhi
  Nepal 27°19N 85°29E 125 F11
Harim, Jabal al *Oman* 25°58N 56°14E 129 E8
Haringhata → *Bangla.* 22°0N 89°58E 125 J13
Hārirūd → *Asia* 37°24N 60°38E 129 B9
Harīr, W. al → *Syria* 32°44N 35°59E 130 C4
Härjedalen *Sweden* 62°22N 13°5E 60 F13
Harlan *Iowa, U.S.A.* 41°39N 95°19W 172 E6
Harlan *Ky., U.S.A.* 36°51N 83°19W 173 G12
Hārlău *Romania* 47°28N 26°52E 81 B8
Harlech *U.K.* 52°52N 4°6W 66 E3
Harlem *U.S.A.* 33°25N 82°19W 178 C6
Harlem *Mont., U.S.A.* 48°32N 108°47W 168 B9
Härlöv *Denmark* 55°21N 12°14E 63 H8
Harleyville *U.S.A.* 33°13N 80°27W 178 C8
Harlingen *Neths.* 53°11N 5°25E 69 A5
Harlingen *U.S.A.* 26°12N 97°42W 177 H8
Harlow *U.K.* 51°46N 0°8E 67 F8
Harlowton *U.S.A.* 46°26N 109°50W 168 C9
Harmanck *Turkey* 39°41N 29°9E 99 C12
Harmånger *Sweden* 61°55N 17°20E 62 C11
Harnai *India* 17°48N 73°6E 126 F1
Harnai *Pakistan* 30°6N 67°56E 124 D3
Harney, L. *U.S.A.* 28°45N 81°3W 179 G8
Harney Basin *U.S.A.* 43°0N 119°30W 168 E4
Harney L. *U.S.A.* 43°14N 119°8W 168 E4
Harney Peak *U.S.A.* 43°52N 103°32W 168 D2
Härnösand *Sweden* 62°36N 18°0E 62 B11
Haro *Spain* 42°35N 2°55W 73 C4
Harold L. *Canada* 55°5N 61°50W 165 B7
Haroldswick *U.K.* 60°48N 0°50W 65 A8
Harp L. *Canada* 55°5N 61°50W 165 B7
Harpanahalli *India* 14°47N 76°2E 127 G3
Harper *Liberia* 4°25N 7°43W 138 E3
Harper, Mt. *U.S.A.* 64°14N 143°51W 166 C5
Harplinge *Sweden* 56°45N 12°45E 63 H6
Harrai *India* 22°37N 79°13E 124 H8
Harrand *Pakistan* 29°28N 70°3E 124 E4
Harricana → *Canada* 50°56N 79°32W 164 B4
Harriman *U.S.A.* 35°56N 84°33W 177 D12
Harrington Harbour
  Canada 50°31N 59°30W 165 B8
Harris *U.K.* 57°50N 6°55W 65 D2
Harris, L. *Australia* 31°10S 135°10E 152 B1
Harris, Sd. of *U.K.* 57°44N 7°6W 65 D1
Harris Mts. *N.Z.* 44°49S 168°49E 155 D2
Harris Pt. *Canada* 43°6N 82°9W 174 C2
Harrisburg *Ill., U.S.A.* 37°44N 88°32W 172 G9
Harrisburg *Nebr.,
  U.S.A.* 41°33N 103°44W 168 F2
Harrismith *S. Africa* 28°15S 29°8E 145 D4
Harrison *Ark., U.S.A.* 36°14N 93°7W 176 C8
Harrison *Nebr., U.S.A.* 42°41N 103°53W 168 F2
Harrison, C. *Canada* 54°55N 57°55W 165 B8
Harrison Bay *U.S.A.* 70°40N 151°0W 166 A4
Harrison L. *Canada* 49°33N 121°50W 162 D4
Harrisonburg *U.S.A.* 38°27N 78°52W 173 F14
Harrisonville *U.S.A.* 38°39N 94°21W 172 F6
Harriston *Canada* 43°57N 80°53W 174 C4
Harrisville *Mich.,
  U.S.A.* 44°39N 83°17W 174 B2
Harrisville *N.Y., U.S.A.* 44°9N 75°19W 175 B9
Harrisville *Pa., U.S.A.* 41°8N 80°0W 174 E5
Harrogate *U.K.* 54°0N 1°33W 66 D6
Harrow *Canada* 42°2N 82°55W 174 D2
Harrow □ *U.K.* 51°35N 0°21W 67 F7
Harrowsmith *Canada* 44°24N 76°40W 175 C8
Harry S. Truman Res.
  U.S.A. 38°16N 93°24W 172 F7
Harsefeld *Germany* 53°27N 9°30E 76 B5
Harsewinkel *Germany* 51°58N 8°14E 76 C4
Harşin *Iran* 34°18N 47°33E 105 E12
Hârșova *Romania* 44°40N 27°59E 81 D8
Harstad *Norway* 68°48N 16°30E 60 B17
Harsud *India* 22°6N 76°44E 124 H7
Hart *U.S.A.* 43°42N 86°22W 172 D9
Hart, L. *Australia* 31°10S 136°25E 152 B2
Hartbees → *S. Africa* 28°45S 20°32E 144 D3
Hartberg *Austria* 47°17N 15°58E 78 D9
Hartford *Ala., U.S.A.* 31°6N 85°42W 177 F12
Hartford *Conn., U.S.A.* 41°46N 72°41W 175 E12
Hartford *Ky., U.S.A.* 37°27N 86°55W 172 G10
Hartford *S. Dak., U.S.A.* 43°38N 96°57W 172 D5
Hartford *Vt., U.S.A.* 43°40N 72°20W 175 C12
Hartford *Wis., U.S.A.* 43°19N 88°22W 172 D8
Hartford City *U.S.A.* 40°27N 85°22W 172 E11
Hartland *Canada* 46°20N 67°32W 165 D6
Hartland Pt. *U.K.* 51°1N 4°32W 67 F3
Hartlepool *U.K.* 54°42N 1°13W 66 C6
Hartlepool □ *U.K.* 54°42N 1°17W 66 C6
Hartley Bay *Canada* 53°25N 129°15W 162 C3
Hartmannberge *Namibia* 17°0S 13°0E 144 B1
Hartmannsdorf *Namibia* 23°56S 18°8E 144 B2
Hårtop *Moldova* 46°39N 28°40E 81 B12
Harts → *S. Africa* 28°24S 24°17E 144 D3
Harts Range *Australia* 23°6S 134°55E 150 C1
Hartsfield-Jackson Atlanta Int. ✈
  (ATL) *U.S.A.* 33°38N 84°26W 178 B4
Hartshorne *U.S.A.* 34°51N 95°34W 176 D6
Hartsville *U.S.A.* 34°23N 80°4W 178 D7
Hartswater *S. Africa* 27°34S 24°43E 144 D3
Hartwell *U.S.A.* 34°21N 82°56W 178 D6
Harunabad *Pakistan* 29°35N 73°8E 124 E5
Harur *India* 12°3N 78°29E 127 H4
Harvand *Iran* 28°25N 55°43E 129 D7
Harvey *Australia* 33°5S 115°54E 149 H2
Harvey *Ill., U.S.A.* 41°36N 87°50W 172 E10
Harvey *N. Dak., U.S.A.* 47°47N 99°56W 172 B4

...vich *U.K.* 51°56N 1°17E **67 F9**
...ana □ *India* 29°0N 76°10E **124 E7**
...na → *Belarus* 52°7N 27°17E **75 B14**
...Germany 51°38N 10°44E **76 D6**
...Germany 51°40N 10°18E **76 D6**
...gerode *Germany* 51°38N 11°8E **76 D7**
...△ *Germany* 51°40N 10°18E **76 D6**
...W. al → *Jordan* 31°4N 35°29E **130 D4**
...Si. Arabia 25°50N 49°0E **129 E6**
...nābād *Iran* 32°8N 52°44E **127 C7**
...nkeyf *Turkey* 37°42N 41°24E **105 D9**
...nparti *India* 18°4N 79°32E **126 E4**
...W. → *Iraq* 31°45N 44°17E **128 D5**
...nne 21°44N 82°44E **125 J10**
...ünne *Germany* 52°29N 9°27E **76 C3**
...imoto *Japan* 34°19N 135°37E **113 G7**
...tjerd *Iran* 35°52N 50°40E **129 C6**
...tpur = Tälesh
 37°58N 48°58E **105 D13**
...trud *Iran* 37°28N 47°4E **105 D12**
...ell *U.S.A.* 33°10N 99°44W **176 E5**
...ovo = Khaskovo
 Bulgaria 41°56N 25°30E **97 E9**
...öy *Turkey* 41°38N 26°52E **97 E11**
...ach *Germany* 48°16N 8°5E **77 G4**
...e *Denmark* 55°11N 14°44E **63 J8**
...mere *U.K.* 51°5N 0°43W **67 F7**
...n *Denmark* 55°18N 11°57E **63 J5**
...arren *France* 43°24N 1°18W **72 E2**
...a *Turkey* 36°48N 36°29E **104 D7**
...an *India* 13°0N 76°5E **127 H3**
...perge △ *Germany* 50°38N 10°45E **77 E6**
...ela *Sweden* 62°7N 16°42E **62 B10**
...lt *Belgium* 50°56N 5°21E **69 D5**
...urt *Germany* 50°2N 10°30E **77 E6**
...bel Guebbour
 Algeria 28°30N 6°41E **136 C5**
...bou Khelala
 Algeria
...Bourachet *Algeria* 27°26N 9°19E **136 C5**
...Djafou *Algeria* 27°26N 3°35E **136 B4**
...el Hadjar *Algeria* 28°18N 4°45E **136 B4**
...Imoulaye *Algeria* 29°54N 9°10E **136 C5**
...Inifeg *Algeria* 28°15N 1°30W **136 C3**
...Inifel *Algeria* 29°50N 3°41E **136 C4**
...Mana *Algeria* 28°48N 2°37W **136 C3**
...Marroket *Algeria* 30°10N 3°0E **136 B4**
...Mengoub *Algeria* 29°49N 5°26W **136 C2**
...Messaoud *Algeria* 31°51N 6°1E **136 B5**
...Sougoued *Algeria* 26°50N 6°28E **136 C5**
...Tartrat *Algeria* 30°51N 3°56W **136 B3**
...Zguilma *Morocco* 30°57N 3°41E **136 C4**
...eholm *Sweden* 56°10N 13°46E **63 H7**
...ö *Sweden* 56°7N 15°28E **63 H9**
...och *Germany* 49°22N 8°16E **77 F4**
...nolmen *Sweden* 58°17N 14°38E **63 F8**
...ngs *Australia* 38°18S 145°12E **153 F6**
...ngs *N.Z.* 39°39S 176°52E **154 F5**
...ngs *Fla., U.S.A.* 29°43N 81°31W **178 F8**
...ngs *Mich., U.S.A.* 42°39N 85°17W **173 D3**
...ngs *Nebr., U.S.A.* 40°35N 98°23W **172 E4**
...ngs Ra.
 Australia 31°15S 152°14E **153 A10**
...reda *Sweden* 56°17N 13°55E **63 H7**
...kraine 48°19N 22°38E **80 B7**
...Mead △ *Australia* 31°3S 153°1E **153 A10**
...ot *Vietnam* 21°15N 104°7E **120 B5**
...ai *Thailand* 7°1N 100°27E **121 J3**
...nbulag = Ergel
 Mongolia 43°8N 109°5E **114 C5**
...y □ *Turkey* 36°14N 36°10E **104 D7**
...y □ *Turkey* 36°25N 36°15E **104 D7**
...net L. *Canada* 32°40N 107°9W **169 K10**
...Romania 27°36N 78°6E **124 F8**
...ruma-Shima
 Japan 24°3N 123°47E **113 M1**
...ngolia 43°8N 109°5E **114 C5**
...eld *Australia* 33°54S 143°49E **152 B5**
...al *Mongolia* 52°6N 100°9E **110 A9**
...ras *India* 27°36N 78°6E **124 F8**
...h *Bangla.* 22°30N 91°5E **123 H17**
...Nepal 28°43N 87°21E **125 F12**
...ah, Ra's *Si. Arabia* 21°55N 58°57E **137 C4**
...India 17°17N 75°3E **126 F2**
...Mayor *Dom. Rep.* 18°46N 69°15W **183 C6**
...= Al Ḥaḍr *Iraq* 35°35N 42°44E **105 D10**
...India 24°7N 79°36E **125 G8**
...U.A.E. 24°45N 56°4E **129 E8**
...h Kulkyne △
 Australia 34°48S 142°17E **152 C5**
...ras, C. *U.S.A.* 35°14N 75°32W **177 D17**
...ras Abyssal Plain
 Atl. Oc. 28°0N 72°0W **56 D4**
...esburg *U.S.A.* 31°20N 89°17W **177 F10**
...sa *Hungary* 40°0N 34°37E **104 B6**
...ana *Hungary* 47°40N 19°45E **80 C4**
...→ *Vietnam* 9°30N 106°13E **121 H6**
...esund *Norway* 59°23N 5°13E **61 G11**
...ungaroa Ra. *N.Z.*
 38°42S 175°40E **154 E4**
...kipudas *Finland* 65°12N 25°20E **60 D21**
...ona *Canada* 55°51N 106°46W **163 B7**
...aki G. *N.Z.* 36°35S 175°5E **154 C4**
...oko L. *N.Z.* 45°5S 167°21E **155 F2**
...bruck *Austria* 48°6N 13°30E **78 C6**
...Atlas *Morocco* 32°30N 5°0W **136 B3**
...-Jura □ *France* 46°25N 2°43E **71 F9**
...-Languedoc □
 France 43°30N 2°43E **72 E6**
...e-Corse □ *France* 42°30N 9°30E **73 F13**
...e-Garonne □ *France* 43°23N 1°30E **72 E5**
...e-Loire □ *France* 45°30N 3°50E **72 C7**
...e-Marne □ *France* 48°10N 5°20E **71 D12**
...-Normandie □
 France 49°20N 1°0E **70 C4**
...e-Saône □ *France* 47°45N 6°10E **71 E13**
...-Savoie □ *France* 46°0N 6°20E **73 C10**
...-Alpes □ *France* 44°42N 6°20E **73 D10**
...es Fagnes = Hohes Venn
 Belgium 50°30N 6°5E **69 D6**
...es-Pyrénées □ *France* 43°0N 0°10E **72 F4**
...éville-Lompnès
 France 45°49N 5°36E **73 C9**

Hautmont *France* 50°15N 3°55E **71 B10**
Hauts-de-Seine □ *France* 48°52N 2°15E **71 D9**
Hauts Plateaux *Algeria* 35°0N 1°0E **136 B4**
Hauzenberg *Germany* 48°40N 13°37E **77 G9**
Havana = La Habana
 Cuba 23°8N 82°22W **182 B3**
Havana *Fla., U.S.A.* 30°37N 84°25W **178 E5**
Havana *Ill., U.S.A.* 40°18N 90°4W **172 E8**
Havant *U.K.* 50°51N 0°58W **67 G7**
Havârna *Romania* 48°4N 26°43E **81 B11**
Havasor = Kiğzı *Turkey* 38°18N 43°25E **128 B4**
Havasu, L. *U.S.A.* 34°18N 114°28W **171 L12**
Havdhem *Sweden* 57°10N 18°20E **63 G12**
Havel → *Germany* 52°50N 12°3E **76 C8**
Havelian *Pakistan* 34°2N 73°10E **124 B5**
Havelock *Canada* 44°26N 77°53W **174 E7**
Havelock *N.Z.* 41°17S 173°48E **155 B8**
Havelock *U.S.A.* 34°53N 76°54W **177 D16**
Havelock I. *India* 11°58N 93°0E **127 J11**
Havelock North *N.Z.* 39°40S 176°53E **154 F5**
Haverfordwest *U.K.* 51°48N 4°58W **67 F3**
Haverhill *U.K.* 52°5N 0°28E **67 E8**
Haverhill *Fla., U.S.A.* 26°42N 80°7W **179 J9**
Haverhill *Mass., U.S.A.* 42°47N 71°5W **175 D13**
Haveri *India* 14°53N 75°24E **126 G2**
Havern *Sweden* 62°18N 15°7E **62 B9**
Haverstraw *U.S.A.* 41°12N 73°58W **175 E11**
Håverud *Sweden* 58°50N 12°28E **63 F6**
Havirga *Mongolia* 45°41N 113°5E **114 B7**
Havířov *Czech Rep.* 49°46N 18°20E **79 B11**
Havlíčkův Brod
 Czech Rep. 49°36N 15°33E **78 B8**
Havneby *Denmark* 55°5N 8°34E **63 J2**
Havran *Turkey* 39°33N 27°6E **99 B9**
Havre *U.S.A.* 48°33N 109°41W **168 B9**
Havre-Aubert *Canada* 47°12N 61°56W **165 C7**
Havre-St.-Pierre
 Canada 50°18N 63°33W **165 B7**
Havsa *Turkey* 41°31N 26°48E **97 E10**
Havza *Turkey* 41°0N 35°35E **104 B6**
Haw → *U.S.A.* 35°36N 79°3W **177 D15**
Hawai'i *U.S.A.* 19°30N 155°30W **167 M8**
Hawai'i □ *U.S.A.* 19°30N 156°30W **167 M8**
Hawaiian Is. *Pac. Oc.* 20°30N 156°0W **157 E12**
Hawaiian Ridge
 Pac. Oc. 24°0N 165°0W **157 E11**
Hawarden *U.S.A.* 43°0N 96°29W **172 D5**
Hawea, L. *N.Z.* 44°28S 169°19E **155 E4**
Hawea Flat *N.Z.* 44°40S 169°19E **155 E4**
Hawera *N.Z.* 39°35S 174°19E **154 F4**
Hawi *U.S.A.* 20°14N 155°50W **167 L8**
Hawick *U.K.* 55°26N 2°47W **65 F6**
Hawk Junction *Canada* 48°5N 84°38W **164 C3**
Hawke B. *N.Z.* 39°25S 177°20E **154 F6**
Hawkdun Ra. *N.Z.* 44°53S 170°5E **155 E5**
Hawke *Australia* 31°59S 138°22E **152 A3**
Hawke's Bay *Canada* 50°36N 57°10W **165 B8**
Hawke's Bay □ *N.Z.* 39°45S 176°35E **154 F5**
Hawkesbury *Canada* 45°37N 74°37W **165 C1**
Hawkesbury I. *Canada* 53°37N 129°3W **162 C3**
Hawkesbury Pt.
 Australia 11°55S 134°5E **150 A1**
Hawkinsville *U.S.A.* 32°17N 83°28W **178 C6**
Hawks Nest *Australia* 32°41S 152°11E **153 B10**
Hawley *Minn., U.S.A.* 46°53N 96°19W **172 B5**
Hawley *Pa., U.S.A.* 41°28N 75°11W **175 E9**
Hawran, W. → *Iraq* 33°58N 42°34E **105 F10**
Hawsh Mūssá *Lebanon* 33°45N 35°55E **130 B4**
Hawthorne *U.S.A.* 29°36N 82°5W **179 F7**
Hawthorne *Nev., U.S.A.*
 38°32N 118°38W **168 G4**
Hay *Australia* 34°30S 144°51E **153 C6**
Hay → *Australia* 24°50S 138°0E **152 C2**
Hay → *Canada* 60°50N 116°26W **162 A5**
Hay, C. *Australia* 14°5S 129°29E **148 B4**
Hay I. *Canada* 44°53N 80°58W **174 B4**
Hay L. *Canada* 58°50N 118°50W **162 B5**
Hay-on-Wye *U.K.* 52°5N 3°8W **67 E4**
Hay Point *Australia* 21°18S 149°17E **150 C4**
Hay River *Canada* 60°51N 115°44W **162 A5**
Hay Springs *U.S.A.* 42°41N 102°41W **172 D2**
Hayachine-San *Japan* 39°34N 141°29E **112 E10**
Hayange *France* 49°20N 6°2E **71 C13**
Hayastan = Armenia ■
 Asia 40°20N 45°0E **87 K7**
Haydān, W. al →
 Jordan 31°29N 35°34E **130 D4**
Haydarlı *Turkey* 38°16N 30°23E **99 C12**
Hayden *U.S.A.* 40°30N 107°16W **168 F10**
Hayes → *U.S.A.* 44°23N 101°1W **172 C3**
Hayes → *Canada* 57°3N 92°12W **164 A1**
Hayes, Mt. *U.S.A.* 63°37N 146°43W **166 C10**
Hayes Creek *Australia* 13°43S 131°22E **148 B5**
Hayle *U.K.* 50°11N 5°26W **67 G2**
Hayling I. *U.K.* 50°48N 0°59W **67 G7**
Hayman I. *Australia* 20°4S 148°53E **150 b**
Haymana *Turkey* 39°26N 32°31E **104 C5**
Hayneville *U.S.A.* 32°11N 86°35W **178 C3**
Hayrabolu *Turkey* 41°12N 27°5E **97 E11**
Hays *Canada* 50°6N 111°48W **162 C6**
Hays *U.S.A.* 38°53N 99°20W **172 F4**
Haysyn *Ukraine* 48°57N 29°25E **81 B14**
Hayvoron *Ukraine* 48°22N 29°52E **81 B14**
Hayward *Calif., U.S.A.* 37°40N 122°4W **170 H4**
Hayward *Wis., U.S.A.* 46°1N 91°29W **172 B8**
Haywards Heath *U.K.* 51°0N 0°5W **67 G7**
Hazafon □ *Israel* 32°40N 35°20E **130 C4**
Hazar *Turkmenistan* 39°34N 53°16E **108 E4**
Hazárán, Kúh-e *Iran* 29°35N 57°20E **129 D8**
Hazard *U.S.A.* 37°15N 83°12W **173 G12**
Hazaribag *India* 23°58N 85°26E **125 H11**
Hazaribag Road *India* 24°12N 85°57E **125 G11**
Hazebrouck *France* 50°42N 2°31E **71 B9**
Hazelton *Canada* 55°20N 127°42W **162 B3**
Hazelton *U.S.A.* 46°29N 100°17W **172 B3**
Hazen, L. *Canada* 81°47N 71°1W **57 A3**
Hazen *Canada* 81°47N 71°1W **57 A3**
Hazlehurst *Ga., U.S.A.* 31°52N 82°36W **178 D7**
Hazlehurst *Miss.,
 U.S.A.* 31°52N 90°24W **177 F9**
Hazlet *U.S.A.* 40°25N 74°12W **175 F10**
Hazleton *U.S.A.* 40°57N 75°59W **175 F9**
Hazlett, L. *Australia* 21°30S 128°48E **148 D4**
Hazro *Turkey* 38°15N 40°47E **128 B4**
He Xian = Hezhou
 China 24°27N 111°30E **117 E8**
He Xian *China* 31°45N 118°20E **117 B12**
Head of Bight *Australia* 31°30S 131°25E **149 F5**
Head-Smashed-In Buffalo Jump
 Canada 49°44N 113°37W **162 D6**
Headland *U.S.A.* 31°21N 85°21W **178 D4**

Headlands *Zimbabwe* 18°15S 32°2E **143 F3**
Healdsburg *U.S.A.* 38°37N 122°52W **170 G4**
Healdton *U.S.A.* 34°14N 97°29W **176 D6**
Healesville *Australia* 37°35S 145°30E **153 D6**
Healy *U.S.A.* 63°52N 148°58W **166 C10**
Heany Junction
 Zimbabwe 20°6S 28°54E **145 B4**
Heard I. *Ind. Oc.* 53°6S 72°36E **146 K6**
Hearne *U.S.A.* 30°53N 96°36W **176 F6**
Hearst *Canada* 49°40N 83°41W **164 C3**
Heart → *U.S.A.* 46°46N 100°50W **172 B3**
Heart's Content
 Canada 47°54N 53°27W **165 C9**
Heath → *Bolivia* 12°31S 68°38W **188 C4**
Heath, Pte. *Canada* 49°8N 61°40W **165 C7**
Heath Mts. *N.Z.* 45°39S 167°9E **155 F2**
Heathcote *Australia* 36°56S 144°45E **153 D6**
Heathrow, London ✈ (LHR)
 U.K. 51°28N 0°27W **67 F7**
Heavener *U.S.A.* 34°53N 94°36W **176 D7**
Hebbronville *U.S.A.* 27°18N 98°41W **176 H5**
Hebei □ *China* 39°0N 116°0E **114 E9**
Hebel *Australia* 28°58S 147°47E **151 D4**
Heber *U.S.A.* 32°44N 115°32W **171 N11**
Heber Springs *U.S.A.* 35°30N 92°2W **176 D8**
Hebgen L. *U.S.A.* 44°52N 111°20W **168 D8**
Hebi *China* 35°57N 114°7E **114 G8**
Hebrides *U.K.* 57°30N 7°0W **58 D4**
Hebrides, Sea of the *U.K.* 57°5N 7°0W **65 D2**
Hebron = Al Khalīl
 West Bank 31°32N 35°6E **130 D4**
Hebron *Canada* 58°5N 62°30W **161 F19**
Hebron *N. Dak., U.S.A.* 46°54N 102°3W **172 B2**
Hebron *Nebr., U.S.A.* 40°10N 97°35W **172 E5**
Heby *Sweden* 59°56N 16°53E **62 E10**
Hecate Str. *Canada* 53°10N 130°30W **162 C2**
Hechi *China* 24°40N 108°2E **116 E7**
Hechingen *Germany* 48°21N 8°57E **77 G4**
Hechuan *China* 30°2N 106°12E **116 B6**
Hecla *U.S.A.* 45°53N 98°9W **172 C4**
Hecla I. *Canada* 51°10N 96°43W **163 C9**
Hedal *Norway* 60°37N 9°41E **62 D3**
Hédé *France* 48°18N 1°49W **70 D5**
Hede *Sweden* 62°23N 13°30E **62 B6**
Hedemora *Sweden* 60°18N 15°58E **62 D9**
Hedensted *Denmark* 55°46N 9°42E **63 J3**
Hedesunda *Sweden* 60°24N 17°0E **62 D10**
Hedgehope *N.Z.* 46°12S 168°34E **155 G3**
Heerde *Neths.* 52°24N 6°2E **69 B6**
Heerenveen *Neths.* 52°57N 5°55E **69 B5**
Heerhugowaard *Neths.* 52°40N 4°51E **69 B4**
Heerlen *Neths.* 50°55N 5°58E **69 D5**
Ḥefa *Israel* 32°46N 35°0E **130 C4**
Ḥefa □ *Israel* 32°40N 35°0E **130 C4**
Hefei *China* 31°52N 117°18E **117 B11**
Hefeng *China* 29°55N 109°52E **116 C7**
Heflin *U.S.A.* 33°39N 85°35W **178 B4**
Hegang *China* 47°20N 130°19E **111 B15**
Hegig *Sudan* 10°0N 29°2E **135 G11**
Hei Ling Chau *China* 22°15N 114°2E **111 a**
Heichengzhen *China* 36°24N 106°3E **114 F4**
Heide *Germany* 54°11N 9°6E **76 A5**
Heidelberg *Germany* 49°24N 8°42E **77 F4**
Heidelberg *S. Africa* 34°6S 20°59E **144 E3**
Heidelberg *S. Africa* 26°30S 28°21E **145 D4**
Heidenau *Germany* 50°57N 13°52E **76 E9**
Heidenheim *Germany* 48°41N 10°9E **77 G6**
Heihe *China* 50°10N 127°30E **111 A14**
Heijing *China* 25°22N 101°44E **116 E3**
Heilbad Heiligenstadt
 Germany 51°22N 10°8E **76 D6**
Heilbron *S. Africa* 27°16S 27°59E **145 D4**
Heilbronn *Germany* 49°9N 9°13E **77 F5**
Heiligenblut *Austria* 47°2N 12°51E **78 B5**
Heiligenhafen *Germany* 54°22N 10°59E **76 A6**
Heilongjiang □ *China* 48°0N 126°0E **111 B14**
Heilunkiang = Heilongjiang □
 China 48°0N 126°0E **111 B14**
Heimaey *Iceland* 63°26N 20°17W **60 E3**
Heinola *Finland* 61°13N 26°2E **84 B4**
Heinze Chaung *Burma* 14°42N 97°52E **120 E1**
Heinze Kyun *Burma* 14°25N 97°45E **120 E1**
Heishan *China* 41°40N 122°5E **115 D12**
Heishui *Liaoning, China* 42°8N 119°30E **115 C10**
Heishui *Sichuan, China* 32°4N 103°2E **116 A4**
Hejaz = Ḥijāz *Si. Arabia* 24°0N 40°0E **128 E3**
Hejian *China* 38°25N 116°5E **114 E9**
Hejiang *China* 28°43N 105°46E **116 C5**
Hejin *China* 35°35N 110°42E **114 G6**
Hejing *China* 42°18N 86°22E **109 D11**
Hekimhan *Turkey* 38°50N 37°55E **104 C7**
Hekla *Iceland* 63°56N 19°35W **60 E4**
Hekou *Gansu, China* 36°10N 103°26E **114 F2**
Hekou *Guangdong,
 China* 23°13N 112°45E **117 F9**
Hekou *Yunnan, China* 22°30N 103°59E **116 F4**
Hel *Poland* 54°37N 18°47E **82 D5**
Helagsfjället *Sweden* 62°54N 12°25E **62 B6**
Helan Shan *China* 38°30N 105°55E **114 E3**
Helechosa de los Montes
 Spain 39°22N 4°53W **89 F6**
Helen Atoll *Palau* 2°40N 132°0E **119 D8**
Helena *U.S.A.* 34°32N 90°36W **177 D9**
Helena *Mont., U.S.A.* 46°36N 112°2W **168 C7**
Helena -West Helena
 U.S.A. 34°32N 90°36W **177 D9**
Helendale *U.S.A.* 34°44N 117°19W **171 L9**
Helensburgh *Australia* 34°11S 151°1E **153 C9**
Helensburgh *U.K.* 56°1N 4°43W **65 E4**
Helensville *N.Z.* 15°43S 145°14E **150 B4**
Helgeland *Norway* 66°7N 13°29E **60 C15**
Helgoland *Germany* 54°10N 7°53E **76 A3**
Heligoland = Helgoland
 Germany 54°10N 7°53E **76 A3**
Heligoland B. = Deutsche Bucht
 Germany 54°15N 8°0E **76 A4**
Heliopolis = Masr el Gedida
 Egypt 30°5N 31°21E **137 E7**
Hell Hole Gorge △
 Australia 25°31S 144°12E **150 D3**
Hella *Iceland* 63°50N 20°24W **60 E3**
Hellendoorn *Neths.* 52°24N 6°27E **69 B6**

Hellespont = Çanakkale Boğazı
 Turkey 40°17N 26°32E **97 F10**
Hellevoetsluis *Neths.* 51°50N 4°8E **69 C4**
Hellín *Spain* 38°31N 1°40W **91 G3**
Hells Canyon △
 U.S.A. 45°30N 117°45W **168 D5**
Hell's Gate △ *Kenya* 0°54S 36°19E **142 C4**
Helmand □ *Afghan.* 31°20N 64°0E **122 D4**
Helmand → *Afghan.* 31°12N 61°34E **122 D2**
Helme → *Germany* 51°20N 11°21E **76 D7**
Helmeringhausen
 Namibia 25°54S 16°57E **144 C2**
Helmond *Neths.* 51°29N 5°41E **69 C5**
Helmsdale *U.K.* 58°7N 3°39W **65 C5**
Helmsdale → *U.K.* 58°8N 3°43W **65 C5**
Helmstedt *Germany* 52°12N 11°0E **76 C7**
Helong *China* 42°40N 129°0E **115 C15**
Helper *U.S.A.* 39°41N 110°51W **168 G8**
Helsingborg *Sweden* 56°3N 12°42E **63 H6**
Helsinge *Denmark* 56°2N 12°12E **63 H6**
Helsingfors = Helsinki
 Finland 60°10N 24°55E **84 B3**
Helsingør *Denmark* 56°2N 12°35E **63 H6**
Helsinki *Finland* 60°10N 24°55E **84 B3**
Helska, Mierzeja *Poland* 54°45N 18°40E **82 D5**
Helston *U.K.* 50°6N 5°17W **67 G2**
Helvellyn *U.K.* 54°32N 3°1W **66 C4**
Helvetinjärvi △ *Finland* 62°5N 23°47E **60 E20**
Ḥelwân *Egypt* 29°50N 31°20E **137 F7**
Hemavati → *India* 12°30N 76°20E **127 H3**
Hemel Hempstead *U.K.* 51°44N 0°28W **67 F7**
Hemet *U.S.A.* 33°45N 116°58W **171 M10**
Hemingford *U.S.A.* 42°19N 103°4W **172 D2**
Hemis △ *India* 34°10N 77°15E **124 B7**
Hemmingford *Canada* 45°3N 73°35W **175 A11**
Hempstead *N.Y.,
 U.S.A.* 40°42N 73°37W **175 F11**
Hempstead *Tex., U.S.A.* 30°6N 96°5W **176 F6**
Hemse *Sweden* 57°15N 18°22E **63 G12**
Hemsön *Sweden* 62°42N 18°5E **62 B12**
Hen and Chickens Is.
 N.Z. 35°58S 174°45E **154 B3**
Henån *Sweden* 58°14N 11°40E **63 F5**
Henan □ *China* 34°0N 114°0E **114 H8**
Henares → *Spain* 40°24N 3°30W **88 E7**
Henashi-Misaki *Japan* 40°37N 139°51E **112 D9**
Hendaye *France* 43°23N 1°47W **72 E2**
Hendek *Turkey* 40°48N 30°44E **104 B4**
Henderson *Argentina* 36°18S 61°43W **190 D3**
Henderson *Ga., U.S.A.* 32°21N 83°47W **178 C6**
Henderson *Ky.,
 U.S.A.* 37°50N 87°35W **172 G10**
Henderson *N.C.,
 U.S.A.* 36°20N 78°25W **177 C15**
Henderson *N.Y.,
 U.S.A.* 43°50N 76°10W **175 C8**
Henderson *Nev.,
 U.S.A.* 36°2N 114°58W **171 J12**
Henderson *Tenn.,
 U.S.A.* 35°26N 88°38W **177 D10**
Henderson *Tex., U.S.A.* 32°9N 94°48W **176 E7**
Henderson I. *Pac. Oc.* 24°22S 128°19W **157 K15**
Hendersonville *N.C.,
 U.S.A.* 35°19N 82°28W **177 C11**
Hendersonville *Tenn.,
 U.S.A.* 36°18N 86°37W **177 C11**
Hendijān *Iran* 30°14N 49°43E **129 D6**
Hendorābī *Iran* 26°40N 53°37E **129 E7**
Hendrik Verwoerd Dam = Gariep Dam
 S. Africa 30°40N 25°40E **144 B5**
Hendrina *S. Africa* 26°9S 29°42E **145 D4**
Hengch'un *Taiwan* 22°0N 120°44E **117 F13**
Hengdaohezi *China* 44°52N 129°0E **115 B15**
Hengduan Shan *China* 28°30N 98°50E **116 C2**
Hengelo *Neths.* 52°16N 6°48E **69 B6**
Henggang *China* 22°39N 114°12E **111 a**
Hengmen *China* 22°33N 113°35E **111 a**
Hengshan *Hunan,
 China* 27°16N 112°45E **117 D9**
Hengshan *Shaanxi,
 China* 37°58N 109°5E **114 F5**
Hengshui *China* 37°41N 115°40E **114 F8**
Hengyang *China* 26°59N 112°22E **117 D9**
Henichesk *Ukraine* 46°12N 34°50E **85 J8**
Hénin-Beaumont *France* 50°25N 2°58E **71 B9**
Henley-on-Thames *U.K.* 51°32N 0°54W **67 F7**
Henlopen, C. *U.S.A.* 38°48N 75°6W **173 F16**
Hennan *Sweden* 47°49N 3°19W **70 E3**
Hennebont *France* 47°49N 3°19W **70 E3**
Hennenman *S. Africa* 27°59S 27°1E **144 C4**
Hennessey *U.S.A.* 36°6N 97°54W **176 C6**
Hennigsdorf *Germany* 52°38N 13°12E **76 C9**
Henri Pittier △
 Venezuela 10°26N 67°37W **183 D6**
Henrietta *N.Y., U.S.A.* 43°4N 77°37W **174 C7**
Henrietta *Tex., U.S.A.* 33°49N 98°12W **176 E5**
Henrietta, Ostrov = Genriyetty,
 Ostrov *Russia* 77°6N 156°30E **107 B16**
Henrietta Maria, C.
 Canada 55°9N 82°20W **164 A3**
Henry *U.S.A.* 41°7N 89°22W **172 E9**
Henry Ice Rise
 Antarctica 80°35S 62°0W **55 E17**
Henry Lawrence I. *India* 12°9N 93°5E **127 H11**
Henryetta *U.S.A.* 35°27N 95°59W **176 D7**
Henryville *Canada* 45°8N 73°11W **175 A11**
Hensall *Canada* 43°26N 81°30W **174 C3**
Henstedt-Ulzburg
 Germany 53°47N 10°0E **76 B6**
Hentiesbaai *Namibia* 22°8S 14°18E **144 B1**
Hentiyn Nuruu
 Mongolia 48°30N 108°30E **111 B10**
Henty *Australia* 35°30S 147°3E **153 C7**
Henzada *Burma* 17°38N 95°26E **123 L19**
Hephaestia *Greece* 39°55N 25°14E **99 B7**
Hephzibah *U.S.A.* 33°18N 82°6W **178 C7**
Heping *China* 24°29N 115°0E **117 E10**
Heppner *U.S.A.* 45°21N 119°33W **168 D4**
Hepu *China* 21°40N 109°12E **116 F7**
Hepworth *Canada* 44°37N 81°9W **174 B3**
Heqing *China* 26°30N 100°12E **116 D3**
Hequ *China* 39°20N 111°15E **114 E6**
Héraðsflói *Iceland* 65°42N 14°12W **60 D6**
Héraðsvötn → *Iceland* 65°45N 19°25W **60 D4**
Heraklion = Iraklio
 Greece 35°20N 25°12E **101 D7**
Herald Cays *Australia* 16°58S 149°9E **150 B4**
Herangi Ra. *N.Z.* 38°33S 174°48E **154 E3**
Herāt *Afghan.* 34°20N 62°7E **108 F6**
Herāt □ *Afghan.* 35°0N 62°0E **122 D2**

Hérault → *France* 43°17N 3°26E **72 E7**
Herault *France* 47°36N 1°8E **70 E8**
Herbert *Canada* 50°30N 107°10W **163 C7**
Herbert → *Australia* 18°31S 146°17E **150 B4**
Herbertabad *India* 11°43N 92°37E **127 J11**
Herberton *Australia* 17°20S 145°25E **150 B4**
Herbertsdale *S. Africa* 34°1S 21°46E **144 E3**
Herbertville *N.Z.* 40°30S 176°33E **154 G5**
Herbignac *France* 47°27N 2°18W **70 E4**
Herborn *Germany* 50°40N 8°18E **76 E4**
Herby *Poland* 50°45N 18°50E **83 H5**
Herceg-Novi *Montenegro* 42°30N 18°33E **96 D2**
Herchmer *Canada* 57°22N 94°10W **163 B10**
Herðubreið *Iceland* 65°11N 16°21W **60 D5**
Hereford *U.K.* 52°4N 2°43W **67 E5**
Hereford *U.S.A.* 34°49N 102°24W **176 D4**
Herefordshire □ *U.K.* 52°8N 2°40W **67 E5**
Herekino *N.Z.* 35°18S 173°11E **154 B2**
Herencia *Spain* 39°21N 3°22W **89 F7**
Herentals *Belgium* 51°12N 4°51E **69 C4**
Herford *Germany* 52°7N 8°39E **76 C4**
Héricourt *France* 47°32N 6°45E **71 E13**
Herington *U.S.A.* 38°40N 96°57W **172 F5**
Heris *Iran* 38°14N 47°6E **105 C12**
Herisau *Switz.* 47°22N 9°17E **77 H5**
Hérisson *France* 46°32N 2°42E **71 F9**
Herkimer *U.S.A.* 43°2N 74°59W **175 D10**
Herlen → *Asia* 48°48N 117°0E **111 B8**
Herlong *U.S.A.* 40°8N 120°8W **170 E6**
Herm *U.K.* 49°30N 2°28W **67 H5**
Hermakivka *Ukraine* 48°42N 26°11E **81 B11**
Hermann *U.S.A.* 38°42N 91°27W **172 F8**
Hermannsburg
 Australia 23°57S 132°45E **148 D5**
Hermannsburg *Germany* 52°50N 10°5E **76 C6**
Hermanus *S. Africa* 34°27S 19°12E **144 D2**
Herment *France* 45°45N 2°24E **72 D6**
Hermidale *Australia* 31°30S 146°42E **153 A7**
Hermiston *U.S.A.* 45°51N 119°17W **168 D4**
Hermitage *N.Z.* 43°44S 170°5E **155 E3**
Hermon *U.S.A.* 44°28N 75°14W **175 B9**
Hermon, Mt. = Shaykh, J. ash
 Lebanon 33°25N 35°50E **130 B4**
Hermosillo *Mexico* 29°10N 111°0W **180 B2**
Hernád → *Hungary* 47°56N 21°8E **80 C6**
Hernandarias
 Paraguay 25°20S 54°40W **191 B5**
Hernandez *U.S.A.* 36°24N 120°46W **170 J6**
Hernando *Argentina* 32°28S 63°40W **190 C3**
Hernando *Fla., U.S.A.* 28°54N 82°23W **179 F7**
Hernando *Miss., U.S.A.* 34°50N 90°0W **177 D10**
Hernando de Magallanes △
 Chile 54°0S 72°40W **192 D2**
Hernani *Spain* 43°16N 1°58W **90 B3**
Herndon *U.S.A.* 40°43N 76°51W **174 F8**
Herne *Germany* 51°32N 7°14E **76 D3**
Herne Bay *U.K.* 51°21N 1°8E **67 F9**
Herning *Denmark* 56°8N 8°58E **63 H2**
Herod *U.S.A.* 34°32N 84°26W **178 D5**
Heroica Caborca = Caborca
 Mexico 30°37N 112°6W **180 A2**
Heroica Nogales = Nogales
 Mexico 31°19N 110°56W **180 A2**
Heron Bay *Canada* 48°40N 86°25W **164 C2**
Heron I. *Australia* 23°27S 151°55E **150 C5**
Herradura, Pta. de la
 Canary Is. 28°26N 14°8W **100 F5**
Herreid *U.S.A.* 45°50N 100°4W **172 C3**
Herrenberg *Germany* 48°35N 8°52E **77 G4**
Herrera *Spain* 37°26N 4°55W **89 H6**
Herrera de Alcántara
 Spain 39°39N 7°25W **89 F3**
Herrera de Pisuerga
 Spain 42°35N 4°20W **88 C6**
Herrera del Duque *Spain* 39°10N 5°3W **89 F5**
Herrestad *Sweden* 58°21N 11°50E **63 F5**
Herrin *U.S.A.* 37°48N 89°2W **172 G9**
Herriot *Canada* 56°22N 101°16W **163 B8**
Herrljunga *Sweden* 58°5N 13°1E **63 F7**
Hersbruck *Germany* 49°30N 11°26E **77 F7**
Herschel I. *Canada* 69°35S 139°5W **54 C1**
Hershey *U.S.A.* 40°17N 76°39W **175 F8**
Herso = Cherso *Greece* 41°5N 22°47E **96 C6**
Herstal *Belgium* 50°40N 5°38E **69 D5**
Hertford *U.K.* 51°48N 0°4W **67 F7**
Hertford *U.S.A.* 36°11N 76°28W **177 C16**
's-Hertogenbosch *Neths.* 51°42N 5°17E **69 C5**
Hertsa *Ukraine* 48°9N 26°15E **81 B11**
Hertzogville *S. Africa* 28°9S 25°30E **144 C4**
Hervás *Spain* 40°16N 5°52W **88 E5**
Hervey B. *Australia* 25°0S 152°52E **150 D5**
Herzberg *Brandenburg,
 Germany* 51°41N 13°14E **76 D9**
Herzberg *Niedersachsen,
 Germany* 51°38N 10°20E **76 D6**
Herzliyya *Israel* 32°10N 34°50E **130 C3**
Herzogenburg *Austria* 48°17N 15°41E **78 D8**
Ḥeşār *Fārs, Iran* 29°52N 50°16E **129 D6**
Ḥeşār *Markazī, Iran* 35°50N 49°12E **129 C6**
Hesdin *France* 50°21N 2°2E **71 B9**
Heshan *Guangdong,
 China* 22°34N 113°4E **117 F9**
Heshan *Guangxi Zhuangzu,
 China* 23°50N 108°53E **116 E7**
Heshui *China* 35°48N 108°0E **114 G5**
Heshun *China* 37°22N 113°32E **114 F7**
Hesperia *U.S.A.* 34°25N 117°18W **171 L9**
Hesse = Hessen □
 Germany 50°30N 9°0E **76 E4**
Hessen □ *Germany* 50°30N 9°0E **76 E4**
Hessenreuther und Manteler
 Wald △ *Germany* 49°45N 12°1E **77 F8**
Hesso *Australia* 32°8S 137°27E **152 B2**
Hestra *Sweden* 57°31N 13°20E **63 H7**
Hetauda *Nepal* 27°25N 85°2E **125 F11**
Hetch Hetchy Aqueduct
 U.S.A. 37°29N 122°19W **170 H5**
Hetta Enontekiö
 Finland 68°23N 23°37E **60 B20**
Hettinger *U.S.A.* 46°0N 102°42W **172 B2**
Hettstedt *Germany* 51°39N 11°31E **76 D7**
Heuksando *S. Korea* 34°40N 125°30E **115 G13**
Heunghae *S. Korea* 36°4N 129°22E **115 E15**
Heuvelton *U.S.A.* 44°37N 75°25W **175 B9**
Heves *Hungary* 47°36N 20°18E **80 C5**
Heves □ *Hungary* 47°50N 20°0E **80 C5**
Hewitt *U.S.A.* 31°28N 97°12W **176 F6**
Hexham *U.K.* 54°58N 2°4W **66 C5**
Hexi *Yunnan, China* 24°9N 102°38E **116 E4**
Hexi *Zhejiang, China* 27°58N 119°38E **117 D12**
Hexigten Qi *China* 43°18N 117°30E **115 C9**

Ḥeydarābād *Iran* 30°33N 55°38E **129 D7**
Heyfield *Australia* 37°59S 146°47E **153 D7**
Heysham *U.K.* 54°3N 2°53W **66 C5**
Heyuan *China* 23°39N 114°40E **117 F10**
Heywood *Australia* 38°8S 141°37E **152 E4**
Heze *China* 35°14N 115°20E **114 G8**
Hezhang *China* 27°8N 104°41E **116 D5**
Hezhou *China* 24°27N 111°30E **117 E8**
Hi Vista *U.S.A.* 34°45N 117°46W **171 L9**
Hialeah *U.S.A.* 25°51N 80°16W **179 K9**
Hiawatha *U.S.A.* 39°51N 95°32W **172 F6**
Hibbing *U.S.A.* 47°25N 92°56W **172 B7**
Hibernia Reef *Australia* 12°0S 123°23E **148 B3**
Hickman *U.S.A.* 36°34N 89°11W **172 G9**
Hickory *U.S.A.* 35°44N 81°21W **177 D14**
Hicks, Pt. *Australia* 37°49S 149°17E **153 D8**
Hicks Bay *N.Z.* 37°34S 178°21E **154 E7**
Hicksville *U.S.A.* 40°46N 73°25W **175 F11**
Hicpochee, L. *U.S.A.* 26°48N 81°9W **179 J8**
Hida *Romania* 47°10N 23°19E **81 C8**
Hida-Gawa → *Japan* 35°26N 137°3E **113 G8**
Hida-Sammyaku
 Japan 36°30N 137°40E **113 F8**
Hidaka *Japan* 42°30N 142°10E **112 C11**
Hidaka-Sammyaku
 Japan 42°35N 142°45E **112 C11**
Hidalgo □ *Mexico* 20°30N 99°0W **181 C5**
Hidalgo del Parral
 Mexico 26°56N 105°40W **180 B3**
Hiddensee *Germany* 54°32N 13°6E **76 A9**
Hieflau *Austria* 47°36N 14°46E **78 D7**
Hiendelaencina *Spain* 41°5N 3°0W **90 D2**
Hierapolis-Pamukkale
 Turkey 37°55N 29°7E **99 D11**
Hierro *Canary Is.* 27°44N 18°0W **100 G1**
Higashiajima-San
 Japan 37°40N 140°10E **112 F10**
Higashiōsaka *Japan* 34°39N 135°37E **113 G7**
Higgins *U.S.A.* 36°7N 100°2W **176 C4**
Higgins Corner *U.S.A.* 39°2N 121°5W **170 F5**
High Bridge *U.S.A.* 40°40N 74°54W **175 F10**
High Desert *U.S.A.* 43°0N 120°20W **168 E3**
High Island Res. *China* 22°21N 114°21E **111 a**
High Level *Canada* 58°31N 117°8W **162 B5**
High Point *U.S.A.* 35°57N 80°0W **177 D15**
High Prairie *Canada* 55°30N 116°30W **162 B5**
High River *Canada* 50°30N 113°50W **162 C6**
High Springs *U.S.A.* 29°50N 82°36W **178 F7**
High Veld *Africa* 27°0S 27°0E **132 J6**
High Wycombe *U.K.* 51°37N 0°45W **67 F7**
Highbank *N.Z.* 43°37S 171°45E **155 D6**
Highland □ *U.K.* 57°17N 4°21W **65 D4**
Highland City *U.S.A.* 27°58N 81°53W **179 H8**
Highland Home *U.S.A.* 31°57N 86°19W **178 D3**
Highland Mills *U.S.A.* 33°17N 84°17W **178 D4**
Highland Park *U.S.A.* 42°11N 87°48W **172 D10**
Highland View *U.S.A.* 29°50N 85°19W **178 F4**
Highmore *U.S.A.* 44°31N 99°27W **172 C4**
Highrock L. *Canada* 55°45N 100°30W **163 B8**
Higüey *Dom. Rep.* 18°37N 68°42W **183 C6**
Hihya *Egypt* 30°40N 31°36E **137 E7**
Hiidenportti △ *Finland* 63°53N 29°0E **60 E23**
Hiiumaa *Estonia* 58°50N 22°45E **84 C2**
Híjar *Spain* 41°10N 0°27W **90 D4**
Ḥijārah, Ṣaḥrā' al *Iraq* 30°25N 44°30E **128 D5**
Ḥijāz *Si. Arabia* 24°0N 40°0E **128 E3**
Hijo = Tagum *Phil.* 7°33N 125°53E **119 C7**
Hikari *Japan* 33°58N 131°58E **113 H5**
Hikkaduwa *Sri Lanka* 6°8N 80°6E **127 L5**
Hikmak, Ras el *Egypt* 31°15N 27°51E **137 A2**
Hiko *U.S.A.* 37°32N 115°14W **170 H11**
Hikone *Japan* 35°15N 136°10E **113 G8**
Hikurangi *Gisborne,
 N.Z.* 37°55S 178°4E **154 E7**
Hikurangi *Northland,
 N.Z.* 35°36S 174°17E **154 B3**
Hiland Park *U.S.A.* 30°12N 85°33W **178 F4**
Hilsbay, Mt. *Barbados* 13°12N 59°35W **183 g**
Hillared *Sweden* 57°37N 13°10E **63 G7**
Hillcrest *Barbados* 13°13N 59°31W **183 g**
Hillegom *Neths.* 52°18N 4°35E **69 B4**
Hillerød *Denmark* 55°56N 12°19E **63 H6**
Hillerstorp *Sweden* 57°20N 13°52E **63 G7**
Hilliard *U.S.A.* 30°41N 81°55W **178 E7**
Hillsboro *Kans., U.S.A.* 38°21N 97°12W **172 F5**
Hillsboro *N. Dak., U.S.A.* 47°24N 97°4W **172 B5**
Hillsboro *Ohio, U.S.A.* 39°12N 83°37W **173 F12**
Hillsboro *Oreg., U.S.A.* 45°31N 122°59W **170 E4**
Hillsboro *Tex., U.S.A.* 32°1N 97°8W **176 E6**
Hillsboro Canal *U.S.A.* 26°30N 80°5W **179 J9**
Hillsboro Grenada 12°28N 61°28W **183 D7**
Hillsborough *U.S.A.* 43°47N 71°54W **175 C13**
Hillsborough Channel
 Australia 20°56S 149°15E **150 b**
Hillsdale *Mich., U.S.A.* 41°56N 84°38W **173 E11**
Hillsport *Canada* 49°27N 85°34W **164 C2**
Hillston *Australia* 33°30S 145°31E **153 B6**
Hilltonia *U.S.A.* 32°53N 81°40W **178 C8**
Hilo *U.S.A.* 19°44N 155°5W **167 M9**
Hilton *U.S.A.* 43°17N 77°48W **174 C7**
Hilton Head Island
 U.S.A. 32°13N 80°45W **178 C9**
Hilvan *Turkey* 37°34N 38°58E **105 D7**
Hilversum *Neths.* 52°14N 5°10E **69 B5**
Himachal Pradesh □
 India 31°30N 77°0E **124 D7**
Himalaya *Asia* 29°0N 84°0E **125 E11**
Himanka *Finland* 64°4N 23°39E **60 E20**
Himarë *Albania* 40°8N 19°43E **96 F3**
Himatnagar *India* 23°37N 72°57E **124 H8**
Himeji *Japan* 34°50N 134°40E **113 G7**
Himi *Japan* 36°50N 136°55E **113 F8**
Himmerland *Denmark* 56°58N 9°40E **63 H3**
Ḥimṣ *Syria* 34°40N 36°45E **130 A5**
Ḥimṣ □ *Syria* 34°30N 37°0E **130 A6**
Hin Khom, Laem *Thailand* 9°25N 99°56E **121 b**

Hinche *Haiti* 19°9N 72°1W **183** C5
Hinchinbrook I.
  Australia 18°20S 146°15E **150** B4
Hinchinbrook Island △
  Australia 18°14S 146°6E **150** B4
Hinckley *U.K.* 52°33N 1°22W **67** E6
Hinckley *U.S.A.* 46°1N 92°56W **172** B7
Hindaun *India* 26°44N 77°5E **124** F7
Hindol *India* 20°40N 85°10E **126** D7
Hinds *N.Z.* 43°59S 171°36E **155** D6
Hindsholm *Denmark* 55°30N 10°40E **63** A4
Hindmarsh, L. *Australia* 36°5S 141°55E **152** D4
Hindu Bagh *Pakistan* 30°56N 67°50E **124** D2
Hindu Kush *Asia* 36°0N 71°0E **109** E8
Hindupur *India* 13°49N 77°32E **127** H3
Hines Creek *Canada* 56°20N 118°40W **162** B5
Hinesville *U.S.A.* 31°51N 81°36W **178** D8
Hinganghat *India* 20°30N 78°52E **126** D4
Hingham *U.S.A.* 48°33N 110°25W **168** B8
Hingir *India* 21°57N 83°41E **125** J10
Hingoli *India* 19°41N 77°15E **126** E3
Hinis *Turkey* 39°22N 41°43E **105** C9
Hinna = Imi *Ethiopia* 6°28N 42°10E **131** F3
Hinna *Nigeria* 10°25N 11°35E **139** C7
Hinnerup *Denmark* 56°16N 10°4E **63** H4
Hinnøya *Norway* 68°35N 15°50E **60** B16
Hinojosa del Duque *Spain* 38°30N 5°9W **89** G5
Hinsdale *U.S.A.* 42°47N 72°29W **175** D12
Hinterrhein → *Switz.* 46°40N 9°25E **77** J5
Hinthada = Henzada
  Burma 17°38N 95°26E **123** L19
Hinton *Canada* 53°26N 117°34W **162** C5
Hinton *U.S.A.* 37°40N 80°54W **173** G13
Hios = Chios *Greece* 38°27N 26°9E **99** C8
Hirado *Japan* 33°22N 129°33E **113** H4
Hirakud Dam *India* 21°32N 83°45E **126** D6
Hiran → *India* 23°6N 79°21E **125** H8
Hirapur *India* 24°22N 79°13E **125** G8
Hirara = Miyakojima
  Japan 24°48N 125°17E **113** M2
Hiratsuka *Japan* 35°19N 139°21E **113** G9
Hirekerur *India* 14°28N 75°23E **127** G2
Hirfanlı Baraji *Turkey* 39°18N 33°31E **104** C5
Hirhafok *Algeria* 23°49N 5°45E **136** D5
Hiroo *Japan* 42°17N 143°19E **112** C11
Hirosaki *Japan* 40°34N 140°28E **112** D10
Hiroshima *Japan* 34°24N 132°30E **113** G6
Hiroshima □ *Japan* 34°50N 133°0E **113** G6
Hirson *France* 49°55N 4°4E **71** C11
Hirtshals *Denmark* 57°36N 9°57E **63** G3
Hisar *India* 29°12N 75°45E **124** E6
Hisarcık *Turkey* 39°15N 29°14E **99** B11
Hisaria *Bulgaria* 42°30N 24°44E **97** D8
Hisb, Sha'ib → = Ḥasb, W. →
  Iraq 31°45N 44°17E **128** D5
Ḥismá *Si. Arabia* 28°30N 36°0E **128** D3
Hispaniola *W. Indies* 19°0N 71°0W **183** C5
Hīt *Iraq* 33°38N 42°49E **105** F10
Hita *Japan* 33°20N 130°58E **113** H5
Hitachi *Japan* 36°36N 140°39E **113** F10
Hitan, W. el *Egypt* 29°19N 30°10E **137** F7
Hitchin *U.K.* 51°58N 0°16W **67** F7
Hitiaa *Tahiti* 17°36S 149°18W **155** b
Hitoyoshi *Japan* 32°13N 130°45E **113** H5
Hitra *Norway* 63°30N 8°45E **60** E13
Hitzacker *Germany* 53°9N 11°2E **76** B7
Hiva Oa
  French Polynesia 9°45S 139°0W **157** H14
Hixon *Canada* 53°25N 122°35W **162** C4
Ḥiyyon, N. → *Israel* 30°25N 35°10E **130** E4
Hjalmar L. *Canada* 61°33N 109°25W **163** A7
Hjälmaren *Sweden* 59°18N 15°40E **62** E9
Hjältevad *Sweden* 57°38N 15°20E **63** G9
Hjo *Sweden* 58°22N 14°17E **63** F8
Hjørring *Denmark* 57°29N 9°59E **63** G3
Hjort Trench *S. Ocean* 58°0S 157°30E **55** B10
Hjortkvarn *Sweden* 58°54N 15°26E **63** F9
Hkakabo Razi *Burma* 28°25N 97°23E **116** C1
Hkamti *Burma* 26°0N 95°39E **123** G19
Hlinsko *Czech Rep.* 49°45N 15°54E **78** B8
Hlobane *S. Africa* 27°42S 31°0E **145** C5
Hlohovec *Slovak Rep.* 48°26N 17°49E **79** C10
Hluchín *Czech Rep.* 49°54N 18°11E **79** B11
Hluhluwe *S. Africa* 28°1S 32°15E **145** D5
Hluhluwe → *S. Africa* 22°10S 32°45E **145** D5
Hlukhiv *Ukraine* 51°40N 33°58E **85** G7
Hlyboka *Ukraine* 48°5N 25°56E **81** B10
Hlybokaye *Belarus* 55°10N 27°45E **84** E4
Hnúšťa *Slovak Rep.* 48°35N 19°58E **79** C12
Ho *Ghana* 6°37N 0°27E **139** D5
Ho Chi Minh City = Thanh Pho
  Ho Chi Minh
  Vietnam 10°58N 106°40E **121** G6
Ho Hoa Binh *Vietnam* 20°50N 105°0E **116** G5
Ho Thac Ba *Vietnam* 21°42N 105°0E **116** A5
Ho Thuong *Vietnam* 19°32N 105°48E **120** C5
Hoa Binh *Vietnam* 20°50N 105°20E **116** G5
Hoa Hiep *Vietnam* 11°34N 105°51E **121** G5
Hoai Nhon *Vietnam* 14°28N 109°1E **120** E7
Hoang Lien △ *Vietnam* 21°30N 105°32E **120** B5
Hoang Lien Son *Vietnam* 22°20N 104°0E **116** F4
Hoang Sa, Dao = Paracel Is.
  S. China Sea 15°50N 112°0E **118** A4
Hoanib → *Namibia* 19°27S 12°46E **144** A2
Hoare B. *Canada* 65°17N 62°30W **161** D19
Hoarusib → *Namibia* 19°3S 12°36E **144** A2
Hobart *Australia* 42°50S 147°21E **151** G4
Hobart *U.S.A.* 35°1N 99°6W **180** B3
Hobbs *U.S.A.* 32°42N 103°8W **169** K12
Hobbs Coast *Antarctica* 74°50S 131°0W **55** D14
Hobe Sound *U.S.A.* 27°4N 80°8W **179** H9
Hoboken *Ga., U.S.A.* 31°11N 82°8W **178** D7
Hoboken *N.J., U.S.A.* 40°44N 74°3W **175** F10
Hobro *Denmark* 56°39N 9°46E **63** H3
Hoburgen *Sweden* 56°55N 18°7E **63** H11
Hobyo *Somalia* 5°25N 48°30E **131** F4
Hocalar *Turkey* 38°36N 30°10E **99** C11
Hochfeld *Namibia* 21°28S 17°58E **144** B2
Hochharz △ *Germany* 51°48N 10°38E **76** D6
Hochschwab *Austria* 47°35N 15°7E **78** D8
Höchstadt *Germany* 49°42N 10°47E **77** F6
Hochtaunus △ *Germany* 50°19N 8°32E **77** F4
Hockenheim *Germany* 49°19N 8°33E **77** F4
Hodaka-Dake *Japan* 36°17N 137°39E **113** F8
Hodeida = Al Ḥudaydah
  Yemen 14°50N 43°0E **131** E3
Hodgeville *Canada* 50°7N 106°58W **163** C7
Hodgson *Canada* 51°13N 97°36W **163** C9
Hodh El Gharbi □
  Mauritania 16°30N 10°0W **138** B3

Hódmezővásárhely
  Hungary 46°28N 20°22E **80** D5
Hodna, Chott el *Algeria* 35°26N 4°43E **136** A4
Hodonín *Czech Rep.* 48°50N 17°10E **79** C10
Hœdic, Î. de *France* 47°20N 2°53W **70** E4
Hoek van Holland *Neths.* 52°0N 4°7E **69** C4
Hoengseong *S. Korea* 37°29N 127°59E **115** F14
Hoeryong *N. Korea* 42°30N 129°45E **115** C15
Hoeyang *N. Korea* 38°43N 127°36E **115** E14
Hof *Germany* 50°19N 11°55E **77** E7
Hofgeismar *Germany* 51°29N 9°23E **76** D5
Hofheim *Germany* 50°5N 8°26E **77** E4
Hofmeyr *S. Africa* 31°39S 25°50E **144** D4
Höfn *Iceland* 64°15N 15°13W **60** D6
Hofors *Sweden* 60°31N 16°15E **62** D10
Hofsjökull *Iceland* 64°49N 18°48W **60** D4
Höfu *Japan* 34°3N 131°34E **113** G5
Hogan Group *Australia* 39°13S 147°1E **151** F4
Höganäs *Sweden* 56°12N 12°33E **63** H6
Hogansville *U.S.A.* 33°10N 84°55W **178** B5
Hogarth, Mt. *Australia* 21°48S 136°58E **150** C2
Hoge Kempen △ *Belgium* 51°6N 5°35E **69** C5
Hoge Veluwe △ *Neths.* 52°5N 5°46E **69** B5
Hogenakal Falls *India* 12°6N 77°50E **127** H3
Hoggar = Ahaggar
  Algeria 23°0N 6°30E **136** D5
Högsäter *Sweden* 58°38N 12°5E **63** F6
Högsby *Sweden* 57°10N 16°1E **63** G10
Högsjö *Sweden* 59°4N 15°44E **62** E9
Hogsty Reef *Bahamas* 21°41N 73°48W **183** B5
Hoh → *U.S.A.* 47°45N 124°29W **170** C2
Hoh Xil Shan *China* 36°30N 89°0E **110** D6
Hohd ech Chargui □
  Mauritania 19°0N 7°15W **138** B3
Hohe Acht *Germany* 50°22N 7°0E **77** E3
Hohe Tauern *Austria* 47°11N 12°40E **78** C5
Hohe Tauern △ *Austria* 47°5N 12°30E **78** C5
Hohenau *Austria* 48°36N 16°55E **79** C9
Hohenems *Austria* 47°22N 9°42E **78** D2
Hohenloher Ebene
  Germany 49°14N 9°36E **77** F5
Hohenwald *U.S.A.* 35°33N 87°33W **177** D11
Hohenwestedt *Germany* 54°5N 9°40E **76** A5
Hoher Rhön △
  Germany 50°24N 9°58E **76** E5
Hoher Vogelsberg △
  Germany 51°45N 9°35E **76** D5
Hohes Venn *Belgium* 50°30N 6°5E **69** D6
Hohes Venn-Eifel △
  Europe 50°30N 6°10E **76** E2
Hohhot *China* 40°52N 111°40E **114** D6
Hohoe *Ghana* 7°8N 0°32E **139** D5
Hoi An *Vietnam* 15°30N 108°19E **120** E7
Hoi Xuan *Vietnam* 20°25N 105°9E **116** G5
Hoisington *U.S.A.* 38°31N 98°47W **172** F4
Hojambaz *Turkmenistan* 38°7N 65°0E **108** E6
Højer *Denmark* 54°58N 8°42E **63** K2
Hōjō *Japan* 33°58N 132°46E **113** H6
Hok *Sweden* 57°31N 14°16E **63** G8
Hökensås *Sweden* 58°0N 14°5E **63** F8
Hökerum *Sweden* 57°51N 13°16E **63** G7
Hokianga Harbour
  N.Z. 35°31S 173°22E **154** B2
Hokitika *N.Z.* 42°42S 171°0E **155** D3
Hokkaidō □ *Japan* 43°30N 143°0E **112** C11
Hokuto *Japan* 41°49N 140°39E **112** D10
Hola *Kenya* 1°29S 40°2E **142** B4
Hola Prystan *Ukraine* 46°29N 32°32E **85** J7
Holakas *Greece* 35°57N 27°53E **100** D9
Holalkere *India* 14°2N 76°11E **127** G3
Holašovice *Czech Rep.* 48°57N 14°15E **78** C7
Holbæk *Denmark* 55°43N 11°43E **63** J5
Holbrook *Australia* 35°42S 147°18E **153** C4
Holbrook *U.S.A.* 34°54N 110°10W **169** J8
Holden *U.S.A.* 39°6N 112°16W **168** G7
Holdenville *U.S.A.* 35°5N 96°24W **176** D6
Holdich *Argentina* 45°57S 68°13W **192** C3
Holdrege *U.S.A.* 40°26N 99°23W **172** E4
Hole-Narsipur *India* 12°48N 76°16E **127** H3
Holešov *Czech Rep.* 49°20N 17°35E **79** B10
Holetown *Barbados* 13°11N 59°38W **183** g
Holguín *Cuba* 20°50N 76°20W **182** B4
Holíč *Slovak Rep.* 48°49N 17°10E **79** C9
Holice *Czech Rep.* 50°5N 16°0E **78** A8
Holiday *U.S.A.* 28°11N 82°44W **179** G7
Höljes *Sweden* 60°50N 12°35E **62** D6
Hollabrunn *Austria* 48°34N 16°5E **78** C9
Hollams Bird I. *Namibia* 24°40S 14°30E **144** B1
Holland = Netherlands ■
  Europe 52°0N 5°30E **69** C5
Holland *Mich., U.S.A.* 42°47N 86°7W **172** D10
Holland *N.Y., U.S.A.* 42°38N 78°32W **174** D6
Holland Centre *Canada* 44°23N 80°47W **174** B4
Hollandale *U.S.A.* 33°10N 90°51W **177** D9
Holley *U.S.A.* 43°14N 78°2W **174** C6
Hollfeld *Germany* 49°56N 11°18E **77** F7
Hollidaysburg *U.S.A.* 40°26N 78°24W **174** F6
Hollis *U.S.A.* 34°41N 99°55W **176** D5
Hollister *Calif., U.S.A.* 36°51N 121°24W **170** J5
Hollister *Idaho, U.S.A.* 42°21N 114°35W **168** E6
Höllviken = Höllviken
  Sweden 55°26N 12°58E **63** J6
Höllviksnäs = Höllviken
  Sweden 55°26N 12°58E **63** J6
Holly Hill *Fla., U.S.A.* 29°16N 81°3W **179** F9
Holly Hill *S.C., U.S.A.* 33°19N 80°25W **178** B9
Holly Springs *Ga.,*
  U.S.A. 34°10N 84°30W **178** A5
Holly Springs *Miss.,*
  U.S.A. 34°46N 89°27W **177** D10
Hollywood *Ireland* 53°6N 6°35W **64** B6
Hollywood *U.S.A.* 26°0N 80°8W **179** J9
Holman *Canada* 70°44N 117°44W **160** C8
Hólmavík *Iceland* 65°42N 21°40W **60** D3
Holmen *U.S.A.* 43°58N 91°15W **172** D8
Holmes Beach *U.S.A.* 27°31N 82°43W **179** H7
Holmes Cr. → *U.S.A.* 30°30N 85°50W **178** E4
Holmes Reefs *Australia* 16°27S 148°0E **150** B4
Holmsjö *Sweden* 56°23N 15°20E **63** H9
Holmsjön *Västernorrland,*
  Sweden 62°41N 16°33E **62** B10
Holmsjön *Västernorrland,*
  Sweden 62°26N 15°20E **62** B9
Holmsland Klit *Denmark* 56°0N 8°5E **63** H2
Holmsund *Sweden* 63°41N 20°20E **60** E19
Holod *Romania* 46°49N 22°8E **80** C5
Holon *Israel* 32°2N 34°46E **130** C3
Holopaw *U.S.A.* 28°8N 81°5W **179** G8
Holovne *Ukraine* 51°20N 24°5E **83** G11
Holoybyntsi *Ukraine* 48°5N 25°56E **81** B11

Holroyd → *Australia* 14°10S 141°36E **150** A3
Holstebro *Denmark* 56°22N 8°37E **63** H2
Holsteinische Schweiz △
  Germany 54°8N 10°30E **76** A6
Holsteinsborg = Sisimiut
  Greenland 66°40N 53°30W **57** D5
Holsworthy *U.K.* 50°48N 4°22W **67** G3
Holt *U.S.A.* 30°43N 86°45W **179** E3
Holton *Canada* 54°31N 57°12W **165** B8
Holton *U.S.A.* 39°28N 95°44W **172** F6
Holtville *U.S.A.* 32°49N 115°23W **171** N11
Holwerd *Neths.* 53°22N 5°54E **69** A5
Holy Cross *U.S.A.* 62°12N 159°46W **166** C8
Holy I. *Anglesey, U.K.* 53°17N 4°37W **66** D3
Holy I. *Northumberland,*
  U.K. 55°40N 1°47W **67** F6
Holyhead *U.K.* 53°18N 4°38W **66** D3
Holyoke *Colo., U.S.A.* 40°35N 102°18W **168** F12
Holyoke *Mass., U.S.A.* 42°12N 72°37W **175** D12
Holyrood *Canada* 47°27N 53°8W **165** C9
Holzkirchen *Germany* 47°52N 11°42E **77** H7
Holzminden *Germany* 51°50N 9°28E **76** D5
Homa Bay *Kenya* 0°36S 34°30E **142** C3
Homalin *Burma* 24°55N 95°0E **123** G19
Homand *Iran* 32°28N 59°37E **129** C8
Homathko → *Canada* 51°0N 124°56W **162** C4
Homberg *Germany* 51°2N 9°25E **76** D5
Hombori *Mali* 15°20N 1°38W **138** B5
Hombori Tondo *Mali* 15°16N 1°40W **139** B4
Homburg *Germany* 49°19N 7°18E **77** F3
Home B. *Canada* 68°40N 67°10W **161** D18
Home Hill *Australia* 19°43S 147°25E **150** B4
Homedale *U.S.A.* 43°37N 116°56W **168** E5
Homeland *U.S.A.* 30°51N 82°1W **178** F7
Homer *Alaska, U.S.A.* 59°39N 151°33W **166** D1
Homer *La., U.S.A.* 32°48N 93°4W **176** E7
Homer *N.Y., U.S.A.* 42°38N 76°10W **175** D8
Homer City *U.S.A.* 40°32N 79°10W **174** F5
Homert △ *Germany* 51°15N 8°0E **76** D4
Homerville *U.S.A.* 31°2N 82°45W **178** D7
Homestead *Australia* 20°20S 145°40E **150** C4
Homestead *U.S.A.* 25°28N 80°29W **179** K9
Homestead △ *U.S.A.* 40°17N 96°50W **172** E5
Homnabad *India* 17°45N 77°11E **126** F3
Homoine *Mozam.* 23°55S 35°8E **145** B6
Homoljske Planina
  Serbia 44°10N 21°45E **96** B5
Homorod *Romania* 46°5N 25°15E **81** D10
Homosassa Springs
  U.S.A. 28°48N 82°35W **179** G7
Homs = Ḥimş *Syria* 34°40N 36°45E **130** A5
Homyel *Belarus* 52°28N 31°0E **75** D16
Homyel □ *Belarus* 52°40N 30°10E **85** F6
Hon Chong *Vietnam* 10°25N 104°30E **121** G5
Hon Hai *Vietnam* 10°0N 109°0E **121** H7
Hon Me *Vietnam* 19°23N 105°56E **120** C5
Honan = Henan □
  China 34°0N 114°0E **114** H8
Honavar *India* 14°17N 74°27E **127** G2
Honaz *Turkey* 37°46N 29°18E **99** D11
Honbetsu *Japan* 43°7N 143°37E **112** C11
Honcut *U.S.A.* 39°20N 121°32W **170** F5
Hondarribia *Spain* 43°22N 1°47W **90** B3
Hondeklipbaai *S. Africa* 30°19S 17°17E **144** D2
Hondo *Japan* 32°27N 130°12E **113** H5
Hondo *U.S.A.* 29°21N 99°9W **176** G5
Hondo, Río → *Belize* 18°25N 88°21W **181** D7
Honduras ■
  Cent. Amer. 14°40N 86°30W **182** D2
Honduras, G. de
  Caribbean 16°50N 87°0W **182** C2
Hønefoss *Norway* 60°10N 10°18E **61** F14
Honesdale *U.S.A.* 41°34N 75°16W **175** E9
Honey Harbour
  Canada 44°52N 79°49W **174** B5
Honey L. *U.S.A.* 40°15N 120°19W **170** E6
Honfleur *France* 49°25N 0°13E **70** C7
Høng *Denmark* 55°31N 11°18E **63** J5
Hong → *Vietnam* 20°16N 106°34E **120** B5
Hong Gai *Vietnam* 20°57N 107°5E **116** G6
Hong He → *China* .32°25N 115°35E **117** A10
Hong Hu *China* 29°54N 113°24E **117** C9
Hong Kong □ *China* 22°11N 114°14E **111** a
Hong Kong I. *China* 22°16N 114°12E **111** a
Hong Kong Int. ✈ (HKG)
  China 22°19N 113°57E **111** a
Hong'an *China* 31°20N 114°40E **117** B10
Hongcheon *S. Korea* 37°44N 127°53E **115** F14
Honghai Wan *China* 22°40N 115°0E **117** F10
Honghe *China* 23°25N 102°25E **116** F4
Honghu *China* 29°50N 113°30E **117** C9
Hongjiang *China* 27°7N 109°59E **116** D7
Hongliu He → *China* 38°0N 109°50E **114** F5
Hongor *Mongolia* 45°45N 112°50E **114** B7
Hongseong *S. Korea* 36°37N 126°38E **115** F14
Hongshan *China* 36°38N 117°58E **115** F9
Hongshui He →
  China 23°48N 109°30E **116** F7
Hongtong *China* 36°16N 111°40E **114** F6
Honguedo, Détroit d'
  Canada 49°15N 64°0W **165** C7
Hongwon *N. Korea* 40°0N 127°56E **115** E14
Hongya *China* 29°57N 103°22E **116** C4
Hongyuan *China* 32°10N 102°40E **116** A4
Hongze Hu *China* 33°15N 118°35E **115** H10
Honiara *Solomon Is.* 9°27S 159°57E **147** B8
Honiton *U.K.* 50°47N 3°11W **67** G4
Honjō = Yurihonjō
  Japan 39°23N 140°3E **112** E10
Honkorâb, Ras *Egypt* 24°35N 35°10E **137** C4
Honnali *India* 14°15N 75°40E **127** G2
Honningsvåg *Norway* 70°59N 25°59E **60** A21
Hönö *Sweden* 57°42N 11°39E **63** G5
Honolulu *U.S.A.* 21°19N 157°52W **167** L8
Honshū *Japan* 36°0N 138°0E **113** F9
Hontoria del Pinar *Spain* 41°50N 3°10W **90** D1
Hood, Mt. *U.S.A.* 45°23N 121°42W **168** D3
Hood, Pt. *Australia* 34°23S 119°34W **149** F2
Hood River *U.S.A.* 45°43N 121°31W **168** D3
Hoodsport *U.S.A.* 47°24N 123°9W **170** C3
Hooge *Germany* 54°34N 8°33E **76** A4
Hoogeveen *Neths.* 52°44N 6°28E **69** B6
Hoogezand-Sappemeer
  Neths. 53°9N 6°45E **69** A6
Hooghly = Hugli →
  India 21°56N 88°4E **125** J13
Hooghly-Chinsura = Chunchura
  India 22°53N 88°27E **125** H13
Hook Hd. *Ireland* 52°7N 6°56W **64** D5
Hook I. *Australia* 20°4S 149°0E **150** b

Hook of Holland = Hoek van
  Holland *Neths.* 52°0N 4°7E **69** C4
Hooker *U.S.A.* 36°52N 101°13W **176** C4
Hooker Creek = Lajamanu
  Australia 18°23S 130°38E **148** C5
Hooker Creek ○
  Australia 18°6S 130°23E **148** C5
Hoonah *U.S.A.* 58°7N 135°27W **162** B1
Hooper Bay *U.S.A.* 61°32N 166°6W **166** D5
Hoopeston *U.S.A.* 40°28N 87°40W **172** E10
Hoopstad *S. Africa* 27°50S 25°55E **144** C4
Höör *Sweden* 55°56N 13°33E **63** J7
Hoorn *Neths.* 52°38N 5°4E **69** B5
Hoover *U.S.A.* 33°24N 86°49W **177** E11
Hoover Dam *U.S.A.* 36°1N 114°44W **171** K12
Hooversville *U.S.A.* 40°9N 78°55W **174** F6
Hop Bottom *U.S.A.* 41°42N 75°46W **175** E9
Hopa *Turkey* 41°28N 41°30E **105** B9
Hope *Canada* 49°25N 121°25W **162** D4
Hope *Ariz., U.S.A.* 33°43N 113°42W **171** M13
Hope *Ark., U.S.A.* 33°40N 93°36W **176** E8
Hope, L. *S. Austral.,*
  Australia 28°24S 139°18E **151** D2
Hope, L. *W. Austral.,*
  Australia 32°35S 120°15E **149** F3
Hope, Pt. *U.S.A.* 68°21N 166°47W **158** C3
Hope I. *Canada* 44°55N 80°11W **174** B4
Hope Town *Bahamas* 26°35N 76°57W **182** A4
Hope Vale ○ *Australia* 15°16S 145°20E **150** B4
Hope Vale *Australia* 15°8S 145°0E **150** B4
Hopedale *Canada* 55°28N 60°13W **165** A7
Hopedale *U.S.A.* 42°8N 71°33W **175** D13
Hopefield *S. Africa* 33°3S 18°22E **144** D2
Hopei = Hebei □ *China* 39°0N 116°0E **114** E9
Hopelchén *Mexico* 19°46N 89°51W **181** D7
Hopetoun *Vic.,*
  Australia 35°42S 142°22E **152** C5
Hopetoun *W. Austral.,*
  Australia 33°57S 120°7E **149** F3
Hopetown *S. Africa* 29°34S 24°3E **144** C3
Hopewell *U.S.A.* 37°18N 77°17W **173** G15
Hopfgarten *Austria* 47°27N 12°10E **78** D5
Hopkins, L. *Australia* 24°15S 128°35E **148** D4
Hopkinsville *U.S.A.* 36°52N 87°29W **172** G10
Hopland *U.S.A.* 38°58N 123°7W **170** G3
Hora Hoverla *Ukraine* 48°7N 24°41E **81** B9
Horana *Sri Lanka* 6°43N 80°4E **127** L5
Horasan *Turkey* 40°3N 42°11E **105** B10
Horažďovice *Czech Rep.* 49°19N 13°42E **78** B6
Horb *Germany* 48°26N 8°47E **77** G4
Hörby *Sweden* 55°51N 13°40E **63** J7
Horcajo de Santiago *Spain* 39°50N 3°1W **90** F1
Hordern Hills *Australia* 21°35S 130°0E **148** D5
Horezu *Romania* 45°6N 24°0E **81** E8
Horgen *Switz.* 47°15N 8°35E **77** H4
Horgoš *Serbia* 46°10N 20°0E **80** D4
Hořice *Czech Rep.* 50°21N 15°39E **78** A8
Horinchove *Ukraine* 48°16N 23°26E **81** B8
Horinger *China* 40°28N 111°48E **114** D6
Horizontina *Brazil* 27°37S 54°19W **191** B5
Horki *Belarus* 54°17N 30°59E **84** E6
Horlick Mts. *Antarctica* 84°0S 102°0W **55** E15
Horlivka *Ukraine* 48°19N 38°5E **85** H10
Hormak *Iran* 29°58N 60°51E **129** D9
Hormoz *Iran* 27°35N 55°0E **129** E7
Hormoz, Jaz.-ye *Iran* 27°8N 56°28E **129** E8
Hormozgān □ *Iran* 27°30N 56°0E **129** E8
Hormuz, Kūh-e *Iran* 27°27N 55°10E **129** E7
Hormuz, Str. of *The Gulf* 26°30N 56°30E **129** E8
Horn *Austria* 48°39N 15°40E **78** C8
Horn *Sweden* 57°54N 15°51E **63** G9
Horn → *Canada* 61°30N 118°1W **162** A5
Horn, Cape = Hornos, C. de
  Chile 55°50S 67°30W **192** H3
Horn Head *Ireland* 55°14N 8°0W **64** A3
Horn I. *Australia* 10°37S 142°17E **150** A3
Horn Plateau *Canada* 62°15N 119°15W **162** A5
Hornavan *Sweden* 66°15N 17°30E **60** C17
Hornbeck *U.S.A.* 31°20N 93°24W **176** F8
Hornbrook *U.S.A.* 41°55N 122°33W **168** F2
Hornby *N.Z.* 43°33S 172°33E **155** D7
Horncastle *U.K.* 53°13N 0°7W **66** D7
Horndal *Sweden* 60°18N 16°23E **62** D10
Hornell *U.S.A.* 42°20N 77°40W **174** D7
Hornell L. *Canada* 62°20N 119°25W **162** A5
Hornepayne *Canada* 49°14N 84°48W **164** D3
Horní Planá *Czech Rep.* 48°46N 14°2E **78** C7
Hornings Mills *Canada* 44°9N 80°12W **174** B4
Hornitos *U.S.A.* 37°30N 120°14W **170** H6
Hornopirén △ *Chile* 41°58S 72°17W **192** E2
Hornos, C. de *Chile* 55°50S 67°30W **192** H3
Hornoy-le-Bourg *France* 49°50N 1°54E **71** C8
Hornsby *Australia* 33°42S 151°2E **153** B9
Hornsea *U.K.* 53°55N 0°11W **66** D7
Hornslandet *Sweden* 61°35N 17°37E **62** C11
Hörnum *Germany* 54°45N 8°17E **76** A4
Horobetsu = Noboribetsu
  Japan 42°24N 141°6E **112** C10
Horodenka *Ukraine* 48°41N 25°29E **81** B10
Horodnya *Ukraine* 51°55N 31°33E **85** G6
Horodok *Khmelnytskyy,*
  Ukraine 49°10N 26°34E **75** D14
Horodok *Lviv, Ukraine* 49°46N 23°32E **75** D12
Horodyshche *Ukraine* 49°17N 31°27E **85** H6
Horokhiv *Ukraine* 50°30N 24°45E **75** C13
Horovice *Czech Rep.* 49°48N 13°53E **78** B6
Horqin Youyi Qianqi
  China 46°5N 122°3E **115** A12
Horqin Zuoyi Zhongqi
  China 44°8N 123°18E **115** B12
Horqueta *Paraguay* 23°15S 56°55W **190** A4
Horred *Sweden* 57°22N 12°28E **63** G6
Høyanger *Norway* 61°13N 6°4E **60** F12
Horse → *U.S.A.* 41°57N 103°58W **168** E12
Horse I. *Canada* 53°20N 99°6W **163** C9
Horsefly L. *Canada* 52°25N 121°0W **162** C4
Horseheads *U.S.A.* 42°10N 76°49W **174** D8
Horsens *Denmark* 55°52N 9°51E **63** H3
Horseshoe Bend
  U.S.A. 32°59N 85°49W **178** B5
Horseshoe Lake
  Canada 45°17N 79°51W **174** A5
Horsham *Australia* 36°44S 142°13E **152** D5
Horsham *U.K.* 51°4N 0°20W **67** F7
Horšovský Týn
  Czech Rep. 49°31N 12°58E **78** B5
Horta *Azores* 38°32N 28°38W **134** a
Horten *Norway* 59°25N 10°32E **61** G14

Hortense *U.S.A.* 31°20N 81°57W **178** D8
Horti *India* 17°7N 75°47E **126** F2
Hortobágy → *Hungary* 47°30N 21°6E **80** C6
Hortobágyi △ *Hungary* 47°36N 21°10E **80** C6
Horton *U.S.A.* 39°40N 95°32W **172** F6
Horton → *Canada* 69°56N 126°52W **160** D6
Horwood L. *Canada* 48°5N 82°20W **164** C3
Hosaina = Hosapete
  India 15°15N 76°20E **127** G3
Hosdrug = Kanhangad
  India 12°21N 74°58E **127** H2
Hoshangabad *India* 22°45N 77°45E **124** H6
Hoshiarpur *India* 31°30N 75°58E **124** D5
Hoskote *India* 13°4N 77°48E **127** H3
Hospet *India* 15°15N 76°20E **127** G3
Hossegor *France* 43°39N 1°25W **72** E2
Hoste, I. *Chile* 55°0S 69°0W **192** H3
Hostens *France* 44°30N 0°40W **72** D3
Hosur *India* 12°43N 77°49E **127** H3
Hot *Thailand* 18°8N 98°29E **120** C2
Hot Creek Range
  U.S.A. 38°40N 116°20W **168** G5
Hot Springs *Ark., U.S.A.* 34°31N 93°3W **176** D8
Hot Springs *S. Dak.,*
  U.S.A. 43°26N 103°29W **172** D2
Hot Springs △ *U.S.A.* 34°31N 93°3W **176** D8
Hotagen *Sweden* 63°59N 14°12E **60** E16
Hotan *China* 37°25N 79°55E **110** D3
Hotan He → *China* 40°22N 80°56E **110** D4
Hotazel *S. Africa* 27°17S 22°58E **144** C3
Hotchkiss *U.S.A.* 38°48N 107°43W **168** G10
Hotham, C. *Australia* 12°2S 131°18E **148** B5
Hoting *Sweden* 64°8N 16°15E **60** D17
Hotolisht *Albania* 41°10N 20°25E **96** E4
Hotspur Seamount
  Atl. Oc. 17°55S 35°55W **56** H8
Hotte, Massif de la
  Haiti 18°30N 73°45W **183** C5
Hottentotsbaai *Namibia* 26°8S 14°59E **144** B1
Hou Hai *China* 22°32N 113°56E **111** a
Houat, Î. de *France* 47°24N 2°58W **70** E4
Houdan *France* 48°48N 1°35E **71** D8
Houei Sai *Laos* 20°18N 100°26E **116** G3
Houeillès *France* 44°12N 0°2E **72** D4
Houffalize *Belgium* 50°8N 5°48E **69** D5
Houghton *Mich., U.S.A.* 47°7N 88°34W **172** B9
Houghton *N.Y., U.S.A.* 42°25N 78°9W **174** D6
Houghton L. *U.S.A.* 44°21N 84°44W **173** C11
Houghton-le-Spring
  U.K. 54°51N 1°28W **66** C6
Houhora Heads *N.Z.* 34°49S 173°9E **154** A2
Houlton *U.S.A.* 46°8N 67°51W **173** B20
Houma *China* 35°36N 111°21E **114** G6
Houma *China* 35°36N 111°0E **114** G6
Houma *U.S.A.* 29°36N 90°43W **177** F9
Houndé *Burkina Faso* 11°34N 3°31W **138** C4
Hourn, L. *U.K.* 57°7N 5°35W **66** A4
Hourtin *France* 45°11N 1°4W **72** C2
Hourtin-Carcans, L. d'
  France 45°10N 1°6W **72** C2
Housatonic → *U.S.A.* 41°10N 73°7W **175** E11
Houston *Canada* 54°25N 126°39W **162** C3
Houston *Fla., U.S.A.* 30°15N 82°54W **178** F7
Houston *Mo., U.S.A.* 37°22N 91°58W **172** G8
Houston *Tex., U.S.A.* 29°45N 95°21W **176** G7
Hout = Mogwadi →
  S. Africa 23°4S 29°36E **145** A4
Houtkraal *S. Africa* 30°23S 24°5E **144** D3
Houtman Abrolhos
  Australia 28°43S 113°48E **149** E1
Hovd = Dund-Us
  Mongolia 48°1N 91°38E **109** C12
Hovd □ *Mongolia* 48°2N 91°37E **109** C12
Hove *U.K.* 50°50N 0°10W **67** G7
Hovedstaden □ *Denmark* 56°0N 10°0E **63** J6
Hovenweep △ *U.S.A.* 37°20N 109°0W **169** H9
Hoveyzeh *Iran* 31°27N 48°4E **129** D6
Hovgaard Ø *Greenland* 79°55N 18°50W **57** B9
Hovmantorp *Sweden* 56°47N 15°7E **63** H9
Hövsgöl *Mongolia* 43°37N 109°9E **114** C5
Hövsgöl Nuur *Mongolia* 51°0N 100°30E **110** A9
Hovsta *Sweden* 59°22N 15°15E **62** E9
Howar, Wadi → *Sudan* 17°30N 27°8E **135** E11
Howard *Australia* 25°16S 152°32E **151** D5
Howard *Pa., U.S.A.* 41°1N 77°40W **174** E7
Howard *S. Dak., U.S.A.* 44°1N 97°32W **172** D5
Howe *U.S.A.* 43°48N 113°0W **168** E7
Howe, C. *Australia* 37°30S 150°0E **153** D9
Howe, West Cape
  Australia 35°8S 117°36E **149** G2
Howell *U.S.A.* 42°36N 83°56W **173** D12
Howick *Canada* 45°11N 73°51W **175** A11
Howick *N.Z.* 36°54S 174°56E **154** B3
Howick *S. Africa* 29°28S 30°14E **145** C5
Howick Group
  Australia 14°20S 145°30E **150** A4
Howitt, L. *Australia* 27°40S 138°40E **151** D2
Howland I. *Pac. Oc.* 0°48N 176°38W **156** G10
Howlong *Australia* 35°59S 146°38E **153** C7
Howrah = Haora
  India 22°34N 88°11E **125** H13
Höxter *Germany* 51°46N 9°22E **76** D5
Hoxtolgay *China* 46°35N 85°59E **110** B6
Hoxud *China* 42°5N 86°51E **110** C7
Hoy *U.K.* 58°50N 3°15W **65** C5
Høyanger *Norway* 61°13N 6°4E **60** F12
Hoyerswerda *Germany* 51°26N 14°14E **76** D10
Hoylake *U.K.* 53°24N 3°10W **66** D4
Hoyos *Spain* 40°9N 6°45W **88** E4
Hoyran Gölü *Turkey* 38°12N 30°38E **99** C12
Hoyos *Spain* 40°9N 6°45W **88** E4

Hrodna □ *Belarus* 53°20N 24°45E |
Hrodzyanka *Belarus* 53°31N 28°42E **75** |
Hron → *Slovak Rep.* 47°49N 18°45E **79** |
Hrubieszów *Poland* 50°49N 23°51E **8** |
Hrubý Jeseník *Czech Rep.* 50°5N 17°10E **7** |
Hrvatska = Croatia ■
  Europe 45°20N 16°0E **9** |
Hrymayliv *Ukraine* 49°20N 26°5E **7** |
Hrynyava *Ukraine* 47°59N 24°53E |
Hsenwi *Burma* 23°22N 97°55E **12** |
Hsiamen = Xiamen
  China 24°25N 118°4E **11** |
Hsian = Xi'an *China* 34°15N 109°0E **1** |
Hsinchu *Taiwan* 24°48N 120°58E **11** |
Hsinhailien = Lianyungang
  China 34°40N 119°11E **11** |
Hsinkai = Bhamo
  Burma 24°15N 97°15E **12** |
Hsinying *Taiwan* 23°11N 98°26E **1** |
Hsopket *Burma* 23°11N 98°26E **1** |
Hsüchou = Xuzhou
  China 34°18N 117°10E **11** |
Htawei = Tavoy *Burma* 14°2N 98°12E **1** |
Hu Xian *China* 34°8N 108°42E **1** |
Hua Hin *Thailand* 12°34N 99°58E **12** |
Hua Muang *Laos* 20°13N 103°52E **1** |
Hua Shan *China* 34°28N 110°4E **1** |
Hua Xian *Henan, China* 35°30N 114°30E **1** |
Hua Xian *Shaanxi,*
  China 34°30N 109°48E **1** |
Hua'an *China* 25°1N 117°32E **11** |
Huab → *Namibia* 20°52S 13°25E **1** |
Huachacalla *Bolivia* 18°45S 68°17W **1** |
Huacheng *China* 24°4N 115°37E **1** |
Huachinera *Mexico* 30°9N 108°55W **1** |
Huacho *Peru* 11°10S 77°35W **1** |
Huachón *Peru* 10°35S 76°0W **1** |
Huade *China* 41°55N 113°59E **1** |
Huadian *China* 43°0N 126°40E **1** |
Huadu *China* 23°22N 113°12E **1** |
Huahine, Î.
  French Polynesia 16°46S 150°58W **15** |
Huai Thad = Thailand* 16°52N 104°17E **12** |
Huai He → *China* 33°0N 118°30E **11** |
Huai Kha Khaeng △
  Thailand 15°20N 98°55E **1** |
Huai Nam Dang △
  Thailand 19°30N 98°30E **1** |
Huai Yot *Thailand* 7°45N 99°37E **1** |
Huai'an *Hebei, China* 40°30N 114°20E **1** |
Huai'an *Jiangsu,*
  China 33°30N 119°10E **11** |
Huaibei *China* 34°0N 116°48E **11** |
Huaibin *China* 32°32N 115°27E **11** |
Huaide = Gongzhuling
  China 43°30N 124°40E **1** |
Huaidezhen *China* 43°48N 124°50E **1** |
Huaihua *China* 27°32N 109°57E **1** |
Huaiji *China* 23°55N 112°12E **1** |
Huainan *China* 32°38N 116°58E **1** |
Huaining *China* 30°28N 116°35E **1** |
Huairen *China* 39°48N 113°20E **1** |
Huairou *China* 40°20N 116°35E **1** |
Huaiyang *China* 33°40N 114°52E **1** |
Huaiyin *China* 33°30N 119°2E **1** |
Huaiyuan *Anhui,*
  China 32°55N 117°10E **11** |
Huaiyuan *Guangxi Zhuangzu,*
  China 24°31N 108°22E **1** |
Huajuápan de León
  Mexico 17°48N 97°46W **1** |
Hualapai Peak *U.S.A.* 35°5N 113°54W **17** |
Hualien *Taiwan* 23°59N 121°36E **1** |
Huallaga → *Peru* 5°15S 75°30W **1** |
Huallanca *Peru* 8°50S 77°36W **1** |
Huamachuco *Peru* 7°50S 78°5W **1** |
Huambo *Angola* 12°42S 15°54E **1** |
Huan Jiang → *China* 34°28N 109°0E **1** |
Huan Xian *China* 36°33N 107°7E **1** |
Huancabamba *Peru* 5°10S 79°15W **1** |
Huancane *Peru* 15°10S 69°44W **1** |
Huancapi *Peru* 13°40S 74°0W **1** |
Huancavelica *Peru* 12°50S 75°5W **1** |
Huancavelica □ *Peru* 13°0S 75°0W **1** |
Huancayo *Peru* 12°5S 75°12W **1** |
Huanchaca *Bolivia* 20°15S 66°40W **1** |
Huang Hai = Yellow Sea
  China 35°0N 123°0E **11** |
Huang He → *China* 37°55N 118°50E **11** |
Huang Xian *China* 37°38N 120°30E **1** |
Huangchuan *China* 32°15N 115°10E **1** |
Huanggang *China* 30°0N 114°50E **11** |
Huangdao *China* 36°0N 120°7E **11** |
Huanggang *China* 30°12N 114°20E **1** |
Huangguoshu *China* 26°0N 105°40E **1** |
Huanghua *China* 38°15N 117°20E **1** |
Huanghuagang *China* 35°34N 109°15E **1** |
Huangling *China* 35°34N 109°15E **1** |
Huanglong *China* 35°30N 109°59E **1** |
Huangmei *China* 30°5N 115°56E **1** |
Huangpi *China* 30°50N 114°22E **1** |
Huangping *China* 26°56N 107°54E **1** |
Huangshan *Anhui,*
  China 30°8N 118°9E **11** |
Huangshan *Anhui,*
  China 29°42N 118°25E **11** |
Huangshi *China* 30°10N 115°3E **1** |
Huangsongdian
  China 43°45N 127°25E **1** |
Huangyan *China* 28°38N 121°19E **1** |
Huangyangsi *China* 26°33N 111°39E **1** |
Huanien *China* 24°17N 102°56E **1** |
Huanren *China* 41°23N 125°20E **1** |
Huanta *Peru* 12°55S 74°0W **1** |
Huantai *China* 36°58N 117°56E **1** |
Huánuco *Peru* 9°55S 76°15W **1** |
Huanuni *Bolivia* 18°16S 66°48W **1** |
Huanzo, Cordillera de
  Peru 14°35S 73°0W **1** |
Huara *Chile* 19°59S 69°46W **1** |
Huaral *Peru* 11°32S 77°13W **1** |
Huaraz *Peru* 9°14S 77°14W **1** |
Huarmey *Peru* 10°5S 78°5W **1** |
Huarochiri *Peru* 12°5S 76°22W **1** |
Huarong *China* 29°15S 73°29W **1** |
Huascarán, Nevado *Peru* 9°7S 77°37W **1** |

sco Chile 28°30S 71°15W **190** B1
sco → Chile 28°27S 71°13W **190** B1
sna U.S.A. 35°6N 120°24W **171** K6
tabampo Mexico 26°50N 109°38W **180** B3
achinano Mexico 20°12N 98°3W **181** C5
tla de Jiménez
Mexico 18°9N 96°51W **181** D5
xi China 26°25N 106°40E **116** D6
yuash, Cordillera
Peru 10°30S 76°45W **188** B2
ying China 34°35N 110°5E **116** G6
ying China 30°8N 106°44E **116** B6
yllay Peru 11°3S 76°21W **188** C2
yuan China 28°37N 109°29E **116** C7
zhou China 21°33N 110°33E **117** G8
alli = Hubli India 15°22N 75°15E **127** G2
ard Ohio U.S.A. 41°9N 80°34W **174** E4
ard Tex., U.S.A. 31°51N 96°48W **176** F6
ard Glacier
nada 60°18N 139°22W **160** B2
art Pt. Canada 59°21N 94°41W **163** B10
í China 31°0N 112°0E **117** B9
i India 15°22N 75°15E **127** G2
r'ang N. Korea 41°25N 127°2E **115** D14
knall U.K. 53°3N 1°13W **66** D6
lersfield U.K. 53°39N 1°47W **66** D6
linge Sweden 59°14N 18°0E **62** E12
r Germany 53°7N 8°26E **76** B4
ksvall Sweden 61°43N 17°10E **62** C11
son Canada 50°6N 92°9W **164** B1
son Fla., U.S.A. 28°22N 82°42W **179** G7
son Mass., U.S.A. 42°23N 71°34W **175** D13
son N.Y., U.S.A. 42°15N 73°46W **175** D11
son Wis., U.S.A. 44°58N 92°45W **172** C7
son Wyo., U.S.A. 42°54N 108°35W **168** E9
son → U.S.A. 40°42N 74°2W **175** F10
son, C. Antarctica 68°21S 153°45E **5** C10
son, Vol. Chile 46°4S 72°55W **192** C2
son Bay Nunavut,
nada 60°0N 86°0W **161** F14
son Bay Sask.,
nada 52°51N 102°23W **163** C8
son Falls U.S.A. 43°18N 73°35W **175** C11
son Mts. Antarctica 71°45S 99°20W **5** D16
son Str. Canada 62°0N 70°0W **161** E18
son's Hope Canada 56°0N 121°54W **162** B4
í Vietnam 16°30N 107°35E **120** D6
ra → Japan 41°2N 6°48W **88** B2
lin Romania 46°52N 23°2E **80** D8
quetenango
atemala 15°20N 91°28W **182** C1
icar Mexico 22°21N 103°13W **180** C4
amo Spain 40°17N 1°48W **90** E3
goat France 48°22N 3°46W **70** D3
va Spain 37°39N 3°28W **89** H1
va Spain 37°18N 6°57W **89** H4
va → Spain 37°40N 7°0W **89** H5
va → Spain 37°27N 6°0W **89** H5
atelauquén Chile 37°38S 71°33W **190** C1
cal-Overa Spain 37°24N 1°45W **89** H3
quehue △ Chile 39°6S 71°42W **192** A2
la, Sa. de la
gentina 31°10S 67°30W **190** C2
tas, C. de las Spain 38°21N 0°24W **91** G4
a → Spain 39°0N 0°52W **90** C4
ca Spain 42°8N 0°25W **90** C4
ca Spain 42°20N 0°1E **90** C5
icar Spain 37°44N 2°35W **91** H2
amo Mexico 18°35N 100°53W **180** D4
e Spain 40°10N 2°43W **90** E2
va → Australia 33°6N 79°48W **178** B10
r → Australia 25°1S 134°1E **150** D1
enden Australia 20°52S 144°10E **150** C3
nesville U.S.A. 41°14N 76°44W **175** E8
i → India 21°56N 88°4E **125** J13
n Colo., U.S.A. 39°8N 103°28W **168** G2
n Okla., U.S.A. 34°1N 95°31W **176** D7
n → U.S.A. 37°11N 101°21W **172** G3
Xian = Huixian
China 35°27N 113°12E **114** G7
Xian China 33°50N 106°4E **114** H4
an China 25°1N 118°43E **117** E12
anbu China 37°28N 106°38E **114** F4
rau Ra. N.Z. 38°45S 176°55E **154** E5
hang China 25°32N 115°45E **117** E10
hapan Mexico 20°23N 99°39W **181** C5
hon N. Korea 40°10N 126°16E **115** D14
ong Guangdong,
ina 22°58N 114°43E **117** F10
ong Sichuan,
ina 26°34N 102°35E **116** D4
a He → China 43°0N 127°50E **115** C14
a, Nevado del
ombia 3°0N 76°0W **186** C2
í China 23°0N 116°18E **117** F11
nin China 26°35N 102°17E **116** D4
an China 27°40N 126°2E **115** C14
ca Renancó
gentina 34°51S 64°22W **190** C3
ong China 35°38N 105°0E **114** G3
ong China 39°5N 106°35E **114** E4
u N.Z. 39°15S 174°30E **154** F3
ne → France 47°59N 0°11E **70** E7
ong China 34°5N 116°5E **114** G9
ong China 26°51N 109°45E **116** D7
ong China 35°27N 113°12E **114** G7
tla Mexico 15°9N 92°28W **181** D6
e China 26°24N 103°15E **116** D4
e China 20°0N 114°23E **117** F10
awng Valley
ma 26°30N 96°30W **123** F20
ri India 16°14N 74°36E **127** L9
umtsi Botswana 23°58S 21°54E **144** B3
yfâ' Si. Arabia 25°58N 40°45E **111** B3
í He → China 45°48N 132°59E **111** B15
í He → China 45°0N 122°10E **115** B12
= Kingston upon Hull
U.K. 53°45N 0°21W **66** D7
sö Canada 45°26N 75°43W **175** A9
Neths. 51°17N 4°2E **69** C4
fred Sweden 57°30N 15°52E **63** G9
dao China 40°45N 120°50E **115** D11
n Nur China 41°0N 117°30E **111** B12
nbuir = Hailar
aypole Ukraine 49°10N 119°38E **111** B12
aypole Ukraine 47°45N 36°21E **85** J9

Huma, Tanjung
Malaysia 5°29N 100°16E **121** c
Humacao Puerto Rico 18°9N 65°50W **183** d
Humahuaca Argentina 23°10S 65°25W **190** A2
Humaitá Brazil 7°35S 63°1W **186** E6
Humaitá Paraguay 27°2S 58°31W **190** B4
Humansdorp S. Africa 34°2S 24°46E **144** D3
Humbe Angola 16°40S 14°55E **144** A1
Humber → U.K. 53°42N 0°27W **66** D7
Humberside □ U.K. 53°50N 0°30W **66** D7
Humboldt Canada 52°15N 105°9W **163** C7
Humboldt Iowa, U.S.A. 42°44N 94°13W **172** D6
Humboldt Tenn.,
U.S.A. 35°50N 88°55W **177** D10
Humboldt → U.S.A. 39°59N 118°36W **168** G4
Humboldt Gletscher =
Sermersuaq Greenland 79°30N 62°0W **57** B4
Humboldt Mts. N.Z. 44°30S 168°15E **155** E3
Hume U.S.A. 36°48N 118°54W **170** J8
Hume, L. Australia 36°0S 147°5E **153** D7
Humen China 22°50N 113°40E **111** a
Humenné Slovak Rep. 48°55N 21°50E **79** C14
Humphreys, Mt.
U.S.A. 37°17N 118°40W **170** H8
Humphreys Peak
U.S.A. 35°21N 111°41W **169** J8
Humpolec Czech Rep. 49°31N 15°20E **78** D8
Humptulips U.S.A. 47°14N 123°57W **170** C3
Humula Australia 35°30S 147°46E **153** C7
Hūn Libya 29°2N 16°0E **137** C9
Húnaflói Iceland 65°50N 20°50W **60** D3
Hunan □ China 27°30N 112°0E **117** D9
Hunchun China 42°52N 130°28E **115** C16
Hundested Denmark 55°58N 11°52E **63** J5
Hundewali Pakistan 31°55N 72°38E **124** D5
Hundred Mile House
Canada 51°38N 121°18W **162** C4
Hunedoara Romania 45°40N 22°50E **80** E7
Hunedoara □ Romania 45°50N 22°54E **80** E7
Hünfeld Germany 50°39N 9°46E **76** E5
Hung Yen Vietnam 20°39N 106°4E **116** G6
Hungary ■ Europe 47°20N 19°20E **79** D12
Hungary, Plain of Europe 47°0N 20°0E **58** F10
Hungerford Australia 28°58S 144°24E **151** D3
Hüngnam N. Korea 39°49N 127°45E **115** E14
Hungt'ou Hsü = Lan Yü
Taiwan 22°4N 121°25E **117** F13
Huni Valley Ghana 5°33N 1°56W **138** D4
Hunjiang China 41°54N 126°26E **115** D14
Hunneberg Sweden 58°18N 12°30E **63** F6
Hunnebostrand Sweden 58°27N 11°18E **63** F5
Hunsberge Namibia 27°45S 17°12E **144** C2
Hunsrück Germany 49°56N 7°27E **77** F3
Hunstanton U.K. 52°56N 0°29E **66** E8
Hunsur India 12°16N 76°16E **127** H3
Hunte → Germany 52°30N 8°28E **76** B4
Hunter N.Z. 44°36S 171°2E **155** E6
Hunter U.S.A. 42°13N 74°13W **175** D10
Hunter → Australia 32°52S 151°46E **153** B9
Hunter → N.Z. 44°21S 169°27E **155** E4
Hunter Hills, The N.Z. 44°26S 170°46E **155** E5
Hunter I. Australia 40°30S 144°45E **151** G3
Hunter I. Canada 51°55N 128°0W **162** C3
Hunter Mts. N.Z. 45°43S 167°25E **155** F2
Hunter Ra. Australia 32°45S 150°15E **153** B9
Hunterville N.Z. 39°56S 175°35E **154** F4
Huntingburg U.S.A. 38°18N 86°57W **172** F10
Huntingdon U.K. 52°20N 0°11W **67** E7
Huntingdon U.S.A. 40°30N 78°1W **174** F6
Huntington Ind.,
U.S.A. 40°53N 85°30W **173** E11
Huntington N.Y.,
U.S.A. 40°52N 73°26W **175** F11
Huntington Oreg.,
U.S.A. 44°21N 117°16W **168** D5
Huntington Utah,
U.S.A. 39°20N 110°58W **168** G8
Huntington W. Va.,
U.S.A. 38°25N 82°27W **173** F12
Huntington Beach
U.S.A. 33°40N 118°5W **171** M9
Huntly N.Z. 37°34S 175°11E **154** D4
Huntly U.K. 57°27N 2°47W **65** D6
Huntsville Canada 45°20N 79°14W **174** B5
Huntsville Ala., U.S.A. 34°44N 86°35W **177** D11
Huntsville Tex., U.S.A. 30°43N 95°33W **176** F7
Hunyani → Zimbabwe 15°57S 30°39E **143** F3
Hunyuan China 39°42N 113°42E **114** E7
Hunza → India 35°54N 74°20E **125** B6
Huo Shan China 36°20N 111°52E **114** F6
Huo Xian = Huozhou
China 36°36N 111°42E **114** F6
Huocheng China 44°0N 80°48E **109** D10
Huolin Gol China 45°32N 119°38E **115** B10
Huong Khe Vietnam 18°13N 105°41E **120** C5
Huonville Australia 43°0S 147°5E **151** G4
Huoqiu China 32°20N 116°12E **117** A11
Huoshan China 31°25N 116°20E **117** B11
Huoshao Dao = Lütao
Taiwan 22°40N 121°30E **117** F13
Huozhou China 36°36N 111°42E **114** F6
Hupeh = Hubei □ China 31°0N 112°0E **117** B9
Ḥūr Iran 30°50N 57°7E **129** D8
Hurand Iran 38°51N 47°22E **105** C12
Ḥuraymila Si. Arabia 25°8N 46°8E **128** E5
Hurbanovo Slovak Rep. 47°51N 18°11E **79** D11
Hurd, C. Canada 45°13N 81°44W **174** A3
Hure Qi China 42°45N 121°45E **115** C11
Hurezani Romania 44°49N 23°40E **81** F8
Hurghada Egypt 27°15N 33°50E **137** C13
Hurley N. Mex., U.S.A. 32°42N 108°8W **169** K9
Hurley Wis., U.S.A. 46°27N 90°11W **172** B8
Huron Calif., U.S.A. 36°12N 120°6W **170** J6
Huron Ohio, U.S.A. 41°24N 82°33W **174** E2
Huron S. Dak., U.S.A. 44°22N 98°13W **172** C4
Huron, L. U.S.A. 44°30N 82°40W **174** B2
Huron East Canada 43°37N 81°18W **174** B3
Hurricane U.S.A. 37°11N 113°17W **169** H7
Hurtsboro U.S.A. 32°15N 85°25W **177** E12
Hurungwe □ Zimbabwe 16°7S 29°5E **143** F2
Hurunui → N.Z. 42°54S 173°18E **155** C6
Hurup Denmark 56°46N 8°25E **63** H2
Húsavík Iceland 66°3N 17°21W **60** C5
Huşi Romania 46°41N 28°7E **81** D13
Huskisson Australia 35°1S 150°41E **153** C9
Huskvarna Sweden 57°47N 14°15E **63** G8
Hustadvika Norway 63°0N 7°0E **60** E12
Hustontown U.S.A. 40°3N 78°2W **174** F6
Hustopeče Czech Rep. 48°57N 16°43E **79** C9

Husum Germany 54°28N 9°4E **76** A5
Husum Sweden 63°21N 19°12E **62** A13
Hutchinson Kans.,
U.S.A. 38°5N 97°56W **172** F5
Hutchinson Minn.,
U.S.A. 44°54N 94°22W **172** C6
Hutiao Xia China 27°13N 100°9E **116** D3
Hutte Sauvage, L. de la
Canada 56°15N 64°45W **165** A7
Hüttenberg Austria 46°56N 14°33E **78** E7
Hüttener Berge △
Germany 54°24N 9°40E **76** A5
Hutton, Mt. Australia 25°51S 148°20E **151** D4
Huwaki Indonesia 7°55S 126°30E **119** F7
Huy Belgium 50°31N 5°15E **69** D5
Huzhou China 30°51N 120°8E **117** B13
Huzurabad India 18°12N 79°25E **126** E4
Huzurnagar India 16°54N 79°53E **126** F4
Hvalpsund Denmark 56°42N 9°11E **63** H3
Hvammstangi Iceland 65°24N 20°57W **60** D3
Hvar Croatia 43°11N 16°28E **93** E13
Hvarski Kanal Croatia 43°15N 16°35E **93** E13
Hvítá → Iceland 64°30N 21°58W **60** D3
Hvizdets Ukraine 48°35N 25°7E **81** B10
Hwacheon-Cheosuji
S. Korea 38°5N 127°50E **115** E14
Hwang Ho = Huang He →
China 37°55N 118°50E **115** F10
Hwange Zimbabwe 18°18S 26°30E **143** F2
Hwange Nat. Park
Zimbabwe 19°0S 26°30E **143** F2
Hwlffordd = Haverfordwest
U.K. 51°48N 4°58W **67** F3
Hyannis Mass., U.S.A. 41°39N 70°17W **173** E14
Hyannis Nebr., U.S.A. 42°0N 101°46W **172** E3
Hyargas Nuur Mongolia 49°0N 93°0E **109** C12
Hybo Sweden 61°49N 16°15E **62** C10
Hydaburg U.S.A. 55°15N 132°50W **162** C2
Hyde N.Z. 45°18S 170°16E **155** F5
Hyde Park U.S.A. 41°47N 73°56W **175** E11
Hyden Australia 32°24S 118°53E **149** F2
Hyder U.S.A. 55°55N 130°5W **162** B2
Hyderabad India 17°22N 78°29E **126** F4
Hyderabad Pakistan 25°23N 68°24E **124** G3
Hydra Greece 37°20N 23°28E **98** D5
Hyères France 43°8N 6°9E **73** E10
Hyères, Îs. d' France 43°0N 6°20E **73** F10
Hyesan N. Korea 41°20N 128°10E **115** D15
Hyland → Canada 59°52N 128°12W **162** B3
Hyltebruk Sweden 56°59N 13°15E **63** H7
Hyndman Peak U.S.A. 43°45N 114°8W **168** E6
Hyōgo □ Japan 35°15N 134°50E **113** G7
Hyrum U.S.A. 41°38N 111°51W **168** F8
Hysham U.S.A. 46°18N 107°14W **168** C10
Hythe U.K. 51°4N 1°5E **67** F9
Hyūga Japan 32°25N 131°35E **113** H5
Hyvinge = Hyvinkää
Finland 60°38N 24°50E **84** B3
Hyvinkää Finland 60°38N 24°50E **84** B3

I

I-n-Akhmed Mali 19°49N 0°56W **139** B4
I-n-Azaoua Algeria 25°42N 6°54E **136** D6
I-n-Ezzane Algeria 23°29N 11°15E **136** D6
I-n-Gall Niger 16°51N 7°1E **139** B6
I-n-Kelemet Algeria 26°57N 5°47E **136** C5
I-n-Oudad Algeria 20°17N 4°38E **139** A5
I-n-Ouzzal Algeria 20°41N 2°34E **139** A5
I-n-Tadreft Niger 19°5N 6°38E **139** B6
Iablès, Erg Algeria 27°30N 2°2W **136** C3
Iablaniţa Romania 44°57N 22°19E **80** F7
Iaco → Brazil 9°3S 68°34W **188** B4
Iacobeni Romania 47°25N 25°20E **81** C10
Iaçu Brazil 12°45S 40°13W **189** C2
Ialissos Greece 36°24N 28°10E **101** C10
Ialomiţa □ Romania 44°30N 27°30E **81** F13
Ialomiţa → Romania 44°42N 27°51E **81** F12
Ialpug → Moldova 45°41N 28°35E **81** F15
Iamonia L. U.S.A. 30°38N 84°14W **178** E5
Ianca Romania 45°6N 27°29E **81** E12
Iara Romania 46°31N 23°35E **81** D8
Iargara Moldova 46°24N 28°23E **81** D13
Iaşi Romania 47°10N 27°40E **81** C12
Iaşi □ Romania 47°20N 27°0E **81** C12
Iasmos Greece 41°8N 25°11E **97** E9
Ib → India 21°34N 83°48E **125** J10
Iba Phil. 15°22N 120°0E **119** A6
Ibadan Nigeria 7°22N 3°58E **139** D5
Ibagué Colombia 4°20N 75°20W **186** C2
Iballë Albania 42°12N 20°2E **96** B4
Ibănești Botoşani,
Romania 48°4N 26°22E **81** B11
Ibănești Mureş, Romania 46°45N 24°57E **81** D9
Ibar → Serbia 43°43N 20°45E **96** C4
Ibaraki □ Japan 36°10N 140°10E **113** F10
Ibara Ecuador 0°21N 78°7W **186** C2
Ibb Yemen 14°2N 44°10E **131** E3
Ibbenbüren Germany 52°16N 7°43E **76** C3
Ibembo
Dem. Rep. of the Congo 2°35S 23°35E **142** B1
Ibenga → Congo 2°19N 18°9E **142** B3
Ibera, L. Argentina 28°30S 57°9W **190** B4
Iberia Peru 11°21S 69°35W **188** C5
Iberian Peninsula Europe 40°0N 5°0W **58** H5
Iberville Canada 45°19N 73°17W **175** A11
Iberville, Mt. d'
Canada 58°50N 63°50W **161** F19
Ibeto Nigeria 10°29N 5°8E **139** C6
Ibi Nigeria 8°15N 9°44E **139** D6
Ibiá Brazil 19°30S 46°30W **189** D1
Ibiapaba, Sa. da Brazil 4°0S 41°30W **189** A2
Ibicaraí Brazil 14°51S 39°36W **189** C3
Ibicuí → Brazil 29°25S 56°47W **191** B4
Ibicuy Argentina 33°55S 59°10W **190** C4
Ibiza = Eivissa Spain 38°54N 1°26E **100** C7
Ibiza ✈ (IBZ) Spain 38°53N 1°22E **100** C7
Íblei, Monti Italy 37°15N 14°45E **95** E7
Ibo Mozam. 12°22S 40°40E **143** G5
Ibonma Indonesia 3°29S 133°31E **119** E8
Ibotirama Brazil 12°13S 43°12W **189** C2
Ibrāhīm → Lebanon 34°4N 35°38E **108** A4
'Ibrī Oman 23°14N 56°30E **131** C6
Ibshawâi Egypt 29°21N 30°40E **137** F7
Ibu Indonesia 1°35N 127°33E **119** D7
Ibusuki Japan 31°12N 130°40E **113** J5

Ica Peru 14°0S 75°48W **188** C2
Ica □ Peru 14°0S 75°30W **188** C2
Iça → Brazil 2°55S 67°58W **186** A4
Içana Brazil 0°21N 67°19W **186** C5
Içana → Brazil 0°26N 67°19W **186** C5
Icatu Brazil 2°46S 44°4W **189** A2
İçel Turkey 36°51N 34°36E **104** D6
İçel □ Turkey 36°45N 34°0E **104** D5
Iceland ■ Europe 64°45N 19°0W **60** D4
Iceland Basin Atl. Oc. 60°10N 19°0W **54** C7
Icelandic Plateau Arctic 64°0N 10°0W **54** C7
İçeriçumra Turkey 37°34N 32°39E **104** D5
İçhalkaranji India 16°40N 74°33E **126** F2
Ich'ang = Yichang
China 30°40N 111°20E **117** B8
Ichchapuram India 19°10N 84°40E **126** E7
Ichhawar India 23°1N 77°1E **124** H7
Ichigat Muja-Cordillera del
Condor △ Peru 4°20S 77°30W **188** A2
Ichihara Japan 35°28N 140°5E **113** G10
Ichikawa Japan 35°43N 139°54E **113** G9
Ichilo → Bolivia 15°57S 64°50W **188** G6
Ichinomiya Japan 35°18N 136°48E **113** G8
Ichinoseki Japan 38°55N 141°8E **112** E10
Ichkeul △ Tunisia 37°9N 9°37E **136** A5
Ichnya Ukraine 50°52N 32°24E **85** G7
Icht Morocco 29°6N 8°54W **136** C2
Icó Brazil 6°24S 38°51W **189** B3
Icod Canary Is. 28°22N 16°43W **100** F3
Içoguz Turkmenistan 40°11N 58°24E **108** D5
Icy C. U.S.A. 70°20N 161°52W **158** B3
Ida Grove U.S.A. 42°21N 95°28W **172** D6
Idabel U.S.A. 33°54N 94°50W **176** E7
Idah Nigeria 7°5N 6°40E **139** D6
Idaho □ U.S.A. 45°0N 115°0W **168** D6
Idaho City U.S.A. 43°50N 115°50W **168** E6
Idaho Falls U.S.A. 43°30N 112°2W **168** E7
Idalia △ Australia 24°49S 144°36E **150** C3
Idanha-a-Nova Portugal 39°50N 7°15W **88** F3
Idar-Oberstein Germany 49°43N 7°16E **77** F3
Idelès Algeria 23°50N 5°53E **136** D5
Idensalmi = Iisalmi
Finland 63°32N 27°10E **60** E22
Idfū Egypt 24°55N 32°49E **137** C3
Idhra = Hydra Greece 37°20N 23°28E **98** D5
Idi, Oros = Psiloritis, Oros
Greece 35°15N 24°45E **101** D6
Idil Turkey 37°20N 41°53E **105** D9
Idiofa
Dem. Rep. of the Congo 4°55S 19°42E **140** E3
Idkerberget Sweden 60°22N 15°15E **62** D9
Idku Egypt 31°18N 30°17E **137** E7
Idku, Bahra el Egypt 31°18N 30°18E **137** E7
Idlib Syria 35°55N 36°36E **104** C4
Idlib □ Syria 35°45N 36°45E **104** C4
Idre Sweden 61°52N 12°42E **62** C6
Idria U.S.A. 36°25N 120°41W **170** J6
Idrija Slovenia 46°0N 14°5E **93** C11
Idritsa Russia 56°17N 28°53E **84** D5
Idlek Russia 51°32N 53°21E **108** B4
Idlemi Africa 32°8S 28°18E **145** D4
Ieper Belgium 50°51N 2°53E **69** D2
Ierapetra Greece 35°1N 25°44E **101** E7
Ierissos Greece 40°22N 23°52E **96** D7
Ierissos Kolpos Greece 40°27N 23°57E **96** F7
Iernut Romania 46°27N 24°16E **81** D9
Iesi Italy 43°31N 13°14E **93** E10
Ifac, Penyal d' Spain 38°38N 0°5E **91** G5
Ifakara Tanzania 8°8S 36°41E **140** F7
'Ifāl, W. al → Si. Arabia 28°7N 35°3E **128** D2
Ife Nigeria 7°30N 4°31E **139** D5
Iférouâne Niger 19°5N 8°24E **139** B6
Ifetesene Algeria 25°30N 4°33E **136** D4
Iffley Australia 18°53S 141°12E **150** B3
Ifon Nigeria 6°58N 5°40E **139** D6
Iforas, Adrar des Africa 19°40N 1°40E **139** B5
Ifould, L. Australia 30°52S 132°6E **149** F5
Ifrane Morocco 33°33N 5°7W **136** B2
Igalo Montenegro 42°28N 18°30E **96** D2
Iganga Uganda 0°37N 33°28E **142** B3
Igarapava Brazil 20°3S 47°47W **189** E1
Igarka Russia 67°30N 86°33E **106** C9
Igatpuri India 19°40N 73°35E **126** E1
Igbetti Nigeria 8°44N 4°8E **139** D5
Igbo-Ora Nigeria 7°29N 3°15E **139** D5
Igboho Nigeria 8°53N 3°50E **139** D5
Igbor Nigeria 7°27N 8°34E **139** D6
Iğdır Turkey 39°55N 44°2E **105** C11
Igelfors Sweden 58°52N 15°41E **63** F9
Iggesund Sweden 61°39N 17°10E **62** C11
Ighil Izane = Relizane
Algeria 35°44N 0°31E **136** A4
Iglésias Italy 39°19N 8°32E **94** C1
Igli Algeria 30°25N 2°19W **136** B3
Igloolik = Iglulik
Canada 69°20N 81°49W **161** D15
Ibben → India
Igluligaarjuk = Chesterfield Inlet
Canada 63°30N 90°45W **160** E13
Iglulik Canada 69°20N 81°49W **161** D15
'Igma, G. el Egypt 28°55N 34°0E **137** F8
Ignace Canada 49°30N 91°40W **164** C1
Iğneada Turkey 41°52N 27°59E **97** E11
Iğneada Burnu Turkey 41°53N 28°2E **97** E12
Igoumenitsa Greece 39°32N 20°18E **98** B2
Igrim Russia 63°12N 64°30E **108** C7
Iguaçu → Brazil 25°36S 54°36W **191** B5
Iguaçu, Cat. del Brazil 25°41S 54°26W **191** B5
Iguaçu △ Brazil 25°30S 54°0W **191** B5
Iguaçu Falls = Iguaçu, Cat. del
Brazil 25°41S 54°26W **191** B5
Iguala Mexico 18°21N 99°32W **181** D5
Igualada Spain 41°37N 1°37E **90** D6
Iguassu = Iguaçu →
Brazil 25°36S 54°36W **191** B5
Iguatu Brazil 6°20S 39°18W **189** B3
Iguazú △ Argentina 25°42S 54°22W **191** B5
Iguidi, Erg Africa 27°0N 6°0W **136** C3
Iharana Madag. 13°25S 50°0E **145** A9
Ihbulag Mongolia 43°11N 107°10E **114** C4
Iheya-Shima Japan 27°4N 127°58E **113** L3
Ihiala Nigeria 5°51N 6°55E **139** D6
Ihosy Madag. 22°24S 46°8E **145** C8
Ihugh Nigeria 7°1N 9°7E **139** D6
Ii Finland 65°19N 25°22E **60** D21
Ii-Shima Japan 26°43N 127°47E **113** L3
Iida Japan 35°35N 137°50E **113** G8
Iijoki → Finland 65°20N 25°20E **60** D21
Iisalmi Finland 63°32N 27°10E **60** E22

Iiyama Japan 36°51N 138°22E **113** F9
Iizuka Japan 33°38N 130°42E **113** H5
Ijâfene Mauritania 20°40N 8°0W **134** D4
Ijebu-Igbo Nigeria 6°56N 4°1E **139** D5
Ijebu-Ode Nigeria 6°47N 3°58E **139** D5
Ijevan Armenia 40°52N 45°8E **87** K7
IJmuiden Neths. 52°28N 4°35E **69** B4
Ijo älv = Iijoki →
Finland 65°20N 25°20E **60** D21
IJssel → Neths. 52°35N 5°50E **69** B5
IJsselmeer Neths. 52°45N 5°20E **69** B5
Ijuí Brazil 28°23S 53°55W **191** B5
Ijuí → Brazil 27°58S 55°20W **191** B4
Iménas Mali 16°20N 0°40E **139** B5
imeni 26 Bakinskikh
Komissarov = Neftçala
Azerbaijan 39°19N 49°12E **105** C13
imeni 26 Bakinskikh Komissarov
Turkmenistan 39°22N 54°10E **129** B7
imeni Ismail Samani, Pik
Tajikistan 39°0N 72°2E **109** F8
imeni Karl Libknekhta
Russia 51°40N 35°35E **85** G8
Imeri, Serra Brazil 0°50N 65°25W **186** C5
Imfolozi △ S. Africa 28°18S 31°50E **145** C5
Imi Ethiopia 6°28N 42°10E **131** F3
Imişli Azerbaijan 39°55N 48°4E **87** L9
Imitek Morocco 29°43N 8°10W **136** C2
Imlay U.S.A. 40°40N 118°9W **168** F4
Imlay City U.S.A. 43°2N 83°5W **174** D1
Immenstadt Germany 47°33N 10°13E **77** H6
Immingham U.K. 53°37N 0°13W **66** D7
Immokalee U.S.A. 26°25N 81°25W **179** J8
Imo □ Nigeria 5°30N 7°10E **139** D6
Imo → Nigeria 4°36N 7°35E **139** E6
Ímola Italy 44°20N 11°42E **93** D8
Imotski Croatia 43°27N 17°12E **93** E14
Imperatriz Amazonas,
Brazil 5°18S 67°11W **188** B4
Imperatriz Maranhão,
Brazil 5°30S 47°29W **189** B1
Impéria Italy 43°53N 8°3E **92** E5
Imperial Canada 51°21N 105°28W **163** C7
Imperial Peru 13°45 76°21W **188** C2
Imperial Calif.,
U.S.A. 32°51N 115°34W **171** N11
Imperial Nebr., U.S.A. 40°31N 101°39W **172** E3
Imperial Beach U.S.A. 32°35N 117°6W **171** N9
Imperial Dam U.S.A. 32°55N 114°25W **171** N12
Imperial Res. U.S.A. 32°53N 114°28W **171** N12
Imperial Valley
U.S.A. 33°0N 115°30W **171** N11
Imperieuse Reef
Australia 17°36S 118°50E **148** C2
Impfondo Congo 1°40N 18°0E **140** D3
Imphal India 24°48N 93°56E **123** G18
Imphy France 46°55N 3°16E **71** F10
Imranli Turkey 39°54N 38°7E **105** C8
İmroz = Gökçeada
Turkey 40°10N 25°50E **97** F8
Imst Austria 47°15N 10°44E **78** D3
İmuris Mexico 30°47N 110°52W **180** A2
Imuruan B. Phil. 10°40N 119°10E **119** B5
In Aleï Mali 17°42N 2°30W **138** C4
In Amenas Algeria 28°5N 9°30E **136** C6
In Amguel Algeria 23°41N 5°9E **136** D5
In Belbel Algeria 27°55N 1°12E **136** C4
In Delimane Mali 15°52N 1°31E **139** B5
In Ghar Algeria 27°10N 1°59E **136** C4
In Guezzam Algeria 19°37N 5°52E **139** A6
In Koufi Mali 27°0N 2°32E **136** C4
In Salah Algeria 27°10N 2°32E **136** C4
In Tallak Mali 16°19N 3°15E **139** B5
In Tebezas Mali 17°49N 1°53E **139** B5
Ina Japan 35°50N 137°55E **113** G8
Inaccessible I. Atl. Oc. 37°18S 12°40W **56** K10
Inagua △ Bahamas 21°5N 73°24W **183** B5
Inajá Brazil 8°54S 37°49W **189** B3
Inambari → Peru 12°41S 69°43W **188** C4
Inangahua N.Z. 41°52S 171°59E **155** D4
Inanwatan Indonesia 2°8S 132°10E **119** E8
Iñapari Peru 11°0S 69°40W **188** C5
Inari Finland 68°54N 27°1E **60** B22
Inarijärvi Finland 69°0N 28°0E **60** B23
Inawashiro-Ko Japan 37°29N 140°6E **112** F10
Inbhear Mór, An = Arklow
Ireland 52°48N 6°10W **64** D5
Inca Spain 39°43N 2°54E **100** B9
Inca de Oro Chile 26°45S 69°54W **190** B2
Incahuasi Argentina 27°2S 68°18W **190** B2
Ince Burun Turkey 42°7N 34°56E **104** A6
İncekum Burnu Turkey 36°13N 33°57E **104** D5
İncesu Turkey 38°38N 35°11E **104** C6
Incheon S. Korea 37°27N 126°40E **115** F14
İnciri □ Mauritania 20°0N 13°0W **134** D3
Incio = A Cruz de Incio
Spain 42°39N 7°21W **88** C3
İncirliova Turkey 37°50N 27°41E **99** D9
Incline Village U.S.A. 39°10N 119°58W **170** F7
Incomáti → Mozam. 25°46S 32°43E **145** C5
Incudine, Mte. France 41°50N 9°12E **73** G13
Indal Sweden 62°35N 17°5E **62** B11
Indalsälven → Sweden 62°36N 17°30E **62** B11
Indaw Burma 24°15N 96°5E **123** G20
Independence Calif.,
U.S.A. 36°48N 118°12W **170** J8
Independence Iowa,
U.S.A. 42°28N 91°54W **172** D8
Independence Kans.,
U.S.A. 37°14N 95°42W **172** G6
Independence Ky.,
U.S.A. 38°57N 84°33W **173** F11
Independence Mo.,
U.S.A. 39°6N 94°25W **172** F6
Independence Fjord
Greenland 82°10N 29°0W **57** A8
Independence Mts.
U.S.A. 41°20N 116°0W **168** F5
Independência Brazil 5°23S 40°19W **189** B2
Independência I. Peru 14°15S 76°21W **188** C2
Inderbor Kazakhstan 48°30N 51°42E **87** H10
Index U.S.A. 47°50N 121°33W **170** C5
Indi India 17°10N 75°58E **126** F2
India ■ Asia 20°0N 78°0E **122** K11
Indialantic U.S.A. 28°6N 80°34W **179** G9
Indian → U.S.A. 28°46N 80°52W **179** G9
Indian Cabins Canada 59°52N 117°40W **162** B5
Indian Harbour
Canada 54°27N 57°13W **165** B8
Indian Harbour Beach
U.S.A. 28°10N 80°35W **179** G9

Indian Head *Canada* 50°30N 103°41W **163** C8
Indian L. *U.S.A.* 43°46N 74°16W **175** C10
Indian Lake *U.S.A.* 43°47N 74°16W **175** C10
Indian Ocean 5°0S 75°0E **146** E6
Indian Rocks Beach
U.S.A. 27°52N 82°51W **179** H7
Indian Springs
U.S.A. 36°35N 115°40W **171** J11
Indiana *U.S.A.* 40°37N 79°9W **174** F5
Indiana □ *U.S.A.* 40°0N 86°0W **173** F11
Indianapolis *U.S.A.* 39°46N 86°9W **172** F10
Indianola *Iowa, U.S.A.* 41°22N 93°34W **172** E7
Indianola *Miss., U.S.A.* 33°27N 90°39W **177** E9
Indiantown *U.S.A.* 27°1N 80°28W **179** H9
Indigirka → *Russia* 70°48N 148°54E **107** B15
Indija *Serbia* 45°6N 20°7E **80** E5
Indio *U.S.A.* 33°43N 116°13W **171** M10
Indira Gandhi Canal
India 28°0N 72°0E **124** F5
Indira Pt. *India* 6°44N 93°49E **127** L11
Indira Sagar *India* 22°15N 76°40E **124** H7
Indo-China *Asia* 15°0N 102°0E **102** G12
Indonesia ■ *Asia* 5°0S 115°0E **118** F5
Indore *India* 22°42N 75°53E **124** H6
Indramayu *Indonesia* 6°20S 108°19E **119** G13
Indravati → *India* 19°20N 80°20E **126** E5
Indre □ *France* 46°50N 1°39E **71** F8
Indre → *France* 47°16N 0°11E **70** E7
Indre-et-Loire □ *France* 47°20N 0°40E **70** E7
Indrio *U.S.A.* 27°31N 80°21W **179** H9
Indulkana *Australia* 26°58S 133°5E **151** D1
Indura *Belarus* 53°26N 23°53E **82** E10
Indus → *Pakistan* 24°20N 67°47E **124** G2
Indus, Mouths of the
Pakistan 24°0N 68°0E **124** H3
İnebolu *Turkey* 41°55N 33°40E **104** B5
İnecik *Turkey* 40°56N 27°16E **97** F11
İnegöl *Turkey* 40°5N 29°31E **97** F13
Inés, Mt. *Argentina* 48°30S 69°40W **192** C3
Ineu *Romania* 46°26N 21°51E **80** D6
Inezgane *Morocco* 30°25N 9°29W **136** B2
Infantes = Villanueva de los
Infantes *Spain* 38°43N 3°1W **89** G7
Infiernillo, Presa del
Mexico 18°35N 101°50W **180** D4
Infiesto *Spain* 43°21N 5°21W **88** B5
Inga, Barrage d'
Dem. Rep. of the Congo 5°39S 13°39E **140** F2
Ingaro *Sweden* 59°12N 18°45E **62** E12
Ingelstad *Sweden* 56°45N 14°56E **63** H8
Ingeniero Jacobacci
Argentina 41°20S 69°36W **192** B3
Ingenio *Canary Is.* 27°55N 15°26W **100** G4
Ingenio Santa Ana
Argentina 27°25S 65°40W **190** B2
Ingersoll *Canada* 43°4N 80°55W **174** C4
Ingham *Australia* 18°43S 146°10E **150** B4
Ingleborough *U.K.* 54°10N 2°22W **66** C5
Inglefield Land *Greenland* 78°30N 70°0W **57** B4
Inglewood *Queens.,*
Australia 28°25S 151°2E **151** D5
Inglewood *Vic.,*
Australia 36°29S 143°53E **152** D5
Inglewood *N.Z.* 39°9S 174°14E **154** F3
Inglewood *U.S.A.* 33°58N 118°21W **171** M8
Inglis *U.S.A.* 29°2N 82°40W **179** F7
Ingolf Fjord *Greenland* 80°35N 17°30W **57** A9
Ingólfshöfði *Iceland* 63°48N 16°39W **60** E5
Ingolstadt *Germany* 48°46N 11°26E **77** G7
Ingomar *U.S.A.* 46°35N 107°23W **168** C10
Ingonish *Canada* 46°42N 60°18W **165** C7
Ingore *Guinea-Biss.* 12°24N 15°48W **138** C1
Ingraj Bazar *India* 24°58N 88°10E **125** G13
Ingrid Christensen Coast
Antarctica 69°30S 76°0E **55** C6
Ingul = Inhul → *Ukraine* 46°50N 32°0E **85** J7
Ingulec = Inhulec
Ukraine 47°42N 33°14E **85** J7
Ingulets = Inhulets →
Ukraine 46°46N 32°47E **85** J7
Inguri = Enguri →
Georgia 42°27N 41°38E **87** J5
Ingushetia □ *Russia* 43°20N 44°50E **87** J7
Ingwavuma *S. Africa* 27°9S 31°59E **145** C5
Inhaca *Mozam.* 26°1S 32°57E **145** C5
Inhaca Pen. *Mozam.* 26°13S 32°55E **145** C5
Inhafenga *Mozam.* 20°36S 33°53E **145** B5
Inhambane *Mozam.* 23°54S 35°30E **145** B6
Inhambane □ *Mozam.* 22°30S 34°20E **145** B5
Inhambupe *Brazil* 11°47S 38°21W **189** C3
Inhaminga *Mozam.* 18°26S 35°0E **143** F4
Inharrime *Mozam.* 24°30S 35°0E **145** B6
Inharrime → *Mozam.* 24°30S 35°0E **145** B6
Inhisar *Turkey* 40°3N 30°23E **99** A12
Inhul → *Ukraine* 46°50N 32°0E **85** J7
Inhulec *Ukraine* 47°42N 33°14E **85** J7
Inhulets → *Ukraine* 46°46N 32°47E **85** J7
Inhuma *Brazil* 6°40S 41°42W **189** B2
Iniesta *Spain* 39°27N 1°45W **91** F3
Ining = Yining *China* 43°58N 81°10E **109** D10
Inírida → *Colombia* 3°55N 67°52W **186** C5
Inis = Ennis *Ireland* 52°51N 8°59W **64** D3
Inishbofin *Ireland* 53°37N 10°13W **64** C1
Inisheer *Ireland* 53°3N 9°32W **64** C2
Inishfree B. *Ireland* 55°4N 8°23W **64** A3
Inishkea North *Ireland* 54°9N 10°11W **64** B1
Inishkea South *Ireland* 54°7N 10°12W **64** B1
Inishmaan *Ireland* 53°5N 9°35W **64** C2
Inishmore *Ireland* 53°8N 9°45W **64** C2
Inishmurray *Ireland* 54°26N 8°39W **64** B3
Inishowen Pen. *Ireland* 55°14N 7°15W **64** A4
Inishshark *Ireland* 53°37N 10°16W **64** C1
Inishturk *Ireland* 53°42N 10°7W **64** C1
Inishvickillane *Ireland* 52°3N 10°37W **64** D1
Injāna *Iraq* 34°29N 44°38E **105** E11
Injinoo ✪ *Australia* 10°56S 142°15E **150** A3
Injune *Australia* 25°53S 148°32E **151** D4
Inklin → *N. Amer.* 58°50N 133°10W **162** B2
Inland Kaikoura Ra.
N.Z. 41°59S 173°41E **155** B8
Inland Sea = Setonaikai
Japan 34°20N 133°30E **113** G6
Inle L. *Burma* 20°30N 96°58E **123** J20
Inlet *U.S.A.* 43°45N 74°48W **175** C10
Inn → *Austria* 48°35N 13°28E **78** C6
Innamincka *Australia* 27°44S 140°46E **151** D3
Inner Hebrides *U.K.* 57°0N 6°30W **65** E2
Inner Mongolia = Nei Mongol
Zizhiqu □ *China* 42°0N 112°0E **114** D7
Inner Sound *U.K.* 57°30N 5°55W **65** D3
Innerkip *Canada* 43°13N 80°42W **174** C4
Innes △ *Australia* 35°52S 136°53E **152** C2
Innetalling I. *Canada* 56°0N 79°0W **164** A4
Innisfail *Australia* 17°33S 146°5E **150** B4
Innisfail *Canada* 52°2N 113°57W **162** C6
In'noshima *Japan* 34°19N 133°10E **113** G6
Innsbruck *Austria* 47°16N 11°23E **78** D4
Innviertel *Austria* 48°15N 13°15E **78** C6
Inny → *Ireland* 53°32N 7°51W **64** C4
Inongo
Dem. Rep. of the Congo 1°55S 18°30E **140** E3
İnönü *Turkey* 39°48N 30°9E **99** B12
Inoucdjouac = Inukjuak
Canada 58°25N 78°15W **161** F16
Inousses *Greece* 38°33N 26°14E **99** C8
Inowrocław *Poland* 52°50N 18°12E **83** F5
Inquisivi *Bolivia* 16°50S 67°10W **188** D4
Inscription, C.
Australia 25°29S 112°59E **149** E1
Insein *Burma* 16°50N 96°5E **123** L20
Insjön *Sweden* 60°41N 15°6E **62** D9
Ińsko *Poland* 53°25N 15°32E **82** E2
Însurăţei *Romania* 44°50N 27°40E **81** F12
Inta *Russia* 66°5N 60°8E **106** C6
Intendente Alvear
Argentina 35°12S 63°32W **190** D3
İntepe *Turkey* 40°1N 26°20E **99** A8
Interlachen *U.S.A.* 29°37N 81°53W **179** F8
Interlaken *Switz.* 46°41N 7°50E **77** J3
Interlaken *U.S.A.* 42°37N 76°44W **175** D8
International Falls
U.S.A. 48°36N 93°25W **172** A7
Interview I. *India* 12°55N 92°43E **127** H11
Intiyaco *Argentina* 28°43S 60°5W **190** B3
Întorsura Buzăului
Romania 45°41N 26°2E **81** E11
Inukjuak *Canada* 58°25N 78°15W **161** F16
Inútil, B. *Chile* 53°30S 70°15W **192** D2
Inuvik *Canada* 68°16N 133°40W **160** D5
Inveraray *U.K.* 56°14N 5°5W **65** E3
Inverbervie *U.K.* 56°51N 2°17W **65** E6
Invercargill *N.Z.* 46°24S 168°24E **155** G3
Inverclyde □ *U.K.* 55°55N 4°49W **65** F4
Inverell *Australia* 29°45S 151°8E **151** D5
Invergordon *U.K.* 57°41N 4°10W **65** D4
Inverleigh *Australia* 38°6S 144°3E **152** E6
Inverloch *Australia* 38°38S 145°45E **151** F4
Invermere *Canada* 50°30N 116°2W **162** C5
Inverness *Canada* 46°15N 61°19W **165** C7
Inverness *U.K.* 57°29N 4°13W **65** D4
Inverness *Ala., U.S.A.* 32°1N 85°45W **178** C4
Inverness *Fla., U.S.A.* 28°50N 82°20W **179** G7
Inverurie *U.K.* 57°17N 2°23W **65** D6
Investigator Group
Australia 34°45S 134°20E **151** E1
Investigator Ridge
Ind. Oc. 11°30S 98°10E **146** F8
Investigator Str.
Australia 35°30S 137°0E **152** C2
Inya *Russia* 50°28N 86°37E **109** B11
Inyanga *Zimbabwe* 18°12S 32°40E **143** F3
Inyangani *Zimbabwe* 18°5S 32°50E **143** F3
Inyantue *Zimbabwe* 18°33S 26°39E **144** A4
Inyo Mts. *U.S.A.* 36°40N 118°0W **170** J9
Inyokern *U.S.A.* 35°39N 117°49W **171** K9
Inyonga *Tanzania* 6°45S 32°5E **142** D3
Inza *Russia* 53°55N 46°25E **86** D8
Inzhavino *Russia* 52°22N 42°30E **86** D6
Iō-Jima *Japan* 30°48N 130°18E **113** J5
Ioannina *Greece* 39°42N 20°47E **98** B2
Iola *U.S.A.* 37°55N 95°24W **172** G6
Ion Corvin *Romania* 44°7N 27°50E **81** F12
Iona *U.K.* 56°20N 6°25W **65** E2
Ione *U.S.A.* 38°21N 120°56W **170** G6
Ionia *U.S.A.* 42°59N 85°4W **173** D11
Ionian Is. = Ionioi Nisoi
Greece 38°40N 20°0E **98** C2
Ionian Sea *Medit. S.* 37°30N 17°30E **58** H9
Ionioi Nisoi *Greece* 38°40N 20°0E **98** C2
Ionioi Nisoi □ *Greece* 38°40N 20°0E **98** C2
Iony, Ostrov *Russia* 56°24N 143°22E **107** D15
Ios *Greece* 36°41N 25°20E **99** E7
Iowa □ *U.S.A.* 42°18N 93°30W **172** D7
Iowa → *U.S.A.* 41°10N 91°1W **172** E8
Iowa City *U.S.A.* 41°40N 91°32W **172** E8
Iowa Falls *U.S.A.* 42°31N 93°16W **172** D7
Iowa Park *U.S.A.* 33°57N 98°40W **176** E5
Ipala *Tanzania* 4°30S 32°52E **142** C3
Ipameri *Brazil* 17°44S 48°9W **189** D1
Ipanema *Brazil* 19°47S 41°44W **189** D2
Iparía *Peru* 9°17S 74°29W **188** B3
Ipati *Greece* 38°52N 22°14E **98** C4
Ipatinga *Brazil* 19°32S 42°30W **189** D2
Ipatovo *Russia* 45°45N 42°50E **87** H6
Ipel' → *Europe* 47°48N 18°53E **79** D11
Ipiales *Colombia* 0°50N 77°37W **186** C3
Ipiaú *Brazil* 14°8S 39°44W **189** C3
Ipin = Yibin *China* 28°45N 104°32E **116** C5
Ipirá *Brazil* 12°10S 39°44W **189** C3
Ipixuna *Brazil* 7°0S 71°40W **188** B3
Ipixuna → *Brazil* 7°11S 71°51W **188** B3
Ipoh *Malaysia* 4°35N 101°5E **121** K3
Ippy *C.A.R.* 6°5N 21°7E **140** C4
İpsala *Turkey* 40°55N 26°23E **97** F10
Ipsario, Oros *Greece* 40°40N 24°40E **97** F8
Ipswich *Australia* 27°35S 152°40E **151** D5
Ipswich *U.K.* 52°4N 1°10E **67** E9
Ipswich *Mass., U.S.A.* 42°41N 70°50W **175** D14
Ipswich *S. Dak., U.S.A.* 45°27N 99°2W **172** C4
Ipu *Brazil* 4°23S 40°44W **189** A2
Ipueiras *Brazil* 4°33S 40°43W **189** A2
Ipupiara *Brazil* 11°49S 42°37W **189** C2
Iqaluit *Canada* 63°44N 68°31W **161** E18
Iqaluktuutiaq = Cambridge Bay
Canada 69°10N 105°0W **160** D11
Iquique *Chile* 20°19S 70°5W **188** E3
Iquitos *Peru* 3°45S 73°10W **186** D4
Irabu-Jima *Japan* 24°50N 125°10E **113** M2
Iracoubo *Fr. Guiana* 5°30N 53°10W **187** B8
Īrafshān *Iran* 26°42N 61°56E **129** E9
Iraklia *Cyclades, Greece* 36°50N 25°28E **99** E7
Iraklia *Serres, Greece* 41°10N 23°16E **96** E7
Iraklio *Greece* 35°20N 25°12E **101** D7
Iráklion = Iraklio
Greece 35°20N 25°12E **101** D7
Irakliou, Kolpos *Greece* 35°23N 25°8E **101** D7
Irala *Paraguay* 25°55S 54°35W **191** B5
Iran ■ *Asia* 33°0N 53°0E **129** C7
Iran, Pegunungan
Malaysia 2°20N 114°50E **118** D4
Iran Ra. = Iran, Pegunungan
Malaysia 2°20N 114°50E **118** D4
Iranamadu Tank
Sri Lanka 9°23N 80°29E **127** K5
Īrānshahr *Iran* 27°15N 60°40E **129** E9
Irapuato *Mexico* 20°41N 101°28W **180** C4
Iraq ■ *Asia* 33°0N 44°0E **105** F10
Irati *Brazil* 25°25S 50°38W **191** B5
Irazú, Volcan
Costa Rica 10°28N 84°42W **182** D3
Irbes saurums *Latvia* 57°45N 22°5E **82** A9
Irbid *Jordan* 32°35N 35°48E **130** C4
Irbid □ *Jordan* 32°30N 35°50E **130** C5
Irebu
Dem. Rep. of the Congo 0°40S 17°46E **140** E3
Irecê *Brazil* 11°18S 41°52W **189** C2
Iregua → *Spain* 42°27N 2°24E **90** C7
Ireland ■ *Europe* 53°50N 7°52W **64** C4
Irele *Nigeria* 7°40N 5°40E **139** D6
Irgiz = Yrghyz
Kazakhstan 48°37N 61°16E **108** C6
Irgiz = Yrghyz →
Kazakhstan 48°6N 62°30E **108** C6
Irgiz, Bolshaya →
Russia 52°10N 49°10E **86** D9
Irharrhar, O. → *Algeria* 28°3N 6°15E **136** C5
Irherm *Morocco* 30°7N 8°18W **136** B2
Irhil M'Goun *Morocco* 31°30N 6°28W **136** B2
Iri = Iksan *S. Korea* 35°59N 127°0E **115** G14
Irian Jaya = Papua □
Indonesia 4°0S 137°0E **119** E9
Irian Jaya Barat □
Indonesia 2°5S 132°50E **119** E8
Irié *Guinea* 8°15N 9°10W **138** D3
Iriklinskoye Vdkhr.
Russia 52°0N 59°0E **108** B5
Iringa *Tanzania* 7°48S 35°43E **142** D4
Iringa □ *Tanzania* 7°48S 35°43E **142** D4
Irinjalakuda *India* 10°21N 76°14E **127** J3
Iriomote △ *Japan* 24°29N 123°53E **113** M1
Iriomote-Jima *Japan* 24°19N 123°48E **113** M1
Iriona *Honduras* 15°57N 85°11W **182** C2
Iriri → *Brazil* 3°52S 52°37W **187** D8
Irish Sea *Europe* 53°38N 4°48W **66** D3
Irkeshtam Pass = Erkech-Tam
Pass Asia 39°46N 74°2E **109** E8
Irkutsk *Russia* 52°18N 104°20E **110** A9
Irğanlı *Turkey* 37°53N 29°12E **99** D11
Irma *Canada* 52°55N 111°14W **163** C6
Irō-Zaki *Japan* 34°36N 138°51E **113** G9
Iroise, Mer d' *France* 48°15N 4°45W **70** D2
Iron Baron *Australia* 32°58S 137°11E **152** B2
Iron Gate = Portile de Fier
Europe 44°44N 22°30E **80** F7
Iron Knob *Australia* 32°46S 137°8E **152** B2
Iron Mountain *U.S.A.* 45°49N 88°4W **172** C9
Iron Range △
Australia 12°34S 143°18E **150** A3
Iron River *U.S.A.* 46°6N 88°39W **172** B9
Irondequoit *U.S.A.* 43°13N 77°35W **174** C7
Ironton *Mo., U.S.A.* 37°36N 90°38W **172** G8
Ironton *Ohio, U.S.A.* 38°32N 82°41W **173** F12
Ironwood *U.S.A.* 46°27N 90°9W **172** B8
Ironwood Forest ⌂
U.S.A. 32°32N 111°28W **169** K8
Iroquois *Canada* 44°51N 75°19W **175** B9
Iroquois Falls *Canada* 48°46N 80°41W **164** C3
Irpin *Ukraine* 50°30N 30°15E **75** C16
Irrara Cr. → *Australia* 29°35S 145°31E **151** D4
Irrawaddy □ *Burma* 17°0N 95°0E **123** L19
Irrawaddy → *Burma* 15°50N 95°6E **123** M19
Irrawaddy, Mouths of the
Burma 15°30N 95°0E **123** M19
Irricana *Canada* 51°19N 113°37W **162** C6
Irrunytju *Australia* 26°3S 128°56E **149** E4
Irshava *Ukraine* 48°19N 23°3E **80** B8
Irsina *Italy* 40°45N 16°14E **95** B9
Irtysh → *Russia* 61°4N 68°52E **106** C7
Irumu
Dem. Rep. of the Congo 1°32N 29°53E **142** B2
Irún *Spain* 43°20N 1°52W **90** B3
Irunea = Pamplona-Iruña
Spain 42°48N 1°38W **90** C3
Irurzun *Spain* 42°55N 1°50W **90** C3
Irvine *Canada* 49°57N 110°16W **163** D6
Irvine *U.K.* 55°37N 4°41W **65** F4
Irvine *Calif., U.S.A.* 33°41N 117°46W **171** M9
Irvine *Ky., U.S.A.* 37°42N 83°58W **173** G12
Irvinestown *U.K.* 54°28N 7°39W **64** B4
Irving *U.S.A.* 32°48N 96°56W **176** E6
Irvona *U.S.A.* 40°46N 78°33W **174** F6
Irwin → *Australia* 29°15S 114°54E **149** E1
Irwinton *U.S.A.* 32°49N 83°10W **178** C6
Irwinville *U.S.A.* 31°39N 83°23W **178** D6
Irymple *Australia* 34°14S 142°8E **152** C5
Is, Jebel *Sudan* 22°3N 35°28E **137** C4
Is-sur-Tille *France* 47°30N 5°8E **71** E12
Isa *Nigeria* 13°14N 6°24E **139** C6
Isa Khel *Pakistan* 32°41N 71°17E **124** C4
Isaac → *Australia* 22°55S 149°20E **150** C4
Isabel *U.S.A.* 45°24N 101°26W **172** C3
Isabel, I. *Mexico* 21°51N 105°55W **180** C3
Isabela *Phil.* 6°40N 121°59E **119** C6
Isabela *Puerto Rico* 18°30N 67°2W **183** d
Isabella, Cord. *Nic.* 13°30N 85°25W **182** D2
Isabella Ra. *Australia* 21°0S 121°4E **148** D3
Isaccea *Romania* 45°16N 28°28E **81** E13
Isachsen, C. *Canada* 79°20N 105°28W **161** B10
Isachsen Mt. *Antarctica* 72°8S 26°5E **55** D4
Ísafjarðardjúp *Iceland* 66°10N 23°0W **60** C2
Ísafjörður *Iceland* 66°5N 23°9W **60** C2
Isagarh *India* 24°48N 77°51E **124** G7
Isahaya *Japan* 32°52N 130°2E **113** H5
Isaka *Tanzania* 3°56S 32°59E **142** C3
İşalniţa *Romania* 44°24N 23°44E **81** F8
Isan → *India* 26°51N 80°7E **125** F9
Isana = Içana → *Brazil* 0°26N 67°19W **186** C5
Isangano △ *Zambia* 11°8S 30°35E **143** E3
Isanlu Makutu *Nigeria* 8°20N 5°50E **139** D6
Isar → *Germany* 48°48N 12°57E **77** G8
Isarco → *Italy* 46°27N 11°18E **93** B8
Isaris *Greece* 37°22N 22°0E **98** D3
Īsavī *Iran* 41°22N 4°32W **88** D6
Iscar *Spain* 41°22N 4°32W **88** D6
İscehisar *Turkey* 38°51N 30°45E **99** C12
Ischia *Italy* 40°44N 13°57E **94** B6
Ischigualasto △
Argentina 30°0S 68°0W **190** B2
Isdell → *Australia* 16°27S 124°51E **148** C3
Ise *Japan* 34°25N 136°45E **113** G8
Ise-Shima △ *Japan* 34°25N 136°48E **113** G8
Ise-Wan *Japan* 34°43N 136°43E **113** G8
Isefjord *Denmark* 55°53N 11°50E **63** J5
Isel → *Austria* 46°50N 12°47E **78** E5
Iseo *Italy* 45°39N 10°3E **92** C7
Iseo, L. d' *Italy* 45°43N 10°4E **92** C7
Iseramagazi *Tanzania* 4°37S 32°10E **142** C3
Isère □ *France* 45°15N 5°40E **73** C9
Isère → *France* 44°59N 4°51E **73** D8
Iserlohn *Germany* 51°22N 7°41E **76** D3
Isérnia *Italy* 41°36N 14°14E **95** A7
Iseyin *Nigeria* 8°0N 3°36E **139** D5
Isfahan = Eşfahān *Iran* 32°39N 51°43E **129** C6
Ishëm *Albania* 41°33N 19°34E **96** E3
Ishigaki *Japan* 24°26N 124°10E **113** M2
Ishigaki-Shima *Japan* 24°20N 124°10E **113** M2
Ishikari *Japan* 43°20N 141°15E **112** C10
Ishikari-Gawa →
Japan 43°15N 141°23E **112** C10
Ishikari-Sammyaku
Japan 43°30N 143°0E **112** C11
Ishikari-Wan *Japan* 43°25N 141°1E **112** C10
Ishikawa *Japan* 26°25N 127°49E **113** L3
Ishikawa □ *Japan* 36°30N 136°30E **113** F8
Ishim *Russia* 56°10N 69°30E **106** D7
Ishim → *Russia* 57°45N 71°10E **106** D8
Ishimbay *Russia* 53°28N 56°2E **108** B5
Ishinomaki *Japan* 38°32N 141°20E **112** E10
Ishioka *Japan* 36°11N 140°16E **113** F10
Ishkashim *Tajikistan* 36°44N 71°37E **109** E8
Ishkoman *Pakistan* 36°30N 73°50E **125** A5
Ishpeming *U.S.A.* 46°29N 87°40W **172** B10
Isigny-sur-Mer *France* 49°19N 1°6W **70** C5
Işıklar Dağı *Turkey* 40°45N 27°15E **97** F11
Işıklı *Turkey* 38°19N 29°51E **99** C11
Isil Kul *Russia* 54°55N 71°16E **109** B8
Ísili *Italy* 39°44N 9°6E **94** C2
iSimangaliso ⌂
S. Africa 27°50S 32°32E **145** C5
Isiolo *Kenya* 0°24N 37°33E **142** B4
Isiro
Dem. Rep. of the Congo 2°53N 27°40E **142** B2
Isisford *Australia* 24°15S 144°21E **150** C3
İskele = Trikomo
Cyprus 35°17N 33°52E **101** D12
İskenderun *Turkey* 36°32N 36°10E **104** D7
İskenderun Körfezi
Turkey 36°40N 35°50E **104** D6
İskilip *Turkey* 40°45N 34°29E **104** B6
Iskitim *Russia* 54°38N 83°18E **109** B10
Iskŭr → *Bulgaria* 43°45N 24°25E **97** C8
Iskŭr, Yazovir *Bulgaria* 42°23N 23°30E **96** D7
Iskut → *Canada* 56°45N 131°49W **162** B2
Isla → *U.K.* 56°32N 3°20W **65** E5
Isla Coiba △ *Panama* 7°33N 81°36W **182** E3
Isla Cristina *Spain* 37°13N 7°17W **89** H3
Isla de Salamanca △
Colombia 10°59N 74°40W **183** D5
Isla Gorge △ *Australia* 25°10S 149°57E **150** D4
Isla Guamblin △ *Chile* 44°50S 75°4W **192** B1
Isla Isabel △ *Mexico* 21°54N 105°58W **180** C3
Isla Magdalena △
Chile 44°20S 73°13W **192** B2
Isla Tiburón y San Esteban ⌂
Mexico 29°0N 112°27W **180** B2
Isla Vista *U.S.A.* 34°25N 119°53W **171** L7
İslahiye *Turkey* 37°0N 36°35E **104** D7
Islam Headworks
Pakistan 29°49N 72°33E **124** E5
Islamabad *Pakistan* 33°40N 73°10E **124** C5
Islamgarh *Pakistan* 27°51N 70°48E **124** F4
Islamkot *Pakistan* 24°42N 70°13E **124** G4
Islamorada *U.S.A.* 24°56N 80°37W **179** L9
Islampur *Bihar, India* 25°9N 85°12E **125** G11
Islampur *Maharashtra,*
India 17°2N 74°20E **126** F2
Islampur *Paschimbanga,*
India 26°16N 88°12E **125** F13
Island = Iceland ■
Europe 64°45N 19°0W **60** D4
Island L. *Canada* 53°47N 94°25W **163** C10
Island Lagoon
Australia 31°30S 136°40E **152** A2
Island Pond *U.S.A.* 44°49N 71°53W **175** B13
Islands, B. of *Canada* 49°11N 58°15W **165** C8
Islands, B. of *N.Z.* 35°15S 174°6E **154** B3
Islas Atlánticas de Galicia △
Spain 42°23N 8°55W **88** C2
Islay *U.K.* 55°46N 6°10W **65** F2
Isle → *France* 44°55N 0°15W **72** D3
Isle aux Morts *Canada* 47°35N 59°0W **165** C8
Isle of Hope *U.S.A.* 31°58N 81°5W **178** D8
Isle of Wight □ *U.K.* 50°41N 1°17W **67** G6
Isle Royale △ *U.S.A.* 48°0N 88°55W **172** B9
Isleton *U.S.A.* 38°10N 121°37W **170** G5
Ismail = Izmayil
Ukraine 45°22N 28°46E **81** E13
Ismâ'ilîya *Egypt* 30°37N 32°18E **137** E8
Ismaning *Germany* 48°13N 11°40E **77** G7
Isna *Egypt* 25°17N 32°30E **137** B3
Isojärvi △ *Finland* 61°40N 25°0E **60** F21
Ísola del Liri *Italy* 41°41N 13°34E **93** G10
Ísola della Scala *Italy* 45°16N 11°0E **92** C7
Ísola di Capo Rizzuto
Italy 38°58N 17°6E **95** D10
Isparta *Turkey* 37°47N 30°30E **99** D12
Isparta □ *Turkey* 38°0N 31°0E **104** D4
Isperikh *Bulgaria* 43°43N 26°50E **97** C10
Íspica *Italy* 36°47N 14°55E **95** F7
İspir *Turkey* 40°28N 40°59E **105** B9
Israel ■ *Asia* 32°0N 34°50E **130** D3
Issakly *Russia* 54°8N 51°32E **86** C10
Issaouane, Erg *Algeria* 26°58N 8°42E **136** C5
Issia *Ivory C.* 6°33N 6°33W **138** D3
Issoire *France* 45°32N 3°15E **72** C7
Issoudun *France* 46°57N 1°59E **71** F8
Issyk-Kul = Balykchy
Kyrgyzstan 42°26N 76°12E **109** D9
Issyk-Kul, Ozero = Ysyk-Köl
Kyrgyzstan 42°25N 77°15E **109** D9
Ist *Croatia* 44°17N 14°47E **93** D11
Istállós-kő *Hungary* 48°4N 20°26E **80** B5
İstanbul *Turkey* 41°0N 28°58E **97** E12
İstanbul □ *Turkey* 41°0N 29°0E **97** E12
İstanbul ✈ (IST) *Turkey* 40°59N 28°49E **97** F12
İstanbul Boğazı *Turkey* 41°5N 29°3E **97** E13
Istaravshan *Tajikistan* 39°55N 69°1E **109** E7
Istiea *Greece* 38°57N 23°9E **98** C5
Isto, Mt. *U.S.A.* 69°12N 143°48W **166** B11
Istok = Burim *Kosovo* 42°45N 20°24E **96** D4
Istokpoga, L. *U.S.A.* 27°23N 81°17W **179** H8
Istra *Croatia* 45°10N 14°0E **93** C10
Istres *France* 43°31N 4°59E **73** E8
Istria = Istra *Croatia* 45°10N 14°0E **93** C10
Itá *Paraguay* 25°29S 57°21W **190** B4
Itabaiana *Paraíba, Brazil* 7°18S 35°19W **189** B3
Itabaiana *Sergipe,*
Brazil 10°41S 37°37W **189** C3
Itabaianinha *Brazil* 11°16S 37°47W **189** C3
Itaberaba *Brazil* 12°32S 40°18W **189** C2
Itabira *Brazil* 19°37S 43°13W **189** D2
Itabirito *Brazil* 20°15S 43°48W **189** E2
Itabuna *Brazil* 14°48S 39°16W **189** C3
Itacajá *Brazil* 8°19S 47°46W **189** B1
Itacaunas → *Brazil* 5°21S 49°8W **187** E9
Itacoatiara *Brazil* 3°8S 58°25W **186** D7
Itaguari → *Brazil* 14°11S 44°40W **189** C2
Itaguatins *Brazil* 5°47S 47°29W **189** B1
Itaim → *Brazil* 7°2S 42°2W **189** B2
Itainópolis *Brazil* 7°24S 41°31W **189** B2
Itaipú, Represa de
Brazil 25°30S 54°30W **191** B5
Itäisen Suomenlahti △
Finland 60°25N 27°15E **60** F22
Itaituba *Brazil* 4°10S 55°50W **187** D7
Itajaí *Brazil* 27°50S 48°39W **191** B6
Itajubá *Brazil* 22°24S 45°30W **191** A6
Itajuípe *Brazil* 14°41S 39°22W **189** C3
Itaka *Tanzania* 8°50S 32°49E **143** D3
Itala ⌂ *S. Africa* 27°30S 31°7E **145** C5
Italy ■ *Europe* 42°0N 13°0E **59** G8
Itamaraju *Brazil* 17°4S 39°32W **189** D3
Itamarati *Brazil* 6°24S 68°15W **188** B4
Itamataré *Brazil* 2°16S 46°24W **189** A1
Itambacuri *Brazil* 18°1S 41°42W **189** D2
Itambé *Brazil* 15°15S 40°37W **189** D2
Itanhém *Brazil* 17°9S 40°20W **189** D2
Itapagé *Brazil* 3°41S 39°34W **189** A3
Itaparica, I. de *Brazil* 12°54S 38°42W **189** C3
Itaparica, Represa de
Brazil 11°3S 42°47W **189** C2
Itapebi *Brazil* 15°56S 39°32W **189** D3
Itapecuru Mirim *Brazil* 3°24S 44°20W **189** A2
Itaperuna *Brazil* 21°10S 41°54W **191** A7
Itapetinga *Brazil* 15°15S 40°15W **189** D2
Itapetininga *Brazil* 23°36S 48°7W **191** A6
Itapeva *Brazil* 23°59S 48°59W **191** A6
Itapicuru → *Bahia,*
Brazil 11°47S 37°32W **189** C3
Itapicuru → *Maranhão,*
Brazil 2°52S 44°12W **189** A2
Itapipoca *Brazil* 3°30S 39°35W **189** A3
Itapiúna *Brazil* 4°33S 38°57W **189** A3
Itaporanga *Brazil* 7°18S 38°0W **189** B3
Itapuá □ *Paraguay* 26°40S 55°40W **191** B4
Itaquai → *Brazil* 4°20S 70°12W **188** A3
Itaquí *Maranhão, Brazil* 2°34S 44°22W **189** A2
Itaquí *Rio Grande do S.,*
Brazil 29°8S 56°30W **190** B4
Itararé *Brazil* 24°6S 49°23W **191** A6
Itarsi *India* 22°36N 77°51E **124** H7
Itatí *Argentina* 27°16S 58°15W **190** B4
Itatiaia △ *Brazil* 22°22S 44°38W **191** A7
Itatira *Brazil* 4°30S 39°37W **189** A3
Itaueira *Brazil* 7°36S 43°2W **189** B2
Itaueira → *Brazil* 6°41S 42°55W **189** B2
Itaúna *Brazil* 20°4S 44°34W **189** E2
Itchen → *U.K.* 50°55N 1°22W **67** G6
Ite *Peru* 17°55S 70°57W **188** D3
Itea *Greece* 38°25N 22°25E **98** C4
Itezhi Tezhi, L. *Zambia* 15°30S 25°30E **143** F2
Ithaca = Ithaki *Greece* 38°25N 20°40E **98** C2
Ithaca *U.S.A.* 42°27N 76°30W **175** D8
Ithaki *Greece* 38°25N 20°40E **98** C2
Iti △ *Greece* 38°50N 22°15E **98** C4
Itinga *Brazil* 16°36S 41°47W **189** D2
Itiquira → *Brazil* 17°18S 56°44W **187** G7
Itiruçu *Brazil* 13°31S 40°9W **189** C2
Itiúba *Brazil* 10°43S 39°51W **189** C3
Itiyuro → *Argentina* 22°40S 63°50W **190** A3
Itō *Japan* 34°58N 139°5E **113** G9
Itoigawa *Japan* 37°2N 137°51E **113** F8
Iton → *France* 49°9N 1°12E **70** C8
Itonamas → *Bolivia* 12°28S 64°24W **186** F6
Itri *Italy* 41°17N 13°32E **94** A6
Itsa *Egypt* 29°15N 30°47E **137** F7
Íttiri *Italy* 40°36N 8°34E **94** B1
Ittoqqortoormiit
Greenland 70°20N 23°0W **57** C8
Itu *Brazil* 23°17S 47°15W **191** A6
Itu *Nigeria* 5°10N 7°58E **139** D6
Itu Aba I. *S. China Sea* 10°23N 114°21E **118** B4
Ituaçu *Brazil* 13°50S 41°18W **189** C2
Ituiutaba *Brazil* 19°0S 49°25W **187** G9
Itumbiara *Brazil* 18°20S 49°10W **187** G9
Ituna *Canada* 51°10N 103°24W **163** C8
Itunge Port *Tanzania* 9°40S 33°55E **143** D3
Iturbe *Argentina* 23°0S 65°25W **190** A2
Ituri →
Dem. Rep. of the Congo 1°40N 27°1E **142** B2
Iturup, Ostrov *Russia* 45°0N 148°0E **107** E15
Ituverava *Brazil* 20°20S 47°47W **189** E1
Ituxi → *Brazil* 7°18S 64°51W **186** E6
Itzehoe *Germany* 53°55N 9°31E **76** B5
Ivaí → *Brazil* 23°18S 53°42W **191** A5
Ivalo *Finland* 68°38N 27°35E **60** B22
Ivalojoki → *Finland* 68°40N 27°40E **60** B22
Ivanava *Belarus* 52°7N 25°29E **75** B13
Ivančice *Czech Rep.* 49°6N 16°23E **79** B9
Ivane-Puste *Ukraine* 48°39N 26°10E **81** B11
Ivăneşti *Romania* 46°39N 27°27E **81** D12
Ivangorod *Russia* 59°27N 28°13E **84** C5
Ivanhoe *N.S.W.,*
Australia 32°56S 144°20E **152** B6
Ivanhoe *Vic., Australia* 37°45S 145°3E **153** D6
Ivanhoe *Canada* 44°23N 77°28W **174** B7
Ivanhoe *Calif., U.S.A.* 36°23N 119°13W **170** J7
Ivanhoe *Minn., U.S.A.* 44°28N 96°15W **172** C5
Ivanhorod *Ukraine* 48°48N 29°50E **81** B14
Ivanić Grad *Croatia* 45°41N 16°25E **93** C13
Ivanjica *Serbia* 43°35N 20°12E **96** C4
Ivanjska *Bos.-H.* 44°55N 17°4E **80** F2
Ivankoyskoye Vdkhr.
Russia 56°37N 36°32E **84** D9
Ivano-Frankivsk
Ukraine 48°40N 24°40E **81** B9
Ivano-Frankivsk □
Ukraine 48°45N 24°30E **81** B9
Ivanovo = Ivanava
Belarus 52°7N 25°29E **75** B13
Ivanovo *Bulgaria* 43°43N 25°58E **97** C9
Ivanovo *Russia* 57°5N 41°0E **84** D11
Ivanovo □ *Russia* 57°10N 41°50E **86** B5
Ivanšćica *Croatia* 46°12N 16°13E **93** B13
Ivatsevichy *Belarus* 52°43N 25°21E **75** B13
Ivaylovgrad *Bulgaria* 41°32N 26°8E **97** E10
Iveragh Pen. *Ireland* 51°52N 10°15W **6**
Ivinheima → *Brazil* 23°14S 53°42W **19**
Ivinhema *Brazil* 22°10S 53°37W **19**
Ivittuut *Greenland* 61°14N 48°12W **5**
Ivory Coast *W. Afr.* 4°20N 5°0W **13**
Ivory Coast ■ *Africa* 7°30N 5°0W **13**
Ivösjön *Sweden* 56°8N 14°25E **6**
Ivrea *Italy* 45°28N 7°52E **9**
İvrindi *Turkey* 39°34N 27°30E **9**
Ivujivik *Canada* 62°24N 77°55W **161**
Ivvavik △ *Canada* 69°6N 139°30W **16**
Ivybridge *U.K.* 50°23N 3°56W **6**
Iwaizumi *Japan* 39°50N 141°45E **112**
Iwaki *Japan* 37°3N 140°55E **113**
Iwakuni *Japan* 34°15N 132°8E **11**
Iwamizawa *Japan* 43°12N 141°46E **112**
Iwanai *Japan* 42°58N 140°30E **112**
Iwata *Japan* 34°42N 137°51E **11**
Iwate □ *Japan* 39°30N 141°30E **112**
Iwate-San *Japan* 39°51N 141°0E **112**
Iwo *Nigeria* 7°39N 4°9E **13**
Iwŏn *N. Korea* 40°19N 128°39E **115**
Iwonicz-Zdrój *Poland* 49°37N 21°47E **8**
Ixiamas *Bolivia* 13°50S 68°5W **18**
Ixopo *S. Africa* 30°11S 30°5E **14**
Ixtepec *Mexico* 16°34N 95°6W **18**
Ixtlán del Río *Mexico* 21°2N 104°22W **18**
Iyo *Japan* 33°45N 132°45E **11**
Izabal, L. de *Guatemala* 15°30N 89°10W **18**
Izamal *Mexico* 20°56N 89°1W **18**
Izberbash *Russia* 42°35N 47°52E **8**
Izbica *Poland* 50°53N 23°10E **83**
Izbica Kujawska *Poland* 52°25N 18°40E **8**
Izbiceni *Romania* 43°45N 24°40E **8**
Izena-Shima *Japan* 26°56N 127°56E **11**
Izgrev *Bulgaria* 43°36N 26°58E **97**
Izhevsk *Russia* 56°51N 53°14E **10**
Izmayil *Ukraine* 45°22N 28°46E **81**
İzmir *Turkey* 38°25N 27°8E **9**
İzmir □ *Turkey* 38°15N 27°40E **9**
İzmir Adnan Menderes ✈ (ADB)
Turkey 38°23N 27°6E **9**
İzmir Körfezi *Turkey* 38°30N 26°50E **9**
İzmit = Kocaeli *Turkey* 40°45N 29°50E **97**
Iznájar *Spain* 37°15N 4°19W **8**
Iznalloz *Spain* 37°24N 3°30W **8**
İznik *Turkey* 40°23N 29°46E **10**
İznik Gölü *Turkey* 40°27N 29°30E **97**
Izobil'nyy *Russia* 45°25N 41°44E **8**
Izola *Slovenia* 45°32N 13°39E **93**
Izra *Syria* 32°51N 36°15E **13**
Iztochni Rodopi *Bulgaria* 41°45N 25°30E **9**
Izu-Hantō *Japan* 34°45N 139°0E **11**
Izu-Shotō *Japan* 34°30N 140°0E **113**
Izúcar de Matamoros
Mexico 18°36N 98°28W **18**
Izumi *Japan* 32°5N 130°22E **11**
Izumi-Sano *Japan* 34°23N 135°18E **11**
Izumo *Japan* 35°20N 132°46E **11**
Izyaslav *Ukraine* 50°5N 26°50E **75**
Izyum *Ukraine* 49°12N 37°19E **8**

J

J.F.K. Int. ✈ (JFK)
U.S.A. 40°38N 73°47W **175**
J.P. Koch Fjord *Greenland* 82°45N 44°0W **5**
J. Strom Thurmond L.
U.S.A. 33°40N 82°12W **17**
Ja-ela *Sri Lanka* 7°5N 79°53E **12**
Jabalón → *Spain* 38°53N 4°5W **8**
Jabalpur *India* 23°9N 79°58E **12**
Jabālya *Gaza Strip* 31°32N 34°29E **13**
Jabbūl *Syria* 36°4N 37°30E **12**
Jabiru *Australia* 12°40S 132°53E **14**
Jablah *Syria* 35°20N 36°0E **10**
Jablanac *Croatia* 44°42N 14°56E **93**
Jablanica *Bos.-H.* 43°40N 17°45E **8**
Jablonec nad Nisou
Czech Rep. 50°43N 15°10E **7**
Jablonica *Slovak Rep.* 48°37N 17°26E **79**
Jabłonowo Pomorskie
Poland 53°23N 19°10E **8**
Jablunkov *Czech Rep.* 49°35N 18°46E **79**
Jaboatão *Brazil* 8°7S 35°1W **18**
Jabotabek = Jakarta
Indonesia 6°9S 106°52E **11**
Jaboticabal *Brazil* 21°15S 48°17W **19**
Jabukovac *Serbia* 44°22N 22°21E **9**
Jaca *Spain* 42°35N 0°33W **9**
Jacaré → *Brazil* 10°3S 42°13W **18**
Jacareí *Brazil* 23°20S 46°0W **19**
Jacarèzinho *Brazil* 23°5S 49°58W **19**
Jacinto *Brazil* 16°10S 40°17W **18**
Jack River △ *Australia* 14°58S 144°19E **15**
Jackman *U.S.A.* 45°37N 70°15W **17**
Jacksboro *U.S.A.* 33°13N 98°10W **17**
Jackson *Barbados* 13°7N 59°36W **1**
Jackson *Ala., U.S.A.* 31°31N 87°53W **17**
Jackson *Calif., U.S.A.* 38°21N 120°46W **17**
Jackson *Ga., U.S.A.* 33°20N 83°57W **17**
Jackson *Ky., U.S.A.* 37°33N 83°23W **17**
Jackson *Mich., U.S.A.* 42°15N 84°24W **17**
Jackson *Minn., U.S.A.* 43°37N 95°1W **17**
Jackson *Miss., U.S.A.* 32°18N 90°12W **1**
Jackson *Mo., U.S.A.* 37°23N 89°40W **17**
Jackson *N.H., U.S.A.* 44°10N 71°11W **17**
Jackson *Ohio, U.S.A.* 39°3N 82°39W **17**
Jackson *S.C., U.S.A.* 33°20N 81°47W **1**
Jackson *Tenn., U.S.A.* 35°37N 88°49W **17**
Jackson *Wyo., U.S.A.* 43°29N 110°46W **16**
Jackson, C. *N.Z.* 40°59S 174°20E **15**
Jackson B. *N.Z.* 43°58S 168°42E **15**
Jackson Hd. *N.Z.* 43°58S 168°37E **15**
Jackson L. *Fla., U.S.A.* 30°30N 84°17W **17**
Jackson L. *Ga., U.S.A.* 33°19N 83°50W **17**
Jackson L. *Wyo.,*
U.S.A. 43°52N 110°36W **16**
Jacksons *N.Z.* 42°46S 171°32E **15**
Jackson's Arm *Canada* 49°52N 56°47W **16**
Jacksonville *Ala.,*
U.S.A. 33°49N 85°46W **17**
Jacksonville *Ark.,*
U.S.A. 34°52N 92°7W **17**
Jacksonville *Calif.,*
U.S.A. 37°52N 120°24W **17**
Jacksonville *Fla.,*
U.S.A. 30°20N 81°39W **17**
Jacksonville *Ga.,*
U.S.A. 31°49N 82°59W **17**

sonville Ill., U.S.A. 39°44N 90°14W 172 F8
sonville N.C.,
.S.A. 34°45N 77°26W 177 D16
sonville Tex.,
.S.A. 31°58N 95°17W 176 F7
sonville Beach
.S.A. 30°17N 81°24W 178 E8
sonville Int. ✕ (JAX)
.S.A. 30°30N 81°41W 178 E8
nel Haiti 18°14N 72°32W 183 C5
b Lake U.S.A. 36°43N 112°13W 169 H7
babad Pakistan 28°20N 68°29E 124 E3
bina Brazil 11°11S 40°30W 189 C2
ues-Cartier, Dét. de
anada 50°0N 63°30W 165 C7
ues-Cartier, Mt.
anada 48°57N 66°0W 165 C6
ues-Cartier △
anada 47°15N 71°33W 165 C5
ueville Ivory C. 5°12N 4°25W 138 D4
í → Brazil 30°2S 51°15W 191 C5
mba U.S.A. 32°37N 116°11W 171 N10
ndá → Brazil 1°57S 50°26W 187 D8
herla India 16°46N 78°9E 126 F4
Germany 53°20N 8°14E 76 B4
, Côte de France 46°40N 2°0W 70 F4
City Canada 59°15N 129°37W 162 B3
Dragon Snow Mt. = Yulong
ueshan China 27°6N 100°10E 116 D3
Mt. = Yü Shan
iwan 23°25N 120°52E 117 F13
busen Germany 53°29N 8°12E 76 B4
vnik Serbia 43°20N 19°45E 96 C3
aque Spain 40°55N 2°55W 90 E2
Peru 5°25S 78°40W 188 B2
Spain 37°44N 3°43W 89 H7
□ Spain 37°50N 3°30W 89 H7
abad India 20°52N 71°22E 124 J4
= Tel Aviv-Yafo
rael 32°4N 34°48E 130 C3
, C. Australia 36°58S 139°40E 152 D3
a Sri Lanka 9°45N 80°2E 127 K5
ey U.S.A. 42°49N 72°2W 175 D12
dhri India 30°10N 77°20E 124 D7
dishpur India 25°30N 84°21E 125 G11
t Nepal 28°19N 84°53E 125 E11
alpur India 19°3N 82°0E 126 E6
aqi China 50°25N 124°7E 111 A13
rsfontein S. Africa 29°44S 25°27E 144 C4
in → Iran 27°17N 57°13E 129 E8
dina Serbia 44°5N 21°15E 96 B5
on India 30°50N 75°25E 124 D6
→ Germany 49°14N 9°10E 77 F5
al India 18°50N 79°0E 126 E4
aquara Brazil 13°32S 39°58W 189 C3
ariaíva Brazil 24°10S 49°50W 191 A6
aribe Brazil 5°53S 38°37W 189 B3
aribe → Brazil 4°25S 37°45W 189 A3
aruana Brazil 4°50S 37°47W 189 A3
ey Grande Cuba 22°35N 81°7W 182 B3
gal, Mt. Australia 36°8S 148°22E 153 D8
nabad India 25°13N 84°59E 125 G11
zpur India 25°37N 75°17E 124 G6
om Iran 28°30N 53°31E 129 D7
os Brazil 7°21S 41°8W 189 B2
rh India 17°17N 73°13E 126 F1
n India 31°21N 76°9E 124 D7
lo Indonesia 1°5N 127°30E 119 D7
lo, Selat Indonesia 0°5N 129°5E 119 D7
r India 27°0N 75°50E 124 F6
India 26°15N 81°32E 125 F9
lmer India 26°55N 70°54E 124 F4
ghnagar India 23°38N 78°34E 125 H8
ran India 26°12N 73°56E 124 F5
ari India 23°14N 78°37E 125 H8
kot Nepal 28°42N 82°14E 125 E10
m Iran 36°58N 56°27E 129 B8
e Bos.-H. 44°19N 17°17E 80 F2
r India 20°53N 86°22E 126 D8
r → India 23°54N 74°13E 124 H6
rta Indonesia 6°9S 106°52E 118 F3
al India 29°48N 75°50E 124 E6
au India 23°13N 68°43E 124 H3
bshavn = Ilulissat
eenland 69°12N 51°10W 57 D5
bstad = Pietarsaari
nland 63°40N 22°43E 60 E20
pica Macedonia 41°45N 21°22E 96 E5
.S.A. 32°7N 103°12W 169 K12
il Si. Arabia 25°40N 45°27E 128 E5
-Abad Kyrgyzstan 40°56N 73°0E 109 D8
-Abad □
yrgyzstan 41°30N 72°30E 109 D8
ābād Afghan. 34°30N 70°29E 124 B4
abad India 27°41N 79°42E 125 F8
pur Jattan Pakistan 32°38N 74°11E 124 C6
na U.S.A. 34°29N 120°29W 171 L6
ndhar = Jullundur
dia 31°20N 75°40E 124 D6
pa Guatemala 14°39N 89°59W 182 D2
pa Enríquez = Xalapa
exico 19°32N 96°55W 181 D5
sjärvi Finland 62°29N 22°47E 60 E20
un India 26°8N 79°25E 125 F8
naka → Bangla. 26°16N 89°16E 125 F13
sar India 27°29N 78°19E 124 F8
swar Nepal 26°38N 85°48E 125 F11
on India 21°0N 75°42E 126 D2
ah Iraq 30°35N 46°32E 128 D5
go Nigeria 8°55N 11°25E 139 D7
co □ Mexico 20°20N 103°40W 180 D4
ot Pakistan 35°14N 73°24E 125 B5
a India 19°48N 75°38E 126 E2
n → Spain 41°47N 1°4W 90 D3
India 25°21N 72°37E 124 G5
a Mexico 21°38N 102°58W 180 C4
aiguri India 26°32N 88°46E 123 F16
an Mexico 21°14N 99°29W 181 C5
it I. Marshall Is. 6°0N 169°30E 156 G8
lā Iraq 34°16N 45°10E 105 E11
aame Somalia 0°4N 42°44E 131 G3
aari Nigeria 11°44N 9°53E 139 C6
aica ■ W. Indies 18°10N 77°30W 182 a
alpur Bangla. 24°52N 89°56E 123 G16
alpur India 25°18N 86°28E 125 G12
alpurganj India 23°2N 87°59E 125 H13
anxim → Brazil 4°43S 56°18W 187 D7
bewangi Indonesia 8°17S 114°7E 119 J17
bi Indonesia 1°38S 103°30E 118 E2
bi □ Indonesia 1°30S 102°30E 118 E2
Jambongan, Pulau
Malaysia 6°45N 117°20E 118 C5
Jambusar India 22°3N 72°51E 124 H5
James U.S.A. 32°58N 83°29W 178 C6
James → S. Dak.,
U.S.A. 42°52N 97°18W 172 D5
James → Va., U.S.A. 36°56N 76°27W 173 G15
James B. Canada 54°0N 80°0W 164 B3
James I. Gambia 13°19N 16°21W 138 C1
James Island U.S.A. 32°45N 79°55W 178 C10
James Ranges
Australia 24°10S 132°30E 148 D5
James Ross I.
Antarctica 63°58S 57°50W 55 C18
James Ross Str.
Canada 69°40N 96°10W 160 D12
Jamesabad Pakistan 25°17N 69°15E 124 G3
Jameson Land Greenland 71°0N 23°30W 57 C8
Jamestown Australia 33°10S 138°32E 152 B3
Jamestown S. Africa 31°6S 26°45E 144 D4
Jamestown N. Dak.,
U.S.A. 46°54N 98°42W 172 B4
Jamestown N.Y., U.S.A. 42°6N 79°14W 174 D5
Jamestown Pa., U.S.A. 41°29N 80°27W 174 E4
Jamestown S.C.,
U.S.A. 33°17N 79°42W 178 B10
Jamīlābād Iran 34°24N 48°28E 129 C6
Jamira → India 21°35N 88°28E 125 J13
Jämjö Sweden 56°12N 15°49E 63 H9
Jamkhandi India 16°30N 75°15E 126 F2
Jamkhed India 18°43N 75°19E 126 E2
Jammalamadugu India 14°51N 78°25E 127 G4
Jammerbugten Denmark 57°15N 9°20E 63 G3
Jammu India 32°43N 74°54E 124 C6
Jammu & Kashmir □
India 34°25N 77°0E 125 B7
Jamnagar India 22°30N 70°6E 124 H4
Jamner India 20°45N 75°52E 126 D2
Jamni → India 25°13N 78°35E 125 G8
Jampur Pakistan 29°39N 70°40E 124 E4
Jamrud Pakistan 33°59N 71°24E 124 C4
Jämsä Finland 61°53N 25°10E 84 B3
Jamshedpur India 22°44N 86°12E 125 H12
Jamtara India 23°59N 86°49E 125 H12
Jämtland Sweden 63°31N 14°0E 60 E16
Jämtlands län □ Sweden 63°0N 14°40E 62 B7
Jan L. Canada 54°56N 102°55W 163 C8
Jan Mayen Arctic 71°0N 9°0W 54 B7
Janakkala Finland 60°54N 24°36E 84 B3
Janakpur Nepal 26°42N 85°55E 125 F11
Janaúba Brazil 15°48S 43°19W 189 D2
Jand Pakistan 33°30N 72°6E 124 C5
Jandanku ✪ Australia 16°20S 135°45E 150 B2
Jandaq Iran 34°3N 54°22E 129 C7
Jandía Canary Is. 28°6N 14°21W 100 F5
Jandía, Pta. de
Canary Is. 28°3N 14°31W 100 F5
Jandía △ Canary Is. 28°4N 14°19W 100 F5
Jandola Pakistan 32°20N 70°9E 124 C4
Jandowae Australia 26°45S 151°7E 151 D5
Jándula → Spain 38°3N 4°6W 89 G6
Jane Pk. N.Z. 45°15S 168°20E 155 F3
Janesville U.S.A. 42°41N 89°1W 172 D9
Janga Ghana 10°5N 1°0W 139 C4
Jangamo Mozam. 24°6S 35°21E 145 B6
Janghai India 25°33N 82°19E 125 G10
Jangheung S. Korea 34°41N 126°52E 115 G14
Jangipur India 24°28N 88°4E 125 G13
Jangoon India 17°44N 79°5E 126 F4
Janikowo Poland 52°45N 18°7E 83 F5
Janja Bos.-H. 44°40N 19°14E 80 F4
Janjanbureh Gambia 13°30N 14°47W 138 C2
Janjevë Kosovo 42°35N 21°19E 96 D5
Janjgir India 22°1N 82°34E 125 J10
Janjina Croatia 42°58N 17°25E 93 F14
Janos Mexico 30°54N 108°10W 180 A3
Jánoshalma Hungary 46°18N 19°21E 80 D4
Jánosháza Hungary 47°8N 17°12E 80 C2
Jánossomorja Hungary 47°47N 17°11E 80 C2
Janów Poland 50°44N 19°27E 83 H6
Janów Lubelski Poland 50°48N 22°23E 83 H9
Janów Podlaski Poland 52°11N 23°11E 83 F10
Janowiec Wielkopolski
Poland 52°45N 17°30E 83 F4
Januária Brazil 15°25S 44°25W 189 D2
Janūb Sīnī □ Egypt 29°30N 33°50E 130 F2
Janubio Canary Is. 28°56N 13°50W 100 F6
Janville France 48°10N 1°50E 71 D8
Janwada India 18°0N 77°29E 126 E3
Janzé France 47°55N 1°28W 70 E5
Jaora India 23°40N 75°10E 124 H6
Japan ■ Asia 36°0N 136°0E 113 G8
Japan, Sea of Asia 40°0N 135°0E 112 E7
Japan Trench Pac. Oc. 32°0N 142°0E 156 D6
Japen = Yapen Indonesia 1°50S 136°0E 119 E9
Japiim Brazil 7°37S 72°54W 188 B3
Japla India 24°33N 84°1E 125 G11
Japurá → Brazil 3°8S 65°46W 186 D5
Jaquarão Brazil 32°34S 53°23W 191 C5
Jaqué Panama 7°27N 78°8W 182 E4
Jarābulus Syria 36°49N 38°1E 105 D8
Jaraguá do Sul Brazil 26°29S 49°4W 191 B6
Jaraicejo Spain 39°40N 5°49W 89 F5
Jaraíz de la Vera Spain 40°4N 5°45W 88 E5
Jarama → Spain 40°24N 3°32W 88 E7
Jaramānah Syria 33°29N 36°21E 104 F7
Jaramillo Argentina 47°10S 67°7W 192 C3
Jarandilla de la Vera Spain 40°8N 5°39W 88 E5
Jaranwala Pakistan 31°15N 73°26E 124 D5
Jarash Jordan 32°17N 35°54E 130 C4
Jarash □ Jordan 32°17N 35°54E 130 C4
Järbo Sweden 60°43N 16°36E 62 D10
Jardim Brazil 21°28S 56°2W 190 A4
Jardín → Spain 38°50N 2°10W 91 G2
Jardín América
Argentina 27°3S 55°14W 191 B4
Jardine River △
Australia 11°9S 142°21E 150 A3
Jardines de la Reina, Arch. de los
Cuba 20°50N 78°50W 182 B4
Jargalang China 43°5N 122°55E 115 C12
Jari → Brazil 1°9S 51°54W 187 D8
Jarīr, W. al →
Si. Arabia 25°38N 42°30E 128 E4
Järlåsa Sweden 59°53N 17°12E 62 E11
Jarmen Germany 53°54N 13°20E 76 B9
Järna Sweden 59°6N 17°34E 62 E11
Jarnac France 45°40N 0°11W 72 C3
Jarny France 49°9N 5°53E 71 C12
Jarocin Poland 51°59N 17°29E 83 G4
Jaroměř Czech Rep. 50°22N 15°52E 78 A8
Jarosław Poland 50°2N 22°42E 83 H9
Järpås Sweden 58°23N 12°57E 63 F6
Järpen Sweden 63°21N 13°26E 62 A7
Jarrahdale Australia 32°24S 116°5E 149 F2
Jarrahi → Iran 30°49N 48°48E 129 D6
Jartai China 39°45N 105°48E 114 E3
Jarud Qi China 44°28N 120°50E 115 B11
Järvenpää Finland 60°29N 25°5E 84 B3
Jarvis Canada 42°53N 80°6W 174 D4
Jarvis I. Pac. Oc. 0°15S 160°5W 157 H11
Jarvorník Czech Rep. 50°23N 17°2E 79 A10
Järvsö Sweden 61°43N 16°10E 62 C10
Jarwa India 27°38N 82°30E 125 F10
Jaša Tomić Serbia 45°26N 20°50E 80 E5
Jasdan India 22°2N 71°12E 124 H4
Jashpurnagar India 22°54N 84°9E 125 H11
Jasidih India 24°31N 86°39E 125 G12
Jasień Poland 51°46N 15°0E 83 G2
Jāsimīyah Iraq 33°45N 44°41E 105 F11
Jasin Malaysia 2°20N 102°26E 121 L4
Jāsk Iran 25°38N 57°45E 129 E8
Jasło Poland 49°45N 21°30E 83 J8
Jasmund Germany 54°32N 13°35E 76 A9
Jasmund △ Germany 54°31N 13°38E 76 A9
Jaso India 24°30N 80°29E 125 G9
Jason Is. Falk. Is. 51°0S 61°0W 192 D4
Jasper Alta., Canada 52°55N 118°5W 162 C5
Jasper Ont., Canada 44°52N 75°57W 175 B9
Jasper Ala., U.S.A. 33°50N 87°17W 177 E11
Jasper Fla., U.S.A. 30°31N 82°57W 178 E7
Jasper Ind., U.S.A. 38°24N 86°56W 172 F10
Jasper Tex., U.S.A. 30°56N 94°1W 176 F7
Jasper △ Canada 52°50N 118°8W 162 C5
Jasrasar India 27°43N 73°49E 124 F5
Jassān Iraq 32°58N 45°52E 105 G11
Jastarnia Poland 54°42N 18°40E 82 D5
Jastrebarsko Croatia 45°41N 15°39E 93 C12
Jastrowie Poland 53°26N 16°49E 82 E3
Jastrzębie Zdrój Poland 49°57N 18°35E 83 J5
Jász-Nagykun-Szolnok □
Hungary 47°15N 20°30E 80 C5
Jászapáti Hungary 47°32N 20°10E 80 C5
Jászárokszállás Hungary 47°39N 19°58E 80 C4
Jászberény Hungary 47°30N 19°55E 80 C4
Jászkisér Hungary 47°27N 20°20E 80 C5
Jászladány Hungary 47°23N 20°10E 80 C5
Jataí Brazil 17°58S 51°48W 187 G8
Jath India 17°3N 75°13E 126 F2
Jati Pakistan 24°20N 68°19E 124 G3
Jatibarang Indonesia 6°28S 108°18E 119 G13
Jatiluwih Indonesia 8°23S 115°8E 119 J18
Jatinegara Indonesia 6°13S 106°52E 119 G12
Játiva = Xátiva Spain 38°59N 0°32W 91 G4
Jättendal Sweden 61°58N 17°15E 62 C11
Jaú Brazil 22°10S 48°30W 191 A6
Jauja Peru 11°45S 75°15W 188 C2
Jaunpur India 25°46N 82°44E 125 G10
Java = Jawa Indonesia 7°0S 110°0E 118 F3
Java Sea Indonesia 4°35S 107°15E 118 E3
Java Trench Ind. Oc. 9°0S 105°0E 118 F3
Javadi Hills India 12°40N 78°40E 127 H4
Javalambre, Sa. de Spain 40°6N 1°0W 90 E4
Javānrud Iran 34°47N 46°31E 105 E12
Jávea Spain 38°48N 0°10E 91 G5
Javier, I. Chile 47°5S 74°25W 192 C2
Javla India 17°18N 75°9E 126 F2
Jawa Indonesia 7°0S 110°0E 118 F3
Jawa Barat □ Indonesia 7°0S 107°0E 119 G12
Jawa Tengah □
Indonesia 7°0S 110°0E 119 G14
Jawa Timur □ Indonesia 8°0S 113°0E 119 G15
Jawad India 24°36N 74°51E 124 G6
Jawhar India 19°55N 73°14E 126 E1
Jawhar Somalia 2°48N 45°30E 131 G4
Jawor Poland 51°4N 16°11E 83 G3
Jaworzno Poland 50°13N 19°11E 83 H6
Jaworzyna Śląska
Poland 50°55N 16°28E 83 H3
Jawoyn ✪ Australia 14°16S 132°28E 148 B5
Jay U.S.A. 30°57N 87°9W 179 E2
Jay Peak U.S.A. 44°55N 72°32W 175 B12
Jaya, Puncak Indonesia 3°57S 137°17E 119 E9
Jayanca Peru 6°24S 79°50W 188 B2
Jayanti India 26°45N 89°40E 123 F16
Jayapura Indonesia 2°28S 140°38E 119 E10
Jayawijaya, Pegunungan
Indonesia 5°0S 139°0E 119 F9
Jaynagar India 26°43N 86°9E 125 F12
Jaypur = Jeypore India 18°50N 82°38E 126 E6
Jayrūd Syria 33°49N 36°44E 104 F7
Jayton U.S.A. 33°15N 100°34W 176 E4
Jāz Mūrīān, Hāmūn-e
Iran 27°20N 58°55E 129 E8
Jazīreh-ye Shīf Iran 29°4N 50°54E 129 D6
Jazminal Mexico 24°52N 101°24W 180 C4
Jazzīn Lebanon 33°31N 35°35E 130 B4
Jean U.S.A. 35°47N 115°20W 171 K11
Jean Marie River
Canada 61°32N 120°38W 162 A4
Jean-Rabel Haiti 19°50N 73°5W 183 C5
Jeanerette U.S.A. 29°55N 91°40W 176 G9
Jeanette, Ostrov = Zhannetty,
Ostrov Russia 76°43N 158°0E 107 B16
Jeannette U.S.A. 40°20N 79°36W 174 F5
Jebāl Bārez, Kūh-e Iran 28°30N 58°20E 129 D8
Jebba Nigeria 9°9N 4°48E 139 D5
Jebel, Bahr el →
South Sudan 9°30N 30°25E 135 G12
Jebel Ali = Minā' Jabal 'Alī
U.A.E. 25°2N 55°8E 129 E7
Jebel Elba △ Egypt 22°11N 36°22E 137 C4
Jeberos Peru 5°15S 76°10W 188 B2
Jecheon S. Korea 37°8N 128°12E 115 F15
Jedburgh U.K. 55°29N 2°33W 65 F6
Jedda = Jiddah
Si. Arabia 21°29N 39°10E 131 C2
Jeddore L. Canada 48°3N 55°55W 165 C8
Jedlicze Poland 49°43N 21°40E 83 J8
Jędrzejów Poland 50°35N 20°15E 83 H7
Jedwabne Poland 53°17N 22°18E 83 E9
Jeetzel → Germany 53°9N 11°3E 76 B7
Jefferson Ga., U.S.A. 34°7N 83°35W 178 A6
Jefferson Iowa, U.S.A. 42°1N 94°23W 172 D6
Jefferson Ohio, U.S.A. 41°44N 80°46W 174 E4
Jefferson Tex., U.S.A. 32°46N 94°21W 176 E7
Jefferson, Mt. Nev.,
U.S.A. 38°47N 116°56W 168 G5
Jefferson, Mt. Oreg.,
U.S.A. 44°41N 121°48W 168 D3
Jefferson City Mo.,
U.S.A. 38°34N 92°10W 172 F7
Jefferson City Tenn.,
U.S.A. 36°7N 83°30W 177 C13
Jeffersontown U.S.A. 38°12N 85°35W 173 F11
Jeffersonville Ga.,
U.S.A. 32°41N 83°20W 178 C6
Jeffersonville Ind.,
U.S.A. 38°17N 85°44W 173 F11
Jeffrey City U.S.A. 42°30N 107°49W 168 E10
Jega Nigeria 12°15N 4°23E 139 C5
Jeju S. Korea 33°31N 126°32E 115 H14
Jeju-do S. Korea 33°29N 126°34E 115 H14
Jeju Haehyop
S. Korea 33°50N 126°30E 115 H14
Jēkabpils Latvia 56°29N 25°57E 84 D3
Jekyll I. U.S.A. 31°4N 81°25W 178 D8
Jelcz-Laskowice Poland 51°2N 17°19E 83 G4
Jelenia Góra Poland 50°50N 15°45E 83 H2
Jelgava Latvia 56°41N 23°49E 82 B10
Jelgava □ Latvia 56°35N 23°45E 82 B10
Jelica Serbia 43°50N 20°17E 96 C4
Jelšava Slovak Rep. 48°37N 20°15E 79 C13
Jemaluang Malaysia 2°16N 103°52E 121 L4
Jember Indonesia 8°11S 113°41E 119 H15
Jena Germany 50°54N 11°35E 76 E7
Jena U.S.A. 31°41N 92°8W 176 F8
Jenbach Austria 47°24N 11°47E 78 D4
Jendouba Tunisia 36°29N 8°47E 136 A5
Jendouba □ Tunisia 36°34N 8°52E 136 A5
Jengish Chokoso = Pobedy, Pik
Kyrgyzstan 42°0N 79°58E 109 D9
Jenīn West Bank 32°28N 35°18E 130 C4
Jenkins U.S.A. 37°10N 82°38W 173 G12
Jenner U.S.A. 38°27N 123°7W 170 G3
Jennings Fla., U.S.A. 30°36N 83°6W 178 E6
Jennings La., U.S.A. 30°13N 92°40W 176 F8
Jensen Beach U.S.A. 27°15N 80°14W 179 H9
Jeong-eup S. Korea 35°35N 126°50E 115 G14
Jeongseon S. Korea 37°20N 128°45E 115 F15
Jeonju S. Korea 35°50N 127°4E 115 G14
Jepara Indonesia 7°40S 109°14E 119 G14
Jeparit Australia 36°8S 142°1E 152 D5
Jequié Brazil 13°51S 40°5W 189 C2
Jequitaí → Brazil 17°4S 44°50W 189 D2
Jequitinhonha Brazil 16°30S 41°0W 189 D2
Jequitinhonha →
Brazil 15°51S 38°53W 189 D3
Jerada Morocco 34°17N 2°10W 136 B3
Jerantut Malaysia 3°56N 102°22E 121 L4
Jerejak, Pulau Malaysia 5°19N 100°19E 121 c
Jérémie Haiti 18°40N 74°10W 183 C5
Jeremoabo Brazil 10°4S 38°21W 189 C3
Jerez, Pta. Mexico 22°58N 97°40W 181 C5
Jerez de García Salinas
Mexico 22°39N 103°0W 180 C4
Jerez de la Frontera Spain 36°41N 6°7W 89 J4
Jerez de los Caballeros
Spain 38°20N 6°45W 89 G4
Jericho = El Arīḥā
West Bank 31°52N 35°27E 130 D4
Jericho Australia 23°38S 146°6E 150 C4
Jerichow Germany 52°30N 12°1E 76 C8
Jerid, Chott el = Djerid, Chott
Tunisia 33°42N 8°30E 136 B5
Jerilderie Australia 35°20S 145°41E 153 C6
Jermyn U.S.A. 41°32N 75°33W 175 E9
Jerome U.S.A. 42°44N 114°31W 168 E6
Jerramungup Australia 33°55S 118°55E 149 F2
Jersey U.K. 49°11N 2°7W 67 H5
Jersey City U.S.A. 40°42N 74°4W 175 F10
Jersey Shore U.S.A. 41°12N 77°15W 174 E7
Jerseyville U.S.A. 39°7N 90°20W 172 F8
Jerumenha Brazil 7°5S 43°30W 189 B2
Jerusalem
Israel/West Bank 31°47N 35°10E 130 D4
Jervis B. Australia 35°8S 150°46E 153 C9
Jervis Bay △ Australia 35°9S 150°40E 153 C9
Jervis Inlet Canada 50°0N 123°57W 162 C4
Jerzu Italy 39°47N 9°31E 94 C2
Jesenice Slovenia 46°28N 14°3E 93 B11
Jeseník Czech Rep. 50°14N 17°8E 79 A10
Jesenké Slovak Rep. 48°20N 20°10E 79 C13
Jesi = Iesi Italy 43°31N 13°14E 93 E10
Jésolo Italy 45°32N 12°38E 93 C9
Jessnitz Germany 51°40N 12°18E 76 D8
Jessore Bangla. 23°10N 89°10E 123 H16
Jesup U.S.A. 31°36N 81°53W 178 D8
Jesup, L. U.S.A. 28°43N 81°14W 179 G8
Jesús Peru 7°15S 78°25W 188 B2
Jesús Carranza Mexico 17°26N 95°2W 181 D5
Jesús María Argentina 30°59S 64°5W 190 C3
Jetmore U.S.A. 38°4N 99°54W 172 F4
Jetpur India 21°45N 70°10E 124 J4
Jeumont France 50°18N 4°6E 71 B11
Jevnaker Norway 60°15N 10°26E 61 F14
Jewett U.S.A. 40°22N 81°2W 174 F3
Jewett City U.S.A. 41°36N 71°59W 175 E13
Jeyḥūnābād Iran 34°58N 48°59E 129 C6
Jeypore India 18°50N 82°38E 126 E6
Jeziorak, Jezioro Poland 53°40N 19°35E 82 E6
Jeziorany Poland 53°58N 20°46E 82 E7
Jeziorka → Poland 52°8N 21°9E 83 F8
Jha Jha India 24°46N 86°22E 125 G12
Jhaarkand = Jharkhand □
India 24°0N 85°50E 125 H11
Jhabua India 22°46N 74°36E 124 H6
Jhajjar India 28°37N 76°42E 124 E7
Jhal Pakistan 28°17N 67°27E 124 E2
Jhal Jhao Pakistan 26°20N 65°35E 122 F4
Jhalawar India 24°40N 76°10E 124 G7
Jhalida India 23°22N 85°58E 125 H11
Jhalrapatan India 24°33N 76°10E 124 G7
Jhang Maghiana
Pakistan 31°15N 72°22E 124 D5
Jhang Sadr = Jhang Maghiana
Pakistan 31°15N 72°22E 124 D5
Jhansi India 25°30N 78°36E 125 G8
Jhargram India 22°27N 86°59E 125 H12
Jharia India 23°45N 86°26E 125 H12
Jharkhand □ India 24°0N 85°50E 125 H11
Jharsuguda India 21°56N 84°5E 126 D7
Jhelum Pakistan 33°0N 73°45E 124 C5
Jhelum → Pakistan 31°20N 72°10E 124 D5
Jhilmilli India 23°24N 82°51E 125 H10
Jhudo Pakistan 24°58N 69°18E 124 G3
Jhunjhunun India 28°10N 75°30E 124 E6
Ji-Paraná Brazil 10°52S 62°57W 186 F6
Ji Xian China 36°7N 110°40E 114 F6
Jia Xian Henan, China 33°59N 113°12E 114 H7
Jia Xian Shaanxi, China 38°12N 110°28E 114 E6
Jiahe China 25°38N 112°19E 117 E9
Jiaji = Qionghai China 19°15N 110°26E 117 a
Jialing Jiang → China 29°30N 106°20E 116 C6
Jiamusi China 46°40N 130°26E 111 B15
Ji'an Jiangxi, China 27°6N 114°59E 117 D10
Ji'an Jilin, China 41°5N 126°10E 115 D14
Jianchang China 40°55N 120°35E 115 D11
Jianchuan China 26°38N 99°55E 116 D2
Jiande China 29°23N 119°15E 117 C12
Jiang'an China 28°40N 105°3E 116 C5
Jiangbei China 29°40N 106°34E 116 C6
Jiangcheng China 22°36N 101°52E 116 F3
Jiangchuan China 24°8N 102°39E 116 E4
Jiangdi China 26°57N 103°37E 116 D4
Jiangdu China 32°27N 119°36E 117 A12
Jiange China 32°4N 105°32E 116 A5
Jianghua China 25°0N 111°47E 117 E8
Jiangjin China 29°14N 106°14E 116 C6
Jiangkou China 27°40N 108°49E 116 D7
Jiangle China 26°42N 117°23E 117 D11
Jiangmen China 22°32N 113°0E 117 F9
Jiangning China 31°55N 118°50E 117 B12
Jiangshan China 28°40N 118°37E 117 C12
Jiangsu □ China 33°0N 120°0E 115 H11
Jiangxi □ China 27°30N 116°0E 117 D11
Jiangyan China 32°30N 120°7E 117 A13
Jiangyin China 31°54N 120°17E 117 B13
Jiangyong China 25°20N 111°22E 117 E8
Jiangyou China 31°44N 104°43E 116 B5
Jiangyuan China 42°2N 126°34E 115 C14
Jianhe China 26°37N 108°31E 116 D7
Jianli China 29°46N 112°56E 117 C9
Jianning China 26°50N 116°50E 117 D11
Jian'ou China 27°3N 118°17E 117 D12
Jianping China 41°53N 119°42E 115 D10
Jianshi China 30°37N 109°38E 116 B7
Jianshui China 23°36N 102°43E 116 F4
Jianyang Fujian, China 27°20N 118°5E 117 D12
Jianyang Sichuan,
China 30°24N 104°33E 116 B5
Jiao Xian = Jiaozhou
China 36°18N 120°1E 115 F11
Jiaohe Hebei, China 38°2N 116°20E 114 E9
Jiaohe Jilin, China 43°40N 127°22E 115 C14
Jiaoling China 24°41N 116°12E 117 E11
Jiaonan China 35°52N 119°58E 115 G10
Jiaozhou China 36°18N 120°1E 115 F11
Jiaozhou Wan China 36°5N 120°10E 115 F11
Jiaozuo China 35°16N 113°12E 114 G7
Jiawang China 34°28N 117°26E 115 G9
Jiaxiang China 35°25N 116°20E 114 G9
Jiaxing China 30°49N 120°45E 117 B13
Jiayi = Chiai Taiwan 23°29N 120°25E 117 F13
Jiayu China 29°55N 113°55E 117 C9
Jiayuguan China 39°49N 98°18E 110 D8
Jibão, Serra do Brazil 14°48S 45°0W 189 C2
Jibiya Nigeria 13°5N 7°12E 139 C6
Jibou Romania 47°15N 23°17E 81 C8
Jibuti = Djibouti ■ Africa 12°0N 43°0E 131 E3
Jicarón, I. Panama 7°10N 81°50W 182 E3
Jičín Czech Rep. 50°25N 15°28E 78 A8
Jiddah Si. Arabia 21°29N 39°10E 131 C2
Jido India 29°2N 94°58E 123 E19
Jieshou China 33°18N 115°22E 114 H8
Jiexiu China 37°2N 111°55E 114 F6
Jieyang China 23°35N 116°21E 117 F11
Jigalong Australia 23°21S 120°47E 148 D3
Jigalong ✪ Australia 23°21S 120°46E 148 D3
Jigawa □ Nigeria 12°0N 9°45E 139 C6
Jigni India 25°45N 79°25E 125 G8
Jihlava Czech Rep. 49°28N 15°35E 78 B8
Jihlava → Czech Rep. 48°55N 16°36E 79 C9
Jihlavský □ Czech Rep. 49°30N 15°30E 78 B8
Jihočeský □ Czech Rep. 49°8N 14°35E 78 B7
Jihomoravský □
Czech Rep. 49°5N 16°30E 79 B9
Jijel Algeria 36°52N 5°50E 136 A5
Jijel □ Algeria 36°45N 6°0E 136 A5
Jijiga Ethiopia 9°20N 42°50E 131 F3
Jikamshi Nigeria 12°12N 7°45E 139 C6
Jilib Somalia 0°29N 42°46E 131 G3
Jilin China 43°44N 126°30E 115 C14
Jilin □ China 44°0N 127°0E 115 C14
Jiloca → Spain 41°21N 1°39W 90 D3
Jilong = Chilung
Taiwan 25°3N 121°45E 117 E13
Jim Thorpe U.S.A. 40°52N 75°44W 175 F9
Jima Ethiopia 7°40N 36°47E 131 F2
Jimbaran, Teluk
Indonesia 8°46S 115°9E 119 K18
Jimbolia Romania 45°47N 20°43E 80 E5
Jimena de la Frontera
Spain 36°27N 5°24W 89 J5
Jiménez Mexico 27°8N 104°54W 180 B4
Jimeta Nigeria 9°17N 12°28E 139 D7
Jimo China 36°23N 120°30E 115 F11
Jimsar China 43°59N 89°4E 109 D11
Jin Jiang → China 28°24N 115°48E 117 C10
Jin Xian = Jinzhou
China 38°55N 121°42E 115 E11
Jinan China 36°38N 117°1E 114 F9
Jinchang China 38°30N 102°10E 110 D9
Jincheng China 35°29N 112°50E 114 G7
Jinchuan China 31°30N 102°3E 116 B4
Jind India 29°19N 76°22E 124 E7
Jindabyne Australia 36°25S 148°35E 153 D8
Jinding China 22°22N 113°33E 111 a
Jindo S. Korea 34°28N 126°15E 115 G14
Jindřichův Hradec
Czech Rep. 49°10N 15°2E 78 B8
Jing He → China 34°27N 109°4E 114 G5
Jing Shan China 31°20N 111°35E 117 B8
Jing Xian China 30°38N 118°25E 117 B12
Jing'an China 28°50N 115°17E 117 C10
Jingbian China 37°20N 108°30E 114 F5
Jingchuan China 35°20N 107°20E 114 G4
Jingde China 30°15N 118°27E 117 B12
Jingdezhen China 29°20N 117°11E 117 C11
Jingdong China 24°23N 100°47E 116 E3
Jinggangshan China 26°58N 114°15E 117 D10
Jinggu China 23°35N 100°41E 116 F3
Jinghai Guangdong,
China 22°59N 116°31E 117 F11
Jinghai Tianjin, China 38°55N 116°55E 114 E9
Jinghong China 22°0N 100°45E 116 G3
Jinghong Dam China 22°10N 100°46E 116 F3
Jingjiang China 32°2N 120°16E 117 A13
Jingle China 38°20N 111°55E 114 E6
Jingmen China 31°0N 112°10E 117 B9
Jingning China 35°30N 105°43E 114 G3
Jingpo Hu China 43°55N 128°55E 115 C15
Jingshan China 31°1N 113°7E 117 B9
Jingtai China 37°10N 104°6E 114 F3
Jingtang China 39°10N 119°5E 115 E10
Jingxi China 23°8N 106°27E 116 F6
Jingyang China 34°30N 108°50E 114 G5
Jingyu China 42°25N 126°45E 115 C14
Jingyuan China 36°30N 104°40E 114 F3
Jingzhou Hubei, China 30°21N 112°11E 117 B9
Jingzhou Hunan, China 26°33N 109°40E 116 D7
Jingziguan China 33°15N 111°0E 114 H6
Jinhua China 29°8N 119°38E 117 C12
Jining Nei Monggol Zizhiqu,
China 41°5N 113°0E 114 D7
Jining Shandong, China 35°22N 116°34E 114 G9
Jinja Uganda 0°25N 33°12E 142 B3
Jinjang Malaysia 3°13N 101°39E 121 L3
Jinji China 37°58N 106°8E 114 F4
Jinjiang Fujian, China 24°43N 118°33E 117 E12
Jinjiang Yunnan, China 26°14N 100°34E 116 D3
Jinjini Ghana 7°26N 2°42W 138 D4
Jinju S. Korea 35°12N 128°2E 115 G15
Jinkou China 30°20N 114°8E 117 B10
Jinkouhe China 29°18N 103°4E 116 C4
Jinmu Jiao China 18°9N 109°34E 117 a
Jinnah Barrage
Pakistan 32°58N 71°33E 124 C4
Jinning China 24°38N 102°38E 116 E4
Jinotega Nic. 13°6N 85°59W 182 D2
Jinotepe Nic. 11°50N 86°10W 182 D2
Jinping Guizhou, China 26°41N 109°10E 116 D7
Jinping Yunnan, China 22°45N 103°18E 116 F4
Jinsha China 27°29N 106°12E 116 D6
Jinsha Jiang → China 28°50N 104°36E 116 C5
Jinshi China 29°40N 111°50E 117 C8
Jintan China 31°42N 119°36E 117 B12
Jintur India 19°37N 76°42E 126 E3
Jinxi Jiangxi, China 27°56N 116°45E 117 D11
Jinxi Liaoning, China 40°52N 120°50E 115 D11
Jinxian China 28°26N 116°17E 117 C11
Jinxiang China 35°5N 116°22E 114 G9
Jinyang China 27°28N 103°5E 116 D4
Jinyun China 28°35N 120°5E 117 C13
Jinzhai China 31°40N 115°53E 117 B10
Jinzhong China 37°42N 112°46E 114 F7
Jinzhou Liaoning,
China 38°55N 121°42E 115 E11
Jinzhou Liaoning, China 41°5N 121°3E 115 D11
Jiparaná → Brazil 8°3S 62°52W 186 E6
Jipijapa Ecuador 1°0S 80°40W 186 D2
Jiquilpan Mexico 19°59N 102°43W 180 D4
Jirisan S. Korea 35°20N 127°44E 115 G14
Jiroft Iran 28°45N 57°50E 129 D8
Jishan China 35°34N 110°58E 114 G6
Jishou China 28°21N 109°43E 116 C7
Jishui China 27°12N 115°8E 117 D10
Jisr ash Shughūr Syria 35°49N 36°18E 104 E7
Jitarning Australia 32°48S 117°57E 149 F2
Jitra Malaysia 6°16N 100°25E 121 J3
Jiu → Romania 43°47N 23°48E 81 G8
Jiudengkou China 39°56N 106°40E 114 E4
Jiujiang Guangdong,
China 22°50N 113°0E 117 F9
Jiujiang Jiangxi, China 29°42N 115°58E 117 C10
Jiuling Shan China 28°40N 114°40E 117 C10
Jiulong = Kowloon
China 22°19N 114°11E 117 F10
Jiulong China 28°57N 101°31E 116 C3
Jiuquan China 39°50N 98°20E 110 D8
Jiutai China 44°10N 125°50E 115 B13
Jiuxincheng China 39°17N 115°59E 114 E8
Jiuzhaigou △ China 33°8N 103°52E 116 A4
Jiwani Pakistan 25°1N 61°44E 122 G2
Jixi Anhui, China 30°5N 118°34E 117 B12
Jixi Heilongjiang, China 45°20N 130°50E 115 B16
Jiyang China 37°0N 117°12E 115 F9
Jiyuan China 35°7N 112°57E 114 G7
Jīzān Si. Arabia 17°0N 42°20E 131 D3
Jize China 36°54N 114°56E 114 F8
Jizera → Czech Rep. 50°10N 14°43E 78 A7
Jizhou China 37°35N 115°30E 114 F8
Jizl, Wādī al →
Si. Arabia 25°39N 38°25E 128 E3
Jizō-Zaki Japan 35°34N 133°20E 113 G6
Jizzax Uzbekistan 40°6N 67°50E 109 D7
Jizzax □ Uzbekistan 40°20N 67°40E 109 D7
Joaçaba Brazil 27°5S 51°31W 191 B5
Joaíma Brazil 16°39S 41°2W 189 D2
Joal Fadiout Senegal 14°9N 16°50W 138 C1
João Amaro Brazil 12°46S 40°22W 189 C2
João Câmara Brazil 5°32S 35°48W 189 B3
João Neiva Brazil 19°45S 40°24W 189 D2
João Pessoa Brazil 7°10S 34°52W 189 B4
João Pinheiro Brazil 17°45S 46°10W 189 D1
Joaquín V. González
Argentina 25°10S 64°0W 190 B3
Jobat India 22°25N 74°34E 124 H6
Jobourg, Nez de France 49°41N 1°57W 70 C5
Jódar Spain 37°50N 3°21W 89 H7
Jodhpur India 26°23N 73°8E 124 F5
Jodiya India 22°42N 70°18E 124 H4
Joensuu Finland 62°37N 29°49E 60 E23
Jōetsu Japan 37°12N 138°10E 113 F9
Jœuf France 49°12N 6°0E 71 C12
Jofane Mozam. 21°15S 34°18E 145 B5
Jog Falls = Gersoppa Falls
India 14°12N 74°46E 127 G2
Jogbani India 26°25N 87°15E 125 F12
Jõgeva Estonia 58°45N 26°24E 84 C4
Jogjakarta = Yogyakarta
Indonesia 7°49S 110°22E 118 F4
Johannesburg S. Africa 26°11S 28°2E 145 C4
Johannesburg U.S.A. 35°22N 117°38W 171 K9
Johansfors Sweden 56°42N 15°32E 63 H9
Johilla → India 23°37N 81°14E 125 H9
John Crow Mts. Jamaica 18°5N 76°25W 182 a
John Day U.S.A. 44°25N 118°57W 168 D4
John Day → U.S.A. 45°44N 120°39W 168 D3
John Day Fossil Beds △
U.S.A. 44°33N 119°38W 168 D4
John D'or Prairie
Canada 58°30N 115°8W 162 B5
John F. Kennedy Space Center
U.S.A. 28°40N 80°42W 179 G9
John H. Kerr Res.
U.S.A. 36°36N 78°18W 177 C15
John o' Groats U.K. 58°38N 3°4W 65 C5
Johnnie U.S.A. 36°25N 116°5W 171 J10
Johns Creek U.S.A. 34°2N 84°12W 178 A5
Johns I. U.S.A. 32°47N 80°7W 178 C9
John's Ra. Australia 21°55S 133°23E 150 C1
Johnson U.S.A. 44°38N 72°41W 175 B12
Johnson City Kans.,
U.S.A. 37°34N 101°45W 172 G3

Johnson City N.Y., U.S.A. 42°7N 75°58W **175** D9
Johnson City Tenn., U.S.A. 36°19N 82°21W **177** C13
Johnson City Tex., U.S.A. 30°17N 98°25W **176** F5
Johnsonburg U.S.A. 41°29N 78°41W **174** E6
Johnsondale U.S.A. 35°58N 118°32W **171** K8
Johnsons Crossing Canada 60°29N 133°18W **162** A2
Johnsonville N.Z. 41°13S 174°48E **154** H3
Johnston U.S.A. 33°50N 81°48W **178** B8
Johnston, L. Australia 32°25S 120°30E **149** F3
Johnston Falls = Mambilima Falls Zambia 10°31S 28°45E **143** E2
Johnston I. Pac. Oc. 17°10N 169°8W **157** F11
Johnstone Str. Canada 50°28N 126°0W **162** C3
Johnstown Ireland 52°45N 7°33W **64** D4
Johnstown N.Y., U.S.A. 43°0N 74°22W **175** C10
Johnstown Ohio, U.S.A. 40°9N 82°41W **174** F2
Johnstown Pa., U.S.A. 40°20N 78°55W **174** F6
Johor □ Malaysia 2°5N 103°20E **121** M4
Johor, Selat Asia 1°28N 103°47E **121** d
Johor Bahru Malaysia 1°28N 103°46E **121** d
Jõhvi Estonia 59°22N 27°27E **84** C4
Joigny France 47°58N 3°20E **71** E10
Joinville France 48°27N 5°10E **71** D12
Joinville I. Antarctica 65°0S 55°30W **55** C18
Jojutla Mexico 18°37N 99°11W **181** D5
Jøkelbugten Greenland 78°25N 20°20W **57** B9
Jokkmokk Sweden 66°35N 19°50E **60** C18
Jökulsá á Bru → Iceland 65°40N 14°16W **60** D6
Jökulsá á Fjöllum → Iceland 66°10N 16°30W **60** C5
Jökulsárgljúfur △ Iceland 65°56N 16°31W **60** D5
Jolfa Āzarbājān-e Sharqī, Iran 38°57N 45°38E **105** C11
Jolfa Esfahan, Iran 32°58N 51°37E **129** C6
Joliet U.S.A. 41°32N 88°5W **172** E9
Joliette Canada 46°3N 73°24W **164** C5
Jolo Phil. 6°0N 121°0E **119** C6
Jolon U.S.A. 35°58N 121°9W **170** K5
Jombang Indonesia 7°33S 112°14E **119** G15
Jomda China 31°28N 98°12E **116** B2
Jonåker Sweden 58°45N 16°45E **63** F10
Jonava Lithuania 55°8N 24°12E **84** E3
Jones Sound Canada 76°0N 85°0W **161** B15
Jonesboro Ark., U.S.A. 35°50N 90°42W **177** D9
Jonesboro Ga., U.S.A. 33°31N 84°22W **178** B5
Jonesboro La., U.S.A. 32°15N 92°43W **176** E8
Jong → S. Leone 7°32N 12°33W **138** D2
Joniškis Lithuania 56°13N 23°35E **82** B10
Jönköping Sweden 57°45N 14°8E **63** G8
Jönköpings län □ Sweden 57°30N 14°30E **63** G8
Jonquière Canada 48°27N 71°14W **165** C5
Jonsered Sweden 57°45N 12°10E **63** G6
Jonzac France 45°27N 0°28W **72** C3
Joplin U.S.A. 37°6N 94°31W **172** G6
Jora India 26°20N 77°49E **124** F6
Jordan Mont., U.S.A. 47°19N 106°55W **168** C10
Jordan N.Y., U.S.A. 43°4N 76°29W **175** C8
Jordan ■ Asia 31°0N 36°0E **130** E5
Jordan → Asia 31°48N 35°32E **130** D4
Jordan Valley U.S.A. 42°59N 117°3W **168** E5
Jordânia Brazil 15°55S 40°11W **189** D2
Jordanów Poland 49°41N 19°49E **83** J6
Jorge, C. Chile 51°40S 75°35W **192** D1
Jørgen Brønlund Fjord Greenland 82°30N 31°0W **57** A7
Jorhat India 26°45N 94°12E **123** F19
Jori → Norway 62°4N 9°5E **62** B3
Jörn Sweden 65°4N 20°1E **60** D19
Jorong Indonesia 3°58S 114°56E **118** E4
Jørpeland Norway 59°3N 6°1E **61** G12
Jorquera → Chile 28°3S 69°58W **190** B2
Joru S. Leone 7°41N 11°9W **138** D2
Jos Nigeria 9°53N 8°51E **139** D6
Jos Plateau Nigeria 9°55N 9°0E **139** D6
Jošanička Banja Serbia 43°24N 20°47E **96** C4
José Battle y Ordóñez Uruguay 33°20S 55°10W **191** C4
José de San Martín Argentina 44°4S 70°26W **192** B2
Joseni Romania 46°42N 25°29E **81** D10
Joseph, L. Canada 45°10N 79°44W **174** A5
Joseph Banks Group Australia 34°36S 136°16E **152** C2
Joseph Bonaparte G. Australia 14°35S 128°50E **148** B4
Joseph L. Canada 52°45N 65°18W **165** B6
Joshinath India 30°34N 79°34E **125** D8
Joshinetsu-Kōgen △ Japan 36°42N 138°32E **113** F9
Joshua Tree U.S.A. 34°8N 116°19W **171** L10
Joshua Tree △ U.S.A. 33°55N 116°0W **171** M10
Josselin France 47°57N 2°33W **70** E4
Jost Van Dyke I. Br. Virgin Is. 18°29N 64°47W **183** e
Jostedalsbreen Norway 61°40N 6°59E **60** F12
Jotunheimen Norway 61°35N 8°25E **60** F13
Joubertberge Namibia 18°30S 14°0E **144** A1
Joué-lès-Tours France 47°21N 0°40E **70** E7
Jourdanton U.S.A. 28°55N 98°33W **176** L5
Joutseno Finland 61°7N 28°31E **84** B5
Jovellanos Cuba 22°40N 81°10W **182** B3
Jowkār Iran 34°25N 48°40E **105** E13
Jowzjan □ Afghan. 36°10N 66°0E **117** A9
Joyeuse France 44°29N 4°16E **73** D8
Józefów Lubelskie, Poland 50°28N 23°2E **83** H10
Józefów Mazowieckie, Poland 52°10N 21°11E **83** F8
Ju Xian China 36°35N 118°20E **115** F10
Juan Aldama Mexico 24°19N 103°21W **180** C4
Juan Bautista Alberdi Argentina 34°26S 61°48W **190** C3
Juan de Fuca, Str of. N. Amer. 48°15N 124°0W **170** B3
Juan de Nova Ind. Oc. 17°3S 43°45E **145** A7
Juan Fernández, Arch. de Pac. Oc. 33°50S 80°0W **184** G2
Juan José Castelli Argentina 25°27S 60°57W **190** B3
Juan L. Lacaze Uruguay 34°26S 57°25W **190** C4
Juanjuí Peru 7°10S 76°45W **188** B2
Juankoski Finland 63°3N 28°19E **60** E23

Juárez Mexico 27°37N 100°44W **180** B4
Juárez, Sa. de Mexico 32°0N 115°50W **180** A1
Juàzeiro Brazil 9°30S 40°30W **189** B2
Juàzeiro do Norte Brazil 7°10S 39°18W **189** B3
Juazohn Liberia 5°22N 8°50W **138** D3
Juba South Sudan 5°0N 31°35E **135** H12
Juba → Somalia 1°30N 42°35E **131** G3
Jubail = Al Jubayl Si. Arabia 27°0N 49°50E **129** E6
Jubany Antarctica 62°30S 58°0W **55** C18
Jubayl Lebanon 34°5N 35°39E **130** A4
Jubbah Si. Arabia 28°2N 40°56E **128** D4
Jubbal India 31°5N 77°40E **124** D7
Jubbulpore = Jabalpur India 23°9N 79°58E **125** H8
Jübek Germany 54°33N 9°22E **76** A5
Jubga Russia 44°19N 38°48E **87** H4
Jubilee L. Australia 29°0S 126°50E **149** E4
Júcar = Xúquer → Spain 39°5N 0°10W **91** F4
Júcaro Cuba 21°37N 78°51W **182** B4
Juchitán de Zaragoza Mexico 16°26N 95°1W **181** D5
Judea = Har Yehuda Israel 31°35N 34°57E **130** D3
Judenburg Austria 47°12N 14°38E **78** D7
Judith → U.S.A. 47°44N 109°39W **168** C9
Judith, Pt. U.S.A. 41°22N 71°29W **175** E13
Judith Gap U.S.A. 46°41N 109°45W **168** C9
Juelsminde Denmark 55°43N 10°1E **63** J4
Juigalpa Nic. 12°6N 85°26W **182** D2
Juiz de Fora Brazil 21°43S 43°19W **191** A7
Jujuy □ Argentina 23°20S 65°40W **190** A2
Julesburg U.S.A. 40°59N 102°16W **168** F12
Juli Peru 16°10S 69°25W **188** D4
Julia Cr. → Australia 20°0S 141°11E **150** C3
Julia Creek Australia 20°39S 141°44E **150** C3
Juliaca Peru 15°25S 70°10W **188** D3
Julian U.S.A. 33°4N 116°38W **171** M10
Julian, L. Canada 54°25N 77°57W **164** B4
Julian Alps = Julijske Alpe Slovenia 46°15N 14°1E **93** B11
Julianatop Suriname 3°40N 56°30W **187** C7
Julianehåb = Qaqortoq Greenland 60°43N 46°0W **57** E6
Jülich Germany 50°55N 6°22E **76** E3
Juliette, L. U.S.A. 33°2N 83°50W **178** B6
Julijske Alpe Slovenia 46°15N 14°1E **93** B11
Julimes Mexico 28°25N 105°27W **180** B3
Jullundur India 31°20N 75°40E **124** D6
Julu China 37°15N 115°2E **114** F8
Jumbo Zimbabwe 17°30S 30°58E **143** F3
Jumbo Pk. U.S.A. 36°12N 114°11W **171** J12
Jumentos Cays Bahamas 23°0N 75°40W **182** B4
Jumilla Spain 38°28N 1°19W **91** G3
Jumla Nepal 29°15N 82°13E **125** E10
Jumna = Yamuna → India 25°30N 81°53E **125** G9
Jumunjin S. Korea 37°55N 128°54E **115** F15
Junagadh India 21°30N 70°30E **124** J3
Junan China 35°12N 118°53E **115** G10
Junction Tex., U.S.A. 30°29N 99°46W **176** F5
Junction Utah, U.S.A. 38°14N 112°13W **169** G7
Junction B. Australia 11°52S 133°55E **150** A1
Junction City Ga., U.S.A. 32°36N 84°28W **178** C5
Junction City Kans., U.S.A. 39°2N 96°50W **172** F5
Junction City Oreg., U.S.A. 44°13N 123°12W **168** D2
Junction Pt. Australia 11°45S 133°50E **150** A1
Jundah Australia 24°46S 143°2E **150** C3
Jundiaí Brazil 24°30S 47°0W **191** A6
Juneau U.S.A. 58°18N 134°25W **162** B2
Junee Australia 34°53S 147°35E **153** C7
Jungar Qi China 39°49N 110°57E **114** E6
Jungfrau Switz. 46°32N 7°58E **77** J3
Junggar Pendi China 44°30N 86°0E **109** D11
Jungshahi Pakistan 24°52N 67°44E **124** G2
Juniata → U.S.A. 40°24N 77°1W **174** F7
Junín Argentina 34°33S 60°57W **190** C3
Junín Peru 11°12S 76°0W **188** C2
Junín □ Peru 11°30S 75°0W **188** C2
Junín, L. de Peru 11°0S 76°6W **188** C2
Junín de los Andes Argentina 39°45S 71°0W **192** A2
Jūniyah Lebanon 33°59N 35°38E **130** B4
Junkerdal △ Norway 66°50N 15°0E **60** C16
Junlian China 28°8N 104°29E **116** D5
Junnar India 19°12N 73°58E **126** E1
Juno Beach U.S.A. 26°52N 80°3W **179** J9
Juntas Chile 28°24S 69°58W **190** B2
Juntura U.S.A. 43°45N 118°5W **168** E4
Juparanã, L. Brazil 19°16S 40°8W **189** D2
Jupiter U.S.A. 26°57N 80°6W **179** J9
Jur → South Sudan 8°45N 29°15E **135** G11
Jura = Jura, Mts. du Europe 46°40N 6°5E **71** F13
Jura = Schwäbische Alb Germany 48°20N 9°30E **77** G5
Jura U.K. 56°0N 5°50W **65** F3
Jura □ France 46°47N 5°45E **71** F12
Jura □ Switz. 47°20N 7°10E **77** H3
Jūra → Lithuania 55°3N 22°9E **82** C9
Jura, Sd. of U.K. 55°57N 5°45W **65** F3
Jura, Mts. du Europe 46°40N 6°5E **71** F13
Jurbarkas Lithuania 55°4N 22°46E **82** C9
Jurien Bay Australia 30°18S 115°2E **149** F2
Jurilovca Romania 44°46N 28°52E **81** F13
Jūrmala Latvia 56°58N 23°34E **84** B3
Jurong China 31°57N 119°9E **117** B12
Jurong Singapore 1°19N 103°42E **121** d
Juruá → Brazil 2°37S 65°44W **186** D5
Juruena Brazil 13°0S 58°10W **186** E7
Juruena → Brazil 7°20S 58°3W **186** E7
Juruti Brazil 2°9S 56°4W **187** D7
Jussey France 47°50N 5°55E **71** E12
Justo Daract Argentina 33°52S 65°12W **190** C2
Jutaí Brazil 5°11S 68°54W **186** E5
Jutaí → Brazil 2°43S 66°57W **186** D5
Jüterbog Germany 51°59N 13°6E **76** D9
Juticalpa Honduras 14°40N 86°12W **182** D2
Jutland = Jylland Denmark 56°25N 9°30E **63** H3
Juuka Finland 63°13N 29°17E **60** E23
Juventud, I. de la Cuba 21°40N 82°40W **182** B3
Juvigny-sous-Andaine France 48°32N 0°30W **70** D6

Juye China 35°22N 116°5E **114** G9
Juzennecourt France 48°10N 4°58E **71** D11
Jvari Georgia 42°42N 42°4E **87** A6
Jwaneng Botswana 24°45S 24°50E **141** J4
Jyderup Denmark 55°40N 11°26E **63** J5
Jylland Denmark 56°25N 9°30E **63** H3
Jyväskylä Finland 62°14N 25°50E **84** A3

K

K2 Pakistan 35°58N 76°32E **125** B7
Ka → Nigeria 11°40N 4°10E **139** C5
Kaakha = Kaka Turkmenistan 37°21N 59°36E **129** B8
Kaapkruis Namibia 21°55S 13°57E **144** B1
Kaapstad = Cape Town S. Africa 33°55S 18°22E **144** D2
Kaba Guinea 10°9N 11°40W **138** C2
Kabaena Indonesia 5°15S 122°0E **119** F6
Kabala S. Leone 9°38N 11°37W **138** D2
Kabale Uganda 1°15S 30°0E **142** C3
Kabalo Dem. Rep. of the Congo 6°0S 27°0E **142** D2
Kabambare Dem. Rep. of the Congo 4°41S 27°39E **142** C2
Kabango Dem. Rep. of the Congo 8°35S 28°30E **143** D2
Kabanjahe Indonesia 3°6N 98°30E **118** D1
Kabankalan Phil. 9°59N 122°49E **119** C6
Kabara Fiji 18°59S 178°56W **154** a
Kabara Mali 16°40N 2°50W **138** B4
Kabardinka Russia 44°40N 37°57E **85** K10
Kabardino-Balkaria □ Russia 43°30N 43°30E **87** A6
Kabarega Falls = Murchison Falls Uganda 2°15N 31°30E **142** B3
Kabarnet Kenya 0°30N 35°45E **142** B4
Kabasalan Phil. 7°47N 122°44E **119** C6
Kabat Indonesia 8°16S 114°19E **119** J17
Kabba Nigeria 7°50N 6°3E **139** D6
Kabbani → India 12°13N 76°54E **127** H3
Kabin Buri Thailand 13°57N 101°43E **120** F3
Kabinakagami L. Canada 48°54N 84°25W **164** C3
Kabinda Dem. Rep. of the Congo 6°19S 24°20E **140** F4
Kabna Sudan 19°6N 32°40E **137** D3
Kabompo Zambia 13°36S 24°14E **143** E1
Kabompo → Zambia 14°11S 23°11E **141** G4
Kabondo Dem. Rep. of the Congo 8°58S 25°40E **143** D2
Kabongo Dem. Rep. of the Congo 7°22S 25°33E **142** D2
Kabot Guinea 10°48N 14°57W **138** C2
Kabrît, G. el Egypt 29°42N 33°16E **130** F2
Kabrousse Senegal 12°25N 16°45W **138** C1
Kabūd Gonbad Iran 37°5N 59°45E **129** B8
Kabudar Ahang Iran 35°11N 48°43E **105** E13
Kābul □ Afghan. 34°28N 69°11E **124** B3
Kābul □ Afghan. 34°30N 69°0E **109** F7
Kābul → Pakistan 33°55N 72°14E **124** C5
Kabunga Dem. Rep. of the Congo 1°38S 28°3E **142** C2
Kaburuang Indonesia 3°50N 126°30E **119** D7
Kabwe Zambia 14°30S 28°29E **143** E2
Kaçanik Kosovo 42°13N 21°12E **96** D5
Kačerginė Lithuania 54°54N 23°42E **82** D10
Kachchh, Gulf of India 22°50N 69°15E **124** H3
Kachchh, Rann of India 24°0N 70°0E **124** H4
Kachchhidhana India 21°44N 78°46E **125** J8
Kachebera Zambia 13°50S 32°50E **143** E3
Kachia Nigeria 9°50N 7°55E **139** D6
Kachikau Botswana 18°8S 24°26E **144** A3
Kachin □ Burma 26°0N 97°30E **116** G1
Kachira, L. Uganda 0°40S 31°7E **142** C3
Kachīry Kazakhstan 53°10N 75°50E **109** D9
Kachot Cambodia 11°30N 103°3E **121** G4
Kadaiyanallur India 9°3N 77°22E **127** G3
Kadam, Mt. Uganda 1°45N 34°45E **142** B3
Kadan Kyun Burma 12°30N 98°20E **120** F2
Kadanai → Afghan. 31°22N 65°45E **124** D1
Kadavu Fiji 19°0S 178°15E **154** a
Kadavu Passage Fiji 18°45S 178°0E **154** a
Kade Ghana 6°7N 0°56W **139** D4
Kadhimain = Al Kāzimīyah Iraq 33°22N 44°18E **105** F11
Kadi India 23°18N 72°23E **124** H5
Kadiana Mali 10°45N 6°30W **138** C3
Kadina Australia 33°55S 137°43E **152** B2
Kadınhanı Turkey 38°14N 32°13E **104** C5
Kadiolo Mali 10°30N 7°41W **138** C3
Kadipur India 26°10N 82°23E **125** F10
Kadirli Turkey 37°23N 36°5E **104** D7
Kadiyevka = Stakhanov Ukraine 48°35N 38°40E **85** H10
Kadmat I. India 11°14N 72°47E **127** G12
Kadoka U.S.A. 43°50N 101°31W **172** D3
Kadom Russia 54°37N 42°30E **86** C6
Kadoma Zimbabwe 18°20S 29°52E **143** F2
Kadugli Sudan 11°0N 29°45E **135** F11
Kaduna Nigeria 10°30N 7°21E **139** C6
Kaduna □ Nigeria 11°0N 7°30E **139** C6
Kadur India 13°34N 76°1E **127** H3
Kaduru Russia 59°12N 97°? **102** A4
Kaédi Mauritania 16°9N 13°28W **138** B2
Kaélé Cameroon 10°7N 14°27E **139** C7
Kaeng Khoi Thailand 14°35N 101°0E **120** E3
Kaeng Krachan △ Thailand 12°57N 99°23E **120** F2
Kaeng Krung △ Thailand 9°30N 98°50E **121** H2
Kaeng Tana △ Thailand 15°25N 105°32E **120** E5
Kaesŏng N. Korea 37°58N 126°35E **115** F14
Kāf Si. Arabia 31°25N 37°29E **128** D3
Kafan = Kapan Armenia 39°18N 46°27E **105** C12
Kafanchan Nigeria 9°40N 8°20E **139** D6

Kafareti Nigeria 10°25N 11°12E **139** C7
Kaffrine Senegal 14°8N 15°36W **138** C1
Kafia Nigeria 9°30N 7°4E **139** D6
Kafin Madaki Nigeria 10°41N 9°46E **139** C6
Kafinda Zambia 12°32S 30°20E **143** E3
Kafireos, Stenon Greece 37°55N 24°35E **98** D6
Kafr el Battikh Egypt 31°25N 31°44E **137** E7
Kafr el Dauwâr Egypt 31°8N 30°8E **137** E7
Kafr el Sheikh Egypt 31°15N 30°50E **137** E7
Kafr el Zaiyât Egypt 30°49N 30°48E **137** E7
Kafue Zambia 15°46S 28°9E **143** F2
Kafue → Zambia 15°30S 29°0E **141** H5
Kafue △ Zambia 15°12S 25°38E **143** F2
Kafue Flats Zambia 15°40S 27°25E **143** F2
Kafulwe Zambia 9°0S 29°1E **143** D2
Kaga Afghan. 34°14N 70°10E **124** B4
Kaga Bandoro C.A.R. 7°0N 19°10E **140** C3
Kagawa □ Japan 34°15N 134°0E **113** G7
Kagera □ Tanzania 2°0S 31°30E **142** C3
Kagera → Uganda 0°57S 31°47E **142** C3
Kagoro Nigeria 9°36N 8°23E **139** C6
Kagoshima Japan 31°35N 130°33E **113** J5
Kagoshima □ Japan 31°30N 130°30E **113** J5
Kagul = Cahul Moldova 45°50N 28°15E **81** E13
Kahak Iran 36°6N 49°46E **129** B6
Kahama Tanzania 4°8S 32°30E **142** C3
Kahan Pakistan 29°18N 68°54E **124** E3
Kahang Malaysia 2°12N 103°32E **121** L4
Kahayan → Indonesia 3°40S 114°0E **118** E4
Kahe Tanzania 3°30S 37°25E **142** C4
Kahemba Dem. Rep. of the Congo 7°18S 18°55E **140** F3
Kaherekoau Mts. N.Z. 45°45S 167°15E **155** F2
Kahil, Djebel bou Algeria 34°26N 4°0E **136** B4
Kahnūj Iran 27°55N 57°40E **129** E8
Kahoka U.S.A. 40°25N 91°44W **172** E8
Kaho'olawe U.S.A. 20°33N 156°37W **167** L8
Kahramanmaraş Turkey 37°37N 36°53E **104** D7
Kahramanmaraş □ Turkey 37°35N 36°33E **104** D7
Kâhta Turkey 37°46N 38°36E **105** D8
Kahul, Ozero Ukraine 45°24N 28°24E **81** E13
Kahului U.S.A. 20°54N 156°28W **167** L8
Kahurangi △ N.Z. 41°10S 172°32E **155** D4
Kahurangi Pt. N.Z. 40°50S 172°10E **155** A7
Kahuta Pakistan 33°35N 73°24E **124** C5
Kahuzi-Biega △ Dem. Rep. of the Congo 1°50S 27°55E **142** C2
Kai, Kepulauan Indonesia 5°55S 132°45E **119** F8
Kai Besar Indonesia 5°35S 133°0E **119** F8
Kai Is. = Kai, Kepulauan Indonesia 5°55S 132°45E **119** F8
Kai Kecil Indonesia 5°45S 132°40E **119** F8
Kai Xian China 31°11N 108°21E **116** B7
Kaiama Nigeria 9°36N 4°1E **139** D5
Kaiapoi N.Z. 43°24S 172°40E **155** E4
Kaidu He → China 41°46N 86°31E **110** C6
Kaieteur Falls Guyana 5°1N 59°10W **187** B6
Kaifeng China 34°48N 114°21E **114** G8
Kaihua China 29°12N 118°20E **117** C12
Kaijiang China 31°7N 107°55E **116** B6
Kaikohe N.Z. 35°25S 173°49E **154** B6
Kaikoura N.Z. 42°25S 173°43E **155** C8
Kaikoura Pen. N.Z. 42°25S 173°43E **155** C8
Kailahun S. Leone 8°18N 10°39W **138** D2
Kailash = Kangrinboqê Feng China 31°0N 81°25E **125** D9
Kaili China 26°33N 107°59E **116** D6
Kailu China 43°38N 121°18E **115** C11
Kailua Kona U.S.A. 19°39N 155°59W **167** M8
Kaimaktsalan Oros = Voras Oros Greece 40°57N 21°45E **96** F5
Kaimana Indonesia 3°39S 133°45E **119** E8
Kaimanawa Mts. N.Z. 39°15S 175°56E **154** F4
Kaimata N.Z. 42°34S 171°28E **155** C6
Kaimganj India 27°33N 79°24E **125** F8
Kaimur Hills India 24°30N 82°0E **125** G10
Kainab → Namibia 28°32S 19°34E **144** C2
Kainji Dam Nigeria 9°55N 4°35E **139** C5
Kainji L. = Jebba → Nigeria 10°1N 4°40E **139** C5
Kainuu □ Finland 64°30N 29°7E **60** D23
Kaipara Harbour N.Z. 36°25S 174°14E **154** C5
Kaiping China 22°23N 112°42E **117** F9
Kaipokok B. Canada 54°54N 59°47W **165** B8
Kaira India 22°45N 72°50E **124** H5
Kairana India 29°24N 77°15E **124** E7
Kaironi Indonesia 0°47S 133°40E **119** E8
Kairouan Tunisia 35°45N 10°5E **136** A6
Kairouan □ Tunisia 35°30N 9°46E **136** A5
Kaiserslautern Germany 49°26N 7°45E **77** F3
Kaiserstuhl Germany 48°4N 7°40E **77** G3
Kaitaia N.Z. 35°8S 173°17E **154** B6
Kaitangata N.Z. 46°17S 169°51E **155** G4
Kaithal India 29°48N 76°26E **124** E7
Kaitu → Pakistan 33°10N 70°30E **124** C4
Kaiwi Channel U.S.A. 21°15N 157°30W **167** L8
Kaiyang China 27°4N 106°59E **116** D6
Kaiyuan Liaoning, China 42°28N 124°1E **115** C13
Kaiyuan Yunnan, China 23°40N 103°12E **116** F4
Kaiyuh Mts. U.S.A. 64°30N 158°0W **166** C8
Kajaani Finland 64°17N 27°46E **60** D22
Kajabbi Australia 20°0S 140°1E **150** C3
Kajana = Kajaani Finland 64°17N 27°46E **60** D22
Kajang Malaysia 2°59N 101°48E **121** L3
Kajaran Armenia 39°9N 46°9E **105** C12
Kajiado Kenya 1°53S 36°48E **142** C4
Kajo Kaji South Sudan 3°58N 31°40E **135** H12
Kajuru Nigeria 10°19N 7°44E **139** C6
Kaka Turkmenistan 37°21N 59°36E **129** B8
Kakabeka Falls Canada 48°24N 89°37W **164** C2
Kakadu △ Australia 12°0S 132°3E **148** B5
Kakamas S. Africa 28°45S 20°33E **144** D3
Kakamega Kenya 0°20N 34°46E **142** B3
Kakanj Bos.-H. 44°4N 18°4E **80** F3
Kakanui Mts. N.Z. 45°10S 170°30E **155** F3
Kakata Liberia 6°25N 10°35W **138** D2
Kakdwip India 21°53N 88°11E **125** J13
Kake = Akiōta Japan 34°36N 132°19E **113** G6
Kake U.S.A. 56°59N 133°57W **162** B2
Kakegawa Japan 34°45N 138°1E **113** G9
Kakeroma-Jima Japan 28°8N 129°14E **113** K4

Kākhak Iran 34°9N 58°38E **129** C8
Kakhib Russia 42°28N 46°34E **87** J8
Kakhovka Ukraine 46°45N 33°30E **85** J7
Kakhovske Vdskh. Ukraine 47°5N 34°0E **85** J7
Kakinada India 16°57N 82°11E **126** F6
Kakisa → Canada 61°3N 118°10W **162** A5
Kakisa L. Canada 60°56N 117°43W **162** A5
Kakogawa Japan 34°46N 134°51E **113** G7
Kakum △ Ghana 5°24N 1°20W **139** D4
Kakwa → Canada 54°37N 118°28W **162** C5
Kala Nigeria 12°2N 14°40E **139** C7
Kala Oya → Sri Lanka 8°20N 79°45E **127** K4
Kalaallit Nunaat = Greenland ☐ N. Amer. 66°0N 45°0W **57** D6
Kalabagh Pakistan 33°0N 71°28E **124** C4
Kalabahi Indonesia 8°13S 124°31E **119** F6
Kalabana Mali 14°10N 8°35W **138** C3
Kalabo Zambia 14°58S 22°33E **143** E1
Kalach Russia 50°22N 41°0E **86** E5
Kalach na Donu Russia 48°43N 43°32E **87** F6
Kalachinsk Russia 55°3N 74°33E **109** A8
Kaladan → Burma 20°20N 93°5E **123** J18
Kaladar Canada 44°37N 77°5W **174** B7
Kalahari S. Africa 24°0S 21°30E **144** B3
Kalahari Gemsbok △ S. Africa 25°30S 20°30E **144** C3
Kalaikhum Tajikistan 38°28N 70°46E **109** F8
Kalajoki Finland 64°12N 24°10E **60** D21
Kalakamati Botswana 20°40S 27°25E **145** B4
Kalakan Russia 55°15N 116°45E **107** D12
Kalama Dem. Rep. of the Congo 2°52S 28°35E **142** C2
Kalama U.S.A. 46°1N 122°51W **170** E4
Kalamaria Greece 40°33N 22°55E **98** D4
Kalamata Greece 37°3N 22°10E **98** E4
Kalamazoo U.S.A. 42°17N 85°35W **173** D11
Kalamazoo → U.S.A. 42°40N 86°10W **172** D10
Kalambaka Greece 39°42N 21°39E **98** B3
Kalambo Falls Tanzania 8°37S 31°35E **143** D3
Kalamnuri India 19°40N 77°20E **126** E3
Kalamos, Attiki, Greece 38°17N 23°52E **98** C5
Kalamos, Lefkada, Greece 38°37N 20°55E **98** C2
Kalan Turkey 39°7N 39°32E **128** B3
Kalangadoo Australia 37°34S 140°41E **152** D4
Kalannie Australia 30°22S 117°5E **149** F2
Kalāntarī Iran 32°10N 54°8E **129** C7
Kalao Indonesia 7°21S 121°0E **119** F6
Kalaotoa Indonesia 7°20S 121°50E **119** F6
Kalārne Sweden 62°59N 16°5E **62** B10
Kalasin Thailand 16°26N 103°30E **120** D4
Kālat Iran 25°29N 59°22E **129** E9
Kalāteh Iran 36°33N 55°41E **129** B7
Kalāteh-ye Ganj Iran 27°31N 57°55E **129** E8
Kalathos Greece 36°9N 28°8E **99** E13
Kalaus → Russia 45°40N 44°7E **87** H7
Kalavrita Greece 38°3N 22°8E **98** C4
Kalbā U.A.E. 25°5N 56°22E **129** E8
Kalbarri Australia 27°40S 114°10E **149** E1
Kalbarri △ Australia 27°51S 114°30E **149** E1
Kalburgi = Gulbarga India 17°20N 76°50E **126** F3
Kalce Slovenia 45°54N 14°13E **74** F8
Kale Antalya, Turkey 36°14N 30°0E **104** D4
Kale Denizli, Turkey 37°27N 28°49E **99** D10
Kaleburnu = Galinoporni Cyprus 35°31N 34°18E **101** D13
Kalecik Turkey 40°4N 33°26E **104** B5
Kaledupa Indonesia 5°50S 123°50E **119** F6
Kalehe Dem. Rep. of the Congo 2°6S 28°50E **142** C2
Kalema Tanzania 1°12S 31°55E **142** C3
Kalemie Dem. Rep. of the Congo 5°55S 29°9E **142** D2
Kalewa Burma 23°10N 94°15E **123** H19
Kaleybar Iran 38°47N 47°2E **105** C12
Kalghatgi India 15°11N 74°58E **127** G2
Kalgoorlie-Boulder Australia 30°40S 121°22E **149** F3
Kali → India 27°6N 79°15E **125** F8
Kali Sindh → India 25°32N 76°17E **124** G6
Kaliakra, Nos Bulgaria 43°21N 28°30E **97** C12
Kalianda Indonesia 5°50S 105°45E **118** F3
Kalibo Phil. 11°43N 122°22E **119** B6
Kalima Dem. Rep. of the Congo 2°33S 26°32E **142** C2
Kalimantan Indonesia 0°0 114°0E **118** D4
Kalimantan Barat □ Indonesia 0°0 110°30E **118** D4
Kalimantan Selatan □ Indonesia 2°30S 115°30E **118** E5
Kalimantan Tengah □ Indonesia 2°0S 113°30E **118** E4
Kalimantan Timur □ Indonesia 1°30N 116°30E **118** D5
Kálimnos Greece 37°0N 27°0E **99** E8
Kalimpong India 27°4N 88°35E **125** F13
Kalinadi → India 14°50N 74°7E **127** G2
Kaliningrad Russia 54°42N 20°32E **84** J2
Kaliningrad × (KGD) Russia 54°45N 20°33E **82** C?
Kalininsk Russia 51°30N 44°12E **86** E7
Kalinkavichy Belarus 52°12N 29°20E **75** D15
Kalinkovichi = Kalinkavichy Belarus 52°12N 29°20E **75** D15
Kalinovik Bos.-H. 43°31N 18°25E **96** C3
Kaliro Uganda 0°56N 33°30E **142** B3
Kalispell U.S.A. 48°12N 114°19W **168** B6
Kalisz Poland 51°45N 18°8E **83** H5
Kalisz Pomorski Poland 53°17N 15°55E **83** B3
Kalithea Greece 35°57N 23°43E **98** D5
Kaliua Tanzania 5°5S 31°48E **142** D3
Kalivia Thorikou Greece 37°44N 24°1E **98** D6
Kalix Sweden 65°53N 23°12E **60** D20
Kalixälven → Sweden 65°50N 23°11E **60** D20
Kalka India 30°46N 76°57E **124** D7

Kalkan Turkey 36°15N 29°23E **99**
Kalkarindji Australia 17°30S 130°47E **54**
Kalkaska U.S.A. 44°44N 85°11W **173**
Kalkfeld Namibia 20°57S 16°14E **14**
Kalkfontein Botswana 22°4S 20°57E **14**
Kalkrand Namibia 24°1S 17°35E **14**
Kallakurichchi India 11°44N 79°1E **12**
Kallam India 18°36N 76°2E **1**
Kållandsö Sweden 58°40N 13°5E **6**
Kallavesi Finland 62°58N 27°30E **6**
Källby Sweden 58°30N 13°8E **6**
Kållered Sweden 57°32N 12°4E **6**
Kallidaikurichi India 8°38N 77°31E **12**
Kallimasia Greece 38°18N 26°6E **9**
Kallinge Sweden 56°15N 15°18E **6**
Kallmet Albania 41°51N 19°42E **9**
Kallsjön Sweden 63°38N 13°0E **6**
Kalmalo Nigeria 13°40N 5°20E **13**
Kalmar Sweden 56°40N 16°20E **63**
Kalmar län □ Sweden 57°25N 16°0E **63**
Kalmar sund Sweden 56°40N 16°25E **63**
Kalmunai Sri Lanka 7°25N 81°49E **12**
Kalmykia □ Russia 46°5N 46°1E **8**
Kalna India 23°13N 88°25E **125**
Kalnai India 22°46N 83°30E **125**
Kalni → Bangla. 24°30N 91°25E **1**
Kalo Nero Greece 37°20N 21°38E **9**
Kalocsa Hungary 46°32N 19°0E **8**
Kalofer Bulgaria 42°37N 24°59E **9**
Kalokhorio Cyprus 34°51N 33°2E **10**
Kaloko Dem. Rep. of the Congo 6°47S 25°48E **14**
Kalol Gujarat, India 22°37N 73°31E **12**
Kalol Gujarat, India 23°15N 72°33E **12**
Kalolimnos Greece 37°4N 27°8E
Kalomo Zambia 17°0S 26°30E **14**
Kaloni Greece 39°14N 26°12E **9**
Kaloni, Kolpos Greece 39°10N 26°10E **9**
Kalpeni I. India 10°5N 73°38E **12**
Kalpi India 26°8N 79°47E **12**
Kalpitiya Sri Lanka 8°14N 79°46E **12**
Kalputhi I. India 10°49N 72°10E **12**
Kalrayan Hills India 11°45N 78°40E **12**
Kalsubai India 19°35N 73°45E **12**
Kaltag U.S.A. 64°20N 158°43W **16**
Kaltern = Caldaro Italy 46°25N 11°14E **7**
Kaltukatjara Australia 24°52S 129°5E **14**
Kaltungo Nigeria 9°48N 11°19E **13**
Kalu Pakistan 25°5N 67°39E **12**
Kaluga Russia 54°35N 36°10E **8**
Kaluga □ Russia 54°15N 34°50E **8**
Kalulushi Zambia 12°50S 28°3E **14**
Kalumburu Australia 13°55S 126°35E **14**
Kalumburu ◎ Australia 14°17S 126°38E **14**
Kalundborg Denmark 55°41N 11°5E **6**
Kalush Ukraine 49°3N 24°23E **7**
Kaluszyn Poland 52°13N 21°52E **8**
Kalutara Sri Lanka 6°35N 80°0E **12**
Kalvarija Lithuania 54°24N 23°14E **8**
Kalwakurti India 16°41N 78°30E **12**
Kalyan Maharashtra, India 20°30N 74°3E **12**
Kalyan Maharashtra, India 19°15N 73°9E **12**
Kalyandurg India 14°33N 77°6E **12**
Kalyani India 17°52N 76°57E **12**
Kalyansingapuram India 19°30N 83°19E **12**
Kalyazin Russia 57°15N 37°55E **8**
Kam Albania 42°17N 20°18E **9**
Kam → Nigeria 8°15N 11°0E **13**
Kama Dem. Rep. of the Congo 3°30S 27°5E **14**
Kama Japan 33°33N 130°40E **11**
Kama → Russia 55°45N 52°0E **8**
Kamachumu Tanzania 1°37S 31°37E **14**
Kamaishi Japan 39°16N 141°53E **11**
Kamalapuram India 14°35N 78°39E **12**
Kamalia India 30°44N 72°42E **12**
Kaman India 27°39N 77°16E **12**
Kaman Turkey 39°22N 33°44E **10**
Kamanjab Namibia 19°35S 14°51E **14**
Kamapanda Zambia 12°5S 24°0E **14**
Kamaran Yemen 15°21N 42°35E **13**
Kamareddi India 18°19N 78°21E **12**
Kamativi Zimbabwe 18°15S 27°0E **14**
Kamba Nigeria 11°50N 3°45E **13**
Kambalda West Australia 31°10S 121°37E **14**
Kambam India 9°45N 77°16E **12**
Kambangan, Nusa Indonesia 7°40S 108°10E **11**
Kambar Pakistan 27°37N 68°1E **12**
Kambia S. Leone 9°3N 12°53W **13**
Kambo-san = Kwanmo-bong N. Korea
Kambolé Togo 8°43N 1°9E **13**
Kambolé Zambia 8°47S 30°48E **14**
Kambos Cyprus 35°2N 32°44E **10**
Kambove Dem. Rep. of the Congo 10°51S 26°33E **14**
Kamchatka, Poluostrov Russia 57°0N 160°0E **10**
Kamchatka Pen. = Kamchatka, Poluostrov Russia 57°0N 160°0E **10**
Kamchiya → Bulgaria 43°4N 27°44E **9**
Kame Ruins Zimbabwe 20°7S 28°25E **14**
Kameda-Hantō Japan 41°50N 141°0E **11**
Kamen Russia 53°50N 81°30E **10**
Kamen-Rybolov Russia 44°46N 132°2E **11**
Kamenica Serbia 43°27N 22°27E **9**
Kamenica Serbia 44°25N 19°45E **9**
Kamenice nad Lipou Czech Rep. 49°18N 15°2E **7**
Kamenjak, Rt Croatia 44°47N 13°55E **7**
Kamenka = Kamyanka Ukraine 49°3N 32°6E
Kamenka Kazakhstan 51°7N 50°19E **8**
Kamenka Penza, Russia 53°10N 44°5E **8**
Kamenka Voronezh, Russia 50°47N 39°20E **8**
Kamenka Bugskaya = Kamyanka-Buzka Ukraine 50°8N 24°16E **7**
Kamenka Dneprovskaya = Kamyanka-Dniprovska Ukraine 47°29N 34°28E
Kamennomostskiy Russia 44°18N 40°13E **8**
Kameno Bulgaria 42°34N 27°18E **9**
Kamenolomni Russia 47°40N 40°14E **8**

amensk-Shakhtinskiy
  Russia 48°23N 40°20E **87** F5
amensk Uralskiy
  Russia 56°25N 62°2E **106** D7
amenskiy Russia 50°48N 45°25E **86** E7
amenskoye Russia 56°16N 165°30E **107** C17
amenyak Bulgaria 43°24N 26°57E **97** C12
amenz Germany 51°15N 14°5E **76** D10
ameoka Japan 35°0N 135°35E **113** G7
amet India 30°55N 79°35E **125** D8
amiah U.S.A. 46°14N 116°2W **168** C5
amień Krajeński
  Poland 53°32N 17°32E **82** E4
amień Pomorski
  Poland 53°57N 14°43E **82** E1
amienna → Poland 51°6N 21°47E **83** G8
amienna Góra Poland 50°47N 16°2E **83** H3
amieński Poland 51°21N 19°29E **83** G6
amieskroon S. Africa 30°9S 17°56E **144** D2
amilukuak L.
  Canada 62°22N 101°40W **163** A8
amin-Kashyrskyy
  Ukraine 51°39N 24°56E **75** C13
amina
  Dem. Rep. of the Congo 8°45S 25°0E **143** D2
aminak L. Canada 62°10N 95°0W **163** A10
aminoyama Japan 38°9N 140°17E **112** E10
amiros Greece 36°20N 27°56E **101** C9
amituga
  Dem. Rep. of the Congo 3°2S 28°10E **142** C2
amla → India 25°55N 86°36E **125** G12
amloops Canada 50°40N 120°20W **162** C4
amnik Slovenia 46°14N 14°37E **93** B11
amo Armenia 40°21N 45°7E **87** K7
amo Japan 37°39N 139°3E **112** F9
amo N.Z. 35°42S 174°20E **154** B4
amoke Pakistan 32°4N 74°4E **124** C6
ampa → Austria 48°23N 15°42E **78** C8
ampala Uganda 0°20N 32°32E **142** B3
ampar → Indonesia 4°18N 101°9E **121** K3
ampar → Indonesia 0°30N 103°8E **118** D2
ampen Neths. 52°33N 5°53E **69** B5
ampene
  Dem. Rep. of the Congo 3°36S 26°40E **140** C1
amphaeng Phet
  Thailand 16°28N 99°30E **120** D2
ampinoski △ Poland 52°21N 20°40E **83** F7
ampolombo, L.
  Zambia 11°37S 29°42E **143** E2
ampong Cham
  Cambodia 12°0N 105°30E **121** G5
ampong Chhnang
  Cambodia 12°20N 104°35E **121** F5
ampong Pengerang
  Malaysia 1°22N 104°7E **121** d
ampong Punggai
  Malaysia 1°27N 104°18E **121** d
ampong Saom
  Cambodia 10°38N 103°30E **121** G4
ampong Saom, Chaak
  Cambodia 10°50N 103°32E **121** G4
ampong Tanjong Langsat
  Malaysia 1°28N 104°1E **121** d
ampong Telok Ramunia
  Malaysia 1°22N 104°15E **121** d
ampot Cambodia 10°36N 104°10E **121** G5
ampti Burkina Faso 10°7N 3°25W **138** C4
ampuchea = Cambodia ■
  Asia 12°15N 105°0E **120** F5
ampung Air Putih
  Malaysia 4°15N 103°10E **121** K4
ampung Jerangau
  Malaysia 4°50N 103°10E **121** K4
ampung Raja
  Malaysia 5°45N 102°35E **121** K4
ampungbaru = Tolitoli
  Indonesia 1°5N 120°50E **119** D6
mrau, Teluk
  Indonesia 3°30S 133°36E **119** E8
msack Canada 51°34N 101°54W **163** C8
msar Guinea 10°40N 14°36W **138** C2
mskoye Ustye Russia 55°10N 49°20E **86** C9
mthi India 21°9N 79°19E **126** D4
muchawie L.
  Canada 56°18N 101°59W **163** B8
mui-Misaki Japan 43°20N 140°21E **112** C10
myanets-Podilskyy
  Ukraine 48°45N 26°40E **81** B11
myanka Ukraine 49°3N 32°6E **85** H7
myanka-Buzka
  Ukraine 50°8N 24°16E **75** C13
myanka-Dniprovska
  Ukraine 47°29N 34°28E **85** J8
myanets Belarus 52°23N 23°49E **83** F10
myanyuki Belarus 52°23N 23°49E **83** F10
myārān Iran 34°47N 46°56E **105** E12
nyshin Russia 50°10N 45°24E **86** E7
nyzyak Russia 46°4N 48°10E **87** G9
naaupscow →
  anada 54°2N 76°30W **164** B4
nab U.S.A. 37°3N 112°32W **169** H7
nab Cr. → U.S.A. 36°24N 112°38W **169** H7
nacea Lau Group, Fiji 17°15S 179°6W **154** a
nacea Taveuni, Fiji 16°59S 179°56E **154** a
naga I. U.S.A. 51°45N 177°22W **166** E4
nagi Japan 40°54N 140°27E **112** D10
nairiktok →
  Canada 55°2N 60°18W **165** A7
nakapura India 39°30N 22°53E **98** B4
nalia Greece
nanga
  Dem. Rep. of the Congo 5°55S 22°18E **140** F4
nangra-Boyd △
  ustralia 33°57S 150°15E **153** B9
nash Russia 33°57S 150°15E **153** B9
nask U.S.A. 47°19N 121°54W **170** C5
nastraion, Ákra = Paliouri,
  kra Greece 39°23N 23°45E **96** G7
nawha → U.S.A. 38°50N 82°9W **173** F12
nazawa Japan 38°30N 136°38E **113** F8
nchanaburi Thailand 14°2N 99°31E **120** E2
nchenjunga Nepal 27°50N 88°10E **125** F13
nchenjunga △ India 27°42N 88°8E **125** F13
nchipuram India 12°52N 79°45E **127** H4
nczuga Poland 49°59N 22°25E **83** J9
ndaghat India 30°59N 77°7E **124** D7
ndahār Afghan. 31°32N 65°43E **122** D2
ndahar India 21°49N 77°12E **126** D3
ndahār △ Afghan. 31°0N 65°0E **122** D4
ndalaksha Russia 67°9N 32°30E **60** C25
ndangan Indonesia 2°50S 115°20E **118** E5
ndanos Greece 35°19N 23°44E **101** D5

Kandava Latvia 57°2N 22°46E **82** A9
Kandavu = Kadavu Fiji 19°0S 178°15E **154** a
Kandavu Passage = Kadavu
  Passage Fiji 18°45S 178°0E **154** a
Kandé = Kanté Togo 9°57N 1°3E **139** D5
Kandhkot Pakistan 28°16N 69°8E **124** E3
Kandhla India 29°18N 77°19E **124** E7
Kandi Benin 11°7N 2°55E **139** C5
Kandi India 23°58N 88°5E **125** H13
Kandiaro Pakistan 27°4N 68°13E **124** F3
Kandıra Turkey 41°4N 30°9E **104** B4
Kandla India 23°0N 70°10E **124** H6
Kandos Australia 32°45S 149°58E **153** B8
Kandy Sri Lanka 7°18N 80°43E **127** L5
Kane U.S.A. 41°40N 78°49E **174** E6
Kane Basin Greenland 79°1N 70°0W **57** B4
Kanevskaya Russia 46°3N 38°57E **87** G4
Kanfanar Croatia 45°7N 13°50E **92** C10
Kang Botswana 23°41S 22°50E **144** B3
Kangaamiut Greenland 65°50N 53°20W **57** D5
Kangaatsiaq Greenland 68°18N 53°20W **57** D5
Kangaba Mali 11°56N 8°25W **138** C3
Kangal Turkey 39°14N 37°23E **104** C7
Kangān Fārs, Iran 27°50N 52°3E **129** E7
Kangān Hormozgān,
  Iran 25°48N 57°28E **129** E8
Kangar Malaysia 6°27N 100°12E **121** J3
Kangaré Mali 11°36N 8°4W **138** C3
Kangaroo I. Australia 35°45S 137°0E **152** C2
Kangaroo Mts.
  Australia 23°29S 141°51E **150** C3
Kangasala Finland 61°28N 24°4E **64** B3
Kangāvar Iran 34°40N 48°0E **105** E12
Kangding China 30°2N 101°57E **116** B3
Kangdong N. Korea 39°9N 126°5E **115** E14
Kangean, Kepulauan
  Indonesia 6°55S 115°23E **118** F5
Kangean Is. = Kangean,
  Kepulauan Indonesia 6°55S 115°23E **118** F5
Kangerdlugssuak
  Greenland 68°10N 32°20W **57** D7
Kangerluarsoruseq
  Greenland 63°45N 51°27W **57** E5
Kangerluarsoruset =
  Kangerluarsoruseq
  Greenland 63°45N 51°27W **57** E5
Kangerlussuaq
  Greenland 66°59N 50°40W **57** D5
Kangertittivaq = Scoresby Sund
  Greenland 70°28N 21°46W **57** C8
Kanggye N. Korea 41°0N 126°35E **115** D14
Kangikajik Greenland 70°7N 22°0W **57** C8
Kangilinnguit Greenland 61°20N 47°57W **57** E6
Kangiqliniq = Rankin Inlet
  Canada 62°30N 93°0W **160** E13
Kangiqsualujjuaq
  Canada 58°30N 65°59W **161** F18
Kangiqsujuaq Canada 61°30N 72°0W **161** E17
Kangiqtugaapik = Clyde River
  Canada 70°30N 68°30W **161** C18
Kangirsuk Canada 60°0N 70°0W **161** F18
Kangka Chemaran
  Malaysia 1°34N 104°12E **121** d
Kangkar Sungai Tiram
  Malaysia 1°35N 103°55E **121** d
Kangkar Teberau
  Malaysia 1°32N 103°51E **121** d
Kangping China 42°43N 123°18E **115** C12
Kangra India 32°6N 76°16E **124** C7
Kangrinboqe Feng
  China 31°0N 81°25E **125** D9
Kanha △ India 22°15N 80°40E **125** H9
Kanhan → India 21°4N 79°34E **126** D4
Kanhangad India 12°21N 74°58E **127** K2
Kanhar → India 24°28N 83°8E **125** G10
Kani Ivory C. 8°29N 6°36W **138** D3
Kaniama
  Dem. Rep. of the Congo 7°30S 24°12E **142** D1
Kaniapiskau = Caniapiscau →
  Canada 56°40N 69°30W **165** A6
Kaniapiskau, L. = Caniapiscau, L.
  Canada 54°10N 69°55W **165** B6
Kaniere, L. N.Z. 42°50S 171°10E **155** C6
Kanigiri India 15°24N 79°13E **127** G4
Kanin Nos, Mys Russia 68°39N 43°32E **106** C5
Kanin Pen. = Kanin, Poluostrov
  Russia 68°0N 45°0E **58** B14
Kaninė Albania 40°23N 19°30E **96** F3
Kaniva Australia 36°22S 141°18E **152** C4
Kanjiža Serbia 46°3N 20°4E **80** D5
Kanjut Sar Pakistan 36°7N 75°25E **126** A6
Kankaanpää Finland 61°44N 22°50E **64** B2
Kankakee U.S.A. 41°7N 87°52W **172** E10
Kankakee → U.S.A. 41°23N 88°15W **172** E9
Kankan Guinea 10°23N 9°15W **138** C3
Kankendy = Xankändi
  Azerbaijan 39°52N 46°49E **105** C12
Kankesanturai Sri Lanka 9°50N 80°2E **127** K5
Kankossa Mauritania 15°54N 11°31W **138** B2
Kankroli India 25°4N 73°53E **124** G5
Kanmaw Kyun Burma 11°40N 98°28E **121** G2
Kannapolis U.S.A. 35°30N 80°37W **177** D14
Kanniyakumari India 8°3N 77°40E **127** L3
Kannod India 22°45N 76°40E **122** H10
Kannur India 11°53N 75°27E **127** J2
Kannyakumari India 8°3N 77°40E **127** K3
Kano Nigeria 12°2N 8°30E **139** C6
Kan'onji Japan 34°7N 133°39E **113** G6
Kanoroba Ivory C. 9°7N 6°8W **138** D3
Kanowna Australia 30°32S 121°31E **149** F3
Kanowit Malaysia 2°14N 112°20E **118** D4
Kanoya Japan 31°25N 130°50E **113** J5
Kanpetlet Burma 21°10N 93°59E **123** J18
Kanpur India 26°28N 80°20E **125** F9
Kansas □ U.S.A. 38°30N 99°0W **174** F6
Kansas → U.S.A. 39°7N 94°37W **172** F6
Kansas City Kans.,
  U.S.A. 39°7N 94°38W **172** F6
Kansas City Mo., U.S.A. 39°6N 94°35W **172** F6
Kansenia
  Dem. Rep. of the Congo 10°20S 26°0E **143** E2
Kansk Russia 56°20N 95°37E **107** D10
Kansu = Gansu □ China 36°0N 104°0E **114** C3
Kantaphor India 22°35N 76°34E **124** H7
Kantchari Burkina Faso 12°37N 1°31E **139** C5

Kantché Niger 13°31N 8°30E **139** C6
Kanté Togo 9°57N 1°3E **139** D5
Kantemirovka Russia 49°43N 39°55E **85** H10
Kantharalak Thailand 14°39N 104°39E **120** E5
Kanthi = Contai India 21°54N 87°46E **125** J12
Kantli → India 28°20N 75°30E **124** E6
Kantō □ Japan 36°15N 139°30E **113** F9
Kantō-Sanchi Japan 35°59N 138°50E **113** G9
Kanturk Ireland 52°11N 8°54W **64** D3
Kanuma Japan 36°34N 139°42E **113** F9
Kanus Namibia 27°50S 18°39E **144** D2
Kanye Botswana 24°55S 25°28E **144** B4
Kanzenze
  Dem. Rep. of the Congo 10°30S 25°12E **143** D2
Kanzi, Ras Tanzania 7°1S 39°33E **142** D4
Kao Phara Thailand 8°3N 98°22E **121** a
Kaohsiung Taiwan 22°35N 120°16E **117** F13
Kaokoveld Namibia 19°15S 14°30E **144** A1
Kaolack Senegal 14°5N 16°8W **138** C1
Kaolack □ Senegal 14°5N 15°10W **138** C1
Kaoshan China 44°38N 124°50E **115** B13
Kapa'a U.S.A. 22°5N 159°19W **167** L8
Kapadvanj India 23°5N 73°0E **124** H5
Kapan Armenia 39°18N 46°27E **105** C12
Kapanga
  Dem. Rep. of the Congo 8°30S 22°40E **140** F4
Kapchagai = Qapshaghay
  Kazakhstan 43°51N 77°14E **109** D9
Kapchagaiskoye Vdkhr. =
  Qapshaghay Bögeni
  Kazakhstan 43°45N 77°50E **109** D9
Kapedo Kenya 1°10N 36°6E **142** B4
Kapela = Velika Kapela
  Croatia 45°10N 15°5E **93** C12
Kapellskär Sweden 59°44N 19°2E **62** E13
Kapelo, Akra Greece 36°9N 23°3E **98** E5
Kapema
  Dem. Rep. of the Congo 10°45S 28°22E **143** E2
Kapenguria Kenya 1°14N 35°7E **142** B4
Kapfenberg Austria 47°26N 15°18E **78** D8
Kapıdağ Turkey 40°28N 27°50E **97** F11
Kapiri Mposhi Zambia 13°59S 28°43E **143** E2
Kāpīsā □ Afghan. 35°0N 69°20E **122** B6
Kapiskau → Canada 52°47N 81°55W **164** B3
Kapit Malaysia 2°0N 112°55E **118** D4
Kapiti I. N.Z. 40°50S 174°56E **154** G3
Kaplan U.S.A. 30°0N 92°17W **176** F8
Kaplica = Davlos
  Cyprus 35°25N 33°54E **101** D12
Kaplice Czech Rep. 48°42N 14°30E **78** C7
Kapoe Thailand 9°34N 98°32E **121** H2
Kapoeta South Sudan 4°50N 33°35E **135** H12
Kápolnásnyék Hungary 47°16N 18°41E **80** C3
Kaponga N.Z. 39°29S 174°9E **154** F3
Kapos → Hungary 46°44N 18°30E **80** D3
Kaposvár Hungary 46°25N 17°47E **80** D2
Kapowsin U.S.A. 46°59N 122°13W **170** D4
Kappeln Germany 54°40N 9°55E **76** A5
Kappelshamn Sweden 57°52N 18°47E **63** G12
Kapps Namibia 22°32S 17°18E **144** B2
Kaprije Croatia 43°42N 15°43E **93** E12
Kapsabet Kenya 0°12N 35°6E **142** B4
Kapsan N. Korea 41°4N 128°19E **115** D15
Kapsukas = Marijampolė
  Lithuania 54°33N 23°19E **82** D10
Kaptai L. Bangla. 22°40N 92°20E **123** H18
Kapuas → Indonesia 0°25S 109°20E **118** E3
Kapuas Hulu, Pegunungan
  Malaysia 1°30N 113°30E **118** D4
Kapuas Hulu Ra. = Kapuas Hulu,
  Pegunungan
  Malaysia 1°30N 113°30E **118** D4
Kapulo
  Dem. Rep. of the Congo 8°18S 29°15E **143** D2
Kapunda Australia 34°20S 138°56E **152** C3
Kapuni N.Z. 39°29S 174°8E **154** F3
Kapurthala India 31°23N 75°25E **124** D6
Kapuskasing Canada 49°25N 82°30W **164** C3
Kapuskasing →
  Canada 49°49N 82°0W **164** C3
Kapustin Yar Russia 48°37N 45°40E **87** F8
Kaputar, Mt. Australia 30°15S 150°10E **151** E5
Kaputir Kenya 2°5N 35°28E **142** B4
Kapuvár Hungary 47°36N 17°1E **80** C2
Kara Russia 69°10N 65°0E **106** C7
Kará, W. → Si. Arabia 20°45N 41°42E **137** C5
Kara Ada Turkey 36°58N 27°28E **99** E9
Kara-Balta Kyrgyzstan 42°50N 73°49E **109** D8
Kara Bogaz Gol, Zaliv =
  Garabogazköl Aylagy
  Turkmenistan 41°0N 53°30E **108** D4
Kara Burun Turkey 36°32N 27°58E **99** E9
Kara-Kala = Garrygala
  Turkmenistan 38°31N 56°29E **129** B8
Kara Kalpak Republic =
  Qoraqalpoghiston □
  Uzbekistan 43°0N 58°0E **108** D5
Kara-Köl Kyrgyzstan 41°30N 72°43E **109** D8
Kara Kum = Garagum
  Turkmenistan 39°30N 60°0E **129** B8
Kara Sea Russia 75°0N 70°0E **106** B8
Karaadilli Turkey 38°18N 30°37E **99** C12
Karabiğa Turkey 40°23N 27°17E **97** F11
Karabük Turkey 41°12N 32°37E **104** B5
Karabük □ Turkey 41°10N 32°30E **104** B5
Karaburun Albania 40°25N 19°20E **96** F3
Karabutak = Qarabutaq
  Kazakhstan 50°0N 60°14E **108** C6
Karacabey Turkey 40°12N 28°21E **97** F12
Karacakılavuz Turkey 41°8N 27°21E **97** E11
Karacaköy Turkey 41°24N 28°22E **97** E12
Karachala = Qaraçala
  Azerbaijan 39°45N 48°53E **87** J9
Karachayevsk Russia 43°40N 41°55E **87** J5
Karachey-Cherkessia □
  Russia 43°40N 41°30E **87** J5
Karachi Pakistan 24°50N 67°0E **124** G2
Karad India 17°15N 74°10E **124** G2
Karadirek Turkey 38°34N 30°11E **99** C12
Karaga Ghana 9°58N 0°28W **139** D4
Karaganda = Qaraghandy
  Kazakhstan 49°50N 73°10E **108** C8
Karagayly = Qaraghayly
  Kazakhstan 49°26N 76°0E **108** C8
Karaginskiy, Ostrov
  Russia 58°45N 164°0E **107** D17
Karagola Road India 25°29N 87°23E **125** G12

Karagüney Dağları
  Turkey 40°30N 34°40E **104** B6
Karahallı Turkey 38°21N 29°33E **99** C11
Karaikal India 10°59N 79°50E **128** J4
Karaikkudi India 10°5N 78°45E **127** J4
Karaitivu I. Sri Lanka 9°45N 79°52E **127** K4
Karaj Iran 35°48N 51°0E **129** C6
Karajarri ○ Australia 19°0S 122°30E **148** C3
Karak Malaysia 3°25N 102°2E **121** L4
Karakalpakstan =
  Qoraqalpoghiston □
  Uzbekistan 43°0N 58°0E **108** D5
Karakaya Barajı
  Turkey 38°31N 38°23E **105** C8
Karakelong Indonesia 4°35N 126°50E **119** D7
Karakitang Indonesia 3°14N 125°28E **119** D7
Karakoçan Turkey 38°57N 40°2E **105** C9
Karakol Kyrgyzstan 42°30N 78°20E **109** D9
Karakoram Pass Asia 35°33N 77°50E **125** B7
Karakoram Ra. Pakistan 35°30N 77°0E **125** B7
Karakul = Qarakol
  Uzbekistan 39°32N 63°50E **108** E6
Karakul Tajikistan 39°20N 73°33E **109** E8
Karakul, Ozero
  Tajikistan 39°5N 73°25E **109** E8
Karakurt Turkey 40°10N 42°37E **105** B10
Karakuwisa Namibia 18°56S 19°40E **144** A2
Karalon Russia 57°5N 115°50E **107** D12
Karama Jordan 31°57N 35°35E **130** D4
Karaman Balıkesir, Turkey 39°39N 28°0E **99** B9
Karaman Konya, Turkey 37°14N 33°13E **104** D5
Karamanlı Turkey 37°23N 29°47E **99** D11
Karamay China 45°30N 84°58E **109** C10
Karambu Indonesia 3°53S 116°6E **118** E5
Karamea N.Z. 41°14S 172°6E **155** B7
Karamea → N.Z. 41°13S 172°26E **155** B7
Karamea Bight N.Z. 41°22S 171°40E **155** B6
Karamnasa → India 25°31N 83°52E **125** G10
Karamürsel Turkey 40°41N 29°36E **97** F13
Karān Si. Arabia 27°43N 49°49E **129** E6
Karand Iran 34°16N 46°15E **105** C12
Karanganyar
  Indonesia 7°38S 109°37E **119** G13
Karangasem = Amlapura
  Indonesia 8°25S 115°37E **119** J18
Karanja Maharashtra,
  India 21°11N 78°24E **126** D4
Karanja Maharashtra,
  India 20°29N 77°31E **126** D3
Karanjia India 21°47N 85°58E **125** J11
Karankasso
  Burkina Faso 10°50N 3°53W **138** C4
Karaova Turkey 37°5N 27°40E **99** D9
Karapınar Turkey 37°41N 33°0E **104** D5
Karapiro N.Z. 37°53S 175°32E **154** D4
Karas □ Namibia 27°0S 17°30E **144** C2
Karasburg Namibia 28°0S 18°44E **144** D2
Karasino Russia 66°50N 86°50E **106** C9
Karasjok Norway 69°27N 25°30E **60** B21
Karasu → Turkey 41°4N 30°46E **104** B4
Karasu Turkey 41°4N 30°46E **104** B4
Karasu → Turkey 39°41N 42°54E **105** C10
Karasuyama Japan 36°39N 140°9E **113** F10
Karatas Adana, Turkey 36°36N 35°21E **104** D6
Karataş Manisa, Turkey 38°35N 28°16E **99** C10
Karatau, Khrebet = Qarataū
  Kazakhstan 43°30N 69°30E **109** D7
Karatax Shan China 35°57N 81°0E **109** E10
Karateki Shan China 40°40N 77°0E **109** D9
Karativu Sri Lanka 8°22N 79°47E **127** K4
Karatoprak Turkey 37°2N 27°15E **99** D9
Karatsu Japan 33°26N 129°58E **113** H5
Karaul Russia 70°6N 82°15E **106** B9
Karauli India 26°30N 77°4E **124** F7
Karavastasë, L. e Albania 40°55N 19°30E **96** F3
Karavia Greece 36°49N 23°37E **98** E5
Karavostasi Cyprus 35°8N 32°50E **101** D11
Karawang Indonesia 6°30S 107°15E **119** G12
Karawanken Europe 46°30N 14°40E **78** B7
Karayazı Turkey 39°41N 42°9E **105** C10
Karazhal = Qarazhal
  Kazakhstan 48°2N 70°49E **106** E8
Karbalā’ Iraq 32°36N 44°3E **105** F11
Karbalā □ Iraq 32°30N 44°0E **105** F11
Kårböle Sweden 61°59N 15°22E **62** D7
Karcag Hungary 47°19N 20°57E **80** C5
Karcha → Pakistan 34°45N 76°10E **125** B7
Karchana India 25°17N 81°56E **125** G9
Karczew Poland 52°5N 21°15E **83** F8
Kardam Bulgaria 43°45N 28°6E **97** C12
Kardamaina Greece 36°47N 27°9E **99** E9
Kardamili Greece 36°53N 22°13E **98** E4
Kardeljovo = Ploče
  Croatia 43°4N 17°26E **93** E14
Kardhitsa Greece 39°23N 21°54E **98** B3
Kärdla Estonia 59°0N 22°45E **84** C2
Kardzhali = Kŭrdzhali
  Bulgaria 41°38N 25°21E **97** E9
Karea Sea Russia 75°0N 70°0E **106** B8
Kareeberge S. Africa 30°59S 21°50E **144** D3
Kareha → India 25°44N 86°21E **125** G12
Kareima Sudan 18°30N 31°49E **137** D3
Karelia □ Russia 65°30N 32°30E **106** C4
Karelian Republic = Karelia □
  Russia 65°30N 32°30E **106** C4
Karera India 25°32N 78°9E **124** G8
Kārevāndar Iran 27°53N 60°44E **129** E9
Kargasok Russia 59°3N 80°53E **106** D9
Kargat Russia 55°10N 80°15E **106** D9
Kargı Kenya 2°31N 37°34E **142** B4
Kargi Turkey 41°11N 34°30E **104** B6
Kargil India 34°32N 76°12E **124** B7
Kargopol Russia 61°30N 38°58E **84** B10
Kargué Niger 13°27N 10°28E **139** C8
Kari Nigeria 11°12N 10°28E **139** C8
Karia ba Mohammed
  Morocco 34°22N 5°12W **136** B2
Kariān Iran 26°57N 57°14E **129** E8
Kariba Zimbabwe 16°28S 28°50E **143** F2
Kariba, L. Zimbabwe 16°40S 28°25E **143** F2
Kariba Dam Zimbabwe 16°30S 28°35E **143** F2
Kariba Gorge Zambia 16°30S 28°50E **143** F2
Karibib Namibia 22°0S 15°56E **144** B2
Karies Greece 40°14N 24°19E **98** A6
Karijini △ Australia 23°8S 118°15E **148** D2
Karijini, C. N.Z. 34°46S 173°24E **154** A4
Karimata, Kepulauan
  Indonesia 1°25S 109°0E **118** E3

Karimata, Selat
  Indonesia 2°0S 108°40E **118** E3
Karimata Is. = Karimata,
  Kepulauan Indonesia 1°25S 109°0E **118** E3
Karimnagar India 18°26N 79°10E **126** E4
Karimun, Pulau Indonesia 1°3N 103°22E **121** d
Karimun Kecil, Pulau
  Indonesia 1°8N 103°22E **121** d
Karimunjawa, Kepulauan
  Indonesia 5°50S 110°30E **118** F4
Karin Somalia 10°50N 45°52E **131** E4
Karistos Greece 38°1N 24°29E **98** C6
Karīt Iran 33°29N 56°55E **129** C8
Kariya Japan 34°58N 137°1E **113** G8
Karkal India 13°15N 74°56E **127** H2
Karkaralinsk = Qarqaraly
  Kazakhstan 49°26N 75°30E **109** C9
Karkheh → Iran 31°2N 47°29E **128** D5
Karki Azerbaijan 39°47N 44°57E **105** C11
Karkinitska Zatoka
  Ukraine 45°56N 33°0E **85** K7
Karkinitskiy Zaliv = Karkinitska
  Zatoka Ukraine 45°56N 33°0E **85** K7
Karkuk = Kirkūk
  Iraq 35°30N 44°21E **105** E11
Karkur Tohl Egypt 22°5N 25°5E **137** C2
Karl Liebknecht = imeni Karl
  Libknekhta Russia 51°40N 35°35E **85** G8
Karl-Marx-Stadt = Chemnitz
  Germany 50°51N 12°54E **76** C7
Karla, L. = Volvi, L.
  Greece 40°40N 23°34E **96** F7
Karlholmsbruk Sweden 60°31N 17°37E **62** D11
Karlino Poland 54°3N 15°53E **82** D2
Karlıova Turkey 39°17N 41°0E **105** C10
Karlobag Croatia 44°32N 15°5E **93** D12
Karlovac Croatia 45°31N 15°36E **93** C12
Karlovasi Greece 37°45N 26°42E **99** D8
Karlovo Bulgaria 42°38N 24°47E **97** D8
Karlovy Vary Czech Rep. 50°13N 12°51E **78** A5
Karlsbad = Karlovy Vary
  Czech Rep. 50°13N 12°51E **78** A5
Karlsborg Sweden 58°33N 14°33E **63** F6
Karlsena, Mys Russia 77°0N 67°42E **106** B7
Karlshamn Sweden 56°10N 14°51E **63** H8
Karlskoga Sweden 59°28N 14°33E **62** E8
Karlskrona Sweden 56°10N 15°35E **63** H9
Karlsruhe Germany 49°0N 8°23E **77** F4
Karlstad Sweden 59°23N 13°30E **62** E7
Karlstad U.S.A. 48°35N 96°31W **172** A5
Karlstadt Germany 49°57N 9°46E **76** F5
Karmala India 18°25N 75°12E **126** E2
Karmel’el Israel 32°55N 35°18E **130** C4
Karmi Egypt 25°43N 32°39E **137** B3
Karnal India 29°42N 77°2E **124** E7
Karnali → Nepal 28°45N 81°16E **125** E9
Karnaphuli Res. = Kaptai L.
  Bangla. 22°40N 92°20E **123** H18
Karnaprayag India 30°16N 79°15E **125** D8
Karnataka □ India 13°15N 77°0E **127** H3
Karnes City U.S.A. 28°53N 97°54W **176** G6
Karnische Alpen Europe 46°36N 13°0E **78** E6
Karnobat Bulgaria 42°39N 26°57E **97** D10
Kärnten □ Austria 46°52N 13°30E **78** E6
Karo Mali 12°16N 3°18W **138** C4
Karoi Zimbabwe 16°48S 29°45E **143** F2
Karon, Ao Thailand 7°51N 98°17E **121** a
Karonga Malawi 9°57S 33°55E **143** D3
Karoo △ S. Africa 32°18S 22°27E **144** D3
Karoonda Australia 35°1S 139°59E **152** C3
Karor Pakistan 31°15N 70°59E **124** D4
Karora Sudan 17°44N 38°15E **135** E13
Karounga Mali 15°20N 7°35W **138** B3
Karousades Greece 39°47N 19°45E **98** B1
Karpasia Cyprus 35°32N 34°15E **101** D13
Karpathos Greece 35°37N 27°10E **99** F10
Karpathou, Stenon
  Greece 36°0N 27°30E **99** F9
Karpatsky △ Ukraine 48°20N 24°35E **81** B9
Karpenisi Greece 38°55N 21°40E **98** C3
Karpuz Burnu = Apostolos
  Andreas, C. Cyprus 35°42N 34°35E **101** D13
Karpuzlu Turkey 37°33N 27°46E **99** D9
Karratha Australia 20°45S 116°52E **148** D2
Kars Turkey 40°40N 43°5E **105** B10
Kars □ Turkey 40°40N 43°0E **105** B10
Karsakpay Kazakhstan 47°55N 66°40E **109** C7
Karsha Kazakhstan 49°45N 51°35E **86** F10
Karshi = Qarshi
  Uzbekistan 38°53N 65°48E **109** F7
Karsiyang India 26°56N 88°18E **125** F13
Karsog India 31°23N 77°12E **124** D7
Karst = Kras Croatia 45°35N 14°0E **93** C10
Kartala Comoros Is. 11°45S 43°21E **141** a
Kartaly Russia 53°3N 60°40E **108** D6
Kartapur India 31°27N 75°32E **124** D6
Karthaus U.S.A. 41°8N 78°9W **174** E6
Kartuzy Poland 54°22N 18°10E **82** D5
Karufa Indonesia 3°50S 133°20E **119** E8
Karula △ Estonia 57°43N 26°34E **84** D4
Karumba Australia 17°31S 140°50E **150** B3
Karumo Tanzania 2°25S 32°50E **142** C3
Karumwa Tanzania 3°12S 32°38E **142** C3
Kārūn → Iran 30°26N 48°10E **128** D5
Karungu Kenya 0°50S 34°10E **142** C3
Karup Denmark 56°19N 9°10E **63** H3
Karviná Czech Rep. 49°53N 18°31E **79** B11
Karwan → India 27°26N 78°4E **124** F7
Karwar India 14°55N 74°13E **127** G2
Karwendel △ Austria 47°29N 11°36E **78** E4
Karwi India 25°12N 80°57E **125** G9
Karymskoye Russia 51°36N 114°21E **107** D12

Kasaba Turkey 36°18N 29°44E **99** E11
Kasache Malawi 13°25S 34°20E **143** E3
Kasai →
  Dem. Rep. of the Congo 3°30S 16°10E **140** D3
Kasai-Oriental □
  Dem. Rep. of the Congo 5°0S 24°30E **142** D1
Kasaji
  Dem. Rep. of the Congo 10°25S 23°27E **143** E1
Kasama Zambia 10°16S 31°9E **143** E3
Kasan-dong N. Korea 41°18N 126°55E **115** D14
Kasane Namibia 40°0N 23°30E **96** F7
Kasanda Kolpos Greece 40°5N 23°30E **96** F7
Kasandras, Akra Greece 39°57N 23°30E **96** F7
Kasane Namibia 17°34S 24°50E **144** A3
Kasanka △ Zambia 11°34S 30°15E **143** E3
Kasar, Ras Sudan 18°2N 38°36E **137** D4
Kasaragod India 12°30N 74°58E **127** H2
Kasba L. Canada 60°20N 102°10W **163** A8
Kasba Tadla Morocco 32°36N 6°17W **136** B2
Kāseh Garān Iran 34°5N 46°2E **128** C5
Kasempa Zambia 13°30S 25°44E **143** E2
Kasenga
  Dem. Rep. of the Congo 10°20S 28°45E **143** E2
Kasese Uganda 0°13N 30°3E **142** B3
Kasganj India 27°48N 78°42E **125** F8
Kashabowie Canada 48°40N 90°26W **164** C1
Kashaf Iran 35°58N 61°7E **129** C9
Kāshān Iran 34°5N 51°30E **129** C6
Kashechewan Canada 52°18N 81°37W **164** B3
Kashgān → Iran 33°5N 47°31E **105** F12
Kashgar = Kashi China 39°30N 76°2E **109** E6
Kashi China 39°30N 76°2E **109** E6
Kashimbo
  Dem. Rep. of the Congo 11°12S 26°19E **143** E2
Kashin Russia 57°20N 37°36E **84** D9
Kashipur Odisha, India 19°16N 83°3E **126** E6
Kashipur Uttarakhand,
  India 29°15N 79°0E **125** E8
Kashira Russia 54°45N 38°10E **84** E10
Kashiwazaki Japan 37°22N 138°33E **113** F9
Kashk-e Kohneh
  Afghan. 34°55N 62°30E **122** B3
Kashksaray Iran 38°4N 45°34E **105** C11
Kashkū’īyeh Iran 30°31N 55°40E **129** D7
Kāshmar Iran 35°16N 58°26E **129** C8
Kashmir Asia 34°0N 76°0E **125** C7
Kashmor Pakistan 28°28N 69°32E **124** E3
Kashpirovka Russia 53°0N 48°30E **86** D9
Kashun Noerh = Gaxun Nur
  China 42°22N 100°30E **110** C9
Kasiari India 22°8N 87°14E **125** H12
Kasimov Russia 54°55N 41°20E **86** C6
Kasinge
  Dem. Rep. of the Congo 6°15S 26°58E **142** D2
Kasiruta Indonesia 0°25S 127°12E **119** E7
Kaskaskia → U.S.A. 37°58N 89°57W **172** G9
Kaskattama → Canada 57°3N 90°4W **163** B10
Kaskinen Finland 62°22N 21°15E **60** E19
Kaskö = Kaskinen
  Finland 62°22N 21°15E **60** E19
Kaslo Canada 49°55N 116°55E **163** D8
Kasmere L. Canada 59°34N 101°10W **163** B8
Kasongo
  Dem. Rep. of the Congo 4°30S 26°33E **142** C2
Kasongo Lunda
  Dem. Rep. of the Congo 6°35S 16°49E **140** F3
Kasos Greece 35°20N 26°55E **99** F8
Kasou, Stenon Greece 35°30N 26°30E **99** F8
Kaspi Georgia 41°59N 44°26E **87** K7
Kaspichan Bulgaria 43°18N 27°11E **97** C11
Kaspiysk Russia 42°52N 47°40E **87** J8
Kaspiyskiy Russia 45°22N 47°23E **87** H8
Kassabá Egypt 22°40N 29°55E **137** C2
Kassalâ Sudan 15°30N 36°0E **135** E13
Kassandrino Greece 40°1N 23°27E **96** F7
Kassel Germany 51°18N 9°26E **76** D5
Kasserine Tunisia 35°10N 8°50E **136** A5
Kassiopi Greece 39°48N 19°53E **101** A3
Kasson U.S.A. 44°2N 92°45W **172** C7
Kastamonu Turkey 41°20N 34°0E **104** B5
Kastamonu □ Turkey 41°20N 34°0E **104** B5
Kastav Croatia 45°22N 14°20E **93** C11
Kasteli Greece 35°12N 23°38E **101** D5
Kastélli = Kissamos
  Greece 35°30N 23°38E **101** D5
Kastellórizo = Megisti
  Greece 36°8N 29°34E **99** E11
Kastelo, Akra Greece 35°30N 27°15E **99** F9
Kasterlee Belgium 51°15N 4°59E **69** C4
Kastlösa Sweden 56°26N 16°25E **63** H10
Kastoria Greece 40°30N 21°19E **96** F5
Kastorias, L. Greece 40°30N 21°19E **96** F5
Kastorio Greece 37°10N 22°17E **98** D4
Kastornoye Russia 51°55N 38°2E **85** G10
Kastos Greece 38°35N 20°55E **98** C2
Kastrom Mefa'a = Umm al Rasas
  Jordan 31°30N 35°55E **130** D4
Kastrosikia Greece 39°6N 20°38E **98** B2
Kastrup, København × (CPH)
  Denmark 55°37N 12°39E **63** J6
Kastsyukovichy Belarus 53°20N 32°4E **85** F7
Kasubi Tombs Uganda 0°20N 32°30E **142** B3
Kasulu Tanzania 4°37S 30°5E **142** C3
Kasumi Japan 35°38N 134°38E **113** G7
Kasumkent Russia 41°47N 48°15E **87** K9
Kasungu Malawi 13°0S 33°29E **143** E3
Kasungu △ Malawi 12°53S 33°9E **143** E3
Kasur Pakistan 31°5N 74°25E **124** D6
Kata, Ao Thailand 7°48N 98°18E **121** J2
Kata Archanes Greece 35°15N 25°10E **101** D7
Kata Zambia 16°5S 25°10E **143** F2
Katagum Nigeria 12°17N 10°16E **139** C8
Katahdin, Mt. U.S.A. 45°54N 68°56W **173** C19
Kataka = Cuttack
  India 20°25N 85°57E **126** D7
Katako Kombe
  Dem. Rep. of the Congo 3°25S 24°20E **142** C1
Katakolo Greece 37°38N 21°19E **98** D3
Katale
  Dem. Rep. of the Congo 0°55S 29°21E **142** C2
Katamatite Australia 36°5S 145°41E **153** D6
Katanda Katanga,
  Dem. Rep. of the Congo 7°52S 24°13E **142** D1
Katanda Nord-Kivu,
  Dem. Rep. of the Congo 0°55S 29°21E **142** C2
Katanga □
  Dem. Rep. of the Congo 8°0S 25°0E **142** D2
Katangi India 21°56N 79°50E **126** D4
Katanning Australia 33°40S 117°33E **149** F2

Katastari *Greece* 37°50N 20°45E **98** D2
Katavi △ *Tanzania* 6°51S 31°3E **142** D3
Katavi Swamp *Tanzania* 6°50S 31°10E **142** D3
Katchall *India* 7°57N 93°22E **127** L11
Katerini *Greece* 40°18N 22°37E **96** F6
Katghora *India* 22°30N 82°33E **125** H10
Katha *Burma* 24°10N 96°30E **123** G20
Katherina, Gebel *Egypt* 28°30N 33°57E **128** D2
Katherine *Australia* 14°27S 132°20E **148** B5
Katherine Gorge = Nitmiluk △
  Australia 14°6S 132°15E **148** B5
Kathi *India* 21°47N 74°3E **124** J6
Kathiawar *India* 22°20N 71°0E **124** H4
Kathikas *Cyprus* 34°55N 32°25E **101** E11
Kathleen *U.S.A.* 28°7N 82°2W **179** G7
Kathua *India* 32°23N 75°34E **124** C6
Kati *Mali* 12°41N 8°4W **138** C3
Katihar *India* 25°34N 87°36E **125** G12
Katikati *N.Z.* 37°32S 175°57E **154** D4
Katima Mulilo *Namibia* 17°28S 24°13E **144** A3
Katimbira *Malawi* 12°40S 34°0E **143** E3
Katingan = Mendawai →
  Indonesia 3°30S 113°0E **118** E4
Katiola *Ivory C.* 8°10N 5°10W **138** D3
Katiti △ *Australia* 25°1S 131°11E **149** E5
Katlabukh, Ozero
  Ukraine 45°28N 29°0E **81** E14
Katlanovo *Macedonia* 41°52N 21°40E **96** E5
Katmandu = Kathmandu
  Nepal 27°45N 85°20E **125** F11
Katni *India* 23°51N 80°24E **125** H9
Kato Achaia *Greece* 38°8N 21°33E **98** C3
Kato Chorio *Greece* 35°3N 25°47E **101** D7
Kato Korakiana *Greece* 39°42N 19°45E **101** A3
Kato Pyrgos *Cyprus* 35°11N 32°41E **101** D11
Katochi *Greece* 38°26N 21°5E **98** C3
Katol *India* 21°17N 78°38E **126** D4
Katompe
  Dem. Rep. of the Congo 6°2S 26°23E **142** D2
Katong *Singapore* 1°18N 103°53E **121** d
Katonga → *Uganda* 0°34N 31°50E **142** B3
Katoomba *Australia* 33°41S 150°19E **153** B9
Katouna *Greece* 38°47N 21°7E **98** C3
Katowice *Poland* 50°17N 19°5E **83** H6
Katrancı Dağı *Turkey* 37°27N 30°20E **99** E12
Katrine, L. *U.K.* 56°15N 4°30W **65** E4
Katrineholm *Sweden* 59°0N 16°12E **62** E10
Katsina *Nigeria* 13°0N 7°32E **139** C6
Katsina □ *Nigeria* 12°30N 7°30E **139** C6
Katsina Ala *Nigeria* 7°10N 9°30E **139** D6
Katsina Ala → *Nigeria* 7°10N 9°20E **139** D6
Katsumoto *Japan* 33°51N 129°42E **113** H4
Katsuura *Japan* 35°10N 140°20E **113** G10
Katsuyama *Japan* 36°3N 136°30E **113** F8
Kattaqŭrghon
  Uzbekistan 39°55N 66°15E **109** E7
Kattavia *Greece* 35°57N 27°46E **101** D9
Kattegat *Denmark* 56°40N 11°0E **63** H5
Katthammarsvik
  Sweden 57°26N 18°51E **63** G12
Katumba
  Dem. Rep. of the Congo 7°40S 25°17E **142** D2
Katun → *Russia* 52°25N 85°1E **109** D11
Katwa *India* 23°30N 88°5E **125** H13
Katwijk *Neths.* 52°12N 4°24E **69** B4
Kąty Wrocławskie
  Poland 51°2N 16°45E **83** G3
Kau-Ye Kyun *Burma* 11°1N 98°32E **121** a2
Kaua'i *U.S.A.* 22°3N 159°30W **167** L8
Kaub *Germany* 50°5N 7°46E **77** E3
Kaudom △ *Namibia* 18°45S 20°51E **144** A3
Kaufbeuren *Germany* 47°53N 10°37E **77** H6
Kaufman *U.S.A.* 32°35N 96°19W **176** E6
Kauhajoki *Finland* 62°25N 22°10E **60** E20
Kauhaneva-Pohjankangas △
  Finland 62°13N 22°20E **60** E20
Kaukauna *U.S.A.* 44°17N 88°17W **172** C9
Kaukauveld *Namibia* 20°0S 20°15E **144** B3
Ka'ula I. *U.S.A.* 21°40N 160°33W **167** L7
Kaunas *Lithuania* 54°54N 23°54E **82** D10
Kaunas ✈ (KUN)
  Lithuania 54°57N 24°3E **82** D11
Kaunia *Bangla.* 25°46N 89°26E **125** G13
Kaunos *Turkey* 36°49N 28°39E **99** E10
Kaura Namoda *Nigeria* 12°37N 6°33E **139** C6
Kauru *Nigeria* 10°33N 8°12E **139** C6
Kautokeino *Norway* 69°0N 23°4E **60** B20
Kauwapur *India* 27°31N 82°18E **125** F10
Kavacha *Russia* 60°16N 169°51E **107** C17
Kavadarci *Macedonia* 41°26N 22°3E **96** E6
Kavajë *Albania* 41°11N 19°33E **96** E3
Kavak *Turkey* 41°4N 36°3E **104** B7
Kavak Dağı *Turkey* 37°27N 28°12E **99** D10
Kavaklı *Turkey* 41°39N 27°10E **97** E11
Kavaklıdere *Turkey* 37°27N 28°21E **99** D10
Kavala *Greece* 40°57N 24°28E **97** F8
Kavala Kolpos *Greece* 40°50N 24°25E **97** F8
Kavalerovo *Russia* 44°15N 135°4E **112** B7
Kavali *India* 14°55N 80°1E **127** G5
Kavār *Iran* 29°11N 52°44E **131** D7
Kavaratti *India* 10°33N 72°37E **127** J1
Kavaratti I. *India* 10°33N 72°38E **127** J1
Kavarna *Bulgaria* 43°26N 28°22E **97** C12
Kavi *India* 22°12N 72°38E **124** H5
Kavimba *Botswana* 18°2S 24°38E **144** A3
Kavīr, Dasht-e *Iran* 34°30N 55°0E **129** C7
Kavīr △ *Iran* 34°40N 52°0E **129** C7
Kavkaz *Russia* 45°20N 36°40E **85** K9
Kävlinge *Sweden* 55°47N 13°9E **63** J7
Kavos *Greece* 39°23N 20°3E **101** B4
Kavousi *Greece* 35°7N 25°51E **101** D7
Kaw *Fr. Guiana* 4°30N 52°15W **187** C8
Kawagama L. *Canada* 45°18N 78°45W **174** A6
Kawagoe *Japan* 35°55N 139°29E **113** G9
Kawaguchi *Japan* 35°52N 139°45E **113** G9
Kawah Ijen △ *Indonesia* 8°3S 114°14E **119** H15
Kawakawa *N.Z.* 35°23S 174°6E **154** B3
Kawambwa *Zambia* 9°48S 29°3E **143** D2
Kawanoe = Shikokuchūō
  Japan 34°1N 133°34E **113** G6
Kawardha *India* 22°0N 81°17E **125** J9
Kawasaki *Japan* 35°31N 139°43E **113** G9
Kawasi *Indonesia* 1°38S 127°28E **119** E7
Kawau I. *N.Z.* 36°25S 174°52E **154** C3
Kawawachikamach
  Canada 54°48N 66°50W **165** B6
Kaweka Ra. *N.Z.* 39°17S 176°19E **154** F5
Kawerau *N.Z.* 38°4S 176°42E **154** F5
Kawhia *N.Z.* 38°4S 174°49E **154** E3
Kawhia Harbour *N.Z.* 38°5S 174°51E **154** E3

Kawio, Kepulauan
  Indonesia 4°30N 125°30E **119** D7
Kawthaung *Burma* 10°5N 98°36E **121** H2
Kawthoolei = Kayin □
  Burma 18°0N 97°30E **123** L20
Kawthule = Kayin □
  Burma 18°0N 97°30E **123** L20
Kaxgar He → *China* 39°45N 78°24E **109** E9
Kaxholmen *Sweden* 57°51N 14°19E **63** G8
Kaya *Burkina Faso* 13°4N 1°10W **139** C4
Kayah □ *Burma* 19°15N 97°15E **123** K20
Kayak I. *U.S.A.* 59°56N 144°23W **168** D11
Kayalıköy Baraji *Turkey* 41°30N 27°55E **97** E11
Kayamkulam *India* 9°10N 76°33E **127** K3
Kayan → *Indonesia* 2°55N 117°35E **118** D5
Kaycee *U.S.A.* 43°43N 106°38W **168** E10
Kayeli *Indonesia* 3°20S 127°10E **119** E7
Kayenta *U.S.A.* 36°44N 110°15W **169** H8
Kayes *Mali* 14°25N 11°30W **138** C2
Kayes □ *Mali* 14°0N 11°0W **138** C2
Kayı *Turkey* 39°12N 30°46E **99** B12
Kayima *S. Leone* 8°54N 11°15W **138** D2
Kayin □ *Burma* 18°0N 97°30E **123** L20
Kaymakçı *Turkey* 38°10N 28°8E **99** C10
Kaymaz *Turkey* 39°41N 31°20E **99** B12
Kayoa *Indonesia* 0°1N 127°28E **119** D7
Kayomba *Zambia* 13°11S 24°2E **143** E1
Kaysatskoye *Russia* 49°47N 46°49E **86** F8
Kayseri *Turkey* 38°45N 35°30E **104** C6
Kayseri □ *Turkey* 38°40N 36°0E **104** C7
Kaysville *U.S.A.* 41°2N 111°56W **168** F8
Kayts *Sri Lanka* 9°42N 79°51E **127** K4
Kaz Dağı *Turkey* 39°42N 26°50E **99** B8
Kazachye *Russia* 70°52N 135°58E **107** B14
Kazaly = Qazaly
  Kazakhstan 45°45N 62°6E **108** C6
Kazan *Russia* 55°50N 49°10E **86** C9
Kazan → *Canada* 64°2N 95°29W **163** A9
Kazan-Rettō *Pac. Oc.* 25°0N 141°0E **156** E6
Kazanlak *Bulgaria* 42°38N 25°20E **97** D9
Kazanskaya *Russia* 49°50N 41°10E **86** F5
Kazatin = Kozyatyn
  Ukraine 49°45N 28°50E **75** D15
Kazaure *Nigeria* 12°42N 8°28E **139** C6
Kazbek *Russia* 42°42N 44°30E **87** J7
Kāzerūn *Iran* 29°38N 51°40E **129** D6
Kazi Magomed = Qazimämmäd
  Azerbaijan 40°3N 49°0E **87** K9
Kazimierz Dolny *Poland* 51°19N 21°57E **83** G8
Kazimierza Wielka
  Poland 50°15N 20°30E **83** H7
Kazincbarcika *Hungary* 48°17N 20°36E **80** B5
Kazipet *India* 17°58N 79°30E **126** F4
Kazlų Rūda *Lithuania* 54°46N 23°30E **82** D10
Kaztalovka *Kazakhstan* 49°47N 48°43E **86** F9
Kazuma Pan △
  Zimbabwe 18°20S 25°48E **143** F2
Kazuno *Japan* 40°10N 140°45E **112** D10
Kazym → *Russia* 63°54N 65°50E **106** C7
Kcynia *Poland* 53°0N 17°30E **83** F4
Ké-Macina *Mali* 13°58N 5°22W **138** C3
Kea *Greece* 37°35N 24°22E **98** D6
Keady *U.K.* 54°15N 6°42W **64** B5
Kearney *U.S.A.* 40°42N 99°5W **172** E4
Kearney □ *Australia* 20°10S 128°4E **148** D4
Kearny *U.S.A.* 33°3N 110°55W **169** K8
Kearsarge, Mt. *U.S.A.* 43°20N 71°50W **175** C13
Keban *Turkey* 38°50N 38°50E **105** C8
Keban Baraji *Turkey* 38°41N 38°33E **105** C8
Kebbi □ *Nigeria* 11°35N 4°0E **139** C5
Kébémèr *Senegal* 15°23N 16°34W **138** B1
Kébi *Ivory C.* 9°18N 6°37W **138** D3
Kebili *Tunisia* 33°47N 9°0E **136** B5
Kebili □ *Tunisia* 33°30N 8°50E **136** B5
Kebri Dehar *Ethiopia* 6°45N 44°17E **131** F3
Kebumen *Indonesia* 7°42S 109°40E **119** G13
Kecel *Hungary* 46°31N 19°16E **80** D4
Kechika → *Canada* 59°41N 127°12W **162** B3
Keçiborlu *Turkey* 37°57N 30°18E **99** D12
Kecskemét *Hungary* 46°57N 19°42E **80** D4
Kedah □ *Malaysia* 5°50N 100°40E **121** K3
Kédainiai *Lithuania* 55°15N 24°2E **82** C11
Kedarnath *India* 30°44N 79°4E **125** D8
Kedgwick *Canada* 47°40N 67°20W **165** C6
Kediri *Indonesia* 7°51S 112°1E **118** F4
Kedjebi *Ghana* 8°12N 0°25E **139** D5
Kédougou *Senegal* 12°35N 12°10W **138** C2
Kedros Oros *Greece* 35°11N 24°37E **101** D6
Kedvavom *India* 54°20N 122°40W **162** C4
Kędzierzyn-Koźle *Poland* 50°20N 18°12E **83** H5
Keeler *U.S.A.* 36°29N 117°52W **170** J9
Keeley L. *Canada* 54°54N 108°8W **167** C7
Keeling Is. = Cocos Is.
  Ind. Oc. 12°10S 96°55E **146** F8
Keelung = Chilung
  Taiwan 25°3N 121°45E **117** E13
Keene *Canada* 44°15N 78°10W **174** B6
Keene *Calif., U.S.A.* 35°13N 118°33W **171** K8
Keene *N.H., U.S.A.* 42°56N 72°17W **175** D12
Keene *N.Y., U.S.A.* 44°16N 73°46W **175** B11
Keep River △ *Australia* 15°49S 129°8E **148** C4
Keeper Hill *Ireland* 52°45N 8°16W **64** D3
Keepit, L. *Australia* 30°50S 150°30E **153** A9
Keer-weer, C. *Australia* 14°0S 141°32E **150** A3
Keeseville *U.S.A.* 44°29N 73°30W **175** B11
Keetmanshoop *Namibia* 26°35S 18°8E **144** C2
Keewatin *Canada* 49°46N 94°34W **163** D10
Keewatin □ *Canada* 63°20N 95°0W **163** B9
Kefalonia *Greece* 38°15N 20°30E **98** C2
Kefalos *Greece* 36°44N 26°57E **97** F10
Kefamenanu *Indonesia* 9°28S 124°29E **119** F6
Kefar Sava *Israel* 32°11N 34°54E **130** C3
Keffi *Nigeria* 8°55N 7°43E **139** D6
Keffin Hausa *Nigeria* 12°13N 9°59E **139** C6
Keflavík *Iceland* 64°2N 22°35W **60** D2
Keg River *Canada* 57°54N 117°55W **162** B5
Kegalla *Sri Lanka* 7°15N 80°21E **127** L5
Kegaska *Canada* 50°9N 61°18W **165** B7
Kehancha *Kenya* 1°11S 34°37E **142** C3
Kehoila *Sudan* 19°25N 32°50E **137** D3
Kehl *Germany* 48°34N 7°50E **77** G2
Keighley *U.K.* 53°52N 1°54W **66** D6
Keila *Estonia* 59°18N 24°25E **84** C1
Keimoes *S. Africa* 28°41S 20°59E **144** D3
Keita *Niger* 14°46N 5°56E **139** C6
Keitele *Finland* 63°10N 26°20E **60** E22
Keith *Australia* 36°5S 140°0E **152** D4
Keith *U.K.* 57°32N 2°57W **65** D6
Keiyasi *Fiji* 17°53S 177°46E **154** a
Keizer *U.S.A.* 44°57N 123°1W **168** D2
Kejimkujik △ *Canada* 44°25N 65°25W **165** D6

Kejserr Franz Joseph Fd.
  Greenland 73°30N 24°30W **57** C8
Kekri *India* 25°50N 75°10E **124** G6
Kelan *China* 38°43N 111°31E **114** E6
Kelang = Klang
  Malaysia 3°2N 101°26E **121** L3
Kelani Ganga →
  Sri Lanka 6°58N 79°50E **127** L4
Kelantan □ *Malaysia* 5°10N 102°0E **121** K3
Kelantan → *Malaysia* 6°13N 102°14E **121** J4
Kĕlcyrĕ *Albania* 40°20N 20°12E **96** F4
Kelekçi *Turkey* 37°15N 29°20E **99** D11
Keles *Turkey* 39°54N 29°14E **97** G13
Keleti-főcsatorna
  Hungary 47°45N 21°20E **80** C6
Kelheim *Germany* 48°54N 11°52E **77** G7
Kelibia *Tunisia* 36°50N 11°3E **136** A6
Kellé *Niger* 14°16N 10°7E **137** C7
Keller *U.S.A.* 31°56N 81°15W **178** D8
Kellerberrin *Australia* 31°36S 117°38E **149** F2
Kellett, C. *Canada* 72°0N 126°0W **54** B1
Kelleys I. *U.S.A.* 41°36N 82°42W **174** E2
Kellogg *U.S.A.* 47°32N 116°7W **168** C5
Kells = Ceanannus Mor
  Ireland 53°44N 6°53W **64** C5
Kélo *Chad* 9°10N 15°45E **135** G9
Kelokedhara *Cyprus* 34°48N 32°39E **101** E11
Kelowna *Canada* 49°50N 119°25W **162** D5
Kelsey Creek *Australia* 20°26S 148°31E **150** b
Kelseyville *U.S.A.* 38°59N 122°50W **170** G4
Kelso *N.Z.* 45°54S 169°15E **155** F4
Kelso *U.K.* 55°36N 2°26W **65** F6
Kelso *U.S.A.* 46°9N 122°54W **170** D4
Keluang = Kluang
  Malaysia 2°3N 103°18E **121** L4
Kelud *Indonesia* 7°56N 112°18E **119** H15
Kelvington *Canada* 52°10N 103°30E **167** C8
Kem *Russia* 65°0N 34°38E **106** C4
Kem-Kem *Morocco* 30°40N 4°30W **136** B3
Kema *Indonesia* 1°22N 125°8E **119** D7
Kemaliye *Erzincan,*
  Turkey 39°16N 38°29E **105** C8
Kemaliye *Manisa,*
  Turkey 38°27N 28°25E **99** C10
Kemalpaşa *Turkey* 38°25N 27°27E **99** C9
Kemaman *Malaysia* 4°12N 103°18E **121** K4
Kemano *Canada* 53°35N 128°0W **162** C3
Kemasik *Malaysia* 4°25N 103°27E **121** K4
Kemer *Antalya, Turkey* 36°36N 30°34E **99** E12
Kemer *Burdur, Turkey* 37°21N 30°4E **99** D12
Kemer *Muğla, Turkey* 36°40N 29°22E **99** E11
Kemer Baraji *Turkey* 37°30N 28°37E **99** D10
Kemerovo *Russia* 55°20N 86°5E **106** D9
Kemerovo □ *Russia* 55°0N 86°0E **109** D11
Kemi *Finland* 65°44N 24°34E **60** D21
Kemi älv = Kemijoki →
  Finland 65°47N 24°32E **60** D21
Kemi träsk = Kemijärvi
  Finland 66°43N 27°22E **60** C22
Kemijärvi *Finland* 66°43N 27°22E **60** C22
Kemijoki → *Finland* 65°47N 24°32E **60** D21
Kemmerer *U.S.A.* 41°48N 110°32W **168** F8
Kemmuna = Comino
  Malta 36°1N 14°20E **101** C1
Kemp, L. *U.S.A.* 33°46N 99°9W **176** E5
Kemp Land *Antarctica* 69°0S 55°0E **55** C5
Kempas *Malaysia* 1°33N 103°42E **121** d
Kempsey *Australia* 31°1S 152°50E **153** A10
Kempt, L. *Canada* 47°25N 74°22W **164** C5
Kempten *Germany* 47°45N 10°17E **77** H6
Kemptville *Canada* 45°0N 75°38W **175** B9
Ken → *India* 25°13N 80°27E **125** G9
Kenadsa *Algeria* 31°48N 2°26W **136** B3
Kenai *U.S.A.* 60°33N 151°16W **168** C1
Kenai Mts. *U.S.A.* 60°0N 150°0W **166** D9
Kenamuke Swamp
  South Sudan 5°55N 33°48E **142** A3
Kenansville *U.S.A.* 27°53N 80°59W **179** H9
Kendal *Indonesia* 6°56S 110°14E **119** G14
Kendal *U.K.* 54°20N 2°44W **66** C5
Kendall *Australia* 31°35S 152°44E **153** A10
Kendall → *Australia* 14°4S 141°35E **150** A3
Kendallville *U.S.A.* 41°27N 85°16W **173** E11
Kendari *Indonesia* 3°50S 122°30E **119** E6
Kendawangan *Indonesia* 2°32S 110°17E **118** E4
Kende *Nigeria* 11°30N 4°12E **139** C5
Kendi, Pulau *Malaysia* 5°13N 100°11E **121** c
Kendrapara *India* 20°35N 86°30E **126** D8
Kĕndrevicēs, Maja e
  Albania 40°15N 19°52E **96** F3
Kendrew *S. Africa* 32°32S 24°30E **144** D3
Kendrick *U.S.A.* 46°37N 116°39W **168** C5
Kene Thao *Laos* 17°44N 101°10E **120** D3
Kenedy *U.S.A.* 28°49N 97°51W **176** G6
Kenema *S. Leone* 7°50N 11°14W **138** D2
Keng Kok *Laos* 16°26N 105°12E **120** D5
Keng Tawng *Burma* 20°45N 98°18E **123** J21
Keng Tung *Burma* 21°0N 99°30E **120** B2
Kengeja *Tanzania* 5°26S 39°45E **142** D4
Kenhardt *S. Africa* 29°19S 21°12E **144** D3
Kéniéba *Mali* 12°5N 11°14W **138** C2
Kenitra *Morocco* 34°15N 6°40W **136** B3
Kenli *China* 37°30N 118°20E **115** F10
Kenmare *Ireland* 51°53N 9°36W **64** E2
Kenmare *U.S.A.* 48°41N 102°5W **172** A2
Kenmare River →
  Ireland 51°48N 9°51W **64** E2
Kennebago Lake
  U.S.A. 45°4N 70°40W **175** A14
Kennebec *U.S.A.* 43°54N 99°52W **172** D4
Kennebec → *U.S.A.* 43°45N 69°46W **173** D19
Kennebunk *U.S.A.* 43°23N 70°33W **175** D14
Kennedy *Zimbabwe* 18°52S 27°10E **144** A4
Kennedy Channel *Arctic* 80°50N 66°0W **57** A4
Kennedy Range △
  Australia 24°34S 115°2E **149** D2
Kennedy Space Center
  U.S.A. 28°40N 80°42W **179** G9
Kennedy Taungdeik *Burma* 23°15N 93°45E **125** H17

Kennedy, U.S.A. 34°1N 84°37W 178 A5
Kennet → U.K. 51°27N 0°57W 67 F7
Kenneth Ra. Australia 23°50S 117°8E 149 D2
Kennett U.S.A. 36°14N 90°3W 172 G8
Kennewick U.S.A. 46°12N 119°7W 168 C4
Kennisis Lake Canada 45°13N 78°36W 174 A6
Kenogami → Canada 51°6N 84°28W 164 B2
Kenora Canada 49°47N 94°29W 163 D10
Kenosha U.S.A. 42°35N 87°49W 172 D10
Kenozersky △ Russia 62°5N 38°10E 106 C6
Kensington Canada 46°28N 63°34W 165 C7
Kent Ohio, U.S.A. 41°9N 81°22W 174 E3
Kent Tex., U.S.A. 31°4N 104°13W 176 F2
Kent Wash., U.S.A. 47°22N 122°14W 170 C4
Kent □ U.K. 51°12N 0°40E 67 F8
Kent Group Australia 39°30S 147°20E 152 E4
Kent Pen. Canada 68°30N 107°0W 160 C10
Kentau Kazakhstan 43°32N 68°36E 108 E7
Kentland U.S.A. 40°46N 87°27W 172 E10
Kenton U.S.A. 40°39N 83°37W 173 E12
Kentucky □ U.S.A. 37°0N 84°0W 173 G11
Kentucky → U.S.A. 38°41N 85°11W 173 F11
Kentucky L. U.S.A. 37°1N 88°16W 172 G9
Kentville Canada 45°6N 64°29W 165 C7
Kentwood U.S.A. 30°56N 90°31W 179 F8
Kenya ■ Africa 1°0N 38°0E 142 B4
Kenya, Mt. Kenya 0°10S 37°18E 142 C4
Kenyir, Tasik Malaysia 5°1N 102°54E 121 K4
Keo Neua, Deo
  Vietnam 18°23N 105°10E 120 C5
Keokuk U.S.A. 40°24N 91°24W 172 E8
Keoladeo △ India 27°0N 77°20E 124 F7
Keonjhargarh India 21°28N 85°35E 125 J11
Kep Cambodia 10°29N 104°19E 121 G5
Kep Vietnam 21°24N 106°16E 120 B6
Kep △ Cambodia 10°30N 104°18E 121 G5
Kepala Batas Malaysia 5°31N 100°26E 121 c
Kepez Turkey 40°5N 26°24E 97 F10
Kępi Indonesia 6°32S 139°19E 119 F9
Kępice Poland 54°16N 16°51E 82 D3
Kepler Mts. N.Z. 45°25S 167°20E 155 F2
Kepno Poland 51°18N 17°58E 83 G4
Kepsut Turkey 39°40N 28°9E 99 B10
Kerala □ India 11°0N 76°15E 127 J3
Kerama-Rettō Japan 26°5N 127°15E 113 L3
Keran India 34°35N 73°59E 125 B5
Keran △ Togo 10°9N 0°41E 139 C5
Kerang Australia 35°40S 143°55E 152 C5
Keratea Greece 37°48N 23°58E 98 D5
Keraudren, C.
  Australia 19°58S 119°45E 148 C2
Kerava Finland 60°25N 25°5E 84 B3
Kerch Ukraine 45°20N 36°20E 85 K9
Kerchenskiy Proliv
  Black Sea 45°20N 36°20E 85 K9
Kerchoual Mali 17°12N 0°20E 139 B5
Kerempe Burnu Turkey 42°22N 33°0E 104 A5
Kerepakupai-Meru = Angel Falls
  Venezuela 5°57N 62°30W 186 B6
Kerewan Gambia 13°29N 16°10W 138 C1
Kerguelen Ind. Oc. 49°15S 69°10E 146 K5
Kerguelen Plateau
  S. Ocean 55°0S 75°0E 146 K6
Keri Greece 37°40N 20°49E 98 D2
Kerian, Kuala Malaysia 5°10N 100°25E 121 c
Kericho Kenya 0°22S 35°15E 142 C4
Kerikeri N.Z. 35°12S 173°59E 154 B2
Kerinci Indonesia 1°40S 101°15E 118 E2
Keriya He → China 39°5N 79°20E 109 E9
Keriya Shankou China 35°51N 89°49W 125 B10
Kerkennah, Is. Tunisia 34°48N 11°11E 136 B6
Kerki = Atamyrat
  Turkmenistan 37°50N 65°12E 109 F7
Kerkini, L. Greece 41°12N 23°10E 96 E7
Kerkouane Tunisia 36°58N 11°2E 94 F4
Kerkrade Neths. 50°53N 6°4E 69 D6
Kerkyra Greece 39°38N 19°50E 101 A3
Kerkyra ✈ (CFU) Greece 39°35N 19°54E 98 B1
Kerkyras, Notio Steno
  Greece 39°34N 20°0E 101 A4
Kerma Sudan 19°33N 30°32E 137 D3
Kermadec Is. Pac. Oc. 30°0S 178°15W 147 E11
Kermadec Trench
  Pac. Oc. 30°30S 176°0W 156 L10
Kermān Iran 30°15N 57°1E 129 D8
Kermān □ Iran 30°0N 57°0E 129 D8
Kermān, Bīābān-e Iran 28°45N 59°45E 129 D8
Kermān □ Iran 30°0N 57°0E 129 D8
Kermānshāh = Bākhtarān
  Iran 34°23N 47°0E 128 C5
Kermānshāh □ Iran 34°0N 46°30E 128 C5
Kermen Bulgaria 42°30N 26°16E 97 D10
Kermit U.S.A. 31°52N 103°6W 176 F3
Kern → U.S.A. 35°16N 119°18W 171 K7
Kernavė Lithuania 54°53N 24°49E 84 E3
Kernhof Austria 47°49N 15°32E 78 D8
Kernow = Cornwall □
  U.K. 50°26N 4°40W 67 G3
Kernville U.S.A. 35°45N 118°26W 171 K8
Keroh Malaysia 5°43N 101°1E 121 K3
Keros Greece 36°54N 25°40E 97 F9
Kérou Benin 10°50N 2°5E 139 C5
Kérouane Guinea 9°15N 9°0W 138 D3
Kerpen Germany 50°51N 6°41E 76 D2
Kerrera U.K. 56°24N 5°33W 65 E3
Kerrobert Canada 51°56N 109°8W 167 C7
Kerrville U.S.A. 30°3N 99°8W 176 F5
Kerry □ Ireland 52°7N 9°35W 64 D2
Kerry Hd. Ireland 52°25N 9°56W 64 D2
Kerulen = Herlen →
  Asia 48°48N 117°0E 111 B12
Kervo = Kerava Finland 60°25N 25°5E 84 B3
Kerzaz Algeria 29°29N 1°37W 136 C4
Kesagami L. Canada 50°23N 80°15W 164 B4
Kesagami → Canada 51°30N 79°45W 164 B4
Keşan Turkey 40°49N 26°38E 97 F10
Kesennuma Japan 38°54N 141°35E 112 E10
Keshit Iran 29°43N 58°17E 129 D8
Kesigi = Kosgi India 16°58N 77°59E 126 F3
Keşiş Dağ Turkey 39°47N 39°56E 105 C9
Keskal India 20°5N 81°35E 126 D5
Keskin Turkey 39°41N 33°36E 104 C5
Kestenga Russia 65°50N 31°45E 106 C4
Keswick U.K. 54°36N 3°8W 66 C4
Keszthely Hungary 46°50N 17°15E 80 D3
Ket → Russia 58°55N 81°32E 106 D9
Keta Ghana 5°49N 1°0E 139 D5
Keta Lagoon Ghana 5°55N 1°1°0E 139 D5
Ketapang Jawa Timur,
  Indonesia 8°9S 114°23E 119 J17
Ketapang Kalimantan Barat,
  Indonesia 1°55S 110°0E 118 E4

Ketchenery Russia 47°18N 44°32E 87 G7
Ketchikan U.S.A. 55°21N 131°39W 162 B2
Ketchum U.S.A. 43°41N 114°22W 168 E6
Kete Krachi Ghana 7°46N 0°1W 139 D4
Ketef, Khalîg Umm el
  Egypt 23°40N 35°35E 128 F2
Keti Bandar Pakistan 24°8N 67°27E 124 G2
Ketri India 28°1N 75°50E 124 E6
Ketrzyn Poland 54°7N 21°22E 82 D8
Kettering U.K. 52°24N 0°43W 67 E7
Kettering U.S.A. 39°41N 84°10W 173 F11
Kettle → Canada 56°40N 89°34W 163 B11
Kettle Falls U.S.A. 48°37N 118°3W 168 B4
Kettle Point Canada 43°10N 82°1W 174 C2
Kettle Pt. Canada 43°13N 82°1W 174 C2
Kettleman City U.S.A. 36°1N 119°58W 170 J7
Keţy Poland 49°51N 19°16E 83 K5
Keuka L. U.S.A. 42°30N 77°9W 174 D7
Keuruu Finland 62°16N 24°41E 84 A3
Kevelaer Germany 51°36N 6°15E 76 D2
Kewanee U.S.A. 41°14N 89°56W 172 E9
Keweenaw B. U.S.A. 47°0N 88°15W 172 B9
Keweenaw Pen.
  U.S.A. 47°15N 88°15W 172 B9
Keweenaw Pt. U.S.A. 47°25N 87°43W 172 B10
Key, L. Ireland 54°0N 8°15W 64 C3
Key Colony Beach
  U.S.A. 24°45N 80°57W 179 L9
Key Lake Mine Canada 57°5N 105°32W 163 B7
Key Largo U.S.A. 25°5N 80°27W 179 K9
Key West U.S.A. 24°33N 81°48W 179 K9
Keynsham U.K. 51°24N 2°29W 67 F5
Keyser U.S.A. 39°26N 78°59W 173 F14
Keystone Heights
  U.S.A. 29°47N 82°2W 178 F7
Kezhma Russia 58°59N 101°9E 107 D11
Kezi Zimbabwe 20°58S 28°32E 145 B4
Kežmarok Slovak Rep. 49°10N 20°28E 79 B10
Kgalagadi □ Botswana 24°30S 22°0E 144 B3
Kgalagadi Transfrontier □
  Africa 25°10S 21°0E 144 C3
Khabarovsk Russia 48°30N 135°5E 111 B16
Khabr △ Iran 28°51N 56°22E 129 D8
Khābūr → Syria 35°17N 40°35E 105 E9
Khachmas = Xaçmaz
  Azerbaijan 41°31N 48°42E 87 K9
Khachrod India 23°25N 75°20E 124 H6
Khadro Pakistan 26°11N 68°50E 124 F3
Khadyzhensk Russia 44°26N 39°32E 87 H4
Khadzhilyangar = Dahongliutan
  China 35°45N 79°20E 125 B8
Khaga India 25°47N 81°7E 125 G9
Khagaria India 25°30N 86°32E 125 G12
Khaipur India 29°34N 72°17E 124 E5
Khair India 27°57N 77°46E 124 F7
Khairabad India 27°33N 80°47E 125 F9
Khairagarh India 21°27N 81°2E 125 J9
Khairpur Pakistan 27°32N 68°49E 124 F3
Khairpur Nathan Shah
  Pakistan 27°6N 67°44E 124 F2
Khairwara India 23°58N 73°38E 124 H5
Khaisor → Pakistan 31°17N 68°59E 124 D3
Khajuraho India 24°51N 79°55E 125 G8
Khajuri Kach Pakistan 32°4N 69°51E 124 C3
Khakassia □ Russia 53°0N 90°0E 109 B12
Khakhea Botswana 24°48S 23°22E 144 B3
Khalafābād Iran 30°54N 49°24E 129 D6
Khalīlābād India 26°48N 83°5E 125 F10
Khalīlī Iran 27°38N 53°17E 129 E7
Khalkhāl Iran 37°37N 48°32E 105 D13
Khalkis = Chalkida
  Greece 38°27N 23°42E 98 C5
Khalmer Yu Russia 67°58N 65°1E 106 C7
Khalūf Oman 20°30N 58°13E 131 C6
Kham Keut Laos 18°15N 104°43E 120 C5
Khamaria India 23°5N 80°48E 125 H9
Khambhaliya India 22°14N 69°41E 124 H3
Khambhat India 22°23N 72°33E 124 H5
Khambhat, G. of India 20°45N 72°30E 124 J5
Khamgaon India 20°42N 76°37E 126 D3
Khami Ruins = Kame Ruins
  Zimbabwe 20°7S 28°25E 143 G2
Khamir India 17°38N 78°5E 126 F4
Khamīr Iran 26°57N 55°36E 129 E7
Khamīr Yemen 16°2N 44°0E 131 D3
Khamīs Mushayt
  Si. Arabia 18°18N 42°44E 131 D3
Khammam India 17°11N 80°6E 126 F5
Khamsa Egypt 30°27N 32°23E 130 E1
Khan → Namibia 22°37S 14°56E 144 B2
Khān Abū Shāmat
  Syria 33°39N 36°53E 130 B5
Khān al Baghdādī
  Iraq 33°51N 42°32E 105 G10
Khān al Ḥammād
  Iraq 32°19N 44°16E 105 G11
Khān Azād Iraq 33°7N 44°22E 128 C5
Khān Mujiddah Iraq 32°21N 43°48E 128 C4
Khān Shaykhūn Syria 35°26N 36°38E 104 E7
Khan Tengri, Pik Asia 42°12N 80°10E 109 D10
Khān Yūnis Gaza Strip 31°21N 34°18E 130 D3
Khanai Pakistan 30°30N 67°8E 124 D2
Khānaqīn Iraq 34°23N 45°25E 128 C5
Khānbāghī Iran 36°10N 55°25E 129 B7
Khandwa India 21°49N 76°22E 124 J7
Khandyga Russia 62°42N 135°35E 107 C14
Khanewal Pakistan 30°20N 71°55E 124 D4
Khangah Dogran
  Pakistan 31°50N 73°37E 124 D5
Khangchendzonga =
  Kanchenjunga △
  India 27°42N 88°8E 125 F13
Khanh Duong
  Vietnam 12°44N 108°44E 120 F7
Khaniá = Chania Greece 35°30N 24°4E 101 D6
Khaniadhana India 25°1N 78°8E 124 G8
Khanka, L. Asia 45°0N 132°24E 111 B15
Khankendy = Xankändi
  Azerbaijan 39°52N 46°49E 105 C12
Khanna India 30°42N 76°16E 124 D7
Khanozai Pakistan 30°37N 67°19E 124 D2
Khanpur Pakistan 28°42N 70°35E 124 E4
Khanty-Mansiysk Russia 61°0N 69°0E 106 C7
Khao Khitchakut △
  Thailand 12°50N 102°12E 120 F4
Khao Laem △ Thailand 14°56N 98°31E 120 D1
Khao Laem Res.
  Thailand 14°50N 98°30E 120 D2
Khao Lak △ Malaysia 8°38N 98°18E 121 H2

Khao Luang △ Thailand 8°34N 99°42E 121 H2
Khao Nam Khang △
  Thailand 6°32N 100°35E 121 J3
Khao Phlu Thailand 9°29N 99°59E 121 b
Khao Pu -Khao Ya △
  Thailand 7°26N 99°57E 121 J2
Khao Sam Roi Yot △
  Thailand 12°13N 99°57E 121 F2
Khao Yai △ Thailand 14°21N 101°29E 120 E3
Khaoen Si Nakarin △
  Thailand 14°47N 99°0E 120 E2
Khapalu Pakistan 35°10N 76°20E 125 B7
Khapcheranga
  Russia 49°42N 112°24E 107 E12
Khaptao △ Nepal 29°20N 81°10E 125 E9
Kharabali Russia 47°25N 47°15E 87 G8
Kharagauli Georgia 42°1N 43°12E 87 F7
Kharaghoda India 23°11N 71°46E 124 H4
Kharagpur India 22°20N 87°25E 125 H12
Kharan Kalat Pakistan 28°34N 65°21E 124 E3
Kharānaq Iran 32°20N 54°45E 129 C7
Kharda India 18°40N 75°34E 126 E2
Khardung La India 34°20N 77°43E 125 B7
Kharg = Khārk, Jazīreh-ye
  Iran 29°15N 50°28E 129 D6
Khârga, El Wâhât el
  Egypt 25°10N 30°35E 137 C3
Khargon India 21°45N 75°40E 124 J6
Khari → India 25°54N 74°31E 124 G6
Kharian Pakistan 32°49N 73°52E 124 C5
Khariar India 20°17N 82°46E 125 J9
Kharit, Wadi el →
  Egypt 24°26N 33°3E 137 C3
Khārk, Jazīreh-ye Iran 29°15N 50°28E 129 D6
Kharkiv Ukraine 49°58N 36°20E 75 D9
Kharkov = Kharkiv
  Ukraine 49°58N 36°20E 75 D9
Kharmanli Bulgaria 41°55N 25°55E 97 E9
Kharovsk Russia 59°56N 40°13E 86 C6
Kharsawangarh India 22°48N 85°50E 125 H11
Kharta Turkey 40°59N 29°7E 97 F13
Khartoum = El Khartûm
  Sudan 15°31N 32°35E 135 E3
Khartum Canada 45°15N 77°5W 174 A7
Khasan Russia 42°25N 130°40E 112 C5
Khasavyurt Russia 43°16N 46°40E 87 J8
Khāsh Iran 28°15N 61°15E 124 C2
Khashm el Girba
  Sudan 14°59N 35°58E 135 F4
Khashuri Georgia 42°1N 43°35E 87 F7
Khaskovo Bulgaria 41°56N 25°30E 97 E9
Khaskovo □ Bulgaria 42°0N 25°40E 97 E9
Khat, Laem Thailand 8°6N 98°26E 121 a
Khatanga Russia 72°0N 102°20E 107 B11
Khatanga → Russia 72°55N 106°0E 107 B11
Khatauli India 29°17N 77°43E 124 E7
Khatlon □ Tajikistan 37°50N 69°0E 125 B5
Khatra India 22°59N 86°51E 125 H12
Khātūnābād Iran 30°1N 55°25E 129 D7
Khatyrka Russia 62°3N 175°15E 107 C18
Khavda India 23°51N 69°43E 124 H2
Khawr Fakkān U.A.E. 25°21N 56°22E 131 E8
Khay' Si. Arabia 18°45N 41°24E 131 D3
Khaybar, Ḥarrat
  Si. Arabia 25°30N 39°45E 128 E4
Khāzimiyah Iraq 34°46N 43°37E 128 C4
Khe Bo Vietnam 19°8N 104°41E 120 C5
Khe Long Vietnam 21°29N 104°46E 120 B5
Khe Sanh Vietnam 16°37N 106°45E 120 D6
Khed Maharashtra, India 17°43N 73°27E 126 F1
Khed Maharashtra, India 18°51N 73°56E 126 F2
Khed Brahma India 24°7N 73°5E 124 G5
Khekra India 28°52N 77°20E 124 E7
Khemarak Phouminville = Krong
  Kaoh Kong
  Cambodia 11°37N 102°59E 120 G4
Khemisset Morocco 33°50N 6°1W 136 B3
Khemmarat Thailand 16°10N 105°15E 120 D5
Khenāmān Iran 30°27N 56°29E 129 D8
Khenchela Algeria 35°28N 7°11E 136 A7
Khenchela □ Algeria 35°0N 7°0E 94 A6
Khenifra Morocco 32°58N 5°46W 136 B3
Kherrata Algeria 36°27N 5°31E 136 A7
Khersān → Iran 31°33N 50°22E 129 D6
Kherson Ukraine 46°35N 32°35E 75 E8
Kherson □ Ukraine 46°15N 33°10E 75 E8
Kheta → Russia 71°54N 102°6E 107 B11
Khewari Pakistan 26°36N 68°52E 124 F3
Khilchipur India 24°2N 76°34E 124 G7
Khilok Russia 51°30N 110°45E 107 D12
Khimki Russia 55°50N 37°20E 86 E9
Khíos = Chios Greece 38°27N 26°9E 97 G10
Khirsadoh India 22°11N 78°47E 124 H8
Khiuma = Hiiumaa
  Estonia 58°50N 22°45E 84 C1
Khiva = Xiva
  Uzbekistan 41°30N 60°18E 108 E6
Khlebarovo Bulgaria 43°37N 26°15E 97 C10
Khlong Khlung
  Thailand 16°12N 99°43E 120 D2
Khlong Lan △ Thailand 16°12N 99°17E 120 D2
Khlong Phanom △
  Thailand 8°49N 98°38E 121 H2
Khmelnik Ukraine 49°33N 27°58E 75 D4
Khmelnytskyy Ukraine 49°23N 27°0E 75 D4
Khmelnytskyy □
  Ukraine 49°50N 26°40E 75 D4
Khmer Rep. = Cambodia ■
  Asia 12°15N 105°0E 120 F5
Khoai, Hon Vietnam 8°26N 104°50E 121 d
Khobar = Al Khubar
  Si. Arabia 26°17N 50°12E 129 E6
Khodoriv Ukraine 49°24N 24°19E 75 D3
Khodzent = Khŭjand
  Tajikistan 40°17N 69°37E 109 E7
Khojak Pass Afghan. 30°51N 66°34E 124 D2
Khojayli = Xo'jayli
  Uzbekistan 42°30N 59°30E 108 E6
Khok Kloi Thailand 8°17N 98°19E 121 a
Khok Pho Thailand 6°43N 101°6E 121 J3
Khok Samrong
  Thailand 15°3N 100°43E 120 E3
Kholm Afghan. 36°45N 67°40E 123 A2
Kholm Russia 57°10N 31°15E 84 D8
Kholmsk Russia 47°40N 142°5E 107 E15
Khomârlu Iran 38°40N 47°0E 105 C12
Khomas □ Namibia 22°40S 16°0E 144 B2
Khomas Hochland
  Namibia 22°40S 16°0E 144 B2

hombole *Senegal* 14°43N 16°42W **138** C1
homeyn *Iran* 33°40N 50°7E **129** C6
homodino *Botswana* 22°46S 23°52E **144** B3
hong ← *Cambodia* 13°32N 105°58E **120** F5
hong Sedone *Laos* 15°34N 105°49E **120** E5
honuu *Russia* 66°30N 143°12E **107** C15
hoper → *Russia* 49°30N 42°20E **86** F6
horāsān-e Janūb □
Iran 32°0N 59°0E **129** C8
horāsān-e Razavī □
Iran 35°0N 59°0E **129** C8
horāsān-e Shemālī □
Iran 37°0N 57°0E **129** B8
horat = Nakhon Ratchasima
Thailand 14°59N 102°12E **120** E4
horat, Cao Nguyen
Thailand 15°30N 102°50E **120** E4
horazm = Xorazm □
Uzbekistan 43°0N 60°0E **108** A6
horb el Ethel *Algeria* 28°30N 6°17W **136** C2
horixas *Namibia* 20°16S 14°59E **144** B1
horol *Ukraine* 49°48N 33°15E **85** H7
Iran 35°6N 57°57E **129** C8
horramābād *Khorāsān,*
Iran 33°30N 48°25E **105** C6
horramdarreh *Iran* 36°11N 49°11E **105** D13
horramshahr *Iran* 30°29N 48°15E **129** D6
horugh *Tajikistan* 37°30N 71°36E **109** E8
hosravī *Iran* 30°48N 51°28E **129** D6
hosrowābād *Khuzestān,*
Iran 30°10N 48°25E **129** D6
hosrowābād *Kordestān,*
Iran 35°31N 47°38E **105** E12
host *Pakistan* 30°13N 67°35E **124** D2
hosūyeh *Iran* 28°32N 54°26E **129** D7
hotang *Nepal* 27°1N 86°51E **125** F12
hotyn *Ukraine* 48°31N 26°27E **81** B11
houribga *Morocco* 32°58N 6°57W **136** B2
howst *Afghan.* 33°22N 69°58E **124** C3
howst □ *Afghan.* 33°20N 70°0E **122** C6
hoyniki *Belarus* 51°54N 29°55E **75** C15
hram, Ko *Thailand* 12°42N 100°47E **120** F3
hrami → *Georgia* 41°25N 45°0E **87** K7
hrenovoye *Russia* 51°4N 40°16E **86** E5
hromtaū *Kazakhstan* 50°17N 58°27E **108** B5
hrysokhou B. *Cyprus* 35°6N 32°25E **101** D11
huan Wa *Thailand* 7°53N 98°17E **121** a

hudzhand = Khūjand □
Tajikistan 40°17N 69°37E **109** D7
uff *Si. Arabia* 24°55N 44°53E **128** E5
ūjiānī *Afghan.* 31°34N 66°32E **124** D2
uis *Botswana* 26°40S 21°49E **144** C3
uiyala *India* 27°9N 70°25E **124** F4
ujner *India* 23°47N 76°36E **124** H7
ukhan *Thailand* 14°42N 104°12E **120** E5
ulna *Bangla.* 22°45N 89°34E **123** H16
ulna □ *Bangla.* 22°25N 89°35E **123** H16
ulo *Georgia* 41°33N 42°19E **87** K6
umago *Botswana* 20°26S 24°32E **144** B3
unjerab △ *Pakistan* 36°40N 75°25E **125** A6
unjerab Pass = Kinjirap Daban
Asia 36°40N 75°25E **109** E9
ünsorkh *Iran* 27°9N 56°7E **129** E8
unti *India* 23°5N 85°17E **125** H11
ūr *Iran* 32°55N 58°18E **129** C8
urai *India* 24°3N 78°23E **124** G8
uraya *Si. Arabia* 25°6N 48°2E **128** E6
urda *India* 20°11N 85°37E **126** D7
urda *India* 28°15N 77°58E **124** E7
ūrmal *Iraq* 35°18N 46°2E **105** E12
ushab *Pakistan* 32°20N 72°20E **124** C5
ust *Ukraine* 48°10N 23°18E **81** B8
utse → *Botswana* 23°31S 24°12E **144** B3
uzdar *Pakistan* 27°52N 66°30E **124** F2
īzestān □ *Iran* 31°0N 49°0E **129** D6
vāf *Iran* 34°33N 60°8E **129** C9
vājeh *Iran* 38°9N 46°35E **128** B5
valynsk *Russia* 52°30N 48°2E **86** D9
valynsky △ *Russia* 52°30N 48°0E **86** D9
vānsar *Iran* 29°56N 54°8E **129** D7
vatovka *Russia* 52°24N 46°32E **86** D8
var *Iran* 33°45N 55°0E **129** C7
vorgū *Iran* 27°34N 56°27E **129** E8
vormūj *Iran* 28°40N 51°30E **129** D6
voy *Iran* 38°35N 45°0E **105** C11
voynaya *Russia* 58°58N 34°28E **84** C8
vae Noi → *Thailand* 14°1N 99°32E **120** E2
ber Pakhtunkhwa □
Pakistan 34°0N 72°0E **124** C4
ber Pass *Afghan.* 34°10N 71°8E **124** B4
riv *Ukraine* 49°32N 22°30E **83** J9
Fiji 16°16S 179°58E **154** a
ukwa
Dem. Rep. of the Congo 8°40S 24°48E **143** D1
lho → *India* 19°37N 77°40E **126** E3
na *Australia* 34°40S 150°50E **153** D9
nba *Phil.* 6°2N 124°46E **119** C6
nbi
Dem. Rep. of the Congo 7°15S 28°0E **142** D2
ng West △ *Gambia* 13°25N 15°50W **138** C1
ngxi = Jiangxi □
China 27°30N 116°0E **117** D11
ng = Jiangsu □
China 33°0N 120°0E **115** H11
o *Greece* 38°1N 22°45E **98** E4
ek *Denmark* 56°2N 8°51E **63** H2
le □ *Tanzania* 0°16N 30°18E **142** B3
nga Port *Uganda* 0°58N 31°45E **142** B3
mbo
Dem. Rep. of the Congo 3°57S 25°53E **142** C2
ndo *Tanzania* 3°35S 30°45E **142** C2
e *Mengist Ethiopia* 3°48N 38°59E **131** F2
ngo *Rwanda* 2°10S 30°32E **142** C3
ye *Burundi* 2°10S 30°32E **142** C2
ye *Rwanda* 2°3S 29°21E **142** C2
yesa *Tanzania* 6°30S 29°58E **142** D2
zi *Kenya* 2°37S 37°57E **142** C4
salih *Turkey* 41°23N 26°48E **97** E10

Kičevo *Macedonia* 41°34N 20°59E **96** E4
Kichha → *India* 28°41N 79°18E **125** E8
Kicking Horse Pass
Canada 51°28N 116°16W **162** C5
Kidal *Mali* 18°26N 1°22E **139** B5
Kidal □ *Mali* 19°55N 1°5E **139** B5
Kidderminster *U.K.* 52°24N 2°15W **67** E5
Kidete *Tanzania* 6°25S 37°17E **142** D4
Kidnappers, C. *N.Z.* 39°38S 177°5E **154** D7
Kidsgrove *U.K.* 53°5N 2°14W **66** D5
Kidston *Australia* 18°52S 144°8E **150** B3
Kidugallo *Tanzania* 6°49S 38°15E **142** D4
Kiel *Germany* 54°19N 10°8E **76** A6
Kiel Canal = Nord-Ostsee-Kanal
Germany 54°12N 9°32E **76** A5
Kielce *Poland* 50°52N 20°42E **77** E11
Kielder Water *U.K.* 55°11N 2°31W **66** B5
Kieler Bucht *Germany* 54°35N 10°25E **76** A6
Kiembara *Burkina Faso* 13°15N 2°44W **138** C4
Kienge
Dem. Rep. of the Congo 10°30S 27°30E **143** E2
Kiessé *Niger* 13°29N 4°1E **139** C5
Kiev = Kyyiv *Ukraine* 50°30N 30°28E **75** C16
Kifaya *Guinea* 12°10N 13°4W **138** C2
Kiffa *Mauritania* 16°37N 11°24W **138** B2
Kifisós → *Greece* 38°35N 23°20E **98** C5
Kifrī *Iraq* 34°45N 45°0E **105** E11
Kigali *Rwanda* 1°59S 30°4E **142** C3
Kigarama *Tanzania* 1°1S 31°50E **142** C3
Kigezi □ *Uganda* 0°34S 29°55E **142** C2
Kiği *Turkey* 39°18N 40°21E **105** D9
Kigoma □ *Tanzania* 5°0S 30°0E **142** D2
Kigoma-Ujiji *Tanzania* 4°55S 29°36E **142** C2
Kigomasha, Ras
Tanzania 4°58S 38°58E **142** C4
Kigosi □ *Tanzania* 4°10S 31°45E **142** C3
Kiğzı *Turkey* 38°18N 43°25E **128** B4
Kihikihi *N.Z.* 38°2S 175°22E **154** E4
Kii-Sanchi *Japan* 34°20N 136°0E **113** G8
Kii-Suidō *Japan* 33°40N 134°45E **113** H7
Kiira Dam *Uganda* 0°25N 33°0E **142** B3
Kikaiga-Shima *Japan* 28°19N 129°59E **113** K4
Kikiak = Rigolet
Canada 54°10N 58°23W **165** B8
Kikinda *Serbia* 45°50N 20°30E **80** E5
Kikládhes = Kyklades
Greece 37°0N 24°30E **98** E6
Kikoira *Australia* 33°39S 146°40E **153** B7
Kikuchi *Japan* 32°59N 130°47E **113** H5
Kikuyu *Kenya* 1°15S 36°40E **142** C4
Kikwit
Dem. Rep. of the Congo 5°0S 18°45E **140** C3
Kil *Sweden* 59°30N 13°20E **62** E7
Kilafors *Sweden* 61°14N 16°36E **62** C10
Kilakkarai *India* 9°12N 78°47E **127** K4
Kilar *India* 33°6N 76°25E **124** C7
Kilbeggan *Ireland* 53°22N 7°30W **64** C4
Kilbrannan Sd. *U.K.* 55°37N 5°26W **65** F3
Kilbuck Mts. *U.S.A.* 60°36N 159°53W **166** C8
Kilchu *N. Korea* 40°57N 129°25E **115** D15
Kilcoy *Australia* 26°59S 152°30E **151** D5
Kildare *Ireland* 53°9N 6°55W **64** C5
Kildare □ *Ireland* 53°10N 6°50W **64** C5
Kildinstroy *Russia* 68°48N 33°6E **60** B25
Kilfinnane *Ireland* 52°21N 8°28W **64** D3
Kilgarvan *Ireland* 51°54N 9°27W **64** E2
Kilgore *U.S.A.* 32°23N 94°53W **176** E7
Kilgoris *Kenya* 1°0S 34°53E **142** C3
Kilibo *Benin* 8°32N 2°38E **139** D5
Kilifi *Kenya* 3°40S 39°48E **142** C4
Kilimanjaro □ *Tanzania* 3°7S 37°20E **142** C4
Kilimanjaro □ *Tanzania* 4°0S 38°0E **142** C4
Kilimanjaro △ *Tanzania* 3°4S 37°19E **142** C4
Kilimli *Turkey* 41°28N 31°50E **104** B4
Kilindini *Kenya* 4°4S 39°40E **142** C4
Kilinochchi *Sri Lanka* 9°24N 80°25E **127** K5
Kilis *Turkey* 36°42N 37°6E **104** D7
Kilis □ *Turkey* 36°50N 37°10E **104** D7
Kiliya *Ukraine* 45°28N 29°16E **81** E14
Kilkee *Ireland* 52°41N 9°39W **64** D2
Kilkeel *U.K.* 54°7N 5°55W **64** B5
Kilkenny *Ireland* 52°39N 7°15W **64** D4
Kilkenny □ *Ireland* 52°35N 7°15W **64** D4
Kilkieran B. *Ireland* 53°20N 9°41W **64** C2
Kilkis *Greece* 40°58N 22°57E **96** F6
Killala *Ireland* 54°13N 9°13W **64** B2
Killala B. *Ireland* 54°16N 9°8W **64** B2
Killaloe *Canada* 45°33N 77°25W **174** A7
Killaloe *Ireland* 52°48N 8°28W **64** D3
Killarney *Australia* 28°20S 152°18E **151** D5
Killarney *Canada* 49°10N 99°40W **163** D9
Killarney *Ireland* 52°4N 9°30W **64** D2
Killarney △ *Ireland* 52°0N 9°33W **64** D2
Killary Harbour *Ireland* 53°38N 9°52W **64** C2
Killdeer *U.S.A.* 47°22N 102°45W **172** B2
Killeberg *Sweden* 56°29N 14°8E **63** H8
Killeen *U.S.A.* 31°7N 97°44W **176** F6
Killin *U.K.* 56°28N 4°19W **65** E4
Killiney *Ireland* 53°15N 6°7W **64** C5
Killington Pk. *U.S.A.* 43°36N 72°49W **175** C12
Killini = Kyllini *Greece* 37°55N 21°8E **98** D3
Killini *Greece* 37°54N 22°25E **98** D3
Killini I. *Canada* 60°24N 64°37W **161** E19
Killorglin *Ireland* 52°6N 9°47W **64** D2
Killybegs *Ireland* 54°38N 8°26W **64** B3
Kilmarnock *U.K.* 55°37N 4°29W **65** F4
Kilmez *Russia* 56°58N 50°55E **86** B10
Kilmez → *Russia* 56°58N 50°28E **86** B10
Kilmore *Australia* 37°25S 144°53E **153** D6
Kilmore Quay *Ireland* 52°10N 6°36W **64** D5
Kilondo
Dem. Rep. of the Congo 9°45S 34°20E **143** D3
Kilosa *Tanzania* 6°48S 37°0E **142** D4
Kiltan I. *India* 11°29N 73°0E **127** J1
Kilwa Kisiwani *Tanzania* 8°58S 39°32E **143** D4
Kilwa Kivinje *Tanzania* 8°45S 39°25E **143** D4
Kilwa Masoko *Tanzania* 8°55S 39°30E **143** D4
Kilwinning *U.K.* 55°39N 4°43W **65** F4
Kim *U.S.A.* 37°15N 103°21W **169** H12
Kim → *Cameroon* 5°28N 11°17E **139** D7
Kimaam *Indonesia* 7°58S 138°53E **119** F9
Kimamba *Tanzania* 6°45S 37°10E **142** D4
Kimba *Australia* 33°8S 136°23E **153** B2
Kimball *Nebr., U.S.A.* 41°14N 103°40W **172** E2
Kimball *S. Dak., U.S.A.* 43°45N 98°57W **172** D4
Kimberley *Australia* 16°20S 127°0E **148** C4

Kimberley *B.C.,*
Canada 49°40N 115°59W **162** D5
Kimberley *Ont., Canada* 44°23N 80°32W **174** B4
Kimberley *S. Africa* 28°43S 24°46E **144** C3
Kimberly *U.S.A.* 42°32N 114°22W **168** E6
Kimch'aek *N. Korea* 40°40N 129°10E **115** D15
Kimhae = Gimhae
S. Korea 35°14N 128°53E **115** G15
Kimi *Greece* 38°38N 24°6E **98** C6
Kimmirut *Canada* 62°50N 69°50W **161** E18
Kimolos *Greece* 36°48N 24°37E **98** E6
Kimovsk *Moskva, Russia* 55°21N 37°28E **84** E9
Kimovsk *Tula, Russia* 54°0N 38°29E **84** E10
Kimparana *Mali* 12°48N 5°0W **138** C4
Kimpese
Dem. Rep. of the Congo 5°35S 14°26E **140** F2
Kimry *Russia* 56°55N 37°15E **84** D9
Kimstad *Sweden* 58°35N 15°58E **63** F9
Kinabalu, Gunung
Malaysia 6°3N 116°14E **118** C5
Kinango *Kenya* 4°8S 39°19E **142** C4
Kinard *U.S.A.* 30°16N 85°15W **178** E4
Kinaros *Greece* 36°59N 26°15E **99** E8
Kinaskan L. *Canada* 57°38N 130°8W **162** D2
Kinbasket L. *Canada* 52°0N 118°10W **162** C5
Kincardine *Canada* 44°10N 81°40W **174** B3
Kinchafoonee Cr. →
U.S.A. 31°38N 84°10W **178** D5
Kinchega △ *Australia* 32°27S 142°15E **152** B4
Kincolith *Canada* 55°0N 129°57W **162** C3
Kinda
Dem. Rep. of the Congo 9°18S 25°4E **143** D2
Kindberg *Austria* 47°30N 15°27E **78** D8
Kinde *U.S.A.* 43°56N 83°0W **174** C2
Kinder Scout *U.K.* 53°24N 1°52W **66** D6
Kindersley *Canada* 51°30N 109°10W **163** C7
Kindia *Guinea* 10°0N 12°52W **138** D2
Kindu
Dem. Rep. of the Congo 2°55S 25°50E **142** C2
Kinel *Russia* 53°15N 50°40E **86** D10
Kineshma *Russia* 57°30N 42°5E **86** B6
Kinesi *Tanzania* 1°25S 33°50E **142** C3
King, L. *Australia* 33°10S 119°35E **149** F2
King, Mt. *Australia* 25°10S 147°30E **150** D4
King Christian I.
Canada 77°48N 101°40W **161** B11
King City *U.S.A.* 36°13N 121°8W **170** J5
King Cr. → *Australia* 24°35S 139°30E **150** C2
King Edward →
Australia 14°14S 126°35E **148** B4
King Edward Point
S. Georgia 54°17S 36°30W **55** B1
King Frederick VI Land = Kong
Frederik VI.s Kyst
Greenland 63°0N 43°0W **57** E6
King George B.
Falk. Is. 51°30S 60°30W **192** D4
King George I. *Antarctica* 60°0S 60°0W **55** C18
King George Is.
Canada 57°20N 80°30W **161** F15
King George Sd.
Australia 35°5S 118°0E **149** G2
King I. = Kadan Kyun
Burma 12°30N 98°20E **120** F2
King I. *Australia* 39°50S 144°0E **151** F3
King I. *Canada* 52°10N 127°40W **162** C3
King Khalid Military City =
Madinat al Malik Khālid al
Askariyah *Si. Arabia* 27°54N 45°31E **128** E5
King Leopold Ranges
Australia 17°30S 125°45E **148** C4
King of Prussia *U.S.A.* 40°5N 75°23W **175** F9
King Sd. *Australia* 16°50S 123°20E **148** C3
King Sejong *Antarctica* 62°30S 58°0W **55** C18
King Shaka = Durban ✈ (DIA)
S. Africa 29°37S 31°7E **145** C5
King William I.
Canada 69°10N 97°25W **160** D12
King William's Town
S. Africa 32°51S 27°22E **144** D4
Kingaok = Bathurst Inlet
Canada 66°50N 108°1W **160** D10
Kingaroy *Australia* 26°32S 151°51E **151** D5
Kingfisher *U.S.A.* 35°52N 97°56W **176** D6
Kingirbān *Iraq* 34°40N 44°54E **128** C5
Kingisepp = Kuressaare
Estonia 58°15N 22°30E **84** C2
Kingisepp *Russia* 59°25N 28°40E **84** C5
Kinglake △ *Australia* 37°30S 145°22E **153** D6
Kingman *Ariz., U.S.A.* 35°12N 114°4W **171** K12
Kingman *Kans., U.S.A.* 37°39N 98°7W **172** G4
Kingoonya *Australia* 30°55S 135°19E **151** E2
Kingri *Pakistan* 30°27N 69°49E **124** D3
Kings → *U.S.A.* 36°3N 119°50W **170** J7
Kings Canyon
Australia 24°15S 131°34E **148** D5
Kings Canyon △
U.S.A. 36°50N 118°40W **170** J8
King's Lynn *U.K.* 52°45N 0°24E **66** E8
Kings Park *U.S.A.* 40°53N 73°16W **175** F11
Kings Peak *U.S.A.* 40°46N 110°23W **168** F8
King's Trough *Atl. Oc.* 43°48N 22°0W **56** B9
Kingsbridge *U.K.* 50°17N 3°47W **67** G4
Kingsburg *U.S.A.* 36°31N 119°33W **170** J7
Kingscote *Australia* 35°40S 137°38E **152** C2
Kingscourt *Ireland* 53°54N 6°48W **64** C5
Kingsford *U.S.A.* 45°48N 88°4W **172** C9
Kingsland *U.S.A.* 30°48N 81°41W **178** E4
Kingsport *U.S.A.* 36°33N 82°33W **177** C13
Kingston *Canada* 44°14N 76°30W **175** B8
Kingston *Jamaica* 17°55N 76°50W **182** a
Kingston *N.Z.* 45°20S 168°43E **155** F2
Kingston *N.H., U.S.A.* 42°56N 71°3W **175** D13
Kingston *N.Y., U.S.A.* 41°56N 73°59W **175** E11
Kingston *Pa., U.S.A.* 41°16N 75°54W **175** E9
Kingston *R.I., U.S.A.* 41°29N 71°30W **175** E13
Kingston Pk. *U.S.A.* 35°44N 115°55W **171** K11
Kingston South East
Australia 36°51S 139°55E **152** C3
Kingston upon Hull
U.K. 53°45N 0°21W **66** D7
Kingston upon Hull □
U.K. 53°45N 0°21W **66** D7
Kingston-upon-Thames □
U.K. 51°24N 0°17W **67** F7
Kingstown *Australia* 30°29S 151°6E **153** A5
Kingstown *St. Vincent* 13°10N 61°10W **183** D7
Kingstree *U.S.A.* 33°40N 79°50W **178** D6
Kingsville *Canada* 42°2N 82°45W **174** D2
Kingsville *U.S.A.* 27°31N 97°52W **176** H6
Kingussie *U.K.* 57°6N 4°2W **65** D4

Kingwood *U.S.A.* 30°2N 95°16W **176** F7
Kınık *Antalya, Turkey* 36°20N 29°20E **99** E11
Kınık *İzmir, Turkey* 39°6N 27°24E **99** B9
Kinistino *Canada* 52°57N 105°2W **163** C7
Kinkala *Congo* 4°18S 14°49E **140** E2
Kinki □ *Japan* 33°45N 136°0E **113** H8
Kinleith *N.Z.* 38°20S 175°56E **154** E4
Kinlochleven *U.K.* 56°43N 5°0W **65** E4
Kinmount *Canada* 44°48N 78°45W **174** B6
Kinna *Sweden* 57°32N 12°42E **63** G6
Kinnairds Hd. *U.K.* 57°43N 2°1W **65** D6
Kinnared *Sweden* 57°2N 13°7E **63** G7
Kinnarodden = Nordkinn
Norway 71°8N 27°40E **60** A22
Kinnarp *Sweden* 58°1N 13°12E **63** F7
Kinneviken *Sweden* 58°35N 13°15E **63** F7
Kinngait *Canada* 64°14N 76°32W **161** E16
Kinniyai *Sri Lanka* 8°29N 81°11E **127** K5
Kino Nuevo *Mexico* 28°52N 112°3W **180** B2
Kinoje → *Canada* 52°8N 81°25W **164** B3
Kinomoto *Japan* 35°30N 136°13E **113** G8
Kinoni *Uganda* 0°41S 30°28E **142** C2
Kinoosao *Canada* 57°5N 102°1W **163** B8
Kinross *U.K.* 56°13N 3°25W **65** E5
Kinsale *Ireland* 51°42N 8°31W **64** E3
Kinsale, Old Hd. of
Ireland 51°37N 8°33W **64** E3
Kinsha = Chang Jiang →
China 31°48N 121°10E **117** B13
Kinshasa
Dem. Rep. of the Congo 4°20S 15°15E **140** E3
Kinsley *U.S.A.* 37°55N 99°25W **172** G4
Kinsman *U.S.A.* 41°26N 80°35W **174** E4
Kinston *Ala., U.S.A.* 31°13N 86°10W **178** F4
Kinston *N.C., U.S.A.* 35°16N 77°35W **177** D16
Kintampo *Ghana* 8°5N 1°41W **139** D4
Kintore *U.K.* 57°14N 2°20W **65** D6
Kintore Ra. *Australia* 23°15S 128°47E **148** D4
Kintyre *U.K.* 55°30N 5°35W **65** F3
Kintyre, Mull of *U.K.* 55°17N 5°47W **65** F3
Kinushseo → *Canada* 55°15S 83°45W **164** A3
Kinuso *Canada* 55°20N 115°25W **162** B5
Kinvarra *Ireland* 53°8N 8°56W **64** C3
Kinwat *India* 19°38N 78°12E **126** E4
Kinyangiri *Tanzania* 4°25S 34°37E **142** C3
Kinyeti *South Sudan* 3°57N 32°54E **132** G11
Kinzig → *Germany* 48°36N 7°49E **77** G3
Kinzua *U.S.A.* 41°52N 78°58W **174** E6
Kioni *Greece* 38°27N 20°41E **98** C2
Kiosk *Canada* 46°6N 78°53W **164** C4
Kiowa *Kans., U.S.A.* 37°1N 98°29W **172** G4
Kiowa *Okla., U.S.A.* 34°43N 95°54W **176** D7
Kipahigan L. *Canada* 55°20N 101°55W **163** B8
Kipanga *Tanzania* 6°15S 35°20E **142** D4
Kiparissia *Greece* 37°15N 21°40E **98** D3
Kiparissiakos Kolpos
Greece 37°25N 21°25E **98** D3
Kipawa, L. *Canada* 46°50N 79°0W **164** C4
Kipembawe *Tanzania* 7°38S 33°27E **142** D3
Kipengere Ra. *Tanzania* 9°12S 34°15E **143** D3
Kipili *Tanzania* 7°28S 30°32E **142** D3
Kipini *Kenya* 2°30S 40°32E **142** C5
Kipling *Canada* 50°6N 102°38W **163** C8
Kippure *Ireland* 53°11N 6°21W **64** C5
Kipushi
Dem. Rep. of the Congo 11°48S 27°12E **143** E2
Kira *Uganda* 0°24N 32°38E **142** B3
Kira Panagia *Greece* 39°17N 24°4E **98** B6
Kirandul *India* 18°33N 81°10E **126** E5
Kirane *Mali* 15°20N 10°20W **138** B2
Kirazli *Turkey* 40°2N 26°41E **97** F10
Kirchhain *Germany* 50°47N 8°56E **76** E4
Kirchheim *Germany* 48°39N 9°27E **77** D5
Kirchheimbolanden
Germany 49°40N 8°0E **77** F3
Kirchschlag *Austria* 47°30N 16°19E **79** D9
Kireç *Turkey* 39°33N 28°22E **99** B10
Kirensk *Russia* 57°50N 107°55E **107** D11
Kirghiz Range *Asia* 42°0N 73°40E **109** D8
Kirghizia = Kyrgyzstan ■
Asia 42°0N 75°0E **109** D9
Kirgiziya Steppe *Eurasia* 50°0N 55°0E **108** C5
Kiri Buru *India* 22°0N 85°0E **126** D7
Kiribati ■ *Pac. Oc.* 3°0S 180°0E **147** B10
Kirikhan *Turkey* 36°31N 36°21E **104** D7
Kırıkkale *Turkey* 39°51N 33°32E **104** C5
Kirikopuni *N.Z.* 35°50S 174°1E **154** B3
Kirin = Jilin *China* 43°44N 126°30E **115** C14
Kirindi Oya → *Sri Lanka* 6°15N 81°20E **127** L5
Kirinyaga = Kenya, Mt.
Kenya 0°10S 37°18E **142** C4
Kirirom △ *Cambodia* 11°18N 104°5E **121** G5
Kirishi *Russia* 59°28N 32°0E **84** C6
Kirishima *Japan* 31°44N 130°46E **113** J5
Kirishima Yaku △
Japan 31°24N 130°50E **113** J5
Kiritimati *Kiribati* 1°58N 157°27W **157** G12
Kırka *Turkey* 39°21N 30°31E **99** B12
Kırkağaç *Turkey* 39°4N 27°30E **99** B9
Kirkby *U.K.* 53°30N 2°54W **66** D5
Kirkby-in-Ashfield *U.K.* 53°6N 1°14W **66** D6
Kirkby Lonsdale *U.K.* 54°12N 2°36W **66** C5
Kirkby Stephen *U.K.* 54°29N 2°21W **66** C5
Kirkcaldy *U.K.* 56°7N 3°9W **65** E5
Kirkcudbright *U.K.* 54°50N 4°2W **65** G4
Kirkcudbright *U.K.* 54°52N 4°2W **65** G4
Kirkenes *Norway* 69°40N 30°5E **60** B24
Kirkfield *Canada* 44°34N 78°59W **174** B6
Kirkintilloch *U.K.* 55°56N 4°8W **65** F4
Kirkjubæjarklaustur
Iceland 63°47N 18°4W **60** E4
Kirkkonummi *Finland* 60°8N 24°26E **63** B21
Kirkland *U.S.A.* 47°40N 122°12W **170** C4
Kirkland Lake *Canada* 48°9N 80°2W **164** C3
Kırklareli *Turkey* 41°44N 27°15E **97** E11
Kırklareli □ *Turkey* 41°45N 27°15E **97** E11
Kirkliston R. *N.Z.* 44°25S 170°34E **155** L3
Kirksville *U.S.A.* 40°12N 92°35W **172** E7
Kirkūk *Iraq* 35°30N 44°21E **105** E11
Kirkwall *U.K.* 58°59N 2°58W **65** C6
Kirkwood *S. Africa* 33°22S 25°15E **144** D4
Kırlampudi *India* 17°12N 82°12E **126** F6
Kirn *Germany* 49°47N 7°29E **77** F3
Kirov *Kaluga, Russia* 54°3N 34°20E **84** E9
Kirov *Kirov, Russia* 58°35N 49°40E **86** D5

Kirovabad = Gäncä
Azerbaijan 40°45N 46°20E **87** K8
Kirovograd = Kirovohrad
Ukraine 48°35N 32°20E **85** H7
Kirovohrad *Ukraine* 48°35N 32°20E **85** H7
Kirovohrad □ *Ukraine* 48°30N 31°30E **85** H6
Kirovskiy = Balpyq Bī
Kazakhstan 44°52N 78°12E **109** D8
Kirovskiy *Astrakhan,*
Russia 45°51N 48°11E **87** H9
Kirovskiy *Kamchatka,*
Russia 54°27N 155°42E **107** D16
Kirovskiy *Primorsk,*
Russia 45°7N 133°30E **112** B6
Kirriemuir *U.K.* 56°41N 3°1W **65** E5
Kirsanov *Russia* 52°35N 42°40E **86** E6
Kırşehir *Turkey* 39°14N 34°5E **104** C6
Kirtachi *Niger* 12°52N 2°10E **139** C5
Kirthar Range *Pakistan* 27°0N 67°0E **124** F2
Kirtland *U.S.A.* 36°44N 108°21W **169** H9
Kiruna *Sweden* 67°52N 20°15E **60** C19
Kirundu
Dem. Rep. of the Congo 0°50S 25°35E **142** C2
Kirya *Russia* 55°8N 46°55E **86** C8
Kiryū *Japan* 36°24N 139°20E **113** F9
Kisa *Sweden* 58°0N 15°39E **63** G9
Kisaga *Tanzania* 4°30S 34°23E **142** C3
Kisalföld *Hungary* 47°30N 17°0E **80** C2
Kisanga
Dem. Rep. of the Congo 2°30N 26°35E **142** B2
Kisangani
Dem. Rep. of the Congo 0°35N 25°15E **142** B2
Kisar *Indonesia* 8°5S 127°10E **119** F7
Kisaran *Indonesia* 2°47N 99°29E **118** D1
Kisarawe *Tanzania* 6°53S 39°0E **142** D4
Kisarazu *Japan* 35°23N 139°55E **113** G9
Kisbér *Hungary* 47°30N 18°2E **80** C3
Kiselevsk *Russia* 54°5N 86°39E **109** B11
Kish = Qeys *Iran* 26°32N 53°58E **129** E7
Kishanganga →
Pakistan 34°18N 73°28E **125** B5
Kishanganj *India* 26°3N 88°14E **125** F13
Kishangarh *Raj., India* 26°34N 74°52E **124** F6
Kishangarh *Raj., India* 27°50N 70°30E **124** F4
Kishi *Nigeria* 9°1N 3°52E **139** D5
Kishinev = Chişinău
Moldova 47°2N 28°50E **81** C13
Kishiwada *Japan* 34°28N 135°22E **113** G7
Kishkeneköl
Kazakhstan 53°38N 72°20E **109** B8
Kishtwar *India* 33°20N 75°48E **124** B6
Kisielice *Poland* 53°36N 19°16E **82** E6
Kisigo □ *Tanzania* 6°27S 34°17E **142** D3
Kisii *Kenya* 0°40S 34°45E **142** C3
Kisiju *Tanzania* 7°23S 39°19E **142** D4
Kisir *Turkey* 41°0N 43°5E **105** B10
Kisizi *Uganda* 1°0S 29°58E **142** C2
Kiska I. *U.S.A.* 51°59N 177°30E **166** E3
Kiskomárom = Zalakomár
Hungary 46°33N 17°10E **80** D2
Kiskörei-víztároló
Hungary 47°31N 20°36E **80** C5
Kiskőrös *Hungary* 46°37N 19°20E **80** D4
Kiskundorozsma
Hungary 46°16N 20°5E **80** D5
Kiskunfélegyháza
Hungary 46°42N 19°53E **80** D4
Kiskunhalas *Hungary* 46°28N 19°37E **80** D4
Kiskunmajsa *Hungary* 46°30N 19°48E **80** D4
Kiskunsági □ *Hungary* 46°39N 19°30E **80** D4
Kislovodsk *Russia* 43°50N 42°45E **87** J6
Kiso-Gawa → *Japan* 35°20N 136°45E **113** G8
Kiso-Sammyaku
Japan 35°45N 137°45E **113** G8
Kisofukushima *Japan* 35°52N 137°43E **113** G8
Kisoro *Uganda* 1°17S 29°48E **142** C2
Kissamos = Kasteli
Greece 35°29N 23°38E **101** D5
Kissamos, Kolpos
Greece 35°30N 23°38E **101** D5
Kissidougou *Guinea* 9°5N 10°5W **138** D2
Kissimmee *U.S.A.* 28°18N 81°24W **179** G4
Kissimmee → *U.S.A.* 27°9N 80°52W **179** H4
Kississing L. *Canada* 55°10N 101°20W **163** B8
Kissónerga *Cyprus* 34°49N 32°24E **101** E11
Kissu, J. *Sudan* 21°37N 25°10E **137** C2
Kistanje *Croatia* 43°58N 15°55E **93** E12
Kisújszállás *Hungary* 47°12N 20°50E **80** C5
Kisumu *Kenya* 0°3S 34°45E **142** C3
Kisvárda *Hungary* 48°14N 22°4E **80** B7
Kiswani *Tanzania* 4°5S 37°57E **142** C4
Kiswere *Tanzania* 9°27S 39°30E **143** D4
Kit Carson *U.S.A.* 38°46N 102°48W **168** G12
Kita *Mali* 13°5N 9°25W **138** C3
Kitaibaraki *Japan* 36°50N 140°45E **113** F10
Kitakami *Japan* 39°20N 141°10E **112** D10
Kitakami-Gawa →
Japan 38°25N 141°19E **112** E10
Kitakami-Sammyaku
Japan 39°30N 141°30E **112** D10
Kitakata *Japan* 37°39N 139°52E **112** F9
Kitakyūshū *Japan* 33°50N 130°50E **113** H5
Kitale *Kenya* 1°0N 35°0E **142** B4
Kitami *Japan* 43°48N 143°54E **112** C11
Kitami-Sammyaku
Japan 44°22N 142°43E **112** B11
Kitangiri, L. *Tanzania* 4°5S 34°20E **142** C3
Kitaya *Tanzania* 10°38S 40°8E **143** E5
Kitchener *Canada* 43°27N 80°29W **174** C4
Kitee *Finland* 62°5N 30°8E **84** A6
Kitega = Gitega *Burundi* 3°26S 29°56E **142** C2
Kitengo
Dem. Rep. of the Congo 7°17N 25°32E **142** D1
Kitgum *Uganda* 3°17N 32°52E **142** B3
Kíthira = Kythira *Greece* 36°23N 23°0E **98** E5
Kithnos = Kythnos
Greece 37°26N 24°27E **98** D6
Kiti *Cyprus* 34°50N 33°34E **101** E12
Kiti, C. *Cyprus* 34°48N 33°36E **101** E12
Kitimat *Canada* 54°3N 128°38W **162** C3
Kitinen → *Finland* 67°14N 27°27E **60** C22
Kitros *Greece* 40°22N 22°34E **100** B5
Kitsman *Ukraine* 48°26N 25°46E **81** B10
Kittakittaooloo, L.
Australia 28°3S 138°14E **151** D2
Kittanning *U.S.A.* 40°49N 79°31W **174** E5
Kittatinny Mt. *U.S.A.* 41°19N 74°39W **175** F11
Kittery *U.S.A.* 43°5N 70°45W **175** D14

Kittilä *Finland* 67°40N 24°51E **60** C21
Kitui *Kenya* 1°17S 38°0E **142** C4
Kitwanga *Canada* 55°6N 128°4W **162** B3
Kitwe *Zambia* 12°54S 28°13E **143** E2
Kitzbühel *Austria* 47°27N 12°24E **78** D5
Kitzbühler Alpen
Austria 47°20N 12°20E **78** D5
Kitzingen *Germany* 49°44N 10°9E **77** F6
Kiunga Marine △ *Kenya* 2°1S 41°14E **142** C5
Kivarli *India* 24°33N 72°46E **124** G5
Kivertsi *Ukraine* 50°50N 25°28E **75** C13
Kividhes *Cyprus* 34°46N 32°51E **101** E11
Kivik *Sweden* 55°41N 14°13E **63** J8
Kivotos *Greece* 40°13N 21°26E **96** F5
Kivu, L.
Dem. Rep. of the Congo 1°48S 29°0E **142** C2
Kiwirrkurra *Australia* 22°49S 127°45E **148** D4
Kiwirrkurra ⊚
Australia 22°49S 127°45E **148** D4
Kiyev = Kyyiv *Ukraine* 50°30N 30°28E **75** C16
Kiyevskoye Vdkhr. = Kyyivske
Vdskh. *Ukraine* 51°0N 30°25E **75** C16
Kıyıköy *Turkey* 41°38N 28°5E **97** E12
Kizhi, Ostrov *Russia* 62°4N 35°13E **84** B8
Kiziba-Baluba △ *Congo* 11°50S 28°0E **143** E2
Kiziguru *Rwanda* 1°46S 30°23E **142** C3
Kızıl Adalar *Turkey* 40°52N 29°5E **97** F13
Kızıl Irmak → *Turkey* 41°44N 35°58E **104** B6
Kizil Jilga *China* 35°26N 78°50E **125** B8
Kizil Yurt *Russia* 43°13N 46°54E **87** J8
Kızılcabölük *Turkey* 37°37N 29°1E **99** D11
Kızılcadağ *Turkey* 37°1N 29°58E **99** D11
Kızılcahamam *Turkey* 40°30N 32°30E **104** B5
Kızıldağ △ *Turkey* 38°5N 31°10E **128** B1
Kızılhisar *Turkey* 37°32N 29°11E **104** D3
Kızılırmak *Turkey* 40°21N 33°59E **104** B5
Kızılkaya *Turkey* 37°18N 30°27E **99** D12
Kızılören *Turkey* 38°15N 30°0E **99** C12
Kızıltepe *Turkey* 37°12N 40°35E **105** D9
Kizimkazi *Tanzania* 6°28S 39°30E **142** D4
Kızlyar *Russia* 43°51N 46°40E **87** J8
Kizyl-Arvat = Serdar
Turkmenistan 39°4N 56°23E **129** B8
Kjellerup *Denmark* 56°17N 9°25E **63** H3
Kjölur *Iceland* 64°50N 19°25W **60** D4
Kladanj *Bos.-H.* 44°14N 18°42E **80** F3
Kladnica *Serbia* 43°23N 20°2E **96** C4
Kladno *Czech Rep.* 50°10N 14°7E **78** A7
Kladovo *Serbia* 44°36N 22°33E **96** B6
Klaeng *Thailand* 12°47N 101°39E **120** F3
Klagenfurt *Austria* 46°38N 14°20E **78** E7
Klaipėda *Lithuania* 55°43N 21°10E **82** C2
Klaipėda □ *Lithuania* 55°43N 21°7E **82** C2
Klaksvík *Færoe Is.* 62°14N 6°35W **60** E9
Klamath → *U.S.A.* 41°33N 124°5W **168** F1
Klamath Falls *U.S.A.* 42°13N 121°46W **168** E1
Klamath Mts. *U.S.A.* 41°50N 123°20W **168** F2
Klamono *Indonesia* 1°8S 131°30E **119** E8
Klang *Malaysia* 3°2N 101°26E **121** L3
Klanjec *Croatia* 46°3N 15°45E **93** B12
Klappan → *Canada* 58°0N 129°43W **162** B3
Klarälven → *Sweden* 59°23N 13°32E **62** E7
Klässbol *Sweden* 59°33N 12°45E **62** E6
Klatovy *Czech Rep.* 49°23N 13°18E **78** B6
Klawer *S. Africa* 31°44S 18°36E **144** D2
Klazienaveen *Neths.* 52°44N 7°0E **69** B6
Klé *Mali* 12°0N 6°28W **138** C3
Klecko *Poland* 52°38N 17°25E **83** F4
Kleczew *Poland* 52°22N 18°9E **83** F5
Kleena Kleene *Canada* 52°0N 124°59W **162** C4
Klein-Karas *Namibia* 27°33S 18°7E **144** C2
Kleinbegin *S. Africa* 28°45S 19°49E **144** C3
Klekovača *Bos.-H.* 44°25N 16°32E **93** D13
Klembivka *Ukraine* 48°23N 28°25E **81** B13
Klenovec *Macedonia* 41°32N 20°49E **96** E4
Klenovec *Slovak Rep.* 48°36N 19°54E **79** C12
Klerksdorp *S. Africa* 26°53S 26°38E **144** D4
Kleszczele *Poland* 52°35N 23°19E **83** F10
Kletnya *Russia* 53°23N 33°12E **84** F7
Kletsk = Klyetsk *Belarus* 53°5N 26°45E **75** B14
Kletskiy *Russia* 49°16N 43°11E **87** F7
Kleve *Germany* 51°47N 6°7E **76** D2
Klickitat *U.S.A.* 45°49N 121°9W **168** D3
Klickitat → *U.S.A.* 45°42N 121°17W **170** E5
Klidhes *Cyprus* 35°42N 34°36E **101** D13
Klimovichi *Belarus* 53°36N 32°0E **84** F6
Klin *Russia* 56°20N 36°48E **84** D9
Klinaklini → *Canada* 51°21N 125°40W **162** C3
Klině *Kosovo* 42°37N 20°35E **96** C4
Klintehamn *Sweden* 57°24N 18°12E **63** G12
Klintsy *Russia* 52°50N 32°10E **85** F7
Klip → *S. Africa* 27°3S 29°3E **145** C4
Klipdale *S. Africa* 34°19S 19°57E **144** D2
Klippan *Sweden* 56°8N 13°10E **63** H7
Klipplaat *S. Africa* 33°1S 24°22E **144** D3
Klishkivtsi *Ukraine* 48°26N 26°16E **81** B11
Klisura *Bulgaria* 42°40N 24°28E **97** C8
Kljajićevo *Serbia* 45°45N 19°17E **80** E4
Ključ *Bos.-H.* 44°32N 16°48E **80** F2
Klobuck *Poland* 50°55N 18°55E **83** H5
Klockestrand *Sweden* 62°53N 17°55E **62** B11
Kłodawa *Poland* 52°15N 18°55E **83** F5
Kłodzko *Poland* 50°28N 16°38E **83** H3
Klondike *Canada* 64°0N 139°26W **160** E4
Klong Wang Chao △
Thailand 16°20N 99°9E **120** D2
Klos *Albania* 41°28N 20°10E **96** E4
Klosterneuburg *Austria* 48°19N 16°19E **78** C9
Klosters *Switz.* 46°52N 9°52E **77** J5
Klötze *Germany* 52°37N 11°10E **76** B7
Klouto *Togo* 6°57N 0°44E **139** D5
Klövsjö *Sweden* 62°30N 14°11E **62** B8
Kluane △ *Canada* 60°45N 139°30W **162** A1
Kluane L. *Canada* 61°15N 138°40W **160** E4
Kluczbork *Poland* 50°58N 18°12E **83** H5
Klukwan *U.S.A.* 59°24N 135°54W **162** B1
Klungkung *Indonesia* 8°32S 115°24E **119** K18
Klyetsk *Belarus* 53°5N 26°45E **75** B14
Klyuchevskaya, Sopka
Russia 55°50N 160°30E **107** D17
Klyuchi *Russia* 56°18N 160°51E **107** D17
Knäred *Sweden* 56°31N 13°19E **63** H7
Knaresborough *U.K.* 54°1N 1°28W **66** C6
Knee L. *Man., Canada* 55°3N 94°45W **164** A1
Knee L. *Sask., Canada* 55°51N 107°0W **163** B7
Kneïss, Îs. *Tunisia* 34°22N 10°18E **136** B6
Knezha *Bulgaria* 43°30N 24°5E **97** C8
Knight Inlet *Canada* 50°45N 125°40W **162** C3
Knighton *U.K.* 52°21N 3°3W **67** E4
Knights Ferry *U.S.A.* 37°50N 120°40W **170** H6

Knights Landing
 U.S.A. 38°48N 121°43W 170 G5
Knin *Croatia* 44°3N 16°17E 93 D13
Knislinge *Sweden* 56°12N 14°5E 63 H8
Knittelfeld *Austria* 47°13N 14°51E 78 D7
Knivsta *Sweden* 59°43N 17°48E 62 E11
Knob, C. *Australia* 34°32S 119°16E 149 F2
Knock *Ireland* 53°48N 8°55W 64 C3
Knockmealdown Mts.
 Ireland 52°14N 7°56W 64 D4
Knokke-Heist *Belgium* 51°21N 3°17E 69 C3
Knossos *Greece* 35°16N 25°10E 101 D7
Knowlton *Canada* 45°13N 72°31W 175 A12
Knox *U.S.A.* 41°18N 86°37W 172 E10
Knox Coast *Antarctica*
 66°30S 108°0E 55 C8
Knoxville, Ga., *U.S.A.* 32°47N 83°59W 178 D5
Knoxville *Iowa, U.S.A.* 41°19N 93°6W 172 E7
Knoxville *Pa., U.S.A.* 41°57N 77°27W 174 E7
Knoxville *Tenn.,*
 U.S.A. 35°58N 83°55W 177 D13
Knud Rasmussen Land
 Greenland 78°0N 60°0W 57 B4
Knysna *S. Africa* 34°2S 23°2E 144 D3
Knyszyn *Poland* 53°20N 22°56E 82 E9
Ko Kha *Thailand* 18°11N 99°24E 120 C2
Ko Tarutao △ *Thailand* 6°31N 99°26E 121 J2
Ko Yao *Thailand* 8°7N 98°35E 121 a
Koartac = Quaqtaq
 Canada 60°55N 69°40W 161 E18
Koba *Indonesia* 6°37S 134°37E 119 F8
Kobarid *Slovenia* 46°15N 13°30E 93 B10
Kobayashi *Japan* 31°56N 130°59E 113 J5
Kōbe *Japan* 34°41N 135°13E 113 G7
Kobelyaky *Ukraine* 49°11N 34°9E 85 H8
København *Denmark* 55°40N 12°26E 63 J6
København ✕ (CPH)
 Denmark 55°37N 12°39E 63 J6
Kobenni *Mauritania* 15°58N 9°24W 138 B3
Kobi-Sho *E. China Sea* 25°56N 123°41E 113 M1
Koblenz *Germany* 50°21N 7°36E 77 E3
Kobryn *Belarus* 52°15N 24°22E 75 B13
Kobuk → *U.S.A.* 66°54N 160°38W 166 B7
Kobuleti *Georgia* 41°55N 41°45E 87 K5
Kobyletska Polyana
 Ukraine 48°3N 24°4E 81 B9
Kobylin *Poland* 51°43N 17°12E 83 G4
Kobyłka *Poland* 52°20N 21°10E 83 F8
Kobylkino *Russia* 54°8N 43°56E 86 C6
Koca → *Turkey* 40°8N 27°57E 97 F11
Kocaeli *Turkey* 40°45N 29°50E 97 F13
Kocaeli □ *Turkey* 40°45N 29°50E 97 F13
Kočane *Serbia* 43°12N 21°52E 96 C5
Koçarlı *Turkey* 41°55N 22°25E 96 E6
Koçarlı *Turkey* 37°45N 27°43E 99 D9
Koceljevo *Serbia* 44°28N 19°50E 96 B3
Kočevje *Slovenia* 45°39N 14°50E 93 C11
Koch Bihar *India* 26°22N 89°29E 123 F16
Kochas *India* 25°15N 83°56E 125 G10
Kocher → *Germany* 49°13N 9°12E 77 F5
Kōchi *Japan* 9°58N 76°20E 127 K3
Kōchi *Japan* 33°30N 133°35E 113 H6
Kōchi □ *Japan* 33°40N 133°30E 113 H6
Kochiu = Gejiu *China* 23°20N 103°10E 116 F4
Kochkor *Kyrgyzstan* 42°13N 75°46E 109 D9
Kochubey *Russia* 44°23N 46°32E 87 H8
Kock *Poland* 51°38N 22°27E 83 G9
Kodala *India* 19°38N 84°57E 126 E7
Kodarma *India* 24°28N 85°36E 125 G11
Koddiyar B. *Sri Lanka* 8°33N 81°15E 127 K5
Kode *Sweden* 57°57N 11°51E 63 G5
Kodiak *U.S.A.* 57°47N 152°24W 166 D9
Kodiak I. *U.S.A.* 57°30N 152°45W 166 D9
Kodikkarai = Point Calimere
 India 10°17N 79°49E 127 J4
Kodinar *India* 20°46N 70°46E 124 J4
Kodinsk *Russia* 58°40N 99°10E 107 D10
Kodlipet *India* 12°48N 75°53E 127 H2
Kodori → *Georgia* 42°47N 41°10E 87 J5
Kodungallur = Cranganore
 India 10°13N 76°13E 127 J3
Kodyma *Ukraine* 48°6N 29°7E 81 B14
Koedoesberge *S. Africa* 32°40S 20°11E 144 D3
Koes *Namibia* 26°0S 19°15E 144 C2
Kofarnihon *Tajikistan* 38°33N 69°1E 109 E7
Kolçaz *Turkey* 41°58N 27°12E 97 F11
Koffiefontein *S. Africa* 29°30S 25°0E 144 C4
Kofiau *Indonesia* 1°11S 129°50E 119 E7
Köflach *Austria* 47°4N 15°5E 78 D8
Koforidua *Ghana* 6°3N 0°17W 139 D4
Kōfu *Japan* 35°40N 138°30E 113 G9
Koga *Japan* 36°11N 139°43E 113 F9
Kogaluc → *Canada* 56°12N 61°44W 165 A7
Køge *Denmark* 55°27N 12°11E 63 J6
Køge Bugt *Denmark* 55°34N 12°24E 63 J6
Kogi □ *Nigeria* 7°45N 6°45E 139 D6
Kogin Baba *Nigeria* 7°55N 11°35E 139 D7
Kogon *Uzbekistan* 39°43N 64°33E 108 E6
Koh-i-Khurd *Afghan.* 33°30N 65°59E 124 C1
Koh-i-Maran *Pakistan* 29°18N 66°50E 124 E2
Koh Ker *Cambodia* 13°48N 104°32E 120 F5
Koh Wai *Thailand* 11°54N 102°25E 121 H4
Kohat *Pakistan* 33°40N 71°29E 124 C4
Kohima *India* 25°35N 94°10E 123 G19
Kohkīlūyeh va Būyer Aḩmadī □
 Iran 31°30N 50°30E 129 D6
Kohler Ra. *Antarctica* 77°0S 110°0W 55 D15
Kohlu *Pakistan* 29°54N 69°15E 124 E3
Kohtla-Järve *Estonia* 59°20N 27°20E 84 C4
Kohukohu *N.Z.* 35°22S 173°38E 154 B2
Kohylnyk → *Ukraine* 45°49N 29°40E 81 E14
Koi Sanjaq *Iraq* 36°5N 44°38E 105 D11
Koidu □ *S. Leone* 8°38N 10°59E 138 D2
Koihoa *India* 8°12N 93°29E 127 K11
Koilkuntla *India* 15°14N 78°19E 127 G3
Koillismaa *Finland* 65°44N 28°36E 60 D23
Koin *N. Korea* 40°28N 126°18E 115 D14
Koinare *Bulgaria* 43°14N 24°8E 97 C8
Koindu *S. Leone* 8°26N 10°19W 138 D2
Kojetín *Czech Rep.* 49°21N 17°20E 79 B10
Kojō *N. Korea* 38°58N 127°58E 115 E14
Kojonup *Australia* 33°48S 117°10E 149 F2
Kojūr *Iran* 36°23N 51°43E 129 B6
Kokand = Qŭqon
 Uzbekistan 40°31N 70°56E 109 D8
Kokang *Burma* 23°45N 98°30E 116 F2
Kokas *Indonesia* 2°42S 132°26E 119 E8
Kokava *Slovak Rep.* 48°35N 19°50E 79 C12
Kokcha → *Afghan.* 37°9N 69°24E 109 E7

Kokchetav = Kökshetaü
 Kazakhstan 53°20N 69°25E 109 B7
Kokemäenjoki →
 Finland 61°32N 21°44E 84 B1
Kokhma *Russia* 56°57N 41°18E 86 B5
Koki *Senegal* 15°30N 15°59W 138 B1
Kokkilai *Sri Lanka* 9°0N 80°57E 127 K5
Kokkola *Finland* 63°50N 23°8E 60 E20
Koko *Nigeria* 11°28N 4°29E 139 C5
Koko Kyunzu *Burma* 14°7N 93°22E 127 G1
Kokologo *Burkina Faso* 12°11N 1°53W 138 C4
Kokolopozo *Ivory C.* 5°8N 6°5W 138 D3
Komoro *U.S.A.* 40°29N 86°8W 172 E10
Kokopo *Papua N. G.* 4°22S 152°19E 156 H7
Kokoro *Niger* 14°12N 0°55E 139 C5
Koksan *N. Korea* 38°46N 126°40E 115 E14
Kökshetaü *Kazakhstan* 53°20N 69°25E 109 B7
Koksoak → *Canada* 58°30N 68°10W 161 F18
Kokstad *S. Africa* 30°32S 29°29E 145 D4
Köktal *Kazakhstan* 44°8N 79°48E 109 D9
Kokubu = Kirishima
 Japan 31°44N 130°46E 113 J5
Kokyar *China* 37°23N 77°10E 109 E9
Kola *Indonesia* 5°35S 134°30E 119 F8
Kola *Russia* 68°45N 33°8E 60 B25
Kola Pen. = Kolskiy Poluostrov
 Russia 67°30N 38°0E 58 B13
Kolachel *India* 8°10N 77°15E 127 K3
Kolachi → *Pakistan* 27°8N 67°2E 124 F2
Kolahoi *India* 34°12N 75°22E 125 B6
Kolahun *Liberia* 8°15N 10°4W 138 D2
Kolaka *Indonesia* 4°3S 121°46E 119 E6
Kolar *India* 13°12N 78°15E 127 H4
Kolar Gold Fields *India* 12°58N 78°16E 127 H4
Kolaras *India* 25°14N 77°36E 124 G6
Kolari *Finland* 67°20N 23°48E 60 C20
Kolárovo *Slovak Rep.* 47°54N 18°0E 79 D10
Kolasib *India* 24°15N 92°45E 123 G18
Kolašin *Montenegro* 42°50N 19°31E 96 D3
Kolayat *India* 27°50N 72°50E 124 F5
Kolbäck *Sweden* 59°34N 16°15E 62 E10
Kolbäcken → *Sweden* 59°36N 16°16E 62 E10
Kolbermoor *Germany* 47°51N 12°4E 77 H8
Kolbuszowa *Poland* 50°15N 21°46E 83 H8
Kolchugino *Russia* 56°17N 39°22E 84 D10
Kolda *Senegal* 12°55N 14°57W 138 C2
Kolda □ *Senegal* 13°5N 14°50W 138 C2
Kolding *Denmark* 55°30N 9°29E 63 J3
Koléa *Algeria* 36°38N 2°46E 136 C4
Kolepom = Dolak, Pulau
 Indonesia 8°0S 138°30E 119 F9
Kolguyev, Ostrov
 Russia 69°20N 48°30E 106 C5
Kolhapur *India* 16°43N 74°15E 126 F2
Kolia *Ivory C.* 9°46N 6°28W 138 D3
Kolimbia *Greece* 36°15N 28°10E 101 C10
Kolín *Czech Rep.* 50°2N 15°9E 78 A8
Kolind *Denmark* 56°21N 10°34E 63 H4
Kolkas rags *Latvia* 57°46N 22°37E 82 A9
Kolkata *India* 22°34N 88°21E 125 H13
Kollam *India* 8°50N 76°38E 127 K3
Kölleda *Germany* 51°11N 11°15E 76 D7
Kollegal *India* 12°9N 77°9E 127 H3
Kolleru L. *India* 16°40N 81°10E 126 F5
Kollum *Neths.* 53°17N 6°10E 69 A6
Kolmanskop *Namibia* 26°45S 15°14E 144 C2
Köln *Germany* 50°56N 6°57E 76 E2
Kolno *Poland* 53°25N 21°56E 82 E8
Kolo *Poland* 52°14N 18°40E 83 F5
Kołobrzeg *Poland* 54°10N 15°35E 82 D2
Kolochava *Ukraine* 48°26N 23°41E 81 B8
Kolokani *Mali* 13°35N 7°45W 138 C3
Koloko *Burkina Faso* 11°5N 5°19W 138 C3
Kolomna *Russia* 55°8N 38°45E 84 D10
Kolomyya *Ukraine* 48°31N 25°2E 81 B10
Kolondiéba *Mali* 11°5N 6°54W 138 C3
Kolonodale *Indonesia* 2°3S 121°19E 119 E6
Kolonowskie *Poland* 50°39N 18°22E 83 H5
Kolpashevo *Russia* 58°20N 83°5E 106 D9
Kolpino *Russia* 59°44N 30°39E 84 C6
Kolpny *Russia* 52°17N 37°1E 85 F9
Kolskiy Poluostrov
 Russia 67°30N 38°0E 58 B13
Kolskiy Zaliv *Russia* 69°23N 34°0E 60 B26
Kolsva *Sweden* 59°36N 15°51E 62 E9
Kolubara → *Serbia* 44°35N 20°15E 96 B4
Koluszki *Poland* 51°45N 19°46E 83 G6
Kolwezi
 Dem. Rep. of the Congo 10°40S 25°25E 143 E2
Kolyma → *Russia* 69°30N 161°0E 107 C17
Kolymskoye Nagorye
 Russia 63°0N 157°0E 107 C16
Kôm Hamâda *Egypt* 30°46N 30°41E 137 C7
Kôm Ombo *Egypt* 24°25N 32°52E 137 C3
Koma Tou Yialou
 Cyprus 35°25N 34°8E 101 D13
Komadugu Gana →
 Nigeria 13°5N 12°24E 139 C7
Komandorskiye Is. =
 Komandorskiye Ostrova
 Russia 55°0N 167°0E 107 D17
Komandorskiye Ostrova
 Russia 55°0N 167°0E 107 D17
Komárno *Slovak Rep.* 47°49N 18°5E 79 D11
Komarnyky *Ukraine* 48°59N 23°3E 80 B8
Komárom *Hungary* 47°43N 18°7E 80 C3
Komárom-Esztergom □
 Hungary 47°35N 18°20E 80 C3
Komatipoort *S. Africa* 25°25S 31°55E 145 C5
Komatsu *Japan* 36°25N 136°30E 113 F8
Komatsushima *Japan* 34°0N 134°35E 113 H7
Kombissiri *Burkina Faso* 12°4N 1°20W 139 C4
Kombori *Burkina Faso* 13°26N 3°56W 138 C4
Komboti *Greece* 39°6N 21°5E 98 B3
Kome Channel *Uganda* 0°10S 32°5E 142 C3
Komen *Slovenia* 45°49N 13°45E 93 C10
Komenda *Ghana* 5°4N 1°28W 139 D4
Komi □ *Russia* 64°0N 55°0E 106 C6
Komi *Cyprus* 35°24N 34°0E 101 D13
Komiža *Croatia* 43°3N 16°11E 93 D13
Komló *Hungary* 46°15N 18°16E 80 D3
Kommamur Canal *India* 15°30N 80°20E 127 G5
Kommunarsk = Alchevsk
 Ukraine 48°30N 38°45E 85 H10
Kommunizma, Pik = imeni Ismail
 Samani, Pik *Tajikistan* 39°0N 72°2E 109 E8
Komodo *Indonesia* 8°37S 119°20E 119 F5
Komoran, Pulau
 Indonesia 8°18S 138°45E 119 F9
Komoro *Japan* 36°19N 138°26E 113 F9
Komotini *Greece* 41°9N 25°26E 97 E9

Komovi *Montenegro* 42°41N 19°39E 96 D3
Kompasberg *S. Africa* 31°45S 24°32E 144 D3
Kompong Chhnang = Kampong
 Chhnang *Cambodia* 12°20N 104°35E 121 F5
Kompong Chikreng
 Cambodia 13°5N 104°18E 120 F5
Kompong Kleang
 Cambodia 13°6N 104°8E 120 F5
Kompong Luong
 Cambodia 11°49N 104°48E 121 G5
Kompong Pranak
 Cambodia 13°35N 104°55E 120 F5
Kompong Som = Kampong Saom
 Cambodia 10°38N 103°30E 121 G4
Kompong Som, Chhung =
 Kampong Saom, Chaak
 Cambodia 10°50N 103°32E 121 G4
Kompong Speu
 Cambodia 11°26N 104°32E 121 G5
Kompong Sralau
 Cambodia 14°5N 105°46E 120 E5
Kompong Thom
 Cambodia 12°35N 104°51E 120 F5
Kompong Trabeck
 Cambodia 13°6N 105°14E 120 F5
Kompong Trach
 Cambodia 11°25N 105°48E 121 G5
Kompong Tralach
 Cambodia 11°54N 104°47E 121 G5
Komrat = Comrat
 Moldova 46°18N 28°40E 81 C13
Komsberg *S. Africa* 32°40S 20°45E 144 D3
Komsomolets = Qarabalyq
 Kazakhstan 53°45N 62°2E 108 B6
Komsomolets, Ostrov
 Russia 80°30N 95°0E 107 A10
Komsomolsk *Russia* 47°28N 46°50E 87 G8
Komsomolsk *Ukraine* 49°1N 33°38E 85 H7
Komsomolsk-na-Amur
 Russia 50°30N 137°0E 111 A16
Komsomolskiy *Russia* 54°27N 45°33E 86 C7
Komsomolskoe
 Kazakhstan 50°25N 60°5E 108 B6
Kömür Burnu *Turkey* 38°39N 26°12E 99 C8
Kon Ka Kinh △
 Vietnam 14°19N 107°23E 120 E6
Kon Tum *Vietnam* 14°24N 108°0E 120 E7
Kon Tum, Plateau du
 Vietnam 14°30N 108°30E 120 E7
Kona *Mali* 14°57N 3°53W 138 C4
Kona *Nigeria* 8°57N 11°21E 139 D7
Konakovo *Russia* 56°40N 36°51E 84 D9
Konar □ *Afghan.* 34°30N 71°3E 122 B7
Konarak *India* 19°54N 86°7E 126 E8
Konārī *Iran* 28°13N 51°36E 129 D6
Konch *India* 26°0N 79°10E 125 G8
Kondagaon *India* 19°35N 81°35E 126 E5
Konde *Tanzania* 4°57S 39°45E 142 C4
Kondias *Greece* 39°49N 25°10E 99 B7
Kondinin *Australia* 32°34S 118°8E 149 F2
Kondoa *Tanzania* 4°55S 35°50E 142 C4
Kondopoga *Russia* 62°12N 34°17E 84 A3
Kondoz *Afghan.* 36°50N 68°50E 109 E7
Kondoz → *Afghan.* 37°0N 68°16E 109 E7
Kondratyevo *Russia* 57°22N 98°15E 107 D10
Kondrovo *Russia* 54°48N 35°56E 84 E8
Konduga *Nigeria* 11°35N 13°26E 139 C7
Kondukur *India* 15°12N 79°57E 127 G4
Kondūz □ *Afghan.* 36°50N 68°50E 109 E7
Köneürgench
 Turkmenistan 42°19N 59°10E 108 D5
Konevo *Russia* 62°8N 39°20E 84 A11
Kong = Khong →
 Cambodia 13°32N 105°58E 120 F5
Kong *Ivory C.* 8°54N 4°36W 138 D4
Kong, Koh *Cambodia* 11°20N 103°0E 121 G4
Kong Christian IX.s Land
 Greenland 68°0N 36°0W 57 D7
Kong Christian X.s Land
 Greenland 74°0N 29°0W 57 C8
Kong Frederik IX.s Land
 Greenland 67°0N 52°0W 57 D5
Kong Frederik VI.s Kyst
 Greenland 63°0N 43°0W 57 E6
Kong Frederik VIII.s Land
 Greenland 78°30N 26°0W 57 B8
Kong Karls Land *Svalbard* 79°0N 28°0E 57 B13
Kong Oscar Fjord
 Greenland 72°20N 24°0W 57 C8
Kongeå → *Denmark* 55°23N 8°39E 63 J2
Kongernes Nordsjælland △
 Denmark 56°5N 12°15E 63 H6
Kongerslev *Denmark* 56°54N 10°6E 63 H4
Konglu *Burma* 27°13N 97°57E 123 F20
Kongola *Namibia* 17°45S 23°20E 144 A3
Kongolo *Kasai-Or..*
 Dem. Rep. of the Congo 5°26S 24°49E 142 D1
Kongolo *Katanga,*
 Dem. Rep. of the Congo 5°22S 27°0E 142 D2
Kongossambougou □
 Mali 14°0N 8°30W 138 C3
Kongoussi *Burkina Faso* 13°19N 1°32W 138 C4
Kongsberg *Norway* 59°39N 9°39E 61 G13
Kongsvinger *Norway* 60°12N 12°2E 61 F15
Kongur Shan *China* 38°34N 75°18E 109 F9
Kongwa *Tanzania* 6°11S 36°26E 142 D4
Koni
 Dem. Rep. of the Congo 10°40S 27°11E 143 E2
Koniakari *Mali* 14°35N 10°50W 138 C2
Koniecpol *Poland* 50°46N 19°40E 83 H6
Königs Wusterhausen
 Germany 52°19N 13°38E 76 C9
Königsbrunn *Germany* 48°16N 10°54E 77 G6
Königslutter *Germany* 52°15N 10°49E 76 C6
Konin *Poland* 52°12N 18°15E 83 F5
Konispol *Albania* 39°42N 20°10E 98 B2
Konitsa *Greece* 40°5N 20°48E 98 A2
Konjic *Bos.-H.* 43°42N 17°58E 96 C7
Konkiep *Namibia* 26°49S 17°15E 144 C2
Konkouré → *Guinea* 9°50N 13°42W 138 D2
Konnur *India* 16°14N 74°49E 127 F2
Kono *S. Leone* 8°30N 11°5W 138 D2
Konongo *Ghana* 6°40N 1°15W 139 D4
Konosha *Russia* 61°0N 40°5E 84 B11
Konosu *Japan* 36°3N 139°31E 113 F9
Konotop *Ukraine* 51°12N 33°7E 85 G7
Konqi He → *China* 41°0N 86°0E 109 E12
Konsankoro *Guinea* 9°2N 9°0W 138 D3
Końskie *Poland* 51°15N 20°23E 83 G7

Konstancin-Jeziorna
 Poland 52°5N 21°7E 83 F8
Konstantinovka =
 Kostyantynivka
 Ukraine 48°32N 37°39E 85 H9
Konstantinovsk *Russia* 47°33N 41°10E 87 G5
Konstantynów Łódżki
 Poland 51°45N 19°20E 83 G6
Konstanz *Germany* 47°40N 9°10E 77 H5
Kont *Iran* 26°55N 61°50E 129 E9
Konta *India* 17°48N 81°23E 126 F5
Kontagora *Nigeria* 10°23N 5°27E 139 C6
Kontcha *Cameroon* 7°59N 12°15E 139 D7
Kontiolahti *Finland* 62°46N 29°50E 60 E23
Kontokali *Greece* 39°38N 19°51E 101 A3
Konya *Turkey* 37°52N 32°35E 104 D5
Konya □ *Turkey* 37°46N 32°20E 104 D5
Konya Ovası *Turkey* 38°9N 33°5E 104 C5
Konz *Germany* 49°42N 6°34E 77 F7
Konza *Kenya* 1°45S 37°7E 142 C4
Koo-wee-rup *Australia* 38°13S 145°28E 153 E6
Koocanusa, L. *Canada* 49°20N 115°15W 168 B6
Kookynie *Australia* 29°17S 121°22E 149 E3
Koolyanobbing
 Australia 30°48S 119°36E 149 F2
Koondrook *Australia* 35°33S 144°8E 152 C6
Koonibba *Australia* 31°54S 133°25E 151 E1
Koorawatha *Australia* 34°2S 148°33E 153 C8
Koorda *Australia* 30°48S 117°35E 149 F2
Kooskia *U.S.A.* 46°9N 115°59W 168 C6
Kootenay → *U.S.A.* 49°19N 117°39W 162 D5
Kootenay L. *Canada* 51°0N 116°0W 162 D5
Kootenay L. *Canada* 49°45N 116°50W 168 B5
Kootingal *Australia* 31°3S 151°4E 153 A9
Kootjieskolk *S. Africa* 31°15S 20°21E 144 D3
Kopanovka *Russia* 47°28N 46°50E 87 G8
Kopaonik *Serbia* 43°10N 20°50E 96 C4
Kopaonik △ *Serbia* 43°20N 20°50E 96 C4
Kopargaon *India* 19°51N 74°28E 126 D8
Kópavogur *Iceland* 64°6N 21°55W 60 D3
Koper *Slovenia* 45°31N 13°44E 93 C10
Kopervik *Norway* 59°17N 5°17E 61 G11
Kopet Dagh *Asia* 38°0N 58°0E 129 B8
Kopeysk *Russia* 55°7N 61°37E 108 A6
Kopi *Australia* 33°24S 135°40E 151 E2
Köping *Sweden* 59°31N 16°3E 62 E10
Köpingsvik *Sweden* 56°53N 16°43E 63 H10
Kopište *Croatia* 42°48N 16°42E 93 F13
Koplik *Albania* 42°15N 19°25E 96 D3
Köpmanholmen
 Sweden 63°10N 18°35E 62 A12
Koppa *India* 13°33N 75°21E 127 H2
Koppal *India* 15°23N 76°5E 127 G3
Kopparberg *Sweden* 59°52N 15°0E 62 E9
Koppeh Dägh = Kopet Dagh
 Asia 38°0N 58°0E 129 B8
Koppies *S. Africa* 27°20S 27°30E 145 C4
Koppom *Sweden* 59°43N 12°10E 62 E6
Koprivlen *Bulgaria* 41°31N 23°53E 96 E7
Koprivnica *Croatia* 46°12N 16°45E 93 B13
Koprivnice *Czech Rep.* 49°36N 18°9E 79 B11
Koprivshtitsa *Bulgaria* 42°40N 24°19E 97 D8
Köprübaşı *Turkey* 38°43N 28°23E 99 C11
Köprülü △ *Turkey* 37°20N 31°5E 128 B1
Kopychyntsi *Ukraine* 49°7N 25°58E 75 D13
Kora △ *Kenya* 0°14S 38°44E 142 C4
Korab *Macedonia* 41°44N 20°40E 96 E4
Koral *India* 21°50N 73°12E 124 J5
Korangal *India* 17°6N 77°38E 126 F3
Koraput *India* 18°50N 82°40E 126 F5
Korarou, L. *Mali* 15°15N 3°15W 138 B4
Korba *India* 22°20N 82°45E 125 H10
Korbach *Germany* 51°16N 8°57E 76 D4
Korbu, Gunung
 Malaysia 4°41N 101°18E 121 K3
Korçë *Albania* 40°37N 20°50E 96 F4
Korčula *Croatia* 42°56N 16°57E 93 F13
Korčulanski Kanal
 Croatia 43°3N 16°40E 93 F13
Kord Kūy *Iran* 36°48N 54°7E 129 B7
Kord Sheykh *Iran* 28°31N 52°53E 129 D7
Kordestan = Kurdistan
 Asia 37°20N 43°30E 105 D10
Kordestän □ *Iran* 36°0N 47°0E 128 C5
Kordié *Burkina Faso* 12°36N 2°22W 138 C4
Kordofân □ *Sudan* 13°0N 19°0E 135 F11
Koré Mayroua *Niger* 13°18N 3°55E 139 C5
Korea, North ■ *Asia* 40°0N 127°0E 115 E14
Korea, South ■ *Asia* 36°0N 128°0E 115 G15
Korea Bay *Korea* 39°0N 124°0E 115 E13
Korea Strait *Asia* 34°0N 129°30E 115 H15
Koregaon *India* 17°40N 74°10E 126 F2
Korenevo *Russia* 51°27N 34°55E 85 G8
Korenovsk *Russia* 45°30N 39°22E 87 H4
Korets *Ukraine* 50°40N 27°5E 75 C14
Korfantów *Poland* 50°29N 17°36E 83 H4
Korff Ice Rise *Antarctica* 79°0S 59°0W 55 D17
Korgalzhyn = Qorghalzhyn
 Kazakhstan 50°35N 69°11E 109 B7
Korgan *Turkey* 40°44N 37°13E 104 B7
Korgus *Sudan* 19°16N 33°29E 137 D3
Korhogo *Ivory C.* 9°29N 5°28W 138 D3
Koribundu *S. Leone* 7°41N 11°46W 138 D2
Korienzé *Mali* 15°22N 3°50W 138 B4
Korinthiakos Kolpos
 Greece 38°16N 22°30E 98 C4
Korinthos *Greece* 37°56N 22°55E 98 D4
Korioumé *Mali* 16°35N 3°0W 138 B4
Korissia *Greece* 39°27N 19°53E 101 B3
Köriyama *Japan* 37°24N 140°23E 112 F10
Korkino *Russia* 54°54N 61°23E 108 B6
Korkuteli *Turkey* 37°4N 30°13E 99 D12
Korla *China* 41°45N 86°4E 109 E11
Kormakiti, C. *Cyprus* 35°19N 32°56E 101 D11
Kormend *Hungary* 47°5N 16°35E 78 E9
Kornat *Iraq* 35°8N 44°50E 105 D11
Kornat △ *Croatia* 43°50N 15°12E 93 E12
Korneshty = Cornești
 Moldova 47°21N 28°1E 81 C13
Korneuburg *Austria* 48°20N 16°20E 78 C9
Kórnik *Poland* 52°15N 17°6E 83 F4
Koro *Fiji* 17°19S 179°23E 154 a
Koro *Ivory C.* 8°32N 7°30W 138 D3
Koro *Mali* 14°1N 2°58W 138 C4
Koro Sea *Fiji* 17°30S 179°45W 154 a
Korocha *Russia* 50°55N 37°30E 85 G9
Köroğlu Dağları *Turkey* 40°38N 31°0E 104 B5
Korogwe *Tanzania* 5°5S 38°25E 142 D4

Koroit *Australia* 38°18S 142°24E 152 E5
Koroleve *Ukraine* 48°9N 23°8E 81 B8
Korolevu *Fiji* 18°12S 177°46E 154 a
Koronadal *Phil.* 6°12N 124°51E 119 C6
Korong Vale *Australia* 36°22S 143°45E 152 D5
Koroni *Greece* 36°48N 21°57E 98 E3
Koronia, L. *Greece* 40°47N 23°10E 96 F7
Koronos *Greece* 37°12N 25°35E 99 D7
Koronowo *Poland* 53°19N 17°55E 83 E4
Korosten *Ukraine* 50°54N 28°36E 75 C15
Korostyshev *Ukraine* 50°19N 29°4E 81 B11
Korotoyak *Russia* 51°1N 39°2E 85 G10
Korovou *Fiji* 17°32S 178°31E 154 a
Koroyanitu △ *Fiji* 17°40S 177°35E 154 a
Korsakov *Russia* 46°36N 142°42E 107 E15
Korsberga *Sweden* 57°19N 15°7E 63 G9
Korshiv *Ukraine* 48°39N 25°1E 81 B10
Korshunovo *Russia* 58°37N 110°10E 107 D12
Korsør *Denmark* 55°20N 11°9E 63 J5
Korsun Shevchenkovskiy
 Ukraine 49°26N 31°16E 85 H6
Korsze *Poland* 54°11N 21°9E 82 D8
Korti *Sudan* 18°6N 31°33E 137 D3
Kortrijk *Belgium* 50°50N 3°17E 69 D3
Korucu *Turkey* 39°28N 27°22E 99 C9
Korumburra *Australia* 38°26S 145°50E 153 E6
Korwai *India* 24°7N 78°5E 124 G6
Koryakskoye Nagorye
 Russia 61°0N 171°0E 107 C18
Koryukivka *Ukraine* 51°46N 32°16E 85 G7
Kos *Greece* 36°50N 27°15E 99 E9
Kosan *N. Korea* 38°52N 127°25E 115 E14
Kosaya Gora *Russia* 54°10N 37°30E 84 E9
Kościan *Poland* 52°5N 16°40E 83 F3
Kościerzyna *Poland* 54°8N 17°59E 82 D4
Kosciusko *U.S.A.* 33°4N 89°35W 177 E10
Kosciuszko, Mt.
 Australia 36°27S 148°16E 153 D8
Kosciuszko △
 Australia 36°30S 148°20E 153 D8
Kösély → *Hungary* 47°25N 21°5E 80 C6
Kosgi *Andhra Pradesh,*
 India 16°58N 77°43E 126 F3
Kosgi *Andhra Pradesh,*
 India 15°51N 77°16E 127 G3
Kosha *Sudan* 20°50N 30°30E 137 C3
Koshava *Bulgaria* 44°4N 23°2E 96 B7
K'oshih = Kashi *China* 39°30N 76°2E 109 F9
Koshiki-Rettō *Japan* 31°45N 129°49E 113 J4
Koshim → *Kazakhstan* 49°20N 50°30E 86 F10
Kosi *India* 27°48N 77°29E 124 F7
Kosi → *India* 26°41N 78°57E 124 G6
Košice *Slovak Rep.* 48°42N 21°15E 79 C14
Košický □ *Slovak Rep.* 48°45N 21°0E 79 C14
Kosiv *Ukraine* 48°19N 25°5E 81 B10
Kosjerić *Serbia* 44°0N 19°55E 96 B3
Köşk *Turkey* 37°50N 28°3E 99 D10
Koskinou *Greece* 36°23N 28°13E 101 C10
Koslan *Russia* 63°34N 49°14E 106 C5
Kosma → *Russia* 66°19N 55°26E 86 A9
Kosmach *Ukraine* 48°20N 24°50E 81 B9
Kosŏng *N. Korea* 38°40N 128°22E 115 E16
Kosovo ■ *Europe* 42°30N 21°0E 96 C4
Kosovo Polje = Fushë Kosovë
 Kosovo 42°32N 21°7E 96 C5
Kosovska Kamenica = Dardanë
 Kosovo 42°33N 21°25E 96 C5
Kosovska Mitrovica = Mitrovicë
 Kosovo 42°54N 20°52E 96 C4
Kossou, L. de *Ivory C.* 7°0S 5°31W 138 D3
Kosta *Sweden* 56°50N 15°24E 63 H9
Kostajnica *Croatia* 45°51N 16°33E 93 C13
Kostanjevica *Slovenia* 45°51N 15°27E 93 C12
Kostenets *Bulgaria* 42°15N 23°52E 96 D7
Koster *S. Africa* 25°52S 26°54E 144 C4
Kôstî *Sudan* 13°8N 32°43E 135 F12
Kostinbrod *Bulgaria* 42°49N 23°13E 96 D7
Kostolac *Serbia* 44°37N 21°15E 96 B5
Kostopil *Ukraine* 50°51N 26°22E 75 C14
Kostroma *Russia* 57°50N 40°58E 84 C11
Kostromo □ *Russia* 58°0N 44°0E 84 C7
Kostromskoye Vdkhr.
 Russia 57°52N 40°49E 84 C11
Kostrzyn *Poland* 52°24N 17°14E 83 F4
Kostyantynivka *Ukraine* 48°32N 37°39E 85 H9
Kostryn Lubuskie, *Poland* 52°35N 14°39E 83 F1
Kostrzyn Wielkopolskie,
 Poland 52°24N 17°14E 83 F4
Kostyantynivka *Ukraine* 48°32N 37°39E 85 H9
Kostyukovichi = Kastsyukovichy
 Belarus 53°10N 32°4E 84 D5
Koszalin *Poland* 54°11N 16°8E 82 D3
Kőszeg *Hungary* 47°23N 16°33E 80 C1
Kot Addu *Pakistan* 30°30N 71°0E 124 D4
Kot Kapura *India* 30°35N 74°50E 124 D6
Kot Moman *Pakistan* 32°13N 73°0E 124 C5
Kot Sultan *Pakistan* 30°46N 70°56E 124 D4
Kota *India* 25°14N 75°49E 124 G6
Kota Barrage *India* 25°6N 75°51E 126 G6
Kota Belud *Malaysia* 6°21N 116°26E 118 C5
Kota Bharu *Malaysia* 6°7N 102°14E 121 J4
Kota = Loaita I.
 S. China Sea 10°41N 114°25E 118 B4
Kota Kinabalu *Malaysia* 6°0N 116°4E 118 C5
Kota Tinggi *Malaysia* 1°44N 103°53E 121 M4
Kotaagung *Indonesia* 5°38S 104°29E 118 F2
Kotabaru *Indonesia* 3°20S 116°20E 118 E5
Kotabumi *Indonesia* 4°49S 104°54E 118 E2
Kotamobagu *Indonesia* 0°57N 124°31E 119 D6
Kotapad *India* 19°9N 82°21E 126 E6
Kotapinang *Indonesia* 1°53N 100°5E 121 M3
Kotcho L. *Canada* 59°7N 121°12W 162 B4
Kotdwara *India* 29°45N 78°32E 125 E8
Kotel *Bulgaria* 42°52N 26°26E 97 D10
Kotelnich *Russia* 58°22N 48°24E 86 A9
Kotelnikovo *Russia* 47°38N 43°8E 87 G6
Kotelnyy, Ostrov
 Russia 75°10N 139°0E 107 B14
Kothagudem *India* 17°30N 80°40E 126 F5
Kothapet *India* 19°21N 79°28E 126 E4
Kothari → *India* 25°20N 75°4E 124 G6
Kothen *Germany* 51°45N 11°59E 76 D7
Kothi *Chhattisgarh, India* 23°21N 82°3E 125 H10
Kothi *Mad. P., India* 24°45N 80°40E 125 G9
Kotiro *India* 26°17N 67°13E 124 F2
Kotka *Finland* 60°28N 26°58E 63 B24
Kotlas *Russia* 61°17N 46°43E 106 C5
Kotlenska Planina
 Bulgaria 42°56N 26°30E 97 D10

Kotli *Pakistan* 33°30N 73°55E 124
Kotli *U.S.A.* 63°2N 163°33W 166
Kotma *India* 23°12N 81°58E 125
Koton-Karifi *Nigeria* 8°0N 6°48E 139
Kotonkoro *Nigeria* 11°3N 5°58E 139
Kotor *Montenegro* 42°25N 18°47E 96
Kotor Varoš *Bos.-H.* 44°38N 17°22E 8
Kotoriba *Croatia* 46°23N 16°48E 93
Kotovsk *Russia* 50°22N 44°45E 8
Kotovsk *Russia* 52°36N 41°32E 8
Kotovsk *Ukraine* 47°45N 29°35E 75
Kotputli *India* 27°43N 76°12E 12
Kotri *Pakistan* 25°22N 68°22E 124
Kotri → *India* 19°15N 80°35E 12
Kotronas *Greece* 36°38N 22°29E 9
Kötschach-Mauthen
 Austria 46°41N 13°1E 7
Kottagudem *India* 17°30N 80°40E 12
Kottayam *India* 9°35N 76°33E 12
Kotto → *C.A.R.* 4°14N 22°2E 14
Kottur *India* 10°34N 76°56E 12
Kotturu *India* 14°45N 76°10E 12
Kotuy → *Russia* 71°54N 102°6E 107
Kotuzhany *Ukraine* 48°48N 27°42E 81
Kotzebue *U.S.A.* 66°53N 162°39W 166
Kotzebue Sound
 U.S.A. 66°20N 163°0W 166
Kouchibouguac △
 Canada 46°50N 65°0W 16
Koudougou
 Burkina Faso 12°10N 2°20W 13
Koufonisi *Iraklio, Greece* 34°56N 26°8E 10
Koufonisi *Notio Aigaio,*
 Greece 36°57N 25°35E
Kougaberge *S. Africa* 33°48S 23°50E 14
Kouibli *Ivory C.* 7°15N 7°14W 13
Kouilou → *Congo* 4°10S 12°5E 14
Koukdjuak → *Canada* 66°43N 73°0W 161
Koula *Greece* 41°23N 24°44E 9
Koula Moutou *Gabon* 1°15S 12°25E 14
Koulen = Kulen
 Cambodia 13°50N 104°40E 12
Koulikoro *Mali* 12°40N 7°50W 13
Koulikoro □ *Mali* 14°0N 7°45W 13
Kouloura *Greece* 39°42N 19°54E 10
Koumala *Australia* 21°38S 149°15E 15
Koumankou *Mali* 11°58N 6°6W 13
Koumbia *Burkina Faso* 11°10N 3°50W 13
Koumbia *Guinea* 11°48N 13°29W 13
Koumboum *Guinea* 10°25N 13°0W 13
Koumpentoum
 Senegal 13°59N 14°34W 13
Koumra *Chad* 8°50N 17°35E 13
Koun-Fao *Ivory C.* 7°30N 3°15W 13
Koundara *Guinea* 12°29N 13°18W 13
Koungheul *Senegal* 14°0N 14°50W 13
Kountze *U.S.A.* 30°22N 94°19W 17
Koupéla *Burkina Faso* 12°11N 0°21W 13
Kourémalé *Mali* 11°59N 8°42W 13
Kouris → *Cyprus* 34°38N 32°54E 10
Kourou *Fr. Guiana* 5°9N 52°39W 18
Kouroaba *Mali* 12°0N 10°57W 13
Koûroudjél *Mauritania* 16°12N 11°30W 13
Kouroukoto *Mali* 12°35N 10°5W 13
Kouroumo *Burkina Faso* 11°35N 4°50W 13
Kourouninkoto *Mali* 13°52N 9°35W 13
Kouroussa *Guinea* 10°45N 9°45W 13
Koussanar *Senegal* 13°52N 14°5W 13
Koussané *Mali* 14°53N 11°14W 13
Koussané *Senegal* 14°10N 12°22W 13
Kousseri *Cameroon* 12°0N 14°55E 13
Koutiala *Mali* 12°25N 5°23W 13
Kouto *Ivory C.* 9°53N 6°25W 13
Kouvé *Togo* 6°25N 1°25E 13
Kouvola *Finland* 60°52N 26°43E 6
Kovačica *Serbia* 45°5N 20°38E 8
Kovdor *Russia* 67°34N 30°24E 6
Kovel *Ukraine* 51°11N 24°38E 75
Kovilpatti *India* 9°10N 77°50E 12
Kovin *Serbia* 44°44N 20°59E 9
Kovrov *Russia* 56°25N 41°25E 8
Kovur *Andhra Pradesh,*
 India 17°3N 81°39E 12
Kovur *Andhra Pradesh,*
 India 14°30N 80°1E 12
Kowal *Poland* 52°32N 19°7E 8
Kowalewo Pomorskie
 Poland 53°10N 18°52E 8
Kowanyama *Australia* 15°29S 141°44E 15
Kowanyama □
 Australia 15°20S 141°47E 15
Kowloon *China* 22°19N 114°11E 117
Kowŏn *N. Korea* 39°26N 127°14E 115
Koyampattur = Coimbatore
 India 11°2N 76°59E 12
Köyceğiz *Turkey* 36°57N 28°40E 9
Köyceğiz Gölü *Turkey* 36°55N 28°36E 9
Koyuk *U.S.A.* 64°55N 157°32W 16
Koyulhisar *Turkey* 40°20N 37°52E 10
Koyunyeri *Turkey* 40°50N 26°26E 9
Koza = Okinawa
 Japan 26°19N 127°46E 11
Kozak *Turkey* 39°15N 27°6E 9
Kozaklı *Turkey* 39°13N 34°49E 10
Kozan *Turkey* 37°26N 35°50E 10
Kozani *Greece* 40°19N 21°47E 9
Kozara *Bos.-H.* 45°0N 17°0E 9
Kozara △ *Bos.-H.* 45°0N 17°0E 9
Kozarac *Bos.-H.* 44°58N 16°48E 9
Kozelsk *Russia* 54°2N 35°48E 8
Kozhikode *India* 11°15N 75°43E 12
Koziegłowy *Poland* 50°37N 19°9E 8
Kozienice *Poland* 51°35N 21°34E
Kozje *Slovenia* 46°5N 15°35E 9
Kozloduy *Bulgaria* 43°45N 23°42E 9
Kozlovets *Bulgaria* 43°30N 25°20E
Kozludere *Turkey* 41°52N 34°18E 1
Kozlu *Turkey* 41°26N 31°45E 1
Kozluk *Turkey* 38°11N 41°33E 1
Koźmin *Poland* 51°48N 17°27E
Koźminek *Poland* 51°49N 18°17E 8
Koźmodemyansk *Russia* 56°20N 46°36E 8
Kōzu-Shima *Japan* 34°13N 139°10E 11
Kozova *Ukraine* 49°25N 25°9E 81
Kozyatyn *Ukraine* 49°45N 28°50E 81
Kozyrevsk *Russia* 56°3N 159°51E 107
Kpabia *Ghana* 9°10N 0°20W 13
Kpalimé *Togo* 6°57N 0°44E 13
Kpandae *Ghana* 8°30N 0°2W 13
Kpessi *Togo* 8°4N 1°16E 13

Isthmus of = Kra, Kho Khot
tiland   10°15N 99°30E **121** G2
Kho Khot *Thailand* 10°15N 99°30E **121** G2
Buri *Thailand* 10°22N 98°46E **121** G2
i → *S. Africa* 30°40S 26°54E **144** D4
i *Thailand* 8°4N 98°55E **121** H2
heh = Kratie
ambodia 12°32N 106°10E **120** F6
a *Indonesia* 6°43S 111°38E **119** G14
erø *Norway* 58°52N 9°25E **61** G13
ujevac *Serbia* 44°2N 20°56E **96** B4
enka *Poland* 53°18N 16°59E **83** E3
atau = Rakata, Pulau
onesia 6°10S 105°20E **119** G11
atoa = Rakata, Pulau
onesia 6°10S 105°20E **119** G11
or *Cambodia* 12°32N 104°12E **120** F5
ów *Poland* 54°9N 19°57E **83** H6
ów ✈ (KRK) *Poland* 50°5N 19°52E **83** H6
saan *Indonesia* 7°43S 113°23E **119** G16
anh *Cambodia* 13°35N 103°25E **120** F4
ky *Czech Rep.* 50°6N 16°45E **79** A9
evo *Serbia* 43°44N 20°41E **96** C4
ovéhradecký □
ch Rep. 50°25N 15°50E **78** A8
ovský Chlmec
vak Rep. 48°27N 22°0E **79** C14
upy nad Vltavou
ch Rep. 50°13N 14°20E **78** A7
anatorsk *Ukraine* 48°50N 37°30E **85** H9
nfors *Sweden* 62°55N 17°48E **62** B11
ia *Greece* 39°57N 22°2E **98** B4
idi *Greece* 39°23N 23°10E **98** D5
j *Slovenia* 46°16N 14°22E **93** B11
jska Gora *Slovenia* 46°29N 13°48E **93** B10
kskop *S. Africa* 28°0S 30°47E **145** C5
ina *Croatia* 46°10N 15°52E **93** B12
ina → *Croatia* 45°50N 15°50E **93** C12
kowice *Poland* 50°29N 17°56E **83** H4
Croatia 45°35N 14°0E **93** C10
eo *Res. Thailand* 14°49N 99°30E **120** F2
kino *Russia* 52°44N 130°48E **112** C5
lava *Latvia* 55°54N 27°10E **84** E4
lice *Czech Rep.* 50°19N 12°31E **78** A5
naya Gorbatka
ssia 55°52N 41°45E **84** C7
naya Polyana
ssia 43°40N 40°13E **87** J5
ne *Ukraine* 46°7N 29°15E **81** D14
ni Okny *Ukraine* 47°32N 29°27E **81** C14
nik *Poland* 50°55N 22°5E **83** H9
noarmeisk *Ukraine* 48°18N 37°11E **85** H9
noarmeysk = Tayynsha
akhstan 53°50N 69°45E **109** B7
noarmeysk *Russia* 51°0N 45°42E **86** E7
nobrod *Russia* 50°33N 23°12E **83** H10
nodar *Russia* 45°5N 39°0E **87** H4
nodar □ *Russia* 46°30N 39°30E **87** G4
nodarskoye Vdkhr.
ssia 45°1N 39°23E **87** H4
nodon *Ukraine* 48°17N 39°44E **85** H10
nogorskiy *Russia* 56°10N 48°28E **86** B9
nograd = Krasnohrad
raine 49°27N 35°27E **85** H8
nogvardeysk
raine 45°32N 34°16E **85** K8
nogvardeyskoye
ssia 45°52N 41°33E **87** H5
nohrad *Ukraine* 49°27N 35°27E **85** H8
nokamensk
ssia 50°3N 118°0E **107** D12
nokutsk *Ukraine* 50°10N 34°50E **85** G8
nolesnyy *Russia* 51°53N 39°35E **85** G10
noperekopsk *Ukraine* 46°0N 33°54E **85** J7
norechenskiy
ssia 44°41N 135°14E **112** B7
noselkup *Russia* 65°20N 82°10E **106** C9
noslobodsk *Mordvinia,*
ssia 54°25N 43°45E **86** C6
noslobodsk *Volgograd,*
ssia 48°42N 44°33E **87** F7
noturinsk *Russia* 59°46N 60°12E **106** D7
noyarsk *Russia* 56°8N 93°0E **107** D10
noyarskoye *Russia* 54°31N 21°56E **82** D8
noyarskoye Vdkhr.
ssia 56°0N 92°30E **107** D10
noye = Krasnyy
ssia 54°25N 31°30E **84** E6
noyilsk *Ukraine* 47°59N 35°28E **81** C10
noznamensk *Russia* 56°27N 38°25E **84** D10
noznamensk
ssia 54°57N 22°30E **82** D9
ny Sulin *Russia* 47°52N 40°8E **87** G5
aystaw *Poland* 50°57N 23°5E **83** H10
nyy *Russia* 54°25N 31°30E **84** E6
nyy Kholm *Russia* 58°10N 37°10E **84** C9
nyy Kut *Russia* 50°50N 47°0E **86** E8
nyy Liman *Ukraine* 48°58N 37°50E **85** H9
nyy Luch *Ukraine* 48°13N 39°0E **85** H10
nyy Profintern
ssia 57°45N 40°27E **84** D11
nyy Yar *Astrakhan,*
ssia 46°43N 48°23E **87** G9
nyy Yar *Samara,*
ssia 53°30N 50°22E **86** D10
nyy Yar *Volgograd,*
ssia 50°42N 44°45E **86** E7
nyye Baki *Russia* 57°8N 45°10E **86** B7
nyyoskolske Vdskh.
ssia 50°42N 37°40E **85** H9
ne *Cambodia* 12°32N 104°12E **120** F6
Indonesia 3°19S 140°5E **119** E10

Kremmen *Germany* 52°45N 13°1E **76** C9
Kremmling *U.S.A.* 40°4N 106°24W **168** F10
Kremnica *Slovak Rep.* 48°45N 18°50E **79** C11
Krems *Austria* 48°25N 15°36E **78** C8
Kremsmünster *Austria* 48°3N 14°8E **78** C7
Krestena *Greece* 37°35N 21°37E **98** D3
Kretinga *Lithuania* 55°53N 21°15E **82** C8
Krettamia *Algeria* 28°47N 3°27W **136** C3
Krettsy *Russia* 58°15N 32°30E **84** C7
Kreuzberg *Germany* 50°22N 9°58E **77** E5
Kreuzbal *Germany* 50°57N 8°0E **76** E4
Kria Vrisi *Greece* 40°41N 22°18E **96** F6
Kribi *Cameroon* 2°57N 9°56E **139** E6
Krichem *Bulgaria* 42°8N 24°28E **97** D8
Krichev = Krychaw
Belarus 53°40N 31°41E **75** B16
Kril'on, Mys *Russia* 45°53N 142°5E **112** B11
Krim *Slovenia* 45°53N 14°30E **93** C11
Krios, Akra *Greece* 35°13N 23°34E **101** D5
Krishna → *India* 15°57N 80°59E **127** G5
Krishnagiri *India* 12°32N 78°16E **127** H4
Krishnanagar *India* 23°24N 88°33E **125** H13
Krishnaraja Sagar
India 12°20N 76°30E **127** H3
Kristdala *Sweden* 57°24N 16°13E **63** G10
Kristiansand *Norway* 58°8N 8°1E **63** G13
Kristiansted *Sweden* 56°2N 14°9E **63** H8
Kristiansund *Norway* 63°7N 7°45E **60** E12
Kristiinankaupunki
Finland 62°16N 21°21E **60** E19
Kristinehamn *Sweden* 59°18N 14°7E **62** E8
Kristinestad =
Kristiinankaupunki
Finland 62°16N 21°21E **60** E19
Kriti *Greece* 35°15N 25°0E **101** D7
Kritsa *Greece* 35°10N 25°41E **101** D7
Kriva → *Macedonia* 42°5N 21°47E **96** D5
Kriva Palanka
Macedonia 42°11N 22°19E **96** D6
Krivaja → *Bos.-H.* 44°27N 18°9E **80** F3
Krivelj *Serbia* 44°10N 22°5E **96** B6
Křivoklátsko △
Czech Rep. 50°1N 13°51E **78** A6
Krivoy Rog = Kryvyy Rih
Ukraine 47°51N 33°20E **85** J7
Križevci *Croatia* 46°3N 16°32E **93** B13
Krk *Croatia* 45°8N 14°40E **93** C11
Krka → *Slovenia* 45°50N 15°30E **93** C12
Krka △ *Croatia* 43°53N 15°56E **93** E12
Krkonoše *Czech Rep.* 50°50N 15°35E **78** A8
Krkonoše △ *Czech Rep.* 50°43N 15°39E **78** A8
Krnov *Czech Rep.* 50°5N 17°40E **79** A10
Krobia *Poland* 51°47N 16°59E **83** G3
Krokees *Greece* 36°53N 22°32E **98** E4
Krokek *Sweden* 58°40N 16°24E **63** F10
Krokodil = Umgwenya →
Mozam. 25°14S 32°18E **145** C5
Krokom *Sweden* 63°20N 14°30E **62** A8
Krokowa *Poland* 54°47N 18°9E **82** D5
Krolevets *Ukraine* 51°35N 33°20E **85** G7
Krompachy *Slovak Rep.* 48°54N 20°52E **79** B10
Kromy *Russia* 52°48N 35°48E **85** F8
Kronach *Germany* 50°14N 11°19E **77** E7
Krong Kaoh Kong
Cambodia 11°37N 102°59E **121** G4
Kronobergs län □
Sweden 56°45N 14°30E **63** H8
Kronprins Christian Land
Greenland 80°30N 22°0W **57** A8
Kronprins Frederik Land
Greenland 81°0N 45°0W **57** A6
Kronprins Olav Kyst
Antarctica 69°0S 42°0E **55** C5
Kronprinsesse Märtha Kyst
Antarctica 73°30S 10°0W **55** D2
Kronshtadt *Russia* 59°57N 29°51E **84** C5
Kroonstad *S. Africa* 27°43S 27°19E **144** C4
Kröpelin *Germany* 54°4N 11°47E **76** A7
Kropotkin *Russia* 45°28N 40°28E **87** H5
Kropp *Germany* 54°24N 9°31E **76** A5
Krosna *Lithuania* 54°23N 23°33E **82** D10
Krośniewice *Poland* 52°15N 19°11E **83** F6
Krosno *Poland* 49°42N 21°46E **83** J8
Krosno Odrzańskie *Poland* 52°3N 15°7E **83** F2
Krotoszyn *Poland* 51°42N 17°23E **83** G4
Krotovka *Russia* 53°18N 51°10E **86** D10
Krousonas *Greece* 35°13N 24°59E **101** D6
Krrabë *Albania* 41°13N 20°0E **96** E3
Krško *Slovenia* 45°57N 15°30E **93** C12
Krstača *Serbia* 42°57N 20°8E **96** C4
Kruger △ *S. Africa* 24°50S 26°10E **145** B4
Krugersdorp *S. Africa* 26°5S 27°46E **145** C4
Kruisfontein *S. Africa* 33°59S 24°43E **144** D3
Krujë *Albania* 41°32N 19°46E **96** E3
Krulevshchina =
Krulyewshchyna
Belarus 55°5N 27°45E **84** E4
Krulyewshchyna *Belarus* 55°5N 27°45E **84** E4
Krumbach *Germany* 48°13N 10°22E **77** G6
Krumë *Albania* 42°14N 20°28E **96** D4
Krumovgrad *Bulgaria* 41°29N 25°38E **97** E9
Krung Thep = Bangkok
Thailand 13°45N 100°35E **120** F3
Krupanj *Serbia* 44°25N 19°22E **96** B3
Krupina *Slovak Rep.* 48°22N 19°5E **79** C12
Krupinica → *Slovak Rep.* 48°4N 18°55E **79** C11
Krupki *Belarus* 54°19N 29°8E **75** A15
Kruševac *Serbia* 43°35N 21°28E **96** C5
Kruševo *Macedonia* 41°23N 21°19E **96** D5
Krushë e Madhe *Kosovo* 42°19N 20°39E **96** D4
Krushelnyksya *Ukraine* 49°7N 23°23E **83** J10
Kruszwica *Poland* 52°40N 18°20E **83** F5
Kruzenshterna, Proliv
Russia 48°0N 154°0E **107** E16
Krychav *Belarus* 53°40N 31°41E **75** B16
Krymsk *Russia* 44°50N 38°0E **85** K10
Krymskiy Poluostrov =
Kremmskyy Pivostriv
Ukraine 45°0N 34°0E **85** K8
Krymskyy Pivostriv
Ukraine 45°0N 34°0E **85** K8
Krynica *Poland* 49°25N 20°57E **83** J7
Krynica Morska *Poland* 54°23N 19°28E **82** D6
Krynki *Poland* 53°17N 23°43E **83** E10
Krynychne *Ukraine* 45°33N 28°40E **81** E13
Kryvyy Rih *Ukraine* 47°51N 33°20E **85** J7
Kryzhopil *Ukraine* 48°23N 28°53E **81** D13
Krzepice *Poland* 50°58N 18°50E **83** H5
Krzeszów *Poland* 50°24N 22°21E **83** H9
Krzna → *Poland* 52°8N 23°3E **83** F10

Krzywiń *Poland* 51°58N 16°50E **83** G3
Krzyż Wielkopolski
Poland 52°52N 16°0E **83** F2
Ksabi *Morocco* 32°51N 4°13W **136** B5
Ksar Chellala *Algeria* 35°13N 2°19E **136** A4
Ksar el Boukhari *Algeria* 35°51N 2°52E **136** A4
Ksar el Kebir *Morocco* 35°0N 6°0W **136** B2
Ksar es Souk = Er Rachidia
Morocco 31°58N 4°20W **136** B3
Ksar Rhilane *Tunisia* 33°0N 9°39E **136** B5
Ksiąz Wielkopolski
Poland 52°4N 17°14E **83** F4
Ksour, Mts. des *Algeria* 32°45N 0°30W **136** B3
Ksovo *Russia* 56°12N 44°13E **86** B7
Ku-Ring-Gai Chase △
Australia 33°39S 151°14E **153** B9
Kuah *Malaysia* 6°19N 99°51E **121** J2
Kuala Belait *Malaysia* 4°35N 114°11E **118** D4
Kuala Berang *Malaysia* 5°5N 103°1E **121** K4
Kuala Dungun = Dungun
Malaysia 4°45N 103°25E **121** K4
Kuala Kangsar
Malaysia 4°46N 100°56E **121** K3
Kuala Kelawang
Malaysia 2°56N 102°5E **121** L4
Kuala Kerai *Malaysia* 5°30N 102°12E **121** K4
Kuala Kubu Bharu
Malaysia 3°34N 101°39E **121** L3
Kuala Lipis *Malaysia* 4°10N 102°3E **121** K4
Kuala Lumpur *Malaysia* 3°9N 101°41E **121** L3
Kuala Nerang *Malaysia* 6°16N 100°37E **121** J3
Kuala Pilah *Malaysia* 2°45N 102°15E **121** L4
Kuala Rompin
Malaysia 2°49N 103°29E **121** L4
Kuala Selangor
Malaysia 3°20N 101°15E **121** L3
Kuala Sepetang
Malaysia 4°49N 100°28E **121** K3
Kuala Terengganu
Malaysia 5°20N 103°8E **121** K4
Kualajelai *Indonesia* 2°58N 110°46E **118** E4
Kualakapuas *Indonesia* 2°55S 114°20E **118** E4
Kualakurun *Indonesia* 1°10S 113°50E **118** E4
Kualapembuang
Indonesia 3°14S 112°38E **118** E4
Kualasimpang *Indonesia* 4°17N 98°3E **118** D1
Kuancheng *China* 40°37N 118°30E **115** D10
Kuandang *Indonesia* 0°56N 123°1E **119** D6
Kuandian *China* 40°45N 124°45E **115** D13
Kuangchou = Guangzhou
China 23°6N 113°13E **117** F9
Kuanshan *Taiwan* 23°3N 121°9E **117** F13
Kuantan *Malaysia* 3°49N 103°20E **121** L4
Kuba = Quba *Azerbaijan* 41°21N 48°32E **87** K9
Kuban Depression =
Prikubanskaya Nizmennost
Russia 45°40N 38°33E **87** H4
Kubaysah *Iraq* 33°35N 42°37E **105** D10
Kubenskoye, Ozero
Russia 59°40N 39°25E **84** C10
Kubokawa = Shimanto
Japan 33°12N 133°8E **113** H6
Kubrat *Bulgaria* 43°49N 26°31E **97** C10
Kubu *Indonesia* 8°16S 115°35E **119** J18
Kubutambahan
Indonesia 8°5S 115°10E **119** J18
Kucar, Tanjung
Indonesia 8°39S 114°34E **119** K18
Kučevo *Serbia* 44°30N 21°40E **96** B5
Kuchaman *India* 27°13N 74°47E **124** F6
Kuchchaveli *Sri Lanka* 8°49N 81°6E **127** K5
Kuchenspitze *Austria* 47°0N 10°12E **78** D3
Kuchinda *India* 21°44N 84°21E **125** J11
Kuching *Malaysia* 1°33N 110°25E **118** D4
Kuchino-eruba-Jima
Japan 30°28N 130°12E **113** J5
Kuchino-Shima *Japan* 29°57N 129°55E **113** K4
Kuchinotsu *Japan* 32°36N 130°11E **113** H5
Kuchl *Austria* 47°37N 13°9E **78** D6
Kuchurhan → *Ukraine* 46°33N 29°57E **81** D14
Kucing = Kuching
Malaysia 1°33N 110°25E **118** D4
Kuçovë *Albania* 40°47N 19°57E **96** F3
Küçükbahçe *Turkey* 38°33N 26°24E **99** C8
Küçükköy *Turkey* 39°16N 26°42E **99** B8
Küçükkuyu *Turkey* 39°35N 26°27E **99** B8
Küçükmenderes →
Turkey 37°50N 27°16E **99** D9
Kud → *Pakistan* 26°5N 66°20E **124** F2
Kuda *India* 23°10N 71°15E **124** H4
Kudal *India* 16°2N 73°41E **127** F1
Kudalier → *India* 18°35N 79°48E **126** E4
Kudat *Malaysia* 6°55N 116°55E **118** C5
Kudirkos Naumiestis
Lithuania 54°46N 22°53E **82** D9
Kudowa-Zdrój *Poland* 50°27N 16°15E **83** H3
Kudremukh *India* 13°15N 75°20E **127** H2
Kudus *Indonesia* 6°48S 110°51E **119** G14
Kudymkar *Russia* 59°1N 54°39E **106** D6
Kueiyang = Guiyang
China 26°32N 106°40E **116** D6
Kufra Oasis = Al Kufrah
Libya 24°17N 23°15E **135** D10
Kufstein *Austria* 47°35N 12°11E **78** D5
Kugaaruk = Pelly Bay
Canada 68°38N 89°50W **161** C14
Kugluktuk *Canada* 67°50N 115°5W **160** D8
Kugong I. *Canada* 56°18N 79°50W **164** A4
Küh Dasht *Iran* 33°32N 47°36E **105** F12
Küh-e Sorkh *Iran* 35°30N 58°45E **108** E5
Kühak *Iran* 27°12N 63°10E **129** E9
Kühan *Pakistan* 28°19N 67°14E **124** E2
Kühbonān *Iran* 31°23N 56°19E **129** D8
Kui Buri *Thailand* 12°11N 99°37E **121** F2
Kuiburi △ *Thailand* 12°10N 99°37E **121** F2
Kuichong *China* 22°38N 114°25E **111** a
Kuiseb → *Namibia* 22°59S 14°31E **144** B1
Kuito *Angola* 12°22S 16°55E **141** G3
Kuiu I. *U.S.A.* 57°45N 134°10W **162** B2

Kujalleq □ *Greenland* 61°0N 44°0W **57** E6
Kujang *N. Korea* 39°57N 126°1E **115** E14
Kujawsko-Pomorskie □
Poland 53°20N 18°30E **82** E5
Kuji *Japan* 40°11N 141°46E **112** D10
Kujū-San *Japan* 33°5N 131°15E **113** H5
Kukawa *Ukraine* 48°37N 27°43E **81** B12
Kuk
e Kebir *Morocco* 35°0N 6°0W **136** B2
Kukawa *Nigeria* 12°58N 13°27E **139** C7
Kukês *Albania* 42°5N 20°27E **96** D4
Kukmor *Russia* 56°11N 50°54E **86** B10
Kukup *Malaysia* 1°20N 103°27E **121** d
Kukup, Pulau *Malaysia* 1°18N 103°25E **121** d
Kukvidze *Russia* 50°40N 43°0E **86** E6
Kula *Bulgaria* 43°52N 22°36E **96** C6
Kula *Serbia* 45°37N 19°32E **80** E4
Kula *Turkey* 38°32N 28°40E **99** C10
Kula *Turkey* 38°33N 28°40E **99** C10
Kulachi *Pakistan* 31°56N 70°27E **124** D4
Kulai *Malaysia* 1°44N 103°35E **121** M4
Kulaly, Ostrov *Kazakhstan* 45°0N 50°5E **87** H10
Kulasekarappattinam
India 8°22N 78°5E **127** K4
Kulautuva *Lithuania* 54°56N 23°36E **82** D10
Kuldiga *Latvia* 56°58N 21°59E **88** B2
Kuldīga □ *Latvia* 56°55N 22°0E **82** B8
Kulebaki *Russia* 55°22N 42°25E **86** C6
Kulen *Cambodia* 13°50N 104°40E **120** F5
Kulen Vakuf *Bos.-H.* 44°35N 16°2E **93** D13
Kulgam *India* 33°36N 75°2E **125** C6
Kulgera *Australia* 25°50S 133°18E **150** D1
Kulim *India* 5°22N 100°34E **121** K3
Kulin *Australia* 32°40S 118°2E **149** F2
Kulittalai *India* 10°55N 78°25E **127** J4
Kulkayu = Hartley Bay
Canada 53°25N 129°15W **162** C3
Kullen *Sweden* 56°18N 12°26E **63** H6
Kullu *India* 31°58N 77°6E **124** D7
Kulmbach *Germany* 50°6N 11°26E **77** E7
Kulob *Tajikistan* 37°55N 69°50E **108** B4
Kulp *Turkey* 38°29N 41°2E **105** C9
Kulpawn → *Ghana* 10°20N 1°5W **139** D4
Kulsary = Qulsary
Kazakhstan 46°59N 54°1E **108** C4
Kulti *India* 23°43N 86°50E **125** H12
Kulu *Turkey* 39°5N 33°5E **104** C5
Kulunda *Russia* 52°35N 78°57E **109** B9
Kulundinskoye, Ozero
Russia 53°0N 79°36E **109** B9
Kulungar *Afghan.* 34°0N 69°2E **124** C3
Kulvand *Iran* 31°21N 54°35E **129** D7
Kulwin *Australia* 35°2S 142°42E **152** C5
Kulyab = Kulob
Tajikistan 37°55N 69°50E **108** B4
Kuma → *Russia* 44°55N 47°0E **87** H8
Kumaganum *Nigeria* 13°8N 10°38E **139** C7
Kumagaya *Japan* 36°9N 139°22E **113** F9
Kumai *Indonesia* 2°44S 111°43E **118** E4
Kumalar Dağı *Turkey* 38°15N 30°20E **99** C12
Kumamba, Kepulauan
Indonesia 1°36S 138°45E **119** E9
Kumamoto *Japan* 32°45N 130°45E **113** H5
Kumamoto □ *Japan* 32°55N 130°55E **113** H5
Kumanovo *Macedonia* 42°9N 21°42E **96** D5
Kumara → *Afghan.* 34°30N 70°28E **109** F8
Kumara *N.Z.* 42°37S 171°12E **155** C6
Kumarina Roadhouse
Australia 24°41S 119°32E **149** D2
Kumasi *Ghana* 6°41N 1°38W **138** D4
Kumba *Cameroon* 27°13N 74°47E **124** F6
Kumbag *Turkey* 40°51N 27°27E **97** F11
Kumbakonam *India* 10°58N 79°25E **127** J4
Kumbarilla *Australia* 27°15S 150°55E **151** D5
Kumbhraj *India* 24°22N 77°3E **124** G7
Kumbia *Australia* 26°41S 151°39E **151** D5
Kumbo *Cameroon* 6°15N 10°36E **139** D7
Kumbukkan Oya →
Sri Lanka 6°35N 81°40E **127** L5
Kümch'on *N. Korea* 38°10N 126°29E **115** E14
Kume-Shima *Japan* 26°20N 126°47E **113** L3
Kumeny *Russia* 58°10N 49°47E **86** A9
Kumertau *Russia* 52°45N 55°57E **108** B5
Kumharsain *India* 31°19N 77°27E **124** D7
Kumi *Uganda* 1°30N 33°58E **142** B3
Kumkale *Turkey* 39°59N 26°11E **97** G10
Kumla *Sweden* 59°8N 15°10E **62** E9
Kumluca *Turkey* 36°22N 30°20E **99** E12
Kummerower See
Germany 53°49N 12°51E **76** B8
Kumo *Nigeria* 10°1N 11°12E **139** C7
Kumo älv = Kokemäenjoki →
Finland 61°32N 21°44E **84** B1
Kumon Bum *Burma* 26°30N 97°15E **123** F20
Kumta *India* 14°29N 74°25E **127** G2
Kumtag Shamo *China* 39°40N 92°0E **110** D7
Kumyalı = Koma Tou Yialou
Cyprus 35°25N 34°8E **101** D13
Kumylzhenskaya *Russia* 49°51N 42°38E **86** F6
Kuna *U.S.A.* 43°30N 116°25W **168** E5
Kunashir, Ostrov
Russia 44°0N 146°0E **107** E15
Kunchha *Nepal* 28°8N 84°20E **125** E11
Kunda *Estonia* 59°30N 26°34E **84** C4
Kunda *India* 25°43N 81°31E **125** G9
Kundar → *Pakistan* 31°56N 69°19E **124** D3
Kundelungu △
Dem. Rep. of the Congo 10°30S 27°40E **143** E2
Kundelungu Ouest △
Dem. Rep. of the Congo 9°55S 27°17E **143** D2
Kundian *Pakistan* 32°27N 71°28E **124** C4
Kundla *India* 21°21N 71°25E **124** J4
Kunene □ *Namibia* 20°0S 14°0E **144** A1
Kung, Ao *Thailand* 8°5N 98°24E **121** a
Kunga → *Bangla.* 21°46N 89°30E **125** J13
Kunghit I. *Canada* 52°6N 131°3W **162** C2
Kungrad = Qünghirot
Uzbekistan 43°2N 58°50E **108** D5
Kungsängen *Sweden* 59°29N 17°46E **62** E11
Kungsbacka *Sweden* 57°30N 12°5E **63** H5
Kungsgården *Sweden* 60°37N 16°35E **62** D10
Kungsör *Sweden* 59°25N 16°5E **62** E10
Kungur *Russia* 57°25N 56°57E **86** C11
Kunhar → *Pakistan* 34°20N 73°30E **125** B5
Kunhegyes *Hungary* 47°22N 20°36E **80** C5

Kuningan *Indonesia* 6°59S 108°29E **119** G13
Kunlara *Australia* 34°54S 139°55E **152** C3
Kunlong *Burma* 23°20N 98°50E **116** F2
Kunlun Shan *Asia* 36°0N 86°30E **109** E11
Kunlun Shankou *China* 35°38N 94°4E **110** D7
Kunmadaras *Hungary* 47°28N 20°45E **80** C5
Kunming *China* 25°1N 102°41E **116** E4
Kunmunya ○
Australia 15°26S 124°42E **148** C3
Kunnamkulam *India* 10°39N 76°4E **127** J3
Kunów *Poland* 50°57N 21°17E **83** H8
Kunshan *China* 31°22N 120°58E **117** B13
Kunszentmárton
Hungary 46°50N 20°20E **80** C5
Kunszentmiklós *Hungary* 47°2N 19°8E **80** C4
Kuntaur *Senegal* 13°40N 14°58E **138** C2
Kununurra *Australia* 15°40S 128°50E **148** C4
Kunwari → *India* 26°26N 79°11E **125** F8
Kunya-Urgench = Köneürgench
Turkmenistan 42°19N 59°10E **108** D5
Künzelsau *Germany* 49°17N 9°42E **77** F5
Kuopio *Finland* 62°53N 27°35E **60** E22
Kupa → *Croatia* 45°28N 16°24E **93** C13
Kupang *Indonesia* 10°19S 123°39E **119** F6
Kupino *Russia* 54°21N 77°18E **109** B9
Kupreanof I. *U.S.A.* 56°50N 133°30W **162** B2
Kupres *Bos.-H.* 43°56N 17°15E **80** G2
Kupyansk *Ukraine* 49°52N 37°35E **85** H9
Kupyansk-Uzlovoi
Ukraine 49°40N 37°43E **85** H9
Kuqa *China* 41°35N 82°30E **109** D10
Kür → *Azerbaijan* 39°29N 49°15E **105** C13
Kür Dili *Azerbaijan* 39°3N 49°13E **105** C13
Kura = Kür → *Azerbaijan* 39°29N 49°15E **105** C13
Kuranda *Australia* 16°48S 145°35E **150** B4
Kuranga *India* 22°4N 69°10E **124** H3
Kurashiki *Japan* 34°40N 133°50E **113** G6
Kurayin *Si. Arabia* 27°39N 49°50E **129** E6
Kurayoshi *Japan* 35°26N 133°50E **113** G6
Kürchatov *Kazakhstan* 50°45N 78°32E **109** B9
Kürdämir *Azerbaijan* 40°25N 48°3E **87** K9
Kurdistan *Asia* 37°20N 43°30E **105** D10
Kurduvadi *India* 18°8N 75°29E **126** E2
Kürdzhali *Bulgaria* 41°38N 25°21E **97** E9
Kürdzhali □ *Bulgaria* 41°38N 25°21E **97** E9
Kure *Japan* 34°14N 132°32E **113** G6
Küre Dağları *Turkey* 41°48N 33°43E **104** B5
Kure I. *U.S.A.* 28°25N 178°25W **167** K4
Kuressaare *Estonia* 58°15N 22°30E **84** C2
Kurgan *Russia* 55°26N 65°18E **108** A7
Kurgan-Tyube = Qürghonteppa
Tajikistan 37°50N 68°47E **109** F7
Kurganinsk *Russia* 44°54N 40°34E **87** H5
Kurgannaya = Kurganinsk
Russia 44°54N 40°34E **87** H5
Kuri *India* 26°37N 70°43E **124** F4
Kuria Maria Is. = Ḩallāniyat,
Jazā'ir al *Oman* 17°30N 55°58E **131** D6
Kurichchi *India* 11°36N 77°35E **127** J3
Kuridala *Australia* 21°16S 140°29E **150** C3
Kurigram *Bangla.* 25°49N 89°39E **123** G16
Kurikka *Finland* 62°36N 22°24E **60** E20
Kuril Basin *Pac. Oc.* 47°0N 150°0E **54** E15
Kuril Is. = Kurilskiye Ostrova
Russia 45°0N 150°0E **107** E16
Kuril-Kamchatka Trench
Pac. Oc. 44°0N 153°0E **156** C7
Kurilsk *Russia* 45°14N 147°53E **107** E15
Kurilskiye Ostrova
Russia 45°0N 150°0E **107** E16
Kurino *Japan* 31°57N 130°43E **113** J5
Kurinskaya Kosa = Kür Dili
Azerbaijan 39°3N 49°13E **105** C13
Kurkheda *India* 20°37N 80°12E **126** D5
Kurkur *Egypt* 23°50N 32°0E **137** C3
Kurla *India* 19°4N 72°52E **124** H6
Kurlkuta ○ *Australia* 22°45S 127°45E **148** D4
Kurlovskiy *Russia* 55°25N 40°40E **86** C6
Kurnool *India* 15°45N 78°0E **127** G4
Kuro-Shima *Kagoshima,*
Japan 30°50N 129°57E **113** J4
Kuro-Shima *Okinawa,*
Japan 24°14N 124°1E **113** M2
Kuror, J. *Sudan* 20°27N 31°30E **137** C3
Kurow *N.Z.* 44°44S 170°29E **155** E5
Kurów *Poland* 51°23N 22°12E **83** G9
Kurrajong *Australia* 33°33S 150°42E **153** B9
Kurram → *Pakistan* 32°36N 71°20E **124** C4
Kurri Kurri *Australia* 32°50S 151°28E **153** B9
Kurrimine *Australia* 17°47S 146°6E **150** B4
Kurse Korhi *India* 20°14N 80°46E **126** D5
Kurseong = Karsiyang
India 26°56N 88°18E **125** F13
Kürshim *Kazakhstan* 48°34N 83°39E **109** C10
Kurshskaya Kosa △
Russia 55°7N 20°45E **82** C7
Kurshskiy Zaliv *Russia* 55°9N 21°6E **82** C8
Kurşiu Nerijos △
Lithuania 55°30N 21°6E **82** C8
Kursk *Russia* 51°42N 36°11E **85** G8
Kursk □ *Russia* 51°50N 36°10E **85** G8
Kursumlija *Serbia* 43°9N 21°19E **96** C5
Kurşumlijska Banja
Serbia 43°3N 21°11E **96** C5
Kurşunlu *Bursa, Turkey* 40°12N 29°6E **97** F13
Kurşunlu *Çankırı,*
Turkey 40°51N 33°15E **104** B5
Kurtalan *Turkey* 37°58N 41°36E **105** D9
Kurtbey *Turkey* 41°9N 26°30E **97** E10
Kurucaşile *Turkey* 41°50N 32°44E **104** A5
Kuruçay *Turkey* 39°39N 38°29E **105** C7
Kurukshetra = Thanesar
India 30°1N 76°52E **124** D7
Kuruktag *China* 41°0N 89°0E **110** C6
Kuruman *S. Africa* 27°28S 23°28E **144** C3
Kuruman → *S. Africa* 26°56S 20°39E **144** C3
Kurume *Japan* 33°15N 130°30E **113** H5
Kurunegala *Sri Lanka* 7°30N 80°23E **127** L5
Kurya *Russia* 61°42N 57°9E **106** C6
Kus Gölü *Turkey* 40°10N 27°55E **97** F11
Kuşadası *Turkey* 37°56N 27°15E **99** D9
Kuşadası Körfezi *Turkey* 37°56N 27°0E **99** D8
Kusatsu *Japan* 35°3N 135°57E **113** G7
Kusawa L. *Canada* 60°20N 136°13W **162** A1
Kusel *Germany* 49°32N 7°24E **77** F3
Kushalgarh *India* 23°10N 74°27E **124** H6

Kushalnagar *India* 12°14N 75°57E **127** H2
Kushchevskaya *Russia* 46°33N 39°35E **87** G4
Kusheriki *Nigeria* 10°33N 6°28E **139** C6
Kushikino *Japan* 31°44N 130°16E **113** J5
Kushima *Japan* 31°29N 131°14E **113** J5
Kushimoto *Japan* 33°28N 135°47E **113** H7
Kushiro *Japan* 43°0N 144°25E **112** C12
Kushiro-Gawa →
Japan 42°59N 144°23E **112** C12
Kushiro Shitsugen △
Japan 43°9N 144°26E **112** C12
Kūshk *Iran* 28°46N 56°51E **129** D8
Kushka = Serhetabat
Turkmenistan 35°20N 62°18E **129** C9
Kushnytsya *Ukraine* 48°27N 23°15E **81** B8
Kushol *India* 33°40N 76°36E **125** C7
Kushtia *Bangla.* 23°55N 89°5E **125** H16
Kuskokwim → *U.S.A.* 60°5N 162°25W **167** C7
Kuskokwim B.
U.S.A. 59°45N 162°25W **166** D7
Kuskokwim Mts.
U.S.A. 62°30N 156°0W **166** C8
Kusmi *India* 23°17N 83°55E **125** H10
Kusŏng *N. Korea* 39°59N 125°15E **115** E13
Kussharo-Ko *Japan* 43°38N 144°21E **112** C12
Kustanay = Qostanay
Kazakhstan 53°10N 63°35E **108** B6
Kut, Ko *Thailand* 11°40N 102°35E **121** G4
Kuta *Indonesia* 8°43S 115°11E **119** K18
Kütahya *Turkey* 39°30N 30°2E **99** B12
Kütahya □ *Turkey* 39°10N 29°30E **99** B11
Kutaisi *Georgia* 42°19N 42°40E **87** J6
Kutaraja = Banda Aceh
Indonesia 5°35N 95°20E **118** C1
Kutch, Gulf of = Kachchh, Gulf of
India 22°50N 69°15E **124** H3
Kutch, Rann of = Kachchh, Rann
of *India* 24°0N 70°0E **124** H4
Kutina *Croatia* 45°29N 16°48E **93** C13
Kutiyana *India* 21°36N 70°2E **124** J4
Kutjevo *Croatia* 45°23N 17°55E **80** E2
Kutkashen = Qäbälä
Azerbaijan 40°58N 47°47E **87** K8
Kutná Hora *Czech Rep.* 49°57N 15°16E **78** B8
Kutno *Poland* 52°15N 19°23E **83** F6
Kutru *India* 19°5N 80°46E **126** E5
Kutse *Botswana* 21°7S 22°16E **144** B3
Kuttabul *Australia* 21°1S 148°54E **150** b
Kutu
Dem. Rep. of the Congo 2°40S 18°11E **140** E3
Kutum *Sudan* 14°10N 24°40E **135** F10
Kúty *Slovak Rep.* 48°40N 17°3E **79** C10
Kuty *Ukraine* 48°16N 25°11E **81** B9
Kuujjuaq *Canada* 58°6N 68°15W **161** F18
Kuujjuarapik *Canada* 55°20N 77°35W **164** A4
Kuusamo *Finland* 65°57N 29°8E **60** D23
Kuusankoski *Finland* 60°55N 26°38E **84** B4
Kuvshinovo *Russia* 57°2N 34°11E **84** D8
Kuwait = Al Kuwayt
Kuwait 29°30N 48°0E **128** D5
Kuwait ■ *Asia* 29°30N 47°30E **128** D5
Kuwana *Japan* 35°5N 136°43E **113** G8
Kuwana → *India* 26°25N 83°15E **125** F10
Kuybyshev = Samara
Russia 53°8N 50°6E **86** D10
Kuybyshev *Russia* 55°27N 78°19E **106** D8
Kuybyshev *Ukraine* 47°25N 36°40E **85** J9
Kuybyshevskoye Vdkhr.
Russia 55°2N 49°30E **86** C9
Kuye He → *China* 38°23N 110°46E **114** E6
Küyeh *Iran* 38°45N 47°57E **128** B5
Kuyto, Ozero *Russia* 65°6N 31°20E **60** D24
Kuytun *China* 44°25N 85°0E **110** B3
Kuyucak *Turkey* 37°55N 28°39E **99** D10
Kuyumba *Russia* 60°58N 96°59E **107** C10
Kuzey Anadolu Dağları
Turkey 41°30N 35°0E **104** B7
Kuzhitturai *India* 8°18N 77°11E **127** L3
Kuzmin *Serbia* 45°2N 19°25E **80** E4
Kuznetsk *Russia* 53°12N 46°40E **86** D8
Kuzomen *Russia* 66°22N 36°50E **106** C4
Kvænangen *Norway* 70°5N 21°15E **60** A19
Kværndrup *Denmark* 55°10N 10°31E **63** A4
Kvänum *Sweden* 58°18N 13°11E **63** F7
Kvaløya *Norway* 69°40N 18°30E **62** B17
Kvaløya *Norway* 58°18N 13°11E **62** A17
Kvareli = Qvareli
Georgia 41°57N 45°47E **87** K7
Kvarner *Croatia* 44°50N 14°10E **93** D11
Kvarnerič *Croatia* 44°43N 14°37E **93** D11
Kvicksund *Sweden* 59°27N 16°19E **62** E10
Kvillsfors *Sweden* 57°24N 15°29E **63** G9
Kvismare kanal *Sweden* 59°10N 15°29E **62** E9
Kvissleby *Sweden* 62°18N 17°22E **62** B11
Kvitøya *Svalbard* 80°0N 32°35E **57** A14
Kwabhaca *S. Africa* 30°51S 29°0E **145** D4
Kwai = Khwae Noi →
Thailand 14°1N 99°32E **120** E2
Kwajalein *Marshall Is.* 9°5N 167°20E **156** G8
Kwakhanai *Botswana* 21°39S 21°16E **144** B3
Kwakoegron *Surinam* 5°12N 55°25W **187** B7
Kwale *Kenya* 4°15S 39°31E **142** C4
Kwale *Nigeria* 5°46N 6°26E **138** D6
KwaMashu *S. Africa* 29°45S 30°58E **145** D5
Kwando → *Africa* 18°27S 23°32E **144** A3
Kwangchow = Guangzhou
China 23°6N 113°13E **117** F9
Kwangdaeri *N. Korea* 40°34N 127°33E **115** D14
Kwango →
Dem. Rep. of the Congo 3°14S 17°22E **140** E3
Kwangsi-Chuang = Guangxi
Zhuangzu Zizhiqu □
China 24°0N 109°0E **116** F7
Kwangtung = Guangdong □
China 23°0N 113°0E **117** F9
Kwara □ *Nigeria* 8°45N 4°30E **138** D6
Kwataboahegan →
Canada 51°9N 80°50W **164** B3
Kwatisore *Indonesia* 3°18S 134°50E **119** E8
KwaZulu Natal □
S. Africa 29°0S 30°0E **145** C5
Kweichow = Guizhou □
China 27°0N 107°0E **116** D5
Kwekwe *Zimbabwe* 18°58S 29°48E **143** F2
Kwemg
Botswana 24°4S 25°12E **144** C3
Kwidzyn *Poland* 53°44N 18°55E **82** E5
Kwilu →
Dem. Rep. of the Congo 3°22S 17°22E **140** E3
Kwinana *Australia* 32°15S 115°47E **149** F2
Kwisa → *Poland* 51°34N 15°24E **83** G2

Kwoka *Indonesia* 0°31S 132°27E **119** E8
Kwolla *Nigeria* 9°0N 9°15E **139** D6
Kwun Tong *China* 22°19N 114°13E **111** a
Kyabra Cr. →
  Australia 25°36S 142°55E **151** D3
Kyabram *Australia* 36°19S 145°4E **153** D6
Kyaikto *Burma* 17°20N 97°3E **120** D1
Kyaing Tong = Keng Tung
  Burma 21°18N 99°39E **120** B2
Kyakhta *Russia* 50°30N 106°25E **107** D11
Kyambura △ *Uganda* 0°7S 30°9E **142** C3
Kyancutta *Australia* 33°8S 135°33E **151** E2
Kyaukpadaung *Burma* 20°52N 95°8E **123** J19
Kyaukpyu *Burma* 19°28N 93°30E **123** K18
Kyaukse *Burma* 21°36N 96°10E **123** J20
Kybartai *Lithuania* 54°39N 22°45E **82** D9
Kyburz *U.S.A.* 38°47N 120°18W **190** G6
Kyelang *India* 32°35N 77°2E **124** C7
Kyenjojo *Uganda* 0°40N 30°37E **142** B3
Kyjov *Czech Rep.* 49°1N 17°7E **79** B10
Kyklades *Greece* 37°0N 24°30E **98** E6
Kyle *Canada* 50°50N 108°2W **163** C7
Kyle *U.S.A.* 29°59N 97°53W **176** G6
Kyle Dam *Zimbabwe* 20°15S 31°0E **143** G3
Kyle of Lochalsh *U.K.* 57°17N 5°44W **65** D3
Kyll → *Germany* 49°48N 6°41E **77** F2
Kyllburg *Germany* 50°2N 6°34E **77** E2
Kyllini *Greece* 37°55N 21°8E **98** D3
Kymijoki → *Finland* 60°30N 26°55E **84** B4
Kymmene älv = Kymijoki →
  Finland 60°30N 26°55E **84** B4
Kyneton *Australia* 37°10S 144°29E **152** D6
Kynuna *Australia* 21°37S 141°55E **150** C3
Kyō-ga-Saki *Japan* 35°45N 135°15E **113** G7
Kyoga, L. *Uganda* 1°35N 33°0E **142** B3
Kyogle *Australia* 28°40S 153°0E **151** D5
Kyŏngju = Gyeongju
  S. Korea 35°51N 129°14E **115** G15
Kyŏngsŏng *N. Korea* 41°35N 129°36E **115** D15
Kyonpyaw *Burma* 17°12N 95°10E **123** L19
Kyōto *Japan* 35°0N 135°45E **113** G7
Kyōto □ *Japan* 35°15N 135°45E **113** G7
Kyparissovouno
  Cyprus 35°19N 33°10E **101** D12
Kyperounda *Cyprus* 34°56N 32°58E **101** E11
Kypros = Cyprus ■ *Asia* 35°0N 33°0E **101** L12
Kyrenia *Cyprus* 35°20N 33°20E **101** D12
Kyrgyzstan ■ *Asia* 42°0N 75°0E **109** D9
Kyritz *Germany* 52°56N 12°24E **76** C8
Kyrkhult *Sweden* 56°22N 14°34E **63** H8
Kyrnasivka *Ukraine* 48°35N 28°58E **81** D15
Kyrnychky *Ukraine* 45°42N 29°4E **81** E14
Kyro älv = Kyrönjoki →
  Finland 63°14N 21°45E **60** E19
Kyrönjoki → *Finland* 63°14N 21°45E **60** E19
Kystatyam *Russia* 67°20N 123°10E **107** C13
Kysucké Nové Mesto
  Slovak Rep. 49°18N 18°47E **79** B11
Kytay, Ozero *Ukraine* 45°40N 29°13E **81** E14
Kythira *Greece* 36°8N 23°0E **98** E5
Kythnos *Greece* 37°26N 24°27E **98** D6
Kythréa *Cyprus* 35°15N 33°29E **101** D12
Kyunhla *Burma* 23°25N 95°15E **123** H19
Kyuquot Sound
  Canada 50°2N 127°22W **162** D3
Kyurdamir = Kürdämir
  Azerbaijan 40°25N 48°3E **87** K9
Kyūshū *Japan* 33°0N 131°0E **113** H5
Kyūshū □ *Japan* 33°0N 131°0E **113** H5
Kyūshū-Palau Ridge
  Pac. Oc. 20°0N 136°0E **156** E5
Kyūshū-Sanchi *Japan* 32°35N 131°17E **113** H5
Kyustendil *Bulgaria* 42°16N 22°41E **96** D6
Kyustendil □ *Bulgaria* 42°16N 22°41E **96** D6
Kyusyur *Russia* 70°19N 127°30E **107** B13
Kywong *Australia* 34°58S 146°44E **153** C7
Kyyiv *Ukraine* 50°30N 30°28E **75** C16
Kyyiv □ *Ukraine* 50°5N 30°45E **85** G6
Kyyivske Vdskh.
  Ukraine 51°0N 30°16E **75** C16
Kyzyl *Russia* 51°50N 94°30E **109** B12
Kyzyl-Adyr *Kyrgyzstan* 42°39N 71°35E **109** D8
Kyzyl Kum *Uzbekistan* 42°30N 65°0E **109** D7
Kyzyl-Kyya *Kyrgyzstan* 40°16N 72°8E **109** D8
Kyzyl Orda = Qyzylorda
  Kazakhstan 44°48N 65°28E **108** D7
Kyzyl-Suu *Kyrgyzstan* 42°20N 78°0E **109** D9

L

La Albuera *Spain* 38°45N 6°49W **89** G4
La Alcarria *Spain* 40°31N 2°45W **90** E2
La Almarcha *Spain* 39°41N 2°24W **90** F2
La Almunia de Doña Godina
  Spain 41°29N 1°23W **90** D3
La Amistad △
  Cent. Amer. 9°28N 83°18W **182** E3
La Asunción *Venezuela* 11°2N 63°51W **186** A6
La Baie *Canada* 48°19N 70°53W **165** C5
La Banda *Argentina* 27°45S 64°10W **190** B3
La Bañeza *Spain* 42°17N 5°54W **88** C5
La Barca *Mexico* 20°17N 102°34W **180** C4
La Barge *U.S.A.* 42°16N 110°12W **168** E8
La Barra *Nic.* 12°54N 83°33W **182** D3
La Bastide-Puylaurent
  France 44°35N 3°52E **73** D7
La Baule *France* 47°17N 2°24W **70** E4
La Belle *U.S.A.* 26°46N 81°26W **179** J8
La Biche → *Canada* 59°57N 123°50W **162** B4
La Biche, L. *Canada* 54°50N 112°3W **162** C6
La Bisbal d'Empordà *Spain* 41°58N 3°2E **92** D8
La Brea *Peru* 4°40S 81°7W **188** A1
La Brea *Trin. & Tob.* 10°15N 61°37W **187** K15
La Brède *France* 44°41N 0°32W **72** D3
La Bresse *France* 48°2N 6°53E **71** D13
La Bureba *Spain* 42°36N 3°24W **88** C1
La Calera *Chile* 32°50S 71°10W **190** C1
La Campana △ *Chile* 32°58S 71°14W **190** C1
La Campiña *Spain* 37°45N 4°45W **89** H6
La Canal = Sa Canal
  Spain 38°51N 1°23E **100** C7
La Cañiza = A Cañiza
  Spain 42°13N 8°16W **88** C2
La Canourgue *France* 44°26N 3°13E **72** D7
La Capelle *France* 49°59N 3°50E **71** C10
La Carlota *Argentina* 33°30S 63°20W **190** C3
La Carlota *Spain* 37°40N 4°56W **89** H6
La Carolina *Spain* 38°17N 3°38W **89** G7
La Cavalerie *France* 44°1N 3°10E **72** D7
La Ceiba *Honduras* 15°40N 86°50W **182** C2

La Chaise-Dieu *France* 45°18N 3°42E **72** C7
La Chapelle d'Angillon
  France 47°21N 2°25E **71** E9
La Chapelle-St-Luc
  France 48°20N 4°3E **71** D11
La Chapelle-sur-Erdre
  France 47°18N 1°34W **70** E5
La Charité-sur-Loire
  France 47°10N 3°1E **71** E10
La Chartre-sur-le-Loir
  France 47°44N 0°34E **70** E7
La Châtaigneraie *France* 46°39N 0°44E **72** B3
La Châtre *France* 46°35N 2°0E **71** F9
La Chaux-de-Fonds *Switz.* 47°7N 6°50E **77** H2
La Chorrera *Panama* 8°53N 79°47W **182** E4
La Ciotat *France* 43°10N 5°37E **73** E9
La Clayette *France* 46°17N 4°19E **71** F11
La Cocha *Argentina* 27°50S 65°40W **190** B2
La Concepción *Panama* 8°31N 82°37W **182** E3
La Concordia *Mexico* 16°5N 92°38W **181** D6
La Coruña = A Coruña
  Spain 43°20N 8°25W **88** B2
La Côte-St-André *France* 45°24N 5°15E **73** C9
La Courtine *France* 45°41N 2°15E **72** C6
La Crau *Bouches-du-Rhône,*
  France 43°32N 4°40E **73** E8
La Crau *Var, France* 43°9N 6°4E **73** E10
La Crescent *U.S.A.* 43°50N 91°18W **172** D8
La Crete *Canada* 58°11N 116°24W **162** B5
La Crosse *Fla., U.S.A.* 29°51N 82°24W **178** F7
La Crosse *Kans., U.S.A.* 38°32N 99°18W **172** F4
La Crosse *Wis., U.S.A.* 43°48N 91°15W **172** D8
La Cruz *Costa Rica* 11°4N 85°39W **182** D2
La Cruz *Mexico* 23°55N 106°54W **180** C3
La Désirade *Guadeloupe* 16°18N 61°3W **182** b
La Digue *Seychelles* 4°20S 55°51E **141** b
La Esperanza *Argentina* 40°26S 68°42W **192** B3
La Esperanza *Cuba* 22°46N 83°44W **182** B3
La Esperanza *Honduras* 14°15N 88°10W **182** D2
La Estrada = A Estrada
  Spain 42°43N 8°27W **88** C2
La Fayette *U.S.A.* 34°42N 85°17W **177** D12
La Fé *Cuba* 22°2N 84°15W **182** B3
La Fère *France* 49°39N 3°21E **71** C10
La Ferté-Bernard *France* 48°10N 0°40E **70** D7
La Ferté-Gaucher *France* 48°47N 3°19E **71** D10
La Ferté-Macé *France* 48°35N 0°22W **70** D6
La Ferté-St-Aubin *France* 47°42N 1°57E **71** E8
La Ferté-sous-Jouarre
  France 48°56N 3°8E **71** D10
La Ferté-Vidame *France* 48°37N 0°53E **70** D7
La Flèche *France* 47°42N 0°4W **70** E6
La Follette *U.S.A.* 36°23N 84°7W **177** C12
La Fregeneda *Spain* 40°58N 6°54W **88** E4
La Fuente de San Esteban
  Spain 40°49N 6°15W **88** E4
La Gacilly *France* 47°45N 2°9W **70** E4
La Gi *Vietnam* 10°40N 107°45E **121** G6
La Gineta *Spain* 39°8N 1°59W **91** F2
La Goulette *Tunisia* 36°53N 10°18E **94** F3
La Grand'Combe *France* 44°13N 4°2E **73** D8
La Grande → *U.S.A.* 45°20N 118°5W **168** D4
La Grande → *Canada* 53°50N 79°0W **164** B5
La Grande 3, Rés.
  Canada 53°40N 75°10W **164** B4
La Grande 4, Rés.
  Canada 54°0N 73°15W **164** B5
La Grande-Motte *France* 43°23N 4°5E **73** E8
La Grange *Calif.,*
  U.S.A. 37°42N 120°27W **170** H6
La Grange *Ga., U.S.A.* 33°2N 85°2W **178** B4
La Grange *Ky., U.S.A.* 38°24N 85°22W **173** F11
La Grange *Tex., U.S.A.* 29°54N 96°52W **176** G6
La Grave *France* 45°3N 6°18E **73** C10
La Guaira *Venezuela* 10°36N 66°56W **186** A5
La Guardia = A Guarda
  Spain 41°56N 8°52W **88** D2
La Gudiña = A Gudiña
  Spain 42°4N 7°8W **88** C3
La Guerche-de-Bretagne
  France 47°57N 1°16W **70** E5
La Guerche-sur-l'Aubois
  France 46°58N 2°56E **71** F9
La Habana *Cuba* 23°8N 82°22W **182** B3
La Haute Vallée de Chevreuse
  France 48°43N 1°58E **71** D8
La Haye-du-Puits *France* 49°17N 1°33W **70** C5
La Horra *Spain* 41°44N 3°53W **88** D7
La Independencia
  Mexico 16°15N 92°1W **181** D6
La Isabela *Dom. Rep.* 19°58N 71°2W **183** C5
La Jonquera *Spain* 42°25N 2°53E **90** C7
La Joya *Peru* 16°35N 71°52W **188** D3
La Junta *U.S.A.* 37°59N 103°33W **168** H12
La Laguna *Canary Is.* 28°28N 16°18W **100** F3
La Libertad = Puerto Libertad
  Mexico 29°55N 112°43W **180** B2
La Libertad *Guatemala* 16°47N 90°7W **182** C1
La Libertad *Peru* 8°0S 78°30W **188** B2
La Ligua *Chile* 32°30S 71°16W **190** C1
La Línea de la Concepción
  Spain 36°15N 5°23W **89** J5
La Loche *Canada* 56°29N 109°26W **163** B7
La Londe-les-Maures
  France 43°8N 6°14E **73** E10
La Lora *Spain* 42°45N 4°0W **88** C7
La Loupe *France* 48°29N 1°0E **70** D8
La Louvière *Belgium* 50°27N 4°10E **69** D4
La Lune *Trin. & Tob.* 10°27N 61°32W **187** K15
La Machine *France* 46°54N 3°27E **71** F10
La Maddalena *Italy* 41°13N 9°24E **94** A2
La Malbaie *Canada* 47°40N 70°10W **165** C5
La Malinche △ *Mexico* 19°14N 98°3W **181** D5
La Mancha *Spain* 39°10N 2°54W **91** F2
La Mariña *Spain* 43°30N 7°40W **88** B3
La Martre, L. *Canada* 63°15N 117°55W **162** A5
La Merced *Peru* 11°3S 75°19W **188** C2
La Mercy = Durban ✕ (DIA)
  S. Africa 29°37S 31°7E **145** C5
La Mesa *Mexico* 32°6N 116°30W **180** A1
La Mesa *U.S.A.* 32°46N 117°1W **171** N9
La Mesilla *U.S.A.* 32°16N 106°48W **169** K10
La Mothe-Achard *France* 46°37N 1°40W **70** F5
La Motte-Chalançon
  France 44°30N 5°21E **73** D9
La Motte-du-Caire *France* 44°20N 6°3E **73** D10
La Motte-Servolex *France* 45°35N 5°53E **73** C9
La Moure *U.S.A.* 46°21N 98°18W **172** B4
La Muela *Spain* 41°36N 1°7W **90** D3
La Mure *France* 44°54N 5°48E **73** D9

La Negra *Chile* 23°46S 70°18W **190** A1
La Oliva *Canary Is.* 28°36N 13°57W **100** F6
La Oraya *Peru* 11°32S 75°54W **188** C2
La Orotava *Canary Is.* 28°22N 16°31W **100** F3
La Oroya *Peru* 11°32S 75°54W **188** C2
La Pacaudière *France* 46°11N 3°52E **71** F10
La Palma *Canary Is.* 28°40N 17°50W **100** F2
La Palma *Panama* 8°15N 78°0W **182** E4
La Palma del Condado
  Spain 37°21N 6°38W **89** H4
La Palmyre *France* 45°43N 1°9W **72** C2
La Paloma *Chile* 30°35S 71°0W **190** C1
La Pampa □ *Argentina* 36°50S 66°0W **190** D2
La Paragua *Venezuela* 6°50N 63°20W **186** B6
La Paz *Entre Ríos,*
  Argentina 30°50S 59°45W **190** C4
La Paz *San Luis,*
  Argentina 33°30S 67°20W **190** C2
La Paz *Bolivia* 16°20S 68°10W **188** D4
La Paz *Honduras* 14°20N 87°47W **182** D2
La Paz *Mexico* 24°10N 110°18W **180** C2
La Paz □ *Bolivia* 15°30S 68°0W **188** D4
La Paz Centro *Nic.* 12°20N 86°41W **182** D2
La Pedrera *Colombia* 1°18S 69°43W **186** D5
La Pérade *Canada* 46°35N 72°12W **165** C5
La Perla *Mexico* 28°18N 104°32W **180** B4
La Perouse Str. *Asia* 45°40N 142°0E **112** B11
La Pesca *Mexico* 23°46N 97°47W **181** C5
La Piedad *Mexico* 20°21N 102°0W **180** C4
La Pine *U.S.A.* 43°40N 121°30W **168** E3
La Plata *Argentina* 35°0S 57°55W **190** D4
La Plata, L. *Argentina* 44°55S 71°50W **192** B2
La Pobla de Lillet *Spain* 42°16N 1°59E **90** C6
La Pobla de Segur *Spain* 42°15N 0°58E **90** C6
La Pocatière *France* 47°22N 70°2W **165** C5
La Pola de Gordón *Spain* 42°51N 5°41W **88** C5
La Porta *France* 42°25N 9°21E **73** F13
La Porte *U.S.A.* 29°40N 95°1W **176** G7
La Presanella *Italy* 46°13N 10°40E **92** B7
La Puebla = Sa Pobla
  Spain 39°46N 3°1E **90** F8
La Puebla de Cazalla
  Spain 37°10N 5°20W **89** H5
La Puebla de los Infantes
  Spain 37°47N 5°24W **89** H5
La Puebla de Montalbán
  Spain 39°52N 4°22W **88** F6
La Puebla del Río *Spain* 37°16N 6°3W **89** H4
La Puerta de Segura
  Spain 38°22N 2°45W **89** G8
La Purísima *Mexico* 26°10N 112°4W **180** B2
La Push *U.S.A.* 47°55N 124°38W **170** C2
La Quiaca *Argentina* 22°5S 65°35W **190** A2
La Réole *France* 44°35N 0°1W **72** D3
La Restinga *Canary Is.* 27°38N 17°59W **100** G2
La Rinconada *Peru* 14°38S 69°27W **188** D4
La Rioja *Argentina* 29°20S 67°0W **190** B2
La Rioja □ *Argentina* 29°30S 67°0W **190** B2
La Rioja □ *Spain* 42°20N 2°20W **88** C2
La Robla *Spain* 42°50N 5°41W **88** C5
La Roche-Bernard
  France 47°31N 2°19W **70** E4
La Roche-Canillac *France* 45°12N 1°57E **72** C5
La Roche-en-Ardenne
  Belgium 50°11N 5°35E **69** D5
La Roche-sur-Foron
  France 46°4N 6°19E **71** F13
La Roche-sur-Yon
  France 46°40N 1°25W **70** F5
La Rochefoucauld *France* 45°44N 0°24E **72** C4
La Rochelle *France* 46°10N 1°9W **72** B2
La Roda *Spain* 39°13N 2°15W **91** F2
La Roda de Andalucía
  Spain 37°12N 4°46W **89** H6
La Romaine *Canada* 50°13N 60°40W **165** B7
La Romana *Dom. Rep.* 18°27N 68°57W **183** C6
La Ronge *Canada* 55°5N 105°20W **163** B7
La Rumorosa *Mexico* 32°34N 116°6W **171** N10
La Sabina = Sa Savina
  Spain 38°44N 1°25E **100** C7
La Sagra *Spain* 37°57N 2°35W **91** H2
La Salle *U.S.A.* 41°20N 89°6W **172** E9
La Sanabria *Spain* 42°0N 6°30W **88** D4
La Santa *Canary Is.* 29°5N 13°40W **100** E6
La Sarre *Canada* 48°45N 79°15W **164** C4
La Scie *Canada* 49°57N 55°36W **165** C8
La Selva *Spain* 41°21N 0°11E **90** D6
La Selva Beach *U.S.A.* 36°56N 121°51W **170** J5
La Selva del Camp *Spain* 41°13N 1°8E **90** D6
La Serena *Chile* 29°55S 71°10W **190** B1
La Serena *Spain* 38°45N 5°40W **89** G5
La Seu d'Urgell *Spain* 42°22N 1°23E **90** C6
La Seyne-sur-Mer *France* 43°7N 5°52E **73** E9
La Sila *Italy* 39°15N 16°35E **95** C9
La Solana *Spain* 38°59N 3°14W **89** G7
La Soufrière *St. Vincent* 13°20N 61°11W **183** D7
La Souterraine *France* 46°15N 1°30E **71** F8
La Spézia *Italy* 44°7N 9°50E **92** D6
La Suze-sur-Sarthe *France* 47°53N 0°2E **70** E6
La Tagua *Colombia* 0°3N 74°40W **186** C4
La Teste-de-Buch *France* 44°37N 1°8W **72** D2
La Tortuga, I. *Venezuela* 11°0N 65°22W **183** D6
La Tour-du-Pin *France* 45°33N 5°27E **73** C9
La Tranche-sur-Mer
  France 46°20N 1°27W **70** F5
La Tremblade *France* 45°46N 1°8W **72** C2
La Trinité *Martinique* 14°45N 60°58W **182** c
La Tuque *Canada* 47°30N 72°50W **165** C5
La Unión *Chile* 40°10S 73°0W **192** B2
La Unión *El Salv.* 13°20N 87°50W **182** D2
La Unión *Spain* 37°38N 0°53W **91** H4
La Urbana *Venezuela* 7°8N 66°56W **186** B5
La Vache Pt.
  Trin. & Tob. 10°47N 61°28W **187** K15
La Vall d'Uixó *Spain* 39°49N 0°15W **90** F4
La Vecilla *Spain* 42°51N 5°27W **88** C5
La Vega *Dom. Rep.* 19°20N 70°30W **183** C5
La Vega *Peru* 10°41S 77°44W **188** C2
La Vela de Coro
  Venezuela 11°27N 69°34W **186** A5
La Veleta *Spain* 37°1N 3°22W **89** H7
La Venta *Mexico* 18°5N 94°3W **181** D6
La Vergne *U.S.A.* 36°1N 86°35W **177** C11
La Villa Joiosa = Villajoyosa
  Spain 38°30N 0°12W **91** G4
La Voulte-sur-Rhône
  France 44°48N 4°46E **73** D8
Laa an der Thaya
  Austria 48°43N 16°23E **79** C9

Laaber, Grosse →
  Germany 48°55N 12°30E **77** G8
Laage *Germany* 53°55N 12°21E **76** B8
Laascaanood = Las Anod
  Somalia 8°26N 47°19E **131** F4
Laatzen *Germany* 52°19N 9°48E **76** C5
Laba → *Russia* 45°11N 39°42E **87** H4
Labasa *Fiji* 16°30S 179°27E **154** a
Labastide-Murat *France* 44°39N 1°33E **72** D5
Labastide-Rouairoux
  France 43°28N 2°39E **72** E6
Labbézenga *Mali* 15°2N 0°48E **139** B5
Labdah = Leptis Magna
  Libya 32°40N 14°12E **135** B8
Labe = Elbe → *Europe* 53°50N 9°0E **76** B4
Labé *Guinea* 11°24N 12°16W **138** C2
Laberge, L. *Canada* 61°11N 135°12W **162** A1
Labin *Croatia* 45°5N 14°8E **93** C11
Labinsk *Russia* 44°40N 40°48E **87** H5
Labis *Malaysia* 2°22N 103°2E **121** L4
Łabiszyn *Poland* 52°57N 17°54E **83** F4
Laboe *Germany* 54°24N 10°13E **76** A6
Laborec → *Slovak Rep.* 48°37N 21°58E **79** C14
Laborie *St. Lucia* 13°45N 61°2W **183** f
Labouheyre *France* 44°13N 0°55W **72** D3
Laboulaye *Argentina* 34°10S 63°30W **190** C3
Labrador *Canada* 53°20N 61°0W **165** B7
Labrador City *Canada* 52°57N 66°55W **165** B6
Labrador Sea *Atl. Oc.* 57°0N 54°0W **161** F21
Lábrea *Brazil* 7°15S 64°51W **186** E6
Labruguière *France* 43°31N 2°16E **72** E6
Labuan □ *Malaysia* 5°20N 115°12E **118** C4
Labuha *Indonesia* 0°30S 127°30E **119** E7
Labuhan *Indonesia* 6°22S 105°50E **119** G11
Labuhanbajo *Indonesia* 8°28S 119°54E **119** F6
Labuhanbilik *Indonesia* 2°31N 100°10E **121** L3
Labuk, Telok *Malaysia* 6°10N 117°50E **118** C5
Labyrinth, L. *Australia* 30°40S 135°11E **151** E2
Labytnangi *Russia* 66°39N 66°21E **106** C7
Laç *Albania* 41°38N 19°43E **96** E3
Lac-Bouchette *Canada* 48°16N 72°11W **165** C5
Lac-Édouard *Canada* 47°40N 72°16W **165** C5
Lac La Biche *Canada* 54°45N 111°58W **162** C6
Lac La Martre = Wha Ti
  Canada 63°8N 117°16W **160** E8
Lac La Ronge △
  Canada 55°9N 104°41W **163** B7
Lac-Mégantic *Canada* 45°35N 70°53W **165** C5
Lac Thien *Vietnam* 12°25N 108°11E **120** F7
Lacanau *France* 44°58N 1°5W **72** D2
Lacanau, L. de *France* 44°58N 1°7W **72** D2
Lacantún → *Mexico* 16°36N 90°39W **181** D6
Lácara → *Spain* 38°55N 6°25W **89** G4
Lacaune *France* 43°43N 2°40E **72** E6
Lacaune, Mts. de *France* 43°43N 2°50E **72** E6
Laccadive Is. = Lakshadweep Is.
  India 10°0N 72°30E **127** J1
Lacepede B. *Australia* 36°40S 139°40E **152** D3
Lacepede Is. *Australia* 16°55S 122°0E **148** C3
Lacerdónia *Mozam.* 18°3S 35°35E **143** F4
Lacey *U.S.A.* 47°7N 122°49W **170** C4
Lachania *Greece* 35°58N 27°54E **101** D9
Lachay, Pta. *Peru* 11°17S 77°44W **188** C2
Lachhmangarh *India* 27°50N 75°4E **124** F6
Lachi *Pakistan* 33°25N 71°20E **124** C4
Lachine *Canada* 45°26N 73°42W **164** C5
Lachlan → *Australia* 34°22S 143°55E **152** C5
Lachoc *Peru* 12°50S 75°6W **188** C2
Lachute *Canada* 45°39N 74°21W **164** C5
Laçın *Azerbaijan* 39°38N 46°33E **105** C12
Lackagh Hills *Ireland* 54°16N 8°10W **64** B3
Lackawanna *U.S.A.* 42°50N 78°50W **174** D6
Lackawaxen *U.S.A.* 41°29N 74°59W **175** E10
Lacolle *Canada* 45°5N 73°22W **175** A11
Lacombe *Canada* 52°30N 113°44W **162** C6
Lacona *U.S.A.* 43°39N 76°10W **175** C8
Láconi *Italy* 39°54N 9°4E **94** C2
Laconia = Lakonia
  Greece 36°55N 22°30E **98** E4
Laconia *U.S.A.* 43°32N 71°28W **175** C13
Lacoochee *U.S.A.* 28°28N 82°11W **179** G7
Lacq *France* 43°25N 0°35W **72** E3
Lacs □ *Ivory C.* 6°50N 5°0W **138** D3
Ladakh Ra. *India* 34°0N 78°0E **125** C8
Lądek-Zdrój *Poland* 50°21N 16°53E **83** H3
Lādīk *Turkey* 40°57N 35°58E **104** B6
Ladismith *S. Africa* 33°28S 21°15E **144** D3
Ladispoli *Italy* 41°56N 12°5E **94** D5
Lādīz *Iran* 28°55N 61°15E **129** D9
Ladnun *India* 27°38N 74°25E **124** F6
Ladoga, L. = Ladozhskoye Ozero
  Russia 61°15N 30°30E **84** B6
Ladonas → *Greece* 37°40N 21°50E **98** D3
Ladozhskoye Ozero
  Russia 61°15N 30°30E **84** B6
Ladrillero, G. *Chile* 49°20S 75°35W **192** C1
Ladson *U.S.A.* 32°59N 80°6W **178** C9
Ladushkin *Russia* 54°34N 20°10E **82** D7
Lady Elliott I. *Australia* 24°7S 152°42E **150** C5
Lady Frere *S. Africa* 31°42S 27°14E **144** D4
Lady Grey *S. Africa* 30°43S 27°13E **144** D4
Lady Lake *U.S.A.* 28°55N 81°55W **179** G8
Ladybrand *S. Africa* 29°9S 27°29E **144** C4
Ladysmith *Canada* 49°0N 123°49W **170** B3
Ladysmith *S. Africa* 28°32S 29°46E **145** C4
Ladysmith *U.S.A.* 45°28N 91°12W **172** C8
Ladyzhyn *Ukraine* 48°40N 29°15E **81** B14
Lae *Papua N. G.* 6°40S 147°2E **147** B7
Laem Ngop *Thailand* 12°10N 102°26E **121** F4
Laem Son △ *Thailand* 9°29N 98°24E **121** H2
Laerma *Greece* 36°9N 27°57E **101** D9
Læsø *Denmark* 57°15N 11°5E **63** G5
Læso Rende *Denmark* 57°20N 10°45E **63** G4
Lafayette *Ala., U.S.A.* 32°54N 85°24W **178** C4
Lafayette *Colo., U.S.A.* 39°59N 105°6W **168** G11
Lafayette *La., U.S.A.* 30°14N 92°1W **176** F8
Lafayette *Tenn., U.S.A.* 36°31N 86°2W **177** C11
Laferte → *Canada* 61°53N 117°44W **162** A5
Lafia *Nigeria* 8°30N 8°34E **139** D6
Lafiagi *Nigeria* 8°52N 5°20E **139** D6
Lafkos *Greece* 39°9N 23°14E **98** B5
Lafleche *Canada* 49°45N 106°40W **163** D7
Laful *India* 7°10N 93°52E **127** L11
Lagan *Sweden* 56°56N 13°58E **63** H7
Lagan → *U.K.* 54°36N 5°55W **64** B6
Lagarfljót → *Iceland* 65°40N 14°18W **60** D6
Lagarto *Brazil* 10°54S 37°41W **189** D12
Lagdo, L. de *Cameroon* 8°40N 14°0E **135** G7
Lage *Germany* 51°59N 8°48E **76** D4

Lågen → *Oppland,*
  Norway 61°8N 10°25E **60** F14
Lågen → *Vestfold, Norway* 59°3N 10°3E **61** G14
Lägerdorf *Germany* 53°53N 9°34E **76** B5
Lages *Brazil* 27°48S 50°0W **191** C5
Laghouat *Algeria* 33°50N 2°59E **136** B4
Laghouat □ *Algeria* 33°35N 2°40E **136** B4
Lagnieu *France* 45°55N 5°20E **73** C9
Lagny-sur-Marne *France* 48°52N 2°44E **71** D9
Lago *Italy* 39°10N 16°9E **95** C9
Lake District □ *U.K.* 54°30N 3°21W
Lago de Sanabria y Entorno △
  Spain 42°9N 6°45W **88** C4
Lago Posadas
  Argentina 47°30S 71°40W **192** C2
Lago Puela △
  Argentina 42°1N 71°55W **192** B2
Lago Ranco *Chile* 40°19S 72°30W **192** B2
Lagôa *Portugal* 37°8N 8°27W **89** H2
Lagoa do Peixe △
  Brazil 31°12S 50°55W **191** C5
Lagoa Vermelha *Brazil* 28°13S 51°32W **191** C5
Lagoaça *Portugal* 41°11N 6°44W **88** D4
Lagodekhi *Georgia* 41°50N 46°22E **87** H8
Lagónegro *Italy* 40°8N 15°45E **95** B8
Lagonoy G. *Phil.* 13°50N 123°50E **119** E6
Lagos *Greece* 41°1N 25°6E **97** E9
Lagos *Nigeria* 6°25N 3°27E **139** D5
Lagos *Portugal* 37°5N 8°41W **89** H2
Lagos □ *Nigeria* 6°28N 3°25E **139** D5
Lagos de Moreno
  Mexico 21°21N 101°55W **180** C4
Lagrange = Bidyadanga
  Australia 18°45S 121°43E **148** C3
Lagrange B. *Australia* 18°38S 121°42E **148** C3
Laguardia *Spain* 42°35N 2°35W **90** C2
Laguépie *France* 44°8N 1°57E **72** D5
Laguna *Brazil* 28°30S 48°50W **191** B6
Laguna *U.S.A.* 35°2N 107°25W **169** J10
Laguna, Sa. de la
  Mexico 23°35N 109°55W **180** C3
Laguna Beach *U.S.A.* 33°33N 117°47W **171** M9
Laguna Blanca △
  Argentina 39°0S 70°5W **192** A2
Laguna de Duero *Spain* 41°35N 4°43W **88** D6
Laguna de la Restinga △
  Venezuela 10°58N 64°0W **183** D6
Laguna de Lachuá △
  Guatemala 15°55N 90°40W **182** C1
Laguna del Laja △
  Chile 37°27S 71°20W **190** D1
Laguna del Tigre △
  Guatemala 17°32N 90°56W **182** C1
Laguna Limpia
  Argentina 26°32S 59°45W **190** B4
Laguna San Rafael △
  Chile 46°54S 73°31W **192** C2
Lagunas *Peru* 5°10S 75°35W **188** B2
Lagunas de Chacahua △
  Mexico 16°0N 97°43W **181** D5
Lagunas de Montebello △
  Mexico 16°4N 91°42W **181** D6
Lagunas de Ruidera △
  Spain 38°57N 2°52W **91** G2
Lagunes □ *Ivory C.* 5°30N 4°0W **138** D4
Lahad Datu *Malaysia* 5°0N 118°20E **119** D5
Lahad Datu, Telok
  Malaysia 4°50N 118°20E **119** D5
Lahan Sai *Thailand* 14°25N 102°52E **120** E4
Lahanam *Laos* 16°16N 105°16E **120** D5
Lahar *India* 26°12N 78°57E **125** F8
Laharpur *India* 27°43N 80°56E **125** F9
Lahat *Indonesia* 3°45S 103°30E **118** E2
Lahewa *Indonesia* 1°22N 97°12E **118** C1
Lāhījān *Iran* 37°10N 50°6E **129** B6
Lahn → *Germany* 50°19N 7°37E **77** E3
Laholm *Sweden* 56°30N 13°2E **63** H7
Laholmsbukten *Sweden* 56°30N 12°45E **63** H6
Lahore *Pakistan* 31°32N 74°22E **124** D6
Lahr *Germany* 48°20N 7°53E **77** G3
Lahri *Pakistan* 29°11N 68°13E **124** E3
Lahti *Finland* 60°58N 25°40E **84** B3
Lahtis = Lahti *Finland* 60°58N 25°40E **84** B3
Lahugala Kitulana △
  Sri Lanka 6°50N 81°40E **127** L5
Laï *Chad* 9°25N 16°18E **135** G9
Lai'an *China* 32°28N 118°30E **117** A12
Laibin *China* 23°42N 109°14E **116** F7
Laifeng *China* 29°27N 109°20E **116** C7
L'Aigle *France* 48°46N 0°38E **70** D7
Laignes *France* 47°50N 4°20E **71** E11
L'Aiguillon-sur-Mer
  France 46°20N 1°18W **72** B2
Laila = Layla *Si. Arabia* 22°10N 46°40E **131** C4
Laingsburg *S. Africa* 33°9S 20°52E **144** D3
Lainioälven → *Sweden* 67°35N 22°40E **60** C20
Lairg *U.K.* 58°2N 4°24W **65** C4
Laisamis *Kenya* 1°36N 37°48E **142** B4
Laissac *France* 44°23N 2°50E **72** D6
Láíves *Italy* 46°26N 11°20E **92** B8
Laiwu *China* 36°15N 117°40E **115** F9
Laixi *China* 36°50N 120°31E **115** F11
Laiyang *China* 36°59N 120°45E **115** F11
Laiyuan *China* 39°20N 114°40E **114** E8
Laizhou *China* 37°8N 119°57E **115** F10
Laizhou Wan *China* 37°30N 119°30E **115** F10
Lajamanu *Australia* 18°23S 130°38E **148** C5
Lajere *Nigeria* 12°10N 11°25E **139** C7
Lajes *Brazil* 5°41S 36°14W **189** D11
Lajinha *Brazil* 20°9S 41°37W **189** E12
Lajosmizse *Hungary* 47°3N 19°32E **80** C4
Lak Sao *Laos* 18°11N 104°59E **120** C5
Lakaband *Pakistan* 31°2N 69°15E **124** D3
Lakamané *Mali* 14°35N 9°40W **138** C3
Lake Alfred *U.S.A.* 28°6N 81°44W **179** G8
Lake Alpine *U.S.A.* 38°29N 120°0W **170** G7
Lake Andes *U.S.A.* 43°9N 98°32W **172** D4
Lake Arthur *U.S.A.* 30°5N 92°41W **176** G8
Lake Bindegolly △
  Australia 28°0S 144°12E **151** D3
Lake Boga *Australia* 35°26S 143°38E **153** C5
Lake Butler *U.S.A.* 30°1N 82°21W **178** F7
Lake Cargelligo
  Australia 33°15S 146°22E **153** E4
Lake Charles *U.S.A.* 30°14N 93°13W **176** F8
Lake City *Colo., U.S.A.* 38°2N 107°19W **169** G10

Lake City *Fla., U.S.A.* 30°11N 82°38W **17**...
Lake City *Mich.,*
  U.S.A. 44°20N 85°13W **17**...
Lake City *Minn., U.S.A.* 44°27N 92°16W **17**...
Lake City *Pa., U.S.A.* ...
Lake City *S.C., U.S.A.* 33°52N 79°45W **17**...
Lake Coleridge *N.Z.* 43°17S 171°30E **1**...
Lake Cowichan
  Canada 48°49N 124°3W **17**...
Lake District □ *U.K.* 54°30N 3°21W
Lake Eildon △
  Australia 37°10S 145°56E **1**...
Lake Elsinore *U.S.A.* 33°38N 117°20W **17**...
Lake Eyre △ *Australia* 28°45S 137°51E **1**...
Lake Gairdner △
  Australia 31°41S 135°51E **1**...
Lake George *U.S.A.* 43°26N 73°43W **17**...
Lake Grace *Australia* 33°7S 118°28E **1**...
Lake Harbor *U.S.A.* 26°42N 80°48W **1**...
Lake Harbour = Kimmirut
  Canada 62°50N 69°50W **16**...
Lake Havasu City
  U.S.A. 34°27N 114°22W **17**...
Lake Helen *U.S.A.* 28°59N 81°14W **1**...
Lake Hughes *U.S.A.* 34°41N 118°26W **1**...
Lake Isabella *U.S.A.* 35°38N 118°28W **1**...
Lake Jackson *U.S.A.* 29°3N 95°27W **17**...
Lake King *Australia* 33°5S 119°45E **1**...
Lake Lenore *Canada* 52°24N 104°59W **1**...
Lake Louise *Canada* 51°30N 116°10W **1**...
Lake Mackay ○
  Australia 21°48S 129°46E **1**...
Lake Mburo △ *Uganda* 0°33S 30°56E **1**...
Lake Mead △ *U.S.A.* 36°30N 114°22W **17**...
Lake Meredith △
  U.S.A. 35°50N 101°50W **1**...
Lake Mills *U.S.A.* 43°25N 93°32W **1**...
Lake Nakuru △ *Kenya* 0°21S 36°8E **1**...
Lake Park *Fla., U.S.A.* 26°48N 80°3W **1**...
Lake Park *U.S.A.* 30°41N 83°11W **1**...
Lake Placid *Fla.,*
  U.S.A. 27°18N 81°22W **1**...
Lake Placid *N.Y.,*
  U.S.A. 44°17N 73°59W **17**...
Lake Pleasant *U.S.A.* 43°28N 74°25W **17**...
Lake Providence
  U.S.A. 32°48N 91°10W **1**...
Lake Pukaki *N.Z.* 44°11S 170°8E **1**...
Lake Roosevelt △
  U.S.A. 48°5N 118°14W **1**...
Lake St. Peter *Canada* 45°18N 78°2W **1**...
Lake Stevens *U.S.A.* 48°1N 122°4W **1**...
Lake Superior △
  Canada 47°45N 84°45W **1**...
Lake Tekapo *N.Z.* 44°0S 170°30E **1**...
Lake Torrens △
  Australia 30°55S 137°40E **1**...
Lake Village *U.S.A.* 33°20N 91°17W **1**...
Lake Wales *U.S.A.* 27°54N 81°35W **1**...
Lake Worth *U.S.A.* 26°37N 80°3W **1**...
Lakeba *Fiji* 18°13S 178°47W **1**...
Lakeba Passage *Fiji* 18°0S 178°45W **1**...
Lakefield *Canada* 44°25N 78°16W **1**...
Lakefield △ *Australia* 15°24S 144°26E **1**...
Lakehurst *U.S.A.* 40°1N 74°19W **17**...
Lakeland *Australia* 15°49S 144°57E **1**...
Lakeland *Fla., U.S.A.* 28°3N 81°57W **1**...
Lakeland *Ga., U.S.A.* 31°2N 83°4W **1**...
Lakemba = Lakeba
  Fiji 18°13S 178°47W **1**...
Lakeport *Calif., U.S.A.* 39°3N 122°55W **1**...
Lakeport *Mich., U.S.A.* 43°7N 82°30W **1**...
Lakes Entrance
  Australia 37°50S 148°0E **1**...
Lakeside *Calif.,*
  U.S.A. 32°52N 116°55W **17**...
Lakeside *Nebr., U.S.A.* 42°3N 102°26W **1**...
Lakeview *U.S.A.* 42°11N 120°21W **1**...
Lakeville *U.S.A.* 44°39N 93°14W **1**...
Lakewood *Colo.,*
  U.S.A. 39°42N 105°4W **1**...
Lakewood *N.J., U.S.A.* 40°6N 74°13W **17**...
Lakewood *N.Y., U.S.A.* 42°6N 79°19W **1**...
Lakewood *Ohio, U.S.A.* 41°28N 81°47W **1**...
Lakewood *Wash.,*
  U.S.A. 47°11N 122°32W **1**...
Lakewood Park *U.S.A.* 27°33N 80°24W **1**...
Lakha *India* 26°9N 70°54E **1**...
Lakhimpur *India* 27°57N 80°46E **1**...
Lakhisarai *India* 25°11N 86°5E **12**...
Lakhnadon *India* 22°36N 79°36E **1**...
Lakhnau = Lucknow
  India 26°50N 81°0E **1**...
Lakhonpheng *Laos* 15°54N 105°34E **1**...
Lakhpat *India* 23°48N 68°47E **1**...
Laki *Azerbaijan* 40°34N 47°22E **1**...
Lakin *U.S.A.* 37°57N 101°15W **1**...
Lakitusaki → *Canada* 54°21N 82°25W **1**...
Lakki *Greece* 35°24N 23°57E **1**...
Lakki *Pakistan* 32°36N 70°55E **1**...
Lakonia □ *Greece* 36°55N 22°30E **1**...
Lakonikos Kolpos
  Greece 36°40N 22°40E **1**...
Lakor *Indonesia* 8°15S 128°17E **1**...
Lakota *Ivory C.* 5°50N 5°30W **1**...
Lakota *U.S.A.* 48°2N 98°21W **1**...
Laksar *India* 29°46N 78°3E **1**...
Laksefjorden *Norway* 70°45N 26°50E **1**...
Lakselv *Norway* 70°2N 25°0E **1**...
Lakshadweep □ *India* 10°0N 72°30E **1**...
Lakshadweep Is. *India* 10°0N 72°30E **1**...
Lakshmanpur *India* 22°58N 83°3E **12**...
Lakshmikantapur
  India 22°5N 88°20E **12**...
Lala Musa *Pakistan* 32°40N 73°57E **1**...
Lalaghat *India* 24°30N 92°40E **12**...
Lalago *Tanzania* 3°28S 33°58E **1**...
Lalapanzi *Zimbabwe* 19°20S 30°15E **1**...
Lalapaşa *Turkey* 41°49N 26°44E **1**...
Lalbenque *France* 44°19N 1°33E **1**...
L'Albert *Australia* 35°38S 143°0E **1**...
L'Albufera *Spain* 39°20N 0°21W **1**...
L'Alcora *Spain* 40°5N 0°14W **1**...
L'Alfàs del Pi *Spain* 38°35N 0°6E **1**...
Lalganj *India* 25°52N 85°13E **12**...
Lalgola *India* 24°25N 88°15E **12**...
Lālī *Iran* 32°21N 49°6E **1**...

bela *Ethiopia*	12°3N 39°0E	**131** E2
China	45°12N 127°0E	**115** B14
He → *China*	45°32N 125°40E	**115** B13
nde *France*	44°50N 0°44E	**72** D4
pur *India*	24°42N 78°28E	**125** G8
pur *Nepal*	27°40N 85°20E	**125** F11
ua *India*	29°5N 79°31E	**125** E8
ot *India*	26°34N 76°20E	**124** F7
ailand	17°55N 100°28E	**120** D3
Pao Res. *Thailand*	16°50N 103°15E	**120** D4
a Kara *Togo*	9°30N 1°15E	**139** D5
ar *Mo., U.S.A.*	37°30N 94°16W	**172** G6
arque *Argentina*	39°24S 65°40W	**192** D3
as *Peru*	6°28S 76°31W	**188** B2
ayuru *India*	34°25N 76°56E	**125** B7
bach *Austria*	48°6N 13°51E	**78** C6
balle *France*	48°29N 2°31W	**70** D4
baréné *Gabon*	0°41S 10°12E	**140** E2
basa = Labasa *Fiji*	16°30S 179°27E	**154** a
bay I. *Ireland*	53°29N 6°1W	**64** C5
bayeque *Peru*	6°45S 80°0W	**188** B2
bert's Bay *S. Africa*	32°55S 18°17E	**144** D2
besc *France*	43°39N 5°16E	**73** E9
beth *Canada*	42°54N 81°18W	**174** D3
bia *Greece*	37°52N 21°53E	**98** D3
bro → *Italy*	45°8N 9°32E	**92** C6
e *Nigeria*	10°30N 9°20E	**139** C6
e Deer *Canada*	45°37N 106°40W	**168** D10
ego *Portugal*	41°5N 7°52W	**88** D3
èque *France*	47°45N 64°38W	**165** C7
eroo *Australia*	35°19S 140°33E	**152** C4
esa *U.S.A.*	32°44N 101°58W	**176** E4
netlla de Mar *Spain*	40°53N 0°48E	**90** E5
ezia Terme *Italy*	38°55N 16°26E	**95** D9
a *Greece*	38°55N 22°26E	**98** C4
ington □		
stralia	28°13S 153°12E	**151** D5
ma I. *China*	22°12N 114°7E	**111** a
mermuir Hills *U.K.*	55°50N 2°40W	**66** F6
mhult *Sweden*	56°10N 14°35E	**63** G8
oille → *U.S.A.*	44°38N 73°13W	**175** B11
on B. *Phil.*	14°30N 122°20E	**119** D4
ont *Canada*	53°46N 112°50W	**162** C6
ont *Calif., U.S.A.*	35°15N 118°55W	**171** K8
ont *Fla., U.S.A.*	30°23N 83°49W	**178** E6
ont *Wyo., U.S.A.*	42°13N 107°29W	**168** E10
tte-Beuvron *France*	47°36N 2°2E	**71** E9
a *Peru*	15°22S 70°22W	**188** D3
pang *Thailand*	18°16N 99°52E	**120** C2
pasas *U.S.A.*	31°4N 98°11W	**176** F5
pazos de Naranjo		
exico	27°1N 100°31W	**180** B4
pertheim *Germany*	49°35N 8°27E	**77** F4
peter *U.K.*	52°7N 4°4W	**67** E3
phun *Thailand*	15°8N 104°54E	**120** D4
oman *Canada*	49°25N 102°50W	**163** D8
prechtshausen		
stria	48°0N 12°58E	**78** D5
pung □ *Indonesia*	5°30S 104°30E	**118** F2
a *India*	22°8N 80°7E	**125** H9
a *Kenya*	2°16S 40°55E	**142** C5
eal *Peru*	6°10S 77°57W	**188** B2
y *U.S.A.*	35°29N 105°53W	**169** J11
Xian *China*	38°15N 111°35E	**114** E6
u'ū *Taiwan*	22°4N 121°25E	**117** F13
'i *U.S.A.*	20°50N 156°55W	**167** L8
k La *China*	34°27N 79°32E	**125** B8
k'o Shank'ou = Lanak La		
na	34°27N 79°32E	**125** B8
rk *Canada*	45°1N 76°22W	**175** A8
rk *U.K.*	55°40N 3°47W	**65** F5
i Kyun *Burma*	10°50N 98°20E	**121** G2
ang Jiang →		
na	21°40N 101°10E	**116** G3
nashire □ *U.K.*	53°50N 2°48W	**66** D5
aster *Canada*	45°10N 74°30W	**175** A10
aster *U.K.*	54°3N 2°48W	**66** C5
aster *Calif., U.S.A.*	34°42N 118°8W	**171** L8
aster *Ky., U.S.A.*	37°37N 84°35W	**173** G11
aster *N.H.,*		
.A.	44°29N 71°34W	**175** B13
aster *Ohio, U.S.A.*	39°43N 82°36W	**173** F12
aster *Pa., U.S.A.*	40°2N 76°19W	**175** F8
aster *S.C., U.S.A.*	34°43N 80°46W	**179** H5
aster *Wis., U.S.A.*	42°51N 90°43W	**172** D8
aster Sd. *Canada*	74°13N 84°0W	**161** C15
elin *Australia*	31°0S 115°18E	**149** F2
how = Lanzhou		
na	36°1N 103°52E	**114** F2
hyn *Ukraine*	48°33N 24°45E	**81** B9
ano *Italy*	44°14N 7°23E	**93** F11
o *Chile*	39°24S 72°46W	**192** A2
ones *Peru*	4°30S 80°30W	**188** A1
un *China*	36°25N 120°10E	**115** F11
Between the Lakes △		
.A.	36°25N 88°0W	**177** C11
au *Bayern, Germany*	48°40N 12°41E	**77** G8
au *Rhld-Pfz., Germany*	49°12N 8°6E	**77** F4
eck *Austria*	47°9N 10°34E	**78** D3
er *U.S.A.*	42°50N 108°44W	**168** E9
erneau *France*	48°28N 4°17W	**70** D2
eryd *Sweden*	57°7N 13°15E	**63** G7
es *France*	44°0N 1°0W	**72** D2
es *France*	43°57N 0°48W	**72** E3
nce		
u de Gascogne △		
nce	44°23N 0°50W	**72** D3
all I. *Canada*	59°56N 1°29W	**65** a
Kotal *Pakistan*	34°7N 71°6E	**124** B4
sburg *U.S.A.*	40°21N 77°19W	**174** F7
visiau *France*	48°31N 4°6W	**70** D2
mannalaugar		
land	63°59N 19°4W	**60** E4
quart *Switz.*	46°58N 9°32E	**77** J5
ecies *France*	50°7N 3°40E	**71** B10
s End *U.K.*	50°4N 5°44W	**67** G2
sberg *Germany*	48°2N 10°53E	**77** G6
sborough Cr. →		
stralia	22°28S 144°35E	**150** C3
sbro *Sweden*	57°24N 14°56E	**63** G8
shut *Germany*	48°34N 12°8E	**77** G8
skrona *Sweden*	55°53N 12°50E	**63** J6

Landstuhl *Germany*	49°24N 7°33E	**77** F3
Landvetter *Sweden*	57°41N 12°17E	**63** G6
Lane *U.S.A.*	33°32N 79°53W	**178** B10
Lanesboro *U.S.A.*	41°57N 75°34W	**175** E9
Lanester *France*	47°46N 3°22W	**70** E3
Lanett *U.S.A.*	32°52N 85°12W	**178** C4
Lang Shan *China*	41°0N 106°30E	**114** D4
Lang Son *Vietnam*	21°52N 106°42E	**116** G6
Lang Suan *Thailand*	9°57N 99°4E	**121** H2
Langå *Denmark*	56°23N 9°54E	**63** H3
La'nga Co *China*	30°45N 81°15E	**125** D9
Langadás *Greece*	40°46N 23°3E	**100** A5
Langádhia *Greece*	37°43N 22°1E	**98** D4
Langar → *Sudan*	6°19N 14°42E	**142** B1
Langar *Iran*	35°23N 60°25E	**129** C9
Langarūd *Iran*	37°11N 50°8E	**129** B6
Långås *Sweden*	56°58N 12°26E	**63** H6
Langdai *China*	26°6N 105°21E	**116** D5
Langdon *U.S.A.*	48°45N 98°22W	**172** A4
Lange Jan = Ölands södra udde		
Sweden	56°12N 16°23E	**63** H10
Langeac *France*	45°7N 3°29E	**72** C7
Langeais *France*	47°20N 0°24E	**70** E7
Langeb Baraka →		
Sudan	17°28N 36°50E	**137** D4
Langeberg *S. Africa*	33°55S 21°0E	**144** D3
Langeberge *S. Africa*	28°15S 22°33E	**144** C3
Langeland *Denmark*	54°56N 10°48E	**63** K4
Langelands Bælt		
Denmark	54°50N 10°55E	**63** K4
Langen *Hessen, Germany*	49°59N 8°40E	**77** F4
Langen *Niedersachsen,*		
Germany	53°36N 8°36E	**76** B4
Langenburg *Canada*	50°51N 101°43W	**163** C8
Langeneß *Germany*	54°38N 8°36E	**76** A4
Langenlois *Austria*	48°29N 15°40E	**78** C8
Langeoog *Germany*	53°45N 7°32E	**76** B3
Langeskov *Denmark*	55°22N 10°35E	**63** J4
Langfang *China*	39°30N 116°41E	**114** E9
Länghem *Sweden*	57°36N 13°14E	**63** G7
Langhirano *Italy*	44°37N 10°16E	**92** D7
Langholm *U.K.*	55°9N 3°0W	**65** F5
Langjökull *Iceland*	64°39N 20°12W	**60** D3
Langkawi, Pulau		
Malaysia	6°25N 99°45E	**121** J2
Langklip *S. Africa*	28°12S 20°20E	**144** C3
Langkon *Malaysia*	6°30N 116°40E	**118** C5
Langley *Canada*	49°7N 122°39W	**170** A4
Langnau *Switz.*	46°56N 7°47E	**77** J3
Langogne *France*	44°43N 3°50E	**72** D7
Langon *France*	44°33N 0°16W	**72** D3
Langoya *Norway*	68°45N 14°50E	**60** B16
Langreo *Spain*	43°18N 5°40W	**88** B5
Langres *France*	47°52N 5°20E	**71** E12
Langres, Plateau de		
France	47°45N 5°3E	**71** E12
Langsa *Indonesia*	4°30N 97°57E	**118** D1
Långsele *Sweden*	63°12N 17°4E	**62** A11
Långshyttan *Sweden*	60°27N 16°2E	**62** D10
Langtang → *Nepal*	28°35N 85°25E	**125** E11
Langtou *China*	40°1N 124°19E	**115** D13
Langtry *U.S.A.*	29°49N 101°34W	**176** G4
Langu *Thailand*	6°53N 99°47E	**121** J2
Langue de Barbarie △		
Senegal	14°54N 16°30W	**138** C1
Languedoc *France*	43°58N 3°55E	**72** E7
Languedoc-Roussillon □		
France	43°25N 3°0E	**72** E6
Langwang *China*	22°38N 113°27E	**111** a
Langxi *China*	31°10N 119°12E	**117** B12
Langzhong *China*	31°38N 105°58E	**116** B5
Lanigan *Canada*	51°51N 105°2W	**163** C7
Lanín △ *Argentina*	40°0S 71°58W	**192** A2
Lanjigarh *India*	19°43N 83°23E	**124** K6
Lankao *China*	34°48N 114°50E	**114** G8
Länkäran *Azerbaijan*	38°48N 48°52E	**105** C13
Lanmeur *France*	48°39N 3°43W	**70** D3
Lannemezan *France*	43°8N 0°23E	**72** E4
Lannilis *France*	48°35N 4°32W	**70** D2
Lannion *France*	48°46N 3°29W	**70** D3
L'Annonciation		
Canada	46°25N 74°55W	**164** C5
Lanouaille *France*	45°24N 1°9E	**72** C5
Lanping *China*	26°28N 99°15E	**116** D2
Lansang △ *Thailand*	16°45N 99°0E	**120** D2
Lansdale *U.S.A.*	40°14N 75°17W	**175** F9
Lansdowne *Australia*	31°48S 152°30E	**153** A10
Lansdowne *Canada*	44°24N 76°1W	**175** B8
Lansdowne *India*	29°50N 78°41E	**125** E8
Lansdowne House = Neskantaga		
Canada	52°14N 87°53W	**164** B2
L'Anse *U.S.A.*	46°45N 88°27W	**172** B9
L'Anse au Loup		
Canada	51°32N 56°50W	**165** B8
L'Anse aux Meadows		
Canada	51°36N 55°32W	**165** B8
Lansford *U.S.A.*	40°50N 75°53W	**175** F9
Lanshan *China*	25°24N 112°10E	**117** E9
Lanshantou *China*	35°5N 119°20E	**115** G10
Länsi-Turunmaa		
Finland	60°18N 22°18E	**63** E8
Lansing *U.S.A.*	42°44N 84°33W	**173** D11
Lanslebourg-Mont-Cenis		
France	45°17N 6°52E	**73** C10
Lanta, Ko *Thailand*	7°35N 99°3E	**121** J2
Lantana *U.S.A.*	26°35N 80°3W	**179** J9
Lantau I. *China*	22°15N 113°56E	**111** a
Lantewa *Nigeria*	12°16N 11°44E	**139** C7
Lantian *China*	34°11N 109°20E	**114** G5
Lanus *Argentina*	34°42S 58°23W	**190** C4
Lanusei *Italy*	39°52N 9°34E	**94** C2
Lanxi *China*	29°13N 119°28E	**117** C12
Lanzarote *Canary Is.*	29°0N 13°40W	**100** F6
Lanzarote ✈ (ACE)		
Canary Is.	28°57N 13°40W	**100** F6
Lanzhou *China*	36°1N 103°52E	**114** F2
Lanzo Torinese *Italy*	45°16N 7°29E	**92** C4
Lao → *Italy*	39°47N 15°48E	**95** C8
Lao Cai *Vietnam*	22°30N 103°57E	**116** F4
Laoag *Phil.*	18°7N 120°34E	**119** B4
Laoang *Phil.*	12°32N 125°8E	**119** E7
Laoha He → *China*	43°25N 120°35E	**115** C11
Laohekou *China*	32°22N 111°38E	**114** H6
Laois □ *Ireland*	52°57N 7°36W	**64** D4
Laon *France*	49°33N 3°35E	**71** C10
Laona *U.S.A.*	45°34N 88°40W	**172** C9
Laos ■ *Asia*	17°45N 105°0E	**120** D5
Lapa *Brazil*	25°46S 49°44W	**191** B6
Lapai *Nigeria*	9°5N 6°32E	**139** D6
Lapalisse *France*	46°15N 3°38E	**71** F10

Lapeer *U.S.A.*	43°3N 83°19W	**173** D12
Lapeyrade *France*	44°4N 0°3W	**72** D3
Lapithos *Cyprus*	35°21N 33°11E	**101** D12
Lapland = Lappland		
Europe	68°7N 24°0E	**60** B21
LaPorte *Ind., U.S.A.*	41°36N 86°43W	**172** E10
Laporte *Pa., U.S.A.*	41°25N 76°30W	**175** E8
Lapovo *Serbia*	44°10N 21°7E	**96** B5
Lappeenranta *Finland*	61°3N 28°12E	**84** B5
Lappland *Europe*	68°7N 24°0E	**60** B21
Lappo = Lapua *Finland*	62°58N 23°0E	**60** E20
Laprida *Argentina*	37°34S 60°45W	**190** D3
Lâpseki *Turkey*	40°20N 26°41E	**97** F10
Lapta = Lapithos		
Cyprus	35°21N 33°11E	**101** D12
Laptev Sea *Russia*	76°0N 125°0E	**107** B13
Lapua *Finland*	62°58N 23°0E	**60** E20
Lâpuş → *Romania*	47°25N 23°40E	**81** C8
Lăpuş, Munţii *Romania*	47°20N 23°50E	**81** C8
Lăpuşna *Moldova*	46°53N 28°25E	**81** D13
Lapy *Poland*	52°59N 22°52E	**83** F9
Laqiya Arba'in *Sudan*	20°1N 28°1E	**137** C2
Laqiya Umran *Sudan*	19°55N 28°18E	**137** D2
L'Aquila *Italy*	42°22N 13°22E	**93** F10
Lār *Iran*	27°40N 54°14E	**129** E7
Lara *Australia*	38°2S 144°26E	**152** E6
Larabanga *Ghana*	9°16N 1°56W	**138** D4
Larache *Morocco*	35°10N 6°5W	**136** A4
Laragne-Montéglin		
France	44°18N 5°49E	**73** D9
Laramie *U.S.A.*	41°19N 105°35W	**168** F11
Laramie Mts. *U.S.A.*	42°0N 105°30W	**168** F11
Laranda = Karaman		
Turkey	37°14N 33°13E	**104** D5
Laranjeiras do Sul		
Brazil	25°23S 52°23W	**191** B5
Larantuka *Indonesia*	8°21S 122°55E	**119** F6
Larat *Indonesia*	7°0S 132°0E	**119** F8
L'Arbresle *France*	45°50N 4°36E	**73** C8
Lärbro *Sweden*	57°47N 18°50E	**63** G12
Larde *Mozam.*	16°28S 39°43E	**143** F4
Larder Lake *Canada*	48°5N 79°40W	**164** C4
Lardos *Greece*	36°6N 28°1E	**101** C10
Lardos, Akra = Lindos, Akra		
Greece	36°4N 28°10E	**101** C10
Lardos, Órmos *Greece*	36°4N 28°2E	**101** C10
Lare *Kenya*	0°20N 37°56E	**142** C4
Laredo *Spain*	43°26N 3°28W	**88** B7
Laredo *U.S.A.*	27°30N 99°30W	**176** H5
Laredo Sd. *Canada*	52°30N 128°53W	**162** C2
Largentière *France*	44°34N 4°18E	**73** D8
L'Argentière-la-Bessée		
France	44°47N 6°33E	**73** D10
Largo *U.S.A.*	27°54N 82°47W	**179** M7
Largo, Key *U.S.A.*	25°15N 80°15W	**179** N9
Largs *U.K.*	55°47N 4°52W	**65** F4
Lari *Italy*	43°34N 10°35E	**92** E7
Lariang *Indonesia*	1°26S 119°17E	**119** E5
Larimore *U.S.A.*	47°54N 97°38W	**172** B5
Larino *Italy*	41°48N 14°54E	**93** G11
Lário, Il = Como, L. di		
Italy	46°0N 9°11E	**92** B6
Lárisa *Greece*	39°36N 22°27E	**98** B4
Larkana *Pakistan*	27°32N 68°18E	**124** F3
Larnaca *Cyprus*	34°55N 33°38E	**101** E12
Larnaca Bay *Cyprus*	34°53N 33°45E	**101** E12
Larne *U.K.*	54°51N 5°51W	**64** B6
Larned *U.S.A.*	38°11N 99°6W	**172** F4
Laroquebrou *France*	44°58N 2°12E	**72** D6
Larose *U.S.A.*	29°34N 90°23W	**177** G9
Larrimah *Australia*	15°35S 133°12E	**148** C5
Larsen Ice Shelf		
Antarctica	67°0S 62°0W	**55** C17
Laruns *France*	43°0N 0°26W	**72** E3
Larvik *Norway*	59°4N 10°2E	**61** G14
Larzac, Causse du *France*	43°50N 3°17E	**72** E7
Las Alpujarras *Spain*	36°55N 3°20W	**91** J1
Las Animas *U.S.A.*	38°4N 103°13W	**168** G12
Las Anod *Somalia*	8°26N 47°19E	**131** F4
Las Arenas *Spain*	43°17N 4°50W	**88** B6
Las Batuecas △ *Spain*	40°32N 6°5W	**88** E4
Las Brenãs *Argentina*	27°5S 61°7W	**190** B3
Las Cabezas de San Juan		
Spain	36°57N 5°58W	**89** J5
Las Cañadas del Teide △		
Canary Is.	28°15N 16°37W	**100** F3
Las Cejas *Argentina*	26°53S 64°44W	**190** B3
Las Chimeneas *Mexico*	32°8N 116°5W	**171** N10
Las Coloradas		
Argentina	39°34S 70°36W	**192** A2
Las Cruces *U.S.A.*	32°19N 106°47W	**169** K10
Las Flores *Argentina*	36°10S 59°7W	**190** D4
Las Gabias = Gabia la Grande		
Spain	37°8N 3°40W	**89** H7
Las Heras *Mendoza,*		
Argentina	32°51S 68°49W	**190** C2
Las Heras *Santa Cruz,*		
Argentina	46°33S 68°57W	**192** C3
Las Horquetas		
Argentina	48°14S 71°11W	**192** C2
Las Lajas *Argentina*	38°30S 70°25W	**192** A2
Las Lomas *Peru*	4°40S 80°10W	**188** A1
Las Lomitas *Argentina*	24°43S 60°35W	**190** A3
Las Manos, Cueva de		
Argentina	47°35S 70°40W	**192** C2
Las Marismas *Spain*	37°5S 6°20W	**89** H4
Las Médulas *Spain*	42°28N 6°46W	**88** C4
Las Minas *Spain*	38°20N 1°41W	**91** G3
Las Navas de la Concepción		
Spain	37°56N 5°30W	**89** H5
Las Navas del Marqués		
Spain	40°36N 4°20W	**88** E6
Las Palmas *Argentina*	27°8S 58°45W	**190** B4
Las Palmas *Canary Is.*	28°7N 15°26W	**100** F4
Las Palmas →		
Mexico	32°31N 116°58W	**171** N10
Las Palmas ✈ (LPA)		
Canary Is.	27°55N 15°25W	**100** G4
Las Pedroñeras *Spain*	39°27N 2°40W	**91** F2
Las Piedras *Uruguay*	34°44S 56°14W	**191** C4
Las Pipinas *Argentina*	35°30S 57°19W	**190** D4
Las Plumas *Argentina*	43°40S 67°15W	**192** B3
Las Rosas *Argentina*	32°30S 61°35W	**190** C3
Las Rozas *Spain*	40°29N 3°52W	**88** E7
Las Tablas *Panama*	7°49N 80°14W	**182** E3
Las Toscas *Argentina*	28°21S 59°18W	**190** B4
Las Tunas *Cuba*	20°58N 76°59W	**182** B4
Las Varillas *Argentina*	31°50S 62°50W	**190** C3
Las Vegas *N. Mex.,*		
U.S.A.	35°36N 105°13W	**169** J11
Las Vegas *Nev., U.S.A.*	36°10N 115°9W	**171** J11

Las Vegas McCarran Int. ✈ (LAS)		
U.S.A.	36°5N 115°9W	**171** J11
Lasarte-Oria *Spain*	43°16N 2°1W	**90** B2
Lascano *Uruguay*	33°35S 54°12W	**191** C5
Lascelles *Australia*	35°34S 142°34E	**152** C5
Lashburn *Canada*	53°10N 109°40W	**163** C7
Lashio *Burma*	22°56N 97°45E	**123** H20
Lashkar *India*	26°10N 78°10E	**124** F8
Lashkar *Poland*	53°30N 19°2E	**83** E10
Lasithi *Greece*	35°11N 25°31E	**101** D7
Läsjerd *Iran*	35°24N 53°4E	**129** C7
Lask *Poland*	51°34N 19°8E	**83** D10
Laskarzew *Poland*	51°48N 21°36E	**83** D9
Lassance *Brazil*	17°54S 44°34W	**189** D2
Lassen Pk. *U.S.A.*	40°29N 121°30W	**168** F3
Lassen Volcanic △		
U.S.A.	40°30N 121°20W	**168** F3
Last Mountain L.		
Canada	51°5N 105°14W	**163** C7
Lastchance Cr. →		
U.S.A.	40°2N 121°15W	**170** E5
Lastoursville *Gabon*	0°55S 12°38E	**140** E2
Lastovo *Croatia*	42°46N 16°55E	**93** F13
Lastovski Kanal *Croatia*	42°50N 17°0E	**93** F14
Lat Yao *Thailand*	15°45N 99°48E	**120** E2
Latacunga *Ecuador*	0°50S 78°35W	**186** D3
Latади I. *Antarctica*	70°45S 74°35W	**55** D17
Latakia = Al Lādhiqīyah		
Syria	35°30N 35°45E	**104** E6
Latchford *Canada*	47°20N 79°50W	**164** C4
Latehar *India*	23°45N 84°30E	**125** H11
Laterza *Italy*	40°37N 16°48E	**95** B9
Latham *Australia*	29°44S 116°20E	**149** E2
Lathen *Germany*	52°52N 7°19E	**76** C3
Lathi *India*	27°43N 71°23E	**124** F4
Lathrop Wells *U.S.A.*	36°39N 116°24W	**171** J10
Latiano *Italy*	40°33N 17°43E	**95** B10
Latina *Italy*	41°28N 12°52E	**94** A5
Latisana *Italy*	45°47N 13°0E	**93** C10
Latium = Lazio □ *Italy*	42°10N 12°30E	**93** F9
Laton *U.S.A.*	36°26N 119°41W	**170** J7
Latorytsya →		
Slovak Rep.	48°28N 21°50E	**79** C14
Latouche Treville, C.		
Australia	18°27S 121°49E	**148** C3
Latrobe *Australia*	41°14S 146°30E	**151** G4
Latrobe *U.S.A.*	40°19N 79°23W	**174** F5
Latrónico *Italy*	40°5N 16°1E	**95** B9
Latur *India*	18°25N 76°40E	**126** E3
Latvia ■ *Europe*	56°50N 24°0E	**84** D2
Lau *Nigeria*	9°11N 11°19E	**139** D7
Lau Group *Fiji*	17°0S 178°30W	**154** a
Lauca → *Bolivia*	19°9S 68°10W	**188** D4
Lauchhammer *Germany*	51°29N 13°47E	**76** D9
Lauda-Königshofen		
Germany	49°33N 9°42E	**77** F5
Laudio = Llodio *Spain*	43°9N 2°58W	**90** B2
Lauenburg *Germany*	53°22N 10°32E	**76** B6
Lauenburgische Seen △		
Germany	53°38N 10°45E	**76** B6
Lauf *Germany*	49°30N 11°16E	**77** F7
Lauge Koch Kyst		
Greenland	75°45N 57°45W	**161** B20
Laughlin *U.S.A.*	35°10N 114°34W	**171** K12
Lauhanvuori △ *Finland*	62°24N 22°10E	**60** E20
Laujar de Andarax *Spain*	37°0N 2°54W	**91** H2
Laukaa *Finland*	62°24N 25°56E	**62** E21
Launceston *Australia*	41°24S 147°8E	**151** G4
Launceston *U.K.*	50°38N 4°22W	**67** G3
Laune → *Ireland*	52°7N 9°47W	**64** D2
Launglon Bok *Burma*	13°50N 97°54E	**121** F1
Laupheim *Germany*	48°14N 9°52E	**77** G5
Laura *Queens.,*		
Australia	15°32S 144°32E	**150** B3
Laura *S. Austral.,*		
Australia	33°10S 138°18E	**152** B3
Laureana di Borrello		
Italy	38°30N 16°5E	**95** D9
Laurel *Fla., U.S.A.*	27°8N 82°27W	**179** H7
Laurel *Miss., U.S.A.*	31°41N 89°8W	**177** F10
Laurel *Mont., U.S.A.*	45°40N 108°46W	**168** D9
Laurel Bay *U.S.A.*	32°27N 80°47W	**178** C9
Laurencekirk *U.K.*	56°50N 2°28W	**65** E6
Laurens *U.S.A.*	34°30N 82°1W	**177** D13
Laurentian Plateau		
Canada	52°0N 70°0W	**165** B6
Lauria *Italy*	40°2N 15°50E	**95** B8
Laurie L. *Canada*	56°35N 101°57W	**163** B8
Laurinburg *U.S.A.*	34°47N 79°28W	**177** D15
Laurium *U.S.A.*	47°14N 88°27W	**172** B9
Lausanne *Switz.*	46°32N 6°38E	**77** J2
Laut *Indonesia*	4°45N 108°0E	**118** D3
Laut, Pulau *Indonesia*	3°40S 116°10E	**118** E5
Laut Kecil, Kepulauan		
Indonesia	4°45S 115°40E	**118** E5
Lautaro *Chile*	38°31S 72°27W	**192** A2
Lauterbach *Germany*	50°37N 9°24E	**76** E5
Lauterecken *Germany*	49°39N 7°35E	**77** F3
Lautoka *Fiji*	17°37S 177°27E	**154** a
Lauwersmeer △ *Neths.*	53°22N 6°11E	**69** A6
Lauzès *France*	44°34N 1°33E	**72** D5
Lava → *Russia*	54°21N 21°14E	**82** D8
Lava Beds △ *U.S.A.*	41°40N 121°30W	**168** F3
Lavagh More *Ireland*	54°46N 8°6W	**64** B3
Lavagna *Italy*	44°18N 9°22E	**92** D6
Laval *France*	48°4N 0°48W	**70** D6
Laval-des-Rapides		
Canada	45°33N 73°42W	**164** C5
Lavalle *Argentina*	28°15S 65°15W	**190** B3
Lāvān *Iran*	26°48N 53°22E	**129** E7
Lavant *Canada*	45°3N 76°42W	**175** A8
Lavar Meydān *Iran*	30°20N 54°30E	**129** D7
Lavara *Greece*	41°19N 26°22E	**97** E10
Lavardac *France*	44°12N 0°20E	**72** D4
Lavaur *France*	43°40N 1°49E	**72** E5
Lavelanet *France*	42°57N 1°51E	**72** F5
Lavello *Italy*	41°3N 15°48E	**95** A8
Lavers Hill *Australia*	38°40S 143°25E	**152** E5
Laverton *Australia*	28°44S 122°29E	**149** E3
Lavezzi, Is. *France*	41°22N 9°16E	**93** G13
Lavis *Italy*	46°8N 11°7E	**92** B8
Lavos *Portugal*	40°6N 8°49W	**88** E2
Lavradio *Portugal*	38°46N 9°3W	**89** C1
Lavras *Brazil*	21°20S 45°0W	**191** A7
Lavre *Portugal*	38°46N 8°22W	**89** C2
Lavrio *Greece*	37°40N 24°4E	**98** D6

Lavris *Greece*	35°25N 24°40E	**101** D6
Lavumisa *Swaziland*	27°20S 31°55E	**145** C5
Lavushi Manda △		
Zambia	12°46S 31°0E	**143** E3
Lawak I. = Nanshan I.		
S. China Sea	10°45N 115°49E	**118** C5
Lawaki *Fiji*	17°40S 178°35E	**154** a
Lawas *Malaysia*	4°55N 115°25E	**118** D5
Lawele *Indonesia*	5°13S 122°57E	**119** F6
Lawn Hill = Boodjamulla △		
Australia	18°15S 138°6E	**150** B2
Lawqah *Si. Arabia*	29°49N 42°45E	**128** D4
Lawra *Ghana*	10°39N 2°51W	**138** C4
Lawrence *N.Z.*	45°55S 169°41E	**155** F4
Lawrence *Ind., U.S.A.*	39°50N 86°2W	**172** F10
Lawrence *Kans., U.S.A.*	38°58N 95°14W	**172** F6
Lawrence *Mass.,*		
U.S.A.	42°43N 71°10W	**175** D13
Lawrenceburg *Ind.,*		
U.S.A.	39°6N 84°52W	**173** F11
Lawrenceburg *Tenn.,*		
U.S.A.	35°14N 87°20W	**177** D11
Lawrenceville *Ga.,*		
U.S.A.	33°57N 83°59W	**178** B6
Lawrenceville *Pa.,*		
U.S.A.	41°59N 77°8W	**174** E7
Laws *U.S.A.*	37°24N 118°20W	**170** H8
Lawtey *U.S.A.*	30°3N 82°5W	**178** F7
Lawton *U.S.A.*	34°37N 98°25W	**176** D5
Lawu *Indonesia*	7°40S 111°13E	**119** G14
Lawz, J. al *Si. Arabia*	28°30N 35°18E	**130** D2
Laxá *Sweden*	58°59N 14°37E	**63** F8
Laxford, L. *U.K.*	58°24N 5°6W	**65** C3
Laxiwa Dam *China*	36°4N 101°11E	**110** D9
Laxou *France*	48°41N 6°8E	**71** D13
Lay → *France*	46°18N 1°17W	**72** B2
Layla *Si. Arabia*	22°10N 46°40E	**131** C4
Laylān *Iraq*	35°18N 44°31E	**128** C5
Layon → *France*	47°20N 0°45W	**70** E6
Laysan I. *U.S.A.*	25°50N 171°50W	**167** K5
Layton *Fla., U.S.A.*	24°50N 80°47W	**179** L9
Layton *Utah, U.S.A.*	41°4N 111°58W	**168** F8
Laytonville *U.S.A.*	39°41N 123°29W	**168** G2
Lazarev *Russia*	52°13N 141°30E	**107** D15
Lazarev Sea *S. Ocean*	67°30S 3°0W	**55** C2
Lazarevac *Serbia*	44°23N 20°17E	**96** B4
Lazarevskoye *Russia*	43°55N 39°21E	**87** J4
Lázaro Cárdenas		
Mexico	17°55N 102°11W	**180** D4
Lazdijai *Lithuania*	54°14N 23°31E	**82** D10
Lazhuglung *China*	34°52N 81°24E	**109** F10
Lazio □ *Italy*	42°10N 12°30E	**93** F9
Lazo *Moldova*	47°33N 28°2E	**81** C13
Lazo *Russia*	43°25N 133°55E	**112** C6
Le Beausset *France*	43°12N 5°48E	**73** E9
Le Bic *France*	48°20N 68°41W	**165** C6
Le Blanc *France*	46°37N 1°3E	**72** B5
Le Bleymard *France*	44°30N 3°42E	**72** D7
Le Bourgneuf-la-Fôret		
France	48°10N 0°59W	**70** D6
Le Bugue *France*	44°55N 0°56E	**72** D4
Le Cateau Cambrésis		
France	50°7N 3°32E	**71** B10
Le Caylar *France*	43°51N 3°19E	**72** E7
Le Chambon-Feugerolles		
France	45°24N 4°19E	**73** C8
Le Châtelet *France*	46°38N 2°16E	**71** F9
Le Chesne *France*	49°30N 4°45E	**71** C11
Le Cheylard *France*	44°55N 4°25E	**73** D8
Le Conquet *France*	48°21N 4°46W	**70** D2
Le Creusot *France*	46°48N 4°24E	**71** F11
Le Croisic *France*	47°18N 2°30W	**70** E4
Le Donjon *France*	46°22N 3°48E	**71** F10
Le Dorat *France*	46°14N 1°5E	**72** B5
Le François *Martinique*	14°38N 60°57W	**182** c
Le Gosier *Guadeloupe*	16°14N 61°29W	**182** b
Le Grand-Lucé *France*	47°52N 0°28E	**70** E7
Le Grand-Pressigny		
France	46°55N 0°48E	**70** F7
Le Gris Gris *Mauritius*	20°35S 57°32E	**141** d
Le Havre *France*	49°30N 0°5E	**70** C7
Le Lamentin *Martinique*	14°35N 61°2W	**182** c
Le Lavandou *France*	43°8N 6°22E	**73** E10
Le Lion-d'Angers *France*	47°37N 0°43W	**70** E6
Le Louroux-Béconnais		
France	47°30N 0°55W	**70** E6
Le Luc *France*	43°23N 6°21E	**73** E10
Le Maire, Estr. de		
Argentina	54°50S 65°0W	**192** D4
Le Mans *France*	48°0N 0°10E	**70** E7
Le Marin *Martinique*	14°27N 60°55W	**182** c
Le Mars *U.S.A.*	42°47N 96°10W	**172** D5
Le Mayet-de-Montagne		
France	46°4N 3°40E	**71** F10
Le Mêle-sur-Sarthe		
France	48°31N 0°22E	**70** D7
Le Monastier-sur-Gazeille		
France	44°57N 3°59E	**72** D7
Le Monêtier-les-Bains		
France	44°58N 6°30E	**73** D10
Le Mont-Dore *France*	45°35N 2°49E	**72** C6
Le Mont-St-Michel		
France	48°40N 1°30W	**70** D5
Le Moule *Guadeloupe*	16°20N 61°22W	**182** b
Le Moyne, L. *Canada*	56°45N 68°47W	**165** A6
Le Muy *France*	43°28N 6°34W	**73** E10
Le Palais *France*	47°20N 3°10W	**70** E3
Le Perthus *France*	42°30N 2°53E	**72** F6
Le Port *Réunion*	20°56S 55°19E	**141** c
Le Pêcheur *Martinique*	14°50N 61°12W	**182** c
Le Puy-en-Velay *France*	45°3N 3°52E	**72** C7
Le Raysville *U.S.A.*	41°50N 76°10W	**175** E8
Le Robert *Martinique*	14°40N 60°56W	**182** c
Le Roy *U.S.A.*	42°58N 77°59W	**174** D7
Le St-Esprit *Martinique*	14°34N 60°56W	**182** c
Le Sueur *U.S.A.*	44°28N 93°55W	**172** C7
Le Tampon *Réunion*	21°16S 55°32E	**141** c
Le Teil *France*	44°33N 4°40E	**73** D8
Le Teilleul *France*	48°30N 0°53W	**70** D6
Le Theil *France*	48°16N 0°42E	**70** D7
Le Thillot *France*	47°53N 6°46E	**71** E13
Le Thuy *Vietnam*	17°14N 106°49E	**120** D6
Le Touquet-Paris-Plage		
France	50°30N 1°36E	**71** B8
Le Tréport *France*	50°3N 1°20E	**70** B8
Le Val-d'Ajol *France*	47°55N 6°31E	**71** E13
Le Verdon-sur-Mer		
France	45°33N 1°4W	**72** C2

Le Vigan *France*	43°59N 3°36E	**72** E7
Lea → *U.K.*	51°31N 0°1E	**67** F8
Leach *Cambodia*	12°21N 103°46E	**121** F4
Lead *U.S.A.*	44°21N 103°46W	**172** C2
Leader *Canada*	50°50N 109°30W	**163** C7
Leadville *U.S.A.*	39°15N 106°18W	**168** G10
Leaf → *U.S.A.*	30°59N 88°44W	**177** F10
Leaf Rapids *Canada*	56°30N 99°59W	**163** B9
Leaghur, L. *Australia*	33°35S 143°3E	**152** B5
League City *U.S.A.*	29°31N 95°6W	**176** C7
Leamington *Canada*	42°3N 82°36W	**174** D2
Leamington *N.Z.*	37°55S 175°30E	**154** B6
Leamington *U.S.A.*	39°32N 112°17W	**168** G7
Leamington Spa = Royal		
Leamington Spa *U.K.*	52°18N 1°31W	**67** E6
Le'an *China*	27°22N 115°48E	**117** D10
Leandro Norte Alem		
Argentina	27°34S 55°15W	**191** B4
Leane, L. *Ireland*	52°2N 9°32W	**64** D2
Learmonth *Australia*	22°13S 114°10E	**148** D1
Leary *U.S.A.*	31°29N 84°31W	**178** D5
Leask *Canada*	53°5N 106°45W	**163** C7
Leatherhead *U.K.*	51°18N 0°20W	**67** F7
Leavdnja = Lakselv		
Norway	70°2N 25°0E	**60** A21
Leavenworth *Kans.,*		
U.S.A.	39°19N 94°55W	**172** F6
Leavenworth *Wash.,*		
U.S.A.	47°36N 120°40W	**168** C3
Leawood *U.S.A.*	38°58N 94°37W	**172** F6
Łeba *Poland*	54°45N 17°32E	**82** A4
Łeba → *Poland*	54°46N 17°33E	**82** A4
Lebach *Germany*	49°25N 6°54E	**77** F2
Lebak *Phil.*	6°32N 124°5E	**119** C6
Lebane *Serbia*	42°56N 21°44E	**96** D5
Lebanon *Ind., U.S.A.*	40°3N 86°28W	**172** E10
Lebanon *Kans., U.S.A.*	39°49N 98°33W	**172** F4
Lebanon *Ky., U.S.A.*	37°34N 85°15W	**173** G11
Lebanon *Mo., U.S.A.*	37°41N 92°40W	**172** G7
Lebanon *N.H., U.S.A.*	43°39N 72°15W	**175** C12
Lebanon *Oreg., U.S.A.*	44°32N 122°55W	**168** D2
Lebanon *Pa., U.S.A.*	40°20N 76°26W	**175** F8
Lebanon *Tenn., U.S.A.*	36°12N 86°18W	**177** C11
Lebanon ■ *Asia*	34°0N 36°0E	**130** B3
Lebap □ *Turkmenistan*	40°0N 63°0E	**108** D6
Lebec *U.S.A.*	34°51N 118°52W	**171** L8
Lebedyan *Russia*	53°0N 39°10E	**85** F10
Lebedyn *Ukraine*	50°35N 34°30E	**86** F4
Lebel-sur-Quévillon		
Canada	49°3N 76°59W	**164** C4
Lebomboberge *S. Africa*	24°30S 32°0E	**145** B5
Lębork *Poland*	54°33N 17°46E	**82** D4
Lebowakgomo *S. Africa*	24°12S 29°30E	**145** B4
Lebrija *Spain*	36°53N 6°5W	**89** J4
Lebsko, Jezioro *Poland*	54°40N 17°25E	**82** A4
Lebu *Chile*	37°40S 73°47W	**190** D1
Leça da Palmeira		
Portugal	41°12N 8°42W	**88** D2
Lecce *Italy*	40°23N 18°11E	**95** B11
Lecco *Italy*	45°51N 9°23E	**92** C6
Lecco, L. di *Italy*	45°55N 9°19E	**92** C6
Lécera *Spain*	41°13N 0°43W	**90** D4
Lech *Austria*	47°13N 10°9E	**78** D3
Lech → *Germany*	48°43N 10°56E	**77** G6
Lechang *China*	25°10N 113°20E	**117** E9
Lechena *Greece*	37°57N 21°16E	**98** D3
Lechtaler Alpen *Austria*	47°15N 10°30E	**78** D3
Lecontes Mills *U.S.A.*	41°5N 78°17W	**174** E6
Lectoure *France*	43°56N 0°38E	**72** E4
Łęczna *Poland*	51°18N 22°53E	**83** G9
Łęczyca *Poland*	52°5N 19°15E	**83** F6
Ledang, Gunung		
Malaysia	2°22N 102°37E	**121** L4
Ledesma *Spain*	41°6N 5°59W	**88** D5
Lednice *Czech Rep.*	48°46N 16°48E	**79** C9
Ledong *China*	18°41N 109°5E	**117** a
Leduc *Canada*	53°15N 113°30W	**162** C6
Lee *Fla., U.S.A.*	30°25N 83°18W	**178** E6
Lee *Mass., U.S.A.*	42°19N 73°15W	**175** D11
Lee → *Ireland*	51°53N 8°56W	**64** E3
Lee Vining *U.S.A.*	37°58N 119°7W	**170** H7
Leech L. *U.S.A.*	47°10N 94°24W	**172** B6
Leechburg *U.S.A.*	40°37N 79°36W	**174** F5
Leeds *U.K.*	53°48N 1°33W	**66** D6
Leeds *U.S.A.*	33°33N 86°33W	**177** E11
Leek *Neths.*	53°10N 6°24E	**69** A6
Leek *U.K.*	53°7N 2°1W	**66** D5
Leeman *Australia*	29°57S 114°58E	**149** E1
Leeper *U.S.A.*	41°22N 79°18W	**174** E5
Leer *Germany*	53°13N 7°26E	**76** B3
Leesburg *Fla., U.S.A.*	28°49N 81°53W	**179** G8
Leesburg *U.S.A.*	39°7N 77°34W	**174** F7
Leeston *N.Z.*	43°45S 172°19E	**155** D7
Leesville *U.S.A.*	31°8N 93°16W	**176** F8
Leeton *Australia*	34°33S 146°23E	**153** C7
Leetonia *U.S.A.*	40°53N 80°45W	**174** F4
Leeu Gamka *S. Africa*	32°47S 21°59E	**144** D3
Leeuwarden *Neths.*	53°15N 5°48E	**69** A5
Leeuwin, C. *Australia*	34°20S 115°9E	**149** F2
Leeuwin Naturaliste △		
Australia	34°6S 115°3E	**149** F2
Leeward Is. *Atl. Oc.*	16°30N 63°30W	**183** C7
Lefka *Cyprus*	35°6N 32°51E	**101** D11
Lefkada *Greece*	38°40N 20°43E	**98** C2
Lefkimi *Greece*	39°25N 20°3E	**101** A4
Lefkimis, Akra *Greece*	39°29N 20°4E	**101** A4
Lefkonko *Cyprus*	35°18N 33°44E	**101** D12
Lefkosia = Nicosia		
Cyprus	35°10N 33°25E	**101** D12
Lefroy *Canada*	44°16N 79°34W	**174** B5
Lefroy, L. *Australia*	31°21S 121°40E	**149** F3
Leg → *Poland*	50°42N 21°50E	**83** H8
Leganés *Spain*	40°19N 3°45W	**88** E7
Legazpi *Phil.*	13°10N 123°45E	**119** E5
Lège-Cap-Ferret *France*	44°48N 1°9W	**72** D2
Legendre I. *Australia*	20°22S 116°55E	**148** D2
Leghorn = Livorno *Italy*	43°33N 10°19E	**92** E7
Legian *Indonesia*	8°42S 115°10E	**119** K18
Legionowo *Poland*	52°25N 20°50E	**83** F7
Legnago *Italy*	45°11N 11°18E	**92** C8
Legnano *Italy*	45°36N 8°54E	**92** C5
Legnica *Poland*	51°12N 16°10E	**83** G3
Legrad *Croatia*	46°17N 16°51E	**92** B13
Leh *India*	34°9N 77°35E	**125** B7
Lehigh Acres *U.S.A.*	26°36N 81°39W	**179** H8
Lehighton *U.S.A.*	40°50N 75°43W	**175** F9
Lehliu *Romania*	44°29N 26°50E	**81** F11
Lehrte *Germany*	52°22N 9°58E	**76** C5

Lehututu *Botswana* 23°54S 21°55E 144 B3
Lei Shui → *China* 26°55N 112°35E 117 C9
Leiah *Pakistan* 30°58N 70°58E 124 D4
Leibnitz *Austria* 46°47N 15°34E 78 E8
Leibo *China* 28°11N 103°54E 116 C4
Leicester *U.K.* 52°38N 1°8W 67 E6
Leicester City □ *U.K.* 52°38N 1°8W 67 E6
Leicestershire □ *U.K.* 52°41N 1°17W 67 E6
Leichhardt →
  Australia 17°35S 139°48E 150 B2
Leichhardt Ra.
  Australia 20°46S 147°40E 150 C4
Leiden *Neths.* 52°9N 4°30E 69 B4
Leie → *Belgium* 51°2N 3°45E 69 C3
Leifers = Láives *Italy* 46°26N 11°20E 93 B8
Leigh → *Australia* 38°18S 144°30E 152 E6
Leigh Creek *Australia* 30°38S 138°26E 152 A3
Leimen *Germany* 49°21N 8°41E 77 F4
Leimus *Nic.* 14°40N 84°3W 182 D3
Leine → *Germany* 52°43N 9°36E 76 C5
Leinefelde *Germany* 51°23N 10°19E 76 D6
Leinster *Australia* 27°51S 120°36E 149 E3
Leinster □ *Ireland* 53°3N 7°8W 64 C4
Leinster, Mt. *Ireland* 52°37N 6°46W 64 D5
Leipalingis *Lithuania* 54°5N 23°51E 82 D10
Leipzig *Germany* 51°18N 12°22E 76 D8
Leiria *Portugal* 39°46N 8°53W 88 F2
Leiria □ *Portugal* 39°46N 8°53W 88 F2
Leirvik *Norway* 59°47N 5°28E 61 G11
Leishan *China* 26°15N 108°20E 116 D7
Leisler, Mt. *Australia* 23°23S 129°20E 148 D4
Leisure City *U.S.A.* 25°30N 80°26W 179 K9
Leith *U.K.* 55°59N 3°11W 65 F5
Leith Hill *U.K.* 51°11N 0°22W 67 F7
Leitha → *Europe* 47°50N 17°15E 79 D10
Leitir Ceanainn = Letterkenny
  Ireland 54°57N 7°45W 64 B4
Leitrim *Ireland* 54°0N 8°5W 64 B3
Leitrim □ *Ireland* 54°8N 8°0W 64 B4
Leitza *Spain* 43°5N 1°55W 90 B3
Leixlip *Ireland* 53°22N 6°30W 64 C5
Leiyang *China* 26°27N 112°45E 117 D9
Leizhou *China* 20°52N 110°8E 117 G8
Leizhou Bandao *China* 21°0N 110°0E 116 G7
Leizhou Wan *China* 20°50N 110°20E 117 G8
Lek → *Neths.* 51°54N 4°35E 69 C4
Leka *Norway* 65°5N 11°35E 60 D14
Lekani *Greece* 41°10N 24°35E 97 E8
Lekbibaj *Albania* 42°17N 19°56E 96 D3
Lekeitio *Spain* 43°20N 2°32W 90 B2
Lekki Lagoon *Nigeria* 6°30N 4°7E 139 D5
Léko *Mali* 13°37N 9°2W 138 C3
Lekoui *Burkina Faso* 12°37N 3°40W 138 C4
Leksand *Sweden* 60°44N 15°1E 62 D9
Leland *Mich., U.S.A.* 45°1N 85°45W 173 C11
Leland *Miss., U.S.A.* 33°24N 90°54W 177 E9
Lelâng *Sweden* 59°10N 12°5E 62 E6
Leleque *Argentina* 42°28S 71°0W 192 B2
Leling *China* 37°44N 117°13E 115 F9
Lélouma *Guinea* 11°11N 12°56W 138 C2
Lelystad *Neths.* 52°30N 5°25E 69 B5
Lem *Denmark* 56°1N 8°24E 63 H2
Lema *Nigeria* 12°58N 4°13E 139 C5
Léman, L. *Europe* 46°26N 6°30E 71 F13
Lembar *Indonesia* 8°45S 116°4E 148 A2
Lembongan, Nusa
  Indonesia 8°40S 115°27E 119 K18
Lembuak *Indonesia* 8°36S 116°11E 119 K19
Lemera
  Dem. Rep. of the Congo 3°0S 28°55E 142 C2
Lemesós = Limassol
  Cyprus 34°42N 33°1E 101 E12
Lemhi Ra. *U.S.A.* 44°30N 113°30W 168 D7
Lemmenjoki △ *Finland* 68°40N 25°30E 60 B21
Lemmer *Neths.* 52°51N 5°43E 69 B5
Lemmon *U.S.A.* 45°57N 102°10W 172 C2
Lemon Grove *U.S.A.* 32°44N 117°1W 171 N9
Lemoore *U.S.A.* 36°18N 119°46W 170 J7
Lempdes-sur-Allagnon
  France 45°22N 3°17E 72 C7
Lemvig *Denmark* 56°33N 8°20E 63 H2
Lena → *Russia* 72°52N 126°40E 107 B13
Lena Pillars = Lenskiy Stolby
  Russia 60°55N 126°0E 107 C13
Lenadoon Pt. *Ireland* 54°18N 9°3W 64 B2
Lenart *Slovenia* 46°36N 15°48E 93 B12
Lenartovce *Slovak Rep.* 48°18N 20°19E 79 C13
Lencloître *France* 46°50N 0°20E 70 F7
Lençóis *Brazil* 12°35S 41°24W 189 C2
Lençóis Maranhenses △
  Brazil 2°30S 43°0W 189 A2
Lendava *Slovenia* 46°35N 16°25E 93 B13
Lendinara *Italy* 45°5N 11°36E 93 C8
Lenger *Kazakhstan* 42°12N 69°54E 109 D7
Lengerich *Germany* 52°11N 7°52E 76 C3
Lenggong *Malaysia* 5°6N 100°58E 121 K3
Lenggries *Germany* 47°41N 11°35E 77 H7
Lengshuijiang *China* 27°40N 111°26E 117 D8
Lengshuitan *China* 26°27N 111°35E 117 D8
Lengua de Vaca, Pta.
  Chile 30°14S 71°38W 190 C1
Lengwe △ *Malawi* 16°14S 34°45E 143 F3
Lengyeltóti *Hungary* 46°40N 17°40E 80 D2
Lenhovda *Sweden* 57°0N 15°16E 63 G9
Lenina, Kanal → *Russia* 43°44N 45°17E 87 J7
Lenine *Ukraine* 45°17N 35°46E 85 K8
Leningrad □ *Russia* 59°40N 32°0E 84 C7
Leningorsk = Ridder
  Kazakhstan 50°20N 83°30E 109 B10
Leninogorsk *Russia* 54°36N 52°30E 108 B4
Leninsk *Russia* 48°40N 45°15E 87 F7
Leninsk-Kuznetskiy
  Russia 54°44N 86°10E 109 B11
Leninskoye *Russia* 58°23N 47°3E 86 A8
Lenk *Switz.* 46°27N 7°28E 77 J3
Lenkoran = Länkäran
  Azerbaijan 38°48N 48°52E 105 C13
Lenmalu *Indonesia* 1°45S 130°15E 118 E7
Lennartsfors *Sweden* 59°20N 11°55E 62 E5
Lenne → *Germany* 51°25N 7°29E 76 D3
Lennestadt *Germany* 51°8N 8°2E 76 D4
Lennox *U.S.A.* 43°21N 96°53W 172 D5
Lennox, I. *Chile* 55°18S 66°50W 192 E4
Lennoxville *Canada* 45°22N 71°51W 175 A13
Leno *Italy* 45°22N 10°13E 92 C7
Lenoir *U.S.A.* 35°55N 81°32W 177 D14
Lenoir City *U.S.A.* 35°48N 84°16W 177 D12
Lenore L. *Canada* 52°30N 104°59W 167 C8
Lenox *U.S.A.* 31°16N 83°28W 178 D6
Lenox *Mass., U.S.A.* 42°22N 73°17W 175 D11
Lens *France* 50°26N 2°50E 71 B9

Lensahn *Germany* 54°13N 10°53E 76 A6
Lensk *Russia* 60°48N 114°55E 107 C12
Lenskiy Stolby *Russia* 60°55N 126°0E 107 C13
Lentas *Greece* 34°56N 24°56E 101 E6
Lentekhi *Georgia* 42°47N 42°45E 87 J6
Lenti *Hungary* 46°37N 16°33E 80 D1
Lentini *Italy* 37°17N 15°0E 95 E8
Lenwood *U.S.A.* 34°53N 117°7W 171 L9
Lenya *Burma* 11°33N 98°57E 121 G2
Lenzen *Germany* 53°6N 11°26E 76 B7
Léo *Burkina Faso* 11°3N 2°2W 138 C4
Leoben *Austria* 47°22N 15°5E 78 E8
Leodhais = Lewis *U.K.* 58°9N 6°40W 65 C2
Leola *U.S.A.* 45°43N 98°56W 172 C4
Leominster *U.K.* 52°14N 2°43W 67 E5
Leominster *U.S.A.* 42°32N 71°46W 175 D13
Léon *France* 43°53N 1°18W 72 E2
León *Mexico* 21°6N 101°41W 180 C4
León *Nic.* 12°27N 86°51W 182 D2
León *Spain* 42°38N 5°34W 88 D5
Leon *U.S.A.* 40°44N 93°45W 172 E7
León □ *Spain* 42°40N 5°55W 88 C5
Leon → *U.S.A.* 31°14N 97°28W 176 F6
León, Montes de *Spain* 42°30N 6°18W 88 C4
Leonardo da Vinci, Roma ✈ (FCO)
  Italy 41°48N 12°15E 93 G9
Leonardtown *U.S.A.* 38°17N 76°38W 173 F15
Leonardville *Namibia* 23°29S 18°49E 144 D2
Leonárisso *Cyprus* 35°28N 34°8E 101 D13
Leonberg *Germany* 48°49N 9°1E 77 G5
Léoncel *France* 44°50N 5°13E 73 D9
Leonessa *Italy* 42°34N 12°58E 93 F9
Leonforte *Italy* 37°38N 14°23E 95 E7
Leongatha *Australia* 38°30S 145°58E 153 E6
Leonia *U.S.A.* 30°55N 86°11W 178 E3
Leonídio *Greece* 37°9N 22°52E 98 D4
Leonora *Australia* 28°49S 121°19E 149 E3
Leopoldina *Brazil* 21°28S 42°40W 191 A7
Leopoldo Bulhões
  Brazil 16°37S 48°46W 189 D1
Leopoldsburg *Belgium* 51°7N 5°13E 69 C5
Leoti *U.S.A.* 38°29N 101°21W 172 F3
Leova *Moldova* 46°28N 28°15E 81 D13
Leoville *Canada* 53°39N 107°33W 167 C7
Lepe *Spain* 37°15N 7°12W 89 H3
Lepel = Lyepyel *Belarus* 54°50N 28°40E 84 E5
Lepenou *Greece* 38°42N 21°17E 98 C3
Leping *China* 28°47N 117°7E 117 C11
Lépo, L. do *Angola* 17°0S 19°0E 144 A2
Lepontine, Alpi *Italy* 46°22N 8°27E 92 B5
Leposavić *Kosovo* 43°6N 20°48E 96 C4
Lepsény *Hungary* 47°0N 18°15E 80 D3
Leptis Magna *Libya* 32°40N 14°12E 135 B8
Lequeitio = Lekeitio
  Spain 43°20N 2°32W 90 B2
Lercara Friddi *Italy* 37°45N 13°36E 94 E6
Léré *Chad* 9°39N 14°13E 139 D7
Léré *Mali* 15°45N 4°55W 138 B4
Lere *Bauchi, Nigeria* 9°43N 9°18E 139 D6
Lere *Kaduna, Nigeria* 10°23N 8°35E 139 C6
Léribe *Lesotho* 28°51S 28°3E 145 C4
Lérici *Italy* 44°4N 9°55E 92 D6
Lérida = Lleida *Spain* 41°37N 0°39E 90 D5
Lérins, Îs. de *France* 43°31N 7°3E 73 E11
Lerma *Spain* 42°0N 3°47W 88 C7
Leros *Greece* 37°10N 26°50E 99 D8
Lérouville *France* 48°44N 5°30E 71 D12
Lerum *Sweden* 57°46N 12°16E 63 G6
Lerwick *U.K.* 60°9N 1°9W 65 A7
Leş *Romania* 46°58N 21°50E 80 D6
Les Abrets *France* 45°32N 5°35E 73 C9
Les Andelys *France* 49°15N 1°25E 70 C8
Les Borges Blanques
  Spain 41°31N 0°52E 90 D5
Les Cayes *Haiti* 18°15N 73°46W 183 C5
Les Coteaux *Canada* 45°15N 74°13W 175 A10
Les Escoumins *Canada* 48°21N 69°24W 165 C6
Les Essarts *France* 46°47N 1°12W 70 F5
Les Herbiers *France* 46°52N 1°1W 70 F5
Les Minquiers, Plateau des
  Chan. Is. 48°58N 2°8W 70 D4
Les Pieux *France* 49°30N 1°48W 70 C5
Les Ponts-de-Cé *France* 47°25N 0°30W 70 E6
Les Riceys *France* 47°59N 4°22E 71 E11
Les Sables-d'Olonne
  France 46°30N 1°45W 72 B2
Les Vans *France* 44°25N 4°7E 73 D8
L'Escala *Spain* 42°7N 3°8E 90 C8
Leshan *China* 29°33N 103°41E 116 C4
Leshwe △
  Dem. Rep. of the Congo 12°45S 29°30E 143 E2
Lésina *Italy* 41°52N 15°21E 93 G12
Lésina, L. di *Italy* 41°53N 15°26E 93 G12
Lesjöfors *Sweden* 59°58N 14°11E 62 E8
Lesko *Poland* 49°30N 22°23E 83 J9
Leskov I. *Antarctica* 56°0S 28°0W 55 B1
Leskovac *Serbia* 43°0N 21°58E 96 C5
Leskovik *Albania* 40°10N 20°34E 96 F4
Leslie *U.S.A.* 31°57N 84°5W 178 D5
Leśna *Poland* 51°1N 15°15E 83 G2
Lesneven *France* 48°35N 4°20W 70 D2
Leśnica *Poland* 50°26N 18°11E 83 H5
Leśnica *Serbia* 44°39N 19°20E 96 B3
Lesnoye *Russia* 58°15N 35°18E 84 C8
Lesopilnoye *Russia* 46°44N 134°20E 112 A7
Lesotho ■ *Africa* 29°0S 28°0E 145 C4
Lesozavodsk *Russia* 45°30N 133°29E 112 B6
Lesparre-Médoc *France* 45°18N 0°57W 72 C3
L'Espluga de Francolí
  Spain 41°24N 1°7E 90 D6
Lessay *France* 49°14N 1°30W 70 C5
Lesse → *Belgium* 50°8N 5°9E 69 D5
Lesse et Lomme △ *Belgium* 50°8N 5°9E 69 D5
Lessebo *Sweden* 56°45N 15°16E 63 G9
Lesser Antilles *W. Indies* 15°0N 61°0W 183 D7
Lesser Slave L. *Canada* 55°30N 115°25W 167 B5
Lesser Sunda Is. *Indonesia* 8°0S 120°0E 119 F6
Lessines *Belgium* 50°42N 3°50E 69 D3
Lester B. Pearson Int., Toronto ✈
  (YYZ) *Canada* 43°46N 79°35W 174 C5
Lestock *Canada* 51°19N 103°59W 167 C8
Lesueur △ *Australia* 30°11S 115°10E 149 F2
Lésvos = Lesbos *Greece* 39°10N 26°20E 99 B8
Leszno *Poland* 51°50N 16°30E 83 G3
Letaba → *S. Africa* 23°59S 31°50E 145 B5
Letälven → *Sweden* 59°5N 14°20E 62 E8
Letchworth *U.K.* 51°59N 0°13W 67 F7

Letea, Ostrov *Romania* 45°18N 29°20E 81 E14
Lethbridge *Canada* 49°45N 112°45W 162 D6
Lethem *Guyana* 3°20N 59°50W 186 C7
Leti, Kepulauan
  Indonesia 8°10S 128°0E 119 F7
Leti Is. = Leti, Kepulauan
  Indonesia 8°10S 128°0E 119 F7
Letiahau → *Botswana* 21°16S 24°0E 144 B3
Leticia *Colombia* 4°9S 70°0W 186 D5
Leting *China* 39°23N 118°55E 115 E10
Letjiesbos *S. Africa* 32°34S 22°16E 144 D3
Letlhakane *Botswana* 21°27S 25°30E 144 B4
Letlhakeng *Botswana* 24°0S 24°59E 144 B3
Letpadan *Burma* 17°45N 95°45E 123 L19
Letpan *Burma* 19°28N 94°10E 123 K19
Letsôk-aw Kyun
  Burma 11°30N 98°25E 121 G2
Letterkenny *Ireland* 54°57N 7°45W 64 B4
Leu *Romania* 44°10N 24°0E 81 F7
Leucadia *U.S.A.* 33°4N 117°18W 171 M9
Leucate *France* 42°56N 3°3E 72 F7
Leucate, Étang de *France* 42°50N 3°0E 72 F7
Leuchars *U.K.* 56°24N 2°53W 65 E5
Leuk *Switz.* 46°19N 7°37E 77 J3
Leuşeni *Moldova* 46°49N 28°12E 81 D13
Leuser, Gunung
  Indonesia 3°46N 97°12E 118 D1
Leutkirch *Germany* 47°49N 10°1E 77 H6
Leuven *Belgium* 50°52N 4°42E 69 D4
Leuze-en-Hainaut
  Belgium 50°36N 3°37E 69 D3
Lev Tolstoy *Russia* 53°13N 39°29E 84 F10
Levan *Albania* 40°40N 19°28E 96 F3
Levanger *Norway* 63°45N 11°19E 60 E14
Levant, Î. du *France* 43°3N 6°28E 73 E10
Levante, Riviera di *Italy* 44°10N 9°7E 92 D6
Lévanto *Italy* 44°10N 9°38E 92 D6
Lévanzo *Italy* 38°0N 12°20E 94 E5
Levelland *U.S.A.* 33°35N 102°23W 176 E3
Leven *U.K.* 56°12N 3°0W 65 E5
Leven, L. *U.K.* 56°12N 3°22W 65 E5
Leveque C. *Australia* 16°20S 123°0E 148 C3
Leverano *Italy* 40°17N 18°0E 95 B10
Leverkusen *Germany* 51°1N 7°1E 76 D3
Levice *Slovak Rep.* 48°13N 18°35E 79 C11
Lévico Terme *Italy* 46°0N 11°18E 93 C8
Levie *France* 41°40N 9°7E 73 G13
Levier *France* 46°58N 6°8E 71 F13
Levin *N.Z.* 40°37S 175°18E 154 C4
Levis *Canada* 46°48N 71°9W 165 C5
Levis, L. *Canada* 62°37N 117°58W 162 A5
Levitha *Greece* 37°0N 26°28E 99 D8
Levittown *N.Y.,*
  U.S.A. 40°44N 73°31W 175 F11
Levittown *Pa., U.S.A.* 40°9N 74°51W 175 F10
Levka *Bulgaria* 41°52N 26°15E 97 E10
Levka Oros *Greece* 35°18N 24°3E 101 D6
Levkás = Lefkada *Greece* 38°40N 20°43E 98 C2
Levočá *Slovak Rep.* 49°2N 20°35E 83 K8
Levroux *France* 46°59N 1°38E 71 F8
Levski *Bulgaria* 43°21N 25°10E 97 C9
Levskigrad = Karlovo
  Bulgaria 42°38N 24°47E 97 D8
Levuka *Fiji* 17°34S 179°0E 154 a
Lewes *U.K.* 50°52N 0°1E 67 G8
Lewes *U.S.A.* 38°46N 75°9W 173 F16
Lewin Brzeski *Poland* 50°45N 17°37E 83 H4
Lewis *U.K.* 58°9N 6°40W 65 C2
Lewis → *U.S.A.* 45°51N 122°48W 170 E4
Lewis, Butt of *U.K.* 58°31N 6°16W 65 C2
Lewis and Clark △
  U.S.A. 46°8N 123°53W 170 D3
Lewis Pass *N.Z.* 42°31S 172°11E 155 C7
Lewis Ra. *Australia* 20°3S 128°50E 148 D4
Lewis Range *U.S.A.* 48°5N 113°5W 168 B7
Lewis Run *U.S.A.* 41°52N 78°40W 174 E6
Lewisburg *Pa., U.S.A.* 40°58N 76°54W 174 F8
Lewisburg *Tenn.,*
  U.S.A. 35°27N 86°48W 177 D11
Lewisburg *W. Va.,*
  U.S.A. 37°48N 80°27W 173 G13
Lewisporte *Canada* 49°15N 55°3W 165 C8
Lewiston *Idaho, U.S.A.* 46°25N 117°1W 168 C5
Lewiston *Maine, U.S.A.* 44°6N 70°13W 173 C18
Lewiston *N.Y., U.S.A.* 43°11N 79°3W 174 C5
Lewistown *Mont.,*
  U.S.A. 47°4N 109°26W 168 C9
Lewistown *Pa., U.S.A.* 40°36N 77°34W 174 F7
Lewisville *U.S.A.* 33°52N 83°7W 178 B6
Lexington *Ga., U.S.A.* 33°52N 83°7W 178 B6
Lexington *Ill., U.S.A.* 39°6N 84°30W 172 E10
Lexington *Ky., U.S.A.* 38°3N 84°30W 173 F11
Lexington *Mich.,*
  U.S.A. 43°16N 82°32W 174 C2
Lexington *Mo., U.S.A.* 39°11N 93°52W 172 F7
Lexington *N.C.,*
  U.S.A. 35°49N 80°15W 177 D14
Lexington *Nebr., U.S.A.* 40°47N 99°45W 172 E4
Lexington *Ohio, U.S.A.* 40°41N 82°35W 174 F2
Lexington *Tenn.,*
  U.S.A. 35°39N 88°24W 177 D10
Lexington *Va., U.S.A.* 37°47N 79°27W 173 G14
Lexington Park
  U.S.A. 38°16N 76°27W 173 F15
Leyburn *U.K.* 54°19N 1°48W 66 C6
Leye *China* 24°48N 106°29E 116 E6
Leyland *U.K.* 53°42N 2°43W 66 D5
Leyte □ *Phil.* 11°0N 125°0E 119 F7
Lezajsk *Poland* 50°16N 22°25E 83 H9
Lezay *France* 46°15N 0°1W 72 B3
Lezhë *Albania* 41°47N 19°39E 96 E3
Lezhi *China* 30°19N 104°58E 116 B5
Lézignan-Corbières
  France 43°13N 2°43E 72 E6
Lézignan-Corbières *France* 45°49N 3°21E 72 E6
Lgov *Russia* 51°42N 35°16E 85 G8
Lhasa *China* 29°25N 90°58E 110 F7
Lhazê *China* 29°5N 87°38E 110 F6
L'Hermite, I. *Chile* 55°50S 68°0W 192 E3
Lessines *Belgium* 50°42N 3°50E 69 D3
Lhokseumawe *Indonesia* 5°10N 97°10E 118 C1
L'Hospitalet de Llobregat
  Spain 41°21N 2°6E 90 D7
Li *Thailand* 17°48N 98°57E 120 D2
Li Jiang → *China* 24°40N 110°40E 117 E8
Li Jiang △ *China* 24°38N 110°38E 117 E8
Li Shan *China* 35°30N 111°56E 114 G6
Li Shui → *China* 29°24N 112°1E 117 C9
Li Xian *Gansu, China* 34°10N 105°5E 114 H3
Li Xian *Hebei, China* 38°30N 115°35E 114 E8

Li Xian *Hunan, China* 29°36N 111°42E 117 C8
Liadi *Greece* 36°50N 26°11E 99 E8
Liancheng *China* 25°42N 116°40E 117 E11
Liancourt Rocks *Asia* 37°15N 131°52E 113 F5
Lianga *Phil.* 8°38N 126°6E 119 C7
Liangcheng *Nei Monggol Zizhiqu,*
  China 40°28N 112°25E 114 D7
Liangcheng *Shandong,*
  China 35°32N 119°37E 115 G10
Liangdang *China* 33°56N 106°18E 114 H4
Lianghe *China* 24°50N 98°20E 116 C2
Lianghekou *China* 21°37N 98°52E 116 C2
Liangping *China* 30°38N 107°47E 116 B6
Liangpran *Indonesia* 1°4N 114°23E 118 D4
Lianhua *China* 27°3N 113°54E 117 D9
Lianhua Shan *China* 23°40N 115°48E 117 F10
Lianjiang *Fujian,*
  China 26°12N 119°27E 117 D12
Lianjiang *Guangdong,*
  China 21°40N 110°0E 117 G8
Lianping *China* 24°26N 114°30E 117 E10
Lianshan *China* 24°38N 112°8E 117 E9
Lianshanguan *China* 40°53N 123°43E 115 D12
Lianshui *China* 33°42N 119°20E 115 H10
Lianyuan *China* 27°40N 111°38E 117 D8
Lianyungang *China* 34°40N 119°11E 115 G10
Lianzhou *China* 24°51N 112°22E 117 E9
Liao He → *China* 41°0N 121°50E 115 D11
Liaocheng *China* 36°28N 115°58E 114 F8
Liaodong Bandao
  China 40°0N 122°30E 115 E12
Liaodong Wan *China* 40°20N 121°10E 115 D11
Liaoning □ *China* 41°40N 122°30E 115 D11
Liaotung, G. of = Liaodong Wan
  China 40°20N 121°10E 115 D11
Liaoyang *China* 41°15N 122°58E 115 D12
Liaoyuan *China* 42°58N 125°2E 115 C13
Liaozhong *China* 41°23N 122°50E 115 D12
Liapades *Greece* 39°42N 19°40E 101 A3
Liard → *Canada* 61°51N 121°18W 162 A4
Liard River *Canada* 59°25N 126°5W 162 B3
Liari *Pakistan* 25°37N 66°30E 124 G2
Libanggaon *Nepal* 28°18N 82°38E 125 E10
Libau = Liepāja *Latvia* 56°30N 21°0E 82 B8
Libby *U.S.A.* 48°23N 115°33W 168 B6
Libenge
  Dem. Rep. of the Congo 3°40N 18°55E 140 D3
Liberal *U.S.A.* 37°3N 100°55W 172 G3
Liberdade *Brazil* 10°5S 70°20W 188 C3
Liberec *Czech Rep.* 50°47N 15°7E 78 A8
Liberecký □ *Czech Rep.* 50°45N 15°0E 78 A8
Liberia *Costa Rica* 10°40N 85°30W 182 D2
Liberia ■ *W. Afr.* 6°30N 9°30W 138 D3
Libertad *Brazil* 34°15S 70°45W 190 C1
Liberty *Mo., U.S.A.* 39°15N 94°25W 172 F7
Liberty *N.Y., U.S.A.* 41°48N 74°45W 175 E10
Liberty *Pa., U.S.A.* 41°34N 77°6W 174 E7
Liberty *Tex., U.S.A.* 30°3N 94°48W 176 F7
Liberty-Newark Int. ✈ (EWR)
  U.S.A. 40°42N 74°10W 175 F10
Líbïaž *Poland* 50°7N 19°21E 83 H6
Libîya, Sahrâ' *Africa* 25°0N 25°0E 135 C10
Libo *China* 25°22N 107°53E 116 E6
Liboobo, Tanjung
  Indonesia 0°54S 128°28E 119 E7
Libode *S. Africa* 31°33S 29°2E 145 D4
Libohovë *Albania* 40°3N 20°10E 96 F4
Libong, Ko *Thailand* 7°15N 99°23E 121 J2
Libourne *France* 44°55N 0°14W 72 D3
Libramont *Belgium* 49°55N 5°23E 69 E5
Libramont *Belgium* 41°12N 20°22E 96 B4
Libreville *Gabon* 0°25N 9°26E 140 D1
Libya ■ *N. Afr.* 27°0N 17°0E 135 C9
Libyan Desert = Libîya, Sahrâ'
  Africa 25°0N 25°0E 135 C10
Libyan Plateau = Ed Déffa
  Egypt 30°40N 26°30E 137 A2
Licantén *Chile* 35°55S 72°0W 190 D1
Licata *Italy* 37°6N 13°56E 94 E6
Lice *Turkey* 38°27N 40°39E 105 C9
Licheng *China* 36°28N 113°20E 114 F7
Lichfield *U.K.* 52°41N 1°49W 67 E6
Lichinga *Mozam.* 13°13S 35°11E 143 E4
Lichtenburg *S. Africa* 26°8S 26°8E 144 C4
Lichtenfels *Germany* 50°8N 11°4E 77 E7
Lichuan *Hubei, China* 30°18N 108°57E 116 B7
Lichuan *Jiangxi,*
  China 27°18N 116°55E 117 D11
Licking → *U.S.A.* 39°6N 84°30W 172 F11
Licosa, Punta *Italy* 40°15N 14°54E 95 B7
Licungo → *Mozam.* 17°40S 37°15E 143 F4
Lida *Belarus* 53°53N 25°15E 75 B13
Liden *Sweden* 62°42N 16°48E 62 B10
Lidhult *Sweden* 56°50N 13°27E 63 G7
Lidköping *Sweden* 58°31N 13°7E 63 F7
Lido *Niger* 12°54N 3°44E 139 C5
Lido di Roma = Ostia, Lido di
  Italy 41°43N 12°17E 93 G9
Lidoriki *Greece* 38°32N 22°12E 98 C4
Lidzbark *Poland* 53°15N 19°49E 83 E6
Lidzbark Warmiński
  Poland 54°7N 20°34E 82 D7
Liebenwalde *Germany* 52°52N 13°24E 76 C9
Lieberose *Germany* 51°59N 14°17E 76 D10
Liebig, Mt. *Australia* 23°18S 131°22E 148 D5
Liebling *Romania* 45°36N 21°20E 80 E6
Liechtenstein ■ *Europe* 47°8N 9°35E 77 H5
Liège *Belgium* 50°38N 5°35E 69 D5
Liège □ *Belgium* 50°32N 5°35E 69 D5
Liegnitz = Legnica
  Poland 51°12N 16°10E 83 G3
Lieksa *Finland* 63°18N 30°2E 60 E24
Lienart
  Dem. Rep. of the Congo 3°3N 25°31E 142 B2
Lienyünchiangshih =
  Lianyungang
  China 34°40N 119°11E 115 G10
Lienz *Austria* 46°50N 12°46E 78 E5
Liepāja *Latvia* 56°30N 21°0E 82 B8
Liepājas ezers *Latvia* 56°27N 21°3E 82 B8
Lier *Belgium* 51°7N 4°34E 69 C4
Lierne △ *Norway* 64°20N 13°50E 60 D15
Lieşti *Romania* 45°38N 27°34E 81 E12
Lietuva = Lithuania ■
  Europe 55°30N 24°0E 84 E2
Liévin *France* 50°24N 2°47E 71 B9
Lièvre → *Canada* 45°31N 75°26W 164 C4
Liezen *Austria* 47°34N 14°15E 78 E7
Liffey → *Ireland* 53°21N 6°13W 64 C5

Lifford *Ireland* 54°51N 7°29W 64 B4
Liffré *France* 48°12N 1°30W 70 D5
Lifudzin *Russia* 44°21N 134°58E 112 B7
Lighthouse Point *U.S.A.* 26°15N 80°7W 179 F9
Lighthouse Pt. *U.S.A.* 29°54N 84°21W 178 F5
Lightning Ridge
  Australia 29°22S 148°0E 151 D4
Lignano Sabbiadoro
  Italy 45°42N 13°9E 93 C10
Ligny-en-Barrois *France* 48°36N 5°20E 71 D12
Ligonha → *Mozam.* 16°54S 39°9E 143 F4
Ligonier *U.S.A.* 40°15N 79°14W 174 F5
Ligua, La → *Chile* 32°30S 71°16W 190 C1
Ligueil *France* 47°2N 0°49E 70 E7
Liguória *Greece* 37°37N 23°4E 98 D5
Liguria □ *Italy* 44°30N 8°50E 92 D5
Ligurian Sea *Medit. S.* 43°20N 9°0E 92 E5
Lihou Reefs and Cays
  Australia 17°25S 151°40E 150 B5
Lihué Calel △ *Argentina* 38°0S 65°10W 190 D2
Lijiang *China* 26°55N 100°20E 116 D3
Lik → *Laos* 18°31N 101°3E 120 C4
Likasi
  Dem. Rep. of the Congo 10°55S 26°48E 143 E2
Likenäs *Sweden* 60°37N 13°3E 62 D7
Likhoslavl *Russia* 57°12N 35°30E 84 D8
Likhovskoy *Russia* 48°10N 40°10E 87 F5
Likoma I. *Malawi* 12°3S 34°45E 143 E3
Likumburu *Tanzania* 9°43S 35°8E 143 D4
Liling *China* 27°42N 113°29E 117 D9
Lilla Edet *Sweden* 58°9N 12°8E 63 F6
Lille *France* 50°38N 3°3E 71 B10
Lille Bælt *Denmark* 55°20N 9°45E 63 J3
Lillebonne *France* 49°30N 0°32E 70 C7
Lillehammer *Norway* 61°8N 10°30E 60 F14
Lillesand *Norway* 58°15N 8°23E 61 G13
Lillhärdal *Sweden* 61°51N 14°4E 62 C8
Lilliam Pt. *Australia* 27°40S 126°6E 149 E4
Lillo *Spain* 39°45N 3°20W 88 F7
Lilloet *Canada* 50°44N 121°57W 162 C4
Lillooet → *Canada* 49°15N 121°57W 162 C4
Lilongwe *Malawi* 14°0S 33°48E 143 E3
Liloy *Phil.* 8°4N 122°39E 119 C6
Lim → *Europe* 43°45N 19°15E 96 C3
Lim Chu Kang *Singapore* 1°26N 103°43E 121 d
Lima *Indonesia* 3°39S 127°58E 119 E7
Lima *Peru* 12°3S 77°2W 188 C2
Lima *Mont., U.S.A.* 44°38N 112°36W 168 D7
Lima *N.Y., U.S.A.* 42°54N 77°36W 174 D7
Lima *Ohio, U.S.A.* 40°44N 84°6W 173 E11
Lima □ *Peru* 12°3S 77°2W 188 C2
Lima → *Portugal* 41°41N 8°50W 88 D2
Liman *Russia* 45°45N 47°12E 87 H8
Limanowa *Poland* 49°42N 20°22E 83 J7
Limassol *Cyprus* 34°42N 33°1E 101 E12
Limavady *U.K.* 55°3N 6°56W 64 A5
Limay → *Argentina* 39°0S 68°0W 192 A3
Limay Mahuida
  Argentina 37°10S 66°45W 190 D2
Limbach-Oberfrohna
  Germany 50°52N 12°43E 76 E8
Limbang *Malaysia* 4°42N 115°6E 118 D5
Limbara, Mte. *Italy* 40°51N 9°10E 94 D2
Limbaži *Latvia* 57°31N 24°42E 84 D3
Limbdi *India* 22°34N 71°51E 124 H4
Limbe *Cameroon* 4°1N 9°10E 139 E6
Limburg *Germany* 50°22N 8°4E 77 E4
Limburg □ *Belgium* 51°2N 5°25E 69 C5
Limburg □ *Neths.* 51°20N 5°55E 69 C5
Limedsforsen *Sweden* 60°52N 13°25E 62 D7
Limeira *Brazil* 22°35S 47°28W 191 A6
Limenaria *Greece* 40°38N 24°32E 97 F8
Limenas Chersonisou
  Greece 35°18N 25°21E 99 F7
Limerick *Ireland* 52°40N 8°37W 64 D3
Limerick *U.S.A.* 43°41N 70°48W 175 C14
Limerick □ *Ireland* 52°30N 8°50W 64 D3
Limestone *U.S.A.* 42°2N 78°38W 174 D6
Limestone → *Canada* 56°31N 94°7W 163 B10
Limfjorden *Denmark* 56°55N 9°0E 63 H3
Limia = Lima →
  Portugal 41°41N 8°50W 88 D2
Limingen *Norway* 64°48N 13°35E 60 D15
Limmared *Sweden* 57°34N 13°20E 63 G7
Limmen △ *Australia* 15°15S 135°30E 150 B2
Limmen Bight
  Australia 14°40S 135°35E 150 A2
Limmen Bight →
  Australia 15°7S 135°44E 150 B2
Limni *Greece* 38°43N 23°18E 98 C5
Limnos *Greece* 39°50N 25°5E 99 B7
Limoeiro *Brazil* 7°52S 35°27W 189 B3
Limoeiro do Norte *Brazil* 5°5S 38°0W 189 B3
Limoges *Canada* 45°20N 75°16W 175 A9
Limoges *France* 45°50N 1°15E 72 C5
Limón *Costa Rica* 10°0N 83°2W 182 E3
Limon *U.S.A.* 39°16N 103°41W 168 G12
Limone *Italy* 45°48N 10°47E 92 C7
Limone Piemonte *Italy* 44°12N 7°34E 92 D4
Limousin *France* 45°30N 1°30E 72 C5
Limousin, Plateaux du
  France 45°45N 1°15E 72 C5
Limoux *France* 43°4N 2°12E 72 E6
Limpopo □ *S. Africa* 24°5S 29°0E 145 B4
Limpopo → *Africa* 25°5S 33°30E 145 C5
Limuru *Kenya* 1°2S 36°35E 140 E7
Lin Xian *China* 37°57N 110°58E 114 F6
Lin'an *China* 30°15N 119°42E 117 B12
Linares *Chile* 35°50S 71°40W 190 D1
Linares *Mexico* 24°52N 99°34W 181 C5
Linares *Spain* 38°10N 3°40W 89 G7
Linaria *Greece* 38°55N 24°31E 98 C6
Linaro, Capo *Italy* 42°2N 11°50E 93 F8
Linate, Milano ✈ (LIN)
  Italy 45°28N 9°16E 92 C5
Lincang *China* 23°58N 100°1E 116 F3
Lincheng *China* 37°25N 114°30E 114 F8
Linchuan *China* 27°57N 116°15E 117 D11
Lincoln = Beamsville
  Canada 43°12N 79°28W 174 C5
Lincoln *Argentina* 34°55S 61°30W 190 C4
Lincoln *N.Z.* 43°38S 172°30E 155 D7
Lincoln *U.K.* 53°14N 0°32W 66 D7
Lincoln *Ill., U.S.A.* 40°9N 89°22W 172 E9
Lincoln *Kans., U.S.A.* 39°3N 98°9W 172 F4
Lincoln *Maine, U.S.A.* 45°22N 68°30W 173 B19
Lincoln *N.H., U.S.A.* 44°3N 71°40W 175 B13

Lincoln *N. Mex.,*
  U.S.A. 33°30N 105°23W 169
Lincoln *Nebr., U.S.A.* 40°49N 96°41W 172
Lincoln City *U.S.A.* 44°57N 124°1W 168
Lincoln Hav = Lincoln Sea
  Arctic 84°0N 55°0W
Lincoln Park *U.S.A.* 32°52N 84°20W 178
Lincoln Sea *Arctic* 84°0N 55°0W
Lincolnshire □ *U.K.* 53°14N 0°32W 66
Lincolnshire Wolds *U.K.* 53°26N 0°13W 66
Lincolnton *Ga., U.S.A.* 33°48N 82°29W 178
Lincolnton *N.C.,*
  U.S.A. 35°29N 81°16W 178
Lind *U.S.A.* 46°58N 118°37W 168
Linda *U.S.A.* 39°8N 121°34W 172
Lindale *U.S.A.* 34°11N 85°11W 178
Lindau *Germany* 47°33N 9°42E 77
Lindeman I. *Australia* 20°27S 149°3E 150
Lindeman Islands △
  Australia 20°28S 149°5E
Linden *Guyana* 6°0N 58°10W 186
Linden *Ala., U.S.A.* 32°18N 87°48W 178
Linden *Calif., U.S.A.* 38°1N 121°5W 172
Linden *Tex., U.S.A.* 33°1N 94°22W 176
Lindenhurst *U.S.A.* 40°41N 73°23W 175
Lindenow Fjord
  Greenland 60°30N 43°25W
Lindesberg *Sweden* 59°36N 15°15E
Lindesnes *Norway* 57°58N 7°3E 61
Lindi *Tanzania* 9°58S 39°38E 14
Lindi □ *Tanzania* 9°40S 38°30E 14
Lindi →
  Dem. Rep. of the Congo 0°33N 25°5E 14
Lindley *U.S.A.* 42°1N 77°8W 17
Lindö *Sweden* 58°37N 16°15E 6
Lindome *Sweden* 57°35S 12°5E
Lindos *Greece* 36°6N 28°4E 10
Lindos, Akra *Greece* 36°4N 28°10E 10
Lindoso *Portugal* 41°52N 8°11W
Lindow *Germany* 52°58N 12°59E
Lindsay *Canada* 44°22N 78°43W 1
Lindsay *Calif., U.S.A.* 36°12N 119°5W 1
Lindsay *Okla., U.S.A.* 34°50N 97°38W 1
Lindsborg *U.S.A.* 38°35N 97°40W 1
Lindsdal *Sweden* 56°44N 16°18E 6
Line Islands *Pac. Oc.* 7°0N 160°0W 15
Linesville *U.S.A.* 41°39N 80°26W 1
Lineville *U.S.A.* 33°19N 85°45W 1
Linfen *China* 36°3N 111°30E 1
Ling Xian *Hunan,*
  China 26°29N 113°48E 1
Ling Xian *Shandong,*
  China 37°22N 116°30E 1
Lingal *India* 16°17N 78°31E 1
Linganamakki Res.
  India 14°6N 74°52E 1
Lingao *China* 19°56N 109°42E
Lingayen *Phil.* 16°1N 120°14E 1
Lingayen G. *Phil.* 16°10N 120°15E 1
Lingbao *China* 34°31N 110°51E 1
Lingbi *China* 33°33N 117°33E 1
Lingbo *Sweden* 61°3N 16°41E 6
Lingchuan *Guangxi Zhuangzu,*
  China 25°26N 110°21E 1
Lingchuan *Shanxi,*
  China 35°45N 113°12E 1
Lingding Yang *China* 22°25N 113°44E
Lingen *Germany* 52°31N 7°19E
Lingga *Indonesia* 0°12S 104°37E 1
Lingga, Kepulauan
  Indonesia 0°10S 104°30E 1
Lingga Arch. = Lingga,
  Kepulauan *Indonesia* 0°10S 104°30E 1
Linghai *China* 41°11N 121°22E 11
Linghed *Sweden* 60°48N 15°55E
Linghem *Sweden* 58°26N 15°47E
Lingle *U.S.A.* 42°8N 104°21W 1
Lingqiu *China* 39°28N 114°22E 1
Lingshan *China* 22°25N 109°18E 1
Lingshou *China* 38°20N 114°20E 1
Lingshui *China* 18°27N 110°0E
Lingsugur *India* 16°10N 76°31E 1
Lingtai *China* 35°0N 107°40E 1
Linguère *Senegal* 15°25N 15°5W 1
Lingui *China* 25°12N 110°2E 1
Lingwu *China* 38°6N 106°20E 1
Lingyuan *China* 41°10N 119°15E 11
Lingyun *China* 25°2N 106°35E 1
Linhai *China* 28°50N 121°8E 11
Linhares *Brazil* 19°25S 40°4W 1
Linhe *China* 40°48N 107°20E 1
Linjiang *China* 41°50N 127°0E 1
Linköping *Sweden* 58°28N 15°36E
Linkou *China* 45°15N 130°18E 1
Linli *China* 29°27N 111°30E 1
Linnansaari △ *Finland* 62°3N 28°40E 1
Linnhe, L. *U.K.* 56°36N 5°25E
Linqi *China* 35°45N 113°52E 1
Linqing *China* 36°50N 115°42E 1
Linqu *China* 36°25N 118°30E 1
Linru *China* 33°5N 112°17E 11
Lins *Brazil* 21°40S 49°44W 1
Linshu *China* 34°53N 118°38E 1
Linshui *China* 30°21N 106°57E 1
Linstead *Jamaica* 18°8N 77°2W
Lintao *China* 35°26N 103°58E 1
Linth → *Switz.* 47°7N 9°7E
Linthal *Switz.* 46°54N 9°0E
Lin Xian *China* 37°57N 110°58E 114 F6
Linton *Canada* 47°15N 72°16W 1
Linton *N. Dak., U.S.A.* 46°16N 100°14W 1
Linton *Ind., U.S.A.* 39°2N 87°10W 1
Lintong *China* 34°20N 109°10E 1
Linwood *Canada* 43°35N 80°43W 1
Linwu *China* 25°19N 112°31E 1
Linxi *Hebei, China* 39°42N 118°26E 1
Linxi *Liaoning, China* 43°36N 118°2E 1
Linxia *China* 35°36N 103°10E 1
Linxiang *China* 29°28N 113°23E 1
Linyanti → *Africa* 17°50S 25°5E 1
Linyi *Shandong, China* 37°13N 116°54E 1
Linyi *Shandong, China* 35°5N 118°21E 1
Linying *China* 33°48N 113°56E 1
Linz *Austria* 48°18N 14°18E
Linz *Germany* 50°34N 7°17E 1
Linzhenzhen *China* 36°30N 109°59E 1
Linzhou *China* 36°4N 113°49E 1
Lion, G. du *France* 43°10N 4°0E 1
Lions, G. of = Lion, G. du
  France 43°10N 4°0E

's Den *Zimbabwe* 17°15S 30°5E **143** F3
's Head *Canada* 44°58N 81°15W **174** B3
no = Lyozna *Belarus* 55°0N 30°50E **84** E6
a *Phil.* 13°57N 121°10E **119** B6
ali *Mozam.* 15°50S 35°50E **143** F4
any *Slovak Rep.* 49°9N 20°58E **79** B13
ari *Italy* 38°26N 14°58E **95** D7
ari, I. *Italy* 38°29N 14°56E **95** D7
aly *Is. = Éolie, Ís.*
38°30N 14°57E **95** D7
cani *Moldova* 48°14N 26°48E **81** M1
eri *Finland* 62°31N 29°24E **60** E23
tsk *Russia* 52°37N 39°35E **85** F10
tsk □ *Russia* 52°50N 38°50E **86** D4
any *Poland* 53°2N 14°58E **83** E1
ing *China* 26°15N 109°7E **116** D7
si *Greece* 37°19N 26°50E **99** D8
ani *Kosovo* 42°31N 21°7E **96** D5
Moldova
a 48°14N 26°48E **81** B11
n Poland
czech Rep. 49°32N 17°36E **79** B10
o Poland 52°49N 19°15E **82** B9
va Romania 46°8N 21°42E **80** D6
vets Ukraine 49°12N 29°1E **75** D15
e → Germany 51°39N 6°36E **76** D2
idstadt Germany 51°41N 8°22E **76** D4
comb U.S.A. 36°14N 100°16W **176** C4
k Poland 53°44N 23°24E **82** E10
ko Poland 51°9N 21°40E **83** G8
ovský Hrádok
Slovak Rep. 49°2N 19°44E **79** B12
ovský Mikuláš
Slovak Rep. 49°6N 19°35E **79** B12
rap, C. Australia 38°50S 145°55E **153** E6
a China 24°30N 110°22E **117** E8
→ Uganda 2°17N 32°57E **142** B3
→ Italy 41°25N 13°52E **94** A6
a = Lliria Spain 39°37N 0°35W **91** F4
kovsk Kazakhstan 52°26N 67°37E **108** B6
la
em. Rep. of the Congo 2°12N 21°38E **140** D4
 la
oa Portugal 38°42N 9°8W **91** C1
oa Portugal 39°0N 9°12W **89** F1
on (LIS) Portugal 38°46N 9°8W **89** G1
on = Lisboa Portugal 38°42N 9°8W **89** G1
n Dak., U.S.A. 46°27N 97°41W **172** B5
on N.H., U.S.A. 44°13N 71°55W **175** B13
on N.Y., U.S.A. 44°43N 75°19W **175** B9
on Ohio, U.S.A. 40°46N 80°46W **174** F4
on Falls U.S.A. 44°0N 70°4W **173** D18
urn U.K. 54°31N 6°3W **64** B5
urne, C. U.S.A. 68°53N 166°13W **166** B6
annor B. Ireland 52°55N 9°24W **64** D2
a → Italy 41°11N 9°9E **94** A2
oonvarna Ireland 53°2N 9°18W **64** C2
e Jiang → China 24°15N 101°35E **116** E3
ni China 37°31N 111°8E **114** F6
u China 43°20N 124°18E **115** C13
ui Jiangsu, China 31°38N 119°2E **117** B12
ui Zhejiang, China 28°28N 119°54E **117** C12
chansk = Lysychansk
kraine 48°55N 38°30E **85** H10
eux France 49°1N 0°12E **70** C7
i Russia 21°0N 74°0W **167** K5
e-Jourdain Gers, France 43°36N 1°5E **72** E5
e-Jourdain Vienne,
France 46°13N 0°31E **72** B4
e-sur-la-Sorgue France 43°54N 5°2E **73** E9
e-sur-Tarn France 43°52N 1°49E **72** E5
nore Australia 28°44S 153°21E **151** D5
more Ireland 52°8N 7°55W **64** D4
os → Greece 41°15N 25°40E **97** E9
a Norway 58°7N 6°39E **63** D2
er, Mt. Antarctica 78°0S 162°0E **55** D11
on Australia 28°39S 152°6E **151** D5
owel Australia 43°44N 80°58W **174** C4
owel Ireland 52°27N 9°29W **64** D2
owel Ireland 52°27N 9°29W **64** D2
Sweden 63°19N 14°51E **62** A8
et-Mixe France 44°2N 1°15W **72** D2
hina Guangxi Zhuangzu,
hina 23°12N 109°8E **116** F7
ng Sichuan, China 30°1N 100°17E **116** B3
ng Qu → China 28°4N 101°32E **116** C3
ni → Lebanon 33°20N 35°15E **130** B4
field Australia 36°18S 142°52E **152** D5
field Calif., U.S.A. 40°24N 120°23W **170** G6
hfield Conn.,
S.A. 41°45N 73°11W **175** E11
field Ill., U.S.A. 39°11N 89°39W **172** F9
hfield Minn., U.S.A. 45°6N 94°32W **172** C6
hfield △ Australia 13°14S 131°1E **148** B5
ni Romania 47°32N 26°32E **81** C11
gow Australia 33°25S 150°8E **153** B9
ino, Akra Greece 55°30N 24°0E **84** E2
uania ■ Europe 55°30N 24°0E **84** E2
a Slovenia 46°3N 14°50E **93** B11
z U.S.A. 40°9N 76°18W **175** F8
choro Greece 40°8N 22°34E **96** F6
měřice Czech Rep. 50°33N 14°10E **78** A7
mýsl Czech Rep. 49°52N 16°20E **78** B9
chau Austria 48°58N 15°4E **78** C8
e Abaco Bahamas 26°50N 77°30W **182** A4
e Andaman I.
dia 10°45N 92°30E **127** J11
= Aral Sea = Northern Aral
a Kazakhstan 46°20N 60°30E **108** C6
e Barrier I. N.Z. 36°12S 175°8E **154** C4
e Basses Sri Lanka 6°24N 81°43E **127** L5
e Belt Mts. U.S.A. 46°40N 110°45W **176** C8
e Bighorn Battlefield ○
S.A. 45°34N 107°25W **168** D10
e Blue → U.S.A. 39°42N 96°41W **172** F5
e Buffalo →
hada 61°0N 113°46W **162** A6
e Cayman
yman Is. 19°41N 80°3W **182** C3
e Churchill →
hada 57°30N 95°22W **163** B9
e Coco I. Burma 14°10N 93°13E **127** H11
e Colorado →
S.A. 36°12N 111°48W **169** H8
e Current Canada 55°59N 82°0W **164** D3
e Current →
S.A. 36°56N 90°15W **172** G8
e Desert △
stralia 27°25S 141°30E **152** D4
e Diomede I.
S.A. 65°45N 168°56W **166** B6

Little Falls *Minn.*,
U.S.A. 45°59N 94°22W **172** C6
Little Falls *N.Y., U.S.A.* 43°3N 74°51W **175** C10
Little Fork → *U.S.A.* 48°31N 93°35W **172** A7
Little Grand Rapids
Canada 52°0N 95°29W **163** C9
Little Humboldt →
U.S.A. 41°1N 117°43W **168** F5
Little Inagua I.
Bahamas 21°40N 73°50W **183** B5
Little Karoo *S. Africa* 33°45S 21°0E **144** D3
Little Khingan Mts. = Xiao
Hinggan Ling *China* 49°0N 127°0E **111** B14
Little Lake *U.S.A.* 35°56N 117°55W **171** K9
Little Laut Is. = Laut Kecil,
Kepulauan *Indonesia* 4°45S 115°40E **118** E5
Little Mecatina = Petit-
Mécatina → *Canada* 50°40N 59°30W **165** B8
Little Minch *U.K.* 57°35N 6°45W **65** D2
Little Missouri →
U.S.A. 47°36N 102°25W **172** B2
Little Nicobar *India* 7°20N 93°40E **127** L11
Little Ouse → *U.K.* 52°22N 1°12E **67** E9
Little Rann *India* 23°25N 71°25E **124** H4
Little Red → *U.S.A.* 35°11N 91°27W **176** D9
Little River *N.Z.* 43°45S 172°49E **155** D7
Little Rock *U.S.A.* 34°45N 92°17W **176** D8
Little Ruaha → *Tanzania* 7°57S 37°53E **142** D4
Little Sable Pt. *U.S.A.* 43°38N 86°33W **172** D10
Little Scarcies →
S. Leone 8°50N 13°10W **138** D2
Little Sioux → *U.S.A.* 41°48N 96°4W **172** E5
Little Smoky →
Canada 54°44N 117°11W **162** C5
Little Snake →
U.S.A. 40°27N 108°26W **168** F9
Little Tobago
Trin. & Tob. 11°18N 60°30W **187** J16
Little Valley *U.S.A.* 42°15N 78°48W **174** D6
Little Wabash →
U.S.A. 37°55N 88°5W **172** G9
Little White →
U.S.A. 43°40N 100°40W **172** D3
Little Zab = Zāb aş Şaghīr →
Iraq 35°17N 43°29E **105** E10
Littlefield *U.S.A.* 33°55N 102°20W **176** E3
Littlehampton *U.K.* 50°49N 0°32W **67** G7
Littleton *U.S.A.* 44°18N 71°46W **175** B13
Littoral □ *Cameroon* 4°0N 10°0E **139** E7
Litvínov *Czech Rep.* 50°36N 13°37E **78** A6
Liu He → *China* 40°55N 121°35E **115** D11
Liu Jiang → *China* 23°55N 109°30E **116** F7
Liuba *China* 33°38N 106°55E **116** A6
Liucheng *China* 24°38N 109°14E **116** E7
Liugou *China* 40°57N 118°15E **115** D10
Liuhe *China* 42°17N 125°43E **115** C13
Liuheng Dao *China* 29°40N 122°5E **117** C14
Liujiang *China* 24°26N 109°11E **116** E7
Liukang Tenggaja = Sabalana,
Kepulauan *Indonesia* 6°45S 118°50E **119** F5
Liuli *Tanzania* 11°3S 34°38E **143** E3
Liupan Shan *China* 35°39N 106°12E **114** G4
Liupanshui *China* 26°38N 104°48E **116** D5
Liuwa Plain *Zambia* 14°20S 22°30E **141** G4
Liuyang *China* 28°10N 113°37E **117** C9
Liuzhou *China* 24°22N 109°22E **116** E7
Liuzhuang *China* 33°12N 120°18E **115** H11
Livada *Romania* 47°52N 23°5E **80** C8
Livadero *Greece* 40°2N 21°57E **96** F5
Livadhia *Cyprus* 34°57N 33°38E **101** E12
Livadi *Greece* 40°8N 22°29E **98** A4
Livadia *Greece* 38°27N 22°54E **98** C4
Livarot *France* 48°58N 0°9E **70** D7
Live Oak *Calif., U.S.A.* 39°17N 121°40W **170** F5
Live Oak *Fla., U.S.A.* 30°18N 82°59W **177** F13
Lively *Canada* 46°26N 81°9W **173** B13
Liveras *Cyprus* 35°23N 32°57E **101** D11
Livermore *U.S.A.* 37°41N 121°47W **170** H5
Livermore, Mt. *U.S.A.* 30°38N 104°11W **176** F2
Livermore Falls
U.S.A. 44°29N 70°11W **173** D18
Liverpool *Australia* 33°54S 150°58E **153** B9
Liverpool *Canada* 44°5N 64°41W **165** D7
Liverpool *U.K.* 53°25N 3°0W **66** D4
Liverpool *U.S.A.* 43°6N 76°13W **175** C8
Liverpool B. *U.K.* 53°30N 3°20W **66** D4
Liverpool Plains
Australia 31°15S 150°15E **153** A9
Liverpool Ra. *Australia* 31°50S 150°30E **153** A9
Livigno *Italy* 46°35N 10°10E **92** B7
Livingston *U.K.* 55°54N 3°30W **65** F5
Livingston *Ala.*,
U.S.A. 32°35N 88°11W **177** E10
Livingston *Calif.*,
U.S.A. 37°23N 120°43W **170** H6
Livingston *Mont.*,
U.S.A. 45°40N 110°34W **168** D8
Livingston *S.C., U.S.A.* 33°32N 81°7W **177** D13
Livingston *Tenn.*,
U.S.A. 36°23N 85°19W **177** C12
Livingston *Tex., U.S.A.* 30°43N 94°56W **176** F7
Livingston, L. *U.S.A.* 30°50N 95°10W **176** F7
Livingston Manor
U.S.A. 41°54N 74°50W **175** E10
Livingstone *Zambia* 17°46S 25°52E **143** F2
Livingstone △
Australia 33°22S 147°22E **153** C7
Livingstone Mts. *N.Z.* 45°15S 168°9E **155** F3
Livingstone Mts.
Tanzania 9°40S 34°20E **143** D3
Livingstonia *Malawi* 10°38S 34°5E **143** E3
Livno *Bos.-H.* 43°50N 17°1E **80** G2
Livny *Russia* 52°30N 37°30E **85** F9
Livonia *Mich., U.S.A.* 42°23N 83°21W **174** D1
Livonia *N.Y., U.S.A.* 42°49N 77°40W **174** D7
Livorno *Italy* 43°33N 10°19E **92** E7
Livradois-Forez △ *France* 45°40N 3°40E **72** E7
Livramento *Brazil* 30°55S 55°30W **191** C4
Livramento do Brumado
Brazil 13°39S 41°50W **189** C2
Livron-sur-Drôme *France* 44°46N 4°51E **73** D8
Livyntsi *Ukraine* 48°25N 26°37E **81** B11
Liwale *Tanzania* 9°48S 37°58E **143** D4
Liwiec → *Poland* 52°36N 21°34E **83** F8
Liwonde *Malawi* 15°4S 35°13E **143** E4
Liwonde △ *Malawi* 14°48S 35°20E **143** E4
Lixi *China* 26°19N 101°59E **116** D3
Lixian *China* 31°23N 103°13E **116** B4
Lixin *China* 33°8N 116°13E **117** A11
Lixouri *Greece* 38°12N 20°26E **98** C2

Liyang *China* 31°26N 119°28E **117** B12
Lizard I. *Australia* 14°42S 145°30E **150** A4
Lizard Pt. *U.K.* 49°57N 5°13W **67** H2
Lizarda *Brazil* 9°36S 46°41W **189** B1
Lizzano *Italy* 40°23N 17°27E **95** B10
Ljig *Serbia* 44°13N 20°18E **96** B4
Ljubija *Bos.-H.* 44°55N 16°35E **96** B3
Ljubinje *Bos.-H.* 42°58N 18°5E **96** C3
Ljubišnja *Europe* 43°18N 19°9E **96** C3
Ljubljana *Slovenia* 46°4N 14°33E **93** B11
Ljubljana × (LJU)
Slovenia 46°14N 14°33E **93** B11
Ljubno *Slovenia* 46°25N 14°46E **93** B11
Ljubovija *Serbia* 44°11N 19°22E **96** B3
Ljugarn *Sweden* 57°20N 18°43E **63** G12
Ljung *Sweden* 57°59N 13°3E **63** F7
Ljungan → *Sweden* 62°18N 17°23E **62** B11
Ljungaverk *Sweden* 62°30N 16°5E **62** B10
Ljungby *Sweden* 56°49N 13°55E **63** H7
Ljungbyholm *Sweden* 56°39N 16°5E **63** H10
Ljungdalen *Sweden* 62°51N 12°47E **62** B6
Ljungsbro *Sweden* 58°31N 15°30E **63** F9
Ljungskile *Sweden* 58°14N 11°55E **63** F5
Ljusdal *Sweden* 61°46N 16°3E **62** C10
Ljusfallshammar *Sweden* 58°48N 15°30E **63** F9
Ljusnan → *Sweden* 61°12N 17°8E **62** C11
Ljusne *Sweden* 61°13N 17°7E **62** C11
Ljusterö *Sweden* 59°31N 18°37E **62** E12
Ljutomer *Slovenia* 46°31N 16°11E **93** B13
Llagostera *Spain* 41°50N 2°54E **90** D7
Llamellín *Peru* 9°0S 76°54W **188** B2
Llançà *Spain* 42°22N 3°9E **90** C8
Llancanelo, Salina
Argentina 35°40S 69°8W **190** D2
Llandeilo *U.K.* 51°53N 3°59W **67** F4
Llandovery *U.K.* 51°59N 3°48W **67** F4
Llandrindod Wells *U.K.* 52°14N 3°22W **67** E4
Llandudno *U.K.* 53°19N 3°50W **66** D4
Llanelli *U.K.* 51°41N 4°10W **67** F3
Llanes *Spain* 43°25N 4°50W **88** B6
Llanfair-ym-Muallt = Builth Wells
U.K. 52°9N 3°25W **67** E4
Llangollen *U.K.* 52°58N 3°11W **66** E4
Llanidloes *U.K.* 52°27N 3°31W **67** E4
Llano *U.S.A.* 30°45N 98°41W **176** F5
Llano → *U.S.A.* 30°39N 98°26W **176** F5
Llano Estacado *U.S.A.* 33°30N 103°0W **176** E3
Llanos *S. Amer.* 5°0N 71°35W **186** C4
Llanos de Challe △ *Chile* 28°8S 71°1W **190** B1
Llanquihue, L. *Chile* 41°10S 72°50W **192** B1
Llanwrtyd Wells *U.K.* 52°7N 3°38W **67** E4
Llata *Peru* 9°25S 76°47W **188** B2
Llebeig, C. des *Spain* 39°33N 2°18E **100** B9
Lleida *Spain* 41°37N 0°39E **90** D5
Lleida □ *Spain* 42°6N 1°0E **90** C6
Llentrisca, C. *Spain* 38°52N 1°15E **100** C7
Llera de Canales *Mexico* 23°19N 99°1W **181** C5
Llerena *Spain* 38°17N 6°0W **89** C5
Lleyn Peninsula *U.K.* 52°51N 4°36W **66** E3
Llica *Bolivia* 19°52S 68°16W **188** D4
Llico *Chile* 34°46S 72°5W **190** C1
Llívia *Spain* 42°28N 1°59E **72** F5
Llobregat → *Spain* 41°19N 2°9E **90** D7
Llodio *Spain* 43°9N 2°58W **90** B2
Lloret de Mar *Spain* 41°41N 2°53E **90** D7
Lloseta *Spain* 39°43N 2°52E **100** B9
Lloyd B. *Australia* 12°45S 143°27E **150** A3
Lloyd L. *Canada* 57°22N 108°57W **163** B7
Lloydminster *Canada* 53°17N 110°0W **163** C7
Llubí *Spain* 39°42N 3°0E **100** B10
Llucena del Cid *Spain* 40°9N 0°17W **90** E4
Llucmajor *Spain* 39°29N 2°53E **100** B9
Llullaillaco, Volcán
S. Amer. 24°43S 68°30W **190** A2
Llullaillaco △ *Chile* 24°50S 68°51W **190** A2
Lo → *Vietnam* 21°18N 105°25E **120** B5
Loa *U.S.A.* 38°24N 111°39W **168** G8
Loa → *Chile* 21°26S 70°41W **190** A1
Loaita I. *S. China Sea* 10°41N 114°25E **118** B4
Loange →
Dem. Rep. of the Congo 4°17S 20°2E **140** E4
Loano *Italy* 44°8N 8°15E **92** D5
Lobamba *Swaziland* 26°28S 31°12E **145** C5
Lobatse *Botswana* 25°12S 25°40E **144** D4
Löbau *Germany* 51°5N 14°40E **76** D10
Lobenstein *Germany* 50°25N 11°39E **76** E7
Lobería *Argentina* 38°10S 58°40W **190** D4
Loberöd *Sweden* 55°47N 13°31E **63** J7
Lobez *Poland* 53°38N 15°39E **82** E2
Lobito *Angola* 12°18S 13°35E **141** G2
Lobo → *Ivory C.* 6°9N 6°45E **138** D4
Lobos *Argentina* 35°10S 59°0W **190** D4
Lobos, I. *Mexico* 27°20N 110°36W **180** B2
Lobos, I. de *Canary Is.* 28°45N 13°50W **100** F6
Lobos de Afuera, Islas
Peru 6°57S 80°42W **188** B1
Lobos de Tierra, I. *Peru* 6°27S 80°52W **188** B1
Łobżenica *Poland* 53°18N 17°15E **83** B4
Loc Binh *Vietnam* 21°46N 106°54E **120** B6
Loc Ninh *Vietnam* 11°50N 106°34E **120** G6
Locarno *Switz.* 46°10N 8°47E **77** J4
Loch Garman = Wexford
Ireland 52°20N 6°28W **64** D5
Loch Lomond and the
Trossachs △ *U.K.* 56°10N 4°40W **65** E4
Lochaber *U.K.* 56°59N 5°1W **65** E3
Locharbriggs *U.K.* 55°7N 3°35W **65** F5
Lochboisdale *U.K.* 57°9N 7°20W **65** D1
Loche, L. La *Canada* 56°30N 109°30W **163** B7
Lochem *Neths.* 52°9N 6°26E **69** B6
Loches *France* 47°7N 1°0E **70** E7
Lochgilphead *U.K.* 56°2N 5°26W **65** E3
Lochinvar △ *Zambia* 15°55S 27°15E **143** F2
Lochinver *U.K.* 58°9N 5°14W **65** C3
Lochloosa L. *U.S.A.* 29°30N 82°7W **177** F13
Lochmaddy *U.K.* 57°36N 7°10W **65** D1
Lochnagar *Australia* 23°33S 145°38E **150** C4
Lochnagar *U.K.* 56°57N 3°15W **65** E5
Łochów *Poland* 52°33N 21°42E **83** F8
Lochy, L. *U.K.* 57°0N 4°53W **65** E4
Lock *Australia* 33°34S 135°46E **151** E2
Lock Haven *U.S.A.* 41°8N 77°28W **174** E7
Lockeford *U.S.A.* 38°10N 121°9W **170** G5
Lockeport *Canada* 43°47N 65°4W **165** D6
Lockerbie *U.K.* 55°7N 3°21W **65** F5
Lockhart *Australia* 35°14S 146°40E **153** C7
Lockhart *U.S.A.* 29°53N 97°40W **176** G6

Lockhart, L. *Australia* 33°15S 119°3E **149** F2
Lockhart River
Australia 12°58S 143°30E **150** A3
Lockhart River ○
Australia 12°47S 143°20E **150** A3
Lockney *U.S.A.* 34°7N 101°27W **176** D4
Lockport *U.S.A.* 43°10N 78°42W **174** C6
Locminé *France* 47°54N 2°51W **70** E4
Locri *Italy* 38°14N 16°16E **95** D9
Locronan *France* 48°7N 4°15W **70** D2
Locust Grove *U.S.A.* 33°21N 84°7W **178** B5
Lod *Israel* 31°57N 34°54E **130** D3
Lodeinoye Pole *Russia* 60°44N 33°33E **84** B7
Lodève *France* 43°44N 3°19E **72** E7
Lodge Bay *Canada* 52°14N 55°51W **165** B8
Lodge Grass *U.S.A.* 45°19N 107°22W **168** D10
Lodhran *Pakistan* 29°32N 71°30E **124** E4
Lodi *Italy* 45°19N 9°30E **92** C6
Lodi *Calif., U.S.A.* 38°8N 121°16W **170** G5
Lodi *Ohio, U.S.A.* 41°2N 82°1W **174** E3
Lodja
Dem. Rep. of the Congo 3°30S 23°23E **142** C1
Lodosa *Spain* 42°25N 2°4W **90** C2
Lödöse *Sweden* 58°2N 12°9E **63** F6
Lodwar *Kenya* 3°7N 35°36E **142** B4
Łódź *Poland* 51°45N 19°27E **83** G6
Łódzkie □ *Poland* 51°30N 19°30E **83** G6
Loei *Thailand* 17°29N 101°35E **120** D3
Loengo
Dem. Rep. of the Congo 4°48S 26°30E **142** C2
Loeriesfontein *S. Africa* 31°0S 19°26E **144** D2
Lofa → *Liberia* 6°35N 11°8W **138** D2
Lofa Mano △ *Liberia* 7°55N 10°25W **138** D2
Lofer *Austria* 47°35N 12°41E **78** D5
Lofoten *Norway* 68°30N 13°59E **60** B16
Lofsdalen *Sweden* 62°10N 13°20E **62** B7
Lofsen → *Sweden* 62°7N 13°57E **62** B7
Loftahammar *Sweden* 57°54N 16°41E **63** G10
Loga *Niger* 13°40N 3°15E **139** C5
Logan *Iowa, U.S.A.* 41°39N 95°47W **172** E6
Logan *Ohio, U.S.A.* 39°32N 82°25W **173** F12
Logan *Utah, U.S.A.* 41°44N 111°50W **168** F8
Logan *W. Va., U.S.A.* 37°51N 81°59W **173** G13
Logan, Mt. *Canada* 60°34N 140°23W **160** C3
Logan Martin L.
U.S.A. 33°26N 86°20W **178** B3
Logandale *U.S.A.* 36°36N 114°29W **171** J12
Logansport *Ind.*,
U.S.A. 40°45N 86°22W **172** E10
Logansport *La., U.S.A.* 31°58N 94°0W **176** F8
Loganville *U.S.A.* 33°50N 83°54W **178** B5
Logatec *Slovenia* 45°56N 14°15E **93** C11
Logne → *Chad* 12°6N 15°2E **135** F9
Logone → *Chad* 12°6N 15°2E **135** F9
Logroño *Spain* 42°28N 2°27W **90** C2
Logrosán *Spain* 39°20N 5°32W **89** F5
Løgstør *Denmark* 56°58N 9°14E **63** H3
Logumkloster *Denmark* 55°4N 8°57E **63** J2
Lohals *Denmark* 55°8N 10°55E **63** J4
Lohardaga *India* 23°27N 84°45E **125** H11
Loharia *India* 23°45N 74°14E **124** H6
Loharu *India* 28°27N 75°49E **124** E6
Lohja *Finland* 60°12N 24°5E **63** F21
Löhne *Germany* 52°11N 8°40E **76** C4
Lohr *Germany* 49°59N 9°35E **77** F5
Lohri Wah → *Pakistan* 27°27N 67°37E **124** F2
Loikaw *Burma* 19°40N 97°17E **123** K20
Loimaa *Finland* 60°50N 23°5E **63** E20
Loir → *France* 47°33N 0°32W **70** E5
Loir-et-Cher □ *France* 47°40N 1°20E **70** E4
Loire □ *France* 45°40N 4°5E **73** C8
Loire → *France* 47°16N 2°10W **70** E4
Loire-Anjou-Touraine △
France 47°14N 0°5W **70** E6
Loire-Atlantique □
France 47°25N 1°40W **70** E5
Loiret □ *France* 47°55N 2°30E **71** E9
Loitz *Germany* 53°58N 13°8E **76** B9
Loja *Ecuador* 3°59S 79°16W **188** A2
Loja *Spain* 37°10N 4°9W **89** H6
Loji = Kawasi *Indonesia* 1°38S 127°28E **119** E7
Lojo = Lohja *Finland* 60°12N 24°5E **63** F21
Løjt Kirkeby *Denmark* 55°7N 9°26E **63** J3
Lojung *China* 24°27N 109°36E **116** E7
Lokandu
Dem. Rep. of the Congo 2°30S 25°45E **142** C2
Lokeren *Belgium* 51°6N 3°59E **69** C3
Lokgwabe *Botswana* 24°10S 21°50E **144** C3
Lokhvytsya *Ukraine* 50°25N 33°18E **85** G7
Lokichar *Kenya* 2°23N 35°39E **142** B4
Lokichokio *Kenya* 4°19N 34°13E **142** B3
Lokitaung *Kenya* 4°12N 35°48E **142** B4
Lokkan tekojärvi
Finland 67°55N 27°35E **60** C22
Løkken *Denmark* 57°22N 9°41E **63** G3
Loknya *Russia* 56°49N 30°4E **84** D6
Loko *Nigeria* 8°1N 7°53E **139** D6
Lokoja *Nigeria* 7°47N 6°45E **139** D6
Lokolo →
Dem. Rep. of the Congo 1°43S 18°23E **140** E3
Lokot *Russia* 52°34N 34°36E **85** F8
Lola *Guinea* 7°52N 8°29W **138** D3
Lola, Mt. *U.S.A.* 39°26N 120°22W **170** F6
Lolgorien *Kenya* 1°14S 34°48E **142** C3
Loliondo *Tanzania* 2°2S 35°39E **142** C4
Lolland *Denmark* 54°45N 11°30E **63** K5
Lollar *Germany* 50°37N 8°43E **76** E4
Lolo *U.S.A.* 46°45N 114°5W **168** C6
Lolodorf *Cameroon* 3°16N 10°49E **139** E7
Lom *Bulgaria* 43°48N 23°12E **96** C7
Lom → *Bulgaria* 43°45N 23°15E **96** C7
Lom Kao *Thailand* 16°53N 101°14E **120** D3
Lom Sak *Thailand* 16°47N 101°15E **120** D3
Loma *U.S.A.* 47°56N 110°30W **168** C8
Loma Linda *U.S.A.* 34°3N 117°16W **171** L9
Loma Mansa *S. Leone* 9°13N 11°7W **138** D2
Loma Mts. *S. Leone* 9°10N 11°7W **138** D2
Lomaloma *Fiji* 17°17S 178°59W **154** a
Lomami →
Dem. Rep. of the Congo 0°46N 24°16E **142** B1
Lomas de Zamora
Argentina 34°45S 58°25W **190** C5
Lomblen *Indonesia* 8°30S 123°32E **119** F6
Lombardia □ *Italy* 45°40N 9°30E **92** C6
Lombardy = Lombárdia □
Italy 45°40N 9°30E **92** C6
Lombez *France* 43°29N 0°55E **72** E9
Lomblen *Indonesia* 8°30S 123°32E **119** F6
Lombok, Selat
Indonesia 8°30S 116°30E **118** F5
Lombok, Selat
Indonesia 8°30S 115°50E **119** K18

Lomé *Togo* 6°9N 1°20E **139** D5
Lomela
Dem. Rep. of the Congo 2°19S 23°15E **140** E4
Lomela →
Dem. Rep. of the Congo 0°15S 20°40E **140** E4
Lomianki *Poland* 52°21N 20°54E **83** F7
Lomma *Sweden* 55°43N 13°6E **63** J7
Lommel *Belgium* 51°14N 5°19E **69** C5
Lomond *Canada* 50°24N 112°36W **162** D6
Lomond, L. *U.K.* 56°8N 4°38W **65** E4
Lomonosov Ridge *Arctic* 88°0N 140°0E **54** A
Lomphat *Cambodia* 13°30N 106°59E **120** F6
Lompobatang *Indonesia* 5°24S 119°56E **119** F5
Lompoc *U.S.A.* 34°38N 120°28W **171** L6
Łomża *Poland* 53°10N 22°2E **83** E9
Lon, Ko *Thailand* 7°47N 98°23E **121** a
Lonavale *India* 18°46N 73°29E **126** E1
Loncoche *Chile* 39°20S 72°50W **192** A2
Loncopué *Argentina* 38°4S 70°37W **192** A2
Londa *India* 15°30N 74°30E **127** G2
Londiani *Kenya* 0°10S 35°33E **142** C4
Londinières *France* 49°50N 1°25E **70** C8
London *Canada* 42°59N 81°15W **174** D3
London *U.K.* 51°30N 0°3W **67** F7
London *Ky., U.S.A.* 37°8N 84°5W **173** G11
London *Ohio, U.S.A.* 39°53N 83°27W **173** F12
London, Greater □ *U.K.* 51°36N 0°5W **67** F7
London Gatwick × (LGW)
U.K. 51°10N 0°11W **67** F7
London Heathrow × (LHR)
U.K. 51°28N 0°27W **67** F7
London Stansted × (STN)
U.K. 51°54N 0°14E **67** F8
Londonderry *U.K.* 55°0N 7°20W **64** B4
Londonderry □ *U.K.* 55°0N 7°20W **64** B4
Londonderry, C.
Australia 13°45S 126°55E **148** B4
Londonderry, I. *Chile* 55°0S 71°0W **192** D2
Londres *Argentina* 27°43S 67°7W **190** B2
Londrina *Brazil* 23°18S 51°10W **191** A5
Lone Pine *U.S.A.* 36°36N 118°4W **170** J8
Lonely Mine *Zimbabwe* 19°30S 28°49E **145** A4
Long B. *U.S.A.* 33°35N 78°45W **177** E15
Long Beach *Calif.*,
U.S.A. 33°46N 118°11W **171** M8
Long Beach *N.Y.*,
U.S.A. 40°35N 73°39W **175** F11
Long Beach *Wash.*,
U.S.A. 46°21N 124°3W **170** D2
Long Branch *U.S.A.* 40°18N 74°0W **175** F11
Long Creek *U.S.A.* 44°43N 119°6W **168** D4
Long Eaton *U.K.* 52°53N 1°15W **66** E6
Long I. *Australia* 20°22S 148°51E **150** b
Long I. *Bahamas* 23°20N 75°10W **183** B4
Long I. *Canada* 54°50N 79°20W **164** B4
Long I. *Ireland* 51°30N 9°34W **64** E2
Long I. *U.S.A.* 40°45N 73°30W **175** F11
Long Island Sd. *U.S.A.* 41°10N 73°0W **175** E12
Long L. *Canada* 49°30N 86°50W **164** C2
Long L. *U.S.A.* 44°0N 74°23W **175** C10
Long Lake *U.S.A.* 43°58N 74°25W **175** C10
Long Point *Canada* 42°34N 80°25W **174** D4
Long Point B. *Canada* 42°40N 80°10W **174** D4
Long Prairie *U.S.A.* 45°59N 94°52W **172** C6
Long Prairie → *U.S.A.* 46°20N 94°36W **172** B6
Long Pt. *Ont., Canada* 42°35N 80°2W **174** D4
Long Pt. *Ont., Canada* 42°40N 80°10W **174** D4
Long Pt. *N.Z.* 46°34S 169°36E **155** G4
Long Range Mts.
Canada 49°30N 57°30W **165** C8
Long Reef *Australia* 14°1S 125°48E **148** B4
Long Sault *Canada* 45°2N 74°53W **175** A10
Long Str. = Longa, Proliv
Russia 70°0N 175°0E **107** C18
Long Thanh *Vietnam* 10°47N 106°57E **121** G6
Long Xian *China* 34°55N 106°55E **114** G4
Long Xuyen *Vietnam* 10°19N 105°28E **121** G5
Longa *Greece* 36°53N 21°55E **98** E3
Long'an *China* 23°10N 107°40E **116** F6
Longarone *Italy* 46°16N 12°18E **93** B9
Longbenton *U.K.* 55°1N 1°31W **66** B6
Longboat Key *U.S.A.* 27°23N 82°39W **179** H7
Longburn *N.Z.* 40°23S 175°35E **154** G4
Longchang *China* 29°18N 105°15E **116** C5
Longchuan *Guangdong*,
China 24°5N 115°17E **117** E10
Longchuan *Yunnan*,
China 24°23N 97°58E **116** E1
Longde *China* 35°30N 106°20E **114** G4
Longeau-Percey *France* 47°47N 5°20E **71** E12
Longford *Australia* 41°32S 147°3E **150** e
Longford *Ireland* 53°43N 7°49W **64** C4
Longford □ *Ireland* 53°42N 7°45W **64** C4
Longfort, An = Longford
Ireland 53°43N 7°49W **64** C4
Longhai *China* 24°25N 117°46E **117** E11
Longhua *Guangdong*,
China 22°39N 114°0E **111** a
Longhua *Hebei, China* 41°18N 117°45E **115** D9
Longhua *China* 27°7N 111°27E **117** D8
Longido *Tanzania* 2°43S 36°42E **142** C4
Longiram *Indonesia* 0°5S 115°45E **118** E5
Longjiang *China* 42°46N 129°25E **115** C15
Longjing *China* 42°46N 129°25E **115** C15
Longkou *Jiangxi, China* 26°8N 115°10E **117** D10
Longkou *Shandong*,
China 37°40N 120°18E **115** F11
Longlac *Canada* 49°45N 86°25W **164** C2
Longli *China* 26°25N 106°58E **116** D6
Longlin *China* 24°35N 105°18E **116** E5
Longmeadow *U.S.A.* 42°3N 72°34W **175** D12
Longmen *China* 23°40N 114°18E **117** F10
Longmen Shiku *China* 34°28N 112°28E **114** G7
Longmont *U.S.A.* 40°10N 105°6W **168** E11
Longnan *China* 24°40N 114°53E **117** E10
Longnawan *Indonesia* 1°51N 114°55E **118** D4
Longobucco *Italy* 39°27N 16°37E **95** C9
Longquan *China* 28°7N 119°10E **117** C12
Longreach *Australia* 23°28S 144°14E **150** C3
Longshan *China* 29°29N 109°25E **116** C7
Longsheng *China* 25°48N 110°0E **117** E8
Longtan Dam *China* 25°0N 107°0E **116** E6
Longué-Jumelles *France* 47°22N 0°8W **70** E6
Longueau *France* 49°52N 2°21E **71** C9
Longueuil *Canada* 45°31N 73°29W **175** A11
Longuyon *France* 49°27N 5°35E **71** C12
Longvic *France* 47°17N 5°4E **71** E12
Longview *Tex., U.S.A.* 32°30N 94°44W **176** E7
Longview *Wash.*,
U.S.A. 46°8N 122°57W **170** D4
Longwood *U.S.A.* 28°42N 81°21W **179** G8
Longwy *France* 49°30N 5°46E **71** C12
Longxi *China* 34°53N 104°40E **114** G3
Longxue Dao *China* 22°41N 113°38E **111** a
Longyan *China* 25°10N 117°0E **117** E11
Longyearbyen *Svalbard* 78°13N 15°40E **54** B8
Longyou *China* 29°1N 119°8E **117** C12
Longzhou *China* 22°22N 106°50E **116** F6
Lonigo *Italy* 45°23N 11°23E **93** C8
Löningen *Germany* 52°44N 7°46E **76** C3
Lonja → *Croatia* 45°22N 16°40E **93** C13
Lonoke *U.S.A.* 34°47N 91°54W **176** D9
Lonquimay *Chile* 38°26S 71°14W **192** A2
Lons-le-Saunier *France* 46°40N 5°31E **71** F12
Lönsboda *Sweden* 56°24N 14°19E **63** H8
Looe *U.K.* 50°22N 4°28W **67** G3
Lookout, C. *Canada* 55°18N 83°56W **164** A3
Lookout, C. *U.S.A.* 34°35N 76°32W **177** D16
Loolmalasin *Tanzania* 3°0S 35°53E **142** C4
Loon → *Alta., Canada* 57°8N 115°3W **162** B5
Loon → *Man., Canada* 55°53N 101°59W **163** B8
Loon Lake *Canada* 54°2N 109°10W **163** C7
Loongana *Australia* 30°52S 127°5E **149** F4
Loop Hd. *Ireland* 52°34N 9°56W **64** D2
Lop *China* 37°3N 80°11E **109** E10
Lop Nor = Lop Nur
China 40°20N 90°10E **109** E12
Lop Nur *China* 40°20N 90°10E **109** D12
Lopare *Bos.-H.* 44°39N 18°46E **80** F3
Lopatin *Russia* 43°50N 47°35E **87** J8
Lopatina, Gora
Russia 50°47N 143°10E **107** D15
Lopatka, Mys *Russia* 50°52N 156°40E **107** D16
Lopburi *Thailand* 14°48N 100°37E **120** E3
Lopez *U.S.A.* 41°27N 76°20W **175** E8
Lopez, C. *Gabon* 0°47S 8°40E **140** E1
Lopphavet *Norway* 70°27N 21°15E **60** A19
Lora → *Afghan.* 31°35N 66°32E **122** D4
Lora, Hāmūn-i-
Pakistan 29°38N 64°58E **122** E4
Lora Cr. → *Australia* 28°10S 135°22E **151** D2
Lora del Río *Spain* 37°39N 5°33W **89** H5
Lorain *U.S.A.* 41°28N 82°11W **174** E2
Loralai *Pakistan* 30°20N 68°41E **124** D3
Lorca *Spain* 37°41N 1°42W **91** H3
Lord Howe I. *Pac. Oc.* 31°33S 159°6E **147** E8
Lord Howe Rise *Pac. Oc.* 30°0S 162°30E **156** L8
Lord Loughborough I.
Burma 10°25N 97°54E **121** G1
Lordsburg *U.S.A.* 32°21N 108°43W **169** K9
Lorestān □ *Iran* 33°30N 48°40E **129** C6
Loreto *Brazil* 7°5S 45°10W **189** B1
Loreto *Italy* 43°26N 13°36E **93** E10
Loreto *Mexico* 26°0N 111°21W **180** B2
Lorgues *France* 43°28N 6°22E **73** E10
Lorhosso = Loropéni
Burkina Faso 10°17N 3°38W **138** C4
Lorient *France* 47°45N 3°23W **70** E3
Lőrinci *Hungary* 47°44N 19°41E **80** C4
Lormi *India* 22°17N 81°41E **125** H9
Lorn *U.K.* 56°26N 5°10W **65** E3
Lorn, Firth of *U.K.* 56°20N 5°40W **65** E3
Lorne *Australia* 38°33S 143°59E **152** E5
Loropéni *Burkina Faso* 10°17N 3°38W **138** C4
Lorovouno *Cyprus* 35°8N 32°36E **101** D11
Lörrach *Germany* 47°36N 7°40E **77** H3
Lorraine □ *France* 48°53N 6°0E **71** D13
Lorraine △ *France* 48°55N 5°50E **71** D12
Los, Îles de *Guinea* 9°30N 13°50W **138** D2
Los Alamos *Calif.*,
U.S.A. 34°44N 120°17W **171** L6
Los Alamos *N. Mex.*,
U.S.A. 35°53N 106°19W **169** J10
Los Alcornocales △
Spain 36°21N 5°32W **89** J5
Los Alerces △
Argentina 42°55S 71°55W **192** B2
Los Altos *Chile* 37°23S 72°7W **190** D1
Los Andes *Chile* 32°50S 70°40W **190** C1
Los Angeles *Chile* 37°28S 72°23W **190** D1
Los Angeles *U.S.A.* 34°4N 118°15W **171** M8
Los Angeles Aqueduct
U.S.A. 35°22N 118°5W **171** K9
Los Angeles Int. × (LAX)
U.S.A. 33°57N 118°25W **171** M8
Los Antiguos *Argentina* 46°35S 71°40W **192** C2
Los Banos *U.S.A.* 37°4N 120°51W **170** H6
Los Barrios *Spain* 36°11N 5°30W **89** J5
Los Blancos *Argentina* 23°40S 62°30W **190** A3
Los Cabos Int. × (SJD)
Mexico 23°9N 109°43W **180** C3
Los Cardones △
Argentina 25°8S 65°55W **190** B2
Los Chiles *Costa Rica* 11°2N 84°43W **182** D3
Los Corrales de Buelna
Spain 43°16N 4°4W **88** B6
Los Cristianos *Canary Is.* 28°3N 16°42W **100** F3
Los Gallardos *Spain* 37°10N 1°57W **91** H3
Los Gatos *U.S.A.* 37°14N 121°59W **170** H5
Los Glaciares △
Argentina 50°0S 73°55W **192** C2
Los Haitíses △
Dom. Rep. 19°4N 69°36W **183** C6
Los Hermanos, Is.
Venezuela 11°45N 64°25W **183** D7
Los Huemules △ *Chile* 46°10S 73°23W **192** C2
Los Islotes *Canary Is.* 29°33N 13°44W **100** E6
Los Lagos *Chile* 39°51S 72°50W **192** A2
Los Llanos de Aridane
Canary Is. 28°38N 17°54W **100** F2
Los Loros *Chile* 27°50S 70°6W **190** B1
Los Lunas *U.S.A.* 34°48N 106°44W **169** J10
Los Menucos *Argentina* 40°50S 68°10W **192** B3
Los Mochis *Mexico* 25°45N 108°57W **180** B3
Los Monegros *Spain* 41°29N 0°13W **90** D4
Los Monos *Argentina* 44°24S 73°29W **192** C2
Los Muermos *Chile* 41°24S 73°29W **192** B1
Los Nietos *Spain* 37°39N 0°47W **91** H4
Los Olivos *U.S.A.* 34°40N 120°7W **171** L6
Los Palacios *Cuba* 22°35N 83°15W **182** B3
Los Palacios y Villafranca
Spain 37°10N 5°55W **89** H5
Los Quẽnes *Chile* 35°1S 70°48W **190** C1
Los Reyes de Salgado
Mexico 19°35N 102°29W **180** D4
Los Roques, Is.
Venezuela 11°50N 66°45W **183** D6

242 Los Santos de Maimona INDEX TO WORLD MA

Los Santos de Maimona Spain 38°27N 6°22W 89 G4
Los Teques Venezuela 10°21N 67°2W 186 A5
Los Testigos, Is. Venezuela 11°23N 63°6W 186 A6
Los Vilos Chile 32°10S 71°30W 190 C1
Los Yébenes Spain 39°36N 3°55W 89 F7
Losice Poland 52°13N 22°43E 83 F9
Lošinj Croatia 44°30N 14°30E 93 D11
Loskop Dam S. Africa 25°23S 29°20E 145 C4
Løsning Denmark 55°48N 9°42E 63 J3
Lossiemouth U.K. 57°42N 3°17W 65 D5
Lossnen Sweden 62°26N 12°45E 62 B6
Lostwithiel U.K. 50°24N 4°41W 67 G3
Lot □ France 44°39N 1°40E 72 D5
Lot → France 44°18N 0°20E 72 D4
Lot-et-Garonne □ France 44°22N 0°30E 72 D4
Lota Chile 37°5S 73°10W 190 D1
Loṭfābād Iran 37°32N 59°20E 129 B8
Lothair S. Africa 26°22S 30°27E 145 C5
Lotorp Sweden 58°44N 15°50E 63 F9
Lötschbergtunnel Switz. 46°26N 7°43E 77 J3
Lotta → Europe 68°42N 31°6E 60 B24
Lottefors Sweden 61°25N 16°24E 62 C10
Löttorp Sweden 57°10N 17°0E 63 G11
Lotung Taiwan 24°41N 121°46E 117 E13
Loubomo Congo 4°9S 12°47E 140 E2
Loudéac France 48°11N 2°47W 70 D4
Loudi China 27°42N 111°59E 117 D8
Loudonville U.S.A. 40°38N 82°14W 174 F2
Loudun France 47°3N 0°5E 70 E7
Loue → France 47°1N 5°28E 71 E12
Louga Senegal 15°45N 16°5W 138 B1
Louga □ Senegal 15°20N 15°35W 138 B1
Loughborough U.K. 52°47N 1°11W 66 E6
Lougheed I. Canada 77°26N 105°6W 161 B10
Loughman U.S.A. 28°14N 81°34W 179 G8
Loughrea Ireland 53°12N 8°33W 64 C3
Loughros More B. Ireland 54°48N 8°32W 64 B3
Louhans France 46°38N 5°12E 71 F12
Louis Trichardt S. Africa 23°1S 29°43E 145 B4
Louis XIV, Pte. Canada 54°37N 79°45W 164 B4
Louisa U.S.A. 38°7N 82°36W 173 F12
Louisbourg Canada 45°55N 60°0W 165 C8
Louisburgh Ireland 53°46N 9°49W 64 C2
Louise I. Canada 52°55N 131°50W 162 C2
Louiseville Canada 46°20N 72°56W 164 C5
Louisiade Arch. Papua N. G. 11°10S 153°0E 147 C8
Louisiana U.S.A. 39°27N 91°3W 172 F8
Louisiana □ U.S.A. 30°50N 92°0W 176 F9
Louisville Ala., U.S.A. 31°47N 85°33W 178 D4
Louisville Ga., U.S.A. 33°0N 82°25W 178 B7
Louisville Ky., U.S.A. 38°15N 85°46W 173 F11
Louisville Miss., U.S.A. 33°7N 89°3W 177 E10
Louisville Ohio, U.S.A. 40°50N 81°16W 174 F3
Louisville Ridge Pac. Oc. 31°0S 172°30W 156 L10
Loulay France 46°3N 0°30W 72 B3
Loulé Portugal 37°9N 8°0W 89 H3
Loulouni Mali 10°54N 5°36W 138 C3
Loum Cameroon 4°42N 9°44E 139 E6
Louny Czech Rep. 50°20N 13°48E 78 A6
Loup City U.S.A. 41°17N 98°58W 172 E4
Loups Marins, Lacs des Canada 56°30N 73°45W 164 A5
Lourdes France 43°6N 0°3W 72 E3
Lourdes-de-Blanc-Sablon Canada 51°24N 57°12W 165 B8
Lourinhã Portugal 39°14N 9°17W 89 F1
Louroujina Cyprus 35°0N 33°28E 101 E12
Lousã Portugal 40°7N 8°14W 88 E2
Louta Burkina Faso 13°30N 3°10W 138 C4
Louth Australia 30°30S 145°8E 153 A6
Louth Ireland 53°58N 6°32W 64 C5
Louth U.K. 53°22N 0°1W 66 D7
Louth □ Ireland 53°56N 6°34W 64 C5
Louth B. Australia 34°33S 135°56E 152 C1
Loutra Edipsou Greece 38°54N 23°2E 98 C5
Loutraki Greece 37°58N 22°57E 98 D4
Loutropoli Thermis Greece 39°11N 26°29E 99 B8
Louvain = Leuven Belgium 50°52N 4°42E 69 D4
Louvale U.S.A. 32°10N 84°50W 178 C5
Louviers France 49°12N 1°10E 70 C8
Louwsburg S. Africa 27°37S 31°7E 145 C5
Lovat → Russia 58°14N 31°28E 84 C6
Lovćen Montenegro 42°23N 18°51E 96 D2
Lovćen △ Montenegro 42°20N 18°50E 96 D2
Lovech Bulgaria 43°8N 24°42E 97 C8
Lovech □ Bulgaria 43°0N 24°45E 97 D8
Loveland U.S.A. 40°24N 105°5W 168 F11
Lovell U.S.A. 44°50N 108°24W 168 D9
Lovelock U.S.A. 40°11N 118°28W 168 F4
Lóvere Italy 45°49N 10°4E 92 C7
Lövestad Sweden 55°40N 13°54E 63 J7
Loviisa Finland 60°28N 26°12E 84 B4
Lovina Indonesia 8°9S 115°1E 119 J18
Loving U.S.A. 32°17N 104°6W 169 K11
Lovington U.S.A. 32°57N 103°21W 169 K12
Lovisa = Loviisa Finland 60°28N 26°12E 84 B4
Lovosice Czech Rep. 50°30N 14°2E 78 A7
Lovran Croatia 45°18N 14°15E 93 C11
Lovrin Romania 45°58N 20°48E 80 E5
Lövstabruk Sweden 60°25N 17°53E 62 D11
Lövstabukten Sweden 60°35N 17°45E 62 D11
Low, L. Canada 52°29N 76°17W 164 B4
Low Pt. Australia 32°25S 127°25E 149 F4
Low Tatra = Nízke Tatry Slovak Rep. 48°55N 19°30E 79 C12
Lowa Dem. Rep. of the Congo 1°25S 25°47E 142 C2
Lowa → Dem. Rep. of the Congo 1°24S 25°51E 142 C2
Lowell U.S.A. 42°38N 71°19W 175 D13
Lowellville U.S.A. 41°2N 80°32W 174 E4
Löwen → Namibia 26°51S 18°17E 144 C2
Lower Alkali L. U.S.A. 41°16N 120°2W 168 F3
Lower Arrow L. Canada 49°40N 118°5W 162 D5
Lower Austria = Niederösterreich □ Austria 48°25N 15°40E 78 C8
Lower California = Baja California Mexico 31°10N 115°12W 180 A1
Lower Glenelg △ Australia 38°4S 141°41E 152 E4
Lower Hutt N.Z. 41°10S 174°55E 154 H3
Lower Lake U.S.A. 38°55N 122°37W 170 G4
Lower Manitou L. Canada 49°15N 93°0W 163 D10
Lower Post Canada 59°58N 128°30W 162 B3
Lower Red L. U.S.A. 47°58N 95°0W 172 B6
Lower Saxony = Niedersachsen □ Germany 52°50N 9°0E 76 C4
Lower Tunguska = Tunguska, Nizhnyaya → Russia 65°48N 88°4E 107 C9
Lower Zambezi △ Zambia 15°25S 29°40E 143 F2
Lowestoft U.K. 52°29N 1°45E 67 E9
Lowgar □ Afghan. 34°0N 69°0E 122 B6
Łowicz Poland 52°6N 19°55E 83 F6
Lowly, Pt. Australia 33°0S 137°46E 152 B2
Lowther I. Canada 74°33N 97°30W 161 C12
Lowville U.S.A. 43°47N 75°29W 175 C9
Loxton Australia 34°28S 140°31E 152 C4
Loxton S. Africa 31°30S 22°22E 144 D3
Loyalton U.S.A. 39°41N 120°14W 170 F6
Loyalty Is. = Loyauté, Îs. N. Cal. 20°50S 166°30E 147 D9
Loyang = Luoyang China 34°40N 112°26E 114 G7
Loyauté, Îs. N. Cal. 20°50S 166°30E 147 D9
Loyev = Loyew Belarus 51°56N 30°46E 75 C16
Loyew Belarus 51°56N 30°46E 75 C16
Loyoro Uganda 3°22N 34°14E 142 B3
Lož Slovenia 45°43N 14°30E 93 C11
Lozère □ France 44°35N 3°30E 72 D7
Loznica Serbia 44°32N 19°12E 96 B3
Lozova Ukraine 49°0N 36°20E 85 H9
Ltalaltuma ☉ Australia 23°57S 132°25E 148 D5
Lü Shan China 29°30N 115°55E 117 C10
Lü Shan △ China 29°26N 115°52E 117 C10
Lu Wo China 22°33N 114°6E 111 a
Luachimo Angola 7°23S 20°48E 140 F4
Luajan → India 24°44N 85°1E 125 G11
Lualaba → Dem. Rep. of the Congo 0°26N 25°20E 142 B2
Luambe △ Zambia 12°30S 32°15E 143 E3
Luampa Zambia 15°4S 24°20E 143 F1
Lu'an China 31°45N 116°29E 117 B11
Luan Chau Vietnam 21°38N 103°24E 116 G4
Luan He → China 39°20N 119°5E 115 E10
Luan Xian China 39°40N 118°40E 115 E10
Luancheng Guangxi Zhuangzu, China 22°48N 108°55E 116 F7
Luancheng Hebei, China 37°53N 114°40E 114 F8
Luanco Spain 43°37N 5°48W 88 B5
Luanda Angola 8°50S 13°15E 140 F2
Luang, Doi Thailand 18°30N 101°15E 120 C3
Luang, Thale Thailand 7°30N 100°15E 121 J3
Luang Nam Tha Laos 20°58N 101°30E 116 G3
Luang Prabang Laos 19°52N 102°10E 116 H4
Luangwa Zambia 15°35S 30°16E 143 F3
Luangwa → Zambia 14°25S 30°25E 143 E3
Luangwa Valley Zambia 13°30S 31°30E 143 E3
Luangwe = Loange → Dem. Rep. of the Congo 4°17S 20°2E 140 E4
Luanne China 40°55N 117°40E 115 D9
Luanping China 40°53N 117°23E 115 D9
Luanshya Zambia 13°3S 28°28E 143 E2
Luapula □ Zambia 11°0S 29°0E 143 E2
Luapula → Africa 9°26S 28°33E 143 D2
Luarca Spain 43°32N 6°32W 88 B4
Luashi Dem. Rep. of the Congo 10°50S 23°36E 143 E1
Luau Angola 10°40S 22°10E 140 G4
Lubaczów Poland 50°10N 23°8E 83 H10
Lubań Poland 51°5N 15°15E 83 G2
Lubana, Ozero = Lubānas Ezers Latvia 56°45N 27°0E 84 D4
Lubānas Ezers Latvia 56°45N 27°0E 84 D4
Lubang Is. Phil. 13°50N 120°12E 119 B6
Lubango Angola 14°55S 13°30E 141 G2
Lubao Dem. Rep. of the Congo 5°17S 25°42E 142 D2
Lubartów Poland 51°28N 22°42E 83 G9
Lubawa Poland 53°30N 19°48E 82 E6
Lübbecke Germany 52°18N 8°37E 76 C4
Lübben Germany 51°56N 13°54E 76 D9
Lübbenau Germany 51°52N 13°57E 76 D9
Lubbock U.S.A. 33°35N 101°51W 176 E4
Lübeck Germany 53°52N 10°40E 76 B6
Lübecker Bucht Germany 54°3N 10°54E 76 A6
Lubefu Dem. Rep. of the Congo 4°47S 24°27E 142 C1
Lubefu → Dem. Rep. of the Congo 4°10S 23°0E 142 C1
Lubelskie □ Poland 51°20N 22°50E 83 G9
Lubero = Luofu Dem. Rep. of the Congo 0°10S 29°15E 142 C2
Luberon ⌂ France 43°52N 5°25E 73 E9
Lubersac France 45°26N 1°23E 72 C5
Lubicon L. Canada 56°23N 115°56W 162 B5
Lubień Kujawski Poland 52°23N 19°9E 83 F6
Lubilash → Dem. Rep. of the Congo 6°2S 23°45E 140 F4
Lubin Poland 51°24N 16°11E 83 G3
Lublin Poland 51°12N 22°38E 83 G9
Lubliniec Poland 50°43N 18°45E 83 H5
Lubnān = Lebanon ■ Asia 34°0N 36°0E 130 B5
Lubnān, Jabal Lebanon 33°45N 35°40E 130 B4
Lubniewice Poland 52°31N 15°15E 83 F2
Lubny Ukraine 50°3N 32°58E 85 G7
Lubomierz Poland 51°1N 15°31E 83 G2
Luboń Poland 52°21N 16°51E 83 F3
Lubongola Dem. Rep. of the Congo 2°35S 27°50E 142 C2
L'ubotín Slovak Rep. 49°17N 20°53E 79 B13
Lubraniec Poland 52°33N 18°50E 83 F5
Lubsko Poland 51°45N 14°57E 83 G1
Lübtheen Germany 53°18N 11°5E 76 B7
Lubudi Dem. Rep. of the Congo 9°57S 25°58E 140 F5
Lubudi → Dem. Rep. of the Congo 9°0S 25°35E 143 D2
Lubuklinggau Indonesia 3°15S 102°55E 118 E2
Lubuksikaping Indonesia 0°10N 100°15E 118 D2
Lubumbashi Dem. Rep. of the Congo 11°40S 27°28E 143 E2
Lubunda Dem. Rep. of the Congo 5°12S 26°41E 142 D2
Lubungu Zambia 14°35S 26°24E 143 E2
Lubuskie □ Poland 52°10N 15°20E 83 F2
Lubutu Dem. Rep. of the Congo 0°45S 26°30E 142 C2
Luc-en-Diois France 44°36N 5°28E 73 D9
Lucan Canada 43°11N 81°24W 174 C3
Lucan Ireland 53°22N 6°28W 64 C5
Lucania, Mt. Canada 61°1N 140°27W 160 E3
Lucas Channel = Main Channel Canada 45°21N 81°45W 174 A3
Lucca Italy 43°50N 10°29E 92 E7
Lucé France 48°26N 1°27E 70 D8
Luce Bay U.K. 54°45N 4°48W 65 G4
Lucea Jamaica 18°27N 78°10W 182 a
Lucedale U.S.A. 30°56N 88°35W 177 F10
Lucena Phil. 13°56N 121°37E 119 B6
Lucena Spain 37°27N 4°31W 89 H6
Lučenec Slovak Rep. 48°18N 19°42E 79 C12
Lucera Italy 41°30N 15°20E 95 A8
Lucerne = Luzern Switz. 47°3N 8°18E 77 H4
Lucerne U.S.A. 39°6N 122°48W 170 F4
Lucerne Valley U.S.A. 34°27N 116°57W 171 L10
Luchena → Spain 37°44N 1°50W 91 H3
Lucheng China 36°20N 113°11E 114 F7
Lucheringo → Mozam. 11°43S 36°17E 143 E4
Lüchow Germany 52°58N 11°8E 76 C7
Luchuan China 22°21N 110°12E 117 F8
Lucia U.S.A. 36°2N 121°33W 170 J5
Lucinda Australia 18°32S 146°20E 150 B4
Lucindale Australia 36°58S 140°22E 152 D4
Luckau Germany 51°50N 13°42E 76 D9
Luckenwalde Germany 52°5N 13°10E 76 C9
Luckhoff S. Africa 29°44S 24°43E 144 C3
Lucknow Canada 43°57N 81°31W 174 C3
Lucknow India 26°50N 81°0E 125 F9
Luçon France 46°28N 1°10W 72 B2
Lüda = Dalian China 38°50N 121°40E 115 E11
Luda Kamchiya → Bulgaria 43°3N 27°29E 97 C11
Ludbreg Croatia 46°15N 16°38E 93 B13
Lüdenscheid Germany 51°13N 7°37E 76 D3
Lüderitz Namibia 26°41S 15°8E 144 C2
Lüderitzbaai Namibia 26°36S 15°8E 144 C2
Ludhiana India 30°57N 75°56E 124 D6
Ludian China 27°10N 103°33E 116 D4
Luding Qiao China 29°53N 102°12E 116 C4
Lüdinghausen Germany 51°46N 7°27E 76 D3
Ludington U.S.A. 43°57N 86°27W 172 D10
Ludlow U.K. 52°22N 2°42W 67 E5
Ludlow Calif., U.S.A. 34°43N 116°10W 171 L10
Ludlow Pa., U.S.A. 41°43N 78°56W 174 E6
Ludlow Vt., U.S.A. 43°24N 72°42W 175 C12
Ludowici U.S.A. 31°43N 81°45W 178 D8
Luduş Romania 46°29N 24°5E 81 D9
Ludvika Sweden 60°8N 15°14E 62 D9
Ludwigsburg Germany 48°53N 9°11E 77 G5
Ludwigsfelde Germany 52°17N 13°17E 76 C9
Ludwigshafen Germany 49°29N 8°26E 77 F4
Ludwigslust Germany 53°19N 11°30E 76 B7
Ludza Latvia 56°32N 27°43E 84 D4
Lue Australia 32°38S 149°50E 153 B8
Lueki Dem. Rep. of the Congo 3°20S 25°48E 142 C2
Luena Dem. Rep. of the Congo 9°28S 25°43E 143 D2
Luena Zambia 10°40S 30°25E 143 E3
Luena Flats Zambia 14°47S 23°17E 141 G4
Luenha = Ruenya → Africa 16°24S 33°48E 143 F3
Lüeyang China 33°22N 106°10E 116 A6
Lufeng Guangdong, China 22°57N 115°38E 117 F10
Lufeng Yunnan, China 25°0N 102°5E 116 E4
Lufira → Dem. Rep. of the Congo 9°30S 27°0E 143 D2
Lufkin U.S.A. 31°21N 94°44W 176 F7
Lufupa Dem. Rep. of the Congo 10°37S 24°56E 143 E1
Luga Russia 58°40N 29°55E 84 C5
Luga → Russia 59°40N 28°18E 84 C5
Lugano Switz. 46°1N 8°57E 77 J4
Lugano, L. di Switz. 46°0N 9°0E 92 C6
Lugansk = Luhansk Ukraine 48°38N 39°15E 85 H10
Lugard's Falls Kenya 3°6S 38°41E 142 C4
Lugela Mozam. 16°25S 36°43E 143 F4
Lugenda → Mozam. 11°25S 38°33E 143 E4
Lugh = Luuq Somalia 3°48N 42°34E 131 G3
Lugnaquilla Ireland 52°58N 6°28W 64 D5
Lugnvik Sweden 62°56N 17°55E 62 B11
Lugo Italy 44°25N 11°54E 93 D8
Lugo Spain 43°2N 7°35W 88 B3
Lugo □ Spain 43°0N 7°30W 88 C3
Lugoj Romania 45°42N 21°57E 80 E6
Lugovoy = Qulan Kazakhstan 42°55N 72°43E 106 E8
Luhansk Ukraine 48°38N 39°15E 85 H10
Luhansk □ Ukraine 49°10N 38°40E 85 H10
Luhe China 32°19N 118°50E 117 A12
Luhe → Germany 53°23N 10°13E 76 B6
Luhuo China 31°21N 100°48E 116 B3
Lui → Angola 8°21S 17°33E 140 F3
Luiana Angola 17°25S 22°59E 144 A3
Luiana → Angola 17°24S 23°3E 141 H4
Luichow Pen. = Leizhou Bandao China 21°0N 110°0E 116 G7
Luimneach = Limerick Ireland 52°40N 8°37W 64 D3
Luing U.K. 56°14N 5°39W 65 E3
Luino Italy 45°59N 8°44E 92 C5
Luís Correia Brazil 3°0S 41°35W 189 A2
Luitpold Coast Antarctica 78°30S 32°0W 55 D1
Luiza Dem. Rep. of the Congo 7°40S 22°30E 140 F4
Luizi Dem. Rep. of the Congo 6°0S 27°25E 142 D2
Luján Argentina 34°45S 59°5W 190 C4
Lujiang China 31°20N 117°15E 117 B11
Lukang Taiwan 24°1N 120°22E 117 E13
Lukanga Swamp Zambia 14°30S 27°40E 143 E2
Lukavac Bos.-H. 44°33N 18°32E 80 F3
Lukenie → Dem. Rep. of the Congo 3°0S 18°50E 140 E3
Lŭki Bulgaria 41°50N 24°43E 97 E8
Lukla Nepal 27°42N 86°43E 125 F12
Lukolela Dem. Rep. of the Congo 5°23S 24°32E 142 D1
Lukosi Zimbabwe 18°30S 26°30E 143 F2
Lukovë Albania 39°59N 19°54E 96 G3
Lukovit Bulgaria 43°13N 24°11E 97 C8
Łuków Poland 51°55N 22°23E 83 G9
Lukoyanov Russia 55°2N 44°29E 86 C7
Lukusuzi △ Zambia 12°43S 32°36E 143 E3
Lülang Shan China 38°0N 111°15E 114 F6
Luleå Sweden 65°35N 22°10E 60 D20
Luleälven → Sweden 65°35N 22°10E 60 D20
Lüleburgaz Turkey 41°23N 27°22E 97 E11
Luliang China 25°0N 103°40E 116 E4
Lulimba Dem. Rep. of the Congo 4°12S 25°36E 142 C2
Luling U.S.A. 29°41N 97°39W 176 G6
Lulong China 39°53N 118°51E 115 E10
Lulonga → Dem. Rep. of the Congo 1°0N 18°10E 140 D3
Lulu U.S.A. 30°7N 82°29W 178 E7
Lulua → Dem. Rep. of the Congo 4°30S 20°30E 140 E4
Lumajang Indonesia 8°8S 113°13E 119 H15
Lumār Iran 33°33N 46°49E 105 F12
Lumbala N'guimbo Angola 14°18S 21°18E 141 G4
Lumber City U.S.A. 31°56N 82°41W 178 D7
Lumberton N.C., U.S.A. 34°37N 79°0W 177 D15
Lumberton Tex., U.S.A. 30°16N 94°12W 176 F7
Lumière, Côte de France 46°50N 2°10W 70 F4
Lumpkin U.S.A. 32°3N 84°48W 178 C5
Lumsden Canada 50°39N 104°52W 163 C8
Lumsden N.Z. 45°44S 168°27E 155 F3
Lumut Malaysia 4°13N 100°37E 121 K3
Lumut, Tanjung Indonesia 3°50S 105°58E 118 E3
Lumwana Zambia 11°50S 25°8E 143 E2
Luna India 23°43N 69°16E 124 H3
Lunan China 24°40N 103°18E 116 E4
Lunavada India 23°8N 73°37E 124 H5
Lunca Romania 47°22N 25°1E 81 C10
Lunca Corbului Romania 44°42N 24°45E 81 F9
Lund Sweden 55°44N 13°12E 63 J7
Lundazi Zambia 12°20S 33°7E 143 E3
Lunde Sweden 62°53N 17°51E 62 B11
Lunderskov Denmark 55°29N 9°19E 63 J3
Lundi → Zimbabwe 21°43S 32°34E 143 G3
Lundu Malaysia 1°40N 109°50E 118 D3
Lundy U.K. 51°10N 4°41W 67 F3
Lune → U.K. 54°0N 2°51W 66 C5
Lüneburg Germany 53°15N 10°24E 76 B6
Lüneburg Heath = Lüneburger Heide Germany 53°10N 10°12E 76 B6
Lüneburger Heide Germany 53°10N 10°12E 76 B6
Lunel France 43°39N 4°9E 73 E8
Lünen Germany 51°37N 7°32E 76 D3
Lunenburg Canada 44°22N 64°18W 165 D7
Lunéville France 48°36N 6°30E 71 D13
Lunga → Zambia 14°34S 26°25E 143 E2
Lunga Lunga Kenya 4°33S 39°7E 142 C4
Lungi S. Leone 8°40N 13°17W 138 D2
Lunglei India 22°55N 92°45E 123 H18
Luni India 26°0N 73°6E 124 G5
Luni → India 24°41N 71°14E 124 G4
Luninets = Luninyets Belarus 52°15N 26°50E 75 B14
Luning U.S.A. 38°30N 118°11W 168 G4
Lunino Russia 53°38N 45°18E 86 D7
Luninyets Belarus 52°15N 26°50E 75 B14
Lunkaransar India 28°29N 73°44E 124 E5
Lunsar S. Leone 8°41N 12°32W 138 D2
Lunsemfwa → Zambia 14°54S 30°12E 143 E3
Lunsemfwa Falls Zambia 14°30S 29°6E 143 E2
Luntai China 41°46N 84°14E 109 D10
Luo He → China 34°35N 110°20E 114 G6
Luocheng China 24°48N 108°53E 116 E7
Luochuan China 35°45N 109°26E 114 G5
Luoci China 25°19N 102°18E 116 E4
Luodian China 25°24N 106°43E 116 E6
Luoding China 22°45N 111°40E 117 F8
Luofu Dem. Rep. of the Congo 0°10S 29°15E 142 C2
Luohe China 33°32N 114°2E 114 H8
Luojiang China 31°18N 104°33E 116 B5
Luonan China 34°5N 110°10E 114 G6
Luoning China 34°35N 111°40E 114 G6
Luoshan China 32°13N 114°30E 117 A10
Luotian China 30°46N 115°22E 117 B10
Luoxiao Shan China 26°30N 114°1E 117 D10
Luoyang China 34°40N 112°26E 114 G7
Luoyuan China 26°28N 119°30E 117 D12
Luozigou China 43°42N 130°18E 115 C16
Lupeni Romania 45°21N 23°13E 81 E8
Lupilichi Mozam. 11°47S 35°13E 143 E4
Łupków Poland 49°15N 22°4E 83 J9
Lupoing China 24°53N 104°21E 116 E5
Luquan Hebei, China 38°4N 114°17E 114 E8
Luquan Yunnan, China 25°35N 102°25E 116 E4
Luque Paraguay 25°19S 57°25W 190 B4
Luquillo, Sierra de Puerto Rico 18°20N 65°47W 183 d
Lúras Italy 40°56N 9°10E 94 B2
Luray U.S.A. 38°40N 78°28W 173 F14
Lure France 47°40N 6°30E 71 E13
Lurgan U.K. 54°27N 6°20W 64 B5
Luribay Bolivia 17°6S 67°39W 188 D4
Lurín Peru 12°17S 76°52W 188 C2
Lúrio Mozam. 13°32S 40°30E 143 E5
Lusaka Zambia 15°28S 28°16E 143 F2
Lusaka □ Zambia 15°30S 29°0E 143 F2
Lusambo Dem. Rep. of the Congo 4°58S 23°28E 142 C1
Lusangaye Dem. Rep. of the Congo 4°54S 26°0E 142 C2
Luseland Canada 52°5N 109°24W 163 C7
Lusenga Plain △ Zambia 9°22S 29°14E 143 D2
Lushan Henan, China 33°45N 112°55E 114 H7
Lushan Sichuan, China 30°12N 102°52E 116 B4
Lushi China 34°3N 111°3E 114 G6
Lushnjë Albania 40°55N 19°41E 96 F3
Lushoto Tanzania 4°47S 38°20E 142 C4
Lushui China 25°58N 98°44E 116 E2
Lüshun China 38°45N 121°15E 115 E11
Lusignan France 46°26N 0°8E 72 B4
Lusigny-sur-Barse France 48°16N 4°15E 71 D11
Lusk U.S.A. 42°46N 104°27W 168 E11
Luso Portugal 40°23N 8°23W 88 E2
Lussac-les-Châteaux France 46°24N 0°43E 72 B4
Lustenau Austria 47°26N 9°39E 78 D2
Lūt, Dasht-e Iran 31°30N 58°0E 129 D8
Luta = Dalian China 38°50N 121°40E 115 E11
Lutao Taiwan 22°40N 121°30E 117 F13
Lutherstadt Wittenberg Germany 51°53N 12°39E 76 D8
Luthersville U.S.A. 33°13N 84°45W 178 B5
Luton U.K. 51°53N 0°24W 67 F7
Luton □ U.K. 51°53N 0°24W 67 F7
Lutselk'e Canada 62°24N 110°44W 163 A6
Lutsk Ukraine 50°50N 25°15E 75 C13
Lutto = Lotta → Europe 68°42N 31°6E 60 B24
Lutz U.S.A. 28°9N 82°28W 179 G7
Lützow Holmbukta Antarctica 69°10S 37°30E 55 C4
Lutzputs S. Africa 28°3S 20°40E 144 C3
Luuq Somalia 3°48N 42°34E 131 G3
Luverne Ala., U.S.A. 31°43N 86°16W 178 D3
Luverne Minn., U.S.A. 43°39N 96°13W 172 D5
Luvua Dem. Rep. of the Congo 8°48S 25°17E 143 D2
Luvua → Dem. Rep. of the Congo 6°50S 27°30E 142 D2
Luvuvhu → S. Africa 22°25S 31°18E 145 B5
Luwegu → Tanzania 8°31S 37°23E 143 D4
Luwero Uganda 0°50N 32°28E 142 B3
Luwuk Indonesia 0°56S 122°47E 119 E6
Luxembourg Lux. 49°37N 6°9E 69 E6
Luxembourg □ Belgium 49°58N 5°30E 69 E5
Luxembourg ■ Europe 49°45N 6°0E 69 E5
Luxembourg ✕ (LUX) Lux. 49°37N 6°10E 69 E6
Luxeuil-les-Bains France 47°49N 6°24E 71 E13
Luxi Hunan, China 28°20N 110°7E 117 C8
Luxi Yunnan, China 24°40N 103°55E 116 E4
Luxi Yunnan, China 24°27N 98°36E 116 E2
Luxian China 29°9N 105°24E 116 C5
Luxor = El Uqsur Egypt 25°41N 32°38E 137 B3
Luy-de-Béarn → France 43°39N 0°48W 72 E3
Luy-de-France → France 43°39N 0°48W 72 E3
Luyi China 33°50N 115°35E 114 H8
Luykau = Loikaw Burma 19°40N 97°17E 123 K20
Luz-St-Sauveur France 42°53N 0°0 72 F4
Luzern Switz. 47°3N 8°18E 77 H4
Luzern □ Switz. 47°2N 7°55E 77 H3
Luzhai China 24°29N 109°42E 116 E7
Luzhany Ukraine 48°22N 25°47E 81 B10
Luzhi China 26°21N 105°16E 116 D5
Luzhou China 28°52N 105°20E 116 C5
Luziânia Brazil 16°20S 48°0W 189 D1
Luzilândia Brazil 3°28S 42°22W 189 A2
Lužnice → Czech Rep. 49°14N 14°23E 78 B7
Luzon Phil. 16°0N 121°0E 119 A6
Luzon Strait Asia 21°0N 120°40E 117 G13
Luzy France 46°47N 3°58E 71 F10
Luzzi Italy 39°27N 16°17E 95 C9
Lviv Ukraine 49°50N 24°0E 75 D13
Lviv □ Ukraine 49°30N 23°45E 75 D13
Lvov = Lviv Ukraine 49°50N 24°0E 75 D13
Lwówek Poland 52°28N 16°10E 83 F3
Lwówek Śląski Poland 51°7N 15°38E 83 G2
Lyakhavichy Belarus 53°2N 26°32E 75 B14
Lyakhovskiye, Ostrova Russia 73°40N 141°0E 107 B15
Lyaki = Läki Azerbaijan 40°34N 47°22E 87 K8
Lyal I. Canada 44°57N 81°24W 174 B3
Lyall Mt. N.Z. 45°16S 167°32E 155 F2
Lyaskovets Bulgaria 43°6N 25°44E 97 C9
Lyasnaya → Belarus 52°9N 23°31E 83 F10
Lybster U.K. 58°18N 3°15W 65 C5
Lycaonia Turkey 38°0N 33°0E 104 D5
Lychen Germany 53°12N 13°18E 76 B9
Lychkova Russia 57°55N 32°24E 84 D7
Lycia Turkey 36°30N 29°30E 99 E11
Lyckebyån → Sweden 56°12N 15°39E 63 H9
Lycksele Sweden 64°38N 18°40E 60 D18
Lycosura Greece 37°20N 22°3E 98 D4
Lydda = Lod Israel 31°57N 34°54E 130 D3
Lyddan I. Antarctica 74°0S 21°0W 55 D2
Lydenburg S. Africa 25°10S 30°29E 145 C5
Lydia Turkey 38°48N 28°19E 99 C10
Łydynia → Poland 52°43N 20°26E 83 F7
Lyell N.Z. 41°48S 172°4E 155 B7
Lyell I. Canada 52°40N 131°35W 162 C2
Lyepyel Belarus 54°50N 28°40E 84 E5
Lygnern Sweden 57°30N 12°15E 63 G6
Lykens U.S.A. 40°34N 76°42W 175 F8
Lyman Ukraine 45°41N 29°45E 81 E14
Lyman U.S.A. 41°20N 110°18W 168 F8
Lymanske Ukraine 46°40N 29°58E 81 D14
Lyme B. U.K. 50°42N 2°53W 67 G4
Lyme Regis U.K. 50°43N 2°57W 67 G5
Lymington U.K. 50°45N 1°32W 67 G6
Łyna → Poland 54°37N 21°14E 82 D8
Lynchburg S.C., U.S.A. 34°3N 80°4W 178 A9
Lynchburg Va., U.S.A. 37°25N 79°9W 173 G14
Lynd → Australia 16°28S 143°18E 150 B3
Lynd Ra. Australia 25°30S 149°20E 151 D4
Lynden Canada 43°14N 80°9W 174 C4
Lynden U.S.A. 48°57N 122°27W 170 B4
Lyndhurst Australia 30°15S 138°18E 151 E2
Lyndon → Australia 23°29S 114°6E 149 D1
Lyndonville N.Y., U.S.A. 43°20N 78°23W 174 C6
Lyndonville Vt., U.S.A. 44°31N 72°1W 175 B12
Lyngen Norway 69°45N 20°30E 60 B19
Lynher Reef Australia 15°27S 121°55E 148 C3
Lynn U.S.A. 42°28N 70°57W 175 D14
Lynn Canal U.S.A. 58°50N 135°15W 166 D12
Lynn Haven U.S.A. 30°15N 85°39W 178 E4
Lynn Lake Canada 56°51N 101°3W 163 B8
Lynne U.S.A. 29°12N 81°55W 179 F8
Lynnwood U.S.A. 47°49N 122°18W 170 C4
Lynton U.K. 51°13N 3°50W 67 F4
Lyntupy Belarus 55°4N 26°23E 84 E4
Lynx L. Canada 62°25N 106°15W 163 A7
Lyon France 45°46N 4°50E 73 C8
Lyon St-Exupery ✕ (LYS) France 45°44N 5°2E 73 C9
Lyonnais France 45°45N 4°15E 73 C8
Lyons = Lyon France 45°46N 4°50E 73 C8
Lyons Ga., U.S.A. 32°12N 82°19W 178 C7
Lyons Kans., U.S.A. 38°21N 98°12W 172 F4
Lyons N.Y., U.S.A. 43°5N 77°0W 174 C8
Lyons → Australia 25°2S 115°9E 149 E2
Lyons Falls U.S.A. 43°37N 75°22W 175 C9
Lyozna Belarus 55°0N 30°50E 84 E6
Lys = Leie → Belgium 51°2N 3°45E 69 C3
Lysá nad Labem Czech Rep. 50°11N 14°51E 78 A7
Lysekil Sweden 58°17N 11°26E 63 F5
Lysi Cyprus 35°6N 33°41E 101 D12
Lyskovo Russia 56°0N 45°3E 86 B7
Lystrup Denmark 56°14N 10°14E 63 H4
Lysvik Sweden 60°1N 13°9E 62 D7
Lysychansk Ukraine 48°55N 38°30E 85 H10
Lytham St. Anne's U.K. 53°45N 3°0W 66 D4
Lyttelton N.Z. 43°35S 172°44E 155 D7
Lytton Canada 50°13N 121°31W 16
Lyuban Russia 59°16N 31°18E 8
Lyubertsy Russia 55°40N 37°51E 8
Lyubim Russia 58°20N 40°39E 8
Lyubimets Bulgaria 41°50N 26°5E 9
Lyuboml Ukraine 51°11N 24°4E 8
Lyubotyn Ukraine 50°0N 36°0E
Lyubytino Russia 58°50N 33°16E
Lyudinovo Russia 53°52N 34°28E

M

M.R. Štefánik, Bratislava ✕ (BTS) Slovak Rep. 48°11N 17°9E 7
Ma → Vietnam 19°47N 105°56E 1
Ma, O. el → Algeria 27°45N 7°52W 1
Ma On Shan China 22°24N 114°10E
Ma'adaba Jordan 31°43N 35°47E 1
Ma'alot-Tarshiha Israel 33°1N 35°17E 1
Maamba Zambia 17°17S 26°28E 1
Ma'ān Jordan 30°12N 35°44E 1
Ma'ān □ Jordan 30°0N 36°0E 1
Maanselkä Finland 63°52N 28°32E 6
Ma'anshan China 31°44N 118°29E 1
Maarianhamina = Mariehamn Finland 60°5N 19°55E 6
Maarmorilik Greenland 71°3N 51°0W
Ma'arrat an Nu'mān Syria 35°43N 36°43E 1
Maas → Neths. 51°45N 4°32E
Maaseik Belgium 51°6N 5°45E
Maasin Phil. 10°8N 124°50E 1
Maastricht Neths. 50°50N 5°40E
Maave Mozam. 21°4S 34°47E 1
Mababe Depression Botswana 18°50S 24°15E 1
Mabalane Mozam. 23°37S 32°31E 1
Mabel L. Canada 50°35N 118°43W 1
Mabenge Dem. Rep. of the Congo 4°15N 24°12E 1
Maberly Canada 44°50N 76°32W 1
Mabesi, L. S. Leone 7°10N 11°42W 1
Mabian China 28°47N 103°37E 1
Mablethorpe U.K. 53°20N 0°15E
Mableton U.S.A. 33°49N 84°35W 1
Mably France 46°5N 4°4E 7
Maboma Dem. Rep. of the Congo 2°30N 28°10E 1
Mabonto S. Leone 8°53N 11°50W 1
Mabrouk Mali 19°29N 1°15W 1
Mabuasehube ⌂ Botswana 25°5S 21°10E 1
Mabuiag Australia 9°57S 142°11E
Mac Bac Vietnam 9°46N 106°7E 1
Macachín Argentina 37°10S 63°43W 1
Macaé Brazil 22°20S 41°43W 1
Macael Spain 37°20N 2°18W
Macaíba Brazil 5°51S 35°21W 1
Macajuba Brazil 12°9S 40°22W 1
McAlester U.S.A. 34°56N 95°46W 1
McAllen U.S.A. 26°12N 98°14W 1
McAlpin U.S.A. 30°8N 82°57W 1
MacAlpine L. Canada 66°32N 102°45W 16
Macamic Canada 48°45N 79°0W 1
Macao = Macau China 22°12N 113°33E 1
Macão Portugal 39°35N 7°59W
Macapá Brazil 0°5N 51°4W 1
Macarani Brazil 15°33S 40°24W 1
Macarao △ Venezuela 10°22N 67°7W 1
Macarthur Australia 38°5S 142°0E 1
McArthur → Australia 15°54S 136°40E 1
McArthur, Port Australia 16°4S 136°23E 1
Macate Peru 8°48S 78°7W 1
Macau Brazil 5°15S 36°40W 1
Macau China 22°12N 113°33E 1
Macaúbas Brazil 13°2S 42°42W 1
McBride Canada 53°20N 120°19W 1
McCall U.S.A. 44°55N 116°6W 1
McCamey U.S.A. 31°8N 102°14W 1
McCammon U.S.A. 42°39N 112°12W 1
McCarran Int., Las Vegas ✕ (LAS) U.S.A. 36°5N 115°9W 17
McCauley I. Canada 53°40N 130°15W 1
McCleary U.S.A. 47°3N 123°16W 1
Macclenny U.S.A. 30°17N 82°7W 1
Macclesfield U.K. 53°15N 2°8W
Macclesfield Bank S. China Sea 16°0N 114°30E 1
M'Clintock Chan. Canada 72°0N 102°0W 16
McClintock Ra. Australia 18°44S 127°38E 1
McCloud U.S.A. 41°15N 122°8W 1
McCluer I. Australia 11°5S 133°0E 1
McClure U.S.A. 40°42N 77°19W 1
McClure, L. U.S.A. 37°35N 120°16W 1
M'Clure Str. Canada 75°0N 119°0W 1
McClusky U.S.A. 47°29N 100°27W 1
McComb U.S.A. 31°15N 90°27W 1
McCook U.S.A. 40°12N 100°38W 1
McCormick U.S.A. 33°55N 82°17W 1
McCreary Canada 50°47N 99°29W 1
McCullough Mt. U.S.A. 35°35N 115°13W 17
McCusker → Canada 55°32N 108°39W 1
McDavid U.S.A. 30°52N 87°19W 1
McDermitt U.S.A. 41°59N 117°43W 1
McDonald U.S.A. 40°22N 80°14W 1
Macdonald, L. Australia 23°30S 129°0E 1
McDonald Is. Ind. Oc. 53°0S 73°0E 1
MacDonnell Ranges Australia 23°40S 133°0E 1
McDonough U.S.A. 33°27N 84°9W 1
McDougalls Well Australia 31°8S 141°15E 1
MacDowell L. Canada 52°15N 92°45W 1
Macduff U.K. 57°40N 2°31W 1
Maceda Spain 42°16N 7°39W
Macedonia U.S.A. 41°19N 81°31W
Macedonia ■ Europe 41°53N 21°40E
Maceió Brazil 9°40S 35°41W 1
Maceira Portugal 39°41N 8°55W
Macenta Guinea 8°35N 9°32W 1
Macerata Italy 43°18N 13°27E 9
McFarland U.S.A. 35°41N 119°14W 1
McFarlane → Canada 59°12N 107°58W 1

arlane, L. *Australia* 32°0S 136°40E **152** B2
hee *U.S.A.* 33°38N 91°24W **176** E9
l *U.S.A.* 39°23N 114°47W **168** G6
illycuddy's Reeks
and 51°58N 9°45W **64** E2
aw *U.S.A.* 42°36N 76°8W **175** D8
egor *U.S.A.* 43°1N 91°11W **172** D8
egor Ra. *Australia* 27°0S 142°45E **151** D3
ire, Mt. *Australia* 20°18S 148°23E **150** b
Pakistan 29°50N 67°20E **124** E2
Kowr *Iran* 25°48N 61°28E **129** E9
acalis *Brazil* 17°55S 40°45W **189** D2
ado = Jiparaná →
zil 8°3S 62°52W **186** E6
agai *Argentina* 26°56S 60°2W **190** B3
akos *Kenya* 1°30S 37°15E **142** C4
ala *Ecuador* 3°20S 79°57W **186** D3
anga *Mozam.* 20°59S 35°0E **145** B6
attie, L. *Australia* 24°50S 139°48E **150** C2
ault *France* 49°21N 4°29E **71** C11
ava *Mozam.* 25°54S 32°28E **145** C5
ecoul *France* 47°0N 1°49W **70** F5
eke *Zimbabwe* 18°5S 31°51E **145** A5
eng *China* 31°12N 115°2E **117** B10
erla *India* 16°29N 79°26E **126** F4
ero *Spain* 39°21N 4°20W **89** F6
gaon *India* 20°5N 86°17E **126** D8
hu → *India* 23°6N 70°46E **124** H4
iaro △ *Pakistan* 34°40N 73°30E **124** B5
ias *Maine,*
.A. 44°43N 67°28W **173** C20
ias *N.Y., U.S.A.* 42°25N 78°29W **174** D6
ichi → *Canada* 57°3N 92°6W **163** B10
ico *Madeira* 32°43N 16°44W **100** D3
ilipatnam *India* 16°12N 81°8E **127** F5
iques *Venezuela* 10°4N 72°34W **186** A4
u Picchu *Peru* 13°8S 72°30W **188** C3
ynlleth *U.K.* 52°35N 3°50W **67** E4
Mozam. 25°2S 33°8E **145** C5
ejowice *Poland* 51°36N 21°26E **83** G8
wraith Ra.
tralia 13°50S 143°20E **150** A3
Romania 45°16N 28°8E **81** E13
Mali 14°50N 5°0W **138** C4
nes L. *Canada* 52°13N 93°45W **163** C10
tosh *U.S.A.* 45°55N 101°21W **172** C3
tosh L. *Canada* 55°45N 105°0W **163** B8
ntosh Ra.
tralia 27°39S 125°32E **149** E4
ntyre →
tralia 28°37S 150°47E **151** D5
zo Galaico *Spain* 42°30N 7°30W **88** C3
a *Turkey* 40°49N 39°36E **105** B8
ay *Australia* 21°8S 149°11E **150** K7
ay *U.S.A.* 43°55N 113°37W **168** E7
ay → *Canada* 57°10N 111°38W **162** B6
ay, L. *Australia* 22°30S 129°0E **148** D4
y Ra. *Australia* 23°0S 122°30E **148** D3
eesport *U.S.A.* 40°20N 79°51W **174** F5
ellar *Canada* 45°30N 79°55W **174** A5
enna *U.S.A.* 46°56N 122°33W **170** D4
enzie = Linden
ana 6°0N 58°10W **186** B7
enzie *Canada* 55°20N 123°5W **162** B4
enzie *U.S.A.* 36°8N 88°31W **177** C10
enzie →
tralia 23°38S 149°46E **150** C4
enzie → *Canada* 69°10N 134°20W **160** D5
enzie → *U.S.A.* 44°7N 123°6W **168** D2
enzie Bay *Canada* 69°0N 137°30W **158** C6
enzie King I.
ada 77°45N 111°0W **161** B9
enzie Mts. *Canada* 64°0N 130°0W **158** C6
enzie Plains *N.Z.* 44°10S 170°25E **155** E5
errow, L. *N.Z.* 44°25S 168°5E **155** E3
inac, Straits of
.A. 45°50N 84°40W **173** C11
inaw City
.A. 45°47N 84°44W **173** C11
nlay *Australia* 21°16S 141°18E **150** C3
nlay → *Australia* 20°50S 141°28E **150** C3
nley, Mt. *U.S.A.* 63°4N 151°0W **160** E1
nley Sea *Arctic* 82°0N 0°0 **57** A11
nney *U.S.A.* 33°12N 96°37W **176** E6
innon Road *Kenya* 3°40S 39°1E **142** C4
ttrick *U.S.A.* 35°18N 119°37W **171** K7
lin *Canada* 52°20N 109°56W **163** C7
sville *Australia* 30°40S 152°56E **153** A10
ren Vale
tralia 35°13S 138°31E **152** C3
ughlin *U.S.A.* 45°49N 100°49W **172** C3
ean *Australia* 29°26S 153°16E **151** D5
an *U.S.A.* 35°14N 100°36W **176** D4
ansboro *U.S.A.* 38°6N 88°32W **172** F9
ear *S. Africa* 31°2S 28°23E **145** D4
ear, C. *Malawi* 13°58S 34°49E **143** E3
eay → *Australia* 30°56S 153°0E **153** A10
nnan *Canada* 55°42N 116°50W **162** B5
eod → *Canada* 54°9N 115°44W **162** C5
eod, L. *Australia* 24°9S 113°47E **149** D1
eod B. *Canada* 62°53N 110°0W **163** A7
eod Lake *Canada* 54°58N 123°0W **162** C4
ughlin, Mt.
.A. 42°27N 122°19W **168** E2
echen *U.S.A.* 39°57N 80°44W **174** G4
innville *Oreg.,*
.A. 45°13N 123°12W **168** D2
innville *Tenn.,*
.A. 35°41N 85°46W **177** D12
urdo *Antarctica* 77°51S 166°37E **55** D11
urdo Sd. *Antarctica* 77°0S 170°0E **55** D11
urray = Fort McMurray
ada 56°44N 111°7W **162** B6
urray *U.S.A.* 48°19N 122°14W **170** B4
ere *Mozam.* 21°13S 32°47E **143** G3
doene *Mozam.* 23°32S 35°5E **145** B6
mb *U.S.A.* 40°27N 90°40W **172** E8
mer *Italy* 40°16N 8°47E **94** B1
n *France* 46°19N 4°50E **71** F11
n *Ga., U.S.A.* 32°51N 83°38W **178** C6
n *Miss., U.S.A.* 33°7N 88°34W **177** E10
n *Mo., U.S.A.* 39°44N 92°28W **172** F7
ssa *Mozam.* 17°55S 33°56E **143** F3
un L. *Canada* 56°32N 103°40W **163** B8
vane *Mozam.* 21°30S 35°2E **145** B6
herson *U.S.A.* 38°22N 97°40W **172** F5
herson Pk.
.A. 34°53N 119°53W **171** L7
herson Ra.
stralia 28°15S 153°15E **151** D5
uarie → *Australia* 30°7S 147°24E **153** A7
Macquarie Harbour
Australia 42°15S 145°23E **151** G4
Macquarie I. *Pac. Oc.* 54°36S 158°55E **156** N7
Macquarie Ridge
S. Ocean 57°0S 159°0E **55** B10
McRae *U.S.A.* 32°4N 82°54W **178** C7
MacRobertson Land
Antarctica 71°0S 64°0E **55** D6
Macroom *Ireland* 51°54N 8°57W **64** E3
MacTier *Canada* 45°8N 79°47W **174** A5
Macubela *Mozam.* 16°53S 37°49E **143** F4
Macugnaga *Italy* 45°58N 7°58E **92** C4
Macuira △ *Colombia* 12°9N 71°21W **183** D5
Macumba →
Australia 27°52S 137°12E **151** D2
Macuro *Venezuela* 10°42N 61°55W **187** K15
Macusani *Peru* 14°4S 70°29W **188** C3
Macuse *Mozam.* 17°45S 37°10E **143** F4
Macuspana *Mexico* 17°46N 92°36W **181** D6
Macusse *Angola* 17°48S 20°23E **144** A3
Mada → *Nigeria* 7°59N 7°55E **139** D6
Ma'dabā □ *Jordan* 31°43N 35°47E **130** D4
Madadeni *S. Africa* 27°43S 30°3E **145** C5
Madagali *Nigeria* 10°56N 13°33E **139** C7
Madagascar ■ *Africa* 20°0S 47°0E **141** J9
Madā'in Sālih *Si. Arabia* 26°46N 37°57E **128** E3
Madakasira *India* 13°56N 77°16E **127** H3
Madama *Niger* 22°0N 13°40E **135** D8
Madame, I. *Canada* 45°30N 60°58W **165** C7
Madan *Bulgaria* 41°30N 24°57E **97** E8
Madanapalle *India* 13°33N 78°28E **127** H4
Madang *Papua N. G.* 5°12S 145°49E **147** B7
Madaoua *Niger* 14°5N 6°27E **139** C6
Madara *Bulgaria* 43°17N 27°8E **97** C11
Madara *Nigeria* 11°45N 10°35E **139** C7
Madaripur *Bangla.* 23°19N 90°15E **123** H17
Madauk *Burma* 17°56N 96°52E **123** L20
Madawaska *Canada* 45°30N 78°0W **174** A7
Madawaska →
Canada 45°27N 76°21W **174** A7
Madaya *Burma* 22°12N 96°10E **123** H20
Maddalena *Italy* 41°16N 9°23E **94** A2
Maddaloni *Italy* 41°2N 14°23E **95** A7
Maddur *India* 12°36N 77°4E **127** H3
Madeira *Atl. Oc.* 32°50N 17°0W **100** D3
Madeira → *Brazil* 3°22S 58°45W **186** D7
Madeleine, Îs. de la
Canada 47°30N 61°40W **165** C7
Maden *Turkey* 38°23N 39°40E **105** C8
Madera *Mexico* 29°12N 108°7W **180** B3
Madera *Calif., U.S.A.* 36°57N 120°3W **170** J6
Madera *Pa., U.S.A.* 40°49N 78°26W **174** F6
Madgaon *India* 15°12N 73°58E **127** G1
Madha *India* 18°0N 75°30E **126** F2
Madhavpur *India* 21°15N 69°58E **124** J3
Madhepura *India* 26°11N 86°23E **125** F12
Madhira *India* 16°55N 80°22E **126** F5
Madhubani *India* 26°21N 86°7E **125** F12
Madhugiri *India* 13°40N 77°12E **127** H3
Madhupur *India* 24°16N 86°39E **125** G12
Madhya Pradesh □
India 22°50N 78°0E **124** J8
Madidi → *Bolivia* 12°32S 66°52W **188** C4
Madikeri *India* 12°30N 75°45E **127** H2
Madikwe △ *S. Africa* 27°38S 32°15E **145** C5
Madill *U.S.A.* 34°6N 96°46W **176** D6
Madimba
Dem. Rep. of the Congo 4°58S 15°5E **140** E3
Ma'din *Syria* 35°45N 39°36E **105** E8
Madina *Mali* 13°25N 8°50W **138** C3
Madinani *Ivory C.* 9°37N 6°57W **138** D3
Madinat al Malik Khālid al
Askarīyah *Si. Arabia* 27°54N 45°31E **128** E5
Madīnat ath Thawrah
Syria 35°50N 38°32E **105** E8
Madīnat Masdar
U.A.E. 24°26N 54°37E **129** E7
Madingou *Congo* 4°10S 13°33E **140** E2
Madison *Calif., U.S.A.* 38°41N 121°59W **170** G5
Madison *Fla., U.S.A.* 30°28N 83°25W **178** E6
Madison *Ga., U.S.A.* 33°36N 83°28W **178** B6
Madison *Ind., U.S.A.* 38°44N 85°23W **173** F11
Madison *Nebr., U.S.A.* 41°50N 97°27W **172** E5
Madison *Ohio, U.S.A.* 41°46N 81°3W **174** E3
Madison *S. Dak., U.S.A.* 44°0N 97°7W **172** C5
Madison *Wis., U.S.A.* 43°4N 89°24W **172** D9
Madison → *U.S.A.* 45°56N 111°31W **168** D8
Madison Heights
U.S.A. 37°25N 79°8W **173** G14
Madisonville *Ky.,*
U.S.A. 37°20N 87°30W **172** G10
Madisonville *Tex.,*
U.S.A. 30°57N 95°55W **176** F7
Madista *Botswana* 21°15S 25°6E **144** B4
Madiun *Indonesia* 7°38S 111°32E **118** F4
Mado Gashi *Kenya* 0°44N 39°10E **142** B4
Madoc *Canada* 44°30N 77°28W **174** B7
Madoi *China* 34°46N 98°18E **110** E8
Madon → *France* 48°36N 6°6E **71** D13
Madona *Latvia* 56°53N 26°5E **84** D4
Madonie *Italy* 37°50N 13°50E **94** E6
Madonna di Campiglio
Italy 46°14N 10°49E **92** B7
Madra Dağı *Turkey* 39°23N 27°12E **99** B9
Madrakah, Ra's al
Oman 19°0N 57°50E **131** D6
Madras = Chennai *India* 13°8N 80°19E **127** H5
Madras = Tamil Nadu □
India 11°0N 77°0E **127** J3
Madras *U.S.A.* 44°38N 121°8W **168** D3
Madre, L. *U.S.A.* 25°15N 97°30W **176** J6
Madre, Sierra *Phil.* 17°0N 122°0E **119** A6
Madre de Dios □ *Peru* 12°0S 70°15W **188** C3
Madre de Dios →
Bolivia 10°59S 66°8W **188** C4
Madre de Dios, I. *Chile* 50°20S 75°10W **192** D1
Madre del Sur, Sierra
Mexico 17°30N 100°0W **181** D5
Madre Occidental, Sierra
Mexico 27°0N 107°0W **180** B3
Madre Oriental, Sierra
Mexico 25°0N 100°0W **180** C5
Madri *India* 24°16N 73°32E **124** G5
Madrid *Spain* 40°24N 3°42W **88** E7
Madrid *Ala., U.S.A.* 31°2N 85°24W **178** D4
Madrid *N.Y., U.S.A.* 44°45N 75°8W **175** B9
Madrid □ *Spain* 40°30N 3°45W **88** E7
Madrid Barajas ✕ (MAD)
Spain 40°26N 3°34W **88** E7
Madridejos *Spain* 39°28N 3°33W **89** F7
Madrigal de las Altas Torres
Spain 41°5N 5°0W **88** D6
Madrona, Sierra *Spain* 38°27N 4°16W **89** G6
Madroñera *Spain* 39°26N 5°42W **89** F5
Madula
Dem. Rep. of the Congo 0°27N 25°22E **142** B2
Madura *Australia* 31°55S 127°0E **149** F4
Madura *Indonesia* 7°30S 114°0E **119** G15
Madura, Selat
Indonesia 7°30S 113°20E **119** G15
Madura Oya △ *Sri Lanka* 7°20N 81°10E **127** L5
Madurai *India* 9°55N 78°10E **127** K4
Madurantakam *India* 12°30N 79°50E **127** H4
Madzhalis *Russia* 42°9N 47°47E **87** J8
Mae Chan *Thailand* 20°9N 99°52E **120** B2
Mae Charim △
Thailand 18°17N 100°59E **120** C3
Mae Hong Son *Thailand* 19°16N 97°56E **120** C2
Mae Khlong →
Thailand 13°24N 100°0E **120** F3
Mae Moei △ *Thailand* 17°26N 98°7E **120** D2
Mae Phang △ *Thailand* 19°7N 99°13E **120** C2
Mae Phrik *Thailand* 17°27N 99°7E **120** D2
Mae Ping △ *Thailand* 17°37N 98°51E **120** D2
Mae Ramat *Thailand* 16°58N 98°31E **120** D2
Mae Rim *Thailand* 18°54N 98°57E **120** C2
Mae Sai *Thailand* 20°20N 99°55E **116** G2
Mae Sot *Thailand* 16°43N 98°34E **120** D2
Mae Suai *Thailand* 19°39N 99°33E **116** H2
Mae Tha *Thailand* 18°28N 99°8E **120** C2
Mae Tup Res. *Thailand* 17°52N 98°45E **120** D2
Mae Wa △ *Thailand* 17°23N 99°16E **120** D2
Mae Wong △ *Thailand* 15°54N 99°12E **120** E2
Mae Yom △ *Thailand* 18°43N 100°15E **120** C3
Maebaru *Japan* 33°33N 130°12E **113** H5
Maebashi *Japan* 36°24N 139°4E **113** F9
Maella *Spain* 41°8N 0°7E **90** D5
Maelpaeg L. *Canada* 48°20N 56°30W **165** C8
Maesteg *U.K.* 51°36N 3°40W **67** F4
Maestra, Sierra *Cuba* 20°15N 77°0W **182** B4
Maevatanana *Madag.* 16°56S 46°49E **141** H9
Mafadi *S. Africa* 29°12S 29°21E **145** C4
Mafeking = Mafikeng
S. Africa 25°50S 25°38E **144** C4
Mafeking *Canada* 52°40N 101°10W **163** C8
Maféré *Ivory C.* 5°30N 3°2W **138** D4
Mafeteng *Lesotho* 29°51S 27°15E **144** C4
Maffra *Australia* 37°53S 146°58E **153** D7
Mafia I. *Tanzania* 7°45S 39°50E **142** D4
Mafikeng *S. Africa* 25°50S 25°38E **144** C4
Mafra *Brazil* 26°10S 49°55W **191** B6
Mafra *Portugal* 38°55N 9°20W **89** G1
Mafungabusi Plateau
Zimbabwe 18°30S 29°8E **143** F2
Magadan *Russia* 59°38N 150°50E **107** D16
Magadi *India* 12°58N 77°14E **127** H3
Magadi *Kenya* 1°54S 36°19E **142** C4
Magadi, L. *Kenya* 1°54S 36°19E **142** C4
Magaliesburg *S. Africa* 26°0S 27°32E **145** C4
Magallanes □ *Chile* 52°0S 72°0W **192** D2
Magallanes, Estrecho de
Chile 52°30S 75°0W **192** D2
Magaluf *Spain* 39°29N 2°32E **91** F7
Magangué *Colombia* 9°14N 74°45W **186** B4
Magaria *Niger* 13°4N 9°5E **139** C6
Magburaka *S. Leone* 8°47N 12°0W **138** D2
Magdagachi *Russia* 53°27N 125°48E **107** D13
Magdalen Is. = Madeleine, Îs. de
la *Canada* 47°30N 61°40W **165** C7
Magdalena *Argentina* 35°5S 57°30W **190** D4
Magdalena *Bolivia* 13°13S 63°57W **186** F6
Magdalena *U.S.A.* 34°7N 107°15W **169** J10
Magdalena → *Colombia* 11°6N 74°51W **186** A4
Magdalena, B. *Mexico* 24°35N 112°0W **180** C2
Magdalena, I. *Chile* 44°40S 73°0W **192** B2
Magdalena, I. *Mexico* 24°40N 112°15W **180** C2
Magdalena, Llano de
Mexico 25°0N 111°25W **180** C2
Magdalena de Kino
Mexico 30°38N 110°57W **180** A2
Magdeburg *Germany* 52°7N 11°38E **76** C7
Magdelaine Cays
Australia 16°33S 150°18E **150** B5
Magee *U.S.A.* 31°52N 89°44W **177** F10
Magelang *Indonesia* 7°29S 110°13E **118** F4
Magellan's Str. = Magallanes,
Estrecho de *Chile* 52°30S 75°0W **192** D2
Magenta *Italy* 45°28N 8°53E **92** C5
Magenta, L. *Australia* 33°30S 119°2E **149** F2
Magerøya *Norway* 71°3N 25°40E **60** A21
Maggea *Australia* 34°28S 140°2E **152** C4
Maggia → *Switz.* 46°18N 8°36E **77** J4
Maggiorasca, Mte. *Italy* 44°33N 9°29E **92** D6
Maggiore, L. *Italy* 45°57N 8°39E **92** B5
Maggotty *Jamaica* 18°9N 77°46W **182** a
Maghâgha *Egypt* 28°38N 30°50E **137** F7
Maghama *Mauritania* 15°32N 12°57W **138** B2
Maghera *U.K.* 54°51N 6°41W **64** B5
Magherafelt *U.K.* 54°45N 6°37W **64** B5
Maghnia *Algeria* 34°50N 1°43W **136** B3
Maghreb *N. Afr.* 32°0N 4°0W **132** C3
Magione *Italy* 43°8N 12°12E **93** E9
Magistralnyy *Russia* 56°16N 107°36E **107** D11
Maglaj *Bos.-H.* 44°33N 18°7E **80** F3
Magliano in Toscana
Italy 42°36N 11°17E **93** F8
Máglie *Italy* 40°7N 18°18E **95** B11
Magnac-Laval *France* 46°13N 1°11E **72** B5
Magnesia = Magnisia
Greece 39°15N 23°0E **98** B5
Magnetic Pole (North)
Arctic 82°18N 113°24W **54** A2
Magnetic Pole (South)
Antarctica 64°8S 138°8E **55** C9
Magnisia *Greece* 39°15N 23°0E **98** B5
Magnitogorsk *Russia* 53°27N 59°4E **108** B5
Magnolia *Ark., U.S.A.* 33°16N 93°14W **176** E8
Magnolia *Miss., U.S.A.* 31°9N 90°28W **177** F9
Magny-en-Vexin *France* 49°9N 1°47E **71** C8
Mago *Fiji* 17°26S 179°8W **154** a
Magog *Canada* 45°18N 72°9W **175** A12
Magoro *Uganda* 1°45N 34°12E **142** B3
Magoulades *Greece* 39°45N 19°42E **101** A3
Magoye *Zambia* 16°1S 27°30E **143** F2
Magpie, L. *Canada* 51°0N 64°41W **165** B7
Magrath *Canada* 49°25N 112°50W **162** D6
Magre → *Spain* 39°11N 0°25W **91** F4
Magta Lahjar
Mauritania 17°28N 13°17W **138** B2
Magu *Tanzania* 2°30S 33°30E **142** C3
Maguan *China* 23°0N 104°21E **116** F5
Maguarinho, C. *Brazil* 0°15S 48°30W **187** D9
Magude *Mozam.* 25°2S 32°40E **145** C5
Magurski △ *Poland* 49°30N 21°30E **83** J8
Mağusa = Famagusta
Cyprus 35°8N 33°55E **101** D12
Maguse L. *Canada* 61°37N 95°10W **163** A9
Maguse Pt. *Canada* 61°20N 93°50W **163** A10
Magvana *India* 23°13N 69°22E **124** H3
Magwe *Burma* 20°10N 95°0E **123** J19
Magyarorszag = Hungary ■
Europe 47°20N 19°20E **79** D12
Maha Oya *Sri Lanka* 7°31N 81°22E **127** L5
Maha Sarakham
Thailand 16°12N 103°16E **120** D4
Mahābād *Iran* 36°50N 45°45E **105** D11
Mahabaleshwar *India* 17°58N 73°43E **126** F1
Mahabalipuram *India* 12°37N 80°11E **127** H5
Mahabharat Lekh
Nepal 28°30N 82°0E **125** E10
Mahabo *Madag.* 20°23S 44°40E **141** J8
Mahad *India* 18°6N 73°29E **126** E1
Mahadeo Hills *India* 22°20N 78°30E **125** H8
Mahadeopur *India* 18°48N 80°0E **126** E5
Mahaffey *U.S.A.* 40°53N 78°44W **174** F6
Mahagi
Dem. Rep. of the Congo 2°20N 31°0E **142** B3
Mahajan *India* 28°48N 73°56E **124** E5
Mahajanga *Madag.* 15°40S 46°25E **141** H9
Mahakam → *Indonesia* 0°35N 117°17E **118** E5
Mahalapye *Botswana* 23°1S 26°51E **144** B4
Mahale Mts. *Tanzania* 6°20S 30°0E **142** D3
Mahale Mts. △ *Tanzania* 6°10S 29°50E **142** D2
Maḩallāt *Iran* 33°55N 50°30E **129** C6
Māhān *Iran* 30°5N 57°18E **129** D8
Mahan → *India* 23°30N 82°50E **125** H10
Mahanadi → *India* 20°20N 86°25E **126** D8
Mahananda → *India* 25°12N 87°52E **125** G12
Mahanoro *Madag.* 19°54S 48°48E **141** H9
Mahanoy City *U.S.A.* 40°49N 76°9W **175** F8
Maharashtra □ *India* 20°30N 75°30E **126** D2
Maharès *Tunisia* 34°32N 10°29E **136** B6
Mahasamund *India* 21°6N 82°6E **126** D6
Mahasham, W. →
Egypt 30°15N 34°10E **130** E3
Mahattat ash Shīdīyah
Jordan 29°55N 35°55E **130** F4
Mahattat 'Unayzah
Jordan 30°30N 35°47E **130** E4
Mahaweli Ganga →
Sri Lanka 8°27N 81°13E **127** K5
Mahaxay *Laos* 17°22N 105°12E **120** D5
Mahbubabad *India* 17°42N 80°2E **126** F5
Mahbubnagar *India* 16°45N 77°59E **126** F3
Mahda *U.A.E.* 25°20N 56°15E **129** E8
Maḩḑah *Oman* 24°24N 55°59E **129** E7
Mahdia *Tunisia* 35°28N 11°0E **136** A6
Mahdia □ *Tunisia* 35°20N 10°35E **136** A6
Mahe *Jammu & Kashmir,*
India 33°10N 78°32E **125** C8
Mahé *Pondicherry, India* 11°42N 75°34E **127** J2
Mahé *Seychelles* 5°0S 55°30E **141** b
Mahé ✕ (SEZ) *Seychelles* 4°40S 55°31E **141** b
Mahébourg *Mauritius* 20°24S 57°42E **141** d
Mahendra Giri *India* 8°20N 77°30E **127** K3
Mahendragarh *India* 28°17N 76°14E **124** E7
Mahendranagar *Nepal* 28°55N 80°20E **125** E9
Mahenge *Tanzania* 8°45S 36°41E **143** D4
Maheno *N.Z.* 45°10S 170°50E **155** F5
Mahesana *India* 23°39N 72°26E **124** H5
Maheshwar *India* 22°11N 75°35E **124** H6
Mahgawan *India* 26°29N 78°37E **125** F8
Mahi → *India* 22°15N 72°55E **124** H5
Mahia Pen. *N.Z.* 39°9S 177°55E **154** F6
Mahikeng = Mafikeng
S. Africa 25°50S 25°38E **144** C4
Mahilyow *Belarus* 53°55N 30°18E **75** B16
Mahilyow □ *Belarus* 54°10N 30°50E **84** E6
Mahim *India* 19°39N 72°44E **126** E1
Mahina *Tahiti* 17°30S 149°27W **155** b
Mahirija *Morocco* 34°0N 3°16W **136** B3
Mahmud Kot *Pakistan* 30°16N 71°0E **124** D4
Mahmudia *Romania* 45°5N 29°5E **81** E14
Mahmudiye *Turkey* 39°48N 30°15E **99** B12
Mahmutbey *Turkey* 41°3N 28°49E **97** E12
Māhneshān *Iran* 36°44N 47°39E **105** D12
Mahnomen *U.S.A.* 47°19N 95°58W **172** B6
Maho *Sri Lanka* 7°49N 80°16E **127** L5
Mahoba *India* 25°15N 79°55E **125** G8
Mahón = Maó *Spain* 39°53N 4°16E **100** B11
Mahón, Menorca ✕ (MAH)
Spain 39°50N 4°16E **90** F9
Mahone Bay *Canada* 44°27N 64°23W **165** D7
Mahongo △ *Namibia* 18°0S 23°15E **144** B3
Mahopac *U.S.A.* 41°22N 73°45W **175** E11
Mahuta *Nigeria* 11°32N 4°58E **139** C5
Mahuva *India* 21°5N 71°48E **124** J4
Mahya Dağı *Turkey* 41°47N 27°36E **97** E11
Mai-Ndombe, L.
Dem. Rep. of the Congo 2°0S 18°20E **140** E3
Mai Thon, Ko *Thailand* 7°40N 98°28E **121** a
Maia *Portugal* 41°14N 8°37W **88** D2
Maials *Spain* 41°22N 0°30E **90** D5
Maîche *France* 47°16N 6°48E **71** E13
Maicuru → *Brazil* 2°14S 54°17W **187** D8
Máida *Italy* 38°51N 16°22E **95** D9
Maidan Khula *Afghan.* 33°36N 69°50E **124** C3
Maidenhead *U.K.* 51°31N 0°42W **67** F7
Maidstone *Canada* 53°5N 109°20W **163** C7
Maidstone *U.K.* 51°16N 0°32E **67** F8
Maiduguri *Nigeria* 12°0N 13°20E **139** C7
Maiella △ *Italy* 42°5N 14°5E **93** F11
Măieruş *Romania* 45°53N 25°31E **81** E10
Maigatari *Nigeria* 12°46N 9°27E **139** C6
Maigh Nuad = Maynooth
Ireland 53°23N 6°34W **64** C5
Maignelay Montigny
France 49°32N 2°30E **71** C9
Maihar *India* 24°16N 80°45E **125** G9
Maikala Ra. *India* 22°0N 81°0E **126** D5
Maiko △
Dem. Rep. of the Congo 0°30S 27°50E **142** C2
Mailani *India* 28°17N 80°21E **125** E9
Maillezais *France* 46°22N 0°45W **72** B3
Mailsi *Pakistan* 29°48N 72°15E **124** E5
Main → *Germany* 50°0N 8°18E **77** F4
Main → *U.K.* 54°48N 6°18W **64** B5
Main Channel *Canada* 45°21N 81°45W **174** A3
Main Range △
Australia 28°11S 152°27E **151** D5
Main Ridge
Trin. & Tob. 11°16N 60°40W **187** J16
Mainburg *Germany* 48°38N 11°47E **77** G7
Maindargi *India* 17°28N 76°18E **126** F3
Maine *France* 48°20N 0°15W **70** D6
Maine □ *U.S.A.* 45°20N 69°0W **173** C19
Maine → *Ireland* 52°9N 9°45W **64** D2
Maine, G. of *U.S.A.* 43°0N 68°30W **167** G26
Maine-et-Loire □ *France* 47°31N 0°30W **70** E6
Maïne-Soroa *Niger* 13°13N 12°2E **139** C7
Maingkwan *Burma* 26°15N 96°37E **123** F20
Mainistir na Corann = Midleton
Ireland 51°55N 8°10W **64** E3
Mainit, L. *Phil.* 9°31N 125°30E **119** C7
Mainland *Orkney, U.K.* 58°59N 3°8W **65** C5
Mainland *Shet., U.K.* 60°15N 1°22W **65** A7
Mainpuri *India* 27°18N 79°4E **125** F8
Maintal *Germany* 50°7N 8°52E **77** E4
Maintenon *France* 48°35N 1°35E **71** D8
Maintirano *Madag.* 18°3S 44°1E **141** H8
Mainz *Germany* 50°1N 8°14E **77** E4
Maio *C. Verde Is.* 15°10N 23°10W **134** b
Maipú *Argentina* 36°52S 57°50W **190** D4
Maiquetía *Venezuela* 10°36N 66°57W **186** A5
Máira → *Italy* 44°49N 7°38E **92** D4
Mairabari *India* 26°30N 92°22E **123** F18
Mairena del Aljarafe
Spain 37°20N 6°6W **89** H4
Maisi *Cuba* 20°17N 74°9W **183** B5
Maisí, Pta. de *Cuba* 20°10N 74°10W **183** B5
Maitland *N.S.W.,*
Australia 32°33S 151°36E **153** B9
Maitland *S. Austral.,*
Australia 34°23S 137°40E **152** C2
Maitland → *Canada* 43°45N 81°43W **174** C3
Maitri *Antarctica* 70°0S 3°0W **55** D3
Maiyema *Nigeria* 12°5N 4°25E **139** C5
Maiyuan *China* 25°34N 117°28E **117** E11
Maíz, Is. del *Nic.* 12°15N 83°4W **182** D3
Maizuru *Japan* 35°25N 135°22E **113** G7
Majalengka *Indonesia* 6°50S 108°13E **119** G13
Majanji *Uganda* 0°16N 34°0E **142** B3
Majella = Maiella △ *Italy* 42°5N 14°5E **93** F11
Majene *Indonesia* 3°38S 118°57E **119** E5
Majete △ *Malawi* 15°54S 34°34E **143** F3
Majevica *Bos.-H.* 44°45N 18°50E **80** F3
Majiang *China* 26°28N 107°32E **116** D6
Majorca = Mallorca
Spain 39°30N 3°0E **100** B10
Majors Creek *Australia* 35°33S 149°45E **153** C8
Majuro *Marshall Is.* 7°9N 171°12E **156** G9
Mak, Ko *Thailand* 11°49N 102°29E **121** G4
Maka *Senegal* 13°40N 14°10W **138** C2
Makaha *Zimbabwe* 17°20S 32°39E **145** A5
Makak *Cameroon* 3°36N 11°0E **139** E7
Makalamabedi
Botswana 20°19S 23°51E **144** B3
Makale *Indonesia* 3°6S 119°51E **119** E5
Makalu *Asia* 27°55N 87°8E **125** F12
Makalu-Barun △
Nepal 27°45N 87°10E **125** F12
Makamba *Burundi* 4°8S 29°49E **142** C2
Makarewa Junction
N.Z. 46°20S 168°21E **155** G3
Makari *Cameroon* 12°35N 14°28E **139** C7
Makarikari = Makgadikgadi Salt
Pans *Botswana* 20°40S 25°45E **144** B4
Makarov Basin *Arctic* 87°0N 150°0W **54** A
Makarovo *Russia* 57°40N 107°45E **107** D11
Makarska *Croatia* 43°20N 17°2E **93** E14
Makaryev *Russia* 57°52N 43°50E **86** B6
Makassar *Indonesia* 5°10S 119°20E **119** F5
Makassar, Selat
Indonesia 1°0S 118°20E **119** E5
Makassar, Str. of = Makassar,
Selat *Indonesia* 1°0S 118°20E **119** E5
Makat = Maqat
Kazakhstan 47°39N 53°19E **108** C4
Makedonija = Macedonia ■
Europe 41°53N 21°40E **96** E5
Makeni *S. Leone* 8°55N 12°5W **138** D2
Makeyevka = Makiyivka
Ukraine 48°0N 38°0E **85** H9
Makgadikgadi △
Botswana 20°27S 24°47E **144** B3
Makgadikgadi Salt Pans
Botswana 20°40S 25°45E **144** B4
Makhachkala *Russia* 43°0N 47°30E **87** J8
Makhado = Louis Trichardt
S. Africa 23°1S 29°43E **145** B4
Makham, Ao *Thailand* 7°51N 98°25E **121** a
Makharadze = Ozurgeti
Georgia 41°55N 42°0E **87** K5
Makhfar al Buşayyah
Iraq 30°0N 46°10E **128** D5
Makhmūr *Iraq* 35°46N 43°35E **105** E10
Makhtal *India* 16°30N 77°31E **127** E3
Makian *Indonesia* 0°20N 127°20E **119** D7
Makindu *Kenya* 2°18S 37°50E **142** C4
Makinsk *Kazakhstan* 52°37N 70°26E **109** B8
Makira = San Cristóbal
Solomon Is. 10°30S 161°0E **147** C9
Makiyivka *Ukraine* 48°0N 38°0E **85** H9
Makkah *Si. Arabia* 21°30N 39°54E **137** C4
Makkovik *Canada* 55°10N 59°10W **165** A8
Makó *Hungary* 46°14N 20°33E **80** D5
Mako *Senegal* 12°52N 12°20W **138** C2
Makogai *Fiji* 17°28S 179°0E **154** a
Makokou *Gabon* 0°40N 12°50E **140** D2
Makongo
Dem. Rep. of the Congo 3°25N 26°17E **142** B2
Makoro
Dem. Rep. of the Congo 3°10N 29°59E **142** B2
Maków Mazowiecki
Poland 52°52N 21°6E **83** F8
Maków Podhalański
Poland 49°43N 19°45E **83** J6
Makra *Greece* 36°15N 25°54E **99** E7
Makrai *India* 22°2N 77°0E **124** H7
Makran Coast Range
Pakistan 25°40N 64°0E **122** G4
Makrana *India* 27°2N 74°46E **124** F6
Makrany *Belarus* 51°48N 24°17E **83** G11
Makri *Greece* 40°52N 25°40E **97** F9
Makri *India* 19°46N 81°55E **126** E5
Makrigialos *Greece* 35°2N 25°59E **101** D7
Makthar *Tunisia* 35°48N 9°12E **136** A5
Mākū *Iran* 39°15N 44°31E **105** C11
Makunda *Botswana* 22°30S 20°7E **144** B3
Makung *Taiwan* 23°34N 119°34E **117** F12
Makurazaki *Japan* 31°15N 130°20E **113** J5
Makurdi *Nigeria* 7°43N 8°35E **139** D6
Makushin Volcano
U.S.A. 53°53N 166°55W **166** E6
Mākūyeh *Iran* 28°7N 53°9E **129** D7
Makwassie *S. Africa* 27°17S 26°0E **144** C4
Makwiro *Zimbabwe* 17°58S 30°25E **145** A5
Mâl *Mauritania* 16°58N 13°23W **138** B2
Mal B. *Ireland* 52°50N 9°30W **64** D2
Mala = Mallow *Ireland* 52°8N 8°39W **64** D3
Mala *Peru* 12°40S 76°38W **188** C2
Mala ✪ *Australia* 21°39S 130°45E **148** D5
Mala, Pta. *Panama* 7°28N 80°2W **182** E3
Mala Belozërka *Ukraine* 47°12N 34°56E **85** J8
Malá Fatra △ *Slovak Rep.* 49°10N 19°0E **79** B12
Mala Kapela *Croatia* 44°45N 15°30E **93** D12
Mala Panew → *Poland* 50°43N 17°54E **83** H4
Mala Vyska *Ukraine* 48°39N 31°36E **85** H6
Malabar *U.S.A.* 28°0N 80°34W **179** H9
Malabar Coast *India* 11°0N 75°0E **127** J2
Malabu *Nigeria* 9°32N 12°48E **139** D7
Malacca, Straits of
Indonesia 3°0N 101°0E **121** L3
Malacky *Slovak Rep.* 48°27N 17°0E **79** C10
Malad City *U.S.A.* 42°12N 112°15W **168** E7
Maladeta *Spain* 42°39N 0°39E **90** C5
Maladzyechna *Belarus* 54°20N 26°50E **75** A14
Málaga *Spain* 36°43N 4°23W **89** J6
Málaga □ *Spain* 36°38N 4°58W **89** J6
Malagarasi *Tanzania* 5°5S 30°50E **142** D3
Malagarasi → *Tanzania* 5°12S 29°47E **142** D2
Malagasy Rep. = Madagascar ■
Africa 20°0S 47°0E **141** J9
Malagón *Spain* 39°11N 3°52W **89** F7
Malagón → *Spain* 37°35N 7°29W **89** H3
Malahide *Ireland* 53°26N 6°9W **64** C5
Malaimbandy *Madag.* 20°20S 45°36E **141** J9
Malaita *Solomon Is.* 9°0S 161°0E **147** B9
Malakal *South Sudan* 9°33N 31°40E **135** G12
Malakanagiri *India* 18°21N 81°54E **126** E5
Malakand *Pakistan* 34°40N 71°55E **124** B4
Malakula *Vanuatu* 16°15S 167°30E **147** C9
Malakwal *Pakistan* 32°34N 73°13E **124** C5
Malamala *Indonesia* 3°21S 120°55E **119** E6
Malanda *Australia* 17°22S 145°35E **150** B4
Malang *Indonesia* 7°59S 112°45E **118** F4
Malanga *Mozam.* 13°28S 36°7E **143** E4
Malangen *Norway* 69°24N 18°37E **60** B18
Malangwa *Nepal* 26°52N 85°34E **125** F11
Malanje *Angola* 9°36S 16°17E **140** F3
Malappuram *India* 11°7N 76°11E **127** J3
Mälaren *Sweden* 59°30N 17°10E **62** E11
Malargüe *Argentina* 35°32S 69°30W **190** D2
Malartic *Canada* 48°9N 78°9W **164** C4
Malaryta *Belarus* 51°50N 24°3E **83** G11
Malaspina Glacier
U.S.A. 59°50N 140°30W **166** D11
Malatya *Turkey* 38°25N 38°20E **105** C8
Malatya □ *Turkey* 38°15N 38°0E **104** C7
Malawi ■ *Africa* 11°55S 34°0E **143** E3
Malawi, L. *Africa* 12°30S 34°30E **143** E3
Malay Pen. *Asia* 7°25N 100°0E **121** J3
Malaya Belozërka = Mala
Belozërka *Ukraine* 47°12N 34°56E **85** J8
Malaya Vishera *Russia* 58°55N 32°25E **84** C7
Malaya Viska = Mala Vyska
Ukraine 48°39N 31°36E **85** H6
Malaybalay *Phil.* 8°5N 125°7E **119** C7
Malāyer *Iran* 34°19N 48°51E **105** E13
Malaysia ■ *Asia* 5°0N 110°0E **121** K4
Malazgirt *Turkey* 39°10N 42°33E **105** C10
Malbaza *Niger* 13°59N 5°38E **139** C6
Malbon *Australia* 21°5S 140°17E **150** C3
Malbooma *Australia* 30°41S 134°11E **151** E1
Malbork *Poland* 54°3N 19°1E **82** D6
Malcésine *Italy* 45°46N 10°48E **92** C7
Malchin *Germany* 53°44N 12°44E **76** B8
Malchow *Germany* 53°28N 12°26E **76** B8
Malcolm *Australia* 28°51S 121°25E **149** E3
Malcolm, Pt. *Australia* 33°48S 123°45E **149** F3
Malczyce *Poland* 51°14N 16°29E **83** G3
Maldah *India* 25°2N 88°9E **125** G13
Maldegem *Belgium* 51°14N 3°26E **69** C3
Malden *Mass., U.S.A.* 42°26N 71°3W **175** D13
Malden *Mo., U.S.A.* 36°34N 89°57W **172** G9
Malden I. *Kiribati* 4°3S 155°1W **157** H12
Maldives ■ *Ind. Oc.* 5°0N 73°0E **103** H9
Maldon *Australia* 37°0S 144°6E **152** D6
Maldon *U.K.* 51°44N 0°42E **67** F8
Maldonado *Uruguay* 34°59S 55°0W **191** C5
Maldonado, Pta.
Mexico 16°20N 98°33W **181** D5
Malè *Italy* 46°21N 10°55E **92** B7
Malé *Maldives* 4°10N 73°28E **146** D6
Malé Karpaty
Slovak Rep. 48°30N 17°20E **79** C10
Maleas, Akra *Greece* 36°28N 23°7E **98** E5
Malebo, Pool *Africa* 4°17S 15°20E **140** E3
Malegaon *India* 20°30N 74°38E **126** D2
Malei *Mozam.* 17°12S 36°58E **143** F4
Malek Kandī *Iran* 37°9N 46°6E **105** D12
Malela
Dem. Rep. of the Congo 4°22S 26°8E **142** C2
Malema *Mozam.* 14°57S 37°20E **143** E4
Maleme *Greece* 35°31N 23°49E **101** D5
Maler Kotla *India* 30°32N 75°58E **124** D6
Malerås *Sweden* 56°54N 15°34E **63** H9
Males *Greece* 35°6N 25°35E **101** D7
Malesherbes *France* 48°15N 2°24E **71** D9
Maleshevska Planina
Europe 41°38N 23°7E **96** E7
Malesina *Greece* 38°37N 23°14E **98** C5
Malestroit *France* 47°49N 2°25W **70** E4
Malfa *Italy* 38°35N 14°50E **95** D7
Malgobek *Russia* 43°30N 44°34E **87** J7
Malgomaj *Sweden* 64°40N 16°30E **60** D17
Malgrat de Mar *Spain* 41°39N 2°46E **90** D7
Malha *Sudan* 15°8N 25°10E **135** E11
Malhada *Brazil* 14°21S 43°47W **189** C2
Malhargarh *India* 24°17N 74°59E **124** G6
Malheur → *U.S.A.* 44°4N 116°59W **168** D5
Malheur L. *U.S.A.* 43°20N 118°48W **168** E4
Mali *Guinea* 12°10N 12°20W **138** C2
Mali ■ *Africa* 17°0N 3°0W **138** B4
Mali → *Burma* 25°42N 97°30E **123** G20
Mali Kanal *Serbia* 45°36N 19°24E **80** E4
Mali Kyun *Burma* 13°0N 98°20E **120** F2
Malia *Greece* 35°17N 25°32E **101** D7
Malia, Kolpos *Greece* 35°19N 25°27E **101** D7
Malibu *U.S.A.* 34°2N 118°41W **171** L8
Maliku = Minicoy I.
India 8°17N 73°2E **127** K1
Maliku *Indonesia* 0°39S 123°16E **119** E6

Malili Indonesia 2°42S 121°6E 119 E6
Mälilla Sweden 57°23N 15°48E 63 G9
Malimba, Mts.
  Dem. Rep. of the Congo 7°30S 29°30E 142 D2
Malin Hd. Ireland 55°23N 7°23W 64 A4
Malin Pen. Ireland 55°20N 7°17W 64 A4
Malindi Kenya 3°12S 40°5E 142 C5
Malindi Marine △ Kenya 3°15S 40°7E 142 C5
Malines = Mechelen
  Belgium 51°2N 4°29E 69 C4
Malino Indonesia 1°0N 121°0E 119 D6
Malinyi Tanzania 8°56S 36°0E 143 D4
Malipo China 23°7N 104°42E 116 F5
Maliq Albania 40°45N 20°48E 96 F4
Malita Phil. 6°19N 125°39E 119 C7
Maliwun Burma 10°17N 98°40E 121 G2
Maliya India 23°5N 70°46E 124 H7
Maljenik Serbia 43°54N 21°43E 96 C5
Malka Mari △ Kenya 4°11N 40°46E 142 B5
Malkapur India 20°53N 76°12E 126 D3
Malkara Turkey 40°53N 26°53E 97 F10
Malkhangiri = Malakanagiri
  India 18°21N 81°54E 126 E5
Malkinia Górna Poland 52°42N 22°5E 83 F9
Malko Tŭrnovo
  Bulgaria 41°59N 27°31E 97 E11
Mallacoota Australia 37°40S 149°40E 153 D8
Mallacoota Inlet
  Australia 37°34S 149°40E 153 D8
Mallaig U.K. 57°0N 5°50W 65 D3
Mallala Australia 34°26S 138°30E 152 C3
Mallawan India 13°2N 9°36E 139 C6
Mallawan India 27°4N 80°12E 125 F9
Mallawi Egypt 27°44N 30°44E 137 B3
Mallee Cliffs △
  Australia 34°16S 142°32E 152 C5
Mallemort France 43°43N 5°11E 73 E9
Málles Venosta Italy 46°41N 10°32E 92 B7
Mallicolo = Malakula
  Vanuatu 16°15S 167°30E 147 C9
Mallorca Spain 39°30N 3°0E 100 B10
Mallorytown Canada 44°29N 75°53W 175 B9
Mallow Ireland 52°8N 8°39W 64 D3
Malmbäck Sweden 57°34N 14°28E 63 G8
Malmberget Sweden 67°11N 20°40E 60 C19
Malmédy Belgium 50°25N 6°2E 69 D6
Malmesbury S. Africa 33°28S 18°41E 144 D2
Malmivaara = Malmberget
  Sweden 67°11N 20°40E 60 C19
Malmköping Sweden 59°8N 16°44E 62 E10
Malmö Sweden 55°36N 12°59E 63 J7
Malmslätt Sweden 58°27N 15°33E 63 F9
Malmyzh Russia 56°31N 50°41E 86 B10
Malnas Romania 46°2N 25°49E 81 D10
Malo Konare Bulgaria 42°12N 24°24E 97 D8
Maloarkhangelsk
  Russia 52°28N 36°30E 85 F9
Malolo Fiji 17°45S 177°11E 154 a
Malolos Phil. 14°50N 120°49E 119 B6
Malolotja △ Swaziland 26°4S 31°6E 145 C5
Malombe L. Malawi 14°40S 35°15E 143 E4
Malomice Poland 51°34N 15°29E 83 G2
Malomir Bulgaria 42°16N 26°32E 97 D10
Malone Fla., U.S.A. 30°57N 85°10W 178 E4
Malone N.Y., U.S.A. 44°51N 74°18W 175 B10
Malong China 25°24N 103°34E 116 E4
Malopolskie □ Poland 49°50N 20°20E 83 J7
Malorad Bulgaria 43°28N 23°41E 96 C7
Maløy Norway 61°57N 5°6E 60 F11
Maloyaroslovets Russia 55°2N 36°20E 84 E9
Malpartida de Cáceres
  Spain 39°26N 6°30W 89 F4
Malpaso Canary Is. 27°43N 18°3W 100 G1
Malpaso, Presa =
  Netzahualcóyotl, Presa
  Mexico 17°8N 93°35W 181 D6
Malpelo, I. de Colombia 4°3N 81°35W 186 C2
Malpica de Bergantiños
  Spain 43°19N 8°50W 88 B2
Malprabha → India 16°2N 76°5E 127 F3
Malpur India 23°21N 73°27E 124 H5
Malpura India 26°17N 75°23E 124 F6
Mals = Málles Venosta
  Italy 46°41N 10°32E 92 B7
Malsiras India 17°52N 74°55E 126 F2
Malta Brazil 6°54S 37°31W 189 B3
Malta Idaho, U.S.A. 42°18N 113°22W 168 E7
Malta Mont., U.S.A. 48°21N 107°52W 166 B10
Malta ■ Europe 35°55N 14°26E 101 D2
Maltahöhe Namibia 24°55S 17°0E 144 B2
Maltepe Turkey 40°55N 29°8E 97 F13
Malton Canada 43°42N 79°38W 174 C5
Malton U.K. 54°8N 0°49W 66 C7
Maluku □ Indonesia 1°0S 127°0E 119 E7
Maluku □ Indonesia 3°0S 128°0E 119 E7
Maluku Sea = Molucca Sea
  Indonesia 0°0 125°0E 119 E6
Malumfashi Nigeria 11°48N 7°39E 139 C6
Malung Sweden 60°42N 13°44E 62 D7
Malungsfors Sweden 60°44N 13°33E 62 D7
Malur India 13°0N 77°55E 127 H3
Maluwe Ghana 8°40N 2°17W 138 D4
Malvalli India 12°28N 77°8E 127 H3
Malvan India 16°2N 73°30E 127 F1
Malvern U.S.A. 34°22N 92°49W 176 D8
Malvern Hills U.K. 52°0N 2°19W 67 E5
Malvinas, Is. = Falkland Is. ☒
  Atl. Oc. 51°30S 59°0W 192 D5
Malý Dunaj →
  Slovak Rep. 47°45N 18°9E 79 D11
Malya Tanzania 3°5S 33°38E 142 C3
Malye Derbety Russia 47°57N 44°42E 87 G7
Malyn Ukraine 50°46N 29°3E 75 C15
Malyy Lyakhovskiy, Ostrov
  Russia 74°7N 140°36E 107 B15
Malyy Taymyr, Ostrov
  Russia 78°6N 107°15E 107 B11
Mama Russia 58°18N 112°54E 107 D12
Mamaku N.Z. 38°5S 176°8E 154 E5
Mamanguape Brazil 6°50S 35°4W 189 B3
Mamanuca Group Fiji 17°35S 177°5E 154 a
Mamarr Mitlâ Egypt 30°2N 32°54E 130 E1
Mamasa Indonesia 2°55S 119°20E 119 E5
Mambasa
  Dem. Rep. of the Congo 1°22N 29°3E 142 B2
Mamberamo →
  Indonesia 2°0S 137°50E 119 E9
Mambilima Falls
  Zambia 10°31S 28°45E 143 E2
Mambirima
  Dem. Rep. of the Congo 11°25S 27°33E 143 E2

Mambo Tanzania 4°52S 38°22E 142 C4
Mambrui Kenya 3°5S 40°5E 142 C5
Mamburao Phil. 13°13N 120°39E 119 B6
Mamedkala Russia 42°10N 48°7E 87 J9
Mameigwess L. Canada 52°35N 87°50W 164 B2
Mamers France 48°21N 0°22E 70 D7
Mamfé Cameroon 5°50N 9°15E 139 D6
Mamili △ Namibia 18°23N 24°1E 144 A3
Mamiña Chile 20°5S 69°14W 188 E4
Mamlyutka Kazakhstan 54°58N 68°32W 109 B7
Mammoth U.S.A. 32°43N 110°39W 169 K8
Mammoth Cave △
  U.S.A. 37°8N 86°13W 172 G10
Mammoth Lakes
  U.S.A. 37°39N 118°59W 170 H8
Mamonovo Russia 54°28N 19°55E 82 D6
Mamoré → Bolivia 10°23S 65°53W 186 F5
Mamou Guinea 10°15N 12°0W 138 C2
Mamoudzou Mayotte 12°48S 45°14E 141 a
Mampong Ghana 7°6N 1°26W 139 D4
Mamry, Jezioro Poland 54°5N 21°50E 82 D8
Mamuil Malal, Paso
  S. Amer. 39°35S 71°28W 192 A2
Mamuju Indonesia 2°41S 118°50E 119 E5
Mamuno Botswana 22°16S 20°1E 144 B3
Mamuras Albania 41°34N 19°41E 96 E3
Man Ivory C. 7°30N 7°40W 138 D3
Man → India 17°31N 75°32E 126 F2
Man, I. of India 8°28N 93°36E 127 K11
Man, I. of U.K. 54°15N 4°30W 66 C3
Man-Bazar India 23°4N 86°39E 125 H12
Mänä U.S.A. 22°2N 159°47W 167 L8
Mana → Fr. Guiana 5°45N 53°55W 187 B8
Mana Pools △
  Zimbabwe 15°56S 29°25E 143 F2
Manaar, G. of = Mannar, G. of
  Asia 8°30N 79°0E 127 K4
Manacapuru Brazil 3°16S 60°37W 186 D6
Manacor Spain 39°34N 3°13E 100 B10
Manado Indonesia 1°29N 124°51E 119 D6
Managua Nic. 12°6N 86°20W 182 D2
Managua, L. de Nic. 12°20N 86°30W 182 D2
Manaia N.Z. 39°33S 174°8E 154 D5
Manakara Madag. 22°8S 48°1E 141 J9
Manakau N.Z. 40°41S 175°14W 175 C8
Manali India 32°16N 77°10E 124 C7
Manama = Al Manāmah
  Bahrain 26°10N 50°30E 129 E6
Manambato Australia 35°15S 142°54E 152 C5
Mananjary Madag. 21°13S 48°20E 141 J9
Manankoro Mali 10°28N 7°25W 138 C3
Manantali, L. de Mali 13°12N 10°08W 138 C2
Manantavadi India 11°49N 76°1E 127 J3
Manantenina Madag. 24°17S 47°19E 141 K9
Manaos = Manaus Brazil 3°0S 60°0W 186 D7
Manapire → Venezuela 7°42N 66°7W 186 B5
Manapouri N.Z. 45°34S 167°39E 155 F2
Manapouri, L. N.Z. 45°32S 167°32E 155 F2
Manapparai India 10°36N 78°25E 127 J4
Manar → India 18°50N 77°20E 126 E3
Manār, Jabal Yemen 14°2N 44°17E 131 E3
Manas China 44°17N 86°10E 110 B6
Manas → India 26°12N 90°40E 123 F17
Manas He → China 45°38N 85°12E 110 B6
Manas Hu China 45°45N 85°55E 109 C11
Manaslu Nepal 28°33N 84°33E 125 E11
Manasquan U.S.A. 40°8N 74°3W 175 F10
Manassa U.S.A. 37°11N 105°56W 169 H11
Manassas U.S.A. 38°47N 77°28W 174 F8
Manatí Puerto Rico 18°26N 66°29W 183 d
Manaus Brazil 3°0S 60°0W 186 D7
Manavgat Turkey 36°47N 31°26E 104 D4
Manawan L. Canada 55°24N 103°14W 163 B8
Manawatu → N.Z. 40°28S 175°12E 154 G4
Manawatu-Wanganui □
  N.Z. 39°50S 175°30E 154 F4
Manbij Syria 36°31N 37°57E 104 D7
Mancha Real Spain 37°48N 3°39W 89 H7
Manche □ France 49°10N 1°20W 70 C5
Manchegorsk Russia 67°54N 32°58E 106 C4
Manchester U.K. 53°29N 2°12W 66 D5
Manchester Calif.,
  U.S.A. 38°58N 123°41W 170 G3
Manchester Conn.,
  U.S.A. 41°47N 72°31W 175 E12
Manchester Ga., U.S.A. 32°51N 84°37W 178 C5
Manchester Iowa,
  U.S.A. 42°29N 91°27W 172 D8
Manchester Ky.,
  U.S.A. 37°9N 83°46W 173 G12
Manchester N.H.,
  U.S.A. 42°59N 71°28W 175 D13
Manchester N.Y.,
  U.S.A. 42°56N 77°16W 174 D7
Manchester Pa., U.S.A. 40°4N 76°43W 175 F8
Manchester Tenn.,
  U.S.A. 35°29N 86°5W 177 D11
Manchester Vt., U.S.A. 43°10N 73°5W 175 C11
Manchester Int. ✈ (MAN)
  U.K. 53°21N 2°17W 66 D5
Manchester L. Canada 61°28N 107°29W 163 A7
Manchhar L. Pakistan 26°25N 67°39E 124 F2
Manchuria = Dongbei
  China 45°0N 125°0E 115 D13
Manchurian Plain
  China 47°0N 124°0E 102 D14
Manciano Italy 42°35N 11°31E 93 F8
Máncora Peru 4°9S 81°1W 188 A1
Mand → India 21°42N 83°15E 125 J10
Mand → Iran 28°20N 52°30E 129 D7
Manda Ludewe, Tanzania 10°30S 34°40E 143 E3
Manda Mbeya, Tanzania 7°58S 32°29E 142 D3
Manda Mbeya, Tanzania 8°30S 32°49E 143 D3
Mandaguari Brazil 23°32S 51°42W 191 A5
Mandah = Töhöm
  Mongolia 44°27N 108°2E 114 B5
Mandal Norway 58°2N 7°25E 61 G12
Mandala, Puncak
  Indonesia 4°44S 140°20E 119 E10
Mandalay = Mandalay
  Burma 22°0N 96°4E 123 J20
Mandale = Mandalay
  Burma 22°0N 96°4E 123 J20
Mandalgarh India 25°12N 75°6E 124 G6
Mandalgovĭ Mongolia 45°45N 106°10E 114 B4
Mandalī Iraq 33°43N 45°28E 105 F11
Mandan U.S.A. 46°50N 100°54W 172 B3
Mandar, Teluk
  Indonesia 3°32S 119°21E 119 E5
Mándas Italy 39°40N 9°8E 94 C2
Mandaue Phil. 10°20N 123°56E 119 B6

Mandelieu-la-Napoule
  France 43°34N 6°57E 73 E10
Mandera Kenya 3°55N 41°53E 142 B5
Mandeville Jamaica 18°2N 77°31W 182 a
Mandi India 31°39N 76°58E 124 D7
Mandi Burewala
  Pakistan 30°9N 72°41E 124 D5
Mandi Dabwali India 29°58N 74°42E 124 E6
Mandiana Guinea 10°37N 8°39W 138 C3
Mandimba Mozam. 14°20S 35°40E 143 E4
Mandioli Indonesia 0°40S 127°20E 119 E7
Mandla India 22°39N 80°30E 125 H9
Mandø Denmark 55°18N 8°33E 63 J2
Mandorah Australia 12°32S 130°42E 148 B5
Mandoudi Greece 38°48N 23°29E 98 C5
Mandra Greece 38°4N 23°30E 98 C5
Mandra Pakistan 33°23N 73°12E 124 C5
Mandraki Greece 36°36N 27°11E 99 E9
Mandritsara Madag. 15°50S 48°49E 141 H9
Mandsaur India 24°3N 75°8E 124 G6
Mandurah Australia 32°36S 115°48E 149 F2
Mandúria Italy 40°24N 17°38E 95 B10
Mandvi India 22°51N 69°22E 124 H3
Mandya India 12°30N 77°0E 127 H3
Mandzai Pakistan 30°55N 67°6E 124 D2
Mané Burkina Faso 12°59N 1°21W 139 C4
Maneh Iran 37°39N 57°7E 129 B8
Manengouba, Mts.
  Cameroon 5°0N 9°50E 139 E6
Maner → India 18°30N 79°40E 126 E4
Manérbio Italy 45°21N 10°8E 92 C7
Maneroo Cr. →
  Australia 23°21S 143°53E 150 C3
Manfalût Egypt 27°20N 30°52E 137 B3
Manfred Australia 33°19S 143°45E 152 B5
Manfredónia Italy 41°38N 15°55E 93 G12
Manfredónia, G. di Italy 41°35N 16°5E 93 G13
Manga Brazil 14°46S 43°56W 189 C2
Manga Burkina Faso 11°40N 1°4W 139 C4
Manga Niger 15°0N 14°0E 139 C7
Mangabeiras, Chapada das
  Brazil 10°0S 46°30W 189 C1
Mangaia Cook Is. 21°55S 157°55W 157 K12
Mangakino N.Z. 38°22S 175°47E 154 E4
Mangalagiri India 16°26N 80°36E 127 F5
Mangalia Romania 43°50N 28°35E 81 G13
Mangalore India 12°55N 74°47E 127 H2
Mangaluru = Mangalore
  India 12°55N 74°47E 127 H2
Mangalvedha India 17°31N 75°28E 126 F2
Mangan India 27°31N 88°32E 125 F13
Mangaon India 18°15N 73°20E 126 E1
Mangarrayi ◇
  Australia 15°5S 133°10E 150 B1
Mangawan India 24°41N 81°33E 125 G9
Mangaweka N.Z. 39°48S 175°47E 154 F4
Mangaweka, Mt. N.Z. 39°49S 176°5E 154 F5
Manggar Indonesia 2°50S 108°10E 118 E3
Manggawitu Indonesia 4°8S 133°32E 119 E8
Mangghystaū
  Kazakhstan 43°40N 51°13E 108 D4
Mangghystaū □
  Kazakhstan 45°0N 53°0E 108 D4
Mangghystaū Tübegi
  Kazakhstan 44°30N 52°30E 108 D4
Manggis Indonesia 8°29S 115°31E 119 J18
Mangkalihat, Tanjung
  Indonesia 1°2N 118°59E 119 D5
Mangkururrpa ◇
  Australia 20°35S 129°43E 148 D4
Mangla Pakistan 33°7N 73°39E 124 C5
Mangla Dam Pakistan 33°9N 73°44E 124 C5
Manglaur India 29°44N 77°49E 124 E7
Manglisi Georgia 41°41N 44°22E 87 K7
Mangnai China 37°52N 91°43E 110 D7
Mangnai Zhen China 38°24N 90°14E 109 E12
Mango Togo 10°20N 0°30E 139 C5
Mangoche Malawi 14°25S 35°16E 143 E4
Mangoky → Madag. 21°29S 43°41E 141 J8
Mangole Indonesia 1°50S 125°55E 119 E6
Mangombe
  Dem. Rep. of the Congo 1°20S 26°48E 142 C2
Mangonui N.Z. 35°1S 173°32E 154 B2
Mangrol Mad. P., India 21°7N 70°7E 124 J4
Mangrol Raj., India 25°20N 76°31E 124 G6
Mangrul Pir India 20°19N 77°21E 126 D3
Manguéigne Portugal 40°38N 7°48W 88 E3
Mangueira, L. da Brazil 33°0S 52°50W 191 C5
Mangum U.S.A. 34°53N 99°30W 176 D5
Manguri Australia 28°58S 134°22E 151 A1
Mangyshlak, Poluostrov =
  Mangghystaū Tübegi
  Kazakhstan 44°30N 52°30E 108 D4
Manhattan U.S.A. 39°11N 96°35W 172 F5
Manhiça Mozam. 25°23S 32°49E 145 C5
Manhuaçu Brazil 20°15S 42°2W 189 E2
Manhumirim Brazil 20°22S 41°57W 189 E2
Maniago Italy 46°10N 12°43E 93 B9
Manica Mozam. 18°58S 32°59E 145 A5
Manica □ Mozam. 19°10S 33°45E 145 A5
Manicaland □ Zimbabwe 19°0S 32°30E 145 A5
Manicoré Brazil 5°48S 61°16W 186 E6
Manicouagan →
  Canada 49°30N 68°30W 165 C6
Manicouagan, Rés.
  Canada 51°5N 68°40W 165 B6
Maniema □
  Dem. Rep. of the Congo 3°0S 26°0E 142 C2
Manīfah Si. Arabia 27°44N 49°0E 129 E6
Manifold, C. Australia 22°41S 150°50E 150 C5
Maniganggo China 31°56N 99°12E 116 B2
Manigotagan Canada 51°6N 96°18W 163 C9
Manigotagan →
  Canada 51°7N 96°20W 163 C9
Manihari India 25°21N 87°38E 125 G12
Manihiki Cook Is. 10°24S 161°1W 157 J11
Manika, Plateau de la
  Dem. Rep. of the Congo 10°0S 25°5E 143 E2
Manikpur India 25°4N 81°7E 125 G9
Manila Phil. 14°35N 120°58E 119 B6
Manila U.S.A. 40°59N 109°43W 168 F9
Manila B. Phil. 14°40N 120°35E 119 B6
Manildra Australia 33°11S 148°41E 153 B8
Manilla Australia 30°45S 150°43E 153 A9
Maninjau Indonesia 0°15S 100°55E 118 E1
Maningrida Australia 12°3S 134°13E 150 A1
Maninian Ivory C. 10°3N 7°52W 138 C3

Manipa, Selat Indonesia 3°20S 127°25E 119 E7
Manipur □ India 25°0N 94°0E 123 G19
Manipur → Burma 23°45N 94°20E 123 H19
Manisa Turkey 38°38N 27°30E 99 C9
Manisa □ Turkey 38°40N 28°0E 99 C9
Manistee U.S.A. 44°15N 86°19W 172 C10
Manistee → U.S.A. 44°15N 86°21W 172 C10
Manistique U.S.A. 45°57N 86°15W 172 C10
Manitoba □ Canada 53°30N 97°0W 163 B9
Manitoba, L. Canada 51°0N 98°45W 163 C9
Manitou Canada 49°15N 98°32W 163 D9
Manitou, L. U.S.A. 50°55N 65°17W 165 B6
Manitou Is. U.S.A. 45°8N 86°0W 172 C10
Manitou L. Canada 52°43N 109°43W 163 C7
Manitou Springs
  U.S.A. 38°52N 104°55W 168 G11
Manitoulin I. Canada 45°40N 82°30W 164 C3
Manitouwadge Canada 49°8N 85°48W 164 C2
Manitowoc U.S.A. 44°5N 87°40W 172 C10
Maniwaki Canada 46°23N 75°58W 165 C9
Manizales Colombia 5°5N 75°32W 186 B3
Manja Madag. 21°26S 44°20E 141 J8
Manjacaze Mozam. 24°45S 34°0E 145 B5
Manjakandriana
  Madag. 18°55S 47°47E 141 H9
Manjhand Pakistan 25°50N 68°10E 124 G3
Manjil Iran 36°46N 49°30E 129 B6
Manjimup Australia 34°15S 116°6E 149 F2
Manjra → India 18°49N 77°52E 126 E3
Mankato Kans., U.S.A. 39°47N 98°13W 172 F4
Mankato Minn., U.S.A. 44°10N 94°0W 172 C6
Mankayane Swaziland 26°40S 31°4E 145 C5
Mankera Pakistan 31°23N 71°26E 124 D4
Mankim Cameroon 5°6N 12°3E 139 D7
Mankono Ivory C. 8°1N 6°10W 138 D3
Mankota Canada 49°25N 107°5W 163 D7
Mankulam Sri Lanka 9°8N 80°26E 127 K5
Manlay = Üydzin
  Mongolia 44°9N 107°0E 114 B4
Manlleu Spain 42°2N 2°17E 90 C7
Manly Australia 33°47S 151°17E 153 B9
Mann Ranges Australia 26°6S 130°5E 149 E5
Mann → India 4°25S 102°55E 118 E2
Mannahill Australia 32°25S 140°0E 152 B4
Mannar Sri Lanka 9°1N 79°54E 127 K4
Mannar, G. of Asia 8°30N 79°0E 127 K4
Mannar I. Sri Lanka 9°5N 79°45E 127 K4
Mannargudi India 10°45N 79°51E 127 J4
Mannheim Germany 49°29N 8°29E 77 F4
Manning Canada 56°53N 117°39W 162 B5
Manning Oreg., U.S.A. 45°45N 123°13W 170 E3
Manning S.C., U.S.A. 33°42N 80°13W 178 B9
Manning →
  Australia 31°52S 152°43E 153 A10
Mannu → Italy 39°16N 9°0E 94 C2
Mannu, C. Italy 40°3N 8°21E 94 B1
Mannum Australia 34°50S 139°20E 152 C3
Mano S. Leone 8°3N 12°2W 138 D2
Mano → Liberia 6°56N 11°30W 138 D2
Mano River Liberia 7°20N 11°6W 138 D2
Manohurpur India 22°23N 85°12E 125 H11
Manokwari Indonesia 0°54S 134°0E 119 E8
Manolada Greece 38°4N 21°21E 98 C3
Manombo Madag. 22°57S 43°28E 141 J8
Manono
  Dem. Rep. of the Congo 7°15S 27°25E 142 D2
Manoppello Italy 42°15N 14°3E 93 F11
Manorhamilton Ireland 54°18N 8°11W 64 B3
Manosque France 43°49N 5°47E 73 E9
Manotick Canada 45°13N 75°41W 174 A9
Manouane → Canada 49°30N 71°10W 165 C5
Manouane, L. Canada 50°45N 70°45W 165 B5
Manp'o N. Korea 41°6N 126°24E 115 D14
Manpojin = Manp'o
  N. Korea 41°6N 126°24E 115 D14
Manpur Chhattisgarh,
  India 23°17N 83°35E 125 H10
Manpur Chhattisgarh,
  India 20°22N 80°43E 125 J9
Manpur Mad. P., India 22°26N 75°37E 124 H6
Manresa Spain 41°48N 1°50E 90 D6
Mansa Gujarat, India 23°27N 72°45E 124 H5
Mansa Punjab, India 30°0N 75°27E 124 E6
Mansa Zambia 11°13S 28°55E 143 E2
Mansa Konko Gambia 13°28N 15°33W 138 C1
Mânsåsen Sweden 63°4N 14°18E 62 A8
Mansehra Pakistan 34°20N 73°15E 124 B5
Mansel I. Canada 62°0N 80°0W 161 C15
Mansfield Australia 37°4S 146°6E 153 D7
Mansfield U.K. 53°9N 1°11W 66 D6
Mansfield Ga., U.S.A. 33°31N 83°44W 178 B6
Mansfield La., U.S.A. 32°2N 93°43W 176 E8
Mansfield Mass.,
  U.S.A. 42°2N 71°13W 175 D13
Mansfield Ohio, U.S.A. 40°45N 82°31W 174 E2
Mansfield Pa., U.S.A. 41°48N 77°5W 174 E7
Mansfield Wash.,
  U.S.A. 47°49N 119°38W 170 D7
Mansfield, Mt. U.S.A. 44°33N 72°49W 175 B12
Mansião Brazil 10°43S 44°2W 189 C2
Mansilla de las Mulas
  Spain 42°30N 5°25W 88 C5
Mansle France 45°52N 0°12E 72 C4
Manso → Brazil 13°50S 47°0W 189 C1
Mansôa Guinea-Biss. 12°0N 15°20W 138 C1
Manson Creek
  Canada 55°37N 124°32W 162 B4
Mansoura Algeria 36°1N 4°31E 136 A4
Manta Ecuador 1°0S 80°40W 186 D2
Mantalingajan, Mt.
  Phil. 8°55N 117°45E 118 C5
Mantare Tanzania 2°42S 33°13E 142 C3
Mantaro → Peru 12°15S 73°57E 186 D3
Manteca U.S.A. 37°48N 121°13W 170 H5
Manteo U.S.A. 35°55N 75°40W 177 D17
Mantes-la-Jolie France 48°58N 1°41E 71 D8
Manthani India 19°40N 79°35E 126 E4
Manti U.S.A. 39°16N 111°38W 168 G8
Mantiqueira, Serra da
  Brazil 22°0S 44°0W 191 A7
Manton U.S.A. 44°25N 85°24W 173 C11
Mantorp Sweden 58°21N 15°20E 63 F9
Mántova Italy 45°9N 10°48E 92 C7
Mänttä Vilppula Finland 62°0N 24°40E 64 A9
Mantua = Mántova Italy 45°9N 10°48E 92 C7
Manturovo Russia 34°35S 140°3E 152 C4
Manú Peru 12°10S 70°51W 186 D3
Manú → Peru 12°16S 70°55W 186 D3

Manuel Alves →
  Brazil 11°19S 48°28W 189 C1
Manuel Alves Grande →
  Brazil 7°27S 47°35W 189 B1
Manuel Urbano Brazil 8°53S 69°18W 188 B4
Manui Indonesia 3°35S 123°5E 119 E6
Manukau N.Z. 37°0S 174°52E 154 D3
Manukau Harbour
  N.Z. 37°3S 174°45E 154 D3
Manunui N.Z. 38°54S 175°21E 154 E4
Manuoha N.Z. 38°39S 177°7E 154 E6
Manuripi → Bolivia 11°6S 67°36W 188 C4
Manvi India 15°57N 76°59E 127 G3
Manwath India 19°19N 76°32E 126 E3
Many U.S.A. 31°34N 93°29W 176 F8
Manyallaluk ◇
  Australia 14°16S 132°49E 148 B5
Manyani Kenya 3°35S 38°33E 142 C5
Manyara □ Tanzania 4°5S 37°10E 142 C4
Manyara, L. Tanzania 3°40S 35°50E 142 C4
Manyara △ Tanzania 3°35S 35°50E 142 C4
Manyas Turkey 40°2N 27°59E 97 F11
Manyava Ukraine 48°39N 24°21E 81 B9
Manych → Russia 47°13N 40°40E 87 G5
Manych-Gudilo, Ozero
  Russia 46°24N 42°38E 87 G6
Manyonga → Tanzania 4°10S 34°15E 142 C3
Manyoni Tanzania 5°45S 34°55E 142 D3
Manzai Pakistan 32°12N 70°15E 124 C4
Manzala, Bahra el
  Egypt 31°10N 31°56E 137 E7
Manzanar △ U.S.A. 36°44N 118°9W 170 J7
Manzanares Spain 39°2N 3°22W 89 F7
Manzaneda Spain 42°12N 7°15W 88 C3
Manzanillo Cuba 20°20N 77°31W 182 B4
Manzanillo Mexico 19°3N 104°20W 180 D4
Manzanillo, Pta.
  Panama 9°30N 79°40W 182 E4
Manzano Mts.
  U.S.A. 34°40N 106°20W 169 J10
Manzariyeh Iran 34°53N 50°50E 129 C6
Manzhouli China 49°35N 117°25E 111 B12
Manzini Swaziland 26°30S 31°25E 145 C5
Manzouli = Manzhouli
  China 49°35N 117°25E 111 B12
Manzur Vadisi △
  Turkey 39°10N 39°30E 128 B3
Mao Chad 14°4N 15°19E 135 F9
Maó Spain 39°53N 4°16E 100 B11
Maoke, Pegunungan
  Indonesia 3°40S 137°30E 119 E9
Maolin China 43°58N 123°30E 115 C12
Maoming China 21°50N 110°54E 117 G8
Maopi T'ou China 21°56N 120°43E 117 G13
Maouri, Dallol → Niger 12°5N 3°30E 139 C5
Maoxian China 31°41N 103°49E 116 B4
Maoxing China 45°28N 124°40E 115 B13
Mapam Yumco China 30°45N 81°28E 125 D9
Mapastepec Mexico 15°26N 92°54W 181 D6
Maphrao, Ko Thailand 7°56N 98°26E 121 a
Mapia, Kepulauan
  Indonesia 0°50N 134°20E 119 D8
Mapimí Mexico 25°49N 103°51W 180 B4
Mapimí, Bolsón de
  Mexico 27°0N 104°15W 180 B4
Maping China 31°34N 113°32E 117 B9
Mapinga Tanzania 6°40S 39°12E 142 D4
Mapinhane Mozam. 22°20S 35°0E 145 B6
Maple Creek Canada 49°55N 109°29W 163 D7
Maple Valley U.S.A. 47°25N 122°3W 170 C4
Mapleton U.S.A. 44°2N 123°52W 168 D2
Mapoon ◇ Australia 11°44S 142°8E 150 A3
Mapourika, L. N.Z. 43°18S 170°12E 155 D5
Mapuca India 15°36N 73°46E 127 G1
Mapuera → Brazil 1°5S 57°2W 186 D7
Mapulanguene Mozam. 24°29S 32°6E 145 B5
Mapungubwe △
  S. Africa 22°12S 29°23E 145 B4
Maputo Mozam. 25°58S 32°32E 145 C5
Maputo □ Mozam. 26°0S 32°25E 145 C5
Maputo, B. de Mozam. 25°50S 32°45E 145 C5
Maqat Kazakhstan 47°39N 53°19E 87 E10
Maqên China 34°24N 100°6E 110 E9
Maqên Gangri China 34°55N 99°18E 110 E8
Maqiaohe China 44°40N 130°30E 115 B16
Maqnā Si. Arabia 28°25N 34°50E 130 D2
Maqteïr Mauritania 21°50N 11°40W 134 D3
Maqu China 33°52N 101°42E 110 E9
Maquan He = Brahmaputra →
  Asia 23°40N 90°35E 125 H13
Maquela do Zombo
  Angola 6°0S 15°15E 140 F3
Maquinchao Argentina 41°15S 68°50W 192 B3
Maquoketa U.S.A. 42°4N 90°40W 172 D8
Mar Canada 44°49N 81°12W 174 B3
Mar, Serra do Brazil 25°30S 49°0W 191 B6
Mar Chiquita, L.
  Argentina 30°40S 62°50W 190 C3
Mar del Plata Argentina 38°0S 57°30W 190 D4
Mar Menor Spain 37°40N 0°45W 91 H4
Mara □ Tanzania 1°45S 34°20E 142 C3
Maraã Brazil 1°52S 65°25W 186 D5
Maraa Tahiti 17°46S 149°34W 155 b
Marabá Brazil 5°20S 49°5W 187 E9
Maraboon, L. Australia 23°41S 148°0E 150 C4
Maracá, I. de Brazil 2°10S 50°30W 187 D8
Maracaibo Venezuela 10°40N 71°37W 186 A4
Maracaibo, L. de
  Venezuela 9°40N 71°30W 186 B4
Maracaju Brazil 21°38S 55°9W 191 A4
Maracanã Brazil 0°46S 47°27W 187 D9
Maracás Brazil 13°26S 40°18W 189 C2
Maracas Bay Village
  Trin. & Tob. 10°46N 61°28W 187 K15
Maracay Venezuela 10°15N 67°28W 186 A5
Maracena Spain 37°12N 3°38W 89 H7
Marādah Libya 29°15N 19°15E 135 C9
Maradi Niger 13°29N 7°20E 139 C6
Marāgheh Iran 37°30N 46°12E 105 D12
Maragogipe Brazil 12°46S 38°55W 189 C3
Marāh Si. Arabia 25°0N 45°35E 128 E5
Marahuaca, Cerro
  Venezuela 3°34N 65°27W 186 C5
Marais du Cotentin et du Bessin
  France 49°10N 1°30W 70 C5

Marais Poitevin, Val de Sèvre et
  Vendée △ France 46°18N 0°35W
Marajó, I. de Brazil 1°0S 49°30W
Marākand Iran 38°51N 45°16E
Marakele △ S. Africa 24°30S 25°30E
Maralal Kenya 1°0N 36°38E
Maralinga Australia 30°13S 131°32E
Maralinga Tjarutja ◇
  Australia 29°30S 131°0E
Marama Australia 35°10S 140°10E
Maramaereğlisi
  Turkey 40°57N 27°57E
Marambio Antarctica 64°0S 56°0W
Maramureş □ Romania 47°45N 24°0E
Maran Malaysia 3°35N 102°45E
Maranboy Australia 14°40S 132°39E
Maranchón Spain 41°6N 2°15W
Marand Iran 38°30N 45°45E
Maranello Italy 44°32N 10°52E
Marang Malaysia 5°12N 103°13E
Maranguape Brazil 3°55S 38°50W
Maranhão = São Luís
  Brazil 2°39S 44°15W
Maranhão □ Brazil 5°0S 46°0W
Maranoa → Australia 27°50S 148°37E
Marañón → Peru 4°30S 73°35W
Marão Mozam. 24°18S 34°2E
Marari Brazil 5°43S 67°47W
Maraş = Kahramanmaraş
  Turkey 37°37N 36°53E
Mărăşeşti Romania 45°52N 27°14E
Maratea Italy 39°59N 15°43E
Marateca Portugal 38°34N 8°40W
Marathasa Cyprus 34°59N 32°51E
Marathókambos Greece 37°43N 26°42E
Marathon Australia 20°51S 143°32E
Marathon Canada 48°44N 86°23W
Marathon Fla., U.S.A. 24°43N 81°5W
Marathon N.Y., U.S.A. 42°27N 76°2W
Marathon Tex., U.S.A. 30°12N 103°15W
Marathónas Greece 38°11N 23°58E
Marathóvounos
  Cyprus 35°13N 33°37E
Maratua Indonesia 2°10N 118°35E
Maraú Brazil 14°6S 39°0W
Maraval Trin. & Tob. 10°42N 61°31W
Maravatío Mexico 19°54N 100°27W
Marāwih U.A.E. 24°18N 53°18E
Marazliyivka Ukraine 46°8N 30°3E
Marble Bar Australia 21°9S 119°44E
Marblehead Mass.,
  U.S.A. 42°29N 70°51W
Marblehead Ohio,
  U.S.A. 41°32N 82°44W
Marburg Germany 50°47N 8°46E
Marca, Pta. do Angola 16°31S 11°43E
Marcal → Hungary 47°41N 17°40E
Marcali Hungary 46°35N 17°25E
Marcapata Peru 13°31S 70°52W
Marcaria Italy 45°7N 10°32E
Mărcăuţi Moldova 48°20N 27°14E
March U.K. 52°33N 0°5E
Marchand = Rommani
  Morocco 33°34N 6°40W
Marche France 46°5N 1°20E
Marche □ Italy 43°30N 13°15E
Marche-en-Famenne
  Belgium 50°14N 5°19E
Marchena Spain 37°18N 5°23W
Marches = Marche □
  Italy 43°30N 13°15E
Marchesale △ Italy 38°32N 16°13E
Marciana Marina Italy 42°48N 10°12E
Marcianise Italy 41°2N 14°17E
Marcigny France 46°17N 4°2E
Marcillat-en-Combraille
  France 46°12N 2°38E
Marck France 50°57N 1°57E
Marckolsheim France 48°10N 7°30E
Marco Island U.S.A. 25°58N 81°44W
Marcona Peru 15°10S 75°0W
Marcos Juárez Argentina 32°42S 62°5W
Mărculeşti Moldova 47°52N 28°14E
Marcus Baker, Mt.
  U.S.A. 61°26N 147°45W
Marcus I. = Minami-Tori-Shima
  Pac. Oc. 24°20N 153°58E
Marcy, Mt. U.S.A. 44°7N 73°56W
Mardan Pakistan 34°20N 72°0E
Mardarivka Ukraine 47°32N 29°44E
Mardie Australia 21°12S 115°59E
Mardin Turkey 37°20N 40°43E
Mârdsjö Sweden 63°18N 15°35E
Marecchia → Italy 44°4N 12°34E
Maree, L. U.K. 57°40N 5°26W
Mareeba Australia 16°59S 145°28E
Mareetsane S. Africa 26°9S 25°25E
Maremma Italy 42°30N 11°30E
Marengo Italy 44°54N 8°33E
Maréna Kayes, Mali 14°36N 10°45W
Maréna Koulikouro, Mali 13°55N 7°20W
Marennes France 45°49N 1°7W
Marerano Madag. 21°23S 44°52E
Maréttimo Italy 37°58N 12°4E
Mareuil France 45°26N 0°29E
Marfa U.S.A. 30°19N 104°1W
Marfa Pt. Malta 35°59N 14°19E

gherita di Savóia
ly 41°22N 16°9E 95 A9
gherita Pk. Uganda 0°22N 29°51E 142 B3
ghilon Uzbekistan 40°27N 71°42E 109 D8
ghita Romania 47°22N 22°22E 80 C7
gonin Poland 52°58N 17°55E 83 F4
gow, Dasht-e
ghan. 30°40N 62°30E 122 D3
guerite Canada 52°30N 122°25W 162 C4
hanets Ukraine 47°40N 34°40E 85 J8
houm Algeria 34°27N 0°11W 136 B3
i El □ Russia 56°30N 48°0E 86 B8
i Indus Pakistan 32°57N 71°34E 124 C4
i Republic = Mari El □
ssia 56°30N 48°0E 86 B8
a, Sa. de Spain 37°39N 2°14W 91 H2
a de la Salut Spain 39°40N 3°5E 100 B10
a Elena Chile 22°18S 69°40W 190 A2
a Grande
gentina 31°45S 59°55W 190 C4
a I. N. Terr.,
stralia 14°52S 135°45E 150 A2
a I. Tas., Australia 42°35S 148°0E 151 G4
a Island △
stralia 42°38S 148°5E 151 G4
a van Diemen, C.
Z. 34°29S 172°40E 154 A1
ager Denmark 56°40N 9°59E 63 H3
ager Fjord Denmark 56°42N 10°19E 63 H4
akani Kenya 3°50S 39°27E 142 C4
ala △ Australia 25°57S 145°2E 151 D4
an Australia 21°9S 148°57E 150 b
an L. Canada 63°0N 116°15W 162 A5
ana Trench Pac. Oc. 13°0N 145°0E 156 F6
anna Ark., U.S.A. 34°46N 90°46W 177 D9
anna Fla., U.S.A. 30°46N 85°14W 178 E4
annelund Sweden 57°37N 15°35E 63 G9
ánské Lázně
ch Rep. 49°58N 12°41E 78 B5
as → U.S.A. 47°56N 110°30W 168 C8
as, Is. Mexico 21°25N 106°28W 180 C3
ato, Punta Panama 7°12N 80°52W 182 E3
azell Austria 47°47N 15°19E 78 D8
bo Denmark 54°48N 11°30E 63 K5
bor Slovenia 46°36N 15°40E 93 B12
co → Africa 23°35S 26°57E 144 B4
copa Ariz., U.S.A. 33°4N 112°3W 169 K7
copa Calif., U.S.A. 35°4N 119°24W 171 K7
é → Brazil 0°27S 66°26W 186 D5
e Byrd Land
tarctica 79°30S 125°0W 55 D14
e-Galante
adeloupe 15°56N 61°16W 182 b
ecourt = Kangiqsujuaq
nada 61°30N 72°0W 161 E17
efred Sweden 59°15N 17°12E 62 E11
ehamn Finland 60°5N 19°55E 61 F18
eholm Sweden 55°53N 13°10E 63 J7
embourg Belgium 50°6N 4°31E 69 D4
enbad = Mariánské Lázně
ch Rep. 49°58N 12°41E 78 B5
enberg Germany 50°39N 13°9E 76 E9
ental Namibia 24°36S 18°0E 144 B2
enville U.S.A. 41°28N 79°8W 174 E5
estad Sweden 58°43N 13°50E 63 F7
etta Ga., U.S.A. 33°57N 84°33W 178 B5
etta Ohio, U.S.A. 39°25N 81°27W 173 F13
eville Canada 45°26N 73°10W 175 A11
ga → Nigeria 9°40N 5°55E 139 C6
gnane France 43°25N 5°13E 73 E9
insk Russia 56°10N 87°20E 106 D9
inskiy Posad Russia 56°10N 47°45E 86 B8
jampolė Lithuania 54°33N 23°19E 82 D10
jampolė □
huania 54°34N 23°21E 82 D10
lia Brazil 22°13S 50°0W 191 A6
n Spain 42°23N 8°42W 88 C2
na U.S.A. 36°41N 121°48W 170 J5
nduque Phil. 13°25N 122°0E 119 B6
ne City U.S.A. 42°43N 82°30W 174 D2
neland U.S.A. 29°40N 81°13W 178 F8
neo Italy 37°57N 13°25E 94 E6
nette U.S.A. 45°6N 87°38W 172 C10
ngá Brazil 23°26S 52°2W 191 A5
rtugal 39°45N 8°56W 88 F2
nho dos Abrolhos △
zil 17°50S 39°0W 189 D3
no Italy 41°46N 12°39E 93 G9
no di Campo Italy 42°46N 10°11E 92 F7
on Ala., U.S.A. 32°38N 87°19W 177 E11
on Ark., U.S.A. 35°13N 90°12W 172 H8
on Ill., U.S.A. 37°44N 88°56W 172 G9
on Ind., U.S.A. 40°32N 85°40W 173 E11
on Iowa, U.S.A. 42°2N 91°36W 172 D8
on Kans., U.S.A. 38°21N 97°1W 172 F5
on N.C., U.S.A. 35°41N 82°1W 177 D13
on Ohio, U.S.A. 40°35N 83°8W 173 E12
on S.C., U.S.A. 34°11N 79°24W 177 D15
on Va., U.S.A. 36°50N 81°31W 173 G13
on, L. U.S.A. 33°28N 80°10W 178 B9
on Bay Australia 35°12S 136°59E 152 C2
on I. Ind. Oc. 47°0S 38°0E 146 J2
posa U.S.A. 37°29N 119°58W 170 H7
scal Estigarribia
raguay 22°3S 60°40W 190 A3
time Alps = Maritimes, Alpes
rope 44°10N 7°10E 73 D11
times, Alpes Europe 44°10N 7°10E 73 D11
tsa = Evros →
eece 41°40N 26°34E 97 F10
tsa Greece 36°22N 28°10E 101 C10
upol Ukraine 47°5N 37°31E 85 J9
usa △ Venezuela 9°24N 61°27W 183 E7
y Chodra △ Russia 56°10N 48°30E 86 B9
vān Iran 35°30N 46°25E 105 E12
'Uyūn Lebanon 33°21N 35°34E 130 B4
ka Si. Arabia 18°14N 41°19E 137 D5
ka Somalia 1°48N 44°50E 131 G3
kam China 29°42N 98°38E 116 C2
kapur India 15°44N 79°19E 127 G4
karyd Sweden 56°28N 13°35E 63 H7
kazī □ Iran 34°0N 49°30E 129 C6
kdale Canada 44°19N 80°39W 174 B4
ked Tree U.S.A. 35°32N 90°25W 177 D9
kelsdorfer Huk
rmany 54°33N 11°4E 76 A7
ket Drayton U.K. 52°54N 2°29W 66 E5
ket Harborough
K. 52°29N 0°55W 67 E7
ket Rasen U.K. 53°24N 0°20W 66 D7
Markham Canada 43°52N 79°16W 174 C5
Markham, Mt.
Antarctica 83°0S 164°0E 55 E11
Marki Poland 52°19N 21°6E 83 F8
Märkische Schweiz △
Germany 52°34N 14°2E 76 C10
Markit China 38°54N 77°40E 109 E9
Markkleeberg Germany 51°16N 12°23E 76 D8
Markleeville U.S.A. 38°42N 119°47W 170 G7
Markopoulo Greece 37°53N 23°57E 98 D5
Markovac Serbia 44°14N 21°7E 96 B5
Markovo Russia 64°40N 170°24E 107 C17
Markoye Burkina Faso 14°39N 0°2E 139 C5
Marks Russia 51°45N 46°50E 86 E8
Marksville U.S.A. 31°8N 92°4W 176 F8
Markt Schwaben
Germany 48°11N 11°52E 77 G7
Marktoberdorf Germany 47°45N 10°37E 77 H6
Marktredwitz Germany 50°1N 12°6E 77 E8
Marl Germany 51°39N 7°4E 76 D3
Marla Australia 27°19S 133°33E 151 D1
Marlbank Canada 44°26N 77°6W 174 B7
Marlboro U.S.A. 41°36N 73°59W 175 E11
Marlborough Australia 22°46S 149°52E 150 C4
Marlborough U.K. 51°25N 1°43W 67 F6
Marlborough U.S.A. 42°21N 71°33W 175 D13
Marlborough □ N.Z. 41°40S 173°50E 155 B8
Marlborough Downs
U.K. 51°27N 1°53W 67 F6
Marle France 49°43N 3°47E 71 C10
Marlin U.S.A. 31°18N 96°54W 176 F6
Marlow Germany 54°9N 12°33E 76 A8
Marlow U.K. 51°34N 0°46W 67 F7
Marlow U.S.A. 34°39N 97°58W 176 D6
Marmagao India 15°25N 73°56E 127 G1
Marmande France 44°30N 0°10E 72 D4
Marmara Turkey 40°35N 27°34E 97 F11
Marmara, Sea of = Marmara
Denizi Turkey 40°45N 28°15E 97 F12
Marmara Denizi Turkey 40°45N 28°15E 97 F12
Marmara Gölü Turkey 38°37N 28°2E 99 C10
Marmaris Turkey 36°50N 28°14E 99 E10
Marmaris Limanı
Turkey 36°50N 28°19E 99 E10
Marmion, Mt.
Australia 29°16S 119°50E 149 E2
Marmion L. Canada 48°55N 91°20W 164 C1
Marmolada, Mte. Italy 46°26N 11°51E 93 B8
Marmolejo Spain 38°3N 4°13W 89 G6
Marmora Canada 44°28N 77°41W 174 B7
Mármora, La Italy 39°59N 9°20E 94 C2
Marnay France 47°16N 5°48E 71 E12
Marne Germany 53°56N 9°2E 76 B5
Marne □ France 48°50N 4°10E 71 D11
Marne → France 48°47N 2°29E 71 D9
Marneuli Georgia 41°30N 44°48E 87 K7
Marnoo Australia 36°40S 142°52E 152 D5
Maro Reef U.S.A. 25°25N 170°35W 167 K5
Maroantsetra Madag. 15°26S 49°44E 141 H9
Maroelaboom Namibia 19°15S 18°53E 144 A2
Marondera Zimbabwe 18°5S 31°42E 143 F3
Maroni → Fr. Guiana 5°30N 54°0W 187 B8
Maronia Greece 40°53N 25°30E 97 F9
Maronne → France 45°5N 1°56E 72 C5
Maroochydore
Australia 26°29S 153°5E 151 D5
Maroona Australia 37°27S 142°54E 152 D5
Maros → Hungary 46°15N 20°13E 80 D5
Maróstica Italy 45°44N 11°40E 93 C8
Maroua Cameroon 10°40N 14°20E 139 C7
Marovoay Madag. 16°6S 46°39E 141 H9
Marqaköl Kazakhstan 48°45N 85°45E 109 C11
Marquard S. Africa 28°40S 27°28E 144 C4
Marquesas Fracture Zone
Pac. Oc. 9°0S 125°0W 157 H15
Marquesas Is. = Marquises, Îs.
French Polynesia 9°30S 140°0W 157 H14
Marquesas Keys
U.S.A. 24°35N 82°10W 179 L7
Marquette U.S.A. 46°33N 87°24W 172 B10
Marquis St. Lucia 14°2N 60°54W 183 f
Marquise France 50°50N 1°40E 71 B8
Marquises, Îs.
French Polynesia 9°30S 140°0W 157 H14
Marra, Djebel Sudan 13°10N 24°22E 135 F10
Marra Cr. → Australia 30°8S 147°15E 153 A7
Marra-Marra △
Australia 33°30S 151°4E 153 B9
Marracuene Mozam. 25°45S 32°35E 145 C5
Marradi Italy 44°4N 11°37E 93 D8
Marrakech Morocco 31°9N 8°0W 136 B2
Marratxí Spain 39°39N 2°48E 90 F7
Marrawah Australia 40°55S 144°42E 151 G3
Marrecas, Serra das
Brazil 9°0S 41°0W 189 B2
Marree Australia 29°39S 138°1E 151 D2
Marrero U.S.A. 29°53N 90°6W 177 G9
Marrimane Mozam. 22°58S 33°34E 145 B5
Marromeu Mozam. 18°15S 36°25E 145 A6
Marromeu △ Mozam. 19°0S 36°0E 145 A6
Marroquí, Punta Spain 36°0N 5°37W 89 K5
Marrowie Cr. →
Australia 33°23S 145°40E 153 B6
Marrubane Mozam. 18°0S 37°0E 143 F4
Marrúbiu Italy 39°40N 8°35E 94 C1
Marrupa Mozam. 13°8S 37°30E 143 E4
Mars Hill U.S.A. 46°31N 67°52W 173 B20
Marsá 'Alam Egypt 25°5N 34°54E 137 B3
Marsá Matrûh Egypt 31°19N 27°9E 137 A2
Marsá Sha'b Sudan 22°52N 35°47E 137 C4
Marsabit Kenya 2°18N 38°0E 142 B4
Marsabit △ Kenya 2°23N 37°56E 142 B4
Marsala Italy 37°48N 12°26E 94 E5
Marsalforn Malta 36°4N 14°16E 101 C1
Mârşani Romania 44°1N 24°1E 81 F9
Marsberg Germany 51°28N 8°52E 76 D4
Marsciano Italy 42°54N 12°20E 93 F9
Marsden Australia 33°47S 147°32E 153 B7
Marsden Point N.Z. 35°50S 174°31E 154 B3
Marseillan France 43°23N 3°31E 72 E7
Marseille France 43°18N 5°23E 73 E9
Marseille-Marignane ✕ (MRS)
France 43°26N 5°14E 73 E9
Marseilles = Marseille
France 43°18N 5°23E 73 E9
Marsh I. U.S.A. 29°34N 91°53W 176 G9
Marshall Liberia 6°8N 10°22W 138 D2
Marshall Ark., U.S.A. 35°55N 92°38W 176 D8
Marshall Mich.,
U.S.A. 42°16N 84°58W 173 D11
Marshall Minn., U.S.A. 44°27N 95°47W 172 C6
Marshall Mo., U.S.A. 39°7N 93°12W 172 F7
Marshall Tex., U.S.A. 32°33N 94°23W 176 E7
Marshall → Australia 22°59S 136°59E 150 C2
Marshall Is. ■ Pac. Oc. 9°0N 171°0E 156 G9
Marshalltown U.S.A. 42°3N 92°55W 172 D7
Marshallville U.S.A. 32°27N 83°56W 178 C6
Marshbrook Zimbabwe 18°33S 31°9E 145 A5
Marshfield Mo., U.S.A. 37°15N 92°54W 172 G7
Marshfield Vt., U.S.A. 44°20N 72°20W 175 B12
Marshfield Wis., U.S.A. 44°40N 90°10W 172 C8
Marshūn Iran 36°19N 49°23E 129 B6
Mársico Nuovo Italy 40°25N 15°44E 95 B8
Märsta Sweden 59°37N 17°52E 62 E11
Marstal Denmark 54°51N 10°30E 63 K4
Marstrand Sweden 57°53N 11°35E 63 G5
Mart U.S.A. 31°33N 96°50W 176 F6
Marta → Italy 42°14N 11°42E 93 F8
Martaban Burma 16°30N 97°35E 123 L20
Martaban, G. of Burma 16°5N 96°30E 123 L20
Martano Italy 40°12N 18°18E 95 B11
Martapura Kalimantan Selatan,
Indonesia 3°22S 114°47E 118 E4
Martapura Sumatera Selatan,
Indonesia 4°19S 104°22E 118 E2
Marte Nigeria 12°23N 13°46E 139 C7
Marte R. Gómez, Presa
Mexico 26°10N 99°0W 181 B5
Martel France 44°57N 1°37E 72 D5
Martelange Belgium 49°49N 5°43E 69 E5
Martellago Italy 45°33N 12°9E 93 C9
Martés, Sierra Spain 39°20N 1°0W 91 F4
Martfű Hungary 47°1N 20°17E 80 C5
Marthaguy Cr. →
Australia 30°16S 147°35E 153 A7
Marthapal India 19°24N 81°37E 126 E5
Martha's Vineyard
U.S.A. 41°25N 70°38W 175 E14
Martigné-Ferchaud
France 47°50N 1°20W 70 E5
Martigny Switz. 46°6N 7°3E 77 J3
Martigues France 43°24N 5°4E 73 E9
Martil Morocco 35°36N 5°15W 136 A2
Martin Slovak Rep. 49°6N 18°58E 79 B11
Martin S. Dak., U.S.A. 43°11N 101°44W 172 D3
Martin Tenn., U.S.A. 36°21N 88°51W 177 C10
Martín → Spain 41°18N 0°19W 90 D4
Martin L. U.S.A. 32°41N 85°55W 178 C4
Martin Vaz Atl. Oc. 20°30S 28°51W 56 J9
Martina Franca Italy 40°42N 17°20E 95 B10
Martinborough N.Z. 41°14S 175°29E 154 H4
Martinez Calif., U.S.A. 38°1N 122°8W 170 G4
Martinez Ga., U.S.A. 33°31N 82°5W 178 B7
Martinho Campos
Brazil 19°20S 45°13W 189 D1
Martinique ☑ W. Indies 14°40N 61°0W 182 c
Martinique Passage
W. Indies 15°15N 61°0W 183 C7
Martino Greece 38°35N 23°12E 98 C5
Martinópolis Brazil 22°11S 51°12W 191 A5
Martins Bay Barbados 13°12N 59°29W 183 g
Martins Ferry U.S.A. 40°6N 80°44W 174 F4
Martinsberg Austria 48°22N 15°9E 78 C8
Martinsburg Pa.,
U.S.A. 40°19N 78°20W 174 F6
Martinsburg W. Va.,
U.S.A. 39°27N 77°58W 173 F15
Martinsicuro Italy 42°54N 13°54E 93 F10
Martinsville Ind.,
U.S.A. 39°26N 86°25W 172 F10
Martinsville Va.,
U.S.A. 36°41N 79°52W 173 G14
Marton N.Z. 40°4S 175°23E 154 G4
Martorell Spain 41°28N 1°56E 90 D6
Martos Spain 37°44N 3°58W 89 H7
Martu ✪ Australia 22°30S 122°30E 148 D3
Martuni Armenia 40°8N 45°20E 87 K7
Maru Nigeria 12°22N 6°22E 139 C6
Marudi Malaysia 4°11N 114°19E 118 D4
Maruf Afghan. 31°30N 67°6E 122 D5
Marugame Japan 34°15N 133°40E 113 G6
Maruia → N.Z. 41°47S 172°13E 155 B7
Maruim Brazil 10°45S 37°5W 189 C3
Marulan Australia 34°43S 150°3E 153 C9
Marunga Angola 17°28S 20°2E 144 A3
Marungu, Mts.
Dem. Rep. of the Congo 7°30S 30°0E 142 D3
Maruwa ✪ Australia 22°30S 127°30E 148 D4
Marv Dasht Iran 29°50N 52°40E 129 D7
Marvão Portugal 39°24N 7°20W 89 F3
Marvast Iran 30°30N 54°15E 129 D7
Marvejols France 44°33N 3°19E 72 D7
Marvel Loch Australia 31°28S 119°29E 149 F2
Marwar India 25°43N 73°45E 124 G5
Mary Turkmenistan 37°40N 61°50E 129 B9
Mary Esther U.S.A. 30°25N 86°40W 179 E3
Maryborough = Portlaoise
Ireland 53°2N 7°18W 64 C4
Maryborough Queens.,
Australia 25°31S 152°37E 151 D5
Maryborough Vic.,
Australia 37°3S 143°44E 152 D5
Maryfield Canada 49°50N 101°35W 163 D8
Maryland □ U.S.A. 39°0N 76°30W 173 F15
Maryland Junction
Zimbabwe 17°45S 30°31E 143 F3
Maryport U.K. 54°44N 3°28W 66 C4
Mary's Harbour
Canada 52°18N 55°51W 165 B8
Marystown Canada 47°10N 55°10W 165 C8
Marysville Calif., U.S.A. 39°9N 121°35W 170 F5
Marysville Kans.,
U.S.A. 39°51N 96°39W 172 F5
Marysville Mich.,
U.S.A. 42°54N 82°29W 174 D2
Marysville Ohio,
U.S.A. 40°14N 83°22W 173 E12
Marysville Wash.,
U.S.A. 48°3N 122°11W 170 B4
Maryville Mo., U.S.A. 40°21N 94°52W 172 E6
Maryville Tenn.,
U.S.A. 35°46N 83°58W 177 D13
Masada Israel 31°18N 35°21E 130 D4
Masahunga Tanzania 2°6S 33°18E 142 C3
Masai Malaysia 1°29N 103°55E 121 d
Masai Mara △ Kenya 1°25S 35°5E 142 C4
Masai Steppe Tanzania 4°30S 36°30E 142 C4
Masaka Uganda 0°21S 31°45E 142 C3
Masāl Iran 37°23N 49°8E 105 D12
Masalembo, Kepulauan
Indonesia 5°35S 114°30E 118 F4
Masalima, Kepulauan
Indonesia 5°4S 117°5E 118 F5
Masallı Azerbaijan 39°3N 48°40E 105 C13
Masamba Indonesia 2°30S 120°15E 119 E6
Masan S. Korea 35°11N 128°32E 115 G15
Masandam, Ra's Oman 26°30N 56°30E 129 E8
Masasi Tanzania 10°45S 38°52E 143 E4
Masaya Nic. 12°0N 86°7W 182 D2
Masba Nigeria 11°35N 13°1E 139 C7
Masbate Phil. 12°21N 123°36E 119 B6
Máscali Italy 37°45N 15°12E 95 E8
Mascara Algeria 35°26N 0°6E 136 A4
Mascara □ Algeria 35°25N 0°10E 136 A4
Mascarene Is. Ind. Oc. 22°0S 55°0E 132 J9
Mascota Mexico 20°32N 104°49W 180 C4
Masdar City = Madīnat Masdar
U.A.E. 24°26N 54°37E 129 E7
Masela Indonesia 8°9S 129°51E 119 F7
Maseru Lesotho 29°18S 27°30E 144 C4
Mashaba Zimbabwe 20°2S 30°29E 143 G3
Mashābih Si. Arabia 25°35N 36°30E 128 E3
Mashan China 23°40N 108°11E 116 F7
Mashang China 36°48N 117°57E 115 F9
Mashatu △ Botswana 22°45S 29°5E 145 B4
Mashegu Nigeria 10°0N 5°35E 139 D6
Masherbrum Pakistan 35°38N 76°18E 125 B7
Mashhad Iran 36°20N 59°35E 129 B8
Mashi Nigeria 13°0N 7°54E 139 C6
Mashīz Iran 29°56N 56°37E 129 D8
Māshkel, Hāmūn-i-
Pakistan 28°20N 62°56E 129 D9
Mashki Chāh Pakistan 29°5N 62°30E 122 E3
Mashonaland Zimbabwe 16°30S 31°0E 141 H6
Mashonaland Central □
Zimbabwe 17°30S 31°0E 145 A5
Mashonaland East □
Zimbabwe 18°0S 32°0E 145 A5
Mashonaland West □
Zimbabwe 17°30S 29°30E 145 A4
Mashrakh India 26°7N 84°48E 125 F11
Masi Manimba
Dem. Rep. of the Congo 4°40S 17°54E 140 E3
Masig Australia 9°45S 143°24E 150 a
Masindi Uganda 1°40N 31°43E 142 B3
Masindi Port Uganda 1°43N 32°2E 142 B3
Masinga Res. Kenya 0°58S 37°38E 142 C4
Maşīrah, Jazīrat Oman 21°0N 58°50E 131 C6
Maşīrah, Khalīj Oman 20°10N 58°10E 131 C6
Masisea Peru 8°35S 74°22W 188 B3
Masisi
Dem. Rep. of the Congo 1°23S 28°49E 142 C2
Masjed Soleyman Iran 31°55N 49°18E 129 D6
Mask, L. Ireland 53°36N 9°22W 64 C2
Maski India 15°56N 76°46E 127 G3
Maskin Oman 23°44N 56°52E 129 F8
Maslen Nos Bulgaria 42°18N 27°48E 97 D11
Maslinica Croatia 43°24N 16°13E 93 E13
Masnou = El Masnou
Spain 41°28N 2°20E 90 D7
Masoala, Tanjon' i
Madag. 15°59S 50°13E 141 H10
Masohi = Amahai
Indonesia 3°20S 128°55E 119 E7
Mason Nev., U.S.A. 38°56N 119°8W 170 G7
Mason Tex., U.S.A. 30°45N 99°14W 176 F5
Mason B. N.Z. 46°55S 167°45E 155 G2
Mason City U.S.A. 43°9N 93°12W 172 D7
Maspalomas Canary Is. 27°46N 15°35W 100 G4
Maspalomas, Pta.
Canary Is. 27°43N 15°36W 100 G4
Masqat Oman 23°37N 58°36E 131 C6
Masr el Gedida Egypt 30°5N 31°21E 137 E7
Massa Italy 44°1N 10°9E 92 D7
Massa, O. → Morocco 30°2N 9°40W 136 B2
Massa e Carrara □ Italy 44°10N 10°10E 92 D7
Massa Marittima Italy 43°3N 10°52E 92 E7
Massachusetts □
U.S.A. 42°30N 72°0W 175 D13
Massachusetts B.
U.S.A. 42°25N 70°50W 175 D14
Massafra Italy 40°35N 17°7E 95 B10
Massakory Chad 13°0N 15°49E 135 F9
Massamba Mozam. 15°58S 33°31E 143 F3
Massanella Spain 39°48N 2°51E 100 B9
Massangena Mozam. 21°34S 33°0E 145 B5
Massango Angola 8°2S 16°21E 140 F3
Massapê Brazil 3°31S 40°19W 189 A2
Massat France 42°53N 1°21E 72 F5
Massawa = Mitsiwa
Eritrea 15°35N 39°25E 131 D2
Massena U.S.A. 44°56N 74°54W 175 B10
Massenya Chad 11°21N 16°9E 135 F9
Masset Canada 54°2N 132°10W 162 C2
Masseube France 43°25N 0°34E 72 E4
Massiac France 45°15N 3°11E 72 C7
Massiah Street Barbados 13°9N 59°29W 183 g
Massif Central France 44°55N 3°0E 72 D7
Massif des Bauges △
France 45°40N 6°10E 71 G13
Massigui Mali 11°48N 6°50W 138 C3
Massillon U.S.A. 40°48N 81°32W 174 F3
Massine, O. → Algeria 36°13N 2°12E 136 A4
Massinga Mozam. 23°15S 35°22E 145 B6
Massingir Mozam. 23°51S 32°4E 145 B5
Masson-Angers
Canada 45°32N 75°25W 175 A9
Masson I. Antarctica 66°10S 93°20E 55 C7
Maştağa Azerbaijan 40°35N 50°1E 87 K10
Mastanli = Momchilgrad
Bulgaria 41°33N 25°23E 97 E9
Masterton N.Z. 40°56S 175°39E 154 G4
Mastic U.S.A. 40°47N 72°54W 175 F12
Mastuj Pakistan 36°20N 72°36E 125 A5
Mastung Pakistan 29°50N 66°56E 122 E5
Mastūrah Si. Arabia 23°7N 38°52E 137 C4
Masty Belarus 53°27N 24°38E 75 B13
Masuda Japan 34°40N 131°51E 113 G5
Masuku = Franceville
Gabon 1°40S 13°32E 140 E2
Masurian Lakes = Mazurski,
Pojezierze Poland 53°50N 21°0E 82 E7
Masvingo Zimbabwe 20°8S 30°49E 143 G3
Masvingo □ Zimbabwe 21°0S 31°30E 143 G3
Maswa △ Tanzania 2°58S 34°19E 142 C3
Maşyāf Syria 35°4N 36°20E 104 E7
Maszewo Poland 53°29N 15°3E 82 E2
Mat → Albania 41°40N 19°35E 96 E3
Mata-au = Clutha →
N.Z. 46°20S 169°49E 155 G4
Mata de São João
Brazil 12°31S 38°17W 189 C3
Matabeleland Zimbabwe 18°0S 27°0E 141 H5
Matabeleland North □
Zimbabwe 19°0S 28°0E 143 F2
Matabeleland South □
Zimbabwe 21°0S 29°0E 143 G2
Matachel → Spain 38°50N 6°17W 89 G4
Matachewan Canada 47°56N 80°39W 164 C3
Matadi
Dem. Rep. of the Congo 5°52S 13°31E 140 F2
Matagalpa Nic. 13°0N 85°58W 182 D2
Matagami Canada 49°45N 77°34W 164 C4
Matagami, L. Canada 49°50N 77°40W 164 C4
Matagorda B. U.S.A. 28°40N 96°12W 176 G6
Matagorda I. U.S.A. 28°15N 96°30W 176 G6
Mataiea Tahiti 17°46S 149°25W 155 b
Matak Indonesia 3°18N 106°16E 118 D3
Matakana Australia 32°59S 145°54E 153 B6
Matakana N.Z. 36°21S 174°43E 154 C3
Matala Greece 34°59N 24°45E 101 E6
Matalaque Peru 16°26S 70°49W 188 D3
Matale Sri Lanka 7°30N 80°37E 127 L5
Matam Senegal 15°34N 13°17W 138 B2
Matam □ Senegal 15°37N 13°19W 138 B2
Matamata N.Z. 37°48S 175°47E 154 D4
Matameye Niger 13°26N 8°28E 139 C6
Matamoros Coahuila,
Mexico 25°32N 103°15W 180 B4
Matamoros Tamaulipas,
Mexico 25°53N 97°30W 181 B5
Ma'ţan as Sarra Libya 21°45N 22°0E 135 D10
Matandu → Tanzania 8°45S 34°19E 143 D3
Matane Canada 48°50N 67°33W 165 C6
Matang China 23°30N 104°7E 116 F5
Matankari Niger 13°46N 4°1E 139 C5
Matanomadh India 23°33N 68°57E 124 H3
Matanzas Cuba 23°0N 81°40W 182 B3
Matapa Botswana 23°11S 24°39E 144 B3
Matapan, C. = Tenaro, Akra
Greece 36°22N 22°27E 98 E4
Matapédia Canada 48°0N 66°59W 165 C6
Matapo △ Zimbabwe 20°30S 29°40E 143 G2
Mataporquera Spain 42°52N 4°10W 88 C6
Matara Sri Lanka 5°58N 80°30E 127 M5
Mataram Indonesia 8°35S 116°7E 118 F5
Matarani Peru 17°0S 72°10W 188 D3
Mataranka Australia 14°55S 133°4E 148 B5
Matarma, Râs Egypt 30°27N 32°44E 130 E1
Mataró Spain 41°32N 2°29E 90 D7
Matarraña → Spain 41°14N 0°22E 90 D5
Mataruška Banja Serbia 43°40N 20°40E 96 C4
Matata N.Z. 37°54S 176°48E 154 D5
Matatiele S. Africa 30°20S 28°49E 145 D4
Matatila Dam India 25°0N 78°22E 126 B4
Mataura N.Z. 46°11S 168°51E 155 G3
Mataura → N.Z. 46°34S 168°44E 155 G3
Matavai, B. de Tahiti 17°30S 149°23W 155 b
Matehuala Mexico 23°39N 100°39W 180 C4
Mateke Hills Zimbabwe 21°48S 31°0E 143 G3
Matelot Trin. & Tob. 10°50N 61°7W 187 K15
Matera Italy 40°40N 16°36E 95 B9
Matese, Monti del Italy 41°27N 14°22E 95 A7
Matese △ Italy 41°24N 14°23E 95 A7
Mátészalka Hungary 47°58N 22°20E 80 C7
Matetsi Zimbabwe 18°12S 26°0E 143 F2
Mateur Tunisia 37°0N 9°40E 136 A5
Matfors Sweden 62°21N 17°2E 62 B11
Matha France 45°52N 0°20W 72 C3
Matheniko △ Uganda 2°49N 34°27E 142 B3
Mathis U.S.A. 28°6N 97°50W 176 G6
Mathoura Australia 35°50S 144°55E 153 C6
Mathraki Greece 39°48N 19°31E 101 A3
Mathura India 27°30N 77°40E 124 F7
Mati Phil. 6°55N 126°15E 119 C7
Matiakoali Burkina Faso 12°28N 1°2E 139 C5
Matiali India 26°56N 88°49E 125 F13
Matías Romero Mexico 16°53N 95°2W 181 D5
Matibane Mozam. 14°49S 40°45E 143 E5
Matiri Ra. N.Z. 41°38S 172°20E 155 B7
Matjiesfontein S. Africa 33°14S 20°35E 144 D3
Matla → India 21°40N 88°40E 125 J13
Matlamanyane
Botswana 19°33S 25°57E 144 A4
Matli Pakistan 25°2N 68°39E 124 G3
Matlock U.K. 53°9N 1°33W 66 D6
Matmata Tunisia 33°37N 9°59E 136 B5
Mato Grosso □ Brazil 14°0S 55°0W 187 F8
Mato Grosso, Planalto do
Brazil 15°0S 55°0W 187 G8
Mato Grosso do Sul □
Brazil 18°0S 55°0W 187 G8
Matobo = Matapo △
Zimbabwe 20°30S 29°40E 143 G2
Matochkin Shar, Proliv
Russia 73°23N 55°12E 106 B6
Matola Mozam. 25°57S 32°27E 145 C5
Matopo Hills Zimbabwe 20°36S 28°20E 143 G2
Matopos Zimbabwe 20°20S 28°29E 143 G2
Matosinhos Portugal 41°11N 8°42W 88 D2
Matour France 46°19N 4°29E 71 F11
Matroosberg S. Africa 33°23S 19°40E 144 D2
Maţruḩ Oman 23°37N 58°30E 131 C6
Matsalu △ Estonia 58°45N 23°36E 84 C2
Matsena Nigeria 13°5N 10°5E 139 C7
Matsesta Russia 43°34N 39°51E 87 J4
Matsu Tao Taiwan 26°8N 119°56E 117 D12
Matsue Japan 35°25N 133°10E 113 G6
Matsum, Ko Thailand 9°22N 99°59E 121 b
Matsumae Japan 41°26N 140°7E 112 D10
Matsumae-Hantō
Japan 41°30N 140°15E 112 D10
Matsumoto Japan 36°15N 138°0E 113 F9
Matsusaka Japan 34°34N 136°32E 113 G8
Matsushima Japan 38°20N 141°10E 112 E10
Matsuura Japan 33°20N 129°49E 113 H4
Matsuyama Japan 33°45N 132°45E 113 H6
Mattagami → Canada 50°43N 81°29W 164 B3
Mattancheri India 9°50N 76°15E 127 K3
Mattawa Canada 46°20N 78°45W 164 C4
Matterhorn Switz. 45°58N 7°39E 77 K3
Mattersburg Austria 47°44N 16°24E 79 D9
Matthew Town
Bahamas 20°57N 73°40W 183 B5
Matthews Ridge
Guyana 7°37N 60°10W 186 B6
Mattice Canada 49°40N 83°20W 164 C3
Mattili India 18°33N 82°12E 126 E6
Mattituck U.S.A. 40°59N 72°32W 175 F12
Mattō = Hakusan
Japan 36°31N 136°34E 113 F8
Mattoon U.S.A. 39°29N 88°23W 172 F9
Matuba Mozam. 24°28S 32°49E 145 B5
Matucana Peru 11°55S 76°25W 188 C2
Matugama Sri Lanka 6°31N 80°7E 127 L5
Matuku Fiji 19°10S 179°44E 154 a
Matūn = Khowst
Afghan. 33°22N 69°58E 124 C3
Matura B. Trin. & Tob. 10°39N 61°1W 187 K15
Maturín Venezuela 9°45N 63°11W 186 B6
Matusadona △
Zimbabwe 16°58S 28°42E 143 F2
Matveyev Kurgan
Russia 47°35N 38°57E 85 J10
Matxitxako, C. Spain 43°28N 2°47W 90 B2
Mau Mad. P., India 26°17N 78°41E 125 F8
Mau Ut. P., India 25°56N 83°33E 125 G10
Mau Ut. P., India 25°17N 81°23E 125 G9
Mau Escarpment Kenya 0°40S 36°0E 142 C4
Mau Ranipur India 25°16N 79°8E 125 G8
Maua Kenya 0°14N 37°56E 142 C4
Maua Mozam. 13°53S 37°10E 143 E4
Maubeuge France 50°17N 3°57E 71 B10
Maubin Burma 16°44N 95°39E 123 L19
Maubourguet France 43°29N 0°1E 72 E4
Maud, Pt. Australia 23°6S 113°45E 148 D1
Maud Rise S. Ocean 66°0S 3°0E 55 C3
Maude Australia 34°29S 144°18E 152 C6
Maudin Sun Burma 16°0N 94°30E 123 M19
Maués Brazil 3°20S 57°45W 186 D7
Mauganj India 24°50N 81°55E 125 G9
Maughold Hd. I. of Man 54°18N 4°18W 66 C3
Mauguio France 43°37N 4°1E 72 E7
Maui U.S.A. 20°48N 156°20W 167 L8
Maulamyaing = Moulmein
Burma 16°30N 97°40E 123 L20
Maule □ Chile 36°5S 72°30W 190 D1
Mauléon-Licharre
France 43°14N 0°54W 72 E3
Maullín Chile 41°38S 73°37W 192 B2
Maumee U.S.A. 41°34N 83°39W 173 E12
Maumee → U.S.A. 41°42N 83°28W 173 E12
Maumere Indonesia 8°38S 122°13E 119 F6
Maumusson, Pertuis de
France 45°48N 1°14W 72 C2
Maun Botswana 20°0S 23°26E 144 B3
Mauna Kea U.S.A. 19°50N 155°28W 167 M8
Mauna Loa U.S.A. 19°30N 155°35W 167 M8
Maunath Bhanjan = Mau
India 25°56N 83°33E 125 G10
Maungaturoto N.Z. 36°6S 174°23E 154 C3
Maungmagan Kyunzu
Burma 14°0N 97°48E 120 E1
Maungu Kenya 3°33S 38°45E 142 C4
Maupin U.S.A. 45°11N 121°5W 168 D3
Maure-de-Bretagne
France 47°59N 1°58W 70 E5
Maurepas, L. U.S.A. 30°15N 90°30W 177 F9
Maures France 43°15N 6°15E 73 E10
Mauriac France 45°13N 2°19E 72 C6
Maurice, L. Australia 29°30S 131°0E 149 E5
Mauriceville N.Z. 40°45S 175°42E 154 G4
Mauricie △ Canada 46°45N 73°0W 164 C5
Maurienne France 45°13N 6°30E 73 C10
Mauritania ■ Africa 20°50N 10°0W 134 E3
Mauritius ■ Ind. Oc. 20°0S 57°0E 141 d
Mauron France 48°9N 2°18W 70 D4
Maurs France 44°43N 2°12E 72 D6
Mauston U.S.A. 43°48N 90°5W 172 D8
Mauterndorf Austria 47°9N 13°40E 78 D6
Mauthen Austria 46°40N 13°0E 78 E6
Mauvezin France 43°44N 0°53E 72 E4
Mauzé-sur-le-Mignon
France 46°12N 0°41W 72 B3
Mavli India 24°45N 73°55E 124 G5
Mavoko = Athi River
Kenya 1°28S 36°58E 142 C4
Mavrovë Albania 40°26N 19°32E 96 F3
Mavrovo △ Macedonia 41°36N 20°45E 96 E4
Mavuradonha Mts.
Zimbabwe 16°30S 31°30E 143 F3
Mawa
Dem. Rep. of the Congo 2°45N 26°40E 142 B2
Mawai India 22°30N 81°4E 125 H9
Mawana India 29°6N 77°58E 124 E7
Mawand Pakistan 29°33N 68°38E 124 E3
Mawat Iraq 35°54N 45°24E 105 E11
Mawjib, W. al →
Jordan 31°28N 35°36E 130 D4
Mawkmai Burma 20°14N 97°37E 123 J20
Mawlaik Burma 23°40N 94°26E 123 H19
Mawlamyine = Moulmein
Burma 16°30N 97°40E 123 L20
Mawqaq Si. Arabia 27°25N 41°8E 128 E4
Mawson Antarctica 67°30S 62°53E 55 C6
Mawson Coast Antarctica 68°30S 63°0E 55 C6
Mawson Pk. Heard I. 53°6S 73°31E 146 K6
Max U.S.A. 47°49N 101°18W 172 B3
Maxcanú Mexico 20°35N 90°0W 181 C6
Maxesibeni S. Africa 30°49S 29°23E 145 D4
Maxeys U.S.A. 33°45N 83°11W 178 B6
Maxhamish L. Canada 59°50N 123°17W 162 B4
Maxixe Mozam. 23°54S 35°17E 145 B6
Maxville Canada 45°17N 74°51W 175 A10
Maxwell N.Z. 39°51S 174°49E 154 F3
Maxwell U.S.A. 39°17N 122°11W 170 F4
Maxwelton Australia 20°43S 142°41E 150 C3
May, C. U.S.A. 38°56N 74°58W 173 F16
May Pen Jamaica 17°58N 77°15W 182 a
Maya → Russia 60°28N 134°28E 107 D14
Maya, Costa Mexico 18°44N 87°42W 181 D7
Maya Mts. Belize 16°30N 89°0W 181 D7
Mayabandar India 12°56N 92°56E 127 H11
Mayaguana I.
Bahamas 22°30N 72°44W 183 B5
Mayaguana Passage
Bahamas 22°32N 73°15W 183 B5
Mayagüez Puerto Rico 18°12N 67°9W 183 d
Mayahi Niger 13°58N 7°40E 139 C6
Mayaky Ukraine 47°26N 29°33E 81 C14
Mayals = Maials Spain 41°22N 0°30E 90 D5
Mayāmey Iran 36°24N 55°42E 129 B7
Mayang China 27°53N 109°49E 116 D7
Mayanup Australia 33°57S 116°27E 149 F2
Mayapán Mexico 20°29N 89°11W 181 C7
Mayarí Cuba 20°40N 75°41W 183 B4
Mayaro Trin. & Tob. 10°17N 61°0W 187 K15
Mayaro B.
Trin. & Tob. 10°14N 60°59W 187 K16
Mayavaram = Mayiladuthurai
India 11°3N 79°42E 127 J4
Maybell U.S.A. 40°31N 108°5W 168 F9
Maybole U.K. 55°21N 4°42W 65 F4
Maydān Iraq 34°55N 45°37E 105 E11

Maydan *Ukraine* 48°36N 23°29E **81** B8
Mayen *Germany* 50°19N 7°13E **77** E3
Mayenne *France* 48°20N 0°38W **70** D6
Mayenne □ *France* 48°10N 0°40W **70** D6
Mayenne → *France* 47°30N 0°32W **70** E6
Mayer *U.S.A.* 34°24N 112°14W **169** J7
Mayerthorpe *Canada* 53°57N 115°8W **162** C5
Mayesville *U.S.A.* 34°0N 80°12W **178** A9
Mayfield *Ky., U.S.A.* 36°44N 88°38W **172** G9
Mayfield *N.Y., U.S.A.* 43°6N 74°16W **175** C10
Mayhill *U.S.A.* 32°53N 105°29W **169** K11
Mayiladuthurai *India* 11°3N 79°42E **127** J4
Maykop *Russia* 44°35N 40°10E **87** H5
Mayma *Russia* 52°3N 85°55E **109** B11
Maymyo *Burma* 22°2N 96°28E **120** A1
Maynard *Mass.,
U.S.A.* 42°26N 71°27W **175** D13
Maynard *Wash.,
U.S.A.* 47°59N 122°55W **170** C4
Maynard Hills
Australia 28°28S 119°49E **149** E2
Mayne → *Australia* 23°40S 141°55E **150** C3
Maynooth *Canada* 45°13N 77°56W **174** A7
Maynooth *Ireland* 53°23N 6°34W **64** C5
Mayo *Canada* 63°38N 135°57W **160** E4
Mayo *U.S.A.* 30°3N 83°10W **178** E6
Mayo □ *Ireland* 53°53N 9°3W **64** C2
Mayo → *Argentina* 45°45S 69°45W **192** C2
Mayo → *Peru* 6°38S 76°15W **188** B2
Mayo Daga *Nigeria* 6°59N 11°25E **139** D7
Mayo Faran *Nigeria* 8°57N 12°4E **139** D7
Mayon Volcano *Phil.* 13°15N 123°41E **119** B6
Mayor Buratovich
Argentina 39°15S 62°37W **192** A4
Mayor I. *N.Z.* 37°16S 176°17E **154** D5
Mayorga *Spain* 42°10N 5°16W **88** C5
Mayotte ☑ *Ind. Oc.* 12°50S 45°10E **141** a
Mayqayyng *Kazakhstan* 51°27N 75°47E **109** B9
Maysān □ *Iraq* 31°55N 47°15E **128** D5
Mayskiy *Russia* 43°47N 44°2E **87** J7
Maysville *U.S.A.* 38°39N 83°46W **173** F12
Mayu *Indonesia* 1°30N 126°30E **119** D7
Mayuram = Mayiladuthurai
India 11°3N 79°42E **127** J4
Mayville *N. Dak.,
U.S.A.* 47°30N 97°20W **172** B5
Mayville *N.Y., U.S.A.* 42°15N 79°30W **174** D5
Mazabuka *Zambia* 15°52S 27°44E **143** F2
Mazagán = El Jadida
Morocco 33°11N 8°17W **136** B2
Mazagão *Brazil* 0°7S 51°16W **187** D8
Mazamet *France* 43°30N 2°20E **72** E6
Mazán *Peru* 3°30S 73°0W **186** D4
Māzandarān □ *Iran* 36°30N 52°0E **129** B7
Mazapil *Mexico* 24°39N 101°34W **180** C4
Mazar *China* 36°32N 77°1E **109** E9
Mazar, O. → *Algeria* 31°50N 1°36E **136** B4
Mazār-e Sharīf *Afghan.* 36°41N 67°0E **128** B2
Mazara del Vallo *Italy* 37°39N 12°35E **94** E5
Mazarredo *Argentina* 47°10S 66°50W **192** C3
Mazarrón *Spain* 37°38N 1°19W **91** H3
Mazarrón, G. de *Spain* 37°27N 1°19W **91** H3
Mazaruni → *Guyana* 6°25N 58°35W **186** B7
Mazatán *Mexico* 29°0N 110°8W **180** B2
Mazatenango
Guatemala 14°35N 91°30W **182** D1
Mazatlán *Mexico* 23°13N 106°25W **180** C3
Mažeikiai *Lithuania* 56°20N 22°20E **82** B9
Māzhān *Iran* 32°30N 59°0E **129** C8
Mazinān *Iran* 36°19N 56°56E **129** B8
Mazo Cruz *Peru* 16°45S 69°44W **188** G5
Mazoe *Mozam.* 16°42S 33°7E **143** F3
Mazoe → *Mozam.* 16°20S 33°30E **143** F3
Mazowe *Zimbabwe* 17°28S 30°58E **143** F3
Mazowieckie □ *Poland* 52°40N 21°0E **83** F8
Mazurski, Pojezierze
Poland 53°50N 21°0E **82** E7
Mazyr *Belarus* 51°59N 29°15E **75** B15
Mba *Fiji* 17°33S 177°41E **154** a
Mbaba *Senegal* 14°59N 16°44W **138** C1
Mbabane *Swaziland* 26°18S 31°6E **145** D5
Mbagne *Mauritania* 16°6N 14°47W **138** B2
M'bahiakro *Ivory C.* 7°33N 4°19W **138** D4
Mbaïki *C.A.R.* 3°53N 18°1E **140** D3
Mbala *Zambia* 8°46S 31°24E **143** D3
Mbalabala *Zimbabwe* 20°27S 29°3E **145** B4
Mbale *Uganda* 1°8N 34°12E **142** B3
Mbalmayo *Cameroon* 3°33N 11°33E **139** E7
Mbam → *Cameroon* 4°24N 11°17E **139** D7
Mbamba Bay *Tanzania* 11°13S 34°49E **143** E3
Mbandaka
Dem. Rep. of the Congo 0°1N 18°18E **140** D3
Mbanga *Cameroon* 4°30N 9°33E **139** E6
Mbanza Congo *Angola* 6°18S 14°16E **140** F2
Mbanza Ngungu
Dem. Rep. of the Congo 5°12S 14°53E **140** F2
Mbarangandu *Tanzania* 10°11S 36°48E **143** D4
Mbarara *Uganda* 0°35S 30°40E **142** C3
Mbatto *Ivory C.* 6°28N 4°22W **138** D4
Mbengga = Beqa *Fiji* 18°23S 178°8E **154** a
Mbenkuru → *Tanzania* 9°25S 39°50E **143** D4
Mberengwa *Zimbabwe* 20°29S 29°57E **145** B4
Mberengwa, Mt.
Zimbabwe 20°37S 29°55E **143** G2
Mberubu *Nigeria* 6°10N 7°38E **139** D6
Mbesuma *Zambia* 10°0S 32°2E **143** E3
Mbeya *Tanzania* 8°54S 33°29E **143** D3
Mbeya □ *Tanzania* 8°15S 33°30E **142** D3
Mbhashe → *S. Africa* 32°15S 28°54E **145** E4
Mbinga *Tanzania* 10°50S 35°0E **143** E4
Mbini = Río Muni □
Eq. Guin. 1°30N 10°0E **140** D2
Mbizi *Zimbabwe* 21°23S 31°1E **143** G3
Mbombela *S. Africa* 25°49S 30°30E **145** D5
M'bonge *Cameroon* 4°33N 9°5E **139** E6
Mboro *Senegal* 15°9N 16°54W **138** C1
Mbouda *Cameroon* 5°38N 10°15E **139** D7
M'boukou, L. de
Cameroon 6°23N 12°50E **139** D7
Mboune *Senegal* 14°42N 13°34W **138** C2
Mbour *Senegal* 14°22N 16°54W **138** C1
Mbout *Mauritania* 16°1N 12°38W **138** B2
Mbuji-Mayi
Dem. Rep. of the Congo 6°9S 23°40E **142** D1
Mbulu *Tanzania* 3°45S 35°30E **142** C4
Mburucuyá *Argentina* 28°1S 58°14W **190** B4
Mburucuyá △
Argentina 28°1S 58°12W **190** B4
Mcherrah *Algeria* 27°0N 4°30W **136** C3
Mchinga *Tanzania* 9°44S 39°45E **143** D4

Mchinji *Malawi* 13°47S 32°58E **143** E3
Mdantsane *S. Africa* 32°56S 27°46E **145** D4
Mead, L. *U.S.A.* 36°0N 114°44W **171** J12
Meade *U.S.A.* 37°17N 100°20W **172** G3
Meade River = Atqasuk
U.S.A. 70°28N 157°24W **166** A8
Meadow Lake *Canada* 54°10N 108°26W **163** C7
Meadow Lake △
Canada 54°27N 109°0W **163** C7
Meadow Valley Wash →
U.S.A. 36°40N 114°34W **171** J12
Meadville *U.S.A.* 41°39N 80°9W **174** E4
Meaford *Canada* 44°36N 80°35W **174** B4
Meakan Dake *Japan* 45°15N 144°0E **112** C11
Mealhada *Portugal* 40°22N 8°27W **88** E2
Mealy Mts. *Canada* 53°10N 58°0W **165** B8
Meander River *Canada* 59°2N 117°42W **162** B5
Mearim → *Brazil* 3°4S 44°35W **189** A2
Meath □ *Ireland* 53°40N 6°57W **64** C5
Meath Park *Canada* 53°27N 105°22W **163** C7
Meaulne *France* 46°36N 2°36E **71** F9
Meaux *France* 48°58N 2°50E **71** D9
Mebechi-Gawa →
Japan 40°31N 141°31E **112** D10
Mebulu, Tanjung
Indonesia 8°50S 115°5E **119** K18
Mecanhelas *Mozam.* 15°12S 35°54E **143** F4
Mecca = Makkah
Si. Arabia 21°30N 39°54E **137** C4
Mecca *U.S.A.* 33°34N 116°5W **171** M10
Mechanicsburg *U.S.A.* 40°13N 77°1W **174** F8
Mechanicville *U.S.A.* 42°54N 73°41W **175** D11
Mechelen *Belgium* 51°2N 4°29E **69** C4
Mecheria *Algeria* 33°35N 0°18W **136** B3
Mechernich *Germany* 50°35N 6°39E **76** E2
Mechetinskaya *Russia* 46°45N 40°32E **87** G5
Mechra Bel Ksiri
Morocco 34°34N 5°57W **136** B2
Mechra Benâbbou
Morocco 32°39N 7°48W **136** B2
Mecidiye *Turkey* 40°38N 26°32E **97** F10
Mecitözü *Turkey* 40°32N 35°17E **104** B6
Mecklenburg *Germany* 53°33N 11°40E **74** B7
Mecklenburg-Vorpommern □
Germany 53°45N 12°15E **76** B8
Mecklenburger Bucht
Germany 54°20N 11°40E **76** A7
Meconta *Mozam.* 14°59S 39°50E **143** E4
Mecsek *Hungary* 46°10N 18°18E **80** D3
Mecubúri *Mozam.* 14°39S 38°54E **143** E4
Mecúfi *Mozam.* 13°20S 40°32E **143** E5
Mēda *Portugal* 40°57N 7°18W **88** E3
Medak *India* 18°1N 78°15E **126** E4
Medan *Indonesia* 3°40N 98°38E **118** D1
Médanos *Argentina* 38°50S 62°42W **192** A4
Médanos de Coro △
Venezuela 11°35N 69°44W **183** D6
Medanosa, Pta.
Argentina 48°8S 66°0W **192** C3
Medart *U.S.A.* 30°5N 84°23W **178** E5
Medawachchiya
Sri Lanka 8°30N 80°30E **127** K5
Medchal *India* 17°37N 78°29E **126** F4
Mede *Italy* 45°6N 8°44E **92** C5
Médéa *Algeria* 36°12N 2°50E **136** A4
Médéa □ *Algeria* 36°0N 3°0E **136** A4
Mededa *Bos.-H.* 43°44N 19°10E **80** G4
Medeiros Neto *Brazil* 17°20S 40°14W **189** D2
Medellín *Colombia* 6°15N 75°35W **186** B3
Medelpad *Sweden* 62°33N 16°30E **62** B10
Medemblik *Neths.* 52°46N 5°8E **69** B5
Médenine *Tunisia* 33°21N 10°30E **136** B6
Médenine □ *Tunisia* 32°20N 10°0E **136** B6
Mederdra *Mauritania* 17°0N 15°38W **138** B1
Medford *Mass., U.S.A.* 42°25N 71°7W **175** D13
Medford *Oreg., U.S.A.* 42°19N 122°52W **168** E2
Medford *Wis., U.S.A.* 45°9N 90°20W **172** C8
Medgidia *Romania* 44°15N 28°19E **81** F13
Media Agua *Argentina* 31°58S 68°25W **190** C2
Media Luna *Argentina* 34°45S 66°44W **190** C2
Medianeira *Brazil* 25°17S 54°5W **191** B5
Mediaș *Romania* 46°9N 24°22E **81** D9
Medicina *Italy* 44°28N 11°38E **93** D8
Medicine Bow
U.S.A. 41°54N 106°12W **168** F10
Medicine Bow Mts.
U.S.A. 40°40N 106°0W **168** F10
Medicine Hat *Canada* 50°0N 110°45W **163** D6
Medicine Lake
U.S.A. 48°30N 104°30W **168** B11
Medicine Lodge *U.S.A.* 37°17N 98°35W **172** G4
Medina = Al Madīnah
Si. Arabia 24°35N 39°52E **128** E3
Medina *Brazil* 16°15S 41°29W **189** D2
Medina *N. Dak., U.S.A.* 46°54N 99°18W **172** B4
Medina *N.Y., U.S.A.* 43°13N 78°23W **174** C6
Medina *Ohio, U.S.A.* 41°8N 81°52W **174** E3
Medina → *U.S.A.* 29°16N 98°29W **176** G5
Medina de Pomar *Spain* 42°56N 3°29W **88** C7
Medina de Ríoseco *Spain* 41°53N 5°3W **88** D5
Medina del Campo *Spain* 41°18N 4°55W **88** D6
Médina Gounas *Senegal* 13°8N 13°49W **138** C2
Medina L. *U.S.A.* 29°32N 98°56W **176** G5
Medina Sidonia *Spain* 36°28N 5°57W **89** J5
Medinaceli *Spain* 41°12N 2°30W **90** D2
Medinipur *India* 22°25N 87°21E **125** H12
Medio-Campidano □
Italy 39°30N 8°30E **94** C1
Mediterranean Sea *Europe* 35°0N 15°0E **58** H7
Médoc *France* 45°10N 0°50W **72** D3
Medulin *Croatia* 44°49N 13°55E **92** D10
Medveda *Serbia* 42°50N 21°32E **81** C10
Medvedevo *Russia* 56°37N 47°47E **86** B8
Medveditsa → *Tver,
Russia* 57°5N 37°30E **84** D9
Medveditsa → *Volgograd,
Russia* 49°35N 42°41E **86** F6
Medvedok *Russia* 57°20N 50°1E **86** B10
Medvezhi, Ostrava
Russia 71°0N 161°0E **107** B17
Medvezhyegorsk *Russia* 63°0N 34°25E **106** C4
Medway □ *U.K.* 51°25N 0°32E **67** F8
Medway → *U.K.* 51°27N 0°46E **67** F8
Medzev *Slovak Rep.* 48°43N 20°55E **79** C13

Meeker *U.S.A.* 40°2N 107°55W **168** F10
Meeniyan *Australia* 38°35S 146°3E **153** E7
Meersburg *Germany* 47°41N 9°16E **77** H5
Meerut *India* 29°1N 77°42E **124** E7
Meeteetse *U.S.A.* 44°9N 108°52W **168** D9
Mega *Ethiopia* 3°57N 38°19E **131** G2
Megalo Chorio *Greece* 36°27N 27°24E **99** E9
Megalonisos *Greece* 38°0N 24°15E **98** D6
Megalopoli *Greece* 37°25N 22°7E **98** D4
Meganisi *Greece* 38°38N 20°46E **98** C2
Megara *Greece* 37°58N 23°22E **98** D5
Megasini *India* 21°38N 86°21E **125** J12
Megdovas = Tavropos →
Greece 39°10N 21°45E **98** B3
Megève *France* 45°51N 6°37E **73** C10
Meghalaya □ *India* 25°50N 91°0E **123** G17
Meghna → *Bangla.* 22°50N 90°50E **123** H17
Megion *Russia* 61°3N 76°6E **106** C8
Mégiscane, L. *Canada* 48°35N 75°55W **164** C4
Megisti *Greece* 36°8N 29°34E **99** E11
Megra *Russia* 60°11N 37°14E **84** B9
Mehadia *Romania* 44°56N 22°23E **80** F7
Mehaïguene, O. →
Algeria 32°15N 2°59E **136** B4
Meharry, Mt.
Australia 22°59S 118°35E **148** D2
Mehedeby *Sweden* 60°27N 17°25E **62** D11
Mehedinți □ *Romania* 44°40N 22°45E **80** F7
Meheisa *Sudan* 19°38N 32°57E **137** D3
Mehekar *India* 20°9N 76°34E **126** D3
Mehlville *U.S.A.* 38°31N 90°19W **172** F8
Mehmetçik = Galateia
Cyprus 35°25N 34°4E **101** D13
Mehndawal *India* 26°58N 83°5E **125** F10
Mehr Jān *Iran* 33°50N 55°6E **129** C7
Mehrābād *Iran* 36°53N 47°55E **105** C12
Mehrābān *Iran* 38°4N 47°7E **105** C12
Mehrān *Iran* 33°7N 46°10E **105** F12
Mehrān → *Iran* 26°45N 55°26E **129** E7
Mehrgarh *Pakistan* 29°30N 67°30E **124** E2
Mehrīz *Iran* 31°35N 54°28E **129** D7
Mehun-sur-Yèvre *France* 47°10N 2°13E **71** E9
Mei Jiang → *China* 24°25N 116°35E **117** E11
Mei Xian *China* 34°18N 107°55E **114** G4
Meicheng *China* 29°29N 119°16E **117** C12
Meichengzhen *China* 28°9N 111°40E **117** C8
Meichuan *China* 30°8N 115°31E **117** B10
Meighen I. *Canada* 80°0N 99°30W **161** B12
Meigs *U.S.A.* 31°4N 84°6W **178** D5
Meigu *China* 28°16N 103°20E **116** C4
Meihekou *China* 42°32N 125°40E **115** C13
Meiktila *Burma* 20°53N 95°54E **123** J19
Meili Xue Shan *China* 28°30N 98°39E **116** C2
Meimyu = Maymyo
Burma 22°2N 96°28E **120** A1
Meinerzhagen *Germany* 51°6N 7°38E **76** D3
Meiningen *Germany* 50°34N 10°25E **76** E6
Meio → *Brazil* 13°36S 44°7W **189** D3
Meiringen *Switz.* 46°43N 8°12E **77** J4
Meishan *China* 30°3N 103°23E **116** B4
Meissen *Germany* 51°9N 13°29E **76** D9
Ménaka *Mali* 15°59N 2°18E **139** B5
Meissner-Kaufunger Wald ○
Germany 51°16N 9°45E **76** D5
Meitan *China* 27°45N 107°29E **116** D6
Meizhou *China* 24°16N 116°6E **117** E11
Meja *India* 25°9N 82°7E **125** G10
Mejillones *Chile* 23°10S 70°30W **190** A1
Mekele *Ethiopia* 13°33N 39°30E **131** E2
Mekerghene, Sebkra
Algeria 26°21N 1°30E **136** C4
Mékhé *Senegal* 15°7N 16°38W **138** C1
Mekhtar *Pakistan* 30°30N 69°15E **122** D6
Meknès *Morocco* 33°57N 5°33W **136** B2
Meknès-Tafilalet □
Morocco 33°3N 5°35W **136** B2
Meko *Nigeria* 7°27N 2°52E **139** D5
Mekong → *Asia* 9°30N 106°15E **121** H6
Mekongga *Indonesia* 3°39S 121°15E **119** E6
Mekrou → *Benin* 12°25N 2°50E **139** C5
Mekvari = Kür →
Azerbaijan 39°29N 49°15E **105** C13
Mel *Italy* 46°4N 12°5E **93** B9
Melagiri Hills *India* 12°20N 77°30E **127** H3
Melah, Oued el →
Algeria 32°20N 2°28E **136** B4
Melaka *Malaysia* 2°15N 102°15E **121** L4
Melaka □ *Malaysia* 2°15N 102°15E **121** L4
Melambes *Greece* 35°8N 24°40E **101** D6
Melanesia *Pac. Oc.* 4°0S 155°0E **156** H7
Melanesian Basin
Pac. Oc. 0°5N 160°35E **156** G8
Melapalaiyam *India* 8°39N 77°44E **127** K3
Melaya *Indonesia* 8°17S 114°30E **119** J17
Melbourne *Australia* 37°48S 144°58E **153** E6
Melbourne *U.S.A.* 28°5N 80°37W **179** G9
Melchor Múzquiz
Mexico 27°53N 101°31W **180** B4
Melchor Ocampo
Mexico 24°51N 101°39W **180** C4
Mēldola *Italy* 44°7N 12°5E **93** D9
Meldorf *Germany* 54°5N 9°5E **76** A5
Melegnano *Italy* 45°21N 9°19E **92** C6
Melekeok *Palau* 7°27N 134°38E **156** G5
Melenci *Serbia* 45°32N 20°20E **80** E5
Melenki *Russia* 55°20N 41°37E **86** C5
Meleuz *Russia* 52°58N 55°55E **108** B5
Mélèzes → *Canada* 57°40N 69°29W **164** A5
Melfi *Italy* 41°0N 15°39E **95** B8
Melfort *Canada* 52°50N 104°37W **163** C8
Melfort *Zimbabwe* 18°0S 31°25E **143** F3
Melgaço *Portugal* 42°2N 8°18E **88** B2
Melgar de Fernamental
Spain 42°27N 4°17W **88** C6
Melhus *Norway* 63°17N 10°18E **60** E14
Melide *Spain* 42°55N 8°1W **88** C2
Meligales *Greece* 37°15N 21°59E **98** D3
Melilla *N. Afr.* 35°21N 2°57W **134** A5
Melilli *Italy* 37°11N 15°7E **95** E8
Melipilla *Chile* 33°42S 71°15W **190** C1
Melissa *Canada* 46°4N 79°49W **174** A6
Melissa, Akra *Greece* 35°6N 24°33E **101** D6
Melissa Oros *Greece* 39°26N 26°4E **99** D8
Melita *Canada* 49°15N 101°0W **163** D8

Mellbystrand *Sweden* 56°30N 12°56E **63** H6
Melle *France* 46°14N 0°10W **72** B3
Melle *Germany* 52°12N 8°20E **76** C4
Mellègue, O. → *Tunisia* 36°36N 9°14E **136** A5
Mellen *U.S.A.* 46°20N 90°40W **172** B8
Mellerud *Sweden* 58°41N 12°28E **63** F6
Mellette *U.S.A.* 45°9N 98°30W **172** C4
Mellid = Melide *Spain* 42°55N 8°1W **88** C2
Mellizo Sur, Cerro
Chile 48°33S 73°10W **192** C2
Mellrichstadt *Germany* 50°25N 10°17E **76** E6
Melnik *Bulgaria* 41°30N 23°25E **96** E7
Mělník *Czech Rep.* 50°22N 14°23E **78** A7
Melo *Uruguay* 32°20S 54°10W **191** C5
Melolo *Indonesia* 9°53S 120°40E **119** F6
Melouprey *Cambodia* 13°48N 105°16E **120** F5
Melrhir, Chott *Algeria* 34°13N 6°30E **136** B5
Melrose *Australia* 32°42S 146°57E **153** E7
Melrose *U.K.* 55°36N 2°43W **65** F6
Melrose *Minn., U.S.A.* 45°40N 94°49W **172** C6
Melrose *N. Mex.,
U.S.A.* 34°26N 103°38W **169** J12
Melstone *U.S.A.* 46°36N 107°52W **168** C10
Melton *Australia* 37°41S 144°35E **152** B6
Melton Mowbray *U.K.* 52°47N 0°54W **66** E7
Melun *France* 48°32N 2°39E **71** D9
Melur *India* 10°2N 78°23E **127** J4
Melut *Sudan* 10°27N 32°13E **137** F3
Melville *Canada* 50°55N 102°50W **163** C8
Melville, C. *Australia* 14°11S 144°30E **150** A3
Melville B. *Australia* 12°0S 136°45E **150** A2
Melville B. *Greenland* 75°30N 63°0W **57** B4
Melville I. *Australia* 11°30S 131°0E **148** B5
Melville I. *Canada* 75°30N 112°0W **161** B9
Melville Pen. *Canada* 68°0N 84°0W **161** D15
Melvin, Lough *Ireland* 54°26N 8°10W **64** B3
Mélykút *Hungary* 46°11N 19°25E **80** D4
Memaliaj *Albania* 40°25N 19°56E **98** B3
Memba *Mozam.* 14°11S 40°30E **143** E5
Memboro *Indonesia* 9°30S 119°30E **148** A2
Membrilla *Spain* 38°59N 3°21W **89** G7
Memel = Klaipėda
Lithuania 55°43N 21°10E **82** C8
Memel *S. Africa* 27°38S 29°36E **145** C4
Memmingen *Germany* 47°58N 10°10E **77** H6
Mempawah *Indonesia* 0°30N 109°5E **118** D3
Memphis *Egypt* 29°52N 31°12E **137** F7
Memphis *Mich., U.S.A.* 42°54N 82°46W **174** D2
Memphis *Tenn., U.S.A.* 35°8N 90°2W **177** D9
Memphis *Tex., U.S.A.* 34°44N 100°33W **176** D4
Memphrémagog, L.
N. Amer. 45°8N 72°17W **175** B12
Mena *Ukraine* 51°31N 32°13E **85** G7
Mena *U.S.A.* 34°35N 94°15W **176** D7
Menado = Manado
Indonesia 1°29N 124°51E **119** D6
Menai Strait *U.K.* 53°11N 4°13W **66** D3
Menan = Chao Phraya →
Thailand 13°32N 100°36E **120** F3
Menard *U.S.A.* 30°55N 99°47W **176** F5
Menard Fracture Zone
Pac. Oc. 43°0S 97°0W **157** M18
Mendaña Fracture Zone
Pac. Oc. 16°0S 91°0W **157** J18
Mendawai → *Indonesia* 3°30S 113°0E **118** E4
Mende *France* 44°31N 3°30E **72** D7
Mendeleyev Ridge
Arctic 80°0N 178°0W **54** B17
Menden *Germany* 51°26N 7°47E **76** D3
Menderes *Turkey* 38°14N 27°8E **99** C9
Mendhar *India* 33°35N 74°10E **125** C6
Mendip Hills *U.K.* 51°17N 2°40W **67** F5
Mendocino *U.S.A.* 39°19N 123°48W **168** G2
Mendocino, C. *U.S.A.* 40°26N 124°25W **168** F1
Mendocino Fracture Zone
Pac. Oc. 40°0N 142°0W **157** D13
Mendooran *Australia* 31°50S 149°6E **153** A8
Mendota *Calif., U.S.A.* 36°45N 120°23W **170** J6
Mendota *Ill., U.S.A.* 41°33N 89°7W **172** E9
Mendoyo *Indonesia* 8°23S 114°42E **119** J17
Mendoza *Argentina* 32°50S 68°52W **190** C2
Mendoza □ *Argentina* 33°0S 69°0W **190** C2
Mene Grande *Venezuela* 9°49N 70°56W **186** B4
Menemen *Turkey* 38°34N 27°3E **99** C9
Menen *Belgium* 50°47N 3°7E **69** D3
Menéndez, L. *Argentina* 42°40S 71°51W **192** B2
Menfi *Italy* 37°36N 12°58E **94** E5
Mengcheng *China* 33°12N 116°36E **116** H9
Mengdingjie *China* 23°31N 98°58E **116** F2
Mengeš *Slovenia* 46°10N 14°35E **93** B11
Menggala *Indonesia* 4°30S 105°15E **118** E3
Menghai *China* 21°49N 100°33E **116** G3
Mengibar *Spain* 37°58N 3°48W **89** H7
Mengjin *China* 34°55N 112°45E **116** G7
Mengla *China* 21°20N 101°25E **116** G3
Menglian *China* 22°21N 99°27E **116** F2
Mengshan *China* 24°14N 110°55E **117** E8
Mengyin *China* 35°40N 117°58E **115** G9
Mengzhe *China* 22°15N 100°15E **116** G3
Mengzi *China* 23°20N 103°22E **116** F5
Menifee *U.S.A.* 33°41N 117°10W **171** M9
Menihek *Canada* 54°28N 56°36W **165** B6
Menihek L. *Canada* 54°0N 67°0W **165** B6
Menin = Menen *Belgium* 50°47N 3°7E **69** D3
Menindee *Australia* 32°20S 142°25E **152** B5
Menindee L. *Australia* 32°20S 142°25E **152** B5
Menjangan, Pulau
Indonesia 8°7S 114°31E **119** J17
Menkrour *Algeria* 26°27N 8°9E **136** C5
Menlo Park *U.S.A.* 37°27N 122°12W **170** H4
Menominee *U.S.A.* 45°6N 87°37W **172** C10
Menominee → *U.S.A.* 45°6N 87°36W **172** C10
Menomonie *U.S.A.* 44°53N 91°55W **172** C8
Menongue *Angola* 14°48S 17°52E **141** H3
Menorca *Spain* 40°0N 4°0E **100** B11
Menorca ✈ **(MAH)** *Spain* 39°50N 4°16E **100** B11
Mentakab *Malaysia* 3°29N 102°21E **121** L4
Mentawai, Kepulauan
Indonesia 2°0S 99°0E **118** E1
Menton *France* 43°50N 7°29E **73** E11
Mentor *U.S.A.* 41°40N 81°21W **174** E3
Menzel-Bourguiba
Tunisia 37°9N 9°49E **136** A5

Menzel-Chaker *Tunisia* 35°0N 10°26E **136** B6
Menzies *Australia* 29°40S 121°2E **149** E3
Meob B. *Namibia* 24°25S 14°34E **144** B1
Meoqui *Mexico* 28°17N 105°29W **180** B3
Mepaco *Mozam.* 15°57S 30°48E **143** F3
Meppel *Neths.* 52°42N 6°12E **69** B6
Meppen *Germany* 52°42N 7°17E **76** C3
Mequinenza *Spain* 41°22N 0°17E **90** D5
Mequinenza, Embalse de
Spain 41°25N 0°15E **90** D5
Mer *France* 47°42N 1°30E **70** E8
Merak *Indonesia* 6°10N 106°26E **119** F12
Meramangye, L.
Australia 28°25S 132°13E **149** E5
Meran = Merano *Italy* 46°40N 11°9E **93** B8
Merano *Italy* 46°40N 11°9E **93** B8
Merate *Italy* 45°42N 9°25E **92** C6
Merauke *Indonesia* 8°29S 140°24E **119** F10
Merbein *Australia* 34°10S 142°2E **153** E5
Merca = Marka *Somalia* 1°48N 44°50E **131** G3
Mercantour △ *France* 44°16N 6°43E **73** D10
Mercato Saraceno *Italy* 43°57N 12°12E **93** E9
Merced *U.S.A.* 37°18N 120°29W **170** H6
Merced → *U.S.A.* 37°21N 120°59W **170** H6
Merced Pk. *U.S.A.* 37°36N 119°24W **170** H7
Mercedes *B. Aires.,
Argentina* 34°40S 59°30W **190** C4
Mercedes *Corrientes,
Argentina* 29°10S 58°5W **190** B4
Mercedes *San Luis,
Argentina* 33°40S 65°21W **190** C2
Mercedes *Uruguay* 33°12S 58°0W **190** C4
Merceditas *Chile* 28°20S 70°35W **190** B1
Mercer *N.Z.* 37°16S 175°5E **154** D4
Mercer *U.S.A.* 41°14N 80°15W **174** E4
Mercer Island *U.S.A.* 47°34N 122°13W **170** C4
Mercier *Bolivia* 10°42S 68°5W **188** C4
Mercury *U.S.A.* 36°40N 115°59W **171** J11
Mercury B. *N.Z.* 36°48S 175°45E **154** C4
Mercury Is. *N.Z.* 36°37S 175°52E **154** C4
Mercy, C. *Canada* 65°0N 63°30W **161** E19
Merdrignac *France* 48°11N 2°27W **70** D4
Mere *U.K.* 51°6N 2°16W **67** F5
Merebuk, Gunung
Indonesia 8°13S 114°39E **119** J17
Meredith *Australia* 37°49S 144°5E **152** B6
Meredith, C. *Falk. Is.* 52°15S 60°40W **192** D4
Meredith, L. *U.S.A.* 35°43N 101°33W **176** D4
Merefa *Ukraine* 49°48N 36°3E **85** H9
Merei *Romania* 45°7N 26°43E **81** E11
Merga = Nukheila
Sudan 19°1N 26°21E **137** D2
Mergui *Burma* 12°26N 98°34E **120** F2
Mergui Arch. = Myeik Kyunzu
Burma 11°30N 97°30E **121** G1
Meriabah *Australia* 34°43S 140°51E **152** C4
Méribel-les-Allues
France 45°25N 6°34E **73** C10
Meric *Turkey* 41°11N 26°25E **97** F10
Meriç → *Turkey* 40°52N 26°12E **97** F10
Mérida *Mexico* 20°58N 89°37W **181** C7
Mérida *Spain* 38°55N 6°25W **89** G4
Mérida *Venezuela* 8°24N 71°8W **186** B4
Mérida, Cord. de
Venezuela 9°0N 71°0W **186** B4
Meriden *U.K.* 52°26N 1°38W **67** E6
Meriden *U.S.A.* 41°32N 72°48W **175** E12
Meridian *Calif., U.S.A.* 39°9N 121°55W **170** F5
Meridian *Ga., U.S.A.* 31°27N 81°23W **178** D8
Meridian *Idaho, U.S.A.* 43°37N 116°24W **168** E5
Meridian *Miss., U.S.A.* 32°22N 88°42W **177** E10
Merimbula *Australia* 36°53S 149°54E **153** E8
Merinda *Australia* 20°2S 148°11E **150** C4
Mering *Germany* 48°16N 10°59E **77** G6
Meringa *Nigeria* 10°44N 12°9E **139** D7
Meringur *Australia* 34°20S 141°19E **152** C4
Merir *Palau* 4°10N 132°30E **119** D8
Merimá *Brazil* 1°15N 54°50W **187** C8
Merke *Kazakhstan* 42°52N 73°6E **108** D8
Merkel *U.S.A.* 32°28N 100°1W **176** E4
Mermaid Reef *Australia* 17°6S 119°36E **148** C2
Meroe *India* 7°33N 93°32E **127** L11
Merowe *Sudan* 18°29N 31°46E **137** D3
Merowe Dam *Sudan* 18°35N 31°56E **137** D3
Merredin *Australia* 31°28S 118°18E **149** F2
Merrick *U.K.* 55°8N 4°28W **65** F4
Merrickville *Canada* 44°55N 75°50W **175** B9
Merrill *Oreg., U.S.A.* 42°1N 121°36W **168** E3
Merrill *Wis., U.S.A.* 45°11N 89°41W **172** C9
Merrimack → *U.S.A.* 42°49N 70°49W **175** D14
Merriman *U.S.A.* 42°55N 101°42W **172** D3
Merritt *Canada* 50°10N 120°45W **162** C4
Merritt Island *U.S.A.* 28°21N 80°42W **179** G9
Merriwa *Australia* 32°6S 150°22E **153** A9
Merriwagga *Australia* 33°47S 145°43E **153** B8
Merry I. *Canada* 55°29N 77°31W **164** A4
Merryville *U.S.A.* 30°45N 93°33W **176** F7
Mersch *Lux.* 49°44N 6°7E **69** E6
Merse → *Italy* 43°5N 11°22E **93** E8
Mersea I. *U.K.* 51°47N 0°58E **67** F8
Merseburg *Germany* 51°22N 11°59E **76** D7
Mersey → *U.K.* 53°25N 3°1W **66** D4
Merseyside □ *U.K.* 53°31N 3°2W **66** D4
Mersin = İçel *Turkey* 36°51N 34°36E **104** D6
Mersing *Malaysia* 2°25N 103°50E **121** L4
Merta *India* 26°39N 74°4E **124** F5
Merta Road *India* 26°43N 73°55E **124** F5
Merthyr Tydfil *U.K.* 51°45N 3°22W **67** F4
Merthyr Tydfil □ *U.K.* 51°46N 3°21W **67** F4
Merti *Kenya* 1°4N 38°40E **142** B4
Mértola *Portugal* 37°40N 7°40W **89** H3
Mertz Glacier
Antarctica 67°30S 144°45E **55** C10
Mertzon *U.S.A.* 31°16N 100°49W **176** F4
Méru *France* 49°13N 2°8E **71** C9
Meru *Tanzania* 3°15S 36°46E **142** C4
Meru △ *Kenya* 0°5N 38°10E **142** B4
Meru Betiri △
Indonesia 8°27S 113°51E **119** H15
Merville *France* 50°38N 2°38E **69** D2
Méry-sur-Seine *France* 48°31N 3°54E **71** D10
Merzifon *Turkey* 40°53N 35°32E **104** B6
Merzig *Germany* 49°26N 6°37E **77** F2
Merzouga, Erg Tin
Algeria 24°0N 11°4E **136** D6
Mesa *U.S.A.* 33°25N 111°50W **169** K8
Mesa Verde △ *U.S.A.* 37°11N 108°29W **169** H9
Mesada = Masada
Israel 31°18N 35°21E **130** D4

Mesagne *Italy* 40°34N 17°48E **95**
Mesanagros *Greece* 36°1N 27°49E **9**
Mesaoria *Cyprus* 35°12N 33°14E **10**
Meschede *Germany* 51°20N 8°18E **7**
Mescit *Turkey* 40°21N 41°11E **10**
Mesgouez, L. *Canada* 51°20N 75°0W **1**
Meshchovsk *Russia* 54°22N 35°17E **8**
Meshchyora △ *Russia* 55°30N 40°0E **8**
Meshchyorsky △ *Russia* 54°50N 41°0E **8**
Meshed = Mashhad
Iran 36°20N 59°35E **1**
Meshgīn Shahr *Iran* 38°30N 47°45E **1**
Meshoppen *U.S.A.* 41°36N 76°3W **1**
Mesilinka → *Canada* 56°6N 124°30W **1**
Meslay-du-Maine *France* 47°58N 0°33W **7**
Mesocco *Switz.* 46°23N 9°12E **7**
Mesopotamia = Al Jazirah
Iraq 33°30N 44°0E **1**
Mesopotamia *U.S.A.* 41°27N 80°57W **1**
Mesopotamo *Greece* 39°14N 20°32E **9**
Mesoraca *Italy* 39°5N 16°48E **9**
Mésou Volimais = Volimes
Greece 37°52N 20°39E **9**
Mesquite *U.S.A.* 36°48N 114°4W **1**
Messaad *Algeria* 34°8N 3°30E **1**
Messac *France* 47°49N 1°50W **7**
Messalo → *Mozam.* 12°25S 39°15E **1**
Messaména *Cameroon* 3°48N 12°49E **1**
Messara, Kolpos *Greece* 35°6N 24°47E **1**
Messier, Canal *Chile* 48°20S 74°33W **1**
Messina = Musina
S. Africa 22°20S 30°5E **1**
Messina *Italy* 38°11N 15°34E **9**
Messina, Str. di *Italy* 38°15N 15°35E **9**
Messina, Stretto di *Italy* 38°15N 15°35E **9**
Messíni *Greece* 37°4N 22°1E **9**
Messiniakos Kolpos
Greece 36°45N 22°5E **9**
Messkirch *Germany* 47°59N 9°7E **7**
Messlingen *Sweden* 62°40N 12°50E **6**
Mesta = Nestos →
Europe 40°54N 24°49E **9**
Mesta, Akra *Greece* 38°16N 25°53E **9**
Mestanza *Spain* 38°35N 4°4W **8**
Mestersvig *Greenland* 72°10N 23°40W **5**
Mestre *Italy* 45°29N 12°15E **9**
Mestre, Espigão *Brazil* 12°30S 46°10W **1**
Mesudiye *Turkey* 40°28N 37°46E **1**
Meta → *S. Amer.* 6°12N 67°28W **1**
Meta Incognita Pen.
Canada 62°45N 68°30W **1**
Metabetchouan
Canada 48°26N 71°52W **1**
Metairie *U.S.A.* 29°59N 90°9W **1**
Metalici, Munţii
Romania 46°15N 22°50E **8**
Metaline Falls *U.S.A.* 48°52N 117°22W **1**
Metallifere, Colline *Italy* 43°10N 11°0E **9**
Metán *Argentina* 25°30S 65°0W **1**
Metangula *Mozam.* 12°40S 34°50E **1**
Metauro → *Italy* 43°50N 13°3E **9**
Metcalf *U.S.A.* 30°43N 83°59W **1**
Metcalfe *Canada* 45°14N 75°28W **1**
Metema *Ethiopia* 12°58N 36°12E **1**
Metengobalame
Mozam. 14°49S 34°30E **1**
Meteora *Greece* 39°43N 21°37E **9**
Methana *Greece* 37°35N 23°23E **9**
Methoni *Greece* 36°49N 21°42E **9**
Methven *N.Z.* 43°38S 171°40E **1**
Metil *Mozam.* 16°24S 39°0E **1**
Metkovets *Bulgaria* 43°37N 23°10E **9**
Metković *Croatia* 43°6N 17°39E **9**
Metlakatla *U.S.A.* 55°8N 131°35W **1**
Metlaoui *Tunisia* 34°24N 8°24E **1**
Metlika *Slovenia* 45°40N 15°20E **9**
Metlili Chaamba *Algeria* 32°5N 3°42E **1**
Metropolis *U.S.A.* 37°9N 88°44W **1**
Metropolitana □ *Chile* 33°30S 70°50W **1**
Metsovo *Greece* 39°48N 21°12E **9**
Metter *U.S.A.* 32°24N 82°3W **1**
Mettuppalaiyam *India* 11°18N 76°59E **1**
Mettur *India* 11°48N 77°47E **1**
Metu *Ethiopia* 8°18N 35°35E **1**
Metz *France* 49°8N 6°10E **7**
Metzingen *Germany* 48°31N 9°17E **7**
Meulaboh *Indonesia* 4°11N 96°3E **1**
Meung-sur-Loire *France* 47°50N 1°40E **7**
Meureudu *Indonesia* 5°19N 96°10E **1**
Meurthe → *France* 48°47N 6°9E **7**
Meurthe-et-Moselle □
France 48°52N 6°0E **7**
Meuse □ *France* 49°8N 5°25E **7**
Meuse → *Europe* 50°45N 5°41E **7**
Meuselwitz *Germany* 51°2N 12°17E **7**
Mexia *U.S.A.* 31°41N 96°29W **1**
Mexiana, I. *Brazil* 0°0 49°30W **1**
Mexicali *Mexico* 32°40N 115°30W **1**
Mexican Plateau
Mexico 25°0N 104°0W **1**
Mexican Water
U.S.A. 36°57N 109°32W **1**
Mexico *Maine, U.S.A.* 44°34N 70°33W **1**
Mexico *Mo., U.S.A.* 39°10N 91°53W **1**
Mexico *N.Y., U.S.A.* 43°28N 76°14W **1**
México □ *Mexico* 19°20N 99°30W **1**
México, Ciudad de
Mexico 19°24N 99°9W **1**
Mexico, G. of *Cent. Amer.* 25°0N 90°0W **1**
Mexico B. *U.S.A.* 43°35N 76°20W **1**
Mexico Beach *U.S.A.* 29°57N 85°25W **1**
Meydān-e Naftūn *Iran* 31°56N 49°18E **1**
Meydānī, Ra's-e *Iran* 25°24N 59°6E **1**
Meyenburg *Germany* 53°19N 12°15W **7**
Meyers Chuck *U.S.A.* 55°45N 132°15W **1**
Meymac *France* 45°32N 2°10E **7**
Meymaneh *Afghan.* 35°53N 64°38E **1**
Meyrueis *France* 44°12N 3°27E **7**
Meyssac *France* 45°3N 1°40E **7**
Mezdra *Bulgaria* 43°12N 23°42E **9**
Mèze *France* 43°25N 3°36E **7**
Mezen *Russia* 65°50N 44°20E **8**
Mezen → *Russia* 65°44N 44°22E **8**
Mézenc, Mt. *France* 44°54N 4°11E **7**
Mezeş, Munţii *Romania* 47°5N 23°5E **8**
Mézin *France* 44°4N 0°16E **7**
Mezhdurechensk
Russia 53°41N 88°3E **1**

hdurechenskiy
ussia 59°36N 65°56E 106 D7
idon-Canon France 49°5N 0°1W 70 C6
ières-en-Brenne
rance 46°49N 1°13E 72 B5
ilhac France 44°49N 4°21E 73 D8
in France 44°4N 0°16E 72 D4
őberény Hungary 46°49N 21°3E 80 D6
őfalva Hungary 46°55N 18°49E 80 D3
őhegyes Hungary 46°19N 20°49E 80 D5
őkövácsháza
ungary 46°25N 20°57E 80 D5
őkövesd Hungary 47°49N 20°35E 80 C5
os France 44°5N 1°10W 72 D2
őtúr Hungary 47°1N 20°41E 80 C5
quital Mexico 23°29N 104°23W 180 C4
zolombardo Italy 46°13N 11°5E 92 B8
lozi → S. Africa 28°25S 32°26E 145 C5
ta Tanzania 8°22S 36°6E 143 D4
in Russia 53°2N 32°50E 85 F7
amid Morocco 29°49N 5°43W 136 C2
aba Hills Zimbabwe 18°30S 30°30E 143 F3
w India 22°33N 75°50E 124 H6
huatlán Mexico 16°20N 96°36W 181 D5
adas Spain 39°9N 5°54W 89 F5
mi Fla., U.S.A. 25°46N 80°11W 179 K9
mi Okla., U.S.A. 36°53N 94°53W 176 C7
mi Tex., U.S.A. 35°42N 100°38W 176 D4
mi Beach U.S.A. 25°47N 80°7W 179 K9
mi Canal U.S.A. 25°45N 80°12W 179 K9
mi Gardens U.S.A. 25°56N 80°15W 179 C1
mi Int. ✈ (MIA)
S.A. 25°48N 80°17W 179 K9
mi Shores U.S.A. 25°51N 80°11W 179 K9
mi Springs U.S.A. 25°49N 80°17W 179 K9
n Xian China 33°10N 106°32E 116 A6
nchi China 34°48N 111°48E 114 G6
ndarreh Iran 35°37N 53°39E 129 C7
ndowāb Iran 37°0N 46°5E 105 D12
ndrivazo Madag. 19°31S 45°29E 141 H9
neh Iran 37°30N 47°40E 105 D12
nning China 28°32N 102°9E 116 C4
nwali Pakistan 32°38N 71°28E 124 C4
nyang China 31°22N 104°47E 116 B5
nzhu China 31°22N 104°47E 116 B5
Ling China 26°5N 107°30E 116 D6
odao Qundao
ina 38°10N 120°45E 115 E11
oli Taiwan 24°37N 120°49E 117 E13
ss Russia 54°59N 60°6E 108 B6
steczko Krajeńskie
land 53°7N 17°1E 83 E4
stko Poland 54°0N 16°58E 82 E3
S. Africa 24°10S 30°48E 145 B5
anopy U.S.A. 29°30N 82°17W 179 F7
isasa Romania 46°7N 24°7E 81 D9
co U.S.A. 27°53N 80°30W 179 H9
cosukee U.S.A. 30°36N 84°3W 178 E5
cosukee, L. U.S.A. 30°33N 83°53W 178 E6
halovce Slovak Rep. 48°47N 21°58E 79 C14
nigan □ U.S.A. 44°0N 85°0W 173 C11
nigan, L. U.S.A. 44°0N 87°0W 172 D10
nigan City U.S.A. 41°43N 86°54W 172 E10
nika Nigeria 10°36N 13°23E 139 C7
nipicoten I. Canada 47°40N 85°40W 164 C2
noacán □ Mexico 19°10N 101°50W 180 D4
nurin Bulgaria 42°9N 27°51E 97 D11
nurinsk Russia 52°58N 40°27E 86 D5
oud St. Lucia 13°49N 60°54W 183 f
onesia Pac. Oc. 11°0N 160°0E 156 G7
onesia, Federated States of ■
c. Oc. 9°0N 150°0E 156 G7
Atlantic Ridge Atl. Oc. 0°0 20°0W 56 J10
Indian Ocean Basin
d. Oc. 10°0S 80°0E 146 F7
Indian Ridge Ind. Oc. 30°0S 75°0E 146 H6
Oceanic Ridge
l. Oc. 42°0S 90°0E 156 M1
Pacific Seamounts
c. Oc. 18°0N 177°0W 156 F10
ai Indonesia 3°0N 107°47E 118 D3
ale Canada 49°25N 103°20W 163 D8
delburg Neths. 51°30N 3°36E 69 C3
delburg Eastern Cape,
Africa 31°30S 25°0E 144 D4
delburg Mpumalanga,
Africa 25°49S 29°28E 145 C4
delfart Denmark 55°30N 9°43E 63 J3
delpos S. Africa 31°55S 20°13E 144 D3
delwit S. Africa 24°51S 27°3E 144 B4
dle Alkali L. U.S.A. 41°27N 120°5W 168 F3
dle America Trench =
uatemala Trench
c. Oc. 14°0N 95°0W 158 H10
dle Andaman I.
dia 12°30N 92°50E 127 H11
dle Bass I. U.S.A. 41°41N 82°48W 174 E2
dle East Asia 35°0N 40°0E 102 E5
dle Fork Feather →
S.A. 38°33N 121°30W 170 F5
dle I. Australia 34°6S 123°11E 149 F3
dle Loup → U.S.A. 41°17N 98°24W 172 E4
dleboro U.S.A. 41°54N 70°55W 175 E14
dleburg Fla., U.S.A. 30°4N 81°52W 178 E8
dleburg Pa., U.S.A. 40°47N 77°3W 174 F7
dleburgh U.S.A. 42°36N 74°20W 175 D10
dlebury U.S.A. 44°1N 73°10W 175 B11
dlefield U.S.A. 41°27N 81°4W 174 E3
dlemarch N.Z. 45°30S 170°9E 155 F5
dlemount
stralia 22°50S 148°40E 150 C4
dleport N.Y.,
S.A. 43°13N 78°29W 174 C6
dleport Ohio, U.S.A. 39°0N 82°3W 173 F12
dlesboro U.S.A. 36°36N 83°43W 173 G12
dlesbrough U.K. 54°35N 1°13W 66 C6
dlesbrough □ U.K. 54°28N 1°13W 66 C6
dlesex Belize 17°2N 88°31W 182 C2
dlesex N.J., U.S.A. 40°36N 74°30W 175 F10
dlesex N.Y., U.S.A. 42°42N 77°16W 174 D7
dleton Australia 22°22S 141°32E 150 C3
dleton Canada 44°57N 65°4W 165 D6
dleton Cr. →
stralia 22°35S 141°51E 150 C3
dleton I. U.S.A. 59°26N 146°20W 166 D10
dletown U.K. 54°17N 6°51W 64 B5
dletown Calif.,
S.A. 38°45N 122°37W 170 G4
dletown Conn.,
S.A. 41°34N 72°39W 175 E12
Middletown N.Y., U.S.A. 41°27N 74°25W 175 E10
Middletown Ohio, U.S.A. 39°31N 84°24W 173 F11
Middletown Pa., U.S.A. 40°12N 76°44W 175 F8
Midelt Morocco 32°46N 4°44W 136 B3
Midge Point Australia 20°39S 148°42E 150 b
Midhirst N.Z. 39°17S 174°18E 154 F3
Midhurst Canada 44°26N 79°43W 174 B5
Midhurst U.K. 50°59N 0°44W 67 G7
Midi, Canal du → France 43°45N 1°21E 72 E5
Midi d'Ossau, Pic du France 42°50N 0°26W 72 F3
Midi-Pyrénées □ France 43°55N 1°45E 72 E5
Midland Australia 31°54S 116°1E 149 F2
Midland Canada 44°45N 79°50W 174 B5
Midland Calif., U.S.A. 33°52N 114°48W 171 M12
Midland Mich., U.S.A. 43°37N 84°14W 173 D11
Midland Pa., U.S.A. 40°39N 80°27W 174 F4
Midland Tex., U.S.A. 32°0N 102°3W 176 F3
Midlands □ Zimbabwe 19°40S 29°0E 143 F2
Midleton Ireland 51°55N 8°10W 64 E3
Midlothian □ U.K. 55°51N 3°5W 65 F5
Midnapore = Medinipur India 22°25N 87°21E 125 H12
Midou → France 43°54N 0°30W 72 E3
Midouze → France 43°48N 0°51W 72 E3
Midtjylland □ Denmark 56°30N 9°0E 63 H2
Midu China 25°18N 100°30E 116 E3
Midville U.S.A. 32°49N 82°14W 178 C7
Midway Ala., U.S.A. 32°5N 85°31W 178 C4
Midway Fla., U.S.A. 30°30N 84°27W 178 E5
Midway Is. Pac. Oc. 28°13N 177°22W 167 K4
Midway Wells U.S.A. 32°41N 115°7W 171 N11
Midwest U.S.A. 42°0N 90°0W 167 G22
Midwest Wyo., U.S.A. 43°25N 106°16W 168 E10
Midwest City U.S.A. 35°27N 97°24W 176 D6
Midyat Turkey 37°25N 41°23E 105 D9
Midžor Bulgaria 43°24N 22°40E 96 C6
Mie □ Japan 34°30N 136°10E 113 G8
Miechów Poland 50°21N 20°5E 83 H7
Miedwie, Jezioro Poland 53°17N 14°54E 83 E1
Międzybórz Poland 51°25N 17°34E 83 G4
Międzychód Poland 52°35N 15°53E 83 F2
Międzylesie Poland 50°8N 16°40E 83 H3
Międzyrzec Podlaski Poland 51°58N 22°45E 83 G9
Międzyrzecz Poland 52°26N 15°35E 83 F2
Międzyzdroje Poland 53°56N 14°26E 82 E1
Miejska Górka Poland 51°39N 16°58E 83 G3
Miélan France 43°27N 0°19E 72 E4
Mielec Poland 50°15N 21°25E 83 H8
Mienga Angola 17°12S 19°48E 144 A2
Miercurea-Ciuc Romania 46°21N 25°48E 81 D10
Miercurea Sibiului Romania 45°53N 23°48E 81 E8
Mieres Spain 43°18N 5°48W 88 B5
Mieroszów Poland 50°40N 16°11E 83 H3
Mieszkowice Poland 52°47N 14°30E 83 F1
Mifflintown U.S.A. 40°34N 77°24W 174 F7
Mifraz Hefa Israel 32°52N 35°0E 130 C4
Migang Shan China 35°32N 106°13E 114 G4
Migennes France 47°58N 3°31E 71 E10
Migliarino Italy 44°46N 11°56E 93 D8
Migliarino-San Rossore-Massaciuccoli ⌓ Italy 43°44N 10°20E 92 E7
Migori Kenya 1°4S 34°28E 142 C3
Miguasha ⌓ Canada 48°5N 66°26W 165 C6
Miguel Alemán, Presa Mexico 18°15N 96°32W 181 D5
Miguel Alves Brazil 4°11S 42°55W 189 A2
Miguel Calmon Brazil 11°26S 40°36W 189 C2
Miguel Hidalgo, Presa Mexico 26°30N 108°34W 180 B3
Miguelturra Spain 38°58N 3°53W 89 G7
Mihăileni Romania 47°58N 26°9E 81 C11
Mihăileşti Romania 44°20N 25°54E 81 F10
Mihailovca Moldova 46°33N 28°56E 81 D13
Mihalgazi Turkey 40°2N 30°34E 99 A12
Mihalıççık Turkey 39°53N 31°30E 104 C4
Mihara Japan 34°24N 133°5E 113 G6
Miheşu de Cîmpie Romania 46°41N 24°9E 81 D9
Mijas Spain 36°36N 4°40W 89 J6
Mikese Tanzania 6°48S 37°55E 142 D4
Mikha-Tskhakaya = Senaki Georgia 42°15N 42°1E 87 J6
Mikhailovka = Mykhaylivka Ukraine 47°12N 35°15E 85 J8
Mikhaylov Russia 54°14N 39°0E 84 E10
Mikhaylovgrad = Montana Bulgaria 43°27N 23°16E 96 C7
Mikhaylovka Russia 50°3N 43°5E 86 E6
Mikhnevo Russia 55°4N 37°59E 84 E9
Mikines Greece 37°43N 22°46E 98 D4
Mikkeli Finland 61°43N 27°15E 84 B4
Mikkwa → Canada 58°25N 114°46W 162 B6
Mikołajki Poland 53°49N 21°37E 82 E8
Míkonos = Mykonos Greece 37°30N 25°25E 99 D7
Mikri Prespa, L. Greece 40°47N 21°3E 96 F5
Mikro Derio Greece 41°19N 26°6E 97 E10
Mikstat Poland 51°32N 17°59E 83 G4
Mikulov Czech Rep. 48°48N 16°39E 79 C9
Mikumi Tanzania 7°26S 37°0E 142 D4
Mikumi △ Tanzania 7°35S 37°15E 142 D4
Mila Algeria 36°27N 6°16E 136 A5
Mila □ Algeria 36°25N 6°10E 136 A5
Milaca U.S.A. 45°45N 93°39W 172 C7
Milagro Ecuador 2°11S 79°36W 186 D3
Milan = Milano Italy 45°28N 9°10E 92 C6
Milan Ga., U.S.A. 32°1N 83°4W 178 C6
Milan Mo., U.S.A. 40°12N 93°7W 172 E7
Milan Tenn., U.S.A. 35°55N 88°46W 177 D10
Milang Australia 35°24S 138°58E 152 C3
Milange Mozam. 16°3S 35°45E 143 F4
Milano Italy 45°28N 9°10E 92 C6
Milano Linate ✈ (LIN) Italy 45°27N 9°16E 92 C6
Milâs Turkey 37°20N 27°50E 99 D9
Milatos Greece 35°18N 25°34E 101 D7
Milazzo Italy 38°13N 15°15E 95 D8
Milbank U.S.A. 45°13N 96°38W 172 C5
Milbanke Sd. Canada 52°19N 128°33W 162 C3
Milden Canada 51°29N 107°32W 163 C7
Mildenhall U.K. 52°21N 0°32E 67 E8
Mildmay Canada 44°3N 81°7W 174 B3
Mildura Australia 34°13S 142°9E 152 C5
Mile China 24°28N 103°20E 116 E4
Miles Australia 26°40S 150°9E 151 D5
Miles City U.S.A. 46°25N 105°51W 168 C11
Mileşti Moldova 47°13N 28°3E 81 C13
Milestone Canada 49°59N 104°31W 163 D8
Mileto Italy 38°36N 16°4E 95 D9
Miletto, Mte. Italy 41°27N 14°22E 95 A7
Miletus Turkey 37°30N 27°18E 99 D9
Milevsko Czech Rep. 49°27N 14°21E 78 B7
Milford Calif., U.S.A. 40°10N 120°22W 170 E6
Milford Conn., U.S.A. 41°14N 73°3W 175 E11
Milford Del., U.S.A. 38°55N 75°26W 173 F16
Milford Mass., U.S.A. 42°8N 71°31W 175 D13
Milford N.H., U.S.A. 42°50N 71°39W 175 D13
Milford N.Y., U.S.A. 42°35N 74°56W 175 D10
Milford Pa., U.S.A. 41°19N 74°48W 175 E10
Milford Utah, U.S.A. 38°24N 113°1W 168 G7
Milford Haven U.K. 51°42N 5°7W 67 F2
Milford Sd. N.Z. 44°41S 167°47E 155 E2
Milh, Bahr al = Razāzah, Buhayrat ar Iraq 32°40N 43°35E 105 F10
Miliana Aïn Salah, Algeria 27°20N 2°32E 136 C4
Miliana Médéa, Algeria 36°20N 2°15E 136 A4
Milicz Poland 51°31N 17°19E 83 G4
Milies Greece 39°20N 23°9E 98 B5
Milikapiti Australia 11°26S 130°40E 148 B5
Miling Australia 30°30S 116°17E 149 F2
Militello in Val di Catánia Italy 37°16N 14°48E 95 E7
Milk, Wadi el → Sudan 17°55N 30°20E 137 D3
Milk River Canada 49°10N 112°5W 162 D6
Mill → U.S.A. 42°57N 83°23W 174 D1
Mill I. Antarctica 66°0S 101°30E 55 C8
Mill I. Canada 63°58N 77°47W 161 E16
Mill Valley U.S.A. 37°54N 122°32W 170 H4
Millárs → Spain 39°55N 0°1W 90 F4
Millau France 44°8N 3°4E 72 D7
Millbridge Canada 44°41N 77°36W 174 B7
Millbrook Canada 44°10N 78°29W 174 B6
Millbrook Ala., U.S.A. 32°29N 86°22W 177 E11
Millbrook N.Y., U.S.A. 41°47N 73°42W 175 E11
Mille Lacs, L. des Canada 48°45N 90°35W 164 C1
Mille Lacs L. U.S.A. 46°15N 93°39W 172 B7
Milledgeville U.S.A. 33°5N 83°14W 178 B6
Millen U.S.A. 32°48N 81°57W 178 C8
Millennium I. = Caroline I. Kiribati 9°58S 150°13W 157 H12
Miller U.S.A. 44°31N 98°59W 172 C4
Miller Lake Canada 45°6N 81°26W 174 A3
Millerovo Russia 48°57N 40°28E 87 F5
Miller's Flat N.Z. 45°39S 169°23E 155 F4
Millersburg Ohio, U.S.A. 40°33N 81°55W 174 F3
Millersburg Pa., U.S.A. 40°32N 76°58W 174 F8
Millerton N.Z. 41°39S 171°54E 155 B6
Millerton U.S.A. 41°57N 73°31W 175 E11
Millerton L. U.S.A. 37°1N 119°41W 170 J7
Millet St. Lucia 13°55N 60°59W 183 f
Millevaches, Plateau de France 45°45N 2°0E 72 C6
Millheim U.S.A. 40°54N 77°29W 174 F7
Millicent Australia 37°34S 140°21E 152 D4
Milligan U.S.A. 30°45N 86°38W 179 E3
Millington U.S.A. 35°20N 89°53W 177 D10
Millinocket U.S.A. 45°39N 68°43W 173 C19
Millmerran Australia 27°53S 151°16E 151 D5
Millom U.K. 54°13N 3°16W 66 C4
Mills L. Canada 61°30N 118°20W 162 A5
Millsboro U.S.A. 40°0N 80°0W 174 G5
Millstream Chichester △ Australia 21°35S 117°6E 148 D2
Millstreet Ireland 52°4N 9°4W 64 D2
Millthorpe Australia 33°26S 149°12E 153 B8
Milltown Malbay Ireland 52°52N 9°24W 64 D2
Millville N.J., U.S.A. 39°24N 75°2W 173 F16
Millville Pa., U.S.A. 41°7N 76°32W 175 E8
Millwood L. U.S.A. 33°42N 93°58W 176 E8
Milna Croatia 43°20N 16°28E 93 E13
Milne → Australia 21°10S 137°33E 150 C2
Milne Land Greenland 70°40N 26°30W 57 C8
Milo U.S.A. 45°15N 68°59W 173 C19
Milo → Guinea 8°52N 9°0W 138 D3
Milon, Akra Greece 36°15N 28°11E 101 C10
Milos Greece 36°44N 24°25E 98 E6
Miłosław Poland 52°12N 17°32E 83 F4
Milot Albania 41°41N 19°43E 96 E3
Milparinka Australia 29°46S 141°57E 151 D3
Milpitas U.S.A. 37°26N 121°55W 170 H5
Miltenberg Germany 49°41N 9°16E 77 F5
Milton Australia 35°20S 150°27E 153 C9
Milton N.S., Canada 44°4N 64°45W 165 D7
Milton Ont., Canada 43°31N 79°53W 174 C5
Milton N.Z. 46°7S 169°59E 155 G4
Milton Calif., U.S.A. 38°3N 120°51W 170 G6
Milton Fla., U.S.A. 30°38N 87°3W 179 E2
Milton Pa., U.S.A. 41°1N 76°51W 174 F8
Milton Vt., U.S.A. 44°38N 73°7W 175 B11
Milton-Freewater U.S.A. 45°56N 118°23W 168 D4
Milton Keynes U.K. 52°1N 0°44W 67 E7
Milton Keynes □ U.K. 52°1N 0°44W 67 E7
Miluo China 29°0N 112°59E 117 C9
Milverton Canada 43°34N 80°55W 174 C4
Milwaukee U.S.A. 43°2N 87°54W 172 D10
Milwaukee Deep Atl. Oc. 19°50N 68°0W 183 C6
Milwaukie U.S.A. 45°26N 122°38W 170 E4
Mim Ghana 6°57N 2°33W 138 D4
Mimili Australia 27°0S 132°42E 149 E5
Mimizan France 44°12N 1°13W 72 D2
Mimoň Czech Rep. 50°38N 14°43E 78 A7
Mimoso Brazil 15°10S 48°5W 189 D1
Mims U.S.A. 28°40N 80°51W 179 G9
Min Jiang → Fujian, China 26°0N 119°35E 117 E12
Min Jiang → Sichuan, China 28°45N 104°40E 116 C5
Min Xian China 34°25N 104°5E 114 G3
Mīnā' al Aḩmadī Kuwait 29°5N 48°10E 129 D6
Mīnā' Jebel 'Alī U.A.E. 25°2N 55°8E 129 E7
Mina Pirquitas Argentina 22°40S 66°30W 190 A2
Mīnā Su'ud Si. Arabia 28°45N 48°28E 129 D6
Minago → Canada 54°33N 98°59W 163 C9
Minaki Canada 49°59N 94°40W 163 D10
Minamata Japan 32°10N 130°30E 113 H5
Minami-Arapusa △ Japan 35°30N 138°9E 113 G9
Minami-Tori-Shima Pac. Oc. 24°20N 153°58E 156 E7
Minamiaizu Japan 37°12N 139°46E 113 F9
Minamiawaji Japan 34°10N 134°42E 113 G7
Minamisōma Japan 37°38N 140°58E 112 F10
Minas Uruguay 34°20S 55°10W 191 C4
Minas, Sierra de las Guatemala 15°9N 89°31W 182 C2
Minas Basin Canada 45°20N 64°12W 165 C7
Minas de Riotinto Spain 37°42N 6°35W 89 H4
Minas Gerais □ Brazil 18°50S 46°0W 189 D1
Minas Novas Brazil 17°15S 42°36W 189 D2
Minatitlán Mexico 17°59N 94°31W 181 D6
Minbu Burma 20°10N 94°52E 123 J19
Minchinabad Pakistan 30°10N 73°34E 124 D5
Mincio → Italy 45°4N 10°59E 92 C7
Minčol Slovak Rep. 49°15N 20°58E 79 B13
Mindanao Phil. 8°0N 125°0E 119 C7
Mindanao Sea = Bohol Sea Phil. 9°0N 124°0E 119 C6
Mindanao Trench Pac. Oc. 12°0N 126°6E 119 B7
Mindel → Germany 48°31N 10°23E 77 G6
Mindelheim Germany 48°2N 10°29E 77 G6
Mindelo C. Verde Is. 16°24N 25°0W 134 b
Minden Canada 44°55N 78°43W 174 B6
Minden Germany 52°17N 8°55E 76 C4
Minden La., U.S.A. 32°37N 93°17W 176 E8
Minden Nev., U.S.A. 38°57N 119°46W 170 G7
Mindibungu = Billiluna Australia 19°37S 127°41E 148 C4
Mindiptana Indonesia 5°55S 140°22E 119 F10
Mindona L. Australia 33°6S 142°6E 152 B5
Mindoro Phil. 13°0N 121°0E 119 B6
Mindoro Str. Phil. 12°30N 120°30E 119 B6
Mine Japan 34°12N 131°7E 113 G5
Minehead U.K. 51°12N 3°29W 67 F4
Mineola N.Y., U.S.A. 40°44N 73°38W 175 F11
Mineola Tex., U.S.A. 32°40N 95°29W 176 E7
Mineral King U.S.A. 36°27N 118°36W 170 J8
Mineral Wells U.S.A. 32°48N 98°7W 176 E5
Mineralnyye Vody Russia 44°15N 43°8E 87 H6
Miners Bay Canada 44°49N 78°46W 174 B6
Minersville U.S.A. 40°41N 76°16W 175 F8
Minerva N.Y., U.S.A. 43°47N 73°59W 175 C11
Minerva Ohio, U.S.A. 40°44N 81°6W 174 F3
Minervino Murge Italy 41°5N 16°5E 95 A9
Minetto U.S.A. 43°24N 76°28W 175 C8
Minfeng China 37°4N 82°46E 109 E10
Ming-Kush Kyrgyzstan 41°40N 74°28E 109 D8
Mingäçevir Azerbaijan 40°45N 47°0E 87 K8
Mingäçevir Su Anbarı Azerbaijan 40°57N 46°50E 87 K8
Mingan Canada 50°20N 64°0W 165 B7
Mingary Australia 32°8S 140°45E 152 B4
Mingechaur = Mingäçevir Azerbaijan 40°45N 47°0E 87 K8
Mingechaurskoye Vdkhr. = Mingäçevir Su Anbarı Azerbaijan 40°57N 46°50E 87 K8
Mingela Australia 19°52S 146°38E 150 B4
Mingenew Australia 29°12S 115°21E 149 E2
Mingera Cr. → Australia 20°38S 137°45E 150 C2
Minggang China 32°24N 114°3E 117 A10
Mingguang China 32°46N 117°59E 117 A11
Mingin Burma 22°50N 94°30E 123 H19
Mingir Moldova 46°40N 28°20E 81 D13
Minglanilla Spain 39°34N 1°38W 91 F3
Minglun China 25°10N 108°21E 116 E7
Mingo Junction U.S.A. 40°19N 80°37W 174 F4
Mingora Pakistan 34°48N 72°22E 125 B5
Mingorría Spain 40°45N 4°40W 88 E6
Mingshan China 30°6N 103°10E 116 B4
Mingteke Daban = Mintaka Pass Pakistan 37°0N 74°58E 125 A6
Mingxi China 26°18N 117°12E 117 D11
Mingyuegue China 43°2N 128°50E 115 C15
Minhe China 36°9N 102°45E 110 D9
Minho = Miño → Spain 41°52N 8°40W 88 D2
Minhou China 26°0N 119°15E 117 E12
Miničevo Serbia 43°42N 22°18E 80 G7
Minicoy I. India 8°17N 73°2E 127 K1
Minidoka U.S.A. 42°45N 113°29W 168 E7
Minigwal, L. Australia 29°31S 123°14E 149 E3
Minilya → Australia 23°45S 114°0E 149 D1
Minilya Roadhouse Australia 23°55S 114°0E 149 D1
Mininera Australia 37°37S 142°58E 152 D5
Minipi L. Canada 52°25N 60°45W 165 B7
Minjilang Australia 11°8S 132°33E 148 B5
Mink L. Canada 61°54N 117°40W 162 A5
Minlaton Australia 34°45S 137°35E 152 C2
Minna Nigeria 9°37N 6°30E 139 D6
Minneapolis Kans., U.S.A. 39°8N 97°42W 172 F5
Minneapolis Minn., U.S.A. 44°57N 93°16W 172 C7
Minnedosa Canada 50°14N 99°50W 163 C9
Minnesota □ U.S.A. 46°0N 94°15W 172 B6
Minnesota → U.S.A. 44°54N 93°9W 172 C7
Minnewaukan U.S.A. 48°4N 99°15W 172 A4
Minnipa Australia 32°51S 135°9E 151 E2
Minnitaki L. Canada 49°57N 92°10W 164 C1
Miño = A Carreira Spain 43°21N 8°12W 88 B2
Mino Japan 35°32N 136°55E 113 G8
Miño → Spain 41°52N 8°40W 88 D2
Minoa Greece 35°6N 25°45E 99 F7
Minorca = Menorca Spain 40°0N 4°0E 100 B11
Minore Australia 32°14S 148°27E 153 B8
Minot U.S.A. 48°14N 101°18W 172 A3
Minqin China 38°38N 103°20E 114 E2
Minqing China 26°15N 118°50E 117 D12
Minsen Germany 53°41N 7°58E 76 B3
Minsk Belarus 53°52N 27°30E 75 B14
Minsk □ Belarus 53°15N 27°30E 84 F4
Mińsk Mazowiecki Poland 52°10N 21°33E 83 F8
Mintabie Australia 27°15S 133°7E 151 D1
Mintaka Pass Pakistan 37°0N 74°58E 125 A6
Minto Canada 46°5N 66°5W 165 C6
Minto, L. Canada 57°13N 75°0W 164 A5
Minton Canada 49°10N 104°35W 163 D8
Minturn U.S.A. 39°35N 106°26W 168 G10
Minturno Italy 41°15N 13°45E 94 A6
Minudasht Iran 37°17N 56°7E 129 B8
Minûf Egypt 30°26N 30°52E 137 E7
Minusinsk Russia 53°43N 91°20E 109 B12
Minutang India 28°15N 96°30E 123 E20
Minvoul Gabon 2°9N 12°8E 140 D2
Minya el Qamh Egypt 30°31N 31°21E 137 E7
Minya Konka = Gongga Shan China 29°40N 101°55E 116 C3
Minyip Australia 36°29S 142°36E 152 D5
Minzhong China 22°37N 113°30E 111 a
Mionica Bos.-H. 44°51N 18°29E 80 F3
Mionica Serbia 44°14N 20°6E 96 B4
Mioveni Romania 44°56N 24°54E 81 F9
Miquan China 43°58N 87°42E 109 D11
Miquelon Canada 49°25N 76°27W 164 C4
Miquelon St-P. & M. 47°8N 56°22W 165 C8
Mir Belarus 53°27N 26°28E 75 B14
Mir Niger 14°5N 11°59E 139 C7
Mīr Kūh Iran 26°22N 58°55E 129 E8
Mīr Shahdād Iran 26°15N 58°29E 129 E8
Mira Italy 45°26N 12°8E 93 C9
Mira Portugal 40°26N 8°44W 88 E2
Mira → Portugal 37°43N 8°47W 89 H2
Mira por vos Cay Bahamas 22°9N 74°30W 183 B5
Mirabella Eclano Italy 41°2N 14°59E 95 A7
Mirabello, Kolpos Greece 35°10N 25°50E 101 D7
Miracema do Norte Brazil 9°33S 48°24W 189 B1
Mirador Brazil 6°22S 44°22W 189 B2
Mirador-Río Azul △ Guatemala 17°45N 89°50W 182 C2
Miraj India 16°50N 74°45E 126 F2
Miram Shah Pakistan 33°0N 70°2E 124 C4
Miramar Argentina 38°15S 57°50W 190 D4
Miramar Mozam. 23°50S 35°35E 145 B6
Miramas France 43°33N 4°59E 73 E8
Mirambeau France 45°23N 0°35W 72 C3
Miramichi Canada 47°2N 65°28W 165 C6
Miramichi B. Canada 47°15N 65°0W 165 C7
Miramont-de-Guyenne France 44°37N 0°21E 72 D4
Miranda Brazil 20°10S 56°15W 187 H7
Miranda → Brazil 19°25S 57°20W 186 G7
Miranda de Ebro Spain 42°41N 2°57W 90 C2
Miranda do Corvo Portugal 40°6N 8°20W 88 E2
Miranda do Douro Portugal 41°30N 6°16W 88 D4
Mirande France 43°31N 0°25E 72 E4
Mirandela Portugal 41°32N 7°10W 88 D3
Mirándola Italy 44°53N 11°4E 92 D8
Mirandópolis Brazil 21°9S 51°6W 191 A5
Mirango Malawi 13°32S 34°58E 143 E3
Mirani Australia 21°8S 148°53E 150 b
Mirano Italy 45°30N 12°7E 93 C9
Miras Albania 40°30N 20°56E 96 F4
Mirassol Brazil 20°46S 49°28W 191 A6
Mirbāţ Oman 17°0N 54°45E 131 D5
Mirboo North Australia 38°24S 146°10E 153 E7
Mirear Egypt 23°15N 35°41E 137 C4
Mirebeau France 46°49N 0°10E 70 F7
Mirebeau-sur-Bèze France 47°25N 5°20E 71 E12
Mirecourt France 48°20N 6°10E 71 D13
Mires Greece 35°4N 24°56E 101 D6
Mirgorod = Myrhorod Ukraine 49°58N 33°37E 85 H7
Miri Malaysia 4°23N 113°59E 118 D4
Mirialguda India 16°52N 79°35E 126 F4
Miriam Vale Australia 24°20S 151°33E 150 C5
Miribel France 45°50N 4°57E 71 G11
Mirigama Sri Lanka 7°15N 80°8E 127 L5
Mirim, L. S. Amer. 32°45S 52°50W 191 C5
Miriuwung Gajerrong ✪ Australia 15°0S 128°45E 148 C4
Mīrjāveh Iran 29°1N 61°30E 129 D9
Mirnyy Antarctica 66°50S 92°30E 55 C14
Mirnyy Russia 62°33N 113°53E 107 C12
Miroč Serbia 44°32N 22°16E 96 B6
Mirokhan Pakistan 27°46N 68°6E 124 F3
Mirond L. Canada 55°6N 102°47W 163 B8
Mirosławiec Poland 53°20N 16°5E 82 E3
Mirpur Pakistan 33°32N 73°56E 125 C5
Mirpur Batoro Pakistan 24°44N 68°16E 124 G3
Mirpur Bibiwari Pakistan 28°33N 67°44E 124 E2
Mirpur Khas Pakistan 25°30N 69°0E 124 G3
Mirpur Sakro Pakistan 24°33N 67°41E 124 G2
Mirria Niger 13°43N 9°7E 139 C6
Mirrool Australia 34°19S 147°10E 153 C7
Mirs Bay = Tai Pang Wan China 22°33N 114°24E 111 a
Mirsk Poland 50°58N 15°23E 83 H2
Mirtağ Turkey 38°23N 41°56E 128 B4
Mirtoo Sea Greece 37°0N 23°20E 98 D5
Miryang S. Korea 35°31N 128°44E 115 G15
Mirzaani Georgia 41°24N 46°5E 87 K8
Mirzapur India 25°10N 82°34E 125 G10
Mirzapur-cum-Vindhyachal = Mirzapur India 25°10N 82°34E 125 G10
Misantla Mexico 19°56N 96°50W 181 D5
Misawa Japan 40°41N 141°24E 112 D10
Miscou I. Canada 47°57N 64°31W 165 C7
Misha India 7°59N 93°20E 127 L10
Mish'āb, Ra's al Si. Arabia 28°15N 48°43E 129 D6
Mishagua → Peru 11°12S 72°58W 188 C3
Mishamo Tanzania 5°41S 30°41E 142 D3
Mishan China 45°37N 131°48E 112 B5
Mishawaka U.S.A. 41°40N 86°11W 172 E10
Mishbih, Gebel Egypt 22°38N 34°44E 137 C3
Mishima Japan 35°10N 138°52E 113 G9
Misión Mexico 32°6N 116°53W 171 N10
Misión Fagnano Argentina 54°32S 67°17W 192 D3
Misiones □ Argentina 27°0S 55°0W 191 B5
Misiones □ Paraguay 27°0S 56°0W 190 B4
Miskah Si. Arabia 24°49N 42°56E 128 E4
Miskitos, Cayos Nic. 14°26N 82°50W 182 D3
Miskolc Hungary 48°7N 20°50E 80 B5
Misoke Dem. Rep. of the Congo 0°42S 28°2E 142 C2
Misool Indonesia 1°52S 130°10E 119 E8
Mişr = Egypt ■ Africa 28°0N 31°0E 137 F7
Mişrātah Libya 32°24N 15°3E 135 B9
Missanabie Canada 48°20N 84°6W 164 C3
Missão Velha Brazil 7°15S 39°10W 189 B3
Missinaibi → Canada 50°43N 81°29W 164 B3
Missinaibi L. Canada 48°23N 83°40W 164 C3
Mission Canada 49°10N 122°15W 162 D4
Mission S. Dak., U.S.A. 43°18N 100°39W 172 D3
Mission Tex., U.S.A. 26°13N 98°20W 176 H5
Mission Beach Australia 17°53S 146°6E 150 B4
Mission Viejo U.S.A. 33°36N 117°40W 171 M9
Missirah Senegal 13°40N 16°30W 138 C1
Missisa L. Canada 52°20N 85°7W 164 B2
Missisicabi → Canada 51°14N 79°31W 164 B4
Mississagi → Canada 46°15N 83°9W 164 C3
Mississauga Canada 43°32N 79°35W 174 C5
Mississippi □ U.S.A. 33°0N 90°0W 177 E10
Mississippi → U.S.A. 29°9N 89°15W 177 G10
Mississippi L. Canada 45°5N 76°10W 175 A8
Mississippi River Delta U.S.A. 29°10N 89°15W 177 G10
Mississippi Sd. U.S.A. 30°20N 89°0W 177 F10
Missoula U.S.A. 46°52N 114°1W 168 C6
Missour Morocco 33°3N 4°0W 136 B3
Missouri □ U.S.A. 38°25N 92°30W 172 F7
Missouri → U.S.A. 38°49N 90°7W 172 F8
Missouri City U.S.A. 29°37N 95°32W 176 G7
Missouri Valley U.S.A. 41°34N 95°53W 172 E6
Mist U.S.A. 45°59N 123°15W 170 E3
Mistassibi → Canada 48°53N 72°13W 165 B5
Mistassini Canada 48°53N 72°12W 165 C5
Mistassini → Canada 48°42N 72°20W 165 C5
Mistassini, L. Canada 51°0N 73°30W 164 B5
Mistastin L. Canada 55°57N 63°20W 165 A7
Mistelbach Austria 48°34N 16°34E 79 C9
Misterbianco Italy 37°31N 15°1E 95 E8
Misti, Volcán Peru 16°18S 71°24W 188 D3
Mistinibi, L. Canada 55°56N 64°17W 165 A7
Mistissini Canada 48°53N 72°12W 165 C5
Mistras = Mystras Greece 37°4N 22°22E 98 D4
Mistretta Italy 37°56N 14°22E 95 E7
Misty L. Canada 58°53N 101°40W 163 B8
Misurata = Mişrātah Libya 32°24N 15°3E 135 B9
Mît Ghamr Egypt 30°42N 31°12E 137 E7
Mitande Mozam. 14°6S 35°58E 143 E4
Mitchell Australia 26°29S 147°58E 151 D4
Mitchell Canada 43°28N 81°12W 174 C3
Mitchell Ga., U.S.A. 33°13N 82°42W 178 B7
Mitchell Nebr., U.S.A. 41°57N 103°49W 172 E2
Mitchell Oreg., U.S.A. 44°34N 120°9W 168 D3
Mitchell S. Dak., U.S.A. 43°43N 98°2W 172 D4
Mitchell → Australia 15°12S 141°35E 150 B3
Mitchell, Mt. U.S.A. 35°46N 82°16W 177 D13
Mitchell-Alice Rivers △ Australia 15°28S 142°5E 150 B3
Mitchell Ra. Australia 12°49S 135°36E 150 A2
Mitchell River △ Australia 37°37S 147°22E 153 D7
Mitchelstown Ireland 52°15N 8°16W 64 D3
Mitha Tiwana Pakistan 32°13N 72°6E 124 C5
Mithi Pakistan 24°44N 69°48E 124 G3
Mithimna Greece 39°20N 26°12E 99 B8
Mithrao Pakistan 27°28N 69°40E 124 F3
Mitiamo Australia 36°12S 144°15E 152 D6
Mitilini Greece 39°6N 26°35E 99 B8
Mitilinii Greece 37°42N 26°56E 99 D8
Mitla Pass = Mamarr Mitlā Egypt 30°2N 32°54E 130 E1
Mito Japan 36°20N 140°30E 113 F10
Mitre, Mt. N.Z. 40°50S 175°30E 154 G4
Mitrofanovka Russia 49°58N 39°42E 85 H10
Mitrovicë Kosovo 42°54N 20°52E 96 D4
Mitsamiouli Comoros Is. 11°20S 43°16E 141 a
Mitsiwa Eritrea 15°35N 39°25E 131 D2
Mitsukaidō Japan 36°1N 139°59E 113 F9
Mittagong Australia 34°28S 150°29E 153 C9
Mittelberg Austria 47°20N 10°10E 78 D3
Mittelfranken □ Germany 49°25N 10°40E 77 F6
Mittellandkanal → Germany 52°20N 8°28E 76 C4
Mittenwalde Germany 52°15N 13°31E 76 C9
Mittersill Austria 47°16N 12°29E 78 D5
Mitterteich Germany 49°57N 12°14E 77 F8
Mittimatalik = Pond Inlet Canada 72°40N 77°0W 161 C16
Mittweida Germany 50°59N 12°59E 76 E8
Mitú Colombia 1°15N 70°13W 186 C4
Mitumba Tanzania 7°8S 31°2E 142 D3
Mitumba, Mts. Dem. Rep. of the Congo 7°0S 27°30E 142 D2
Mitwaba Dem. Rep. of the Congo 8°2S 27°17E 143 D2
Mityana Uganda 0°23N 32°2E 142 B3
Mixteco → Mexico 18°11N 98°30W 181 D5
Miyagi □ Japan 38°15N 140°45E 112 E10
Miyāh, W. el → Egypt 25°0N 33°23E 137 C3
Miyāh, W. el → Syria 34°44N 39°57E 128 C3
Miyake-Jima Japan 34°5N 139°30E 113 G9
Miyako Japan 39°40N 141°59E 112 E10
Miyako-Jima Japan 24°45N 125°20E 113 M2
Miyako-Rettō Japan 24°24N 125°0E 113 M2
Miyakojima Japan 24°48N 125°17E 113 M2
Miyakonojō Japan 31°40N 131°5E 113 J5
Miyān Rahan Iran 34°34N 47°26E 105 E12
Miyani India 21°50N 69°26E 124 J3
Miyanoura-Dake Japan 30°20N 130°31E 113 J5
Miyazaki Japan 31°56N 131°30E 113 J5
Miyazaki □ Japan 32°30N 131°30E 113 H5
Miyazu Japan 35°35N 135°10E 113 G7
Miyet, Bahr el = Dead Sea Asia 31°30N 35°30E 130 D4
Miyi China 26°47N 102°9E 116 D4
Miyoshi Japan 34°48N 132°51E 113 G6
Miyun China 40°28N 116°50E 114 D9
Miyun Shuiku China 40°30N 117°0E 115 D9
Mizdah Libya 31°30N 13°0E 135 B8
Mizen Hd. Cork, Ireland 51°27N 9°50W 64 E2
Mizen Hd. Wicklow, Ireland 52°51N 6°4W 64 D5
Mizhhirya Ukraine 48°32N 23°30E 81 B8
Mizhi China 37°47N 110°12E 114 F6
Mizil Romania 44°59N 26°29E 81 F11
Mizoram □ India 23°30N 92°40E 123 H18
Mizpe Ramon Israel 30°34N 34°49E 130 E3
Mizuho Antarctica 70°30S 41°0E 55 D5
Mizusawa = Ōshū Japan 39°8N 141°8E 112 E10
Mjällby Sweden 56°3N 14°40E 63 H8
Mjöbäck Sweden 57°28N 12°53E 63 G6
Mjölby Sweden 58°20N 15°10E 63 F9
Mjörn Sweden 57°55N 12°25E 63 G6
Mjøsa Norway 60°40N 11°0E 60 F14
Mkata Tanzania 5°45S 38°20E 142 D4
Mkhaya ⌓ Swaziland 26°34S 31°45E 145 C5
Mkhuze ⌓ S. Africa 29°27S 29°30E 145 C4
Mkokotoni Tanzania 5°55S 39°15E 142 D4
Mkomazi Tanzania 4°40S 38°7E 142 C4
Mkomazi → S. Africa 30°12S 30°50E 145 D5
Mkomazi ⌓ Tanzania 4°4S 30°2E 142 C3

Mkulwe *Tanzania* 8°37S 32°20E **143** D3
Mkumbi, Ras *Tanzania* 7°38S 39°55E **142** D4
Mkushi *Zambia* 14°25S 29°15E **143** E2
Mkushi River *Zambia* 13°32S 29°45E **143** E2
Mkuze *S. Africa* 27°10S 32°0E **145** C5
Mladá Boleslav
  Czech Rep. 50°27N 14°53E **78** A7
Mladenovac *Serbia* 44°28N 20°44E **96** B4
Mlala Hills *Tanzania* 6°50S 31°40E **142** D3
Mlange = Mulanje, Mt.
  Malawi 16°2S 35°33E **143** F4
Mlava → *Serbia* 44°45N 21°13E **96** B5
Mława *Poland* 53°9N 20°25E **83** E7
Mławula △ *Swaziland* 26°12S 32°2E **145** C5
Mlinište *Bos.-H.* 44°15N 16°50E **93** D13
Mljet *Croatia* 42°43N 17°30E **93** F14
Mljet △ *Croatia* 42°45N 17°25E **93** F14
Mljetski Kanal *Croatia* 42°48N 17°35E **93** F14
Mlynary *Poland* 54°12N 19°46E **83** D6
Mmabatho *S. Africa* 25°49S 25°30E **144** C4
Mme *Cameroon* 6°18N 10°14E **139** D7
Mnichovo Hradiště
  Czech Rep. 50°32N 14°59E **78** A7
Mo i Rana *Norway* 66°20N 14°7E **60** C16
Moa *Australia* 10°11S 142°16E **150** a
Moa *Cuba* 20°40N 74°56W **183** B4
Moa *Indonesia* 8°0S 128°0E **119** F7
Moa → *S. Leone* 6°59N 11°36W **138** D2
Moab *U.S.A.* 38°35N 109°33W **168** G9
Moaco → *Brazil* 7°41S 68°18W **188** B4
Moala *Fiji* 18°36S 179°53E **154** a
Moama *Australia* 36°7S 144°46E **151** F3
Moamba *Mozam.* 25°36S 32°15E **145** C5
Moapa *U.S.A.* 36°40N 114°37W **171** J12
Moate *Ireland* 53°24N 7°44W **64** C4
Moba
  Dem. Rep. of the Congo 7°0S 29°48E **142** D2
Mobārakābād *Iran* 28°24N 53°20E **129** D7
Mobaye *C.A.R.* 4°25N 21°5E **140** D4
Moberly *U.S.A.* 39°25N 92°26W **172** F7
Moberly Lake *Canada* 55°50N 121°44W **162** B4
Mobile *U.S.A.* 30°41N 88°3W **177** F10
Mobile B. *U.S.A.* 30°30N 88°0W **177** F11
Mobridge *U.S.A.* 45°32N 100°26W **172** C3
Moc Chau *Vietnam* 20°50N 104°38E **120** B5
Moc Hoa *Vietnam* 10°46N 105°56E **121** G5
Mocabe Kasari
  Dem. Rep. of the Congo 9°58S 26°12E **143** D2
Moçambique = Mozambique ■
  Africa 19°0S 35°0E **143** F4
Moçâmedes *Mozam.* 15°3S 40°42E **143** F5
Mocanaqua *U.S.A.* 41°9N 76°8W **175** E8
Moce *Fiji* 18°40S 178°29W **154** a
Mocha, I. *Chile* 38°22S 73°56W **192** A2
Mochima △ *Venezuela* 10°30N 64°5W **183** D7
Mochos *Greece* 35°16N 25°27E **101** D7
Mochudi *Botswana* 24°27S 26°7E **144** B4
Mocimboa da Praia
  Mozam. 11°25S 40°20E **143** E5
Mociu *Romania* 46°46N 24°3E **81** D9
Möckeln *Sweden* 56°40N 14°15E **63** H8
Mockfjärd *Sweden* 60°40N 14°57E **62** D8
Moclips *U.S.A.* 47°14N 124°13W **170** C2
Mocoa *Colombia* 1°7N 76°35W **186** C3
Mococa *Brazil* 21°28S 47°0W **191** A6
Mocorito *Mexico* 25°29N 107°55W **180** B3
Moctezuma *Mexico* 29°48N 109°42W **180** B3
Moctezuma → *Mexico* 21°59N 98°34W **181** C5
Mocuba *Mozam.* 16°54S 36°57E **143** F4
Modane *France* 45°12N 6°40E **73** C10
Modasa *India* 23°30N 73°21E **124** H5
Modder → *S. Africa* 29°2S 24°37E **144** C3
Modderrivier *S. Africa* 29°2S 24°38E **144** C3
Módena *Italy* 44°40N 10°55E **92** D7
Modena *U.S.A.* 37°48N 113°56W **169** H7
Modesto *U.S.A.* 37°39N 121°0W **170** H6
Módica *Italy* 36°52N 14°46E **95** F7
Modimolle *S. Africa* 24°42S 28°22E **145** B4
Modjadjiskloof *S. Africa* 23°42S 30°10E **145** B5
Mödling *Austria* 48°5N 16°17E **79** C9
Modoc *U.S.A.* 33°44N 82°13W **178** B7
Modra *Slovak Rep.* 48°19N 17°20E **79** C10
Modriča *Bos.-H.* 44°57N 18°17E **80** F3
Moe *Australia* 38°12S 146°19E **153** E7
Moebase *Mozam.* 17°3S 38°41E **143** F4
Moëlan-sur-Mer *France* 47°49N 3°38W **70** E3
Moengo *Suriname* 5°45N 54°20W **187** B8
Moenjodaro = Mohenjodaro
  Pakistan 27°19N 68°7E **124** F3
Moerewa *N.Z.* 35°8S 174°1E **154** B3
Moffat *U.K.* 55°21N 3°27W **65** F5
Moga *India* 30°48N 75°8E **124** D6
Mogadishu = Muqdisho
  Somalia 2°2N 45°25E **131** G4
Mogador = Essaouira
  Morocco 31°32N 9°42W **136** B2
Mogadouro *Portugal* 41°22N 6°47W **88** D4
Mogalakwena →
  S. Africa 22°38S 28°40E **145** B4
Mogami-Gawa →
  Japan 38°45N 140°0E **112** E10
Mogán *Canary Is.* 27°53N 15°43W **100** G4
Mogaung *Burma* 25°20N 97°0E **123** G20
Mogente = Moixent
  Spain 38°52N 0°45W **91** G4
Mogi-Mirim *Brazil* 22°29S 47°0W **187** H9
Mogielnica *Poland* 51°42N 20°41E **83** G7
Mogilev = Mahilyow
  Belarus 53°55N 30°18E **75** B16
Mogilev-Podolskiy = Mohyliv-
  Podilskyy *Ukraine* 48°26N 27°48E **81** B12
Mogilno *Poland* 52°39N 17°55E **83** F4
Mogincual *Mozam.* 15°35S 40°25E **143** F5
Mogliano Véneto *Italy* 45°33N 12°14E **92** C5
Mogocha *Russia* 53°40N 119°50E **107** D12
Mogoditshane
  Botswana 24°25S 25°51E **144** B4
Mogok *Burma* 23°0N 96°40E **123** H20
Mogollon Rim *U.S.A.* 34°10N 110°50W **169** J8
Mógoro *Italy* 39°41N 8°47E **94** C1
Mograt *Sudan* 19°28N 33°11E **137** D12
Moguer *Spain* 37°15N 6°52W **89** H4
Mogumber *Australia* 31°2S 116°3E **149** F2
Mogwadi → *S. Africa* 23°4S 29°36E **145** B5
Mohács *Hungary* 45°58N 18°41E **80** E3
Mohaka → *N.Z.* 39°7S 177°12E **154** F6
Mohala *India* 20°35N 80°44E **126** D5
Mohall *U.S.A.* 48°46N 101°31W **172** A3
Moḥammadābād *Iran* 37°52N 59°5E **129** B8

Mohammadia *Algeria* 35°33N 0°3E **136** A4
Mohammedia *Morocco* 33°44N 7°21W **136** B2
Mohana *India* 19°27N 84°16E **126** D7
Mohana → *India* 24°43N 85°0E **125** G11
Mohanlalganj *India* 26°41N 80°58E **125** D11
Mohave, L. *U.S.A.* 35°12N 114°34W **171** K12
Mohawk → *U.S.A.* 42°47N 73°41W **175** D11
Moheda *Sweden* 57°1N 14°35E **63** G8
Mohéli *Comoros Is.* 12°20S 43°40E **141** a
Mohenjodaro *Pakistan* 27°19N 68°7E **124** F3
Moher, Cliffs of *Ireland* 52°58N 9°27W **64** D2
Mohicanville Res.
  U.S.A. 40°45N 82°9W **174** F2
Möhne → *Germany* 51°29N 7°57E **76** D3
Mohns Ridge *Arctic* 72°30N 5°0W **54** B7
Mohoro *Tanzania* 8°6S 39°8E **142** D4
Mohsenābād *Iran* 36°40N 59°35E **129** B8
Mohyliv-Podilskyy
  Ukraine 48°26N 27°48E **81** B12
Moidart, L. *U.K.* 56°47N 5°52W **65** E3
Moinabad *India* 17°44N 77°16E **126** F1
Moineşti *Romania* 46°28N 26°31E **81** D11
Moira → *Canada* 44°21N 77°24W **174** B7
Moirans *France* 45°20N 5°33E **73** C9
Moirans-en-Montagne
  France 46°26N 5°43E **71** F12
Moisaküla *Estonia* 58°3N 25°12E **84** C3
Moisie *Canada* 50°12N 66°1W **165** B6
Moisie → *Canada* 50°14N 66°5W **165** B6
Moissac *France* 44°7N 1°5E **72** D5
Moita *Portugal* 38°38N 8°58W **89** G2
Moixent *Spain* 38°52N 0°45W **91** G4
Möja *Sweden* 59°26N 18°55E **62** E12
Mojácar *Spain* 37°6N 1°55W **91** H3
Mojados *Spain* 41°26N 4°40W **88** D6
Mojave *U.S.A.* 35°3N 118°10W **171** K8
Mojave → *U.S.A.* 35°7N 115°32W **171** K11
Mojave Desert *U.S.A.* 35°0N 116°30W **171** L10
Moji das Cruzes *Brazil* 23°31S 46°11W **191** A6
Moji-Guaçu → *Brazil* 20°53S 48°10W **191** A6
Mojiang *China* 23°37N 101°35E **116** F3
Mojkovac *Montenegro* 42°58N 19°35E **96** D3
Mojo *Bolivia* 21°48S 65°33W **190** A2
Mojokerto *Indonesia* 7°28S 112°26E **119** G15
Mokai *N.Z.* 38°32S 175°56E **154** E4
Mokala △ *S. Africa* 29°10S 24°10E **144** C3
Mokambo
  Dem. Rep. of the Congo 12°25S 28°20E **143** E2
Mokameh *India* 25°24N 85°55E **125** G11
Mokau *N.Z.* 38°42S 174°39E **154** E3
Mokau → *N.Z.* 38°35S 174°35E **154** E3
Mokelumne →
  U.S.A. 38°13N 121°28W **170** G5
Mokelumne Hill
  U.S.A. 38°18N 120°43W **170** G6
Mokhotlong *Lesotho* 29°22S 29°2E **145** C4
Mokihinui → *N.Z.* 41°33S 171°58E **155** B6
Möklinta *Sweden* 60°4N 16°33E **62** D10
Moknine *Tunisia* 35°35N 10°58E **136** A6
Mokoan, L. *Australia* 36°27S 146°5E **153** C7
Mokokchung *India* 26°15N 94°30E **123** F19
Mokolo *Cameroon* 10°49N 13°54E **139** C7
Mokolo → *S. Africa* 23°14S 27°43E **145** B4
Mokopane *S. Africa* 24°10S 28°55E **145** B4
Mokpo *S. Korea* 34°50N 126°25E **115** G14
Mokra Gora *Europe* 42°50N 20°30E **96** D4
Mokronog *Slovenia* 45°57N 15°9E **93** C12
Moksha → *Russia* 54°45N 41°53E **86** C6
Mokshan *Russia* 53°25N 44°35E **86** D7
Mokwa *Nigeria* 9°19N 5°0E **139** D6
Mol *Belgium* 51°11N 5°5E **76** C5
Mola di Bari *Italy* 41°4N 17°5E **95** A10
Molai *Greece* 36°49N 22°56E **98** E4
Molakalmuru *India* 14°55N 76°50E **127** G3
Molaly *Kazakhstan* 45°27N 78°18E **109** C9
Molara *Italy* 40°52N 9°43E **94** B2
Molat *Croatia* 44°15N 14°50E **93** D11
Molchanovo *Russia* 57°40N 83°50E **106** D9
Mold *U.K.* 53°9N 3°8W **66** D4
Moldava nad Bodvou
  Slovak Rep. 48°38N 21°0E **79** C14
Moldavia = Moldova ■
  Europe 47°0N 28°0E **81** C13
Moldavia *Romania* 46°30N 27°0E **81** D12
Molde *Norway* 62°45N 7°9E **60** E12
Moldova ■ *Europe* 47°0N 28°0E **81** C13
Moldova Nouă *Romania* 44°45N 21°41E **80** F6
Moldoveanu, Vf.
  Romania 45°36N 24°45E **81** E9
Moldoviţa *Romania* 47°41N 25°32E **81** C10
Mole → *U.K.* 51°24N 0°21W **67** F7
Mole → *Ghana* 9°43N 1°44W **139** D4
Molepolole *Botswana* 24°28S 25°28E **144** B4
Molesworth *N.Z.* 42°5S 173°16E **155** C5
Molfetta *Italy* 41°12N 16°36E **95** A9
Molina de Aragón *Spain* 40°46N 1°52W **90** E3
Molina de Segura *Spain* 38°3N 1°12W **91** G3
Moline *U.S.A.* 41°30N 90°31W **172** E8
Molinella *Italy* 44°37N 11°40E **93** D8
Molino *U.S.A.* 30°43N 87°20W **177** F11
Molinos *Argentina* 25°28S 66°15W **190** B2
Moliro
  Dem. Rep. of the Congo 8°12S 30°30E **142** D3
Moliterno *Italy* 40°14N 15°52E **95** B8
Molkom *Sweden* 59°37N 13°44E **62** E7
Mölle *Sweden* 56°17N 12°31E **63** H6
Molledo *Spain* 43°9N 4°6W **88** B6
Mollendo *Peru* 17°0S 72°0W **188** D3
Mollerin, L. *Australia* 30°30S 117°35E **149** F2
Mollerussa *Spain* 41°37N 0°54E **90** D5
Mollina *Spain* 37°8N 4°38W **89** H6
Mölln *Germany* 53°37N 10°41E **76** B6
Mölltorp *Sweden* 58°30N 14°26E **63** F8
Mölndal *Sweden* 57°40N 12°3E **63** G6
Mölnlycke *Sweden* 57°40N 12°8E **63** G6
Molo *Kenya* 0°15S 35°44E **142** C4
Molochansk *Ukraine* 47°15N 35°35E **85** J8
Molochnoye, Ozero
  Ukraine 46°30N 35°20E **85** J8
Molodechno = Maladzyechna
  Belarus 54°20N 26°50E **75** A14
Molodezhnaya
  Antarctica 26°41N 40°58E **5** C5
Molodove *Ukraine* 46°11N 29°39E **81** D14
Moloka'i *U.S.A.* 21°8N 157°0W **167** L8
Molokai Fracture Zone
  Pac. Oc. 28°0N 125°0W **157** E15
Molong *Australia* 33°5S 148°54E **153** E8
Molopo → *Africa* 28°30S 20°12E **144** C3
Molos *Greece* 38°47N 22°37E **98** C4
Molsheim *France* 48°33N 7°29E **71** D14

Molson L. *Canada* 54°22N 96°40W **163** C9
Molteno *S. Africa* 31°22S 26°22E **144** E4
Molu *Indonesia* 6°45S 131°40E **119** F8
Molucca Sea *Indonesia* 0°0 125°0E **119** E6
Moluccas = Maluku
  Indonesia 1°0S 127°0E **119** E7
Moma
  Dem. Rep. of the Congo 1°35S 23°52E **142** C1
Moma *Mozam.* 16°47S 39°4E **143** F4
Momba *Australia* 30°58S 143°30E **152** A5
Mombaça *Brazil* 5°43S 39°45W **189** B3
Mombasa *Kenya* 4°3S 39°40E **142** C4
Mombetsu *Japan* 44°21N 143°22E **112** B11
Mombuey *Spain* 42°3N 6°20W **88** C4
Momchilgrad *Bulgaria* 41°33N 25°23E **97** E9
Momi
  Dem. Rep. of the Congo 1°42S 27°0E **142** C2
Mompós *Colombia* 9°14N 74°26W **186** B4
Mon □ *Burma* 16°0N 97°30E **123** L20
Mona, Canal de la = Mona
  Passage *W. Indies* 18°30N 67°45W **183** C6
Mona, Isla *Puerto Rico* 18°5N 67°54W **183** C6
Mona, Pta. *Costa Rica* 9°37N 82°36W **182** E3
Mona Passage
  W. Indies 18°30N 67°45W **183** C6
Monaca *U.S.A.* 40°41N 80°17W **174** F4
Monaco ■ *Europe* 43°46N 7°23E **73** E11
Monadhliath Mts. *U.K.* 57°10N 4°4W **65** D4
Monadnock, Mt.
  U.S.A. 42°52N 72°7W **175** D12
Monaghan *Ireland* 54°15N 6°57W **64** B5
Monaghan □ *Ireland* 54°11N 6°56W **64** B5
Monahans *U.S.A.* 31°36N 102°54W **176** F3
Monar, L. *U.K.* 57°26N 5°8W **65** D3
Monaragala *Sri Lanka* 6°52N 81°22E **127** L5
Monarch Mt. *Canada* 51°55N 125°57W **162** C3
Monashee Mts. *Canada* 51°0N 118°43W **162** C5
Monastir = Bitola
  Macedonia 41°1N 21°20E **96** C5
Monastir *Tunisia* 35°50N 10°49E **136** A6
Monastir □ *Tunisia* 35°37N 10°45E **136** A6
Monbetsu = Hidaka
  Japan 42°30N 142°10E **112** C11
Moncalieri *Italy* 45°0N 7°41E **92** D4
Moncalvo *Italy* 45°3N 8°16E **92** C5
Monção *Portugal* 42°4N 8°27W **88** C2
Moncarapacho *Portugal* 37°5N 7°46W **89** H3
Moncayo, Sierra del
  Spain 41°48N 1°50W **90** D3
Monchegorsk *Russia* 67°54N 32°58E **60** C25
Mönchengladbach
  Germany 51°11N 6°27E **76** D2
Monchique *Portugal* 37°19N 8°38W **89** H2
Moncks Corner *U.S.A.* 33°12N 80°1W **178** B9
Monclova *Mexico* 26°54N 101°25W **180** B4
Moncontour *France* 48°22N 2°38W **70** D4
Moncton *Canada* 46°7N 64°51W **165** C7
Mondariz *Spain* 42°14N 8°27W **88** C2
Mondego → *Portugal* 40°9N 8°52W **88** E2
Mondego, C. *Portugal* 40°11N 8°54W **88** E2
Mondeodo *Indonesia* 3°34S 122°9E **119** E6
Mondeville *France* 49°10N 0°18W **70** C6
Mondlo *S. Africa* 27°59S 30°43E **145** C5
Mondolfo *Italy* 43°45N 13°6E **93** E10
Mondoñedo *Spain* 43°25N 7°23W **88** B3
Mondovi *Italy* 44°23N 7°49E **92** D4
Mondragon = Arrasate
  Spain 43°3N 2°35W **90** B3
Mondragone *Italy* 41°7N 13°53E **94** A6
Mondrain I. *Australia* 34°9S 122°14E **149** F3
Moneague *Jamaica* 18°16N 77°7W **182** a
Monemvasia *Greece* 36°41N 23°3E **98** E5
Moneron, Ostrov
  Russia 46°15N 141°16E **112** A10
Monessen *U.S.A.* 40°9N 79°54W **174** F5
Monesterio *Spain* 38°6N 6°15W **89** G4
Monestier-de-Clermont
  France 44°55N 5°38E **73** D9
Monett *U.S.A.* 36°55N 93°55W **172** G7
Moneymore *U.K.* 54°41N 6°40W **64** B5
Monflanquin *France* 44°32N 0°47E **72** D4
Monforte *Portugal* 39°6N 7°25W **89** F3
Monforte de Lemos *Spain* 42°31N 7°33W **88** C3
Monfragüe △ *Spain* 39°48N 5°52W **89** F5
Mong Hpayak *Burma* 20°52N 99°55E **120** B2
Mong Hsat *Shan,
  Burma* 21°54N 98°30E **116** G2
Mong Hsat *Shan,
  Burma* 20°31N 99°15E **120** B2
Mong Kung *Burma* 21°35N 97°35E **123** J20
Mong Nai *Burma* 20°32N 97°46E **123** J20
Mong Ping *Burma* 21°22N 99°2E **116** G2
Mong Tai = Shan □
  Burma 21°30N 98°30E **123** J21
Mong Ton *Burma* 20°17N 98°45E **123** J21
Mong Yai *Burma* 22°21N 98°3E **123** H21
Mong Yang *Burma* 21°50N 99°41E **120** B2
Mongalla *South Sudan* 5°8N 31°42E **135** G12
Mongers, L. *Australia* 29°25S 117°5E **149** E2
Monghyr = Munger
  India 25°23N 86°30E **125** G12
Mongibello = Etna *Italy* 37°50N 14°55E **95** E7
Mongo *Chad* 12°14N 18°43E **135** F9
Mongo → *S. Leone* 9°35N 12°10W **138** D2
Mongolia ■ *Asia* 47°0N 103°0E **110** B9
Mongolia, Plateau of
  Asia 45°0N 105°0E **102** D12
Mongonu *Nigeria* 12°40N 13°32E **139** C7
Mongu *Zambia* 15°16S 23°12E **141** H4
Môngua *Angola* 16°43S 15°20E **144** A2
Moniac *U.S.A.* 30°31N 82°14W **178** F7
Monifieth *U.K.* 56°30N 2°48W **65** E6
Monistrol-sur-Loire
  France 45°17N 4°11E **73** D8
Monkey Bay *Malawi* 14°7S 35°1E **143** E4
Monkey Mia *Australia* 25°48S 113°43E **149** E1
Monkey River *Belize* 16°22N 88°29W **181** D7
Monki *Poland* 53°23N 22°48E **83** E9
Monkland *Canada* 45°11N 74°52W **175** A10
Monkoto
  Dem. Rep. of the Congo 1°38S 20°35E **140** E4
Monkton *Canada* 43°35N 81°5W **174** C3
Monmouth *U.K.* 51°48N 2°42W **67** F5
Monmouth *Ill., U.S.A.* 40°55N 90°39W **172** E8
Monmouth *Oreg.,
  U.S.A.* 44°51N 123°14W **168** D2
Monmouthshire □ *U.K.* 51°48N 2°54W **67** F5

Mono → *Togo* 6°17N 1°51E **139** D5
Mono, Pta. *Nic.* 12°0N 83°30W **182** D3
Mono L. *U.S.A.* 38°1N 119°1W **170** H7
Monolith *U.S.A.* 35°7N 118°22W **171** K8
Monolithos *Greece* 36°7N 27°45E **101** C9
Monongahela *U.S.A.* 40°12N 79°56W **174** F5
Monópoli *Italy* 40°57N 17°18E **95** B10
Monor *Hungary* 47°21N 19°27E **80** C4
Monos I. *Trin. & Tob.* 10°42N 61°44W **187** K15
Monóvar *Spain* 38°28N 0°53W **91** G4
Monowai *N.Z.* 45°53S 167°31E **155** F2
Monowai, L. *N.Z.* 45°53S 167°25E **155** F2
Monreal del Campo
  Spain 40°47N 1°20W **90** E3
Monreale *Italy* 38°5N 13°17E **94** D6
Monroe *Ga., U.S.A.* 33°47N 83°43W **178** B6
Monroe *La., U.S.A.* 32°30N 92°7W **176** E8
Monroe *Mich., U.S.A.* 41°55N 83°24W **173** E12
Monroe *N.C., U.S.A.* 34°59N 80°33W **177** D14
Monroe *N.Y., U.S.A.* 41°20N 74°11W **175** E10
Monroe *Utah, U.S.A.* 38°38N 112°7W **168** G7
Monroe *Wash., U.S.A.* 47°51N 121°58W **170** C5
Monroe *Wis., U.S.A.* 42°36N 89°38W **172** D9
Monroe, L. *U.S.A.* 28°50N 81°19W **179** G8
Monroe City *U.S.A.* 39°39N 91°44W **172** F8
Monroeton *U.S.A.* 41°43N 76°29W **175** E8
Monroeville *Ala.,
  U.S.A.* 31°31N 87°20W **177** F11
Monroeville *Pa., U.S.A.* 40°26N 79°45W **174** F5
Monrovia *Liberia* 6°18N 10°47W **138** D2
Mons *Belgium* 50°27N 3°58E **69** D3
Møns Klint *Denmark* 54°57N 12°33E **63** K6
Monsaraz *Portugal* 38°28N 7°22W **89** G3
Monse *Indonesia* 4°7S 123°15E **119** E6
Monségur *France* 44°38N 0°4E **72** D4
Monşelice *Italy* 45°14N 11°45E **93** C8
Mönsterås *Sweden* 57°3N 16°26E **63** H10
Mont Cenis, Col du
  France 45°15N 6°55E **73** C10
Mont-de-Marsan *France* 43°54N 0°31W **72** E3
Mont-Joli *Canada* 48°37N 68°10W **165** C6
Mont-Laurier *Canada* 46°35N 75°30W **164** C4
Mont-Louis *Canada* 49°15N 65°44W **165** C6
Mont Peko △ *Ivory C.* 9°5N 7°15W **138** D3
Mont-roig del Camp *Spain* 41°5N 0°58E **90** D5
Mont-St-Michel, Le
  France 48°40N 1°30W **70** D5
Mont Sangbé △ *Ivory C.* 8°0N 7°10W **138** D3
Mont-Tremblant □
  Canada 46°30N 74°30W **164** C5
Montabaur *Germany* 50°25N 7°50E **76** E3
Montagnac *France* 43°29N 3°28E **72** E7
Montagnana *Italy* 45°14N 11°29E **93** C8
Montagne de Reims △
  France 49°8N 4°0E **71** C11
Montagu *S. Africa* 33°45S 20°8E **144** E3
Montagu I. *Antarctica* 58°25S 26°20W **5** B1
Montague *Canada* 46°10N 62°39W **165** C7
Montague *I., Mexico* 31°45N 114°48W **180** A2
Montague I. *Australia* 36°16S 150°13E **153** D9
Montague I. *U.S.A.* 60°0N 147°30W **166** D10
Montague Ra.
  Australia 27°15S 119°30E **149** E2
Montague Sd.
  Australia 14°28S 125°20E **148** B4
Montaigu *France* 46°59N 1°18W **70** F5
Montalbán *Spain* 40°50N 0°45W **90** E4
Montalbano Iónico *Italy* 40°17N 16°34E **95** B9
Montalbo *Spain* 39°53N 2°42W **90** F2
Montalcino *Italy* 43°3N 11°29E **93** E8
Montalegre *Portugal* 41°49N 7°47W **88** D3
Montalto *Italy* 38°10N 15°55E **95** D8
Montalto di Castro *Italy* 42°21N 11°37E **93** F8
Montalto Uffugo *Italy* 39°24N 16°9E **95** C9
Montalvo *U.S.A.* 34°15N 119°12W **171** L7
Montamarta *Spain* 41°39N 5°49W **88** D5
Montana *Bulgaria* 43°27N 23°16E **96** C7
Montana *Peru* 6°0S 73°0W **188** B3
Montana □ *Bulgaria* 43°30N 23°0E **96** C7
Montana □ *U.S.A.* 47°0N 110°0W **168** C9
Montaña Clara, I.
  Canary Is. 29°17N 13°33W **100** E6
Montañas de Malaga △
  Spain 36°48N 4°32W **89** J6
Montánchez *Spain* 39°15N 6°8W **89** F4
Montargil *Portugal* 39°5N 8°10W **89** F2
Montargis *France* 47°59N 2°43E **71** E9
Montauban *France* 44°2N 1°21E **72** E5
Montauk *U.S.A.* 41°3N 71°57W **175** E13
Montauk Pt. *U.S.A.* 41°4N 71°51W **175** E13
Montbard *France* 47°38N 4°20E **71** E11
Montbarrey *France* 47°1N 5°39E **71** E12
Montbéliard *France* 47°31N 6°48E **71** E13
Montblanc *Spain* 41°23N 1°4E **90** D6
Montbrison *France* 45°36N 4°3E **73** C8
Montcalm, Pic de *France* 42°40N 1°25E **72** F5
Montceau-les-Mines
  France 46°40N 4°23E **71** F11
Montcenis *France* 46°47N 4°23E **73** B8
Montchanin *France* 46°45N 4°28E **73** B8
Montclair *U.S.A.* 40°49N 74°12W **175** F10
Montcornet *France* 49°40N 4°1E **71** C11
Montcuq *France* 44°21N 1°13E **72** D5
Montdidier *France* 49°38N 2°35E **71** C9
Monte Albán *Mexico* 17°2N 96°46W **181** D5
Monte Alegre *Brazil* 2°0S 54°0W **187** D8
Monte Alegre de Goiás
  Brazil 13°14S 47°10W **189** E9
Monte Alegre do Piauí
  Brazil 9°46S 45°18W **189** B1
Monte Azul *Brazil* 15°9S 42°53W **189** E10
Monte-Carlo *Monaco* 43°44N 7°25E **73** E11
Monte Carmelo *Brazil* 18°43S 47°29W **189** E9
Monte Caseros
  Argentina 30°10S 57°50W **190** C4
Monte Comán
  Argentina 34°40S 67°53W **190** C3
Monte Cristi *Dom. Rep.* 19°52N 71°39W **183** C5
Monte Cucco △ *Italy* 43°22N 12°43E **93** E9
Monte Dinero
  Argentina 52°15S 68°33W **192** G3
Monte León *Argentina* 50°15S 69°0W **192** F3
Monte Lindo →
  Paraguay 23°56S 57°12W **190** A4
Monte Pascoal △
  Brazil 16°51S 39°21W **189** E10
Monte Patria *Chile* 30°42S 70°58W **190** C2
Monte Quemado
  Argentina 25°53S 62°41W **190** B3
Monte Redondo *Portugal* 39°53N 8°50W **88** F2

Monte Rio *U.S.A.* 38°28N 123°0W **170** G4
Monte San Giovanni Campano
  Italy 41°38N 13°31E **94** A6
Monte San Savino *Italy* 43°20N 11°43E **93** E8
Monte Sant'Ángelo
  Italy 41°42N 15°59E **93** G12
Monte Santu, C. di *Italy* 40°5N 9°44E **94** B2
Monte Subasio △ *Italy* 43°5N 12°40E **93** E9
Monte Vista *U.S.A.* 37°35N 106°9W **169** H10
Monteagudo *Argentina* 27°14S 54°8W **191** B5
Montealegre del Castillo
  Spain 38°48N 1°17W **91** G3
Montebello *Canada* 45°40N 74°55W **164** C5
Montebello Iónico *Italy* 37°59N 15°45E **95** E8
Montebello Is.
  Australia 20°30S 115°45E **148** D2
Montebelluna *Italy* 45°47N 12°3E **93** C9
Montebourg *France* 49°30N 1°20W **70** C5
Montecarlo *Argentina* 26°34S 54°47W **191** B5
Montecastrilli *Italy* 42°39N 12°29E **93** F9
Montecatini Terme *Italy* 43°53N 10°46E **92** E7
Montecito *U.S.A.* 34°26N 119°40W **171** L7
Montecristo *Italy* 42°20N 10°19E **92** F7
Montefalco *Italy* 42°53N 12°39E **93** F9
Montefiascone *Italy* 42°32N 12°2E **93** F9
Montefrío *Spain* 37°20N 4°0W **89** H7
Montegiórgio *Italy* 43°6N 13°33E **93** E10
Montego Bay *Jamaica* 18°28N 77°55W **182** a
Montehermoso *Spain* 40°5N 6°21W **88** E4
Monteiro *Brazil* 7°48S 37°2W **189** B3
Montejícar *Spain* 37°33N 3°30W **89** H7
Montélimar *France* 44°33N 4°45E **73** D8
Montella *Italy* 40°51N 15°1E **95** B8
Montellano *Spain* 36°59N 5°29W **89** J5
Montello *U.S.A.* 43°48N 89°20W **172** D9
Montemayor, Meseta de
  Argentina 44°20S 66°10W **192** E3
Montemor-o-Novo
  Portugal 38°40N 8°12W **89** G2
Montemor-o-Velho
  Portugal 40°11N 8°40W **88** E2
Montemorelos *Mexico* 25°12N 99°49W **181** B5
Montendre *France* 45°16N 0°26W **72** C3
Montenegro *Brazil* 29°39S 51°29W **191** B5
Montenegro ■ *Europe* 42°40N 19°20E **96** D3
Montenero di Bisáccia
  Italy 41°57N 14°47E **93** G11
Montepuez *Mozam.* 13°8S 38°59E **143** E4
Montepuez → *Mozam.* 12°32S 40°27E **143** E5
Montepulciano *Italy* 43°5N 11°47E **93** E8
Montereale *Italy* 42°31N 13°15E **93** F10
Montereau-Faut-Yonne
  France 48°22N 2°57E **71** D9
Monterey *U.S.A.* 36°37N 121°55W **170** J5
Monterey B. *U.S.A.* 36°45N 122°0W **170** J5
Montería *Colombia* 8°46N 75°53W **186** B3
Monteros *Argentina* 27°11S 65°30W **190** B2
Monterotondo *Italy* 42°3N 12°37E **93** F9
Monterrey *Mexico* 25°40N 100°19W **180** B4
Montes Altos *Brazil* 5°50S 47°4W **189** B1
Montes Azules △
  Mexico 16°21N 91°3W **181** D6
Montes Claros *Brazil* 16°30S 43°50W **189** E10
Montes Universales *Spain* 40°15N 1°35W **90** E3
Montesano sulla Marcellana
  Italy 40°16N 15°42E **95** B8
Montesárchio *Italy* 41°4N 14°38E **95** A7
Montescaglioso *Italy* 40°33N 16°40E **95** B9
Montesilvano *Italy* 42°28N 14°8E **93** F11
Montevarchi *Italy* 43°31N 11°34E **93** E8
Montevideo *Uruguay* 34°50S 56°11W **191** C4
Montevideo *U.S.A.* 44°57N 95°43W **172** C6
Montezuma *Ga., U.S.A.* 32°18N 84°2W **178** D5
Montezuma *Iowa,
  U.S.A.* 41°35N 92°32W **172** E7
Montezuma Castle △
  U.S.A. 34°39N 111°45W **169** J8
Montfaucon *France* 47°6N 1°7W **70** E5
Montfaucon-d'Argonne
  France 49°16N 5°8E **71** C12
Montfaucon-en-Velay
  France 45°11N 4°20E **73** C8
Montfort-le-Gesnois
  France 48°0N 0°25E **70** D7
Montfort-sur-Meu *France* 48°9N 1°58W **70** D5
Montgenèvre *France* 44°56N 6°43E **73** D10
Montgó △ *Spain* 38°48N 0°7W **91** G5
Montgomery *U.K.* 52°34N 3°8W **67** E4
Montgomery *Ala.,
  U.S.A.* 32°23N 86°19W **178** C3
Montgomery *Pa.,
  U.S.A.* 41°10N 76°53W **174** E8
Montgomery *W. Va.,
  U.S.A.* 38°11N 81°19W **173** F13
Montgomery City
  U.S.A. 38°59N 91°30W **172** F8
Montguyon *France* 45°12N 0°12W **72** C3
Monthermé *France* 49°52N 4°43E **71** C11
Monthey *Switz.* 46°15N 6°56E **77** J2
Monthois *France* 49°18N 4°43E **71** C11
Monti *Italy* 40°48N 9°19E **94** B2
Monti Lucrétili △ *Italy* 42°5N 12°50E **93** F9
Monti Picentini △ *Italy* 40°45N 15°2E **95** B8
Monti Sibillini △ *Italy* 42°55N 13°15E **93** F10
Monti Simbruini △
  Italy 41°55N 13°19E **93** G10
Monticelli d'Ongina *Italy* 45°5N 9°56E **92** C6
Monticello *Ark., U.S.A.* 33°38N 91°47W **176** E8
Monticello *Fla., U.S.A.* 30°33N 83°52W **178** F6
Monticello *Ga., U.S.A.* 33°18N 83°41W **178** B6
Monticello *Ill.,
  U.S.A.* 40°1N 88°34W **172** E9
Monticello *Ind.,
  U.S.A.* 40°45N 86°46W **172** E10
Monticello *Iowa,
  U.S.A.* 42°15N 91°12W **172** E8
Monticello *Ky., U.S.A.* 36°50N 84°51W **173** G11
Monticello *Minn.,
  U.S.A.* 45°18N 93°48W **172** C7
Monticello *Miss., U.S.A.* 31°33N 90°7W **177** F9
Monticello *N.Y.,
  U.S.A.* 41°39N 74°42W **175** E10
Monticello *Utah,
  U.S.A.* 37°52N 109°21W **169** H9
Montichiari *Italy* 45°28N 10°23E **92** C7
Montier-en-Der *France* 48°30N 4°45E **71** D11
Montignac *France* 45°4N 1°10E **72** C5
Montigny-les-Metz
  France 49°6N 6°10E **71** C13
Montigny-sur-Aube
  France 47°57N 4°45E **71** E11
Montijo *Portugal* 38°41N 8°54W **89** G2

Montijo *Spain* 38°52N 6°39W **89** [cut]
Montilla *Spain* 37°36N 4°40W **89** [cut]
Montivilliers *France* 49°33N 0°12E **70** [cut]
Montluçon *France* 46°22N 2°36E **7** [cut]
Montmagny *Canada* 46°58N 70°34W **16** [cut]
Montmarault *France* 46°19N 2°57E **7** [cut]
Montmartre *Canada* 50°14N 103°27W **16** [cut]
Montmédy *France* 49°30N 5°20E **71** [cut]
Montmélian *France* 45°30N 6°4E **73** [cut]
Montmirail *France* 48°51N 3°30E **71** [cut]
Montmoreau-St-Cybard
  France 45°23N 0°8E **7** [cut]
Montmorillon *France* 46°26N 0°50E **7** [cut]
Montmort-Lucy *France* 48°55N 3°49E **71** [cut]
Monto *Australia* 24°52S 151°6E **15** [cut]
Montoire-sur-le-Loir
  France 47°45N 0°52E **7** [cut]
Montongbuwoh
  Indonesia 8°33S 116°4E **11** [cut]
Montório al Vomano
  Italy 42°35N 13°38E **93** [cut]
Montoro *Spain* 38°1N 4°27W **8** [cut]
Montour Falls *U.S.A.* 42°21N 76°51W **17** [cut]
Montoursville *U.S.A.* 41°15N 76°55W **17** [cut]
Montpelier *Idaho,
  U.S.A.* 42°19N 111°18W **16** [cut]
Montpelier *Vt., U.S.A.* 44°16N 72°35W **175** [cut]
Montpellier *France* 43°37N 3°52E **7** [cut]
Montpezat-de-Quercy
  France 44°15N 1°30E **7** [cut]
Montpon-Ménestérol
  France 45°0N 0°11E **7** [cut]
Montréal *Canada* 45°30N 73°33W **175** [cut]
Montréal *Aude, France* 43°13N 2°8E **7** [cut]
Montréal *Gers, France* 43°56N 0°11E **7** [cut]
Montreal → *Canada* 47°14N 84°39W **16** [cut]
Montreal L. *Canada* 54°20S 66°10W **192** [cut]
Montreal Lake *Canada* 54°3N 105°46W **16** [cut]
Montredon-Labessonnié
  France 43°45N 2°18E **7** [cut]
Montrésor *France* 47°10N 1°10E **7** [cut]
Montret *France* 46°40N 5°7E **71** [cut]
Montreuil *Pas-de-Calais,
  France* 50°27N 1°45E **7** [cut]
Montreuil *Seine-St-Denis,
  France* 48°51N 2°27E **7** [cut]
Montreuil-Bellay *France* 47°8N 0°9W **7** [cut]
Montreux *Switz.* 46°26N 6°55E **7** [cut]
Montrevel-en-Bresse
  France 46°21N 5°8E **71** [cut]
Montrichard *France* 47°20N 1°10E **7** [cut]
Montrose *U.K.* 56°44N 2°27W **6** [cut]
Montrose *Colo.,
  U.S.A.* 38°29N 107°53W **168** [cut]
Montrose *Pa., U.S.A.* 41°50N 75°53W **17** [cut]
Monts, Pte. des *Canada* 49°20N 67°12W **16** [cut]
Montsalvy *France* 44°41N 2°30E **7** [cut]
Montsant, Serra de *Spain* 41°17N 1°0E **9** [cut]
Montsauche-les-Settons
  France 47°13N 4°2E **71** [cut]
Montsec, Serra del *Spain* 42°5S 0°45E **9** [cut]
Montseny △ *Spain* 41°43N 2°29E **9** [cut]
Montserrat *Spain* 41°36N 1°49E **9** [cut]
Montserrat ☑
  W. Indies 16°40N 62°10W **18** [cut]
Montuenga *Spain* 41°3N 4°38W **8** [cut]
Montuïri *Spain* 39°34N 2°59E **10** [cut]
Monywa *Burma* 22°7N 95°11E **123** [cut]
Monza *Italy* 45°35N 9°16E **9** [cut]
Monze *Zambia* 16°17S 27°29E **14** [cut]
Monze, C. *Pakistan* 24°47N 66°37E **12** [cut]
Monzón *Spain* 41°52N 0°10E **9** [cut]
Mooers *U.S.A.* 44°58N 73°35W **175** [cut]
Mooi → *S. Africa* 28°45S 30°34E **14** [cut]
Mooi River *S. Africa* 29°13S 29°50E **14** [cut]
Mookgopong *S. Africa* 24°31S 28°44E **14** [cut]
Moomba *Australia* 28°6S 140°12E **15** [cut]
Moonah → *Australia* 22°3S 138°33E **15** [cut]
Moonda, L. *Australia* 25°52S 140°25E **15** [cut]
Moonie *Australia* 27°46S 150°19E **15** [cut]
Moonie → *Australia* 29°19S 148°43E **15** [cut]
Moora *Australia* 30°37S 115°58E **14** [cut]
Moorcroft *U.S.A.* 44°16N 104°57W **168** [cut]
Moore, L. *Australia* 29°50S 117°35E **14** [cut]
Moore, L. *Australia* 30°3S 117°35E **14** [cut]
Moore Falls *Canada* 44°48N 78°48W **17** [cut]
Moore Haven *U.S.A.* 26°50N 81°6W **17** [cut]
Moore Park *Australia* 24°42S 152°12E **15** [cut]
Moore Res. *U.S.A.* 44°20N 71°53W **175** [cut]
Moore River →
  Australia 31°7S 115°39E **14** [cut]
Moorefield *U.S.A.* 39°4N 78°58W **173** [cut]
Moorfoot Hills *U.K.* 55°44N 3°8W **6** [cut]
Moorhead *U.S.A.* 46°53N 96°45W **17** [cut]
Moornanyah L.
  Australia 33°15S 143°42E **15** [cut]
Mooroopna *Australia* 36°25S 145°22E **15** [cut]
Moorpark *U.S.A.* 34°17N 118°53W **17** [cut]
Moorreesburg *S. Africa* 33°6S 18°38E **14** [cut]
Moosburg *Germany* 48°27N 11°56E **7** [cut]
Moose → *Canada* 51°20N 80°25W **16** [cut]
Moose Creek *Canada* 45°15N 74°58W **175** [cut]
Moose Factory *Canada* 51°16N 80°32W **16** [cut]
Moose Jaw *Canada* 50°24N 105°30W **16** [cut]
Moose Jaw → *Canada* 50°34N 105°18W **16** [cut]
Moose Lake *Canada* 53°46N 100°8W **16** [cut]
Moose Lake *U.S.A.* 46°27N 92°46W **17** [cut]
Moose Mountain △
  Canada 49°48N 102°25W **16** [cut]
Moosehead L. *U.S.A.* 45°38N 69°40W **17** [cut]
Mooselookmeguntic L.
  U.S.A. 44°55N 70°49W **17** [cut]
Moosilauke, Mt.
  U.S.A. 44°3N 71°40W **17** [cut]
Moosomin *Canada* 50°9N 101°40W **16** [cut]
Moosonee *Canada* 51°17N 80°39W **16** [cut]
Moosup *U.S.A.* 41°43N 71°53W **17** [cut]
Mootwingee △
  Australia 31°1S 142°25E **15** [cut]
Mopane *S. Africa* 22°37S 29°52E **14** [cut]
Mopeia Velha *Mozam.* 17°30S 35°40E **14** [cut]
Mopipi *Botswana* 21°6S 24°55E **14** [cut]
Mopoi *C.A.R.* 5°6N 26°54E **14** [cut]
Mopti *Mali* 14°30N 4°0W **13** [cut]
Moqor *Afghan.* 32°50N 67°42E **12** [cut]
Moquegua *Peru* 17°15S 70°46W **18** [cut]

juegua □ *Peru* 16°50S 70°55W **188** D3
ˈHungary 47°52N 18°12E **80** C3
ˈa *Cameroon* 11°2N 14°7E **139** C7
ˈa *Portugal* 38°55N 8°10W **89** G2
ˈa *Sweden* 61°2N 14°38E **62** C4
ˈa *Minn., U.S.A.* 45°53N 93°18W **172** C7
ˈa *N. Mex., U.S.A.* 35°58N 105°20W **169** J11
ˈa de Rubielos *Spain* 40°15N 0°45W **90** C4
ˈd'Ebre *Spain* 41°9N 0°38E **90** D5
ˈa la Nova *Spain* 41°7N 0°39E **90** D5
ˈaca = *Montenegro* 42°20N 19°9E **96** D3
ˈada Nova *Brazil* 5°7S 38°23W **189** B3
ˈada Nova de Minas
  Brazil 18°37S 45°22W **189** D1
ˈadabad *India* 28°50N 78°50E **125** E8
ˈafenobe *Madag.* 17°50S 44°54E **141** H8
ˈag *Poland* 53°55N 19°56E **82** E6
ˈal de Calatrava
  Spain 38°51N 3°33W **89** G7
ˈaleda, Canal *Chile* 44°30S 73°30W **192** B2
ˈaleja *Spain* 40°6N 6°43W **88** E4
ˈamanga *Madag.* 18°56S 48°12E **141** H9
ˈano Cálabro *Italy* 38°10N 16°8E **95** C9
ˈant Bay *Jamaica* 17°53N 76°25W **182** a
ˈant Cays *Jamaica* 17°22N 76°9W **182** a
ˈant Pt. *Jamaica* 17°55N 76°12W **182** a
ˈar *India* 26°14N 78°14E **124** F8
ˈatalla *Spain* 38°14N 1°49W **91** G3
ˈatuwa *Sri Lanka* 6°45N 79°55E **127** L4
ˈavia = *Slovak Rep.* 48°10N 16°59E **79** C9
ˈavia *U.S.A.* 42°43N 76°29W **175** D8
ˈavian Hts. = Českomoravská
  vrchovina *Czech Rep.* 49°30N 15°40E **78** B8
ˈavica = *Serbia* 43°52N 20°8E **96** C4
ˈavița *Romania* 45°17N 21°14E **80** E6
ˈavská Třebová
  Czech Rep. 49°45N 16°40E **79** B9
ˈavské Budějovice
  Czech Rep. 49°4N 15°49E **78** B4
ˈawa *Australia* 29°13S 116°0E **149** F2
ˈawanha *Guyana* 8°30N 59°40W **186** B7
ˈawa *U.S.A.* 57°31N 3°18W **65** D5
ˈay Firth *U.K.* 57°40N 3°52W **65** D5
ˈbach *Germany* 49°48N 7°6E **77** F3
ˈbegno *Italy* 46°8N 9°34E **92** B6
ˈbi *India* 22°50N 70°42E **124** H4
ˈbihan □ *France* 47°55N 2°50W **70** E4
ˈbylånga *Sweden* 56°32N 16°22E **63** H10
ˈcenx *France* 44°3N 0°55W **72** D3
ˈcone *Italy* 41°20N 14°40E **95** A7
ˈdelles *France* 48°5N 1°52W **70** D5
ˈden *Canada* 49°15N 98°10W **163** D9
ˈdovian Republic =
  Mordvinia □ *Russia* 54°20N 44°30E **86** C7
ˈdovo *Russia* 52°6N 40°50E **86** D5
ˈdvinia □ *Russia* 54°20N 44°30E **86** C7
ˈdy *Nepal* 52°13N 22°31E **83** F9
ˈeau ← *U.S.A.* 45°18N 100°43W **172** C3
ˈebeng *S. Africa* 23°30S 29°55E **145** B4
ˈecambe *U.K.* 54°5N 2°52W **66** C5
ˈecambe B. *U.K.* 54°7N 3°0W **66** C5
ˈee *Australia* 29°28S 149°54E **151** D4
ˈehead *U.S.A.* 38°11N 83°26W **173** F12
ˈehead *U.S.A.* 34°43N 76°43W **177** D16
ˈel ← *India* 26°13N 76°36E **124** F7
ˈeland *U.S.A.* 33°17N 84°46W **178** B5
ˈelia *Mexico* 19°42N 101°7W **180** D4
ˈella *Australia* 33°45S 122°8E **150** C3
ˈella *Spain* 40°35N 0°5W **90** E4
ˈelos *Mexico* 26°42N 107°40W **180** B3
ˈeı □ *Mexico* 18°45N 99°0W **181** D5
ˈemi □ *Botswana* 19°18S 23°10E **144** A3
ˈena, Sierra *Spain* 38°20N 4°0W **89** G7
ˈeni *Romania* 44°59N 25°36E **81** F10
ˈeno *Bolivia* 11°9S 66°15W **188** C4
ˈeno Valley
  U.S.A. 33°56N 117°14W **171** M10
ˈesby I. *Canada* 52°30N 131°40W **162** C2
ˈeton *France* 45°40N 5°28E **73** C9
ˈeton I. *Australia* 27°10S 153°25E **151** D5
ˈeton Island △
  Australia 27°2S 153°24E **151** D5
ˈeuil *France* 49°46N 2°30E **71** C9
ˈez *France* 46°31N 6°2E **71** F13
ˈgan *Australia* 34°2S 139°35E **152** C3
ˈga, G.A., U.S.A.* 31°32N 84°36W **178** D5
ˈgan Utah, U.S.A.* 41°2N 111°41W **168** F8
ˈgan City *U.S.A.* 29°42N 91°12W **176** G9
ˈgan Hill *U.S.A.* 37°8N 121°39W **170** H5
ˈganfield *U.S.A.* 37°41N 87°55W **172** G10
ˈgantown *U.S.A.* 35°45N 81°41W **177** D14
ˈgantown *U.S.A.* 39°38N 79°57W **173** F14
ˈgenzon *S. Africa* 26°45S 29°36E **145** C4
ˈges *Switz.* 46°31N 6°29E **77** J2
ˈghak *Iran* 29°7N 57°54E **129** D8
ˈgongáva *Sweden* 59°57N 16°58E **62** E10
ˈhange *France* 48°55S 6°38E **71** C13
ˈhar ← *India* 25°29N 85°11E **125** G11
ˈhioka *Japan* 43°49N 90°11E **112** C10
ˈi *Japan* 42°6N 140°35E **112** C10
ˈiarty *U.S.A.* 34°59N 106°3W **169** J10
ˈibaya *Guinea* 9°53N 9°32W **138** D3
ˈice L. *Canada* 53°50N 127°40W **162** C3
ˈiki *Nigeria* 12°52N 6°30E **139** C6
ˈinville *Canada* 53°49N 113°41W **162** C6
ˈioka *Japan* 39°45N 141°8E **112** E10
ˈis *Mexico* 28°10N 108°32W **180** B3
ˈisset *Australia* 33°6S 151°30E **153** B9
ˈlaix *France* 48°36N 3°52W **70** D3
ˈlunda *Sweden* 57°19N 15°52E **63** H10
ˈmanno *Italy* 39°53N 15°59E **95** C8
ˈmant *France* 48°37N 2°52E **71** D9
ˈmugao = Marmagao
  India 15°25N 73°56E **127** G1
ˈnington *Australia* 38°15S 145°5E **153** E6
ˈnington, I. *Chile* 49°50S 75°30W **192** C1
ˈnington I.
  Australia 16°30S 139°30E **150** B4
ˈnington Peninsula △
  Australia 38°25S 144°53E **153** E6
ˈnos ← *Greece* 38°25N 21°50E **98** C3

Moro *Pakistan* 26°40N 68°0E **124** F2
Moro ← *Pakistan* 29°42N 67°22E **124** E2
Moro G. *Phil.* 6°30N 123°0E **119** C6
Morocco ■ *N. Afr.* 32°0N 5°50W **134** B4
Morococha *Peru* 11°40S 76°5W **188** C2
Morogoro *Tanzania* 6°50S 37°40E **142** D4
Morogoro □ *Tanzania* 8°0S 37°0E **142** D4
Moroleón *Mexico* 20°8N 101°12W **180** C4
Morombe *Madag.* 21°45S 43°22E **141** J8
Moron *Argentina* 34°39S 58°37W **190** C4
Morón *Cuba* 22°8N 78°39W **182** B4
Mörön *Mongolia* 49°38N 100°9E **110** B9
Morón de Almazán
  Spain 41°29N 2°27W **90** D2
Morón de la Frontera
  Spain 37°6N 5°28W **89** H5
Morona ← *Peru* 4°40S 77°10W **188** D3
Morondava *Madag.* 20°17S 44°17E **141** J8
Moroni *Comoros Is.* 11°40S 43°16E **141** a
Moroni *U.S.A.* 39°32N 111°35W **168** G8
Moronou *Ivory C.* 6°16N 4°59W **138** D4
Morotai *Indonesia* 2°10N 128°30E **119** D7
Moroto *Uganda* 2°28N 34°42E **142** B3
Moroto, Mt. *Uganda* 2°30N 34°43E **142** B3
Morozov *Bulgaria* 42°30N 25°10E **97** D9
Morozovsk *Russia* 48°25N 41°50E **87** F5
Morpeth *Canada* 42°23N 81°50W **174** D3
Morpeth *U.K.* 55°10N 1°41W **66** B6
Morphou *Cyprus* 35°12N 32°59E **101** D11
Morphou Bay *Cyprus* 35°15N 32°50E **101** D11
Morrilton *U.S.A.* 35°9N 92°44W **176** D8
Morrinhos *Ceará, Brazil* 3°14S 40°7W **189** A2
Morrinhos *Minas Gerais,*
  Brazil 17°45S 49°10W **187** D9
Morrinsville *N.Z.* 37°40S 175°32E **154** D4
Morris *Canada* 49°25N 97°22W **163** D9
Morris *Ill., U.S.A.* 41°22N 88°26W **172** E9
Morris *Minn., U.S.A.* 45°35N 95°55W **172** C6
Morris *N.Y., U.S.A.* 42°33N 75°15W **175** D9
Morris *Pa., U.S.A.* 41°35N 77°17W **174** E7
Morris, Mt. *Australia* 26°9S 131°4E **149** E5
Morris Jesup, Kap
  Greenland 83°40N 34°0W **57** A7
Morrisburg *Canada* 44°55N 75°7W **175** B9
Morristown *Ariz.,*
  U.S.A. 33°51N 112°37W **169** K7
Morristown *N.J.,*
  U.S.A. 40°48N 74°29W **175** F10
Morristown *N.Y.,*
  U.S.A. 44°35N 75°39W **175** B9
Morristown *Tenn.,*
  U.S.A. 36°13N 83°18W **177** C13
Morrisville *N.Y.,*
  U.S.A. 42°53N 75°35W **175** D9
Morrisville *Pa., U.S.A.* 40°13N 74°47W **175** F10
Morrisville *Vt., U.S.A.* 44°34N 72°36W **175** B12
Morro, Pta. *Chile* 27°6S 71°0W **190** B1
Morro Bay *U.S.A.* 35°22N 120°51W **170** K6
Morro Chico *Chile* 52°2S 71°26W **192** D2
Morro del Jable
  Canary Is. 28°3N 14°23W **100** F5
Morro do Chapéu *Brazil* 11°33S 41°9W **189** C2
Morro Jable, Pta. de
  Canary Is. 28°2N 14°20W **100** F5
Morrocoy △ *Venezuela* 10°48N 68°13W **183** D6
Morros *Brazil* 2°52S 44°3W **189** A2
Morrosquillo, G. de
  Colombia 9°35N 75°40W **182** E4
Mörrum *Sweden* 56°12N 14°45E **63** H6
Morrumbene *Mozam.* 23°31S 35°16E **145** B6
Mörrumsån ← *Sweden* 56°10N 14°45E **63** H6
Mors *Denmark* 56°50N 8°45E **63** H2
Morshansk *Russia* 53°28N 41°50E **86** D5
Morsi *India* 21°21N 78°0E **126** D4
Mörsil *Sweden* 63°19N 13°40E **62** A7
Mortagne ← *France* 48°33N 6°27E **71** D13
Mortagne-au-Perche
  France 48°31N 0°33E **70** D7
Mortagne-sur-Gironde
  France 45°28N 0°47W **72** C3
Mortagne-sur-Sèvre
  France 47°0N 0°57W **70** F6
Mortain *France* 48°40N 0°57W **70** D6
Mortara *Italy* 45°15N 8°44E **92** C5
Morteau *France* 47°3N 6°35E **71** F13
Morteros *Argentina* 30°50S 62°0W **190** C3
Mortlach *Canada* 50°27N 106°4W **163** C7
Mortlake *Australia* 38°5S 142°50E **152** E5
Morton *Tex., U.S.A.* 33°44N 102°46W **176** E3
Morton *Wash., U.S.A.* 46°34N 122°17W **170** D4
Moruga *Trin. & Tob.* 10°4N 61°16W **187** K15
Morundah *Australia* 34°57S 146°19E **153** C7
Moruya *Australia* 35°58S 150°3E **153** C9
Morvan *France* 47°5N 4°3E **71** E11
Morvan □ *France* 47°12N 4°3E **71** E11
Morven *Australia* 26°22S 147°5E **151** D4
Morven *N.Z.* 44°50S 171°6E **155** E6
Morvern *U.K.* 56°38N 5°44W **65** E3
Morwell △ *Australia* 38°14S 146°23E **153** E7
Moryń *Poland* 52°51N 14°22E **83** F1
Morzine *France* 46°11N 6°42E **71** F13
Mosakahiken = Moose Lake
  Canada 53°46N 100°8W **163** C8
Mosalsk *Russia* 54°30N 34°55E **84** E4
Mosbach *Germany* 49°21N 9°9E **77** F5
Moščenice *Croatia* 45°17N 14°16E **93** C11
Mosciano Sant' Angelo
  Italy 42°42N 13°52E **93** F10
Moscos Is. *Burma* 14°0N 97°30E **120** F1
Moscow = Moskva
  Russia 55°45N 37°37E **84** E9
Moscow *Idaho, U.S.A.* 46°44N 117°0W **168** C5
Moscow *Pa., U.S.A.* 41°20N 75°31W **175** E9
Mosel ← *Europe* 50°22N 7°36E **71** B14
Moselle = Mosel ←
  Europe 50°22N 7°36E **71** B14
Moselle □ *France* 48°59N 6°33E **71** D13
Moses Lake *U.S.A.* 47°8N 119°17W **168** C4
Mosgiel *N.Z.* 45°53S 170°21E **155** F5
Moshaweng ←
  S. Africa 26°35S 22°50E **144** C3
Moshchnyy, Ostrov
  Russia 60°1N 27°50E **84** B4
Moshi *Tanzania* 3°22S 37°18E **142** C4
Moshi ← *Nigeria* 9°18N 4°38E **139** D5

Moshupa *Botswana* 24°46S 25°29E **144** B4
Mosi-oa-Tunya = Victoria Falls
  Zimbabwe 17°58S 25°52E **143** F2
Mosina *Poland* 52°15N 16°50E **83** F3
Mosjøen *Norway* 65°51N 13°12E **60** D15
Moskenesøya *Norway* 67°58N 13°0E **60** C15
Moskenstraumen
  Norway 67°47N 12°45E **60** C15
Moskva *Russia* 55°45N 37°37E **84** E9
Moskva □ *Russia* 55°20N 37°20E **84** E9
Moskva ← *Russia* 55°5N 38°51E **84** E10
Moslavačka Gora
  Croatia 45°40N 16°37E **93** C13
Mosomane *Botswana* 24°2S 26°19E **144** B4
Mosonmagyaróvár
  Hungary 47°52N 17°18E **80** C2
Mošorin *Serbia* 45°19N 20°4E **80** E5
Mospyne *Ukraine* 47°52N 38°0E **85** J9
Mosquera *Colombia* 2°35N 78°24W **186** C3
Mosquero *U.S.A.* 35°47N 103°58W **169** J12
Mosqueruela *Spain* 40°21N 0°27W **90** E4
Mosquitia *Honduras* 15°20N 84°10W **182** C3
Mosquito Creek L.
  U.S.A. 41°18N 80°46W **174** E4
Mosquito L. *Canada* 62°35N 103°20W **163** A8
Mosquitos, G. de los
  Panama 9°15N 81°10W **182** E3
Moss *Norway* 59°27N 10°40E **61** G14
Moss Vale *Australia* 34°32S 150°25E **153** C9
Mossaka *Congo* 1°15S 16°45E **140** E3
Mossbank *Canada* 49°56N 105°56W **163** D7
Mossburn *N.Z.* 45°41S 168°15E **155** F3
Mosselbaai *S. Africa* 34°11S 22°8E **144** E3
Mossendjo *Congo* 2°55S 12°42E **140** E2
Mossgiel *Australia* 33°15S 144°5E **152** B6
Mossingen *Germany* 48°24N 9°4E **77** G5
Mossman *Australia* 16°21S 145°15E **150** B4
Mossoró *Brazil* 5°10S 37°15W **189** B3
Mossuril *Mozam.* 14°58S 40°42E **143** E5
Mossy Head *U.S.A.* 30°45N 86°19W **179** D3
Mossy Point *Australia* 35°50S 150°11E **153** C9
Most *Czech Rep.* 50°31N 13°38E **78** A6
Mosta *Malta* 35°55N 14°26E **101** D1
Mostaganem *Algeria* 35°54N 0°5E **136** A4
Mostaganem □ *Algeria* 35°40N 0°15E **136** A4
Mostar *Bos.-H.* 43°22N 17°50E **80** G2
Mostardas *Brazil* 31°2S 50°51W **191** C5
Mostiska = Mostyska
  Ukraine 49°48N 23°4E **83** J10
Móstoles *Spain* 40°19N 3°53W **88** B7
Mosty = Masty *Belarus* 53°27N 24°38E **75** B13
Mostyska *Ukraine* 49°48N 23°4E **83** J10
Mosul = Al Mawşil
  Iraq 36°15N 43°5E **105** D10
Mota del Cuervo *Spain* 39°30N 2°52W **91** F2
Mota del Marqués *Spain* 41°38N 5°11W **88** D5
Motagua ← *Guatemala* 15°44N 88°14W **182** C2
Motala *Sweden* 58°32N 15°1E **63** F9
Motaze *Mozam.* 24°48S 32°52E **145** B5
Motça *Romania* 47°15N 26°37E **81** C11
Moth *India* 25°43N 78°57E **125** G8
Motherwell *U.K.* 55°47N 3°58W **65** F5
Motihari *India* 26°30N 84°55E **125** F11
Motilla del Palancar
  Spain 39°34N 1°55W **91** F3
Motiti I. *N.Z.* 37°38S 176°25E **154** D5
Motnik *Slovenia* 46°14N 14°54E **93** B11
Motovun *Croatia* 45°20N 13°50E **93** C10
Motozintla de Mendoza
  Mexico 15°22N 92°14W **181** D6
Motril *Spain* 36°31N 3°37W **89** J7
Motru *Romania* 44°48N 22°59E **80** F7
Motru ← *Romania* 44°32N 23°31E **81** F8
Mott *U.S.A.* 46°23N 102°20W **172** B2
Móttola *Italy* 40°38N 17°2E **95** B10
Motu ← *N.Z.* 37°52S 177°36E **154** D6
Motueka *N.Z.* 41°7S 173°1E **155** B8
Motueka ← *N.Z.* 41°5S 173°1E **155** B8
Motul *Mexico* 21°6N 89°17W **181** C7
Mouchalagane ←
  Canada 50°56N 68°41W **165** B6
Mouding *China* 25°20N 101°28E **116** E3
Moudjéria *Mauritania* 17°50N 12°28W **138** B2
Moudon *Switz.* 46°40N 6°49E **77** J2
Moudros *Greece* 39°50N 25°18E **99** B7
Mougins *France* 43°36N 7°0E **73** E10
Mouhoun = Black Volta ←
  Africa 8°41N 1°33W **138** D4
Mouila *Gabon* 1°50S 11°0E **140** E2
Moulamein *Australia* 35°3S 144°1E **152** C6
Moule à Chique, C.
  St. Lucia 13°43N 60°57W **183** f
Mouliana *Greece* 35°10N 25°59E **101** D7
Moulins *France* 46°35N 3°19E **71** F10
Moulmein *Burma* 16°30N 97°40E **123** L20
Moulouya, O. ←
  Morocco 35°5N 2°25W **136** A3
Moultrie *U.S.A.* 31°11N 83°47W **178** D6
Moultrie, L. *U.S.A.* 33°20N 80°5W **178** B9
Mound City *Mo., U.S.A.* 40°7N 95°14W **172** E6
Mound City *S. Dak.,*
  U.S.A. 45°44N 100°4W **172** C3
Moundou *Chad* 8°40N 16°10E **135** G9
Moundsville *U.S.A.* 39°55N 80°44W **174** G4
Moung *Cambodia* 12°46N 103°27E **120** F4
Mount Airy *U.S.A.* 36°31N 80°37W **177** C14
Mount Albert *Canada* 44°8N 79°19W **174** B5
Mount Aspiring △
  N.Z. 44°19S 168°47E **155** E3
Mount Barker *S. Austral.,*
  Australia 35°5S 138°52E **152** C3
Mount Barker *W. Austral.,*
  Australia 34°38S 117°40E **149** F2
Mount Barnett Roadhouse
  Australia 16°25S 125°57E **148** C4
Mount Beauty
  Australia 36°47S 147°10E **153** D7
Mount Brydges *Canada* 42°54N 81°29W **174** D3
Mount Buffalo △
  Australia 36°43S 146°46E **153** D7
Mount Burr *Australia* 37°36S 140°20E **152** E4
Mount Carmel = Ha Karmel △
  Israel 32°45N 35°5E **130** C4
Mount Carmel *Ill.,*
  U.S.A. 38°25N 87°46W **172** F9
Mount Carmel *Pa.,*
  U.S.A. 40°47N 76°26W **175** F8
Mount Clemens *U.S.A.* 42°35N 82°53W **174** D2
Mount Coolon

Mount Coolon
  Australia 21°25S 147°25E **150** C4
Mount Darwin
  Zimbabwe 16°47S 31°38E **143** F3
Mount Desert I.
  U.S.A. 44°21N 68°20W **173** C19
Mount Dora *U.S.A.* 28°48N 81°38W **179** G5
Mount Ebenezer
  Australia 25°6S 132°34E **149** E5
Mount Eccles △
  Australia 38°5S 141°54E **152** E4
Mount Edziza △
  Canada 57°30N 130°45W **162** B2
Mount Elgon △ *E. Afr.* 1°4N 34°42E **142** B3
Mount Field △
  Australia 42°39S 146°35E **151** G4
Mount Fletcher
  S. Africa 30°40S 28°30E **145** D4
Mount Forest *Canada* 43°59N 80°43W **174** C4
Mount Frankland △
  Australia 31°47S 116°37E **149** F2
Mount Frederick ○
  Australia 19°39S 129°18E **148** C4
Mount Gambier
  Australia 37°50S 140°46E **152** D4
Mount Garnet *Australia* 17°37S 145°6E **150** B4
Mount Holly *U.S.A.* 39°59N 74°47W **175** G10
Mount Holly Springs
  U.S.A. 40°7N 77°12W **174** F7
Mount Hope *N.S.W.,*
  Australia 32°51S 145°51E **153** B6
Mount Hope *S. Austral.,*
  Australia 34°7S 135°23E **151** E2
Mount Isa *Australia* 20°42S 139°26E **150** C2
Mount James ○
  Australia 24°51S 116°54E **149** D2
Mount Jewett *U.S.A.* 41°44N 78°39W **174** E6
Mount Kaputar △
  Australia 30°16S 150°10E **151** E5
Mount Kenya △ *Kenya* 0°1S 37°21E **142** C4
Mount Kisco *U.S.A.* 41°12N 73°44W **175** E11
Mount Laguna
  U.S.A. 32°52N 116°25W **171** N10
Mount Larcom
  Australia 23°48S 150°59E **150** C5
Mount Lofty Ranges
  Australia 34°35S 139°5E **152** C3
Mount Magnet
  Australia 28°2S 117°47E **149** E2
Mount Manara
  Australia 32°29S 143°58E **152** B5
Mount Maunganui
  N.Z. 37°40S 176°14E **154** D5
Mount Molloy
  Australia 16°42S 145°20E **150** B4
Mount Morgan
  Australia 23°40S 150°25E **150** C5
Mount Morris *U.S.A.* 42°44N 77°52W **174** D7
Mount Pearl *Canada* 47°31N 52°47W **165** C9
Mount Penn *U.S.A.* 40°20N 75°54W **175** F9
Mount Perry *Australia* 25°13S 151°42E **151** D5
Mount Pleasant *Iowa,*
  U.S.A. 40°58N 91°33W **172** E8
Mount Pleasant *Mich.,*
  U.S.A. 43°36N 84°46W **173** D11
Mount Pleasant *Pa.,*
  U.S.A. 40°9N 79°33W **174** F5
Mount Pleasant *S.C.,*
  U.S.A. 32°47N 79°52W **178** C10
Mount Pleasant *Tenn.,*
  U.S.A. 35°32N 87°12W **177** D11
Mount Pleasant *Tex.,*
  U.S.A. 33°9N 94°58W **176** E7
Mount Pleasant *Utah,*
  U.S.A. 39°33N 111°27W **168** G8
Mount Pocono *U.S.A.* 41°7N 75°22W **175** E9
Mount Rainier △
  U.S.A. 46°55N 121°50W **170** D5
Mount Remarkable △
  Australia 32°47S 138°3E **152** B3
Mount Revelstoke △
  Canada 51°5N 118°30W **162** C5
Mount Robson △
  Canada 53°0N 119°0W **162** C5
Mount St. Helens ○
  U.S.A. 46°14N 122°11W **170** D4
Mount Selinda
  Zimbabwe 20°24S 32°43E **145** B5
Mount Shasta *U.S.A.* 41°19N 122°19W **168** F2
Mount Signal *U.S.A.* 32°39N 115°37W **171** N11
Mount Somers *U.S.A.* 43°45S 171°27E **155** D6
Mount Sterling *Ill.,*
  U.S.A. 39°59N 90°45W **172** F8
Mount Sterling *Ky.,*
  U.S.A. 38°4N 83°56W **173** F12
Mount Surprise
  Australia 18°10S 144°17E **150** B3
Mount Union *U.S.A.* 40°23N 77°53W **174** F7
Mount Upton *U.S.A.* 42°26N 75°23W **175** D9
Mount Vernon *Ga.,*
  U.S.A. 32°11N 82°36W **178** D7
Mount Vernon *Ill.,*
  U.S.A. 38°19N 88°55W **172** F9
Mount Vernon *Ind.,*
  U.S.A. 37°56N 87°54W **167** H22
Mount Vernon *N.Y.,*
  U.S.A. 40°54N 73°49W **175** F11
Mount Vernon *Ohio,*
  U.S.A. 40°23N 82°29W **174** F2
Mount Vernon *Wash.,*
  U.S.A. 48°25N 122°20W **170** B4
Mount Victor
  Australia 32°11S 139°44E **152** B3
Mount Wellington
  N.Z. 36°55S 174°52E **154** C4
Mount William △
  Australia 40°56S 148°14E **151** G4
Mounta, Akra *Greece* 38°3N 20°47E **98** C2
Mountain Ash *U.K.* 51°40N 3°23W **67** F4
Mountain Center
  U.S.A. 33°42N 116°44W **171** M10
Mountain City *Nev.,*
  U.S.A. 41°50N 115°58W **168** F6
Mountain City *Tenn.,*
  U.S.A. 36°29N 81°48W **177** C14
Mountain Dale
  U.S.A. 41°41N 74°32W **175** E10
Mountain Grove *U.S.A.* 37°8N 92°16W **172** G7
Mountain Home *Ark.,*
  U.S.A. 36°20N 92°23W **176** C8

Mountain Home *Idaho,*
  U.S.A. 43°8N 115°41W **168** E6
Mountain Iron *U.S.A.* 47°32N 92°37W **172** B7
Mountain Pass
  U.S.A. 35°29N 115°35W **171** K11
Mountain View *Ark.,*
  U.S.A. 35°52N 92°7W **176** D8
Mountain View *Calif.,*
  U.S.A. 37°23N 122°5W **170** H4
Mountain Zebra △
  S. Africa 32°14S 25°27E **144** D4
Mountainair *U.S.A.* 34°31N 106°15W **169** J10
Mountbellew *Ireland* 53°28N 8°31W **64** C3
Mountlake Terrace
  U.S.A. 47°47N 122°18W **170** C4
Mountmellick *Ireland* 53°7N 7°20W **64** C4
Mountrath *Ireland* 53°0N 7°28W **64** C4
Moura *Australia* 24°35S 149°58E **150** C4
Moura *Brazil* 1°32S 61°38W **186** D6
Moura *Portugal* 38°7N 7°30W **89** G3
Mourão *Portugal* 38°22N 7°22W **89** G3
Mourdi, Dépression du
  Chad 18°10N 23°0E **135** E10
Mourdiah *Mali* 14°35N 7°25W **138** C3
Moure ← *France* 43°22N 0°38W **72** E3
Mouri *Ghana* 5°6N 1°14W **139** D4
Mourilyan *Australia* 17°35S 146°3E **150** B4
Mourmelon-le-Grand
  France 49°8N 4°22E **71** C11
Mourne ← *U.K.* 54°52N 7°26W **64** B4
Mourne Mts. *U.K.* 54°10N 6°0W **64** B5
Mournies *Greece* 35°29N 24°1E **101** D6
Mouscron *Belgium* 50°45N 3°12E **69** D3
Moussoro *Chad* 13°41N 16°35E **135** F9
Mouthe *France* 46°44N 6°12E **71** F13
Moutier *Switz.* 47°16N 7°21E **77** H3
Moûtiers *France* 45°29N 6°32E **73** C10
Moutong *Indonesia* 0°28N 121°13E **119** D6
Mouy *France* 49°18N 2°20E **71** C9
Mouydir, Monts du
  Algeria 25°30N 4°10E **136** C4
Mouzaki *Greece* 39°25N 21°37E **98** B3
Mouzon *France* 49°36N 5°5E **71** C12
Movas *Mexico* 28°10N 109°25W **180** B3
Moville *Ireland* 55°11N 7°3W **64** A4
Mowandjum *Australia* 17°22S 123°40E **148** C3
Moxotó ← *Brazil* 9°19S 38°14W **189** B3
Moy ← *Ireland* 54°8N 9°8W **64** B2
Moya *Comoros Is.* 12°18S 44°18E **141** a
Moyale *Ethiopia* 3°34N 39°5E **142** B4
Moyale *Kenya* 3°30N 39°4E **142** B4
Moyamba *S. Leone* 8°4N 12°30W **138** D2
Moyen Atlas *Morocco* 33°0N 5°0W **136** B3
Moyen-Cavally □
  Ivory C. 6°45N 7°30W **138** D3
Moyen-Comoé □
  Ivory C. 6°40N 3°25W **138** D4
Moyo *Indonesia* 8°10S 117°40E **118** F5
Moyobamba *Peru* 6°0S 77°0W **188** B2
Moyowosi □ *Tanzania* 3°50S 31°0E **142** C3
Møysalen △ *Norway* 68°32N 15°29E **60** B16
Moyu *China* 37°15N 79°44E **109** E9
Moyynqum *Zhambyl,*
  Kazakhstan 44°17N 72°57E **109** D8
Moyynqum *Zhambyl,*
  Kazakhstan 44°12N 71°0E **109** D8
Moyynty *Kazakhstan* 47°10N 73°18E **109** C8
Mozambique ■ *Africa* 19°0S 35°0E **143** F4
Mozambique = Moçambique
  Mozam. 15°3S 40°42E **143** F5
Mozambique Basin
  Ind. Oc. 30°0S 40°0E **146** G2
Mozambique Chan.
  Africa 17°30S 42°30E **145** A7
Mozdok *Russia* 43°45N 44°48E **87** J7
Mozdūrān *Iran* 36°9N 60°35E **129** B9
Mozhaysk *Russia* 55°30N 36°2E **84** E9
Mozhga *Russia* 56°26N 52°15E **86** B11
Mozhnābād *Iran* 34°7N 60°6E **129** C9
Mozirje *Slovenia* 46°22N 14°58E **93** B11
Mozyr = Mazyr *Belarus* 51°59N 29°15E **75** B15
Mpanda *Tanzania* 6°23S 31°1E **142** D3
Mpésoba *Mali* 12°31N 5°39W **138** C3
Mphoeng *Zimbabwe* 21°10S 27°51E **143** G2
Mpika *Zambia* 11°51S 31°25E **143** E3
Mpulungu *Zambia* 8°51S 31°5E **143** D3
Mpumalanga *S. Africa* 29°50S 30°33E **145** D5
Mpumalanga □ *S. Africa* 26°0S 30°0E **145** D5
Mpwapwa *Tanzania* 6°23S 36°30E **142** D4
Mqanduli *S. Africa* 31°49S 28°45E **145** E4
Mqinvartsveri = Kazbek
  Russia 42°42N 44°30E **87** J7
Mragowo *Poland* 53°52N 21°18E **82** E8
Mramor *Serbia* 43°20N 21°45E **96** C5
Mrimina *Morocco* 29°50N 7°9W **136** C3
Mrkonjić Grad *Bos.-H.* 44°26N 17°4E **80** F2
Mrkopalj *Croatia* 45°21N 14°52E **93** C11
Mrocza *Poland* 53°16N 17°35E **83** E4
Msaken *Tunisia* 35°49N 10°33E **136** A6
Msambansovu *Zimbabwe* 15°50S 30°3E **143** F3
M'sila *Algeria* 35°46N 4°30E **136** A4
M'sila □ *Algeria* 35°20N 4°20E **136** A4
Msoro *Zambia* 13°35S 31°50E **143** E3
Msta ← *Russia* 58°25N 31°20E **84** C6
Mstislavl = Mstsislaw
  Belarus 54°0N 31°50E **75** A16
Mstsislaw *Belarus* 54°0N 31°50E **75** A16
Mszana Dolna *Poland* 49°41N 20°5E **83** J7
Mszczonów *Poland* 51°58N 20°33E **83** G7
Mtama *Tanzania* 10°17S 39°21E **143** E4
Mtamvuna = Mthamvuna ←
  S. Africa 31°6S 30°12E **145** D5
Mthamvuna ← *S. Africa* 31°6S 30°12E **145** D5
Mthatha *S. Africa* 31°36S 28°49E **145** D4
Mtilikwe ← *Zimbabwe* 21°9S 31°30E **143** G3
Mtirala △ *Georgia* 41°50N 42°2E **87** K6
Mtito Andei *Kenya* 2°41S 38°10E **142** C4
Mtsensk *Russia* 53°17N 36°34E **84** F9
Mtskheta *Georgia* 41°52N 44°45E **87** K7
Mtubatuba *S. Africa* 28°30S 32°8E **145** D5
Mtwalume *S. Africa* 30°30S 30°38E **145** D5
Mtwara-Mikindani
  Tanzania 10°20S 40°20E **143** E5
Mu Gia, Deo *Vietnam* 17°40N 105°47E **120** D5
Mu Ko Chang △
  Thailand 11°59N 102°22E **121** G4
Mu Ko Surin *Thailand* 9°30N 97°55E **121** H1
Mu Us Shamo *China* 39°0N 109°0E **114** E5
Muang Beng *Laos* 20°23S 101°46E **116** G3

Muang Chiang Rai = Chiang Rai
  Thailand 19°52N 99°50E **116** H2
Muang Et *Laos* 20°49N 104°1E **120** B5
Muang Hiam *Laos* 20°5N 103°22E **120** B4
Muang Hongsa *Laos* 19°43N 101°20E **120** C3
Muang Houn *Laos* 20°8N 101°23E **116** G3
Muang Kau *Laos* 15°6N 105°47E **120** E5
Muang Khao *Laos* 19°38N 103°32E **120** C4
Muang Khong *Laos* 14°7N 105°51E **120** E5
Muang Khoua *Laos* 21°5N 102°31E **116** G4
Muang Liap *Laos* 18°29N 101°40E **120** C3
Muang Mai *Thailand* 8°5N 98°21E **121** a
Muang May *Laos* 14°49N 106°56E **120** E6
Muang Na Mo *Laos* 20°36N 101°3E **116** G3
Muang Ngeun *Laos* 20°36N 101°3E **116** G3
Muang Ngoi *Laos* 20°43N 102°41E **116** G4
Muang Nong *Laos* 16°22N 106°30E **120** D6
Muang Ou Neua *Laos* 22°18N 101°48E **116** F3
Muang Ou Tay *Laos* 22°7N 101°48E **116** F3
Muang Pak Beng *Laos* 19°54N 101°8E **116** G3
Muang Phalane *Laos* 16°39N 105°34E **120** D5
Muang Phiang *Laos* 19°6N 101°32E **120** C3
Muang Phine *Laos* 16°32N 106°2E **120** D6
Muang Phonhong
  Laos 18°30N 102°25E **120** C4
Muang Saiapoun *Laos* 18°24N 101°31E **120** C3
Muang Sing *Laos* 21°11N 101°9E **116** G3
Muang Son *Laos* 20°27N 103°19E **120** B4
Muang Soui *Laos* 19°33N 102°52E **120** C4
Muang Va *Laos* 21°53N 102°19E **116** F4
Muang Va *Laos* 18°18N 101°20E **120** C3
Muang Xai *Laos* 20°42N 101°59E **116** G3
Muang Xamteu *Laos* 19°59N 104°38E **120** C5
Muar *Malaysia* 2°3N 102°34E **121** L4
Muarabungo *Indonesia* 1°28S 102°52E **118** E2
Muaraenim *Indonesia* 3°40S 103°50E **118** E2
Muarajuloi *Indonesia* 0°12S 114°3E **118** E4
Muarakaman *Indonesia* 0°2S 116°45E **118** E5
Muaratebo *Indonesia* 1°30S 102°26E **118** E2
Muaratembesi *Indonesia* 1°42S 103°8E **118** E2
Muarateweh *Indonesia* 0°58S 114°52E **118** E4
Mubarakpur *India* 26°6N 83°18E **125** F10
Mubarraz = Al Mubarraz
  Si. Arabia 25°30N 49°40E **129** E6
Mubende *Uganda* 0°33N 31°22E **142** B3
Mubi *Nigeria* 10°18N 13°16E **139** C7
Mucajaí ← *Brazil* 2°25N 60°52W **186** C6
Muchachos, Roque de los
  Canary Is. 28°44N 17°52W **100** F2
Mücheln *Germany* 51°17N 11°47E **76** D7
Muchinga □ *Zambia* 12°0S 31°30E **143** E3
Muchinga Mts. *Zambia* 11°30S 31°30E **143** E3
Muchkapskiy *Russia* 51°52N 42°28E **86** E6
Muchuan *China* 28°57N 103°55E **116** C5
Muck *U.K.* 56°50N 6°15W **65** E2
Muckadilla *Australia* 26°35S 148°23E **151** D4
Muckalee Cr. ← *U.S.A.* 31°38N 84°9W **178** D5
Muckaty ○ *Australia* 18°37S 133°52E **150** B1
Muckle Flugga *U.K.* 60°51N 0°54W **65** A8
Mucugé *Brazil* 13°0S 41°23W **189** C2
Mucur *Turkey* 39°3N 34°22E **104** C6
Mucuri *Brazil* 18°0S 39°36W **189** D3
Mucurici *Brazil* 18°6S 40°31W **189** D3
Mucusso *Angola* 18°1S 21°25E **144** A3
Muda ← *China* 34°3N 135°7W **100** F6
Mudanjiang *China* 44°38N 129°30E **115** B15
Mudanya *Turkey* 40°25N 28°50E **97** F12
Muddebihal *India* 16°20N 76°8E **127** F2
Muddus ← *Sweden* 66°58N 20°15E **60** C19
Muddy Cr. ← *U.S.A.* 38°24N 110°42W **168** G8
Mudgee *Australia* 32°32S 149°31E **153** B8
Mudhol *Andhra Pradesh,*
  India 18°58N 77°55E **126** C3
Mudhol *Karnataka, India* 16°21N 75°17E **127** F2
Mudigere *India* 13°8N 75°38E **127** H1
Mudjatik ← *Canada* 56°1N 107°36W **163** B7
Mudumu △ *Namibia* 18°5S 23°29E **144** A3
Mudurnu *Turkey* 40°27N 31°12E **104** B4
Mudurnu ← *Turkey* 40°31N 31°18E **104** B4
Muecate *Mozam.* 14°55S 39°40E **143** E4
Mueda *Mozam.* 11°36S 39°28E **143** E4
Mueller Ranges
  Australia 18°18S 126°46E **148** C4
Muende *Mozam.* 14°28S 33°0E **143** E3
Muerto, Mar *Mexico* 16°10N 94°10W **181** D6
Mufu Shan *China* 29°20N 114°30E **117** C10
Mufulira *Zambia* 12°32S 28°15E **143** E2
Mufumbiro Range
  Africa 1°25S 29°30E **142** C2
Mugardos *Spain* 43°27N 8°15W **88** B2
Muge ← *Portugal* 39°8N 8°44W **89** F2
Múggia *Italy* 45°36N 13°46E **93** C10
Mughal Sarai *India* 25°18N 83°7E **125** G10
Mughayrā Taŭy
  Kazakhstan 49°0N 58°40E **108** C7
Mughayrā' *Si. Arabia* 29°17N 37°41E **128** D3
Mugi *Japan* 33°40N 134°25E **113** H7
Mugia = Muxía *Spain* 43°3N 9°10W **88** B1
Mugila, Mts.
  Dem. Rep. of the Congo 7°0S 28°50E **142** D2
Muğla *Turkey* 37°15N 28°22E **99** D10
Muğla □ *Turkey* 37°15N 28°22E **99** D10
Müglizh *Bulgaria* 42°37N 25°32E **97** D9
Mugodzhary = Mughalzhar Taŭy
  Kazakhstan 49°0N 58°40E **108** C7
Mugu *Nepal* 29°45N 82°30E **125** E10
Mugu Karnali ←
  Nepal 29°38N 81°51E **125** E9
Muhala *Congo* 5°40S 28°43E **142** D2
Muhammad, Râs *Egypt* 27°44N 34°16E **128** E2
Muhammad Qol *Sudan* 20°53N 37°9E **137** C4
Muhammadabad *India* 26°4N 83°25E **125** F10
Muḥaiyil *Si. Arabia* 18°33N 42°3E **131** D3
Muhesi ← *Tanzania* 7°0S 35°20E **142** D4
Mühlacker *Germany* 48°57N 8°51E **77** G4
Mühldorf *Germany* 48°14N 12°32E **77** G8
Mühlhausen *Germany* 51°12N 10°27E **76** D6
Mühlig Hofmann fjell
  Antarctica 72°30S 5°0E **55** D3
Mühlviertel *Austria* 48°30N 14°10E **78** D7
Muhos *Finland* 64°47N 25°59E **60** D21
Muhu *Estonia* 58°36N 23°11E **63** F8
Muhutwe *Tanzania* 1°35S 31°45E **142** C3
Mui Wo *China* 22°16N 113°59E **111** a
Muileann gCearr, An = Mullingar
  Ireland 53°31N 7°21W **64** C4
Muine Bheag = Bagenalstown
  Ireland 52°42N 6°58W **64** D5
Muineachán = Monaghan
  Ireland 54°15N 6°57W **64** B5
Muir, L. *Australia* 34°30S 116°40E **149** F2

Muir of Ord *U.K.* 57°32N 4°28W **65** G4
Mujeres, I. *Mexico* 21°13N 86°43W **182** B2
Muka, Tanjung
  Malaysia 5°8N 100°11E **121** c
Mukacheve *Ukraine* 48°27N 22°45E **80** B7
Mukacheve = Mukacheve
  Ukraine 48°27N 22°45E **80** B7
Mukah *Malaysia* 2°55N 112°5E **118** D4
Mukandwara *India* 24°49N 75°59E **124** G6
Mukawwa, Geziret
  Egypt 23°55N 35°53E **128** F2
Mukawwar *Sudan* 20°50N 37°17E **137** C4
Mukdahan *Thailand* 16°32N 104°43E **120** D5
Mukdahan △ *Thailand* 16°26N 104°45E **120** D5
Mukden = Shenyang
  China 41°48N 123°27E **115** D12
Mukerian *India* 31°57N 75°37E **124** D6
Mukhavyets → *Belarus* 52°5N 23°39E **83** F10
Mukher *India* 18°42N 77°22E **126** E3
Mukhtolovo *Russia* 55°29N 43°15E **86** C6
Mukinbudin *Australia* 30°55S 118°5E **149** F2
Mukishi
  Dem. Rep. of the Congo 8°30S 24°44E **143** D1
Muko Phetra △ *Thailand* 6°57N 99°33E **121** J2
Mukomuko *Indonesia* 2°30S 101°10E **118** E2
Mukomwenze
  Dem. Rep. of the Congo 6°49S 27°15E **142** D2
Mukono *Uganda* 0°21N 32°45E **142** B3
Muktinath *Nepal* 28°49N 83°53E **125** E10
Muktsar *India* 30°30N 74°30E **124** D6
Mukur = Moqor
  Afghan. 32°50N 67°42E **124** C2
Mukutuwa → *Canada* 53°10N 97°24W **163** C9
Mukwela *Zambia* 17°0S 26°40E **143** F2
Mul *India* 20°4N 79°40E **126** E4
Mula *Spain* 38°3N 1°33W **91** G3
Mula → *India* 18°34N 74°21E **126** E2
Mula → *Pakistan* 27°57N 67°36E **124** F2
Mulanje
  Dem. Rep. of the Congo 3°40S 27°10E **142** C2
Mulanje, Mt. *Malawi* 16°2S 35°33E **143** F4
Mulbagal *India* 13°10N 78°24E **127** H4
Mulchatna → *U.S.A.* 59°40N 157°7W **166** D8
Mulchén *Chile* 37°45S 72°20W **190** D1
Mulde → *Germany* 51°53N 12°15E **76** D8
Mule Creek Junction
  U.S.A. 43°23N 104°13W **168** E11
Muleba *Tanzania* 1°50S 31°37E **142** C3
Mulegé *Mexico* 26°53N 111°59W **180** B2
Muleshoe *U.S.A.* 34°13N 102°43W **176** D3
Mulgrave *Canada* 45°38N 61°31W **165** C7
Mulgrave I. = Badu
  Australia 10°7S 142°11E **150** a
Mulhacén *Spain* 37°4N 3°20W **89** H7
Mülheim *Germany* 51°25N 6°54E **76** D2
Mulhouse *France* 47°40N 7°20E **71** E14
Muli *China* 29°2N 101°8E **116** D3
Muling *China* 44°35N 130°10E **115** B16
Mulki *India* 13°6N 74°48E **127** H2
Mull *U.K.* 56°25N 5°56W **65** E3
Mull, Sound of *U.K.* 56°30N 5°50W **65** E3
Mullach Íde = Malahide
  Ireland 53°26N 6°9W **64** C5
Mullaittivu *Sri Lanka* 9°15N 80°49E **127** K5
Mullen *U.S.A.* 42°3N 101°1W **172** D3
Mullengudgery
  Australia 31°43S 147°23E **151** B4
Mullens *U.S.A.* 37°35N 81°23W **173** G13
Muller, Pegunungan
  Indonesia 0°30N 113°30E **118** D4
Mullet Pen. *Ireland* 54°13N 10°2W **64** B1
Mullewa *Australia* 28°29S 115°30E **149** E2
Müllheim *Germany* 47°47N 7°36E **77** H3
Mulligan → *Australia* 25°0S 139°0E **150** D2
Mullingar *Ireland* 53°31N 7°21W **64** C4
Mullins *U.S.A.* 34°12N 79°15W **177** D15
Mullsjö *Sweden* 57°56N 13°55E **63** G7
Mullumbimby
  Australia 28°30S 153°30E **151** D5
Mulobezi *Zambia* 16°45S 25°7E **143** F2
Mulonga Plain *Zambia* 16°20S 22°40E **141** H4
Mulroy B. *Ireland* 55°15N 7°46W **64** A4
Mulshi L. *India* 18°30N 73°48E **126** E1
Multai *India* 21°50N 78°21E **126** D4
Multan *Pakistan* 30°15N 71°36E **124** D4
Mulug *India* 18°11N 79°57E **126** E4
Mulumbe, Mts.
  Dem. Rep. of the Congo 8°40S 27°30E **143** D2
Mulungushi Dam
  Zambia 14°48S 28°48E **143** E2
Mulurulu L. *Australia* 33°15S 143°20E **152** B5
Mulvane *U.S.A.* 37°29N 97°15W **172** G5
Mulwad *Sudan* 18°45N 30°39E **137** D3
Mulwala *Australia* 35°59S 146°0E **153** C7
Mulwala, L. *Australia* 35°59S 146°0E **151** C4
Mumbai *India* 18°56N 72°50E **126** E1
Mumbwa *Zambia* 15°0S 27°0E **143** F2
Mumias *Kenya* 0°20N 34°29E **142** C4
Mummel Gulf △
  Australia 31°17S 151°51E **153** A9
Mumra *Russia* 45°45N 47°41E **87** H8
Mun → *Thailand* 15°19N 105°30E **120** E5
Muna *Indonesia* 5°0S 122°30E **119** F6
Munabao *India* 25°45N 70°17E **124** G4
Munamagi *Estonia* 57°43N 27°4E **84** D4
Munaung *Burma* 18°45N 93°40E **123** K18
Munaung = Cheduba I.
  Burma 18°45N 93°40E **123** K18
Muncan *Indonesia* 8°34S 115°11E **119** K18
Muncar *Indonesia* 8°26S 114°20E **119** J17
Müncheberg *Germany* 50°11N 11°47E **77** E7
Müncheberg *Germany* 52°30N 14°9E **76** C10
München *Germany* 48°8N 11°34E **77** G7
München Franz Josef Strauss
  Int. ✈ (MUC)
  Germany 48°21N 11°47E **77** G7
Munchen-Gladbach =
  Mönchengladbach
  Germany 51°11N 6°27E **76** D2
Muncho Lake *Canada* 59°0N 125°50W **162** B3
Munch'ŏn *N. Korea* 39°14N 127°19E **115** E14
Muncie *U.S.A.* 40°12N 85°23W **173** E11
Muncoonie L. West
  Australia 25°12S 138°40E **150** D2
Mundabbera *Australia* 25°36S 151°18E **151** D5
Mundakayam *India* 9°30N 76°50E **127** K3
Mundal *Sri Lanka* 7°48N 79°48E **127** L4
Munday *U.S.A.* 33°27N 99°38W **176** E5
Mundemba *Cameroon* 4°57N 8°52E **139** E6
Münden *Germany* 51°25N 9°38E **76** D5

Münden ⌂ *Germany* 51°28N 9°42E **76** D5
Mundiwindi *Australia* 23°47S 120°9E **148** D3
Mundo → *Spain* 38°30N 2°15W **91** G2
Mundo Novo *Brazil* 11°50S 40°29W **189** D2
Mundra *India* 22°54N 69°48E **124** H3
Mundrabilla *Australia* 31°52S 127°51E **149** F4
Munera *Spain* 39°2N 2°29W **91** F2
Muneru → *India* 16°45N 80°3E **126** F5
Mungallala *Australia* 26°28S 147°34E **151** D4
Mungallala Cr. →
  Australia 28°53S 147°5E **151** D4
Mungana *Australia* 17°8S 144°27E **150** B3
Mungaoli *India* 24°24N 78°7E **124** G8
Mungari *Mozam.* 17°12S 33°30E **143** F3
Mungbere
  Dem. Rep. of the Congo 2°36N 28°28E **142** B2
Mungeli *India* 22°4N 81°41E **125** H9
Munger *India* 25°23N 86°30E **125** G12
Mungeranie *Australia* 28°1S 138°39E **151** A2
Mungilli △ *Australia* 25°14S 124°17E **149** E3
Mungkan Kandju △
  Australia 13°35S 142°52E **150** A3
Mungkarta ⊙ *Australia* 20°22S 134°2E **150** C1
Mungo, L. *Australia* 33°45S 143°0E **152** B5
Mungo △ *Australia* 33°44S 143°6E **152** B5
Munich = München
  Germany 48°8N 11°34E **77** G7
Munising *U.S.A.* 46°25N 86°40W **172** B10
Munka-Ljungby *Sweden* 56°16N 12°58E **63** H6
Munkebo *Denmark* 55°27N 10°34E **63** J4
Munkedal *Sweden* 58°28N 11°40E **63** F5
Munkfors *Sweden* 59°47N 13°30E **62** E7
Munku-Sardyk
  Russia 51°45N 100°20E **107** D11
Münnerstadt *Germany* 50°14N 10°12E **77** E6
Munnsville *U.S.A.* 42°58N 75°35W **175** D9
Muñoz Gamero, Pen.
  Chile 52°30S 73°5W **192** G2
Munroe L. *Canada* 59°13N 98°35W **163** B9
Munsan *S. Korea* 37°51N 126°48E **115** F14
Munson *U.S.A.* 30°52N 86°52W **179** E3
Munster *France* 48°2N 7°8E **71** D14
Münster *Niedersachsen,*
  Germany 52°58N 10°5E **76** C6
Münster *Nordrhein-Westfalen,*
  Germany 51°58N 7°37E **76** D3
Munster □ *Ireland* 52°18N 8°44W **64** D3
Muntadgin *Australia* 31°45S 118°33E **149** F2
Muntele Mare, Vf.
  Romania 46°30N 23°12E **81** D8
Muntok *Indonesia* 2°5S 105°10E **118** E3
Munzur Dağları *Turkey* 39°30N 39°10E **105** C8
Muong Hiem *Vietnam* 22°12N 102°28E **116** F4
Muong Sen *Vietnam* 19°24N 104°8E **116** C5
Muong Te *Vietnam* 22°24N 102°49E **116** F4
Muong Xia *Vietnam* 20°19N 104°50E **120** B5
Muonio *Finland* 67°57N 23°40E **60** C20
Muonio älv = Muonionjoki →
  Finland 67°11N 23°34E **60** C20
Muonioälven = Muonionjoki →
  Finland 67°11N 23°34E **60** C20
Muonionjoki →
  Finland 67°11N 23°34E **60** C20
Mupa → *Mozam.* 18°58S 35°54E **143** F4
Muping *China* 37°22N 121°36E **115** F11
Muqdisho *Somalia* 2°2N 45°25E **131** G4
Mur → *Austria* 46°18N 16°52E **79** E9
Mûr-de-Bretagne *France* 48°12N 3°0W **70** D4
Muradiye *Manisa, Turkey* 38°39N 27°21E **99** C9
Muradiye *Van, Turkey* 39°0N 43°44E **105** C10
Murakami *Japan* 38°14N 139°29E **112** E9
Muralag = Prince of Wales I.
  Australia 10°40S 142°10E **150** A3
Murallón, Cerro *Chile* 49°48S 73°30W **192** C2
Muranda *Rwanda* 1°52S 29°20E **142** C2
Murang'a *Kenya* 0°45S 37°9E **142** C4
Murashi *Russia* 59°30N 49°0E **106** D5
Murat *France* 45°7N 2°53E **72** C6
Murat → *Turkey* 38°46N 40°0E **105** C9
Murat Dağı *Turkey* 38°55N 29°43E **99** C11
Muratlı *Turkey* 41°10N 27°29E **97** E11
Murato *France* 42°35N 9°20E **73** F13
Murau *Austria* 47°6N 14°10E **78** D7
Murava *Belarus* 52°39N 24°15E **83** F11
Muravera *Italy* 39°25N 9°34E **94** C2
Murayama *Japan* 38°30N 140°25E **112** E10
Murça *Portugal* 41°24N 7°28W **88** D3
Murchison *N.Z.* 41°49S 172°21E **155** B7
Murchison → *Australia* 27°45S 114°0E **149** E1
Murchison, Mt.
  Antarctica 73°15S 166°20E **55** D11
Murchison, Mt. *N.Z.* 43°0S 171°22E **155** D4
Murchison Falls *Uganda* 2°15N 31°30E **142** B3
Murchison Falls △
  Uganda 2°17N 31°48E **142** B3
Murchison Mts. *N.Z.* 45°13S 167°23E **155** F2
Murchison Ra.
  Australia 20°0S 134°10E **150** C1
Murchison Rapids
  Malawi 15°55S 34°35E **143** F3
Murchison Roadhouse
  Australia 27°39S 116°14E **149** E2
Murcia *Spain* 38°5N 1°10W **91** G3
Murcia □ *Spain* 37°50N 1°30W **91** H3
Murdo *U.S.A.* 43°53N 100°43W **172** D3
Murdoch Pt. *Australia* 14°37S 144°55E **150** A3
Mures → *Romania* 46°15N 20°13E **80** D5
Mureş → *Romania* 46°15N 20°13E **80** D5
Muret *France* 43°30N 1°20E **72** E4
Murewa *Zimbabwe* 17°39S 31°47E **145** A5
Murfreesboro *N.C.,*
  U.S.A. 36°27N 77°6W **177** C16
Murfreesboro *Tenn.,*
  U.S.A. 35°51N 86°24W **177** D11
Murgab = Morghāb →
  Turkmenistan 38°18N 61°12E **129** B9
Murgenella *Australia* 11°34S 132°56E **148** B5
Murgeni *Romania* 46°12N 28°1E **81** D13
Murgha Kibzai
  Pakistan 30°44N 69°25E **124** D3
Murghob = Murgab
  Tajikistan 38°10N 74°2E **109** F8
Murgon *Australia* 26°15S 151°54E **151** D5
Muri *India* 23°22N 85°52E **125** H11
Muria *Indonesia* 6°36S 110°53E **119** G14
Muriaé *Brazil* 21°8S 42°23W **191** A7
Murias de Paredes *Spain* 42°52N 6°11W **88** C4

Murici *Brazil* 9°19S 35°56W **189** B3
Muriel Mine *Zimbabwe* 17°14S 30°40E **143** F3
Müritz *Germany* 53°25N 12°42E **76** B8
Müritz △ *Germany* 53°22N 12°57E **76** B8
Muriwai Beach *N.Z.* 36°50S 174°26E **154** C3
Murliganj *India* 25°54N 86°59E **125** G12
Murmansk *Russia* 68°57N 33°10E **60** B25
Murmashi *Russia* 68°47N 32°42E **60** B25
Murnau *Germany* 47°40N 11°12E **77** H7
Muro *Spain* 39°44N 3°3E **100** B10
Muro, C. di *France* 41°44N 8°37E **73** G12
Muro de Alcoy *Spain* 38°46N 0°26W **91** G4
Muro Lucano *Italy* 40°45N 15°29E **95** B8
Murom *Russia* 55°35N 42°3E **86** C6
Muroran *Japan* 42°25N 141°0E **112** C10
Muros *Spain* 42°45N 9°5W **88** C1
Muros e Noya, Ría de →
  Spain 42°45N 9°0W **88** C1
Muroto *Japan* 33°18N 134°9E **113** H7
Muroto-Misaki *Japan* 33°15N 134°10E **113** H7
Murovani Kurylivtsi
  Ukraine 48°44N 27°31E **81** B12
Murowana Goślina
  Poland 52°35N 17°0E **83** F3
Murphy *U.S.A.* 43°13N 116°33W **168** E5
Murphys *U.S.A.* 38°8N 120°28W **170** G6
Murrat *Sudan* 18°51N 29°33E **137** D2
Murrat Wells *Sudan* 21°3N 32°55E **137** C3
Murray *Australia* 9°56S 144°2E **150** a
Murray *Ky., U.S.A.* 36°37N 88°19W **172** G9
Murray *Utah, U.S.A.* 40°40N 111°53W **168** F8
Murray → *Australia* 35°20S 139°22E **152** C3
Murray → *U.S.A.* 34°3N 81°13W **178** A8
Murray, L. *U.S.A.* 34°3N 81°13W **178** A8
Murray Bridge
  Australia 35°6S 139°14E **152** C3
Murray Fracture Zone
  Pac. Oc. 35°0N 130°0W **157** D14
Murray Harbour
  Canada 46°0N 62°28W **165** C7
Murray River △
  Australia 34°23S 140°32E **151** E3
Murray-Sunset △
  Australia 34°45S 141°30E **152** C4
Murraysburg *S. Africa* 31°58S 23°47E **144** D3
Murree *Pakistan* 33°56N 73°28E **124** C5
Murrieta *U.S.A.* 33°33N 117°13W **171** M9
Murro di Porco, Capo
  Italy 37°0N 15°20E **95** F8
Murrumbateman
  Australia 34°58S 149°0E **153** C8
Murrumbidgee →
  Australia 34°43S 143°12E **152** C5
Murrumburrah
  Australia 34°32S 148°22E **153** C8
Murrurundi *Australia* 31°42S 150°51E **153** A9
Murshid *Sudan* 21°40N 31°10E **137** D3
Murshidabad *India* 24°11N 88°19E **125** G13
Murska Sobota
  Slovenia 46°39N 16°12E **93** B13
Murtazapur *India* 20°40N 77°25E **126** D3
Murtle L. *Canada* 52°8N 119°38W **162** C5
Murtoa *Australia* 36°35S 142°28E **152** D5
Murtosa *Portugal* 40°44N 8°40W **88** E2
Muru → *Brazil* 8°9S 70°45W **188** E3
Murud *India* 18°19N 72°58E **126** E1
Murungu *Tanzania* 4°12S 31°10E **142** C3
Murupara *N.Z.* 38°28S 176°42E **154** E5
Mururoa
  French Polynesia 21°52S 138°55W **157** K14
Murwara *India* 23°46N 80°28E **125** H9
Murwillumbah
  Australia 28°18S 153°27E **151** D5
Mürz → *Austria* 47°30N 15°25E **78** D8
Murzūq *Libya* 25°53N 13°57E **135** C8
Murzūq, Idehān *Libya* 24°50N 13°51E **135** D8
Mürzzuschlag *Austria* 47°36N 15°41E **78** D8
Mus *Indonesia* 9°1N 92°47E **127** K11
Muş *Turkey* 38°45N 41°30E **105** C9
Muş □ *Turkey* 38°45N 41°30E **105** C9
Mûsa, Gebel *Egypt* 28°33N 33°59E **128** D2
Musa Khel *Pakistan* 30°59N 69°52E **124** D3
Mûsa Qal'eh *Afghan.* 32°20N 64°50E **122** C4
Musafirkhana *India* 26°22N 81°48E **125** F9
Musala *Bulgaria* 42°13N 23°37E **96** D7
Musala *Indonesia* 1°41N 98°28E **118** D1
Musan *N. Korea* 42°12N 129°12E **115** C15
Musangu
  Dem. Rep. of the Congo 10°28S 23°55E **143** E1
Musasa *Tanzania* 3°25S 31°30E **142** C3
Muscat = Masqaṭ
  Oman 23°37N 58°36E **131** C6
Muscatine *U.S.A.* 41°25N 91°3W **172** E8
Muscle Shoals *U.S.A.* 34°45N 87°40W **177** D11
Musgrave Harbour
  Canada 49°27N 53°58W **165** C9
Musgrave Ranges
  Australia 26°0S 132°0E **149** E5
Mushie
  Dem. Rep. of the Congo 2°56S 16°55E **140** D3
Mushin *Nigeria* 6°31N 3°21E **139** D5
Musi → *India* 16°41N 79°40E **126** F4
Musi → *Indonesia* 2°20S 104°56E **118** E2
Musina *S. Africa* 22°20S 30°5E **145** B5
Musiri *India* 10°58N 78°25E **127** F3
Muskauer Park *Europe* 51°34N 14°43E **76** D10
Muskeg → *Canada* 60°20N 123°20W **162** A4
Muskegon *U.S.A.* 43°14N 86°16W **172** D10
Muskegon → *U.S.A.* 43°14N 86°21W **172** D10
Muskegon Heights
  U.S.A. 43°12N 86°16W **172** D10
Muskoka, L. *Canada* 45°0N 79°25W **174** B5
Muskoka Falls *Canada* 44°59N 79°17W **174** B5
Muskwa → *Canada* 58°47N 122°48W **162** B4
Muslīmiyah *Syria* 36°19N 37°12E **106** B3
Musmar *Sudan* 18°13N 35°40E **137** D4
Musofu *Zambia* 13°30S 29°0E **143** E2
Musoma *Tanzania* 1°30S 33°48E **142** C3
Musquaro, L. *Canada* 50°38N 61°5W **165** B7
Musquodoboit Harbour
  Canada 44°50N 63°9W **165** D7
Musselburgh *U.K.* 55°57N 3°2W **65** F5
Musselshell →
  U.S.A. 47°21N 107°57W **168** C10
Mussende *Angola* 10°32S 16°5E **140** G3
Mussidan *France* 45°2N 0°22E **72** C4
Mussomeli *Italy* 37°35N 13°45E **94** E6
Mussoorie *India* 30°27N 78°6E **124** D8

Mussuco *Angola* 17°2S 19°3E **144** A2
Mustafakemalpaşa
  Turkey 40°2N 28°24E **97** F12
Mustang *Nepal* 29°10N 83°55E **125** E10
Musters, L. *Argentina* 45°20S 69°25W **192** C3
Musudan *N. Korea* 40°50N 129°43E **115** D15
Muswellbrook
  Australia 32°16S 150°56E **153** B9
Mustafakemalpaşa
  Turkey 49°22N 20°55E **83** J7
Mût *Egypt* 25°28N 28°58E **137** B2
Mut *Turkey* 36°40N 33°28E **104** C5
Mutanda *Mozam.* 21°0S 33°34E **145** B5
Mutanda *Zambia* 12°24S 26°13E **143** E2
Mutare *Zimbabwe* 18°58S 32°38E **143** F3
Mutawintji △
  Australia 31°10S 142°30E **152** B5
Mutha *Kenya* 1°48S 38°26E **142** C4
Muting *Indonesia* 7°23S 140°20E **119** F10
Mutki → *Turkey* 38°23N 41°56E **128** B4
Mutoko *Zimbabwe* 17°24S 32°13E **145** A5
Mutomo *Kenya* 1°51S 38°12E **142** C4
Mutoray *Russia* 60°56N 101°0E **107** C12
Mutsamudu *Comoros Is.* 12°10S 44°25E **141** a
Mutsu *Japan* 41°5N 140°55E **112** C10
Mutsu-Wan *Japan* 41°5N 140°55E **112** D10
Muttaburra *Australia* 22°38S 144°29E **150** C3
Muttalip *Turkey* 39°50N 30°32E **99** B12
Mutton I. *Ireland* 52°49N 9°32W **64** D2
Muttukuru *India* 14°16N 80°6E **127** G5
Mutuáli *Mozam.* 14°55S 37°0E **143** E4
Mutum Biyu *Nigeria* 8°40N 10°50E **139** D7
Mutumba *Burundi* 3°25S 29°21E **142** C2
Mutur *Sri Lanka* 8°27N 81°16E **127** K5
Muweilih *Egypt* 30°42N 34°19E **130** E3
Muxía *Spain* 43°3N 9°10W **88** B1
Muy Muy *Nic.* 12°39N 85°36W **182** D2
Muyinga *Burundi* 3°14S 30°33E **142** C3
Muynak *Uzbekistan* 43°44N 59°10E **108** D5
Muyunkum, Peski = Moyynqum
  Kazakhstan 44°12N 71°0E **109** D8
Muz Tag *China* 36°25N 87°25E **109** E11
Muzaffarabad *Pakistan* 34°25N 73°30E **125** B5
Muzaffargarh *Pakistan* 30°5N 71°14E **124** D4
Muzaffarnagar *India* 29°26N 77°40E **124** E7
Muzaffarpur *India* 26°7N 85°23E **125** F11
Muzafirpur *Pakistan* 30°58N 69°9E **124** D3
Mużakowski, Park = Muskauer
  Park *Europe* 51°34N 14°43E **76** D10
Muzhi *Russia* 65°25N 64°40E **106** C7
Muzillac *France* 47°35N 2°30W **70** E4
Muztag-Ata *China* 38°17N 75°7E **109** E9
Muzūra *Egypt* 24°39N 33°38E **137** F7
Mvuma *Zimbabwe* 19°16S 30°30E **143** F3
Mvurwi *Zimbabwe* 17°0S 30°57E **143** F3
Mwabvi △ *Malawi* 16°42S 35°0E **143** F3
Mwadui *Tanzania* 3°26S 33°32E **142** C3
Mwali = Mohéli
  Comoros Is. 12°20S 43°40E **141** a
Mwambo *Tanzania* 10°30S 40°22E **143** E5
Mwandi *Zambia* 17°30S 24°51E **143** F1
Mwanza
  Dem. Rep. of the Congo 7°55S 26°43E **142** D2
Mwanza *Tanzania* 2°30S 32°58E **142** C3
Mwanza *Zambia* 16°58S 24°28E **143** F1
Mwanza □ *Tanzania* 2°0S 33°0E **142** C3
Mwaya *Tanzania* 9°32S 33°55E **143** D3
Mweelrea *Ireland* 53°39N 9°49W **64** C2
Mweka
  Dem. Rep. of the Congo 4°50S 21°34E **140** E4
Mwene-Ditu
  Dem. Rep. of the Congo 6°35S 22°27E **140** F4
Mwenezi *Zimbabwe* 21°15S 30°48E **143** G3
Mwenezi → *Mozam.* 22°40S 31°50E **143** G3
Mwenga
  Dem. Rep. of the Congo 3°1S 28°28E **142** C2
Mweru, L. *Zambia* 9°0S 28°40E **143** D2
Mweru Wantipa △
  Zambia 8°39S 29°25E **143** D2
Mweza Range *Zimbabwe* 21°0S 30°0E **143** G3
Mwilambwe
  Dem. Rep. of the Congo 8°7S 25°5E **142** D2
Mwimbi *Tanzania* 8°38S 31°39E **143** D3
Mwingi *Kenya* 0°56S 38°4E **142** C4
Mwinilunga *Zambia* 11°43S 24°25E **143** E1
My Son *Vietnam* 15°48N 108°7E **120** E7
My Tho *Vietnam* 10°29N 106°23E **121** G6
Mya, O. → *Algeria* 30°46N 4°54E **136** B4
Myajlar *India* 26°15N 70°20E **124** F4
Myakka → *U.S.A.* 26°56N 82°11W **179** J7
Myall Lakes △
  Australia 32°25S 152°30E **153** B10
Myanaung *Burma* 18°18N 95°22E **123** K19
Myanmar = Burma ■
  Asia 21°0N 96°30E **123** J20
Myaungmya *Burma* 16°30N 94°40E **123** L19
Mycenae = Mikines
  Greece 37°43N 22°46E **98** D4
Myedna *Belarus* 51°52N 23°42E **83** E10
Myeik = Mergui *Burma* 12°26N 98°34E **120** F2
Myeik Kyunzu *Burma* 11°30N 97°30E **121** G1
Myerstown *U.S.A.* 40°22N 76°19W **175** F8
Myingyan *Burma* 21°30N 95°20E **123** J19
Myitkyina *Burma* 25°24N 97°26E **123** G20
Myjava *Slovak Rep.* 48°41N 17°37E **79** C10
Mykhaylivka *Ukraine* 47°16N 35°15E **87** J9
Mykines *Færoe Is.* 62°7N 7°35W **60** E9
Mykolayiv *Ukraine* 46°58N 32°0E **85** J7
Mykolayiv □ *Ukraine* 47°20N 31°50E **85** J6
Mykonos *Greece* 37°30N 25°25E **99** D7
Mylius Erichsen Land
  Greenland 81°30N 27°0W **57** A8
Mymensingh *Bangla.* 24°45N 90°24E **123** G17
Mynydd Du *U.K.* 51°52N 3°50W **67** F4
Mýrdalsjökull *Iceland* 63°40N 19°6W **60** E4
Myrhorod *Ukraine* 50°19N 33°37E **85** H7
Myrtle Beach *U.S.A.* 33°42N 78°53W **177** D15
Myrtle Creek *U.S.A.* 43°1N 123°17W **168** E2
Myrtle Grove *U.S.A.* 30°24N 87°19W **179** E2
Myrtle Point *U.S.A.* 43°4N 124°8W **168** E1
Myrtleford *Australia* 36°34S 146°44E **153** D7
Myrtoan Sea = Mirtoo Sea
  Greece 37°0N 23°20E **98** D5
Mýrtou *Cyprus* 35°18N 33°4E **101** D12
Myrviken *Sweden* 62°58N 14°20E **62** B8
Mysia *Turkey* 39°50N 27°0E **97** G11
Myślenice *Poland* 49°51N 19°57E **83** J6
Myślibórz *Poland* 52°55N 14°50E **83** F1
Myślowice *Poland* 50°15N 19°12E **83** H6

Mysore = Karnataka □
  India 13°15N 77°0E **127** H3
Mysore *India* 12°17N 76°41E **127** H3
Mystic *U.S.A.* 41°21N 71°58W **175** E13
Mystras *Greece* 37°4N 22°22E **98** D4
Mysuru = Mysore
  India 12°17N 76°41E **127** H3
Myszków *Poland* 50°45N 19°22E **83** H6
Myszyniec *Poland* 53°23N 21°21E **82** E8
Mytishchi *Russia* 55°50N 37°50E **84** E9
Mývatn *Iceland* 65°36N 17°0W **60** D5
Mzab, Oued → = M'zab, Oued
  Algeria 32°15N 5°0E **136** B5
Mzimba *Malawi* 11°55S 33°39E **143** E3
Mzimkulu → *S. Africa* 30°44S 30°28E **145** D5
Mzimvubu → *S. Africa* 31°38S 29°33E **145** D4
Mzuzu *Malawi* 11°30S 33°55E **143** E3

N

Na Clocha Liatha = Greystones
  Ireland 53°9N 6°5W **64** C5
Na Haeo △ *Thailand* 17°31N 100°58E **120** D3
Na Hearadh = Harris
  U.K. 57°50N 6°55W **65** D2
Na Hearadh, Caolas = Harris, Sd.
  of *U.K.* 57°44N 7°6W **65** D1
Na Noi *Thailand* 18°19N 100°43E **120** C3
Na Phao *Laos* 17°35N 105°44E **120** D5
Na Sam *Vietnam* 22°3N 106°37E **116** F6
Na Sceirí = Skerries
  Ireland 53°35N 6°8W **64** C5
Na Thon *Thailand* 9°32N 99°56E **121** b
Naab → *Germany* 49°1N 12°2E **77** F8
Naama *Algeria* 33°16N 0°19E **136** B4
Naama □ *Algeria* 33°15N 0°45E **136** B4
Naantali *Finland* 60°29N 22°2E **84** B1
Naas *Ireland* 53°12N 6°40W **64** C5
Nababeep *S. Africa* 29°36S 17°46E **144** C2
Nabadwip = Navadwip
  India 23°34N 88°20E **125** H13
Nabawa *Australia* 28°30S 114°48E **149** E1
Nabberu, L. *Australia* 25°50S 120°30E **149** E3
Nabburg *Germany* 49°27N 12°11E **77** F8
Naberezhnyye Chelny
  Russia 55°42N 52°19E **86** C11
Nabeul *Tunisia* 36°30N 10°44E **136** A6
Nabha *India* 30°26N 76°14E **124** D7
Nabī Rūbā, W. → *Egypt* 29°40N 33°0E **128** F2
Nabībūr *Indonesia* 3°15S 135°26E **119** E9
Nabisar *Pakistan* 25°8N 69°40E **124** G3
Nabisipi → *Canada* 50°14N 62°13W **165** B7
Nabiswera *Uganda* 1°27N 32°15E **142** B3
Nablus = Nābulus
  West Bank 32°14N 35°15E **130** C4
Naboomspruit *S. Africa* 24°32S 28°40E **145** B4
Nabou *Burkina Faso* 11°25N 2°50W **138** C4
Nabouwalu *Fiji* 17°0S 178°45E **154** a
Nābulus *West Bank* 32°14N 35°15E **130** C4
Nacala *Mozam.* 14°32S 40°34E **143** E5
Nacaome *Honduras* 13°31N 87°30W **182** D2
Nacaroa *Mozam.* 14°22S 39°56E **143** E4
Naches *U.S.A.* 46°44N 120°42W **168** C3
Naches → *U.S.A.* 46°38N 120°31W **170** D6
Nachicapau, L. *Canada* 56°40N 68°5W **165** A6
Nachingwea *Tanzania* 10°23S 38°49E **143** E4
Nachna *India* 27°34N 71°41E **124** F4
Náchod *Czech Rep.* 50°25N 16°8E **78** A9
Nachuge *India* 10°47N 92°21E **127** J11
Nacimiento, L. *U.S.A.* 35°46N 120°53W **170** K6
Nacka *Sweden* 59°19N 18°10E **62** E12
Nackara *Australia* 32°48S 139°12E **152** B3
Naco *Mexico* 31°19N 109°56W **180** A3
Nacogdoches *U.S.A.* 31°36N 94°39W **176** F7
Nácori Chico *Mexico* 29°40N 108°57W **180** B3
Nacozari de García
  Mexico 30°25N 109°38W **180** A3
Nacula *Fiji* 16°54S 177°27E **154** a
Nada = Danzhou *China* 19°31N 109°33E **117** a
Nådendal = Naantali
  Finland 60°29N 22°2E **84** B1
Nadi *Fiji* 17°42S 177°20E **154** a
Nadī *Sudan* 18°40N 33°41E **137** D3
Nadiad *India* 22°41N 72°56E **124** H5
Nădlac *Romania* 46°10N 20°50E **80** D5
Nador *Morocco* 35°14N 2°58W **136** A5
Nadur *Malta* 36°2N 14°18E **101** C1
Nadūshan *Iran* 32°2N 53°35E **129** C7
Naduvattam *India* 11°32N 76°33E **127** G3
Nadvirna *Ukraine* 48°37N 24°30E **81** B9
Nadvoitsy *Russia* 63°52N 34°14E **86** B5
Nadvornaya = Nadvirna
  Ukraine 48°37N 24°30E **81** B9
Nadym *Russia* 65°35N 72°42E **106** C8
Nadym → *Russia* 66°12N 72°0E **106** C8
Nærbo *Norway* 58°40N 5°39E **61** G11
Næstved *Denmark* 55°13N 11°44E **63** J5
Nafada *Nigeria* 11°8N 11°20E **139** C7
Nafarroa = Navarra □
  Spain 42°40N 1°40W **90** C3
Nafpaktos *Greece* 38°24N 21°50E **98** C3
Nafplio *Greece* 37°33N 22°50E **98** D4
Naft-e Safid *Iran* 31°40N 49°17E **130** D5
Naftshahr *Iran* 34°0N 45°30E **128** C5
Nafud Desert = An Nafūd
  Si. Arabia 28°15N 41°0E **128** D4
Nag Hammâdi *Egypt* 26°2N 32°18E **137** B3
Naga *Phil.* 13°38N 123°15E **119** B6
Naga, Kreb en *Africa* 24°12N 6°0W **136** D3
Nagagami → *Canada* 50°23N 84°20W **164** B3
Nagahama *Japan* 35°23N 136°16E **113** G8
Nagai *Japan* 38°6N 140°2E **112** E10
Nagaland □ *India* 26°0N 94°30E **123** G19
Nagambie *Australia* 36°47S 145°10E **153** D6
Nagano *Japan* 36°40N 138°10E **113** F9
Nagano □ *Japan* 36°15N 138°0E **113** F9
Nagaoka *Japan* 37°27N 138°51E **113** E9
Nagaon *India* 26°20N 92°50E **125** F18
Nagappattinam *India* 10°46N 79°51E **127** G4
Nagar → *Bangla.* 24°27N 89°12E **125** G16
Nagar Karnul *India* 16°29N 78°19E **126** F4
Nagar Parkar *Pakistan* 24°28N 70°46E **124** G4
Nagasaki *Japan* 32°47N 129°50E **113** H4
Nagasaki □ *Japan* 32°50N 129°40E **113** H4
Nagato *Japan* 34°19N 131°5E **113** G5

Nagaur *India* 27°15N 73°45E **124**
Nagbhir *India* 20°34N 79°55E **126**
Nagda *India* 23°27N 75°25E **124**
Nagercoil *India* 8°12N 77°26E **127**
Nagina *India* 29°30N 78°30E **125**
Nagineh *Iran* 34°20N 57°15E **129**
Nagir *Pakistan* 36°12N 74°42E **125**
Naglarby *Sweden* 60°25N 15°34E **62**
Nagles Mts. *Ireland* 52°8N 8°30W **64**
Nagod *India* 24°34N 80°36E **125**
Nagold *Germany* 48°32N 8°43E **77**
Nagold → *Germany* 48°55N 8°41E **77**
Nagoorin *Australia* 24°17S 151°15E **150**
Nagorno-Karabakh □
  Azerbaijan 39°55N 46°45E **128**
Nagornyy *Russia* 55°58N 124°57E **107**
Nagoya *Japan* 35°10N 136°50E **113**
Nagoya ✈ (NGO)
  Japan 34°53N 136°45E **113**
Nagpur *India* 21°8N 79°10E **126**
Nagqu *China* 31°29N 92°3E **110**
Nagua *Dom. Rep.* 19°23N 69°50W **183**
Naguabo *Puerto Rico* 18°13N 65°44W **18**
Nagurunguru
  Australia 16°45S 129°45E **148**
Nagyatád *Hungary* 46°14N 17°22E **80**
Nagyecsed *Hungary* 47°53N 22°24E **80**
Nagykálló *Hungary* 47°53N 21°51E **80**
Nagykanizsa *Hungary* 46°28N 17°0E **80**
Nagykáta *Hungary* 47°25N 19°48E **80**
Nagykőrös *Hungary* 47°5N 19°48E **80**
Naha *Japan* 26°13N 127°42E **113**
Nahan *India* 30°33N 77°18E **124**
Nahanni △ *Canada* 61°36N 125°41W **162**
Nahanni Butte *Canada* 61°2N 123°31W **162**
Nahargarh *Mad. P.,*
  India 24°10N 75°14E **124**
Nahargarh *Raj., India* 24°55N 76°50E **124**
Nahariyya *Israel* 33°1N 35°5E **104**
Nahāvand *Iran* 34°10N 48°22E **105**
Nahe → *Germany* 49°58N 7°54E **77**
Nahīrne *Ukraine* 45°26N 28°27E **81**
Nahīya, W. → *Egypt* 28°55N 31°0E **137**
Nahuel Huapi, L.
  Argentina 41°0S 71°32W **192**
Nahuel Huapi △
  Argentina 41°3S 71°59W **192**
Nahuelbuta △ *Chile* 37°44S 72°57W **190**
Nahunta *U.S.A.* 31°12N 81°59W **177**
Nai Yong *Thailand* 8°14N 98°22E **121**
Naicá *Mexico* 27°53N 105°31W **180**
Naicam *Canada* 52°30N 104°30W **163**
Naikoon △ *Canada* 53°55N 131°55W **162**
Naikul *India* 21°20N 84°58E **125**
Naila *Germany* 50°19N 11°42E **77**
Naimisharanya *India* 27°21N 80°30E **125**
Naimona'nyi Feng
  China 30°26N 81°18E **125**
Nain *Canada* 56°34N 61°40W **165**
Nā'īn *Iran* 32°54N 53°0E **129**
Naini Tal *India* 29°30N 79°30E **125**
Nainpur *India* 22°30N 80°10E **125**
Naintré *France* 46°46N 0°29E **70**
Nainwa *India* 25°46N 75°51E **124**
Naipu *Romania* 44°12N 25°47E **81**
Nairai *Fiji* 17°49S 179°15E **15**
Nairn *U.K.* 57°35N 3°53W **65**
Nairobi *Kenya* 1°17S 36°48E **142**
Nairobi □ *Kenya* 1°22S 36°50E **142**
Naissaar *Estonia* 59°34N 24°29E **84**
Naitaba *Fiji* 17°0S 179°16W **15**
Naivasha *Kenya* 0°40S 36°30E **142**
Naivasha, L. *Kenya* 0°48S 36°30E **142**
Najac *France* 44°14N 1°58E **72**
Najaf = An Najaf *Iraq* 32°3N 44°15E **105**
Najafābād *Iran* 32°40N 51°15E **129**
Najd *Si. Arabia* 26°30N 42°0E **131**
Nájera *Spain* 42°26N 2°48W **90**
Najerilla → *Spain* 42°32N 2°48W **90**
Najibabad *India* 29°40N 78°20E **124**
Najin *N. Korea* 42°12N 130°15E **115**
Najmah *Si. Arabia* 26°42N 42°0E **131**
Najrān *Si. Arabia* 17°34N 44°18E **131**
Naju *S. Korea* 35°3N 126°43E **115**
Nakadōri-Shima *Japan* 32°57N 129°4E **113**
Nakalagba
  Dem. Rep. of the Congo 2°50N 27°58E **142**
Nakambé = White Volta →
  Ghana 9°10N 1°15W **138**
Nakaminato *Japan* 36°21N 140°36E **113**
Nakamura = Shimanto
  Japan 32°59N 132°56E **113**
Nakano *Japan* 36°45N 138°22E **113**
Nakano-Shima *Japan* 29°51N 129°52E **113**
Nakashibetsu *Japan* 43°33N 144°59E **112**
Nakfa *Eritrea* 16°40N 38°32E **13**
Nakha Yai, Ko *Thailand* 8°3N 98°28E **12**
Nakhichevan = Naxçıvan
  Azerbaijan 39°12N 45°15E **105**
Nakhichevan Rep. = Naxçıvan □
  Azerbaijan 39°25N 45°26E **105**
Nakhl *Egypt* 29°55N 33°43E **13**
Nakhl-e Taqī *Iran* 27°28N 52°36E **13**
Nakhodka *Russia* 42°53N 132°54E **11**
Nakhon Nayok
  Thailand 14°12N 101°13E **12**
Nakhon Pathom
  Thailand 13°49N 100°3E **12**
Nakhon Phanom
  Thailand 17°23N 104°43E **12**
Nakhon Ratchasima
  Thailand 14°59N 102°12E **12**
Nakhon Sawan
  Thailand 15°35N 100°10E **12**
Nakhon Si Thammarat
  Thailand 8°29N 100°0E **12**
Nakhon Thai *Thailand* 17°5N 100°44E **12**
Nakhtarana *India* 23°20N 69°15E **12**
Nakina *Canada* 50°10N 86°40W **16**
Nakło nad Notecią *Poland* 53°9N 17°38E **8**
Nako *Burkina Faso* 10°40N 3°4W **13**
Nakodar *India* 31°8N 75°31E **12**
Nakskov *Denmark* 54°50N 11°8E **6**
Naktong → *S. Korea* 35°7N 128°57E **11**
Nakuru *Kenya* 0°15S 36°4E **14**
Nakuru, L. *Kenya* 0°23S 36°5E **14**
Nakusp *Canada* 50°20N 117°45W **16**
Nal → *Pakistan* 25°20N 65°30E **12**
Nalázi *Mozam.* 24°3S 33°20E **14**
Nalchik *Russia* 43°30N 43°33E **8**

eczów *Poland*	51°17N 22°9E **83** G9	Nanbu *China*	31°18N 106°3E **116** B6	Napier Pen. *Australia*	12°4S 135°48E **150** A2	Nasrīān-e Pā'īn *Iran*	32°52N 46°52E **128** C5	Nawabshah *Pakistan*	26°15N 68°25E **124** F3	Neeses *U.S.A.*	33°33N 81°7W **178** B8
erigu *Ghana*	10°35N 0°25W **139** C4	Nanchang *China*	28°42N 115°55E **117** C10	Napierville *Canada*	45°11N 73°25W **175** A11	Nass → *Canada*	55°0N 129°40W **162** C3	Nawada *India*	24°50N 85°33E **125** G11	Nefta *Tunisia*	33°53N 7°50E **136** B6
hati *India*	24°17N 87°52E **125** G12	Nanching = Nanjing		Naples = Nápoli *Italy*	40°50N 14°15E **95** B7	Nassarawa *Nigeria*	8°32N 7°41E **139** D6	Nawakot *Nepal*	27°55N 85°10E **125** F11	Neftçala *Azerbaijan*	39°19N 49°12E **105** C13
iya *India*	23°16N 68°50E **124** H3	*China*	32°2N 118°47E **117** A12	Naples Park *U.S.A.*	26°17N 81°46W **179** J8	Nassarawa □ *Nigeria*	8°30N 8°20E **139** D6	Nawalgarh *India*	27°50N 75°15E **124** F6	Neftegorsk *Krasnodar,*	
gonda *India*	17°6N 79°15E **126** F4	Nanchong *China*	30°43N 106°2E **116** B6	Naples *U.S.A.*	26°8N 81°48W **179** J8	Nassau *Bahamas*	25°5N 77°20W **184** A4	Nawapara *India*	20°46N 82°33E **126** D6	*Russia*	44°25N 39°45E **87** H4
lamalai Hills *India*	15°30N 78°50E **127** G4	Nanchuan *China*	29°9N 107°6E **116** C6	Napo → *Peru*	3°20S 72°40W **186** D4	Nassau *U.S.A.*	42°31N 73°37W **175** D11	Nawar, Dasht-i- *Afghan.*	33°52N 68°0E **124** C3	Neftegorsk *Sakhalin,*	
lón → *Spain*	43°32N 6°4W **88** B4	Nancowry *India*	7°59N 93°32E **127** L11	Napoleon N. Dak.,		Nassau, B. *Chile*	55°20S 68°0W **192** E3	Nawāşīf, Ḥarrat		*Russia*	53°1N 142°58E **107** D15
ubaale Dam *Uganda*	0°30N 33°5E **142** B3	Nancy *France*	48°42N 6°12E **71** D13	*U.S.A.*	46°30N 99°46W **172** B4	Nasser, L. = Naser, Buheirat en		*Si. Arabia*	21°20N 42°10E **137** C5	Neftekumsk *Russia*	44°46N 44°50E **87** H7
umasortoq		Nanda Devi *India*	30°23N 79°59E **125** D8	Napoleon *Ohio, U.S.A.*	41°23N 84°8W **173** E11	*Egypt*	23°0N 32°30E **137** C3	Nawi *Sudan*	18°32N 30°50E **137** D3	Neftyugansk *Russia*	61°5N 72°42E **106** C8
reenland	60°23N 44°28W **57** E6	Nanda Devi △ *India*	30°30N 79°50E **125** D8	Nápoli *Italy*	40°50N 14°15E **95** B7	Nassian *Ivory C.*	8°28N 3°28E **138** D4	Nawoiy = Navoi		Nefyn *U.K.*	52°56N 4°31W **66** E3
n Can *Vietnam*	18°46N 104°59E **121** H5	Nanda Kot *India*	30°17N 80°5E **125** D9	Nápoli, G. di *Italy*	40°40N 14°10E **95** B7	Nässjö *Sweden*	57°39N 14°42E **63** G8	*Uzbekistan*	40°9N 65°22E **108** D7	Négala *Mali*	12°52N 8°30W **138** C2
n Co *China*	30°30N 90°45E **125** F7	Nandan = Minamiawaji		Napopo		Nastapoka → *Canada*	56°55N 76°33W **164** A4	Naxçıvan *Azerbaijan*	39°12N 45°15E **105** C11	Negapatam = Nagappattinam	
n Dinh *Vietnam*	20°25N 106°5E **116** G6	*Japan*	34°10N 134°42E **113** G7	*Dem. Rep. of the Congo*	4°15N 28°0E **142** B2	Nastapoka, Is. *Canada*	56°55N 76°50W **164** A4	Naxçıvan □ *Azerbaijan*	39°25N 45°26E **105** C11	*India*	10°46N 79°51E **127** G4
n Du, Quan Dao		Nandan *China*	24°58N 107°29E **116** E6	Napperby *Australia*	33°9S 138°7E **152** B3	Nasugbu *Phil.*	14°6N 120°35E **117** E6	Naxos *Greece*	37°8N 25°25E **99** D7	Negara *Indonesia*	8°22S 114°37E **119** J17
Vietnam	9°41N 104°21E **121** H5	Nandewar Ra.		Naqadeh *Iran*	36°57N 45°23E **105** D11	Nata → *Botswana*	20°14S 26°10E **144** B4	Nay *France*	43°10N 0°18W **72** E3	Negaunee *U.S.A.*	46°30N 87°36E **172** B2
n Hka → *Burma*	21°34N 95°41E **116** G2	*Australia*	30°15S 150°35E **151** E5	Naqb, Ra's an *Jordan*	29°48N 35°44E **130** F4	Nata *Botswana*	20°12S 26°12E **144** C4	Nay, Mui *Vietnam*	12°55N 109°23E **120** F7	Negele *Ethiopia*	5°20N 39°36E **131** F2
n Loi → *Burma*	21°3N 98°27E **116** G3	Nandgaon *India*	20°19N 74°39E **126** D2	Naqqāsh *Iran*	35°40N 49°6E **129** C6	Natal *Brazil*	5°47S 35°13W **189** D4	Nãy Band *Büshehr, Iran*	27°20N 52°40E **129** E7	Negeri Sembilan □	
n Nao △ *Thailand*	16°44N 101°32E **120** D3	Nandi = Nadi *Fiji*	17°42S 177°20E **154** a	Nãr *Sweden*	57°15N 18°35E **63** G10	Natal *Indonesia*	0°35N 99°7E **118** D1	Nãy Band *Khorãsãn,*		*Malaysia*	2°45N 102°10E **121** L4
n Ngum Res. *Laos*	18°35N 102°34E **120** C4	Nandigama *India*	16°47N 80°18E **126** F5	Nara *Japan*	34°40N 135°49E **113** G7	Natal □ *S. Africa*	28°30S 30°30E **145** D5	*Iran*	32°20N 57°34E **129** C8	Negev Desert = Hanegev	
n-Phan *Vietnam*	10°30N 106°0E **121** G6	Nandikotkur *India*	15°52N 78°18E **127** G4	Nara *Mali*	15°10N 7°20W **138** B3	Natal Drakensberg =		Nay Pyi Taw = Naypyidaw		*Israel*	30°50N 35°0E **130** E4
n Phong *Thailand*	16°42N 102°52E **120** D4	Nandura *India*	20°52N 76°25E **126** D3	Nara □ *Japan*	34°30N 136°0E **113** G8	uKhahlamba Drakensberg △		*Burma*	19°44N 96°12E **110** H8	Negoiul, Vf. *Romania*	45°38N 24°35E **81** E9
n Theun Res. *Laos*	17°51N 105°3E **120** D5	Nandurbar *India*	21°20N 74°15E **126** D2	Nara Canal *Pakistan*	24°30N 69°20E **124** G3	*S. Africa*	29°27S 29°30E **145** C4	Nayagarh *India*	20°7N 85°6E **126** D7	Negombo *Sri Lanka*	7°12N 79°50E **127** L4
n Tok *Thailand*	14°21N 99°4E **120** E2	Nandyal *India*	15°30N 78°30E **127** G4	Nara Visa *U.S.A.*	35°37N 103°6W **169** J12	Natalinci *Serbia*	44°15N 20°49E **80** F5	Nayakhan *Russia*	61°56N 159°0E **107** C16	Negotin *Serbia*	44°16N 22°37E **96** B6
n Un Res. *Thailand*	17°13N 103°44E **120** D4	Nanfeng *Guangdong,*		Naracoorte *Australia*	36°58S 140°45E **152** D4	Natanz *Iran*	33°30N 51°55E **129** C6	Nayarit □ *Mexico*	22°0N 105°0W **180** C4	Negotino *Macedonia*	41°29N 22°7E **96** E6
nacunde *Angola*	17°18S 15°50E **144** A2	*China*	23°45N 111°47E **117** F8	Naradhan *Australia*	33°34S 146°17E **153** B7	Natashquan *Canada*	50°14N 61°46W **165** B7	Nayau *Fiji*	18°6S 178°10E **154** a	Negra, Peña *Spain*	42°11N 6°30W **88** C4
nacurra *Mozam.*	17°30S 36°50E **145** B6	Nanfeng *Jiangxi,*		Naraini *India*	25°11N 80°29E **125** G9	Natashquan → *Canada*	50°7N 61°50W **165** B7	Nayé *Senegal*	14°28N 12°12W **138** C2	Negra, Pta. *Mauritania*	22°54N 16°18W **134** D2
nadgi △ *Australia*	35°42S 149°0E **153** C8	*China*	27°12N 116°28E **117** D11	Naranjos *Mexico*	21°21N 97°41W **181** C5	Natchez *U.S.A.*	31°34N 91°24W **176** F9	Nayong *China*	26°50N 105°20E **116** D5	Negra, Pta. *Peru*	6°6S 81°10W **188** B1
nak, Daryācheh-ye		Nang Rong *Thailand*	14°38N 102°48E **120** E4	Naranjos *India*	18°25N 84°3E **126** E7	Natchitoches *U.S.A.*	31°46N 93°5W **176** F8	Nayoro *Japan*	44°21N 142°28E **112** B11	Negrais, C. = Maudin Sun	
Iran	34°30N 52°0E **129** C7	Nanga-Eboko *Cameroon*	4°41N 12°22E **139** E7	Narasannapeta *India*	18°25N 84°3E **126** E7	Nathalia *Australia*	36°1S 145°13E **153** D6	Nayudupeta *India*	13°54N 79°54E **127** H4	*Burma*	16°0N 94°30E **123** M19
nak, Kavir-e *Iran*	34°30N 57°30E **129** C8	Nanga Parbat *Pakistan*	35°10N 74°35E **125** B6	Narasapur *India*	16°26N 81°40E **127** F5	Nathdwara *India*	24°55N 73°50E **124** G5	Nayyāl, W. → *Si. Arabia*	28°35N 39°4E **128** D3	Negreşti *Romania*	46°50N 27°30E **81** D12
nakkal *India*	11°30N 78°13E **127** J4	Nangade *Mozam.*	11°5S 39°36E **143** E4	Narasaraopet *India*	16°14N 80°4E **127** F5	Nati, Pta. *Spain*	40°3N 3°50E **100** A10	Nazar Kahrizi *Iran*	37°20N 46°45E **105** D12	Negreşti-Oaş *Romania*	47°52N 23°26E **81** C8
nakzār, Daryācheh-ye		Nangapinoh *Indonesia*	0°20S 111°44E **118** E4	Narathiwat *Thailand*	6°30N 101°48E **121** J3	Natimuk *Australia*	36°42S 142°0E **152** D5	Nazaré *Bahia, Brazil*	13°2S 39°0W **189** D3	Negril *Jamaica*	18°22N 78°20W **182** a
Iran	34°0N 60°30E **129** C9	Nangar △ *Australia*	33°23S 148°3E **153** B8	Narayangadh = Bharatpur		Nation → *Canada*	55°30N 123°32W **162** B4	Nazaré *Tocantins, Brazil*	6°23S 47°40W **189** E1	Négrine *Algeria*	34°30N 7°30E **136** B6
naland *Namibia*	26°0S 17°0E **144** B2	Nangarhār □ *Afghan.*	34°20N 70°0E **122** B7	*Nepal*	27°34N 84°10E **125** F11	National City *U.S.A.*	32°40N 117°5W **171** N9	Nazaré *Portugal*	39°36N 9°4W **89** F1	Negro → *Argentina*	41°2S 62°47W **192** B4
nanga *Kenya*	2°35S 36°47E **142** C4	Nangatayap *Indonesia*	1°32S 110°34E **118** E4	Narayanganj *Bangla.*	23°40N 90°33E **125** H17	Natividad, I. *Mexico*	27°52N 115°11W **180** B1	Nazareth = Nazerat		Negro → *Brazil*	3°0S 60°0W **186** D7
nangan *Uzbekistan*	41°0N 71°40E **109** D8	Nangeya Mts. *Uganda*	3°30N 33°30E **142** B3	Narayanpet *India*	16°45N 77°30E **126** F3	Natividade *Brazil*	11°43S 47°47W **189** C1	*Israel*	32°42N 35°17E **130** C4	Negro → *Uruguay*	33°24S 58°22W **190** C4
nangan □ *Uzbekistan*	41°0N 71°15E **109** D8	Nangong *China*	37°23N 115°22E **114** F8	Narberth *U.K.*	51°47N 4°44W **67** F3	Natkyizin *Burma*	14°57N 97°59E **120** E1	Nazarovo *Russia*	56°2N 90°40E **107** D10	Negro, C. = Tarf, Ras	
napa *Mozam.*	13°43S 39°50E **143** E4	Nanhua *China*	25°2N 100°21E **116** E3	Narcea → *Spain*	43°33N 6°44W **88** B4	Natron, L. *Tanzania*	2°20S 36°0E **142** C4	Nazas *Mexico*	25°14N 104°8W **180** B4	*Morocco*	35°40N 5°11W **136** A2
naqua △ *S. Africa*	30°0S 17°30E **144** D2	Nanhuang *China*	36°58N 121°48E **115** F11	Narcondam I. *India*	13°20N 94°16E **127** H12	Natrona Heights		Nazas → *Mexico*	25°35N 104°11W **180** B4	Negros *Phil.*	9°30N 122°40E **117** C6
naqualand *S. Africa*	30°0S 17°25E **144** D2	Nanjangud *India*	12°6N 76°43E **127** H3	Nardin *Iran*	37°3N 55°59E **129** B7	*U.S.A.*	40°37N 79°44W **174** F5	Nazca = Nasca *Peru*	14°50S 74°57W **188** C3	Negru Vodă *Romania*	43°47N 28°21E **81** G13
nasagali *Uganda*	1°2S 33°0E **142** B3	Nanji Shan *China*	27°27N 121°4E **117** D13	Nardò *Italy*	40°11N 18°2E **95** B11	Natron, L. *Tanzania*	2°20S 36°0E **142** C4	Naze, The *U.K.*	51°53N 1°18E **67** F9	Neguac *Canada*	47°15N 65°5W **165** C6
nber *Indonesia*	1°2S 134°49E **119** E8	Nanjiang *China*	32°28N 106°51E **116** A6	Narembeen *Australia*	32°7S 118°24E **149** F2	Natrûn, W. el → *Egypt*	30°25N 30°13E **137** E7	Nazerat *Israel*	32°42N 35°17E **130** C4	Nehalem → *U.S.A.*	45°40N 123°56E **174** D2
nbour *Australia*	26°32S 152°58E **151** D5	Nanjing *Fujian, China*	24°25N 117°20E **117** E11	Nares Abyssal Plain		Nattai △ *Australia*	34°12S 150°22E **153** C9	Nazerat *Israel*	32°42N 35°17E **130** C4	Nehãvand *Iran*	35°56N 49°31E **129** C6
nbouwalu = Nabouwalu		Nanjing *Jiangsu, China*	32°2N 118°47E **117** A12	*Atl. Oc.*	22°0N 67°0W **56** D5	Nättraby *Sweden*	56°13N 15°31E **63** H9	Näzik *Iran*	39°1N 45°4E **105** C11	Nehbandãn *Iran*	31°35N 60°5E **129** D9
iji	17°0S 178°45E **154** a	Nanjirinji *Tanzania*	9°41S 39°5E **143** D4	Nares Str. *Arctic*	80°0N 70°0W **57** B3	Natukanaaka Pan		Nazilli *Turkey*	37°55N 28°15E **99** D10	Nehe *China*	48°29N 124°50E **111** B13
nbucca Heads		Nankana Sahib		Naretha *Australia*	31°0S 124°45E **149** F3	*Namibia*	18°40S 15°45E **144** A2	Nazir Hat *India*	39°1N 45°4E **105** C11	Nehoiu *Romania*	45°24N 26°20E **81** E11
ustralia	30°37S 153°0E **153** A10	*Pakistan*	31°27N 73°38E **124** D5	Narew → *Poland*	52°26N 20°41E **83** F7	Nau Qala *Afghan.*	34°5N 68°5E **124** B3	Nazko *Canada*	53°1N 123°37W **162** C4	Nei Mongol Zizhiqu □	
nburg △ *Australia*	30°30S 115°5E **149** F2	Nankang *China*	25°40N 114°45E **117** E10	Narin *Afghan.*	36°5N 69°0E **122** A6	Naucelle *France*	44°13N 2°20E **72** D6	Nazko → *Canada*	53°7N 123°34W **162** C4	*China*	42°0N 112°0E **114** D7
nche Barwa *China*	29°40N 95°10E **110** F8	Nanking = Nanjing		Narmada → *India*	21°38N 72°36E **124** J5	Nauders *Austria*	46°54N 10°30E **78** E3	Näzlu *Iran*	37°41N 45°0E **105** D11	Neijiang *China*	29°35N 104°55E **116** C5
nche Bazar *Nepal*	25°51N 86°47E **125** F12	*China*	32°2N 118°47E **117** A12	Narmada Canal *India*	23°45N 73°45E **126** C1	Nauen *Germany*	52°36N 12°52E **80** A7	Nazret *Ethiopia*	8°32N 39°22E **131** F2	Neillsville *U.S.A.*	44°34N 90°36W **172** C8
nchonjôm = Nam-ch'on		Nankoku *Japan*	33°39N 133°44E **113** H6	Narman *Turkey*	40°26N 41°57E **105** B9	Naugatuck *U.S.A.*	41°30N 73°3W **175** E11	Nchanga *Zambia*	12°30S 27°49E **143** E2	Neilton *U.S.A.*	47°25N 123°53W **170** C3
. Korea	38°15N 126°26E **115** E14	Nanling *China*	30°55N 118°20E **117** B12	Naro *Ghana*	10°22N 2°27W **138** C4	Naujaat = Repulse Bay		Ncheu *Malawi*	14°50S 34°47E **143** E3	Neiqiu *China*	37°15N 114°30E **114** F8
necunda *Mozam.*	14°54S 37°37E **143** E4	Nannine *Australia*	26°51S 118°18E **149** E2	Naro Fominsk *Russia*	55°23N 36°43E **84** E9	*Canada*	66°30N 86°30W **161** D14	Ndala *Tanzania*	4°45S 33°15E **142** C3	Neiva *Colombia*	2°56N 75°18W **186** C3
nenalala *Fiji*	17°8S 179°9E **154** a	Nannup *Australia*	33°59S 115°48E **149** F2	Narochanski △ *Belarus*	54°55N 26°50E **84** E4	Naujoji Akmenė		Ndali *Benin*	9°50N 2°46E **139** D5	Neixiang *China*	33°10N 111°52E **114** H6
neponda *Mozam.*	15°50S 39°50E **143** F4	Nanortalik *Greenland*	60°10N 45°17W **57** E6	Narón *Spain*	43°32N 8°9W **88** B2	*Lithuania*	56°19N 22°55E **82** B9	Ndareda *Tanzania*	4°12S 35°30E **142** C4	Nejanilini L. *Canada*	59°33N 97°48E **163** B9
něst' nad Oslavou		Nanpan Jiang → *China*	25°0N 106°0E **116** F6	Narooma *Australia*	36°14S 150°4E **153** D9	Naumburg *Germany*	51°9N 11°47E **76** D7	Ndélé *C.A.R.*	8°25N 20°36E **140** G8	Nejd = Najd *Si. Arabia*	26°30N 42°0E **131** B3
zech Rep.	49°12N 16°10E **79** B9	Nanpara *India*	27°52N 81°33E **125** F9	Narowal *Pakistan*	32°6N 74°52E **124** C6	Nauru ■ *Pac. Oc.*	1°0S 166°0E **147** B9	Ndiael △ *Senegal*	16°15N 16°0W **138** B1	Nekã *Iran*	36°39N 53°19E **129** B7
nestovo *Slovak Rep.*	49°24N 19°25E **79** B12	Nanping *Fujian,*		Narrabri *Australia*	30°19S 149°46E **151** E4	Naushahra = Nowshera		Nd		Nekemte *Ethiopia*	9°4N 36°30E **131** F2
netil *Mozam.*	15°40S 39°21E **143** F4	*China*	26°38N 118°10E **117** D12	Narran → *Australia*	28°37S 148°12E **151** D4	*Pakistan*	34°0N 72°0E **122** C8	Ndikinimeki *Cameroon*	4°46N 10°50E **139** E7	Nékhel *Egypt*	25°10N 32°48E **137** B3
new L. *Canada*	54°14N 101°56W **163** C8	Nanri Dao *China*	25°15N 119°25E **117** E12	Narrandera *Australia*	34°42S 146°31E **153** B8	Naushahro *Pakistan*	26°50N 68°7E **124** F3	N'Dioum *Senegal*	16°31N 14°39W **138** B2	Nekso *Denmark*	55°4N 15°8E **63** B9
ngia *India*	31°48N 78°40E **125** D8	Nansei-Shotô = Ryūkyū-Rettō		Narrogin *Australia*	32°58S 117°14E **149** F2	Naushon I. *U.S.A.*	41°29N 70°45W **175** E14	Ndjamena *Chad*	12°10N 15°0E **135** F8	Nelamangala *India*	13°6N 77°24E **127** H3
nhkam *Burma*	23°50N 97°41E **116** G1	*Japan*	26°0N 126°0E **117** M3	Narromine *Australia*	32°12S 148°12E **153** B8	Nausori *Fiji*	18°2S 178°32E **154** a	Ndola *Zambia*	13°0S 28°34E **143** E2	Nelas *Portugal*	40°32N 7°52W **88** E3
nialo *Mozam.*	14°55S 39°59E **143** E4	Nansha Port *China*	22°45N 113°34E **111** a	Nannial *India*	19°4N 79°38E **126** E4	Nauta *Peru*	4°31S 73°35W **186** D4	Nduguti *Tanzania*	4°18S 34°41E **142** C3	Nelia *Australia*	20°39S 142°12E **150** C3
nib Desert *Namibia*	22°30S 15°0E **144** B2	Nanshan I.		Naro → *Kenya*	1°55S 35°52E **142** C4	Nautanwa *India*	27°20N 83°25E **125** F10	Nea Alikarnassos *Greece*	35°18N 25°13E **99** F7	Nelidovo *Russia*	56°13N 32°49E **84** D7
nib-Nauklooft △		*S. China Sea*	10°45N 115°49E **118** B5	Nanortalik *Greenland*	60°10N 45°17W **57** E6	Nautla *Mexico*	20°13N 96°47W **181** C5	Nea Anchialos *Greece*	39°16N 22°49E **98** B4	Neligh *U.S.A.*	42°8N 98°2W **172** D4
amibia	24°40S 15°16E **144** B2	Nansio *Tanzania*	2°3S 33°4E **142** C3	Nanpanjiang → *China*	25°0N 106°0E **116** F6	Nava *Mexico*	28°25N 100°45W **180** B4	Nea Ionia *Greece*	39°21N 22°56E **98** B4	Nelkan *Russia*	57°40N 136°4E **107** D14
nibe *Angola*	15°7S 12°11E **141** H2	Nant *France*	44°1N 3°18E **72** D7	Narrabri *Australia*	30°19S 149°46E **151** E4	Nava del Rey *Spain*	41°22N 5°6W **88** D5	Nea Kalikratia *Greece*	40°21N 23°3E **96** F7	Nellikuppam *India*	11°46N 79°43E **127** J4
nibe □ *Angola*	16°35S 12°30E **144** A1	Nanterre *France*	48°53N 2°12E **71** D9	Narrandera *Australia*	34°42S 146°31E **153** B8	Navadwip *India*	23°34N 88°20E **125** H13	Nea Makri *Greece*	38°5N 23°59E **98** B5	Nellore *India*	14°27N 79°59E **127** G4
nibia ■ *Africa*	22°0S 18°9E **144** B2	Nantes *France*	47°12N 1°33W **70** E5	Narrogin *Australia*	32°58S 117°14E **149** F2	Navahermosa *Spain*	39°41N 4°28W **89** F6	Nea Moudania *Greece*	40°15N 23°17E **96** F7	Nelson *Canada*	49°30N 117°20W **162** D5
nibia Abyssal Plain		Nanteuil *France*	46°11N 1°11E **72** B5	Narrow Hills △ *Canada*	54°20N 104°37W **163** C8	Navahrudak *Belarus*	53°40N 25°50E **75** B13	Nea Peramos *Attiki,*		Nelson *N.Z.*	41°18S 173°16E **155** B8
tl. Oc.	30°0S 5°30E **56** J12	Nantiat *France*	46°1N 1°11E **72** B5	Narsampet *India*	17°57N 79°58E **126** F4	Navajo Res. *U.S.A.*	36°48N 107°36W **169** H10	*Greece*	38°0N 23°26E **98** C5	Nelson *U.K.*	53°50N 2°13W **66** D5
nibwoestyn = Namib Desert		Nanticoke *U.S.A.*	41°12N 76°0W **175** E8	Narsaq *Greenland*	60°57N 46°4W **57** E6	Navalcarnero *Spain*	40°17N 4°5W **88** E6	Nea Peramos *Kavala,*		Nelson *Ariz., U.S.A.*	35°31N 113°19W **169** J7
amibia	22°30S 15°0E **144** B2	Nanton *Canada*	50°21N 113°46W **162** C6	Narsimhapur *India*	22°54N 79°14E **125** H8	Navalgund *India*	15°34N 75°27E **127** G2	*Greece*	40°50N 24°18E **97** F8	Nelson *Nev., U.S.A.*	35°42N 114°49W **171** K12
nin *Iran*	38°25N 48°30E **105** C13	Nantong *China*	32°1N 120°52E **117** A13	Narsinghgarh *India*	23°54N 77°14E **124** H6	Navalmoral de la Mata		Nea Visa *Greece*	41°34N 26°33E **97** E10	Nelson □ *N.Z.*	42°11S 172°15E **155** B7
njeju *S. Korea*	33°14N 126°33E **115** H14	Nantou *China*	22°32N 113°55E **111** a	Narsinghpur *India*	20°28N 85°5E **126** D7	*Spain*	39°52N 5°33W **88** F5	Nea Zichni *Greece*	41°2N 23°49E **96** E7	Nelson, C. *Australia*	38°26S 141°32E **152** E4
nlea *Indonesia*	3°18S 127°5E **119** F7	Nant'ou *Taiwan*	23°55N 120°41E **117** F13	Narsipatnam *India*	17°40N 82°37E **126** F6	Navan = An Uaimh		Neagh, Lough *U.K.*	54°37N 6°25W **64** B5	Nelson, Estrecho *Chile*	51°30S 75°0W **192** D2
nnoi → *Australia*	30°12S 149°30E **153** A9	Nantua *France*	46°10N 5°35E **71** F12	Nartes, L. e *Albania*	40°41N 19°25E **96** F3	*Ireland*	53°39N 6°41W **64** C5	Neah Bay *U.S.A.*	48°22N 124°37W **170** B2	Nelson Bay *Australia*	32°43S 152°9E **153** B10
nous, O. en →		Nantucket *U.S.A.*	41°17N 70°6W **173** E18	Nartkala *Russia*	43°33N 43°51E **87** J6	Navarino, I. *Chile*	55°0S 67°40W **192** E3	Neale, L. *Australia*	24°15S 130°0E **148** D5	Nelson Forks *Canada*	59°30N 124°0W **162** B4
lgeria	31°0N 0°15W **136** B3	Nantucket I. *U.S.A.*	41°16N 70°5W **173** E18	Naruto = Sanmu		Navarra □ *Spain*	42°40N 1°40W **93** C2	Neales → *Australia*	28°8S 136°47E **151** A2	Nelson House *Canada*	55°47N 98°51W **163** B9
npala *Mali*	15°20N 5°30W **138** B3	Nantulo *Mozam.*	12°32S 38°45E **143** E4	*Japan*	34°11N 134°37E **113** G7	Navarre *U.S.A.*	40°43N 81°31W **174** F3	Neamţ □ *Romania*	46°56N 26°20E **81** C11	Nelson L. *Canada*	55°48N 100°7W **163** B8
np'o *N. Korea*	38°52N 125°10E **115** E13	Nantwich *U.K.*	53°4N 2°31W **66** D5	Narva *Estonia*	59°23N 28°12E **84** B4	Navarre *Fla., U.S.A.*	30°24N 86°52W **179** D3	Neapoli *Kozani, Greece*	40°20N 21°24E **96** F5	Nelson Lakes △ *N.Z.*	41°55S 172°44E **155** B7
namp'o-Shotô *Japan*	32°0N 140°0E **113** J12	Nanty Glo *U.S.A.*	40°28N 78°50W **174** F6	Narva → *Russia*	59°27N 28°2E **84** C4	Navarre, Ohio, U.S.A.	40°43N 81°31W **174** F3	Neapoli *Kriti, Greece*	35°15N 25°37E **99** G7	Nelspoort *S. Africa*	32°7S 23°0E **144** D3
npula *Mozam.*	15°6S 39°15E **143** F4	Nanuque *Brazil*	17°50S 40°21W **189** D2	Narva Bay = Narva Laht		Navas de San Juan *Spain*	38°30N 3°19W **89** G7	Neapoli *Lakonia, Greece*	36°31N 23°4E **98** D5	Nelspruit = Mbombela	
nrode *Indonesia*	3°46S 126°46E **119** E7	Nanusa, Kepulauan		*Estonia*	59°35N 27°35E **61** G22	Navasota *U.S.A.*	30°23N 96°5W **176** F6	Near Is. *U.S.A.*	52°30N 174°0E **166** E2	*S. Africa*	25°29S 30°59E **145** D5
nse Shankou *China*	30°0N 80°25E **125** D10	*Indonesia*	4°45N 127°1E **119** D7	Narva → *Russia*	59°27N 28°2E **84** C4	Navassa I. *W. Indies*	18°30N 75°0W **183** C5	Neath *U.K.*	51°39N 3°48W **67** F4	Néma *Mauritania*	16°40N 7°15W **138** B3
nsen → *Norway*	64°28N 11°37E **60** D14	Nanutarra Roadhouse		Narva Laht *Estonia*	59°35N 27°35E **61** G22	Navasvkern *Sweden*	58°38N 16°49E **63** F10	Neath → *U.K.*	51°39N 3°48W **67** F4	Neman = Nemunas →	
nsos *Norway*	64°29N 11°30E **60** D14	*Australia*	22°32S 115°30E **148** D2	Narvik *Norway*	68°28N 17°26E **60** B9	Navenby *U.K.*	53°6N 0°31W **66** E7	Neath Port Talbot □		*Lithuania*	55°25N 21°10E **82** G3
ntok Chat Trakan △		Nanxi *China*	28°54N 104°59E **116** C5	Narvskoye Vdkhr.		Navi Mumbai *India*	19°5N 73°0E **126** E1	*U.K.*	51°42N 3°45W **67** F4	Neman *Russia*	55°2N 22°2E **82** G3
hailand	17°17N 100°40E **120** D3	Nanxiong *China*	25°6N 114°15E **117** E10	*Russia*	59°18N 28°14E **84** C5	Navia *Spain*	43°35N 6°42W **88** B4	Nebbi *Uganda*	2°24N 31°26E **142** B3	Nembrala *Indonesia*	10°53S 122°58E **148** B3
ntok Huay Yang △		Nanyang *China*	33°11N 112°30E **114** H7	Narwana *India*	29°39N 76°6E **124** E7	Navia → *Spain*	43°35N 6°42W **88** B4	Nebbou *Burkina Faso*	11°9N 1°51W **138** C4	Nemea *Greece*	37°49N 22°40E **98** C4
hailand	11°35N 99°30E **121** G2	Nanyi Hu *China*	31°5N 119°0E **117** B12	Narwiński △ *Poland*	52°5N 22°55E **83** F9	Navidad *Chile*	33°57S 71°50W **190** C1	Nebine Cr. →		Nemeiben L. *Canada*	55°20N 105°20W **163** B7
ntok Mae Surin △		Nanyuan *China*	39°47N 116°24E **114** E9	Narwinbi △ *Australia*	16°7S 136°17E **150** B2	Navidade *Brazil*	23°0S 47°10W **189** E1	*Australia*	29°27S 146°56E **151** D4	Nemé9crçkë, Mal *Albania*	40°15N 20°15E **96** F4
hailand	18°55N 98°2E **120** C2	Nanzhang *China*	31°45N 111°50E **114** H7	Naryan-Mar *Russia*	67°42N 53°12E **106** D6	Navidad *Bank W. Indies*	20°35N 69°0W **183** C5	Nebitdag = Balkanabat		Nemira, Vf. *Romania*	46°17N 26°19E **81** D11
ntok Ngao △		Nanzhao *China*	33°30N 112°20E **114** H7	Narym *Russia*	59°0N 81°30E **106** D9	Navin, Mys *Russia*	62°15N 179°5E **107** C18	*Turkmenistan*	39°30N 54°22E **129** B7	Nemirv = Nemyriv *Ukraine*	48°58N 26°30E **81** A11
hailand	9°58N 98°46E **121** H2	Nao, C. de la *Spain*	38°44N 0°14E **91** G5	Naryn *Kyrgyzstan*	41°26N 75°58E **109** D9	Navlakhi *India*	22°58N 70°28E **124** H4	Nebo, Mt. *U.S.A.*	39°49N 111°46W **169** G8	Nemiscau *Canada*	51°18N 76°54W **164** B4
ntok Phlew △		Naococane, L. *Canada*	52°50N 70°45W **165** B5	Naryn → *Uzbekistan*	40°52N 71°36E **109** D8	Navlya *Russia*	52°53N 34°30E **85** F8	Nebo *Australia*	21°42S 148°42E **150** C4	Nemiscau, L. *Canada*	51°25N 76°40W **164** B4
hailand	12°32N 102°13E **120** F4	Naoussa *Cyclades, Greece*	37°7N 25°14E **99** D7	Narva Qum *Kazakhstan*	47°30N 49°0E **87** E9	Navoi = Nawoiy *Uzbekistan*	40°9N 65°22E **108** D7	Nebolchi *Russia*	59°8N 33°18E **84** C7	Nemours *France*	48°16N 2°40E **71** D9
ntok Yong △		Naoussa *Imathia, Greece*	40°42N 22°9E **96** F6	Narooma *Australia*	36°14S 150°4E **153** D9	Navojoa *Mexico*	27°0N 109°30W **180** B3	Nebraska □ *U.S.A.*	41°30N 99°30W **172** E5	Nemrut Daği △ *Turkey*	38°0N 38°55E **105** D8
hailand	8°15N 98°45E **121** H2	Naozhou Dao *China*	20°55N 110°20E **117** G8	Nashik = Nasik *India*	19°58N 73°50E **126** D1	Navolato *Mexico*	24°47N 107°42W **180** C3	Nebraska City *U.S.A.*	40°41N 95°52W **172** E6	Nemšová *Slovak Rep.*	48°58N 18°7E **79** C11
ntsy *Russia*	62°43N 129°37E **107** C13	Napa *U.S.A.*	38°18N 122°17W **170** G4	Nashua *Mont., U.S.A.*	48°8N 106°22W **168** B10	Navrongo *Ghana*	10°51N 1°3W **139** C4	Nébrodi, Monti *Italy*	37°54N 14°35E **95** F7	Nemunas → *Lithuania*	55°25N 21°10E **82** G2
ntu *Burma*	23°5N 97°28E **123** H20	Napa → *U.S.A.*	38°10N 122°19W **170** G4	Nashua *N.H., U.S.A.*	42°45N 71°28W **175** D13	Navsari *India*	20°57N 72°59E **124** J8	Necedah *U.S.A.*	44°2N 90°4W **172** C8	Nemuro *Japan*	43°20N 145°35E **112** C12
ntumbo *Tanzania*	10°30S 36°4E **143** E4	Napanoch *U.S.A.*	41°44N 74°22W **175** E10	Nashville *Ga., U.S.A.*	31°12N 83°15W **178** E6	Nawa Kot *Pakistan*	28°21N 71°24E **124** E4	Nechako → *Canada*	53°55N 122°42W **162** C4	Nemuro-Kaikyō	
nu *Canada*	51°52N 127°50W **162** C3	Nanpa *Laos*	18°18N 105°6E **120** C5	Nashville *Tenn.,*		Nawa Kot *India*	28°21N 71°24E **124** E4	Neches → *U.S.A.*	29°58N 93°51W **176** G8	*Japan*	43°30N 145°30E **112** C12
nuka-i-Lau *Fiji*	18°53S 178°37W **154** a	Nape Pass = Keo Neua, Deo		*U.S.A.*	36°10N 86°47W **177** C11	Nawabganj Ut. P., India	26°56N 81°14E **125** F9	Neckar → *Germany*	49°27N 8°29E **79** F8	Nemyriv *Ukraine*	48°58N 26°30E **81** A11
tu *Burma*	23°5N 97°28E **123** H20	*Vietnam*	18°23N 105°10E **120** C5	Nashville *Ark., U.S.A.*	33°57S 71°50W **190** C1	Nawabganj Ut. P., India	26°56N 81°14E **125** F9	Neckartal-Odenwald △		Nen Jiang → *China*	45°28N 124°30E **115** B13
nwala *Zambia*	15°44S 26°30E **143** F2	Napier *N.Z.*	39°30S 176°56E **154** F5	Naselle *U.S.A.*	46°22N 123°49W **170** D3	Nawab Khan *Pakistan*	30°17N 69°12E **124** D3	*Germany*	49°30N 9°5E **77** F5	Nenagh *Ireland*	52°52N 8°11W **64** D3
nwon *S. Korea*	35°23N 127°23E **115** G14	Napier Broome B.		Naser, Buheirat en		Nawabganj Ut. P., India	28°32N 79°40E **125** E8	Necochea *Argentina*	38°30S 58°50W **190** D4	Nenana *U.S.A.*	64°34N 149°5W **166** C10
nyil I. *S. China Sea*	10°11N 114°22E **118** C4	*Australia*	14°2S 126°37E **148** B4	*Egypt*	23°0N 32°30E **137** C3	Nawab B. *Australia*	39°43N 111°56W **168** G8	Nene → *U.K.*	52°49N 0°11E **67** E8	Nene *Greece*	38°14N 26°16E **99** C8
nysłów *Poland*	51°6N 17°42E **83** G4	Napier Pen. *Australia*	12°4S 135°43E **150** A2	Nashik = Nasik *India*	19°58N 73°50E **126** D1			Nenita *Greece*	38°14N 26°16E **99** C8
→ *Thailand*	18°48N 100°46E **120** C3			Nasik *India*	19°58N 73°50E **126** D1			Nenjiang *China*	49°10N 125°10E **111** B13
-ch'ang = Nanchang				Nasikabad = Nasriabad *India*				Neno *Malawi*	15°25S 34°40E **143** F3
ina	28°42N 115°55E **117** C10			Nasiriyah = An Nāşirīyah				Neo Chori *Greece*	39°4N 21°16E **98** B3
Ling *China*	25°0N 112°30E **117** F8			*Iraq*	31°0N 46°15E **128** D5			Neodesha *U.S.A.*	37°25N 95°41W **172** G6
Xian *China*	29°20N 112°22E **117** C9			Naskaupi → *Canada*	53°47N 60°51W **165** B7			Neópolis *Brazil*	10°18S 36°35W **189** C3
a *Romania*	44°17N 26°34E **81** F11			Naso *Italy*	38°7N 14°47E **95** D7			Neora Valley △ *India*	27°0N 88°30E **125** F13
a Kru *Liberia*	4°35N 8°45W **138** E3			Naşrābād *Iran*	34°8N 51°26E **129** C6			Nepal ■ *Asia*	28°0N 84°30E **125** F11
aimo *Canada*	49°10N 124°0W **162** D4							Nepalganj *Nepal*	28°5N 81°40E **125** E9
akuli *U.S.A.*	21°24N 158°9W **167** L8							Nepalganj Road *India*	28°1N 81°41E **125** E9
am *N. Korea*	41°44N 129°40E **115** D15							Nephin *Ireland*	54°1N 9°22W **64** B2
'an *China*	24°59N 118°21E **117** E12							Nephin Beg Range *Ireland*	54°0N 9°40W **64** C2

Nepi Italy 42°14N 12°21E 93 F9
Nepomuk Czech Rep. 49°29N 13°35E 78 B6
Neptune U.S.A. 40°13N 74°2W 175 F10
Neptune Is. Australia 35°17S 136°10E 152 C2
Neqāb Iran 36°42N 57°25E 129 B8
Nera → Italy 42°26N 12°24E 93 F9
Nera → Romania 44°48N 21°25E 80 F6
Nérac France 44°8N 0°21E 72 D4
Nerang Australia 27°58S 153°20E 151 D5
Neratovice Czech Rep. 50°16N 14°31E 78 A7
Nerchinsk Russia 52°0N 116°39E 107 D12
Nereju Romania 45°43N 26°43E 81 E11
Nerekhta Russia 57°26N 40°38E 84 D11
Neresnytsya Ukraine 48°7N 23°46E 81 B8
Néret, L. Canada 54°45N 70°44W 165 B15
Neretvanski Kanal Croatia 43°7N 17°10E 93 E14
Neringa Lithuania 55°20N 21°5E 82 C8
Neris → Lithuania 55°8N 24°16E 84 E3
Nerja Spain 36°43N 3°55W 89 J7
Nerl → Russia 56°11N 40°34E 84 D11
Nerpio Spain 38°11N 2°16W 91 G2
Nerva Spain 37°42N 6°30W 89 H4
Nervi Italy 44°23N 9°2E 92 D6
Neryungri Russia 57°38N 124°28E 107 D13
Nescopeck U.S.A. 41°3N 76°12W 175 E8
Nesebŭr Bulgaria 42°41N 27°46E 97 D11
Neskantaga Canada 52°14N 87°53W 164 B2
Neskaupstaður Iceland 65°9N 13°42W 60 D7
Ness, L. U.K. 57°15N 4°32W 65 D4
Ness City U.S.A. 38°27N 99°54W 172 F4
Nessebar = Nesebŭr Bulgaria 42°41N 27°46E 97 D11
Nesterov = Zhovkva Ukraine 50°4N 23°58E 75 C12
Nesterov Russia 54°38N 22°41E 82 D9
Nestorio Greece 40°24N 21°5E 96 F5
Nestos → Europe 40°54N 24°49E 97 F8
Nesvady Slovak Rep. 47°56N 18°7E 79 D11
Nesvizh = Nyasvizh Belarus 53°14N 26°38E 75 B14
Netanya Israel 32°20N 34°51E 130 C3
Netarhat India 23°29N 84°16E 125 H11
Nete → Belgium 51°6N 4°14E 69 C4
Netherdale Australia 21°10S 148°33E 150 b
Netherlands ■ Europe 52°0N 5°30E 69 C5
Netherlands Antilles = ABC Islands W. Indies 12°15N 69°0W 183 D6
Neto → Italy 39°12N 17°9E 95 C10
Netrang India 21°39N 73°21E 124 J5
Nettancourt France 48°51N 4°57E 71 D11
Nettetal Germany 51°19N 6°12E 76 D2
Nettilling L. Canada 66°30N 71°0W 161 D17
Nettuno Italy 41°27N 12°39E 94 A5
Netzahualcóyotl, Presa Mexico 17°8N 93°35W 181 D6
Neu-Isenburg Germany 50°3N 8°42E 77 E4
Neu-Ulm Germany 48°22N 10°0E 77 G6
Neubrandenburg Germany 53°33N 13°15E 76 B9
Neubukow Germany 54°2N 11°39E 76 A7
Neuburg Germany 48°44N 11°11E 77 G7
Neuchâtel Switz. 47°0N 6°55E 77 J2
Neuchâtel □ Switz. 47°0N 6°55E 77 J2
Neuchâtel, Lac de Switz. 46°53N 6°50E 77 J2
Neudau Austria 47°11N 16°6E 78 D9
Neuenhagen Germany 52°32N 13°38E 76 C9
Neuenhaus Germany 52°30N 6°58E 76 C2
Neuf-Brisach France 48°1N 7°30E 71 D14
Neufahrn Bayern, Germany 48°41N 12°11E 77 G8
Neufahrn Bayern, Germany 48°18N 11°40E 77 G7
Neufchâteau Belgium 49°50N 5°25E 69 E5
Neufchâteau France 48°21N 5°40E 71 D12
Neufchâtel-en-Bray France 49°44N 1°26E 70 C8
Neufchâtel-sur-Aisne France 49°26N 4°1E 71 C11
Neuhaus Germany 53°17N 10°56E 76 B6
Neuillé-Pont-Pierre France 47°33N 0°33E 70 E7
Neuilly-St-Front France 49°10N 3°15E 71 C10
Neukalen Germany 53°49N 12°46E 76 B8
Neumarkt Germany 49°26N 11°27E 77 F7
Neumayer Antarctica 71°0S 68°30W 55 D17
Neumünster Germany 54°4N 9°58E 76 A5
Neung-sur-Beuvron France 47°30N 1°50E 71 E8
Neunkirchen Austria 47°43N 16°4E 78 D9
Neunkirchen Germany 49°20N 7°9E 77 F3
Neuquén Argentina 38°55S 68°0W 192 A3
Neuquén □ Argentina 38°0S 69°50W 190 D2
Neuquén → Argentina 38°59S 68°0W 192 A3
Neuruppin Germany 52°55N 12°48E 76 C8
Neusäss Germany 48°24N 10°50E 77 G6
Neuse → U.S.A. 35°6N 76°29W 177 D16
Neusiedl Austria 47°57N 16°50E 79 D9
Neusiedler See Austria 47°50N 16°47E 79 D9
Neusiedler See-Seewinkel △ Austria 47°50N 16°45E 79 D9
Neuss Germany 51°11N 6°42E 76 D2
Neussargues-Moissac France 45°9N 3°0E 72 C7
Neustadt Bayern, Germany 49°44N 12°10E 77 F8
Neustadt Bayern, Germany 48°48N 11°46E 77 G7
Neustadt Bayern, Germany 49°34N 10°37E 77 F6
Neustadt Bayern, Germany 50°19N 11°7E 77 E7
Neustadt Brandenburg, Germany 52°50N 12°27E 76 C8
Neustadt Hessen, Germany 50°51N 9°9E 76 E5
Neustadt Niedersachsen, Germany 52°30N 9°30E 76 C5
Neustadt Rhld-Pfz., Germany 49°21N 8°10E 77 F4
Neustadt Sachsen, Germany 51°2N 14°12E 76 D10
Neustadt Schleswig-Holstein, Germany 54°6N 10°49E 76 A6
Neustadt Thüringen, Germany 50°45N 11°43E 76 E7
Neustrelitz Germany 53°21N 13°4E 76 B8
Neuvic France 45°23N 2°16E 72 C6
Neuville-sur-Saône France 45°52N 4°51E 73 C8
Neuvy-le-Roi France 47°36N 0°36E 70 E7
Neuvy-St-Sépulchre France 46°35N 1°48E 71 F8

Neuvy-sur-Barangeon France 47°20N 2°15E 71 E9
Neuwerk Germany 53°55N 8°30E 76 B4
Neuwied Germany 50°26N 7°29E 76 E3
Neva → Russia 59°56N 30°20E 84 C6
Nevada Iowa, U.S.A. 42°1N 93°27W 172 D7
Nevada Mo., U.S.A. 37°51N 94°22W 172 G6
Nevada □ U.S.A. 39°0N 117°0W 168 G5
Nevada City U.S.A. 39°16N 121°1W 170 F6
Nevado, Cerro Argentina 35°30S 68°32W 190 D2
Nevado de Colima = Volcán de Colima △ Mexico 19°30N 103°40W 180 D4
Nevado de Tres Cruces △ Chile 27°13S 69°5W 190 B2
Nevasa India 19°34N 75°0E 126 E2
Nevel Russia 56°0N 29°55E 84 D5
Nevelsk Russia 46°40N 141°51E 107 E15
Nevers France 47°0N 3°9E 71 F10
Nevertire Australia 31°50S 147°44E 153 A7
Nevesinje Bos.-H. 43°14N 18°6E 96 C2
Neville Canada 49°58N 107°39W 163 D7
Nevinnomyssk Russia 44°40N 42°0E 87 H6
Nevis St. Kitts & Nevis 17°0N 62°30W 183 C7
Nevrokop = Gotse Delchev Bulgaria 41°36N 23°46E 96 E7
Nevşehir Turkey 38°33N 34°40E 104 C6
Nevşehir □ Turkey 38°50N 34°40E 104 C6
Nevskoye Russia 54°32N 22°39E 82 D9
New → U.S.A. 38°10N 81°12W 173 F13
New Aiyansh Canada 55°12N 129°4W 162 B3
New Albany Ind., U.S.A. 38°18N 85°49W 173 F11
New Albany Miss., U.S.A. 34°29N 89°0W 177 D10
New Albany Pa., U.S.A. 41°36N 76°27W 175 E8
New Amsterdam Guyana 6°15N 57°36W 186 B7
New Atlas = Akhali Atoni Georgia 43°7N 40°50E 87 J5
New Baltimore U.S.A. 42°41N 82°44W 174 D2
New Bedford U.S.A. 41°38N 70°56W 175 E14
New Berlin N.Y., U.S.A. 42°37N 75°20W 175 D9
New Berlin Pa., U.S.A. 40°50N 76°57W 174 F8
New Bern U.S.A. 35°7N 77°3W 177 D16
New Bethlehem U.S.A. 41°0N 79°20W 174 F5
New Bight Bahamas 24°19N 75°24W 183 B4
New Bloomfield U.S.A. 40°25N 77°11W 174 F7
New Boston U.S.A. 33°28N 94°25W 176 E7
New Braunfels U.S.A. 29°42N 98°8W 176 G5
New Brighton N.Z. 43°29S 172°43E 155 D7
New Brighton U.S.A. 40°42N 80°19W 174 F4
New Britain Papua N. G. 5°50S 150°20E 147 B8
New Britain U.S.A. 41°40N 72°47W 175 E12
New Brockton U.S.A. 31°23N 85°56W 178 D4
New Brunswick U.S.A. 40°30N 74°27W 175 F10
New Brunswick □ Canada 46°50N 66°30W 165 C6
New Bussa Nigeria 9°53N 4°31E 139 D5
New Caledonia ☑ Pac. Oc. 21°0S 165°0E 147 D9
New Caledonia Trough Pac. Oc. 30°0S 165°0E 156 L8
New Castile = Castilla-La Mancha □ Spain 39°30N 3°30W 89 F7
New Castle Ind., U.S.A. 39°55N 85°22W 173 F11
New Castle Pa., U.S.A. 41°0N 80°21W 174 F4
New City U.S.A. 41°9N 73°59W 175 E11
New Concord U.S.A. 39°59N 81°54W 174 G3
New Cumberland U.S.A. 40°30N 80°36W 174 F4
New Cuyama U.S.A. 34°57N 119°38W 171 L7
New Delhi India 28°36N 77°11E 124 E7
New Denver Canada 50°0N 117°25W 162 D5
New Don Pedro Res. U.S.A. 37°43N 120°24W 170 H6
New Ellenton U.S.A. 33°28N 81°41W 178 B8
New England U.S.A. 43°0N 71°0W 167 G25
New England N. Dak. 46°32N 102°52W 172 B2
New England △ Australia 30°25S 152°30E 153 A10
New England Ra. Australia 30°20S 151°45E 151 E5
New England Seamounts Atl. Oc. 38°0N 63°0W 56 C5
New Forest △ U.K. 50°53N 1°34W 67 G6
New Galloway U.K. 55°5N 4°9W 65 F4
New Glasgow Canada 45°35N 62°36W 165 C7
New Guinea Oceania 4°0S 136°0E 147 B6
New Hamburg Canada 43°23N 80°42W 174 C4
New Hampshire □ U.S.A. 44°0N 71°30W 175 C13
New Hampton U.S.A. 43°3N 92°19W 172 D7
New Hanover S. Africa 29°22S 30°31E 145 C5
New Hartford U.S.A. 43°4N 75°18W 175 C9
New Haven Conn., U.S.A. 41°18N 72°55W 175 E12
New Haven Mich., U.S.A. 42°44N 82°48W 174 D2
New Haven N.Y., U.S.A. 43°28N 76°18W 175 C8
New Hazelton Canada 55°20N 127°30W 162 B3
New Hebrides = Vanuatu ■ Pac. Oc. 15°0S 168°0E 147 C9
New Holland U.S.A. 40°6N 76°5W 175 F8
New Iberia U.S.A. 30°1N 91°49W 176 F9
New Ireland Papua N. G. 3°20S 151°50E 147 B8
New Jersey □ U.S.A. 40°0N 74°30W 173 F16
New Kensington U.S.A. 40°34N 79°46W 174 F5
New Lexington U.S.A. 39°43N 82°13W 173 F12
New Liskeard Canada 47°31N 79°41W 164 C4
New London Conn., U.S.A. 41°22N 72°6W 175 E12
New London Ohio, U.S.A. 41°5N 82°24W 174 E2
New London Wis., U.S.A. 44°23N 88°45W 172 C9
New Madrid U.S.A. 36°36N 89°32W 172 G9
New Martinsville U.S.A. 39°39N 80°52W 173 F13
New Meadows U.S.A. 44°58N 116°18W 168 D5
New Melones L. U.S.A. 37°57N 120°31W 170 H6

New Mexico □ U.S.A. 34°30N 106°0W 169 J11
New Milford Conn., U.S.A. 41°35N 73°25W 175 E11
New Milford Pa., U.S.A. 41°52N 75°44W 175 E9
New Mumbai = Navi Mumbai India 19°5N 73°0E 126 E1
New Norcia Australia 30°57S 116°13E 149 F2
New Norfolk Australia 42°46S 147°2E 151 G4
New Orleans U.S.A. 29°57N 90°4W 177 G9
New Philadelphia U.S.A. 40°30N 81°27W 174 F3
New Plymouth N.Z. 39°4S 174°5E 154 F3
New Plymouth U.S.A. 43°58N 116°49W 168 E5
New Port Richey U.S.A. 28°16N 82°43W 179 G7
New Providence Bahamas 25°25N 77°35W 182 A4
New Quay U.K. 52°13N 4°21W 67 E3
New Radnor U.K. 52°15N 3°9W 67 E4
New Richmond Canada 48°15N 65°45W 165 C6
New Richmond U.S.A. 45°7N 92°32W 172 C7
New River Gorge ○ U.S.A. 37°53N 81°5W 173 G13
New Roads U.S.A. 30°42N 91°26W 176 F9
New Rochelle U.S.A. 40°55N 73°46W 175 F11
New Rockford U.S.A. 47°41N 99°8W 172 B4
New Romney U.K. 50°59N 0°57E 67 G8
New Ross Ireland 52°23N 6°57W 64 D5
New Salem U.S.A. 46°51N 101°25W 172 B3
New Scone = Scone U.K. 56°25N 3°24W 65 E5
New Siberian I. = Novaya Sibir, Ostrov Russia 75°10N 150°0E 107 B16
New Siberian Is. = Novosibirskiye Ostrova Russia 75°0N 142°0E 107 B15
New Smyrna Beach U.S.A. 29°1N 80°56W 179 F9
New South Wales □ Australia 33°0S 146°0E 153 B7
New Tecumseth = Alliston Canada 44°9N 79°52W 174 B5
New Town U.S.A. 47°59N 102°30W 172 B2
New Tredegar U.K. 51°44N 3°16W 67 F4
New Ulm U.S.A. 44°19N 94°28W 172 C6
New Waterford Canada 46°13N 60°4W 165 C7
New Westminster Canada 49°13N 122°55W 170 A4
Newaj → India 24°24N 76°49E 124 G7
Newala Tanzania 10°58S 39°18E 143 E4
Newark Del., U.S.A. 39°41N 75°46W 173 F16
Newark N.J., U.S.A. 40°44N 74°10W 175 F10
Newark N.Y., U.S.A. 43°3N 77°6W 174 C7
Newark Ohio, U.S.A. 40°3N 82°24W 174 F2
Newark Liberty Int. ✈ (EWR) U.S.A. 40°42N 74°10W 175 F10
Newark Valley U.S.A. 42°14N 76°11W 175 D8
Newberg U.S.A. 45°18N 122°58W 168 D2
Newberry Fla., U.S.A. 29°39N 82°37W 179 F7
Newberry Mich., U.S.A. 46°21N 85°30W 173 B11
Newberry S.C., U.S.A. 34°17N 81°37W 178 B6
Newberry Springs U.S.A. 34°50N 116°41W 171 L10
Newboro L. Canada 44°38N 76°20W 175 B8
Newbridge Ireland 53°11N 6°48W 64 C5
Newburgh Canada 44°19N 76°52W 174 B8
Newburgh U.S.A. 41°30N 74°1W 175 E10
Newbury U.K. 51°24N 1°20W 67 F6
Newbury N.H., U.S.A. 43°19N 72°3W 175 B12
Newbury Vt., U.S.A. 44°5N 72°4W 175 B13
Newburyport U.S.A. 42°49N 70°53W 175 D14
Newcastle Australia 33°0S 151°46E 153 B9
Newcastle N.B., Canada 47°1N 65°38W 165 C6
Newcastle Ont., Canada 43°55N 78°35W 164 D4
Newcastle Ireland 52°27N 9°3W 64 D2
Newcastle S. Africa 27°45S 29°58E 145 C4
Newcastle U.K. 54°13N 5°54W 64 B6
Newcastle Calif., U.S.A. 38°53N 121°8W 170 G5
Newcastle Wyo., U.S.A. 43°50N 104°11W 168 E11
Newcastle Emlyn U.K. 52°2N 4°28W 67 E3
Newcastle Ra. Australia 15°45S 130°15E 148 C5
Newcastle-under-Lyme U.K. 53°1N 2°14W 66 D5
Newcastle-upon-Tyne U.K. 54°58N 1°36W 66 C6
Newcastle Waters Australia 17°30S 133°28E 150 B1
Newcomb U.S.A. 43°58N 74°10W 175 C10
Newcomerstown U.S.A. 40°16N 81°36W 174 F3
Newdegate Australia 33°6S 119°0E 149 F2
Newell Australia 16°20S 145°16E 150 B4
Newell U.S.A. 44°43N 103°25W 172 C2
Newenham, C. U.S.A. 58°39N 162°11W 166 D7
Newfane U.S.A. 43°17N 78°43W 174 C6
Newfield U.S.A. 42°18N 76°33W 175 D8
Newfound L. U.S.A. 43°40N 71°47W 175 C13
Newfoundland Canada 49°0N 55°0W 165 C8
Newfoundland & Labrador □ Canada 52°0N 58°0W 165 B8
Newhaven U.K. 50°47N 0°3E 67 G8
Newington U.S.A. 32°35N 81°30W 178 C8
Newkirk U.S.A. 36°53N 97°3W 176 C6
Newlyn U.K. 50°6N 5°34W 67 G2
Newman Australia 23°18S 119°45E 149 D2
Newman U.S.A. 37°19N 121°1W 170 H5
Newmarket Canada 44°3N 79°28W 174 B5
Newmarket Ireland 52°13N 9°0W 64 D2
Newmarket U.K. 52°15N 0°25E 67 E8
Newnan U.S.A. 33°23N 84°48W 178 B5
Newport I. of W., U.K. 50°42N 1°17W 67 G6
Newport Newport, U.K. 51°35N 3°0W 67 F4
Newport Fla., U.S.A. 30°11N 84°10W 178 E5
Newport Ky., U.S.A. 39°5N 84°29W 173 F11
Newport N.H., U.S.A. 43°22N 72°10W 175 C12
Newport N.Y., U.S.A. 43°11N 75°1W 175 C9
Newport Oreg., U.S.A. 44°39N 124°3W 168 D1

Newport Pa., U.S.A. 40°29N 77°8W 174 F7
Newport R.I., U.S.A. 41°29N 71°19W 175 E13
Newport Tenn., U.S.A. 35°58N 83°11W 177 D13
Newport Vt., U.S.A. 44°56N 72°13W 175 B12
Newport Wash., U.S.A. 48°11N 117°3W 168 B5
Newport □ U.K. 51°33N 3°1W 67 F4
Newport Beach U.S.A. 33°37N 117°56W 171 M9
Newport News U.S.A. 36°58N 76°25W 173 G15
Newport Pagnell U.K. 52°5N 0°43W 67 E7
Newquay U.K. 50°25N 5°6W 67 G2
Newry U.K. 54°11N 6°21W 64 B5
Newry Islands △ Australia 20°51S 148°56E 150 b
Newton Ga., U.S.A. 31°19N 84°20W 178 D5
Newton Ill., U.S.A. 38°59N 88°10W 172 F9
Newton Iowa, U.S.A. 41°42N 93°3W 172 E7
Newton Kans., U.S.A. 38°3N 97°21W 172 F5
Newton Mass., U.S.A. 42°21N 71°12W 175 D13
Newton Miss., U.S.A. 32°19N 89°10W 177 E10
Newton N.C., U.S.A. 35°40N 81°13W 177 D14
Newton Tex., U.S.A. 30°51N 93°46W 176 F8
Newton Abbot U.K. 50°32N 3°37W 67 G4
Newton Aycliffe U.K. 54°37N 1°34W 66 C6
Newton Falls N.Y., U.S.A. 44°12N 74°59W 175 B10
Newton Falls Ohio, U.S.A. 41°11N 80°59W 174 E4
Newton Stewart U.K. 54°57N 4°30W 65 G4
Newtonmore U.K. 57°4N 4°8W 65 D4
Newtontoppen Svalbard 79°0N 17°30E 57 B12
Newtown U.K. 52°31N 3°19W 67 E4
Newtownabbey U.K. 54°40N 5°56W 64 B6
Newtownards U.K. 54°36N 5°42W 64 B6
Newtownbarry = Bunclody Ireland 52°39N 6°40W 64 D5
Newtownstewart U.K. 54°43N 7°23W 64 B4
Newville U.S.A. 40°10N 77°24W 174 F7
Nexon France 45°41N 1°11E 72 C5
Neya Russia 58°21N 43°49E 86 A6
Neyrīz Iran 29°15N 54°19E 129 D7
Neyshābūr Iran 36°10N 58°50E 129 B8
Neyveli India 11°32N 79°29E 127 J4
Neyyattinkara India 8°26N 77°5E 127 K3
Nezhin = Nizhyn Ukraine 51°5N 31°55E 85 G6
Nezperce U.S.A. 46°14N 116°14W 168 C5
Nezvysko Ukraine 48°46N 25°15E 81 B10
Nga, Laem Thailand 7°55N 98°27E 121 a
Ngaanyatjarra ◌ Australia 22°40S 127°0E 148 D4
Ngabang Indonesia 0°23N 109°55E 118 D3
Ngabordamlu, Tanjung Indonesia 6°56S 134°11E 119 F8
N'Gage Angola 7°46S 15°15E 140 F3
Ngala Nigeria 12°20N 14°11E 139 C7
Ngaliwurru Nungali ◌ Australia 15°42S 130°4E 148 C5
Ngalurrtju ◌ Australia 22°44S 132°5E 148 D5
Ngambé Centre, Cameroon 5°48N 11°29E 139 D7
Ngambé Littoral, Cameroon 4°21N 10°40E 139 E7
Ngami Depression Botswana 20°30S 22°46E 144 B3
Ngamo Zimbabwe 19°3S 27°32E 143 F2
Nganglong Kangri China 33°0N 81°0E 125 C9
Ngao Thailand 18°46N 99°59E 120 C2
Ngaoundéré Cameroon 7°15N 13°35E 140 C2
Ngapara N.Z. 44°57S 170°46E 155 E3
Ngara Tanzania 2°29S 30°40E 142 C3
Ngarluma ◌ Australia 21°30S 118°30E 148 D2
Ngaruawahia N.Z. 37°42S 175°11E 154 B5
Ngaruroro → N.Z. 39°34S 176°55E 154 F5
Ngatapa N.Z. 38°32S 177°45E 154 E6
Ngauruhoe, Mt. N.Z. 39°13S 175°45E 154 F4
Ngawi Indonesia 7°24S 111°26E 119 G14
Ngcobo S. Africa 31°37S 28°0E 145 D4
Ngeru Uganda 0°27N 31°12E 142 B3
Ngerulmud = Melekeok Palau 7°27N 134°38E 156 G5
Nghia Lo Vietnam 21°33N 104°28E 116 G5
Ngoma Malawi 13°8S 33°45E 143 E3
Ngomahura Zimbabwe 20°26S 30°43E 143 G3
Ngomba Tanzania 8°20S 32°53E 143 D3
Ngomeni, Ras Kenya 2°59S 40°14E 142 C5
Ngong Kenya 1°22S 36°39E 142 C4
Ngongotaha N.Z. 38°5S 176°12E 154 E5
Ngoring Hu China 34°55N 97°5E 110 F8
Ngorkou Mali 15°40N 3°41W 138 B4
Ngorongoro Tanzania 3°11S 35°32E 142 C4
Ngorongoro △ Tanzania 2°40S 35°30E 142 C4
Ngozi Burundi 2°54S 29°50E 142 C2
Ngudu Tanzania 2°58S 33°25E 142 C3
Nguigmi Niger 14°20N 13°20E 135 F8
Nguila Cameroon 4°41N 11°43E 139 D7
Nguiu Australia 11°46S 130°38E 148 B5
Ngukurr Australia 14°44S 134°44E 150 A1
Ngum → Laos 18°31N 102°32E 120 C4
Ngundu Zimbabwe 18°11S 31°15E 143 F3
Ngunga Tanzania 3°37S 33°37E 142 C3
Nguru Nigeria 12°56N 10°29E 139 C7
Nguru Mts. Tanzania 6°0S 37°30E 142 D4
Ngusi Malawi 14°0S 34°50E 143 E3
Nguyen Binh Vietnam 22°39N 105°56E 116 F5
Ngwaketse ◌ Botswana 25°0S 25°0E 144 C3
Nha Bang Vietnam 10°37N 105°0E 121 G5
Nha Trang Vietnam 12°16N 109°10E 121 F7
Nhacoongo Mozam. 24°18S 35°14E 145 C6
Nhamaabué Mozam. 17°25S 35°5E 143 F4
Nhamundá → Brazil 2°12S 56°41W 187 D7
Nhangulaze, L. Mozam. 24°0S 34°30E 145 C5
Nharnuwangga, Wajarri and Ngarlawangga ◌ Australia 24°50S 118°0E 149 D2
Nhill Australia 36°18S 141°40E 152 D4
Nho Quan Vietnam 20°18N 105°45E 116 G5
Nhulunbuy Australia 12°10S 137°20E 150 A2
Nia-nia Dem. Rep. of the Congo 1°30N 27°40E 142 B2
Niafounké Mali 16°0N 4°5W 138 B4
Niagara Falls Canada 43°7N 79°5W 174 C5
Niagara Falls U.S.A. 43°5N 79°4W 174 C6
Niagara-on-the-Lake Canada 43°15N 79°4W 174 C5
Niah Malaysia 3°58N 113°46E 118 D4
Niamey Niger 13°27N 2°6E 139 C5
Niamtougou Togo 9°46N 1°16E 139 D5
Niandan-Koro Guinea 9°37N 9°15W 138 C3

Nianforando Guinea 9°37N 10°36W 138 D2
Niangara Dem. Rep. of the Congo 3°42N 27°50E 142 B2
Niangay, L. Mali 15°50N 3°0W 138 B4
Niangbo Ivory C. 8°49N 5°10W 138 D3
Niangoloko Burkina Faso 10°15N 4°55W 138 C4
Niantic U.S.A. 41°20N 72°11W 175 E12
Nias Indonesia 1°0N 97°30E 118 D1
Niassa □ Mozam. 13°30S 36°0E 143 E4
Niassa △ Mozam. 12°4S 36°57E 143 E4
Nibāk Si. Arabia 24°25N 50°50E 129 E7
Nibe Denmark 56°59N 9°38E 63 H3
Nicaragua ■ Cent. Amer. 11°40N 85°30W 182 D2
Nicaragua, L. de Nic. 12°0N 85°30W 182 D2
Nicastro Italy 38°59N 16°19E 95 D9
Nice France 43°42N 7°14E 73 E11
Nice-Côte-d'Azur ✈ (NCE) France 43°41N 7°12E 73 E11
Niceville U.S.A. 30°31N 86°30W 179 E3
Nichicun, L. Canada 53°5N 71°0W 165 B5
Nichinan Japan 31°38N 131°23E 113 J5
Nicholás, Canal Caribbean 23°30N 80°5W 182 B3
Nicholas Channel = Nicholás, Canal Caribbean 23°30N 80°5W 182 B3
Nicholasville U.S.A. 37°53N 84°34W 173 G11
Nicholls U.S.A. 31°31N 82°38W 178 D7
Nichols U.S.A. 42°1N 76°22W 175 E8
Nicholson Australia 18°2S 128°54E 148 C4
Nicholson U.S.A. 41°37N 75°47W 175 E9
Nicholson → Australia 17°31S 139°36E 150 B2
Nicholson L. Canada 62°40N 102°40W 163 A8
Nicholson Ra. Australia 27°15S 116°45E 149 E2
Nicholville U.S.A. 44°41N 74°39W 175 B10
Nicobar Is. Ind. Oc. 8°0N 93°30E 127 L11
Nicola Canada 50°12N 120°40W 162 C4
Nicolls Town Bahamas 25°8N 78°0W 182 A4
Nicosia Cyprus 35°10N 33°25E 101 D12
Nicosia Italy 37°45N 14°24E 95 E7
Nicótera Italy 38°33N 15°56E 95 D8
Nicoya Costa Rica 10°9N 85°27W 182 D2
Nicoya, G. de Costa Rica 10°0N 85°0W 182 E3
Nicoya, Pen. de Costa Rica 9°45N 85°40W 182 E2
Nida Lithuania 55°20N 21°4E 82 C8
Nidd → U.K. 53°59N 1°23W 66 D6
Nidda Germany 50°23N 9°1E 77 E5
Nidda → Germany 50°17N 8°48E 77 E4
Nidwalden □ Switz. 46°50N 8°25E 77 J4
Nidzica Poland 53°25N 20°28E 83 E7
Niebüll Germany 54°46N 8°48E 76 A4
Nied → Germany 49°23N 6°40E 71 C13
Niederaula Germany 50°47N 9°36E 76 E5
Niederbayern □ Germany 48°40N 12°50E 77 G8
Niederbronn-les-Bains France 48°57N 7°39E 71 D14
Niedere Tauern Austria 47°20N 14°0E 78 D7
Niederlausitz Germany 51°42N 13°56E 76 D9
Niederösterreich □ Austria 48°25N 15°40E 78 C8
Niedersachsen □ Germany 52°50N 9°0E 76 C4
Niedersächsisches Wattenmeer △ Germany 53°45N 7°30E 76 B3
Niekerkshoop S. Africa 29°19S 22°51E 144 C3
Niellé Ivory C. 10°5N 5°38W 138 C3
Niemba Dem. Rep. of the Congo 5°58S 28°24E 142 D2
Niemen = Nemunas → Lithuania 55°25N 21°10E 82 C8
Niemodlin Poland 50°38N 17°38E 83 H4
Niemur Australia 35°17S 144°9E 152 C6
Nienburg Germany 52°39N 9°13E 76 C5
Niepolomice Poland 50°3N 20°13E 83 H7
Niers → Germany 51°43N 5°57E 76 D1
Niesky Germany 51°17N 14°49E 76 D10
Nieszawa Poland 52°52N 18°50E 83 F5
Nieu Bethesda S. Africa 31°51S 24°34E 144 D3
Nieuw Amsterdam Suriname 5°53N 55°5W 187 B7
Nieuw Nickerie Suriname 6°0N 56°59W 187 B7
Nieuwoudtville S. Africa 31°23S 19°7E 144 D2
Nieuwpoort Belgium 51°8N 2°45E 69 C2
Nieves, Pico de las Canary Is. 27°57N 15°35W 100 G4
Nièvre □ France 47°10N 3°40E 71 E10
Niğde Turkey 37°58N 34°40E 104 C6
Niğde □ Turkey 38°0N 34°30E 104 C6
Nigel S. Africa 26°27S 28°25E 145 C4
Niger □ Nigeria 10°0N 5°30E 139 D6
Niger ■ W. Afr. 17°30N 10°0E 139 B7
Niger → W. Afr. 5°33N 6°33E 139 D6
Niger Delta Africa 4°50N 6°0E 139 D6
Nigeria ■ W. Afr. 8°30N 8°0E 139 D6
Nightcaps N.Z. 45°57S 168°2E 155 F3
Nigrita Greece 40°56N 23°29E 96 F7
Nihoa U.S.A. 23°6N 161°58W 167 L7
Nihon = Japan ■ Asia 36°0N 136°0E 113 G8
Nii-Jima Japan 34°20N 139°15E 113 G9
Niigata Japan 37°58N 139°0E 112 F9
Niigata □ Japan 37°15N 138°45E 113 F9
Niihama Japan 33°55N 133°16E 113 H6
Ni'ihau U.S.A. 21°54N 160°9W 167 L7
Niimi Japan 34°59N 133°28E 113 G6
Niitsu Japan 37°48N 139°7E 112 F9
Nijar Spain 36°53N 2°15W 91 J2
Nijil Jordan 30°32N 35°33E 130 E4
Nijkerk Neths. 52°13N 5°30E 69 B5
Nijmegen Neths. 51°50N 5°52E 69 C5
Nijverdal Neths. 52°22N 6°28E 69 B6
Nik Pey Iran 36°50N 48°10E 105 D13
Nikaweratiya Sri Lanka 7°45N 80°7E 127 L5
Nike Nigeria 6°26N 7°29E 139 D6
Nikel Russia 69°24N 30°13E 60 B24
Nikiniki Indonesia 9°49S 124°30E 148 A3
Nikki Benin 9°58N 3°12E 139 D5
Nikítí Greece 40°13N 23°43E 96 F7
Nikkō Japan 36°45N 139°35E 113 F9
Nikkō △ Japan 36°56N 139°37E 113 F9
Nikolayev = Mykolayiv Ukraine 46°58N 32°0E 85 J7
Nikolayevsk Russia 50°0N 45°35E 86 E7
Nikolayevsk-na-Amur Russia 53°8N 140°44E 107 D15

Nikolsk Russia 53°49N 46°4E 86
Nikolskoye Russia 55°12N 166°0E 107
Nikopol Bulgaria 43°43N 24°54E 97
Nikopol Ukraine 47°35N 34°25E 85
Nikopolis Greece 39°5N 20°43E 96
Niksar Turkey 40°31N 37°2E 104
Nikshahr Iran 26°15N 60°10E 129
Nikšić Montenegro 42°50N 18°57E 96
Nîl, Nahr en → Africa 30°10N 31°6E 137
Nîl el Abyad → Sudan 15°38N 32°31E 135
Nîl el Azraq → Sudan 15°38N 32°31E 135
Nila Indonesia 6°44S 129°31E 119
Nilakkottai India 10°10N 77°52E 127
Niland U.S.A. 33°14N 115°31W 171
Nilanga India 18°6N 76°46E 126
Nile = Nîl, Nahr en → Africa 30°10N 31°6E 137
Nile Delta Egypt 31°40N 31°0E 137
Niles Mich., U.S.A. 41°50N 86°15W 172
Niles Ohio, U.S.A. 41°11N 80°46W 174
Nileshwar India 12°15N 75°6E 127
Nilgiri Hills India 11°30N 76°30E 127
Nilo Peçanha Brazil 13°37S 39°6W 189
Nilüfer → Turkey 40°18N 28°27E 97
Nim Ka Thana India 27°44N 75°48E 124
Nimach India 24°30N 74°56E 124
Nimba, Mt. Africa 7°37N 8°25W 138
Nimbahera India 24°37N 74°45E 124
Nîmes France 43°50N 4°23E 72
Nimfaion, Ákra = Pines, Akra Greece 40°5N 24°20E 97
Nimmitabel Australia 36°29S 149°15E 153
Nin Croatia 44°16N 15°12E 93
Nînawá Iraq 36°25N 43°10E 105
Nînawá □ Iraq 36°15N 43°0E 128
Nindigully Australia 28°21S 148°50E 151
Nine Degree Channel India 9°0N 73°0E 127
Ninepin Group China 22°16N 114°21E 111
Ninety Mile Beach N.Z. 34°48S 173°0E 154
Ninety Mile Beach, The Australia 38°15S 147°24E 153
Ninety Six U.S.A. 34°11N 82°1W 178
Ninetyeast Ridge Ind. Oc. 1°0S 90°0E 144
Nineveh = Nînawá Iraq 36°25N 43°10E 105
Ning Xian China 35°30N 107°58E 114
Ning'an China 44°22N 129°20E 115
Ningbo China 29°51N 121°28E 117
Ningcheng China 41°32N 119°53E 115
Ningde China 26°38N 119°23E 117
Ningdu China 26°25N 115°59E 117
Ninggang China 26°42N 113°55E 117
Ningguo China 30°35N 119°0E 117
Ninghai China 29°15N 121°27E 117
Ninghua China 26°14N 116°45E 117
Ningi Nigeria 10°55N 9°30E 139
Ningjin China 37°35N 114°57E 114
Ningjing Shan China 31°0N 98°20E 114
Ninglang China 27°20N 100°55E 116
Ningling China 34°25N 115°22E 114
Ningming China 22°8N 107°4E 114
Ningnan China 27°4N 102°37E 116
Ningpo = Ningbo China 29°51N 121°28E 117
Ningqiang China 32°47N 106°15E 114
Ningshan China 33°21N 108°21E 116
Ningsia Hui A.R. = Ningxia Huizu Zizhiqu □ China 38°0N 106°0E 114
Ningwu China 39°0N 112°18E 114
Ningxia Huizu Zizhiqu □ China 38°0N 106°0E 114
Ningxiang China 28°15N 112°30E 117
Ningyang China 35°47N 116°45E 114
Ningyuan China 25°37N 111°57E 117
Ninh Binh Vietnam 20°15N 105°55E 116
Ninh Giang Vietnam 20°44N 106°24E 116
Ninh Hoa Vietnam 12°30N 109°7E 120
Ninh Ma Vietnam 12°48N 109°21E 120
Nini-Suhien △ Ghana 5°20N 2°34W 138
Ninove Belgium 50°51N 4°2E 69
Nioaque Brazil 21°5S 55°50W 188
Niobrara U.S.A. 42°45N 98°2W 172
Niobrara → U.S.A. 42°46N 98°3W 172
Niokolo-Koba △ Senegal 13°3N 13°2W 138
Niono Mali 14°15N 6°0W 138
Nionsamoridougou Guinea 8°45N 8°50W 138
Nioro du Rip Senegal 13°40N 15°50W 138
Nioro du Sahel Mali 15°15N 9°30W 138
Niort France 46°19N 0°29W 72
Nipani India 16°20N 74°25E 124
Nipawin Canada 53°20N 104°0W 163
Nipfjället Sweden 61°59N 12°50E 63
Nipigon Canada 49°0N 88°17W 164
Nipigon, L. Canada 49°50N 88°30W 164
Nipishish L. Canada 54°12N 60°45W 165
Nipissing, L. Canada 46°20N 80°0W 164
Nipomo U.S.A. 35°3N 120°29W 171
Nippon = Japan ■ Asia 36°0N 136°0E 113
Nipton U.S.A. 35°28N 115°16W 171
Niquelândia Brazil 14°33S 48°23W 188
Nīr Iran 38°2N 47°59E 105
Nira → India 17°58N 75°3E 124
Nirasaki Japan 35°42N 138°27E 113
Nirmal India 19°3N 78°20E 122
Nirmali India 26°20N 86°35E 125
Niš Serbia 43°19N 21°58E 96
Nisa Portugal 39°30N 7°41W 89
Nisa Turkmenistan 37°59N 58°11E 129
Nişāb Si. Arabia 29°11N 44°43E 128
Nişāb Yemen 14°25N 46°29E 132
Nišava → Serbia 43°20N 21°46E 96
Niscemi Italy 37°9N 14°23E 95
Nishinomiya Japan 34°45N 135°20E 113
Nishino'omote Japan 30°43N 130°59E 113
Nishiwaki Japan 34°59N 134°58E 113
Niška Banja Serbia 43°18N 22°1E 96
Niskibi → Canada 56°29N 88°9W 164
Nisko Poland 50°35N 22°7E 83
Nisporeni Moldova 47°4N 28°10E 81
Nisqually → U.S.A. 47°7N 122°42W 170
Nissaki Greece 39°43N 19°52E 96
Nissan → Sweden 56°40N 12°51E 63
Nissiros Greece 36°35N 27°12E 97
Nissum Bredning Denmark 56°40N 8°20E 63
Nissum Fjord Denmark 56°20N 8°11E 63

ru = Dnister → urope 46°18N 30°17E 75 E16
atlin → Canada 60°14N 132°34W 162 A2
hequon Canada 53°10N 70°58W 165 B5
rói Brazil 22°53S 43°7W 191 A7
→ Canada 43°12N 80°23W 174 C4
→ U.K. 55°14N 3°33W 65 F5
niluk △ Australia 14°6S 132°15E 148 B5
a Slovak Rep. 48°19N 18°4E 79 C11
a → Slovak Rep. 47°46N 18°10E 79 D11
iansky □ ovak Rep. 48°10N 18°30E 79 C11
enau Germany 49°12N 12°16E 77 F8
e ☑ Pac. Oc. 19°2S 169°54W 157 J11
an Jiang → China 27°30N 103°5E 116 D4
Indonesia 0°55N 109°54E 118 D4
tou Shan China 29°5N 121°59E 117 C13
zhuang China 40°58N 122°28E 115 D12
ala Finland 63°56N 24°57E 60 E21
elles Belgium 50°35N 4°20E 69 D4
ernais France 47°15N 3°30E 71 E10
erville Canada 49°36N 97°3W 163 D9
as India 23°3N 80°26E 125 H9
U.S.A. 37°3N 93°18W 172 G7
on U.S.A. 29°16N 97°46W 176 G6
m Sagar India 18°10N 77°58E 126 E3
mabad India 18°45N 78°7E 126 E4
mghat India 28°20N 95°45E 123 E19
ne-Kolymsk ussia 68°34N 160°55E 107 C17
ne-Svirskiy ⌂ ussia 60°30N 32°55E 84 B7
negorskiy = Nyzhnohirskyy kraine 45°27N 34°38E 85 K8
nekamsk Russia 55°38N 51°49E 86 C10
neudinsk Russia 54°54N 99°3E 107 D10
nevartovsk Russia 60°56N 76°38E 106 C8
niy Bestyakh ussia 61°57N 129°54E 107 C13
niy Chir Russia 48°22N 43°5E 87 F6
niy Lomov Russia 53°34N 43°38E 86 D6
niy Novgorod Russia 56°20N 44°0E 86 B7
niy Novgorod □ ussia 56°30N 44°20E 86 B7
niy Tagil Russia 57°55N 59°57E 106 D6
yn Ukraine 51°5N 31°55E 85 G6
na Mazowiecka land 52°30N 21°0E 83 F8
Turkey 37°5N 37°50E 104 D7
é Tatry Slovak Rep. 48°55N 19°30E 79 C12
é Tatry △ ovak Rep. 48°55N 19°37E 79 C12
ý Jeseník ech Rep. 49°50N 17°30E 79 B10
vá Oman 22°56N 57°32E 131 C6
a Monferrato Italy 44°46N 8°21E 92 D5
wa Malawi 11°1S 33°56E 143 E3
idja = Grande Comore omoros Is. 11°35S 43°20E 141 a
oš Montenegro 42°53N 18°45E 96 D2
jo Tanzania 8°48S 38°54E 143 D4
nbe Tanzania 9°20S 34°50E 143 D3
nbe → Tanzania 6°56S 35°6E 142 D4
rundabommen veden 62°15N 17°25E 62 B11
mbe Cameroon 6°35N 10°40E 139 D7
na Zambia 12°50S 28°8E 143 E2
ndla S. Africa 28°37S 31°5E 145 C5
wkaw Ghana 6°36N 0°49W 139 D4
yi Zimbabwe 19°41S 29°20E 143 F2
otakota Malawi 12°56S 34°15E 143 E3
otakota ⌂ Malawi 12°50S 34°0E 143 E3
ndwe Tanzania 5°51S 30°51E 142 D3
ngsamba Cameroon 4°55N 9°55E 139 E6
teng Cameroon 4°31N 12°2E 139 E7
renkuru Namibia 17°42S 18°32E 144 A2
vanta Ghana 6°10N 2°10W 138 D4
ai → Burma 25°30N 97°25E 116 F2
khali Bangla. 22°48N 91°10E 123 H17
el Canada 45°25N 80°6W 174 A4
eoka Japan 32°36N 131°41E 113 H5
lejas Spain 39°58N 3°26W 88 F7
lesville U.S.A. 40°3N 86°1W 172 E10
oribetsu Japan 42°24N 141°6E 112 C10
atee U.S.A. 27°10N 81°53W 179 H8
cundra Australia 27°50S 142°36E 151 D3
→ Italy 46°9N 11°4E 92 B8
era Inferiore Italy 40°44N 14°38E 95 B7
era Umbra Italy 43°5N 12°47E 93 E9
Italy 40°48N 17°7E 95 B10
ona U.S.A. 33°47N 97°44W 176 E6
rich Romania 45°55N 24°26E 81 E9
a Japan 35°56N 139°52E 113 G9
ales Mexico 31°19N 110°56W 180 A2
ales U.S.A. 31°21N 110°56W 169 L8
aro France 43°45N 0°2W 72 E3
at → Poland 54°17N 19°17E 82 D6
ata Japan 33°48N 130°44E 113 H5
ent France 48°1N 5°20E 71 D12
ent-le-Rotrou France 48°20N 0°50E 70 D7
ent-sur-Seine ance 48°30N 3°30E 71 D10
gerup Australia 33°32S 116°5E 149 F2
nsk Russia 64°30N 90°50E 107 C10
iki Russia 51°50N 143°10E 107 D15
oa → Australia 23°40S 147°55E 150 C4
oyá Argentina 32°24S 59°48W 190 C4
rád □ Hungary 48°0N 19°30E 80 C4
uera Pallaresa → ain 41°55N 0°55E 90 D5
uera Ribagorçana → ain 41°40N 0°43E 90 D5
ar India 29°11N 74°49E 124 E6
felden Germany 49°35N 7°7E 77 F3
ta India 23°40N 79°34E 125 H8
Spain 42°48N 8°53W 88 C2
a India 28°36N 77°19E 124 E7
e, Montagne France 43°28N 2°18E 72 E6
es, Mts. France 48°11N 3°40W 70 D3
étable France 45°48N 3°46E 72 C7
moutier, Î. de France 46°58N 2°10W 70 F4
moutier-en-l'Île ance 47°0N 2°14W 70 F4
ne Botswana 23°15S 20°14E 144 B3
ma-Zaki Japan 34°54N 139°53E 113 G9
Kundi Pakistan 28°50N 62°45E 122 E3
Ta Phao, Ko ailand 9°23N 99°40E 121 b
aneng Botswana 19°40S 22°17E 144 A3
a Finland 61°30N 23°30E 84 B2
omis Canada 51°35N 105°0W 163 C8
Nokomis U.S.A. 27°7N 82°27W 179 H7
Nokomis L. Canada 57°0N 103°0W 163 B8
Nola C.A.R. 3°35N 16°4E 140 D3
Nola Italy 40°55N 14°33E 95 B7
Nolay France 46°58N 4°35E 71 F11
Noli, C. di Italy 44°12N 8°25E 92 D5
Nolinsk Russia 57°28N 49°57E 86 B9
Noma U.S.A. 30°59N 85°37W 178 E4
Noma Omuramba → Namibia 18°52S 20°53E 144 A3
Nombre de Dios Panama 9°34N 79°28W 182 E4
Nome U.S.A. 64°30N 165°25W 166 C6
Nomgon Mongolia 42°50N 105°8E 114 C3
Nomo-Zaki Japan 32°35N 129°44E 113 H4
Nonacho L. Canada 61°42N 109°40W 163 A7
Nonancourt France 48°47N 1°11E 70 D8
Nonda Australia 20°40S 142°28E 150 C3
None Italy 44°56N 7°32E 92 D4
Nong Chang Thailand 15°23N 99°51E 120 E2
Nong Han Res. Thailand 17°11N 104°9E 120 D5
Nong Het Laos 19°29N 103°59E 120 C4
Nong Khai Thailand 17°50N 102°46E 120 D4
Nong'an China 44°25N 125°5E 115 B13
Nongoma S. Africa 27°58S 31°35E 145 C5
Nongsa Indonesia 1°11N 104°8E 121 d
Nonoava Mexico 27°28N 106°44W 180 B3
Nonsan S. Korea 36°12N 127°5E 115 F14
Nonthaburi Thailand 13°50N 100°29E 120 F3
Nontron France 45°31N 0°40E 72 C4
Nonza France 42°47N 9°21E 73 F13
Noonamah Australia 12°40S 131°4E 148 B5
Noondie, L. Australia 28°30S 119°30E 149 E2
Noonkanbah ☼ Australia 18°30S 124°50E 148 C3
Noord Brabant □ Neths. 51°40N 5°0E 69 C5
Noord Holland □ Neths. 52°30N 4°45E 69 B4
Noordbeveland Neths. 51°35N 3°50E 69 C3
Noordoostpolder Neths. 52°45N 5°45E 69 B5
Noordwijk Neths. 52°14N 4°26E 69 B4
Noosa Heads Australia 26°25S 153°6E 151 D5
Nootka I. Canada 49°32N 126°42W 162 D3
Nopiming ⌂ Canada 50°30N 95°37W 163 C9
Nora Sweden 59°32N 15°2E 62 E9
Noralee Canada 53°59N 126°26W 162 C3
Noranda = Rouyn-Noranda Canada 48°20N 79°0W 164 C4
Norberg Sweden 60°4N 15°56E 62 D9
Nórcia Italy 42°48N 13°5E 93 F10
Norco U.S.A. 33°56N 117°33W 171 M9
Norcross U.S.A. 33°56N 84°13W 178 B5
Nord □ Cameroon 8°30N 14°0E 139 D7
Nord □ France 50°15N 3°30E 71 B10
Nord-Kivu □ Dem. Rep. of the Congo 1°0S 29°0E 142 C2
Nord-Ostsee-Kanal Germany 54°12N 9°32E 76 A5
Nord-Ouest □ Cameroon 6°20N 10°30E 139 D7
Nord-Pas-de-Calais □ France 50°30N 2°50E 71 B9
Nordaustlandet Svalbard 79°14N 23°0E 54 B9
Nordborg Denmark 55°5N 9°50E 63 J3
Nordby Denmark 55°27N 8°24E 63 J2
Norddeich Germany 53°36N 7°9E 76 B3
Nordegg Canada 52°29N 116°5W 162 C5
Norden Germany 53°35N 7°12E 76 B3
Nordenham Germany 53°30N 8°30E 76 B4
Norderney Germany 53°42N 7°9E 76 B3
Norderstedt Germany 53°42N 10°1E 76 B6
Nordfjord Norway 61°55N 5°30E 60 F11
Nordfriesische Inseln Germany 54°40N 8°20E 76 A4
Nordhausen Germany 51°30N 10°47E 76 D6
Nordhorn Germany 52°26N 7°4E 76 C3
Norðoyar Færoe Is. 62°17N 6°35W 60 E9
Nördinge-Nol Sweden 57°56N 12°5E 63 G6
Nordingrå Sweden 62°56N 18°17E 62 B12
Nordjylland □ Denmark 57°0N 9°30E 63 G3
Nordkapp Norway 71°10N 25°50E 60 A21
Nordkapp Svalbard 80°31N 20°0E 54 A9
Nordkinn Norway 71°8N 27°40E 60 A22
Nordkinnhalvøya Norway 70°55N 27°40E 60 A22
Nördlicher Teutoburger Wald-Wiehengebirge ⌂ Germany 52°18N 8°10E 76 C4
Nördlingen Germany 48°48N 10°30E 77 G6
Nordostrundingen Greenland 81°22N 11°40W 57 A9
Nordre Strømfjord Greenland 67°10N 53°35W 57 D5
Nordrhein-Westfalen □ Germany 51°45N 7°30E 76 D3
Nordstrand Germany 54°30N 8°52E 76 A4
Nordvik Russia 74°2N 111°32E 107 B12
Nore → Ireland 52°25N 6°58W 64 D4
Noreland Canada 44°43N 78°48W 174 B6
Norfolk = Simcoe Canada 42°50N 80°23W 174 D4
Norfolk N.Y., U.S.A. 44°48N 74°59W 175 B10
Norfolk Nebr., U.S.A. 42°2N 97°25W 172 D5
Norfolk Va., U.S.A. 36°50N 76°17W 173 G15
Norfolk □ U.K. 52°39N 0°54E 67 E8
Norfolk Broads △ U.K. 52°45N 1°30E 67 E9
Norfolk I. Pac. Oc. 28°58S 168°3E 147 D9
Norfolk Ridge Pac. Oc. 29°0S 168°0E 156 K8
Norfork L. U.S.A. 36°15N 92°14W 176 C8
Norge = Norway ■ Europe 63°0N 11°0E 60 E14
Norilsk Russia 69°20N 88°6E 107 C9
Norma, Mt. Australia 20°55S 140°42E 150 C3
Normal U.S.A. 40°31N 88°59W 172 E9
Norman U.S.A. 35°13N 97°26W 176 D6
Norman → Australia 19°18S 141°51E 150 B3
Norman Park U.S.A. 31°16N 83°41W 178 D6
Norman Wells Canada 65°17N 126°51W 160 D6
Normanby N.Z. 39°32S 174°18E 154 F3
Normanby → Australia 14°23S 144°10E 150 A3
Normandie-Maine ⌂ France 48°30N 0°20W 70 D6
Normandin Canada 48°49N 72°31W 164 C5
Normanhurst, Mt. Australia 25°4S 122°30E 149 E3
Normanton Australia 17°40S 141°10E 150 B3
Normanville Australia 35°27S 138°18E 152 C3
Normétal Canada 49°0N 79°22W 164 C4
Norquay Canada 51°53N 102°5W 163 C8
Norquinco Argentina 41°51S 70°55W 192 B2
Norra Kvill △ Sweden 57°46N 15°35E 63 G9
Norra Ulvön Sweden 63°3N 18°40E 62 A12
Norrahammar Sweden 57°43N 14°7E 63 G8
Norrbottens län □ Sweden 66°50N 20°0E 60 C19
Norrdellen Sweden 61°53N 16°43E 62 C10
Nørre Åby Denmark 55°27N 9°52E 63 J3
Nørre Alslev Denmark 54°54N 11°52E 63 K5
Nørresundby Denmark 57°5N 9°52E 63 G3
Norrhult-Klavreström Sweden 57°7N 15°10E 63 G9
Norris Point Canada 49°31N 57°53W 165 C8
Norristown Ga., U.S.A. 32°30N 82°30W 178 C7
Norristown Pa., U.S.A. 40°7N 75°21W 175 F9
Norrköping Sweden 58°37N 16°11E 63 F10
Norrland Sweden 62°15N 15°45E 60 E16
Norrsundet Sweden 60°56N 17°8E 62 D11
Norrtälje Sweden 59°46N 18°42E 62 E12
Norseman Australia 32°8S 121°43E 149 F3
Norsewood N.Z. 40°3S 176°13E 154 G5
Norsk Russia 52°30N 130°5E 107 D14
Norte, Pta. Argentina 42°5S 63°46W 192 B4
Norte, Pta. del Canary Is. 27°51N 17°57W 100 G2
Norte, Serra do Brazil 11°20S 59°0W 186 F7
North U.S.A. 33°37N 81°6W 178 B8
North, C. Canada 47°2N 60°20W 165 C7
North Adams U.S.A. 42°42N 73°7W 175 D11
North America 40°0N 100°0W 158 F10
North Andaman I. India 13°15N 92°55E 127 H11
North Arm Canada 62°0N 114°30W 162 A5
North Augusta U.S.A. 33°30N 81°59W 178 B8
North Australian Basin Ind. Oc. 14°30S 116°30E 146 F10
North Ayrshire □ U.K. 55°45N 4°44W 65 F4
North Bass I. U.S.A. 41°40N 82°56W 174 E2
North Battleford Canada 52°50N 108°17W 163 C7
North Bay Canada 46°20N 79°30W 164 C4
North Belcher Is. Canada 56°50N 79°50W 164 A4
North Bend Oreg., U.S.A. 43°24N 124°14W 168 E1
North Bend Pa., U.S.A. 41°20N 77°42W 174 E7
North Bend Wash., U.S.A. 47°30N 121°47W 170 C5
North Bennington U.S.A. 42°56N 73°15W 175 D11
North Berwick U.K. 56°4N 2°42W 65 E6
North Berwick U.S.A. 43°18N 70°44W 175 C14
North Brother I. India 10°59N 92°40E 127 J11
North Bruce Canada 44°22N 81°26W 174 B3
North C. Canada 47°5N 64°0W 165 C7
North C. N.Z. 34°23S 173°4E 154 A2
North Canadian → U.S.A. 35°22N 95°37W 176 D7
North Canton U.S.A. 40°53N 81°24W 174 F3
North Cape = Nordkapp Norway 71°10N 25°50E 60 A21
North Caribou L. Canada 52°50N 90°40W 164 B1
North Carolina □ U.S.A. 35°30N 80°0W 177 D15
North Cascades △ U.S.A. 48°45N 121°10W 168 B3
North Channel Canada 46°0N 83°0W 164 C3
North Channel U.K. 55°13N 5°52W 65 F3
North Charleston U.S.A. 32°53N 79°58W 178 C10
North Chicago U.S.A. 42°19N 87°51W 172 D10
North Collins U.S.A. 42°35N 78°56W 174 D6
North Creek U.S.A. 43°42N 73°59W 175 C11
North Dakota □ U.S.A. 47°30N 100°15W 172 B3
North Downs U.K. 51°19N 0°21E 67 F8
North East U.S.A. 42°13N 79°50W 174 D5
North East □ Botswana 20°45S 27°30E 145 B4
North East Frontier Agency = Arunachal Pradesh □ India 28°0N 95°0E 123 F19
North East Lincolnshire □ U.K. 53°34N 0°2W 66 D7
North Eastern □ Kenya 1°30N 40°0E 142 B5
North Esk → U.K. 56°46N 2°24W 65 E6
North European Plain Europe 55°0N 25°0E 58 E10
North Foreland U.K. 51°22N 1°28E 67 F9
North Fork U.S.A. 37°14N 119°21W 170 H7
North Fork American → U.S.A. 38°57N 120°59W 170 G5
North Fork Edisto → U.S.A. 33°16N 80°54W 178 B9
North Fork Feather → U.S.A. 38°33N 121°30W 170 F5
North Fork Grand → U.S.A. 45°47N 102°16W 172 C2
North Fork Red → U.S.A. 34°24N 99°14W 176 D5
North Fort Myers U.S.A. 26°41N 81°53W 179 J8
North Frisian Is. = Nordfriesische Inseln Germany 54°40N 8°20E 76 A4
North Gower Canada 45°8N 75°43W 175 A9
North Hd. Australia 30°14S 114°59E 149 F1
North Henik L. Canada 61°45N 97°40W 163 A9
North Highlands U.S.A. 38°40N 121°23W 170 G5
North Horr Kenya 3°20N 37°8E 142 B4
North I. India 10°8N 72°20E 127 J1
North I. Kenya 4°5N 36°5E 142 B4
North I. N.Z. 38°0S 175°0E 154 E4
North I. Seychelles 4°25S 55°13E 141 b
North Kingsville U.S.A. 41°54N 80°42W 174 E4
North Kitui ⌂ Kenya 0°15S 38°29E 142 C4
North Knife → Canada 58°53N 94°45W 163 B10
North Koel → India 24°45N 83°50E 125 G10
North Korea ■ Asia 40°0N 127°0E 115 E14
North L. Australia 32°30S 143°5E 152 B5
North Lakhimpur India 27°14N 94°7E 123 F19
North Lanarkshire □ U.K. 55°52N 3°56W 65 F5
North Las Vegas U.S.A. 36°11N 115°7W 171 J11
North Lincolnshire □ U.K. 53°36N 0°30W 66 D7
North Little Rock U.S.A. 34°45N 92°16W 176 D8
North Loup → U.S.A. 41°17N 98°24W 172 E4
North Luangwa △ Zambia 11°49S 32°9E 143 E3
North Magnetic Pole Arctic 82°18N 113°24W 54 A2
North Mankato U.S.A. 44°10N 94°2W 172 C6
North Miami U.S.A. 25°53N 80°11W 179 K9
North Miami Beach U.S.A. 25°55N 80°9W 179 K9
North Minch U.K. 58°5N 5°55W 65 C3
North Moose L. Canada 54°4N 100°12W 163 C8
North Myrtle Beach U.S.A. 33°48N 78°42W 177 E15
North Nahanni → Canada 62°15N 123°20W 162 A4
North Naples U.S.A. 26°12N 81°48W 179 J8
North New River Canal U.S.A. 26°30N 80°30W 179 J9
North Olmsted U.S.A. 41°25N 81°56W 174 E3
North Ossetia-Alaniya □ Russia 43°30N 44°30E 87 J7
North Pagai, I. = Pagai Utara, Pulau Indonesia 2°35S 100°0E 118 E2
North Palisade U.S.A. 37°6N 118°31W 170 H8
North Platte U.S.A. 41°8N 100°46W 172 E3
North Platte → U.S.A. 41°7N 100°42W 172 E3
North Point U.S.A. 27°4N 82°10W 179 H7
North Pole Arctic 90°0N 0°0 54 A
North Portal Canada 49°0N 102°33W 163 D8
North Powder U.S.A. 45°2N 117°55W 168 D5
North Pt. Barbados 13°20N 59°37W 183 g
North Pt. Trin. & Tob. 11°21N 60°31W 187 J16
North Pt. U.S.A. 45°2N 83°16W 174 A1
North Reef I. India 13°5N 92°43E 127 H11
North Rhine Westphalia = Nordrhein-Westfalen □ Germany 51°45N 7°30E 76 D3
North River Canada 53°49N 57°6W 165 B8
North Ronaldsay U.K. 59°22N 2°26W 65 B6
North Saskatchewan → Canada 53°15N 105°5W 163 C7
North Sea Europe 56°0N 4°0E 58 D6
North Seal → Canada 58°50N 98°7W 163 B9
North Sentinel I. India 11°33N 92°15E 127 J11
North Shields Australia 34°38S 135°52E 152 C1
North Slope U.S.A. 69°15N 152°0W 166 B9
North Somerset □ U.K. 51°24N 2°45W 67 F5
North Sydney Canada 46°12N 60°15W 165 C7
North Syracuse U.S.A. 43°8N 76°7W 175 C8
North Taranaki Bight N.Z. 38°50S 174°15E 154 E3
North Thompson → Canada 50°40N 120°20W 162 C4
North Tonawanda U.S.A. 43°2N 78°53W 174 C6
North Troy U.S.A. 45°0N 72°24W 175 B12
North Twin I. Canada 53°20N 80°0W 164 B4
North Tyne → U.K. 55°0N 2°8W 66 B5
North Uist U.K. 57°40N 7°15W 65 D1
North Vancouver Canada 49°19N 123°4W 170 A3
North Vernon U.S.A. 39°0N 85°38W 173 F11
North Wabasca L. Canada 56°0N 113°55W 162 B6
North Walsham U.K. 52°50N 1°22E 66 E9
North West = Severo-Zapadnyy □ Russia 65°0N 40°0E 106 C4
North West □ Botswana 19°0S 22°30E 144 A3
North-West □ S. Africa 27°0S 25°0E 144 C4
North West C. Australia 21°45S 114°9E 148 D1
North West Christmas I. Ridge Pac. Oc. 6°30N 165°0W 157 F11
North West Frontier = Khyber Pakhtunkhwa □ Pakistan 34°0N 72°0E 124 C4
North West Highlands U.K. 57°33N 4°58W 65 D4
North West River Canada 53°30N 60°10W 165 B7
North Western □ Zambia 13°30S 25°30E 143 E2
North Wildwood U.S.A. 39°0N 74°48W 173 F16
North York Moors U.K. 54°23N 0°53W 66 C7
North York Moors △ U.K. 54°27N 0°51W 66 C7
North Yorkshire □ U.K. 54°15N 1°25W 66 C6
Northallerton U.K. 54°20N 1°26W 66 C6
Northam Australia 31°35S 116°42E 149 F2
Northam S. Africa 24°56S 27°18E 144 B4
Northampton Australia 28°27S 114°33E 149 E1
Northampton U.K. 52°15N 0°53W 67 E7
Northampton Mass., U.S.A. 42°19N 72°38W 175 D12
Northampton Pa., U.S.A. 40°41N 75°30W 175 F9
Northamptonshire □ U.K. 52°16N 0°55W 67 E7
Northbridge U.S.A. 42°9N 71°39W 175 D13
Northbrook Canada 44°44N 77°9W 174 B7
Northcliffe Australia 34°39S 116°7E 149 F2
Northeast Pacific Basin Pac. Oc. 32°0N 145°0W 157 D13
Northeast Providence Channel W. Indies 26°0N 76°0W 182 A4
Northeim Germany 51°42N 10°0E 76 D6
Northern = Limpopo □ S. Africa 24°5S 29°0E 145 B4
Northern □ Ghana 9°30N 1°0W 139 D4
Northern □ Malawi 11°0S 34°0E 143 E3
Northern □ S. Leone 9°15N 11°30W 138 D2
Northern □ Zambia 10°30S 30°30E 143 E3
Northern Aral Sea Kazakhstan 46°20N 60°30E 108 C6
Northern Areas = Gilgit-Baltistan □ Pakistan 36°30N 73°0E 125 A5
Northern Cape □ S. Africa 30°0S 20°0E 144 C3
Northern Circars India 17°30N 82°30E 126 F6
Northern Dvina = Dvina, Severnaya → Russia 64°32N 40°30E 58 C14
Northern Indian L. Canada 57°20N 97°20W 163 B9
Northern Ireland □ U.K. 54°45N 7°0W 64 B5
Northern Lau Group Fiji 17°30S 178°59W 154 a
Northern Light L. Canada 48°15N 90°39W 164 C1
Northern Marianas ☑ Pac. Oc. 17°0N 145°0E 156 F6
Northern Province □ S. Africa 24°0S 29°0E 145 B4
Northern Range Trin. & Tob. 10°46N 61°15W 187 K15
Northern Sporades = Voreios Sporades Greece 39°15N 23°30E 98 B5
Northern Territory □ Australia 20°0S 133°0E 148 D5
Northfield Minn., U.S.A. 44°27N 93°9W 172 C7
Northfield Vt., U.S.A. 44°9N 72°40W 175 B12
Northgate Canada 49°0N 102°16W 163 D8
Northland □ N.Z. 35°30S 173°30E 154 B2
Northome U.S.A. 47°52N 94°17W 172 B6
Northport Ala., U.S.A. 33°14N 87°35W 177 E11
Northport Wash., U.S.A. 48°55N 117°48W 168 B5
Northumberland □ U.K. 55°12N 2°0W 66 B6
Northumberland, C. Australia 38°5S 140°40E 152 E4
Northumberland Is. Australia 21°30S 149°50E 150 C4
Northumberland Str. Canada 46°20N 64°0W 165 C7
Northville Canada 43°10N 81°56W 174 C3
Northville U.S.A. 43°13N 74°11W 175 C10
Northwest Atlantic Mid-Ocean Canyon Atl. Oc. 54°0N 48°0W 56 A7
Northwest Pacific Basin Pac. Oc. 32°0N 165°0E 156 D8
Northwest Providence Channel W. Indies 26°0N 78°0W 182 A4
Northwest Territories □ Canada 63°0N 118°0W 160 E8
Northwich U.K. 53°15N 2°31W 66 D5
Northwood Iowa, U.S.A. 43°27N 93°13W 172 D7
Northwood N. Dak., U.S.A. 47°44N 97°34W 172 B5
Norton U.S.A. 39°50N 99°53W 172 F4
Norton Zimbabwe 17°52S 30°40E 143 F3
Norton Sd. U.S.A. 63°50N 164°0W 166 C7
Nortorf Germany 54°10N 9°50E 76 A5
Norwalk Calif., U.S.A. 33°54N 118°4W 171 M8
Norwalk Conn., U.S.A. 41°7N 73°22W 175 E11
Norwalk Iowa, U.S.A. 41°29N 93°41W 172 E7
Norwalk Ohio, U.S.A. 41°15N 82°37W 174 E2
Norway Maine, U.S.A. 44°13N 70°32W 173 C18
Norway Mich., U.S.A. 45°47N 87°55W 172 C10
Norway ■ Europe 63°0N 11°0E 60 E14
Norway House Canada 53°59N 97°50W 163 C9
Norwegian B. Canada 77°30N 90°0W 161 B14
Norwegian Basin Atl. Oc. 68°0N 2°0W 54 C7
Norwegian Sea Atl. Oc. 66°0N 1°0E 58 B6
Norwich Canada 42°59N 80°36W 174 D4
Norwich U.K. 52°38N 1°18E 67 E9
Norwich Conn., U.S.A. 41°31N 72°5W 175 E12
Norwich N.Y., U.S.A. 42°32N 75°32W 175 D9
Norwood Canada 44°23N 77°59W 174 B7
Norwood U.S.A. 44°45N 75°0W 175 B10
Nosappu-Misaki Japan 45°26N 141°39E 112 C12
Noshiro Japan 40°12N 140°0E 112 D10
Nosivka Ukraine 50°50N 31°37E 85 G6
Nosovka = Nosivka Ukraine 50°50N 31°37E 85 G6
Noşratābād Iran 29°55N 60°0E 129 D8
Noss Hd. U.K. 58°28N 3°3W 65 C5
Nossa Senhora da Glória Brazil 10°14S 37°25W 189 C3
Nossa Senhora das Dores Brazil 10°29S 37°13W 189 C3
Nossa Senhora do Socorro Brazil 10°52S 37°7W 189 C3
Nossebro Sweden 58°12N 12°43E 63 F6
Nossob → S. Africa 26°55S 20°45E 144 C3
Nossombougou Mali 13°5N 7°55W 138 C3
Nosy Varika Madag. 20°35S 48°32E 141 J9
Notasulga U.S.A. 32°34N 85°41W 178 C4
Noteć → Poland 52°44N 15°26E 83 F2
Notikewin → Canada 57°2N 117°38W 162 B5
Notio Aigaio □ Greece 36°52N 25°34E 99 E7
Notios Aiyaíon = Notio Aigaio □ Greece 36°52N 25°34E 99 E7
Notios Evvoikos Kolpos Greece 38°20N 24°0E 98 C5
Noto Italy 36°53N 15°4E 95 F8
Noto, G. di Italy 36°50N 15°12E 95 F8
Noto, Val di Italy 37°14N 14°31E 95 E7
Noto-Hantō Japan 37°15N 136°40E 113 F8
Notodden Norway 59°35N 9°17E 61 G13
Notre Dame B. Canada 49°45N 55°30W 165 C8
Notre-Dame-de-Koartac = Quaqtaq Canada 60°55N 69°40W 161 E18
Notre-Dame-des-Bois Canada 45°24N 71°4W 175 A13
Notre-Dame-d'Ivugivic = Ivujivik Canada 62°24N 77°55W 161 E16
Notre-Dame-du-Nord Canada 47°36N 79°30W 164 C4
Notsé Togo 7°0N 1°17E 139 D5
Nottawasaga B. Canada 44°35N 80°15W 174 B4
Nottaway → Canada 51°22N 78°55W 164 B4
Nottingham U.K. 52°58N 1°10W 66 E6
Nottingham, City of □ U.K. 52°58N 1°10W 66 E6
Nottingham I. Canada 63°20N 77°55W 161 E16
Nottinghamshire □ U.K. 53°10N 1°3W 66 D6
Nottoway → U.S.A. 36°33N 76°55W 173 G15
Notwane → Botswana 23°35S 26°58E 144 B4
Nouâdhibou Mauritania 20°54N 17°0W 134 D2
Nouâdhibou, Râs Mauritania 20°50N 17°0W 134 D2
Nouakchott Mauritania 18°9N 15°58W 138 B1
Nouâmghâr Mauritania 19°20N 16°20W 138 B1
Nouméa N. Cal. 22°17S 166°30E 147 D9
Nouna Burkina Faso 12°45N 3°52W 138 C4
Noupoort S. Africa 31°10S 24°57E 144 D3
Nouveau Comptoir = Wemindji Canada 53°0N 78°49W 164 B4
Nouvelle Amsterdam, Î. Ind. Oc. 38°30S 77°30E 146 H6
Nouvelle-Calédonie = New Caledonia ☑ Pac. Oc. 21°0S 165°0E 147 D9
Nouzonville France 49°48N 4°44E 71 C11
Nová Baňa Slovak Rep. 48°28N 18°39E 79 C11
Nová Bystřice Czech Rep. 49°2N 15°8E 78 B8
Nova Cruz Brazil 6°28S 35°25W 189 B3
Nova Era Brazil 19°45S 43°3W 189 D2
Nova Esperança Brazil 23°8S 52°24W 191 A5
Nova Friburgo Brazil 22°16S 42°30W 191 A7
Nova Gorica Slovenia 45°57N 13°39E 93 C10
Nova Gradiška Croatia 45°17N 17°28E 80 E2
Nova Iguaçu Brazil 22°45S 43°28W 191 A7
Nova Iorque Brazil 7°0S 44°5W 189 B2
Nova Kakhovka Ukraine 46°42N 33°27E 85 J7
Nova Lamego Guinea-Biss. 12°19N 14°11W 138 C2
Nova Lusitânia Mozam. 19°50S 34°34E 143 F3
Nova Mambone Mozam. 21°0S 35°3E 145 B6
Nova Odesa Ukraine 47°19N 31°47E 85 J6
Nová Paka Czech Rep. 50°29N 15°30E 78 A8
Nova Pavova Serbia 44°56N 20°14E 80 F5
Nova Ponte Brazil 19°8S 47°41W 189 D1
Nova Russas Brazil 4°42S 40°34W 189 A2
Nova Scotia □ Canada 45°10N 63°0W 165 C7
Nova Siri Italy 40°10N 16°35E 95 B9
Nova Sofala Mozam. 20°7S 34°42E 145 B5
Nova Ushytsya Ukraine 48°50N 27°17E 81 B12
Nova Varoš Serbia 43°29N 19°48E 96 C3
Nova Venécia Brazil 18°45S 40°24W 189 D2
Nova Zagora Bulgaria 42°32N 26°1E 97 D10
Novaci Macedonia 41°5N 21°29E 96 E5
Novaci Romania 45°10N 23°42E 81 E8
Novaféltria Italy 43°53N 12°17E 93 E9
Novannenskiy = Novoannenskiy Russia 50°32N 42°39E 86 E6
Novar Canada 45°27N 79°15W 174 A5
Novara Italy 45°28N 8°38E 92 C5
Novato U.S.A. 38°6N 122°35W 170 G4
Novaya Kakhovka = Nova Kakhovka Ukraine 46°42N 33°27E 85 J7
Novaya Kazanka = Zhangaqala Kazakhstan 48°56N 49°36E 87 F9
Novaya Ladoga Russia 60°7N 32°16E 84 B7
Novaya Lyalya Russia 59°4N 60°45E 106 D7
Novaya Sibir, Ostrov Russia 75°10N 150°0E 107 B16
Novaya Zemlya Russia 75°0N 56°0E 106 B6
Nové Město Slovak Rep. 48°45N 17°50E 79 C10
Nové Město na Moravě Czech Rep. 49°34N 16°5E 78 B9
Nové Město nad Metují Czech Rep. 50°20N 16°10E 79 A9
Nové Zámky Slovak Rep. 48°2N 18°8E 79 C11
Novelda Spain 38°24N 0°45W 91 G4
Novellara Italy 44°51N 10°44E 92 D7
Noventa Vicentina Italy 45°17N 11°32E 93 C8
Novgorod = Velikiy Novgorod Russia 58°30N 31°25E 84 C6
Novgorod □ Russia 58°50N 32°30E 84 C7
Novgorod-Severskiy = Novhorod-Siverskyy Ukraine 52°2N 33°10E 85 G7
Novhorod-Siverskyy Ukraine 52°2N 33°10E 85 G7
Novi Bečej Serbia 45°36N 20°10E 80 E5
Novi Iskar Bulgaria 42°48N 23°21E 96 D7
Novi Kneževac Serbia 46°4N 20°8E 80 D5
Novi Lígure Italy 44°46N 8°47E 92 D5
Novi Pazar Bulgaria 43°25N 27°15E 97 C11
Novi Pazar Serbia 43°12N 20°28E 96 C4
Novi Sad Serbia 45°18N 19°52E 80 E4
Novi Slankamen Serbia 45°8N 20°15E 80 E5
Novi Travnik Bos.-H. 44°10N 17°40E 80 F2
Novi Vinodolski Croatia 45°10N 14°48E 93 C11
Novigrad Istra, Croatia 45°19N 13°33E 93 C10
Novigrad Zadar, Croatia 44°10N 15°32E 93 D12
Novigradsko More Croatia 44°12N 15°33E 93 D12
Novo Acôrdo Brazil 10°10S 46°48W 189 C1
Novo Cruzeiro Brazil 17°29S 41°53W 189 D2
Novo Hamburgo Brazil 29°37S 51°7W 191 B5
Novo Ivanivka Ukraine 45°55N 29°5E 81 E14
Novo Mesto Slovenia 45°47N 15°12E 93 C12
Novo Miloševo Serbia 45°42N 20°20E 80 E5
Novoaleksandrovsk Russia 45°29N 41°17E 87 H5
Novoaleksandrovskaya = Novoaleksandrovsk Russia 45°29N 41°17E 87 H5
Novoaltaysk Russia 53°30N 84°0E 109 B10
Novoannenskiy Russia 50°32N 42°39E 86 E6
Novoazovsk Ukraine 47°15N 38°4E 85 J10
Novocheboksarsk Russia 56°5N 47°27E 86 B8
Novocherkassk Russia 47°27N 40°15E 87 G5
Novodevichye Russia 53°37N 48°50E 86 D9
Novodvinsk Russia 64°25N 40°42E 106 C5
Novogrudok = Navahrudak Belarus 53°40N 25°50E 75 B13
Novohrad-Volynskyy Ukraine 50°34N 27°35E 75 C14
Novokachalinsk Russia 45°5N 132°0E 112 B5
Novokhopersk Russia 51°5N 41°39E 86 E5
Novokuybyshevsk Russia 53°7N 49°58E 86 D9
Novokuznetsk Russia 53°45N 87°10E 109 B11
Novolazarevskaya Antarctica 71°0S 12°0E 55 D3
Novomoskovsk Russia 54°5N 38°15E 84 E10
Novomoskovsk Ukraine 48°33N 35°17E 85 H8
Novomyrhorod Ukraine 48°45N 31°33E 85 H6
Novopolotsk = Navapolatsk Belarus 55°32N 28°37E 84 E5
Novorossiysk Russia 44°43N 37°46E 85 K9
Novorybnoye Russia 72°50N 105°50E 107 B11
Novorzhev Russia 57°3N 29°25E 84 D5
Novosej Albania 41°56N 20°35E 96 E4
Novoselytsya Ukraine 48°14N 26°15E 81 B11
Novoshakhtinsk Russia 47°46N 39°58E 85 J10
Novosibirsk Russia 55°0N 83°5E 109 B10
Novosibirskiye Ostrova Russia 75°0N 142°0E 107 B15
Novosibirskoye Vdkhr. Russia 54°35N 82°35E 109 B10
Novosil Russia 52°59N 37°2E 85 F9
Novosokolniki Russia 56°20N 30°2E 84 D6
Novotitarovskaya Russia 45°17N 39°2E 87 H4
Novotroitsk Russia 51°10N 58°15E 108 B5
Novotroitskoye = Töle Bī Kazakhstan 43°42N 73°46E 109 D8
Novoukrayinka Ukraine 48°25N 31°30E 85 H6
Novoulyanovsk Russia 54°8N 48°24E 86 C9
Novouzensk Russia 50°32N 48°17E 86 E9
Novovolynsk Ukraine 50°45N 24°4E 83 H11
Novovoronezhskiy Russia 51°19N 39°13E 85 G10
Novoyavoriske Ukraine 49°53N 23°33E 83 J10
Novozybkov Russia 52°30N 32°0E 85 F6
Novska Croatia 45°19N 17°0E 93 C14
Nový Bor Czech Rep. 50°46N 14°35E 78 A7

Novy Bug = Novyy Buh
Ukraine 47°34N 32°29E **85** J7
Nový Bydžov *Czech Rep.* 50°14N 15°29E **78** A8
Novy Dvor *Belarus* 52°50N 24°21E **83** F11
Nowy Dwór Mazowiecki
Poland 52°26N 20°44E **83** F7
Nový Jičín *Czech Rep.* 49°30N 18°2E **79** B11
Novyy Buh *Ukraine* 47°34N 32°29E **85** J7
Novyy Oskol *Russia* 50°44N 37°55E **85** G9
Novyy Port *Russia* 67°40N 72°30E **106** C8
Novyy Urengoy *Russia* 65°48N 76°52E **106** C8
Nowa Deba *Poland* 50°26N 21°41E **83** H8
Nowa Ruda *Poland* 50°35N 16°30E **83** H3
Nowa Sarzyna *Poland* 50°21N 22°21E **83** H9
Nowa Sól *Poland* 51°48N 15°44E **83** G2
Nowata *U.S.A.* 36°42N 95°38W **176** C7
Nowbarān *Iran* 35°8N 49°42E **129** C6
Nowe *Poland* 53°41N 18°44E **82** E5
Nowe Miasteczko
Poland 51°42N 15°42E **83** G2
Nowe Miasto *Poland* 51°38N 20°34E **83** G7
Nowe Miasto Lubawskie
Poland 53°27N 19°33E **82** E6
Nowe Skalmierzyce
Poland 51°43N 18°0E **83** G4
Nowe Warpno *Poland* 53°42N 14°18E **82** E1
Nowendoc *Australia* 31°32S 151°44E **153** A9
Nowendoc △ *Australia* 31°33S 151°45E **153** A9
Nowghāb *Iran* 33°53N 59°4E **129** C8
Nowgong = Nagaon
India 26°20N 92°50E **123** F18
Nowgong *India* 25°4N 79°27E **125** G8
Nowogard *Poland* 53°41N 15°10E **82** E2
Nowogród *Poland* 53°14N 21°53E **83** E8
Nowogród Bobrzanski
Poland 51°48N 15°15E **83** G2
Nowogrodziec *Poland* 51°12N 15°24E **83** G2
Nowra *Australia* 34°53S 150°35E **153** C9
Nowrangapur *India* 19°14N 82°32E **126** E6
Nowshera *Pakistan* 34°0N 72°0E **122** C8
Nowy Dwór Gdański
Poland 54°13N 19°7E **82** D6
Nowy Sącz *Poland* 49°40N 20°41E **83** J7
Nowy Staw *Poland* 54°13N 19°2E **82** D6
Nowy Targ *Poland* 49°29N 20°2E **83** J7
Nowy Tomyśl *Poland* 52°19N 16°10E **83** F3
Nowy Wiśnicz *Poland* 49°55N 20°28E **83** J7
Noxen *U.S.A.* 41°25N 76°4W **175** E8
Noyabr'sk *Russia* 64°34N 76°21E **106** C8
Noyant *France* 47°30N 0°6E **70** E7
Noyers *France* 47°40N 4°0E **71** E10
Noyon *France* 49°34N 2°59E **71** C9
Noyon *Mongolia* 43°2N 102°4E **114** C2
Nozay *France* 47°34N 1°38W **70** E5
Nqutu *S. Africa* 28°13S 30°32E **145** C5
Nsa, O. en → *Algeria* 32°28N 5°24E **136** B5
Nsanje *Malawi* 16°55S 35°12E **143** F4
Nsawam *Ghana* 5°50N 0°24W **139** D4
Nseluka *Zambia* 9°58S 31°16E **143** D3
Nsomba *Zambia* 10°45S 29°51E **143** E2
Nsukka *Nigeria* 6°51N 7°29E **139** D6
Ntaria ○ *Australia* 24°0S 132°41E **148** D5
Ntui *Cameroon* 4°27N 11°38E **139** E7
Ntungamo *Uganda* 0°56S 30°17E **142** C3
Nu Jiang → *China* 29°58N 97°25E **116** E2
Nu Shan *China* 26°0N 99°20E **116** E2
Nuba Mts. = Nubah, Jibalan
Sudan 12°0N 31°0E **135** F12
Nubah, Jibalan *Sudan* 12°0N 31°0E **135** F12
Nubia *Africa* 21°0N 32°0E **132** D7
Nubian Desert = Nûbiya, Es Sahrâ
en *Sudan* 21°30N 33°30E **137** C3
Nûbiya, Es Sahrâ en
Sudan 21°30N 33°30E **137** C3
Nubledo *Spain* 43°31N 5°52W **88** B5
Nuboai *Indonesia* 2°10S 136°30E **119** E9
Nubra → *India* 34°35N 77°35E **123** B7
Nucet *Romania* 46°28N 22°35E **80** D7
Nueces → *U.S.A.* 27°51N 97°30W **176** H6
Nueltin L. *Canada* 60°30N 99°30W **163** A9
Nuestra Señora del Rosario de
Caá-Catí *Argentina* 27°45S 57°36W **190** B4
Nueva, I. *Chile* 55°13S 66°30W **192** E4
Nueva Carteya *Spain* 37°35N 4°28W **89** H6
Nueva Ciudad Guerrero
Mexico 26°34N 99°12W **181** B5
Nueva Gerona *Cuba* 21°53N 82°49W **182** B3
Nueva Imperial *Chile* 38°45S 72°58W **192** A2
Nueva Palmira
Uruguay 33°52S 58°20W **190** C4
Nueva Rosita *Mexico* 27°57N 101°13W **180** B4
Nueva San Salvador
El Salv. 13°40N 89°18W **182** D2
Nueva Tabarca *Spain* 38°17N 0°30W **91** G4
Nuéve de Julio
Argentina 35°30S 61°0W **190** D3
Nuevitas *Cuba* 21°30N 77°20W **182** B4
Nuevo, G. *Argentina* 43°0S 64°30W **192** B4
Nuevo Casas Grandes
Mexico 30°25N 107°55W **180** A3
Nuevo Laredo *Mexico* 27°30N 99°31W **181** B5
Nuevo León □ *Mexico* 25°20N 100°0W **180** C5
Nuevo Mundo, Cerro
Bolivia 21°55S 66°53W **188** E4
Nuevo Rocafuerte
Ecuador 0°55S 75°27W **186** D3
Nugget Pt. *N.Z.* 46°27S 169°50E **155** G4
Nugrus, Gebel *Egypt* 24°47N 34°53E **137** C3
Nuhaka *N.Z.* 39°3S 177°45E **154** F6
Nuits-St-Georges *France* 47°10N 4°56E **71** E11
Nukey Bluff *Australia* 32°26S 135°29E **151** E2
Nukhayb *Iraq* 32°4N 42°3E **105** F10
Nukheila *Sudan* 19°1N 26°21E **137** D2
Nuku Hiva
French Polynesia 8°54S 140°6W **157** H13
Nuku'alofa *Tonga* 21°10S 175°12W **147** D11
Nukus *Uzbekistan* 42°27N 59°41E **108** D5
Nulato *U.S.A.* 64°43N 158°6W **166** C4
Nules *Spain* 39°51N 0°9W **90** F4
Nullagine *Australia* 21°53S 120°7E **148** C6
Nullagine → *Australia* 21°20S 120°20E **148** D3
Nullarbor *Australia* 31°28S 130°55E **149** F2
Nullarbor △ *Australia* 32°33S 130°10E **149** F2
Nullarbor Plain
Australia 31°10S 129°0E **149** F4
Numalla, L. *Australia* 28°43S 144°20E **151** D3
Numan *Nigeria* 9°29N 12°3E **139** D8
Numata *Japan* 36°45N 139°4E **113** F9
Numaykoos Lake ○
Canada 57°52N 95°58W **163** B9

Numazu *Japan* 35°7N 138°51E **113** G9
Numbulwar *Australia* 14°15S 135°45E **150** A2
Numfoor *Indonesia* 1°0S 134°50E **119** E8
Numurkah *Australia* 36°5S 145°26E **153** D6
Nunaksaluk I. *Canada* 55°49N 60°20W **165** A7
Nunap Isua *Greenland* 59°48N 43°55W **57** D6
Nunavik *Greenland* 71°50N 54°25W **57** C5
Nunavut □ *Canada* 66°0N 85°0W **161** D15
Nunda *U.S.A.* 42°35N 77°56W **174** D7
Nuneaton *U.K.* 52°32N 1°27W **67** E6
Nungarin *Australia* 31°12S 118°6E **149** F2
Nungo *Mozam.* 13°23S 37°43E **143** E4
Nungwe *Tanzania* 2°48S 32°2E **142** C3
Nunivak I. *U.S.A.* 60°10N 166°30W **166** C6
Nunkun *India* 33°57N 76°2E **125** C7
Núoro *Italy* 40°20N 9°20E **94** B2
Nuozhadu Dam *China* 22°39N 100°25E **116** F3
Nûr *Iran* 36°33N 52°1E **129** B7
Nura → *Kazakhstan* 51°45N 69°22E **108** D8
Nūrābād *Hormozgān,*
Iran 27°47N 57°12E **129** E8
Nūrābād *Lorestān, Iran* 34°4N 47°58E **105** E12
Nurabad *Uzbekistan* 39°36N 66°17E **109** E7
Nure → *Italy* 45°3N 9°49E **92** C6
Nuremberg = Nürnberg
Germany 49°27N 11°3E **77** F7
Nuri *Mexico* 28°5N 109°22W **180** B3
Nuri *Sudan* 18°29N 31°58E **137** D3
Nuriootpa *Australia* 34°27S 139°0E **152** C3
Nuristan ◇ *Afghan.* 35°20N 71°0E **109** E8
Nurlat *Russia* 54°29N 50°45E **86** C10
Nurmes *Finland* 63°33N 29°10E **60** E23
Nürnberg *Germany* 49°27N 11°3E **77** F7
Nurpur *Pakistan* 31°53N 71°54E **124** D4
Nurra, La *Italy* 40°45N 8°15E **94** B1
Nurran, L. = Terewah, L.
Australia 29°52S 147°35E **151** D4
Nurrari Lakes *Australia* 29°1S 130°5E **149** E5
Nurri *Italy* 39°43N 9°14E **94** C2
Nürtingen *Germany* 48°37N 9°19E **77** G5
Nurzec → *Poland* 52°37N 22°25E **83** F9
Nus *Italy* 45°45N 7°28E **92** C4
Nusa Dua *Indonesia* 8°48S 115°14E **119** K18
Nusa Tenggara Barat □
Indonesia 8°50S 117°30E **118** F5
Nusa Tenggara Timur □
Indonesia 9°30S 122°0E **119** F6
Nusaybin *Turkey* 37°3N 41°10E **105** D9
Nuşeirat *Gaza Strip* 31°27N 34°24E **108** D3
Nushki *Pakistan* 29°35N 66°0E **124** E2
Nuuk *Greenland* 64°10N 51°35W **57** C5
Nuwara Eliya *Sri Lanka* 6°58N 80°48E **127** L5
Nuwaybʽ, W. an →
Si. Arabia 29°18N 34°57E **130** F3
Nuweiba' *Egypt* 28°58N 34°39E **130** F3
Nuwerus *S. Africa* 31°8S 18°24E **144** D2
Nuweveldberge
S. Africa 32°10S 21°45E **144** D3
Nuyts, Pt. *Australia* 35°4S 116°38E **149** G2
Nuyts Arch. *Australia* 32°35S 133°20E **151** E1
Nxai Pan △ *Botswana* 19°50S 24°46E **144** A3
Nxaunxau *Botswana* 18°57S 21°4E **144** A3
Nyaake *Liberia* 4°52N 7°37W **138** E3
Nyabing *Australia* 33°33S 118°9E **149** F2
Nyack *U.S.A.* 41°5N 73°55W **175** E11
Nyagan *Russia* 62°30N 65°38E **106** C7
Nyah West *Australia* 35°16S 143°21E **152** C5
Nyahanga *Tanzania* 2°20S 33°37E **142** C3
Nyahua *Tanzania* 5°25S 33°23E **142** D3
Nyahururu *Kenya* 0°2N 36°27E **142** B4
Nyainqêntanglha Shan
China 30°0N 90°0E **110** F7
Nyakanazi *Tanzania* 3°2S 31°10E **142** C3
Nyakrom *Ghana* 5°40N 0°50W **139** D4
Nyálâ *Sudan* 12°2N 24°58E **135** F10
Nyalam *China* 28°32N 86°4E **110** F6
Nyamandhlovu
Zimbabwe 19°55S 28°16E **143** F2
Nyambiti *Tanzania* 2°48S 33°27E **142** C3
Nyamira *Kenya* 0°36S 34°52E **142** C3
Nyamwaga *Tanzania* 1°27S 34°33E **142** C3
Nyandekwa *Tanzania* 3°57S 32°32E **142** C3
Nyandoma *Russia* 61°40N 40°12E **84** B11
Nyanga △ *Zimbabwe* 18°17S 32°46E **143** F3
Nyangana *Namibia* 18°0S 20°40E **144** A3
Nyanguge *Tanzania* 2°30S 33°12E **142** C3
Nyanji *Zambia* 14°25S 31°46E **143** E3
Nyankpala *Ghana* 9°21N 0°58W **139** D4
Nyanza *Rwanda* 2°20S 29°42E **142** C2
Nyanza □ *Kenya* 0°10S 34°15E **142** C3
Nyanza-Lac *Burundi* 4°21S 29°36E **142** C2
Nyasa, L. = Malawi, L.
Africa 12°0S 34°30E **143** E3
Nyasvizh *Belarus* 53°14N 26°38E **75** B14
Nyaungdon = Yandoon
Burma 17°0N 95°40E **123** L19
Nyazura *Zimbabwe* 18°40S 32°16E **143** F3
Nyazwidzi → *Zimbabwe* 20°0S 31°17E **143** G3
Nyborg *Denmark* 55°18N 10°47E **63** J4
Nybro *Sweden* 56°44N 15°55E **63** H9
Nyda *Russia* 66°40N 72°58E **106** C8
Nyeboe Land *Greenland* 82°0N 57°0W **57** A5
Nyeri *Kenya* 0°23S 36°56E **142** C4
Nyhammar *Sweden* 60°17N 14°58E **62** D8
Nyika △ *Malawi* 10°30S 33°53E **143** E3
Nyimba *Zambia* 14°33S 30°50E **143** E3
Nyinahin *Ghana* 6°43N 2°3W **138** D4
Nyingchi *China* 29°32N 94°25E **110** F7
Nyíregyháza *Hungary* 47°58N 21°47E **80** C6
Nyiru, Mt. *Kenya* 2°36N 36°50E **142** B4
Nykarleby = Uusikaarlepyy
Finland 63°32N 22°31E **60** E20
Nykøbing *Nordjylland,*
Denmark 56°48N 8°51E **63** H2
Nykøbing *Sjælland,*
Denmark 54°56N 11°52E **63** K5
Nykøbing *Sjælland,*
Denmark 55°55N 11°40E **63** J5
Nyköping *Sweden* 58°45N 17°1E **63** G7
Nykroppa *Sweden* 59°37N 14°18E **62** G8
Nykvarn *Sweden* 59°11N 17°25E **62** E11
Nyland *Sweden* 63°1N 17°45E **62** A11
Nylstroom = Modimolle
S. Africa 24°42S 28°22E **145** B4
Nymagee *Australia* 32°7S 146°20E **153** B7

Nymboida △ *Australia* 29°38S 152°26E **151** D5
Nymburk *Czech Rep.* 50°10N 15°1E **78** A8
Nynäshamn *Sweden* 58°54N 17°57E **63** F11
Nyngan *Australia* 31°30S 147°8E **153** A7
Nyoma Rap *India* 33°10N 78°40E **125** C8
Nyoman = Nemunas →
Lithuania 55°25N 21°10E **82** C8
Nyong → *Cameroon* 3°17N 9°54E **139** E6
Nyons *France* 44°22N 5°10E **73** D9
Nyou *Burkina Faso* 12°42N 2°1W **139** C4
Nýrsko *Czech Rep.* 49°18N 13°9E **78** B6
Nysa *Poland* 50°30N 17°22E **83** H4
Nysa → *Europe* 52°4N 14°46E **76** C10
Nysa Kłodzka → *Poland* 50°49N 17°40E **83** H4
Nysäter *Sweden* 59°17N 12°47E **62** E6
Nyssa *U.S.A.* 43°53N 117°0W **168** E5
Nystad = Uusikaupunki
Finland 60°47N 21°25E **84** B1
Nysted *Denmark* 54°40N 11°44E **63** K5
Nyunzu
Dem. Rep. of the Congo 5°57S 27°58E **142** D2
Nyurba *Russia* 63°17N 118°28E **107** C12
Nyzhankovychi *Ukraine* 49°40N 22°49E **83** J9
Nyzhnohirskyy *Ukraine* 45°27N 34°38E **85** K8
Nyzhny Vorota *Ukraine* 48°46N 23°5E **80** B8
Nzébéla *Guinea* 8°9N 9°7W **138** D3
Nzérékoré *Guinea* 7°49N 8°48W **138** D3
Nzeto *Angola* 7°10S 12°52E **140** F2
N'zi-Comoé □ *Ivory C.* 7°0N 4°30W **138** D4
Nzilo, Chutes de
Dem. Rep. of the Congo 10°18S 25°27E **143** E2
N'zo → *Ivory C.* 6°15N 7°3W **138** D3
N'zo → *Ivory C.* 6°15N 7°15W **138** D3
Nzubuka *Tanzania* 4°45S 32°50E **142** C3
Nzwani = Anjouan
Comoros Is. 12°15S 44°20E **141** a

O

O Barco *Spain* 42°23N 6°58W **88** C4
O Carballiño *Spain* 42°26N 8°5W **88** C2
O Castro de Ferreira
Spain 42°31N 7°37W **88** C3
O Convento *Spain* 42°28N 8°41W **88** C2
O Corgo *Spain* 42°56N 7°25W **88** C3
O Pedrouzo *Spain* 42°56N 8°20W **88** C2
O Pino = O Pedrouzo
Spain 42°56N 8°20W **88** C2
O Porriño *Spain* 42°10N 8°37W **88** C2
O Real *Spain* 43°20N 8°19W **88** B2
O Seixo *Spain* 41°59N 8°46W **88** D2
Ō-Shima *Hokkaidō,*
Japan 41°30N 139°22E **112** D9
Ō-Shima *Shizuoka,*
Japan 34°44N 139°24E **113** G9
Oa, Mull of *U.K.* 55°35N 6°20W **65** F2
Oacoma *U.S.A.* 43°48N 99°24W **172** D4
Oahe, L. *U.S.A.* 44°27N 100°24W **172** C3
Oahe Dam *U.S.A.* 44°27N 100°24W **172** C3
O'ahu *U.S.A.* 21°28N 157°58W **167** L8
Oak Harbor *U.S.A.* 48°18N 122°39W **170** B4
Oak Hill *Fla., U.S.A.* 28°52N 80°51W **179** G9
Oak Hill *W. Va., U.S.A.* 37°59N 81°9W **173** G6
Oak Island *U.S.A.* 33°55N 78°10W **177** E15
Oak Park *U.S.A.* 41°53N 87°47W **172** E2
Oak Ridge *U.S.A.* 36°1N 84°16W **177** C12
Oak View *U.S.A.* 34°24N 119°18W **171** L7
Oakan-Dake *Japan* 43°27N 144°10E **112** C12
Oakbank *Australia* 33°4S 140°33E **152** B4
Oakdale *Calif., U.S.A.* 37°46N 120°51W **170** H6
Oakdale *La., U.S.A.* 30°49N 92°40W **176** F8
Oakes *U.S.A.* 46°8N 98°6W **172** B4
Oakesdale *U.S.A.* 47°8N 117°15W **168** C5
Oakey *Australia* 27°25S 151°43E **151** D5
Oakfield *Ga., U.S.A.* 31°47N 83°58W **178** D6
Oakfield *N.Y., U.S.A.* 43°4N 78°16W **174** C6
Oakham *U.K.* 52°40N 0°43W **67** E7
Oakhurst *U.S.A.* 37°19N 119°40W **170** H7
Oakland *Calif., U.S.A.* 37°48N 122°18W **170** H4
Oakland Park *U.S.A.* 26°10N 80°7W **179** H9
Oaklands *Australia* 35°34S 146°10E **153** C7
Oakley *Idaho, U.S.A.* 42°15N 113°53W **168** E7
Oakley *Kans., U.S.A.* 39°8N 100°51W **172** F3
Oakover → *Australia* 21°0S 120°40E **148** C3
Oakridge *U.S.A.* 43°45N 122°28W **168** E2
Oaks, The *Australia* 34°3S 150°34E **153** C9
Oakville *Canada* 43°27N 79°41W **174** C5
Oakville *U.S.A.* 46°51N 123°14W **170** D3
Oamaru *N.Z.* 45°5S 170°59E **155** F3
Oancea *Romania* 45°21N 27°42E **81** C12
Oasis *Calif., U.S.A.* 37°29N 117°55W **170** H9
Oasis *Calif., U.S.A.* 33°28N 116°6W **171** M10
Oates Land *Antarctica* 69°0S 160°0E **5** C11
Oatman *U.S.A.* 35°1N 114°19W **171** K12
Oaxaca *Mexico* 17°3N 96°43W **181** D5
Oaxaca □ *Mexico* 17°0N 96°30W **181** D5
Ob → *Russia* 66°45N 69°30E **106** C7
Oba *Canada* 49°4N 84°7W **164** C3
Obala *Cameroon* 4°9N 11°32E **139** E7
Obama *Japan* 35°30N 135°45E **113** G7
Oban *Nigeria* 5°17N 8°33E **139** D6
Oban *N.Z.* 46°54S 168°8E **155** G2
Oban *U.K.* 56°25N 5°29W **65** E3
Obbia = Hobyo *Somalia* 5°30N 48°30E **132** F4
Oberá *Argentina* 27°21S 55°2W **191** B4
Oberammergau *Germany* 47°36N 11°4E **77** H7
Oberasbach *Germany* 49°25N 10°57E **77** F6
Oberbayern □ *Germany* 48°5N 11°50E **77** G7
Oberdrauburg *Austria* 46°45N 12°59E **78** E5
Obere Donau △ *Germany* 48°5N 9°0E **77** G5
Oberer Bayerischer Wald △
Germany 49°15N 12°40E **77** F8
Oberfranken □ *Germany* 50°10N 11°20E **77** E7
Oberhausen *Germany* 51°28N 6°51E **76** D2
Oberkirch *Germany* 48°31N 8°4E **77** G4
Oberlausitz *Germany* 51°16N 14°18E **76** D10
Oberlin *Kans., U.S.A.* 39°49N 100°32W **172** F3
Oberlin *Ohio, U.S.A.* 41°18N 82°13W **174** E2
Obernai *France* 48°28N 7°30E **71** D14
Oberndorf *Germany* 48°17N 8°34E **77** G4
Oberon *Australia* 33°45S 149°52E **153** B8
Oberösterreich □ *Austria* 48°10N 14°0E **78** C7
Oberpfalz □ *Germany* 49°30N 12°10E **77** F8
Oberpfälzer Wald △
Germany 49°30N 12°25E **77** F8

Oberpfälzer Wald △
Germany 49°30N 12°20E **77** F8
Oberstdorf *Germany* 47°24N 10°15E **77** H6
Obertyn *Ukraine* 48°42N 25°10E **81** B10
Oberursel *Germany* 50°11N 8°35E **77** E4
Oberwart *Austria* 47°17N 16°12E **78** D9
Obi, Kepulauan
Indonesia 1°23S 127°45E **119** E7
Obiaruku *Nigeria* 5°51N 6°9E **139** D6
Óbidos *Brazil* 1°50S 55°30W **187** D7
Óbidos *Portugal* 39°19N 9°10W **89** F1
Obihiro *Japan* 42°56N 143°12E **112** C11
Obilatu *Indonesia* 1°25S 127°20E **119** E7
Obilnoye *Russia* 47°32N 44°30E **87** G7
Obing *Germany* 48°0N 12°24E **77** G8
Objat *France* 45°16N 1°24E **72** C5
Obluchye *Russia* 49°1N 131°4E **107** E14
Obninsk *Russia* 55°8N 36°37E **84** E9
Obo *C.A.R.* 5°20N 26°32E **142** A2
Obodivka *Ukraine* 48°24N 29°15E **81** B14
Oborniki *Poland* 52°39N 16°50E **83** F3
Oborniki Śląskie *Poland* 51°17N 16°53E **83** G3
Oboyan *Russia* 51°15N 36°21E **85** G9
Obozerskaya = Obozerskiy
Russia 63°34N 40°21E **106** C5
Obozerskiy *Russia* 63°34N 40°21E **106** C5
Obrenovac *Serbia* 44°40N 20°11E **96** B4
O'Brien *U.S.A.* 31°58N 82°57W **178** E7
Obrovac *Croatia* 44°11N 15°41E **93** D12
Obruk *Turkey* 38°7N 33°12E **104** C5
Obrzycko *Poland* 52°42N 16°32E **83** F3
Observatory Inlet
Canada 55°10N 129°54W **162** B3
Obshchi Syrt *Russia* 52°0N 53°0E **58** E16
Obskaya Guba *Russia* 69°0N 73°0E **106** C8
Obuasi *Ghana* 6°17N 1°40W **139** D4
Obubra *Nigeria* 6°8N 8°20E **139** D6
Obudu *Nigeria* 6°38N 9°5E **139** D6
Obwalden □ *Switz.* 46°55N 8°15E **77** J4
Obzor *Bulgaria* 42°50N 27°52E **97** D11
Ocala *U.S.A.* 29°11N 82°8W **179** F7
Ocampo *Chihuahua,*
Mexico 28°11N 108°23W **180** B3
Ocampo *Tamaulipas,*
Mexico 22°50N 99°20W **181** C5
Ocaña *Spain* 39°55N 3°30W **89** F7
Occidental, Cordillera
Colombia 5°0N 76°0W **186** C3
Occidental, Cordillera
Peru 14°0S 74°0W **188** C3
Occidental, Grand Erg
Algeria 30°20N 1°0E **136** B4
Ocean City *Md., U.S.A.* 38°20N 75°5W **173** F16
Ocean City *N.J.,*
U.S.A. 39°17N 74°35W **173** F16
Ocean City *Wash.,*
U.S.A. 47°4N 124°10W **170** C2
Ocean Falls *Canada* 52°18N 127°48W **162** C3
Ocean I. = Banaba
Kiribati 0°45S 169°50E **156** H8
Ocean Park *U.S.A.* 46°30N 124°3W **170** D2
Oceano *U.S.A.* 35°6N 120°37W **171** K6
Oceanport *U.S.A.* 40°19N 74°3W **175** F10
Oceanside *U.S.A.* 33°12N 117°23W **171** M9
Ochagavía *Spain* 42°55N 1°5W **89** G3
Ochakiv *Ukraine* 46°37N 31°33E **85** J6
Ochamchire *Georgia* 42°46N 41°32E **87** J5
Ochi, Oros *Greece* 38°5N 24°25E **98** C6
Ochil Hills *U.K.* 56°14N 3°40W **65** E5
Ochlockonee →
U.S.A. 29°59N 84°26W **178** F5
Ocho Rios *Jamaica* 18°24N 77°6W **182** a
Ochopee *U.S.A.* 25°54N 81°19W **179** H7
Ochsenfurt *Germany* 49°40N 10°4E **77** F6
Ochsenhausen *Germany* 48°4N 9°57E **77** G5
Ocilla *U.S.A.* 31°36N 83°15W **178** E6
Ockelbo *Sweden* 60°54N 16°45E **62** D10
Ocmulgee → *U.S.A.* 31°58N 82°33W **178** D7
Ocmulgee ○ *U.S.A.* 32°49N 83°37W **178** C6
Ocna Mureş *Romania* 46°23N 23°55E **81** C8
Ocna Sibiului *Romania* 45°52N 24°2E **81** E9
Ocnele Mari *Romania* 45°8N 24°18E **81** D9
Ocnița *Moldova* 48°25N 27°30E **81** B15
Ocoee *U.S.A.* 28°34N 81°32W **179** G7
Ocoña *Peru* 16°26S 73°8W **188** D3
Ocoña → *Peru* 16°28S 73°8W **188** D3
Oconee → *U.S.A.* 31°58N 82°33W **178** D7
Oconomowoc *U.S.A.* 43°7N 88°30W **172** D9
Oconto *U.S.A.* 44°53N 87°52W **172** C9
Oconto Falls *U.S.A.* 44°52N 88°9W **172** C9
Ocosingo *Mexico* 16°53N 92°6W **181** D6
Ocotal *Nic.* 13°41N 86°31W **182** D2
Ocotlán *Jalisco,*
Mexico 20°21N 102°46W **180** C4
Ocotlán *Oaxaca, Mexico* 16°48N 96°40W **181** D5
Ocreza → *Portugal* 39°32N 7°50W **89** F3
Ócsa *Hungary* 47°17N 19°15E **80** E5
Oda *Ghana* 5°50N 0°51W **139** D4
Ōda *Japan* 35°11N 132°30E **113** G6
Oda, J. *Sudan* 20°21N 36°39E **137** C4
Ódáðahraun *Iceland* 65°5N 17°0W **60** D5
Ödaejin *N. Korea* 41°34N 129°40E **112** D4
Odawara *Japan* 35°20N 139°6E **113** G9
Odda *Norway* 60°3N 6°35E **63** E11
Odder *Denmark* 55°58N 10°10E **63** J4
Odei → *Canada* 56°6N 96°54W **163** B9
Odemira *Portugal* 37°35N 8°40W **89** H2
Ödemiş *Turkey* 38°15N 28°0E **99** C9
Odendaalsrus *S. Africa* 27°48S 26°45E **144** C4
Odense *Denmark* 55°22N 10°23E **63** J4
Odenwald *Germany* 49°30N 9°0E **77** F5
Oder → *Europe* 53°33N 14°38E **76** B10
Oder-Havel Kanal
Germany 52°52N 14°2E **76** C10
Oderzo *Italy* 45°47N 12°29E **93** C9
Odesa *Ukraine* 46°30N 30°45E **85** J6
Ódeshög *Sweden* 58°14N 14°39E **63** F8
Odessa = Odesa *Ukraine* 46°30N 30°45E **85** J6
Odessa *Tex., U.S.A.* 31°52N 102°23W **176** F3
Odessa *Wash., U.S.A.* 47°20N 118°41W **168** C4
Odiakwe *Botswana* 20°12S 25°17E **144** B4
Odiel → *Spain* 37°10N 6°55W **89** H4

Odienné *Ivory C.* 9°30N 7°34W **138** D3
Odintsovo *Russia* 55°40N 37°16E **84** E9
Odisha □ *India* 20°0N 84°0E **126** E7
Odobeşti *Romania* 45°43N 27°4E **81** E12
Odolanów *Poland* 51°34N 17°40E **83** G4
O'Donnell *U.S.A.* 32°58N 101°50W **176** E4
O'Donnell Pt. *Canada* 45°5N 80°5W **174** A4
Odoyevo *Russia* 53°56N 36°42E **84** F9
Odra = Oder → *Europe* 53°33N 14°38E **76** B10
Odra → *Spain* 42°14N 4°17W **88** C6
Odum *U.S.A.* 31°40N 82°2W **178** D7
Odžaci *Serbia* 45°30N 19°17E **80** E4
Odžak *Bos.-H.* 45°3N 18°18E **80** E3
Odzi *Zimbabwe* 19°0S 32°20E **145** A5
Odzi → *Zimbabwe* 19°45S 32°23E **145** A5
Oecusse = Pante Macassar
E. Timor 9°30S 123°58E **119** F7
Oeiras *Brazil* 7°0S 42°8W **189** D7
Oeiras *Portugal* 38°41N 9°18W **89** G1
Oelrichs *U.S.A.* 43°11N 103°14W **172** D2
Oelwein *U.S.A.* 42°41N 91°55W **172** D8
Oeno I. *Pac. Oc.* 24°0S 131°0W **157** K14
Oenpelli = Gunbalanya
Australia 12°20S 133°4E **148** B5
Oetz *Austria* 47°13N 10°53E **78** D3
Of *Turkey* 40°59N 40°23E **105** B9
Ofanto → *Italy* 41°22N 16°13E **95** A9
Offa *Nigeria* 8°13N 4°42E **139** D5
Offaly □ *Ireland* 53°15N 7°30W **64** C4
Offenbach *Germany* 50°6N 8°44E **77** E4
Offenburg *Germany* 48°28N 7°56E **77** G3
Officer Cr. → *Australia* 27°46S 132°30E **149** E5
Offida *Italy* 42°56N 13°41E **93** F10
Ofidousa *Greece* 36°33N 26°8E **99** E8
Ofotfjorden *Norway* 68°27N 17°0E **60** B17
Ōfunato *Japan* 39°4N 141°43E **112** E10
Oga *Japan* 39°55N 139°50E **112** E9
Oga-Hantō *Japan* 39°58N 139°47E **112** E9
Ōgaki *Japan* 35°21N 136°37E **113** G8
Ogallala *U.S.A.* 41°8N 101°43W **172** E3
Ogasawara Gunto
Pac. Oc. 27°0N 142°0E **156** E6
Ogbomosho *Nigeria* 8°1N 4°11E **139** D5
Ogden *U.S.A.* 41°13N 111°58W **168** F8
Ogdensburg *U.S.A.* 44°42N 75°30W **175** B9
Ogea Driki *Fiji* 19°12S 178°27W **154** a
Ogea Levu *Fiji* 19°8S 178°24W **154** a
Ogeechee → *U.S.A.* 31°50N 81°3W **178** D8
Ogilby *U.S.A.* 32°49N 114°50W **171** N12
Oglat Beraber *Algeria* 30°15N 3°34W **136** B4
Oglethorpe *U.S.A.* 32°18N 84°4W **178** D5
Ogliastra □ *Italy* 39°50N 9°35E **94** C2
Óglio → *Italy* 45°2N 10°39E **92** C7
Óglio Sud □ *Italy* 45°7N 10°24E **92** C7
Ogmore *Australia* 22°37S 149°35E **150** C4
Ognon → *France* 47°20N 5°29E **71** E12
Ogoja *Nigeria* 6°38N 8°39E **139** D6
Ogoki → *Canada* 51°38N 85°58W **164** B2
Ogoki L. *Canada* 50°50N 87°10W **164** B2
Ogoki Res. *Canada* 50°45N 88°15W **164** B2
Ogooué → *Gabon* 1°0S 9°0E **140** E1
Ogosta → *Bulgaria* 43°48N 23°55E **96** C7
Ogou → *Togo* 7°50N 1°19E **139** D5
Ogražden *Macedonia* 41°30N 22°50E **96** E6
Ogre *Latvia* 56°49N 24°36E **84** D3
Ogulin *Croatia* 45°16N 15°16E **93** C12
Ogun □ *Nigeria* 7°0N 3°0E **139** D5
Ogurja Ada
Turkmenistan 38°55N 53°2E **129** B7
Oguta *Nigeria* 5°44N 6°44E **139** D6
Ogwashi-Uku *Nigeria* 6°15N 6°30E **139** D6
Ogwe *Nigeria* 5°0N 7°14E **139** E6
Ohai *N.Z.* 45°55S 168°0E **155** F1
Ohakune *N.Z.* 39°24S 175°24E **154** F4
Ohanet *Algeria* 28°44N 8°46E **136** C6
Ohangwena □ *Namibia* 17°30S 17°0E **144** A2
Ohata *Japan* 41°24N 141°10E **112** D10
Ohatchee *U.S.A.* 33°47N 86°0W **178** D4
Ohau, L. *N.Z.* 44°15S 169°53E **155** F2
Ohaupo *N.Z.* 37°56S 175°19E **154** C5
Ohio □ *U.S.A.* 40°15N 82°45W **174** F2
Ohio → *U.S.A.* 36°59N 89°8W **173** G3
Ohiwa Harbour *N.Z.* 37°59S 177°10E **154** C6
Ohře → *Czech Rep.* 50°30N 14°10E **78** A7
Ohrid *Macedonia* 41°8N 20°52E **96** E4
Ohridsko Jezero
Macedonia 41°8N 20°52E **96** E4
Ohrigstad *S. Africa* 24°39S 30°36E **145** B5
Öhringen *Germany* 49°12N 9°31E **77** F5
Oi Qu → *China* 28°37N 98°16E **116** C2
Oiapoque *Brazil* 3°50N 51°50W **187** C8
Oikou *China* 38°35N 117°42E **114** E9
Oil City *U.S.A.* 41°26N 79°42W **174** E5
Oil Springs *Canada* 42°47N 82°7W **174** D2
Oildale *U.S.A.* 35°25N 119°1W **171** K7
Oinousa = Inousses
Greece 38°33N 26°14E **99** C8
Oise □ *France* 49°28N 2°30E **71** C9
Oise → *France* 49°0N 2°4E **71** C9
Öita *Japan* 33°14N 131°36E **113** H5
Öita □ *Japan* 33°15N 131°30E **113** H5
Oiticica *Brazil* 5°3S 41°5W **189** D7
Ojacastro *Spain* 42°20N 2°54W **89** F7
Ojai *U.S.A.* 34°27N 119°15W **171** L7
Ojinaga *Mexico* 29°34N 104°25W **180** B4
Ojiya *Japan* 37°18N 138°48E **113** F9
Ojo Caliente *Mexico* 21°51N 102°37W **180** C4
Ojo de Liebre, L.
Mexico 27°45N 114°15W **180** B2
Ojos del Salado, Cerro
Argentina 27°0S 68°40W **190** B3
Oka → *Russia* 56°20N 43°59E **86** C7
Okaba *Indonesia* 8°6S 139°42E **119** F10
Okahandja *Namibia* 22°0S 16°59E **144** B2
Okahukura *N.Z.* 38°48S 175°14E **154** C5
Okanagan L. *Canada* 50°0N 119°30W **162** D5

Okakarara *Namibia* 20°35S 17°27E **144**
Okanagan L. *Canada* 50°0N 119°30W **162**
Okandja *Gabon* 0°35S 13°45E **140**
Okanogan *U.S.A.* 48°22N 119°35W **168**
Okanogan → *U.S.A.* 48°6N 119°44W **168**
Okanogan Range
N. Amer. 49°0N 120°0W **162**
Okány *Hungary* 46°52N 21°21E **80**
Okapi ○
Dem. Rep. of the Congo 2°30N 27°20E **142**
Okaputa *Namibia* 20°5S 17°0E **144**
Okara *Pakistan* 30°50N 73°31E **124**
Okarito *N.Z.* 43°15S 170°9E **155**
Okato *N.Z.* 39°12S 173°53E **154**
Okaukuejo *Namibia* 19°10S 16°0E **144**
Okavango □ *Namibia* 18°45S 22°45E **144**
Okavango Delta
Botswana 18°45S 22°45E **144**
Okavango Swamp = Okavango
Delta Botswana 18°45S 22°45E **144**
Okaya *Japan* 36°5S 138°10E **113**
Okayama *Japan* 34°40N 133°54E **113**
Okayama □ *Japan* 35°0N 133°50E **113**
Okazaki *Japan* 34°57N 137°10E **113**
Okęcie, Warszawa ✈ (WAW)
Poland 52°9N 20°59E **8**
Okeechobee *U.S.A.* 27°15N 80°50W **179**
Okeechobee, L. *U.S.A.* 27°0N 80°50W **179**
Okefenokee △ *U.S.A.* 30°40N 82°20W **179**
Okefenokee Swamp
U.S.A. 30°40N 82°20W **179**
Okehampton *U.K.* 50°44N 4°0W **67**
Okene *Nigeria* 7°32N 6°11E **139**
Oker → *Germany* 52°32N 10°22E **77**
Okha *India* 22°27N 69°4E **124**
Okha *Russia* 53°40N 143°0E **107**
Okhotsk *Russia* 59°20N 143°10E **107**
Okhotsk, Sea of *Asia* 55°0N 145°0E **107**
Okhotskiy Perevoz
Russia 61°52N 135°35E **107**
Okhtyrka *Ukraine* 50°25N 35°0E **85**
Oki-Shotō *Japan* 36°5N 133°15E **113**
Okiep *S. Africa* 29°39S 17°53E **144**
Okigwi *Nigeria* 5°52N 7°20E **139**
Okija *Nigeria* 5°54N 6°55E **139**
Okinawa *Japan* 26°19N 127°46E **113**
Okinawa □ *Japan* 26°40N 128°0E **113**
Okinawa-Guntō *Japan* 26°40N 128°0E **113**
Okinawa-Jima *Japan* 26°32N 128°0E **113**
Okino-erabu-Shima
Japan 27°21N 128°33E **113**
Okitipupa *Nigeria* 6°31N 4°50E **139**
Oklahoma □ *U.S.A.* 35°20N 97°30W **176**
Oklahoma City *U.S.A.* 35°30N 97°30W **176**
Oklawaha → *U.S.A.* 29°26N 81°41W **179**
Okmulgee *U.S.A.* 35°37N 95°58W **176**
Oknitsa = Ocnița
Moldova 48°25N 27°30E **81**
Oko, W. → *Sudan* 21°15N 35°56E **137**
Okolo *Uganda* 2°37N 31°8E **142**
Okolona *U.S.A.* 34°0N 88°45W **177**
Okombahe *Namibia* 21°23S 15°22E **144**
Okonek *Poland* 53°32N 16°51E **83**
Okotoks *Canada* 50°43N 113°58W **162**
Okrika *Nigeria* 4°40N 7°10E **139**
Oktyabrsk = Qandyaghash
Kazakhstan 49°28N 57°25E **108**
Oktyabrsk *Russia* 53°11N 48°40E **86**
Oktyabrskiy = Aktsyabrski
Belarus 52°38N 28°53E **75**
Oktyabrskiy *Bashkortostan,*
Russia 54°28N 53°28E **86**
Oktyabrskiy *Kamchatka,*
Russia 52°39N 156°14E **107**
Oktyabrskiy *Rostov.,*
Russia 47°56N 40°32E **87**
Oktyabrskoy Revolyutsii, Ostrov
Russia 79°30N 97°0E **107**
Oktyabrskoye = Zhovtneve
Ukraine 46°54N 32°3E **85**
Okulovka *Russia* 58°25N 33°19E **84**
Okuru *N.Z.* 43°55S 168°55E **155**
Okushiri-Tō *Japan* 42°15N 139°30E **112**
Okuta *Nigeria* 9°14N 3°12E **139**
Okwa → *Botswana* 22°30S 23°0E **144**
Ola *Russia* 59°35N 151°17E **107**
Ólafsfjörður *Iceland* 66°4N 18°39W **60**
Ólafsvík *Iceland* 64°53N 23°43W **60**
Olaine *Latvia* 56°47N 23°59E **84**
Olancha *U.S.A.* 36°17N 118°1W **171**
Olancha Pk. *U.S.A.* 36°16N 118°7W **171**
Olanchito *Honduras* 15°30N 86°30W **182**
Öland *Sweden* 56°45N 16°38E **63**
Ölands norra udde
Sweden 57°22N 17°5E **63**
Ölands södra udde
Sweden 56°12N 16°23E **63**
Olanta *U.S.A.* 33°56N 79°56W **178**
Olar *U.S.A.* 33°11N 81°11W **178**
Olargues *France* 43°34N 2°53E **72**
Olary *Australia* 32°18S 140°19E **152**
Olascoaga *Argentina* 35°15S 60°39W **190**
Olathe *U.S.A.* 38°53N 94°49W **172**
Olavarría *Argentina* 36°55S 60°20W **190**
Oława *Poland* 50°57N 17°20E **83**
Olbernhau *Germany* 50°40N 13°19E **76**
Ólbia *Italy* 40°55N 9°31E **94**
Ólbia, G. di *Italy* 40°55N 9°35E **94**
Olching *Germany* 48°12N 11°21E **77**
Olcott *U.S.A.* 43°20N 78°42W **174**
Old Bahama Chan. = Bahama,
Canal Viejo de
W. Indies 22°10N 77°30W **182**
Old Baldy Pk. = San Antonio, Mt.
U.S.A. 34°17N 117°38W **171**
Old Bar *Australia* 31°58S 152°38E **153**
Old Bridge *U.S.A.* 40°25N 74°22W **175**
Old Castile = Castilla y Leon □
Spain 42°0N 5°0W **89**
Old Crow *Canada* 67°30N 139°55W **166**
Old Dale *U.S.A.* 34°8N 115°47W **171**
Old Forge *N.Y., U.S.A.* 43°43N 74°58W **175**
Old Forge *Pa., U.S.A.* 41°22N 75°45W **175**
Old Mapoon ○
Australia 11°5S 142°22E **150**
Old Perlican *Canada* 48°5N 53°1W **165**
Old Shinyanga *Tanzania* 3°33S 33°27E **142**
Old Speck Mt. *U.S.A.* 44°34N 70°57W **175**
Old Town *U.S.A.* 44°56N 68°39W **175**

Town Maine, S.A. 44°56N 68°39W 173 C19
Washington U.S.A. 40°2N 81°27W 174 F3
Wives L. Canada 50°5N 106°0W 163 C17
bury U.K. 51°38N 2°33W 67 F5
astle Ireland 53°46N 7°10W 64 C4
ani Tanzania 3°22S 35°35E 142 C4
nburg Niedersachsen, rmany 53°9N 8°13E 76 B4
rmany Schleswig-Holstein, rmany 54°17N 10°52E 76 A6
nzaal Neths. 52°19N 6°53E 69 B6
am U.K. 53°33N 2°7W 66 D5
an → Canada 49°57N 111°42W 174 F3
meldrum U.K. 57°20N 2°19W 65 D6
Canada 51°50N 114°10W 162 C6
mar U.S.A. 28°2N 82°39W 179 G7
avai Gorge Tanzania 2°57S 35°23E 142 C4
Tanzania 44°40N 109°1E 114 B5
Romer Land reenland 74°10N 24°30W 57 C8
n U.S.A. 42°5N 78°26W 174 D6
y Sweden 60°8N 13°2E 62 D7
ko Poland 54°2N 22°31E 82 D9
talo Italy 38°9N 13°8E 92 C5
ros = O Real Spain 43°20N 8°19W 88 B2
ros Portugal 39°56N 7°56W 88 F3
ma → Russia 60°22N 120°42E 107 C13
minsk Russia 60°25N 120°30E 107 C13
sandriya Ukraine 48°55N 32°20E 85 H7
sandriya Kirovohrad, raine 48°42N 33°3E 85 H7
raine 50°37N 26°19E 75 C14
na U.S.A. 38°3N 122°47W 170 G4
egorsk Russia 68°9N 33°18E 60 B25
ek Russia 68°28N 112°18E 107 C12
ek → Russia 73°0N 120°10E 107 B13
ino Russia 56°15N 33°30E 84 D7
on, Î. d' France 45°55N 1°15W 72 C2
k Ukraine 51°6N 24°11E 83 G11
n Poland 50°51N 18°26E 83 H5
sk Ukraine 51°12N 27°39E 75 C14
, L. Canada 49°47N 77°15W 164 C4
stralia 25°20S 130°50E 149 E5
Mongolia 48°56N 89°57E 109 C11
d Denmark 55°49N 8°36E 63 J2
o Portugal 37°3N 7°48W 89 H3
pil Ukraine 48°12N 29°30E 81 D4
vatka Russia 54°30N 22°18E 82 D9
Croatia 44°23N 14°44E 93 D11
a Italy 40°16N 9°24E 94 B2
e Spain 41°1N 0°41W 90 D4
nts = Elefantes →
rica 24°10S 32°40E 145 B5
rica → Namibia 25°30S 19°30E 144 B2
ntshoek S. Africa 27°57S 22°42E 144 C3
bos Greece 35°44N 27°11E 99 E9
The = Kata Tjuta

Olvega Spain 41°47N 2°0W 90 D2
Olvera Spain 36°55N 5°18W 89 J5
Olymbos Cyprus 35°21N 33°45E 101 D12
Olymbos Oros Greece 40°6N 22°23E 96 F6
Olympia Greece 37°39N 21°39E 98 D3
Olympia U.S.A. 47°3N 122°53W 170 D4
Olympic △ U.S.A. 47°45N 123°43W 170 C3
Olympic Dam Australia 30°30S 136°55E 152 A2
Olympic Mts. U.S.A. 47°55N 123°45W 170 C3
Olympus Cyprus 34°56N 32°52E 101 E11
Olympus, Mt. = Olymbos Oros Greece 40°6N 22°23E 96 F6
Olympus, Mt. = Uludağ Turkey 40°4N 29°13E 97 F13
Olympus, Mt. U.S.A. 47°48N 123°43W 170 C3
Olyphant U.S.A. 41°27N 75°36W 175 E9
Olyutorskiy, Mys Russia 59°55N 170°27E 107 D18
Om → Russia 54°59N 73°22E 109 B8
Om Koi Thailand 17°48N 98°22E 120 D2
Ōma Japan 41°45N 141°5E 112 D10
Ōmachi Japan 36°30N 137°50E 113 F8
Omae-Zaki Japan 34°36N 138°14E 113 G9
Ōmagari = Daisen Japan 39°27N 140°29E 112 E10
Omagh U.K. 54°36N 7°19W 64 B4
Omagh □ U.K. 54°35N 7°15W 64 B4
Omaha U.S.A. 41°17N 95°58W 172 E6
Omaheke □ Namibia 21°30S 19°0E 144 B2
Omak U.S.A. 48°25N 119°31W 168 B4
Omalos Greece 35°19N 23°55E 101 D5
Omalur India 11°44N 78°4E 127 J4
Oman ■ Asia 23°0N 58°0E 131 C6
Oman, G. of Asia 24°30N 58°30E 129 E8
Omapere N.Z. 35°37S 173°25E 154 B2
Omaruru Namibia 21°26S 16°0E 144 B2
Omaruru → Namibia 22°7S 14°15E 144 B1
Omate Peru 16°45S 71°0W 188 D3
Ombai, Selat Indonesia 8°30S 124°50E 119 F6
Omboué Gabon 1°35S 9°15E 140 E1
Ombrone → Italy 42°42N 11°5E 92 F8
Omdurmân Sudan 15°40N 32°28E 135 E12
Omega U.S.A. 31°21N 83°36W 179 D6
Omegna Italy 45°53N 8°24E 92 C5
Omemee Canada 44°18N 78°33W 174 B6
Omeo Australia 37°6S 147°36E 153 D7
Omeonga Dem. Rep. of the Congo 3°40S 24°22E 142 C1
Ometepe, I. de Nic. 11°32N 85°35W 182 D2
Ometepec Mexico 16°41N 98°25W 181 D5
Ominato Japan 41°17N 141°10E 112 D10
Omineca → Canada 56°3N 124°16W 162 B4
Omineca Mts. Canada 56°30N 125°30W 162 B3
Omiš Croatia 43°28N 16°40E 93 E13
Omišalj Croatia 45°13N 14°32E 93 C11
Omitara Namibia 22°16S 18°2E 144 B2
Ōmiya = Saitama Japan 35°54N 139°38E 113 G9
Omme Å → Denmark 55°56N 8°32E 63 J2
Ommen Neths. 52°31N 6°26E 69 B6
Omnögovï □ Mongolia 43°15N 104°0E 114 C3
Omo → Ethiopia 6°25N 36°10E 131 F2
Omodeo, L. Italy 40°8N 8°56E 94 B1
Omodhos Cyprus 34°51N 32°48E 101 E11
Omoko Nigeria 5°19N 6°40E 139 D6
Omolon → Russia 68°42N 158°36E 107 C16
Omono-Gawa → Japan 39°46N 140°3E 112 E10
Ompha Canada 45°0N 76°50W 175 B8
Omsk Russia 55°0N 73°12E 109 B8
Omsukchan Russia 62°32N 155°48E 107 C16
Ōmu Japan 44°34N 142°58E 112 B11
Omul, Vf. Romania 45°27N 25°29E 81 E10
Omulew → Poland 53°5N 21°33E 83 E8
Ōmura Japan 32°56N 129°57E 113 H4
Omuramba Omatako → Namibia 17°45S 20°25E 144 A2
Omuramba Ovambo → Namibia 18°45S 16°59E 144 A2
Omurtag Bulgaria 43°8N 26°26E 97 C10
Omusati □ Namibia 18°30S 15°0E 144 A1
Ōmuta Japan 33°5N 130°26E 113 H5
Omuthiya Namibia 17°43S 16°13E 144 A2
Oña Spain 42°43N 3°25W 88 C7
Ona U.S.A. 27°29N 81°55W 179 H8
Onaga U.S.A. 39°29N 96°10W 172 F5
Onalaska U.S.A. 43°53N 91°14W 172 D8
Onancock U.S.A. 37°43N 75°45W 173 G16
Onangue, L. Gabon 0°57S 10°4E 140 E2
Onaping L. Canada 47°3N 81°30W 164 C3
Oñati Spain 43°3N 2°25W 90 B2
Onavas Mexico 28°31N 109°35W 180 B3
Onawa U.S.A. 42°2N 96°6W 172 D5
Oncócua Angola 16°30S 13°25E 144 A1
Onda Spain 39°55N 0°17W 90 F4
Ondangwa Namibia 17°57S 16°4E 144 A2
Ondarroa Spain 43°19N 2°25W 90 B2
Ondas → Brazil 12°8S 44°55W 189 F9
Ondava → Slovak Rep. 48°27N 21°48E 79 C14
Ondjiva Angola 16°48S 15°50E 144 A2
Ondo Nigeria 7°4N 4°47E 139 D5
Ondo □ Nigeria 6°45N 5°0E 139 D6
Öndörhaan Mongolia 47°19N 110°39E 111 B11
Öndverðarnes Iceland 64°52N 24°0W 60 D2
One Arm Point Australia 16°26S 123°3E 148 C3
One Arm Point ○ Australia 16°31S 122°53E 148 C3
One Tree Australia 34°11S 144°43E 151 E3
Oneata Fiji 18°26S 178°25W 154 a
Oneco U.S.A. 27°25N 82°31W 179 H7
Onega Russia 63°58N 38°2E 58 C13
Onega → Russia 63°58N 38°0E 58 C13
Onega, L. = Onezhskoye Ozero Russia 61°44N 35°22E 84 B8
Onehunga N.Z. 36°55S 174°48E 154 C3
Oneida U.S.A. 43°6N 75°39W 175 C9
Oneida L. U.S.A. 43°12N 75°54W 175 C9
O'Neill U.S.A. 42°27N 98°39W 172 D4
Onekotan, Ostrov Russia 49°25N 154°45E 107 E16
Onema Dem. Rep. of the Congo 4°35S 24°30E 142 C1
Oneonta U.S.A. 42°27N 75°4W 175 D9
Onerahi N.Z. 35°45S 174°22E 154 B3
Oneşti Romania 46°17N 26°47E 81 D11
Onezhskoye Ozero Russia 61°44N 35°22E 84 B8
Ongarue N.Z. 38°42S 175°19E 154 E4

Ongea Levu = Ogea Levu Fiji 19°8S 178°24W 154 a
Ongers → S. Africa 31°4S 23°13E 144 D3
Ongerup Australia 33°58S 118°28E 149 F2
Ongi Mongolia 45°27N 103°54E 114 B2
Ongjin N. Korea 37°56N 125°21E 115 F13
Ongkharak Thailand 14°8N 101°1E 120 E3
Ongniud Qi China 42°58N 118°38E 115 C12
Ongoka Dem. Rep. of the Congo 1°20S 26°0E 142 C2
Ongole India 15°33N 80°2E 127 G5
Ongon = Havirga Mongolia 45°41N 113°5E 114 B7
Ongtüstik Qazaqstan □ Kazakhstan 43°0N 68°0E 109 D7
Ongwediva Namibia 17°47S 15°44E 144 A2
Oni Georgia 42°33N 43°26E 87 J6
Onilahy → Madag. 23°34S 43°45E 141 J8
Onitsha Nigeria 6°6N 6°42E 139 D6
Ono Fiji 18°55S 178°29E 154 a
Onoda Japan 33°59N 131°11E 113 G5
Onoke, L. N.Z. 41°22S 175°8E 154 H4
Ons, I. de Spain 42°23N 8°55W 88 C2
Onsala Sweden 57°26N 12°0E 63 G6
Onslow Australia 21°40S 115°12E 148 D2
Onslow B. U.S.A. 34°20N 77°15W 177 D16
Ontake-San Japan 35°53N 137°29E 113 G8
Ontario Calif., U.S.A. 34°4N 117°39W 171 L9
Ontario Oreg., U.S.A. 44°2N 116°58W 168 D5
Ontario □ Canada 48°0N 83°0W 164 B2
Ontario, L. N. Amer. 43°20N 78°0W 174 C7
Ontinyent Spain 38°50N 0°35W 91 G4
Ontonagon U.S.A. 46°52N 89°19W 172 B9
Ontur Spain 38°38N 1°29W 91 G3
Onyx U.S.A. 35°41N 118°14W 171 K8
Oodaaq Greenland 83°40N 30°40W 57 A8
Oodnadatta Australia 27°33S 135°30E 151 D2
Ooldea Australia 30°27S 131°50E 149 F5
Oombulgurri Australia 15°15S 127°45E 148 C4
Oombulgurri ○ Australia 15°10S 127°50E 148 C4
Oorindi Australia 20°40S 141°1E 150 C3
Oost-Vlaanderen □ Belgium 51°5N 3°50E 69 C3
Oostende Belgium 51°15N 2°54E 69 C2
Oosterhout Neths. 51°39N 4°47E 69 C4
Oosterschelde → Neths. 51°33N 4°0E 69 C4
Oosterwolde Neths. 53°0N 6°17E 69 B6
Oosterschelde △ Neths. 51°40N 3°40E 69 C3
Ootacamund = Udagamandalam India 11°30N 76°44E 127 J3
Ootha Australia 33°6S 147°29E 153 E4
Ootsa L. Canada 53°50N 126°2W 162 C3
Ooty = Udagamandalam India 11°30N 76°44E 127 J3
Op Luang △ Thailand 18°12N 98°32E 120 C2
Opaka Bulgaria 43°28N 26°10E 97 C10
Opala Dem. Rep. of the Congo 0°40S 24°20E 142 C1
Opâle, Côte d' France 50°30N 1°30E 70 B8
Opalenica Poland 52°18N 16°24E 83 F3
Opan Bulgaria 42°13N 25°41E 97 D9
Opanake Sri Lanka 6°35N 80°40E 127 L5
Opapa N.Z. 39°47S 176°42E 154 F5
Opasatika Canada 49°30N 82°50W 164 C3
Opasquia △ Canada 53°33N 93°5W 164 B1
Opatija Croatia 45°21N 14°17E 93 C11
Opatów Poland 50°50N 21°27E 83 H8
Opava Czech Rep. 49°57N 17°58E 79 B10
Opelika U.S.A. 32°39N 85°23W 178 C4
Opelousas U.S.A. 30°32N 92°5W 176 F8
Opémisca, L. Canada 49°56N 74°52W 164 C5
Opheim U.S.A. 48°51N 106°24W 168 B10
Ophthalmia Ra. Australia 23°15S 119°30E 148 D2
Opi Nigeria 6°36N 7°28E 139 D6
Opinaca → Canada 52°15N 78°2W 164 B4
Opinaca, Rés. Canada 52°39N 76°20W 164 B4
Opinnagau → Canada 54°12N 82°25W 164 B3
Opiscotéo, L. Canada 53°10N 68°10W 165 B6
Opobo Nigeria 4°35N 7°34E 139 E6
Opochka Russia 56°42N 28°45E 84 D5
Opoczno Poland 51°22N 20°18E 83 G7
Opole Poland 50°42N 17°58E 83 H4
Opole Lubelskie Poland 51°9N 21°58E 83 H9
Opolskie □ Poland 50°30N 18°0E 83 H5
Oponono L. Namibia 18°8S 15°45E 144 A2
Opornyy = Borankul Kazakhstan 46°11N 54°25E 108 C7
Oporto = Porto Portugal 41°8N 8°40W 88 D2
Opotiki N.Z. 38°1S 177°19E 154 E6
Opp U.S.A. 31°17N 86°16W 178 D3
Oppdal Norway 62°35N 9°41E 60 E13
Opportunity U.S.A. 47°39N 117°15W 168 C5
Opnişor Romania 44°17N 23°5E 80 F8
Oprtalj Croatia 45°23N 13°50E 80 F8
Opua N.Z. 35°19S 174°9E 154 B3
Opunake N.Z. 39°26S 173°52E 154 F2
Opuwo Namibia 18°3S 13°45E 144 A1
Opuzen Croatia 43°1N 17°34E 93 E14
Or → Russia 51°11N 58°32E 108 B5
Or, Côte d' France 47°10N 4°50E 71 E11
Ora Cyprus 34°51N 33°12E 101 E12
Oracle U.S.A. 32°37N 110°46W 169 K8
Oradea Romania 47°2N 21°58E 80 C6
Öræfajökull Iceland 64°2N 16°39W 60 D5
Orahovac = Rahovec Kosovo 42°24N 20°40E 96 C4
Orahovica Croatia 45°35N 17°52E 80 E2
Orai India 25°58N 79°30E 125 G8
Oraison France 43°55N 5°55E 73 E9
Oral = Zhayyq → Kazakhstan 47°0N 51°48E 108 C4
Oral Kazakhstan 51°20N 51°20E 86 E10
Oran Algeria 35°45N 0°39W 136 A4
Orange Australia 33°15S 149°7E 153 E8
Orange France 44°8N 4°47E 73 D8
Orange Calif., U.S.A. 33°47N 117°51W 171 M9
Orange Mass., U.S.A. 42°35N 72°19W 175 D12
Orange Tex., U.S.A. 30°6N 93°44W 176 F4
Orange Va., U.S.A. 38°15N 78°7W 173 F14
Orange → S. Africa 28°41S 16°28E 144 C2
Orange, C. Brazil 4°20N 51°30W 187 C8
Orange City U.S.A. 28°57N 81°18W 179 G7
Orange Cove U.S.A. 36°38N 119°19W 170 J7
Orange Free State = Free State □ S. Africa 28°30S 27°0E 144 C4
Orange Grove U.S.A. 27°58N 97°56W 176 H6

Orange L. U.S.A. 29°25N 82°13W 179 F7
Orange Park U.S.A. 30°10N 81°42W 178 E8
Orange Walk Belize 18°6N 88°33W 181 D7
Orangeburg U.S.A. 33°30N 80°52W 178 B9
Orangeville Canada 43°55N 80°5W 174 C4
Orango Guinea-Biss. 11°5N 16°0W 138 C1
Orani Italy 40°15N 9°11E 94 B2
Oranienburg Germany 52°45N 13°14E 76 C9
Oranje = Orange → S. Africa 28°41S 16°28E 144 C2
Oranjemund Namibia 28°38S 16°29E 144 C2
Oranjerivier S. Africa 29°40S 24°12E 144 C3
Oranjestad Aruba 12°32N 70°2W 183 D5
Orapa Botswana 21°15S 25°30E 141 J5
Oras Phil. 12°9N 125°28E 119 B7
Orašje Bos.-H. 45°1N 18°42E 80 E3
Orăştie Romania 45°50N 23°10E 81 E8
Orava → Slovak Rep. 49°9N 19°18E 79 B12
Orava, Vodna nádrž Slovak Rep. 49°25N 19°35E 79 B12
Oravița Romania 45°6N 21°43E 80 E6
Orawia N.Z. 46°1S 167°50E 155 G2
Orb → France 43°15N 3°18E 72 E7
Orba → Italy 44°53N 8°37E 92 D5
Ørbæk Denmark 55°17N 10°39E 63 J4
Orbe Switz. 46°43N 6°32E 77 J2
Orbec France 49°1N 0°23E 70 C7
Orbetello Italy 42°27N 11°13E 93 F8
Órbigo → Spain 42°5N 5°42W 88 C5
Orbisonia U.S.A. 40°15N 77°54W 174 F7
Orbost Australia 37°40S 148°29E 153 D8
Ørbyhus Sweden 60°15N 17°43E 62 D11
Orcadas Antarctica 60°44S 44°37W 55 C18
Orcas I. U.S.A. 48°42N 122°56W 178 B4
Orce Spain 37°44N 2°28W 91 H2
Orce → Spain 37°44N 2°28W 91 H2
Orchard City U.S.A. 38°50N 107°58W 168 G10
Orchard Homes U.S.A. 46°55N 114°4W 168 C6
Orchid = Lan Yü Taiwan 22°4N 121°25E 117 F13
Orchies France 50°28N 3°14E 71 B10
Orchila, I. Venezuela 11°48N 66°10W 183 D6
Orchilla, Pta. Canary Is. 27°42N 18°10W 100 G1
Órcia → Italy 42°58N 11°21E 93 F8
Orco → Italy 45°10N 7°52E 92 C4
Orcopampa Peru 15°20S 72°23W 188 D3
Orcutt U.S.A. 34°52N 120°27W 171 L6
Ord → Australia 15°33S 128°15E 148 C4
Ord, Mt. Australia 17°20S 125°34E 148 C4
Ord Mts. U.S.A. 34°39N 116°45W 171 L10
Ordenes = Ordes Spain 43°5N 8°29W 88 B2
Orderville U.S.A. 37°17N 112°38W 169 H7
Ordes Spain 43°5N 8°29W 88 B2
Ordesa y Monte Perido △ Spain 42°40N 0°10W 90 C4
Ording = Sankt Peter-Ording Germany 54°20N 8°36E 76 A4
Ordos = Mu Us Shamo China 39°0N 109°0E 114 E5
Ordu Turkey 40°55N 37°53E 104 B7
Ordu □ Turkey 41°0N 37°50E 104 B7
Ordubad Azerbaijan 38°54N 46°1E 105 C12
Orduña Álava, Spain 42°58N 2°58W 88 B7
Orduña Granada, Spain 37°20N 3°30W 89 H7
Ordzhonikidze = Denisovka Kazakhstan 52°27N 61°39E 108 D6
Ordzhonikidze Ukraine 47°39N 34°3E 85 J8
Ore Dem. Rep. of the Congo 3°17N 29°30E 142 B2
Ore Mts. = Erzgebirge Germany 50°27N 12°55E 76 E8
Orebić Croatia 43°0N 17°11E 93 F14
Örebro Sweden 59°20N 15°18E 62 G9
Orebro län □ Sweden 59°27N 15°0E 62 E8
Orecchiella △ Italy 44°16N 10°22E 92 D7
Oregon U.S.A. 42°1N 89°20W 172 D9
Oregon □ U.S.A. 44°0N 121°0W 168 E3
Oregon City U.S.A. 45°21N 122°36W 170 E4
Oregon Dunes △ U.S.A. 43°40N 124°10W 168 E1
Orehova → Orikhiv Ukraine 47°30N 35°48E 85 J8
Orekhovo-Zuyevo Russia 55°50N 38°55E 84 E10
Orel Russia 52°57N 36°3E 85 F9
Orel → Russia 52°30N 36°40E 85 F9
Orellana, Canal de Spain 39°2N 6°0W 89 F5
Orellana, Embalse de Spain 39°5N 5°10W 89 F5
Orellana la Vieja Spain 39°1N 5°32W 89 F5
Orem U.S.A. 40°19N 111°42W 168 F8
Ören Turkey 37°3N 27°57E 99 D9
Orenburg Russia 51°45N 55°6E 108 D6
Örencik Turkey 39°16N 29°33E 99 B11
Orense = Ourense Spain 42°19N 7°55W 88 C3
Orepuki N.Z. 46°19S 167°46E 155 G1
Orestes Pereyra Mexico 26°30N 105°39W 180 B3
Orestiada Greece 41°30N 26°33E 97 E10
Øresund Europe 55°45N 12°40E 63 J6
Oreti → N.Z. 46°28S 168°14E 155 G2
Orfanos Kolpos Greece 40°33N 24°0E 96 F7
Orford Ness U.K. 52°5N 1°35E 67 E9
Organ Pipe Cactus △ U.S.A. 32°0N 112°52W 169 K7
Organos, Pta. de los Canary Is. 28°12N 17°17W 100 F2
Organyà Spain 42°13N 1°20E 90 C6
Orgaz Spain 39°39N 3°53W 89 F7

Oriente Argentina 38°44S 60°37W 190 D3
Orihuela Spain 38°7N 0°55W 91 G4
Orihuela del Tremedal Spain 40°33N 1°39W 90 E3
Orikhiv Ukraine 47°30N 35°48E 85 J8
Orikum Albania 40°20N 19°30E 98 D2
Oril → Ukraine 48°40N 34°39E 85 H8
Orillia Canada 44°40N 79°24W 174 B5
Orinoco → Venezuela 9°15N 61°30W 186 B6
Orion Canada 49°27N 110°49W 163 D8
Orissa = Odisha □ India 20°0N 84°0E 126 E7
Orissaare Estonia 58°34N 23°5E 84 C12
Oristano Italy 39°54N 8°36E 94 C1
Oristano, G. di Italy 39°50N 8°29E 94 C1
Orizaba Mexico 18°51N 97°6W 181 D5
Orizaba, Pico de Mexico 18°58N 97°15W 181 D5
Orizare Bulgaria 42°44N 27°39E 97 D11
Orizona Brazil 17°3S 48°18W 191 G9
Orjen Bos.-H. 42°35N 18°34E 96 D2
Orjiva = Órgiva Spain 36°53N 3°24W 89 J7
Orkanger Norway 63°18N 9°52E 60 E13
Örkelljunga Sweden 56°17N 13°17E 63 H7
Örken Sweden 57°6N 15°1E 63 H8
Örkény Hungary 47°9N 19°26E 80 C4
Orkhon = Orhon Gol → Mongolia 50°21N 106°0E 110 A10
Orkla → Norway 63°18N 9°51E 60 E13
Orkney S. Africa 26°58S 26°40E 144 C4
Orkney □ U.K. 59°2N 3°13W 65 B5
Orkney Is. U.K. 59°0N 3°0W 65 B6
Orland U.S.A. 39°45N 122°12W 170 F4
Orlando U.S.A. 28°32N 81°22W 179 G8
Orlando, C. d' Italy 38°10N 14°43E 95 D7
Orlando Int. ✈ (MCO) U.S.A. 28°26N 81°19W 179 G8
Orléanais France 48°0N 2°0E 71 E9
Orléans France 47°54N 1°52E 71 E8
Orleans U.S.A. 44°49N 72°12W 175 B12
Orléans, Î. d' Canada 46°54N 70°58W 165 C5
Orlice → Czech Rep. 50°13N 15°50E 78 A8
Orlivka Ukraine 45°19N 28°27E 81 E13
Orlov Slovak Rep. 49°17N 20°51E 79 B13
Orlov Gay Russia 50°56N 48°19E 86 E9
Orlová Czech Rep. 49°51N 18°26E 79 B11
Orlovat Serbia 45°14N 20°33E 80 E5
Orly, Paris ✈ (ORY) France 48°44N 2°23E 71 D9
Ormara Pakistan 25°16N 64°33E 122 G4
Ormea Italy 44°9N 7°54E 92 D4
Ormília Greece 40°16N 23°39E 96 F7
Ormoc Phil. 11°0N 124°37E 119 B6
Ormond N.Z. 38°33S 177°56E 154 E6
Ormond Beach U.S.A. 29°17N 81°3W 179 F8
Ormond-by-the-Sea U.S.A. 29°21N 81°4W 179 F8
Ormondville N.Z. 40°5S 176°19E 154 G5
Ormož Slovenia 46°25N 16°10E 93 B13
Ormskirk U.K. 53°35N 2°54W 66 D5
Ormstown Canada 45°8N 74°0W 175 A11
Ornans France 47°7N 6°10E 71 E13
Orne □ France 48°40N 0°5E 70 D7
Orne → France 49°18N 0°15W 70 C6
Orneta Poland 54°8N 20°9E 82 D7
Ornö Sweden 59°4N 18°24E 62 E12
Örnsköldsvik Sweden 63°17N 18°40E 62 A12
Oro → N. Korea 40°1N 127°27E 115 D14
Oro → Mexico 25°35N 105°2W 180 B3
Oro Grande U.S.A. 34°36N 117°20W 171 L9
Oro Valley U.S.A. 32°26N 110°58W 169 K8
Orobie, Alpi Italy 46°7N 10°0E 92 B7
Orobie Bergamasche △ Italy 46°0N 9°45E 92 C6
Orobie Valtellinesi △ Italy 46°5N 9°45E 92 B6
Orocué Colombia 4°48N 71°20W 186 C4
Orodara Burkina Faso 11°0N 4°55W 138 C4
Orodo Nigeria 5°34N 7°4E 139 D6
Orofino U.S.A. 46°29N 116°15W 168 C5
Orohena, Mt. Tahiti 17°37S 149°28W 155 b
Oromocto Canada 45°54N 66°29W 165 D6
Oron Nigeria 4°48N 8°14E 139 E7
Orono Canada 43°59N 78°37W 174 C6
Orono U.S.A. 44°53N 68°40W 173 C19
Oronsay U.K. 56°1N 6°15W 65 E2
Oropesa Spain 39°57N 5°10W 89 F5
Oroquieta Phil. 8°32N 123°44E 119 C6
Orós Brazil 6°15S 38°55W 189 E11
Orosei Italy 40°23N 9°42E 94 B2
Orosei, G. di Italy 40°15N 9°44E 94 B2
Orosháza Hungary 46°32N 20°42E 80 D5
Oroszlány Hungary 47°29N 18°19E 80 C3
Orotukan Russia 62°16N 151°42E 107 C16
Oroville Calif., U.S.A. 39°31N 121°33W 170 F5
Oroville Wash., U.S.A. 48°56N 119°26W 168 B4
Oroville, L. U.S.A. 39°33N 121°29W 170 F5
Orrefors Sweden 56°50N 15°45E 63 H9
Orroroo Australia 32°43S 138°38E 152 B3
Orrville U.S.A. 40°50N 81°46W 174 F3
Orša Belarus 54°30N 30°25E 84 E6

Ortona Italy 42°21N 14°24E 93 F11
Ortonville U.S.A. 45°19N 96°27W 172 C5
Orūmiyeh Iran 37°40N 45°0E 105 D11
Orūmiyeh, Daryācheh-ye Iran 37°50N 45°30E 105 D11
Orune Italy 40°24N 9°22E 94 B2
Oruro Bolivia 18°0S 67°9W 188 D4
Orust Sweden 58°10N 11°40E 63 F5
Oruzgān □ Afghan. 33°0N 66°0E 122 C5
Orvault France 47°17N 1°38W 70 E5
Orvieto Italy 42°43N 12°7E 93 F9
Orwell N.Y., U.S.A. 43°35N 75°50W 175 C9
Orwell Ohio, U.S.A. 41°32N 80°52W 174 E4
Orwell → U.K. 51°59N 1°18E 67 F9
Orwigsburg U.S.A. 40°38N 76°6W 175 F8
Oryakhovo Bulgaria 43°40N 23°57E 96 C7
Orynyn Ukraine 48°46N 26°24E 81 H1
Oryol = Orel Russia 52°57N 36°3E 85 F9
Orzinuovi Italy 45°24N 9°55E 92 C6
Orzyc → Poland 52°46N 21°14E 83 F8
Orzysz Poland 53°50N 21°58E 82 E8
Osa → Poland 53°33N 18°46E 82 E5
Osa, Pen. de Costa Rica 8°0N 84°0W 182 E3
Osage U.S.A. 43°17N 92°49W 172 D7
Osage → U.S.A. 38°36N 91°57W 172 F8
Osage City U.S.A. 38°38N 95°50W 172 F6
Ōsaka Japan 34°42N 135°30E 113 G7
Osakarovka Kazakhstan 50°33N 72°34E 109 D8
Ōsaki Japan 38°34N 140°58E 112 E10
Osawatomie U.S.A. 38°31N 94°57W 172 F6
Osborn Plateau Ind. Oc. 14°45S 87°0E 146 F7
Osborne U.S.A. 39°26N 98°42W 172 F3
Osby Sweden 56°23N 13°59E 63 H7
Osceola Ark., U.S.A. 35°42N 89°58W 177 D10
Osceola Iowa, U.S.A. 41°2N 93°46W 172 E7
Oschatz Germany 51°17N 13°8E 76 D9
Oschersleben Germany 52°2N 11°14E 76 C7
Öschiri Italy 40°43N 9°6E 94 B2
Oscoda U.S.A. 44°26N 83°20W 174 B1
Osečina Serbia 44°23N 19°34E 96 B3
Ösel = Saaremaa Estonia 58°30N 22°30E 84 C2
Osery Russia 54°52N 38°28E 84 E10
Osgoode Canada 45°8N 75°36W 175 A9
Osh Kyrgyzstan 40°37N 72°49E 109 D8
Osh □ Kyrgyzstan 40°0N 73°0E 109 D8
Oshakati Namibia 17°45S 15°40E 141 H3
Oshawa Canada 43°50N 78°50W 174 C6
Oshika-Hantō Japan 38°20N 141°30E 112 E10
Oshikoto □ Namibia 18°30S 17°0E 144 A2
Oshivelo Namibia 18°37S 17°10E 144 A2
Oshkosh Nebr., U.S.A. 41°24N 102°21W 172 E2
Oshkosh Wis., U.S.A. 44°1N 88°33W 172 C9
Oshmyany = Ashmyany Belarus 54°26N 25°52E 75 A13
Oshnovīyeh Iran 37°2N 45°6E 105 D11
Oshogbo Nigeria 7°48N 4°37E 139 D5
Oshtorīnān Iran 34°1N 48°38E 105 C13
Ōshū Japan 39°8N 141°9E 112 E10
Oshwe Dem. Rep. of the Congo 3°25S 19°28E 140 E3
Osi Nigeria 8°8N 5°14E 139 D6
Osieczna Poland 51°55N 16°40E 83 G3
Osijek Croatia 45°34N 18°41E 80 E3
Ósilo Italy 40°45N 8°41E 94 B1
Osimo Italy 43°28N 13°30E 93 E10
Osintorf Belarus 54°40N 30°39E 84 E6
Osipovichi = Asipovichy Belarus 53°19N 28°33E 75 B15
Osiyan India 26°43N 72°55E 124 F5
Osizweni S. Africa 27°49S 30°7E 145 C5
Oskaloosa U.S.A. 41°18N 92°39W 172 E7
Oskarshamn Sweden 57°15N 16°27E 63 H10
Oskarström Sweden 56°48N 12°58E 63 H6
Oskélanéo Canada 48°5N 75°15W 164 C4
Öskemen Kazakhstan 50°0N 82°36E 109 E9
Oskol → Ukraine 49°6N 37°25E 85 H9
Osku Iran 37°54N 46°8E 105 D12
Oslo Norway 59°54N 10°43E 61 G14
Oslofjorden Norway 59°20N 10°35E 61 G14
Osmanabad India 18°5N 76°10E 126 E3
Osmancık Turkey 40°58N 34°50E 104 B6
Osmaniye Turkey 37°5N 36°10E 104 D7
Osmannagar India 18°32N 79°13E 126 E4
Osnabrück Germany 52°17N 8°3E 76 C4
Ośno Lubuskie Poland 52°28N 14°51E 83 F1
Osoblaha Czech Rep. 50°17N 17°44E 79 A10
Osogbo = Oshogbo Nigeria 7°48N 4°37E 139 D5
Osogovska Planina Macedonia 42°10N 22°30E 96 D8
Osório Brazil 29°53S 50°17W 191 B5
Osorno Chile 40°25S 73°0W 192 E2
Osorno Spain 42°24N 4°22W 88 C6
Osorno, Vol. Chile 41°0S 72°30W 192 E2
Osoyoos Canada 49°0N 119°30W 162 D5
Osøyro Norway 60°9N 5°30E 60 F11
Ospika → Canada 56°20N 124°0W 162 B4
Osprey U.S.A. 27°12N 82°29W 179 H7
Osprey Reef Australia 13°52S 146°36E 150 A4
Oss Neths. 51°46N 5°32E 69 C5
Ossa, Mt. Australia 41°52S 146°3E 151 G4
Ossa de Montiel Spain 38°58N 2°45W 91 G2
Ossabaw I. U.S.A. 31°50N 81°5W 179 D8
Ossabaw Sd. U.S.A. 31°50N 81°6W 178 D8
Osse → France 44°7N 0°17E 72 D4
Ossett U.K. 53°41N 1°34W 66 E6
Ossi Italy 40°40N 8°35E 94 B1
Ossining U.S.A. 41°10N 73°55W 175 E11
Ossipee U.S.A. 43°41N 71°7W 175 C13
Ossokmanuan L. Canada 53°25N 65°0W 165 B7
Ossora Russia 59°20N 163°13E 107 D17
Östavall Sweden 62°26N 15°22E 62 A9
Oste → Germany 53°30N 9°12E 76 B5
Ostend = Oostende Belgium 51°15N 2°54E 69 C2
Ostend N.Z. 36°48S 175°2E 154 C4
Österbotten = Pohjanmaa Finland 62°58N 22°50E 60 E20
Osterburg Germany 52°47N 11°45E 76 C7

Osterburg *U.S.A.* 40°16N 78°31W **174** F6
Osterburken *Germany* 49°25N 9°26E **77** F5
Österbybruk *Sweden* 60°13N 17°55E **62** D11
Österbymo *Sweden* 57°49N 15°15E **63** G9
Österdalälven → *Sweden* 60°30N 15°7E **62** C7
Østerdalen *Norway* 61°40N 10°50E **62** C4
Österforse *Sweden* 63°9N 17°3E **62** A11
Östergötlands län □
   Sweden 58°35N 15°45E **63** F9
Osterholz-Scharmbeck
   Germany 53°13N 8°47E **76** B4
Østerild *Denmark* 57°2N 8°51E **63** G2
Östermyra = Seinäjoki
   Finland 62°40N 22°51E **60** E20
Osterode *Germany* 51°43N 10°15E **76** D6
Österreich = Austria ■
   Europe 47°0N 14°0E **78** E7
Östersund *Sweden* 63°10N 14°38E **62** A8
Österväla *Sweden* 60°11N 17°11E **62** D11
Ostfriesische Inseln
   Germany 53°42N 7°0E **76** B3
Ostfriesland *Germany* 53°20N 7°30E **76** B3
Östhammar *Sweden* 60°16N 18°22E **62** D12
Òstia, Lido di *Italy* 41°43N 12°17E **93** G9
Ostíglia *Italy* 45°4N 11°9E **93** C8
Östmark *Sweden* 60°17N 12°45E **62** D6
Östra Husby *Sweden* 58°35N 16°33E **63** F10
Ostrava *Czech Rep.* 49°51N 18°18E **79** B11
Ostravský □ *Czech Rep.* 49°55N 17°58E **79** B10
Ostróda *Poland* 53°42N 19°58E **82** E6
Ostrogozhsk *Russia* 50°55N 39°7E **85** G10
Ostroh *Ukraine* 50°20N 26°30E **75** C14
Ostrołęka *Poland* 53°4N 21°32E **83** E8
Ostrov *Bulgaria* 43°40N 24°9E **97** C8
Ostrov *Czech Rep.* 50°18N 12°57E **78** A5
Ostrov *Romania* 44°6N 27°24E **81** F12
Ostrov *Russia* 57°25N 28°20E **84** D5
Ostrów Lubelski *Poland* 51°29N 22°51E **83** G9
Ostrów Mazowiecka
   Poland 52°50N 21°51E **83** F8
Ostrów Wielkopolski
   Poland 51°36N 17°44E **83** G4
Ostrowiec-Świętokrzyski
   Poland 50°55N 21°22E **83** H8
Ostrožac *Bos.-H.* 43°43N 17°49E **80** G2
Ostrzeszów *Poland* 51°25N 17°52E **83** G4
Ostseebad Kühlungsborn
   Germany 54°8N 11°44E **76** A7
Osttirol □ *Austria* 46°50N 12°30E **78** E5
Ostuni *Italy* 40°44N 17°35E **95** B10
Osum → *Albania* 40°40N 20°10E **96** F4
Osŭm → *Bulgaria* 43°40N 24°50E **97** C8
Ōsumi-Kaikyō *Japan* 30°55N 131°0E **113** J5
Ōsumi-Shotō *Japan* 30°30N 130°0E **113** J5
Osun □ *Nigeria* 7°30N 4°30E **139** D5
Osuna *Spain* 37°14N 5°8W **89** H5
Oswegatchie →
   U.S.A. 44°42N 75°30W **175** B9
Oswego *U.S.A.* 43°27N 76°31W **175** C8
Oswego → *U.S.A.* 43°27N 76°30W **175** C8
Oswestry *U.K.* 52°52N 3°3W **66** E4
Oświęcim *Poland* 50°2N 19°11E **83** H6
Otaci *Moldova* 48°27N 27°47E **81** B12
Otago □ *N.Z.* 45°15S 170°0E **155** F5
Otago Harbour *N.Z.* 45°47S 170°42E **155** F5
Otago Pen. *N.Z.* 45°48S 170°39E **155** F5
Otaheite B.
   Trin. & Tob. 10°15N 61°30W **187** K15
Otahuhu *N.Z.* 36°56S 174°51E **154** C3
Ōtake *Japan* 34°12N 132°13E **113** G6
Otaki *N.Z.* 40°45S 175°10E **154** G4
Otane *N.Z.* 39°54S 176°39E **154** F5
Otaru *Japan* 43°10N 141°0E **112** C10
Otaru-Wan = Ishikari-Wan
   Japan 43°25N 141°1E **112** C10
Otautau *N.Z.* 46°9S 168°1E **155** G3
Otava → *Czech Rep.* 49°26N 14°12E **78** B7
Otavalo *Ecuador* 0°13N 78°20W **186** C3
Otavi *Namibia* 19°40S 17°24E **144** A2
Ōtawara *Japan* 36°50N 140°5E **113** F10
Otego *U.S.A.* 42°23N 75°10W **175** D9
Otelec *Romania* 45°36N 20°50E **80** E5
Otelnuk, L. *Canada* 56°9N 68°12W **165** A6
Oţelu Roşu *Romania* 45°32N 22°22E **80** E7
Otero de Rey = Outeiro de Rei
   Spain 43°6N 7°36W **88** B3
Othello *U.S.A.* 46°50N 119°10W **168** C4
Othoni *Greece* 39°52N 19°22E **98** B1
Othris, Oros *Greece* 39°2N 22°37E **98** B4
Oti → *Africa* 7°48N 0°19E **139** D5
Oti □ *Togo* 10°40N 0°35E **139** D5
Otira *N.Z.* 42°49S 171°33E **155** C6
Otira Gorge *N.Z.* 42°53S 171°33E **155** C6
Otish, Mts. *Canada* 52°22N 70°30W **165** B5
Otishi △ *Peru* 11°40S 73°5W **188** C3
Otjinene *Namibia* 21°8S 18°46E **144** B2
Otjiwarongo *Namibia* 20°30S 16°33E **144** B2
Otjozondjupa □ *Namibia* 21°0S 17°0E **144** B2
Otmuchów *Poland* 50°28N 17°10E **83** H4
Otočac *Croatia* 44°53N 15°12E **93** D12
Otoineppu *Japan* 44°44N 142°16E **112** B11
Otok *Croatia* 43°42N 16°44E **93** E13
Otopeni, Bucureşti × (OTP)
   Romania 44°26N 26°11E **81** F11
Otorohanga *N.Z.* 38°12S 175°14E **154** E4
Otoskwin → *Canada* 52°13N 88°6E **164** B2
Otra → *Norway* 58°9N 8°1E **61** G13
Otradnyy *Russia* 53°22N 51°21E **86** D10
Otranto *Italy* 40°9N 18°28E **95** B11
Otranto, C. d' *Italy* 40°7N 18°30E **95** B11
Otranto, Str. of *Italy* 40°15N 18°40E **95** B11
Otrokovice *Czech Rep.* 49°12N 17°31E **79** B9
Otse *S. Africa* 25°2S 25°45E **144** C4
Otsego L. *U.S.A.* 42°45N 74°53W **175** D10
Ōtsu *Japan* 35°0N 135°50E **113** G7
Ōtsuki *Japan* 35°36N 138°57E **113** G9
Ottappalam *India* 10°46N 76°23E **127** J3
Ottawa = Outaouais →
   Canada 45°27N 74°8W **164** C5
Ottawa *Canada* 45°26N 75°42W **175** A9
Ottawa *Ill., U.S.A.* 41°21N 88°51W **172** E9
Ottawa *Kans., U.S.A.* 38°37N 95°16W **172** F7
Ottawa Is. *Canada* 59°35N 80°10W **161** F15

Otterndorf *Germany* 53°48N 8°53E **76** B4
Otterup *Denmark* 55°30N 10°22E **63** J4
Otterville *Canada* 42°55N 80°36W **174** D4
Ottery St. Mary *U.K.* 50°44N 3°17W **67** G4
Otto Beit Bridge
   Zimbabwe 15°59S 28°56E **143** F2
Ottosdal *S. Africa* 26°46S 25°59E **144** C4
Ottumwa *U.S.A.* 41°1N 92°25W **172** E7
Otukpa *Nigeria* 7°9N 7°41E **139** D6
Oturkpo *Nigeria* 7°16N 8°8E **139** D6
Otway, B. *Chile* 53°30S 74°0W **192** D2
Otway, C. *Australia* 38°52S 143°30E **152** F5
Otway, Seno de *Chile* 53°0S 71°30W **192** D2
Otway □ *Australia* 38°47S 143°34E **152** E5
Otwock *Poland* 52°5N 21°20E **83** F8
Otyniya *Ukraine* 48°44N 24°51E **81** B9
Ötztaler Ache →
   Austria 47°14N 10°50E **78** D3
Ötztaler Alpen *Austria* 46°56N 11°0E **78** E3
Ou → *Laos* 20°4N 102°13E **120** B4
Ou-Sammyaku *Japan* 39°20N 140°35E **112** C10
Ouachita → *U.S.A.* 31°38N 91°49W **176** F9
Ouachita, L. *U.S.A.* 34°34N 93°12W **176** D8
Ouachita Mts. *U.S.A.* 34°30N 94°30W **176** D7
Ouagadougou
   Burkina Faso 12°25N 1°30W **139** C4
Ouahigouya
   Burkina Faso 13°31N 2°25W **138** C4
Ouahran = Oran
   Algeria 35°45N 0°39W **136** A3
Oualâta *Mauritania* 17°20N 6°55W **138** B3
Ouallam *Niger* 14°23N 2°10E **139** C5
Ouallene *Algeria* 24°41N 1°11E **136** D4
Ouarâne *Mauritania* 21°0N 10°30W **134** D3
Ouargaye *Burkina Faso* 11°40N 0°5E **139** C5
Ouargla *Algeria* 31°59N 5°16E **136** B5
Ouargla □ *Algeria* 30°30N 6°10E **136** B5
Ouarkoye *Burkina Faso* 12°5N 3°40W **138** C4
Ouarkziz, Jebel *Algeria* 28°50N 8°0W **136** C2
Ouarra → *C.A.R.* 5°6N 24°26E **140** C4
Ouarzazate *Morocco* 30°55N 6°50W **136** B2
Ouassoulou *Mali* 16°10N 1°23E **139** B5
Ouatagouna *Mali* 15°11N 0°43E **139** B5
Oubangi →
   Dem. Rep. of the Congo 0°30S 17°50E **140** E3
Oubarakai, O. → *Algeria* 27°20N 9°10E **136** C7
Ouche → *France* 47°6N 5°16E **71** E12
Ouddorp *Neths.* 51°50N 3°57E **69** C3
Oude Rijn → *Neths.* 52°12N 4°24E **69** B4
Oudeïka *Mali* 17°30N 1°40W **139** B4
Oudenaarde *Belgium* 50°50N 3°37E **69** D3
Oudon → *France* 47°41N 0°53W **70** E6
Oudtshoorn *S. Africa* 33°35S 22°14E **144** D3
Oued Zem *Morocco* 32°52N 6°34W **136** B2
Ouella *Niger* 14°48N 3°38E **139** C5
Ouellé *Ivory C.* 7°26N 4°1W **138** D4
Ouenza *Algeria* 35°57N 8°4E **136** A5
Ouessa *Burkina Faso* 11°4N 2°47W **138** C4
Ouessant, Î. d' *France* 48°28N 5°6W **70** D1
Ouesso *Congo* 1°37N 16°5E **140** D3
Ouest, Pte. de l' *Canada* 49°52N 64°40W **165** C7
Ouezzane *Morocco* 34°51N 5°35W **136** B2
Ougarou *Burkina Faso* 12°10N 0°58E **139** C5
Oughter, L. *Ireland* 54°1N 7°28W **64** B4
Oughterard *Ireland* 53°26N 9°18W **64** C2
Ouidah *Benin* 6°25N 2°0E **139** D5
Ouidi *Niger* 14°10N 13°0E **139** C7
Ouistreham *France* 49°17N 0°18W **70** C6
Oujda *Morocco* 34°41N 1°55W **136** B3
Oujeft *Mauritania* 20°2N 13°0W **138** A2
Oulad-Teïma *Morocco* 30°24N 9°12W **136** B2
Oulainen *Finland* 64°17N 24°47E **60** D21
Ould Yenjé *Mauritania* 15°38N 12°16W **138** B2
Ouled Djellal *Algeria* 34°28N 5°2E **136** B5
Ouled Naïl, Mts. des
   Algeria 34°30N 3°30E **136** B4
Oullins *France* 45°43N 4°49E **73** C8
Oulmès *Morocco* 33°17N 6°0W **136** B2
Oulu *Finland* 65°1N 25°29E **60** D21
Oulujärvi *Finland* 64°25N 27°15E **60** D22
Oulujoki → *Finland* 65°1N 25°30E **60** D21
Oulx *Italy* 45°2N 6°50E **92** C4
Oum Chalouba *Chad* 15°48N 20°46E **135** E10
Oum-el-Bouaghi *Algeria* 35°55N 7°6E **136** A5
Oum-el-Bouaghi □
   Algeria 35°50N 7°5E **136** A5
Oum el Ksi *Algeria* 29°4N 6°59W **136** C2
Oum-er-Rbia, O. →
   Morocco 33°19N 8°21W **136** B2
Oum Hadjer *Chad* 13°18N 19°41E **135** F9
Oumé *Ivory C.* 6°21N 5°27W **138** D3
Ounane, Dj. *Algeria* 25°4N 7°19E **136** C5
Ounasjoki → *Finland* 66°31N 25°40E **60** C21
Ounguati *Namibia* 22°0S 15°46E **144** B2
Ouninga Kébir *Chad* 19°4N 20°29E **135** E10
Our → *Lux.* 49°55N 6°5E **69** E6
Oura, Akra *Greece* 38°10N 26°2E **99** C8
Ouranoupoli *Greece* 40°20N 23°59E **96** F7
Ourârene *Niger* 19°30N 7°20E **139** B6
Ouray *U.S.A.* 38°1N 107°40W **169** G10
Ourcq → *France* 49°1N 3°1E **71** C10
Ourém *Portugal* 39°40N 8°35W **88** F2
Ourense *Spain* 42°19N 7°55W **88** C3
Ourense □ *Spain* 42°15N 7°51W **88** C3
Ouricuri *Brazil* 7°53S 40°5W **189** B2
Ourinhos *Brazil* 23°0S 49°54W **191** A6
Ourique *Portugal* 37°38N 8°16W **89** H2
Ouro Fino *Brazil* 22°16S 46°25W **191** A6
Ouro-Ndia *Mali* 15°8N 4°35W **138** B4
Ouro Prêto *Brazil* 20°20S 43°30W **191** A7
Oursi *Burkina Faso* 14°41N 0°27W **138** B4
Ourthe → *Belgium* 50°29N 5°35E **69** D5
Ouse → *E. Susx., U.K.* 50°47N 0°4E **67** G8
Ouse → *N. Yorks., U.K.* 53°44N 0°55W **66** D7
Oust *France* 42°52N 1°13E **72** F5
Oust → *France* 47°35N 2°6W **70** E4
Outaouais → *Canada* 45°27N 74°8W **164** C5
Outardes → *Canada* 49°24N 69°30W **165** C6
Outat Oulad el Haj
   Morocco 33°22N 3°42W **136** B3
Outeiro de Rei *Spain* 43°6N 7°36W **88** B3
Outer Hebrides *U.K.* 57°30N 7°15W **65** D1
Outes = A Serra de Outes
   Spain 42°52N 8°55W **88** C2

Outjo *Namibia* 20°5S 16°7E **144** B2
Outlook *Canada* 51°30N 107°0W **163** C7
Outokumpu *Finland* 62°43N 29°1E **60** E23
Outreau *France* 50°40N 1°36E **71** B8
Ouvèze → *France* 43°59N 4°51E **73** E8
Ouyen *Australia* 35°1S 142°22E **152** C5
Ouzouer-le-Marché
   France 47°54N 1°32E **71** E8
Ovada *Italy* 44°38N 8°38E **92** D5
Ovalau *Fiji* 17°40S 178°48E **154** a
Ovalle *Chile* 30°33S 71°18W **190** C1
Ovamboland = Ovamboland
   Namibia 18°30S 16°0E **144** A2
Ovanåker *Sweden* 61°22N 15°53E **62** C9
Ovar *Portugal* 40°51N 8°40W **88** E2
Overath *Germany* 50°56N 7°17E **76** E3
Overflakkee *Neths.* 51°44N 4°10E **69** C4
Overijssel □ *Neths.* 52°25N 6°35E **69** B6
Overland Park *U.S.A.* 38°58N 94°40W **172** F6
Overlander Roadhouse
   Australia 26°19S 114°28E **149** E1
Overton *U.S.A.* 36°33N 114°27W **171** J12
Övertorneå *Sweden* 66°23N 23°38E **60** C20
Överum *Sweden* 58°0N 16°20E **63** F10
Ovid *U.S.A.* 42°41N 76°49W **175** D8
Ovidiopol *Ukraine* 46°15N 30°30E **81** C16
Ovidiu *Romania* 44°16N 28°34E **81** F13
Oviedo *Spain* 43°25N 5°50W **88** B5
Oviedo □ *Spain* 28°40N 81°13W **179** G8
Oviksfjällen *Sweden* 63°0N 13°49E **62** A7
Ovišrags *Latvia* 57°33N 21°44E **62** A8
Ovoot *Mongolia* 45°21N 113°45E **114** B7
Övör Hangay □
   Mongolia 45°0N 102°30E **114** B2
Ovoro *Nigeria* 5°26N 7°16E **139** D6
Øvre Anárjohka △
   Norway 68°30N 24°40E **60** B21
Øvre Årdal *Norway* 61°19N 7°48E **60** F12
Øvre Dividal △ *Norway* 68°43N 19°50E **60** B18
Øvre Fryken *Sweden* 60°0N 13°7E **62** E7
Øvre Pasvik △ *Norway* 69°6N 28°54E **60** B23
Ovruch *Ukraine* 51°25N 28°45E **75** C15
Owaka *N.Z.* 46°27S 169°40E **155** G4
Owambo = Ovamboland
   Namibia 18°30S 16°0E **144** A2
Owasco L. *U.S.A.* 42°50N 76°31W **175** D8
Owase *Japan* 34°7N 136°12E **113** G8
Owatonna *U.S.A.* 44°5N 93°14W **172** C7
Owbeh *Afghan.* 34°28N 63°10E **122** B3
Owego *U.S.A.* 42°6N 76°16W **175** D8
Owen *Australia* 34°15S 138°32E **152** C2
Owen, Mt. *N.Z.* 41°35S 172°33E **155** B7
Owen Falls Dam = Nalubaale
   Dam *Uganda* 0°30N 33°5E **142** B3
Owen Sound *Canada* 44°35N 80°55W **174** B4
Owen Stanley Ra.
   Papua N.G. 8°30S 147°0E **147** B7
Oweniny → *Ireland* 54°8N 9°34W **64** B2
Owens → *U.S.A.* 36°32N 117°59W **170** J9
Owens L. *U.S.A.* 36°26N 117°57W **171** J9
Owensboro *U.S.A.* 37°46N 87°7W **172** G10
Owerri *Nigeria* 5°29N 7°0E **139** D6
Owhango *N.Z.* 39°0S 175°23E **154** F4
Owl → *Canada* 57°51N 92°44W **163** B10
Owo *Nigeria* 7°10N 5°39E **139** D6
Owosso *U.S.A.* 43°0N 84°10W **173** D11
Owyhee *U.S.A.* 41°57N 116°6W **168** F5
Owyhee → *U.S.A.* 43°49N 117°2W **168** E5
Owyhee, L. *U.S.A.* 43°38N 117°14W **168** E5
Ox Mts. = Slieve Gamph
   Ireland 54°6N 9°0W **64** B3
Oxapampa *Peru* 10°33S 75°2W **188** C2
Öxarfjörður *Iceland* 66°15N 16°45W **60** C5
Oxbow *Canada* 49°14N 102°10W **163** D8
Oxelösund *Sweden* 58°43N 17°15E **63** F11
Oxford *N.Z.* 43°18S 172°11E **155** D7
Oxford *U.K.* 51°46N 1°15W **67** F6
Oxford *Ala., U.S.A.* 33°36N 85°51W **178** B4
Oxford *Mass., U.S.A.* 42°7N 71°52W **175** D13
Oxford *Miss., U.S.A.* 34°22N 89°31W **177** D10
Oxford *N.C., U.S.A.* 36°19N 78°35W **177** C15
Oxford *N.Y., U.S.A.* 42°27N 75°36W **175** D9
Oxford *Ohio, U.S.A.* 39°31N 84°45W **173** F11
Oxford L. *Canada* 54°51N 95°37W **163** C10
Oxfordshire □ *U.K.* 51°48N 1°16W **67** F6
Oxia *Greece* 38°18N 21°6E **98** C3
Oxie *Sweden* 55°33N 13°6E **63** J7
Oxílithos *Greece* 38°35N 24°7E **98** C6
Oxley *Australia* 34°11S 144°6E **152** C6
Oxley Wild Rivers △
   Australia 30°57S 152°12E **153** A10
Oxnard *U.S.A.* 34°12N 119°11W **171** L7
Oxsjövälen *Sweden* 62°34N 13°57E **62** B7
Oxus = Amudarya →
   Uzbekistan 43°58N 59°34E **108** C3
Oya *Malaysia* 2°55N 111°55E **118** D4
Oyama *Japan* 36°18N 139°48E **113** F9
Oyambre △ *Spain* 43°22N 4°21W **88** B6
Oyem *Gabon* 1°34N 11°31E **140** D2
Oyen *Canada* 51°22N 110°28W **163** C6
Oykel → *U.K.* 57°56N 4°26W **65** D4
Oymyakon *Russia* 63°25N 142°44E **107** C15
Oyo *Nigeria* 7°46N 3°56E **139** D5
Oyo *Sudan* 21°58N 36°10E **137** C4
Oyo □ *Nigeria* 8°15N 3°30E **139** D5
Oyón *Peru* 10°37S 76°47W **188** C2
Oyonnax *France* 46°16N 5°40E **71** F12
Oyster Bay *U.S.A.* 40°52N 73°32W **175** F11
Øyubari *Japan* 43°1N 142°5E **112** C11
Oyyl → *Kazakhstan* 49°4N 54°40E **108** C4
Özalp *Turkey* 38°39N 43°59E **105** C10
Ozamiz *Phil.* 8°15N 123°50E **119** C6
Ozar = Ojhar *India* 20°6N 73°56E **126** D1
Ozark *Ala., U.S.A.* 31°28N 85°39W **178** D4
Ozark *Ark., U.S.A.* 35°29N 93°50W **176** D8
Ozark *Mo., U.S.A.* 37°1N 93°12W **172** G7
Ozark Plateau *U.S.A.* 37°20N 91°40W **172** H8
Ozarks, L. of the *U.S.A.* 38°12N 92°38W **172** F7
Ožd *Hungary* 48°14N 20°15E **80** B5
Ozernyy *Russia* 51°30N 156°31E **107** D16
Ozernoye *Russia* 51°46N 51°28E **86** E11
Ozersk *Russia* 54°25N 22°0E **62** D8
Ozette, L. *U.S.A.* 48°6N 124°38W **170** B2
Ozieri *Italy* 40°35N 9°0E **94** B2
Ozimek *Poland* 50°41N 18°11E **83** H5
Ozona *U.S.A.* 30°43N 101°12W **176** F4
Ozorków *Poland* 51°57N 19°16E **83** G6
Ozren, Bos.-H. *Bos.-H.* 44°35N 18°20E **80** G3
Ozuluama *Mexico* 21°40N 97°51W **181** C5
Ozun *Romania* 45°47N 25°50E **81** E10
Ozurgeti *Georgia* 41°55N 42°0E **87** K5

P

Pa *Burkina Faso* 11°33N 3°19W **138** C4
Pa-an *Burma* 16°51N 97°40E **123** L20
Pa Mong Dam *Thailand* 18°0N 102°22E **120** D4
Pa Sak → *Thailand* 15°30N 101°0E **120** E3
Paamiut *Greenland* 62°0N 49°43W **57** E6
Paanayarvi △ *Russia* 66°16N 30°10E **60** C24
Paar → *Germany* 48°37N 10°56E **75** G7
Paarl *S. Africa* 33°45S 18°56E **144** D2
Pab Hills *Pakistan* 26°30N 66°45E **124** F2
Pabaidh = Pabbay *U.K.* 57°46N 7°14W **65** D1
Pabbay *U.K.* 57°46N 7°1W **65** D1
Pabianice *Poland* 51°40N 19°20E **83** G6
Pabna *Bangla.* 24°1N 89°18E **123** G16
Pabo *Uganda* 3°1N 32°10E **142** B3
Pacaipampa *Peru* 5°35S 79°39W **188** B2
Pacaja → *Brazil* 1°56S 50°50W **187** D8
Pacajus *Brazil* 4°10S 38°31W **189** A3
Pacaraima, Sa. *S. Amer.* 4°0N 62°30W **186** C6
Pacarán *Peru* 12°55S 76°42W **188** C2
Pacaraos *Peru* 11°12S 76°42W **188** C2
Pacasmayo *Peru* 7°20S 79°35W **188** B2
Pace *U.S.A.* 30°36N 87°10W **179** F2
Paceco *Italy* 37°59N 12°33E **94** E5
Pachacamac *Peru* 12°14S 77°53W **188** C2
Pachino *Italy* 36°43N 15°4E **95** F8
Pachino *Italy* 36°43N 15°5E **95** F8
Pachitea → *Peru* 8°46S 74°33W **188** B3
Pachiza *Peru* 7°16S 76°46W **188** B2
Pachmarhi *India* 22°28N 78°26E **125** H8
Pachnes *Greece* 35°16N 24°4E **101** D6
Pachora *India* 20°38N 75°29E **126** D2
Pachpadra *India* 25°58N 72°10E **124** G5
Pachuca *Mexico* 20°7N 98°44W **181** C5
Pacific Antarctic Ridge
   Pac. Oc. 43°0S 115°0W **55** B13
Pacific Grove *U.S.A.* 36°38N 121°56W **170** J5
Pacific Ocean 10°0N 140°0W **157** G14
Pacific Rim △ *Canada* 48°40N 124°45W **170** B2
Pacifica *U.S.A.* 37°37N 122°27W **170** H4
Pacitan *Indonesia* 8°12S 111°7E **119** H14
Packsaddle *Australia* 30°36S 141°58E **152** A4
Packwood *U.S.A.* 46°36N 121°40W **170** D5
Pacov *Czech Rep.* 49°27N 15°0E **78** B8
Pacui → *Brazil* 16°46S 45°1W **189** D1
Pacy-sur-Eure *France* 49°1N 1°23E **70** C8
Padaido, Kepulauan
   Indonesia 1°15S 136°30E **119** E9
Padampur *India* 20°59N 83°4E **126** D6
Padang *Riau, Indonesia* 1°30N 102°30E **121** M4
Padang *Sumatera Barat,
   Indonesia* 1°0S 100°20E **118** E2
Padang Endau
   Malaysia 2°40N 103°38E **121** L4
Padangpanjang
   Indonesia 0°40S 100°20E **118** E2
Padangsidempuan
   Indonesia 1°30N 99°15E **118** D1
Padborg *Denmark* 54°49N 9°21E **63** K3
Paddle Prairie *Canada* 57°57N 117°29W **162** B5
Paderborn *Germany* 51°42N 8°45E **76** D4
Paderoo *India* 18°5N 82°42E **126** E6
Padeş, Vf. *Romania* 45°40N 22°22E **80** E7
Padina *Romania* 44°50N 27°8E **81** F12
Padjelanta △ *Sweden* 67°20N 16°5E **60** C17
Padma *India* 24°12N 85°22E **125** G11
Pádova *Italy* 45°25N 11°53E **93** C8
Padra *India* 22°15N 73°7E **124** H5
Padrauna *India* 26°54N 83°59E **125** F10
Padre I. *U.S.A.* 27°10N 97°25W **176** H6
Padre Island △ *U.S.A.* 27°0N 97°25W **176** H6
Padrón *Spain* 42°41N 8°39W **88** C2
Padstow *U.K.* 50°33N 4°58W **67** G3
Padthaway *Australia* 36°35S 140°31E **152** D4
Padua = Pádova *Italy* 45°25N 11°53E **93** C8
Paducah *Ky., U.S.A.* 37°5N 88°37W **172** G9
Paducah *Tex., U.S.A.* 34°1N 100°18W **176** D4
Padukka *Sri Lanka* 6°50N 80°5E **127** L5
Padul *Spain* 37°2N 3°37W **89** H7
Padwa *India* 18°27N 82°47E **126** E6
Paea *Tahiti* 17°41S 149°35W **155** b
Paekakariki *N.Z.* 41°0S 174°56E **154** G4
Paektu-san *N. Korea* 41°59N 128°4E **115** D15
Paengaroa *N.Z.* 37°23S 176°29E **154** D5
Paeroa *N.Z.* 37°23S 175°41E **154** D5
Paesana *Italy* 44°41N 7°16E **92** D4
Pafúri *Mozam.* 22°28S 31°17E **145** B5
Pag *Croatia* 44°25N 15°3E **93** D12
Paga *Ghana* 11°1N 1°8W **139** C4
Pagadian *Phil.* 7°55N 123°30E **119** C6
Pagai Selatan, Pulau
   Indonesia 3°0S 100°15W **118** E2
Pagai Utara, Pulau
   Indonesia 2°35S 100°0E **118** E2
Pagalu = Annobón
   Atl. Oc. 1°25S 5°36E **133** G4
Pagan *Burma* 21°22N 80°1E **125** G9
Pagastikos Kolpos *Greece* 39°15S 23°0E **98** B5
Pagatan *Indonesia* 3°33S 115°59E **118** E5
Page *U.S.A.* 36°57N 111°27W **169** H8
Pagēgiai *Lithuania* 55°9N 21°57E **63** J8
Pagerungan Besar
   Indonesia 6°57S 115°59E **118** F5
Pago Pago *Amer. Samoa* 14°16S 170°43W **155** b
Pagosa Springs
   U.S.A. 37°16N 107°1W **169** H10
Pagri *China* 27°45N 89°10E **116** F6
Pagwa River *Canada* 50°2N 85°14W **164** B2
Pähala *U.S.A.* 19°12N 155°29W **182** J17
Pahang □ *Malaysia* 3°30N 102°45E **121** K4
Pahang → *Malaysia* 3°30N 103°9E **121** L4
Pahiatua *N.Z.* 40°27S 175°50E **154** G4
Pahokee *U.S.A.* 26°50N 80°40W **179** H9
Pahrump *U.S.A.* 36°12N 115°59W **171** J11
Pahute Mesa *U.S.A.* 37°20N 116°45W **171** H10
Pai *Thailand* 19°19N 98°27E **120** C2
Paicines *U.S.A.* 36°44N 121°17W **170** J5
Paide *Estonia* 58°53N 25°33E **84** C3
Paignton *U.K.* 50°26N 3°35W **67** G4
Paihia *N.Z.* 35°17S 174°6E **154** B3
Paiho *Taiwan* 23°10N 120°23E **117** F13
Paiján *Peru* 7°42S 79°20W **188** B2
Päijänne *Finland* 61°30N 25°30E **63** E22
Pailani *India* 25°45N 80°26E **125** G9
Pailin *Cambodia* 12°46N 102°36E **120** F4

Painan *Indonesia* 1°21S 100°34E **118** E2
Paine Grande, Cerro
   Chile 50°59S 73°4W **192** D2
Painesville *U.S.A.* 41°43N 81°15W **174** E3
Paint Hills = Wemindji
   Canada 53°0N 78°49W **164** B4
Paint L. *Canada* 55°28N 97°57W **163** B9
Painted Desert *U.S.A.* 36°0N 111°0W **169** H8
Paintsville *U.S.A.* 37°49N 82°48W **173** G12
País Vasco □ *Spain* 42°50N 2°45W **90** C2
Paisley *Canada* 44°18N 81°16W **174** B3
Paisley *U.K.* 55°50N 4°25W **65** F4
Paita *Peru* 5°11S 81°9W **188** B1
Paithan *India* 19°29N 75°23E **126** E2
Paiva → *Portugal* 41°4N 8°16W **88** D2
Paizhou *China* 30°12N 113°55E **117** F9
Pajares *Spain* 43°1N 5°46W **88** B5
Pajares, Puerto de *Spain* 42°58N 5°46W **88** C5
Pajęczno *Poland* 51°10N 19°0E **83** G5
Pak Lay *Laos* 18°15N 101°27E **120** C3
Pak Ou *Laos* 20°3N 102°12E **120** B4
Pak Phanang *Thailand* 8°21N 100°12E **121** H3
Pak Sane *Laos* 18°22N 103°39E **120** C4
Pak Song *Laos* 15°11N 106°14E **120** E6
Pak Suang *Laos* 19°58N 102°15E **116** H4
Pak Tam Chung *China* 22°24N 114°19E **111** a
Pak Thong Chai
   Thailand 14°43N 102°1E **120** E4
Pakala *India* 13°29N 79°8E **127** H4
Pakaur *India* 24°38N 87°51E **125** G12
Pakch'ŏn *N. Korea* 39°44N 125°35E **115** E13
Pakenham *Australia* 38°6S 145°30E **153** E6
Pakenham *Canada* 45°18N 76°18W **175** A8
Pakhuis *S. Africa* 32°9S 19°5E **144** D2
Pakistan ■ *Asia* 30°0N 70°0E **124** E5
Pakkading *Laos* 18°19N 103°59E **120** C4
Paklenica △ *Croatia* 44°20N 15°39E **93** D12
Pakokku *Burma* 21°20N 95°0E **123** J19
Pakość *Poland* 52°48N 18°6E **83** F5
Pakowki L. *Canada* 49°20N 111°0W **163** D6
Pakpattan *Pakistan* 30°25N 73°27E **124** D5
Pakrac *Croatia* 45°27N 17°12E **80** E2
Pakruojis *Lithuania* 55°58N 23°52E **82** C10
Paks *Hungary* 46°38N 18°55E **80** D3
Paktiä □ *Afghan.* 33°0N 69°15E **122** C6
Paktīkā □ *Afghan.* 32°30N 69°0E **122** C6
Pakwach *Uganda* 2°28N 31°27E **142** B3
Pakxe *Laos* 15°5N 105°52E **120** E5
Pal Lahara *India* 21°27N 85°11E **125** J11
Pala *Chad* 9°25N 15°5E **135** G8
Pala
   Dem. Rep. of the Congo 6°45S 29°30E **142** D2
Pala *U.S.A.* 33°22N 117°5W **171** M9
Palabek *Uganda* 3°22N 32°33E **142** B3
Palacios *U.S.A.* 28°42N 96°13W **176** G6
Palafrugell *Spain* 41°55N 3°10E **90** D8
Palagiano *Italy* 40°35N 17°2E **95** B10
Palagonía *Italy* 37°19N 14°45E **95** E7
Palagruža *Croatia* 42°24N 16°15E **93** F13
Palaiseau *France* 48°42N 2°14E **71** D9
Palakkad *India* 10°46N 76°42E **127** J3
Palakol *India* 16°31N 81°46E **127** F5
Palalankwe *India* 10°52N 92°29E **127** J11
Palam *India* 19°0N 77°0E **126** E3
Palamás *Greece* 39°26N 22°1E **98** B4
Palamós *Spain* 41°50N 3°10E **90** D8
Palampur *India* 32°10N 76°30E **124** C7
Palamut *Turkey* 38°59N 27°41E **99** C9
Palana *Australia* 39°45S 147°55E **151** F4
Palana *Russia* 59°10N 159°59E **107** D16
Palanan *Phil.* 17°8N 122°29E **119** A6
Palanan Pt. *Phil.* 17°17N 122°30E **119** A6
Palandri *Pakistan* 33°42N 73°40E **124** C5
Palanga *Lithuania* 55°58N 21°3E **63** J8
Palangkaraya *Indonesia* 2°16S 113°56E **118** E4
Palani *India* 10°30N 77°30E **127** J3
Palani Hills *India* 10°14N 77°33E **127** J3
Palanpur *India* 24°10N 72°25E **124** G5
Palapye *Botswana* 22°30S 27°7E **144** B4
Palar → *India* 12°27N 80°13E **127** H5
Palas de Rei *Spain* 42°52N 7°52W **88** C3
Palasponga *India* 21°47N 85°34E **125** J11
Palatka *Russia* 60°6N 150°54E **107** C16
Palatka *U.S.A.* 29°39N 81°38W **178** F14
Palau ■ *Palau* 7°30N 134°30E **156** G5
Palauk *Burma* 13°10N 98°40E **120** F2
Palaw *Burma* 12°58N 98°39E **120** F2
Palawan *Phil.* 9°30N 118°30E **118** C5
Palayankottai *India* 8°45N 77°45E **127** K3
Palazzo, Pte. *France* 42°28N 8°30E **73** E12
Palazzo San Gervásio
   Italy 40°53N 15°59E **95** B8
Palazzolo Acréide *Italy* 37°4N 14°54E **95** E7
Palca *Chile* 19°45S 69°9W **188** G5
Paldiski *Estonia* 59°23N 24°9E **84** C2
Pale *Bos.-H.* 43°50N 18°38E **80** G3
Palekastro *Greece* 35°12N 26°15E **101** D8
Paleleh *Indonesia* 1°10N 121°50E **119** D6
Palembang *Indonesia* 3°0S 104°50E **118** E2
Palena → *Chile* 43°55S 71°40W **192** B2
Palena, L. *Chile* 43°55S 71°40W **192** B2
Palencia *Spain* 42°1N 4°34W **88** C6
Palencia □ *Spain* 42°31N 4°33W **88** C6
Palenque *Mexico* 17°39N 91°58W **182** D6
Paleochora *Greece* 35°16N 23°39E **101** D5
Paleokastrítsa *Greece* 39°40N 19°41E **98** B1
Paleometokho *Cyprus* 35°7N 33°11E **101** D12
Paleopoli *Greece* 37°49N 24°50E **98** D6
Palermo *Italy* 38°7N 13°22E **94** D6
Palermo *U.S.A.* 39°26N 121°33W **170** F5
Palermo × (PMO) *Italy* 38°10N 13°5E **94** D6
Paleros *Greece* 38°47N 20°53E **98** C2
Palestina *Chile* 23°10S 69°0W **190** A2
Palestine *Asia* 32°0N 35°0E **130** D4
Paletwa *Burma* 21°10N 92°50E **123** J18
Palghat = Palakkad
   India 10°46N 76°42E **127** J3
Palgrave, Mt.
   Australia 23°22S 115°58E **148** D2
Pali *India* 25°50N 73°20E **124** G5
Pali-Aike △ *Chile* 52°6S 69°44W **192** D3
Palikir *Micronesia* 6°55N 158°9E **156** G7
Palinuro *Italy* 40°3N 15°16E **95** B7
Palinuro, C. *Italy* 40°2N 15°16E **95** B7
Paliouri, Akra *Greece* 39°57N 23°45E **96** G7

Palisades Res. *U.S.A.* 43°20N 111°12W **168** E8
Paliseul *Belgium* 49°54N 5°8E
Palitana *India* 21°32N 71°49E
Palizada *Mexico* 18°15N 92°5W
Palk Bay *Asia* 9°30N 79°15E
Palk Strait *Asia* 10°0N 79°45E
Palkānah *Iraq* 35°49N 44°26E
Palkonda *India* 18°36N 83°48E
Palkonda Ra. *India* 13°50N 79°20E
Palkot *India* 22°53N 84°39E
Pallanza = Verbánia
   Italy 45°56N 8°33E
Pallarenda *Australia* 19°12S 146°46E
Pallas-Yllästunturi △
   Finland 68°8N 24°15E
Palleru → *India* 16°45N 80°2E
Pallès, Bishti i *Albania* 41°24N 19°24E
Pallinup → *Australia* 34°27S 118°50E
Pallisa *Uganda* 1°12N 33°43E
Palliser, C. *N.Z.* 41°26S 175°5E
Palliser B. *N.Z.* 41°26S 175°5E
Pallu *India* 28°59N 74°14E
Palm Bay *U.S.A.* 28°2N 80°35W
Palm Beach *U.S.A.* 26°43N 80°2W
Palm Coast *U.S.A.* 29°35N 81°12W
Palm Desert *U.S.A.* 33°43N 116°22W
Palm-Grove △
   Australia 24°57S 149°21E
Palm Harbor *U.S.A.* 28°5N 82°46W
Palm Is. *Australia* 18°40S 146°35E
Palm Springs *U.S.A.* 33°50N 116°33W
Palm Valley *U.S.A.* 30°11N 81°23W
Palma *Mozam.* 10°46S 40°29E
Palma → *Brazil* 12°33S 47°52W
Palma, B. de *Spain* 39°30N 2°39E
Palma de Mallorca
   Spain 39°35N 2°39E
Palma de Mallorca × (PMI)
   Spain 39°33N 2°44E
Palma del Río *Spain* 37°43N 5°17W
Palma di Montechiaro
   Italy 37°11N 13°46E
Palma Nova = Palmanova
   Spain 39°32N 2°34E
Palma Soriano *Cuba* 20°15N 76°0W
Palmanova *Spain* 39°32N 2°34E
Palmaner *India* 13°12N 78°45E
Palmanova *Italy* 45°54N 13°19E
Palmares *Brazil* 8°41S 35°28W
Palmarola *Italy* 40°57N 12°50E
Palmas *Paraná, Brazil* 26°29S 52°0W
Palmas *Tocantins, Brazil* 10°13S 48°16W
Pálmas, C. *Liberia* 4°27N 7°46W
Pálmas, G. di *Italy* 39°0N 8°30E
Palmas de Monte Alto
   Brazil 14°16S 43°10W
Palmdale *Calif., U.S.A.* 34°35N 118°7W
Palmdale *Fla., U.S.A.* 26°57N 81°19W
Palmeira das Missões
   Brazil 27°55S 53°17W
Palmeira dos Índios
   Brazil 9°25S 36°37W
Palmeirais *Brazil* 6°0S 43°0W
Palmeiras → *Brazil* 12°31S 41°34W
Palmeiras → *Brazil* 12°2S 48°48W
Palmela *Portugal* 38°32N 8°57W
Palmer *Antarctica* 64°3S 64°0W
Palmer *U.S.A.* 61°36N 149°7W
Palmer → *Australia* 16°0S 142°26E
Palmer Arch. *Antarctica* 64°15S 65°0W
Palmer Lake *U.S.A.* 39°7N 104°55W
Palmer Land *Antarctica* 73°0S 63°0W
Palmerston *Australia* 12°31S 130°59E
Palmerston *Canada* 43°50N 80°51W
Palmerston *N.Z.* 45°29S 170°43E
Palmerston North
   N.Z. 40°21S 175°39E
Palmerton *U.S.A.* 40°48N 75°37W
Palmetto *Fla., U.S.A.* 27°31N 82°34W
Palmetto *Ga., U.S.A.* 33°31N 84°40W
Palmi *Italy* 38°21N 15°51E
Palmira *Argentina* 32°59S 68°34W
Palmira *Colombia* 3°32N 76°16W
Palmyra = Tudmur
   Syria 34°36N 38°15E
Palmyra *Mo., U.S.A.* 39°48N 91°32W
Palmyra *N.J., U.S.A.* 40°0N 75°1W
Palmyra *N.Y., U.S.A.* 43°5N 77°18W
Palmyra Is. *Pac. Oc.* 5°52N 162°5W
Palmyras Pt. *India* 20°46N 87°11E
Palo Alto *U.S.A.* 37°27N 122°10W
Palo Seco *Trin. & Tob.* 10°4N 61°36W
Palo Verde *U.S.A.* 33°26N 114°44W
Palo Verde △
   Costa Rica 10°21N 85°21W
Palomar Mt. *U.S.A.* 33°22N 116°50W
Palopo *Indonesia* 3°0S 120°16E
Palos, C. de *Spain* 37°38N 0°40W
Palos de la Frontera
   Spain 37°14N 6°53W
Palos Verdes, Pt.
   U.S.A. 33°46N 118°23W
Palos Verdes Estates
   U.S.A. 33°48N 118°23W
Palpa *Peru* 14°30S 75°15W
Pålsboda *Sweden* 59°3N 15°22E
Palu *Indonesia* 1°0S 119°52E
Palu *Turkey* 38°45N 40°0E
Paluke *Liberia* 5°23N 8°5W
Paluma Ra. *Australia* 19°9S 146°22E
Paluzza *Italy* 46°32N 13°0E
Palwal *India* 28°8N 77°19E
Pama *Burkina Faso* 11°19N 0°44E
Pama □ *Burkina Faso* 11°27N 0°40E
Pamanukan *Indonesia* 6°16S 107°49E
Pamban I. *India* 9°15N 79°20E
Pamekasan *Indonesia* 7°10S 113°28E
Pamenang *Indonesia* 8°24S 116°6E
Pamiers *France* 43°7N 1°39E
Pamir *Tajikistan* 37°40N 73°0E
Pamlico → *U.S.A.* 35°20N 76°28W
Pamlico Sd. *U.S.A.* 35°20N 76°0W
Pampa *U.S.A.* 35°32N 100°58W
Pampa de Agma
   Argentina 43°45S 69°40W
Pampa de las Salinas
   Argentina 32°1S 66°58W
Pampa Hermosa *Peru* 7°7S 75°41W
Pampanua *Indonesia* 4°16S 120°8E
Pampas *Argentina* 35°0S 63°0W

pas Peru 12°20S 74°50W 188 C3
pas → Peru 13°24S 73°12W 188 C3
phylia Turkey 37°0N 31°20E 104 D4
plona Colombia 7°23N 72°39W 186 B4
plona-Iruña Spain 42°48N 1°38W 90 C3
poenpoort S. Africa 31°3S 22°40E 144 D3
ukçu Turkey 39°30N 27°54E 99 B9
ukkale Turkey 37°55N 29°8E 99 D11
de Azúcar Chile 24°5S 68°10W 190 A2
de Azúcar △ Chile 26°0S 70°40W 190 B1
Xian China 25°46N 104°38E 116 E5
a U.S.A. 39°23N 89°5W 172 F9
aca U.S.A. 37°47N 114°23W 169 H6
acea U.S.A. 30°2N 84°23W 178 E5
adura Sri Lanka 6°47N 79°53E 127 L4
agyurishte Bulgaria 42°30N 24°15E 97 D8
aitan Indonesia 6°36S 105°12E 119 G11
aji India 15°25N 73°50E 127 G1
amá Panama 9°0N 79°25W 182 E4
ama Sri Lanka 6°45N 81°48E 127 L5
ama ■ Cent. Amer. 8°48N 79°55W 182 E4
amá, G. de Panama 8°4N 79°20W 182 E4
ama, Isthmus of
nt. Amer. 9°0N 79°0W 182 E4
ama Basin Pac. Oc. 5°0N 83°30W 157 G19
ama Canal Panama 9°10N 79°37W 182 E4
ama City U.S.A. 30°10N 85°40W 178 E4
ama City Beach
S.A. 30°11N 85°48W 178 E4
amint Range
S.A. 36°20N 117°20W 171 J9
amint Springs
S.A. 36°20N 117°28W 171 J9
ão Peru 9°55S 75°55W 188 B2
are Thailand 6°51N 101°30E 121 J3
area Italy 38°38N 15°4E 95 D8
aro → Italy 44°55N 11°25E 93 D8
ay Phil. 11°10N 122°30E 119 B6
ay G. Phil. 11°0N 122°30E 119 B6
čevo Serbia 44°52N 20°41E 80 F5
ch'iao Taiwan 25°1N 121°27E 117 E13
ciu Romania 45°54N 27°8E 81 E12
corbo, Desfiladero
ain 42°32N 3°5W 88 C7
cota Romania 46°20N 21°45E 80 D6
da Mozam. 24°2S 34°45E 145 B5
dan Malaysia 1°32N 103°46E 121 d
dan Phil. 11°45N 122°10E 119 B6
dan, Selat Singapore 1°15N 103°44E 121 d
dan Tampoi = Tampoi
alaysia 1°30N 103°39E 121 d
degelang Indonesia 6°25S 106°5E 119 G12
dhana India 21°42N 76°13E 124 J7
dharkawada India 20°1N 78°32E 126 D4
dharpur India 17°41N 75°20E 126 F2
dhurna India 21°36N 78°35E 126 D4
do Uruguay 34°44S 56°0W 191 C4
do □ Bolivia 11°20S 67°40W 188 C4
do, L. = Hope, L.
stralia 28°24S 139°18E 151 D2
dokratoras Greece 39°45N 19°50E 101 A3
dora Costa Rica 9°43N 83°3W 182 E3
drup Denmark 57°14N 9°40E 63 G3
evéggio-Pale di San
artino ⌓ Italy 46°14N 11°46E 93 B8
evėžys Lithuania 55°42N 24°25E 84 E3
filovo Russia 50°25N 42°46E 86 E6
g Sida △ Thailand 14°5N 102°17E 120 E4
ga
m. Rep. of the Congo 1°52N 26°18E 142 B2
gaíon Óros Greece 40°50N 24°0E 97 F8
gandaran
donesia 7°40S 108°39E 119 G13
gandaran △
donesia 7°43S 108°42E 119 G13
gani Tanzania 5°25S 38°58E 142 D4
gani → Tanzania 5°26S 38°58E 142 D4
gar Djeréme ⌓
meroon 5°50N 13°10E 139 D7
gfou = Bengbu
ina 32°58N 117°20E 117 A11
gga, Tanjung
donesia 8°54S 116°2E 119 K19
ghsang = Bangkang
rma 22°4N 99°1E 116 F2
gil
m. Rep. of the Congo 3°10S 26°35E 142 C2
gjiabu China 40°38N 115°26E 114 D8
gkah, Tanjung
donesia 6°51S 112°33E 119 G15
gkai Burma 22°49N 98°39E 116 F2
gkajene Indonesia 4°46S 119°34E 119 E5
gkalanbrandan
donesia 4°1N 98°20E 118 D1
gkalanbuun
donesia 2°41S 111°37E 118 E4
gkalpinang
donesia 2°10S 106°10E 118 E3
gkor, Pulau
alaysia 4°13N 100°34E 121 K3
gniqtuuq = Pangnirtung
nada 66°8N 65°43W 161 D18
gnirtung Canada 66°8N 65°43W 161 D18
gody Russia 65°52N 74°27E 106 C8
gong Tso = Bangong Co
ina 33°45N 78°43E 125 C8
guipulli Chile 39°38S 72°20W 192 A2
guitch U.S.A. 37°50N 112°26W 169 H7
gutaran Group
il. 6°18N 120°34E 119 C6
hala India 16°49N 74°7E 126 F2
handle U.S.A. 35°21N 101°23W 176 D4
Mines India 22°29N 73°50E 124 H5
a-Mutombo
m. Rep. of the Congo 5°11S 23°51E 142 D1
kota I. India 20°46N 71°21E 124 J4
pat India 29°25N 77°2E 124 E7
akent Tajikistan 39°29N 67°37E 109 E7
al Range = Pir Panjal Range
dia 32°30N 76°50E 124 C7
gur Pakistan 27°0N 64°5E 122 F4
hra → India 21°13N 74°57E 126 D2
im = Panaji India 15°25N 73°50E 127 G1
in China 41°3N 122°2E 115 D12
nad → Pakistan 28°57N 70°30E 124 E4
nad Barrage
kistan 29°22N 71°15E 124 E4
shīr □ Afghan. 35°50N 69°45E 109 E7
wai Afghan. 31°26N 65°27E 124 D1
kisi Gorge = Pankisis Kheoba
orgia 42°7N 45°15E 87 J7

Pankisis Kheoba Georgia 42°7N 45°15E 87 J7
Pankshin Nigeria 9°16N 9°25E 139 D6
Panmunjŏm N. Korea 37°59N 126°38E 115 F14
Panna India 24°40N 80°15E 125 G9
Panna △ India 24°40N 80°0E 125 G8
Panna Hills India 24°40N 81°15E 125 G9
Pannawonica Australia 21°39S 116°19E 148 D2
Pano Akil Pakistan 27°51N 69°7E 124 F3
Pano Lefkara Cyprus 34°53N 33°20E 101 E12
Pano Panayia Cyprus 34°55N 32°38E 101 E11
Panorama Brazil 21°21S 51°51W 191 A5
Panormos Greece 35°25N 24°41E 101 D6
Panruti India 11°46N 79°35E 127 J4
Pansemal India 21°39N 74°42E 124 J6
Panshan = Panjin China 41°3N 122°2E 115 D12
Panshi China 42°58N 126°5E 115 C14
Pantanal Brazil 17°30S 57°40W 186 H7
Pantanos de Centla ⌓ Mexico 18°25N 92°25W 181 D6
Pantar Indonesia 8°28S 124°10E 119 F6
Pante Macassar E. Timor 9°30S 123°58E 119 F6
Pantelleria Italy 36°50N 11°57E 94 F4
Pantón = O Castro de Ferreira Spain 42°31N 7°37W 88 C3
Pánuco Mexico 22°3N 98°10W 181 C5
Panvel India 18°59N 73°4E 126 E1
Panyam Nigeria 9°27N 9°8E 139 D6
Panyu China 23°1N 113°21E 117 F9
Panzhihua China 26°33N 101°44E 116 D3
Páola Italy 39°21N 16°2E 95 C9
Paola Malta 35°52N 14°30E 101 D2
Paola U.S.A. 38°35N 94°53W 172 F6
Paonia U.S.A. 38°52N 107°36W 168 G10
Paoting = Baoding China 38°50N 115°28E 114 E8
Paot'ou = Baotou China 40°32N 110°2E 114 D6
Paoua C.A.R. 7°9N 16°20E 140 C3
Pápa Hungary 47°22N 17°30E 80 C2
Papa Stour U.K. 60°20N 1°42W 65 A7
Papa Westray U.K. 59°20N 2°55W 65 B6
Papagayo → Mexico 16°46N 99°43W 181 D5
Papagayo, G. de Costa Rica 10°30N 85°50W 182 D2
Papagni → India 15°35N 77°45E 127 G3
Papakura N.Z. 37°4S 174°59E 154 D3
Papantla Mexico 20°27N 97°19W 181 C5
Papar Malaysia 5°45N 116°0E 118 C5
Papara Tahiti 17°43S 149°31W 155 b
Paparoa N.Z. 36°6S 174°16E 154 C3
Paparoa △ N.Z. 42°7S 171°26E 155 C6
Paparoa Ra. N.Z. 42°5S 171°35E 155 C6
Papas, Akra Greece 38°13N 21°20E 98 C3
Papatoetoe N.Z. 36°59S 174°51E 154 C3
Papeete Tahiti 17°32S 149°34W 155 b
Papenburg Germany 53°5N 7°23E 76 B3
Papenoo Tahiti 17°30S 149°25W 155 b
Papenoo → Tahiti 17°30S 149°25W 155 b
Paphlagonia Turkey 41°30N 33°0E 104 B5
Paphos Cyprus 34°46N 32°25E 101 E11
Papikio Oros Greece 41°15N 25°13E 97 E9
Paposo Chile 25°0S 70°30W 190 B1
Papoutsa Cyprus 34°54N 33°4E 101 E12
Papua □ Indonesia 4°0S 137°0E 119 E9
Papua, G. of Papua N. G. 9°0S 144°50E 147 B7
Papua New Guinea ■ Oceania 8°0S 145°0E 147 B7
Papudo Chile 32°29S 71°27W 190 C1
Papuk Croatia 45°30N 17°30E 80 E2
Papun Burma 18°2N 97°30E 123 K20
Papunya Australia 23°15S 131°54E 148 D5
Pará = Belém Brazil 1°20S 48°30W 187 D9
Pará □ Brazil 3°20S 52°0W 187 D8
Paraburdoo Australia 23°14S 117°32E 148 D2
Paracas, Pen. de Peru 13°53S 76°20W 188 C2
Paracatu Brazil 17°10S 46°50W 189 D1
Paracatu → Brazil 16°30S 45°4W 189 D1
Paracel Is. S. China Sea 15°50N 112°0E 118 A4
Parachilna Australia 31°10S 138°21E 152 A3
Parachinar Pakistan 33°55N 70°5E 124 C4
Paraćin Serbia 43°54N 21°27E 96 C5
Paracuru Brazil 3°24S 39°4W 189 A3
Parada, Punta Peru 15°22S 75°11W 188 D2
Paradas Spain 37°18N 5°29W 89 H5
Paradela Spain 42°44N 7°37W 88 C3
Paradip India 20°15N 86°35E 126 D8
Paradise Calif., U.S.A. 39°46N 121°37W 170 F5
Paradise Nev., U.S.A. 36°5N 115°8W 171 J11
Paradise → Canada 53°27N 57°19W 165 B8
Paradise Hill Canada 53°32N 109°28W 163 C7
Paradise River Canada 53°27N 57°17W 165 B8
Paradise Valley U.S.A. 41°30N 117°32W 168 F5
Paradisi Greece 36°18N 28°7E 101 C10
Paragould U.S.A. 36°3N 90°29W 177 C9
Paragua → Venezuela 6°55N 62°55W 186 B6
Paraguaçú → Brazil 12°45S 38°54W 189 C3
Paraguaçu Paulista Brazil 22°22S 50°35W 191 A5
Paraguaná, Pen. de Venezuela 12°0N 70°0W 186 A5
Paraguarí Paraguay 25°36S 57°0W 190 B4
Paraguarí □ Paraguay 26°0S 57°10W 190 B4
Paraguay ■ S. Amer. 23°0S 57°0W 190 A4
Paraguay → Paraguay 27°18S 58°38W 190 B4
Paraíba = João Pessoa Brazil 7°10S 34°52W 189 B4
Paraíba □ Brazil 7°0S 36°0W 189 B3
Paraíba do Sul → Brazil 21°37S 41°3W 191 A7
Paraíso Mexico 18°24N 93°14W 181 D6
Parak Iran 27°38N 52°25E 129 E7
Parakhino Paddubye Russia 58°26N 33°10E 84 C7
Parakou Benin 9°25N 2°40E 139 D5
Parakylia Australia 30°24S 136°25E 152 A2
Paralimni Cyprus 35°2N 33°58E 101 D12
Paralio Astros Greece 37°25N 22°45E 98 D4
Paralkote India 19°47N 80°41E 126 E5
Paramaribo Suriname 5°50N 55°10W 187 B7
Parambu Brazil 6°13S 40°43W 189 B2
Paramirim Brazil 13°26S 42°15W 189 C2
Paramirim → Brazil 11°34S 43°18W 189 C2
Paramithia Greece 39°30N 20°35E 98 B2
Paramonga Peru 10°40S 77°50W 188 C2
Páramos del Batallón y La Negra △ Venezuela 8°2N 71°55W 183 E5

Paramushir, Ostrov Russia 50°24N 156°0E 107 D16
Paran → Israel 30°20N 35°10E 130 E4
Paraná Argentina 31°45S 60°30W 190 C3
Paraná Brazil 12°30S 47°48W 189 C1
Paraná □ Brazil 24°30S 51°0W 191 A5
Paraná → Argentina 33°43S 59°15W 190 C4
Paraná → Brazil 12°30S 48°14W 189 C1
Paranaguá Brazil 25°30S 48°30W 191 B6
Paranaíba Brazil 19°40S 51°11W 187 G8
Paranaíba → Brazil 20°6S 51°4W 187 H8
Paranapanema → Brazil 22°40S 53°9W 191 A5
Paranapiacaba, Serra do Brazil 24°31S 48°35W 191 A6
Paranavaí Brazil 23°4S 52°56W 191 A5
Parang Maguindanao, Phil. 7°23N 124°16E 119 C6
Parang Sulu, Phil. 5°55N 120°54E 119 C6
Parangippettai India 11°30N 79°38E 127 J4
Parângul Mare, Vf. Romania 45°20N 23°37E 81 E8
Paranthan Sri Lanka 9°26N 80°24E 127 K5
Paraparaumu N.Z. 40°57S 175°3E 154 G4
Paraspori, Akra Greece 35°55N 27°15E 99 F9
Paratinga Brazil 12°40S 43°10W 189 C2
Paratoo Australia 32°42S 139°20E 152 B3
Parauapebas Brazil 6°4S 49°54W 187 E9
Paray-le-Monial France 46°27N 4°7E 71 F11
Parbati → Mad. P., India 25°50N 76°30E 124 G7
Parbati → Raj., India 26°54N 77°53E 124 F7
Parbhani India 19°8N 76°52E 126 E3
Parchim Germany 53°26N 11°52E 76 B7
Parczew Poland 51°40N 22°52E 83 G9
Pardes Hanna-Karkur Israel 32°28N 34°57E 130 C3
Pardilla Spain 41°33N 3°43W 88 D7
Pardo → Bahia, Brazil 15°40S 39°0W 189 D3
Pardo → Mato Grosso, Brazil 21°46S 52°9W 191 A5
Pardo → Minas Gerais, Brazil 15°48S 44°48W 189 D2
Pardoo Roadhouse Australia 20°6S 119°3E 148 D2
Pardubice Czech Rep. 50°3N 15°45E 78 A8
Pardubický □ Czech Rep. 49°50N 16°0E 78 B8
Pare Indonesia 7°43S 112°12E 119 G15
Pare Mts. Tanzania 4°0S 37°45E 142 C4
Parecis, Serra dos Brazil 13°0S 60°0W 186 F7
Paredes de Nava Spain 42°9N 4°42W 88 C6
Parelhas Brazil 6°41S 36°39W 189 B3
Paren Russia 62°30N 163°15E 107 C17
Parenda India 18°16N 75°28E 126 E2
Parengarenga Harbour N.Z. 34°31S 173°0E 154 A2
Parent Canada 47°55N 74°35W 164 C5
Parent, L. Canada 48°31N 77°1W 164 C4
Parentis-en-Born France 44°21N 1°4W 72 D2
Parepare Indonesia 4°0S 119°40E 119 E5
Parfino Russia 57°59N 31°34E 84 D6
Parga Greece 39°15N 20°29E 98 B2
Pargas = Länsi-Turunmaa Finland 60°18N 22°18E 84 B2
Pargi India 17°11N 77°53E 126 E3
Pargo, Pta. do Madeira 32°49N 17°17W 100 D2
Parham Canada 44°39N 76°43W 175 B8
Paria → U.S.A. 36°52N 111°36W 169 H8
Paria, G. de Venezuela 10°30N 61°40W 187 K14
Pariaguán Venezuela 8°51N 64°34W 186 B6
Paricutín, Cerro Mexico 19°28N 102°15W 180 D4
Parigi Indonesia 0°50S 120°5E 119 E6
Parika Guyana 6°50N 58°20W 186 B7
Parikia Greece 37°6N 25°11E 99 D7
Parikkala Finland 61°33N 29°31E 84 B5
Parima, Serra Brazil 2°30N 64°0W 186 C6
Parinari Peru 4°35S 74°25W 188 A3
Pariñas, Pta. Peru 4°30S 82°0W 188 A1
Parincea Romania 46°27N 27°9E 81 D12
Paringa Australia 34°10S 140°46E 152 C4
Parintins Brazil 2°40S 56°50W 187 D7
Pariparit Kyun Burma 14°52N 93°41E 127 G11
Paris Canada 43°12N 80°25W 174 C4
Paris France 48°53N 2°20E 71 D9
Paris Idaho, U.S.A. 42°14N 111°24W 168 E8
Paris Ky., U.S.A. 38°13N 84°15W 173 F11
Paris Tenn., U.S.A. 36°18N 88°19W 177 C10
Paris Tex., U.S.A. 33°40N 95°33W 176 E7
Paris, Ville de □ France 48°50N 2°20E 71 D9
Paris Charles de Gaulle ✈ (CDG) France 49°0N 2°32E 71 D9
Paris Orly ✈ (ORY) France 48°44N 2°23E 71 D9
Parish U.S.A. 43°25N 76°8W 175 C8
Parishville U.S.A. 44°38N 74°49W 175 B10
Pariti Indonesia 10°1S 123°45E 148 B3
Park U.S.A. 48°45N 122°18W 170 B4
Park City U.S.A. 37°48N 97°20W 172 G5
Park Falls U.S.A. 45°56N 90°27W 172 C8
Park Head Canada 44°36N 81°9W 174 B3
Park Hills U.S.A. 37°51N 90°51W 172 G8
Park Range U.S.A. 40°41N 106°41W 168 F10
Park Rapids U.S.A. 46°55N 95°4W 172 B6
Park River U.S.A. 48°24N 97°45W 172 A5
Park Rynie S. Africa 30°25S 30°45E 145 D5
Parkā Bandar Iran 25°55N 59°35E 129 E8
Parkal India 18°12N 79°43E 126 E4
Parkano Finland 62°1N 23°0E 84 A2
Parkent Uzbekistan 41°18N 69°40E 109 D7
Parker Ariz., U.S.A. 34°9N 114°17W 171 L12
Parker Pa., U.S.A. 41°5N 79°41W 174 E5
Parker Dam U.S.A. 34°18N 114°8W 171 L12
Parkersburg U.S.A. 39°16N 81°34W 173 F13
Parkes Australia 33°9S 148°11E 153 B8
Parkfield U.S.A. 35°54N 120°26W 170 K6
Parkhill Canada 43°15N 81°38W 174 C3
Parkland U.S.A. 47°9N 122°26W 170 C4
Parkston U.S.A. 43°24N 97°59W 172 D5
Parksville Canada 49°20N 124°21W 162 D4
Parkway U.S.A. 38°32N 121°26W 170 G5
Parla Spain 40°14N 3°46W 88 E7
Parlakimidi India 18°45N 84°5E 126 E7
Parli India 18°50N 76°35E 126 E3
Pârliţa Moldova 47°19N 27°52E 81 C12
Parma Italy 44°48N 10°20E 92 D7
Parma Idaho, U.S.A. 43°47N 116°57W 168 E5
Parma Ohio, U.S.A. 41°24N 81°43W 174 E3
Parma → Italy 44°56N 10°26E 92 D7
Parnaguá Brazil 10°10S 44°38W 189 C2
Parnaíba Brazil 2°54S 41°47W 189 A2

Parnaíba → Brazil 3°0S 41°50W 189 A2
Parnamirim Pernambuco, Brazil 8°5S 39°34W 189 B3
Parnamirim Rio Grande do N., Brazil 5°55S 35°15W 189 B3
Parnarama Brazil 5°31S 43°6W 189 B2
Parnassos Greece 38°35N 22°30E 98 C4
Parnassus N.Z. 42°42S 173°23E 155 C8
Parndana Australia 35°48S 137°12E 152 C2
Parner India 19°0N 74°26E 126 E2
Parnitha Greece 38°14N 23°45E 98 C5
Parnitha △ Greece 38°12N 23°44E 98 C5
Parnonas Oros Greece 37°15N 22°45E 98 D4
Pärnu Estonia 58°28N 24°33E 84 C3
Pärnu → Estonia 58°28N 24°33E 84 C3
Paro Dzong Bhutan 27°32N 89°53E 125 F13
Parola India 20°47N 75°7E 126 D2
Paroo → Australia 31°28S 143°32E 152 A5
Paros Greece 37°5N 25°12E 99 D7
Parowan U.S.A. 37°51N 112°50W 169 H7
Parpaillon France 44°30N 6°40E 73 D10
Parral Chile 36°10S 71°52W 190 D1
Parramatta Australia 33°48S 151°1E 153 B9
Parras Mexico 25°25N 102°11W 180 B4
Parrett → U.K. 51°12N 3°1W 67 F4
Parris I. U.S.A. 32°20N 80°41W 178 C9
Parrish U.S.A. 27°35N 82°26W 179 H7
Parrott U.S.A. 31°54N 84°31W 178 D5
Parrsboro Canada 45°30N 64°25W 165 C7
Parry Channel Canada 74°15N 94°0W 161 C13
Parry I. Canada 45°18N 80°10W 174 A4
Parry Is. Canada 77°0N 110°0W 161 B10
Parry Sound Canada 45°20N 80°0W 174 A5
Parsābād Iran 39°39N 47°50E 105 C12
Parsaloi Kenya 1°16N 36°51E 142 B4
Parsberg Germany 49°10N 11°43E 77 F7
Parsęta → Poland 54°11N 15°34E 82 D2
Parsnip → Canada 55°10N 123°2W 162 B4
Parsons U.S.A. 37°20N 95°16W 172 G6
Parsons Ra. Australia 13°30S 135°15E 150 A2
Partabpur India 20°0N 80°42E 126 E5
Partanna Italy 37°43N 12°53E 94 E5
Partenio ⌓ Italy 40°56N 14°38E 95 B7
Parthenay France 46°38N 0°16W 70 F6
Partinico Italy 38°3N 13°7E 94 D6
Partizansk Russia 43°8N 133°9E 107 E14
Partizánske Slovak Rep. 48°38N 18°23E 79 C11
Partridge I. Canada 55°59N 87°37W 164 A2
Partry Mts. Ireland 53°40N 9°28W 64 C2
Partur India 19°40N 76°14E 126 E3
Paru → Brazil 1°33S 52°38W 187 D8
Parur India 10°13N 76°14E 127 J3
Paruro Peru 13°45S 71°50W 188 C3
Parvān □ Afghan. 35°0N 69°0E 109 F7
Parvatipuram India 18°50N 83°25E 126 E6
Parvatsar India 26°52N 74°49E 124 F6
Påryd Sweden 56°34N 15°55E 63 H9
Parys S. Africa 26°52S 27°29E 144 C4
Pas, Pta. des Spain 38°46N 1°26E 100 C7
Pas, The Canada 53°45N 101°15W 163 C8
Pas-de-Calais □ France 50°30N 2°10E 71 B9
Pasada Spain 43°23N 5°40W 88 B5
Pasadena Canada 49°1N 57°36W 165 C8
Pasadena Calif., U.S.A. 34°9N 118°8W 171 L8
Pasadena Tex., U.S.A. 29°43N 95°13W 176 G7
Pasaje → Argentina 25°39S 63°56W 190 B3
Paşalimanı Turkey 40°29N 27°36E 97 F11
Pasar Indonesia 8°27S 114°54E 119 J17
Pasargadae Iran 30°11N 53°10E 129 D7
Pascagoula U.S.A. 30°21N 88°33W 177 F10
Pascagoula → U.S.A. 30°23N 88°37W 177 F10
Paşcani Romania 47°14N 26°45E 81 C11
Paschimbanga □ India 23°0N 88°0E 125 H13
Pasco U.S.A. 46°14N 119°6W 168 C4
Pasco □ Peru 10°40S 75°0W 188 C3
Pasco I. Australia 20°57S 115°20E 148 D2
Pascoag U.S.A. 41°57N 71°42W 175 E13
Pascua, I. de Chile 27°7S 109°23W 157 K17
Pasewalk Germany 53°30N 13°58E 76 B9
Pasfield L. Canada 58°24N 105°20W 163 B7
Pasha → Russia 60°29N 32°55E 84 B7
Pasinler Turkey 39°59N 41°41E 105 C9
Pasir Mas Malaysia 6°2N 102°8E 121 J4
Pasir Panjang Singapore 1°18N 103°46E 121 d
Pasir Putih Malaysia 5°50N 102°24E 121 K4
Påskallavik Sweden 57°10N 16°26E 63 G10
Paskūh Iran 27°34N 61°39E 129 E9
Pasłęk Poland 54°3N 19°41E 82 D6
Pasłęka → Poland 54°26N 19°46E 82 D6
Pasley, C. Australia 33°52S 123°35E 149 F3
Pašman Croatia 43°58N 15°20E 93 E12
Pasmore → Australia 31°5S 139°49E 152 A3
Pasni Pakistan 25°15N 63°27E 122 G3
Paso Bravo △ Paraguay 22°32S 57°5W 190 A4
Paso Cantinela Mexico 32°33N 115°47W 171 N11
Paso de Indios Argentina 43°55S 69°0W 192 B3
Paso de los Indios Argentina 38°32S 69°25W 192 A3
Paso de los Libres Argentina 29°44S 57°10W 190 B4
Paso de los Toros Uruguay 32°45S 56°30W 190 C4
Paso Flores Argentina 40°35S 70°38W 192 B2
Paso Robles U.S.A. 35°38N 120°41W 170 K6
Paspébiac Canada 48°3N 65°17W 165 C6
Pasrur Pakistan 32°16N 74°43E 124 C6
Passage East Ireland 52°14N 7°0W 64 D5
Passage West Ireland 51°52N 8°21W 64 E3
Passaic U.S.A. 40°51N 74°7W 175 F10
Passau Germany 48°34N 13°28E 77 G9
Passero, C. Italy 36°41N 15°10E 95 F8
Passo Fundo Brazil 28°10S 52°20W 191 B5
Passos Brazil 20°45S 46°37W 189 E1
Passow Germany 53°8N 14°6E 76 B10
Passy France 45°55N 6°41E 73 C10
Pastavy Belarus 55°4N 26°50E 84 E4
Pastaza → Peru 4°50S 76°52W 186 D3
Pasto Colombia 1°13N 77°17W 186 C3
Pastos Bons Brazil 6°36S 44°5W 189 B2
Pastrana Spain 40°27N 2°53W 90 E2
Pasuruan Indonesia 7°40S 112°44E 119 G15
Pasym Poland 53°48N 20°49E 82 E7
Pásztó Hungary 47°52N 19°43E 80 C4
Patag I. = Flat I. S. China Sea 10°49N 115°49E 118 B5
Patagonia Argentina 45°0S 69°0W 192 C3
Patagonia U.S.A. 31°33N 110°45W 169 L8
Patambar Iran 29°45N 60°17E 129 D9
Patan = Lalitpur Nepal 27°40N 85°20E 125 F11
Patan = Somnath India 20°53N 70°22E 124 J4

Patan Gujarat, India 23°54N 72°14E 124 H5
Patan Maharashtra, India 17°22N 73°57E 126 F1
Patani Indonesia 0°20N 128°50E 119 D7
Pătârlagele Romania 45°19N 26°21E 81 E11
Pataudi India 28°18N 76°48E 124 E7
Patchewollock Australia 35°22S 142°12E 152 C5
Patchogue U.S.A. 40°46N 73°1W 175 F11
Pate Kenya 2°10S 41°0E 142 C5
Patea N.Z. 39°45S 174°30E 154 F3
Pategi Nigeria 8°50N 5°45E 139 D6
Patensie S. Africa 33°46S 24°49E 144 D3
Paterna Spain 39°30N 0°26W 91 F4
Paternion Austria 46°43N 13°38E 78 E6
Paternò Italy 37°34N 14°54E 95 E7
Pateros U.S.A. 48°3N 119°54W 168 B4
Paterson Australia 32°35S 151°36E 153 B9
Paterson U.S.A. 40°54N 74°9W 175 F10
Paterson Inlet N.Z. 46°56S 168°12E 155 G3
Paterson Ra. Australia 21°45S 122°10E 148 D3
Pathankot India 32°18N 75°45E 124 C6
Pathardi India 19°10N 75°11E 126 E2
Pathein = Bassein Burma 16°45N 94°30E 123 L19
Pathfinder Res. U.S.A. 42°28N 106°51W 168 E10
Pathiu Thailand 10°42N 99°19E 121 G2
Pathri India 19°15N 76°27E 126 E3
Pathum Thani Thailand 14°1N 100°32E 120 E3
Pati Indonesia 6°45S 111°1E 119 G14
Patía → Colombia 2°13N 78°40W 186 C3
Patiala Punjab, India 30°23N 76°26E 124 D7
Patiala Ut. P., India 27°43N 79°1E 125 F8
Patine Kouka Senegal 12°45N 13°45W 138 C2
Patitiri Greece 39°8N 23°50E 98 B5
Patkai Bum India 27°0N 95°30E 123 F19
Patmos Greece 37°21N 26°36E 99 D8
Patna India 25°35N 85°12E 125 G11
Patnagarh India 20°43N 83°9E 126 D6
Patnos Turkey 39°13N 42°51E 105 C10
Pato Branco Brazil 26°13S 52°40W 191 B5
Patong, Ao Thailand 7°54N 98°17E 121 a
Patonga Uganda 2°45N 33°15E 142 B3
Patos Albania 40°42N 19°38E 96 F3
Patos Brazil 6°55S 37°16W 189 B3
Patos, L. dos Brazil 31°20S 51°0W 191 C5
Patos, Río de los → Argentina 31°18S 69°25W 190 C2
Patos de Minas Brazil 18°35S 46°32W 189 D1
Patquía Argentina 30°2S 66°55W 190 C2
Patra Greece 38°14N 21°47E 98 C3
Patraikos Kolpos Greece 38°17N 21°30E 98 C3
Patras = Patra Greece 38°14N 21°47E 98 C3
Patricio Lynch, I. Chile 48°35S 75°30W 192 C1
Patriot Hills Antarctica 82°20S 81°25W 55 E16
Patrocínio Brazil 18°57S 47°0W 189 D1
Pattada Italy 40°35N 9°6E 94 B2
Pattadakal India 16°1N 75°42E 127 F2
Pattani Thailand 6°48N 101°15E 121 J3
Pattaya Thailand 12°52N 100°55E 120 F3
Patten U.S.A. 46°0N 68°38W 173 B19
Patterson Calif., U.S.A. 37°28N 121°8W 170 H5
Patterson Ga., U.S.A. 31°23N 82°8W 178 D7
Patterson La., U.S.A. 29°42N 91°18W 176 G9
Patterson, Mt. U.S.A. 38°29N 119°20W 170 G7
Patti Punjab, India 31°17N 74°54E 124 D6
Patti Ut. P., India 25°55N 82°12E 125 G10
Patti Italy 38°8N 14°58E 95 D7
Pattoki Pakistan 31°5N 73°52E 124 D5
Patton U.S.A. 40°38N 78°39W 174 F6
Pattukkattai India 10°25N 79°20E 127 J4
Patu Brazil 6°6S 37°38W 189 B3
Patuakhali Bangla. 22°20N 90°25E 123 H17
Patuanak Canada 55°55N 107°43W 163 B7
Patuca → Honduras 15°50N 84°18W 182 C3
Patuca, Punta Honduras 15°49N 84°14W 182 C3
Patuca △ Honduras 14°30N 85°30W 182 D2
Pătulele Romania 44°21N 22°47E 80 F7
Patur India 20°27N 76°56E 126 D3
Patvinsuo △ Finland 63°7N 30°45E 60 E24
Pátzcuaro Mexico 19°31N 101°38W 180 D4
Pau France 43°19N 0°25W 72 E3
Pau, Gave de → France 43°33N 1°12W 72 E2
Pau dos Ferros Brazil 6°7S 38°10W 189 B3
Pauanui N.Z. 37°1S 175°52E 154 D4
Paucartambo Peru 13°19S 71°35W 188 C3
Paudash Canada 44°59N 77°58W 174 B7
Pauillac France 45°11N 0°46W 72 C3
Pauini Brazil 7°40S 66°58W 188 B4
Pauk Burma 21°27N 94°30E 123 J19
Paul I. Canada 56°30N 61°20W 165 A7
Paul Smiths U.S.A. 44°26N 74°15W 175 B10
Paulatuk Canada 69°25N 124°0W 160 D7
Paulding Bay S. Ocean 66°0S 118°0E 55 C8
Paulhan France 43°33N 3°28E 72 E7
Paulista Brazil 7°57S 34°53W 189 B4
Paulistana Brazil 8°9S 41°9W 189 B2
Paulistrōm Sweden 57°28N 15°31E 63 G9
Paulo Afonso Brazil 9°21S 38°15W 189 B3
Paulpietersburg S. Africa 27°23S 30°50E 145 C5
Pauls Valley U.S.A. 34°44N 97°13W 176 D6
Pauma Valley U.S.A. 33°16N 116°58W 171 M10
Pauni India 20°48N 79°40E 126 D4
Pauri India 30°9N 78°47E 125 D8
Pausa Peru 15°16S 73°22W 188 D3
Pavagada India 14°6N 77°16E 127 G3
Pāveh Iran 35°3N 46°22E 105 E12
Pavelets Russia 53°49N 39°14E 84 F10
Pavia Italy 45°7N 9°8E 92 C6
Pavilion U.S.A. 42°52N 78°1W 174 D6
Pavilly France 49°34N 0°57E 70 C7
Pāvilosta Latvia 56°53N 21°14E 82 B8
Pavlikeni Bulgaria 43°14N 25°20E 97 C9
Pavlodar Kazakhstan 52°33N 77°0E 109 B9
Pavlograd = Pavlohrad Ukraine 48°30N 35°52E 85 H8
Pavlohrad Ukraine 48°30N 35°52E 85 H8
Pavlovo Russia 55°58N 43°5E 86 C6
Pavlovsk Russia 50°26N 40°5E 86 E5
Pavlovskaya Russia 46°17N 39°47E 87 G4
Pavlovskiy-Posad Russia 55°47N 38°42E 84 E10
Pavo U.S.A. 30°58N 83°45W 178 E6
Pavullo nel Frignano Italy 44°20N 10°50E 92 D7
Pawai, Pulau Singapore 1°11N 103°44E 121 d
Pawayan India 28°4N 80°6E 125 E9

Pawhuska U.S.A. 36°40N 96°20W 176 C6
Pawling U.S.A. 41°34N 73°36W 175 E11
Pawnee U.S.A. 36°20N 96°48W 176 C6
Pawnee City U.S.A. 40°7N 96°9W 172 E5
Pawtucket U.S.A. 41°53N 71°23W 175 E13
Paxi Greece 39°14N 20°12E 98 B2
Paximadia Greece 35°0N 24°35E 101 E6
Paxton U.S.A. 40°27N 88°6W 172 E9
Payakumbuh Indonesia 0°20S 100°35E 118 E2
Payerne Switz. 46°49N 6°56E 77 J2
Payette U.S.A. 44°5N 116°56W 168 D5
Paymogo Spain 37°44N 7°21W 89 H3
Payne Bay = Kangirsuk Canada 60°0N 70°0W 161 F18
Payne L. Canada 59°30N 74°30W 161 F17
Paynes Find Australia 29°15S 117°42E 149 E2
Paynesville Liberia 6°20N 10°45W 138 D2
Paynesville U.S.A. 45°23N 94°43W 172 C6
Pays de la Loire □ France 47°45N 0°25W 70 E6
Paysandú Uruguay 32°19S 58°8W 190 C4
Payson Ariz., U.S.A. 34°14N 111°20W 169 J8
Payson Utah, U.S.A. 40°3N 111°44W 168 F8
Paz → Guatemala 13°44N 90°10W 182 D1
Paz, B. de la Mexico 24°9N 110°25W 180 C2
Pāzanān Iran 30°35N 49°59E 129 D6
Pazar Turkey 41°10N 40°50E 105 B9
Pazarcık Turkey 37°30N 37°17E 104 D7
Pazardzhik Bulgaria 42°12N 24°20E 97 D8
Pazardzhik □ Bulgaria 42°12N 24°20E 97 D8
Pazarköy Turkey 39°51N 27°24E 99 B9
Pazarlar Turkey 39°0N 29°7E 99 C11
Pazaryeri Turkey 40°0N 29°56E 99 B11
Pazaryolu Turkey 40°21N 40°47E 105 B9
Pazin Croatia 45°14N 13°56E 93 C10
Pazña Bolivia 18°36S 66°55W 188 D4
Pčinja → Macedonia 41°50N 21°45E 96 E5
Pe Ell U.S.A. 46°34N 123°18W 170 D3
Pea → U.S.A. 31°1N 85°51W 178 D4
Peabody U.S.A. 42°31N 70°56W 175 D14
Peace → Canada 59°0N 111°25W 162 B6
Peace → U.S.A. 26°56N 82°6W 179 J7
Peace Point Canada 59°7N 112°27W 162 B6
Peace River Canada 56°15N 117°18W 162 B5
Peach Springs U.S.A. 35°32N 113°25W 169 J7
Peachland Canada 49°47N 119°45W 162 D5
Peachtree City U.S.A. 33°25N 84°35W 178 B5
Peak, The = Kinder Scout U.K. 53°24N 1°52W 66 D6
Peak Charles △ Australia 32°42S 121°10E 149 F3
Peak District △ U.K. 53°24N 1°46W 66 D6
Peak Hill Australia 32°47S 148°11E 153 B8
Peak Ra. Australia 22°50S 148°20E 150 C4
Peake Australia 35°25S 139°55E 152 C3
Peake Cr. → Australia 28°2S 136°7E 151 D2
Peal de Becerro Spain 37°55N 3°7W 89 H7
Peale, Mt. U.S.A. 38°26N 109°14W 168 G9
Pearblossom U.S.A. 34°30N 117°55W 171 L9
Pearl → U.S.A. 30°11N 89°32W 177 F10
Pearl and Hermes Reef U.S.A. 27°55N 175°45W 167 K4
Pearl Banks Sri Lanka 8°45N 79°45E 127 K4
Pearl River = Zhu Jiang → China 22°45N 113°37E 117 F9
Pearl River U.S.A. 41°4N 74°2W 175 E10
Pearl River Bridge China 22°15N 113°48E 111 a
Pearsall U.S.A. 28°54N 99°6W 176 G5
Pearson U.S.A. 31°18N 82°51W 178 D7
Pearson Int. Toronto ✈ (YYZ) Canada 43°46N 79°35W 174 C5
Peary Chan. Canada 79°40N 101°30W 161 B11
Peary Land Greenland 82°40N 33°0W 57 A7
Pease → U.S.A. 34°12N 99°2W 176 D5
Peawanuck Canada 55°15N 85°12W 164 A2
Pebane Mozam. 17°10S 38°8E 143 F4
Pebas Peru 3°10S 71°46W 186 D4
Pebble, I. Falk. Is. 51°20S 59°40W 192 D5
Pebble Beach U.S.A. 36°34N 121°57W 170 J5
Peć = Pejë Kosovo 42°40N 20°17E 96 D4
Peçanha Brazil 18°33S 42°34W 189 D2
Péccioli Italy 43°33N 10°43E 92 E7
Pechea Romania 45°36N 27°49E 81 E12
Pechenga Russia 69°29N 31°4E 60 B24
Pechenizhyn Ukraine 48°30N 24°48E 81 B9
Pechiguera, Pta. Canary Is. 28°51N 13°53W 100 F6
Pechnezhskoye Vdkhr. Ukraine 50°5N 36°54E 85 G9
Pechora Russia 65°10N 57°11E 106 C6
Pechora → Russia 68°13N 54°15E 58 B16
Pechorskaya Guba Russia 68°40N 54°0E 106 C6
Pechory Russia 57°48N 27°40E 84 D4
Pecica Romania 46°10N 21°3E 80 D6
Pecka Serbia 44°18N 19°33E 96 B3
Pécora, C. Italy 39°27N 8°23E 94 C1
Pecos N. Mex., U.S.A. 35°35N 105°41W 169 J11
Pecos Tex., U.S.A. 31°26N 103°30W 176 F3
Pecos → U.S.A. 29°42N 101°22W 176 G4
Pécs Hungary 46°5N 18°15E 80 D3
Pedasí Panama 7°32N 80°2W 182 E3
Pedda Bellala India 19°4N 78°49E 126 E4
Peddapalli India 18°40N 79°24E 126 E4
Peddapuram India 17°6N 82°8E 126 F6
Pedder, L. Australia 42°55S 146°10E 151 G4
Peddie S. Africa 33°14S 27°7E 145 D4
Pedernales Dom. Rep. 18°2N 71°44W 183 C5
Pedieos → Cyprus 35°10N 33°54E 101 D12
Pedirka Desert Australia 26°47S 134°11E 151 A1
Pedra Azul Brazil 16°2S 41°17W 189 D2
Pedra Grande, Recifes de Brazil 17°45S 38°58W 189 D3
Pedra Lume C. Verde Is. 16°40N 22°52W 134 b
Pedreguer Spain 38°48N 0°3E 91 G5
Pedreiras Brazil 4°32S 44°40W 189 A2
Pedro Afonso Brazil 9°0S 48°10W 189 B1
Pedro Cays Jamaica 17°5N 77°48W 182 C4
Pedro de Valdivia Chile 22°55S 69°38W 190 A2
Pedro Juan Caballero Paraguay 22°30S 55°40W 191 A4
Pedro Muñoz Spain 39°25N 2°56W 89 F8
Pedrógão Grande Portugal 39°55N 8°9W 88 F2
Pee Dee = Great Pee Dee → U.S.A. 33°21N 79°10W 177 E15
Peebinga Australia 34°52S 140°57E 152 C4
Peebles U.K. 55°40N 3°11W 65 F5
Peekskill U.S.A. 41°17N 73°55W 175 E11
Peel I. of Man 54°13N 4°40W 66 C3
Peel → Australia 30°50S 150°29E 153 A9

Peel → Canada 67°0N 135°0W 160 D5
Peel Sd. Canada 73°0N 96°0W 160 C12
Peene → Germany 54°9N 13°46E 76 A9
Peera Peera Poolanna L. Australia 26°30S 138°0E 151 D2
Peerless Lake Canada 56°37N 114°40W 162 B6
Peers Canada 53°40N 116°0W 162 C5
Peery L. Australia 30°45S 143°35E 152 A5
Pegasus Bay N.Z. 43°20S 173°10E 155 D8
Peggau Austria 47°12N 15°21E 78 D8
Pegnitz Germany 49°44N 11°31E 77 F7
Pegnitz → Germany 49°30N 10°59E 77 F6
Pego Spain 38°51N 0°8W 91 G4
Pegu Burma 17°20N 96°29E 123 L20
Pegu Yoma Burma 19°0N 96°0E 123 K20
Pehčevo Macedonia 41°41N 22°55E 96 E6
Pehlivanköy Turkey 41°20N 26°55E 97 E10
Pehuajó Argentina 35°45S 62°0W 190 D3
Pei Xian China 34°44N 116°55E 114 G9
Peikang Taiwan 23°34N 120°18E 117 F13
Peine Chile 23°45S 68°8W 190 A2
Peine Germany 52°19N 10°14E 76 C6
Pei'ing = Beijing China 39°53N 116°21E 114 E9
Peipus, L. = Chudskoye, Ozero Russia 58°13N 27°30E 84 C4
Peissenberg Germany 47°48N 11°4E 77 H7
Peitz Germany 51°51N 14°24E 76 D10
Peixe Brazil 12°0S 48°40W 189 C1
Peixe → Brazil 21°31S 51°58W 187 H8
Pejë Kosovo 42°40N 20°17E 96 D4
Pek → Serbia 44°45N 21°29E 96 B5
Pekalongan Indonesia 6°53S 109°40E 118 F3
Pekan Malaysia 3°30N 103°25E 121 L4
Pekan Nenas Malaysia 1°31N 103°31E 121 d
Pekanbaru Indonesia 0°30N 101°15E 118 D2
Pekin U.S.A. 40°35N 89°40W 172 E9
Peking = Beijing China 39°53N 116°21E 114 E9
Pekutatan Indonesia 8°25S 114°49E 119 J17
Pela Greece 40°46N 22°23E 96 F6
Pelabuhan Ratu, Teluk Indonesia 7°5S 106°30E 119 G12
Pélagos = Kira Panagia Greece 39°17N 24°4E 98 B6
Pelaihari Indonesia 3°55S 114°45E 118 E4
Pelat, Mt. France 44°16N 6°42E 73 D10
Pelczyce Poland 53°3N 15°16E 83 E2
Peleaga, Vf. Romania 45°22N 22°55E 80 E7
Pelechuco Bolivia 14°48S 69°4W 188 C4
Pelée, Mt. Martinique 14°48N 61°10W 182 c
Pelee, Pt. Canada 41°54N 82°31W 164 D3
Pelee I. Canada 41°47N 82°40W 174 E2
Pelejo Peru 6°10S 75°49W 188 B2
Pelekech Kenya 3°52N 35°8E 142 B4
Peleng Indonesia 1°20S 123°30E 119 E6
Pelentong Malaysia 1°32N 103°49E 121 d
Pélézi Ivory C. 7°17N 6°54W 138 D3
Pelham U.S.A. 31°8N 84°9W 178 D5
Pelhřimov Czech Rep. 49°24N 15°12E 78 B8
Pelican U.S.A. 57°58N 136°14W 162 B1
Pelican L. Canada 52°28N 100°20W 163 C8
Pelican Narrows Canada 55°10N 102°56W 163 B8
Pelion U.S.A. 33°46N 81°15W 178 B8
Pelister △ Macedonia 41°0N 21°10E 96 F5
Peljesac Croatia 42°55N 17°25E 93 F14
Pelkosenniemi Finland 67°6N 27°28E 60 C22
Pell City U.S.A. 33°35N 86°17W 178 B3
Pella Greece 40°52N 22°0E 96 F6
Pella S. Africa 29°1S 19°6E 144 C2
Pella U.S.A. 41°25N 92°55W 172 E7
Pello Finland 66°47N 23°59E 60 C20
Pellworm Germany 54°31N 8°39E 76 A4
Pelly → Canada 62°47N 137°19W 162 A1
Pelly Bay Canada 68°38N 89°50W 161 D14
Peloponnesos □ Greece 37°10N 22°0E 98 D4
Peloritani, Monti Italy 38°3N 15°20E 95 D8
Pelorus → N.Z. 41°16S 173°45E 155 B8
Pelorus Sd. N.Z. 40°59S 173°59E 155 A8
Pelotas Brazil 31°42S 52°23W 191 C5
Pelotas → Brazil 27°28S 51°55W 191 B5
Pelovo Bulgaria 43°26N 24°17E 97 C8
Pelplin Poland 53°55N 18°42E 82 E5
Pelvoux, Massif du France 44°52N 6°20E 73 D10
Pemalang Indonesia 6°53S 109°23E 119 G13
Pemanggil, Pulau Malaysia 2°37N 104°21E 121 L5
Pematangsiantar Indonesia 2°57N 99°5E 118 D1
Pemba Mozam. 12°58S 40°30E 143 E5
Pemba Zambia 16°30S 27°28E 143 F2
Pemba Channel Tanzania 5°0S 39°37E 142 D4
Pemba I. Tanzania 5°0S 39°45E 142 D4
Pemberton Australia 34°30S 116°0E 149 F2
Pemberton Canada 50°25N 122°50W 162 C4
Pembina → Canada 54°45N 114°17W 162 C6
Pembroke Canada 45°50N 77°7W 164 C4
Pembroke U.K. 51°41N 4°55W 67 F3
Pembroke U.S.A. 32°8N 81°37W 178 C8
Pembroke Pines U.S.A. 26°0N 80°13W 179 J9
Pembrokeshire □ U.K. 51°52N 4°56W 67 F3
Pembrokeshire Coast △ U.K. 51°50N 5°2W 67 F2
Pen India 18°45N 73°5E 126 E1
Pen-y-bont ar Ogwr = Bridgend U.K. 51°30N 3°34W 67 F4
Pen-y-Ghent U.K. 54°10N 2°14W 66 C5
Peña, Sierra de la Spain 42°32N 0°45W 90 C4
Peña de Francia, Sierra de la Spain 40°32N 6°10W 88 E4
Penafiel Portugal 41°12N 8°17W 88 D2
Peñafiel Spain 41°35N 4°7W 88 D6
Peñaflor Spain 37°43N 5°21W 89 H5
Penal Trin. & Tob. 10°9N 61°29W 187 K15
Peñalara Spain 40°51N 3°57W 88 E7
Penalva Brazil 3°18S 45°10W 189 A1
Penamacôr Portugal 40°10N 7°10W 88 E3
Penang = Pinang Malaysia 5°25N 100°15E 121 c
Penápolis Brazil 21°30S 50°0W 191 A6
Peñaranda de Bracamonte Spain 40°53N 5°13W 88 E5
Peñarroya Spain 40°25N 0°40W 90 E4
Peñarroya-Pueblonuevo Spain 38°19N 5°16W 89 G5
Penarth U.K. 51°26N 3°11W 67 F4
Peñas, C. de Spain 43°42N 5°52W 88 B5
Peñas, G. de Chile 47°0S 75°0W 192 C2
Peñas de San Pedro Spain 38°44N 2°0W 91 G3
Peñas del Chache Canary Is. 29°6N 13°33W 100 E6
Peñausende Spain 41°17N 5°52W 88 D5
Pench → India 21°17N 79°10E 126 D4
Pench △ India 21°45N 79°20E 125 J8
Pench'i = Benxi China 41°20N 123°48E 115 D12
Pend Oreille → U.S.A. 49°4N 117°37W 168 B5
Pend Oreille, L. U.S.A. 48°10N 116°21W 168 B5
Pendalofos Greece 40°14N 21°12E 96 F5
Pendembu Eastern, S. Leone 8°10N 10°42W 138 D2
Pendembu Northern, S. Leone 9°7N 11°14W 138 D2
Pendências Brazil 5°15S 36°43W 189 B3
Pender B. Australia 16°45S 122°42E 148 C3
Pendik Turkey 40°53N 29°13E 97 F13
Pendjari → Benin 10°55N 0°50E 139 C5
Pendjari △ Benin 11°15N 1°32E 139 C5
Pendleton U.S.A. 45°40N 118°47W 168 D4
Pendra India 22°46N 81°57E 125 H9
Pendzhikent = Panjakent Tajikistan 39°29N 67°37E 109 E7
Peneda-Gerês △ Portugal 41°57N 8°15W 88 D2
Penedo Brazil 10°15S 36°36W 189 C3
Penelokan Indonesia 8°17S 115°22E 119 J18
Penetanguishene Canada 44°50N 79°55W 174 B5
Penfield U.S.A. 41°13N 78°35W 174 E6
Penfro = Pembroke U.K. 51°41N 4°55W 67 F3
Peng Chau China 22°17N 114°2E 111 a
Peng'an China 31°2N 106°22E 116 B6
Penganga → India 19°53N 79°9E 126 E4
Penge Kasai-Or., Dem. Rep. of the Congo 5°30S 24°33E 142 D1
Penge Sud-Kivu, Dem. Rep. of the Congo 4°27S 28°25E 142 C2
P'enghu Ch'üntou Taiwan 23°34N 119°30E 117 F12
Penglai China 37°48N 120°42E 115 F11
Pengshan China 30°14N 103°58E 116 B4
Pengshui China 29°17N 108°12E 116 C7
Penguin Australia 41°8S 146°6E 151 G4
Pengxi China 30°44N 105°45E 116 B5
Pengze China 29°52N 116°32E 117 C11
Pengzhou China 31°4N 103°32E 116 B4
Penhalonga Zimbabwe 18°52S 32°40E 143 F3
Peniche Portugal 39°19N 9°22W 89 F1
Penicuik U.K. 55°50N 3°13W 65 F5
Penida, Nusa Indonesia 8°45S 115°30E 118 F5
Peninnes, Alpes = Pennine, Alpi Alps 46°4N 7°30E 77 J3
Peninsular Malaysia □ Malaysia 4°0N 102°0E 121 L4
Peñíscola Spain 40°22N 0°24E 90 E5
Penitente, Serra do Brazil 8°45S 46°20W 189 B1
Pënjwīn Iraq 35°37N 45°56E 105 E11
Penkridge U.K. 52°44N 2°6W 66 E5
Penmarch France 47°49N 4°21W 70 E2
Penmarch, Pte. de France 47°48N 4°22W 70 E2
Penn Hills U.S.A. 40°28N 79°52W 174 F5
Penn Yan U.S.A. 42°40N 77°3W 174 D7
Penna, Punta della Italy 42°10N 14°43E 93 F11
Pennant Canada 50°32N 108°14W 163 C7
Penne Italy 42°27N 13°55E 93 F10
Penner → India 14°35N 80°10E 127 G5
Penneshaw Australia 35°44S 137°56E 152 C2
Pennine, Alpi Alps 46°4N 7°30E 77 J3
Pennines U.K. 54°45N 2°27W 66 C5
Pennington U.S.A. 39°15N 121°47W 170 F5
Pennington → Nigeria 4°45N 5°35E 139 E6
Pennino, Mte. Italy 43°6N 12°53E 93 E9
Pennsburg U.S.A. 40°23N 75°29W 175 F9
Pennsylvania □ U.S.A. 40°45N 77°30W 173 E15
Penny Canada 53°51N 121°20W 162 C4
Peno Russia 57°2N 32°49E 84 D7
Penobscot → U.S.A. 44°30N 68°48W 173 C19
Penobscot B. U.S.A. 44°35N 68°50W 173 C19
Penola Australia 37°25S 140°48E 152 D4
Penong Australia 31°56S 133°1E 149 F5
Penonomé Panama 8°31N 80°21W 182 E3
Penrhyn Cook Is. 9°0S 158°0W 157 H12
Penrith Australia 33°43S 150°38E 153 B9
Penrith U.K. 54°40N 2°45W 66 C5
Penryn U.K. 50°9N 5°7W 67 G2
Pensacola U.S.A. 30°25N 87°13W 179 E2
Pensacola B. U.S.A. 30°25N 87°5W 179 E2
Pensacola Mts. Antarctica 84°0S 40°0W 55 E1
Pense Canada 50°25N 104°59W 163 C8
Penshurst Australia 37°49S 142°20E 152 D5
Pentadaktylos Cyprus 35°20N 33°20E 101 D12
Pentecostes Brazil 3°48S 39°17W 189 A3
Penticton Canada 49°30N 119°38W 162 D5
Pentland Australia 20°32S 145°25E 150 C4
Pentland Firth U.K. 58°43N 3°10W 65 C5
Pentland Hills U.K. 55°48N 3°25W 65 F5
Penukonda India 14°5N 77°38E 127 G3
Penza Russia 53°15N 45°5E 86 D7
Penza □ Russia 52°50N 44°50E 86 D7
Penzance U.K. 50°7N 5°33W 67 G2
Penzberg Germany 47°45N 11°22E 77 H7
Penzhino Russia 63°30N 167°55E 107 C17
Penzhinskaya Guba Russia 61°30N 163°0E 107 C17
Penzlin Germany 53°30N 13°5E 76 B9
Peoria Ariz., U.S.A. 33°43N 112°14W 169 K7
Peoria Ill., U.S.A. 40°42N 89°36W 172 E9
Pepacton Res. U.S.A. 42°5N 74°58W 175 D10
Pepani → S. Africa 25°49S 22°47E 144 C3
Pepel S. Leone 8°40N 13°5W 138 D2
Peqin Albania 41°3N 19°44E 96 E3
Pera Hd. Australia 12°55S 141°37E 150 A3
Perabumulih Indonesia 3°27S 104°15E 118 E2
Perachora Greece 38°2N 22°56E 98 C4
Perak □ Malaysia 5°0N 101°0E 121 K3
Perak → Malaysia 4°0N 100°50E 121 K3
Perales del Alfambra Spain 40°38N 1°0W 90 E4
Perales del Puerto Spain 40°10N 6°40W 88 E4
Peralta Spain 42°20N 1°48W 90 C3
Perama Kerkyra, Greece 39°34N 19°54E 101 A3
Perama Kriti, Greece 35°20N 24°40E 101 D6
Perämeri △ Finland 65°35N 24°22E 60 D21
Perancak Indonesia 8°24S 114°37E 119 J17
Peräpohjola Finland 66°16N 26°10E 60 C22
Perast Montenegro 42°31N 18°47E 96 D2
Percé Canada 48°31N 64°13W 165 C7
Perche France 48°31N 1°1E 70 D8
Perche ⌂ France 48°24N 0°46E 70 D7
Perchtoldsdorf Austria 48°7N 16°17E 79 C9
Percival Lakes Australia 21°25S 125°0E 148 D4
Percy France 48°55N 1°11W 70 D5
Percy Is. Australia 21°39S 150°16E 150 C5
Perdido → Argentina 42°55S 67°0W 192 B3
Perdido, Mte. Spain 42°40N 0°5E 90 C5
Perdu, Mt. = Perdido, Mte. Spain 42°40N 0°5E 90 C5
Perechyn Ukraine 48°44N 22°28E 80 B7
Perehinske Ukraine 48°49N 24°11E 81 B9
Pereira Colombia 4°49N 75°43W 186 C3
Perejil Spain 35°55N 5°25W 89 K5
Perelazovskiy Russia 49°8N 42°35E 87 F6
Peremul Par India 11°10N 72°4E 127 J1
Perené → Peru 11°9S 74°14W 188 C3
Perenjori Australia 29°26S 116°16E 149 E2
Peresecina Moldova 47°16N 28°46E 81 C13
Pereslavl-Zalesskiy Russia 56°45N 38°50E 84 D10
Peretu Romania 44°3N 25°5E 81 F10
Pereyaslav-Khmelnytskyy Ukraine 50°3N 31°28E 85 G6
Pereyma Ukraine 48°4N 29°30E 81 B14
Pérez, I. Mexico 22°24N 89°42W 181 C7
Perg Austria 48°15N 14°38E 78 C7
Pergamino Argentina 33°52S 60°30W 190 C3
Pergau → Malaysia 5°23N 102°2E 121 K3
Pérgine Valsugana Italy 46°4N 11°14E 93 B8
Pérgola Italy 43°34N 12°50E 93 E9
Perham U.S.A. 46°36N 95°34W 172 B6
Perhentian, Kepulauan Malaysia 5°54N 102°42E 121 K4
Peri → Turkey 38°53N 39°52E 105 C8
Periam Romania 46°2N 20°52E 80 D5
Péribonka → Canada 48°45N 72°5W 165 C5
Péribonka, L. Canada 50°1N 71°10W 165 B5
Péribonka, La Centrale de Canada 49°30N 71°10W 165 C5
Perico Argentina 24°20S 65°5W 190 A2
Pericos Mexico 25°3N 107°42W 180 B3
Périers France 49°11N 1°25W 70 C5
Périgord France 45°0N 0°40E 72 D4
Périgord-Limousin ⌂ France 45°40N 0°50E 72 C4
Périgueux France 45°10N 0°42E 72 C4
Perijá, Sierra de Colombia 9°30N 73°3W 186 B4
Perijá △ Venezuela 9°30N 72°55W 183 E5
Peringat Malaysia 6°2N 102°17E 121 J4
Perisher Valley Australia 36°27S 148°25E 153 D8
Peristera Greece 39°15N 23°58E 98 B5
Peristerona → Cyprus 35°8N 33°5E 101 D12
Perito Moreno Argentina 46°36S 70°56W 192 C2
Perito Moreno △ Argentina 47°49S 72°17W 192 C2
Peritoró Brazil 4°20S 44°18W 189 A2
Perivol = Dragovishtitsa Bulgaria 42°22N 22°39E 96 D6
Periyakulam India 10°5N 77°30E 127 J3
Periyar → India 10°15N 76°10E 127 J3
Periyar, L. India 9°25N 77°10E 127 K3
Periyar △ India 9°25N 77°10E 127 K3
Perkasie U.S.A. 40°22N 75°18W 175 F9
Perković Croatia 43°41N 16°10E 93 E13
Perlas, Arch. de las Panama 8°41N 79°7W 182 E4
Perlas, Punta de Nic. 12°30N 83°30W 182 D3
Perleberg Germany 53°5N 11°52E 76 B7
Perlez Serbia 45°11N 20°22E 80 E5
Perlis □ Malaysia 6°30N 100°15E 121 J2
Perm Russia 58°0N 56°10E 106 D6
Përmet Albania 40°15N 20°21E 96 F4
Pernambuco = Recife Brazil 8°0S 35°0W 189 B4
Pernambuco □ Brazil 8°0S 37°0W 189 B3
Pernambuco Abyssal Plain Atl. Oc. 5°0S 24°0W 56 G9
Pernatty Lagoon Australia 31°30S 137°12E 152 A2
Pernik Bulgaria 42°35N 23°2E 96 D7
Pernik □ Bulgaria 42°35N 23°2E 96 D7
Peron Is. Australia 13°9S 130°4E 148 B5
Peron Pen. Australia 26°0S 113°10E 149 E1
Péronne France 49°55N 2°57E 71 C9
Perosa Argentina Italy 44°58N 7°10E 92 D4
Perow Canada 54°35N 126°10W 162 C3
Perpignan France 42°42N 2°53E 72 F6
Perrine U.S.A. 25°36N 80°21W 179 K9
Perris U.S.A. 33°47N 117°14W 171 M9
Perros-Guirec France 48°49N 3°28W 70 D3
Perry Fla., U.S.A. 30°7N 83°35W 178 E6
Perry Ga., U.S.A. 32°28N 83°44W 178 C6
Perry Iowa, U.S.A. 41°51N 94°6W 172 E6
Perry N.Y., U.S.A. 42°42N 78°0W 174 D7
Perry Okla., U.S.A. 36°17N 97°14W 176 C6
Perryton U.S.A. 36°24N 100°48W 176 C4
Perryville U.S.A. 37°43N 89°52W 172 G9
Persan France 49°9N 2°16E 71 C9
Persberg Sweden 59°47N 14°15E 62 E8
Perşembe Turkey 41°5N 37°46E 104 B7
Persepolis Iran 29°55N 52°50E 129 D7
Pershotravensk Ukraine 50°13N 27°40E 75 C14
Persia = Iran ■ Asia 33°0N 53°0E 129 C7
Persian Gulf Asia 27°0N 50°0E 129 E6
Perstorp Sweden 56°10N 13°25E 63 H7
Pertek Turkey 38°51N 39°19E 105 C8
Perth Australia 31°57S 115°52E 149 F2
Perth Canada 44°55N 76°15W 175 B8
Perth U.K. 56°24N 3°26W 65 E5
Perth & Kinross □ U.K. 56°45N 3°55W 65 E5
Perth Amboy U.S.A. 40°30N 74°15W 175 F10
Perth-Andover Canada 46°44N 67°42W 165 C6
Perth Basin Ind. Oc. 30°0S 108°0E 156 L2
Pertuis France 43°42N 5°30E 73 E9
Pertusato, C. France 41°21N 9°11E 73 G13
Peru Ind., U.S.A. 40°45N 86°4W 172 E10
Peru N.Y., U.S.A. 44°35N 73°32W 175 B11
Peru ■ S. Amer. 4°0S 75°0W 186 D4
Peru Basin Pac. Oc. 20°0S 95°0W 157 J18
Peru-Chile Trench Pac. Oc. 20°0S 72°0W 186 G3
Perúgia Italy 43°7N 12°23E 93 E9
Perušić Croatia 44°40N 15°22E 93 D12
Pervomaisk Russia 54°56N 43°58E 86 C6
Pervomaysk Ukraine 48°10N 30°46E 85 H6
Pervomayskïy Kazakhstan 50°16N 82°0E 109 B10
Pervouralsk Russia 56°59N 59°59E 106 D6
Pésaro Italy 43°54N 12°55E 93 E9
Pésaro e Urbino □ Italy 43°45N 12°40E 93 E9
Pescadores = P'enghu Ch'üntou Taiwan 23°34N 119°30E 117 F12
Pescara Italy 42°28N 14°13E 93 F11
Pescara → Italy 42°28N 14°13E 93 F11
Peschanokopskoye Russia 46°14N 41°4E 87 G5
Pescia Italy 43°54N 10°41E 92 E7
Pescina Italy 42°2N 13°39E 93 F10
Peshawar Pakistan 34°2N 71°37E 124 B4
Peshkopi Albania 41°41N 20°25E 96 E4
Peshtera Bulgaria 42°2N 24°18E 97 D8
Peshtigo U.S.A. 45°3N 87°45W 172 C10
Peski Russia 51°14N 42°29E 86 E6
Peski Turkmenistan 38°11N 62°59E 108 E6
Pêso da Régua Portugal 41°10N 7°47W 88 D3
Pesqueira Brazil 8°20S 36°42W 189 B3
Pessac France 44°48N 0°37W 72 D3
Pest □ Hungary 47°29N 19°5E 80 C4
Pestovo Russia 58°33N 35°42E 84 C8
Pestravka Russia 52°28N 49°57E 86 D9
Petah Tiqwa Israel 32°6N 34°53E 130 C3
Petalidi Greece 36°57N 21°55E 98 E3
Petaling Jaya Malaysia 3°4N 101°42E 121 L3
Petaloudes Greece 36°18N 28°5E 101 C10
Petaluma U.S.A. 38°14N 122°39W 170 G4
Pétange Lux. 49°33N 5°55E 69 E5
Petaro Pakistan 25°31N 68°18E 124 G3
Petas Greece 39°10N 21°2E 98 B3
Petatlán Mexico 17°31N 101°16W 180 D4
Petauke Zambia 14°14S 31°20E 143 E3
Petawawa Canada 45°54N 77°17W 164 C4
Petén Itzá, L. Guatemala 16°58N 89°50W 182 C2
Peter I. Br. Virgin Is. 18°22N 64°35W 183 e
Peter I. Øy Antarctica 69°0S 91°0W 55 C16
Peter Pond L. Canada 55°55N 108°44W 163 B7
Peterbell Canada 48°36N 83°21W 164 C3
Peterborough Australia 32°58S 138°51E 152 B3
Peterborough Canada 44°20N 78°20W 174 B6
Peterborough U.K. 52°35N 0°15W 67 E7
Peterborough U.S.A. 42°53N 71°57W 175 D13
Peterborough □ U.K. 52°35N 0°15W 67 E7
Peterculter U.K. 57°6N 2°16W 65 D6
Peterhead U.K. 57°31N 1°48W 65 D7
Peterlee U.K. 54°47N 1°20W 66 C6
Petermann ◎ Australia 24°58S 130°0E 149 E4
Petermann Bjerg Greenland 73°7N 28°25W 57 C8
Petermann Gletscher Greenland 80°30N 60°0W 57 A4
Petermann Ranges Australia 26°0S 130°30E 149 E5
Petersburg Alaska, U.S.A. 56°48N 132°58W 160 F5
Petersburg Pa., U.S.A. 40°34N 78°3W 174 F6
Petersburg Va., U.S.A. 37°14N 77°24W 173 G15
Petersburg W. Va., U.S.A. 39°1N 79°5W 173 F14
Petersfield U.K. 51°1N 0°56W 67 F7
Petershagen Germany 52°23N 8°58E 76 C4
Petilia Policastro Italy 39°7N 16°48E 95 C9
Petilla de Aragón Spain 42°28N 1°6W 90 C3
Petit-Canal Guadeloupe 16°25N 61°31W 182 b
Petit-Goâve Haiti 18°27N 72°51W 183 C5
Petit Lac Manicouagan Canada 51°25N 67°40W 165 B6
Petit-Mécatina → Canada 50°40N 59°30W 165 B8
Petit-Mécatina, Î. du Canada 50°30N 59°25W 165 B8
Petit Piton St. Lucia 13°51N 61°5W 183 f
Petit-Saguenay Canada 48°15N 70°4W 165 C5
Petit Saint Bernard, Col du Italy 45°40N 6°52E 73 C10
Petitcodiac Canada 45°57N 65°11W 165 C6
Petite Terre, Îles de la Guadeloupe 16°13N 61°9W 182 b
Petitot → Canada 60°14N 123°29W 162 A4
Petitsikapau L. Canada 54°37N 66°25W 165 B6
Petlad India 22°30N 72°45E 124 H5
Peto Mexico 20°8N 88°55W 181 C7
Petone N.Z. 41°13S 174°53E 154 H3
Petorca Chile 32°15S 70°56W 190 C1
Petoskey U.S.A. 45°22N 84°57W 173 C11
Petra Jordan 30°20N 35°22E 130 E4
Petra Spain 39°37N 3°6E 100 B10
Petra, Ostrov Russia 76°15N 118°30E 107 B12
Petra Velikogo, Zaliv Russia 42°40N 132°0E 112 C6
Petre, Pt. Canada 43°50N 77°9W 174 C7
Petrel = Petrer Spain 38°30N 0°46W 91 G4
Petrella, Monte Italy 41°18N 13°40E 94 A6
Petrer Spain 38°30N 0°46W 91 G4
Petreto-Bicchisano France 41°47N 8°58E 73 G12
Petrich Bulgaria 41°24N 23°13E 96 E7
Petrified Forest △ U.S.A. 35°0N 109°30W 169 J9
Petrijanec Croatia 46°23N 16°17E 93 B13
Petrikov = Pyetrykaw Belarus 52°11N 28°29E 75 B15
Petrila Romania 45°29N 23°29E 81 E8
Petrinja Croatia 45°28N 16°18E 93 C13
Petrodvorets Russia 59°52N 29°54E 84 C5
Petrolândia Brazil 9°5S 38°20W 189 B3
Petrolia Canada 42°54N 82°9W 174 D2
Petrolina Brazil 9°24S 40°30W 189 B2
Petropavl Kazakhstan 54°53N 69°13E 109 B7
Petropavlovsk = Petropavl Kazakhstan 54°53N 69°13E 109 B7
Petropavlovsk-Kamchatskiy Russia 53°3N 158°43E 107 D16
Petropavlovskiy = Akhtubinsk Russia 48°13N 46°7E 87 F8
Petrópolis Brazil 22°33S 43°9W 191 A7
Petroşani Romania 45°28N 23°20E 81 E8
Petrova Gora Croatia 45°15N 15°45E 93 C12
Petrovac Montenegro 42°13N 18°57E 96 D2
Petrovac Serbia 44°22N 21°26E 96 B5
Petrovaradin Serbia 45°16N 19°55E 80 E4
Petrovsk Russia 52°22N 45°19E 86 D7
Petrovsk-Zabaykalskiy Russia 51°20N 108°55E 107 D11
Petrovskaya Russia 45°25N 37°58E 85 K9
Petrozavodsk Russia 61°41N 34°20E 84 B8
Petrus Steyn S. Africa 27°38S 28°8E 145 C4
Petrusburg S. Africa 29°4S 25°26E 144 C4
Petukhovo Russia 55°6N 67°58E 109 A7
Petzeck Austria 46°57N 12°48E 78 E5
Peumo Chile 34°21S 71°12W 190 C1
Peureulak Indonesia 4°48N 97°45E 118 D1
Pevek Russia 69°41N 171°19E 107 C18
Peveragno Italy 44°20N 7°37E 92 D4
Peyrehorade France 43°34N 1°7W 72 E2
Peyruis France 44°1N 5°56E 73 D9
Pézenas France 43°28N 3°24E 72 E7
Pezinok Slovak Rep. 48°17N 17°17E 79 C10
Pfaffenhofen Germany 48°31N 11°31E 77 G7
Pfälzerwald ⌂ Germany 49°18N 9°55E 77 F5
Pfarrkirchen Germany 48°25N 12°56E 77 G8
Pfeffenhausen Germany 48°39N 11°58E 77 G7
Pforzheim Germany 48°52N 8°41E 77 G4
Pfullendorf Germany 47°55N 9°15E 77 H5
Pfungstadt Germany 49°48N 8°35E 77 F4
Pha Taem △ Thailand 15°32N 105°30E 120 E5
Phaestos Greece 35°2N 24°50E 101 D6
Phagwara India 31°10N 75°40E 124 D6
Phala Botswana 23°45S 26°50E 144 B4
Phalaborwa S. Africa 23°57S 31°7E 145 B5
Phalera = Phulera India 26°52N 75°16E 124 F6
Phalodi India 27°12N 72°24E 124 F5
Phalsbourg France 48°46N 7°15E 71 D14
Phaltan India 17°59N 74°26E 126 F2
Phaluai, Ko Thailand 9°32N 99°41E 121 b
Phan Thailand 19°28N 99°43E 120 C2
Phan Rang-Thap Cham Vietnam 11°34N 109°0E 121 G7
Phan Ri Cua Vietnam 11°16N 108°40E 121 G7
Phan Si Pan Vietnam 22°18N 103°46E 120 A4
Phan Thiet Vietnam 11°1N 108°9E 121 G7
Phan Thiet, Vinh Vietnam 10°53N 108°5E 121 G7
Phan Wa, Laem Thailand 7°47N 98°25E 121 a
Phanae Greece 38°8N 25°57E 99 C7
Phanat Nikhom Thailand 13°27N 101°11E 120 F3
Phangan, Ko Thailand 9°45N 100°0E 121 H3
Phangnga Thailand 8°28N 98°30E 121 H2
Phangnga, Ao Thailand 8°16N 98°33E 121 a
Phanom Sarakham Thailand 13°45N 101°21E 120 F3
Phaphund India 26°36N 79°28E 125 F8
Pharenda India 27°5N 83°17E 125 F10
Pharr U.S.A. 26°12N 98°11W 176 H5
Phatthalung Thailand 7°39N 100°6E 121 J3
Phayam, Ko Thailand 9°44N 98°25E 121 H2
Phayao Thailand 19°11N 99°55E 120 C2
Phelps U.S.A. 42°58N 77°3W 174 D7
Phelps L. Canada 59°15N 103°15W 163 B8
Phenix City U.S.A. 32°28N 85°1W 178 C4
Phet Buri = Phetchaburi Thailand 13°1N 99°55E 120 F2
Phetchabun Thailand 16°25N 101°8E 120 D3
Phetchabun, Thiu Khao Thailand 16°0N 101°20E 120 E3
Phetchaburi Thailand 13°1N 99°55E 120 F2
Phi Phi, Ko Thailand 7°45N 98°46E 121 J2
Phiafay Laos 14°48N 106°0E 120 E6
Phibun Mangsahan Thailand 15°14N 105°14E 120 E5
Phichai Thailand 17°22N 100°10E 120 D3
Phichit Thailand 16°26N 100°22E 120 D3
Philadelphia Miss., U.S.A. 32°46N 89°7W 177 E10
Philadelphia N.Y., U.S.A. 44°9N 75°43W 175 B9
Philadelphia Pa., U.S.A. 39°57N 75°9W 175 G9
Philip U.S.A. 44°2N 101°40W 172 C3
Philip Smith Mts. U.S.A. 68°0N 148°0W 166 B10
Philipi Greece 41°1N 24°16E 97 E8
Philippeville Belgium 50°12N 4°33E 69 D4
Philippi U.S.A. 39°9N 80°3W 173 F13
Philippi L. Australia 24°20S 138°55E 150 C2
Philippine Basin Pac. Oc. 17°0N 132°0E 156 F5
Philippine Sea Pac. Oc. 18°0N 125°0E 156 F4
Philippine Trench = Mindanao Trench Pac. Oc. 12°0N 126°6E 119 B7
Philippines ■ Asia 12°0N 123°0E 119 B6
Philippolis S. Africa 30°15S 25°16E 144 D4
Philippopolis = Plovdiv Bulgaria 42°8N 24°44E 97 D8
Philipsburg Canada 45°2N 73°5W 175 A11
Philipsburg Mont., U.S.A. 46°20N 113°18W 168 C7
Philipsburg Pa., U.S.A. 40°54N 78°13W 174 F6
Philipstown = Daingean Ireland 53°18N 7°17W 64 C4
Philipstown S. Africa 30°28S 24°30E 144 D3
Phillip I. Australia 38°30S 145°12E 153 E6
Phillips U.S.A. 45°42N 90°24W 172 C8
Phillipsburg Ga., U.S.A. 31°25N 83°30W 178 D6
Phillipsburg Kans., U.S.A. 39°45N 99°19W 172 F4
Phillipsburg N.J., U.S.A. 40°42N 75°12W 175 F9
Philmont U.S.A. 42°15N 73°39W 175 D11
Philomath Ga., U.S.A. 33°44N 82°59W 178 B7
Philomath Oreg., U.S.A. 44°32N 123°22W 168 D2
Phimai Thailand 15°13N 102°30E 120 E4
Phitsanulok Thailand 16°50N 100°12E 120 D3
Phnom Kulen △ Cambodia 13°38N 104°15E 120 F5
Phnom Penh Cambodia 11°33N 104°55E 121 G5
Phnum Penh = Phnom Penh Cambodia 11°33N 104°55E 121 G5
Pho, Laem Thailand 6°55N 101°19E 121 J3
Phocis = Fokida Greece 38°30N 22°15E 98 C4
Phoenicia U.S.A. 42°5N 74°14W 175 D10
Phoenix Mauritius 20°17S 57°30E 141 d
Phoenix Ariz., U.S.A. 33°26N 112°4W 169 K7
Phoenix N.Y., U.S.A. 43°14N 76°18W 175 C8
Phoenix Is. Kiribati 3°30S 172°0W 156 H10
Phoenixville U.S.A. 40°8N 75°31W 175 F9
Phon Thailand 15°49N 102°36E 120 E4
Phong → Thailand 16°23N 102°56E 120 D4
Phong Nha -Ke Bang △ Vietnam 17°30N 106°10E 120 D6
Phong Saly Laos 21°42N 102°9E 116 G4
Phong Tho Vietnam 22°32N 103°21E 120 A4
Phonsavan Laos 19°27N 103°10E 120 C4
Phonum Thailand 8°49N 98°48E 121 H2
Phosphate Hill Australia 21°53S 139°58E
Photharam Thailand 13°41N 99°51E
Phra Nakhon Si Ayutthaya Thailand 14°25N 100°30E
Phra Pradaeng Thailand 13°39N 100°33E
Phra Thong, Ko Thailand 9°5N 98°17E
Phrae Thailand 18°7N 100°9E
Phrom Phiram Thailand 17°2N 100°12E
Phrom Thep, Laem Thailand 7°45N 98°19E
Phrygia Turkey 38°40N 30°0E
Phthiotis = Fthiotida Greece 38°50N 22°25E
Phu Bia Laos 19°10N 103°0E
Phu Chong -Na Yoi △ Thailand 14°25N 105°30E
Phu Hin Rong Kla △ Thailand 17°0N 100°59E
Phu Kao -Phu Phan Kham △ Thailand 16°53N 102°31E
Phu Kradung △ Thailand 17°2N 101°44E
Phu Loi Laos 20°14N 103°14E
Phu Luang △ Thailand 17°15N 101°29E
Phu Ly Vietnam 20°35N 105°50E
Phu My Vietnam 14°15N 109°5E
Phu Pha Man △ Thailand 16°44N 101°50E
Phu Phan △ Thailand 17°0N 103°56E
Phu Quoc, Dao Vietnam 10°20N 104°0E
Phu Sa Dok Bua △ Thailand 16°11N 104°45E
Phu Sang △ Thailand 19°35N 100°19E
Phu Tho Vietnam 21°24N 105°13E
Phu Wiang △ Thailand 16°39N 102°23E
Phuc Yen Vietnam 21°16N 105°45E
Phuket Thailand 7°53N 98°24E
Phuket, Ko Thailand 8°0N 98°22E
Phul India 30°19N 75°14E
Phulad India 25°38N 73°49E
Phulbani India 20°28N 84°14E
Phulchari Bangla. 25°11N 89°37E
Phulera India 26°52N 75°16E
Phulpur India 25°31N 82°49E
Phunphin Thailand 9°7N 99°12E
Phuntsholing Bhutan 26°51N 89°23E
Phuphrabat Thailand 17°40N 102°45E
Phuthaditjhaba S. Africa 28°29S 28°48E
Phyu = Pyu Burma 18°30N 96°28E
Pia ◎ Australia 27°7S 116°23E
Piaçabuçu Brazil 10°24S 36°25W
Piacenza Italy 45°1N 9°40E
Piai, Tanjung Malaysia 1°17N 103°30E
Piako → N.Z. 37°12S 175°30E
Pian Cr. → Australia 30°2S 148°12E
Pian-Upe ⌂ Uganda 1°44N 34°20E
Piana France 42°15N 8°34E
Pianella Italy 42°24N 14°2E
Piangil Australia 35°5S 143°20E
Pianosa Puglia, Italy 42°12N 15°44E
Pianosa Toscana, Italy 42°35N 10°5E
Piao'ertun China 41°50N 123°47E
Piapot Canada 49°59N 109°8W
Pias Portugal 38°1N 7°29W
Piaseczno Poland 52°5N 21°2E
Piaski Poland 51°8N 22°52E
Piastów Poland 52°12N 20°48E
Piatã Brazil 13°9S 41°48W
Piatra Romania 43°51N 25°9E
Piatra Craiului △ Romania 45°30N 25°12E
Piatra Neamţ Romania 46°56N 26°21E
Piatra Olt Romania 44°22N 24°16E
Piauí □ Brazil 7°0S 43°0W
Piauí → Brazil 6°38S 42°42W
Piave → Italy 45°32N 12°44E
Piazza Ármerina Italy 37°21N 14°20E
Pibor Post South Sudan 6°47N 33°3E
Pic St-Loup France 43°47N 3°48E
Pica Chile 20°35S 69°25W
Picardie □ France 49°50N 3°0E
Picardie, Plaine de France 50°0N 2°0E
Picardy = Picardie □ France 49°50N 3°0E
Picayune U.S.A. 30°32N 89°41W
Picerno Italy 40°38N 15°38E
Pichhor India 25°58N 78°20E
Pichilemu Chile 34°22S 72°0W
Pichor India 25°11N 78°11E
Pickerel L. Canada 48°40N 91°25W
Pickering U.K. 54°15N 0°46W
Pickering, Vale of U.K. 54°14N 0°45W
Pickle Lake Canada 51°30N 90°12W
Pickwick L. U.S.A. 35°4N 88°15W
Pico Azores 38°28N 28°20W
Pico Bonito △ Honduras 15°34N 86°48W
Pico Truncado Argentina 46°40S 68°0W
Picos Brazil 7°5S 41°28W
Picos, Pta. dos Spain 41°52N 8°53W
Picos de Europa △ Spain 43°14N 4°59W
Picota Peru 6°54S 76°24W
Picton Australia 34°12S 150°34E
Picton Canada 44°1N 77°9W
Picton N.Z. 41°18S 174°3E
Picton, I. Chile 55°2S 66°57W
Pictou Canada 45°41N 62°42W
Picture Butte Canada 49°55N 112°45W
Pictured Rocks ⌂ U.S.A. 46°30N 86°30W
Picuí Brazil 6°31S 36°21W
Picún Leufú Argentina 39°30S 69°5W
Pidbuzh Ukraine 49°19N 23°14E
Pidurutalagala Sri Lanka 7°10N 80°50E
Piechowice Poland 50°51N 15°36E
Piedimonte Matese Italy 41°22N 14°22E
Piedmont = Piemonte □ Italy 45°0N 8°0E
Piedmont Ala., U.S.A. 33°55N 85°37W
Piedmont S.C., U.S.A. 34°42N 82°28W
Piedra → Spain 41°18N 1°47W
Piedra del Águila Argentina 40°2S 70°4W

ira del Águila, Embalse
  argentina 40°15S 70°4W 192 B2
rabuena Spain 39°0N 4°10W 89 G6
rahita Spain 40°28N 5°23W 88 E5
ralaves Spain 40°19N 4°42W 88 E6
ras, R. de las →
  eru 12°30S 69°15W 188 C4
ras Blancas Spain 43°33N 5°58W 88 B5
ras Negras
  exico 28°42N 100°31W 180 B4
cary Śląskie Poland 50°24N 18°57E 83 H5
säämäki Finland 62°18N 27°10E 84 A4
nen Finland 63°15N 29°40E 60 E23
ekaise S. Africa 66°20N 16°45E 60 C17
iezno Poland 54°14N 20°8E 82 D7
monte □ Italy 45°0N 8°0E 92 D5
ras S. Africa 25°15S 28°18E 145 C4
inský △ Europe 49°25N 20°28E 79 B13
ask Poland 51°16N 15°2E 82 D2
aza Italy 43°4N 11°40E 93 E8
cefield U.S.A. 44°13N 74°35W 175 B10
celand Canada 52°20N 109°46W 163 C7
ia Greece 40°13N 22°25E 96 F6
pont U.S.A. 41°45N 80°34W 174 E4
re U.S.A.
re-Buffière France 45°41N 1°22E 72 C5
re-de-Bresse France 46°54N 5°13E 71 F12
refonds Canada 45°32N 73°51W 175 A11
refontaine-les-Varans
  ance 47°14N 6°32E 71 E13
refort France 44°55N 2°50E 72 D6
relatte France 44°23N 4°43E 73 D8
son U.S.A. 29°14N 81°28W 179 F8
tany Slovak Rep. 48°38N 17°55E 79 C10
i Austria 46°36N 16°40E 79 C9
yzce Poland 50°43N 16°33E 83 H3
Retief S. Africa 27°1S 30°50E 145 C5
arsaari Finland 63°40N 22°43E 60 E20
ermaritzburg
  Africa 29°35S 30°25E 145 C5
ersburg = Polokwane
  Africa 23°54S 29°25E 145 B4
ragalla Italy 40°45N 15°53E 95 B8
rasanta Italy 43°57N 10°14E 92 E7
roşiţa Romania 45°11N 25°26E 81 E10
rosul, Vf. Maramureş,
  omania 47°35N 24°43E 81 C9
rosul, Vf. Suceava,
  omania 47°12N 25°18E 81 C10
e di Campera Italy 46°26N 12°22E 93 B9
e di Teco Italy 44°3N 7°56E 92 D4
epélago Italy 44°12N 10°37E 92 D7
aditsa Greece 39°59N 21°23E 96 G5
on I. India 14°2N 74°20E 127 G2
on L. Canada 44°27N 78°30W 174 B6
s Greece 39°17N 21°25E 98 B3
gott U.S.A. 36°23N 90°11W 177 C9
ia Italy 43°56N 7°40E 92 E4
e Argentina 37°36S 62°25W 190 D3
i U.S.A. 36°57S 174°28E 154 C3
ani India 27°36N 80°15E 125 F9
ajavesi Finland 61°45N 28°45E 84 B5
iapan Mexico 15°42N 93°14W 181 D6
wa Canada 59°37N 34°9E 84 C8
angikum Canada 51°49N 94°0W 163 C10
s Peak U.S.A. 38°50N 105°3W 168 G2
tberg S. Africa 32°55S 18°40E 144 D2
ville U.S.A. 37°29N 82°31W 173 G12
ou China 39°18N 122°22E 115 E12
witonei Canada 55°35N 97°9W 163 B9
Poland 53°10N 16°48E 83 C4
Spain 38°16N 1°11W 91 G3
nesberg △ S. Africa 25°15S 27°4E 144 B5
ani India 28°22N 75°33E 124 E6
Brazil 9°36S 35°56W 189 B3
Paraguay 26°50S 58°20W 190 B4
de la Horadada
  pain 37°52N 0°47W 91 H4
t, Dune du France 44°35N 1°13W 72 D2
t France 45°20N 4°30E 73 C8
wa Poland 51°57N 21°32E 83 D8
a → Bolivia 20°55S 64°4W 186 H6
ara Australia 21°15S 118°16E 148 D2
omaya →
  araguay 25°21S 57°42W 190 B4
a Greece 40°32N 22°59E 96 F6
rim's Rest S. Africa 24°55S 30°44E 145 B5
rimstad Sweden 56°50N 27°15E 62 B9
hit India 28°40N 79°50E 125 E8
a, → Oros Greece 39°27N 23°3E 98 B5
inas = Philippines ■
  sia 12°0N 123°0E 119 B6
sia Hungary 47°17N 19°35E 80 C4
vörösmarty Hungary 47°8N 18°42E 80 C3
hawa India 28°43N 77°42E 124 E7
ga Australia 30°21S 148°54E 151 E4
s Greece 36°55N 21°42E 98 D4
Mound Canada 49°15N 98°54W 163 D9
Point U.S.A. 33°24N 96°58W 176 E6
Rock U.S.A. 45°29N 118°50W 168 D4
anj Slovenia 46°8N 15°39E 93 B12
a Latvia 57°13N 21°40E 82 A8
no Poland 50°51N 21°16E 83 A8
a U.S.A. 32°54N 109°50W 169 K9
enta Bueno Brazil 11°35S 61°10W 186 B6
entel Peru 6°45S 79°55W 188 B2
pri Chinchwad
  dia 18°37N 73°47E 126 E1
Valley △ India 31°50N 77°50E 124 D7
de Ebro Spain 41°29N 0°33W 90 D4
ang □ Malaysia 5°20N 100°15E 121 c1
ng □ Malaysia 5°20N 100°20E 121 K3
ar, C. des Spain 39°53N 3°12E 100 B10
ar del Río Cuba 22°26N 83°40W 182 B3
arbaşı Çanakkale,
  urkey 39°53N 26°15E 99 B8
arbaşı Kayseri,
  urkey 38°43N 36°23E 104 C7
arhisar Turkey 41°37N 27°30E 97 E11
atubo, Mt. Phil. 15°8N 120°21E 119 A6
wa Canada 50°9N 95°50W 163 C9
ehely Hungary 46°41N 18°27E 80 D3
chang China 34°38N 107°30E 116 B6
her Creek Canada 49°30N 113°57W 162 D6
hi L. Canada 54°38N 124°30W 162 C4
kneyville U.S.A. 38°5N 89°23W 172 F9
zów Poland 50°32N 20°32E 83 H7

Pind Dadan Khan
  Pakistan 32°36N 73°7E 109 F8
Pindar Australia 28°30S 115°47E 149 E2
Pindaré → Brazil 3°17S 44°47W 189 A2
Pindaré-Mirim Brazil 3°37S 45°21W 189 A1
Pindera Downs ○
  Australia 29°24S 142°37E 151 A3
Pindi Gheb Pakistan 33°14N 72°21E 124 C5
Pindiga Nigeria 9°58N 10°53E 139 D7
Pindos △ Greece 39°52N 21°11E 98 B3
Pindos Oros Greece 40°0N 21°0E 98 B3
Pindus Mts. = Pindos Oros
  Greece 40°0N 21°0E 98 B3
Pine → B.C., Canada 56°8N 120°43W 162 B4
Pine → Sask., Canada 58°50N 105°38W 163 B7
Pine Bluff U.S.A. 34°13N 92°1W 176 D8
Pine Bluffs U.S.A. 41°11N 104°4W 168 F11
Pine City U.S.A. 45°50N 92°59W 172 C7
Pine Cr. → U.S.A. 41°10N 77°16W 174 E7
Pine Creek Australia 13°50S 131°50E 148 B5
Pine Falls Canada 50°34N 96°11W 163 C9
Pine Flat L. U.S.A. 36°50N 119°20W 170 J7
Pine Grove U.S.A. 40°33N 76°23W 175 F8
Pine Hill Australia 23°38S 146°57E 150 C4
Pine Hills U.S.A. 28°33N 81°27W 179 G8
Pine Island Glacier
  Antarctica 76°0S 100°0W 55 D15
Pine Level U.S.A. 32°4N 86°4W 178 C3
Pine Mountain U.S.A. 32°49N 84°51W 178 C5
Pine Pass Canada 55°25N 122°42W 162 B4
Pine Ridge Australia 31°30S 150°28E 153 A9
Pine Ridge U.S.A. 43°2N 102°33W 172 D2
Pine River Canada 51°45N 100°30W 163 C8
Pine River U.S.A. 46°43N 94°24W 172 B6
Pine Valley U.S.A. 32°50N 116°32W 171 N10
Pinecrest U.S.A. 38°12N 120°1W 170 G6
Pineda de Mar Spain 41°37N 2°42E 90 D7
Pinedale Calif., U.S.A. 36°50N 119°48W 170 J7
Pinedale Wyo., U.S.A. 42°52N 109°52W 168 E9
Pinega → Russia 64°30N 44°19E 106 C5
Pinehouse L. Canada 55°32N 106°35W 163 B7
Pineimuta → Canada 52°8N 88°33W 164 B1
Pinellas Park U.S.A. 27°50N 82°41W 179 H7
Pinerolo Italy 44°53N 7°21E 92 D4
Pines, Akra Greece 40°5N 24°20E 97 F8
Pineto Italy 42°36N 14°4E 93 F11
Pinetop-Lakeside
  U.S.A. 34°9N 109°58W 169 J9
Pinetown S. Africa 29°48S 30°54E 145 C5
Pinetta U.S.A. 30°36N 83°21W 178 E6
Pineview U.S.A. 32°7N 83°30W 178 C6
Pineville La., U.S.A. 31°19N 92°26W 176 F8
Pineville S.C., U.S.A. 33°26N 80°1W 178 B9
Pinewood U.S.A. 33°44N 80°27W 178 B9
Piney France 48°22N 4°21E 71 D11
Ping → Thailand 15°42N 100°9E 120 E3
Pingaring Australia 32°40S 118°32E 149 F2
Pingba China 26°23N 106°12E 116 F6
Pingchuan China 27°35N 101°55E 116 D3
Pingding China 37°47N 113°38E 114 F7
Pingdingshan China 33°43N 113°27E 114 H7
Pingdu China 36°42N 119°59E 115 F10
Pingelly Australia 32°32S 117°5E 149 F2
Pingguo China 23°19N 107°36E 116 F6
Pinghe China 24°17N 117°21E 117 E11
Pinghu China 30°40N 121°2E 117 B13
Pingjiang China 28°45N 113°36E 117 C9
Pingle China 24°40N 110°40E 117 E8
Pingli China 32°27N 109°22E 116 A7
Pingliang China 35°35N 106°31E 114 G4
Pinglu China 39°31N 112°30E 114 E7
Pingluo China 38°52N 106°30E 114 E4
Pingnan Fujian, China 26°55N 119°0E 117 D12
Pingnan Guangxi Zhuangzu,
  China 23°33N 110°22E 117 F8
Pingquan China 41°1N 118°37E 115 D10
Pingrup Australia 33°32S 118°29E 149 F2
Pingshan China 28°39N 104°3E 116 C5
Pingtan China 25°31N 119°47E 117 E12
Pingtang China 25°49N 107°17E 116 E6
P'ingtung Taiwan 22°38N 120°30E 117 F13
Pingwu China 32°25N 104°30E 114 H3
Pingxiang Guangxi Zhuangzu,
  China 22°6N 106°46E 116 F6
Pingxiang Jiangxi,
  China 27°43N 113°48E 117 D9
Pingyao China 37°12N 112°10E 114 F7
Pingyi China 35°30N 117°35E 115 G9
Pingyin China 36°20N 116°25E 114 F9
Pingyuan Guangdong,
  China 24°24N 115°57E 117 E10
Pingyuanjie China 23°45N 103°48E 116 F4
Pinhal Novo Portugal 38°38N 8°55W 89 G2
Pinheiro Brazil 2°31S 45°5W 189 A1
Pinheiro Machado
  Brazil 31°34S 53°23W 191 C5
Pinhel Portugal 40°50N 7°1W 88 E3
Pini Indonesia 0°10N 98°40E 118 D1
Pinios → Ilía, Greece 37°48N 21°20E 98 D3
Pinios → Trikala, Greece 39°55N 22°41E 98 B4
Pinjarra Australia 32°37S 115°52E 149 F2
Pink Mountain Canada 57°3N 122°52W 162 B4
Pinkafeld Austria 47°22N 16°9E 79 D9
Pinnacle Is. = Senkaku-Shotō
  E. China Sea 25°45N 123°30E 113 M1
Pinnacles Australia 36°25N 121°12W 170 J5
Pinnaroo Australia 35°17S 140°53E 152 C4
Pinrang Indonesia 3°46S 119°41E 119 D5
Pins, Pte. aux Canada 42°15N 81°51W 174 D3
Pinsk Belarus 52°10N 26°1E 75 B14
Pintados Chile 20°35S 69°40W 188 E4
Pinturas → Argentina 47°35S 69°40W 192 C3
Pinyang China 27°42N 120°31E 117 D13
Pinyug Russia 60°5N 48°0E 106 C8
Pio XII Brazil 3°53S 45°17W 189 A1
Pioche U.S.A. 37°56N 114°27W 169 H6
Piombino Italy 42°55N 10°32E 92 F7

Piombino, Canale di
  Italy 42°53N 10°30E 92 F7
Pioner, Ostrov Russia 79°50N 92°0E 107 B10
Pionerskiy Russia 54°56N 20°14E 82 D7
Pionki Poland 51°29N 21°28E 83 G8
Piopiotaki = Milford Sd.
  N.Z. 44°41S 167°47E 155 E2
Piorini, L. Brazil 3°15S 62°35W 186 D6
Piotrków Trybunalski
  Poland 51°23N 19°43E 83 G6
Piove di Sacco Italy 45°18N 12°2E 93 C9
Pip Iran 26°45N 60°10E 129 E9
Pipar India 26°25N 73°31E 124 F5
Pipar Road India 26°27N 73°27E 124 F5
Piparia Mad. P., India 21°49N 77°37E 124 J7
Piparia Mad. P., India 22°45N 78°23E 124 H8
Piperi Greece 39°20N 24°19E 98 B6
Pipestone U.S.A. 44°0N 96°19W 172 D5
Pipestone → Canada 52°53N 89°23W 164 B2
Pipestone Cr. →
  Canada 49°38N 100°15W 163 D8
Pipiriki N.Z. 39°28S 175°5E 154 F4
Piplan Pakistan 32°17N 71°21E 124 C4
Piploda India 23°37N 74°56E 124 H6
Pipmuacan, Rés.
  Canada 49°45N 70°30W 165 C5
Pippingarra Australia 20°27S 118°42E 148 D2
Pipriac France 47°59N 1°58W 70 E5
Piqua U.S.A. 40°9N 84°15W 173 E11
Piquet Carneiro Brazil 5°48S 39°25W 189 D4
Piquiri → Brazil 24°3S 54°14W 191 A5
Pīr Panjal Range India 32°30N 76°50E 124 C7
Pīr Sohrāb Iran 25°44N 60°54E 129 E9
Pira Benin 8°28N 1°48E 139 D5
Piracicaba Brazil 22°45S 47°40W 191 A6
Piracuruca Brazil 3°50S 41°50W 189 A2
Pirae Tahiti 17°31S 149°32W 155 b
Piraeus = Piraiévs Greece 37°57N 23°42E 98 D5
Piraiévs = Piraiévs Greece 37°57N 23°42E 98 D5
Pirajuí Brazil 21°59S 49°29W 191 A6
Piram I. India 21°36N 72°21E 124 J5
Piran = Pirano Slovenia 45°31N 13°33E 93 C10
Pirané Argentina 25°42S 59°6W 190 B4
Piranhas Brazil 9°27S 37°46W 189 B3
Pirano = Piran Slovenia 45°31N 13°33E 93 C10
Pīrānshahr Iran 36°41N 45°8E 105 D11
Pirapemas Brazil 3°43S 44°14W 189 A2
Pirapora Brazil 17°20S 44°56W 189 D2
Pirawa India 24°10N 76°2E 124 G7
Pirdop Bulgaria 42°40N 24°10E 97 D8
Pireas Greece 37°57N 23°42E 98 D5
Pires do Rio Brazil 17°18S 48°17W 189 D1
Pirgi Greece 38°13N 25°59E 99 C7
Pirgos Ilía, Greece 37°40N 21°27E 98 D3
Pirgos Kríti, Greece 35°0N 25°9E 99 F7
Pirgovo Bulgaria 43°44N 25°43E 97 C9
Piribebuy Paraguay 25°26S 57°2W 190 B4
Pirimapun Indonesia 6°20S 138°24E 119 F9
Pirin △ Bulgaria 41°48N 23°22E 96 E7
Pirin Planina Bulgaria 41°40N 23°30E 96 E7
Pirineos = Pyrénées
  Europe 42°45N 0°18E 72 F4
Piripiri Brazil 4°15S 41°46W 189 A2
Pirlangimpi Australia 11°24S 130°26E 148 B5
Pirmasens Germany 49°12N 7°36E 77 F3
Pirna Germany 50°57N 13°56E 76 E9
Pirot Serbia 43°9N 22°33E 96 C6
Piru Indonesia 3°4S 128°12E 119 E7
Pisa Italy 43°43N 10°23E 92 E7
Pisa → Poland 53°14N 21°52E 83 E8
Pisa, Firenze ✈ (PSA)
  Italy 43°40N 10°22E 92 E7
Pisa Ra. N.Z. 44°52S 169°12E 155 E4
Pisac Peru 13°25S 71°50W 188 C3
Pisagua Chile 19°40S 70°15W 188 D3
Pisarovina Croatia 45°35N 15°50E 93 C12
Pisco Peru 13°50S 76°12W 188 C2
Piscu Romania 45°30N 27°43E 81 E12
Písek Czech Rep. 49°19N 14°10E 78 B7
Pishan China 37°30N 78°33E 109 E9
Pishchanka Ukraine 51°35N 23°50E 83 G10
Pishchanka Ukraine 48°12N 28°54E 81 B13
Pishin Iran 26°6N 61°47E 129 E9
Pishin Pakistan 30°35N 67°0E 124 C1
Pishin Lora → Pakistan 29°9N 64°5E 124 E1
Pisidia Turkey 37°30N 31°40E 104 D4
Pising Indonesia 5°8S 121°53E 119 F6
Pismo Beach U.S.A. 35°9N 120°38W 170 K6
Piso, L. Liberia 6°50N 11°15W 138 D2
Pisogne Italy 45°48N 10°6E 92 C7
Pissila Burkina Faso 13°7N 0°50W 138 C4
Pissis, Cerro Argentina 27°45S 68°48W 190 B3
Pissos France 44°19N 0°49W 72 D3
Pissouri Cyprus 34°40N 32°42E 101 E11
Pisticci Italy 40°23N 16°33E 95 B9
Pistóia Italy 43°55N 10°54E 92 E7
Pistol B. Canada 62°25N 92°37W 163 A10
Pisuerga → Spain 41°33N 4°52W 88 D6
Piszki Poland 53°38N 21°49E 82 E8
Pit → U.S.A. 40°47N 122°6W 168 F2
Pitangui Brazil 19°40S 44°54W 189 D2
Pitarpunga L.
  Australia 34°24S 143°30E 152 C5
Pitcairn I. Pac. Oc. 25°5S 130°5W 157 K14
Pitch L. Trin. & Tob. 10°14N 61°39W 187 K15
Piteå Sweden 65°20N 21°25E 60 D19
Piteälven → Sweden 65°20N 21°25E 60 D19
Piterka Russia 50°41N 47°29E 84 E8
Piteşti Romania 44°52N 24°54E 81 F9
Pithapuram India 17°10N 82°15E 125 L13
Pithara Australia 30°20S 116°35E 149 F2
Pithio Greece 41°24N 26°40E 97 E10
Pithiviers France 48°10N 2°13E 70 D5
Pithora India 21°16N 82°31E 126 D6
Pithoragarh India 29°35N 80°13E 125 E9
Pithoro Pakistan 25°31N 69°23E 124 G3
Pitigliano Italy 42°38N 11°40E 92 F8
Pitkyaranta Russia 61°34N 31°57E 84 B6
Pitlochry U.K. 56°42N 3°44W 65 E5
Pitnak = Drujba
  Uzbekistan 41°13N 61°18E 108 D6
Pitrufquén Chile 38°59S 72°39W 190 D2
Pitsilia Cyprus 34°55N 33°0E 101 E12
Pitsunda = Bichvinta
  Georgia 43°9N 40°21E 87 J5
Pitt I. Canada 53°30N 129°50W 162 C3
Pitti I. India 10°50N 72°38E 127 J1

Pittsburg Calif., U.S.A. 38°2N 121°53W 170 G5
Pittsburg Kans., U.S.A. 37°25N 94°42W 172 G6
Pittsburg Tex., U.S.A. 33°0N 94°59W 176 E7
Pittsburgh U.S.A. 40°26N 79°58W 174 F5
Pittsfield Ill., U.S.A. 39°36N 90°49W 172 F8
Pittsfield Maine,
  U.S.A. 44°47N 69°23W 173 C19
Pittsfield Mass., U.S.A. 42°27N 73°15W 175 D11
Pittsfield N.H., U.S.A. 43°18N 71°20W 175 C13
Pittston U.S.A. 41°19N 75°47W 175 E9
Pittsview U.S.A. 32°11N 85°10W 178 C4
Pittsworth Australia 27°41S 151°37E 151 D5
Pituri → Australia 22°35S 138°30E 150 C2
Piumhi Brazil 20°28S 45°58W 189 E1
Piura Peru 5°15S 80°38W 188 B1
Piura □ Peru 5°10S 80°0W 188 B2
Piuthan Nepal 28°7N 82°56E 125 E10
Pixian China 30°48N 103°52E 116 B4
Pixley U.S.A. 35°58N 119°18W 170 K7
Pizarra Spain 36°36N 4°42W 89 J6
Pizhou = Pei Xian
  China 34°44N 116°55E 114 G9
Pizhou China 34°18N 117°57E 115 G9
Pizzo Italy 38°44N 16°10E 95 D9
Placentia Canada 47°20N 54°0W 165 C9
Placentia B. Canada 47°0N 54°40W 165 C9
Placerville U.S.A. 38°44N 120°48W 170 G6
Placetas Cuba 22°15N 79°44W 182 B4
Plácido de Castro
  Brazil 10°20S 67°11W 188 C4
Plačkovica Macedonia 41°45N 22°30E 96 E6
Plaine des Jarres Laos 19°27N 103°10E 120 C4
Plainfield N.J., U.S.A. 40°37N 74°25W 175 F10
Plainfield Ohio, U.S.A. 40°13N 81°43W 174 F3
Plainfield Vt., U.S.A. 44°17N 72°26W 175 B12
Plains Ga., U.S.A. 32°2N 84°24W 178 C5
Plains Mont., U.S.A. 47°28N 114°53W 168 C6
Plains Tex., U.S.A. 33°11N 102°50W 176 D3
Plainview Nebr., U.S.A. 42°21N 97°47W 172 D5
Plainview Tex., U.S.A. 34°11N 101°43W 176 D4
Plainwell U.S.A. 42°27N 85°38W 173 D11
Plaisance France 43°36N 0°3E 72 E4
Plaistow U.S.A. 42°50N 71°6W 175 D13
Plaka Greece 40°0N 25°24E 99 B7
Plaka, Akra Greece 35°11N 26°19E 101 D8
Plakenska Planina
  Macedonia 41°14N 21°2E 96 E5
Planá Czech Rep. 49°50N 12°44E 78 B5
Plana Cays Bahamas 22°38N 73°30W 183 B5
Planada U.S.A. 37°16N 120°19W 170 H6
Planchón Peru 12°14S 69°11W 188 C4
Plancoët France 48°32N 2°13W 70 D4
Plandište Serbia 45°16N 21°10E 80 E6
Plano U.S.A. 33°1N 96°42W 176 E6
Plant City U.S.A. 28°1N 82°7W 179 G7
Plantation U.S.A. 26°7N 80°41W 179 J9
Plaquemine U.S.A. 30°17N 91°14W 176 F9
Plasencia Spain 40°3N 6°8W 88 E4
Plaški Croatia 45°4N 15°22E 93 C12
Plast Russia 54°22N 60°58E 108 D7
Plaster City U.S.A. 32°47N 115°51W 171 N11
Plaster Rock Canada 46°53N 67°22W 165 C6
Plastun Russia 44°45N 136°19E 112 B8
Plasy Czech Rep. 49°56N 13°24E 78 B6
Plata, Río de la →
  S. Amer. 34°45S 57°30W 190 C4
Plátani → Italy 37°23N 13°16E 94 E6
Platanos Greece 35°28N 23°33E 101 D5
Plateau □ Nigeria 8°30N 9°0E 139 D6
Platja d'Aro Spain 41°49N 3°4E 90 D8
Platte → Mo., U.S.A. 39°16N 94°50W 172 F6
Platte → Nebr., U.S.A. 41°4N 95°53W 172 E6
Platteville U.S.A. 42°44N 90°29W 172 D8
Plattling Germany 48°46N 12°53E 77 G8
Plattsburgh U.S.A. 44°42N 73°28W 175 B11
Plattsmouth U.S.A. 41°1N 95°53W 172 E6
Plau Germany 53°27N 12°16E 76 B8
Plauen Germany 50°30N 12°8E 76 E8
Plauer See Germany 53°28N 12°17E 76 B8
Plav Montenegro 42°38N 19°57E 96 D3
Plavinas Latvia 56°35N 25°46E 84 D3
Plavnica Montenegro 42°20N 19°13E 96 D3
Plavno Croatia 44°9N 16°10E 93 D13
Plavsk Russia 53°40N 37°18E 84 F9
Playa Blanca Canary Is. 28°51N 13°50W 100 F6
Playa de las Americas
  Canary Is. 28°5N 16°43W 100 F3
Playa de Mogán
  Canary Is. 27°48N 15°47W 100 G4
Playa del Carmen
  Mexico 20°37N 87°4W 181 C7
Playa del Inglés
  Canary Is. 27°45N 15°33W 100 G4
Playa Esmeralda
  Canary Is. 28°8N 14°16W 100 F5
Playgreen L. Canada 54°0N 98°15W 163 C9
Pleasant Bay Canada 46°51N 60°48W 165 C7
Pleasant Hill U.S.A. 38°47N 94°16W 172 F6
Pleasant Mount U.S.A. 41°44N 75°26W 175 E9
Pleasanton Calif.,
  U.S.A. 37°39N 121°52W 170 H5
Pleasanton Tex., U.S.A. 28°58N 98°29W 176 G5
Pleasantville N.J.,
  U.S.A. 39°24N 74°32W 173 F16
Pleasantville Pa.,
  U.S.A. 41°35N 79°34W 174 E5
Pléaux France 45°8N 2°13E 72 C6
Plei Ku Vietnam 13°57N 108°0E 120 F7
Plélan-le-Grand France 48°0N 2°7W 70 D4
Pleniţa Romania 44°14N 23°10E 81 F8
Plenty □ Australia 23°25S 136°31E 150 C2
Plenty, B. of N.Z. 37°45S 177°0E 154 F6
Plentywood U.S.A. 48°47N 104°34W 168 B11
Plérin France 48°32N 2°46W 70 D4
Pleshcheyevo Ozero △
  Russia 56°45N 38°50E 84 D10
Plessisville Canada 46°14N 71°47W 165 C5
Plestin-les-Grèves France 48°40N 3°39W 70 D3
Pleszew Poland 51°53N 17°47E 83 G4
Pleternica Croatia 45°17N 17°48E 93 D14
Plétipi, L. Canada 51°44N 70°6W 165 B5
Pleven Bulgaria 43°26N 24°37E 97 C8
Plevlja = Pljevlja
  Montenegro 43°21N 19°21E 96 C3
Plevna Canada 44°58N 76°59W 174 B8
Plitvice Lakes = Plitvička Jezera △
  Croatia 44°50N 15°45E 93 D12
Plitvička Jezera △
  Croatia 44°54N 15°35E 93 D12

Plješevica Croatia 44°45N 15°45E 93 D12
Pljevlja Montenegro 43°21N 19°21E 96 C3
Ploaghe Italy 40°40N 8°45E 94 B1
Ploče Croatia 43°4N 17°26E 93 E14
Płock Poland 52°32N 19°40E 83 F6
Plöckenpass 46°37N 12°57E 93 B9
Plöckenstein Germany 48°46N 13°51E 77 G9
Ploemeur France 47°44N 3°26E 70 E3
Ploërmel France 47°55N 2°26W 70 E4
Ploieşti Romania 44°57N 26°5E 81 F11
Plomari Greece 38°59N 26°24E 99 C8
Plombières-les-Bains
  France 47°58N 6°27E 71 E13
Plomin Croatia 45°8N 14°10E 93 C11
Plön Germany 54°9N 10°22E 76 A6
Plonge, Lac la Canada 55°8N 107°20W 163 B7
Płońsk Poland 52°37N 20°21E 83 F7
Plopeni Romania 45°4N 25°59E 81 E10
Plopșului, Munţii
  Romania 47°5N 22°30E 80 C7
Ploty Poland 53°48N 15°18E 82 E2
Plouaret France 48°37N 3°28W 70 D3
Plouay France 47°55N 3°21W 70 E3
Ploučnice → Czech Rep. 50°46N 14°13E 78 A7
Ploudalmézeau France 48°34N 4°41W 70 D2
Plouescat France 48°39N 4°0W 70 D2
Plougasnou France 48°42N 3°49W 70 D3
Plougastel-Daoulas
  France 48°22N 4°17W 70 D2
Plouguerneau France 48°36N 4°34W 70 D2
Plouha France 48°41N 2°57W 70 D4
Plouhinec France 48°0N 4°29W 70 E2
Plovdiv Bulgaria 42°8N 24°44E 97 D8
Plovdiv □ Bulgaria 42°15N 24°30E 97 D8
Plover Cove Res. China 22°30N 114°15E 111 a
Plum U.S.A. 40°29N 79°47W 174 F5
Plum I. U.S.A. 41°11N 72°12W 175 E12
Plumas U.S.A. 39°45N 120°4W 170 F6
Plummer U.S.A. 47°20N 116°53W 168 C5
Plumridge Lakes
  Australia 29°26S 125°16E 149 E4
Plumtree Zimbabwe 20°27S 27°55E 143 G2
Plunge Lithuania 55°53N 21°59E 82 C8
Pluvigner France 47°46N 3°1W 70 E3
Plužine Montenegro 43°8N 18°51E 96 C2
Plymouth Trin. & Tob. 11°14N 60°48W 187 J16
Plymouth U.K. 50°22N 4°10W 67 G3
Plymouth Calif.,
  U.S.A. 38°29N 120°51W 170 G6
Plymouth Ind., U.S.A. 41°21N 86°19W 172 E10
Plymouth Mass.,
  U.S.A. 41°57N 70°40W 175 D14
Plymouth N.C.,
  U.S.A. 35°52N 76°43W 177 B16
Plymouth N.H.,
  U.S.A. 43°46N 71°41W 175 C13
Plymouth Wis.,
  U.S.A. 43°45N 87°59W 172 D10
Plympton-Wyoming = Wyoming
  Canada 42°57N 82°7W 174 D2
Plynlimon = Pumlumon Fawr
  U.K. 52°28N 3°46W 67 E4
Plyusa Russia 58°28N 29°27E 84 C5
Plyusa → Russia 59°4N 28°6E 84 C5
Plzeň Czech Rep. 49°45N 13°22E 78 B6
Plzeňský □ Czech Rep. 49°35N 13°0E 78 B6
Pmere Nyente ○
  Australia 24°15S 136°10E 150 C2
Pniewy Poland 52°31N 16°16E 83 F3
Pô Burkina Faso 11°14N 1°5W 139 C4
Po → Italy 44°57N 12°4E 93 C9
Po, Delta del Italy 44°55N 12°30E 93 C9
Po → B. Burkina Faso 11°25N 1°5W 139 C4
Po Hai = Bo Hai China 39°0N 119°0E 115 E10
Po Toi China 22°10N 114°16E 111 a
Pobè Benin 7°0N 2°56E 139 D5
Pobé Burkina Faso 11°25N 1°42W 139 C4
Pobeda Russia 65°12N 146°12E 107 C15
Pobedy, Pik Kyrgyzstan 42°0N 79°58E 109 D9
Pobiedziska Poland 52°29N 17°11E 83 F4
Pobladura del Valle Spain 42°6N 5°44W 88 C5
Poblet, Monasterio de
  Spain 41°22N 1°4E 90 D6
Pobra de Trives Spain 42°20N 7°6W 88 C3
Pocahontas Ark.,
  U.S.A. 36°16N 90°58W 177 C9
Pocahontas Iowa,
  U.S.A. 42°44N 94°40W 172 D6
Pocatello U.S.A. 42°52N 112°27W 168 E7
Počátky Czech Rep. 49°15N 15°14E 78 B8
Pochep Russia 52°58N 33°29E 86 F7
Pochinki Russia 54°41N 44°59E 86 C7
Pochinok Russia 54°28N 32°29E 86 C7
Pöchlarn Austria 48°12N 15°12E 78 C8
Pocinhos Brazil 7°4S 36°3W 189 B3
Pocking Germany 48°24N 13°19E 77 G9
Poções Brazil 14°31S 40°21W 189 D3
Pocomoke City U.S.A. 38°5N 75°34W 173 F16
Poços de Caldas Brazil 21°50S 46°33W 191 A6
Podbořany Czech Rep. 50°14N 13°24E 78 A6
Poddębice Poland 51°54N 18°58E 83 G5
Poddorie Russia 57°30N 31°36E 84 D5
Podensac France 44°40N 0°22W 72 D3
Podgorač Croatia 45°27N 18°13E 80 E3
Podgorica Montenegro 42°30N 19°19E 96 D3
Podile India 15°37N 79°37E 127 G4
Podilska Vysochyna
  Ukraine 49°0N 28°0E 81 B13
Podkarpackie □ Poland 50°0N 22°0E 83 H9
Podkova Bulgaria 41°24N 25°24E 97 E9
Podlaskie □ Poland 53°0N 23°0E 83 E9
Podoleni Romania 46°26N 26°39E 81 D11
Podolínec Slovak Rep. 49°16N 20°31E 83 J8
Podolsk Russia 55°25N 37°30E 84 D9
Podor Senegal 16°40N 15°2W 138 B1
Podporozhye Russia 60°55N 34°2E 84 B8
Podu Turcului Romania 46°11N 27°25E 81 D12
Podujevo Kosovo 42°54N 21°10E 96 D6
Podyjí △ Czech Rep. 48°51N 15°55E 78 B8
Poel Germany 54°0N 11°25E 76 A7
Pofadder S. Africa 29°10S 19°22E 144 C2
Pogamasing Canada 46°55N 81°50W 164 C2
Poggiardo Italy 40°3N 18°23E 95 B11
Poggibonsi Italy 43°28N 11°9E 92 E8
Póggio Mirteto Italy 42°16N 12°41E 93 F9
Pogoanele Romania 44°55N 27°0E 81 F12

Pogorzela Poland 51°50N 17°12E 83 G4
Pogradec Albania 40°54N 20°37E 96 F4
Pogranichnyy Russia 44°25N 131°24E 112 B5
Poh Indonesia 0°46S 122°51E 119 E6
Pohang S. Korea 36°1N 129°23E 115 F15
Pohjanmaa □ Finland 62°58N 22°50E 60 E20
Pohnpei Micronesia 6°55N 158°10E 156 G7
Pohorelá Slovak Rep. 48°46N 19°59E 83 G10
Pohořelice Czech Rep. 48°59N 16°31E 79 C9
Pohorje Slovenia 46°30N 15°2E 93 B12
Pohri India 25°32N 77°22E 124 G6
Poiana Mare Romania 43°57N 23°5E 80 G8
Poiana Ruscăi, Munţii
  Romania 45°45N 22°25E 80 E7
Poiana Stampei Romania 47°19N 25°8E 81 C10
Poinsett, C. Antarctica 65°42S 113°18E 55 C8
Point Baker U.S.A. 56°21N 133°37W 162 B2
Point Calimere India 10°17N 79°49E 127 J4
Point Fortin
  Trin. & Tob. 10°10N 61°42W 187 K15
Point Hope U.S.A. 68°21N 166°47W 166 B6
Point L. Canada 65°15N 113°4W 160 D9
Point Lisas
  Trin. & Tob. 10°24N 61°29W 187 K15
Point Pedro Sri Lanka 9°50N 80°15E 127 K5
Point Pelee △ Canada 41°57N 82°31W 174 E2
Point Pleasant N.J.,
  U.S.A. 40°5N 74°4W 175 F10
Point Pleasant W. Va.,
  U.S.A. 38°51N 82°8W 173 F12
Point Reyes △ U.S.A. 38°10N 122°55W 170 G2
Pointe-à-Pitre
  Guadeloupe 16°15N 61°32W 182 b
Pointe-au-Pic = La Malbaie
  Canada 47°40N 70°10W 165 C5
Pointe-Claire Canada 45°26N 73°50W 175 A11
Pointe-Gatineau
  Canada 45°27N 75°41W 175 A9
Pointe-Noire Congo 4°48S 11°53E 140 E2
Pointe-Noire Guadeloupe 16°14N 61°47W 182 b
Poio = O Convento Spain 42°26N 8°41W 88 C2
Poipet Cambodia 13°39N 102°33E 120 F4
Poirino Italy 44°56N 7°48E 92 D4
Poisonbush Ra.
  Australia 22°30S 121°30E 148 D3
Poissonnier Pt.
  Australia 19°57S 119°10E 148 C2
Poitiers France 46°35N 0°20E 70 F7
Poitou France 46°40N 0°10W 72 B3
Poitou-Charentes □
  France 46°10N 0°15E 72 B4
Poix-de-Picardie France 49°47N 1°58E 71 C8
Poix-Terron France 49°38N 4°38E 71 C11
Pojoaque U.S.A. 35°54N 106°1W 169 J10
Pokaran India 27°0N 71°50E 124 F4
Pokataroo Australia 29°30S 148°36E 151 D4
Pokhara Nepal 28°14N 83°58E 125 E10
Pokhvistnevo Russia 53°36N 52°0E 86 D11
Poko
  Dem. Rep. of the Congo 3°7N 26°52E 142 B2
Pokrov Russia 55°55N 39°7E 84 E10
Pokrovka = Kyzyl-Suu
  Kyrgyzstan 42°20N 78°0E 109 D9
Pokrovsk Russia 61°29N 129°0E 107 C13
Pokrovskoye Russia 47°25N 38°54E 85 J10
Pol-e Dokhtar Iran 33°9N 47°42E 105 C13
Pol-e Zahāb Iran 34°27N 45°51E 105 C11
Pola = Pula Croatia 44°54N 13°57E 93 D10
Pola Russia 57°55N 32°0E 84 D7
Pola de Allande Spain 43°16N 6°37W 88 B4
Pola de Lena Spain 43°10N 5°49W 88 B5
Pola de Siero Spain 43°24N 5°39W 88 B5
Pola de Somiedo Spain 43°5N 6°15W 88 B4
Polacca U.S.A. 35°50N 110°23W 169 J8
Polan Iran 25°30N 61°10E 129 E9
Pol'ana Slovak Rep. 48°38N 19°29E 79 C12
Poland ■ Europe 52°0N 20°0E 83 F8
Polanica-Zdrój Poland 50°24N 16°32E 83 H3
Polaniec Poland 50°26N 21°17E 83 H8
Polar Bear △ Canada 55°0N 83°45W 164 A2
Polatlı Turkey 39°36N 32°9E 104 C5
Polatsk Belarus 55°30N 28°50E 84 E5
Polavaram India 17°15N 81°32E 126 C5
Polcura Chile 37°17S 71°43W 190 D1
Polczyn-Zdrój Poland 53°47N 16°5E 82 E3
Poldasht Iran 39°20N 45°4E 105 C11
Poleski □ Poland 51°29N 23°5E 83 G10
Polessk Russia 54°50N 21°8E 82 D8
Polesye = Pripet Marshes
  Europe 52°10N 27°10E 75 B15
Polgar Hungary 47°54N 21°6E 80 C6
Poli Cameroon 8°34N 13°15E 139 D7
Policastro, G. di Italy 40°0N 15°35E 95 C8
Police Poland 53°33N 14°33E 82 E1
Police, Pte. Seychelles 4°51S 55°32E 141 b
Polichnitos Greece 39°6N 26°10E 99 C8
Polička Czech Rep. 49°43N 16°15E 79 B9
Policoro Italy 40°13N 16°40E 95 B9
Poliegos Greece 36°45N 24°38E 98 E6
Polignano a Mare Italy 41°0N 17°13E 95 A10
Poligny France 46°50N 5°42E 71 F12
Polillo Is. Phil. 14°56N 122°0E 119 B6
Polis Cyprus 35°2N 32°26E 101 D11
Polistena Italy 38°24N 16°4E 95 D9
Políyiros Greece 40°23N 23°25E 96 F7
Polk U.S.A. 41°22N 79°56W 174 E5
Polkowice Poland 51°29N 16°3E 83 G3
Polla Italy 40°31N 15°28E 95 B8
Pollachi India 10°35N 77°0E 127 F3
Pollença Spain 39°54N 3°1E 100 B10
Pollença, B. de Spain 39°53N 3°8E 100 B10
Póllica Italy 40°11N 15°3E 95 B8
Pollino, Mte. Italy 39°54N 16°13E 95 C9
Polna Russia 58°31N 28°5E 84 C5
Polo U.S.A. 41°59N 89°35W 172 E9
Pology Ukraine 47°29N 36°15E 85 J8
Polokwane S. Africa 23°54S 29°25E 145 B4
Polokwane → S. Africa 22°25S 30°5E 145 A5
Polonne Ukraine 50°6N 27°30E 81 A11
Polonnaruwa Sri Lanka 7°56N 81°0E 127 L5
Polonnoye = Polonne
  Ukraine 50°6N 27°30E 81 A11
Polski Trŭmbesh
  Bulgaria 43°20N 25°38E 97 C9
Polsko Kosovo Bulgaria 43°23N 25°10E 97 C9
Polson U.S.A. 47°41N 114°9W 168 C6
Poltár Slovak Rep. 48°26N 19°48E 79 C12

Poltava Ukraine 49°35N 34°35E 85 H8
Poltava □ Ukraine 50°15N 33°15E 85 G7
Põltsamaa Estonia 58°39N 25°58E 84 C3
Polunochnoye Russia 60°52N 60°25E 106 C7
Polur India 12°32N 79°11E 127 H4
Põlva Estonia 58°3N 27°3E 84 C4
Polyana Ukraine 48°38N 22°58E 80 B7
Polyarny Russia 69°8N 33°20E 60 B25
Polyarnyye Zori Russia 67°22N 32°30E 60 C25
Polynesia Pac. Oc. 10°0S 162°0W 157 F11
Polynésie française = French Polynesia ☒ Pac. Oc. 20°0S 145°0W 157 J13
Pomabamba Peru 8°50S 77°28W 188 B2
Pomarance Italy 43°18N 10°52E 92 E7
Pombal Brazil 6°45S 37°50W 189 B3
Pombal Portugal 39°55N 8°40W 88 F2
Pombia Greece 35°0N 24°51E 101 E6
Pomene Mozam. 22°53S 35°33E 145 B6
Pomeroy Ohio, U.S.A. 39°2N 82°2W 173 F12
Pomeroy Wash., U.S.A. 46°28N 117°36W 168 C5
Pomézia Italy 41°40N 12°30E 94 A5
Pomichna Ukraine 48°13N 31°36E 85 H6
Pomona Australia 26°22S 152°52E 151 D5
Pomona U.S.A. 34°4N 117°45W 171 L9
Pomona Park U.S.A. 29°30N 81°36W 179 F8
Pomorie Bulgaria 42°32N 27°41E 97 D11
Pomorskie □ Poland 54°30N 18°0E 82 D5
Pomorskie, Pojezierze Poland 53°40N 16°37E 82 E3
Pomos Cyprus 35°9N 32°33E 101 D11
Pomos, C. Cyprus 35°10N 32°33E 101 D11
Pompano Beach U.S.A. 26°14N 80°7W 179 J9
Pompei Italy 40°45N 14°30E 95 B7
Pompey France 48°46N 6°6E 71 D13
Pompeys Pillar U.S.A. 45°59N 107°57W 168 D10
Pompeys Pillar ⌂ U.S.A. 46°0N 108°0W 168 D10
Pompton Lakes U.S.A. 41°0N 74°17W 175 F10
Ponape = Pohnpei Micronesia 6°55N 158°10E 156 G7
Ponask L. Canada 54°0N 92°41W 164 B1
Ponca U.S.A. 42°34N 96°43W 172 D5
Ponca City U.S.A. 36°42N 97°5W 176 C6
Ponce Puerto Rico 18°1N 66°37W 183 d
Ponce de Leon U.S.A. 30°44N 85°56W 178 E4
Ponce de Leon B. U.S.A. 25°15N 81°10W 179 K8
Ponchatoula U.S.A. 30°26N 90°26W 177 F9
Poncheville, L. Canada 50°10N 76°55W 164 B4
Pond U.S.A. 35°43N 119°20W 171 K7
Pond Inlet Canada 72°40N 77°0W 161 C16
Pondicherry = Puducherry India 11°59N 79°50E 127 J4
Ponds, I. of Canada 53°27N 55°52W 165 B8
Ponferrada Spain 42°32N 6°35W 88 C4
Poniatowa Poland 51°11N 22°3E 83 G9
Poniec Poland 51°48N 16°50E 83 G3
Ponikva Slovenia 46°16N 15°26E 93 B12
Ponnaiyar → India 11°50N 79°45E 127 J4
Ponnani India 10°45N 75°59E 127 J2
Ponneri India 13°20N 80°15E 127 H5
Ponnuru India 16°5N 80°34E 127 F5
Ponoka Canada 52°42N 113°40W 162 C6
Ponorogo Indonesia 7°52S 111°27E 119 G14
Pons = Ponts Spain 41°55N 1°12E 90 D6
Pons France 45°35N 0°34W 72 C3
Ponsul → Portugal 39°40N 7°31W 88 F3
Pont-à-Mousson France 48°54N 6°1E 71 D13
Pont-Audemer France 49°21N 0°30E 70 C7
Pont-Aven France 47°51N 3°47W 70 E3
Pont Canavese Italy 45°25N 7°36E 92 C4
Pont-d'Ain France 46°3N 5°21E 71 F12
Pont-de-Roide France 47°23N 6°45E 71 E13
Pont-de-Salars France 44°18N 2°44E 72 D6
Pont-de-Vaux France 46°26N 4°56E 71 F11
Pont-de-Veyle France 46°17N 4°53E 71 F11
Pont-du-Château France 45°47N 3°15E 71 G10
Pont du Gard France 43°57N 4°32E 73 E8
Pont du Gard Gard, France 43°56N 4°32E 73 E8
Pont-l'Abbé France 47°52N 4°15W 70 E2
Pont-l'Évêque France 49°18N 0°11E 70 C7
Pont-St-Esprit France 44°16N 4°40E 73 D8
Pont-St-Martin Italy 45°36N 7°48E 92 C4
Pont-Ste-Maxence France 49°18N 2°36E 71 C9
Pont-sur-Yonne France 48°18N 3°10E 71 D10
Ponta Delgada Azores 37°44N 25°40W 134 a
Ponta do Sol Madeira 32°42N 17°7W 100 D2
Ponta Grossa Brazil 25°7S 50°10W 191 B5
Ponta Porã Brazil 22°20S 55°35W 191 A4
Pontacq France 43°11N 0°8W 72 E3
Pontailler-sur-Saône France 47°13N 5°25E 71 E12
Pontal → Brazil 9°8S 40°12W 189 B2
Pontarlier France 46°54N 6°20E 71 F13
Pontassieve Italy 43°46N 11°26E 93 E8
Pontaumur France 45°52N 2°40E 72 C6
Pontcharra France 45°26N 6°1E 73 C10
Pontchartrain, L. U.S.A. 30°5N 90°5W 177 F9
Pontchâteau France 47°25N 2°5W 70 E4
Ponte Alta, Serra do Brazil 19°42S 47°40W 189 D1
Ponte Alta do Norte Brazil 10°45S 47°34W 189 C1
Ponte da Barca Portugal 41°48N 8°25W 88 D2
Ponte de Lima Portugal 41°46N 8°35W 88 D2
Ponte de Sor Portugal 39°17N 8°1W 89 F2
Ponte dell'Ólio Italy 44°52N 9°39E 92 D6
Ponte di Legno Italy 46°16N 10°31E 92 B7
Ponte do Pungué Mozam. 19°30S 34°33E 143 F3
Ponte-Leccia France 42°28N 9°13E 73 F13
Ponte nelle Alpi Italy 46°11N 12°16E 93 B9
Ponte Nova Brazil 20°25S 42°54W 189 E2
Ponte Vedra Beach U.S.A. 30°15N 81°23W 178 E8
Ponteareas Spain 42°10N 8°28W 88 C2
Pontebba Italy 46°30N 13°18E 93 B10
Ponteceso Spain 43°15N 8°54W 88 B2
Pontecorvo Italy 41°27N 13°40E 94 A6
Pontedeume Spain 43°24N 8°10W 88 B2
Ponteix Canada 49°46N 107°29W 163 D7
Pontevedra Spain 42°26N 8°40W 88 C2
Pontevedra □ Spain 42°25N 8°39W 88 C2
Pontevedra, R. de → Spain 42°22N 8°45W 88 C2
Pontevico Italy 45°16N 10°5E 92 C7
Pontiac Ill., U.S.A. 40°53N 88°38W 172 E9
Pontiac Mich., U.S.A. 42°38N 83°18W 173 D12
Pontian Kechil Malaysia 1°29N 103°23E 121 d
Pontianak Indonesia 0°3S 109°15E 118 E3
Pontine Is. = Ponziane, Ísole Italy 40°55N 12°57E 94 B5
Pontine Mts. = Kuzey Anadolu Dağları Turkey 41°0N 36°45E 104 B7
Pontínia Italy 41°25N 13°2E 94 A6
Pontivy France 48°5N 2°58W 70 D4
Pontoise France 49°3N 2°5E 71 C9
Ponton → Canada 58°27N 116°11W 162 B5
Pontorson France 48°34N 1°30W 70 D5
Pontrémoli Italy 44°22N 9°53E 92 D6
Pontrieux France 48°42N 3°10W 70 D3
Ponts Spain 41°55N 1°12E 90 D6
Pontypool Canada 44°6N 78°38W 174 B6
Pontypool U.K. 51°42N 3°2W 67 F4
Ponza Italy 40°54N 12°58E 94 B5
Ponziane, Ísole Italy 40°55N 12°57E 94 B5
Poochera Australia 32°43S 134°51E 151 E1
Poole U.K. 50°43N 1°59W 67 G6
Poole □ U.K. 50°43N 1°59W 67 G6
Pooler U.S.A. 32°7N 81°15W 178 C8
Poona = Pune India 18°29N 73°57E 126 E1
Poonamallee India 13°3N 80°10E 127 H5
Pooncarie Australia 33°22S 142°31E 152 B5
Poopelloe L. Australia 31°40S 144°0E 152 A6
Poopó Bolivia 18°23S 66°59W 188 D4
Poopó, L. de Bolivia 18°30S 67°35W 188 D4
Poor Knights Is. N.Z. 35°29S 174°43E 154 B3
Popayán Colombia 2°27N 76°36W 186 C3
Poperinge Belgium 50°51N 2°42E 69 D2
Popiltah L. Australia 33°10S 141°42E 152 B4
Popina Bulgaria 44°7N 26°57E 97 B10
Popio L. Australia 33°10S 141°52E 152 B4
Poplar U.S.A. 48°7N 105°12W 168 B11
Poplar → Canada 53°0N 97°19W 163 C9
Poplar Bluff U.S.A. 36°46N 90°24W 172 G8
Poplarville U.S.A. 30°51N 89°32W 177 F10
Popocatépetl, Volcán Mexico 19°2N 98°38W 181 D5
Popokabaka Dem. Rep. of the Congo 5°41S 16°40E 140 F3
Pópoli Italy 42°10N 13°50E 93 F10
Popovača Croatia 45°30N 16°41E 93 C13
Popovo Bulgaria 43°21N 26°18E 97 C10
Poppberg Germany 49°26N 11°37E 77 F7
Poppi Italy 43°43N 11°46E 93 E8
Poprad Slovak Rep. 49°3N 20°18E 79 B13
Poprad → Slovak Rep. 49°38N 20°42E 79 B13
Porali → Pakistan 25°58N 66°26E 124 G2
Porangaba Brazil 8°48S 70°36W 188 B3
Porangahau N.Z. 40°17S 176°37E 154 G5
Porbandar India 21°44N 69°43E 124 J3
Porcher I. Canada 53°50N 130°30W 162 C2
Porcos → Brazil 12°42S 45°7W 189 C1
Porcuna Spain 37°52N 4°11W 89 H6
Porcupine → Canada 59°11N 104°46W 163 B8
Porcupine → U.S.A. 66°34N 145°19W 160 D2
Porcupine Abyssal Plain Atl. Oc. 48°0N 8°0W 56 B10
Porcupine Gorge △ Australia 20°22S 144°26E 150 C3
Pordenone Italy 45°57N 12°39E 93 C9
Pordim Bulgaria 43°23N 24°51E 97 C8
Poreč Croatia 45°14N 13°36E 93 C10
Poretskoye Russia 55°9N 46°21E 86 C8
Pori Finland 61°29N 21°48E 84 B1
Pori Greece 35°58N 23°13E 98 F5
Porkhov Russia 57°45N 29°38E 84 D5
Porlamar Venezuela 10°57N 63°51W 186 A6
Porlezza Italy 46°2N 9°7E 92 B6
Porma → Spain 42°49N 5°28W 88 C5
Pormpuraaw Australia 14°59S 141°26E 150 A3
Pormpuraaw ۞ Australia 14°55S 141°47E 150 A3
Pornic France 47°7N 2°5W 70 E4
Poronaysk Russia 49°13N 143°0E 111 B17
Poros Greece 37°30N 23°30E 98 D5
Poroshiri-Dake Japan 42°41N 142°52E 112 C11
Poroszló Hungary 47°39N 20°40E 80 C5
Poroto Mts. Tanzania 9°0S 33°30E 143 D3
Porpoise B. Antarctica 66°0S 127°0E 55 C9
Porquerolles, Î. de France 43°0N 6°13E 73 F10
Porrentruy Switz. 47°25N 7°6E 77 H3
Porreres Spain 39°31N 3°2E 100 B10
Porsangerfjorden Norway 70°40N 25°40E 60 A21
Porsgrunn Norway 59°10N 9°40E 61 G13
Port Adelaide Australia 34°50S 138°30E 152 C3
Port Alberni Canada 49°14N 124°50W 162 D4
Port Albert Australia 38°42S 146°42E 153 E7
Port Alfred S. Africa 33°36S 26°55E 144 D4
Port Alice Canada 50°20N 127°25W 162 C3
Port Allegany U.S.A. 41°48N 78°17W 174 E6
Port Allen U.S.A. 30°27N 91°12W 176 F9
Port Alma Australia 23°38S 150°53E 150 C5
Port Alma Canada 42°10N 82°14W 174 D2
Port Angeles U.S.A. 48°7N 123°27W 170 B3
Port Antonio Jamaica 18°10N 76°26W 182 a
Port Aransas U.S.A. 27°50N 97°4W 176 H6
Port Arthur Australia 43°7S 147°50E 151 G4
Port Arthur U.S.A. 29°54N 93°56W 176 G8
Port au Choix Canada 50°43N 57°22W 165 B8
Port au Port B. Canada 48°40N 58°50W 165 C8
Port-au-Prince Haiti 18°40N 72°20W 183 C5
Port Augusta Australia 32°30S 137°50E 152 B2
Port Austin U.S.A. 44°3N 83°1W 174 B2
Port-aux-Français Kerguelen 49°21S 70°13E 146 J6
Port Blair India 11°40N 92°45E 127 J11
Port Blandford Canada 48°20N 54°10W 165 C9
Port-Bouët Ivory C. 5°16N 3°57W 138 D4
Port Bradshaw Australia 12°30S 137°20E 150 A2
Port Broughton Australia 33°37S 137°56E 152 B2
Port Bruce Canada 42°39N 81°0W 174 D4
Port Burwell Canada 42°40N 80°48W 174 D4
Port Campbell Australia 38°37S 143°1E 152 E5
Port Campbell India 11°56N 92°37E 127 J11
Port Campbell △ Australia 38°8S 143°6E 152 E5
Port Canning India 22°23N 88°40E 125 H13
Port Carling Canada 45°7N 79°35W 174 A5
Port-Cartier Canada 50°2N 66°50W 165 B6
Port Chalmers N.Z. 45°49S 170°30E 155 F5
Port Charles N.Z. 36°33S 175°30E 154 C4
Port Charlotte U.S.A. 26°59N 82°6W 179 J7
Port Chester U.S.A. 41°0N 73°40W 175 F11
Port Clements Canada 53°40N 132°10W 162 C2
Port Clinton U.S.A. 41°31N 82°56W 173 E12
Port Colborne Canada 42°50N 79°10W 174 D5
Port Coquitlam Canada 49°15N 122°45W 170 A4
Port Cornwallis India 13°17N 93°5E 127 H11
Port Credit Canada 43°33N 79°35W 174 C5
Port-Cros △ France 43°0N 6°24E 73 F10
Port Curtis Australia 23°57S 151°20E 150 C5
Port d'Alcúdia Spain 39°50N 3°7E 100 B10
Port Dalhousie Canada 43°13N 79°16W 174 C5
Port d'Andratx Spain 39°32N 2°23E 100 B9
Port Darwin Australia 12°24S 130°45E 148 B5
Port Darwin Falk. Is. 51°50S 59°0W 192 D5
Port Davey Australia 43°16S 145°55E 151 G4
Port-de-Bouc France 43°24N 4°59E 73 E8
Port-de-Paix Haiti 19°50N 72°50W 183 C5
Port de Pollença Spain 39°54N 3°4E 100 B10
Port de Sóller Spain 39°48N 2°42E 100 B9
Port Dickson Malaysia 2°30N 101°49E 121 L3
Port Douglas Australia 16°30S 145°30E 150 B4
Port Dover Canada 42°47N 80°12W 174 D4
Port Edward Canada 54°12N 130°10W 162 C2
Port Elgin Canada 44°25N 81°25W 174 B3
Port Elizabeth S. Africa 33°58S 25°40E 144 D4
Port Ellen U.K. 55°38N 6°11W 65 F2
Port Elliot Australia 35°32S 138°41E 152 C3
Port-en-Bessin-Huppain France 49°21N 0°45W 70 C6
Port Erin I. of Man 54°5N 4°45W 66 C3
Port Essington Australia 11°15S 132°10E 148 B5
Port Ewen U.S.A. 41°54N 73°59W 175 E11
Port Fairy Australia 38°22S 142°12E 152 E5
Port Fitzroy N.Z. 36°8S 175°20E 154 C4
Port Fouâd = Bûr Fuad Egypt 31°15N 32°20E 137 E8
Port Gamble U.S.A. 47°51N 122°34W 170 C4
Port-Gentil Gabon 0°40S 8°50E 140 E1
Port Germein Australia 33°1S 138°1E 151 E2
Port Ghalib Egypt 25°20N 34°50E 128 E2
Port Gibson U.S.A. 31°58N 90°59W 176 F9
Port Glasgow U.K. 55°56N 4°41W 65 F4
Port Harcourt Nigeria 4°40N 7°10E 139 E6
Port Hardy Canada 50°41N 127°30W 162 C3
Port Harrison = Inukjuak Canada 58°25N 78°15W 161 F16
Port Hawkesbury Canada 45°36N 61°22W 165 C7
Port Hedland Australia 20°25S 118°35E 148 D2
Port Henry U.S.A. 44°3N 73°28W 175 B11
Port Hood Canada 46°0N 61°32W 165 C7
Port Hope Canada 43°56N 78°20W 174 C6
Port Hope U.S.A. 43°57N 82°43W 174 C2
Port Hope Simpson Canada 52°33N 56°18W 165 B8
Port Hueneme U.S.A. 34°7N 119°12W 171 L7
Port Huron U.S.A. 42°58N 82°26W 174 D2
Port Iliç Azerbaijan 38°53N 48°47E 105 C13
Port Jefferson U.S.A. 40°57N 73°3W 175 F11
Port Jervis U.S.A. 41°22N 74°41W 175 E10
Port-Joinville France 46°45N 2°23W 70 F4
Port Katon Russia 46°52N 38°46E 85 J10
Port Kembla Australia 34°52S 150°49E 153 C9
Port Kenny Australia 33°10S 134°41E 151 E1
Port-la-Nouvelle France 43°1N 3°3E 72 E7
Port Láirge = Waterford Ireland 52°15N 7°8W 64 D4
Port Lavaca U.S.A. 28°37N 96°38W 176 G6
Port Leyden U.S.A. 43°35N 75°21W 175 C9
Port Lincoln Australia 34°42S 135°52E 152 C1
Port Loko S. Leone 8°48N 12°46W 138 D2
Port Louis France 47°42N 3°22W 70 E3
Port-Louis Guadeloupe 16°28N 61°32W 182 b
Port Louis Mauritius 20°10S 57°30E 141 d
Port MacDonnell Australia 38°5S 140°48E 152 E4
Port McNeill Canada 50°35N 127°6W 162 C3
Port Macquarie Australia 31°25S 152°25E 153 A10
Port Maria Jamaica 18°22N 76°54W 182 a
Port Mathurin Rodrigues 19°41S 63°25E 146 F5
Port Matilda U.S.A. 40°48N 78°3W 174 F6
Port Mayaca U.S.A. 26°59N 80°36W 179 J9
Port McNicoll Canada 44°44N 79°48W 174 B5
Port Mellon Canada 49°32N 123°31W 162 D4
Port-Menier Canada 49°51N 64°15W 165 C7
Port Moody Canada 49°17N 122°51W 170 A4
Port Morant Jamaica 17°54N 76°19W 182 a
Port Moresby Papua N. G. 9°24S 147°8E 147 B7
Port Musgrave Australia 11°55S 141°50E 150 A3
Port-Navalo France 47°34N 2°54W 70 E4
Port Neches U.S.A. 30°0N 93°59W 176 G8
Port Nicholson N.Z. 41°20S 174°52E 154 H3
Port Nolloth S. Africa 29°17S 16°52E 144 C2
Port Nouveau-Québec = Kangiqsualujjuaq Canada 58°30N 65°59W 161 F18
Port of Climax Canada 49°10N 108°20W 163 D7
Port of Coronach Canada 49°7N 105°31W 163 D7
Port of Spain Trin. & Tob. 10°40N 61°31W 183 D7
Port Orange U.S.A. 29°9N 80°59W 179 F9
Port Orchard U.S.A. 47°32N 122°38W 170 C4
Port Orford U.S.A. 42°45N 124°30W 168 E1
Port Pegasus N.Z. 47°12S 167°41E 155 H2
Port Perry Canada 44°6N 78°56W 174 B6
Port Phillip B. Australia 38°10S 144°50E 153 E6
Port Pirie Australia 33°10S 138°1E 152 B3
Port Renfrew Canada 48°30N 124°20W 170 B2
Port Roper Australia 14°45S 135°25E 150 A2
Port Rowan Canada 42°40N 80°30W 174 D4
Port Royal Sd. U.S.A. 32°15N 80°40W 178 C9
Port Safaga = Bûr Safâga Egypt 26°43N 33°57E 128 E2
Port Said = Bûr Sa'îd Egypt 31°16N 32°18E 137 E8
Port St. Joe U.S.A. 29°49N 85°18W 178 F4
Port St. John U.S.A. 28°29N 80°47W 179 G9
Port St. Johns = Umzimvubu S. Africa 31°38S 29°33E 145 D4
Port-St-Louis-du-Rhône France 43°23N 4°49E 73 E8
Port St. Lucie U.S.A. 27°18N 80°21W 179 H9
Port-Ste-Marie France 44°15N 0°25E 72 D4
Port Salerno U.S.A. 27°9N 80°12W 179 H9
Port Sanilac U.S.A. 43°26N 82°33W 174 C2
Port Severn Canada 44°48N 79°43W 174 B5
Port Shepstone S. Africa 30°44S 30°28E 145 D5
Port Simpson Canada 54°30N 130°20W 162 C2
Port Stanley = Stanley Falk. Is. 51°40S 59°51W 192 D5
Port Stanley Canada 42°40N 81°10W 174 D3
Port Sudan = Bûr Sûdân Sudan 19°32N 37°9E 137 D4
Port Sulphur U.S.A. 29°29N 89°42W 177 G10
Port-sur-Saône France 47°42N 6°2E 71 E13
Port Talbot U.K. 51°35N 3°47W 67 F4
Port Taufiq = Bûr Taufiq Egypt 29°54N 32°32E 137 F8
Port Townsend U.S.A. 48°7N 122°45W 170 B4
Port-Vendres France 42°32N 3°8E 72 F7
Port Victoria Australia 34°30S 137°29E 152 C2
Port Vila Vanuatu 17°45S 168°18E 147 C9
Port Vladimir Russia 69°25N 33°6E 60 B25
Port Wakefield Australia 34°12S 138°10E 152 C3
Port Washington U.S.A. 43°23N 87°53W 172 D10
Port Wentworth U.S.A. 32°9N 81°10W 178 C8
Porta Orientalis Romania 45°6N 22°18E 75 F12
Portacloy Ireland 54°20N 9°46W 64 B2
Portadown U.K. 54°25N 6°27W 64 B5
Portaferry U.K. 54°23N 5°33W 64 B6
Portage Pa., U.S.A. 40°23N 78°41W 174 F6
Portage Wis., U.S.A. 43°33N 89°28W 172 D9
Portage la Prairie Canada 49°58N 98°18W 163 D9
Portageville U.S.A. 36°26N 89°42W 172 G9
Portal U.S.A. 32°33N 81°56W 178 C8
Portalegre Portugal 39°19N 7°25W 89 F3
Portalegre □ Portugal 39°20N 7°40W 89 F3
Portales U.S.A. 34°11N 103°20W 169 J12
Portarlington Ireland 53°9N 7°14W 64 C4
Portbou Spain 42°25N 3°9E 90 C8
Porteirinha Brazil 15°44S 43°2W 189 D2
Portel Portugal 38°19N 7°41W 89 G3
Portela, Lisboa ✈ (LIS) Portugal 38°46N 9°8W 89 G1
Porter L. N.W.T., Canada 61°41N 108°5W 163 A7
Porter L. Sask., Canada 56°20N 107°20W 163 B7
Porterville S. Africa 33°0S 19°0E 144 D2
Porterville U.S.A. 36°4N 119°1W 170 J8
Portes-lès-Valence France 44°52N 4°54E 73 D8
Porth Tywyn = Burry Port U.K. 51°41N 4°15W 67 F3
Porthcawl U.K. 51°29N 3°42W 67 F4
Porthill U.S.A. 48°59N 116°30W 168 B5
Porthmadog U.K. 52°55N 4°8W 66 E3
Portile de Fier Europe 44°44N 22°30E 80 F7
Portimão Portugal 37°8N 8°32W 89 H2
Portishead U.K. 51°29N 2°46W 67 F5
Portiţei, Gura Romania 44°41N 29°0E 81 F14
Portknockie U.K. 57°42N 2°51W 65 D6
Portland N.S.W., Australia 33°20S 150°0E 153 B9
Portland Vic., Australia 38°20S 141°35E 152 E4
Portland Canada 44°42N 76°12W 175 B8
Portland Conn., U.S.A. 41°34N 72°38W 175 E12
Portland Fla., U.S.A. 30°31N 86°12W 178 E3
Portland Maine, U.S.A. 43°39N 70°16W 173 D18
Portland Mich., U.S.A. 42°52N 84°54W 173 D11
Portland Oreg., U.S.A. 45°32N 122°37W 170 E4
Portland Pa., U.S.A. 40°55N 75°6W 175 F9
Portland Tex., U.S.A. 27°53N 97°20W 176 H6
Portland, I. of U.K. 50°33N 2°26W 67 G5
Portland B. Australia 38°15S 141°45E 152 E4
Portland Bight Jamaica 17°52N 77°5W 182 a
Portland Bill U.K. 50°31N 2°28W 67 G5
Portland Canal U.S.A. 55°56N 130°0W 162 B2
Portland I. N.Z. 39°20S 177°51E 154 F6
Portland Int. ✈ (PDX) U.S.A. 45°35N 122°36W 170 E4
Portland Pt. Jamaica 17°42N 77°11W 182 a
Portlaoise Ireland 53°2N 7°18W 64 C4
Portmadoc = Porthmadog U.K. 52°55N 4°8W 66 E3
Portmore Jamaica 17°53N 76°53W 182 a
Porto Brazil 3°54S 42°42W 189 A2
Porto France 42°16N 8°42E 73 F12
Porto Portugal 41°8N 8°40W 88 D2
Porto □ Portugal 41°8N 8°20W 88 D2
Porto, G. de France 42°17N 8°34E 73 F12
Porto Acre Brazil 9°34S 67°31W 188 B4
Pôrto Alegre Brazil 30°5S 51°10W 191 C5
Porto Azzurro Italy 42°46N 10°24E 92 F7
Porto Cervo Italy 41°8N 9°33E 94 A2
Porto Colom Spain 39°26N 3°15E 100 B10
Porto Cristo Spain 39°33N 3°20E 100 B10
Pôrto da Fôlha Brazil 9°55S 37°17W 189 B3
Porto de Moz Brazil 1°41S 52°13W 187 D8
Porto de Pedras Brazil 9°10S 35°17W 189 B3
Porto Empédocle Italy 37°17N 13°32E 94 E6
Porto Esperança Brazil 19°37S 57°29W 186 G7
Porto Franco Brazil 6°20S 47°24W 189 B1
Porto Inglês C. Verde Is. 15°21N 23°10W 134 b
Porto Mendes Brazil 24°30S 54°15W 191 A5
Porto Moniz Madeira 32°52N 17°11W 100 D2
Porto Murtinho Brazil 21°45S 57°55W 186 H7
Porto Nacional Brazil 10°40S 48°30W 189 C1
Porto-Novo Benin 6°23N 2°42E 139 D5
Porto Primavera, Represa Brazil 22°10S 52°45W 191 A5
Porto San Giórgio Italy 43°11N 13°48E 93 E10
Porto Sant' Elpídio Italy 43°15N 13°43E 93 E10
Porto Santo, I. de Madeira 33°45N 16°25W 134 B2
Porto Santo Stéfano Italy 42°26N 11°7E 92 F8
Porto São José Brazil 22°43S 53°10W 191 A5
Porto Seguro Brazil 16°26S 39°5W 189 D3
Porto Tolle Italy 44°56N 12°22E 93 D9
Porto Tórres Italy 40°50N 8°24E 94 B1
Porto União Brazil 26°10S 51°10W 191 B5
Porto-Vecchio France 41°35N 9°16E 73 G13
Porto Velho Brazil 8°46S 63°54W 186 E6
Porto Viro Italy 45°1N 12°13E 93 C9
Porto Walter Brazil 8°15S 72°40W 188 B3
Portobelo Panama 9°35N 79°42W 182 E4
Portoferráio Italy 42°48N 10°20E 92 F7
Portofino Italy 44°18N 9°12E 92 D6
Portogruaro Italy 45°47N 12°50E 93 C9
Portola U.S.A. 39°49N 120°28W 170 F6
Portomaggiore Italy 44°42N 11°48E 93 D8
Portopetro Spain 39°22N 3°13E 100 B10
Portoscuso Italy 39°12N 8°24E 94 C1
Portovénere Italy 44°3N 9°51E 92 D6
Portoviejo Ecuador 1°7S 80°28W 186 D2
Portpatrick U.K. 54°51N 5°7W 65 G3
Portree U.K. 57°25N 6°12W 65 D2
Portrush U.K. 55°12N 6°40W 64 A5
Portsmouth Dominica 15°34N 61°27W 183 C7
Portsmouth U.K. 50°48N 1°6W 67 G6
Portsmouth N.H., U.S.A. 43°5N 70°45W 175 C14
Portsmouth Ohio, U.S.A. 38°44N 82°57W 173 F12
Portsmouth R.I., U.S.A. 41°36N 71°15W 175 E13
Portsmouth Va., U.S.A. 36°58N 76°23W 173 G15
Portsmouth □ U.K. 50°48N 1°6W 67 G6
Portsoy U.K. 57°41N 2°41W 65 D6
Portstewart U.K. 55°11N 6°43W 64 A5
Porttipahdan tekojärvi Finland 68°5N 26°40E 60 B22
Portugal ■ Europe 40°0N 8°0W 88 F3
Portugalete Spain 43°19N 3°4W 90 B1
Portumna Ireland 53°6N 8°14W 64 C3
Portville U.S.A. 42°3N 78°20W 174 D6
Poruma Australia 10°2S 143°4E 150 a
Porvenir Bolivia 11°10S 68°50W 188 C4
Porvenir Chile 53°10S 70°16W 192 D2
Porvoo Finland 60°24N 25°40E 84 B3
Porzuna Spain 39°9N 4°9W 89 F6
Posada Italy 40°38N 9°43E 94 B2
Posada → Italy 40°39N 9°45E 94 B2
Posadas Argentina 27°30S 55°50W 191 B4
Posadas Spain 37°47N 5°11W 89 H5
Poschiavo Switz. 46°19N 10°4E 77 J6
Posets Spain 42°39N 0°25E 90 C5
Posht-e Badam Iran 33°2N 55°23E 129 C7
Posidium Greece 35°30N 27°10E 99 F9
Poso Indonesia 1°20S 120°55E 119 E6
Poso, Danau Indonesia 1°52S 120°35E 119 E6
Posof Turkey 41°30N 42°43E 105 B10
Pospelikha Russia 51°57N 81°46E 109 B10
Posse Brazil 14°4S 46°18W 189 C1
Possession I. Antarctica 72°4S 172°0E 55 D11
Pössneck Germany 50°42N 11°35E 76 E7
Possum Kingdom L. U.S.A. 32°52N 98°26W 176 E5
Post U.S.A. 33°12N 101°23W 176 E4
Post Falls U.S.A. 47°43N 116°57W 168 C5
Postavy = Pastavy Belarus 55°4N 26°50E 84 E4
Poste-de-la-Baleine = Kuujjuarapik Canada 55°20N 77°35W 164 A4
Postmasburg S. Africa 28°18S 23°5E 144 C3
Postojna Slovenia 45°46N 14°12E 93 C11
Poston U.S.A. 34°0N 114°24W 171 M12
Postville Canada 54°54N 59°47W 165 B8
Posyet Russia 42°39N 130°48E 112 C5
Potamos Antikythira, Greece 35°52N 23°15E 98 F5
Potamos Kythira, Greece 36°15N 22°58E 98 E4
Potchefstroom S. Africa 26°41S 27°7E 144 C4
Potcoava Romania 44°30N 24°39E 81 F9
Poté Brazil 17°49S 41°49W 189 D2
Poteau U.S.A. 35°3N 94°37W 176 D7
Poteet U.S.A. 29°2N 98°35W 176 G5
Potenza Italy 40°38N 15°48E 95 B8
Potenza → Italy 43°25N 13°40E 93 E10
Potenza Picena Italy 43°22N 13°37E 93 E10
Poteriteri, L. N.Z. 46°5S 167°10E 155 G2
Potgietersrus = Mokopane S. Africa 24°10S 28°55E 145 B4
Poti Georgia 42°10N 41°38E 87 J5
Potiraguá Brazil 15°36S 39°53W 189 D3
Potiskum Nigeria 11°39N 11°2E 139 C7
Potlogi Romania 44°34N 25°34E 81 F10
Potomac → U.S.A. 38°0N 76°23W 173 F14
Potosí Bolivia 19°38S 65°50W 186 G5
Potosi Mt. U.S.A. 35°57N 115°29W 171 K11
Pototan Phil. 10°54N 122°38E 119 B6
Potrerillos Chile 26°30S 69°30W 190 B2
Potsdam Germany 52°23N 13°3E 76 C9
Potsdam U.S.A. 44°40N 74°59W 175 B10
Pottangi India 18°34N 82°58E 126 E6
Pottenstein Germany 49°46N 11°24E 77 F7
Pottersville U.S.A. 43°43N 73°50W 175 C11
Pottstown U.S.A. 40°15N 75°39W 175 F9
Pottsville U.S.A. 40°41N 76°12W 175 F8
Pottuvil Sri Lanka 6°55N 81°50E 127 L5
P'otzu Taiwan 23°28N 120°15E 117 F13
Pouancé France 47°44N 1°10W 70 E5
Pouce Coupé Canada 55°40N 120°10W 162 B4
Poughkeepsie U.S.A. 41°42N 73°56W 175 E11
Pouilly-sur-Loire France 47°17N 2°57E 71 E9
Poulan U.S.A. 31°31N 83°47W 178 D6
Poulaphouca Res. Ireland 53°8N 6°30W 64 C5
Poulsbo U.S.A. 47°44N 122°38W 170 C4
Poultney U.S.A. 43°31N 73°14W 175 C11
Poulton-le-Fylde U.K. 53°51N 2°58W 66 D5
Pouso Alegre Brazil 22°14S 45°57W 191 A6
Pout Senegal 14°45N 17°0W 138 C1
Pouthisat Cambodia 12°34N 103°50E 120 F4
Pouytenga Burkina Faso 12°15N 0°25W 139 C4
Pouzauges France 46°47N 0°50W 70 F6
Považská Bystrica Slovak Rep. 49°8N 18°27E 79 B11
Poverty B. N.Z. 38°43S 178°2E 154 E7
Povlen Serbia 44°9N 19°44E 96 B3
Póvoa de Lanhosa Portugal 41°33N 8°15W 88 D2
Póvoa de Santa Iria Portugal 38°51N 9°4W 89 G1
Póvoa de Varzim Portugal 41°25N 8°46W 88 D2
Povorino Russia 51°12N 42°5E 86 E6
Povorotnyy, Mys Russia 42°40N 133°2E 112 C6
Povungnituk = Puvirnituq Canada 60°2N 77°10W 161 E16
Powassan Canada 46°5N 79°25W 164 C4
Poway U.S.A. 32°58N 117°2W 171 N9
Powder → U.S.A. 46°45N 105°26W 168 C11
Powder River U.S.A. 43°2N 106°59W 168 E10
Powder Springs U.S.A. 33°52N 84°41W 178 B5
Powell U.S.A. 44°45N 108°46W 168 D9
Powell, L. U.S.A. 36°57N 111°29W 169 H8
Powell River Canada 49°50N 124°35W 162 D4
Powelton U.S.A. 33°26N 82°52W 178 B7
Powers U.S.A. 45°41N 87°32W 172 C10
Pownal U.S.A. 42°45N 73°14W 175 D11
Powys □ U.K. 52°20N 3°20W 67 E4
Poyang Hu China 29°5N 116°20E 117 C11
Poyarkovo Russia 49°36N 128°41E 107
Poysdorf Austria 48°40N 16°37E 7
Poza de la Sal Spain 42°35N 3°31W 8
Poza Rica Mexico 20°33N 97°27W 18
Pozantı Turkey 37°25N 34°50E 10
Požarevac Serbia 44°35N 21°18E 9
Pozazal, Puerto Spain 42°56N 4°10W 8
Požega Croatia 45°20N 17°40E 8
Požega Serbia 43°53N 20°2E 9
Poznań Poland 52°25N 16°55E 8
Poznań ✈ (POZ) Poland 52°26N 16°45E 8
Pozo U.S.A. 35°20N 120°24W 17
Pozo Alcón Spain 37°42N 2°56W 8
Pozo Almonte Chile 20°10S 69°50W 18
Pozo Colorado Paraguay 23°30S 58°45W 19
Pozoblanco Spain 38°23N 4°51W 8
Pozuzo Peru 10°5S 75°35W 18
Pozzallo Italy 36°43N 14°51E 9
Pozzomaggiore Italy 40°24N 8°39E 9
Pozzuoli Italy 40°49N 14°7E 9
Pra → Ghana 5°1N 1°37W 13
Prabuty Poland 53°47N 19°15E 8
Prača Bos.-H. 43°47N 18°43E 8
Prachatice Czech Rep. 49°1N 14°0E 7
Prachin Buri Thailand 14°0N 101°25E 12
Prachuap Khirikhan Thailand 11°49N 99°48E 12
Pradelles France 44°46N 3°52E 7
Prades France 42°38N 2°23E 7
Prado Brazil 17°20S 39°13W 18
Prado del Rey Spain 36°48N 5°33W
Præstø Denmark 55°8N 12°2E
Pragersko Slovenia 46°27N 15°42E 93
Prague = Praha Czech Rep. 50°4N 14°25E 7
Praha Czech Rep. 50°4N 14°25E 7
Praha ✈ (PRG) Czech Rep. 50°6N 14°16E 7
Prahecq France 46°19N 0°26W 7
Prahita → India 19°0N 79°55E 12
Prahova □ Romania 45°10N 26°0E 81
Prahova → Romania 44°50N 25°50E 81
Prahovo Serbia 44°18N 22°39E 9
Praia C. Verde Is. 15°2N 23°34W 1
Praia a Mare Italy 39°50N 15°45E 9
Praid Romania 46°32N 25°10E 81
Prainha Brazil 1°45S 53°30W 18
Prainha Nova Brazil 7°10S 60°30W 1
Prairie Australia 20°50S 144°35E 15
Prairie City U.S.A. 44°28N 118°43W 16
Prairie Dog Town Fork Red → U.S.A. 34°34N 99°58W 17
Prairie du Chien U.S.A. 43°3N 91°9W 17
Prairies, L. of the Canada 51°16N 101°32W 16
Pramanda Greece 39°32N 21°8E 9
Prambanan △ Indonesia 7°45S 110°28E 119
Prampram Ghana 5°43N 0°8E 13
Pran Buri Thailand 12°23N 99°55E 12
Prang Ghana 8°1N 0°56W 13
Prapat Indonesia 2°41N 98°58E 11
Praslin Seychelles 4°18S 55°45E
Prasonisi, Akra Greece 35°42N 27°46E 10
Praszka Poland 51°5N 18°31E 8
Prata Brazil 19°25S 48°54W 18
Pratabpur India 23°28N 83°15E 125
Pratapgarh Raj., India 24°2N 74°40E 12
Pratapgarh Ut. P., India 25°56N 81°59E 12
Pratas I. = Dongsha Dao S. China Sea 20°45N 116°43E 11
Prato Italy 43°53N 11°6E
Prátola Peligna Italy 42°6N 13°52E 9
Prats-de-Mollo-la-Preste France 42°25N 2°27E
Pratt U.S.A. 37°39N 98°44W 17
Prattville U.S.A. 32°28N 86°29W 17
Pravara → India 19°35N 74°45E 1
Pravdinsk Kaliningrad, Russia 54°27N 21°1E 8
Pravdinsk Nizhniy Novgorod, Russia 56°29N 43°28E
Pravets Bulgaria 42°53N 23°55E
Pravia Spain 43°30N 6°12W
Praya Indonesia 8°39S 116°17E 1
Prayag = Allahabad India 25°25N 81°58E 1
Pre-delta △ Argentina 32°10S 60°40W 1
Pré-en-Pail France 48°28N 0°12W 7
Preah Vihear Cambodia 14°23N 104°41E 1
Preble U.S.A. 42°44N 76°8W 17
Precipice △ Australia 25°18S 150°5E 15
Precordillera Argentina 30°0S 69°1W 1
Predáppio Italy 44°6N 11°59E
Predazzo Italy 46°19N 11°36E
Predeal Romania 45°30N 25°34E 8
Predejane Serbia 42°51N 22°9E
Preeceville Canada 51°57N 102°40W 1
Preetz Germany 54°14N 10°18E
Pregolya → Russia 54°41N 20°22E 8
Pregrada Croatia 46°11N 15°45E 93
Preiļi Latvia 56°18N 26°43E 8
Preko Croatia 44°7N 15°10E 93
Prelog Croatia 46°18N 16°32E 93
Premer Australia 31°29S 149°56E 15
Prémery France 47°10N 3°18E 7
Premià de Mar Spain 41°29N 2°22E
Premont U.S.A. 27°22N 98°7W 17
Premuda Croatia 44°20N 14°36E 93
Prentice U.S.A. 45°33N 90°17W 17
Prenzlau Germany 53°19N 13°50E 7
Preobrazheniye Russia 42°54N 133°54E 11
Preparis I. = Pariparit Kyun Burma 14°52N 93°41E 12
Preparis North Channel Ind. Oc. 15°27N 94°5E 12
Preparis South Channel Ind. Oc. 14°33N 93°30E 12
Přerov Czech Rep. 49°28N 17°27E 7
Prescott Canada 44°45N 75°30W 1
Prescott Ariz., U.S.A. 34°33N 112°28W 1
Prescott Ark., U.S.A. 33°48N 93°23W 1
Prescott Valley U.S.A. 34°40N 112°18W 1
Preservation Inlet N.Z. 46°8S 166°35E 1
Preševo Serbia 42°19N 21°39E
Presho U.S.A. 43°54N 100°3W 1
Presicce Italy 39°54N 18°16E 9
Presidencia de la Plaza Argentina 27°0S 59°50W 1

idencia Roque Saenz Peña
rgentina 26°45S 60°30W 190 B3
idente Dutra Brazil 5°15S 44°30W 189 B2
idente Epitácio
razil 21°56S 52°6W 187 H8
idente Hayes □
raguay 24°0S 59°0W 190 A4
idente Prudente
razil 22°5S 51°25W 191 A5
idente Ríos, L.
hile 46°28S 74°25W 192 C2
idio U.S.A. 29°34N 104°22W 176 G2
lav Bulgaria 43°10N 26°52E 97 C10
lavska Planina
lgaria 43°10N 26°45E 97 C10
ov Slovak Rep. 49°0N 21°15E 79 B14
ovský □ Slovak Rep. 49°10N 21°0E 79 B13
pa Bulgaria 41°44N 24°55E 97 E8
pa, L. = Prespansko Jezero
acedonia 40°55N 21°0E 96 F5
pa △ Greece 40°48N 21°4E 96 F5
pansko Jezero
acedonia 40°55N 21°0E 96 F5
que I. U.S.A. 42°10N 80°6W 174 D4
que Isle U.S.A. 46°41N 68°1W 173 B19
tatyn U.K. 53°20N 3°24W 66 D4
tea Ghana 5°22N 2°7W 138 D4
teigne U.K. 52°17N 3°0W 67 E5
tice Czech Rep. 49°34N 13°20E 78 B6
ton Canada 43°23N 80°21W 174 C4
ton U.K. 53°46N 2°42W 66 D5
ton Ga., U.S.A. 32°4N 84°32W 178 C5
ton Idaho, U.S.A. 42°6N 111°53W 168 E8
ton Minn., U.S.A. 43°40N 92°5W 172 D7
ton, C. Australia 20°51S 116°12E 148 D2
tonsburg U.S.A. 37°40N 82°47W 173 G12
tranda Norway 59°6N 9°4E 62 E3
twick U.K. 55°29N 4°37W 65 F4
o → Brazil 11°21S 43°52W 189 C2
oria S. Africa 25°44S 28°12E 145 C4
illy-sur-Claise France 46°51N 0°56E 70 F7
eza Greece 38°57N 20°45E 98 C2
Veng Cambodia 11°35N 105°29E 121 G5
zovskoye Ukraine 46°44N 35°40E 85 J8
aykalsky △
ussia 52°30N 106°0E 107 D11
ilof Is. U.S.A. 57°0N 170°0W 166 D6
oj Serbia 43°35N 19°32E 96 C3
ram Czech Rep. 49°41N 14°2E 78 B7
e U.S.A. 39°36N 110°49W 168 G8
e, C. India 13°34N 93°3E 127 H11
e I. Canada 52°23N 128°41W 162 C3
hard U.S.A. 30°44N 88°5W 177 F10
go Spain 40°26N 2°21W 90 E2
go de Córdoba Spain 37°27N 4°12W 89 H6
kule Latvia 56°26N 21°35E 82 B8
kule Lithuania 55°33N 21°19E 82 C8
lbrusye △ Russia 43°20N 42°37E 87 J6
n Germany 47°51N 12°20E 77 H8
nai Lithuania 54°38N 23°57E 82 D10
ska S. Africa 29°40S 22°42E 144 C3
st L. U.S.A. 48°35N 116°52W 168 B5
st River U.S.A. 48°11N 116°55W 168 B5
st Valley U.S.A. 36°10N 120°39W 170 J6
vidza Slovak Rep. 48°46N 18°36E 79 C11
nitz Germany 53°6N 11°45E 76 B7
edor Bos.-H. 44°58N 16°41E 93 D13
epolje Serbia 43°27N 19°40E 96 C3
aspiyskaya Nizmennost =
aspian Depression
urasia 47°0N 48°0E 87 G9
ro Ivory C. 7°40N 3°59W 138 D4
ubanskaya Nizmennost
ussia 45°39N 38°33E 87 H4
ep Macedonia 41°21N 21°32E 96 E5
ıki = Pryluky
kraine 50°30N 32°24E 85 G7
e Seal I. Australia 40°3S 147°43E 151 G4
eira Cruz Brazil 2°30S 43°26W 189 A2
no Tapia Mexico 32°16N 116°54W 171 N10
orsk Kaliningrad,
ussia 54°44N 20°0E 82 D6
orsk St. Petersburg,
ussia 60°22N 28°37E 84 B5
orskiy Kray □
ussia 45°0N 135°0E 112 B7
orsko Bulgaria 42°15N 27°44E 97 D11
orsko-Akhtarsk
ussia 46°2N 38°10E 85 J10
rose L. Canada 54°55N 109°45W 163 C7
ce Albert Canada 53°15N 105°50W 163 C7
ce Albert S. Africa 33°12S 22°2E 144 D3
ce Albert △
anada 54°0N 106°25W 163 C7
ce Albert Mts.
ntarctica 76°0S 161°30E 55 D11
ce Albert Pen.
anada 72°30N 116°0W 160 C8
ce Albert Sd.
anada 70°25N 115°0W 160 C9
ce Alfred, C.
anada 74°20N 124°40W 54 B1
ce Charles I.
anada 67°47N 76°12W 161 D16
ce Charles Mts.
ntarctica 72°0S 67°0E 55 D6
ce Edward Fracture Zone
d. Oc. 46°0S 35°0E 55 A4
ce Edward I. □
anada 46°20N 63°20W 165 C7
ce Edward Is.
d. Oc. 46°35S 38°0E 146 J2
ce George Canada 53°55N 122°50W 162 C4
ce of Wales, C.
.S.A. 65°36N 168°5W 166 B6
ce of Wales I.
ustralia 10°40S 142°10E 150 A3
ce of Wales I.
anada 73°0N 99°0W 160 C12
ce of Wales I.
.S.A. 55°47N 132°50W 160 F5
ce of Wales Icefield
anada 78°15N 79°0W 161 B16
ce of Wales Str.
anada 73°0N 117°0W 160 C8
ce Patrick I. Canada 77°0N 120°0W 161 B8
ce Regent Inlet
anada 73°0N 90°0W 161 C14
ce Rupert Canada 54°20N 130°20W 162 C2
ce William Sd.
.S.A. 60°40N 147°0W 160 E2
Princes Town
Trin. & Tob. 10°16N 61°23W 187 K15
Princesa Isabel Brazil 7°44S 38°0W 189 B3
Princess Charlotte B.
Australia 14°25S 144°0E 150 A3
Princess Elizabeth Trough
S. Ocean 64°10S 83°0E 55 C7
Princess May Ranges
Australia 15°30S 125°30E 148 C4
Princess Royal I.
Canada 53°0N 128°40W 162 C3
Princeton Canada 49°27N 120°30W 162 D4
Princeton Calif., U.S.A. 39°24N 122°1W 170 F4
Princeton Ill., U.S.A. 41°23N 89°28W 172 E9
Princeton Ind., U.S.A. 38°21N 87°34W 172 F10
Princeton Ky., U.S.A. 37°7N 87°53W 172 G10
Princeton Mo., U.S.A. 40°24N 93°35W 172 E7
Princeton N.J., U.S.A. 40°21N 74°39W 175 F10
Princeton W. Va.,
U.S.A. 37°22N 81°6W 173 G13
Príncipe
São Tomé & Príncipe 1°37N 7°25E 132 F4
Príncipe da Beira
Brazil 12°20S 64°30W 186 F6
Prineville U.S.A. 44°18N 120°51W 168 D3
Prins Christian Sund
Greenland 60°4N 43°10W 57 E6
Prins Harald Kyst
Antarctica 70°0S 35°1E 55 D4
Prins Karls Forland
Svalbard 78°30N 11°0E 57 B12
Prinsesse Astrid Kyst
Antarctica 70°45S 12°30E 55 D3
Prinsesse Ragnhild Kyst
Antarctica 70°15S 27°30E 55 D4
Prinzapolca Nic. 13°20N 83°35W 182 D3
Prior, C. Spain 43°34N 8°17W 88 B2
Priozersk Russia 61°2N 30°7E 84 B6
Pripet = Prypyat →
Europe 51°20N 30°15E 75 C16
Pripet Marshes Europe 52°10N 27°10E 75 B15
Pripyat Marshes = Pripet Marshes
Europe 52°10N 27°10E 75 B15
Pripyats = Prypyat →
Europe 51°20N 30°15E 75 C16
Prishtinë Kosovo 42°40N 21°13E 96 D5
Prislop, Pasul Romania 47°37N 24°48E 81 C9
Pristen Russia 51°15N 36°44E 85 G9
Priština = Prishtinë
Kosovo 42°40N 21°13E 96 D5
Pritzwalk Germany 53°9N 12°10E 76 B8
Privas France 44°45N 4°37E 73 D8
Priverno Italy 41°28N 13°11E 94 A6
Privolzhsk Russia 57°23N 41°16E 86 B5
Privolzhskaya Vozvyshennost
Russia 51°0N 46°0E 86 E7
Privolzhskiy Russia 51°25N 46°3E 86 E8
Privolzhskiy □ Russia 56°0N 50°0E 106 D6
Privolzhye Russia 52°52N 48°33E 86 D9
Privutnoye Russia 46°12N 43°40E 87 G6
Prizren Kosovo 42°13N 20°45E 96 D4
Prizzi Italy 37°43N 13°26E 94 E6
Prnjavor Bos.-H. 44°52N 17°43E 80 F2
Probolinggo Indonesia 7°46S 113°13E 119 G15
Prochowice Poland 51°17N 16°20E 83 G3
Proctor U.S.A. 43°40N 73°2W 175 C11
Proddatur India 14°45N 78°30E 127 G4
Prodhromos Cyprus 34°57N 32°50E 101 E11
Proença-a-Nova Portugal 39°45N 7°54W 88 F3
Profilia Greece 36°5N 27°51E 101 C9
Profondeville Belgium 50°23N 4°52E 69 D4
Progreso Coahuila,
Mexico 27°28N 100°59W 180 B4
Progreso Yucatán,
Mexico 21°20N 89°40W 181 C7
Progress Antarctica 66°22S 76°22E 55 C12
Progress Russia 49°45N 129°37E 107 E13
Prokhladnyy Russia 43°50N 44°2E 87 J7
Prokhorovka Russia 51°2N 36°44E 86 E3
Prokletije Albania 42°30N 19°45E 96 D3
Prokopyevsk Russia 54°0N 86°45E 109 B11
Prokuplje Serbia 43°16N 21°36E 96 C5
Proletarsk Russia 46°42N 41°50E 87 G5
Prome Burma 18°49N 95°13E 123 K19
Prophet → Canada 58°48N 122°40W 162 B4
Prophet River Canada 58°6N 122°43W 162 B4
Propriá Brazil 10°13S 36°51W 189 C3
Propriano France 41°41N 8°52E 73 G12
Proserpine Australia 20°21S 148°36E 150 b
Prosna → Poland 52°6N 17°44E 83 F4
Prospect U.S.A. 43°18N 75°9W 175 C9
Prosperity U.S.A. 30°51N 85°56W 178 E4
Prosser U.S.A. 46°12N 119°46W 168 C4
Prostějov Czech Rep. 49°30N 17°9E 79 B10
Prostki Poland 53°42N 22°25E 82 E9
Proston Australia 26°8S 151°32E 151 D5
Proszowice Poland 50°13N 20°16E 83 H7
Proti Greece 37°5N 21°32E 98 D3
Provadiya Bulgaria 43°12N 27°30E 97 C11
Provadiyska →
Bulgaria 43°12N 27°42E 97 C11
Provence France 43°40N 5°46E 73 E9
Provence-Alpes-Côte d'Azur □
France 44°0N 6°15E 73 D10
Providence Ky.,
U.S.A. 37°24N 87°46W 172 G10
Providence R.I.,
U.S.A. 41°49N 71°24W 175 E13
Providence, C. N.Z. 45°59S 166°29E 155 F1
Providence Bay
Canada 45°41N 82°15W 164 C3
Providence Mts.
U.S.A. 35°10N 115°15W 171 K11
Providencia, I. de
Colombia 13°25N 81°26W 182 D3
Provideniya Russia 64°23N 173°18W 107 C19
Provincetown U.S.A. 42°3N 70°11W 173 D18
Provins France 48°33N 3°15E 71 D10
Provo U.S.A. 40°14N 111°39W 168 F8
Provost Canada 52°25N 110°20W 163 C6
Prozor Bos.-H. 43°50N 17°34E 80 G2
Prrenjas Albania 41°4N 20°32E 96 E4
Prudhoe Bay U.S.A. 70°18N 148°22W 166 A10
Prudhoe I. Australia 21°19S 149°41E 150 C4
Prud'homme Canada 52°20N 105°54W 163 C7
Prudnik Poland 50°20N 17°38E 83 H4
Prüm Germany 50°12N 6°25E 77 E2
Prundu Romania 44°6N 26°14E 81 F11
Prundu Bârgăului
Romania 47°13N 24°46E 81 C9
Pruszcz Gdański Poland 54°17N 18°40E 82 D5
Pruszków Poland 52°9N 20°49E 83 F7
Prut → Romania 45°28N 28°10E 81 E13
Pruzhany Belarus 52°33N 24°28E 75 B13
Prvič Croatia 44°55N 14°47E 93 D11
Prydz B. Antarctica 69°0S 74°0E 55 C6
Pryluky Ukraine 50°30N 32°24E 85 G7
Prymorske Ukraine 46°48N 36°20E 85 J9
Pryor U.S.A. 36°19N 95°19W 176 C7
Prypyat → Europe 51°20N 30°15E 75 C16
Prypyatsky △ Belarus 52°0N 28°0E 75 C14
Przasnysz Poland 53°2N 20°54E 83 E7
Przedbórz Poland 51°6N 19°53E 83 G6
Przedecz Poland 52°20N 18°53E 83 F5
Przemków Poland 51°31N 15°48E 83 G2
Przemyśl Poland 49°50N 22°45E 83 J9
Przeworsk Poland 50°6N 22°32E 83 H9
Przewóz Poland 51°28N 14°57E 83 G1
Przhevalsk = Karakol
Kyrgyzstan 42°30N 78°20E 109 D9
Przysucha Poland 51°22N 20°38E 83 G7
Psachna Greece 38°34N 23°35E 98 C5
Psara Greece 38°37N 25°38E 99 C7
Psathoura Greece 39°30N 24°12E 98 B6
Pserimos Greece 36°56N 27°8E 99 E9
Psiloritis, Oros Greece 35°15N 24°45E 101 D6
Psira Greece 35°12N 25°52E 101 D7
Pskov Russia 57°50N 28°25E 84 D5
Pskov □ Russia 57°20N 29°0E 84 D5
Pskovskoye, Ozero
Russia 58°0N 27°58E 84 D5
Psol → Ukraine 49°10N 33°37E 85 H7
Psunj Croatia 45°25N 17°19E 80 E2
Pteleos Greece 39°3N 22°57E 98 B4
Ptich = Ptsich →
Belarus 52°9N 28°52E 75 B15
Ptichia = Vidos Greece 39°38N 19°55E 101 A3
Ptolemaida Greece 40°30N 21°43E 96 F5
Ptsich → Belarus 52°9N 28°52E 75 B15
Ptuj Slovenia 46°28N 15°50E 93 B12
Ptujska Gora Slovenia 46°23N 15°47E 93 B12
Pu Xian China 36°24N 111°6E 114 F6
Pua Thailand 19°11N 100°55E 120 C3
Puán Argentina 37°30S 62°45W 190 D3
Pu'an China 25°46N 104°57E 116 E5
Pubei China 22°16N 109°31E 116 F7
Pucallpa Peru 8°25S 74°30W 188 B3
Pucará Cajamarca, Peru 6°0S 79°7W 188 B2
Pucará Puno, Peru 15°5S 70°24W 188 D3
Pucarani Bolivia 16°23S 68°30W 188 D4
Pucheng China 27°59N 118°31E 117 D12
Pucheni Romania 45°12N 25°17E 81 E10
Puchheim Germany 48°9N 11°21E 77 G7
Puch'on = Bucheon
S. Korea 37°28N 126°45E 115 F14
Púchov Slovak Rep. 49°8N 18°20E 79 B11
Pucioasa Romania 45°5N 25°25E 81 E10
Pučišća Croatia 43°22N 16°43E 93 E13
Puck Poland 54°45N 18°23E 82 D5
Pucka, Zatoka Poland 54°30N 18°40E 82 D5
Puçol Spain 39°37N 0°18W 91 F4
Pudasjärvi Finland 65°23N 26°53E 60 D22
Puding China 26°18N 105°44E 116 D5
Pudozh Russia 61°48N 36°32E 84 B9
Pudu = Suizhou China 31°42N 113°24E 117 B9
Puducherry India 11°59N 79°50E 127 J4
Pudukkottai India 10°28N 78°47E 127 J4
Puebla Mexico 19°3N 98°12W 181 D5
Puebla □ Mexico 18°50N 98°0W 181 D5
Puebla de Alcocer Spain 38°59N 5°14W 89 G5
Puebla de Don Fadrique
Spain 37°58N 2°25W 91 H2
Puebla de Don Rodrigo
Spain 39°5N 4°37W 89 F6
Puebla de Guzmán Spain 37°37N 7°15W 89 H3
Puebla de la Calzada
Spain 38°54N 6°37W 89 G4
Puebla de Sanabria Spain 42°4N 6°38W 88 C4
Puebla de Trives = Pobra de
Trives Spain 42°20N 7°10W 88 C3
Pueblo U.S.A. 38°16N 104°37W 168 G11
Puelches Argentina 38°5S 65°51W 190 D2
Puelén Argentina 37°32S 67°38W 190 D2
Puente Alto Chile 33°32S 70°35W 190 C1
Puente-Genil Spain 37°22N 4°47W 89 H6
Puente la Reina Spain 42°40N 1°49W 90 C3
Puente San Miguel Spain 43°21N 4°5W 88 B6
Puenteareas = Ponteareas
Spain 42°10N 8°28W 88 C2
Puentedeume = Pontedeume
Spain 43°24N 8°10W 88 B2
Puentes de García Rodríguez = As
Pontes de García Rodríguez
Spain 43°27N 7°50W 88 B3
Pu'er China 23°0N 101°15E 116 F3
Puerca, Pta. Puerto Rico 18°13N 65°36W 183 d
Puerco → U.S.A. 34°22N 107°50W 169 J10
Puerto Acosta Bolivia 15°32S 69°15W 188 D4
Puerto Aisén Chile 45°27S 73°0W 192 C2
Puerto Ángel Mexico 15°40N 96°29W 181 D5
Puerto Arista Mexico 15°56N 93°48W 181 D6
Puerto Armuelles
Panama 8°20N 82°51W 182 E3
Puerto Ayacucho
Venezuela 5°40N 67°35W 186 B5
Puerto Barrios
Guatemala 15°40N 88°32W 182 C2
Puerto Bermejo
Argentina 26°55S 58°34W 190 B4
Puerto Bermúdez Peru 10°20S 74°58W 188 C3
Puerto Bolívar Ecuador 3°19S 79°55W 186 D3
Puerto Cabello
Venezuela 10°28N 68°1W 186 A5
Puerto Cabezas Nic. 14°0N 83°30W 182 D3
Puerto Cabo Gracias á Dios
Nic. 15°0N 83°10W 182 D3
Puerto Carreño
Colombia 6°12N 67°22W 186 B5
Puerto Castilla Honduras 16°0N 86°0W 182 C2
Puerto Chicama Peru 7°45S 79°20W 188 B2
Puerto Cisnes Chile 44°45S 72°42W 192 B2
Puerto Coig Argentina 50°54S 69°15W 192 D3
Puerto Cortés Honduras 15°51N 88°0W 182 C2
Puerto Cumarebo
Venezuela 11°29N 69°30W 186 A5
Puerto de Alcudia = Port
d'Alcúdia Spain 39°50N 3°7E 100 B10
Puerto de Cabrera Spain 39°8N 2°56E 100 B9
Puerto de Gran Tarajal
Canary Is. 28°13N 14°1W 100 F5
Puerto de la Cruz
Canary Is. 28°24N 16°32W 100 F3
Puerto de los Angeles ⌂
Mexico 23°39N 105°45W 180 C3
Puerto de Mazarrón
Spain 37°34N 1°15W 91 H3
Puerto de Pozo Negro
Canary Is. 28°19N 13°55W 100 F6
Puerto de Sóller = Port de Sóller
Spain 39°48N 2°42E 100 B9
Puerto de Somosierra
Spain 41°9N 3°35W 88 D7
Puerto del Carmen
Canary Is. 28°55N 13°38W 100 F6
Puerto del Rosario
Canary Is. 28°30N 13°52W 100 F6
Puerto Deseado
Argentina 47°55S 66°0W 192 C3
Puerto Escondido
Mexico 15°50N 97°3W 181 D5
Puerto Heath Bolivia 12°34S 68°39W 188 C4
Puerto Inca Peru 9°22S 74°54W 188 B3
Puerto Inírida Colombia 3°53N 67°52W 186 C5
Puerto Juárez Mexico 21°11N 86°49W 181 C7
Puerto La Cruz
Venezuela 10°13N 64°38W 186 A6
Puerto Leguízamo
Colombia 0°12S 74°46W 186 D4
Puerto Lempira
Honduras 15°16N 83°46W 182 C3
Puerto Libertad
Mexico 29°55N 112°43W 180 B2
Puerto Limón Colombia 3°23N 73°30W 186 C4
Puerto Lobos Argentina 42°0S 65°3W 192 B3
Puerto Lumbreras Spain 37°34N 1°48W 91 H3
Puerto Madryn
Argentina 42°48S 65°4W 192 B3
Puerto Maldonado
Peru 12°30S 69°10W 188 C4
Puerto Manatí Cuba 21°22N 76°50W 182 B4
Puerto Montt Chile 41°28S 73°0W 192 B2
Puerto Morazán Nic. 12°51N 87°11W 182 D2
Puerto Morelos Mexico 20°50N 86°52W 181 C7
Puerto Natales Chile 51°45S 72°15W 192 D2
Puerto Oscuro Chile 31°24S 71°35W 190 C1
Puerto Padre Cuba 21°13N 76°35W 182 B4
Puerto Páez Venezuela 6°13N 67°28W 186 B5
Puerto Peñasco
Mexico 31°20N 113°33W 180 A2
Puerto Pinasco
Paraguay 22°36S 57°50W 190 A4
Puerto Pirámides
Argentina 42°35S 64°20W 192 B4
Puerto Plata Dom. Rep. 19°48N 70°45W 183 C5
Puerto Pollensa = Port de
Pollença Spain 39°54N 3°4E 100 B10
Puerto Portillo Peru 9°45S 72°42W 188 B3
Puerto Princesa Phil. 9°46N 118°45E 119 C5
Puerto Quepos Costa Rica 9°29N 84°6W 182 E3
Puerto Real Spain 36°33N 6°12W 89 J4
Puerto Rico Bolivia 11°5S 67°38W 188 C4
Puerto Rico Canary Is. 27°47N 15°42W 100 G4
Puerto Rico ☑ W. Indies 18°15N 66°45W 183 d
Puerto Rico Trench
Atl. Oc. 19°50N 66°0W 183 C6
Puerto Saavedra Chile 38°47S 73°24W 192 A2
Puerto San Julián
Argentina 49°15S 67°45W 192 C3
Puerto Santa Cruz
Argentina 50°0S 68°32W 192 D3
Puerto Sastre Paraguay 22°2S 57°55W 190 A4
Puerto Serrano Spain 36°56N 5°33W 89 J5
Puerto Suárez Bolivia 18°58S 57°52W 186 G7
Puerto Supe Peru 11°0S 77°30W 188 C2
Puerto Vallarta
Mexico 20°37N 105°15W 180 C3
Puerto Varas Chile 41°19S 72°59W 192 B2
Puerto Wilches
Colombia 7°21N 73°54W 186 B4
Puerto Williams Chile 54°56S 67°37W 192 E3
Puertollano Spain 38°43N 4°7W 89 G6
Pueu Tahiti 17°44S 149°13W 155 b
Pueyrredón, L.
Argentina 47°20S 72°0W 192 C2
Púez Odle ⌂ Italy 46°37N 11°48E 93 B8
Puffin I. Ireland 51°50N 10°24W 64 E1
Pugachev Russia 52°0N 48°49E 86 D9
Pugal India 28°30N 72°48E 124 E5
Puge China 27°20N 102°31E 116 D4
Puge Tanzania 4°45S 33°11E 142 C3
Puget Sound U.S.A. 47°50N 122°30W 170 C4
Puget-Théniers France 43°58N 6°53E 73 E10
Púglia □ Italy 41°15N 16°15E 95 A9
Pugŏdong N. Korea 42°5N 130°0E 115 C16
Pugu Tanzania 6°55S 39°4E 142 D4
Pūgūnzī Iran 25°49N 59°10E 129 E8
Puha N.Z. 38°30S 177°50E 154 E6
Pui Romania 45°30N 23°4E 80 E8
Puica Peru 15°0S 72°33W 188 D3
Puiești Romania 46°25N 27°33E 81 D12
Puig Major Spain 39°48N 2°47E 100 B9
Puigcerdà Spain 42°24N 1°50E 90 C6
Puigmal Spain 42°23N 2°7E 90 C7
Puigpunyent Spain 39°38N 2°32E 100 B9
Pujiang China 30°14N 103°30E 116 B4
Puisaye, Collines de la
France 47°37N 3°20E 71 E10
Puiseaux France 48°11N 2°30E 71 D9
Pujehun S. Leone 7°23N 11°45W 138 D2
Pujiang China 29°29N 119°54E 117 C12
Pujols France 44°48N 0°2W 72 D3
Pujon-ho N. Korea 40°35N 127°35E 115 D14
Pukaki, L. N.Z. 44°4S 170°1E 155 E5
Pukapuka Cook Is. 10°53S 165°49W 157 J11
Pukaskwa △ Canada 48°20N 86°0W 164 C2
Pukatawagan Canada 55°45N 101°20W 163 B8
Pukchin N. Korea 40°12N 125°45E 115 D13
Pukch'ŏng N. Korea 40°14N 128°10E 115 D15
Pukë Albania 42°2N 19°53E 96 D3
Pukearuhe N.Z. 38°55S 174°31E 154 E3
Pukekohe N.Z. 37°12S 174°55E 154 D3
Puketeraki Ra. N.Z. 42°58S 172°13E 155 C7
Puketoi Ra. N.Z. 40°30S 176°5E 154 G5
Pukeuri N.Z. 45°4S 171°2E 155 F6
Pukhrayan India 26°14N 79°51E 125 F8
Puksubaek-san
N. Korea 40°42N 127°45E 115 D14
Pula Croatia 44°54N 13°57E 93 D10
Pula Italy 39°1N 9°0E 94 C1
Pulacayo Bolivia 20°25S 66°41W 188 E4
Pulandian China 39°25N 121°58E 115 E11
Pulaski N.Y., U.S.A. 43°34N 76°8W 175 C8
Pulaski Tenn., U.S.A. 35°12N 87°2W 177 D11
Pulaski Va., U.S.A. 37°3N 80°47W 173 G13
Pulau → Indonesia 5°50S 138°15E 119 F9
Pulau Gili Indonesia 8°21S 116°1E 119 J19
Puławy Poland 51°23N 21°59E 83 G8
Pulga U.S.A. 39°48N 121°29W 170 F5
Pulgaon India 20°44N 78°21E 126 D4
Pulicat India 13°25N 80°19E 127 H5
Pulicat L. India 13°40N 80°15E 127 H5
Pulivendla India 14°25N 78°14E 127 G4
Puliyangudi India 9°11N 77°24E 127 K3
Pullman U.S.A. 46°44N 117°10W 168 C5
Pulog, Mt. Phil. 16°40N 120°50E 119 A6
Pulpí Spain 37°24N 1°44W 91 H3
Pultusk Poland 52°43N 21°6E 83 F8
Pülümür Turkey 39°30N 39°51E 105 C8
Pumlumon Fawr U.K. 52°28N 3°46W 67 E4
Puná, I. Ecuador 2°55S 80°5W 186 D2
Punaauia Tahiti 17°37S 149°34W 155 b
Punakha Dzong
Bhutan 27°42N 89°52E 123 F16
Punalur India 9°0N 76°56E 127 K3
Punasar India 27°6N 73°6E 124 F5
Punata Bolivia 17°32S 65°50W 186 G5
Punch India 33°48N 74°4E 125 C6
Punch → Pakistan 33°12N 73°40E 124 C5
Punda Maria S. Africa 22°40S 31°5E 145 B5
Pune India 18°29N 73°57E 126 E1
P'ungsan N. Korea 40°50N 128°9E 115 D15
Pungue, Ponte de Mozam. 19°0S 34°0E 143 F3
Puning China 23°20N 116°12E 117 F11
Punjab □ India 31°0N 76°0E 124 D7
Punjab □ Pakistan 32°0N 72°30E 124 E6
Puno Peru 15°55S 70°3W 188 D3
Puno □ Peru 15°0S 70°0W 188 C3
Punpun → India 25°31N 85°18E 125 G11
Punta, Cerro de
Puerto Rico 18°10N 66°37W 183 d
Punta Alta Argentina 38°53S 62°4W 192 A4
Punta Arenas Chile 53°10S 71°0W 192 D2
Punta Coles Peru 17°43S 71°23W 188 D3
Punta de Bombón
Peru 17°10S 71°48W 188 D3
Punta del Díaz Chile 28°0S 70°45W 190 B1
Punta del Hidalgo
Canary Is. 28°33N 16°19W 100 F3
Punta Delgado
Argentina 42°43S 63°38W 192 B4
Punta Gorda Belize 16°10N 88°45W 181 D7
Punta Gorda U.S.A. 26°56N 82°3W 179 J7
Punta Prieta Mexico 28°58N 114°17W 180 B2
Punta Prima Spain 39°48N 4°16E 100 B11
Punta Umbría Spain 37°10N 6°56W 89 H4
Puntarenas Costa Rica 10°0N 84°50W 182 E3
Puntland Somalia 9°0N 50°0E 131 F4
Punto Fijo Venezuela 11°50N 70°13W 186 A4
Punxsutawney U.S.A. 40°57N 78°59W 174 F6
Pupuan Indonesia 8°19S 115°0E 119 J18
Puqi China 29°40N 113°50E 117 C9
Puquio Peru 14°45S 74°10W 188 C3
Pur → Russia 67°31N 77°55E 106 C8
Puracé, Vol. Colombia 2°21N 76°23W 186 C3
Puračić Bos.-H. 44°33N 18°28E 80 F3
Puralia = Puruliya
India 23°17N 86°24E 125 H12
Puranpur India 28°31N 80°9E 125 E9
Purbalingga Indonesia 7°23S 109°21E 119 G13
Purbeck, Isle of U.K. 50°39N 1°59W 67 G5
Purcell U.S.A. 35°1N 97°22W 176 D6
Purcell Mts. Canada 49°55N 116°15W 162 D5
Purdy Canada 45°19N 77°44W 174 A7
Puri India 19°50N 85°58E 126 E7
Purmerend Neths. 52°32N 4°58E 69 B4
Purna → India 19°6N 77°2E 126 E3
Purnia India 25°45N 87°31E 125 G12
Purnululu △ Australia 17°20S 128°20E 148 C4
Pursat = Pouthisat
Cambodia 12°34N 103°50E 120 F4
Purukcahu Indonesia 0°35S 114°35E 118 E4
Puruliya India 23°17N 86°24E 125 H12
Purus → Brazil 3°42S 61°28W 186 D6
Puruvesi Finland 61°50N 29°30E 84 B5
Purvis U.S.A. 31°9N 89°25W 177 F10
Pŭrvomay Bulgaria 42°8N 25°17E 97 D9
Purwa India 26°28N 80°47E 125 F9
Purwakarta Indonesia 6°35S 107°29E 119 G12
Purwo, Tanjung
Indonesia 8°44S 114°21E 119 K18
Purwodadi Indonesia 7°7S 110°55E 119 G14
Purwokerto Indonesia 7°25S 109°14E 119 G13
Puryŏng N. Korea 42°5N 129°43E 115 C15
Pus → India 19°55N 77°55E 126 E3
Pusa India 25°59N 85°41E 125 G11
Pusad India 19°56N 77°36E 126 E3
Pusan = Busan
S. Korea 35°5N 129°0E 115 G15
Pushkin Russia 59°45N 30°25E 84 C6
Pushkino Moskva, Russia 56°2N 37°49E 84 D9
Pushkino Saratov, Russia 51°16N 47°0E 86 E8
Püspökladány Hungary 47°19N 21°6E 80 C6
Pustoshka Russia 56°20N 29°30E 84 D5
Puszczykowo Poland 52°18N 16°49E 83 F3
Put-in-Bay U.S.A. 41°39N 82°49W 174 E2
Putahow L. Canada 59°54N 100°40W 163 B8
Putao Burma 27°28N 97°30E 123 F20
Putaruru N.Z. 38°2S 175°50E 154 E4
Putbus Germany 54°22N 13°28E 76 A9
Puteran Indonesia 7°5S 114°0E 119 G15
Putian China 25°23N 119°0E 117 E12
Putignano Italy 40°51N 17°7E 95 B10
Putina Peru 14°55S 69°55W 188 C4
Puting, Tanjung
Indonesia 3°31S 111°46E 118 E4
Putlitz Germany 53°15N 12°2E 76 B8
Putna Romania 47°50N 25°33E 81 C10
Putna → Romania 45°42N 27°26E 81 E12
Putnam U.S.A. 41°55N 71°55W 175 E13
Putney U.S.A. 31°29N 84°8W 178 D5
Putnok Hungary 48°18N 20°26E 80 B5
Putorana, Gory Russia 69°0N 95°0E 107 C10
Putorino N.Z. 39°4S 176°58E 154 F5
Putrajaya Malaysia 2°55N 101°40E 121 L3
Putre Chile 18°12S 69°35W 188 D4
Puttalam Sri Lanka 8°1N 79°55E 127 K5
Puttalam Lagoon
Sri Lanka 8°15N 79°45E 127 K4
Puttgarden Germany 54°30N 11°10E 76 A7
Püttlingen Germany 49°17N 6°53E 77 F2
Puttur Andhra Pradesh,
India 13°27N 79°33E 127 H4
Puttur Karnataka, India 12°46N 75°12E 127 H2
Putty Australia 32°57S 150°42E 153 B9
Putumayo → S. Amer. 3°7S 67°58W 186 D5
Putuo China 29°56N 122°20E 117 C14
Putussibau Indonesia 0°50N 112°56E 118 D4
Pututahi N.Z. 38°39S 177°53E 154 E6
Putyla Ukraine 48°0N 25°5E 81 B10
Puvirnituq Canada 60°2N 77°10W 161 E16
Puy-de-Dôme France 45°46N 2°57E 72 C6
Puy-de-Dôme □ France 45°40N 3°5E 72 C7
Puy-l'Évêque France 44°31N 1°9E 72 D5
Puyallup U.S.A. 47°12N 122°18W 170 C4
Puyang China 35°40N 115°1E 114 G8
Puyehue Chile 40°40S 72°37W 192 B2
Puyehue △ Chile 40°27S 72°6W 192 B2
Puylaurens France 43°35N 2°0E 72 E6
Puysegur Pt. N.Z. 46°9S 166°37E 155 G1
Pūzeh Rīg Iran 27°20N 58°40E 129 E8
Puzhaykove Ukraine 48°7N 29°50E 81 B14
Pwani □ Tanzania 7°0S 39°0E 142 D4
Pweto
Dem. Rep. of the Congo 8°25S 28°51E 143 D2
Pwllheli U.K. 52°53N 4°25W 66 E3
Pyana → Russia 55°43N 46°1E 86 C8
Pyaozero, Ozero Russia 66°5N 30°58E 60 C24
Pyapon Burma 16°20N 95°40E 123 L19
Pyasina → Russia 73°30N 87°0E 107 B9
Pyatigorsk Russia 44°2N 43°6E 87 H6
Pyatykhatky Ukraine 48°28N 33°38E 85 H7
Pyay = Prome Burma 18°49N 95°13E 123 K19
Pydna Greece 40°20N 22°34E 96 F6
Pye = Prome Burma 18°49N 95°13E 123 K19
Pyeongtaek S. Korea 37°1N 127°4E 115 F14
Pyetrikaw Belarus 52°11N 28°29E 75 B15
Pyhäjoki → Finland 64°28N 24°14E 60 D21
Pyhätunturi △ Finland 66°58N 27°5E 60 C22
Pyin-Oo-Lwin = Maymyo
Burma 22°2N 96°28E 120 A1
Pyinmana Burma 19°45N 96°12E 123 K20
Pyla, C. Cyprus 34°56N 33°51E 101 E12
Pymatuning Res.
U.S.A. 41°30N 80°28W 174 E4
Pyŏktong N. Korea 40°50N 125°50E 115 D13
Pyŏnggang N. Korea 38°24N 127°17E 115 E14
P'yŏngsong N. Korea 39°14N 125°52E 115 E13
P'yŏngyang N. Korea 39°0N 125°30E 115 E13
Pyote U.S.A. 31°32N 103°8W 176 F3
Pyramid L. U.S.A. 40°1N 119°35W 168 F4
Pyramid Pk. U.S.A. 36°25N 116°37W 171 J10
Pyramids Egypt 29°58N 31°9E 137 F7
Pyrénées Europe 42°45N 0°18E 72 F4
Pyrénées △ France 42°52N 0°10W 72 F3
Pyrénées-Atlantiques □
France 43°10N 0°50W 72 E3
Pyrénées-Orientales □
France 42°35N 2°26E 72 F6
Pyryatyn Ukraine 50°15N 32°25E 85 G7
Pyrzyce Poland 53°10N 14°55E 83 E1
Pyskowice Poland 50°24N 18°38E 83 H5
Pytalovo Russia 57°5N 27°55E 84 D4
Pyu Burma 18°30N 96°28E 123 K20
Pyzdry Poland 52°11N 17°42E 83 F4

Q

Qaanaaq Greenland 77°30N 69°10W 57 B4
Qaasuitsup □ Greenland 74°0N 52°0W 57 C5
Qäbälä Azerbaijan 40°58N 47°47E 87 K8
Qabanbay Kazakhstan 45°50N 80°37E 109 C10
Qabirri → Azerbaijan 41°3N 46°17E 87 K8
Qachasnek S. Africa 30°6S 28°42E 145 D4
Qādisiyah, Buhayrat al
Iraq 34°20N 42°12E 105 E10
Qa'el Jafr Jordan 30°20N 36°25E 130 E5
Qa'emābād Iran 31°44N 60°2E 129 D9
Qā'emshahr Iran 36°30N 52°53E 129 B7
Qagan Nur Jilin,
China 45°15N 124°18E 115 B13
Qagan Nur Nei Monggol Zizhiqu,
China 43°30N 114°55E 114 C8
Qahar Youyi Zhongqi
China 41°12N 112°40E 114 D7
Qahremānshahr = Kermānshāh
Iran 34°23N 47°0E 105 E12
Qaidam Pendi China 37°0N 95°0E 110 D8
Qaiyara Iraq 35°48N 43°17E 105 E10
Qajarīyeh Iran 31°1N 48°22E 129 D6
Qala, Ras il Malta 36°2N 14°20E 101 C1
Qala-i-Jadid = Spīn Būldak
Afghan. 31°1N 66°25E 124 D2
Qala Point = Qala, Ras il
Malta 36°2N 14°20E 101 C1
Qala Viala Pakistan 30°49N 67°17E 124 D2
Qala Yangi Afghan. 34°20N 66°30E 124 B2
Qalaikhum = Kalaikhum
Tajikistan 38°28N 70°46E 109 E8
Qal'at al Akhḍar
Si. Arabia 28°4N 37°9E 128 E3
Qal'at Bīshah Si. Arabia 20°0N 42°36E 137 C5
Qal'at Dīzah Iraq 36°11N 45°7E 105 D11
Qal'at Şāliḥ Iraq 31°31N 47°16E 128 D5
Qal'at Sukkar Iraq 31°51N 46°5E 105 G12
Qal'eh-ye Now Afghan. 35°0N 63°5E 108 F6
Qalyûb Egypt 30°12N 31°11E 137 E7
Qamani'tuaq = Baker Lake
Canada 64°20N 96°3W 160 E12
Qamdo China 31°15N 97°6E 116 B1
Qamea Fiji 16°45S 179°45W 154 a
Qamruddin Karez
Pakistan 31°45N 68°20E 124 D3
Qandahār = Kandahār
Afghan. 31°32N 65°43E 122 D4
Qandahār = Kandahār □
Afghan. 31°0N 65°0E 122 D4
Qandyaghash
Kazakhstan 49°28N 57°25E 108 C5
Qapān Iran 37°40N 55°47E 129 B7
Qapqal China 43°48N 81°5E 109 D10
Qapshaghay
Kazakhstan 43°51N 77°14E 109 D9
Qapshaghay Bögeni
Kazakhstan 43°45N 77°50E 109 D9
Qaqortoq Greenland 60°43N 46°0W 57 E6
Qâra Egypt 29°38N 26°30E 137 B2
Qara Dāgh Iraq 35°18N 45°18E 105 E11
Qara Qash → China 35°0N 78°30E 125 B8
Qarabalyq Kazakhstan 53°45N 62°2E 108 B6
Qarabutaq Kazakhstan 50°0N 60°14E 108 C6
Qaraçala Azerbaijan 39°45N 48°53E 87 L9
Qaraçuxur Azerbaijan 40°25N 50°1E 87 K10
Qaraghandy
Kazakhstan 49°50N 73°10E 109 C8

Qaraghayly Kazakhstan 49°26N 76°0E 106 E8
Qārah Si. Arabia 29°55N 40°3E 128 D4
Qarah Āghāj Iran 37°8N 46°58E 105 D12
Qarakol Uzbekistan 39°32N 63°50E 108 E6
Qaraoba Kazakhstan 47°6N 56°15E 108 C5
Qaraqīya Oyysy Kazakhstan 43°27N 51°45E 108 D4
Qaraqosh Iraq 36°16N 43°22E 105 D10
Qarataū Ongtüstik Qazaqstan, Kazakhstan 43°30N 69°30E 109 D7
Qarataū Zhambyl, Kazakhstan 43°10N 70°28E 109 D8
Qarazhal Kazakhstan 48°2N 70°49E 106 E8
Qarchak Iran 35°25N 51°34E 129 C6
Qardho Somalia 9°30N 49°6E 131 F4
Qareh → Iran 39°25N 47°22E 105 C12
Qareh Tekān Iran 36°38N 49°29E 129 B6
Qarnein U.A.E. 24°56N 52°52E 129 E7
Qarokŭl = Karakul, Ozero Tajikistan 39°5N 73°25E 109 E8
Qarqan He → China 39°30N 88°30E 109 E11
Qarqaraly Kazakhstan 49°26N 75°30E 109 C9
Qarshi Uzbekistan 38°53N 65°48E 109 E7
Qartabā Lebanon 34°4N 35°50E 130 A4
Qārūh Kuwait 28°49N 48°46E 129 D6
Qaryat al Gharab Iraq 31°27N 44°48E 128 D5
Qaryat al 'Ulyā Si. Arabia 27°33N 47°42E 128 E5
Qarynzharyq Oyysy Kazakhstan 42°55N 54°25E 108 D4
Qashqadaryo □ Uzbekistan 38°35N 66°0E 109 E7
Qasigiannguit Greenland 68°50N 51°18W 57 D5
Qasr 'Amra Jordan 31°48N 36°35E 128 D3
Qaşr-e Qand Iran 26°15N 60°45E 129 E9
Qaşr-e Shīrīn Iran 34°31N 45°35E 105 E11
Qasr Farâfra Egypt 27°0N 28°1E 137 B2
Qasuittuq = Resolute Canada 74°42N 94°54W 161 C13
Qatanā Syria 33°26N 36°4E 130 B5
Qatar ■ Asia 25°30N 51°15E 129 E6
Qatlīsh Iran 37°50N 57°19E 129 B8
Qattâra Egypt 30°12N 27°3E 137 A2
Qattâra, Munkhafed el Egypt 29°30N 27°30E 137 B2
Qattâra Depression = Qattâra, Munkhafed el Egypt 29°30N 27°30E 137 B2
Qawām al Ḩamzah = Al Ḩamzah Iraq 31°43N 44°58E 128 D5
Qāyen Iran 33°40N 59°10E 129 C8
Qaynar Kazakhstan 49°12N 77°22E 109 C9
Qazaly Kazakhstan 45°45N 62°6E 108 C6
Qazaqstan = Kazakhstan ■ Asia 50°0N 70°0E 109 C8
Qazaqtyng Usaqshogylyghy Kazakhstan 50°0N 72°0E 109 C8
Qazax Azerbaijan 41°5N 45°21E 87 K7
Qazımämmäd Azerbaijan 40°3N 49°0E 87 K9
Qazvīn Iran 36°15N 50°0E 129 B6
Qazvīn □ Iran 36°20N 50°0E 129 B6
Qazyghurt Kazakhstan 41°45N 69°23E 109 D7
Qena Egypt 26°10N 32°43E 137 B3
Qena, W. → Egypt 26°12N 32°44E 137 B3
Qeqertarsuaq Qaasuitsup, Greenland 69°45N 53°30W 57 D5
Qeqertarsuaq Qaasuitsup, Greenland 69°15N 53°38W 57 D5
Qeqertarsuatsiaat Greenland 63°5N 50°45W 57 E5
Qeqqata □ Greenland 66°30N 48°0W 57 D6
Qeshlāq Iran 34°55N 46°28E 105 E12
Qeshm Iran 26°55N 56°10E 129 E8
Qeydār Iran 36°6N 48°35E 105 D13
Qeys Iran 26°32N 53°58E 129 E7
Qezel Owzen → Iran 36°45N 49°22E 129 B6
Qezi'ot Israel 30°52N 34°26E 130 E3
Qi Xian China 34°40N 114°48E 114 G8
Qian Gorlos China 45°5N 124°42E 115 B13
Qian Hai China 22°32N 113°54E 111 a
Qian Xian China 34°31N 108°15E 114 G5
Qian'an China 40°0N 118°41E 115 E10
Qiancheng China 27°12N 109°50E 116 D7
Qianjiang Guangxi Zhuangzu, China 23°38N 108°58E 116 F7
Qianjiang Hubei, China 30°24N 112°55E 117 B9
Qianjiang Sichuan, China 29°33N 108°47E 116 C7
Qianjin China 47°34N 133°4E 111 B15
Qianshan Anhui, China 30°37N 116°35E 117 B11
Qianshan Guangdong, China 22°15N 113°31E 111 a
Qianwei China 29°13N 103°56E 116 C4
Qianxi China 27°3N 106°3E 116 D6
Qianyang Hunan, China 27°18N 110°10E 117 D8
Qianyang Shaanxi, China 34°40N 107°8E 114 G4
Qianyang Zhejiang, China 30°11N 119°25E 117 B12
Qi'ao China 22°25N 113°39E 111 a
Qi'ao Dao China 22°25N 113°38E 111 a
Qiaocun China 39°56N 112°55E 114 E7
Qiaojia China 26°56N 102°58E 116 D4
Qichun China 30°18N 115°25E 117 B10
Qidong Hunan, China 26°49N 112°7E 117 D9
Qidong Jiangsu, China 31°48N 121°38E 117 B13
Qiemo China 38°8N 85°32E 109 E11
Qijiang China 28°57N 106°35E 116 C6
Qijiaojing China 43°28N 91°36E 109 D12
Qikiqtarjuaq Canada 67°33N 63°0W 161 D19
Qila Saifullāh Pakistan 30°45N 68°17E 124 D3
Qilian Shan China 38°30N 96°0E 110 D8
Qimen China 29°50N 117°42E 117 C11
Qin He → China 35°1N 113°22E 114 G7
Qin Jiang → Guangxi Zhuangzu, China 21°53N 108°35E 116 F7
Qin Jiang → Jiangxi, China 26°15N 115°55E 117 D10
Qin Ling = Qinling Shandi China 33°50N 108°10E 114 H5
Qin'an China 34°48N 105°40E 114 G3
Qing Xian China 38°35N 116°45E 114 E9
Qingcheng China 37°15N 117°40E 115 F9
Qingcheng Shan China 30°58N 103°31E 116 B4
Qingchuan China 32°36N 105°9E 114 H3
Qingdao China 36°5N 120°20E 115 F11
Qingfeng China 35°52N 115°8E 114 G8
Qinghai □ China 36°0N 98°0E 110 D8
Qinghai Hu China 36°40N 100°10E 110 D9
Qinghe China 46°37N 90°25E 109 C12
Qinghecheng China 41°28N 124°15E 115 D13
Qinghemen China 41°48N 121°25E 115 D11
Qingjian China 37°8N 110°8E 114 F6
Qingjiang = Huaiyin China 33°30N 119°2E 115 H10
Qingliu China 26°11N 116°48E 117 D11
Qinglong China 25°49N 105°12E 116 E5
Qingping China 26°39N 107°47E 116 D6
Qingshui China 34°48N 106°8E 114 G4
Qingshuihe China 39°55N 111°35E 114 E6
Qingtian China 28°12N 120°15E 117 C13
Qingtongxia China 38°2N 106°3E 114 E4
Qingtongxia Shuiku China 37°50N 105°58E 114 F3
Qingxi China 27°8N 108°43E 116 D7
Qingxu China 37°34N 112°22E 114 F7
Qingyang Anhui, China 30°38N 117°50E 117 B11
Qingyang Gansu, China 36°2N 107°55E 114 F4
Qingyi Jiang → China 29°32N 103°44E 116 C4
Qingyuan Guangdong, China 23°40N 112°59E 117 F9
Qingyuan Liaoning, China 42°10N 124°55E 115 C13
Qingyuan Zhejiang, China 27°36N 119°3E 117 D12
Qingyun China 37°45N 117°20E 115 F9
Qingzhen China 26°31N 106°25E 116 D6
Qinhuangdao China 39°56N 119°30E 115 E10
Qinling Shandi China 33°50N 108°10E 114 H5
Qinshui China 35°40N 112°8E 114 G7
Qinyang = Jiyuan China 35°7N 112°57E 114 G7
Qinyang China 35°5N 112°56E 114 G7
Qinyuan China 36°29N 112°20E 114 F7
Qinzhou China 21°58N 108°38E 116 G7
Qionghai China 19°15N 110°26E 117 a
Qionglai China 30°25N 103°31E 116 B4
Qionglai Shan China 31°0N 102°30E 116 B4
Qiongshan China 19°51N 110°26E 117 a
Qiongzhou Haixia China 20°10N 110°15E 117 a
Qiqihar China 47°26N 124°0E 111 B13
Qira China 37°0N 80°48E 109 E10
Qiraîya, W. → Egypt 30°27N 34°0E 130 E3
Qiryat Ata Israel 32°47N 35°6E 130 C4
Qiryat Gat Israel 31°32N 34°46E 130 D3
Qiryat Mal'akhi Israel 31°44N 34°44E 130 D3
Qiryat Shemona Israel 33°13N 35°35E 130 B4
Qiryat Yam Israel 32°51N 35°4E 130 C4
Qishan China 34°25N 107°38E 114 G4
Qitai China 44°2N 89°35E 109 D11
Qitaihe China 45°48N 130°51E 112 B5
Qiubei China 24°2N 104°12E 116 E5
Qixia China 37°17N 120°52E 115 F11
Qiyang China 26°35N 111°50E 117 D8
Qızılağac Körfäzi Azerbaijan 39°9N 49°0E 105 C13
Qobda Kazakhstan 50°55N 54°31E 108 B4
Qods Iran 35°45N 51°15E 129 C6
Qojūr Iran 36°12N 47°55E 128 B5
Qom Iran 34°40N 51°0E 129 C6
Qom □ Iran 34°40N 51°0E 129 C6
Qomolangma Feng = Everest, Mt. Nepal 28°5N 86°58E 125 E12
Qomsheh Iran 32°0N 51°55E 129 D6
Qong Muztag China 35°42N 82°22E 109 E10
Qoqek = Tacheng China 46°40N 82°58E 109 C10
Qoqon = Qŭqon Uzbekistan 40°31N 70°56E 109 D8
Qoraqalpoghistan □ Uzbekistan 43°0N 58°0E 108 D5
Qorghalzhyn Kazakhstan 50°25N 69°11E 109 B7
Qorveh Iran 35°10N 47°48E 105 E12
Qosshaghyl Kazakhstan 46°40N 54°0E 108 C4
Qostanay Kazakhstan 53°10N 63°35E 108 B6
Qotanqaraghay Kazakhstan 49°10N 85°36E 109 C11
Qoṭūr Iran 38°28N 44°25E 105 C11
Qu Jiang → China 30°1N 106°24E 116 B6
Qu Xian China 30°48N 106°58E 116 B6
Quabbin Res. U.S.A. 42°20N 72°20W 175 D12
Quairading Australia 32°0S 117°21E 149 F2
Quakenbrück Germany 52°41N 7°57E 76 C3
Quakertown U.S.A. 40°26N 75°21W 175 F9
Qualicum Beach Canada 49°22N 124°26W 162 D4
Quambatook Australia 35°49S 143°34E 152 C5
Quambone Australia 30°57S 147°53E 153 A7
Quamby Australia 20°22S 140°17E 150 C3
Quan Long = Ca Mau Vietnam 9°7N 105°8E 121 H5
Quanah U.S.A. 34°18N 99°44W 176 D5
Quandialla Australia 34°1S 147°47E 153 C7
Quang Ngai Vietnam 15°13N 108°58E 120 E7
Quang Tri Vietnam 16°45N 107°13E 120 D6
Quang Yen Vietnam 20°56N 106°52E 116 G6
Quannan China 24°45N 114°33E 117 E10
Quantock Hills U.K. 51°8N 3°10W 67 F4
Quanyang China 42°21N 127°32E 115 C14
Quanzhou Fujian, China 24°55N 118°34E 117 E12
Quanzhou Guangxi Zhuangzu, China 25°57N 111°5E 117 E8
Qu'Appelle → Canada 50°33N 103°53W 163 C8
Quaqtaq Canada 60°55N 69°40W 161 E18
Quaraí Brazil 30°15S 56°20W 190 C4
Quarré-les-Tombes France 47°21N 4°0E 71 E11
Quarteira Portugal 37°4N 8°6W 89 H2
Quartu Sant'Élena Italy 39°15N 9°10E 94 C2
Quartzsite U.S.A. 33°40N 114°13W 171 M12
Quatre Bornes Mauritius 20°15S 57°28E 141 d
Quatsino Sd. Canada 50°25N 127°58W 162 C3
Quba Azerbaijan 41°21N 48°32E 87 K9
Qūchān Iran 37°10N 58°27E 129 B8
Queanbeyan Australia 35°17S 149°14E 153 C8
Québec Canada 46°52N 71°13W 165 C5
Québec □ Canada 48°0N 74°0W 165 B6
Quebo Guinea-Biss. 11°20N 14°56W 138 C2
Quebrada del Condorito △ Argentina 31°49S 64°40W 190 C3
Quedlinburg Germany 51°47N 11°8E 76 D7
Queen Alexandra Ra. Antarctica 85°0S 170°0E 55 E11
Queen Charlotte B. Falk. Is. 51°50S 60°40W 192 D4
Queen Charlotte City Canada 53°15N 132°2W 162 C2
Queen Charlotte Is. = Haida Gwaii Canada 53°20N 132°10W 162 C2
Queen Charlotte Sd. Canada 51°0N 128°0W 162 C3
Queen Charlotte Sd. N.Z. 41°10S 174°15E 155 B9
Queen Charlotte Strait Canada 50°45N 127°10W 162 C3
Queen Elizabeth △ Uganda 0°0 30°0E 142 C3
Queen Elizabeth Is. Canada 76°0N 95°0W 161 B13
Queen Elizabeth Land Antarctica 85°0S 60°0W 55 E17
Queen Mary Land Antarctica 70°0S 95°0E 55 D7
Queen Maud G. Canada 68°15N 102°30W 160 D11
Queen Maud Land = Dronning Maud Land Antarctica 72°30S 12°0E 55 D3
Queen Maud Mts. Antarctica 86°0S 160°0W 55 E12
Queens Channel Australia 15°0S 129°30E 148 C4
Queenscliff Australia 38°16S 144°39E 152 E6
Queensland U.S.A. 31°46N 83°14W 178 D6
Queensland □ Australia 22°0S 142°0E 150 C3
Queenstown Australia 42°4S 145°35E 151 G4
Queenstown N.Z. 45°1S 168°40E 155 F3
Queenstown Singapore 1°18N 103°48E 121 d
Queenstown S. Africa 31°52S 26°52E 144 D4
Queets U.S.A. 47°32N 124°19W 170 C2
Queguay Grande → Uruguay 32°9S 58°9W 190 C4
Queimadas Brazil 11°0S 39°38W 189 C3
Quelimane Mozam. 17°53S 36°58E 143 F4
Quellón Chile 43°7S 73°37W 192 B2
Quelpart = Jeju-do S. Korea 33°29N 126°34E 115 H14
Queluz Portugal 38°45N 9°14W 89 G1
Quemado N. Mex., U.S.A. 34°20N 108°30W 169 J9
Quemado Tex., U.S.A. 28°56N 100°37W 176 G4
Quemoy = Chinmen Taiwan 24°26N 118°19E 117 E12
Quemú-Quemú Argentina 36°3S 63°36W 190 D3
Quepem India 15°13N 74°3E 127 G2
Quequén Argentina 38°30S 58°30W 190 D4
Querco Peru 13°50S 74°52W 188 C3
Querétaro Mexico 20°36N 100°23W 180 C4
Querétaro □ Mexico 21°0N 99°55W 180 C5
Querfurt Germany 51°23N 11°35E 76 D7
Quérigut France 42°42N 2°6E 72 F6
Querqueville France 49°40N 1°42W 70 C5
Quesada Spain 37°51N 3°4W 89 H7
Queshan China 32°55N 114°2E 117 A10
Quesnel Canada 53°0N 122°30W 162 C4
Quesnel → Canada 52°58N 122°29W 162 C4
Quesnel L. Canada 52°30N 121°20W 162 C4
Questa U.S.A. 36°42N 105°36W 169 H11
Questembert France 47°40N 2°28W 70 E4
Quetico ⌂ Canada 48°30N 91°45W 164 C1
Quetrequile Argentina 41°33S 69°22W 192 B3
Quetta Pakistan 30°15N 66°55E 124 D2
Quetzaltenango Guatemala 14°50N 91°30W 182 D1
Queulat △ Chile 44°29S 72°24W 192 B2
Queyras ⌂ France 44°45N 6°50E 73 D10
Quezon City Phil. 14°37N 121°2E 119 B6
Qufār Si. Arabia 27°26N 41°37E 128 E4
Qufu China 35°36N 116°58E 114 G9
Qui Nhon Vietnam 13°40N 109°13E 120 F7
Quibala Angola 10°46S 14°59E 140 G2
Quibaxe Angola 8°24S 14°27E 140 F2
Quibdó Colombia 5°42N 76°40W 186 B3
Quiberon France 47°29N 3°9W 70 E3
Quiberon, Presqu'île de France 47°30N 3°8W 70 E3
Quickborn Germany 53°42N 9°52E 76 B5
Quiet L. Canada 61°5N 133°5W 162 A2
Quiindy Paraguay 25°58S 57°14W 190 B4
Quilá Mexico 24°23N 107°13W 180 C3
Quilán, C. Chile 43°15S 74°30W 192 B2
Quilcene U.S.A. 47°49N 122°53W 170 C4
Quilimarí Chile 32°5S 71°30W 190 C1
Quilino Argentina 30°14S 64°29W 190 C3
Quillabamba Peru 12°50S 72°50W 188 C3
Quillagua Chile 21°40S 69°40W 190 A2
Quillan France 42°53N 2°10E 72 F6
Quillota Chile 32°54S 71°16W 190 C1
Quilmes Argentina 34°43S 58°15W 190 C4
Quilon = Kollam India 8°50N 76°38E 127 K3
Quilpie Australia 26°35S 144°11E 151 D3
Quilpué Chile 33°5S 71°33W 190 C1
Quilua Mozam. 16°17S 39°54E 143 F4
Quime Bolivia 17°2S 67°15W 188 D4
Quimilí Argentina 27°40S 62°30W 190 B3
Quimper France 48°0N 4°9W 70 E2
Quimperlé France 47°53N 3°33W 70 E3
Quinault → U.S.A. 47°21N 124°18W 170 C2
Quince Mil Peru 13°15S 70°40W 188 C3
Quincy Calif., U.S.A. 39°56N 120°57W 170 F6
Quincy Fla., U.S.A. 30°35N 84°34W 178 E5
Quincy Ill., U.S.A. 39°56N 91°23W 172 F8
Quincy Mass., U.S.A. 42°14N 71°0W 175 D14
Quincy Wash., U.S.A. 47°14N 119°51W 168 C4
Quines Argentina 32°13S 65°48W 190 C2
Quinga Mozam. 15°49S 40°15E 143 F5
Quingey France 47°7N 5°52E 71 E12
Quinhámel Guinea-Biss. 11°53N 15°51W 138 C1
Quintana de la Serena Spain 38°45N 5°40W 89 G5
Quintana Roo □ Mexico 19°40N 88°30W 181 D7
Quintanar de la Orden Spain 39°36N 3°5W 89 F7
Quintanar de la Sierra Spain 41°57N 2°55W 90 D2
Quintanar del Rey Spain 39°21N 1°56W 91 F3
Quintero Chile 32°45S 71°30W 190 C1
Quintin France 48°26N 2°56W 70 D4
Quinto Spain 41°25N 0°32W 90 D4
Quípar → Spain 38°15N 1°40W 91 G3
Quirihue Chile 36°15S 72°35W 190 D1
Quirimbas △ Mozam. 12°30S 40°15E 143 E5
Quirindi Australia 31°28S 150°40E 153 A9
Quirinópolis Brazil 18°32S 50°30W 187 G8
Quiroga Spain 42°28N 7°18W 88 C3
Quiruvilca Peru 8°1S 78°19W 188 B2
Quissac France 43°55N 4°0E 73 E8
Quissanga Mozam. 12°24S 40°28E 143 E5
Quissico Mozam. 24°42S 34°44E 145 B5
Quitilipi Argentina 26°50S 60°13W 190 B3
Quitman U.S.A. 30°47N 83°34W 178 E6
Quito Ecuador 0°15S 78°35W 186 D3
Quitralco △ Chile 45°43S 73°25W 192 C2
Quixadá Brazil 4°55S 39°0W 189 A3
Quixaxe Mozam. 15°17S 40°4E 143 F5
Quixeramobim Brazil 5°12S 39°17W 189 B3
Qujing China 25°32N 103°41E 116 E4
Qulan Kazakhstan 42°55N 72°43E 106 E8
Qul'ân, Jazâ'ir Egypt 24°22N 35°31E 128 E2
Qulsary Kazakhstan 46°59N 54°1E 108 C4
Qumbu S. Africa 31°10S 28°48E 145 D4
Quneitra = Al Qunayṭirah Syria 33°5N 35°45E 130 B4
Qŭnghirot Uzbekistan 43°2N 58°50E 108 D5
Qu'nyido China 31°15N 98°6E 116 B2
Quoin I. Australia 14°54S 129°32E 148 B4
Quoin Pt. S. Africa 34°46S 19°37E 144 D2
Quorn Australia 32°25S 138°5E 152 B3
Qŭqon Uzbekistan 40°31N 70°56E 109 D8
Qŭrghonteppa Tajikistan 37°50N 68°47E 109 E7
Qurimbas △ Mozam. 12°20S 40°10E 143 E5
Qurnat as Sawdā' Lebanon 34°18N 36°6E 130 A5
Quryq Kazakhstan 43°12N 51°39E 108 D4
Qûs Egypt 25°55N 32°50E 137 B3
Qusar Azerbaijan 41°25N 48°26E 87 K9
Quşaybā' Si. Arabia 26°53N 43°35E 128 E4
Qusaybah Iraq 34°24N 40°59E 105 E9
Quseir Egypt 26°7N 34°16E 128 E2
Quseir Amra = Qasr 'Amra Jordan 31°48N 36°35E 128 D3
Qūshchī Iran 37°59N 45°3E 105 D11
Qusmuryn Kazakhstan 52°27N 64°36E 108 B6
Qusmuryn Köli Kazakhstan 52°41N 64°48E 108 B6
Qutang Gorge = Qutang Xia China 31°0N 109°40E 116 B7
Qutang Xia China 31°0N 109°40E 116 B7
Quthing Lesotho 30°25S 27°36E 145 D4
Qūṭīābād Iran 35°47N 48°30E 105 E13
Quttinirpaaq △ Canada 82°13N 72°13W 161 A17
Quwo China 35°38N 111°25E 114 G6
Quyang China 38°35N 114°40E 114 E8
Quynh Nhai Vietnam 21°49N 103°33E 120 B4
Quyon Canada 45°31N 76°14W 175 A8
Quzhou China 28°57N 118°54E 117 C12
Quzi China 36°20N 107°20E 114 F4
Qvareli Georgia 41°57N 45°47E 87 K7
Qyzylorda Kazakhstan 44°48N 65°28E 108 D7
Qyzylorda □ Kazakhstan 45°0N 65°0E 108 D6
Qyzylzhar Kazakhstan 48°17N 69°38E 109 C7

R

Ra, Ko Thailand 9°13N 98°16E 121 H2
Raab Austria 48°21N 13°39E 78 C6
Raahe Finland 64°40N 24°28E 60 D21
Raalte Neths. 52°23N 6°16E 69 B6
Raas Indonesia 7°8S 114°33E 119 G16
Raasay U.K. 57°25N 6°4W 65 D2
Raasay, Sd. of U.K. 57°30N 6°8W 65 D2
Raasepori Finland 60°0N 23°26E 84 B2
Rab Croatia 44°45N 14°45E 93 D11
Rába → Hungary 47°38N 17°38E 80 C2
Raba → Poland 50°8N 20°30E 83 H7
Rabaçal → Portugal 41°30N 7°12W 88 D3
Rabah Nigeria 13°5N 5°30E 139 C6
Rabai Kenya 3°50S 39°31E 142 C4
Rabastens France 43°50N 1°43E 72 E5
Rabastens-de-Bigorre France 43°23N 0°9E 72 E4
Rabat = Victoria Malta 36°3N 14°14E 101 C1
Rabat Malta 35°53N 14°24E 101 D1
Rabat Morocco 34°2N 6°48W 136 B2
Rabat □ Morocco 34°10N 6°45W 136 B2
Rabaul Papua N. G. 4°24S 152°18E 147 B8
Rabbit Flat Australia 20°11S 130°1E 148 D5
Rabbit Lake Mine Canada 58°4N 104°5W 163 B8
Rabi Fiji 16°30S 179°59W 154 a
Rābigh Si. Arabia 22°50N 39°5E 131 C2
Rabka Poland 49°37N 19°59E 83 J6
Râbnița Moldova 47°45N 29°0E 81 C14
Rābor Iran 29°17N 56°55E 129 D8
Rabwah = Chenab Nagar Pakistan 31°45N 72°55E 124 D5
Rača Serbia 44°14N 21°0E 96 B4
Răcăciuni Romania 46°20N 26°59E 81 D11
Răcășdia Romania 44°59N 21°36E 80 F6
Racconigi Italy 44°46N 7°46E 92 D4
Race, C. Canada 46°40N 53°5W 165 C9
Race Pond U.S.A. 31°1N 82°8W 178 D7
Rach Gia Vietnam 10°5N 105°5E 121 G5
Rach Soi Vietnam 9°57N 105°7E 121 H5
Racha Noi, Ko Thailand 7°30N 98°19E 121 J2
Racha Yai, Ko Thailand 7°36N 98°21E 121 J2
Rachid Mauritania 18°45N 11°35W 138 B2
Raciąż Poland 52°46N 20°10E 83 F7
Racibórz Poland 50°7N 18°18E 83 H5
Racichy Belarus 53°44N 23°42E 82 E10
Racine U.S.A. 42°44N 87°47W 172 D10
Rackerby U.S.A. 39°26N 121°22W 170 F5
Råda Sweden 60°0N 13°36E 62 E7
Radan Serbia 42°59N 21°29E 96 D5
Rădăuți Romania 47°50N 25°59E 81 C10
Rădăuți-Prut Romania 48°14N 26°48E 81 B11
Radbuza → Czech Rep. 49°45N 13°22E 78 B6
Radcliff U.S.A. 37°51N 85°57W 173 G11
Radeberg Germany 51°7N 13°53E 76 D9
Radebeul Germany 51°6N 13°39E 76 D9
Radeče Slovenia 46°5N 15°14E 93 B12
Radekhiv Ukraine 50°25N 24°32E 75 C13
Radekhov = Radekhiv Ukraine 50°25N 24°32E 75 C13
Radenthein Austria 46°48N 13°43E 78 E6
Radew → Poland 54°2N 15°52E 82 D2
Radford U.S.A. 37°8N 80°34W 173 G13
Radhanpur India 23°50N 71°38E 124 H4
Radhwa, Jabal Si. Arabia 24°34N 38°18E 128 E3
Radika → Macedonia 41°38N 20°37E 96 E4
Radisson Qué., Canada 53°47N 77°37W 164 B4
Radisson Sask., Canada 52°30N 107°20W 163 C7
Radium Hot Springs Canada 50°35N 116°2W 162 C5
Radlje ob Dravi Slovenia 46°38N 15°13E 93 B12
Radnevo Bulgaria 42°17N 25°58E 97 D9
Radnice Czech Rep. 49°51N 13°35E 78 B6
Radnor Forest U.K. 52°17N 3°10W 67 E4
Radolfzell Germany 47°39N 8°59E 77 H4
Radom Poland 51°23N 21°12E 83 G8
Radomir Bulgaria 42°37N 22°59E 96 D6
Radomka → Poland 51°43N 21°28E 83 G8
Radomsko Poland 51°5N 19°28E 83 G6
Radomyshl Ukraine 50°30N 29°12E 75 C15
Radomyśl Wielki Poland 50°14N 21°15E 83 H8
Radoszyce Poland 51°4N 20°15E 83 G7
Radoviš Macedonia 41°38N 22°28E 96 E6
Radovljica Slovenia 46°22N 14°12E 93 B11
Radstadt Austria 47°24N 13°28E 78 D6
Radstock, C. Australia 33°12S 134°20E 151 E1
Răducăneni Romania 46°58N 27°54E 81 D12
Raduša Macedonia 42°7N 21°15E 96 D5
Raduzhnyy Russia 62°5N 77°28E 106 C8
Radvanichy Belarus 52°1N 24°0E 83 F11
Radviliškis Lithuania 55°49N 23°33E 82 C10
Radville Canada 49°30N 104°15W 163 D8
Raḍwá, J. Si. Arabia 24°34N 38°18E 137 C4
Radymno Poland 49°59N 22°52E 83 J9
Radzanów Poland 52°56N 20°8E 83 F7
Radziejów Poland 52°40N 18°30E 83 F5
Radzyń Chełmiński Poland 53°23N 18°55E 82 E5
Radzyń Podlaski Poland 51°47N 22°37E 83 G9
Rae Canada 62°50N 116°3W 162 A5
Rae Bareli India 26°18N 81°20E 125 F9
Rae Isthmus Canada 66°40N 87°30W 161 D14
Raeren Belgium 50°41N 6°7E 69 D6
Raeside, L. Australia 29°20S 122°0E 149 E3
Raetihi N.Z. 39°25S 175°17E 154 F4
Rafaela Argentina 31°10S 61°30W 190 C3
Rafah Gaza Strip 31°18N 34°14E 130 D3
Rafai C.A.R. 4°59N 23°58E 142 B1
Raffadali Italy 37°24N 13°32E 94 E6
Rafḩā Si. Arabia 29°35N 43°35E 128 D4
Rafina Greece 38°2N 24°0E 98 C6
Rafsanjān Iran 30°30N 56°5E 129 D8
Raft Pt. Australia 16°4S 124°26E 148 C3
Râgâ South Sudan 8°28N 25°41E 135 G11
Ragachow Belarus 53°8N 30°5E 75 B16
Ragama Sri Lanka 7°0N 79°50E 122 R11
Ragged, Mt. Australia 33°27S 123°25E 149 F3
Ragged Pt. Barbados 13°10N 59°26W 183 g
Raghunathpalli India 22°14N 84°48E 125 H11
Raghunathpur India 23°33N 86°40E 125 H12
Raglan N.Z. 37°55S 174°55E 154 D3
Raglan Harbour N.Z. 37°47S 174°50E 154 D3
Ragland U.S.A. 33°45N 86°9W 178 B3
Ragusa Italy 36°55N 14°44E 95 F7
Raha Indonesia 4°55S 123°0E 119 E6
Rahaeng = Tak Thailand 16°52N 99°8E 120 D2
Rahat Israel 31°24N 34°45E 130 D3
Rahat, Ḩarrat Si. Arabia 23°0N 40°5E 137 C5
Rahatgarh India 23°47N 78°22E 125 H8
Rahden Germany 52°26N 8°36E 76 C4
Rahimyar Khan Pakistan 28°30N 70°25E 124 E4
Rāhjerd Iran 34°22N 50°22E 129 C6
Rahole ⌂ Kenya 0°5N 38°57E 142 B4
Rahon India 31°3N 76°7E 124 D7
Rahotu N.Z. 39°20S 173°49E 154 F2
Rahovec Kosovo 42°24N 20°40E 96 D4
Rahuri India 19°23N 74°39E 126 E2
Rai, Hon Vietnam 9°48N 104°38E 121 H5
Raiatéa, Î. French Polynesia 16°50S 151°25W 157 J12
Raichur India 16°10N 77°20E 127 F3
Raiford U.S.A. 30°4N 82°14W 178 E7
Raiganj India 25°37N 88°10E 125 G13
Raigarh India 21°56N 83°25E 126 D6
Raighar India 19°51N 82°6E 126 E6
Raijua Indonesia 10°37S 121°36E 119 F6
Raikot India 30°41N 75°42E 124 D6
Railton Australia 41°25S 146°28E 151 G4
Rainbow Bridge ⌂ U.S.A. 37°5N 110°58W 169 H8
Rainbow City U.S.A. 33°57N 86°5W 178 B3
Rainbow Lake Canada 58°30N 119°23W 162 B5
Rainier U.S.A. 46°53N 122°41W 170 D4
Rainier, Mt. U.S.A. 46°52N 121°46W 170 D5
Rainy L. Canada 48°42N 93°10W 163 D10
Rainy River Canada 48°43N 94°29W 163 D10
Raippaluoto Finland 63°13N 21°14E 60 E19
Raipur India 21°17N 81°45E 126 D5
Rairakhol India 21°4N 84°21E 126 D7
Ra'is Si. Arabia 23°33N 38°43E 137 C4
Raisen India 23°20N 77°48E 124 H8
Raisio Finland 60°28N 22°11E 84 B2
Raj Nandgaon India 21°5N 81°5E 126 D5
Raj Nilgiri India 21°28N 86°46E 125 J12
Raja, Ujung Indonesia 3°40N 96°25E 118 D1
Raja Ampat, Kepulauan Indonesia 0°30S 130°0E 119 E8
Rajahmundry India 17°1N 81°48E 126 F5
Rajaji △ India 30°10N 78°20E 124 D8
Rajampet India 14°11N 79°10E 127 G4
Rajang → Malaysia 2°30N 112°0E 118 D4
Rajanpur Pakistan 29°6N 70°19E 124 E4
Rajapalaiyam India 9°25N 77°35E 127 K3
Rajapur India 16°40N 73°31E 126 F1
Rajasthan □ India 26°45N 73°30E 124 F5
Rajasthan Canal = Indira Gandhi Canal India 28°0N 72°0E 124 F5
Rajauri India 33°25N 74°21E 125 C6
Rajendranagar India 17°18N 78°27E 126 F4
Rajgarh Mad. P., India 24°2N 76°45E 124 G7
Rajgarh Raj., India 27°14N 76°38E 124 F7
Rajgarh Raj., India 28°40N 75°25E 124 E6
Rajghat Dam India 24°45N 78°20E 126 B4
Rajgir India 25°2N 85°25E 125 G11
Rajgród Poland 53°42N 22°42E 82 E9
Rajim India 20°58N 81°53E 126 D5
Rajkot India 22°15N 70°56E 124 H4
Rajmahal Hills India 24°30N 87°30E 125 G12
Rajpipla India 21°50N 73°30E 126 D1
Rajpur India 22°18N 74°21E 124 H6
Rajpura India 30°25N 76°32E 124 D7
Rajsamand = Kankroli India 25°4N 73°53E 124 G5
Rajshahi Bangla. 24°22N 88°39E 123 G16
Rajshahi □ Bangla. 25°0N 89°0E 12
Rajula India 21°3N 71°26E 1
Rajur India 20°7N 78°55E 1
Rajura India 19°47N 79°22E 1
Rakaia N.Z. 43°45S 172°1E 1
Rakaia → N.Z. 43°36S 172°15E 1
Rakan, Ra's Qatar 26°10N 51°20E 1
Rakaposhi Pakistan 36°10N 74°25E 1
Rakata, Pulau Indonesia 6°10S 105°20E 11
Rakbah, Sahl Si. Arabia 22°15N 41°0E 1
Rakhine □ Burma 19°0N 94°15E 12
Rakhiv Ukraine 48°3N 24°12E
Rakhni Pakistan 30°4N 69°56E 1
Rakhni → Pakistan 29°31N 69°36E 1
Rakhny-Lisovi Ukraine 48°47N 28°29E 8
Rakiraki Fiji 17°22S 178°11E
Rakitnoye Russia 45°36N 134°17E 1
Rakitovo Bulgaria 41°59N 24°5E
Rakiura = Stewart I. N.Z. 46°58S 167°54E 1
Rakoniewice Poland 52°10N 16°16E
Rakops Botswana 21°1S 24°28E 1
Rakovica Croatia 44°59N 15°38E 9
Rakovník Czech Rep. 50°6N 13°42E
Rakovski Bulgaria 42°21N 24°57E
Rakvere Estonia 59°20N 26°25E
Raleigh Fla., U.S.A. 29°25N 82°32W 1
Raleigh N.C., U.S.A. 35°47N 78°39W 17
Ralik Chain Pac. Oc. 8°0N 168°0E 1
Ralja Serbia 44°33N 20°34E
Rälla Sweden 56°40N 16°30E 6
Ralls U.S.A. 33°41N 101°24W 1
Ralston U.S.A. 41°30N 76°57W 1
Ram → Canada 62°1N 123°41W 1
Rām Allāh West Bank 31°55N 35°10E 1
Rama Nic. 12°9N 84°15W 1
Ramacca Italy 37°23N 14°42E
Ramachandrapuram India 16°50N 82°4E 1
Ramagiri Udayagiri India 19°5N 84°18E 1
Ramagundam India 18°55N 79°15E 1
Ramakona India 21°43N 78°50E 1
Ramalho, Serra do Brazil 13°45S 44°0W 1
Rāmallāh = Rām Allāh West Bank 31°55N 35°10E 1
Raman Thailand 6°29N 101°18E 1
Ramanathapuram India 9°25N 78°55E 1
Ramanujganj India 23°48N 83°42E 12
Ramas C. India 15°5N 73°55E 1
Ramat Gan Israel 32°4N 34°48E 1
Ramatlhabama S. Africa 25°37S 25°33E 1
Ramban India 33°14N 75°12E 1
Rambervillers France 48°20N 6°38E 7
Rambi = Rabi Fiji 16°30S 179°59W
Rambipuji Indonesia 8°12S 113°37E 11
Rambouillet France 48°39N 1°50E
Ramdurg India 15°58N 75°22E 1
Rame Hd. Australia 37°47S 149°30E 1
Ramechhap Nepal 27°25N 86°10E 12
Ramenskoye Russia 55°32N 38°15E 8
Ramer U.S.A. 32°3N 86°13W 1
Rameswaram India 9°17N 79°18E 1
Ramganga → India 27°5N 79°58E 1
Ramgarh Jharkhand, India 23°40N 85°35E 12
Ramgarh Raj., India 27°16N 75°14E 1
Ramgarh Raj., India 27°30N 70°36E 1
Rāmhormoz Iran 31°15N 49°35E 1
Ramīān Iran 37°3N 55°16E 1
Ramingining Australia 12°19S 135°3E 1
Ramla Israel 31°55N 34°52E 1
Ramm = Rum Jordan 29°39N 35°26E 1
Ramm, Jabal Jordan 29°35N 35°24E 1
Râmna → Romania 45°36N 27°3E 8
Ramnad = Ramanathapuram India 9°25N 78°55E 1
Ramnagar Jammu & Kashmir, India 32°47N 75°18E 1
Ramnagar Uttarakhand, India 29°24N 79°7E 1
Ramnäs Sweden 59°46N 16°12E 6
Râmnicu Sărat Romania 45°26N 27°3E 8
Râmnicu Vâlcea Romania 45°9N 24°21E
Ramnous Greece 38°12N 24°3E
Ramon Russia 51°55N 39°21E 8
Ramona U.S.A. 33°2N 116°52W 17
Ramonville-St-Agne France 43°33N 1°28E
Ramore Canada 48°30N 80°25W 1
Ramos → Nigeria 5°8N 5°22E 1
Ramotswa Botswana 24°50S 25°52E 1
Rampur H.P., India 31°26N 77°43E 1
Rampur Mad. P., India 23°25N 73°53E 1
Rampur Odisha, India 21°48N 83°58E 1
Rampur Ut. P., India 28°50N 79°5E 1
Rampur Hat India 24°10N 87°50E 12
Rampura India 24°30N 75°27E 1
Ramrama Tola India 21°52N 79°55E 1
Ramree I. Burma 19°0N 93°40E 12
Rāmsar Iran 36°53N 50°41E 1
Ramsey I. of Man 54°20N 4°22W
Ramsey U.S.A. 41°4N 74°9W 17
Ramsey L. Canada 47°13N 82°15W 1
Ramsgate U.K. 51°20N 1°25E
Ramsjö Sweden 62°11N 15°37E
Ramstein Germany 49°27N 7°32E
Ramtek India 21°20N 79°15E 1
Ramu Kenya 3°55N 41°10E 1
Ramvik Sweden 62°49N 17°51E 6
Rana Pratap Sagar Dam India 24°58N 75°38E 1
Ranaghat India 23°15N 88°35E 12
Ranahu Pakistan 25°55N 69°45E 1
Ranau Malaysia 6°2N 116°40E 1
Rancagua Chile 34°10S 70°50W 1
Rance → France 48°34N 1°59W
Rancheria → Canada 60°13N 129°7W 1
Ranchester U.S.A. 44°54N 107°10W 16
Ranchi India 23°19N 85°27E 12
Rancho Cordova U.S.A. 38°36N 121°18W 1
Rancho Cucamonga U.S.A. 34°10N 117°30W 1
Ranco, L. Chile 40°15S 72°25W 1
Rand Australia 35°33S 146°32E 1
Randalstown U.K. 54°45N 6°19W
Randan France 46°2N 3°21E 7

ıdazzo *Italy* 37°53N 14°57E **95** E7
ıder *India* 21°14N 72°47E **126** D1
ıders *Denmark* 56°29N 10°1E **63** H4
ıders Fjord *Denmark* 56°37N 10°20E **63** H4
ıdfontein *S. Africa* 26°8S 27°45E **145** C4
ıdle *U.S.A.* 46°32N 121°57W **170** D5
ıdolph *Mass., U.S.A.* 42°10N 71°2W **175** D13
ıdolph *N.Y., U.S.A.* 42°10N 78°59W **174** D6
ıdolph *Utah, U.S.A.* 41°40N 111°11W **168** F8
ıdolph *Vt., U.S.A.* 43°55N 72°40W **175** C12
ıdsburg *U.S.A.* 35°22N 117°39W **171** K9
ıeälven → *Sweden* 65°50N 22°20E **60** D20
ıfurly *N.Z.* 45°7S 170°6E **155** F5
ıgae *Thailand* 6°19N 101°44E **121** J3
ıgataua *N.Z.* 39°26S 175°28E **154** F4
ıgaunu B. *N.Z.* 34°51S 173°15E **154** A2
ıge, The *Zimbabwe* 19°2S 31°2E **143** F3
ıgeley *U.S.A.* 44°58N 70°39W **175** B14
ıgeley L. *U.S.A.* 44°55N 70°43W **175** B14
ıgely *U.S.A.* 40°5N 108°48W **168** F9
ıger *U.S.A.* 32°28N 98°41W **176** E5
ıgia *India* 26°28N 91°38E **123** F17
ıgiora *N.Z.* 43°19S 172°36E **155** D7
ıgitaiki *N.Z.* 38°52S 176°24E **154** E5
ıgitaiki → *N.Z.* 37°54S 176°49E **154** D5
ıgitata → *N.Z.* 43°45S 171°15E **155** D6
ıgitikei → *N.Z.* 40°17S 175°15E **154** G4
ıgitoto ke te tonga = D'Urville *N.Z.* 40°50S 173°55E **155** A8
ıgitoto Ra. *N.Z.* 38°25S 175°35E **154** E4
ıgkasbitung *ıdonesia* 6°21S 106°15E **119** G12
ıgoon *Burma* 16°45N 96°20E **123** L20
ıgpur *Bangla.* 25°42N 89°22E **123** G16
ıgsang *Indonesia* 1°20N 103°5E **121** M4
ıibennur *India* 14°35N 75°30E **127** G2
ıiganj *Paschimbanga, ıdia* 23°40N 87°5E **123** H15
ıiganj *Ut. P., India* 27°3N 82°13E **125** F9
ıikhet *India* 29°39N 79°25E **125** E8
ıippettai *India* 12°56N 79°23E **127** H4
ıiwara *India* 24°50N 72°10E **124** G5
ıiyah *Iraq* 36°15N 44°53E **105** D11
ıka *India* 23°59N 83°47E **125** H10
ıken → *Australia* 20°31S 137°36E **150** C2
ıkin *U.S.A.* 31°13N 101°56W **176** F4
ıkin Inlet *Canada* 62°30N 93°0W **160** E13
ıkins Springs *ustralia* 33°49S 146°14E **153** B7
ıkweil *Austria* 47°17N 9°39E **78** D2
ınoch, L. *U.K.* 56°41N 4°20W **65** E4
ınoch Moor *U.K.* 56°38N 4°48W **65** E4
ıohira *Madag.* 22°29S 45°24E **141** J9
ıong *Thailand* 9°56N 98°40E **121** H2
ıpur *India* 20°5N 85°20E **126** D7
ısa *Iran* 33°39N 48°18E **129** C6
ısiki *Indonesia* 1°30S 134°10E **119** E8
ıtau Abang *Ialaysia* 4°52N 103°24E **121** K4
ıtauprapat *Indonesia* 2°15N 99°50E **118** D1
ıtemario *Indonesia* 3°15S 119°57E **119** E5
ıthambore △ *India* 26°10N 76°30E **124** F7
ıtoul *U.S.A.* 40°19N 88°9W **172** E9
ıum *Denmark* 56°54N 9°14E **63** H3
ıyah, W. → *. Arabia* 21°18N 43°20E **137** C5
ıhe *China* 46°47N 134°0E **112** A7
ın l'Étape *France* 48°24N 6°50E **71** D13
ıping *China* 23°42N 117°1E **117** F11
ıui, Erg er *Algeria* 29°0N 2°0W **136** C3
ıyang *China* 38°15N 115°45E **114** E8
ı, Ko *Thailand* 9°19N 99°58E **121** b
ıa *French Polynesia* 27°35S 144°20W **157** K13
ıa Nui = Pascua, I. de *hile* 27°7S 109°23W **157** K17
ıallo *Italy* 44°21N 9°14E **92** D6
ıar *India* 23°34N 70°38E **124** H4
ıch *Iran* 25°40N 59°15E **129** E8
ıel, Lago *Chile* 34°20S 71°14W **190** C1
ıer, C. *Canada* 69°44N 67°6W **161** D18
ıid City *U.S.A.* 44°5N 103°14W **172** C2
ıid River *U.S.A.* 45°55N 86°58W **172** C10
ıla *Estonia* 59°1N 24°52E **84** C3
ıti → *India* 26°18N 83°41E **125** F10
ıuette → *U.S.A.* 45°0N 74°42W **175** B10
ıuette Lake *U.S.A.* 43°49N 74°40W **175** C10
ıa △ *Nepal* 29°30N 82°10E **125** E10
ıotonga *Cook Is.* 21°30S 160°0W **157** K12
ıs al 'Ayn *Syria* 36°45N 40°12E **105** D9
ıs al Khaymah *.A.E.* 25°50N 55°59E **129** E7
ıs aţ Tib *Tunisia* 37°1N 11°2E **136** A6
ıel Ma *Algeria* 34°26N 0°50W **136** B3
ıel Mâ *Mali* 16°35N 4°30W **138** B4
ıel Oued *Algeria* 35°57N 5°2E **136** A5
ı Ghârib *Egypt* 28°6N 33°18E **137** F8
ı Muhammad △ *gypt* 27°45N 34°16E **137** B3
ı Sudr *Egypt* 29°40N 32°42E **137** F8
ıa, Pta. *B. Aires, rgentina* 36°20S 56°41W **190** D4
ıa, Pta. *Río Negro, rgentina* 40°50S 62°15W **192** B4
ıca, Pta. de la *ınary Is.* 27°59N 16°41W **100** G3
ıcani *Moldova* 47°58N 27°33E **81** C12
ıeiniai *Lithuania* 55°25N 23°5E **82** C10
ıhîd *Egypt* 31°21N 30°22E **137** E7
ıhîd, Masabb *Egypt* 31°22N 30°17E **137** E7
ıhmi *India* 25°4N 74°22E **124** G6
ıht *Iran* 37°20N 49°40E **105** D13
ı Salai *Thailand* 15°20N 104°9E **120** E5
ıipuram *India* 11°30N 78°15E **127** J4
ıka *Serbia* 43°19N 20°39E **96** C4
ıkot *Nepal* 29°14N 81°39E **125** E9
ınov *Romania* 45°35N 25°27E **81** E10
ıon L. *Australia* 28°45S 124°25E **149** E3
ıova *Romania* 44°15N 27°55E **81** F12
ıovo *Bulgaria* 43°42N 23°17E **96** C7
ıra *India* 25°50N 83°50E **125** G10
ıskazovo *Russia* 52°35N 41°50E **86** D5
ı *Romania* 43°53N 23°16E **81** G8
ıtatt *Germany* 48°50N 8°11E **77** G4
ıtede *Germany* 53°15N 8°12E **76** B4
ıolița *Romania* 46°59N 24°58E **81** D9
ıua Garhi *Nepal* 28°17N 85°23E **125** E11
ıul *Pakistan* 32°42N 73°34E **124** C5
ıków *Poland* 51°43N 17°40E **83** G4
ı → *Canada* 49°35N 97°10W **163** D9
Rat Buri = Ratchaburi *Thailand* 13°30N 99°54E **120** F2
Rat Islands *U.S.A.* 52°0N 178°0E **166** E3
Rat L. *Canada* 56°10N 99°40W **163** B9
Ratak Chain *Pac. Oc.* 1°0N 170°0E **156** G8
Rätan *Sweden* 62°29N 14°33E **62** B8
Ratangarh *India* 28°5N 74°35E **124** E6
Raţāwī *Iraq* 30°38N 47°13E **128** D5
Ratcatchers L. *Australia* 32°30S 143°12E **152** B5
Ratchaburi *Thailand* 13°30N 99°54E **120** F2
Rath *India* 25°36N 79°37E **125** G8
Rath Luirc = Charleville *Ireland* 52°21N 8°40W **64** D3
Rathangan *Ireland* 53°14N 7°0W **64** C4
Rathdrum *Ireland* 52°56N 6°14W **64** D5
Rathenow *Germany* 52°37N 12°19E **76** C8
Rathkeale *Ireland* 52°32N 8°56W **64** D3
Rathlin I. *U.K.* 55°18N 6°14W **64** A5
Rathmelton *Ireland* 55°2N 7°39W **64** A4
Ratibor = Racibórz *Poland* 50°7N 18°18E **83** H5
Rätikon *Austria* 47°0N 9°55E **78** D2
Ratingen *Germany* 51°18N 6°52E **76** D2
Ratlam *India* 23°20N 75°0E **124** H6
Ratmanova Ostrov *Russia* 65°46N 169°6W **166** B6
Ratnagiri *India* 16°57N 73°18E **126** F1
Ratnapura *Sri Lanka* 6°40N 80°20E **127** L5
Ratodero *Pakistan* 27°48N 68°18E **124** F3
Raton *U.S.A.* 36°54N 104°24W **169** H11
Rattaphum *Thailand* 7°8N 100°16E **121** J3
Ratten *Austria* 47°28N 15°44E **78** D8
Rattray Hd. *U.K.* 57°38N 1°50W **65** D7
Rättvik *Sweden* 60°52N 15°7E **62** D9
Ratz, Mt. *Canada* 57°23N 132°12W **162** B2
Ratzeburg *Germany* 53°40N 10°46E **76** B6
Raub *Malaysia* 3°47N 101°52E **121** L3
Rauch *Argentina* 36°45S 59°5W **190** D4
Raudales *Mexico* 17°27N 93°39W **181** D6
Raufarhöfn *Iceland* 66°27N 15°57W **60** C6
Raufoss *Norway* 60°44N 10°37E **60** F14
Raukumara Ra. *N.Z.* 38°5S 177°55E **154** E6
Raul Soares *Brazil* 20°5S 42°22W **189** E2
Rauma *Finland* 61°10N 21°30E **84** B1
Raumo = Rauma *Finland* 61°10N 21°30E **84** B1
Raung, Gunung *Indonesia* 8°8S 114°3E **119** J17
Raurkela *India* 22°14N 84°50E **125** H11
Rausu-Dake *Japan* 44°4N 145°7E **112** B12
Răut → *Moldova* 47°15N 29°9E **81** C14
Rava-Ruska *Ukraine* 50°15N 23°42E **83** H10
Rava Russkaya = Rava-Ruska *Ukraine* 50°15N 23°42E **83** H10
Ravalli *U.S.A.* 47°17N 114°11W **168** C6
Ravānsar *Iran* 34°43N 46°40E **105** E12
Ravanusa *Italy* 37°16N 13°58E **94** E6
Rāvar *Iran* 31°20N 56°51E **129** D8
Ravena *U.S.A.* 42°28N 73°49W **175** D11
Ravenel *U.S.A.* 32°46N 80°15W **178** C9
Ravenna *Italy* 44°25N 12°12E **93** D9
Ravenna *Nebr., U.S.A.* 41°1N 98°55W **172** E4
Ravenna *Ohio, U.S.A.* 41°9N 81°15W **174** E3
Ravensburg *Germany* 47°46N 9°36E **77** H5
Ravenshoe *Australia* 17°37S 145°29E **150** B4
Ravensthorpe *Australia* 33°35S 120°2E **149** F3
Ravenswood *Australia* 20°6S 146°54E **150** C4
Ravenswood *U.S.A.* 38°57N 81°46W **173** F13
Ravensworth *Australia* 32°26S 151°4E **153** B9
Raver *India* 21°15N 76°2E **126** D3
Ravi → *Pakistan* 30°35N 71°49E **124** D4
Ravna Gora *Croatia* 45°24N 14°50E **93** C11
Ravna Reka *Serbia* 44°1N 21°35E **96** B5
Ravne na Koroškem *Slovenia* 46°36N 14°59E **93** B11
Rawa Mazowiecka *Poland* 51°46N 20°12E **83** G7
Rawalpindi *Pakistan* 33°38N 73°8E **124** C5
Rawang *Malaysia* 3°20N 101°35E **121** L3
Rawene *N.Z.* 35°25S 173°32E **154** B2
Rawi, Ko *Thailand* 6°33N 99°14E **121** J2
Rawicz *Poland* 51°36N 16°52E **83** G3
Rawka → *Poland* 52°9N 20°8E **83** F7
Rawlinna *Australia* 30°58S 125°28E **149** F4
Rawlins *U.S.A.* 41°47N 107°14W **168** F10
Rawlinson Ra. *Australia* 24°40S 128°30E **149** D4
Rawson *Argentina* 43°15S 65°5W **192** B3
Raxaul *India* 26°59N 84°51E **125** F11
Ray *U.S.A.* 48°21N 103°10W **172** A2
Ray, C. *Canada* 47°33N 59°15W **165** C8
Ray City *U.S.A.* 31°5N 83°11W **178** D6
Ray Mts. *U.S.A.* 66°0N 152°0W **166** B9
Raya Ring, Ko *Thailand* 8°18N 98°29E **121** a
Rayachoti *India* 14°4N 78°50E **127** G4
Rayadurg *India* 14°40N 76°50E **127** G3
Rayagada *India* 19°15N 83°20E **126** E6
Raychikhinsk *Russia* 49°46N 129°25E **107** E13
Rāyen *Iran* 29°34N 57°26E **129** D8
Rayle *U.S.A.* 33°48N 82°54W **178** B7
Rayleigh *U.K.* 51°36N 0°37E **67** F8
Raymond *Canada* 49°30N 112°35W **162** D6
Raymond *Calif., U.S.A.* 37°13N 119°54W **170** H7
Raymond *N.H., U.S.A.* 43°2N 71°11W **175** C13
Raymond *Wash., U.S.A.* 46°41N 123°44W **170** D3
Raymond Terrace *Australia* 32°45S 151°44E **153** B9
Raymondville *U.S.A.* 26°29N 97°47W **176** H6
Raymore *Canada* 51°25N 104°31W **163** C8
Rayón *Mexico* 29°43N 110°35W **180** B2
Rayong *Thailand* 12°40N 101°20E **120** F3
Raystown L. *U.S.A.* 40°25N 78°5W **174** F6
Rayville *U.S.A.* 32°29N 91°46W **176** E9
Raz, Pte. du *France* 48°2N 4°47W **70** D2
Razan *Iran* 35°23N 49°2E **105** E13
Ražana *Serbia* 44°6N 19°55E **96** B3
Ražanj *Serbia* 43°40N 21°31E **96** C5
Razāzah, Buḩayrat ar *Iraq* 32°40N 43°35E **105** F10
Razazah, L. = Razāzah, Buḩayrat ar *Iraq* 32°40N 43°35E **105** F10
Razdelna *Bulgaria* 43°13N 27°41E **97** C11
Razdel'naya = Rozdilna *Ukraine* 46°50N 30°2E **81** D15
Razdolnoye *Russia* 43°30N 131°52E **112** C5
Razdolnoye *Ukraine* 45°46N 33°29E **85** K7
Razeh *Iran* 32°47N 48°9E **129** C6
Razgrad *Bulgaria* 43°33N 26°34E **97** C10
Razgrad □ *Bulgaria* 43°33N 26°34E **97** C10
Razim, Lacul *Romania* 44°50N 29°0E **81** F14
Razlog *Bulgaria* 41°53N 23°28E **96** E7
Razmak *Pakistan* 32°45N 69°50E **124** C3
Rāznas Ezers △ *Latvia* 56°30N 27°30E **84** D4
Re, Cu Lao *Vietnam* 15°22N 109°8E **120** E7
Ré, Î. de *France* 46°12N 1°30W **72** B2
Reading *U.K.* 51°27N 0°58W **67** F7
Reading *U.S.A.* 40°20N 75°56W **175** F9
Reading □ *U.K.* 51°27N 0°58W **67** F7
Real, Cordillera *Bolivia* 17°0S 67°10W **188** D4
Realicó *Argentina* 35°0S 64°15W **190** D3
Réalmont *France* 43°48N 2°10E **72** E6
Ream *Cambodia* 10°34N 103°39E **121** G4
Ream △ *Cambodia* 10°30N 103°45E **121** G4
Reay Forest *U.K.* 58°22N 4°55W **65** C4
Rebais *France* 48°50N 3°10E **71** D10
Rebecca, L. *Australia* 30°0S 122°15E **149** F3
Rebi *Indonesia* 6°23S 134°7E **119** F8
Rebiana, Sahrâ' *Libya* 24°30N 21°0E **135** D10
Reboly *Russia* 63°49N 30°47E **60** E24
Rebun-Tō *Japan* 45°23N 141°2E **112** B10
Recanati *Italy* 43°24N 13°32E **93** E10
Recaş *Romania* 45°46N 21°30E **80** E6
Recco *Italy* 44°22N 9°9E **92** D6
Recherche, Arch. of the *Australia* 34°15S 122°50E **149** F3
Rechna Doab *Pakistan* 31°35N 73°30E **124** D5
Rechytsa *Belarus* 52°21N 30°24E **75** B16
Recife *Brazil* 8°0S 35°0W **189** B4
Recife *Seychelles* 4°36S 55°42E **141** b
Recklinghausen *Germany* 51°37N 7°12E **76** D3
Reckong Peo *India* 31°32N 78°16E **124** D8
Reconquista *Argentina* 29°10S 59°45W **190** B4
Recreo *Argentina* 29°25S 65°10W **190** B2
Recuay *Peru* 9°43S 77°28W **188** B2
Recz *Poland* 53°16N 15°31E **83** E2
Red = Hong → *Vietnam* 20°16N 106°34E **120** B5
Red → *U.S.A.* 31°1N 91°45W **176** F9
Red Bank *U.S.A.* 40°21N 74°5W **175** F10
Red Bay *Canada* 51°44N 56°25W **165** B8
Red Bluff *U.S.A.* 40°11N 122°15W **168** F2
Red Bluff Res. *U.S.A.* 31°54N 103°55W **169** L12
Red Cliffs *Australia* 34°19S 142°11E **152** C5
Red Cloud *U.S.A.* 40°5N 98°32W **172** E4
Red Creek *U.S.A.* 43°14N 76°45W **175** C8
Red Deer *Canada* 52°20N 113°50W **162** C6
Red Deer → *Alta., Canada* 50°58N 110°0W **163** C7
Red Deer → *Man., Canada* 52°53N 101°1W **163** C8
Red Deer L. *Canada* 52°55N 101°20W **163** C8
Red Hook *U.S.A.* 41°55N 73°53W **175** E11
Red Indian L. *Canada* 48°35N 57°0W **165** C8
Red L. *Canada* 51°3N 93°49W **163** C10
Red Lake *Canada* 51°3N 93°49W **163** C10
Red Lake Falls *U.S.A.* 47°53N 96°16W **172** B5
Red Lake Road *Canada* 49°59N 93°25W **163** C10
Red Lodge *U.S.A.* 45°11N 109°15W **168** D9
Red Mountain *U.S.A.* 35°37N 117°38W **171** K9
Red Oak *U.S.A.* 41°1N 95°14W **172** E6
Red River of the North → *N. Amer.* 49°0N 97°15W **172** A5
Red Rock *Canada* 48°55N 88°15W **164** C2
Red Rock, L. *U.S.A.* 41°22N 92°59W **172** E7
Red Rocks Pt. *Australia* 32°13S 127°32E **149** F4
Red Sea *Asia* 25°0N 36°0E **131** C2
Red Slate Mt. *U.S.A.* 37°31N 118°52W **170** H8
Red Sucker L. *Canada* 54°9N 93°40W **164** B1
Red Tower Pass = Turnu Roşu, P. *Romania* 45°33N 24°17E **81** E9
Red Volta → *Africa* 10°34N 0°30W **139** C4
Red Wing *U.S.A.* 44°34N 92°31W **172** C7
Reda *Poland* 54°40N 18°19E **82** D5
Redang, Pulau *Malaysia* 5°49N 103°2E **121** K4
Redange *Lux.* 49°46N 5°52E **69** E5
Redcar *U.K.* 54°37N 1°4W **66** C6
Redcar & Cleveland □ *U.K.* 54°29N 1°0W **66** C7
Redcliff *Canada* 50°10N 110°50W **168** A8
Redcliffe *Australia* 27°12S 153°6E **151** D5
Redcliffe, Mt. *Australia* 28°30S 121°30E **149** E3
Reddersburg *S. Africa* 29°41S 26°10E **144** C4
Reddick *U.S.A.* 29°22N 82°12W **179** F7
Redding *U.S.A.* 40°35N 122°24W **168** F2
Redditch *U.K.* 52°18N 1°55W **67** E6
Redenção *Brazil* 4°13S 38°43W **189** A3
Redfield *U.S.A.* 44°53N 98°31W **172** C4
Redford *U.S.A.* 44°38N 73°48W **175** B11
Redhead *Trin. & Tob.* 10°44N 60°58W **187** K16
Redkino *Russia* 56°39N 36°16E **84** D9
Redlands *U.S.A.* 34°4N 117°11W **171** M9
Redmond *Oreg., U.S.A.* 44°17N 121°11W **168** D3
Redmond *Wash., U.S.A.* 47°40N 122°7W **170** C4
Redon *France* 47°40N 2°6W **70** E4
Redonda *Antigua & B.* 16°58N 62°19W **183** C7
Redondela *Spain* 42°15N 8°38W **88** C2
Redondo *Portugal* 38°39N 7°37W **89** G3
Redondo Beach *U.S.A.* 33°50N 118°23W **171** M8
Redoubt Volcano *U.S.A.* 60°29N 152°45W **166** C9
Redruth *U.K.* 50°14N 5°14W **67** G2
Redvers *Canada* 49°35N 101°40W **163** D8
Redwater *Canada* 53°55N 113°6W **162** C6
Redwood *U.S.A.* 44°18N 75°48W **175** B9
Redwood △ *U.S.A.* 41°40N 124°5W **168** F1
Redwood City *U.S.A.* 37°30N 122°15W **170** H4
Redwood Falls *U.S.A.* 44°32N 95°7W **172** C6
Ree, L. *Ireland* 53°35N 8°0W **64** C3
Reed City *U.S.A.* 43°53N 85°31W **173** D11
Reed L. *Canada* 54°38N 100°30W **163** C8
Reedley *U.S.A.* 36°36N 119°27W **170** J7
Reedsburg *U.S.A.* 43°32N 90°0W **172** D8
Reedsport *U.S.A.* 43°42N 124°6W **168** E1
Reedsville *U.S.A.* 40°39N 77°35W **174** F7
Reedy Creek *Australia* 36°58S 140°2E **152** D4
Reefton *N.Z.* 42°6S 171°51E **155** C6
Rees *Germany* 51°46N 6°24E **76** D2
Reese → *U.S.A.* 40°48N 117°4W **168** F5
Refahiye *Turkey* 39°54N 38°47E **105** C8
Reftele *Sweden* 57°11N 13°35E **63** G7
Refugio *U.S.A.* 28°18N 97°17W **176** G6
Rega → *Poland* 54°10N 15°18E **82** D2
Regalbuto *Italy* 37°39N 14°38E **95** E7
Regana, C. de *Spain* 39°25N 2°43E **100** B9
Regen *Germany* 48°58N 13°8E **77** G9
Regen → *Germany* 49°1N 12°6E **77** F8
Regeneração *Brazil* 6°15S 42°41W **189** B2
Regensburg *Germany* 49°1N 12°6E **77** F8
Regenstauf *Germany* 49°7N 12°8E **77** F8
Reggâne = Zaouiet Reggâne *Algeria* 26°32N 0°3E **136** C4
Reggello *Italy* 43°41N 11°32E **93** E8
Réggio di Calábria *Italy* 38°6N 15°39E **95** D8
Réggio nell'Emília *Italy* 44°43N 10°36E **92** D7
Reghin *Romania* 46°46N 24°42E **81** D9
Regina *Canada* 50°27N 104°35W **163** C8
Regina Beach *Canada* 50°47N 105°0W **163** C8
Register *U.S.A.* 32°22N 81°53W **178** C8
Registro *Brazil* 24°29S 47°49W **191** A6
Reguengos de Monsaraz *Portugal* 38°25N 7°32W **89** G3
Rehar → *India* 23°55N 82°40E **125** H10
Rehli *India* 23°38N 79°5E **125** H8
Rehoboth *Namibia* 23°15S 17°4E **144** B2
Rehovot *Israel* 31°54N 34°48E **130** D3
Rei, Costa *Italy* 39°15N 9°40E **94** C2
Reichenbach *Germany* 50°37N 12°17E **76** E8
Reid *Australia* 30°49S 128°26E **149** F4
Reidsville *Ga., U.S.A.* 32°6N 82°7W **178** C7
Reidsville *N.C., U.S.A.* 36°21N 79°40W **177** C15
Reigate *U.K.* 51°14N 0°12W **67** F7
Reillo *Spain* 39°54N 1°53W **90** F3
Reims *France* 49°15N 4°1E **71** C11
Reina Adelaida, Arch. *Chile* 52°20S 74°0W **192** D2
Reina Sofia, Tenerife ✕ (TFS) *Canary Is.* 28°3N 16°33W **100** F3
Reinbek *Germany* 53°30N 10°16E **76** B6
Reindeer → *Canada* 55°36N 103°11W **163** B8
Reindeer I. *Canada* 52°30N 98°0W **163** C9
Reindeer L. *Canada* 57°15N 102°15W **163** B8
Reinga, C. *N.Z.* 34°25S 172°43E **154** A1
Reinheimen △ *Norway* 62°10N 7°45E **60** E12
Reinosa *Spain* 43°2N 4°15W **88** B6
Reitz *S. Africa* 27°48S 28°29E **145** C4
Reivilo *S. Africa* 27°36S 24°8E **144** C3
Rejmyre *Sweden* 58°50N 15°55E **63** F9
Rejowiec Fabryczny *Poland* 51°5N 23°17E **83** G10
Reka → *Slovenia* 45°40N 14°0E **93** C11
Rekovac *Serbia* 43°51N 21°3E **96** C5
Reliance *Canada* 63°0N 109°20W **163** A7
Relizane *Algeria* 35°44N 0°31E **136** A4
Relizane □ *Algeria* 35°45N 0°55E **136** A4
Remad, Oued → *Algeria* 33°28N 1°20W **136** B3
Rémalard *France* 48°26N 0°47E **70** D7
Remanso *Brazil* 9°41S 42°4W **189** B2
Remarkable, Mt. *Australia* 32°48S 138°10E **152** B3
Remarkables, The *N.Z.* 45°10S 168°50E **155** F3
Rembang *Indonesia* 6°42S 111°21E **119** G14
Rembert *U.S.A.* 34°6N 80°32W **178** A9
Remchi *Algeria* 35°2N 1°26W **136** A3
Remedios *Panama* 8°15N 81°50W **182** E3
Remeshk *Iran* 26°55N 58°50E **129** E8
Remetea *Romania* 46°45N 25°29E **81** D10
Remich *Lux.* 49°32N 6°22E **69** E6
Remiremont *France* 48°2N 6°36E **71** D13
Remontnoye *Russia* 46°34N 43°37E **87** G6
Remoulins *France* 43°55N 4°35E **73** E8
Remscheid *Germany* 51°11N 7°12E **76** D3
Ren Xian *China* 37°8N 114°40E **114** F8
Rendang *Indonesia* 8°26S 115°25E **119** J18
Rende *Italy* 39°20N 16°11E **95** C9
Rendina *Greece* 39°4N 21°58E **98** B3
Rendsburg *Germany* 54°17N 9°39E **76** A5
Renfrew *Canada* 45°30N 76°40W **175** A8
Renfrewshire □ *U.K.* 55°49N 4°38W **65** F4
Renfroe *U.S.A.* 32°14N 84°43W **178** C5
Rengat *Indonesia* 0°30S 102°45E **118** E2
Rengo *Chile* 34°24S 70°50W **190** C1
Renhua *China* 25°5N 113°40E **117** E9
Renhuai *China* 27°48N 106°24E **116** D6
Reni = Taranagar *India* 28°43N 74°50E **124** E6
Reni *Ukraine* 45°28N 28°15E **81** E13
Renigunta *India* 13°38N 79°30E **127** H4
Renland *Greenland* 71°10N 26°30W **57** C8
Renmark *Australia* 34°11S 140°43E **152** C4
Rennell Sd. *Canada* 53°23N 132°35W **162** C2
Renner Springs *Australia* 18°20S 133°47E **150** B1
Rennes *France* 48°7N 1°41W **70** D5
Rennick Glacier *Antarctica* 70°30S 161°45E **55** D11
Rennie L. *Canada* 61°32N 105°35W **163** A7
Reno *U.S.A.* 39°31N 119°48W **170** F7
Reno → *Italy* 44°38N 12°16E **93** D9
Renovo *U.S.A.* 41°20N 77°45W **174** E7
Renqiu *China* 38°43N 116°5E **114** E9
Rens *Denmark* 54°54N 9°5E **63** K3
Renshou *China* 29°59N 104°9E **116** C5
Rensselaer *Ind., U.S.A.* 40°57N 87°9W **172** E10
Rensselaer *N.Y., U.S.A.* 42°38N 73°45W **175** D11
Renton *U.S.A.* 47°28N 122°12W **170** C4
Renukoot *India* 24°12N 83°2E **125** G10
Renwick *N.Z.* 41°30S 173°51E **155** B8
Réo *Burkina Faso* 12°28N 2°35W **138** C4
Reocín = Puente San Miguel *Spain* 43°21N 4°5W **88** B6
Reotipur *India* 25°33N 83°45E **125** G10
Repalle *India* 16°2N 80°45E **127** F5
Répcelak *Hungary* 47°24N 17°1E **80** C2
Republic *Mo., U.S.A.* 37°7N 93°29W **172** G7
Republic *Wash., U.S.A.* 48°39N 118°44W **168** B4
Republican → *U.S.A.* 39°4N 96°48W **172** F5
Republika Srpska □ *Bos.-H.* 44°56N 17°11E **93** D14
Repulse B. *Australia* 20°35S 148°46E **150** b
Repulse Bay *Canada* 66°30N 86°30W **161** D14
Requena *Peru* 5°5S 73°52W **188** B3
Requena *Spain* 39°30N 1°4W **91** F3
Réquista *France* 44°1N 2°32E **72** D6
Reşadiye *Muğla, Turkey* 36°45N 27°39E **99** E9
Reşadiye *Tokat, Turkey* 40°23N 37°20E **104** B7
Reşadiye Yarımadası *Turkey* 36°40N 27°45E **99** E9
Resavica *Serbia* 44°4N 21°31E **96** B5
Resen *Macedonia* 41°5N 21°0E **96** E5
Reserve *U.S.A.* 33°43N 108°45W **169** K9
Resht = Rasht *Iran* 37°20N 49°40E **105** D13
Resistencia *Argentina* 27°30S 59°0W **190** B4
Reşiţa *Romania* 45°18N 21°53E **80** E6
Resko *Poland* 53°47N 15°25E **82** E2
Reso = Raisio *Finland* 60°28N 22°11E **84** B2
Resolute *Canada* 74°42N 94°54W **161** C13
Resolution I. *Canada* 61°30N 65°0W **161** E19
Resolution I. *N.Z.* 45°40S 166°40E **155** F1
Resplandes *Brazil* 6°17S 45°13W **189** B1
Resplendor *Brazil* 19°20S 41°15W **189** D2
Ressano Garcia *Mozam.* 25°25S 32°0E **145** C5
Reston *Canada* 49°33N 101°6W **163** D8
Reszel *Poland* 54°4N 21°10E **82** D8
Retalhuleu *Guatemala* 14°33N 91°46W **182** D1
Retenue, L. de *Dem. Rep. of the Congo* 11°0S 27°0E **143** E2
Retezat, Munţii *Romania* 45°25N 23°0E **80** E8
Retezat △ *Romania* 45°23N 22°56E **80** E7
Retford *U.K.* 53°19N 0°56W **66** D7
Rethel *France* 49°30N 4°20E **71** C11
Rethem *Germany* 52°47N 9°22E **76** C5
Rethimno *Greece* 35°18N 24°30E **101** D6
Reti *Pakistan* 28°5N 69°48E **124** E3
Retiche, Alpi *Switz.* 46°30N 10°0E **77** J6
Retiers *France* 47°55N 1°23W **70** E5
Retortillo *Spain* 40°48N 6°21W **88** E4
Retournac *France* 45°12N 4°2E **73** C8
Rétság *Hungary* 47°58N 19°10E **80** C4
Réunion ☑ *Ind. Oc.* 21°0S 56°0E **141** c
Reus *Spain* 41°10N 1°5E **90** D6
Reuterstadt Stavenhagen *Germany* 53°42N 12°54E **76** B8
Reutlingen *Germany* 48°29N 9°12E **77** G5
Reutte *Austria* 47°29N 10°42E **78** D3
Reval = Tallinn *Estonia* 59°22N 24°48E **84** C3
Revel *France* 43°28N 2°1E **72** E6
Revelganj *India* 25°50N 84°40E **125** G11
Revelstoke *Canada* 51°0N 118°10W **162** C5
Reventazón *Peru* 6°10S 80°58W **188** B1
Revigny-sur-Ornain *France* 48°49N 4°59E **71** D11
Revillagigedo, Is. de *Pac. Oc.* 18°40N 112°0W **180** D2
Revin *France* 49°55N 4°39E **71** C11
Revúca *Slovak Rep.* 48°41N 20°7E **79** C13
Revuè → *Mozam.* 19°50S 34°0E **143** F3
Rewa *India* 24°33N 81°25E **125** G9
Rewari *India* 28°15N 76°40E **124** E7
Rexburg *U.S.A.* 43°49N 111°47W **168** E8
Rey *Iran* 35°35N 51°25E **108** E4
Rey, I. del *Panama* 8°20N 78°30W **182** E4
Rey, L. del *Mexico* 27°1N 103°26W **180** B4
Rey Malabo *Eq. Guin.* 3°45N 8°50E **139** E6
Reyðarfjörður *Iceland* 65°2N 14°13W **60** D6
Reyes *Bolivia* 14°19S 67°23W **188** C4
Reyes, Pt. *U.S.A.* 38°0N 123°0W **170** H3
Reyhanlı *Turkey* 36°16N 36°35E **104** D7
Reykjahlið *Iceland* 65°40N 16°55W **60** D5
Reykjanes *Iceland* 63°48N 22°40W **60** E2
Reykjanes Ridge *Atl. Oc.* 59°0N 31°0W **56** A8
Reykjavík *Iceland* 64°10N 21°57W **60** D3
Reynolds *U.S.A.* 32°33N 84°6W **178** C5
Reynolds Ra. *Australia* 22°30S 133°0E **148** D5
Reynoldsville *Ga., U.S.A.* 30°51N 84°47W **178** E5
Reynoldsville *Pa., U.S.A.* 41°6N 78°53W **174** E6
Reynosa *Mexico* 26°7N 98°18W **181** B5
Rēzekne *Latvia* 56°30N 27°17E **84** D4
Rezina *Moldova* 47°45N 28°58E **81** C13
Rezovo *Bulgaria* 42°0N 28°0E **97** D12
Rezvān *Iran* 27°34N 56°6E **129** E8
Rezvānshahr *Iran* 37°32N 49°7E **105** D13
Rgotina *Serbia* 44°1N 22°17E **96** B6
Rharbi, Zahrez *Algeria* 34°50N 2°55E **136** B4
Rharis, O. → *Algeria* 26°0N 5°4E **136** C5
Rhayader *U.K.* 52°18N 3°29W **67** E4
Rheda-Wiedenbrück *Germany* 51°50N 8°20E **76** D4
Rhede *Germany* 51°50N 6°42E **76** D2
Rhein → *Europe* 51°52N 6°2E **69** C6
Rhein-Main-Donau-Kanal *Germany* 49°1N 11°27E **77** F7
Rhein-Ruhr, Düsseldorf ✕ (DUS) *Germany* 51°17N 6°46E **76** D2
Rhein-Taunus ⌓ *Germany* 50°10N 8°10E **77** E4
Rhein-Westerwald ⌓ *Germany* 50°32N 7°20E **76** E3
Rheinbach *Germany* 50°38N 6°57E **76** E2
Rheine *Germany* 52°17N 7°26E **76** C3
Rheinfelden *Germany* 47°33N 7°47E **77** H3
Rheinland-Pfalz □ *Germany* 50°0N 7°0E **77** E2
Rheinsberg *Germany* 53°6N 12°54E **76** B8
Rheris, Oued → *Morocco* 30°50N 4°34W **136** B3
Rhin = Rhein → *Europe* 51°52N 6°2E **69** C6
Rhine = Rhein → *Europe* 51°52N 6°2E **69** C6
Rhine *U.S.A.* 31°59N 83°12W **178** D6
Rhinebeck *U.S.A.* 41°56N 73°55W **175** E11
Rhineland-Palatinate = Rheinland-Pfalz □ *Germany* 50°0N 7°0E **77** E2
Rhinelander *U.S.A.* 45°38N 89°25W **172** C9
Rhinns Pt. *U.K.* 55°40N 6°29W **65** F2
Rhino Camp *Uganda* 3°0N 31°22E **142** B3
Rhir, Cap *Morocco* 30°38N 9°54W **136** B2
Rho *Italy* 45°31N 9°2E **92** C6
Rhode Island □ *U.S.A.* 41°40N 71°30W **175** E13
Rhodes *Greece* 36°15N 28°10E **101** C10
Rhodes ✕ (RHO) *Greece* 36°23N 28°12E **99** E10
Rhodope Mts. = Rhodopi Planina *Bulgaria* 41°40N 24°20E **97** E8
Rhodopi Planina *Bulgaria* 41°40N 24°20E **97** E8
Rhön *Germany* 50°24N 9°58E **76** E5
Rhondda *U.K.* 51°39N 3°31W **67** F4
Rhondda Cynon Taff □ *U.K.* 51°42N 3°27W **67** F4
Rhône □ *France* 45°54N 4°35E **73** C8
Rhône → *France* 43°28N 4°42E **73** E8
Rhône-Alpes □ *France* 45°40N 6°0E **73** C9
Rhum = Rùm *U.K.* 57°0N 6°20W **65** E2
Rhydaman = Ammanford *U.K.* 51°48N 3°59W **67** F4
Rhyl *U.K.* 53°20N 3°29W **66** D4
Ri-Aba *Eq. Guin.* 3°28N 8°40E **139** E6
Ria Formosa ⌓ *Portugal* 37°1N 7°48W **89** H3
Riachão *Brazil* 7°20S 46°37W **189** B1
Riacho de Santana *Brazil* 13°37S 42°57W **189** C2
Riang, Laem *Thailand* 8°7N 98°27E **121** a
Riaño *Spain* 42°59N 4°59W **88** C6
Rians *France* 43°37N 5°44E **73** E9
Riansáres → *Spain* 39°32N 3°18W **89** F7
Riasi *India* 33°10N 74°50E **125** C6
Riau □ *Indonesia* 0°0 102°35E **118** E2
Riau, Kepulauan □ *Indonesia* 0°30N 104°20E **118** D2
Riau Arch. = Riau, Kepulauan □ *Indonesia* 0°30N 104°20E **118** D2
Riaza *Spain* 41°18N 3°30W **88** D7
Riaza → *Spain* 41°42N 3°55W **88** D7
Riba de Saelices *Spain* 40°55N 2°17W **90** E2
Riba-roja de Túria *Spain* 39°33N 0°34W **91** F4
Ribadavia *Spain* 42°17N 8°8W **88** C2
Ribadeo *Spain* 43°35N 7°5W **88** B3
Ribadesella *Spain* 43°30N 5°7W **88** B5
Ribado *Nigeria* 9°16N 12°47E **139** D7
Ribamar *Brazil* 2°33S 44°3W **189** A2
Ribao *Cameroon* 6°32N 11°30E **139** D7
Ribas = Ribes de Freser *Spain* 42°19N 2°15E **90** C7
Ribas do Rio Pardo *Brazil* 20°27S 53°46W **187** H8
Ribauè *Mozam.* 14°57S 38°17E **143** E4
Ribble → *U.K.* 53°52N 2°25W **66** D5
Ribe *Denmark* 55°19N 8°44E **63** J2
Ribeauvillé *France* 48°10N 7°20E **71** D14
Ribécourt-Dreslincourt *France* 49°30N 2°55E **71** C9
Ribeira *Spain* 42°36N 8°58W **88** C2
Ribeira Brava *Madeira* 32°41N 17°4W **100** D2
Ribeira do Pombal *Brazil* 10°50S 38°32W **189** C3
Ribeira Grande *C. Verde Is.* 17°0N 25°4W **134** b
Ribeirão Prêto *Brazil* 21°10S 47°50W **191** A6
Ribeiro Gonçalves *Brazil* 7°32S 45°14W **189** B1
Ribemont *France* 49°47N 3°27E **71** C10
Ribera *Italy* 37°30N 13°16E **94** E6
Ribérac *France* 45°15N 0°20E **72** C4
Riberalta *Bolivia* 11°0S 66°0W **186** F5
Ribes de Freser *Spain* 42°19N 2°15E **90** C7
Ribnica *Slovenia* 45°45N 14°45E **93** C11
Ribnitz-Damgarten *Germany* 54°15N 12°27E **76** A8
Ričany *Czech Rep.* 50°0N 14°40E **78** B7
Riccarton *N.Z.* 43°32S 172°37E **155** D7
Ríccia *Italy* 41°30N 14°50E **95** A7
Riccione *Italy* 43°59N 12°39E **93** E9
Rice *U.S.A.* 34°5N 114°51W **171** L12
Rice L. *Canada* 44°12N 78°10W **174** B6
Rice Lake *U.S.A.* 45°30N 91°44W **172** C8
Riceboro *U.S.A.* 31°44N 81°26W **178** D8
Rich, C. *Canada* 44°43N 80°38W **174** B4
Richard Toll *Senegal* 16°25N 15°42W **138** B1
Richards Bay *S. Africa* 28°48S 32°6E **145** C5
Richardson → *Canada* 58°25N 111°14W **163** B6
Richardson Lakes *U.S.A.* 44°46N 70°58W **173** C18
Richardson Mts. *N.Z.* 44°49S 168°34E **155** E3
Richardson Springs *U.S.A.* 39°51N 121°46W **170** F5
Riche, C. *Australia* 34°36S 118°47E **149** F2
Richelieu *France* 47°1N 0°20E **70** E7
Richey *U.S.A.* 47°39N 105°4W **168** C11
Richfield *U.S.A.* 38°46N 112°5W **168** G7
Richfield Springs *U.S.A.* 42°51N 74°59W **175** D10
Richford *U.S.A.* 45°0N 72°40W **175** B12
Richibucto *Canada* 46°42N 64°54W **165** C7
Richland *Ga., U.S.A.* 32°5N 84°40W **178** C5
Richland *Wash., U.S.A.* 46°17N 119°18W **168** C4
Richland Center *U.S.A.* 43°21N 90°23W **172** D8
Richlands *U.S.A.* 37°6N 81°48W **173** G13
Richmond *N.S.W., Australia* 33°35S 150°42E **153** B9
Richmond *Queens., Australia* 20°43S 143°8E **150** C3
Richmond *N.Z.* 41°20S 173°12E **155** B8
Richmond *U.K.* 54°25N 1°43W **66** C6
Richmond *Calif., U.S.A.* 37°56N 122°21W **170** H4
Richmond *Ind., U.S.A.* 39°50N 84°53W **173** F11
Richmond *Ky., U.S.A.* 37°45N 84°18W **173** G11
Richmond *Mich., U.S.A.* 42°49N 82°45W **174** D2
Richmond *Mo., U.S.A.* 39°17N 93°58W **172** F7
Richmond *Tex., U.S.A.* 29°35N 95°46W **176** G7
Richmond *Utah, U.S.A.* 41°56N 111°48W **168** F8
Richmond *Va., U.S.A.* 37°33N 77°27W **173** G15
Richmond *Vt., U.S.A.* 44°24N 72°59W **175** B12
Richmond, Mt. *N.Z.* 41°32S 173°22E **155** B8
Richmond Hill *Canada* 43°52N 79°27W **174** C5
Richmond Hill *U.S.A.* 31°56N 81°18W **178** D8
Richmond Ra. *Australia* 29°0S 152°45E **151** D5
Richmond Ra. *N.Z.* 41°32S 173°22E **155** B8
Richmondville *U.S.A.* 42°38N 74°33W **175** D10
Richtersveld △ *S. Africa* 28°15S 17°10E **144** C2
Richville *U.S.A.* 44°25N 75°23W **175** B9
Richwood *U.S.A.* 38°14N 80°32W **173** F13
Ricla *Spain* 41°31N 1°24W **90** D3
Ridder *Kazakhstan* 50°20N 83°30E **109** B10
Riddlesburg *U.S.A.* 40°9N 78°15W **174** F6
Rideau → *Canada* 45°27N 75°42W **175** A9
Ridge Spring *U.S.A.* 33°51N 81°40W **178** B8
Ridgecrest *U.S.A.* 35°38N 117°40W **171** K9
Ridgefield *Conn., U.S.A.* 41°17N 73°30W **175** E11
Ridgefield *Wash., U.S.A.* 45°49N 122°45W **170** E4
Ridgeland *Miss., U.S.A.* 32°26N 90°8W **177** E9
Ridgeland *S.C., U.S.A.* 32°29N 80°59W **178** C9
Ridgetown *Canada* 42°26N 81°52W **174** D3
Ridgeville *U.S.A.* 33°6N 80°19W **178** B9
Ridgewood *U.S.A.* 40°59N 74°7W **175** F10
Ridgway *U.S.A.* 41°25N 78°44W **174** E6
Riding Mountain △ *Canada* 50°50N 100°0W **163** C9
Ridley, Mt. *Australia* 33°12S 122°7E **149** F3
Riebeek-Oos *S. Africa* 33°10S 26°10E **144** D4
Ried *Austria* 48°14N 13°30E **78** C6
Riedlingen *Germany* 48°9N 9°28E **77** G5
Riedstadt *Germany* 49°45N 8°30E **77** F4
Rienza → *Italy* 46°49N 11°47E **93** B8
Riesa *Germany* 51°17N 13°17E **76** D9
Riesco, I. *Chile* 52°55S 72°40W **192** D2
Riesi *Italy* 37°17N 14°5E **95** E7
Riet → *S. Africa* 29°0S 23°54E **144** C3
Rietavas *Lithuania* 55°44N 21°56E **82** C8

Rietbron *S. Africa* 32°54S 23°10E **144** D3
Rietfontein *Namibia* 21°58S 20°58E **144** B3
Rieti *Italy* 42°24N 12°51E **93** F9
Rieupeyroux *France* 44°19N 2°12E **72** D6
Riez *France* 43°49N 6°6E **73** E10
Rif = Er Rif *Morocco* 35°1N 4°1W **136** A3
Riffe L. *U.S.A.* 46°32N 122°26W **170** D4
Rifle *U.S.A.* 39°32N 107°47W **168** G10
Rift Valley *Africa* 7°0N 30°0E **132** G7
Rift Valley □ *Kenya* 0°20N 36°0E **142** B4
Rīga *Latvia* 56°53N 24°8E **82** B11
Rīga ✕ (RIX) *Latvia* 56°54N 23°59E **82** B10
Riga, G. of *Latvia* 57°40N 23°45E **82** A10
Rigacikun *Nigeria* 10°40N 7°28E **139** C6
Rīgān *Iran* 28°37N 58°58E **129** D8
Rīgas Jūras Līcis = Riga, G. of
  Latvia 57°40N 23°45E **82** A10
Rigaud *Canada* 45°29N 74°18W **175** A10
Rigby *U.S.A.* 43°40N 111°55W **168** E8
Rīgestān *Afghan.* 30°15N 65°0E **122** D4
Riggins *U.S.A.* 45°25N 116°19W **168** D5
Rignac *France* 44°25N 2°16E **72** D6
Rigolet *Canada* 54°10N 58°23W **165** B8
Rigu *Ghana* 9°59N 0°48W **139** D4
Rihand Dam *India* 24°9N 83°2E **125** G10
Riihimäki *Finland* 60°45N 24°48E **84** B3
Riiser-Larsen-halvøya
  Antarctica 68°0S 35°0E **55** C4
Riiser-Larsen Ice Shelf
  S. Ocean 74°0S 19°0W **55** D2
Riiser-Larsen Sea *S. Ocean* 67°30S 22°0E **55** C4
Riisitunturi △ *Finland* 66°27N 28°27E **60** C23
Rijau *Nigeria* 11°8N 5°17E **139** C6
Rijeka *Croatia* 45°20N 14°21E **93** C11
Rijeka Crnojevića
  Montenegro 42°24N 19°1E **96** C3
Rijssen *Neths.* 52°19N 6°31E **69** B6
Rika → *Ukraine* 48°11N 23°16E **81** B8
Rikuchū-Kaigan △
  Japan 39°20N 142°0E **112** E11
Rikuzentakada *Japan* 39°0N 141°40E **112** E10
Rila *Bulgaria* 42°7N 23°7E **96** D7
Rila Planina *Bulgaria* 42°10N 23°20E **96** D7
Riley *U.S.A.* 43°32N 119°28W **168** E4
Rima → *Nigeria* 13°4N 5°10E **139** C6
Rimah, Wadi ar →
  Si. Arabia 26°5N 41°30E **128** E4
Rimau, Pulau *Malaysia* 5°15N 100°16E **121** c
Rimavská Sobota
  Slovak Rep. 48°22N 20°2E **79** C13
Rimbey *Canada* 52°35N 114°15W **162** C6
Rimbo *Sweden* 59°44N 18°21E **62** E12
Rimersburg *U.S.A.* 41°3N 79°30W **174** E5
Rimforsa *Sweden* 58°6N 15°43E **63** F9
Rímini *Italy* 44°3N 12°33E **93** D9
Rimouski *Canada* 48°27N 68°30W **165** C6
Rimrock *U.S.A.* 46°40N 121°7W **170** D5
Rinca *Indonesia* 8°45S 119°35E **119** F5
Rincon *U.S.A.* 32°18N 81°14W **178** C8
Rincón de Anchuras = Anchuras
  Spain 39°29N 4°50W **89** F6
Rincón de la Victoria
  Spain 36°43N 4°18W **89** J6
Rincón de Romos
  Mexico 22°14N 102°18W **180** C4
Rinconada *Argentina* 22°26S 66°10W **190** A2
Rind → *India* 26°30N 80°33E **125** G9
Ringarum *Sweden* 58°21N 16°26E **63** F10
Ringas *India* 27°21N 75°34E **124** F6
Ringe *Denmark* 55°13N 10°28E **63** J4
Ringgold Is. *Fiji* 16°15S 179°25W **154** a
Ringim *Nigeria* 12°13N 9°10E **139** C6
Ringkøbing *Denmark* 56°5N 8°15E **63** H2
Ringkøbing Fjord *Denmark* 56°0N 8°15E **63** H2
Ringsjön *Sweden* 55°55N 13°30E **63** J7
Ringsted *Denmark* 55°25N 11°46E **63** J5
Ringvassøya *Norway* 69°56N 19°15E **60** B18
Ringwood *U.S.A.* 41°7N 74°15W **175** E10
Rinia *Greece* 37°23N 25°13E **99** D7
Rinjani, Gunung
  Indonesia 8°24S 116°28E **118** F5
Rinteln *Germany* 52°10N 9°8E **76** C5
Río, Punta del *Spain* 36°49N 2°24W **91** J2
Rio Branco *Brazil* 9°58S 67°49W **188** B4
Rio Branco *Uruguay* 32°40S 53°40W **191** C5
Río Bravo *Mexico* 25°59N 98°6W **181** B5
Rio Bravo → *N. Amer.* 29°2N 102°45W **180** B4
Rio Bravo del Norte →
  Mexico 29°2N 102°45W **180** B4
Rio Brilhante *Brazil* 21°48S 54°33W **191** A5
Rio Bueno *Chile* 40°19S 72°58W **192** B2
Rio Claro *Brazil* 22°19S 47°35W **191** A6
Rio Claro *Trin. & Tob.* 10°20N 61°10W **183** D7
Río Colorado *Argentina* 39°0S 64°0W **192** A4
Río Cuarto *Argentina* 33°10S 64°25W **190** C3
Rio das Pedras *Mozam.* 23°8S 35°28E **145** B6
Rio de Contas *Brazil* 13°36S 41°48W **189** D2
Rio de Janeiro *Brazil* 23°0S 43°12W **191** A7
Rio de Janeiro □ *Brazil* 22°50S 43°0W **191** A7
Rio do Prado *Brazil* 16°35S 40°34W **189** C2
Rio do Sul *Brazil* 27°13S 49°37W **191** B6
Rio Dulce △ *Guatemala* 15°43N 88°50W **182** C2
Río Gallegos *Argentina* 51°35S 69°15W **192** D3
Rio Grande *Argentina* 53°50S 67°45W **192** D3
Rio Grande *Bolivia* 20°51S 67°17W **188** E4
Rio Grande *Brazil* 32°0S 52°20W **191** C5
Río Grande *Mexico* 23°50N 103°2W **180** C4
Río Grande *Puerto Rico* 18°23N 65°50W **183** d
Rio Grande → *N. Amer.* 25°58N 97°9W **176** J6
Rio Grande City *U.S.A.* 26°23N 98°49W **176** H5
Rio Grande de Santiago →
  Mexico 21°36N 105°26W **180** C3
Rio Grande do Norte □
  Brazil 5°40S 36°0W **189** B3
Rio Grande do Sul □
  Brazil 30°0S 53°0W **191** C5
Rio Grande Rise *Atl. Oc.* 31°0S 35°0W **56** K8
Río Hato *Panama* 8°22N 80°10W **182** E3
Río Lagartos *Mexico* 21°36N 88°10W **181** C7
Rio Largo *Brazil* 9°28S 35°50W **189** B3
Rio Maior *Portugal* 39°19N 8°57W **91** F2
Rio Marina *Italy* 42°49N 10°25E **92** F7
Rio Mayo *Argentina* 45°24S 70°23W **192** B2
Rio Mulatos *Bolivia* 19°40S 66°50W **188** D4
Rio Muni □ *Eq. Guin.* 1°30N 10°0E **140** D2
Rio Negro *Brazil* 26°0S 49°55W **191** B6
Rio Negro *Chile* 40°47S 73°14W **192** B2
Rio Pardo *Brazil* 30°0S 52°30W **191** C5
Rio Pico *Argentina* 44°0S 70°22W **192** B2
Rio Pilcomayo △
  Argentina 25°5S 58°5W **190** B4

Río Plátano △ *Honduras* 15°45N 85°0W **182** C3
Rio Rancho *U.S.A.* 35°14N 106°41W **169** J10
Rio Real *Brazil* 11°28S 37°56W **189** C3
Río Segundo *Argentina* 31°40S 63°59W **190** C3
Río Simpson △ *Chile* 45°27S 73°30W **192** C2
Río Tercero *Argentina* 32°15S 64°8W **190** C3
Rio Tinto *Brazil* 6°48S 35°5W **189** B3
Rio Tinto *Portugal* 41°11N 8°34W **88** D2
Río Turbio *Argentina* 51°32S 72°18W **192** D2
Río Verde *Brazil* 17°50S 51°0W **187** G8
Río Verde *Mexico* 21°56N 99°59W **181** C5
Río Vista *U.S.A.* 38°10N 121°42W **170** G5
Riobamba *Ecuador* 1°50S 78°45W **186** D3
Riohacha *Colombia* 11°33N 72°55W **186** A4
Rioja *Peru* 6°11S 77°5W **188** B2
Riom *France* 45°54N 3°7E **72** C7
Riom-ès-Montagnes
  France 45°17N 2°39E **72** C6
Rion-des-Landes *France* 43°55N 0°56W **72** E3
Rionero in Vúlture *Italy* 40°55N 15°40E **95** B8
Rioni → *Georgia* 42°14N 41°44E **87** J5
Ríos *Spain* 41°58N 7°16W **88** D3
Riosucio *Colombia* 7°27N 77°7W **186** B3
Riou L. *Canada* 59°7N 106°25W **163** B7
Rioz *France* 47°26N 6°5E **71** E13
Ripatransone *Italy* 42°59N 13°46E **93** F10
Ripley *Canada* 44°4N 81°35W **174** B3
Ripley Calif., U.S.A.* 33°32N 114°39W **171** M12
Ripley N.Y., U.S.A.* 42°16N 79°43W **174** D5
Ripley Tenn., U.S.A.* 35°45N 89°32W **177** D10
Ripley W. Va., U.S.A.* 38°49N 81°43W **173** F13
Ripoll *Spain* 42°15N 2°13E **90** C7
Ripon *U.K.* 54°9N 1°31W **66** C6
Ripon Calif., U.S.A.* 37°44N 121°7W **170** H5
Ripon Wis., U.S.A.* 43°51N 88°50W **172** D9
Ríposto *Italy* 37°44N 15°12E **95** E8
Risan *Montenegro* 42°32N 18°42E **96** D2
Riscle *France* 43°39N 0°5W **72** E3
Rishā', W. ar →
  Si. Arabia 25°33N 44°5E **128** E5
Rishikesh *India* 30°7N 78°19E **124** D8
Rishiri-Rebun-Sarobetsu △
  Japan 45°26N 141°30E **112** B10
Rishiri-Tō *Japan* 45°11N 141°15E **112** B10
Rishon le Ziyyon *Israel* 31°58N 34°48E **130** D3
Risle → *France* 49°26N 0°23E **70** C7
Risnjak △ *Croatia* 45°34E **93** C11
Rison *U.S.A.* 33°58N 92°11W **174** D8
Risør *Norway* 58°43N 9°13E **61** G13
Rita Blanca Cr. →
  U.S.A. 35°40N 102°29W **176** D3
Ritchie's Arch. *India* 12°14N 93°10E **127** H11
Riti *Nigeria* 7°57N 9°41E **139** D6
Ritter, Mt. *U.S.A.* 37°41N 119°12W **170** H7
Rittman *U.S.A.* 40°58N 81°47W **174** F3
Ritzville *U.S.A.* 47°8N 118°23W **168** C4
Riva del Garda *Italy* 45°53N 10°50E **92** C7
Riva Lígure *Italy* 43°50N 7°50E **92** E4
Rivadavia *B. Aires,*
  Argentina 35°29S 62°59W **190** D3
Rivadavia *Mendoza,*
  Argentina 33°13S 68°30W **190** C2
Rivadavia *Salta,*
  Argentina 24°5S 62°54W **190** A3
Rivadavia *Chile* 29°57S 70°35W **190** B1
Rivarolo Canavese *Italy* 45°19N 7°43E **92** C4
Rivas *Nic.* 11°30N 85°50W **182** D2
Rivash *Iran* 35°28N 58°26E **129** C8
Rive-de-Gier *France* 45°32N 4°37E **73** C8
River Cess *Liberia* 5°30N 9°32W **138** D3
River Jordan *Canada* 48°26N 124°3W **170** B2
Rivera *Argentina* 37°12S 63°14W **190** D3
Rivera *Uruguay* 31°0S 55°50W **191** C4
Riverbank *U.S.A.* 37°44N 120°56W **170** H6
Riverdale Calif., U.S.A.* 36°26N 119°52W **170** J7
Riverdale Ga., U.S.A.* 33°34N 84°25W **178** B4
Riverhead *U.S.A.* 40°55N 72°40W **175** F12
Riverhurst *Canada* 50°55N 106°50W **163** C7
Rivers *Canada* 50°2N 100°14W **163** C8
Rivers □ *Nigeria* 4°30N 7°10E **139** E6
Rivers Inlet *Canada* 51°42N 127°15W **162** C3
Riverside Canada* 44°5N 81°20W **174** B3
Riverside N.Z.* 45°54S 168°44E **155** F3
Riverside S. Africa* 34°7S 21°15E **144** D3
Riverside U.S.A.* 33°59N 117°22W **171** M9
Riversleigh *Australia* 19°5S 138°40E **150** B2
Riverton *Australia* 34°10S 138°46E **152** C3
Riverton Canada* 51°1N 97°0W **163** C9
Riverton N.Z.* 46°21S 168°0E **155** G2
Riverton U.S.A.* 43°2N 108°23W **168** E9
Riverview Fla., U.S.A.* 27°52N 82°20W **179** H7
Riverview Fla., U.S.A.* 30°32N 87°12W **179** E2
Rives *France* 45°21N 5°31E **73** C9
Rivesaltes *France* 42°47N 2°50E **72** F6
Riviera = Azur, Côte d'
  France 43°25N 7°10E **73** E11
Riviera *U.S.A.* 35°4N 114°35W **171** K12
Riviera Beach *U.S.A.* 26°47N 80°3W **179** J9
Riviera di Levante *Italy* 44°15N 9°30E **92** D6
Riviera di Ponente *Italy* 44°10N 8°20E **92** D5
Rivière-au-Renard
  Canada 48°59N 64°23W **165** C7
Rivière-du-Loup
  Canada 47°50N 69°30W **165** C6
Rivière-Pentecôte
  Canada 49°57N 67°1W **165** C6
Rivière-Pilote
  Martinique 14°26N 60°53W **182** c
Rivière-St-Paul *Canada* 51°28N 57°45W **165** B8
Rivière-Salée *Martinique* 14°31N 61°0W **182** c
Rivne, Odesa, Ukraine* 46°1N 29°10E **81** D14
Rivne □ Ukraine* 51°15N 26°30E **75** C14
Rívoli *Italy* 45°3N 7°31E **92** C4
Rívoli B. *Australia* 37°32S 140°3E **152** C3
Riwaka *N.Z.* 41°5S 172°59E **155** B7
Rixheim *France* 47°40N 7°24E **71** E14
Riyadh = Ar Riyāḍ
  Si. Arabia 24°41N 46°42E **128** E5
Riza *Greece* 40°31N 23°16E **100** D3
Rize *Turkey* 41°0N 40°30E **105** B9
Rize □ *Turkey* 41°0N 40°30E **105** B9
Rizhao *China* 35°25N 119°30E **115** G10
Rizokarpaso *Cyprus* 35°36N 34°23E **101** D13
Rizzuto, C. *Italy* 38°53N 17°5E **95** C10
Rjukan *Norway* 59°54N 8°33E **61** G13
Rkîz, L. *Mauritania* 16°55N 15°50W **138** B2
Ro *Greece* 36°9N 29°33E **99** E11
Roa *Norway* 60°17N 10°37E **63** D4
Roa *Spain* 41°41N 3°56W **88** D7
Road Town *Br. Virgin Is.* 18°27N 64°37W **183** e

Roan Plateau *U.S.A.* 39°20N 109°20W **168** G9
Roanne *France* 46°3N 4°4E **71** F11
Roanoke *Ala., U.S.A.* 33°9N 85°22W **178** B4
Roanoke *Va., U.S.A.* 37°16N 79°56W **173** G14
Roanoke → *U.S.A.* 35°57N 76°42W **177** D17
Roanoke I. *U.S.A.* 35°53N 75°39W **177** D17
Roanoke Rapids
  U.S.A. 36°28N 77°40W **177** C16
Roatán *Honduras* 16°18N 86°35W **182** C2
Robāt *Iran* 34°16N 64°47E **105** E12
Robāt Sang *Iran* 35°35N 59°10E **129** C8
Robāṭkarīm *Iran* 35°25N 50°59E **129** C6
Robbah *Algeria* 33°4N 4°13E **138** B5
Robbins I. *Australia* 40°42S 145°0E **151** G4
Róbbio *Italy* 45°17N 8°35E **92** C5
Robe *Australia* 37°11S 139°45E **152** C3
Robe → *Australia* 21°42S 116°15E **148** D2
Röbel *Germany* 53°22N 12°35E **76** B8
Robert Bourassa, Rés.
  Canada 53°40N 76°55W **164** B4
Robert Lee *U.S.A.* 31°54N 100°29W **176** F4
Roberta *U.S.A.* 32°43N 84°1W **178** C5
Robertsbridge *U.K.* 40°11N 78°6W **174** F6
Robertsganj *India* 24°44N 83°4E **125** G10
Robertson *S. Africa* 33°46S 19°50E **144** D2
Robertson I. *Antarctica* 65°15S 59°30W **55** C18
Robertson Ra. *Australia* 23°15S 121°0E **148** D3
Robertstown *Australia* 33°58S 139°5E **152** B3
Roberval *Canada* 48°32N 72°15W **165** C5
Robeson Chan. *N. Amer.* 82°0N 61°30W **57** A4
Robesonia *U.S.A.* 40°21N 76°8W **175** F8
Robinson *U.S.A.* 39°0N 87°44W **172** F10
Robinson → *Australia* 16°3S 137°16E **150** B2
Robinson Crusoe I.
  Pac. Oc. 33°38S 78°52W **184** F2
Robinson Ra. *Australia* 25°40S 119°0E **149** E2
Robinvale *Australia* 34°40S 142°45E **152** C5
Robledo *Spain* 38°46N 2°26W **91** G2
Roblin *Canada* 51°14N 101°21W **163** C8
Roboré *Bolivia* 18°10S 59°45W **186** G7
Robson, Mt. *Canada* 53°10N 119°10W **162** C5
Robstown *U.S.A.* 27°47N 97°40W **176** H6
Roca, C. da *Portugal* 38°40N 9°31W **89** G1
Roca Partida, I. *Mexico* 19°1N 112°2W **180** D2
Rocamadour *France* 44°48N 1°37E **72** D5
Rocas, Atol das *Brazil* 4°0S 34°1W **187** D12
Rocca San Casciano *Italy* 44°3N 11°50E **93** D8
Roccadáspide *Italy* 40°27N 15°10E **95** B8
Roccastrada *Italy* 43°0N 11°10E **93** F8
Roccella Iónica *Italy* 38°19N 16°24E **95** D9
Rocha *Uruguay* 34°30S 54°25W **191** C5
Rochdale *U.K.* 53°38N 2°9W **66** D5
Roche Melon = Rocciamelone,
  Mte. Italy 45°12N 7°5E **73** C11
Rochechouart *France* 45°50N 0°49E **72** C4
Rochefort *Belgium* 50°9N 5°12E **69** D5
Rochefort *France* 45°56N 0°57W **72** C3
Rochefort-en-Terre
  France 47°42N 2°22W **70** E4
Rochelle *U.S.A.* 31°57N 83°27W **178** D6
Rochelle *Ill., U.S.A.* 41°56N 89°4W **172** E9
Rocher River *Canada* 61°23N 112°44W **162** A6
Rocheservière *France* 46°57N 1°30W **70** F4
Rochester *Australia* 36°22S 144°41E **152** D6
Rochester *U.K.* 51°23N 0°31E **67** F8
Rochester *Ind., U.S.A.* 41°4N 86°13W **172** E10
Rochester *Minn., U.S.A.* 44°1N 92°28W **172** C7
Rochester *N.H.,*
  U.S.A. 43°18N 70°59W **175** C14
Rochester *N.Y., U.S.A.* 43°10N 77°37W **174** C7
Rociu *Romania* 44°43N 25°2E **81** F10
Rock → *Canada* 60°7N 127°7W **162** A3
Rock, The *Australia* 35°15S 147°2E **153** C7
Rock Creek *U.S.A.* 41°40N 80°52W **174** E4
Rock Falls *U.S.A.* 41°47N 89°41W **172** E9
Rock Flat *Australia* 36°21S 149°13E **153** D8
Rock Hill *U.S.A.* 34°56N 81°1W **177** D13
Rock Island *U.S.A.* 41°30N 90°34W **172** E8
Rock Port *U.S.A.* 40°25N 95°31W **172** E6
Rock Rapids *U.S.A.* 43°26N 96°10W **172** D5
Rock Sound *Bahamas* 24°54N 76°12W **182** B4
Rock Springs *Mont.,*
  U.S.A. 46°49N 106°15W **168** C10
Rock Springs *Wyo.,*
  U.S.A. 41°35N 109°14W **168** F9
Rock Valley *U.S.A.* 43°12N 96°18W **172** D5
Rockall *U.K.* 57°37N 13°42W **58** D3
Rockall Trough *Atl. Oc.* 57°0N 12°0W **56** D4
Rockdale *Tex., U.S.A.* 30°39N 97°0W **176** F6
Rockdale *Wash.,*
  U.S.A. 47°23N 121°28W **170** C5
Rockeby = Mungkan Kandju △
  Australia 13°35S 142°53E **150** A3
Rockefeller Plateau
  Antarctica 76°0S 130°0W **55** E14
Rockford *U.S.A.* 42°53N 86°13W **172** D3
Rockford *Ill., U.S.A.* 42°16N 89°6W **172** D9
Rockglen *Canada* 49°11N 105°57W **163** D7
Rockhampton
  Australia 23°22S 150°32E **150** C5
Rockhampton *Australia* 32°15S 115°38E **149** F2
Rockingham N.C.,*
  U.S.A. 34°57N 79°46W **177** D15
Rockingham Vt.,*
  U.S.A. 43°11N 72°29W **175** C12
Rockingham B.
  Australia 18°5S 146°10E **150** B4
Rocklake *U.S.A.* 48°47N 99°15W **172** A4
Rockland *Canada* 45°33N 75°17W **175** A9
Rockland *Idaho,*
  U.S.A. 42°34N 112°53W **168** E7
Rockland *Maine, U.S.A.* 44°6N 69°7W **173** B19
Rockland *Mich., U.S.A.* 46°44N 89°11W **172** B9
Rocklands Reservoir
  Australia 37°15S 142°5E **152** C5
Rockledge *U.S.A.* 28°20N 80°43W **179** G9
Rockly B. *Trin. & Tob.* 11°9N 60°46W **187** J16
Rockmart *U.S.A.* 34°1N 85°3W **178** A4
Rockport *Mass.,*
  U.S.A. 42°39N 70°37W **175** D14
Rockport *Tex., U.S.A.* 28°2N 97°3W **176** H6
Rocksprings *U.S.A.* 30°1N 100°13W **176** F4
Rockville *Conn.,*
  U.S.A. 41°52N 72°28W **175** E12
Rockville *Md.,*
  U.S.A. 39°5N 77°9W **174** F7
Rockwall *U.S.A.* 32°56N 96°28W **176** E6
Rockwell City *U.S.A.* 42°24N 94°38W **172** D6
Rockwood *Canada* 43°37N 80°8W **174** C4

Rockwood *Maine,*
  U.S.A. 45°41N 69°45W **173** C19
Rockwood *Tenn.,*
  U.S.A. 35°52N 84°41W **177** D12
Rocky Ford *U.S.A.* 38°3N 103°43W **168** G12
Rocky Gully *Australia* 34°30S 116°57E **149** F2
Rocky Harbour
  Canada 49°36N 57°55W **165** C8
Rocky Island L. *Canada* 46°55N 83°0W **164** C3
Rocky Lane *Canada* 58°31N 116°22W **162** B5
Rocky Mount *U.S.A.* 35°57N 77°48W **177** D16
Rocky Mountain △
  U.S.A. 40°25N 105°45W **168** F11
Rocky Mountain House
  Canada 52°22N 114°55W **162** C6
Rocky Mts. *N. Amer.* 49°0N 115°0W **168** B6
Rocky Point *Namibia* 19°3S 12°30E **144** A2
Rocroi *France* 49°55N 4°30E **71** C11
Rod *Pakistan* 28°10N 63°5E **122** E3
Roda *Greece* 39°48N 19°46E **101** A3
Rødby *Denmark* 54°41N 11°23E **63** K5
Rødbyhavn *Denmark* 54°39N 11°22E **63** K5
Roddickton *Canada* 50°51N 56°8W **165** B8
Rødding *Denmark* 55°23N 9°3E **63** J3
Rødekro *Denmark* 55°4N 9°20E **63** J3
Rodeo *Mexico* 25°11N 104°34W **180** B4
Rodez *France* 44°21N 2°33E **72** D6
Ródhos = Rhodes
  Greece 36°15N 28°10E **101** C10
Rodi Gargánico *Italy* 41°55N 15°53E **93** G12
Rodinó *Kazakhstan* 52°28N 104°50E **109** D11
Roding → *U.K.* 51°31N 0°6E **67** F8
Rodna *Romania* 47°25N 24°50E **81** C9
Ródney *Canada* 42°34N 81°41W **174** D3
Rodney, C. *N.Z.* 36°17S 174°50E **154** C3
Rodniki *Russia* 57°7N 41°47E **86** B5
Rodolivos *Greece* 40°55N 24°0E **96** F7
Rodonit, Kepi i *Albania* 41°35N 19°27E **96** E3
Rodopi □ *Greece* 41°5N 25°30E **97** E7
Rodopos *Greece* 35°34N 23°45E **101** D5
Rodrigues *Ind. Oc.* 19°45S 63°20E **145** G4
Roe → *U.K.* 55°6N 6°59W **64** A5
Roebling *U.S.A.* 40°7N 74°47W **175** F10
Roebourne *Australia* 20°44S 117°9E **148** D2
Roebuck B. *Australia* 18°5S 122°20E **148** C3
Roebuck Roadhouse
  Australia 17°59S 122°36E **148** C3
Roermond *Neths.* 51°12N 6°0E **69** C6
Roes Welcome Sd.
  Canada 65°0N 87°0W **161** E14
Roeselare *Belgium* 50°57N 3°7E **69** D3
Rogachev = Ragachow
  Belarus 53°8N 30°5E **75** B16
Rogačica *Serbia* 44°4N 19°40E **96** B4
Rogagua, L. *Bolivia* 13°43S 66°50W **188** C4
Rogaška Slatina
  Slovenia 46°15N 15°42E **93** B12
Rogatec *Slovenia* 46°15N 15°46E **93** B12
Rogatica *Bos.-H.* 43°47N 19°0E **80** G4
Rogatyn *Ukraine* 49°24N 24°36E **75** D13
Rogen *Sweden* 62°20N 12°20E **62** B6
Rogers *U.S.A.* 36°20N 94°7W **176** C7
Rogers City *U.S.A.* 45°25N 83°49W **173** C12
Rogersville *Canada* 46°44N 65°26W **165** C6
Roggan → *Canada* 54°24N 79°25W **164** B4
Roggan L. *Canada* 54°8N 77°50W **164** B4
Roggeveen Basin
  Pac. Oc. 31°30S 95°30W **157** L18
Roggeveldberge
  S. Africa 32°10S 20°10E **144** D3
Rogliano *France* 42°57N 9°30E **73** F13
Rogliano *Italy* 39°10N 16°19E **95** C9
Rogoaguado, L. *Bolivia* 13°0S 65°30W **186** F5
Rogojampi *Indonesia* 8°19S 114°17E **119** J17
Rogozno *Poland* 52°45N 16°59E **77** B3
Rogue → *U.S.A.* 42°26N 124°26W **168** E1
Roha *India* 18°26N 73°7E **126** E1
Rohan *France* 48°4N 2°45W **70** D4
Rohnert Park *U.S.A.* 38°16N 122°40W **170** G4
Rohri *Pakistan* 27°45N 68°51E **124** F3
Rohri Canal *Pakistan* 26°15N 68°27E **124** F3
Rohtak *India* 28°55N 76°43E **124** E7
Roi Et *Thailand* 16°4N 103°40E **120** D4
Roja *Latvia* 57°29N 22°43E **88** A9
Rojas *Argentina* 34°10S 60°45W **190** C3
Rojište *Romania* 44°4N 23°56E **81** F8
Rojo, C. *Mexico* 21°33N 97°20W **181** C5
Rokan → *Indonesia* 2°0N 100°50E **118** D2
Rokel → *S. Leone* 8°30N 12°48W **138** D2
Rokiškis *Lithuania* 55°55N 25°35E **84** E3
Rokitno *Russia* 50°57N 35°56E **86** B5
Rokua ○ *Finland* 64°30N 26°15E **62** D9
Rokycany *Czech Rep.* 49°43N 13°35E **78** D6
Rolândia *Brazil* 23°18S 51°23W **191** A5
Rolla *N. Dak., U.S.A.* 48°52N 99°37W **172** A4
Rolla *U.S.A.* 37°57N 91°46W **172** G8
Rolleston *Australia* 24°28S 148°35E **150** C4
Rolleston *N.Z.* 43°35S 172°24E **155** D7
Rollingstone *Australia* 19°2S 146°24E **150** B4
Roma *Australia* 26°32S 148°49E **151** D4
Roma *Italy* 41°54N 12°28E **93** G9
Roma *Sweden* 57°32N 18°26E **63** G12
Roma Fiumicino ✕ (FCO)
  Italy 41°48N 12°15E **93** G9
Roma-Los Saenz *U.S.A.* 26°24N 99°1W **176** H5
Romain, C. *U.S.A.* 33°0N 79°22W **177** E15
Romaine → *Canada* 50°18N 63°47W **165** B7
Roman *Bulgaria* 43°8N 23°54E **96** C7
Roman *Romania* 46°57N 26°55E **81** D11
Roman-Kosh, Gora
  Ukraine 44°37N 34°15E **85** K8
Romanche → *France* 45°5N 5°43E **73** C9
Romang *Indonesia* 7°30S 127°20E **119** F7
Români *Egypt* 30°59N 32°38E **130** E1
Romania ■ *Europe* 46°0N 25°0E **81** D9
Romanija *Bos.-H.* 43°50N 18°45E **80** G3
Romano, C. *U.S.A.* 25°51N 81°41W **179** H7
Romano, Cayo *Cuba* 22°0N 77°30W **182** B4
Romanovka = Bessarabka
  Moldova 46°21N 28°58E **81** E15
Romans-sur-Isère *France* 45°3N 5°3E **73** C9
Romanshorn *Switz.* 47°33N 9°22E **78** E5
Romanzof C. *U.S.A.* 61°49N 166°6W **166** C6
Romblon *Phil.* 12°33N 122°17E **119** E6
Rome = Roma *Italy* 41°54N 12°28E **93** G9
Rome *Ga., U.S.A.* 34°15N 85°10W **177** D12
Rome *N.Y., U.S.A.* 43°13N 75°27W **175** C9
Rome *Pa., U.S.A.* 41°51N 76°21W **175** E8
Rometta *Italy* 38°10N 15°25E **95** D8

Romilly-sur-Seine
  France 48°31N 3°44E **71** D10
Romny *Ukraine* 50°48N 33°28E **85** G7
Rømø *Denmark* 55°10N 8°30E **63** J2
Romodan *Ukraine* 49°55N 33°15E **85** G7
Romodanovo *Russia* 54°26N 45°23E **86** C7
Romont *Switz.* 46°42N 6°54E **77** J2
Romorantin-Lanthenay
  France 47°21N 1°45E **71** E8
Rompin → *Malaysia* 2°49N 103°29E **121** L4
Romsdalen *Norway* 62°25N 7°52E **60** E12
Romsey *U.K.* 51°0N 1°29W **67** G6
Ron *Vietnam* 17°53N 106°27E **120** D6
Ron *India* 15°40N 75°44E **127** G2
Ronan *U.S.A.* 47°32N 114°6W **168** C6
Roncador, Cayos
  Colombia 13°32N 80°4W **182** D3
Roncador, Serra do
  Brazil 12°30S 52°30W **187** F8
Ronciglione *Italy* 42°17N 12°13E **93** F9
Ronco → *Italy* 44°24N 12°12E **93** D9
Ronda *Spain* 36°46N 5°12W **89** J5
Ronda, Serranía de *Spain* 36°44N 5°3W **89** J5
Rondane *Norway* 61°57N 9°50E **60** F13
Rondônia □ *Brazil* 11°0S 63°0W **186** F6
Rondonópolis *Brazil* 16°28S 54°38W **187** G8
Rong, Koh *Cambodia* 10°45N 103°15E **121** G4
Rong Jiang → *China* 24°35N 109°20E **116** E7
Rong Xian *China* 22°50N 110°31E **117** F8
Rong'an *China* 25°14N 109°22E **116** E7
Rongcheng *China* 29°20N 105°32E **116** C5
Rongjiang *China* 25°57N 108°28E **116** E7
Rongshui *China* 25°5N 109°12E **116** E7
Rongxian *China* 29°23N 104°22E **116** C5
Rønne *Denmark* 55°6N 14°43E **63** J8
Ronne Ice Shelf
  Antarctica 77°30S 60°0W **55** D18
Ronneby *Sweden* 56°12N 15°17E **63** H9
Ronnebyån → *Sweden* 56°11N 15°18E **63** H9
Rönneshytta *Sweden* 58°56N 15°2E **63** F9
Ronsard, C. *Australia* 24°46S 113°10E **149** D1
Ronse *Belgium* 50°45N 3°35E **69** D3
Roodepoort *S. Africa* 26°11S 27°54E **145** C4
Roof Butte *U.S.A.* 36°28N 109°5W **169** H9
Rooiboklaagte →
  Namibia 20°50S 21°0E **144** B3
Rooniu, Mt. *Tahiti* 17°49S 149°12W **155** b
Roopville *U.S.A.* 33°27N 85°8W **178** B4
Roorkee *India* 29°52N 77°59E **124** E7
Roosendaal *Neths.* 51°32N 4°29E **69** C4
Roosevelt *U.S.A.* 40°18N 109°59W **168** F9
Roosevelt → *Brazil* 7°35S 60°20W **186** E6
Roosevelt, Mt. *Canada* 58°26N 125°20W **162** B3
Roosevelt I. *Antarctica* 79°30S 162°0W **55** D12
Ropczyce *Poland* 50°4N 21°38E **83** H8
Roper → *Australia* 14°43S 135°27E **150** A2
Roper Bar *Australia* 14°44S 134°44E **150** A1
Roper River = St. Vidgeon's ○
  Australia 14°47S 134°53E **150** A1
Roque Pérez *Argentina* 35°25S 59°24W **190** D4
Roquefort *France* 44°2N 0°20W **72** D3
Roquemaure *France* 44°3N 4°48E **73** D8
Roquetas de Mar *Spain* 36°46N 2°36W **91** J2
Roquetes *Spain* 40°50N 0°30E **90** E5
Roraima □ *Brazil* 2°0N 61°30W **186** C6
Roraima, Mt. *Venezuela* 5°10N 60°40W **186** B6
Røros *Norway* 62°35N 11°23E **60** E14
Rorschach *Switz.* 47°28N 9°28E **78** E5
Ros Comáin = Roscommon
  Ireland 53°38N 8°11W **64** C3
Ros Mhic Thriúin = New Ross
  Ireland 52°23N 6°57W **64** D5
Rosa *Zambia* 9°33S 31°15E **143** D3
Rosa, C. *Algeria* 37°0N 8°16E **95** F6
Rosa, Monte *Europe* 45°57N 7°53E **92** C4
Rosal de la Frontera
  Spain 37°59N 7°13W **89** H3
Rosalia *U.S.A.* 47°14N 117°22W **168** C5
Rosamond *U.S.A.* 34°52N 118°10W **171** L8
Rosans *France* 44°24N 5°29E **73** D9
Rosário *Brazil* 3°0S 44°15W **189** B2
Rosario *Mexico* 22°58N 105°53W **180** C3
Rosario *Paraguay* 24°30S 57°35W **190** A4
Rosario de la Frontera
  Argentina 25°50S 65°0W **190** B3
Rosario de Lerma
  Argentina 24°59S 65°35W **190** A2
Rosario del Tala
  Argentina 32°20S 59°10W **190** C4
Rosarito *Baja Calif.,*
  Mexico 32°20N 117°2W **171** N9
Rosarito *Baja Calif.,*
  Mexico 28°38N 114°1W **180** B2
Rosário do Sul *Brazil* 30°15S 54°55W **191** C5
Rosas = Roses *Spain* 42°19N 3°10E **90** C8
Roscoe *U.S.A.* 41°56N 74°55W **175** E10
Roscoff *France* 48°44N 3°58W **70** D3
Roscommon *Ireland* 53°38N 8°11W **64** C3
Roscommon □ *Ireland* 53°49N 8°23W **64** C3
Roscrea *Ireland* 52°57N 7°49W **64** D4
Rose → *Australia* 14°16S 135°45E **150** A2
Rose Belle *Mauritius* 20°24S 57°36E **141** d
Rose Blanche *Canada* 47°38N 58°45W **165** C8
Rose Hill *Mauritius* 20°14S 57°27E **141** d
Rose Pt. *Canada* 54°11N 131°39W **162** C2
Rose Valley *Canada* 52°19N 103°49W **163** C8
Roseau *Dominica* 15°17N 61°24W **183** C7
Roseau *U.S.A.* 48°51N 95°46W **172** A6
Rosebery *Australia* 41°46S 145°33E **151** G4
Rosebud → *Australia* 14°16S 135°45E **150** A2
Rosebud *S. Dak.,*
  U.S.A. 43°14N 100°51W **172** D3
Rosebud *Tex., U.S.A.* 31°4N 96°59W **176** F6
Roseburg *U.S.A.* 43°13N 123°20W **168** E2
Rosedale *Australia* 24°38S 151°53E **150** C5
Rosedale *U.S.A.* 33°51N 91°2W **174** D8
Rosehearty *U.K.* 57°42N 2°7W **65** D9
Roseires Res. *Sudan* 11°51N 34°23E **137** E2
Roseland *U.S.A.* 38°25N 122°43W **170** G4

und Mountain U.S.A. 38°43N 117°4W 168 G5
und Mt. Australia 30°26S 152°16E 153 A10
und Rock U.S.A. 30°31N 97°41W 176 F6
undup U.S.A. 46°27N 108°33W 168 D9
usay U.K. 59°10N 3°2W 65 B5
uses Point U.S.A. 41°28N 79°42W 175 D11
useville U.S.A. 41°28N 79°42W 174 E5
use = Ruse Bulgaria 43°48N 25°59E 97 C9
ussenski Lom △
  Bulgaria 43°40N 26°10E 97 C10
ussillon Isère, France 45°24N 4°49E 73 C8
ussillon Pyrénées-Or.,
  France 42°30N 2°53E 72 F6
uxville S. Africa 30°25S 26°50E 144 D4
uyn-Noranda Canada 48°20N 79°0W 164 C4
vaniemi Finland 66°29N 25°41E 60 C21
venki Ukraine 45°34N 10°0E 92 C7
vereto Italy 45°53N 11°3E 92 C8
vigo Italy 45°4N 11°47E 93 C8
vinj Croatia 45°5N 13°40E 93 C10
vno = Rivne Ukraine 50°40N 26°10E 75 C13
vnoye Russia 50°52N 46°3E 86 E8
vuma = Ruvuma →
  Tanzania 10°29S 40°28E 143 E5
w'ān Iran 35°8N 48°51E 129 C6
wena Australia 29°48S 148°55E 151 D4
wley I. Canada 69°6N 77°52W 161 D16
wley Shoals
  Australia 17°30S 119°0E 148 C2
wley Sound
  Australia
xboro Trin. & Tob. 11°15N 60°35W 187 D7
xburgh N.Z. 45°33S 169°19E 155 F4
xbury N.Y., U.S.A. 42°17N 74°33W 175 D10
xbury Pa., U.S.A. 40°6N 77°39W 174 F7
xby Downs
  Australia 30°43S 136°46E 151 E2
xen Sweden 58°30N 15°40E 63 F7
x Mont., U.S.A. 47°20N 108°58W 168 C9
x N. Mex., U.S.A. 35°57N 104°12W 169 J11
x Utah, U.S.A. 41°10N 112°2W 168 F7
yal △ Australia 34°5S 151°5E 153 C4
yal Bardia △ Nepal 28°20N 81°20E 125 E9
yal Canal Ireland 53°30N 7°13W 64 C4
yal Chitawan △
  Nepal 26°30N 84°30E 125 F11
yal Geographical Society Is.
  Canada 68°56N 100°15W 160 D11
yal Leamington Spa
  U.K. 52°18N 1°31W 67 E6
yal Natal △ S. Africa 28°43S 28°51E 145 C4
yal Palm Beach
  U.S.A. 26°42N 80°14W 179 J9
yal Tunbridge Wells
  U.K. 51°7N 0°16E 67 E8
yale, Isle U.S.A. 48°0N 88°54W 172 B9
yalla Australia 35°30S 149°9E 153 C4
yan France 45°37N 1°2W 72 C2
ye France 49°42N 2°48E 71 C9
yston U.K. 52°3N 0°0 67 E7
zaj Montenegro 42°50N 20°11E 96 D4
zan Poland 52°52N 21°25E 83 F8
zay-en-Brie France 48°41N 2°58E 71 D9
zdilna Ukraine 46°50N 30°2E 81 D15
zhnyatyn Ukraine 48°56N 24°9E 81 D9
zhyshche Ukraine 50°54N 25°15E 75 C13
zmitál pod Třemšínem
  Czech Rep. 49°36N 13°53E 78 B6
zogi Poland 53°26N 21°19E 82 E8
zoy-sur-Serre France 49°40N 4°8E 71 C11
ztoczański △ Poland 50°37N 23°0E 83 H10
zzano Italy 44°40N 9°10E 92 C6
zshen Albania 41°47N 19°49E 96 E1
zgoghine Albania 41°47N 19°50E 96 E1
zanj Serbia 43°45N 21°50E 96 C5
zm, O. er → Algeria 33°29N 5°38E 136 B5
za = A Rúa Spain 42°24N 7°6W 88 C3
zaha Namibia 17°27S 14°21E 144 A1
zaha △ Tanzania 7°41S 34°30E 142 D3
zahine Ra. N.Z. 37°55S 176°7E 154 H4
zamahanga → N.Z. 41°24S 175°8E 154 H4
zapuke I. N.Z. 46°4S 168°31E 155 G3
zāq, W. → Egypt 30°0N 33°49E 130 F2
zatoria N.Z. 37°55S 178°0E 154 C7
zawai A. N.Z. 36°58S 173°59E 154 C4
bezhnoye = Rubizhne
  Ukraine 49°6N 38°25E 85 H10
bh a'Mhail U.K. 55°56N 6°8W 65 F2
bha Hunish U.K. 57°42N 6°20W 65 D2
bha Robhanais = Lewis, Butt of
  U.K. 58°31N 6°16W 65 C2
bi Spain 41°29N 2°6E 90 D7
bicon → Italy 44°8N 12°28E 93 D9
bik Albania 41°46N 19°47E 96 E3
bino Ivory C. 6°4N 4°18W 138 D4
bio Venezuela 7°43N 72°22W 186 B4
bizhne Ukraine 49°6N 38°25E 85 H10
bondo △ Tanzania 2°18S 31°58E 142 C3
btsovsk Russia 51°30N 81°10E 109 D10
by L. U.S.A. 40°10N 115°28W 168 F6
by Mts. U.S.A. 40°30N 115°20W 168 F6
byvale Australia 23°25S 147°42E 150 C4
cheng China 25°33N 113°38E 117 E9
ciane-Nida Poland 50°16N 17°44E 83 E3
d Sar 37°38N 50°18E 129 B6
da Sweden 61°16N 17°7E 63 G10
da Śląska Poland 50°16N 18°50E 83 H5
dall → Australia 33°43S 136°17E 152 B2
dall River △
  Australia 22°34S 122°13E 148 D3
dbar Iran 36°48N 49°23E 129 B6
dersdorf Germany 52°27N 13°37E 76 C9
dewa Tanzania 10°7S 34°40E 143 E3
dhendaløse Denmark 54°56N 10°14E 63 B3
dky Ukraine 48°39N 23°29E 83 D11
dki Ukraine 51°30N 16°17E 83 G3
dnik Bulgaria 42°7N 27°20E 97 D11
dnik Poland 50°26N 22°15E 83 H9
dnik Serbia 44°0N 20°35E 96 B4
dnisa Russia 54°55N 31°7E 84 E6

Rudnytsia Ukraine 48°16N 28°54E 81 B13
Rudnyy Kazakhstan 52°57N 63°7E 108 B6
Rudo Bos.-H. 43°41N 19°23E 80 G4
Rudolfa, Ostrov Russia 81°45N 58°30E 106 A6
Rudolstadt Germany 50°44N 11°19E 76 E7
Rudong China 32°0N 121°12E 117 A13
Rudozem Bulgaria 41°29N 24°51E 97 E8
Rudrapur India 28°59N 79°24E 125 E8
Rudyard U.S.A. 46°14N 84°36W 173 B11
Rue France 50°15N 1°40E 71 B8
Ruenya → Africa 16°24S 33°48E 143 F3
Ruffin U.S.A. 33°0N 80°49W 179 F5
Ruffling Pt. Br. Virgin Is. 18°44N 64°27W 183 e
Rufino Argentina 34°20S 62°50W 190 C3
Rufisque Senegal 14°40N 17°15W 138 C1
Rufunsa Zambia 15°4S 29°34E 143 F2
Rugao China 32°23N 120°31E 117 A13
Rugby U.K. 52°23N 1°16W 67 E6
Rugby U.S.A. 48°22N 100°0W 172 A4
Rügen Germany 54°22N 13°24E 76 A9
Rügen △ Germany 54°25N 13°25E 76 A9
Rugles France 48°50N 0°40E 70 D7
Ruhengeri Rwanda 1°30S 29°36E 142 C2
Ruhla Germany 50°54N 10°23E 76 E6
Ruhland Germany 51°27N 13°51E 76 D9
Ruhnu Estonia 57°48N 23°15E 82 A10
Ruhr → Germany 51°27N 6°43E 76 D2
Ruhuhu → Tanzania 10°31S 34°34E 143 E3
Rui Barbosa Brazil 12°18S 40°27W 189 E3
Rui'an China 27°47N 120°40E 117 D13
Ruichang China 29°40N 115°39E 117 C10
Ruidoso U.S.A. 33°20N 105°41W 169 K11
Ruijin China 25°48N 116°0E 117 D10
Ruili China 24°6N 97°46E 116 E1
Ruiru Kenya 1°9S 36°58E 142 C4
Ruivo, Pico Madeira 32°45N 16°56W 100 D3
Ruj Bulgaria 42°52N 22°34E 96 D6
Rujen Macedonia 42°9N 22°30E 96 D6
Rujm Tal'at al Jamā'ah
  Jordan 30°24N 35°30E 130 E4
Ruk Pakistan 27°50N 68°42E 124 F3
Rukhla Pakistan 32°27N 71°57E 124 C4
Ruki →
  Dem. Rep. of the Congo 0°5N 18°17E 140 E3
Rukumkot Nepal 28°37N 82°37E 125 E10
Rukwa △ Tanzania 7°0S 31°30E 142 D3
Rukwa, L. Tanzania 8°0S 32°20E 142 D3
Rulenge Burundi 2°43S 30°37E 142 C3
Rulhieres, C. Australia 13°56S 127°22E 148 B4
Rum Jordan 29°39N 35°26E 130 F4
Rùm U.K. 57°0N 6°20W 65 E2
Rum Cay Bahamas 23°40N 74°58W 183 B5
Rum Jungle Australia 13°0S 130°59E 148 B5
Ruma Serbia 45°0N 19°50E 80 E4
Ruma △ Kenya 0°39S 34°18E 142 C3
Rumāḥ Si. Arabia 25°29N 47°10E 128 E5
Rumania = Romania ■
  Europe 46°0N 25°0E 81 D10
Rumaylah Iraq 30°47N 47°37E 128 D5
Rumaylah, 'Urūq ar
  Si. Arabia 22°0N 48°30E 131 C4
Rumbek South Sudan 6°54N 29°37E 135 G11
Rumburk Czech Rep. 50°57N 14°32E 78 A7
Rumford U.S.A. 44°33N 70°33W 175 B14
Rumia Poland 54°37N 18°25E 83 A10
Rumilly France 45°53N 5°56E 73 C9
Rumoi Japan 43°56N 141°39E 112 C10
Rumonge Burundi 3°59S 29°26E 142 C2
Rumphi Malawi 11°1S 33°52E 143 E3
Rumson U.S.A. 40°23N 74°0W 175 F11
Rumuruti Kenya 0°17N 36°32E 142 B4
Runan China 33°0N 114°30E 117 A10
Runanga N.Z. 42°25S 171°15E 155 C6
Runaway, C. N.Z. 37°32S 177°59E 154 D6
Runaway Bay Jamaica 18°27N 77°20W 182 a
Runcorn U.K. 53°21N 2°44W 66 D5
Rundu Namibia 17°52S 19°43E 144 A2
Rungwa Tanzania 6°55S 33°32E 142 D3
Rungwa → Tanzania 7°36S 31°50E 142 D3
Rungwa △ Tanzania 6°53S 34°2E 142 D3
Rungwe Tanzania 9°11S 33°32E 143 D3
Rungwe, Mt. Tanzania 9°8S 33°40E 140 F6
Runka Nigeria 12°28N 7°20E 139 C6
Runton Ra. Australia 23°31S 123°6E 148 D3
Ruo Shui → China 41°0N 100°16E 110 C9
Ruokolahti Finland 61°17N 28°50E 84 B5
Ruoqiang China 38°55N 88°10E 109 E11
Rupa India 27°15N 92°21E 123 F18
Rupar India 31°2N 76°38E 124 D7
Rupat Indonesia 1°45N 101°40E 118 D2
Rupea Romania 46°2N 25°13E 81 D10
Rupen → India 23°28N 71°31E 124 H4
Rupert U.S.A. 42°37N 113°41W 168 E7
Rupert → Canada 51°29N 78°45W 164 B4
Rupert B. Canada 51°35N 79°0W 164 B4
Rupert House = Waskaganish
  Canada 51°30N 78°40W 164 B4
Rupsa India 21°37N 87°1E 125 J12
Rur → Germany 51°11N 5°59E 76 D1
Rurrenabaque Bolivia 14°30S 67°32W 188 C4
Rus → Spain 39°30N 2°30W 91 F2
Rusambo Zimbabwe 16°30S 32°4E 143 F3
Rusape Zimbabwe 18°35S 32°8E 143 F3
Ruschuk = Ruse
  Bulgaria 43°48N 25°59E 97 C9
Ruse Bulgaria 43°48N 25°59E 97 C9
Ruse □ Bulgaria 43°35N 25°40E 97 C9
Ruşeţu Romania 44°57N 27°14E 81 F12
Rush Ireland 53°31N 6°6W 64 C5
Rushan China 36°56N 121°30E 115 F11
Rushden U.K. 52°18N 0°35W 67 E7
Rushikulya → India 19°23N 85°5E 126 F8
Rushmore, Mt.
  U.S.A. 43°53N 103°28W 172 D2
Rushville Ill., U.S.A. 40°7N 90°34W 172 E8
Rushville Nebr.,
  U.S.A. 42°43N 102°28W 172 D2
Rushworth Australia 36°32S 145°1E 153 D6
Ruskin U.S.A. 27°43N 82°26W 179 H7
Russas Brazil 5°0S 37°50W 189 D4
Russell Canada 50°50N 101°20W 163 C8
Russell N.Z. 35°16S 174°10E 154 B3
Russell Fla., U.S.A. 30°3N 81°45W 178 E7
Russell Kans., U.S.A. 38°54N 98°52W 172 F4
Russell N.Y., U.S.A. 44°27N 75°9W 175 B9
Russell Pa., U.S.A. 41°56N 79°8W 174 E5
Russell Cave △
  U.S.A. 34°59N 85°49W 177 D12

Russell L. Man.,
  Canada 56°15N 101°30W 163 B8
Russell L. N.W.T.,
  Canada 63°5N 115°44W 162 A5
Russellkonda India 19°57N 84°42E 126 E7
Russellville Ala.,
  U.S.A. 34°30N 87°44W 177 D11
Russellville Ark., U.S.A. 35°17N 93°8W 176 D8
Russellville Ky.,
  U.S.A. 36°51N 86°53W 172 G10
Rüsselsheim Germany 49°59N 8°23E 77 F4
Russi Italy 44°22N 12°2E 93 D9
Russia ■ Eurasia 62°0N 105°0E 107 C11
Russian → U.S.A. 38°27N 123°8W 170 G3
Russkaya Arktika △
  Russia 73°40N 55°55E 106 B6
Russkiy, Ostrov Russia 43°0N 131°50E 112 C5
Russky Sever △ Russia 59°57N 38°34E 84 B10
Rust Austria 47°49N 16°42E 78 D9
Rüstam Shahr Pakistan 26°58N 66°6E 124 F2
Rustavi Georgia 41°30N 45°0E 87 K7
Rustenburg S. Africa 25°41S 27°14E 144 C4
Ruston U.S.A. 32°32N 92°38W 176 E8
Rutana Burundi 3°55S 30°0E 142 C3
Rute Spain 37°19N 4°23W 89 H6
Rutenga Zimbabwe 21°15S 30°44E 143 G3
Ruth U.S.A. 43°42N 82°45W 174 C2
Rutherford U.S.A. 38°26N 122°24W 170 G4
Rutherglen Australia 36°5S 146°29E 153 D6
Rutland U.S.A. 43°37N 72°58W 175 C12
Rutland □ U.K. 52°38N 0°40W 67 E7
Rutland I. India 11°25N 92°10E 127 J11
Rutland Water U.K. 52°39N 0°38W 67 E7
Rutledge → Canada 61°4N 112°0W 163 A6
Rutledge L. Canada 61°33N 110°47W 163 A6
Rutog China 33°27N 79°42E 109 F9
Rutqa, W. → Syria 34°30N 41°3E 105 E9
Rutshuru
  Dem. Rep. of the Congo 1°13S 29°25E 142 C2
Ruvo di Púglia Italy 41°7N 16°29E 95 A9
Ruvu Tanzania 6°49S 38°43E 142 D4
Ruvu → Tanzania 6°23S 38°52E 142 D4
Ruvuma □ Tanzania 10°20S 36°0E 143 E4
Ruvuma → Tanzania 10°29S 40°28E 143 E5
Ruwais U.A.E. 24°5N 52°50E 129 E7
Ruwenzori Africa 0°30N 29°55E 142 B2
Ruwenzori △ Uganda 0°20N 30°0E 142 B2
Ruya → Zimbabwe 16°27S 32°5E 145 A5
Ruyang China 34°9N 112°27E 114 G7
Ruyigi Burundi 3°29S 30°15E 142 C3
Ruyuan China 24°46N 113°16E 117 E9
Rūzaevka Kazakhstan 52°49N 66°56E 108 B7
Ruzayevka Russia 54°4N 45°0E 86 C7
Růžhevo Konare
  Bulgaria 42°23N 24°46E 97 D8
Ruzhou China 34°11N 112°52E 114 G7
Ružomberok Slovak Rep. 49°3N 19°17E 83 D10
Ruzyne, Praha ✈ (PRG)
  Czech Rep. 50°6N 14°16E 78 A7
Rwanda ■ Africa 2°0S 30°0E 142 C2
Ryakhovo Bulgaria 43°58N 26°18E 97 C10
Ryan, L. U.K. 55°0N 5°2W 66 G3
Ryazan Russia 54°40N 39°40E 84 D11
Ryazan □ Russia 54°5N 39°30E 86 C4
Ryazhsk Russia 53°45N 40°3E 84 F11
Rybachiy Russia 55°10N 20°50E 82 C7
Rybachiy Poluostrov
  Russia 69°43N 32°0E 60 B25
Rybachye = Balykchy
  Kyrgyzstan 42°26N 76°12E 109 D9
Rybinsk Russia 58°5N 38°50E 84 C11
Rybinskoye Vdkhr.
  Russia 58°30N 38°25E 84 C10
Rybnik Poland 50°6N 18°32E 83 H5
Rybnitsa = Rãbniţa
  Moldova 47°45N 29°0E 81 C14
Rybnoye Russia 54°45N 39°30E 84 E10
Rychnov nad Kněžnou
  Czech Rep. 50°10N 16°17E 79 A9
Rychwal Poland 52°4N 18°10E 83 F5
Rycroft Canada 55°45N 118°40W 162 B5
Ryd Sweden 56°27N 14°42E 63 H8
Rydaholm Sweden 56°59N 14°18E 63 H8
Ryde U.K. 50°43N 1°9W 67 G6
Ryderwood U.S.A. 46°23N 123°3W 170 D3
Rydzyna Poland 51°47N 16°39E 83 G3
Rye U.K. 50°57N 0°45E 67 G8
Rye → U.K. 54°11N 0°44W 66 C7
Rye Bay U.K. 50°52N 0°49E 67 G8
Rye Patch Res. U.S.A. 40°28N 118°19W 168 F4
Ryegate U.S.A. 46°18N 109°15W 168 C9
Ryki Poland 51°38N 21°56E 83 G8
Ryley Canada 53°17N 112°26W 162 C6
Rylsk Russia 51°36N 34°43E 86 G8
Rylstone Australia 32°46S 149°58E 153 B8
Rymanów Poland 49°35N 21°51E 83 J8
Ryn Poland 53°57N 21°34E 82 E8
Ryn Peski = Naryn Qum
  Kazakhstan 47°30N 49°0E 87 G9
Ryōtsu Japan 38°5N 138°26E 112 E9
Rypin Poland 53°3N 19°25E 83 E6
Ryssby Sweden 56°52N 14°0E 63 H8
Rysy Europe 49°10N 20°4E 79 B13
Ryūgasaki Japan 35°54N 140°11E 113 G10
Ryukyu Is. = Ryūkyū-Rettō
  Japan 26°0N 126°0E 113 M3
Ryūkyū-Rettō Japan 26°0N 126°0E 113 M3
Rzepin Poland 52°20N 14°49E 83 F1
Rzeszów Poland 50°5N 21°58E 83 H8
Rzhev Russia 56°20N 34°20E 84 D18

S

Sa Cabaneta Spain 39°37N 2°45E 100 B9
Sa Canal Spain 38°51N 1°23E 100 C7
Sa Conillera Spain 38°59N 1°13E 100 C7
Sa Dec Vietnam 10°20N 105°46E 121 G5
Sa Dragonera Spain 39°35N 2°19E 100 B9
Sa Kaeo Thailand 13°49N 102°4E 120 F4
Sa Mesquida Spain 39°55N 4°16E 100 B11
Sa Pa Vietnam 22°20N 103°47W 118 A4
Sa Pobla Spain 39°46N 3°1E 100 B10
Sa Savina Spain 38°44N 1°25E 100 C7
Sa'ādat Shahr Iran 30°10N 53°5E 129 D7
Sa'ādatābād Hormozgan,
  Iran 28°3N 55°53E 129 D7

Sa'ādatābād Kermān,
  Iran 29°40N 55°51E 129 D7
Saale → Germany 51°56N 11°54E 76 D7
Saaler Bodden Germany 54°20N 12°27E 76 A8
Saalfeld Germany 50°38N 11°21E 76 E6
Saalfelden Austria 47°25N 12°51E 78 D5
Saane → Switz. 47°8N 7°10E 77 H3
Saanich Canada 48°29N 123°26W 170 B3
Saar → Germany 49°41N 6°32E 69 E6
Saarbrücken Germany 49°14N 6°59E 77 F2
Saarburg Germany 49°36N 6°32E 77 F2
Saaremaa Estonia 58°30N 22°30E 84 C2
Saarijärvi Finland 62°43N 25°16E 60 E21
Saarland □ Germany 49°20N 7°0E 77 F2
Saarlouis Germany 49°18N 6°45E 77 F2
Saatḩ Azerbaijan 39°55N 48°22E 105 C13
Sab 'Abar Syria 33°46N 37°41E 104 F7
Saba W. Indies 17°38N 63°14W 183 C7
Sabac Serbia 44°48N 19°42E 96 B3
Sabadell Spain 41°28N 2°7E 90 D7
Sabah □ Malaysia 6°0N 117°0E 118 C5
Sabak Bernam
  Malaysia 3°46N 100°58E 121 L3
Sabalān, Kūhhā-ye
  Iran 38°15N 47°45E 105 C12
Sabalana, Kepulauan
  Indonesia 6°45S 118°50E 119 F5
Sabana de la Mar
  Dom. Rep. 19°7N 69°24W 183 C6
Sábanalarga Colombia 10°38N 74°55W 186 A4
Sabang Indonesia 5°50N 95°15E 118 C1
Sabattin → Turkey 40°28N 33°16E 104 B5
Sabari → India 17°35N 81°16E 126 F5
Sabarmati → India 22°18N 72°22E 124 H5
Sabattis U.S.A. 44°6N 74°40W 175 B10
Sabáudia Italy 41°18N 13°1E 94 A6
Sabaya Bolivia 19°1S 68°23W 188 D4
Saberania Indonesia 2°5S 138°18E 119 E9
Sabhā Libya 27°9N 14°29E 135 C8
Sabhā Jordan 32°19N 36°29E 104 F8
Sabidana, J. Sudan 18°4N 36°50E 137 D4
Sabie S. Africa 25°10S 30°48E 145 C5
Sabile Latvia 57°21N 22°15E 84 C2
Sabinal Mexico 29°19N 99°28W 176 G5
Sabiñánigo Spain 42°31N 0°22W 90 C4
Sabinas Turkey 40°28N 33°16E 104 B5
Sabinas Mexico 27°51N 101°7W 180 B4
Sabinas → Mexico 27°37N 100°42W 180 B4
Sabinas Hidalgo
  Mexico 26°30N 100°10W 180 B4
Sabine → U.S.A. 29°59N 93°47W 176 G8
Sabine L. U.S.A. 29°53N 93°51W 176 G8
Sabine Pass U.S.A. 29°44N 93°54W 176 H8
Sablanqan Phil. 12°50N 120°50E 119 B6
Sable Canada 55°30N 68°21W 165 A6
Sable, C. Canada 43°29N 65°38W 165 D6
Sable, C. U.S.A. 25°9N 81°8W 179 K8
Sable I. Canada 44°0N 60°0W 165 D8
Sable-sur-Sarthe France 47°50N 0°20W 70 E6
Saboeiro Brazil 6°32S 39°54W 189 E3
Sabonkafi Niger 14°40N 5°50E 139 C6
Sabor → Portugal 41°10N 7°7W 88 D3
Sabou Burkina Faso 12°1N 2°15W 138 C4
Sabres France 44°9N 0°43W 72 D3
Sabrina Coast Antarctica 68°0S 120°0E 5 C9
Sabugal Portugal 40°20N 7°5W 88 E3
Sabulubek Indonesia 1°36S 98°40E 118 E1
Sabuncu Turkey 39°33N 30°12E 99 B12
Sabzevār Iran 36°15N 57°40E 129 B8
Sabzvārān = Jiroft Iran 28°45N 57°45E 129 D8
Sac City U.S.A. 42°25N 95°0W 172 D6
Sacedón Spain 40°29N 2°41W 90 E2
Săcele Romania 45°37N 25°41E 81 E10
Sacheon S. Korea 35°0N 128°6E 115 G15
Sachigo → Canada 55°6N 88°58W 164 A2
Sachigo, L. Canada 53°50N 92°12W 164 B1
Sachimbo Angola 9°14S 20°16E 140 F4
Sachin India 21°5N 72°53E 126 D1
Sachkhere Georgia 42°25N 43°28E 87 K6
Sachsen □ Germany 50°55N 13°10E 76 E9
Sachsen-Anhalt □
  Germany 52°0N 12°0E 76 D7
Sächsische Schweiz △
  Germany 50°55N 14°10E 76 E10
Sacile Italy 45°57N 12°30E 93 C9
Sackets Harbor U.S.A. 43°57N 76°7W 175 C8
Sackville Canada 45°54N 64°22W 165 C7
Saco Maine, U.S.A. 43°30N 70°27W 175 C14
Saco Mont., U.S.A. 48°28N 107°21W 168 B10
Sacramento Brazil 19°53S 47°27W 189 D1
Sacramento U.S.A. 38°35N 121°29W 170 G5
Sacramento → U.S.A. 38°3N 121°56W 170 G5
Sacramento Mts.
  U.S.A. 32°30N 105°30W 169 K11
Sacramento Valley
  U.S.A. 39°30N 122°0W 170 G5
Sacratif, C. Spain 36°42N 3°28W 89 J7
Săcueni Romania 47°20N 22°5E 80 C7
Sada Spain 43°22N 8°15W 88 B2
Sada-Misaki Japan 33°20N 132°1E 113 H6
Sádaba Spain 42°19N 1°12W 90 C3
Sadani Tanzania 6°0S 38°35E 142 D4
Sadao Thailand 6°38N 100°26E 121 J3
Sadaoeng India 17°38N 77°59E 126 F3
Sadd el Aali Egypt 23°54N 32°54E 137 D3
Saddle Pk. India 13°9N 93°1E 127 H11
Sade U.S.A. 20°12N 105°45E 139 D7
Sadimi
  Dem. Rep. of the Congo 9°25S 23°32E 143 D1
Sadiola Mali 13°50N 11°40W 138 C2
Sa'diyah, Hawr as
  Iraq 32°15N 46°30E 105 F12
Sado Japan 38°0N 138°25E 112 F9
Sado → Portugal 38°29N 8°55W 89 G2
Sadon Russia 42°52N 43°58E 87 J6
Sadovoye Russia 47°47N 44°31E 87 G7
Sadra India 23°21N 72°43E 124 H5
Sadri India 25°11N 73°26E 124 G5
Sæby Denmark 57°21N 10°30E 63 E4
Saegertown U.S.A. 41°43N 80°9W 174 E4

Saelices Spain 39°55N 2°49W 90 F2
Safaalan Turkey 41°26N 28°6E 97 E12
Şafājah Si. Arabia 26°25N 39°0E 128 E3
Šafárikovo = Tornal'a
  Slovak Rep. 48°25N 20°20E 79 C13
Säffle Sweden 59°8N 12°55E 62 E6
Safford U.S.A. 32°50N 109°43W 169 K9
Saffron Walden U.K. 52°1N 0°16E 67 E8
Safi Morocco 32°18N 9°20W 136 B2
Safiabad Iran 36°45N 57°58E 129 B8
Şafīd Dasht Iran 33°27N 48°11E 129 C6
Safīd Kūh Afghan. 34°45N 63°0E 108 F6
Safīd Rūd → Iran 37°23N 50°11E 129 B6
Safipur India 26°44N 80°21E 125 F9
Şafītā Syria 34°48N 36°7E 104 E7
Safonovo Russia 55°4N 33°16E 84 D9
Safranbolu Turkey 41°15N 32°41E 104 B5
Saft Rashīn Egypt 28°58N 30°55E 137 F7
Şafwān Iraq 30°7N 47°43E 128 D5
Sag Harbor U.S.A. 41°0N 72°18W 175 F12
Saga Japan 33°15N 130°16E 113 H5
Saga □ Japan 33°15N 130°20E 113 H5
Sagae Japan 38°22N 140°17E 112 E10
Sagaing Burma 21°52N 95°59E 123 J19
Sagala Mali 14°9N 6°38W 138 C3
Sagamore U.S.A. 40°46N 79°14W 174 F5
Saganaga L. Canada 48°15N 90°53W 164 C1
Saganthit Kyun Burma 11°56N 98°29E 121 G2
Sagar Karnataka, India 16°38N 76°48E 126 F3
Sagar Karnataka, India 14°14N 75°6E 127 G2
Sagar Mad. P., India 23°50N 78°44E 125 H8
Sagara, L. Tanzania 5°20S 31°0E 142 D3
Sagarejo Georgia 41°44N 45°19E 87 K7
Sagarmatha = Everest, Mt.
  Nepal 28°5N 86°58E 125 F12
Sagarmatha △ Nepal 27°55N 86°45E 125 F12
Saginaw U.S.A. 43°26N 83°56W 173 D12
Saginaw B. U.S.A. 43°50N 83°40W 173 D12
Saglouc = Salluit
  Canada 62°14N 75°38W 161 E16
Sagone France 42°7N 8°42E 73 F12
Sagone, G. de France 42°4N 8°40E 73 F12
Sagres Portugal 37°0N 8°58W 89 J2
Sagua la Grande Cuba 22°50N 80°10W 182 B3
Saguache U.S.A. 38°5N 106°8W 168 G10
Saguaro △ U.S.A. 32°12N 110°38W 169 K8
Saguenay → Canada 48°22N 71°0W 165 C5
Sagunto = Sagunt Spain 39°42N 0°18W 90 F4
Sagunt Spain 39°42N 0°18W 90 F4
Sagwara India 23°41N 74°1E 124 H6
Sahaba Sudan 18°57N 30°25E 137 D3
Sahagún Spain 42°18N 5°2W 88 C5
Saham al Jawlān Syria 32°45N 35°55E 130 C4
Sahand, Kūh-e Iran 37°44N 46°27E 105 D12
Sahara Africa 23°0N 5°0E 134 D6
Saharan Atlas = Saharien, Atlas
  Algeria 33°30N 1°0E 136 B4
Saharanpur India 29°58N 77°33E 124 E7
Saharien, Atlas Algeria 33°30N 1°0E 136 B4
Saharsa India 25°53N 86°36E 125 G12
Sahaswan India 28°5N 78°45E 124 E8
Saheira, W. el → Egypt 30°5N 33°25E 130 E2
Sahel Africa 16°0N 5°0E 134 E5
Sahel, Canal du Mali 14°20N 6°0W 138 C4
Sahibganj India 25°12N 87°40E 125 G12
Sāḩiliyah Iraq 33°43N 42°42E 105 F10
Sahiwal Pakistan 30°45N 73°8E 124 D8
Şaḩneh Iran 34°29N 47°41E 105 E12
Sahrawi = Western Sahara ■
  Africa 25°0N 13°0W 134 D3
Sahuaripa Mexico 29°3N 109°14W 180 B3
Sahuarita U.S.A. 31°57N 110°58W 169 L8
Sahuayo de Díaz
  Mexico 20°4N 102°43W 180 C4
Šahy Slovak Rep. 48°4N 18°55E 79 C11
Sai → India 26°3N 81°10E 125 F9
Sai Buri Thailand 6°43N 101°45E 121 J3
Sai Kung China 22°23N 114°16E 111 a
Sai Thong △ Thailand 15°54N 101°18E 120 E3
Sai Yok △ Thailand 14°25N 98°40E 120 E2
Saibai I. Australia 9°25S 142°40E 150 a
Sa'id Bundâs
  South Sudan 8°24N 24°48E 135 G10
Saïda Algeria 34°50N 0°11E 136 B6
Saïda □ Algeria 34°40N 0°20E 136 B6
Sa'īdābād = Sīrjān Iran 30°30N 55°45E 129 D7
Sa'īdābād Iran 36°8N 54°11E 129 B7
Saïdia Morocco 35°5N 2°14W 136 A5
Saidpur Bangla. 25°48N 89°0E 123 G16
Saidpur India 25°33N 83°11E 125 G10
Saidu Sharif Pakistan 34°43N 72°24E 125 B5
Saignes France 45°20N 2°31E 72 C6
Saigō Japan 36°12N 133°20E 113 F6
Saigon = Thanh Pho Ho Chi Minh
  Vietnam 10°58N 106°40E 121 G6
Saijō Japan 33°55N 133°11E 113 H6
Saikai △ Japan 33°5N 129°30E 113 H4
Saikhoa Ghat India 27°50N 95°40E 123 F19
Saiki Japan 32°58N 131°51E 113 H5
Sailana India 23°28N 74°55E 124 H6
Saillans France 44°42N 5°12E 73 D9
Sailolof Indonesia 1°15S 130°46E 119 E8
Sailu India 19°28N 76°28E 126 E3
Saimaa Finland 61°15N 28°15E 84 B5
Saimbeyli Turkey 37°59N 36°6E 104 D7
Saimen = Saimaa
  Finland 61°15N 28°15E 84 B5
Şa'in Dezh Iran 36°40N 46°25E 105 D12
St. Abb's Head U.K. 55°55N 2°9W 65 F6
St. Affrique France 43°57N 2°53E 72 E6
St-Agrève France 45°0N 4°23E 73 C8
St-Aignan France 47°16N 1°22E 70 E8
St. Alban's Canada 47°51N 55°50W 165 C8
St. Albans U.K. 51°45N 0°19W 67 F7
St. Albans Vt., U.S.A. 44°49N 73°5W 175 B11
St. Albans W. Va.,
  U.S.A. 38°23N 81°50W 173 F13
St. Alban's Head U.K. 50°34N 2°4W 67 G5
St. Albert Canada 53°37N 113°32W 162 C6
St-Amand-en-Puisaye
  France 47°32N 3°5E 71 E10
St-Amand-les-Eaux
  France 50°27N 3°25E 71 B10
St-Amand-Montrond
  France 46°43N 2°30E 71 F9
St-Amarin France 47°54N 7°1E 71 E14
St-Amour France 46°26N 5°21E 73 B9
St-André Réunion 20°57S 55°39E 141 c

St-André-de-Cubzac
  France 44°59N 0°26W 72 D3
St-André-les-Alpes
  France 43°58N 6°30E 73 E10
St. Andrew Sd. U.S.A. 30°58N 81°25W 178 E8
St. Andrew's Canada 47°45N 59°15W 165 C8
St. Andrews N.Z. 44°33S 171°10E 155 C6
St. Andrews U.K. 56°20N 2°47W 65 E6
St. Andrews U.S.A. 32°47N 80°0W 178 D6
St-Anicet Canada 45°8N 74°22W 175 A10
St. Annes Canada 49°40N 96°39W 163 D9
St. Anns B. Canada 46°22N 60°25W 165 C7
St. Ann's Bay Jamaica 18°26N 77°12W 182 a
St. Anthony Canada 51°22N 55°35W 165 B8
St. Anthony U.S.A. 43°58N 111°41W 168 E8
St-Antonin-Noble-Val
  France 44°10N 1°45E 72 D5
St. Arnaud Australia 36°40S 143°16E 153 C3
St. Arnaud Ra. N.Z. 42°1S 172°53E 155 C7
St-Astier France 45°8N 0°31E 72 C4
St-Aubin-du-Cormier
  France 48°15N 1°26W 70 D5
St-Augustin Canada 51°13N 58°38W 165 B8
St-Augustin →
  Canada 51°16N 58°40W 165 B8
St. Augustine U.S.A. 29°54N 81°19W 178 E7
St. Augustine Beach
  U.S.A. 29°51N 81°16W 178 E7
St-Aulaye France 45°12N 0°9E 72 C4
St. Austell U.K. 50°20N 4°47W 67 G3
St-Avold France 49°6N 6°43E 71 C13
St. Barbe Canada 51°12N 56°46W 165 B8
St-Barthélemy ☒
  W. Indies 17°50N 62°50W 183 C7
St. Barts = St-Barthélemy ☒
  W. Indies 17°50N 62°50W 183 C7
St. Bathans N.Z. 44°53S 169°50E 155 C6
St. Bathan's, Mt. N.Z. 44°53S 169°50E 155 C6
St-Béat France 42°55N 0°41E 72 F4
St. Bees Hd. U.K. 54°31N 3°38W 66 C4
St. Bees I. Australia 20°56S 149°26E 150 b
St-Benoît Réunion 21°2S 55°43E 141 c
St-Benoît-du-Sault
  France 46°26N 1°24E 72 B5
St-Brevin-les-Pins France 47°14N 2°10W 70 E4
St. Bride's Canada 46°56N 54°10W 165 C9
St. Brides B. U.K. 51°49N 5°9W 67 F2
St-Brieuc France 48°30N 2°46W 70 D4
St-Calais France 47°55N 0°45E 70 E7
St-Cast-le-Guildo France 48°37N 2°18W 70 D4
St. Catharines Canada 43°10N 79°15W 174 D5
St. Catherine's I. U.S.A. 31°40N 81°10W 178 E8
St. Catherine's Pt. U.K. 50°34N 1°18W 67 G6
St-Céré France 44°51N 1°54E 72 D5
St-Cergue Switz. 46°27N 6°10E 77 J2
St-Cernin France 45°5N 2°25E 72 C6
St-Chamond France 45°28N 4°31E 73 C8
St. Charles Ill., U.S.A. 41°54N 88°19W 172 E9
St. Charles Md.,
  U.S.A. 38°36N 76°56W 173 F15
St. Charles Mo., U.S.A. 38°47N 90°29W 172 F8
St. Charles Va., U.S.A. 36°48N 83°4W 173 G12
St-Chély-d'Apcher France 44°48N 3°17E 72 D7
St-Chinian France 43°25N 2°56E 72 E6
St. Christopher-Nevis = St. Kitts &
  Nevis ■ W. Indies 17°20N 62°40W 183 C7
St-Ciers-sur-Gironde
  France 45°17N 0°37W 72 C3
St. Clair Ga., U.S.A. 33°9N 82°13W 178 D5
St. Clair Mich., U.S.A. 42°50N 82°29W 174 D2
St. Clair Pa., U.S.A. 40°43N 76°12W 175 F8
St. Clair → U.S.A. 42°38N 82°31W 174 D2
St. Clair, L. Australia 37°20S 139°32E 152 C3
St. Clair, L. N. Amer. 42°30N 82°45W 174 D2
St. Clairsville U.S.A. 40°5N 80°54W 174 F4
St-Claud France 45°54N 0°28E 72 C4
St. Claude Canada 49°40N 98°20W 163 D9
St-Claude France 46°22N 5°52E 73 B9
St. Clears U.K. 51°49N 4°31W 67 F3
St-Clet Canada 45°21N 74°13W 175 A10
St. Cloud Fla., U.S.A. 28°15N 81°17W 179 G8
St. Cloud Minn., U.S.A. 45°34N 94°10W 172 C7
St. Cricq, C. Australia 25°17S 113°6E 149 E1
St. Croix → U.S. Virgin Is. 17°45N 64°45W 183 C7
St. Croix → U.S.A. 44°45N 92°48W 172 C7
St. Croix Falls U.S.A. 45°24N 92°38W 172 C8
St-Cyprien France 42°37N 3°2E 72 F7
St-Cyr-sur-Mer France 43°11N 5°43E 73 E9
St. David's Canada 48°12N 58°52W 165 C8
St. David's U.K. 51°53N 5°16W 67 F2
St. David's Head U.K. 51°54N 5°19W 67 F2
St-Denis Réunion 20°52S 55°27E 141 c
St-Denis ✈ (RUN)
  Réunion 20°53S 55°32E 141 c
St-Dié-des-Vosges France 48°17N 6°56E 71 D13
St-Dizier France 48°38N 4°56E 71 D11
St-Égrève France 45°14N 5°41E 73 C9
St. Elias, Mt. U.S.A. 60°18N 140°56W 160 B5
St. Elias Mts. N. Amer. 60°33N 139°28W 162 A1
St-Eloy-les-Mines France 46°10N 2°51E 71 F9
St-Émilion France 44°53N 0°9W 72 D3
St-Étienne France 45°27N 4°22E 73 C8
St-Étienne-de-Tinée
  France 44°16N 6°56E 73 D10
St-Étienne-du-Rouvray
  France 49°23N 1°6E 70 C7
St. Eugène Canada 45°30N 74°28W 175 A10
St. Eustatius W. Indies 17°20N 63°0W 183 C7
St-Exupery, Lyon ✈ (LYS)
  France 45°44N 5°2E 73 C9
St-Fargeau France 47°39N 3°4E 71 E10
St-Félicien Canada 48°40N 72°25W 164 C5
St-Florent France 42°41N 9°18E 73 F13
St-Florent, G. de France 42°47N 9°12E 73 F13
St-Florent-sur-Cher
  France 46°59N 2°15E 71 F9
St-Florentin France 48°0N 3°45E 71 E10
St-Flour France 45°2N 3°6E 72 C7
St. Francis U.S.A. 39°47N 101°48W 172 F3
St. Francis → U.S.A. 34°38N 90°36W 176 D9
St. Francis, C. S. Africa 34°14S 24°49E 144 D3
St. Francisville U.S.A. 30°47N 91°23W 176 F9
St-François, L. Canada 45°10N 74°22W 175 A10
St. Fulgent France 46°50N 1°10W 70 F5
St-Gabriel Canada 46°17N 73°24W 164 C5

St. Gallen = Sankt Gallen Switz. 47°26N 9°22E 77 H5
St-Galmier France 45°35N 4°19E 71 G11
St-Gaudens France 43°6N 0°44E 72 E4
St-Gaultier France 46°39N 1°26E 70 F8
St-Gengoux-le-National France 46°37N 4°40E 71 F11
St-Geniez-d'Olt France 44°27N 2°58E 72 D6
St. George Australia 28°1S 148°30E 151 D4
St. George N.B., Canada 45°11N 66°50W 165 C6
St. George Ont., Canada 43°15N 80°15W 174 C4
St. George Ga., U.S.A. 30°31N 82°2W 178 E7
St. George S.C., U.S.A. 33°11N 80°35W 178 B9
St. George Utah, U.S.A. 37°6N 113°35W 169 H7
St. George, C. Canada 48°30N 59°16W 165 C8
St. George, C. U.S.A. 29°40N 85°5W 178 F4
St. George I. Alaska, U.S.A. 56°35N 169°35W 166 D6
St. George I. Fla., U.S.A. 29°35N 84°55W 178 F5
St. George Ra. Australia 18°40S 125°0E 148 C4
St. George's Canada 48°26N 58°31W 165 C8
St-Georges Canada 46°8N 70°40W 165 C5
St. George's Grenada 12°5N 61°43W 183 D7
St. George's B. Canada 48°24N 58°53W 165 C8
St. Georges Basin N.S.W., Australia 35°7S 150°36E 153 C9
St. Georges Basin W. Austral., Australia 15°23S 125°2E 148 C4
St. George's Channel Europe 52°0N 6°0W 64 E6
St. George's Channel India 7°15N 93°43E 127 L11
St. Georges Hd. Australia 35°12S 150°42E 153 C9
St-Georges-lès-Baillargeaux France 46°41N 0°22E 72 B4
St-Germain-de-Calberte France 44°13N 3°48E 72 D7
St-Germain-en-Laye France 48°53N 2°4E 71 D9
St-Germain-Lembron France 45°27N 3°14E 72 C7
St-Gervais-d'Auvergne France 46°4N 2°50E 71 F9
St-Gervais-les-Bains France 45°53N 6°42E 73 C10
St-Gildas, Pte. de France 47°8N 2°14W 70 E4
St-Gilles France 43°40N 4°26E 73 E8
St-Girons France 42°59N 1°8E 72 F5
St. Gotthard P. = San Gottardo, P. del Switz. 46°33N 8°33E 77 J4
St. Helena Atl. Oc. 15°58S 5°42W 132 H3
St. Helena U.S.A. 38°30N 122°28W 170 G4
St. Helena, Mt. U.S.A. 38°40N 122°36W 170 G4
St. Helena B. S. Africa 32°40S 18°10E 144 D2
St. Helena Sd. U.S.A. 32°15N 80°25W 178 C9
St. Helens Australia 41°20S 148°15E 151 G4
St. Helens U.K. 53°27N 2°44W 66 D5
St. Helens U.S.A. 45°52N 122°48W 170 E4
St. Helens, Mt. U.S.A. 46°12N 122°12W 170 D4
St. Helier U.K. 49°10N 2°7W 67 H5
St-Herblain France 47°13N 1°40W 70 E5
St-Hilaire-du-Harcouët France 48°35N 1°5W 70 D5
St-Hillaire-de-Riez France 46°43N 1°57W 72 B2
St-Hippolyte France 47°19N 6°50E 71 E13
St-Hippolyte-du-Fort France 43°58N 3°52E 72 E7
St-Honoré-les-Bains France 46°54N 3°50E 71 F10
St-Hubert Canada 45°29N 73°25W 175 A11
St-Hyacinthe Canada 45°40N 72°58W 164 C5
St. Ignace U.S.A. 45°52N 84°44W 173 C11
St. Ignace I. Canada 48°45N 88°0W 164 C2
St. Ignatius U.S.A. 47°19N 114°6W 168 C6
St-Imier Switz. 47°9N 6°58E 77 H2
St. Ives Cambs., U.K. 52°20N 0°4W 67 E7
St. Ives Corn., U.K. 50°12N 5°30W 67 G2
St-James France 48°31N 1°20W 70 D5
St. James U.S.A. 43°59N 94°38W 172 D6
St-Jean → Canada 50°17N 64°20W 165 B7
St-Jean, L. Canada 48°40N 72°0W 165 C5
St-Jean-d'Angély France 45°57N 0°31W 72 C3
St-Jean-de-Braye France 47°53N 1°58E 71 E8
St-Jean-de-Luz France 43°23N 1°39W 72 E2
St-Jean-de-Maurienne France 45°16N 6°21E 73 C10
St-Jean-de-Monts France 46°47N 2°4W 70 F4
St-Jean-du-Gard France 44°7N 3°52E 72 D7
St-Jean-en-Royans France 45°1N 5°18E 73 C9
St-Jean-Pied-de-Port France 43°10N 1°14W 72 E2
St-Jean-Port-Joli Canada 47°15N 70°13W 165 C5
St-Jean-sur-Richelieu Canada 45°20N 73°20W 175 A11
St-Jérôme Canada 45°47N 74°0W 164 C5
St. John Canada 45°20N 66°8W 165 C6
St. John U.S.A. 38°0N 98°46W 172 F4
St. John → Liberia 6°40N 9°10W 138 D2
St. John → N. Amer. 45°12N 66°5W 173 C20
St. John, C. Canada 50°0N 55°32W 165 C8
St. John I. U.S. Virgin Is. 18°20N 64°42W 183 e
St. John's Antigua & B. 17°6N 61°51W 183 C7
St. John's Canada 47°35N 52°40W 165 C9
St. Johns Ariz., U.S.A. 34°30N 109°22W 169 J9
St. Johns Mich., U.S.A. 43°0N 84°33W 173 D11
St. Johns → U.S.A. 30°24N 81°24W 178 E8
St. John's Pt. Ireland 54°34N 8°27W 64 B3
St. Johnsbury U.S.A. 44°25N 72°1W 175 B12
St. Johnsville U.S.A. 43°0N 74°43W 175 C10
St. Joseph Canada 43°24N 81°42W 174 C3
St-Joseph Martinique 14°39N 61°4W 182 c
St-Joseph Réunion 21°22S 55°37E 141 c
St. Joseph La., U.S.A. 31°55N 91°14W 176 F9
St. Joseph Mo., U.S.A. 39°46N 94°50W 172 F6
St. Joseph → U.S.A. 42°7N 86°29W 172 D10
St. Joseph, I. Canada 46°12N 83°58W 164 C3
St. Joseph, L. Canada 51°10N 90°35W 164 B1
St. Joseph Pt. U.S.A. 29°52N 85°24W 178 F4
St-Juéry France 43°57N 2°12E 72 E6
St-Julien-Chapteuil France 45°2N 4°4E 73 C8
St-Julien-de-Vouvantes France 47°38N 1°13W 70 E5
St-Julien-en-Genevois France 46°9N 6°5E 71 F13
St-Junien France 45°53N 0°55E 72 C4
St-Just-en-Chaussée France 49°30N 2°25E 71 C9
St-Just-en-Chevalet France 45°55N 3°50E 72 C7
St. Kilda N.Z. 45°53S 170°31E 155 F5
St. Kilda U.K. 57°49N 8°34W 68 C2
St. Kitts & Nevis ■ W. Indies 17°20N 62°40W 183 C7
St. Laurent Canada 50°25N 97°58W 163 C9
St-Laurent-de-la-Salanque France 42°46N 2°59E 72 F6
St-Laurent-du-Pont France 45°23N 5°45E 73 C9
St-Laurent-en-Grandvaux France 46°35N 5°58E 71 F12
St-Laurent-Médoc France 45°8N 0°49W 72 C3
St. Lawrence Australia 22°16S 149°31E 150 C4
St. Lawrence Canada 46°54N 55°23W 165 C8
St. Lawrence → Canada 49°30N 66°0W 165 C6
St. Lawrence, Gulf of Canada 48°25N 62°0W 165 C7
St. Lawrence I. U.S.A. 63°30N 170°30W 166 C5
St. Lawrence Islands △ Canada 44°27N 75°52W 175 B9
St. Léonard Canada 47°12N 67°58W 165 C6
St-Léonard-de-Noblat France 45°49N 1°29E 72 C5
St-Leu Réunion 21°9S 55°18E 141 c
St. Lewis → Canada 52°26N 56°11W 165 B8
St-Lô France 49°7N 1°5W 70 C5
St-Louis France 47°30N 7°34E 71 E14
St-Louis Guadeloupe 15°56N 61°19W 182 b
St-Louis Réunion 21°16S 55°25E 141 c
St-Louis Senegal 16°8N 16°27W 138 B1
St. Louis U.S.A. 38°37N 90°11W 172 F8
St-Louis □ Senegal 16°20N 15°0W 138 B2
St. Louis → U.S.A. 46°44N 92°9W 172 B7
St-Loup-sur-Semouse France 47°53N 6°16E 71 E13
St-Luc Canada 45°22N 73°18W 175 A11
St. Lucia ■ W. Indies 14°0N 60°57W 183 f
St. Lucia, L. S. Africa 28°5S 32°30E 145 C5
St. Lucia △ S. Africa 28°6S 32°27E 145 C5
St. Lucia Channel W. Indies 14°15N 61°0W 183 D7
St. Lucie U.S.A. 27°29N 80°20W 179 H9
St. Lucie Canal U.S.A. 27°10N 80°18W 179 H9
St. Maarten ☒ W. Indies 18°2N 63°5W 183 C7
St. Magnus B. U.K. 60°25N 1°35W 65 A7
St-Maixent-l'École France 46°24N 0°12W 72 B3
St-Malo France 48°39N 2°1W 70 D4
St-Malo, G. de France 48°50N 2°30W 70 D4
St-Mandrier-sur-Mer France 43°4N 5°57E 73 E9
St-Marc Haiti 19°10N 72°41W 183 C5
St-Marcellin France 45°9N 5°20E 73 C9
St-Marcouf, Îs. France 49°30N 1°10W 70 C5
St. Maries U.S.A. 47°19N 116°35W 168 C5
St. Marks U.S.A. 30°9N 84°12W 178 E5
St-Martin ☒ W. Indies 18°5N 63°5W 183 C7
St-Martin, C. Martinique 14°52N 61°14W 182 c
St. Martin, L. Canada 51°40N 98°30W 163 C9
St-Martin-de-Crau France 43°38N 4°48E 73 E8
St-Martin-de-Ré France 46°12N 1°21W 72 B2
St-Martin-d'Hères France 45°9N 5°45E 73 C9
St-Martin-Vésubie France 44°4N 7°15E 73 D11
St. Martins Barbados 13°5N 59°28W 183 g
St-Martory France 43°9N 0°56E 72 E4
St. Mary Is. India 13°20N 74°35E 127 H2
St. Mary Pk. Australia 31°32S 138°34E 152 A3
St. Marys Australia 41°35S 148°11E 151 G4
St. Marys Canada 43°20N 81°10W 174 C3
St. Mary's Corn., U.K. 49°55N 6°18W 67 H1
St. Mary's Orkney, U.K. 58°54N 2°54W 65 C6
St. Marys Ga., U.S.A. 30°44N 81°33W 178 E8
St. Marys Pa., U.S.A. 41°26N 78°34W 174 E6
St. Marys → U.S.A. 30°43N 81°27W 178 E8
St. Mary's, C. Canada 46°50N 54°12W 165 C9
St. Mary's B. Canada 46°50N 53°50W 165 C9
St. Mary's Bay Canada 44°25N 66°10W 165 D6
St-Mathieu, Pte. France 48°20N 4°45W 70 D2
St. Matthew I. U.S.A. 60°24N 172°42W 166 C5
St. Matthews U.S.A. 33°40N 80°46W 178 B9
St-Maurice → Canada 46°21N 72°31W 164 C5
St. Mawes U.K. 50°10N 5°2W 67 G2
St-Maximin-la-Ste-Baume France 43°27N 5°52E 73 E9
St-Médard-en-Jalles France 44°53N 0°43W 72 D3
St-Méen-le-Grand France 48°11N 2°12W 70 D4
St-Mihiel France 48°54N 5°32E 71 D12
St-Nazaire France 47°17N 2°12W 70 E4
St. Neots U.K. 52°14N 0°15W 67 E7
St-Nicolas-de-Port France 48°38N 6°18E 71 D13
St-Omer France 50°45N 2°15E 71 B9
St-Palais-sur-Mer France 45°38N 1°5W 72 C2
St-Pamphile Canada 46°58N 69°48W 165 C6
St-Pardoux-la-Rivière France 45°29N 0°45E 72 C4
St-Pascal Canada 47°32N 69°48W 165 C6
St. Paul Canada 54°0N 111°17W 162 C6
St-Paul Réunion 20°59S 55°17E 141 c
St. Paul Minn., U.S.A. 44°56N 93°5W 172 C7
St. Paul Nebr., U.S.A. 41°13N 98°27W 172 E4
St-Paul → Canada 51°27N 57°42W 165 B8
St. Paul → Liberia 6°25N 10°48W 138 D2
St. Paul, Î. Ind. Oc. 38°55S 77°34E 146 H6
St-Paul-de-Fenouillet France 42°48N 2°30E 72 F6
St. Paul I. Canada 47°12N 60°9W 165 C7
St. Paul I. U.S.A. 57°10N 170°15W 166 D5
St-Paul-lès-Dax France 43°44N 1°3W 72 E2
St-Paul-sur-Ubaye France 44°31N 6°45E 73 D10
St-Péray France 44°57N 4°50E 73 D8
St. Pete Beach U.S.A. 27°43N 82°44W 179 H7
St. Peter U.S.A. 44°20N 93°57W 172 C7
St. Peter Port U.K. 49°26N 2°33W 67 H5
St. Peters N.S., Canada 45°40N 60°53W 165 C7
St. Peters P.E.I., Canada 46°25N 62°35W 165 C7
St. Petersburg = Sankt-Peterburg Russia 59°55N 30°20E 84 C6
St. Petersburg U.S.A. 27°46N 82°40W 179 H7
St-Philbert-de-Grand-Lieu France 47°2N 1°39W 70 E5
St-Phillippe Réunion 21°21S 55°44E 141 c
St-Pie Canada 45°30N 72°54W 175 A12
St-Pierre Martinique 14°45N 61°10W 182 c
St-Pierre Réunion 21°19S 55°28E 141 c
St-Pierre St-P. & M. 46°46N 56°12W 165 C8
St-Pierre, L. Canada 46°12N 72°52W 164 C5
St-Pierre-d'Oléron France 45°57N 1°19W 72 C2
St-Pierre-en-Port France 49°48N 0°30E 70 C7
St-Pierre-et-Miquelon ☒ N. Amer. 46°55N 56°10W 165 C8
St-Pierre-le-Moûtier France 46°47N 3°7E 71 F10
St-Pierre-sur-Dives France 49°2N 0°1W 70 C6
St-Pol-de-Léon France 48°41N 4°0W 70 D3
St-Pol-sur-Mer France 51°1N 2°20E 71 A9
St-Pol-sur-Ternoise France 50°23N 2°20E 71 B9
St-Pons France 43°30N 2°45E 72 E6
St-Pourçain-sur-Sioule France 46°18N 3°18E 71 F10
St-Priest France 45°42N 4°57E 73 C8
St-Quay-Portrieux France 48°39N 2°51W 70 D4
St-Quentin Canada 47°30N 67°23W 165 C6
St-Quentin France 49°50N 3°16E 71 C10
St-Rambert-d'Albon France 45°17N 4°49E 73 C8
St-Raphaël France 43°25N 6°46E 73 E10
St. Regis U.S.A. 47°18N 115°6W 168 C6
St. Regis Falls U.S.A. 44°40N 74°32W 175 B10
St-Renan France 48°26N 4°37W 70 D2
St-Saëns France 49°41N 1°16E 70 C8
St-Savin France 46°34N 0°53E 72 B4
St-Savinien France 45°53N 0°42W 72 C3
St-Seine-l'Abbaye France 47°26N 4°47E 71 E11
St-Sernin-sur-Rance France 43°54N 2°35E 72 E6
St-Sever France 43°45N 0°35W 72 E3
St-Siméon Canada 47°51N 69°54W 165 C6
St. Simons I. U.S.A. 31°12N 81°15W 178 D8
St. Simons Island U.S.A. 31°9N 81°22W 178 D8
St. Stephen Canada 45°16N 67°17W 165 C6
St. Stephen U.S.A. 33°24N 79°55W 178 B10
St-Sulpice France 43°46N 1°41E 72 E5
St-Sulpice-Laurière France 46°3N 1°29E 72 B5
St-Sulpice-les-Feuilles France 46°19N 1°21E 72 B5
St-Syprien = St-Cyprien France 42°37N 3°2E 72 F7
St. Teresa U.S.A. 29°55N 84°27W 178 F5
St-Thégonnec France 48°31N 3°57W 70 D3
St. Thomas Canada 42°45N 81°10W 174 D3
St. Thomas I. U.S. Virgin Is. 18°20N 64°55W 183 e
St-Tite Canada 46°45N 72°34W 164 C5
St-Trond = Sint-Truiden Belgium 50°48N 5°10E 69 D5
St-Tropez France 43°17N 6°38E 73 E10
St-Vaast-la-Hougue France 49°35N 1°17W 70 C5
St-Valery-en-Caux France 49°52N 0°43E 70 C7
St-Valéry-sur-Somme France 50°11N 1°38E 71 B8
St-Vallier France 46°38N 4°22E 71 F11
St-Vallier-de-Thiey France 43°42N 6°51E 73 E10
St-Varent France 46°53N 0°13W 70 F6
St-Vaury France 46°12N 1°46E 72 B5
St. Vidgeon's ✪ Australia 14°47S 134°53E 150 A1
St. Vincent = São Vicente C. Verde Is. 17°0N 25°0W 134 b
St. Vincent Italy 45°45N 7°39E 92 C4
St. Vincent, G. Australia 35°0S 138°0E 152 C3
St. Vincent & the Grenadines ■ W. Indies 13°0N 61°10W 183 D7
St-Vincent-de-Tyrosse France 43°39N 1°19W 72 E2
St. Vincent I. U.S.A. 29°42N 85°3W 179 F4
St. Vincent Passage W. Indies 13°30N 61°0W 183 D7
St-Vith Belgium 50°17N 6°9E 69 D6
St-Vivien-de-Médoc France 45°25N 1°2W 72 C2
St. Walburg Canada 53°39N 109°12W 163 C7
St-Yrieix-la-Perche France 45°31N 1°12E 72 C5
Saintala India 20°26N 83°20E 126 D6
Ste-Adresse France 49°31N 0°5E 70 C7
Ste-Agathe-des-Monts Canada 46°3N 74°17W 164 C5
Ste-Anne Guadeloupe 16°13N 61°24W 182 b
Ste-Anne Seychelles 4°36S 55°31E 141 b
Ste-Anne, L. Canada 50°0N 67°42W 165 B6
Ste-Anne-des-Monts Canada 49°8N 66°30W 165 C6
Ste-Croix Switz. 46°49N 6°34E 77 J2
Ste-Enimie France 44°22N 3°26E 72 D7
Ste-Foy-la-Grande France 44°50N 0°13E 72 D4
Ste. Genevieve U.S.A. 37°59N 90°2W 172 G8
Ste-Hermine France 46°32N 1°4W 72 B2
Ste-Livrade-sur-Lot France 44°24N 0°36E 72 D4
Ste-Marguerite → Canada 50°9N 66°36W 165 B6
Ste-Marie Canada 46°26N 71°0W 165 C5
Ste-Marie Martinique 14°48N 61°1W 182 c
Ste-Marie Réunion 20°53S 55°33E 141 c
Ste-Marie, Ile = Boraha, Nosy Madag. 16°50S 49°55E 141 H9
Ste-Marie-aux-Mines France 48°15N 7°12E 71 D14
Ste-Maure-de-Touraine France 47°7N 0°37E 70 E7
Ste-Maxime France 43°19N 6°39E 73 E10
Ste-Menehould France 49°5N 4°54E 71 C11
Ste-Mère-Église France 49°24N 1°19W 70 C5
Ste-Rose Guadeloupe 16°20N 61°45W 182 b
Ste-Rose Réunion 21°8S 55°45E 141 c
Ste. Rose du Lac Canada 51°4N 99°30W 163 C9
Ste-Savine France 48°18N 4°3E 71 D11
Ste-Sigolène France 45°15N 4°14E 73 C8
Saintes France 45°45N 0°37W 72 C3
Saintes, Îs. des Guadeloupe 15°50N 61°35W 182 b
Stes-Maries-de-la-Mer France 43°26N 4°26E 73 E8
Saintfield U.K. 54°28N 5°49W 64 B6
Saintonge France 45°40N 0°50W 72 C3
Saipal Nepal 29°50N 81°40E 125 E9
Saipan N. Marianas 15°12N 145°45E 156 F6
Sairang India 23°50N 92°45E 123 H18
Sairecábur, Cerro Bolivia 22°43S 67°54W 190 A2
Sāitah Si. Arabia 16°36N 42°56E 131 D3
Saitama Japan 35°54N 139°38E 113 G9
Saitama □ Japan 36°25N 139°30E 113 F9
Saiteli = Kadınhanı Turkey 38°14N 32°13E 104 C5
Saiţi Moldova 46°30N 29°24E 81 D14
Saiyid Pakistan 33°7N 73°2E 124 C5
Saja-Besaya △ Spain 43°10N 4°9W 88 B6
Sajama Bolivia 18°7S 69°0W 188 D4
Sajama, Nevado Bolivia 18°6S 68°54W 188 D4
Sajan Serbia 45°50N 20°20E 80 E5
Sajó → Hungary 47°56N 21°7E 80 C6
Sajószentpéter Hungary 48°12N 20°44E 80 B5
Sajum India 33°20N 79°0E 125 C8
Sak → S. Africa 30°52S 20°25E 144 D3
Saka Kenya 0°9S 39°20E 142 B4
Sakaba Nigeria 11°4N 5°35E 139 C6
Sakai Japan 34°34N 135°27E 113 G7
Sakaide Japan 34°19N 133°50E 113 G6
Sakaiminato Japan 35°38N 133°11E 113 G6
Sakākah Si. Arabia 30°0N 40°8E 128 D4
Sakakawea, L. U.S.A. 47°30N 101°25W 172 B3
Sakami → Canada 53°40N 76°40W 164 B4
Sakami, L. Canada 53°15N 77°0W 164 B4
Sâkâne, 'Erg i-n Mali 20°30N 1°30W 139 A4
Sakania Dem. Rep. of the Congo 12°43S 28°30E 143 E2
Sakartvelo = Georgia ■ Asia 42°0N 43°0E 87 J6
Sakarya Turkey 40°48N 30°25E 104 B4
Sakarya □ Turkey 40°45N 30°25E 104 B4
Sakarya → Turkey 41°7N 30°39E 104 B4
Sakashima-Guntō Japan 24°46N 124°0E 113 M2
Sakassou Ivory C. 7°29N 5°19W 138 D3
Sakata Japan 38°55N 139°50E 112 E9
Sakchu N. Korea 40°23N 125°2E 115 D13
Sakété Benin 6°40N 2°45E 139 D5
Sakha □ Russia 66°0N 130°0E 107 C14
Sakhalin Russia 51°0N 143°0E 107 D15
Sakhalinskiy Zaliv Russia 54°0N 141°0E 107 D15
Sakhi Gopal India 19°58N 85°50E 126 E7
Şaki Azerbaijan 41°10N 47°5E 87 K8
Šakiai Lithuania 54°59N 23°2E 82 D10
Sakmara → Russia 51°46N 55°1E 108 B5
Sakoli India 21°5N 79°59E 126 D4
Sakon Nakhon Thailand 17°10N 104°9E 120 D5
Sakrand Pakistan 26°10N 68°15E 124 F3
Sakri Maharashtra, India 26°13N 86°5E 125 F12
Sakri Maharashtra, India 21°2N 74°20E 126 D2
Sakrivier S. Africa 30°54S 20°28E 144 D3
Sakskøbing Denmark 54°49N 11°39E 63 K5
Sakti India 22°2N 82°58E 125 H10
Sakuma Japan 35°3N 137°49E 113 G8
Sakurai Japan 34°30N 135°51E 113 G7
Saky Ukraine 45°9N 33°34E 85 K7
Sal C. Verde Is. 16°45N 22°55W 134 b
Sal → Russia 47°31N 40°45E 87 G5
Sal Rei C. Verde Is. 16°11N 22°53W 134 b
Šal'a Slovak Rep. 48°10N 17°50E 79 C10
Sala Sweden 59°58N 16°35E 62 E10
Sala Consilina Italy 40°23N 15°36E 95 B8
Sala-y-Gómez Pac. Oc. 26°28S 105°28W 157 K17
Sala-y-Gómez Ridge Pac. Oc. 25°0S 98°0W 157 K18
Salaberry-de-Valleyfield Canada 45°15N 74°8W 175 A10
Salacgrīva Latvia 57°45N 24°21E 82 A11
Salada, L. Mexico 32°20N 115°40W 169 K6
Saladas Argentina 28°15S 58°40W 190 B4
Saladillo Argentina 35°40S 59°55W 190 D4
Salado → B. Aires, Argentina 35°44S 57°22W 190 D4
Salado → La Pampa, Argentina 37°30S 67°0W 192 A3
Salado → Río Negro, Argentina 41°34S 65°3W 192 B3
Salado → Santa Fe, Argentina 31°40S 60°41W 190 C3
Salado → Mexico 26°52N 99°19W 176 H5
Salaga Ghana 8°31N 0°31W 139 D4
Şalāh Syria 32°40N 36°45E 130 C5
Şalāḩ ad Dīn □ Iraq 34°35N 43°35E 128 C4
Sălaj □ Romania 47°15N 23°0E 80 C8
Salakos Greece 36°17N 27°57E 101 C9
Salala Liberia 6°42N 10°7W 138 D2
Salala Sudan 21°17N 36°16E 137 C4
Salālah Oman 16°56N 53°59E 131 D5
Salamajärvi △ Finland 63°12N 24°50E 60 E21
Salamanca Chile 31°46S 70°59W 190 C1
Salamanca Spain 40°58N 5°39W 88 E5
Salamanca U.S.A. 42°10N 78°43W 174 D6
Salamanca □ Spain 40°57N 5°40W 88 E5
Salāmatābād Iran 35°39N 47°50E 128 C5
Salamina Greece 37°56N 23°30E 98 D5
Salamis Cyprus 35°11N 33°54E 101 D12
Salar de Atacama Chile 23°30S 68°25W 190 A2
Salar de Uyuni Bolivia 20°30S 67°45W 188 E4
Sălard Romania 47°12N 22°3E 80 C7
Salas Spain 43°25N 6°15W 88 B4
Salas de los Infantes Spain 42°2N 3°17W 88 C7
Salatiga Indonesia 7°19S 110°30E 119 G14
Salavat Russia 53°21N 55°55E 108 B5
Salaverry Peru 8°15S 79°0W 188 B2
Salawati Indonesia 1°7S 130°52E 119 E8
Salawin △ Thailand 18°18N 97°40E 120 C1
Salaya India 22°19N 69°35E 124 H3
Salayar Indonesia 6°7S 120°30E 119 F6
Salazar → Spain 42°40N 1°20W 90 C3
Salbris France 47°25N 2°3E 71 E9
S'Albufera Spain 39°47N 3°7E 100 B10
Salcantay, Nevado Peru 13°19S 72°33W 188 C3
Salcia Romania 43°56N 24°55E 81 G9
Sălciua Romania 46°24N 23°26E 81 D8
Salcombe U.K. 50°14N 3°47W 67 G4
Saldaña Spain 42°32N 4°48W 88 C6
Saldanha S. Africa 33°0S 17°58E 144 D2
Saldanha B. S. Africa 33°6S 18°0E 144 D2
Saldus Latvia 56°38N 22°30E 82 B9
Saldus □ Latvia 56°35N 22°30E 82 B9
Sale Australia 38°6S 147°6E 153 E7
Sale Italy 44°59N 8°48E 92 D5
Salé Morocco 34°3N 6°48W 136 B2
Sale U.K. 53°26N 2°19W 66 D5
Sale City U.S.A. 31°16N 84°1W 178 D5
Salekhard Russia 66°30N 66°35E 106 C7
Salem India 11°40N 78°11E 127 J4
Salem Fla., U.S.A. 29°53N 83°25W 178 F6
Salem Ill., U.S.A. 38°38N 88°57W 172 F9
Salem Ind., U.S.A. 38°36N 86°6W 172 F10
Salem Mass., U.S.A. 42°31N 70°53W 175 D14
Salem Mo., U.S.A. 37°39N 91°32W 172 G8
Salem N.H., U.S.A. 42°45N 71°12W 175 D13
Salem N.J., U.S.A. 39°34N 75°28W 173 F16
Salem N.Y., U.S.A. 43°10N 73°20W 175 C11
Salem Ohio, U.S.A. 40°54N 80°52W 174 F4
Salem Oreg., U.S.A. 44°56N 123°2W 168 D2
Salem S. Dak., U.S.A. 43°44N 97°23W 172 D5
Salem Va., U.S.A. 37°18N 80°3W 173 G13
Salemi Italy 37°49N 12°48E 94 E5
Sälen Sweden 61°20N 13°10E 62 C7
Salernes France 43°34N 6°15E 73 E10
Salerno Italy 40°41N 14°47E 95 B7
Salerno, G. di Italy 40°32N 14°42E 95 B7
Salford U.K. 53°30N 2°18W 66 D5
Salgótarján Hungary 48°5N 19°47E 80 B4
Salgueiro Brazil 8°4S 39°6W 189 B3
Salher India 20°40N 73°55E 126 D1
Salhyr → Ukraine 45°38N 35°1E 85 K8
Salibabu Indonesia 3°51N 126°40E 119 D7
Salibea = Salybia Trin. & Tob. 10°43N 61°2W 187 K15
Salida U.S.A. 38°32N 106°0W 168 G11
Salies-de-Béarn France 43°28N 0°56W 72 E3
Salihli Turkey 38°28N 28°8E 104 C3
Salihorsk Belarus 52°51N 27°27E 75 B14
Salima Malawi 13°47S 34°28E 141 G6
Salina Italy 38°34N 14°50E 95 D7
Salina Kans., U.S.A. 38°50N 97°37W 172 F5
Salina Utah, U.S.A. 38°58N 111°51W 168 G8
Salina Cruz Mexico 16°10N 95°12W 181 D5
Salina di Margherita di Savóia △ Italy 41°23N 16°4E 95 A9
Salinas Brazil 16°10S 42°10W 189 D2
Salinas Ecuador 2°10S 80°58W 186 D2
Salinas U.S.A. 36°40N 121°39W 170 J5
Salinas → Guatemala 16°28N 90°31W 181 D6
Salinas → U.S.A. 36°45N 121°48W 170 J5
Salinas, B. de Nic. 11°4N 85°45W 182 D2
Salinas, Pampa de las Argentina 31°58S 66°42W 190 C2
Salinas Ambargasta Argentina 29°0S 65°0W 190 B3
Salinas de Hidalgo Mexico 22°38N 101°43W 180 C4
Salinas Grandes Argentina 30°0S 65°0W 190 C3
Salinas Pueblo Missions △ U.S.A. 34°6N 106°4W 169 J10
Salinas Valley U.S.A. 36°15N 121°15W 170 J5
Saline → Ark., U.S.A. 33°10N 92°8W 176 E8
Saline → Kans., U.S.A. 38°52N 97°30W 172 F5
Saline di Trapani e Paceco △ Italy 37°59N 12°28E 94 E5
Salines, C. de ses Spain 39°16N 3°4E 100 B10
Salinópolis Brazil 0°40S 47°20W 187 D9
Salins-les-Bains France 46°58N 5°52E 71 F12
Salir Portugal 37°14N 8°2W 89 H2
Salisbury Australia 34°46S 138°38E 152 C3
Salisbury U.K. 51°4N 1°47W 67 F6
Salisbury Md., U.S.A. 38°22N 75°36W 173 F16
Salisbury N.C., U.S.A. 35°40N 80°29W 177 D14
Salisbury I. Canada 63°30N 77°0W 161 E16
Salisbury Plain U.K. 51°14N 1°55W 67 F6
Săliște Romania 45°45N 23°56E 81 E8
Salitre → Brazil 9°29S 40°39W 189 B2
Salkehatchie → U.S.A. 32°37N 80°53W 178 C9
Şalkhad Syria 32°29N 36°43E 130 C5
Salkove Ukraine 48°15N 29°59E 81 B14
Salla Finland 66°50N 28°49E 60 C23
Sallanches France 45°55N 6°38E 73 C10
Sallent Spain 41°49N 1°54E 90 D6
Salles France 44°33N 0°52W 72 D3
Salles-Curan France 44°11N 2°48E 72 D6
Salling Denmark 56°40N 8°55E 63 H2
Salliq = Coral Harbour Canada 64°8N 83°10W 161 E15
Sallisaw U.S.A. 35°28N 94°47W 176 D7
Sallom Sudan 19°17N 37°6E 137 D4
Salluit Canada 62°14N 75°38W 161 E16
Sallyana Nepal 28°22N 82°10E 125 E10
Salmān Pak Iraq 33°6N 44°34E 105 G11
Salmās Iran 38°11N 44°47E 105 C11
Salmerón Spain 40°33N 2°29W 90 E2
Salmo Canada 49°10N 117°20W 162 D5
Salmon U.S.A. 45°11N 113°54W 168 D7
Salmon → Canada 54°3N 122°40W 162 C4
Salmon → U.S.A. 45°51N 116°47W 168 D5
Salmon Arm Canada 50°40N 119°15W 162 C5
Salmon Gums Australia 32°59S 121°38E 149 F3
Salmon Pt. Canada 43°52N 77°15W 174 C7
Salmon River Mts. U.S.A. 44°50N 115°30W 168 D6
Salmon River Res. U.S.A. 43°32N 75°55W 175 C9
Salo Finland 60°22N 23°10E 84 B2
Salò Italy 45°36N 10°31E 92 C7
Salobreña Spain 36°44N 3°35W 89 J7
Salome U.S.A. 33°47N 113°37W 171 M13
Salon India 26°2N 81°27E 125 F9
Salon-de-Provence France 43°39N 5°6E 73 E9
Salonica = Thessaloniki Greece 40°38N 22°58E 96 F6
Salonta Romania 46°49N 21°42E 80 D6
Salor → Spain 39°39N 7°3W 89 F3
Salou Spain 41°4N 1°8E 90 D6
Salou, C. de Spain 41°3N 1°10E 90 D6
Saloum → Senegal 13°50N 16°45W 138 C1
Salpausselkä Finland 61°3N 26°15E 84 B4
Salsacate Argentina 31°20S 65°5W 190 C2
Salses France 42°50N 2°55E 72 F6
Salsette I. India 19°2N 72°52E 126 E1
Salsk Russia 46°28N 41°30E 87 G5
Salso → Italy 37°6N 13°57E 94 E6
Salsomaggiore Terme Italy 44°49N 9°59E 92 D6
Salt Spain 41°59N 2°47E 90 D7
Salt → Canada 60°0N 112°25W 162 B6
Salt → U.S.A. 33°23N 112°19W 169 K7
Salt Fork Red → U.S.A. 34°27N 99°21W 176 D5
Salt L. Australia 30°6S 142°8E 151 E3
Salt Lake City U.S.A. 40°45N 111°53W 168 F8
Salt Range Pakistan 32°30N 72°25E 124
Salt Springs U.S.A. 29°21N 81°44W 179
Salta Argentina 24°57S 65°25W 190 A
Salta □ Argentina 24°48S 65°30W 190
Saltara Italy 43°45N 12°56E 93
Saltash U.K. 50°24N 4°14W 67 G
Saltburn by the Sea U.K. 54°35N 0°58W 66
Saltcoats U.K. 55°38N 4°47W 65
Saltee Is. Ireland 52°7N 6°37W 64
Salters U.S.A. 33°36N 79°51W 178 B
Saltfjellet Norway 66°40N 15°15E 60 C
Saltfjellet-Svartisen △ Norway 66°45N 15°10E 60 C
Saltfjorden Norway 67°15N 14°10E 60 C
Saltholm Denmark 55°38N 12°43E 63
Saltillo Mexico 25°25N 101°0W 180
Salto Argentina 34°20S 60°15W 190
Salto Uruguay 31°27S 57°50W 190
Salto da Divisa Brazil 16°0S 39°57W 189
Salto del Guaíra Paraguay 24°3S 54°17W 191
Salton City U.S.A. 33°18N 115°57W 171 M
Salton Sea U.S.A. 33°15N 115°45W 171 M
Saltpond Ghana 5°15N 1°3W 139
Saltsburg U.S.A. 40°29N 79°27W 174
Saltsjöbaden Sweden 59°15N 18°20E 62 E
Saluda U.S.A. 34°0N 81°46W 178
Saluda → U.S.A. 34°1N 81°4W 178
Salue Timpaus, Selat Indonesia 1°50S 123°50E 119
Salûm Egypt 31°31N 25°7E 137
Salûm, Khâlig el Egypt 31°35N 25°24E 137
Salur India 18°27N 83°18E 126
Saluzzo Italy 44°39N 7°29E 92
Salvación, B. Chile 50°50S 75°10W 192
Salvador Brazil 13°0S 38°30W 189
Salvador Canada 52°10N 109°32W 163
Salvador, El ■ Cent. Amer. 13°50N 89°0W 182
Salvador, L. U.S.A. 29°43N 90°15W 177
Salvaterra de Magos Portugal 39°1N 8°47W 89
Sálvora, I. de Spain 42°30N 8°58W 88
Salween → Burma 16°31N 97°37E 123 L
Salyan Azerbaijan 39°33N 48°59E 105 C
Salybia Trin. & Tob. 10°43N 61°2W 187 K
Salza → Austria 47°40N 14°43E 78
Salzach → Austria 48°12N 12°56E 78
Salzburg Austria 47°48N 13°2E 78
Salzburg □ Austria 47°15N 13°0E 78
Salzgitter Germany 52°9N 10°19E 76
Salzkotten Germany 51°40N 8°37E 76
Salzwedel Germany 52°52N 11°10E 76
Sam India 26°50N 70°31E 124
Sam Neua Laos 20°29N 104°5E 116
Sam Ngao Thailand 17°18N 99°0E 120
Sam Rayburn Res. U.S.A. 31°4N 94°5W 176
Sam Rong, Laem Thailand 9°35N 100°4E 121
Sam Son Vietnam 19°44N 105°54E 120
Sama de Langreo = Langreo Spain 43°18N 5°40W 88
Samagaltay Russia 50°36N 95°3E 109 B
Samales Group Phil. 6°0N 122°0E 119
Samalga Pass U.S.A. 52°50N 169°0W 166
Samalkot India 17°3N 82°13E 126
Samâlût Egypt 28°20N 30°42E 137
Samana India 30°10N 76°13E 124
Samana Cays Bahamas 23°3N 73°45W 183
Samandağ Turkey 36°5N 35°59E 104
Samandıra Turkey 40°59N 29°13E 97 F
Samanga Tanzania 8°20S 39°13E 143
Samangān □ Afghan. 36°15N 68°3E 109
Samangwa Dem. Rep. of the Congo 4°23S 24°10E 142
Samani Japan 42°7N 142°56E 112 C
Samanli Dağları Turkey 40°32N 29°10E 97 F
Samar Phil. 12°0N 125°0E 119
Samara Russia 53°8N 50°6E 86
Samara → Russia 53°10N 50°4E 86
Samara → Ukraine 48°28N 35°7E 85
Samaria = Shōmrōn West Bank 32°15N 35°13E 130
Samaria △ Greece 35°17N 23°58E 101
Samarinda Indonesia 0°30S 117°9E 118
Samarkand = Samarqand Uzbekistan 39°40N 66°55E 109
Samarqand Uzbekistan 39°40N 66°55E 109
Samarqand □ Uzbekistan 39°35N 66°35E 109
Sāmarrā' Iraq 34°12N 43°52E 105 E
Samarskaya Luka △ Russia 53°30N 49°30E 86
Samastipur India 25°50N 85°50E 125 G
Şamaxı Azerbaijan 40°38N 48°37E 87
Samba Dem. Rep. of the Congo 4°38S 26°22E 142
Samba India 32°32N 75°10E 125
Sambaíba Brazil 7°8S 45°21W 189
Sambalpur India 21°28N 84°4E 126
Sambar, Tanjung Indonesia 2°59S 110°19E 118
Sambas Indonesia 1°20N 109°20E 118
Sambawizi Zimbabwe 18°24S 26°13E 143
Sambhajinagar = Aurangabad India 19°50N 75°23E 126
Sambhal India 28°35N 78°37E 125
Sambhar India 26°52N 75°6E 124
Sambhar L. India 26°55N 75°12E 124
Sambiase Italy 38°58N 16°17E 95
Sambir Ukraine 49°30N 23°10E 83
Sambor Cambodia 12°46N 106°0E 120
Sambor Prei Kuk Cambodia 12°46N 105°58E 120
Samborombón, B. Argentina 36°5S 57°20W 190
Sambuca di Sicilia Italy 37°39N 13°7E 94
Samburu △ Kenya 0°37N 37°31E 142
Samcheok S. Korea 37°30N 129°10E 115
Same Tanzania 4°2S 37°38E 142
Samer France 50°38N 1°44E 71
Samet, Ko Thailand 12°34N 101°27E 120
Samfya Zambia 11°22S 29°31E 143
Sami Greece 38°15N 20°39E 98
Şämkir Azerbaijan 40°50N 46°0E 87
Samland = Zemlandskiy Poluostrov Russia 54°50N 20°20E 82
Şamlı Turkey 39°48N 27°51E 99
Sammanturai Sri Lanka 7°36N 81°39E 127
Samnah Si. Arabia 25°10N 37°15E 128
Samo Alto Chile 30°22S 71°0W 190

NDEX TO WORLD MAPS Sankt-Peterburg 267

moa ■ Pac. Oc. 14°0S 172°0W 147 C11
mobor Croatia 45°47N 15°44E 93 C12
moëns France 46°5N 6°45E 71 F13
mokov Bulgaria 42°18N 23°35E 96 D7
morín Slovak Rep. 48°2N 17°19E 79 C10
morogouan Burkina Faso 11°21N 4°57W 138 C4
mos Greece 37°45N 26°50E 99 D8
moš Serbia 45°13N 20°46E 80 E5
mos Spain 42°44N 7°20W 88 C3
moset U.S.A. 27°28N 82°33W 179 H7
mothráki = Mathraki Greece 39°48N 19°31E 101 A3
mothraki Greece 40°28N 25°28E 97 F9
moylovka Russia 51°12N 43°43E 86 E6
mpa Ghana 8°0N 2°36W 138 D4
mpacho Argentina 33°20S 64°50W 190 C3
mpalan Indonesia 8°41S 115°34E 119 K18
mpang Indonesia 7°11S 113°13E 119 G15
mper de Calanda Spain 41°11N 0°28W 90 D4
mpéyre Italy 44°34N 7°11E 92 D4
mpit Indonesia 2°34S 113°0E 118 E4
mpit, Teluk Indonesia 3°5S 113°3E 118 E4
mrong Cambodia 14°15N 103°30E 120 E4
msø Denmark 55°50N 10°35E 63 J4
msø Bælt Denmark 55°45N 10°45E 63 J4
mson U.S.A. 31°7N 86°3W 178 D3
msun Turkey 41°15N 36°22E 104 B7
msun □ Turkey 41°10N 36°10E 104 B7
mtredia Georgia 42°7N 42°24E 87 J6
mui, Ko Thailand 9°30N 100°0E 121 b
mur ➔ Russia 41°53N 48°32E 87 K9
murskiy Khrebet Russia 41°55N 47°11E 87 K8
musole Dem. Rep. of the Congo 10°2S 24°0E 143 E1
mut Prakan Thailand 13°40N 100°36E 120 F3
mut Sakhon Thailand 13°32N 100°17E 120 F3
mut Songkhram Thailand 13°24N 100°1E 120 F3
nwari Pakistan 28°30N 66°46E 124 E2
n Mali 13°15N 4°57W 138 C4
n ➔ Cambodia 13°32N 105°57E 120 F5
n ➔ Poland 50°45N 21°51E 83 H8
n Adrián Spain 42°20N 1°56W 90 C3
n Adrián, C. de Spain 43°21N 8°50W 88 B2
n Agustín, C. Phil. 6°20N 126°13E 119 C7
n Agustín de Valle Fértil Argentina 30°35S 67°30W 190 C2
n Ambrosio Pac. Oc. 26°28S 79°53W 184 F3
n Andreas U.S.A. 38°12N 120°41W 170 G6
n Andrés, I. de Caribbean 12°42N 81°46W 182 D3
n Andrés del Rabanedo Spain 42°37N 5°36W 88 C5
n Andres Mts. U.S.A. 33°0N 106°30W 169 K10
n Andrés Tuxtla Mexico 18°27N 95°13W 181 D5
n Angelo U.S.A. 31°28N 100°26W 176 F4
n Anselmo U.S.A. 37°59N 122°34W 170 H4
n Antonio Belize 16°15N 89°2W 181 D7
n Antonio Chile 33°40S 71°40W 190 C1
n Antonio N. Mex., U.S.A. 33°55N 106°52W 169 K10
n Antonio Tex., U.S.A. 29°25N 98°29W 176 G5
n Antonio ➔ U.S.A. 28°30N 96°54W 176 G6
n Antonio, C. Argentina 36°15S 56°40W 190 D4
n Antonio, C. de Cuba 21°50N 84°57W 182 B3
n Antonio, C. de Spain 38°48N 0°12E 91 G5
n Antonio, Mt. U.S.A. 34°17N 117°38W 171 L9
n Antonio de los Baños Cuba 22°54N 82°31W 182 B3
n Antonio de los Cobres Argentina 24°10S 66°17W 190 A2
n Antonio Oeste Argentina 40°40S 65°0W 192 B4
n Arcángelo Italy 40°14N 16°14E 95 B9
n Ardo U.S.A. 36°1N 120°54W 170 J6
n Augustín Canary Is. 27°47N 15°32W 100 G4
n Augustine U.S.A. 31°32N 94°7W 176 F7
n Bartolomé Canary Is. 28°59N 13°37W 100 F6
n Bartolomé de Tirajana Canary Is. 27°54N 15°34W 100 G4
n Bartolomeo in Galdo Italy 41°24N 15°1E 95 A8
n Benedetto del Tronto Italy 42°57N 13°53E 93 F10
n Benedetto Po Italy 45°2N 10°55E 92 C7
n Benedicto, I. Mexico 19°18N 110°49W 180 D2
n Benito U.S.A. 26°8N 97°38W 176 H6
n Benito ➔ U.S.A. 36°53N 121°34W 170 J5
n Benito Mt. U.S.A. 36°22N 120°37W 170 J6
n Bernardino U.S.A. 34°7N 117°19W 171 L9
n Bernardino Mts. U.S.A. 34°10N 116°45W 171 L10
n Bernardino Str. Phil. 12°30N 124°10E 119 B7
n Bernardo Chile 33°40S 70°50W 190 C1
n Bernardo, I. de Colombia 9°45N 75°50W 186 B3
n Blas Mexico 26°5N 108°46W 180 B3
n Blas, Arch. de Panama 9°50N 78°31W 182 E4
n Blas, C. U.S.A. 29°40N 85°21W 178 F4
n Bonifacio Italy 45°24N 11°16E 93 C8
n Borja Bolivia 14°50S 66°52W 188 C4
n Buenaventura = Ventura U.S.A. 34°17N 119°18W 171 L7
n Buenaventura Bolivia 14°28S 67°35W 188 C4
n Buenaventura Mexico 27°5N 101°32W 180 B4
n Carlos = Sant Carles Spain 39°3N 1°34E 100 B8
n Carlos Argentina 33°50S 69°0W 190 C2
n Carlos Chile 36°10S 72°0W 190 D1
n Carlos Baja Calif. S., Mexico 24°47N 112°7W 180 C2
San Carlos Coahuila, Mexico 29°1N 100°51W 180 B4
San Carlos Nic. 11°12N 84°50W 182 D3
San Carlos Phil. 10°29N 123°25E 119 B6
San Carlos Uruguay 34°46S 54°58W 191 C5
San Carlos U.S.A. 33°21N 110°27W 169 K8
San Carlos Venezuela 9°40N 68°36W 186 B5
San Carlos de Bariloche Argentina 41°10S 71°25W 192 B2
San Carlos de Bolívar Argentina 36°15S 61°6W 190 D3
San Carlos de la Rápita = Sant Carles de la Ràpita Spain 40°37N 0°35E 90 E5
San Carlos del Zulia Venezuela 9°1N 71°55W 186 B4
San Carlos L. U.S.A. 33°11N 110°32W 169 K8
San Carlos Park U.S.A. 26°28N 81°49W 179 J8
San Cataldo Italy 37°29N 13°59E 94 E6
San Celoni = Sant Celoni Spain 41°42N 2°30E 90 D7
San Clemente Chile 35°30S 71°29W 190 D1
San Clemente Spain 39°24N 2°25W 91 F2
San Clemente U.S.A. 33°26N 117°37W 171 M9
San Clemente I. U.S.A. 32°53N 118°29W 171 N8
San Cristóbal = Es Migjorn Gran Spain 39°57N 4°3E 100 B11
San Cristóbal Argentina 30°20S 61°10W 190 C3
San Cristóbal Dom. Rep. 18°25N 70°6W 183 C5
San Cristóbal Solomon Is. 10°30S 161°0E 147 C9
San Cristóbal Venezuela 7°46N 72°14W 186 B4
San Cristóbal de La Laguna = La Laguna Canary Is. 28°28N 16°18W 100 F3
San Cristóbal de las Casas Mexico 16°45N 92°38W 181 D6
San Damiano d'Asti Italy 44°50N 8°4E 92 D5
San Daniele del Friuli Italy 46°9N 13°1E 93 B10
San Diego Calif., U.S.A. 32°42N 117°9W 171 N9
San Diego Tex., U.S.A. 27°46N 98°14W 176 H5
San Diego, C. Argentina 54°40S 65°10W 192 D3
San Diego de la Unión Mexico 21°28N 100°52W 180 C4
San Diego Int. ✕ (SAN) U.S.A. 32°44N 117°11W 171 N9
San Dimitri, Ras Malta 36°4N 14°11E 101 C1
San Dimitri Point = San Dimitri, Ras Malta 36°4N 14°11E 101 C1
San Donà di Piave Italy 45°38N 12°34E 93 C9
San Estanislao Paraguay 24°39S 56°26W 190 A4
San Esteban de Gormaz Spain 41°34N 3°13W 90 D1
San Felice Circeo Italy 41°14N 13°5E 94 A6
San Felice sul Panaro Italy 44°50N 11°8E 93 D8
San Felipe Chile 32°43S 70°42W 190 C1
San Felipe Mexico 31°1N 114°52W 180 A2
San Felipe Venezuela 10°20N 68°44W 186 A5
San Felipe ➔ U.S.A. 33°10N 115°49W 171 M11
San Félix Chile 28°56S 70°28W 190 B1
San Félix Pac. Oc. 26°23S 80°0W 184 F2
San Fernando = Sant Ferran Spain 38°42N 1°28E 100 C7
San Fernando Chile 34°30S 71°0W 190 C1
San Fernando Mexico 24°51N 98°10W 181 C5
San Fernando La Union, Phil. 16°40N 120°23E 119 A6
San Fernando Pampanga, Phil. 15°5N 120°37E 119 A6
San Fernando Spain 36°28N 6°17W 89 J4
San Fernando Trin. & Tob. 10°16N 61°28W 183 D7
San Fernando U.S.A. 34°17N 118°26W 171 L8
San Fernando de Apure Venezuela 7°54N 67°15W 186 B5
San Fernando de Atabapo Venezuela 4°3N 67°42W 186 C5
San Fernando di Púglia Italy 41°18N 16°5E 95 A9
San Francisco Argentina 31°30S 62°5W 190 C3
San Francisco Peru 12°36S 73°49W 188 C3
San Francisco U.S.A. 37°46N 122°23W 170 H4
San Francisco ➔ U.S.A. 32°59N 109°22W 169 K9
San Francisco, C. de Colombia 6°18N 77°29W 184 C3
San Francisco, Paso de S. Amer. 27°0S 68°0W 190 B2
San Francisco de Macorís Dom. Rep. 19°19N 70°15W 183 C5
San Francisco del Monte de Oro Argentina 32°36S 66°8W 190 C2
San Francisco del Oro Mexico 26°52N 105°51W 180 B3
San Francisco Int. ✕ (SFO) U.S.A. 37°37N 122°22W 170 H4
San Francisco Javier = Sant Francesc de Formentera Spain 38°42N 1°26E 100 C7
San Fratello Italy 38°1N 14°36E 95 D7
San Gabriel Chile 33°47S 70°15W 190 C1
San Gabriel Chilac Mexico 18°19N 97°21W 181 D5
San Gabriel Mts. U.S.A. 34°17N 117°38W 171 L9
San Gavino Monreale Italy 39°33N 8°47E 94 C1
San German Puerto Rico 18°4N 67°4W 183 d
San Gimignano Italy 43°28N 11°2E 92 E8
San Giórgio di Nogaro Italy 45°50N 13°13E 93 C10
San Giórgio Iónico Italy 40°27N 17°23E 95 B10
San Giovanni Bianco Italy 45°52N 9°39E 92 C6
San Giovanni in Fiore Italy 39°15N 16°42E 95 C9
San Giovanni in Persiceto Italy 44°38N 11°11E 93 D8
San Giovanni Rotondo Italy 41°42N 15°44E 93 G12
San Giovanni Valdarno Italy 43°34N 11°32E 93 E8
San Giuliano Terme Italy 43°46N 10°26E 92 E7
San Gorgonio Mt. U.S.A. 34°6N 116°50W 171 L10
San Gottardo, P. del Switz. 46°33N 8°33E 77 J4
San Gregorio Uruguay 32°37S 55°40W 191 C4
San Gregorio U.S.A. 37°20N 122°23W 170 H4
San Guillermo △ Argentina 27°50S 69°45W 190 B2
San Guiseppe Jato Italy 37°57N 13°11E 94 E6
San Ignacio Belize 17°10N 89°5W 181 D7
San Ignacio Bolivia 16°20S 60°55W 186 G6
San Ignacio Mexico 27°27N 112°51W 180 B2
San Ignacio Paraguay 26°52S 57°3W 190 B4
San Ignacio Peru 5°8S 78°59W 188 B2
San Ignacio, L. Mexico 26°54N 113°13W 180 B2
San Ildefonso, C. Phil. 16°0N 122°1E 119 A6
San Isidro Argentina 34°29S 58°31W 190 C4
San Jacinto U.S.A. 33°47N 116°57W 171 M10
San Jaime = Sant Jaume Spain 39°54N 4°4E 100 B11
San Javier Misiones, Argentina 27°55S 55°5W 191 B4
San Javier Santa Fe, Argentina 30°40S 59°55W 190 C4
San Javier Bolivia 16°18S 62°30W 186 G6
San Javier Chile 35°40S 71°45W 190 D1
San Javier Spain 37°49N 0°50W 91 H4
San Jerónimo Taviche Mexico 16°44N 96°35W 181 D5
San Joaquin U.S.A. 36°36N 120°11W 170 J6
San Joaquin ➔ U.S.A. 38°4N 121°51W 170 G5
San Joaquin Valley U.S.A. 37°20N 121°0W 170 J6
San Jon U.S.A. 35°6N 103°20W 169 J12
San Jordi = Sant Jordi Spain 39°33N 2°46E 100 B9
San Jorge Argentina 31°54S 61°50W 190 C3
San Jorge, B. Mexico 31°20N 113°20W 180 A2
San Jorge, G. Argentina 46°0S 66°0W 192 C3
San José = San Josep Spain 38°55N 1°18E 100 C7
San José Argentina 32°12S 58°15W 190 C4
San José Costa Rica 9°55N 84°2W 182 E3
San José Guatemala 14°0N 90°50W 182 D1
San Jose Mind. Occ., Phil. 12°27N 121°4E 119 B6
San Jose Nueva Ecija, Phil. 15°45N 120°55E 119 A6
San Jose U.S.A. 37°20N 121°53W 170 H5
San Jose ➔ U.S.A. 34°25N 106°45W 169 J10
San José, G. Argentina 42°20S 64°18W 192 B4
San José, I. Mexico 25°0N 110°38W 180 C2
San Jose de Buenavista Phil. 10°45N 121°56E 119 B6
San José de Chiquitos Bolivia 17°53S 60°50W 186 G6
San José de Feliciano Argentina 30°26S 58°46W 190 C4
San José de Jáchal Argentina 30°15S 68°46W 190 C2
San José de Mayo Uruguay 34°27S 56°40W 190 C4
San José de Uchapiamonas Bolivia 14°13S 68°5W 188 C4
San José del Cabo Mexico 23°3N 109°41W 180 C3
San José del Guaviare Colombia 2°35N 72°38W 186 C4
San Josep Spain 38°55N 1°18E 100 C7
San Juan Argentina 31°30S 68°30W 190 C2
San Juan Peru 15°22S 75°7W 188 D2
San Juan Puerto Rico 18°28N 66°7W 183 d
San Juan Trin. & Tob. 10°39N 61°29W 187 K15
San Juan □ Argentina 31°9S 69°0W 190 C2
San Juan ➔ Argentina 32°20S 67°25W 190 C2
San Juan ➔ Nic. 10°56N 83°42W 182 D3
San Juan ➔ U.S.A. 37°16N 110°26W 169 H8
San Juan, C. Argentina 54°44S 63°44W 192 D4
San Juan Bautista = Sant Joan de Labritja Spain 39°5N 1°31E 100 B8
San Juan Bautista Paraguay 26°37S 57°6W 190 B4
San Juan Bautista U.S.A. 36°51N 121°32W 170 J5
San Juan Capistrano U.S.A. 33°30N 117°40W 171 M9
San Juan Cr. ➔ U.S.A. 35°40N 120°22W 170 J5
San Juan de Guadelupe Mexico 24°38N 102°44W 180 C4
San Juan de la Costa Mexico 24°20N 110°41W 180 C2
San Juan de los Lagos Mexico 21°15N 102°18W 180 C4
San Juan de los Morros Venezuela 9°55N 67°21W 186 B5
San Juan del Norte Nic. 10°58N 83°40W 182 D3
San Juan del Norte, B. de Nic. 11°0N 83°40W 182 D3
San Juan del Río Mexico 20°23N 100°0W 181 C5
San Juan del Sur Nic. 11°20N 85°51W 182 D2
San Juan I. U.S.A. 48°32N 123°5W 170 B3
San Juan Island ⌂ U.S.A. 48°35N 123°8W 170 B4
San Juan Mts. U.S.A. 37°30N 107°0W 169 H10
San Just, Sierra de Spain 40°45N 0°49W 90 E4
San Justo Argentina 30°47S 60°30W 190 C3
San Kamphaeng Thailand 18°45N 99°8E 120 C2
San Lázaro, C. Mexico 24°50N 112°18W 180 C2
San Leandro U.S.A. 37°42N 122°9W 170 H4
San Leonardo de Yagüe Spain 41°51N 3°5W 90 D1
San Lorenzo = Sant Llorenç des Cardassar Spain 39°37N 3°17E 100 B10
San Lorenzo Argentina 32°45S 60°45W 190 C3
San Lorenzo Ecuador 1°15N 78°50W 186 C3
San Lorenzo Paraguay 25°20S 57°32W 190 B4
San Lorenzo ➔ Mexico 24°15N 107°24W 180 C3
San Lorenzo, I. Mexico 28°38N 112°51W 180 B2
San Lorenzo, I. Peru 12°7S 77°15W 188 C2
San Lorenzo, Mte. Argentina 47°40S 72°20W 192 C2
San Lorenzo de la Parrilla Spain 39°51N 2°22W 90 F2
San Lorenzo de Morunys = Sant Llorenç de Morunys Spain 42°8N 1°35E 90 C6
San Lucas = Cabo San Lucas Mexico 22°53N 109°54W 180 C3
San Lucas Bolivia 20°5S 65°7W 186 H5
San Lucas Mexico 27°10N 112°14W 180 B2
San Lucas U.S.A. 36°8N 121°1W 170 J5
San Lucas, C. Mexico 22°52N 109°53W 180 C3
San Lúcido Italy 39°18N 16°3E 95 C9
San Luis Argentina 33°20S 66°20W 190 C2
San Luis Cuba 22°17N 83°46W 182 B3
San Luis Guatemala 16°14N 89°27W 182 C2
San Luis Ariz., U.S.A. 32°29N 114°47W 169 K6
San Luis Colo., U.S.A. 37°12N 105°25W 169 H11
San Luis □ Argentina 34°0S 66°0W 190 C2
San Luis, I. Mexico 29°58N 114°26W 180 B2
San Luis, Sierra de Argentina 32°30S 66°10W 190 C2
San Luis de la Paz Mexico 21°18N 100°31W 180 C4
San Luis Obispo U.S.A. 35°17N 120°40W 171 K6
San Luis Potosí Mexico 22°9N 100°59W 180 C4
San Luis Potosí □ Mexico 23°0N 101°0W 180 C4
San Luis Res. U.S.A. 37°4N 121°5W 170 H5
San Luis Río Colorado Mexico 32°29N 114°58W 180 A2
San Manuel U.S.A. 32°36N 110°38W 169 K8
San Marco, C. Italy 39°51N 8°26E 94 C1
San Marco Argentano Italy 39°33N 16°7E 95 C9
San Marco in Lámis Italy 41°43N 15°38E 93 G12
San Marcos Calif., U.S.A. 33°9N 117°10W 171 M9
San Marcos Tex., U.S.A. 29°53N 97°56W 176 G6
San Marcos, I. Mexico 27°13N 112°6W 180 B2
San Marino San Marino 43°55N 12°30E 93 E9
San Marino ■ Europe 43°56N 12°25E 93 E9
San Martín Antarctica 68°11S 67°0W 55 C17
San Martín Argentina 33°5S 68°28W 190 C2
San Martín □ Peru 7°0S 76°50W 188 B2
San Martín ➔ Bolivia 13°8S 63°43W 186 F6
San Martín, L. Argentina 48°50S 72°50W 192 C2
San Martín de la Vega Spain 40°13N 3°34W 88 E7
San Martín de los Andes Argentina 40°10S 71°20W 192 B2
San Martín de Valdeiglesias Spain 40°21N 4°24W 88 E6
San Mateo = Sant Mateu Baleares, Spain 39°3N 1°23E 100 B7
San Mateo = Sant Mateu Valencia, Spain 40°28N 0°10E 90 E5
San Mateo U.S.A. 37°34N 122°19W 170 H4
San Matías Bolivia 16°25S 58°20W 186 G7
San Matías, G. Argentina 41°30S 64°0W 192 B4
San Miguel = Sant Miquel Spain 39°3N 1°26E 100 B7
San Miguel El Salv. 13°30N 88°12W 182 D2
San Miguel Panama 8°27N 78°55W 182 E4
San Miguel U.S.A. 35°45N 120°42W 170 K6
San Miguel ➔ Bolivia 13°52S 63°56W 186 F6
San Miguel de Huachi Bolivia 15°40S 67°15W 188 D4
San Miguel de Tucumán Argentina 26°50S 65°20W 190 B2
San Miguel del Monte Argentina 35°23S 58°50W 190 D4
San Miguel I. U.S.A. 34°2N 120°23W 171 L6
San Millán de la Cogolla Spain 42°19N 2°51W 90 C2
San Miniato Italy 43°41N 10°51E 92 E7
San Nicandro Gargánico Italy 41°50N 15°34E 93 G12
San Nicolás Canary Is. 27°58N 15°47W 100 G4
San Nicolás de los Arroyos Argentina 33°25S 60°10W 190 C3
San Nicolas I. U.S.A. 33°15N 119°30W 171 M7
San Onofre U.S.A. 33°22N 117°34W 171 M9
San Pablo Bolivia 21°43S 66°38W 190 A2
San Pablo U.S.A. 37°58N 122°21W 170 H4
San Páolo di Civitate Italy 41°44N 15°15E 93 G12
San Pedro B. Aires, Argentina 33°40S 59°40W 190 C4
San Pedro Misiones, Argentina 26°30S 54°10W 191 B5
San Pedro Chile 33°54S 71°28W 190 C1
San Pedro Ivory C. 4°50N 6°33W 138 E3
San Pedro Mexico 23°55N 110°17W 180 C2
San Pedro Peru 14°49S 74°5W 188 C3
San Pedro □ Paraguay 24°0S 57°0W 190 A4
San Pedro ➔ Chihuahua, Mexico 28°21N 105°25W 180 B3
San Pedro ➔ Nayarit, Mexico 21°45N 105°30W 180 C3
San Pedro ➔ U.S.A. 32°59N 110°47W 169 K8
San Pedro, Pta. Chile 25°30S 70°38W 190 B1
San Pedro, Sierra de Spain 39°18N 6°40W 89 F4
San Pedro Channel U.S.A. 33°30N 118°25W 171 M8
San Pedro de Atacama Chile 22°55S 68°15W 190 A2
San Pedro de Jujuy Argentina 24°12S 64°55W 190 A3
San Pedro de las Colonias Mexico 25°45N 102°59W 180 B4
San Pedro de Lloc Peru 7°15S 79°28W 188 B2
San Pedro de Macorís Dom. Rep. 18°30N 69°18W 183 C6
San Pedro del Norte Nic. 13°4N 84°33W 182 D3
San Pedro del Paraná Paraguay 26°43S 56°13W 190 B4
San Pedro del Pinatar Spain 37°50N 0°50W 91 H4
San Pedro Mártir, Sa. de Mexico 30°45N 115°13W 180 A1
San Pedro Ocampo = Melchor Ocampo Mexico 24°51N 101°39W 180 C4
San Pedro Pochutla Mexico 15°44N 96°28W 181 D5
San Pedro Sula Honduras 15°30N 88°0W 182 C2
San Pedro Tututepec Mexico 16°9N 97°38W 181 D5
San Pietro Italy 39°8N 8°17E 94 C1
San Pietro Vernótico Italy 40°29N 18°0E 95 B11
San Rafael Argentina 34°40S 68°21W 190 C2
San Rafael Calif., U.S.A. 37°58N 122°32W 170 H4
San Rafael N. Mex., U.S.A. 35°7N 107°53W 169 J10
San Rafael Mt. U.S.A. 34°41N 119°52W 171 L7
San Rafael Mts. U.S.A. 34°40N 119°50W 171 L7
San Ramón de la Nueva Orán Argentina 23°10S 64°20W 190 A3
San Remo Italy 43°49N 7°46E 92 E4
San Roque Argentina 28°25S 58°45W 190 B4
San Roque Spain 36°17N 5°21W 89 J5
San Rosendo Chile 37°16S 72°43W 190 D1
San Saba U.S.A. 31°12N 98°43W 176 F5
San Salvador El Salv. 13°40N 89°10W 182 D2
San Salvador de Jujuy Argentina 24°10S 64°48W 190 A3
San Salvador I. Bahamas 24°0N 74°30W 183 B5
San Salvo Italy 42°3N 14°44E 93 F11
San Sebastián = Donostia-San Sebastián Spain 43°17N 1°58W 90 B3
San Sebastián Argentina 53°10S 68°30W 192 D3
San Sebastián Puerto Rico 18°20N 66°59W 183 d
San Sebastián de la Gomera Canary Is. 28°5N 17°7W 100 F2
San Serra = Son Serra Spain 39°43N 3°13E 100 B10
San Serverino Marche Italy 43°13N 13°10E 93 E10
San Severo Italy 41°41N 15°23E 93 G12
San Simeon U.S.A. 35°39N 121°11W 170 K5
San Simon U.S.A. 32°16N 109°14W 169 K9
San Stéfano di Cadore Italy 46°34N 12°33E 93 B9
San Stino di Livenza Italy 45°44N 12°41E 93 C9
San Telmo = Sant Elm Spain 39°35N 2°21E 100 B9
San Telmo Mexico 30°58N 116°6W 180 A1
San Teodoro Italy 40°46N 9°40E 94 B2
San Tiburcio Mexico 24°8N 101°32W 180 C4
San Valentin, Mte. Chile 46°30S 73°30W 192 C2
San Vicente de Alcántara Spain 39°22N 7°8W 89 F3
San Vicente de Cañete Peru 13°8S 76°30W 188 C2
San Vicente de la Barquera Spain 43°23N 4°29W 88 B6
San Vicenzo Spain 42°58N 8°46W 88 C2
San Vincenzo Italy 43°6N 10°32E 92 E7
San Vito Costa Rica 8°50N 82°58W 182 E3
San Vito Italy 39°26N 9°32E 94 C2
San Vito, C. Italy 38°11N 12°41E 94 D5
San Vito al Tagliamento Italy 45°54N 12°52E 93 C9
San Vito Chietino Italy 42°18N 14°27E 93 F11
San Vito dei Normanni Italy 40°39N 17°42E 95 B10
Sana' = Şan'ā' Yemen 15°27N 44°12E 131 D3
Saña Peru 6°54S 79°36W 188 B2
Şan'ā' Yemen 15°27N 44°12E 131 D3
Sana ➔ Bos.-H. 45°3N 16°23E 93 C13
Sanaa = Şan'ā' Yemen 15°27N 44°12E 131 D3
Sanaba Burkina Faso 12°25N 3°47W 138 C4
Sanae IV Antarctica 70°20S 9°0W 55 D2
Şanāfīr Si. Arabia 27°56N 34°42E 137 B3
Sanaga ➔ Cameroon 3°35N 9°38E 139 E6
Sanak I. U.S.A. 54°25N 162°40W 166 E7
Sanalona, Presa Mexico 24°49N 107°7W 180 C3
Sanana Indonesia 2°4S 125°58E 119 E7
Sanand India 22°59N 72°25E 124 H5
Sanandaj Iran 35°18N 47°1E 105 E12
Sanandita Bolivia 21°40S 63°45W 190 A3
Sanary-sur-Mer France 43°7N 5°49E 73 E9
Sanawad India 22°11N 76°5E 124 H7
Sancellas = Sencelles Spain 39°39N 2°54E 100 B9
Sancergues France 47°10N 2°54E 71 E9
Sancerre France 47°20N 2°50E 71 E9
Sancerrois, Collines du France 47°20N 2°40E 71 E9
Sancha He ➔ China 26°48N 106°7E 116 D6
Sanchahe China 44°50N 126°2E 115 B14
Sánchez Dom. Rep. 19°15N 69°36W 183 C6
Sanchi India 23°28N 77°44E 124 H7
Sanchor India 24°45N 71°55E 124 G4
Sancoins France 46°47N 2°55E 71 F9
Sancti Spíritus Cuba 21°52N 79°33W 182 B4
Sancy, Puy de France 45°32N 2°50E 72 C6
Sand = Polokwane ➔ S. Africa 22°25S 30°5E 145 B5
Sand Hills U.S.A. 42°10N 101°30W 172 D3
Sand Lakes ⌂ Canada 57°51N 98°32W 163 B9
Sand Springs U.S.A. 36°9N 96°7W 176 C6
Sanda Japan 34°53N 135°14E 113 G7
Sandakan Malaysia 5°53N 118°4E 118 C5
Sandalwood Australia 34°55S 140°9E 152 C4
Sandan = Sambor Cambodia 12°46N 106°0E 120 F6
Sandanski Bulgaria 41°35N 23°16E 96 E7
Sandaré Mali 14°40N 10°15W 138 C2
Sandared Sweden 57°43N 12°47E 63 G6
Sandarne Sweden 61°16N 17°9E 62 C11
Sanday U.K. 59°16N 2°31W 65 B6
Sande Norway 59°36N 10°12E 62 E4
Sandefjord Norway 59°10N 10°15E 61 G14
Sanders U.S.A. 35°13N 109°20W 169 J9
Sanderson Fla., U.S.A. 30°15N 82°16W 178 E7
Sanderson Tex., U.S.A. 30°9N 102°24W 176 F3
Sandersville U.S.A. 32°59N 82°48W 178 C7
Sandfire Roadhouse Australia 19°45S 121°15E 148 C3
Sandfly L. Canada 55°43N 106°6W 163 B7
Sandfontein Namibia 23°48S 19°1E 144 B2
Sandhammaren Sweden 55°23N 14°14E 63 J8
Sandheads, The India 21°10N 88°20E 125 J13
Sandía Peru 14°10S 69°30W 188 C4
Sandıklı Turkey 38°28N 30°17E 99 C12
Sandila India 27°5N 80°31E 125 F9
Sandnes Norway 58°50N 5°45E 61 G11
Sandnessjøen Norway 66°2N 12°38E 60 C15
Sandoa Dem. Rep. of the Congo 9°41S 23°0E 140 F4
Sandomierz Poland 50°40N 21°43E 83 H8
Sândominic Romania 46°35N 25°47E 81 D10
Sandover ➔ Australia 21°43S 136°32E 150 C2
Sandoway = Thandwe Burma 18°20N 94°30E 123 K19
Sandoy Færoe Is. 61°52N 6°46W 60 F9
Sandpoint U.S.A. 48°17N 116°33W 168 B5
Sandray U.K. 56°53N 7°31W 65 E1
Sandringham U.K. 52°51N 0°31E 66 E8
Sandstone Australia 27°59S 119°16E 149 E2
Sandu China 26°0N 107°52E 116 E6
Sandur India 15°6N 76°33E 127 F3
Sandusky Mich., U.S.A. 43°25N 82°50W 174 C2
Sandusky Ohio, U.S.A. 41°27N 82°42W 174 E2
Sandveld Namibia 21°25S 20°0E 144 B3
Sandvig Denmark 55°18N 14°47E 63 J8
Sandviken Sweden 60°38N 16°46E 62 D10
Sandwich, C. Australia 18°14S 146°18E 150 B4
Sandwich B. Canada 53°40N 57°15W 165 B8
Sandwich B. Namibia 23°25S 14°20E 144 B1
Sandy Oreg., U.S.A. 45°24N 122°16W 170 E4
Sandy Pa., U.S.A. 41°6N 78°46W 174 E6
Sandy Utah, U.S.A. 40°32N 111°50W 168 F8
Sandy Bay Canada 55°31N 102°19W 163 B8
Sandy Bight Australia 33°50S 123°20E 149 F3
Sandy C. Queens., Australia 24°42S 153°15E 150 C5
Sandy C. Tas., Australia 41°25S 144°45E 151 G3
Sandy Cay Bahamas 23°13N 75°18W 183 B4
Sandy Cr. ➔ Australia 31°54S 145°18E 151 B4
Sandy Cr. ➔ U.S.A. 41°51N 109°47W 168 F9
Sandy Creek U.S.A. 43°38N 76°5W 175 C8
Sandy L. Canada 53°2N 93°0W 164 B1
Sandy Lake Canada 53°0N 93°15W 164 B1
Sandy Point India 10°32N 92°22E 127 J11
Sandy Springs U.S.A. 33°56N 84°23W 178 B5
Sandy Valley U.S.A. 35°49N 115°38W 171 K11
Sånfjället △ Sweden 62°17N 13°35E 62 B7
Sanford Fla., U.S.A. 28°48N 81°16W 179 G8
Sanford Maine, U.S.A. 43°27N 70°47W 175 C14
Sanford N.C., U.S.A. 35°29N 79°10W 177 D15
Sanford ➔ Australia 27°22S 115°53E 149 E2
Sanford, Mt. U.S.A. 62°13N 144°8W 160 E3
Sang-i-Masha Afghan. 33°8N 67°27E 124 C2
Sanga Mozam. 12°22S 35°21E 143 E4
Sanga ➔ Congo 1°5S 17°0E 140 E3
Sangamner India 19°37N 74°15E 126 E2
Sangān Iran 34°23N 60°15E 129 C9
Sanganeb Atoll △ Sudan 19°33N 37°11E 137 D4
Sangar Afghan. 32°56N 65°30E 124 C1
Sangar Russia 64°2N 127°31E 107 C13
Sangar Sarai Afghan. 34°27N 70°35E 124 B4
Sangareddi India 17°38N 78°7E 126 F4
Sangaredi Guinea 11°7N 13°52W 138 C2
Sangarh ➔ Pakistan 30°43N 70°44E 124 D4
Sangasso Mali 12°5N 5°35W 138 C3
Sangatte France 50°56N 1°44E 71 B8
Sangāw Iraq 35°17N 45°10E 105 E11
Sangay Ecuador 2°0S 78°20W 186 D3
Sangbé Cameroon 6°3N 12°28E 139 D7
Sange Dem. Rep. of the Congo 6°58S 28°21E 142 D2
Sangeang Indonesia 8°12S 119°6E 119 F5
Sângeorz-Băi Romania 47°22N 24°41E 81 C9
Sanger U.S.A. 36°42N 119°33W 170 J7
Sângera Moldova 46°55N 28°58E 81 D13
Sangerhausen Germany 51°28N 11°18E 76 D7
Sanggan He ➔ China 38°12N 117°15E 114 E9
Sanggau Indonesia 0°5N 110°30E 118 D4
Sanghar Pakistan 26°2N 68°57E 124 F3
Sangihe, Kepulauan Indonesia 3°0N 125°30E 119 D7
Sangihe, Pulau Indonesia 3°35N 125°30E 119 D7
Sangiran △ Indonesia 7°27S 110°50E 119 G14
Sangju S. Korea 36°25N 128°10E 115 F15
Sangkapura Indonesia 5°52S 112°40E 118 F4
Sangkha Thailand 14°37N 103°52E 120 E4
Sangkhla Buri Thailand 14°57N 98°28E 120 E2
Sangkulirang Indonesia 0°59N 117°58E 118 D5
Sangla Pakistan 31°43N 73°23E 124 D5
Sangli India 16°55N 74°33E 126 F2
Sangmélima Cameroon 2°57N 12°1E 139 E7
Sango Zimbabwe 18°44S 31°44E 143 F3
Sangod India 24°55N 76°17E 124 G7
Sangole India 17°26N 75°12E 126 F2
Sangre de Cristo Mts. U.S.A. 37°30N 105°20W 169 H11
Sangre Grande Trin. & Tob. 10°35N 61°8W 187 K15
Sangro ➔ Italy 42°14N 14°32E 93 F11
Sangrur India 30°14N 75°50E 124 D6
Sangudo Canada 53°50N 114°54W 162 C6
Sangue ➔ Brazil 11°1S 58°39W 186 F7
Sangüesa Spain 42°37N 1°17W 90 C3
Sanguinaires, Îs. France 41°51N 8°36E 73 G12
Sangzhi China 29°25N 110°12E 117 C8
Sanhala Ivory C. 10°3N 6°51W 138 C3
Sanibel U.S.A. 26°27N 82°1W 179 J7
Sanibel I. U.S.A. 26°26N 82°6W 179 J7
Sanikluaq Canada 56°32N 79°14W 164 A4
Sanin-Kaigan △ Japan 35°39N 134°37E 113 G7
Sanirajak = Hall Beach Canada 68°46N 81°12W 161 D15
Sanjawi Pakistan 30°17N 68°21E 124 D3
Sanje Uganda 0°49S 31°30E 142 C3
Sanjiang China 25°48N 109°37E 116 E7
Sanjo Japan 37°37N 138°57E 112 F9
Sankarankovil India 9°10N 77°35E 127 K3
Sankeshwar India 16°23N 74°32E 127 F2
Sankh ➔ India 22°15N 84°48E 125 H11
Sankt Andrä Austria 46°46N 14°50E 78 E7
Sankt Anton Austria 47°8N 10°16E 77 H6
Sankt Augustin Germany 50°45N 7°10E 76 E3
Sankt Blasien Germany 47°47N 8°7E 77 H4
Sankt Gallen Switz. 47°26N 9°22E 77 H5
Sankt Gallen □ Switz. 47°25N 9°22E 77 H5
Sankt Goar Germany 50°12N 7°43E 77 E3
Sankt Ingbert Germany 49°16N 7°6E 77 F3
Sankt Johann im Pongau Austria 47°22N 13°12E 78 D6
Sankt Johann in Tirol Austria 47°30N 12°25E 78 D5
Sankt Michel = Mikkeli Finland 61°43N 27°15E 84 B4
Sankt Moritz Switz. 46°30N 9°51E 77 J5
Sankt Peter-Ording Germany 54°20N 8°36E 76 A4
Sankt-Peterburg Russia 59°55N 30°20E 84 C6

Sankt Pölten *Austria* 48°12N 15°38E **78** C8
Sankt Ulrich = Ortisei
  Italy 46°34N 11°40E **93** B8
Sankt Valentin *Austria* 48°11N 14°33E **78** C7
Sankt Veit an der Glan
  Austria 46°47N 14°22E **78** E7
Sankt Wendel *Germany* 49°27N 7°9E **77** F3
Sankt Wolfgang *Austria* 47°43N 13°27E **78** D6
Sankuru →
  Dem. Rep. of the Congo 4°17S 20°25E **140** E4
Sanliurfa *Turkey* 37°12N 38°50E **105** D8
Sanliurfa □ *Turkey* 37°0N 39°0E **105** D8
Sanlúcar de Barrameda
  Spain 36°46N 6°21W **89** J4
Sanluri *Italy* 39°34N 8°54E **94** C1
Sânmartin *Romania* 46°19N 25°58E **81** D10
Sanmen *China* 29°5N 121°35E **117** C13
Sanmenxia *China* 34°47N 111°12E **114** G6
Sanming *China* 26°15N 117°40E **117** D11
Sanmu *Japan* 34°11N 134°37E **113** G7
Sanndraigh = Sandray
  U.K. 56°53N 7°31W **65** E1
Sânnicolau Mare
  Romania 46°5N 20°39E **80** D5
Sannieshof *S. Africa* 26°30S 25°47E **144** C4
Sannîn, J. *Lebanon* 33°57N 35°52E **130** B4
Sanniquellie *Liberia* 7°19N 8°38W **138** D3
Sannûr, W. → *Egypt* 28°59N 31°3E **137** F7
Sano *Japan* 36°19N 139°35E **113** F9
Sanok *Poland* 49°35N 22°10E **83** J9
Sanqingshan △ *China* 28°54N 118°3E **117** C12
Sanquhar *U.K.* 55°22N 3°54W **65** F5
Sans Souci *Trin. & Tob.* 10°50N 61°0W **187** K16
Sansando *Mali* 13°48N 6°0W **138** C3
Sansané *Niger* 13°50N 1°36E **139** C5
Sansepolcro *Italy* 43°34N 12°8E **93** E9
Sansha *China* 26°58N 120°12E **117** D13
Sanshui *China* 23°10N 112°56E **117** F9
Sansui *China* 26°58N 108°39E **116** D7
Sant Antoni de Portmany
  Spain 38°59N 1°19E **100** C7
Sant Boi de Llobregat
  Spain 41°20N 2°2E **90** D7
Sant Carles *Spain* 39°3N 1°34E **100** B8
Sant Carles de la Ràpita
  Spain 40°37N 0°35E **90** E5
Sant Celoni *Spain* 41°42N 2°30E **90** D7
Sant Elm *Spain* 39°35N 2°21E **100** B9
Sant Feliu de Guíxols
  Spain 41°45N 3°1E **90** D8
Sant Feliu de Llobregat
  Spain 41°22N 2°2E **90** D7
Sant Ferran *Spain* 38°42N 1°28E **100** C7
Sant Francesc de Formentera
  Spain 38°42N 1°26E **100** C7
Sant Jaume *Spain* 39°54N 4°4E **100** B11
Sant Joan *Spain* 39°36N 3°4E **100** B10
Sant Joan d'Alacant
  Spain 38°24N 0°26W **91** G4
Sant Joan de Labritja
  Spain 39°5N 1°31E **100** B8
Sant Jordi *Ibiza, Spain* 38°53N 1°24E **100** C7
Sant Jordi *Mallorca, Spain* 39°33N 2°46E **100** B9
Sant Jordi, G. de *Spain* 40°53N 1°2E **90** E6
Sant Llorenç de Morunys
  Spain 42°8N 1°35E **90** C6
Sant Llorenç del Munt y l'Obac △
  Spain 41°39N 1°55W **90** D3
Sant Llorenç des Cardassar
  Spain 39°37N 3°17E **100** B10
Sant Mateu *Baleares,*
  Spain 39°3N 1°23E **100** B7
Sant Mateu *Valencia,*
  Spain 40°28N 0°10E **90** E5
Sant Miquel *Spain* 39°3N 1°26E **100** B7
Sant Pere de Ribes *Spain* 41°16N 1°46E **90** D6
Sant Salvador *Spain* 39°27N 3°11E **100** B10
Sant Vicent del Raspeig
  Spain 38°24N 0°31W **91** G4
Santa *Peru* 8°59S 78°40W **188** E2
Sant' Ágata Militello *Italy* 38°2N 14°8E **95** D7
Santa Agnés *Spain* 39°3N 1°21E **100** B7
Santa Ana *Beni, Bolivia* 13°50S 65°40W **186** F5
Santa Ana La Paz,
  Bolivia 15°31S 67°30W **188** D4
Santa Ana *El Salv.* 14°0N 89°31W **182** D2
Santa Ana *Mexico* 30°33N 111°7W **180** A2
Santa Ana *U.S.A.* 33°46N 117°52W **171** M9
Santa Ana de los Ríos de Cuenca
  = Cuenca *Ecuador* 2°50S 79°9W **186** D3
Sant' Ángelo Lodigiano
  Italy 45°14N 9°25E **92** C6
Sant' Antíoco *Italy* 39°4N 8°27E **94** C1
Santa Bárbara *Chile* 37°40S 72°1W **190** D1
Santa Bárbara
  Honduras 14°53N 88°14W **182** D2
Santa Bárbara *Mexico* 26°48N 105°49W **180** B3
Santa Bárbara *Spain* 40°42N 0°29E **90** E5
Santa Barbara *U.S.A.* 34°25N 119°42W **171** L7
Santa Bárbara, Mt.
  Spain 37°23N 2°50W **91** H2
Santa Barbara Channel
  U.S.A. 34°15N 120°0W **171** L7
Santa Barbara I.
  U.S.A. 33°29N 119°2W **171** M7
Santa Catalina, Gulf of
  U.S.A. 33°10N 117°50W **171** N9
Santa Catalina, I.
  Mexico 25°40N 110°47W **180** B2
Santa Cataliña de Armada
  Spain 43°2N 8°49W **88** B2
Santa Catalina I.
  U.S.A. 33°23N 118°25W **171** M8
Santa Catarina □
  Brazil 27°25S 48°30W **191** B6
Santa Catarina, I. de
  Brazil 27°30S 48°40W **191** B6
Santa Caterina di Pittinuri
  Italy 40°6N 8°27E **94** B1
Santa Caterina Villarmosa
  Italy 37°35N 14°1E **95** E7
Santa Cecilia *Brazil* 26°56S 50°18W **191** B5
Santa Clara *Cuba* 22°20N 80°0W **182** B4
Santa Clara *Calif.,*
  U.S.A. 37°21N 121°57W **170** H6
Santa Clara *N.Y.,*
  U.S.A. 44°38N 74°27W **175** B10
Santa Clara *Utah,*
  U.S.A. 37°8N 113°39W **169** H7
Santa Clara → *Mexico* 29°51N 107°6W **180** A3

Santa Clara de Olimar
  Uruguay 32°50S 54°54W **191** C5
Santa Clara Valley
  U.S.A. 36°50N 121°30W **170** J5
Santa Clarita *U.S.A.* 34°24N 118°33W **171** L8
Santa Clotilde *Peru* 2°33S 73°45W **186** D4
Santa Coloma de Farners
  Spain 41°50N 2°39E **90** D7
Santa Coloma de Gramenet
  Spain 41°27N 2°13E **90** D7
Santa Comba = Santa Catalíña de
  Armada *Spain* 43°2N 8°49W **88** B2
Santa Croce Camerina
  Italy 36°50N 14°31E **95** F7
Santa Croce di Magliano
  Italy 41°42N 14°59E **93** G11
Santa Cruz *Bolivia* 17°43S 63°10W **186** G6
Santa Cruz *Brazil* 6°13S 36°1W **189** B3
Santa Cruz *Chile* 34°38S 71°27W **190** C1
Santa Cruz *Costa Rica* 10°15N 85°35W **182** D2
Santa Cruz *Madeira* 32°42N 16°46W **100** D3
Santa Cruz *Peru* 5°40S 75°56W **188** E2
Santa Cruz *Phil.* 14°20N 121°24E **119** B6
Santa Cruz *U.S.A.* 36°58N 122°1W **170** J4
Santa Cruz □ *Argentina* 49°0S 70°0W **192** C3
Santa Cruz →
  Argentina 50°10S 68°20W **192** D3
Santa Cruz Cabrália
  Brazil 16°17S 39°2W **189** D3
Santa Cruz de la Palma
  Canary Is. 28°41N 17°46W **100** F2
Santa Cruz de la Palma ✈ (SPC)
  Canary Is. 28°40N 17°45W **100** F2
Santa Cruz de Mompox =
  Mompós *Colombia* 9°14N 74°26W **186** B4
Santa Cruz de Mudela
  Spain 38°39N 3°28W **89** G7
Santa Cruz de Tenerife
  Canary Is. 28°28N 16°15W **100** F3
Santa Cruz del Norte
  Cuba 23°9N 81°55W **182** B3
Santa Cruz del Retamar
  Spain 40°8N 4°14W **88** E6
Santa Cruz del Sur *Cuba* 20°44N 78°0W **182** B4
Santa Cruz do Rio Pardo
  Brazil 22°54S 49°37W **191** A6
Santa Cruz do Sul
  Brazil 29°42S 52°25W **191** B5
Santa Cruz I. *U.S.A.* 34°1N 119°43W **171** M7
Santa Cruz Is.
  Solomon Is. 10°30S 166°0E **147** C9
Santa Cruz Mts. *Jamaica* 17°58N 77°43W **182** a
Sant' Egidio alla Vibrata
  Italy 42°49N 13°42E **93** F10
Santa Elena *Argentina* 30°58S 59°47W **190** C4
Santa Elena, C.
  Costa Rica 10°54N 85°56W **182** D2
Sant' Eufémia, G. di *Italy* 38°51N 16°4E **95** D9
Santa Eulària des Riu
  Spain 38°59N 1°32E **100** C8
Santa Fé *Argentina* 31°35S 60°41W **190** C3
Santa Fé *Spain* 37°11N 3°43W **89** H7
Santa Fe *U.S.A.* 35°41N 105°57W **169** J11
Santa Fé □ *Argentina* 31°50S 60°55W **190** C3
Santa Fé do Sul *Brazil* 20°13S 50°56W **187** H8
Santa Filomena *Brazil* 9°6S 45°50W **189** B1
Santa Fiora *Italy* 42°50N 11°35E **93** F8
Santa Gertrudis *Spain* 39°0N 1°26E **100** C7
Santa Giulia *France* 41°32N 9°17E **73** G13
Santa Giustina *Italy* 46°10N 12°5E **93** B9
Santa Helena *Brazil* 2°14S 45°18W **189** A1
Santa Inês *Bahia, Brazil* 13°17S 39°48W **189** C3
Santa Inês *Maranhão,*
  Brazil 3°39S 45°20W **189** A1
Santa Inés *Spain* 38°32N 5°37W **89** G5
Santa Inés, I. *Chile* 54°0S 73°0W **192** D2
Santa Isabel *Argentina* 36°10S 66°54W **190** D2
Santa Isabel do Morro
  Brazil 11°34S 50°40W **187** F8
Santa Lucía *Corrientes,*
  Argentina 28°58S 59°5W **190** B4
Santa Lucía *San Juan,*
  Argentina 31°30S 68°30W **190** C2
Santa Lucía *Spain* 37°35N 0°58W **91** H4
Santa Lucía *Uruguay* 34°27S 56°24W **190** C4
Santa Lucia Range
  U.S.A. 36°0N 121°20W **170** K5
Santa Luzia *Brazil* 19°47S 43°52W **189** D2
Santa Luzia *C. Verde Is.* 16°50N 24°35W **134** b
Santa Margalida *Spain* 39°42N 3°6E **100** B10
Santa Margarita
  Argentina 38°28S 61°35W **190** D3
Santa Margarita
  U.S.A. 35°23N 120°37W **170** K6
Santa Margarita →
  U.S.A. 33°13N 117°23W **171** M9
Santa Margarita, I.
  Mexico 24°27N 111°50W **180** C2
Santa Margherita Ligure
  Italy 44°20N 9°11E **92** D6
Santa María *Argentina* 26°40S 66°0W **190** B2
Santa María *Azores* 36°58N 25°6W **134** a
Santa Maria *Brazil* 29°40S 53°48W **191** B5
Santa Maria *C. Verde Is.* 16°31N 22°53W **134** b
Santa Maria →
  Mexico 31°0N 107°14W **180** A3
Santee *U.S.A.* 32°50N 116°58W **171** N10
Santee → *U.S.A.* 33°7N 79°17W **177** E15
Santéramo in Colle *Italy* 40°49N 16°45E **95** B9
Santerno → *Italy* 44°34N 11°58E **93** D8
Santhià *Italy* 45°22N 8°10E **92** C5
Santi-Quaranta = Sarandë
  Albania 39°52N 19°55E **96** G3
Santiago = Rio Grande de
  Santiago →
  Mexico 21°36N 105°26W **180** C3
Santiago = São Tiago
  C. Verde Is. 15°0N 23°40W **134** b
Santiago *Brazil* 29°11S 54°52W **191** B5
Santiago *Canary Is.* 28°2N 17°12W **100** F2
Santiago *Chile* 33°26S 70°40W **190** C1
Santiago *Panama* 8°0N 81°0W **182** E3
Santiago *Peru* 14°11S 75°43W **188** C2
Santiago *Phil.* 16°41N 121°33E **119** A6
Santiago □ *Chile* 33°30S 70°50W **190** C1
Santiago → *Peru* 4°27S 77°38W **186** D3
Santiago, C. *Chile* 50°46S 75°27W **192** D1
Santiago, Punta de
  Eq. Guin. 3°12N 8°40E **138** D6
Santiago de Chuco *Peru* 8°9S 78°11W **188** B2
Santiago de Compostela
  Spain 42°52N 8°37W **88** C2

Santa Marta *Colombia* 11°15N 74°13W **186** A4
Santa Marta, Sierra Nevada de
  Colombia 10°55N 73°50W **186** A4
Santa Marta de Tormes
  Spain 40°57N 5°38W **88** E5
Santa Marta Grande, C.
  Brazil 28°43S 48°50W **191** B6
Santa Maura = Lefkada
  Greece 38°40N 20°43E **98** C2
Santa Monica *U.S.A.* 34°1N 118°29W **171** M8
Santa Monica Mts. △
  U.S.A. 34°4N 118°44W **171** L8
Santa Olalla *Spain* 40°2N 4°25W **88** E6
Santa Olalla del Cala
  Spain 37°54N 6°14W **89** H4
Santa Paula *U.S.A.* 34°21N 119°4W **171** L7
Santa Pola *Spain* 38°13N 0°35W **91** G4
Santa Ponça *Spain* 39°30N 2°28E **100** B9
Santa Quitéria *Brazil* 4°20S 40°10W **189** A4
Santa Rita *Brazil* 7°8S 34°58W **189** B4
Santa Rita de Cássia
  Brazil 11°0S 44°32W **189** C2
Santa Rosa *La Pampa,*
  Argentina 36°40S 64°17W **190** D3
Santa Rosa *San Luis,*
  Argentina 32°21S 65°10W **190** C2
Santa Rosa *Beni,*
  Bolivia 14°10S 66°50W **188** B3
Santa Rosa *Pando,*
  Bolivia 10°36S 67°20W **188** C4
Santa Rosa *Brazil* 27°52S 54°29W **191** B5
Santa Rosa *Puno, Peru* 14°30S 70°50W **188** C3
Santa Rosa *San Martín,*
  Peru 6°41S 76°37W **188** B2
Santa Rosa *Calif.,*
  U.S.A. 38°26N 122°43W **170** G4
Santa Rosa *N. Mex.,*
  U.S.A. 34°57N 104°41W **169** J11
Santa Rosa and San Jacinto
  Mts. ○ *U.S.A.* 33°28N 116°20W **171** M10
Santa Rosa Beach
  U.S.A. 30°22N 86°14W **178** E3
Santa Rosa de Copán
  Honduras 14°47N 88°46W **182** D2
Santa Rosa de Río Primero
  Argentina 31°8S 63°20W **190** C3
Santa Rosa del Sara
  Bolivia 17°7S 63°35W **186** G6
Santa Rosa I. *Calif.,*
  U.S.A. 33°58N 120°6W **171** M6
Santa Rosa I. *Fla.,*
  U.S.A. 30°20N 86°50W **179** E3
Santa Rosa Range
  U.S.A. 41°45N 117°40W **168** F5
Santa Rosalía *Mexico* 27°19N 112°17W **180** B2
Santa Sylvina
  Argentina 27°50S 61°10W **190** B3
Santa Tecla = Nueva San
  Salvador *El Salv.* 13°40N 89°18W **182** D2
Santa Teresa *Argentina* 33°25S 60°47W **190** C3
Santa Teresa *Australia* 24°8S 134°22E **150** C1
Santa Teresa *Brazil* 19°55S 40°36W **189** D3
Santa Teresa *Mexico* 25°17N 97°51W **181** B5
Santa Teresa △
  Uruguay 33°57S 53°31W **191** C5
Santa Teresa di Riva
  Italy 37°57N 15°22E **95** E8
Santa Teresa Gallura
  Italy 41°14N 9°11E **94** A2
Santa Teresita
  Argentina 36°32S 56°41W **190** D4
Santa Uxía de Ribeira = Ribeira
  Spain 42°36N 8°58W **88** C2
Santa Vitória do Palmar
  Brazil 33°32S 53°25W **191** C5
Santa Ynez → *U.S.A.* 34°41N 120°36W **171** L6
Santa Ynez Mts.
  U.S.A. 34°30N 120°0W **171** L6
Santa Ysabel *U.S.A.* 33°7N 116°40W **171** M10
Santadi *Italy* 39°5N 8°43E **94** C1
Santaella *Spain* 37°34N 4°51W **89** H6
Santai *China* 31°5N 104°58E **116** B5
Santaluz *Brazil* 11°15S 39°22W **189** C3
Santana *Brazil* 13°2S 44°5W **189** C2
Santana *Madeira* 32°48N 16°52W **100** D3
Sântana *Romania* 46°20N 21°30E **80** D6
Santana, Coxilha de
  Brazil 30°50S 55°35W **191** C4
Santana do Ipanema
  Brazil 9°22S 37°14W **189** B3
Santana do Livramento
  Brazil 30°55S 55°30W **191** C4
Santander *Spain* 43°27N 3°51W **88** B7
Santander Jiménez
  Mexico 24°13N 98°28W **181** C5
Santanilla, Is.
  Honduras 17°22N 83°57W **182** C3
Santanyí *Spain* 39°20N 3°5E **100** B10
Santaquin *U.S.A.* 39°59N 111°47W **168** G8
Santarcángelo di Romagna
  Italy 44°4N 12°26E **93** E9
Santarém *Brazil* 2°25S 54°42W **187** D8
Santarém *Portugal* 39°12N 8°42W **89** F2
Santarém □ *Portugal* 39°10N 8°40W **89** F2
Santaren Channel
  W. Indies 24°0N 79°30W **182** B4

Santiago de Cuba *Cuba* 20°0N 75°49W **182** C4
Santiago de los Caballeros
  Dom. Rep. 19°30N 70°40W **183** C5
Santiago del Estero
  Argentina 27°50S 64°15W **190** B3
Santiago del Estero □
  Argentina 27°40S 63°15W **190** B3
Santiago del Teide
  Canary Is. 28°17N 16°48W **100** F3
Santiago do Cacém
  Portugal 38°1N 8°42W **89** G2
Santiago Ixcuintla
  Mexico 21°49N 105°13W **180** C3
Santiago Jamiltepec
  Mexico 16°17N 97°49W **181** D5
Santiago Papasquiaro
  Mexico 25°3N 105°25W **180** C3
Santiago Pinotepa Nacional
  Mexico 16°19N 98°1W **181** D5
Santiaguillo, L. de
  Mexico 24°48N 104°48W **180** C4
Santiguila *Mali* 12°42N 7°25W **138** C3
Santillana del Mar *Spain* 43°24N 4°6W **88** B7
Santisteban del Puerto
  Spain 38°17N 3°15W **89** G7
Santo → *Peru* 8°56S 78°37W **188** B2
Santo Amaro *Brazil* 12°30S 38°43W **189** C3
Santo Anastácio *Brazil* 21°58S 51°39W **191** A5
Santo André *Brazil* 23°39S 46°29W **191** A6
Santo Ângelo *Brazil* 28°15S 54°15W **191** B5
Santo Antão *C. Verde Is.* 16°52N 25°10W **134** b
Santo Antônio de Jesus
  Brazil 12°58S 39°16W **189** C3
Santo Antônio do Içá
  Brazil 3°5S 67°57W **186** D5
Santo Antônio do Leverger
  Brazil 15°52S 56°5W **187** G7
Santo Domingo
  Dom. Rep. 18°30N 69°59W **183** C6
Santo Domingo
  Mexico 25°29N 111°55W **180** B2
Santo Domingo *Nic.* 12°14N 84°59W **182** D3
Santo Domingo, Cay
  Bahamas 21°25N 75°45W **182** B4
Santo Domingo de la Calzada
  Spain 42°26N 2°57W **90** C2
Santo Domingo de los Colorados
  Ecuador 0°15S 79°9W **186** D3
Santo Domingo Pueblo
  U.S.A. 35°31N 106°22W **169** J10
Santo Domingo Tehuantepec =
  Tehuantepec
  Mexico 16°21N 95°13W **181** D5
Santo Stéfano di Camastro
  Italy 38°1N 14°22E **95** D7
Santo Tirso *Portugal* 41°21N 8°28W **88** D2
Santo Tomás *Mexico* 31°33N 116°24W **180** A1
Santo Tomás *Peru* 14°26S 72°8W **186** F4
Santo Tomé *Argentina* 28°40S 56°5W **191** B4
Santo Tomé de Guayana = Ciudad
  Guayana *Venezuela* 8°0N 62°30W **186** B6
Santomera *Spain* 38°6N 1°3W **91** G3
Santoña *Spain* 43°29N 3°27W **88** B7
Santorini *Greece* 36°23N 25°27E **99** E7
Santos *Brazil* 24°0S 46°20W **191** A6
Santos, Sierra de los *Spain* 38°7N 5°12W **89** G5
Santos Dumont *Brazil* 22°55S 43°10W **191** A7
Santuario de Aves Laguna
  Colorada △ *Bolivia* 22°10S 67°45W **190** A2
Sanuki *Japan* 34°19N 134°10E **113** G7
Sanur *Indonesia* 8°41S 115°15E **119** K18
Sanwer *India* 22°59N 75°50E **124** H6
Sanxenxo *Spain* 42°24N 8°49W **88** C2
Sanxia Shuiku *China* 30°3N 107°58E **116** B6
Sanxiang *China* 22°21N 113°25E **111** a
Sanya *China* 18°14N 109°29E **117** a
Sanyuan *China* 34°35N 108°58E **114** G5
São Bartolomeu de Messines
  Portugal 37°15N 8°17W **89** H2
São Benedito *Brazil* 4°3S 40°53W **189** A4
São Bento *Brazil* 2°42S 44°50W **189** A2
São Bento do Norte *Brazil* 5°4S 36°2W **189** B3
São Bernardo do Campo
  Brazil 23°45S 46°34W **191** A6
São Borja *Brazil* 28°39S 56°0W **191** B4
São Brás de Alportel
  Portugal 37°8N 7°37W **89** H3
São Caetano *Brazil* 8°21S 36°6W **189** B3
São Carlos *Brazil* 22°0S 47°50W **191** A6
São Cristóvão *Brazil* 11°1S 37°15W **189** C3
São Domingos *Brazil* 13°25S 46°19W **189** C1
São Domingos
  Guinea-Biss. 12°19N 16°13W **138** C1
São Domingos do Maranhão
  Brazil 5°42S 44°22W **189** B2
São Filipe *C. Verde Is.* 15°2N 24°30W **134** b
São Francisco
  Brazil 10°30S 36°24W **189** E3
São Francisco →
  Brazil 10°30S 36°24W **189** E3
São Francisco do Maranhão
  Brazil 6°15S 42°52W **189** B2
São Francisco do Sul
  Brazil 26°15S 48°36W **191** B6
São Gabriel *Brazil* 30°20S 54°20W **191** C5
São Gabriel da Palha
  Brazil 18°47S 40°39W **189** D2
São Gonçalo *Brazil* 22°48S 43°5W **191** A7
São Gotardo *Brazil* 19°19S 46°3W **189** D1
São Hill *Tanzania* 8°20S 35°12E **143** D4
São João *Guinea-Biss.* 11°32N 15°25W **138** C1
São João da Boa Vista
  Brazil 22°0S 46°52W **191** A6
São João da Madeira
  Portugal 40°54N 8°30W **88** D2
São João da Pesqueira
  Portugal 41°8N 7°24W **88** D3
São João da Ponte
  Brazil 15°56S 44°1W **189** D2
São João do Araguaia
  Brazil 5°23S 48°46W **187** E9
São João do Paraíso
  Brazil 15°19S 42°1W **189** D2
São João do Piauí *Brazil* 8°21S 42°15W **189** B3
São João dos Patos
  Brazil 6°30S 43°42W **189** B3
São Joaquim *Brazil* 28°18S 49°56W **191** B6
São Joaquim △ *Brazil* 28°12S 49°37W **191** B6
São Joaquim da Barra
  Brazil 20°55S 47°53W **189** E1

São Jorge, Pta. de
  Madeira 32°50N 16°53W **100** D3
São José *Brazil* 27°38S 48°39W **191** B5
São José da Laje *Brazil* 9°1S 36°3W **189** B3
São José de Mipibu *Brazil* 6°5S 35°15W **189** B3
São José do Norte *Brazil* 32°1S 52°3W **191** C5
São José do Peixe *Brazil* 7°24S 42°34W **189** B2
São José do Rio Preto
  Brazil 20°50S 49°20W **191** A6
São José dos Campos
  Brazil 23°7S 45°52W **191** A6
São Leopoldo *Brazil* 29°50S 51°10W **191** B5
São Lourenço *Brazil* 22°7S 45°3W **191** A6
São Lourenço →
  Brazil 17°53S 57°27W **187** G7
São Lourenço, Pta. de
  Madeira 32°44N 16°39W **100** D3
São Lourenço do Sul
  Brazil 31°22S 51°58W **191** C5
São Luís *Brazil* 2°39S 44°15W **189** A2
São Luís do Curu *Brazil* 3°40S 39°14W **189** A3
São Luís Gonzaga *Brazil* 28°25S 55°0W **191** B5
São Marcos → *Brazil* 18°15S 47°37W **189** D1
São Marcos, B. de *Brazil* 2°0S 44°0W **189** A2
São Martinho da Cortiça
  Portugal 40°18N 8°8W **88** E2
São Mateus *Brazil* 18°44S 39°50W **189** D3
São Mateus → *Brazil* 18°35S 39°44W **189** D3
São Mateus do Sul
  Brazil 25°52S 50°23W **191** B5
São Miguel *Azores* 37°47N 25°30W **134** a
São Miguel do Oeste
  Brazil 26°45S 53°34W **191** B5
São Miguel dos Campos
  Brazil 9°47S 36°5W **189** B3
São Nicolau *C. Verde Is.* 16°20N 24°20W **134** b
São Nicolau → *Brazil* 5°45S 42°2W **189** B2
São Paulo *Atl. Oc.* 0°56N 29°22W **56** F9
São Paulo *Brazil* 23°32S 46°38W **191** A6
São Paulo □ *Brazil* 22°0S 49°0W **191** A6
São Paulo de Olivença
  Brazil 3°27S 68°48W **186** D5
São Pedro *Atl. Oc.* 0°56N 29°22W **56** F9
São Pedro do Sul *Portugal* 40°46N 8°4W **88** E2
São Rafael *Brazil* 5°47S 36°55W **189** B3
São Raimundo das Mangabeiras
  Brazil 7°1S 45°29W **189** B1
São Raimundo Nonato
  Brazil 9°1S 42°42W **189** B2
São Romão *Brazil* 16°22S 45°4W **189** D1
São Roque *Madeira* 32°46N 16°48W **100** D3
São Roque, C. de *Brazil* 5°30S 35°16W **189** B3
São Sebastião, I. de
  Brazil 23°50S 45°18W **191** A6
São Sebastião do Paraíso
  Brazil 20°54S 46°59W **191** A6
São Teotónio *Portugal* 37°30N 8°42W **89** H2
São Tiago *C. Verde Is.* 15°0N 23°40W **134** b
São Tomé *Argentina* 28°40S 56°5W **191** B4
São Tomé *Brazil* 5°58S 36°4W **189** B3
São Tomé
  São Tomé & Príncipe 0°10N 6°39E **132** F4
São Tomé *São Tomé* 0°20S 40°59W **189** E2
São Tomé & Príncipe ■
  Africa 0°12N 6°39E **133** F4
São Vicente *Brazil* 23°57S 46°23W **191** A6
São Vicente *C. Verde Is.* 17°0N 25°0W **134** b
São Vicente *Madeira* 32°48N 17°3W **100** D2
São Vicente, C. de *Portugal* 37°0N 9°0W **89** H1
Saona, I. *Dom. Rep.* 18°10N 68°40W **183** C6
Saône → *France* 45°44N 4°50E **71** C11
Saône-et-Loire □ *France* 46°30N 4°50E **71** F11
Saonek *Indonesia* 0°22S 130°55E **119** E8
Saoura, O. → *Algeria* 29°0N 0°55W **136** C3
Sapam, Ao *Thailand* 8°0N 98°26E **121** a
Sapanca *Turkey* 40°41N 30°16E **104** B4
Sapê *Brazil* 7°6S 35°13W **189** B4
Sape *Indonesia* 8°34S 118°59E **119** F5
Sapele *Nigeria* 5°50N 5°40E **138** D6
Sapelo I. *U.S.A.* 31°25N 81°12W **178** E5
Sapelo Sound *U.S.A.* 31°30N 81°10W **178** E5
Sapes *Greece* 41°2N 25°43E **97** E9
Saphane *Turkey* 39°1N 29°13E **99** B11
Sapi △ *Zimbabwe* 15°48S 29°42E **143** F2
Sapiéntza *Greece* 36°45N 21°43E **98** E3
Sapone *Burkina Faso* 12°3N 1°35W **139** C4
Saposoa *Peru* 6°55S 76°45W **188** B2
Sapotskina *Belarus* 53°49N 23°40E **82** E10
Sapozhok *Russia* 53°59N 40°41E **86** D5
Sapphire *Australia* 23°28S 147°43E **150** C4
Sappho *U.S.A.* 48°4N 124°16W **168** B1
Sapporo *Japan* 43°0N 141°21E **112** C10
Sapt Kosi → *Nepal* 26°32N 86°56E **125** F12
Sapudi *Indonesia* 7°6S 114°20E **119** G16
Sapulpa *U.S.A.* 35°59N 96°5W **176** D6
Saqqez *Iran* 36°15N 46°20E **105** D12
Sar Dasht *Āzarbāyjān-e Gharbī,*
  Iran 36°9N 45°28E **105** D11
Sar Dasht *Khuzestān,*
  Iran 32°32N 48°52E **129** C6
Sar-e Pol *Afghan.* 36°10N 66°0E **128** B4
Sar-e Pol □ *Afghan.* 36°20N 65°50E **128** B4
Sar Gachīneh = Yāsūj
  Iran 30°31N 51°31E **129** D6
Sar Planina *Macedonia* 42°0N 21°0E **96** E4
Šar Planina *Serbia* 42°10N 21°0E **96** D5
Sara *Burkina Faso* 11°40N 3°53W **138** C4
Šara → *Serbia* 42°12N 21°0E **96** D5
Sara Buri = Saraburi
  Thailand 14°30N 100°55E **120** E3
Sarāb *Iran* 37°55N 47°40E **105** D12
Sarābādī *Iran* 33°1N 44°48E **128** C5
Sarābleh *Iran* 33°44N 46°34E **105** F12
Saraburi *Thailand* 14°30N 100°55E **120** E3
Saradiya *India* 21°34N 70°2E **124** J4
Saraféré *Mali* 15°50N 3°40W **138** B4
Saragossa = Zaragoza
  Spain 41°39N 0°53W **90** D3
Saragosso *Ecuador* 3°35S 79°16W **186** D3
Sarahs *Turkmenistan* 36°32N 61°13E **128** B9
Sarai Naurang *Pakistan* 32°50N 70°47E **124** C4
Saraikela *India* 22°42N 85°56E **125** H11
Saraipali *India* 21°20N 82°59E **126** D6
Saraiú *Romania* 44°43N 28°10E **81** F13
Sarajevo *Bos.-H.* 43°52N 18°26E **96** C3
Sarakhs = Sarahs
  Turkmenistan 36°32N 61°13E **128** B9
Sarakhs *Iran* 36°32N 61°9E **108** E8

Saran, Gunung
  Indonesia 0°30S 111°25E **118**
Saranac Lake *U.S.A.* 44°20N 74°10W **175**
Saranac Lakes *U.S.A.* 44°20N 74°28W **175**
Saranda *Tanzania* 5°45S 34°59E **142**
Sarandë *Albania* 39°52N 19°55E **96**
Sarandí del Yi *Uruguay* 33°18S 55°38W **191**
Sarandí Grande
  Uruguay 33°44S 56°20W **190**
Sarangani B. *Phil.* 6°0N 125°13E **119**
Sarangani Is. *Phil.* 5°25N 125°25E **119**
Sarangarh *India* 21°30N 83°5E **126**
Saransk *Russia* 54°10N 45°10E **86**
Sarapul *Russia* 56°28N 53°48E **86**
Sarasota *U.S.A.* 27°20N 82°32W **179**
Sarata *Ukraine* 45°51N 29°41E **81**
Sarata → *Ukraine* 45°51N 29°41E **81**
Saratoga *Calif., U.S.A.* 37°16N 122°2W **170**
Saratoga *Wyo.,*
  U.S.A. 41°27N 106°49W **168**
Saratoga *U.S.A.* 43°0N 73°38W **175**
Saratoga L. *U.S.A.* 43°1N 73°44W **175**
Saratoga Springs
  U.S.A. 43°5N 73°47W **175**
Saratok *Malaysia* 1°55N 111°17E **118**
Saratov *Russia* 51°30N 46°2E **86**
Saratov □ *Russia* 51°50N 46°20E **86**
Saratovskoye Vdkhr.
  Russia 53°10N 48°35E **86**
Sarāvān *Iran* 27°25N 62°15E **129**
Saravane *Laos* 15°43N 106°25E **120**
Sarawak □ *Malaysia* 2°0N 113°0E **118**
Saray *Tekirdağ, Turkey* 41°26N 27°55E **97**
Saray *Van, Turkey* 38°38N 44°9E **105**
Saraya *Senegal* 12°50N 11°45W **138**
Saraycık *Turkey* 39°1N 29°49E **99**
Sarayköy *Turkey* 37°55N 28°54E **99**
Saraylar *Turkey* 40°39N 27°40E **97**
Sarayönü *Turkey* 38°16N 32°24E **104**
Sarbāz *Iran* 26°38N 61°19E **129**
Sarbīsheh *Iran* 32°30N 59°40E **127**
Sárbogárd *Hungary* 46°50N 18°40E **84**
Sarca → *Italy* 45°52N 10°52E **92**
Sarcelles *France* 48°58N 2°23E **73**
Sarda → *India* 27°21N 81°23E **124**
Sardar Sarovar Dam
  India 21°50N 73°50E **124**
Sardarshahr *India* 28°30N 74°29E **124**
Sardegna □ *Italy* 40°0N 9°0E **94**
Sardhana *India* 29°9N 77°39E **124**
Sardina, Pta. *Canary Is.* 28°9N 15°44W **100**
Sardinia = Sardegna □
  Italy 40°0N 9°0E **94**
Sardis *Turkey* 38°28N 27°58E **99**
Sardis *U.S.A.* 32°58N 81°46W **178**
Sārdūīyeh = Dar Mazār
  Iran 29°14N 57°20E **127**
Sarek △ *Sweden* 67°22N 17°35E **60**
Saren *Indonesia* 8°26S 115°34E **119**
S'Arenal *Spain* 39°30N 2°45E **100**
Sarentino *Italy* 46°38N 11°21E **92**
Sarera, G. of *Indonesia* 2°0S 135°0E **146**
Saréyamou *Mali* 16°7N 3°10W **138**
Sargasso Sea *Atl. Oc.* 27°0N 72°0W **158**
Sargent *U.S.A.* 33°26N 84°52W **177**
Sargodha *Pakistan* 32°10N 72°40E **124**
Sarh *Chad* 9°5N 18°23E **134**
Sarhala *Ivory C.* 8°22N 6°8W **138**
Sarhro, Jebel *Morocco* 31°6N 5°0W **136**
Sāri *Iran* 36°30N 53°4E **127**
Sari d'Orcino *France* 42°3N 8°49E **73**
Saria *Greece* 35°54N 27°17E **99**
Saria *India* 21°38N 83°22E **125**
Sariab *Pakistan* 30°6N 66°59E **124**
Saribeyler *Turkey* 39°24N 27°33E **99**
Sarıgöl *Turkey* 38°14N 28°41E **99**
Sarıkamış *Turkey* 40°22N 42°35E **105**
Sarıkaya *Turkey* 39°29N 35°22E **104**
Sarikei *Malaysia* 2°8N 111°30E **118**
Sarıköy *Turkey* 40°12N 27°37E **99**
Sarila *India* 25°46N 79°41E **124**
Sarina *Australia* 21°22S 149°13E **150**
Sariñena *Spain* 41°47N 0°10W **90**
Sariogölan *Turkey* 39°5N 35°59E **104**
Sarita *U.S.A.* 27°13N 97°47W **176**
Sariwon *N. Korea* 38°31N 125°46E **115**
Sariyar Barajı *Turkey* 40°2N 31°33E **104**
Sarıyer *Turkey* 41°10N 29°3E **97**
Sarız *Turkey* 38°16N 36°30E **104**
Sarju → *India* 27°21N 81°23E **124**
Sark *U.K.* 49°25N 2°22W **67**
Sarkad *Hungary* 46°47N 21°23E **84**
Sarkari Tala *India* 27°39N 70°52E **124**
Şarkikaraağaç *Turkey* 38°5N 31°25E **104**
Şarköy *Turkey* 40°36N 27°6E **97**
Sarlat-la-Canéda *France* 44°54N 1°13E **72**
Sărmaşag *Romania* 47°21N 22°50E **84**
Sărmaşu *Romania* 46°45N 24°13E **84**
Sarmi *Indonesia* 1°49S 138°44E **146**
Sarmiento *Argentina* 45°35S 69°5W **192**
Sarmiento, Mt. *Chile* 54°27S 70°50W **192**
Sarmizegetusa *Romania* 45°31N 22°47E **84**
Särna *Sweden* 61°41N 13°8E **64**
Sarnano *Italy* 43°2N 13°18E **93**
Sarnen *Switz.* 46°53N 8°13E **84**
Sarnia *Canada* 42°58N 82°23W **174**
Sarno *Italy* 40°49N 14°37E **95**
Sarnthein = Sarentino
  Italy 46°38N 11°21E **92**
Särö *Sweden* 57°31N 11°57E **66**
Sarolangun *Indonesia* 2°19S 102°42E **118**
Saronikos Kolpos *Greece* 37°45N 23°45E **98**
Saronno *Italy* 45°37N 9°2E **92**
Saros Körfezi *Turkey* 40°30N 26°15E **97**
Sárospatak *Hungary* 48°18N 21°33E **84**
Sarpsborg *Norway* 59°16N 11°7E **63**
Sarqan *Kazakhstan* 45°24N 79°55E **108**
Sarracín *Spain* 42°15N 3°45W **88**
Sarralbe *France* 49°0N 7°1E **71**
Sarre = Saar → *Europe* 49°41N 6°32E **71**
Sarre *Italy* 45°44N 7°14E **92**
Sarre-Union *France* 48°57N 7°4E **71**
Sarrebourg *France* 48°43N 7°3E **71**
Sarreguemines *France* 49°5N 7°4E **71**
Sarria *Spain* 42°49N 7°29W **88**
Sarrión *Spain* 40°9N 0°49W **90**
Sarro *Mali* 13°40N 5°15W **138**
Sarroch *Italy* 39°4N 9°1E **94**
Sarsing *Iraq* 37°3N 43°20E **105**
Sarstedt *Germany* 52°14N 9°52E **76**
Sartell *U.S.A.* 45°37N 94°12W **172**

ène France 41°38N 8°58E 73 G12
he ◻ France 48°10N 0°10E 70 D7
he → France 47°33N 0°31W 70 E6
illy France 48°45N 1°28W 70 D5
hanlı Turkey 38°44N 27°36E 99 C9
leşti Romania 44°25N 26°39E 81 F11
na → Pakistan 26°31N 67°7E 124 F2
r Azerbaijan 39°22N 45°5E 105 C11
ár Hungary 47°15N 16°56E 80 C1
ar India 26°4N 75°0E 124 F6
estān Iran 29°20N 53°10E 129 D7
fjället Sweden 62°42N 13°30E 62 B7
iz → Hungary 46°24N 18°41E 80 D3
-Tash Kyrgyzstan 39°44N 73°15E 109 E8
ch, Mys Ukraine 44°25N 33°45E 85 K7
esik-Atyraū Qumy
zakhstan 45°30N 76°0E 109 C9
kamyshskoye, Ozero =
aryqamysh Köli
rkmenistan 41°56N 57°25E 108 D5
kemer Kazakhstan 43°0N 71°30E 109 D8
kenggir →
zakhstan 48°22N 67°59E 109 C7
köl Kazakhstan 53°20N 65°12E 108 B7
kolskiy Khrebet
jikistan 38°30N 74°30E 109 E8
özek Kazakhstan 44°22N 77°59E 109 D9
qamysh Köli
rkmenistan 41°56N 57°25E 108 D5
shaghan
zakhstan 46°12N 73°38E 109 C8
sū → Kazakhstan 45°12N 66°36E 109 C7
ana Italy 44°7N 9°58E 92 D6
eau France 47°31N 2°48W 70 E4
n Gir India 21°10N 70°36E 124 J4
ram India 24°57N 84°5E 125 G11
bo Japan 33°10N 129°43E 113 H4
r Kangri India 34°50N 77°50E 125 B7
atchewan ◻
nada 54°40N 106°0W 163 C7
atchewan →
nada 53°37N 100°40W 163 C8
atoon Canada 52°10N 106°38W 163 C7
ylakh Russia 71°55N 114°1E 107 B12
aya △ Nic. 13°45N 85°4W 182 D2
lburg S. Africa 26°46S 27°49E 145 C4
n Turkey 38°19N 41°24E 105 C9
vo Russia 54°25N 41°55E 86 C5
andra Ivory C. 4°55N 6°8W 138 E3
andra → Ivory C. 4°58N 6°5W 138 E3
ari Italy 40°43N 8°34E 94 B1
ie Australia 10°2S 142°51E 150 a
nitz Germany 54°29N 13°39E 76 A9
o Marconi Italy 44°24N 11°15E 93 D8
ocorvaro Italy 43°47N 12°30E 93 E9
oferrato Italy 43°26N 12°51E 93 E9
uolo Italy 44°33N 10°47E 92 D7
ago Spain 41°19N 0°21W 90 D4
amala Finland 61°20N 22°54E 84 B2
own Liberia 4°45N 8°27W 138 E3
ad India 18°20N 74°2E 126 E2
k, Ozero Ukraine 45°45N 29°40E 81 E14
qköl Kazakhstan 46°35N 81°0E 109 C10
-Misaki Japan 31°0N 130°40E 113 J5
dougou Mali 12°25N 11°25W 138 C2
kunta ◻ Finland 61°45N 23°0E 60 F20
ma-Soukoura
ory C. 7°55N 4°27W 138 D4
ra India 17°44N 73°58E 126 F1
ra S. Africa 24°29S 31°47E 145 B5
aev Kazakhstan 48°10N 67°31E 109 C7
arwa India 23°55N 84°16E 125 H11
llite Beach U.S.A. 28°10N 80°36W 179 G9
r Sweden 60°21N 15°45E 62 D9
vó Mexico 27°57N 106°7W 180 B3
la → U.S.A. 30°59N 81°29W 178 E8
oo Peru 11°15S 74°25W 188 C3
a Russia 55°3N 59°1E 108 A5
ıala Hills Andhra Pradesh,
dia 19°45N 78°45E 126 E4
ıala Hills Maharashtra,
dia 20°15N 74°40E 126 D2
a India 24°35N 80°50E 125 G9
r Bos.-H. 44°11N 16°37E 93 D13
raljaújhely Hungary 48°25N 21°41E 80 B6
ura △ India 22°40N 78°15E 124 H8
ura Ra. India 21°25N 76°10E 126 D3
up Germany 54°41N 9°36E 76 A5
uma-Sendai Japan 31°50N 130°20E 113 J5
unan-Shotō Japan 30°0N 130°0E 113 K5
ahip Thailand 12°41N 100°54E 120 F3
enapalle India 16°25N 80°6E 127 F5
Mare Romania 47°46N 22°55E 80 C7
Mare ◻ Romania 47°45N 23°0E 80 C8
i Indonesia 3°50S 115°27E 118 E5
n Thailand 6°43N 100°2E 121 J3
rnina → Brazil 12°15S 58°10W 186 F7
ce Argentina 30°5S 58°46W 190 C4
ceda Mexico 25°46N 101°19W 180 B4
cillo Mexico 28°1N 105°17W 180 B3
da Norway 59°40N 6°20E 61 G12
de Brazil 10°56S 40°24W 189 C2
Darkrókur Iceland 65°45N 19°40W 60 D4
di Arabia ■ Asia 26°0N 44°0E 128 B3
erland Germany 51°12N 7°59E 74 C4
geen → Canada 44°30N 81°22W 174 B3
gerties U.S.A. 42°5N 73°57W 175 D11
gues France 44°58N 3°32E 72 D7
gus U.S.A. 34°25N 118°32W 171 L8
ion France 45°41N 0°55W 72 C3
k Centre U.S.A. 45°44N 94°57W 172 C6
k Rapids U.S.A. 45°35N 94°10W 172 C6
gau Germany 48°1N 9°29E 77 G5
ieu France 47°17N 4°14E 71 E11
t France 44°6N 5°24E 73 D9
t Ste. Marie
nada 46°30N 84°20W 164 C3
lt Ste. Marie
S.A. 46°30N 84°21W 173 B11
malkol Kazakhstan 53°17N 68°6E 109 B7
mlaki Indonesia 7°55S 131°20E 119 F8
mur France 47°15N 0°5W 70 E6
ndatti India 15°47N 75°7E 127 G2
nders, C. N.Z. 45°53S 170°45E 155 F5
nders I. Antarctica 57°48S 26°28W 55 B1
nders Pt. Australia 27°52S 125°38E 149 E4
ri Nigeria 11°42N 6°44E 139 C6
rimo Angola 9°40S 20°12E 140 F4
salito U.S.A. 37°51N 122°29W 170 H4
vage, Côte France 45°50N 1°30W 72 C2
Sauveterre-de-Béarn
France 43°24N 0°57W 72 E3
Sauzé-Vaussais France 46°8N 0°8E 72 B4
Savá Honduras 15°32N 86°15W 182 C2
Sava Italy 40°24N 17°33E 95 B10
Sava → Serbia 44°50N 20°26E 80 F5
Savage U.S.A. 47°27N 104°21W 168 C11
Savage I. = Niue ⊠
Pac. Oc. 19°2S 169°54W 157 J11
Savage River Australia 41°31S 145°14E 151 G4
Savai'i Samoa 13°28S 172°24W 147 C11
Savalou Benin 7°57N 1°58E 139 D5
Savane Mozam. 19°37S 35°8E 143 F4
Savanes ◻ Ivory C. 9°30N 6°0W 138 D3
Savanna U.S.A. 42°5N 90°8W 172 D8
Savanna-la-Mar
Jamaica 18°10N 78°10W 182 a
Savannah Ga., U.S.A. 32°5N 81°6W 178 C8
Savannah Mo., U.S.A. 39°56N 94°50W 172 F6
Savannah Tenn.,
U.S.A. 35°14N 88°15W 177 D10
Savannah → U.S.A. 32°2N 80°53W 178 C9
Savannah Beach = Tybee Island
U.S.A. 32°1N 80°51W 178 C9
Savannakhet Laos 16°30N 104°49E 120 D5
Savant L. Canada 50°16N 90°44W 164 B1
Savant Lake Canada 50°14N 90°40W 164 B1
Savantvadi India 15°55N 73°54E 127 G1
Savanur India 14°59N 75°21E 127 G2
Savarkundla = Kundla
India 21°21N 71°25E 124 J4
Săvârşin Romania 46°1N 22°14E 80 D7
Savaştepe Turkey 39°22N 27°42E 99 B9
Savda India 21°9N 75°56E 126 D2
Savé Benin 8°2N 2°29E 139 D5
Save → France 43°47N 1°17E 72 E5
Save → Mozam. 21°16S 34°0E 145 B5
Sāveh Iran 35°2N 50°20E 129 C6
Savelugu Ghana 9°38N 0°54W 139 D4
Savenay France 47°20N 1°55W 70 E5
Săveni Romania 47°57N 26°52E 81 C11
Saverdun France 43°14N 1°34E 72 E5
Saverne France 48°43N 7°20E 71 D14
Savigliano Italy 44°38N 7°40E 92 D4
Savigny-sur-Braye
France 47°53N 0°49E 70 E7
Sávio → Italy 44°19N 12°20E 93 D9
Šavnik Montenegro 42°59N 19°10E 96 D3
Savo Finland 62°45N 27°30E 60 E22
Savoie ◻ France 45°26N 6°25E 73 C10
Savolax = Savo Finland 62°45N 27°30E 60 E22
Savona Italy 44°17N 8°30E 92 D5
Savona U.S.A. 42°17N 77°13W 174 D7
Savonlinna Finland 61°52N 28°53E 84 B5
Savoy = Savoie ◻
France 45°26N 6°25E 73 C10
Şavşat Turkey 41°15N 42°20E 105 B10
Sävsjö Sweden 57°20N 14°40E 63 G8
Savur Turkey 37°34N 40°53E 128 B4
Savusavu Fiji 16°34S 179°15E 154 a
Savusavu B. Fiji 16°45S 179°15E 154 a
Sawahlunto Indonesia 0°40S 100°52E 118 E2
Sawai Indonesia 3°0S 129°5E 119 E7
Sawai Madhopur India 26°0N 76°25E 124 G7
Sawaleke Fiji 17°59S 179°18E 154 a
Sawang Daen Din
Thailand 17°28N 103°28E 120 D4
Sawankhalok Thailand 17°19N 99°50E 120 D2
Sawara Japan 35°55N 140°30E 113 G10
Sawatch Range
U.S.A. 39°0N 106°30W 168 G10
Sawel Mt. U.K. 54°50N 7°2W 64 B4
Sawi Thailand 10°14N 99°5E 121 G2
Sawla Ghana 9°17N 2°25W 138 D4
Sawmills Zimbabwe 19°30S 28°2E 143 F2
Sawtell Australia 30°19S 153°6E 153 A10
Sawtooth ⌓ U.S.A. 44°0N 114°50W 168 D6
Sawtooth Range
U.S.A. 44°3N 114°58W 168 D6
Sawu Indonesia 10°35S 121°50E 119 F6
Sawu Sea Indonesia 9°30S 121°50E 119 F6
Saxby → Australia 18°25S 140°53E 150 B3
Saxmundham U.K. 52°13N 1°30E 67 E9
Saxon Switzerland = Sächsische
Schweiz △ Germany 50°55N 14°10E 76 E10
Saxony = Sachsen ◻
Germany 50°55N 13°10E 76 E9
Saxony, Lower =
Niedersachsen ◻
Germany 52°50N 9°0E 76 C4
Saxton U.S.A. 40°13N 78°15W 174 F6
Say Mali 13°50N 4°57W 138 C4
Say Niger 13°8N 2°22E 139 C5
Saya Nigeria 9°30N 3°18E 139 D5
Sayabec Canada 48°35N 67°41W 165 C6
Sayaboury Laos 19°15N 101°45E 120 C3
Sayán Peru 11°8S 77°12W 188 C2
Sayan, Vostochnyy
Russia 54°0N 96°0E 107 D10
Sayan, Zapadnyy
Russia 52°30N 94°0E 109 B12
Sayanogorsk Russia 53°5N 91°23E 107 D10
Saydā Lebanon 33°35N 35°25E 130 B4
Sayhandulaan = Öldziyt
Mongolia 44°40N 109°1E 114 B5
Sayḩūt Yemen 15°12N 51°10E 131 D5
Saykhin Kazakhstan 48°50N 46°47E 87 F8
Saylac Somalia 11°21N 43°30E 131 E3
Saynshand = Buyant-Uhaa
Mongolia 44°55N 110°11E 114 B6
Sayre Okla., U.S.A. 35°18N 99°38W 176 D5
Sayre Pa., U.S.A. 41°59N 76°32W 175 E8
Sayreville U.S.A. 40°28N 74°22W 175 F10
Sayula Mexico 19°52N 103°36W 180 D4
Say'ūn Yemen 15°56N 48°47E 131 D4
Sayward Canada 50°21N 125°55W 162 C3
Sazanit Albania 40°30N 19°20E 96 F3
Sázava → Czech Rep. 49°53N 14°24E 78 B7
Sazin Pakistan 35°35N 73°30E 125 B5
Sazlika → Bulgaria 41°59N 25°50E 97 E9
Sbeïtla Tunisia 35°12N 9°7E 136 A5
Scaër France 48°2N 3°42W 70 D3
Scafell Pike U.K. 54°27N 3°14W 66 C4
Scalea Italy 39°49N 15°47E 95 C8
Scalloway U.K. 60°9N 1°17W 65 A7
Scalpay U.K. 57°18N 6°0W 65 D3
Scandia Canada 50°20N 112°2W 162 C6
Scandiano Italy 44°36N 10°43E 92 D7
Scandicci Italy 43°45N 11°11E 93 E8
Scandinavia Europe 64°0N 12°0E 60 E15
Scansano Italy 42°41N 11°20E 93 F8
Scapa Flow U.K. 58°53N 3°3W 65 C5
Scappoose U.S.A. 45°45N 122°53W 170 E4
Scarámia, Capo Italy 36°47N 14°29E 95 F7
Scarba U.K. 56°11N 5°43W 65 E3
Scarborough
Trin. & Tob. 11°11N 60°42W 183 D7
Scarborough U.K. 54°17N 0°24W 66 C7
Scargill N.Z. 42°56S 172°58E 155 C7
Scariff I. Ireland 51°44N 10°15W 64 E1
Scarp U.K. 58°1N 7°8W 65 C1
Scarpe-Escaut ⌓ France 50°26N 3°23E 71 B10
Scarsdale Australia 37°41S 143°39E 152 D5
Scebeli = Shabeelle →
Somalia 2°0N 44°0E 131 G3
Šćedro Croatia 43°6N 16°43E 93 E13
Schaal See Germany 53°36N 10°55E 76 B6
Schaalsee ⌓ Germany 53°40N 10°59E 76 B6
Schaffhausen Switz. 47°42N 8°39E 77 H4
Schagen Neths. 52°49N 4°48E 69 B4
Schaghticoke U.S.A. 42°54N 73°35W 175 D11
Schärding Austria 48°27N 13°27E 78 C6
Scharhörn Germany 53°57N 8°24E 76 B4
Scheessel Germany 53°10N 9°29E 76 B5
Schefferville Canada 54°48N 66°50W 165 B6
Scheibbs Austria 48°1N 15°9E 78 C8
Schelde → Belgium 51°15N 4°16E 69 C4
Schell Creek Ra.
U.S.A. 39°25N 114°40W 168 G6
Schellsburg U.S.A. 40°3N 78°39W 174 F6
Schenectady U.S.A. 42°49N 73°57W 175 D11
Schenevus U.S.A. 42°33N 74°50W 175 D10
Scherfede Germany 51°32N 9°2E 76 D5
Schesslitz Germany 49°58N 11°1E 77 F7
Schiedam Neths. 51°55N 4°25E 69 C4
Schiermonnikoog Neths. 53°30N 6°15E 69 A6
Schiermonnikoog △
Neths. 53°30N 6°15E 69 A6
Schiltigheim France 48°35N 7°45E 71 D14
Schinousa Greece 36°53N 25°31E 99 E7
Schio Italy 45°43N 11°21E 93 C8
Schiphol, Amsterdam ✈ (AMS)
Neths. 52°18N 4°45E 69 B4
Schladming Austria 47°23N 13°41E 78 D6
Schlanders = Silandro
Italy 46°38N 10°46E 92 B7
Schlei → Germany 54°40N 10°0E 76 A5
Schleiden Germany 50°31N 6°28E 76 E2
Schleiz Germany 50°35N 11°49E 76 E7
Schleswig Germany 54°31N 9°34E 76 A5
Schleswig-Holstein ◻
Germany 54°30N 9°30E 76 A5
Schlüchtern Germany 50°20N 9°32E 77 E5
Schmalkalden Germany 50°44N 10°26E 76 E6
Schmölln Germany 50°54N 12°19E 76 E8
Schneeberg Austria 47°47N 15°48E 78 D8
Schneeberg Germany 50°35N 12°38E 76 E8
Schneverdingen Germany 53°7N 9°48E 76 B5
Schœlcher Martinique 14°36N 61°7W 182 c
Schoharie U.S.A. 42°40N 74°19W 175 D10
Schoharie Cr. →
U.S.A. 42°57N 74°18W 175 D10
Schokland Neths. 52°38N 5°46E 69 B5
Scholls U.S.A. 45°24N 122°56W 170 E4
Schönberg
Mecklenburg-Vorpommern,
Germany 53°52N 10°56E 76 B6
Schönberg Schleswig-Holstein,
Germany 54°23N 10°21E 76 A6
Schönbuch ⌓ Germany 48°35N 9°2E 77 G5
Schönebeck Germany 52°2N 11°44E 76 C7
Schöngau Germany 47°47N 10°53E 77 H6
Schöningen Germany 52°8N 10°56E 76 C6
Schopfheim Germany 47°38N 7°50E 77 H3
Schorndorf Germany 48°47N 9°32E 77 G5
Schortens Germany 53°31N 7°56E 76 B3
Schouten I. Australia 42°20S 148°20E 151 G4
Schouten Is. = Supiori
Indonesia 1°0S 136°0E 119 E9
Schouwen Neths. 51°43N 3°45E 69 C3
Schramberg Germany 48°13N 8°22E 77 G4
Schrankogel Austria 47°3N 11°7E 78 D4
Schreiber Canada 48°45N 87°20W 164 C2
Schrems Austria 48°47N 15°4E 78 C8
Schrobenhausen
Germany 48°34N 11°16E 77 G7
Schroffenstein Namibia 27°11S 18°42E 144 C2
Schroon Lake U.S.A. 43°50N 73°46W 175 C11
Schruns Austria 47°5N 9°56E 78 D2
Schuler Canada 50°20N 110°6W 163 C6
Schumacher Canada 48°30N 81°16W 164 C3
Schurz U.S.A. 38°57N 118°49W 168 G4
Schuyler U.S.A. 41°27N 97°4W 172 E5
Schuylerville U.S.A. 43°6N 73°35W 175 C11
Schuylkill → U.S.A. 39°53N 75°12W 175 G9
Schuylkill Haven
U.S.A. 40°37N 76°11W 175 F8
Schwabach Germany 49°19N 11°2E 77 F7
Schwaben ◻ Germany 48°15N 10°30E 77 G6
Schwäbisch-Fränkischer Wald ⌓
Germany 49°0N 9°30E 77 G5
Schwäbisch Gmünd
Germany 48°48N 9°47E 77 G5
Schwäbisch Hall Germany 49°6N 9°44E 77 F5
Schwäbische Alb
Germany 48°20N 9°30E 77 G5
Schwabmünchen
Germany 48°10N 10°46E 77 G6
Schwalmstadt Germany 50°55N 9°10E 76 E5
Schwandorf Germany 49°20N 12°7E 77 F8
Schwaner, Pegunungan
Indonesia 1°0S 112°30E 118 E4
Schwanewede Germany 53°14N 8°35E 76 B4
Schwarmstedt Germany 52°39N 9°38E 76 C5
Schwarze Elster →
Germany 51°48N 12°50E 76 D8
Schwarzenberg Germany 50°32N 12°47E 76 E8
Schwarzrand Namibia 25°37S 16°50E 144 C2
Schwarzwald Germany 48°30N 8°20E 77 G4
Schwatka Mts.
U.S.A. 67°20N 156°30W 166 B8
Schwaz Austria 47°20N 11°44E 78 D4
Schwechat Austria 48°8N 16°28E 79 C9
Schwechat, Wien ✈ (VIE)
Austria 48°7N 16°35E 79 C9
Schwedt Germany 53°3N 14°16E 76 B10
Schweinfurt Germany 50°3N 10°14E 77 E6
Schweiz = Switzerland ■
Europe 46°30N 8°0E 77 J4
Schweizer-Reneke
S. Africa 27°11S 25°18E 144 C4
Schwenningen = Villingen-
Schwenningen Germany 48°3N 8°26E 77 G4
Schwerin Germany 53°36N 11°22E 76 B7
Schweriner See Germany 53°43N 11°28E 76 B7
Schwetzingen Germany 49°23N 8°35E 77 F4
Schwyz Switz. 47°2N 8°39E 77 H4
Schwyz ◻ Switz. 47°2N 8°39E 77 H4
Sciacca Italy 37°31N 13°3E 94 E6
Scicli Italy 36°47N 14°42E 95 F7
Sciliar-Catinaccio ⌓
Italy 46°28N 11°35E 93 B8
Scilla Italy 38°15N 15°43E 95 D8
Scilly, Isles of U.K. 49°56N 6°22W 67 H1
Ścinawa Poland 51°25N 16°26E 83 G3
Scione Greece 39°57N 23°36E 96 G7
Scioto → U.S.A. 38°44N 83°1W 173 F12
Scituate U.S.A. 42°12N 70°44W 175 D14
Scobey U.S.A. 48°47N 105°25W 168 B11
Scone Australia 32°5S 150°52E 153 B9
Scone U.K. 56°25N 3°24W 65 E5
Scordia Italy 37°18N 14°51E 95 E7
Scoresby Sund
Greenland 70°28N 21°46W 57 C8
Scoresbysund = Ittoqqortoormiit
Greenland 70°20N 23°0W 57 C8
Scorniceşti Romania 44°34N 24°33E 81 F9
Scotia Calif., U.S.A. 40°29N 124°6W 168 F1
Scotia N.Y., U.S.A. 42°50N 73°58W 175 D11
Scotia Sea Antarctica 56°5S 56°0W 55 B18
Scotland Canada 43°1N 80°22W 174 C4
Scotland ◻ U.K. 57°0N 4°0W 65 E5
Scott Antarctica 77°50S 166°45E 55 D11
Scott, C. Australia 13°30S 129°49E 148 B4
Scott City U.S.A. 38°29N 100°54W 172 F3
Scott Glacier Antarctica 66°15S 100°5E 55 C8
Scott I. Antarctica 67°0S 179°0E 55 C11
Scott Is. Canada 50°48N 128°40W 162 C3
Scott L. Canada 59°55N 106°18W 163 B7
Scott Reef Australia 14°0S 121°50E 148 B3
Scottburgh S. Africa 30°15S 30°47E 145 D5
Scottdale U.S.A. 40°6N 79°35W 174 F5
Scottish Borders ◻ U.K. 55°35N 2°50W 65 F6
Scotts Head Australia 30°45S 153°0E 153 A10
Scotts Valley U.S.A. 37°3N 122°1W 170 H4
Scottsbluff U.S.A. 41°52N 103°40W 172 E2
Scottsboro U.S.A. 34°40N 86°2W 177 D11
Scottsburg U.S.A. 38°41N 85°47W 173 F11
Scottsdale Australia 41°9S 147°31E 151 G4
Scottsdale U.S.A. 33°40N 111°53W 169 K8
Scottsville Ky., U.S.A. 36°45N 86°11W 172 G10
Scottsville N.Y., U.S.A. 43°2N 77°47W 174 C7
Scottville U.S.A. 43°58N 86°17W 172 D10
Scranton U.S.A. 41°25N 75°40W 175 E9
Screven U.S.A. 31°29N 82°1W 178 D7
Scugog, L. Canada 44°10N 78°55W 174 B6
Sculeni Moldova 47°20N 27°37E 81 C12
Scunthorpe U.K. 53°36N 0°39W 66 D7
Scuol Schuls Switz. 46°48N 10°17E 77 J6
Scutari = Shkodër
Albania 42°4N 19°32E 96 D3
Scutari = Üsküdar Turkey 41°1N 29°0E 97 F13
Sea Is. U.S.A. 31°30N 81°7W 178 D9
Sea Lake Australia 35°28S 142°55E 152 C5
Seabra Brazil 12°25S 41°46W 189 C2
Seabrook, L. Australia 30°55S 119°40E 149 F2
Seaford U.K. 50°47N 0°7E 67 G8
Seaford U.S.A. 38°39N 75°37W 173 F16
Seaforth Australia 20°55S 148°57E 150 b
Seaforth Canada 43°35N 81°25W 174 C3
Seaforth, L. U.K. 57°52N 6°36W 65 D2
Seagraves U.S.A. 32°57N 102°34W 176 E3
Seaham U.K. 54°50N 1°20W 66 C6
Seal → Canada 59°4N 94°48W 163 B10
Seal L. Canada 54°20N 61°30W 165 B7
Seale U.S.A. 32°18N 85°10W 178 C4
Sealy U.S.A. 29°47N 96°9W 176 G6
Searchlight U.S.A. 35°28N 114°55W 171 K12
Searcy U.S.A. 35°15N 91°44W 176 D9
Searles L. U.S.A. 35°44N 117°21W 171 K9
Seascale U.K. 54°24N 3°29W 66 C4
Seaside Calif., U.S.A. 36°37N 121°50W 170 J5
Seaside Oreg., U.S.A. 46°0N 123°56W 170 E3
Seaspray Australia 38°25S 147°15E 153 E7
Seattle U.S.A. 47°36N 122°19W 170 C4
Seattle-Tacoma Int. ✈ (SEA)
U.S.A. 47°27N 122°18W 170 C4
Seaward Kaikoura Ra.
N.Z. 42°10S 173°44E 155 C8
Seba Indonesia 10°29S 121°50E 148 B3
Sebago L. U.S.A. 43°52N 70°34W 175 C14
Sebago Lake U.S.A. 43°51N 70°34W 175 C14
Sebastian U.S.A. 27°49N 80°28W 179 H9
Sebastián Vizcaíno, B.
Mexico 28°0N 114°30W 180 B2
Sebastopol = Sevastopol
Ukraine 44°35N 33°30E 85 K7
Sebastopol U.S.A. 38°24N 122°49W 170 G4
Sebba Burkina Faso 13°35N 0°32E 139 C5
Sebdou Algeria 34°38N 1°19W 136 B3
Sébékoro Mali 12°58N 9°0W 138 C3
Seben Turkey 40°24N 31°34E 104 B4
Sebeş Romania 45°58N 23°34E 81 E8
Sebeşului, Munţii
Romania 45°36N 23°40E 81 E8
Sebewaing U.S.A. 43°44N 83°27W 173 D12
Sebezh Russia 56°14N 28°22E 84 D5
Sebezhsky △ Russia 56°16N 28°30E 84 D5
Sebha = Sabhā Libya 27°9N 14°29E 135 C8
Sébi Mali 15°50N 4°12W 138 B4
Şebinkarahisar Turkey 40°22N 38°28E 105 B8
Sebino, L. di = Iseo, L. d'
Italy 45°43N 10°4E 92 C7
Sebiş Romania 46°23N 22°13E 80 D7
Sebnitz Germany 50°58N 14°15E 76 E10
Sebou, Oued →
Morocco 34°16N 6°40W 136 B2
Sebring Fla., U.S.A. 27°30N 81°27W 179 H8
Sebring Ohio, U.S.A. 40°55N 81°2W 174 F3
Sebringville Canada 43°24N 81°4W 174 C3
Sebta = Ceuta N. Afr. 35°52N 5°18W 134 A4
Sebuku Indonesia 3°30S 116°25E 118 E5
Sečanj Serbia 45°25N 20°47E 80 E5
Secchia → Italy 45°4N 11°0E 92 C8
Sechelt Canada 49°25N 123°42W 162 D4
Sechura Peru 5°39S 80°50W 188 B1
Sechura, Desierto de
Peru 6°0S 80°30W 188 B1
Seclin France 50°33N 3°2E 71 B10
Secondigny France 46°37N 0°26W 70 F6
Sečovce Slovak Rep. 48°42N 21°40E 79 C14
Secretary I. N.Z. 45°15S 166°56E 155 F1
Secunderabad India 17°28N 78°30E 126 F4
Security U.S.A. 38°45N 104°45W 168 G11
Sedalia U.S.A. 38°42N 93°14W 172 F7
Sedam India 17°11N 77°17E 126 E3
Sedan Australia 34°34S 139°19E 152 C3
Sedan France 49°43N 4°57E 71 C11
Sedan U.S.A. 37°8N 96°11W 172 G5
Sedano Spain 42°43N 3°49W 88 C7
Sedbergh U.K. 54°20N 2°31W 66 C5
Seddon N.Z. 41°40S 174°7E 155 B9
Seddonville N.Z. 41°33S 172°1E 155 B7
Sedé Boqér Israel 30°52N 34°47E 130 E3
Sedeh Fārs, Iran 30°45N 52°11E 129 D7
Sedeh Khorāsān, Iran 33°20N 59°14E 129 C8
Séderon France 44°12N 5°32E 73 D9
Sederot Israel 31°32N 34°37E 130 D3
Sédhiou Senegal 12°44N 15°30W 138 C1
Sedico Italy 46°8N 12°6E 93 B9
Sedlčany Czech Rep. 49°40N 14°25E 78 B7
Sedley Canada 50°10N 104°0W 163 C8
Sedona U.S.A. 34°52N 111°46W 169 J8
Sedova, Pik Russia 73°29N 54°58E 106 B6
Sedrata Algeria 36°7N 7°31E 136 A5
Sedro-Woolley U.S.A. 48°30N 122°14W 170 B4
Šeduva Lithuania 55°45N 23°45E 82 C10
Sędziszów Poland 50°35N 20°4E 83 H7
Sędziszów Małapolski
Poland 50°5N 21°45E 83 H8
Seebad Ahlbeck
Germany 53°56N 14°10E 76 B10
Seefeld in Tirol Austria 47°19N 11°13E 78 D4
Seehausen Germany 52°54N 11°45E 76 C7
Seeheim Namibia 26°50S 17°45E 144 C2
Seeheim-Jugenheim
Germany 49°49N 8°40E 77 F4
Seeis Namibia 22°29S 17°39E 144 B2
Seekoei → S. Africa 30°18S 25°1E 144 D4
Seeley's Bay Canada 44°29N 76°14W 175 B8
Seelow Germany 52°32N 14°23E 76 C10
Sées France 48°38N 0°10E 70 D7
Seesen Germany 51°54N 10°10E 76 D6
Seevetal Germany 53°26N 10°1E 76 B6
Seewinkel = Neusiedler See-
Seewinkel △ Austria 47°50N 16°45E 79 D9
Şefaatli Turkey 39°30N 34°45E 104 C6
Seferihisar Turkey 38°10N 26°50E 99 C8
Séféto Mali 14°8N 9°49W 138 C3
Sefophe Botswana 22°11S 27°58E 145 B4
Sefrou Morocco 33°52N 4°52W 136 B3
Sefton N.Z. 43°15S 172°41E 155 D7
Sefwi Bekwai Ghana 6°10N 2°25W 138 D4
Segamat Malaysia 2°30N 102°50E 121 L4
Şegarcea Romania 44°6N 23°43E 81 F8
Ségbana Benin 10°55N 3°42E 139 C5
Segbwema S. Leone 8°0N 11°0W 138 D2
Segersta Sweden 61°16N 16°39E 62 C10
Segesta Italy 37°56N 12°50E 94 E5
Seget Indonesia 1°24S 130°58E 119 E8
Seggueur, O. → Algeria 32°14N 1°48E 136 B4
Segmon Sweden 59°17N 13°3E 62 E7
Segonzac France 45°36N 0°14W 72 C3
Segorbe Spain 39°50N 0°30W 90 F4
Ségou Mali 13°30N 6°16W 138 C3
Ségou ◻ Mali 14°0N 6°0W 138 C3
Segovia = Coco →
Cent. Amer. 15°0N 83°8W 182 D3
Segovia Spain 40°57N 4°10W 88 E6
Segovia ◻ Spain 40°55N 4°10W 88 E6
Segré France 47°40N 0°52W 70 E6
Segre → Spain 41°40N 0°43E 90 D5
Seguam I. U.S.A. 52°19N 172°30W 166 E5
Séguéla Ivory C. 7°55N 6°40W 138 D3
Séguélon Ivory C. 9°13N 7°7W 138 D3
Séguénéga Burkina Faso 13°25N 1°58W 139 C4
Seguin U.S.A. 29°34N 97°58W 176 G6
Segundo → Argentina 30°53S 62°44W 190 C3
Segura → Spain 38°3N 0°44W 91 G4
Segura, Sierra de Spain 38°5N 2°45W 91 G2
Seh Konj, Kūh-e Iran 30°6N 57°30E 129 D8
Seh Qal'eh Iran 33°40N 58°24E 129 C8
Sehitwa Botswana 20°30S 22°30E 144 B3
Sehlabathebe △ Lesotho 29°53S 29°7E 145 C4
Sehore India 23°10N 77°5E 124 H7
Sehwan Pakistan 26°28N 67°53E 124 F2
Seia Portugal 40°25N 7°42W 88 E3
Şeica Mare Romania 46°1N 24°7E 81 D9
Seikan Tunnel Japan 41°28N 140°10E 112 D10
Seil U.K. 56°18N 5°38W 65 E3
Seiland Norway 70°25N 23°15E 60 A20
Seilhac France 45°22N 1°43E 72 C5
Seiling U.S.A. 36°9N 98°56W 176 C5
Seille → Moselle, France 49°7N 6°11E 71 C13
Seille → Saône-et-Loire,
France 46°31N 4°57E 71 F11
Sein, Î. de France 48°2N 4°52W 70 D2
Seinäjoki Finland 62°40N 22°51E 60 E20
Seine → France 49°26N 0°26E 70 C7
Seine, B. de la France 49°40N 0°40W 70 C6
Seine-et-Marne ◻ France 48°45N 3°0E 71 D10
Seine-Maritime ◻ France 49°40N 1°0E 70 C7
Seine-St-Denis ◻ France 48°58N 2°24E 71 D9
Seini Romania 47°44N 23°21E 81 C8
Seirijai Lithuania 54°14N 23°49E 82 D10
Seistan = Sīstān Asia 30°50N 61°0E 129 D9
Seistan, Daryācheh-ye = Sīstan,
Daryācheh-ye Iran 31°0N 61°0E 129 D9
Seitseminen △ Finland 61°55N 23°25E 60 F20
Sejerø Denmark 55°54N 11°9E 63 J5
Sejerø Bugt Denmark 55°53N 11°15E 63 J5
Sejny Poland 54°6N 23°21E 82 D10
Sekayu Indonesia 2°51S 103°51E 118 E2
Seke Tanzania 3°20S 33°31E 142 C3
Sekenke Tanzania 4°18S 34°11E 142 C3
Sekhira Tunisia 34°20N 10°5E 136 B6
Seki Turkey 36°48N 29°33E 99 E11
Sekondi-Takoradi Ghana 4°58N 1°45W 138 E4
Sekseūil Kazakhstan 47°5N 61°9E 108 C6
Seksna Russia 59°13N 38°30E 84 C10
Sekudai Malaysia 1°32N 103°39E 121 d
Sekuma Botswana 24°36S 23°50E 144 B3
Selah U.S.A. 46°39N 120°32W 168 C3
Selama Malaysia 5°12N 100°42E 121 K3
Selangor ◻ Malaysia 3°10N 101°30E 121 L3
Selárgius Italy 39°16N 9°10E 94 C2
Selaru Indonesia 8°9S 131°0E 119 F8
Selatan, Selat Malaysia 5°15N 100°20E 121 c
Selawik L. U.S.A. 66°30N 160°45W 166 B7
Selb Germany 50°10N 12°7E 77 E8
Selby U.K. 53°47N 1°5W 66 D6
Selby U.S.A. 45°31N 100°2W 172 C3
Selca Croatia 43°20N 16°50E 93 E13
Selçuk Turkey 37°56N 27°22E 99 D9
Selden U.S.A. 39°33N 100°34W 172 F3
Sele → Italy 40°29N 14°56E 95 B7
Selebi-Phikwe
Botswana 21°58S 27°48E 145 B4
Selemdzha → Russia 51°42N 128°53E 107 D13
Selendi Manisa, Turkey 38°43N 28°50E 99 C10
Selendi Manisa, Turkey 38°46N 27°53E 99 C9
Selenga = Selenge Mörön →
Asia 52°16N 106°16E 110 A10
Selenge Mörön →
Asia 52°16N 106°16E 110 A10
Selenicë Albania 40°33N 19°39E 96 F3
Selenter See Germany 54°18N 10°26E 76 A6
Sélestat France 48°16N 7°26E 71 D14
Seletan, Tanjung
Indonesia 4°10S 114°40E 118 E4
Selevac Serbia 44°28N 20°52E 96 B4
Sélibabi Mauritania 15°10N 12°15W 138 B2
Seliger, Ozero Russia 57°15N 33°0E 84 D7
Seligman U.S.A. 35°20N 112°53W 169 J7
Şelim Turkey 40°30N 42°46E 105 B10
Selîma Sudan 21°22N 29°19E 137 C2
Selimiye Turkey 37°24N 27°40E 99 D9
Selinda Spillway →
Botswana 18°35S 23°10E 144 A3
Sélingué, L. de Mali 11°37N 8°14W 138 C3
Selinsgrove U.S.A. 40°48N 76°52W 174 F8
Selizharovo Russia 56°51N 33°27E 84 D7
Selkirk Man., Canada 50°10N 96°55W 163 C9
Selkirk Ont., Canada 42°49N 79°56W 174 D5
Selkirk U.K. 55°33N 2°50W 65 F6
Selkirk I. = Horse I.
Canada 53°20N 99°6W 163 C9
Selkirk Mts. Canada 51°15N 117°40W 160 G8
Sellafield U.K. 54°25N 3°29W 66 C4
Sellia Greece 35°12N 24°23E 101 D6
Sellières France 46°50N 5°32E 71 F12
Sells U.S.A. 31°55N 111°53W 169 L8
Sellye Hungary 45°52N 17°51E 80 E2
Selma Ala., U.S.A. 32°25N 87°1W 177 E11
Selma Calif., U.S.A. 36°34N 119°37W 170 J7
Selma N.C., U.S.A. 35°32N 78°17W 177 D15
Selmer U.S.A. 35°10N 88°36W 177 D10
Selongey France 47°36N 5°11E 71 E12
Selouane Morocco 35°7N 2°57W 136 A3
Selous ⌓ Tanzania 8°37S 37°42E 143 D4
Selowandoma Falls
Zimbabwe 21°15S 31°50E 143 G3
Selpele Indonesia 0°1S 130°5E 119 E8
Selsey Bill U.K. 50°43N 0°47W 67 G7
Seltso Russia 53°22N 34°4E 84 F8
Seltz France 48°54N 8°4E 71 D15
Selu Indonesia 7°32S 130°55E 119 F8
Sélune → France 48°38N 1°22W 70 D5
Selva = La Selva del Camp
Spain 41°13N 1°8E 90 D6
Selva Argentina 29°50S 62°0W 190 B3
Selva Spain 39°46N 2°54E 100 B9
Selva Lancandona = Montes
Azules ⌓ Mexico 16°21N 91°3W 181 D6
Selvagens, Ilhas
Madeira 30°5N 15°55W 134 B2
Selvas Brazil 6°30S 67°0W 188 B4
Selwyn L. Canada 60°0N 104°30W 163 B8
Selwyn Mts. Canada 63°0N 130°0W 160 E5
Selwyn Ra. Australia 21°10S 140°0E 150 C3
Selyatyn Ukraine 47°50N 25°12E 81 C10
Seman → Albania 40°47N 19°30E 96 F3
Semarang Indonesia 7°0S 110°26E 118 F4
Semarapura = Klungkung
Indonesia 8°32S 115°24E 119 K18
Sembabule Uganda 0°4S 31°25E 142 C3
Sembawang Singapore 1°27N 103°50E 121 d
Sembung Indonesia 8°28S 115°11E 119 J18
Şemdinli Turkey 37°18N 44°35E 105 D11
Sémé Senegal 15°4N 13°41W 138 B2
Semenic-Cheile Caraşului △
Romania 45°8N 22°5E 80 E7
Semenivka Chernihiv,
Ukraine 52°8N 32°36E 85 F7
Semenivka Kremenchuk,
Ukraine 49°37N 33°10E 85 H7
Semenov Russia 56°43N 44°30E 86 B7
Semeru Indonesia 8°4S 112°55E 119 H15
Semey Kazakhstan 50°30N 80°10E 109 B10
Semikarakorskiy Russia 47°31N 40°48E 87 G5
Semiluki Russia 51°41N 39°2E 85 G10
Seminoe Res. U.S.A. 42°9N 106°55W 168 E10
Seminole Fla., U.S.A. 27°50N 82°47W 179 H7
Seminole Okla., U.S.A. 35°14N 96°41W 176 D6
Seminole Tex., U.S.A. 32°43N 102°39W 176 E3
Seminole, L. U.S.A. 30°43N 84°52W 178 E5
Seminole Draw →
U.S.A. 32°27N 102°20W 176 E3
Semipalatinsk = Semey
Kazakhstan 50°30N 80°10E 109 B10
Semirara Is. Phil. 12°0N 121°20E 119 B6
Semisopochnoi I.
U.S.A. 51°55N 179°36E 166 E3
Semitau Indonesia 0°29N 111°57E 118 D4
Semliki △ Uganda 0°49N 30°4E 142 B3
Semmering P. Austria 47°41N 15°45E 78 D8
Semnān Iran 35°40N 53°23E 129 C7
Semnān ◻ Iran 36°0N 54°0E 129 C7
Semporna Malaysia 4°30N 118°33E 119 D5
Semuda Indonesia 2°51S 112°58E 118 E4
Semur-en-Auxois France 47°30N 4°20E 71 E11
Sen → Cambodia 12°32N 104°28E 120 F5
Sena Bolivia 11°32S 67°11W 188 C4
Senā Iran 28°27N 51°36E 129 D6
Sena Mozam. 17°25S 35°0E 143 F4
Sena → Bolivia 11°31S 67°11W 188 C4
Sena Madureira Brazil 9°5S 68°45W 188 B4
Senador Pompeu Brazil 5°40S 39°20W 189 B3
Senaki Georgia 42°15N 42°1E 87 J6
Senang, Pulau Singapore 1°11N 103°52E 121 d
Senanga Zambia 16°7S 23°16E 141 H4
Senatobia U.S.A. 34°37N 89°58W 177 D10
Sencelles Spain 39°39N 2°54E 100 B9
Sendai = Satsuma-Sendai
Japan 31°50N 130°20E 113 J5
Sendai Japan 38°15N 140°53E 112 E10
Sendai-Wan Japan 38°15N 141°0E 112 E10
Senden Bayern, Germany 48°19N 10°4E 77 G6
Senden Nordrhein-Westfalen,
Germany 51°52N 7°22E 76 D3
Sendhwa India 21°41N 75°6E 124 J6
Sendurjana India 21°32N 78°17E 126 D4
Sene → Ghana 7°30N 0°33W 139 D4
Senec Slovak Rep. 48°12N 17°23E 79 C10

Seneca *U.S.A.* 34°41N 82°57W **177** D13
Seneca Falls *U.S.A.* 42°55N 76°48W **175** D8
Seneca L. *U.S.A.* 42°40N 76°54W **174** D8
Senecaville L. *U.S.A.* 39°55N 81°25W **174** G3
Senegal ■ *W. Afr.* 14°30N 14°30W **138** C2
Sénégal → *W. Afr.* 15°48N 16°32W **138** B1
Senegambia *Africa* 12°45N 12°0W **132** E2
Senekal *S. Africa* 28°20S 27°36E **145** C4
Senftenberg *Germany* 51°32N 14°0E **76** D10
Senga Hill *Zambia* 9°19S 31°11E **143** D3
Senge Khambab = Indus →
  Pakistan 24°20N 67°47E **124** G2
Sengerema *Tanzania* 2°42S 32°35E **142** C3
Senggigi *Indonesia* 8°29S 116°2E **119** J19
Sengiley *Russia* 53°58N 48°46E **86** D9
Sengua → *Zimbabwe* 17°7S 28°5E **143** F2
Senguerr → *Argentina* 45°35S 68°50W **192** C3
Senhor-do-Bonfim
  Brazil 10°30S 40°10W **189** C2
Senica *Slovak Rep.* 48°41N 17°25E **79** C10
Senigállia *Italy* 43°43N 13°13E **93** E10
Senio → *Italy* 44°35N 12°15E **93** D9
Senirkent *Turkey* 38°6N 30°33E **99** C12
Senise *Italy* 40°9N 16°17E **95** B9
Senj *Croatia* 45°0N 14°58E **93** D11
Senja *Norway* 69°25N 17°30E **60** B7
Senkaku-Shotō
  E. China Sea 25°45N 123°30E **113** M1
Senlis *France* 49°13N 2°35E **71** C9
Senmonorom
  Cambodia 12°27N 107°12E **120** F6
Senneterre *Canada* 48°25N 77°15W **164** C4
Senno *Belarus* 54°45N 29°43E **84** E5
Sénnori *Italy* 40°47N 8°35E **94** B1
Seno *Laos* 16°35N 104°50E **120** D5
Senoia *U.S.A.* 33°18N 84°33W **178** B5
Senonches *France* 48°34N 1°2E **70** D8
Senorbì *Italy* 39°32N 9°8E **94** C2
Senožeče *Slovenia* 45°43N 14°3E **93** C11
Senqu = Orange →
  S. Africa 28°41S 16°28E **144** C2
Sens *France* 48°11N 3°15E **71** D10
Senta *Serbia* 45°55N 20°3E **80** E5
Sentery = Lubao
  Dem. Rep. of the Congo 5°17S 25°42E **142** D2
Sentinel *U.S.A.* 32°52N 113°13W **169** K7
Šentjur *Slovenia* 46°14N 15°24E **93** B12
Sentosa *Singapore* 1°16N 103°50E **121** d2
Senwabarana *S. Africa* 23°17S 29°7E **145** B4
Senya Beraku *Ghana* 5°28N 0°31W **139** D4
Seo de Urgel = La Seu d'Urgell
  Spain 42°22N 1°23E **90** C6
Seogwipo *S. Korea* 33°13N 126°34E **115** H14
Seohara *India* 29°15N 78°33E **125** E8
Seonath → *India* 21°44N 82°28E **125** J10
Seondha *India* 26°9N 78°48E **125** F8
Seongnam *S. Korea* 37°26N 127°8E **115** F14
Seoni *India* 22°5N 79°30E **125** H8
Seoni Malwa *India* 22°27N 77°28E **124** H8
Seonsan *S. Korea* 36°14N 128°17E **115** F15
Seoriuarayan *India* 21°45N 82°34E **126** D6
Seosan *S. Korea* 36°47N 126°27E **115** F14
Seoul *S. Korea* 37°31N 126°58E **115** F14
Separation Pt. *N.Z.* 40°47S 172°59E **155** A7
Sepīdān *Iran* 30°20N 52°5E **129** D7
Sepo-ri *N. Korea* 38°57N 127°25E **115** E14
Sępólno Krajeńskie
  Poland 53°26N 17°30E **82** E4
Sepone *Laos* 16°45N 106°13E **120** D6
Sępopol *Poland* 54°16N 21°2E **82** D8
Sept-Îles *Canada* 50°13N 66°22W **165** B6
Septemvri *Bulgaria* 42°13N 24°6E **97** D8
Sepúlveda *Spain* 41°18N 3°45W **88** D7
Sequeros *Spain* 40°31N 6°2W **88** E4
Sequim *U.S.A.* 48°5N 123°6W **170** B3
Sequoia ∆ *U.S.A.* 36°30N 118°30W **170** J8
Serafimovich *Russia* 49°36N 42°43E **86** F6
Seraing *Belgium* 50°35N 5°32E **69** D5
Serakhis → *Cyprus* 35°13N 32°55E **101** D11
Seram *Indonesia* 3°10S 129°0E **119** E7
Seram Sea *Indonesia* 2°30S 128°30E **119** E7
Serampore = Shrirampur
  India 22°44N 88°21E **125** H13
Serang *Indonesia* 6°8S 106°10E **119** G12
Serangoon *Singapore* 1°23N 103°54E **121** d2
Serasan *Indonesia* 2°29N 109°4E **118** D3
Seravezza *Italy* 43°59N 10°13E **92** E7
Şerbettar *Turkey* 41°27N 26°46E **97** E10
Serbia ■ *Europe* 43°20N 20°0E **96** C4
Šercaia *Romania* 45°49N 25°9E **81** E10
Serdar *Turkmenistan* 39°4N 56°23E **128** B8
Serdobsk *Russia* 52°28N 44°10E **86** D7
Serebryansk
  Kazakhstan 49°41N 83°17E **109** C10
Sered *Slovak Rep.* 48°17N 17°44E **79** C10
Seredka *Russia* 58°12N 28°10E **84** C5
Serednye *Ukraine* 48°32N 22°30E **80** B7
Şereflikoçhisar *Turkey* 38°56N 33°32E **104** C5
Seregno *Italy* 45°39N 9°12E **92** C6
Seremban *Malaysia* 2°43N 101°53E **121** L3
Serengeti ∆ *Tanzania* 2°11S 35°0E **142** C3
Serengeti Plain *Tanzania* 2°40S 35°0E **142** C4
Serenje *Zambia* 13°14S 30°15E **143** E3
Seret → *Ukraine* 48°37N 25°52E **81** B10
Sereth = Siret →
  Romania 45°24N 28°1E **81** E12
Sergach *Russia* 55°30N 45°30E **86** C7
Sergeevka *Kazakhstan* 53°52N 67°24E **109** B7
Sergen *Turkey* 41°41N 27°42E **97** E11
Sergeya Kirova, Ostrova
  Russia 77°30N 89°0E **107** B10
Sergino *Russia* 62°25N 65°12E **106** C7
Sergipe □ *Brazil* 10°30S 37°30W **189** D3
Sergiyev Posad *Russia* 56°20N 38°10E **84** D10
Serhetabat
  Turkmenistan 35°20N 62°18E **128** C9
Seria *Brunei* 4°37N 114°23E **118** D4
Serian *Malaysia* 1°10N 110°31E **118** D4
Seriate *Italy* 45°41N 9°43E **92** C6
Sericho *Kenya* 1°5N 39°5E **142** B4
Sérifontaine *France* 49°20N 1°45E **71** C8
Serifos *Greece* 37°9N 24°30E **98** D6
Sérignan *France* 43°17N 3°17E **72** E7
Sérigny → *Canada* 56°47N 66°0W **165** A6
Serik *Turkey* 36°55N 31°7E **104** D4
Seringapatam Reef
  Australia 13°38S 122°5E **148** B3
Serinhisar *Turkey* 37°15N 29°19E **99** D11
Seririt *Indonesia* 8°12S 114°56E **119** J17
Serishābād *Iran* 35°14N 47°36E **105** E12
Serkout *Algeria* 23°56N 6°47E **136** D5

Sermaize-les-Bains
  France 48°47N 4°54E **71** D11
Sermata *Indonesia* 8°15S 128°50E **119** F7
Sermersooq □ *Greenland* 68°0N 40°0W **57** D7
Sermersuaq *Greenland* 79°30N 62°0W **57** B4
Sérmide *Italy* 45°0N 11°18E **93** D8
Sernovodsk *Russia* 53°58N 51°16E **86** D10
Sernur *Russia* 56°52N 49°2E **86** B9
Serock *Poland* 52°31N 21°4E **83** F8
Serón *Spain* 37°20N 2°29W **91** H2
Seròs *Spain* 41°27N 0°24E **90** D5
Serouenout *Algeria* 24°18N 7°25E **136** D5
Serov *Russia* 59°29N 60°35E **106** D7
Serowe *Botswana* 22°25S 26°43E **144** B4
Serpa *Portugal* 37°57N 7°38W **89** H3
Serpeddì, Pta. *Italy* 39°22N 9°18E **94** C2
Serpentara *Italy* 39°8N 9°36E **94** C2
Serpentine Lakes
  Australia 28°30S 129°10E **149** E4
Serpent's Mouth = Sierpe, Bocas
  de la *Venezuela* 10°0N 61°30W **187** L15
Serpis → *Spain* 38°59N 0°9W **91** G4
Serpneve *Ukraine* 46°18N 29°1E **81** D14
Serpukhov *Russia* 54°55N 37°28E **84** E9
Serra *Brazil* 20°7S 40°18W **189** E2
Serra da Canastra ∆
  Brazil 20°3S 46°50W **189** E1
Serra da Capivara ∆
  Brazil 8°42S 42°15W **189** B2
Serra da Estrela ≃
  Portugal 40°27N 7°33W **88** E3
Serra das Confusões ∆
  Brazil 8°50S 43°50W **189** B2
Serra de Mesa, Barragem de
  Brazil 14°30S 48°30W **189** C1
Serra do Cipó ∆ *Brazil* 19°14S 43°23W **189** D2
Serra do Divisor ∆ *Brazil* 8°3S 73°29W **188** B3
Serra do Navio *Brazil* 0°59N 52°3W **187** C8
Serra do Salitre *Brazil* 19°6S 46°41W **189** E1
Serra São Bruno *Italy* 38°35N 16°20E **95** D9
Serra Talhada *Brazil* 7°59S 38°18W **189** B3
Serradilla *Spain* 39°50N 6°9W **88** F4
Serramanna *Italy* 39°25N 8°55E **94** C1
Serrania San Luis ∆
  Paraguay 22°35S 57°22W **190** A4
Serrania San Rafael ∆
  Paraguay 26°30S 56°0W **191** B4
Serras d'Aire e Candeeiros ∆
  Portugal 39°31N 8°48W **89** F2
Serrat, C. *Tunisia* 37°14N 9°10E **136** A5
Serravalle Scrívia *Italy* 44°43N 8°51E **92** D5
Serre-Ponçon, L. de
  France 44°22N 6°20E **73** D10
Serrejón *Spain* 39°49N 5°48W **88** F5
Serres *France* 44°26N 5°43E **73** D9
Serres *Greece* 41°5N 23°31E **96** E7
Serrezuela *Argentina* 30°40S 65°20W **190** C2
Serrinha *Brazil* 11°39S 39°0W **189** C3
Serrita *Brazil* 7°56S 39°19W **189** B3
Sersale *Italy* 39°1N 16°43E **95** C9
Sertã *Portugal* 39°48N 8°6W **88** F2
Sertânia *Brazil* 8°5S 37°20W **189** B3
Sertanópolis *Brazil* 23°4S 51°2W **191** A5
Sêrtar *China* 32°20N 100°41E **116** A3
Serua *Indonesia* 6°18S 130°1E **119** F8
Serui *Indonesia* 1°53S 136°10E **119** E9
Serule *Botswana* 21°57S 27°20E **144** B4
Servia *Greece* 40°11N 22°0E **96** F6
Serzedelo *Portugal* 41°24N 8°14W **88** D2
Ses Salines *Spain* 39°21N 3°3E **100** B10
Sese Is. *Uganda* 0°20S 32°20E **142** C3
Sesepe *Indonesia* 1°30S 127°59E **119** E7
Sesfontein *Namibia* 19°7S 13°39E **144** A1
Sesheke *Zambia* 17°29S 24°13E **144** A3
Sésia → *Italy* 45°5N 8°37E **92** C5
Sesimbra *Portugal* 38°28N 9°6W **89** G1
S'Espalmador *Spain* 38°47N 1°26E **100** C7
S'Espardell *Spain* 38°48N 1°29E **100** C7
Sessa Aurunca *Italy* 41°14N 13°56E **94** A6
S'Estanyol *Spain* 39°22N 2°54E **100** B9
Sestao *Spain* 43°18N 3°0W **90** B2
Sesto Calende *Italy* 45°43N 8°37E **92** C5
Sesto San Giovanni *Italy* 45°31N 9°13E **92** C6
Sestri Levante *Italy* 44°16N 9°24E **92** D6
Sestriere *Italy* 44°57N 6°53E **92** D3
Sestroretsk *Russia* 60°5N 29°58E **84** A6
Sestrunj *Croatia* 44°10N 15°0E **93** D11
Sestu *Italy* 39°18N 9°5E **94** C2
Setana *Japan* 42°26N 139°51E **112** C9
Sète *France* 43°25N 3°42E **72** E7
Sete Cidades ∆ *Brazil* 4°0S 41°37W **189** A2
Sete Lagoas *Brazil* 19°27S 44°16W **189** D2
Seti → *Nepal* 28°59N 81°8E **125** E9
Sétif *Algeria* 36°9N 5°26E **136** A5
Sétif □ *Algeria* 36°10N 5°0E **136** A5
Seto *Japan* 35°14N 137°6E **113** G8
Setonaikai *Japan* 34°20N 133°30E **113** G6
Setonaikai ∆ *Japan* 34°15N 133°15E **113** G6
Settat *Morocco* 33°0N 7°40W **136** B2
Séttimo Torinese *Italy* 45°9N 7°46E **92** C4
Setting L. *Canada* 55°0N 98°38W **163** C9
Settle *U.K.* 54°5N 2°16W **66** C5

Settlement, The
  Br. Virgin Is. 18°43N 64°22W **183** e
Settlers *S. Africa* 25°2S 28°30E **145** C4
Setúbal *Portugal* 38°30N 8°58W **89** G2
Setúbal □ *Portugal* 38°25N 8°35W **89** G2
Setúbal, B. de *Portugal* 38°40N 8°56W **89** G2
Seugne → *France* 45°42N 0°32W **72** C3
Seul, Lac *Canada* 50°20N 92°30W **164** B1
Seurre *France* 47°0N 5°8E **71** F12
Sevan *Armenia* 40°33N 44°56E **87** K7
Sevan, Ozero = Sevana Lich
  Armenia 40°30N 45°20E **87** K7
Sevana Lich *Armenia* 40°30N 45°20E **87** K7
Sevastopol *Ukraine* 44°35N 33°30E **87** K9
Seven Sisters *Canada* 54°56N 128°10W **162** C3
Sever → *Spain* 39°40N 7°32W **89** F3
Sévérac-le-Château *France* 44°20N 3°5E **72** D7
Severn → *Canada* 56°2N 87°36W **164** A2
Severn → *U.K.* 51°35N 2°40W **67** F5
Severnaya Zemlya
  Russia 79°0N 100°0E **107** B11
Severo Kosovo *Kosovo* 43°29N 21°27E **96** C4
Severo-Kurilsk *Russia* 50°40N 156°8E **107** D16
Severo-Yenlseyskiy
  Russia 60°22N 93°1E **107** C10
Severo-Zapadnyy □
  Russia 65°0N 40°0E **106** C4
Severobaykalsk
  Russia 55°39N 109°19E **107** D11

Severočeský □ *Czech Rep.* 50°30N 14°0E **78** A7
Severodonetsk = Syeverodonetsk
  Ukraine 48°58N 38°35E **85** H10
Severodvinsk *Russia* 64°27N 39°58E **106** C4
Severomoravský □
  Czech Rep. 49°38N 17°40E **79** B10
Severomorsk *Russia* 69°5N 33°27E **60** B25
Seversk *Russia* 56°36N 84°49E **106** D9
Sevier → *U.S.A.* 39°4N 113°6W **168** G7
Sevier Desert *U.S.A.* 39°40N 112°45W **168** G7
Sevier L. *U.S.A.* 38°54N 113°9W **168** G7
Sevilla *Spain* 37°23N 5°58W **89** H5
Sevilla □ *Spain* 37°25N 5°30W **89** H5
Seville = Sevilla *Spain* 37°23N 5°58W **89** H5
Seville, Ga., U.S.A. 31°58N 83°36W **178** D6
Seville, S.C., U.S.A. 33°58N 83°36W **178** D6
Sevlievo *Bulgaria* 43°2N 25°6E **97** C9
Sèvre-Nantaise →
  France 47°12N 1°33W **70** E5
Sèvre-Niortaise →
  France 46°28N 0°50W **72** B3
Sevsk *Russia* 52°10N 34°30E **85** F8
Sewa → *S. Leone* 7°20N 12°10W **138** D2
Sewani *India* 28°58N 75°39E **124** E6
Seward, Alaska, U.S.A. 60°7N 149°27W **160** E2
Seward, Nebr., U.S.A. 40°55N 97°6W **172** E5
Seward, Pa., U.S.A. 40°25N 79°1W **174** F5
Seward Peninsula
  U.S.A. 65°30N 166°0W **166** B6
Sewell *Chile* 34°10S 70°23W **190** C1
Sewer *Indonesia* 5°53S 134°40E **119** F8
Sewickley *U.S.A.* 40°32N 80°12W **174** F4
Sexsmith *Canada* 55°21N 118°47W **162** B5
Seychelles ■ *Ind. Oc.* 5°0S 56°0E **141** b
Seyðisfjörður *Iceland* 65°16N 13°57W **60** D7
Seydişehir *Turkey* 37°25N 31°51E **104** D4
Seydvān *Iran* 38°34N 45°2E **105** C11
Seyhan → *Turkey* 36°43N 34°53E **104** D6
Seyhan Baraji *Turkey* 37°2N 35°18E **104** D6
Seyitgazi *Turkey* 39°27N 30°43E **99** C12
Seyitömer *Turkey* 39°34N 29°52E **99** B11
Seym → *Ukraine* 51°27N 32°34E **85** G7
Seymour *Turkey* 41°6N 27°57E **97** E11
Seymour, *Australia* 37°2S 145°10E **153** D6
Seymour, *S. Africa* 32°33S 26°46E **145** D4
Seymour, Conn., U.S.A. 41°24N 73°4W **175** E11
Seymour, Ind., U.S.A. 38°58N 85°53W **173** F11
Seymour, Tex., U.S.A. 33°35N 99°16W **176** E5
Seyne *France* 44°21N 6°22E **73** D10
Seyssel *France* 45°57N 5°50E **73** C9
Sežana *Slovenia* 45°43N 13°41E **93** C10
Sézanne *France* 48°40N 3°40E **71** D10
Sezze *Italy* 41°30N 13°3E **94** A6
Sfântu Gheorghe *Covasna,*
  Romania 45°52N 25°48E **81** E10
Sfântu Gheorghe *Tulcea,*
  Romania 44°53N 29°36E **81** F14
Sfântu Gheorghe, Brațul →
  Romania 44°51N 29°36E **81** F14
Sfax *Tunisia* 34°49N 10°48E **136** B6
Sfax □ *Tunisia* 34°40N 10°20E **136** B6
Sha Tau Kok *China* 22°33N 114°13E **111** a
Sha Tin *China* 22°23N 114°12E **111** a
Sha Xi → *China* 26°35N 118°0E **117** D12
Sha Xian *China* 26°23N 117°45E **117** D11
Shaanxi □ *China* 35°0N 109°0E **114** G5
Shaba = Katanga □
  Dem. Rep. of the Congo 8°0S 25°0E **142** D2
Shaba ∆ *Kenya* 0°38N 37°48E **142** B4
Shabeelle → *Somalia* 2°0N 44°0E **131** G3
Shabestar *Iran* 38°11N 45°41E **105** C11
Shabla *Bulgaria* 43°31N 28°32E **97** C12
Shabogamo L. *Canada* 53°15N 66°30W **165** B6
Shabunda
  Dem. Rep. of the Congo 2°40S 27°16E **142** C2
Shache *China* 38°20N 77°10E **109** E9
Shackleton Fracture Zone
  S. Ocean 60°0S 60°0W **55** B18
Shackleton Ice Shelf
  Antarctica 66°0S 100°0E **55** C8
Shackleton Inlet
  Antarctica 83°0S 160°0E **55** E11
Shādegān *Iran* 30°40N 48°38E **129** D6
Shadi *China* 26°7N 114°47E **117** D10
Shadi *India* 33°24N 77°14E **125** C7
Shadrinsk *Russia* 56°5N 63°32E **106** D7
Shady Dale *U.S.A.* 33°24N 83°36W **178** B6
Shady Grove *U.S.A.* 30°17N 83°38W **178** F6
Shadyside *U.S.A.* 39°58N 80°45W **174** G4
Shaffa *Nigeria* 10°30N 12°6E **139** C7
Shafter *U.S.A.* 35°30N 119°16W **171** K7
Shaftesbury *U.K.* 51°0N 2°11W **67** F5
Shaftsbury *U.S.A.* 43°0N 73°11W **175** D11
Shag Pt. *N.Z.* 45°29S 170°52E **155** F5
Shag Rocks *Atl. Oc.* 53°0S 41°0W **56** M7
Shagamu *Nigeria* 6°51N 3°39E **139** D5
Shagram *Pakistan* 36°24N 72°20E **124** A6
Shah Alam *Malaysia* 3°5N 101°32E **121** L3
Shah Alizai *Pakistan* 29°25N 66°33E **124** E7
Shah Bunder *Pakistan* 24°13N 67°56E **124** G2
Shahabad *Karnataka,*
  India 17°10N 76°54E **126** F3
Shahabad, Punjab, India 30°10N 76°55E **124** D7
Shahabad, Raj., India 25°15N 77°11E **124** G7
Shahabad, Ut. P., India 27°36N 79°56E **125** F8
Shahada *India* 21°33N 74°30E **126** D2
Shahadpur *Pakistan* 25°55N 68°35E **124** G3
Shahapur *India* 15°50N 74°34E **127** G2
Shahbā *Syria* 32°52N 36°38E **130** C5
Shahdād *Iran* 30°30N 57°40E **129** D8
Shahdād, Namakzār-e
  Iran 30°20N 58°20E **129** D8
Shahdadkot *Pakistan* 27°50N 67°55E **124** F6
Shahdol *India* 23°19N 81°26E **125** H9
Shahe *China* 37°0N 114°32E **114** F8
Shahganj *India* 26°3N 82°44E **125** F10
Shahgarh *India* 27°15N 69°50E **124** F3
Shahid Rajaee Port = Bandar
  Shahid Rajaee *Iran* 27°5N 56°7E **129** E8
Shāhīn Shahr *Iran* 32°49N 51°32E **129** C6
Shahjahanpur *India* 27°54N 79°57E **125** F8
Shahpur = Salmās
  Iran 38°11N 44°47E **105** C11
Shahpur, Karnataka,
  India 16°40N 76°48E **126** F3
Shahpur, Mad. P., India 22°12N 77°58E **124** H7
Shahpur, Baluchistan,
  Pakistan 28°46N 68°27E **124** E6
Shahpur, Punjab,
  Pakistan 32°17N 72°26E **124** C5

Shahpur Chakar
  Pakistan 26°9N 68°39E **124** F3
Shahpura *Mad. P., India* 23°10N 80°45E **125** H9
Shahpura *Raj., India* 25°38N 74°56E **124** G5
Shahr-e Bābak *Iran* 30°7N 55°9E **129** D7
Shahr-e Kord *Iran* 32°15N 50°55E **129** C6
Shāhrakht *Iran* 33°38N 60°16E **129** C10
Shāhrezā = Qomsheh
  Iran 32°0N 51°55E **129** D6
Shahrig *Pakistan* 30°15N 67°40E **124** D7
Shahrisabz *Uzbekistan* 39°3N 66°50E **109** E7
Shāhrud = Emāmrūd
  Iran 36°30N 55°0E **129** B7
Shahukou *China* 40°20N 112°18E **114** D7
Shaikhabad *Afghan.* 34°2N 68°45E **124** B3
Shajapur *India* 23°27N 76°21E **124** H7
Shajing *China* 22°44N 113°48E **111** a
Shakargarh *Pakistan* 32°17N 75°10E **124** C6
Shakawe *Botswana* 18°28S 21°49E **144** A3
Shaker Heights *U.S.A.* 41°28N 81°32W **174** E3
Shakhrisyabz = Shahrisabz
  Uzbekistan 39°3N 66°50E **109** E7
Shakhtersk *Russia* 49°10N 142°8E **107** E15
Shakhtīnsk *Kazakhstan* 49°42N 72°35E **109** C8
Shakhty *Russia* 47°40N 40°16E **87** G5
Shakhunya *Russia* 57°40N 46°46E **86** B8
Shaki *Nigeria* 8°41N 3°21E **139** D5
Shākir *Egypt* 27°30N 33°59E **137** B3
Shakotan-Hantō
  Japan 43°10N 140°30E **112** C10
Shaksam Valley *Asia* 36°0N 76°20E **125** A7
Shali *Russia* 43°9N 45°55E **87** J7
Shalkar Köli
  Kazakhstan 50°35N 51°47E **86** E10
Shallow Lake *Canada* 44°36N 81°5W **174** B3
Shalqar *Kazakhstan* 47°48N 59°39E **108** C5
Shalqar Köli *Kazakhstan* 50°5N 51°40E **108** B4
Shalskiy *Russia* 61°48N 35°58E **84** B8
Shaluli Shan *China* 30°40N 99°55E **116** B2
Shām *Iran* 26°39N 57°21E **129** E8
Shām, Bādiyat ash *Asia* 32°0N 40°0E **128** C3
Shamāl Sīnî □ *Egypt* 30°30N 34°0E **130** E2
Shamattawa *Canada* 55°51N 92°5W **164** A1
Shamattawa → *Canada* 55°1N 85°23W **164** A2
Shamīl *Iran* 27°30N 56°55E **129** E8
Shamkhor = Şämkir
  Azerbaijan 40°50N 46°0E **87** K8
Shāmkūh *Iran* 35°47N 57°50E **129** C8
Shamli *India* 29°32N 77°18E **124** E7
Shammar, Jabal
  Si. Arabia 27°40N 41°0E **128** E4
Shamo = Gobi *Asia* 44°0N 110°0E **114** C6
Shamo, L. *Ethiopia* 5°45N 37°30E **131** F2
Shamokin *U.S.A.* 40°47N 76°34W **175** F8
Shamrock, Canada 50°23N 106°50W **163** C7
Shamrock, U.S.A. 35°13N 100°15W **176** D4
Shamva *Zimbabwe* 17°20S 31°32E **143** F3
Shan □ *Burma* 21°30N 98°30E **123** J21
Shan Xian *China* 34°50N 116°5E **114** G9
Shanchengzhen
  China 42°20N 125°20E **115** C13
Shāndak *Iran* 28°28N 60°27E **129** D9
Shandan *China* 38°45N 101°15E **110** D9
Shandon *U.S.A.* 35°39N 120°23W **170** K6
Shandong □ *China* 36°0N 118°0E **115** F10
Shandong Bandao
  China 37°0N 121°0E **115** F11
Shandur Pass *Pakistan* 36°4N 72°31E **125** A5
Shang Xian = Shangzhou
  China 33°50N 109°58E **114** H5
Shangalowe
  Dem. Rep. of the Congo 10°50S 26°30E **143** E2
Shangani *Zimbabwe* 19°41S 29°20E **145** A4
Shangani → *Zimbabwe* 18°41S 27°10E **143** F2
Shangbancheng
  China 40°50N 118°1E **115** D10
Shangcheng *China* 31°47N 115°26E **117** B10
Shangchuan Dao
  China 21°40N 112°50E **117** G9
Shanggao *China* 28°17N 114°55E **117** C10
Shanghai *China* 31°15N 121°26E **117** B13
Shanghai Shi □ *China* 31°0N 121°30E **117** B13
Shanghang *China* 25°12N 116°33E **117** E11
Shanghe *China* 37°20N 117°10E **115** F9
Shanglin *China* 23°27N 108°33E **116** E7
Shangnan *China* 33°32N 110°50E **114** H6
Shangqiu *China* 34°26N 115°36E **114** G8
Shangrao *China* 28°25N 117°59E **117** C11
Shangri-La = Zhongdian
  China 27°48N 99°42E **116** D2
Shangshui *China* 33°42N 114°35E **114** H8
Shangsi *China* 22°8N 107°58E **116** F6
Shangyi *China* 41°4N 113°57E **114** D7
Shangyou *China* 25°48N 114°32E **117** E10
Shangzhi *China* 45°22N 127°56E **115** B14
Shangzhou *China* 33°50N 109°58E **114** H5
Shanhetun *China* 44°33N 127°15E **115** B14
Shani *Nigeria* 10°14N 12°2E **139** C7
Shānidar *Iraq* 36°46N 44°41E **105** D11
Shanklin *U.K.* 50°38N 1°11W **67** G6
Shannon *N.Z.* 40°33S 175°25E **154** G4
Shannon → *Ireland* 52°35N 9°30W **64** D2
Shannon ✈ (SNN)
  Ireland 52°42N 8°57W **64** D3
Shannon, Mouth of the
  Ireland 52°30N 9°55W **64** D2
Shannon △ *Australia* 34°35S 116°25E **149** F2
Shannon Ø *Greenland* 75°10N 18°30W **57** B9
Shannonbridge *Ireland* 53°17N 8°3W **64** C3
Shannontown *U.S.A.* 33°53N 80°21W **178** B9
Shanshan *China* 42°52N 90°10E **109** D12
Shansi = Shanxi □
  China 37°0N 112°0E **114** F7
Shantar, Ostrov Bolshoy
  Russia 55°9N 137°40E **107** D14
Shantipur *India* 23°17N 88°25E **125** H13
Shantou *China* 23°18N 116°40E **117** F11
Shantung = Shandong □
  China 36°0N 118°0E **115** F10
Shanwei *China* 22°48N 115°22E **117** F10
Shanxi □ *China* 37°0N 112°0E **114** F7
Shanyang *China* 33°31N 109°55E **114** H5
Shanyin *China* 39°25N 112°56E **114** E7
Shaodong *China* 27°15N 111°43E **117** D8
Shaoguan *China* 24°48N 113°27E **117** E9
Shaoshan *China* 27°55N 112°33E **117** D9
Shaowu *China* 27°22N 117°28E **117** D11
Shaoxing *China* 30°0N 120°35E **117** C13

Shaoyang *Hunan,*
  China 26°59N 111°20E **117** D8
Shaoyang *Hunan,*
  China 27°14N 111°25E **117** D8
Shap *U.K.* 54°32N 2°40W **66** C5
Shapinsay *U.K.* 59°3N 2°51W **65** B6
Shaqlāwah *Iraq* 36°23N 44°20E **105** D11
Shaqra' *Si. Arabia* 25°15N 45°16E **128** E5
Shar *Kazakhstan* 49°35N 81°2E **109** C10
Sharafkhāneh *Iran* 38°11N 45°29E **105** C11
Sharashova *Belarus* 52°34N 24°12E **83** F11
Sharavati → *India* 14°20N 74°25E **127** G2
Sharbaqty *Kazakhstan* 51°23N 78°17E **109** B9
Sharbot Lake *Canada* 44°46N 76°41W **175** B8
Shardara, Step
  Kazakhstan 42°20N 68°0E **109** D7
Sharhorod *Ukraine* 48°45N 28°5E **81** B13
Shari *Japan* 43°55N 144°40E **112** C12
Sharjah = Ash Shāriqah
  U.A.E. 25°23N 55°26E **129** E7
Shark B. *Australia* 25°15N 113°32E **149** E1
Shark Bay ∆ *Australia* 25°30S 113°30E **149** E1
Sharm el Sheikh *Egypt* 27°53N 34°18E **137** B3
Sharon *Canada* 44°6N 79°26W **174** B5
Sharon, Mass., U.S.A. 42°7N 71°11W **175** D13
Sharon, Pa., U.S.A. 41°14N 80°31W **174** E4
Sharon Springs Kans.,
  U.S.A. 38°54N 101°45W **172** F3
Sharon Springs N.Y.,
  U.S.A. 42°48N 74°37W **175** D10
Sharp Pt. *Australia* 10°58S 142°43E **150** A3
Sharpe L. *Canada* 54°24N 93°40W **164** B1
Sharpes *U.S.A.* 28°26N 80°46W **179** G9
Sharpsville *U.S.A.* 41°15N 80°29W **174** E4
Sharqi, Al Jabal ash
  Lebanon 33°40N 36°10E **130** B5
Sharr Kosovo 42°5N 20°41E **96** D4
Sharya *Russia* 58°22N 45°20E **86** A7
Shashemene *Ethiopia* 7°13N 38°33E **131** F2
Shashi *Botswana* 21°15S 27°27E **145** A4
Shashi → *Africa* 21°14S 29°20E **143** G2
Shasta, Mt. *U.S.A.* 41°25N 122°12W **168** F2
Shasta L. *U.S.A.* 40°43N 122°25W **168** F2
Shatsk *Russia* 54°0N 41°45E **86** C5
Shatsk *Ukraine* 51°29N 23°58E **83** G10
Shatsky Rise *Pac. Oc.* 34°0N 157°0E **156** D7
Shatskyy □ *Ukraine* 51°30N 23°52E **83** G10
Shatt al Arab *Asia* 29°57N 48°34E **129** D6
Shatura *Russia* 55°33N 39°21E **84** E10
Shaumyani = Shulaveri
  Georgia 41°22N 44°45E **87** K7
Shaunavon *Canada* 49°35N 108°25W **163** D7
Shaver L. *U.S.A.* 37°9N 119°18W **170** H7
Shaw → *Australia* 20°21S 119°17E **148** D2
Shaw I. *Australia* 20°30S 149°2E **150** b
Shawanaga *Canada* 45°31N 80°17W **174** A4
Shawano *U.S.A.* 44°47N 88°36W **172** C9
Shawinigan *Canada* 46°35N 72°50W **164** C5
Shawmari, J. ash
  Jordan 30°35N 36°35E **130** E5
Shawnee, Ga., U.S.A. 32°29N 81°25W **178** C8
Shawnee, Okla., U.S.A. 35°20N 96°55W **176** D6
Shay Gap *Australia* 20°30S 120°10E **148** D3
Shayang *China* 30°42N 112°29E **117** B9
Shaybārā *Si. Arabia* 25°26N 36°47E **128** E3
Shayib el Banat, Gebel
  Egypt 26°59N 33°39E **137** B3
Shaykh, J. ash *Lebanon* 33°25N 35°50E **130** B4
Shaykh Miskīn *Syria* 32°49N 36°9E **130** C5
Shaykh Sa'd *Iraq* 32°34N 46°17E **105** F12
Shaykh 'Uthmān
  Yemen 12°52N 44°59E **131** E3
Shāzand *Iran* 33°56N 49°24E **129** C6
Shazud *Tajikistan* 37°45N 72°10E **109** F8
Shchekino *Russia* 54°1N 37°34E **84** E9
Shchigry *Russia* 51°55N 36°58E **85** G9
Shchors *Ukraine* 51°48N 31°56E **85** G6
Shchuchinsk
  Kazakhstan 52°56N 70°12E **108** H8
She Xian *Anhui,*
  China 29°50N 118°25E **117** C12
She Xian *Hebei,* China 36°30N 113°40E **114** F7
Shebekino *Russia* 50°28N 36°54E **85** G10
Shebele = Shabeelle →
  Somalia 2°0N 44°0E **131** G3
Sheberghān *Afghan.* 36°40N 65°45E **109** F7
Sheboygan *U.S.A.* 43°46N 87°45W **172** D10
Shebshi Mts. *Nigeria* 8°30N 12°0E **139** D7
Shediac *Canada* 46°14N 64°32W **165** C7
Sheelin, L. *Ireland* 53°48N 7°20W **64** C4
Sheenjek → *U.S.A.* 66°45N 144°33W **166** B11
Sheep Haven *Ireland* 55°11N 7°52W **64** A4
Sheep Range *U.S.A.* 36°35N 115°15W **171** J11
Sheerness *U.K.* 51°26N 0°47E **67** F8
Sheet Harbour *Canada* 44°56N 62°31W **165** D7
Sheffield *N.Z.* 43°23S 172°1E **155** D7
Sheffield *U.K.* 53°23N 1°28W **66** D6
Sheffield, Ala., U.S.A. 34°46N 87°41W **177** D11
Sheffield, Mass., U.S.A. 42°5N 73°21W **175** D11
Sheffield, Pa., U.S.A. 41°42N 79°3W **174** E5
Shegaon *India* 20°48N 76°47E **126** D3
Shehong *China* 30°54N 105°18E **116** B5
Sheikh Zayed Canal
  Egypt 23°30N 30°15E **137** C2
Sheikhpura *India* 25°9N 85°53E **125** G11
Shekhupura *Pakistan* 31°42N 73°58E **124** D5
Sheki = Şaki *Azerbaijan* 41°10N 47°5E **87** K8
Shekou *China* 22°29N 113°55E **111** a
Shelburne, N.S., Canada 43°47N 65°20W **165** D6
Shelburne, Ont., Canada 44°4N 80°15W **174** B4
Shelburne, U.S.A. 44°23N 73°14W **175** B11
Shelburne B. *Australia* 11°50S 142°50E **150** A3
Shelburne Falls
  U.S.A. 42°36N 72°45W **175** D12

Shelek *Kazakhstan* 43°33N 78°17E **109** ...
Shelikhova, Zaliv
  Russia 59°30N 157°0E **107** ...
Shelikof Strait *U.S.A.* 57°30N 155°0W **16** ...
Shell Lakes *Australia* 29°20S 127°30E **14** ...
Shellbrook *Canada* 53°13N 106°24W **16** ...
Shellharbour *Australia* 34°31S 150°51E **15** ...
Shellman *U.S.A.* 31°46N 84°37W **17** ...
Shelon → *Russia* 58°13N 30°47E **8** ...
Shelter I. *U.S.A.* 41°4N 72°20W **17** ...
Shelter, Conn., U.S.A. 41°19N 73°5W **175** ...
Shelton, Wash., U.S.A. 47°13N 123°6W **17** ...
Shemakha = Şamaxı
  Azerbaijan 40°38N 48°37E **8** ...
Shemonaīkha
  Kazakhstan 50°37N 81°54E **10** ...
Shēmri Albania 42°7N 20°13E **9** ...
Shemsi *Sudan* 19°2N 29°57E **13** ...
Shen Xian *China* 36°15N 115°40E **11** ...
Shenandoah Iowa,
  U.S.A. 40°46N 95°22W **17** ...
Shenandoah Pa.,
  U.S.A. 40°49N 76°12W **17** ...
Shenandoah Va.,
  U.S.A. 38°29N 78°37W **173** ...
Shenandoah → *U.S.A.* 39°19N 77°44W **173** ...
Shenandoah △
  U.S.A. 38°35N 78°22W **173** ...
Shenchi *China* 39°8N 112°10E **11** ...
Shencottah *India* 8°59N 77°18E **12** ...
Shendam *Nigeria* 8°49N 9°30E **13** ...
Shendî *Sudan* 16°46N 33°22E **135** ...
Shendurni *India* 20°39N 75°36E **12** ...
Shenge *S. Leone* 7°54N 12°55W **13** ...
Shengfang *China* 39°3N 116°42E **11** ...
Shēngjergj *Albania* 41°17N 20°10E **9** ...
Shēngjin *Albania* 41°50N 19°35E **9** ...
Shengzhou *China* 29°35N 120°50E **117** ...
Shenjingzi *China* 44°40N 124°30E **115** ...
Shenmu *China* 38°50N 110°29E **11** ...
Shennongjia *China* 31°43N 110°44E **11** ...
Shenqiu *China* 33°25N 115°5E **11** ...
Shensi = Shaanxi □
  China 35°0N 109°0E **11** ...
Shenyang *China* 41°48N 123°27E **115** ...
Shenzhen *China* 22°32N 114°5E **117** ...
Shenzhen Bao'an Int. ✈ (SZX)
  China 22°39N 113°48E **11** ...
Shenzhen Wan *China* 22°27N 113°56E **11** ...
Sheo *India* 26°11N 71°15E **12** ...
Sheopur Kalan *India* 25°40N 76°40E **12** ...
Shepetivka *Ukraine* 50°10N 27°10E **75** ...
Shepparton *Australia* 36°23S 145°26E **15** ...
Sheppey, I. of *U.K.* 51°25N 0°48E **6** ...
Shepton Mallet *U.K.* 51°11N 2°33W **6** ...
Sheqi *China* 33°12N 112°57E **11** ...
Sher Qila *Pakistan* 36°7N 74°2E **12** ...
Sherabad *Uzbekistan* 37°40N 67°1E **10** ...
Sherborne *U.K.* 50°57N 2°31W **6** ...
Sherbro I. *S. Leone* 7°45N 12°55W **13** ...
Sherbro I. *S. Leone* 7°30N 12°40W **13** ...
Sherbrooke N.S., Canada 45°8N 61°59W **16** ...
Sherbrooke Qué.,
  Canada 45°28N 71°57W **175** ...
Sherburne *U.S.A.* 42°41N 75°30W **17** ...
Shereik *Sudan* 18°44N 33°47E **13** ...
Shergarh *India* 26°20N 72°18E **12** ...
Sherghati *India* 24°34N 84°47E **125** ...
Sheridan Ark., U.S.A. 34°19N 92°24W **17** ...
Sheridan Wyo.,
  U.S.A. 44°48N 106°58W **16** ...
Sheringham *U.K.* 52°56N 1°13E **6** ...
Sherkin I. *Ireland* 51°28N 9°26W **6** ...
Sherkot *India* 29°22N 78°35E **12** ...
Sherlovaya Gora
  Russia 50°34N 116°15E **10** ...
Sherman N.Y., U.S.A. 42°9N 79°35W **17** ...
Sherman Tex., U.S.A. 33°38N 96°36W **17** ...
Sherpur *India* 25°34N 83°47E **12** ...
Sherridon *Canada* 55°8N 101°5W **16** ...
Shertallai = Cherthala
  India 9°42N 76°20E **12** ...
Sherwood Forest *U.K.* 53°6N 1°7W **6** ...
Sherwood Park
  Canada 53°31N 113°19W **16** ...
Sheslay → *Canada* 58°48N 132°5W **16** ...
Shethanei L. *Canada* 58°48N 97°50W **16** ...
Shetland □ *U.K.* 60°30N 1°30W **6** ...
Shetland Is. *U.K.* 60°30N 1°30W **6** ...
Shetpe *Kazakhstan* 44°10N 52°7E **10** ...
Sheung Shui *China* 22°30N 114°7E **11** ...
Shevaroy Hills *India* 11°58N 78°12E **12** ...
Shevchenkovo *Ukraine* 45°33N 29°20E **81** ...
Shevgaon *India* 19°21N 75°14E **12** ...
Shevishen *Iran* 35°21N 46°40E **10** ...
Shey-Phoksundo △
  Nepal 29°30N 82°45E **125** ...
Sheyenne → *U.S.A.* 47°2N 96°50W **17** ...
Shiashkotan, Ostrov
  Russia 48°49N 154°6E **107** ...
Shibām *Yemen* 15°59N 48°36E **13** ...
Shibata *Japan* 37°57N 139°20E **11** ...
Shibecha *Japan* 43°17N 144°36E **11** ...
Shibetsu *Hokkaidō,*
  Japan 44°10N 142°23E **11** ...
Shibetsu *Hokkaidō,*
  Japan 43°30N 145°10E **11** ...
Shibīn el Kôm *Egypt* 30°31N 30°55E **13** ...
Shibīn el Qanâtir *Egypt* 30°19N 31°19E **13** ...
Shibogama L. *Canada* 53°35N 88°15W **16** ...
Shibushi *Japan* 31°25N 131°8E **11** ...
Shicheng *China* 26°22N 116°20E **11** ...
Shickshinny *U.S.A.* 41°9N 76°9W **17** ...
Shickshock Mts. = Chic-Chocs,
  Mts. *Canada* 48°55N 66°0W **16** ...
Shidao *China* 36°50N 122°25E **11** ...
Shiderti → *Kazakhstan* 52°3N 74°54E **10** ...
Shidian *China* 24°40N 99°6E **11** ...
Shido = Sanuki *Japan* 34°19N 134°10E **11** ...
Shiel, L. *U.K.* 56°48N 5°34W **6** ...
Shield, C. *Australia* 13°20S 136°20E **15** ...
Shīeli *Kazakhstan* 44°20N 66°45E **10** ...
Shifang *China* 31°6N 104°0E **11** ...
Shiga □ *Japan* 35°20N 136°0E **11** ...
Shigu *China* 26°51N 99°56E **11** ...
Shiguaigou *China* 40°52N 110°15E **11** ...

hchiachuangi = Shijiazhuang
China 38°2N 114°28E **114** E8
hezi *China* 44°15N 86°2E **109** D11
jak *Albania* 41°21N 19°33E **96** E3
jiazhuang *China* 38°2N 114°28E **114** E8
jiu Hu *China* 31°25N 118°50E **117** B12
karpur *India* 28°17N 78°7E **124** E8
karpur *Pakistan* 27°57N 68°39E **124** F3
kohabad *India* 27°6N 78°36E **125** F8
kokochūō *Japan* 34°1N 133°30E **113** G6
koku □ *Japan* 33°30N 133°30E **113** H6
kotan, Ostrov
Asia 43°47N 146°44E **107** L15
kotsu-Ko *Japan* 42°45N 141°25E **112** C10
kotsu-Tōya △ *Japan* 44°4N 145°8E **112** C10
liguri *India* 26°45N 88°25E **123** F16
liu = Changjiang
China 19°2ON 108°55E **117** a
Ika *Russia* 52°0N 115°55E **107** D12
Ika → *Russia* 53°2ON 121°26E **107** D13
lelagh *Ireland* 52°45N 6°32W **64** D5
llington U.S.A. 40°18N 75°58W **175** F9
llong *India* 25°35N 91°53E **123** G17
lo *West Bank* 32°4N 35°18E **130** C4
long *China* 23°5N 113°52E **117** F9
lou *China* 37°0N 110°48E **114** F6
lovo *Russia* 54°25N 40°57E **86** C5
mabara *Japan* 32°48N 130°20E **113** H5
mada *Japan* 34°49N 138°10E **113** G9
mane □ *Japan* 35°0N 132°30E **113** G6
manovski *Japan* 52°15N 127°30E **113** H3
manto *Kōchi, Japan* 33°12N 133°8E **113** H6
manto *Kōchi, Japan* 42°59N 132°56E **113** H6
mba Hills △ *Kenya* 4°14S 39°25E **142** C4
mbiris *Somalia* 10°44N 47°14E **131** E4
men *China* 29°35N 111°20E **117** C8
menjie *China* 29°29N 116°48E **117** C11
mian *China* 29°17N 102°23E **116** C4
mizu *Japan* 35°0N 138°30E **113** G9
mla *India* 31°2N 77°9E **124** D7
modate *Japan* 36°20N 139°55E **113** F9
moga *India* 13°57N 75°32E **127** H2
mokita-Hantō
Japan 41°2ON 141°0E **112** D10
moni *Kenya* 4°38S 39°20E **142** C4
monoseki *Japan* 33°58N 130°55E **113** H5
mpuru Rapids
Zambia 17°45S 19°55E **144** A2
msha → *India* 13°15N 77°10E **127** H3
msk *Russia* 58°15N 30°50E **84** C6
n, L. U.K. 58°5N 4°30W **65** C4
an *China* 24°2N 109°53E **116** F7
nano-Gawa →
Japan 36°50N 138°30E **113** F9
nāş *Oman* 24°46N 56°28E **129** E8
ndand *Afghan.* 33°12N 62°8E **122** C3
nglehouse U.S.A. 41°58N 78°12W **174** E6
ngji *S. Africa* 23°5S 31°25E **145** B5
njō *Japan* 38°46N 140°18E **112** E10
nkolobwe
Dem. Rep. of the Congo 11°10S 26°40E **140** G5
nshār *Syria* 34°36N 36°43E **130** A5
ntuya *Peru* 12°41S 71°15W **188** D3
nyanga *Tanzania* 3°45S 33°27E **142** C3
nyanga □ *Tanzania* 3°50S 34°0E **142** C3
o-no-Misaki *Japan* 33°25N 135°45E **113** H7
ogama *Japan* 38°19N 141°1E **112** E10
ojiri *Japan* 36°6N 137°58E **113** F8
ochenski Prokhod
Bulgaria 42°45N 25°15E **97** D9
phoirt, L. = Seaforth, L.
.K. 57°52N 6°36W **65** D2
ping *China* 23°45N 102°23E **116** F4
ppagan *Canada* 47°45N 64°45W **165** C7
ppensburg U.S.A. 40°3N 77°31W **174** F7
ppenville U.S.A. 41°15N 79°28W **174** E5
prock U.S.A. 36°47N 108°41W **169** H9
qian *China* 27°32N 108°13E **116** D7
qma, N. → *Israel* 31°37N 34°30E **130** D3
quan *China* 33°55N 108°13E **116** A7
quan He = Indus →
Pakistan 24°20N 67°47E **124** G2
rabad *Afghan.* 31°39N 54°3E **129** D7
ra'awh *Qatar* 25°2N 52°2E **129** E7
rabad = Sherabad
Uzbekistan 37°40N 67°1E **109** E7
ragami-Misaki
Japan 41°24N 140°12E **112** D10
rakawa *Fukushima,*
Japan 37°7N 140°13E **113** F10
rakawa *Gifu, Japan* 36°17N 136°56E **113** F8
rane-San *Gumma,*
Japan 36°48N 139°22E **113** F9
rane-San *Yamanashi,*
Japan 35°42N 138°9E **113** G9
raoi *Japan* 42°33N 141°21E **112** C10
rāz *Iran* 29°42N 52°30E **129** D7
rbīn *Egypt* 31°11N 31°32E **137** E7
re → *Africa* 17°42S 35°19E **143** F4
ren *China* 41°57N 126°34E **115** D14
retoko △ *Japan* 44°15N 145°15E **112** B12
retoko-Misaki
Japan 44°21N 145°20E **112** B12
rinab → *Pakistan* 30°15N 66°28E **124** D2
riya-Zaki *Japan* 41°25N 141°13E **112** D10
oishi *Japan* 38°0N 140°37E **113** F10
ol *India* 16°47N 74°41E **126** F2
oro Res. *Nigeria* 9°56N 6°54E **139** D6
show Ridge *Pac. Oc.* 58°0N 170°0E **156** B8
vān *Iran* 32°30N 57°50E **129** D8
wa, L. = Chilwa, L.
Malawi 15°15S 35°40E **143** F4
haldin Volcano
S.A. 54°45N 163°58W **166** F7
hi *China* 24°44N 118°37E **117** E12
hou *China* 29°38N 112°22E **117** C9
häthah *Iraq* 30°12N 117°25E **117** B11
amogga = Shimoga
India 13°57N 75°32E **127** H2
puri *India* 25°6N 77°42E **124** G7
ian *China* 43°5N 129°50E **115** C15
ing *China* 24°46N 114°5E **117** E10
an *China* —
an *Guangdong,*
China 22°42N 113°56E **111** a
an *Hubei, China* 32°35N 110°45E **114** A7
an Shuiku *China* 32°42N 113°54E **111** a

Shiyata *Egypt* 29°25N 25°7E **137** B2
Shizhu *China* 29°58N 108°7E **116** C7
Shizong *China* 24°50N 104°0E **116** E5
Shizuishan *China* 39°15N 106°50E **114** E4
Shizuoka *Japan* 34°57N 138°24E **113** G9
Shizuoka □ *Japan* 35°15N 138°40E **113** G9
Shkhara *Georgia* 43°0N 43°8E **105** A10
Shklov = Shklow
Belarus 54°16N 30°15E **75** A16
Shklow *Belarus* 54°16N 30°15E **75** A16
Shkodër *Albania* 42°4N 19°32E **96** D3
Shkumbini → *Albania* 41°2N 19°31E **96** E3
Shmidta, Ostrov *Russia* 81°0N 91°0E **107** A10
Shoal L. *Canada* 49°33N 95°1W **163** D9
Shoal Lake *Canada* 50°30N 100°35W **163** C8
Shoalhaven →
Australia 34°54S 150°42E **153** C9
Shōdo-Shima *Japan* 34°30N 134°15E **113** G7
Sholapur = Solapur
India 17°43N 75°56E **126** F2
Shōmrōn *West Bank* 32°15N 35°13E **130** C4
Shonzhy *Kazakhstan* 43°32N 79°28E **109** D9
Shoranur *India* 10°46N 76°19E **127** J3
Shorapur *India* 16°31N 76°48E **127** F3
Shoreham U.S.A. 43°53N 73°18W **175** C11
Shoreham by Sea U.K. 50°50N 0°16W **67** G7
Shori → *Pakistan* 28°29N 69°44E **124** E3
Shorkot *Pakistan* 30°50N 72°2E **124** D4
Shorkot Road *Pakistan* 30°47N 72°15E **124** D4
Shorsky △ *Russia* 52°40N 88°0E **109** B11
Shorter *U.S.A.* 32°24N 85°57W **178** C4
Shorterville U.S.A. 31°34N 85°6W **178** D4
Shortt's I. *India* 20°47N 87°4E **126** D8
Shoshone *Calif.,*
U.S.A. 35°58N 116°16W **171** K10
Shoshone *Idaho,*
U.S.A. 42°56N 114°25W **168** E6
Shoshone L. U.S.A. 44°22N 110°43W **168** D8
Shoshone Mts. U.S.A. 39°20N 117°25W **168** G5
Shoshong *Botswana* 22°56S 26°31E **144** B4
Shoshoni U.S.A. 43°14N 108°7W **168** E9
Shostka *Ukraine* 51°57N 33°32E **85** G7
Shot *Iran* 31°22N 44°49E **105** C11
Shotover → *N.Z.* 44°59S 168°41E **155** E3
Shou Xian *China* 32°37N 116°42E **117** A11
Shouchang *China* 28°18N 119°12E **117** C12
Shouguang *China* 37°52N 118°45E **115** F10
Shouning *China* 27°27N 119°31E **117** D12
Shouyang *China* 37°54N 113°8E **114** F7
Show Low U.S.A. 34°15N 110°2W **169** J9
Shpola *Ukraine* 49°1N 31°30E **85** H6
Shpykiv *Ukraine* 48°47N 28°34E **81** B13
Shqipëria = Albania ■
Europe 41°0N 20°0E **96** E4
Shreveport U.S.A. 32°31N 93°45W **176** E8
Shrewsbury U.K. 52°43N 2°45W **67** E5
Shri Mohangarh *India* 27°17N 71°18E **124** F4
Shrigonda *India* 18°37N 74°41E **126** E2
Shrirampur *India* 22°44N 88°21E **125** F19
Shropshire □ *U.K.* 52°36N 2°45W **67** E5
Shtërpcë *Kosovo* 42°14N 21°1E **96** D5
Shū *Kazakhstan* 43°36N 73°42E **109** D8
Shū → *Kazakhstan* 45°0N 67°44E **109** D7
Shuangbai *China* 24°42N 101°38E **116** E4
Shuangcheng *China* 45°20N 126°15E **115** B14
Shuangfeng *China* 27°29N 112°11E **117** D9
Shuanggou *China* 34°2N 117°30E **115** G9
Shuangjiang *China* 23°26N 99°58E **116** F2
Shuangliao *China* 43°29N 123°30E **115** C12
Shuangshanzi *China* 40°20N 119°8E **115** D10
Shuangyang *China* 43°28N 125°40E **115** C13
Shuangyashan *China* 46°28N 131°5E **111** B15
Shubarqudyq
Kazakhstan 49°13N 56°34E **108** C5
Shubarshi *Kazakhstan* 48°35N 57°11E **108** C5
Shubrā el Kheima *Egypt* 30°4N 31°14E **137** E7
Shubrā Khit *Egypt* 31°2N 30°42E **137** E7
Shucheng *China* 31°28N 116°57E **117** B11
Shugozero *Russia* 59°54N 34°10E **84** C8
Shuguri Falls *Tanzania* 8°33S 37°22E **142** D4
Shuiding = Huocheng
China 44°0N 80°48E **109** D10
Shuiji *China* 27°13N 118°20E **117** D12
Shujalpur *India* 23°18N 76°46E **124** H7
Shukpa Kunzang *India* 34°22N 78°22E **125** B8
Shulan *China* 44°28N 127°0E **115** B14
Shule *China* 39°25N 76°3E **109** E9
Shule Ne → *China* 40°20N 92°50E **116** A1
Shumanay *Uzbekistan* 42°38N 58°55E **108** D6
Shumen *Bulgaria* 43°18N 26°55E **97** C10
Shumerlya *Russia* 55°30N 46°25E **86** C8
Shumikha *Russia* 55°10N 63°15E **106** D7
Shunan *Japan* 34°3N 131°50E **113** G5
Shunchang *China* 26°54N 117°48E **117** D11
Shunde *China* 22°42N 113°14E **117** F9
Shungay *Kazakhstan* 48°30N 46°45E **87** F8
Shungnak *U.S.A.* 66°52N 157°9W **166** B8
Shuo Xian = Shuozhou
China 39°20N 112°33E **114** E7
Shuozhou *China* 39°20N 112°33E **114** E7
Shuqrā' *Yemen* 13°22N 45°44E **131** E4
Shūr → *Fārs, Iran* 28°30N 55°0E **129** D7
Shūr → *Kermān, Iran* 30°52N 57°37E **129** D8
Shūr → *Yazd, Iran* 31°45N 55°15E **129** D7
Shūr Āb *Iran* 34°23N 51°11E **129** C6
Shūr Gaz *Iran* 29°10N 59°20E **129** D8
Shūrāb *Iran* 33°43N 56°29E **129** C8
Shūrjestān *Iran* 31°24N 52°25E **129** D7
Shurugwi *Zimbabwe* 19°40S 30°0E **143** F3
Shūsf *Iran* 31°50N 60°5E **129** D9
Shūsh *Iran* 32°11N 48°15E **105** F13
Shusha *Azerbaijan* 39°32N 46°40E **105** B13
Shushenskoye *Russia* 53°19N 91°55E **109** B12
Shushtar *Iran* 32°0N 48°50E **129** D6
Shuswap L. *Canada* 50°55N 119°3W **162** C5
Shute Harbour △
Australia 20°17S 148°47E **150** b
Shuya *Russia* 56°50N 41°28E **86** B5
Shuyang *China* 34°10N 118°42E **115** G10
Shūzū *Iran* 29°52N 54°30E **129** D7
Shwebo *Burma* 22°30N 95°45E **123** H19
Shwegu *Burma* 24°15N 96°26E **123** G20
Shweli → *Burma* 23°45N 96°45E **123** H20
Shyamnagar *India* 13°21N 92°57E **127** H11
Shyghys *Kazakhstan* 45°6N 73°58E **109** D8

Shyghys Qazaqstan □
Kazakhstan 48°30N 82°0E **109** D10
Shymkent *Kazakhstan* 42°18N 69°36E **109** D7
Shyok *India* 34°13N 78°12E **125** B8
Shyok → *Pakistan* 35°13N 75°53E **125** B6
Shyroke *Odesa, Ukraine* 45°59N 30°5E **81** E15
Shyroke *Ternopil, Ukraine* 48°13N 23°6E **80** B8
Si Kiang = Xi Jiang →
China 22°5N 113°20E **117** F9
Si Lanna △ *Thailand* 19°17N 99°12E **120** C2
Si Nakarin Res. *Thailand* 14°35N 99°0E **120** E2
Si-ngan = Xi'an *China* 34°15N 109°0E **114** G5
Si Phangnga *Thailand* 9°8N 98°29E **121** H2
Si Prachan *Thailand* 14°37N 100°9E **120** E3
Si Racha *Thailand* 13°10N 100°48E **120** F3
Si Sa Ket *Thailand* 15°8N 104°23E **120** E5
Siachen Glacier *Asia* 35°20N 77°30E **125** B7
Sīāh Chashmeh *Iran* 39°3N 44°25E **105** C11
Siahaf → *Pakistan* 29°3N 68°57E **124** E3
Siahan Range *Pakistan* 27°30N 64°40E **122** F4
Siak Sri Indrapura
Indonesia 0°51N 102°0E **118** D2
Sialkot *Pakistan* 32°32N 74°30E **124** C5
Siam = Thailand ■ *Asia* 16°0N 102°0E **120** E4
Sian = Xi'an *China* 34°15N 109°0E **114** G5
Sian Ka'an *Mexico* 19°35N 87°40W **181** D7
Siantan *Indonesia* 3°10N 106°15E **118** D3
Sīāreh *Iran* 28°5N 60°14E **129** D9
Siargao I. *Phil.* 9°52N 126°3E **119** C7
Siasi *Phil.* 5°34N 120°50E **119** C6
Siatista *Greece* 40°15N 21°33E **96** F5
Siau *Indonesia* 2°50N 125°25E **119** D7
Šiauliai *Lithuania* 55°56N 23°15E **82** C10
Šiauliai □ *Lithuania* 55°56N 23°15E **82** C10
Siavonga *Zambia* 16°33S 28°42E **145** A4
Siazan = Siyäzän
Azerbaijan 41°3N 49°10E **87** K9
Sībā, Gebel el *Egypt* 25°45N 34°10E **128** E2
Sibang *Indonesia* 8°34S 115°13E **119** K18
Sibay *Russia* 52°42N 58°39E **108** D6
Sibayi, L. *S. Africa* 27°20S 32°45E **145** C5
Šibenik *Croatia* 43°48N 15°54E **93** E12
Siberia = Sibirskiy □
Russia 58°0N 90°0E **107** D10
Siberia *Indonesia* 60°0N 100°0E **102** D2
Siberut *Indonesia* 1°30S 99°0E **118** E1
Sibi *Pakistan* 29°30N 67°54E **124** E2
Sibiloi △ *Kenya* 4°0N 36°20E **142** B4
Sibirskiy □ *Russia* 58°0N 90°0E **107** D10
Sibirtsevo *Russia* 44°12N 132°26E **112** B5
Sibiti *Congo* 3°38S 13°19E **140** E2
Sibiu *Romania* 45°45N 24°9E **81** E9
Sibiu □ *Romania* 45°50N 24°15E **81** E9
Sibley U.S.A. 43°24N 95°45W **172** D6
Sibolga *Indonesia* 1°42N 98°45E **118** D1
Siborongborong
Indonesia 2°13N 98°58E **121** L2
Sibsagar *India* 27°0N 94°36E **123** F19
Sibu *Malaysia* 2°18N 111°49E **118** D4
Sibuco *Phil.* 7°20N 122°10E **119** C6
Sibuguey B. *Phil.* 7°50N 122°45E **119** C6
Sibut *C.A.R.* 5°46N 19°10E **140** C3
Sibutu *Phil.* 4°45N 119°30E **119** D5
Sibutu Passage *E. Indies* 4°50N 120°0E **119** D6
Sibuyan I. *Phil.* 12°25N 122°40E **119** B6
Sibuyan Sea *Phil.* 12°30N 122°20E **119** B6
Sic *Romania* 46°56N 23°53E **81** D8
Sicamous *Canada* 50°49N 119°0W **162** C5
Sicasica *Bolivia* 17°22S 67°45W **188** G5
Siccus → *Australia* 31°55S 139°17E **152** A3
Sichon *Thailand* 9°0N 99°54E **121** H2
Sichuan □ *China* 30°30N 103°0E **116** B5
Sichuan Pendi *China* 31°0N 105°0E **116** C5
Sicilia *Italy* 37°30N 14°30E **95** E7
Sicily = Sicilia *Italy* 37°30N 14°30E **95** E7
Sicily, Str. of *Medit. S.* 37°35N 11°56E **94** E4
Sico → *Honduras* 15°58N 84°58W **182** C3
Sicuani *Peru* 14°21S 71°10W **188** D3
Sidaouet *Niger* 18°34N 8°3E **139** B6
Sidári *Greece* 39°47N 19°41E **101** A3
Siddapur *India* 14°20N 74°53E **127** G2
Siddhapur *India* 23°56N 72°25E **124** H5
Siddipet *India* 18°5N 78°51E **126** B4
Sidéradougou
Burkina Faso 10°42N 4°12W **138** C4
Siderno *Italy* 38°16N 16°18E **95** D9
Sideros, Akra *Greece* 35°19N 26°19E **101** D8
Sidhauli *India* 27°17N 80°50E **125** F9
Sidhi *India* 24°25N 81°53E **125** G9
Sīdī 'Abd al Rahmān
Egypt 30°55N 28°41E **137** E6
Sīdī Barrāni *Egypt* 31°38N 25°58E **137** A2
Sidi-bel-Abbès *Algeria* 35°13N 0°39W **136** A3
Sidi-bel-Abbès □
Algeria 34°50N 0°30W **136** B3
Sidi Bennour *Morocco* 32°40N 8°25W **136** B2
Sidi Bou Zid *Tunisia* 35°9N 9°16E **136** B5
Sidi Bou Zid □ *Tunisia* 35°0N 9°30E **136** B5
Sidi Boubekeur *Algeria* 35°1N 0°4E **136** A4
Sidi Haneish *Egypt* 31°10N 27°35E **137** A2
Sidi Ifni *Morocco* 29°29N 10°12W **134** C3
Sidi Kacem *Morocco* 34°11N 5°49W **136** B3
Sidi Omar *Egypt* 31°24N 24°57E **137** A1
Sidi Slimane *Morocco* 34°16N 5°56W **136** B3
Sidi Smaïl *Morocco* 32°50N 8°31W **136** B3
Sidikalang *Indonesia* 2°45N 98°19E **121** L2
Sidlaw Hills *U.K.* 56°32N 3°2W **65** E5
Sidley, Mt. *Antarctica* 77°2S 126°2W **55** D14
Sidmouth *U.K.* 50°40N 3°15W **67** G4
Sidmouth, C. *Australia* 13°25S 143°36E **150** A3
Sidoarjo *Indonesia* 7°27S 112°43E **119** G15
Sidon = Saydā *Lebanon* 33°35N 35°25E **130** B4
Sidra, G. of = Surt, Khalīj
Libya 31°40N 18°30E **135** B9

Siem Pang *Cambodia* 14°7N 106°23E **120** E6
Siem Reap = Siemreab
Cambodia 13°20N 103°52E **120** F4
Siemiatycze *Poland* 52°27N 22°53E **83** F9
Siemreab *Cambodia* 13°20N 103°52E **120** F4
Siena *Italy* 43°19N 11°21E **93** E8
Sieniawa *Poland* 50°11N 22°38E **83** H9
Sieradz *Poland* 51°37N 18°41E **83** G5
Sieraków *Poland* 52°39N 16°2E **83** F3
Sierck-les-Bains *France* 49°26N 6°20E **71** C13
Sierning *Austria* 48°2N 14°18E **78** C7
Sierpc *Poland* 52°55N 19°43E **83** F6
Sierpe, Bocas de la
Venezuela 10°0N 61°30W **187** L15
Sierra Blanca U.S.A. 31°11N 105°22W **176** F2
Sierra Blanca Peak
U.S.A. 33°23N 105°49W **169** K11
Sierra City U.S.A. 39°34N 120°38W **170** F6
Sierra Colorada
Argentina 40°35S 67°50W **192** B3
Sierra de Agalta △
Honduras 15°1N 85°48W **182** C2
Sierra de Andújar ○
Spain 38°20N 3°50W **89** G7
Sierra de Aracena y Picos de
Aroche ○ *Spain* 37°53N 6°41W **89** H4
Sierra de Bahoruco △
Dom. Rep. 18°10N 71°25W **183** C5
Sierra de Baza ○ *Spain* 37°20N 2°48W **91** H2
Sierra de Castril ○ *Spain* 37°54N 2°50W **91** H2
Sierra de España ○
Spain 37°50N 1°31W **91** H3
Sierra de Grazalema ○
Spain 36°31N 5°28W **89** J5
Sierra de Gredos ○ *Spain* 40°17N 5°17W **88** E5
Sierra de Hornachuelos ○
Spain 37°50N 5°10W **89** H5
Sierra de Huétor ○ *Spain* 37°14N 3°30W **89** H7
Sierra de La Culata △
Venezuela 8°45N 71°10W **183** E5
Sierra de Lancandón △
Guatemala 16°59N 90°23W **182** C1
Sierra de las Nieves ○
Spain 36°42N 5°0W **89** J6
Sierra de las Quijadas △
Argentina 32°29S 67°5W **190** C2
Sierra de María-Los Vélez ○
Spain 37°41N 2°10W **91** H2
Sierra de San Luis △
Venezuela 11°20N 69°43W **183** D6
Sierra de San Pedro Mártir △
Mexico 31°10N 115°30W **180** A1
Sierra de Yeguas *Spain* 37°7N 4°52W **89** H6
Sierra del São Mamede ○
Portugal 39°17N 7°18W **89** F3
Sierra Gorda *Chile* 22°50S 69°15W **190** A2
Sierra Grande
Argentina 41°36S 65°22W **192** B3
Sierra Leone ■ *W. Afr.* 9°0N 12°0W **138** D2
Sierra Leone Basin *Atl. Oc.* 5°0N 17°0W **56** F10
Sierra Leone Rise *Atl. Oc.* 7°0N 22°0W **56** F9
Sierra Madre *Mexico* 16°0N 93°0W **181** D6
Sierra Madre Occidental
Mexico 27°0N 107°0W **180** B3
Sierra Madre Oriental
Mexico 25°0N 100°0W **180** C5
Sierra Mágina ○ *Spain* 37°44N 3°28W **89** H7
Sierra Mojada *Mexico* 27°18N 103°41W **180** B4
Sierra Nevada *U.S.A.* 39°0N 120°30W **170** H8
Sierra Nevada *Spain* 37°3N 3°15W **89** H7
Sierra Nevada △ *U.S.A.* 39°0N 120°30W **170** H8
Sierra Nevada ○
Venezuela 8°35N 70°45W **183** E5
Sierra Nevada de Santa Marta △
Colombia 10°56N 73°36W **183** D5
Sierra Norte de Sevilla ○
Spain 37°55N 5°46W **89** H5
Sierra Subbéticas ○
Spain 37°26N 4°18W **89** H6
Sierra Vista U.S.A. 31°33N 110°18W **169** L8
Sierras de Cardeña y Montoro ○
Spain 38°13N 4°15W **89** G6
Sierras de Cazorla, Segura y las
Villas ○ *Spain* 37°0N 2°45W **91** J2
Sierraville U.S.A. 39°36N 120°22W **170** F6
Sierre *Switz.* 46°17N 7°31E **77** J3
Sifié *Ivory C.* 8°0N 7°5W **138** D3
Sifnos *Greece* 37°0N 24°45E **98** E6
Sifton *Canada* 51°21N 100°8W **163** C8
Sifton Pass *Canada* 57°52N 126°15W **162** B3
Sig *Algeria* 35°32N 0°12W **136** A3
Sigatoka *Fiji* 18°8S 177°32E **154** a
Sigean *France* 43°2N 2°58E **72** E6
Sighetu-Marmaţiei
Romania 47°57N 23°52E **81** C8
Sighişoara *Romania* 46°12N 24°50E **81** D9
Sigiriya *Sri Lanka* 7°57N 80°45E **127** L5
Sigli *Indonesia* 5°25N 96°0E **118** C1
Siglufjörður *Iceland* 66°12N 18°55W **60** C4
Sigmaringen *Germany* 48°5N 9°12E **77** G5
Signa *Italy* 43°45N 11°10E **92** E8
Signakhi = Tsnori
Georgia 41°40N 45°57E **87** K7
Signal de Botrang *Belgium* 50°29N 6°4E **69** D6
Signal Pk. *U.S.A.* 33°20N 114°2W **171** M12
Signy I. *Antarctica* 60°43S 45°36W **55** C18
Signy-l'Abbaye *France* 49°40N 4°25E **71** C11
Sigsbee Deep
Gulf of Mexico 25°0N 92°0W **56** D1
Sigsig *Ecuador* 3°0S 78°50W **186** D3
Sigtuna *Sweden* 59°36N 17°44E **62** E11
Sigüenza *Spain* 41°3N 2°40W **90** D2
Siguiri *Guinea* 11°31N 9°10W **138** C3
Sigulda *Latvia* 57°10N 24°55E **84** D3
Siguniangshan *China* 31°15N 103°0E **116** B4
Sihawa *India* 20°19N 81°55E **126** D5
Sihong *China* 33°27N 118°16E **115** H10
Sihora *India* 23°29N 80°6E **125** H9
Sihui *China* 23°24N 112°40E **117** F9
Siikajoki → *Finland* 64°50N 24°43E **60** D21
Siilinjärvi *Finland* 63°4N 27°39E **62** B22
Sijarira Ra. = Chizarira
Zimbabwe 17°36S 27°45E **143** F2
Sika *India* 22°26N 69°47E **124** H3
Sikanni Chief →
Canada 57°47N 122°15W **162** B4
Sikao *Thailand* 7°34N 99°21E **121** J2

Sikar *India* 27°33N 75°10E **124** F6
Sikasso *Mali* 11°18N 5°35W **138** C3
Sikasso □ *Mali* 10°55N 7°0W **138** C3
Sikeston U.S.A. 36°53N 89°35W **172** G9
Sikhote Alin, Khrebet
Russia 45°0N 136°0E **112** B8
Sikhote Alin Ra. = Sikhote Alin,
Khrebet *Russia* 45°0N 136°0E **112** B8
Sikia *Greece* 40°2N 23°56E **96** F7
Sikinos *Greece* 36°40N 25°8E **99** E7
Sikkim □ *India* 27°50N 88°30E **123** F16
Sil → *Spain* 42°27N 7°43W **88** C3
Silacayoapan *Mexico* 17°30N 98°9W **181** D5
Silalè *Lithuania* 55°28N 22°12E **84** C9
Silandro *Italy* 46°38N 10°46E **92** B7
Silawad *India* 21°54N 74°54E **124** J6
Silba *Croatia* 44°24N 14°41E **93** D11
Silchar *India* 24°49N 92°48E **123** G18
Şile *Turkey* 41°10N 29°37E **97** E13
Silent Valley △ *India* 11°10N 76°20E **127** J3
Siler City *U.S.A.* 35°44N 79°28W **177** D15
Sileru → *India* 17°49N 81°24E **126** C5
Silesia = Śląsk *Poland* 51°0N 16°30E **74** C9
Silgarhi Doti *Nepal* 29°15N 81°0E **125** E9
Silghat *India* 26°35N 93°0E **123** F18
Silhouette *Seychelles* 4°29S 55°12E **141** b
Sili *Burkina Faso* 11°37N 2°30W **138** C4
Siliana *Tunisia* 36°5N 9°22E **136** A5
Siliana □ *Tunisia* 36°0N 9°20E **136** A5
Silicon Valley = Santa Clara
Valley U.S.A. 36°50N 121°30W **170** J5
Silifke *Turkey* 36°22N 33°58E **104** D5
Siliguri = Shiliguri
India 26°45N 88°25E **123** F16
Siling Co *China* 31°50N 89°20E **110** E6
Silistea Nouă *Romania* 44°23N 25°1E **81** F10
Silistra *Bulgaria* 44°6N 27°19E **97** B11
Silistra □ *Bulgaria* 44°6N 27°19E **97** B11
Silivri *Turkey* 41°4N 28°14E **97** C12
Siljan *Sweden* 60°55N 14°45E **62** D8
Siljansnäs *Sweden* 60°47N 14°52E **62** D8
Silkeborg *Denmark* 56°10N 9°32E **63** H3
Silkwood *Australia* 17°45S 146°2E **150** B4
Silla *Spain* 39°22N 0°25W **91** F4
Sillajhuay, Cordillera
Chile 19°46S 68°40W **188** G5
Sillamäe *Estonia* 59°24N 27°45E **84** C4
Sillé-le-Guillaume *France* 48°10N 0°8W **70** D6
Silleda *Spain* 42°42N 8°14W **88** C2
Sillod *India* 20°17N 75°39E **126** D2
Silloth *U.K.* 54°52N 3°23W **66** C4
Sillustani *Peru* 15°50S 70°7W **188** D3
Silo *Greece* 41°10N 25°53E **97** E9
Siloam Springs U.S.A. 36°11N 94°32W **176** C7
Silopi *Turkey* 37°15N 42°27E **105** D10
Siluko *Nigeria* 6°35N 5°10E **139** D6
Šilutė *Lithuania* 55°21N 21°33E **84** C8
Silvan *Turkey* 38°7N 41°2E **105** C9
Silvani *India* 23°45N 78°4E **125** H8
Silvassa *India* 20°16N 73°1E **126** D1
Silver City *U.S.A.* 32°46N 108°17W **169** K9
Silver Cr. → *U.S.A.* 43°16N 119°13W **168** E4
Silver L. *U.S.A.* 38°39N 120°6W **170** G6
Silver Lake *Calif.,*
U.S.A. 35°21N 116°7W **171** K10
Silver Lake *Oreg., U.S.A.* 43°8N 121°3W **168** E3
Silver Springs U.S.A. 39°25N 119°13W **170** F4
Silverdale *Sweden* 57°32N 15°45E **63** G9
Silvermine Mts. *Ireland* 52°47N 8°15W **64** D3
Silverton *Australia* 31°52S 141°10E **152** A4
Silverton *Colo.,*
U.S.A. 37°49N 107°40W **169** H10
Silverton *Tex., U.S.A.* 34°28N 101°19W **176** D4
Silves *Portugal* 37°11N 8°26W **89** H2
Silvi Marina *Italy* 42°34N 14°5E **93** F11
Silvies → *U.S.A.* 43°34N 119°2W **168** E4
Silvretta Horn *Switz.* 46°50N 10°6E **78** E2
Silwa Bahari *Egypt* 24°45N 32°55E **137** D3
Silz *Austria* 47°16N 10°56E **78** D3
Sim, C. *Morocco* 31°26N 9°51W **136** B2
Simaltala *India* 24°43N 86°33E **125** G12
Simanggang = Bandar Sri Aman
Malaysia 1°15N 111°32E **118** D4
Simao *China* 22°47N 101°5E **116** F3
Simão Dias *Brazil* 10°44S 37°49W **189** E11
Simard, L. *Canada* 47°40N 78°40W **164** C4
Şimareh → *Iran* 33°1N 47°17E **105** C12
Simav *Turkey* 39°4N 28°58E **97** E13
Simav *Turkey* 40°23N 28°31E **97** E12
Simav Dağları *Turkey* 39°30N 28°50E **99** B10
Simba *Tanzania* 2°10S 37°36E **142** C4
Simbach *Germany* 48°16N 13°3E **77** G9
Simbirsk = Ulyanovsk
Russia 54°20N 48°25E **86** C9
Simcoe *Canada* 42°50N 80°20W **174** D4
Simcoe, L. *Canada* 44°25N 79°20W **174** B5
Simdega *India* 22°37N 84°31E **125** H11
Simeonovgrad *Bulgaria* 42°1N 25°50E **97** D8
Simeria *Romania* 45°51N 23°1E **81** E8
Simeto → *Italy* 37°25N 15°10E **95** E8
Simeulue *Indonesia* 2°45N 95°45E **118** D1
Simferopol *Ukraine* 44°55N 34°3E **85** K8
Simi *Greece* 36°35N 27°50E **99** E9
Simi Valley *U.S.A.* 34°16N 118°47W **171** L8
Simikot *Nepal* 30°0N 81°50E **125** E9
Simmeri → *Iran* 36°59N 45°54E **105** C11
Simitli *Bulgaria* 41°52N 23°7E **97** D7
Simla = Shimla *India* 31°2N 77°9E **124** D7
Şimleu-Silvaniei
Romania 47°17N 22°50E **81** C7
Simlipal △ *India* 21°36N 86°20E **125** J12
Simmer *Germany* 49°58N 7°30E **77** F4
Simmie *Canada* 49°56N 108°6W **162** D6
Simmler U.S.A. 35°21N 119°59W **171** K7
Simnas *Lithuania* 54°24N 23°39E **82** D10
Simo älv = Simojoki →
Finland 65°35N 25°1E **60** D21
Simões *Brazil* 7°30S 40°49W **189** B2
Simojoki → *Finland* 65°35N 25°1E **60** D21
Simojovel *Mexico* 17°12N 92°38W **181** D6
Simonette → *Canada* 55°9N 118°15W **162** B5
Simonstown *S. Africa* 34°14S 18°26E **144** E2
Simontornya *Hungary* 46°45N 18°33E **80** D3
Simpang Empat
Malaysia 5°27N 100°29E **121** c

Simplício Mendes *Brazil* 7°51S 41°54W **189** B2
Simplonpass *Switz.* 46°15N 8°3E **77** J4
Simplontunnel *Switz.* 46°15N 8°7E **77** J4
Simpson Desert
Australia 25°0S 137°0E **150** D2
Simpson Desert △
Australia 25°0S 137°0E **150** D2
Simpson Pen. *Canada* 68°34N 88°45W **161** D14
Simrishamn *Sweden* 55°33N 14°22E **63** J8
Simsbury *U.S.A.* 41°53N 72°48W **175** E12
Simushir, Ostrov
Russia 46°50N 152°30E **107** E16
Sin Cowe I. *S. China Sea* 9°53N 114°19E **118** C4
Sina → *India* 17°30N 75°55E **126** F2
Sina Dhaqa *Somalia* 5°50N 47°0E **131** F4
Sinabang *Indonesia* 2°30N 96°24E **118** D1
Sinai = Es Sînâ' *Egypt* 29°0N 34°0E **130** F2
Sinai, Mt. = Mûsa, Gebel
Egypt 28°33N 33°59E **128** D2
Sinaia *Romania* 45°21N 25°38E **81** E10
Sinaloa □ *Mexico* 25°0N 107°30W **180** C3
Sinaloa de Leyva
Mexico 25°50N 108°14W **180** B3
Sinalunga *Italy* 43°12N 11°44E **93** E8
Sinan *China* 27°56N 108°13E **116** D7
Sinandrei *Romania* 45°52N 21°13E **80** E6
Sinarades *Greece* 39°34N 19°51E **101** A3
Sincan *Turkey* 40°0N 32°36E **104** B5
Sincanlı *Turkey* 38°45N 30°15E **99** C12
Sincelejo *Colombia* 9°18N 75°24W **186** B3
Sinch'ang *N. Korea* 40°7N 128°28E **115** D15
Sinch'ŏn *N. Korea* 38°17N 125°21E **115** E13
Sinclair *U.S.A.* 41°47N 107°7W **168** F10
Sinclair, L. *U.S.A.* 33°8N 83°12W **178** B4
Sinclair Mills *Canada* 54°5N 121°40W **162** C4
Sinclair's B. *U.K.* 58°31N 3°5W **65** C5
Sinclairville *U.S.A.* 42°16N 79°16W **174** D5
Sincorá, Serra do
Brazil 13°10S 41°20W **189** C2
Sind = Sindh □ *Pakistan* 26°0N 69°0E **124** G3
Sind → *Jammu & Kashmir,*
India 34°18N 74°45E **125** B6
Sind → *Mad. P., India* 26°26N 79°13E **125** F8
Sind Sagar Doab
Pakistan 32°0N 71°30E **124** C4
Sindal *Denmark* 57°28N 10°10E **63** G4
Sindangan *Phil.* 8°10N 123°5E **119** C6
Sindangbarang
Indonesia 7°27S 107°1E **119** G12
Sinde *Zambia* 17°28S 25°51E **143** F2
Sindelfingen *Germany* 48°42N 9°0E **77** G4
Sindewahni *India* 20°17N 79°39E **126** D4
Sindgi *India* 16°55N 76°14E **126** F3
Sindh □ *Pakistan* 26°0N 69°0E **124** G3
Sindh □ *Pakistan* 26°0N 69°0E **124** G3
Sindhnur *India* 15°47N 76°46E **127** G3
Sindhuli Garhi *Nepal* 27°16N 85°58E **125** F11
Sindi *India* 20°48N 78°52E **126** D4
Sindirgi *Turkey* 39°13N 28°10E **99** B10
Sindou *Burkina Faso* 10°35N 5°4W **138** C3
Sine → *Senegal* 14°10N 16°28W **138** C1
Sinegorskiy *Russia* 47°55N 40°52E **87** G5
Sinekli *Turkey* 41°14N 28°12E **97** E12
Sinelnikovo = Synelnykove
Ukraine 48°25N 35°30E **85** H8
Sinendé *Benin* 10°20N 2°22E **139** C5
Sines *Portugal* 37°56N 8°51W **89** H2
Sines, C. de *Portugal* 37°58N 8°53W **89** H2
Sineu *Spain* 39°38N 3°1E **100** B10
Sinfra *Ivory C.* 6°35N 5°56W **138** D3
Sing Buri *Thailand* 14°53N 100°25E **120** E3
Singa *Sudan* 13°10N 33°57E **135** F12
Singalila △ *India* 11°2N 77°6E **127** J3
Singanallur *India* 11°2N 77°1E **127** J3
Singapore ■ *Asia* 1°17N 103°51E **121** d
Singapore, Straits of *Asia* 1°15N 104°0E **121** d
Singapore Changi × (SIN)
Singapore 1°23N 103°59E **121** M4
Singaraja *Indonesia* 8°7S 115°6E **118** F5
Singatoka = Sigatoka
Fiji 18°8S 177°32E **154** a
Singen *Germany* 47°45N 8°50E **77** H4
Singida *Tanzania* 4°49S 34°48E **142** C3
Singida □ *Tanzania* 6°0S 34°30E **142** D3
Singitikos Kolpos
Greece 40°6S 24°0E **96** D7
Singkaling Hkamti *Burma* 26°0N 95°39E **123** G19
Singkang *Indonesia* 4°8S 120°1E **119** E6
Singkawang *Indonesia* 1°0N 108°57E **118** D3
Singkep *Indonesia* 0°30S 104°25E **118** E2
Singkil *Indonesia* 2°17N 97°49E **121** L1
Singleton *Australia* 32°33S 151°0E **153** B5
Singleton, Mt. *N. Terr.,*
Australia 22°0S 130°46E **148** D5
Singleton, Mt. *W. Austral.,*
Australia 29°27S 117°15E **149** E2
Singö *Sweden* 60°12N 18°45E **62** D12
Singora = Songkhla
Thailand 7°13N 100°37E **121** J3
Singrauli *India* 24°7N 82°23E **125** G10
Sinh Ton, Dao = Sin Cowe I.
S. China Sea 9°53N 114°19E **118** C4
Sinhoi *Brazil* 13°25N 105°41E **189** C2
Sinhkhkamti *Burma* 27°50N 95°39E **123** G19
Sinhung *N. Korea* 40°11N 127°34E **115** D14
Sinisúcola *Italy* 40°34N 9°41E **94** B2
Sinj *Croatia* 43°42N 16°39E **93** E13
Sinjai *Indonesia* 5°7S 120°20E **119** F6
Sinjajevina *Montenegro* 42°57N 19°22E **96** C3
Sinjār *Iraq* 36°19N 41°52E **105** B10
Sinjār, Jabal *Iraq* 36°23N 41°44E **105** D9
Sinkiang = Xinjiang Uygur
Zizhiqu □ *China* 42°0N 86°0E **109** D11
Sinkö *Guinea* 8°53N 8°16W **138** D3
Sinmak *N. Korea* 38°25N 126°14E **115** E14
Sinmi-do *N. Korea* 39°33N 124°53E **115** E13
Sinnai *Italy* 39°18N 9°13E **94** C2
Sinnamary *Fr. Guiana* 5°25N 52°57W **187** B8
Sinnar *India* 19°48N 74°0E **126** E2
Sinni → *Italy* 40°8N 16°41E **95** B9
Sinnuris *Egypt* 29°26N 30°31E **137** F7
Sinoie, Lacul *Romania* 44°35N 28°56E **81** F13
Sinop *Turkey* 42°1N 35°11E **104** A6
Sinop □ *Turkey* 42°0N 35°0E **104** A6
Sinp'o *N. Korea* 40°0N 128°13E **115** E15
Sinsheim *Germany* 49°15N 8°52E **77** F4
Sinsk *Russia* 61°8N 126°48E **107** C13

Sint-Hubert *Belgium* 50°2N 5°23E **69** D5
Sint-Niklaas *Belgium* 51°10N 4°8E **69** C4
Sint-Truiden *Belgium* 50°48N 5°10E **69** D5
Sintang *Indonesia* 0°5N 111°35E **118** D4
Sinton *U.S.A.* 28°2N 97°31W **176** G6
Sintra *Portugal* 38°47N 9°25W **89** G1
Sintra-Cascais △

Portugal 38°50N 9°25W **89** G1
Sinŭiju *N. Korea* 40°5N 124°24E **115** D13
Sinyukha → *Ukraine* 48°3N 30°51E **85** H6
Sinzig *Germany* 50°32N 7°14E **76** E3
Sio → *Hungary* 46°23N 18°53E **80** D3
Siocon *Phil.* 7°40N 122°10E **119** C6
Siófok *Hungary* 46°54N 18°3E **80** D3
Sion *Switz.* 46°14N 7°20E **77** J3
Sion Mills *U.K.* 54°48N 7°29W **64** B4
tSionainn, An = Shannon →

Ireland 52°35N 9°30W **64** D2
Sioux Center *U.S.A.* 43°5N 96°11W **172** D5
Sioux City *U.S.A.* 42°30N 96°24W **172** D5
Sioux Falls *U.S.A.* 43°33N 96°44W **172** D5
Sioux Lookout *Canada* 50°10N 91°50W **164** B1
Sioux Narrows

Canada 49°25N 94°10W **163** D10
Sipadan *Malaysia* 4°6N 118°38E **119** D5
Šipan *Croatia* 42°45N 17°52E **96** D1
Siparia *Trin. & Tob.* 10°8N 61°31W **187** K15
Sipil Dağı △ *Turkey* 38°35N 27°30E **99** C9
Siping *China* 43°8N 124°21E **115** C13
Sipiwesk L. *Canada* 55°5N 97°35W **163** B9
Siple I. *Antarctica* 73°40S 125°10W **55** D14
Sipra → *India* 23°55N 75°28E **124** H6
Sipsongpanna = Xishuangbanna

China 22°5N 101°1E **116** F3
Sipur *India* 21°11N 85°9E **126** D7
Sipura *Indonesia* 2°18S 99°40E **118** E1
Siquia → *Nic.* 12°10N 84°20W **182** D3
Siquijor *Phil.* 9°12N 123°35E **119** C6
Siquirres *Costa Rica* 10°6N 83°30W **182** D3
Şīr Abū Nu'ayr *U.A.E.* 25°20N 54°20E **129** E7
Şīr Banī Yās *U.A.E.* 24°19N 52°37E **129** E7
Sir Edward Pellew Group

Australia 15°40S 137°10E **150** B2
Sir Graham Moore Is.

Australia 13°53S 126°34E **148** B4
Sir James MacBrien, Mt.

Canada 62°7N 127°41W **160** E6
Sira *India* 13°41N 76°49E **127** H3
Sira → *Norway* 58°23N 6°34E **61** G12
Siracusa *Italy* 37°4N 15°17E **95** E8
Sirajganj *Bangla.* 24°25N 89°47E **125** G13
Sirakoro *Mali* 12°41N 9°14W **138** C3
Şiran *Turkey* 40°11N 39°7E **105** B8
Sirasso *Ivory C.* 9°16N 6°6W **138** D3
Sirathu *India* 25°39N 81°19E **125** G9
Şīrdān *Iran* 36°39N 49°12E **105** D13
Sirdaryo □ *Uzbekistan* 40°30N 68°45E **109** D7
Siren *U.S.A.* 45°47N 92°24W **172** C7
Sirente-Velino △ *Italy* 42°10N 13°32E **93** F10
Sirer *Spain* 38°56N 1°22E **100** C7
Siret *Romania* 47°55N 26°5E **81** C11
Siret → *Romania* 45°24N 28°1E **81** E12
Sirghāyā *Syria* 33°51N 36°8E **130** B5
Şiria *Romania* 46°16N 21°38E **80** D6
Sirikit Res. *Thailand* 17°45N 100°34E **120** C3
Sirinat △ *Thailand* 8°6N 98°17E **121** a
Sirino, Mte. *Italy* 40°7N 15°50E **95** B8
Şīrjān *Iran* 29°30N 55°45E **129** D7
Sirkali = Sirkazhi *India* 11°15N 79°41E **127** J4
Sirkazhi *India* 11°15N 79°41E **127** J4
Sirmans *U.S.A.* 30°21N 83°39W **178** E6
Sirmaur *India* 24°51N 81°23E **125** G9
Sirmilik △ *Canada* 72°50N 80°35W **161** C15
Sirmione *Italy* 45°30N 10°36E **92** C7
Sirna *Greece* 36°22N 26°42E **99** E8
Şirnak *Turkey* 37°31N 42°28E **105** D10
Sirohi *India* 24°52N 72°53E **124** G5
Sironj *India* 24°5N 77°39E **124** G7
Siros = Ermoupoli

Greece 37°28N 24°57E **98** D6
Sirpur *India* 19°29N 79°36E **126** E4
Sirr, Nafud as *Si. Arabia* 25°33N 44°35E **128** E5
Sirretta Pk. *U.S.A.* 35°56N 118°19W **171** K8
Şīrrī *Iran* 25°55N 54°32E **129** E7
Sirsa *India* 29°33N 75°4E **124** E6
Sirsa → *India* 26°51N 79°4E **125** F8
Sirsi *India* 14°40N 74°49E **127** G2
Sirsilla *India* 18°23N 78°50E **126** E4
Sirte = Surt *Libya* 31°11N 16°39E **135** B9
Siruela *Spain* 38°58N 5°3W **89** G5
Siruguppa *India* 15°38N 76°54E **127** F3
Sirur *India* 18°50N 74°23E **126** E2
Şirvan *Azerbaijan* 39°59N 48°52E **87** L9
Sirvān → *Iran* 35°4N 46°50E **105** E12
Sisak *Croatia* 45°30N 16°21E **93** C13
Sisante *Spain* 39°25N 2°12W **91** F2
Sisargas, Is. *Spain* 43°21N 8°50W **88** B2
Sishen *S. Africa* 27°47S 22°59E **144** C3
Sishui *China* 35°42N 117°18E **115** G9
Sisian *Armenia* 39°31N 46°1E **105** C12
Sisimiut *Greenland* 66°40N 53°30W **57** D5
Sisipuk L. *Canada* 55°45N 101°50W **163** B8
Sisophon *Cambodia* 13°38N 102°59E **120** F4
Sisseton *U.S.A.* 45°40N 97°3W **172** C5
Sissonne *France* 49°34N 3°51E **71** C10
Sīstān *Asia* 30°50N 61°0E **129** D9
Sīstān, Daryācheh-ye

Iran 31°0N 61°0E **129** D9
Sīstān va Balūchestān □

Iran 27°0N 62°0E **129** E9
Sisteron *France* 44°12N 5°57E **73** D9
Sisters, The *Seychelles* 4°16S 55°52E **141** b
Siswa Bazar *India* 27°9N 83°46E **125** F10
Sitakili *Mali* 13°7N 11°14W **138** C2
Sitamarhi *India* 26°37N 85°30E **125** F11
Sitapur *India* 27°38N 80°45E **125** F9
Siteki *Swaziland* 26°32S 31°58E **145** D5
Sitges *Spain* 41°17N 1°47E **90** D6
Sithonia *Greece* 40°0N 23°45E **96** F7
Sitia *Greece* 35°11N 26°10E **101** D8
Sitio da Abadia *Brazil* 14°48S 46°16W **189** G9
Sitito-Ozima Ridge

Pac. Oc. 23°0N 143°0E **156** E6
Sitka *U.S.A.* 57°3N 135°20W **170** B1
Sitkaing = Sagaing

Burma 21°52N 95°59E **123** J19
Sitoti *Botswana* 23°15S 23°40E **144** B3
Sitra *Egypt* 28°40N 26°53E **137** B2

Sittang Myit →

Burma 17°20N 96°45E **123** L20
Sittard *Neths.* 51°0N 5°52E **69** C5
Sittensen *Germany* 53°17N 9°32E **76** B5
Sittingbourne *U.K.* 51°21N 0°45E **67** F8
Sittoung = Sittang Myit →

Burma 17°20N 96°45E **123** L20
Sittwe *Burma* 20°18N 92°45E **123** J18
Situbondo *Indonesia* 7°42S 113°56E **119** G16
Siuna *Nic.* 13°37N 84°45W **182** D3
Siuri *India* 23°50N 87°34E **125** H12
Siutghiol, Lacul

Romania 44°15N 28°35E **81** F13
Sivaganga *India* 9°50N 78°28E **127** K4
Sivagiri *India* 9°16N 77°26E **127** K3
Sivakasi *India* 9°24N 77°47E **127** K3
Sīvand *Iran* 30°5N 52°55E **129** D7
Sivas *Turkey* 39°43N 36°58E **104** C7
Sivas □ *Turkey* 39°45N 37°0E **104** C7
Sivasamudram *India* 12°17N 77°10E **127** H3
Sivaslı *Turkey* 38°31N 29°42E **99** C11
Siverek *Turkey* 37°50N 39°19E **105** D8
Sivrihisar *Turkey* 39°30N 31°35E **104** C4
Sīwa *Egypt* 29°11N 25°31E **137** B2
Sīwa, El Wâhât es

Egypt 29°10N 25°30E **137** B2
Siwa Oasis = Sīwa, El Wâhât es

Egypt 29°10N 25°30E **137** B2
Siwalik Range *Nepal* 28°0N 83°0E **125** F10
Siwan *India* 26°13N 84°21E **125** F11
Siwana *India* 25°38N 72°25E **124** G5
Six Cross Roads *Barbados* 13°7N 59°28W **183** g
Six-Fours-les-Plages

France 43°6N 5°49E **73** E9
Sixian *China* 33°30N 117°50E **115** H9
Sixmilebridge *Ireland* 52°44N 8°46W **64** D3
Sixth Cataract *Sudan* 16°20N 32°42E **135** E12
Siyabuswa *S. Africa* 25°7S 29°3E **145** C4
Siyah Kuh, Kavīr-e

Iran 32°55N 53°55E **129** C7
Siyāl, Jazā'ir *Egypt* 22°49N 36°12E **137** C4
Siyang *China* 33°42N 118°40E **115** H10
Siyāzän *Azerbaijan* 41°3N 49°10E **87** K9
Siziwang Qi *China* 41°25N 111°40E **114** D6
Sjælland *Denmark* 55°30N 11°30E **63** D5
Sjælland □ *Denmark* 55°30N 11°30E **63** J5
Sjællands Odde *Denmark* 55°58N 11°24E **63** J5
Sjenica *Serbia* 43°16N 20°0E **96** C3
Sjöbo *Sweden* 55°37N 13°45E **63** J7
Sjötofta *Sweden* 57°22N 13°17E **63** G7
Sjötorp *Sweden* 58°50N 14°0E **63** F7
Sjumen = Shumen

Bulgaria 43°18N 26°55E **97** C10
Sjuntorp *Sweden* 58°12N 12°13E **63** F6
Skadarsko Jezero *Europe* 42°10N 19°20E **96** D3
Skadarsko Jezero △

Montenegro 42°10N 19°20E **96** D3
Skadovsk *Ukraine* 46°17N 32°52E **85** J7
Skælskør *Denmark* 55°15N 11°18E **63** J5
Skærbæk *Denmark* 55°9N 8°45E **63** J2
Skaftafell *Iceland* 64°1N 17°0W **60** D5
Skaftafell △ *Iceland* 64°9N 16°50W **60** D5
Skagafjörður *Iceland* 65°54N 19°35W **60** D4
Skagastølstindane

Norway 61°28N 7°52E **60** F12
Skagaströnd *Iceland* 65°50N 20°19W **60** D3
Skagen *Denmark* 57°43N 10°35E **63** G4
Skagern *Sweden* 59°0N 14°20E **62** E8
Skagerrak *Denmark* 57°30N 9°0E **63** G2
Skagit → *U.S.A.* 48°23N 122°22W **170** B4
Skagway *U.S.A.* 59°28N 135°19W **160** F4
Skala-Podilska *Ukraine* 48°50N 26°15E **81** B11
Skalat *Ukraine* 49°23N 25°55E **75** D13
Skalbmierz *Poland* 50°20N 20°25E **83** H7
Skälderviken *Sweden* 56°22N 12°30E **63** H6
Skalica *Slovak Rep.* 48°50N 17°15E **79** C10
Skallingen *Denmark* 55°32N 8°13E **63** J2
Skalni Dol = Kamenyak

Bulgaria 43°24N 26°57E **97** C10
Skanderborg *Denmark* 56°2N 9°55E **63** H3
Skåne *Sweden* 55°59N 13°30E **63** J7
Skåne □ *Sweden* 56°15N 14°0E **63** H7
Skaneateles *U.S.A.* 42°57N 76°26W **175** D8
Skaneateles L. *U.S.A.* 42°51N 76°22W **175** D8
Skänninge *Sweden* 58°24N 15°5E **63** F9
Skanör med Falsterbo

Sweden 55°24N 12°50E **63** J6
Skantzoura *Greece* 39°5N 24°6E **98** B6
Skara *Sweden* 58°25N 13°30E **63** F7
Skärblacka *Sweden* 58°35N 15°54E **63** F9
Skardu *Pakistan* 35°20N 75°44E **125** B6
Skåre *Sweden* 59°26N 13°26E **63** F7
Skärhamn *Sweden* 57°59N 11°34E **63** F5
Skarszewy *Poland* 54°4N 18°25E **82** D5
Skarvan og Roltdalen △

Norway 63°16N 11°31E **60** E14
Skaryszew *Poland* 51°19N 21°15E **83** G8
Skarżysko-Kamienna

Poland 51°7N 20°52E **83** G7
Skattkärr *Sweden* 59°25N 13°40E **62** E7
Skattungbyn *Sweden* 61°10N 14°56E **62** C8
Skawina *Poland* 49°59N 19°50E **83** J6
Skebobruk *Sweden* 59°58N 18°36E **62** E12
Skee *Sweden* 58°56N 11°19E **63** F5
Skeena → *Canada* 54°9N 130°5W **162** C2
Skeena Mts. *Canada* 56°40N 128°30W **162** B3
Skegness *U.K.* 53°9N 0°20E **66** D8
Skeleton Coast *Namibia* 20°0S 13°0E **141** J2
Skeleton Coast △

Namibia 20°0S 13°20E **144** B1
Skellefteå *Sweden* 64°45N 20°50E **60** D19
Skellefteälven →

Sweden 64°45N 21°10E **60** D19
Skelleftehamn *Sweden* 64°40N 21°9E **60** D19
Skellig Michael = Great Skellig

Ireland 51°47N 10°33W **64** E1
Skender Vakuf *Bos.-H.* 44°29N 17°22E **80** F2
Skënderaj *Kosovo* 42°45N 20°47E **96** C5
Skerries *Ireland* 53°35N 6°8W **64** C5
Skerries, The *U.K.* 53°25N 4°36W **66** D3
Skhidnytsya *Ukraine* 49°17N 23°18E **83** J10
Skhiza *Greece* 36°41N 21°40E **98** E3
Ski *Norway* 59°43N 10°52E **63** E14
Skiathos *Greece* 39°12N 23°30E **98** B5
Skibbereen *Ireland* 51°33N 9°16W **64** F3
Skiddaw *U.K.* 54°39N 3°9W **66** C4
Skidegate *Canada* 53°15N 132°1W **162** C2
Skidra *Greece* 40°46N 22°10E **96** F6
Skien *Norway* 59°12N 9°35E **61** G13
Skierniewice *Poland* 51°58N 20°10E **83** G7
Skihist, Mt. *Canada* 50°12N 121°54W **162** C4

Skikda *Algeria* 36°50N 6°58E **136** A5
Skikda □ *Algeria* 36°45N 6°50E **136** A5
Skillingaryd *Sweden* 57°27N 14°5E **63** G8
Skillinge *Sweden* 55°30N 14°16E **63** J8
Skilloura *Cyprus* 35°14N 33°10E **101** D12
Skinari, Akra *Greece* 37°56N 20°42E **98** D2
Skinnskatteberg *Sweden* 59°50N 15°42E **62** E9
Skipton *Australia* 37°39S 143°40E **152** D5
Skipton *U.K.* 53°58N 2°3W **66** D5
Skiring, C. *Senegal* 12°26N 16°46W **138** C1
Skirmish Pt. *Australia* 11°59S 134°17E **150** A1
Skíros = Skyros *Greece* 38°55N 24°34E **98** C6
Skivarp *Sweden* 55°23N 13°34E **63** J7
Skive *Denmark* 56°33N 9°2E **63** H3
Skjálfandafljót →

Iceland 65°59N 17°25W **60** D5
Skjálfandi *Iceland* 66°5N 17°30W **60** C5
Skjern *Denmark* 55°57N 8°30E **63** J2
Skjern Å △ *Denmark* 55°50N 8°30E **63** H2
Škocjanske Jame

Slovenia 45°40N 14°0E **93** C10
Skoczów *Poland* 49°49N 18°45E **83** J5
Škofja Loka *Slovenia* 46°9N 14°19E **93** B11
Skoghall *Sweden* 59°20N 13°30E **62** E7
Skogstorp *Sweden* 59°19N 16°29E **62** E10
Skoki *Poland* 52°40N 17°11E **83** F4
Skole *Ukraine* 49°3N 23°30E **75** D12
Skopelos *Greece* 39°9N 23°47E **98** B5
Skopi *Greece* 35°11N 26°2E **101** D8
Skopin *Russia* 53°55N 39°32E **84** F10
Skopje *Macedonia* 42°1N 21°26E **96** D5
Skopje ✈ (SKP)

Macedonia 41°59N 21°29E **96** E5
Skórcz *Poland* 53°47N 18°30E **82** E5
Skørping *Denmark* 56°50N 9°53E **63** H3
Skövde *Sweden* 58°24N 13°50E **63** F7
Skovorodino *Russia* 54°0N 124°0E **107** D13
Skowhegan *U.S.A.* 44°46N 69°43W **173** C19
Skradin *Croatia* 43°52N 15°53E **93** E12
Skrea *Sweden* 56°53N 12°34E **63** H6
Skrunda *Latvia* 56°41N 22°1E **82** B9
Skurup *Sweden* 55°28N 13°30E **63** J7
Skutskär *Sweden* 60°37N 17°25E **62** D11
Skvyra *Ukraine* 49°44N 29°40E **75** D15
Skye *U.K.* 57°15N 6°10W **65** D2
Skykomish *U.S.A.* 47°42N 121°22W **168** C3
Skyring, Seno *Chile* 52°35S 72°0W **192** D3
Skyropoula *Greece* 38°50N 24°23E **98** C6
Skyros = Skyros *Greece* 38°55N 24°34E **98** C6
Skyros *Greece* 38°55N 24°34E **98** C6
Skyttorp *Sweden* 60°5N 17°44E **62** D11
Slade Point *Australia* 21°4S 149°13E **150** b
Slade Pt. *Australia* 21°5S 149°13E **150** b
Slættaratindur *Faroe Is.* 62°18N 7°1W **60** E9
Slagelse *Denmark* 55°23N 11°19E **63** J5
Slamet *Indonesia* 7°16S 109°8E **119** G13
Slane *Ireland* 53°42N 6°33W **64** C5
Slaney → *Ireland* 52°26N 6°33W **64** D5
Slangberge *S. Africa* 31°32S 20°48E **144** D3
Slănic *Romania* 45°14N 25°58E **81** E10
Slano *Croatia* 42°48N 17°53E **96** D1
Slantsy *Russia* 59°7N 28°5E **84** C5
Slaný *Czech Rep.* 50°13N 14°6E **78** A7
Śląsk □ *Poland* 51°0N 16°30E **74** D9
Śląskie □ *Poland* 50°30N 19°0E **83** H6
Slate Is. *Canada* 48°40N 87°0W **164** C2
Slatina *Croatia* 45°42N 17°45E **80** E2
Slatina *Romania* 44°28N 24°22E **81** F9
Slatina Timiş *Romania* 45°15N 22°17E **80** E7
Slatington *U.S.A.* 40°45N 75°37W **175** F9
Slaton *U.S.A.* 33°26N 101°39W **176** E4
Slave → *Canada* 61°18N 113°39W **162** A6
Slave Coast *W. Afr.* 6°0N 2°30E **139** D5
Slave Lake *Canada* 55°17N 114°43W **162** B6
Slave Pt. *Canada* 61°11N 115°56W **162** A5
Slavgorod *Russia* 53°1N 78°37E **109** D9
Slavinja *Serbia* 43°9N 22°50E **96** C6
Slavkov u Brna

Czech Rep. 49°10N 16°52E **79** B9
Slavkovský Les △

Czech Rep. 50°5N 12°44E **78** A5
Slavonija *Europe* 45°0N 18°0E **80** E2
Slavonski Brod *Croatia* 45°11N 18°1E **80** E3
Slavsk *Russia* 55°3N 21°41E **82** D8
Slavske *Ukraine* 48°51N 23°27E **81** B8
Slavskoye *Russia* 54°30N 20°27E **82** D7
Slavuta *Ukraine* 50°15N 27°2E **75** C14
Slavyanka *Russia* 42°53N 131°21E **112** C5
Slavyanovo *Bulgaria* 43°28N 24°52E **97** C8
Slavyansk = Slovyansk

Ukraine 48°55N 37°36E **85** H9
Slavyansk-na-Kubani

Russia 45°15N 38°11E **85** K10
Sława *Poland* 51°52N 16°2E **83** G3
Sławharad *Belarus* 53°27N 31°0E **75** B16
Sławno *Poland* 54°20N 16°41E **82** D3
Sławoborze *Poland* 53°55N 15°42E **82** E2
Slea Hd. *Ireland* 52°6N 10°27W **64** D1
Sleaford *U.K.* 53°0N 0°24W **66** D7
Sleaford B. *Australia* 34°55S 135°45E **151** E2
Sleat, Sd. of *U.K.* 57°5N 5°47W **65** D3
Sleeper Is. *Canada* 58°30N 81°0W **161** F15
Sleeping Bear Dunes △

U.S.A. 44°50N 86°5W **172** C10
Sleepy Eye *U.S.A.* 44°18N 94°43W **172** C6
Slemon L. *Canada* 63°13N 116°4W **162** A5
Slide Mt. *U.S.A.* 42°0N 74°25W **175** E10
Sliedrecht *Neths.* 51°50N 4°45E **69** C4
Sliema *Malta* 35°55N 14°30E **101** D2
Slieve Aughty *Ireland* 53°4N 8°30W **64** C3
Slieve Bloom *Ireland* 53°4N 7°40W **64** C4
Slieve Donard *U.K.* 54°11N 5°55W **64** B6
Slieve Gamph *Ireland* 54°6N 9°0W **64** B3
Slieve Gullion *U.K.* 54°7N 6°26W **64** B5
Slieve League *Ireland* 54°40N 8°42W **64** B3
Slieve Mish *Ireland* 52°12N 9°50W **64** D2
Slievenamon *Ireland* 52°25N 7°34W **64** D4
Sligeach = Sligo *Ireland* 54°16N 8°28W **64** B3
Sligo *Ireland* 54°16N 8°28W **64** B3
Sligo □ *Ireland* 54°8N 8°42W **64** B3

Sligo B. *Ireland* 54°18N 8°40W **64** B3
Slippery Rock *U.S.A.* 41°4N 80°3W **174** E4
Slite *Sweden* 57°42N 18°48E **63** G12
Sliven *Bulgaria* 42°42N 26°19E **97** D10
Sliven □ *Bulgaria* 42°42N 26°19E **97** D10
Sljeme *Croatia* 45°57N 15°58E **93** C12
Sloan *U.S.A.* 35°57N 115°13W **171** K11
Sloansville *U.S.A.* 42°45N 74°22W **175** D10
Slobidka *Ukraine* 47°54N 29°21E **81** C14
Slobozia *Moldova* 46°45N 29°42E **81** C14
Slobozia Argeş, *Romania* 44°30N 25°14E **81** F9
Slobozia Ialomiţa,

Romania 44°34N 27°23E **81** F12
Slocan *Canada* 49°48N 117°28W **162** D5
Slocomb *U.S.A.* 31°7N 85°36W **178** D4
Słomniki *Poland* 50°16N 20°4E **83** H7
Slonim *Belarus* 53°4N 25°19E **75** B13
Slough *U.K.* 51°30N 0°36W **67** F7
Slough □ *U.K.* 51°30N 0°36W **67** F7
Sloughhouse *U.S.A.* 38°26N 121°12W **170** G5
Slovak Rep. ■ *Europe* 48°30N 20°0E **79** C13
Slovakia = Slovak Rep. ■

Europe 48°30N 20°0E **79** C13
Slovakian Ore Mts. = Slovenské

Rudohorie *Slovak Rep.* 48°45N 20°0E **79** C12
Slovenia ■ *Europe* 45°58N 14°30E **93** C11
Slovenija = Slovenia ■

Europe 45°58N 14°30E **93** C11
Slovenj Gradec *Slovenia* 46°31N 15°5E **93** B12
Slovenska = Slovak Rep. ■

Europe 48°30N 20°0E **79** C13
Slovenska Bistrica

Slovenia 46°24N 15°35E **93** B12
Slovenske Konjice

Slovenia 46°20N 15°28E **93** B12
Slovenské Rudohorie

Slovak Rep. 48°45N 20°0E **79** C12
Slovenský Kras △

Slovak Rep. 48°40N 20°20E **79** C13
Slovenský Raj △

Slovak Rep. 48°53N 20°25E **79** C13
Slovyansk *Ukraine* 48°55N 37°36E **85** H9
Słowiński △ *Poland* 54°43N 17°26E **82** D4
Słubice *Poland* 52°22N 14°35E **83** F1
Sluch → *Ukraine* 51°37N 26°38E **75** C14
Sluis *Neths.* 51°18N 3°23E **69** C3
Slŭnchev Bryag

Bulgaria 42°40N 27°41E **97** D11
Slunj *Croatia* 45°6N 15°33E **93** C12
Slupca *Poland* 52°15N 17°52E **83** F4
Słupia → *Poland* 54°35N 16°51E **82** D3
Słupsk *Poland* 54°30N 17°3E **82** D4
Slurry *S. Africa* 25°49S 25°42E **144** C4
Slutsk *Belarus* 53°2N 27°31E **75** B14
Slyne Hd. *Ireland* 53°25N 10°10W **64** C1
Slyudyanka *Russia* 51°40N 103°40E **107** D11
Småland *Sweden* 57°15N 15°25E **63** G9
Smålandsfarvandet

Denmark 55°10N 11°20E **63** J5
Smålandsstenar *Sweden* 57°10N 13°25E **63** G7
Smalltree L. *Canada* 61°0N 105°0W **163** A8
Smallwood Res. *Canada* 54°5N 64°30W **165** B7
Smarhon *Belarus* 54°20N 26°24E **75** A14
Smarje *Slovenia* 46°15N 15°34E **93** B12
Smartt Syndicate Dam

S. Africa 30°45S 23°10E **144** D3
Smartville *U.S.A.* 39°13N 121°18W **170** F5
Smeaton *Canada* 53°30N 104°49W **163** C8
Smederevo *Serbia* 44°40N 20°57E **96** B4
Smederevska Palanka

Serbia 44°22N 20°58E **96** B4
Smedjebacken *Sweden* 60°8N 15°25E **62** D9
Smela = Smila *Ukraine* 49°15N 31°58E **85** H6
Smeralda, Costa *Italy* 41°5N 9°35E **94** A2
Smerwick Harbour

Ireland 52°12N 10°23W **64** D1
Smethport *U.S.A.* 41°49N 78°27W **174** E6
Smidovich *Russia* 48°36N 133°49E **107** E14
Śmigiel *Poland* 52°1N 16°32E **83** F3
Smila *Ukraine* 49°15N 31°58E **85** H6
Smilyan *Bulgaria* 41°29N 24°46E **97** E8
Smith *Canada* 55°10N 114°0W **162** B6
Smith Center *U.S.A.* 39°47N 98°47W **172** F4
Smith I. *Canada* 60°45N 78°25W **161** E16
Smith I. *India* 13°20N 93°4E **127** H11
Smith Islands △

Australia 20°40S 149°9E **150** b
Smith River *U.S.A.* 41°55N 124°0W **168** F7
Smith Sd. *N. Amer.* 78°25N 74°0W **57** B3
Smithburne →

Australia 17°3S 140°57E **150** B3
Smithers *Canada* 54°45N 127°10W **162** C3
Smithfield *S. Africa* 30°9S 26°30E **145** D4
Smithfield N.C.,

U.S.A. 35°31N 78°21W **177** D15
Smithfield Utah,

U.S.A. 41°50N 111°50W **168** F8
Smiths Falls *Canada* 44°55N 76°0W **175** B8
Smithton *Australia* 40°53S 145°6E **151** G4
Smithton *Canada* 56°41N 16°13E **63** H8
Smithville *Ga., U.S.A.* 31°54N 84°15W **178** D5
Smithville *Tex., U.S.A.* 30°1N 97°10W **176** F6
Smoke Creek Desert

U.S.A. 40°30N 119°40W **168** F4
Smoky → *Canada* 56°10N 117°21W **162** B5
Smoky Bay *Australia* 32°22S 134°13E **151** E1
Smoky Hill → *U.S.A.* 39°4N 96°48W **172** F6
Smoky Hills *U.S.A.* 39°15N 99°30W **172** F4
Smoky Lake *Canada* 54°10N 112°30W **162** C6
Smøla *Norway* 63°23N 8°3E **60** E13
Smolensk *Russia* 54°45N 32°5E **84** E7
Smolikas, Oros *Greece* 40°9N 20°58E **96** F4
Smolník *Slovak Rep.* 48°43N 20°44E **79** C13
Smolny → *Russia* 53°54N 47°10E **86** C17
Smolyan *Bulgaria* 41°36N 24°38E **97** E8
Smolyan □ *Bulgaria* 41°36N 24°38E **97** E8
Smooth Rock Falls

Canada 49°17N 81°37W **164** C3
Smoothstone L.

Canada 54°40N 106°50W **163** C7
Smorgon = Smarhon

Belarus 54°20N 26°24E **75** A14
Smotrych *Ukraine* 48°57N 26°39E **85** H3
Smotrych → *Ukraine* 48°34N 26°39E **81** B11

Smulţi *Romania* 45°57N 27°44E **81** E12
Smyadovo *Bulgaria* 43°2N 27°1E **97** C10
Smygehamn *Sweden* 55°21N 13°22E **63** J7
Smygehuk *Sweden* 55°20N 13°20E **63** J7
Smyley I. *Antarctica* 72°55S 78°0W **55** D17
Smyrna = İzmir *Turkey* 38°25N 27°8E **99** C9
Smyrna *Del., U.S.A.* 39°18N 75°36W **173** F16
Smyrna *Ga., U.S.A.* 33°53N 84°31W **178** B5
Snaefell *I. of Man* 54°16N 4°27W **66** C3
Snæfell *Iceland* 64°48N 15°34W **60** D6
Snæfellsjökull *Iceland* 64°49N 23°46W **60** D2
Snake → *Canada* 46°12N 119°2W **168** C4
Snake I. *Australia* 38°47S 146°33E **153** E7
Snake Range *U.S.A.* 39°0N 114°20W **168** G6
Snake River Plain

U.S.A. 42°50N 114°0W **168** E7
Snåsahögarna *Sweden* 63°13N 12°21E **62** A6
Snåsavatnet *Norway* 64°12N 12°0E **60** D15
Snedsted *Denmark* 56°55N 8°32E **63** H2
Sneek *Neths.* 53°2N 5°40E **69** A5
Sneem *Ireland* 51°50N 9°54W **64** E2
Sneeuberge *S. Africa* 31°46S 24°20E **144** D3
Snejbjerg *Denmark* 56°8N 8°54E **63** H2
Snelling *Calif., U.S.A.* 37°31N 120°26W **170** H6
Snelling *S.C., U.S.A.* 33°15N 81°27W **178** B8
Snells Beach *N.Z.* 36°25S 174°44E **154** C3
Sneznoye *Ukraine* 48°0N 38°58E **85** J10
Snežka *Europe* 50°41N 15°50E **83** A8
Snežnik *Slovenia* 45°36N 14°35E **93** C11
Śniadowo *Poland* 53°0N 22°0E **83** E8
Śniardwy, Jezioro *Poland* 53°48N 21°50E **82** E8
Snieżka *Europe* 50°44N 15°44E **78** A8
Snigirevka = Snihurivka

Ukraine 47°2N 32°49E **85** J7
Snihurivka *Ukraine* 47°2N 32°49E **85** J7
Snina *Slovak Rep.* 48°58N 22°9E **79** C15
Snizort, L. *U.K.* 57°33N 6°28W **65** D2
Snøhetta *Norway* 62°19N 9°16E **60** E13
Snohomish *U.S.A.* 47°55N 122°6W **170** C4
Snoqualmie *U.S.A.* 47°31N 121°49W **170** C5
Snoqualmie Pass

U.S.A. 47°25N 121°25W **170** C5
Snoul *Cambodia* 12°4N 106°26E **121** F6
Snover *U.S.A.* 43°27N 82°58W **174** C2
Snow Hill *U.S.A.* 38°11N 75°24W **173** F16
Snow Lake *Canada* 54°52N 100°3W **163** C8
Snow Mt. *Calif.,*

U.S.A. 39°23N 122°45W **170** F4
Snow Mt. *Maine,*

U.S.A. 45°18N 70°48W **175** A14
Snow Shoe *U.S.A.* 41°2N 77°57W **174** E7
Snowbird L. *Canada* 60°45N 103°0W **163** A8
Snowdon *U.K.* 53°4N 4°5W **66** D3
Snowdonia △ *U.K.* 53°7N 3°59W **66** D4
Snowdrift = Lutsel K'e

Canada 62°24N 110°44W **163** A6
Snowdrift → *Canada* 62°24N 110°44W **163** A6
Snowflake *U.S.A.* 34°30N 110°5W **169** J8
Snowshoe Pk. *U.S.A.* 48°13N 115°41W **168** B6
Snowtown *Australia* 33°46S 138°14E **152** B3
Snowville *U.S.A.* 41°58N 112°43W **168** F7
Snowy → *Australia* 37°46S 148°30E **153** E8
Snowy Mt. *U.S.A.* 43°42N 74°23W **175** C10
Snowy Mts. *Australia* 36°30S 148°20E **153** D8
Snowy River △

Australia 37°15S 147°29E **153** D7
Snug Corner *Bahamas* 22°33N 73°52W **183** B5
Snug Harbour *Canada* 45°22N 80°17W **174** A4
Snyatyn *Ukraine* 48°27N 25°38E **81** B10
Snyder *Okla., U.S.A.* 34°40N 98°57W **176** D5
Snyder *Tex., U.S.A.* 32°44N 100°55W **176** E4
Soalala *Madag.* 16°6S 45°20E **145** H9
Soan → *Pakistan* 33°1N 71°44E **124** C4
Soars *Romania* 45°24N 24°55E **81** E9
Soba *Nigeria* 10°58N 8°4E **139** C6
Sobat → *South Sudan* 9°22N 31°33E **135** G12
Sobėslav *Czech Rep.* 49°16N 14°45E **78** B7
Sobinka *Russia* 56°0N 40°0E **84** E11
Sobolevo *Russia* 54°20N 155°30E **107** D17
Sobótka *Poland* 50°54N 16°44E **83** H3
Sobradinho, Represa de

Brazil 9°30S 42°0W **189** E10
Sobral *Brazil* 3°50S 40°20W **189** D10
Sobrance *Slovak Rep.* 48°45N 22°11E **79** C15
Sobreira Formosa

Portugal 39°46N 7°51W **88** F3
Soc Giang *Vietnam* 22°54N 106°1E **116** F6
Soc Trang *Vietnam* 9°37N 105°50E **121** H5
Soča → *Europe* 46°20N 13°40E **78** E6
Socastee *U.S.A.* 33°41N 78°59W **177** E15
Sochaczew *Poland* 52°25N 20°13E **83** F7
Soch'e = Shache *China* 38°20N 77°10E **109** E9
Sochi *Russia* 43°35N 39°40E **85** K9
Sochi ✈ (AER) *Russia* 43°27N 39°57E **87** J4
Sochos *Greece* 40°48N 23°22E **96** F7
Social Circle *U.S.A.* 33°39N 83°43W **178** B6
Société, Îs. de la

French Polynesia 17°0S 151°0W **157** J12
Society Hill *U.S.A.* 34°31N 79°51W **177** D15
Society Is. = Société, Îs. de la

French Polynesia 17°0S 151°0W **157** J12
Socompa, Portezuelo de

Chile 24°27S 68°18W **190** A2
Socorro *N. Mex.,*

U.S.A. 34°4N 106°54W **169** J10
Socorro *Tex., U.S.A.* 31°39N 106°18W **176** F1
Socorro, I. *Mexico* 18°45N 110°58W **180** D2
Socotra *Yemen* 12°30N 54°0E **131** E5
Socovos *Spain* 38°20N 1°58W **91** G3
Soda L. *U.S.A.* 35°10N 116°4W **171** K10
Soda Plains *India* 35°30N 79°0E **125** B8
Soda Springs *U.S.A.* 42°39N 111°36W **168** E8
Sodankylä *Finland* 67°29N 26°40E **60** C22
Soddy-Daisy *U.S.A.* 35°17N 85°10W **178** B3
Söderala *Sweden* 61°17N 16°55E **62** C10
Söderbärke *Sweden* 60°13N 15°55E **62** D9
Söderfors *Sweden* 60°23N 17°25E **62** D11
Söderhamn *Sweden* 61°18N 17°10E **62** C11
Söderköping *Sweden* 58°31N 16°35E **63** F10
Södermanlands län □

Sweden 59°10N 16°30E **62** E10
Södertälje *Sweden* 59°12N 17°39E **62** E11
Sodiri *Sudan* 14°27N 29°0E **135** F11
Södra Finnskoga *Sweden* 60°42N 12°34E **62** D6
Södra Sandby *Sweden* 55°43N 13°21E **63** J7

Södra Ulvön *Sweden* 62°59N 18°38E **62** [?]
Södra Vi *Sweden* 57°45N 15°45E **63** [?]
Sodražica *Slovenia* 45°45N 14°39E **93** [?]
Sodus *U.S.A.* 43°14N 77°4W **174** [?]
Sodwana Bay △

S. Africa 27°35S 32°43E **145** [?]
Soe *Indonesia* 9°52S 124°17E **146** [?]
Soekmekaar = Morebeng

S. Africa 23°30S 29°55E **145** [?]
Soest *Germany* 51°34N 8°7E **76** [?]
Soest *Neths.* 52°9N 5°19E **69** [?]
Sofades *Greece* 39°20N 22°4E **98** [?]
Sofala □ *Mozam.* 19°30S 34°30E **145** [?]
Sofala *Mali* 13°59N 4°9W **138** [?]
Sofia = Sofiya *Bulgaria* 42°45N 23°20E **96** [?]
Sofia → *Madag.* 15°27S 47°23E **145** [?]
Sofievka *Ukraine* 48°6N 33°55E **85** [?]
Sofiko *Greece* 37°47N 23°3E **98** [?]
Sofiya *Bulgaria* 42°45N 23°20E **96** [?]
Sofiya □ *Bulgaria* 42°45N 23°20E **96** [?]
Sofiya ✈ (SOF) *Bulgaria* 42°46N 23°28E **96** [?]
Sofrana *Greece* 36°5N 26°24E **99** [?]
Sōfu-Gan *Japan* 29°49N 140°21E **113** [?]
Sogakofe *Ghana* 6°2N 0°39E **139** [?]
Sogamoso *Colombia* 5°43N 72°56W **186** [?]
Sogār *Iran* 25°53N 58°6E **129** [?]
Sögel *Germany* 52°50N 7°31E **76** [?]
Sogndalsfjøra *Norway* 61°14N 7°5E **60** [?]
Søgne *Norway* 58°5N 7°48E **61** [?]
Sognefjorden *Norway* 61°10N 5°50E **60** [?]
Söğüt *Bilecik, Turkey* 40°2N 30°11E **99** [?]
Söğüt *Burdur, Turkey* 37°2N 29°50E **99** [?]
Söğüt Dağı △ *Turkey* 37°50N 29°55E **99** [?]
Söğütlü *Turkey* 38°26N 31°27E **99** [?]
Soh *Iran* 33°26N 51°27E **129** [?]
Sohâg *Egypt* 26°33N 31°43E **137** [?]
Sohagpur *India* 22°42N 78°12E **124** [?]
Sohar = Şuḩār *Oman* 24°20N 56°40E **129** [?]
Sohela *India* 21°18N 83°24E **126** [?]
Soheuksando *S. Korea* 34°4N 125°7E **115** [?]
Sohm Abyssal Plain

Atl. Oc. 36°0N 55°0W **9** [?]
Soignies *Belgium* 50°35N 4°5E **69** [?]
Soin *Burkina Faso* 12°47N 3°50W **138** [?]
Soissons *France* 49°25N 3°19E **71** [?]
Sōja *Japan* 34°40N 133°45E **113** [?]
Sojat *India* 25°55N 73°45E **124** [?]
Sok → *Russia* 53°24N 50°8E **86** [?]
Sokal *Ukraine* 50°31N 24°15E **75** [?]
Sokcho *S. Korea* 38°12N 128°36E **115** [?]
Söke *Turkey* 37°48N 27°28E **99** [?]
Sokelo

Dem. Rep. of the Congo 9°55S 24°36E **142** [?]
Sokhumi *Georgia* 43°0N 41°0E **87** [?]
Sokki, Oued In →

Algeria 29°30N 3°42E **13[?]**
Soko Banja *Serbia* 43°40N 21°51E **96** [?]
Soko Is. *China* 22°10N 113°54E **1[?]**
Sokodé *Togo* 9°0N 1°11E **139** [?]
Sokol *Russia* 59°30N 40°5E **84** [?]
Sokolac *Bos.-H.* 43°56N 18°48E **80** [?]
Sokółka *Poland* 53°25N 23°30E **82** [?]
Sokolo *Mali* 14°53N 6°8W **138** [?]
Sokolo *Ségou, Mali* 10°52S 6°59W **13[?]**
Sokolov *Czech Rep.* 50°12N 12°40E **7[?]**
Sokołów Malopolski

Poland 50°12N 22°7E **8[?]**
Sokołów Podlaski

Poland 52°25N 22°15E **8[?]**
Sokoly *Poland* 52°59N 22°42E **8[?]**
Sokoto *Nigeria* 13°2N 5°16E **13[?]**
Sokoto □ *Nigeria* 12°30N 6°0E **13[?]**
Sokyrnytsya *Ukraine* 48°7N 23°23E **8[?]**
Sokyryany *Ukraine* 48°27N 27°25E **8[?]**
Sol, Costa del *Spain* 36°30N 4°30W **8[?]**
Sol Iletsk *Russia* 51°10N 55°0E **1[?]**
Sola → *Poland* 50°4N 19°15E **8[?]**
Solai *Kenya* 0°2N 36°12E **14[?]**
Solan *India* 30°55N 77°7E **12[?]**
Solana Beach *U.S.A.* 32°58N 117°16W **17[?]**
Solander I. *N.Z.* 46°34S 166°54E **15[?]**
Solapur *India* 17°43S 75°56E **12[?]**
Solca *Romania* 47°40N 25°50E **8[?]**
Solda Gölü *Turkey* 37°33N 29°42E **99** [?]
Soldănești *Moldova* 47°49N 28°58E **8[?]**
Soldeu *Andorra* 42°35N 1°40E **9[?]**
Soledad *U.S.A.* 60°29N 151°3W **17[?]**
Soléa *Cyprus* 35°5N 33°4E **10[?]**
Solec Kujawski *Poland* 53°5N 18°14E **8[?]**
Soledad *Colombia* 10°55N 74°46W **18[?]**
Soledad *U.S.A.* 36°26N 121°20W **17[?]**
Soledad *Venezuela* 8°10N 63°34W **18[?]**
Solent, The *U.K.* 50°45N 1°25W **6[?]**
Solenzara *France* 41°53N 9°23E **7[?]**
Solferino *Italy* 45°22N 10°34E **9[?]**
Solfonntaggen *Norway* 60°2N 6°57E **6[?]**
Solhan *Turkey* 38°57N 41°3E **10[?]**
Soligalich = Salihorsk

Belarus 52°51N 27°27E **7[?]**
Solihull *U.K.* 52°26N 1°47W **6[?]**
Solikamsk *Russia* 59°38N 56°50E **10[?]**
Solimões = Amazonas →

S. Amer. 0°5S 50°0W **1[?]**
Solin *Croatia* 43°33N 16°30E **9[?]**
Solingen *Germany* 51°10N 7°5E **7[?]**
Söll *Austria* 47°30N 12°11E **7[?]**
Sollebrunn *Sweden* 58°8N 12°32E **6[?]**
Sollefteå *Sweden* 63°12N 17°20E **6[?]**
Sollentuna *Sweden* 59°26N 17°56E **6[?]**
Sóller *Spain* 39°46N 2°43E **1[?]**
Sollerön *Sweden* 60°54N 14°34E **6[?]**
Solling *Germany* 51°44N 9°36E **7[?]**
Solling-Vogler △

Germany 51°45N 9°32E **7[?]**
Solnechnogorsk *Russia* 56°10N 36°57E **8[?]**
Solo → *Indonesia* 6°47S 112°22E **11[?]**
Sologne *France* 47°40N 1°45E **7[?]**
Solok *Indonesia* 0°45S 100°40E **1[?]**
Sololá *Guatemala* 14°49N 91°10W **18[?]**
Solok *Kenya* 3°33N 38°39E **14[?]**
Solomon, N. Fork →

U.S.A. 39°29N 98°26W **17[?]**
Solomon, S. Fork →

U.S.A. 39°25N 99°12W **17[?]**
Solomon Is. ■ *Pac. Oc.* 6°0S 155°0E **15[?]**
Solomon Rise *Pac. Oc.* 1°0N 157°0E **15[?]**
Solon *China* 46°32N 121°10E **11[?]**
Solon Springs *U.S.A.* 46°22N 91°49W **17[?]**

nôpole Brazil 5°44S 39°1W 189 B3
r Indonesia 8°27S 123°0E 119 F6
tcha Russia 54°48N 39°53E 84 E10
thurn Switz. 47°13N 7°32E 77 H3
thurn □ Switz. 47°18N 7°40E 77 H3
tvyn Ukraine 48°42N 24°51E 81 B9
ona Spain 42°0N 1°31E 90 D4
a Croatia 43°24N 16°15E 93 E13
inābād Khorāsān, an 34°13N 59°58E 129 C8
inābād Khorāsān, an 36°29N 58°5E 129 B8
iniyeh Iran 36°26N 48°47E 105 D13
au Germany 52°59N 9°50W 76 C5
sy Russia 58°10N 30°30E 84 C6
istik Qazaqstan □ azakhstan 54°0N 70°0E 109 B8
nska Glava acedonia 41°44N 21°31E 96 E5
ay U.S.A. 34°36N 120°8E 171 L6
aug Sweden 56°5N 14°55E 63 B8
ay Firth U.K. 54°49N 3°35W 66 C4
ezi Zambia 12°11S 26°21E 143 E12
bor Serbia 45°46N 19°9E 80 E4
a Japan 37°40N 140°50E 112 F10
a Turkey 39°10N 27°35E 99 B9
abhula Zimbabwe 19°42S 29°40E 145 A4
ali Pen. Africa 7°0N 46°0E 132 F8
alia ■ Africa 7°0N 47°0E 131 F4
aliland □ Somalia 10°0N 46°0E 131 F4
bernon France 47°20N 4°40E 71 E11
brero Mexico 23°38N 103°39W 180 C4
brero Anguilla 18°37N 63°30W 183 C7
brero Channel dia 7°41N 93°35E 127 L11
cuta Mare Romania 47°31N 23°28E 81 C8
dari India 25°47N 72°38E 124 G5
eido □ Spain 43°5N 6°11W 88 B4
ers U.S.A. 48°5N 114°13W 168 B6
erset Ky., U.S.A. 37°5N 84°36W 173 G11
erset Mass., 40°1N 79°5W 174 F5
erset Pa., U.S.A. 40°1N 79°5W 174 F5
erset East S. Africa 32°42S 25°35E 144 D4
erset I. Canada 73°30N 93°0W 160 C13
erset West S. Africa 34°8S 18°50E 144 D2
ersworth U.S.A. 43°16N 70°52W 175 C14
erton U.S.A. 32°36N 114°43W 169 K6
erville U.S.A. 38°58N 74°38W 175 F10
es ➤ Romania 47°49N 22°43E 80 C7
eşul Mare mania 47°59N 23°55E 81 C8
me □ France 49°57N 2°20E 71 C9
me ➤ France 50°11N 1°38E 71 B8
me, B. de la France 50°14N 1°33E 70 B8
men Jönköping, 58°12N 14°58E 63 F8
men Östergötland, 58°0N 15°15E 63 F9
mepy-Tahure ance 49°15N 4°31E 71 C11
merda Germany 51°9N 11°7E 76 D7
mesous France 48°44N 4°12E 71 D11
mières France 43°47N 4°6E 73 E8
nath India 20°53N 70°22E 124 J4
ogy □ Hungary 46°19N 17°30E 80 D2
ogyszob Hungary 46°18N 17°50E 80 D2
osomo Fiji 16°45S 179°58W 154 a
osomo Str. Fiji 16°0S 180°0E 154 a
oto Nic. 13°28N 86°37W 182 D2
polno Poland 52°26N 18°30E 83 F5
port, Túnel de Spain 42°48N 0°31W 90 C4
gentina 41°30S 67°0W 192 B3
varpet India 12°36N 75°52E 127 H7
➤ India 25°42N 84°52E 125 G11
Laem Thailand 7°59N 98°16E 121 a
Ha Vietnam 15°3N 108°34E 120 D7
La Vietnam 21°20N 103°50E 116 A4
Morrell Spain 39°44N 3°20E 100 B10
Rapinya Spain 39°35N 2°37E 100 B9
Sardina Spain 39°37N 2°40E 100 B9
Serra Spain 39°43N 3°13E 100 B10
Servera Spain 39°37N 3°21E 90 F8
Tay Vietnam 21°8N 105°30E 116 G5
Tinh Vietnam 15°10N 108°40E 120 F7
Panama 8°0N 81°20W 182 E3
amarg India 34°18N 75°21E 125 B6
amukhi India 23°18N 87°27E 125 H12
ar ➤ India 24°24N 79°56E 125 G8
ch'ŏn N. Korea 39°48N 124°55E 115 E13
dags ➤ S. Africa 33°44S 25°51E 144 D4
dalo Israel 32°30N 35°22E 108 C4
er Felding Denmark 55°57N 8°47E 63 J2
er Omme Denmark 55°50N 8°54E 63 J2
derborg Denmark 54°55N 9°49E 63 K3
dershausen Germany 51°22N 10°51E 76 D6
dre Strømfjord = angerlussuaq reenland 66°59N 50°40W 57 D5
lrio Italy 46°10N 9°52E 92 B6
lur ➤ India 20°40N 82°12E 126 D6
n Mozam. 17°23S 34°55E 143 F3
epur India 20°55N 83°50E 126 D6
im Brazil 6°0S 67°52W 188 E4
g Nigeria 9°49N 12°9E 139 D7
Thailand 18°28N 100°11E 120 C3
Cau Vietnam 13°27N 109°18E 120 F7
Ma Vietnam 20°56N 103°53E 116 G4
Xian China 34°21N 112°8E 114 G7
gadh India 21°9N 73°33E 126 D1
gan Indonesia 8°13S 115°24E 119 J18
aga Tanzania 10°40S 35°40E 145 E3
geons France 49°32N 1°50E 71 C8
ggang China 22°46N 113°50E 111 a
ghua Hu China 43°35N 126°50E 115 C14
hua Jiang ➤ China 47°45N 132°30E 111 B15
imvelo ➤ S. Africa 25°50S 31°2E 145 C5
jiang China 31°1N 121°12E 117 B13
jianghe China 32°10N 127°29E 115 C14
jin = Kimch'aek Korea 40°40N 129°10E 115 D15
gkan China 28°35N 106°52E 116 C6
gkhla Thailand 7°13N 100°37E 121 J3
gming China 25°12N 103°2E 116 E4
nim N. Korea 38°45N 125°39E 115 E13

Songo Mozam. 15°34S 32°38E 145 A5
Songpan China 32°40N 103°30E 116 A4
Songtao China 28°11N 109°10E 116 C7
Songwe Dem. Rep. of the Congo 3°20S 26°16E 142 C2
Songwe ➤ Africa 9°44S 33°58E 143 D3
Songxi China 27°31N 118°44E 117 D12
Songzi China 30°12N 111°45E 117 B8
Sonhat India 23°29N 82°31E 125 H10
Sonid Youqi China 42°45N 112°48E 114 C7
Sonid Zuoqi China 43°50N 113°42E 114 C7
Sonipat India 29°0N 77°5E 124 E7
Sonkach India 22°59N 76°21E 124 H7
Sonkovo Russia 57°50N 37°5E 84 D9
Sonmiani Pakistan 25°25N 66°40E 124 G2
Sonmiani B. Pakistan 25°15N 66°30E 124 G2
Sonnino Italy 41°25N 13°14E 94 A6
Sono ➤ Minas Gerais, Brazil 17°2S 45°32W 189 D1
Sono ➤ Tocantins, Brazil 9°58S 48°11W 189 B1
Sonoma U.S.A. 38°18N 122°28W 170 G4
Sonora Calif., U.S.A. 37°59N 120°23W 170 H6
Sonora Tex., U.S.A. 30°34N 100°39W 176 F4
Sonora □ Mexico 29°20N 110°40W 180 B2
Sonora ➤ Mexico 29°5N 110°55W 180 B2
Sonoran Desert 33°40N 113°30W 171 L12
Sonoyta Mexico 31°51N 112°50W 180 A2
Sonqor Iran 34°47N 47°36E 105 E12
Sonseca Spain 39°42N 3°57W 89 F7
Sonsonate El Salv. 13°43N 89°44W 182 D2
Sonsorol Is. Pac. Oc. 5°30N 132°13E 119 D8
Sonstorp Sweden 58°44N 15°38E 63 F9
Sonthofen Germany 47°30N 10°16E 77 H6
Soochow = Suzhou China 31°19N 120°38E 117 B13
Sooke Canada 48°13N 123°43W 170 B3
Soomaa △ Estonia 58°30N 28°5E 84 C3
Soomaaliya = Somalia ■ Africa 7°0N 47°0E 131 F4
Sop Hao Laos 20°33N 104°27E 116 G5
Sop Prap Thailand 17°53N 99°20E 120 D2
Sopchoppy U.S.A. 30°4N 84°29W 178 E5
Sopelana Spain 43°23N 2°58W 90 B2
Soperton U.S.A. 32°23N 82°35W 178 C7
Sopi Indonesia 2°34N 128°28E 119 D7
Sopot Bulgaria 42°39N 24°45E 97 D8
Sopot Poland 54°27N 18°31E 82 D5
Sopot Serbia 44°29N 20°36E 96 B4
Sopotnica Macedonia 41°18N 21°13E 96 E5
Sopron Hungary 47°45N 16°32E 80 C1
Sopur India 34°18N 74°27E 125 B6
Sør-Rondane Antarctica 72°0S 25°0E 55 D4
Sora Italy 41°43N 13°37E 93 G10
Sorab India 14°23N 75°6E 127 G2
Sorada India 19°45N 84°26E 126 E7
Sorah Pakistan 27°13N 68°56E 124 F3
Söråker Sweden 62°30N 17°32E 62 B11
Sorang Kazakhstan 49°46N 72°51E 109 C8
Sorano Italy 42°41N 11°43E 93 F8
Soraon India 25°37N 81°51E 125 G9
Sorata Bolivia 15°50S 68°40W 188 D4
Sorbas Spain 37°6N 2°7W 91 H2
Sörbygden Sweden 62°48N 16°12E 62 B10
Sord = Swords Ireland 53°28N 6°13W 64 C5
Sordellen Sweden 61°48N 16°43E 62 C10
Sore France 44°18N 0°35W 72 D3
Sorel-Tracy Canada 46°0N 73°10W 164 C5
Soresina Italy 45°17N 9°51E 92 C6
Sörforsa Sweden 61°43N 16°58E 62 C10
Sórgono Italy 40°1N 9°6E 94 B2
Sorgues France 44°1N 4°53E 73 D8
Sorgun Turkey 39°46N 35°11E 104 C6
Soria Spain 41°43N 2°32W 90 D2
Soria □ Spain 41°46N 2°28W 90 D2
Soriano Uruguay 33°24S 58°19W 190 C4
Soriano nel Cimino Italy 42°25N 12°14E 93 F9
Sorkh, Kuh-e Iran 35°30N 58°30E 129 C8
Sorø Denmark 55°26N 11°32E 63 J5
Soro Guinea 10°9N 9°48W 138 C3
Soroca Moldova 48°8N 28°12E 81 B13
Sorocaba Brazil 23°31S 47°27W 191 A6
Sorochinsk Russia 52°26N 53°10E 108 B4
Soroki = Soroca Moldova 48°8N 28°12E 81 B13
Sorong Indonesia 0°55S 131°15E 119 E8
Soroni Greece 36°21N 28°1E 101 C10
Soroti Uganda 1°43N 33°35E 142 B3
Sørøya Norway 70°40N 22°30E 60 A20
Sørøysundet Norway 70°25N 23°0E 60 A20
Sorraia ➤ Portugal 38°55N 8°53W 89 G2
Sorrell Australia 42°47S 147°34E 151 G4
Sorrento Italy 40°37N 14°22E 95 B7
Sorsele Sweden 65°31N 17°30E 60 D17
Sörsjön Sweden 61°24N 13°5E 62 C7
Sorso Italy 40°48N 8°34E 94 B1
Sorsogon Phil. 13°0N 124°0E 119 B6
Sortavala Russia 61°42N 30°41E 84 B6
Sortland Norway 68°42N 15°25E 60 B16
Sortot Sudan 19°3N 30°28E 137 D3
Sorvizhi Russia 57°52N 48°32E 86 B9
Sos del Rey Católico Spain 42°30N 1°13W 90 C3
Soscumica, L. Canada 50°15N 77°27W 164 B4
Sösdala Sweden 56°2N 13°41E 63 C7
Sosna ➤ Russia 52°42N 38°55E 85 F10
Sosnovka Kirov, Russia 56°17N 51°17E 86 B10
Sosnovka Murmansk, Russia 53°13N 41°24E 86 D5
Sosnovyy Bor Russia 59°55N 29°6E 84 C5
Sosnowiec Poland 50°20N 19°10E 83 H6
Sospel France 43°52N 7°27E 73 E11
Sossus Vlei Namibia 24°40S 15°23E 144 B2
Šoštanj Slovenia 46°23N 15°4E 93 B12
Šóstura N. Korea 42°16N 130°36E 115 C16
Sot ➤ India 27°27N 79°37E 125 F8
Sotavento C. Verde Is. 15°0N 24°0W 134 b
Sotkamo Finland 64°8N 28°23E 60 D23
Soto Spain 43°32N 6°4W 88 B4
Soto la Marina Mexico 23°46N 98°13W 181 C5
Soto la Marina ➤ Mexico 23°45N 97°45W 181 C5
Soto y Amío Spain 42°46N 5°53W 88 C5
Sotouboua Togo 8°34N 0°59E 139 D5
Sotrondio Spain 43°17N 5°36E 88 B5
Sotuta Mexico 20°36N 89°1W 181 C7
Souanké Congo 2°10N 14°3E 140 D2
Soubré Ivory C. 5°50N 6°35W 138 D3
Souda Greece 35°29N 24°4E 101 D6
Soudas, Ormos Greece 35°25N 24°10E 101 D6
Souderton U.S.A. 40°19N 75°19W 175 F9

Soufli Greece 41°12N 26°18E 97 E10
Soufrière Guadeloupe 16°5N 61°40W 182 b
Soufrière St. Lucia 13°51N 61°3W 183 f
Soufrière Bay Dominica 15°13N 61°22W 183 f
Souillac France 44°53N 1°29E 72 D5
Souilly France 49°3N 5°17E 71 C12
Souk-Ahras Algeria 36°23N 7°57E 136 A5
Souk-Ahras □ Algeria 36°23N 7°57E 136 A5
Souk el Arba du Rharb Morocco 34°43N 5°59W 136 B2
Soukhouma Laos 14°38N 105°48E 120 E5
Sŏul = Seoul S. Korea 37°31N 126°58E 115 F14
Soulac-sur-Mer France 45°30N 1°7W 72 C2
Soulougou Burkina Faso 13°1N 0°25E 139 C5
Soultz-sous-Forêts France 48°57N 7°52E 71 D14
Sound, The = Øresund Europe 55°45N 12°40E 63 J6
Sound, The U.K. 55°45N 12°40E 63 J6
Sound I. India 12°58N 92°59E 127 H11
Sounio, Akra Greece 37°37N 24°1E 98 D6
Sour el Ghozlane Algeria 36°10N 3°45E 136 A4
Sources, Mt. aux Lesotho 28°45S 28°50E 145 C4
Soure Brazil 0°35S 48°30W 187 D9
Soure Portugal 40°4N 8°38W 88 E2
Souris Man., Canada 49°40N 100°20W 163 D8
Souris P.E.I., Canada 46°21N 62°15W 165 C7
Souris ➤ N. Amer. 49°40N 99°34W 172 A4
Sourou ➤ Africa 12°45N 3°25W 138 C4
Sourpi Greece 39°6N 22°54E 98 B4
Sous, O. ➤ Morocco 30°27N 9°31W 136 B2
Sous-Massa △ Morocco 30°26N 9°35W 136 B2
Sous-Massa-Drâa □ Morocco 30°45N 6°30W 136 B2
Sousa Brazil 6°45S 38°10W 189 B3
Sousel Portugal 38°57N 7°40W 89 G3
Sousse Tunisia 35°50N 10°38E 136 A6
Sousse □ Tunisia 35°40N 10°30E 136 A6
Soustons France 43°45N 1°19W 72 E2
Sout ➤ S. Africa 31°35S 18°24E 144 D2
South Africa ■ Africa 32°0S 23°0E 144 D3
South America 10°0S 60°0W 184 E5
South Andaman India 11°45N 92°10E 127 J11
South Aulatsivik I. Canada 56°45N 61°30W 165 A7
South Australia □ Australia 32°0S 139°0E 152 B3
South Australian Basin Ind. Oc. 38°0S 126°0E 156 L4
South Ayrshire □ U.K. 55°18N 4°41W 65 F4
South Baldy Pk. U.S.A. 34°6N 107°11W 169 J10
South Bass I. U.S.A. 41°39N 82°49W 174 E2
South Bay Canada 25°40N 80°43W 179 J9
South Bend Ind., U.S.A. 41°41N 86°15W 172 E10
South Bend Wash., U.S.A. 46°40N 123°48W 170 D3
South Boston U.S.A. 36°42N 78°54W 173 G14
South Branch Canada 47°55N 59°2W 165 C8
South Brook Canada 49°26N 56°5W 165 C8
South Brother I. India 10°56N 92°37E 127 J11
South Bruny I. Australia 43°20S 147°15E 151 G4
South Carolina □ U.S.A. 34°0N 81°0W 177 E14
South Charleston U.S.A. 38°22N 81°44W 173 F13
South China Sea Asia 10°0N 113°0E 118 C4
South Congaree U.S.A. 33°53N 81°9W 178 B8
South Cumberland Is. △ Australia 20°42S 149°11E 150 b
South Dakota □ U.S.A. 44°15N 100°0W 172 C4
South Dayton U.S.A. 42°21N 79°3W 174 D5
South Daytona U.S.A. 29°10N 81°0W 179 F8
South Deerfield U.S.A. 42°29N 72°37W 175 D12
South Downs U.K. 50°52N 0°25W 67 G7
South Downs △ U.K. 50°50N 0°50W 67 G7
South East □ Botswana 25°0S 25°40E 144 C4
South East C. Australia 43°40S 146°50E 151 G4
South East Forest △ Australia 37°0S 149°30E 153 D8
South East Is. Australia 34°17S 123°30E 149 F3
South Esk ➤ U.K. 56°43N 2°31W 65 E6
South Fiji Basin Pac. Oc. 27°0S 178°0E 156 K9
South Foreland U.K. 51°8N 1°24E 67 F9
South Fork American ➤ U.S.A. 38°57N 120°59W 170 G5
South Fork Edisto ➤ U.S.A. 33°16N 80°54W 178 B9
South Fork Feather ➤ U.S.A. 39°17N 121°36W 170 F5
South Fork Grand ➤ U.S.A. 45°43N 102°17W 172 C2
South Fork Milk ➤ U.S.A. 48°4N 106°19W 168 B10
South Fork Republican ➤ U.S.A. 39°10N 101°31W 172 E3
South Georgia Antarctica 54°30S 37°0W 55 B1
South Gloucestershire □ U.K. 51°32N 2°28W 67 F5
South Hadley U.S.A. 42°16N 72°35W 175 D12
South Haven U.S.A. 42°24N 86°16W 172 D10
South Henik L. Canada 61°30N 97°20W 163 A9
South Horr Kenya 2°12N 36°56E 142 B4
South I. India 10°3N 72°17E 127 J1
South I. Kenya 2°35N 36°35E 142 B4
South I. N.Z. 44°0S 170°0E 155 E5
South Indian Lake Canada 56°47N 98°56W 163 B9
South Invercargill N.Z. 46°26S 168°23E 155 G3
South Island △ Kenya 2°35N 36°35E 142 B4
South Kitui △ Kenya 1°48S 38°46E 142 C4
South Knife ➤ Canada 58°55N 94°37W 163 B10
South Koel ➤ India 22°32N 85°14E 125 H11
South Korea ■ Asia 36°0N 128°0E 115 G15
South Lake Tahoe U.S.A. 38°57N 119°59W 170 G6
South Lanarkshire □ U.K. 55°37N 3°53W 65 F5
South Loop ➤ U.S.A. 41°4N 98°39W 172 E4
South Luangwa △ Zambia 13°0S 31°20E 143 E3
South Magnetic Pole Antarctica 64°8S 138°8E 55 C9
South Miami U.S.A. 25°42N 80°17W 179 K9

South Milwaukee U.S.A. 42°55N 87°52W 172 D10
South Molton U.K. 51°1N 3°51W 67 F4
South Moose L. Canada 53°49N 100°1W 163 C8
South Nahanni ➤ Canada 61°3N 123°21W 162 A4
South Nation ➤ Canada 45°34N 75°6W 175 A9
South Natuna Is. = Natuna Selatan, Kepulauan Indonesia 2°45N 109°0E 118 D3
South Negril Pt. Jamaica 18°16N 78°22W 182 a
South Newport U.S.A. 31°38N 81°24W 178 D8
South Orkney Is. Antarctica 63°0S 45°0W 55 C18
South Ossetia □ Georgia 42°21N 44°2E 87 J7
South Otselic U.S.A. 42°38N 75°46W 175 D9
South Pagai, I. = Pagai Selatan, Pulau Indonesia 3°0S 100°15E 118 E2
South Paris U.S.A. 44°14N 70°31W 175 B14
South Pittsburg U.S.A. 35°1N 85°42W 177 D12
South Platte ➤ U.S.A. 41°7N 100°42W 172 E3
South Pole Antarctica 90°0S 0°0 55 E
South Ponte Vedra Beach U.S.A. 30°3N 81°20W 178 E8
South Porcupine Canada 48°30N 81°12W 164 C3
South Portland U.S.A. 43°38N 70°15W 173 D18
South Pt. Barbados 13°2N 59°32W 183 g
South Pt. U.S.A. 44°52N 83°19W 174 B1
South River Canada 45°52N 79°23W 164 C4
South River U.S.A. 40°27N 74°23W 175 F10
South Ronaldsay U.K. 58°48N 2°58W 65 C6
South Rukuru Malaysia 10°44S 34°14E 143 E3
South Sandwich Is. Antarctica 57°0S 27°0W 55 B1
South Sandwich Trench Atl. Oc. 56°0S 24°0W 55 B1
South Saskatchewan ➤ Canada 53°15N 105°5W 163 C7
South Seal ➤ Canada 58°48N 98°8W 163 B9
South Sentinel I. India 10°59N 92°14E 127 J11
South Shetland Is. Antarctica 62°0S 59°0W 55 C18
South Shields U.K. 55°0N 1°25W 66 C6
South Sioux City U.S.A. 42°28N 96°24W 172 D5
South Sister U.S.A. 44°4N 121°51W 168 D3
South Sudan ■ Africa 8°0N 30°0E 135 G11
South Taranaki Bight N.Z. 39°40S 174°5E 154 F3
South Tasman Rise S. Ocean 48°0S 146°0E 55 A10
South Thompson ➤ Canada 50°40N 120°20W 162 C4
South Twin I. Canada 53°7N 79°52W 164 B4
South Tyne ➤ U.K. 54°59N 2°8W 66 C5
South Uist U.K. 57°20N 7°15W 65 D1
South Valley U.S.A. 35°1N 106°41W 169 J10
South Venice U.S.A. 27°3N 82°25W 179 H7
South Wellesley Is. Australia 16°58S 139°17E 150 B2
South West □ Botswana 43°34S 146°3E 151 G4
South West C. N.Z. 47°17S 167°28E 155 H2
South West Rocks Australia 30°52S 153°3E 153 A10
South Williamsport U.S.A. 41°13N 77°0W 174 E8
South Yorkshire □ U.K. 53°27N 1°36W 66 D6
Southampton Canada 44°30N 81°25W 164 C3
Southampton U.K. 50°54N 1°23W 67 G6
Southampton U.S.A. 40°53N 72°23W 175 F12
Southampton I. Canada 64°30N 84°0W 161 E15
Southaven U.S.A. 34°59N 90°0W 177 D9
Southbank U.S.A. 31°25N 85°46W 178 D5
Southbridge N.Z. 43°48S 172°16E 155 D7
Southbridge U.S.A. 42°5N 72°2W 175 D12
Southeast Indian Ridge Ind. Oc. 43°0S 80°0E 146 J10
Southend Canada 56°19N 103°22W 163 B8
Southend-on-Sea U.K. 51°32N 0°44E 67 F8
Southend-on-Sea □ U.K. 51°32N 0°44E 67 F8
Southern □ Malawi 15°0S 35°0E 143 F4
Southern □ S. Leone 8°0N 12°0W 138 D2
Southern □ Zambia 16°20S 26°20E 143 F2
Southern Alps N.Z. 43°41S 170°11E 155 D5
Southern Cross Australia 31°12S 119°15E 149 F2
Southern Indian L. Canada 57°10N 98°30W 163 B9
Southern Lau Group Fiji 18°40S 178°40W 154 a
Southern Ocean 62°0S 60°0E 55 C6
Southern Pines U.S.A. 35°11N 79°24W 177 D15
Southern Uplands U.K. 55°28N 3°52W 65 F5
Southington U.S.A. 41°36N 72°53W 175 E12
Southland □ N.Z. 45°30S 168°0E 155 F3
Southold U.S.A. 41°4N 72°26W 175 E12
Southport Australia 27°58S 153°25E 153 D5
Southport U.K. 53°39N 3°0W 66 D4
Southport Fla., U.S.A. 30°17N 85°38W 178 E4
Southport N.Y., U.S.A. 42°3N 76°49W 174 D8
Southwest □ Australia 43°8S 146°5E 151 G4
Southwest Pacific Basin Pac. Oc. 40°0S 140°0W 55 M12
Southwood △ Australia 27°48S 150°8E 151 D5
Soutpansberg S. Africa 23°0S 29°30E 145 C4
Souvigny France 46°33N 3°10E 71 F10
Sovata Romania 46°35N 25°3E 81 D10
Soverato Italy 38°41N 16°33E 95 D9
Sovetsk Kaliningrad, Russia 55°6N 21°50E 62 C8
Sovetsk Kirov, Russia 57°38N 48°53E 86 B9
Sovetskaya Gavan Russia 48°58N 140°18E 107 E15
Sovicille Italy 43°17N 11°13E 93 E8
Soweto S. Africa 26°14S 27°52E 145 D4
Sowma'eh Sarā Iran 37°17N 49°18E 105 D13
Sõya-Kaikyõ = La Perouse Str. Asia 45°40N 142°0E 112 B11
Sõya-Misaki Japan 45°30N 141°55E 112 B11
Soyaux France 45°39N 0°12E 72 C4
Soyo Angola 6°13S 12°20E 140 F2
Sozaq Kazakhstan 44°8N 68°28E 109 D7

Sozh ➤ Belarus 51°57N 30°48E 75 B16
Sozopol Bulgaria 42°23N 27°42E 97 D11
Spa Belgium 50°29N 5°53E 68 E7
Spaatz I. Antarctica 73°10S 75°0W 55 D17
Spain ■ Europe 39°0N 4°0W 90 H5
Spalding Australia 33°30S 138°37E 152 B3
Spalding U.K. 52°48N 0°9W 66 E7
Spanaway U.S.A. 47°6N 122°26W 170 C4
Spangler U.S.A. 40°39N 78°48W 174 F6
Spanish Canada 46°12N 82°20W 164 C3
Spanish Fork U.S.A. 40°7N 111°39W 168 F8
Spanish Town Br. Virgin Is. 18°26N 64°26W 183 e
Spanish Town Jamaica 18°0N 76°57W 182 a
Sparks Nev., U.S.A. 39°32N 119°45W 170 F7
Sparreholm Sweden 59°4N 16°49E 62 E10
Sparta = Sparti Greece 37°5N 22°25E 98 D4
Sparta Ga., U.S.A. 33°17N 82°58W 178 C7
Sparta Mich., U.S.A. 43°10N 85°42W 173 D11
Sparta N.J., U.S.A. 41°2N 74°38W 175 E10
Sparta Wis., U.S.A. 43°56N 90°49W 172 D8
Spartanburg U.S.A. 34°56N 81°57W 177 D14
Spartel, C. Morocco 35°47N 5°56W 136 A2
Sparti Greece 37°5N 22°25E 98 D4
Spartivento, C. Calabria, Italy 37°55N 16°4E 95 E9
Spartivento, C. Sard., Italy 38°53N 8°50E 94 D1
Sparwood Canada 49°44N 114°53W 162 D6
Spas-Demensk Russia 54°20N 34°0E 84 E7
Spas-Klepiki Russia 55°10N 40°10E 84 E11
Spassk-Dalniy Russia 44°40N 132°48E 112 B6
Spassk-Ryazanskiy Russia 54°24N 40°25E 84 E11
Spatha, Akra Greece 35°42N 23°43E 101 D5
Spatsizi ➤ Canada 57°42N 128°7W 162 B3
Spatsizi Plateau Wilderness △ Canada 57°40N 128°0W 162 B3
Spean ➤ U.K. 56°55N 4°59W 65 E4
Spearfish U.S.A. 44°30N 103°52W 172 C2
Spearman U.S.A. 36°12N 101°12W 176 C4
Speculator U.S.A. 43°30N 74°22W 175 C10
Speed U.S.A. 35°21S 142°27E 153 C3
Speia Moldova 46°59N 29°19E 81 D14
Speightstown Barbados 13°15N 59°39W 183 g
Speke Gulf Tanzania 2°20S 32°50E 142 C3
Spello Italy 42°59N 12°40E 93 F9
Spence Bay = Taloyoak Canada 69°32N 93°32W 160 D13
Spencer Idaho, U.S.A. 44°22N 112°11W 168 D7
Spencer Iowa, U.S.A. 43°9N 95°9W 172 D6
Spencer N.Y., U.S.A. 42°13N 76°30W 175 D8
Spencer Nebr., U.S.A. 42°53N 98°42W 172 D4
Spencer, C. Australia 35°20S 136°53E 152 C1
Spencer B. Namibia 25°30S 14°47E 144 C1
Spencer G. Australia 34°0S 137°20E 152 C2
Spencerville Canada 44°51N 75°33W 175 A9
Spences Bridge Canada 50°25N 121°20W 162 C4
Spennymoor U.K. 54°42N 1°36W 66 C6
Spenser Mts. N.Z. 42°15S 172°45E 155 C7
Spentrup Denmark 56°33N 10°2E 63 H4
Sperchios ➤ Greece 38°57N 22°3E 98 C4
Sperrin Mts. U.K. 54°50N 7°0W 64 B5
Spessart Germany 49°56N 9°18E 77 F5
Spetses Greece 37°15N 23°10E 98 D5
Spey ➤ U.K. 57°40N 3°6W 65 D5
Speyer Germany 49°29N 8°25E 77 F4
Spezand Pakistan 29°59N 67°0E 124 E2
Spezzano Albanese Italy 39°40N 16°19E 95 C9
Spiddle Ireland 53°15N 9°18W 64 C2
Spiekeroog Germany 53°46N 7°42E 76 B3
Spiez Switz. 46°40N 7°40E 76 C4
Spili Greece 35°13N 24°31E 101 D6
Spilimbergo Italy 46°7N 12°54E 93 B9
Spin Búldak Afghan. 31°1N 66°25E 124 D2
Spinalonga Greece 35°18N 25°44E 101 D7
Spinazzola Italy 40°58N 16°5E 95 B9
Spineni Romania 44°43N 24°37E 81 F9
Spinifex ◊ Australia 28°30S 128°30E 149 E4
Spirit Lake U.S.A. 46°15N 122°9W 170 D4
Spirit River Canada 55°45N 118°50W 162 B5
Spiritwood Canada 53°24N 107°33W 163 C7
Spišská Nová Ves Slovak Rep. 48°58N 20°34E 79 C13
Spišské Podhradie Slovak Rep. 49°0N 20°48E 79 B13
Spital Austria 47°6N 15°26E 80 D7
Spithead U.K. 50°45N 1°10W 67 G6
Spitsbergen = Svalbard Arctic 78°0N 17°0E 57 B7
Spittal an der Drau Austria 46°48N 13°31E 80 B6
Spjelkavik Norway 62°28N 6°22E 60 E12
Split Croatia 43°31N 16°26E 93 E13
Split ✈ (SPU) Croatia 43°33N 16°15E 93 E13
Split L. Canada 56°8N 96°15W 163 B9
Split Lake Canada 56°8N 96°15W 163 B9
Splitski Kanal Croatia 43°31N 16°20E 93 E13
Splügenpass Switz. 46°30N 9°20E 77 J5
Spofford U.S.A. 29°10N 100°25W 176 G4
Spokane U.S.A. 47°40N 117°24W 168 C5
Spoleto Italy 42°44N 12°44E 93 F9
Spooner U.S.A. 45°50N 91°53W 172 C8
Sporyy Navolok, Mys Russia 75°50N 68°40E 106 B7
Sprague U.S.A. 47°18N 117°59W 168 C5
Spratly I. S. China Sea 8°38N 111°55E 118 C4
Spratly Is. S. China Sea 8°20N 112°0E 118 C4
Spray U.S.A. 44°50N 119°48W 168 D4
Spree ➤ Germany 52°32N 13°12E 76 B9
Spreewald Germany 51°54N 14°22E 76 C10
Spremberg Germany 51°34N 14°22E 76 C10
Sprengisandur Iceland 64°52N 18°7W 60 D6
Spring Cr. ➤ U.S.A. 30°54N 84°45W 178 E5
Spring Creek U.S.A. 40°44N 115°35W 168 F6
Spring Garden U.S.A. 39°52N 120°47W 170 F6
Spring Hill Barbados 13°18N 59°35W 183 g
Spring Hill U.S.A. 28°27N 82°41W 179 G7
Spring Hill Fla., U.S.A. 28°27N 82°41W 179 G7
Spring Mts. U.S.A. 36°0N 115°45W 171 J11
Spring Valley Calif., U.S.A. 32°44N 116°59W 171 N10
Spring Valley Nev.,

Springdale U.S.A. 36°11N 94°8W 176 C7
Springe Germany 52°13N 9°33E 76 C5
Springer U.S.A. 36°22N 104°36W 169 H11
Springerville U.S.A. 34°8N 109°17W 169 J9
Springfield Canada 42°50N 80°56W 174 D3
Springfield N.Z. 43°19S 171°56E 155 D6
Springfield Colo., U.S.A. 37°24N 102°37W 169 H12
Springfield Fla., U.S.A. 30°10N 85°37W 178 E4
Springfield Ga., U.S.A. 32°22N 81°18W 178 C8
Springfield Ill., U.S.A. 39°48N 89°39W 172 F9
Springfield Mass., U.S.A. 42°6N 72°35W 175 D12
Springfield Mo., U.S.A. 37°13N 93°17W 172 G7
Springfield Ohio, U.S.A. 39°55N 83°49W 173 F12
Springfield Oreg., U.S.A. 44°3N 123°1W 168 D2
Springfield S.C., U.S.A. 33°30N 81°17W 178 B8
Springfield Tenn., U.S.A. 36°31N 86°53W 177 C11
Springfield Vt., U.S.A. 43°18N 72°29W 175 C12
Springfontein S. Africa 30°15S 25°40E 144 D4
Springhill Canada 45°40N 64°4W 165 C7
Springhill U.S.A. 33°0N 93°28W 176 E7
Springhouse Canada 51°56N 122°7W 162 C4
Springlands = Corriverton Guyana 5°55N 57°20W 186 B7
Springs S. Africa 26°13S 28°25E 145 D4
Springsure Australia 24°8S 148°6E 150 C4
Springvale La., U.S.A. 31°50N 84°53W 178 D5
Springvale Maine, U.S.A. 43°28N 70°48W 175 C14
Springville Calif., U.S.A. 36°8N 118°49W 170 J8
Springville N.Y., U.S.A. 42°31N 78°40W 174 D6
Springville Utah, U.S.A. 40°10N 111°37W 168 F8
Springwater U.S.A. 42°38N 77°35W 174 D7
Spruce-Creek U.S.A. 40°36N 78°9W 174 F6
Spruce Knob-Seneca Rocks △ U.S.A. 38°50N 79°30W 173 F14
Spruce Mt. U.S.A. 44°12N 72°19W 175 B12
Sprucedale Canada 45°29N 79°28W 174 A5
Spur U.S.A. 33°28N 100°52W 176 E4
Spurn Hd. U.K. 53°35N 0°8E 66 D8
Spuž Montenegro 42°32N 19°10E 96 D3
Spuzzum Canada 49°37N 121°23W 162 D4
Squam L. U.S.A. 43°45N 71°32W 175 C13
Squamish Canada 49°45N 123°10W 162 D4
Square Islands Canada 52°47N 55°47W 165 B8
Squillace, G. di Italy 38°45N 16°50E 95 D9
Squinzano Italy 40°26N 18°2E 95 B11
Squires, Mt. Australia 26°14S 127°28E 149 E4
Srbac Bos.-H. 45°7N 17°30E 80 E2
Srbica = Skënderaj Kosovo 42°45N 20°47E 96 D4
Srbija = Serbia ■ Europe 43°20N 20°0E 96 C4
Srbobran Serbia 45°32N 19°48E 80 E4
Sre Ambel Cambodia 11°8N 103°46E 121 G4
Sre Khtum Cambodia 12°10N 106°52E 121 F6
Sre Umbell = Sre Ambel Cambodia 11°8N 103°46E 121 G4
Srebarna Bulgaria 44°6N 27°4E 97 D11
Srebrenica Bos.-H. 44°6N 19°18E 80 F4
Sredinnyy Khrebet Russia 57°0N 160°0E 107 D17
Sredinnyy Ra. = Sredinnyy Khrebet Russia 57°0N 160°0E 107 D17
Središče Slovenia 46°24N 16°17E 93 B13
Sredna Gora Bulgaria 42°40N 24°20E 97 D8
Srednekolymsk Russia 67°27N 153°40E 107 C16
Sredni Rodopi Bulgaria 41°40N 24°45E 97 E8
Srednogorie Bulgaria 42°33N 24°10E 97 D8
Šrem Poland 52°6N 17°2E 83 F4
Sremska Mitrovica Serbia 44°59N 19°38E 80 E4
Sremski Karlovci Serbia 45°13N 19°56E 80 E4
Srepok ➤ Cambodia 13°33N 106°16E 120 F6
Sretensk Russia 52°10N 117°40E 107 D12
Sri Aman = Bandar Sri Aman Malaysia 1°15N 111°32E 118 D4
Sri Kalahasti India 13°45N 79°44E 127 H4
Sri Lanka ■ Asia 7°30N 80°50E 127 L5
Sri Pada = Adam's Peak Sri Lanka 6°48N 80°30E 127 L5
Srikakulam India 18°14N 83°58E 126 E6
Srinagar India 34°5N 74°50E 125 B6
Srivardhan India 18°4N 73°3E 126 C1
Srivilliputhur India 9°31N 77°40E 127 K3
Środa Śląska Poland 51°10N 16°36E 83 G3
Środa Wielkopolski Poland 52°15N 17°19E 83 F4
Srono Indonesia 8°24S 114°16E 119 J17
Srpska Crnja Serbia 45°38N 20°44E 80 E5
Srpski Itebej Serbia 45°35N 20°44E 80 E5
Srungavarapukota India 18°7N 83°10E 126 E6
Ssese Is. = Sese Is. Uganda 0°20S 32°20E 142 C3
Staaten ➤ Australia 16°24S 141°17E 150 B3
Staaten River △ Australia 16°15S 142°40E 150 B3
Stabbursdalen △ Norway 70°5N 24°15E 60 A21
Staberhuk Germany 54°23N 11°18E 76 A7
Stade Germany 53°35N 9°29E 76 B5
Stadskanaal Neths. 53°4N 6°55E 68 A6
Stadtallendorf Germany 50°48N 9°1E 76 E5
Stadthagen Germany 52°19N 9°13E 76 C5
Stadtlohn Germany 51°59N 6°52E 76 C3
Stadtroda Germany 50°52N 11°44E 76 E7
Staffa U.K. 56°27N 6°21W 65 E2
Staffanstorp Sweden 55°38N 13°13E 63 C6
Stafford U.K. 52°49N 2°7W 66 E5
Stafford U.S.A. 37°58N 98°36W 172 G4
Stafford Springs U.S.A. 41°57N 72°18W 175 E12
Staffordshire □ U.K. 52°53N 2°10W 66 E5
Stagnone di Marsala Italy 37°52N 12°26E 94 E5
Staines U.K. 51°26N 0°29W 67 F7
Stainz Austria 46°53N 15°17E 78 E8
Stakhanov Ukraine 48°35N 38°40E 85 H10
Stalač Serbia 43°43N 21°28E 96 C5
Stalida Greece 35°17N 25°25E 101 D7
Stallarholmen Sweden 59°22N 17°12E 62 E11
Ställdalen Sweden 59°56N 14°56E 62 E8
Stalowa Wola Poland 50°34N 22°3E 83 H9

Stalybridge *U.K.* 53°28N 2°3W **66** D5
Stamford *Australia* 21°15S 143°46E **150** C3
Stamford *U.K.* 52°39N 0°29W **67** E7
Stamford *Conn., U.S.A.* 41°3N 73°32W **175** E11
Stamford *N.Y., U.S.A.* 42°25N 74°38W **175** D10
Stamford *Tex., U.S.A.* 32°57N 99°48W **176** E5
Stampriet *Namibia* 24°20S 18°28E **144** B2
Stamps *U.S.A.* 33°22N 93°30W **176** E8
Stančevo = Kalipetrovo *Bulgaria* 44°5N 27°14E **97** B11
Standerton *S. Africa* 26°55S 29°7E **145** C4
Standish *U.S.A.* 43°59N 83°57W **173** D12
Stanford *S. Africa* 34°26S 19°29E **144** D2
Stanford *U.S.A.* 47°9N 110°13W **168** C8
Stånga *Sweden* 57°17N 18°29E **63** G12
Stanger *S. Africa* 29°27S 31°14E **145** C5
Stängselåsen = Salpausselkä *Finland* 61°3N 26°15E **84** B4
Stanhope *Australia* 36°27S 144°59E **153** D6
Stanišić *Serbia* 45°56N 19°10E **80** E4
Stanislaus → *U.S.A.* 37°40N 121°14W **170** H5
Stanisławów *Poland* 52°18N 21°33E **83** F8
Stanley *Australia* 40°46S 145°19E **151** G4
Stanley *China* 22°13N 114°12E **111** a
Stanley *Falk. Is.* 51°40S 59°51W **192** D5
Stanley *U.K.* 54°53N 1°41W **66** C6
Stanley *Idaho, U.S.A.* 44°13N 114°56W **168** D6
Stanley *N. Dak., U.S.A.* 48°19N 102°23W **172** A2
Stanley *N.Y., U.S.A.* 42°48N 77°6W **174** D7
Stanley Mission *Canada* 55°25N 104°33W **163** B8
Stanley Res. *India* 11°50N 77°40E **127** J3
Stannards *U.S.A.* 42°5N 77°55W **174** D7
Stanovoy Khrebet *Russia* 55°0N 130°0E **107** D14
Stanovoy Ra. = Stanovoy Khrebet *Russia* 55°0N 130°0E **107** D14
Stansmore Ra. *Australia* 21°23S 128°33E **148** D4
Stansted, London ✈ (STN) *U.K.* 51°54N 0°14E **67** F8
Stanthorpe *Australia* 28°36S 151°59E **151** D5
Stanton *U.S.A.* 32°8N 101°48W **176** E4
Stanwood *U.S.A.* 48°15N 122°23W **170** B4
Staples *Canada* 42°10N 82°35W **174** D2
Staples *U.S.A.* 46°21N 94°48W **172** B6
Stapleton *U.S.A.* 41°29N 100°31W **172** E3
Stąporków *Poland* 51°9N 20°31E **83** G7
Star City *Canada* 52°50N 104°20W **163** C8
Star Lake *U.S.A.* 44°10N 75°2W **175** B9
Stará L'ubovňa *Slovak Rep.* 49°18N 20°42E **79** B13
Stara Moravica *Serbia* 45°50N 19°30E **80** E4
Stara Pazova *Serbia* 44°58N 20°10E **80** F5
Stara Planina *Bulgaria* 43°15N 23°0E **96** C7
Stara Sil *Ukraine* 49°29N 22°58E **83** J9
Stará Turá *Slovak Rep.* 48°47N 17°42E **79** C10
Stara Ushytsya *Ukraine* 48°35N 27°8E **81** B12
Stara Zagora *Bulgaria* 42°26N 25°39E **97** D9
Stara Zagora □ *Bulgaria* 42°26N 25°39E **97** D9
Starachowice *Poland* 51°3N 21°2E **83** G8
Staraya Russa *Russia* 57°58N 31°23E **84** D6
Starbuck I. *Kiribati* 5°37S 155°55W **157** H12
Starchiojd *Romania* 45°19N 26°11E **81** E11
Starcke △ *Australia* 14°56S 145°2E **150** A4
Stargard Szczeciński *Poland* 53°20N 15°0E **82** E2
Stari Bar *Montenegro* 42°7N 19°10E **96** D3
Stari Grad *Croatia* 43°10N 16°38E **93** E13
Stari Trg *Slovenia* 45°29N 15°7E **93** C12
Staritsa *Russia* 56°33N 34°55E **84** D8
Starke *U.S.A.* 29°57N 82°7W **178** F7
Starkville *U.S.A.* 33°28N 88°49W **177** E10
Starnberg *Germany* 48°0N 11°21E **77** H7
Starnberger See *Germany* 47°54N 11°19E **77** H7
Staro Oryakhovo *Bulgaria* 42°59N 27°47E **97** D11
Starobilsk *Ukraine* 49°16N 39°0E **85** H10
Starodub *Russia* 52°30N 32°50E **85** F7
Starogard Gdański *Poland* 53°59N 18°30E **82** E5
Starokonstantinov = Starokonstyantyniv *Ukraine* 49°48N 27°10E **75** D14
Starokonstyantyniv *Ukraine* 49°48N 27°10E **75** D14
Starokozache *Ukraine* 46°20N 29°59E **81** D14
Starominskaya *Russia* 46°33N 39°0E **87** G4
Staroshcherbinovskaya *Russia* 46°40N 38°53E **87** G4
Starrs Mill *U.S.A.* 33°19N 84°31W **178** B5
Start Pt. *U.K.* 50°13N 3°39W **67** G4
Stary Sącz *Poland* 49°33N 20°35E **83** J7
Staryy Biryuzyak *Russia* 44°46N 46°50E **87** H8
Staryy Chartoriysk *Ukraine* 51°15N 25°54E **75** C13
Staryy Krym *Ukraine* 45°3N 35°8E **85** K8
Staryy Oskol *Russia* 51°19N 37°55E **85** G9
Staryy Sambir *Ukraine* 49°27N 22°59E **83** J9
Stassfurt *Germany* 51°51N 11°35E **76** D7
Staszów *Poland* 50°33N 21°10E **83** H8
State College *U.S.A.* 40°48N 77°52W **174** F7
Stateline *U.S.A.* 38°57N 119°56W **170** G7
Staten, I. = Estados, I. de Los *Argentina* 54°40S 64°30W **192** D4
Staten I. *U.S.A.* 40°35N 74°9W **175** F10
Statenville *U.S.A.* 30°42N 83°2W **178** E6
Statesboro *U.S.A.* 32°27N 81°47W **178** C8
Statesville *U.S.A.* 35°47N 80°53W **177** D14
Statham *U.S.A.* 33°58N 83°35W **178** B6
Statia = St. Eustatius *W. Indies* 17°20N 63°0W **183** C7
Stauffer *U.S.A.* 34°45N 119°3W **171** L7
Staunton *Ill., U.S.A.* 39°1N 89°47W **172** F9
Staunton *Va., U.S.A.* 38°9N 79°4W **173** F14
Stavanger *Norway* 58°57N 5°40E **61** G11
Stavelot *Belgium* 50°23N 5°55E **69** D5
Stavern *Norway* 59°0N 10°1E **61** G14
Stavoren *Neths.* 52°53N 5°22E **69** B5
Stavropol *Russia* 45°5N 42°0E **87** H6
Stavropol □ *Russia* 47°20N 42°50E **87** G6
Stavros *Cyprus* 35°1N 32°38E **101** D11
Stavros *Kriti, Greece* 35°12N 24°45E **101** D6
Stavros *Thessaloniki, Greece* 40°39N 23°43E **96** F7
Stavros, Akra *Greece* 35°26N 24°58E **101** D6
Stavroupoli *Greece* 41°12N 24°45E **97** E8
Stawell *Australia* 37°5S 142°47E **152** D5
Stawell → *Australia* 20°20S 142°55E **150** C3
Stawiski *Poland* 53°22N 22°9E **82** E9
Stawiszyn *Poland* 51°56N 18°4E **83** G5
Stayner *Canada* 44°25N 80°5W **174** B4
Stayton *U.S.A.* 44°48N 122°48W **168** D2
Steamboat Springs *U.S.A.* 40°29N 106°50W **168** F10
Steblevë *Albania* 41°23N 20°33E **96** E4
Steele *Ala., U.S.A.* 33°56N 86°12W **178** B3
Steele *N. Dak., U.S.A.* 46°51N 99°55W **172** B4
Steelton *U.S.A.* 40°14N 76°50W **174** F8
Steen River *Canada* 59°40N 117°12W **162** B5
Steens Mt. *U.S.A.* 42°35N 118°40W **168** E4
Steenstrup Gletscher *Greenland* 75°15N 57°0W **57** B5
Steenwijk *Neths.* 52°47N 6°7E **69** B6
Steep Pt. *Australia* 26°8S 113°8E **149** E1
Steep Rock *Canada* 51°30N 98°48W **163** C9
Ştefan Vodă *Moldova* 46°27N 29°42E **81** D14
Ştefăneşti *Romania* 47°44N 27°15E **81** C12
Stefanie L. = Chew Bahir *Ethiopia* 4°40N 36°50E **131** G2
Stefansson Bay *Antarctica* 67°20S 59°8E **55** C5
Stefansson I. *Canada* 73°20N 105°45W **161** C10
Stege *Denmark* 54°59N 12°18E **63** K6
Ştei *Romania* 46°32N 22°27E **80** D7
Steiermark □ *Austria* 47°26N 15°0E **78** D8
Steigerwald *Germany* 49°44N 10°26E **77** F6
Steigerwald ⌓ *Germany* 49°50N 10°30E **77** F6
Steilacoom *U.S.A.* 47°10N 122°36W **170** C4
Steilrandberge *Namibia* 17°45S 13°20E **144** A1
Steinbach *Canada* 49°32N 96°40W **163** D9
Steinfurt *Germany* 52°9N 7°20E **76** C3
Steinhatchee *U.S.A.* 29°40N 83°23W **178** F6
Steinhausen *Namibia* 21°49S 18°20E **144** B2
Steinheim *Germany* 51°51N 9°5E **76** D5
Steinhuder Meer *Germany* 52°29N 9°21E **76** C5
Steinhuder Meer ⌓ *Germany* 52°30N 9°16E **76** C5
Steinkjer *Norway* 64°1N 11°31E **60** D14
Steinkopf *S. Africa* 29°18S 17°43E **144** C2
Steinwald ⌓ *Germany* 49°55N 12°8E **77** F8
Stellarton *Canada* 45°32N 62°30W **165** C7
Stellenbosch *S. Africa* 33°58S 18°50E **144** D2
Stélvio, Paso dello *Italy* 46°32N 10°27E **92** B7
Stenay *France* 49°29N 5°12E **71** C12
Stendal *Germany* 52°36N 11°53E **76** C7
Stende *Latvia* 57°11N 22°33E **82** A9
Stenhamra *Sweden* 59°20N 17°41E **62** E11
Stenshuvud △ *Sweden* 55°39N 14°15E **63** J8
Stenstorp *Sweden* 58°17N 13°45E **63** F7
Stenungsund *Sweden* 58°6N 11°50E **63** F5
Steornabhaigh = Stornoway *U.K.* 58°13N 6°23W **65** C2
Stepanakert = Xankändi *Azerbaijan* 39°52N 46°49E **105** C12
Stepanavan *Armenia* 41°1N 44°23E **87** K7
Stephens, C. *N.Z.* 40°42S 173°58E **155** A8
Stephens Creek *Australia* 31°50S 141°30E **152** A4
Stephens I. *Canada* 54°10N 130°45W **162** C2
Stephens I. *N.Z.* 40°40S 174°1E **155** A9
Stephens L. *Canada* 56°32N 95°0W **163** B9
Stephenville *Canada* 48°31N 58°35W **165** C8
Stephenville *U.S.A.* 32°13N 98°12W **176** E5
Stepnica *Poland* 53°38N 14°36E **82** E1
Stepnogorsk *Kazakhstan* 52°21N 71°53E **109** B8
Steppe *Asia* 50°0N 50°0E **102** C7
Sterea Ellas □ *Greece* 38°50N 23°0E **98** C4
Sterkstroom *S. Africa* 31°32S 26°32E **144** D4
Sterling *Colo., U.S.A.* 40°37N 103°13W **168** F12
Sterling *Ga., U.S.A.* 31°16N 81°34W **178** D8
Sterling *Ill., U.S.A.* 41°48N 89°42W **172** E9
Sterling *Kans., U.S.A.* 38°13N 98°12W **172** F4
Sterling City *U.S.A.* 31°51N 101°0W **176** F4
Sterling Heights *U.S.A.* 42°35N 83°2W **173** D12
Sterling Run *U.S.A.* 41°25N 78°12W **174** E6
Sterlitamak *Russia* 53°40N 56°0E **108** B5
Sternberg *Germany* 53°42N 11°50E **76** B7
Šternberk *Czech Rep.* 49°45N 17°15E **79** B10
Sternes *Greece* 35°30N 24°9E **101** D6
Sterzing = Vipiteno *Italy* 46°54N 11°26E **93** B8
Stettin = Szczecin *Poland* 53°27N 14°27E **82** E1
Stettiner Haff *Germany* 53°47N 14°15E **76** B10
Stettler *Canada* 52°19N 112°40W **162** C6
Steubenville *U.S.A.* 40°22N 80°37W **174** F4
Stevenage *U.K.* 51°55N 0°13W **67** F7
Stevens Point *U.S.A.* 44°31N 89°34W **172** C9
Stevens Pottery *U.S.A.* 32°57N 83°17W **178** C6
Stevenson *U.S.A.* 45°42N 121°53W **170** E5
Stevenson → *Australia* 27°6S 135°33E **151** D2
Stevenson L. *Canada* 53°55N 96°0W **163** C9
Stevensville *U.S.A.* 46°30N 114°5W **168** C6
Stevns Klint *Denmark* 55°17N 12°28E **63** J6
Stewart *Canada* 55°56N 129°57W **162** B3
Stewart *Ga., U.S.A.* 33°25N 83°52W **178** B6
Stewart *Nev., U.S.A.* 39°5N 119°46W **170** F7
Stewart → *Canada* 63°19N 139°26W **160** E4
Stewart, C. *Australia* 11°57S 134°56E **150** A1
Stewart, I. *Chile* 54°50S 71°15W **192** D2
Stewart I. *N.Z.* 46°58S 167°54E **155** G2
Stewarts Point *U.S.A.* 38°39N 123°24W **170** G3
Stewartville *U.S.A.* 43°51N 92°29W **172** D7
Stewiacke *Canada* 45°9N 63°22W **165** C7
Steynsburg *S. Africa* 31°15S 25°49E **144** D4
Steyr *Austria* 48°3N 14°25E **78** C7
Steyr → *Austria* 48°3N 14°25E **78** C7
Steytlerville *S. Africa* 33°17S 24°19E **144** D3
Stia *Italy* 43°48N 11°42E **93** E8
Stigler *U.S.A.* 35°15N 95°8W **176** D7
Stigliano *Italy* 40°24N 16°14E **95** B9
Stigtomta *Sweden* 58°47N 16°48E **63** F10
Stikine → *Canada* 56°40N 132°30W **162** B2
Stilfontein *S. Africa* 26°51S 26°50E **144** C4
Stilida *Greece* 38°55N 22°47E **98** C4
Stillmore *U.S.A.* 32°27N 82°13W **178** C7
Stillwater *N.Y., U.S.A.* 42°55N 73°41W **175** D11
Stillwater *Okla., U.S.A.* 36°7N 97°4W **176** C6
Stillwater Range *U.S.A.* 39°50N 118°5W **168** G4
Stillwater Res. *U.S.A.* 43°54N 75°3W **175** C9
Stilo, Pta. *Italy* 38°25N 16°35E **95** D9
Stilwell *U.S.A.* 35°49N 94°38W **176** D7
Stînga Nistrului □ *Moldova* 47°20N 29°15E **81** C14
Štip *Macedonia* 41°42N 22°10E **96** E6
Stira *Greece* 38°9N 24°14E **98** C6
Stirling *Canada* 44°18N 77°33W **174** B7
Stirling *N.Z.* 46°14S 169°49E **155** G4
Stirling *U.K.* 56°8N 3°57W **65** E5
Stirling □ *U.K.* 56°12N 4°18W **65** E4
Stirling Ra. *Australia* 34°23S 118°0E **149** F2
Stirling Range △ *Australia* 34°26S 118°20E **149** F2
Stittsville *Canada* 45°15N 75°55W **175** A9
Stjernøya *Norway* 70°20N 22°40E **60** A20
Stjørdalshalsen *Norway* 63°29N 10°51E **60** E14
Stock Island *U.S.A.* 24°32N 81°34W **179** L8
Stocka *Sweden* 61°53N 17°20E **62** C11
Stockach *Germany* 47°50N 9°1E **77** H5
Stockaryd *Sweden* 57°19N 14°36E **63** G8
Stockbridge *U.S.A.* 33°33N 84°14W **178** B5
Stockerau *Austria* 48°24N 16°12E **79** C9
Stockholm *Sweden* 59°19N 18°4E **62** E12
Stockholm Arlanda ✈ (ARN) *Sweden* 59°41N 17°56E **62** E11
Stockholms län □ *Sweden* 59°30N 18°20E **62** E12
Stockport *U.K.* 53°25N 2°9W **66** D5
Stocksbridge *U.K.* 53°29N 1°35W **66** D6
Stockton *Calif., U.S.A.* 37°58N 121°17W **170** H5
Stockton *Kans., U.S.A.* 39°26N 99°16W **172** F4
Stockton *Mo., U.S.A.* 37°42N 93°48W **172** G7
Stockton-on-Tees *U.K.* 54°35N 1°19W **66** C6
Stockton-on-Tees □ *U.K.* 54°35N 1°19W **66** C6
Stockton Plateau *U.S.A.* 30°30N 102°30W **176** F3
Stoczek Łukowski *Poland* 51°58N 21°58E **83** G8
Stöde *Sweden* 62°28N 16°35E **62** B10
Stoeng Treng *Cambodia* 13°31N 105°58E **120** F5
Stoer, Pt. of *U.K.* 58°16N 5°23W **65** C3
Stogovo *Macedonia* 41°31N 20°38E **96** E4
Stoholm *Denmark* 56°30N 9°8E **63** H3
Stoke *N.Z.* 41°19S 173°14E **155** B8
Stoke-on-Trent *U.K.* 53°1N 2°11W **66** D5
Stoke-on-Trent □ *U.K.* 53°1N 2°11W **66** D5
Stokes △ *Australia* 33°45S 121°11E **149** F3
Stokes Bay *Canada* 45°0N 81°28W **174** B3
Stokes Pt. *Australia* 40°10S 143°56E **151** G3
Stokes Ra. *Australia* 15°50S 130°50E **148** C5
Stokksnes *Iceland* 64°14N 14°58W **60** D6
Stokmarknes *Norway* 68°34N 14°54E **60** B16
Stolac *Bos.-H.* 43°5N 17°59E **96** C1
Stolberg *Germany* 50°47N 6°13E **76** E2
Stolbovoy, Ostrov *Russia* 74°44N 135°14E **107** B14
Stolbtsy = Stowbtsy *Belarus* 53°30N 26°43E **75** B14
Stolin *Belarus* 51°53N 26°50E **75** C14
Stöllet *Sweden* 60°26N 13°15E **62** D7
Stolnici *Romania* 44°31N 24°48E **81** F9
Stomio *Greece* 35°21N 23°32E **101** D5
Ston *Croatia* 42°51N 17°43E **93** F14
Stone *U.K.* 52°55N 2°9W **66** E5
Stone Mountain *U.S.A.* 33°49N 84°10W **178** B5
Stoneboro *U.S.A.* 41°20N 80°7W **174** E4
Stonehaven *U.K.* 56°59N 2°12W **65** E6
Stonehenge *Australia* 24°22S 143°17E **150** C3
Stonehenge *U.K.* 51°9N 1°45W **67** F6
Stonewall *Canada* 50°10N 97°19W **163** C9
Stony I. *U.S.A.* 43°53N 76°19W **175** C8
Stony L. *Man., Canada* 58°51N 98°40W **163** B9
Stony L. *Ont., Canada* 44°30N 78°5W **174** B6
Stony Point *U.S.A.* 41°14N 73°59W **175** E11
Stony Pt. *U.S.A.* 43°50N 76°18W **175** C8
Stony Rapids *Canada* 59°16N 105°50W **163** B7
Stony Tunguska = Tunguska, Podkamennaya → *Russia* 61°50N 90°13E **107** C10
Stonyford *U.S.A.* 39°23N 122°33W **170** F4
Stopnica *Poland* 50°27N 20°57E **83** H7
Storå *Sweden* 59°42N 15°6E **62** E9
Storå → *Denmark* 56°20N 8°19E **63** H2
Stora Gla *Sweden* 59°30N 12°30E **62** E6
Stora Le *Sweden* 59°5N 11°55E **62** E5
Stora Lulevatten *Sweden* 67°10N 19°30E **60** C18
Stora Sjöfallet △ *Sweden* 67°36N 17°45E **60** C17
Storavan *Sweden* 65°45N 18°10E **60** D18
Stord *Norway* 59°52N 5°23E **61** G11
Store Bælt *Denmark* 55°20N 11°0E **63** J4
Store Heddinge *Denmark* 55°18N 12°23E **63** J6
Store Koldewey *Greenland* 76°30N 19°0W **57** B9
Store Mosse △ *Sweden* 57°18N 13°55E **63** G7
Storebro *Sweden* 57°35N 15°52E **63** G9
Storfors *Sweden* 59°32N 14°17E **62** E8
Storkerson Pen. *Canada* 72°30N 106°30W **160** C10
Storlien *Sweden* 63°19N 12°6E **62** A6
Storm B. *Australia* 43°10S 147°30E **151** G4
Storm Lake *U.S.A.* 42°39N 95°13W **172** D6
Stormberge *S. Africa* 31°16S 26°17E **144** D4
Stormsrivier *S. Africa* 33°59S 23°52E **144** D3
Stornoway *U.K.* 58°13N 6°23W **65** C2
Storo *Italy* 45°51N 10°35E **92** C7
Storozhinets = Storozhynets *Ukraine* 48°14N 25°45E **81** B10
Storozhynets *Ukraine* 48°14N 25°45E **81** B10
Storrs *U.S.A.* 41°49N 72°15W **175** E12
Storsjön *Gävleborg, Sweden* 60°35N 16°45E **62** D10
Storsjön *Jämtland, Sweden* 62°48N 13°7E **62** B7
Storsjön *Jämtland, Sweden* 63°9N 14°30E **62** A8
Storstrømmen *Greenland* 76°17N 22°25W **57** B8
Storuman *Sweden* 65°5N 17°10E **60** D17
Storuman, L. *Sweden* 65°13N 16°50E **60** D17
Storvätteshågna *Sweden* 62°6N 12°30E **62** B6
Storvik *Sweden* 60°35N 16°33E **62** D10
Storvreta *Sweden* 59°58N 17°44E **62** E11
Stouffville *Canada* 43°58N 79°15W **174** C5
Stoughton *Canada* 49°40N 103°0W **163** D8
Stour → *Dorset, U.K.* 50°43N 1°47W **67** G6
Stour → *Kent, U.K.* 51°18N 1°22E **67** F9
Stour → *Suffolk, U.K.* 51°57N 1°4E **67** F9
Stourbridge *U.K.* 52°28N 2°8W **67** E5
Stout L. *Canada* 52°0N 94°40W **163** C10
Stove Pipe Wells Village *U.S.A.* 36°35N 117°11W **171** J9
Støvring *Denmark* 56°54N 9°50E **63** H3
Stow *U.S.A.* 41°10N 81°27W **174** E3
Stowbtsy *Belarus* 53°30N 26°43E **75** B14
Stowmarket *U.K.* 52°12N 1°0E **67** E9
Strabane *U.K.* 54°50N 7°27W **64** B4
Stracin *Macedonia* 42°13N 22°2E **96** D6
Stradella *Italy* 45°5N 9°18E **92** C6
Strahan *Australia* 42°9S 145°20E **151** G4
Strajitsa *Bulgaria* 43°14N 25°58E **97** C9
Strakonice *Czech Rep.* 49°15N 13°53E **78** B6
Straldzha *Bulgaria* 42°35N 26°40E **97** D10
Stralsund *Germany* 54°18N 13°4E **76** A9
Strand *S. Africa* 34°9S 18°48E **144** D2
Stranda *Møre og Romsdal, Norway* 62°19N 6°58E **60** E12
Stranda *Nord-Trøndelag, Norway* 63°33N 10°14E **60** E14
Strandby *Denmark* 57°30N 10°29E **63** G4
Strangford L. *U.K.* 54°30N 5°37W **64** B6
Strängnäs *Sweden* 59°23N 17°2E **62** E11
Stranorlar *Ireland* 54°48N 7°46W **64** B4
Stranraer *U.K.* 54°54N 5°1W **65** G3
Strasbourg *Canada* 51°4N 104°55W **163** C8
Strasbourg *France* 48°35N 7°42E **71** D14
Strasburg *Germany* 53°30N 13°43E **76** B9
Strășeni *Moldova* 47°8N 28°36E **81** C13
Stråssa *Sweden* 59°44N 15°12E **62** E9
Stratford *N.S.W., Australia* 32°7S 151°55E **153** B9
Stratford *Vic., Australia* 37°59S 147°7E **153** D7
Stratford *Canada* 43°23N 81°0W **174** C4
Stratford *N.Z.* 39°20S 174°19E **154** F3
Stratford *Calif., U.S.A.* 36°11N 119°49W **170** J7
Stratford *Conn., U.S.A.* 41°12N 73°8W **175** E11
Stratford *Tex., U.S.A.* 36°20N 102°4W **176** C3
Stratford-upon-Avon *U.K.* 52°12N 1°42W **67** E6
Strath Spey *U.K.* 57°9N 3°49W **65** D5
Strathalbyn *Australia* 35°13S 138°53E **152** C3
Strathaven *U.K.* 55°40N 4°5W **65** F4
Strathcona ⌓ *Canada* 49°38N 125°40W **162** D3
Strathmore *Canada* 51°5N 113°18W **162** C6
Strathmore *U.K.* 56°37N 3°7W **65** E5
Strathmore *U.S.A.* 36°9N 119°4W **170** J7
Strathnaver *Canada* 53°20N 122°33W **162** C4
Strathpeffer *U.K.* 57°35N 4°32W **65** D4
Strathroy *Canada* 42°58N 81°38W **174** D3
Strathy Pt. *U.K.* 58°36N 4°1W **65** C4
Strattanville *U.S.A.* 41°12N 79°19W **174** E5
Stratton *U.S.A.* 45°8N 70°26W **175** A14
Stratton Mt. *U.S.A.* 43°4N 72°55W **175** C12
Straubing *Germany* 48°52N 12°34E **77** G8
Straumnes *Iceland* 66°26N 23°8W **60** C2
Strausberg *Germany* 52°35N 13°54E **76** C9
Strawberry → *U.S.A.* 40°10N 110°24W **168** F8
Strážnice *Czech Rep.* 48°54N 17°19E **79** C10
Streaky B. *Australia* 32°48S 134°13E **151** E1
Streaky Bay *Australia* 32°51S 134°18E **151** E1
Streator *U.S.A.* 41°8N 88°50W **172** E9
Středočeský □ *Czech Rep.* 49°55N 14°30E **78** B7
Streetsboro *U.S.A.* 41°14N 81°21W **174** E3
Streetsville *Canada* 43°35N 79°42W **174** C5
Strehaia *Romania* 44°37N 23°10E **81** F8
Strelcha *Bulgaria* 42°25N 24°19E **97** D8
Streng → *Cambodia* 13°12N 103°37E **120** F4
Stresa *Italy* 45°52N 8°28E **92** C5
Streymoy *Færoe Is.* 62°8N 7°5W **60** E9
Strezhevoy *Russia* 60°42N 77°34E **106** C8
Stříbro *Czech Rep.* 49°44N 13°0E **78** A6
Strilky *Ukraine* 49°20N 22°59E **83** J9
Strimonas → *Greece* 40°46N 23°51E **96** F7
Stroeder *Argentina* 40°12S 62°37W **192** B4
Strofades *Greece* 37°15N 21°0E **98** D3
Strokestown *Ireland* 53°47N 8°5W **64** C3
Stroma *U.K.* 58°41N 3°7W **65** C5
Stromberg-Heuchelberg ⌓ *Germany* 49°2N 8°50E **77** F4
Strómboli *Italy* 38°47N 15°13E **95** D8
Stromeferry *U.K.* 57°21N 5°33W **65** D3
Stromness *U.K.* 58°58N 3°17W **65** C5
Strömsbruk *Sweden* 61°52N 17°18E **62** C11
Stromsburg *U.S.A.* 41°7N 97°36W **172** E5
Strömsnäsbruk *Sweden* 56°35N 13°45E **63** H7
Strömstad *Sweden* 58°56N 11°10E **63** F5
Strömsund *Sweden* 63°51N 15°33E **60** E16
Strongili *Greece* 36°6N 29°42E **99** E11
Stróngoli *Italy* 39°16N 17°3E **95** C10
Strongsville *U.S.A.* 41°19N 81°50W **174** E3
Stronie Śląskie *Poland* 50°18N 16°53E **83** H3
Stronsay *U.K.* 59°7N 2°35W **65** B6
Stropkov *Slovak Rep.* 49°13N 21°39E **79** B14
Stroud *U.K.* 51°45N 2°13W **67** F5
Stroud Road *Australia* 32°18S 151°57E **153** B9
Stroudsburg *U.S.A.* 40°59N 75°12W **175** F9
Stroumbi *Cyprus* 34°53N 32°29E **101** E11
Štrpce = Shtërpcë *Kosovo* 42°14N 21°1E **96** D5
Struer *Denmark* 56°30N 8°35E **63** H2
Struga *Macedonia* 41°11N 20°44E **96** E4
Strugi Krasnyye *Russia* 58°21N 29°1E **84** C5
Strumica *Macedonia* 41°28N 22°41E **96** E6
Strumica → *Europe* 41°20N 23°22E **96** E7
Strumok *Ukraine* 45°43N 29°27E **81** E14
Struthers *U.S.A.* 41°4N 80°39W **174** E4
Stryama *Bulgaria* 42°16N 24°54E **97** D8
Stryker *U.S.A.* 48°41N 114°46W **168** B6
Stryków *Poland* 51°55N 19°33E **83** G6
Stryy *Ukraine* 49°16N 23°48E **75** D12
Strzegom *Poland* 50°58N 16°20E **83** H3
Strzelce Krajeńskie *Poland* 52°52N 15°33E **83** F2
Strzelce Opolskie *Poland* 50°31N 18°18E **83** H5
Strzelecki Cr. → *Australia* 29°37S 139°59E **151** D2
Strzelecki Desert *Australia* 29°30S 140°0E **151** D3
Strzelin *Poland* 50°46N 17°2E **83** H4
Strzelno *Poland* 52°35N 18°9E **83** F5
Strzybnica *Poland* 50°28N 18°48E **83** H5
Strzyżów *Poland* 49°52N 21°47E **83** J8
Stuart *Fla., U.S.A.* 27°12N 80°15W **179** H9
Stuart *Nebr., U.S.A.* 42°36N 99°8W **172** D4
Stuart → *Canada* 54°0N 123°35W **162** C4
Stuart Bluff Ra. *Australia* 22°50S 131°52E **148** D5
Stuart I. *U.S.A.* 63°35N 162°30W **166** C7
Stuart L. *Canada* 54°30N 124°30W **162** C4
Stuart Mts. *N.Z.* 45°2S 167°39E **155** F2
Stuart Ra. *Australia* 29°10S 134°56E **151** D1
Stubbekøbing *Denmark* 54°53N 12°9E **63** K6
Stuben *Austria* 47°10N 10°8E **78** D3
Studen Kladenets, Yazovir *Bulgaria* 41°37N 25°30E **97** E9
Studenica *Serbia* 43°29N 20°32E **96** C4
Studenka *Czech Rep.* 49°44N 18°5E **79** B11
Studholme *N.Z.* 44°42S 171°9E **155** E6
Stugun *Sweden* 63°10N 15°40E **62** A9
Stuhr *Germany* 53°5N 8°44E **76** B4
Stull L. *Canada* 54°24N 92°34W **164** B1
Stung Treng = Stoeng Treng *Cambodia* 13°31N 105°58E **120** F5
Stupart → *Canada* 56°0N 93°25W **164** A1
Stupava *Slovak Rep.* 48°17N 17°2E **79** C10
Stupino *Russia* 54°57N 38°2E **84** E10
Sturge I. *Antarctica* 67°26S 164°47E **55** C11
Sturgeon B. *Canada* 52°0N 97°50W **163** C9
Sturgeon Bay *U.S.A.* 44°50N 87°23W **172** C10
Sturgeon Falls *Canada* 46°25N 79°57W **164** C4
Sturgeon L. *Alta., Canada* 55°6N 117°32W **162** B5
Sturgeon L. *Ont., Canada* 50°0N 90°45W **164** C1
Sturgeon L. *Ont., Canada* 44°28N 78°43W **174** B6
Sturgis *Canada* 51°56N 102°36W **163** C8
Sturgis *Mich., U.S.A.* 41°48N 85°25W **173** E11
Sturgis *S. Dak., U.S.A.* 44°25N 103°31W **172** C2
Sturkö *Sweden* 56°5N 15°42E **63** H9
Štúrovo *Slovak Rep.* 47°48N 18°41E **79** D11
Sturt △ *Australia* 27°17S 141°37E **151** D3
Sturt Cr. → *Australia* 19°8S 127°50E **148** C4
Sturt Stony Desert *Australia* 28°30S 141°0E **151** D3
Sturts Meadows *Australia* 31°18S 141°42E **152** A4
Stutterheim *S. Africa* 32°33S 27°28E **144** D4
Stuttgart *Germany* 48°48N 9°11E **77** G5
Stuttgart *U.S.A.* 34°30N 91°33W **176** D9
Stuttgart Echterdingen ✈ (STR) *Germany* 48°42N 9°11E **77** G5
Stuyvesant *U.S.A.* 42°23N 73°45W **175** D11
Stykkishólmur *Iceland* 65°2N 22°40W **60** D2
Styria = Steiermark □ *Austria* 47°26N 15°0E **78** D8
Styrsö *Sweden* 57°37N 11°46E **63** G5
Su Xian = Suzhou *China* 33°41N 116°59E **114** H9
Suakin *Sudan* 19°8N 37°20E **137** D4
Suakin Archipelago *Sudan* 18°42N 38°30E **137** D4
Suamico *U.S.A.* 44°38N 88°2W **172** C9
Suan *N. Korea* 38°42N 126°22E **115** E14
Suana *Indonesia* 8°44S 115°36E **119** K18
Suape *Brazil* 8°24S 35°0W **189** B3
Suar *India* 29°2N 79°3E **125** E8
Şubā *Si. Arabia* 27°10N 35°40E **128** E2
Subang *Indonesia* 6°34S 107°45E **119** G12
Subansiri → *India* 26°48N 93°50E **123** F18
Subarnagiri *India* 19°50N 83°51E **126** E6
Subarnarekha → *India* 22°34N 87°24E **125** H12
Subay', Urūq *Si. Arabia* 22°15N 43°5E **137** C5
Subayhah *Si. Arabia* 30°2N 38°50E **128** D3
Subcetate *Romania* 45°36N 23°0E **80** E8
Subi *Indonesia* 2°58N 108°50E **118** D3
Subiaco *Italy* 41°56N 13°5E **93** G10
Subotica *Serbia* 46°6N 19°39E **80** D4
Suceava *Romania* 47°38N 26°16E **81** C11
Suceava □ *Romania* 47°37N 25°40E **81** C10
Suceava → *Romania* 47°32N 26°32E **81** C11
Sucha-Beskidzka *Poland* 49°44N 19°35E **83** J6
Suchan = Partizansk *Russia* 43°8N 133°9E **107** E14
Suchań *Poland* 53°18N 15°18E **83** E2
Suchedniów *Poland* 51°3N 20°49E **83** G7
Suchil *Mexico* 23°39N 103°54W **180** C4
Suchou = Suzhou *China* 31°19N 120°38E **117** B13
Süchow = Xuzhou *China* 34°18N 117°10E **115** G9
Suchowola *Poland* 53°33N 23°3E **82** E10
Suck → *Ireland* 53°17N 8°3W **64** C3
Sucre *Bolivia* 19°0S 65°15W **186** G5
Sućuraj *Croatia* 43°10N 17°8E **93** E14
Sucuriú → *Brazil* 20°47S 51°38W **187** H8
Sud □ *Cameroon* 2°30N 11°45E **139** E7
Sud, Pte. du *Canada* 49°3N 62°14W **165** C7
Sud-Bandama □ *Ivory C.* 6°0N 5°15W **138** D3
Sud-Comoé □ *Ivory C.* 5°30N 3°0W **138** D4
Sud-Kivu □ *Dem. Rep. of the Congo* 3°0S 28°30E **142** C2
Sud-Ouest □ *Cameroon* 5°25N 9°20E **139** D6
Sud-Ouest, Pte. *Canada* 49°23N 63°36W **165** C7
Sud Ouest, Pte. *Mauritius* 20°28S 57°18E **141** d
Suda → *Russia* 59°0N 37°40E **84** C9
Sudak *Ukraine* 44°51N 34°57E **85** K8
Sudan *U.S.A.* 34°4N 102°31W **176** D3
Sudan ■ *Africa* 15°0N 30°0E **135** E11
Sudbury *Canada* 46°30N 81°0W **164** C3
Sudbury *U.K.* 52°2N 0°45E **67** E8
Sudd *South Sudan* 8°20N 30°0E **135** G12
Sudeifel = Deutsch-Luxemburgischer ⌓ *Germany* 49°58N 6°12E **77** F2
Süderbrarup *Germany* 54°38N 9°45E **76** A5
Süderlügum *Germany* 54°52N 8°54E **76** A4
Süderoogsand *Germany* 54°27N 8°28E **76** A4
Sudeten Mts. = Sudety *Europe* 50°20N 16°45E **79** A9
Sudety *Europe* 50°20N 16°45E **79** A9
Südheide ⌓ *Germany* 52°46N 10°10E **76** C6
Suðuroy *Færoe Is.* 61°32N 6°50W **60** F9
Sudi *Tanzania* 10°11S 39°57E **143** E4
Sudirman, Pegunungan *Indonesia* 4°30S 137°0E **119** E9
Sudiţi *Romania* 44°35N 27°38E **81** F12
Sudogda *Russia* 55°55N 40°50E **86** C5
Sudong, Pulau *Singapore* 1°13N 103°44E **121** d
Sudova Vyshnya *Ukraine* 49°46N 23°22E **83** J10
Sudzha *Russia* 51°14N 35°17E **85** G8
Sueca *Spain* 39°12N 0°21W **91** F4
Sŭedinenie *Bulgaria* 42°16N 24°33E **97** D8
Suemez I. *U.S.A.* 55°15N 133°20W **162** B2
Suez = El Suweis *Egypt* 29°58N 32°31E **137** F8
Suez, G. of = Suweis, Khalîg el *Egypt* 28°40N 33°0E **137** F8
Suez Canal = Suweis, Qanâ es *Egypt* 31°0N 32°20E **137** E8
Suffield *Canada* 50°12N 111°10W **162** C6
Suffolk *U.S.A.* 36°44N 76°35W **173** G15
Suffolk □ *U.K.* 52°16N 1°0E **67** E9
Şufiān *Iran* 38°16N 45°58E **105** C11
Şugag *Romania* 45°47N 23°37E **81** E8
Sugaing = Sagaing *Burma* 21°52N 95°59E **123** J19
Sugar Grove *U.S.A.* 41°59N 79°20W **174** E5
Sugar Hill *U.S.A.* 34°6N 84°2W 1
Sugarcreek *U.S.A.* 41°25N 79°52W 1
Sugarive → *India* 26°16N 86°24E 12
Sughd □ *Tajikistan* 40°0N 69°0E 1
Suğla Gölü *Turkey* 37°20N 32°0E 1
Sugluk = Salluit *Canada* 62°14N 75°38W 16
Sugun *China* 39°53N 76°47E 1
Suha Reke = Therandë *Kosovo* 42°21N 20°50E
Suhaia, Lacul *Romania* 43°45N 25°15E 8
Şuḩār *Oman* 24°20N 56°40E 1
Sühbaatar *Mongolia* 50°17N 106°10E 11
Sühbaatar □ *Mongolia* 45°30N 114°0E 1
Suheli Par *India* 10°5N 72°17E 1
Suhl *Germany* 50°36N 10°42E
Şuhut *Turkey* 38°31N 30°32E 9
Sui *Pakistan* 28°37N 69°19E 1
Sui Xian *China* 34°25N 115°2E 1
Šuica *Bos.-H.* 43°52N 17°11E
Suichang *China* 28°29N 119°15E 11
Suichuan *China* 26°20N 114°32E 11
Suide *China* 37°30N 110°12E 1
Suifenhe *China* 44°25N 131°10E 11
Suihua *China* 46°32N 126°55E 11
Suijiang *China* 28°40N 103°59E 1
Suining *Hunan, China* 26°35N 110°10E 1
Suining *Jiangsu, China* 33°56N 117°58E 1
Suining *Sichuan, China* 30°26N 105°35E 1
Suiping *China* 33°10N 113°59E 1
Suippes *France* 49°8N 4°30E 7
Suir → *Ireland* 52°16N 7°9W
Suisse = Switzerland ■ *Europe* 46°30N 8°0E
Suisun City *U.S.A.* 38°15N 122°2W 1
Suixi *China* 21°19N 110°18E 1
Suiyang *Guizhou, China* 27°58N 107°18E 1
Suiyang *Heilongjiang, China* 44°30N 130°56E 11
Suizhong *China* 40°21N 120°20E 11
Suizhou *China* 31°42N 113°24E 1
Sujangarh *India* 27°42N 74°31E 1
Sujiatun *China* 41°39N 123°20E 11
Sukabumi *Indonesia* 6°56S 106°50E 11
Sukadana *Indonesia* 1°10S 110°0E 1
Sukagawa *Japan* 37°17N 140°23E 11
Sukamade *Indonesia* 8°30S 113°52E 11
Sukaraja *Indonesia* 2°28S 110°25E 1
Sukawati *Indonesia* 8°35S 115°17E 11
Sukch'ŏn *N. Korea* 39°22N 125°35E 11
Sukhindol *Bulgaria* 43°11N 25°10E
Sukhinichi *Russia* 54°8N 35°10E
Sukhona → *Russia* 61°15N 46°39E 1
Sukhothai *Thailand* 17°1N 99°49E 1
Sukhumi = Sokhumi *Georgia* 43°0N 41°0E
Sukkertoppen = Maniitsoq *Greenland* 65°26N 52°55W
Sukkur *Pakistan* 27°42N 68°54E 1
Sukkur Barrage *Pakistan* 27°40N 68°50E 1
Sukma *India* 18°24N 81°45E 1
Sukovo *Serbia* 43°4N 22°37E
Sukri → *India* 25°4N 71°43E 1
Sukumo *Japan* 32°56N 132°44E 1
Sukunka → *Canada* 55°45N 121°15W 1
Sula → *Ukraine* 49°40N 32°41E
Sula, Kepulauan *Indonesia* 1°45S 125°0E 1
Sulaco → *Honduras* 15°2N 87°44W 1
Sulaiman Range *Pakistan* 30°30N 69°50E 1
Sulaiman-Too *Kyrgyzstan* 40°31N 72°46E 1
Sulak → *Russia* 43°20N 47°34E
Sulakyurt *Turkey* 40°9N 33°43E 1
Sūlār *Iran* 31°53N 51°54E 1
Sulawesi *Indonesia* 2°0S 120°0E 1
Sulawesi Barat □ *Indonesia* 3°0S 119°0E 1
Sulawesi Sea = Celebes Sea *Indonesia* 3°0N 123°0E 1
Sulawesi Selatan □ *Indonesia* 2°30S 120°0E 1
Sulawesi Tengah □ *Indonesia* 1°30S 121°0E 1
Sulawesi Tenggara □ *Indonesia* 3°50S 122°0E 1
Sulawesi Utara □ *Indonesia* 1°0N 124°0E 1
Sulechów *Poland* 52°5N 15°40E
Sulęcin *Poland* 52°26N 15°10E
Suleja *Nigeria* 9°10N 7°10E 1
Sulejów *Poland* 51°26N 19°53E
Sulejówek *Poland* 52°13N 21°17E
Süleymanlı *Turkey* 38°58N 27°47E
Sulima *S. Leone* 6°58N 11°32W 1
Sulina *Romania* 45°10N 29°40E 8
Sulina, Braţul → *Romania* 45°10N 29°40E 8
Sulingen *Germany* 52°41N 8°48E
Suliţa *Romania* 47°39N 26°59E 8
Sulitjelma *Norway* 67°9N 16°3E 6
Sułkowice *Poland* 49°50N 19°49E
Sullana *Peru* 4°52S 80°39W 1
Süller *Turkey* 38°9N 29°29E 9
Sullivan *Ill., U.S.A.* 39°36N 88°37W 1
Sullivan *Ind., U.S.A.* 39°6N 87°24W 17
Sullivan *Mo., U.S.A.* 38°13N 91°10W 1
Sullivan Bay *Canada* 50°55N 126°50W 1
Sullivan I. = Lanbi Kyun *Burma* 10°50N 98°20E 1
Sullom Voe *U.K.* 60°27N 1°20W
Sullorsuaq *Greenland* 70°5N 53°0W
Sully-sur-Loire *France* 47°45N 2°20E
Sulmierzyce *Poland* 51°37N 17°32E
Sulmona *Italy* 42°3N 13°55E 9
Süloğlu *Turkey* 41°44N 26°53E 9
Sulphur *La., U.S.A.* 30°14N 93°23W 1
Sulphur *Okla., U.S.A.* 34°31N 96°58W 1
Sulphur Pt. *Canada* 60°56N 114°48W 1
Sulphur Springs *U.S.A.* 33°8N 95°36W 1
Sultan *Canada* 47°36N 82°47W 1
Sultan *U.S.A.* 47°52N 121°49W 1
Sultan Dağları *Turkey* 38°20N 31°20E 1
Sultan Hamud *Kenya* 2°1S 37°22E 1
Sultanābād = Arāk *Iran* 34°0N 49°40E 1
Sultanhisar *Turkey* 37°53N 28°9E 9
Sultaniça *Turkey* 40°37N 26°8E 9
Sultaniye *Turkey* 40°11N 28°12E 9

anpur Mad. P., India 23°9N 77°56E 124 H8
anpur Punjab, India 31°13N 75°11E 124 D6
anpur Ut. P., India 26°18N 82°4E 125 F10
. Arch. Phil. 6°0N 121°0E 119 C6
Sea E. Indies 8°0N 120°0E 119 C6
klü Turkey 38°53N 32°20E 104 C5
ova Turkey 40°46N 35°32E 104 B6
q Libya 31°44N 20°14E 135 B10
ru India 13°42N 80°1E 127 H5
bach Germany 49°18N 7°3E 77 F3
bach-Rosenberg
rmany 49°30N 11°44E 77 F7
berger Ice Shelf
tarctica 78°0S 150°0W 55 E13
alata Indonesia 1°0N 122°31E 119 D6
ampa Argentina 29°25S 63°29W 190 B3
atera Indonesia 0°40N 100°20E 118 D2
atera Barat □
donesia 1°0S 101°0E 118 E2
atera Selatan □
donesia 3°0S 104°0E 118 E2
atera Utara □
donesia 2°30N 98°0E 118 D1
atra = Sumatera
donesia 0°40N 100°20E 118 D2
atra U.S.A. 30°1N 84°59W 178 E5
ava △ Czech Rep. 49°0N 13°49E 78 C6
ba Indonesia 9°45S 119°35E 119 F5
ba, Selat Indonesia 9°0S 118°40E 119 F5
bawa Indonesia 8°26S 117°30E 118 F5
bawa Besar
donesia 8°30S 117°26E 118 F5
bawanga □ Tanzania 8°0S 31°30E 140 F6
be Angola 11°10S 13°48E 140 G2
bu △ Zambia 8°43S 30°22E 143 D3
burgh Hd. U.K. 59°52N 1°17W 65 B7
deo India 31°26N 78°44E 125 D8
do China 35°6N 78°41E 125 B8
é Brazil 7°39S 36°55W 189 B3
edang Indonesia 6°52S 107°55E 119 G12
eg Hungary 46°59N 17°20E 80 D2
en = Shumen
lgaria 43°18N 26°55E 97 C10
enep Indonesia 7°1S 113°52E 119 G15
gait = Sumqayıt
erbaijan 40°34N 49°38E 87 K9
mer L. U.S.A. 42°50N 120°45W 168 E3
merland Canada 49°32N 119°41W 162 D5
merland Key
S.A. 24°40N 81°27W 179 L8
merside Canada 46°24N 63°47W 165 C7
mersville U.S.A. 38°17N 80°51W 173 F13
merton U.S.A. 33°36N 80°20W 178 B9
mertown U.S.A. 32°45N 82°16W 178 C7
merville Ga.,
S.A. 34°29N 85°21W 177 D12
merville S.C.,
S.A. 33°1N 80°11W 178 B9
mit Lake Canada 54°20N 122°40W 162 C4
mit Peak U.S.A. 37°21N 106°42W 169 H10
ner N.Z. 43°35S 172°48E 155 D7
ner Iowa, U.S.A. 42°51N 92°6W 172 D7
ner Wash., U.S.A. 47°12N 122°14W 170 C4
ner, L. N.Z. 42°42S 172°15E 155 C7
oto Japan 34°21N 134°54E 113 G7
perk Czech Rep. 49°59N 16°59E 79 B9
qayıt Azerbaijan 40°34N 49°38E 87 K9
ter U.S.A. 33°55N 80°21W 178 B9
xi China 34°35N 80°22E 109 F10
y Ukraine 50°57N 34°50E 85 G8
y □ Ukraine 50°50N 33°50E 85 G7
City S. Africa 25°17S 27°3E 144 C4
City Center U.S.A. 27°43N 82°21W 179 H7
Kosi → Nepal 26°59N 87°8E 125 F12
Lakes U.S.A. 33°10N 111°52W 169 K8
Valley U.S.A. 43°42N 114°21W 168 E6
agawa Japan 43°29N 141°55E 112 C10
an N. Korea 39°15N 125°40E 115 E13
art, L. U.K. 56°42N 5°43W 65 E3
burst U.S.A. 48°53N 111°55W 168 B8
bury Australia 37°35S 144°44E 153 D6
bury U.S.A. 40°52N 76°48W 175 F8
chales Argentina 30°58S 61°35W 190 C3
cheon S. Korea 34°52N 127°31E 115 G14
cho Corral
gentina 27°55S 63°27W 190 B3
ch'on N. Korea 39°25N 125°56E 115 E13
cook U.S.A. 43°8N 71°27W 175 C13
da, Selat Indonesia 6°20S 105°30E 118 F3
da Is. Indonesia 5°0S 105°0E 156 H2
da Str. = Sunda, Selat
donesia 6°20S 105°30E 118 F3
da Trench = Java Trench
d. Oc. 9°0S 105°0E 118 F3
dance Canada 56°32N 94°4W 163 B10
dance U.S.A. 44°24N 104°23W 168 D11
dar Nagar India 31°32N 76°53E 124 D7
darbans Asia 22°0N 89°0E 123 J16
darbans △ India 22°0N 88°45E 125 J13
dargarh India 22°4N 84°5E 126 C7
days = Sondags →
Africa 33°44S 25°51E 144 D4
derland Canada 44°16N 79°4W 174 B5
derland U.K. 54°55N 1°23W 66 C6
down △ Australia 28°49S 151°38E 151 D5
dre Canada 51°49N 114°38W 162 C6
ds Denmark 56°13N 9°1E 63 H3
dsvall Sweden 62°23N 17°17E 62 B11
dsvallsbukten
weden 62°21N 17°25E 62 B11
gai Acheh Malaysia 5°8N 100°30E 121 c
gai Kolok Thailand 6°2N 101°58E 121 J3
gai Lembing
alaysia 3°55N 103°3E 121 L4
gai Petani Malaysia 5°37N 100°30E 121 K3
gaigerong Indonesia 2°59S 104°52E 118 E2
gailiat Indonesia 1°51S 106°8E 118 E3
gaipenuh Indonesia 2°1S 101°20E 118 E2
gari = Songhua Jiang →
ina 47°45N 132°30E 111 B15
ghua Chiang = Songhua
→ China 47°45N 132°30E 111 B15
gurlu Turkey 40°12N 34°21E 104 B6
ja Croatia 45°21N 16°35E 93 C13
land Park U.S.A. 31°50N 106°40W 169 L10
nansjö Sweden 60°13N 14°58E 62 D8
ndalsøra Norway 62°40N 8°33E 60 E13
ne Sweden 59°52N 13°5E 62 E7
nemo Sweden 59°53N 13°44E 62 E7
nyside U.S.A. 46°20N 120°0W 168 C4
nyvale U.S.A. 37°23N 122°2W 170 H4
Sunrise U.S.A. 26°8N 80°14W 179 J9
Sunrise Manor U.S.A. 36°12N 115°4W 171 J11
Suntar Russia 62°15N 117°30E 107 C12
Sunyani Ghana 7°21N 2°22W 138 D4
Suomenselkä Finland 62°52N 24°0E 60 E21
Suomi = Finland ■
Europe 63°0N 27°0E 60 E22
Suomussalmi Finland 64°54N 29°10E 60 D23
Suoyarvi Russia 62°3N 32°20E 84 A7
Supai U.S.A. 36°15N 112°41W 169 H7
Supaul India 26°10N 86°40E 125 F12
Superior Ariz., U.S.A. 33°18N 111°6W 169 K8
Superior Mont., U.S.A. 47°12N 114°53W 168 C6
Superior Nebr., U.S.A. 40°1N 98°4W 172 E4
Superior Wis., U.S.A. 46°44N 92°6W 172 B7
Superior, L. N. Amer. 47°0N 87°0W 164 C2
Supetar Croatia 43°25N 16°32E 93 E13
Suphan Buri Thailand 14°14N 100°10E 120 E3
Suphan Dağı Turkey 38°54N 42°48E 105 C10
Supiori Indonesia 1°0S 136°0E 119 E9
Supraśl Poland 53°13N 23°19E 83 E10
Supraśl → Poland 53°11N 22°57E 83 E9
Supsa Georgia 42°2N 41°49E 87 J5
Supung Shuiku
China 40°35N 124°50E 115 D13
Sūq ash Shuyūkh Iraq 30°53N 46°28E 128 D5
Sūq Suwayq Si. Arabia 24°23N 38°27E 128 E3
Suqian China 33°54N 118°8E 115 H10
Suquṭra = Socotra
Yemen 12°30N 54°0E 131 E5
Sūr Lebanon 33°19N 35°16E 130 B4
Şūr Oman 22°34N 59°32E 131 C6
Sur, Pt. U.S.A. 36°18N 121°54W 170 J5
Sura → Russia 56°6N 46°0E 86 C8
Surab Pakistan 28°25N 66°15E 124 E2
Surabaja = Surabaya
Indonesia 7°17S 112°45E 118 F4
Surabaya Indonesia 7°17S 112°45E 118 F4
Surahammar Sweden 59°43N 16°13E 62 E10
Suraia Romania 45°40N 27°25E 81 E12
Surakarta Indonesia 7°35S 110°48E 118 F4
Šurany Slovak Rep. 48°6N 18°10E 79 C11
Surat Australia 27°10S 149°6E 151 D4
Surat India 21°12N 72°55E 126 D1
Surat Thani Thailand 9°6N 99°20E 121 H2
Suratgarh India 29°18N 73°55E 124 E5
Surathkal India 12°58N 74°46E 127 H2
Suraxanı = Qaraçuxar
Azerbaijan 40°25N 50°1E 87 K10
Şuraymilā Si. Arabia 25°7N 46°7E 128 E5
Suraż Poland 52°57N 22°57E 83 F9
Surazh Belarus 55°25N 30°44E 84 E6
Surazh Russia 53°5N 32°27E 85 F7
Surduc Romania 47°15N 23°25E 81 C8
Surduc Pasul Romania 45°21N 23°23E 81 E8
Surdulica Serbia 42°41N 22°11E 96 D6
Surendranagar India 22°45N 71°40E 124 H4
Surf U.S.A. 34°41N 120°36W 171 L6
Surfers Paradise
Australia 28°0S 153°25E 151 D5
Surfside U.S.A. 25°52N 80°7W 179 K9
Surgana India 20°34N 73°37E 126 D1
Surgères France 46°7N 0°47W 72 B3
Surgut Russia 61°14N 73°20E 106 C8
Sùria Spain 41°50N 1°45E 90 D6
Suriapet India 17°10N 79°40E 126 F4
Surigao Phil. 9°47N 125°29E 119 C7
Surin Thailand 14°50N 103°34E 120 E4
Surinam = Suriname ■
S. Amer. 4°0N 56°0W 187 C7
Suriname ■ S. Amer. 4°0N 56°0W 187 C7
Suriname → Suriname 5°50N 55°15W 187 B7
Surjagarh India 19°36N 80°25E 126 E5
Sūrmaq Iran 31°3N 52°48E 129 D7
Sürmene Turkey 41°0N 40°1E 105 B9
Surovikino Russia 48°32N 42°55E 87 F6
Surprise U.S.A. 33°38N 112°19W 169 K7
Surrey Canada 49°7N 122°45W 170 A4
Surrey □ U.K. 51°15N 0°31W 67 F7
Sursand India 26°39N 85°43E 125 F11
Sursar → India 26°14N 87°3E 125 F12
Sursee Switz. 47°11N 8°6E 77 H4
Sursk Russia 53°3N 45°40E 86 D7
Surskoye Russia 54°30N 46°44E 86 C8
Surt Libya 31°11N 16°39E 135 B9
Surt, Khalīj Libya 31°40N 18°30E 135 B9
Surtanahu Pakistan 26°22N 70°0E 124 F4
Surte Sweden 57°50N 12°1E 63 G6
Surtsey Iceland 63°20N 20°30W 60 E3
Surubim Brazil 7°50S 35°45W 189 B3
Sürüç Turkey 36°58N 38°25E 105 D8
Suruga-Wan Japan 34°45N 138°30E 113 G9
Surxondaryo □
Uzbekistan 38°0N 67°30E 109 E7
Susa Italy 45°8N 7°3E 92 C4
Susă → Denmark 55°12N 11°42E 63 J5
Sušac Croatia 42°46N 16°30E 93 F13
Sūsah Libya 32°52N 21°59E 135 B10
Susak Croatia 44°30N 14°18E 93 D11
Susaki Japan 33°22N 133°17E 113 H6
Sūsangerd Iran 31°35N 48°6E 105 G13
Susanville U.S.A. 40°25N 120°39W 168 F3
Susch Switz. 46°46N 10°5E 77 J6
Suşehri Turkey 40°10N 38°6E 105 B8
Sušice Czech Rep. 49°17N 13°30E 78 B6
Susleni Moldova 47°25N 28°59E 81 C13
Susner India 23°57N 76°5E 124 H7
Susong China 30°10N 116°5E 117 B11
Susquehanna U.S.A. 41°57N 75°36W 175 E9
Susquehanna →
U.S.A. 39°33N 76°5W 175 G8
Susques Argentina 23°35S 66°25W 190 A2
Sussex Canada 45°45N 65°37W 165 C6
Sussex U.S.A. 41°13N 74°37W 175 E10
Sussex, East □ U.K. 51°0N 0°20E 67 G8
Sussex, West □ U.K. 51°0N 0°30W 67 G7
Sussex Inlet Australia 35°10S 150°36E 153 C9
Sustut → Canada 56°20N 127°30W 162 B3
Susuman Russia 62°47N 148°10E 107 C15
Susunu Indonesia 3°7S 133°39E 119 E8
Susurluk Turkey 39°54N 28°8E 99 B10
Susuz Turkey 40°46N 43°8E 105 B10
Susz Poland 53°44N 19°20E 82 E6
Sutay Uul Asia 46°35N 93°38E 110 B7
Sütçüler Turkey 37°29N 30°57E 104 D4
Şuţeşti Romania 45°13N 27°27E 81 E12
Sutherland Australia 34°2S 151°4E 153 C9
Sutherland S. Africa 32°24S 20°40E 144 D3
Sutherland U.K. 58°12N 4°50W 65 C4
Sutherland U.S.A. 41°10N 101°8W 172 E3
Sutherland Falls N.Z. 44°48S 167°46E 155 E2
Sutherlin U.S.A. 43°23N 123°19W 168 E2
Suthri India 23°3N 68°55E 124 H3
Sutjeska △ Bos.-H. 43°50N 18°32E 80 G3
Sutlej → Pakistan 29°23N 71°3E 124 E4
Sutter U.S.A. 39°10N 121°45W 170 F5
Sutter Buttes U.S.A. 39°12N 121°49W 170 F5
Sutter Creek U.S.A. 38°24N 120°48W 170 G6
Sutton Canada 45°6N 72°37W 175 A12
Sutton N.Z. 45°34S 170°8E 155 F5
Sutton Nebr., U.S.A. 40°36N 97°52W 172 E5
Sutton W. Va., U.S.A. 38°40N 80°43W 173 F13
Sutton → Canada 55°15N 83°45W 164 A3
Sutton Coldfield U.K. 52°35N 1°49W 67 E6
Sutton in Ashfield U.K. 53°8N 1°16W 66 D6
Sutton L. Canada 54°15N 84°42W 164 B3
Suttor → Australia 21°36S 147°2E 150 C4
Suttsu Japan 42°48N 140°14E 112 C10
Sutwik I. U.S.A. 56°34N 157°12W 166 D8
Suva Fiji 18°6S 178°30E 154 a
Suva Gora Macedonia 41°45N 21°3E 96 E5
Suva Planina Serbia 43°10N 22°5E 96 C6
Suva Reka = Therandë
Kosovo 42°21N 20°50E 96 D4
Suvorov Russia 54°7N 36°30E 84 E9
Suvorov Is. = Suwarrow Is.
Cook Is. 13°15S 163°5W 157 J11
Suvorove Ukraine 45°35N 28°59E 81 E13
Suvorovo Bulgaria 43°20N 27°35E 97 C11
Suwałki Poland 54°8N 22°59E 82 D9
Suwannaphum
Thailand 15°33N 103°47E 120 E4
Suwannee U.S.A. 29°20N 83°9W 179 F6
Suwannee → U.S.A. 29°17N 83°10W 179 F6
Suwannee Sd. U.S.A. 29°20N 83°15W 179 F6
Suwanose-Jima Japan 29°38N 129°43E 113 K4
Suwarrow Is. Cook Is. 13°15S 163°5W 157 J11
Suwayqīyah, Hawr as
Iraq 32°40N 46°3E 105 G12
Suweis, Khalîg el Egypt 28°40N 33°0E 137 F8
Suweis, Qanâ es Egypt 31°0N 32°20E 137 E8
Suwon S. Korea 37°17N 127°1E 115 F14
Suzdal Russia 56°29N 40°26E 84 D11
Suzhou Anhui, China 33°41N 116°59E 114 H9
Suzhou Jiangsu, China 31°19N 120°38E 117 B13
Suzu Japan 37°25N 137°17E 113 F8
Suzu-Misaki Japan 37°31N 137°21E 113 F8
Suzuka Japan 34°55N 136°36E 113 G8
Suzun Russia 53°47N 82°18E 109 B10
Suzzara Italy 44°59N 10°45E 92 D7
Svalbard Arctic 78°0N 17°0E 57 B12
Svalbard Radio = Longyearbyen
Svalbard 78°13N 15°40E 54 B8
Svalöv Sweden 55°57N 13°8E 63 J7
Svalyava Ukraine 48°33N 22°59E 80 B7
Svaneke Denmark 55°8N 15°8E 63 J9
Svaneti Georgia 42°50N 42°45E 105 A10
Svängsta Sweden 56°16N 14°47E 63 H8
Svanskog Sweden 59°11N 12°33E 62 E6
Svappavaara Sweden 67°40N 21°3E 60 C19
Svärdsjö Sweden 60°45N 15°54E 62 D9
Svartå Sweden 59°8N 14°32E 62 E8
Svartisen Norway 66°40N 13°59E 60 C15
Svartvik Sweden 62°19N 17°24E 62 B11
Svatove Ukraine 49°22N 38°15E 85 H10
Svatovo = Svatove
Ukraine 49°22N 38°15E 85 H10
Svay Chek Cambodia 13°48N 102°58E 120 F4
Svay Rieng Cambodia 11°9N 105°45E 121 G5
Svealand Sweden 60°20N 15°0E 62 D9
Svedala Sweden 55°30N 13°15E 63 J7
Sveg Sweden 62°2N 14°21E 62 B8
Svendborg Denmark 55°4N 10°35E 63 J4
Svenljunga Sweden 57°29N 13°5E 63 G7
Svenstavik Sweden 62°45N 14°26E 62 B8
Svenstrup Denmark 56°58N 9°50E 63 H3
Svenyhorodka Ukraine 49°4N 30°56E 85 H6
Sverdlovsk Ukraine 48°5N 39°47E 85 H10
Sverdrup Chan.
Canada 79°56N 96°25W 161 B12
Sverdrup Is. Canada 79°0N 97°0W 158 B10
Sverige = Sweden ■
Europe 57°0N 15°0E 61 H16
Sveshtari Bulgaria 43°40N 26°40E 97 C10
Svetac Croatia 43°3N 15°43E 93 E12
Sveti Nikola, Prokhad
Europe 43°27N 22°6E 96 C6
Sveti Nikole Macedonia 41°51N 21°56E 96 E5
Sveti Rok Croatia 44°22N 15°39E 93 D12
Svetlaya Russia 46°33N 138°18E 112 A9
Svetlogorsk = Svyetlahorsk
Belarus 52°38N 29°46E 75 B15
Svetlogorsk Russia 54°56N 20°10E 82 D7
Svetlograd Russia 45°25N 42°58E 87 H6
Svetlovodsk = Svitlovodsk
Ukraine 49°2N 33°13E 85 H7
Svetlyy Kaliningrad, Russia 54°41N 20°8E 82 D7
Svetlyy Orenburg, Russia 50°48N 60°51E 108 B6
Svidník Slovak Rep. 49°20N 21°37E 79 B14
Svilaja Planina Croatia 43°49N 16°31E 93 E13
Svilajnac Serbia 44°15N 21°11E 96 B5
Svilengrad Bulgaria 41°49N 26°12E 97 E10
Svir → Russia 60°30N 32°48E 84 B7
Sviritsa Russia 60°29N 32°51E 84 B7
Svishtov Bulgaria 43°36N 25°23E 97 C9
Svislach Belarus 53°3N 24°2E 83 E11
Svitava → Czech Rep. 49°11N 16°37E 79 B9
Svitavy Czech Rep. 49°47N 16°28E 79 B9
Svitlovodsk Ukraine 49°2N 33°13E 85 H7
Svityaz, Ozero Ukraine 51°30N 23°50E 83 G10
Svizzera = Switzerland ■
Europe 46°30N 8°0E 77 J4
Svobodnyy Russia 51°20N 128°0E 107 D13
Svoge Bulgaria 42°59N 23°23E 96 D7
Svolvær Norway 68°15N 14°34E 60 B16
Svratka → Czech Rep. 49°11N 16°38E 79 B9
Svrljig Serbia 43°25N 22°6E 96 C6
Svyetlahorsk Belarus 52°38N 29°46E 75 B15
Swabian Alps = Schwäbische Alb
Germany 48°20N 9°30E 77 G5
Swaffham U.K. 52°39N 0°42E 67 E8
Swains I. Amer. Samoa 11°11S 171°4W 157 J11
Swainsboro U.S.A. 32°36N 82°20W 178 C7
Swakop → Namibia 22°38S 14°36E 144 B2
Swakopmund Namibia 22°37S 14°30E 144 B1
Swale → U.K. 54°5N 1°20W 66 C6
Swamihalli India 14°52N 76°38E 127 G3
Swan → Australia 32°3S 115°45E 149 F2
Swan → Canada 52°30N 100°45W 163 C8
Swan Hill Australia 35°20S 143°33E 152 C5
Swan Hills Canada 54°43N 115°24W 162 C5
Swan Is. = Santanilla, Is.
Honduras 17°22N 83°57W 182 C3
Swan L. Man., Canada 52°30N 100°40W 163 C8
Swan L. Ont., Canada 54°16N 91°11W 164 B1
Swan Ra. U.S.A. 48°0N 113°45W 168 C7
Swan Reach Australia 34°35S 139°37E 152 C3
Swan River Canada 52°10N 101°16W 163 C8
Swanage U.K. 50°36N 1°58W 67 G6
Swansea N.S.W.,
Australia 33°3S 151°35E 153 B9
Swansea Tas., Australia 42°8S 148°4E 151 G4
Swansea Canada 43°38N 79°28W 174 C5
Swansea U.K. 51°37N 3°57W 67 F4
Swansea U.S.A. 33°44N 81°6W 178 B8
Swansea □ U.K. 51°38N 4°3W 67 F3
Swartberge S. Africa 33°20S 22°0E 144 D3
Swartmodder S. Africa 28°1S 20°32E 144 C3
Swartnossob → Namibia 23°8S 18°42E 144 B2
Swartruggens S. Africa 25°39S 26°42E 144 C4
Swarzędz Poland 52°25N 17°4E 83 F4
Swastika Canada 48°7N 80°6W 164 C3
Swat → Pakistan 34°40N 72°5E 125 B5
Swatow = Shantou
China 23°18N 116°40E 117 F11
Swaziland ■ Africa 26°30S 31°30E 145 C5
Sweden ■ Europe 57°0N 15°0E 61 H16
Swedru Ghana 5°32N 0°41W 139 D4
Sweet Grass U.S.A. 48°59N 111°58W 168 B8
Sweet Home U.S.A. 44°24N 122°44W 168 D2
Sweetwater Nev.,
U.S.A. 38°27N 119°9W 170 G7
Sweetwater Tenn.,
U.S.A. 35°36N 84°28W 177 D12
Sweetwater Tex.,
U.S.A. 32°28N 100°25W 176 E4
Sweetwater →
U.S.A. 42°31N 107°2W 168 E10
Swellendam S. Africa 34°1S 20°26E 144 D3
Swider → Poland 52°6N 21°14E 83 F8
Świdnica Poland 50°50N 16°30E 83 H3
Świdnik Poland 51°13N 22°39E 83 G9
Świdwin Poland 53°47N 15°49E 82 E2
Świebodzice Poland 50°51N 16°20E 83 H3
Świebodzin Poland 52°15N 15°31E 83 F2
Świecie Poland 53°25N 18°30E 82 E5
Świerzawa Poland 51°1N 15°54E 83 G2
Świętokrzyski △ Poland 50°53N 20°59E 83 H7
Świętokrzyskie □
Poland 50°45N 20°45E 83 H7
Świętokrzyskie, Góry
Poland 51°0N 20°30E 83 H7
Swift Current Canada 50°20N 107°45W 163 C7
Swift Current →
Canada 50°38N 107°44W 163 C7
Swifts Creek Australia 37°17S 147°44E 153 D7
Swilly, L. Ireland 55°12N 7°33W 64 A4
Swindon U.K. 51°34N 1°46W 67 F6
Swindon □ U.K. 51°34N 1°46W 67 F6
Swinemünde = Świnoujście
Poland 53°54N 14°16E 82 E1
Swinford Ireland 53°57N 8°58W 64 C3
Świnoujście Poland 53°54N 14°16E 82 E1
Switzerland ■ Europe 46°30N 8°0E 77 J4
Swords Ireland 53°28N 6°13W 64 C5
Swoyerville U.S.A. 41°18N 75°53W 175 E9
Syasstroy Russia 60°9N 32°33E 84 B7
Sychevka Russia 55°59N 34°16E 84 E8
Syców Poland 51°19N 17°40E 83 G4
Syddanmark □ Denmark 55°30N 9°0E 63 J2
Sydenham → Canada 42°33N 82°25W 174 D2
Sydney Australia 33°52S 151°12E 153 B9
Sydney Canada 46°7N 60°7W 165 C7
Sydney L. Canada 50°41N 94°25W 163 C10
Sydney Mines Canada 46°18N 60°15W 165 C7
Sydprøven = Alluitsup Paa
Greenland 60°30N 45°35W 57 E6
Sydra, G. of = Surt, Khalīj
Libya 31°40N 18°30E 135 B9
Syeverodonetsk
Ukraine 48°58N 38°35E 85 H10
Syke Germany 52°55N 8°50E 76 C4
Sykesville U.S.A. 41°3N 78°50W 174 E6
Syktyvkar Russia 61°45N 50°40E 106 C6
Sylacauga U.S.A. 33°10N 86°15W 178 B3
Sylarna Sweden 63°2N 12°13E 60 E15
Sylhet Bangla. 24°54N 91°52E 123 G17
Sylhet □ Bangla. 24°50N 91°50E 123 G17
Sylt Germany 54°54N 8°22E 76 A4
Sylvan Beach U.S.A. 43°12N 75°44W 175 C9
Sylvan Lake Canada 52°20N 114°3W 162 C6
Sylvania Ga., U.S.A. 32°45N 81°38W 178 C8
Sylvania Ohio, U.S.A. 41°43N 83°42W 173 E12
Sylvester U.S.A. 31°32N 83°50W 178 D6
Sym Russia 60°20N 88°18E 106 C9
Synelnykove Ukraine 48°25N 35°30E 85 H8
Synevyr △ Ukraine 48°30N 23°40E 81 B8
Synevyrska Polyana
Ukraine 48°35N 23°41E 81 B8
Synnot Ra. Australia 16°30S 125°20E 148 C4
Synyak Ukraine 48°35N 22°51E 80 B7
Syöte △ Finland 65°44N 27°58E 60 D22
Syowa Antarctica 68°50S 12°0E 55 C5
Syracuse Kans.,
U.S.A. 37°59N 101°45W 172 G3
Syracuse N.Y., U.S.A. 43°3N 76°9W 175 C8
Syracuse Nebr., U.S.A. 40°39N 96°11W 172 E5
Syrdarya → Kazakhstan 46°3N 61°0E 108 C6
Syria ■ Asia 35°0N 38°0E 105 E8
Syrian Desert = Shām, Bādiyat
ash Asia 32°0N 40°0E 128 C3
Syros = Ermoupoli
Greece 37°28N 24°57E 98 D6
Sysslebäck Sweden 60°44N 12°52E 62 D6
Syzran Russia 53°12N 48°30E 86 D9
Szabolcs-Szatmár-Bereg □
Hungary 48°2N 21°45E 80 B6
Szadek Poland 51°41N 18°59E 83 G5
Szamocin Poland 53°2N 17°7E 83 E4
Szamos → Hungary 48°7N 22°20E 80 B7
Szamotuły Poland 52°37N 16°33E 83 F3
Száraz → Hungary 46°10N 21°15E 80 D6
Szarvas Hungary 46°50N 20°38E 80 D5
Százhalombatta
Hungary 47°20N 18°58E 80 C3
Szczawnica Poland 49°26N 20°30E 83 J7
Szczebrzeszyn Poland 50°42N 22°59E 83 H9
Szczecin Poland 53°27N 14°27E 82 E1
Szczecinek Poland 53°43N 16°41E 82 E3
Szczeciński, Zalew = Stettiner Haff
Germany 53°47N 14°15E 76 B10
Szczekociny Poland 50°38N 19°48E 83 H6
Szczucin Poland 50°18N 21°4E 83 H8
Szczuczyn Poland 53°36N 22°19E 82 E9
Szczyrk Poland 49°43N 19°2E 83 J6
Szczytna Poland 50°25N 16°28E 83 H3
Szczytno Poland 53°33N 21°0E 82 E7
Szechuan = Sichuan □
China 30°30N 103°0E 116 B5
Szechuan Basin = Sichuan Pendi
China 31°0N 105°0E 116 B5
Szécsény Hungary 48°7N 19°30E 80 B4
Szeged Hungary 46°16N 20°10E 80 D5
Szeghalom Hungary 47°1N 21°10E 80 C6
Székesfehérvár Hungary 47°15N 18°25E 80 C3
Szekszárd Hungary 46°22N 18°42E 80 D3
Szendrő Hungary 48°24N 20°41E 80 B5
Szentendre Hungary 47°39N 19°4E 80 C4
Szentes Hungary 46°39N 20°21E 80 D5
Szentgotthárd Hungary 46°58N 16°19E 80 D1
Szentlőrinc Hungary 46°3N 18°1E 80 D3
Szerencs Hungary 48°10N 21°12E 80 B6
Szigetszentmiklós
Hungary 47°21N 19°3E 80 C4
Szigetvár Hungary 46°3N 17°46E 80 D2
Szikszó Hungary 48°12N 20°56E 80 B5
Szklarska Poreba Poland 50°50N 15°33E 83 H2
Szkwa → Poland 53°11N 21°43E 83 E8
Szlichtyngowa Poland 51°42N 16°15E 83 G3
Szob Hungary 47°48N 18°53E 80 C3
Szolnok Hungary 47°10N 20°15E 80 C5
Szombathely Hungary 47°14N 16°38E 80 C1
Szprotawa Poland 51°33N 15°35E 83 G2
Sztum Poland 53°55N 19°1E 82 E6
Sztutowo Poland 54°20N 19°15E 82 D6
Szubin Poland 53°1N 17°45E 83 E4
Szydłowiec Poland 51°15N 20°51E 83 G7
Szypliszki Poland 54°17N 23°2E 82 D10

T

Ta Khli Thailand 15°15N 100°21E 120 E3
Ta Lai Vietnam 11°24N 107°23E 121 G6
Ta Phraya △ Thailand 14°11N 102°49E 120 E4
Taal Volcano Phil. 14°7N 120°59E 119 B6
Taamisaari = Raasepori
Finland 60°0N 23°26E 84 B2
Tab Hungary 46°44N 18°2E 80 D3
Tabacal Argentina 23°15S 64°15W 190 A3
Tabaco Phil. 13°22N 123°44E 119 B6
Tabagné Ivory C. 7°59N 3°4W 138 D4
Ţābah Si. Arabia 26°55N 42°38E 128 E4
Tabalos Peru 6°26S 76°37W 188 B2
Tabanan Indonesia 8°32S 115°8E 119 K18
Tabankort Niger 17°44N 0°20E 139 B5
Tabarka Tunisia 36°56N 8°46E 136 A5
Ţabas Khorāsān, Iran 32°48N 60°12E 129 C9
Ţabas Yazd, Iran 33°35N 56°55E 129 C8
Tabasará, Serranía de
Panama 8°35N 81°40W 182 E3
Tabasco □ Mexico 18°0N 92°40W 181 D6
Tabāsīn Iran 31°12N 57°54E 129 D8
Tabatinga Brazil 4°16S 69°56W 188 A4
Tabatinga, Serra da
Brazil 10°30S 44°0W 189 C2
Tabelbala Algeria 29°24N 3°15W 136 C3
Tabelbala, Kahal de
Algeria 28°47N 2°0W 136 C3
Tabelembila Algeria 24°43N 4°16E 136 D4
Taber Canada 49°47N 112°8W 162 D6
Taberg Sweden 57°40N 14°5E 63 G8
Tabira Brazil 7°35S 37°33W 189 B3
Tabla Niger 13°46N 3°1E 139 C5
Tablas de Daimiel △ Spain 39°9N 3°40W 89 F7
Tablas I. Phil. 12°25N 122°2E 119 B6
Table, Pte. de la Réunion 21°14S 55°48E 141 c
Table B. Canada 53°40N 56°25W 165 B8
Table B. S. Africa 33°35S 18°25E 144 D2
Table C. N.Z. 39°6S 178°0E 154 F7
Table I. Burma 14°12N 93°22E 127 G11
Table Mountain △
S. Africa 33°58S 18°28E 144 D2
Table Mt. S. Africa 33°58S 18°26E 144 D2
Table Rock L. U.S.A. 36°36N 93°19W 172 G7
Tabletop, Mt. Australia 23°24S 147°11E 150 C4
Tábor Czech Rep. 49°25N 14°39E 78 B7
Tabora Tanzania 5°2S 32°50E 142 D3
Tabora □ Tanzania 5°0S 33°0E 142 D3
Tabou Ivory C. 4°30N 7°20W 138 E3
Tabrīz Iran 38°7N 46°20E 105 C12
Tabuaeran Kiribati 3°51N 159°22W 157 G12
Tabuenca Spain 41°42N 1°33W 90 D3
Tabūk Si. Arabia 28°23N 36°36E 128 D3
Tabūk □ Si. Arabia 27°40N 36°50E 128 E3
Taburno-Camposauro ⌂
Italy 41°8N 14°37E 95 A7
Täby Sweden 59°26N 18°2E 62 E12
Tacámbaro de Codallos
Mexico 19°14N 101°28W 180 D4
Tacheng China 46°40N 82°58E 109 C10
Tach'i Taiwan 24°53N 121°17E 117 E13
Tachia Taiwan 24°25N 120°28E 117 E13
Tachilek Burma 20°26N 99°52E 120 B2
Tach'ing Shan = Daqing Shan
China 40°40N 111°0E 114 D6
Tachov Czech Rep. 49°47N 12°39E 78 B5
Tácina → Italy 38°57N 16°55E 95 D9
Tacloban Phil. 11°15N 124°58E 119 B6
Tacna Peru 18°0S 70°20W 188 D3
Tacna □ Peru 17°40S 70°20W 188 D3
Tacoma U.S.A. 47°14N 122°26W 170 C4
Tacuarembó Uruguay 31°45S 56°0W 191 C4
Tademaït, Plateau du
Algeria 28°30N 2°30E 136 C4
Tādepallegudem India 16°50N 81°30E 126 F5
Tadio, L. Ivory C. 5°10N 5°15W 138 D3
Tadjerdjeri, O. → Algeria 26°0N 8°0E 136 C5
Tadjerouna Algeria 33°31N 2°3E 136 B4
Tadjmout Laghouat,
Algeria 33°52N 2°30E 136 B4
Tadjmout Saoura, Algeria 25°37N 3°48E 136 C4
Tadjoura Djibouti 11°50N 42°55E 131 E3
Tadla-Azilal □ Morocco 32°0N 6°30W 136 B2
Tadmor N.Z. 41°27S 172°45E 155 B7
Tadoba △ India 20°30N 78°20E 126 D4
Tadoule L. Canada 58°36N 98°20W 163 B9
Tadoussac Canada 48°11N 69°42W 165 C6
Tadpatri India 14°55N 78°1E 127 G4
Tadrés ⌂ Niger 16°0N 7°10E 139 B6
Tadzhikistan = Tajikistan ■
Asia 38°30N 70°0E 109 E8
Taegu = Daegu
S. Korea 35°50N 128°37E 115 G15
Taegwan N. Korea 40°13N 125°12E 115 D13
Taejŏn = Daejeon
S. Korea 36°20N 127°28E 115 F14
Taen, Ko Thailand 9°22N 99°57E 121 b
Tafalla Spain 42°30N 1°41W 90 C3
Tafelbaai = Table B.
S. Africa 33°35S 18°25E 144 D2
Tafelney, C. Morocco 31°3N 9°51W 136 B2
Tafermaar Indonesia 6°47S 134°10E 119 F8
Taffermit Morocco 29°37N 9°15W 136 C2
Tafi Viejo Argentina 26°43S 65°17W 190 B2
Tafihān Iran 29°25N 52°39E 129 D7
Tafilalet Morocco 31°20N 4°45W 136 B3
Tafiré Ivory C. 9°4N 5°4W 138 D3
Tafo Ghana 6°15N 0°20W 139 D4
Tafraoute Morocco 29°50N 8°58W 136 C2
Tafresh Iran 34°45N 49°57E 129 C6
Taft Iran 31°45N 54°14E 129 D7
Taft Phil. 11°57N 125°30E 119 B7
Taft U.S.A. 35°8N 119°28W 171 K7
Taftan Pakistan 29°0N 61°30E 122 E2
Taftān, Kūh-e Iran 28°40N 61°0E 129 D9
Tafwap India 7°23N 93°43E 127 L11
Taga Dzong Bhutan 27°5N 89°55E 123 F16
Taganay △ Russia 55°15N 59°48E 108 B5
Taganrog Russia 47°12N 38°50E 85 J10
Taganrogskiy Zaliv
Russia 47°0N 38°30E 85 J10
Tagânt □ Mauritania 19°0N 10°0W 138 B3
Tagbilaran Phil. 9°39N 123°51E 119 C6
Tággia Italy 43°52N 7°51E 92 E4
Taghit Algeria 30°58N 2°0W 136 B3
Tagish Canada 60°19N 134°16W 162 A2
Tagish L. Canada 60°10N 134°20W 162 A2
Tagliacozzo Italy 42°4N 13°15E 93 F10
Tagliamento → Italy 45°38N 13°6E 93 C10
Táglio di Po Italy 45°0N 12°12E 93 D9
Tagomago Spain 39°2N 1°39E 100 B8
Tagourăret Mauritania 17°45N 7°45W 138 B3
Taguatinga Distrito Federal,
Brazil 15°51S 48°4W 189 D1
Taguatinga Tocantins,
Brazil 12°27S 46°22W 189 C1
Tagum Phil. 7°33N 125°53E 119 C7
Tagus = Tejo → Europe 38°40N 9°24W 89 F2
Tahakopa N.Z. 46°30S 169°23E 155 G4
Tahala Morocco 34°0N 4°28W 136 B3
Tahan, Gunung
Malaysia 4°34N 102°17E 121 K4
Tahat Algeria 23°18N 5°33E 136 D5
Tāherī Iran 27°43N 52°20E 129 E7
Tahifet Algeria 22°58N 6°0E 136 D5
Tahiti French Polynesia 17°37S 149°27W 155 b
Tahiti, I. Tahiti 17°37S 149°27W 155 b
Tahlequah U.S.A. 35°55N 94°58W 176 D7
Tahoe, L. U.S.A. 39°6N 120°2W 170 G6
Tahoe City U.S.A. 39°10N 120°9W 170 F6
Tahoka U.S.A. 33°10N 101°48W 176 E4
Taholah U.S.A. 47°21N 124°17W 170 C2
Tahora N.Z. 39°2S 174°49E 154 F3
Tahoua Niger 14°57N 5°16E 139 C6
Tahrūd Iran 29°26N 57°49E 129 D8
Tahsis Canada 49°55N 126°40W 162 D3
Tahta Egypt 26°44N 31°32E 137 B3
Tahtaköprü Turkey 39°57N 29°39E 97 G13
Tahtalı Dağları Turkey 38°20N 36°0E 104 C7
Tahuamanú → Bolivia 11°6S 67°36W 188 C4
Tahulandang Indonesia 2°27N 125°23E 119 D7
Tahuna Indonesia 3°38N 125°30E 119 D7
Taï Ivory C. 5°55N 7°30W 138 D3
Taï △ Ivory C. 5°25N 7°5W 138 D3
Tai Hu China 31°5N 120°10E 117 B13
Tai Mo Shan China 22°25N 114°7E 111 a
Tai O China 22°15N 113°52E 111 a
Tai Pang Wan China 22°33N 114°24E 111 a
Tai Po China 22°27N 114°10E 111 a
Tai Rom Yen △ Thailand 8°45N 99°30E 121 H2
Tai Yue Shan = Lantau I.
China 22°15N 113°56E 111 a
Tai'an China 36°12N 117°8E 115 F9
Taiarapu, Presqu'île de
Tahiti 17°47S 149°14W 155 b
Taibai Shan China 33°57N 107°45E 114 H4
Taibei = T'aipei
Taiwan 25°4N 121°29E 117 E13
Taibique Canary Is. 27°42N 17°58W 100 G2
Taibus Qi China 41°54N 115°22E 114 D8
Taicang China 31°30N 121°5E 117 B13
T'aichung Taiwan 24°9N 120°37E 117 E13
Taieri → N.Z. 46°3S 170°12E 155 G5
Taigu China 37°28N 112°30E 114 F7
Taihang Shan China 36°0N 113°30E 114 G7
Taihape N.Z. 39°41S 175°48E 154 F4
Taihe Anhui, China 33°20N 115°42E 114 H8
Taihe Jiangxi, China 26°47N 114°52E 117 D10
Taihu China 30°22N 116°20E 117 B11
Taijiang China 26°39N 108°21E 116 D7
Taikang China 34°5N 114°50E 114 G8
Tailem Bend Australia 35°12S 139°29E 152 C3
Taillfingen Germany 48°15N 9°1E 77 G5
T'ailuko Taiwan 24°9N 121°37E 117 E13
Taimyr Peninsula = Taymyr,
Poluostrov Russia 75°0N 100°0E 107 B11
Tain U.K. 57°49N 4°4W 65 D4
T'ainan Taiwan 23°0N 120°10E 117 F13
Taining China 26°54N 117°9E 117 D11
Taiobeiras Brazil 15°49S 42°14W 189 D2
Taipa China 22°10N 113°35E 111 a
T'aipei Taiwan 25°4N 121°29E 117 E13
Taiping China 30°15N 118°6E 117 B12
Taiping Malaysia 4°51N 100°44E 121 K3
Taiping Dao = Itu Aba I.
S. China Sea 10°23N 114°21E 118 B4
Taipingchuan China 44°23N 123°11E 115 B12
Taipingzhen China 33°35N 111°42E 114 H6
Taipu Brazil 5°37S 35°36W 189 B3
Tairua N.Z. 37°0S 175°51E 154 D4
Taishan Guangdong,
China 22°14N 112°41E 117 F9
Taishan Shandong,
China 36°25N 117°20E 115 F9
Taishun China 27°30N 119°42E 117 D12
Taita Hills Kenya 3°25S 38°15E 142 C4
Taitao, C. Chile 45°53S 75°5W 192 C1
Taitao, Pen. de Chile 46°30S 75°0W 192 C2
T'aitung Taiwan 22°43N 121°4E 117 F13
Taivalkoski Finland 65°33N 28°12E 60 D23
Taiwan ■ Asia 23°30N 121°0E 117 F13
Taiwan Strait Asia 24°40N 120°0E 117 E12

276 Taixing INDEX TO WORLD MAP

Taixing China 32°11N 120°0E 117 A13
Taiyiba Israel 32°36N 35°27E 130 C4
Taiyuan China 37°52N 112°33E 114 F7
Taizhong = T'aichung Taiwan 24°9N 120°37E 117 E13
Taizhou Jiangsu, China 32°28N 119°55E 117 A12
Taizhou Zhejiang, China 28°40N 121°24E 117 C13
Taizhou Liedao China 28°30N 121°55E 117 C13
Ta'izz Yemen 13°35N 44°2E 131 E3
Taj Mahal India 27°10N 78°2E 124 F8
Tājābād Iran 30°2N 54°24E 129 D7
Tajikistan ■ Asia 38°30N 70°0E 109 E8
Tajima = Minamiaizu Japan 37°12N 139°46E 113 F9
Tajo = Tejo → Europe 38°40N 9°24W 89 F2
Tajrīsh Iran 35°48N 51°25E 129 C6
Tak Thailand 16°52N 99°8E 120 D2
Takāb Iran 36°24N 47°7E 105 D12
Takachiho Japan 32°42N 131°18E 113 H5
Takachu Botswana 22°37S 21°58E 144 B3
Takada Japan 37°7N 138°15E 113 F9
Takahagi Japan 36°43N 140°45E 113 F10
Takaka N.Z. 40°51S 172°50E 155 A7
Takamaka Seychelles 4°50S 55°30E 141 b
Takamatsu Japan 34°20N 134°5E 113 G7
Takaoka Japan 36°47N 137°0E 113 F8
Takapau N.Z. 40°2S 176°21E 154 G5
Takapuna N.Z. 36°47S 174°47E 154 C3
Takasaki Japan 36°20N 139°0E 113 F9
Takatsuki Japan 34°51N 135°37E 113 G7
Takaungu Kenya 3°38S 39°52E 142 C4
Takayama Japan 36°18N 137°11E 113 F8
Take-Shima Japan 30°49N 130°26E 113 J5
Takefu = Echizen Japan 35°50N 136°10E 113 G8
Takengon Indonesia 4°45N 96°50E 118 D1
Takeo Cambodia 10°59N 104°47E 121 G5
Takeo Japan 33°12N 130°1E 113 H5
Tåkern Sweden 58°22N 14°45E 63 F8
Takeshima = Liancourt Rocks Asia 37°15N 131°52E 113 F5
Tākestān Iran 36°0N 49°40E 129 C6
Taketa Japan 32°58N 131°24E 113 H5
Takh India 33°6N 77°32E 125 C7
Takhār □ Afghan. 36°40N 70°0E 109 E7
Takhiatash Uzbekistan 42°20N 59°33E 108 D5
Takhmau Cambodia 11°29N 104°57E 121 G5
Takht-e Soleyman Iran 36°36N 47°14E 105 D12
Takht-Sulaiman Pakistan 31°40N 69°58E 124 D3
Takiéta Niger 13°41N 8°32E 139 C6
Takikawa Japan 43°33N 141°54E 112 C10
Takla L. Canada 55°15N 125°45W 162 B3
Takla Landing Canada 55°30N 125°50W 162 B3
Taklamakan China 38°0N 83°0E 109 E10
Taklamakan Shamo = Taklamakan China 38°0N 83°0E 109 E10
Taksimo Russia 56°20N 114°52E 107 D12
Taku → Canada 58°30N 133°50W 162 B2
Takua Thung Thailand 8°24N 98°27E 121 a
Takum Nigeria 7°18N 9°36E 139 D6
Tal Halāl Iran 28°54N 55°1E 129 D7
Tala Uruguay 34°21S 55°46W 191 C4
Talachyn Belarus 54°25N 29°42E 84 E5
Talagang Pakistan 32°55N 72°25E 124 C5
Talagante Chile 33°40S 70°50W 190 C1
Talahouhait Algeria 24°52N 1°5E 136 D4
Talaimannar Sri Lanka 9°6N 79°43E 127 K4
Talaïnt Morocco 29°41N 9°40W 136 C2
Talak Niger 18°0N 5°0E 139 B6
Talamanca, Cordillera de Cent. Amer. 9°20N 83°20W 182 E3
Talampaya △ Argentina 29°43S 67°42W 190 B2
Talant France 47°19N 4°58E 71 E11
Talara Peru 4°38S 81°18W 188 A1
Talas Kyrgyzstan 42°30N 72°13E 109 D8
Talas Turkey 38°41N 35°33E 104 C6
Talas □ Kyrgyzstan 42°20N 72°0E 109 D8
Talas → Kazakhstan 44°0N 70°20E 109 D8
Talas Ala Too Kyrgyzstan 42°15N 72°0E 109 D8
Talasskiy Alatau = Talas Ala Too Kyrgyzstan 42°15N 72°0E 109 D8
Talâta Egypt 30°36N 32°20E 130 E1
Talata Mafara Nigeria 12°38N 6°4E 139 C6
Talaud, Kepulauan Indonesia 4°30N 126°50E 119 D7
Talaud Is. = Talaud, Kepulauan Indonesia 4°30N 126°50E 119 D7
Talavera de la Reina Spain 39°55N 4°46W 88 F6
Talavera la Real Spain 38°53N 6°46W 89 G4
Talayan Phil. 6°52N 124°24E 119 C6
Talayuela Spain 39°59N 5°36W 88 F5
Talbandh India 22°3N 86°20E 125 H12
Talbert, Sillon de France 48°53N 3°5W 70 D3
Talbot Australia 37°10S 143°44E 152 D5
Talbot, C. Australia 13°48S 126°43E 148 B4
Talbotton U.S.A. 32°41N 84°32W 178 C5
Talbragar → Australia 32°12S 148°37E 153 B8
Talca Chile 35°28S 71°40W 190 D1
Talcahuano Chile 36°40S 73°10W 190 D1
Talcher India 21°0N 85°18E 126 D7
Talcho Niger 14°44N 3°28E 139 C5
Taldy Kurgan = Taldyqorghan Kazakhstan 45°10N 78°45E 109 C9
Taldyqorghan Kazakhstan 45°10N 78°45E 109 C9
Tālesh Iran 37°58N 48°58E 105 D13
Tālesh, Kūhhā-ye Iran 37°42N 48°55E 105 D13
Talgar = Talghar Kazakhstan 43°19N 77°15E 109 D9
Talghar Kazakhstan 43°19N 77°15E 109 D9
Talguharai Sudan 18°19N 35°56E 137 D4
Talguppa India 14°13N 74°56E 127 G2
Tali Post South Sudan 5°55N 30°44E 135 G12
Taliabu Indonesia 1°50S 125°0E 119 E6
Talibon Phil. 10°9N 124°20E 119 B6
Talihina U.S.A. 34°45N 95°3W 176 D7
Talikota India 16°29N 76°17E 127 F3
Talipparamba India 12°3N 75°21E 127 H2
Taliwang Indonesia 8°50S 116°55E 118 F5
Talkha Egypt 31°3N 31°22E 137 E7
Talkot Nepal 29°37N 81°19E 125 E9
Tall 'Afar Iraq 36°22N 42°27E 105 D10
Tall Kalakh Syria 34°41N 36°15E 130 A5
Tall Kayf Iraq 36°29N 43°7E 105 D10
Talla Egypt 28°5N 30°43E 137 F7
Talladega U.S.A. 33°26N 86°6W 178 B3
Tallaganda △ Australia 35°29S 149°37E 153 C8
Tallahassee U.S.A. 30°27N 84°17W 178 E5
Tallangatta Australia 36°15S 147°19E 153 D7
Tallapoosa U.S.A. 33°45N 85°17W 178 B4
Tallapoosa → U.S.A. 32°30N 86°16W 178 C3
Tallard France 44°28N 6°3E 73 D10
Tallarook Australia 37°5S 145°6E 153 D6
Tallassee U.S.A. 32°32N 85°54W 178 C4
Tällberg Sweden 60°51N 15°2E 62 D9
Tallering Pk. Australia 28°6S 115°37E 149 E2
Talli Pakistan 29°32N 68°8E 124 E3
Tallinn Estonia 59°22N 24°48E 84 C3
Tallmadge U.S.A. 41°6N 81°27W 174 E3
Tallulah U.S.A. 32°25N 91°11W 176 E9
Tălmaciu Romania 45°38N 24°19E 81 E9
Talmest Morocco 31°48N 9°21W 136 B2
Talmont-St-Hilaire France 46°27N 1°37W 72 B2
Talnakh Russia 69°29N 88°22E 107 C9
Talne Ukraine 48°50N 30°44E 85 H6
Talnoye = Talne Ukraine 48°50N 30°44E 85 H6
Taloda India 21°34N 74°11E 126 D2
Tāloqān Afghan. 36°44N 69°33E 109 E7
Talovaya Russia 51°6N 40°45E 86 E5
Taloyoak Canada 69°32N 93°32W 160 D13
Talpa de Allende Mexico 20°23N 104°51W 180 C4
Talparo Trin. & Tob. 10°30N 61°17W 187 K15
Talquin, L. U.S.A. 30°23N 84°39W 178 E5
Talsi Latvia 57°10N 22°30E 82 A9
Talsi □ Latvia 57°20N 22°40E 82 A9
Talsinnt Morocco 32°33N 3°27W 136 B3
Taltal Chile 25°23S 70°33W 190 B1
Taltson → Canada 61°24N 112°46W 162 A6
Talwood Australia 28°29S 149°29E 151 D4
Talyawalka Cr. → Australia 32°28S 142°22E 152 B5
Tam Dao △ Vietnam 21°45N 105°45E 120 B5
Tam Ky Vietnam 15°34N 108°29E 120 E7
Tam Quan Vietnam 14°35N 109°3E 120 E7
Tama U.S.A. 41°58N 92°35W 172 E7
Tama Abu, Banjaran Malaysia 3°50N 115°5E 118 D5
Tamale Ghana 9°22N 0°50W 139 D4
Taman Russia 45°14N 36°41E 85 K9
Taman Negara △ Malaysia 4°38N 102°26E 121 K4
Tamanar Morocco 31°1N 9°46W 136 B2
Tamani Mali 13°20N 6°50W 138 C3
Tamano Japan 34°29N 133°59E 113 G6
Tamanrasset Algeria 22°50N 5°30E 136 D5
Tamanrasset □ Algeria 23°45N 4°40E 136 D4
Tamaqua U.S.A. 40°48N 75°58W 175 F9
Tamar → U.K. 50°27N 4°15W 67 G3
Tamarac U.S.A. 26°12N 80°15W 179 J9
Tamarin Mauritius 20°19S 57°20E 141 d
Tamarinda Spain 39°55N 3°49E 100 B10
Tamarite de Litera Spain 41°52N 0°25E 90 D5
Tamashima Japan 34°32N 133°40E 113 G6
Tamási Hungary 46°40N 18°18E 80 D3
Tamaské Niger 14°49N 5°43E 139 C6
Tamatave = Toamasina Madag. 18°10S 49°25E 141 H9
Tamaulipas □ Mexico 24°0N 98°45W 181 C5
Tamaulipas, Sierra de Mexico 23°30N 98°20W 181 C5
Tamazula Mexico 24°57N 106°57W 180 C3
Tamazunchale Mexico 21°16N 98°47W 181 C5
Tamba-Dabatou Guinea 11°50N 10°40W 138 C2
Tambach Kenya 0°36N 35°31E 142 B4
Tambacounda Senegal 13°45N 13°40W 138 C2
Tambacounda □ Senegal 14°0N 13°0W 138 C2
Tambaram India 12°55N 80°7E 127 H5
Tambelan, Kepulauan Indonesia 1°0N 107°30E 118 D3
Tambellup Australia 34°4S 117°37E 149 F2
Tambo Australia 24°54S 146°14E 150 C4
Tambo Peru 12°57S 74°1W 188 C3
Tambo → Peru 10°42S 73°47W 188 C3
Tambo de Mora Peru 13°30S 76°8W 188 C2
Tambobamba Peru 13°54S 72°8W 188 C3
Tambopata → Peru 13°21S 69°36W 188 C4
Tambora Indonesia 8°12S 118°5E 118 F5
Tamboritha, Mt. Australia 37°31S 146°40E 153 D7
Tamboura C.A.R. 5°10N 25°12E 142 A2
Tambov Russia 52°45N 41°28E 86 D5
Tambov □ Russia 52°50N 41°20E 86 D5
Tambre → Spain 42°49N 8°53W 88 C2
Tambuku Indonesia 7°8S 113°40E 119 G15
Tâmchekket Mauritania 17°25N 10°40W 138 B2
Tâmega → Portugal 41°5N 8°21W 88 D2
Tamegroute Morocco 30°15N 5°39W 136 B2
Tamelelt Morocco 31°50N 7°32W 136 B2
Tamenglong India 25°0N 93°35E 123 G18
Tamerza Tunisia 34°23N 7°58E 136 B5
Tamgué, Massif du Guinea 12°0N 12°18W 138 C2
Tamiahua, L. de Mexico 21°35N 97°35W 181 C5
Tamiami Canal U.S.A. 25°50N 81°0W 179 K8
Tamil Nadu □ India 11°0N 77°0E 127 J3
Tamis → Serbia 44°51N 20°39E 80 F5
Tamiya Egypt 29°29N 30°58E 137 F7
Tamlelt, Plaine de Morocco 32°30N 2°20W 136 B3
Tamluk India 22°18N 87°58E 125 H12
Tammerfors = Tampere Finland 61°30N 23°50E 84 B2
Tämnaren Sweden 60°10N 17°25E 62 D11
Tampa U.S.A. 27°56N 82°27W 179 H7
Tampa, Tanjung Indonesia 8°55S 116°12E 119 K19
Tampa B. U.S.A. 27°50N 82°30W 179 H7
Tampa Int. ✈ (TPA) U.S.A. 27°59N 82°32W 179 H7
Tampere Finland 61°30N 23°50E 84 B2
Tampico Mexico 22°13N 97°51W 181 C5
Tampin Malaysia 2°28N 102°13E 121 L4
Tampoi Malaysia 1°30N 103°39E 121 d
Tamri Morocco 30°49N 9°50W 136 B2
Tamsagbulag Mongolia 47°14N 117°21E 111 B12
Tamsweg Austria 47°7N 13°49E 78 D6
Tamu Burma 24°13N 94°12E 123 G19
Tamuja → Spain 39°38N 6°29W 89 F4
Tamworth Australia 31°7S 150°58E 153 A9
Tamworth Canada 44°29N 77°0W 174 B8
Tamworth U.K. 52°39N 1°41W 67 E6
Tan An Vietnam 10°32N 106°25E 121 G6
Tan Chau Vietnam 10°48N 105°12E 121 G5
Tan Hiep Vietnam 10°27N 106°21E 121 G6
Tan Iddah Algeria 26°33N 9°42E 136 C5
Tan-Tan Morocco 28°29N 11°1W 134 C3
Tan Yen Vietnam 22°4N 105°3E 120 A5
Tana → Kenya 2°32S 40°31E 142 C5
Tana → Norway 70°30N 28°14E 60 A23
Tana, L. Ethiopia 13°5N 37°30E 131 E2
Tana River Primate ⌓ Kenya 1°55S 40°7E 142 C5
Tanabe Japan 33°44N 135°22E 113 H7
Tanafjorden Norway 70°45N 28°25E 60 A23
Tanaga I. U.S.A. 51°48N 177°53W 166 E4
Tanah Merah Malaysia 5°48N 102°9E 121 K4
Tanahbala Indonesia 0°30S 98°30E 118 E1
Tanahgrogot Indonesia 1°55S 116°15E 118 E5
Tanahjampea Indonesia 7°10S 120°35E 119 F6
Tanahmasa Indonesia 0°12S 98°39E 118 E1
Tanahmerah Indonesia 6°5S 140°16E 119 F10
Tanakpur India 29°5N 80°7E 125 E9
Tanamalwila Sri Lanka 6°26N 81°8E 127 L5
Tanami Desert Australia 18°50S 132°0E 148 C5
Tanana U.S.A. 65°10N 152°4W 166 B9
Tanana → U.S.A. 65°10N 151°58W 160 D1
Tananarive = Antananarivo Madag. 18°55S 47°31E 141 H9
Tanannt Morocco 31°54N 6°56W 136 B2
Tánaro → Italy 44°55N 8°40E 92 D5
Tancheng China 34°25N 118°20E 115 G10
Tanch'ŏn N. Korea 40°27N 128°54E 115 D15
Tanda Ut. P., India 26°33N 82°35E 125 F10
Tanda Ut. P., India 28°57N 78°56E 125 E8
Tanda Ivory C. 7°48N 3°10W 138 D4
Tandag Phil. 9°4N 126°9E 119 C7
Tandaia Tanzania 9°25S 34°15E 143 D3
Tăndărei Romania 44°39N 27°40E 81 F12
Tandaué Angola 16°58S 18°5E 144 A2
Tandil Argentina 37°15S 59°6W 190 D4
Tandil, Sa. del Argentina 37°30S 59°0W 190 D4
Tandlianwala Pakistan 31°3N 73°9E 124 D5
Tando Adam Pakistan 25°45N 68°40E 124 G3
Tando Allahyar Pakistan 25°28N 68°43E 124 G3
Tando Bago Pakistan 24°47N 68°58E 124 G3
Tando Mohommed Khan Pakistan 25°8N 68°32E 124 G3
Tandou L. Australia 32°40S 142°5E 152 B5
Tandoureh △ Iran 37°50N 59°0E 129 B8
Tandragee U.K. 54°21N 6°24W 64 B5
Tandsjöborg Sweden 61°42N 14°43E 62 C8
Tandula → India 21°6N 81°14E 126 D5
Tandula Tank India 20°40N 81°12E 126 D5
Tandur Andhra Pradesh, India 19°11N 79°30E 126 E4
Tandur Andhra Pradesh, India 17°14N 77°35E 126 F3
Tane-ga-Shima Japan 30°30N 131°0E 113 J5
Taneatua N.Z. 38°4S 177°1E 154 E6
Tanen Tong Dan = Dawna Ra. Burma 16°30N 98°30E 120 D2
Tanew → Poland 50°29N 22°16E 83 H9
Tanezrouft Algeria 23°9N 0°11E 134 D6
Tang, Koh Cambodia 10°16N 103°7E 121 G4
Tang, Ra's-e Iran 25°21N 59°52E 129 E8
Tang Krasang Cambodia 12°34N 105°3E 120 F5
Tanga Tanzania 5°5S 39°2E 142 D4
Tanga □ Tanzania 5°20S 38°0E 142 D4
Tangalla Sri Lanka 6°1N 80°48E 127 L5
Tanganyika, L. Africa 6°40S 30°0E 142 D3
Tangasseri India 8°53N 76°35E 127 K3
Tangaza Nigeria 13°19N 4°55E 139 C5
Tanger Morocco 35°50N 5°49W 136 A2
Tanger-Med Morocco 35°53N 5°30W 89 K5
Tanger-Tétouan □ Morocco 35°50N 5°50W 136 A2
Tangerang Indonesia 6°11S 106°37E 119 G12
Tangerhütte Germany 52°26N 11°48E 76 C7
Tangermünde Germany 52°33N 11°58E 76 C7
Tanggu China 39°2N 117°40E 115 E9
Tanggula Shan China 32°40N 92°10E 110 E7
Tanggula Shankou China 32°42N 92°27E 110 E7
Tanghe China 32°47N 112°50E 117 A9
Tanghla Range = Tanggula Shan China 32°40N 92°10E 110 E7
Tangi India 19°56N 85°24E 126 E7
Tangier = Tanger Morocco 35°50N 5°49W 136 A2
Tangjia China 22°22N 113°35E 111 a
Tangjia Wan China 22°21N 113°36E 111 a
Tangorin Australia 21°47S 144°12E 150 C3
Tangra Yumco China 31°0N 86°38E 110 E6
Tangshan China 39°38N 118°10E 115 E10
Tangtou China 35°28N 118°30E 115 G10
Tanguen-Dassouri Burkina Faso 12°16N 1°42W 139 C4
Tanguiéta Benin 10°35N 1°21E 139 C5
Tangxi China 29°3N 119°25E 117 C12
Tangyan He → China 28°54N 108°19E 116 C7
Tangyin China 35°54N 114°21E 114 G8
Taniantaweng Shan China 31°20N 98°0E 116 B2
Tanimbar, Kepulauan Indonesia 7°30S 131°30E 119 F8
Tanimbar Is. = Tanimbar, Kepulauan Indonesia 7°30S 131°30E 119 F8
Tanintharyi = Tenasserim Burma 12°6N 99°3E 121 F2
Tanjay Phil. 9°30N 123°5E 119 C6
Tanjong Pelepas Malaysia 1°21N 103°33E 121 d
Tanjore = Thanjavur India 10°48N 79°12E 127 J4
Tanjung Kalimantan Selatan, Indonesia 2°10S 115°25E 118 E5
Tanjung Nusa Tenggara Barat, Indonesia 8°21S 116°9E 119 J19
Tanjung Malim Malaysia 3°42N 101°31E 121 L3
Tanjung Tokong Malaysia 5°28N 100°18E 121 c
Tanjungbalai Indonesia 2°55N 99°44E 118 D1
Tanjungbatu Indonesia 2°23N 118°3E 118 D5
Tanjungkarang Telukbetung = Bandar Lampung Indonesia 5°20S 105°10E 118 F3
Tanjungpandan Indonesia 2°43S 107°38E 118 E3
Tanjungpinang Indonesia 1°5N 104°30E 118 D2
Tanjungredeb Indonesia 2°9N 117°29E 118 D5
Tanjungselor Indonesia 2°55N 117°25E 118 D5
Tank Pakistan 32°14N 70°25E 124 C4
Tankhala India 21°58N 73°47E 124 J5
Tankwa-Karoo △ S. Africa 32°14S 19°50E 144 D2
Tännäs Sweden 62°26N 12°42E 62 B6
Tannersville U.S.A. 41°3N 75°18W 175 E9
Tannis Bugt Denmark 57°40N 10°15E 63 G4
Tannu Ola Asia 51°0N 94°0E 109 B12
Tannum Sands Australia 23°57S 151°22E 150 C5
Tano → Ghana 5°7N 2°56W 138 D4
Tanombella Algeria 25°30N 5°49E 136 C5
Tanout Niger 14°50N 8°55E 139 C6
Tanquinho Brazil 11°58S 39°6W 189 C3
Tanshui Taiwan 25°10N 121°28E 117 E13
Tansilla Burkina Faso 12°25N 4°23W 138 C4
Tansing Nepal 27°52N 83°33E 125 F10
Tanta Egypt 30°45N 30°57E 137 E7
Tantoyuca Mexico 21°21N 98°14W 181 C5
Tantung = Dandong China 40°10N 124°20E 115 D13
Tanuku India 16°45N 81°44E 126 F5
Tanumshede Sweden 58°42N 11°20E 63 F5
Tanunda Australia 34°30S 139°0E 152 C3
Tanur India 11°1N 75°52E 127 J2
Tanus France 44°8N 2°19E 72 D6
Tanzania ■ Africa 6°0S 34°0E 142 D3
Tanzhou China 22°16N 113°28E 111 a
Tanzilla → Canada 58°8N 130°43W 162 B2
Tao, Ko Thailand 10°5N 99°52E 121 G2
Tao'an = Taonan China 45°22N 122°40E 115 B12
Tao'er He → China 45°45N 124°5E 115 B13
Taohua Dao China 29°50N 122°20E 117 C14
Taolanaro Madag. 25°2S 47°0E 141 K9
Taole China 38°48N 106°40E 114 E4
Taonan China 45°22N 122°40E 115 B12
Taormina Italy 37°51N 15°17E 95 E8
Taos U.S.A. 36°24N 105°35W 169 H11
Taoudenni Mali 22°40N 3°55W 134 D5
Taoudrart, Adrar Algeria 24°25N 2°24E 136 D4
Taounate Morocco 34°25N 4°41W 136 B3
Taourirt Algeria 26°37N 0°20E 136 C4
Taourirt Morocco 34°25N 2°53W 136 B3
Taouz Morocco 30°53N 4°0W 136 B3
Taoyuan China 28°55N 111°16E 117 C8
T'aoyüan Taiwan 25°0N 121°4E 117 E13
Tapa Estonia 59°15N 25°50E 61 G21
Tapa Shan = Daba Shan China 32°0N 109°0E 116 B7
Tapachula Mexico 14°54N 92°17W 181 E6
Tapah Malaysia 4°12N 101°15E 121 K3
Tapajós → Brazil 2°24S 54°41W 187 D8
Tapaktuan Indonesia 3°15N 97°10E 118 D1
Tapanahoni → Suriname 4°20N 54°25W 187 C8
Tapanui N.Z. 45°56S 169°18E 155 F4
Tapauá → Brazil 5°40S 64°21W 186 E6
Tapes Brazil 30°40S 51°23W 191 C5
Tapeta Liberia 6°29N 8°52W 138 D3
Taphan Hin Thailand 16°13N 100°26E 120 D3
Tapia de Casariego Spain 43°34N 6°56W 88 B4
Tapiraí Brazil 19°52S 46°1W 189 D1
Tapirapecó, Serra Venezuela 1°10N 65°0W 186 C6
Taplan Australia 34°33S 140°52E 152 C4
Taplejung Nepal 27°1N 86°16E 125 F12
Tapo-Capara △ Venezuela 7°55N 71°15W 183 E5
Tapolca Hungary 46°53N 17°29E 80 D2
Tapti → India 21°8N 72°41E 126 D1
Tapuae-o-Uenuku N.Z. 42°0S 173°39E 155 C8
Tapul Group Phil. 5°35N 120°50E 119 C6
Tapurucuará Brazil 0°24S 65°2W 186 D5
Ţaqţaq Iraq 35°53N 44°35E 105 E11
Taquara Brazil 29°36S 50°46W 191 B5
Taquari → Brazil 19°15S 57°17W 186 G7
Tara Australia 27°17S 150°31E 151 D5
Tara Canada 44°28N 81°9W 174 B3
Tara Russia 56°55N 74°24E 106 D8
Tara Zambia 16°58S 26°45E 143 F2
Tara → Montenegro 43°21N 18°51E 96 C2
Tara △ Serbia 43°55N 19°30E 96 C3
Taraba □ Nigeria 8°0N 10°30E 139 D7
Taraba → Nigeria 8°30N 10°15E 139 D7
Tarābulus Lebanon 34°31N 35°50E 130 A4
Tarābulus Libya 32°49N 13°7E 135 B8
Tarābulus □ Libya 31°0N 13°0E 135 B8
Taraclia Taraclia, Moldova 45°54N 28°40E 81 E13
Taraclia Tighina, Moldova 46°34N 29°7E 81 D14
Taradale N.Z. 39°33S 176°53E 154 F5
Taradehi India 23°18N 79°21E 125 H8
Tarajalejo Canary Is. 28°12N 14°7W 100 F5
Tarakan Indonesia 3°20N 117°35E 118 D5
Tarakit, Mt. Kenya 2°2N 35°10E 142 B4
Taralga Australia 34°26S 149°52E 153 C8
Tarama-Jima Japan 24°39N 124°42E 113 M2
Taramakau → N.Z. 42°34S 171°8E 155 C6
Taran, Mys Russia 54°56N 19°59E 82 D6
Taranagar India 28°43N 74°50E 124 E6
Taranaki □ N.Z. 39°25S 174°30E 154 F3
Taranaki, Mt. N.Z. 39°17S 174°5E 154 F3
Tarancón Spain 40°1N 3°1W 90 E1
Tarangire △ Tanzania 4°21S 36°7E 142 C4
Taransay U.K. 57°54N 7°0W 65 D1
Táranto Italy 40°28N 17°14E 95 B10
Táranto, G. di Italy 40°8N 17°20E 95 B10
Tarapacá Colombia 2°56S 69°46W 186 D5
Tarapacá □ Chile 20°45S 69°30W 190 A2
Tarapoto Peru 6°30S 76°20W 188 B2
Tarare France 45°54N 4°26E 73 C8
Tararua Ra. N.Z. 40°45S 175°25E 154 G4
Tarasaigh = Taransay U.K. 57°54N 7°0W 65 D1
Tarascon France 43°48N 4°39E 73 E8
Tarascon-sur-Ariège France 42°50N 1°36E 72 F5
Tarashcha Ukraine 49°30N 30°31E 75 D16
Tarata Peru 17°27S 70°2W 188 D3
Tarauacá Brazil 8°6S 70°48W 188 B3
Tarauacá → Brazil 6°42S 69°48W 188 B4
Taravao Tahiti 17°43S 149°18W 155 b
Taravao, Isthme de Tahiti 17°43S 149°19W 155 b
Taravo → France 41°42N 8°49E 73 G12
Tarawa Kiribati 1°30N 173°0E 156 G9
Tarawera N.Z. 39°2S 176°36E 154 F5
Tarawera, L. N.Z. 38°13S 176°27E 154 E5
Tarawera, Mt. N.Z. 38°14S 176°32E 154 E5
Taraz Kazakhstan 42°54N 71°22E 109 D8
Tarazona Spain 41°55N 1°43W 90 D3
Tarazona de la Mancha Spain 39°16N 1°55W 91 F3
Tarbagatay, Khrebet Kazakhstan 48°0N 83°0E 109 C10
Tarbat Ness U.K. 57°52N 3°47W 65 D5
Tarbela Dam Pakistan 34°8N 72°52E 124 B5
Tarbert Ireland 52°34N 9°22W 64 D2
Tarbert Argyll & Bute, U.K. 55°52N 5°25W 65 F3
Tarbert W. Isles, U.K. 57°54N 6°49W 65 D2
Tarbes France 43°15N 0°3E 72 E4
Tarboro U.S.A. 35°54N 77°32W 177 D16
Tărcău, Munţii Romania 46°39N 26°7E 81 D11
Tarcento Italy 46°13N 13°13E 93 B10
Tarcoola Australia 30°44S 134°36E 151 E1
Tarcoon Australia 30°15S 146°43E 151 E4
Tarcutta Australia 35°16S 147°44E 153 C7
Tardets-Sorholus France 43°8N 0°52W 72 E3
Tardoire → France 45°52N 0°14E 72 C4
Taredjerdja Algeria 25°12N 2°32E 136 C4
Taree Australia 31°50S 152°30E 153 A10
Tarella Australia 31°2S 143°2E 152 A5
Tarf, Ras Morocco 35°40N 5°11W 136 A2
Tarfa, W. el → Egypt 28°25N 30°50E 137 F7
Tarfaya Morocco 27°55N 12°55W 134 C3
Târgovişte Romania 44°55N 25°27E 81 F10
Târgu Bujor Romania 45°52N 27°54E 81 E12
Târgu Cărbuneşti Romania 44°57N 23°31E 81 F8
Târgu Frumos Romania 47°12N 27°2E 81 C12
Târgu Jiu Romania 45°5N 23°19E 81 E8
Târgu Lăpuş Romania 47°27N 23°52E 81 C8
Târgu Mureş Romania 46°31N 24°38E 81 D9
Târgu Neamţ Romania 47°12N 26°25E 81 C11
Târgu Ocna Romania 46°16N 26°39E 81 D11
Târgu Secuiesc Romania 46°0N 26°10E 81 E11
Targuist Morocco 34°59N 4°14W 136 B3
Târguşor Romania 44°27N 28°25E 81 F13
Târhăus, Vf. Romania 46°40N 26°8E 81 D11
Tarhbalt Morocco 30°39N 5°20W 136 B2
Ţarif U.A.E. 24°3N 53°46E 129 E7
Tarifa Spain 36°1N 5°36W 89 J5
Tarija Bolivia 21°30S 64°40W 190 A3
Tarija □ Bolivia 21°30S 63°30W 190 A3
Tariku → Indonesia 2°55S 138°26E 119 E9
Tarīm Yemen 16°3N 49°0E 131 D4
Tarim Basin = Tarim Pendi China 40°0N 84°0E 109 E10
Tarim He → China 39°30N 88°30E 109 E11
Tarim Pendi China 40°0N 84°0E 109 E10
Taritatu → Indonesia 2°54S 138°27E 119 E9
Tarka → S. Africa 32°10S 26°0E 144 D4
Tarka La Bhutan 27°12N 89°44E 125 F13
Tarkastad S. Africa 32°0S 26°16E 144 D4
Tarkhankut, Mys Ukraine 45°25N 32°30E 85 K7
Tarko Sale Russia 64°55N 77°50E 106 C8
Tarkwa Ghana 5°20N 2°0W 138 D4
Tarlac Phil. 15°29N 120°35E 119 A6
Tarm Denmark 55°56N 8°31E 63 J2
Tarma Peru 11°25S 75°45W 188 C2
Tarmiya Iraq 33°40N 44°23E 105 G11
Tarn □ France 43°49N 2°8E 72 E6
Tarn → France 44°5N 1°6E 72 D5
Tarn-et-Garonne □ France 44°8N 1°20E 72 D5
Tarna → Hungary 47°31N 19°59E 80 C4
Târnava Mare → Romania 46°10N 23°43E 81 D8
Târnava Mică → Romania 46°9N 23°55E 81 D8
Târnăveni Romania 46°19N 24°13E 81 D9
Tarnica Poland 49°4N 22°44E 83 J9
Tarnobrzeg Poland 50°35N 21°41E 83 H8
Tarnogród Poland 50°22N 22°45E 83 H9
Tarnos France 43°32N 1°28W 72 E2
Târnova Moldova 48°10N 27°40E 81 B12
Târnova Romania 45°23N 21°59E 80 E6
Tarnów Poland 50°3N 21°0E 83 H8
Tarnowskie Góry Poland 50°27N 18°54E 83 H5
Tärnsjö Sweden 60°9N 16°56E 62 D10
Táro → Italy 45°2N 10°15E 92 C7
Ţārom Iran 28°11N 55°46E 129 D7
Taroom Australia 25°36S 149°48E 151 D4
Taroudannt Morocco 30°30N 8°52W 136 B2
Tarp Germany 54°39N 9°24E 76 A5
Tarpeena Australia 37°37S 140°47E 152 D4
Tarpon Springs U.S.A. 28°9N 82°45W 179 G7
Tarquínia Italy 42°15N 11°45E 93 F8
Tarra Bulga △ Australia 38°27S 146°31E 153 E7
Tarrafal C. Verde Is. 15°18N 23°39W 134 b
Tarragona Spain 41°5N 1°17E 90 D6
Tarragona □ Spain 41°5N 1°0E 90 D6
Tarraleah Australia 42°17S 146°26E 151 G4
Tarrasa = Terrassa Spain 41°34N 2°1E 90 D7
Tàrrega Spain 41°39N 1°9E 90 D6
Tarrytown Ga., U.S.A. 32°19N 82°34W 178 C7
Tarrytown N.Y., U.S.A. 41°4N 73°52W 175 E11
Tårs Denmark 57°23N 10°7E 63 G4
Tarsus Turkey 36°58N 34°55E 104 D6
Tartagal Argentina 22°30S 63°50W 190 A3
Tärtär Azerbaijan 40°20N 46°58E 87 K8
Tärtär → Azerbaijan 40°26N 47°20E 87 K8
Tartas France 43°50N 0°49W 72 E3
Tartu Estonia 58°20N 26°44E 84 C4
Ţarţūs Syria 34°55N 35°55E 104 E6
Ţarţūs □ Syria 35°0N 36°0E 130 A5
Tarumirim Brazil 19°16S 41°59W 189 D2
Tarumizu Japan 31°29N 130°42E 113 J5
Tarussa Russia 54°44N 37°10E 84 E9
Tarutao = Ko Tarutao △ Thailand 6°31N 99°26E 121 J2
Tarutao, Ko Thailand 6°33N 99°40E 121 J2
Tarutung Indonesia 2°0N 98°54E 118 D1
Tarutyne Ukraine 46°12N 29°9E 81 D14
Tarvísio Italy 46°30N 13°35E 93 B10
Tasaret, O. → Algeria 26°25N 1°59E 136 C4
Tasböget Kazakhstan 44°46N 65°33E 108 D7
Taseko → Canada 52°8N 123°45W 162 C4
Tasgaon India 17°2N 74°39E 12
Tash-Kömür Kyrgyzstan 41°40N 72°10E 10
Tashauz = Daşoguz Turkmenistan 41°49N 59°58E 10
Tashi Chho Dzong = Thimphu Bhutan 27°31N 89°45E 12
Ţashk, Daryācheh-ye Iran 29°45N 53°35E 12
Tashkent = Toshkent Uzbekistan 41°20N 69°10E 10
Tashtagol Russia 52°47N 87°53E 10
Tasiilaq Greenland 65°40N 37°20W 5
Tasikmalaya Indonesia 7°18S 108°12E 11
Tåsinge Denmark 55°0N 10°35E 6
Tåsjön Sweden 64°15N 15°40E 6
Task Niger 14°56N 10°46E 13
Taskan Russia 62°59N 150°20E 10
Taşkent Turkey 36°55N 32°29E 1
Taşköprü Turkey 41°30N 34°15E 1
Taşlâc Moldova 47°4N 29°24E 8
Taşlıçay Turkey 39°38N 43°22E 10
Tasman □ N.Z. 41°30S 172°40E 1
Tasman → N.Z. 43°48S 170°8E 1
Tasman, Mt. N.Z. 43°34S 170°12E 1
Tasman B. N.Z. 40°59S 173°25E 1
Tasman Basin Pac. Oc. 46°0S 158°0E 1
Tasman Glacier N.Z. 43°37S 170°12E 1
Tasman Mts. N.Z. 41°3S 172°25E 1
Tasman Pen. Australia 43°10S 148°0E 1
Tasman Sea Pac. Oc. 36°0S 160°0E 1
Tasmania □ Australia 42°0S 146°30E 1
Tasmanian Wilderness World Heritage Area △ Australia 43°0S 146°0E 1
Tăşnad Romania 47°30N 22°33E 8
Taşova Turkey 40°45N 36°19E 1
Tassili n'Ajjer Algeria 25°47N 8°1E 13
Tassili n'Ajjer △ Algeria 26°5N 6°0E 13
Tassili-Oua-n-Ahaggar Algeria 20°41N 5°30E 13
Tassili Tin-Rerhoh Algeria 20°5N 3°55E 13
Tasuj Iran 38°18N 45°23E 10
Tat Ton △ Thailand 15°57N 102°2E 1
Tata Hungary 47°37N 18°19E 8
Tata Morocco 29°46N 7°56W 13
Tatabánya Hungary 47°32N 18°25E 8
Tataouine Tunisia 32°57N 10°29E 13
Tataouine □ Tunisia 32°0N 10°0E 13
Tatar Republic = Tatarstan □ Russia 55°30N 51°30E 8
Tatarbunary Ukraine 45°50N 29°39E 8
Tatarsk Russia 55°14N 76°0E 1
Tatarskiy Proliv Russia 50°0N 141°0E 10
Tatarstan □ Russia 55°30N 51°30E 8
Tatatua, Pte. Tahiti 17°44S 149°8W 1
Tateyama Japan 35°0N 139°50E 1
Tathlina L. Canada 60°33N 117°39W 1
Tathra Australia 36°44S 149°59E 1
Tatinnai L. Canada 60°55N 97°40W 1
Tatla Lake Canada 52°0N 124°20W 1
Tatlısu = Akanthou Cyprus 35°22N 33°45E 10
Tatlısu Turkey 40°24N 27°55E 9
Tatnam, C. Canada 57°16N 91°0W 16
Tatra = Tatry Slovak Rep. 49°20N 20°0E 7
Tatranský △ Slovak Rep. 49°10N 20°0E 7
Tatry Slovak Rep. 49°20N 20°0E 7
Tatshenshini → Canada 59°28N 137°45W 1
Tatshenshini-Alsek ⌓ Canada 59°55N 137°45W 1
Tatsuno Japan 34°52N 134°33E 1
Tatta = Thatta Pakistan 24°42N 67°55E 1
Tatuí Brazil 23°25S 47°53W 1
Tatum U.S.A. 33°16N 103°19W 16
Tat'ung = Datong China 40°6N 113°18E 1
Tatura Australia 36°29S 145°16E 1
Tatvan Turkey 38°31N 42°15E 10
Tauá Brazil 6°1S 40°26W 1
Taubaté Brazil 23°0S 45°36W 1
Tauberbischofsheim Germany 49°37N 9°39E 7
Taucha Germany 51°23N 12°29E 7
Tauern Austria 47°15N 12°40E 7
Tauern-tunnel Austria 47°0N 13°12E 7
Taulé France 48°37N 3°55W 7
Taumarunui N.Z. 38°53S 175°15E 1
Taumaturgo Brazil 8°54S 72°51W 1
Taung S. Africa 27°33S 24°47E 1
Taungdwingyi Burma 20°1N 95°40E 12
Taunggyi Burma 20°50N 97°0E 12
Taungoo = Tounggoo Burma 19°0N 96°30E 12
Taungup Burma 18°51N 94°14E 12
Taunsa Pakistan 30°42N 70°39E 12
Taunsa Barrage Pakistan 30°42N 70°50E 12
Taunton U.K. 51°1N 3°5W 6
Taunton U.S.A. 41°54N 71°6W 17
Taunus Germany 50°13N 8°34E 7
Taupo N.Z. 38°41S 176°7E 1
Taupo, L. N.Z. 38°46S 175°55E 1
Tauragė Lithuania 55°14N 22°16E 8
Tauragė □ Lithuania 55°15N 22°17E 8
Tauranga N.Z. 37°42S 176°11E 1
Tauranga Harb. N.Z. 37°30S 176°5E 1
Taureau, Rés. Canada 46°46N 73°50W 16
Taurianova Italy 38°21N 16°1E 9
Tauroa Pt. N.Z. 35°10S 173°4E 1
Taurus Mts. = Toros Dağları Turkey 37°0N 32°30E 10
Tauste Spain 41°58N 1°18W 9
Tautira Tahiti 17°44S 149°9W 1
Tauyskaya Guba Russia 59°20N 150°20E 10
Tauz = Tovuz Azerbaijan 41°0N 45°40E 8
Tavan Bogd Uul Mongolia 49°10N 87°49E 10
Tavares U.S.A. 28°48N 81°44W 1
Tavas Turkey 37°34N 29°4E 9
Tavastehus = Hämeenlinna Finland 61°0N 24°28E 8
Tavda Russia 58°7N 65°8E 1
Tavda → Russia 57°47N 67°18E 1
Taverner B. Canada 67°12N 72°25W 16
Tavernes de la Valldigna Spain 39°5N 0°13W 9

ernier *U.S.A.* 25°1N 80°31W **179** K9
eta *Kenya* 3°23S 37°37E **142** C4
euni *Fiji* 16°51S 179°58W **154** a
iano *Italy* 39°59N 18°5E **95** C11
ignano → *France* 42°7N 9°33E **73** F13
a *Portugal* 37°8N 7°40W **89** H3
istock *Canada* 43°19N 80°50W **174** C4
istock *U.K.* 50°33N 4°9W **67** G3
olara *Italy* 40°54N 9°42E **94** B2
ora → *Portugal* 41°8N 7°35W **88** D3
oy *Burma* 14°2N 98°12E **120** E2
oy Pt. *Burma* 13°32N 98°10E **120** F2
richanka *Russia* 43°18N 131°59E **112** C5
ropos → *Greece* 39°10N 21°45E **98** B3
şanlı *Turkey* 39°32N 29°30E **99** B11
uki *Fiji* 17°37S 177°5E **154** a
uki *Fiji* 19°7S 178°8E **154** a
ra → *India* 51°4N 4°4W **67** F3
ra → *India* 22°48N 77°48E **124** H8
a Res. *India* 22°35N 78°5E **126** C4

istock City *U.S.A.* 44°16N 83°31W **173** C12
itawi I. *Phil.* 4°20N 117°55E **118** D5
ru *Taiwan* 22°22N 120°54E **117** F13
rüq *Iraq* 35°8N 44°26E **105** F11
co *Mexico* 18°33N 99°36W **181** D5
ila *Pakistan* 33°42N 72°52E **124** C5

korgan Tajik Zizhixian
   China 39°4N 75°14E **109** E9
→ *U.K.* 56°37N 3°38W **65** E5
L. *Australia* 32°55S 120°48E **149** F3
I. *U.K.* 56°32N 4°8W **65** E4
→ *U.K.* 56°43N 3°59W **65** E5
Ninh *Vietnam* 11°20N 106°5E **121** G6
abamba *Peru* 8°15S 77°16W **188** B2
getos Oros *Greece* 37°0N 22°23E **98** D4
akova *Russia* 59°13N 74°0E **106** D8
lor *Canada* 56°13N 120°40W **162** B4
lor Fla., *U.S.A.* 30°26N 82°18W **177** D7
lor Nebr., *U.S.A.* 41°46N 99°23W **172** E4
lor Pa., *U.S.A.* 41°23N 75°43W **175** E9
lor Tex., *U.S.A.* 34°30N 97°25W **176** H6
lor, Mt. *N.Z.* 43°30S 171°20E **155** D6
lor, Mt. *U.S.A.* 35°14N 107°37W **169** J10
lorville *U.S.A.* 39°33N 89°18W **172** F9
māā *Si. Arabia* 27°35N 38°45E **128** E3
myr, Oz. *Russia* 74°20N 102°0E **107** B11
myr, Poluostrov
   Russia 75°0N 100°0E **107** B11
port *U.K.* 56°27N 2°52W **65** E6
rona △ *Colombia* 11°20N 74°2W **183** D5
shet *Russia* 55°58N 98°1E **107** D10
tay *Phil.* 10°45N 119°30E **119** F5
yebād *Iran* 34°45N 60°45E **129** C9
yebād *Iran* 34°44N 60°44E **129** C9
ynsha *Kazakhstan* 50°53N 69°45E **109** B7
a → *Russia* 67°32N 78°40E **106** C8
a-Al Hoceïma-Taounate □
   Morocco 34°15N 3°20W **136** B3
a Khurmātū *Iraq* 35°18N 44°20E **105** E11
a-Taou □ *Morocco* 34°15N 4°10W **136** B3
awa-Ko *Japan* 39°43N 140°40E **112** E10
erbo *Libya* 25°45N 21°0E **135** C10
n → *Canada* 59°48N 109°55W **163** B7
n L. *Canada* 59°44N 108°42W **163** B7
ault *Algeria* 35°29N 6°11E **136** A5
ovskiy *Russia* 67°30N 78°44E **106** C8
isi *Georgia* 41°43N 44°50E **87** K7
an = Chad ■ *Africa* 15°0N 17°15E **135** F8
ad, L. *Chad* 13°30N 14°30E **135** F8
aourou *Benin* 8°58N 2°40E **139** D5
eng-tou = Chengdu
   China 30°38N 104°2E **116** B5
entok L. *Canada* 55°15N 125°0W **162** B4
etti *Benin* 7°50N 1°40E **139** D5
sbanza *Gabon* 2°45S 11°0E **140** E2
ien *Liberia* 5°59N 8°15W **138** D3
n Tabaraden *Niger* 15°58N 5°56E **139** B6
ogha Zanbil = Choghā Zanbīl
   Iran 32°1N 48°32E **129** C6
ong-k'ing = Chongqing
   China 29°35N 106°25E **116** C6
ew Poland 54°8N 18°50E **62** D5
anau *N.Z.* 45°25S 167°43E **155** F2
anau *N.Z.* 45°15S 167°45E **155** F2
araroa *N.Z.* 37°39S 178°25E **154** D7
aroa *N.Z.* 37°32S 175°44E **154** D4
awamutu *N.Z.* 38°1S 175°20E **154** E4
ka a Maui = North I.
   N.Z. 38°0S 175°0E **154** E4
aha *N.Z.* 37°44S 177°52E **154** D5
araka *N.Z.* 38°26S 177°53E **154** E6
auwhata *N.Z.* 37°25S 175°9E **154** D4
opuru *N.Z.* 35°23S 173°56E **154** C2
uiti *N.Z.* 38°20S 175°11E **154** E4
-Dghâmcha, Sebkhet
   Mauritania 18°30N 15°55W **138** B1
Puke *N.Z.* 37°46S 176°22E **154** D5
Teko *N.Z.* 38°2S 176°48E **154** E5
Waewae B. *N.Z.* 46°15S 167°33E **155** G2
Wai Pounamu = South I.
   N.Z. 44°0S 170°0E **155** E5
za *Romania* 46°55N 24°30E **81** D9
egue *U.S.A.* 31°38N 96°17W **176** F6
hupoo *Tahiti* 17°50S 149°16W **155** b
na *Italy* 41°15N 14°4E **95** A7
pa *Mexico* 17°33N 92°57W **181** D6
a *Spain* 36°59N 4°55W **89** J6
akang *Malaysia* 1°6N 110°30E **118** D4
araut *Niger* 14°51N 5°43E **139** C6
erau → *Malaysia* 1°30N 103°42E **121** d
erda *Russia* 43°30N 41°46E **87** J5
essa □ *Algeria* 35°0N 7°50E **136** B5
essa *Algeria* 35°0N 7°50E **136** B5
icuary → *Paraguay* 26°36S 58°16W **190** B4
ingtinggi *Riau,*
   Indonesia 1°0N 102°45E **118** E2
ingtinggi *Sumatera Utara,*
   Indonesia 3°20N 99°9E **118** D1
ourba *Tunisia* 36°49N 9°51E **136** A4
oursouk *Tunisia* 36°29N 9°10E **136** A4
ates *Georgia* 42°5N 45°17E **87** J7
ate *Mexico* 32°34N 116°38W **171** N10
a *Spain* 36°59N 4°55W **89** J6

Tecka *Argentina* 43°29S 70°48W **192** B2
Tecomán *Mexico* 18°55N 103°53W **180** D4
Tecopa *U.S.A.* 35°51N 116°13W **171** K10
Tecoripa *Mexico* 28°37N 109°57W **180** B3
Tecuala *Mexico* 22°23N 105°27W **180** C3
Tecuci *Romania* 45°51N 27°27E **81** E12
Tecumseh Mich.,
   U.S.A. 42°0N 83°57W **173** D12
Tecumseh Okla., *U.S.A.* 35°15N 96°56W **176** D6
Tedzhen = Tejen
   Turkmenistan 37°23N 60°31E **108** E6
Tees → *U.K.* 54°37N 1°10W **66** C6
Tees B. *U.K.* 54°40N 1°9W **66** C6
Teeswater *Canada* 43°59N 81°17W **174** C3
Tefé *Brazil* 3°25S 64°50W **186** D6
Tefenni *Turkey* 37°18N 29°45E **99** D11
Tegal *Indonesia* 6°52S 109°8E **118** F3
Tegallalang *Indonesia* 8°27S 115°17E **119** J18
Tegalsari *Indonesia* 8°25S 114°8E **119** J17
Tegernsee *Germany* 47°43N 11°46E **77** H7
Tegid, L. = Bala, L. *U.K.* 52°53N 3°37W **66** E4
Tegina *Nigeria* 10°5N 6°11E **139** C6
Tegucigalpa *Honduras* 14°5N 87°14W **182** D2
Teguidda i-n-Tessoum
   Niger 17°25N 6°37E **139** B6
Tehachapi *U.S.A.* 35°8N 118°27W **171** K8
Tehachapi Mts. *U.S.A.* 35°0N 118°30W **171** L8
Tehamiyam *Sudan* 18°20N 36°32E **137** D4
Tehéni *Ivory C.* 9°39N 3°40W **138** D4
Tehoru *Indonesia* 3°23S 129°30E **119** E7
Tehrān = Tehrān *Iran* 35°41N 51°25E **129** C6
Tehran □ *Iran* 35°30N 51°30E **129** C6
Tehri *India* 30°23N 78°29E **125** D8
Tehuacán *Mexico* 18°27N 97°23W **181** D5
Tehuantepec *Mexico* 16°21N 95°13W **181** D5
Tehuantepec, G. de
   Mexico 15°50N 95°12W **181** D5
Tehuantepec, Istmo de
   Mexico 17°15N 94°30W **181** D6
Teide, Pico de
   Canary Is. 28°15N 16°38W **100** F3
Teifi → *U.K.* 52°5N 4°41W **67** E3
Teigebyen *Norway* 60°12N 11°0E **62** D5
Teign → *U.K.* 50°32N 3°32W **67** G4
Teignmouth *U.K.* 50°33N 3°31W **67** G4
Teinainano = Tarawa
   Kiribati 1°30N 173°0E **156** G9
Teius *Romania* 46°12N 23°40E **81** D8
Teixeira *Brazil* 7°13S 37°15W **189** B3
Teixeira Pinto
   Guinea-Biss. 12°3N 16°0W **138** C1
Tejakula *Indonesia* 8°8S 115°20E **119** J18
Tejen *Turkmenistan* 37°23N 60°31E **108** E6
Tejen → *Turkmenistan* 37°24N 60°38E **108** E6
Tejo → *Europe* 38°40N 9°24W **89** F2
Tejon Pass *U.S.A.* 34°49N 118°53W **171** L8
Tekamah *U.S.A.* 41°47N 96°13W **172** E5
Tekapo → *N.Z.* 44°13S 170°21E **155** F5
Tekapo, L. *N.Z.* 43°53S 170°33E **155** F4
Tekax *Mexico* 20°12N 89°17W **181** C7
Teke *Turkey* 41°4N 29°39E **97** E13
Tekeli *Kazakhstan* 44°50N 79°0E **109** D9
Tekeze Dam *Ethiopia* 13°10N 38°45E **131** E2
Tekija *Serbia* 44°42N 22°26E **96** B6
Tekirdağ *Turkey* 40°58N 27°30E **97** F11
Tekirdağ □ *Turkey* 41°0N 27°0E **97** F11
Tekirova *Turkey* 36°30N 30°32E **99** E12
Tekkali *India* 18°37N 84°15E **126** E7
Tekke *Turkey* 40°42N 36°12E **104** B7
Tekman *Turkey* 39°38N 41°29E **105** C9
Tekoa *U.S.A.* 47°14N 117°4W **168** C5
Tekong Besar, Pulau
   Singapore 1°25N 104°3E **121** d
Tel → *India* 20°50N 83°54E **126** D6
Tel Aviv ✈ (TLV) *Israel* 32°5N 34°49E **130** C3
Tel Aviv-Yafo *Israel* 32°4N 34°48E **130** C3
Tel Lakhish *Israel* 31°34N 34°51E **130** D3
Tel Megiddo *Israel* 32°35N 35°11E **130** C4
Tela *Honduras* 15°40N 87°28W **182** C2
Télagh *Algeria* 34°51N 0°32W **136** B3
Telanaipura = Jambi
   Indonesia 1°38S 103°30E **118** E2
Telangana *India* 17°30N 78°30E **126** F4
Telašćica △ *Croatia* 43°55N 15°10E **82** G5
Telavi *Georgia* 42°0N 45°30E **87** J7
Telč *Czech Rep.* 49°11N 15°28E **78** B8
Telciu *Romania* 47°25N 24°24E **81** C9
Telde *Canary Is.* 27°59N 15°25W **100** G4
Telegraph Creek
   Canada 58°0N 131°10W **162** B2
Telekhany = Tsyelyakhany
   Belarus 52°30N 25°46E **75** B13
Telemark *Norway* 59°15N 7°40E **60** G12
Télemsès *Niger* 15°37N 4°44E **139** B5
Telén *Argentina* 36°15N 65°31W **190** D2
Teleneşti *Moldova* 47°30N 28°22E **81** C13
Teleng *Iran* 25°47N 61°3E **129** E9
Teleño *Spain* 42°23N 6°22W **88** C4
Teleorman □ *Romania* 44°0N 25°0E **81** G10
Teleorman → *Romania* 43°52N 25°26E **81** G9
Telerhteba, Djebel
   Algeria 24°10N 6°51E **136** D5
Teles Pires → *Brazil* 7°21S 58°3W **186** E7
Telescope Pk. *U.S.A.* 36°10N 117°5W **171** J9
Teletaye *Mali* 16°31N 1°30E **139** B5
Teletskoye, Oz. *Russia* 51°40N 87°30E **109** B11
Telford *U.K.* 52°40N 2°27W **67** E5
Telford and Wrekin □
   U.K. 52°45N 2°27W **66** E5
Telkwa *Canada* 54°41N 127°5W **162** C3
Tell City *U.S.A.* 37°57N 86°46W **172** G10
Teller *U.S.A.* 65°16N 166°22W **166** C6
Tellicherry = Thalassery
   India 11°45N 75°30E **127** J2
Telluride *U.S.A.* 37°56N 107°49W **169** H10
Teloloapán *Mexico* 18°21N 99°51N **181** D5
Telpos Iz *Russia* 63°16N 59°13E **58** C17
Telsen *Argentina* 42°30S 66°50W **192** B3
Telšiai *Lithuania* 55°53N 22°14E **62** C9
Telšiai □ *Lithuania* 55°59N 22°15E **62** C9
Telukbutun *Indonesia* 52°23N 13°17E **76** B9
Teluk Anson = Teluk Intan
   Malaysia 4°3N 101°0E **121** K3
Teluk Bahang *Malaysia* 5°28N 100°13E **121** c
Teluk Betung = Bandar Lampung
   Indonesia 5°20S 105°10E **118** F3

Teluk Intan *Malaysia* 4°3N 101°0E **121** K3
Teluk Kumbar *Malaysia* 5°18N 100°14E **121** c
Telukbutun *Indonesia* 4°13N 108°12E **118** D3
Telukdalam *Indonesia* 0°33N 97°50E **118** D1
Tema *Ghana* 5°41N 0°0 **139** D5
Temagami, L. *Canada* 47°0N 80°10W **164** C3
Temax *Mexico* 21°9N 88°56W **181** C7
Temba *S. Africa* 25°20S 28°17E **145** C4
Tembagapura *Indonesia* 4°20S 137°0E **119** E9
Tembe
   Dem. Rep. of the Congo 0°16S 28°14E **142** C2
Tembe △ *S. Africa* 26°51S 32°24E **145** C5
Tembleque *Spain* 39°41N 3°30W **88** F7
Temblor Range
   U.S.A. 35°20N 119°50W **171** K7
Teme → *U.K.* 52°11N 2°13W **67** E5
Temecula *U.S.A.* 33°30N 117°9W **171** M9
Temengor, Tasik
   Malaysia 5°24N 101°18E **121** K3
Temerloh *Malaysia* 3°27N 102°25E **121** L4
Teminabuan *Indonesia* 1°26S 132°1E **119** E8
Temir *Kazakhstan* 49°1N 57°14E **108** C5
Temirtau *Kazakhstan* 50°5N 72°56E **109** D8
Temirtau *Russia* 53°10N 87°30E **109** B11
Témiscamie → *Canada* 50°59N 73°5W **165** B5
Témiscaming *Canada* 46°44N 79°5W **164** C4
Témiscamingue, L.
   Canada 47°10N 79°25W **164** C4
Temnikov *Russia* 54°40N 43°11E **86** C9
Temo → *Italy* 40°17N 8°28E **94** B1
Temora *Australia* 34°30S 147°30E **153** C7
Temosachic *Mexico* 28°57N 107°51W **180** B3
Tempe *U.S.A.* 33°24N 111°54W **169** K8
Tempio Pausánia *Italy* 40°54N 9°6E **94** B2
Tempiute *U.S.A.* 37°39N 115°38W **170** H11
Temple *U.S.A.* 31°6N 97°21W **176** F6
Temple B. *Australia* 12°15S 143°3E **150** A3
Temple Terrace *U.S.A.* 28°2N 82°23W **179** G7
Templemore *Ireland* 52°47N 7°51W **64** D4
Templeton *U.S.A.* 35°33N 120°42W **170** K6
Templeton → *Australia* 21°0S 138°40E **150** C2
Templin *Germany* 53°7N 13°28E **76** B9
Tempoal de Sánchez
   Mexico 21°31N 98°23W **181** C5
Temryuk *Russia* 45°15N 37°24E **85** K9
Temska → *Serbia* 43°17N 22°33E **96** C6
Temuco *Chile* 38°45S 72°40W **192** A2
Temuka *N.Z.* 44°14S 171°17E **155** E6
Ten Degree Channel
   India 10°0N 92°30E **127** K11
Ten Thousand Is.
   U.S.A. 25°55N 81°45W **179** K8
Tenabo *Mexico* 20°3N 90°14W **181** C6
Tenaha *U.S.A.* 31°57N 94°15W **176** F7
Tenakee Springs
   U.S.A. 57°47N 135°13W **162** B1
Tenali *India* 16°15N 80°35E **127** F5
Tenancingo *Mexico* 18°58N 99°38W **181** D5
Tenango del Valle
   Mexico 19°7N 99°33W **181** D5
Tenaro, Akra *Greece* 36°22N 22°27E **98** E4
Tenasserim *Burma* 12°6N 99°3E **121** F2
Tenasserim □ *Burma* 14°0N 98°30E **121** F2
Tenasserim → *Burma* 12°24N 98°37E **121** F2
Tenby *U.K.* 51°40N 4°42W **67** F3
Tenda, Colle di *France* 44°7N 7°36E **73** D11
Tendaho *Ethiopia* 11°48N 40°54E **131** E3
Tende *France* 44°5N 7°35E **73** D11
Tendjedi, Adrar *Algeria* 23°41N 7°32E **136** D5
Tendō *Japan* 38°20N 140°30E **112** E10
Tendrara *Morocco* 33°3N 1°58W **136** B3
Tendrovskaya Kosa
   Ukraine 46°16N 31°35E **85** J6
Tendukhera *India* 23°24N 79°33E **125** H8
Teneguía, Volcanes de
   Canary Is. 28°28N 17°51W **100** F2
Teneida *Egypt* 25°30N 29°19E **137** B2
Tenenkou *Mali* 14°28N 4°55W **138** C4
Ténéré *Niger* 19°0N 10°30E **139** B7
Tenerife *Canary Is.* 28°15N 16°35W **100** F3
Tenerife, Pico *Canary Is.* 27°43N 18°1W **100** G1
Tenerife Norte ✈ (TFN)
   Canary Is. 28°28N 16°17W **100** F3
Tenerife Sur ✈ (TFS)
   Canary Is. 28°3N 16°33W **100** F3
Ténès *Algeria* 36°31N 1°14E **136** A4
Teng Xian *Guangxi Zhuangzu,*
   China 23°21N 110°56E **117** F8
Teng Xian *Shandong,*
   China 35°5N 117°10E **115** G9
Tengah, Kepulauan
   Indonesia 7°5S 118°15E **118** F5
Tengchong *China* 25°0N 98°28E **116** E2
Tengchowfu = Penglai
   China 37°48N 120°42E **115** F11
Tenggarong *Indonesia* 0°24S 116°58E **118** E5
Tengger Feng *China* 42°12N 86°48E **109** D11
Tengger Shamo *China* 38°0N 104°10E **114** F3
Tenggol, Pulau
   Malaysia 4°48N 103°41E **121** K4
Tengiz Köli *Kazakhstan* 50°30N 69°0E **108** D7
Tengzhou *China* 35°4N 117°9E **115** G9
Tenhult *Sweden* 57°41N 14°20E **63** G8
Teniente Enciso △
   Paraguay 21°5S 61°8W **190** A3
Tenille *U.S.A.* 29°46N 83°19W **178** F2
Tenino *U.S.A.* 46°51N 122°51W **170** D4
Tenkasi *India* 8°55N 77°20E **127** K3
Tenke *Katanga,*
   Dem. Rep. of the Congo 11°22S 26°40E **143** E2
Tenke *Katanga,*
   Dem. Rep. of the Congo 10°32S 26°7E **143** E2
Tenkodogo *Burkina Faso* 11°54N 0°19W **138** C4
Tenna → *Italy* 43°14N 13°47E **93** C10
Tennant Creek
   Australia 19°30S 134°15E **150** B1
Tennessee □ *U.S.A.* 36°0N 86°30W **177** D11
Tennessee → *U.S.A.* 37°4N 88°34W **177** C10
Tennille *U.S.A.* 32°56N 82°48W **178** E3
Teno, Pta. de *Canary Is.* 28°21N 16°55W **100** F3
Tenojoki = Tana →
   Norway 70°30N 28°14E **60** A23
Tenom *Malaysia* 5°4N 115°57E **118** C5
Tenosique *Mexico* 17°29N 91°26W **181** D6
Tenryū-Gawa →
   Japan 35°39N 137°48E **113** G8
Tensift, Oued →
   Morocco 32°3N 9°28W **136** B2
Tenterden *U.K.* 51°4N 0°42E **67** F8
Tenterfield *Australia* 29°0S 152°0E **151** D5

Teo = A Ramallosa *Spain* 42°45N 8°30W **88** C2
Teófilo Otoni *Brazil* 17°50S 41°30W **189** D2
Tepa *Indonesia* 7°52S 129°31E **119** F7
Tepalcatepec →
   Mexico 18°35N 101°59W **180** D4
Tepecik *Bursa, Turkey* 40°7N 28°25E **97** F12
Tepecik *Kütahya, Turkey* 39°2N 29°25E **99** B11
Tepehuanes *Mexico* 25°21N 105°44W **180** B3
Tepelenë *Albania* 40°17N 20°2E **96** F4
Tepetongo *Mexico* 22°28N 103°9W **180** C4
Tepic *Mexico* 21°30N 104°54W **180** C4
Teplá *Czech Rep.* 49°59N 12°52E **78** B5
Teplice *Czech Rep.* 50°40N 13°48E **78** A6
Teplyk *Ukraine* 48°40N 29°44E **81** D14
Ter → *Spain* 42°2N 3°12E **90** C8
Ter Apel *Neths.* 52°53N 7°5E **69** B7
Téra *Niger* 14°0N 0°45E **139** C5
Tera → *Spain* 41°54N 5°44W **88** D5
Teraina *Kiribati* 4°43N 160°25W **157** G12
Téramo *Italy* 42°39N 13°42E **93** F10
Terang *Australia* 38°15S 142°55E **152** E5
Terang, Teluk *Indonesia* 8°44S 116°0E **119** K19
Terawhiti, C. *N.Z.* 41°16S 174°38E **154** H3
Terazit, Massif de *Niger* 20°2N 8°30E **139** A6
Tercan *Turkey* 39°47N 40°23E **105** C9
Terceira *Azores* 38°43N 27°13W **134** a
Tercero → *Argentina* 32°58S 61°47W **190** C3
Terdal *India* 16°33N 75°3E **126** F2
Terebovlya *Ukraine* 49°18N 25°44E **75** D13
Teregova *Romania* 45°10N 22°16E **80** E7
Terek → *Russia* 44°0N 47°30E **87** J8
Terengganu □ *Malaysia* 4°55N 103°0E **121** K4
Terepaima △ *Venezuela* 9°58N 69°17W **183** E6
Tereshka → *Russia* 51°48N 46°26E **86** E8
Teresina *Brazil* 5°9S 42°45W **189** B2
Terespol *Poland* 52°5N 23°37E **63** F15
Teressa *India* 8°15N 93°10E **127** K11
Teresva → *Ukraine* 48°0N 23°42E **81** B8
Terewah, L. *Australia* 29°52S 147°35E **151** D4
Terges → *Portugal* 37°49N 7°41W **89** H3
Tergnier *France* 49°40N 3°17E **71** C10
Terhazza
   Australia 30°25S 148°50E **153** A8
Terlizzi *Italy* 41°8N 16°32E **95** A9
Termas de Río Hondo
   Argentina 27°29S 64°52W **190** B3
Terme *Turkey* 41°11N 37°0E **104** B7
Términi Imerese *Italy* 37°59N 13°42E **94** E6
Términos, L. de *Mexico* 18°37N 91°33W **181** D6
Térmiz *Uzbekistan* 37°15N 67°15E **109** F7
Térmoli *Italy* 42°0N 15°0E **93** F12
Ternate *Indonesia* 0°45N 127°25E **119** D7
Terneuzen *Neths.* 51°20N 3°50E **69** C3
Terney *Russia* 45°3N 136°37E **112** B8
Terni *Italy* 42°34N 12°37E **93** F9
Ternitz *Austria* 47°43N 16°2E **78** D9
Ternivka *Ukraine* 48°32N 29°58E **81** B14
Ternopil *Ukraine* 49°30N 25°40E **75** D13
Ternopil □ *Ukraine* 49°10N 25°10E **75** D13
Ternopol = Ternopil
   Ukraine 49°30N 25°40E **75** D13
Terowie *Australia* 33°8S 138°55E **152** B2
Terpni *Greece* 40°55N 23°26E **96** F7
Terra Bella *U.S.A.* 35°58N 119°3W **171** K7
Terra Nova △ *Canada* 48°33N 53°55W **165** C9
Terrace *Canada* 54°30N 128°35W **162** C3
Terrace Bay *Canada* 48°47N 87°5W **164** C2
Terracina *Italy* 41°17N 13°15E **94** A6
Terralba *Italy* 39°43N 8°39E **94** C1
Terrassini *Italy* 38°10N 13°4E **94** D6
Terrassa *Spain* 41°34N 2°1E **90** D7
Terrasson-la-Villedieu
   France 45°8N 1°18E **72** C5
Terre Haute *U.S.A.* 39°28N 87°25W **172** F10
Terrebonne B. *U.S.A.* 29°5N 90°35W **177** D9
Terrecht *Mali* 19°35N 0°22E **139** B5
Terrell *U.S.A.* 32°44N 96°17W **176** E6
Terrenceville *Canada* 47°40N 54°44W **165** C9
Terrick Terrick △
   Australia 36°8S 144°13E **152** D6
Terry *U.S.A.* 46°47N 105°19W **168** C11
Terryville *U.S.A.* 41°41N 73°3W **175** E11
Terschelling *Neths.* 53°25N 5°20E **69** A5
Tersko-Kumskiy Kanal
   Russia 44°32N 44°38E **87** H7
Tertenia *Italy* 39°42N 9°34E **94** C2
Terter = Tärtär △
   Azerbaijan 40°26N 47°22E **87** K8
Teruel *Spain* 40°22N 1°8W **90** E3
Teruel □ *Spain* 40°48N 1°0W **90** E4
Tervel *Bulgaria* 43°45N 27°28E **97** C11
Tervola *Finland* 66°6N 24°49E **60** C21
Teryaweynya L.
   Australia 32°18S 143°22E **152** B5
Teşani *Bos.-H.* 44°38N 18°1E **80** F3
Tesha → *Russia* 55°38N 42°0E **86** C6
Teshio *Japan* 44°53N 141°44E **112** B10
Teshio-Gawa →
   Japan 44°53N 141°45E **112** B10
Tešica *Serbia* 43°27N 21°45E **96** C5
Tesiyn Gol → *Mongolia* 50°40N 93°20E **110** A7
Teslić *Bos.-H.* 44°37N 17°54E **80** F2
Teslin *Canada* 60°10N 132°43W **162** A2
Teslin → *Canada* 61°34N 134°35W **162** A2
Teslin L. *Canada* 60°15N 132°57W **162** A2
Tessalit *Mali* 20°12N 1°0E **139** A5
Tessaoua *Niger* 13°47N 7°56E **139** C6
Tessin *Germany* 54°2N 12°26E **76** A8
Tessit *Mali* 15°13N 0°18E **139** B5
Test → *U.K.* 50°56N 1°29W **67** G6
Testa del Gargano *Italy* 41°50N 16°10E **93** G13
Testigos, Is. Los
   Venezuela 11°23N 63°7W **183** D7
Têt → *France* 42°44N 3°2E **72** E7
Tetachuck L. *Canada* 53°18N 125°55W **162** C3
Tetas, Pta. *Chile* 23°31S 70°38W **190** A1
Tete *Mozam.* 16°13S 33°33E **143** F3
Tete □ *Mozam.* 15°15S 32°40E **143** F3
Teterev → *Ukraine* 51°1N 30°5E **75** C16
Teterow *Germany* 53°46N 12°34E **76** B8
Teteven *Bulgaria* 42°58N 24°17E **97** D8
Tethul → *Canada* 60°35N 112°12W **162** A6
Tetiyev *Ukraine* 49°22N 29°38E **75** D15
Tetlin *U.S.A.* 63°8N 142°30W **166** C5
Tetlin Zheh = Fort McPherson
   Canada 67°30N 134°55W **166** C6
Teton → *U.S.A.* 47°56N 110°31W **168** C8
Tétouan *Morocco* 35°35N 5°21W **136** A3
Tetovo *Macedonia* 42°1N 20°59E **96** D4
Tetufera, Mt. *Tahiti* 17°40S 149°26W **155** b

Tetyushi *Russia* 54°55N 48°49E **86** C9
Teuco → *Argentina* 25°35S 60°11W **190** B3
Teulada *Italy* 38°58N 8°46E **94** D1
Teulon *Canada* 50°23N 97°16W **163** C9
Teun *Indonesia* 6°59S 129°8E **119** F7
Teuri-Tō *Japan* 44°26N 141°19E **112** B10
Teutoburger Wald
   Germany 52°5N 8°22E **76** C4
Tevere → *Italy* 41°44N 12°14E **93** G9
Tevere △ *Italy* 42°46N 12°14E **93** F9
Teverya *Israel* 32°47N 35°32E **130** C4
Teviot → *U.K.* 55°29N 2°38E **65** F6
Tewantin *Australia* 26°27S 153°3E **151** D5
Tewkesbury *U.K.* 51°59N 2°9W **67** F5
Texada I. *Canada* 49°40N 124°25W **162** D4
Texarkana Ark., *U.S.A.* 33°26N 94°2W **176** E7
Texarkana Tex., *U.S.A.* 33°26N 94°3W **176** E7
Texas *Australia* 28°49S 151°9E **151** D5
Texas □ *U.S.A.* 31°40N 98°30W **176** F5
Texas City *U.S.A.* 29°24N 94°54W **176** G7
Texel *Neths.* 53°5N 4°50E **69** A4
Texline *U.S.A.* 36°23N 103°2W **176** C3
Texoma, L. *U.S.A.* 33°50N 96°34W **176** E6
Teyateyaneng *Lesotho* 29°7S 27°34E **145** C4
Teykovo *Russia* 56°55N 40°30E **84** C11
Teza → *Russia* 56°32N 41°53E **86** C5
Tezin *Afghan.* 34°24N 69°30E **124** B3
Teziutlán *Mexico* 19°49N 97°21N **181** D5
Tezpur *India* 26°40N 92°45E **123** F18
Tezzeron L. *Canada* 54°43N 124°30W **162** C4
Tha-anne → *Canada* 60°31N 94°37W **163** A10
Tha Deua *Laos* 17°57N 102°53E **120** D4
Tha Deua *Laos* 19°26N 101°50E **120** C3
Tha Li *Thailand* 17°37N 101°25E **120** D3
Tha Pla *Thailand* 17°48N 100°32E **120** D3
Tha Rua *Thailand* 14°34N 100°44E **120** E3
Tha Sala *Thailand* 8°40N 99°56E **121** H2
Tha Song Yang
   Thailand 17°34N 97°55E **120** D1
Thaba Putsoa *Lesotho* 29°45S 28°0E **145** C4
Thaba-Tseka *Lesotho* 29°32S 28°36E **145** C4
Thabana Ntlenyana
   Lesotho 29°30S 29°16E **145** C4
Thabazimbi *S. Africa* 24°40S 27°21E **145** C4
Thädig *Si. Arabia* 25°18N 45°52E **128** E5
Thai Binh *Vietnam* 20°35N 106°1E **116** G6
Thai Muang *Thailand* 8°24N 98°16E **121** H2
Thai Nguyen *Vietnam* 21°35N 105°55E **116** G5
Thailand ■ *Asia* 16°0N 102°0E **120** E4
Thailand, G. of *Asia* 11°30N 101°0E **121** G3
Thakhek *Laos* 17°25N 104°45E **120** D5
Thal *Pakistan* 33°28N 70°33E **124** C4
Thal Desert *Pakistan* 31°10N 71°30E **124** D4
Thala *Tunisia* 35°35N 8°40E **136** A5
Thala La = Hkakabo Razi
   Burma 28°25N 97°23E **116** C1
Thalabarivat *Cambodia* 13°33N 105°57E **120** F5
Thalang = Amphoe Thalang
   Thailand 8°1N 98°20E **121** a
Thalang *Thailand* 8°1N 98°20E **121** a
Thalara *Nepal* 29°29N 80°59E **125** D9
Thalassery *India* 11°45N 75°30E **127** J2
Thale Sap Songkhla
   Thailand 7°12N 100°28E **121** J3
Thallon *Australia* 28°39S 148°49E **151** D4
Thalu, Ko *Thailand* 9°26N 99°54E **121** b
Thalwil *Switz.* 47°17N 8°35E **77** H4
Tham Lot *Thailand* 19°34N 98°16E **120** C2
Thamarït *Oman* 17°39N 54°2E **131** D5
Thames → *N.Z.* 37°7S 175°34E **154** D4
Thames → *Canada* 42°20N 82°25W **174** D2
Thames → *U.K.* 51°29N 0°34E **67** F8
Thames, Firth of *N.Z.* 37°0S 175°25E **154** D4
Thames Estuary *U.K.* 51°29N 0°52E **67** F8
Thamesford *Canada* 43°4N 81°0W **174** C3
Thamesville *Canada* 42°33N 81°59W **174** D3
Than *India* 22°34N 71°11E **124** H4
Than Kyun *Burma* 9°49N 98°4E **121** H1
Than Uyen *Vietnam* 22°0N 103°54E **116** G4
Thana Gazi *India* 27°25N 76°19E **124** F7
Thandla *India* 23°0N 74°34E **124** H6
Thandwe *Burma* 18°20N 94°30E **123** K19
Thane *India* 19°12N 72°59E **124** G8
Thanesar *India* 30°1N 76°52E **124** D7
Thanet, I. of *U.K.* 51°21N 1°20E **67** F9
Thangool *Australia* 24°38S 150°42E **150** C5
Thanh Hoa *Vietnam* 19°48N 105°46E **116** G5
Thanh Pho Ho Chi Minh
   Vietnam 10°58N 106°40E **121** G6
Thanh Thuy *Vietnam* 22°55N 104°51E **120** C5
Thanjavur *India* 10°48N 79°12E **127** J4
Thanlwin = Salween →
   Burma 16°31N 97°37E **123** L20
Thann *France* 47°48N 7°5E **71** E14
Thano Bula Khan
   Pakistan 25°22N 67°50E **124** G2
Thanya Buri *Thailand* 14°1N 100°45E **120** E3
Thaoge → *Botswana* 20°27S 22°36E **144** B3
Thaolintoa L. *Canada* 61°30N 96°25W **163** A9
Thaon-les-Vosges
   France 48°15N 6°24E **71** D13
Thap Lan △ *Thailand* 14°15N 102°16E **120** E4
Thap Sakae *Thailand* 11°30N 99°37E **121** G2
Thap Than *Thailand* 15°27N 99°54E **120** E2
Thar Desert *India* 28°0N 72°0E **124** F5
Tharad *India* 24°30N 71°44E **124** G4
Thargomindah
   Australia 27°58S 143°46E **151** D3
Tharp Fracture Zone
   S. Ocean 54°0S 135°0W **55** B14
Tharrawaddy *Burma* 17°38N 95°48E **123** L19
Tharthār, Buhayrat ath
   Iraq 34°0N 43°15E **105** E10
Tharthār, L. = Tharthār,
   Buhayrat ath *Iraq* 34°0N 43°15E **105** E10
Tharthār, W. ath →
   Iraq 34°32N 43°4E **105** C10
Thasopoula *Greece* 40°49N 24°45E **97** F8
Thásos *Greece* 40°40N 24°40E **97** F8
That Khe *Vietnam* 22°16N 106°28E **116** F6
Thatcher *Ariz., U.S.A.* 32°51N 109°46W **169** K9
Thatcher *Colo., U.S.A.* 37°33N 104°7W **169** H11
Thaton *Burma* 16°55N 97°22E **123** L20
Thatta *Pakistan* 24°42N 67°55E **124** G2
Thaungdut *Burma* 24°30N 94°40E **123** G19
Thayawthadangy Kyun
   Burma 12°19N 98°0E **120** F1
Thayer *U.S.A.* 36°31N 91°33W **172** G8

Thayetmyo *Burma* 19°20N 95°10E **123** K19
Thazi *Burma* 21°0N 96°5E **123** J20
Thbeng Meanchey
   Cambodia 13°49N 104°58E **120** F5
The Bahamas ■
   N. Amer. 24°0N 75°0W **183** B5
The Broads *U.K.* 52°45N 1°30E **66** E9
The Everglades *U.S.A.* 25°50N 81°0W **179** K9
The Gambia ■ *W. Afr.* 13°25N 16°0W **138** C1
The Gulf = Persian Gulf
   Asia 27°0N 50°0E **129** E6
The Hague = 's-Gravenhage
   Neths. 52°7N 4°17E **69** B4
The Pas *Canada* 53°45N 101°15W **163** C8
The Wash *U.K.* 52°58N 0°20E **66** E8
The Weald *U.K.* 51°4N 0°20E **67** F8
Thebes = Thiva *Greece* 38°19N 23°19E **98** C5
Thebes *Egypt* 25°40N 32°35E **137** B3
Thedford *U.S.A.* 41°59N 100°35W **172** E3
Theebine *Australia* 25°57S 152°34W **151** D5
Thekulthili L. *Canada* 61°3N 110°0W **163** A7
Thelon → *Canada* 64°16N 96°4W **163** A8
Thénézay *France* 46°44N 0°2W **70** F6
Thenon *France* 45°9N 1°4E **72** C5
Theodore *Australia* 24°55S 150°3E **150** C5
Theodore *Canada* 51°26N 102°55W **163** C8
Theodore *U.S.A.* 30°33N 88°10W **177** F10
Theodore Roosevelt △
   U.S.A. 47°0N 103°25W **172** B2
Theodore Roosevelt L.
   U.S.A. 33°40N 111°10W **169** K8
Thepha *Thailand* 6°52N 100°58E **121** J3
Thérain → *France* 49°15N 2°27E **71** C9
Therandë *Kosovo* 42°21N 20°50E **96** D4
Theresa *U.S.A.* 44°13N 75°48E **175** B9
Theressa *U.S.A.* 29°50N 82°4W **178** F7
Thermopolis *U.S.A.* 43°39N 108°13W **168** D9
Thermopylae *Greece* 38°48N 22°35E **98** C4
Thesprotia *Greece* 39°27N 20°22E **98** B2
Thessalon *Canada* 46°20N 83°30W **164** C3
Thessalonica, Gulf of =
   Thessaloniki Kolpos
   Greece 40°15N 22°45E **96** F6
Thessaloniki *Greece* 40°38N 22°58E **96** F6
Thessaloniki ✈ (SKG)
   Greece 40°30N 23°0E **96** F7
Thessaloniki Kolpos
   Greece 40°15N 22°45E **96** F6
Thessaly □ *Greece* 39°25N 22°0E **98** B4
Thetford *U.K.* 52°25N 0°45E **67** E8
Thetford Mines *Canada* 46°8N 71°18W **165** C5
Theun → *Laos* 18°19N 104°0E **120** C5
Theunissen *S. Africa* 28°26S 26°43E **144** C4
Thevenard *Australia* 32°9S 133°38E **151** E1
Thiamis → *Greece* 39°15N 20°6E **98** B2
Thibodaux *U.S.A.* 29°48N 90°49W **177** G9
Thicket Portage
   Canada 55°19N 97°42W **163** B9
Thief River Falls *U.S.A.* 48°7N 96°10W **172** A5
Thiel Mts. *Antarctica* 85°15S 91°0W **55** E16
Thiene *Italy* 45°42N 11°29E **93** C8
Thiérache *France* 49°51N 3°45E **71** C10
Thiers *France* 45°52N 3°33E **72** C7
Thiès *Senegal* 14°50N 16°51W **138** C1
Thiès □ *Senegal* 14°45N 16°50W **138** C1
Thiesi *Italy* 40°31N 8°43E **94** B1
Thika *Kenya* 1°1S 37°5E **142** C4
Thille-Boubacar *Senegal* 16°31N 15°5W **138** B1
Thimphu *Bhutan* 27°31N 89°45E **123** F16
Thira *Greece* 31°18S 29°13E **145** D4
Þingvallavatn *Iceland* 64°11N 21°9W **60** D3
Thionville *France* 49°20N 6°10E **71** C13
Thíra = Santorini *Greece* 36°23N 25°27E **99** E7
Thirasia *Greece* 36°26N 25°21E **99** E7
Third Cataract *Sudan* 19°42N 30°37E **137** D3
Thirsk *U.K.* 54°14N 1°19W **66** C6
Thiruvananthapuram
   India 8°41N 77°0E **127** K3
Thiruvarur *India* 10°46N 79°38E **127** J4
Thisted *Denmark* 56°58N 8°40E **63** H2
Thistle I. *Australia* 35°0S 136°8E **152** C2
Thithia = Cicia *Fiji* 17°45S 179°18W **154** a
Thitu I. *S. China Sea* 11°3N 114°17E **118** B4
Thiva *Greece* 38°19N 23°19E **98** C5
Thiviers *France* 45°25N 0°54E **72** C4
Thizy *France* 46°2N 4°18E **71** F11
Þjórsá → *Iceland* 63°47N 20°48W **60** D3
Thlewiaza → *Canada* 60°29N 94°40W **163** A10
Thmar Puok *Cambodia* 13°57N 103°4E **120** F4
Tho Chu, Dao *Vietnam* 9°20N 103°28E **121** H4
Tho Vinh *Vietnam* 19°16N 105°42E **120** C5
Thoa → *Canada* 60°31N 109°47W **163** A7
Thoen *Thailand* 17°43N 99°12E **120** D2
Thoeng *Thailand* 19°41N 100°12E **120** C3
Thohoyandou *S. Africa* 22°58S 30°29E **141** J6
Thomas, L. *Australia* 35°45S 98°45W **176** D5
Thomas, L. *Australia* 26°4S 137°58E **151** D2
Thomas Hubbard, C.
   Canada 82°0N 94°25W **161** A13
Thomaston *U.S.A.* 32°53N 84°20W **178** E3
Thomasville *Ala.,
   U.S.A.* 31°55N 87°44W **177** F11
Thomasville *Ga.,
   U.S.A.* 30°50N 83°59W **178** F3
Thomasville *N.C.,
   U.S.A.* 35°53N 80°5W **177** D14
Thompson *Canada* 55°48N 97°34W **163** B9
Thompson *U.S.A.* 41°52N 75°31W **175** E9
Thompson → *Canada* 50°15N 121°24W **162** C4
Thompson → *U.S.A.* 39°46N 93°37W **172** F7
Thompson Falls
   U.S.A. 47°36N 115°21W **168** C6
Thompson Pk. *U.S.A.* 41°0N 123°2W **168** F2
Thompson Sd. *N.Z.* 45°8S 166°46E **155** F1
Thompson Springs
   U.S.A. 38°58N 109°43W **168** G9
Thompsontown *U.S.A.* 40°33N 77°14W **174** F7
Thomson *U.S.A.* 33°28N 82°30W **178** E4
Thomson → *Australia* 25°11S 142°53E **150** C3
Thon Buri *Thailand* 13°43N 100°20E **120** F3
Thônes *France* 45°54N 6°18E **73** C10
Thong Yang *Thailand* 9°28N 99°56E **121** b
Thonon-les-Bains
   France 46°22N 6°29E **71** F13
Thoothukudi = Tuticorin
   India 8°50N 78°12E **127** K4
Þórisvatn *Iceland* 64°20N 18°55W **60** D4
Thornaby on Tees *U.K.* 54°33N 1°18W **66** C6
Thornbury *Canada* 44°34N 80°26W **174** B4

Thornbury *N.Z.* 46°17S 168°9E **155** G3
Thorne *U.K.* 53°37N 0°57W **66** D7
Thornton *Canada* 44°16N 79°43W **174** B5
Thornton *U.S.A.* 39°52N 104°58W **168** G11
Thorold *Canada* 43°7N 79°12W **174** C5
Þórshöfn *Iceland* 66°12N 15°20W **60** C6
Thouarcé *France* 47°17N 0°30W **70** E6
Thouars *France* 47°0N 0°15W **70** F6
Thouet → *France* 47°17N 0°6W **70** E6
Thouin, C. *Australia* 20°20S 118°10E **148** D2
Thousand Islands
  U.S.A. 44°20N 76°0W **175** B9
Thousand Oaks
  U.S.A. 34°10N 118°50W **171** L8
Thrace *Turkey* 41°0N 27°0E **97** F10
Thrace, Sea of *Greece* 40°30N 25°0E **97** F8
Thredbo *Australia* 36°31S 148°20E **153** D8
Three Forks *U.S.A.* 45°54N 111°33W **168** D8
Three Gorges Dam
  China 30°45N 111°15E **117** B8
Three Gorges Res. = Sanxia
  Shuiku *China* 30°3N 107°58E **116** B6
Three Hills *Canada* 51°43N 113°15W **162** C6
Three Hummock I.
  Australia 40°25S 144°55E **151** G3
Three Pagodas Pass
  Asia 15°20N 98°30E **120** E2
Three Points, C. *Ghana* 4°42N 2°6W **138** E4
Three Rivers *Calif.,*
  U.S.A. 36°26N 118°54W **170** J8
Three Rivers *Tex.,*
  U.S.A. 28°28N 98°11W **176** G5
Three Springs
  Australia 29°32S 115°45E **149** E2
Thrissur *India* 10°30N 76°18E **127** J3
Throssell, L. *Australia* 27°33S 124°10E **149** E3
Throssell Ra. *Australia* 22°3S 121°43E **148** D3
Thrushton △ *Australia* 27°47S 147°40E **151** D4
Thu Dau Mot *Vietnam* 10°58N 106°39E **121** G6
Thua → *Kenya* 1°31S 39°30E **142** C4
Thuamal Rampur *India* 19°23N 82°56E **126** E6
Thuan Hoa *Vietnam* 8°58N 105°30E **121** H5
Thubun Lakes *Canada* 61°30N 112°0W **163** A6
Thueyts *France* 44°41N 4°9E **73** D8
Thugga = Dougga
  Tunisia 36°25N 9°13E **136** A5
Thuin *Belgium* 50°20N 4°17E **69** D4
Thuir *France* 42°38N 2°45E **72** F6
Thule = Qaanaaq
  Greenland 77°30N 69°10W **57** B4
Thule Air Base = Uummannaq
  Greenland 77°33N 68°52W **57** B4
Thun *Switz.* 46°45N 7°38E **77** J3
Thunder B. *U.S.A.* 45°0N 83°20W **174** B1
Thunder Bay *Canada* 48°20N 89°15W **164** C2
Thunderbolt *U.S.A.* 32°3N 81°4W **178** C8
Thunersee *Switz.* 46°43N 7°39E **77** J3
Thung Salaeng Luang △
  Thailand 16°43N 100°50E **120** D3
Thung Song *Thailand* 8°10N 99°40E **121** H2
Thungyai △ *Thailand* 15°20N 98°55E **120** E2
Thunkar *Bhutan* 27°55N 91°0E **123** F17
Thuong Tra *Vietnam* 16°2N 107°42E **120** D6
Thur → *Switz.* 47°32N 9°10E **77** H5
Thurgau □ *Switz.* 47°34N 9°10E **77** H5
Thüringen □ *Germany* 51°0N 11°0E **76** D6
Thüringer Wald *Germany* 50°35N 11°0E **76** E6
Thuringowa △
  Australia 19°18S 146°43E **150** B4
Thurles *Ireland* 52°41N 7°49W **64** D4
Thurn P. *Austria* 47°20N 12°25E **78** D5
Thurrock □ *U.K.* 51°31N 0°23E **67** F8
Thursday I. *Australia* 10°30S 142°3E **150** A3
Thurso *Canada* 45°36N 75°15W **164** C4
Thurso *U.K.* 58°36N 3°32W **65** C5
Thurso → *U.K.* 58°36N 3°32W **65** C5
Thurston I. *Antarctica* 72°0S 100°0W **55** D16
Thury-Harcourt *France* 48°59N 0°30W **70** D6
Thutade L. *Canada* 57°0N 126°55W **162** B3
Thy *Denmark* 56°52N 8°25E **63** H2
Thy △ *Denmark* 56°55N 8°25E **63** H2
Thyborøn *Denmark* 56°42N 8°12E **63** H2
Thyolo *Malawi* 16°7S 35°5E **143** F4
Ti-n-Amzi → *Niger* 18°20N 4°32E **139** B5
Ti-n-Barraouene, O. →
  Africa 18°40N 4°5E **139** B5
Ti-n-Tanetfirt *Algeria* 24°49N 3°48E **136** D4
Ti-n-Zaouatene *Algeria* 19°55N 2°55E **139** B5
Ti-Tree *Australia* 22°5S 133°22E **150** C1
Tiadiaye *Senegal* 14°25N 16°40W **138** C1
Tiahuanaco *Bolivia* 16°33S 68°42W **188** D4
Tian Shan *Asia* 40°30N 76°0E **109** D9
Tianchang *China* 32°40N 119°0E **117** A12
Tiandeng *China* 23°6N 107°3E **116** F6
Tiandong *China* 23°36N 107°8E **116** F6
Tian'e *China* 25°1N 107°9E **116** E6
Tiangua *Brazil* 3°44S 40°59W **189** A2
Tianhe *China* 24°48N 108°40E **116** E7
Tianjin *China* 39°7N 117°12E **115** E9
Tianjin Shi □ *China* 39°8N 117°12E **115** E9
Tianjun *China* 38°0N 98°30E **110** D8
Tiankoura *Burkina Faso* 10°47N 3°17W **138** C4
Tianlin *China* 24°21N 106°12E **116** E6
Tianmen *China* 30°39N 113°9E **117** B9
Tianquan *China* 30°7N 102°43E **116** B4
Tianshifu *China* 41°17N 124°22E **115** D13
Tianshui *China* 34°32N 105°40E **114** G3
Tiantai *China* 29°10N 121°2E **117** C13
Tianya *China* 18°18N 109°20E **117** a
Tianyang *China* 23°42N 106°53E **116** F6
Tianyar *Indonesia* 8°12S 115°30E **119** J18
Tianzhen *China* 40°24N 114°5E **114** D8
Tianzhu *China* 26°54N 109°11E **116** D7
Tianzhuangtai *China* 40°43N 122°5E **115** D12
Tiarei *Tahiti* 17°32S 149°20W **155** b
Tiaret *Algeria* 35°20N 1°21E **136** A5
Tiaret □ *Algeria* 34°30N 1°30E **136** B4
Tiassalé *Ivory C.* 5°58N 4°57W **138** D4
Tibagi *Brazil* 24°30S 50°24W **191** A5
Tibagi → *Brazil* 22°47S 51°1W **191** A5
Tibastī, Sarīr *Libya* 22°50N 18°30E **135** D9
Tibati *Cameroon* 6°22N 12°30E **139** D7
Tiber = Tevere → *Italy* 41°44N 12°14E **93** G9
Tiber Res. *U.S.A.* 48°19N 111°6W **168** B8
Tiberias = Teverya
  Israel 32°47N 35°32E **130** C4
Tiberias, L. = Yam Kinneret
  Israel 32°45N 35°35E **130** C4
Tibesti *Chad* 21°0N 17°30E **135** D9
Tibet = Xizang Zizhiqu □
  China 32°0N 88°0E **110** E6

Tibet, Plateau of *Asia* 32°0N 86°0E **102** E10
Tibiri *Niger* 13°34N 7°4E **139** C6
Ţibleş, Vf. *Romania* 47°32N 24°15E **81** C9
Ţibleşului, Munţii
  Romania 47°38N 24°5E **81** C9
Tibni *Syria* 35°36N 39°50E **105** E8
Tibooburra *Australia* 29°26S 142°1E **151** D3
Tibrikot *Nepal* 29°3N 82°42E **125** E10
Tibro *Sweden* 58°28N 14°10E **63** F8
Tiburón, I. *Mexico* 29°0N 112°25W **180** B2
Tice *U.S.A.* 26°40N 81°49W **179** J8
Tîchît *Mauritania* 18°21N 9°29W **138** B3
Ticino □ *Switz.* 46°20N 8°45E **77** J4
Ticino → *Italy* 45°9N 9°14E **92** C6
Ticleni *Romania* 44°53N 23°24E **81** F8
Ticonderoga *U.S.A.* 43°51N 73°26W **175** C11
Ticul *Mexico* 20°24N 89°32W **181** C7
Tidaholm *Sweden* 58°12N 13°58E **63** F7
Tidan *Sweden* 58°34N 14°1E **63** F8
Tiddim *Burma* 23°28N 93°45E **123** H18
Tiden *India* 7°15N 93°33E **127** L4
Tidikelt *Algeria* 26°58N 1°30E **136** C4
Tidioute *U.S.A.* 41°41N 79°24W **174** E5
Tidjikja *Mauritania* 18°29N 11°35W **138** B2
Tidore *Indonesia* 0°40N 127°25E **119** D7
Tiébissou *Ivory C.* 7°9N 5°10W **138** D3
Tiefa *China* 42°28N 123°26E **115** C12
Tiegang Shuiku *China* 22°37N 113°53E **111** a
Tiel *Neths.* 51°53N 5°26E **69** C5
Tiel *Senegal* 14°55N 15°5W **138** C1
Tieli *China* 46°57N 128°3E **111** B14
Tieling *China* 42°20N 123°55E **115** C12
Tielt *Belgium* 51°0N 3°20E **69** C3
Tien Shan = Tian Shan
  Asia 40°30N 76°0E **109** D9
Tien-tsin = Tianjin
  China 39°7N 117°12E **115** E9
Tien Yen *Vietnam* 21°20N 107°24E **120** B6
T'ienching = Tianjin
  China 39°7N 117°12E **115** E9
Tienen *Belgium* 50°48N 4°57E **69** D4
Tiénigbé *Ivory C.* 8°11N 5°43W **138** D3
Tientsin = Tianjin
  China 39°7N 117°12E **115** E9
Tieri *Australia* 23°2S 148°21E **150** C4
Tierp *Sweden* 60°20N 17°30E **64** F8
Tierra Amarilla *Chile* 27°28S 70°18W **190** B1
Tierra Amarilla
  U.S.A. 36°42N 106°33W **169** H10
Tierra Colorada
  Mexico 17°11N 99°32W **181** D5
Tierra de Barros *Spain* 38°40N 6°30W **89** G4
Tierra de Campos *Spain* 42°10N 4°50W **88** C6
Tierra del Fuego □
  Argentina 54°0S 67°45W **192** D3
Tierra del Fuego, I. Grande de
  Argentina 54°0S 69°0W **192** D3
Tierra del Fuego △
  Argentina 54°50S 68°23W **192** D3
Tiétar → *Spain* 39°50N 6°1W **88** F4
Tieté → *Brazil* 20°40S 51°35W **191** A5
Tiffin *U.S.A.* 41°7N 83°11W **173** E13
Tiflèt *Morocco* 33°54N 6°20W **136** B2
Tifton *U.S.A.* 31°27N 83°31W **178** D6
Tifu *Indonesia* 3°39S 126°24E **119** E7
Tiga Res. *Nigeria* 11°35N 8°30E **139** C6
Tiger Leaping Gorge = Hutiao Xia
  China 27°13N 100°9E **116** D3
Tighina *Moldova* 46°50N 29°30E **81** D14
Tigil *Russia* 57°49N 158°40E **107** D16
Tigiria *India* 20°29N 85°31E **126** D7
Tignall *U.S.A.* 33°52N 82°44W **178** D7
Tignish *Canada* 46°58N 64°2W **165** C7
Tigre → *Peru* 4°30S 74°10W **188** A3
Tigre → *Venezuela* 9°20N 62°30W **186** B6
Tigris = Dijlah, Nahr →
  Asia 31°0N 47°25E **128** D5
Tiguentourine *Algeria* 27°52N 9°8E **136** C7
Tigyeni *Romania* 45°10N 24°31E **81** E9
Tigyaing *Burma* 23°45N 96°10E **123** H20
Tîh, Gebel el *Egypt* 29°32N 33°26E **137** F8
Tihāmah *Asia* 15°3N 41°55E **131** D3
Tihodaine, Erg de
  Algeria 25°15N 7°15E **136** C5
Tijara *India* 27°56N 76°31E **124** F7
Tijuana *Mexico* 32°32N 117°1W **171** N9
Tikal *Guatemala* 17°13N 89°24W **182** C2
Tikal △ *Guatemala* 17°23N 89°34W **182** C2
Tikamgarh *India* 24°44N 78°50E **125** G8
Tikaré *Burkina Faso* 13°15N 1°43W **139** C4
Tikchik Lakes *U.S.A.* 60°0N 159°0W **166** D8
Tikhoretsk *Russia* 45°56N 40°5E **87** H5
Tikhvin *Russia* 59°35N 33°30E **84** C7
Tikirarjuaq = Whale Cove
  Canada 62°10N 92°34W **163** A10
Tikkadouine, Adrar
  Algeria 24°28N 1°30E **136** D4
Tikmehdāsh *Iran* 37°16N 46°54E **105** D12
Tiko *Cameroon* 4°4N 9°20E **139** E6
Tikrīt *Iraq* 34°35N 43°37E **105** E10
Tiksi *Russia* 71°40N 128°45E **107** B13
Tilal 'al 'Alī *Jordan* 32°0N 35°52E **130** D4
Tilamuta *Indonesia* 0°32N 122°23E **119** D6
Tilburg *Neths.* 51°31N 5°6E **69** C5
Tilbury *Canada* 42°17N 82°23W **174** D2
Tilbury *U.K.* 51°27N 0°22E **67** F8
Tilcara *Argentina* 23°36S 65°23W **190** A2
Tilden *U.S.A.* 42°3N 97°50W **172** D5
Tilemsi, Vallée du *Mali* 17°42N 0°15E **139** B5
Tilhar *India* 28°0N 79°45E **125** F8
Tilia, O. → *Algeria* 27°32N 0°55E **136** C4
Tilichiki *Russia* 60°27N 166°5E **107** C17
Tililane *Algeria* 27°49N 0°6W **136** C4
Tilissos *Greece* 35°20N 25°1E **101** D7
Till → *U.K.* 55°41N 2°13W **66** B5
Tillabéri *Niger* 14°28N 1°28E **139** C5
Tillamook *U.S.A.* 45°27N 123°51W **168** D2
Tillanchong I. *India* 8°30N 93°37E **127** K1
Tillberga *Sweden* 59°40N 16°39E **62** E10
Tillia *Niger* 16°8N 4°47E **139** B5
Tillman *U.S.A.* 32°28N 81°6W **178** D8
Tillsonburg *Canada* 42°53N 80°44W **174** D4
Tillyeria *Cyprus* 35°6N 32°40E **101** D11
Tilos *Greece* 36°27N 27°27E **97** F8
Tilpa *Australia* 30°57S 144°24E **152** A6
Tilrhemt *Algeria* 33°9N 3°22E **136** B6
Tilt → *U.K.* 56°46N 3°51W **65** E5
Tilton *U.S.A.* 43°27N 71°36W **175** C13
Tiltonsville *U.S.A.* 40°10N 80°41W **174** F4

Tim *Denmark* 56°12N 8°19E **63** H2
Tima *Egypt* 26°54N 31°25E **137** B3
Timanfaya ○ *Canary Is.* 29°0N 13°46W **100** F6
Timaru *N.Z.* 44°23S 171°14E **155** E6
Timashevo *Russia* 53°22N 51°9E **86** D10
Timashevsk *Russia* 45°35N 39°0E **87** H4
Timau *Kenya* 0°4N 37°15E **142** B4
Timbaki *Greece* 35°4N 24°45E **101** D6
Timbaúba *Brazil* 7°31S 35°19W **189** B3
Timbedgha *Mauritania* 16°17N 8°16W **138** B3
Timber Creek
  Australia 15°40S 130°29E **148** C5
Timber Lake *U.S.A.* 45°26N 101°5W **172** C3
Timber Mt. *U.S.A.* 37°6N 116°28W **170** H10
Timbo *Guinea* 10°35N 11°50W **138** C2
Timbo *Liberia* 5°35N 9°45W **138** D2
Timboon *Australia* 38°30S 142°58E **152** E5
Timbué, Ponta *Mozam.* 18°47S 36°22E **143** F4
Timbuktu = Tombouctou
  Mali 16°50N 3°0W **138** B4
Timeïaoulne *Algeria* 20°27N 1°50E **139** A5
Timellouline *Algeria* 29°22N 8°55E **136** C5
Timétrin *Mali* 19°19N 0°34W **139** B4
Timétrine, Mts. *Mali* 19°25N 0°34W **139** B4
Timfi Oros *Greece* 39°59N 20°45E **98** B2
Timfristos, Oros *Greece* 38°57N 21°50E **98** C3
Timgad *Algeria* 35°29N 6°28E **136** A5
Timhadit *Morocco* 33°15N 5°4W **136** B4
Timi *Cyprus* 34°44N 32°31E **101** E11
Tîmia *Niger* 18°4N 8°40E **139** B6
Timika *Indonesia* 4°47S 136°32E **119** E9
Timimoun *Algeria* 29°14N 0°16E **136** C4
Timimoun, Sebkha de
  Algeria 28°50N 0°46E **136** C4
Timiris, Râs *Mauritania* 19°21N 16°30W **138** B1
Timiş = Tamiš → *Serbia* 44°51N 20°39E **80** F5
Timiş □ *Romania* 45°40N 21°30E **80** E6
Timiskaming, L. =
  Témiscamingue, L.
  Canada 47°10N 79°25W **164** C4
Timişoara *Romania* 45°43N 21°15E **80** E6
Timmersdala *Sweden* 58°32N 13°46E **63** F7
Timmins *Canada* 48°28N 81°25W **164** C3
Timmonsville *U.S.A.* 34°8N 79°57W **178** D10
Timok → *Serbia* 44°10N 22°40E **96** B6
Timoleague *Ireland* 51°39N 8°46W **64** E3
Timon *Brazil* 5°8S 42°52W **189** B2
Timor *Asia* 9°0S 125°0E **119** F7
Timor Leste = East Timor ■
  Asia 8°50S 126°0E **119** F7
Timor Sea *Ind. Oc.* 12°0S 127°0E **148** B4
Timrå *Sweden* 62°29N 17°18E **62** B11
Timucuan △ *U.S.A.* 30°28N 81°27W **178** E8
Tin Alkoum *Algeria* 24°42N 10°17E **136** D7
Tin Atanai *Algeria* 25°52N 1°37E **136** C4
Tin Can Bay *Australia* 25°56S 153°0E **151** D5
Tin Ethisane *Mali* 19°3N 0°52W **139** B4
Tin Gornai *Mali* 16°38N 0°38W **139** B4
Tin Mt. *U.S.A.* 36°50N 117°10W **170** J9
Tin Shui Wai *China* 22°28N 114°0E **111** a
Tina → *Thina →
  S. Africa 31°18S 29°13E **145** D4
Tina, Khalîg el *Egypt* 31°10N 32°40E **130** D1
Tinaca Pt. *Phil.* 5°30N 125°25E **119** C7
Tinajo *Canary Is.* 29°4N 13°42W **100** E6
Tinca *Romania* 46°46N 21°58E **80** D6
Tindal *Australia* 14°31S 132°22E **148** B5
Tindivanam *India* 12°15N 79°41E **127** H4
Tindouf *Algeria* 27°42N 8°10W **136** C3
Tindouf □ *Algeria* 27°25N 5°50W **136** C2
Tinée → *France* 43°55N 7°11E **73** E11
Tineo *Spain* 43°21N 6°27W **88** A4
Tinerhir *Morocco* 31°29N 5°31W **136** B2
Tinfouchi *Algeria* 28°52N 5°49W **136** C2
Tinfunque △ *Paraguay* 23°55S 60°17W **190** A3
Ting Jiang → *China* 25°0N 117°20E **117** D11
Tingi Mts. *S. Leone* 8°55N 10°47W **138** D2
Tingi Mts. *S. Leone* 8°55N 10°47W **138** D2
Tingley *Denmark* 54°57N 9°13E **63** K3
Tingo María *Peru* 9°10S 75°54W **188** B2
Tingrela *Ivory C.* 10°27N 6°25W **138** C3
Tingri *China* 28°34N 86°38E **110** F6
Tingsryd *Sweden* 56°31N 15°0E **63** H6
Tinh Bien *Vietnam* 10°36N 104°57E **121** G5
Tinharé, I. de *Brazil* 13°30S 38°58W **189** C3
Tinian *N. Marianas* 15°0N 145°38E **156** F6
Tinkisso → *Guinea* 11°21N 9°10W **138** C2
Tinnevelly = Tirunelveli
  India 8°45N 77°45E **127** K3
Tinogasta *Argentina* 28°5S 67°32W **190** B2
Tinos *Greece* 37°33N 25°8E **99** D7
Tiñoso, C. *Spain* 37°32N 1°6W **91** H3
Tinpahar *India* 24°59N 87°44E **125** G12
Tinta *Peru* 14°9S 71°20W **188** C3
Tintâne *Mauritania* 16°18N 10°10W **138** B2
Tintina *Argentina* 27°2S 62°45W **190** B3
Tintinara *Australia* 35°48S 140°2E **152** C4
Tintioulé *Guinea* 12°2N 9°12W **138** C2
Tinto → *Spain* 37°12N 6°55W **89** H4
Ti'zi N'Isli *Morocco* 32°28N 5°47W **136** B2
Tiobraid Árann = Tipperary
  Ireland 52°28N 8°10W **64** D3
Tioga *N. Dak., U.S.A.* 48°24N 102°56W **172** A2
Tioga *Pa., U.S.A.* 41°55N 77°8W **174** E7
Tioman, Pulau
  Malaysia 2°50N 104°10E **121** L5
Tione di Trento *Italy* 46°2N 10°43E **92** B7
Tionesta *U.S.A.* 41°30N 79°28W **174** E5
Tioulilne *Algeria* 27°1N 0°2W **136** C4
Tipasa *Algeria* 36°35N 2°25E **136** A6
Tipasa □ *Algeria* 36°35N 2°25E **136** A6
Tipperary *Ireland* 52°28N 8°10W **64** D3
Tipperary □ *Ireland* 52°37N 7°55W **64** D4
Tipton *Calif., U.S.A.* 36°4N 119°19W **170** J7
Tipton *Iowa, U.S.A.* 41°46N 91°8W **172** E8
Tipton *Mt., U.S.A.* 35°32N 114°12W **171** K12
Tiptonville *U.S.A.* 36°23N 89°29W **177** C10
Tiptur *India* 13°15N 76°26E **127** H3
Tiquina *Bolivia* 16°13S 68°50W **188** D4
Tiracambu, Serra do
  Brazil 3°15S 46°30W **189** A1
Tirahart, O. → *Algeria* 23°45S 3°10E **136** D4
Tīrān *Iran* 32°45N 51°8E **107** C6
Tīrān, Si. Arabia* 27°57N 34°32E **137** B3
Tiranë *Albania* 41°18N 19°49E **96** E3
Tiranë ✈ (TIA) *Albania* 41°57N 19°42E **96** E3
Tirano *Italy* 46°13N 10°10E **92** B7

Tirari Desert *Australia* 28°22S 138°7E **151** D2
Tiraspol *Moldova* 46°55N 29°35E **81** D14
Tiratimine *Algeria* 25°56N 3°37E **136** C4
Tirau *N.Z.* 37°58S 175°46E **154** D4
Tirdout *Mali* 16°7N 1°5W **139** B4
Tire *Turkey* 38°5N 27°45E **99** C9
Tirebolu *Turkey* 40°58N 38°45E **105** B8
Tiree *U.K.* 56°31N 6°55W **65** E2
Tiree, Passage of *U.K.* 56°30N 6°30W **65** E2
Tîrgovişte = Târgovişte
  Romania 44°55N 25°27E **81** F10
Tîrgu Jiu = Târgu Jiu
  Romania 45°5N 23°19E **81** E8
Tîrgu Mureş = Târgu Mureş
  Romania 46°31N 24°38E **81** D9
Tirich Mir *Pakistan* 36°15N 71°55E **109** E8
Tiriolo *Italy* 38°57N 16°30E **95** D9
Tiris Zemmour □
  Mali 21°0N 8°40W **138** C3
Tirititri o te Moana = Southern
  Alps *N.Z.* 43°41S 170°11E **155** D5
Tirna → *India* 18°4N 76°57E **126** E3
Tirnavos *Greece* 39°45N 22°18E **98** B4
Tirodi *India* 21°40N 79°44E **126** D4
Tirol □ *Austria* 47°3N 10°43E **78** D3
Tiros *Brazil* 19°0S 45°58W **189** D1
Tirrukkovil *Sri Lanka* 7°7N 81°51E **127** L5
Tirschenreuth *Germany* 49°53N 12°19E **77** F8
Tirso → *Italy* 39°53N 8°32E **94** C1
Tirstrup *Denmark* 56°18N 10°42E **63** H4
Tirtagangga *Indonesia* 8°24S 115°35E **119** J18
Tirthahalli *India* 13°42N 75°14E **127** H2
Tirua Pt. *N.Z.* 38°25S 174°40E **154** E3
Tiruchchendur *India* 8°30N 78°11E **127** K4
Tiruchchirappalli *India* 10°45N 78°45E **127** J4
Tirukkoyilur *India* 11°57N 79°12E **127** J4
Tirumangalam *India* 9°49N 77°58E **127** K3
Tirumayam *India* 10°14N 78°45E **127** J4
Tirunelveli *India* 8°45N 77°45E **127** K3
Tirupati *India* 13°39N 79°25E **127** H4
Tiruppattur *Tamil Nadu,*
  India 12°30N 78°30E **127** H4
Tiruppattur *Tamil Nadu,*
  India 9°8N 78°37E **127** J4
Tiruppur *India* 11°5N 77°22E **127** J3
Tirur *India* 10°54N 75°55E **127** J2
Tiruttani *India* 13°11N 79°58E **127** H4
Tirutturaippundi *India* 10°32N 79°41E **127** J4
Tiruvadaimarudur *India* 11°2N 79°27E **127** J4
Tiruvalla *India* 9°23N 76°34E **127** K3
Tiruvallar *India* 13°9N 79°57E **127** H4
Tiruvannamalai *India* 12°15N 79°5E **127** H4
Tiruvettipuram *India* 12°39N 79°33E **127** H4
Tiruvottiyur *India* 13°15N 80°22E **127** H5
Tisa → *Serbia* 45°15N 20°17E **80** E5
Tisa → *Serbia* 45°15N 20°17E **80** E5
Tisdale *Canada* 52°50N 104°0W **163** C8
Tishomingo *U.S.A.* 34°14N 96°41W **176** D6
Tisjön *Sweden* 60°56N 13°0E **62** D7
Tisnaren *Sweden* 58°58N 15°58E **63** F9
Tišnov *Czech Rep.* 49°21N 16°25E **79** B9
Tisovec *Slovak Rep.* 48°41N 19°56E **79** C12
Tissamaharama
  Sri Lanka 6°17N 81°17E **127** L5
Tissemsilt *Algeria* 35°35N 1°50E **136** A4
Tissemsilt □ *Algeria* 35°45N 1°45E **136** A4
Tissint *Morocco* 29°57N 7°16W **136** C2
Tisza = Tisa → *Serbia* 45°15N 20°17E **80** E5
Tiszaföldvár *Hungary* 46°58N 20°14E **80** D5
Tiszafüred *Hungary* 47°38N 20°50E **80** C5
Tiszakécske *Hungary* 46°55N 19°54E **80** D5
Tiszalök *Hungary* 48°1N 21°20E **80** B6
Tiszavasvári *Hungary* 47°58N 21°18E **80** C6
Tit *Ahaggar, Algeria* 23°0N 5°10E **136** D5
Tit *Tademait, Algeria* 27°0N 1°29E **136** C4
Tit-Ary *Russia* 71°55N 127°2E **107** B13
Titaguas *Spain* 39°53N 1°6W **90** F3
Titao *Burkina Faso* 13°45N 2°5W **139** C4
Titel *Serbia* 45°10N 20°18E **80** E5
Tithwal *Pakistan* 34°21N 73°50E **125** B5
Titicaca, L. *S. Amer.* 15°30S 69°30W **188** D4
Titisee *Germany* 47°54N 8°10E **77** H4
Tititira Hd. *N.Z.* 43°35S 169°25E **155** D4
Titiwa *Nigeria* 12°14N 12°53E **139** C8
Titograd = Podgorica
  Montenegro 42°30N 19°19E **96** C3
Titov Veles *Macedonia* 41°46N 21°47E **96** D5
Titova Korenica
  Croatia 44°45N 15°41E **93** D12
Titu *Romania* 44°39N 25°32E **81** F10
Titule
  Dem. Rep. of the Congo 3°15N 25°31E **142** B2
Titusville *Fla., U.S.A.* 28°37N 80°49W **179** G9
Titusville *Pa., U.S.A.* 41°38N 79°41W **174** E5
Tivaouane *Senegal* 14°56N 16°45W **138** C1
Tivat *Montenegro* 42°28N 18°43E **96** D2
Tivedens △ *Sweden* 58°45N 14°35E **63** F8
Tiverton *Canada* 44°16N 81°32W **174** B3
Tiverton *U.K.* 50°54N 3°29W **67** G4
Tívoli *Italy* 41°58N 12°45E **93** G9
Tiwanaku = Tiahuanaco
  Bolivia 16°33S 68°42W **188** D4
Tiwi ○ *Australia* 11°33S 130°42E **148** B5
Tizga *Morocco* 32°1N 5°9W **136** B2
Ti'zi N'Isli *Morocco* 32°28N 5°47W **136** B2
Tizi-Ouzou *Algeria* 36°42N 4°3E **136** A6
Tizi-Ouzou □ *Algeria* 36°35N 4°5E **136** A6
Tizimín *Mexico* 21°9N 88°9W **181** C7
Tiznap He → *China* 38°21N 77°26E **109** E9
Tiznit *Morocco* 29°48N 9°45W **136** C2
Tjæreborg *Denmark* 55°28N 8°36E **63** J2
Tjällmo *Sweden* 58°43N 15°21E **63** F9
Tjeggelvas *Sweden* 66°37N 17°45E **60** C17
Tjeggelvas = Tjeggelvas
  Sweden 66°37N 17°45E **60** C17
Tjirebon = Cirebon
  Indonesia 6°45S 108°32E **118** F3
Tjörn *Sweden* 58°0N 11°35E **63** F5
Tjukayirla Roadhouse
  Australia 27°9S 124°34E **149** E3
Tjurabalan ○ *Australia* 20°32N 127°16E **148** C4
Tkibuli = Tqibuli *Georgia* 42°26N 43°0E **87** A7
Tkvarcheli = Tqvarcheli
  Georgia 42°47N 41°42E **87** A5
Tlacotalpan *Mexico* 18°37N 95°40W **181** D5
Tlahualilo de Zaragoza
  Mexico 26°7N 103°27W **180** B4
Tlaquepaque *Mexico* 20°39N 103°19W **180** C4
Tlaxcala *Mexico* 19°18N 98°14W **181** D5
Tlaxcala □ *Mexico* 19°30N 98°20W **181** D5
Tlaxiaco *Mexico* 17°25N 97°35W **181** D5

Tlemcen *Algeria* 34°52N 1°21W **136** B3
Tlemcen □ *Algeria* 34°38N 1°30W **136** B3
Tleta Sidi Bouguedra
  Morocco 32°16N 9°59W **136** B2
Tlokweng *Botswana* 24°40S 25°58E **144** B4
Tlumach *Ukraine* 48°51N 25°0E **81** B10
Tłuszcz *Poland* 52°25N 21°25E **83** F8
Tlyarata *Russia* 42°9N 46°26E **87** J8
Toad → *Canada* 59°25N 124°57W **162** B4
Toad River *Canada* 58°51N 125°14W **162** B3
Toaca, Montes de *Spain* 39°33N 4°20E **48** c
Toay *Argentina* 36°43S 64°38W **190** D3
Toba *China* 31°19N 97°42E **116** B1
Toba *Japan* 34°30N 136°51E **113** G8
Toba, Danau *Indonesia* 2°30N 98°30E **118** D1
Toba Kakar *Pakistan* 31°30N 69°0E **124** D3
Toba Tek Singh
  Pakistan 30°55N 72°25E **124** D5
Tobago *Trin. & Tob.* 11°10N 60°30W **183** D7
Tobarra *Spain* 38°37N 1°44W **91** G3
Tobelo *Indonesia* 1°45N 127°56E **119** D7
Tobercurry *Ireland* 54°3N 8°44W **64** B3
Tobermory *Canada* 45°12N 81°40W **174** A3
Tobermory *U.K.* 56°38N 6°5W **65** E2
Tobi *Palau* 2°40N 131°10E **119** D8
Tobi-Shima *Japan* 41°12N 139°34E **112** D9
Tobin, L. *Australia* 21°45S 125°49E **148** D4
Tobin, L. *Canada* 53°35N 103°30W **163** C8
Toblach = Dobbiaco
  Italy 46°44N 12°14E **93** B9
Tobol = Tobyl → *Russia* 58°10N 68°12E **106** D7
Tobol → *Russia* 58°10N 68°12E **106** D7
Toboli *Indonesia* 0°38S 120°5E **119** E6
Tobolsk *Russia* 58°15N 68°10E **106** D7
Tobor *Senegal* 12°40N 16°15W **138** C1
Tobruk = Tubruq
  Libya 32°7N 23°55E **135** B10
Tobyhanna *U.S.A.* 41°11N 75°25W **175** E9
Tobyl = Tobol →
  Russia 58°10N 68°12E **106** D7
Tobyl *Kazakhstan* 52°41N 62°34E **108** B6
Tocache Nuevo *Peru* 8°7N 76°26W **188** B2
Tocantínia *Brazil* 9°33S 48°22W **189** B3
Tocantinópolis *Brazil* 6°20S 47°25W **189** B1
Tocantins □ *Brazil* 10°0S 48°0W **187** F9
Tocantins → *Brazil* 1°45S 49°10W **187** D9
Toccoa *U.S.A.* 34°35N 83°19W **177** D13
Toce → *Italy* 45°56N 8°29E **92** C5
Tochi → *Pakistan* 32°49N 70°41E **124** C4
Tochigi *Japan* 36°25N 139°45E **113** F9
Tochigi □ *Japan* 36°45N 139°45E **113** F9
Tocina *Spain* 37°37N 5°44W **89** H5
Töcksfors *Sweden* 59°31N 11°52E **62** E5
Toco *Trin. & Tob.* 10°49N 60°57W **187** K16
Toconao *Chile* 23°11S 68°1W **190** A2
Tocopilla *Chile* 22°5S 70°10W **190** A1
Tocumwal *Australia* 35°51S 145°31E **153** C4
Tocuyo → *Venezuela* 11°3N 68°23W **186** A5
Todd → *Australia* 24°52S 135°48E **150** C2
Todeli *Indonesia* 1°40S 124°29E **119** E6
Todenyang *Kenya* 4°35N 35°56E **142** B4
Todgarh *India* 25°42N 73°58E **124** G5
Todi *Italy* 42°47N 12°24E **93** F9
Todos os Santos, B. de
  Brazil 12°48S 38°38W **189** C3
Todos Santos *Mexico* 23°26N 110°13W **180** C2
Todtnau *Germany* 47°49N 7°56E **77** H3
Toe Hd. *U.K.* 57°50N 7°8W **65** D1
Toecé *Burkina Faso* 11°50N 1°16W **139** C4
Toetoes B. *N.Z.* 46°42S 168°41E **155** G2
Tofield *Canada* 53°25N 112°40W **162** C6
Tofino *Canada* 49°11N 125°55W **162** D3
Tõfsingdalen △ *Sweden* 62°10N 12°28E **62** B6
Tõgane *Japan* 35°33N 140°22E **113** G10
Togba *Mauritania* 17°26N 10°12W **138** B2
Togian, Kepulauan
  Indonesia 0°20S 121°50E **119** E6
Togliatti *Russia* 53°32N 49°24E **86** D9
Togo ■ *W. Afr.* 8°30N 1°35E **139** D5
Tõgrõg *Mongolia* 47°25N 92°13E **109** C12
Togtoh *China* 40°15N 111°10E **114** D6
Tohma → *Turkey* 38°39N 38°23E **104** C8
Tõhõk △ *Japan* 35°50N 141°45E **112** E10
Tõhõku □ *Japan* 39°50N 141°45E **112** E10
Tohopekaliga, East L.
  U.S.A. 28°18N 81°15W **179** G8
Tohopekaliga, L.
  U.S.A. 28°12N 81°24W **179** G8
Toinya *South Sudan* 6°17N 29°46E **135** G11
Toiyabe Range *U.S.A.* 39°30N 117°0W **168** G5
Tojikiston = Tajikistan ■
  Asia 38°30N 70°0E **109** E8
Tõjõ *Japan* 34°53N 133°16E **113** G6
Tok *U.S.A.* 63°20N 142°59W **161** C11
Tokaanu *N.Z.* 38°58S 175°46E **154** E4
Tokachi-Dake *Japan* 43°17N 142°5E **112** C11
Tokachi-Gawa →
  Japan 42°44N 143°42E **112** C11
Tokaj *Hungary* 48°8N 21°27E **80** B6
Tokala *Indonesia* 1°30S 121°40E **119** E6
Tõkamachi *Japan* 37°8N 138°43E **113** E9
Tokanui *N.Z.* 46°34S 168°56E **155** G2
Tokar *Sudan* 18°27N 37°56E **137** D4
Tokara-Rettõ *Japan* 29°37N 129°43E **113** K4
Tokarahi *N.Z.* 44°56S 170°39E **155** E3
Tokashiki-Shima
  Japan 26°11N 127°21E **113** L3
Tokat *Turkey* 40°22N 36°35E **104** B7
Tokat □ *Turkey* 40°15N 36°30E **104** B7
Tokch'õn *N. Korea* 39°45N 126°18E **115** E14
Tokdo = Liancourt Rocks
  Asia 37°15N 131°52E **113** F5
Tokeland *U.S.A.* 46°42N 123°59W **170** D3
Tokelau Is. □ *Pac. Oc.* 9°0S 171°45W **156** H10
Tokmak *Kyrgyzstan* 42°49N 75°15E **108** C8
Tokmak *Ukraine* 47°16N 35°42E **85** J8
Toko Ra. *Australia* 23°5S 138°20E **150** C2
Tokoname *Japan* 34°53N 136°51E **113** G8
Tokoro-Gawa → *Japan* 44°7N 144°5E **112** B12
Tokoroa *N.Z.* 38°13S 175°56E **154** E4
Tokpijaja *Indonesia* 5°10N 95°20E **118** C1
Tokuno-Shima *Japan* 27°56N 128°55E **113** L3
Tokushima *Japan* 34°4N 134°34E **113** G7
Tokushima □ *Japan* 33°55N 134°0E **113** H7
Tokuyama = Shūnan
  Japan 34°3N 131°50E **113** G5

Tõkyõ *Japan* 35°43N 139°45E **113** —
Tolaga Bay *N.Z.* 38°21S 178°20E **154** —
Tolbo *Mongolia* 48°25N 90°17E **109** —
Tolbukhin = Dobrich
  Bulgaria 43°37N 27°49E **97** —
Tolchin Russia 54°30N 25°58E **144** —
Tôle Bī *Kazakhstan* 43°42N 73°46E **108** —
Toledo *Brazil* 24°44S 53°45W **191** —
Tlyarata *Russia* 42°9N 46°26E **87** —
Toledo *Spain* 39°50N 4°2W **89** —
Toledo *Ohio, U.S.A.* 41°39N 83°33W **173** —
Toledo *Oreg., U.S.A.* 44°37N 123°56W **168** —
Toledo *Wash., U.S.A.* 46°26N 122°51W **170** —
Toledo, Montes de *Spain* 39°33N 4°20W **49** —
Toledo Bend Res.
  U.S.A. 31°11N 93°34W **177** —
Tolentino *Italy* 43°12N 13°17E **93** —
Tolfa *Italy* 42°9N 11°57E **93** —
Tolga *Algeria* 34°40N 5°22E **136** —
Tolga *Australia* 17°15S 145°29E **150** —
Tolhuaca △ *Chile* 38°15S 71°50W **190** —
Toli *China* 45°57N 83°37E **109** —
Toliara *Madag.* 23°21S 43°40E **145** —
Tolima *Colombia* 4°40N 75°19W **186** —
Tolitoli *Indonesia* 1°5N 120°50E **119** —
Tolkmicko *Poland* 54°19N 19°31E **83** —
Tollarp *Sweden* 55°55N 13°58E **63** —
Tollensee *Germany* 53°30N 13°13E **76** —
Tollhouse *U.S.A.* 37°1N 119°24W **170** —
Tolmachevo *Russia* 58°56N 29°51E **84** —
Tolmezzo *Italy* 46°24N 13°1E **93** —
Tolmin *Slovenia* 46°11N 13°45E **93** —
Tolna *Hungary* 46°25N 18°48E **80** —
Tolna □ *Hungary* 46°30N 18°30E **80** —
Toloali *Indonesia* 3°0S 106°25E **118** E3
Tobol → *Russia* 58°10N 68°12E **106** —
Tolo Harbour *China* 22°27N 114°12E **111** —
Tolochin = Talachyn
  Belarus 54°25N 29°42E **84** —
Tolosa *Spain* 43°8N 2°5W **90** —
Tolox *Spain* 36°41N 4°54W **89** —
Toltén *Chile* 39°13S 74°14W **190** —
Toluca *Mexico* 19°17N 99°40W **181** —
Tolyatti = Togliatti
  Russia 53°32N 49°24E **86** —
Tom Burke *S. Africa* 23°5S 28°0E **145** —
Tom Price *Australia* 22°40S 117°48E **149** —
Toma *Burkina Faso* 12°45N 2°53W **139** —
Tomah *U.S.A.* 43°59N 90°30W **172** —
Tomahawk *U.S.A.* 45°28N 89°44W **172** —
Tomai *Moldova* 46°34N 28°19E **81** —
Tomakomai *Japan* 42°38N 141°36E **112** —
Tomales *U.S.A.* 38°15N 122°53W **170** —
Tomales B. *U.S.A.* 38°15N 123°58W **170** —
Tomanivi *Fiji* 17°37S 178°1E **155** —
Tomar *Portugal* 39°36N 8°25W **89** —
Tomaros, Oros *Greece* 39°29N 20°48E **98** —
Tomarza *Turkey* 38°27N 35°48E **104** —
Tomás Barrón *Bolivia* 17°35S 67°31W **188** —
Tomashpil *Ukraine* 48°32N 28°31E **81** —
Tomaszów Lubelski
  Poland 50°27N 23°25E **83** —
Tomaszów Mazowiecki
  Poland 51°30N 20°2E **83** —
Tomatlán *Mexico* 19°56N 105°15W **180** —
Tombadonkéa *Guinea* 11°0N 14°25W **138** —
Tombador, Serra do
  Brazil 12°0S 58°0W **187** —
Tombigbee → *U.S.A.* 31°8N 87°57W **177** —
Tombouctou *Mali* 16°50N 3°0W **138** —
Tombouctou □ *Mali* 16°50N 3°0W **138** —
Tombstone *U.S.A.* 31°43N 110°4W **169** —
Tombua *Angola* 15°55S 11°55E **144** —
Tomé *Chile* 36°36S 72°57W **190** —
Tome *Japan* 38°40N 141°20E **112** —
Tomelilla *Sweden* 55°33N 13°58E **63** —
Tomelloso *Spain* 39°10N 3°2W **91** —
Tomingley *Australia* 32°26S 148°16E **153** —
Tomini *Indonesia* 0°30N 120°30E **119** —
Tomini, Teluk *Indonesia* 0°10S 121°0E **119** —
Tominian *Mali* 13°17N 4°35W **138** —
Tomiño = O Seixo *Spain* 41°59N 8°46W **88** —
Tomintoul *U.K.* 57°15N 3°23W **65** —
Tomislavgrad *Bos.-H.* 43°42N 17°13E **95** —
Tomkinson Ranges
  Australia 26°11S 129°5E **149** —
Tommot *Russia* 59°4N 126°20E **107** —
Tomnop Ta Suos
  Cambodia 11°20N 104°15E **120** —
Tomo → *Colombia* 5°20N 67°48W **186** —
Toms Place *U.S.A.* 37°34N 118°41W **170** —
Toms River *U.S.A.* 39°58N 74°12W **175** —
Tomsk *Russia* 56°30N 85°5E **106** —
Tomtabacken *Sweden* 57°30N 14°30E **63** —
Tona *Spain* 41°51N 2°14E **90** —
Tonalá *Chiapas, Mexico* 16°4N 93°45W **181** —
Tonalá *Jalisco, Mexico* 20°37N 103°14W **180** —
Tonale, Passo del *Italy* 46°16N 10°35E **92** —
Tonantins *Brazil* 2°45S 67°45W **186** —
Tonasket *U.S.A.* 48°42N 119°26W **168** —
Tonawanda *U.S.A.* 43°1N 78°53W **174** —
Tonb *Iran* 26°15N 55°15E **131** —
Tonbridge *U.K.* 51°11N 0°17E **67** —
Tondano *Indonesia* 1°35N 124°54E **119** —
Tondela *Portugal* 40°31N 8°5W **88** —
Tønder *Denmark* 54°58N 8°50E **63** —
Tondi *India* 9°45N 79°4E **127** —
Tondi Kiwindi *Niger* 14°28N 2°2E **139** —
Tondibi *Mali* 16°39N 0°14W **139** —
Tondoro *Namibia* 17°45S 18°50E **144** —
Tone → *Australia* 34°25S 116°25E **149** —
Tone-Gawa → *Japan* 35°44N 140°51E **113** —
Tonekābon *Iran* 36°45N 51°12E **107** —
Tong Xian *China* 39°55N 116°35E **114** —
Tong-yeong *S. Korea* 34°50N 128°20E **115** —
Tonga ■ *Pac. Oc.* 19°50S 174°30W **147** —
Tonga Trench *Pac. Oc.* 18°0S 173°0W **146** —
Tongaat *S. Africa* 29°33S 31°9E **145** —
Tongala *Australia* 36°14S 144°56E **153** —
Tongareva = Penrhyn
  Cook Is. 9°0S 158°0W **157** —
Tongariro, Mt. *N.Z.* 39°7S 175°37E **154** —
Tongatapu Group
  Tonga 21°0S 175°0W **147** —
Tongcheng *Anhui,*
  China 31°4N 116°56E **117** —
Tongcheng *Hubei,*
  China 29°15N 113°50E **117** —
Tongchuan *China* 35°6N 109°3E **114** —

ngdao *China* 26°10N 109°42E 116 D7
ngeren *Belgium* 50°47N 5°28E 69 D5
nggu *China* 28°31N 114°20E 117 C10
nggu Jiao *China* 22°22N 113°37E 111 a
nghai *China* 34°40N 110°25E 114 G6
nghua *China* 24°10N 102°53E 116 E4
nghua *Heilongjiang,*
  China 47°40N 132°27E 111 B15
njiang *Heilongjiang,*
  China 47°40N 132°27E 111 B15
njiang *Sichuan,*
  China 31°58N 107°11E 116 B6
ngosŏn Man
  N. Korea 39°30N 128°0E 115 E15
nkling, G. of = Tonkin, G. of
  Asia 20°0N 108°0E 120 C7
ngliao *China* 29°50N 106°3E 116 C6
ngliao *China* 43°38N 122°18E 115 C12
nglu *China* 30°55N 117°48E 117 B11
nglu *China* 29°45N 119°73E 117 C12
ngnan = Anyue
  China 30°9N 105°50E 116 B5
ngoy *Chile* 30°16S 71°31W 190 C1
ngoy *Guizhou,*
  China 27°43N 109°11E 116 D7
ngren *Qinghai, China* 35°25N 102°5E 110 D9
ngres = Tongeren
  Belgium 50°47N 5°28E 69 D5
ngsa Dzong *Bhutan* 27°31N 90°31E 123 F17
ngshi *China* 18°30N 109°20E 117 a
ngue *China* 30°N 105°50E 116 B5
ngue *U.K.* 56°29N 4°25W 65 C4
ngue → *U.S.A.* 46°25N 105°52W 168 C11
ngwei *China* 35°0N 105°5E 114 G3
ngxiang *China* 30°39N 120°34E 117 B13
ngxin *China* 36°59N 105°58E 114 F3
ngyang *N. Korea* 39°9N 126°35E 115 E14
ngyu *China* 44°45N 123°4E 115 B12
ngzhou *China* 32°12N 121°2E 117 A13
ngzi *China* 28°9N 106°49E 116 C6
i *South Sudan* 7°20N 28°44E 135 G11
nk *India* 26°6N 75°54E 124 F6
nkawa *U.S.A.* 36°41N 97°18W 176 C6
nkin = Bac Phan
  Vietnam 22°0N 105°0E 116 G5
nkin, G. of *Asia* 20°0N 108°0E 120 C7
nlê Sap *Cambodia* 13°0N 104°0E 120 F5
nnay-Charente *France* 45°56N 0°55W 72 C3
nneins *France* 44°23N 0°19E 72 D4
nnerre *France* 47°51N 3°59E 71 E10
nning *Germany* 54°19N 8°56E 76 A4
nopah *U.S.A.* 39°19N 141°32E 112 E10
nopah *U.S.A.* 38°4N 117°14W 169 G5
nosi *Panama* 7°20N 80°20W 182 E3
ns → *Haryana, India* 29°30N 77°40E 124 D7
ns → *Ut. P., India* 26°1N 83°33E 125 F10
nsberg River *Russia* 59°19N 10°25E 64 G14
nsen *France* 47°46N 3°4E 71 E10
nya *Turkey* 40°53N 39°16E 105 B8
nzhou *China* 40°32N 118°1W 168 F7
mpine *Australia* 27°15S 144°19E 151 D3
msboro *U.S.A.* 32°50N 83°5W 178 C6
nra *Australia* 38°39S 146°23E 153 E7
nra-Khem *Russia* 52°28N 96°17E 110 A8
nwoomba *Australia* 27°32S 151°56E 151 D5
n Springs *Australia* 16°37S 131°51E 148 C5
nalu *Romania* 44°31N 28°3E 81 F13
naz *U.S.A.* 38°41N 119°30W 172 G7
neka *U.S.A.* 39°3N 95°40W 172 F6
nl'a → *Slovak Rep.* 48°45N 21°45E 79 C14
nley *Canada* 54°49N 126°18W 162 C3
nlica → *Serbia* 43°15N 21°49E 96 C5
niša *Romania* 46°55N 25°2E 81 D10
noitu *Bosnia* 34°10S 72°2W 190 C1
nock *U.S.A.* 36°46N 114°29W 171 L12
nola *Serbia* 44°17N 20°41E 96 B4
nol'čani *Macedonia* 41°14N 21°25E 96 E5
nol'čany *Slovak Rep.* 48°12N 18°12E 79 C11
nolnitsa → *Bulgaria* 42°11N 24°18E 97 D8
nolobampo *Mexico* 25°36N 109°3W 180 B3
noloveni *Romania* 44°49N 25°5E 81 F10
nolovgrad *Bulgaria* 42°5N 26°20E 97 C10
nolvătu Mare
  Romania 45°46N 21°41E 80 E6
nozero, Ozero *Russia* 65°35N 32°0E 60 D25
npenish *U.S.A.* 46°23N 120°19W 168 D3
npraisar *Romania* 44°1N 28°27E 81 F13
pusko *Croatia* 45°18N 15°59E 93 C12
nquepala *Peru* 17°24S 70°25W 188 D3
nyraŭyn →
  Kazakhstan 46°48N 75°24E 109 C9
rà *Spain* 41°49N 1°25E 90 D6
rata *Peru* 38°10N 27°21E 99 C9

Torneträsk *Sweden* 68°24N 19°15E 60 B18
Torngat Mountains Nat. Park △
  Canada 59°0N 63°40W 161 F19
Torngat Mts. *Canada* 59°0N 63°40W 161 F19
Tornio *Finland* 65°50N 24°12E 60 D21
Tornionjoki = Torneälven →
  Europe 65°50N 24°12E 60 D21
Tornquist *Argentina* 38°8S 62°15W 190 D3
Toro *Baleares, Spain* 39°59N 4°8E 100 B11
Toro *Zamora, Spain* 41°35N 5°24W 88 D5
Torö *Sweden* 58°48N 17°50E 63 F11
Toro, Cerro del *Chile* 29°10S 69°50W 190 B2
Toro → *Uganda* 1°5N 30°22E 142 C3
Toro Pk. *U.S.A.* 33°34N 116°24W 171 M10
Torödi *Niger* 13°7N 1°47E 139 C5
Törökszentmiklós
  Hungary 47°11N 20°27E 80 C5
Toronto *Australia* 33°0S 151°30E 153 B9
Toronto *Canada* 43°39N 79°20W 174 C5
Toronto *U.S.A.* 40°28N 80°36W 174 F4
Toronto Lester B. Pearson Int. ✈
  (YYZ) *Canada* 43°39N 79°35W 174 C5
Toropets *Russia* 56°30N 31°40E 84 D6
Tororo *Uganda* 0°45N 34°12E 142 B3
Toros Dağları *Turkey* 37°0N 32°30E 106 D5
Torpa *India* 22°57N 85°6E 125 H11
Torquay *Australia* 38°20S 144°19E 152 E6
Torquay *U.K.* 50°27N 3°32W 67 G4
Torquemada *Spain* 42°2N 4°19W 88 C6
Torrance *U.S.A.* 33°50N 118°20W 171 M8
Torrão *Portugal* 38°16N 8°11W 89 G2
Torre Annunziata *Italy* 40°45N 14°27E 95 B7
Torre de Moncorvo
  Portugal 41°12N 7°8W 88 D3
Torre del Campo *Spain* 37°46N 3°53W 89 H7
Torre del Greco *Italy* 40°47N 14°22E 95 B7
Torre del Mar *Spain* 36°44N 4°6W 89 J6
Torre-Pacheco *Spain* 37°44N 0°57W 91 H4
Torre Péllice *Italy* 44°49N 7°13E 92 D4
Torreblanca *Spain* 40°14N 0°12E 90 E5
Torrecampo *Spain* 38°29N 4°41W 89 G6
Torrecilla en Cameros
  Spain 42°15N 2°38W 90 C2
Torredembarra *Spain* 41°9N 1°24E 90 D6
Torredonjimeno *Spain* 37°46N 3°57W 89 H7
Torrejón de Ardoz *Spain* 40°27N 3°29W 88 E7
Torrejoncillo *Spain* 39°54N 6°28W 88 F4
Torrelaguna *Spain* 40°50N 3°38W 88 E7
Torrelavega *Spain* 43°20N 4°5W 88 B6
Torremaggiore *Italy* 41°41N 15°17E 93 G12
Torremolinos *Spain* 36°38N 4°30W 89 J6
Torrens, L. *Australia* 31°0S 137°50E 152 A2
Torrens Cr. →
  Australia 22°23S 145°9E 150 C4
Torrens Creek *Australia* 20°48S 145°3E 150 C4
Torrent *Spain* 39°27N 0°28W 91 F4
Torrenueva *Spain* 38°38N 3°22W 89 G7
Torreón *Mexico* 25°33N 103°26W 180 B4
Torreperogil *Spain* 38°2N 3°17W 89 G7
Torres *Brazil* 29°21S 49°44W 191 B5
Torres *Mexico* 28°46N 110°47W 180 B2
Torres del Paine △
  Chile 51°3S 72°58W 192 D2
Torres Novas *Portugal* 39°27N 8°33W 89 F2
Torres Strait *Australia* 9°50S 142°20E 150 a
Torres Vedras *Portugal* 39°5N 9°15W 89 F1
Torrevieja *Spain* 37°59N 0°42W 91 H4
Torrey *U.S.A.* 38°18N 111°25W 168 G8
Torridge → *U.K.* 51°0N 4°13W 67 G3
Torridon, L. *U.K.* 57°35N 5°50W 65 D3
Torrijos *Spain* 39°59N 4°18W 88 F6
Torring *Denmark* 55°52N 9°29E 63 J3
Torrington *Conn.,*
  U.S.A. 41°48N 73°7W 175 E11
Torrington *Wyo.,*
  U.S.A. 42°4N 104°11W 168 E11
Torroella de Montgrí *Spain* 42°2N 3°8E 90 C8
Torrox *Spain* 36°46N 3°57W 89 J7
Torsås *Sweden* 56°24N 16°0E 63 H7
Torsby *Sweden* 60°7N 13°0E 62 D6
Torshälla *Sweden* 59°25N 16°28E 62 E10
Tórshavn *Føroe Is.* 62°5N 6°56W 62 F9
Torslanda *Sweden* 57°44N 11°45E 63 G5
Torsö *Sweden* 58°48N 13°45E 63 F7
Tortola *Br. Virgin Is.* 18°19N 64°45W 183 e
Tórtoles de Esgueva *Spain* 41°49N 4°2W 88 D6
Tórtoli *Italy* 39°55N 9°39E 94 C2
Tortona *Italy* 44°54N 8°52E 92 D5
Tortorici *Italy* 38°2N 14°49E 95 D7
Tortosa *Spain* 40°49N 0°31E 90 C5
Tortosa, C. *Spain* 40°41N 0°52E 90 C5
Tortosendo *Portugal* 40°15N 7°31W 88 E3
Tortue, Î. de la *Haiti* 20°5N 72°57W 183 B5
Tortuguero △
  Costa Rica 10°31N 83°29W 182 D3
Tortum *Turkey* 40°19N 41°35E 105 B9
Toröd *Iran* 35°25N 55°5E 129 C7
Torul *Turkey* 40°34N 39°18E 105 B8
Toruń *Poland* 53°2N 18°39E 83 E5
Torun *Ukraine* 48°40N 23°34E 81 B8
Tory Hill *Canada* 44°58N 78°16W 174 B6
Tory I. *Ireland* 55°16N 8°14W 64 A3
Torysa → *Slovak Rep.* 48°39N 21°21E 79 C14
Torzhok *Russia* 57°5N 34°55E 84 D8
Torzym *Poland* 52°19N 15°5E 83 F2
Tosa *Japan* 33°24N 133°23E 113 H6
Tosa-Shimizu *Japan* 32°52N 132°58E 113 H6
Tosa-Wan *Japan* 33°15N 133°30E 113 H6
Toscana □ *Italy* 43°25N 11°0E 92 E8
Toscano, Arcipelago
  Italy 42°30N 10°30E 92 F7
Toshka *Egypt* 22°30N 31°53E 137 D3
Toshka Lakes *Egypt* 22°50N 31°0E 137 C3
Toshkent *Uzbekistan* 41°20N 69°10E 108 E7
Toshkent □ *Uzbekistan* 41°0N 69°40E 108 D7
Tosno *Russia* 59°38N 30°46E 84 C6
Tossa de Mar *Spain* 41°43N 2°56E 90 D7
Tostado *Argentina* 29°15S 61°50W 190 B3
Tostedt *Germany* 53°17N 9°42E 76 B5
Tostón, Pta. de
  Canary Is. 28°42N 14°2W 100 F5
Tosu *Japan* 33°22N 130°31E 113 H5
Tosya *Turkey* 41°1N 34°2E 104 B6
Toszek *Poland* 50°27N 18°32E 83 E4
Totana *Spain* 37°45N 1°30W 91 H3
Totebo *Sweden* 57°44N 16°12E 63 G10
Toteng *Botswana* 20°22S 22°58E 144 B3
Tôtes *France* 49°41N 1°2E 70 C8
Tótkomlós *Hungary* 46°24N 20°45E 80 D5
Totma *Russia* 60°0N 42°40E 106 D5

Totnes *U.K.* 50°26N 3°42W 67 G4
Totness *Suriname* 5°53N 56°19W 187 B7
Toto *Nigeria* 8°26N 7°5E 139 D6
Totonicapán
  Guatemala 14°58N 91°12W 182 D1
Totoya, I. *Fiji* 18°57S 179°50W 154 a
Totten Glacier
  Antarctica 66°45S 116°10E 55 C8
Tottenham *Australia* 32°14S 147°21E 153 B7
Tottenham *Canada* 44°1N 79°49W 174 B5
Tottori *Japan* 35°30N 134°15E 113 G7
Tottori □ *Japan* 35°30N 134°12E 113 G7
Touáret *Niger* 20°17N 7°8E 139 A6
Touat *Algeria* 27°27N 0°30E 136 C4
Touba *Ivory C.* 8°22N 7°40W 138 D3
Touba *Senegal* 14°50N 15°55W 138 C1
Toubkal, Djebel *Morocco* 31°0N 8°0W 136 B2
Toubkal △ *Morocco* 31°0N 8°0W 136 B2
Toucy *France* 47°44N 3°15E 71 E10
Tougan *Burkina Faso* 13°11N 2°58W 138 C4
Touggourt *Algeria* 33°6N 6°4E 136 B5
Tougouri *Burkina Faso* 13°20N 0°30W 139 C4
Tougué *Guinea* 11°25N 11°50W 138 C2
Toukoto *Mali* 13°27N 9°52W 138 C3
Toul *France* 48°40N 5°53E 71 D12
Toulepleu *Ivory C.* 6°32N 8°24W 138 D3
Touliu *Taiwan* 23°42N 120°31E 117 F13
Toulon *France* 43°10N 5°55E 73 E9
Toulouse *France* 43°37N 1°27E 72 E5
Toulouse Blagnac ✈ (TLS)
  France 43°37N 1°22E 72 E5
Toummo *Niger* 22°45N 14°8E 135 D8
Toumodi *Ivory C.* 6°32N 5°4W 138 D3
Tounan *Taiwan* 23°41N 120°28E 117 F13
Tounassine, Hamada
  Algeria 28°48N 5°0W 136 C3
Toungoo *Burma* 19°0N 96°30E 123 K20
Toungo *Nigeria* 8°2N 12°3E 139 D7
Touques → *France* 49°22N 0°8E 70 C7
Touraine *France* 47°20N 0°30E 70 E7
Touran = Tūrān △
  Iran 35°45N 56°30E 129 C8
Tourcoing *France* 50°42N 3°10E 70 B6
Touriñán, C. *Spain* 43°3N 9°18W 88 B1
Tournai *Belgium* 50°35N 3°25E 69 D3
Tournan-en-Brie *France* 48°44N 2°46E 71 D9
Tournay *France* 43°13N 0°13E 72 E4
Tournon-St-Martin
  France 46°45N 0°58E 70 F7
Tournon-sur-Rhône
  France 45°4N 4°50E 73 C8
Tournus *France* 46°35N 4°54E 71 F11
Touros *Brazil* 5°12S 35°28W 189 B3
Tours *France* 47°22N 0°40E 70 E7
Toussoro, Mt. *C.A.R.* 9°7N 23°14E 140 C4
Touws → *S. Africa* 33°45S 21°11E 144 D3
Touwsrivier *S. Africa* 33°20S 20°2E 144 D3
Tovarkovskiy *Russia* 53°40N 38°14E 84 F10
Tovste *Ukraine* 48°50N 25°44E 81 B10
Tovuz *Azerbaijan* 41°0N 45°40E 87 K7
Towada *Japan* 40°37N 141°13E 112 D10
Towada-Hachimantai △
  Japan 40°20N 140°55E 112 D10
Towada-Ko *Japan* 40°28N 140°55E 112 D10
Towanda *U.S.A.* 41°46N 76°27W 175 E8
Towarri △ *Australia* 31°50S 150°37E 153 A9
Tower *U.S.A.* 47°48N 92°17W 172 B7
Towerhill Cr. →
  Australia 22°28S 144°35E 150 C3
Towner *U.S.A.* 48°21N 100°25W 172 A3
Townsend *U.S.A.* 33°33N 81°31W 178 D8
Townsend *Mont.,*
  U.S.A. 46°19N 111°31W 168 C8
Townshend I.
  Australia 22°10S 150°31E 150 C5
Townsville *Australia* 19°15S 146°45E 150 B4
Towot *South Sudan* 6°12N 34°25E 142 A3
Towraghondī *Afghan.* 35°13N 62°16E 108 E6
Towson *U.S.A.* 39°24N 76°36W 173 F15
Towuti, Danau
  Indonesia 2°45S 121°32E 119 E6
Toxkan Ne → *China* 41°8N 80°11E 109 D10
Tōya-Ko *Japan* 42°35N 140°51E 112 C10
Toyama *Japan* 36°40N 137°15E 113 F8
Toyama □ *Japan* 36°45N 137°30E 113 F8
Toyama-Wan *Japan* 37°0N 137°30E 113 F8
Toyapakeh *Indonesia* 8°41S 115°29E 119 K18
Toyohashi *Japan* 34°45N 137°25E 113 G8
Toyokawa *Japan* 34°48N 137°27E 113 G8
Toyonaka *Japan* 34°46N 135°28E 113 G7
Toyooka *Japan* 35°35N 134°48E 113 G7
Toyota *Japan* 35°3N 137°7E 113 G8
Tozeur *Tunisia* 33°56N 8°8E 136 B5
Tozeur *Tunisia* 34°0N 8°0E 136 B5
Tqibuli *Georgia* 42°26N 43°0E 87 J6
Tqvarcheli *Georgia* 42°47N 41°42E 87 J5
Trá Lí = Tralee *Ireland* 52°16N 9°42W 64 D2
Trá Mhór = Tramore
  Ireland 52°10N 7°10W 64 D4
Tra On *Vietnam* 9°58N 105°55E 121 H5
Tra Vinh *Vietnam* 9°50N 106°15E 121 H6
Trabancos → *Spain* 41°36N 5°15W 88 D5
Traben-Trarbach *Germany* 49°57N 7°7E 77 F3
Trabzon *Turkey* 41°0N 39°45E 105 B8
Trabzon □ *Turkey* 41°0N 39°45E 105 B8
Tracadie *Canada* 47°30N 64°55W 165 C7
Tracy *Canada* 46°1N 73°9W 164 C5
Tracy *Calif., U.S.A.* 37°44N 121°26W 170 H5
Tracy *Minn., U.S.A.* 44°14N 95°37W 172 C6
Tradate *Italy* 45°43N 8°54E 92 C5
Trade Town *Liberia* 5°40N 9°50W 138 D3
Trafalgar *Australia* 38°14S 146°12E 153 E7
Trafalgar, C. *Spain* 36°10N 6°2W 89 J4
Tragonisi *Greece* 37°30N 25°20E 99 D11
Traian *Brăila, Romania* 45°11N 27°44E 81 E12
Traian *Tulcea, Romania* 45°2N 28°42E 81 E13
Traiguén *Chile* 38°15S 72°41W 192 A2
Trail *Canada* 49°5N 117°40W 163 F9
Traill Ø *Greenland* 72°30N 23°0W 57 C8
Trainor L. *Canada* 60°24N 120°17W 162 A4
Trakai *Lithuania* 54°30N 25°1E 61 J21
Trákhonas *Cyprus* 35°12N 33°21E 101 D12
Tralee *Ireland* 52°16N 9°42W 64 D2
Tralee B. *Ireland* 52°17N 9°55W 64 D2
Tram Chim △ *Vietnam* 10°43N 105°31E 121 G5
Tramore *Ireland* 52°10N 7°10W 64 D4
Tramore B. *Ireland* 52°9N 7°10W 64 D4
Tramuntana, Serra de
  Spain 39°48N 2°54E 100 B9
Tran Ninh, Cao Nguyen
  Laos 19°30N 103°10E 120 C4

Tranås *Sweden* 58°3N 14°59E 63 F8
Tranbjerg *Denmark* 56°6N 10°9E 63 H4
Trancas *Argentina* 26°11S 65°20W 190 B2
Trancoso *Portugal* 40°49N 7°21W 88 E3
Tranebjerg *Denmark* 55°51N 10°36E 63 J4
Tranemo *Sweden* 57°30N 13°20E 63 G7
Trang *Thailand* 7°33N 99°38E 121 J2
Trangan *Indonesia* 6°40S 134°20E 119 F8
Trangie *Australia* 32°4S 148°0E 153 B8
Trångsviken *Sweden* 63°19N 13°59E 62 A7
Trani *Italy* 41°17N 16°25E 95 A9
Tranoroa *Madag.* 24°42S 45°4E 141 J9
Tranqueras *Uruguay* 31°13S 55°45W 191 C4
Transantarctic Mts.
  Antarctica 85°0S 170°0W 55 E12
Transcarpathia = Zakarpattya □
  Ukraine 48°30N 23°20E 81 B8
Transilvania *Romania* 46°30N 24°0E 81 D9
Transilvanian Alps = Carpații
  Meridionali *Romania* 45°30N 25°0E 81 E9
Transnistria = Stînga Nistrului □
  Moldova 47°20N 29°15E 81 C14
Transtrand *Sweden* 61°6N 13°20E 62 C7
Transtrandsfjällen *Sweden* 61°8N 13°0E 62 C6
Transylvania = Transilvania
  Romania 46°30N 24°0E 81 D9
Trápani *Italy* 38°1N 12°29E 94 D5
Trapper Pk. *U.S.A.* 45°54N 114°18W 168 D6
Traralgon *Australia* 38°12S 146°34E 153 E7
Traryd *Sweden* 56°35N 13°45E 63 H7
Trarza □ *Mauritania* 18°0N 15°0W 138 B2
Trasacco *Italy* 41°57N 13°32E 93 G10
Trăscău, Munţii
  Romania 46°14N 23°14E 81 D8
Trasimeno, L. *Italy* 43°8N 12°6E 93 E9
Träslövsläge *Sweden* 57°4N 12°16E 63 G6
Trasvase Tajo-Segura, Canal de
  Spain 40°15N 2°55W 90 E2
Trat *Thailand* 12°14N 102°33E 121 F4
Tratani → *Pakistan* 29°19N 68°20E 124 E3
Traun *Austria* 48°14N 14°15E 78 C7
Traun → *Austria* 48°9N 14°15E 78 C7
Traunreut *Germany* 47°57N 12°36E 77 H8
Traunsee *Austria* 47°55N 13°50E 78 D6
Traunstein *Germany* 47°52N 12°37E 77 H8
Travellers L. *Australia* 33°20S 142°0E 152 B5
Travemünde *Germany* 53°57N 10°52E 76 B6
Travers, Mt. *N.Z.* 42°1S 172°45E 155 C7
Traverse City *U.S.A.* 44°46N 85°38W 173 C11
Travis, L. *U.S.A.* 30°24N 97°55W 176 F6
Travnik *Bos.-H.* 44°17N 17°39E 80 F2
Trawbreaga B. *Ireland* 55°20N 7°25W 64 A4
Trbovlje *Slovenia* 46°12N 15°5E 78 B5
Treasure Island *U.S.A.* 27°46N 82°46W 179 H7
Trébbia → *Italy* 45°4N 9°41E 92 C6
Trebel → *Germany* 53°54N 13°2E 76 B9
Trébeurden *France* 48°46N 3°35W 70 D3
Trebević △ *Bos.-H.* 43°49N 18°45E 80 G3
Trebević *Czech Rep.* 49°14N 15°55E 78 B8
Trebinje *Bos.-H.* 42°44N 18°22E 96 D2
Trebisacce *Italy* 39°52N 16°32E 95 C9
Trebišnica → *Bos.-H.* 42°47N 18°8E 96 D3
Trebišov *Slovak Rep.* 48°38N 21°41E 79 C14
Trebižat → *Bos.-H.* 43°15N 17°30E 93 E14
Trebnje *Slovenia* 45°54N 15°1E 93 C12
Trebon *Czech Rep.* 49°1N 14°48E 78 B7
Trebonne *Australia* 18°37S 146°5E 150 B4
Trebořov △ *Czech Rep.* 49°1N 14°49E 78 B7
Trebujena *Spain* 36°52N 6°11W 89 J4
Trecate *Italy* 45°26N 8°44E 92 C5
Trefaldwyn = Montgomery
  U.K. 52°34N 3°8W 67 E4
Trefynwy = Monmouth
  U.K. 51°48N 2°42W 67 F5
Tregaron *U.K.* 52°14N 3°56W 67 E4
Tregnago *Italy* 45°31N 11°10E 93 C8
Tregrosse Is. *Australia* 17°41S 150°43E 150 B5
Tréguier *France* 48°47N 3°16W 70 D3
Trégunc *France* 47°51N 3°51W 70 E3
Treherne *Canada* 49°38N 98°42W 163 D9
Tréia *Italy* 43°19N 13°19E 93 E10
Treignac *France* 45°32N 1°48E 72 C5
Treinta y Tres *Uruguay* 33°16S 54°17W 191 C5
Treis-karden *Germany* 50°10N 7°18E 77 E3
Treklyano *Bulgaria* 42°33N 22°36E 97 C9
Trelawney *Zimbabwe* 17°30S 30°30E 145 A5
Trélazé *France* 47°26N 0°30W 70 E6
Trelew *Argentina* 43°10S 65°20W 192 B3
Trélissac *France* 45°11N 0°47E 72 C4
Trelleborg *Sweden* 55°20N 13°10E 63 J7
Tremadog Bay *U.K.* 52°51N 4°18W 66 E3
Trémiti I. *Italy* 42°8N 15°30E 93 F12
Tremonton *U.S.A.* 41°43N 112°10W 168 F7
Tremp *Spain* 42°10N 0°52E 90 C6
Trenche → *Canada* 47°46N 72°53W 164 C5
Trenčiansky □
  Slovak Rep. 48°45N 18°20E 79 C11
Trenčín *Slovak Rep.* 48°52N 18°4E 79 C11
Trengganu □ *Malaysia* 8°3S 111°43E 119 H14
Trenque Lauquen
  Argentina 36°5S 62°45W 190 D3
Trent → *Canada* 44°6N 77°34W 174 B7
Trent → *U.K.* 53°41N 0°42W 66 D7
Trentino-Alto Adige □
  Italy 46°30N 11°20E 93 B8
Trento *Italy* 46°4N 11°8E 92 B8
Trenton *Canada* 44°10N 77°34W 174 B7
Trenton *Fla., U.S.A.* 29°37N 82°49W 179 F7
Trenton *Mo., U.S.A.* 40°5N 93°37W 172 E7
Trenton *N.J., U.S.A.* 40°14N 74°46W 175 F10
Trenton *Nebr., U.S.A.* 40°11N 101°1W 172 E3
Trenton *S.C., U.S.A.* 33°45N 81°51W 178 D8
Trepassey *Canada* 46°43N 53°25W 165 C9
Trepuzzi *Italy* 40°24N 18°4E 95 B11
Tres Arroyos *Argentina* 38°26S 60°20W 190 D3
Três Corações *Brazil* 21°44S 45°15W 191 A6
Três Lagos *Argentina* 49°35S 71°35W 192 C2
Tres Lomas *Argentina* 36°27S 62°51W 190 D3
Três Marias, Represa
  Brazil 18°12S 45°15W 189 D1
Tres Montes, C. *Chile* 46°28N 44°15E 87 G7
Tres Pinos *U.S.A.* 36°48N 121°19W 170 H5
Três Pontas *Brazil* 21°23S 45°29W 191 A6
Tres Puentes *Chile* 27°50S 70°15W 190 B1
Tres Puntas, C. *Argentina* 47°0S 66°0W 192 C3
Três Rios *Brazil* 22°6S 43°15W 191 A7
Tres Valles *Mexico* 18°15N 96°8W 181 D5
Tresco *U.K.* 49°57N 6°20W 67 H1
Treska → *Macedonia* 42°0N 21°20E 96 D5
Treskavica *Bos.-H.* 43°40N 18°20E 80 G3
Trespaderne *Spain* 42°47N 3°24W 88 C7

Tresticklan △ *Sweden* 59°0N 11°42E 63 F5
Trets *France* 43°27N 5°41E 73 E9
Treuchtlingen *Germany* 52°5N 10°54E 77 G6
Treuenbrietzen *Germany* 52°5N 12°52E 76 C8
Trevi *Italy* 42°52N 12°45E 93 F9
Treviglio *Italy* 45°31N 9°35E 92 C6
Trevínca, Peña *Spain* 42°15N 6°46W 88 C4
Treviño *Spain* 42°44N 2°45W 88 C7
Treviso *Italy* 45°40N 12°15E 93 C9
Trévoux *France* 45°57N 4°47E 73 C8
Triabunna *Australia* 42°30S 147°55E 151 G4
Triangle *Zimbabwe* 21°2S 31°28E 145 B5
Triaucourt-en-Argonne
  France 48°59N 5°2E 71 D12
Tribal Areas □ *Pakistan* 33°0N 70°0E 124 C4
Tribsees *Germany* 54°5N 12°44E 76 A8
Tribulation, C. *Australia* 16°5S 145°29E 150 B4
Tribune *U.S.A.* 38°28N 101°45W 172 F3
Tricárico *Italy* 40°37N 16°9E 95 B9
Trichinopoly = Tiruchchirappalli
  India 10°45N 78°45E 127 J4
Trichonida, L. *Greece* 38°34N 21°30E 98 C3
Trichur = Thrissur
  India 10°30N 76°18E 127 J3
Trichy = Tiruchchirappalli
  India 10°45N 78°45E 127 J4
Trida *Australia* 33°1S 145°1E 153 B6
Trier *Germany* 49°45N 6°38E 77 F2
Trieste *Italy* 45°40N 13°46E 93 C10
Trieste, G. di *Italy* 45°40N 13°35E 93 C10
Trieux → *France* 48°43N 3°9W 70 D3
Triggiano *Italy* 41°4N 16°55E 95 A9
Triglav *Slovenia* 46°21N 13°50E 93 B10
Triglavski △ *Slovenia* 46°20N 13°50E 93 B10
Trigno → *Italy* 42°4N 14°48E 93 F11
Trigueros *Spain* 37°24N 6°50W 89 H4
Trikala *Greece* 39°34N 21°47E 98 B3
Trikeri *Greece* 39°6N 23°5E 98 B5
Trikomo *Cyprus* 35°17N 33°52E 101 D12
Trikora, Puncak
  Indonesia 4°15S 138°45E 119 E9
Trilby *U.S.A.* 28°28N 82°12W 179 G7
Trilj *Croatia* 43°38N 16°42E 93 E13
Trillo *Spain* 40°42N 2°35W 90 E2
Trim *Ireland* 53°33N 6°48W 64 C5
Trimbak *India* 19°56N 73°33E 126 E1
Trimmu Dam *Pakistan* 31°10N 72°8E 124 D5
Trincomalee *Sri Lanka* 8°38N 81°15E 127 K5
Trindade *Brazil* 16°40S 49°30W 187 E9
Trindade *Atl. Oc.* 20°20S 29°50W 56 J9
Trinidad *Bolivia* 14°46S 64°50W 188 F6
Trinidad *Cuba* 21°48N 80°0W 182 B4
Trinidad *Trin. & Tob.* 10°30N 61°15W 183 D7
Trinidad *Uruguay* 33°30S 56°50W 191 C4
Trinidad *U.S.A.* 37°10N 104°31W 169 H11
Trinidad, G. *Chile* 49°55S 75°25W 192 D1
Trinidad, I. *Argentina* 39°10S 62°0W 192 A4
Trinidad & Tobago ■
  W. Indies 10°30N 61°20W 186 A6
Trinitápoli *Italy* 41°21N 16°5E 95 A9
Trinity *Canada* 48°59N 53°55W 165 C9
Trinity *U.S.A.* 30°57N 95°22W 176 F7
Trinity →
  Calif., U.S.A. 41°11N 123°42W 168 F2
Trinity → *Tex., U.S.A.* 29°45N 94°43W 176 G7
Trinity B. *Canada* 48°20N 53°10W 165 C9
Trinity Hills *Trin. & Tob.* 10°7N 61°7W 187 K15
Trinity Range *U.S.A.* 40°15N 118°40W 168 F4
Trinkat *India* 8°5N 93°30E 123 L11
Trinkitat *Sudan* 18°45N 37°51E 137 D4
Trino *Italy* 45°12N 8°18E 92 C5
Trinway *U.S.A.* 40°9N 82°1W 174 F2
Triolet *Mauritius* 20°5S 57°32E 141 d
Trionto, C. *Italy* 39°37N 16°47E 95 C9
Triora *Italy* 44°1N 7°46E 92 D4
Tripoli = Tarābulus
  Lebanon 34°31N 35°50E 130 A4
Tripoli = Tarābulus
  Libya 32°49N 13°7E 135 B8
Tripoli *Greece* 37°31N 22°25E 98 D4
Tripolis = Tarābulus
  Libya 31°0N 13°0E 135 B8
Tripolitania = Tarābulus
  Libya 31°0N 13°0E 135 B8
Tripura □ *India* 24°0N 92°0E 123 H18
Tripylos *Cyprus* 34°59N 32°41E 101 E11
Trischen *Germany* 54°4N 8°40E 76 A4
Tristan da Cunha
  Atl. Oc. 37°6S 12°20W 133 K2
Trisul *India* 30°19N 79°47E 125 D8
Triton I. *S. China Sea* 15°47N 111°12E 118 A4
Trivandrum =
  Thiruvananthapuram
  India 8°41N 77°0E 127 K3
Trivento *Italy* 41°47N 14°33E 93 G11
Trizin *Greece* 37°25N 23°15E 98 D5
Trnava *Slovak Rep.* 48°23N 17°35E 79 C10
Trnavský □ *Slovak Rep.* 48°30N 17°35E 79 C10
Troarn *France* 49°11N 0°11W 70 C6
Trochu *Canada* 51°50N 113°13W 162 C6
Trodely I. *Canada* 52°15N 79°26W 164 B4
Troglav *Croatia* 43°56N 16°36E 93 E13
Tróia *Italy* 41°22N 15°18E 95 A8
Troilus, L. *Canada* 50°50N 74°35W 164 B5
Troina *Italy* 37°47N 14°36E 95 E7
Trois Fourches, Cap des
  Morocco 35°26N 2°58W 136 A3
Trois-Pistoles *Canada* 48°5N 69°10W 165 C6
Trois-Rivières *Canada* 46°25N 72°34W 164 C5
Trois-Rivières
  Guadeloupe 15°57N 61°40W 182 b
Troisdorf *Germany* 50°49N 7°11E 76 E3
Troitsk *Russia* 54°10N 61°35E 108 B6
Troitsko-Pechorsk
  Russia 62°40N 56°10E 106 C6
Troitskoye *Russia* 46°26N 44°15E 87 G7
Troll *Antarctica* 72°0S 2°30E 55 D3
Trölladyngja *Iceland* 64°54N 17°16W 60 D5
Trollhättan *Sweden* 58°17N 12°20E 63 F6
Trollheimen *Norway* 62°46N 9°1E 62 C5
Trombetas → *Brazil* 1°55S 55°35W 187 D7
Tromelin I. *Ind. Oc.* 15°52S 54°25E 146 H8
Tromsø *Norway* 69°40N 18°56E 60 B18
Trona *U.S.A.* 35°46N 117°23W 171 K9
Tronador, Mte.
  Argentina 41°10S 71°50W 192 B2

Trøndelag *Norway* 64°17N 11°50E 60 D14
Trondheim *Norway* 63°36N 10°25E 60 E14
Trondheimsfjorden
  Norway 63°35N 10°30E 60 E14
Trönninge *Sweden* 56°37N 12°51E 63 H6
Tronto → *Italy* 42°54N 13°55E 93 F10
Troodos *Cyprus* 34°55N 32°52E 101 E11
Troon *U.K.* 55°33N 4°39W 65 F4
Tropea *Italy* 38°41N 15°54E 95 D8
Tropic *U.S.A.* 37°37N 112°5W 169 H7
Tropojë *Albania* 42°23N 20°10E 96 D4
Trosa *Sweden* 58°54N 17°33E 63 F11
Trostan *U.K.* 55°3N 6°10W 64 A5
Trostberg *Germany* 48°1N 12°33E 77 G8
Trostyanets *Sumy,*
  Ukraine 50°33N 34°59E 85 G8
Trostyanets *Vinnytsya,*
  Ukraine 48°31N 29°11E 81 B9
Trou Gras Pt. *St. Lucia* 13°51N 60°53W 183 f
Trout L. *N.W.T.,*
  Canada 60°40N 121°14W 162 A4
Trout L. *Ont., Canada* 51°20N 93°15W 163 C10
Trout Lake *Canada* 56°30N 114°32W 162 B6
Trout Lake *U.S.A.* 46°0N 121°32W 170 E5
Trout River *Canada* 49°29N 58°8W 165 C8
Trout Run *U.S.A.* 41°23N 77°3W 174 E7
Trouville-sur-Mer *France* 49°21N 0°5E 70 C7
Trowbridge *U.K.* 51°18N 2°12W 67 F5
Troy *Turkey* 39°57N 26°12E 99 B8
Troy *Ala., U.S.A.* 31°48N 85°58W 178 D4
Troy *Kans., U.S.A.* 39°47N 95°5W 172 F6
Troy *Mo., U.S.A.* 38°59N 90°59W 172 F8
Troy *Mont., U.S.A.* 48°28N 115°53W 168 B6
Troy *N.Y., U.S.A.* 42°44N 73°41W 175 D11
Troy *Ohio, U.S.A.* 40°2N 84°12W 173 E11
Troy *Pa., U.S.A.* 41°47N 76°47W 175 E8
Troyan *Bulgaria* 42°57N 24°43E 97 D8
Troyes *France* 48°19N 4°3E 71 D11
Trpanj *Croatia* 43°1N 17°15E 93 E14
Trstenik *Serbia* 43°36N 21°0E 96 C5
Trubchevsk *Russia* 52°33N 33°47E 85 F7
Truchas Pk. *U.S.A.* 35°58N 105°39W 169 J11
Trucial States = United Arab
  Emirates ■ *Asia* 23°50N 54°0E 129 F7
Truckee *U.S.A.* 39°20N 120°11W 170 F6
Trudfront *Russia* 45°56N 47°40E 87 H8
Trudovoye *Russia* 43°17N 132°5E 112 C6
Trujillo *Honduras* 16°0N 86°0W 182 C2
Trujillo *Peru* 8°6S 79°0W 188 B2
Trujillo *Spain* 39°28N 5°55W 89 F5
Trujillo *U.S.A.* 35°32N 104°42W 169 J11
Trujillo *Venezuela* 9°22N 70°38W 186 B4
Truk *Micronesia* 7°25N 151°46E 156 G7
Trumann *U.S.A.* 35°41N 90°31W 177 D9
Trumansburg *U.S.A.* 42°33N 76°40W 175 D8
Trumbull, Mt. *U.S.A.* 36°25N 113°19W 169 H7
Trůn *Bulgaria* 42°51N 22°38E 96 C6
Trun *France* 48°50N 0°2E 70 D7
Trundle *Australia* 32°53S 147°35E 153 B7
Trung Lon, Hon *Vietnam* 8°36N 106°8E 121 H6
Trung-Phan *Vietnam* 17°0N 109°0E 120 C4
Truro *Canada* 45°21N 63°14W 165 C7
Truro *U.K.* 50°16N 5°4W 67 G2
Truskavets *Ukraine* 49°17N 23°30E 75 D12
Trůstenik *Bulgaria* 43°31N 24°28E 97 C8
Trustrup *Denmark* 56°20N 10°46E 63 H4
Trutch *Canada* 57°44N 122°57W 162 B4
Truth or Consequences
  U.S.A. 33°8N 107°15W 169 K10
Trutnov *Czech Rep.* 50°37N 15°54E 78 A8
Truyère → *France* 44°38N 2°34E 72 D6
Tryavna *Bulgaria* 42°54N 25°25E 97 C9
Tryonville *U.S.A.* 41°42N 79°48W 174 E4
Tryphena *N.Z.* 36°18S 175°28E 154 C4
Trzcianka *Poland* 53°3N 16°25E 83 E3
Trzciel *Poland* 52°23N 15°50E 83 F2
Trzcińsko Zdrój *Poland* 52°58N 14°35E 83 F1
Trzebiatów *Poland* 54°4N 15°18E 82 D2
Trzebiez *Poland* 53°38N 14°31E 82 E1
Trzebnica *Poland* 51°20N 17°1E 83 E3
Trzemeszno *Poland* 52°33N 17°48E 83 F4
Tržič *Slovenia* 46°22N 14°18E 93 B11
Tsagaannur *Mongolia* 49°32N 89°42E 109 C11
Tsagan Aman *Russia* 47°34N 46°43E 87 G8
Tsala Apopka L.
  U.S.A. 28°53N 82°19W 179 G7
Tsamandás *Greece* 39°46N 20°21E 98 B2
Tsandi *Namibia* 17°42S 14°50E 144 A1
Tsaratanana *Madag.* 16°47S 47°39E 141 G9
Tsarevo *Bulgaria* 42°8N 25°52E 97 D9
Tsaritsani *Greece* 39°53N 22°14E 98 B4
Tsau *Botswana* 20°8S 22°22E 144 B3
Tsavo *Kenya* 2°59S 38°28E 142 C4
Tsavo East △ *Kenya* 2°44S 38°47E 142 C4
Tsavo West △ *Kenya* 3°19S 37°57E 142 C4
Tsentralen Balkan △
  Bulgaria 42°40N 24°45E 97 D8
Tsentralnyy □ *Russia* 52°0N 40°0E 106 D4
Tses *Namibia* 25°58S 18°8E 144 C2
Tsetserleg *Mongolia* 47°36N 101°32E 110 B9
Tseung Kwan *China* 22°20N 114°15E 111 a
Tsévié *Togo* 6°25N 1°20E 139 D5
Tshabong *Botswana* 26°2S 22°29E 144 C3
Tshane *Botswana* 24°5S 21°54E 144 B3
Tshela
  Dem. Rep. of the Congo 4°57S 13°4E 140 E2
Tshesebe *Botswana* 21°51S 27°32E 145 B4
Tshibeke
  Dem. Rep. of the Congo 2°40S 28°35E 142 C2
Tshibinda
  Dem. Rep. of the Congo 2°23S 28°43E 142 C2
Tshikapa
  Dem. Rep. of the Congo 6°28S 20°48E 140 F4
Tshilenge
  Dem. Rep. of the Congo 6°17S 23°48E 142 D1
Tshinsenda
  Dem. Rep. of the Congo 12°20S 28°0E 143 E2
Tshofa
  Dem. Rep. of the Congo 5°13S 25°16E 142 D2
Tshwane = Pretoria
  S. Africa 25°44S 28°12E 145 D4
Tshwane *Botswana* 22°24S 22°1E 144 B3
Tsigara *Botswana* 20°22S 25°54E 144 B4
Tsiigehtchic *Canada* 67°15N 134°0W 154 B6
Ts'il-os △ *Canada* 51°9N 123°59W 162 C4
Tsimlyansk *Russia* 47°40N 42°6E 87 G6

Tsimlyansk Res. = Tsimlyanskoye
　Vdkhr. *Russia* 48°0N 43°0E **87** F6
Tsimlyanskoye Vdkhr.
　Russia 48°0N 43°0E **87** F6
Tsinan = Jinan *China* 36°38N 117°1E **114** F9
Tsineng *S. Africa* 27°5S 23°5E **144** C3
Tsing Yi *China* 22°21N 114°6E **111** a
Tsinghai = Qinghai □
　China 36°0N 98°0E **110** D8
Tsingtao = Qingdao
　China 36°5N 120°20E **115** F11
Tsirigo = Kythira *Greece* 36°8N 23°0E **98** E5
Tsiteli-Tsqaro = Dedopolis Tsqaro
　Georgia 41°30N 46°0E **87** K8
Tsitsikamma △ *S. Africa* 34°3S 23°40E **144** D3
Tsivilsk *Russia* 55°50N 47°25E **86** C8
Tskhinvali *Georgia* 42°14N 44°1E **87** J7
Tsna → *Russia* 54°55N 41°58E **86** C6
Tsnori *Georgia* 41°40N 45°57E **87** K7
Tso Moriri, L. *India* 32°50N 78°20E **125** C8
Tsobis *Namibia* 19°27S 17°30E **144** A2
Tsodilo Hills *Botswana* 18°49S 21°43E **144** A3
Tsogttsetsiy = Baruunsuu
　Mongolia 43°43N 105°35E **114** C3
Tsolo *S. Africa* 31°18S 28°37E **145** E4
Tsomo *S. Africa* 32°0S 27°42E **145** D4
Tsu *Japan* 34°45N 136°25E **113** G8
Tsu L. *Canada* 60°40N 111°52W **162** A6
Tsuchiura *Japan* 36°5N 140°15E **113** F10
Tsuen Wan *China* 22°22N 114°6E **111** a
Tsugaru-Hantō *Japan* 41°0N 140°30E **112** D10
Tsugaru-Kaikyō
　Japan 41°35N 141°0E **112** D10
Tsumeb *Namibia* 19°9S 17°44E **144** A2
Tsumis *Namibia* 23°39S 17°29E **144** B2
Tsuruga *Japan* 35°45N 136°2E **113** G8
Tsurugi-San *Japan* 33°51N 134°6E **113** H7
Tsuruoka *Japan* 38°44N 139°50E **112** E9
Tsushima *Gifu, Japan* 35°10N 136°43E **113** G8
Tsushima *Nagasaki,*
　Japan 34°20N 129°20E **113** G4
Tsuyama *Japan* 35°3N 134°0E **113** G7
Tsvetkovo *Ukraine* 49°8N 31°33E **85** H6
Tsyelyakhany *Belarus* 52°30N 25°46E **75** E3
Tua → *Portugal* 41°13N 7°26W **88** D3
Tuaheni Pt. *N.Z.* 38°43S 178°4E **154** E7
Tuai *N.Z.* 38°47S 177°10E **154** E6
Tuaim = Tuam *Ireland* 53°31N 8°51W **64** C3
Tuakau *N.Z.* 37°16S 174°59E **154** D3
Tual *Indonesia* 5°38S 132°44E **119** F8
Tualatin *U.S.A.* 45°23N 122°45W **170** E4
Tuam *Ireland* 53°31N 8°51W **64** C3
Tuamarina *N.Z.* 41°25S 173°59E **155** B8
Tuamotu, Îs.
　French Polynesia 17°0S 144°0W **157** J13
Tuamotu Arch. = Tuamotu, Îs.
　French Polynesia 17°0S 144°0W **157** J13
Tuamotu Ridge
　Pac. Oc. 20°0S 138°0W **157** K14
Tuan Giao *Vietnam* 21°35N 103°25E **120** B4
Tuanfeng *China* 30°38N 114°52E **117** B10
Tuanxi *China* 27°28N 107°8E **116** D6
Tuao *Phil.* 17°45N 121°22E **119** A6
Tuapse *Russia* 44°5N 39°10E **87** H4
Tuas *Singapore* 1°19N 103°39E **121** d
Tuatapere *N.Z.* 46°8S 167°41E **155** G2
Tuba City *U.S.A.* 36°8N 111°14W **169** H8
Tuban *Indonesia* 6°54S 112°3E **119** G15
Tubani *Botswana* 24°46S 24°18E **144** B3
Tubarão *Brazil* 28°30S 49°0W **191** B6
Tûbâs *West Bank* 32°20N 35°22E **130** C4
Tubas → *Namibia* 22°54S 14°35E **144** B2
Tübingen *Germany* 48°31N 9°4E **77** G5
Tubou *Fiji* 18°13S 178°48W **154** a
Tubruq *Libya* 32°7N 23°55E **135** B10
Tubuaï, Îs.
　French Polynesia 25°0S 150°0W **157** K13
Tuc Trung *Vietnam* 11°1N 107°12E **121** G6
Tucacas *Venezuela* 10°48N 68°19W **186** A5
Tucano *Brazil* 10°58S 38°48W **189** C3
T'uch'ang *Taiwan* 24°35N 121°29E **117** E13
Tuchitua *Canada* 60°55N 129°13W **162** A3
Tuchodi → *Canada* 58°17N 123°42W **162** B4
Tuchola *Poland* 53°33N 17°52E **82** E4
Tuchów *Poland* 49°54N 21°1E **83** J8
Tuckanarra *Australia* 27°7S 118°5E **149** E2
Tucker *U.S.A.* 33°51N 84°13W **178** B5
Tucson *U.S.A.* 32°13N 110°58W **169** K8
Tucumán □ *Argentina* 26°48S 66°2W **190** B3
Tucumcari *U.S.A.* 35°10N 103°44W **169** J12
Tucupita *Venezuela* 9°2N 62°3W **186** B6
Tucuruí *Brazil* 3°42S 49°44W **187** D9
Tucuruí, Represa de
　Brazil 4°0S 49°30W **187** D9
Tuczno *Poland* 53°13N 16°10E **83** E3
Tudela *Spain* 42°4N 1°39W **90** C3
Tudmur *Syria* 34°36N 38°15E **105** E8
Tudor, L. *Canada* 55°50N 65°25W **165** A6
Tudora *Romania* 47°31N 26°54E **81** C11
Tuella → *Portugal* 41°30N 7°12W **88** D3
Tuen Mun *China* 22°24N 113°59E **111** a
Tufanbeyli *Turkey* 38°15N 36°13E **104** C7
Tug Hill Plateau
　U.S.A. 43°45N 75°50W **175** C9
Tugela → *S. Africa* 29°14S 31°30E **145** D5
Tugela Falls *S. Africa* 28°42S 29°51E **145** D4
Tuguegarao *Phil.* 17°35N 121°42E **119** A6
Tugur *Russia* 53°44N 136°45E **107** D14
Tui *Spain* 42°3N 8°39W **88** C2
Tuineje *Canary Is.* 28°19N 14°3W **100** F5
Tukangbesi, Kepulauan
　Indonesia 6°0S 124°0E **119** F6
Tukarak I. *Canada* 56°15N 78°45W **164** A4
Tukayyid *Iraq* 29°47N 45°21E **126** D5
Tûkh *Egypt* 30°21N 31°12E **137** E7
Tukhla *Ukraine* 48°51N 23°28E **81** B9
Tukituki → *N.Z.* 39°36S 176°58E **154** F5
Tukobo *Ghana* 5°1N 2°47W **138** D4
Tuktoyaktuk *Canada* 69°27N 133°2W **160** D5
Tuktut Nogait △
　Canada 69°15N 122°0W **160** D7
Tukums *Latvia* 56°58N 23°10E **82** B10
Tukums □ *Latvia* 56°55N 23°0E **82** B10
Tukuyu *Tanzania* 9°17S 33°35E **143** D3
Tula *Hidalgo, Mexico* 20°3N 99°21W **181** C5
Tula *Tamaulipas, Mexico* 23°0N 99°43W **181** C5
Tula *Nigeria* 9°51N 11°27E **139** D7
Tula *Russia* 54°13N 37°38E **86** D9
Tula □ *Russia* 53°45N 37°30E **84** F9
Tulach Mhór = Tullamore
　Ireland 53°16N 7°31W **64** C4

Tulancingo *Mexico* 20°5N 98°22W **181** C5
Tulare *Serbia* 42°48N 21°28E **96** D5
Tulare *U.S.A.* 36°13N 119°21W **170** J7
Tulare Lake Bed
　U.S.A. 36°0N 119°48W **170** K7
Tularosa *U.S.A.* 33°5N 106°1W **169** K10
Tulbagh *S. Africa* 33°16S 19°6E **144** D2
Tulcán *Ecuador* 0°48N 77°43W **186** C3
Tulcea *Romania* 45°13N 28°46E **81** E13
Tulcea □ *Romania* 45°0N 28°30E **81** E13
Tulchyn *Ukraine* 48°41N 28°49E **81** B13
Tûledi Araldary
　Kazakhstan 45°2N 50°16E **87** H10
Tûleh *Iran* 34°35N 52°33E **129** C7
Tulemalu L. *Canada* 62°58N 99°25W **163** A9
Tulgheş *Romania* 46°58N 25°45E **81** D10
Tuli *Zimbabwe* 21°58S 29°13E **143** G2
Tulia *U.S.A.* 34°32N 101°46W **176** D4
Tuliszków *Poland* 52°5N 18°18E **83** F5
Tulita *Canada* 64°57N 125°30W **160** E6
Tullahoma *U.S.A.* 35°22N 86°13W **177** D11
Tullamore *Australia* 32°39S 147°36E **153** B7
Tullamore *Ireland* 53°16N 7°31W **64** C4
Tulle *France* 45°16N 1°46E **72** C5
Tulln *Austria* 48°20N 16°4E **78** C9
Tullow *Ireland* 52°49N 6°45W **64** D5
Tully *Australia* 17°56S 145°55E **150** B4
Tully *U.S.A.* 42°48N 76°7W **175** D8
Tulnici *Romania* 45°51N 26°38E **81** E11
Tulovo *Bulgaria* 42°33N 25°32E **97** D9
Tulsa *U.S.A.* 36°10N 95°55W **176** C7
Tulsequah *Canada* 58°39N 133°35W **162** B2
Tuluá *Colombia* 4°6N 76°11W **186** C3
Tulucești *Romania* 45°34N 28°2E **81** E13
Tulum *Mexico* 20°13N 87°28W **181** C7
Tulun *Russia* 54°32N 100°35E **107** D11
Tulungagung *Indonesia* 8°5S 111°54E **119** H14
Tuma → *Nic.* 13°6N 84°35W **182** D3
Tuma *Russia* 55°10N 40°30E **84** E11
Tumaco *Colombia* 1°50N 78°45W **186** C3
Tumacacori △ *U.S.A.* 31°35N 111°6W **169** L8
Tumaku = Tumkur
　India 13°18N 77°6E **127** H3
Tumatumari *Guyana* 5°20N 58°55W **186** B7
Tumba *Sweden* 59°12N 17°48E **62** E11
Tumba, L.
　Dem. Rep. of the Congo 0°50S 18°0E **140** E3
Tumbarumba *Australia* 35°44S 148°0E **153** C8
Tumbaya *Argentina* 23°50S 65°26W **190** A2
Tumbes *Peru* 3°37S 80°27W **188** A1
Tumbes □ *Peru* 3°50S 80°30W **188** A1
Tumbler Ridge *Canada* 55°8N 121°0W **162** B4
Tumbwe
　Dem. Rep. of the Congo 11°25S 27°15E **143** E2
Tumby Bay *Australia* 34°21S 136°8E **152** C2
Tumd Youqi *China* 40°30N 110°30E **114** D6
Tumen *China* 43°0N 129°50E **112** C4
Tumen Jiang →
　China 42°20N 130°35E **115** C16
Tumeremo *Venezuela* 7°18N 61°30W **186** B6
Tumiritinga *Brazil* 18°58S 41°38W **189** D2
Tumkur *India* 13°18N 77°6E **127** H3
Tump *Pakistan* 26°7N 62°16E **122** F3
Tumpat *Malaysia* 6°11N 102°10E **121** J4
Tumsar *India* 21°26N 79°45E **125** D4
Tumu *Ghana* 10°56N 1°56W **138** C4
Tumucumaque, Serra
　Brazil 2°0N 55°0W **187** C8
Tumupasa *Bolivia* 14°9S 67°55W **188** C5
Tumut *Australia* 35°16S 148°13E **153** C8
Tumwater *U.S.A.* 47°1N 122°54W **170** C4
Tun *Sweden* 58°26N 12°43E **63** F6
Tuna *India* 22°59N 70°5E **124** H4
Tunapuna
　Trin. & Tob. 10°38N 61°24W **187** K15
Tunas de Zaza *Cuba* 21°39N 79°34W **182** B4
Tunbridge Wells = Royal
　Tunbridge Wells *U.K.* 51°7N 0°16E **67** F8
Tunçbilek *Turkey* 39°37N 29°29E **99** B11
Tunceli *Turkey* 39°6N 39°31E **105** C8
Tunceli □ *Turkey* 39°5N 39°35E **105** C8
Tunchang *China* 19°21N 110°5E **117** a
Tuncurry *Australia* 32°17S 152°29E **153** B10
Tundla *India* 27°12N 78°17E **124** F8
Tundubai *Sudan* 18°36N 28°33E **137** D2
Tunduru *Tanzania* 11°8S 37°25E **143** E4
Tundzha → *Bulgaria* 41°40N 26°35E **97** E10
Tunga → *India* 15°57N 78°15E **127** G4
Tungabhadra → *India* 15°57N 78°15E **127** G4
Tungabhadra Dam
　India 15°0N 75°50E **127** G3
Tungla *Nic.* 13°24N 84°21W **182** D3
Tungsha Tao = Dongsha Dao
　S. China Sea 20°45N 116°43E **111** G12
Tungshih *Taiwan* 24°12N 120°48E **117** E13
Tungsten *Canada* 61°57N 128°16W **162** A3
Tunguska, Nizhnyaya →
　Russia 65°48N 88°4E **107** C9
Tunguska, Podkamennaya →
　Russia 61°50N 90°13E **107** C10
Tuni *India* 17°22N 82°36E **126** F6
Tunica *U.S.A.* 34°41N 90°23W **177** D9
Tunis *Tunisia* 36°50N 10°11E **136** A6
Tunis, Golfe de *Tunisia* 37°0N 10°30E **136** A6
Tunis ✈ (TUN) *Tunisia* 36°52N 10°14E **94** F3
Tunis, Golfe de *Tunisia* 37°0N 10°30E **136** A6
Tunisia ■ *Africa* 33°30N 9°10E **136** B6
Tunja *Colombia* 5°33S 73°25W **186** B4
Tunkhannock *U.S.A.* 41°32N 75°57W **175** E9
Tunkinsky △ *Russia* 51°30N 102°0E **107** D11
Tunliu *China* 36°13N 112°52E **114** F7
Tunnel Creek △
　Australia 17°41S 125°18E **148** C4
Tunnsjøen *Norway* 64°45N 13°25E **60** D15
Tunø *Denmark* 55°57N 10°27E **63** J4
Tunungayualok I.
　Canada 56°0N 61°0W **165** A7
Tunuyán *Argentina* 33°35S 69°0W **190** C2
Tunuyán → *Argentina* 33°33S 67°30W **190** C2
Tunxi = Huangshan
　China 29°38N 118°19E **117** B12
Tuo Jiang → *China* 28°50N 105°35E **116** C5
Tuolumne *U.S.A.* 37°58N 120°15W **170** H6
Tuolumne → *U.S.A.* 37°36N 121°13W **170** H5
Tüp *Kyrgyzstan* 42°45N 78°20E **109** D9
Tüp Ăghăj *Iran* 36°3N 47°50E **105** D12
Tupã *Brazil* 21°57S 50°28W **191** A5

Tupaciguara *Brazil* 18°35S 48°42W **189** D1
Tupelo *U.S.A.* 34°16N 88°43W **177** D10
Tupik *Russia* 55°42N 33°22E **84** E7
Tupinambarana, I. *Brazil* 3°0S 58°0W **186** D7
Tupirama *Brazil* 8°58S 48°12W **189** B1
Tupiratins *Brazil* 8°23S 48°8W **189** B1
Tupiza *Bolivia* 21°30S 65°40W **190** A2
Tupižnica *Serbia* 43°43N 22°10E **96** C6
Tupman *U.S.A.* 35°18N 119°21W **171** K7
Tupper *Canada* 55°32N 120°1W **162** B4
Tupper L. *U.S.A.* 44°10N 74°32W **175** B10
Tupper L. *U.S.A.* 44°14N 74°28W **175** B10
Tüpqarghan Muyis
　Kazakhstan 44°40N 50°19E **87** H10
Tupungato, Cerro
　S. Amer. 33°15S 69°50W **190** C2
Tuquan *China* 45°18N 121°38E **115** B11
Túquerres *Colombia* 1°5N 77°37W **186** C3
Tura *Russia* 64°20N 100°17E **107** C11
Turabah *Ḥā'il,*
　Si. Arabia 28°20N 43°15E **128** D4
Turabah *Makkah,*
　Si. Arabia 21°15N 41°34E **137** C5
Turakina *N.Z.* 40°3S 175°16E **154** E4
Turakina → *N.Z.* 40°5S 175°8E **154** G4
Turakirae Hd. *N.Z.* 41°26S 174°56E **154** H3
Tūrān *Iran* 35°39N 56°42E **129** C8
Tūrān △ *Iran* 35°45N 56°20E **129** C8
Turan Lowland *Asia* 43°30N 62°0E **108** D6
Ţurayf *Si. Arabia* 31°41N 38°39E **128** D3
Turbaco *Colombia* 10°20N 75°25W **186** A3
Turbacz *Poland* 49°30N 20°8E **83** J7
Turbe *Bos.-H.* 44°15N 17°35E **80** F2
Turberville *U.S.A.* 33°54N 80°1W **178** B9
Turčianske Teplice
　Slovak Rep. 48°52N 18°52E **79** C11
Turco *Bolivia* 18°10S 68°11W **188** D4
Turcoaia *Romania* 45°7N 28°11E **81** E13
Turda *Romania* 46°34N 23°47E **81** D8
Turek *Poland* 52°3N 18°30E **83** F5
Turén *Venezuela* 9°17N 69°6W **186** B5
Turfan = Turpan
　China 43°58N 89°10E **109** D11
Turfan Basin = Turpan Pendi
　China 42°40N 89°25E **109** D11
Turfan Depression = Turpan
　Pendi *China* 42°40N 89°25E **109** D11
Turgayskaya Stolovaya Strana =
　Torghay Ustirti *Asia* 51°0N 63°0E **108** B6
Turgeon → *Canada* 50°0N 78°56W **164** C4
Tŭrgovishte *Bulgaria* 43°17N 26°38E **97** C10
Tŭrgovishte □ *Bulgaria* 43°17N 26°38E **97** C10
Turgut *Turkey* 37°22N 28°4E **99** D10
Turgutlu *Turkey* 38°30N 27°43E **99** C9
Turhal *Turkey* 40°24N 36°5E **104** B7
Turia → *Spain* 39°27N 0°19W **91** F4
Turiaçu *Brazil* 1°40S 45°19W **187** D9
Turiaçu → *Brazil* 1°36S 45°19W **187** D9
Turiec → *Slovak Rep.* 49°7N 18°55E **79** B11
Turin = Torino *Italy* 45°3N 7°40E **92** C4
Turka *Ukraine* 49°10N 23°2E **83** D10
Turkana, L. *Africa* 3°30N 36°5E **142** B4
Türkeli *Turkey* 40°30N 27°30E **97** F11
Turkestan = Türkistan
　Kazakhstan 43°17N 68°16E **109** E7
Turkestan Range *Asia* 39°35N 69°0E **109** E7
Túrkeve *Hungary* 47°6N 20°44E **80** C5
Turkey ■ *Eurasia* 39°0N 36°0E **104** C7
Turkey Creek = Warmun
　Australia 17°2S 128°12E **148** C4
Turki *Russia* 52°0N 43°15E **86** D6
Türkistan *Kazakhstan* 43°17N 68°16E **109** E7
Türkmenabat
　Turkmenistan 39°6N 63°34E **129** B9
Türkmenbashi
　Turkmenistan 40°5N 53°5E **129** A7
Turkmenistan ■ *Asia* 39°0N 59°0E **108** C5
Türkmenli *Turkey* 39°45N 26°30E **99** B8
Türkoğlu *Turkey* 37°23N 36°50E **104** D7
Turks & Caicos Is. ☑
　W. Indies 21°20N 71°20W **183** B5
Turks Island Passage
　Turks & Caicos 21°25N 71°19W **183** B5
Turku *Finland* 60°30N 22°19E **64** B2
Turkwel → *Kenya* 3°6N 36°6E **142** B4
Turlock *U.S.A.* 37°30N 120°51W **170** H6
Turnagain → *Canada* 59°12N 127°35W **162** B3
Turnagain, C. *N.Z.* 40°28S 176°38E **154** G5
Turneffe Is. *Belize* 17°20N 87°50W **181** D7
Turner *Australia* 17°52S 133°35E **150** C1
Turner Pt. *Australia* 11°47S 133°32E **150** A1
Turner Valley *Canada* 50°40N 114°17W **162** D6
Turners Falls *U.S.A.* 42°36N 72°33W **175** D12
Turner's Pen. *S. Leone* 7°22N 12°24W **138** D2
Turnhout *Belgium* 51°19N 4°57E **69** C4
Türnitz *Austria* 47°55N 15°29E **78** D8
Turnor L. *Canada* 56°35N 108°35W **162** B7
Turnov *Czech Rep.* 50°34N 15°10E **78** A8
Tŭrnovo = Veliko Tŭrnovo
　Bulgaria 43°5N 25°41E **97** C9
Turnu Măgurele
　Romania 43°46N 24°56E **81** G9
Turnu Roşu, P. *Romania* 45°33N 24°17E **81** E9
Turobin *Poland* 50°50N 22°44E **83** H9
Tuross Head *Australia* 36°3S 150°8E **153** D9
Turpan *China* 43°58N 89°10E **109** D11
Turpan Pendi *China* 42°40N 89°25E **109** D11
Turrawan *Australia* 30°28S 149°53E **153** A8
Turrës, Kala e *Albania* 41°10N 19°28E **98** B1
Turriff *U.K.* 57°32N 2°27W **65** D6
Tursāq *Iraq* 33°27N 45°47E **105** F11
Tursi *Italy* 40°15N 16°28E **95** D9
Turtle Creek △
　Australia 10°56S 142°37E **150** A3
Turtle Is. *S. Leone* 7°22N 13°0W **138** D2
Turtle L. *Canada* 53°36N 108°38W **163** C7
Turtle Lake *U.S.A.* 47°31N 100°53W **168** B4
Turtleford *Canada* 53°23N 108°57W **163** C7
Turua *N.Z.* 37°14S 175°35E **154** D4
Turuépano △
　Venezuela 10°34N 62°43W **187** K15
Turukhansk *Russia* 65°21N 88°5E **107** C9
Turzovka *Slovak Rep.* 49°25N 18°35E **79** B11
Tuscaloosa *U.S.A.* 33°12N 87°34W **177** E11
Tuscánia *Italy* 42°25N 11°55E **92** F4
Tuscany = Toscana □
　Italy 43°25N 11°0E **92** E8

Tuscarawas → *U.S.A.* 40°24N 81°25W **174** F3
Tuscarora Mt. *U.S.A.* 40°55N 77°55W **174** F7
Tuscola, Ill., *U.S.A.* 39°48N 88°17W **172** F1
Tuscola *Tex., U.S.A.* 32°12N 99°48W **176** E5
Tuscumbia *U.S.A.* 34°44N 87°42W **177** D11
Tuskegee *U.S.A.* 32°25N 85°42W **177** E12
Tuszyn *Poland* 51°36N 19°33E **83** G6
Tutak *Turkey* 39°31N 42°46E **105** C10
Tutayev *Russia* 57°53N 39°32E **84** D10
Tuticorin *India* 8°50N 78°12E **127** K4
Tutin *Serbia* 42°58N 20°20E **96** C4
Tutóia *Brazil* 2°45S 42°20W **189** A2
Tutong *Brunei* 4°47N 114°40E **118** D4
Tutova → *Romania* 46°7N 27°30E **81** D12
Tutrakan *Bulgaria* 44°2N 26°40E **97** B10
Tuttle Creek L. *U.S.A.* 39°15N 96°36W **172** F5
Tuttlingen *Germany* 47°58N 8°48E **77** H4
Tutuala *E. Timor* 8°25S 127°15E **119** F7
Tutuila *Amer. Samoa* 14°19S 170°50W **155** b
Tutume *Botswana* 20°30S 27°5E **141** J5
Tutun *Egypt* 29°9N 30°46E **137** F7
Tuul Gol → *Mongolia* 48°30N 104°25E **110** B9
Tuva □ *Russia* 51°30N 95°0E **109** D12
Tuvalu ■ *Pac. Oc.* 8°0S 178°0E **147** B10
Tuvuca *Fiji* 17°40S 178°48W **154** a
Tuxer Alpen *Austria* 47°10N 11°45E **78** D4
Tuxpan *Mexico* 20°57N 97°24W **181** C5
Tuxtla Gutiérrez *Mexico* 16°45N 93°7W **181** D6
Tuy = Tui *Spain* 42°3N 8°39W **88** C2
Tuy Duc *Vietnam* 12°15N 107°27E **121** F6
Tuy Phong *Vietnam* 11°14N 108°43E **121** G7
Tuy L. *Canada* 59°7N 130°35W **162** B2
Tuyen Hoa *Vietnam* 17°50N 106°10E **120** D6
Tuyen Quang *Vietnam* 21°50N 105°10E **116** G5
Tuymazy *Russia* 54°36N 53°42E **108** B4
Tūysarkān *Iran* 34°33N 48°27E **105** E13
Tuz Gölü *Turkey* 38°42N 33°18E **104** C5
Ţūz Khurmātū *Iraq* 34°56N 44°38E **105** E11
Tuzi *Montenegro* 42°22N 19°20E **96** D3
Tuzigoot △ *U.S.A.* 34°46N 112°2W **169** J7
Tuzla *Bos.-H.* 44°34N 18°41E **80** F3
Tuzlucu *Turkey* 47°17N 39°57E **85** J10
Tuzluca *Turkey* 40°3N 43°39E **105** B10
Tuzly *Ukraine* 45°54N 30°6E **81** E15
Tvååker *Sweden* 57°4N 12°25E **63** G6
Tvärditsa *Bulgaria* 46°9N 28°58E **81** D13
Tver *Russia* 56°55N 35°59E **84** D8
Tver □ *Russia* 56°50N 35°0E **84** D8
Tvrdošin *Slovak Rep.* 49°21N 19°35E **79** B12
Tvrdošovce *Slovak Rep.* 48°6N 18°4E **79** C11
Tvŭrditsa *Bulgaria* 42°42N 25°53E **97** D9
Twain *U.S.A.* 40°1N 121°3W **170** E5
Twain Harte *U.S.A.* 38°2N 120°14W **170** G6
Twardogóra *Poland* 51°23N 17°28E **83** G4
Twee River *Namibia* 25°27S 19°27E **144** C2
Tweed *Canada* 44°29N 77°19W **174** B7
Tweed → *U.K.* 55°45N 2°0W **65** F6
Tweed Heads *Australia* 28°10S 153°31E **151** D5
Tweedsmuir △ *Canada* 53°0N 126°20W **162** C3
Twentynine Palms
　U.S.A. 34°8N 116°3W **171** L10
Twillingate *Canada* 49°42N 54°45W **165** C9
Twin Bridges *U.S.A.* 45°33N 112°20W **168** D7
Twin City *U.S.A.* 32°35N 82°10W **178** D6
Twin Falls *Canada* 53°30N 64°32W **165** B7
Twin Falls *U.S.A.* 42°34N 114°28W **168** E6
Twin Lakes *U.S.A.* 30°43N 83°13W **178** E6
Twin Valley *U.S.A.* 47°16N 96°16W **172** B5
Twinsburg *U.S.A.* 41°19N 81°26W **174** E3
Twistringen *Germany* 52°48N 8°37E **76** C4
Twitchell Res. *U.S.A.* 34°59N 120°19W **171** L6
Two Harbors *U.S.A.* 47°2N 91°40W **172** B8
Two Hills *Canada* 53°43N 111°52W **162** C6
Two Rivers *U.S.A.* 44°9N 87°34W **172** C10
Two Rocks *Australia* 31°30S 115°35E **149** F2
Two Thumb Ra. *N.Z.* 43°45S 170°44E **155** D5
Twofold B. *Australia* 37°8S 149°59E **153** D8
Twyfelfontein *Namibia* 20°34S 14°22E **144** B1
Ty Ty *U.S.A.* 31°28N 83°39W **178** E6
Tyachiv *Ukraine* 48°1N 23°35E **75** D12
Tybee Island *U.S.A.* 32°1N 80°51W **178** D6
Tychy *Poland* 50°9N 18°59E **83** H5
Tyczyn *Poland* 49°58N 22°2E **83** J9
Tykocin *Poland* 53°13N 22°46E **83** E9
Tyler *Minn., U.S.A.* 44°17N 96°8W **172** C5
Tyler *Tex., U.S.A.* 32°21N 95°18W **176** E7
Tyligul → *Ukraine* 46°30N 30°57E **85** J6
Tymanivka *Ukraine* 48°34N 28°50E **81** B13
Týn nad Vltavou
　Czech Rep. 49°13N 14°26E **78** B7
Tynda *Russia* 55°10N 124°43E **107** D13
Tyndall *U.S.A.* 43°0N 97°50W **172** D5
Tyne → *U.K.* 54°59N 1°32W **66** C6
Tyne & Wear □ *U.K.* 55°6N 1°17W **66** B6
Tynemouth *U.K.* 55°1N 1°26W **66** B6
Tyre = Sûr *Lebanon* 33°19N 35°16E **130** B4
Tyresta △ *Sweden* 59°12N 18°14E **62** E12
Tyrifjorden *Norway* 60°2N 10°8E **61** F14
Tyringe *Sweden* 56°9N 13°35E **63** H7
Tyrnyauz *Russia* 43°21N 42°45E **87** J6
Tyrol = Tirol □ *Austria* 47°3N 10°43E **78** D3
Tyrone *U.S.A.* 40°40N 78°14W **174** F6
Tyrone □ *U.K.* 54°38N 7°11W **64** B4
Tyrrell → *Australia* 35°26S 142°51E **153** C3
Tyrrell, L. *Australia* 35°20S 142°50E **153** C3
Tyrrell L. *Canada* 63°7N 105°27W **163** A7
Tyrrhenian Sea *Medit. S.* 40°0N 12°30E **94** C5
Tysfjorden *Norway* 68°7N 16°25E **60** B17
Tysmenytsya *Ukraine* 48°54N 24°51E **81** B9
Tystberga *Sweden* 58°51N 17°15E **63** F11
Tytuvėnai *Lithuania* 55°36N 23°12E **82** C10
Tyub Karagan, Mys =
　Tŭpqarghan Muyis
　Kazakhstan 44°40N 50°19E **87** H10
Tyuleni, Ostrova = Tüledi
　Araldary *Kazakhstan* 45°2N 50°16E **87** H10
Tyuleniy *Russia* 44°28N 47°30E **87** H8
Tyuleniy, Mys
　Azerbaijan 40°12N 50°22E **87** K10
Tyumen *Russia* 57°11N 65°29E **108** C7
Tyup = Tüp *Kyrgyzstan* 42°45N 78°20E **109** D9
Tywi → *U.K.* 51°48N 4°21W **67** F3
Tywyn *U.K.* 52°35N 4°5W **67** E3
Tzaneen *S. Africa* 23°47S 30°9E **145** B5
Tzermiado *Greece* 35°12N 25°29E **101** D7
Tzermiado *Greece* 35°12N 25°29E **101** D7
Tzoumérka, Óros =
　Oros *Greece* 39°30N 21°26E **98** B3
Tzukong = Zigong
　China 29°15N 104°48E **116** C5

U

U.S.A. = United States of
　America ■ *N. Amer.* 37°0N 96°0W **167** H20
U.S. Virgin Is. ☑
　W. Indies 18°20N 65°0W **183** e
Uaimh, An = Navan
　Ireland 53°39N 6°41W **64** C5
Uanle Uen = Wanlweyne
　Somalia 2°37N 44°54E **131** G3
Uatumã → *Brazil* 2°26S 57°37W **186** D7
Uauá *Brazil* 9°50S 39°28W **189** B3
Uaupés *Brazil* 0°8S 67°5W **186** D5
Uaupés → *Brazil* 0°2N 67°16W **186** C5
Ubá *Brazil* 21°8S 43°0W **191** A7
Ubaitaba *Brazil* 14°18S 39°20W **189** C3
Ubajara *Brazil* 3°55S 40°50W **189** A2
Ubangi = Oubangi →
　Dem. Rep. of the Congo 0°30S 17°50E **140** E3
Ubauro *Pakistan* 28°15N 69°45E **124** E3
Ubaye → *France* 44°28N 6°18E **73** D10
Ubayyid, W. al →
　Iraq 32°34N 43°48E **105** F10
Ube *Japan* 33°56N 131°15E **113** H5
Úbeda *Spain* 38°3N 3°23W **89** G7
Uberaba *Brazil* 19°50S 47°55W **189** D1
Uberlândia *Brazil* 19°0S 48°20W **189** D1
Überlingen *Germany* 47°46N 9°10E **77** H5
Ubiaja *Nigeria* 6°41N 6°22E **139** D6
Ubin, Pulau *Singapore* 1°24N 103°57E **121** d
Ubly *U.S.A.* 43°42N 82°55W **174** C2
Ubolratna Res.
　Thailand 16°45N 102°30E **120** D4
Ubombo *S. Africa* 27°31S 32°4E **145** C5
Ubon Ratchathani
　Thailand 15°15N 104°50E **120** E5
Ubondo
　Dem. Rep. of the Congo 0°55S 25°42E **142** C2
Ubort → *Belarus* 52°6N 28°30E **75** E5
Ubrique *Spain* 36°41N 5°27W **89** J5
Ubud *Indonesia* 8°30S 115°16E **119** J18
Ubundu
　Dem. Rep. of the Congo 0°22S 25°30E **142** C2
Ucar *Azerbaijan* 40°31N 47°39E **87** K8
Ucayali → *Peru* 4°30S 73°30W **188** A3
Uchab *Namibia* 19°47S 17°42E **144** A2
Uchiura-Wan *Japan* 42°25N 140°40E **112** C10
Uchiza *Peru* 8°25S 76°20W **188** B3
Uchquduq *Uzbekistan* 41°50N 62°50E **108** E6
Uchte *Germany* 52°30N 8°54E **76** C4
Uchur → *Russia* 58°48N 130°35E **107** D14
Uckermark *Germany* 53°5N 13°30E **76** B9
Ucluelet *Canada* 48°57N 125°32W **162** D3
Uda → *Russia* 54°42N 135°14E **107** D14
Uda Walawe △ *Sri Lanka* 6°20N 81°0E **127** L5
Udachnyy *Russia* 66°25N 112°24E **107** C12
Udagamandalam *India* 11°30N 76°44E **127** J3
Udainagar *India* 22°33N 76°13E **124** H7
Udaipur *India* 24°36N 73°44E **124** G5
Udaipur Garhi *Nepal* 27°0N 86°35E **125** F12
Udala *India* 21°35N 86°34E **125** J12
Udayagiri *Andhra Pradesh,*
　India 14°52N 79°19E **127** G4
Udayagiri *Odisha, India* 20°8N 84°23E **126** D7
Udbina *Croatia* 44°31N 15°47E **93** D12
Uddeholm *Sweden* 60°1N 13°38E **62** D7
Uddevalla *Sweden* 58°21N 11°55E **63** F5
Uddheden *Sweden* 59°57N 12°54E **62** E6
Uddjaure *Sweden* 65°56N 17°49E **60** D17
Udgir *India* 18°25N 77°5E **126** E3
Udhampur *India* 32°55N 75°8E **126** a
Udi *Nigeria* 6°17N 7°21E **139** D6
Udine *Italy* 46°3N 13°14E **93** B10
Udintsev Fracture Zone
　S. Ocean 57°0S 145°0W **55** B13
Udon Thani *Thailand* 17°29N 102°46E **120** D4
Udong *Cambodia* 11°48N 104°45E **121** G5
Udskaya Guba
　Russia 54°50N 135°45E **107** D14
Udu Pt. *Fiji* 16°9S 179°57W **154** a
Udumalaippettai *India* 10°35N 77°15E **127** J3
Udupi *India* 13°25N 74°42E **127** H2
Udva *India* 20°30N 73°0E **126** D1
Udvoy Balkan *Bulgaria* 42°50N 26°50E **97** D10
Udzungwa △ *Tanzania* 7°52S 36°55E **142** D4
Udzungwa Range
　Tanzania 9°30S 35°10E **142** D4
Ueckermünde *Germany* 53°44N 14°1E **76** B10
Uelen *Russia* 66°10N 170°0W **107** C19
Uelzen *Germany* 52°57N 10°32E **76** B6
Uetersen *Germany* 53°40N 9°40E **76** B5
Uetze *Germany* 52°28N 10°11E **76** C6
Ufaq → *Russia* 54°40N 56°0E **108** B5
Uffenheim *Germany* 49°33N 10°14E **77** G6
Ugab → *Namibia* 20°55S 13°30E **144** B1
Ugalla → *Tanzania* 5°8S 30°42E **142** D3
Ugalla River △ *Tanzania* 5°50S 31°54E **142** D3
Uganda ■ *Africa* 2°0N 32°0E **142** B3
Ugento *Italy* 39°56N 18°10E **95** C11
Ugep *Nigeria* 5°53N 8°2E **139** D6
Ughelli *Nigeria* 5°30N 6°0E **139** D6
Ugie *S. Africa* 31°10S 28°13E **145** E4
Ugine *France* 45°45N 6°25E **73** C10
Uglegorsk *Russia* 49°5N 142°2E **107** E15
Uglich *Russia* 57°33N 38°20E **84** D10
Ugljan *Croatia* 44°12N 15°10E **93** D12
Ugljane *Croatia* 43°35N 16°46E **93** E13
Ugolnye Kopi *Russia* 64°44N 177°42E **107** C18
Ugra → *Russia* 54°30N 36°7E **84** E9
Ugúrchin *Bulgaria* 43°6N 24°26E **97** C8
Uh → *Slovak Rep.* 48°7N 22°0E **79** C16
Uherské Hradiště
　Czech Rep. 49°4N 17°30E **79** B9
Uherský Brod *Czech Rep.* 49°1N 17°40E **79** B9
Úhlava → *Czech Rep.* 49°45N 13°24E **78** B6
Uhlenhorst *Namibia* 23°45S 17°55E **144** B2

Uhniv *Ukraine* 50°22N 23°45E **83** H10
Uhrichsville *U.S.A.* 40°24N 81°21W **174** F3
Uibhist a Deas = South Uist
　U.K. 57°20N 7°15W **65** D1
Uibhist a Tuath = North Uist
　U.K. 57°40N 7°15W **65** D1
Uíge *Angola* 7°30S 14°40E **140** F2
Uijeongbu *S. Korea* 37°48N 127°0E **115** F14
Ŭiju *N. Korea* 40°15N 124°35E **115** D13
Uinta Mts. *U.S.A.* 40°45N 110°30W **169** F8
Uis *Namibia* 21°8S 14°49E **144** B1
Uiseong *S. Korea* 36°21N 128°45E **115** F15
Uitenhage *S. Africa* 33°40S 25°28E **144** E3
Uithuizen *Neths.* 53°24N 6°41E **69** A6
Ujazd *Poland* 50°23N 18°21E **83** H5
Újfehértó *Hungary* 47°49N 21°41E **80** C6
Uji *India* 32°10N 75°18E **122** a
Ujhani *India* 28°0N 79°6E **125** E8
Uji-guntō *Japan* 31°15N 129°25E **113** K4
Ujjain *India* 23°9N 75°43E **124** H6
Ujście *Poland* 53°3N 16°45E **83** E3
Ujście Warty △ *Poland* 52°35N 14°44E **83** F2
Újszász *Hungary* 47°19N 20°7E **80** C5
Ujung Kulon △
　Indonesia 6°46S 105°19E **119** G12
Ujung Pandang = Makassar
　Indonesia 5°10S 119°20E **119** F5
Uka *Russia* 57°50N 162°0E **107** d
Ukai Sagar *India* 21°20N 73°43E **124** D1
Ukara I. *Tanzania* 1°50S 33°0E **142** C3
Uke-Shima *Japan* 28°2N 129°14E **113** K4
Ukerewe I. *Tanzania* 2°0S 33°0E **142** C3
uKhahlamba Drakensberg △
　S. Africa 29°27S 29°30E **145** D4
Ukholovo *Russia* 53°47N 40°30E **84** E11
Ukhrul *India* 25°10N 94°25E **125** G19
Ukhta *Russia* 63°34N 53°41E **100** B10
Ukiah *U.S.A.* 39°9N 123°13W **170** F3
Ukkusiksalik △
　Canada 65°20N 89°30W **160** D10
Ukmergė *Lithuania* 55°15N 24°45E **82** C11
Ukraine ■ *Europe* 49°0N 32°0E **84** F5
Ukwi *Botswana* 23°29S 20°30E **144** C3
Ula *Turkey* 37°6N 28°25E **99** D10
Ulaan Nuur *Mongolia* 44°30N 103°40E **114** C3
Ulaan-Uul *Mongolia* 46°4N 100°49E **110** B9
Ulaanbaatar
　Mongolia 47°55N 106°53E **110** B9
Ulaangom *Mongolia* 50°5N 92°10E **110** A7
Ulaanjirem *Mongolia* 45°5N 105°30E **114** C3
Ulak I. *U.S.A.* 51°22N 178°57W **166** E4
Ulamambri *Australia* 31°19S 149°23E **153** B8
Ulamba
　Dem. Rep. of the Congo 9°3S 23°38E **140** F4
Ulan Bator = Ulaanbaatar
　Mongolia 47°55N 106°53E **110** B9
Ulan Erge *Russia* 46°19N 44°53E **87** G7
Ulan Khol *Russia* 45°27N 46°48E **87** G8
Ulan Ude *Russia* 51°45N 107°40E **111** d
Ulanhad = Chifeng
　China 42°18N 118°58E **115** C11
Ulanhot = Horqin Youyi Qianqi
　China 46°5N 122°3E **115** B11
Ulanów *Poland* 50°30N 22°16E **83** H9
Ulansuhai Nur *China* 40°53N 108°51E **114** D5
Ulaş *Sivas, Turkey* 39°27N 37°2E **104** C7
Ulaş *Tekirdağ, Turkey* 41°5N 27°42E **97** F11
Ulaya *Morogoro, Tanzania* 7°3S 36°55E **142** D4
Ulaya *Tabora, Tanzania* 4°25S 33°30E **142** C3
Ulcinj *Montenegro* 41°58N 19°10E **96** D3
Ulco *S. Africa* 28°21S 24°15E **144** D3
Ule älv = Oulujoki →
　Finland 65°1N 25°30E **60** D22
Ule träsk = Oulujärvi
　Finland 64°25N 27°15E **60** D22
Uleåborg = Oulu *Finland* 65°1N 25°29E **60** D21
Ulefoss *Norway* 59°17N 9°16E **61** F13
Ulfborg *Denmark* 56°16N 8°20E **63** H2
Ullhasnagar *India* 19°15N 73°10E **124** K8
Uliastay = Mongolia
　Mongolia 47°56N 97°28E **110** B8
Uljin *S. Korea* 36°59N 129°24E **115** F15
Uljma *Serbia* 45°2N 21°10E **96** B5
Ülken Kazakhstan 45°12N 73°58E **108** E8
Ülken Borsyq Qumy
　Kazakhstan 47°0N 59°11E **108** E6
Ulla → *Spain* 42°39N 8°44W **88** C2
Ulladulla *Australia* 35°21S 150°29E **153** C9
Ullal *India* 12°48N 74°51E **127** H2
Ullapool *U.K.* 57°54N 5°9W **66** a
Ullared *Sweden* 57°8N 12°42E **63** H6
Ulldecona *Spain* 40°36N 0°20E **90** E5
Ulleungdo *S. Korea* 37°30N 130°30E **115** F16
Ullswater *Canada* 45°12N 79°29W **174** A5
Ullswater *U.K.* 54°34N 2°52W **66** C5
Ulm *Germany* 48°23N 9°58E **77** G5
Ulmarra *Australia* 29°37S 153°4E **153** A9
Ulmeni *Buzău, Romania* 45°4N 26°40E **81** E11
Ulmeni *Maramureş,*
　Romania 47°28N 23°18E **81** C8
Ulongue *Mozam.* 14°37S 34°19E **143** E3
Ulricehamn *Sweden* 57°46N 13°26E **63** H7
Ulrika *Sweden* 58°5N 15°23E **63** F7
Ulsan *S. Korea* 35°20N 129°15E **115** G15
Ulsta *U.K.* 60°30N 1°9W **65** a
Ulster □ *U.K.* 54°35N 6°30W **64** B5
Ulstrem *Bulgaria* 42°1N 26°27E **97** D10
Ultima *Australia* 35°30S 143°18E **153** C3
Ulubat Gölü *Turkey* 40°9N 28°35E **97** F12
Ulubey *Turkey* 38°25N 29°18E **99** C11
Uluborlu *Turkey* 38°4N 30°28E **99** C12
Uluçınar *Turkey* 36°24N 35°53E **104** D6
Uludağ *Turkey* 40°4N 29°13E **99** B12
Uludağ △ *Turkey* 40°5N 29°12E **99** B12
Uluguru Mts. *Tanzania* 7°15S 37°40E **142** D4
Ulukışla = Marathóvounos
　Cyprus 35°13N 33°37E **101** D12
Ulundi *S. Africa* 28°20S 31°25E **145** D5
Ulungur He → *China* 47°1N 87°24E **110** B6
Ulungur Hu *China* 47°20N 87°10E **110** B6
Uluru-Kata Tjuta △
　Australia 25°19S 131°1E **149** E5
Uluru = Ayers Rock
　Australia 25°23S 131°5E **149** E5
Ulutau *Kazakhstan* 48°39N 67°1E **108** E7
Uluwatu *Indonesia* 8°50S 115°5E **119** K18
Ulva *U.K.* 56°29N 6°13W **66** a
Ulverston *U.K.* 54°13N 3°5W **66** C4

...erstone *Australia* 41°11S 146°11E **151** G4
...ra *Russia* 59°10N 142°0E **107** D15
...anovo *Russia* 54°50N 22°6E **82** D9
...anovsk *Russia* 54°20N 48°25E **86** C9
...asutay = Uliastay
  Mongolia 47°56N 97°28E **110** B8
...sses *Kans., U.S.A.* 37°35N 101°22W **172** D3
...sses *Pa., U.S.A.* 41°54N 77°46W **174** E7
...sses, Mt. *Canada* 57°20N 124°5W **162** B4
...zhylanshyq ➔
  Kazakhstan 48°51N 63°46E **108** C6
...aag *Croatia* 45°26N 13°31E **93** C10
...aala *Sweden* 17°25S 68°58W **188** D4
...nän = Oman ■ *Asia* 23°0N 58°0E **131** C6
...an *Ukraine* 48°40N 30°12E **75** D16
...aria *India* 23°35N 80°50E **125** H9
...arkhed *India* 19°37N 77°46E **126** E3
...arpada *Pakistan* 25°15N 69°40E **124** G3
...arpada *India* 21°27N 73°30E **124** J5
...atilla *U.S.A.* 45°55N 119°21W **168** D4
...bagog L. *U.S.A.* 44°46N 71°3W **175** B13
...bakumba *Australia* 13°47S 136°56E **150** A2
...bértide *Italy* 43°18N 12°20E **93** E9
...brella Mts. *N.Z.* 45°35S 169°5E **155** F4
...bria □ *Italy* 42°53N 12°30E **93** F9
...neå *Sweden* 63°45N 20°20E **60** E19
...ecälven ➔ *Sweden* 63°45N 20°20E **60** E19
...era *Indonesia* 0°12S 129°37E **119** E7
...fuli ➔ *Zimbabwe* 17°30S 29°23E **143** F2
...furudzi △ *Zimbabwe* 17°6S 31°40E **143** F3
...agusa *Zimbabwe* 19°29S 27°52E **143** F2
...gwenya ➔ *Mozam.* 25°14S 32°18E **145** C5
...niujaq *Canada* 56°33N 76°33W **164** A4
...nka *Serbia* 44°40N 20°19E **96** B4
...nlazi *S. Africa* 29°59S 30°54E **141** L6
...m ad Daraj, J.
  Jordan 32°18N 35°48E **130** C4
...m al Khashab
  Si. Arabia 17°23N 42°32E **137** D5
...m al Qaywayn
  U.A.E. 25°30N 55°35E **129** E7
...m al Qittayn *Jordan* 32°18N 36°40E **130** C5
...m al Rasas *Jordan* 31°30N 35°30E **130** D4
...m Bāb *Qatar* 25°12N 50°48E **129** E6
...m Birkah *Si. Arabia* 27°44N 36°31E **137** B4
...m Durman = Omdurmân
  Sudan 15°40N 32°28E **135** E12
...m el Fahm *Israel* 32°31N 35°9E **130** C4
...m Keddada *Sudan* 13°33N 26°35E **135** F11
...m Lajj *Si. Arabia* 25°0N 37°23E **128** E3
...m Qasr *Iraq* 30°1N 47°58E **128** D5
...m Ruwaba *Sudan* 12°50N 31°20E **135** F12
...m Sa'id *Qatar* 25°0N 51°33E **129** E6
...m Tais □ *Qatar* 26°7N 51°15E **129** E6
...m Urūmah
  Si. Arabia 25°43N 36°35E **137** B4
...m Zehetir *Egypt* 28°48N 32°31E **137** E8
...mak I. *U.S.A.* 53°15N 168°20W **166** E6
...mniati ➔ *Zimbabwe* 16°49S 28°45E **143** F2
...mpqua ➔ *U.S.A.* 43°40N 124°12W **168** E1
...mared *India* 20°51N 79°18E **126** D4
...mreth *India* 22°41N 73°4E **124** H5
...mri *India* 19°2N 77°39E **126** E3
...mtata = Mthatha
  S. Africa 31°36S 28°49E **145** D4
...nuahia *Nigeria* 5°31N 7°26E **139** D6
...nuarama *Brazil* 23°45S 53°20W **191** A5
...nurbey *Turkey* 40°13N 36°28E **97** F10
...nvukwe Ra.
  Zimbabwe 16°45S 30°45E **143** F3
...nzimvubu *S. Africa* 31°38S 29°33E **145** D4
...ngwingwe ➔
  Zimbabwe 22°12S 29°56E **143** G2
...nzinto = eMuziwezinto
  S. Africa 30°15S 30°45E **145** D5
...n *Africa* 20°46N 71°8E **124** A4
...a ➔ *Bos.-H.* 45°0N 16°20E **93** D13
...ac ➔ *Bos.-H.* 45°4N 16°22E **93** D13
...adilla *Ga., U.S.A.* 32°16N 83°44W **178** C4
...adilla *N.Y., U.S.A.* 42°20N 75°19W **175** D9
...aí *Brazil* 16°23S 46°53W **189** D2
...alakleet *U.S.A.* 63°52N 160°47W **166** C7
...alaska *U.S.A.* 53°53N 166°32W **166** E6
...alaska I. *U.S.A.* 53°35N 166°50W **166** E6
...ayzah *Si. Arabia* 26°6N 43°58E **128** E4
...ayzah, J. *Asia* 32°12N 39°18E **105** F8
...cia *Spain* 42°21N 1°8W **90** C3
...cia *Bolivia* 18°25S 66°40W **186** G5
...compahgre Peak
  U.S.A. 38°4N 107°28W **168** G10
...compahgre Plateau
  U.S.A. 38°20N 108°15W **168** G9
...dara Volcanic △
  Australia 18°14S 144°41E **150** B3
...den *Sweden* 58°45N 14°25E **63** F8
...derbool *Australia* 35°10S 141°51E **152** C4
...dersaker *Sweden* 63°19N 13°21E **62** A7
...derwood *Canada* 44°18N 81°29W **174** B3
...echa *Russia* 52°50N 32°37E **86** F7
...garie *Australia* 33°38S 146°56E **153** B7
...garra *Australia* 34°12S 136°2E **152** B2
...gava, Pén. d' *Canada* 60°0N 74°0W **161** F17
...gava B. *Canada* 59°30N 67°30W **161** F18
...geny = Ungheni
  Moldova 47°11N 27°51E **81** C12
...ggi *N. Korea* 42°16N 130°28E **115** C16
...gheni *Moldova* 47°11N 27°51E **81** C12
...gwana B. *Kenya* 2°45S 40°20E **142** C5
...i *Russia* 57°46N 51°13E **86** D10
...iäo *Brazil* 4°35S 42°52W **191** D10
...iäo da Vitória *Brazil* 33°58S 51°5W **191** B5
...iäo dos Palmares
  Brazil 9°10S 36°2W **189** D3
...ičov *Czech Rep.* 49°46N 17°8E **79** B10
...iejów *Poland* 51°59N 18°46E **83** G5
...imak I. *U.S.A.* 54°45N 164°0W **166** E7
...imak Pass. *U.S.A.* 54°15N 164°30W **166** E7
...ion *Miss., U.S.A.* 32°34N 89°7W **177** E10
...ion *Mo., U.S.A.* 38°27N 91°0W **172** F8
...ion *S.C., U.S.A.* 34°43N 81°37W **177** D14
...ion City *Calif.,
  U.S.A.* 37°36N 122°1W **170** H4
...ion City *Ga., U.S.A.* 33°35N 84°33W **178** D3
...ion City *N.J., U.S.A.* 40°45N 74°2W **175** E10
...ion City *Tenn.,
  U.S.A.* 36°26N 89°3W **177** C10
...ion Dale *U.S.A.* 41°43N 75°29W **175** E8

Union Gap *U.S.A.* 46°33N 120°28W **168** C3
Union Park *U.S.A.* 28°34N 81°17W **179** G8
Union Point *U.S.A.* 33°37N 83°4W **178** B6
Union Springs *Ala.,
  U.S.A.* 32°9N 85°43W **178** C4
Union Springs *N.Y.,
  U.S.A.* 42°50N 76°41W **175** D8
Uniondale *S. Africa* 33°39S 23°7E **144** E3
Uniontown *U.S.A.* 39°54N 79°44W **173** F14
Unionville *La., U.S.A.* 31°26N 83°30W **178** D6
Unionville *Mo., U.S.A.* 40°29N 93°1W **172** E7
Unirea *Romania* 44°15N 27°35E **81** F12
United Arab Emirates ■
  Asia 23°50N 54°0E **129** F7
United Kingdom ■ *Europe* 53°0N 2°0W **68** E6
United States of America ■
  N. Amer. 37°0N 96°0W **167** H20
Unity *Canada* 52°30N 109°5W **163** C7
Universales, Mtes. *Spain* 40°18N 1°33W **90** E3
University Park
  U.S.A. 32°17N 106°45W **169** K10
University Place
  U.S.A. 47°14N 122°33W **170** C4
Unjha *India* 23°46N 72°24E **124** H5
Unna *Germany* 51°32N 7°42E **76** D3
Unnao *India* 26°35N 80°30E **125** F9
Uno, Ilha *Guinea-Biss.* 11°15N 16°13W **138** C1
Unsengedsi ➔
  Zimbabwe 15°43S 31°14E **143** F3
Unst *U.K.* 60°44N 0°53W **65** A8
Unstrut ➔ *Germany* 51°10N 11°48E **76** D7
Unterfranken □ *Germany* 50°0N 10°0E **77** F5
Unterschleissheim
  Germany 48°17N 11°34E **77** G7
Unuk ➔ *Canada* 56°5N 131°3W **162** B2
Ünye *Turkey* 41°5N 37°15E **104** B7
Unzen-Amakusa △
  Japan 32°15N 130°10E **113** H5
Unzha *Russia* 58°0N 44°0E **86** C7
Unzha ➔ *Russia* 57°49N 43°47E **86** B6
Uong Bi *Vietnam* 21°2N 106°47E **120** B6
Uotsuri-Shima
  E. China Sea 25°45N 123°29E **113** M1
Uozu *Japan* 36°48N 137°24E **113** F8
Upata *Venezuela* 8°1N 62°24W **186** B6
Upatoi Cr. ➔ *U.S.A.* 32°22N 84°58W **178** C5
Upemba, L.
  Dem. Rep. of the Congo 8°30S 26°20E **143** D2
Upemba △
  Dem. Rep. of the Congo 9°0S 26°35E **143** D2
Upernavik *Greenland* 72°49N 56°20W **57** C5
Upington *S. Africa* 28°25S 21°15E **144** C3
Upleta *India* 21°46N 70°16E **124** J7
'Upolu *Samoa* 13°58S 172°0W **147** C11
Upper Alkali L. *U.S.A.* 41°47N 120°8W **168** F3
Upper Arrow L.
  Canada 50°30N 117°50W **162** C5
Upper Daly ⊙ *Australia* 14°26S 131°3E **148** B5
Upper Darby *U.S.A.* 39°55N 75°16W **173** F16
Upper East □ *Ghana* 10°30N 1°0W **139** C4
Upper Foster L.
  Canada 56°47N 105°20W **163** B7
Upper Hutt *N.Z.* 41°8S 175°5E **154** H4
Upper Klamath L.
  U.S.A. 42°25N 121°55W **168** E3
Upper Lake *U.S.A.* 39°10N 122°54W **170** F4
Upper Liard *Canada* 60°3N 128°54W **162** A3
Upper Manilla
  Australia 30°38S 150°40E **153** A9
Upper Manzanilla
  Trin. & Tob. 10°31N 61°4W **187** K15
Upper Missouri Breaks △
  U.S.A. 47°40N 109°55W **168** C9
Upper Musquodoboit
  Canada 45°10N 62°58W **165** C7
Upper Red L. *U.S.A.* 48°8N 94°45W **172** A6
Upper Sandusky
  U.S.A. 40°50N 83°17W **173** E12
Upper Volta = Burkina Faso ■
  Africa 12°0N 1°0W **138** C4
Upper West □ *Ghana* 10°30N 2°20W **138** C4
Uppharad *Sweden* 58°9N 12°19E **63** F6
Uppland *Sweden* 59°59N 17°48E **62** D12
Upplands-Väsby
  Sweden 59°31N 17°54E **62** E11
Uppsala *Sweden* 59°53N 17°38E **62** E11
Uppsala län □ *Sweden* 60°0N 17°30E **62** D11
Upshi *India* 33°48N 77°52E **125** C7
Upton *U.S.A.* 44°6N 104°38W **168** D11
Uqsuqtuuq = Gjoa Haven
  Canada 68°38N 95°53W **160** D12
Ur *Iraq* 30°55N 46°25E **128** D5
Ura-Tyube = Istaravshän
  Tajikistan 39°55N 69°1E **109** E7
Urad Qianqi *China* 40°40N 108°30E **114** D5
Uraholo *Japan* 42°50N 143°40E **112** C11
Urakawa *Japan* 42°9N 142°47E **112** C11
Ural = Uralskiy □ *Russia* 64°0N 70°0E **106** C7
Ural ➔ *Zhayyq ➔*
  Kazakhstan 47°0N 51°48E **108** C4
Ural *Australia* 33°21S 146°12E **153** B7
Ural Mts. = Uralskie Gory
  Eurasia 60°0N 59°0E **58** C17
Urala *Australia* 30°37S 151°29E **153** A9
Uralsk = Oral
  Kazakhstan 51°20N 51°20E **86** E10
Uralskie Gory *Eurasia* 60°0N 59°0E **58** C17
Uralskiy □ *Russia* 64°0N 70°0E **106** C7
Urambo *Tanzania* 5°4S 32°0E **142** D3
Urana *Australia* 35°15S 146°21E **153** C7
Urana, L. *Australia* 35°16S 146°10E **153** C7
Urandangi *Australia* 21°32S 138°14E **150** C2
Uranga *Australia* 30°31S 153°1E **153** A10
Uranium City *Canada* 59°34N 108°37W **163** B7
Urapuntja = Utopia
  Australia 22°14S 134°33E **150** C1
Uraricoera ➔ *Brazil* 3°2N 60°30W **186** C6
Urasoe *Japan* 26°15N 127°43E **113** L3
Uravakonda *India* 14°57N 77°12E **127** G3
Urawa = Saitama
  Japan 35°54N 139°38E **113** G9
Uray *Russia* 60°5N 65°15E **106** C7
'Uray'irah *Si. Arabia* 25°57N 48°53E **129** E6
Urbana *Ill., U.S.A.* 40°7N 83°45W **173** E11
Urbana *Ohio, U.S.A.* 40°7N 83°45W **173** E12
Urbánia *Italy* 43°40N 12°31E **93** E9
Urbano Santos *Brazil* 3°12S 43°23W **189** B3
Urbel ➔ *Spain* 42°21N 3°40W **88** C7
Urbino *Italy* 43°43N 12°38E **93** E9
Urbión, Picos de *Spain* 42°1N 2°52W **90** C2

Urcos *Peru* 13°40S 71°38W **188** C3
Urdinarrain *Argentina* 32°37S 58°52W **190** C4
Urdos *France* 42°51N 0°35W **72** F3
Ure ➔ *U.K.* 54°5N 1°20W **66** C6
Uren *Russia* 57°35N 45°55E **86** B7
Urengoy *Russia* 65°58N 78°22E **106** C8
Ures *Mexico* 29°26N 110°24W **180** B2
Urewera △ *N.Z.* 38°29S 177°7E **154** E6
Urfa = Şanlıurfa *Turkey* 37°12N 38°50E **105** D8
Urganch *Uzbekistan* 41°40N 60°41E **108** D6
Urgench = Urganch
  Uzbekistan 41°40N 60°41E **108** D6
Ürgüp *Turkey* 38°38N 34°56E **104** C6
Urho Kekkonen △
  Finland 68°20N 27°40E **60** B22
Uri *Switz.* 34°8N 74°2E **125** B6
Uri □ *Switz.* 46°43N 8°35E **77** J4
Uribia *Colombia* 11°43N 72°16W **186** A4
Uricani *Romania* 45°20N 23°9E **80** E8
Uriondo *Bolivia* 21°41S 64°41W **190** A3
Urique *Mexico* 27°13N 107°55W **180** B3
Urique ➔ *Mexico* 26°29N 107°58W **180** B3
Urk *Neths.* 52°39N 5°36E **69** B5
Urkiola △ *Spain* 43°6N 1°20W **90** B3
Urla *Turkey* 38°20N 26°47E **99** C11
Urlaţi *Romania* 44°59N 26°15E **81** F11
Urmia = Orūmīyeh
  Iran 37°40N 45°0E **105** D11
Uromi *Nigeria* 6°42N 6°20E **139** D6
Uroševac = Ferizaj
  Kosovo 42°23N 21°10E **96** D5
Uroyan, Montanas de
  Puerto Rico 18°12N 66°50W **183** d
Urrampinyi Iltjiltarri ⊙
  Australia 24°20S 132°10E **148** D5
Urshult *Sweden* 56°31N 14°50E **63** H8
Uru Uru, L. *Bolivia* 18°6S 67°8W **188** D4
Uruaçu *Brazil* 14°30S 49°10W **187** F9
Uruapan *Mexico* 19°24N 102°3W **180** D4
Urubamba *Peru* 13°20S 72°10W **188** C3
Urubamba ➔ *Peru* 10°43S 73°48W **188** C3
Urucará *Brazil* 2°32S 57°45W **186** D7
Uruçuí, Serra do *Brazil* 9°0S 44°45W **189** D2
Uruçuí Prêto ➔ *Brazil* 7°20S 44°33W **189** D2
Urucuia ➔ *Brazil* 16°8S 45°5W **189** D1
Uruguai ➔ *Brazil* 26°0S 53°30W **191** B5
Uruguaiana *Brazil* 29°50S 57°0W **190** B4
Uruguay ■ *S. Amer.* 32°30S 56°30W **190** C4
Uruguay ➔ *S. Amer.* 34°12S 58°18W **190** C4
Urumchi = Ürümqi
  China 43°45N 87°45E **109** D11
Ürümqi *China* 43°45N 87°45E **109** D11
Uruna ⊙ *Australia* 24°35S 133°1E **148** D5
Urup ➔ *Russia* 45°0N 41°10E **87** H5
Urup, Ostrov *Russia* 46°0N 151°0E **107** E16
Urutaí *Brazil* 17°28S 48°12W **189** D1
Uryupinsk *Russia* 50°45N 41°58E **86** E5
Ürzhar *Kazakhstan* 47°5N 81°38E **109** C10
Urzhum *Russia* 57°10N 49°56E **86** B9
Urziceni *Romania* 44°40N 26°42E **81** F11
Usa ➔ *Russia* 66°16N 59°49E **106** C6
Uşak *Turkey* 38°43N 29°28E **99** C11
Uşak □ *Turkey* 38°30N 29°0E **99** C11
Usakos *Namibia* 21°54S 15°31E **144** B2
Usborne, Mt. *Falk. Is.* 51°40S 58°55W **192** D5
Ušće *Serbia* 43°30N 20°39E **96** C4
Usedom *Germany* 53°55N 14°2E **76** B10
Usedom □ *Germany* 53°55N 14°0E **76** B10
Useless Loop *Australia* 26°8S 113°23E **149** E1
'Usfān *Si. Arabia* 21°58N 39°27E **137** C4
Ushakova, Ostrov *Russia* 82°0N 80°0E **107** A8
Ushakovo *Russia* 54°37N 20°56E **83** A11
Ushant = Ouessant, Î. d'
  France 48°28N 5°6W **70** D1
Üsharal *Kazakhstan* 46°10N 80°56E **109** C10
Ushashi *Tanzania* 1°59S 33°57E **142** C3
'Ushayrim *Ar Riyāḍ,
  Si. Arabia* 25°35N 45°47E **128** E5
'Ushayrah *Makkah,
  Si. Arabia* 21°46N 40°42E **137** C5
Ushibuka *Japan* 32°11N 130°1E **113** H5
Üshtöbe *Kazakhstan* 45°16N 78°0E **109** C9
Ushuaia *Argentina* 54°50S 68°23W **192** D3
Ushumun *Russia* 52°47N 126°32E **107** D13
Ushytsya ➔ *Ukraine* 48°35N 27°8E **81** D12
Usinsk *Russia* 65°57N 57°27E **106** C6
Usk *Canada* 54°38N 128°26W **162** C3
Usk ➔ *U.K.* 51°33N 2°58W **67** F5
Uska *India* 27°12N 83°7E **125** F10
Üsküdar *Turkey* 41°1N 29°0E **97** F13
Uslar *Germany* 51°39N 9°38E **76** D5
Usman *Russia* 52°5N 39°48E **85** F10
Usoke *Tanzania* 5°8S 32°24E **142** D3
Usolye-Sibirskoye
  Russia 52°48N 103°40E **107** D11
Usoro *Nigeria* 5°0N 6°11E **139** D6
Uspallata, P. de
  Argentina 32°37S 69°22W **190** C2
Ussel *France* 45°32N 2°18E **72** D6
Usson-du-Poitou *France* 46°16N 0°31E **72** B4
Ussuriysk *Russia* 43°48N 131°59E **112** C6
Ussurka *Russia* 45°12N 133°31E **112** B6
Ust-Buzulukskaya *Russia* 50°8N 42°11E **86** E6
Ust-Chaun *Russia* 68°47N 170°30E **107** C18
Ust-Chorna *Ukraine* 48°19N 23°56E **81** D8
Ust-Donetskiy *Russia* 47°35N 40°55E **87** G5
Ust-Ilimsk *Russia* 58°3N 102°39E **107** D11
Ust-Ishim *Russia* 57°45N 71°10E **106** D8
Ust-Kamchatsk
  Russia 56°10N 162°28E **107** D17
Ust-Kamenogorsk = Öskemen
  Kazakhstan 50°0N 82°36E **109** C10
Ust-Khayryuzovo
  Russia 57°15N 156°45E **107** D16
Ust-Kut *Russia* 56°50N 105°42E **107** D11
Ust-Kuyga *Russia* 70°1N 135°43E **107** B14
Ust-Labinsk *Russia* 45°15N 39°41E **87** H4
Ust-Luga *Russia* 59°35N 28°20E **84** C5
Ust-Maya *Russia* 60°30N 134°28E **107** C14
Ust-Nera *Russia* 64°35N 143°15E **107** C15
Ust-Nyukzha *Russia* 56°34N 121°37E **107** D13
Ust-Olenek *Russia* 73°0N 120°5E **107** B12
Ust-Omchug *Russia* 61°9N 149°38E **107** C15
Ust-Port *Russia* 69°40N 84°26E **106** C9
Ust-Tsilma *Russia* 65°28N 52°11E **106** C6
Ust-Urt = Ustyurt Plateau
  Asia 44°0N 55°0E **108** D5

Urcos ... V column

Ustaritz *France* 43°24N 1°27W **72** E2
Ustecký □ *Czech Rep.* 50°30N 14°0E **78** A7
Uster *Switz.* 47°22N 8°43E **77** H4
Ústí nad Labem
  Czech Rep. 50°41N 14°3E **78** A7
Ústí nad Orlicí *Czech Rep.* 49°58N 16°24E **79** B9
Ústica *Italy* 38°42N 13°11E **94** D6
Ustinov = Izhevsk
  Russia 56°51N 53°14E **106** D9
Ustka *Poland* 54°35N 16°58E **82** D3
Ustroń *Poland* 49°43N 18°48E **83** J5
Ustrzyki Dolne *Poland* 49°27N 22°40E **83** J9
Ustyuh *Ukraine* 50°51N 24°10E **83** H11
Ustyurt Plateau *Asia* 44°0N 55°0E **108** D5
Ustyuzhna *Russia* 58°50N 36°32E **84** C9
Usu *China* 44°27N 84°40E **109** D10
Usuki *Japan* 33°8N 131°49E **113** H5
Usulután *El Salv.* 13°25N 88°28W **182** D2
Usumacinta ➔
  Mexico 18°24N 92°38W **181** D6
Usumbura = Bujumbura
  Burundi 3°16S 29°18E **142** C2
Usure *Tanzania* 4°40S 34°22E **142** C3
Usutuo ➔ *Mozam.* 26°48S 32°7E **145** C5
Uta *Indonesia* 4°33S 136°0E **119** E9
Utah □ *U.S.A.* 39°20N 111°30W **168** G8
Utah L. *U.S.A.* 40°12N 111°48W **168** F8
Utansjö *Sweden* 62°46N 17°55E **62** B11
Utara, Selat *Malaysia* 5°28N 100°20E **121** c
Utarni *India* 26°5N 71°58E **124** F4
Utatlan *Guatemala* 15°2N 91°11W **182** C1
Ute Creek ➔ *U.S.A.* 35°21N 103°50W **169** J12
Utebo *Spain* 41°43N 1°0W **90** D3
Utena *Lithuania* 55°25N 25°40E **84** E3
Utete *Tanzania* 8°0S 38°45E **142** D4
Uthai Thani *Thailand* 15°22N 100°3E **120** E3
Uthal *Pakistan* 25°44N 66°40E **124** G2
Utiariti *Brazil* 13°0S 58°10W **186** F7
Utica *N.Y., U.S.A.* 43°6N 75°14W **175** C9
Utica *Ohio, U.S.A.* 40°14N 82°27W **174** F2
Utiel *Spain* 39°37N 1°11W **91** F3
Utikuma L. *Canada* 55°50N 115°30W **162** B5
Utila *Honduras* 16°6N 86°56W **182** C2
Utinga *Brazil* 12°6S 41°5W **189** C2
Utkela *India* 20°6N 83°10E **126** D6
Utländen *Sweden* 56°2N 15°48E **63** H9
Utnur *India* 19°22N 78°46E **126** E4
Utö *Sweden* 58°56N 18°16E **62** F12
Utopia *Australia* 22°14S 134°33E **150** C1
Utraula *India* 27°19N 82°25E **125** F10
Utrecht *Neths.* 52°5N 5°8E **69** B5
Utrecht *S. Africa* 27°38S 30°20E **145** D5
Utrecht □ *Neths.* 52°6N 5°7E **69** B5
Utrera *Spain* 37°12N 5°48W **89** H5
Utsjoki ➔ *Finland* 69°51N 26°59E **60** B22
Utsunomiya *Japan* 36°30N 139°50E **113** F9
Uttar Pradesh □ *India* 27°0N 80°0E **125** F9
Uttaradit *Thailand* 17°36N 100°5E **120** D3
Uttarakhand □ *India* 30°0N 79°30E **125** D8
Utterson *Canada* 45°12N 79°19W **174** A5
Uttoxeter *U.K.* 52°54N 1°52W **66** E6
Utuado *Puerto Rico* 18°16N 66°42W **183** d
Uummannaq *Qaasuitsup,
  Greenland* 70°58N 52°17W **54** B5
Uummannaq *Qaasuitsup,
  Greenland* 77°33N 68°52W **57** B4
Uummannarsuaq = Nunap Isua
  Greenland 59°48N 43°55W **57** F6
Uunartoq Qeqertaq
  Greenland 71°33N 21°47W **57** C8
Uusikaarlepyy *Finland* 63°32N 22°31E **60** E20
Uusikaupunki *Finland* 60°47N 21°25E **84** B1
Uva *Russia* 56°59N 52°13E **86** B11
Uvac ➔ *Serbia* 43°35N 19°30E **96** C3
Uvalda *U.S.A.* 32°2N 82°31W **178** C7
Uvalde *U.S.A.* 29°13N 99°47W **176** G5
Uvarovo *Russia* 51°59N 42°14E **86** E6
Uvat *Russia* 59°5N 68°50E **106** D7
Uvinza *Tanzania* 5°5S 30°24E **142** D3
Uvira
  Dem. Rep. of the Congo 3°22S 29°3E **142** C2
Uvs □ *Mongolia* 49°38N 93°0E **109** C12
Uvs Nuur *Mongolia* 50°20N 92°30E **109** B12
'Uwairidh, Ḥarrat al
  Si. Arabia 26°50N 38°0E **128** E3
Uwajima *Japan* 33°10N 132°35E **113** H6
Uwanda ⊙ *Tanzania* 7°46S 32°0E **142** D3
Uweinat, Jebel *Sudan* 21°54N 24°58E **137** C11
Uxbridge *Canada* 44°6N 79°7W **174** B5
Uxin Qi *China* 38°50N 109°5E **114** E5
Uxmal *Mexico* 20°22N 89°46W **181** C7
Uydzin *Mongolia* 44°9N 107°0E **114** B4
Uyo *Nigeria* 5°1N 7°53E **139** D6
Uyüklü Tepe *Turkey* 37°5N 27°21E **99** D9
Uyûn Mûsa *Egypt* 29°53N 32°40E **130** F1
Uyuni *Bolivia* 20°28S 66°47W **188** E4
Uzbekistan ■ *Asia* 41°30N 65°0E **109** D7
Uzboy ➔ *Turkmenistan* 39°30N 55°0E **129** B7
Uzen, Mal ➔ *Kazakhstan* 49°4N 49°44E **87** F9
Uzerche *France* 45°25N 1°34E **72** C5
Uzès *France* 44°1N 4°26E **73** D8
Uzh ➔ *Ukraine* 51°15N 30°12E **75** C16
Uzhgorod = Uzhhorod
  Ukraine 48°36N 22°18E **80** B7
Uzhhorod *Ukraine* 48°36N 22°18E **80** B7
Uzhok *Ukraine* 48°59N 22°52E **80** B7
Uzice *Serbia* 43°55N 19°50E **96** C3
Uzlovaya *Russia* 54°0N 38°5E **84** F10
Üzümlü *Turkey* 36°44N 29°14E **99** E11
Uzunköprü *Turkey* 41°16N 26°43E **97** F10
Uzunkuyu *Turkey* 38°17N 26°23E **99** C8

V

Vaal ➔ *S. Africa* 29°4S 23°38E **144** C3
Vaal Dam *S. Africa* 27°0S 28°14E **145** D4
Vaalwater *S. Africa* 24°15S 28°8E **145** B4
Vaasa *Finland* 63°6N 21°38E **60** E19
Vabre *France* 43°42N 2°24E **72** E6
Vác *Hungary* 47°49N 19°10E **80** A9
Vacaria *Brazil* 28°31S 50°52W **191** B5
Vacaville *U.S.A.* 38°21N 121°59W **170** G5
Vaccarès, Étang de
  France 43°32N 4°34E **73** E8
Vach = Vakh ➔ *Russia* 60°45N 76°45E **106** C8
Vache, Î. à *Haiti* 18°2N 73°35W **183** C5
Väckelsång *Sweden* 56°37N 14°58E **63** H8
Vacoas *Mauritius* 20°18S 57°29E **141** d

Vada *India* 19°39N 73°8E **126** E1
Vadakara *India* 11°35N 75°40E **127** J2
Väddö *Sweden* 60°0N 18°50E **62** D12
Vadehavet △ *Denmark* 55°20N 8°30E **63** J2
Väderstad *Sweden* 58°19N 14°55E **63** F8
Vado Lígure *Italy* 44°17N 8°26E **92** D5
Vadodara *India* 22°20N 73°10E **124** H5
Vadsø *Norway* 70°3N 29°50E **60** A23
Vadstena *Sweden* 58°28N 14°54E **63** F8
Vaduj *India* 17°36N 74°27E **126** F2
Vaduz *Liech.* 47°8N 9°31E **77** H5
Værøy *Norway* 67°40N 12°40E **60** C15
Vågar *Færoe Is.* 62°5N 7°15W **60** E9
Vaggeryd *Sweden* 57°30N 14°10E **63** G8
Vaghia *Greece* 38°19N 23°11E **98** C5
Vagia, Akra *Greece* 36°15N 28°11E **101** C10
Vagney *France* 48°1N 6°43E **71** D13
Vagnhärad *Sweden* 58°57N 17°33E **63** F11
Vagos *Portugal* 40°33N 8°42W **88** E2
Vågsfjorden *Norway* 68°50N 16°50E **60** B17
Váh ➔ *Slovak Rep.* 47°43N 18°7E **79** D11
Vahsel B. *Antarctica* 75°0S 35°0W **55** D1
Váhtjer = Gällivare
  Sweden 67°9N 20°40E **60** C19
Vaï *Greece* 35°15N 26°18E **101** D8
Vaiaku = Fongafale
  Tuvalu 8°31S 179°13E **147** B10
Vaigai ➔ *India* 9°15N 79°10E **127** K4
Vaiges *France* 48°2N 0°30W **70** D6
Vaihingen *Germany* 48°54N 8°57E **77** G4
Vaihiria, L. *Tahiti* 17°43S 149°25W **155** b
Vaijapur *India* 19°58N 74°45E **126** D2
Vaikam *India* 9°45N 76°25E **127** K3
Vail *U.S.A.* 39°40N 106°20W **168** G10
Vailly-sur-Aisne *France* 49°24N 3°31E **71** C10
Vaippar ➔ *India* 9°0N 78°25E **127** K4
Vairao *Tahiti* 17°47S 149°17W **155** b
Vaisali ➔ *India* 26°5N 71°58E **124** F4
Vaison-la-Romaine *France* 44°14N 5°4E **73** D9
Vajpur *India* 21°24N 73°17E **126** D1
Vakarai *Sri Lanka* 8°8N 81°26E **127** K5
Vakarel *Bulgaria* 42°35N 23°40E **96** D7
Vakfıkebir *Turkey* 41°3N 39°17E **105** B8
Vakh ➔ *Russia* 60°45N 76°45E **106** C8
Vakhtan *Russia* 57°53N 46°47E **86** B8
Vál *Hungary* 47°22N 18°40E **80** D3
Val Camónica *Italy* 22°14S 134°33E **150** C1
Val-de-Marne □ *France* 48°45N 2°28E **71** D9
Val-d'Isère *France* 45°27N 6°59E **73** C10
Val-d'Oise □ *France* 49°5N 2°10E **71** C9
Val-d'Or *Canada* 48°7N 77°47W **164** C4
Val Grande △ *Italy* 46°3N 8°25E **92** B5
Val Marie *Canada* 49°15N 107°45W **163** D7
Val Thorens *France* 45°18N 6°33E **73** C10
Valaam *Russia* 61°22N 30°57E **84** B6
Valadares *Portugal* 41°5N 8°38W **88** D2
Valahia *Romania* 44°35N 25°0E **81** F9
Valaichenai *Sri Lanka* 7°54N 81°32E **127** L5
Valais □ *Switz.* 46°12N 7°45E **77** J3
Valais, Alpes du *Switz.* 46°5N 7°35E **77** J3
Valandovo *Macedonia* 41°19N 22°34E **96** B6
Valašské Meziříčí
  Czech Rep. 49°29N 17°59E **79** B10
Valatie *U.S.A.* 42°24N 73°40W **175** D11
Valaxa *Greece* 38°50N 24°29E **98** C6
Vålberg *Sweden* 59°23N 13°11E **62** E7
Valbo *Sweden* 60°40N 17°0E **62** D10
Valbondione *Italy* 46°2N 10°1E **92** B7
Valcamonica = Val Camónica
  Italy 46°0N 10°17E **92** C7
Vâlcani *Romania* 46°0N 20°26E **80** D5
Vâlcea □ *Romania* 45°0N 24°0E **81** F9
Valcheta *Argentina* 40°40S 66°8W **192** B3
Valdagno *Italy* 45°39N 11°18E **92** C8
Valdahon *France* 47°8N 6°21E **71** E13
Valdai Hills = Valdayskaya
  Vozvyshennost *Russia* 57°0N 33°30E **84** D7
Valday *Russia* 57°58N 33°9E **84** D7
Valdayskaya Vozvyshennost
  Russia 57°0N 33°30E **84** D7
Valdaysky △ *Russia* 58°0N 33°0E **84** D7
Valdeazogues ➔ *Spain* 38°45N 4°55W **89** G6
Valdecañas, Embalse de
  Spain 39°45N 5°25W **88** F5
Valdemarsvik *Sweden* 58°14N 16°40E **63** F10
Valdemoro *Spain* 40°12N 3°40W **88** E7
Valdepeñas *Spain* 38°43N 3°25W **89** G7
Valderaduey ➔ *Spain* 41°31N 5°42W **88** D5
Valdérice *Italy* 38°4N 12°37E **94** E5
Valderrobres *Spain* 40°53N 0°9E **90** E5
Valdés, Pen. *Argentina* 42°30S 63°45W **192** B4
Valdez *U.S.A.* 61°7N 146°16W **166** C6
Valdivia *Chile* 39°50S 73°14W **192** A2
Valdivia Abyssal Plain
  S. Ocean 62°30S 70°0E **55** C6
Valdobbiádene *Italy* 45°54N 12°0E **93** C8
Valdosta *U.S.A.* 30°50N 83°17W **178** D6
Valdovíño = Aviño *Spain* 43°36N 8°8W **88** B2
Valdres *Norway* 61°5N 9°5E **63** D5
Vale *Georgia* 41°30N 42°58E **87** K6
Vale *U.S.A.* 43°59N 117°15W **168** E5
Vale of Glamorgan □
  U.K. 51°28N 3°25W **67** F4
Valea lui Mihai *Romania* 47°32N 22°11E **80** A7
Valea Mărului *Romania* 45°49N 27°42E **81** E12
Valemount *Canada* 52°50N 119°17W **162** C5
Valença *Brazil* 13°20S 39°5W **189** C3
Valença do Piauí *Brazil* 6°20S 41°45W **189** D2
Valençay *France* 47°9N 1°34E **71** E8
Valence *France* 44°57N 4°54E **73** D8
Valence d'Agen *France* 44°6N 0°53E **72** D4
Valencia *Spain* 39°27N 0°23W **91** F4
Valencia *Trin. & Tob.* 10°39N 61°11W **187** K15
Valencia *Venezuela* 10°11N 68°0W **186** A5
Valencia □ *Spain* 39°20N 0°40W **91** F4
Valencia ✈ (VLC) *Spain* 39°20N 0°26W **91** F4
Valencia de Alcántara
  Spain 39°25N 7°14W **89** F3
Valencia de Don Juan
  Spain 42°17N 5°31W **88** C5
Valencia I. *Ireland* 51°54N 10°22W **64** G2
Valenciennes *France* 50°20N 3°34E **71** B10
Văleni *Romania* 44°15N 24°45E **81** F9
Vălenii de Munte
  Romania 45°11N 26°3E **81** E11
Valensole *France* 43°50N 5°59E **73** E9

Valentigney *France* 47°27N 6°51E **71** E13
Valentim, Sa. do *Brazil* 6°0S 43°30W **189** B2
Valentin *Russia* 43°8N 134°17E **112** C7
Valentine *Nebr.,
  U.S.A.* 42°52N 100°33W **172** D3
Valentine *Tex., U.S.A.* 30°35N 104°30W **176** F2
Valenza *Italy* 45°1N 8°38E **92** C5
Valera *Venezuela* 9°19N 70°37W **186** B4
Valga *Estonia* 57°47N 26°2E **84** C4
Valguarnera Caropepe
  Italy 37°30N 14°23E **95** E7
Valier *U.S.A.* 48°18N 112°16W **168** B7
Valinco, G. de *France* 41°40N 8°52E **73** G12
Valjevo *Serbia* 44°18N 19°53E **96** B3
Valka *Latvia* 57°46N 26°3E **84** C4
Valkeakoski *Finland* 61°16N 24°2E **84** B2
Valkenswaard *Neths.* 51°21N 5°29E **69** C5
Vall de Uxó = La Vall d'Uixó
  Spain 39°49N 0°15W **90** F4
Valla *Sweden* 59°2N 16°20E **62** E10
Valladolid *Mexico* 20°41N 88°12W **181** C7
Valladolid *Spain* 41°38N 4°43W **88** D6
Valladolid □ *Spain* 41°38N 4°43W **88** D6
Vallata *Italy* 41°2N 15°16E **95** A8
Valldemossa *Spain* 39°43N 2°37E **100** B9
Valle d'Aosta □ *Italy* 45°45N 7°15E **92** C4
Valle de la Pascua
  Venezuela 9°13N 66°0W **186** B5
Valle de las Palmas
  Mexico 32°20N 116°43W **171** N10
Valle de Santiago
  Mexico 20°23N 101°12W **180** C4
Valle de Villaverde *Spain* 43°15N 3°15W **88** B7
Valle de Zaragoza
  Mexico 27°25N 105°50W **180** B3
Valle del Ticino △ *Italy* 45°22N 9°0E **92** C6
Valle Fértil, Sierra del
  Argentina 30°20S 68°0W **190** C2
Valle Gran Rey
  Canary Is. 28°5N 17°20W **100** F2
Valle Hermoso *Mexico* 25°35N 97°40W **181** B5
Valle Nacional *Mexico* 17°47N 96°18W **181** D5
Valledupar *Colombia* 10°29N 73°15W **186** A4
Vallée du Bandama □
  Ivory C. 8°0N 5°0W **138** D3
Vallehermoso
  Canary Is. 28°10N 17°15W **100** F3
Vallejo *U.S.A.* 38°7N 122°14W **170** G4
Vallenar *Chile* 28°30S 70°50W **190** B1
Vallentuna *Sweden* 59°32N 18°5E **62** E12
Valleraugue *France* 44°6N 3°39E **72** D7
Vallet *France* 47°10N 1°15W **70** E5
Valletta *Malta* 35°54N 14°31E **101** D2
Valley Center *U.S.A.* 33°13N 117°2W **171** M9
Valley City *U.S.A.* 46°55N 98°0W **172** B7
Valley Falls *Oreg.,
  U.S.A.* 42°29N 120°17W **168** E3
Valley Falls *R.I.,
  U.S.A.* 41°54N 71°24W **175** E13
Valley of Flowers △
  India 30°50N 79°40E **125** D8
Valley of the Kings
  Egypt 25°41N 32°34E **137** C12
Valley Springs *U.S.A.* 38°12N 120°50W **170** G6
Valley View *U.S.A.* 40°39N 76°33W **175** E8
Valley Wells *U.S.A.* 35°27N 115°46W **171** K11
Valleyview *Canada* 55°5N 117°17W **162** B5
Valli di Comácchio *Italy* 44°40N 12°15E **93** D9
Vallimanca, Arroyo
  Argentina 35°40S 59°10W **190** D4
Vallo della Lucánia *Italy* 40°14N 15°16E **95** B8
Vallon-Pont-d'Arc *France* 44°24N 4°24E **73** D8
Vallorbe *Switz.* 46°42N 6°20E **77** J2
Valls *Spain* 41°18N 1°15E **90** D6
Vallvik *Sweden* 61°11N 17°10E **62** C11
Valmaseda = Balmaseda
  Spain 43°11N 3°12W **90** B1
Valmiera *Latvia* 57°37N 25°29E **84** C3
Valnera *Spain* 43°9N 3°40W **88** B7
Valognes *France* 49°30N 1°28W **70** C5
Valona = Vlorë *Albania* 40°32N 19°28E **96** B3
Valongo *Portugal* 41°8N 8°30W **88** D2
Valozhyn *Belarus* 54°3N 26°30E **75** A14
Valpaços *Portugal* 41°36N 7°17W **88** D3
Valparaí *India* 10°22N 76°58E **127** J3
Valparaíso *Chile* 33°2S 71°40W **190** C1
Valparaíso *Mexico* 22°46N 103°34W **180** C4
Valparaíso Fla., *U.S.A.* 30°29N 86°30W **179** G1
Valparaíso Ind., *U.S.A.* 41°28N 87°4W **172** E10
Valparaíso □ *Chile* 33°2S 71°40W **190** C1
Valpovo *Croatia* 45°39N 18°25E **80** E2
Valpoy *India* 15°32N 74°8E **127** G2
Valréas *France* 44°24N 5°0E **73** D9
Vals *Switz.* 46°39N 9°11E **77** J5
Vals ➔ *S. Africa* 27°23S 26°30E **144** C4
Vals, Tanjung *Indonesia* 8°26S 137°25E **119** F9
Vals-les-Bains *France* 44°40N 4°24E **73** D8
Valsad *India* 20°40N 72°58E **126** D1
Valtellina *Italy* 46°11N 9°55E **92** B6
Valuyki *Russia* 50°10N 38°5E **85** G10
Valverde *Canary Is.* 27°48N 17°55W **100** G2
Valverde del Camino
  Spain 37°35N 6°47W **89** H4
Valverde del Fresno
  Spain 40°15N 6°51W **88** E4
Vama *Romania* 47°34N 25°42E **81** C10
Vambori *India* 19°17N 74°44E **126** D2
Vamdrup *Denmark* 55°25N 9°17E **63** J3
Vámhus *Sweden* 61°7N 14°22E **62** C8
Vamizi, I. *Mozam.* 11°2S 40°40E **143** E5
Vammala = Sastamala
  Finland 61°20N 22°54E **84** B2
Vamos *Greece* 35°24N 24°13E **101** D6
Van □ *Turkey* 38°30N 43°0E **105** C10
Van, L. = Van Gölü
  Turkey 38°30N 43°0E **105** C10
Van Alstyne *U.S.A.* 33°25N 96°35W **176** E6
Van Blommestein Meer
  Suriname 4°45N 55°5W **187** C7
Van Buren *Canada* 47°10N 67°55W **165** C6
Van Buren *Ark., U.S.A.* 35°26N 94°21W **176** D7
Van Buren *Maine,
  U.S.A.* 47°10N 67°58W **173** B20
Van Buren *Mo., U.S.A.* 37°0N 91°1W **172** G8
Van Canh *Vietnam* 13°37N 109°0E **120** F7
Van Diemen, C. *N. Terr.,
  Australia* 11°9S 130°24E **148** B5
Van Diemen, C. *Queens.,
  Australia* 16°30S 139°46E **150** B2

Van Diemen G.
　Australia　11°45S 132°0E 148 B5
Van Gölü Turkey　38°30N 43°0E 105 C10
Van Horn U.S.A.　31°3N 104°50W 176 F2
Van Ninh Vietnam　12°42N 109°14E 120 F7
Van Rees, Pegunungan
　Indonesia　2°35S 138°15E 119 E9
Van Tivu India　8°51N 78°15E 127 K4
Van Wert U.S.A.　40°52N 84°35W 173 E11
Van Yen Vietnam　21°4N 104°42E 116 G5
Van Zylsrus S. Africa　26°52S 22°4E 144 C3
Vanadzor Armenia　40°48N 44°30E 87 K7
Vanavara Russia　60°22N 102°16E 107 C11
Vancouver Canada　49°15N 123°7W 170 A3
Vancouver, C. Australia　35°2S 118°11E 149 G2
Vancouver I. Canada　49°50N 126°0W 170 B2
Vancouver Int. ✈ (YVR)
　Canada　49°10N 123°10W 170 A3
Vanda = Vantaa Finland　60°18N 24°56E 84 B3
Vandalia Ill., U.S.A.　38°58N 89°6W 172 F9
Vandalia Mo., U.S.A.　39°19N 91°29W 172 F8
Vandavasi India　12°30N 79°30E 127 H4
Vandellòs Spain　41°0N 0°55E 90 E5
Vandenberg Village
　U.S.A.　34°43N 120°28W 171 L6
Vandergrift U.S.A.　40°36N 79°34W 174 F5
Vanderhoof Canada　54°0N 124°0W 162 C4
Vanderkloof Dam
　S. Africa　30°4S 24°40E 144 D3
Vanderlin I. Australia　15°44S 137°2E 150 B2
Vänern Sweden　58°47N 13°30E 63 F7
Vänersborg Sweden　58°26N 12°19E 63 F6
Vang Vieng Laos　18°58N 102°32E 120 C4
Vanga Kenya　4°35S 39°12E 142 C4
Vangaindrano Madag.　23°21S 47°36E 141 J9
Vänge Sweden　59°50N 17°20E 62 E11
Vanguard Canada　49°55N 107°20W 163 D7
Vanino Russia　48°50N 140°5E 107 E15
Vanivilasa Sagara
　India　13°45N 76°30E 127 H3
Vaniyambadi India　12°46N 78°44E 127 H4
Vânju Mare Romania　44°25N 22°52E 80 F7
Vankleek Hill Canada　45°32N 74°40W 175 A10
Vännäs Sweden　63°58N 19°48E 60 E18
Vannes France　47°40N 2°47W 70 E4
Vannøya Norway　70°6N 19°50E 60 A18
Vanoise, Massif de la
　France　45°25N 6°40E 73 C10
Vanrhynsdorp S. Africa　31°36S 18°44E 144 D2
Vansada India　20°47N 73°25E 126 D1
Vansbro Sweden　60°32N 14°15E 62 D8
Vansittart B. Australia　14°3S 126°17E 148 B4
Vansittart I. Canada　65°50N 84°0W 161 D15
Vantaa Finland　60°18N 24°56E 84 B3
Vanua Balavu Fiji　17°12S 178°55W 154 a
Vanua Levu Fiji　16°33S 179°15E 154 a
Vanua Vatu Fiji　18°22S 179°15W 154 a
Vanuatu ■ Pac. Oc.　15°0S 168°0E 147 C9
Vanwyksvlei S. Africa　30°18S 21°49E 144 D3
Vapi India　20°22N 72°54E 126 D1
Vapnyarka Ukraine　48°32N 28°45E 81 B13
Var □ France　43°27N 6°18E 73 E10
Var ➤ France　43°39N 7°12E 73 E11
Vara Sweden　58°16N 12°55E 63 F6
Varada ➤ India　15°0N 75°40E 127 G2
Varades France　47°25N 1°1W 70 E5
Varáita ➤ Italy　44°49N 7°53E 92 D4
Varalé Ivory C.　9°40N 3°17W 138 D4
Varallo Italy　45°49N 8°15E 92 C5
Varāmīn Iran　35°20N 51°39E 129 C6
Varāmīn □ Iran　35°18N 51°35E 129 B6
Varanasi India　25°22N 83°0E 125 G10
Varangerfjorden
　Norway　70°3N 29°25E 60 A23
Varangerhalvøya
　Norway　70°25N 29°30E 60 A23
Varano, Lago di Italy　41°53N 15°45E 93 G12
Varaždin Croatia　46°20N 16°20E 93 B13
Varazze Italy　44°22N 8°34E 92 D5
Varberg Sweden　57°6N 12°20E 63 H6
Vardak □ Afghan.　34°0N 68°0E 122 B6
Vardar = Axios ➤
　Greece　40°57N 22°35E 96 F6
Varde Denmark　55°38N 8°29E 63 J2
Varde Å ➤ Denmark　55°35N 8°19E 63 J2
Vardenis Armenia　40°10N 45°43E 87 K7
Vardo Norway　70°23N 31°5E 60 A24
Varel Germany　53°23N 8°8E 76 B4
Varella, Mui = Nay, Mui
　Vietnam　12°54N 109°26E 120 F7
Varèna Lithuania　54°12N 24°30E 84 E3
Varennes-sur-Allier
　France　46°19N 3°24E 71 F10
Varennes-Vauzelles France　47°3N 3°9E 71 E10
Vareš Bos.-H.　44°12N 18°23E 80 F3
Varese Italy　45°48N 8°50E 92 C5
Vârfurile Romania　46°19N 22°31E 80 D7
Vårgårda Sweden　58°2N 12°49E 63 F6
Vargem Bonita Brazil　20°20S 46°22W 189 E1
Vargem Grande Brazil　3°33S 43°56W 189 A2
Varginha Brazil　21°33S 45°25W 191 A6
Vargön Sweden　58°22N 12°20E 63 F6
Varillas Chile　24°0S 70°10W 190 A1
Varkaus Finland　62°19N 27°50E 84 A4
Värmdölandet Sweden　59°20N 18°33E 62 E12
Värmeln Sweden　59°35N 12°54E 62 E6
Värmlands län □ Sweden　60°0N 13°20E 62 D7
Värmlandsbro Sweden　59°11N 13°0E 62 E7
Varna Bulgaria　43°13N 27°56E 97 C11
Varna □ Bulgaria　43°20N 27°30E 97 C11
Varna ➤ India　16°48N 74°32E 126 F2
Värnamo Sweden　57°10N 14°3E 63 H8
Várnjárga = Varangerhalvøya
　Norway　70°25N 29°30E 60 A23
Varnsdorf Czech Rep.　50°55N 14°35E 78 A7
Varnville U.S.A.　32°51N 81°5W 178 C8
Várpalota Hungary　47°12N 18°8E 80 C2
Vars Canada　45°21N 75°21W 175 A9
Vars France　44°37N 6°42E 73 D10
Varto Turkey　39°10N 41°27E 105 C9
Varvarin Serbia　43°43N 21°20E 96 C5
Varysburg U.S.A.　42°46N 78°19W 174 D6
Varzaneh Iran　32°25N 52°40E 129 C7
Varzaqān Iran　38°39N 46°40E 105 C12
Várzea Alegre Brazil　6°47S 39°17W 189 B3
Várzea da Palma
　Brazil　17°36S 44°44W 189 D2
Varzi Italy　44°49N 9°12E 92 D5
Varzo Italy　46°12N 8°15E 92 B5

Varzy France　47°22N 3°20E 71 E10
Vas □ Hungary　47°10N 16°55E 80 C1
Vasa = Vaasa Finland　63°6N 21°38E 60 E19
Vasa Barris ➤ Brazil　11°10S 37°10W 189 C3
Vasai-Virar India　19°28N 72°48E 126 E1
Vásárosnamény Hungary　48°9N 22°19E 80 B7
Vascão ➤ Portugal　37°31N 7°31W 89 H3
Vaşcău Romania　46°28N 22°30E 80 D7
Vascongadas = País Vasco □
　Spain　42°50N 2°45W 90 C2
Vashkivtsi Ukraine　48°23N 25°31E 81 B10
Vasht = Khāsh Iran　28°15N 61°15E 129 D9
Vasilevichi Belarus　52°15N 29°50E 75 B16
Vasiliki Greece　38°37N 20°36E 98 C2
Vasiliko Greece　38°25N 23°40E 98 C5
Vasilkov = Vasylkiv
　Ukraine　50°7N 30°15E 75 C16
Vaslui Romania　46°38N 27°42E 81 D12
Vaslui □ Romania　46°30N 27°45E 81 D12
Väsman Sweden　60°9N 15°5E 62 D9
Vassar Canada　49°10N 95°55W 163 D9
Vassar U.S.A.　43°22N 83°35W 173 D12
Västeras Sweden　59°37N 16°38E 62 E10
Västerbotten Sweden　64°36N 20°4E 60 D19
Västerdalälven ➤
　Sweden　60°30N 15°7E 62 D8
Västergötland Sweden　58°0N 13°0E 63 F7
Västerhaninge Sweden　59°7N 18°6E 62 E12
Västervik Sweden　57°43N 16°33E 63 G10
Västmanland Sweden　59°45N 16°20E 61 G17
Västmanlands län □
　Sweden　59°45N 16°20E 62 E10
Vasto Italy　42°8N 14°40E 93 F11
Västra Götalands Län □
　Sweden　58°0N 13°0E 63 F6
Vasvár Hungary　47°3N 16°47E 80 C1
Vasylivka Ukraine　45°38N 28°50E 81 E13
Vasylkiv Ukraine　50°7N 30°15E 75 C16
Vat Phou Laos　14°51N 105°49E 120 E5
Vatan France　47°4N 1°50E 71 E8
Vatersay U.K.　56°55N 7°32W 65 E1
Vathia Greece　36°29N 22°29E 98 E4
Vati Greece　36°3N 27°53E 100 D12
Vatican City ■ Europe　41°54N 12°27E 93 G9
Vaticano, C. Italy　38°37N 15°50E 95 D8
Vatili Cyprus　35°6N 33°40E 101 D12
Vatin Serbia　45°12N 21°20E 80 E6
Vatiu = Atiu Cook Is.　20°0S 158°10W 157 J12
Vatnajökull Iceland　64°30N 16°48W 60 D5
Vatnajökull △ Iceland　64°24N 16°48W 60 D5
Vato Sweden　59°50N 19°0E 62 E12
Vatolakkos Greece　35°27N 23°53E 101 D5
Vatra-Dornei Romania　47°25N 25°22E 81 C10
Vatrak ➤ India　23°9N 73°2E 124 H5
Vatu Vara Fiji　17°26S 179°31W 154 a
Vatulele Fiji　18°33S 177°37E 154 a
Vaucluse □ France　43°50N 5°20E 73 E9
Vaucouleurs France　48°37N 5°40E 71 D12
Vaud □ Switz.　46°35N 6°30E 77 J2
Vaudreuil-Dorion
　Canada　45°23N 74°3W 175 A10
Vaughn Mont., U.S.A.　47°33N 111°33W 168 C8
Vaughn N. Mex.,
　U.S.A.　34°36N 105°13W 169 J11
Vaujours L. Canada　55°27N 74°15W 164 A5
Vaupés = Uaupés ➤
　Brazil　0°2N 67°16W 186 C5
Vaupés □ Colombia　1°0N 71°0W 186 C4
Vauvert France　43°42N 4°17E 73 E8
Vauxhall Canada　50°5N 112°9W 162 C6
Vav India　24°22N 71°31E 124 G4
Vavoua Ivory C.　7°23N 6°29W 138 D4
Vavuniya Sri Lanka　8°45N 80°30E 127 K5
Vawkavysk Belarus　53°9N 24°30E 75 B13
Vaxholm Sweden　59°25N 18°20E 62 E12
Växjö Sweden　56°52N 14°50E 63 H8
Våxtorp Sweden　56°25N 13°8E 63 H7
Vayalpad India　13°39N 78°38E 127 H4
Vaygach, Ostrov Russia　70°0N 60°0E 106 C7
Veadeiros Brazil　14°7S 47°31W 189 C1
Veaikevárri = Svappavaara
　Sweden　67°40N 21°3E 60 C19
Vechelde Germany　52°16N 10°22E 76 C6
Vechta Germany　52°44N 8°17E 76 C4
Vechte ➤ Neths.　52°34N 6°6E 69 B6
Vecsés Hungary　47°26N 19°19E 80 C4
Vedaranniyam India　10°25N 79°50E 127 J4
Veddige Sweden　57°17N 12°20E 63 H6
Vedea ➤ Romania　43°42N 25°41E 81 G10
Vedi Armenia　39°54N 44°43E 105 C11
Vedia Argentina　34°30S 61°31W 190 C3
Vedrette di Ries-Aurina △
　Italy　46°54N 12°5E 93 B9
Vedum Sweden　58°11N 13°0E 63 F7
Veendam Neths.　53°5N 6°52E 69 A6
Veenendaal Neths.　52°2N 5°34E 69 B5
Vefsna ➤ Norway　65°48N 13°10E 60 D15
Vega Norway　65°40N 11°55E 60 D14
Vega U.S.A.　35°15N 102°26W 176 D3
Vega Baja Puerto Rico　18°27N 66°23W 183 d
Vegadeo Spain　43°27N 7°4W 88 B3
Vegoritida, L. Greece　40°45N 21°45E 96 F5
Vegreville Canada　53°30N 112°5W 162 C6
Veinge Sweden　56°33N 13°4E 63 H7
Veisiejai Lithuania　54°6N 23°42E 84 D3
Vejbystrand Sweden　56°9N 12°45E 63 H6
Vejen Denmark　55°30N 9°9E 63 J3
Vejer de la Frontera
　Spain　36°15N 5°59W 89 J5
Vejle Denmark　55°43N 9°30E 63 J3
Vejle Fjord Denmark　55°40N 9°50E 63 J3
Vela Luka Croatia　42°59N 16°44E 93 F13
Velachha India　21°26N 73°1E 126 D1
Velanai I. Sri Lanka　9°45N 79°45E 127 K4
Velas, C. Costa Rica　10°21N 85°52W 182 D2
Velasco, Sierra de
　Argentina　29°20S 67°10W 190 B2
Velay, Mts. du France　45°0N 3°40E 72 D7
Velbert Germany　51°20N 7°3E 76 D4
Velddrif S. Africa　32°42S 18°11E 144 D2
Velebit Croatia　44°50N 15°20E 93 D12
Velebit Planina Croatia　44°50N 15°20E 93 D12
Velebitski Kanal
　Croatia　44°45N 14°55E 93 D11
Veleka ➤ Bulgaria　42°4N 27°58E 97 D11
Velenci-tó Hungary　47°13N 18°36E 80 C3
Velenje Slovenia　46°23N 15°8E 93 B12
Veles Macedonia　41°46N 21°47E 96 E5
Velestino Greece　39°23N 22°43E 98 B4

Vélez-Málaga Spain　36°48N 4°5W 89 J6
Vélez Rubio Spain　37°41N 2°5W 91 H2
Velhas ➤ Brazil　17°13S 44°49W 189 D2
Velika Croatia　45°27N 17°40E 80 E2
Velika Gorica Croatia　45°44N 16°5E 93 C13
Velika Kapela Croatia　45°10N 15°5E 93 C12
Velika Kladuša Bos.-H.　45°11N 15°48E 93 C12
Velika Kruša = Krushë e Madhe
　Kosovo　42°19N 20°39E 96 D4
Velika Morava ➤ Serbia　44°43N 21°3E 96 B5
Velika Plana Serbia　44°20N 21°1E 96 B5
Velikaya ➤ Russia　57°48N 28°10E 84 C5
Velikaya Kema Russia　45°30N 137°12E 112 B8
Velikonda Range India　14°45N 79°10E 127 G4
Velingara Kolda, Senegal　13°12N 14°55W 138 C2
Velingara Louga, Senegal　15°0N 14°40W 138 B2
Velingrad Bulgaria　42°4N 23°58E 96 D7
Velino, Mte. Italy　42°9N 13°23E 93 F10
Velizh Russia　55°36N 31°11E 84 E6
Vel'ké Kapušany
　Slovak Rep.　48°34N 22°5E 79 C15
Velké Karlovice
　Czech Rep.　49°20N 18°17E 79 B11
Vel'ké Meziříčí Czech Rep.　49°21N 16°1E 78 B9
Vel'ký Javorník
　Slovak Rep.　49°19N 18°22E 79 B11
Vel'ký Krtíš Slovak Rep.　48°12N 19°21E 79 C12
Vel'ký Meder
　Slovak Rep.　47°52N 17°46E 79 D10
Vellar ➤ India　11°30N 79°36E 127 J4
Velletri Italy　41°41N 12°47E 94 A5
Vellinge Sweden　55°29N 13°2E 63 J6
Vellmar Germany　51°22N 9°28E 76 D5
Vellore India　12°57N 79°10E 127 H4
Velopoula Greece　36°55N 23°27E 98 E5
Velsen-Noord Neths.　52°27N 4°40E 69 B4
Velsk Russia　61°10N 42°5E 84 B11
Velten Germany　52°42N 13°10E 76 C9
Veluwezoom △ Neths.　52°5N 6°0E 69 B6
Velva U.S.A.　48°4N 100°56W 172 A3
Velvendos Greece　40°15N 22°6E 96 F6
Velyka Mykhaylivka
　Ukraine　47°4N 29°52E 81 C14
Velyki Luchky Ukraine　48°25N 22°34E 80 B7
Velykyy Bereznyy
　Ukraine　48°54N 22°28E 80 B7
Velykyy Bychkiv Ukraine　47°58N 24°1E 81 C9
Vemb Denmark　56°21N 8°21E 63 H2
Vembanad L. India　9°36N 76°15E 127 K3
Vemdalen Sweden　62°27N 13°51E 62 B7
Ven Sweden　55°55N 12°45E 63 J6
Venaco France　42°14N 9°11E 73 F13
Venado Mexico　22°56N 101°6W 180 C4
Venado Tuerto
　Argentina　33°50S 62°0W 190 C3
Venafro Italy　41°29N 14°2E 95 A7
Venarey-les-Laumes
　France　47°32N 4°26E 71 E11
Venaria Italy　45°8N 7°38E 92 C4
Venčane Serbia　44°24N 20°28E 96 B4
Vence France　43°43N 7°6E 73 E11
Vendas Novas Portugal　38°39N 8°27W 89 G2
Vendée □ France　46°50N 1°35W 70 F5
Vendée ➤ France　46°20N 1°10W 70 F5
Vendeuvre-sur-Barse
　France　48°14N 4°28E 71 D11
Vendôme France　47°47N 1°3E 70 E8
Vendrell = El Vendrell
　Spain　41°10N 1°30E 90 D6
Vendsyssel Denmark　57°22N 10°0E 63 G4
Vendychany Ukraine　48°38N 27°48E 81 B12
Venelles France　43°35N 5°28E 73 E9
Véneta, L. Italy　45°23N 12°25E 93 C9
Véneto □ Italy　45°23N 12°0E 93 C9
Venev Russia　54°22N 38°17E 84 E10
Venézia, G. di Italy　45°15N 13°0E 93 C10
Venézia Lido Italy　45°24N 12°26E 93 C9
Venezuela ■ S. Amer.　8°0N 66°0W 186 B5
Venezuela, G. de
　Venezuela　11°30N 71°0W 186 A4
Vengurla India　15°53N 73°45E 127 G1
Vengurla Rocks India　15°55N 73°22E 127 G1
Venice = Venézia Italy　45°27N 12°21E 93 C9
Venice U.S.A.　27°6N 82°27W 179 H7
Vénissieux France　45°42N 4°53E 73 C8
Venjan Sweden　60°57N 13°55E 62 D7
Venjansjön Sweden　60°57N 13°55E 62 D7
Venkatagiri India　14°0N 79°35E 127 H4
Venkatapuram India　18°20N 80°30E 126 E5
Venlo Neths.　51°22N 6°11E 69 C6
Vennachar Junction
　Canada　45°5N 77°14W 174 A7
Vennesla Norway　58°15N 7°59E 61 G12
Venosa Italy　40°58N 15°49E 95 B8
Venray Neths.　51°31N 6°0E 69 C6
Venta Lithuania　56°15N 22°35E 84 B4
Venta ➤ Latvia　57°24N 21°33E 84 B4
Venta de Baños Spain　41°55N 4°30W 88 D6
Venta de Cardeña = Cardeña
　Spain　38°16N 4°20W 89 G6
Ventana, Sa. de la
　Argentina　38°0S 62°30W 190 D3
Ventanas S. Africa　25°37S 27°9E 144 C4
Venterstad S. Africa　30°47S 25°48E 144 D4
Ventimíglia Italy　43°47N 7°36E 92 E4
Ventnor U.K.　50°36N 1°12W 67 G6
Ventotène, I. Italy　40°47N 13°25E 94 B6
Ventoux, Mt. France　44°10N 5°17E 73 D9
Ventspils Latvia　57°25N 21°32E 84 B3
Ventspils □ Latvia　57°20N 21°50E 82 A8
Ventuari ➤ Venezuela　3°58N 67°2W 186 C5
Ventucopa U.S.A.　34°50N 119°29W 171 L7
Ventura U.S.A.　34°17N 119°18W 171 L7
Venturosa S. Africa　26°19S 27°29E 144 C4
Venus B. Australia　38°40S 145°42E 153 E6
Venustiano Carranza
　Mexico　30°25N 115°53W 180 A1
Venustiano Carranza, Presa
　Mexico　27°30N 100°37W 180 B4
Vera Argentina　29°30S 60°20W 190 B3
Vera Spain　37°15N 1°51W 91 H3
Veracruz Mexico　19°11N 96°8W 181 D5
Veracruz □ Mexico　19°0N 96°15W 181 D5
Veraval India　20°53N 70°27E 124 J4
Verbánia Italy　45°56N 8°33E 92 C5
Verbano, L. di = Maggiore, L.
　Italy　45°57N 8°39E 92 C5
Verbano Cusio Ossola □
　Italy　46°15N 8°20E 92 B5
Verbicaro Italy　39°45N 15°55E 95 C8
Verbier Switz.　46°6N 7°13E 77 J3
Vercelli Italy　45°19N 8°25E 92 C5
Verchovchevo Ukraine　48°32N 34°10E 85 H8
Vercors △ France　45°0N 5°25E 73 D9
Verdalsøra Norway　63°48N 11°16E 60 E14
Verde ➤ Argentina　41°56S 65°5W 192 B3
Verde ➤ Goiás, Brazil　18°1S 50°14W 187 G8
Verde ➤ Mato Grosso do Sul,
　Brazil　21°25S 52°20W 187 H8
Verde ➤ Chihuahua,
　Mexico　26°39N 107°11W 180 B3
Verde ➤ Jalisco,
　Mexico　20°42N 103°14W 180 C4
Verde ➤ Oaxaca,
　Mexico　15°59N 97°50W 181 D5
Verde ➤ Paraguay　23°9S 57°37W 190 A4
Verde ➤ U.S.A.　33°33N 111°40W 169 K8
Verde, Cay Bahamas　23°0N 75°5W 182 B4
Verde Grande ➤
　Brazil　16°13S 43°49W 189 D2
Verde Pequeno ➤
　Brazil　14°48S 43°31W 189 C2
Verden Germany　52°55N 9°14E 76 C5
Verdi U.S.A.　39°31N 119°59W 170 F7
Verdikoussa Greece　39°47N 21°59E 98 B3
Verdon ➤ France　43°43N 5°46E 73 E9
Verdon △ France　43°50N 6°5E 73 E10
Verdun France　49°9N 5°24E 71 C12
Verdun, Lux.　49°9N 1°2E 69 E6
Verdun-sur-le-Doubs
　France　46°54N 5°2E 71 F12
Vereeniging S. Africa　26°38S 27°57E 145 C4
Verga, C. Guinea　10°30N 14°10W 138 C2
Vergara = Bergara Spain　43°9N 2°28W 90 B2
Vergara Uruguay　32°56S 53°57W 191 C5
Vergato Italy　44°17N 11°7E 92 D8
Vergemont Cr. ➤
　Australia　24°16S 143°16E 150 C3
Vergennes U.S.A.　44°10N 73°15W 175 B11
Vergina = Aigai Greece　40°28N 22°19E 96 F6
Vergt France　45°2N 0°43E 72 C4
Veria Greece　40°34N 22°12E 96 F6
Verín Spain　41°57N 7°27W 88 D3
Verkhnedvinsk =
　Vyerkhnyadzvinsk
　Belarus　55°45N 27°58E 84 E4
Verkhnetulomskoye Vdkhr.
　Russia　68°36N 31°12E 60 B24
Verkhnevilyuysk
　Russia　63°27N 120°18E 107 C13
Verkhniy Baskunchak
　Russia　48°14N 46°44E 87 F8
Verkhnya Russia　52°55N 37°15E 85 F9
Verkhovyna Ukraine　48°9N 24°47E 81 B9
Verkhoyansk Russia　67°35N 133°25E 107 C14
Verkhoyansk Ra. =
　Verkhoyanskiy Khrebet
　Russia　66°0N 129°0E 107 C13
Verkhoyanskiy Khrebet
　Russia　66°0N 129°0E 107 C13
Vermeille, Côte France　42°50N 3°20E 72 F7
Vermenton France　47°40N 3°42E 71 E10
Vermilion Canada　53°20N 110°50W 163 C6
Vermilion U.S.A.　41°25N 82°22W 174 E2
Vermilion ➤ Canada　53°22N 110°51W 163 C6
Vermilion B. U.S.A.　29°42N 92°0W 176 G9
Vermilion Bay Canada　49°51N 93°34W 163 D10
Vermilion L. U.S.A.　47°53N 92°26W 172 B7
Vermillion U.S.A.　42°47N 96°56W 172 D5
Vermillion ➤ Canada　47°38N 72°56W 164 C5
Vermont □ U.S.A.　44°0N 73°0W 175 C12
Vermosh Albania　42°33N 19°42E 96 D3
Vernalis U.S.A.　37°36N 121°17W 170 H5
Vernal U.S.A.　40°27N 109°32W 168 F9
Vernazza Italy　44°8N 9°41E 92 D6
Verner Canada　46°25N 80°8W 173 B15
Verneukpan S. Africa　30°0S 21°0E 144 D3
Vernier Switz.　46°11N 6°7E 77 J2
Vernon Canada　50°20N 119°15W 162 C5
Vernon France　49°5N 1°30E 70 C8
Vernon U.S.A.　34°9N 99°17W 176 D5
Vernonia U.S.A.　45°52N 123°11W 170 E3
Vero Beach U.S.A.　27°38N 80°24W 179 H9
Véroia = Veria Greece　40°34N 22°12E 96 F6
Véroli Italy　41°41N 13°25E 93 G10
Verona Italy　45°24N 10°59E 92 C7
Verrès Italy　45°40N 7°42E 92 C4
Versailles France　48°48N 2°7E 70 C9
Versmold Germany　52°3N 8°10E 76 C4
Vert, C. Senegal　14°45N 17°30W 138 C1
Vertou France　47°10N 1°28W 70 E5
Vertus France　48°54N 4°2E 71 D11
Verulam S. Africa　29°38S 31°2E 145 D5
Verviers Belgium　50°37N 5°52E 69 D5
Vervins France　49°50N 3°53E 71 C11
Verwood Canada　49°30N 105°40W 163 D7
Verzy France　49°9N 4°10E 71 C11

Vesuvio Italy　40°49N 14°26E 95 B7
Vesuvius, Mt. = Vesuvio
　Italy　40°49N 14°26E 95 B7
Vesyegonsk Russia　58°40N 37°16E 84 C9
Veszprém Hungary　47°8N 17°57E 80 C2
Veszprém □ Hungary　47°5N 17°55E 80 C2
Vesztő Hungary　46°55N 21°16E 80 D6
Vetapalem India　15°47N 80°18E 127 G5
Vetlanda Sweden　57°24N 15°3E 63 G9
Vetluga Russia　57°53N 45°45E 86 B7
Vetlugu ➤ Russia　56°36N 46°4E 88 B8
Vetovo Bulgaria　43°42N 26°16E 97 C10
Vetralla Italy　42°20N 12°2E 93 F9
Vetren Bulgaria　42°15N 24°3E 97 D8
Vettore, Mte. Italy　42°49N 13°16E 93 F10
Veurne Belgium　51°5N 2°40E 69 C2
Vevey Switz.　46°28N 6°51E 77 J2
Vevi Greece　40°47N 21°38E 96 F5
Veynes France　44°32N 5°49E 73 D9
Veys Iran　31°30N 49°0E 129 D6
Vézelay France　47°27N 3°45E 71 E10
Vézelise France　48°30N 6°5E 71 D13
Vézère ➤ France　44°53N 0°53E 72 D4
Vezhen Bulgaria　42°50N 24°20E 97 D8
Veziröprü Turkey　41°8N 35°27E 104 B6
Vezzani France　42°10N 9°15E 73 F13
Vi Thanh Vietnam　9°42N 105°26E 121 H5
Viacha Bolivia　16°39S 68°18W 188 D4
Viadana Italy　44°56N 10°31E 92 D7
Viamão Brazil　30°5S 51°0W 191 C5
Viana Brazil　3°13S 44°55W 189 A2
Viana Spain　42°31N 2°22W 90 C2
Viana do Alentejo
　Portugal　38°17N 7°59W 89 G3
Viana do Bolo Spain　42°11N 7°6W 88 C3
Viana do Castelo
　Portugal　41°42N 8°50W 88 D2
Viana do Castelo □
　Portugal　41°50N 8°30W 88 D2
Viangchan = Vientiane
　Laos　17°58N 102°36E 120 D4
Vianópolis Brazil　16°40S 48°35W 189 D1
Vianos Greece　35°2N 25°21E 101 D7
Viar ➤ Spain　37°36N 5°50W 89 H5
Viaréggio Italy　43°52N 10°14E 92 E7
Viaur ➤ France　44°8N 1°58E 72 D5
Vibble Sweden　57°37N 18°16E 63 G12
Vibo Valéntia Italy　38°40N 16°6E 95 D9
Viborg Denmark　56°27N 9°23E 63 H3
Vibraye France　48°3N 0°44E 70 D7
Vic Spain　41°58N 2°19E 90 D7
Vic, Étang de France　43°29N 3°50E 72 E7
Vic-en-Bigorre France　43°24N 0°3E 72 E4
Vic-Fezensac France　43°47N 0°19E 72 E4
Vic-le-Comte France　45°39N 3°14E 71 G10
Vic-sur-Cère France　44°59N 2°38E 72 D6
Vicar Spain　36°49N 2°39W 91 J2
Vicente Pérez Rosales △
　Chile　41°11S 72°12W 192 B2
Vicenza Italy　45°33N 11°33E 93 C8
Vich = Vic Spain　41°58N 2°19E 90 D7
Vichada □ Colombia　4°55N 67°50W 186 C5
Vichuga Russia　57°12N 41°55E 86 B5
Vicksburg Ariz.,
　U.S.A.　33°45N 113°45W 171 M13
Vicksburg Miss., U.S.A.　32°21N 90°53W 177 E9
Vico Italy　42°10N 8°49E 73 F12
Vico, L. di Italy　42°19N 12°10E 93 F9
Vico del Gargano Italy　41°54N 15°57E 93 G12
Vicosa Brazil　9°28S 36°14W 189 B3
Viçosa do Ceará Brazil　3°34S 41°5W 189 A2
Vicovu de Sus Romania　47°56N 25°41E 81 C10
Victor India　21°0N 71°30E 124 J4
Victor Harbor
　Australia　35°30S 138°37E 152 C3
Victoria Argentina　32°40S 60°10W 190 C3
Victoria Chile　38°13N 72°20W 192 A2
Victoria China　22°17N 114°9E 111 a
Victoria Guinea　10°50N 14°32W 138 C2
Victoria Malta　36°3N 14°14E 101 C1
Victoria Romania　45°44N 24°41E 81 E9
Victoria Seychelles　4°38S 55°28E 141 b
Victoria U.S.A.　28°48N 96°59W 176 G6
Victoria □ Australia　37°0S 144°0E 153 C2
Victoria ➤ Australia　15°10S 129°40E 148 C4
Victoria, Grand L.
　Canada　47°31N 77°30W 164 C4
Victoria, L. Africa　1°0S 33°0E 142 C3
Victoria, L. Australia　33°57S 141°15E 152 B4
Victoria, Mt. Burma　21°14N 93°55E 123 J18
Victoria Beach Canada　50°40N 96°35W 163 C9
Victoria de Durango = Durango
　Mexico　24°3N 104°39W 180 C4
Victoria de las Tunas = Las Tunas
　Cuba　20°58N 76°59W 182 B4
Victoria Falls Zimbabwe　17°58S 25°52E 143 F2
Victoria Fjord Greenland　82°0N 46°0W 57 A6
Victoria Harbour
　Canada　44°45N 79°45W 174 B5
Victoria I. Canada　71°0N 111°0W 160 C9
Victoria L. Canada　48°20N 57°27W 165 C8
Victoria Ld. Antarctica　75°0S 160°0E 55 D11
Victoria Nile ➤ Uganda　2°14N 31°26E 142 B2
Victoria Pk. Belize　16°48N 88°37W 182 C2
Victoria River Australia　15°12S 129°43E 148 C4
Victoria Str. Canada　69°31N 100°30W 160 D11
Victoria West S. Africa　31°25S 23°4E 144 D3
Victoriaville Canada　46°4N 71°56W 165 C5
Victorica Argentina　36°20S 65°30W 190 D2
Victorville U.S.A.　34°32N 117°18W 171 L9
Vicuña Chile　30°0S 70°50W 190 C1
Vicuña Mackenna
　Argentina　33°53S 64°25W 190 C3
Vidal U.S.A.　34°7N 114°31W 171 L12
Vidalia U.S.A.　32°13N 82°25W 178 D6
Vidauban France　43°25N 6°27E 73 E10
Videbæk Denmark　56°6N 8°38E 63 H2
Videle Romania　44°17N 25°31E 81 F10
Vidette U.S.A.　33°2N 82°15W 178 D7

Vidigueira Portugal　38°12N 7°48W 89 G3
Vidin Bulgaria　43°59N 22°50E 96 C6
Vidin □ Bulgaria　43°59N 22°50E 96 C6
Vidio, C. Spain　43°35N 6°14W 88 B4
Vidisha India　23°28N 77°53E 124 H7
Vidos Greece　39°38N 19°55E 101 A3
Vidra Romania　45°56N 26°55E 81 E11
Viduša Bos.-H.　42°55N 18°21E 96 D3
Vidzy Belarus　55°23N 26°37E 84 E4
Viechtach Germany　49°4N 12°53E 77 D8
Viedma Argentina　40°50S 63°0W 192 B4
Viedma, L. Argentina　49°30S 72°30W 192 C2
Vieira do Minho Portugal　41°38N 8°8W 88 D2
Vielha = Vielha Spain　42°43N 0°44E 90 C6
Viella = Vielha Spain　42°43N 0°44E 90 C6
Vielle St-Girons France　43°56N 1°18W 72 E3
Vielsalm Belgium　50°17N 5°54E 69 D5
Vienenburg Germany　51°57N 10°34E 76 C6
Vieng Pou Kha Laos　20°41N 101°4E 116 G3
Vienna = Wien Austria　48°12N 16°22E 78 C9
Vienna Canada　42°41N 80°48W 174 D3
Vienna Ga., U.S.A.　32°6N 83°47W 178 D4
Vienna Ill., U.S.A.　37°25N 88°54W 172 G9
Vienna Mo., U.S.A.　38°11N 91°57W 172 F8
Vienne France　45°31N 4°53E 73 C8
Vienne □ France　46°30N 0°42E 72 B4
Vienne ➤ France　47°13N 0°5E 70 E7
Vientiane Laos　17°58N 102°36E 120 D4
Vientos, Paso de los
　Caribbean　20°0N 74°0W 183 C5
Vieques Puerto Rico　18°8N 65°25W 183 d
Vierge Pt. St. Lucia　13°49N 60°53W 183 f
Viernheim Germany　49°31N 8°35E 77 D5
Viersen Germany　51°15N 6°23E 76 D3
Vierwaldstättersee Switz.　47°0N 8°30E 77 J5
Vierzon France　47°13N 2°5E 71 E9
Vieste Italy　41°53N 16°10E 93 G13
Viet Quang Vietnam　22°30N 104°48E 116 F5
Viet Tri Vietnam　21°18N 105°25E 116 G5
Vietnam ■ Asia　19°0N 106°0E 120 C5
Vieux-Boucau-les-Bains
　France　43°48N 1°23W 72 E3
Vieux Fort St. Lucia　13°46N 60°58W 183 f
Vif France　45°5N 5°41E 73 C9
Vigan Phil.　17°35N 120°28E 119 A6
Vigévano Italy　45°19N 8°51E 92 C5
Vigia Brazil　0°50S 48°5W 187 D9
Viglas, Akra Greece　35°54N 27°51E 101 E9
Vignemalle France　42°47N 0°10W 72 F3
Vigneulles-lès-Hattonchâtel
　France　48°59N 5°43E 71 C12
Vignola Italy　44°29N 11°1E 92 D8
Vigo Spain　42°12N 8°41W 88 C2
Vigo, Ría de Spain　42°15N 8°45W 88 C2
Vigsø Bugt Denmark　57°8N 8°47E 63 G2
Vihiers France　47°10N 0°30W 70 E6
Vihowa Pakistan　31°8N 70°30E 124 D6
Vihowa ➤ Pakistan　31°8N 70°41E 124 D6
Vijayadurg India　16°30N 73°25E 124 L8
Vijayawada India　16°31N 80°39E 126 F5
Vijosë ➤ Albania　40°37N 19°24E 96 F2
Vik Iceland　63°25N 19°1W 60 D5
Vika Sweden　60°57N 14°28E 62 D8
Vikarabad India　17°20N 77°54E 126 F3
Vikarbyn Sweden　60°55N 15°1E 62 D9
Vikeke = Viqueque
　E. Timor　8°52S 126°23E 119 F7
Viken Skåne, Sweden　56°9N 12°34E 63 H6
Viken Västra Götaland,
　Sweden　58°39N 14°20E 62 F8
Viking Canada　53°7N 111°50W 162 C6
Vikmanshyttan Sweden　60°18N 15°50E 62 D9
Vikna Norway　64°55N 10°58E 60 D14
Vikos-Aoos △ Greece　40°0N 20°45E 98 A2
Vila Bela da Santissima Trindade
　Brazil　15°0S 59°57W 188 D5
Vila da Maganja
　Mozam.　17°18S 37°30E 143 G4
Vila da Ribeira Brava
　C. Verde Is.　16°32N 24°25W 138 b
Vila de Rei Portugal　39°41N 8°9W 88 F2
Vila do Bispo Portugal　37°5N 8°53W 89 H2
Vila do Conde Portugal　41°21N 8°45W 88 D2
Vila Franca de Xira
　Portugal　38°57N 8°59W 89 G2
Vila Gamito Mozam.　14°12S 33°0E 143 G3
Vila Gomes da Costa
　Mozam.　24°20S 33°37E 145 C5
Vila Machado Mozam.　19°15S 34°14E 143 H3
Vila Mouzinho Mozam.　14°48S 34°25E 143 G3
Vila Nova de Famalicão
　Portugal　41°25N 8°32W 88 D2
Vila Nova de Foz Côa
　Portugal　41°5N 7°9W 88 D3
Vila Nova de Gaia
　Portugal　41°8N 8°37W 88 D2
Vila Pouca de Aguiar
　Portugal　41°30N 7°38W 88 D3
Vila Real Portugal　41°17N 7°48W 88 D3
Vila-real Spain　39°55N 0°3W 90 F4
Vila Real □ Portugal　41°36N 7°35W 88 D3
Vila Real de Santo António
　Portugal　37°10N 7°28W 89 H3
Vila-seca Spain　41°7N 1°9E 90 D6
Vila Vasco da Gama
　Mozam.　14°54S 32°14E 143 G3
Vila Velha Espírito Santo,
　Brazil　20°20S 40°17W 189 E3
Vila Velha Sergipe, Brazil　11°20S 38°9W 189 C3
Vila Viçosa Portugal　38°45N 7°27W 89 G3
Vilafranca del Maestrat =
　Villafranca del Cid
　Spain　40°26N 0°16W 90 E4
Vilafranca del Penedès
　Spain　41°21N 1°40E 90 D6
Vilagarcía de Arousa
　Spain　42°34N 8°46W 88 C2
Vilaine ➤ France　47°30N 2°27W 70 E4
Vilanandro, Tanjona
　Madag.　16°11S 44°27E 141 H8
Vilanculos Mozam.　22°1S 35°17E 145 C6
Vilanova i la Geltrú Spain　41°13N 1°40E 90 D6
Vilar Formoso Portugal　40°38N 6°45W 88 E3
Vilaseca-Salou = Vila-seca
　Spain　41°7N 1°9E 90 D6
Vilbjerg Denmark　56°12N 8°46E 63 H2
Vilcabamba, Cordillera
　Peru　13°0S 73°0W 188 D3
Vilcanchos Peru　13°40S 74°25W 188 D3
Vilcheka, Ostrov Russia　80°0N 58°31E 106 A6

cheka, Zemlya
  Russia 80°30N 60°30E **54** A11
ches Spain 38°12N 3°30W **89** G7
eyka Belarus 54°30N 26°53E **75** A14
nelmina Sweden 64°35N 16°39E **60** D17
nena Brazil 12°40S 60°50W **186** F6
ya = Neris ➤
  Lithuania 55°8N 24°16E **84** E3
andi Estonia 58°38N 25°30E **84** D3
aviškis Lithuania 54°39N 23°2E **82** D10
xija Lithuania 55°3N 23°35E **82** C10
kitskogo, Proliv
  Russia 78°0N 103°0E **107** B11
ovo = Vylkove
  Ukraine 45°28N 29°32E **81** E14
a Abecia Bolivia 21°0S 68°18W **190** A2
a Ana Argentina 28°28S 59°40W **190** B4
a Angela Argentina 27°34S 60°45W **190** B3
a Bella Bolivia 29°55S 63°43W **190** B3
a Cañas Argentina 34°0S 61°35W **190** C3
a Constitución
  Argentina 33°15S 60°20W **190** C3
a de Arriaga
  Mexico 21°56N 101°20W **180** C4
a de María
  Argentina 29°55S 63°43W **190** B3
a del Río Argentina 31°58S 65°15W **190** C2
a Dolores Argentina 31°58S 65°15W **190** C2
a Gesell Argentina 37°15S 56°55W **190** D4
a Guillermina
  Argentina 28°15S 59°29W **190** B4
a Hayes Paraguay 25°5S 57°20W **190** B4
a Hidalgo Mexico 24°15N 99°26W **181** C5
a Iris Argentina 38°12S 63°12W **190** D3
a María Argentina 32°20S 63°10W **190** C3
a Mazán Argentina 28°40S 66°30W **190** B2
a Minozzo Italy 44°22N 10°28E **92** D7
a Montes Bolivia 21°10S 63°30W **190** A3
a Ocampo
  Argentina 28°30S 59°20W **190** B4
a Ocampo Mexico 26°27N 105°31W **180** B3
a Ojo de Agua
  Argentina 29°30S 63°44W **190** B3
a Regina Argentina 39°6S 67°4W **192** A3
a Rica U.S.A. 33°44N 84°55W **178** B5
a San Giovanni Italy 38°13N 15°38E **95** D8
a San Martín
  Argentina 28°15S 64°9W **190** B3
a Santina Italy 46°24N 12°55E **93** B9
a Unión Mexico 23°12N 106°14W **180** C3
ablino Spain 42°57N 6°19W **88** C4
acarlos Spain 39°53N 4°17E **100** B11
acarriedo Spain 43°14N 3°48W **88** B7
acarrillo Spain 38°7N 3°3W **89** G7
acastín Spain 40°46N 4°25W **88** E6
ach Austria 46°37N 13°51E **78** E6
acidro Italy 39°27N 8°44E **94** C1
ada Spain 42°15N 4°59W **88** C6
adiego Spain 42°31N 4°1W **88** C6
adóssola Italy 46°4N 8°16E **92** B5
afeliche Spain 41°10N 1°30W **90** D3
afranca Spain 38°35N 6°18W **89** G4
afranca de Bonany
  Spain 39°34N 3°5E **100** B10
afranca de los Barros
  Spain 38°35N 6°18W **89** G4
afranca de los Caballeros
  Spain 39°26N 3°21W **89** F7
afranca del Cid Spain 40°26N 0°16W **90** E4
afranca del Panadés =
  Vilafranca del Penedès
  Spain 41°21N 1°40E **90** D6
afranca di Verona
  Italy 45°21N 10°50E **92** C7
afranca Tirrena Italy 38°20N 15°25E **95** D8
agrán Mexico 24°29N 99°29W **181** C5
aguay Argentina 32°0S 59°0W **190** C4
aharta Spain 38°9N 4°54W **89** G6
ahermosa Mexico 17°59N 92°55W **181** D6
ahermosa Spain 38°46N 2°52W **91** G2
aines-la-Juhel France 48°30N 0°12W **70** D6
ajoyosa Spain 38°30N 0°12W **91** G4
alba Spain 43°22N 7°40W **88** B3
alba de Guardo Spain 42°42N 4°49W **88** C6
alón de Campos Spain 42°5N 5°4W **88** C5
alpando Spain 41°51N 5°25W **88** D5
aluenga de la Sagra
  Spain 40°2N 3°54W **88** E7
amanán Spain 42°19N 5°35W **88** D5
amartín Spain 36°52N 5°38W **89** J5
amayor de Santiago
  Spain 39°50N 2°59W **90** F2
amblard France 45°2N 0°32E **72** C4
anova Monteleone
  Italy 40°30N 8°28E **94** B1
anueva U.S.A. 35°16N 105°22W **169** J11
anueva de Castellón
  Spain 39°5N 0°31W **91** F4
anueva de Córdoba
  Spain 38°20N 4°38W **89** G6
anueva de la Fuente
  Spain 38°42N 2°42W **91** G2
anueva de la Serena
  Spain 38°59N 5°50W **89** G5
anueva de la Sierra
  Spain 40°12N 6°24W **88** E4
anueva de los Castillejos
  Spain 37°30N 7°15W **89** H3
anueva de los Infantes
  Spain 38°43N 3°1W **89** G7
anueva del Arzobispo
  Spain 38°10N 3°0W **91** G2
anueva del Fresno
  Spain 38°23N 7°10W **89** G3
anueva y Geltrú = Vilanova i
  la Geltrú Spain 41°13N 1°40E **90** D6
aputzu Italy 39°26N 9°34E **94** C2
aquilambre Spain 43°3N 5°33W **88** C5
ar del Arzobispo
  Spain 39°44N 0°50W **90** F4
ar del Rey Spain 39°7N 6°50W **89** F4
ard-de-Lans France 45°3N 5°33E **73** C9
arramiel Spain 42°4N 4°55W **88** C6
arreal = Vila-Real
  Spain 39°55N 0°3W **90** F4
arrica Chile 39°15S 72°15W **192** A2
arrica Paraguay 25°40S 56°30W **190** B4
arrica △ Chile 39°24S 71°46W **192** A2
arrobledo Spain 39°18N 2°36W **91** F2

Villarroya de la Sierra
  Spain 41°27N 1°46W **90** D3
Villarrubia de los Ojos
  Spain 39°14N 3°36W **89** F7
Villars-les-Dombes France 46°0N 5°3E **71** F12
Villasayas Spain 41°24N 2°39W **90** D2
Villaseco de los Gamitos
  Spain 41°2N 6°7W **88** D4
Villasimíus Italy 39°8N 9°31E **94** C2
Villastar Spain 40°17N 1°9W **90** E3
Villatobas Spain 39°54N 3°20W **88** F7
Villavicencio Argentina 32°28S 69°0W **190** C2
Villavicencio Colombia 4°9N 73°37W **186** C4
Villaviciosa Spain 43°32N 5°27W **88** B5
Villazón Bolivia 22°0S 65°35W **190** A2
Ville-Marie Canada 47°20N 79°30W **164** C4
Ville Platte U.S.A. 30°41N 92°17W **176** F8
Villedieu-les-Poêles
  France 48°50N 1°13W **70** D5
Villefort France 44°28N 3°56E **72** D7
Villefranche-de-Lauragais
  France 43°25N 1°44E **72** E5
Villefranche-de-Rouergue
  France 44°21N 2°2E **72** D6
Villefranche-du-Périgord
  France 44°38N 1°5E **72** D5
Villefranche-sur-Saône
  France 45°59N 4°43E **73** C8
Villemur-sur-Tarn France 43°51N 1°31E **72** E5
Villena Spain 38°39N 0°52W **91** G4
Villenauxe-la-Grande
  France 48°35N 3°33E **71** D10
Villenave-d'Ornon
  France 44°46N 0°33W **72** D3
Villeneuve-d'Ascq France 50°38N 3°9E **71** B10
Villeneuve-l'Archevêque
  France 48°14N 3°32E **71** D10
Villeneuve-lès-Avignon
  France 43°58N 4°49E **73** E8
Villeneuve-sur-Allier
  France 46°40N 3°13E **71** F10
Villeneuve-sur-Lot
  France 44°24N 0°42E **72** D4
Villeneuve-sur-Yonne
  France 48°5N 3°18E **71** D10
Villeréal France 44°38N 0°45E **72** D4
Villers-Bocage France 49°3N 0°40W **70** C6
Villers-Cotterêts France 49°15N 3°4E **71** C10
Villers-sur-Mer France 49°21N 0°2W **70** C6
Villersexel France 47°33N 6°26E **71** E13
Villerupt France 49°28N 5°55E **71** C12
Villeurbanne France 45°46N 4°55E **73** C8
Villiers S. Africa 27°2S 28°36E **145** C4
Villingen-Schwenningen
  Germany 48°3N 8°26E **77** G4
Villmanstrand = Lappeenranta
  Finland 61°3N 28°12E **84** B5
Villupuram India 11°59N 79°31E **127** J4
Vilna Canada 54°7N 111°55W **162** C6
Vilnius Lithuania 54°38N 25°19E **84** E4
Vils Austria 47°33N 10°38E **78** D3
Vils ➤ Bayern, Germany 48°37N 13°11E **77** G9
Vils ➤ Bayern, Germany 49°10N 11°57E **77** F7
Vilsandi □ Estonia 58°23N 21°52E **84** C1
Vilsbiburg Germany 48°26N 12°22E **77** G8
Vilshofen Germany 48°37N 13°11E **77** G9
Vilusi Montenegro 42°44N 18°34E **96** D2
Vilyuchinsk Russia 52°55N 158°24E **107** D16
Vilyuy ➤ Russia 64°24N 126°26E **107** C13
Vilyuysk Russia 63°40N 121°35E **107** C13
Vilyuyskoye Vdkhr.
  Russia 63°0N 112°0E **107** C12
Vimianzo Spain 43°7N 9°3W **88** A1
Vimioso Portugal 41°35N 6°31W **88** D4
Vimmerby Sweden 57°40N 15°55E **63** G9
Vimoutiers France 48°57N 0°10E **70** D7
Vimperk Czech Rep. 49°3N 13°46E **78** F4
Viña del Mar Chile 33°0S 71°30W **190** C1
Vinarós Spain 40°30N 0°27E **90** E5
Vincennes U.S.A. 38°41N 87°32W **172** F10
Vincennes Bay S. Ocean 66°0S 109°0E **55** C8
Vincent U.S.A. 34°33N 118°11W **171** L8
Vinchina Argentina 28°45S 68°15W **190** B2
Vindelälven ➤ Sweden 63°55N 19°50E **60** E18
Vindeln Sweden 64°12N 19°43E **60** D18
Vindhya Ra. India 22°50N 77°0E **124** H7
Vineland U.S.A. 39°29N 75°2W **173** F16
Vinga Romania 46°1N 21°14E **80** D6
Vingåker Sweden 59°2N 15°52E **62** E9
Vinh Vietnam 18°45N 105°38E **120** C5
Vinh Long Vietnam 10°16N 105°57E **121** G5
Vinh Moc Vietnam 17°18N 105°1E **120** D6
Vinh Yen Vietnam 21°21N 105°35E **116** G5
Vinhais Portugal 41°50N 7°5W **88** D3
Vinica Croatia 46°20N 16°9E **93** B13
Vinica Macedonia 41°53N 22°30E **96** E6
Vinica Slovenia 45°28N 15°16E **93** C12
Vinita U.S.A. 36°39N 95°9W **176** C7
Vinkovci Croatia 45°19N 18°48E **80** E3
Vinnitsa = Vinnytsya
  Ukraine 49°15N 28°30E **75** D15
Vinnytsya Ukraine 49°15N 28°30E **75** D15
Vinnytsya □ Ukraine 49°20N 28°15E **75** D15
Vinslöv Sweden 56°7N 13°55E **63** H7
Vinson Massif
  Antarctica 78°35S 85°25W **55** D16
Vintjärn Sweden 60°50N 16°4E **62** G7
Vinton Calif., U.S.A. 39°48N 120°10W **170** F6
Vinton Iowa, U.S.A. 42°10N 92°1W **172** D8
Vinton La., U.S.A. 30°11N 93°35W **176** F8
Vinukonda India 16°4N 79°45E **127** F3
Viöl Germany 54°34N 9°11E **76** A5
Violet Town Australia 36°38S 145°42E **153** D6
Violet Valley ♦
  Australia 17°10S 127°55E **148** C4
Viooslsdrif S. Africa 28°46S 17°55E **144** C2
Viotía Greece 38°20N 23°0E **98** C5
Vipava Slovenia 45°51N 13°58E **93** C10
Vipiteno Italy 46°54N 11°26E **93** B8
Viqueque E. Timor 8°52S 126°23E **119** F7
Vir Croatia 44°17N 15°3E **93** D12
Virac Phil. 13°30N 124°20E **119** B6
Virachey Cambodia 13°59N 106°55E **120** E6
Virachey △ Cambodia 14°14N 106°55E **120** E6
Virago Sd. Canada 54°0N 132°30E **162** C2

Virajpet = Virarajendrapet
  India 12°10N 75°50E **127** H2
Viramgam India 23°5N 72°0E **124** H5
Viranşehir Turkey 37°13N 39°45E **105** D8
Virarajendrapet India 12°10N 75°50E **127** H2
Virawah Pakistan 24°31N 70°46E **124** G4
Virbalis Lithuania 54°39N 22°49E **84** E3
Virden Canada 49°50N 100°56W **163** D8
Vire France 48°50N 0°53W **70** D6
Vire ➤ France 49°20N 1°7W **70** C5
Virgem da Lapa Brazil 16°49S 42°21W **189** D2
Vírgenes, C. Argentina 52°19S 68°21W **192** D3
Virgin ➤ U.S.A. 36°28N 114°21W **169** H6
Virgin Gorda
  Br. Virgin Is. 18°30N 64°26W **183** a
Virgin Is. (British) ☑
  W. Indies 18°30N 64°30W **183** a
Virgin Is. (U.S.) ☑
  W. Indies 18°20N 65°0W **183** a
Virgin Islands △
  U.S. Virgin Is. 18°21N 64°43W **183** C7
Virginia S. Africa 28°8S 26°55E **144** C4
Virginia U.S.A. 47°31N 92°32W **172** B7
Virginia □ U.S.A. 37°30N 78°45W **173** G14
Virginia Beach U.S.A. 36°49N 76°9W **173** F16
Virginia City Mont.,
  U.S.A. 45°18N 111°56W **168** D8
Virginia City Nev.,
  U.S.A. 39°19N 119°39W **170** F7
Virginia Falls Canada 61°38N 125°42W **162** A3
Virginiatown Canada 48°9N 79°36W **164** C4
Virje Croatia 46°4N 16°59E **93** B13
Viroqua U.S.A. 43°34N 90°53W **172** D8
Virovitica Croatia 45°51N 17°21E **80** E2
Virpazar Montenegro 42°14N 19°6E **96** D3
Virpur India 21°51N 70°42E **124** J4
Virsbo Sweden 59°52N 16°12E **62** E10
Virserum Sweden 57°20N 15°35E **63** G9
Virton Belgium 49°35N 5°32E **69** E5
Virudunagar India 9°30N 77°58E **127** K3
Virú Peru 8°25S 78°45W **188** B2
Virunga △
  Dem. Rep. of the Congo 0°5N 29°38E **142** B2
Vis Croatia 43°4N 16°10E **93** E13
Visalia U.S.A. 36°20N 119°18W **170** J7
Visayan Sea Phil. 11°30N 123°30E **119** B6
Visby Sweden 57°37N 18°18E **63** G12
Viscount Melville Sd.
  Canada 74°10N 108°0W **161** C10
Visé Belgium 50°44N 5°41E **69** D5
Vise, Ostrov Russia 79°33N 76°50E **106** B8
Višegrad Bos.-H. 43°47N 19°17E **80** G4
Viseu Brazil 1°10S 46°5W **187** D9
Viseu Portugal 40°40N 7°55W **88** E3
Viseu □ Portugal 40°40N 7°55W **88** E3
Vișeu de Sus Romania 47°45N 24°25E **81** C9
Vishakhapatnam India 17°45N 83°20E **126** F6
Vișina Romania 43°52N 24°27E **81** G9
Vișineşti Moldova 46°20N 28°27E **81** D13
Visingsö Sweden 58°2N 14°20E **63** F8
Viskafors Sweden 57°37N 12°50E **63** G6
Viskan ➤ Sweden 57°4N 12°12E **63** H6
Viški Kanal Croatia 43°4N 16°5E **93** E13
Vislanda Sweden 56°46N 14°30E **63** H8
Visnagar India 23°45N 72°32E **124** H5
Višnja Gora Slovenia 45°58N 14°45E **93** C11
Viso, Mte. Italy 44°38N 7°5E **92** D4
Viso del Marqués Spain 38°32N 3°34W **89** G7
Visoko Bos.-H. 43°58N 18°10E **80** G3
Visokoi I. Antarctica 56°43S 27°15W **55** B1
Visp Switz. 46°17N 7°52E **77** J3
Vissefjärda Sweden 56°32N 15°35E **63** H9
Visselhövede Germany 52°59N 9°34E **76** C5
Vissenbjerg Denmark 55°23N 10°7E **63** J4
Vista U.S.A. 33°12N 117°14W **171** M9
Vistonida, L. Greece 41°0N 25°7E **97** E9
Vistonikos, Ormos = Vistonida, L.
  Greece 41°0N 25°7E **97** E9
Vistula = Wisła ➤
  Poland 54°22N 18°55E **82** D5
Vit ➤ Bulgaria 43°30N 24°30E **97** C8
Vita India 17°17N 74°33E **126** G2
Vitanje Slovenia 46°25N 15°18E **93** B12
Viterbo Italy 42°25N 12°6E **93** F9
Vitez Bos.-H. 44°10N 17°48E **80** F2
Viti Levu Fiji 17°30S 177°30E **154** a
Vitigudino Spain 41°1N 6°26W **88** D4
Vitim Russia 59°28N 112°35E **107** D12
Vitim ➤ Russia 59°26N 112°34E **107** D12
Vitina Bos.-H. 43°17N 17°29E **93** E14
Vitina Greece 37°40N 22°10E **98** D4
Vitkov Czech Rep. 49°46N 17°45E **79** B10
Vitória Brazil 20°20S 40°22W **189** E2
Vitória da Conquista
  Brazil 14°51S 40°51W **189** D2
Vitória de Santo Antão
  Brazil 8°10S 35°20W **189** B3
Vitoria-Gasteiz Spain 42°50N 2°41W **90** C2
Vitória Seamount Atl. Oc. 20°0S 44°0W **56** J8
Vitorino Freire Brazil 4°10S 45°10W **189** A1
Vitosha △ Bulgaria 42°36N 23°18E **96** D7
Vitré France 48°8N 1°12W **70** D5
Vitry-le-François France 48°43N 4°33E **71** D11
Vitry-sur-Seine France 48°47N 2°23E **71** D9
Vitsand Sweden 60°20N 13°0E **62** D7
Vitsi, Oros Greece 40°40N 21°25E **98** F5
Vitsyebsk Belarus 55°10N 30°15E **84** E6
Vittangi Sweden 67°49N 21°25E **60** C19
Vittaryd Sweden 56°58N 13°57E **63** H7
Vitteaux France 47°24N 4°30E **71** E11
Vittel France 48°12N 5°57E **71** D12
Vittória Italy 36°57N 14°32E **95** F7
Vittório Véneto Italy 45°59N 12°18E **93** C9
Vittsjö Sweden 56°20N 13°40E **63** H7
Viveiro Spain 43°39N 7°38W **88** A3
Vivian U.S.A. 32°53N 93°59W **176** E8
Viviers France 44°30N 4°40E **72** D8
Vivonne Australia 35°59S 137°9E **152** C2
Vivonne France 46°25N 0°15E **72** B4
Vivonne B. Australia 35°59S 137°9E **152** C2
Viwa Fiji 17°10S 177°58E **154** a
Vizcaíno, Desierto de
  Mexico 27°30N 113°45W **180** B2
Vizcaíno, Sierra
  Mexico 27°30N 114°0W **180** B2
Vizcaya □ Spain 43°15N 2°45W **90** B2
Vize Turkey 41°34N 27°45E **97** C11
Vizianagaram India 18°6N 83°30E **126** E6
Vizille France 45°5N 5°46E **73** C9

Viziñada Croatia 45°20N 13°46E **93** C10
Viziru Romania 45°0N 27°43E **81** E12
Vizzini Italy 37°10N 14°45E **95** F7
Vlaardingen Neths. 51°55N 4°21E **69** C4
Vlachiotis Greece 36°52N 22°42E **98** E4
Vladikavkaz Russia 43°0N 44°35E **87** J7
Vladimir Russia 56°15N 40°30E **84** D11
Vladimir ➤ Russia 56°15N 40°30E **84** D11
Vladimir Volynskiy = Volodymyr-
  Volynskyy Ukraine 50°50N 24°18E **75** C13
Vladimirci Serbia 44°36N 19°50E **96** B3
Vladimirovac Serbia 45°1N 20°53E **96** B5
Vladimirovka Russia 48°27N 46°10E **87** F8
Vladimirovo Bulgaria 43°32N 23°22E **96** C7
Vladislavovka Ukraine 45°15N 35°29E **85** K8
Vladivostok Russia 43°10N 131°53E **112** C5
Vlǎhiţa Romania 46°21N 25°31E **81** D10
Vlasenica Bos.-H. 44°11N 18°59E **80** F3
Vlašić Bos.-H. 44°19N 17°37E **80** F2
Vlašim Czech Rep. 49°40N 14°53E **78** B7
Vlasinsko Jezero Serbia 42°44N 22°22E **96** D6
Vlasotince Serbia 42°59N 22°7E **96** D6
Vlieland Neths. 53°16N 4°55E **69** A4
Vlissingen Neths. 51°26N 3°34E **69** C3
Vlóra Albania 40°32N 19°28E **96** F3
Vlorës, Gjiri i Albania 40°29N 19°27E **96** F3
Vltava ➤ Czech Rep. 50°21N 14°30E **78** A7
Vo Dat Vietnam 11°9N 107°31E **121** G6
Vóçin Croatia 45°37N 17°33E **80** E2
Vöcklabruck Austria 48°1N 13°39E **78** C6
Vodice Croatia 43°47N 15°47E **93** E12
Vodlozersky △ Russia 62°40N 37°5E **106** C1
Vodňany Czech Rep. 49°9N 14°11E **78** B7
Vodnjan Croatia 44°59N 13°52E **93** D10
Voe U.K. 60°21N 1°16W **65** A7
Vogan Togo 6°23N 1°30E **139** D5
Vogel Pk. Nigeria 8°24N 11°47E **139** D7
Vogelkop = Doberai, Jazirah
  Indonesia 1°25S 133°0E **119** E8
Vogelsberg Germany 50°31N 9°12E **76** E5
Voghera Italy 44°59N 9°1E **92** D6
Vohibinany Madag. 18°49S 49°4E **141** H9
Vohimarina = Iharana
  Madag. 13°25S 50°0E **141** G10
Vohimena, Tanjon' i
  Madag. 25°36S 45°8E **141** K9
Vohipeno Madag. 22°22S 47°51E **141** J9
Voi Kenya 3°25S 38°32E **142** C4
Void-Vacon France 48°40N 5°36E **71** D12
Voinești Iaşi, Romania 47°5N 27°27E **81** C12
Voinești Prahova,
  Romania 45°5N 25°14E **81** E10
Voinjama Liberia 8°25N 9°44W **138** D3
Voiron France 45°22N 5°35E **73** C9
Voisey B. Canada 56°15N 61°50W **165** A7
Voitsberg Austria 47°3N 15°9E **78** D8
Vojens Denmark 55°16N 9°18E **63** J3
Vojmsjön Sweden 65°0N 16°24E **60** D17
Vojnić Croatia 45°19N 15°43E **93** C12
Vojnik Italy 46°18N 15°19E **93** B12
Vojvodina □ Serbia 45°20N 20°0E **80** E5
Vokhtoga Russia 58°46N 41°8E **84** C11
Volary Czech Rep. 48°54N 13°52E **78** C6
Volborg U.S.A. 45°51N 105°41W **168** D11
Volca Croatia 45°37N 17°33E **80** E2
Volcán de Colima △
  Mexico 19°30N 103°40W **180** D4
Volcano Is. = Kazan-Rettō
  Pac. Oc. 25°0N 141°0E **156** E6
Volcans △ Rwanda 1°30S 29°26E **142** C2
Volcans d'Auvergne △
  France 45°20N 2°40E **72** C6
Volchansk = Vovchansk
  Ukraine 50°17N 36°58E **85** G9
Volchikha Russia 52°2N 80°23E **109** B10
Volchya ➤ Ukraine 48°32N 36°0E **85** H8
Volda Norway 62°9N 6°5E **60** E12
Volga ➤ Russia 46°0N 48°30E **87** G9
Volga Hts. = Privolzhskaya
  Vozvyshennost Russia 51°0N 46°0E **86** E7
Volgodonsk Russia 47°33N 42°5E **87** G6
Volgograd Russia 48°40N 44°25E **87** F7
Volgograd □ Russia 49°40N 44°0E **86** E7
Volgogradskoye Vdkhr.
  Russia 50°0N 45°20E **86** E8
Volgorechensk Russia 57°28N 41°14E **86** B5
Volimes Greece 37°52N 20°39E **98** D2
Volissós Greece 38°29N 25°54E **99** C9
Volkach Germany 49°52N 10°14E **77** F6
Völkermarkt Austria 46°39N 14°39E **78** E7
Volkhov ➤ Russia 59°55N 32°15E **84** C7
Volkhov ➤ Russia 60°8N 32°20E **84** B7
Völklingen Germany 49°15N 6°50E **77** F2
Volkovysk = Vawkavysk
  Belarus 53°9N 24°30E **75** D13
Volksrust S. Africa 27°24S 29°53E **145** C4
Volnovakha Ukraine 47°35N 37°30E **85** J8
Volochanka Russia 71°0N 94°28E **107** B10
Volodarsk Russia 56°12N 43°15E **86** B6
Volodymyr-Volynskyy
  Ukraine 50°50N 24°18E **75** C13
Vologda Russia 59°10N 39°45E **84** C10
Vologda □ Russia 60°15N 39°0E **84** B10
Volokolamsk Russia 56°5N 35°57E **84** D8
Volokonovka Russia 50°33N 37°52E **85** G9
Volos Greece 39°24N 22°59E **98** B4
Volosovo Russia 59°27N 29°32E **84** B5
Volovets Ukraine 48°43N 23°11E **81** B8
Volozhin = Valozhyn
  Belarus 54°3N 26°30E **75** A14
Volsk Russia 52°5N 47°22E **86** D8
Volta ➤ Ghana 5°46N 0°41E **139** D5
Volta, L. Ghana 7°30N 0°0 **139** D5
Volta Blanche = White Volta ➤
  Ghana 9°10N 1°15W **139** D4
Volta Redonda Brazil 22°31S 44°5W **191** A7
Voltaire, C. Australia 14°16S 125°35E **148** B4
Volterra Italy 43°24N 10°51E **92** E7
Voltri Italy 44°26N 8°45E **92** D5

Volturno ➤ Italy 41°1N 13°55E **94** A6
Volubilis Morocco 34°2N 5°33W **136** B4
Volvi, L. Greece 40°40N 23°34E **98** H6
Volyn □ Ukraine 51°15N 24°30E **75** C13
Volynё Czech Rep. 49°10N 13°53E **78** B6
Volzhskiy Russia 48°56N 44°46E **87** F7
Vomo Fiji 17°30S 177°15E **154** a
Vonitsa Greece 38°55N 20°53E **98** C2
Vopnafjörður Iceland 65°45N 14°50W **60** D6
Vorarlberg □ Austria 47°20N 10°0E **78** D2
Voras Óros Greece 40°57S 21°45E **96** F5
Vorbasse Denmark 55°39N 9°6E **63** J3
Vorchdorf Austria 48°0N 13°55E **78** C6
Vorderrhein ➤ Switz. 46°49N 9°25E **77** J5
Vordingborg Denmark 55°0N 11°54E **63** J5
Vorë Albania 41°23N 19°40E **96** E3
Voreio Aigaio □ Greece 38°50N 25°50E **99** C7
Voreíos Sporades Greece 39°15N 23°30E **98** B5
Vóreppe France 45°18N 5°39E **73** C9
Vóri Greece 35°4N 24°49E **98** F6
Vórios Evoikos Kolpos
  Greece 38°45N 23°15E **98** C5
Vorkuta Russia 67°48N 64°20E **106** C7
Vórmsi Estonia 59°1N 23°13E **84** C2
Vorona ➤ Russia 51°26N 42°43E **86** E8
Voronezh Russia 51°40N 39°10E **85** G10
Voronezh Ukraine 51°47N 33°28E **85** G7
Voronezh □ Russia 51°25N 39°0E **86** E4
Vorontsovo-Aleksandrovskoye =
  Zelenokumsk Russia 44°24N 44°0E **87** H6
Vorpommersche
  Boddenlandschaft △
  Germany 54°25N 12°32E **76** A8
Vorskla ➤ Ukraine 48°50N 34°10E **85** H8
Võrts järv Estonia 58°16N 26°3E **84** C4
Võru Estonia 57°48N 26°54E **84** D4
Vosges France 48°12N 6°20E **71** D13
Vosges □ France 48°12N 6°20E **71** D13
Vosges du Nord △ France 49°0N 7°30E **71** D14
Voskopoljë Albania 40°30N 20°33E **96** F4
Voskresensk Russia 55°19N 38°43E **84** E10
Voskresenskoye Russia 56°51N 45°30E **86** B7
Voss Norway 60°38N 6°26E **60** F12
Vostochnyy Port
  Russia 42°44N 133°4E **112** C6
Vostok Antarctica 78°30S 106°54E **55** D8
Vostok I. Kiribati 10°5S 152°23W **157** J12
Votice Czech Rep. 49°38N 14°39E **78** B7
Vouga ➤ Portugal 40°41N 8°40W **88** E2
Vouillé France 46°38N 0°10E **70** F7
Vouxa, Akra Greece 35°37N 23°32E **101** D5
Vouzela Portugal 40°43N 8°7W **88** E2
Vouziers France 49°22N 4°40E **71** C11
Vovchansk Ukraine 50°17N 36°58E **85** G9
Vovchyn Belarus 52°18N 23°18E **83** F10
Voyageurs □ U.S.A. 48°32N 93°0W **172** A7
Voynitsa Russia 65°10N 30°20E **60** D24
Voyvozh Russia 62°56N 54°56E **106** C6
Vozhe, Ozero Russia 60°45N 39°0E **84** B10
Vozhega Russia 60°29N 40°12E **84** B11
Voznesensk Ukraine 47°35N 31°21E **85** J6
Voznesenye Russia 61°0N 35°28E **84** B8
Vrå Denmark 57°21N 9°56E **63** G3
Vráble Slovak Rep. 48°15N 18°16E **79** C11
Vračevšnica Serbia 44°2N 20°34E **96** B4
Vrachneíka Greece 38°10N 21°40E **98** C3
Vrancea □ Romania 45°50N 26°45E **81** E11
Vrancei, Munţii
  Romania 45°50N 26°45E **81** E11
Vrangel Russia 42°43N 133°5E **112** C6
Vrangelya, Ostrov
  Russia 71°0N 180°0E **107** B18
Vranica Bos.-H. 43°55N 17°50E **80** G2
Vranje Serbia 42°34N 21°54E **96** D6
Vranjska Banja Serbia 42°34N 22°1E **96** D6
Vranov nad Topľou
  Slovak Rep. 48°53N 21°40E **79** C14
Vransko Slovenia 46°17N 14°58E **93** B11
Vransko Jezero Croatia 43°53N 15°34E **93** E12
Vrapčíšte Macedonia 41°50N 20°53E **96** E5
Vratsa Bulgaria 43°15N 23°30E **96** C7
Vratsa □ Bulgaria 43°40N 19°40E **80** F4
Vrbas Serbia 45°40N 19°40E **80** E4
Vrbas ➤ Bos.-H. 45°8N 17°29E **80** E2
Vrbnik Croatia 45°4N 14°40E **93** D11
Vrbovec Croatia 45°53N 16°28E **93** C13
Vrbovsko Croatia 45°24N 15°5E **93** C12
Vrchlabí Czech Rep. 50°38N 15°37E **78** A8
Vrede S. Africa 27°24S 29°6E **145** C4
Vredefort S. Africa 27°0S 27°22E **144** C4
Vreden Germany 52°2N 6°59E **76** C2
Vredenburg S. Africa 32°56S 18°0E **144** D2
Vredendal S. Africa 31°41S 18°35E **144** D2
Vretstorp Sweden 59°1N 14°53E **62** E8
Vrgorac Croatia 43°12N 17°20E **93** E14
Vrhnika Slovenia 45°58N 14°15E **93** C11
Vriddhachalam India 11°30N 79°20E **127** J4
Vrindavan India 27°37N 77°40E **124** F7
Vrisses Greece 35°23N 24°13E **101** D6
Vrnograč Bos.-H. 45°10N 15°57E **93** C12
Vrondádes Greece 38°25N 26°7E **99** C8
Vrpolje Croatia 45°13N 18°24E **80** E3
Vršac Serbia 45°8N 21°20E **80** E6
Vrsacki Kanal Serbia 45°15N 21°0E **80** E5
Vrútky Slovak Rep. 49°7N 18°55E **79** B11
Vryburg S. Africa 26°55S 24°45E **144** C3
Vryheid S. Africa 27°45S 30°47E **145** C5
Vsetín Czech Rep. 49°20N 18°0E **79** B10
Vu Liet Vietnam 18°43N 105°23E **120** C5
Vúcha ➤ Russia 58°30N 13°20E **63** D13
Vučitrn = Vushtrri
  Kosovo 42°49N 20°59E **96** D4
Vukovar Croatia 45°21N 18°59E **80** E4
Vuktyl Russia 63°52N 57°20E **106** C6
Vulcan Canada 50°25N 113°15W **162** C6
Vulcan Romania 45°23N 23°17E **81** E8
Vulcăneşti Moldova 45°41N 28°18E **81** F13
Vulcano Italy 38°24N 14°58E **95** E7
Vûlchedruma Bulgaria 43°42N 23°27E **96** C7
Vulkaneşty = Vulcăneşti
  Moldova 45°41N 28°18E **81** F13
Vunduzi ➤ Mozam. 18°56S 34°1E **143** F3
Vung Tau Vietnam 10°21N 107°4E **121** G6
Vunidawa Fiji 17°50S 178°21E **154** a
Vunisea Fiji 19°3S 178°10E **154** a
Vuntut △ Canada 68°25N 139°41W **160** C6
Vûrbitsa Bulgaria 42°59N 26°40E **97** D10

Vurshets Bulgaria 43°13N 23°23E **96** C7
Vutcani Romania 46°26N 27°59E **81** D12
Vuzlove Ukraine 48°22N 22°24E **80** B7
Vwaza △ Malawi 10°58S 33°25E **143** E3
Vyara India 21°8N 73°28E **126** D1
Vyartsilya Russia 62°8N 30°45E **84** A6
Vyatka = Kirov Russia 58°35N 49°40E **106** D5
Vyatka ➤ Russia 55°37N 51°28E **86** C10
Vyatskiye Polyany
  Russia 56°14N 51°5E **86** B10
Vyazemskiy Russia 47°32N 134°45E **107** E14
Vyazma Russia 55°10N 34°15E **84** E8
Vyazniki Russia 56°10N 42°10E **86** B6
Vyborg Russia 60°43N 28°47E **84** B5
Vychegda ➤ Russia 61°18N 46°36E **106** C5
Vychodné Beskydy
  Europe 49°20N 22°0E **79** B15
Vyerkhnyadzvinsk
  Belarus 55°45N 27°58E **84** E4
Vyhoda Ukraine 48°56N 23°55E **81** B8
Vyksa Russia 55°19N 42°11E **86** C6
Vylkove Ukraine 45°28N 29°32E **81** E14
Vylok Ukraine 48°6N 22°50E **80** B7
Vynohradiv Ukraine 48°9N 23°2E **80** B8
Vypin India 10°10N 76°15E **127** J3
Vyrnwy, L. U.K. 52°48N 3°31W **66** E4
Vyshkiv Ukraine 48°44N 23°39E **81** B8
Vyshkove Ukraine 48°3N 23°25E **81** B8
Vyshniy Volochek
  Russia 57°30N 34°30E **84** D8
Vyshnya = imeni 26 Bakinskikh
  Komissarov
  Turkmenistan 39°22N 54°10E **129** B7
Vyškov Czech Rep. 49°17N 17°0E **79** B9
Vysokaye Belarus 52°22N 23°22E **83** F10
Vysoké Mýto Czech Rep. 49°58N 16°10E **79** B9
Vysokovsk Russia 56°22N 36°30E **84** D9
Vyšší Brod Czech Rep. 48°37N 14°19E **78** C7
Vytegra Russia 61°0N 36°27E **84** B9
Vyzhnytsya Ukraine 48°15N 25°11E **81** B9
Vyzhnytsya △ Ukraine 48°7N 25°15E **81** B10

W

W du Benin △ Benin 11°57N 2°43E **139** C5
W du Burkina Faso △
  Burkina Faso 11°52N 2°50E **139** C5
W du Niger △ Niger 13°31N 2°28E **139** C5
W.A.C. Bennett Dam
  Canada 56°2N 122°6W **162** B4
Wa Ghana 10°7N 2°25W **138** C4
Waal ➤ Neths. 51°37N 5°0E **69** C5
Waalwijk Neths. 51°42N 5°4E **69** C5
Waanyi-Garawa ♦
  Australia 18°2S 137°33E **150** B2
Wabakimi △ Canada 50°43N 89°29W **164** B2
Wabana Canada 47°40N 53°0W **165** C9
Wabasca ➤ Canada 58°22N 115°20W **162** B5
Wabasca-Desmarais
  Canada 55°57N 113°56W **162** B6
Wabash U.S.A. 40°48N 85°49W **173** E11
Wabash ➤ U.S.A. 37°48N 88°2W **172** G9
Wabasso U.S.A. 27°45N 80°26W **179** M5
Wabigoon L. Canada 49°44N 92°44W **163** D10
Wabowden Canada 54°55N 98°38W **163** C9
Wąbrzeźno Poland 53°16N 18°57E **83** E5
Wabu Hu China 32°20N 116°50E **117** A11
Wabush Canada 52°55N 66°52W **165** B6
Waccasassa B. U.S.A. 29°10N 82°50W **179** F7
Wachau Austria 48°21N 15°26E **78** E6
Wächock Poland 51°4N 21°11E **83** G8
Wächtersbach Germany 50°14N 9°17E **77** E5
Wacissa U.S.A. 32°40N 58°59W **178** B6
Waco U.S.A. 31°33N 97°9W **178** E6
Waconichi, L. Canada 50°8N 74°0W **165** B5
Wad Hamid Sudan 16°30N 32°45E **135** E12
Wad Medani Sudan 14°28N 33°30E **135** F12
Wad Thana Pakistan 27°22N 66°23E **124** F2
Wadayama Japan 35°19N 134°52E **113** G7
Wadbilliga △ Australia 36°25S 149°36E **153** D8
Waddeneilanden Neths. 53°25N 5°10E **69** A5
Waddenzee Neths. 53°6N 5°10E **69** A5
Waddi, Chappal Nigeria 7°2N 11°43E **139** D7
Waddington U.S.A. 44°52N 75°12W **173** B9
Waddington, Mt.
  Canada 51°23N 125°15W **162** C3
Waddy Pt. Australia 24°58S 153°21E **151** C5
Wadebridge U.K. 50°31N 4°51W **67** G3
Wadena Canada 51°57N 103°47W **163** C8
Wadena U.S.A. 46°26N 95°8W **172** B6
Wädenswil Switz. 47°14N 8°40E **77** J4
Wadern Germany 49°32N 6°53E **77** F2
Wadeye Australia 14°28S 129°52E **148** B4
Wadgaon India 18°44N 73°39E **126** D1
Wadhams Canada 51°30N 127°30W **162** C3
Wadhwan India 22°42N 71°41E **124** H4
Wadi India 17°4N 76°59E **126** F3
Wadi as Sir Jordan 31°56N 35°49E **130** D4
Wadi Gemâl, J. Egypt 24°35N 35°10E **137** C4
Wadi Halfa Sudan 21°53N 31°19E **137** D3
Wadi Rum △ Jordan 29°30N 35°20E **130** F4
Wadian China 32°42N 112°29E **117** A9
Wadlew Poland 51°31N 19°23E **83** G6
Wadley Ala., U.S.A. 33°7N 85°34W **178** B4
Wadley Ga., U.S.A. 32°52N 82°24W **178** B5
Wadowice Poland 49°52N 19°30E **83** J6
Wadsworth Nev.,
  U.S.A. 39°38N 119°17W **168** G4
Wadsworth Ohio, U.S.A. 41°1N 81°44W **174** E3
Waegwan S. Korea 35°59N 128°23E **115** G15
Wafangdian China 39°59N 121°59E **115** E11
Wafrah Kuwait 28°33N 47°56E **128** D5
Wagait ♦ Australia 13°1S 130°6E **148** B5
Wagener U.S.A. 33°39N 81°22W **179** D5
Wagga Wagga
  Australia 35°7S 147°24E **153** C7
Waghai India 20°46N 73°30E **126** D1
Waghete Indonesia 4°10S 135°50E **119** E9
Wagin Australia 33°17S 117°25E **149** H2
Wagner U.S.A. 43°5N 98°18W **172** D5
Wagon Mound
  U.S.A. 36°1N 104°42W **169** H11
Wagoner U.S.A. 35°58N 95°22W **176** C7
Wagrowiec Poland 52°48N 17°11E **83** F4
Wah Pakistan 33°45N 72°40E **124** C5
Wahai Indonesia 2°48S 129°35E **119** E7

Waharoa N.Z. 37°46S 175°45E **154** D4
Wâhid Egypt 30°48N 32°21E **130** E1
Wahnai Afghan. 32°40N 65°50E **124** C1
Wahoo U.S.A. 41°13N 96°37W **172** E5
Wahpeton U.S.A. 46°16N 96°36W **172** B5
Wai India 17°56N 73°57E **126** F1
Waialua U.S.A. 21°34N 158°8W **167** L8
Waiapu → N.Z. 37°47S 178°29E **154** D7
Waiau N.Z. 42°39S 173°5E **155** C8
Waiau → Canterbury, N.Z. 42°47S 173°22E **155** C8
Waiau → Southland, N.Z. 46°12S 167°38E **155** G2
Waiawe Ganga → Sri Lanka 6°15N 81°0E **127** L5
Waibeem Indonesia 0°30S 132°59E **119** E8
Waiblingen Germany 48°49N 9°18E **77** G5
Waidhofen an der Thaya Austria 48°49N 15°17E **78** C8
Waidhofen an der Ybbs Austria 47°57N 14°46E **78** D7
Waigeo Indonesia 0°20S 130°40E **119** E8
Waihao → N.Z. 44°47S 171°10E **155** E6
Waihao Downs N.Z. 44°48S 170°55E **155** E5
Waiheke I. N.Z. 36°48S 175°6E **154** C4
Waihi N.Z. 37°23S 175°52E **154** D4
Waihi Beach N.Z. 37°25S 175°57E **154** D4
Waihola N.Z. 46°1S 170°8E **155** G5
Waihola L. N.Z. 45°59S 170°8E **155** G5
Waihou → N.Z. 37°15S 175°40E **154** D4
Waika Dem. Rep. of the Congo 2°22S 25°42E **142** C2
Waikabubak Indonesia 9°45S 119°25E **119** F5
Waikaia N.Z. 45°44S 168°51E **155** F3
Waikaka N.Z. 45°55S 169°1E **155** F4
Waikare, L. N.Z. 37°26S 175°13E **154** D4
Waikareiti, L. N.Z. 38°43S 177°10E **154** E6
Waikaremoana N.Z. 38°42S 177°12E **154** E6
Waikaremoana, L. N.Z. 38°49S 177°9E **154** E6
Waikari N.Z. 42°58S 172°41E **155** C7
Waikato → N.Z. 37°23S 174°43E **154** D3
Waikelo Indonesia 9°24S 119°19E **148** A2
Waikerie Australia 34°9S 140°0E **152** C4
Waikiekie N.Z. 35°57S 174°16E **154** B3
Waikokopu N.Z. 39°3S 177°52E **154** F6
Waikouaiti N.Z. 45°36S 170°41E **155** F5
Waikouaiti Downs N.Z. 45°30S 170°30E **155** F5
Waimakariri → N.Z. 43°24S 172°42E **155** D7
Waimangaroa N.Z. 41°43S 171°46E **155** B6
Waimarie N.Z. 41°35S 171°56E **155** B6
Waimate N.Z. 44°45S 171°3E **155** E6
Waimea Plain N.Z. 45°55S 168°35E **155** F3
Wainganga → India 18°50N 79°55E **126** E4
Waingapu Indonesia 9°35S 120°11E **119** F6
Waini → Guyana 8°20N 59°50W **186** B7
Wainuiomata N.Z. 41°17S 174°56E **154** H3
Wainwright Canada 52°50N 110°50W **163** C6
Wainwright U.S.A. 70°38N 160°2W **166** A7
Waiotapu N.Z. 38°21S 176°25E **154** E5
Waiouru N.Z. 39°28S 175°41E **154** F4
Waipa → N.Z. 38°16S 175°21E **154** E4
Waipahi N.Z. 46°6S 169°15E **155** G4
Waipapa Pt. N.Z. 46°40S 168°51E **155** G3
Waipara N.Z. 43°3S 172°45E **155** D7
Waipawa N.Z. 39°56S 176°38E **154** F5
Waipiro N.Z. 38°2S 178°22E **154** E7
Waipiro Bay N.Z. 38°1S 178°21E **154** E7
Waipoua Forest N.Z. 35°39S 173°33E **154** B2
Waipu N.Z. 35°59S 174°29E **154** B3
Waipukurau N.Z. 40°1S 176°33E **154** G5
Wairakei N.Z. 38°37S 176°6E **154** E5
Wairarapa, L. N.Z. 41°14S 175°15E **154** H3
Wairau → N.Z. 41°32S 174°7E **155** B9
Wairio N.Z. 45°59S 168°3E **155** F3
Wairoa N.Z. 39°3S 177°25E **154** F6
Wairoa → Hawke's Bay, N.Z. 39°4S 177°25E **154** F6
Wairoa → Northland, N.Z. 36°5S 173°59E **154** C2
Waitaki → N.Z. 44°56S 171°7E **155** E6
Waitaki Plains N.Z. 44°22S 170°0E **155** E5
Waitangi N.Z. 35°16S 174°5E **154** B3
Waitara N.Z. 38°59S 174°15E **154** E3
Waitara → N.Z. 38°59S 174°14E **154** E3
Waitiki Landing N.Z. 34°31S 172°50E **154** A1
Waitoa N.Z. 37°37S 175°35E **154** D4
Waitomo Caves N.Z. 38°16S 175°7E **154** E4
Waitotara N.Z. 39°49S 174°44E **154** F3
Waitotara → N.Z. 39°55S 174°41E **154** F3
Waitsburg U.S.A. 46°16N 118°9W **168** C4
Waiuku N.Z. 37°15S 174°45E **154** D3
Wajima Japan 37°30N 137°0E **113** F8
Wajir Kenya 1°42N 40°5E **142** B5
Wakasa Japan 35°20N 134°24E **113** G7
Wakasa-Wan Japan 35°40N 135°30E **113** G7
Wakatipu, L. N.Z. 45°5S 168°33E **155** F3
Wakaw Canada 52°39N 105°44W **163** C7
Wakaya Fiji 17°37S 179°0E **154** a
Wakayama Japan 34°15N 135°15E **113** G7
Wakayama □ Japan 33°50N 135°30E **113** H7
Wake Forest U.S.A. 35°59N 78°30W **177** D15
Wake I. Pac. Oc. 19°18N 166°36E **156** F8
WaKeeney U.S.A. 39°1N 99°53W **172** F4
Wakefield Jamaica 18°26N 77°42W **182** a
Wakefield U.K. 53°41N 1°29W **66** D6
Wakefield Mass., U.S.A. 42°30N 71°5W **175** D13
Wakefield Mich., U.S.A. 46°29N 89°56W **172** B9
Wakkanai Japan 45°28N 141°35E **112** B10
Wakkerstroom S. Africa 27°24S 30°10E **145** C5
Wakool Australia 35°28S 144°23E **152** C6
Wakool → Australia 35°5S 143°33E **152** C6
Wakre Indonesia 0°19S 131°5E **119** E8
Wakuach, L. Canada 55°34N 67°32W **165** A6
Wakulla U.S.A. 30°14N 84°14W **178** E5
Walagunya ○ Australia 23°0S 120°50E **148** C3
Walamba Zambia 13°30S 28°42E **143** G5
Walbrzych Poland 50°45N 16°18E **83** H3
Walbury Hill U.K. 51°21N 1°28W **67** F6
Walcha Australia 30°55S 151°31E **153** E5
Walcheren Neths. 51°30N 3°35E **69** C3
Walcott U.S.A. 41°46N 106°51W **168** F10
Walcz Poland 53°17N 16°27E **83** E3
Waldbröl Germany 50°52N 7°37E **76** E3
Waldburg Ra. Australia 24°40S 117°35E **149** D2

Waldeck Germany 51°12N 9°4E **76** D5
Walden Colo., U.S.A. 40°44N 106°17W **168** F10
Walden N.Y., U.S.A. 41°34N 74°11W **175** E10
Waldkirch Germany 48°5N 7°58E **77** G3
Waldkirchen Germany 48°43N 13°36E **77** G9
Waldkraiburg Germany 48°11N 12°24E **77** G8
Waldo U.S.A. 29°48N 82°10W **178** F7
Waldport U.S.A. 44°26N 124°4W **168** D1
Waldron U.S.A. 34°54N 94°5W **176** D7
Waldviertel Austria 48°30N 15°30E **78** C8
Walebing Australia 30°41S 116°13E **149** F2
Walembele Ghana 10°30N 1°58W **138** C4
Walensee Switz. 47°7N 9°13E **77** H5
Wales □ U.K. 52°19N 4°43E **67** E3
Wales I. Canada 68°1N 86°40W **161** D14
Walewale Ghana 10°21N 0°50W **139** C4
Walgett Australia 30°0S 148°5E **151** E4
Walgreen Coast Antarctica 75°15S 105°0W **55** D15
Walhalla Australia 37°56S 146°29E **153** D7
Walker U.S.A. 47°6N 94°35W **172** B6
Walker, L. Canada 50°20N 67°11W **165** B6
Walker L. Canada 54°42N 95°57W **163** C9
Walker L. U.S.A. 38°42N 118°43W **168** G4
Walkerston Australia 21°11S 149°8E **150** b
Walkerton U.S.A. 41°28N 86°29W **172** E9
Wall U.S.A. 44°0N 102°8W **172** C2
Walla Walla Australia 35°45S 146°54E **153** C7
Walla Walla U.S.A. 46°4N 118°20W **168** C4
Wallace Idaho, U.S.A. 47°28N 115°56W **168** C6
Wallace N.C., U.S.A. 34°44N 77°59W **177** D16
Wallaceburg Canada 42°34N 82°23W **174** D2
Wallacetown N.Z. 46°21S 168°19E **155** G3
Wallachia = Valahia Romania 44°35N 25°0E **81** F9
Wallal Australia 26°32S 146°7E **151** D4
Wallam Cr. → Australia 28°40S 147°20E **151** D4
Wallambin, L. Australia 30°57S 117°35E **149** F2
Wallan Australia 37°26S 144°59E **153** D6
Wallangarra Australia 28°56S 151°58E **151** D5
Wallaroo Australia 33°56S 137°39E **152** B2
Walldürn Germany 49°34N 9°22E **77** F5
Wallenhorst Germany 52°21N 8°1E **76** C4
Wallenpaupack, L. U.S.A. 41°25N 75°15W **175** E9
Wallerawang Australia 33°25S 150°4E **153** B9
Wallingat → Australia 32°14S 152°25E **153** B10
Wallingford Conn., U.S.A. 41°27N 72°50W **175** E12
Wallingford Vt., U.S.A. 43°28N 72°58W **175** C12
Wallis & Futuna, Îs. ☑ Pac. Oc. 13°18S 176°10W **147** C11
Wallowa U.S.A. 45°34N 117°32W **168** D5
Wallowa Mts. U.S.A. 45°20N 117°30W **168** D5
Walls U.K. 60°14N 1°33W **65** A7
Walls of Jerusalem △ Australia 41°56S 146°15E **151** G4
Wallsend Australia 32°55S 151°40E **153** B9
Wallula U.S.A. 46°5N 118°54W **168** C4
Wallumbilla Australia 26°33S 149°9E **151** D4
Walmsley L. Canada 63°25N 108°36W **163** A7
Walney, I. of U.K. 54°6N 3°15W **66** C4
Walnut Canyon △ U.S.A. 35°15N 111°20W **169** J8
Walnut Creek U.S.A. 37°54N 122°4W **170** H4
Walnut Grove U.S.A. 34°4N 86°18W **178** A3
Walnut Hill U.S.A. 30°53N 87°30W **178** F11
Walnut Ridge U.S.A. 36°4N 90°57W **177** C9
Walpeup Australia 35°7S 142°2E **152** C5
Walpole Australia 34°58S 116°44E **149** F2
Walpole U.S.A. 42°9N 71°15W **175** D13
Walpole-Nornalup △ Australia 35°0S 116°45E **149** G2
Wals Austria 47°44N 12°58E **78** E3
Walsall U.K. 52°35N 1°58W **67** E6
Walsenburg U.S.A. 37°38N 104°47W **169** H11
Walsh U.S.A. 37°23N 102°17W **169** H12
Walsh → Australia 16°31S 143°42E **150** B3
Walsingham Canada 42°40N 80°31W **174** D4
Walsrode Germany 52°51N 9°35E **76** C5
Walt Disney World U.S.A. 28°22N 81°33W **179** G8
Waltair India 17°44N 83°23E **126** F6
Walter F. George Res. U.S.A. 31°38N 85°4W **178** E3
Walterboro U.S.A. 32°55N 80°40W **178** E5
Walters U.S.A. 34°22N 98°19W **176** D5
Waltershausen Germany 50°54N 10°33E **76** E6
Waltershausen Gletscher Greenland 73°54N 24°25W **57** C8
Waltham U.S.A. 42°23N 71°14W **175** D13
Waltman U.S.A. 43°4N 107°12W **168** E10
Walton U.S.A. 42°10N 75°8W **175** D9
Walton-on-the-Naze U.K. 51°51N 1°17E **67** F9
Walvis Bay Namibia 23°0S 14°28E **144** B1
Walvis Ridge Atl. Oc. 26°0S 5°0E **56** J12
Walvisbaai = Walvis Bay Namibia 23°0S 14°28E **144** B1
Walwa Australia 35°59S 147°44E **153** C7
Wamba Dem. Rep. of the Congo 2°10N 27°57E **142** D5
Wamba Kenya 0°58N 37°19E **142** B4
Wamba Nigeria 8°57N 8°42E **139** D6
Wambardi ○ Australia 16°15S 130°15E **148** C5
Wamego U.S.A. 39°12N 96°18W **172** F5
Wamena Indonesia 4°4S 138°57E **119** E9
Wampana Karlantijpa ○ Australia 17°45S 132°10E **148** C5
Wampaya ○ Australia 17°20S 135°0E **150** B2
Wampsville U.S.A. 43°4N 75°42W **175** C9
Wamsutter U.S.A. 41°40N 107°58W **168** F10
Wamulan Indonesia 3°2S 126°7E **119** E7
Wan Tup Burma 21°13N 98°42E **116** C2
Wan Xian China 38°47N 115°7E **114** E8
Wana Pakistan 32°20N 69°32E **124** C3
Wanaaring Australia 29°38S 144°9E **151** D3
Wanaka N.Z. 44°42S 169°9E **155** E2
Wanaka, L. N.Z. 44°33S 169°7E **155** E2
Wan'an China 26°26N 114°49E **117** D10
Wanapitei L. Canada 46°45N 80°40W **172** B12
Wanbi Australia 34°46S 140°17E **152** C4
Wandel Sea = McKinley Sea Arctic 82°0N 0°0E **57** A11
Wandérama Ivory C. 8°37N 4°25W **138** D4
Wandhari Pakistan 27°42N 66°48E **124** F2
Wanding China 24°24S 98°4E **116** E2

Wandoan Australia 26°5S 149°55E **151** D4
Wandur Marine △ India 11°30N 92°30E **127** J11
Wanfu China 40°8N 122°38E **115** D12
Wang → Thailand 17°8N 99°2E **120** D2
Wang Noi Thailand 14°13N 100°44E **120** E3
Wang Saphung Thailand 17°18N 101°46E **120** D3
Wang Thong Thailand 16°50N 100°26E **120** D3
Wanga Dem. Rep. of the Congo 2°58N 29°12E **142** B2
Wanganella Australia 35°6S 144°49E **153** C6
Wanganui N.Z. 39°56S 175°3E **154** F4
Wanganui → W. Coast, N.Z. 43°3S 170°26E **155** D5
Wanganui → Wanganui-Manawatu, N.Z. 39°55S 175°4E **154** F4
Wangaratta Australia 36°21S 146°19E **153** D7
Wangary Australia 34°35S 135°29E **152** B2
Wangcang China 32°18N 106°20E **116** A6
Wangcheng China 28°29N 112°49E **117** C9
Wangcun China 36°41N 117°41E **115** F9
Wangdu China 38°40N 115°7E **114** E8
Wangen Germany 47°41N 9°50E **77** H5
Wangerooge Germany 53°47N 7°54E **76** B3
Wangiwangi Indonesia 5°22S 123°37E **119** F6
Wangjiang China 30°10N 116°42E **117** B11
Wangmo China 25°11N 106°5E **116** E6
Wangolodougou Ivory C. 9°55N 5°10W **138** D3
Wangqing China 43°12N 129°42E **115** C15
Wani India 20°5N 78°55E **126** D4
Wanimiyn ○ Australia 15°50S 130°49E **148** C5
Wanjina Wunggurr Wilinggin ○ Australia 16°0S 127°0E **148** C4
Wankaner India 22°35N 71°0E **124** H4
Wanless Canada 54°11N 101°21W **163** C8
Wanlefeweyne Somalia 2°37N 44°54E **131** G3
Wanneroo Australia 31°42S 115°46E **149** F2
Wannian China 28°42N 117°4E **117** C11
Wanning China 18°48N 110°22E **117** a
Wannoo Billabong Roadhouse Australia 27°25S 115°49E **149** E2
Wanon Niwat Thailand 17°38N 103°46E **120** D4
Wanqinsha China 22°43N 113°33E **111** a
Wanquan China 40°50N 114°40E **114** D8
Wanrong China 35°25N 110°50E **114** G6
Wanshan China 27°30N 109°12E **116** D7
Wanshan Qundao China 21°57N 113°45E **111** a
Wansheng China 28°57N 106°53E **116** C6
Wanstead N.Z. 40°8S 176°30E **154** G5
Wantage U.K. 51°35N 1°25W **67** F6
Wanxian China 30°42N 108°20E **116** B7
Wanxian China 32°4N 108°3E **116** A7
Wanzai Guangdong, China 22°12N 113°31E **111** a
Wanzai Jiangxi, China 28°7N 114°30E **117** C10
Wapakoneta U.S.A. 40°34N 84°12W **173** E11
Wapato U.S.A. 46°27N 120°25W **168** C3
Wapawekka L. Canada 54°55N 104°40W **163** C8
Wapikopa L. Canada 52°56N 87°53W **164** B2
Wapiti → Canada 55°5N 118°18W **162** B5
Wappingers Falls U.S.A. 41°36N 73°55W **175** E11
Wapsipinicon → U.S.A. 41°44N 90°19W **172** E8
Wapusk △ Canada 57°45N 92°22W **163** B10
Warakurna Australia 24°59S 128°17E **149** D4
Warangal India 17°58N 79°35E **126** F4
Waraseoni India 21°45N 80°2E **125** J9
Waratah Australia 41°30S 145°30E **151** G4
Waratah B. Australia 38°54S 146°5E **153** E7
Warburg Germany 51°28N 9°11E **76** D5
Warburton Vic., Australia 37°47S 145°42E **153** D6
Warburton W. Austral., Australia 26°8S 126°35E **149** E4
Warburton ○ Australia 26°7S 126°34E **149** E4
Warburton → Australia 28°4S 137°28E **151** D2
Warburton Groove Australia 28°18S 137°8E **151** A2
Warburton Ra. Australia 25°55S 126°28E **149** E4
Ward N.Z. 41°49S 174°11E **155** B9
Ward → Australia 26°28S 146°6E **151** D4
Ward Mt. U.S.A. 37°12N 118°54W **170** H8
Wardang I. Australia 34°30S 137°20E **152** C2
Warden S. Africa 27°50S 29°0E **145** C4
Wardha India 20°45N 78°39E **126** D4
Wardha → India 19°57N 79°11E **126** D4
Wardsville Canada 42°39N 81°45W **174** D3
Ware U.K. 51°49N 0°0 **67** F8
Ware U.S.A. 42°16N 72°14W **175** D12
Waregem Belgium 50°53N 3°27E **69** D3
Wareham U.S.A. 41°46N 70°43W **175** E14
Waremme Belgium 50°43N 5°15E **69** D5
Waren Germany 53°31N 12°40E **76** B8
Warendorf Germany 51°57N 8°1E **76** D4
Waresboro U.S.A. 31°15N 82°29W **178** E7
Warialda Australia 29°29S 150°33E **151** D5
Warin Chamrap Thailand 15°12N 104°53E **120** E5
Warka Poland 51°47N 21°12E **83** G8
Warkopi Indonesia 1°12S 134°9E **119** E8
Warkworth N.Z. 36°24S 174°41E **154** C3
Warm Springs Ga., U.S.A. 32°53N 84°41W **178** C5
Warm Springs Nev., U.S.A. 38°10N 116°20W **169** G5
Warman Canada 52°19N 106°30W **163** C7
Warmbad = Bela Bela S. Africa 24°51S 28°19E **145** B4
Warmbad Namibia 28°25S 18°42E **144** D2
Warming I. = Uunartoq Qeqertaq Greenland 71°33N 21°47W **57** C8
Warmińsko-Mazurskie □ Poland 54°0N 21°0E **82** D8
Warminster U.K. 51°12N 2°10W **67** F5
Warminster U.S.A. 40°12N 75°6W **175** F9
Warmun Australia 17°2S 128°12E **148** C4
Warnemünde Germany 54°10N 12°4E **76** A8
Warner Mts. U.S.A. 41°40N 120°15W **168** F3
Warner Robins U.S.A. 32°37N 83°36W **178** D6
Warnow → Germany 54°6N 12°9E **76** A8
Waroona Australia 32°50S 115°58E **149** F2
Warora India 20°14N 79°1E **126** D4
Warrabah △ Australia 30°31S 150°56E **153** A10

Warrabri ○ Australia 21°1S 134°19E **150** C1
Warracknabeal Australia 36°9S 142°26E **152** D5
Warragul Australia 38°10S 145°58E **153** E6
Warrego → Australia 30°24S 145°21E **151** E4
Warrego Ra. Australia 24°58S 146°0E **150** C4
Warren Australia 31°42S 147°51E **153** E4
Warren Ark., U.S.A. 33°37N 92°4W **176** E8
Warren Mich., U.S.A. 42°28N 83°1W **173** D12
Warren Minn., U.S.A. 48°12N 96°46W **172** A5
Warren Ohio, U.S.A. 41°14N 80°49W **174** E4
Warren Pa., U.S.A. 41°51N 79°9W **174** E5
Warrenpoint U.K. 54°6N 6°15W **64** B5
Warrensburg Mo., U.S.A. 38°46N 93°44W **172** F7
Warrensburg N.Y., U.S.A. 43°29N 73°46W **175** C11
Warrenton S. Africa 28°9S 24°47E **144** C3
Warrenton Ga., U.S.A. 33°24N 82°40W **178** B7
Warrenton Oreg., U.S.A. 46°10N 123°56W **170** D3
Warrenville U.S.A. 33°33N 81°48W **178** B8
Warri Nigeria 5°30N 5°41E **139** D6
Warrington N.Z. 45°43S 170°35E **155** F5
Warrington U.K. 53°24N 2°35W **66** D5
Warrington U.S.A. 30°23N 87°17W **179** E2
Warrington □ U.K. 53°24N 2°35W **66** D5
Warrnambool Australia 38°25S 142°30E **152** E5
Warroad U.S.A. 48°54N 95°19W **172** A6
Warrumbungle △ Australia 31°18S 149°1E **153** A8
Warruwi Australia 11°36S 133°20E **150** A1
Warsak Dam Pakistan 34°11N 71°19E **124** B4
Warsaw = Warszawa Poland 52°14N 21°0E **83** F8
Warsaw Ind., U.S.A. 41°14N 85°51W **173** E11
Warsaw N.Y., U.S.A. 42°45N 78°8W **174** D6
Warsaw Ohio, U.S.A. 40°20N 82°0W **174** F3
Warstein Germany 51°26N 8°22E **76** D4
Warszawa Poland 52°14N 21°0E **83** F8
Warszawa ✈ (WAW) Poland 52°9N 20°59E **83** F7
Warta Poland 51°43N 18°38E **83** G5
Warta → Poland 52°35N 14°39E **83** F1
Warthe = Warta → Poland 52°35N 14°39E **83** F1
Warthen U.S.A. 33°6N 82°48W **178** B7
Waru Indonesia 3°30S 130°36E **119** E8
Warud India 21°30N 78°16E **126** D4
Warumungu ○ Australia 19°15S 134°44E **150** B1
Warwick Australia 28°10S 152°1E **151** D5
Warwick U.K. 52°18N 1°35W **67** E6
Warwick Ga., U.S.A. 31°50N 83°57W **178** D6
Warwick N.Y., U.S.A. 41°16N 74°22W **175** E10
Warwick R.I., U.S.A. 41°42N 71°28W **175** E13
Warwickshire □ U.K. 52°14N 1°38W **67** E6
Wasaga Beach Canada 44°31N 80°1W **174** B4
Wasagaming Canada 50°39N 99°58W **163** C9
Wasatch Ra. U.S.A. 40°0N 111°30W **168** F8
Wasbank S. Africa 28°15S 30°9E **145** C5
Wasco Calif., U.S.A. 35°36N 119°20W **171** K7
Wasco Oreg., U.S.A. 45°36N 120°42W **168** D3
Wase Nigeria 9°4N 9°54E **139** D6
Waseca U.S.A. 44°5N 93°30W **172** C7
Wasekamio L. Canada 56°45N 108°45W **163** B7
Wash, The U.K. 52°58N 0°20E **66** E8
Washago Canada 44°45N 79°20W **174** B5
Washburn N. Dak., U.S.A. 47°17N 101°2W **172** B3
Washburn Wis., U.S.A. 46°40N 90°54W **172** B8
Washim India 20°3N 77°0E **126** D3
Washington U.K. 54°55N 1°30W **66** C6
Washington D.C., U.S.A. 38°53N 77°2W **173** F15
Washington Ga., U.S.A. 33°44N 82°44W **178** B7
Washington Ind., U.S.A. 38°40N 87°10W **172** F2
Washington Iowa, U.S.A. 41°18N 91°42W **172** E8
Washington Mo., U.S.A. 38°33N 91°1W **172** F8
Washington N.C., U.S.A. 35°33N 77°3W **177** D16
Washington N.J., U.S.A. 40°46N 74°59W **175** F10
Washington Pa., U.S.A. 40°10N 80°15W **174** F4
Washington Utah, U.S.A. 37°8N 113°31W **169** H7
Washington □ U.S.A. 47°30N 120°30W **168** C3
Washington, Mt. U.S.A. 44°16N 71°18W **175** B13
Washington Court House U.S.A. 39°32N 83°26W **173** F12
Washington I. U.S.A. 45°23N 86°54W **172** C10
Washington Land Greenland 80°30N 66°0W **57** A4
Washougal U.S.A. 45°35N 122°21W **170** E4
Washpool △ Australia 29°22S 152°20E **151** D5
Wasian Indonesia 1°47S 133°19E **119** E8
Wasilków Poland 53°12N 23°13E **83** E10
Wasilla U.S.A. 61°35N 149°26W **160** E2
Wasini Marine ○ Kenya 4°33S 39°14E **142** C4
Wasior Indonesia 2°43S 134°30E **119** E8
Wasiri Indonesia 7°30S 126°30E **119** F7
Wāsiṭ □ Iraq 32°50N 45°50E **105** F11
Waskaganish Canada 51°30N 78°40W **164** B4
Waskaiowaka L. Canada 56°33N 96°23W **163** B9
Waskesiu Lake Canada 53°55N 106°5W **163** C7
Wassaw I. U.S.A. 31°53N 80°58W **178** D8
Wassaw Sd. U.S.A. 31°53N 80°58W **178** D8
Wasserburg Germany 48°3N 12°14E **77** G8
Wasserkuppe Germany 50°29N 9°56E **76** E5
Wassy France 48°30N 4°58E **71** D11
Waswanipi Canada 49°40N 76°29W **164** C4
Waswanipi, L. Canada 49°35N 76°40W **164** C4
Watagans △ Australia 33°0S 151°58E **153** B5
Watampone Indonesia 4°29S 120°25E **119** E6
Watamu Kenya 3°23S 40°0E **142** C5
Watarrka △ Australia 24°20S 131°30E **148** D5
Water Park Pt. Australia 22°56S 150°47E **150** C5
Water Valley U.S.A. 34°10N 89°38W **177** D10
Waterberg Plateau Namibia 20°25S 17°18E **144** B2
Waterberge S. Africa 24°10S 28°0E **145** B4

Waterbury Conn., U.S.A. 41°33N 73°3W **175** E11
Waterbury Vt., U.S.A. 44°20N 72°46W **175** B12
Waterbury L. Canada 58°10N 104°22W **163** B8
Waterdown Canada 43°20N 79°53W **174** C5
Wateree → U.S.A. 33°45N 80°37W **178** B9
Waterford Ireland 52°15N 7°8W **64** D4
Waterford Calif., U.S.A. 37°38N 120°46W **170** H6
Waterford Pa., U.S.A. 41°57N 79°59W **174** E5
Waterford □ Ireland 52°10N 7°40W **64** D4
Waterford Harbour Ireland 52°8N 6°58W **64** D5
Waterhen L. Canada 52°10N 99°40W **163** C9
Waterloo Belgium 50°43N 4°25E **69** D4
Waterloo Ont., Canada 43°30N 80°32W **174** C4
Waterloo Qué., Canada 45°22N 72°32W **175** A12
Waterloo S. Leone 8°26N 13°8W **138** D2
Waterloo Ill., U.S.A. 38°20N 90°9W **172** F8
Waterloo Iowa, U.S.A. 42°30N 92°21W **172** D7
Waterloo N.Y., U.S.A. 42°54N 76°52W **174** D8
Watersmeet U.S.A. 46°16N 89°11W **172** B9
Waterton Lakes △ Canada 48°45N 115°0W **162** D6
Watertown Conn., U.S.A. 41°36N 73°7W **175** E11
Watertown N.Y., U.S.A. 43°59N 75°55W **175** C9
Watertown S. Dak., U.S.A. 44°54N 97°7W **172** C5
Watertown Wis., U.S.A. 43°12N 88°43W **172** D9
Waterval-Boven = Emgwenya S. Africa 25°40S 30°18E **145** C5
Waterville Canada 45°16N 71°54W **175** A13
Waterville Maine, U.S.A. 44°33N 69°38W **173** C19
Waterville N.Y., U.S.A. 42°56N 75°23W **175** D9
Waterville Pa., U.S.A. 41°19N 77°21W **174** E7
Waterville Wash., U.S.A. 47°39N 120°4W **168** C3
Watervliet U.S.A. 42°44N 73°42W **175** D11
Wates Indonesia 7°51S 110°10E **119** G14
Watford U.K. 51°40N 0°24W **67** F7
Watford City U.S.A. 47°48N 103°17W **172** B2
Wathaman → Canada 57°16N 102°59W **163** B8
Wathaman L. Canada 56°58N 103°44W **163** B8
Watheroo Australia 30°15S 116°5E **149** F2
Watheroo ○ Australia 30°19S 115°48E **149** F2
Wating China 35°40N 106°38E **114** G4
Watkins Glen U.S.A. 42°23N 76°52W **174** D8
Watkinsville U.S.A. 33°52N 83°25W **178** B6
Watling I. = San Salvador I. Bahamas 24°0N 74°30W **183** B5
Watonga U.S.A. 35°51N 98°25W **176** D5
Watrous Canada 51°40N 105°25W **163** C7
Watrous U.S.A. 35°48N 104°59W **169** J11
Watsa Dem. Rep. of the Congo 3°4N 29°30E **142** B2
Watseka U.S.A. 40°47N 87°44W **172** E10
Watson Canada 52°10N 104°30W **163** C8
Watson Lake Canada 60°6N 128°49W **162** A3
Watsontown U.S.A. 41°5N 76°52W **174** E8
Watsonville U.S.A. 36°55N 121°45W **170** J5
Wattamolla △ Australia 28°57S 136°10E **151** D2
Wattiwarriganna Cr. → Australia 28°57S 136°10E **151** D2
Wattwil Switz. 47°18N 9°6E **77** H5
Watuata = Batuata Indonesia 6°12S 122°42E **119** F6
Watubela, Kepulauan Indonesia 4°28S 131°35E **119** E8
Watubela Is. = Watubela, Kepulauan Indonesia 4°28S 131°35E **119** E8
Wau South Sudan 7°45N 28°1E **135** G11
Waubamik Canada 45°27N 80°1W **174** A4
Waubay U.S.A. 45°20N 97°18W **172** C5
Waubra Australia 37°21S 143°39E **152** D5
Wauchope N.S.W., Australia 31°28S 152°45E **153** A10
Wauchope N. Terr., Australia 20°36S 134°15E **150** C1
Wauchula U.S.A. 27°33N 81°49W **179** H8
Waukarlycarly, L. Australia 21°18S 121°56E **148** D3
Waukeenah U.S.A. 30°25N 83°57W **178** E6
Waukegan U.S.A. 42°22N 87°50W **172** D10
Waukesha U.S.A. 43°1N 88°14W **172** D9
Waukon U.S.A. 43°16N 91°29W **172** D8
Waupaca U.S.A. 44°21N 89°5W **172** C9
Waupun U.S.A. 43°38N 88°44W **172** D9
Waurika U.S.A. 34°10N 98°0W **176** D6
Wausau U.S.A. 44°58N 89°38W **172** C9
Wausau Wis., U.S.A. 44°58N 89°38W **172** C9
Wautoma U.S.A. 44°4N 89°18W **172** C9
Wauwatosa U.S.A. 43°2N 88°0W **172** D9
Wave Hill = Kalkarindji Australia 17°30S 130°47E **148** C5
Wave Rock ○ Australia 32°26S 118°53E **149** F2
Waveney → U.K. 52°35N 1°39E **67** E9
Waverley N.Z. 39°46S 174°37E **154** F3
Waverly Ala., U.S.A. 32°44N 85°35W **178** C4
Waverly Fla., U.S.A. 27°59N 81°37W **179** H8
Waverly Iowa, U.S.A. 42°44N 92°29W **172** D7
Waverly N.Y., U.S.A. 42°1N 76°32W **175** E8
Waverly Hall U.S.A. 32°41N 84°44W **178** C5
Wâw = Wau South Sudan 7°45N 28°1E **135** G11
Wâw al Kabîr Libya 25°20N 16°43E **135** C9
Wawa Canada 47°59N 84°47W **164** C3
Wawa Nigeria 9°54N 4°27E **139** D5
Wawa Sudan 20°30N 30°22E **135** D12
Wawanesa Canada 49°36N 99°40W **163** D9
Wawona U.S.A. 37°32N 119°39W **170** H7
Waxahachie U.S.A. 32°24N 96°51W **176** E6
Waxxari China 38°42N 87°59E **109** E11
Way, L. Australia 26°45S 120°16E **149** E3
Waya Fiji 17°19S 177°10E **154** a
Waycross U.S.A. 31°13N 82°21W **178** E7
Wayland U.S.A. 42°34N 77°35W **174** D7
Wayne Nebr., U.S.A. 42°14N 97°1W **172** D5
Wayne W. Va., U.S.A. 38°13N 82°27W **173** F12
Waynesboro Ga., U.S.A. 33°6N 82°1W **178** B7
Waynesboro Miss., U.S.A. 31°40N 88°39W **177** F10

Waynesboro Pa., U.S.A. 39°45N 77°35W **173**
Waynesboro Va., U.S.A. 38°4N 78°53W **173**
Waynesburg U.S.A. 39°54N 80°11W **173**
Waynesville U.S.A. 35°28N 82°58W **177**
Waynoka U.S.A. 36°35N 98°53W **176**
Wayside U.S.A. 33°4N 83°37W **178**
Wazirabad Pakistan 32°30N 74°8E **124**
Waziristan Pakistan 33°0N 70°0E **124**
Wda → Poland 53°25N 18°29E **82**
We Indonesia 5°51N 95°18E **118**
Weald, The U.K. 51°4N 0°20E **67**
Wear → U.K. 54°55N 1°23W **66**
Weatherford Okla., U.S.A. 35°32N 98°43W **176**
Weatherford Tex., U.S.A. 32°46N 97°48W **176**
Weaverville U.S.A. 40°44N 122°56W **168**
Webb City U.S.A. 37°9N 94°28W **172**
Webequie Canada 52°59N 87°21W **164**
Weber N.Z. 40°24S 176°20E **154**
Webo = Nyaake Liberia 4°52N 7°37W **138**
Webster Mass., U.S.A. 42°3N 71°53W **175**
Webster N.Y., U.S.A. 43°13N 77°26W **174**
Webster S. Dak., U.S.A. 45°20N 97°31W **172**
Webster City U.S.A. 42°28N 93°49W **172**
Webster Springs U.S.A. 38°29N 80°25W **173**
Webuye Kenya 0°37N 34°46E **142**
Weda Indonesia 0°21N 127°50E **119**
Weda, Teluk Indonesia 0°20N 128°0E **119**
Weddell Abyssal Plain S. Ocean 65°0S 20°0W **55**
Weddell I. Falk. Is. 51°50S 61°0W **192**
Weddell Sea Antarctica 72°30S 40°0W **55**
Wedderburn Australia 36°26S 143°33E **152**
Weddin Mts. △ Australia 33°59S 148°0E **153**
Wedel Germany 53°34N 9°42E **76**
Wedemark Germany 52°32N 9°43E **76**
Wedgeport Canada 43°44N 65°59W **165**
Wedowee U.S.A. 33°18N 85°29W **178**
Wedza Zimbabwe 18°40S 31°33E **145**
Wee Waa Australia 30°11S 149°26E **151**
Weed U.S.A. 41°25N 122°23W **168**
Weed Heights U.S.A. 38°59N 119°13W **170**
Weedsport U.S.A. 43°2N 76°33W **175**
Weedville U.S.A. 41°17N 78°30W **174**
Weeki Wachee U.S.A. 28°32N 82°35W **179**
Weenen S. Africa 28°48S 30°7E **148**
Weener Germany 53°9N 7°20E **76**
Weerribben-Weerwielen △ Neths. 52°47N 5°58E **69**
Weert Neths. 51°15N 5°43E **69**
Węgierska-Górka Poland 49°36N 19°7E **83**
Węgliniec Poland 51°18N 15°10E **83**
Węgorzewo Poland 54°13N 21°43E **82**
Węgorzyno Poland 53°32N 15°33E **82**
Węgrów Poland 52°24N 22°0E **83**
Wei He → Hebei, China 36°10N 115°45E **114**
Wei He → Shaanxi, China 34°38N 110°15E **114**
Weichang China 41°58N 117°49E **115**
Weichuan China 34°20N 113°59E **114**
Weida Germany 50°46N 12°2E **76**
Weiden Germany 49°41N 12°10E **77**
Weifang China 36°44N 119°7E **115**
Weihai China 37°30N 122°6E **115**
Weihui China 35°25N 114°3E **114**
Weil Germany 47°35N 7°37E **73**
Weilburg Germany 50°28N 8°17E **76**
Weilheim Germany 47°50N 11°9E **77**
Weimar Germany 50°58N 11°19E **76**
Weinan China 34°31N 109°29E **114**
Weingarten Germany 49°3N 9°31E **72**
Weinheim Germany 49°32N 8°39E **72**
Weining China 26°50N 104°17E **116**
Weipa Australia 12°40S 141°50E **150**
Weir → Australia 28°20S 149°50E **151**
Weir → Canada 56°54N 93°21W **163**
Weir, L. U.S.A. 29°0N 81°57W **179**
Weir River Canada 56°49N 94°6W **163**
Weirsdale U.S.A. 28°59N 81°55W **179**
Weirton U.S.A. 40°24N 80°35W **174**
Weiser U.S.A. 44°15N 116°58W **168**
Weishan Shandong, China 34°47N 117°5E **115**
Weishan Yunnan, China 25°12N 100°20E **116**
Weishan Hu China 34°35N 117°14E **115**
Weissenburg Germany 49°2N 10°58E **77**
Weissenfels Germany 51°11N 12°0E **76**
Weisswasser Germany 51°30N 14°36E **76**
Wéitra Austria 48°41N 14°54E **78**
Weixi China 27°10N 99°10E **116**
Weixin China 27°48N 105°3E **116**
Weiyuan Gansu, China 35°7N 104°10E **114**
Weiyuan Sichuan, China 29°35N 104°36E **116**
Weiz Austria 47°13N 15°39E **78**
Weizhou Dao China 21°0N 109°0E **117**
Wejherowo Poland 54°35N 18°12E **82**
Wekusko L. Canada 54°40N 99°50W **163**
Welch U.S.A. 37°26N 81°35W **173**
Welford △ Australia 25°5S 143°16E **150**
Weligama Sri Lanka 5°58N 80°25E **127**
Welkom S. Africa 28°0S 26°46E **144**
Welland Canada 43°0N 79°15W **174**
Welland → U.K. 52°51N 0°5W **67**
Wellawaya Sri Lanka 6°44N 81°6E **127**
Wellesley Is. = Wellesley Islands Australia 16°42S 139°30E **150**
Wellesley Islands ○ Australia 16°35S 139°30E **150**
Wellingborough U.K. 52°19N 0°41W **67**
Wellington Australia 32°35S 148°59E **153**
Wellington N.Z. 41°19S 174°46E **154**
Wellington S. Africa 33°38S 19°1E **144**
Wellington Somst., U.K. 50°58N 3°13W **67**
Wellington Telford & Wrekin, U.K. 52°42N 2°30W **67**
Wellington Colo., U.S.A. 40°42N 105°0W **168**
Wellington Kans., U.S.A. 37°16N 97°24W **172**
Wellington Nev., U.S.A. 38°45N 119°23W **170**
Wellington Ohio, U.S.A. 41°10N 82°13W **174**

llington *Tex.*,
.S.A. 34°51N 100°13W 176 D4
llington □ *N.Z.* 41°0S 175°30E 154 H4
llington, I. *Chile* 49°30S 75°0W 192 C2
llington, I. *Australia* 38°6S 147°20E 153 E7
anada 75°0N 93°0W 161 C13
ls U.K. 51°13N 2°39W 67 F5
ls Maine, *U.S.A.* 43°20N 70°35W 175 C14
ls N.Y., *U.S.A.* 43°24N 74°17W 175 C10
ls Nev., *U.S.A.* 41°7N 114°58W 168 F6
ls, L. *Australia* 26°44S 123°15E 149 E3
ls, Mt. *Australia* 17°25S 127°8E 148 C4
ls Gray *Canada* 52°30N 120°15W 162 C4
lls-next-the-Sea *U.K.* 52°57N 0°51E 66 E8
ls River *U.S.A.* 44°9N 72°4W 175 B12
lsboro *U.S.A.* 41°45N 77°18W 174 E7
lsburg *U.S.A.* 40°16N 80°37W 174 F4
lsford *U.S.A.* 36°16S 174°32E 154 C3
lsville N.Y., *U.S.A.* 42°7N 77°57W 174 D7
lsville Ohio, *U.S.A.* 40°36N 80°39W 174 F4
lsville Utah, *U.S.A.* 41°38N 111°56W 168 F8
lton *U.S.A.* 32°40N 114°8W 169 K6
ls *Austria* 48°9N 14°1E 78 D7
shpool *Australia* 38°42S 146°26E 153 E7
shpool U.K. 52°39N 3°8W 67 E4
m U.K. 51°48N 0°12W 67 F7
m U.K. 52°52N 2°44W 66 E5
mbere ⮕ *Tanzania* 4°10S 34°15E 142 C3
mindji *Canada* 53°0N 78°49W 164 B4
myss *Canada* 44°52N 76°23W 175 B8
n Xian *Gansu,*
China 32°43N 104°36E 114 H3
n Xian *Henan, China* 33°54N 113°5E 114 G7
matche *U.S.A.* 47°25N 120°19W 168 C3
nchang *China* 19°38N 110°42E 117 a
ncheng *China* 27°46N 120°4E 117 D13
nchi *Ghana* 7°46N 2°8W 138 D4
nchow = *Wenzhou*
China 28°0N 120°38E 117 D13
nchuan *China* 31°22N 103°35E 116 B4
nden *China* 33°49N 113°33W 171 M13
ndeng *China* 37°15N 122°5E 115 F12
ndesi *Indonesia* 2°30S 134°17E 119 E8
ndover *U.S.A.* 40°44N 114°2W 168 F6
n'an *China* 27°5N 107°25E 116 D6
ngcheng *China* 24°22N 113°50E 117 E9
ngen *Switz.* 46°37N 7°55E 71 F14
ngyuan *China* 24°20N 114°9E 117 E10
nling *China* 28°21N 121°20E 117 C13
nlock ⮕ *Australia* 12°2S 141°55E 150 A3
nshan *China* 23°20N 104°18E 116 F5
nshang *China* 35°45N 116°30E 114 G9
nshui *China* 37°26N 112°1E 114 F6
nsleydale *U.K.* 54°17N 2°0W 66 C6
nsu *China* 41°15N 80°10E 109 D10
nsum ⮕ *U.K.* 52°40N 1°15E 66 E8
ntworth *Australia* 34°2S 141°54E 152 C4
ntzel I., *Canada* 59°2N 114°28W 162 B6
nut *Indonesia* 3°11S 133°19E 119 E8
nxi *China* 35°20N 111°10E 114 G6
nzhou *China* 28°0N 120°38E 117 D13
pener *S. Africa* 29°42S 27°3E 144 C4
rda *Botswana* 25°24S 23°15E 144 C3
rdau *Germany* 50°44N 12°22E 76 E8
rder *Germany* 52°23N 12°55E 76 C8
rdohl *Germany* 51°15N 7°46E 76 D3
ri *Indonesia* 3°10S 132°38E 119 E8
rneck *Germany* 49°58N 10°5E 77 F6
rnigerode *Germany* 51°50N 10°47E 76 D6
rra *Germany* 51°24N 9°39E 76 D5
rribee *Australia* 37°54S 144°40E 152 D6
rikimbe △
Australia 31°11S 152°15E 153 A10
rimull *Australia* 34°25S 141°38E 152 C4
ris Creek *Australia* 31°18S 150°38E 153 A9
rtach ⮕ *Germany* 48°22N 10°54E 77 G6
rtheim *Germany* 49°45N 9°32E 77 F5
rtingen *Germany* 48°33N 10°41E 77 G6
sel ⮕ *Germany* 51°39N 6°37E 76 D2
ser ⮕ *Germany* 53°36N 8°28E 76 B4
serbergland *Germany* 52°12N 9°7E 76 C5
serbergland Schaumburg
Hameln ⮕ *Germany* 52°9N 9°20E 76 C5
slaco *Canada* 26°10N 97°58W 176 H6
slemkoon L. *Canada* 44°7N 77°25W 174 A7
sleyville *Canada* 49°9N 53°33W 165 C9
sleyville *U.S.A.* 42°9N 80°1W 174 D4
ssel, C. *Australia* 10°59S 136°46E 150 A2
ssel Is. *Australia* 11°10S 136°45E 150 A2
sselburen *Germany* 54°13N 8°54E 76 A4
ssex U.K. 51°0N 2°0W 67 F5
ssington Springs
.S.A. 44°5N 98°34W 172 C5
st *U.S.A.* 31°48N 97°6W 176 F6
st ⮕ *U.S.A.* 52°26N 72°33W 175 D12
st Allis *U.S.A.* 43°1N 88°0W 172 D9
st Antarctica
ntarctica 80°0S 90°0W 55 D15
st Baines ⮕
ustralia 15°38S 129°59E 148 C4
st Bank ■ *Asia* 32°6N 35°13E 130 C4
st Bend *U.S.A.* 43°25N 88°11W 172 D9
st Bengal = *Paschimbanga* ⮕
dia 23°0N 88°0E 125 H13
st Berkshire □ *U.K.* 51°25N 1°17W 67 F6
st Beskids = *Západné Beskydy*
urope 49°30N 19°0E 79 B12
st Branch *U.S.A.* 44°17N 84°14W 173 C11
st Branch Susquehanna ⮕
U.S.A. 40°53N 76°48W 175 F8
st Bromwich *U.K.* 52°32N 1°59W 66 E5
st Burra *U.K.* 60°5N 1°21W 65 A7
st Canada Cr. ⮕
U.S.A. 43°1N 74°58W 175 C10
st Caroline Basin
ac. Oc. 4°0N 138°0E 156 G5
st Chazy *U.S.A.* 44°49N 73°28W 175 B11
st Chester *U.S.A.* 39°58N 75°36W 175 G9
st Coast □ *N.Z.* 43°15N 170°30E 155 D5
st Coast △ *S. Africa* 33°18S 28°0E 144 D2
st Columbia *S.C.*
U.S.A. 33°59N 81°4W 178 B8
st Columbia *Tex.*,
U.S.A. 29°9N 95°39W 176 G7
st Covina *U.S.A.* 34°4N 117°54W 171 L9
st Des Moines
U.S.A. 41°35N 93°43W 172 E7

West Dunbartonshire □
U.K. 55°59N 4°30W 65 F4
West End *Bahamas* 26°41N 78°58W 182 A4
West Falkland *Falk. Is.* 51°40S 60°0W 192 D5
West Fargo *U.S.A.* 46°52N 96°54W 172 B5
West Fiji Basin *Pac. Oc.* 17°0S 173°0E 156 J9
West Fjord = *Vestfjorden*
Norway 67°55N 14°0E 60 C16
West Fork Trinity ⮕
U.S.A. 32°48N 96°54W 176 E6
West Frankfort *U.S.A.* 37°54N 88°55W 172 G9
West Grand L. *U.S.A.* 45°14N 67°51W 173 C20
West Green *U.S.A.* 31°37N 82°44W 178 D7
West Hartford *U.S.A.* 41°45N 72°44W 175 E12
West Haven *U.S.A.* 41°17N 72°57W 175 E12
West Hazleton *U.S.A.* 40°58N 76°0W 175 F9
West Hurley *U.S.A.* 41°59N 74°7W 175 E11
West I. *India* 13°35N 92°54E 127 H11
West Ice Shelf *Antarctica* 67°0S 85°0E 55 C7
West Indies *Cent. Amer.* 15°0N 65°0W 183 D7
West Jordan *U.S.A.* 40°36N 111°56W 168 F8
West Lamma Channel
China 22°14N 114°4E 111 a
West Linn *U.S.A.* 45°21N 122°36W 170 E4
West Lorne *Canada* 42°36N 81°36W 174 D3
West Lothian □ *U.K.* 55°54N 3°36W 65 F5
West Lunga ⮕ *Zambia* 13°6S 24°39E 143 E1
West MacDonnell △
Australia 23°38S 132°59E 148 D5
West Mariana Basin
Pac. Oc. 15°0N 137°0E 156 F5
West Memphis *U.S.A.* 35°8N 90°10W 177 D9
West Midlands □ *U.K.* 52°26N 2°0W 67 E6
West Mifflin *U.S.A.* 40°21N 79°52W 174 F5
West Milford *U.S.A.* 41°8N 74°22W 175 E10
West Milton *U.S.A.* 41°1N 76°50W 174 E8
West Monroe *U.S.A.* 32°31N 92°9W 176 E8
West Newton *U.S.A.* 40°14N 79°46W 174 F5
West Nicholson
Zimbabwe 21°2S 29°20E 143 G2
West Odessa *U.S.A.* 31°50N 102°30W 176 F3
West Palm Beach
U.S.A. 26°43N 80°3W 179 J9
West Palm Beach Canal
U.S.A. 26°40N 80°15W 179 J9
West Pensacola *U.S.A.* 30°25N 87°16W 179 E2
West Plains *U.S.A.* 36°44N 91°51W 172 G8
West Point Ga., *U.S.A.* 32°53N 85°11W 178 C4
West Point *Miss.*,
U.S.A. 33°36N 88°39W 177 E10
West Point *N.Y.*,
U.S.A. 41°24N 73°58W 175 E11
West Point *Nebr.*,
U.S.A. 41°51N 96°43W 172 E5
West Point *Va.*,
U.S.A. 37°32N 76°48W 173 G15
West Point L. *U.S.A.* 32°58N 85°0W 178 B4
West Pt. = *Ouest, Pte. de l'*
Canada 49°52N 64°40W 165 C7
West Pt. *Australia* 35°1S 135°56E 152 C1
West Road ⮕ *Canada* 53°18N 122°53W 162 C4
West Rutland *U.S.A.* 43°36N 73°3W 175 C11
West Schelde = *Westerschelde* ⮕
Neths. 51°25N 3°25E 69 D2
West Seneca *U.S.A.* 42°51N 78°48W 174 D6
West Siberian Plain
Russia 62°0N 75°0E 102 B9
West Sussex □ *U.K.* 50°55N 0°30W 67 G7
West-Terschelling *Neths.* 53°22N 5°13E 69 A5
West Valley City
U.S.A. 40°42N 111°58W 168 F8
West Virginia □
U.S.A. 38°45N 80°30W 173 F13
West-Vlaanderen □
Belgium 51°0N 3°0E 69 D2
West Walker ⮕
U.S.A. 38°54N 119°9W 170 G7
West Wyalong
Australia 33°56S 147°10E 153 B7
West Yellowstone
U.S.A. 44°40N 111°6W 168 D8
West Yorkshire □ *U.K.* 53°45N 1°40W 66 D6
Westall, Pt. *Australia* 32°55S 134°4E 151 E1
Westbrook *U.S.A.* 43°41N 70°22W 173 D18
Westbury *Australia* 41°30S 146°51E 151 G4
Westby *U.S.A.* 48°52N 104°3W 168 A2
Westend *U.S.A.* 35°42N 117°24W 171 K9
Westerland *Germany* 54°54N 8°17E 76 A4
Westerly *U.S.A.* 41°22N 71°50W 175 E13
Western □ *Ghana* 5°30N 2°30W 138 D4
Western □ *Kenya* 0°30N 34°30E 142 B3
Western □ *S. Leone* 8°30N 13°20W 138 D2
Western □ *Zambia* 15°0S 24°4E 143 F1
Western Australia □
Australia 25°0S 118°0E 149 E2
Western Cape □ *S. Africa* 34°0S 20°0E 144 D3
Western Dvina = *Daugava* ⮕
Latvia 57°4N 24°3E 84 D3
Western Ghats *India* 14°0N 75°0E 127 H2
Western Isles = *Eilean Siar* □
U.K. 57°30N 7°10W 65 D1
Western Sahara ■
Africa 25°0N 13°0W 134 D3
Western Samoa = *Samoa* ■
Pac. Oc. 14°0S 172°0W 147 C11
Western Sierra Madre = *Madre*
Occidental, Sierra
Mexico 27°0N 107°0W 180 B3
Westernport *U.S.A.* 39°29N 79°3W 173 F14
Westerschelde ⮕ *Neths.* 51°25N 3°25E 69 D2
Westerstede *Germany* 53°15N 7°55E 76 B3
Westerwald *Germany* 50°38N 7°56E 76 E3
Westfield *Mass.*, *U.S.A.* 42°7N 72°45W 175 D12
Westfield *N.Y.*, *U.S.A.* 42°20N 79°35W 174 D5
Westfield *Pa.*, *U.S.A.* 41°55N 77°32W 174 E7
Westhill *U.K.* 57°9N 2°19W 65 D6
Westhope *U.S.A.* 48°55N 101°1W 172 A3
Westland □ *N.Z.* 43°16S 170°16E 155 D5
Westland Bight *N.Z.* 42°55S 170°5E 155 C5
Westlock *Canada* 54°9N 113°55W 162 C6
Westmar *U.S.A.* 27°55S 149°44E 151 D4
Westmeath □ *Ireland* 53°33N 7°34W 64 C4
Westminster *Calif.*,
U.S.A. 33°45N 118°0W 171 M8
Westminster *Colo.*,
U.S.A. 39°50N 105°2W 168 G11
Westminster *Md.*,
U.S.A. 39°34N 76°59W 173 F15
Westmont *U.S.A.* 40°19N 78°58W 174 F6
Westmoreland *Barbados* 13°13N 59°37W 183 g

Westmorland *U.S.A.* 33°2N 115°37W 171 M11
Weston *Oreg.*, *U.S.A.* 45°49N 118°26W 168 D4
Weston *W. Va.*, *U.S.A.* 39°2N 80°28W 173 F13
Weston I. *Canada* 52°33N 79°36W 164 B4
Weston-super-Mare
U.K. 51°21N 2°58W 67 F5
Westover *U.S.A.* 40°45N 78°40W 174 F6
Westport *Canada* 44°40N 76°25W 175 B8
Westport *Ireland* 53°48N 9°31W 64 C2
Westport *N.Z.* 41°46S 171°37E 155 B6
Westport N.Y., *U.S.A.* 44°11N 73°26W 175 B11
Westport *Oreg.*, *U.S.A.* 46°8N 123°23W 170 D3
Westport *Wash.*, *U.S.A.* 46°53N 124°6W 170 D2
Westray *Canada* 53°36N 101°24W 163 C8
Westray *U.K.* 59°18N 3°0W 65 B5
Westree *Canada* 47°26N 81°34W 164 C3
Westville *Calif.*, *U.S.A.* 39°8N 120°42W 170 G6
Westville *Fla.*, *U.S.A.* 30°46N 85°51W 178 E4
Westwood *U.S.A.* 40°18N 121°0W 168 F3
Westwood Lake *U.S.A.* 25°44N 80°23W 179 K9
Wetar *Indonesia* 7°48S 126°30E 119 F7
Wetaskiwin *Canada* 52°55N 113°24W 162 C6
Wete *Tanzania* 5°4S 39°43E 140 F7
Wetherby *U.K.* 53°56N 1°23W 66 D6
Wethersfield *U.S.A.* 41°42N 72°40W 175 E12
Wetteren *Belgium* 51°0N 3°53E 69 D3
Wetumpka *U.S.A.* 32°32N 86°13W 178 C3
Wetzlar *Germany* 50°32N 8°31E 76 E4
Wewahitchka *U.S.A.* 30°7N 85°12W 178 E4
Wewoka *U.S.A.* 35°9N 96°30W 176 D6
Wexford *Ireland* 52°20N 6°28W 64 D5
Wexford □ *Ireland* 52°20N 6°25W 64 D5
Wexford Harbour *Ireland* 52°20N 6°25W 64 D5
Weyburn *Canada* 49°40N 103°50W 163 D8
Weyer Markt *Austria* 47°51N 14°40E 78 D7
Weyhe *Germany* 52°58N 8°49E 76 C4
Weymouth *Canada* 44°30N 66°1W 165 D6
Weymouth *U.K.* 50°37N 2°28W 67 G5
Weymouth *U.S.A.* 42°13N 70°58W 175 D14
Weymouth, C.
Australia 12°37S 143°27E 150 A3
Wha Ti *Canada* 63°8N 117°16W 160 E8
Whakaari *N.Z.* 37°30S 177°13E 154 G6
Whakamaru *N.Z.* 38°23S 175°50E 154 G4
Whakatane *N.Z.* 37°57S 177°1E 154 G6
Whakatane ⮕ *N.Z.* 37°55S 177°1E 154 G6
Whale = *Baleine* ⮕
Canada 58°15N 67°40W 165 A6
Whale B. *Burma* 11°37N 98°38E 121 G2
Whale Cove *Canada* 62°10N 92°34W 163 A10
Whale Valley = *Hitan, W. el*
Egypt 29°19N 30°10E 137 F7
Whales, B. of *Antarctica* 78°0S 160°0W 55 D12
Whalsay *U.K.* 60°22N 0°59W 65 A8
Whangaehu ⮕ *N.Z.* 40°3S 175°6E 154 G4
Whangamata *N.Z.* 37°12S 175°53E 154 G5
Whangamomona *N.Z.* 39°8S 174°44E 154 G3
Whanganui ⮕ *N.Z.* 39°1'7S 174°53E 154 F3
Whangaparaoa Pen.
N.Z. 36°40S 174°45E 154 C3
Whangarei *N.Z.* 35°43S 174°21E 154 C3
Whangarei Harb. *N.Z.* 35°45S 174°28E 154 B3
Whangaroa Harb. *N.Z.* 35°4S 173°46E 154 B2
Whangaruru Harb.
N.Z. 35°24S 174°23E 154 B3
Wharanui *N.Z.* 41°55S 174°6E 155 B9
Wharekauri = *Chatham Is.*
Pac. Oc. 44°0S 176°40W 155 c
Wharfe ⮕ *U.K.* 53°51N 1°9W 66 D6
Wharfedale *U.K.* 54°6N 2°1W 66 C5
Wharton *N.J.*, *U.S.A.* 40°54N 74°35W 175 F10
Wharton *Pa.*, *U.S.A.* 41°31N 78°1W 174 E6
Wharton *Tex.*, *U.S.A.* 29°19N 96°6W 176 G6
Wharton Basin *Ind. Oc.* 22°0S 99°0E 146 G9
Whataroa *N.Z.* 43°16S 170°22E 155 D5
Whataroa ⮕ *N.Z.* 43°7S 170°16E 155 D5
Wheatland *Calif.*,
U.S.A. 39°1N 121°25W 170 F5
Wheatland *Wyo.*,
U.S.A. 42°3N 104°58W 168 E11
Wheatley *Canada* 42°6N 82°27W 174 D2
Wheaton *Md.*, *U.S.A.* 39°3N 77°3W 173 F15
Wheaton *Minn.*, *U.S.A.* 45°48N 96°30W 172 C5
Wheelbarrow Pk.
U.S.A. 37°26N 116°5W 170 H10
Wheeler *Oreg.*, *U.S.A.* 45°41N 123°53W 168 D2
Wheeler *Tex.*, *U.S.A.* 35°27N 100°16W 176 D4
Wheeler ⮕ *Canada* 57°2N 67°13W 165 A6
Wheeler L. *U.S.A.* 34°48N 87°23W 177 D11
Wheeler Pk. *N. Mex.*,
U.S.A. 36°34N 105°25W 169 H11
Wheeler Pk. *Nev.*,
U.S.A. 38°57N 114°15W 168 G6
Wheeler Ridge *U.S.A.* 35°0N 118°57W 171 L8
Wheelersburg *U.S.A.* 38°44N 82°51W 173 F12
Wheeling *U.S.A.* 40°4N 80°43W 174 F4
Whernside *U.K.* 54°14N 2°24W 66 C5
Whiddy I. *Ireland* 51°41N 9°31W 64 E2
Whim Creek *Australia* 20°50S 117°49E 148 D2
Whiskey Jack L.
Canada 58°23N 101°55W 163 B8
Whistleduck Cr. ⮕
Australia 20°15S 135°18E 150 C2
Whistler *Canada* 50°7N 122°58W 162 C4
Whitby *Canada* 43°52N 78°56W 174 C6
Whitby *U.K.* 54°29N 0°37W 66 C7
Whitcombe Pass *N.Z.* 43°13S 170°55E 155 D5
White ⮕ *Ark.*, *U.S.A.* 33°57N 91°5W 176 E9
White ⮕ *Ind.*, *U.S.A.* 38°25N 87°45W 172 F10
White ⮕ *S. Dak.*,
U.S.A. 43°42N 99°27W 172 D4
White ⮕ *Tex.*, *U.S.A.* 33°14N 100°56W 176 E4
White ⮕ *Utah*, *U.S.A.* 40°4N 109°41W 168 F9
White ⮕ *Vt.*, *U.S.A.* 43°37N 72°20W 175 C12
White ⮕ *Wash.*,
U.S.A. 47°12N 122°15W 170 C4
White, L. *Australia* 21°9S 128°56E 148 D4
White B. *Canada* 50°0N 56°35W 165 C8
White Bird *U.S.A.* 45°46N 116°18W 168 D5
White Butte *U.S.A.* 46°23N 103°18W 172 B2
White City *Fla.*, *U.S.A.* 29°53N 85°13W 178 F4
White City *Oreg.* 42°26N 122°51W 168 E2
White Cliffs *Australia* 30°50S 143°10E 152 A5
White Desert = *Es Sahrâ el Beida*
Egypt 27°50N 28°45E 137 B2
White Hall *U.S.A.* 39°26N 90°24W 172 F8
White Haven *U.S.A.* 41°4N 75°47W 175 E9

White Horse, Vale of
U.K. 51°37N 1°30W 67 F6
White I. = *Whakaari*
N.Z. 37°30S 177°13E 154 G6
White L. *Canada* 45°18N 76°31W 175 A8
White L. *U.S.A.* 29°44N 92°30W 176 H8
White Lake *U.S.A.* 45°21N 76°29W 175 A8
White Mountain Peak
U.S.A. 37°38N 118°15W 171 H8
White Mts. *Calif.*,
U.S.A. 37°30N 118°15W 170 H8
White Mts. *N.H.*,
U.S.A. 44°15N 71°15W 175 B13
White Mts. △
U.S.A. 20°43S 145°12E 150 C4
White Nile = *Nil el Abyad* ⮕
Sudan 15°38N 32°31E 135 E12
White Oak *U.S.A.* 31°2N 81°43W 178 D8
White Otter L. *Canada* 49°5N 91°55W 164 C1
White Pass *U.S.A.* 46°38N 121°24W 170 D5
White Plains *Ga.*, *U.S.A.* 33°28N 83°1W 178 B6
White Plains N.Y.,
U.S.A. 41°2N 73°46W 175 E11
White River *Canada* 48°35N 85°20W 164 C2
White River *U.S.A.* 43°34N 100°45W 172 D3
White Rock *Canada* 49°2N 122°48W 170 A4
White Rock *U.S.A.* 35°50N 106°12W 169 J10
White Russia = *Belarus* ■
Europe 53°30N 27°0E 75 B14
White Sands *U.S.A.* 32°46N 106°20W 169 K10
White Sea = *Beloye More*
Russia 66°30N 38°0E 58 B13
White Springs *U.S.A.* 30°20N 82°45W 178 E7
White Sulphur Springs *Mont.*,
U.S.A. 46°33N 110°54W 168 C8
White Sulphur Springs *W. Va.*,
U.S.A. 37°48N 80°18W 173 G13
White Swan *U.S.A.* 46°23N 120°44W 170 D6
White Volta ⮕ *Ghana* 9°10N 1°15W 139 D4
Whitecliffs *N.Z.* 43°26S 171°55E 155 D6
Whitecourt *Canada* 54°10N 115°45W 162 C5
Whiteface Mt. *U.S.A.* 44°22N 73°54W 175 B11
Whitefield *U.S.A.* 44°23N 71°37W 175 B13
Whitefish *U.S.A.* 48°25N 114°20W 168 B6
Whitefish *U.S.A.* 48°24N 84°55W 164 C3
Whitefish L. *Canada* 62°41N 106°48W 163 A7
Whitefish Pt. *U.S.A.* 46°45N 84°59W 173 B11
Whitegull, L. = *Goélands, L. aux*
Canada 55°27N 64°17W 165 A7
Whitehall *Mich.*,
U.S.A. 43°24N 86°21W 172 D10
Whitehall *Mont.*,
U.S.A. 45°52N 112°6W 168 D7
Whitehall *N.Y.*,
U.S.A. 43°33N 73°24W 175 C11
Whitehall *Wis.*, *U.S.A.* 44°22N 91°19W 172 C8
Whitehaven *U.K.* 54°33N 3°35W 66 C4
Whitehorse *Canada* 60°43N 135°3W 162 A1
Whitemark *Australia* 40°7S 148°3E 151 G4
Whiteriver *U.S.A.* 33°50N 109°58W 169 K9
Whitesand ⮕ *Canada* 60°9N 115°45W 162 A5
Whitesboro N.Y., *U.S.A.* 43°7N 75°18W 175 C9
Whitesboro *Tex.*,
U.S.A. 33°39N 96°54W 176 E6
Whiteshell △ *Canada* 50°0N 95°40W 163 D9
Whiteside, Canal *Chile* 53°55S 70°15W 192 D2
Whiteville *U.S.A.* 34°20N 78°42W 177 D15
Whitewater *U.S.A.* 42°50N 88°44W 172 D9
Whitewater B. *U.S.A.* 25°15N 81°0W 179 K9
Whitewater Baldy
U.S.A. 33°20N 108°39W 169 K9
Whitewater L. *U.S.A.* 50°50N 89°10W 164 B2
Whitewood *Australia* 21°28S 143°30E 150 C3
Whitewood *Canada* 50°20N 102°20W 163 C8
Whitfield *Australia* 36°42S 146°24E 153 D7
Whithorn *U.K.* 54°44N 4°26W 65 G4
Whitianga *N.Z.* 36°47S 175°41E 154 C4
Whitman *U.S.A.* 42°5N 70°56W 175 D14
Whitmore Mts.
Antarctica 82°35S 104°30W 55 E15
Whitney *Canada* 45°31N 78°14W 174 A6
Whitney, Mt. *U.S.A.* 36°35N 118°18W 170 J8
Whitney Point *U.S.A.* 42°20N 75°58W 175 D9
Whitstable *U.K.* 51°21N 1°3E 67 F9
Whitsunday I. *Australia* 20°15S 149°4E 150 b
Whitsunday Islands △
Australia 20°15S 149°0E 150 b
Whittier *Alaska*,
U.S.A. 60°47N 148°41W 166 C10
Whittier *Calif.*, *U.S.A.* 33°58N 118°2W 171 M8
Whittlesea *Australia* 37°27S 145°9E 153 D6
Wholdaia L. *Canada* 60°43N 104°20W 163 A8
Whyalla *Australia* 33°2S 137°30E 152 B2
Wiang Kosai △
Thailand 17°54N 99°2E 120 D2
Wiang Sa *Thailand* 18°34N 100°45E 120 C3
Wiarton *Canada* 44°40N 81°10W 174 B3
Wiawso *Ghana* 6°10N 2°25W 138 D4
Wiay *U.K.* 57°24N 7°13W 65 D1
Wiązów *Poland* 50°50N 17°10E 83 H4
Wibaux *U.S.A.* 46°59N 104°11W 168 C2
Wichian Buri *Thailand* 15°39N 101°7E 120 E3
Wichita *U.S.A.* 37°42N 97°20W 172 G5
Wichita Falls *U.S.A.* 33°54N 98°30W 176 E5
Wick *U.K.* 58°26N 3°5W 65 C5
Wickenburg *U.S.A.* 33°58N 112°44W 169 K7
Wickepin *Australia* 32°50S 117°30E 149 F2
Wickham *Australia* 20°42S 117°11E 148 D2
Wickham, C. *Australia* 39°35S 143°57E 151 F3
Wickliffe *U.S.A.* 41°36N 81°28W 174 E3
Wicklow *Ireland* 52°59N 6°3W 64 D5
Wicklow □ *Ireland* 52°57N 6°25W 64 D5
Wicklow Hd. *Ireland* 52°58N 6°0W 64 D6
Wicklow Mts. △ *Ireland* 53°6N 6°21W 64 C5
Widawa *Poland* 51°27N 18°51E 83 G5
Widawka ⮕ *Poland* 51°27N 19°52E 83 G5
Widgeegoara Cr. ⮕
Australia 28°51S 146°34E 151 D4
Widgiemooltha *Australia* 31°30S 121°34E 149 F3
Widnes *U.K.* 53°23N 2°45W 66 D5
Więcbork *Poland* 53°21N 17°30E 83 E4
Wiehengebirge = *Nördlicher*
Teutoburger
Wald-Wiehengebirge △
Germany 52°18N 8°10E 76 C4
Wiehl *Germany* 50°56N 7°34E 76 E3

Wiek *Germany* 54°37N 13°17E 76 A9
Wielbark *Poland* 53°24N 20°55E 82 E7
Wieleń *Poland* 52°53N 16°9E 83 E3
Wielichowo *Poland* 52°7N 16°22E 83 F3
Wieliczka *Poland* 50°0N 20°5E 83 J7
Wielkopolski △ *Poland* 52°18N 16°45E 83 F3
Wielkopolskie □ *Poland* 52°10N 17°30E 83 F4
Wieluń *Poland* 51°15N 18°34E 83 G5
Wien *Austria* 48°12N 16°22E 79 C9
Wien-Schwechat ✈ (VIE)
Austria 48°7N 16°35E 79 C9
Wiener Neustadt
Austria 47°49N 16°16E 79 D9
Wieprz ⮕ *Poland* 51°34N 21°49E 83 G8
Wieprza ⮕ *Poland* 54°26N 16°35E 82 D3
Wieruszów *Poland* 51°19N 18°9E 83 G5
Wiesbaden *Germany* 50°4N 8°14E 77 E4
Wiesental *Germany* 49°13N 8°31E 77 F4
Wiesloch *Germany* 49°18N 8°41E 77 F4
Wiesmoor *Germany* 53°24N 7°47E 76 B3
Wieżyca *Poland* 54°14N 18°8E 82 D5
Wigan *U.K.* 53°33N 2°38W 66 D5
Wiggins *Colo.*, *U.S.A.* 40°14N 104°4W 168 F11
Wiggins *Miss.*, *U.S.A.* 30°51N 89°8W 177 F10
Wight, I. of *U.K.* 50°41N 1°17W 67 G6
Wigierski △ *Poland* 54°5N 23°5E 82 D10
Wigry, Jezioro *Poland* 54°2N 23°8E 82 D10
Wigston *U.K.* 52°35N 1°6W 67 E6
Wigton *U.K.* 54°50N 3°10W 66 C4
Wigtown *U.K.* 54°53N 4°27W 65 G4
Wigtown B. *U.K.* 54°46N 4°15W 65 G4
Wik and Wikway People ✥
Australia 13°55S 142°28E 150 A3
Wil *Switz.* 47°28N 9°3E 77 H5
Wilamowice *Poland* 49°55N 19°9E 83 J6
Wilber *U.S.A.* 40°29N 96°58W 172 E5
Wilberforce *Canada* 45°2N 78°13W 174 A6
Wilberforce, C.
Australia 11°54S 136°35E 150 A2
Wilburton *U.S.A.* 34°55N 95°19W 176 D7
Wilcannia *Australia* 31°30S 143°26E 152 A5
Wilcox *U.S.A.* 41°35N 78°41W 174 E6
Wildbad *Germany* 48°44N 8°33E 77 G4
Wildeshausen *Germany* 52°54N 8°27E 76 C4
Wildeshauser Geest △
Germany 52°54N 8°30E 76 C4
Wildomar *U.S.A.* 33°36N 117°16W 171 M9
Wildon *Austria* 46°52N 15°31E 78 E8
Wildrose *U.S.A.* 36°14N 117°11W 171 J9
Wildspitze *Austria* 46°53N 10°53E 78 E3
Wildwood *U.S.A.* 28°52N 82°2W 178 G6
Wilga ⮕ *Poland* 51°52N 21°18E 83 G8
Wilge ⮕ *S. Africa* 27°3S 28°20E 145 C4
Wilhelm II Coast
Antarctica 68°0S 90°0E 55 C7
Wilhelmsburg *Austria* 48°6N 15°36E 78 D8
Wilhelmshaven *Germany* 53°31N 8°7E 76 B4
Wilhelmstal *Namibia* 21°58S 16°21E 144 B2
Wilis *Indonesia* 7°51S 111°48E 119 G15
Wilkes-Barre *U.S.A.* 41°15N 75°53W 175 E9
Wilkes Land *Antarctica* 69°0S 120°0E 55 D9
Wilkie *Canada* 52°27N 108°42W 163 C7
Wilkins Ice Shelf
Antarctica 70°30S 72°0W 55 C17
Wilkinsburg *U.S.A.* 40°26N 79°52W 174 F5
Wilkinson Lakes
Australia 29°40S 132°39E 149 E5
Willacoochee *U.S.A.* 31°20N 83°3W 178 D6
Willandra △ *Australia* 33°12S 145°0E 153 B6
Willandra Creek ⮕
Australia 33°22S 145°52E 152 B6
Willapa B. *U.S.A.* 46°40N 124°0W 170 D3
Willapa Hills *U.S.A.* 46°35N 123°25W 170 D3
Willard *U.S.A.* 41°3N 82°44W 174 E2
Willare Bridge Roadhouse
Australia 17°43S 123°38E 148 C3
Willcox *U.S.A.* 32°15N 109°50W 169 K9
Willemstad *Curaçao* 12°5N 68°55W 183 D6
Willi Willi △
Australia 30°57S 152°27E 153 A10
William ⮕ *Canada* 59°8N 109°19W 163 B7
William, Mt. *Australia* 37°17S 142°35E 152 D5
William Creek
Australia 28°58S 136°22E 151 D2
Williams *Australia* 33°2N 87°24W 177 E11
Williams *Ariz.*, *U.S.A.* 35°15N 112°11W 169 J7
Williams *Calif.*, *U.S.A.* 39°9N 122°9W 170 F4
Williams Harbour
Canada 52°33N 55°47W 165 B8
Williams Lake *Canada* 52°10N 122°10W 162 C4
Williamsburg *Ky.*,
U.S.A. 36°44N 84°10W 173 G11
Williamsburg *Pa.*,
U.S.A. 40°28N 78°12W 174 F6
Williamson W. Va.,
U.S.A. 37°41N 82°17W 173 G12
Williamson N.Y.,
U.S.A. 43°14N 77°11W 174 C7
Williamsport *U.S.A.* 41°15N 77°1W 174 E7
Williamston *U.S.A.* 35°51N 77°4W 177 D16
Williamstown
Australia 37°51S 144°52E 151 F3
Williamstown *Ky.*,
U.S.A. 38°38N 84°34W 173 F11
Williamstown *Mass.*,
U.S.A. 42°43N 73°12W 175 D11
Williamstown N.Y.,
U.S.A. 43°26N 75°53W 175 C9
Willimantic *U.S.A.* 41°43N 72°13W 175 E12
Willingboro *U.S.A.* 40°3N 74°54W 175 F10
Williston *S. Africa* 31°20S 20°53E 144 D3
Williston *Fla.*, *U.S.A.* 29°23N 82°27W 178 F7
Williston *N. Dak.*,
U.S.A. 48°9N 103°37W 172 A2
Williston L. *Canada* 56°0N 124°0W 162 B4
Willits *U.S.A.* 39°25N 123°21W 170 F3
Willmar *U.S.A.* 45°7N 95°3W 172 C6
Willmore Wilderness △
Canada 53°45N 119°30W 162 C5
Willoughby *U.S.A.* 41°39N 81°24W 174 E3
Willow Bunch
Canada 49°20N 105°35W 163 D7
Willow L. *Canada* 62°10N 119°8W 162 A5
Willow Tree *Australia* 31°40S 150°45E 153 A9

Willow Wall, The
China 42°10N 122°0E 115 C12
Willowick *U.S.A.* 41°38N 81°28W 174 E3
Willowlake ⮕ *Canada* 62°42N 123°8W 162 A4
Willowmore *S. Africa* 33°15S 23°30E 144 D3
Willows *U.S.A.* 39°31N 122°12W 170 F4
Willowvale = *Gatyana*
S. Africa 32°16S 28°31E 145 D4
Wills, L. *Australia* 21°25S 128°51E 148 D4
Wills Cr. ⮕ *Australia* 22°43S 140°2E 150 C3
Willsboro *U.S.A.* 44°21N 73°24W 175 B11
Willunga *Australia* 35°15S 138°30E 152 C3
Wilma *U.S.A.* 30°9N 84°58W 178 E5
Wilmette *U.S.A.* 42°4N 87°42W 172 D10
Wilmington *Australia* 32°39S 138°7E 152 B3
Wilmington *Del.*,
U.S.A. 39°45N 75°33W 173 F16
Wilmington N.C.,
U.S.A. 34°14N 77°55W 177 D16
Wilmington Ohio,
U.S.A. 39°27N 83°50W 173 F12
Wilmington *Vt.*,
U.S.A. 42°52N 72°52W 175 D12
Wilmslow *U.K.* 53°19N 2°13W 66 D5
Wilpattu △ *Sri Lanka* 8°20N 79°50E 127 K4
Wilpena Cr. ⮕
Australia 31°25S 139°29E 152 A3
Wilsall *U.S.A.* 45°59N 110°38W 168 D8
Wilson *N.C.*, *U.S.A.* 35°44N 77°55W 177 D16
Wilson *N.Y.*, *U.S.A.* 43°19N 78°50W 174 C6
Wilson *Pa.*, *U.S.A.* 40°41N 75°15W 175 F9
Wilson ⮕ *Australia* 16°48S 128°16E 148 C4
Wilson Bluff *Australia* 31°41S 129°0E 149 F4
Wilson Inlet *Australia* 35°0S 117°22E 149 G2
Wilsons Promontory
Australia 38°59S 146°23E 153 F7
Wilsons Promontory △
Australia 38°55S 146°23E 153 D7
Wilster *Germany* 53°55N 9°23E 76 B5
Wilton *U.S.A.* 47°10N 100°47W 172 B3
Wilton ⮕ *Australia* 14°45S 134°33E 150 A1
Wiltshire □ *U.K.* 51°18N 1°53W 67 F6
Wiltz *Lux.* 49°57N 5°55E 69 E5
Wiluna *Australia* 26°36S 120°14E 149 E3
Wimborne Minster *U.K.* 50°48N 1°59W 67 G6
Wimmera ⮕ *Australia* 36°8S 141°56E 152 D4
Wimereux *France* 50°45N 1°37E 71 F8
Winam G. *Kenya* 0°20S 34°15E 142 C3
Winburg *S. Africa* 28°30S 27°2E 144 C4
Winchelsea *Australia* 38°10S 144°1E 152 D6
Winchendon *U.S.A.* 42°41N 72°3W 175 D12
Winchester *N.Z.* 44°11S 171°17E 155 E6
Winchester *U.K.* 51°4N 1°18W 67 F6
Winchester *Conn.*,
U.S.A. 41°53N 73°9W 175 E11
Winchester *Idaho*,
U.S.A. 46°14N 116°38W 168 C5
Winchester *Ind.*,
U.S.A. 40°10N 84°59W 173 E11
Winchester *Ky.*,
U.S.A. 37°59N 84°11W 173 G11
Winchester *N.H.*,
U.S.A. 42°46N 72°23W 175 D12
Winchester *Nev.*,
U.S.A. 36°7N 115°7W 171 J11
Winchester *Tenn.*,
U.S.A. 35°11N 86°7W 177 D11
Winchester *Va.*,
U.S.A. 39°11N 78°10W 173 F14
Wind ⮕ *U.S.A.* 43°12N 108°12W 168 E9
Wind Cave △ *U.S.A.* 43°32N 103°17W 172 D2
Wind River Range
U.S.A. 43°0N 109°30W 168 E9
Windamere, L.
Australia 32°48S 149°51E 153 B8
Windau = *Ventspils*
Latvia 57°25N 21°32E 82 A8
Windber *U.S.A.* 40°14N 78°50W 174 F6
Winder *U.S.A.* 34°0N 83°45W 178 A6
Windermere *U.S.A.* 54°23N 2°55W 66 C5
Windermere *U.S.A.* 28°29N 81°32W 179 G8
Windhoek *Namibia* 22°35S 17°4E 144 B2
Windidda △ *Australia* 26°23S 122°12E 149 E3
Windischgarsten
Austria 47°42N 14°21E 78 D7
Windjana Gorge △
Australia 17°51S 125°0E 148 C3
Windom *U.S.A.* 43°52N 95°7W 172 D6
Windorah *Australia* 25°24S 142°36E 150 D3
Window Rock *U.S.A.* 35°41N 109°3W 169 J9
Windrush ⮕ *U.K.* 51°43N 1°24W 67 F6
Windsor *Australia* 33°37S 150°50E 153 B9
Windsor *N.S., Canada* 44°59N 64°5W 165 D7
Windsor *Ont., Canada* 42°18N 83°0W 174 D2
Windsor *N.Z.* 44°59S 170°49E 155 E3
Windsor *U.K.* 51°29N 0°36W 67 F7
Windsor *Calif., U.S.A.* 38°33N 122°49W 170 G4
Windsor *Colo., U.S.A.* 40°29N 104°54W 168 F11
Windsor *Conn., U.S.A.* 41°50N 72°39W 175 E12
Windsor *Mo., U.S.A.* 38°32N 93°31W 172 F7
Windsor *N.Y., U.S.A.* 42°5N 75°37W 175 D9
Windsor *Vt., U.S.A.* 43°29N 72°24W 175 C12
Windsor & Maidenhead □
U.K. 51°29N 0°40W 67 F7
Windsorton *S. Africa* 28°16S 24°44E 144 C3
Windward Is. *W. Indies* 13°0N 61°0W 183 D7
Windward Passage = *Vientos,*
Paso de los *Caribbean* 20°0N 74°0W 183 C5
Winefred L. *Canada* 55°30N 110°30W 163 B6
Winfield *U.S.A.* 37°15N 96°59W 172 G5
Wingate Mts.
Australia 14°25S 130°40E 148 B5
Wingellina = *Irrunytju*
Australia 26°3S 128°56E 149 E4
Wingham *Australia* 31°48S 152°22E 153 A10
Wingham *Canada* 43°55N 81°20W 174 C3
Winisk ⮕ *Canada* 55°17N 85°5W 164 A2
Winisk L. *Canada* 52°55N 87°22W 164 B2
Wink *U.S.A.* 31°45N 103°9W 176 F3
Winkler *Canada* 49°10N 97°56W 163 D9
Winklern *Austria* 46°52N 12°52E 78 E5
Winlock *U.S.A.* 46°30N 122°56W 170 D4
Winneba *Ghana* 5°25N 0°36W 139 D4
Winnebago, L. *U.S.A.* 44°0N 88°26W 172 D9
Winnecke Cr. ⮕
Australia 18°35S 131°34E 148 C5
Winnemucca *U.S.A.* 40°58N 117°44W 168 F5
Winnemucca L. *U.S.A.* 40°7N 119°21W 168 F4
Winner *U.S.A.* 43°22N 99°52W 172 D4
Winnett *U.S.A.* 47°0N 108°21W 168 C9

Winnfield U.S.A. 31°56N 92°38W 176 F8
Winnibigoshish, L. U.S.A. 47°27N 94°13W 172 B6
Winnipeg Canada 49°54N 97°9W 163 D9
Winnipeg → Canada 50°38N 96°19W 163 C9
Winnipeg, L. Canada 52°0N 97°0W 163 C9
Winnipeg Beach Canada 50°30N 96°58W 163 C9
Winnipegosis Canada 51°39N 99°55W 163 C9
Winnipegosis L. Canada 52°30N 100°0W 163 C9
Winnipesaukee, L. U.S.A. 43°38N 71°21W 175 C13
Winnisquam L. U.S.A. 43°33N 71°31W 175 C13
Winnsboro La., U.S.A. 32°10N 91°43W 176 E9
Winnsboro S.C., U.S.A. 34°23N 81°5W 177 D14
Winnsboro Tex., U.S.A. 32°58N 95°17W 176 E7
Winokapau, L. Canada 53°15N 62°50W 165 B7
Winona Minn., U.S.A. 44°3N 91°39W 172 C8
Winona Miss., U.S.A. 33°29N 89°44W 177 E10
Winooski U.S.A. 44°29N 73°11W 175 B11
Winooski → U.S.A. 44°32N 73°17W 175 B11
Winschoten Neths. 53°9N 7°3E 69 A7
Winsen Germany 53°22N 10°13E 76 B6
Winsford U.K. 53°12N 2°31W 66 D5
Winslow = Bainbridge Island U.S.A. 47°38N 122°32W 170 C4
Winslow U.S.A. 35°2N 110°42W 169 J8
Winsted U.S.A. 41°55N 73°4W 175 E11
Winston-Salem U.S.A. 36°6N 80°15W 177 C14
Winter Garden U.S.A. 28°34N 81°35W 179 G8
Winter Haven U.S.A. 28°1N 81°44W 179 G8
Winter Park U.S.A. 28°36N 81°20W 179 G8
Winterberg Germany 51°11N 8°33E 76 D4
Winterhaven U.S.A. 32°44N 114°38W 171 N12
Winters U.S.A. 38°32N 121°58W 170 G5
Winterset U.S.A. 41°20N 94°1W 172 E6
Wintersville U.S.A. 40°23N 80°42W 174 F4
Winterswijk Neths. 51°58N 6°43E 69 C6
Winterthur Switz. 47°30N 8°44E 77 H4
Winthrop U.S.A. 48°28N 120°10W 168 B3
Winton Australia 22°24S 143°3E 150 C3
Winton N.Z. 46°8S 168°20E 155 G3
Wipper → Germany 51°16N 11°12E 76 D7
Wirlyajarrayi ✪ Australia 21°45S 132°35E 148 D5
Wirraminna Australia 31°12S 136°13E 152 A2
Wirrulla Australia 32°24S 134°31E 151 E1
Wisbech U.K. 52°41N 0°9E 67 E8
Wisconsin □ U.S.A. 44°45N 89°30W 172 C9
Wisconsin → U.S.A. 43°0N 91°15W 172 D8
Wisconsin Rapids U.S.A. 44°23N 89°49W 172 C9
Wisdom U.S.A. 45°37N 113°27W 168 D7
Wiseman U.S.A. 67°25N 150°6W 166 B9
Wishaw U.K. 55°46N 3°54W 65 F5
Wishek U.S.A. 46°16N 99°33W 172 B4
Wisła Poland 49°38N 18°53E 83 J5
Wisła → Poland 54°22N 18°55E 82 D5
Wisłok → Poland 50°13N 22°32E 83 H9
Wisłoka → Poland 50°27N 21°23E 83 H8
Wismar Germany 53°54N 11°29E 76 B7
Wisner U.S.A. 41°59N 96°55W 172 E5
Wissant France 50°52N 1°40E 71 B8
Wissembourg France 49°2N 7°57E 71 C14
Wisznice Poland 51°48N 23°13E 83 G10
Witbank = eMalahleni S. Africa 25°51S 29°14E 145 C4
Witches Gorge = Wu Xia China 31°2N 110°10E 117 B8
Witdraai S. Africa 26°58S 20°48E 144 C3
Witham U.K. 51°48N 0°40E 67 F8
Witham → U.K. 52°59N 0°2W 66 E7
Withernsea U.K. 53°44N 0°1E 66 D8
Withlacoochee → Fla., U.S.A. 30°24N 83°10W 178 E6
Withlacoochee → Fla., U.S.A. 29°0N 82°45W 179 G7
Witjira △ Australia 26°22S 135°37E 151 D2
Witkowo Poland 52°26N 17°45E 83 F4
Witless Bay Canada 47°17N 52°50W 165 C9
Witney U.K. 51°48N 1°28W 67 F6
Witnica Poland 52°40N 14°54E 83 F1
Witnossob → Namibia 23°55S 18°45E 144 C3
Witriver S. Africa 25°20S 31°0E 145 C5
Wittdün Germany 54°38N 8°23E 76 A4
Wittelsheim France 47°48N 7°14E 71 E14
Witten Germany 51°26N 7°20E 76 D3
Wittenberge Germany 53°0N 11°45E 76 B7
Wittenburg Germany 53°31N 11°4E 76 B7
Wittenoom Australia 22°15S 118°20E 148 D2
Wittingen Germany 52°44N 10°44E 76 C6
Wittlich Germany 49°59N 6°53E 77 F2
Wittmund Germany 53°34N 7°46E 76 B3
Wittow Germany 54°38N 13°20E 76 A9
Wittstock Germany 53°10N 12°28E 76 B8
Witu Kenya 2°23S 40°26E 142 C5
Witvlei Namibia 22°23S 18°32E 144 B2
Witzenhausen Germany 51°20N 9°51E 76 D5
Wiwon N. Korea 40°54N 126°3E 115 D14
Wkra → Poland 52°27N 20°44E 83 F7
Władysławowo Poland 54°48N 18°25E 82 D5
Wleń Poland 51°2N 15°39E 83 G2
Wlingi Indonesia 8°5S 112°25E 119 H15
Włocławek Poland 52°40N 19°3E 83 F6
Włodawa Poland 51°33N 23°31E 83 G10
Włoszczowa Poland 50°50N 19°55E 83 H6
Woburn U.S.A. 42°29N 71°9W 175 D13
Wodian China 32°50N 112°35E 114 H7
Wodonga Australia 36°5S 146°50E 153 D7
Wodzisław Śląski Poland 50°1N 18°26E 83 H5
Wœrth France 48°57N 7°45E 71 D14
Woinbogoin China 32°51N 98°39E 116 A2
Woippy France 49°10N 6°8E 71 C13
Wojcieszów Poland 50°58N 15°55E 83 H2
Wokam Indonesia 5°45S 134°28E 119 F8
Woking U.K. 51°19N 0°34W 67 F7
Wokingham U.K. 51°24N 0°49W 67 F7
Wokingham □ U.K. 51°25N 0°51W 67 F7
Woko △ Australia 31°46S 151°49E 153 A9
Wolbrom Poland 50°24N 19°45E 83 H6
Wołczyn Poland 51°1N 18°3E 83 G5
Woldegk Germany 53°27N 13°34E 76 B9
Wolf → Canada 60°17N 132°33W 162 A2
Wolf Creek U.S.A. 47°0N 112°4W 168 C7
Wolf L. Canada 60°24N 131°40W 162 A2
Wolf Point U.S.A. 48°5N 105°39W 168 B11
Wolfe Creek Crater △ Australia 19°10S 127°47E 148 C4
Wolfe I. Canada 44°7N 76°20W 175 B8
Wolfeboro U.S.A. 43°35N 71°13W 175 C13
Wolfen Germany 51°39N 12°15E 76 D8
Wolfenbüttel Germany 52°10N 10°33E 76 C6
Wolfratshausen Germany 47°54N 11°24E 77 H7
Wolfsberg Austria 46°50N 14°52E 78 E7
Wolfsburg Germany 52°25N 10°48E 76 C6
Wolgast Germany 54°3N 13°46E 76 A9
Wolhusen Switz. 47°4N 8°4E 77 H4
Wolin Poland 53°50N 14°37E 82 E1
Woliński △ Poland 53°57N 14°28E 82 E1
Wollaston, Is. Chile 55°40S 67°30W 192 E3
Wollaston Forland Greenland 74°25N 19°40W 57 C9
Wollaston L. Canada 58°7N 103°10W 163 B8
Wollaston Lake Canada 58°3N 103°33W 163 B8
Wollaston Pen. Canada 69°30N 115°0W 160 D9
Wollemi △ Australia 33°0S 150°30E 153 B9
Wollongong Australia 34°25S 150°54E 153 C9
Wolmaransstad S. Africa 27°12S 25°59E 144 C4
Wolmirstedt Germany 52°14N 11°37E 76 C7
Wołomin Poland 52°19N 21°15E 83 F8
Wołów Poland 51°20N 16°38E 83 G3
Wolseley Australia 36°23S 140°54E 152 D4
Wolseley S. Africa 33°26S 19°7E 144 D2
Wolsey U.S.A. 44°25N 98°28W 172 C4
Wolstenholme, C. Canada 62°35N 77°30W 158 C12
Wolsztyn Poland 52°8N 16°5E 83 F3
Wolvega Neths. 52°52N 6°0E 69 B6
Wolverhampton U.K. 52°35N 2°7W 67 E5
Wondai Australia 26°20S 151°49E 151 D5
Wongalarroo L. Australia 31°32S 144°0E 152 A6
Wongan Hills Australia 30°51S 116°37E 149 F2
Wonju S. Korea 37°22N 127°58E 115 F14
Wonosari Indonesia 7°58S 110°36E 119 G14
Wonosobo Indonesia 7°22S 109°54E 119 G13
Wonowon Canada 56°44N 121°48W 162 B4
Wŏnsan N. Korea 39°11N 127°27E 115 E14
Wonthaggi Australia 38°37S 145°37E 153 E6
Wood Buffalo △ Canada 59°0N 113°41W 162 B6
Wood Is. Australia 16°24S 123°19E 148 C3
Wood L. Canada 55°17N 103°17W 163 B8
Woodah, I. Australia 13°27S 136°10E 150 A2
Woodbine U.S.A. 30°58N 81°44W 178 E8
Woodbourne U.S.A. 41°46N 74°36W 175 E10
Woodbridge Canada 43°47N 79°36W 174 C5
Woodbridge U.K. 52°6N 1°20E 67 E9
Woodburn Australia 29°6S 153°23E 151 A5
Woodburn U.S.A. 45°9N 122°51W 168 D2
Woodbury U.S.A. 32°59N 84°35W 178 C5
Woodenbong Australia 28°24S 152°39E 151 D5
Woodend Australia 37°20S 144°33E 152 D6
Woodford Australia 26°58S 152°47E 151 D5
Woodfords U.S.A. 38°47N 119°50W 170 G7
Woodlake U.S.A. 36°25N 119°6W 170 J7
Woodland Calif., U.S.A. 38°41N 121°46W 170 G5
Woodland Maine, U.S.A. 45°9N 67°25W 173 C20
Woodland Pa., U.S.A. 41°0N 78°21W 174 F6
Woodland Wash., U.S.A. 45°54N 122°45W 170 E4
Woodland Caribou ⌂ Canada 51°0N 94°45W 163 C10
Woodlands Singapore 1°26N 103°46E 121 d
Woodlands, The U.S.A. 30°9N 95°29W 176 F7
Woodonga Australia 36°10S 146°50E 151 F4
Woodridge Canada 49°20N 96°9W 163 D9
Woodroffe, Mt. Australia 26°20S 131°45E 149 E5
Woods, L. Australia 17°50S 133°30E 150 B1
Woods, L. of the N. Amer. 49°15N 94°45W 163 D10
Woods Bay Canada 45°8N 79°59W 174 A5
Woodside S. Austral., Australia 34°58S 138°52E 152 C3
Woodside Vic., Australia 38°31S 146°52E 153 E7
Woodstock N.S.W., Australia 33°45S 148°53E 153 B8
Woodstock Queens., Australia 19°35S 146°50E 150 B4
Woodstock N.B., Canada 46°11N 67°37W 165 C6
Woodstock Ont., Canada 43°10N 80°45W 174 C4
Woodstock U.K. 51°51N 1°20W 67 F6
Woodstock Ill., U.S.A. 42°19N 88°27W 172 D9
Woodstock N.Y., U.S.A. 42°2N 74°7W 175 D10
Woodstock Vt., U.S.A. 43°37N 72°31W 175 C12
Woodsville U.S.A. 44°9N 72°2W 175 B13
Woodview Canada 44°35N 78°8W 174 B6
Woodville N.Z. 40°20S 175°53E 154 G4
Woodville Fla., U.S.A. 30°19N 84°15W 178 E5
Woodville Ga., U.S.A. 33°40N 83°7W 178 B6
Woodville Miss., U.S.A. 31°6N 91°18W 176 F9
Woodville Tex., U.S.A. 30°47N 94°25W 176 F7
Woodward U.S.A. 36°26N 99°24W 176 C5
Woody U.S.A. 35°42N 118°50W 171 K8
Woody → Canada 52°31N 100°51W 163 C8
Woody I. S. China Sea 16°50N 112°20E 118 A4
Woolacombe U.K. 51°10N 4°13W 67 F3
Woolamai, C. Australia 38°30S 145°23E 153 E6
Woolbrook Australia 30°56S 151°25E 153 A9
Wooler U.K. 55°33N 2°1W 66 B5
Woolgoolga Australia 30°6S 153°11E 151 E5
Woomargama △ Australia 35°50S 147°15E 153 C7
Woomera Australia 31°5S 136°50E 152 A2
Woonsocket R.I., U.S.A. 42°0N 71°31W 175 E13
Woonsocket S. Dak., U.S.A. 44°3N 98°17W 172 C4
Wooramel → Australia 25°47S 114°10E 149 E1
Wooramel Roadhouse Australia 25°45S 114°17E 149 E1
Wooroonooran △ Australia 16°25S 146°1E 150 B4
Wooster U.S.A. 40°48N 81°56W 174 F3
Worcester S. Africa 33°39S 19°27E 144 D2
Worcester U.K. 52°11N 2°12W 67 E5
Worcester Mass., U.S.A. 42°16N 71°48W 175 D13
Worcester N.Y., U.S.A. 42°36N 74°45W 175 D10
Worcestershire □ U.K. 52°13N 2°10W 67 E5
Wörgl Austria 47°29N 12°3E 78 D5
Workington U.K. 54°39N 3°33W 66 C4
Worksop U.K. 53°18N 1°7W 66 D6
Workum Neths. 52°59N 5°26E 69 B5
Worland U.S.A. 44°1N 107°57W 168 D10
Wormhout France 50°52N 2°28E 71 B9
Worms Germany 49°37N 8°21E 77 F4
Worodougou □ Ivory C. 8°0N 6°0W 138 D3
Worsley Canada 56°31N 119°8W 162 B5
Wörth Germany 49°1N 12°24E 77 F8
Wortham U.S.A. 31°47N 96°28W 176 F6
Wörther See Austria 46°37N 14°10E 78 E7
Worthing Barbados 13°5N 59°35W 183 g
Worthing U.K. 50°49N 0°21W 67 G7
Worthington Minn., U.S.A. 43°37N 95°36W 172 D6
Worthington Pa., U.S.A. 40°50N 79°38W 174 F5
Wosi Indonesia 0°15S 128°0E 119 E7
Wote Kenya 1°47S 37°38E 142 C4
Wotjalum ✪ Australia 16°30S 123°45E 148 C3
Wotjobaluk ✪ Australia 37°0S 142°0E 151 C3
Wou-han = Wuhan China 30°31N 114°18E 117 B10
Wousi = Wuxi China 31°33N 120°18E 117 B13
Wowoni Indonesia 4°5S 123°5E 119 E6
Woy Woy Australia 33°30S 151°19E 153 B9
Wrangel I. = Vrangelya, Ostrov Russia 71°0N 180°0E 107 B18
Wrangell U.S.A. 56°28N 132°23W 162 B2
Wrangell Mts. U.S.A. 61°30N 142°0W 160 E3
Wrath, C. U.K. 58°38N 5°1W 65 C3
Wray U.S.A. 40°5N 102°13W 168 F12
Wrekin, The U.K. 52°41N 2°32W 67 E5
Wrens U.S.A. 33°12N 82°23W 178 B7
Wrexham U.K. 53°3N 3°0W 66 D4
Wrexham □ U.K. 53°1N 2°58W 66 D5
Wriezen Germany 52°42N 14°7E 76 C10
Wright Fla., U.S.A. 30°27N 86°38W 179 E3
Wright Wyo., U.S.A. 43°45N 105°28W 168 E11
Wright Pt. Canada 43°48N 81°44W 174 C3
Wrightmyo India 11°47N 92°43E 127 J11
Wrighton, Mt. U.S.A. 31°42N 110°51W 169 L8
Wrightsville U.S.A. 32°44N 82°43W 178 C7
Wrightwood U.S.A. 34°22N 117°38W 171 L9
Wrigley Canada 63°16N 123°37W 160 E7
Wrocław Poland 51°5N 17°5E 83 G4
Wronki Poland 52°41N 16°21E 83 F3
Września Poland 52°21N 17°36E 83 F4
Wschowa Poland 51°48N 16°20E 83 G3
Wu Jiang → China 29°40N 107°20E 116 C6
Wu Kau Tang China 22°30N 114°14E 111 a
Wu Xia China 31°2N 110°10E 117 B8
Wu'an China 36°40N 114°15E 114 F8
Wubalawun ✪ Australia 15°28S 133°1E 148 C5
Wubin Australia 30°6S 116°37E 149 F2
Wubu China 37°28N 110°42E 114 F6
Wuchang China 44°55N 127°5E 115 B14
Wucheng China 37°12N 116°20E 114 F9
Wuchuan Guangdong, China 21°33N 110°43E 117 G8
Wuchuan Guizhou, China 28°25N 108°3E 116 C7
Wuchuan Nei Monggol Zizhiqu, China 41°5N 111°28E 114 D6
Wuda China 39°29N 106°42E 114 E4
Wudang Shan China 32°23N 111°2E 117 A8
Wudi China 37°40N 117°35E 115 F9
Wuding China 25°24N 102°21E 116 E4
Wuding He → China 37°2N 110°23E 114 F6
Wudinna Australia 33°0S 135°22E 151 E2
Wudongde Dam China 26°20N 102°15E 116 D4
Wudu China 33°22N 104°54E 114 H3
Wufeng China 30°12N 110°42E 117 B8
Wugang China 26°44N 110°35E 117 D8
Wugong Shan China 27°30N 114°0E 117 D9
Wuguishan China 22°25N 113°25E 111 a
Wugullar = Beswick Australia 14°34S 132°53E 148 B5
Wuhai China 39°39N 106°48E 114 E4
Wuhan China 30°31N 114°18E 117 B10
Wuhe China 33°10N 117°50E 115 H9
Wuhsi = Wuxi China 31°33N 120°18E 117 B13
Wuhu China 31°22N 118°21E 117 B12
Wujiang China 31°10N 120°38E 117 B13
Wukari Nigeria 7°51N 9°42E 139 D6
Wulajie China 44°6N 126°33E 115 B14
Wulanbulang China 41°5N 110°55E 114 D6
Wular L. India 34°20N 74°30E 125 B6
Wulehe Ghana 8°39N 0°0 139 D5
Wulff Land Greenland 82°0N 49°0W 57 A6
Wulian China 35°40N 119°12E 115 G10
Wulian Feng China 27°48N 103°36E 116 D4
Wuliang Shan China 24°30N 100°40E 116 E3
Wuliaru Indonesia 7°27S 131°0E 119 F8
Wuling Shan China 30°0N 110°0E 116 C7
Wulingyuan ⌂ China 29°20N 110°30E 117 C8
Wulong China 29°22N 107°43E 116 C6
Wulong ⌂ China 31°8N 103°5E 116 B4
Wulumuchi = Ürümqi China 43°45N 87°45E 109 D11
Wum Cameroon 6°24N 10°2E 139 D7
Wumeng Shan China 26°48N 104°0E 116 D5
Wuming China 23°12N 108°18E 116 F7
Wundanyi Kenya 3°24S 38°22E 142 C4
Wuning China 29°17N 115°5E 117 C10
Wunna → India 20°18N 78°48E 126 D4
Wunnummin L. Canada 52°55N 89°10W 164 B2
Wunsiedel Germany 50°2N 12°0E 77 E8
Wunstorf Germany 52°25N 9°26E 76 C5
Wuntho Burma 23°55N 95°45E 123 H19
Wupatki ⌂ U.S.A. 35°35N 111°20W 169 J8
Wuping China 25°5N 116°5E 117 E11
Wuppertal Germany 51°16N 7°12E 76 D3
Wuppertal S. Africa 32°13S 19°12E 144 D2
Wuqia China 39°40N 75°7E 109 E9
Wuqing China 39°23N 117°4E 115 E9
Wurralibi ✪ Australia 15°43S 137°1E 150 B2
Wurtsboro U.S.A. 41°35N 74°29W 175 E10
Würzburg Germany 49°46N 9°55E 77 F5
Wurzen Germany 51°22N 12°44E 76 D8
Wushan China 34°43N 104°53E 114 G3
Wushi China 41°9N 79°13E 109 D9
Wushishi Nigeria 9°46N 6°7E 139 D6
Wutach → Germany 47°37N 8°15E 77 H4
Wutai China 38°40N 113°12E 114 E7
Wutai Shan China 39°3N 113°32E 114 E7
Wuting = Huimin China 37°27N 117°28E 115 F9
Wutong China 25°24N 110°4E 117 E8
Wutonghaolai China 42°50N 120°5E 115 C11
Wutongqiao China 29°22N 103°50E 116 C4
Wuwei Anhui, China 31°18N 117°54E 117 B11
Wuwei Gansu, China 37°57N 102°34E 110 D9
Wuxi Jiangsu, China 31°33N 120°18E 117 B13
Wuxi Sichuan, China 31°23N 109°35E 116 B7
Wuxiang China 36°49N 112°50E 114 F7
Wuxuan China 23°34N 109°38E 116 F7
Wuxue China 29°52N 115°30E 117 C10
Wuyang China 33°25N 113°35E 114 H7
Wuyi Hebei, China 37°46N 115°56E 114 F8
Wuyi Zhejiang, China 28°52N 119°50E 117 C12
Wuyi Shan China 27°0N 117°0E 117 D11
Wuyishan China 27°45N 118°0E 117 D12
Wuyishan △ China 27°55N 117°54E 117 D11
Wuyo Nigeria 10°23N 11°50E 139 C7
Wuyuan Jiangxi, China 29°15N 117°50E 117 C11
Wuyuan Nei Monggol Zizhiqu, China 41°2N 108°20E 114 D5
Wuzhai China 38°54N 111°48E 114 E6
Wuzhi Shan China 18°45N 109°45E 117 a
Wuzhishan = Tongshi China 18°30N 109°20E 117 a
Wuzhong China 38°2N 106°12E 114 E4
Wuzhou China 23°30N 111°18E 117 F8
Wyaaba Cr. → Australia 16°27S 141°35E 150 B3
Wyalkatchem Australia 31°8S 117°22E 149 F2
Wyalusing U.S.A. 41°40N 76°16W 175 E8
Wyandotte U.S.A. 42°12N 83°9W 173 D12
Wyandra Australia 27°12S 145°56E 151 D4
Wyangala, L. Australia 33°54S 149°0E 153 B8
Wyara, L. Australia 28°42S 144°14E 151 D3
Wycheproof Australia 36°5S 143°17E 152 D5
Wycliffe Well Australia 20°48S 134°14E 150 C1
Wye → U.K. 51°38N 2°40W 67 F5
Wyemandoo Australia 28°28S 118°29E 149 E2
Wyk Germany 54°41N 8°33E 76 A4
Wymondham U.K. 52°35N 1°7E 67 E9
Wymore U.S.A. 40°7N 96°40W 172 E5
Wyndham Australia 15°33S 128°3E 148 C4
Wyndham N.Z. 46°20S 168°51E 155 G3
Wynne U.S.A. 35°14N 90°47W 177 D9
Wynyard Australia 41°5S 145°44E 151 G4
Wynyard Canada 51°45N 104°10W 163 C8
Wyola L. Australia 29°8S 130°17E 149 E5
Wyoming Canada 42°57N 82°7W 174 D2
Wyoming □ U.S.A. 43°0N 107°30W 168 E10
Wyomissing U.S.A. 40°20N 75°59W 175 F9
Wyong Australia 33°14S 151°24E 153 B9
Wyperfeld △ Australia 35°35S 141°42E 152 C4
Wyrzysk Poland 53°10N 17°17E 83 E4
Wyśmierzyce Poland 51°37N 20°50E 83 G7
Wysoka Poland 53°13N 17°2E 83 E4
Wysokie Poland 50°55N 22°40E 83 H9
Wysokie Mazowieckie Poland 52°55N 22°30E 83 F9
Wyszków Poland 52°36N 21°25E 83 F8
Wyszogród Poland 52°23N 20°9E 83 F7
Wytheville U.S.A. 36°57N 81°5W 173 G13
Wyżyna Małopolska Poland 50°45N 20°0E 83 H7

X

Xaafuun Somalia 10°25N 51°16E 131 E5
Xaafuun, Ras Somalia 10°27N 51°24E 131 E5
Xàbia = Jávea Spain 38°48N 0°10E 91 G5
Xaçmaz Azerbaijan 41°31N 48°42E 87 K9
Xai-Xai Mozam. 25°6S 33°31E 145 C5
Xaidulla China 36°28N 77°59E 109 E9
Xaignabouri = Sayaboury Laos 19°15N 101°45E 120 C3
Xainza China 30°58N 88°35E 110 E6
Xalapa Mexico 19°32N 96°55W 181 D5
Xallas → Spain 42°54N 9°8W 88 C1
Xangongo Angola 16°45S 15°5E 144 A2
Xankändi Azerbaijan 39°52N 46°49E 105 C12
Xanlar = Goygöl Azerbaijan 40°37N 46°12E 87 K8
Xanten Germany 51°39N 6°26E 76 D2
Xanthi Greece 41°10N 24°58E 97 E8
Xanthos Turkey 36°19N 29°18E 99 E11
Xanxerê Brazil 26°53S 52°23W 191 B5
Xapuri Brazil 10°35S 68°35W 188 C4
Xar Moron He → China 43°25N 120°35E 115 C11
Xarrë Albania 39°44N 20°3E 96 G4
Xátiva Spain 38°59N 0°32W 91 G4
Xau, L. Botswana 21°15S 24°44E 144 B3
Xavantina Brazil 21°15S 52°48W 191 A5
Xayar China 41°13N 82°48E 109 D10
Xebert China 44°2N 122°0E 115 B12
Xenia U.S.A. 39°41N 83°56W 173 F12
Xeraco Spain 39°2N 0°13W 91 F4
Xeropotamos → Cyprus 34°42N 32°33E 101 E11
Xertigny France 48°3N 6°24E 71 D13
Xhora S. Africa 31°55S 28°38E 145 D4
Xhumo Botswana 21°7S 24°35E 144 B3
Xi Jiang → China 22°5N 113°20E 117 F9
Xi Ujimqin Qi China 44°32N 117°40E 115 B9
Xi Xian Henan, China 32°20N 114°43E 117 A10
Xi Xian Shanxi, China 36°41N 110°58E 114 F6
Xia Xian China 35°8N 111°12E 114 G6
Xiachengzi China 44°40N 130°18E 115 B16
Xiachuan Dao China 21°40N 112°40E 117 G9
Xiaguan China 25°32N 100°16E 110 F9
Xiajiang China 27°30N 115°10E 117 D10
Xiajin China 36°56N 116°0E 114 F9
Xiamen China 24°25N 118°4E 117 E12
Xi'an China 34°15N 109°0E 114 G5
Xian Xian China 38°12N 116°6E 114 E9
Xianfeng China 29°40N 109°8E 116 C7
Xiang Jiang → China 28°55N 112°50E 117 C9
Xiang Khouang Laos 19°17N 103°25E 120 C4
Xiangcheng Henan, China 33°50N 113°27E 114 H7
Xiangcheng Sichuan, China 28°53N 99°47E 116 C2
Xiangdu China 23°13N 106°58E 116 F6
Xiangfan China 32°2N 112°8E 117 A9
Xianggang = Hong Kong □ China 22°11N 114°14E 111 a
Xianghuang Qi China 42°2N 113°50E 114 C7
Xiangjiaba Dam China 28°37N 104°17E 116 C5
Xiangning China 35°58N 110°50E 114 G6
Xiangquan China 36°30N 113°1E 114 F7
Xiangquan He = Sutlej → Pakistan 29°23N 71°3E 124 E4
Xiangshan China 29°29N 121°51E 117 C13
Xiangshui China 34°12N 119°33E 115 G10
Xiangtan China 27°51N 112°54E 117 D9
Xiangxiang China 27°43N 112°28E 117 D9
Xiangyin China 28°38N 112°54E 117 C9
Xiangyun China 25°34N 100°35E 116 E3
Xiangzhou China 23°58N 109°40E 116 F7
Xianju China 28°51N 120°44E 117 C13
Xianning China 29°51N 114°16E 117 C10
Xianshui He → China 30°10N 100°59E 116 B3
Xiantao China 30°25N 113°25E 117 B9
Xianyang China 34°20N 108°40E 114 G5
Xianyou China 25°22N 118°38E 117 E12
Xiao Hinggan Ling China 49°0N 127°0E 111 B14
Xiao Xian China 34°15N 116°55E 114 G9
Xiaofeng China 30°35N 119°32E 117 B12
Xiaogan China 30°52N 113°55E 117 B9
Xiaojin China 30°59N 102°21E 116 B4
Xiaolan China 22°38N 113°13E 117 F9
Xiaoshan China 30°12N 120°18E 117 B13
Xiaowan Dam China 24°42N 100°5E 116 E3
Xiaowutai Shan China 39°51N 114°59E 114 E8
Xiaoyi China 37°8N 111°48E 114 F6
Xiapu China 26°54N 119°59E 117 D12
Xiashan = Zhanjiang China 21°15N 110°20E 117 G8
Xiawa China 42°35N 120°38E 115 C11
Xiayi China 34°15N 116°10E 114 G9
Xichang China 27°51N 102°19E 116 D4
Xichong China 30°57N 105°54E 116 B5
Xichou China 23°25N 104°42E 116 F5
Xichuan China 33°0N 111°30E 117 A8
Xide China 28°8N 102°19E 116 C4
Xiemahe China 31°38N 111°12E 117 B8
Xifei He → China 32°45N 116°40E 117 A11
Xifeng Gansu, China 35°40N 107°40E 114 G4
Xifeng Guizhou, China 27°7N 106°42E 116 D6
Xifeng Liaoning, China 42°42N 124°45E 115 C13
Xifengzhen = Xifeng China 35°40N 107°40E 114 G4
Xigazê China 29°5N 88°45E 110 F6
Xihe China 34°2N 105°20E 114 G3
Xihua China 33°45N 114°30E 114 H8
Xilagani Greece 40°58N 25°28E 97 F9
Xili Shuiku China 22°36N 113°57E 111 a
Xiliao He → China 43°32N 123°35E 115 C12
Xilin China 24°30N 105°6E 116 E5
Xiling Gorge = Xiling Xia China 30°54N 110°48E 117 B8
Xiling Xia China 30°54N 110°48E 117 B8
Xilinhot China 43°52N 116°2E 114 C9
Xilokastro Greece 38°5N 22°38E 98 C4
Xiluodu Dam China 28°12N 103°34E 116 C4
Ximana Mozam. 19°24S 33°58E 143 F3
Xime Guinea-Biss. 11°59N 14°57W 138 C2
Ximeng China 22°50N 99°27E 116 F2
Ximiao China 40°59N 100°12E 110 C9
Xin Jiang → China 28°45N 116°35E 117 C11
Xin Xian = Xinzhou China 38°22N 112°46E 114 E7
Xin'anjiang Shuiku China 29°33N 118°56E 117 C12
Xinavane Mozam. 25°2S 32°47E 145 C5
Xinbin China 41°40N 125°2E 115 D13
Xincai China 32°43N 114°58E 117 A10
Xinchang China 29°28N 120°52E 117 C13
Xincheng Guangxi Zhuangzu, China 24°5N 108°39E 116 E7
Xincheng Jiangxi, China 26°48N 114°6E 117 D10
Xinfeng Guangdong, China 24°5N 114°16E 117 E10
Xinfeng Jiangxi, China 27°7N 116°11E 117 D11
Xinfeng Jiangxi, China 25°27N 114°58E 117 E10
Xinfengjiang Shuiku China 23°52N 114°30E 117 F10
Xing Xian China 38°27N 111°7E 114 E6
Xing'an Guangxi Zhuangzu, China 25°38N 110°40E 117 E8
Xingan Jiangxi, China 27°46N 115°20E 117 D10
Xingcheng China 40°40N 120°45E 115 D11
Xingguo China 26°21N 115°21E 117 D10
Xinghe China 40°55N 113°55E 114 D7
Xinghua China 32°58N 119°48E 117 A12
Xinghua Wan China 25°15N 119°20E 117 E12
Xinglong China 40°25N 117°30E 115 D9
Xingning China 24°3N 115°42E 117 E10
Xingping China 34°20N 108°28E 114 G5
Xingren China 25°24N 105°11E 116 E5
Xingshan China 31°15N 110°45E 117 B8
Xingtai China 37°3N 114°32E 114 F8
Xingu → Brazil 1°30S 51°53W 187 D8
Xingwen China 28°22N 104°50E 116 C5
Xingxingxia China 41°47N 95°0E 110 C7
Xingyang China 34°45N 112°52E 114 G7
Xingyi China 25°3N 104°59E 116 E5
Xinhe Hebei, China 37°30N 115°15E 114 F8
Xinhe Xinjiang Uygur, China 41°33N 82°37E 109 D10
Xinhua China 27°42N 111°13E 117 D8
Xinhuang China 27°21N 109°12E 116 D7
Xinhui China 22°25N 113°0E 117 F9
Xining China 36°34N 101°40E 110 D9
Xinji China 37°55N 115°13E 114 F8
Xinjian China 28°37N 115°46E 117 C10
Xinjiang China 35°34N 111°11E 114 G6
Xinjiang Uygur Zizhiqu □ China 42°0N 86°0E 109 D11
Xinjin = Pulandian China 39°25N 121°58E 115 E11
Xinjin China 30°24N 103°47E 116 B4
Xinkai He → China 43°32N 123°35E 115 C12
Xinken China 22°39N 113°36E 111 a
Xinle China 38°25N 114°40E 114 E8
Xinlitun China 42°0N 122°8E 115 D12
Xinlong China 30°57N 100°12E 116 B3
Xinmi China 34°30N 113°25E 114 G7
Xinmin China 41°59N 122°50E 115 D12
Xinning China 26°28N 110°50E 117 D8
Xinping China 24°5N 101°59E 116 E3
Xinshao China 27°21N 111°26E 117 D8
Xintai China 35°55N 117°45E 115
Xintian China 25°55N 112°13E 117
Xinwan China 22°47N 113°40E 11
Xinxiang China 35°18N 113°50E 114
Xinxing China 22°35N 112°15E 117
Xinyang China 32°6N 114°3E 117
Xinye China 32°30N 112°21E 117
Xinyi Guangdong, China 22°25N 111°0E 117
Xinyi Nei Monggol Zizhiqu, China 34°23N 118°21E 115
Xinyu China 27°49N 114°58E 117
Xinzhan China 43°50N 127°18E 115
Xinzheng China 34°20N 113°45E 114
Xinzhou Hainan, China 19°43N 109°17E 11
Xinzhou Hubei, China 30°50N 114°48E 117
Xinzhou Shanxi, China 38°22N 112°46E 114
Xinzo de Limia Spain 42°3N 7°47W 88
Xiongyuecheng China 40°12N 122°5E 115
Xiping Henan, China 33°22N 114°5E 114
Xiping Henan, China 33°25N 111°8E 114
Xiping Zhejiang, China 28°16N 119°29E 117
Xique-Xique Brazil 10°50S 42°40W 189
Xiruá → Brazil 6°3S 67°50W 188
Xisha Qundao = Paracel Is. S. China Sea 15°50N 112°0E 118
Xishuangbanna China 22°5N 101°1E 116
Xishui Guizhou, China 28°19N 106°9E 116
Xishui Hubei, China 30°30N 115°15E 117
Xitole Guinea-Biss. 11°43N 14°50W 138
Xiu Shui → China 29°13N 116°0E 117
Xiuning China 29°45N 118°10E 117
Xiuren China 24°27N 110°12E 117
Xiushan China 28°25N 108°57E 116
Xiushui China 29°2N 114°33E 117
Xiuwen China 26°49N 106°32E 116
Xiuyan China 40°18N 123°11E 115
Xiva Uzbekistan 41°30N 60°18E 108
Xixabangma Feng China 28°20N 85°40E 125
Xixia China 33°25N 111°29E 114
Xixiang Guangdong, China 22°34N 113°52E 11
Xixiang Shaanxi, China 33°0N 107°44E 114
Xixón = Gijón Spain 43°32N 5°42W 88
Xiyang China 37°38N 113°38E 114
Xizang Zizhiqu □ China 32°0N 88°0E 11
Xlendi Malta 36°1N 14°12E 101
Xochob Mexico 19°21N 89°48W 181
Xo'jayli Uzbekistan 42°29N 59°31E 108
Xorazm □ Uzbekistan 43°0N 60°0E 108
Xu Jiang → China 28°0N 116°25E 117
Xuan Loc Vietnam 10°56N 107°14E 121
Xuan'en China 30°0N 109°30E 116
Xuanhan China 31°18N 107°38E 116
Xuanhua China 40°40N 115°2E 114
Xuanwei China 26°15N 103°59E 116
Xuanzhou China 30°56N 118°43E 117
Xuchang China 34°2N 113°48E 114
Xudat Azerbaijan 41°38N 48°41E 87
Xuefeng Shan China 27°5N 110°35E 117
Xuejiaping China 31°39N 110°16E 117
Xun Jiang → China 23°35N 111°30E 117
Xun Xian China 35°42N 114°33E 114
Xundian China 25°36N 103°15E 116
Xunwu China 24°54N 115°37E 117
Xunyang China 32°48N 109°22E 114
Xunyi China 35°8N 108°20E 114
Xupu China 27°53N 110°32E 117
Xúquer → Spain 39°5N 0°10W 91
Xushui China 39°2N 115°40E 114
Xuwen China 20°20N 110°10E 117
Xuyi China 32°55N 118°32E 117
Xuyong China 28°10N 105°22E 116
Xuzhou China 34°18N 117°10E 115
Xylophagou Cyprus 34°54N 33°51E 101

Y

Y Drenewydd = Newtown U.K. 52°31N 3°19W 67
Y Fenni = Abergavenny U.K. 51°49N 3°1W 67
Y Gelli Gandryll = Hay-on-Wye U.K. 52°5N 3°8W 67
Y Trallwng = Welshpool U.K. 52°39N 3°8W 67
Ya Xian = Sanya China 18°14N 109°29E 11
Yaamba Australia 23°8S 150°22E 150
Ya'an China 29°58N 103°5E 116
Yaapeet Australia 35°45S 142°3E 152
Yabassi Cameroon 4°30N 9°57E 139
Yabayo Ivory C. 5°56N 6°36W 138
Yablanitsa Bulgaria 43°2N 24°5E 97
Yablonovyy Khrebet Russia 53°0N 114°0E 107
Yablonovyy Ra. = Yablonovyy Khrebet Russia 53°0N 114°0E 107
Yabluniv Ukraine 48°24N 24°57E 81
Yablunytsya Ukraine 48°19N 24°29E 81
Yabrai Shan China 39°40N 103°0E 114
Yabrūd Syria 33°58N 36°39E 130
Yabucoa Puerto Rico 18°3N 65°53W 18
Yacambú △ Venezuela 9°42N 69°27W 183
Yacheng China 18°22N 109°6E 11
Yackandandah Australia 36°18S 146°52E 153
Yacuiba Bolivia 22°0S 63°43W 190
Yacuma → Bolivia 13°38S 65°23W 186
Yacurí △ Ecuador 4°42S 79°20W 188
Yadgir India 16°45N 77°5E 126
Yadkin → U.S.A. 35°23N 80°4W 177
Yadrin Russia 55°57N 46°12E 86
Yadua Fiji 16°49S 178°18E 15
Yaeyama-Rettō Japan 24°30N 123°40E 113
Yagaba Ghana 10°14N 1°20W 139
Yagasa Cluster Fiji 18°57S 178°28W 15
Yağcılar Turkey 39°25N 28°23E 99
Yagodnoye Russia 62°33N 149°40E 107
Yahila Dem. Rep. of the Congo 0°13N 24°28E 142
Yahk Canada 49°6N 116°10W 162
Yahotyn Ukraine 50°17N 31°46E 85
Yahuma Dem. Rep. of the Congo 1°0N 23°10E 140
Yahyalı Turkey 38°5N 35°2E 104
Yaita Japan 36°48N 139°56E 11
Yaiza Canary Is. 28°57N 13°46W 10
Yajiang China 30°2N 100°57E 116
Yajua Nigeria 11°27N 12°49E 139
Yakeshi China 49°17N 120°44E 111

kima U.S.A. 46°36N 120°31W 168 C3
kima ➝ U.S.A. 46°15N 119°14W 168 C4
kishiri-Jima Japan 44°26N 141°25E 112 B10
ko Burkina Faso 12°59N 2°15W 138 C4
kobi I. U.S.A. 58°0N 136°30W 162 B1
koruda Bulgaria 42°1N 23°39E 96 D7
kovlevka Russia 44°26N 133°28E 112 B6
ku-Shima Japan 30°20N 130°30E 113 J5
kumo Japan 42°15N 140°16E 112 C10
kutat U.S.A. 59°33N 139°44W 160 F4
kutat B. U.S.A. 59°45N 140°45W 166 D11
kutia = Sakha □
Russia 66°0N 130°0E 107 C14
kutsk Russia 62°5N 129°50E 107 C13
kymivka Ukraine 46°44N 35°0E 85 J8
la Thailand 6°33N 101°18E 121 J3
la △ Sri Lanka 6°20N 81°30E 127 L5
lata Australia 31°59S 132°26E 149 F5
lata ✪ Australia 31°35S 132°7E 149 F5
lboroo Australia 20°50S 148°40E 150 b
le U.S.A. 43°8N 82°48W 174 C2
lgorup △ Australia 32°39S 115°38E 149 F2
linga C.A.R. 6°33N 23°10E 140 C4
lkabul, Pta. Mexico 21°32N 88°37W 181 C7
lleroi Australia 24°3S 145°42E 150 C4
lobusha ➝ U.S.A. 33°33N 90°10W 177 E9
long China 18°12N 109°42E 117 a
long Jiang ➝
China 26°40N 101°55E 116 D3
lova Turkey 40°41N 29°15E 97 F13
lpirakinu ✪
Australia 22°24S 132°15E 148 D5
puh, Ozero Ukraine 45°30N 28°41E 81 E13
lta Ukraine 44°30N 34°10E 85 K8
lu Jiang ➝ China 39°55N 124°19E 115 E13
lvaç Turkey 38°17N 31°10E 104 C4
m Australia 9°54S 142°46E 150 a
m Ha Melaḥ = Dead Sea
Asia 31°30N 35°30E 130 D4
m Kinneret Israel 32°45N 35°35E 130 C4
mada = Kama
apan 33°33N 130°49E 113 H5
magata Japan 38°15N 140°15E 112 E10
magata □ Japan 38°30N 140°0E 112 E10
maguchi Japan 34°10N 131°32E 113 G5
maguchi □ Japan 34°20N 131°40E 113 G5
mal, Poluostrov Russia 71°0N 70°0E 106 B8
mal Pen. = Yamal, Poluostrov
Russia 71°0N 70°0E 106 B8
manashi □ Japan 35°40N 138°40E 113 G9
mantau, Gora Russia 54°15N 58°6E 108 B5
mato Ridge
Sea of Japan 39°20N 135°0E 112 E7
mba Australia 29°26S 153°23E 151 D5
mbarran Ra.
Australia 15°10S 130°25E 148 C5
mbéring Guinea 11°50N 12°18W 138 C2
mbio South Sudan 4°35N 28°16E 135 H11
mbol Bulgaria 42°30N 26°30E 97 D10
mbol □ Bulgaria 42°30N 26°30E 97 D10
mburg Russia 68°21N 77°8E 106 C8
mdena Indonesia 7°45S 131°20E 119 F8
me Japan 33°13N 130°35E 113 H5
methin Burma 20°29N 96°18E 123 J20
mma Yamma, L.
Australia 26°16S 141°20E 151 D3
moussoukro Ivory C. 6°49N 5°17W 138 D3
mpa ➝ U.S.A. 40°32N 108°59W 168 F9
mpi Sd. Australia 16°8S 123°38E 148 C3
mpil Moldova 48°15N 28°15E 75 D15
mpol = Yampil
Moldova 48°15N 28°15E 75 D15
mrat Nigeria 10°11N 9°55E 139 C6
mrukchal = Botev
Bulgaria 42°44N 24°52E 97 D8
mu, Laem Thailand 7°59N 98°26E 121 a
muna ➝ India 25°30N 81°53E 125 G9
munanagar India 30°7N 77°17E 124 D7
mzho Yumco China 28°48N 90°35E 110 F7
n Nigeria 10°5N 12°11E 139 C7
n Oya ➝ Sri Lanka 9°0N 81°10E 127 K5
na ➝ Russia 71°30N 136°0E 107 B14
nagawa Japan 33°10N 130°24E 113 H5
nai Japan 33°58N 132°7E 113 H6
n'an China 36°35N 109°26E 114 F5
nbian China 26°47N 101°31E 116 D3
nbu 'al Baḥr Si. Arabia 24°5N 38°5E 128 E3
nchang China 36°43N 110°1E 114 F6
ncheng Henan, China 33°35N 114°0E 114 H8
ncheng Jiangsu,
China 33°23N 120°8E 115 H11
nchep Australia 31°33S 115°37E 149 F2
nchi China 37°48N 107°20E 114 F4
nchuan China 36°51N 110°10E 114 F6
nco Australia 34°38S 146°27E 153 C7
nco Cr. ➝ Australia 35°14S 145°35E 153 C6
ndang Shan China 28°0N 120°25E 117 D13
ndeyarra ✪
Australia 21°17S 118°24E 148 D2
ndicoogina
Australia 22°49S 119°12E 148 D2
ndoon Burma 17°0N 95°40E 123 L19
nfeng China 25°52N 101°8E 116 E3
nfolila Mali 11°11N 8°9W 138 C3
ng Xian China 33°15N 107°30E 116 A6
ng-yang S. Korea 38°4N 128°38E 115 E15
ng-Yang Senegal 15°30N 15°20W 138 B1
ngambi
Dem. Rep. of the Congo 0°47N 24°24E 142 B1
ngbi China 25°41N 99°58E 116 E2
ngcheng China 35°28N 112°22E 114 G7
ngch'ü = Taiyuan
China 37°52N 112°33E 114 F7
ngchun China 22°11N 111°48E 117 F8
nggao China 40°21N 113°55E 114 D7
nggu China 36°8N 115°43E 114 F8
ngiyul Uzbekistan 41°0N 69°3E 109 D7
ngjiang China 21°50N 111°59E 117 G8
ngliuqing China 39°2N 117°5E 115 E9
ngon = Rangoon
Burma 16°45N 96°20E 123 L20
ngping China 31°12N 111°25E 117 B8
ngpingguan China 32°58N 106°5E 116 A6
ngquan China 37°58N 113°31E 114 F7
ngshan Guangdong,
China 24°30N 112°40E 117 E9
ngshan Shanghai,
China 30°37N 122°4E 117 B14
ngshuo China 24°48N 110°29E 117 E8
ngtse = Chang Jiang ➝
China 31°48N 121°10E 117 B13
Yangtze Kiang = Chang Jiang ➝
China 31°48N 121°10E 117 B13
Yangxin China 29°50N 115°12E 117 C10
Yangyuan China 40°1N 114°10E 114 D8
Yangzhong China 32°22N 119°22E 117 A12
Yangzhou China 32°21N 119°26E 117 A12
Yanhe China 28°31N 108°29E 116 C7
Yanji China 42°59N 129°30E 115 C15
Yanjin China 28°5N 104°18E 116 C5
Yanjing China 29°7N 98°33E 116 C2
Yankari △ Nigeria 9°50N 10°28E 139 D7
Yankton U.S.A. 42°53N 97°23W 172 D5
Yankunytjatjara-Antakirinja ✪
Australia 27°20S 134°30E 151 A1
Yanonge
Dem. Rep. of the Congo 0°35N 24°38E 142 B1
Yanqi China 42°5N 86°35E 109 D11
Yanqing China 40°30N 115°58E 114 D8
Yanshan Hebei, China 38°4N 117°22E 115 E9
Yanshan Jiangxi,
China 28°15N 117°41E 117 C11
Yanshan Yunnan,
China 23°35N 104°20E 116 F5
Yanshou China 45°28N 128°22E 115 B15
Yantabulla Australia 29°21S 145°0E 151 D4
Yantai China 37°34N 121°22E 115 F11
Yantarnyy Russia 54°52N 19°57E 82 D6
Yantian China 22°35N 114°16E 111 a
Yanting China 31°11N 105°24E 116 B5
Yantongshan China 43°17N 126°0E 115 C14
Yantra ➝ Bulgaria 43°40N 25°37E 97 C9
Yanuca Fiji 18°24S 178°0E 154 a
Yanununbeyan △
Australia 35°29S 149°24E 153 C8
Yanwa China 27°35N 98°55E 116 D2
Yanyuan China 27°25N 101°30E 116 D3
Yanzhou China 35°35N 116°49E 114 G9
Yao Xian China 34°55N 108°59E 114 G5
Yao Yai, Ko Thailand 8°7N 98°37E 121 a
Yao'an China 25°31N 101°18E 116 E3
Yaoundé Cameroon 3°50N 11°35E 139 E7
Yaowan China 34°15N 118°3E 115 G10
Yap Pac. Oc. 9°30N 138°10E 156 G5
Yapei Ghana 9°10N 1°10W 139 D4
Yapen Indonesia 1°50S 136°0E 119 E9
Yapen, Selat Indonesia 1°20S 136°10E 119 E9
Yapero Indonesia 4°59S 137°11E 119 E9
Yappar ➝ Australia 18°22S 141°16E 150 B3
Yapuparra ✪ Australia 27°15S 126°20E 149 E4
Yaqaga Fiji 16°35S 178°36E 154 a
Yaqui ➝ Mexico 27°37N 110°39W 180 B2
Yar-Sale Russia 66°50N 70°50E 106 C8
Yaraka Australia 24°53S 144°3E 150 C3
Yaransk Russia 57°22N 47°49E 86 B8
Yarbasan Turkey 38°59N 28°49E 99 C10
Yardımcı Burnu Turkey 36°13N 30°25E 99 E12
Yare ➝ U.K. 52°35N 1°38E 67 E9
Yaremcha Ukraine 48°27N 24°33E 81 B9
Yarensk Russia 62°11N 49°15E 106 C5
Yarfa Si. Arabia 24°37N 38°35E 137 C4
Yarí ➝ Colombia 0°20S 72°20W 186 D4
Yarkand = Shache
China 38°20N 77°10E 109 E9
Yarkant He ➝ China 40°26N 80°59E 109 D10
Yarker Canada 44°23N 76°46W 175 B8
Yarkhun ➝ Pakistan 36°17N 72°30E 125 A5
Yarlung Ziangbo Jiang =
Brahmaputra ➝
Asia 23°40N 90°35E 125 H13
Yarmouth Canada 43°50N 66°7W 165 D6
Yarmūk ➝ Syria 32°42N 35°40E 130 C4
Yaroslavl Russia 57°35N 39°55E 84 D10
Yaroslavl □ Russia 59°20N 38°50E 84 C10
Yarqa, W. ➝ Egypt 30°0N 33°49E 130 F2
Yarra Ranges △
Australia 37°40S 146°3E 153 D7
Yarra Yarra Lakes
Australia 29°40S 115°45E 149 E2
Yarram Australia 38°29S 146°39E 153 E7
Yarraman Australia 26°50S 152°0E 151 D5
Yarras Australia 31°25S 152°20E 153 A10
Yarrawonga Australia 36°0S 146°0E 153 D7
Yarrie Australia 20°40S 120°12E 148 D3
Yartsevo Sib., Russia 60°20N 90°0E 107 C10
Yartsevo Smolensk, Russia 55°6N 32°43E 84 E7
Yarumal Colombia 6°58N 75°24W 186 B3
Yasawa Fiji 16°47S 177°31E 154 a
Yasawa Group Fiji 17°0S 177°23E 154 a
Yaselda Belarus 52°7N 26°28E 75 B14
Yasen Ukraine 48°45N 24°10E 81 B9
Yashi Nigeria 12°23N 7°54E 139 C6
Yashikera Nigeria 9°44N 3°29E 139 D5
Yashkul Russia 46°11N 45°21E 87 G7
Yasin Pakistan 36°24N 73°23E 125 A5
Yasinovataya Ukraine 48°7N 37°57E 85 H9
Yasinski, L. Canada 53°16N 77°35W 164 B4
Yasinya Ukraine 48°16N 24°21E 81 B9
Yasnyy Russia 51°1N 59°58E 108 B5
Yasothon Thailand 15°50N 104°10E 120 E5
Yass Australia 34°49S 148°54E 153 C8
Yāsūj Iran 30°31N 51°31E 129 D6
Yatağan Turkey 37°20N 28°10E 99 D10
Yatakala Niger 14°50N 0°22E 139 C5
Yates Center U.S.A. 37°53N 95°44W 172 G6
Yates Pt. N.Z. 44°29S 167°49E 155 E2
Yathkyed L. Canada 62°40N 98°0W 163 A9
Yathong Australia 32°37S 145°33E 153 B6
Yatsushiro Japan 32°30N 130°40E 113 H5
Yatta Plateau Kenya 2°0S 38°0E 142 C4
Yauca Peru 15°39S 74°35W 188 D3
Yauco Puerto Rico 18°2N 66°51W 183 d
Yauri Peru 14°47S 71°25W 188 C3
Yauya Peru 8°59S 77°17W 188 B2
Yauyos Peru 12°19S 75°50W 188 C2
Yaval India 21°10N 75°42E 126 D2
Yavarí ➝ Peru 4°21S 70°2W 188 A3
Yávaros Mexico 26°42N 109°31W 180 B3
Yavatmal India 20°20N 78°15E 126 D4
Yavero ➝ Peru 12°6S 72°57W 188 C3
Yavne Israel 31°52N 34°45E 130 D3
Yavoriv Ukraine 49°55N 23°20E 75 D12
Yavorov = Yavoriv
Ukraine 49°55N 23°20E 75 D12
Yavuzeli Turkey 37°18N 37°24E 104 D7
Yawatahama Japan 33°27N 132°24E 113 H6
Yawri B. S. Leone 8°22N 13°0W 138 D2
Yaxi China 27°33N 106°41E 116 D6
Yaxian = Sanya China 18°14N 109°29E 117 a
Yayladağı Turkey 35°54N 36°3E 104 E7
Yazd Iran 31°55N 54°27E 129 D7
Yazd □ Iran 32°0N 55°0E 129 D7
Yazd-e Khvāst Iran 31°31N 52°7E 129 D7
Yazıköy Turkey 36°40N 27°20E 99 E9
Yazman Pakistan 29°8N 71°45E 124 E4
Yazoo ➝ U.S.A. 32°22N 90°54W 177 E9
Yazoo City U.S.A. 32°51N 90°25W 177 E9
Ybbs Austria 48°12N 15°4E 78 C8
Ybycuí △ Paraguay 26°5S 56°46W 190 B4
Ybytyruzú △ Paraguay 25°51S 56°11W 191 B4
Ye Burma 15°15N 97°15E 120 E1
Ye Xian China 33°35N 113°25E 114 H7
Yea Australia 37°14S 145°26E 153 D6
Yebyu Burma 14°15N 98°13E 120 E2
Yecheng China 37°54N 77°26E 109 E9
Yecheon S. Korea 36°39N 128°27E 115 F15
Yecla Spain 38°35N 1°5W 91 G3
Yécora Mexico 28°20N 108°58W 180 B3
Yedigöller △ Turkey 40°55N 31°55E 104 B4
Yedintsy = Edineţ
Moldova 48°9N 27°18E 81 B12
Yedseram ➝ Nigeria 12°30N 14°5E 139 C7
Yefremov Russia 53°8N 38°3E 84 F10
Yeghegnadzor
Armenia 39°44N 45°19E 105 C11
Yegorlyk ➝ Russia 46°35N 41°57E 87 G5
Yegorlykskaya Russia 46°35N 40°35E 87 G5
Yegoryevsk Russia 55°27N 38°55E 84 E10
Yegros Paraguay 26°20S 56°25W 190 B4
Yehbuah Indonesia 8°23S 114°45E 119 J17
Yehuda, Midbar Israel 31°35N 35°15E 130 D4
Yei South Sudan 4°9N 30°40E 135 H12
Yeji Ghana 8°13N 0°39W 139 D4
Yejmiadzin = Ejmiatsin
Armenia 40°12N 44°19E 87 K7
Yekaterinburg Russia 56°50N 60°30E 106 D7
Yekateriny, Proliv
Russia 44°30N 146°30E 107 E15
Yelabuga Russia 55°46N 52°2E 86 C11
Yelan Russia 50°55N 43°43E 86 E6
Yelandur India 12°6N 77°0E 127 H3
Yelarbon Australia 28°33S 150°38E 151 D5
Yelatma Russia 55°0N 41°45E 86 C5
Yelcho, L. Chile 43°18S 72°18W 192 B2
Yelets Russia 52°40N 38°30E 85 F10
Yélimané Mali 15°9N 10°34W 138 B2
Yelin = Lingshui China 18°27N 110°0E 117 a
Yelizavetgrad = Kirovohrad
Ukraine 48°35N 32°20E 85 H7
Yelizovo Russia 53°11N 158°23E 107 D16
Yell U.K. 60°35N 1°5W 65 A7
Yell Sd. U.K. 60°33N 1°15W 65 A7
Yellamanchilli = Elamanchili
India 17°33N 82°50E 126 F6
Yellandu India 17°39N 80°23E 126 F5
Yellapur India 14°58N 74°43E 127 G2
Yellareddi India 18°12N 78°2E 126 E4
Yellow = Huang He ➝
China 37°55N 118°50E 115 F10
Yellow ➝ U.S.A. 30°30N 87°0W 179 E3
Yellow Sea China 35°0N 123°0E 115 G12
Yellowhead Pass
Canada 52°53N 118°25W 162 C5
Yellowknife Canada 62°27N 114°29W 162 A6
Yellowknife ➝
Canada 62°31N 114°19W 162 A6
Yellowstone ➝
U.S.A. 47°59N 103°59W 168 C12
Yellowstone △ U.S.A. 44°40N 110°30W 168 D8
Yellowstone L. U.S.A. 44°27N 110°22W 168 D8
Yelnya Russia 54°35N 33°15E 84 E7
Yelsk Belarus 51°50N 29°10E 75 C15
Yelwa Nigeria 10°49N 4°41E 139 C5
Yemanzhelinsk Russia 54°58N 61°18E 108 B6
Yemassee U.S.A. 32°41N 80°51W 178 C9
Yemen ■ Asia 15°0N 44°0E 131 E3
Yemmiganur India 15°44N 77°29E 127 G3
Yen Bai Vietnam 21°42N 104°52E 116 G5
Yenagoa Nigeria 4°58N 6°16E 139 E6
Yenakiyeve Ukraine 48°15N 38°15E 85 H10
Yenakiyevo = Yenakiyeve
Ukraine 48°15N 38°15E 85 H10
Yenangyaung Burma 20°30N 95°0E 123 J19
Yenbo = Yanbu 'al Baḥr
Si. Arabia 24°5N 38°5E 128 E3
Yenda Australia 34°13S 146°14E 153 C7
Yende Millimou Guinea 8°55N 10°10W 138 D2
Yendéré Burkina Faso 10°12N 4°59W 138 C4
Yendi Ghana 9°29N 0°1W 139 D4
Yengisar China 38°56N 76°9E 109 E9
Yengo △ Australia 33°0S 150°55E 153 B9
Yéni Niger 13°30N 3°1E 139 C5
Yenı Erenköy = Yialousa
Cyprus 35°32N 34°10E 101 D13
Yenıbogaziçi = Áyios Seryios
Cyprus 35°12N 33°53E 101 D12
Yenice Ankara, Turkey 39°14N 32°42E 104 C5
Yenice Aydın, Turkey 37°49N 28°35E 99 D10
Yenice Çanakkale, Turkey 39°55N 27°17E 99 B9
Yenice Edirne, Turkey 40°42N 26°9E 97 F10
Yenice ➝ Turkey 37°37N 35°33E 104 D6
Yenifoça Turkey 38°44N 26°51E 99 C8
Yenihisar = Didim
Turkey 37°22N 27°16E 99 D9
Yeniköy Bursa, Turkey 40°31N 29°22E 97 F13
Yeniköy Çanakkale,
Turkey 39°55N 26°10E 99 B8
Yeniköy Kütahya,
Turkey 38°52N 29°17E 99 C11
Yenipazar Turkey 37°49N 28°11E 99 D10
Yenişehir Turkey 40°16N 29°38E 97 F13
Yenisey ➝ Russia 71°50N 82°40E 106 B9
Yeniseysk Russia 58°27N 92°13E 107 D10
Yeniseyskiy Zaliv Russia 72°20N 81°0E 106 B9
Yenne France 45°43N 5°44E 73 C9
Yenotayevka Russia 47°15N 47°0E 87 G8
Yenyuka Russia 57°57N 121°15E 107 D13
Yeo ➝ U.K. 51°2N 2°49W 67 G5
Yeo, L. Australia 28°0S 124°30E 149 E3
Yeo I. Canada 45°24N 81°48W 174 A3
Yeola India 20°2N 74°30E 126 D2
Yeong-wol S. Korea 37°11N 128°28E 115 F15
Yeongcheon S. Korea 35°58N 128°56E 115 G15
Yeongdeok S. Korea 36°24N 129°22E 115 F15
Yeongdong S. Korea 36°10N 127°46E 115 F14
Yeongju S. Korea 36°50N 128°40E 115 F15
Yeosu S. Korea 34°47N 127°45E 115 G14
Yeotmal = Yavatmal
India 20°20N 78°15E 126 D4
Yeovil U.K. 50°57N 2°38W 67 G5
Yepes Spain 39°55N 3°39W 88 F7
Yeppoon Australia 23°5S 150°47E 150 C5
Yerbent Turkmenistan 39°19N 58°36E 129 B8
Yerbogachen Russia 61°16N 108°0E 107 C11
Yerevan Armenia 40°10N 44°31E 87 K7
Yerington U.S.A. 38°59N 119°10W 168 G4
Yerkesik Turkey 37°7N 28°19E 99 D10
Yerköy Turkey 39°38N 34°28E 104 C6
Yerla ➝ India 16°50N 74°30E 126 F2
Yermo U.S.A. 34°54N 116°50W 171 L10
Yerolakkos Cyprus 35°11N 33°15E 101 D12
Yeropol Russia 65°15N 168°40E 107 C17
Yeroskipos Cyprus 34°46N 32°28E 101 E11
Yershov Russia 51°23N 48°27E 86 E9
Yerupajá, Cerro Peru 10°16S 76°55W 188 C2
Yerushalayim = Jerusalem
Israel/West Bank 31°47N 35°10E 130 D4
Yerville France 49°40N 0°53E 70 C7
Yes Tor U.K. 50°41N 4°0W 67 G4
Yesan S. Korea 36°41N 126°51E 115 F14
Yeşilhisar Turkey 38°20N 35°5E 104 C6
Yeşilırmak ➝ Turkey 41°22N 36°37E 104 B7
Yeşilkent Turkey 36°57N 36°12E 104 D7
Yeşilköy Turkey 40°57N 28°49E 97 F12
Yeşilova Turkey 37°31N 29°46E 99 D11
Yeşilyurt Manisa,
Turkey 38°22N 28°40E 99 C10
Yeşilyurt Muğla, Turkey 37°10N 28°20E 99 D10
Yesnogorsk Russia 54°32N 37°38E 84 E9
Yeso U.S.A. 34°26N 104°37W 169 J11
Yessentuki Russia 44°5N 42°53E 87 H6
Yessey Russia 68°29N 102°10E 107 C11
Yeste Spain 38°22N 2°19W 91 G2
Yetman Australia 28°56S 150°48E 151 D5
Yeu, Î. d' France 46°42N 2°20W 70 F4
Yevlax Azerbaijan 40°39N 47°7E 87 K8
Yevpatoriya Ukraine 45°15N 33°20E 85 K7
Yeya ➝ Russia 46°40N 38°40E 87 G4
Yeysk Russia 46°40N 38°12E 85 J10
Yezd = Yazd Iran 31°55N 54°27E 129 D7
Yezerishche Belarus 55°50N 30°0E 84 E5
Ygatimi Paraguay 24°5S 55°40W 191 A4
Yhati Paraguay 25°45S 56°35W 190 B4
Yhú Paraguay 25°0S 56°0W 191 B4
Yí ➝ Uruguay 33°7S 57°8W 190 C4
Yi 'Allaq, G. Egypt 30°21N 33°31E 130 E2
Yi He ➝ China 34°10N 118°8E 115 G10
Yi Xian Anhui, China 29°55N 117°57E 117 C11
Yi Xian Hebei, China 39°20N 115°30E 114 E8
Yi Xian Liaoning,
China 41°30N 121°22E 115 D11
Yialiás ➝ Cyprus 35°9N 33°44E 101 D12
Yialousa Cyprus 35°32N 34°10E 101 D13
Yibin China 28°45N 104°32E 116 C5
Yichang China 30°40N 111°20E 117 B8
Yicheng Henan, China 31°41N 112°12E 117 B9
Yicheng Shanxi, China 35°42N 111°40E 114 G6
Yichuan China 36°2N 110°10E 114 F6
Yichun Heilongjiang,
China 47°44N 128°52E 111 B14
Yichun Jiangxi, China 27°48N 114°22E 117 D10
Yidu China 36°43N 118°28E 115 F10
Yidun China 30°22N 99°21E 116 B2
Yifeng China 28°22N 114°45E 117 C10
Yihuang China 27°30N 116°12E 117 D11
Yijun China 35°28N 109°8E 114 G5
Yıldız Dağları Turkey 41°48N 27°36E 97 E11
Yıldızeli Turkey 39°51N 36°36E 104 C7
Yilehuli Shan China 51°20N 124°20E 111 A13
Yiliang Yunnan, China 27°38N 104°2E 116 D5
Yiliang Yunnan, China 24°56N 103°11E 116 E4
Yılmazköy = Skilloura
Cyprus 35°14N 33°10E 101 D12
Yilong China 31°34N 106°23E 116 B6
Yima China 34°44N 111°53E 114 G6
Yimen China 24°40N 102°10E 116 E4
Yimianpo China 45°7N 128°2E 115 B15
Yin Xu China 36°7N 114°18E 114 F8
Yi'nan China 35°31N 118°24E 115 G10
Yinchuan China 38°30N 106°15E 114 E4
Yindarlgooda, L.
Australia 30°40S 121°52E 149 F3
Yindjibarndi ✪
Australia 22°0S 118°35E 148 D2
Ying He ➝ China 32°30N 116°30E 117 A11
Ying Xian China 39°32N 113°10E 114 E7
Yingcheng China 30°56N 113°35E 117 B9
Yingde China 24°10N 113°25E 117 E9
Yingjiang China 24°41N 97°55E 116 E1
Yingjing China 29°41N 102°52E 116 C4
Yingkou China 40°37N 122°18E 115 D12
Yingpanshui China 37°26N 104°18E 114 F3
Yingshan Hubei,
China 30°41N 115°32E 117 B10
Yingshan Sichuan,
China 31°4N 106°35E 116 B6
Yingshang China 32°38N 116°12E 117 A11
Yingtan China 28°12N 117°0E 117 C11
Yingualyalya ✪
Australia 18°49S 129°12E 148 C4
Yining China 43°58N 81°10E 109 D10
Yiningarra ✪
Australia 20°53S 129°27E 148 D4
Yinjiang China 28°1N 108°21E 116 C7
Yinmabin Burma 22°10N 94°55E 123 H19
Yioúra = Giaros Greece 37°32N 24°40E 98 D6
Yipinglang China 25°10N 101°52E 116 E3
Yirga Alem Ethiopia 6°48N 38°22E 131 F2
Yirrkala Australia 12°14S 136°56E 150 A2
Yishan China 24°28N 108°38E 116 E7
Yishui China 35°47N 118°30E 115 G10
Yishun Singapore 1°26N 103°51E 121 d
Yitong China 43°13N 125°20E 115 C13
Yiwu China 29°20N 120°3E 117 C13
Yixing China 31°21N 119°48E 117 B12
Yiyang Henan, China 34°27N 112°10E 114 G7
Yiyang Hunan, China 28°35N 112°18E 117 C9
Yiyang Jiangxi, China 28°22N 117°20E 117 C11
Yizhang China 25°27N 112°57E 117 E9
Yizheng China 32°18N 119°10E 117 A12
Yli-Kitka Finland 66°8N 28°30E 60 C23
Yliki, L. Greece 38°24N 23°15E 98 C5
Ylitornio Finland 66°19N 23°39E 60 C20
Ylivieska Finland 64°4N 24°28E 60 D21
Ymer Ø Greenland 73°9N 24°20W 57 C8
Yngaren Sweden 58°50N 16°35E 63 F10
Yoakum U.S.A. 29°17N 97°9W 176 G6
Yobe □ Nigeria 12°0N 11°30E 139 C7
Yog Pt. Phil. 14°6N 124°12E 119 B6
Yoğuntaş Turkey 41°50N 27°4E 97 E11
Yogyakarta Indonesia 7°49S 110°22E 118 F4
Yogyakarta □
Indonesia 7°48S 110°22E 119 G14
Yoho △ Canada 51°25N 116°30W 162 C5
Yojoa, L. de Honduras 14°53N 88°0W 182 D2
Yok Don △ Vietnam 12°50N 107°40E 120 F6
Yokadouma Cameroon 3°26N 14°55E 140 D2
Yokkaichi Japan 34°55N 136°38E 113 G8
Yoko Cameroon 5°32N 12°20E 139 D7
Yokohama Japan 35°27N 139°28E 113 G9
Yokosuka Japan 35°20N 139°40E 113 G9
Yokote Japan 39°20N 140°30E 112 E10
Yola Nigeria 9°10N 12°29E 139 D7
Yolaina, Cordillera de
Nic. 11°30N 84°0W 182 D3
Yölöten Turkmenistan 37°18N 62°21E 129 B9
Yom ➝ Thailand 15°35N 100°1E 120 E3
Yonago Japan 35°25N 133°19E 113 G6
Yonaguni-Jima Japan 24°27N 123°0E 113 M1
Yŏnan N. Korea 37°55N 126°11E 115 F14
Yonezawa Japan 37°57N 140°4E 112 F10
Yong-in S. Korea 37°14N 127°12E 115 F14
Yong Peng Malaysia 2°0N 103°3E 121 M4
Yong Sata Thailand 7°8N 99°41E 121 J2
Yongamp'o N. Korea 39°56N 124°23E 115 E13
Yong'an China 25°59N 117°25E 117 E11
Yongchang China 38°17N 102°7E 110 D9
Yongcheng China 33°55N 116°20E 114 H9
Yongchuan China 29°17N 105°55E 116 C5
Yongchun China 25°16N 118°20E 117 E12
Yongde China 24°5N 99°25E 116 E2
Yongdeng China 36°38N 103°25E 114 F2
Yongding China 24°43N 116°45E 117 E11
Yongfeng China 27°20N 115°22E 117 D10
Yongfu China 24°59N 109°59E 116 E7
Yonghe China 36°46N 110°38E 114 F6
Yŏnghŭng N. Korea 39°31N 127°18E 115 E14
Yongji Jilin, China 43°33N 126°13E 115 C14
Yongji Shanxi, China 34°52N 110°28E 114 G6
Yongjia China 28°10N 120°45E 117 C13
Yongkang Yunnan, China 24°9N 99°20E 116 E2
Yongkang Zhejiang,
China 28°55N 120°2E 117 C13
Yongnian China 36°47N 114°29E 114 F8
Yongning Guangxi Zhuangzu,
China 22°44N 108°28E 116 F7
Yongning Ningxia Huizu,
China 38°15N 106°14E 114 E4
Yongping China 25°27N 99°38E 116 E2
Yongren China 26°4N 101°40E 116 D3
Yongshan China 28°11N 103°35E 116 C4
Yongsheng China 26°38N 100°46E 116 D3
Yongshun China 29°2N 109°51E 116 C7
Yongtai China 25°49N 118°58E 117 E12
Yongxin = Jinggangshan
China 26°58N 114°15E 117 D10
Yongxing China 26°9N 113°8E 117 D9
Yongxing Dao = Woody I.
S. China Sea 16°50N 112°20E 118 A4
Yongxiu China 29°2N 115°42E 117 C10
Yongzhou China 26°17N 111°37E 117 D8
Yonibana S. Leone 8°30N 12°19W 138 D2
Yonkers U.S.A. 40°56N 73°52W 175 F11
Yonne □ France 47°50N 3°40E 71 E10
Yonne ➝ France 48°23N 2°58E 71 D9
York Australia 31°52S 116°47E 149 F2
York U.K. 53°58N 1°6W 66 D6
York Ala., U.S.A. 32°29N 88°18W 177 E10
York Nebr., U.S.A. 40°52N 97°36W 172 E5
York Pa., U.S.A. 39°58N 76°44W 173 F15
York, C. Australia 10°42S 142°31E 150 A3
York, City of □ U.K. 53°58N 1°6W 66 D6
York, Kap Greenland 75°55N 66°25W 57 B4
York, Vale of U.K. 54°15N 1°25W 66 C6
York Sd. Australia 15°0S 125°5E 148 C4
Yorke Pen. Australia 34°50S 137°40E 152 C2
Yorketown Australia 35°2S 137°33E 152 C2
Yorkshire Dales △ U.K. 54°12N 2°10W 66 C5
Yorkshire Wolds U.K. 54°8N 0°31W 66 C7
Yorkton Canada 51°11N 102°28W 163 C8
Yorkville Calif., U.S.A. 38°52N 123°13W 170 G3
Yorkville Ga., U.S.A. 33°55N 84°58W 178 B5
Yoro Honduras 15°9N 87°7W 182 C2
Yoron-Jima Japan 27°2N 128°26E 113 L4
Yorosso Mali 12°17N 4°55W 138 C4
Yos Sudarso, Pulau = Dolak,
Pulau Indonesia 8°0S 138°30E 119 F9
Yosemite △ U.S.A. 37°45N 119°40W 170 H7
Yosemite Village
U.S.A. 37°45N 119°35W 170 H7
Yoshino-Kumano △
Japan 34°12N 135°55E 113 H8
Yoshkar Ola Russia 56°38N 47°55E 86 B8
Yotvata Israel 29°55N 35°2E 130 F4
You Jiang ➝ China 22°50N 108°6E 116 F6
You Xian China 27°1N 113°17E 117 D9
Youbou Canada 48°53N 124°13W 170 B2
Youghal Ireland 51°56N 7°52W 64 E4
Youghal B. Ireland 51°55N 7°49W 64 E4
Youkounkoun Guinea 12°35N 13°11W 138 C2
Young Australia 34°19S 148°18E 153 C8
Young Canada 51°47N 105°45W 163 C7
Young Uruguay 32°44S 57°36W 190 C4
Young I. Antarctica 66°25S 162°24E 55 C11
Young Ra. N.Z. 44°10S 169°30E 155 E4
Younghusband, L.
Australia 30°50S 136°5E 152 A2
Younghusband Pen.
Australia 36°0S 139°25E 152 D3
Youngstown Canada 51°35N 111°10W 163 C6
Youngstown Fla.,
U.S.A. 30°22N 85°26W 178 E4
Youngstown N.Y.,
U.S.A. 43°15N 79°3W 174 C5
Youngstown Ohio,
U.S.A. 41°6N 80°39W 174 E4
Youngsville U.S.A. 41°51N 79°19W 174 E5
Youngwood U.S.A. 40°14N 79°34W 174 F5
Youssoufia Morocco 32°16N 8°31W 136 B2
Youxi China 26°10N 118°13E 117 D12
Youyang China 28°47N 108°42E 116 C7
Youyu China 40°10N 112°20E 114 D7
Yozgat Turkey 39°51N 34°47E 104 C6
Yozgat □ Turkey 39°30N 35°0E 104 C6
Ypacaraí △ Paraguay 25°18S 57°19W 190 B4
Ypané ➝ Paraguay 23°29S 57°19W 190 A4
Yport France 49°45N 0°15E 70 C7
Ypres = Ieper Belgium 50°51N 2°53E 69 D2
Yr Wyddgrug = Mold U.K. 53°9N 3°8W 66 D4
Yreka U.S.A. 41°44N 122°38W 168 F2
Yrghyz Kazakhstan 48°37N 61°16E 108 C6
Yrghyz ➝ Kazakhstan 48°6N 62°30E 108 C6
Yssingeaux France 45°9N 4°8E 73 C8
Ystad Sweden 55°26N 13°50E 63 J7
Ysyk-Köl = Balykchy
Kyrgyzstan 42°26N 76°12E 109 D9
Ysyk-Köl Kyrgyzstan 42°25N 77°15E 109 D9
Ysyk-Köl □ Kyrgyzstan 42°0N 78°0E 109 D9
Ythan ➝ U.K. 57°19N 1°59W 65 D7
Ytteran Sweden 63°16N 14°7E 62 A8
Ytterhogdal Sweden 62°12N 14°56E 62 B8
Yttermalung Sweden 60°35N 13°51E 62 D7
Ytyk-Kyuyel Russia 62°30N 133°45E 107 C14
Yu Jiang ➝ China 23°22N 110°3E 116 F7
Yü Shan Taiwan 23°25N 120°52E 117 F13
Yu Xian = Yuzhou
China 34°10N 113°28E 114 G7
Yu Xian Hebei, China 39°50N 114°35E 114 E8
Yu Xian Shanxi, China 38°5N 113°20E 114 E7
Yuan Jiang ➝ Hunan,
China 28°55N 111°50E 117 C8
Yuan Jiang ➝ Yunnan,
China 22°20N 103°59E 116 F4
Yuan'an China 31°3N 111°34E 117 B8
Yuanjiang Hunan,
China 28°47N 112°21E 117 C9
Yuanjiang Yunnan,
China 23°32N 102°0E 116 F4
Yüanli Taiwan 24°27N 120°39E 117 E13
Yüanlin Taiwan 23°58N 120°30E 117 F13
Yuanling China 28°29N 110°22E 117 C8
Yuanmou China 25°42N 101°53E 116 E3
Yuanping China 38°42N 112°46E 114 E7
Yuanqu China 35°18N 111°40E 114 G6
Yuanyang Henan, China 35°3N 113°58E 114 G7
Yuanyang Yunnan,
China 23°10N 102°43E 116 F4
Yuba ➝ U.S.A. 39°8N 121°36W 170 F5
Yuba City U.S.A. 39°8N 121°37W 170 F5
Yūbari Japan 43°4N 141°59E 112 C10
Yūbetsu Japan 44°13N 143°50E 112 B11
Yucatán □ Mexico 20°50N 89°0W 181 C7
Yucatán, Canal de
Caribbean 22°0N 86°30W 182 B2
Yucatán, Península de
Mexico 19°30N 89°0W 158 H11
Yucatan Basin
Cent. Amer. 19°0N 86°0W 181 D7
Yucatan Channel = Yucatán,
Canal de Caribbean 22°0N 86°30W 182 B2
Yucca U.S.A. 34°52N 114°9W 171 L12
Yucca Valley U.S.A. 34°8N 116°27W 171 L10
Yucheng China 36°55N 116°32E 114 F9
Yuci = Jinzhong China 37°42N 112°46E 114 F7
Yudu China 25°59N 115°30E 117 E10
Yuechi China 30°34N 106°25E 116 B6
Yuen Long China 22°26N 114°2E 111 a
Yuendumu Australia 22°16S 131°49E 148 D5
Yuendumu ✪
Australia 22°21S 131°40E 148 D5
Yueqing China 28°9N 120°59E 117 C13
Yueqing Wan China 28°5N 121°20E 117 C13
Yuexi Anhui, China 30°50N 116°20E 117 B11
Yuexi Sichuan, China 28°37N 102°26E 116 C4
Yueyang China 29°21N 113°5E 117 C9
Yugan China 28°43N 116°37E 117 C11
Yugorenok Russia 59°47N 137°40E 107 D14
Yugyd Va △ Russia 62°25N 58°45E 106 C6
Yuhuan China 28°9N 121°12E 117 C13
Yuhuan Dao China 28°5N 121°15E 117 C13
Yujiang China 28°10N 116°43E 117 C11
Yukhary Askipara
Azerbaijan 41°4N 45°1E 105 B11
Yukhnov Russia 54°44N 35°15E 84 E8
Yukon U.S.A. 35°31N 97°45W 176 D6
Yukon ➝ U.S.A. 62°32N 163°54W 166 C7
Yukon Flats U.S.A. 66°40N 145°45W 166 B10
Yukon Territory □
Canada 63°0N 135°0W 160 E5
Yüksekova Turkey 37°34N 44°16E 105 D11
Yukta Russia 63°26N 105°42E 107 C11
Yukuhashi Japan 33°44N 130°59E 113 H5
Yulara Australia 25°10S 130°55E 149 E5
Yule ➝ Australia 20°41S 118°17E 148 D2
Yuleba Australia 26°37S 149°24E 151 D4
Yulee U.S.A. 30°38N 81°36W 178 E8
Yuli China 41°19N 86°15E 109 D11
Yuli Nigeria 9°44N 10°12E 139 D7
Yüli Taiwan 23°20N 121°18E 117 F13
Yulin Guangxi Zhuangzu,
China 22°40N 110°8E 117 F8
Yulin Hainan, China 18°10N 109°31E 117 a
Yulin Shaanxi, China 38°20N 109°30E 114 E5
Yulong Xueshan China 27°6N 100°10E 116 D3
Yuma Ariz., U.S.A. 32°43N 114°37W 171 N12
Yuma Colo., U.S.A. 40°8N 102°43W 168 F12
Yuma, B. de Dom. Rep. 18°20N 68°35W 183 C6
Yumali Australia 35°32S 139°45E 152 C3
Yumbe Uganda 3°28N 31°15E 142 B3
Yumbi
Dem. Rep. of the Congo 1°12S 26°15E 142 C2
Yumen China 39°50N 97°30E 110 D8
Yumurtalık Turkey 36°45N 35°48E 104 D6
Yun Gui Gaoyuan China 26°0N 104°0E 116 E5
Yun Ling Shan China 27°0N 99°20E 116 D2
Yun Xian Hubei, China 32°50N 110°46E 117 A8
Yun Xian Yunnan,
China 24°27N 100°8E 116 E3
Yuna Australia 28°20S 115°0E 149 E2
Yunak Turkey 38°49N 31°43E 104 C4
Yunan China 23°12N 111°30E 117 F8
Yuncheng Henan,
China 35°36N 115°57E 114 G8
Yuncheng Shanxi, China 35°2N 111°0E 114 G6
Yunfu China 22°50N 112°5E 117 F9
Yungang Shiku China 40°6N 113°7E 114 D7
Yungas Bolivia 17°0S 66°0W 186 G5
Yungay Chile 37°10S 72°5W 190 D1
Yungay Peru 9°2S 77°45W 188 B2
Yunhe China 28°8N 119°33E 117 C12
Yunkai Dashan China 22°30N 111°0E 117 F8
Yunkanjini ✪ Australia 22°33S 131°6E 148 D5
Yunling Shan China 28°30N 98°50E 110 F8
Yunlong China 25°57N 99°13E 116 E2
Yunmeng China 31°2N 113°43E 117 B9
Yunnan □ China 25°0N 102°0E 116 E4
Yunquera de Henares
Spain 40°47N 3°11W 90 E1
Yunt Dağı Turkey 38°56N 27°13E 99 C9
Yunta Australia 32°34S 139°36E 151 E2
Yunxi China 33°0N 110°22E 117 A8
Yunxiao China 23°59N 117°18E 117 F11
Yunyang Chongqing,
China 31°2N 108°51E 116 B7
Yunyang Henan, China 33°26N 112°42E 117 A9

Yupanqui Basin
  Pac. Oc.   19°0S 101°0W **157** J17
Yuping China   27°13N 108°56E **116** D7
Yuqing China   27°13N 107°53E **116** D6
Yuraygir △ Australia   29°45S 153°15E **151** D5
Yurga Russia   55°42N 84°51E **106** D9
Yurihonjō Japan   39°23N 140°3E **112** E10
Yurimaguas Peru   5°55S 76°7W **188** B2
Yurkiyka Ukraine   48°42N 28°35E **81** B13
Yurubí △ Venezuela   10°26N 68°42W **183** D6
Yurungkax He →
  China   38°5N 80°34E **109** E10
Yuryev-Polskiy Russia   56°30N 39°40E **84** D10
Yuryevets Russia   57°25N 43°2E **86** B6
Yuscarán Honduras   13°58N 86°45W **182** D2
Yushan China   28°42N 118°10E **117** C12
Yushanzhen China   29°28N 108°22E **116** C7
Yushe China   37°4N 112°58E **114** F7
Yushu Jilin, China   44°43N 126°38E **115** B14
Yushu Qinghai, China   33°5N 96°55E **110** E8
Yusufeli Turkey   40°50N 41°33E **105** B9
Yutai China   35°0N 116°45E **114** G9
Yutian Hebei, China   39°53N 117°45E **115** E9
Yutian Sinkiang-Uigur,
  China   36°52N 81°42E **109** E10
Yuxarı Qarabağ =
  Nagorno-Karabakh ☐
  Azerbaijan   39°55N 46°45E **105** C12
Yuxi China   24°30N 102°35E **116** E4
Yuyao China   30°3N 121°10E **117** B13
Yuzawa Japan   39°10N 140°30E **112** E10
Yuzha Russia   56°34N 42°1E **86** B6
Yuzhno-Kurilsk
  Russia   44°1N 145°51E **107** E15
Yuzhno-Sakhalinsk
  Russia   46°58N 142°45E **111** B17
Yuzhno-Sukhokumsk
  Russia   44°40N 45°35E **87** H7
Yuzhnouralsk Russia   54°26N 61°15E **108** B6
Yuzhnyy ☐ Russia   44°0N 40°0E **106** E5
Yuzhou China   34°10N 113°28E **114** G7
Yvelines ☐ France   48°40N 1°45E **71** D8
Yverdon-les-Bains Switz.   46°47N 6°39E **77** J2
Yvetot France   49°37N 0°44E **70** C7
Yzeure France   46°33N 3°22E **71** F10

Z

Zaanstad Neths.   52°27N 4°50E **69** B4
Zab, Monts du Algeria   34°55N 5°0E **136** B5
Zāb al Kabīr → Iraq   36°1N 43°24E **105** D10
Zāb aş Şaghīr → Iraq   35°17N 43°29E **105** E10
Zabalj Serbia   45°21N 20°5E **80** E5
Zabari Serbia   44°22N 21°15E **96** B5
Zabarjad Egypt   23°40N 36°12E **137** C4
Zabaykalsk Russia   49°40N 117°25E **107** E12
Zabaykalsky △ Russia   53°40N 109°0E **107** D11
Zabki Poland   52°17N 21°6E **83** F8
Ząbkowice Śląskie
  Poland   50°35N 16°50E **83** H3
Žabljak Montenegro   43°18N 19°5E **96** C3
Zabludów Poland   53°0N 23°19E **83** F9
Żabno Poland   50°9N 20°53E **83** H7
Zābol Iran   31°0N 61°32E **129** D9
Zābol ☐ Afghan.   32°0N 67°0E **122** D5
Zābolī Iran   27°10N 61°35E **129** E9
Zabolotiv Ukraine   48°28N 25°18E **81** B10
Zabolottya Ukraine   51°38N 24°16E **83** G11
Zabré Burkina Faso   11°12N 0°36W **139** C4
Zábřeh Czech Rep.   49°53N 16°52E **79** B9
Zabrze Poland   50°18N 18°50E **83** H5
Zabuzhzhya Ukraine   51°21N 23°42E **83** G10
Zabzuga Ghana   9°20N 0°30E **139** D5
Zacapa Guatemala   14°59N 89°31W **182** D2
Zacapu Mexico   19°50N 101°43W **180** D4
Zacatecas Mexico   22°47N 102°35W **180** C4
Zacatecas ☐ Mexico   23°0N 103°0W **180** C4
Zacatecoluca El Salv.   13°29N 88°51W **182** D2
Zacharo Greece   37°30N 21°39E **98** D3
Zachary U.S.A.   30°39N 91°9W **176** F9
Zachodnio-Pomorskie ☐
  Poland   53°40N 15°50E **82** E2
Zacoalco de Torres
  Mexico   20°14N 103°35W **180** C4
Zacualtipán Mexico   20°39N 98°36W **181** C5
Zadar Croatia   44°8N 15°14E **93** D12
Zadawa Nigeria   11°33N 10°19E **139** C7
Zadetkyi Kyun Burma   10°0N 98°25E **121** G2
Zadonsk Russia   52°25N 38°56E **85** F10
Zafarqand Iran   33°11N 52°29E **129** C7
Zafra Spain   38°26N 6°30W **89** G4
Żagań Poland   51°39N 15°22E **82** D2
Zagaoua Chad   15°30N 22°24E **135** E10
Žagarė Lithuania   56°21N 23°15E **82** B10
Zagazig Egypt   30°40N 31°30E **137** E2
Żăgheh Iran   33°30N 48°42E **129** C6
Zaghouan Tunisia   36°23N 10°10E **136** A6
Zaghouan ☐ Tunisia   36°20N 10°0E **136** A6
Zaglou Algeria   27°17N 0°3W **136** C3
Zagnanado Benin   7°18N 2°28E **139** D5
Zagora Greece   39°27N 23°6E **98** B5
Zagora Morocco   30°22N 5°51W **136** B2
Zagorje Slovenia   46°8N 15°0E **93** B11
Zagórów Poland   52°10N 17°54E **83** F4
Zagórz Poland   49°30N 22°14E **83** J9
Zagreb ☐ (ZAG) Croatia   45°45N 16°4E **93** C13
Zagros Mts. = Zāgros, Kūhhā-ye
  Iran   33°45N 48°5E **129** C6
Zagros, Kūhhā-ye Iran
Zagros Mts. = Zāgros, Kūhhā-ye
Žagubica Serbia   44°15N 21°47E **96** C5
Zaguinaso Ivory C.   10°1N 6°14W **138** D3
Zagyva → Hungary   47°5N 20°1E **78** E11
Zāhedān Fārs, Iran   28°46N 53°52E **129** D7
Zāhedān Sīstān va Balūchestān,
  Iran   29°30N 60°50E **129** D9
Zahirabad India   17°43N 77°37E **126** F3
Zahlah Lebanon   33°52N 35°50E **130** B4
Zahna Germany   51°55N 12°49E **76** D8
Záhony Hungary   48°25N 22°11E **80** D7
Zahrān al Janub
  Si. Arabia   17°40N 43°30E **131** D3
Zainsk Russia   55°18N 52°4E **86** C11
Zaïre = Congo → Africa   6°4S 12°24E **140** F2
Zaječar Serbia   43°53N 22°18E **96** C6
Zaka Zimbabwe   20°20S 31°29E **145** B5
Zakamensk Russia   50°23N 103°17E **107** D11
Zakarpattya ☐ Ukraine   48°30N 23°20E **81** B8

Zakataly = Zaqatala
  Azerbaijan   41°38N 46°35E **87** K8
Zakhodnaya Dzvina =
  Daugava → Latvia   57°4N 24°3E **84** D3
Zākhū Iraq   37°10N 42°50E **105** D10
Zakinthos = Zakynthos
  Greece   37°47N 20°54E **98** D2
Zakopane Poland   49°18N 19°57E **83** J6
Zakroczym Poland   52°26N 20°38E **83** F7
Zakros Greece   35°6N 26°10E **101** D8
Zakynthos Greece   37°47N 20°54E **98** D2
Zala ☐ Hungary   46°42N 16°50E **80** D1
Zala → Hungary   46°43N 17°16E **80** D2
Zalaegerszeg Hungary   46°53N 16°47E **80** D1
Zalakomár Hungary   46°33N 17°10E **80** D2
Zalalövő Hungary   46°51N 16°35E **80** D1
Zalamea de la Serena
  Spain   38°40N 5°38W **89** G5
Zalamea la Real Spain   37°41N 6°38W **89** H4
Zalantun China   48°0N 122°43E **107** D11
Zalău Romania   47°12N 23°3E **80** C8
Žalec Slovenia   46°16N 15°10E **93** B12
Zaleshchiki = Zalishchyky
  Ukraine   48°45N 25°45E **81** B10
Zalesye Russia   54°50N 21°31E **82** D8
Zalew Russia   54°50N 21°31E **82** D8
Zalew Wiślany Poland   54°20N 19°50E **82** D6
Zalewo Poland   53°50N 19°41E **82** E6
Zalingei Sudan   12°51N 23°29E **135** F10
Zalishchyky Ukraine   48°45N 25°45E **81** B10
Zama L. Canada   58°45N 119°5W **162** B5
Zambeke
  Dem. Rep. of the Congo   2°8N 25°17E **142** B2
Zambeze → Africa   18°35S 36°20E **143** F4
Zambezi = Zambeze →
  Africa   18°35S 36°20E **143** F4
Zambezi Zambia   13°30S 23°15E **141** G4
Zambezi △ Zimbabwe   17°54S 25°41E **143** F2
Zambézia ☐ Mozam.   16°15S 37°30E **143** F4
Zambia ■ Africa   15°0S 28°0E **143** F2
Zamboanga Phil.   6°59N 122°3E **119** C6
Zambrów Poland   52°59N 22°14E **83** F9
Zametchino Russia   53°30N 42°30E **86** D6
Zamfara ☐ Nigeria   12°10N 6°0E **139** C6
Zamfara → Nigeria   12°5N 4°2E **139** C5
Zamora Mexico   19°59N 102°16W **180** D4
Zamora Spain   41°30N 5°45W **88** D5
Zamora ☐ Spain   41°30N 5°46W **88** D5
Zamość Poland   50°43N 23°15E **83** H10
Zamtang China   32°26N 101°6E **116** A3
Zan Ghana   9°26N 0°17W **139** D4
Zăncara → Spain   39°18N 3°18W **91** F1
Zanda China   31°32N 79°50E **110** E4
Zandvoort Neths.   52°22N 4°32E **69** B4
Zanesville U.S.A.   39°56N 82°1W **174** G2
Zangābād Iran   38°26N 46°44E **128** B5
Zangliveri Greece   40°36N 23°15E **96** F7
Zangoza = Sangüesa
  Spain   42°37N 1°17W **90** C3
Zangue → Mozam.   17°50S 35°21E **143** F4
Zanjān Iran   36°40N 48°35E **105** D13
Zanjān ☐ Iran   37°20N 49°30E **129** B6
Zanjān → Iran   37°8N 47°47E **129** B6
Zannone Italy   40°58N 13°3E **94** B6
Zante = Zakynthos
  Greece   37°47N 20°54E **98** D2
Zanthus Australia   31°2S 123°34E **149** F3
Zanzan ☐ Ivory C.   8°30N 3°30W **138** D4
Zanzibar Tanzania   6°12S 39°12E **142** D4
Zaouatallaz Algeria   24°52N 8°30E **136** D6
Zaouiet El-Kala = Bordj Omar
  Driss Algeria   28°10N 6°40E **136** C5
Zaouiet Reggâne Algeria   26°32N 0°3E **136** C4
Zaoyang China   32°10N 112°45E **117** A9
Zaozernyy Kazakhstan   53°6N 71°9E **109** B8
Zaozhuang China   34°50N 117°35E **115** G9
Zap Suyu = Zāb al Kabīr →
  Iraq   36°1N 43°24E **105** D10
Zapadna Morava →
  Serbia   43°38N 21°30E **96** C5
Zapadnaya Dvina = Daugava →
  Latvia   57°4N 24°3E **84** D3
Zapadnaya Dvina Russia   56°15N 32°3E **84** D7
Západné Beskydy
  Europe   49°30N 19°0E **79** B12
Zapadni Rodopi Bulgaria   41°50N 24°0E **96** E7
Západočeský ☐
  Czech Rep.   49°35N 13°0E **78** B6
Zapala Argentina   39°0S 70°5W **192** A2
Zapaleri, Cerro Bolivia   22°49S 67°11W **190** A2
Zapata U.S.A.   26°55N 99°16W **176** H5
Zapatón → Spain   39°0N 6°49W **89** F4
Zapiga Chile   19°40S 69°55W **188** D4
Zapolyarnyy Russia   69°26N 30°51E **60** B24
Zapopán Mexico   20°43N 103°24W **180** C4
Zaporizhzhya Ukraine   47°50N 35°10E **85** J8
Zaporizhzhya ☐ Ukraine   46°55N 35°50E **85** J8
Zaporozhye = Zaporizhzhya
  Ukraine   47°50N 35°10E **85** J8
Zaqatala Azerbaijan   41°38N 46°35E **87** K8
Zara Turkey   39°58N 37°43E **104** C7
Zarafshon Uzbekistan   41°34N 64°12E **108** D6
Zaragoza Coahuila,
  Mexico   28°29N 100°55W **180** B4
Zaragoza Nuevo León,
  Mexico   23°58N 99°46W **181** C5
Zaragoza Spain   41°39N 0°53W **90** D4
Zaragoza ☐ Spain   41°35N 1°0W **90** D4
Zarand Kermān, Iran   30°46N 56°34E **129** D8
Zarand Markazī, Iran   35°18N 50°25E **129** C6
Zărăndului, Munții
  Romania   46°14N 22°7E **80** D7
Zarasai Lithuania   55°40N 26°20E **84** E4
Zárate Argentina   34°7S 59°0W **190** C4
Zaragza Spain   41°39N 0°53W **90** D4
Zaraysk Russia   54°48N 38°53E **84** E10
Zard, Kūh-e Iran   32°22N 50°4E **129** C6
Zāreh Iran   35°7N 49°9E **129** C6
Zari Nigeria   13°4N 12°45E **139** C7
Zaria Nigeria   11°0N 7°40E **139** C6
Zarineh → Iran   36°17N 46°2E **105** D12
Zărnești Romania   45°33N 25°18E **81** D11
Żarki Poland   50°38N 19°23E **83** H6
Zarko Greece   39°28N 127°14E **98** D3
Zarneh Iran   33°55N 46°10E **128** C5
Żărnești Romania   45°33N 25°18E **81** D11
Zaros Greece   35°8N 24°54E **101** D6
Żarów Poland   50°56N 16°29E **83** H3
Zarqā' Nahr az →
  Jordan   32°10N 35°37E **130** C4

Zarrīn Iran   32°46N 54°37E **129** C7
Zarrīnābād Iran   36°25N 48°17E **105** D13
Zaruma Ecuador   3°40S 79°38W **186** D3
Zarza de Granadilla Spain   40°14N 6°3W **88** E4
Zarzaïtine Algeria   28°15N 9°34E **136** C5
Zarzis Tunisia   33°31N 11°2E **136** B6
Zashagan Kazakhstan   51°11N 51°20E **108** B4
Zaskar → India   34°13N 77°20E **125** B7
Zaskar Mts. India   33°15N 77°30E **125** C7
Zastavna Ukraine   48°31N 25°51E **81** B10
Zastron S. Africa   30°18S 27°7E **144** D4
Žatec Czech Rep.   50°20N 13°32E **78** A6
Zaterechnyy Russia   44°48N 45°11E **87** H7
Zator Poland   49°59N 19°28E **83** J6
Zatyshshya Ukraine   47°20N 29°51E **81** C14
Zavala Bos.-H.   42°50N 17°59E **96** D1
Zave Zimbabwe   17°6S 30°1E **145** A5
Zavetnoye Russia   47°13N 43°50E **87** G6
Zavidovići Bos.-H.   44°27N 18°10E **80** F3
Zavitinsk Russia   50°10N 129°20E **107** D13
Zavolzhsk Russia   57°30N 42°3E **86** B6
Zavolzhye Russia   56°37N 43°26E **86** B6
Zawadzkie Poland   50°37N 18°28E **83** H5
Zawiercie Poland   50°30N 19°24E **83** H6
Zawidów Poland   51°1N 15°1E **83** G2
Zawiercie Poland   50°48N 21°51E **83** H8
Zawidów Poland   51°1N 15°1E **83** G2
Zāwiyat al Baydā = Al Baydā
  Libya   32°50N 21°44E **135** B10
Zâwyet Shammas
  Egypt   31°30N 26°37E **137** A2
Zâwyet Um el Rakham
  Egypt   31°18N 27°1E **137** A2
Zâwyet Ungeîla Egypt   31°23N 26°42E **137** A2
Zāyā Iraq   33°33N 44°13E **128** C5
Zāyandeh → Iran   32°35N 52°0E **129** C7
Zaysan Kazakhstan   47°28N 84°52E **109** C10
Zaysan Köli Kazakhstan   48°0N 83°0E **109** C10
Zayü China   28°48N 97°27E **123** D20
Zāzrivá Slovak Rep.   49°16N 19°7E **79** B12
Zbarazh Ukraine   49°43N 25°44E **75** D13
Zbąszyń Poland   52°14N 15°56E **83** F2
Zbąszynek Poland   52°16N 15°51E **83** F2
Zblewo Poland   53°56N 18°19E **82** E5
Zbruch → Ukraine   48°32N 26°27E **81** B11
Žďár nad Sázavou
  Czech Rep.   49°34N 15°57E **78** B8
Zdolbuniv Ukraine   50°30N 26°15E **75** C14
Ždrelo Serbia   44°16N 21°28E **96** B5
Zdunska Wola Poland   51°37N 18°59E **83** G5
Zduny Poland   51°39N 17°21E **83** G4
Zeballos Canada   49°59N 126°50W **162** D3
Zebediela S. Africa   24°20S 29°17E **145** B4
Zebila Ghana   10°55N 0°30W **139** C4
Zebulon U.S.A.   33°6N 84°21W **178** B5
Zeebrugge Belgium   51°19N 3°12E **69** C3
Zeehan Australia   41°52S 145°25E **151** G4
Zeeland ☐ Neths.   51°30N 3°50E **69** C3
Zeerust S. Africa   25°31S 26°4E **144** C4
Zefat Israel   32°58N 35°29E **130** C4
Zegdou Algeria   29°51N 4°45W **136** B3
Zeggerene, Irachar Mali   16°49N 2°16E **139** B5
Zégoua Mali   10°32N 5°35W **138** C3
Zehak Iran   30°53N 61°42E **129** D9
Zehdenick Germany   52°58N 13°20E **76** C9
Zeil, Mt. Australia   23°30S 132°23E **148** D5
Zeila = Saylac Somalia   11°21N 43°30E **131** E3
Zeist Neths.   52°5N 5°15E **69** B5
Zeitz Germany   51°2N 12°7E **76** D8
Želechów Poland   51°49N 21°54E **83** G8
Zelena Ukraine   48°3N 24°45E **81** B9
Zelená Hora Czech Rep.   49°34N 15°56E **78** B8
Zelengora Bos.-H.   43°22N 18°30E **96** C2
Zelenodolsk Russia   55°55N 48°30E **86** C9
Zelenogorsk Russia   60°12N 29°43E **84** B5
Zelenograd Russia   56°1N 37°12E **84** D9
Zelenogradsk Russia   54°53N 20°29E **82** D7
Zelenokumsk Russia   44°24N 44°0E **87** H6
Železná Ruda Czech Rep.   49°8N 13°15E **78** B6
Železnik Serbia   44°43N 20°23E **96** B4
Zelfana Algeria   32°27N 4°15E **136** B4
Zelienople U.S.A.   40°48N 80°8W **174** F4
Železnorce Slovak Rep.   38°30N 18°40E **79** C11
Zelina Croatia   45°57N 16°16E **93** C13
Zell Baden-W., Germany   47°42N 7°52E **77** H3
Zell Rhld-Pfz., Germany   50°1N 7°10E **76** E3
Zell am See Austria   47°19N 12°47E **78** D5
Zella-Mehlis Germany   50°39N 10°40E **76** E6
Zelów Poland   51°28N 19°14E **83** G6
Zeltweg Austria   47°11N 14°45E **78** D7
Zémaitijos △ Lithuania   56°2N 21°55E **82** B8
Zémio C.A.R.   5°2N 25°5E **142** A2
Zemlandskiy Poluostrov
  Russia   54°50N 20°20E **82** D7
Zemmora Algeria   35°44N 0°51E **136** A4
Zemoul, O. → Algeria   29°15N 7°0W **136** C2
Zemplén-hegység
  Hungary   48°25N 21°25E **80** B6
Zemplínska Šírava
  Slovak Rep.   48°48N 22°0E **79** C13
Zempoala Mexico   19°27N 96°23W **181** D5
Zemun Serbia   44°51N 20°25E **96** B4
Zengbé Cameroon   5°46N 13°4E **139** D7
Zengcheng China   23°13N 113°52E **117** F9
Zhidan China   36°48N 108°48E **114** F5
Zenica Bos.-H.   44°10N 17°57E **80** F2
Žepče Bos.-H.   44°28N 18°2E **80** F3
Zephyrhills U.S.A.   28°14N 82°11W **179** G7
Zepu China   38°11N 77°16E **109** E9
Zerbst Germany   51°58N 12°5E **76** D8
Zerhamra Algeria   29°58N 2°30W **136** C3
Zermatt Switz.   46°2N 7°46E **77** J3
Zernez Switz.   46°42N 10°7E **77** J6
Zernograd Russia   46°52N 40°19E **87** G5
Zerqan Albania   41°27N 20°20E **96** H4
Zestaponi Georgia   42°6N 43°0E **87** J6
Zetel Germany   53°25N 7°58E **76** B3
Zeulenroda Germany   50°39N 11°59E **76** E7
Zeven Germany   53°17N 9°16E **76** B5
Zevenaar Neths.   51°56N 6°5E **69** C6
Zévio Italy   45°22N 11°8E **92** C8
Zeya Russia   53°48N 127°14E **107** D13
Zeya → Russia   51°42N 128°53E **107** D13
Zeyskoye Vdkhr.
  Russia   54°30N 127°30E **107** D13
Zeytinbağı Turkey   40°24N 28°47E **97** F12
Zeytindağ Turkey   38°58N 27°4E **99** C9
Zgharta Lebanon   34°21N 35°53E **130** A4

Zgierz Poland   51°50N 19°27E **83** G6
Zgorzelec Poland   51°10N 15°0E **83** G2
Zguriţa Moldova   48°1N 28°1E **81** B13
Zhabinka Belarus   52°13N 24°2E **83** F11
Zhabokrych Ukraine   48°23N 28°59E **81** B13
Zhalgiztobe Kazakhstan   49°26N 81°6E **109** C10
Zhalpaqtal Kazakhstan   49°42N 49°25E **86** F9
Zhaltyr Kazakhstan   51°37N 69°49E **109** B7
Zhambyl = Taraz
  Kazakhstan   42°54N 71°22E **108** D8
Zhambyl ☐ Kazakhstan   44°0N 72°0E **109** D8
Zhanatas Kazakhstan   43°35N 69°35E **109** D7
Zhangaly Kazakhstan   47°1N 50°37E **87** G10
Zhangaözen Kazakhstan   43°18N 52°48E **106** E6
Zhangaqala Kazakhstan   48°56N 49°36E **87** F9
Zhangaqazaly
  Kazakhstan   45°48N 62°6E **108** C6
Zhangatas = Zhanatas
  Kazakhstan   43°35N 69°35E **109** D7
Zhangbei China   41°10N 114°45E **114** D8
Zhangguangcai Ling
  China   45°0N 129°0E **115** B15
Zhangjiabian China   22°33N 113°28E **111** a
Zhangjiagang China   31°55N 120°30E **117** B13
Zhangjiakou China   40°48N 114°55E **114** D8
Zhangping China   25°17N 117°23E **117** E11
Zhangpu China   24°8N 117°35E **117** C11
Zhangshu China   28°4N 115°29E **117** C10
Zhangye China   38°50N 100°23E **110** D9
Zhangzhou China   24°30N 117°35E **117** C11
Zhanhua China   37°40N 118°8E **115** F10
Zhänibek Kazakhstan   49°25N 46°50E **86** F8
Zhanjiang China   21°15N 110°20E **117** G8
Zhannetty, Ostrov
  Russia   76°43N 158°0E **107** B16
Zhanyi China   25°38N 103°48E **116** E4
Zhanyu China   44°30N 122°30E **115** B12
Zhao Xian China   37°43N 114°45E **114** F8
Zhao'an China   23°41N 117°10E **117** F11
Zhaocheng China   36°22N 111°38E **114** F6
Zhaodong China   46°4N 125°59E **111** B13
Zhaojue China   28°1N 102°49E **116** C4
Zhaoping China   24°11N 110°48E **117** E8
Zhaoqing China   23°0N 112°20E **117** F9
Zhaotong China   27°20N 103°44E **116** D4
Zhaoyang Hu China   35°4N 116°47E **114** G9
Zhaoyuan Heilongjiang,
  China   45°27N 125°0E **115** B13
Zhaoyuan Shandong,
  China   37°20N 120°23E **115** F11
Zhar, Mali Kosovo   42°20N 21°0E **96** D5
Zhari Namco China   31°6N 85°36E **110** E6
Zharkent China   44°10N 80°0E **109** D10
Zharkovskiy Russia   55°56N 32°19E **84** E7
Zhashkiv Ukraine   49°15N 30°5E **75** D16
Zhashui China   33°40N 109°8E **114** H5
Zhaslyk Uzbekistan   43°58N 57°10E **108** D7
Zhayrang Kazakhstan   48°20N 70°10E **109** C8
Zhayylma Kazakhstan   51°37N 61°33E **108** B6
Zhayyq → Kazakhstan   47°0N 51°48E **108** C4
Zhdanov = Mariupol
  Ukraine   47°5N 37°31E **85** J9
Zhecheng China   34°7N 115°20E **114** G8
Zhegao China   31°46N 117°45E **117** B11
Zhejiang ☐ China   29°0N 120°0E **117** C13
Zheleznodorozhnyy
  Russia   54°22N 21°19E **82** D8
Zheleznogorsk Russia   52°22N 35°23E **85** F8
Zheleznogorsk-Ilimskiy
  Russia   56°34N 104°8E **107** D11
Zheltye Vody = Zhovti Vody
  Ukraine   48°21N 33°31E **85** H7
Zhen'an China   33°27N 109°9E **114** H5
Zhenba China   32°34N 107°58E **116** A6
Zhenfeng China   25°22N 105°40E **116** E5
Zheng'an China   28°32N 107°27E **116** C6
Zhengding China   38°8N 114°32E **114** E8
Zhenghe China   27°20N 118°50E **117** D12
Zhengyang China   32°37N 114°22E **117** A10
Zhengyangguan
  China   32°30N 116°29E **117** A11
Zhenhai China   34°45N 113°34E **114** G7
Zhenjiang China   29°59N 121°42E **117** C13
Zhenkang China   32°11N 105°42E **116** A5
Zhenlai China   45°50N 123°5E **115** B12
Zhenning China   26°4N 105°45E **116** D5
Zhenping Henan, China   33°10N 112°16E **114** H7
Zhenping Shaanxi,
  China   31°59N 109°31E **116** B7
Zhenxiong China   27°27N 104°50E **116** D5
Zhenyuan Gansu,
  China   35°35N 107°30E **114** G4
Zhenyuan Guizhou,
  China   27°4N 108°21E **116** D6
Zherdevka Russia   51°56N 41°29E **85** E7
Zherebkove Ukraine   50°50N 29°52E **81** C14
Zherong China   27°15N 119°52E **117** D12
Zhetiqara Kazakhstan   52°11N 61°12E **108** B6
Zhezdi Kazakhstan   48°3N 67°3E **109** C7
Zhezqazghan
  Kazakhstan   47°44N 67°40E **108** C7
Zhicheng China   30°25N 111°27E **117** B8
Zhidan China   36°48N 108°48E **114** F5
Zhigansk Russia   66°48N 123°27E **107** C13
Zhigulevsk Russia   53°28N 49°30E **86** D9
Zhijiang Hubei, China   30°32N 111°42E **117** B8
Zhijiang Hunan, China   27°7N 109°42E **116** D7
Zhijin China   26°38N 105°45E **116** D5
Zhilinda Russia   70°0N 114°0E **107** C12
Zhilino Russia   54°54N 21°54E **82** D8
Ziway, L. Ethiopia   8°0N 38°50E **131** F2
Zixi China   27°45N 117°4E **117** D11
Zixing China   25°59N 113°21E **117** E9
Ziyamet = Leonarisso
  Cyprus   35°28N 34°8E **101** D13
Ziyang Shaanxi, China   32°32N 108°31E **114** H5
Ziyang Sichuan, China   30°6N 104°40E **116** B5
Ziyun China   25°45N 106°5E **116** E6
Zizhou China   37°18N 109°40E **114** F5
Ziz, Oued → Morocco   31°40N 4°15W **136** B3

Zhongning China   37°29N 105°40E **114** F3
Zhongsha Qundao = Macclesfield
  Bank S. China Sea   16°0N 114°30E **118** A4
Zhongshan Antarctica   69°0S 39°50E **55** C6
Zhongshan Guangdong,
  China   22°26N 113°20E **117** F9
Zhongshan Guangxi Zhuangzu,
  China   24°29N 111°18E **117** E8
Zhongshankang China   13°33N 109°29E **111** a
Zhongtiao Shan China   35°0N 111°10E **114** G6
Zhongwei China   37°30N 105°12E **114** F3
Zhongxian China   30°18N 107°58E **116** B6
Zhongxiang China   31°12N 112°34E **117** B9
Zhorany Ukraine   32°20N 111°11E **117** A8
Zhosaly Kazakhstan   45°29N 64°4E **108** C6
Zhoucun China   36°47N 117°48E **115** F9
Zhoukou China   33°38N 114°58E **114** H8
Zhoukoudian China   39°41N 115°56E **114** E8
Zhouning China   27°12N 119°20E **117** D12
Zhoushan China   30°1N 122°6E **117** B14
Zhoushan Dao China   30°5N 122°10E **117** C14
Zhouzhi China   34°10N 108°12E **114** G5
Zhovkva Ukraine   50°4N 23°58E **75** C12
Zhovti Vody Ukraine   48°21N 33°31E **85** H7
Zhovtneve Lubelskie,
  Ukraine   50°42N 24°12E **83** H11
Zhovtneve Mykolayiv,
  Ukraine   46°54N 32°3E **85** J7
Zhu Jiang → China   22°45N 113°37E **117** F9
Zhuanghe China   39°40N 123°0E **115** E12
Zhucheng China   36°0N 119°27E **115** G10
Zhugqu China   33°40N 104°30E **114** H3
Zhuhai China   22°17N 113°34E **117** F9
Zhuji China   29°40N 120°10E **117** C13
Zhujiang Kou China   22°20N 113°45E **111** a
Zhukovka Russia   53°35N 33°50E **84** F7
Zhumadian China   32°59N 114°2E **117** A10
Zhuo Xian = Zhuozhou
  China   39°28N 115°58E **114** E8
Zhuolu China   40°20N 115°12E **114** D8
Zhuozhou China   39°28N 115°58E **114** E8
Zhuozi China   41°0N 112°25E **114** D7
Zhur Kosovo   42°13N 20°34E **96** G4
Zhushan China   32°15N 110°13E **117** A8
Zhuxi China   32°25N 109°40E **116** A7
Zhuzhou China   27°49N 113°12E **117** D9
Zhvanets Ukraine   48°33N 26°30E **81** B11
Zhympity Kazakhstan   50°16N 52°35E **108** B4
Zhytomyr Ukraine   50°20N 28°40E **75** C15
Zhytomyr ☐ Ukraine   50°50N 28°10E **75** C14
Zi Shui → China   28°40N 112°40E **117** C9
Ziarat Pakistan   30°25N 67°49E **124** D2
Zibo China   36°47N 118°3E **115** F10
Zichang China   37°18N 109°40E **114** F5
Zidarovo Bulgaria   42°20N 27°24E **97** D11
Zidi = Wandhari
  Pakistan   27°42N 66°48E **124** F2
Ziębice Poland   50°37N 17°2E **83** H4
Zielona Góra Poland   51°57N 15°31E **83** G2
Zierikzee Neths.   51°40N 3°55E **69** C3
Ziesar Germany   52°16N 12°17E **76** C8
Žiar nad Hronom
  Slovak Rep.   48°35N 18°53E **79** C11
Zigey Chad   14°43N 15°50E **135** F9
Ziguéy Chad   14°43N 15°50E **135** F9
Zigong China   29°15N 104°48E **116** C5
Ziguinchor Senegal   12°25N 16°20W **138** C1
Ziguinchor ☐ Senegal   12°45N 16°20W **138** C1
Zihuatanejo Mexico   17°39N 101°33W **180** D4
Zile Turkey   40°15N 35°52E **104** B6
Žilina Slovak Rep.   49°12N 18°42E **79** B11
Žilinský ☐ Slovak Rep.   49°10N 19°0E **79** B12
Zillah Libya   28°30N 17°33E **135** C9
Zillertaler Alpen Austria   47°6N 11°45E **78** D4
Zima Russia   54°0N 102°5E **107** D11
Zimapán Mexico   20°45N 99°21W **181** C5
Zimba Zambia   17°20S 26°11E **143** F2
Zimbabwe ■ Africa   19°0S 30°0E **143** F3
Zimbabwe Zimbabwe   20°16S 30°54E **143** G3
Zimmi S. Leone   7°20N 11°20W **138** D2
Zimnicea Romania   43°40N 25°22E **81** G10
Zimovniki Russia   47°10N 42°0E **87** G6
Zinave △ Mozam.   21°35S 33°40E **145** B5
Zinder Niger   13°48N 9°0E **139** C7
Zinder ☐ Niger   15°0N 10°0E **139** C7
Zinga Tanzania   9°16S 38°49E **143** D4
Zíngaro △ Italy   38°6N 12°53E **94** D5
Ziniaré Burkina Faso   12°35N 1°18W **138** C4
Zinnowitz Germany   54°4N 13°54E **76** A9
Zion Nat. Park △ U.S.A.   37°15N 113°5W **169** H7
Zirc Hungary   47°17N 17°42E **80** C2
Zirl Slovenia   46°5N 14°56E **93** B11
Zirl Austria   47°14N 11°14E **78** D4
Zirndorf Germany   49°27N 10°57E **77** F6
Ziros Greece   35°5N 26°8E **101** D8
Zirreh, Gowd-e Afghan.   29°45N 62°0E **122** E3
Zisterdorf Austria   48°33N 16°45E **79** C9
Zitácuaro Mexico   19°24N 100°22W **180** D4
Žitava → Slovak Rep.   48°14N 18°21E **79** C11
Žitište Serbia   45°30N 20°32E **80** E5
Zitong China   31°37N 105°10E **116** B5
Zitsa Greece   39°47N 20°40E **98** B2
Zittau Germany   50°53N 14°48E **76** E10
Zitsa Greece   39°47N 20°40E **98** B2
Zhonggar Dangshan   29°39N 84°10E **110** E7
Zhongdian China   27°48N 99°42E **116** D2
Zhongdong China   24°44N 107°47E **116** E6
Zhongdu China   24°40N 109°40E **116** E7
Zhongjian Dao = Triton I.
  S. China Sea   15°47N 111°12E **118** A4
Zhongjiang China   30°58N 104°45E **116** B5

Zlatitsa Bulgaria   42°41N 24°7E **97** D8
Zlatna Romania   46°8N 23°11E **81** D8
Zlatna Panega Bulgaria   43°5N 24°9E **97** D8
Zlatni Pyasŭtsi Bulgaria   43°17N 28°3E **97** C12
Zlatograd Bulgaria   41°22N 25°7E **97** E8
Zlatoust Russia   55°10N 59°40E **108** D6
Zletovo Macedonia   41°59N 22°17E **96** H5
Zlín Czech Rep.   49°14N 17°40E **79** B9
Zlínský ☐ Czech Rep.   49°20N 17°40E **79** B9
Złocieniec Poland   53°30N 16°1E **82** E3
Złoczew Poland   51°24N 18°35E **83** G5
Zlot Serbia   44°1N 21°58E **96** C5
Złotoryja Poland   51°8N 15°55E **83** G2
Złotów Poland   53°22N 17°2E **82** E3
Zmeinogorsk
  Kazakhstan   51°10N 82°13E **108** B9
Žmiegród Poland   51°28N 16°53E **83** G3
Žmiyev Ukraine   49°39N 36°27E **85** H9
Znamenka = Znamyanka
  Ukraine   48°45N 32°30E **85** H7
Znamensk Russia   54°36N 21°16E **82** D8
Znamyanka Ukraine   48°45N 32°30E **85** H7
Żnin Poland   52°51N 17°44E **83** F4
Znojmo Czech Rep.   48°50N 16°2E **78** C8
Zobeyrī Iran   34°10N 46°40E **128** C5
Zobia
  Dem. Rep. of the Congo   3°0N 25°59E **142** B2
Zoetermeer Neths.   52°3N 4°30E **69** B4
Zogang China   29°55N 97°42E **116** B1
Zogno Italy   45°48N 9°40E **92** C6
Zohreh → Iran   30°16N 51°15E **129** D6
Zolfo Springs U.S.A.   27°30N 81°48W **179** H7
Zolochiv Ukraine   49°45N 24°51E **75** D12
Zolotonosha Ukraine   49°39N 32°5E **85** H7
Zolotyy Potik Ukraine   48°54N 25°20E **81** B10
Zomba Malawi   15°22S 35°19E **143** G4
Zongo
  Dem. Rep. of the Congo   4°20N 18°35E **140** D3
Zonguldak Turkey   41°28N 31°50E **104** A4
Zonguldak ☐ Turkey   41°20N 31°45E **104** A4
Zonqor Pt. Malta   35°52N 14°34E **107** ?
Zonza France   41°45N 9°11E **73** ?
Zorgo Burkina Faso   12°15N 0°35W **139** ?
Zorita Spain   39°17N 5°39W **89** ?
Zorleni Romania   46°14N 27°44E **81** ?
Zornitsa Bulgaria   42°23N 26°58E **97** ?
Zorritos Peru   3°43S 80°40W **188** ?
Żory Poland   50°3N 18°44E **83** ?
Zorzor Liberia   7°46N 9°28W **138** ?
Zossen Germany   52°13N 13°27E **76** ?
Zou Xiang China   35°30N 116°58E **114** ?
Zouan-Hounien Ivory C.   6°55N 8°15W **138** ?
Zouar Chad   20°30N 16°32E **135** ?
Zouérate = Zouîrât
  Mauritania   22°44N 12°21W **134** ?
Zouîrât Mauritania   22°44N 12°21W **134** ?
Zourika Niger   19°16N 7°52E **139** ?
Zourma Burkina Faso   11°20N 0°50W **139** ?
Zousfana, O. → Algeria   31°28N 2°17W **136** ?
Zoutkamp Neths.   53°20N 6°18E **69** ?
Zov Tigra △ Russia   43°25N 134°10E **112** ?
Zrenjanin Serbia   45°22N 20°23E **80** ?
Zuba Nigeria   9°11N 7°12E **139** ?
Zubin Potok Kosovo   42°54N 20°41E **96** ?
Zubtsov Russia   56°10N 34°34E **84** ?
Zuénoula Ivory C.   7°34N 6°3W **138** ?
Zuera Spain   41°51N 0°49W **90** ?
Zufar Oman   17°40N 54°0E **139** ?
Zug Switz.   47°10N 8°31E **77** ?
Zugdidi Georgia   42°30N 41°55E **87** ?
Zugersee Switz.   47°7N 8°35E **77** ?
Zugspitze Germany   47°25N 10°59E **77** ?
Zuid-Holland ☐ Neths.   52°0N 4°35E **69** ?
Zuidbeveland Neths.   51°30N 3°50E **69** ?
Zuidhorn Neths.   53°15N 6°23E **69** ?
Zújar Spain   37°34N 2°50W **89** ?
Zújar → Spain   39°1N 5°47W **89** ?
Żukowo Poland   54°21N 18°22E **82** ?
Zula Eritrea   15°17N 39°40E **131** ?
Zülpich Germany   50°41N 6°39E **76** ?
Zumaia Spain   43°19N 2°15W **90** ?
Zumárraga Spain   43°5N 2°19W **90** ?
Zumbo Mozam.   15°35S 30°26E **143** ?
Zummo Nigeria   9°51N 12°59E **139** ?
Zumpango Mexico   19°48N 99°6W **181** ?
Zungeru Nigeria   9°48N 6°8E **139** ?
Zunhua China   40°18N 117°58E **115** ?
Zuni Pueblo U.S.A.   35°4N 108°51W **165** ?
Zunyi China   27°42N 106°53E **116** ?
Zuo Jiang → China   22°50N 108°6E **116** ?
Zuoquan China   37°1N 113°27E **114** ?
Zuozhou China   22°42N 107°2E **116** ?
Županja Croatia   45°4N 18°43E **80** ?
Zurbāṭīyah Iraq   33°9N 46°3E **128** ?
Zürich Switz.   47°22N 8°32E **77** ?
Zürich ☐ Switz.   47°26N 8°40E **77** ?
Zürichsee Switz.   47°18N 8°40E **77** ?
Żuromin Poland   53°4N 19°51E **82** ?
Żut Croatia   43°52N 15°17E **93** ?
Zutphen Neths.   52°9N 6°12E **69** ?
Zuurberg △ S. Africa   33°12S 25°32E **144** ?
Zuwārah Libya   32°58N 12°1E **135** ?
Žužan Iran   34°22N 59°53E **129** ?
Žužemberk Slovenia   45°52N 14°56E **93** ?
Zvečan Kosovo   42°54N 20°50E **96** ?
Zvenigorodka = Svenyhorodka
  Ukraine   49°4N 30°56E **81** ?
Zvezdets Bulgaria   42°6N 27°26E **97** ?
Zvishavane Zimbabwe   20°17S 30°2E **143** ?
Zvolen Slovak Rep.   48°33N 19°10E **79** ?
Zvonce Serbia   42°57N 22°34E **96** ?
Zvornik Bos.-H.   44°26N 19°7E **80** ?
Zwedru = Tchien Liberia   5°59N 8°15W **138** ?
Zweibrücken Germany   49°15N 7°21E **77** ?
Zwenkau Germany   51°13N 12°20E **76** ?
Zwettl Austria   48°35N 15°9E **78** ?
Zwickau Germany   50°44N 12°30E **76** ?
Zwierzyniec Poland   50°36N 22°58E **83** ?
Zwiesel Germany   49°1N 13°13E **78** ?
Zwoleń Poland   51°21N 21°36E **83** ?
Zwolle Neths.   52°31N 6°6E **69** ?
Zwolle U.S.A.   31°38N 93°39W **176** ?
Żychlin Poland   52°15N 19°37E **83** ?
Żyrardów Poland   52°3N 20°35E **83** ?
Zyryan Kazakhstan   49°43N 84°20E **108** ?
Zyryanka Russia   65°45N 150°51E **107** ?
Zyryanovsk = Zyryan
  Kazakhstan   49°43N 84°20E **108** ?
Żywiec Poland   49°42N 19°10E **83** ?

GREENLAND

KEY TO EUROPEAN MAP PAGES

57

 **Large scale maps**
(>1:2 500 000)

 **Medium scale maps**
(1:2 800 000 – 1:9 900 000)

 **Small scale maps**
(<1:10 000 000)

60

ICELAND

Arctic Circle

WORLD COUNTRY INDEX

Afghanistan	122	**G**ermany	76–77	**O**man	131
Albania	96	Ghana	138–139		
Algeria	136	Greece	96–99	**P**akistan	122, 124
Angola	140–141	Greenland	57	Panama	182
Argentina	190–192	Guadeloupe	183	Papua New Guinea	156
Armenia	105	Guatemala	182	Paraguay	190–191
Australia	148–153	Guinea	138	Peru	188
Austria	78–79	Guinea-Bissau	138	Philippines	119
Azerbaijan	105	Guyana	186	Poland	82–83
				Portugal	88–89
Bahamas	182–183	**H**aiti	183	Puerto Rico	183
Bahrain	129	Honduras	182		
Bangladesh	123	Hungary	80	**Q**atar	129
Barbados	183				
Belarus	84–85	**I**celand	60	**R**omania	80–81
Belgium	69	India	122–127	Russia	84–87, 106–109
Belize	182	Indonesia	118–119	Rwanda	142
Benin	139	Iran	105, 128–129		
Bhutan	123	Iraq	105, 128–129	**S**t. Lucia	183
Bolivia	186	Ireland	64	Samoa	156
Bosnia-Herzegovina	80, 96	Israel	130	Saudi Arabia	128–129, 131
Botswana	144	Italy	92–95	Scotland	65
Brazil	186–187, 189, 191	Ivory Coast	138	Senegal	138
Brunei	118			Serbia	96
Bulgaria	96–97	**J**amaica	182	Sierra Leone	138
Burkina Faso	138–139	Japan	112–113	Singapore	121
Burma (Myanmar)	123	Jordan	130	Slovak Republic	79
Burundi	142			Slovenia	93
		Kazakhstan	108–109	Solomon Is.	156
Cambodia	120–121	Kenya	142	Somalia	131
Canary Is.	100	Korea, North	115	South Africa	144–145
Cameroon	139, 140	Korea, South	115	South Sudan	135
Canada	160–165	Kosovo	96	Spain	88–91
Central African Republic	140	Kuwait	128–129	Sri Lanka	127
Chad	135	Kyrgyzstan	109	Sudan	135
Chile	190, 192			Suriname	186–187
China	110–111, 114–117	**L**aos	120	Swaziland	145
Colombia	186	Latvia	82, 84	Sweden	60–63
Congo	140	Lebanon	130	Switzerland	77
Congo, Dem. Rep.		Lesotho	145	Syria	105, 128
of the	140–143	Liberia	138		
Costa Rica	182	Libya	135	**T**aiwan	117
Croatia	93	Lithuania	82, 84	Tajikistan	109
Cuba	182–183	Luxembourg	69	Tanzania	142–143
Cyprus	101			Thailand	120–121
Czech Republic	78–79	**M**acedonia	96	Togo	139
		Madagascar	141	Tonga	156
Denmark	63	Malawi	143	Trinidad and Tobago	187
Djibouti	131	Malaysia	118–119, 121	Tunisia	134–135
Dominican Republic	183	Mali	134, 138–139	Turkey	104–105
		Malta	101	Turkmenistan	108
East Timor	119	Martinique	183		
Ecuador	186	Mauritania	134	**U**ganda	142
Egypt	137	Mexico	180–181	Ukraine	85
El Salvador	182	Moldova	81	United Arab Emirates	129
England	66–67	Mongolia	110–111	United Kingdom	64–67
Equatorial Guinea	140	Montenegro	96	USA	168–179
Eritrea	131	Morocco	136	Uruguay	190–191
Estonia	84	Mozambique	143, 145	Uzbekistan	108–109
Ethiopia	131				
		Namibia	144	**V**anuatu	156
Fiji	154	Nepal	125	Venezuela	186
Finland	60–61	Netherlands	69	Vietnam	120–121
France	70–73	New Zealand	154–155		
French Guiana	187	Nicaragua	182	**W**ales	66–67
		Niger	134–135, 139		
Gabon	140	Nigeria	139	**Y**emen	131
Gambia	138	Northern Ireland	64		
Georgia	87	Norway	60–62	**Z**ambia	141, 143
				Zimbabwe	145

60

68

65

65

65

66

64

70

74

IRELAND

UNITED KINGDOM

72

FR

88

90

ANDORRA

PORTUGAL

SPAIN

10

MOROCCO